CASES AND MATERIALS

TRADE REGULATION

SIXTH EDITION

by

ROBERT PITOFSKY
Sheehy Professor of Law,
Georgetown University Law Center

HARVEY J. GOLDSCHMID
Dwight Professor of Law,
Columbia University School of Law

DIANE P. WOOD
Circuit Judge, U.S. Court of Appeals,
Seventh Circuit
Senior Lecturer in Law,
University of Chicago Law School

FOUNDATION PRESS
2010

THOMSON REUTERS™

© 1975, 1983, 1990, 1997, 2003 FOUNDATION PRESS
© 2010 By THOMSON REUTERS/FOUNDATION PRESS

     195 Broadway, 9th Floor
     New York, NY 10007
     Phone Toll Free 1–877–888–1330
     Fax (212) 367–6799
     foundation–press.com

Printed in the United States of America

ISBN 978–1–59941–249–8

Mat #40555303

PREFACE

In our Preface to the fifth edition of this casebook, published in 2003, we noted the increased willingness of courts, academics, enforcement officials, and the bar to reconsider almost all aspects of competition policy in the United States. The sixth edition is being published early in a new administration, and at a time when much rethinking and more aggressive antitrust enforcement is expected. The search continues for a middle way in antitrust that respects its role in protecting free markets as well as traditional non-economic values but also is sensitive to preserving and encouraging efficiencies and to protecting incentives to innovate. Reconciliation of competing values, in our view, makes debate about antitrust all the more fascinating to teach and to study.

There are several noteworthy changes in the approach of this edition to the study of antitrust.

First, the tradition of this casebook, going back to Milton Handler's earliest treatment of the subject, was to concentrate on Supreme Court caselaw. Although the Supreme Court remains active in the antitrust area, much law is being made in the Courts of Appeals, in federal (and state) guidelines, and in consent orders. Non–Supreme Court materials have always been included in prior editions, but their proportion has continued to increase. More in-depth essays and notes have been provided to elaborate on current issues and trends.

Second, as we recognized in the fifth edition, as the American economy grows increasingly high-tech, difficult issues at the intersection of antitrust and protection of intellectual property frequently arise. These issues are particularly important because products that are the embodiment of ideas, and therefore candidates for intellectual property protection, are found in the most dynamic and fastest growing sectors of the U.S. economy. There has been an increase in the number of antitrust cases that require reconciliation of antitrust policy on the one hand and patent, copyright and trade secret protection on the other. Differences between intellectual property and other forms of property—and potential antitrust consequences—are examined in an expanded part of Chapter 8.

Third, we commented previously that it is no longer enough to address competition questions in the United States without some knowledge of the antitrust systems of other countries. Comparative insights may lead to policy adjustments and are increasingly important in lawyering major transactions. The volume of comparative materials (mostly from the European Union) has been expanded in this edition in the form of extensive notes—due in large part to the special knowledge and experience of our colleague Diane Wood. We realize these materials are no substitute for a full analysis of foreign law, but expect that many teachers will find them useful in the way they expose first principles and offer alternatives to accepted ways of regulating competition in the United States.

This edition of the casebook retains the fundamental approach of its predecessors. It has been written and edited to be used as a teaching tool. The cases are supplemented with materials from the related fields of economics, history, political science and even law. A continuing feature of this edition is a series of notes prepared in collaboration with Professor Steven C. Salop of Georgetown University Law Center. A new feature is an economic appendix, "Basic Economics for Antitrust," authored by Nirit Sandman Eriksson. This appendix will allow teachers to provide basic economic learning for those students with limited backgrounds and greater depth for those who bring substantial economic backgrounds to the antitrust course.

The casebook again includes hypothetical problems, spaced frequently throughout the chapters. A principal virtue of the problem method—optional, of course, for teachers—is the opportunity afforded students to "synthesize" particular assignments in the context of focused, structured discussion. An additional virtue is the opportunity provided to students to sharpen their lawyering skills with respect to concrete issues of fact and law. Many teachers assign two, four or more students in advance to address each problem, asking them to prepare to argue in class as counsel for defendant, plaintiff or, for example, a government intervenor. In an advanced class, which describes antitrust in virtually every law school, the problems demand all the reconciliation of doctrine, and all the policy scrutiny, of more traditional teaching methods.

Finally, we gratefully acknowledge the valuable assistance of the following individuals who participated in the preparation of this edition: Scott Buell, Jesse Creed, David Hutchinson, Joanna Persio, Michael D. Yanovsky, and Robert A. Yu. In addition we would like to express our very special thanks to Hilda Daniels who worked tirelessly and with enormous skill in the preparation of this manuscript.

ROBERT PITOFSKY
HARVEY J. GOLDSCHMID
DIANE P. WOOD

February 2010

EDITORIAL NOTE

Throughout the casebook omissions are generally indicated by ellipses. However, (i) some footnotes from judicial opinions and secondary sources, (ii) repetitive or unnecessary citations in the text of opinions and secondary sources, and (iii) most parallel citations and many full case names have been omitted without ellipses or other warnings to the reader. Parallel citations appear only for main cases, and in a few other instances, where it appeared likely that students would go to the original opinion. Footnotes that have been retained, whether in judicial opinions or secondary sources, are in their original citation form but have been renumbered. Unless the context clearly indicates otherwise or an "Ed." has been inserted, a footnote found in an opinion or secondary source is the work of the indicated court or commentator.

SUMMARY OF CONTENTS

TABLE OF CONTENTS

TABLE OF CASES

Principal cases are in bold type. Non-principal cases are in roman type. References are to Pages.

CASES AND MATERIALS

TRADE REGULATION

CHAPTER 1

THE OBJECTIVES AND ORIGINS OF ANTITRUST LAW

SECTION 1.   THE GOALS OF ANTITRUST POLICY
A.   THE ROLES OF ANTITRUST AND COMPETITION

A Historical Perspective on Antitrust and the Goals of Competition Policy[1]

From the earliest days of the United States a concern has existed about centralized economic power and the dominant firm. But in the post-Civil War period, as historian Richard Hofstadter put it, "bigness had come with such a rush that its momentum seemed irresistible."[2] Also, during this period, anticompetitive group activity—the fixing of prices and division of markets—was taking a heavy toll. The Sherman Act, enacted in 1890, was intended to be the nation's answer to wrongful group conduct and abuse by dominant firms.

The original targets of Sherman Act enforcement were the improper exercise of monopoly power, price fixing, and market divisions among rivals, but over time, other forms of potentially abusive behavior (*e.g.,* involving distribution practices and boycotts) were incorporated into the antitrust system.

Levels of antitrust enforcement have varied significantly since 1890. In the early years, as Section 2C *infra* demonstrates, there were periods of both activity and passivity. During the 1920's, most of the 1930's, and during World War II, antitrust often appeared to be a "faded passion."[3] But after World War II, the atmosphere began to change. Antitrust enforcers, backed by a sympathetic Congress and Supreme Court, introduced the most aggressive enforcement program in the nation's history. During this period, little or no concern was shown about business's claims that excessive antitrust enforcement was interfering with efficiency.

---

1. Part of this note is taken from Pitofsky, Setting the Stage, in Pitofsky (ed.), How the Chicago School Overshot the Mark 3–6 (2008).

2. Hofstadter, What Happened to the Antitrust Movement?, in The Paranoid Style in American Politics and Other Essays 193 (1965).

3. *Id.* at 188.

In the 1970's, a group of economists, economically trained lawyers, and academics (most notably, Robert Bork and Richard Posner[4]) criticized the government's excessive antitrust enforcement program and the lack of concern about efficiency in Supreme Court decisions by the Warren Court. The basic approach of the so-called "Chicago School" was to examine business behavior from a purely economic point of view and to exclude from consideration any political or social values. Richard Posner explained "[there is no] justification for using the antitrust laws to attain goals unrelated or antithetical to efficiency...."[5]

Chicago School– purely economic (Posner)

Those concerned about antitrust excesses were given a large political boost when President Ronald Reagan famously announced "government is the problem" and not the solution. It is unlikely that President Reagan had antitrust in mind, but aggressive antitrust enforcement ended during his administration. Indeed, antitrust enforcement (other than price-fixing cases and challenges to a few very large mergers) virtually disappeared during the 1980's.

Post–Reagan, there occurred a decade or so (mainly during the Clinton Administration) when there was more rigorous enforcement, which included an effort to find a middle ground between the aggressiveness of the 1960's and the minimal enforcement of the 1980's, but that came to an end during the Administration of George W. Bush. What in effect happened during the Bush Administration was a return to the neglect of the 1920's and 1980's. Antitrust enforcement in the Obama Administration appears as if it will be at least as rigorous as in the Clinton years.

Why does any of this enforcement history matter? There is general agreement today in the United States that a competitive, free market system is the best way to allocates resources. As the Supreme Court put it, "the unrestrained interaction of competitive forces will yield the best allocation of our economic resources, the lowest prices, the highest quality and the greatest material progress."[6] Professors F.M. Scherer and David Ross concluded that in political terms, "competition decentralizes and disburses power"; it solves "the economic problem *impersonally*, and not through the personal control of entrepreneurs and bureaucrats"; and it advances "freedom of opportunity."[7] Alternatives to a competitive, free market system, like central planning, were discredited by the dismal results in the Soviet Union, Maoist China, and North Korea.

But there is also a widely shared view that private interests operating in free markets, and unchecked by effective government antitrust rules, will harm efficiency and consumer welfare. Indeed, as Section 1B *infra* demonstrates, there is now broad global acceptance of both competitive markets (often as a spur to economic growth) and antitrust values. In the

---

4. *See, e.g.*, Bork, The Antitrust Paradox (1978); Posner, Antitrust Law (2d ed. 2001).

5. Posner, *supra* note 4, at 2.

6. Northern Pacific Ry. Co. v. U.S., 356 U.S. 1, 4 (1958).

7. Scherer & Ross, Industrial Market Structure and Economic Performance 18–19 (3d ed. 1990).

monopoly area, for example, it is believed that the evils of dominance include "excessive price, misallocation of resources, and loss of dynamic efficiency."[8]

Set forth below are a series of major statements about antitrust values largely from the Supreme Court. At this early stage of the course, think about those values and carefully note the tensions between various values (*e.g.,* between efficiency and the protection of small business) and the inconsistencies among the various articulations.

NOTES

1.   Northern Pacific Railway Co. v. United States, 356 U.S. 1, 4–5, 78 S.Ct. 514, 517–18, 2 L.Ed.2d 545, 549 (1958). "The Sherman Act was designed to be a comprehensive charter of economic liberty aimed at preserving free and unfettered competition as the rule of trade. It rests on the premise that the unrestrained interaction of competitive forces will yield the best allocation of our economic resources, the lowest prices, the highest quality and the greatest material progress, while at the same time providing an environment conducive to the preservation of our democratic political and social institutions." (Black, J.)

2.   Brown Shoe Co. v. United States, 370 U.S. 294, 344, 82 S.Ct. 1502, 1534, 8 L.Ed.2d 510, 547 (1962). ". . . [W]e cannot fail to recognize Congress' desire to promote competition through the protection of viable, small, locally owned businesses. Congress appreciated that occasional higher costs and prices might result from the maintenance of fragmented industries and markets. It resolved these competing considerations in favor of decentralization. We must give effect to that decision." (Warren, C.J.)

3.   United States v. Aluminum Co. of America, 148 F.2d 416, 427 (2d Cir. 1945). "[I]t is no excuse for 'monopolizing' a market that the monopoly has not been used to extract from the consumer more than a 'fair' profit. The Act has wider purposes. Indeed, even though we disregarded all but economic considerations, it would by no means follow that such concentration of producing power is to be desired, when it has not been used extortionately. Many people believe that possession of unchallenged economic power deadens initiative, discourages thrift and depresses energy; that immunity from competition is a narcotic, and rivalry is a stimulant, to industrial progress; that the spur of constant stress is necessary to counteract an inevitable disposition to let well enough alone. Such people believe that competitors, versed in the craft as no consumer can be, will be quick to detect opportunities for saving and new shifts in production, and be eager to profit by them. In any event the mere fact that a producer, having command of the domestic market, has not been able to make more than a 'fair' profit, is no evidence that a 'fair' profit could not have been made at lower prices. True, it might have been thought adequate to condemn only those monopolies which could not show that they had exercised the highest possible ingenuity, had adopted every possible economy, had anticipated every conceivable improvement, stimulated every possible demand. No doubt, that would be one way of dealing with the matter, although it would imply constant scrutiny and constant supervision, such as courts are unable

---

8.   *See* Goldschmid, Comment on . . . the Dominant Firm, in Pitofsky, *supra* note 1, at 125.

to provide. Be that as it may, that was not the way that Congress chose; it did not condone 'good trusts' and condemn 'bad' ones; it forbad all. Moreover, in so doing it was not necessarily actuated by economic motives alone. It is possible, because of its indirect social or moral effect, to prefer a system of small producers, each dependent for his success upon his own skill and character, to one in which the great mass of those engaged must accept the direction of a few." (L. Hand, J.)

4. National Society of Professional Engineers v. United States, 435 U.S. 679, 688, 695, 98 S.Ct. 1355, 1363, 1367, 55 L.Ed.2d 637, 648, 652 (1978). "Congress . . . did not intend the text of the Sherman Act to delineate the full meaning of the statute or its application in concrete situations. The legislative history makes it perfectly clear that it expected the courts to give shape to the statute's broad mandate by drawing on common-law tradition. The Rule of Reason, with its origins in common-law precedents long antedating the Sherman Act, has served that purpose. It has been used to give the Act both flexibility and definition, and its central principle of antitrust analysis has remained constant. Contrary to its name, the Rule does not open the field of antitrust inquiry to any argument in favor of a challenged restraint that may fall within the realm of reason. Instead . . . it focuses directly on the challenged restraint's impact on competitive conditions.

"The Sherman Act reflects a legislative judgment that ultimately competition will not only produce lower prices, but also better goods and services. . . . The assumption that competition is the best method of allocating resources in a free market recognizes that all elements of a bargain—quality, service, safety, and durability—and not just the immediate cost, are favorably affected by the free opportunity to select among alternative offers. Even assuming occasional exceptions to the presumed consequences of competition, the statutory policy precludes inquiry into the question whether competition is good or bad." (Stevens, J.)

5. Berkey Photo, Inc. v. Eastman Kodak Co., 603 F.2d 263, 273 (2d Cir. 1979), cert. denied, 444 U.S. 1093, 100 S.Ct. 1061, 62 L.Ed.2d 783 (1980). "Because, like all power, it is laden with the possibility of abuse; because it encourages sloth rather than the active quest for excellence; and because it tends to damage the very fabric of our economy and our society, monopoly power is 'inherently evil. . . .' [W]hile proclaiming vigorously that monopoly power is the evil at which § 2 is aimed, courts have declined to take what would have appeared to be the next logical step—declaring monopolies unlawful *per se* unless specifically authorized by law. . . .

"The conundrum was indicated in characteristically striking prose by Judge Hand, who was not able to resolve it. Having stated that Congress 'did not condone' 'good trusts' and condemn 'bad' ones; it forbad all,'" he declared with equal force, 'The successful competitor, having been urged to compete, must not be turned upon when he wins.' Hand, therefore, told us that it would be inherently unfair to condemn success when the Sherman Act itself mandates competition. Such a wooden rule, it was feared, might also deprive the leading firm in an industry of the incentive to exert its best efforts. Further success would yield not rewards but legal castigation. The antitrust laws would thus compel the very sloth they were intended to prevent. We must always be mindful lest the Sherman Act be invoked perversely in favor of those who seek protection against the rigors of competition." (Kaufman, C.J.)

6. Eastman Kodak Co. v. Image Technical Services, Inc., 504 U.S. 451, 482–483, 112 S.Ct. 2072, 2090–2091, 119 L.Ed.2d 265, 294 (1992). "The second element of a § 2 claim is the use of monopoly power 'to foreclose competition, to gain a competitive advantage, or to destroy a competitor. . . .' [R]espondents have present-ed evidence that Kodak took exclusionary action to maintain its parts monopoly and

used its control over parts to strengthen its monopoly share of the Kodak service market. Liability turns, then, on whether 'valid business reasons' can explain Kodak's actions." (Blackmun, J.)

7. Verizon Communications v. Law Offices of Curtis V. Trinko, 540 U.S. 398, 414, 124 S.Ct. 872, 882, 157 L.Ed.2d 823, 840 (2004).

"Under the best of circumstances, applying the requirements of § 2 'can be difficult' because 'the means of illicit exclusion, like the means of legitimate competition, are myriad.'.... The cost of false positives counsels against an undue expansion of § 2 liability." (Scalia, J.)

B. THE SHERMAN ACT AND COMPARATIVE LEGISLATION

Sherman Act[9]

Act of July 2, 1890, ch. 647, 26 Stat. 209.

An Act To Protect Trade and Commerce Against Unlawful Restraints and Monopolies

Section 1. Every contract, combination in the form of trust or otherwise, or conspiracy, in restraint of trade or commerce among the several States, or with foreign nations, is hereby declared to be illegal. Every person who shall make any contract or engage in any combination or conspiracy hereby declared to be illegal shall be deemed guilty of a felony, and, on conviction thereof, shall be punished by fine not exceeding $100,000,000 if a corporation, or, if any other person, $1,000,000[10] or by imprisonment not exceeding ten years, or by both said punishments, in the discretion of the court.

Section 2. Every person who shall monopolize, or attempt to monopolize, or combine or conspire with any other person or persons, to monopolize any part of the trade or commerce among the several States, or with foreign nations, shall be deemed guilty of a felony, and, on conviction thereof, shall be punished by fine not exceeding $100,000,000 if a corporation, or, if any other person,

---

9. The Sherman Act, as amended, appears at 15 U.S.C. §§ 1–7. Only the first two sections are set out above.

10. The ceiling on fines was set at $5,000 in 1890, increased to $50,000 in 1955, and then raised three times in more recent years. The current figures were enacted in 2004. Even greater fines than are available under the Sherman Act may be imposed under the Criminal Fines Improvements Act of 1987, which is applicable to federal felonies, 18 U.S.C. § 3571. The Criminal Fines Improvements Act and private treble damage actions under the Sherman Act are discussed in Chapter 2 *infra*. The maximum term of imprisonment, originally set at one year in 1890, was increased to three years in 1974, and the status of an offense was changed from misdemeanor to felony. In 2004, in the Antitrust Criminal Penalty Enforcement and Reform Act, the current maximum of ten years was established.

$1,000,000, or by imprisonment not exceeding ten years, or by both said punishments, in the discretion of the court.

COMPARATIVE NOTE ON COMPETITION LAW IN OTHER NATIONS AND REGIONS

Although there was a time when antitrust, or competition law as it is more commonly called in international circles, was regarded as a peculiarity of United States legislation, those days are long since past. Today, more than one hundred[11] countries have competition laws, and more are considering enacting such laws every year. In fact, the popularity of competition law has become so great that some scholars and public officials have called for some kind of world competition code to be negotiated under the auspices of the World Trade Organization, to ensure that companies in all countries operate under the same set of rules and to guard against the possibility that private restraints of trade might undo the great strides in global trade liberalization that have taken place during the sixty-five years since World War II.[12] Although the momentum to launch such an ambitious undertaking seems to have faded, those efforts have been replaced with concrete steps to improve international coordination of competition law enforcement. The possibility of the eventual international harmonization of competition law and the current trend toward more effective cooperation both put a premium on understanding how competition law is viewed in other countries and how it differs from or is similar to the law in the United States.

The reasons why competition laws exist vary considerably, as does the vigor with which those laws are enforced. Something as fundamental as the purpose of competition law is still a matter of debate. Over the years, a consensus has developed in the United States that the purpose of the antitrust laws is principally (if not exclusively) to promote consumer welfare, by banning economically inefficient transactions and practices. Other countries, however, without excluding consumer welfare as a goal, also take additional considerations into account, such as the development of the national economy, expansion of opportunities for cross-border trade, or protection of small and medium-sized enterprises. Some countries add a broader "public interest" dimension to antitrust enforcement: South Africa, for example, specifically includes among the purposes of its antitrust law the promotion of employment and the increase of the ownership stakes of historically disadvantaged persons.

Considering the different purposes reflected in these different laws, it is not surprising that this diverse set of legal regimes might not always work harmoniously together. As noted above, one solution to that problem could be some kind of binding agreement, perhaps among the parties to the World Trade Organization, but that is something at this point that is only on the distant horizon. For now, the trend is toward "soft" harmonization of national and regional laws: discussion of specific cases, sharing of expertise, and mutual education about the ways antitrust laws operate, under the auspices of a variety of global fora. The work of groups such as the multilateral International Competition Network, or the Global Competition Forum sponsored by the Organisation for Economic Co-operation and Development, has already begun to create a solid foundation for effective international enforce-

---

11. *See* speech by Angel Gurria, OECD Secretary–General at the 100th Meeting of the Competition Committee. OECD Conference Centre, Feb. 20, 2008.

12. Fox, Competition Law and the Agenda for the WTO: Forging the Links of Competition and Trade, 4 Pacific Rim Law & Policy J. 1 (1995); Petersmann, Proposals for Negotiating International Competition Rules in the GATT–WTO World Trade and Legal System, 49 Aussenwirtschaft 231 (1994).

ment of competition law. In time, it is possible that these efforts will lead to some kind of formal harmonization.

Before World War II, competition laws were quite rare. Aside from the United States, Canada had a narrow law that was enacted in 1889, which established such stringent requirements for liability it was rarely invoked. Isolated instances of anti-cartel rules appeared elsewhere, but again they had little real impact. For example, the 1917 Mexican Constitution and the 1934 Mexican Monopolies Law proscribed monopolies and restraints of trade, with exceptions for labor unions, certain export cartels, intellectual property, and specified strategic activities reserved to the government.[13] Some of the Scandinavian countries also had similar laws. But it is fair to say that competition law as a global phenomenon was born in the years following World War II.

In some cases, the United States simply imposed antitrust laws on the vanquished nations. Thus, the occupational authorities put competition laws into effect in both Germany and Japan. However, interest in competition law was growing more generally. The draft Charter for an International Trade Organization (known as the Havana Charter) included an entire chapter on restrictive business practices that would have required each member country to take steps to prevent such practices when they would have harmful effects on international trade.[14] The European Coal and Steel Treaty of 1952 included competition provisions for the six-nation community it created.[15] In the United Kingdom, in sharp contrast to the rather pro-cartel attitude that had prevailed prior to the war, the post-war government accepted the proposition that monopolies and restrictive practices could have a deleterious effect on output and employment, and it thus sponsored the Monopolies and Restrictive Practices (Inquiry and Control) Act of 1948.[16] Norway enacted its Price Act on June 26, 1953, which established a system of control and supervision of restrictive business practices and dominant enterprises. These examples indicate that competition law was gaining a foothold even in countries that were not in the unusual position of post-war Germany and Japan.

Why this was so is harder to explain. One important factor, which led to the inclusion of the provisions relating to restrictive business practices in the unsuccessful Havana Charter mentioned above, was a general consensus among the founding members of the General Agreement on Tariffs and Trade (the "GATT") that the pre-war cartels in Germany and Japan had contributed to the strength of the fascist or monarchist systems of government. Second, the rampant inflation after the war experienced by so many countries naturally led to a strong interest in any economic policy that focused on lowering prices. Third, the performance of the American economy excited admiration. Antitrust was in its heyday in the United States; the U.S. government was bringing actions to bring down numerous global cartels,[17] and other countries could not help but be impressed by the competitive vigor of the U.S. market.

---

13. Constitution of Mexico, art. 28; Ley Organica del Articulo 28 Constitucional en Material de Monopolios, D.O. Aug. 31, 1934; *see generally* Report of the Task Force of the ABA Section of Antitrust Law on the Competition Dimension of NAFTA 47 (1994).

14. Havana Charter for an International Trade Organization, Ch. V, March 24, 1948, U.S. Dept. of State Publ. No. 3206, Commercial Policy Series 114 (Sept. 1948).

15. Treaty Establishing the European Coal and Steel Community, Articles 65–66, April 18, 1951, 261 UNTS 140.

16. *See generally* Whish, Competition Law (6th ed. 2008).

17. *See, e.g.*, United States v. General Electric Co., 82 F. Supp. 753 (D.N.J.1949) (*Incandescent Lamp*); United States v. National Lead Co., 332 U.S. 319 (1947); Timken Roller

Without a doubt, the most important emulator of American-style antitrust laws proved to be the European Community. The Community itself is now part of the broader European Union, which was inaugurated when the Maastricht Treaty on European Union established a framework for closer cooperation of the Member States of the European Community.[18] In addition, as of November 4, 2009, the Treaty of Lisbon received the approval of member countries of the EU and is thus ready to take effect. Its focus is on institutional reforms designed to make the EU work more effectively; it thus amends the existing treaties without replacing them. For example, the Lisbon Treaty strengthens the role of the European Parliament; it authorizes the Council (*see infra*) to operate by qualified majority in more areas; it introduces a new Charter of Fundamental Rights into the primary law of Europe; and it strengthens the institutions responsible for a unified European foreign policy.

It was the Maastricht Treaty that renamed the European Community the "European Union" and outlined what are now known as the three pillars of the EU: European Community, Common Foreign and Security Policy, and Justice and Home Affairs. The first pillar is responsible for economic and monetary union and relies on a vast body of competition law as one of the primary tools to integrate European markets. Recognizing that the EC is currently only one of the three "pillars" of the EU, we will generally use the term European Union (EU); occasionally, however, we will call it European Community (EC) to refer to historical facts or to emphasize the economic aspect of the cooperation.

In order to understand the nature of EC competition law, it is helpful to look at the broad outline of the European Union's system of governance. There are now five principal institutions in the Union: a European Parliament, a Council, a Commission, a Court of Justice, and a Court of Auditors. Most important is the Council, or the Council of Ministers as it is often called. The Council, according to Article 203 (Article 146 in the original treaty, but we will normally use the numbering inaugurated by the Treaty of Amsterdam effective May 1, 1999) of the Treaty,[19] is composed of ministers representing each Member State.[20] If the

---

Bearing Co. v. United States, 341 U.S. 593 (1951); United States v. United States Alkali Export Ass'n, 86 F. Supp. 59 (S.D.N.Y.1949); United States v. Standard Oil (N.J.), Civ. No. 86–27 (S.D.N.Y.1953) (complaint); 1963 Trade Cas. (CCH) ¶ 70,819 (consent judgt), 1969 Trade Cas. (CCH) ¶¶ 72, 742, 72,743 (superseding consent judgts).

18.   Treaty on European Union, signed at Maastricht on February 7, 1992. Published by the EC Office for Official Publications; reprinted in part at CCH Common Market Law Rept. [1992] 1 CMLR 719, as amended by the Treaty of Amsterdam, October 2, 1997, entered into force on May 1, 1999.

19.   The European Economic Community was established by the Rome Treaty in 1957. The Rome Treaty has been amended several times since then, and the subsequent amendments, along with the initial text, have now been consolidated into a continuously updated version. The current version of the Rome Treaty is referred to as the "Treaty Establishing the European Community." Following a major amendment by the 1997 Treaty of Amsterdam, the previously used numbering of treaty provisions has been changed as well. Because the new numbers have been in use for more than a decade, we will refer to them, using brackets if the original document used the old numbers; a table showing the changes is furnished in the Treaty of Amsterdam.

20.   *See* Treaty of Rome, 298 UNTS 11, as amended. There are now twenty-seven Member States of the European Union: Austria, Belgium, Bulgaria, Cyprus, Czech Republic, Denmark, Estonia, Finland, France, Germany, Greece, Hungary, Ireland, Italy, Latvia, Lithuania, Luxembourg, Malta, the Netherlands, Poland, Portugal, Romania, Slovakia, Slovenia, Spain, Sweden, and the United Kingdom. Several more countries are on the list of candidates to join: Croatia, Turkey, and the Former Yugoslav Republic of Macedonia. Other countries question before the Council is a general one, it is usually composed of the foreign ministers of the twenty-seven Member States, but if it is a specialized question, such as agriculture or finance, the ministers with the relevant portfolios will be in attendance. So constituted, the Council functions both as a head of state for the Union and as its chief legislative body.

The Commission in Brussels is the Union's administrative and executive arm. It now has 27 members (one from each Member State). The Commissioners, according to Article 213 of the Treaty of Rome, are chosen on the grounds of general competence and independence. The Commission is divided into various Directorates–General with responsibility for substantive areas within the Union's competence. The Competition Directorate General, or DG Comp, is responsible for competition policy and enforcement.

The European Court of Justice (ECJ) and the Court of First Instance (CFI), both located in Luxembourg, constitute the EU's judicial branch. The ECJ's function is to review formal decisions of the Commission and to review questions of EC law referred to it by the national courts of the Member States. Since 1988, the ECJ has been assisted by the Court of First Instance, which was established by the Council pursuant to authority granted under Article 225 of the Treaty of Rome.[21] The CFI has always had jurisdiction over competition cases. Over time, its authority has expanded. It currently also has jurisdiction to rule in the first instance on (1) all actions for annulment, for failure to act, and for damages brought by natural or legal persons against the Community, (2) actions brought by Member States against the Commission, (3) actions brought by Member States against the Council relating to state aids, (4) actions seeking compensation for damage caused by the Community institutions or their staff, (5) actions based on contracts made by the Communities that expressly give jurisdiction to the CFI, (6) actions relating to Community trademarks, and (7) appeals (limited to points of law) against the decisions of the Civil Service Tribunal. Competition cases typically fall within the first head of jurisdiction. Over time, the CFI's jurisdiction has expanded; indeed, it is worth noting that the Treaty of Amsterdam, which entered into force on May 1, 1999, contemplates that the CFI may eventually have jurisdiction over all categories of cases now within the jurisdiction of the ECJ except for preliminary references from the national courts made pursuant to Article 234 of the Treaty.

Two principles developed by the ECJ make EC competition law of particular importance: first, the Court has held that it has "direct effect" on individuals and companies, which means that violations can be prosecuted without regard to any measures in national law that may apply; second, the Court has developed an equivalent to the Supremacy Clause of the U.S. Constitution, under which EC competition law has primacy over conflicting Member State legislation.

The European Parliament has been gaining power over the years, and will gain even more once the Treaty of Lisbon is fully implemented, but it is still misleading to think of it as the counterpart to the British Parliament, the French Assemblé Nationale, or the German Bundestag. Since 1979, members of the Parliament have been elected directly by European voters. The Parliament sits in Strasbourg. Its most important role now is to review legislative proposals from the Council and the Commission. If it approves such a proposal, the Council may act by qualified

---

waiting in the wings include Albania, Bosnia and Herzegovina, Montenegro, and Serbia. *See* http://ec.europa.eu/enlargement/index_en.htm.

21.   Article 225 was added by the Single European Act of 1987, which amended the Rome Treaty in a number of significant respects.

majority; if it does not, or if it is not consulted, then the Council must act unanimously. The Parliament also has the power to put questions to the Commission, which must be answered, and it reviews the Commission's annual general report.

The last institution, the Court of Auditors, was introduced by the Maastricht Treaty. It is responsible for examining the accounts of all revenue and expenditure of the Union and its various constituent bodies, and reporting to both the Parliament and the Council.

Through this elaborate set of institutions, the EU has developed one of the most sophisticated bodies of competition law in the world. When the original Treaty of Rome, which established the European Economic Community, was signed on March 25, 1957, it included as one of its fundamental goals "the institution of a system ensuring that competition in the common market is not distorted."[22] In the Consolidated Version of the Treaty Establishing the European Community (Doc. 97/C 340/03), the rules on competition policy are set forth in Title VI, chapter 1. Section 1 contains the rules that apply to "undertakings" (the European term for companies or business entities), and section 2 contains the rules that apply to aids granted by States. Article 81 (formerly Article 85–a point not repeated further in this note) of the Treaty prohibits agreements and other concerted practices that have as their object or effect the prevention, restriction, or distortion of competition, unless the particular agreement should be exempted from the prohibition because it may "contribute to improving the production or distribution of goods or to promoting technical or economic progress, while allowing consumers a fair share of the resulting benefit," as long as its detrimental effects do not outweigh those benefits. (You should note that the extent to which the beneficial effects must relate to efficiencies, as contrasted with effects on employment, regional development, or other industrial policy goals, has been debated for years within European circles.) Article 82 (formerly Article 86) of the Treaty prohibits abuses of a dominant position. The current Article 86 seeks to make the competition rules as fully applicable as possible against both state-operated monopolies and private enterprises to which a State has granted special or exclusive rights. Article 87.1 declares that "any aid granted by a Member State or through State resources in any form whatsoever which distorts or threatens to distort competition by favouring certain undertakings or the production of certain goods shall, insofar as it affects trade between Member States, be incompatible with the common market." The Commission is responsible for reviewing state aids, as they are called, and it has the power to require that incompatible aids be discontinued. Finally, a review of EC competition law would not be complete without reference to the Merger Regulation. The Council adopted the initial version of that regulation in 1989, after seventeen years of debate; it established a system of merger regulation at the Community level for large transactions.[23] Transactions falling below the thresholds specified in the Merger Regulation continue to be regulated at the Member State level.

---

22.   298 UNTS 11.

23.   The original regulation was Council Reg. 4064/89, (1990 O.J. (L257) 14). In 2004, it was replaced by Council Reg. (EC) No. 139/2004 (2004 O.J. L24, 29 Jan. 2004). Roughly, it covers transactions that involve a worldwide turnover of 5 billion Euros, which in 2009 dollars represents about $7.5 billion, and for which the intra-community turnover is 250 million Euros for each of at least two participants, as long as more than two-thirds of the intra-Community turnover is not in one and the same Member State, fall within the Merger Regulation. Other "concentrations" are regulated only at the Member State level. This was the Community's effort to establish a "one-stop shopping" system, under which it would be

The Commission has extensive powers that it can bring to bear on companies that violate the EC's competition rules. Until the reorganization plan described below entered into force, on May 1, 2004, the Commission received extensive information from the business community, through "notifications" filed pursuant to Article 81(1) and Council Regulation 17, through complaints, and through more informal letters seeking "negative clearances."[24] Article 81(2) provides that a failure to notify with respect to an agreement that the Commission later concludes is unlawful under Article 81 means that the agreement is void. In addition, the Commission can and does impose significant fines, sometimes in the millions or even billions of dollars, for violations of Articles 81 or 82. So, for example, in March 2007, the Commission fined Microsoft 899 million Euros for failing to comply with its obligation under an earlier Commission decision to offer complete and accurate interoperability information on reasonable and nondiscriminatory terms.[25]

Important changes in the way that European competition law is administered were enacted in 2002. On November 26, 2002, the Member States agreed on fundamental reforms of the primary regulation that had implemented the competition articles of the Treaties for years, Regulation 17. Under the new system, which took effect on May 1, 2004, agreements and other arrangements falling under Article 81(1) no longer need to be notified, and the Commission no longer has the sole power to make individual Article 81(3) exemption decisions. (It continues, however, to be the entity authorized to issue block exemptions, where these seem appropriate.) Instead, Article 81(3) operates automatically to exempt from Article 81(1) all agreements falling within the scope of subpart (3), without the need for any official decision to that effect. This paves the way for the other significant aspect of the new system: decentralized enforcement. With the Commission's monopoly over the conferral of Article 81(3) exemptions abolished, national authorities and courts have substantially greater responsibility for the enforcement of both Article 81 and Article 82. To ensure that all national institutions are applying the EU law in a consistent way, there is now a network of competition authorities (the European Competition Network) through which the Commission and those authorities exchange information, consult with one another, and to the extent possible, cooperate in their enforcement efforts. Finally, there is a rule providing that when an agreement or practice affects trade between member states, the national authorities and courts will be obliged to apply EU law (*i.e.,* Articles 81 and 82), even if they also apply national law (which cannot in any event be inconsistent with EU law).[26] These changes are far-reaching; they were designed to strengthen the ways in which European competition law is enforced.

---

clear which regulator had jurisdiction over the case. On the whole, it has worked well, although occasionally cases arise where the rules for calculating turnover are unclear, or where it may be possible for a Member State to refer the case to Brussels or vice versa.

24.   *See* Council Reg. 17/62. *See generally* Barry Hawk, Common Market and International Antitrust—A Comparative Guide (ed.); Richard Whish, Competition Law, ch. 9 (3d ed. 1993); Leonard Ritter, Francis Rawlinson, and W. David Braun, EC Competition Law—A Practitioner's Guide (Kluwer 1991).

25.   *See* Commission of the European Communities, Report on Competition Policy 2008 (COM (2009) 374 final), at ¶ 23.

26.   For background on these rules, *see* Proposal for a Council Regulation on the implementation of the rules on competition laid down in Articles 81 and 82 of the Treaty and amending Regulations (EEC) No 1017/68, (EEC) No 2988/74, (EEC) No 4056/86 and (EEC) No 3975/87, Brussels, September 17, 2000, COM (2000) 582 final, available on the website of the Competition Directorate. That website is now found at http://ec.europa.eu/competition/index_en.html.

The near-explosive spread of competition laws around the world in more recent years reflects both the success and the strong influence of the European Union's competition laws, both taken alone and in combination with those in the Americas and the Asia–Pacific region. Throughout Central and Eastern Europe, countries eager to join the EU one day have modeled their new competition laws on those of the EU, in recognition of the fact that accession would mean the acceptance of the full *acquis communautaire* of competition laws, regulations, and court precedents. In addition, the administrative approach taken by the EC appeals to countries that do not share the Anglo–American common-law tradition. For that reason, we allude from time to time throughout this casebook to European rules, both by way of comparison and contrast. The extent to which European law follows efficiency principles, the extent to which it continues to reflect its roots by giving primacy to intra-European market integration goals, and the extent to which it displays more concern for equitable market behavior, all provide a useful perspective for our consideration of U.S. law.

As noted above, the central competition provisions of EC law are Articles 81 and 82 of the Rome Treaty. These provisions are set forth below. At this point, please compare Articles 81 and 82 with the provisions of Sections 1 and 2 of the Sherman Act, pp. 5–6 *supra*.

Treaty Establishing the European Community (Rome Treaty)

Article 81

1. The following shall be prohibited as incompatible with the common market: all agreements between undertakings, decisions by associations of undertakings and concerted practices which may affect trade between Member States and which have as their object or effect the prevention, restriction or distortion of competition within the common market, and in particular those which:

(a) directly or indirectly fix purchase or selling prices or any other trading conditions;

(b) limit or control production, markets, technical development, or investment;

(c) share markets or sources of supply;

(d) apply dissimilar conditions to equivalent transactions with other trading parties, thereby placing them at a competitive disadvantage;

(e) make the conclusion of contracts subject to acceptance by the other parties of supplementary obligations which, by their nature or according to commercial usage, have no connection with the subject of such contracts.

2. Any agreements or decisions prohibited pursuant to this article shall be automatically void.

3.   The provisions of paragraph 1 may, however, be declared inapplicable in the case of:

—any agreement or category of agreements between undertakings,

—any decision or category of decisions by associations of undertakings,

—any concerted practice or category of concerted practices,

which contributes to improving the production or distribution of goods or to promoting technical or economic progress, while allowing consumers a fair share of the resulting benefit, and which does not:

(a) impose on the undertakings concerned restrictions which are not indispensable to the attainment of these objectives;

(b) afford such undertakings the possibility of eliminating competition in respect of a substantial part of the products in question.

Article 82

Any abuse by one or more undertakings of a dominant position within the common market or in a substantial part of it shall be prohibited as incompatible with the common market in so far as it may affect trade between Member States.

Such abuse may, in particular, consist in:

(a) directly or indirectly imposing unfair purchase or selling prices or other unfair trading conditions;

(b) limiting production, markets or technical development to the prejudice of consumers;

(c) applying dissimilar conditions to equivalent transactions with other trading parties, thereby placing them at a competitive disadvantage;

(d) making the conclusion of contracts subject to acceptance by the other parties of supplementary obligations which, by their nature or according to commercial usage, have no connection with the subject of such contracts.[27]

QUESTIONS

1. What are the key substantive words of the Sherman Act and the EC Treaty? What, if any, are the differences between the concepts of "restraint of

---

27. Consolidated version of the Rome Treaty (Treaty Establishing the European Community), March 25, 1957, Arts. 81 and 82, 298 UNTS 11, 48.

trade" and "monopolization," on the one hand, and "prevention, restriction, or distortion of competition" and "abuse of a dominant position," on the other?

2.   What does the Sherman Act mean when it refers to "every ... restraint of trade"? Should this be read literally as meaning without exception? Does Article 81(1) really prohibit *all* agreements setting trading conditions, or controlling technical development, or sharing sources of supply? Is there any room in Section 1 of the Sherman Act or Article 81(1) for a "rule of reason"? If Article 81(1) incorporates a rule of reason, what function is left for Article 81(3)?

3.   *Compare* Article 82 *with* Section 2 of the Sherman Act. What, if any, is the relation between a "dominant position" and "monopolization"? Does Article 82 forbid "dominance" as such? Does Sherman Act Section 2 forbid "monopoly" as such? What is the significance of conduct under both systems of law? Must a dominant firm justify its prices, production policies, and discriminatory treatment of customers to the Commission, or to the European courts? How would you determine what an unfair selling price was, or what constituted prejudice to consumers? How can you tell the difference between vigorous competition that might harm other trading partners and abusive practices that place them at a competitive disadvantage?

SECTION 2.   THE HISTORICAL SOURCES OF ANTITRUST, LEGISLATIVE HISTORY, AND EARLY DEVELOPMENTS

A.   THE EARLY LAW ON MONOPOLY AND CONTRACTS IN RESTRAINT OF TRADE

William L. Letwin, The English Common Law Concerning Monopolies[28]

21 U.Chi.L.Rev. 355 (1954).

It has been widely believed that the common law always favored freedom of trade. When English and American judges during the eighteenth and nineteenth centuries decided cases against monopolists, engrossers, or restrainers of trade, they thought they were continuing a tradition that reached back into "time of which no man hath memory." The congressmen who drafted and passed the Sherman Antitrust Law thought they were merely declaring illegal offenses that the common law had always prohibited. Those judges and legislators, like other lawyers, must have known, or at least would not have doubted, that the common law rules on these subjects had changed in the course of time, for it is taken as axiomatic that the common law "grows." But it is not always recognized that the common law can change its direction, and without much warning begin to prohibit practices it had formerly endorsed, or to protect arrangements it had earlier condemned. Lawyers do not so readily see that the common law at any given time reflects the economic theories and policies then favored by

28.   Reprinted by permission of the University of Chicago Law Review, University of Chicago Law School.

the community, and may change as radically as those theories and policies. As a result they have too easily accepted the mistaken view that the attitude of the common law toward freedom of trade was essentially the same throughout its history.

But the common law did not always defend freedom of trade and abhor monopoly. For a long time it did quite the opposite: it supported an economic order in which the individual's getting and spending were closely controlled by kings, parliaments, and mayors, statutes and customs, and his opportunities limited by the exclusive powers of guilds, chartered companies, and patentees. The common law first began to oppose this system of regulation and privilege at the end of the sixteenth century; it did not do so wholeheartedly until the eighteenth century; and by the middle of the nineteenth century, it had again lost its enthusiasm for the task. It would have been surprising if the pattern of development had been different. Changes in the common law are changes in the attitudes of judges and of lawyers; it would have been remarkable if they had persistently opposed monopoly when the rest of the community did not know the word and considered the phenomenon natural or desirable. It would have been strange if lawyers had upheld laissez-faire policies centuries before any statesman or economist had advocated or stated them, and had continued following them long after they had been abandoned or denied by the rest of the community. In fact, English laws governing monopoly and English policies for the economic organization of society changed together, except for minor differences in timing. The English law of monopoly traditionally includes four branches: the law on monopoly proper, whether by patent, charter, or custom; on forestalling, engrossing, and regrating; on contracts in restraint of trade; and on combinations in restraint of trade. These branches, distinct in form and based on more or less independent bodies of precedent, nevertheless show the same development from an active support of monopolies in the earliest period, through active opposition during an interlude of less than two centuries, to the leniency and indifference which characterized them in 1890.

The idea that the common law opposed monopolies from the earliest time onward was invented largely by Sir Edward Coke, who argued that monopoly was forbidden by the Civil Law,[29] and implicitly by Magna Carta as well as by certain statutes of Edward III's reign.[30] But the earliest common-law precedent he could mention was a case that arose during the fourteenth century,[31] and the modern lawyers and historians who follow his authority continue to cite that case as evidence of the ancient antagonism of common law to monopolies.[32] Yet the case gives at least equally good evidence to the contrary. . . .

---

29. *See* Coke's argument in Davenant v. Hurdis, Moore *576, *580 (K.B., 1599).

30. 2 Coke, Institutes 47, 62–63; 3 ibid., at c. 85.

31. Ed. Pecche's Case, Rot.Parl., 50 Edw. 3, No. 33 (1376).

32. 3 Coke Institutes, 47, 181; 11 Co.Rep. *53, *88a, b. Cf. 4 Holdsworth, History 344, n. 6 (1924). The case was cited in the same sense by Laurence Hyde during the parliamentary debate on monopolies in 1601. Tawney and Power, 2 Tudor Economic Documents 275 (1924).

The great movement against the granting of monopolies by letter-patent began only at the end of the sixteenth century, although it was so strongly supported that within less than a hundred years the principle had been established that Parliament alone could grant a monopoly, and that generally even it could not, as the King had regularly done, sell a patent or award it on a whim or as a friendly gesture. By the end of the seventeenth century the royal letter-patent had been converted into a more or less modern version of the patent, justifiable only by a solid contribution to economic development. The process was not, however, moved by coherent opposition to monopoly; it was brought about mainly by disturbances within the monopolistic system administered largely by the guilds, and by objections not to the broad economic effect of monopolies but to the political power which the crown exercised in granting them. . . .

. . . [P]erhaps the greatest single [step] in creating the modern common law on monopolies was Darcy v. Allen, or *The Case of Monopolies*,[33] decided in 1603. . . . [It] laid down the principle that even a royal grant by patent would be invalid if it [created a monopoly]. . . . In short, Darcy's patent was held void on the argument that it violated the right of others to carry on their trade.

. . . The common-law right to work was predicated on an economic system that would protect the established trades from competition, whether from foreign workmen, improperly qualified English workmen, overly aggressive guilds, or domestic monopolists. The right to work was protected by giving each guild a monopoly, and Darcy's grant was condemned not because it was a monopoly and therefore necessarily bad, but because it was a bad monopoly. . . .

. . . The fact is that the monopolistic powers of guilds, which Coke insisted repeatedly were always void at common law, had really been supported by law. That support first began to be withdrawn in the beginning of the seventeenth century, under the pressure of, among other things, Coke's powerful but inaccurate polemics.

There is no doubt that the series of cases at the turn of the seventeenth century radically changed the attitude of the common law toward monopolies. But it must be borne in mind that this change was also a consequence of the decay of the monopolistic system from within. . . . Darcy v. Allen was not the action of a solitary champion bravely contesting the monopoly of a powerful courtier; it has been shown instead that Allen was supported in the case by the Mayor and Aldermen of London, who, regarding Darcy's patent as an attack on all the trades and privileges of the City, "comforted and animated [Allen] to continue his selling of cards" and promised to pay the costs of any legal action that might follow. . . .

Moreover, the mercantilist system of private and corporate monopolies, though very much weakened by 1600, was still too widespread to be

---

33. 11 Co.Rep. *84, Moore *671 (K.B., 1599), Noy *173. These reports are collated in Gordon, Monopolies by Patents 193–232 (1897).

destroyed by the application of common-law remedies in specific cases. It was seriously limited, and in the end destroyed, by legislation. The first important law contributing to that result was the Statute of Monopolies of 1624, which, however, has a deceptive ring. For though it was certainly directed against monopolies, it was based not on a preference for competition, but on constitutional objections to the power which the Crown presumed in granting monopolies and to the arbitrary reasons for which it had granted them. Parliament did not at this period oppose monopolies in themselves. . . . [In] the final irony in the case of Darcy v. Allen: only a few years after Darcy's monopoly of playing cards was judged void at common law, the same monopoly was given, under authority of the Statute of Monopolies, to the Company of Card Makers.

The Statute of Monopolies soon put an end to the arbitrary granting of private monopolies. But it was not intended to abolish customary monopoly privileges of corporations. Cities and boroughs, guilds, and chartered trading companies continued to exercise their monopoly powers to exclude strangers from various trades. The common law continued to protect them, though with lessening fervor as the influence of economic liberalism grew, and some of these monopolistic controls were finally abolished only by legislation in the nineteenth century.

Throughout these early monopoly cases the complaint is made that practices are objectionable because they tend to raise prices. But even this complaint did not arise from opposition to monopolies. It did not mean that the common law early in the seventeenth century favored competition or endorsed the determination of prices by the free play of the market. The common law favored "low" prices rather than free prices, and accepted as a matter of course that all important prices would be set by political or corporate authorities. The complaint meant only that Englishmen objected to private efforts to raise prices, and that they readily attributed a rise in prices to the evil machinations of profiteers. . . .

The body of law concerning these crimes has been thought to be an integral part of the law on monopolies because forestalling and the associated offenses seem at first sight to be older names for the modern monopolistic tactic known as "cornering the market. . . ." The basic legal difference is that the monopolist had a legal warrant for his activity, whereas the forestaller was justified by no custom, grant, or statute whatsoever. . . . [T]he first statute prohibiting it defined forestallers as those "that buy anything before the due hour, or that pass out of the town to meet such things as come to the market. . . ."

The major objective of laws against forestalling was to keep food prices low. Such laws fit very neatly into the more general price-fixing program administered by medieval and, later, mercantilist governments. Local authorities of manors, cities, and guilds had customary rights to control food prices; kings issued proclamations and parliaments passed statutes for the same end; all these are implicitly confirmed in a statute of 1533 which gave certain members of the Privy Council as well the right to set "reasonable prices" of "cheese, butter, capons, hens, chickens, and other victuals necessary for man's sustenance."[34] The work of surveillance would be much easier if all sales were made publicly in the market, and so forestalling and engrossing, means of evading the market, were seen as attempts to evade price-controls.

But to maintain low food prices was not the sole objective of the laws against forestalling. Just as monopolies by patent were attacked by those who feared to lose their own monopoly powers, so forestalling was abhorred not only by a public which hated high prices but also by those who saw in it an infringement of their privileges as owners of markets. Rights to hold markets were granted or confirmed by the Crown, and established local but powerful monopolies. What was given was not the mere right to hold a market, but an exclusive right....

The objectives of statesmen and the interest of owners of markets coincided with the prejudices of the public. They considered forestalling, engrossing, and regrating the typical tricks of middlemen and speculators, and were convinced that merchants who used such tactics were parasites profiting by the distress of others.... The practices described show no sign of being, properly speaking, monopolistic; they appear on the contrary to have been acts of speculation, arbitrage, or wholesaling; but most men continued to identify the two phenomena until the new economic theory in the eighteenth century taught a few of them at least ... that the community had as much to gain as the merchant from free trade.

The development of laissez-faire economic theory accounted for the abolition of the laws against forestalling.... Parliament in 1844 passed a law repealing all the remaining statutes against it, and utterly abolishing the common-law crimes of forestalling, engrossing, and regrating.

Clearly, then, the laws against forestalling and engrossing, which some have tried to identify as a fount of modern antitrust law, did not have the required character. They were of narrow scope, applying almost exclusively to trade in foodstuffs; they were part of a program to regulate all economic activities; like the common law against monopolies by patent, they were supported by monopolists—in this case, the owners of markets—who found them useful protection; and they were finally repealed by the supporters of free trade and in the name of free trade....

By 1890, what there had been of English common law against monopolies had become quite weak. The common law against monopoly proper had been superseded by the Statute of Monopolies. The common law against forestalling had been abolished by the statute of 1844. The common law against combinations of workmen and of masters had been overruled by the Trade Union Acts. The common law against contracts and combinations in restraint of trade alone remained in force....

---

34.   25 Hen. VIII, c. 2, § 1 (1533).

Anonymous—"Dyer's Case"

Y.B., 2 Hen. V, vol. 5, pl. 26 (1415).

A writ of debt was brought on an obligation by one John Dyer wherein the defendant alleged, by Lod, that, according to a certain indenture which he put forth and on condition that the defendant should not use his art of a dyer's craft within the town where the plaintiff, etc. for a certain time, viz., for half a year, the obligation was to lose its force; and he said that he did not use his art of a dyer's craft within the time limited, which matter he offered to prove and demanded judgment whether the action, etc.

HULL. To my mind you might have demurred on him since the obligation is void because the condition is against the common law, and per Dieu, if the plaintiff were here, he should go to prison till he paid a fine to the king.[35]

Anonymous—"The Schoolmaster Case"

Court of Common Pleas, Hilary Term, 1410.
Y.B., 11 Hen. IV, f. 47, pl. 21.

Two masters of a grammar school at Gloucester brought a writ of trespass against another master, and counted that the defendant had started a school in the same town, so that whereas the plaintiffs had formerly received 40*d.* or two shillings a quarter from each child, now they got only 12*d.*, to their damage, & c.

TILDESLEY. His writ is worthless.

SKRENE. It is a good action on the case, and the plaintiffs have shown well enough how they are damaged; wherefore, & c.

HANKFORD, J. There may be damnum absque injuria. As if I have a mill, and my neighbor builds another mill, whereby the profit of mine is diminished, I shall have no action against him; still I am damaged, quod Thirning, C.J., concessit, and said that the instruction of children is a spiritual matter; and if one retains a master in his house to teach his children, it is a damage to the common master of the town, yet, I think, he will have no action.

SKRENE. The masters of Paul's claim that there shall be no other masters in all London except themselves.

HORTON demurred because the action was not maintainable.

HILL, J. There is no ground to maintain this action, since the plaintiffs have no estate, but a ministry for the time; and though another equally

---

35. Ed. *See* Blake, Employee Agreements Not to Compete, 73 Harv.L.Rev. 625, 632–37 (1960). Consider the plight of an apprentice or journeyman, bound by a covenant not to exercise the only craft for which he had been trained. On the possibility of migration to other towns, consider the conditions of travel during this period, Day, History of Commerce 54–55 (4th ed. 1938), and the position of strangers. On the legislative prohibition of guild exactions of covenants not to engage in trade from apprentices or journeymen, *see* 28 Hen. VIII, c. 5 (1536).

competent with the plaintiffs comes to teach the children, this is a virtuous and charitable thing, and an ease to the people, for which he cannot be punished by our law.

SKRENE. If a market is erected to the nuisance of my market I shall have an assize of nuisance; and in a common case, if those coming to my market be disturbed or beaten, whereby I lose my toll, I shall have a good action on my case; so here.

HANKFORD, J. Not the same case, because in the case put you have a freehold and inheritance in the market; but here the plaintiffs have no estate in the schoolmastership, & c., but for an uncertain time, and it would be against reason for a master to be hindered from keeping school where he pleases, unless where a university was incorporated or a school founded in ancient times.

And the opinion of the court was that the writ would not lie. Wherefore it was awarded that they should take nothing, & c.

The Case of Monopolies

Court of King's Bench, 1602.
11 Coke 84, 77 Eng.Rep. 1260.[36]

Edward Darcy, Esq., a groom of the Privy Chamber to Queen Elizabeth, brought an action on the case against T. Allein, Haberdasher of London, and declared that Queen Elizabeth by her letters patent in 30 Eliz. granted to Ralph Bowes power to buy playing cards overseas and import them, he to enjoy the whole trade, and that Bowes and none other should have the making of playing cards within the realm for twelve years. In 40 Eliz., the grant was extended for 21 years after the end of the former term, he rendering to the Queen 100 marks per annum; and further declared that the defendant, knowing of plaintiff's grant, made and sold cards, to the plaintiff's damage, 200 pounds, whereby the plaintiff was unable to pay his farm to the crown. Defendant, except as to one half gross, pleaded not guilty and as to that pleaded that he is a member of the society of Haberdashers of London, and that by custom all members of that society could freely sell all manner of goods. The plaintiff demurred.

DYER and CROKE argued against the patent that the Queen could not grant a patent to restrain any from their usual trades and that no occupation can be put in monopoly but only such a thing as is newly invented.

FULLER: The Judges in the exposition of the Kings Letters Patents are to be guided not by the precise words of the Patents, but by the Laws of the Realm.

Before, cards were and ought to be sold at reasonable prices, or else be punished as inhauncers of merchandize, now Darcy may sell cards for his

---

36. Abridged from the combined reports in Gordon, Monopolies by Patents 199–232 (1897).

most advantage, as he doth, viz., one gross for 35*s.* where the Haberdashers have offered to sell better for 20*s.* the gross; this is malum in se against the Common Law that cannot be dispensed with by patent as malum prohibitum may be.

Before a person might have reaped the fruits of his skill; now Darcy hath devised a means to take away a man's skill from him, which was never heard of before.

The condition in the *Dyer's* Case, not to use his trade for half a year in the town of Dale, was void; much more so this Patent, restraining men from their trade 21 years throughout the whole realm.

There is no wrong done to the plaintiff by the defendant's selling cards cheaper than the Plaintiff would, though he received losse, and therefore no cause of action lies, as in the *Schoolmaster's* Case. When a miller loses some of his trade to a new mill, this is no wrong though it be damage, and therefore no cause of action.

I.S. hath a pasture where the tenants sometimes put their cattle; another person makes a good pasture where the tenants have cattle cheaper to the damage of I.S. & yet no cause of action, being neither wrong to I.S. nor hurt to the commonwealth.

The Attorney General contra argued that the King can prohibit or license mala prohibita and can restrain matters of pleasure and it is for the public good although it may involve damage to private persons.

Judgment.

Resolved by Popham Chief Justice & per totam curiam that the grant to the plaintiff of the sole making of cards within the realm was utterly void and that for two reasons: 1. That it is a monopoly and against the common law. 2. That it is against divers acts of Parliament. Against the common law for four reasons:

1. All trades which prevent idleness and keep men in labour are profitable to the commonwealth and therefore the grant to the plaintiff to have the sole making is against the common law and the benefit and liberty of the subject.

2. Any monopoly is not only a damage to those that exercise the same trade but also to others, for the end of all these monopolies is the private gain of the patentees. There are three inseparable incidents to every monopoly: (1) That the price will be raised. (2) After the monopoly grant, the commodity is not so good as it was before. (3) It tends to the impoverishment of divers artificers and others who before by their labour had maintained themselves and their families, who now will of necessity be constrained to live in idleness and beggary.

3. The Queen was deceived in her grant.

4. This grant is primae impressionis, for no such was ever seen to pass by letters patent before, and therefore it is a dangerous innovation.

Also such charter of monopoly, against the freedom of trade and traffic, is against divers acts of Parliament, sc. 9 E. 3 c. 1 & 2, which for the advancement of the freedom of trade and traffic extends to all things vendible, notwithstanding any charter to the contrary or usage or custom, which charters are adjudged to be of no force and effect.

Also, the licence to have the sole importation and merchandizing is utterly against law, since Parliament pro bono publico has prohibited the importation of foreign manufactures to the intent that subjects might apply themselves to the making of the said manufactures, and for a private gain to grant the sole importation is a monopoly against the common law, for this is not to maintain the card-makers but to take away their trade, and that without any reason.

And admitting that such grant was valid, yet the plaintiff cannot maintain an action on the case against those who import any foreign goods, but the remedy which the act of 3 Eliz. 4 gives ought to be pursued.[37] And judgment was given, quod querens nihil caperet per billam.[38]

NOTE

The Statute of Monopolies, 21 Jac. I, ch. 3 (1623–34), provided that, with certain exceptions—including one for patents and grants of privileges for "true inventors"—"all monopolies ... are and shall be utterly void ..." unless granted or confirmed by an act of Parliament.

---

37. *I.e.*, forfeiture of the goods, imported in breach of the statute, half to the king, the other half to him who will first seize them for the king.

38. "Allein was not an independent, unsupported protagonist on behalf of the liberty of the subject to pursue lawful and established trades, but rather a freeman of the City actively instigated to resistance to the monopolist by the most influential authorities of the City of London." Davies, Further Light on the Case of Monopolies, 48 L.Q.Rev. 394, 395 (1932).

The practice of granting special monopoly privileges as a means of revenue to the crown or as a reward for services "reached its climax while Elizabeth was in power. A list of her grants includes patents giving the sole rights to sell or manufacture currants, salt, iron, powder, cards, calf-skins, fells, pouldavies, ox-shin bones, train-oil, lists of cloth, potashes, aniseed, vinegar, sea-coals, steel, aquavitae, brushes, pots, saltpetre, bottles, lead, accidences, oil, calamine-stone, oil-of-blubber, glasses, paper, starch, tin, sulphur, new drapery, dried pilchards, beer, horn, leather, Irish yarn, importation of Spanish wool, and transportation of iron-ordinance." Miller, The Case of the Monopolies, 6 Mich.L.Rev. 1, 2 (1907).

Prior to 1601, grants of monopoly had been sustained in Privy Council and Star Chamber as a valid expression of the royal prerogative. In 1601, however, popular opposition to these privileges forced Elizabeth to concede that in the future the validity of such grants was to be determined according to the common law. *See* 4 Holdsworth, History of English Law 346 (1924). For accounts of the Tudor patents and monopolies, *see* Price, English Patents of Monopoly (1906); 3 Lipson, Economic History of England 352–86 (6th ed. 1935); Thorelli, Federal Antitrust Policy 20 (1954); Letwin, English Common Law Concerning Monopolies, 21 U.Chi.L.Rev. 355 (1954); Churchill, Monopolies, 41 L.Q.Rev. 275 (1925); Hulme, Early History of the English Patent System, in 3 Select Essays in Anglo–American Legal History 117–47 (1909).

Mitchel v. Reynolds

1 P.Wms. 181, 24 Eng.Rep. 347 (K.B.1711).

■ PARKER, C.J. . . .

Debt upon a bond. The condition recited that the defendant had assigned to the plaintiff a bakehouse in the parish of St. Andrews Holborn for the term of five years, and that if he did not exercise the trade of baker within that parish during that term, or if he did and paid fifty pounds to the plaintiff within three days after proof thereof, the obligation was to be void. Defendant pleaded that he was a baker by trade and the obligation was void in law. Plaintiff demurred. *Held,* for plaintiff. The general question upon this record is, whether this bond being made in restraint of trade, be good? The resolutions of the books seeming to disagree, I will endeavor to reconcile the jarring opinions. The cases are either of involuntary contracts, or voluntary restraints by agreement of the parties. Voluntary restraints are general or particular, as to places or persons. General restraints are all void. Particular restraints are either without consideration, all of which are void, or upon a good and adequate consideration so as to make it a proper and useful contract. A man may, upon a valuable consideration, by his own consent, and for his own profit, give over his trade, and part with it to another in a particular place. All the books, when carefully examined, seem to concur in the distinctions of restraints general and particular, and with or without consideration, which stand upon very good foundation. *Volenti non fit injuria.* Some observations which may be useful in understanding these cases are: First, that to obtain the sole exercise of any known trade throughout England is a complete monopoly, and against the policy of the law. Secondly, that when restrained to particular places or persons, the same is not a monopoly. Thirdly, that since these restraints may be by custom, and custom must have a good foundation, the thing is not absolutely and in itself unlawful. Fourthly, that it is lawful upon good consideration for a man to part with his trade. Fifthly, that actions on the case will lie for a man's using a trade contrary to custom, or to his own agreement; for there he uses it injuriously. Sixthly, that where the law allows a restraint of trade, it is not unlawful to enforce it with a penalty. Seventhly, that no man can contract not to use his trade at all. Eighthly, that a particular restraint is not good without just reason and consideration. The true reasons for the distinctions in the cases of voluntary restraints are founded on the mischief which may arise from them, to the party by the loss of his livelihood, and to the public by depriving it of an useful member. Another reason is the great abuses they are liable to; from corporations who are perpetually laboring for exclusive advantages in trade, from masters who are apt to give their apprentices much vexation on this account. In a great many instances they can be of no use to the obligee, which holds in all cases of general restraint throughout England; for what does it signify to a tradesman in London what another does at Newcastle? A reason in favour of these contracts is that there may happen instances wherein they may be useful and beneficial, as to prevent a town being overstocked with any particular trade; or in case an old man is likely to be a loser by continuing his trade. The law is not so unreasonable, as to set aside a man's own agreement for fear of an uncertain injury to him, and fix a certain damage upon another; as it must do, if contracts with a consideration were made void. Wherever such a contract \ftnrstcontplain *stat indifferenter,* and for ought appears, may be either good or bad, the law presumes it bad. For there plainly appears a mischief, but the benefit (if any) can only be presumed. There is a sort of presumption, that it is not of any benefit to the obligee himself, it being a general mischief to the publick, everybody is affected thereby. The presumption answers all the difficulties that are to be found in the books. All contracts where there is a bare restraint of trade and no more, must be void; where special matter appears so as to make it a reasonable and useful contract, the presumption is excluded. This shews why promises in restraint of trade have been held good, but the contracts are governed by the special matter shown. The application of this to the case at bar is very plain. The true distinction of this case is, not between promises and bonds, but between contracts with and without consideration. The plaintiff took a baker's house and the question is whether he or the defendant shall have the trade of this neighborhood; the concern of the public is the same on both sides. What makes this the more reasonable is, that the restraint is exactly proportioned to the consideration, viz., the term of five years. To conclude: In all restraints of trade, where nothing more appears, the law presumes them bad; but if the circumstances are set forth, that presumption is excluded, and the court is to judge of those circumstances, and determine accordingly; and if upon them it appears to be a just and honest contract it ought to be maintained.[39]

NOTES AND QUESTIONS

1.   The leading decisions between *Dyer's* Case of 1415 and Mitchel v. Reynolds in 1711 are set forth in full in Oliphant, Cases on Trade Regulation 34–42 (1923).

2.   The "rule of reason" originates with Mitchel v. Reynolds. What are the standards by which the reasonableness of an agreement not to compete may be measured? Should the same test be applicable to the restrictions in contracts of employment and contracts of sale? Contracts ancillary to purchases of property? Naked restrictions which are not ancillary to any major transaction? In general it is desirable to consider the purposes served by the agreements not to engage in a trade or exercise a craft, the reasons why they were exacted from the covenantors, and the factors that might condition their reasonableness. Can the judicial impairment of the voluntary arrangements of the parties be reconciled with the basic tenets of laissez faire?

3.   The English courts considered a different kind of restrictive agreement in Mogul Steamship Co., Ltd. v. McGregor, Gow & Co., Ltd. (1889) 23 Q.B.D. 598,

---

39.   Ed. For discussions of the early common-law cases, *see* Letwin, English Common Law Concerning Monopolies, 21 U.Chi.L.Rev. 355 (1954); Thorelli, Federal Antitrust Policy, Ch. I (1954); Blake, Employee Covenants Not to Compete, 73 Harv.L.Rev. 625, 629 (1960).

aff'd, A.C. 25 (1892). *Mogul Steamship* involved a combination of steamship companies that had fixed rates and divided cargoes among them. When one member of the association attempted to sue for a breach of the agreement, the court concluded that the contract was invalid, because it was in restraint of trade. The court therefore found that the agreement was unenforceable. Third parties, however, could not complain about the agreement, and the court thought that it would not subject the parties to criminal liability. Compare the court's decision to find the agreement void and unenforceable to the consequences of entering into an anticompetitive agreement in the EU, as specified in Article 81.

4. During the late eighteenth and nineteenth centuries, a flood of restrictive covenant cases reached English and American courts.[40] Judges struggled with whether "general restraints" (*e.g.*, covenants not to carry on a given trade anywhere in England), as opposed to "particular restraints" (such as those limited in time and space), could ever be reasonable.[41] They further refined the reasonableness test. Mitchel v. Reynolds, however, remained the starting place for all analyses; cases which failed to cite it are difficult to find. National Society of Professional Engineers v. United States, Chapter 4 *infra*, is a relatively recent (1978) example of its continuing vitality. The Supreme Court cited Mitchel v. Reynolds in the *Professional Engineers* case for the proposition that the rule of reason is not open ended but "focuses directly on the challenged restraint's impact on competition." Later in that case, Justice Stevens states that "the inquiry mandated by the Rule of Reason is whether the challenged agreement is one that promotes competition or one that suppresses competition." Other social values may be irrelevant. Is all this explicit or implicit in Mitchel v. Reynolds?

5. By 1890, when Section 1 of the Sherman Act was adopted to prohibit restraints illegal at common law or "those which are comparable to restraints deemed illegal at common law,"[42] the validity of restrictive covenants was clearly to be measured by a "rule of reason" test.

6. "The true view at the present time I think, is this: The public have an interest in every person's carrying on his trade freely: so has the individual. All interference with individual liberty of action in trading, and all restraints of trade of themselves, if there is nothing more, are contrary to public policy, and therefore void. That is the general rule. But there are exceptions: restraints of trade and interference with individual liberty of action may be justified by the special

---

40. *See, e.g.*, Morse Twist Drill & Mach. Co. v. Morse, 103 Mass. 73 (1869); Diamond Match Co. v. Roeber, 106 N.Y. 473, 13 N.E. 419 (1887); Dunlop v. Gregory, 10 N.Y. 241 (1851); Horner v. Graves, 7 Bing. 735, 131 Eng.Rep. 284 (C.P.1831); N. Moller, Voluntary Covenants in Restraint of Trade 6–14 (1925).

41. The distinction between "general" and "particular" restraints was rejected in a series of cases that took cognizance of industrial and technological change. *See, e.g.*, Diamond Match Co. v. Roeber, 106 N.Y. 473, 13 N.E. 419 (1887); Rousillon v. Rousillon, 14 Ch.D. 351 (1880). General restraints have been upheld if no broader than the business sold. *See, e.g.*, Ace Tackless Corp. v. American Tackless Corp., 3 A.D.2d 672, 158 N.Y.S.2d 635 (1957) (United States); Burton, Parsons & Co. v. Parsons, 146 F. Supp. 114 (D.D.C.1956) (unlimited area interpreted to include only the United States, the area in which the company was doing business). General employment restraints have also been enforced. *See, e.g.*, Hulsenbusch v. Davidson Rubber Co., 344 F.2d 730 (8th Cir. 1965), cert. denied, 382 U.S. 977 (1966); De Long Corp. v. Lucas, 278 F.2d 804 (2d Cir. 1960), cert. denied, 364 U.S. 833 (1960) (worldwide).

42. Apex Hosiery Co. v. Leader, 310 U.S. 469, 498 (1940); *see* Standard Oil Co. v. United States, 221 U.S. 1, 58–59 (1911); United States v. Addyston Pipe & Steel Co., 85 F. 271, 279, 282–83 (6th Cir. 1898), affirmed, 175 U.S. 211 (1899).

circumstances of a particular case. It is a sufficient justification, and indeed it is the only justification, if the restriction is reasonable—reasonable, that is, in reference to the interests of the parties concerned and reasonable in reference to the interests of the public, so framed and so guarded as to afford adequate protection to the party in whose favour it is imposed, while at the same time it is in no way injurious to the public." Lord MacNaghten, in Nordenfelt v. Maxim Nordenfelt Guns and Ammunition Co., [1894] A.C. 535, 565.

B.   THE SHERMAN ACT—SOME LEGISLATIVE HISTORY

William L. Letwin, Congress and the Sherman Antitrust Law: 1887–1890[43]

23 U.Chi.L.Rev. 221 et seq. (1956).

The deceptive simplicity of the Sherman Act has led many historians to believe that the intention of Congress was equally simple. Although they have not agreed on what the intention was.... Some suppose that the congressmen of 1890 were committed to a policy of laissez-faire, interpret that policy as a dogmatic faith in competition, and regard the Sherman Act as an effort to enforce that orthodoxy. Others less trustful maintain that the Act was a fraud, contrived to soothe the public without injuring the trusts, and they insist that no other result was possible because the Republican Party, in control of the 51st Congress, was "itself dominated at the time by many of the very industrial magnates most vulnerable to real antitrust legislation."[44] Both these schools can draw support from distinguished men who lived while the Act was being passed.[45] ...

I

No one denies that Congress passed the Sherman Act in response to real public feeling against the trusts, but at this distance it is difficult to be sure how hostile the public was and why. The intensity of public opposition, difficult though it may be to assess, is of some importance in explaining what Congress did. If public hatred of trusts was violent, or if congressmen thought it was, then they might have felt so pressed to pass the law, whatever their own judgments, as to have done the work hastily and perhaps spitefully. If, on the other hand, the public opposition was firm but calm, then Congress may have felt free to pass the best law it could devise.

---

43. Reprinted by permission of The University of Chicago Law Review, University of Chicago Law School.

44. Fainsod and Gordon, Government and the American Economy 450 (1941). Cochran and Miller, The Age of Enterprise 171–2 (1942). *See also*, Papandreou and Wheeler, Competition and Its Regulation 213 (1954) in which the Sherman Act is described as a measure of "appeasement."

45. Senator Platt said that his colleagues were interested in only one thing, "to get some bill headed: 'A Bill to Punish Trusts' with which to go to the country." Coolidge, An Old-Fashioned Senator: Orville H. Platt 444 (1910). Justice Holmes thought that the Act was "a humbug based on economic ignorance and incompetence." 1 Holmes–Pollock Letters 163 (Howe ed., 1941).

In fact, though the public sentiment may not have been so intense as some believed, yet it was more deeply rooted than many have noticed, and sufficient in any event to persuade Congress that something had to be done; but since the public, despite its hostility, did not and could not suggest any specific solution for the problem, Congress was left very much to its own devices in deciding what was to be done.

In the years immediately before the Sherman Act, between 1888 and 1890, there were few who doubted that the public hated the trusts fervently. Those who fanned the prejudice and those who hoped to smother it agreed that the fire was already blazing. Radical agitators and polite reformers spoke admiringly of the "people's wrath." Apologists for the trust did not deny its unpopularity. . . .

These impressions of the state of public opinion were supported by more nearly impartial contemporaries, including the judges who, with William Howard Taft, took it quite for granted that the Act "was a step taken by Congress to meet what the public had found to be a growing and intolerable evil."[46] Here and there a few doubts were expressed about the public's determination. Some extremists said that the people could solve the trust problem—by establishing government ownership of all industry—if it would only awake and "prove itself worthy to be free."[47] Some free-traders said that trusts could be eradicated by abolishing protective tariffs, if the people would only "open their eyes."[48] A skeptic has since held that government would have destroyed the trusts, if the people had really cared.[49] But these irregular views have not received much notice, and most later commentators have been satisfied to believe that there was a "great public outcry" against the trusts. . . .

Between 1887 and 1890 the tariff question had priority in the newspapers, party platforms, and, as Senator Sherman himself said, in the work of the 51st Congress.[50] But the pre-eminence of the tariff question did not detract from the trust problem, and if the tariff constantly intruded in congressional debate on trusts, so did the trust problem regularly infiltrate discussion of tariffs. . . .

The pervasive antitrust sentiment did not spring up overnight. Hatred of monopoly is one of the oldest American political habits and, like most profound traditions, it consisted of an essentially permanent idea expressed at different times. "Monopoly," as the word was used in America, meant at first a special legal privilege granted by the state; later it came more often to mean exclusive control that a few persons achieved by their own efforts; but it always meant some sort of unjustified power, especially one that raised obstacles to equality of opportunity. The trust was popularly regard-

---

46. Taft, The Anti–Trust Act and the Supreme Court 2 (1914).

47. Lewis, A Talk About "Trusts" 13 (1889).

48. N.Y. Times, p. 4, col. 3 (Dec. 28, 1887) (editorial).

49. Wollman, The Mortality of Trusts, 67 Alb.L.J. 227 (1905).

50. SEN. SHERMAN TO GEN. W.T. SHERMAN, Nov. 9, 1889, THE SHERMAN LETTERS 379 (THORNDIKE ED., 1894).

ed as nothing but a new form of monopoly, and the whole force of the tradition was focused against it immediately. . . .

Trust-building did not begin in earnest until 1887, but then it took hold quickly. That year saw the formation of the Sugar and Whisky Trusts, which until the end of the century contended for unpopularity only with Standard Oil [which became a trust in 1882]. Others, affecting lesser industries or smaller markets, added to the list. . . .

The greater fervor against trusts in 1888, which bursts so unexpectedly on an historian like Clark, was for the people living at the time nothing so sudden or strange. It was simply a familiar feeling raised to a high pitch, intense because the speed with which new trusts were being hatched made it seem that they would overrun everything unless some remedy were found soon. The general disposition of the public was not in doubt. There were numerous objections to the trusts—complaints of a traditional sort as well as newer ones suited to the character of these particular monopolies. Trusts, it was said, threatened liberty, because they corrupted civil servants and bribed legislators; they enjoyed privileges such as protection by tariffs; they drove out competitors by lowering prices; victimized consumers by raising prices; defrauded investors by watering stocks; put laborers out of work by closing down plants; and somehow or other abused everyone. The kind of remedy that the public desired was also clear enough: it wanted a law to destroy the power of the trusts. The alternative suggestion that government should take over the trusts and operate them as public property seems to have had scant support. But the desire was not, and, in the nature of public opinion, could not be expressed in much greater detail. Any law might be acceptable if it really suppressed the worst abuses of the trusts, especially of those like the Standard Oil, Sugar, and Whisky Trusts, that were most noticeable and most important in the everyday life of many people. The public's mandate was clear, but so broad that Congress had to look elsewhere for advice on how to implement it.

II

Expert judgment on how to solve the trust problem would naturally be expected from the two professions most closely concerned with it, the economists and the lawyers. . . .

Although they differed as to the exact action government should take, nearly all the economists were convinced that any attempt to prohibit combinations would be either unnecessary or futile. Since many of the trusts were "natural," the law could not destroy them. . . . Moreover, some economists argued, any combination that was not justified by the underlying conditions of its industry would decay of its own accord or be controlled by what came to be called "the active influence of the potential competitor."[51]

---

51. Gunton, The Economic and Social Aspects of Trusts, 3 Pol.Sci.Q. 385, 403 (1888); Clark, The "Trust," 52 New Englander 223 (1890).

The legal profession was more apt to suggest means that Congress might use in solving the trust problem, since most lawyers believed that laws could prohibit monopolies. Indeed they thought that the common law already did so, although their conviction rested on a somewhat tenuous basis. . . .

To say that monopolies were illegal at common law was one thing, to destroy them by using the common law was another. . . . Active prosecution of trusts was needed, and indeed a few public officials managed to do it. If they could not sue monopolies in any other way, they could and did use the legal weapons provided by their power over corporations. Between 1887 and 1890 the attorneys-general of five states more or less enthusiastically initiated suits to dissolve corporations that exceeded their chartered powers, or to destroy associations that exercised corporate powers without having charters. Most of the lawyers who insisted on the legality of trusts argued that they were either unincorporated joint-stock companies or partnerships of shareholders, both perfectly lawful forms of organization. The public prosecutors set out to prove the opposite, and in every case they won. . . . But in any case, few monopolies had been destroyed in this way by 1890.

Still, these few recent attacks on monopolies, together with the current view that the common law expressed a public policy hostile to monopolies, made lawyers confident that the common law went in the right direction. Some of them thought it went far enough. . . .

The lawyers and the economists offered Congress little specific help and much conflicting advice. Yet, although the economists advocated some sort of public regulation while the lawyers suggested nothing but prohibitory laws, their underlying views were well adapted to each other. The economists thought that both competition and combination should play their parts in the economy. The lawyers saw that the common law permitted combination in some instances and prohibited it in others. Congressmen seized on this hidden agreement, and set out to construct a statute which by the use of common law principles would eliminate excesses but allow "healthy" competition and combination to flourish side by side.

III

The major parties were anything but anxious to appear as champions of the trusts. The Democrats had made the appropriate general statements against monopoly in 1880 and 1884, but they had especially good reasons for carrying these further in 1888. For one thing, they could cite the new offense as additional evidence against their old enemy, protection. President Cleveland, in his annual message to Congress at the end of 1887, said it was "notorious" that the "combinations quite prevalent at this time, and frequently called trusts," strangled competition; he urged that action be taken against them, and suggested that Congress reduce the customs duties protecting them against foreign competitors. Moreover, the trust issue was especially useful for appealing to farmers and laborers who might shift their vote to the third party. . . .

The Republican Party had even more compelling need to condemn the trusts. They had since 1880 achieved the reputation of being the party of the rich, and in 1884 Ben Butler began calling them the "Party of Monopolists." This label became especially current after their presidential candidate was given a banquet by a group of businessmen, among them Gould, Vanderbilt, and Astor, which the New York World titled "The Royal Feast of Belshazzar Blaine and the Money Kings," and during which, it said, the "Millionaires and Monopolists" sealed their allegiance to the party. A party whose policies were subject to so crudely cynical an interpretation and which was undoubtedly supported—as were the others—by some millionaires, must have condemned the trusts in self-defense even if it had not objected to them in principle. In their convention of 1888, the Republicans accordingly condemned "all combinations of capital, organized in trusts or otherwise, to control arbitrarily the conditions of trade among our citizens," and recommended "such legislation as will prevent the execution of all schemes to oppress the people by undue charges on their supplies, or by unjust rates for the transportation of their products to market." Because they elected President Harrison and won decisive control of Congress in the following election, responsibility for carrying out the recommendation became theirs.

Congress began to concern itself with the trust problem in January of 1888. The antitrust bill was brought to the floor of Congress by Senator John Sherman because he wanted to leave one more monument to himself. By 1888 he was aging, at times impatient and confused, but still the most prominent and esteemed Republican in Congress. He had served as representative for eight years, senator for over twenty-five, and had been Secretary of the Treasury under Hayes. He had been a candidate for the presidential nomination since 1880, and seemed finally to be winning it at the convention of 1888 until Harrison took the lead during the seventh ballot. Soon after this defeat he began to take serious interest in the trust question. His seniority and experience gave him great authority on financial questions and his recent disappointment gave him the urge to do something memorable. He began by establishing personal jurisdiction over the antitrust problem. The antitrust bills introduced earlier in the year had been referred to committees, but none had yet been debated, when, on July 10, Sherman successfully introduced a resolution directing the Senate Committee on Finance, of which he was a ranking member, to investigate all antitrust bills. He maintained that the Committee would investigate antitrust bills "in connection with" tariff bills. . . .

Suddenly the situation [*i.e.*, of standstill] changed, and in the last weeks of March 1890, the serious work of preparing an antitrust law was begun. The burst of energy may have come because the Republican congressmen gave up the idea, supposing they ever had it, of treating the trust problem in the McKinley Tariff Bill. To have done so would have given the impression that they agreed with the Democrats about the causes of trusts and the constitutional powers available to destroy them. They may have felt that the public was becoming impatient, for congressmen were receiving an increasing number of petitions advocating antitrust legislation. Or the new activity may have come at Sherman's insistence. He announced a few days before it began that he had revised his bill. . ., having deleted the provisions George had criticized because they would make the law a criminal one and thus oblige the courts to interpret it narrowly. In any case, by the time Sherman submitted his new bill on March 21, the Senate was prepared to concentrate on it and spent the next five days doing little else.

The great debate opened with a long, formal address in which Sherman praised his bill. He began by explaining its political and legal theory. It was intended, he said, to destroy combinations, not all combinations, but all those which the common law had always condemned as unlawful. It was not intended to outlaw all partnerships and corporations, though they were by nature combinations. The corporations had demonstrated their useful- ness by the vast development of railroads and industry, and Sherman added—bearing in mind the lingering prejudice against them—that as long as every man had the right under general laws to form corporations, they were "not in any sense a monopoly."[52] But any combination which sought to restrain trade, any combination of the leading corporations in an industry, organized in a trust to stifle competition, dictate terms to rail- roads, command the price of labor, and raise prices to consumers, was a "substantial monopoly." It smacked of tyranny, "of kingly prerogative," and a nation that "would not submit to an emperor . . . should not submit to an autocrat of trade." Sherman went on to say that all such combina- tions in restraint of trade were prohibited by the common law, wherever it was in force; it had always applied in the states, and the "courts in different States have declared this thing, when it exists in a State, to be unlawful and void." Senator Cullom interrupted to ask, "Everywhere?" "In every case, everywhere,"[53] Sherman replied, and went on to list the recent decisions supporting his view. . . . Once again, he insisted that Congress was authorized alike by the commerce and revenue clauses of the Constitu- tion to regulate combinations affecting interstate and foreign commerce; and he concluded that his bill, based on this constitutional power and declaring the common law rule, would effectively destroy the power of the trusts.

The debate which occupied much of the following week was untidy but not without pattern. Many senators delivered great orations, but few were heard to say that the trusts were desirable or an antitrust law unnecessary. George repeatedly questioned the bill's constitutionality; certain of his Democratic colleagues took occasion to avow their opposition to tariffs. A number of senators tried to substitute their own bills for Sherman's and failing this they attached them to his as amendments. By the end of the third day, the bill before the Senate consisted of sixteen sections. Sher- man's bill now had tailing after it: Reagan's bill, which, instead of relying on common-law formulas, gave a long explicit definition of the term "trust;" Ingall's bill, which was a more or less independent effort to

---

52. Cong.Rec. 2,456 (1890).

53. Ibid.

prohibit speculation in farm products; and George's clause, which exempted labor unions and farmers' organizations from the general prohibitions. Moreover, the constitutional issue was still confused, and George suggested that the bill be referred to the Judiciary Committee, who, chosen for their legal wisdom, might be able to restore order to the law. Sherman, piqued and impatient, objected that it was most unusual to transfer a bill from one committee to another; Reagan, whose original bill had never yet been reported to the floor by the Judiciary Committee, was equally adamant; and Vance called the Judiciary Committee a "grand mausoleum of Senatorial literature" in which this bill would be buried. But after two more days in which further amendments were added and further profound doubts expressed, the matter had become so tangled that little alternative remained, and the bill was referred to the Judiciary Committee with instructions to report within twenty days.

The Judiciary Committee took the matter out of Sherman's hands, much to his regret and anger. But within a week, surprising everyone, the Committee produced a bill of its own. The work was done largely by its chairman, George Edmunds of Vermont. He disposed of the constitutional question very quickly: when the Committee first met to consider the bill, he proposed to his colleagues "that it is competent for Congress to pass laws preventing and punishing contracts etc. in restraint of commerce between the states." And they, including George, who had raised objections to this theory all along, unanimously agreed. Edmunds then presented drafts of the critical sections of the Act, that made it a misdemeanor to engage in any combination in restraint of trade or to "monopolize" trade, and these were agreed to by all the committeemen present. Two of the remaining sections were written by others: George prepared the section authorizing the Attorney General to sue for injunctions against violators, and Hoar wrote the section authorizing private persons to sue violators for triple damages. The Committee's draft was in broad outline the same as Sherman's original bill, yet Sherman was not pleased. He immediately denounced it as "totally ineffective in dealing with combinations and trusts. All corporations can ride through it or over it without fear of punishment or detection."[54] His reaction was particularly ungenerous, since aside from the fact that the new bill was simpler than his, it differed mainly in providing a greater number of more severe penalties. But when the time came, he voted for it, and as a matter of courtesy it bears his name. The Senate as a whole seemed well satisfied, and after hearing Edmunds' plea that they "pass a bill that is clear in its terms, is definite in its definitions, and is broad in its comprehension, without winding it up into infinite details,"[55] they passed it by fifty-two votes to one.

The action of the House was less systematic. Representative Culberson, who was in charge of the debate, tried to limit it to one hour. His colleagues, who had not until now considered any antitrust bill, complained that they could not get printed copies of the one before them. A strong

---

54. N.Y. Times p. 4, col. 4 (April 8, 1890).

55. 21 Cong.Rec. 3,148 (April 8, 1890).

group insisted that a section should be added to the bill specifically aimed at outlawing railroad and meat-packing pools. After a rather desultory debate, the House passed the bill with one amendment, on May 1. During the next two months, conferences were held between the two chambers, and the House was eventually prevailed on to withdraw its amendment.[56] President Harrison signed the bill, and it became law on July 2, 1890.

Hans B. Thorelli, The Federal Antitrust Policy[57]

180–85, 226–29 (1955).

March 21, 1890. Sherman's Defense of Bill. Debate Begun

... Senator Sherman stated that no intelligent person could question, in good faith, the need for some form of congressional action against the trusts....

Calling the proposed measure a "bill of rights" and a "charter of liberty," he said, "Now, Mr. President, what is this bill? A remedial statute to enforce by civil process in the courts of the United States the common law against monopolies...."

The second section offered relief to private parties injured by unlawful combination. Such a party could

... sue for and recover in any court of the United States of competent jurisdiction, of any person or corporation a party to such a combination, all damages sustained by him. The measure of damages, whether merely compensatory, punitive, or vindictive, is a matter of detail depending upon the judgment of Congress. My own opinion is that the damages should be commensurate with the difficulty of maintaining a private suit against a combination such as is described.

The bill did not declare unlawful *all* restraints of trade.... He stated on several occasions that the object of the bill was to make the common law against monopolies and restraint of trade applicable on the federal level. The common law as it had been applied in Britain and in the several states was to be the main guide of the national courts in drawing the line of demarcation between lawful and unlawful combinations....

That Sherman wanted the bill to cover the great industrial trusts proper as well as mergers and other tight combinations when of a monopolistic nature there can be no doubt. With regard to simple agreements, pools and similar loose associations no equally emphatic statement can be made. Only one or two of the cases referred to ... belong to this category.... By implication the bill intended to leave the task of drawing these lines of demarcation to the courts. This brings us back to the common law and the observation that Sherman's general concept of the common law on monopolies and restraint of trade as evidenced in his speech was quite

---

56. Bills and Debates 327–402 (1890).

57. Reprinted by permission of the publisher, the Johns Hopkins Press and the author.

"radical." Thus, either line of reasoning would seem to suggest that Sherman wanted to give the bill a broad coverage with respect to all kinds of combinations "made with a view or which tend to prevent full and free competition."

... There can be no doubt that Sherman's views were typical in the sense that the vast majority of congressmen were sincere proponents of a private enterprise system founded on the principle of "full and free competition." Most of the legislators sponsoring bills or participating in debates with speeches relating to the principal issues involved made vigorous statements to this effect. But, generally speaking, little need was felt to attempt penetrating analyses of the underlying economic theory or to support the prevalent belief by extended argument—the members of Congress proclaimed "the norm of a free competition too self-evident to be debated, too obvious to be asserted." ...

There can be no doubt that the Congress felt that the ultimate beneficiary in this whole process was the consumer, enjoying a continuous increase in production and commodity quality at progressively lowered prices. The immediate beneficiary legislators had in mind, however, was in all probability the small business proprietor or tradesman whose opportunities were to be safeguarded from the dangers emanating from those recently-evolving elements of business that seemed so strange, gigantic, ruthless and awe-inspiring. This is one reason why it was natural to adopt the old doctrines of the common law, doctrines whose meaning had been established largely in cases brought by business or professional people dissatisfied with the behavior of competitors. Perhaps we are even justified in saying that the Sherman Act is not to be viewed exclusively as an expression of economic policy. In safeguarding rights of the "common man" in business "equal" to those of the evolving more "ruthless" and impersonal forms of enterprise the Sherman Act embodies what is to be characterized as an eminently "social" purpose. A moderate limitation of the freedom of contract was expected to yield a maximization of the freedom of enterprise. Sherman himself, furthermore, expressed the idea probably in the minds of many of his colleagues that the legislation contemplated constituted an important means of achieving freedom from corruption and maintaining freedom of independent thinking in political life, a treasured cornerstone of democratic government....

It seems futile and superfluous to discuss whether the Sherman Act was intended to bring the body of common law on the subject within reach of the United States courts. Authors questioning that this was the intent of Congress manifest a striking lack of familiarity with the records of legislative proceedings. There is ample evidence that not only the bills reported by Sherman in the 51st Congress but also the bill finally passed were intended by their sponsors primarily to be federal codifications of the common law of England and the several states....

While available evidence suggests that those members of Congress who had given the matter special consideration felt that the common law was slightly more "radical," generally speaking, than it actually may have been, that evidence also indicates that legislators realized that the doctrines of the common law were far from "perfection" in the sense of clarity and unambiguousness. This may be derived, in part at least, from the recurrent references in the debates to the courts as instrumentalities for the clarification of the law. Moreover, there can be no reasonable doubt that legislators realized that the current meaning of the doctrines might undergo some changes with the evolution of the economy and its institutions. Thus, we are led to agree with Albert M. Kales in his conclusion (not based on the records of congressional proceedings) that in adopting the standard of the common law Congress expected the courts not only to apply a set of somewhat vague doctrines but also in doing so to make use of that "certain technique of judicial reasoning" characteristic of common law courts.[58]

It must be said that the "solution" of the trust problem represented by the Sherman Act was an elegant one. The complexities of the problem were enormous. Under the circumstances two radically different types of legislation would theoretically have been equally plausible. Congress could have tried to define every type of behavior or practice it found reprehensible. This would have necessitated a multitude of detailed provisions. Or it could have gone to what may almost be called the other extreme, enacting a few fundamental principles in the light of which the courts would evaluate the multifarious types of business combinations and methods with which they would be confronted. The former solution might conceivably—not necessarily—have the advantage of great certainty of the meaning of the law in individual cases. On the other hand, available information would hardly allow legislation spelled out in great detail. And, equally important, detailed legislation would run a serious risk of becoming obsolete in a very short time in the dynamics of economic life and its institutions. Congress wanted the law to be flexible to a certain extent. Restrainers of trade were not to be able to find subterfuge behind new forms of combinations or methods. What mattered was whether trade *was restrained* (or monopolized) or not. Thus the second line of action was chosen. And in this realm the evolved doctrines and the "philosophy" of evolution of the common law most nearly met the requirements of the legislator. . . .

C. EARLY DEVELOPMENT OF LEGAL DOCTRINE

1. THE FIRST CARTEL CASES

United States v. Trans–Missouri Freight Association

Supreme Court of the United States, 1897.
166 U.S. 290, 17 S.Ct. 540, 41 L.Ed. 1007.

[Suit in equity by the United States to dissolve the Trans–Missouri Freight Association, and to set aside and to have declared illegal and void the articles of agreement by which the association was formed on March 15, 1889. The association includes among its members eighteen carriers whose

---

58. Albert M. Kales, Contracts and Combinations in Restraint of Trade (1918), 106f.

lines extend from the Mississippi River to the west coast and which, according to the bill, control the freight traffic in this region. The defendants are charged with fixing rates, and establishing rules and regulations for the traffic which they carry. Under the articles of the association, rates are set by a committee, and the members are required to observe the rates thus fixed, with the privilege of withdrawal from the association on thirty days' notice. Members may, in order to meet the competition of non-member roads, change their rates, subject, however, to penalty if the association finds that the change was not actually necessary. Any proposed change in rates must be submitted to the vote of the association, and members must abide by the association's decision unless at least ten days' written notice shall have been given of an intention to make such change notwithstanding the vote of the association. The case was heard on the pleadings and the bill was dismissed by the District Court. The dismissal was affirmed by the Circuit Court of Appeals. Motion is made in the Supreme Court to dismiss the appeal on the ground that the association was dissolved on November 18, 1892.]

■ PECKHAM, J. . . .

[T]he results of trusts, or combinations of that nature, may be different in different kinds of corporations, and yet they all have an essential similarity, and have been induced by motives of individual or corporate aggrandizement as against the public interest. In business or trading combinations they may even temporarily, or perhaps permanently, reduce the price of the article traded in or manufactured, by reducing the expense inseparable from the running of many different companies for the same purpose. Trade or commerce under those circumstances may nevertheless be badly and unfortunately restrained by driving out of business the small dealers and worthy men whose lives have been spent therein, and who might be unable to readjust themselves to their altered surroundings. Mere reduction in the price of the commodity dealt in might be dearly paid for by the ruin of such a class, and the absorption of control over one commodity by an all-powerful combination of capital. In any great and extended change in the manner or method of doing business it seems to be an inevitable necessity that distress and, perhaps, ruin shall be its accompaniment in regard to some of those who were engaged in the old methods. . . .

It takes time to effect a readjustment of industrial life so that those who are thrown out of their old employment, by reason of such changes as we have spoken of, may find opportunities for labor in other departments than those to which they have been accustomed. It is a misfortune, but yet in such cases it seems to be the inevitable accompaniment of change and improvement.

It is wholly different, however, when such changes are effected by combinations of capital, whose purpose in combining is to control the production or manufacture of any particular article in the market, and by such control dictate the price at which the article shall be sold, the effect being to drive out of business all the small dealers in the commodity and to render the public subject to the decision of the combination as to what price shall be paid for the article. In this light it is not material that the price of an article may be lowered. It is in the power of the combination to raise it, and the result in any event is unfortunate for the country by depriving it of the services of a large number of small but independent dealers who were familiar with the business and who had spent their lives in it, and who supported themselves and their families from the small profits realized therein. Whether they be able to find other avenues to earn their livelihood is not so material, because it is not for the real prosperity of any country that such changes should occur which result in transferring an independent business man, the head of his establishment, small though it might be, into a mere servant or agent of a corporation for selling the commodities which he once manufactured or dealt in, having no voice in shaping the business policy of the company and bound to obey orders issued by others. Nor is it for the substantial interests of the country that any one commodity should be within the sole power and subject to the sole will of one powerful combination of capital. Congress has, so far as its jurisdiction extends, prohibited all contracts or combinations in the form of trusts entered into for the purpose of restraining trade and commerce. The results naturally flowing from a contract or combination in restraint of trade or commerce, when entered into by a manufacturing or trading company such as above stated, while differing somewhat from those which may follow a contract to keep up transportation rates by railroads, are nevertheless of the same nature and kind, and the contracts themselves do not so far differ in their nature that they may not all be treated alike and be condemned in common.

    ... [T]he next question to be discussed is as to what is the true construction of the statute, assuming that it applies to common carriers by railroad.... Is it confined to a contract or combination which is only in unreasonable restraint of trade or commerce, or does it include what the language of the act plainly and in terms covers, all contracts of that nature?

    We are asked to regard the title of this act as indicative of its purpose to include only those contracts which were unlawful at common law, but which require the sanction of a Federal statute in order to be dealt with in a Federal court. It is said that when terms which are known to the common law are used in a Federal statute those terms are to be given the same meaning that they received at common law, and that when the language of the title is "to protect trade and commerce against unlawful restraints and monopolies," it means those restraints and monopolies which the common law regarded as unlawful, and which were to be prohibited by the Federal statute. We are of opinion that the language used in the title refers to and includes and was intended to include those restraints and monopolies which are made unlawful in the body of the statute. It is to the statute itself that resort must be had to learn the meaning thereof, though a resort to the title here creates no doubt about the meaning of and does not alter the plain language contained in its text.

    It is now with much amplification of argument urged that the statute, in declaring illegal every combination in the form of trust or otherwise, or conspiracy in restraint of trade or commerce, does not mean what the language used therein plainly imports, but that it only means to declare illegal any such contract which is in unreasonable restraint of trade, while leaving all others unaffected by the provisions of the act; that the common law meaning of the term "contract in restraint of trade" includes only such contracts as are in unreasonable restraint of trade, and when that term is used in the Federal statute it is not intended to include all contracts in restraint of trade, but only those which are in unreasonable restraint thereof.

The term is not of such limited signification. Contracts in restraint of trade have been known and spoken of for hundreds of years both in England and in this country, and the term includes all kinds of those contracts which in fact restrain or may restrain trade. Some of such contracts have been held void and unenforceable in the courts by reason of their restraint being unreasonable, while others have been held valid because they were not of that nature. A contract may be in restraint of trade and still be valid at common law. Although valid, it is nevertheless a contract in restraint of trade, and would be so described either at common law or elsewhere. By the simple use of the term "contract in restraint of trade," all contracts of that nature, whether valid or otherwise, would be included, and not alone that kind of contract which was invalid and unenforceable as being in unreasonable restraint of trade. When, therefore, the body of an act pronounces as illegal every contract or combination in restraint of trade or commerce among the several States, etc., the plain and ordinary meaning of such language is not limited to that kind of contract alone which is in unreasonable restraint of trade, but all contracts are included in such language, and no exception or limitation can be added without placing in the act that which has been omitted by Congress.

Proceeding, however, upon the theory that the statute did not mean what its plain language imported, and that it intended in its prohibition to denounce as illegal only those contracts which were in unreasonable restraint of trade, the courts below have made an exhaustive investigation as to the general rules which guide courts in declaring contracts to be void as being in restraint of trade, and therefore against the public policy of the country. In the course of their discussion of that subject they have shown that there has been a gradual though great alteration in the extent of the liberty granted to the vendor of property in agreeing, as part consideration for his sale, not to enter into the same kind of business for a certain time or within a certain territory. So long as the sale was the bona fide consideration for the promise and was not made a mere excuse for an evasion of the rule itself, the later authorities, both in England and in this country, exhibit a strong tendency towards enabling the parties to make such a contract in relation to the sale of property, including an agreement not to enter into the same kind of business, as they may think proper, and this with the view to granting to a vendor the freest opportunity to obtain the largest consideration for the sale of that which is his own. A contract which is the mere accompaniment of the sale of property, and thus entered into for the purpose of enhancing the price at which the vendor sells it, which in effect is collateral to such sale, and where the main purpose of the whole contract is accomplished by such sale, might not be included, within the letter or spirit of the statute in question. But we cannot see how the statute can be limited, as it has been by the courts below, without reading into its text an exception which alters the natural meaning of the language used, and that, too, upon a most material point, and where no sufficient reason is shown for believing that such alteration would make the statute more in accord with the intent of the law-making body that enacted it....

The plaintiffs are, however, under no obligation in order to maintain this action to show that by the common law all agreements among competing railroad companies to keep up rates to such as are reasonable were void as in restraint of trade or commerce. There are many cases which look in that direction if they do not precisely decide that point.... But assuming that agreements of this nature are not void at common law and that the various cases cited by the learned courts below show it, the answer to the statement of their validity now is to be found in the terms of the statute under consideration....

Reversed, and the case remanded to the Circuit Court for further proceedings in conformity with this opinion.[59]

NOTE

1. The trial court in *Trans–Missouri* had held that the combination was lawful in that its activities served to prevent "unhealthy competition . . . and furnish the public with adequate facilities at . . . reasonable prices." 53 F. 440, 451 (D.Kan. 1892). The Circuit Court of Appeals affirmed, finding "fair, open, and healthy" competition to be necessary, thus rejecting the "plain meaning" approach. 58 F. 58, 69 (8th Cir. 1893).

2. United States v. Joint–Traffic Association, 171 U.S. 505, 567–568 (1898). Justice Peckham retreated from his earlier literal interpretation of the Sherman Act and recognized exceptions for ordinary contracts which might arguably restrain trade including traditional ancillary restraints. He rejected counsel's contention that the statute as construed in *Trans–Missouri* invalidates such agreements, stating: "We are not aware that it has ever been claimed that a lease or purchase by

---

59. The dissenting opinion of White, J., with whom Field, Gray and Shiras, JJ., concurred, is omitted. In his dissent, Justice White expressed the view that:

> "If these obvious rules of interpretation be applied, it seems to me they render it impossible to construe the words 'every restraint of trade' used in the act in any other sense than as excluding reasonable contracts, as the fact that such contracts were not considered to be within the rule of contracts in restraint of trade, was thoroughly established both in England and in this country at the time the act was adopted. It is, I submit, not to be doubted that the interpretation of the words 'every contract in restraint of trade,' so as to embrace within its purview every contract, however reasonable, would certainly work an enormous injustice and operate to the undue restraint of the liberties of the citizen. But there is no canon of interpretation which requires that the letter be followed, when by so doing an unreasonable result is accomplished. On the contrary, the rule is the other way, and exacts that the spirit which vivifies, and not the letter which killeth, is the proper guide, by which to correctly interpret a statute." 166 U.S. at 354.

a farmer, manufacturer, or merchant of an additional farm, manufactory or shop, or the withdrawal from business of any farmer, merchant or manufacturer, restrained commerce or trade within any legal definition of that term; and the sale of a good will of a business with an accompanying agreement not to engage in a similar business was instanced in the *Trans–Missouri* case as a contract not within the meaning of the act; and it was said that such a contract was collateral to the main contract of sale and was entered into for the purpose of enhancing the price at which the vendor sells his business.... An agreement entered into for the purpose of promoting the legitimate business of an individual or corporation, with no purpose to thereby affect or restrain interstate commerce, and which does not directly restrain such commerce, is not, as we think, covered by the act, although the agreement may indirectly and remotely affect that commerce. We also repeat what is said in the case above cited, that 'the act of Congress must have a reasonable construction, or else there would scarcely be an agreement or contract among business men that could not be said to have, indirectly or remotely, some bearing upon interstate commerce, and possibly to restrain it.' "

3. Hopkins v. United States, 171 U.S. 578 (1898), referred to by Justice Peckham in *Joint Traffic,* involved a voluntary association of livestock commission merchants. The rules of the association forbade members from buying from non-members in Kansas City, fixed the commission for selling livestock, prohibited the employment of agents to solicit consignments except upon a stipulated salary, and forbade the sending of prepaid telegrams or telephone messages with information as to the condition of the markets.

Justice Peckham found that the defendants "entered into a voluntary association for the purpose of ... better conducting their business, and that after they entered into such association they still continued their individual business in full competition with each other, and that the association itself ... is simply a means by and through which the individual members who have become thus associated are the better enabled to transact their business; to maintain and uphold a proper way of doing it; and to create the means for preserving business integrity....

To treat as condemned by the act all agreements under which as a result, the cost of conducting an interstate commercial business may be increased would enlarge the application of the act far beyond the fair meaning of the language used. There must be some direct and immediate effect upon interstate commerce in order to come within the act."

4. Anderson v. United States, 171 U.S. 604 (1898), dealt with a livestock exchange similar to that in *Hopkins,* except that exchange members in *Anderson* were purchasers of cattle for their own account. The *Anderson* court followed *Hopkins,* holding that the defendants were not in restraint of interstate commerce, since "the purpose of the agreement was not to regulate, obstruct or restrain that commerce, but ... it was entered into with the object of properly and fairly regulating the transaction of the business in which the parties to the agreement were engaged ... and ... the effect of its formation and enforcement upon interstate trade or commerce is in any event but indirect and incidental, and not its purpose or object."

United States v. Addyston Pipe & Steel Co.

Circuit Court of Appeals of the United States, Sixth Circuit, 1898.
85 F. 271, affirmed, 175 U.S. 211, 20 S.Ct. 96, 44 L.Ed. 136 (1899).

[Suit in equity by the United States against six corporations engaged in the manufacture of cast iron pipe, charging a combination and conspiracy in violation of the Sherman Act. The bill sought a forfeiture of all pipe shipped by the defendants pursuant to the conspiracy and for an injunction against the continuance of the combination. The case was heard upon the pleadings and affidavits. The lower court dismissed the petition on the merits. The government appeals.

The defendants on December 31, 1896, entered into an agreement of two years' duration. A large part of their business consisted of selling pipes to gas and water works. Under this agreement, the gas and water works in designated cities in the southern and central parts of the United States were assigned to each defendant. The price at which pipe was sold in the reserved territories was determined by the association and the member to whom the business was assigned paid a fixed bonus to the association. The other members submitted fictitious bids to the customers in the reserved cities in order to create the appearance of competition. A secret auction pool was conducted for the allocation of business arising outside the reserved cities. The price was determined by the association and the business was assigned to the member who offered the largest bonus to the association. The unsuccessful bidders in the auction pool submitted padded bids to the purchaser to maintain the pretense of competitive bidding. The bonuses were distributed to members in proportion to their respective tonnage capacities. The total tonnage capacity of all the defendants was 220,000 tons annually. In territories in which there was considerable outside competition, members were permitted to sell without restriction and without payment of any bonus to the association. Such territory was called "free" territory as contrasted with "pay" territory, on the sales in which a bonus was paid. Sales in free territory to customers situated more than 500 miles from defendants' foundries were made at lower prices than sales in reserved cities near their mills. The capacity of nonmember mills in pay territory was 170,500 tons, and in free territory 348,000 tons. The evidence was scanty as to rates of freight upon iron pipes, but enough appeared to show that the advantage in freight rates which the defendants had over the large pipe foundries in New York, eastern Pennsylvania, and New Jersey in bidding on contracts to deliver pipe in almost all of the pay territory varied from $2 to $6 a ton, according to the location. The defendants filed the affidavits of their managing officers, in which they stated that the object of their association was not to raise prices beyond what was reasonable, but only to prevent ruinous competition among defendants, which would have carried prices far below a reasonable point; that the bonuses charged were not exorbitant profits and additions to a reasonable price, but they were deductions from a reasonable price, in the nature of a penalty or burden intended to curb the natural disposition of each member to get all the business possible, and more than his due proportion; that the prices fixed by the association were always reasonable, and were always fixed, as they must have been, with reference to the very active competition of other pipe manufacturers for every job; that the reason why they sold pipe at cheaper rates in the free territory than in the pay territory was that they were willing to sell at a loss to keep their mills going rather than to shut them down; that the prices in a city such as St.

[Handwritten margin notes: "pipes. 2 yr agreement - price fixed by assoc, members paid bonus to assoc, fictitious bids"]

[Handwritten margin notes: "Ds arg: preventing "ruinous competition" by fixing prices"]

Louis, in which the specifications were detailed and precise, were higher because pipe had to be made specially for the job, and stock on hand could not be used.]

■ Before HARLAN, CIRCUIT JUSTICE, and TAFT and LURTON, CIRCUIT JUDGES.

■ TAFT, J. . . . Two questions are presented in this case for our decision: First. Was the association of the defendants a contract, combination, or conspiracy in restraint of trade, as the terms are to be understood in the act? Second. Was the trade thus restrained trade between the states?

The contention on behalf of defendants is that the association would have been valid at common law, and that the federal antitrust law was not intended to reach any agreements that were not void and unenforceable at common law. It might be a sufficient answer to this contention to point to the decision of the Supreme Court of the United States in U.S. v. Trans–Missouri Freight Ass'n, 166 U.S. 290, in which it was held that contracts in restraint of interstate transportation were within the statute, whether the restraints would be regarded as reasonable at common law or not. It is suggested, however, that that case related to a quasi public employment necessarily under public control, and affecting public interests, and that a less stringent rule of construction applies to contracts restricting parties in sales of merchandise, which is purely a private business, having in it no element of a public or quasi public character. Whether or not there is substance in such a distinction—a question we do not decide—it is certain that, if the contract of association which bound the defendants was void and unenforceable at the common law because in restraint of trade, it is within the inhibition of the statute if the trade it restrained was interstate. Contracts that were in unreasonable restraint of trade at common law were not unlawful in the sense of being criminal, or giving rise to a civil action for damages in favor of one prejudicially affected thereby, but were simply void, and were not enforced by the courts. The effect of the act of 1890 is to render such contracts unlawful in an affirmative or positive sense, and punishable as a misdemeanor, and to create a right of civil action for damages in favor of those injured thereby, and a civil remedy by injunction in favor of both private persons and the public against the execution of such contracts and the maintenance of such trade restraints.

The argument for defendants is that their contract of association was not, and could not be, a monopoly, because their aggregate tonnage capacity did not exceed 30 per cent of the total tonnage capacity of the country; that the restraints upon the members of the association, if restraints they could be called, did not embrace all the states, and were not unlimited in space; that such partial restraints were justified and upheld at common law if reasonable, and only proportioned to the necessary protection of the parties; that in this case the partial restraints were reasonable, because without them each member would be subjected to ruinous competition by the other, and did not exceed in degree of stringency or scope what was necessary to protect the parties in securing prices for their product that were fair and reasonable to themselves and the public; that competition was not stifled by the association because the prices fixed by it had to be fixed with reference to the very active competition of pipe companies which were not members of the association, and which had more than double the defendants' capacity; that in this way the association only modified and restrained the evils of ruinous competition, while the public had all the benefit from competition which public policy demanded.

From early times it was the policy of Englishmen to encourage trade in England, and to discourage those voluntary restraints which tradesmen were often induced to impose on themselves by contract. Courts recognized this public policy by refusing to enforce stipulations of this character. The objections to such restraints were mainly two. One was that by such contracts a man disabled himself from earning a livelihood with the risk of becoming a public charge, and deprived the community of the benefit of his labor. The other was that such restraints tended to give to the covenantee, the beneficiary of such restraints, a monopoly of the trade, from which he had thus excluded one competitor, and by the same means might exclude others. . . .

Much has been said in regard to the relaxing of the original strictness of the common law in declaring contracts in restraint of trade void as conditions of civilization and public policy have changed, and the argument drawn therefrom is that the law now recognizes that competition may be so ruinous as to injure the public, and, therefore, that contracts made with a view to check such ruinous competition and regulate prices, though in restraint of trade, and having no other purpose, will be upheld. We think this conclusion is unwarranted by the authorities when all of them are considered. It is true that certain rules for determining whether a covenant in restraint of trade ancillary to the main purpose of a contract was reasonably adapted and limited to the necessary protection of a party in the carrying out of such purpose have been somewhat modified by modern authorities. . . . But these cases all involved contracts in which the covenant in restraint of trade was ancillary to the main and lawful purpose of the contract, and was necessary to the protection of the covenantee in the carrying out of that main purpose. They do not manifest any general disposition on the part of the courts to be more liberal in supporting contracts having for their sole object the restraint of trade than did the courts of an earlier time. It is true that there are some cases in which the courts, mistaking, as we conceive, the proper limits of the relaxation of the rules for determining the unreasonableness of restraints of trade, have set sail on a sea of doubt, and have assumed the power to say, in respect to contracts which have no other purpose and no other consideration on either side than the mutual restraint of the parties, how much restraint of competition is in the public interest, and how much is not.

The manifest danger in the administration of justice according to so shifting, vague, and indeterminate a standard would seem to be a strong reason against adopting it. . . .

Upon this review of the law and the authorities, we can have no doubt that the association of the defendants, however reasonable the prices they fixed, however great the competition they had to encounter, and however

great the necessity for curbing themselves by joint agreement from committing financial suicide by ill-advised competition, was void at common law,
because in restraint of trade, and tending to a monopoly. But the facts of
the case do not require us to go so far as this, for they show that the
attempted justification of this association on the grounds stated is without
foundation. . . .[60]

NOTE

1. The Supreme Court had first given its attention to the Sherman Act in
United States v. E.C. Knight Co., 156 U.S. 1 (1895). In that case, the defendant,
which refined and manufactured 65% of the nation's sugar, had completed its
monopoly by acquiring four smaller independent manufacturers. Defendant and the
acquired firms were all located in the same state, indeed, in the same city,
Philadelphia. The government's petition sought cancellation of the contracts by
which the consolidation had taken place. The Court affirmed the decisions of the
lower courts denying relief, asserting that the monopoly of manufacture only
"incidentally and indirectly" affected commerce, and that the Constitution's commerce clause did not reach so far. The Court found nothing to indicate "any
intention to put a restraint on trade. . . ."

2. In *Addyston Pipe,* the trial court had dismissed the government's petition
on the basis of the *E.C. Knight* decision. On appeal, Judge Taft read the *Knight*
decision as drawing "the distinction between a restraint upon the business of
manufacturing and a restraint upon the trade or commerce between the states in
the articles after manufacture, with the manifest purpose of showing that the
regulating power of congress under the Constitution could affect only the latter. . . ." 85 F. 271, 297 (1898). In the Supreme Court, Justice Peckham affirmed:

> The direct purpose of the combination of the *Knight* case was the control of
> the manufacture of sugar. There was no combination or agreement, in
> terms, regarding the future disposition of the manufactured article; noth-
> ing looking to a transaction in the nature of interstate commerce. The
> probable intention on the part of the manufacturer of the sugar to
> thereafter dispose of it by sending it to some market in another State, was
> held to be immaterial and not to alter the character of the combination. . . .
> [T]he case was decided upon the principle that a combination simply to
> control manufacture was not a violation of the act of Congress, because
> such a contract or combination did not directly control or affect interstate
> commerce. . . .

175 U.S. 211, 240 (1899).

3. In Swift & Co. v. United States, 196 U.S. 375 (1905), the Court severely
undercut any remaining force of the distinction between "direct" and "indirect"
effects by holding that price fixing in livestock markets could be reached since the
markets, although themselves each located in a single state, were part of "a current
of commerce among the States. . . ." Id. at 399. Thus, although the *Knight* decision
temporarily placed manufacturing beyond the purview of direct national regulation,

---

60. The court then analyzed the facts and concluded that the members of the combination were not subject to substantial outside competition in the territories in which they
operated.

it did not substantially impede antitrust enforcement. As Chapter 2 *infra* indicates, the narrow view of the reach of the "commerce clause" which gave rise to these early problems has, of course, long since given way to an expansive view, and the reach of the Sherman Act, understood to be as broad as the Constitution permits, has grown accordingly.

NOTE ON RESTRICTIVE COVENANTS UNDER STATE AND FEDERAL LAW

After passage of the Sherman Act, both state and federal courts adopted the principal approaches set forth in *Mitchel v. Reynolds* (*supra*) and *Addyston Pipe* with respect to restrictive covenants. The Restatement (Second) Contracts § 187 (1981), for example, adopted Judge Taft's ancillary/non-ancillary theme by concluding: "A promise to refrain from competition that imposes a restraint that is not ancillary to an otherwise valid transaction or relationship is unreasonably in restraint of trade."

Section 188 of the Restatement (Second) Contracts (1981), which is consistent with the great bulk of state law, explains how to judge the reasonableness of a restrictive covenant:

> (1) A promise to refrain from competition that imposes a restraint that is ancillary to an otherwise valid transaction or relationship is unreasonably in restraint of trade if
>
>> (a) the restraint is greater than is needed to protect the promisee's legitimate interest, or
>>
>> (b) the promisee's need is outweighed by the hardship to the promisor and the likely injury to the public.
>
> (2) Promises imposing restraints that are ancillary to a valid transaction or relationship include the following:
>
>> (a) a promise by the seller of a business not to compete with the buyer in such a way as to injure the value of the business sold;
>>
>> (b) a promise by an employee or other agent not to compete with his employer or other principal;
>>
>> (c) a promise by a partner not to compete with the partnership.

Generally, courts have looked at three dimensions in evaluating whether a restrictive covenant is unnecessarily burdensome. First, they have considered the geographic area covered by the restraint; second, they have reviewed the duration of the covenant; and third, they have considered whether the scope of the restraint is unreasonably broad. *See, e.g.*, Karpinski v. Ingrasci, 28 N.Y.2d 45, 320 N.Y.S.2d 1, 268 N.E.2d 751 (1971).

Courts have tended to apply a more stringent requirement of reasonableness to covenants appearing in contracts of employment, than to contracts for the sale of a business or formation of a partnership, which are more likely to have been fully negotiated. The social policy underlying enforceable post-employment covenants is that they permit an employer greater freedom to use employees' services and to make available to them confidential information; they may increase efficiency. On the other hand, the employer's justifiably protectable interests are apt to be fewer and less broad with respect to employees having less access to trade secrets, customer lists, and the like. As Professor Blake put it:

> From the point of view of the employer, postemployment restraints are regarded as perhaps the only effective method of preventing unscrupulous

competitors or employees from appropriating valuable trade information and customer relationships for their own benefit. . . . The opposite view is that postemployment restraints reduce both the economic mobility of employees and their personal freedom to follow their own interests. These restraints also diminish competition by intimidating potential competitors and by slowing down the dissemination of ideas, processes, and methods. Blake, Employee Agreements Not to Compete, 73 Harv.L.Rev. 625, 627, 638 (1960); *see* Purchasing Associates, Inc. v. Weitz, 13 N.Y.2d 267, 246 N.Y.S.2d 600, 196 N.E.2d 245 (1963).

Today, almost all restrictive covenant cases are handled under state law. But the enforcement, for example, of an overly restrictive covenant by a dominant firm, which prevents a likely innovative new entrant from coming into a concentrated market, may give rise to a Sherman Act violation. *See* Lektro–Vend Corp. v. Vendo Co., 660 F.2d 255 (7th Cir. 1981), cert. denied, 455 U.S. 921 (1982). Such normally privileged conduct will be much more likely to run afoul of the antitrust laws if it is part of a pattern of repetitive litigation or seen to involve intentional harassment. The Seventh Circuit concluded that the restrictive covenant in issue was not unreasonably broad, at least as enforced against the conduct of the plaintiff. In an earlier stage of that litigation, the Supreme Court did not reach the issue. Vendo Co. v. Lektro–Vend Corp., 433 U.S. 623 (1977).

In Newburger, Loeb & Co., Inc. v. Gross, 563 F.2d 1057 (2d Cir. 1977), cert. denied, 434 U.S. 1035 (1978), the Second Circuit indicated some concern about applying the Sherman Act to "employer-employee controversies which individually have only a small impact on commerce and which have traditionally been handled in state courts." But many large employers use "form" restrictive covenants across-the-board with numerous employees, and other businesses have used restrictive covenants in ways that significantly impact commerce. For example, various types of restrictive covenants, most often inserted at the insistence of large department stores or other major tenants, have appeared in the leasing arrangements of major shopping centers. These include: (i) "exclusivity" clauses that insure that the lessee will have limited (or no) competition within the center; (ii) clauses that prevent the lessor from leasing to discount stores or houses; and (iii) "veto" clauses that grant the lessee discretion to disapprove prospective tenants and to limit their floor space and general business operations.[61] Should such covenants receive scrutiny under the Sherman Act? Would state judges be as likely as federal judges to take account of competitive market values? *See* Goldschmid, Antitrust's Neglected Stepchild: A Proposal for Dealing with Restrictive Covenants Under Federal Law, 73 Colum.L.Rev. 1193 (1973); cf. Consultants & Designers, Inc. v. Butler Service Group, Inc., 720 F.2d 1553, 1562–64 (11th Cir. 1983) (restrictive covenant survived a rule of reason analysis under the Sherman Act because covenant did "not have a sufficiently adverse impact on competition").

2. EARLY MERGERS AND THE DEVELOPMENT OF THE "RULE OF REASON"

The early wave of industrial consolidations, which gave rise to the political pressures leading to the Sherman Act, was renewed and intensified

---

61. *See* Dalmo Sales Co. v. Tysons Corner Regional Shopping Center, 308 F. Supp. 988, 993 (D.D.C.), affirmed, 429 F.2d 206 (D.C.Cir. 1970); FTC Complaint, Proposed Order § I, Gimbel Brothers, Inc., Docket No. 8885 (filed May 8, 1972); FTC Complaint ¶ 11, Tysons Corner Regional Shopping Center, Docket No. 8886 (filed May 8, 1972), 3 Trade Reg.Rep. ¶ 20,003.

after 1890. By 1899, the number of major firms absorbed annually by merger had risen to more than one thousand. DuPont, United States Steel, American Tobacco, and International Harvester were products of this wave, which abated only with the government's more vigorous antitrust enforcement activities in the first decade of the new century. *See, e.g.*, Northern Securities Co. v. United States, 193 U.S. 197 (1904); United States v. Union Pacific Railroad Co., 226 U.S. 61 (1912); United States v. Reading Co., 253 U.S. 26 (1920); United States v. Southern Pacific Co., 259 U.S. 214 (1922).

The *Northern Securities* case was one of the most important antitrust cases historically. The government's prosecution of the Northern Securities Company was filed in a politically charged atmosphere involving famous defendants, powerful newspaper editors, and the "trust busting" rhetoric of President Theodore Roosevelt.

The company was formed during a period of large railroad consolidations, and competition by various financial groups to bring together attractive systems of connecting long distance routes. The Northern Pacific Railway Company, controlled by associates of defendant J.P. Morgan, and Great Northern Railway Company, controlled by defendant James J. Hill, were parallel and competing lines connecting St. Paul and other points in Minnesota with the northwest. The two companies jointly acquired the Burlington line, which connected Chicago and St. Paul with Billings, Montana, where it connected with the Northern Pacific. E.H. Harriman, president of the Union Pacific, which also wanted access to the Burlington connections, sought access to the Burlington routes by purchasing large amounts of Northern Pacific stock. In response, the Morgan interests and the Hill interests created Northern Securities Company, a holding company for their stock. Northern Securities almost immediately became a target for action under the Sherman Act. The President and the nation's newspapers held the holding company up as a prototype of the giant "trusts," at which the Sherman Act had been directed.

The trial court ruled that the defendants, in creating the company, had entered into an unlawful combination for the restraint of trade. By a 5–4 margin, the Supreme Court, in an opinion often criticized for leaving important questions unanswered, affirmed the lower court's ruling. Justice Harlan, writing for the majority, listed a number of "propositions" of the Sherman Act, including that the Act "embraces *all* direct *restraints*," that "Congress . . . has prescribed the rule of free competition," and that "*every* combination or conspiracy which would extinguish competition between otherwise competing railroads engaged in *interstate trade or commerce,* and which would *in that way* restrain *such* trade or commerce, is made illegal by the act."

Justice Brewer, who delivered a concurring opinion in *Northern Securities,* expressed the view that Congress intended only to prohibit those contracts which were in "direct restraint of trade, unreasonable and against public policy." Nevertheless, he condemned the combination effected in *Northern Securities,* which, he declared, might be extended until a single corporation would be in control of the whole transportation system of the country.

Justice Holmes' dissent in *Northern Securities* began with the famous language:

> Great cases like hard cases make bad law. For great cases are called great, not by reason of their real importance in shaping the law of the future, but because of some accident of immediate overwhelming interest which appeals to the feelings and distorts the judgment.

Justice Holmes was referring to the extensive public interest in the *Northern Securities* decision which was a result of the notoriety of the defendants and Roosevelt's behind-the-scenes participation in the prosecution.[62]

Holmes felt that the plain meaning of Section 1 of the Sherman Act did not prohibit "partnerships" such as in *Northern Securities* whose effect is to suppress competition.

> The law ... says nothing about competition, and only prevents its suppression by contracts or combinations in restraint of trade, and such contracts or combinations derive their character as restraining trade from other features than the suppression of competition alone....

The *Union Pacific* and *Southern Pacific* cases illustrate the Supreme Court's receptivity to the government's more rigorous antitrust approach. In the *Union Pacific* case, the Supreme Court struck down Union Pacific's acquisition of a controlling interest in Southern Pacific, holding:

> The consolidation of two great competing systems of railroad engaged in interstate commerce by a transfer to one of a dominating stock interest in the other creates a combination which restrains interstate commerce within the meaning of the statute, because, in destroying or greatly abridging the free operation of competition theretofore existing, it tends to higher rates. It directly tends to less activity in furnishing the public with prompt and efficient service in carrying and handling freight and in carrying passengers, and in attention to and prompt adjustment of the demands of patrons for losses, and in these respects puts interstate commerce under restraint. Nor does it make any difference that rates for the time being may not be raised and much money be spent in improvements after the combination is effected. It is the scope of such combinations and their power to suppress or stifle competition or create monopoly which determines the applicability of the act. 226 U.S. at 88.

---

62. *See* Letwin, Law and Economic Policy in America: The Evolution of the Sherman Antitrust Act (Phoenix ed. 1981).

In the *Southern Pacific* case, the Southern Pacific's acquisition of the stock of the Central Pacific was held to violate the Sherman Act. Relying on the earlier railroad cases, the Supreme Court said:

> These cases, collectively, establish that one system of railroad transportation cannot acquire another, nor a substantial and vital part thereof, when the effect of such acquisition is to suppress, or materially reduce the free and normal flow of competition in the channels of interstate trade. 259 U.S. at 230.

In Standard Oil Co. of New Jersey v. United States, 221 U.S. 1 (1911), the government charged that defendants (including John D. and William Rockefeller and 71 corporate defendants) were conspiring to monopolize and restrain domestic and foreign trade in crude oil, refined oil, and other petroleum products. Chief Justice White found unreasonable restraints, including the "slow but resistless methods" by which means of transportation and other aspects of the petroleum business "were absorbed and brought under control." The Supreme Court described the "evils which led to the public outcry against monopolies and to the final denial of the power to make them" as follows:

> (1) The power which the monopoly gave to the one who enjoyed it to fix the price and thereby injure the public; (2) The power which it engendered of enabling a limitation on production; and, (3) The danger of deterioration in quality of the monopolized article which it was deemed was the inevitable resultant of the monopolistic control over its production and sale.

The Supreme Court ordered the dissolution of Standard Oil.

But a renewal of the incidence of large consolidations followed World War I. The Supreme Court's 4–3 decision, in 1920, upholding the organization of United States Steel encouraged this round of mergers. United States Steel had 80% to 90% of the output of iron and steel products when it was established in 1901, but its market share had fallen to roughly 50% by the time the Supreme Court addressed the consolidation in 1920. *See* United States v. United States Steel Corp., 251 U.S. 417 (1920).

As we will see in Chapters 6 and 9 *infra*, it is difficult to reconcile the *United States Steel* case with the *Standard Oil* and the *Railroad* cases. In general, however, it should be recognized that consolidations—unlike price-fixing agreements—may have underlying business purposes and effects (*e.g.*, the closing of inefficient plants, the attainment of manufacturing or distributional efficiencies) that are economically desirable and which must be balanced against the likelihood of public injury arising from an increase of market power. Note also that as a matter of judicial administration, a merger or consolidation is a discrete event that has to be passed upon only once, in contrast with the continuing surveillance of cartels which would be necessary to determine whether or not their prices remain "reasonable" in terms of ever-changing economic conditions.

Also, in the *Standard Oil* case, the Supreme Court—noting that the sweeping language of Section 1 of the Sherman Act was "broad enough to embrace every conceivable contract or combination"—rejected such an interpretation in favor of a reasonableness approach. Justice White concluded that Congress "intended that the standard of reason which had been applied at the common law ... was intended to be the measure used...." 221 U.S. at 60.

In the majority opinion of United States v. American Tobacco Co., 221 U.S. 106, 179 (1911), Chief Justice White affirmed the Court's adoption of the rule of reason and acknowledged its departure from the across-the-board *per se* approach: "[T]he doctrine thus stated [in *Standard Oil*] was in accord with all the previous decisions of this court.... That such a view [of Section 1 as expressed in *Trans–Missouri*] was a mistaken one was fully pointed out in the *Standard Oil Case*...." In the *American Tobacco* case, five firms that together were responsible for 95% of the cigarettes sold in the United States had merged into the American Tobacco Company. The merged entity purchased forty going tobacco concerns and required those concerns' stockholders and managers to bind themselves not to compete with American Tobacco in the future. The combination not only maintained its control of the cigarette market, but also achieved dominance in the manufacture of other tobacco-related products. Upon applying a rule of reason analysis, the Court determined that the defendant combination had in fact violated Section 1, and remanded the case to the lower court to develop a means of "dissolving the combination and of recreating ... a new condition which shall be honestly in harmony with and not repugnant to the law." 221 U.S. at 187.

Although the rule of reason approach to Section 1 analysis continues to be used by courts today, some behavior is considered so plainly anticompetitive that it warrants invocation of the *per se* rule. As we will see in Chapters 4 and 5 *infra*, among the most common examples of such conduct are horizontal agreements among firms to fix prices, divide territories, or to refuse to deal. Generally, however, agreements that do not fall into one of these so-called *per se* categories are evaluated according to the rule of reason.

NOTES AND QUESTIONS

1. Can the "rule of reason" announced by Chief Justice White be reconciled with the view of Justice Peckham or of Judge (later Chief Justice) Taft? Chief Justice Taft attempted a reconciliation in Cline v. Frink Dairy Co., 274 U.S. 445, 460 (1927). *See also* Taft, The Antitrust Act and the Supreme Court (1914).

2. In 1913, the Supreme Court largely put to rest the question of whether the criminal provisions of the Sherman Act could be declared void for vagueness. In Nash v. United States, 229 U.S. 373 (1913), the American Naval Stores Company was engaged in buying, selling, shipping and exporting turpentine in interstate and foreign commerce, and the National Transportation & Terminal Company had warehouses and terminal facilities for handling turpentine and other naval stores in a number of southern states. Of the six officers of American Naval Stores named in

the opinion, three were also officers of National Transportation & Terminal. The two corporations and six officers were indicted in two counts for conspiracy to restrain trade and to monopolize in violation of Sections 1 and 2 of the Sherman Act.

It was alleged that the corporations and individual defendants conspired to restrain commerce in turpentine and naval stores by the following means: (1) bidding down turpentine and rosin so that competitors could sell them only at ruinous prices; (2) causing naval stores receipts to go to ports other than those to which they would normally go; (3) refraining from purchasing supplies at Savannah, the primary market in the United States for naval stores, because purchases there would tend to strengthen prices in the market; (4) refusing to purchase from factors and brokers unless they entered into contracts for the storage and purchase of defendants' receipts, thereby coercing the factors and brokers into such contracts; (5) circulating false statements as to production and stocks of naval stores; (6) issuing fraudulent warehouse receipts; (7) fraudulently grading rosin and gauging turpentine; (8) attempting to bribe rivals' employees to gain information as to their business and stocks; (9) inducing consumers by payments and threats of boycott to delay dates of delivery of contract supplies, enabling defendants to avoid making purchases at times when such purchases would tend to strengthen the market; (10) offering large amounts of naval stores to depress the market, accepting contracts only for small amounts, and purchasing when the market had been depressed by the offers; (11) selling far below cost to compel competitors to meet prices ruinous to everybody; and (12) fixing the price of turpentine below the cost of production—all for the purpose of driving competitors out of business and restraining and monopolizing trade. A jury found five of the individual defendants guilty, one of them not guilty, and rendered no verdict as to the two corporations.

The defendants had demurred to the indictment on the grounds, among others, that the statute was so vague as to be inoperative on its criminal side; that neither count alleged an overt act; and that the contemplated acts would not have constituted an offense if they had been done. With respect to the first issue raised by the demurrer, the Court (per Holmes, J.) rejected the contention that the Sherman Act was too vague, stating that "the law is full of instances where a man's fate depends on his estimating rightly, that is, as the jury subsequently estimates it, some matter of degree. If his judgment is wrong, not only may he incur a fine or a short imprisonment, as here; he may incur the penalty of death." As to the objection that no overt act was alleged, the Court said that "the Sherman Act punishes the conspiracies at which it is aimed on the common law footing—that is to say, it does not make the doing of any act other than the act of conspiring a condition of liability." Then "as to the suggestion that the matters alleged to have been contemplated would not have constituted an offense if they had been done, it is enough to say that some of them conceivably might have been adequate to accomplish the result, and that the intent alleged would convert what on their face might be no more than ordinary acts of competition or the small dishonesties of trade into a conspiracy of wide scope...." But, after upholding the indictment against claims raised by the demurrer, the Court went on to reverse the verdict because of errors in the charge.

SELECTIVE BIBLIOGRAPHY

1. Antitrust Law and Policy

Pitofsky (ed.), How the Chicago School Overshot the Mark (2008). (Essays and analytical dialogues by leading antitrust authorities).

Areeda & Hovenkamp, Antitrust Law: An Analysis of Antitrust Principles and Their Application (22 Vol. 1980–2006 & Supp. 2009). (Highly influential and comprehensive treatise).

Sullivan & Grimes, The Law of Antitrust: An Integrated Handbook (2d ed. 2006). (Thoughtful and forceful analysis of antitrust cases and policy).

Hovenkamp, Federal Antitrust Policy: The Law of Competition and Its Practice (3d ed. 2005). (Both the Hovenkamp and the Gellhorn, Calkins & Kovacic works clearly explain the essentials of antitrust law and microeconomics).

Gellhorn, Calkins & Kovacic, Antitrust Law and Economics in a Nutshell (5th ed. 2004).

Posner, Antitrust Law (2d ed. 2001). (Antitrust policy as viewed by a distinguished jurist and leading member of the so-called Chicago School).

FTC Staff, Anticipating the 21st Century: Competition Policy in the New High–Tech, Global Marketplace (1996).

Ross, Principles of Antitrust Law (1993).

Bork, The Antitrust Paradox (1978). (A statement on antitrust policy as viewed by a leading member of the so-called Chicago School).

Goldschmid, Mann & Weston (eds.), Industrial Concentration: The New Learning (1974).

Kaysen & Turner, Antitrust Policy (1959). (A classic integration of economic and legal analysis with respect to antitrust law and policy).

Report of the Attorney General's National Committee to Study the Antitrust Laws (1955).

Pitofsky, The Political Content of Antitrust, 127 U.Pa.L.Rev. 1051 (1979).

Students should learn to use the Trade Regulation Reporter, published by Commerce Clearing House, as a research tool and particularly for current developments. Antitrust and Trade Regulation Reporter ("ATRR"), a weekly newsletter published by the Bureau of National Affairs, provides a helpful summary of current judicial, administrative, and legislative developments.

2. Primarily Economic Studies

A number of the works noted in the previous section are by economists or contain substantial doses of descriptive or analytical economics. All, however, deal primarily with antitrust policy and cases. Students who care to refresh or repair their education in economics should read Appendix A to this casebook and one or more of the following works:

Kwoka & White (eds.), The Antitrust Revolution (5th ed. 2008).

Scherer & Ross, Industrial Market Structure and Economic Performance (3d ed. 1990). (Recommended as the most comprehensive and analytically useful book for law students.)

Porter, The Competitive Advantage of Nations (1990).

Williamson, Markets and Hierarchies: Analysis and Antitrust Implications (1983).

3. Origins and History of U.S. Antitrust Policy

Peritz, Competition Policy in America: History, Rhetoric, Law (Rev. Ed. 2001).

Letwin, Law and Economic Policy in America: The Evolution of the Sherman Antitrust Act (Phoenix ed. 1981).

Hofstadter, What Happened to the Antitrust Movement, in The Paranoid Style in American Politics and Other Essays (Phoenix ed. 1979).

Thorelli, The Federal Antitrust Policy (1954).

Nevins, John D. Rockefeller 338–574 (1941).

Walker, History of the Sherman Law of the United States of America (1910).

4. General Comparative Materials

Jones & Sufrin, EC Competition Law: Text, Cases, and Materials (3d ed. 2008).

Atwood, Brewster & Waller, Antitrust and American Business Abroad (3d ed. 2006, Supplement until 2008).

Whish, Competition Law (5th ed. 2004).

Goyder, EC Competition law (4th ed. 2003).

Hawk, United States, Common Market and International Antitrust: A Comparative Guide (2d ed., 3 vol., 1985 & Supp. 1996).

Wang, et al., International Harmonization of Competition Laws (1995).

Scherer, Competition Policies for an Integrated World Economy (1994).

The OECD Journal of Competition Law and Policy.

The competition page of the Organisation for Economic Co-operation and Development (OECD) at http://www.oecd.org/competition

The website of the International Competition Network at http://www.internationalcompetitionnetwork.org.

CHAPTER 2

INSTITUTIONAL FRAMEWORK OF ANTITRUST POLICY

SECTION 1. THE THREE-LEVEL ANTITRUST ENFORCEMENT PATTERN

The antitrust laws are administered and enforced by the Antitrust Division of the Department of Justice and by the Federal Trade Commission. Either agency may proceed against violations of the Clayton Act, while the Justice Department alone is charged with enforcement of the Sherman Act. But the FTC may, in effect, enforce the Sherman Act since under Section 5 of the Federal Trade Commission Act it acts against "unfair methods of competition," a phrase which has been interpreted broadly to encompass practices contravening public policy as declared in the Sherman Act and other antitrust laws.

As an addition to governmental proceedings, a third level of antitrust enforcement has assumed increased importance in recent decades—the enforcement of the antitrust laws by state attorneys general and private parties. State attorneys general, usually acting as representatives of those injured as a result of antitrust violations,[1] and private parties can seek not only equitable relief but also treble damages, the cost of suit, and a reasonable attorney's fee.

This section will profile the two principal federal enforcement agencies. It will summarize briefly the nature and extent of antitrust enforcement by state attorneys general and private claimants, and then discuss a variety of procedural and process problems relating to antitrust enforcement. Antitrust administration and enforcement each year generate an increasingly wide range of complex procedural and process problems. Most of these, for example, the proper scope of pretrial discovery in antitrust cases and the limits on proof at trial, are related principally to the fields of civil procedure and judicial administration, or are of marginal significance, and therefore do not merit separate treatment in an antitrust course. Other problem areas, discussed here, are so intimately connected with fundamental questions of antitrust policy that they must be more fully considered.

---

1. *See* discussion, pp. 64–65 *infra*.

SECTION 1 THREE-LEVEL ANTITRUST ENFORCEMENT

A. SOURCES OF ANTITRUST LITIGATION

1. DEPARTMENT OF JUSTICE

Statutory Responsibilities. Within the Department of Justice is the Antitrust Division, headed by an Assistant Attorney General. The Antitrust Division is responsible for enforcing the Sherman and Clayton Acts, and is required or permitted to intervene in some proceedings before federal administrative agencies involving considerations of public policy with respect to competition and monopoly.[2]

Violations of Sections 1 and 2 of the Sherman Act can be enforced in both civil and criminal proceedings. In 2004, Congress passed the Antitrust Criminal Penalty Enforcement and Reform Act. The statute substantially increased civil and criminal penalties for antitrust violations. Congress' purpose was to make criminal penalties for antitrust offenses more consistent with the harsh penalties for white collar crime established in recent legislation. Criminal proceedings can result in imprisonment of individuals for a maximum of ten years (up from three years previously). Criminal fines for corporations were increased from $10 million to $100 million and criminal fines for individuals were increased from $350,000 to $1 million.[3] In addition, under the Criminal Fine Improvements Act of 1987, fines as high as $500 million have been imposed. The Improvements Act, which is applicable to all felonies, reads as follows:

(d) Alternative fine based on gain or loss.

If any person derives pecuniary gain from the offense, or if the offense results in pecuniary loss to a person other than the defendant, the defendant may be fined not more than the greater of twice the gross gain or twice the gross loss, unless imposition of a fine under this subsection would unduly complicate or prolong the sentencing process.[4]

As applied to a Sherman Act offense, this fine is an *alternative* to what would otherwise be the maximum statutory fine. Thus, for example, in a price-fixing case, the alternative fine would be twice the excess profit

---

2. For example, the Antitrust Division has responsibility to intervene before administrative agencies, functioning wholly or in part under regulatory statutes which require an accommodation between their purposes and those of the antitrust laws, such as the Commodities Futures Trading Commission, Federal Reserve Board, FCC, International Trade Commission, and the SEC. In the past few decades, the Antitrust Division has become much more active in this sort of intervention, generally advocating a policy of free competition before these regulatory agencies.

3. Antitrust Criminal Penalty Enhancement and Reform Act of 2004, Pub. L. No. 108–237, 215, 118 Stat. 661, 668; 15 U.S.C. § 1.

4. 18 U.S.C. § 3571(d). An important use of this provision was first made in 1996, in a price-fixing case against Archer Daniels Midland, where a "$100 million criminal fine—the largest criminal antitrust fine ever"—was collected. Department of Justice, Press Release (Oct. 15, 1996). Since 1996, 17 other antitrust defendants have been fined $100 million or more, including a $500 million fine imposed in 1999 on F. Hoffmann–La Roche for its leadership role in an international price-fixing cartel involving vitamins. The second largest fine imposed was $400 million on LG Display Co. in 2009.

derived (*i.e.*, the difference between the fixed price and the price under normal conditions) by each defendant from a conspiracy, which could total hundreds of millions or even billions of dollars. In fiscal 2008, for example, the Antitrust Division obtained fines of over $700 million, which is more than twenty times the average that was being collected in the decade after the alternative fine was enacted. The fines imposed in fiscal 2009 were much higher than in 2008.

When the Sherman Act was enacted in 1890, the criminal sanctions were imprisonment "not to exceed one year" for a misdemeanor and a $5,000 fine. From 1890 until relatively recently, criminal prosecution followed by imprisonment of individuals was rare; fines were seldom large enough to constitute much of a deterrent. This fact frequently was cited by critics of the antitrust system as an instance of weak law enforcement against "white collar" crime.

Beginning in the mid 1970's, the Antitrust Division put new emphasis on criminal prosecutions. In "Guidelines for Sentencing Recommendations in Felony Cases Under the Sherman Act," issued in 1977, the Antitrust Division explained that an antitrust offender "has a clear option to engage or not to engage in criminal activity." Prison sentences for hard-core offenses (*e.g.*, horizontal price fixing or market allocations), therefore,

> are uniquely effective in deterring antitrust violators (who are generally white collar businessmen) who may view a fine as a "license fee" for fixing prices but who view the threat of a substantial prison term more seriously.[5]

This theme has been consistently repeated by Antitrust Division officials through 2009. The significant issues raised by this emphasis on criminal prosecutions are discussed at pages 75–78 *infra*.

Violations of the Clayton Act, including its Robinson–Patman Act amendments, are not treated criminally.[6] Since 1990, the United States has had a right to recover treble damages for injuries resulting from antitrust violations (*e.g.*, because of government purchasing). Not only are defendants in criminal prosecutions entitled to a jury trial, but either party in a civil treble damage action may demand a jury trial as well.

Budget and Personnel. After a period of growth in the mid 1970's, the resources available to the Antitrust Division stabilized through 1980, and then dramatically decreased throughout the rest of the decade. During the 1990's and early years of the new century, the resources increased, but did not reach the level of the late 1970's. In fiscal 1972, the Antitrust Division had about 325 attorneys and a budget of approximately $12 million. In fiscal 1977, the Antitrust Division had about 421 attorneys and a budget of almost $27 million. In fiscal 1989, the Antitrust Division's budget was only

---

5. 803 ATRR at F–1 (1977).

6. Two minor exceptions are § 10 of the Clayton Act which imposes criminal penalties for certain transactions among common carriers, and § 3 of the Robinson–Patman Act which contains criminal penalties for certain price discrimination activities. These sections give rise to almost no enforcement activity.

about $45 million, and because inflation had taken a toll, the number of attorneys was down to 229.[7] For fiscal 2002, the Antitrust Division was authorized to employ about 400 attorneys and had a budget of about $141 million. The Antitrust Division received a total appropriation of $148 million, and had about 345 attorneys, in 2008.

Given the continued growth of the national economy, the increased need for vigilance created by newly deregulated corporations and foreign companies (with different traditions) doing business in the United States in the shrinking global market,[8] the breadth of responsibilities imposed on the Antitrust Division, the technical complexity of the products and services produced by the so-called "new economy," and the economic strength of many antitrust defendants, thoughtful observers worry about whether the resources available to the Antitrust Division in the early years of the 21st century are adequate. A consensus developed that the resources available in the late 1980's were inadequate. In 1989, a blue ribbon ABA "Task Force on the Antitrust Division" reported as follows:

> [T]he Task Force has concluded that the core mission of the Antitrust Division—to preserve competitive markets—cannot be carried out at current reduced levels of resources and morale.... Likelihood of apprehension is a key variable in deterring antitrust violations. Without sufficient antitrust enforcement resources available, the prospects of being caught are reduced substantially. The Task Force does not believe that, at the present time, the Division's enforcement resources and the public perception of the Division's ability and determination to enforce the laws are adequate to achieve antitrust policy objectives.[9]

In 2001, an ABA Task Force on the Federal Antitrust Agencies concluded:

> The Task Force believes that more resources should be devoted to the full range of tasks that are inherent in the broad mission responsibilities of the federal antitrust agencies.... [T]he performance of the U.S. competition policy system today suffers from the failure of budgets to keep pace with legitimate enforcement and policymaking functions assigned to the two federal enforcement agencies.[10]

---

7. These figures are taken from data prepared in 1989 by the Department of Justice for the Subcommittee on Antitrust, Monopolies and Business Restraints of the Senate Judiciary Committee.

8. *See* Goldschmid, Horizontal Restraints in Antitrust: Current Treatment and Future Needs, 75 Cal.L.Rev. 925, 929–30 (1987).

9. Report of the American Bar Association Section of Antitrust Law Task Force on the Antitrust Division of the U.S. Department of Justice 19–20 (1989) (hereinafter ABA 1989 Task Force Report).

10. ABA Section of Antitrust Law, The State of Federal Antitrust Enforcement—2001: Report of the Task Force on the Federal Antitrust Agencies 14–15 (2001) (hereinafter ABA 2001 Task Force Report).

2.   FEDERAL TRADE COMMISSION

Origins of the FTC and Statutory Responsibilities. The FTC is an independent regulatory agency established in 1914 under the Federal Trade Commission Act. That statute together with the Clayton Act was the culmination of several years of congressional debate and represented compromise positions among the provisions in a series of proposed bills. In a general sense, these statutes constituted a response to the *Standard Oil* decision of 1911,[11] where the Supreme Court first enunciated a "rule of reason" approach to antitrust violations. Advocates of a vigorous antitrust policy felt that this flexible approach gave undesirable and unreviewable power over the nation's economic development to the judiciary. On the other hand, businessmen worried about how to stay within the confines of this vague standard.

One result was a series of statutory provisions in the Clayton Act which outlawed specific business practices such as creation of certain holding companies, price discrimination, and tie-in sales. Of course, specificity in describing illegal practices generated the danger that businessmen might skirt the edges of practices declared illegal. To deal with this problem, Congress enacted Section 5 of the FTC Act which declared unlawful "unfair methods of competition"—an exceptionally broad and vague grant of authority to supervise the functioning of the economy. Congress also created a new agency to enforce these laws. The FTC was given concurrent jurisdiction with the Department of Justice to enforce the provisions of the Clayton Act, and exclusive jurisdiction to enforce the FTC Act. Subsequently, Section 5 of the latter Act has been interpreted not only to cover trade practices which violate a particular provision of the antitrust laws but also those "which conflict with the basic policies of the Sherman and Clayton Acts even though such practices may not actually violate these laws."[12] In a classic work on the origins of the FTC, Gerard C. Henderson summarized the 1914 legislation as follows:

> This apparently widespread demand for a new administrative agency to carry out the anti-trust laws concealed, however, two radically divergent policies. Especially among the business interests, support of a federal trade commission rested not only upon the expectation that such a commission would administer a policy more tolerant toward large aggregations of capital, but on the belief that it could give to a group of business men, in advance, authoritative advice as to the legality of a contemplated undertaking. . . . Plans presented to the Senate Committee on Interstate Commerce by Mr. E.H. Gary, Mr. Francis Lynde Stetson, Mr. Victor Morawetz, and Mr. George W. Perkins all had in common this theory of "advice in advance"—in the nature of an administrative "declaratory judgment," to obviate uncertainty and litiga-

---

11.   Standard Oil Co. of New Jersey v. United States, 221 U.S. 1 (1911).

12.   FTC v. Brown Shoe Co., 384 U.S. 316, 321 (1966); *see* FTC v. Sperry & Hutchinson Co., 405 U.S. 233 (1972).

tion. In general these proposals embodied the theory advocated by President Roosevelt, that combinations and consolidations were not of themselves an evil; that there were good as well as bad trusts; and that rather than pursue a policy of indiscriminate warfare against big business, it was the part of wisdom to license big business under competent regulation in the public interest.

Very different were the grounds upon which such men as Senator Newlands, Senator Cummins, and later President Wilson supported a federal trade commission. In their view of the matter such a commission was to be merely a more effective agency for the enforcement of the anti-trust laws. The purpose of the anti-trust laws was to maintain competitive conditions—a field free to all upon equal terms—and this purpose was not to be abandoned. The only object was to eliminate the delays and uncertainties incident to judicial enforcement. . . .

. . . [I]t was the Congressional intention to confer on the Commission, subject to court review, the duty of giving a detailed content to the general principle embodied in the phrase ["unfair methods of competition"], and to employ, in fulfilling this duty, not only the rules and precedents established by the courts at common law and under previous statutes, but the technique of reasoning by analogy and upon principle, with which jurists are familiar. . . .

It will be apparent from this review of the legislation of 1914, that in so far as the proponents of supplemental antitrust legislation had hoped to clarify the law of restraints and monopolies by substituting specific rules of conduct for general principles, they had largely failed. The draftsmen of the Federal Trade Commission Act avowedly chose a phrase embodying a general principle, while the unlawfulness of the practices somewhat inaptly described in the Clayton Act is made to depend upon the construction of a phrase at least as indefinite as the standard of the Sherman Law under the rule of reason. Both statutes were rather a victory for those who doubted the efficacy of legislative codification, and placed their reliance instead upon the development of rules and precedents by the gradual process of interpretation and decision of controversies by administrative and judicial tribunals.[13]

The FTC also has been empowered by legislation subsequent to the Clayton and FTC Acts to enforce laws with respect to a broad variety of other statutes, including fair packaging and labeling legislation.[14] Far more important, however, are those provisions of Section 5 which in effect make the agency the principal regulatory force at the federal level dealing with unfair and deceptive advertising and general consumer exploitation and

---

13. Henderson, The Federal Trade Commission: A Study in Administrative Law and Procedure 21, 48 (1924).

14. 15 U.S.C. §§ 1451–61.

abuse.[15] Partly in response to the consumer movement of the 1970's, FTC activities in the consumer protection area have increased to the point where, in terms of budget and total personnel, they now substantially exceed the agency's antitrust efforts. The FTC also has certain rulemaking powers, regulatory intervention responsibilities, and information gathering functions.

Organization. The FTC is headed by a chair and four other commissioners who are appointed by the President, with the advice and consent of the Senate, for staggered terms of seven years. No more than three members of the Commission may be of the same political party.

Commission proceedings are initiated by an administrative complaint which is then tried before an "administrative law judge." The findings of the administrative law judge are reviewed by the Commission which may dismiss the complaint or issue a cease and desist order. Much criticism over the years has been directed to the fact that the commissioners both issue the complaint and later pass upon the alleged violation of law—a combination of prosecutorial and judicial functions present in many administrative agencies.

Appeal from a Commission order may be taken directly to a Court of Appeals. The Court of Appeals must uphold Commission orders that are in accord with governing law and supported by substantial evidence. This means that a Court of Appeals must approach the Commission's findings of fact with considerable deference.

Budget and Personnel. The budget and personnel trends at the FTC have been similar to those at the Antitrust Division, but the enhanced resources made available to the Antitrust Division during the 1990's for antitrust enforcement were not paralleled at the FTC. In fiscal 1972, the budget for the FTC was somewhat above $25 million; it employed 1,386 persons. In fiscal 1977, the budget for the FTC was $54.7 million; it employed 1,712 persons. In fiscal 1989, the FTC's budget was about $67 million and it employed fewer than 900 persons. The Bush Administration received about $171 million for the FTC in fiscal 2003, but the bulk of this appropriation (*i.e.*, $94 million) went to the Commission's consumer protection mission, and the FTC was able to employ only slightly over 1,000 persons. The Obama Administration has requested about $287 million for the FTC for fiscal 2010, but again the bulk of the appropriation ($165 million) would go to the Commission's consumer protection efforts and the FTC would employ about 1,150 persons. The ABA 2001 Task Force observed:

> Measured by full-time equivalent work years, from 1981 to 1989 outlays for the Antitrust Division and the FTC's competition mission fell by approximately 50 percent. In the 1990s, Congress restored the budget for the Antitrust Division to nearly 80 percent of its level in 1980. The FTC's competition-related activities,

---

15. 15 U.S.C. § 45(a)(1).

however, continued to receive funding at roughly 50 percent of the budget they received in 1980.

The Task Force concluded that by "almost any measure, the resources allocated the federal antitrust agencies in recent years have not kept up with the increasing scope and complexity of their mission responsibilities."[16]

3.   NATURE AND SCOPE OF ANTITRUST ENFORCEMENT EFFORTS BY THE TWO FEDERAL AGENCIES

Until recently, there has been a substantial increase over the years in the number of actions brought by the Antitrust Division and the FTC. From 1890 to 1925, for example, the Antitrust Division brought an average of about 8 cases a year. Between 1926 and 1937, the average number of new actions rose to about 11; for the years 1938 to 1950, the average was about 50. The following chart—which includes the minimal enforcement years of the Bush Administration—indicates the situation through 2008:

FISCAL YEAR*	PRICE FIXING CRIMINAL	MERGER CIVIL	MONOPOLY CIVIL
1952	6	0	8
1962	31	10	9
1972	14	19	13
1977	34	4	2
1983	92	4	1
1993	78	5	0
1998	57	15	3
2003	23	9	0
2008	26	15	0

* Source   Annual Hearings Before the Subcommittee of the House Committee on Appropriations and the Annual Reports of the Attorney General.

Although merger reviews and negotiations (*i.e.*, where no case is actually filed) and unreasonable restraint cases are time-consuming, important, and not reflected on the foregoing chart, it is obvious that criminal price-fixing cases have played a large role in the Antitrust Division's enforcement effort in recent decades, and this role increased sharply during the Reagan and George W. Bush years. Indeed, from 1981 to 1989 and from 2001 to 2009, with the exception of price-fixing cases, and a relatively few other challenges, enforcement activity by the Antitrust Division was virtually nonexistent. Professor Kovacic, writing about the Reagan Administration, but with words that generally could have been used about the Bush Administration, concluded:

> [T]he Reagan enforcement agencies largely removed the government from the business of scrutinizing exclusionary or abusive

---

16.   ABA 2001 Task Force Report at 4, 14.

conduct by dominant firms. From 1981 through 1988, the Justice Department and the Federal Trade Commission initiated three cases enforcing the Sherman Act's ban on monopolization and attempted monopolization. This level of federal enforcement activity was the lowest in any eight-year period since 1900.

[T]he focus of Reagan non-merger enforcement activity shifted heavily to smaller firms. From 1973 through the arrival of Reagan appointees in 1981, the federal antitrust agencies brought a total of 108 non-merger cases involving Fortune 500 companies. From 1981 through 1988, the number fell to 11.... Critics argue that the Reagan administration pursued an aggressive campaign to collar a hapless, economically trivial parade of asphalt suppliers, lawyers for indigent criminal defendants, moving and storage firms, bakeries, individual physicians, obscure trade associations and a host of other commercial pygmies.[17]

Since 1914, a succession of independent investigations and reports have concluded that the performance of the FTC has not measured up to its potential.[18] During the late 1970's and early 1980's the FTC received heavy criticism for "excessive activism" from business groups, segments of the bar, and members of the Reagan Administration.[19] During most of 1980's, critiques of the FTC contained terms like "passivity" and "timidity."[20] Both the Antitrust Division and the FTC began more vigorous enforcement programs during the first Bush Administration, and grew even more rigorous and enforcement-oriented during the Clinton Administration.[21] The ABA 2001 Task Force concluded that the Clinton Administration's antitrust policy was "within the broad mainstream of American antitrust thinking, albeit at the more activist end of the spectrum."[22] Although the FTC was more active during the George W. Bush Administration than the Antitrust Division, the overall effect was similar to the Reagan years.

---

17. Kovacic, Steady Reliever at Antitrust, Wall St.J., Oct. 10, 1989, at A14, col. 4; *see* Handler, Antitrust Review—1988, 115 N.Y.L.J., Dec. 15, 1988, at 1, col. 1.

18. *See* Henderson, The Federal Trade Commission: A Study in Administrative Law and Procedure (1924). Compare Henderson to the strikingly similar criticisms 45 years later in Cox, Fellmeth, & Schultz, The Nader Report on the Federal Trade Commission (1969) and in the ABA Report on the Federal Trade Commission (1969).

19. For example, David Stockman, President Reagan's first Director of the Office of Management and Budget, referred to the FTC as a "passel of ideologues who are hostile to the business system." Impact of OMB–Proposed Budget Cuts for the Federal Trade Commission, Hearing before a Subcommittee of the House Committee on Government Operations, 97th Cong. 1st Sess. 265 (1981).

20. *See, e.g.*, Correia & Rothbard, Consumer Protection: The Federal Trade Commission, in Green & Pinsky (ed.), America's Transition: Blueprints for the 1990's 247–67 (1989).

21. Anne K. Bingaman and Joel I. Klein, who headed the Antitrust Division during the Clinton Administration, were described as "most aggressive trustbusters," and Robert Pitofsky, who became Chairman of the FTC in 1995, received high praise because he "revived an agency whose influence had waned for more than a decade." Bencivenga, Invigorating the FTC, N.Y.L.J., Feb. 1, 1996, at 5.

22. ABA 2001 Task Force Report at 2.

4. PRIVATE ACTIONS AND STATE ATTORNEYS GENERAL

Statutory Authority and Profile of Private Actions. The key legislative provisions authorizing and controlling private treble damage actions are Sections 4 and 5(a) of the Clayton Act which read as follows:[23]

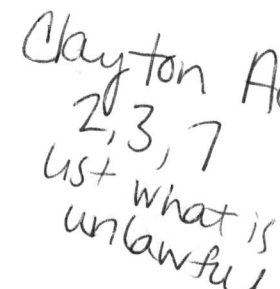

Clayton Act 2, 3, 7 list what is unlawful

> **Sec. 4. Any person who shall be injured in his business or property by reason of anything forbidden in the antitrust laws may sue therefor in any district court of the United States in the district in which the defendant resides, or is found, or has an agent, without respect to the amount in controversy, and shall recover threefold the damages by him sustained, and the cost of suit, including a reasonable attorney's fee. . . .**
>
> **Sec. 5. (a) A final judgment or decree heretofore or hereafter rendered in any civil or criminal proceeding brought by or on behalf of the United States under the antitrust laws to the effect that a defendant has violated said laws shall be prima facie evidence against such defendant in any action or proceeding brought by any other party against such defendant under said laws as to all matters respecting which said judgment or decree would be an estoppel as between the parties thereto: Provided, That this section shall not apply to consent judgments or decrees entered before any testimony has been taken.**

Until the 1960's, very few private plaintiffs were successful. During the period 1890 to 1940, 175 private damage suits proceeded to final adjudication and plaintiffs prevailed in only 13.[24] Between 1952 and 1958, plaintiffs recovered in only 20 of 144 reported cases.[25] In addition, plaintiffs were able to achieve an advantageous settlement in only about 25% of all private suits filed.

The lack of successful private litigation during the first 70 years of antitrust enforcement was particularly remarkable in light of the fact that so many litigants relied on prior government judgments. It has been estimated that approximately 75% of private treble damage suits prior to 1960 were initiated after government suit, and in reliance on prior judgments against defendants.[26] Since 1960, however, the situation has changed, probably largely as a result of a number of Supreme Court decisions easing procedural hurdles and damage standards, and changing substantive norms.[27]

---

23. 15 U.S.C. §§ 15, 16.

24. *See* Att'y Gen. Rep. on the Antitrust Laws 378 (1955).

25. Bicks, The Department of Justice and Private Treble Damage Actions, 4 Antitrust Bull. 5, 11 (1959).

26. Stedman, Consent Decrees and Private Action: An Antitrust Dilemma, 53 Cal.L.Rev. 627, 628 n. 7 (1965).

27. *See* discussion of the "Policy Issues Related to Actions by Private Parties and State Attorneys General," pp. 66–68 *infra*.

A comparison of U.S. government cases and private antitrust cases filed since 1941 indicates that private suits have been the predominant form of antitrust litigation—at least in terms of number of cases filed—for more than 40 years. Professors Salop and White explained:

> Until 1965, with the exception of a "spike" in 1962 due to the electrical conspiracy follow-on cases, the ratio of private to government cases tended to be 6 to 1 or less. From the mid 1960's until the late 1970's the absolute and relative number of private antitrust cases grew, reaching a peak of 1,611 cases in 1977, while the ratio of private to public cases exceeded 20 to 1. In the 1980's, however, both the absolute and relative numbers of antitrust cases have declined, and the private to public ratio has fallen to the 10 to 1 range.[28]

This pattern of private and governmental enforcement appears to have continued into the 21st century.

Statutory Authority and Profile of Enforcement by State Attorneys General. Private actions are also available to states.[29] A state may show damages caused, for example, by overcharges to it resulting from price fixing or other cartel activity or, in its capacity as *parens patriae,* may seek injunctive relief without the need to show damage to its "business or property."[30]

In addition, in September 1976, Congress enacted the Hart–Scott–Rodino Act which contained new *parens patriae* provisions.[31] These permit state attorneys general to bring Sherman Act cases on behalf of natural persons (as opposed to business entities) residing in their states. The attorneys general may seek treble damages, costs, and attorney's fees in addition to injunctive relief. Most importantly, in any action in which it has been determined that a defendant fixed prices in violation of the Sherman Act:

> damages may be proved and assessed in the aggregate by statistical or sampling methods, by the computation of illegal overcharges, or by such other reasonable system of estimating aggregate damages as the court in its discretion may permit without the necessity of separately proving the individual claim of, or amount of damage to, persons on whose behalf the suit was brought.

---

28. Commentary by Salop & White, in White (ed.), Private Antitrust Litigation: New Evidence, New Learning 3 (1988).

29. Under certain circumstances, foreign governments may also recover in treble damage actions. *See* Antitrust Reciprocity Amendment, Pub.L. No. 97–393, 96 Stat. 1964 (1982); Pfizer, Inc. v. Government of India, 434 U.S. 308 (1978).

30. *See* Georgia v. Pennsylvania Railroad Co., 324 U.S. 439 (1945). States, however, may not bring treble damage actions for general injury to their economies. *See* Hawaii v. Standard Oil Co., 405 U.S. 251 (1972) (The Court focused on the danger of double recovery by both a state and individual citizens for the same injury).

31. Hart–Scott–Rodino Antitrust Improvements Act of 1976, Pub.L. No. 94–435, 90 Stat. 1383; 15 U.S.C. §§ 15, 1311–1314.

Where price fixing has been found the Act provides, in essence, for "fluid recoveries." Once aggregate damages have been awarded, each person in the attorney general's class may come forward and prove the extent of his or her injury. Monies not claimed by individuals:

> Shall (1) be distributed in such manner as the district court in its discretion may authorize; or (2) be deemed a civil penalty by the court and deposited with the State as general revenues.

Critics contended that the *parens patriae* provisions improperly focus on "ill-gotten gains rather than on consumer compensation," and would result in unmanageable classes and ruinous exposures. The report of the Senate Judiciary Committee responded:

> The economic burden of most antitrust violations is borne by the consumer in the form of higher prices for goods and services. . . . When everyday consumer purchases are involved (*e.g.*, bread, dairy products, gasoline, etc.), the individual dollar amounts are so small that, as a practical matter, an individual antitrust lawsuit is out of the question. Similarly, consumers have found little relief under the class action provisions of the Federal Rules. . . .
>
> The Committee believes that this title provides a practical remedy for consumers, and that it is necessary to deter antitrust violations, to take the profit out of white collar crime, and to dispense equal justice to the rich and poor alike. The predictions of ruinous liability made by opponents . . . [are unproven and must be rejected].[32]

The *parens patriae* provisions of the Hart–Scott–Rodino Act and the general contractions of antitrust enforcement at the federal level led, as the National Association of Attorneys General describe it, to "a revolution in the patterns of enforcement" during the 1980's. In this decade, state attorney general enforcement:

> experienced first renaissance and then an explosive increase in cases, investigations, and legislative and other policy initiatives. To the traditional attorney general role of *parens patriae* in local cases involving price-fixing and bid-rigging was added a concern with the entire spectrum of competition law and policy.[33]

During the 1990's, with more aggressive enforcement by the Antitrust Division and the FTC, the antitrust activity of state attorneys general somewhat receded. In the early years of the 21st century, it appears that

---

32. S.Rep. No. 803, 94th Cong., 2d Sess. 7 (1976).

33. National Association of Attorneys General, State Attorney General Antitrust Enforcement (i) (1989). The *parens patriae* role of state attorneys general must be viewed in the light of the Supreme Court's decisions in Illinois Brick Co. v. Illinois, 431 U.S. 720 (1977), which may prevent consumers (often indirect purchasers) from proving antitrust damage, and California v. ARC America Corp., 490 U.S. 93 (1989), which acknowledges the right of indirect purchasers to recover under state antitrust statutes. *See* pp. 88–91 *infra*. In general, state antitrust statutes, which usually parallel the federal antitrust laws, are beyond the purview of this casebook.

state antitrust enforcement increased and now remains vigorous by any historic measure. Also, particularly in the late 1990's, state attorneys general worked effectively with the federal enforcement agencies through cooperation agreements and joint proceedings (*e.g.*, state attorneys general joined with the Antitrust Division in the Microsoft case[34] and with the FTC in a merger proceeding against Exxon and Mobil).

Policy Issues Related to Actions by Private Parties and State Attorneys General. One result of the surge of antitrust enforcement activity by private parties and state attorneys general has been to change the balance of potential profit and risk for businessmen contemplating questionable conduct under the antitrust laws. Since the Antitrust Division and the FTC have limited resources, allowing them to bring perhaps 100 to 150 cases even in well-funded years, the question of whether a particular new distribution policy, or other practice questionable under the antitrust laws, will be attempted often comes down to an inquiry about whether or not there is a potential litigant (or a class of litigants) who has the resources and staying power to take its claim to the courts.

In 1982, in several cases, the Supreme Court reemphasized its long-standing recognition of the important role played by private treble damage actions:

> Congress sought to create a private enforcement mechanism that would deter violators and deprive them of the fruits of their illegal actions, and would provide ample compensation to the victims of antitrust violations. . . . Consistent with the congressional purpose, we have refused to engraft artificial limitations on the § 4 remedy. . . . [W]e have applied § 4 in accordance with its plain language and its broad remedial and deterrent objectives.

Blue Shield of Virginia v. McCready, 457 U.S. 465 (1982); *see* American Society of Mechanical Engineers, Inc. v. Hydrolevel Corp., 456 U.S. 556, 571 (1982).

On the other hand, many commentators agree that some private damage claimants, attracted by the possibility of a treble damage "bonanza," have instituted suits with little merit in the hope of at least extracting a settlement. Defendants are often hesitant to go to trial when faced with large damage exposures in complex antitrust litigation. Also, as the Supreme Court noted in Blue Chip Stamps v. Manor Drug Stores, 421 U.S. 723, 742–43 (1975), in the context of securities litigation:

> [I]n this type of litigation . . . the mere existence of an unresolved lawsuit has settlement value to the plaintiff not only because of the possibility that he may prevail on the merits, an entirely legitimate component of settlement value, but because of the threat of extensive discovery and disruption of normal business activities which may accompany a lawsuit which is groundless in any event, but cannot be proved so before trial. . . .

---

34. *See* Section 1 of Chapter 8 *infra.*

Additional problems may be caused by the fact that competitors will sometimes have perverse (anticompetitive) reasons for challenging a practice or opposing a merger, and in antitrust class actions, the plaintiffs' attorney is often the engine (with a large financial stake in the result) of the litigation. These problems create the danger of overenforcement and, in comparison to a government action, leave little room for prosecutorial discretion in the public interest.

Similarly, actions by state attorneys general have been challenged as involving heavy political components or undue concern for special local interests. Nevertheless, during the past twenty-five years or so, a broad consensus appears to have developed in support of vigorous state attorney general action. For example, Charles F. Rule, the last Assistant Attorney in charge of the Antitrust Division during the Reagan years, stated:

> In the ten years since the *parens patriae* remedy was enacted, state antitrust activity has increased greatly. Consumers likely have benefited from having their antitrust damage concerns addressed by those best able to identify and respond to them.

> State attorneys general, being closer to their citizens injured by antitrust violations, have a greater incentive to bring consumer-based damage actions than would the federal government. State attorneys general have been steadily accumulating the expertise needed successfully to pursue complex antitrust damages actions, and are free to hire outside counsel when additional assistance is required. Furthermore, the state attorneys general have shown in several instances that, by coordinating their efforts, they can pursue antitrust actions of multi-state scope that approach the limits on the size of such consumer damage actions that successfully can be litigated.[35]

The ABA 2001 Task Force, however, observed that [t]here "are many enforcers of the American antitrust laws-federal antitrust agencies, state attorneys general, and multiple private attorneys general," and that "our system generates large administrative costs, large legal fees, and haphazard results in terms of victim compensation." It urged careful study of the problem.[36] But in 2007, a bipartisan Antitrust Modernization Commission created by Congress, recommended no statutory change "to the current role of the states in non-merger civil antitrust enforcement or "with respect to reviewing mergers." The Modernization Commission encouraged federal and state antitrust enforcement agencies to "coordinate their activities and to seek to avoid subjecting companies to multiple and possibly inconsistent proceedings.[37] Throughout the course consider the costs and benefits—including the deterrent, resource enhancement, and compensa-

---

35.   Rule, Remarks at an ALI–ABA Course of Study 30 (May 6, 1988).

36.   ABA 2001 Task Force Report at 4–5.

37.   Antitrust Modernization Commission, Report and Recommendations 187 (2007), at http://www.govinfo.library.unt.edu/amc/report (hereinafter Antitrust Modernization Commission Report).

tion advantages—of antitrust's three-level enforcement pattern. In response to the important role in antitrust enforcement that is played by private actions and to the potential for abuse of such actions, the procedural and process rules discussed in Section C *infra* have been developed.

B. SPECIAL ISSUES RELATED TO ENFORCEMENT BY THE FEDERAL AGENCIES

1. COORDINATION BETWEEN THE DEPARTMENT OF JUSTICE AND THE FTC AND THE ISSUE OF DUAL ENFORCEMENT

The Antitrust Division has left to the FTC virtually all enforcement of the price discrimination provisions of the Robinson–Patman Act. The FTC, of course, brings no action of a criminal nature. In other areas of antitrust enforcement, there is a substantial overlap in jurisdiction, and as a result, the two agencies have developed a "liaison" system to avoid duplication of effort and unnecessary harassment of businesses. Investigations are cleared between the two agencies. Some particular antitrust practices appear to fall within the special province of the Antitrust Division, such as "hard-core" price fixing, and some industries, such as data processing and basic metals, also seem to devolve upon the Antitrust Division rather than the FTC. On the other hand, pharmaceutical and food distribution problems are regularly handled by the FTC. There are exceptions to these generalizations. In March 2002, the heads of the Antitrust Division and FTC worked out an agreement to formally allocate industries between the two agencies in order to provide transparency, and to reduce the controversy and delay that can occur when both agencies wish to investigate the same matter. The plan was dropped because of opposition in Congress. Arguably, there are advantages to the overlapping responsibilities; Congress had consciously created the agencies' concurrent jurisdiction. In any event, most former heads of the Antitrust Division and FTC believe the system works well. John H. Shenefield, for example, who was in charge of the Antitrust Division during the Carter Administration, testified as follows:

> The liaison arrangement gives weight to several factors in resolving conflicts between the two agencies. First, the existence within an agency of special industry expertise or a prior case or past investigation concerning the same companies or products should operate presumptively to give that same agency responsibility for any new case. In addition the availability of resources is relevant to the necessity for immediate action. The type of conduct involved may suggest that one or another agency is the more suitable. Finally, the existence within an agency of an investigation or decree that would be interfered with should another agency proceed would be taken into account.

> In general, the liaison arrangement has worked extremely well. In only four or five cases during the two and two-thirds years that I was in charge of the Antitrust Division were liaison disagreements referred to me.... [I was] able easily to resolve the

disputes without delay. Such disputes only seem to arise in cases involving significant mergers, particularly in the conglomerate area where both agencies can legitimately claim involvement or familiarity with one of the merging firms.[38]

Neither the Antitrust Division nor the FTC has been able to resist all outside pressures seeking to influence enforcement policies. The Antitrust Division, as a part of the executive branch, is necessarily somewhat more responsive to pressures exerted by way of the White House. The FTC, as an independent agency relying in the last analysis on Congressional appropriations, is apt to feel more strongly pressures from crucial legislators. In a field where private financial stakes are often high, there is real danger that the public interest will be inadequately represented. In this context, many argue that any inefficiencies arising from overlapping enforcement responsibilities are more than offset by the advantage provided by the different positions of the two agencies in the political and administrative structures. In many ways, the two agencies—with somewhat different focuses and expertise—stimulate and complement each other. For many, the existence of two agencies, with different appointment processes and somewhat different institutional loyalties, provides an important safety valve in so sensitive an area of national policy. In 2007, the Antitrust Modernization Commission recommended "no comprehensive change to the existing system in which both the FTC and the DOJ enforce the antitrust laws."[39]

2. INVESTIGATIVE AUTHORITY AND REQUIRED REPORTING

Most antitrust investigations proceed through informal interviews and questionnaires, with voluntary compliance by the person or firm being investigated. The Antitrust Division may also convene a grand jury with subpoena powers, although the Supreme Court, in United States v. Procter & Gamble Co., 356 U.S. 677 (1958), made it clear that a grand jury may not be used if the Antitrust Division's principal intent is eventually to bring a civil action. Partly in response to that decision, in 1962, the Antitrust Division obtained from Congress broad civil investigatory powers under the Antitrust Civil Process Act.[40] The Act enabled the Antitrust Division to issue a civil investigative demand ("CID") to obtain documentary evidence from non-natural persons (*e.g.*, corporations) suspected of committing a violation.

In 1976, in the Hart–Scott–Rodino Act,[41] the Antitrust Division was empowered to issue a demand (i) for oral testimony or written interrogatories (*i.e.*, in addition to documentary evidence), (ii) to all persons (*i.e.*, non-natural and natural), (iii) including "non-target" third parties, such as

---

38. Impact of OMB–Proposed Budget Cuts for the Federal Trade Commission, Hearing before a Subcommittee of the House Committee on Government Operations, 97th Cong., 1st Sess. 245–46 (1981).

39. Antitrust Modernization Commission Report at 129.

40. 15 U.S.C. §§ 1311–14.

41. Hart–Scott–Rodino Antitrust Improvements Act of 1976, Pub.L. No. 94–435, 90 Stat. 1383; 15 U.S.C. §§ 15, 1311–1314.

competitors, suppliers, customers, and employees, with relevant information. In addition to the authority to investigate past or present violations, the Act also gives investigators authority to inquire into "activities in preparation for a merger, acquisition, joint venture, or similar transaction, which, if consummated, may result in an antitrust violation." Additional amendments to the Act in 1980 further strengthened the Antitrust Division's CID power. The FTC has similar investigative powers.[42] Once an action has been instituted, in general, the usual civil discovery procedures are available, and extensive use of interrogatories and depositions is customary.

The Hart–Scott–Rodino Act also required pre-merger notification. Parties, including foreign interests, involved in a merger must file a pre-merger notification form with the FTC and Antitrust Division. The Hart–Scott–Rodino Act and FTC implementing regulations now require that filings must involve a "size-of-transaction" threshold of over $65 million (up from the original $15 million) for the Act to be applicable. An amendment in 2000, did away with prior "size-of-person" tests for transactions now valued in excess of $260 million, and put into effect a graduated scale for filing fees based on the size of a transaction. An automatic waiting period, prior to the consummation of a merger, is mandated, and the waiting period runs for 15 to at least 50 days, depending on circumstances and the type of merger.

3.   CASE SELECTION AND PROSECUTORIAL DISCRETION

In the past, thoughtful critics of governmental antitrust enforcement have focused on deficiencies in policy planning and case selection at both the Antitrust Division and FTC. Many have urged more systematic policy planning. Effective planning would, for example, involve consideration of available enforcement techniques (*e.g.*, case-by-case litigation, rulemaking, guides, stimulation of industry self-regulation), and selection of cases and litigating theories that would achieve maximum deterrence of anticompetitive activities.

There is evidence that a good deal of public antitrust enforcement in the past has been triggered by complaints by businessmen who felt they were losing out in the competitive battle. When those complaints had the benefit of political support—*e.g.*, suggestions for investigation of particular practices by the administration or powerful legislators—there seems to have been a tendency to satisfy the complainants. A major effort to do the type of policy planning being advocated was carried out by the FTC in 1995–96. After two months of hearings during the fall of 1995, the FTC released a report, dated May 1996, that "analyzes and makes recommendations on how to continue the FTC's mission in light of increased global and innovation-based competition." The report, among other topics, deals with: "competition at the close of the century"; efficiencies; "innovation, intellec-

---

42.   15 U.S.C. §§ 46, 49.

tual property, and competition"; joint ventures; and "themes for the future."[43]

There remains, however, a concern that enforcement priorities shift too sharply with each new Assistant Attorney General in charge of the Antitrust Division, Chair of the FTC, and, of course, with each new administration. Although shifts in emphasis may reflect desirable flexibility and a healthy concern about new developments, serious questions may be raised about *ad hoc* case selection and sharply shifting priorities.

In addition, as discussed earlier, the 1980's and early 2000's saw a significant issue arise as to the proper boundaries of prosecutorial discretion. Enforcement officials stated that they would not enforce certain antitrust rules with which they disagreed. While some prosecutorial discretion is both necessary and desirable, the scope of discretion asserted by recalcitrant officials reemphasized, at least for some observers, the importance of the antitrust roles played by private parties and state attorneys general.

4.   LITIGATION OR SETTLEMENT

The vast majority (*i.e.*, 80% or more) of government cases never go to trial but rather are settled through some sort of voluntary agreement. The Antitrust Division and the FTC both accept "consent" decrees or orders, respectively, which, in effect, are negotiated settlements between the staff of the agency and counsel for the litigants, approved by a federal district court in Antitrust Division proceedings or by the commissioners in FTC matters. In addition, the FTC occasionally will accept assurances of voluntary compliance and informal corrective actions which are written commitments by respondents to discontinue objectionable practices. These have no legal effect, except that the FTC is more likely to take vigorous enforcement action against a company that continues a violation after voluntary compliance has been assured.

Given the great expense and length of many antitrust actions (*see* Section D *infra*), consent agreements often offer advantages to all parties. Defendants can usually avoid the government obtaining its maximum relief, avoid any *prima facie* effect of a pretrial consent decree (*see* pp. 78–80 *infra*), and avoid significant business disruption. The Antitrust Division and FTC may be able to obtain expeditious relief while husbanding scarce enforcement resources.

During the 1960's and early 1970's observers of the antitrust scene increasingly came to realize that major questions of antitrust policy were being resolved in the context of consent negotiations. This led Congress in 1974 to enact the Antitrust Procedures and Penalties Act, known as the Tunney Act, which subjects antitrust settlements made by the Antitrust

---

43. FTC Staff, Anticipating the 21st Century: Competition Policy in the New High–Tech, Global Marketplace (1996). More than 200 business and consumer representatives, practitioners, government officials, and academicians participated in the FTC's hearings.

Division to greater court and public scrutiny.[44] The Act required the Department of Justice to file a detailed "competitive impact statement" with respect to any proposed consent decree and creates a 60–day waiting period (which allows for public comment) between the filing of a proposed consent judgment and the effective date of the decree. The "competitive impact statement" must include descriptions of the nature and purposes of the proceeding and an explanation of the proposed consent decree. The sponsors of the Act suggested these statements would: (i) increase public understanding of, and participation in, consent decree proceedings; (ii) focus government attorneys on the public impact of their case; and (iii) encourage district judges more carefully to review consent decrees in appropriate instances.

Under the Act, a district judge is not to enter a proposed consent judgment unless he or she determines that it is "in the public interest." Congress contemplated that district judges would be more deeply involved in evaluating consent judgments than had previously been the practice, and evidence suggests that district judges are respecting this Congressional mandate.

District judges can, however, carry their mandate too far. In a recent celebrated case, United States v. Microsoft Corp., 56 F.3d 1448 (D.C.Cir. 1995), the district court had refused to enter a proposed consent decree between the Antitrust Division and Microsoft. The Circuit Court concluded that the district court exceeded its authority and reasoned:

> At the heart of this case, then, is the proper scope of the district court's inquiry into the "public interest." Is the district judge entitled to seize hold of the matter—the investigation into the putative defendant's business practices—and decide for himself the appropriate combined response of the executive and judicial branches to those practices? With respect to the specific allegations in the government's complaint, may the court interpose its own views of the appropriate remedy over those the government seeks as a part of its overall settlement? To be sure, Congress, in passing the Tunney Act, intended to prevent "judicial rubber stamping" of the Justice Department's proposed consent decree....

> [Nevertheless, although] the language of section 16(e) is not precise, we think the government is correct in contending that section 16(e)(1)'s reference to the alleged violations suggests that Congress did not mean for a district judge to construct his own hypothetical case and then evaluate the decree against that case. Moreover, in section 16(e)(2), the court is authorized to consider "the public benefit ... of the determination of the issues at trial." Putting aside the perplexing question of how the district judge could insure a trial if the government did not wish one, "the issues" referred to must be those formulated in the complaint.

---

44. Antitrust Procedures and Penalties Act—Expediting Act, Pub.L. No. 93–528, 88 Stat. 1706; 15 U.S.C. § 16.

Congress surely did not contemplate that the district judge would, by reformulating the issues, effectively redraft the complaint himself.[45]

In 2004, in response to the D.C. Circuit's *Microsoft* decision, Congress amended the Tunney Act to clarify (or emphasize) that district courts are to undertake a thorough and independent determination of whether a proposed consent decree is adequate and in the public interest.

Either the government or a defendant may petition for court modification of a previously entered consent decree, but consent decrees have seldom been modified absent the agreement of the original parties. Both the Antitrust Division and the FTC now have active programs for reviewing past consent decrees to determine whether or not they continue to effectuate antitrust objectives.

5.   INTERVENTION

Business conduct at issue in a particular government (or private) antitrust action may have ramifications far beyond the interests of the particular litigants. Accordingly, parties may attempt to intervene, either "of right" under Rule 24(a) or as a matter of discretion under Rule 24(b) of the Federal Rules of Civil Procedure.

Rule 24(a)(2) was amended in 1966 to permit intervention of right when the applicant claims an interest such that disposition of the action as a practical matter may "impair or impede his ability to protect that interest . . ." unless that interest "is adequately represented by existing parties." Prior to 1966, intervention was rarely granted, particularly in government antitrust litigation. Arguably, the Supreme Court might have signaled a change in attitude in this area in Cascade Natural Gas Corp. v. El Paso Natural Gas Co., 386 U.S. 129 (1967), where the Court sustained the right of California, Southern California Edison (a large industrial user of natural gas), and Cascade Natural Gas (a distributor whose sole supplier had been one of the companies in the challenged merger) to intervene in a divestiture proceeding looking toward the breakup of El Paso and Pacific Northwest, two natural gas companies that previously had been held to have merged illegally. Noting that "the United States knuckled under to El Paso," the Court found inadequacy of representation in the divestiture proceedings.

Though many expected the *Cascade* decision would lead to expanded opportunities for intervention in government antitrust litigation,[46] subsequent cases have not borne this out. For example, intervention was denied in United States v. Automobile Manufacturers Ass'n,[47] where the City of New York and others attempted to intervene in proposed consent proceedings to dispose of a pollution conspiracy case against the big four automobile manufacturers. Similarly, Ralph Nader's attempt to intervene to chal-

---

45.   56 F.3d 1448, 1458–59 (D.C.Cir.1995).

46.   *See* 3B J. Moore, Federal Practice, ¶ 24.08[6] at 24–198 (2d ed. 1975).

47.   307 F.Supp. 617 (C.D.Cal.1969), affirmed per curiam sub nom., City of New York v. United States, 397 U.S. 248 (1970).

lenge an *ITT–Hartford* consent decree was denied in United States v. International Telephone & Telegraph Corp.[48]

The judicial tendency to construe *Cascade* narrowly reflects a reluctance to assume that plaintiffs—particularly in government litigation—will inadequately represent the public interest. The current test in determining intervention of right is probably close to the standard announced in United States v. Ciba Corp., 50 F.R.D. 507, 513 (S.D.N.Y.1970), where *Cascade* was distinguished and the district court announced a standard which includes requirements that: (1) the interest justifying intervention be substantial; (2) it "lie at the center" of the controversy; and (3) there be a clear showing that the interest is less than "adequately represented."[49]

Under Rule 24(b), permissive intervention may be granted when there are common questions of law or fact and where the court determines that intervention will not unduly delay or prejudice the adjudication of the rights of individual parties. Requests for permissive intervention are rarely granted in antitrust cases.

Intervention in an adjudicative proceeding at the FTC is at the Commission's discretion. In the past, in several consumer protection cases, intervention by public interest law groups has been permitted.

6. GOVERNMENT ANTITRUST REMEDIES AND THE EMPHASIS ON CRIMINAL PROSECUTIONS

As previously indicated, the Antitrust Division may seek either criminal or civil remedies when challenging anticompetitive activity. Section 4 of the Sherman Act and Section 15 of the Clayton Act confer jurisdiction on the federal courts to "prevent and restrain" violations.[50] The FTC is empowered to issue "cease and desist" orders and may thereby undo or prevent unlawful activity. In fashioning relief, courts and the FTC have considerable discretion and are entitled to enjoin a broad range of possible future violations. The classic statement is found in International Salt Co. v. United States, 332 U.S. 392, 400 (1947):

> The District Court is not obliged to assume, contrary to common experience, that a violator of the antitrust laws will relinquish the fruits of his violation more completely than the court requires him to do. . . . When the purpose to restrain trade appears from a clear violation of law, it is not necessary that all the untraveled roads to that end be left open and that only the worn one be closed.[51]

---

48. 349 F.Supp. 22 (D.Conn.1972), affirmed mem. sub nom., Nader v. United States, 410 U.S. 919 (1973). *See generally* Note, The ITT Dividend: Reform of Department of Justice Consent Decree Procedures, 73 Colum.L.Rev. 594 (1973).

49. *See* United States v. Associated Milk Producers, Inc., 534 F.2d 113 (8th Cir.1976), cert. denied, 429 U.S. 940 (1976); cf. United States v. AT&T, 1981–2 Trade Cas. (CCH) ¶ 64,979 at 73,142 (D.D.C.1982) (intervention permitted).

50. 15 U.S.C. §§ 4, 25.

51. *See, e.g.,* Atlantic Refining Co. v. FTC, 381 U.S. 357 (1965); FTC v. Henry Broch & Co., 368 U.S. 360, 364 (1962).

Until recently, injunctive sanctions, damage claims, and criminal fines were the principal remedies available to the government. Particularly for "hard-core" anticompetitive offenses, these remedies have been inadequate. Indeed, from 1890 to about 30 years ago, private treble damage actions constituted the most significant antitrust sanction. Prison sentences were almost never imposed.

Since the mid 1970's, Congress has played an active role in broadening and strengthening antitrust remedies. Presently, as indicated earlier, violation of the Sherman Act is a felony for which individuals may be sentenced to a prison term of up to ten years and a fine of no more than $1 million. Corporations face a fine of up to $100 million. Even more important in monetary terms, the Criminal Fine Improvements Act of 1987[52] provides for an alternative maximum fine, for both individual and corporate antitrust offenders, of twice the gross pecuniary gain or loss resulting from the violation. Until fiscal 1992, the largest corporate fine ever imposed in an antitrust prosecution was $2 million, and during the late 1980's and early 1990's, annual fines collected by the Antitrust Division averaged about $27 million. By contrast, since the Improvements Act was applied to antitrust (by way of a $100 million fine in a price-fixing case against Archer Daniels Midland in 1996), 17 defendants have been fined $100 million or more (including a $500 million fine and a $400 million fine), and in fiscal 2008, the Antitrust Division obtained fines of over $700 million.[53] On the civil side, the FTC recently obtained a $100 million settlement in an action seeking disgorgement of illicit profits. In FTC v. Mylan, the Commission persuaded a district court, relying on equitable powers in a disgorgement settlement, to require repayment of the $100 million to exploited consumers.[54]

Since the mid 1970's, there has been increasing recognition of the significance of imprisonment as a uniquely important antitrust sanction. Until 1977, the most notable instance of the imposition of prison sentences involved 30–day sentences for General Electric and Westinghouse executives after they pleaded guilty to price fixing on electrical equipment in the early 1960's. But this in no way established a trend. No one convicted of an antitrust violation—no matter how egregious or hard-core—received a prison sentence from fiscal 1962 through 1968. From 1969 to 1977, fewer than a dozen individuals received prison sentences of more than 30 days.[55] Even in the GE–Westinghouse price-fixing cases, most observers concluded that although the 30–day sentences may have made a few executives contrite, the real bite came from the approximately 1,800 private lawsuits

---

52.   *See* discussion p. 55 *supra*.

53.   *See* Sherman Act Violations Chart, Antitrust Division Spring 2009 Update; Hammond, A Review of Recent Cases and Developments in the Antitrust Division's Criminal Enforcement Program (Conference Board program March 7, 2002).

54.   *See* FTC v. Mylan Laboratories, FTC File No. X990015 (2000); FTC v. Mylan Laboratories, Civil 1:98CV03114 (TFH) (D.D.C.1999).

55.   Baker and Reeves, The Paper Label Sentences: Critiques, 86 Yale L.J. 619, 623 n. 16 (1977).

which cost GE and other companies upwards of $350 million to litigate and settle.

In 1974, however, in the Antitrust Procedures and Penalties Act, Congress attempted to alter the antitrust sanctions equation. Congress, in effect, mandated heavier prison sentences for antitrust violators by increasing the maximum prison term to three years and by making violations felonies.[56] A cynical wag suggested that: "Congress decided on three years by adding up all of the time spent in prison by antitrust violators since 1890." There is, of course, truth in the statement, but it misses the point. Congress was really saying that criminal fines, treble damages, and injunctive provisions were not enough; to make antitrust enforcement work, what was needed was the general deterrence created by the threat of imprisonment for meaningful periods of time.

In 1977, the Department of Justice issued sentencing guidelines for felony cases under the Sherman Act. The guidelines indicate that the Antitrust Division had taken Congress' hint. The Antitrust Division said that it would recommend to district judges that antitrust violators—at least where hard-core offenses were involved—should go to jail. The guidelines also indicated that fines were "poor alternatives" to imprisonment and would be recommended only where prison sentences were inappropriate.

Although Nash v. United States, 229 U.S. 373 (1913), largely put to rest the question of whether or not the criminal provisions of the Sherman Act would be declared void for vagueness, critics of criminal enforcement still raise the "vagueness" policy issue: "Is it fair," they ask, "to prosecute a defendant who was understandably confused about the state of the law?" The Antitrust Division's answer is that criminal prosecutions will take place only where hard-core offenses—for example, horizontal price fixing, bid-rigging schemes, and market allocations—are involved. Even in these areas, it is unlikely that criminal cases will be brought if a potential defendant was understandably confused about the state of the law or otherwise acted reasonably and in good faith.

A significant development with respect to sentencing for antitrust offenses came in the Sentencing Guidelines, which took effect on November 1, 1987.[57] The background notes to the antitrust Guideline predicted that prison terms for antitrust offenders would become more common, and usually longer, than was the case under pre-Guidelines practice. This prediction has been verified. From 1984 to 1988, the average sentence for an antitrust felony was 5 months. In the five-year period ending in February 1993, the average sentence was 10 months for offenses under the

---

56. See p. 5 n.10 supra.

57. The Sentencing Reform Act of 1984 (Title II of the Comprehensive Crime Control Act of 1984) established the United States Sentencing Commission in the Judicial Branch. It charged the Commission with developing a set of guidelines that would, while reducing the variance in sentences imposed for similar offenses, also meet the goals of criminal sentencing: respect for the law, deterrence, incapacitation, and rehabilitation. It is important to bear in mind that antitrust offenses are only the smallest part of the overall Sentencing Guidelines, which cover virtually all federal crimes.

Sentencing Guidelines (where judges had more limited discretion) and 7.5 months for non-Guideline offenses.[58] During fiscal 2001, the average prison term had increased to nearly 15 months.[59] Although the Supreme Court made the Sentencing Guidelines, advisory and no longer mandatory in 2005,[60] average prison sentences for pricing fixing have continued to increase. In fiscal 2007 and in fiscal 2008, the average prison sentence was 31 months.[61]

In thinking about sentencing issues, consider the following:

a.   Do you agree with the Antitrust Division that prison sentences are uniquely effective in deterring antitrust violators? There is almost no empirical evidence available to support or refute this view.[62] What about "certainty of punishment"?[63] Are the two mutually exclusive? Since price fixing is a crime that involves rational choice, are not both substantial enforcement efforts and meaningful punishments necessary to create viable deterrence?

b.   Sentencing for the purpose of "general deterrence" makes the character of the offense—rather than the offender—the central focus in the sentencing decision. A defendant's background and peculiar characteristics are given little weight since he or she is not being imprisoned for the purpose of self-improvement. Thus, tailoring sentences to take account of community service, family needs, etc., may actually undermine general deterrence. But what about fairness to the offender and the flexibility that individual tailoring provides?

c.   Evaluate the following view of Judge Renfrew:

> Despite the seriousness of antitrust violations, I find a blanket comparison between these crimes and other felonies inappropriate. I believe that crimes of violence are, in general, much more destructive of the fabric of society than are nonviolent commercial crimes.... While the two kinds of crime may have a similar economic impact, and may both instill some apprehension in the public, the psychological effect of violent crime is clearly more pernicious.[64]

---

58.   *See* 60 Minutes with Anne K. Bingaman, Assistant Attorney General Antitrust, 63 Antitrust L.J. 323, 329 (1994).

59.   *See* Hammond, A Review of Recent Cases and Developments in the Antitrust Division's Criminal Enforcement Program (Conference Board program March 7, 2002).

60.   United States v. Booker, 543 U.S. 220 (2005).

61.   Hammond, Recent Developments, Trends, and Milestones in the Antitrust Division's Criminal Enforcement Program (2008), at http://www.usdoj.gov/atr/public/speeches/232716. htm.

62.   Compare Baker and Reeves, The Paper Label Sentences: Critiques, 86 Yale L.J. 619, 622 (1977) with Wheeler, Critique, 86 Yale L.J. 636 (1977).

63.   *See* United States v. Alton Box Co., ATRR No. 805, P.E.–1 (N.D. Ill. 1977).

64.   Renfrew, The Paper Label Sentences: An Evaluation, 86 Yale L.J. 590, 593 n.8 (1977).

Consider the impact on public confidence in the legal system if the perception grows that blue-collar criminals go to jail but white-collar criminals do not.

d. Are "alternative sentences" (*e.g.*, to provide community service) sufficiently unpleasant or stigmatizing to create general deterrence? What other sanctions (*e.g.*, suspensions or forced resignations of corporate offenders, civil money penalties) might be made available?

e. There has been no study of the level of recidivism among individuals convicted of price fixing. Is it unreasonable to assume that a corporate officer, who is convicted of price fixing and returns to the job after little punishment, may be tempted to engage in price fixing again?

f. Although the United States is not the only country in the world to use criminal sanctions for antitrust offenders, this system is more the exception than the rule. Of our two NAFTA partners, Canada also criminalizes certain conduct, and Mexico does not. The European Union relies exclusively on a system of injunctions and administrative fines, some of which can run into the hundreds of millions of dollars. In light of this, do you regard criminal penalties (fines and imprisonment) as (i) necessary, (ii) desirable, (iii) one optional way to achieve deterrence, on a par with others, or (iv) affirmatively undesirable? Why?[65]

7. LENIENCY PROGRAMS

As will be discussed in Chapter 4 in more detail, in order to induce individuals or corporations involved in price fixing, or other hard-core cartel activity, to come forward and cooperate, the Antitrust Division put in place leniency programs. In this context, leniency means that a qualifying corporation or individual will not be charged criminally for the activity being report. The Antitrust Division first implemented its Corporate Leniency Program in 1978, but revised it in 1993 to create more opportunities for individuals and companies to come forward and to increase their incentives to do so. In recent years, the Antitrust Division has received roughly 25 applications a year and the result has been scores of convictions, billions of dollars of criminal fines, and the dismantling of dozens of large international cartels.[66]

8. INTERFACES BETWEEN GOVERNMENT LITIGATION AND PRIVATE ACTIONS: AFTEREFFECTS AND TOLLING THE STATUTE OF LIMITATIONS

Much private antitrust litigation follows in the wake of victories by the government. Under Section 5(a) of the Clayton Act, a private litigant may use a judgment or decree in a prior civil or criminal action brought by the government as "*prima facie* evidence against such defendant ... as to all matters respecting which said judgment or decree would be an estoppel as

---

65. Price fixing and other hard-core antitrust offenses are considered in Chapter 4 *infra*.

66. *See* Hammond, An Update of the Antitrust Division's Enforcement Program, 2005, at http://www.usdoj.gov/atr/public/speeches/213247.htm.

between the parties thereto." A proviso to this statute, however, excludes "consent judgments or decrees entered before any testimony has been taken."[67]

The exact scope of Section 5(a) has been the subject of some controversy. It clearly permits a private litigant to utilize a final judgment in favor of the government in a prior criminal suit or civil suit for an injunction that proceeded to trial. On the other hand, an action brought by the government under Section 4(a) of the Clayton Act[68] for damages resulting from an antitrust violation may not be used in a subsequent private action. A suit by the government that is terminated by a consent decree before any testimony has been taken is expressly inadmissible in subsequent private litigation. Pleas of *nolo contendere* to criminal indictments, although not specifically mentioned in the statute, also have been deemed unavailable to a private plaintiff. The reasoning is that a *nolo* plea, although an implied confession of guilt upon which criminal penalties can be imposed, is equivalent to a consent decree and is governed by the proviso. There is no doubt that many defendants accept consent decrees or enter *nolo* pleas mainly to avoid the *prima facie* effect risk under Section 5(a).

The courts have not been unanimous in their treatment of guilty pleas. A majority have treated them as *prima facie* evidence under Section 5,[69] but others have rejected that approach on grounds that the overriding purpose of Section 5 was to encourage the quick capitulation of the defendant, and that this policy would be frustrated by permitting subsequent litigants to make use of guilty pleas entered before the taking of testimony.[70]

For many years, FTC orders had been held to be unavailable to private litigants under Section 5(a), but that approach was abandoned by the First Circuit in 1969, when an FTC administrative judgment under the price discrimination provisions of the Robinson–Patman Act was given 5(a) effect.[71] It now appears possible that FTC orders, when based on findings that the Clayton Act or one of the other antitrust laws has been violated, could be given *prima facie* effect.[72] In a recent case, however, an FTC action under Section 5(a), which found that Rambus had violated federal antitrust laws, was not given *prima facie* effect.[73]

---

67. 15 U.S.C. § 16(a).

68. 15 U.S.C. § 15(a).

69. *See* City of Burbank v. General Electric Co., 329 F.2d 825 (9th Cir.1964).

70. *See* Twin Ports Oil Co. v. Pure Oil Co., 26 F.Supp. 366, 374–6 (D.Minn.1939), aff'd, 119 F.2d 747 (8th Cir.), cert. denied, 314 U.S. 644 (1941). On the question of issues as to which a judgment will have *prima facie* effect, see Emich Motors Corp. v. General Motors Corp., 340 U.S. 558 (1951).

71. Farmington Dowel Products Co. v. Forster Manufacturing Co., 421 F.2d 61 (1st Cir.1969). *But see* Proper v. John Bene & Sons, 295 F. 729 (E.D.N.Y.1923).

72. *See* Purex Corp. v. Procter & Gamble Co., 453 F.2d 288 (9th Cir.1971), cert. denied, 405 U.S. 1065 (1972); cf. Sullivan & Grimes, The Law of Antitrust: An Integrated Handbook 963 (2000).

73. *See* Rambus Inc. v. Hynix Semiconductor Inc., 2008–1 Trade Cas. (CCH) ¶ 76,048 (N.D. Cal. 2008).

These "aftereffect" aspects have generated much controversy. Occasionally, the government has succeeded in negotiating special admissions on consent judgments for the benefit of subsequent private litigants.

Prior to 1955, there was no federal statute of limitations for private antitrust actions. The federal courts simply borrowed state rules. In 1955, the Clayton Act was amended to provide for a four-year statute of limitations in both private and government damage actions.[74] Section 5(i) of the Clayton Act provides that where there is pending a civil or criminal proceeding instituted by the government to enforce the "antitrust laws," any private action based in whole or part on any matter complained of in the proceeding shall not be barred until one year after the conclusion of the government's case. Although Section 5(i) speaks of enforcement of the "antitrust laws," the Supreme Court has held that FTC proceedings trigger the section's tolling provisions.[75]

9.   INTERNATIONAL COOPERATION

While the United States had relatively little company in the world of antitrust at the mid-point of the twentieth century, today the field of countries with antitrust laws is quite crowded, with more than 100 participants. As the world is moving steadily toward a more integrated global economy, and the number of countries with competition laws increases, some degree of international cooperation seems to be essential.

Initially, the United States was almost alone in its view that enforcement of its domestic antitrust law to arrangements outside its territory with an effect within the country (so-called extraterritorial enforcement) was an appropriate response to global competition issues. This policy led to a significant number of conflicts with other countries. As time went on, however, more and more countries and regions adopted competition laws, and as they did, their concern with their own domestic consumers led many to accept variants of the effects principle. While on one level this may have been a philosophical victory for the United States, on a pragmatic level it created a more urgent need for more effective coordination and cooperation. A task force of the American Bar Association expressed its concern in 2001 about the complexity, costs, and delays of the present system:

> In today's global economy, American companies are affected
> not only by domestic antitrust enforcement but also by the actions
> of a growing number of foreign competition agencies and regimes.
> This proliferation of competition policy throughout the world is

---

74.   15 U.S.C. § 15b. Although the four-year limitations period applies only to damage actions under Section 4 of the Clayton Act, and not to private actions for equitable relief under Section 16 of the Clayton Act, the defense of laches is applicable to Section 16 claims. See ITT Corp. v. GTE Corp., 518 F.2d 913, 926–29 (9th Cir.1975) (equitable defense of laches may be available in an action under Section 16 of the Clayton Act, and the four-year statutory limitations period should be used as a guideline in determining whether the action was brought within a reasonable time).

75.   Minnesota Mining and Manufacturing Co. v. New Jersey Wood Finishing Co., 381 U.S. 311, 317–18 (1965).

highly desirable in concept, but it matters greatly how those policies are defined and enforced.... The burdens of complying with a growing number of antitrust regimes, particularly in the case of cross-border transactions, are significant and growing; a high priority effort of the U.S. antitrust agencies should be an attempt to find procedural common ground with (at least) the most significant international antitrust regimes.[76]

The earliest and most informal options to accomplish the goal of coordination are commonly known as "soft" measures, while those that would be legally binding on signatories are called "hard" agreements. For the most part, "soft" cooperation has been the preferred form for most countries thus far. This has occurred on two fronts: multilaterally, under the auspices of such organizations as the International Competition Network (ICN) and the Organisation for Economic Co-operation and Development (OECD), and bilaterally. The OECD in particular has served as a gathering place for discussion and exchange of expertise about the enforcement of competition laws. The ICN came into being more recently, having been launched in February 2001 by an inaugural group of antitrust officials from 14 countries. *See* http://ww.internationalcompetitionnetwork.org/index.php/en/about-icn/history. In its brief history, its membership has broadened to include almost all countries with competition laws. Speaking about the ICN, former Chairman Timothy Muris of the U.S. FTC reported as follows:

> International Competition Network will provide a venue where senior antitrust officials from developed and developing countries will work to reach consensus on concrete proposals for procedural and substantive convergence in antitrust enforcement. We hope to make international antitrust enforcement more efficient and effective, to the benefit of consumers and companies around the world. The ICN also will assist developing countries in building a competition culture based on sound economic principles. One of the ICN's first topics is merger review in a multi-jurisdictional context, and includes projects focusing on merger notification and procedures, the framework for analyzing mergers, and merger investigation techniques.[77]

Even without the ICN, bilateral cooperation agreements have grown in number, ambition and importance over the years. *See generally* Chapter 10 *infra*. Many of the early Friendship, Commerce, and Navigation treaties concluded by the United States contain language committing both, treaty partners to prevent anticompetitive and monopolistic practices. In the 1960s, more specific antitrust cooperation agreements began to appear. They offered a framework for conflict management, some general form of cooperation, and regular consultations. (*See*, for example, the agreements concluded with Germany, Australia and Canada that entered into force in

---

76. ABA 2001 Task Force Report at 5.

77. Muris, Prepared Remarks before Brookings Institution Roundtable on Trade and Investment Policy 15 (December 21, 2001).

the seventies and eighties, available at http://www.justice.gov/atr/public/
international/int_arrangements.htm.)

In 1991, the United States and the European Community signed an
antitrust cooperation agreement that broke new ground. (This agreement
was temporarily derailed by the European Court of Justice for technical
reasons relating to EU law, but the agreement later was reaffirmed and is
effective today.) In that agreement, the two parties undertook a new kind
of commitment to one another. This came to be known as "positive
comity," under which each party promised to consider using its own
competition laws to address practices within its territory that were harming the other. If a positive comity request is made and it is legally possible
for the requested party to take action, the requesting party no longer has
any reason to resort to extraterritorial measures. Similar agreements that
commit both parties to the principle of positive comity and cooperation now
exist between the United States and a number of other countries.

Another important breakthrough occurred in 1994, when Congress
passed the International Antitrust Enforcement Assistance Act (IAEAA),
15 U.S.C. §§ 6201 *et seq.* That statute empowers the U.S. Department of
Justice and Federal Trade Commission to enter into binding international
agreements that authorize information sharing between the United States
and a foreign competition agency, with strict protection of any confidential
information that may be exchanged. Joint investigations and prosecutions
are also made possible. At present, one such agreement exists, between the
United States and Australia. Similar cooperation exists between the United
States and Canada with respect to criminal antitrust matters, which fall
under the general U.S.-Canadian Mutual Legal Assistance Treaty.

Finally, the U.S. antitrust agencies have been working with foreign
antitrust authorities in recent years to facilitate parallel investigations, to
conduct operations jointly where legally possible, and to create effective
leniency programs (to encourage the reporting of cartel activities). The
leniency programs have brought results. From 1987–1990, the Antitrust
Division did not bring a single case against foreign-based companies or
foreign individuals. By 2001, "nearly 70 percent of the companies charged
by the Division . . . were foreign-based firms, and roughly 33 percent of the
individual defendants were foreign nationals."[78] The Division prosecuted
international cartels affecting more than $10 billion in U.S. commerce from
1997 through 2001. These prosecutions "dwarfed the domestic and regional
conspiracies that the Division had traditionally prosecuted over the
years."[79] In more recent years, the Division has continued to pursue
violators, whether they are foreign or domestic, and to seek to obtain
penalties stiff enough to deter illegal behavior.[80]

---

78. Hammond, A Review of Recent Cases and Developments in the Antitrust Division's
Criminal Enforcement Program 2 (Conference Board program March 7, 2002).

79. Id.

80. See Hammond, Recent Developments, Trends, and Milestones in the Antitrust
Division's Criminal Enforcement Program, available at http://www.justice.gov/atr/public/
speeches/232716.htm.

C. SPECIAL ISSUES RELATED TO PRIVATE ENFORCEMENT

Private treble damage actions can be big business. For example, as indicated earlier, GE and other companies paid upwards of $350 million, in the early 1960's, to litigate and settle price-fixing cases. Although the Department of Justice stipulated to the dismissal of its monopolization case against IBM in 1982, in 1973 Control Data settled its private monopolization action against IBM for upwards of $100 million (including $15 million to reimburse legal fees and expenses); senior officers of Control Data boasted that the lawsuit had been the best investment the company had ever made. In the early 1980's, private antitrust actions shook the paper industry to its economic foundations; as the result of this series of private actions (through settlements and judgments), over $1 billion changed hands. Similarly, in the 1990's and early 2000's, large litigations and settlements involved actions against pharmaceutical manufacturers, Microsoft, Sotheby's and Christie's auction houses, and an international vitamin cartel.

In general, as Section A *supra* demonstrates, private antitrust enforcement now dwarfs government enforcement in the number of cases brought, and in many areas, because of treble damage provisions, in economic impact. In older cases, the courts often were reluctant to authorize massive recoveries, partly because of the vague line between legal and illegal conduct in many areas of antitrust. In the last fifty years or so, however, a recognition of the importance of the contribution of these "private attorneys general" to an effective national antitrust policy has led the courts to clear many obstacles—procedural, substantive, and related to damages—from the path of private actions. But, particularly during roughly the past thirty years, courts fearful of overdeterrence and self-interested plaintiff's lawyers have also put new obstacles in the path of private litigation. Discussed below are procedural and process issues related to private enforcement that have special antitrust significance.

1. STANDING, CAUSATION, AND ANTITRUST INJURY

Section 4 of the Clayton Act requires that a private treble damage plaintiff be a "person" (defined in the Act to include corporations and associations) who was "injured in his business or property." The Supreme Court noted in Reiter v. Sonotone Corp., 442 U.S. 330, 337 (1979), that Section 4 "contains little in the way of restrictive language." Nevertheless, numerous lower court decisions have restricted the class of plaintiffs who may claim damages under Section 4. For example, a shareholder may not sue in his own right (as opposed to derivatively for his corporation) for a reduction in the value of his stock.[81] Neither a trade association nor a nonprofit institution may maintain private actions to recover damages

---

81. *See* Lovett v. General Motors Corp., 975 F.2d 518, 521 (8th Cir.1992); Peter v. Western Newspaper Union, 200 F.2d 867 (5th Cir.1953).

allegedly inflicted on members,[82] nor according to most cases, may a landlord sue even though it has leased property under terms which include payment of a percentage of the profits.[83] As previously indicated, a state or municipality can sue for treble damages for injuries to its property, but a state may not sue in a *parens patriae* capacity on behalf of its citizens to recover for general damages to the state's economy.[84]

The theory underlying standing cases has often been stated elliptically and without analytical precision. Many of the cases cannot be reconciled. The language of standing cases—*e.g.*, was the injury "direct" or "indirect," was plaintiff within the "target area" of the offense—often obscures underlying policy issues. In general, what courts should be doing in this area is analyzing the purposes of the antitrust laws and the probable costs and benefits to the antitrust system of allowing a particular plaintiff to vindicate its claim to protection against antitrust injuries. At issue will be a series of discrete policy questions such as: Are the injuries to this particular plaintiff too speculative or remote to make it an appropriate antitrust enforcer? Is the injury of a type with which the antitrust laws should be concerned? Is there an excessive risk of duplicative recovery? Would affording standing create unmanageable complexity, and on balance, discourage vigorous private enforcement? A precise analysis of the answers to these questions is what is desirable. In recent years, the Supreme Court has moved in this direction.

Blue Shield of Virginia v. McCready, 457 U.S. 465 (1982), in which the justices split 5–4, illustrates the Supreme Court's approach and the difficult policy issues that lie at the heart of standing cases. Careful note should be taken of the Court's sympathetic attitude towards private enforcement and of its analytical framework for resolving standing issues. McCready's antitrust complaint alleged that Blue Shield's practice of refusing to reimburse subscribers for psychotherapy performed by *psychologists,* while providing reimbursement for comparable treatment by *psychiatrists,* was in furtherance of an unlawful conspiracy to restrain competition in the psychotherapy market. The question presented was "whether a subscriber who employed the services of a psychologist has standing to maintain an action under § 4 of the Clayton Act based upon the plan's failure to provide reimbursement for the costs of that treatment." The Supreme Court held that McCready had standing. Justice Brennan, writing for the majority, emphasized the "broad remedial and deterrent objectives" of Section 4 of the Clayton Act. Nevertheless, he "acknowledged two types of limitation on the availability of the § 4 remedy."

For the first type of limitation Justice Brennan cited Hawaii v. Standard Oil Co., 405 U.S. 251 (1972) (discussed *supra*), and Illinois Brick Co. v. Illinois, 431 U.S. 720 (1977) (discussed *infra*), and explained these cases as

---

82. *See* Buckley Towers Condominium, Inc. v. Buchwald, 533 F.2d 934 (5th Cir.1976), cert. denied, 429 U.S. 1121 (1977); Northern California Monument Dealers Association v. Interment Association, 120 F.Supp. 93 (D.Cal.1954).

83. *See* Calderone Enterprises Corp. v. United Artists Theatre Circuit, Inc., 454 F.2d 1292 (2d Cir.1971), cert. denied, 406 U.S. 930 (1972); Harrison v. Paramount Pictures, 115 F.Supp. 312 (E.D.Pa.1953), aff'd, 211 F.2d 405 (3d Cir.), cert. denied, 348 U.S. 828 (1954); cf. G.K.A. Beverage Corp. v. Honickman, 55 F.3d 762 (2d Cir.), cert. denied, 516 U.S. 944 (1995). But see Congress Building Corp. v. Loew's, Inc., 246 F.2d 587 (7th Cir.1957).

84. Hawaii v. Standard Oil Co., 405 U.S. 251 (1972).

"focused on the risk of duplicative recovery" not present in the *McCready* case. Id. at 474. The Court noted that a subordinate theme in the *Hawaii* and *Illinois Brick* cases involved a concern about "burdening § 4 actions with damages issues giving rise to the need for 'massive evidence and complicated theories,' where the consequence would be to discourage vigorous enforcement." The Court concluded, however, that "our cautious approach to speculative, abstract, or impractical damages theories has no application to McCready's suit." Id. at 475 n.11.

The second type of limitation related to the "conceptually more difficult question 'of which persons have sustained injuries *too remote* . . . to give them standing to sue.' " As to this issue, the Court reasoned:

> An antitrust violation may be expected to cause ripples of harm to flow through the Nation's economy; but "despite the broad wording of § 4 there is a point beyond which the wrongdoer should not be held liable." . . . It is reasonable to assume that Congress did not intend to allow every person tangentially affected by an antitrust violation to maintain an action to recover threefold damages for the injury to his business or property. Of course, neither the statutory language nor the legislative history of § 4 offers any focused guidance on the question of which injuries are too remote from the violation and the purposes of the antitrust laws to form the predicate for a suit under § 4; indeed, the unrestrictive language of the section, and the avowed breadth of the congressional purpose, cautions us not to cabin § 4 in ways that will defeat its broad remedial objective. But the potency of the remedy implies the need for some care in its application. In the absence of direct guidance from Congress, and faced with the claim that a particular injury is too remote from the alleged violation to warrant § 4 standing, the courts are thus forced to resort to an analysis no less elusive than that employed traditionally by courts at common law with respect to the matter of "proximate cause." . . . In applying that elusive concept to this statutory action, we look (1) to the physical and economic nexus between the alleged violation and the harm to the plaintiff, and, (2) more particularly, to the relationship of the injury alleged with those forms of injury about which Congress was likely to have been concerned in making defendant's conduct unlawful and in providing a private remedy under § 4. Id. at 476–78.

In answer to item (1), the "physical and economic nexus," the Court concluded:

> We do not think that because the goal of the conspirators was to halt encroachment by psychologists into a market that physicians and psychiatrists sought to preserve for themselves, McCready's injury is rendered "remote." The availability of the § 4 remedy to some person who claims its benefit is not a question of the specific intent of the conspirators. Here the remedy cannot reasonably be restricted to those competitors whom the conspira-

tors hoped to eliminate from the market. McCready claims that she has been the victim of a concerted refusal to pay on the part of Blue Shield, motivated by a desire to deprive psychologists of the patronage of Blue Shield subscribers. Denying reimbursement to subscribers for the cost of treatment was the very means by which it is alleged that Blue Shield sought to achieve its illegal ends. The harm to McCready and her class was clearly foreseeable; indeed, it was a necessary step in effecting the ends of the illegal conspiracy. Id. at 478–79.

In answer to item (2), the "relationship of the injury" to Congress' antitrust concern, the Court concluded:

> Relying on . . . [language in Brunswick Corp. v. Pueblo Bowl–O–Mat, Inc., 429 U.S. 477, 489 (1977), as to the need to "prove antitrust injury"], petitioners reason that McCready can maintain no action under § 4 because her injury "did not reflect the anticompetitive effect" of the alleged violation.
>
> *Brunswick* is not so limiting. Indeed, as we made clear in a footnote to the relied-upon passage, a § 4 plaintiff need not "prove an actual lessening of competition in order to recover. . . .[C]ompetitors may be able to prove antitrust injury before they actually are driven from the market and competition is thereby lessened." . . . Thus while an increase in price resulting from a dampening of competitive market forces is assuredly one type of injury for which § 4 potentially offers redress, see Reiter v. Sonotone, *supra*, that is not the only form of injury remediable under § 4. We think it plain that McCready's injury was of a type that Congress sought to redress in providing a private remedy for violations of the antitrust laws.
>
>   . . . [W]e think that McCready's injury "flows from that which makes defendants' acts unlawful" within the meaning of *Brunswick*, and falls within the area of congressional concern. Id. at 482–84.

Two dissenting opinions found no " 'antitrust injury' within the meaning of *Brunswick*"(Justices Burger, Rehnquist, and O'Connor) and no injury to plaintiff's "property by reason of the alleged antitrust violation" (Justice Stevens).

The "causality" and "antitrust injury"[85] cases referred to in the *McCready* opinions also use "direct-indirect" and "target area" terminology. These cases appear to have the same conceptual and policy underpinnings as do the standing cases.

---

85.   For a discussion of "antitrust injury" in the merger context, *see* p. 1020 *infra. See* Atlantic Richfield Co. v. USA Petroleum Co., 495 U.S. 328 (1990) ("Although a vertical maximum price-fixing agreement . . . [was then (but not now, see Chapter 7 *infra*) *per se*] unlawful under § 1 of the Sherman Act, it does not cause a competitor injury unless it results in predatory pricing").

In Associated General Contractors v. California State Council of Carpenters, 459 U.S. 519, 537–46 (1983), the Supreme Court decided that the plaintiff union was not a proper party to bring a private antitrust action. The Court focused principally on whether the harm to plaintiff was: (i) the sort that the Sherman Act was designed to protect; (ii) direct or indirect; (iii) intended; (iv) speculative; (v) likely to lead to duplicative recoveries, difficulties of apportionment, or burdensome complex trials; and (vi) likely to be vindicated by more direct victims of the alleged wrongful acts or whether harm was likely to go undetected or unremedied. Cf. Cargill, Inc. v. Monfort of Colorado, Inc., 479 U.S. 104 (1986).

Circuit court opinions, reaching opposite or varying conclusions, illustrate both the interplay among the "standing," "causation," and "antitrust injury" concepts, and the difficult policy judgments that must be made. In Ostrofe v. H.S. Crocker Co., Inc., 670 F.2d 1378, 1382 (9th Cir.1982) (*Ostrofe I*), the Ninth Circuit ruled that an employee who was forced to resign because he refused to participate in an alleged price-fixing and market-allocation scheme by his employer, and others, had standing to bring a treble damage action against his employer.

The Supreme Court vacated the Ninth Circuit's judgment in *Ostrofe I*[86] and directed that on remand the lower court review its decision in light of the Supreme Court's *Associated General Contractors* case, *supra*. In *Ostrofe II,* the Ninth Circuit reaffirmed plaintiff's standing and focused on the fact that he was an "essential participant" in the price-fixing scheme, which "could not succeed without his active cooperation"; moreover, no one had as strong an interest as the discharged employee in vindicating the public interest in effective antitrust enforcement. 740 F.2d 739, 745–47 (9th Cir.1984), cert. dismissed, 469 U.S. 1200 (1985). More recently, the Ninth Circuit dismissed a terminated employee's claim because the "loss of a job is not the type of injury that the antitrust laws were designed to prevent." *Ostrofe II* was distinguished as involving a limited exception for an "essential participant" whose dismissal was a "necessary means" to accomplish the anticompetitive scheme.[87]

Other circuit courts have rejected *Ostrofe I and II*. The Seventh Circuit, for example, in Bichan v. Chemetron Corp., 681 F.2d 514, 519 (7th Cir.1982), concluded that plaintiff had not established "antitrust injury" since he was "not the target of the alleged anticompetitive practices:"

> [A] determination of antitrust standing should focus not only on whether there has been an "antitrust injury," but also on whether the particular plaintiff is the appropriate antitrust enforcer. Thus, the conflicting interests of deterrence through private antitrust enforcement and redress for injury must be balanced against the avoidance of excessive treble damages litigation. An appropriate balance is achieved by granting standing only to those

---

86.   460 U.S. 1007 (1983).

87.   Vinci v. Waste Management Inc., 80 F.3d 1372 (9th Cir.1996); *see* NicSand, Inc. v. 3M Co., 507 F.3d 442 (6th Cir. 2007).

who, as consumers or competitors, suffer immediate injuries with respect to their business or property, while excluding persons whose injuries were more indirectly caused by the antitrust conduct.[88]

In thinking about these employee cases, consider the following: Was not the deterrence of anticompetitive acts a fundamental Congressional concern? Who is in a better position than an employee to prevent—or alleviate *early* the consequences of—unlawful acts? How much danger is there here of duplicative recovery or of any of the other concerns articulated in the Supreme Court's *McCready* and *Associated General Contractors* opinions? There is, of course, real danger of increased litigation (true or untrue allegations of this type may be made by disgruntled present or former employees), and treble damage exposure could lead to unwarranted settlements. How would you draw the policy balance? Is the Ninth Circuit on the right track in concluding that all employees or agents need not be treated alike?

The *Illinois Brick* case,[89] discussed in the *McCready* opinion *supra*, is of large practical importance. *Illinois Brick*, at least as the Supreme Court majority saw it, built upon Hanover Shoe, Inc. v. United Shoe Machinery Corp., 392 U.S. 481 (1968), where a plaintiff's claim that it paid illegally high prices could not be defeated by proof that it recaptured part or all of the extra cost by charging higher prices to its customers, *i.e.*, by "passing-on" the higher prices. In reaching its result in *Hanover Shoe*, the Court took into account that it would be unlikely that large numbers of ultimate consumers would have the economic interest to sue for the relatively small damages each might have suffered.

In *Illinois Brick*, Justice White, writing for the majority, held that pass-on theory could not be used offensively by an indirect purchasing plaintiff (*i.e.*, further down the distribution line) against price-fixing manufacturers. Illinois Brick had sold concrete block to masonry contractors who were employed as subcontractors by general contractors working on construction projects for the plaintiffs, local government entities. The Court saw the plaintiffs' action as an *offensive* use of the passing-on theory rejected as a defense in *Hanover Shoe*.

In rejecting the offensive use of pass-on theory, the Court concluded that whatever rule was applied, it should be applied equally to both defendants and plaintiffs since concerns about "evidentiary complexities and uncertainties" were similar in each instance. The Court feared that the offensive use of pass-on theory might create the possibility of multiple recoveries against a single defendant. Justice White stated:

88. *See, e.g.*, Adams v. Pan American World Airways, Inc., 828 F.2d 24 (D.C.Cir.1987) (employees of defunct airline denied standing); Gregory Marketing Corp. v. Wakefern Food Corp., 787 F.2d 92 (3d Cir.), cert. denied, 479 U.S. 821 (1986). But see Ashmore v. Northeast Petroleum, 843 F.Supp. 759, 767 n. 15 (D.Me.1994) ("providing standing to employees who are coerced to violate the antitrust laws is more likely to provide efficient enforcement").

89. 431 U.S. 720 (1977).

> Permitting the use of pass-on theories under § 4 essentially would transform treble-damage actions into massive efforts to apportion the recovery among all potential plaintiffs ... [and] would add whole new dimensions of complexity to treble-damage suits and seriously undermine their effectiveness.[90]

The Court also indicated its hesitancy to involve the judiciary in measuring market elasticities and pricing policies (*i.e.*, to measure how much, if any, of price increases were passed on), and repeated the concerns expressed in *Hanover Shoe* about a plaintiff's reduced incentive to sue since apportionment would diminish each plaintiff's recovery. The Court concluded that plaintiffs had not sustained legally cognizable "antitrust injury" under Section 4.

Justice Brennan dissented in *Illinois Brick* and argued that the "broad objectives" of Section 4, to "compensate victims of antitrust violations and to deter future violations," were sufficient to allow the plaintiff and defendant to be treated differently:

> [T]he same policies [outlined in *Hanover Shoe*] of insuring the continued effectiveness of the treble-damages action and preventing wrongdoers from retaining the spoils of their misdeeds favor allowing indirect purchasers to prove that overcharges were passed on to them.[91]

Justice Brennan was unconvinced that the complexities of the offensive use of pass-on theory were any different from issues regularly decided in antitrust cases, and was convinced that "existing procedural mechanisms" could largely eliminate the danger of multiple recoveries. He was particularly concerned that "direct purchasers, acting as middlemen, and ordinarily reluctant to sue their suppliers, [would] pass on the bulk of their increased cost to consumers farther along the chain of distribution."

In *Illinois Brick* the majority indicated two possible special circumstances in which an indirect purchaser might be permitted to recover: first, where a "pre-existing cost-plus contract" existed, and second, "where the direct purchaser is owned or controlled by its customer." The first possibility was narrowly construed in Kansas v. UtiliCorp United, Inc., 497 U.S. 199 (1990), where states (asserting *parens patriae* claims under the Hart–Scott–Rodino Act[92]) argued that public utilities (direct buyers) had passed on 100% of inflated prices to their customers.

In a 5–4 decision, the Supreme Court held that no exception to the *Hanover Shoe/Illinois Brick* rulings would be made. Continuing the focus on judicial resources and evidentiary complexities, Justice Kennedy, writing for the majority, was not convinced that proof of the passage of 100% of the overcharge on to utility customers was easily ascertainable under a system of regulated rates:

---

90.   431 U.S. at 737.

91.   431 U.S. at 753.

92.   *See* discussion p. 64 *supra*.

[S]tate regulation does not simplify the problem but instead imports an additional level of complexity. . . . [A] court would have to consider not only the extent to which market conditions would have allowed the utility to raise its rates prior to the overcharge, as in the case of an unregulated business, but also what the state regulators would have allowed. . . . Proof . . . would turn upon the intricacies of state laws. . . . To the extent that the [utility] could have sought and gained permission to raise its rates in the absence of an overcharge, at least some portion of the overcharge is being borne by it.[93]

Justice Kennedy went on to reject the contention that the situation of a regulated utility was identical to the exception for cost-plus contracts:

[W]e might allow indirect purchasers to sue only when, by hypothesis, the direct purchaser will bear no portion of the overcharge and otherwise suffer no injury. That certainty does not exist here. . . . [T]he need to inquire into the precise operation of market forces [in the context of a public utility's market] would negate the simplicity and certainty that could justify a cost-plus contract exception.[94]

The Court also concluded that the Hart–Scott–Rodino Act did not create any new substantive liabilities when it provided for *parens patriae* claims. Claims by state attorneys general may only be brought on behalf of customers who themselves have incurred a Section 4 injury.

Justice White, the author of the majority opinions in *Hanover Shoe* and *Illinois Brick,* dissented on the basis that the difficulties relied upon by the majority were "speculative" and that state regulation made this a case "in which it would be easy to prove the extent to which the overcharge was passed on."[95]

Although the Supreme Court has refused to allow pass-on theory to be used offensively or defensively in federal antitrust cases, California v. ARC America Corp., 490 U.S. 93 (1989), presented the Court with the question of whether state antitrust laws were similarly limited. Justice White, writing for a unanimous Court, held that the federal policies outlined in *Hanover Shoe* and *Illinois Brick* for federal antitrust laws did not preempt the states from allowing indirect purchasers to recover under state antitrust laws. The Court found that "Congress intended the federal antitrust laws to supplement, not displace, state antitrust remedies."[96] In the early 2000's, more than half the states allowed indirect purchasers to sue for antitrust violations under state law.[97] In 2007, the Antitrust Modernization

---

93. 497 U.S. at 209–10.

94. 497 U.S. at 218.

95. 497 U.S. at 220.

96. 409 U.S. at 102.

97. For recent lower court cases dealing with still complex and difficult *Illinois Brick* issues in special circumstances under the federal antitrust laws, *see, e.g.,* Blue Cross & Blue

Commission recommended that Congress overrule both *Hanover Shoe* and *Illinois Brick*. The Commission concluded that different federal and state standards have resulted in "wasteful, duplicative litigation," involving potentially duplicative damage recoveries and inconsistent decisions.[98]

2. CLASS ACTIONS

Antitrust violations frequently cause relatively modest damages to a large number of victims. For example, price fixing on consumer products may raise the price of a commodity only a few cents on each purchase, and only a few dollars per year for individual consumers. In those circumstances, no individual plaintiff ordinarily suffers sufficient damages to justify the expense and inconvenience of private litigation, even where damages may be trebled and attorney's fees and costs returned to the victorious plaintiff.[99]

Under Rule 23(a) of the Federal Rules, plaintiffs may aggregate their claims in a "class action" if (1) the class is so numerous that joinder of all members is impractical, (2) there are common questions of law or fact, (3) claims or defenses of the representative parties are typical, and (4) the representative parties will fairly and adequately protect the interests of the class. In addition, those seeking to maintain class actions must satisfy one of the provisions of 23(b), the most important of which is subsection (3), which requires that common questions of law and fact predominate and that a class action is superior to other available methods of adjudication. All sorts of complicated questions of "manageability" arise under that provision, including requirements of notice to the class, possible opting out of those who do not want to participate in the class action but would rather enforce individual rights, computation of damages, and distribution of any eventual recovery. Class actions in antitrust have increased dramatically in recent years along with complex procedural disputes as to their enforcement and management.

3. POSSIBLE DISQUALIFICATION—UNCLEAN HANDS

Under the doctrines of *in pari delicto* and unclean hands, the courts for many years dismissed private antitrust actions where the plaintiff could be shown either to have participated in the challenged antitrust practice or to have been engaged in some other violation of the antitrust laws. These related doctrines were narrowed, and perhaps almost eliminated, by the Supreme Court in Perma Life Mufflers, Inc. v. International Parts Corp.— at least where the plaintiff did not "aggressively support and further the monopolistic scheme."[1] Justice Black reasoned that while a "plaintiff who

---

Shield United of Wisc. v. Marshfield Clinic, 65 F.3d 1406 (7th Cir.1995); Three Crown Limited Partnership v. Salomon Bros., 1995 WL 422467, 1995–2 Trade Cases ¶ 71,076 (S.D.N.Y.1995).

98. Antitrust Modernization Commission Report 266–67.

99. Antitrust plaintiffs may sue under 28 U.S.C. § 1337 and 15 U.S.C. § 15.

1. 392 U.S. 134 (1968); *see, e.g.,* Sullivan v. NFL, 34 F.3d 1091 (1st Cir.1994); Southwest Marine, Inc. v. Campbell Indus., 732 F.2d 744 (9th Cir.), cert. denied, 469 U.S. 1072 (1984); Memorex Corp. v. IBM Corp., 555 F.2d 1379 (9th Cir.1977).

reaps the reward of treble damages may be no less morally reprehensible than the defendant," the purposes of the antitrust statutes are best served by insuring that the private action will be an ever-present threat to deter anyone contemplating anticompetitive behavior. The Court did not reach the question whether "truly complete involvement" could be a basis for barring a plaintiff's cause of action. The Court was probably influenced in *Perma Life* by the fact that plaintiff was a franchisee—much smaller in terms of assets and market power than defendant—and may have been coerced into accepting otherwise undesirable contractual provisions. Where the plaintiff has the capacity to resist a proffered anticompetitive arrangement but does not do so, the result might be different.[2]

A related situation arises where a defendant resists a non-antitrust action—for example, an effort to collect monies due on a contract—on grounds that the cause of action was tainted with antitrust illegality. For example, in Kelly v. Kosuga,[3] the Court would not prevent collection of the purchase price for onions where the alleged antitrust agreement was independent of the particular purchase-sale transaction. The courts have made clear that they will recognize a defense based on antitrust in those circumstances where failure to do so would in effect make the court a party to implementing the unlawful restraint.

4.   DAMAGES AND EQUITABLE RELIEF

Enormous time and effort in private antitrust litigation is devoted to proof of the fact and amount of damages. Bigelow v. RKO Radio Pictures, Inc.[4] is a landmark case and generally adopted a liberal posture toward plaintiffs' claims. Plaintiffs, owners of a motion picture theater, had alleged that the defendants had discriminated against them in distribution of motion pictures pursuant to a conspiracy, and as a result profits were reduced. To support the damage claim, plaintiffs introduced evidence comparing their profits with those of a competing theater, and also comparing profits during the period of the alleged conspiracy with corresponding receipts for the years immediately preceding. Noting that defendant "by his own wrong has prevented a more precise computation," the Supreme Court affirmed a jury verdict based on those two categories of evidence. "Any other rule would enable the wrongdoer to profit by his wrongdoing at the expense of his victim. It would be an inducement to make wrongdoing so effective and complete in every case as to preclude any recovery, by rendering the measure of damages uncertain."[5]

Today, questions related to damages generally arise after threshold issues are resolved concerning standing, causation, and antitrust injury.[6]

---

2. For the distinction between *in pari delicto* and the equitable doctrine of unclean hands, and an attempt to reconcile the cases in this area, see Handler & Sacks, The Continued Vitality of In Pari Delicto as an Antitrust Defense, 70 Geo.L.J. 1123 (1982).

3. 358 U.S. 516 (1959).

4. 327 U.S. 251 (1946).

5. 327 U.S. at 264.

6. *See* 83 *supra*.

Once these hurdles have been cleared, *Bigelow* remains good law, and proof of the actual amount of damage is treated liberally and realistically.

Particularly difficult damage questions arise where the plaintiff is a party who claims he was prevented from starting a business by the anticompetitive activities of the defendant,[7] since the plaintiff has had no actual experience in the market to use as a basis for assessing what profits might have been earned absent the challenged conduct. The Supreme Court has said the following on the topic of future profits:

> [E]ach separate action that so accrues entitles a plaintiff to recover not only those damages which he has suffered at the date of accrual, but also those which he will suffer in the future from particular invasion.... On the other hand, it is hornbook law, in antitrust actions as in others, that even if injury and a cause of action have accrued as of a certain date, future damages that might arise from the conduct sued on are unrecoverable if the fact of their accrual is speculative or their amount and nature unprovable.[8]

In general, however, if the jury is presented with evidence somewhat beyond pure guesswork, a damage award is likely to be sustained.

Since 1914, Section 16 of the Clayton Act has permitted private plaintiffs to obtain injunctive relief. As in damage actions, plaintiffs asking for injunctive relief must allege "threatened loss or damage 'of the type the antitrust laws were designed to prevent and that flows from that which makes defendant's acts unlawful.' "[9] The Supreme Court has observed: "Section 16 should be construed and applied ... with the knowledge that the remedy it affords, like other equitable remedies, is flexible and capable of nice 'adjustments and reconciliation between the public interest and private needs....' "[10] In general, the courts have exercised their injunctive powers flexibly and appear to grant injunctive relief much more readily to the government than to private plaintiffs. The issue of the availability of divestiture as a remedy in private actions and actions by state attorneys general under Section 7 of the Clayton Act (*i.e.*, where a merger or an acquisition is involved), which the Supreme Court has recently resolved in favor of such relief, is discussed in Chapter 9 *infra*.

5.   THE TREBLE DAMAGE BONANZA, REASONABLE ATTORNEY'S FEES, AND PROPOSED PROCEDURAL REFORMS

In American Society of Mechanical Engineers, Inc. v. Hydrolevel Corp., 456 U.S. 556, 574 (1982), the Supreme Court said the following about treble damages:

---

7.   *See, e.g.*, Dominicus Americana Bohio v. Gulf & Western Industries, Inc., 473 F.Supp. 680 (S.D.N.Y.1979); William Goldman Theatres, Inc. v. Loew's, Inc., 69 F.Supp. 103 (E.D.Pa. 1946), aff'd per curiam, 164 F.2d 1021 (3d Cir.), cert. denied, 334 U.S. 811 (1948).

8.   Zenith Radio Corp. v. Hazeltine Research Inc., 401 U.S. 321, 338–39 (1971).

9.   Cargill, Inc. v. Monfort of Colorado, Inc., 479 U.S. 104, 113 (1986).

10.   Zenith Radio Corp. v. Hazeltine Research, Inc., 395 U.S. 100, 131 (1969).

> It is true that antitrust treble damages were designed in part to
> punish past violations of the antitrust laws.... But treble dam-
> ages were also designed to deter future antitrust violations. More-
> over, the antitrust private action was created primarily as a
> remedy for the victims of antitrust violations.... Treble damages
> "make the remedy meaningful by counter-balancing 'the difficulty
> of maintaining a private suit'" under the antitrust laws. *Bruns-
> wick Corp., supra*, at 486, n. 10, quoting 21 Cong.Rec. 2456 (1890)
> (remarks of Sen. Sherman).

While private treble damage actions undoubtedly have an important
role to play in overall antitrust enforcement, they still have some questionable aspects. Some antitrust rules are vague, and a single misstep by a
company can subject it to liability of disastrous proportions.

During the past thirty years there has been considerable controversy
about antitrust remedies in general and the so-called "treble damage
bonanza" in particular. It was claimed that many private lawsuits:

> were of little merit and were instigated in the hopes of generous
> settlements and generous attorneys' fee awards. Further many
> critics claimed that the fear of private treble damage actions
> deterred companies from taking risks in areas near the uncertain
> line defining legal behavior, for fear of becoming the targets of
> enormous private actions. As a result innovative manufacturing,
> organizational, and distributional techniques were not adopted.[11]

Responding in part to such claims, three times during the 1980's
Congress adjusted antitrust damage rules for specific types of cases. The
Export Trading Company Act of 1982[12] and the National Cooperative
Research Act of 1984[13] basically limited specific types of claims to actual
damages. The Local Government Antitrust Act of 1984,[14] in certain circumstances entirely eliminated antitrust damage recoveries. Numerous general
legislative proposals to "detreble" antitrust damages were made.[15]

A broad consensus developed around the proposition that while there
was "no lack of debate" on treble damage policy issues and on antitrust
remedies generally, "there was a striking absence of hard empirical data
about the cost and benefits of the present system."[16] After extensive
empirical study, however, a Georgetown private treble damage project
provided no definitive policy guidance. The "policy session," at the end of a
conference in 1985, was summarized as follows:

11. Pitofsky & Salop, Foreword, in White (ed.), Private Antitrust Litigation xi (1988).

12. Pub.L. No. 97–290, 96 Stat. 1233 (1982).

13. Pub.L. No. 98–462, 98 Stat. 1815 (1984).

14. Pub.L. No. 98–544, 98 Stat. 2750 (1984).

15. For a comprehensive review of these proposals, see Cavanagh, Detrebling Antitrust
Damages: An Idea Whose Time Has Come?, 61 Tul.L.Rev. 777 (1987).

16. Pitofsky & Salop, Foreword, in White (ed.), Private Antitrust Litigation xi (1988).

In the policy session ... several participants expounded the view that the private treble damage system is not out of control. Private antitrust litigation generally does not appear to be excessively expensive, to consume a large amount of judicial resources, or to result in inappropriate recoveries. They argued that any significant reform proposals would damage a system that is fair and useful, particularly during periods when government antitrust enforcement is lax and pro-business. But other participants in the policy session thought that the present system unduly encourages frivolous suits and deters efficient behavior, and they suggested a variety of ways to reform private enforcement.[17]

The data produced by the Georgetown study did not provide clear answers to basic questions such as: Do mandatory treble damages create excessive deterrence? Are a significant number of weak cases brought, containing large damage claims, which lead to unwarranted, large settlements? How do the considerable advantages of the deterrence associated with treble damages balance against perceived failings in the system? There is, however, substantial evidence that judges are increasingly using summary disposition motions to weed out meritless cases before unwarranted settlements are made.[18]

The debate on treble damages and other remedial issues will clearly continue as we go further into the 21st century. One ameliorating technique with respect to treble damages would be to eliminate mandatory trebling of damages and confer authority on trial courts to award single, double, or triple damages depending on the circumstances of the antitrust violation.[19]

Another approach would be to eliminate mandatory trebling (and permit judicial discretion to award single, double, or triple damages)—in non-*per se* cases—when a defendant can show that it "reasonably believed" that a given act or transaction would not violate the antitrust laws.[20] This second approach would encourage antitrust counseling (in order to be in a position to establish a "reasonable belief") and promote self-policing compliance programs.

Congress' decision to supplement treble-damage recovery with the award of reasonable attorney's fees also provides litigation incentives to potential plaintiffs. The Second Circuit, for example, held that the plaintiffs, including the United States Football League, who were awarded only

---

17. Id. at xiii. See Lande, Are Antitrust "Treble" Damages Really Single Damages?, 54 Ohio St.L.J. 115 (1993).

18. *See* Calkins, Equilibrating Tendencies in the Antitrust System, With Special Attention to Summary Judgment and to Motions to Dismiss, in White (ed.), Private Antitrust Litigation 185–239 (1988).

19. *See* Cavanagh, Detrebling Antitrust Damages: An Idea Whose Time Has Come?, 61 Tul.L.Rev. 777 (1987).

20. Goldschmid, Comment on the Policy Implications of the Georgetown Study, in White (ed.), Private Antitrust Litigation 412–15 (1988).

$3 in treble damages, should be awarded $5.5 million in attorney's fees and $62,221 in costs.[21] The Second Circuit reasoned:

> In the instant case, the jury found that the NFL's monopolization of the United States major league professional football market injured the USFL. An injury having been found, the awarding of attorney's fees to the USFL was compulsory.... That the USFL only received nominal damages is relevant in determining the amount of fees allowed and may be a factor used in reducing a fee award, but it does not affect the entitlement to an award. See Home Placement Serv., 819 F.2d at 1210.

> As the First Circuit has stated, the purpose behind mandatory attorney's fees in antitrust cases is "to encourage private prosecution of antitrust violations by insulating plaintiff's treble damage recoveries from the expense of legal fees." Id. What is important is encouraging the detection and cessation of anticompetitive behavior, not the amount of damages found. Because of the importance of the policy of encouraging private parties to bring antitrust actions, recovery of their reasonable attorney's fees must be sustained regardless of the amount of damages awarded.... [T]here is no requirement in section 4 of the Clayton Act that an antitrust plaintiff be a "prevailing party" to recover attorney's fees. The term "prevailing party" appears nowhere in section 4 of the Clayton Act. All that is required is an injury. As stated *supra*, an injury was found, therefore the award of attorney's fees was automatic.[22]

6. CONTRIBUTION AND CLAIM REDUCTION

In Texas Industries, Inc. v. Radcliff Materials, Inc., 451 U.S. 630 (1981), the Supreme Court held that defendant, against whom damages had been assessed, had no right of contribution from other participants in an unlawful conspiracy under the federal antitrust laws. Since liability for antitrust damage is joint and several, the absence of contribution means that when, for example, a plaintiff releases a defendant in a price-fixing case from liability for damages in a settlement, only the actual amount paid for the release is deducted from the plaintiff's claim against the remaining defendants. Thus, if a plaintiff enters into a settlement with a defendant for an amount that is less than the share of the injury caused by the settling defendant, responsibility for the difference is shifted to the remaining defendants.

---

21. United States Football League v. National Football League, 887 F.2d 408 (2d Cir.1989), cert. denied, 493 U.S. 1071 (1990); Gulfstream III Associates, Inc. v. Gulfstream Aerospace Corp., 995 F.2d 414 (3d Cir.1993); see generally Cavanagh, Attorneys' Fees in Antitrust Litigation: Making the System Fairer, 57 Fordham L.Rev. 51 (1988).

22. The district court had reduced the request for attorney's fees from about $7.7 million to $5.5 million in light of the nominal damage award and this conclusion was sustained by the Second Circuit.

The term "whipsaw" settlement has come to be applied to settlements that build a plaintiff's "war chest" for litigation and raise the perceived liability of nonsettling defendants to the point where they may be forced to abandon meritorious defenses and settle out of fear of facing ruinous liability should they litigate and lose. Since 1979, Congress has been struggling with the question of whether it should legislatively provide for a right of contribution or a right to claim reduction.

In 1987, the arguments for and against contribution were effectively summarized in a Senate report as follows:

> The ultimate result of this restructuring of the defendants relationship to their liability will assure that: (1) every defendant pays an equitable share of the liability; (2) no defendant will be able to get out of the suit so cheaply as to weaken deterrence; and (3) those defendants who wish to defend the suit will not be left with a disproportionately large part of the liability and will be able to put their claim of innocence to the test of the trial.... [T]he counter arguments ... are that [the contribution bill:] (1) will dilute deterrence, (2) will deter settlements, and (3) will unfairly burden the plaintiff's case (and the courts) with unnecessary complexities.[23]

How can it be that both the proponents and opponents of contribution legislation cite improved deterrence as a reason for their positions? If there is no right of contribution, might not some defendants settle early at relatively modest expense, and by helping to finance the plaintiff's lawsuit, also enhance deterrence? Is this fair? Contribution is permitted in the admiralty area, and the Supreme Court there had the following to say about the argument that a contribution right would deter settlement:

> [A]t bottom, [this argument] asks us to continue the operation of an archaic rule because its facile application out of court yields quick, though inequitable, settlements, and relieves the court of some litigation. Congestion in the courts cannot justify a legal rule that produces unjust results in litigation simply to encourage speedy out-of-court accommodations.[24]

After almost a decade of hearings, Congress flirted with passing claim reduction legislation for price-fixing cases in the late 1980's. Claim reduction differs from contribution in that it requires automatic deduction from a plaintiff's remaining claim for the share of damages attributable to the acts of any person released by the plaintiff from liability. Contribution permits liable defendants who have paid more than their share of a plaintiff's damages to sue other liable defendants who have not. Claim reduction would, of course, alleviate "whipsaw" pressures, but would potentially reduce recoveries and, to a degree, deterrence. The difficulty of calculating how much of the loss of a class of plaintiffs is attributable to the

---

23.   Senate Comm. on the Judiciary, Antitrust Equal Enforcement Act of 1979, S.Rep. No. 96–428, 96th Cong., 1st Sess. (1987).

24.   United States v. Reliable Transfer Co., 421 U.S. 397, 408 (1975).

acts of a given defendant has led some to question the wisdom of either contribution or claim reduction legislation and others to suggest that any legislation should deal only with horizontal price fixing.[25] Some defendants have created claim reduction agreements among themselves.[26]

D. SPECIAL ISSUES RELATED TO THE "BIG CASE"

In approaching antitrust policy questions, it is essential to have some appreciation of the size, duration, and complexity of antitrust litigation. In both government and private actions, it is not uncommon for discovery, trial, and appeal to take ten or more years and to involve a vast number of documents. Scores of attorneys often represent the parties to an antitrust litigation. This "big case" problem has always been part of the antitrust scene. In 1953, in the *United Shoe Machinery* case,[27] for example, the government offered 4,600 exhibits at one time; the *Alcoa* case[28] (p. 114 *infra*) involved 15,000 pages of record.

Although there were relatively few large government cases brought during the past thirty years, the combined experience of the 1970's through the early 2000's indicates that the "big case" in antitrust has grown even bigger and more unmanageable. The most "horrible" recent example is the government's monopolization case against IBM. After several years of investigation, the case was filed in 1969. In January 1982, the government stipulated to the dismissal of the case. During the intervening 13 years (including about 6 years of trial) more than 66 million pages of documents were produced; the government's trial presentation took 104,000 pages of transcript; IBM called 856 witnesses and cited 12,280 exhibits. IBM is conservatively estimated to have spent well over $150 million on its defense; the cost to the government is estimated to have been about $20 million.[29] Former Assistant Attorney General Baker (of the Antitrust Division) analyzed the problem as follows:

> From our experience with *IBM* and other such cases, we can draw several conclusions. One of these is that the Division itself shares some of the responsibility for the current state of affairs. First, there is an obvious tendency to broaden and overtry these complicated cases. In such high stakes cases, both parties will naturally attempt to introduce every shred of even marginally probative evidence in the trial of every conceivable theory of antitrust violation.

25. For a comprehensive review of this area, *see* Cavanagh, Contribution, Claim Reduction and Individual Treble Damage Responsibility: Which Path to Reform of Antitrust Remedies?, 40 Vand.L.Rev. 1277 (1987).

26. Kenny & Bassett, Private Enforcement of the Antitrust Laws, in Scher (ed.), Antitrust Adviser ch. 10 (4th ed.1995).

27. United States v. United Shoe Machinery Corp., 110 F.Supp. 295 (D.Mass.1953), affirmed per curiam, 347 U.S. 521 (1954).

28. United States v. Aluminum Co. of America, 148 F.2d 416 (2d Cir.1945).

29. *See* 1051 ATRR 310–11 (1982); N.Y. Times, Jan. 18, 1982, at D 1, col. 5.

Second, it is difficult to manage litigation in the context of budget limitations and bureaucratic requirements. Private parties in big cases draw on mammoth litigation budgets, retain several law firms and multitudes of paralegal assistants and technical advisors, and are able to utilize every form of litigation support system that current technology can make available. By contrast, the Government must rely on fewer resources spread over a wide front as it attempts a trial. . . .

The Antitrust Division often finds itself in a big case with fewer, more overworked and less experienced staff than its private opponents. This inevitably makes the hard-pressed Government attorneys more willing to accede in suggestions of delay. . . . The defendant, who benefits from stringing out litigation in order to preserve the status quo and put off the day on which remedial relief will produce an impact, sees no advantage in litigation efficiency. Delays are thus frequently sought by the parties on both sides, and are acquiesced in by courts that are themselves overworked and reluctant to become mired in swamps of difficult, inaccessible, economic evidence, without adequate assistance to deal with the massive record, multiple witnesses and mammoth briefs.[30]

Similar illustrations are all too evident. In 1990, the FTC began investigating Microsoft's alleged acquisition and maintenance of monopoly power in the market for operating systems. After an extensive investigation, the FTC deadlocked 2–2 on the decision whether to file a complaint. The Antitrust Division then initiated its own investigation using the FTC's extensive investigative files as a starting point. The Antitrust Division reviewed one million pages of documents, conducted over 100 interviews, and deposed 22 persons, including Microsoft Chairman Bill Gates. In July 1994, the Antitrust Division filed a complaint and a settlement with Microsoft. As indicated earlier, the district judge reviewing the settlement under the Tunney Act rejected it because its scope was too narrow, and it did not deal with "certain anticompetitive practices." In 1995, the Circuit Court for the District of Columbia concluded that the district court exceeded its authority; the Circuit Court implicitly suggested that the Antitrust Division should not be forced to take on a huge litigation burden that it wished to avoid.[31]

Litigation between Microsoft and the Antitrust Division continued in 1997–98 when the government filed a civil contempt action against Microsoft for violating a consent decree resulting from 1994 action. The government's claim, however, was rejected by the Circuit Court.[32] Finally, in May

---

30. Oversight of Antitrust Enforcement, Hearings before the Subcommittee on Antitrust and Monopoly of the Senate Committee on the Judiciary, 95th Cong., 1st Sess. 345 (May 5, 1977) (statement of Donald I. Baker).

31. United States v. Microsoft Corp., 56 F.3d 1448 (D.C.Cir.1995). For a discussion of Tunney Act issues, see p. 71 *supra*.

32. *See* United States v. Microsoft Corp., 147 F.3d 935 (D.C.Cir.1998).

1998, the Antitrust Division and a group of states (represented by state attorneys general) took on the "huge litigation burden" (which the government had avoided in 1994–95) by filing broad monopolization suits against Microsoft; the suits were consolidated. The district court scheduled the case on a "fast track," and a bench trial commenced less than four months after the complaints had been filed. Each side was limited to a maximum of 12 trial witnesses, and two rebuttal witnesses, and the trial was completed in 76 days. The D.C. Circuit, when the case was on appeal, said "it is noteworthy that a case of this magnitude and complexity has proceeded from the filing of complaints through trial to appellate decision in a mere three years."[33] The Circuit Court held that district courts have "extraordinarily broad discretion to determine the manner in which they will conduct trials," and "easily disposed" of Microsoft's challenges to the "fast track" process.

Nevertheless, despite the innovative and relatively speedy "fast track" process, the D.C. Circuit observed that in technologically dynamic markets remedies for anticompetitive conduct may not be available "because innovation to a large degree has already rendered the anticompetitive conduct obsolete (although by no means harmless)."[34] In 2004, the last part of the *Microsoft* case was finally settled.[35]

The FTC's "shared monopoly" case against the ready-to-eat cereal manufacturers was commenced in 1972, and after more than two years of trial before an administrative law judge, was dismissed with prejudice by the Commission in 1982.[36] The FTC's case against the oil industry, filed in 1973, was abandoned in 1981 without even progressing beyond the early stages of discovery.[37] A private action, Zenith Radio Corp. v. Matsushita Electric Industrial Co., Ltd., 513 F.Supp. 1100 (E.D.Pa.1981), was filed in 1970; defendants' motions for summary judgment were granted in 1981. In the interim, nearly 30 million pages of documents were exchanged, and in 1980 alone, the parties filed 114 briefs or memoranda estimated to total 7,500 pages.[38] In 1986, in sustaining the grant of defendants' motion for summary judgment, the Supreme Court observed:

> Stating the facts of this case is a daunting task. The opinion of the Court of Appeals for the Third Circuit runs to 69 pages; the primary opinion of the District Court is more than three times as long. 723 F.2d 238 (CA3 1983); 513 F.Supp. 1100 (ED Pa. 1981). Two respected District Judges each have authored a number of opinions in this case; the published ones alone would fill an entire

---

33. For a discussion of the substantive issues resolved in the *Microsoft* case, see p. 767 *infra*.

34. United States v. Microsoft Corp., 253 F.3d 34, 49 (D.C.Cir.), cert. denied, 534 U.S. 952 (2001).

35. *See* Massachusetts v. Microsoft Corp., 373 F.3d 1199 (D.C. Cir. 2004).

36. ATRR No. 1048, pp. 154–182 (1982).

37. ATRR No. 1031, p. A–28 (1981).

38. *See* Judge Becker Cuts 11–Year Monster Down to Size, Legal Times of Washington, May 11, 1981, at 1.

volume for the Federal Supplement. In addition, the parties have filed a forty-volume appendix in this Court that is said to contain the essence of the evidence on which the District Court and the Court of Appeals based their respective decisions.[39]

Vast amounts of time and energy of government officials, judges, lawyers, court administrators, and scholars have been devoted to analyzing techniques to bring these massive proceedings under control. President Carter, for example, in June 1978, appointed a National Commission for the Review of Antitrust Laws and Procedures (the "National Commission"). This twenty-two member National Commission (composed of ten members of Congress, seven public members, and various government officials) proposed managerial and procedural approaches to: (i) limit and speed discovery; (ii) lead to the early refinement of issues; and (iii) encourage aggressive judicial participation in the shaping of complex antitrust cases. See National Commission, Report to the President and the Attorney General 111–112 (1979).[40] The trial judge in the *Microsoft* case made contributions along these lines. How to gain control of these "big cases"—through new procedural, process and/or substantive rules—remains one of the principal antitrust problems of our time.

In reading substantive chapters of this casebook, ask yourself whether courts have taken (or should take) into account this "big case" problem in fashioning substantive rules defining legal or illegal behavior. Should, for example, "shortcut" approaches to proof, or to the definition of an offense, be adopted because full exploration of economic cause and effect would produce unwieldy or unmanageable litigation?

SECTION 2.   THE LIMITS OF ANTITRUST

The free-market model assumes that key economic decisions—(1) what commodities shall be produced and in what quantities, (2) who will produce goods, with what resources, and in what technological manner, and (3) how goods will be distributed among different individuals or factions within a society—will be determined in the competitive market place. In a broad sense, most of antitrust represents a system of rules designed to prevent individuals or groups from interfering unduly in the operations of these market forces. For example, supply and demand factors theoretically determine the prices and amounts of particular commodities to be produced; antitrust laws prohibit conspiracies to increase price or limit production. Antitrust laws limiting mergers and consolidations are designed to prevent the creation or growth of excessive market power which would result in private interference with these economic determinations.

39.   Matsushita Electric Industrial Co. v. Zenith Radio Corp., 475 U.S. 574, 576 (1986).

40.   The National Commission's Report is reprinted at 80 F.R.D. 509 (1979); *see, e.g.,* Judicial Conference of the United States, Report on Procedure in Antitrust and Other Protracted Cases, 13 F.R.D. 62 (1951); McAllister, The Big Case: Procedural Problems in Antitrust Litigation, 64 Harv.L.Rev. 27 (1950).

American political rhetoric tends to exaggerate somewhat the extent to which the free market governs economic decisionmaking in the United States. In certain sectors of the economy, antitrust has been replaced by more intrusive systems of government regulation, while in other segments—for example, organized baseball and insurance—it has been displaced with no other federal government regulation being substituted in its place.

A.   GOVERNMENT OWNERSHIP OF THE MEANS OF PRODUCTION

The most intrusive form of government presence occurs where, as in the former Soviet Union, the government owns outright the principal means of production and makes all relevant economic decisions in those sectors of the economy. Again, political rhetoric in the United States is somewhat deceptive in tending to focus upon delivery of the mails and generating of electric power (*e.g.*, TVA) as prime domestic examples of this approach, but these areas have never been of great significance economically.

More significant instances of federal and state enterprise include the development of major weapons systems within the national defense program, providing public education, and operating a large portion of local urban transit. The federal government also participates in the health care and insurance businesses through, for example, Medicare and programs it operates relating to veterans affairs and agricultural commodities. In these markets, economic decisions are often made through the political process. Measured against the total economy, these federal and state enterprises are relatively small. It should also be noted, however, that as a result of the recent financial crisis, the federal government now owns controlling shares or significant stakes in major financial enterprises (including banks and an insurance company) and industrial (automobile) corporations.

B.   REGULATED INDUSTRIES

Displacement of antitrust can also occur through extensive government regulation falling short of outright ownership of the means of production. Regulatory systems vary widely in the scope and intensity of government intrusion. A useful but arbitrary guideline in distinguishing "free market" sectors from "regulated industries" focuses on entry and price. When both of these are controlled by government processes, the industry often is categorized as "regulated."

The theory underlying government intrusion is that free-market forces will discipline inadequately or will produce otherwise unacceptable results. The beneficiary of a natural monopoly—for example, the owner of a ferry landing at the only point where a river can conveniently be crossed—will neither be permitted to take advantage of that geographic good fortune by charging whatever the market will bear nor be allowed to discriminate among potential customers. As Professor W.K. Jones has noted:

> The unifying characteristic of natural monopoly industries is the ability of a single firm to provide the most economical service to a given area. Within the area reached by the physical facilities of the firm, the introduction of additional suppliers requires a wasteful duplication of plant and a significant increase in cost not normally justified by any benefits to users of the service. Under such circumstances, monopoly is accepted as the most appropriate industry structure and the industry is subjected to regulation as a "public utility."[41]

Federal and state legislatures have, however, sometimes been persuaded to displace competition with regulation in markets that are neither natural monopolies nor even highly concentrated. The statute which until relatively recently gave the Interstate Commerce Commission (which no longer exists) extensive authority to regulate the otherwise highly competitive interstate trucking industry was one example of many at the federal level. Since it passed the Interstate Commerce Act in 1887, Congress has established numerous regulatory agencies charged with supervision of the economic activities of particular industries engaged in interstate commerce. The FCC, FERC, CFTC, and SEC, as well as the Secretary of Agriculture, the Board of Governors of the Federal Reserve System, the Comptroller of the Currency, the Secretary of the Interior, and the Secretary of Transportation, among other agencies and administrators, have been given broad grants of regulatory authority in areas of economic activity related to their broader duties.

In general, each of these regulatory bodies operates under a separate statute, the regulatory criteria of which may or may not include provisions analogous to the proscriptions of the antitrust laws. In some, Congress has incorporated language from the Sherman or Clayton Acts; several of the regulatory bodies are given specific authority to enforce Sections 3, 7, and 8 of the Clayton Act. Some statutes, however, clearly express Congressional acquiescence in activity which would otherwise be subject to antitrust sanction, usually subject to the regulator's review or approval. Thus, the regulatory body may have authority (by its own action or by approval of private transactions) to fix rates or prices, control market entry, or eliminate existing or potential competition.

Some statutes confer an express antitrust exemption. More frequently, no express immunity is granted but the nature of the regulation is such that the courts have implied a limited immunity for certain activities. *See, e.g.*, Gordon v. NYSE, 422 U.S. 659 (1975) (active agency regulation, pursuant to a Congressional directive, implied immunity); United States v. NASD, 422 U.S. 694 (1975) (regulatory scheme so pervasive that immunity assumed). In 2007, in Credit Suisse Securities (USA) LLC v. Billing, 551 U.S. 264 (2007), the Supreme Court analyzed the implied immunity doctrine at some length, and concluded there was "a 'clear repugnancy' between the [extensive] securities laws" related to new issues of shares and

---

41. Jones, Government Price Controls and Inflation: A Prognosis Based on the Impact of Controls in the Regulated Industries, 65 Cornell L.Rev. 303, 304 (1980).

a private antitrust complaint. An issue to be resolved in the future is how to reconcile *Credit Suisse* with the Court's earlier view that repeal of antitrust "is to be regarded as implied only if necessary to make ... [the regulatory scheme] work, and even then only to the minimum extent necessary." Silver v. New York Stock Exchange, 373 U.S. 341, 357 (1963).

An increasingly significant activity of the Antitrust Division and the FTC has been to appear in federal regulatory proceedings as an advocate for competitive policy. In addition, Congress, during the past four decades, has entered into a far-reaching program of deregulation. Significant steps have been taken, for example, with respect to railroads, airlines, trucking, telecommunications, and financial institutions. Deregulation has usually been accompanied by some limitation of the existing scope of antitrust immunity.

At the state level, laws by the thousands assist such professionals or businessmen as lawyers, doctors, druggists, liquor dealers, funeral home operators, barbers, optometrists—an endless list—in combatting the forces of competition, by implementing self-regulation of "ethical standards" or other forms of what can be thought of as cartelization. Local ordinances perform similar functions for other business groups, seldom overlooking the "desirability" of providing a city commission to keep taxis from crowding the streets and to keep their rates at non-competitive (high) levels.[42]

Major regulated industries in the United States are banking, public transportation, provision of gas and electric services, local telephone services, television broadcasting, and portions of agricultural production. In each instance the regulated industry has felt the winds of deregulation during the 1970's, 1980's, 1990's, and early 2000's. A primary policy concern underlying the deregulation movement is that regulation may be less efficient economically than the operation of market forces. Many of these regulatory regimes were instituted during the New Deal, and were designed as a liberal alternative to Marxism. After more than 70 years of experience, however, the conviction has come to be widely shared that many regulatory agencies, particularly those regulating entry and price, no longer serve adequately the public interest and some have, in fact, become captives of the industries they were designed to regulate.[43] As indicated earlier, during the past four decades "deregulation" advocacy has become an increasingly important activity of both the Antitrust Division and the FTC. In the mid 1990's and early 2000's a major new area of competition advocacy involves intellectual property protection for new technologies. In 1996, an important FTC staff report concluded:

> As the Supreme Court has recognized many times, there is a need to balance intellectual property and competition values....

---

42. For a discussion of efforts to influence government action and the so-called "state action" doctrine, see Chapter 5 *infra*.

43. *See, e.g.,* Jones, *supra* note 42, at 313–18; Breyer & MacAvoy, Energy Regulation by the Federal Power Commission 72–88 (1974); Green & Nader, Economic Regulation vs. Competition: Uncle Sam the Monopoly Man, 82 Yale L.J. 871 (1973); Winter, Economic Regulation vs. Competition: Ralph Nader and Creeping Capitalism, 82 Yale L.J. 890 (1973).

Accordingly, in light of testimony and literature on this topic, we believe that the FTC should act to ensure that intellectual property policy and decision makers, including the courts, the PTO [U.S. Patent and Trademark Office], the Registrar of Copyrights, and the legislature, are aware of the potential competitive consequences of intellectual property policy for new technologies such as biotechnology and computer software.[44]

On the other hand, the recent financial crisis has raised a basic question as to whether "deregulation", especially involving safety and soundness (as opposed to price), has gone too far. The crisis has demonstrated an overwhelming need for new or enhanced federal regulatory oversight in many areas. Particularly for financial institutions, reinvigorated oversight of both institutions and financial products appears to be a national imperative. Government regulation of industries is obviously too vast a topic to be treated in an antitrust course. However, Section 3 of Chapter 5 examines the increasingly complex and important interface between federal antitrust policy and state and local business regulation; Section 1 of Chapter 8 deals with the current tension between intellectual property protection and antitrust.

C. INTERSTATE AND FOREIGN COMMERCE

1. INTERSTATE COMMERCE

The Sherman Act prohibits only "restraints of trade or commerce among the several States." During the past seventy years, this language has been interpreted very broadly. In general, today it is unlikely that economic activity of sufficient significance to attract the attention of federal enforcement agencies, or justify private litigation, will not directly involve interstate commerce. Even where involvement is not direct, the courts have developed an expansive "effect on commerce" test to justify federal jurisdiction. In Burke v. Ford, 389 U.S. 320 (1967), a group of Oklahoma liquor dealers sued under Section 1 of the Sherman Act to enjoin an alleged statewide division of markets by all Oklahoma liquor wholesalers. The Supreme Court, without hearing argument, summarily reversed the finding below that the interstate commerce prerequisite of the Sherman Act had not been satisfied, noting that anticompetitive arrangements are likely to lead to increased prices and, therefore, lower unit sales. Accordingly, territorial market division almost certainly resulted in fewer sales to retailers and hence fewer purchases of out-of-state liquor by wholesalers than would have occurred but for the anticompetitive arrangements.

In Goldfarb v. Virginia State Bar, 421 U.S. 773 (1975), the Supreme Court continued its expansive reading of the Sherman Act's commerce clause.[45] The Court of Appeals (Fourth Circuit) had held that real estate

---

44. FTC Staff, Anticipating the 21st Century: Competition Policy in the New High–Tech, Global Marketplace Ch. 8 at 22 (1996).

45. For portions of the *Goldfarb* opinion setting forth the facts of the case and discussing other issues, *see* Chapter 4 *infra*.

title examinations (which had to be performed by lawyers) "are performed wholly intrastate, are essentially local in nature and therefore a restraint with respect to them can never substantially affect interstate commerce." Id. at 783. The Supreme Court reversed, pointing out that a significant portion of the funds for purchasing homes in Fairfax County (a suburb of Washington, D.C.) came from out of state and that significant amounts of loans were guaranteed by the Veterans Administration and HUD, both headquartered in the District of Columbia.

Chief Justice Burger's opinion noted that the "necessary connection between the interstate transactions and the restraint of trade provided by the minimum-fee schedule is present because, in a practical sense, title examinations are necessary in real estate transactions." The Chief Justice continued:

> The fact that there was no showing that home buyers were discouraged by the challenged activities [*i.e.*, price fixing] does not mean that interstate commerce was not affected. Otherwise, the magnitude of the effect would control, and our cases have shown that, once an effect is shown, no specific magnitude need be proved. Nor was it necessary for petitioners to prove that the fee schedule raised fees. Petitioners clearly proved that the fee schedule fixed fees and thus "deprive[d] purchasers or consumers of the advantages which they derive from free competition." Apex Hosiery Co. v. Leader, 310 U.S. 469, 501 (1940).

> Where, as a matter of law or practical necessity, legal services are an integral part of an interstate transaction, a restraint on those services may substantially affect commerce for Sherman Act purposes. Id. at 785.[46]

In McLain v. Real Estate Board of New Orleans, Inc., 444 U.S. 232 (1980), in which a class of private plaintiffs alleged a price-fixing conspiracy among real estate brokers in Greater New Orleans, the Supreme Court reversed a dismissal and reasoned:

> The broad authority of Congress under the Commerce Clause has, of course, long been interpreted to extend beyond activities actually *in* interstate commerce to reach other activities that, while wholly local in nature, nevertheless substantially *affect* interstate commerce....

> To establish the jurisdictional element of a Sherman Act violation it would be sufficient for petitioners to demonstrate a substantial effect on interstate commerce generated by respondents' brokerage activity. Petitioners need not make the more particularized showing of an effect on interstate commerce caused by the alleged conspiracy to fix commission rates, or by those other aspects of respondents' activity that are alleged to be unlawful. The validity of this approach is confirmed by an examination of

---

46. *See* Hospital Building Co. v. Trustees of Rex Hospital, 425 U.S. 738 (1976).

the case law. If establishing jurisdiction required a showing that the unlawful conduct itself had an effect on interstate commerce, jurisdiction would be defeated by a demonstration that the alleged restraint failed to have its intended anticompetitive effect. This is not the rule of our cases. . . .

Nor is jurisdiction defeated in a case relying on anticompetitive effects by plaintiff's failure to quantify the adverse impact of defendant's conduct. . . . Even where there is an inability to prove that concerted activity has resulted in legally cognizable damages, jurisdiction need not be impaired, though such a failure may confine the available remedies to injunctive relief. . . .

. . . Brokerage activities necessarily affect both the frequency and the terms of residential sales transactions. Ultimately, whatever stimulates or retards the volume of residential sales, or has an impact on the purchase price, affects the demand for financing and title insurance, those two commercial activities that on this record are shown to have occurred in interstate commerce. Where, as here, the services of respondent real estate brokers are often employed in transactions in the relevant market, petitioners at trial may be able to show that respondents' activities have a not insubstantial effect on interstate commerce. Id. at 241, 242, 246.

More recently, in Summit Health, Ltd. v. Pinhas, 500 U.S. 322 (1991), an ophthalmologist sued members of a medical center and the hospital itself for revoking his staff privileges and conspiring to prevent him from finding employment in the Los Angeles area. A 5–4 majority of the Supreme Court stated that the Sherman Act was intended to "go as far as the Constitution permits Congress to go." 500 U.S. at 328 n.7. Pointing to general activities of the hospital, the Court noted that as "a 'matter of practical economics' . . . the effect of such a conspiracy on the hospital's 'purchase of out-of-state medicines and supplies as well as its revenues from out-of-state insurance companies' . . . would establish the necessary interstate nexus." 500 U.S. at 329.

The Court rejected the hospital's argument that the elimination of one physician's practice could not affect interstate commerce. First, the Court indicated that a violation of the Sherman Act is not found by looking at the "actual consequences" of the action, but by consideration of the "potential harm that would ensue if the conspiracy were successful." Second, the change in the make-up of the Los Angeles market was stated to have a "market-wide impact and therefore an effect on interstate commerce." The Court reasoned:

The competitive significance of [plaintiff's] exclusion from the market must be measured, not just by a particularized evaluation of his own practice, but rather, by a general evaluation of the impact of the restraint on other participants and potential participants in the market from which he has been excluded. 500 U.S. at 332.

Justices Scalia, O'Connor, Kennedy, and Souter dissented. First, they disagreed with the proposition that the Sherman Act extended to the reach of the Commerce Clause: "[T]he question before us is not whether Congress *could* reach the activity before us here if it wanted to, but whether it *has done* so via the Sherman Act." 500 U.S. at 333 (emphasis in original). The dissent then noted a circuit split on the issue of whether the unlawful activities or merely the general business activities of a defendant need to affect interstate commerce. The dissent stated:

> Today the Court could have cleared up the confusion created by *McLain,* refocused the inquiry along the lines marked by our previous cases (and still adhered to by most Circuits), and [found that there was no jurisdiction under the Sherman Act in this case]. Instead, it compounds the confusion by rejecting the two competing interpretations of *McLain* and adding yet a third candidate to the field.... To determine Sherman Act jurisdiction it looks *neither* to the effect on commerce of the restraint, *nor* to the effect on commerce of the defendants' infected activity, but rather, it seems, to the effect on commerce of the activity from which the plaintiff has been excluded.... This analysis tell us nothing about the substantiality of the impact on interstate commerce generated by the particular conduct at issue here. 500 U.S. at 336.

After *McLain* and *Summit Health* how much room is left for a jurisdictional defense given the Court's willingness to focus on "brokerage activity," or non-litigating "participants and potential participants in the market," as opposed to the "effect on interstate commerce caused by the alleged conspiracy"?

Unlike the Sherman Act, the Clayton Act and the Robinson–Patman Act apply to persons and conduct "in commerce." In two cases, in 1974 and 1975,[47] the Supreme Court limited the jurisdictional reach of this "in commerce" language. In Gulf Oil Corp. v. Copp Paving Co., 419 U.S. 186, 194–195 (1974), the Court said:

> The jurisdictional reach of § 1 [of the Sherman Act] thus is keyed directly to effects on interstate markets and the interstate flow of goods. Moreover, our cases have recognized that in enacting § 1 Congress "wanted to go to the utmost extent of its Constitutional power in restraining trust and monopoly agreements." ...
>
> In contrast to § 1, the distinct "in commerce" language of the Clayton and Robinson–Patman Act provisions with which we are concerned here appears to denote only persons or activities within the flow of interstate commerce—the practical, economic continuity in the generation of goods and services for interstate markets

---

47. *See* United States v. American Building Maintenance Industries, 422 U.S. 271 (1975); Gulf Oil Corp. v. Copp Paving Co., Inc., 419 U.S. 186 (1974). For recent Robinson–Patman cases, *see, e.g.,* Godfrey v. Pulitzer Pub. Co., 161 F.3d 1137 (8th Cir.1998); McCallum v. City of Athens, 976 F.2d 649 (11th Cir.1992).

and their transport and distribution to the consumer. If this is so, the jurisdictional requirements of these provisions cannot be satisfied merely by showing that allegedly anticompetitive acquisitions and activities *affect* commerce.

In 1980, however, Congress amended Section 7 of the Clayton Act to reach mergers involving companies engaged "in any activity affecting commerce."[48] Similarly, in 1975, Congress amended Section 5 of the Federal Trade Commission Act as follows:

> Section 5 [also Sections 6 and 12] of the Federal Trade Commission Act (15 U.S.C. § 45) is amended by striking out "in commerce" wherever it appears and inserting in lieu thereof "in or affecting commerce."[49]

Of course, cases occasionally do arise, particularly in large states like New York, Texas, or California, or physically isolated states like Alaska and Hawaii, where interstate commerce cannot be demonstrated. In those situations, state antitrust statutes or common-law "restraint of trade" provisions may serve objectives parallel to those of the federal laws.

2. FOREIGN COMMERCE

The Sherman Act and other antitrust laws also apply to foreign trade or commerce. Chapter 10 deals with the complex jurisdictional issues presented in the context of foreign trade or commerce, and with the application of United States antitrust laws to the acts and instrumentalities of foreign sovereigns. Various substantive sections of the casebook deal with the subtle and increasingly significant issues related to whether or not antitrust rules should be modified when they are applied to foreign activities.

D. ADDITIONAL EXEMPTIONS, EXCLUSIONS, AND OTHER ASPECTS OF ECONOMIC CONTROL

As indicated, the United States relies only in part on competition to regulate its markets. In addition to government ownership and regulation (*see* A and B *supra*), numerous exemptions and exclusions from the antitrust laws exist, and the influences of various governmental policies and controls on the free-market sector are so varied and widespread as to be impossible to summarize. For example, government policies designed to increase productivity or control inflation—including tax policies, control of monetary supply, intellectual property policy, and spending—powerfully influence free-market economic determinations. Some government programs stimulate arguably desirable economic activity (*e.g.*, housing allowances), while others intervene in order to prevent undesirable social conse-

---

48. 15 U.S.C. § 18.

49. Magnuson–Moss Warranty–Federal Trade Commission Improvement Act § 201, Pub.L. 93–637, 88 Stat. 2183; 15 U.S.C. § 45. This amendment legislatively overruled FTC v. Bunte Brothers, Inc., 312 U.S. 349 (1941).

quences (*e.g.*, pollution control). Collaboration between competitors can be authorized by the President and Department of Defense in the name of national defense,[50] or by the Small Business Administration to assist small entrepreneurs.[51]

The most important legislative exemption from the antitrust laws is in the labor market where national policy—recognized in a statutory exemption and a nonstatutory exemption—permits collective bargaining by employees when negotiating wages and other terms of their employment.[52] The collective bargaining process can produce effects in product markets which would otherwise be impermissible under the antitrust laws—for example, where negotiations result in a combination between labor and some employers to advance mutual interests at the expense of other employer groups. While the labor exemption is not intended to cover these practices,[53] there will be relatively few situations in which unacceptable anticompetitive consequences occurring in the product market could not be justified by some arguably legitimate and allegedly "unilaterally sought" union objective. The labor exemption is applicable to a collective bargaining agreement, and to negotiation-impasse situations involving wages and working conditions.[54]

Another area of antitrust exemption involves agricultural cooperatives. Section 6 of the Clayton Act and the Capper–Volstead Act,[55] in effect, allow farmers organized into agricultural cooperatives to fix prices at which farm produce will be sold without antitrust consequences. Maryland & Virginia Milk Producers Association v. United States, 362 U.S. 458 (1960), contains a useful review of the history and purpose of this statutory scheme. The exemption of most efforts by competitors to influence public officials or engage in "political activities," under the so-called Noerr–Pennington doctrine, is discussed in Chapter 5 *infra*.

Finally, there are a number of "rifle-shot exceptions" which usually reflect successful petitioning by particular groups to Congress for relief from allegedly onerous aspects of antitrust rules or decisions. Although

---

50. Defense Production Act of 1950, 50 U.S.C. § 2158.

51. 15 U.S.C. §§ 638, 640.

52. Section 6 of the Clayton Act (15 U.S.C. § 17) provides that: "The labor of a human being is not a commodity or article of commerce." And Section 20 (29 U.S.C. § 52) prohibits issuance of injunctions to prevent peaceful activities by employees growing out of a labor dispute except under special circumstances. *See* American Steel Erectors, Inc. v. Local Union No. 7, 536 F.3d 68, 76–77 (1st Cir. 2008).

53. The various Supreme Court opinions in United Mine Workers v. Pennington, 381 U.S. 657 (1965), and Local Union No. 189, Amalgamated Meat Cutters v. Jewel Tea Co., 381 U.S. 676 (1965), demonstrate what a complicated matter it is to draw meaningful distinctions in this area. See generally Connell Construction Co. v. Plumbers and Steamfitters Local Union No. 100, 421 U.S. 616 (1975); Gifford, Redefining the Antitrust Labor Exemption, 72 Minn.L.Rev. 1379 (1988).

54. *See, e.g.*, Brown v. Pro Football, Inc., 518 U.S. 231 (1996) (permitting use of the nonstatutory exemption in a negotiation-impasse situation). For a further discussion of the labor exemption, *see* pp. 277–81 *infra*.

55. 7 U.S.C. §§ 291–92.

increasingly subject to question, the McCarran–Ferguson Act exempts insurance activities (other than practices involving boycott, coercion, and intimidation) from the antitrust laws to the extent those activities are regulated by state law.[56] Another example is the Newspaper Preservation Act, discussed at p. 1008 *infra*, which under certain conditions permits newspaper publishers to engage in otherwise illegal joint publishing ventures.

SELECTIVE BIBLIOGRAPHY

1. The Three–Level Enforcement Pattern

1–2 Areeda & Hovenkamp, Antitrust Law: An Analysis of Antitrust Principles and Their Application (3d ed. 2006 & Supp. 2009).

Sullivan & Grimes, The Law of Antitrust: An Integrated Handbook 930–1011 (2d ed. 2006).

ABA Section of Antitrust Law, 2008 Transition Report (2008).

Antitrust Modernization Commission, Report and Recommendations (2007).

ABA Section of Antitrust Law, The State of Federal Antitrust Enforcement—2001: Report of the Task Force on the Federal Antitrust Agencies (2001).

FTC Staff, Anticipating the 21st Century: Competition Policy in the New High–Tech, Global Marketplace (1996).

White (ed.), Private Antitrust Litigation: New Evidence, New Learning (1988).

National Commission for the Review of Antitrust Laws and Procedures, Report to the President and the Attorney General, 80 F.R.D. 509 (1979).

2. The Limits of Antitrust

1A Areeda & Hovenkamp, Antitrust Law: An Analysis of Antitrust Principles and Their Application (3d ed. 2006 & Supp. 2009).

Sullivan & Grimes, The Law of Antitrust: An Integrated Handbook 737–929 (2d ed. 2006).

Kaysen & Turner, Antitrust Policy Chs. 6–7 (1959).

Green & Nader, Economic Regulation vs. Competition: Uncle Sam the Monopoly Man, 82 Yale L.J. 871 (1973).

---

56. 15 U.S.C. §§ 1011–1015. As to what constitutes the business of insurance, *see* Union Labor Life Insur. Co. v. Pireno, 458 U.S. 119 (1982); Group Life & Health Insurance Co. v. Royal Drug Co., 440 U.S. 205 (1979). On the question of what constitutes sufficient state regulation to oust federal jurisdiction, *see* FTC v. Travelers Health Association, 362 U.S. 293 (1960); FTC v. National Casualty Co., 357 U.S. 560 (1958). On the boundaries of the "boycott" non-exemption, see Hartford Fire Insur. Co. v. California, 509 U.S. 764 (1993).

CHAPTER 3

MARKET STRUCTURE AND A FIRST LOOK AT THE PROBLEM OF MONOPOLY POWER

SECTION 1. MONOPOLIZATION AND THE PROBLEM OF MARKET DEFINITION

SCOPE NOTE

The Sherman Act is a composite of two major concepts—restraint of trade and monopoly. The cases in this section are concerned with single firm monopolies. At issue are three interrelated antitrust questions: (i) what is the proper technique for measuring market shares, usually phrased as the problem of "defining relevant market;" (ii) at what point and in what circumstances do large market shares give rise to market power of monopoly dimensions; and (iii) given monopoly power, what kinds of business conduct on the part of the firm will the antitrust laws tolerate?[1]

The measurement problem is best addressed by considering at the outset the purposes of antitrust. With respect to a single firm, one chief evil with which antitrust policy is concerned is power to curtail output and thereby raise prices above the levels that would exist under competitive conditions. A firm's power to raise prices is limited primarily by the existence of other producers who, by failing similarly to raise prices, would take over enough of its business to make a price rise unprofitable. The principal problem in any given case is to determine which existing firms and potential competitors have sufficient restraining influence on the defendant's power over price to warrant their inclusion in the "relevant market."

Three considerations are of primary importance in distinguishing the relevant firms from the irrelevant. Two of these pertain to the "demand" side of the analysis. The first is the nature of the product and the ability or willingness of its users to substitute other products for it. As alternative products become generally less "substitutable," their influence on defendant's price diminishes.

Consider three competitive situations. In the first, we are concerned with a single farmer who produces wheat that is completely fungible with the wheat produced by a large number of other producers. In that situation, the price the seller charges will be determined entirely by the market and will not be significantly

---

1. In this chapter, we will examine some "simple" aspects of the conduct question, and then discuss those issues again in detail in Chapter 8. The remainder of the chapter will address questions (i) and (ii)—related to market definition and the identification of market power of monopoly dimensions. Problems of market definition and market power cut across every area of antitrust. They arise, for example, in many Sherman Act "restraint of trade" cases and are often a decisive factor in merger enforcement.

affected by any individual farmer's decision to expand or curtail his production. Thus, if the market is working perfectly and purchasers are fully informed, the farmer will find that he can sell no wheat at all if he charges even a penny more than the going market price. On the other hand, since the farmer can sell his full supply at the market price, it would be senseless to sell for even a penny less. By contrast, consider the market position of the manufacturer of a patented drug that is far more effective in treating a serious disease than any alternative course of treatment. At least during the period of the patent, the seller can curtail production and raise price considerably in the expectation that consumers will prefer its product to very imperfect existing substitutes.

The common situation is neither of these two—that is, neither perfect competition nor monopoly—but rather one in which a seller or group of sellers offers a product for which there are many close but not perfect substitutes.[2] Coca–Cola could be viewed as a monopolist if in the minds of buyers it is completely different from any other liquid beverage. Its market power would be less if as a result of slight changes in price buyers quickly were willing to switch to other carbonated cola beverages, and its market power would be still less if they would be similarly willing to switch to non-cola carbonated beverages or even to coffee, tea, or milk. A threshold problem in any given case is to determine which existing firms and potential competitors have sufficient restraining influence on the seller's power over price to warrant their inclusion as effective competitors. The process of resolving that set of questions is called "defining the relevant market."

The second consideration is spatial or geographic. One obvious matter that bears on the substitutability of alternatives is their location. If X owns every shoe store in a particular city, his prices are still limited by the presence of independent stores in the suburbs or in shopping centers located on highways leading into the city and by mail-order possibilities. But he may nevertheless be able to raise his prices above the going rate—by a dollar, let us say—on the assumption that relatively few customers would take the trouble to buy elsewhere in order to save so small an amount. Note, however, that this might not be the case if he owned wholesale rather than retail outlets. Even a dollar's difference would cause retail stores to turn to more remote sources since such a differential becomes important to anyone buying in quantity.

The "supply" side of the equation has received less attention in the cases. A firm may not be limited in its power over price solely by the alternative sources of supply (of its product or widely acceptable substitutes) that are at present in existence. It may also be limited by the desire to forestall possible competition that would enter the field if its profits were to rise too high. Any firm with market power approaching monopoly dimensions could be expected to take account of potential competition of this sort. The importance of this factor is hard to assess, however, and will differ from industry to industry. A steel rolling mill may be able to move from one product market (sheets for automobile manufacturers) to another (sheets for metal containers) by a simple adjustment in its processing. At the other extreme, entry into a new market may require construction of completely new production facilities. In either case, the likelihood of a new firm entering a market depends on the expense to the newcomer of obtaining and operating a plant, the availability of raw materials, skilled personnel and production processes, the cost of obtaining a satisfactory share of the market (advertising, sales network, etc.), and so forth—in other words, the cost and other barriers to entry. As these barriers

---

2. An early and extremely influential analysis of these various structural conditions is found in Bain, Industrial Organization, 27–31 (1959).

become more imposing, the likelihood of new competition declines and its influence over the pricing policy of an existing firm diminishes correspondingly.

We start our examination of questions of "monopoly power" by examining the *Alcoa* case—one of the landmark opinions in antitrust. While there are some interesting relevant market definition issues in the case, it is principally concerned with the question of limits on permissible behavior by a company that has achieved or is in the process of achieving monopoly power.

While measurement of market power is critical to enforcement in virtually all areas of antitrust, the very difficult issues can be illustrated best by a comparison in this chapter of three leading cases relating to dominant firms—*Alcoa, DuPont* (often referred to as "the Cellophane case") and *Grinnell*. We therefore start with these three cases and two lengthy notes, one beginning on page 171 and other beginning on page 165. Before applying their teaching (and occasionally their errors) to the issues we will discuss.

Sherman Act, Section 2

[Reprinted pp. 5–6 *supra.*]

Treaty of Rome, Article 82

[Reprinted pp. 12–13 *supra.*]

United States v. Aluminum Co. of America

United States Court of Appeals, Second Circuit, 1945.
148 F.2d 416.

■ Before L. HAND, SWAN and AUGUSTUS N. HAND, CIRCUIT JUDGES.

L. HAND, J. This appeal comes to us by virtue of a certificate of the Supreme Court, under the amendment of 1944 to § 29 of 15 U.S.C.A. The action was brought under § 4 of that title, praying the district court to adjudge that the defendant, Aluminum Company of America, was monopolizing interstate and foreign commerce, particularly in the manufacture and sale of "virgin" aluminum ingot, and that it be dissolved; and further to adjudge that that company and the defendant, Aluminum Limited, had entered into a conspiracy in restraint of such commerce. It also asked incidental relief.... The action came to trial on June 1, 1938.... The judge ... entered final judgment dismissing the complaint on July 23, [1942].... On June 12, 1944, the Supreme Court, declaring that a quorum of six justices qualified to hear the case was wanting, referred the appeal to this court under § 29 of Title 15, already mentioned....

"Alcoa" is a corporation, organized under the laws of Pennsylvania on September 18, 1888; its original name, "Pittsburgh Reduction Company," was changed to its present one on January 1, 1907. It has always been engaged in the production and sale of "ingot" aluminum, and since 1895 also in the fabrication of the metal into many finished and semi-finished articles. It has proliferated into a great number of subsidiaries, created at various times between the years 1900 and 1929, as the business expanded. Aluminum is a chemical element; it is never found in a free state, being always in chemical combination with oxygen. One form of this combination is known as alumina; and for practical purposes the most available material from which alumina can be extracted is an ore called "bauxite." . . . .

The extraction of aluminum from alumina requires a very large amount of electrical energy, which is ordinarily, though not always, most cheaply obtained from waterpower. Beginning at least as early as 1895, "Alcoa" secured such power from several companies by contracts, containing in at least three instances, covenants binding the power companies not to sell or let power to anyone else for the manufacture of aluminum. "Alcoa"—either itself or by a subsidiary—also entered into four successive "cartels" with foreign manufacturers of aluminum by which, in exchange for certain limitations upon its import into foreign countries, it secured covenants from the foreign producers, either not to import into the United States at all, or to do so under restrictions, which in some cases involved the fixing of prices. These "cartels" and restrictive covenants and certain other practices were the subject of a suit filed by the United States against "Alcoa" on May 16, 1912, in which a decree was entered by consent on June 7, 1912, declaring several of these covenants unlawful and enjoining their performance; and also declaring invalid other restrictive covenants obtained before 1903 relating to the sale of alumina. ("Alcoa" failed at this time to inform the United States of several restrictive covenants in waterpower contracts; its justification—which the judge accepted—being that they had been forgotten.) . . . .

None of the foregoing facts are in dispute, and the most important question in the case is whether the monopoly in "Alcoa's" production of "virgin" ingot, secured by the two patents until 1909, and in part perpetuated between 1909 and 1912 by the unlawful practices, forbidden by the decree of 1912, continued for the ensuing twenty-eight years; and whether, if it did, it was unlawful under § 2 of the Sherman Act. It is undisputed that throughout this period "Alcoa" continued to be the single producer of "virgin" ingot in the United States; and the plaintiff argues that this without more was enough to make it an unlawful monopoly. It also takes an alternative position: that in any event during this period "Alcoa" consistently pursued unlawful exclusionary practices, which made its dominant position certainly unlawful, even though it would not have been, had it been retained only by "natural growth." Finally, it asserts that many of these practices were of themselves unlawful, as contracts in restraint of trade under § 1 of the Act. "Alcoa's" position is that the fact that it alone continued to make "virgin" ingot in this country did not, and does not, give it a monopoly of the market; that it was always subject to the competition of imported "virgin" ingot, and of what is called "secondary" ingot; and that even if it had not been, its monopoly would not have been retained by unlawful means, but would have been the result of a growth which the Act does not forbid, even when it results in a monopoly. We shall first consider the amount and character of this competition; next, how far it established a monopoly; and finally, if it did, whether that monopoly was unlawful under § 2 of the Act....

... [The court went on to hold that ingot fabricated by "Alcoa" should be included and "secondary" ingot should be excluded in[3] determining "Alcoa's" control of the aluminum market.[4]]

We conclude therefore that "Alcoa's" control over the ingot market must be reckoned at over ninety per cent; that being the proportion which its production bears to imported "virgin" ingot. If the fraction that it did not supply were the produce of domestic manufacture, there could be no doubt that this percentage gave it a monopoly—lawful or unlawful, as the case might be. The producer of so large a proportion of the supply has complete control within certain limits. It is true that if by raising the price he reduces the amount which can be marketed—as always, or almost always, happens—he may invite the expansion of the small producers who will try to fill the place left open; nevertheless, not only is there an inevitable lag in this, but the large producer is in a strong position to check such competition; and, indeed, if he has retained his old plant and personnel, he can inevitably do so. There are indeed limits to his power; substitutes are available for almost all commodities, and to raise the price enough is to evoke them. [Citing cases.] Moreover, it is difficult and expensive to keep idle any part of a plant or of personnel; and any drastic contraction of the market will offer increasing temptation to the small producers to expand. But these limitations also exist when a single producer occupies the whole market: even then, his hold will depend upon his moderation in exerting his immediate power.

The case at bar is however different, because, for aught that appears, there may well have been a practically unlimited supply of imports as the price of ingot rose. Assuming that there was no agreement between "Alcoa" and foreign producers not to import, they sold what could bear the

---

3. Ed. Ingot fabricated by "Alcoa" was included because it had a direct effect upon the ingot market by virtue of the fact that the intermediate or end products fabricated by "Alcoa" "*pro tanto* reduce the demand for ingot itself." Secondary ingot was excluded because "Alcoa" had originally produced all of the secondary ingot as virgin ingot and it could, therefore, regulate the future return of secondary ingot to the market by controlling the production of virgin ingot. Judge Knox, when he fashioned the decree in 1950, found that, since scrap aluminum no longer necessarily originated with "Alcoa," secondary aluminum would not be excluded from the market. United States v. Aluminum Co. of America, 91 F.Supp. 333, 358 (S.D.N.Y.1950).

4. Ed. In the course of this discussion, Judge Hand asserts: "That percentage [over 90%] is enough to constitute a monopoly; it is doubtful whether 60% or 64% would be enough; and certainly 33% per cent is not." These numbers by Judge Hand were not drawn out of thin air. If secondary ingot had been included rather than excluded from the market, Alcoa's market share would have fallen to around 64%. If the market included self-supply and excluded secondary, which the Court found was the case, Alcoa's market share reached approximately 90%. In addition, there had been previous court decisions where market shares in the 30% range were found not to constitute monopoly power and market shares in 90% and about that were found to constitute monopoly power.

handicap of the tariff and the cost of transportation. For the period of eighteen years—1920–1937—they sold at times a little above "Alcoa's" prices, at times a little under; but there was substantially no gross difference between what they received and what they would have received, had they sold uniformly at "Alcoa's" prices. While the record is silent, we may therefore assume—the plaintiff having the burden—that, had "Alcoa" raised its prices, more ingot would have been imported. Thus there is a distinction between domestic and foreign competition: the first is limited in quantity, and can increase only by an increase in plant and personnel; the second is of producers who, we must assume, produce much more than they import, and who a rise in price will presumably induce immediately to divert to the American market what they have been selling elsewhere. It is entirely consistent with the evidence that it was the threat of greater foreign imports which kept "Alcoa's" prices where they were, and prevented it from exploiting its advantage as sole domestic producer; indeed, it is hard to resist the conclusion that potential imports did put a "ceiling" upon those prices. Nevertheless, within the limits afforded by the tariff and the cost of transportation, "Alcoa" was free to raise its prices as it chose, since it was free from domestic competition, save as it drew other metals into the market as substitutes. Was this a monopoly within the meaning of § 2? The judge found that, over the whole half century of its existence, "Alcoa's" profits upon capital invested, after payment of income taxes, had been only about ten per cent, and, although the plaintiff puts this figure a little higher, the difference is negligible....

But the whole issue is irrelevant anyway, for it is no excuse for "monopolizing" a market that the monopoly has not been used to extract from the consumer more than a "fair" profit. The Act has wider purposes. Indeed, even though we disregarded all but economic considerations, it would by no means follow that such concentration of producing power is to be desired, when it has not been used extortionately. Many people believe that possession of unchallenged economic power deadens initiative, discourages thrift and depresses energy; that immunity from competition is a narcotic, and rivalry is a stimulant, to industrial progress; that the spur of constant stress is necessary to counteract an inevitable disposition to let well enough alone. Such people believe that competitors, versed in the craft as no consumer can be, will be quick to detect opportunities for saving and new shifts in production, and be eager to profit by them. In any event the mere fact that a producer, having command of the domestic market, has not been able to make more than a "fair" profit, is no evidence that a "fair" profit could not have been made at lower prices. United States v. Corn Products Refining Co., [234 F.] 1014, 1015. True, it might have been thought adequate to condemn only those monopolies which could not show that they had exercised the highest possible ingenuity, had adopted every possible economy, had anticipated every conceivable improvement, stimulated every possible demand. No doubt, that would be one way of dealing with the matter, although it would imply constant scrutiny and constant supervision, such as courts are unable to provide. Be that as it may, that was not the way that Congress chose; it did not condone "good trusts" and condemn "bad" ones; it forbade all. Moreover, in so doing it was not necessarily actuated by economic motives alone. It is possible, because of its indirect social or moral effect, to prefer a system of small producers, each dependent for his success upon his own skill and character, to one in which the great mass of those engaged must accept the direction of a few. These considerations, which we have suggested only as possible purposes of the Act, we think the decisions prove to have been in fact its purposes.

It is settled, at least as to § 1, that there are some contracts restricting competition which are unlawful, no matter how beneficent they may be; no industrial exigency will justify them; they are absolutely forbidden. Chief Justice Taft said as much of contracts dividing a territory among producers, in the often quoted passage of his opinion in the Circuit Court of Appeals in United States v. Addyston Pipe and Steel Co., 6 Cir., 85 F. 271, 291. The Supreme Court unconditionally condemned all contracts fixing prices in United States v. Trenton Potteries Company, 273 U.S. 392, 397, 398, and whatever doubts may have arisen as to that decision from Appalachian Coals Inc. v. United States, 288 U.S. 344; they were laid by United States v. Socony–Vacuum Co., 310 U.S. 150, 220–224. It will now scarcely be denied that the same notion originally extended to all contracts—"reasonable," or "unreasonable"—which restrict competition. United States v. Trans–Missouri Freight Association, 166 U.S. 290, 327, 328; United States v. Joint Traffic Association, 171 U.S. 505, 575–577. The decisions in Standard Oil Co. v. United States, 221 U.S. 1, and American Tobacco Company v. United States, 221 U.S. 106, certainly did change this, and since then it has been accepted law that not all contracts which in fact put an end to existing competition are unlawful. Starting, however, with the authoritative premise that all contracts fixing prices are unconditionally prohibited, the only possible difference between them and a monopoly is that while a monopoly necessarily involves an equal, or even greater, power to fix prices, its mere existence might be thought not to constitute an exercise of that power. That distinction is nevertheless purely formal; it would be valid only so long as the monopoly remained wholly inert; it would disappear as soon as the monopoly began to operate; for, when it did—that is, as soon as it began to sell at all—it must sell at some price and the only price at which it could sell is a price which it itself fixed. (Thereafter the power and its exercise must needs coalesce.) Indeed it would be absurd to condemn such contracts unconditionally, and not to extend the condemnation to monopolies; for the contracts are only steps toward that entire control which monopoly confers: they are really partial monopolies.

But we are not left to deductive reasoning. Although in many settings it may be proper to weigh the extent and effect of restrictions in a contract against its industrial or commercial advantages, this is never to be done when the contract is made with intent to set up a monopoly. As much was plainly implied in Swift & Co. v. United States, 196 U.S. 375, 396, where the court spoke of monopoly as being the "result" which the law seeks to prevent; and, although the language on pages 60 and 61 of Standard Oil Co. v. United States, 221 U.S. 1, is not altogether clear, it seems to presuppose as a premise that a monopoly is always an "unreasonable restraint of trade." Again, the opinion in Sugar Institute v. United States, 297 U.S. 553, 598—borrowing from Appalachian Coals Inc. v. United States, *supra*, 288 U.S. 344, 374—said: "Accordingly, we have held that a cooperative enterprise otherwise free from objection which carries with it no monopolistic menace" need not always be condemned....

We have been speaking only of the economic reasons which forbid monopoly; but, as we have already implied, there are others, based upon the belief that great industrial consolidations are inherently undesirable, regardless of their economic results. In the debates in Congress Senator Sherman himself ... showed that among the purposes of Congress in 1890 was a desire to put an end to great aggregations of capital because of the helplessness of the individual before them. Another aspect of the same notion may be found in the language of Mr. Justice Peckham in United States v. Trans–Missouri Freight Association, *supra*, 323 (166 U.S. 290). That Congress is still of the same mind appears in the Surplus Property Act of 1944, and the Small Business Mobilization Act. Not only does § 2(d) of the first declare it to be one aim of that statute "to preserve the competitive position of small business concerns," but § 18 is given over to directions designed to "preserve and strengthen" their position.... Throughout the history of these statutes it has been constantly assumed that one of their purposes was to perpetuate and preserve, for its own sake and in spite of possible cost, an organization of industry in small units which can effectively compete with each other. We hold that "Alcoa's" monopoly of ingot was of the kind covered by § 2.

It does not follow because "Alcoa" had such a monopoly, that it "monopolized" the ingot market; it may not have achieved monopoly; monopoly may have been thrust upon it. If it had been a combination of existing smelters that united the whole industry and controlled the production of all aluminum ingot, it would certainly have "monopolized" the market. In several decisions the Supreme Court has decreed the dissolution of such combinations, although they had engaged in no unlawful trade practices.... We may start therefore with the premise that to have combined ninety per cent of the producers of ingot would have been to "monopolize" the ingot market; and, so far as concerns the public interest, it can make no difference whether an existing competition is put an end to, or whether prospective competition is prevented. The Clayton Act itself speaks in that alternative: "to injure, destroy or prevent competition." Nevertheless, it is unquestionably true that from the very outset the courts have at least kept in reserve the possibility that the origin of a monopoly may be critical in determining its legality; and for this they had warrant in some of the congressional debates which accompanied the passage of the Act. [Citing cases.] This notion has usually been expressed by saying that size does not determine guilt; that there must be some "exclusion" of competitors; that the growth must be something else than "natural" or "normal;" that there must be a "wrongful intent," or some other specific intent; or that some "unduly" coercive means must be used. At times there has been emphasis upon the use of the active verb, "monopolize," as the

[margin note: monopolies can arise by accident]

judge noted in the case at bar. [Citing cases.] What engendered these compunctions is reasonably plain; persons may unwittingly find themselves in possession of a monopoly, automatically so to say: that is, without having intended either to put an end to existing competition, or to prevent competition from arising when none had existed; they may become monopolists by force of accident. Since the Act makes "monopolizing" a crime, as well as a civil wrong, it would be not only unfair, but presumably contrary to the intent of Congress, to include such instances. A market may, for example, be so limited that it is impossible to produce at all and meet the cost of production except by a plant large enough to supply the whole demand. Or there may be changes in taste or in cost which drive out all but one purveyor. A single producer may be the survivor out of a group of active competitors, merely by virtue of his superior skill, foresight and industry. In such cases a strong argument can be made that, although the result may expose the public to the evils of monopoly, the Act does not mean to condemn the resultant of those very forces which it is its prime object to foster: *finis opus coronat*. The successful competitor, having been urged to compete, must not be turned upon when he wins. The most extreme expression of this view is in United States v. United States Steel Corporation, 251 U.S. 417, from which we quote in the margin[5] and which Sanford, J. in part repeated in United States v. International Harvester Co., 274 U.S. 693, 708. It so chances that in both instances the corporation had less than two-thirds of the production in its hands, and the language quoted was not necessary to the decision; so that even if it had not later been modified, it has not the authority of an actual decision. But, whatever authority it does have was modified by the gloss of Cardozo, J. in Swift & Company v. United States, 286 U.S. 106, when he said, at 116: "Mere size ... is not an offense against the Sherman Act unless magnified to the point at which it amounts to a monopoly ... but size carries with it an opportunity for abuse that is not to be ignored when the opportunity is proved to have been utilized in the past." "Alcoa's" size was "magnified" to make it a "monopoly;" indeed, it has never been anything else; and its size, not only offered it an "opportunity for abuse," but it "utilized" its size for "abuse," as can easily be shown.

[margin note: this was not a passive or accidental monopoly]

It would completely misconstrue "Alcoa's" position in 1940 to hold that it was the passive beneficiary of a monopoly, following upon an involuntary elimination of competitors by automatically operative economic forces. Already in 1909, when its last lawful monopoly ended, it sought to

---

5. Justice McKenna for the majority said, 251 U.S. 417, at page 451: "The Corporation is undoubtedly of impressive size and it takes an effort of resolution not to be affected by it or to exaggerate its influence. But we must adhere to the law and the law does not make mere size an offence or the existence of unexerted power an offence. It, we repeat, requires overt acts and trusts to its prohibition of them and its power to repress or punish them. It does not compel competition nor require all that is possible." The minority through Day, J. agreed, 215 U.S. 417, at page 460: "the act offers no objection to the mere size of a corporation nor to the continued exertion of its lawful power, when that size and power have been obtained by lawful means and developed by natural growth, although its resources, capital and strength may give to such corporation a dominating place in the business and industry with which it is concerned. It is entitled to maintain its size and the power that legitimately goes with it, provided no law has been transgressed in obtaining it."

strengthen its position by unlawful practices, and these concededly continued until 1912. In that year it had two plants in New York, at which it produced less than 42 million pounds of ingot; in 1934 it had five plants (the original two, enlarged; one in Tennessee; one in North Carolina; one in Washington), and its production had risen to about 327 million pounds, an increase of almost eight-fold. Meanwhile not a pound of ingot had been produced by anyone else in the United States. This increase and this continued and undisturbed control did not fall undesigned into "Alcoa's" lap; obviously it could not have done so. It could only have resulted, as it did result, from a persistent determination to maintain the control, with which it found itself vested in 1912. There were at least one or two abortive attempts to enter the industry, but "Alcoa" effectively anticipated and forestalled all competition, and succeeded in holding the field alone. True, it stimulated demand and opened new uses for the metal, but not without making sure that it could supply what it had evoked. There is no dispute as to this; "Alcoa" avows it as evidence of the skill, energy and initiative with which it has always conducted its business; as a reason why, having won its way by fair means, it should be commended, and not dismembered. We need charge it with no moral derelictions after 1912; we may assume that all it claims for itself is true. The only question is whether it falls within the exception established in favor of those who do not seek, but cannot avoid, the control of a market. It seems to us that that question scarcely survives its statement. It was not inevitable that it should always anticipate increases in the demand for ingot and be prepared to supply them. Nothing compelled it to keep doubling and redoubling its capacity before others entered the field. It insists that it never excluded competitors; but we can think of no more effective exclusion than progressively to embrace each new opportunity as it opened, and to face every newcomer with new capacity already geared into a great organization, having the advantage of experience, trade connections and the elite of personnel. Only in case we interpret "exclusion" as limited to maneuvers not honestly industrial, but actuated solely by a desire to prevent competition, can such a course indefatigably pursued, be deemed not "exclusionary." So to limit it would in our judgment emasculate the Act; would permit just such consolidations as it was designed to prevent.

"Alcoa" answers that it positively assisted competitors, instead of discouraging them. That may be true as to fabricators of ingot; but what of that? They were its market for ingot, and it is charged only with a monopoly of ingot. We can find no instance of its helping prospective ingot manufacturers....

We disregard any question of "intent." Relatively early in the history of the Act–1905—Holmes, J. in Swift & Company v. United States, *supra* (196 U.S. 375, 396), explained this aspect of the Act in a passage often quoted. Although the primary evil was monopoly, the Act also covered preliminary steps, which, if contained, would lead to it. These may do no harm of themselves; but, if they are initial moves in a plan or scheme which, carried out, will result in monopoly, they are dangerous and the law will nip them in the bud. For this reason conduct falling short of monopoly, is not illegal unless it is part of a plan to monopolize, or to gain such other control of a market as is equally forbidden. To make it so, the plaintiff must prove what in the criminal law is known as a "specific intent;" an intent which goes beyond the mere intent to do the act. By far the greatest part of the fabulous record piled up in the case at bar, was concerned with proving such an intent. The plaintiff was seeking to show that many transactions, neutral on their face, were not in fact necessary to the development of "Alcoa's" business, and had no motive except to exclude others and perpetuate its hold upon the ingot market. Upon that effort success depended in case the plaintiff failed to satisfy the court that it was unnecessary under § 2 to convict "Alcoa" of practices unlawful of themselves. The plaintiff has so satisfied us, and the issue of intent ceases to have any importance; no intent is relevant except that which is relevant to any liability, criminal or civil: *i.e.*, an intent to bring about the forbidden act. Note 59 on page 226 of United States v. Socony–Vacuum Oil Co., *supra* (310 U.S. 150, on page 226), on which "Alcoa" appears so much to rely, is in no sense to the contrary. Douglas, J. was answering the defendants' argument that, assuming that a combination had attempted to fix prices, it had never had the power to do so, for there was too much competing oil. His answer was that the plan was unlawful, even if the parties did not have the power to fix prices, provided that they intended to do so; and it was to drive home this that he contrasted the case then before the court with monopoly, where power was a necessary element. In so doing he said: "An intent and a power ... are then necessary," which he at once followed by quoting the passage we have just mentioned from Swift & Co. v. United States, *supra* (196 U.S. 375). In order to fall within § 2, the monopolist must have both the power to monopolize, and the intent to monopolize. To read the passage as demanding any "specific" intent, makes nonsense of it, for no monopolist monopolizes unconscious of what he is doing. So here, "Alcoa" meant to keep, and did keep, that complete and exclusive hold upon the ingot market with which it started. That was to "monopolize" that market, however innocently it otherwise proceeded. So far as the judgment held that it was not within § 2, it must be reversed.

Judgment reversed, and cause remanded for further proceedings not inconsistent with the foregoing.[6]

NOTES AND QUESTIONS

1. Despite Judge Hand's pronouncement in *Alcoa* on the market share required to sustain the charge of monopolization (*see* note 4, *supra*), no fixed

---

6. On remand, Judge Knox denied the government's prayer for divestiture and ordered that stockholders with shares in both Alcoa and Aluminum Limited, the Canadian producer, sell their interest in one of the companies and that certain patent practices be terminated. United States v. Aluminum Co. of America, 91 F.Supp. 333 (S.D.N.Y.1950). And see Judge Cashin's opinion, finding that during the five-year period set by Judge Knox to determine if further relief was warranted, such competitive conditions had been established that a further extension of time to request relief should be denied. United States v. Aluminum Co. of America, 153 F.Supp. 132 (S.D.N.Y.1957).

percentages have been established under Section 2. The Supreme Court has expressly stated that the "relative effect of percentage command of the market varies with the setting in which that factor is placed." United States v. Columbia Steel Co., 334 U.S. 495, 528 (1948). In Domed Stadium Hotel, Inc. v. Holiday Inns, Inc., 732 F.2d 480, 489–90 (5th Cir. 1984), the Fifth Circuit handled the market share issue as follows:

> The precise market share a defendant must control, absent supporting evidence of monopoly power before he is guilty of monopolization, remains undefined.... Supreme Court cases, as well as cases from this court, suggest that absent special circumstances, a defendant must have a market share of at least fifty percent before he can be guilty of monopolization. Further, undisputed evidence of low market share may make monopolization an impossibility as a matter of law. *Dimmitt,* 679 F.2d 516, 529. Recent cases by this court hold that market shares of between seventeen and twenty-five percent are legally insufficient to uphold a finding of monopolization, at least absent other compelling evidence that the defendant had monopoly power.

See Syufy Enterprises v. American Multicinema, Inc., 793 F.2d 990 (9th Cir. 1986), cert. denied, 479 U.S. 1031 (1987) (market share of 60–69% is sufficient to show monopoly power when coupled with other factors, including the fragmentation of competition and the presence of entry barriers).

What factors other than market share *should* be considered in determining the presence of market power? How much weight should a court place on the presence or absence of entry barriers, abnormal profits, historical trend, fragmented competition, corporate conduct, and other such factors? Could Alcoa have held down its market share by charging exorbitant prices? Would a 49% market share in such circumstances indicate a lack of monopoly power? See Broadway Delivery Corp. v. United Parcel Service of America, Inc., 651 F.2d 122 (2d Cir.), cert. denied, 454 U.S. 968 (1981) (trial court instruction precluding a finding of monopoly power where defendant's market share was less than 50% was in error but was harmless in the circumstances). Conversely, should a corporation with a very large market share *always* be considered a company with monopoly power? In Ball Memorial Hospital, Inc. v. Mutual Hospital Insurance, Inc., 784 F.2d 1325, 1335 (7th Cir. 1986), the Court of Appeals opined as follows:

> Market power comes from the ability to cut back the market's total output and so raise price; consumers bid more in competing against one another to obtain the smaller quantity available. When a firm (or group of firms) controls a significant percentage of the productive assets in the market, the remaining firms may not have the capacity to increase their sales quickly to make up for any reduction by the dominant firm or group of firms. In other cases, however, a firm's share of current sales does not reflect an ability to reduce the total output in the market, and therefore it does not convey power over price. Other firms may be able, for example, to divert production into the market from outside. They may be able to convert productive capacity to the product in question or import the product from out of the area. If firms are able to enter, expand, or import sufficiently quickly, that may counteract a reduction in output by existing firms. And if current sales are not based on the ownership of productive assets—so that entrants do not need to build new plants or otherwise take a long time to supply consumers' wants—the existing firms may have no power at all to cut back the market's output. To put these points a little

differently, the lower the barriers to entry, and the shorter the lags of new entry, the less power existing firms have. When the supply is highly elastic, existing market share does not signify power.

These issues will again be considered in United States v. Grinnell Corp., 384 U.S. 563 (1966), p. 152 *infra*, and Chapter 8, Section 1.

2. If Judge Hand in *Alcoa* had excluded the ingot processed by Alcoa's subsidiaries, (*i.e.*, the self-supply ingot), its share of the market would have been reduced to about 60%. Why was Alcoa's captive production included in the market? Do you agree with the Court's reasoning?

3. Judge Hand apparently assumed that secondary aluminum ingot competed effectively with primary aluminum ingot, but excluded secondary ingot from the relevant market on grounds that Alcoa, in the past, had controlled the commodity. In Judge Hand's view, the monopolist would have been guided "not alone by [the] effect [of its production] at that time upon the market, but by his knowledge that some part of it was likely to be reclaimed and seek the future market. That consideration will to some extent affect its production ... and, if it was as far-sighted as it proclaimed itself, that consideration must have had its share in determining how much to produce." See note 3, p. 116 *supra*.

How could Alcoa's prior control over production give it the capacity to influence competition during any relevant subsequent period? Suppose Alcoa knew in 1927 that 25% of a given year's production would re-enter the market in the form of secondary aluminum about 10 years later. Would Alcoa really be likely to leave demand unsatisfied in 1927, beyond levels that would prevail if aluminum were a fully consumed product, in order to protect its predicted market position in 1937? Would even a far-sighted monopolist have sufficiently reliable information about market conditions a decade later to make that judgment?

4. What exactly did Alcoa do wrong? What must a firm with monopoly power do—or not do—in order to avoid violating Section 2? Were Alcoa's profits too high? Does Judge Hand's opinion provide the answer? Should high profits matter? What if potentially high profits were lost because of what economists call X-inefficiencies— *i.e.*, monopoly power acted as a "narcotic," depressed energy, led to luxurious management perks, and created slack throughout the operation?

Under the *Alcoa* conduct standard, must a firm with monopoly power avoid hiring too many scientists for its research and development department, so as not to exclude competitors through consistently successful product innovation? Must a firm with monopoly power disclose trade secrets or avoid the use of restrictive covenants?

Suppose a monopolist engages in deceptive advertising or some other kind of business tort; would that constitute illegal behavior under Section 2 regardless of whether the conduct bears a direct or significant relationship to the acquisition or maintenance of monopoly power? In other words, does every sort of illegality taint monopoly power?

What if a firm with monopoly power charged relatively low prices and made only a reasonable profit, but, in doing so, drove its few weak competitors from the market? Must a firm with monopoly power price its products in such a way as not to drive out its few remaining competitors or not to discourage new entry?

These questions are meant to raise broad policy issues about the permissible behavior of a firm with monopoly power. The issues are considered again, and in more depth, in Chapter 8, Sections 1–5. For present purposes, however, consider the following decisions, which should help you analyze the *Alcoa* decision and its sweeping language.

(a) Berkey Photo, Inc. v. Eastman Kodak Co., 603 F.2d 263 (2d Cir. 1979), cert. denied, 444 U.S. 1093 (1980). In 1972, Kodak introduced its immensely successful pocket Instamatic 110, a much smaller version of its successful Instamatic line, along with a specially designed film called Kodacolor II. Even before these new developments, Kodak had a monopoly in the sale of "amateur conventional still cameras" and in camera film. The pocket Instamatic was dramatically successful, improving and solidifying its monopoly position, and Berkey's market position, along with all other Kodak competitors, was adversely affected.

Berkey had begun to sell amateur still cameras in 1968 and from 1970 to 1977 accounted for 8.2% of U.S. camera sales. In 1978, Berkey sold its camera division and abandoned the market. Several years earlier Berkey had sued Kodak for treble damages, charging among other things that Kodak had acquired and maintained its monopoly position in camera and films in violation of Section 2 of the Sherman Act.

Among many charges of monopolization and attempt to monopolize leveled by Berkey, one of special interest contended that it was a violation of Section 2 for Kodak to fail to predisclose "sufficient advance information to enable [competitors] to enter the market with copies of the new product on the day of Kodak's introduction." Berkey did not contend that every monopolist had to predisclose innovations but rather that Kodak's related monopolies in camera and film created a special obligation. In fact, Kodak had notified competitors in January 1972 that it would introduce a new camera and offered to sell further information to all camera makers describing the new products, indicating anticipated dates of announcement and commercial introduction, and providing specifications and technical notes about the product. Berkey paid the fee but as a result obtained only about two months' advance knowledge of information needed to compete on the new product.

The Court of Appeals held as a matter of law that Kodak, for policy and practical reasons, did not have a duty to predisclose information about the pocket Instamatic or its new film to competing camera manufacturers. It concluded that even a monopolist has a right to the lead time that follows from success in innovation, and that Kodak's related monopoly position in film, and the simultaneous introduction of a new film type, did not create any additional obligations. If the result were otherwise, the Court observed, aggressive competition in innovation would be discouraged.

The Second Circuit was also concerned about the difficulty of fashioning a workable rule describing where and under what circumstances a monopolist had a duty to disclose:

> But it is difficult to comprehend how a major corporation ... could possess the omniscience to anticipate all the instances in which a jury might one day in the future retrospectively conclude that predisclosure was warranted. And it is equally difficult to discern workable guidelines that a court might set forth to aid the firm's decision. For example, how detailed must the information conveyed be? And how far must research have progressed before it is "ripe" for disclosure? These inherent uncertainties would have an inevitable chilling effect on innovation. They go far, we believe, towards explaining why no court has ever imposed the duty Berkey seeks to create here.

Can you imagine any circumstances in which a monopolist might have some duty to disclose? How does *Berkey's* holding affect Judge Hand's comment in *Alcoa*

(p. 121 *supra*) that "We can find no instance of [Alcoa] helping prospective ingot manufacturers...." Did Judge Hand mean to rely on the failure to assist as a basis for his finding of monopolization?

(b) In Re E.I. du Pont de Nemours & Co., 3 Trade Reg.Rep. (CCH) ¶ 21,770 (FTC Oct. 20, 1980). In the early 1970s, duPont found itself with about a 25% cost advantage in the production of titanium dioxide pigments (TiO2), a chemical used in the manufacture of paint and paper. DuPont had concentrated on a "chloride process" and had constructed two plants in the 1950s based on that technology; all its competitors had built plants based on a competing "sulfate process." In the 1950s and 60s, the sulfate process was equally or more efficient, but in about 1970, a worldwide shortage drove up the price of raw materials used in the sulfate process while environmental regulations imposed costly pollution abatement requirements on sulfate but not chloride manufacturing facilities.

In 1972, duPont accounted for about 30% of TiO2 sales. Recognizing its substantial cost advantage, duPont embarked on a growth strategy that incorporated three elements. First, it expanded its two existing plants and planned to construct a new large-scale facility. Its acknowledged goal was to expand capacity to serve all the expected increase in marketwide demand for TiO2 from the late 1970s into the mid–1980s, but not, according to its expectations, to take much market share away from existing competitors. Second, it priced its TiO2 products high enough to finance its own expansion of capacity, yet low enough to discourage existing rivals from expanding and to discourage new domestic or foreign entry. DuPont earned at all times a reasonable profit on its TiO2 sales. Third, it refused to license its cost-saving chloride technology (patents and know-how) to rivals.

DuPont's market share increased from 30% in 1972 to 42% in 1977, and it anticipated in 1977 that it would achieve 55% by 1985. (At an earlier date in the 1970s, duPont thought its expansion program might achieve for it a 65% market share by 1985.) While not part of its expressed aim, duPont's expansion was to some extent at the expense of existing rivals. Its expansion and construction program produced plants of optimally efficient scale, and there was no evidence of an intention to build excess capacity for strategic competitive reasons. DuPont anticipated that the prices it would charge in the period 1972 to 1980 would be somewhat lower than would be the case if it were not pursuing an expansion strategy, but that profits after 1984 and through 1992 would be higher under the expansion plan.

The FTC's staff counsel argued that duPont's construction program, though not illegal in itself, became illegal when viewed in conjunction with the pricing and non-licensing policies. They argued that duPont's willingness to forego available short-term profits and invest in expansion of capacity would only make sense if noncompetitive profits would become available at a later date, and the combination of duPont's construction/pricing/non-licensing policies therefore constituted an "attempt to monopolize" under Section 2 of the Sherman Act and an unfair practice under Section 5 of the Federal Trade Commission Act.

The full Commission unanimously rejected these staff arguments, emphasizing that duPont's expansion program grew out of legally obtained efficiencies and that its pricing program was rational, earning substantial profits for the company through the entire period of expansion, without regard to any ability to extract monopoly profits in the future. Moreover, the Commission noted there simply is no duty under the antitrust laws for a firm that develops superior products or processes to license or disclose its technology to rivals.

The Commission observed that a different conclusion would have required that the firm with the most efficient process not expand its capacity, or not lower its prices, in order to provide market opportunities or funds to less efficient rivals. The opinion concluded:

> Antitrust policy wisely disfavors monopoly, but it also seeks to promote vigorous competitive behavior. Indeed, the essence of the competitive process is to induce firms to become more efficient and to pass the benefits of the efficiency along to consumers. That process would be ill-served by using antitrust to block hard, aggressive competition that is solidly based on efficiencies and growth opportunities, even if monopoly is a possible result. Such a view, we believe, is entirely consistent with the "superior skill, foresight and industry" exception in *Alcoa* and subsequent cases, for those decisions clearly indicate that monopolies may be lawfully created by superior competitive ability.

(c) Olympia Equipment Leasing Co. v. Western Union Telegraph, 797 F.2d 370, 375–76 (7th Cir. 1986), cert. denied, 480 U.S. 934 (1987). Judge Posner, writing for a panel of the Seventh Circuit, had the following to say about monopoly conduct:

> Opinion about the offense of monopolization has undergone an evolution. Forty years ago it was thought that even a firm with a lawful monopoly (there is no suggestion that Western Union's monopoly of telex service is unlawful) could not be allowed to defend its monopoly against would-be competitors by tactics otherwise legitimate; it had to exercise special restraint—perhaps, indeed, had to hold its prices high, to encourage new entry. So Alcoa was condemned as a monopolist because it had assiduously created enough productive capacity to supply all new increments of demand for aluminum.... Later, as the emphasis of antitrust policy shifted from the protection of competition as a process of rivalry to the protection of competition as a means of promoting economic efficiency ... it became recognized that the lawful monopolist should be free to compete like everyone else; otherwise the antitrust laws would be holding an umbrella over inefficient competitors. "A monopolist, no less than any other competitor, is permitted and indeed encouraged to compete aggressively on the merits...." Foremost Pro Color, Inc. v. Eastman Kodak Co., 703 F.2d 534, 544 (9th Cir.1983). With Judge Hand's opinion in *Alcoa* compare the approach of his successors in Berkey Photo, Inc. v. Eastman Kodak Co., 603 F.2d 263, 274, 276, 287 (2d Cir.1979).
>
> Today it is clear that a firm with lawful monopoly power has no general duty to help its competitors, whether by holding a price umbrella over their heads or by otherwise pulling its competitive punches. *See, e.g.,* MCI Communications Corp. v. AT & T, 708 F.2d 1081, 1149 (7th Cir.1983); Catlin v. Washington Energy Co., 791 F.2d 1343 (9th Cir.1986). "There is a difference between positive and negative duties, and the antitrust laws, like other legal doctrines sounding in tort, have generally been understood to impose only the latter." USM Corp. v. SPS Technologies, Inc., 694 F.2d 505, 512–13 (7th Cir.1982). So if a firm went to a monopolist and said, "Please—for the sake of competition—give me a loan so I can compete with you and make this a competitive market," and it was turned down, it could not invoke the Sherman Act. A monopolist has no duty to reduce its prices in order to help consumers—and no duty to extend a helping hand to new entrants; thus IBM "was under no duty to help CalComp or other peripheral equipment manufacturers survive or expand. IBM need not have

provided its rivals with disk products to examine and copy. . . ." *California Computer Products, Inc. v. IBM,* 613 F.2d 727, 744 (9th Cir.1979) (citation omitted). *Berkey, Foremost* and other cases make clear that a monopolist has no duty to disclose its plans to rivals in order to help the rivals compete with it.

If a monopolist does extend a helping hand, though not required to do so, and later withdraws it as happened in this case, does he incur antitrust liability? We think not.

(d) In re Intel Corporation, 1999 WL 164046 (1999). In 1998, the Federal Trade Commission filed a complaint charging that Intel had monopoly power in the microprocessor product market (it was alleged to have approximately an 80% market share in dollar sales), and had violated Section 2 by denying advance technical information about new microprocessor products, product samples and related technical assistance to customers so that they could perform system testing and debugging on new generations of microprocessors. Microprocessors are sometimes described as the "brains" of computers because they perform major data processing functions.

Intel followed a policy of providing technical data and samples to a group of about a dozen preferred customers. Three of those customers—Digital Equipment, Intergraph and Compaq—became involved in intellectual property (IP) disputes with Intel, essentially complaining that Intel's new microprocessors infringed upon each company's patents. After negotiations proved fruitless, two of the companies sued Intel, and one threatened to sue, for patent infringement. Intel retaliated by cutting each of the three off from product information and samples, allegedly essential to compete effectively in design and sale of new computer systems. The FTC charged that Intel's actions had several anticompetitive effects, the most significant being that coercion by a monopolist that forces customers to license away IP rights on unfavorable terms tends to diminish the customers' incentives to develop new technologies, and thus is likely to harm competition by reducing innovation. Intel defended on grounds that it had the right not to deal with companies that sued it. The Commission's response was that a refusal to continue to do business by a monopolist was unreasonably exclusionary behavior under Section 2 and that IP controversies should be addressed in court rather than by self-help.

The case was settled in 1999 with an agreed-upon consent order acknowledging that Intel was free to decide in the first instance whether to provide or not provide information to customers, and could discontinue business relations on many grounds such as that the customer did not protect the confidentiality of Intel's IP. But it could not discriminate among customers once business arrangements were initiated on grounds that it found itself in an IP dispute. One interesting exception to Intel's obligation to continue providing information and product related to the remedy that the customer sought in court. Customers were free to seek a wide range of legal and equitable remedies, including damages (trebled or otherwise increased in appropriate cases), reasonable royalties and attorneys' fees and costs. On the other hand, if the customer sought a preliminary or permanent injunction to put Intel out of the business of selling microprocessors, then Intel was free to deny the customer information and products. The rationale appears to be that neither party should deny ultimate consumers the benefits of innovation while the parties litigate over their respective views in court.

Digital and Compaq had settled their quarrels with Intel before completion of the FTC action. Intergraph pursued its remedies and, in November 1999, the Court of Appeals for the Federal Circuit found in favor of Intel. The Circuit Court concluded:

> "The remedy of compulsory disclosure of proprietary information and provision of pre-production chips and other commercial and intellectual property is a dramatic remedy for antitrust illegality, and requires violation of antitrust law or the likelihood that such violation would be established. In the proceedings whose record is before us, Intergraph has not shown a substantial likelihood of success in establishing that Intel violated the antitrust laws...." *See*, Intergraph Corp. v. Intel Corp., 195 F.3d 1346 (Fed.Cir.1999).

Should a monopolist that finds itself in legal controversies with other companies that depend on its essential product or services be entitled to use self-help? If self-help is permitted, will it turn out that the monopolist will prevail every time?

Should a monopolist be free to compete like everyone else? What if it controls a facility essential to competitors and refuses them access? What if a monopolist who is a supplier retaliates against a customer—*e.g.*, by refusing to deal—who has the temerity to try to compete with it? Think about other instances where a firm with monopoly power should be treated differently than a company with 4% of a competitive market. In general, *see* Aspen Skiing Co. v. Aspen Highlands Skiing Corp., 472 U.S. 585 (1985), p. 726 *infra*, and other materials in Chapter 8, Section 1A. For a discussion of "attempt to monopolize," *see* Chapter 8, Section 1B.

United States v. E.I. du Pont de Nemours & Co.

Supreme Court of the United States, 1956.
351 U.S. 377, 76 S.Ct. 994, 100 L.Ed. 1264.

■ REED, J. The United States brought this civil action under § 4 of the Sherman Act against E.I. du Pont de Nemours and Company. The complaint ... charged du Pont with monopolizing, attempting to monopolize and conspiracy to monopolize interstate commerce in cellophane and cellulosic caps and bands in violation of § 2 of the Sherman Act. Relief by injunction was sought against defendant and its officers, forbidding monopolizing or attempting to monopolize interstate trade in cellophane. The prayer also sought action to dissipate the effect of the monopolization by divestiture or other steps.... After a lengthy trial, judgment was entered for du Pont on all issues.

The Government's direct appeal here does not contest the findings that relate to caps and bands, nor does it raise any issue concerning the alleged attempt to monopolize or conspiracy to monopolize interstate commerce in cellophane. The appeal, as specifically stated by the Government, "attacks only the ruling that du Pont has not monopolized trade in cellophane." At issue for determination is only this alleged violation by du Pont of § 2 of the Sherman Act.

During the period that is relevant to this action, du Pont produced almost 75% of the cellophane sold in the United States, and cellophane constituted less than 20% of all "flexible packaging material" sales....

The Government contends that, by so dominating cellophane production, du Pont monopolized a "part of the trade or commerce" in violation of *du Pont argues*

§ 2. Respondent agrees that cellophane is a product which constitutes "a 'part' of commerce within the meaning of Section 2." But it contends that the prohibition of § 2 against monopolization is not violated because it does not have the power to control the price of cellophane or to exclude competitors from the market in which cellophane is sold. The court below found that the "relevant market for determining the extent of du Pont's market control is the market for flexible packaging materials," and that competition from those other materials prevented du Pont from possessing monopoly powers in its sales of cellophane.

gov't: cellophane not interchangable w/ other materials shouldn't be considered for monopoly purposes

The Government asserts that cellophane and other wrapping materials are neither substantially fungible nor like priced. For these reasons, it argues that the market for other wrappings is distinct from the market for cellophane and that the competition afforded cellophane by other wrappings is not strong enough to be considered in determining whether du Pont has monopoly powers. Market delimitation is necessary under du Pont's theory to determine whether an alleged monopolist violates § 2. The ultimate consideration in such a determination is whether the defendants control the price and competition in the market for such part of trade or commerce as they are charged with monopolizing. Every manufacturer is the sole producer of the particular commodity it makes but its control in the above sense of the relevant market depends upon the availability of alternative commodities for buyers: *i.e.*, whether there is a cross-elasticity of demand between cellophane and the other wrappings. This interchangeability is largely gauged by the purchase of competing products for similar uses considering the price, characteristics and adaptability of the competing commodities. The court below found that the flexible wrappings afforded such alternatives. This Court must determine whether the trial court erred in its estimate of the competition afforded cellophane by other materials.

Dist ct found there were rees alternative prods

The burden of proof, of course, was upon the Government to establish monopoly. See United States v. Aluminum Co. of America, 2 Cir., 148 F.2d 416, 423, 427. This the trial court held the Government failed to do, upon findings of fact and law stated at length by that court. For the United States to succeed in this Court now, it must show that erroneous legal tests were applied to essential findings of fact or that the findings themselves were "clearly erroneous." . . .

clearly erroneous std

Factual Background.— For consideration of the issue as to monopolization, a general summary of the development of cellophane is useful.

In the early 1900s Jacques Brandenberger, a Swiss chemist, attempted to make tablecloths impervious to dirt by spraying them with liquid viscose (a cellulose solution available in quantity from wood pulp) and by coagulating this coating. His idea failed, but he noted that the coating peeled off in a transparent film. This first "cellophane" was thick, hard, and not perfectly transparent, but Brandenberger apparently foresaw commercial possibilities in his discovery. By 1908 he developed the first machine for the manufacture of transparent sheets of regenerated cellulose. The 1908 product was not satisfactory, but by 1912 Brandenberger was making a saleable thin flexible film used in gas masks. He obtained patents to cover the machinery and the essential ideas of his process.

In 1917 Brandenberger assigned his patents to La Cellophane Societe Anonyme and joined that organization. Thereafter developments in the production of cellophane somewhat paralleled those taking place in artificial textiles. Chemical science furnished the knowledge for perfecting the new products. The success of the artificial products has been enormous. Du Pont was an American leader in the field of synthetics and learned of cellophane's successes through an associate, Comptoir des Textiles Artificiel.

In 1923 du Pont organized with La Cellophane an American company for the manufacture of plain cellophane. The undisputed findings are that:

> "On December 26, 1923, an agreement was executed between duPont Cellophane Company and La Cellophane by which La Cellophane licensed duPont Cellophane Company exclusively under its United States cellophane patents, and granted duPont Cellophane Company the exclusive right to make and sell in North and Central America under La Cellophane's secret processes for cellophane manufacture. DuPont Cellophane Company granted to La Cellophane exclusive rights for the rest of the world under any cellophane patents or processes duPont Cellophane Company might develop."

Subsequently du Pont and La Cellophane licensed several foreign companies, allowing them to manufacture and vend cellophane in limited areas. Technical exchange agreements with these companies were entered into at the same time. However, in 1940, du Pont notified these foreign companies that sales might be made in any country, and by 1948 all the technical exchange agreements were canceled.

Sylvania, an American affiliate of a Belgian producer of cellophane not covered by the license agreements above referred to, began the manufacture of cellophane in the United States in 1930. Litigation between the French and Belgian companies resulted in a settlement whereby La Cellophane came to have a stock interest in Sylvania, contrary to the La Cellophane-du Pont agreement. This resulted in adjustments as compensation for the intrusion into United States of La Cellophane that extended du Pont's limited territory. The details do not here seem important. Since 1934 Sylvania has produced about 25% of United States cellophane.

An important factor in the growth of cellophane production and sales was the perfection of moistureproof cellophane, a superior product of du Pont research and patented by that company through a 1927 application. Plain cellophane has little resistance to the passage of moisture vapor. Moistureproof cellophane has a composition added which keeps moisture in and out of the packed commodity. This patented type of cellophane has had a demand with much more rapid growth than the plain.

In 1931 Sylvania began the manufacture of moistureproof cellophane under its own patents. After negotiations over patent rights, du Pont in

1933 licensed Sylvania to manufacture and sell moistureproof cellophane produced under the du Pont patents at a royalty of 2% of sales. These licenses with the plain cellophane licenses from the Belgian company, made Sylvania a full cellophane competitor, limited on moistureproof sales by the terms of the licenses to 20% of the combined sales of the two companies of that type by the payment of a prohibitive royalty on the excess. There was never an excess production. The limiting clause was dropped on January 1, 1945, and Sylvania was acquired in 1946 by the American Viscose Corporation with assets of over two hundred million dollars.

Between 1928 and 1950, du Pont's sales of plain cellophane increased from $3,131,608 to $9,330,776. Moistureproof sales increased from $603,222 to $89,850,416, although prices were continuously reduced. It could not be said that this immense increase in use was solely or even largely attributable to the superior quality of cellophane or to the technique or business acumen of du Pont, though doubtless those factors were important. The growth was a part of the expansion of the commodity-packaging habits of business, a by-product of general efficient competitive merchandising to meet modern demands. The profits, which were large, apparently arose from this trend in marketing, the development of the industrial use of chemical research and production of synthetics, rather than from elimination of other producers from the relevant market....

The Sherman Act, § 2—Monopolization.— The only statutory language of § 2 pertinent on this review is: "Every person who shall monopolize ... shall be deemed guilty.... Our cases determine that a party has monopoly power if it has, over 'any part of the trade or commerce among the several states,' a power of controlling prices or unreasonably restricting competition."

Senator Hoar, in discussing § 2, pointed out that monopoly involved something more than extraordinary commercial success, "that it involved something like the use of means which made it impossible for other persons to engage in fair competition."[7] This exception to the Sherman Act prohibi-

---

7. 21 Cong.Rec. 3151:

"Mr. Kenna. Mr. President, I have no disposition to delay a vote on the bill, but I would like to ask, with his permission, the Senator from Vermont a question touching the second section:

" 'Every person who shall monopolize, or attempt to monopolize or combine or conspire with any other person or persons, to monopolize any part of the trade, etc.'

"Is it intended by the committee, as the section seems to indicate, that if an individual engaged in trade between States or between States and Territories, or between States or Territories and the District of Columbia, or between a State and a foreign country, by his own skill and energy, by the propriety of his conduct generally, shall pursue his calling in such a way as to monopolize a trade, his action shall be a crime under this proposed act? To make myself understood, if I am not clear—

"Mr. Edmunds. I think I understand the Senator.

"Mr. Kenna. Suppose a citizen of Kentucky is dealing in shorthorn cattle and by virtue of his superior skill in that particular product it turns out that he is the only one in the United States to whom an order comes from Mexico for cattle of that stock for a tions of monopoly power is perhaps the monopoly "thrust upon" one of United States v. Aluminum Co. of America, 2 Cir., 148 F.2d 416, 429, left as an undecided possibility by American Tobacco Co. v. United States, 328 U.S. 781. Compare United States v. United Shoe Machinery Corp., D.C., 110 F.Supp. 295, 342.

If cellophane is the "market" that du Pont is found to dominate, it may be assumed it does have monopoly power over that "market." Monopoly power is the power to control prices or exclude competition. It seems apparent that du Pont's power to set the price of cellophane has been limited only by the competition afforded by other flexible packaging materials. Moreover, it may be practically impossible for anyone to commence manufacturing cellophane without full access to du Pont's technique. However, du Pont has no power to prevent competition from other wrapping materials. The trial court consequently had to determine whether competition from the other wrappings prevented du Pont from possessing monopoly power in violation of § 2. Price and competition are so intimately entwined that any discussion of theory must treat them as one. It is inconceivable that price could be controlled without power over competition or vice versa. This approach to the determination of monopoly power is strengthened by this Court's conclusion in prior cases that, when an alleged monopolist has power over price and competition, an intention to monopolize in a proper case may be assumed.

If a large number of buyers and sellers deal freely in a standardized product, such as salt or wheat, we have complete or pure competition. Patents, on the other hand, furnish the most familiar type of classic monopoly. As the producers of a standardized product bring about signifi-

---

considerable period, so that he is conceded to have a monopoly of that trade with Mexico; is it intended by the committee that the bill shall make that man a culprit?

"Mr. Edmunds. It is not intended by it and the bill does not do it. Anybody who knows the meaning of the word 'monopoly,' as the courts apply it, would not apply it to such a person at all; and I am sure my friend must understand that."

Id., at 3152:

"Mr. Hoar. I put in the committee, if I may be permitted to say so (I suppose there is no impropriety in it), the precise question which has been put by the Senator from West Virginia, and I had that precise difficulty in the first place with this bill, but I was answered, and I think all the other members of the committee agreed in the answer, that 'monopoly' is a technical term known to the common law, and that it signifies—I do not mean to say that they stated what the signification was, but I became satisfied that they were right and that the word 'monopoly' is a merely technical term which has a clear and legal signification, and it is this: It is the sole engrossing to a man's self by means which prevent other men from engaging in fair competition with him.

"Of course a monopoly granted by the King was a direct inhibition of all other persons to engage in that business or calling or to acquire that particular article, except the man who had a monopoly granted him by the sovereign power. I suppose, therefore, that the courts of the United States would say in the case put by the Senator from West Virginia that a man who merely by superior skill and intelligence, a breeder of horses or raiser of cattle, or manufacturer or artisan of any kind, got the whole business because nobody could do it as well as he could was not a monopolist, but that it involved something like the use of means which made it impossible for other persons to engage in fair competition, like the engrossing, the buying up of all other persons engaged in the same business."

cant differentiations of quality, design, or packaging in the product that permit differences of use, competition becomes to a greater or less degree incomplete and the producer's power over price and competition greater over his article and its use, according to the differentiation he is able to create and maintain. A retail seller may have in one sense a monopoly on certain trade because of location, as an isolated country store or filling station, or because no one else makes a product of just the quality or attractiveness of his product, as for example in cigarettes. Thus one can theorize that we have monopolistic competition in every nonstandardized commodity with each manufacturer having power over the price and production of his own product. However, this power that, let us say, automobile or soft-drink manufacturers have over their trademarked products is not the power that makes an illegal monopoly. Illegal power must be appraised in terms of the competitive market for the product.

Determination of the competitive market for commodities depends on how different from one another are the offered commodities in character or use, how far buyers will go to substitute one commodity for another. For example, one can think of building materials as in commodity competition but one could hardly say that brick competed with steel or wood or cement or stone in the meaning of Sherman Act litigation; the products are too different. This is the interindustry competition emphasized by some economists. See Lilienthal, Big Business, c. 5. On the other hand, there are certain differences in the formulae for soft drinks but one can hardly say that each one is an illegal monopoly. Whatever the market may be, we hold that control of price or competition establishes the existence of monopoly power under § 2. Section 2 requires the application of a reasonable approach in determining the existence of monopoly power just as surely as did § 1. This of course does not mean that there can be a reasonable monopoly. Our next step is to determine whether du Pont has monopoly power over cellophane: that is, power over its price in relation to or competition with other commodities. The charge was monopolization of cellophane. The defense, that cellophane was merely a part of the relevant market for flexible packaging materials.

The Relevant Market.—When a product is controlled by one interest, without substitutes available in the market, there is monopoly power. Because most products have possible substitutes, we cannot, as we said in Times–Picayune Pub. Co. v. United States, 345 U.S. 594, 612, give "that infinite range" to the definition of substitutes. Nor is it a proper interpretation of the Sherman Act to require that products be fungible to be considered in the relevant market.

The Government argues:

"We do not here urge that in *no* circumstances may competition of substitutes negative possession of monopolistic power over trade in a product. The decisions make it clear at the least that the courts will not consider substitutes other than those which are substantially fungible with the monopolized product and sell at substantially the same price."

But where there are market alternatives that buyers may readily use for their purposes, illegal monopoly does not exist merely because the product said to be monopolized differs from others. If it were not so, only physically identical products would be a part of the market. To accept the Government's argument, we would have to conclude that the manufacturers of plain as well as moistureproof cellophane were monopolists, and so with films such as Pliofilm, foil, glassine, polyethylene, and Saran, for each of these wrapping materials is distinguishable. These were all exhibits in the case. New wrappings appear, generally similar to cellophane: is each a monopoly? What is called for is an appraisal of the "cross-elasticity" of demand in the trade. See Note, 54 Col.L.Rev. 580. The varying circumstances of each case determine the result. In considering what is the relevant market for determining the control of price and competition, no more definite rule can be declared than that commodities reasonably interchangeable by consumers for the same purposes make up that "part of the trade or commerce," monopolization of which may be illegal. As respects flexible packaging materials, the market geographically is nationwide.

[handwritten margin note: must analyze the cross-elasticity of demand for alt. prods]

[handwritten margin note: reas. interchangeable prods. make up part of the mkt: it's nationwide]

Industrial activities cannot be confined to trim categories. Illegal monopolies under § 2 may well exist over limited products in narrow fields where competition is eliminated.[8] That does not settle the issue here. In determining the market under the Sherman Act, it is the use or uses to which the commodity is put that control. The selling price between commodities with similar uses and different characteristics may vary, so that the cheaper product can drive out the more expensive. Or, the superior quality of higher priced articles may make dominant the more desirable. Cellophane costs more than many competing products and less than a few. But whatever the price, there are various flexible wrapping materials that are bought by manufacturers for packaging their goods in their own plants or are sold to converters who shape and print them for use in the packaging of the commodities to be wrapped.

---

8. The Government notes that the prohibitions of § 2 of the Sherman Act have often been extended to producers of single products and to businesses of limited scope. But the cases to which the Government refers us were not concerned with the problem that is now before the Court. In Story Parchment Co. v. Paterson Parchment Paper Co., 282 U.S. 555, a conspiracy to monopolize trade in vegetable parchment was held to be a violation of § 2. Parchment paper is obviously no larger a part of commerce than cellophane. Recovery, however, was based on proven allegations of combination and conspiracy to monopolize, and the scope of the market was not in issue. 282 U.S. at page 560.... Lorain Journal Co. v. United States, 342 U.S. 143, a case not cited by the Government, was concerned with even a smaller geographical area (dissemination of news in a community and surrounding territory). But the Court held only that defendant had attempted to monopolize, not that he had in fact monopolized.... United States v. Aluminum Co. of America, 2 Cir., 148 F.2d 416, did involve the question of monopolization. Judge Hand found that the relevant market for measuring Alcoa's power was the market for "virgin" aluminum; he refused to consider the close competition offered by "secondary" (used) aluminum. The reason for the narrow definition was that Alcoa's control over virgin aluminum permitted it to regulate the supply of used aluminum even though the latter should be actually sold by a competitor. Consequently, the case is not particularly helpful in the problem of market definition now before the Court.

Cellophane differs from other flexible packaging materials. From some it differs more than from others. The basic materials from which the wrappings are made and the advantages and disadvantages of the products to the packaging industry are summarized in Findings 62 and 63. They are aluminum, cellulose acetate, chlorides, wood pulp, rubber hydrochloride, and ethylene gas. It will adequately illustrate the similarity in characteristics of the various products by noting here Finding 62 as to glassine.[9] Its use is almost as extensive as cellophane and many of its characteristics equally or more satisfactory to users.[10]

It may be admitted that cellophane combines the desirable elements of transparency, strength and cheapness more definitely than any of the others. Comparative characteristics have been noted thus:

"Moistureproof cellophane is highly transparent, tears readily but has high bursting strength, is highly impervious to moisture and gases, and is resistant to grease and oils. Heat sealable, printable, and adapted to use on wrapping machines, it makes an excellent packaging material for both display and protection of commodities.

"Other flexible wrapping materials fall into four major categories: (1) opaque nonmoistureproof wrapping *paper* designed primarily for convenience and protection in handling packages; (2) moistureproof *films* of varying degrees of transparency designed primarily either to protect, or to display and protect, the products they encompass; (3) nonmoistureproof transparent *films* designed primarily to display and to some extent protect, but which obviously do a poor protecting job where exclusion or retention of mois-

---

9. "62. *Greaseproof paper* is made by beating wood pulp in a vat filled with water until the fibers become saturated and gelatinous in texture. Resulting product is translucent and resistant to oil and grease.

10. 63. There are respects in which other flexible packaging materials are as satisfactory as cellophane:

"Glassine

"Glassine is, in some types, about 90% transparent, so printing is legible through it.

"Glassine affords low cost transparency.

"Moisture protection afforded by waxed or lacquered glassine is as good as that of moistureproof cellophane.

"Glassine has greater resistance to tearing and breakage than cellophane.

"Glassine runs on packaging machinery with ease equal to that of cellophane.

"Glassine can be printed faster than cellophane, and can be run faster than moistureproof cellophane on bag machines.

"Glassine has greater resistance than cellophane to rancidity-inducing ultraviolet rays.

"Glassine has dimensional stability superior to cellophane.

"Glassine is more durable in cold weather than cellophane.

"Printed glassine can be sold against cellophane on the basis of appearance.

"Glassine may be more easily laminated than cellophane.

"Glassine is cheaper than cellophane in some types, comparable in others."

ture is important; and (4) moistureproof *materials* other than films of varying degrees of transparency (foils and paper products) designed to protect and display."

But, despite cellophane's advantages, it has to meet competition from other materials in every one of its uses. . . . Food products are the chief outlet, with cigarettes next. The Government makes no challenge to Finding 283 that cellophane furnishes less than 7% of wrappings for bakery products, 25% for candy, 32% for snacks, 35% for meats and poultry, 27% for crackers and biscuits, 47% for fresh produce, and 34% for frozen foods. Seventy-five to eighty per cent of cigarettes are wrapped in cellophane. Thus, cellophane shares the packaging market with others. The over-all result is that cellophane accounts for 17.9% of flexible wrapping materials, measured by the wrapping surface.

Moreover a very considerable degree of functional interchangeability exists between these products. . . . It will be noted, that except as to permeability to gases, cellophane has no qualities that are not possessed by a number of other materials. Meat will do as an example of interchangeability. Although du Pont's sales to the meat industry have reached 19,000,-000 pounds annually, nearly 35%, this volume is attributed "to the rise of self-service retailing of fresh meat." In fact, since the popularity of self-service meats, du Pont has lost "a considerable proportion" of this packaging business to Pliofilm. Pliofilm is more expensive than cellophane, but its superior physical characteristics apparently offset cellophane's price advantage. While retailers shift continually between the two, the trial court found that Pliofilm is increasing its share of the business. One further example is worth noting. Before World War II, du Pont cellophane wrapped between 5 and 10% of baked and smoked meats. The peak year was 1933. Thereafter du Pont was unable to meet the competition of Sylvania and of greaseproof paper. Its sales declined and the 1933 volume was not reached again until 1947. It will be noted that greaseproof paper, glassine, waxed paper, foil and Pliofilm are used as well as cellophane. Findings 209–210 show the competition and 215–216 the advantages that have caused the more expensive Pliofilm to increase its proportion of the business.

An element for consideration as to cross-elasticity of demand between products is the responsiveness of the sales of one product to price changes of the other. If a slight decrease in the price of cellophane causes a considerable number of customers of other flexible wrappings to switch to cellophane, it would be an indication that a high cross-elasticity of demand exists between them; that the products compete in the same market. The court below held that the "[g]reat sensitivity of customers in the flexible packaging markets to price or quality changes" prevented du Pont from possessing monopoly control over price. . . .

We conclude that cellophane's interchangeability with the other materials mentioned suffices to make it a part of this flexible packaging material market.

The Government stresses the fact that the variation in price between cellophane and other materials demonstrates they are noncompetitive. As these products are all flexible wrapping materials, it seems reasonable to consider, as was done at the trial, their comparative cost to the consumer in terms of square area.... Findings as to price competition are set out in the margin.[11] Cellophane costs two or three times as much, surface measure, as its chief competitors for the flexible wrapping market, glassine and greaseproof papers. Other forms of cellulose wrappings and those from other chemical or mineral substances, with the exception of aluminum foil, are more expensive. The uses of these materials ... are largely to wrap small packages for retail distribution. The wrapping is a relatively small proportion of the entire cost of the article. Different producers need different qualities in wrappings and their need may vary from time to time as their products undergo change. But the necessity for flexible wrappings is the central and unchanging demand. We cannot say that these differences in cost gave du Pont monopoly power over prices in view of the findings of fact on that subject.[12]

11. "132. The price of cellophane is today an obstacle to its sales in competition with other flexible packaging materials.

"133. Cellophane has always been higher priced than the two largest selling flexible packaging materials, wax paper and glassine, and this has represented a disadvantage to sales of cellophane.

"134. DuPont considered as a factor in the determination of its prices, the prices of waxed paper, glassine, greaseproof, vegetable parchment, and other flexible packaging materials.

"135. DuPont, in reducing its prices, intended to narrow price differential between cellophane and packaging papers, particularly glassine and waxed paper. The objective of this effort has been to increase the use of cellophane. Each price reduction was intended to open up new uses for cellophane, and to attract new customers who had not used cellophane because of its price."

12. "140. Some users are sensitive to the cost of flexible packaging materials; others are not. Users to whom cost is important include substantial business: for example, General Foods, Armour, Curtiss Candy Co., and smaller users in the bread industry, cracker industry, and frozen food industry. These customers are unwilling to use more cellophane because of its relatively high price, would use more if the price were reduced, and have increased their use as the price of cellophane has been reduced.

"141. The cost factor slips accounts away from cellophane. This hits at the precarious users, whose profit margins on their products are low, and has been put in motion by competitive developments in the user's trade. Examples include the losses of business to glassine in candy bar wraps in the 30's, frozen food business to waxed paper in the late 40's, and recent losses to glassine in cracker packaging.

"142. The price of cellophane was reduced to expand the market for cellophane. DuPont did not reduce prices for cellophane with intent of monopolizing manufacture or with intent of suppressing competitors.

"143. DuPont reduced cellophane prices to enable sales to be made for new uses from which higher prices had excluded cellophane, and to expand sales. Reductions were made as sales volume and market conditions warranted. In determining price reductions, duPont considered relationship between its manufacturing costs and proposed prices, possible additional volume that might be gained by the price reduction, effect of price reduction upon the return duPont would obtain on its investment. It considered the effect its lowered price might have on the manufacture by others, but this possible result of a price reduction was never a motive for the reduction.

"144. DuPont never lowered cellophane prices below cost, and never dropped cellophane prices temporarily to gain a competitive advantage.

It is the variable characteristics of the different flexible wrappings and the energy and ability with which the manufacturers push their wares that determine choice. A glance at "Modern Packaging," a trade journal, will give, by its various advertisements, examples of the competition among manufacturers for the flexible packaging market. The trial judge visited the 1952 Annual Packaging Show at Atlantic City, with the consent of counsel. He observed exhibits offered by "machinery manufacturers, converters and manufacturers of flexible packaging materials." He states that these personal observations confirmed his estimate of the competition between cellophane and other packaging materials. From this wide variety of evidence, the Court reached the conclusion expressed in Finding 838:

> "The record establishes plain cellophane and moistureproof cellophane are each flexible packaging materials which are functionally interchangeable with other flexible packaging materials and sold at same time to same customers for same purpose at competitive prices; there is no cellophane market distinct and separate from the market for flexible packaging materials; the market for flexible packaging materials is the relevant market for determining nature and extent of duPont's market control; and duPont has at all times competed with other cellophane producers and manufacturers of other flexible packaging materials in all aspects of its cellophane business."

[handwritten margin note: there is no sep cellophane mkt - it's interch. w/other pkg materials]

The facts above considered dispose also of any contention that competitors have been excluded by du Pont from the packaging material market. That market has many producers and there is no proof du Pont ever has possessed power to exclude any of them from the rapidly expanding flexible packaging market. The Government apparently concedes as much, for it states that "lack of power to inhibit entry into this so-called market [*i.e.*, flexible packaging materials], comprising widely disparate products, is no indicium of absence of power to exclude competition in the manufacture and sale of cellophane." The record shows the multiplicity of competitors and the financial strength of some with individual assets running to the hundreds of millions. Indeed, the trial court found that du Pont could not exclude competitors even from the manufacture of cellophane, an immaterial matter if the market is flexible packaging material. Nor can we say that du Pont's profits, while liberal (according to the Government 15.9% net after taxes on the 1937–1947 average), demonstrate the existence of a monopoly without proof of lack of comparable profits during those years in other prosperous industries. Cellophane was a leader, over 17%, in the flexible packaging materials market. There is no showing that du Pont's rate of return was greater or less than that of other producers of flexible packaging materials.

"145. As duPont's manufacturing costs declined, 1924 to 1935, duPont reduced prices for cellophane. When costs of raw materials increased subsequent to 1935, it postponed reductions until 1938 and 1939. Subsequent increases in cost of raw material and labor brought about price increases after 1947."

The "market" which one must study to determine when a producer has monopoly power will vary with the part of commerce under consideration. The tests are constant. That market is composed of products that have reasonable interchangeability for the purposes for which they are produced—price, use and qualities considered. While the application of the tests remains uncertain, it seems to us that du Pont should not be found to monopolize cellophane when that product has the competition and interchangeability with other wrappings that this record shows.

On the findings of the District Court, its judgment is affirmed.

■ CLARK and HARLAN, JJ., took no part in the consideration or decision of this case.

■ WARREN, C.J., with whom BLACK and DOUGLAS, JJ., join, dissenting.

This case, like many under the Sherman Act, turns upon the proper definition of the market. In defining the market in which du Pont's economic power is to be measured, the majority virtually emasculate § 2 of the Sherman Act. They admit that "cellophane combines the desirable elements of transparency, strength and cheapness more definitely than any of" a host of other packaging materials. Yet they hold that all of those materials are so indistinguishable from cellophane as to warrant their inclusion in the market. We cannot agree that cellophane, in the language of Times–Picayune Publishing Co. v. United States, 345 U.S. 594, 613, is "the self-same product" as glassine, greaseproof and vegetable parchment papers, waxed papers, sulphite papers, aluminum foil, cellulose acetate, and Pliofilm and other films.[13]

The majority opinion states that "[I]t will adequately illustrate the similarity in characteristics of the various products by noting here Finding 62 as to glassine." But Finding 62 merely states the respects in which the selected flexible packaging materials are as satisfactory as cellophane; it does not compare all the physical properties of cellophane and other materials. The Table incorporated in Finding 59 does make such a comparison, and enables us to note cellophane's unique combination of qualities lacking among less expensive materials in varying degrees.[14] A glance at this Table reveals that cellophane has a high bursting strength while

---

13. In Times–Picayune Publishing Co. v. United States, 345 U.S. 594, 612, note 31, the Court said:

> "For every product, substitutes exist. But a relevant market cannot meaningfully encompass that infinite range. The circle must be drawn narrowly to exclude any other product to which, within reasonable variations in price, only a limited number of buyers will turn; in technical terms, products whose 'cross-elasticities of demand' are small."

14. See 118 F.Supp. at page 64. The majority opinion quotes at length from Stocking and Mueller, The Cellophane Case, XLV Amer.Economic Rev. 29, 48–49, in noting the comparative characteristics of cellophane and other products. Unfortunately, the opinion fails to quote the conclusion reached by these economists. They state: "The [trial] court to the contrary notwithstanding, the market in which cellophane meets the 'competition' of other wrappers is narrower than the market for all flexible packaging materials." Id., at 52. And they conclude that "... cellophane is so differentiated from other flexible wrapping materials that its cross elasticity of demand gives du Pont significant and continuing monopoly power." Id., at 63.

glassine's is low; that cellophane's permeability to gases is lower than that of glassine; and that both its transparency and its resistance to grease and oils are greater than glassine's. Similarly, we see that waxed paper's bursting strength is less than cellophane's and that it is highly permeable to gases and offers no resistance whatsoever to grease and oils. With respect to the two other major products held to be close substitutes for cellophane, Finding 59 makes the majority's market definition more dubious. In contrast to cellophane, aluminum foil is actually opaque and has a low bursting strength. And sulphite papers, in addition to being opaque, are highly permeable to both moisture and gases, have no resistance to grease and oils, have a lower bursting strength than cellophane, and are not even heat sealable. Indeed, the majority go further than placing cellophane in the same market with such products. They also include the transparent films, which are more expensive than cellophane. These bear even less resemblance to the lower priced packaging materials than does cellophane. The juxtaposition of one of these films, Cry–O–Rap, with sulphite in the Table facilitates a comparison which shows that Cry–O–Rap is markedly different and far superior.

If the conduct of buyers indicated that glassine, waxed and sulphite papers and aluminum foil were actually "the self-same products" as cellophane, the qualitative differences demonstrated by the comparison of physical properties in Finding 59 would not be conclusive. But the record provides convincing proof that businessmen did not so regard these products. During the period covered by the complaint (1923–1947) cellophane enjoyed phenomenal growth. Du Pont's 1924 production was 361,249 pounds, which sold for $1,306,662. Its 1947 production was 133,502,858 pounds, which sold for $55,339,626. Yet throughout this period the price of cellophane was far greater than that of glassine, waxed paper or sulphite paper. In 1929 cellophane's price was seven times that of glassine; in 1934, four times, and in 1949 still more than twice glassine's price. . . . [T]he graph upon which Finding 136 is based, shows that cellophane had a similar price relation to waxed paper and that sulphite paper sold at even less than glassine and waxed paper. We cannot believe that buyers, practical businessmen, would have bought cellophane in increasing amounts over a quarter of a century if close substitutes were available at from one-seventh to one-half cellophane's price. That they did so is testimony to cellophane's distinctiveness.

The inference yielded by the conduct of cellophane buyers is reinforced by the conduct of sellers other than du Pont. Sylvania, the only other cellophane producer, absolutely and immediately followed every du Pont price change, even dating back its price list to the effective date of du Pont's change. Producers of glassine and waxed paper, on the other hand, displayed apparent indifference to du Pont's repeated and substantial price cuts. From 1924 to 1932 du Pont dropped the price of plain cellophane 84%, while the price of glassine remained constant. And during the period 1933–1946 the prices for glassine and waxed paper actually increased in the face of a further 21% decline in the price of cellophane. If "shifts of business" due to "price sensitivity" had been substantial, glassine and waxed paper producers who wanted to stay in business would have been compelled by market forces to meet du Pont's price challenge just as Sylvania was. The majority correctly point out that:

> "An element for consideration as to cross-elasticity of demand between products is the responsiveness of the sales of one product to price changes of the other. If a slight decrease in the price of cellophane causes a considerable number of customers of other flexible wrappings to switch to cellophane, it would be an indication that a high cross-elasticity of demand exists between them; that the products compete in the same market."

Cross-elasticity – doesn't seem like there was any

Surely there was more than "a slight decrease in the price of cellophane" during the period covered by the complaint. That producers of glassine and waxed paper remained dominant in the flexible packaging materials market without meeting cellophane's tremendous price cuts convinces us that cellophane was not in effective competition with their products.

Certainly du Pont itself shared our view. From the first, du Pont recognized that it need not concern itself with competition from other packaging materials. For example, when du Pont was contemplating entry into cellophane production, its Development Department reported that glassine "is so inferior that it belongs in an entirely different class and has hardly to be considered as a competitor of cellophane." This was still du Pont's view in 1950 when its survey of competitive prospects wholly omitted reference to glassine, waxed paper or sulphite paper and stated that "Competition for du Pont cellophane will come from competitive cellophane and from non-cellophane films made by us or by others.". . .

As predicted by its 1923 market analysis, du Pont's dominance in cellophane proved enormously profitable from the outset. After only five years of production, when du Pont bought out the minority stock interests in its cellophane subsidiary, it had to pay more than fifteen times the original price of the stock. But such success was not limited to the period of innovation, limited sales and complete domestic monopoly. A confidential du Pont report shows that during the period 1937–1947, despite great expansion of sales, du Pont's "operative return" (before taxes) averaged 31%, while its average "net return" (after deduction of taxes, bonuses, and fundamental research expenditures) was 15.9%. Such profits provide a powerful incentive for the entry of competitors.

Yet from 1924 to 1951 only one new firm, Sylvania, was able to begin cellophane production. And Sylvania could not have entered if La Cellophane's secret process had not been stolen. It is significant that for 15 years Olin Industries, a substantial firm, was unsuccessful in its attempt to produce cellophane, finally abandoning the project in 1944 after having spent about $1,000,000. When the Government brought this suit, du Pont, "to reduce the hazard of being judged to have a monopoly of the U.S. cellophane business," decided to let Olin enter the industry. Despite this demonstration of the control achieved by du Pont through its exclusive dominion over the cellophane process, the District Court found that du Pont could not exclude competitors from the manufacture of cellophane.

Finding 727. This finding is "clearly erroneous." The majority avoid passing upon Finding 727 by stating that it is "immaterial . . . if the market is flexible packaging material." They do not appear to disagree with our conclusion, however, since they concede that . . . "it may be practically impossible for anyone to commence manufacturing cellophane without full access to du Pont's technique."

The trial court found that:

> "Du Pont has no power to set cellophane prices arbitrarily. If prices for cellophane increase in relation to prices of other flexible packaging materials it will lose business to manufacturers of such materials in varying amounts for each of du Pont cellophane's major end uses."

This further reveals its misconception of the antitrust laws. A monopolist seeking to maximize profits cannot raise prices "arbitrarily." Higher prices of course mean smaller sales, but they also mean higher per-unit profit. Lower prices will increase sales but reduce per-unit profit. Within these limits a monopolist has a considerable degree of latitude in determining which course to pursue in attempting to maximize profits. The trial judge thought that, if du Pont raised its price, the market would "penalize" it with smaller profits as well as lower sales. Du Pont proved him wrong. When 1947 operating earnings dropped below 26% for the first time in 10 years, it increased cellophane's price 7% and boosted its earnings in 1948. . . .

The majority opinion purports to reject the theory of "interindustry competition." Brick, steel, wood, cement and stone, it says, are "too different" to be placed in the same market. But cellophane, glassine, wax papers, sulphite papers, greaseproof and vegetable parchment papers, aluminum foil, cellulose, acetate, Pliofilm and other films are not "too different," the opinion concludes. The majority approach would apparently enable a monopolist of motion picture exhibition to avoid Sherman Act consequences by showing that motion pictures compete in substantial measure with legitimate theater, television, radio, sporting events and other forms of entertainment. Here, too, "shifts of business" undoubtedly accompany fluctuations in price and "there are market alternatives that buyers may readily use for their purposes." Yet, in United States v. Paramount Pictures, 334 U.S. 131, where the District Court had confined the relevant market to that for nationwide movie exhibition, this Court remanded the case to the District Court with directions to determine whether there was a monopoly on the part of the five major distributors "in the *first-run* field for the entire country, in the *first-run* field in the 92 largest cities of the country, or in the *first-run* field in separate localities." 334 U.S. at 172. Similarly, it is difficult to square the majority view with United States v. Aluminum Co. of America, 2 Cir., 148 F.2d 416, a landmark § 2 case. There Judge Learned Hand, reversing a district court, held that the close competition which "secondary" (used) aluminum offered to "virgin" aluminum did not justify including the former within the relevant market for measuring Alcoa's economic power. Against these and other precedents, which the Court's opinion approves but does not follow, the formula of "reasonable interchangeability," as applied by the majority, appears indistinguishable from the theory of "interindustry competition." The danger in it is that, as demonstrated in this case, it is "perfectly compatible with a fully monopolized economy."

The majority hold in effect that, because cellophane meets competition for many end uses, those buyers for other uses who need or want only cellophane are not entitled to the benefits of competition within the cellophane industry. For example, the largest single use of cellophane in 1951 was for wrapping cigarettes, and 75 to 80% of all cigarettes are wrapped with cellophane. As the recent report of the Attorney General's National Committee to Study the Antitrust Laws states: "In the interest of rivalry that extends to *all* buyers and *all* uses, competition among rivals within the industry is always important." (Emphasis added.) Furthermore, those buyers who have "reasonable alternatives" between cellophane and other products are also entitled to competition within the cellophane industry, for such competition may lead to lower prices and improved quality.

The foregoing analysis of the record shows conclusively that cellophane is the relevant market. Since du Pont has the lion's share of that market, it must have monopoly power, as the majority concede.[15] This being so, we think it clear that, in the circumstances of this case, du Pont is guilty of "monopolization." The briefest sketch of du Pont's business history precludes it from falling within the "exception to the Sherman Act prohibitions of monopoly power" (majority opinion, 76 S.Ct. 1004) by successfully asserting that monopoly was "thrust upon" it. Du Pont was not "the passive beneficiary of a monopoly" within the meaning of United States v. Aluminum Co. of America, *supra*, 148 F.2d at pages 429–430. It sought and maintained dominance through illegal agreements dividing the world market, concealing and suppressing technological information, and restricting its licensee's production by prohibitive royalties, and through numerous maneuvers which might have been "honestly industrial" but whose necessary effect was nevertheless exclusionary.[16] Du Pont cannot bear "the burden of proving that it owes its monopoly *solely* to superior skill...." (Emphasis supplied.) United States v. United Shoe Machinery Corp., D.C., 110 F.Supp. 295, 342, affirmed per curiam 347 U.S. 521....

If competition is at the core of the Sherman Act, we cannot agree that it was consistent with that Act for the enormously lucrative cellophane industry to have no more than two sellers from 1924 to 1951. The conduct of du Pont and Sylvania illustrates that a few sellers tend to act like one

---

15. If cellophane is the 'market' that du Pont is found to dominate, it may be assumed it does have monopoly power over that 'market.' Monopoly power is the power to control prices or exclude competition. It seems apparent that du Pont's power to set the price of cellophane has only been limited by the competition afforded by other flexible packaging materials. Moreover, it may be practically impossible for anyone to commence manufacturing cellophane without full access to du Pont's technique." Majority opinion, 76 S.Ct. 1005.

16. See United States v. Aluminum Co. of America, 2 Cir., 148 F.2d 416, 431.

[handwritten margin note: thinks cellophane should be relevant mkt and if that's the mkt, duPont is guilty of monopolization]

and that an industry which does not have a competitive structure will not have competitive behavior. The public should not be left to rely upon the dispensations of management in order to obtain the benefits that normally accompany competition. Such beneficence is of uncertain tenure. Only actual competition can assure long-run enjoyment of the goals of a free economy.

We would reverse the decision below and remand the cause to the District Court with directions to determine the relief that should be granted against du Pont.

■ The concurring opinion of FRANKFURTER, J., is omitted.

NOTES AND QUESTIONS

1. In International Boxing Club v. United States, 358 U.S. 242 (1959), the Supreme Court purported to apply the *Cellophane* reasoning where not only actual monopolization but conspiracy to monopolize had been found by the district court.

The complaint alleged, *inter alia,* that Norris and Wirtz, owners of controlling interests in important sports arenas in Chicago, Detroit, and St. Louis, conspired with the management of Madison Square Garden, the foremost sports arena in New York City, to control the promotion, broadcasting and televising of championship boxing contests in the United States. The complaint further alleged that defendants effectuated their conspiracy chiefly by using their control of arenas to coerce contenders for boxing titles into granting exclusive promotional contracts for championship fights, including film and broadcasting rights, for a period of from three to five years.

In the Supreme Court, defendants' chief attack on the findings turned on the contention that the proper relevant market should not have been the promotion of professional championship boxing contests, as found by the district court, but the promotion of all professional boxing contests. Defendants' control of championship boxing contests in the four years immediately succeeding their first championship promotion was approximately 81% of the field, but was much less if all professional boxing contests were considered. With respect to the relevant market issue, the Supreme Court, per Clark, J., wrote:

> Appellants ... rely primarily on United States v. du Pont & Co. That case, involving an alleged monopoly of the market in cellophane, held that the relevant market was not cellophane alone but the entire field of flexible packaging materials. ... The appellants argue that the "physical identity of the products here would seem necessarily to put them in one and the same market." They say that any boxing contest, whether championship or not, always includes one ring, two boxers and one referee, fighting under the same rules before a greater or lesser number of spectators either present at ringside or through the facilities of television, radio, or moving pictures.
>
> We do not feel that this conclusion follows. ... [T]he lower court in the instant case found that there exists a "separate, identifiable market" for championship boxing contests. This general finding is supported by detailed findings to the effect that the average revenue from all sources for

appellants' championship bouts was $154,000, compared to $40,000 for their nonchampionship programs; that television rights to one championship fight brought $100,000, in contrast to $45,000 for a nontitle fight seven months later between the same two fighters; that the average "Nielsen" ratings over a two-and-one-half year period were 74.9% for appellants' championship contests, and 57.7% for their nonchampionship programs (reflecting a difference of several million viewers between the two types of fights); that although the revenues from movie rights for six of appellants' championship bouts totaled over $600,000 no full-length motion picture rights were sold for a nonchampionship contest; and that spectators pay "substantially more" for tickets to championship fights than for nontitle fights. In addition, numerous representatives of the broadcasting, motion picture and advertising industries testified to the general effect that a "particular and special demand exists among radio broadcasting and telecasting [and motion picture] companies for the rights to broadcast and telecast [and make and distribute films of] championship contests in contradistinction to similar rights to non-championship contests."[17]

In view of these findings, we cannot say that the lower court was "clearly erroneous" in concluding that nonchampionship fights are not "reasonably interchangeable for the same purpose" as championship contests....

... [C]hampionship boxing is the "cream" of the boxing business, and, as has been shown above ... is a sufficiently separate part of the trade or commerce to constitute the relevant market for Sherman Act purposes.

2. In Syufy Enterprises v. American Multicinema, Inc., 793 F.2d 990 (9th Cir.1986), cert. denied, 479 U.S. 1031 (1987), Syufy was charged with having a monopoly in the exhibition of certain motion pictures in the area of San Jose, California. The following excerpt from the Ninth Circuit decision illustrates the difficulties inherent in the market definition task:

AMC defined the relevant market as the market for exhibition of industry anticipated top-grossing motion pictures in the San Jose area. Syufy does not dispute the geographic component of this definition—the San Jose area. Nor does it dispute limiting the product market definition to hardtop theaters. The only aspect of AMC's market definition that Syufy disputes is the limitation of the relevant product market to the exhibition of major films, more specifically to industry-anticipated top-grossing films. Syufy argues that this market definition is ex post facto and ad hoc, and that all first run films are in substantial competition with each other.

In evaluating Syufy's challenge, we begin with the principle that assessment of a product market definition must take into account whether products excluded from the definition are "interchangeab[le] in use" with those included in the market and whether there is "cross-elasticity of demand" between excluded and included products. United States v. E.I. duPont de Nemours & Co., 351 U.S. 377, 394–95 (1956). In economic terms, we might recharacterize Syufy's argument as follows: all first run films are interchangeable in use and the price and availability of any one film will affect the demand for all other films. Top-grossing films, Syufy

---

17. Approximately 25% of the revenue produced by the appellants' championship fights during the period covered by the complaint was derived through the sale of radio, television and motion picture rights.

argues, are simply those films that prove to be highly successful in the market place, but they possess no special characteristics that differentiate them from less successful films from an ex ante perspective. Syufy also argues that limiting the product definition to top-grossing films has the effect of irrationally and unfairly penalizing the exhibitor with the prescience to book films that later prove to be big hits with the movie-going public.

AMC's rejoinder is that Syufy's argument mischaracterizes the product market definition. AMC points out that it did not define the market as simply top-grossing films, but as *industry anticipated* top-grossing films. AMC argues that these films can be differentiated from other first run films from an ex ante perspective because they have larger budgets, "name" stars and directors, larger advertising budgets, command large guarantees, and possess other distinctive characteristics which can be identified before the film is released. In economic terms, the viability of AMC's product market definition depends on the proposition that anticipated top-grossing films are not interchangeable with other films in the eyes of consumers and that price increases or supply constrictions for such films do not result in a shift in consumption patterns to other films. In legal terms, the question is whether the films excluded from the definition are "interchangeab[le] in use" with those included in the market and whether there is "cross-elasticity of demand" between excluded and included products. United States v. E.I. duPont de Nemours & Co., 351 U.S. 377, 394–95 (1956). In more colloquial terms, the viability of the proposed definition depends on the argument that if the price for admission to *E.T.* goes up, audiences will not flock to *My Dinner with Andre*.

We conclude that there is sufficient evidence in the record to permit a rational jury to conclude that industry anticipated top-grossing films constitute a distinct product market. The evidence indicates that approximately thirty pictures a year are identifiable as "anticipated top grossing films" on the basis of such criteria as national advertising support, longer playtimes, guaranteed rentals, famous stars, directors and producers, booking in first class theatres, and lucrative terms offered for the pictures by exhibitors. AMC compiled a list of the industry anticipated top-grossing films based on bidding materials submitted by both Syufy and AMC. Although AMC did not present direct evidence going to the "cross-elasticity of demand" between this limited class of pictures and other films, the jury could reasonably have concluded from the evidence presented that the industry anticipated top-grossing films were not in substantial competition with other films.

3.   United States v. Microsoft Corp., 253 F.3d 34 (D.C.Cir. 2001), one of the most widely discussed antitrust cases in recent decades, will be considered at length in Chapter 8. We pause here only to explore briefly the question of definition of relevant market, which turned out not to be a central issue in the proceeding.

The Department of Justice and several state attorneys general had brought suit charging Microsoft, along with other antitrust violations, with illegally maintaining a monopoly in the market for personal computer ("PC") operating systems and attempting to monopolize the market for web browsers—both allegedly illegal under Section 2 of the Sherman Act. The court defined the market as "the licensing of all Intel-compatible PC operating systems worldwide." and concluded that Microsoft had 95% of that market. Microsoft argued that this definition was too narrow and failed to include three product categories: (1) non-Intel PC operating systems (such as Apple computers); (2) operating systems for non-PC devices, such as handheld computers or personal digital assistants; and (3) "middleware" products. Middleware is a software product that exposes other application programs ("APIs") and had the potential to incorporate a consistent set of APIs while running on a variety of operating systems, allowing programs to more easily "port" applications from one system to another. Netscape Navigator and the Java programming language, the most well-known of middleware products, were at issue in the case and had been targets of conduct by Microsoft that formed the basis of liability for monopoly maintenance.

In a unanimous *per curiam* opinion, the Court of Appeals easily dismissed non-Intel PC operating systems and non-PC devices from the market. Other systems like the Apple system cost more, supported fewer applications, and involved considerable effort in transferring files to its format. As to other information appliances like handheld devices, the Court found that they fell short of performing all the functions of a PC, and therefore most consumers would buy them only as a supplement.

The decision of the lower court to exclude "middleware" from the relevant product market raised more serious questions, addressed by the Court of Appeals as follows:

> "This brings us to Microsoft's main challenge to the District Court's market definition: the inclusion of middleware.... Microsoft argues that, because middleware could usurp the operating system's platform function and might eventually take over other operating system functions (for instance, by controlling peripherals), the District Court erred in excluding Navigator and Java from the relevant market. The District Court found, however, that neither Navigator, Java, nor any other middleware product could now, or would soon, expose enough APIs to serve as a platform for popular applications, much less take over all operating system functions. Again, Microsoft fails to challenge these findings, instead simply asserting middleware's "potential" as a competitor.

> "The test of reasonable interchangeability, however, required the District Court to consider only substitutes that constrain pricing in the reasonably foreseeable future, and only products that can enter the market in a relatively short time can perform this function. Whatever middleware's ultimate potential, the District Court found that consumers could not now abandon their operating systems and switch to middleware in response to a sustained price for Windows above the competitive level. Nor is middleware likely to overtake the operating system as the primary platform for software development at any time in the near future.... Because market definition is meant to identify products "reasonably interchangeable by consumers," *du Pont*, 351 U.S. at 395, and because middleware is not now interchangeable with Windows, the District Court had good reason for excluding middleware from the relevant market."

By contrast, the D.C. Circuit found Microsoft was not liable for attempting to monopolize the market for web browsers because the government had failed to define a relevant market. The D.C. Circuit chastised the District Court for "never engag[ing] in an ... analysis [of the browser market] nor enter[ing] detailed findings defining what a browser is or what products might constitute substitutes." Essentially, the D.C. Circuit rejected out of hand the government's effort to define a market for web browsers.

NOTE ON MARKET POWER AND CONSUMER LOSS[18]

The following note explores some economic concepts about the value of competition, and the injuries to competition and to consumers that can result from monopoly or cartel behavior.

Market power is the ability to profitably reduce output below the competitive level of production, and the corresponding power to raise or maintain prices above the competitive level when consumers bid up the price of the constricted supply. Market power can be achieved and exercised either by a "monopolist" (*i.e.*, a single firm) or by a "cartel" (*i.e.*, a group of competitors) directly restricting output and raising price.[19]

Antitrust law is premised on the general principle that competition, as opposed to monopolization or cartelization, tends to maximize the economic performance of a market. Economic performance refers to the economic achievements of the market. Performance involves *economic efficiency,* the degree to which (i) enough output is produced to satisfy all the demand of consumers who value the product in excess of its cost of production ("allocative efficiency") and (ii) output is produced at minimum cost ("productive efficiency"). Performance also involves *wealth distribution,* the degree to which consumers do or do not pay a market price for the product that equals the cost of production. Over time, market performance also involves the speed of innovation in the market ("dynamic efficiency"), the degree to which sellers reduce their costs and design new and superior products to satisfy consumer preferences.[20]

When a monopolist or cartel restricts output and raises price, this exercise of market power injures consumers (as a group) in two separate ways. First, the higher price creates a monopoly overcharge on the quantity sold by the monopolist. This monopoly overcharge involves a transfer of wealth from consumers to the shareholders (or persons) who own the monopoly firm. Second, the higher price chokes off demand somewhat, creating a loss of potential consumption benefits. Although the consumer values units of the commodity in excess of their production cost, the units are not produced and consumed. This "deadweight loss," a term used by economists, is not gained by the shareholders. It is a reduction in the economic efficiency of the market.

A. *Monopoly Overcharge*

Consider the case of a monopoly or cartel taking over an initially perfectly competitive market, restricting output, and raising price. If a particular consumer continues to purchase the product at the higher, monopoly price, this creates a transfer of wealth from that purchaser to the monopolist or cartel. This wealth transfer takes place as the consumer now pays the higher monopoly price for the same product previously purchased at the competitive price. The monopoly overcharge may be compared to theft. Relative to the competitive price, the cartel or monopolist simply expropriates more of the purchaser's money without providing any additional goods or services.

---

18. This note was written in collaboration with Professor Steven C. Salop.

19. Market power also can be achieved and exercised by exclusionary conduct that raises rivals' costs and erects barriers to entry. This is discussed in more detail in Chapter 8, Section 4.

20. *See, e.g.*, Lande, Wealth Transfers as the Original and Primary Concern of Antitrust: The Efficiency Interpretation Challenged, 34 Hastings L.J. 65 (1982).

B.   Deadweight Loss

Some consumers will react to the higher price by purchasing less of the product or eliminating purchases entirely. Pricing above the competitive level thereby reduces economic efficiency by restricting consumption below the efficient level achieved in a perfectly competitive market. The higher prices eliminate consumption by those consumers who value units of the product at more than the (marginal) cost of production but at less than the monopoly price. Those consumers lose the "benefit of the bargain" they might have received on those units no longer purchased. This consumer loss amounts to the difference in the dollar value the consumer places on those foregone units ("willingness to pay") less the competitive price paid for them; this excess of value over price is referred to by economists as "consumer surplus." The loss in consumer surplus is called a "deadweight loss" to denote the fact that the consumer loss is not gained by the monopolist. It is not a wealth transfer, but rather represents wasted resources—that is, a loss in economic efficiency.

An analogous loss in "producer surplus" is borne by the cartel or monopolist when output is restricted below the efficient, competitive level. The sellers lose the incremental profit (or "surplus") they earned by selling some units of output at the competitive price that were produced at a lower "marginal" cost. This reduction in producer surplus harms the seller as well as society. For the seller, of course, this loss is more than counterbalanced by the gains from the monopoly overcharge.

For those students who are interested in a more technical explanation, the monopoly overcharge to consumers and deadweight loss can be seen diagrammatically:

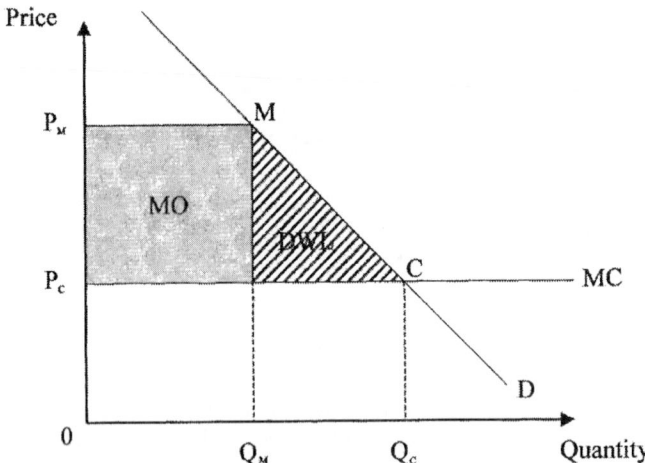

The competitive price and quantity are given by the point C (price P_c and quantity Q_c) and the monopoly price and quantity are given by point M (price P_m and quantity Q_m). The diagram assumes that the competitive price P_c equals marginal cost MC, so that there is no producer surplus. The monopoly overcharge consists of the price overcharge over and above the competitive level paid by consumers on the output they purchase. Diagrammatically, it is illustrated by the "rectangle" labelled MO. (The height of this rectangle is the price overcharge P_m—P_c. The base of the rectangle is the quantity purchased by consumers at the monopoly price Q_m. Thus, the area of the rectangle is the product of the price overcharge times the quantity, or $(P_m - P_c)(Q_m.)$ The deadweight loss in consumer surplus is the loss in surplus resulting from the monopoly output restriction over and above the monopoly overcharge. The deadweight loss is illustrated by the triangle labelled DWL. (The height of this triangle is the price overcharge $P_m - P_c$. The base of the triangle is the reduction in quantity purchased by consumers resulting from the monopoly, or $Q_c - Q_m$. Thus, the area of the rectangle is the product of the price overcharge times the quantity reduction, or (*i.e.*, area = ½(P_m − P_c)($Q_c - Q_m$)). For example, suppose the monopolist raised price from the competitive level of $100 to the monopoly level of $140 (*i.e.*, a price increase of $40) and restricted output from the competitive level of 1,000 units to the monopoly level of 700 (*i.e.*, a reduction of 300 units). In this case, the monopoly overcharge equals $28,000 (*i.e.*, 700 units × $40) and the deadweight loss in consumer surplus equals $6,000 (*i.e.*, ½ × 300 × $40). If the original cost curve were rising, then there also would be a deadweight loss in producer surplus from the output reduction.

C. Comparing the Harms

From the point of view of a single consumer, the per unit wealth transfer from the monopoly overcharge on each unit he or she continues to buy necessarily exceeds the deadweight loss on each unit he or she stops purchasing. This is because the consumer *voluntarily* chooses to forego purchasing those units, implying that reducing consumption necessarily dominates paying the higher price. In effect, the consumer mitigates the damages from the monopoly price by reducing consumption.

However, some argue that, from the point of view of the economy as a whole, the monopoly overcharge is *less* significant than the deadweight loss. This result follows if it is recognized that the cartel or monopolist actually consists of stockholders who are themselves members of society. From this broader vantage point, the monopoly overcharge is "just" a transfer of wealth from one group of society to another. A policymaker not allied with any particular segment of society may have little if any interest in this redistribution of wealth. In contrast, the deadweight efficiency losses represent unrecoverable reductions in social wealth, rather than "simply" a wealth transfer. As a result, some commentators argue that antitrust should be concerned purely with efficiency, not consumer welfare and wealth distribution.[21] Thus, minimization of the deadweight losses, and indifference to the wealth transfer resulting from the monopoly overcharge, should provide the exclusive focus of antitrust policy.[22]

---

21. This is a view advocated by Judge Robert Bork in his book, The Antitrust Paradox, Chapter 5 (1978). Bork actually refers to his pure efficiency view as a "consumer welfare" approach, thereby treating the owners of firms, in effect, as consumers. According to this view, income redistribution should be the concern of tax and expenditure statutes, not antitrust. In contrast, the pure consumer welfare standard would be concerned with the distribution of wealth. In particular, it evaluates conduct on the basis of the impact on consumers, not the owners of the firms.

22. As discussed below, analysis of the long run implications of monopoly pricing is more complex. On the one hand, the monopoly overcharge may be converted into a deadweight loss in the long run as the monopolist expends some of his monopoly profits in order to erect barriers to entry to protect the monopoly. Posner, The Social Costs of Monopoly and Regulation, 83 Journal of Political Economy 807 (1975). On the other hand, the prospect of large monopoly profits provides an added incentive for firms to innovate, in order to achieve the monopoly, with the ultimate effect of providing better or less expensive products that benefit consumers. Schumpeter, Capitalism, Socialism and Democracy (1942). But once the monopoly is achieved, and the monopolist is free of competitive pressures, the monopolist may feel less need to innovate. Scherer & Ross, Industrial Market Structure and Economic Performance, Ch. 17 (3d ed. 1990).

Price fixing both reduces efficiency and harms consumers. The analysis becomes more complicated when a merger or other conduct reduces costs at the same time that it reduces competition. In such cases, the pure efficiency and consumer welfare standards may lead to opposing recommendations.[23]

Are wealth transfers—earlier analogized to theft—a legitimate concern of antitrust policy? From your reading of Chapter 1, what would Congress in 1890 have thought?

United States v. Grinnell Corp.

Supreme Court of the United States, 1966.
384 U.S. 563, 86 S.Ct. 1698, 16 L.Ed.2d 778.

■ DOUGLAS, J. This case presents an important question under § 2 of the Sherman Act, which makes it an offense for any person to "monopolize . . . any part of the trade or commerce among the several States." This is a civil suit brought by the United States against Grinnell Corporation (Grinnell), American District Telegraph Co. (ADT), Holmes Electric Protective Co. (Holmes) and Automatic Fire Alarm Co. of Delaware (AFA). The District Court held for the Government and entered a decree. . . . All parties appeal, the United States because it deems the relief inadequate and the defendants both on the merits and on the relief and on the ground that the District Court denied them a fair trial. . . .

Grinnell manufactures plumbing supplies and fire sprinkler systems. It also owns 76% of the stock of ADT, 89% of the stock of AFA, and 100% of the stock of Holmes. ADT provides both burglary and fire protection services; Holmes provides burglary services alone; AFA supplies only fire protection service. Each offers a central station service under which hazard-detecting devices installed on the protected premises automatically transmit an electric signal to a central station.[24] The central station is manned 24 hours a day. Upon receipt of a signal, the central station, where appropriate, dispatches guards to the protected premises and notifies the police or fire department direct. There are other forms of protective services. But the record shows that subscribers to accredited central station service (*i.e.*, that approved by the insurance underwriters) receive reductions in their insurance premiums that are substantially greater than the

---

23. For the general framework, see Williamson, Economics as an Antitrust Defense: The Welfare Tradeoffs, 58 American Economic Review 18 (1968); Williamson, Economics as an Antitrust Defense Revisited, 125 U.Pa.L.Rev. 699 (1977).

24. Among the various central station services offered are the following:

(1) *automatic burglar alarms.*

(2) *automatic fire alarms.*

(3) *sprinkler supervisory service:* any malfunctions in the fire sprinkler system (*e.g.,* changes in water pressure, dangerously low water temperatures, etc.) are reported to the central station.

(4) *watch signal service:* night watchmen, by operating a key-triggered device on the protected premises, indicate to the central station that they are making their rounds and that all is well; the failure of a watchman to make his electrical report alerts the central station that something may be amiss.

reduction received by the users of other kinds of protection service. In 1961 accredited companies in the central station service business grossed $65,000,000. ADT, Holmes, and AFA are the three largest companies in the business in terms of revenue: ADT (with 121 central stations in 115 cities) has 73% of the business; Holmes (with 12 central stations in three large cities) has 12.5%; AFA (with three central stations in three large cities) has 2%. Thus the three companies that Grinnell controls have over 87% of the business.

Over the years ADT purchased the stock or assets of 27 companies engaged in the business of providing burglar or fire alarm services. Holmes acquired the stock or assets of three burglar alarm companies in New York City using a central station. Of these 30, the officials of seven agreed not to engage in the protective service business in the area for periods ranging from five years to permanently. After Grinnell acquired control of the other defendants, the latter continued in their attempts to acquire central station companies—offers being made to at least eight companies between the years 1955 and 1961, including four of the five largest nondefendant companies in the business. When the present suit was filed, each of those defendants had outstanding an offer to purchase one of the four largest nondefendant companies.

In 1906, prior to the affiliation of ADT and Holmes, they made a written agreement whereby ADT transferred to Holmes its burglar alarm business in a major part of the Middle Atlantic States and agreed to refrain forever from engaging in that business in that area, while Holmes transferred to ADT its watch signal business and agreed to limit its activities to burglar alarm service and night watch service for financial institutions. While this agreement was modified several times and terminated in 1947, in 1961 Holmes still restricted its business to burglar alarm service and operated only in those areas which had been allocated to it under the 1906 agreement. Similarly, ADT continued to refrain from supplying burglar alarm service in those areas earlier allocated to Holmes.

In 1907 Grinnell entered into a series of agreements with the other defendant companies and with Automatic Fire Protection Co. to the following effect:

AFA received the exclusive right to provide central station sprinkler supervisory and waterflow alarm and automatic fire alarm service in New York City, Boston and Philadelphia, and agreed not to provide burglar alarm service in those cities or central station service elsewhere in the United States.

Automatic Fire Protection Co. obtained the exclusive right to provide central station sprinkler supervisory and waterflow alarm service everywhere else in the United States except for the three cities in which AFA received that exclusive right, and agreed not to engage in burglar alarm service.

ADT received the exclusive right to render burglar alarm and nightwatch service throughout the United States. (Under ADT's 1906 agreement with Holmes, however, it could not provide burglar alarm services in the areas for which it had given Holmes the exclusive right to do so.) It agreed not to furnish sprinkler supervisory and waterflow alarm service anywhere in the country and not to furnish automatic fire alarm service in New York City, Boston or Philadelphia (the three cities allocated to AFA). ADT agreed to connect to its central stations the systems installed by AFA and Automatic.

Grinnell agreed to furnish and install all sprinkler supervisory and waterflow alarm actuating devices used in systems that AFA and Automatic would install, and otherwise not to engage in the central station protection business.

AFA and Automatic received 25% of the revenue produced by the sprinkler supervisory waterflow alarm service which they provided in their respective territories; ADT and Grinnell received 50% and 25%, respectively, of the revenue which resulted from such service. The agreements were to continue until February 1954.

The agreements remained substantially unchanged until 1949 when ADT purchased all of Automatic Fire Protection Co.'s rights under it for $13,500,000. After these 1907 agreements expired in 1954, AFA continued to honor the prior division of territories; and ADT and AFA entered into a new contract providing for the continued sharing of revenues on substantially the same basis as before.[25] In 1954 Grinnell and ADT renewed an agreement with a Rhode Island company which received the exclusive right to render central station service within Rhode Island at prices no lower than those of ADT and which agreed to use certain equipment supplied by Grinnell and ADT and to share its revenues with those companies. ADT had an informal agreement with a competing central station company in Washington, D.C., "that we should not solicit each other's accounts."

ADT over the years reduced its minimum basic rates to meet competition and renewed contracts at substantially increased rates in cities where it had a monopoly of accredited central station service. ADT threatened retaliation against firms that contemplated inaugurating central station service. And the record indicates that, in contemplating opening a new central station, ADT officials frequently stressed that such action would deter their competitors from opening a new station in that area.

The District Court found that the defendant companies had committed *per se* violations of § 1 of the Sherman Act as well as § 2 and entered a decree. 236 F.Supp. 244.

---

25. In 1959, ADT complained that AFA's share of the revenues was excessive. AFA replied, in a letter to the president of Grinnell (which by that time controlled both ADT and AFA), that its share was just compensation for its continued observance of the service and territorial restrictions: "*[T]he geographic restrictions placed upon us plus the requirement that we confine our activities to sprinkler and fire alarm services exclusively,* since 1907 and presumably into the future, has definitely retarded our expansion in the past to the benefit of ADT growth.... [AFA's] contribution must also include the many things that helped make ADT big." (Emphasis added.)

The offense of monopoly under § 2 of the Sherman Act has two elements: (1) the possession of monopoly power in the relevant market and (2) the willful acquisition or maintenance of that power as distinguished from growth or development as a consequence of a superior product, business acumen, or historic accident. We shall see that this second ingredient presents no major problem here, as what was done in building the empire was done plainly and explicitly for a single purpose. In United States v. E.I. du Pont De Nemours & Co., 351 U.S. 377, 391, we defined monopoly power as "the power to control prices or exclude competition." The existence of such power ordinarily may be inferred from the predominant share of the market. In American Tobacco Co. v. United States, 328 U.S. 781, 797, we said that "over two-thirds of the entire domestic field of cigarettes and . . . over 80 per cent of the field of comparable cigarettes" constituted "a substantial monopoly." In United States v. Aluminum Co. of America, 2 Cir., 148 F.2d 416, 429, 90% of the market constituted monopoly power. In the present case, 87% of the accredited central station service business leaves no doubt that the congeries of these defendants have monopoly power—power which, as our discussion of the record indicates, they did not hesitate to wield—if that business is the relevant market. The only remaining question therefore is, what is the relevant market?

In case of a product it may be of such a character that substitute products must also be considered, as customers may turn to them if there is a slight increase in the price of the main product. That is the teaching of the du Pont case, viz., that commodities reasonably interchangeable make up that "part" of trade or commerce which § 2 protects against monopoly power.

The District Court treated the entire accredited central station service business as a single market and we think it was justified in so doing. Defendants argue that the different central station services offered are so diverse that they cannot under du Pont be lumped together to make up the relevant market. For example, burglar alarm services are not interchangeable with fire alarm services. They further urge that du Pont requires that protective services other than those of the central station variety be included in the market definition.

But there is here a single use, i.e., the protection of property, through a central station that receives signals. It is that service, accredited, that is unique and that competes with all the other forms of property protection. We see no barrier to combining in a single market a number of different products or services where that combination reflects commercial realities. To repeat, there is here a single basic service—the protection of property through use of a central service station—that must be compared with all other forms of property protection.

In § 2 cases under the Sherman Act, as in § 7 cases under the Clayton Act (Brown Shoe Co. v. United States, 370 U.S. 294, 325), there may be submarkets that are separate economic entities. We do not pursue that question here. First we deal with services, not with products, and second, we conclude that the accredited central station is a type of service that makes up a relevant market and that domination or control of it makes out a monopoly of a "part" of trade or commerce within the meaning of § 2 of the Sherman Act. The defendants have not made out a case for fragmentizing the types of services into lesser units.

Burglar alarm service is in a sense different from fire alarm service; from waterflow alarms; and so on. But it would be unrealistic on this record to break down the market into the various kinds of central station protective services that are available. Central station companies recognize that to compete effectively, they must offer all or nearly all types of service.[26] The different forms of accredited central station service are provided from a single office and customers utilize different services in combination. We held in United States v. Philadelphia Nat'l Bank, 374 U.S. 321, 356, that "the cluster" of services denoted by the term "commercial banking" is "a distinct line of commerce." ... There is, in our view, a comparable cluster of services here. Those bank cases arose under § 7 of the Clayton Act where the question was whether the effect of a merger "in any line of commerce" may be "substantially to lessen competition." We see no reason to differentiate between "line" of commerce in the context of the Clayton Act and "part" of commerce for purposes of the Sherman Act. In the § 7 national bank case just mentioned, *services,* not *products* in the mercantile sense, were involved. In our view the lumping of various kinds of *services* makes for the appropriate market here as it did in the § 7 case.

There are, to be sure, substitutes for the accredited central station service. But none of them appears to operate on the same level as the central station service so as to meet the interchangeability test of the *du Pont* case. Nonautomatic and automatic local alarm systems appear on this record to have marked differences, not the low degree of differentiation required of substitute services as well as substitute articles.

Watchman service is far more costly and less reliable. Systems that set off an audible alarm at the site of a fire or burglary are cheaper but often less reliable. They may be inoperable without anyone knowing it. Moreover, there is a risk that the local ringing of an alarm will not attract the needed attention and help. Proprietary systems that a customer purchases and operates are available; but they can be used only by a very large business or by government and are not realistic alternatives for most concerns. There are also protective services connected directly to a municipal police or fire department. But most cities with an accredited central station do not permit direct, connected service for private businesses. These alternate services and devices differ, we are told, in utility, efficiency, reliability,

---

26. Thus, of the 38 nondefendant firms operating a central service station protective service in the United States in 1961, 24 offered all of the following services: automatic fire alarm; waterflow alarm and sprinkler supervision; watchman's reporting and manual fire alarm; and burglar alarm. Of the other firms, 11 provided no watchman's reporting and manual fire alarm service; six provided no automatic fire alarm service; and two offered no sprinkler supervisory and waterflow alarm service. Moreover, of the 14 firms not providing the full panoply of services, 10 lacked only *one* of the above-described services. Appellant ADT's assertion that "very few accredited central stations furnish the full variety of services" is flatly contradicted by the record.

responsiveness, and continuity, and the record sustains that position. And, as noted, insurance companies generally allow a greater reduction in premiums for accredited central station service than for other types of protection.

Defendants earnestly urge that despite these differences, they face competition from these other modes of protection. They seem to us seriously to overstate the degree of competition, but we recognize that (as the District Court found) they "do not have unfettered power to control the price of their services ... due to the fringe competition of other alarm or watchmen services." 236 F.Supp., at 254. What defendants overlook is that the high degree of differentiation between central station protection and the other forms means that for many customers, only central station protection will do. Though some customers may be willing to accept higher insurance rates in favor of cheaper forms of protection, others will not be willing or able to risk serious interruption to their businesses, even though covered by insurance, and will thus be unwilling to consider anything but central station protection.

The accredited, as distinguished from nonaccredited, service is a relevant part of commerce. Virtually the only central station companies in the status of the nonaccredited are those that have not yet been able to meet the standards of the rating bureau. The accredited ones are indeed those that have achieved, in the eyes of underwriters, superiorities that other central stations do not have. The accredited central station is located in a building of approved design, provided with an emergency lighting system and two alternate main power sources, manned constantly by at least a required minimum of operators, provided with a direct line to fire headquarters and, where possible, a direct line to a police station; and equipped with all the devices, circuits and equipment meeting the requirements of the underwriters. These standards are important as insurance carriers often require accredited central station service as a condition to writing insurance. There is indeed evidence that customers consider the unaccredited service as inferior.

We also agree with the District Court that the geographic market for the accredited central station service is national. The activities of an individual station are in a sense local as it serves, ordinarily, only that area which is within a radius of 25 miles. But the record amply supports the conclusion that the business of providing such a service is operated on a national level. There is national planning. The agreements we have discussed covered activities in many States. The inspection, certification and rate-making is largely by national insurers. The defendant ADT has a national schedule of prices, rates, and terms, though the rates may be varied to meet local conditions. It deals with multi-state businesses on the basis of nationwide contracts. The manufacturing business of ADT is interstate. The fact that Holmes is more nearly local than the others does not save it, for it is part and parcel of the combine presided over and controlled by Grinnell.

rel mkt is one that reflects realities of business

As the District Court found, the relevant market for determining whether the defendants have monopoly power is not the several local areas which the individual stations serve, but the broader national market that reflects the reality of the way in which they built and conduct their business.

We have said enough about the great hold that the defendants have on this market. The percentage is so high as to justify the finding of monopoly. And, as the facts already related indicate, this monopoly was achieved in large part by unlawful and exclusionary practices. The restrictive agreements that preempted for each company a segment of the market where it was free of competition of the others were one device. Pricing practices that contained competitors were another. The acquisition by Grinnell of ADT, AFA, and Holmes were still another. Grinnell long faced a problem of competing with ADT. That was one reason it acquired AFA and Holmes. Prior to settlement of its dispute and controversy with ADT, Grinnell prepared to go into the central station service business. By acquiring ADT in 1953, Grinnell eliminated that alternative. Its control of the three other defendants eliminated any possibility of an outbreak of competition that might have occurred when the 1907 agreements terminated. By those acquisitions it perfected the monopoly power to exclude competitors and fix prices. . . .

The final decree enjoins the defendants in general terms from restraining trade or attempting or conspiring to restrain trade in this particular market, from further monopolizing, and attempting or conspiring to monopolize. The court ordered the alarm companies to file with the Department of Justice standard lists of prices and terms and every quotation to customers that deviated from those lists and enjoined the defendants from acquiring stock, assets, or business of any enterprise in the market. Grinnell was ordered to file, not later than April 1, 1966, a plan of divestiture of its stock in each of the other defendant companies. It was given the option either to sell the stock or distribute it to its stockholders or combine or vary those methods. The court further enjoined any of the defendants from employing in any capacity the President and Chairman of the Board of Grinnell, James D. Fleming. Both the Government and the defendants challenge aspects of the decree.

goal of remedy

We start from the premise that adequate relief in a monopolization case should put an end to the combination and deprive the defendants of any of the benefits of the illegal conduct, and break up or render impotent the monopoly power found to be in violation of the Act. That is the teaching of our cases, notably Schine Theatres v. United States, 334 U.S. 110, 128–129.

We largely agree with the Government's views on the relief aspect of the case. We start with ADT, which presently does 73% of the business done by accredited central stations throughout the country. It is indeed the keystone of the defendants' monopoly power. The mere dissolution of the combination through the divestiture by Grinnell of its interests in the other companies does not reach the root of the evil. In 92 of the 115 cities in which ADT operates there are no other accredited central stations. Perhaps some cities could not support more than one. Defendants recognized prior to trial that at least 13 cities can; the Government urged divestiture in 48 cities. That there should be some divestiture on the part of ADT seems clear; but the details of such divestiture must be determined by the District Court as the matter cannot be resolved on this record.

Two of the means by which ADT acquired and maintained its large share of the market are the requirement that subscribers sign five-year contracts and the retention by ADT of title to the protective services equipment installed on a subscriber's premises. On this record it appears that these practices constitute substantial barriers to competition and that relief against them is appropriate. The *pros* and *cons* are argued with considerable vehemence here.[27] Again, we cannot resolve them on this record. The various aspects of this controversy must be explored by the District Court and suitable protective provisions included in the decree that deprive these two devices of the coercive power that they apparently have had towards restraining competition and creating a monopoly.

The Government proposed that the defendants be required to sell, on nondiscriminatory terms, any devices manufactured by them for use in furnishing central station service. It seems clear that if the competitors are to be able to compete effectively for the existing customers of the defendants when the present service contracts expire, they must be assured of replacement parts to maintain those systems.

. . .

Defendants urge and the Government concedes that the barring of Mr. Fleming from the employment of any of the defendants is unduly harsh and quite unnecessary on this record. While relief of that kind may be appropriate where the predatory conduct is conspicuous, we cannot see that any such case was made out on this record.

. . .

The defendants object to the requirements that Grinnell divest itself of its holdings in the three alarm company defendants, but we think that provision is wholly justified. Dissolution of the combination is essential as indicated by many of our cases, starting with Standard Oil Co. v. United States, 221 U.S. 1, 78. The defendants object to that portion of the decree that bars them from acquiring interests in firms in the accredited central station business. But since acquisition was one of the methods by which the

dissolution totes approp.

----

27. Specifically, the areas of disagreement are: (1) Defendants urge that barring them from offering five-year contracts would put them at a competitive disadvantage *vis-à-vis* nondefendant firms; the Government responds that since they violated the law, they may properly be subjected to restrictions not borne by others. See United States v. Bausch & Lomb Co., 321 U.S. 707, 723–724. (2) Some customers of defendants may wish to have long-term contracts; the Government responds that this may be explored on remand. (3) There is some dispute as to whether, if the central station company cannot retain title to the equipment it installs, the insurance companies will accredit the system. This, too, is a proper subject for inquiry on remand.

defendants acquired their market power and was the method by which Grinnell put the combination together, an injunction against the repetition of the practice seems fully warranted. . . .

The judgment below is affirmed except as to the decree. We remand for further hearings on the nature of the relief. . . .

■ MR. JUSTICE FORTAS, with whom MR. JUSTICE STEWART, joins, dissenting. I agree that the judgment below should be reversed, but I do not agree that the remand should be limited to reshaping the decree. Because I believe that the definition of the relevant market here cannot be sustained, I would reverse and remand for a new determination of this basic issue, subject to proper standards.

We have here a case under both § 1 and § 2 of the Sherman Act, which proscribe combinations in restraint of trade, and monopolies and attempts to monopolize. The judicial task is not difficult to state: Does the record show a combination in restraint of trade or a monopoly or attempt to monopolize? If so, what are its characteristics, scope and effect? And, finally, what is the appropriate remedy for a court of equity to decree?

Each of these inquiries depends upon two basic referents: definition of the geographical area of trade or commerce restrained or monopolized, and of the products or services involved. In § 1 cases this problem ordinarily presents little difficulty because the combination in restraint of trade itself delineates the "market" with sufficient clarity to support the usual injunctive form of relief in those cases. *See, e.g.*, United States v. Griffith, 334 U.S. 100. In the present case, however, the essence of the offense is monopolization, achieved or attempted, and the major relief is divestiture. For these purposes, "market" definition is of the essence, just as in § 7 cases the kindred definition of the "line of commerce" is fundamental. We must define the area of commerce that is allegedly engrossed before we can determine its engrossment; and we must define it before a decree can be shaped to deal with the consequences of the monopoly, and to restore or produce competition.

In § 2 cases, the search for "the relevant market" must be undertaken and pursued with relentless clarity. It is, in essence, an economic task put to the uses of the law. Unless this task is well done, the results will be distorted in terms of the conclusion as to whether the law has been violated and what the decree should contain.

In this case, the relevant geographical and product markets have not been defined on the basis of the economic facts of the industry concerned. They have been tailored precisely to fit defendants' business. The Government proposed and the trial court concluded that the relevant market is not the business of fire protection, or burglary protection, or protection against waterflow, etc., or all of these together. It is not even the business of furnishing these from a central location. It is the business, viewed nationally, of supplying "insurance accredited central station protection services." (CSPS)—that is, fire, burglary and other kinds of protection furnished from a central station that is accredited by insurance companies.

The business of defendants fits neatly into the product and geographic market so defined. In fact, it comes close to filling the market so defined. This Court has now approved this Procrustean definition.

[handwritten: Greek mythology — geo should be local, not nat'l]

The geographical market is defined as nationwide. But the need and the service are intensely local—more local by far, for example, than the market which this Court found to be local in United States v. Philadelphia Nat. Bank, 374 U.S. 321, 357–362. The premises protected do not travel. They are fixed locations. They must be protected where they are. Protection must be provided on the spot. It must be furnished by local personnel able to bring help to the scene within minutes. Even the central stations can provide service only within a 25–mile radius. Where the tenants of the premises turn to central stations for this service, they must make their contracts locally with the central station and purchase their services from it on the basis of local conditions.

But because these defendants, the trial court found, are connected by stock ownership, interlocking management and some degree of national corporate direction, and because there is some national participation in selling as well as national financing, advertising, purchasing of equipment, and the like,[28] the court concluded that the competitive area to be considered is national. This Court now affirms that conclusion.

This is a nonsequitur. It is not permissible to seize upon the nationwide scope of defendants' operation and to bootstrap a geographical definition of the market from this. The purpose of the search for the relevant geographical market is to find the area or areas to which a potential buyer may rationally look for the goods or services that he seeks. The test, as this Court said in United States v. Philadelphia Nat. Bank, is "the geographic structure of supplier-customer relations," 374 U.S. 321, 357, quoting Kaysen and Turner, Antitrust Policy 102 (1959). And as Mr. Justice Clark put it in Tampa Electric Co. v. Nashville Coal Co., 365 U.S. 320, 327, the definition of the relevant market requires "careful selection of the market area in which the seller operates, and to which the purchaser can practicably turn for supplies." The central issue is where does a potential buyer look for potential suppliers of the service—what is the geographical area in which the buyer has, or, in the absence of monopoly, would have, a real choice as to price and alternative facilities? This depends upon the facts of the market place, taking into account such economic factors as the distance over which supplies and services may be feasibly furnished, consistently with cost and functional efficiency.

[handwritten: reason for geo mkt def]

The incidental aspects of defendants' business which the court uses cannot control the outcome of this inquiry. They do not measure the market area in which buyer and sellers meet. They have little impact upon the ascertainment of the geographical areas in which the economic and

---

28. There is a danger that this Court's opinion will be read as somewhat overstating the case. There is neither finding or record to support the implication that rates are to any substantial extent fixed on a nationwide basis, or that there are nationwide contracts with multi-state businesses in any significant degree, or that insurers inspect or certify central stations on a nationwide basis.

legal questions must be answered: have defendants "monopolized" or "restrained" trade; have they eliminated or can they eliminate competitors or prevent or obstruct new entries into the business; have they controlled or can they control price for the services? These are the issues; and, in defendants' business, a finding that the "relevant market" is national is nothing less than a studied failure to assess the effect of defendants' position and practices in the light of the competition which exists, or could exist, in economically defined areas—in the real world.

Here, there can be no doubt that the correct geographic market is local. The services at issue are intensely local: they can be furnished only locally. The business as it is done is local—not nationwide. If, as might well be the case on this record, defendants were found to have violated the Sherman Act in a number of these local areas, a proper decree, directed to those markets, as well as to general corporate features relevant to the condemned practices, could be fashioned. On the other hand, a gross definition of the market as nationwide leads to a gross, nationwide decree which does not address itself to the realities of the market place. This is what happened here: The District Court's finding that the market was *nationwide* logically led it to a decree which operated on the only *national* aspect of the situation, the parent company nexus, instead of on the economically realistic areas—the local situations. This Court now directs the trial court to require "some [unspecified] divestiture" locally by the alarm companies. This is a recognition of the economic reality that the relevant competitive areas are local. In plain terms, the Court's direction to the trial court means a "market-by-market" analysis for the purpose of breaking up defendants' monopoly position and creating competitors and competition wherever feasible in particular cities. In my view, however, by so directing, the Court implies that which it does not command: that the case should be reconsidered at the trial court level because of the improper standard it used to define the relevant geographic markets.

The trial court's definition of the "product" market even more dramatically demonstrates that its action has been Procrustean—that it has tailored the market to the dimensions of the defendants. It recognizes that a person seeking protective services has many alternative sources. It lists "watchmen, watchdogs, automatic proprietary systems confined to one site (often, but not always), alarm systems connected with some local police or fire station, often unaccredited CSPS [central station protective services], and often accredited CSPS." The court finds that even in the same city a single customer seeking protection for several premises may "exercise its option" differently for different locations. It may choose accredited CSPS for one of its locations and a different type of service for another.

But the court isolates from all of these alternatives only those services in which defendants engage. It eliminates all of the alternative sources despite its conscientious enumeration of them. Its definition of the "relevant market" is not merely confined to "central station" protective services, but to those central station protective services which are "accredited" by insurance companies.

There is no pretense that these furnish peculiar services for which there is no alternative in the market place, on either a price or a functional basis. The court relies solely upon its finding that the services offered by accredited central stations are of better quality, and upon its conclusion that the insurance companies tend to give "noticeably larger" discounts to policyholders who are accredited central station protective services. This Court now approved this strange red-haired, bearded, one-eyed man-with-a-limp classification. . . .

. . .

I do not suggest that wide disparities in quality, price and customer appeal could never affect the definition of the market. But this follows only where the disparities are so great that they create separate and distinct categories of buyers and sellers. The record here and the findings do not approach this standard. They fall far short of justifying the narrowing of the market as practiced here. I need refer only to the exclusion of non-accredited central stations, which the court seeks to justify by reference to differentials in insurance discounts. This differential may indeed affect the relative cost to the consumer of the competing modes of protection. But, in the absence of proof that it results in eliminating the competing services from the category of those to which the purchaser "can practicably turn" for supplies, it does not justify their total exclusion. This sort of exclusion of the supposedly not-quite-so-attractive service from the basic definition of the kinds of business and service against which defendants' activity will be measured, is entirely unjustified on this record. . . .[29]

---

29. The dissenting opinion of Harlan, J., is omitted.

The opinion of Wyzanski, J., below, 236 F.Supp. 244, 247–48 (D.R.I.1964), contained the following observations:

With regard to § 2 of the Sherman Act . . . in the two decades since the opinion of Judge Learned Hand in United States v. Aluminum Co. of America, 2nd Cir., 148 F.2d 416 (1945), most of the cognoscenti have expected that a day would come when the Supreme Court would announce that where one or more persons acting jointly had acquired so clear a dominance in a market as to have the power to exclude competition therefrom, there was a *rebuttable* presumption that such power had been criminally acquired and was a monopolizing punishable under § 2. To be sure, the putative offender would be allowed to avoid or defeat this presumption if he bore the burden of proving that this share of the market was the result of superior skill, superior products, natural advantages, technological or economic efficiency, scientific research, low margins of profit maintained permanently and without discrimination, legal licenses, or the like. Cf. United States v. United Shoe Machinery Corp., D.Mass., 110 F.Supp. 295, aff'd 347 U.S. 521. Such a shifting of the burden not merely of going forward, but of proof, such a rebuttable presumption rests on the by-now dozens of court records which make it quite clear that it is the highly exceptional case, a *rara avis* more often found in academic groves than in the thickets of business, where monopoly power was thrust upon an enterprise by the economic character of the industry and by what Judge L. Hand in *Aluminum* called "superior skill, foresight and industry." More than 7 decades of Sherman Act enforcement leave the informed observer with the abiding conviction that durable non-statutory monopolies (ones created without patents or licenses or lasting beyond their term) are, to a moral certainty, due to acquisitions of competitors or restraints of trade prohibited by § 1. They are the achievement of the quiet life after the enemy's capitulation or his defeat in inglorious battle.

NOTES AND QUESTIONS

1. In *Grinnell*, the majority said a violation of Section 2 occurs when a company with monopoly power willfully acquires or maintains that power, "as distinguished from growth or development as a consequence of a superior product, business acumen or historic accident." That language, if read as an acceptance of the *Alcoa* approach, would, of course, make it difficult for any company to obtain a dominant position in any market without violating Section 2.

Why not go the next step and explicitly eliminate the "conduct" element in Section 2 cases? In 1979, the National Commission for the Review of Antitrust Laws and Procedures (NCRALP), a group of antitrust experts under the leadership of the Assistant Attorney General for Antitrust, recommended that Congress conduct hearings to explore the advisability of an amendment to Section 2 to cover "no-fault" violations. No-fault proposals usually provide that substantial, persistent single-firm monopoly power will violate Section 2 regardless of whether it was achieved or maintained by objectionable conduct. The essential point is that monopoly is undesirable in a free market system regardless of how it was achieved, and that enormous time and resources are expended in Section 2 litigation—up to 40% in discovery and trial time according to recent studies—to explore "conduct" issues. Almost all no-fault proposals are limited to government civil suits, have minimum trigger figures (the FTC's submission to NCRALP suggested $500 million in sales in the relevant market), and require a finding of persistent or durable monopoly power (*e.g.*, 5 or 10 years). No-fault proposals usually provide exemptions for natural monopoly (*i.e.*, situations where there is not sufficient demand to support two efficiently operated firms), and some create a defense where it can be shown that the monopoly power derives solely from production and distribution efficiencies.

What's wrong with the concept of a no-fault violation of Section 2? Would such an amendment create undesirable disincentives for aggressive competition; specifically, would large companies avoid aggressive competitive action out of fear that they would become a no-fault monopolist and then be summarily dismembered? Would the cost to society of this kind of anticipatory avoidance be greater than the current cost of monopoly profits? Is the proposal "unfair" to corporate managers and shareholders? Or should those two groups welcome the new career and profit opportunities that could result if a giant company were split into five aggressive competitors?

NCRALP's suggestion that Congress hold hearings on the no-fault issue has been studiously ignored, and the concept is no longer being pursued.

2. Are you satisfied with the majority view that Grinnell operated in a national geographic market? Could individual users rationally seek CSPS protection

---

To this Court it appears that the day has come for it, and more important for counsel, to proceed on the acknowledged principle that once the Government has borne the burden of proving what is the relevant market and how predominant a share of that market defendant has, it follows that there are rebuttable presumptions that defendant has monopoly power and has monopolized in violation of § 2. The Government need not prove, and in a well-conducted trial ought not to be allowed to consume time in needlessly proving, defendant's predatory tactics, if any, or defendant's pricing, or production, or selling, or leasing, or marketing, or financial policies while in this predominant role. If defendant does wish to go forward, it is free to do so and to maintain the burden of showing that its eminence is traceable to such highly respectable causes as superiority in means and methods which are "honestly industrial," as Judge Hand characterized the supposititious socially desirable monopolizer.

from suppliers located throughout the country? Are you satisfied that the factors cited by the court at p. 157 overcome the otherwise local nature of the market, or might the court have been influenced to choose a national market in order to justify the relief it imposed?

KEY ISSUES RAISED BY *CELLOPHANE* AND GRINNELL AND CURRENT VIEWS ON RELEVANT MARKET

As we have seen, definition of relevant market is an analytical tool to assist in estimating the market power of a firm or group of firms. Essentially, it is an attempt to identify those firms that would at once be looked to as offering alternatives if one or more sellers of a product raises its price.

In theory and practice, relevant market definition is as difficult an undertaking as any in antitrust. How do we decide whether Coca–Cola or the New York Times should be regarded as monopolies? The sellers of each of these products have some discretion in setting price—partly because each is in some degree different from all possible substitutes, and partly because buyers perceive the products to be different. But when the sellers of these products seek to exercise that discretion—raising prices and curtailing output—competition from substitutes will soon be encountered.

There is, of course, no such thing as pure monopoly, in the sense of absolute discretion over price, because at some point a further price increase will lead some consumers to switch to less satisfactory products, or to withdraw from the market.

Between the poles of absolute market power and zero market power are an infinite array of market possibilities, on both the demand and supply sides. Thus, market definition involves matters of degree, approximation, and judgment. The Supreme Court's decisions in the *Cellophane* and *Grinnell* cases provide the framework for market analysis under Section 2 of the Sherman Act. The problem, of course, is that the market approaches in the two cases differ and each case—for different reasons—raises significant analytical questions. Added complexity comes by way of market definition precedents from other areas of antitrust (*e.g.*, merger precedents) and developing views on market definition and power articulated by leading economists. Set forth below are critiques of the *Cellophane* and *Grinnell* opinions and appraisals of the adequacy and practicality of various approaches to the task of defining relevant market.

1. **The *Cellophane* and *Grinnell* cases.** In its *Cellophane* decision, the Supreme Court found that cellophane competed with Pliofilm, Saran Wrap, wax paper, and other flexible wrapping materials for a wide range of end uses. It found that if du Pont raised the price of cellophane even slightly, it would lose substantial sales to these other materials. If prices of the other materials changed, cellophane sales would be affected. This competitive feature it denominated "cross-elasticity of demand," borrowing a technical concept of economic analysis.[30] The Court found

---

30. "Elasticity of demand" is the percentage change in the quantity of a product sold resulting from a percentage change in price. If a small percentage change leads to great increases or decreases in the volume of sale, demand is said to be elastic; if it results in only slight changes in volume, demand is said to be inelastic.

Economists attach numbers to these concepts. If the price of product A is increased two per cent and a four per cent decrease in sales results, an economist would describe the elasticity of demand as 2. If a two per cent increase in the price of a product resulted in only a one per cent decrease in demand, the elasticity would be ½.

that even though cellophane costs "two or three times as much, surface measure, as its chief competitors," p. 138 *supra*, and even though there were pronounced differences from the other wrapping materials in functional characteristics, the cross-elasticity of demand between cellophane and the other products was nevertheless sufficient to warrant including them in the same product market. By defining the relevant product market as "flexible wrapping materials," rather than "cellophane," the Court was able to conclude that du Pont had less than 20% rather than about 75% of the relevant market.

One problem with the *Cellophane* approach is that it involves circular reasoning. A firm with significant market power will normally set a price just high enough so that if it raised the price another notch, the price increase would not increase profits because of the business that would be lost. Thus, the fact that du Pont would lose business to other flexible wraps if it raised the current price slightly is entirely consistent with its possessing market power. Du Pont's current price could include an abnormally high profit level.

As we will see in Chapter 9, which deals with mergers, during the 1980s, the Department of Justice adopted merger guidelines which set forth an analytical framework for defining relevant markets and then elaborated a methodology for applying that definition to given cases.[31] Those guidelines have the same failing as the *Cellophane* case when dealing with *exercised* market power. As one group of commentators put it:

> The Justice Department's merger guidelines begin by taking the product of one of the merging firms and asking whether a coordinated, significant price increase above the current level by all the firms making the product would be profitable. The hypothesized increase usually is a five percent price rise lasting one year. If the hypothesized increase would be profitable, those firms constitute a relevant market.
>
> The most obvious problem with this approach ... is that the guidelines will not identify as a relevant market the product of a profit-maximizing monopolist.... A single firm that already is maximizing profits cannot, by definition, increase profits by raising its price further. Thus, this single firm cannot constitute a relevant market under the Justice Department's approach. Consider, for example, the case of a firm charged with monopolization for excluding all other producers of a particular product, but which faces a competitive fringe comprised of a large number of small producers of a substitute product, each of which can produce an unlimited amount at some constant unit cost level. That firm might set its price at the level just below the value consumers place on the substitute, such that any further price increase would eliminate virtually all of its sales. As a result, under the Justice Department's test, the relevant market would include the substitute products. If the firm's share of capacity in that broader market was small, the Justice Department would conclude that it had no market power. Because a finding of market power is a

---

Cross-elasticity—the concept cited by the Supreme Court in *Cellophane*- concerns the relative demand of one product compared to another. If product A is an excellent substitute for product B, then a slight increase in the price of B should lead to a substantial increase in volume of sales of product A at the expense of product B. That situation would be described as one of high cross-elasticity of demand. The Supreme Court in *Cellophane* apparently believed that all products with high cross-elasticities of demand belong in the same relevant product market. As we shall see, that is an incomplete analysis of the market definition issue.

31. *See* Chapter 9, p. 965 *infra*.

prerequisite to a section 2 violation, that firm's exclusionary conduct would be immunized.[32]

In the monopoly context, one way of avoiding the *Cellophane* fallacy is to focus on the degree of cross-elasticity of demand at the price that would provide only normal competitive profits. If current prices are used, the relevant cross-elasticities would be those among alternative products, if any, with price structures that have the same relationship to cost, *i.e.*, whose cost/price ratios are the same.

In *Grinnell* the Supreme Court noted that some buyers had a special preference for accredited central station protective service (CSPS)—for many customers "only central station protection will do," p. 157 *supra*. It defined CSPS as a separate product market, using the concept of "submarket." A Fifth Circuit decision described the submarket concept as follows:

> Antitrust law recognizes that economically significant submarkets may exist which themselves constitute relevant product markets. The fact finder may determine a submarket exists by "examining such practical indicia as industry or public recognition of the sub-market as a separate economic entity, the product's peculiar characteristics and uses, unique production facilities, distinct customers, distinct prices, sensitivity to price changes, and specialized vendors." *Brown Shoe,* 370 U.S. at 325.[33]

In *Grinnell* the Supreme Court focused on the existence of a vulnerable group of buyers. Would it be appropriate to carve out a separate market (*i.e.*, decide that a seller is a monopolist) every time there is a class of purchasers that has a decided preference for a seller's particular product? With almost any consumer product—consider Coca–Cola and the New York Times again—there will be a class of customers who greatly prefer the product. Should the criterion be how large the class? How strong the preference? There was no finding in *Grinnell* as to what percentage of purchasers had a preference for CSPS, or how much more they were being charged or would be willing to pay.

While neither the *Cellophane* nor the *Grinnell* approach is entirely satisfactory, there is an important difference between the market situations in the two cases that may partially explain their outcomes. Most cellophane users did have acceptable alternatives, since most categories of purchasers (produce packers, bakers, etc.) used or could use other wrappings than cellophane. Users for whom substitutes were poor—such as the cigarette manufacturers, reluctant to market their product in Saran Wrap or wax paper—were protected to some extent by the fact that, if need be, they could arrange to buy cellophane from the channels of supply to those other users or in "arbitrage" transactions. For example, if du Pont were to attempt to double the price of cellophane to the cigarette companies ("captive users," because for them there were no reasonable substitutes) while maintaining the price to bakers ("precarious users," because they would shift to other wraps if even a slight price increase were announced), the bakers or their suppliers could offer cellophane at a slight profit to the cigarette companies. Since cigarette companies constituted only a fairly small part of total sales, this possibility would offer them important protection, unless du Pont could prevent such sales by policing channels of distribution.

---

32. Krattenmaker, Lande & Salop, Monopoly Power and Market Power in Antitrust Law, 76 Geo.L.J. 241, 256 (1987).

33. Domed Stadium Hotel, Inc. v. Holiday Inns, Inc., 732 F.2d 480, 487–88 (5th Cir. 1984).

In *Grinnell,* in contrast, customers were buyers of "services," as the Court notes, p. 162 *supra,* and each protection service contract was presumably independently negotiated. If the seller of CSPS could identify users who were strongly attracted to its product, it could raise price to such users without concern that they might be able to protect their position by buying from others who paid a lower price. Since arbitrage in services is usually impossible, it may be necessary to define the market narrowly in such cases if captive users are to be protected against discretionary market power.

2. **Standardized vs. differentiated products.** When products are identical or regarded as perfect substitutes, the real test of market power derives from the relative efficiency (*i.e.,* unit costs of production) of each producer. Suppose there are five producers of identical products, and each has 20% of the market and essentially similar costs. No one seller can significantly increase its market share without being checked by the competitive response of the others. But suppose further, given the same market structure, that unit costs of one of the sellers are 30% below the others. Assuming the low-cost producer has unused capacity, it might lower its price to a point where none of its rivals could respond, and take as much of the market as it chose (unless and until its increased volume resulted in costs increased to a level comparable to those of its rivals). In terms of market power, it is a matter of indifference whether a company earns (or dissipates) a 30% profit on a 20% market share, or a 15% profit on a 90% market share. In the first instance, it is a "latent monopolist" with the power to exclude its competitors; in the latter, it has exercised that power in order to obtain an overwhelming market share.

Where products differ—in physical characteristics or perceived desirability—the problem of market definition is more difficult. A common situation involves a set of producers of competing products that are more or less valued for different attributes by different groups of buyers. For example, cellophane was recognized as having physical properties (transparency, bursting strength, impermeability, etc.) which resulted in its being preferred in different degrees by different classes of purchasers. Du Pont, as the sole producer of cellophane, had some degree of market power with respect to each group of purchasers; its overall market power at any given price level would depend upon: (1) the size of each such group; (2) the strength of each group's preference for cellophane; (3) the relative costs of each substitute product; (4) whether new entrants were expected to appear at a higher price level for cellophane; and (5) the ability of du Pont to discriminate in price among various groups of users.

With data providing answers to all five questions, it would be possible to make at least a preliminary estimate of du Pont's market power. Unfortunately, the kind of information necessary to make such judgments will almost never be available, to say nothing of its being amenable to the judicial process. First, cost of production and profit data are difficult to ascertain and exist, if at all, in the books of defendant companies. Companies tend to resist disclosure efforts and, even when outsiders can obtain access, they must worry about the accuracy of the information. Second, information as to how different groups of purchasers will react at a given time to a price increase at a range of price levels is never available, and estimates are unlikely to be very reliable. If the price of cellophane were raised from $1.00 per surface unit to $1.10, what would tobacco companies, fresh fruit packers, candy companies, frozen food packers, and bakers do? Some would switch immediately to substitutes, others would regard cellophane as a bargain at an even higher price, and a third group might hedge its bets while awaiting future price developments. Since a comparable price rise usually will not actually have occurred, estimates will necessarily be speculative. In any event, the amount and complexity of information necessary to measure market power with a high degree of accuracy would swamp any trial court. This may be the most important reason why the courts, in *Cellophane, Grinnell,* and other cases, have sought more manageable shortcut approaches to relevant market questions.

3. **Added complications.** Even if the cost, price, and customer preference data were adequate to produce some tentative conclusion about market share, there would be other important factors to be taken into account.

(a) *Time.* The foregoing information would provide a somewhat fuzzy snapshot at some point in time of a seller's market power, but markets are dynamic and that position may well be expanding or eroding. New products or production processes may appear at any moment to undercut a dominant market position, or a patent or other temporary advantage may be expiring. Hence, current market power may predictably be transitory. It has occasionally been suggested that monopoly antitrust cases take so long to litigate that market power that may have existed when the complaint was filed will have been dissipated by the time trial is over and appeals exhausted. On the other hand, a superior product or process may be in the early stages of eliminating all rivals so that present market share bears little relationship to reasonably predictable future market power.

(b) *Barriers to entry of potential competition.* The existence of potential entrants may constrain market power; thus they should somehow be encompassed within the definition of relevant market, although they have no current market share. Put another way, if there are insignificant or no barriers to new entry, so that if a seller raised price even a fraction of a cent, it would be swamped by new competition, that seller regardless of its current market share has no market power. For example, suppose a seller dominates the current supply of a specialized kind of unpatented microfilm. Suppose further that three large film manufacturers do not currently make such microfilm but could do so by minor changes in existing machinery or the addition of an inexpensive chemical ingredient. The current market for microfilm might appear to be monopolized, using all the demand and cost data described above, but the existence of substantial potential entrants, capable of cheaply and promptly increasing the availability of the product, sharply limits the market power of the microfilm "monopolist."

Potential competition can derive from a number of sources. As in the example discussed above, existing manufacturers who make a slightly different product can modify their manufacturing process to compete in an adjacent product market (often referred to as "supply substitutability"). Similarly, manufacturers currently serving a remote market can divert their production into the monopolist's market ("geographic diversion"). Firms actively competing in the market but operating at less than full capacity can expand their operations. Finally, companies entirely outside the product and geographic market may be able to invest quickly in new facilities and become competitors ("new entrants") if a current monopolist attempts to exploit its market position by charging excessive prices.

(c) *Countervailing buyer power.* The dominant supplier of a particular ingredient may be a small company whose only customer is an industrial giant. The large company may have bargaining resources that limit the market power of the supplier, regardless of current market share. For example, it might be able to induce small competitors of the dominant firm to deviate from the monopoly price by offering a very large contract. It might also enter into the manufacture of its own supply of the ingredient in question or break down the monopoly price with a credible threat of entry, or it might encourage other firms to enter the market with the offer of a substantial, long-term contract.

(d) *Conduct evidence.* Often an indication of a firm's market power can be obtained inferentially from the way it behaves in the marketplace. A firm may raise prices in a period of declining demand with no loss of sales volume, engage in effective price discrimination, or drive competitors out of the market through product innovation, distribution methods or advertising, even though it enjoys no apparent cost advantage. It may raise or maintain price above competitive levels by raising the costs of its rivals by, for example, exclusionary conduct.[34] In such cases, the behavior itself may demonstrate market power and properly be taken into account. On the other hand, there can be many explanations for an apparent ability to control market price or exclude competitors, and such "conduct" evidence of market power must be handled with a high degree of care.

4. **Conclusion.** Courts often do face extremely close relevant market questions. For example, does domestic sherry compete with imported sauternes? Does a department store at a shopping mall with good public transportation compete with downtown stores three miles away? Does bus transportation compete with subways? Do sales of soft drinks through vending machines compete with sales of the same soft drinks in supermarkets? Do industry anticipated top-grossing motion pictures compete with other first-run films? In these cases it is important for courts to remember that market definition is no more than a tool for estimating market power, not a scientific test that produces precise results.

Difficulties arise in two main ways. First, a trial court, perhaps considering itself required to do so by Supreme Court opinions, permits or requires the parties to exhaust enormous resources, energies, and litigation efforts in an essentially fruitless search for some ideal of relevant market. The case may go on almost endlessly, or the party with fewest resources for pretrial proceedings, expert witnesses, market research, and such paraphernalia, eventually collapses. Second, having invested heavily, often with less than satisfying results, in this unusual fact-finding venture, the court feels impelled to make use of the results in its findings and opinion, perhaps making it appear more cogent and relevant to the decision than it in fact was. The worst outcome is when—as might appear to be the case in *Cellophane*—the market *share* figure thus produced is treated as dispositive and the proceeding is terminated without the ultimate question of market *power* having been adequately dealt with. Having made a close call on market definition, the court usually proceeds to count (or not to count) percentage market shares on an all-or-nothing basis, forgetting the number of difficult judgments involved and the approximate nature of the underlying market decision. This kind of mechanical jurisprudence, more frequently than the application of "wrong" relevant market rules, is what produces so much costly wasted effort in the courtroom and error and confusion in the cases.

Given the difficulties of proof and the dangers of trying to seem more "scientific" than the process warrants, it probably would make more sense in close cases for trial courts (at least where bench trials are involved) to select tentatively a plausible market definition as to which some usable market data are available, and then investigate to determine whether existing or potential substitutes, cost differences among producers, entry conditions, and dynamic factors in the marketplace indicate the existence of durable and significant market power. An important consideration in taking any line of evidence into account is the practical one of assessing the quality of the data available and the nature of problems that will be encountered in introducing such evidence into a legal proceeding. This first-cut approach would

---

34. *See* Krattenmaker, Lande & Salop, Monopoly Power and Market Power in Antitrust Law, 76 Geo.L.J. 241 (1987).

allow trials to proceed without committing judges or the parties to final judgments about the market before all the relevant evidence is in.

PROBLEM 1

THE BATTLE FOR SAWVILLE

For a number of years there have been three "regular" motion picture theaters and one "art" house in Sawville, New York, a suburb of New York City about a 40–minute drive from Times Square. The "art" house—the Frolic—has a policy of showing foreign films and more esoteric films of independent domestic producers not regularly handled by national distributors; the films are almost always "X-rated" or have not been submitted for classification. There has only been sufficient demand for "art films" in Sawville to permit profitable operations by one theater, but the management of the Frolic has noticed that its theater is increasingly filled to capacity and sometimes patrons must be turned away.

The Frolic is locally owned. It charges more than the three regular theaters for general evening admission ($12 as compared to $9), and, unlike the other three, is open every weekday evening for a midnight show. The Frolic is closed all day Sunday. A study for a local newspaper showed that almost all patrons of the Frolic have visited the other three movie theaters at least once in the previous six months, and about 30% of the patrons of the three regular theaters have attended the Frolic at least once in the last six months.

The closest art houses to Sawville are in mid-town New York and they charge, on the average, an admission price of $10. Sawville's local cable company, which is owned by a non-profit corporation with strong moral and ethical commitments, has refused to show "X-rated" films, but such films are available on DVD (at an average rental of $5 per day), for home video use, in Sawville.

The Frolic has earned about 30% on its investment in each of the last three years, while the three regular theaters have earned about 10% on investment. One reason for the difference in profitability is that the Frolic spends little on advertising, new equipment, decor, and maintenance.

There is one empty building in Sawville—an auditorium once used for club meetings and amateur theater productions—that could be converted promptly and without great expense to a movie theater. About six months ago there were rumors that Read Theaters, a large East Coast chain of art houses, was negotiating to purchase the building and convert it into an art house. Whether the rumors were true or not, the Frolic's owners purchased the empty building announcing that they believed demand in Sawville would soon be sufficiently great to support a second profitable art theater operation. To date, however, the building remains dark and the Frolic remains the only art theater in Sawville.

Does the Frolic have monopoly power? Has it violated Section 2 of the Sherman Act?

COMPARATIVE NOTE ON ARTICLE 82 AND THE "ABUSE OF DOMINANT POSITION" IN THE EC

Article 82 of the Treaty of Rome provides that any "abuse by one or more undertakings of a dominant position within the Common Market or in a substantial part of it" is prohibited if it may affect trade between member states. *See* p. 13 *supra*. A "dominant position" for purposes of Article 82 is the analogue to the possession of monopoly power for purposes of Section 2 of the Sherman Act. The European Court of Justice explained the concept of "dominant position" in the early case of Hoffmann–LaRoche v. Commission, 1979 ECR 461, [1978–1979 Transfer Binder] Comm. Mkt. Rep. (CCH) ¶ 8527 at 7542–43 (ECJ 1979):

> Article [82] is an application of the general objective of the activities of the Community laid down in Article [3] of the Treaty, namely, the institution of a system ensuring that competition in the Common Market is not distorted. Article [82] prohibits any abuse by an undertaking of a dominant position in a substantial part of the Common Market in so far as it may affect trade between Member States. The dominant position thus referred to related to a position of economic strength enjoyed by an undertaking which enables it to prevent effective competition being maintained in the relevant market by affording it the power to behave to an appreciable extent independently of its competitors, its customers and ultimately of the consumers.

> Such a position does not preclude some competition, which it does where there is a monopoly or a quasi-monopoly, but enables the undertaking which profits by it, if not to determine at least to have an appreciable influence on the conditions under which that competition will develop, and in any case to act largely in disregard of it so long as such conduct does not operate to its detriment.

More recently, the Court of First Instance had the following to say about the way that a dominant position can be demonstrated, in the case of Amministrazione Autonoma dei Monopoli di Stato (AAMS) v. EC Commission, Case No. T–139/98, [2002] 4 CMLR 10 (CFI 5th Chamber 2001):

> It is settled case law that very large market shares are in themselves, and save in exceptional circumstances, evidence of the existence of a dominant position. An undertaking which has a very large market share and holds it for some time, by means of the volume of production and the scale of the supply for which it stands—without holders of much smaller market shares being able to meet rapidly the demand from those who would like to break away from the undertaking which has the largest market share—is by virtue of that share in a position of strength which makes it an unavoidable trading partner and which, because of this alone, secures for it, at the very least during relatively long periods, that freedom of action which is the special feature of a dominant position. Moreover, a dominant position is a position of economic strength enjoyed by an undertaking which enables it to prevent effective competition being maintained on the relevant market by giving it the power to behave to an appreciable extent independently of its competitors, customers and ultimately of its consumers.

It is also possible for companies collectively to hold a position of dominance. The European Court of Justice noted in Irish Sugar Plc v. EC Commission, Case C–497/99, [2001] CMLR 29 (ECJ 5th Chamber 2001), that

> in order to establish whether the undertakings concerned together constitute a collective entity on a given market, it is necessary to examine the economic links or factors which give rise to a connection between them, and, in particular, whether economic links exist between them which enable them to act together independently of their competitors, their customers and consumers.

See also the Italian Flat Glass case, Societe Italiano Vetro SpA (SIV) v. Commission, Case T–68, 77 & 78/89 (March 10, 1992). In Piau v. Commission, Case T–193/02 (Jan. 26, 2005), a case dealing with the rules adopted by an umbrella association of national football (soccer to an American) associations of clubs, the CFI reconfirmed that "a dominant position may be held by two or more economic entities legally independent of each other, provided that from an economic point of view they present themselves or act together on a particular market as a collective entity." *See also* Chapter 6, section 2, *infra*, comparing the European doctrine of collective dominance to the idea of shared monopoly or tacit collusion in U.S. law.

Whether the dominant position is held by a single firm or a group of firms, it appears that the emphasis of Article 82 is primarily on the abusive nature of the conduct in question when undertaken by the powerful firm or group, rather than on acquisition or maintenance of that power. The Court of Justice defined "abuse" in *Hoffmann–LaRoche* as follows:

> The concept of abuse is an objective concept relating to the behavior of an undertaking in a dominant position which is such as to influence the structure of a market where, as a result of the very presence of the undertaking in question, the degree of competition is weakened and which, through recourse to methods different from those which condition normal competition in products or services on the basis of the transactions of commercial operators, has the effect of hindering the maintenance of the degree of competition still existing in the market or the growth of that competition.

In its ruling of September 17, 2007, in the long-running *Microsoft* litigation, the CFI again noted (at ¶ 239) that "Article 82 EC deals with the conduct of one or more economic actors involving the abuse of a position of economic strength which enables the operator concerned to hinder the maintenance of effective competition on the relevant market by allowing it to behave to an appreciable extent independently of its competitors, its customers, and, ultimately, consumers.... Furthermore, whilst the finding of a dominant position does not in itself imply any criticism of the undertaking concerned, that undertaking has a special responsibility, irrespective of the causes of that position, not to allow its conduct to impair genuine undistorted competition on the common market." See Microsoft v. Commission, Case T–201/04 (CFI, Sept. 17, 2007). The Court ruled there that competitors' operating systems had to be able to interoperate with the Windows domain architecture "on an equal footing" with Windows systems. (¶ ¶ 230, 374.) It therefore upheld most of the Commission's decision finding that Microsoft had abused its dominant position.

An Article 82 proceeding begins, much like a case under Section 2 of the Sherman Act, with the definition of the relevant market. In the earliest case on this subject from the Court of Justice, Europemballage Corp. v. Commission, Case 6/72, [1973] ECR 215, the Court rejected the Commission's effort to define separate markets for light containers for canned meat products, light containers for canned seafood, and metal closures for the food packing industry. It held that the Commission should have considered not only the separate uses to which the products were put, but also production characteristics, possibility of production substitution, and interchangeability of use. See also L'Oreal, ECJ Dec. 11, 1980, 1980 ECR 3775, 1981–2 CMLR 235. Although this result looks familiar to U.S. eyes, there are other examples where the Commission and the European courts have taken a narrower approach to relevant markets. In their book on EC Competition law[35], Ritter, Braun & Rawlinson offer the following examples of that point:

Natural sugar as distinct from sugar substitutes

Cola as distinct from other soft drinks

Bananas, not other fresh fruit

Advance weekly television listings different from daily listings

Spare parts for particular makes of cash registers or particular car models

In its decision in Tetra Laval BV v. EC Commission, Case No. T–5/02, CFI 25 October 2002 (a merger case), the Court of First Instance apparently did not find fault with the idea that there is no single "liquid food packaging industry," but instead different technologies must be regarded separately. (The ultimate result of that case was to reject the Commission's decision to block the merger in question, but the point about relevant market is unaffected by the ultimate outcome of the case.)

Article 82 sweeps more broadly than Section 2 of the Sherman Act in a second way: the degree of market power that suffices to make a firm "dominant" is distinctly less than the degree required for monopolization. One Commission official noted that, in the absence of special circumstances, market shares between 40 and 65% are considered strong evidence of dominance, citing *Hoffmann–LaRoche* (47–66%), *United Brands*, 1978 *ECR* 267 (40–45%), *ECS/Akzo II*, Comm. Dec. 15.12.1985, O.J. L 374/1, p. 18 (50%), and *Sabena*, Com. Dec. 4.11.1988, O.J. L 317, 47, p. 52 (50%). Nacke, Abuse of Dominant Positions: Recent Developments (Taipei, April 19, 1995).

Once the Commission has determined that a firm is dominant within a given market, it must decide whether the conduct amounts to an abuse. It is important to recall in this context that dominance might arise because the firm has been given special privileges by a public body. *See, e.g.*, Re Landing Fees at Portuguese Airports: Portugal v. EC Commission, Case C–163/99, [2002] 4 CMLR 31 (ECJ 6th Chamber 2001). The European courts have made it clear that such firms are equally subject to the rules of Article 82, unless the alleged abuse is an inevitable consequence of the public responsibility. The concept of abuse is elastic, encompassing almost any kind of behavior that would allow the dominant firm to put its rivals at a competitive disadvantage. For example, in the *Portuguese Landing Fees* case just mentioned, the Commission argued that the dominant carriers were abusing their dominant position through certain discounts. The Court had the following to say in response:

> Nonetheless, where as a result of the thresholds of the various discount bands, and the levels of discount offered, discounts (or additional discounts) are enjoyed by only some trading parties, giving them an economic advantage which is not justified by the volume of business they bring or by any economies of scale they allow the supplier to make compared with their competitors, a system of quantity discounts leads to the application of dissimilar conditions to equivalent transactions.

Thus, in European law some kind of objective justification for the dominant firm's conduct is required. As the *Microsoft* case mentioned above well illustrates, it is not enough to say that all firms are entitled to compete. Another recent example is the Commission's decision regarding certain practices of Intel Corporation. *See* Case

---

35. *See* Ritter, Braun & Rawlinson, EC Competition Law 274–75 (Kluwer 1991).

COMP/C–3/37990, May 13, 2009. There, acting on a complaint from one of Intel's competitors, Advanced Micro Devices (AMD), the Commission found that Intel had abused its dominant position in Central Processing Units (CPUs) of x86 machines, both by using conditional rebates and by imposing a number of restrictions (such as payments to OEMs to induce them to postpone the launch of AMD-based products) that it considered to be "naked restraints." Recall that Article 82 itself specifies that abuse may consist in imposing "unfair" purchase or selling prices, limiting production or technical development to the detriment of consumers, applying dissimilar conditions to "equivalent" transactions, and requiring supplemental obligations unconnected to the subject of the contract.

The net result of the EU's approach to market definition, the concept of dominance, and the idea of abuse, is a body of law that reaches more deeply into the internal affairs of companies than Section 2 of the Sherman Act. At first blush, this may seem paradoxical because Europe has generally had a more hospitable attitude toward larger companies than the United States has historically held. On closer examination, however, the differences are more understandable. In part, the European approach has been possible because the Commission controls which cases will be brought for the most part, and what penalty will be imposed. (It is theoretically possible now to bring Article 82 cases in the national courts, and there may be much more of this kind of litigation once the reforms that have been proposed enter into force, but up until the present there has been little private enforcement of the competition laws in Europe.) Thus, the actual field for application of Article 82 is far smaller than the potential field. Second, the European approach here as elsewhere reflects the overall goal of the Treaty to integrate the separate national markets into one. Practices that tend to divide member states from one another are a matter of great concern, and the Community institutions as a whole tend to mobilize against them. Finally, it may be that the Europeans have more experience with the administrative state, and thus more confidence in its operation, than their American counterparts. *See generally* Fox, Monopolization and Dominance in the United States and the European Community: Efficiency, Opportunity, and Fairness, 61 Notre Dame L. Rev. 981 (1986).

SELECTIVE BIBLIOGRAPHY

1. General

Hovenkamp, The Harvard and Chicago Schools and the Dominant Firm, in R. Pitofsky (ed.), How the Chicago School Overshot the Mark 109 (2008).

Goldschmid, Comment on . . . the Dominant Firm, in R. Pitofsky (ed.), How the Chicago School Overshot the Mark 123 (2008).

Areeda, & Hovenkamp, Antitrust Law: An Analysis of Antitrust Principles and Their Application Chs. 4–6 (2006 & Supp. 2009).

Hovenkamp, Federal Antitrust Policy: The Law of Competition and its Practice Ch. 3 (3d ed. 2005).

Posner, Antitrust Law (2d ed. 2001).

Bork, The Antitrust Paradox (1978).

Goldschmid, Mann & Weston (eds.), Industrial Concentration: The New Learning (1974).

Pitofsky, New Definitions of Relevant Market and the Assault on Antitrust, 90 Colum.L.Rev. 1805 (1990).

Krattenmaker, Lande & Salop, Monopoly Power and Market Power in Antitrust Law, 76 Geo.L.J. 241 (1987).

Fox, Monopolization and Dominance in the United States and the European Community: Efficiency, Opportunity, and Fairness, 61 Notre Dame L.Rev. 981 (1986).

Harris & Jorde, Antitrust Market Definition: An Integrated Approach, 72 Cal.L.Rev. 1 (1984).

Kaplow, The Accuracy of Traditional Market Power Analysis and a Direct Adjustment Alternative, 95 Harv.L.Rev. 1817 (1982).

Landes & Posner, Market Power in Antitrust Cases, 94 Harv.L.Rev. 937 (1981).

Pitofsky, The Political Content of Antitrust, 127 U.Pa.L.Rev. 1051 (1979).

2. Economic Materials

Adams (ed.), The Structure of American Industry (10th ed. 2001)

Shepherd, The Economics of Industrial Organization (5th ed. 2004).

Scherer & Ross, Industrial Market Structure and Economic Performance (3d ed. 1990).

Kaysen & Turner, Antitrust Policy Ch. 2 (1959).

See the Selective Bibliographies of Chapters 1, 8, and 9 for additional relevant materials.

3. Comparative Materials

Berry, The Uncertainty of Monopolistic Conduct: A Comparative Review of Three Jurisdictions, 32 Law & Policy in Int'l Bus. 263 (2001)

Jebsen, Assumptions, Goals and Dominant Undertakings: The Regulation of Competition Under Article 86, 64 Antitrust L.J. 443 (1996).

Rodger, The Oligopoly Problem and the Concept of Collective Dominance: EC Developments in Light of US Trends in Antitrust and Policy, 2 Colum. J.Eur. L. 25 (1996).

CHAPTER 4

COMPETITOR COLLABORATION ON PRICE FIXING AND DIVISION OF MARKETS

SECTION 1. CONSPIRACY IN THEORY AND ACTION

SCOPE NOTE

This chapter begins our study of horizontal competitor collaboration under Section 1 of the Sherman Act by focusing on the development of the *per se* rule for price fixing and on more subtle characterization issues. Horizontal collaboration refers to agreements between two or more companies that produce or market the same product. As Section 2C of Chapter 1 indicated, by 1911 the Supreme Court had clearly rejected the plain meaning approach of *Trans–Missouri* (the "plain and ordinary" meaning of every restraint of trade means "all") and substituted a rule of reason analysis. But what if, as is true of "naked" price fixing, conduct is always or almost always anticompetitive? In such circumstances, should a court act summarily or should it deal at length with claims of reasonableness?

In this chapter, first, focus on the policy rationale for a *per se* rule and when to apply it. Second, keep in mind that competitor collaborations can enhance efficiency in compelling ways (*e.g.*, by allowing economies of scale to be obtained). When should allegedly efficient competitor collaboration (often labeled as a joint venture) be characterized as non-*per se* and subject to a "reasonableness" examination? Finally, please remember from Chapter 2 that price fixing and market divisions by horizontal competitors represent a critically important—and highly active—area of antitrust enforcement today.[1]

John S. McGee, Cartels: Organization and Functions[2]
27 U.Chi.L.Rev. 191, 197 (1960).

A. CONDITIONS FAVORING CARTELIZATION

A cartel is an association of firms cooperating to fix price or other terms of trade. To the extent that a cartel is successful, it suppresses competition in those terms about which there is agreement. From the

---

1. *See also* Note on Price Fixing in Action *infra*.

2. This is an excerpt from the article, Ocean Freight Rate Conferences and the American Merchant Marine, reprinted by permission of The University of Chicago Law Review, University of Chicago Law School.

standpoint of any industry, it is desirable to suppress competition entirely, or at least to mitigate it. Such a task is not equally easy or attractive everywhere. Both to predict where cartels are most likely to appear and to understand them better wherever they are found, it would be useful to draw up a brief list of conditions that favor cartelization. First, the costs of organizing and maintaining the cartel should be small; ideally, zero. The number of independent firms to be coordinated will probably influence such costs. On this account alone, a plan to cartelize all of, say, retail trade is more likely to be a vainglorious dream than a scheme to be relied upon. If, however, some smaller portion of the market can be carved out and insulated, there is hope.

Second, it is highly desirable that there not be burdensome size or other diseconomies to plague the cartel once it is organized.[3]

Third, the price elasticity of demand for the product should ideally be very low at the competitive price. The lower it is, the further the cartel can advance prices without suffering a disastrous loss of custom. Put simply, any cartel can make greater profits if, under competition, buyers were not very sensitive to a price increase. This may be roughly equivalent to saying that there is no very good substitute for the service or product, a condition that often appears to be met in the real world.

Fourth, it would be of slight comfort to construct a cartel that scarcely survives its creation. A durable one is what is wanted. Durability will be lessened by centrifugal forces within the combination itself and by the easy creation or expansion of outside supplies. In cartels the first problem is that of defection; the second, of entry and the growth of existing outsiders. Though both are influenced by technological and other natural conditions, both may, nevertheless, be subject to a considerable degree of control, as we shall see.

As the number of participants in a loose confederation rises, the problem of coordination grows, even if all concerned honestly and earnestly seek to preserve that solidarity which is the central object of the coalition. Furthermore, with greater numbers, it becomes somewhat easier for an individual member to defect without appearing to have done so. The difficulties of policing the agreement multiply; the attractiveness of a unilateral policy grows. In sum, large numbers encourage a separation of group and individual interests. In addition is the problem of heterogeneity within the group, which is sometimes a function of the numbers of participants. Cartels are much concerned with these problems, which are multiplied by the uncertainty and wavering confidence that are inherent in human affairs. . . .

Important though these internal problems are, there are also dangers from outside. Entry is the nemesis of cartels. Cartels could rest much more securely if there were natural barriers to entry. These might include scarce

---

3. This is much to be hoped for, not only for the obvious reason that any producer, competitor or cartelist will fare better if he can produce any output at lower cost, but also because if entrants of a more efficient size arise, the cartel would face a somber long run.

resources or a very long gestation period for those resources that must be committed for successful entry. Still another might be economies of size, of various kinds, that compel entry on a scale so large relative to the market that no entry will occur. Every cartel would welcome some check on entry, and some of them have devised policies and institutions to accomplish that objective....

The more subject cartels are to problems of the sort just discussed, the more likely it is that they will require meticulous centralized administration to achieve the desired coordination. Because of the very nature of cartels, we should expect that they will seldom function quite so precisely or reliably as would a single firm operating under like circumstances....

Where cartels operate in a hostile legal climate, which has generally been the case in the United States since the Sherman Law of 1890, it is to be expected that their organizations will be less formal and tight. As a consequence it would not be surprising to find that departures from the "ideal" behavior expected of cartels in theory will be greater than when the law is neutral or promotive. This hypothesis is broadly confirmed by American experience. Before the law intruded, cartels in the United States were often tightly organized, with pools, penalties and other devices to assure precision and solidarity. After the Sherman Law was passed and was found to have some force, it was only natural that a successful cartel would have to function as well as could be, taking into account the need to minimize discovery and punishment.

NOTE ON BARRIERS TO ENTRY AND POTENTIAL COMPETITION[4]

Consideration of conditions of entry is essential to any appraisal of market power[5]—including whatever market power may be created by the organization of a cartel. If entry were completely unimpeded, it would make no sense for companies in a particular market to go to the trouble of setting up a cartel. As soon as the cartel members curtailed output and raised price, potential entrants rapidly would enter the market (and non-members of the cartel in that market would expand existing production) to seek profits by pricing below the cartel price but above the competitive price. Under these conditions of a "perfect contestable market," established sellers would have no market power (to raise price) even though over long intervals actual entry seldom, if ever, took place. *See* Bain, Barriers to New Competition 1–14 (1962); Baumol, Contestable Markets: An Uprising in the Theory of Industry Structure (1982).

Some commentators have questioned the need for Sherman Act enforcement against cartels, arguing that they are inherently unstable and would break down eventually without government intervention (primarily because members of the

---

4. This note was revised by Professor Steven C. Salop from materials appearing in earlier editions of the casebook.

5. For a further discussion of barriers to entry, *see* U.S. Department of Justice and FTC Joint Horizontal Merger Guidelines, § 3, p. 1047 *infra*.

cartel will offer secret discounts), and because new entry will restore competitive conditions as soon as the cartel attempts to extract monopoly profits.[6]

We have seen that cartel "chiseling" is indeed a destabilizing factor, but can often be suppressed over the short run. *See* McGee, p. 177 *supra*. As to new entry, it can be delayed or prevented entirely by "barriers" of various kinds. If the cartel price is high enough, almost all barriers to entry eventually can be overcome. But given delays in entry, there can be short-run monopoly profit and misallocation of resources that make cartel behavior inviting and cartel profits significant.

It is important to recognize that not every economic condition which delays entry or makes it more difficult is a "barrier" in the same sense of the word. Some "barriers" simply reflect costs that existing companies must assume in order to be competitive. If higher-than-competitive prices are being charged (*i.e.*, prices substantially above marginal costs plus a fair return on investment) and potential entrants recognize that fact, they can incur the same costs and eventually compete with the incumbents on roughly equal terms. Other economic conditions are more extreme "barriers" in that they either require the potential entrant to bear *higher* costs than established sellers in the industry or in other ways deter entry by equally efficient competitors. These barriers may be "structural," meaning that they tend to disappear only over a long-run period, or when legal protection is withdrawn. When "barriers" in the strict sense are present, the incumbent can charge a higher-than-competitive price, up to or beyond the level of the challenger's costs, without seeing its sales threatened by a challenger.

The point can be illustrated in connection with capital costs of entry. Suppose it would take a capital investment of $100 million to establish an efficient plant in a particular industry. In one sense, that condition impedes entry. First, it certainly is true that more entry would occur if the necessary investment were smaller. Second, not everyone has access to $100 million to compete in that market. On the other hand, that entry requires investment is a fact of life. It does not reflect lack of competition in any meaningful sense. Moreover, if an established company in another industry or a group of experienced entrepreneurs can show that they have the managerial talent, access to raw materials, potential for a distribution network, and know-how, they may well be able to obtain financing from a bank or from venture capitalists. If they build a plant, they will amortize its costs over the useful life of the facility—say $10 million per year for ten years. A comparable $100 million expense for plant construction is a cost that the incumbent has already paid. In addition, companies ordinarily intend to replace their plants at the end of their useful lives, and put aside an amount annually—in this illustration, the incumbent and the entrant each might reasonably put aside $10 million per year for ten years—to pay the cost of that replacement.

In this case, if established firms tried to price non-competitively, by raising prices above their costs, these "barriers" would not deter entry. In this sense, they are not true barriers to entry.

A more significant type of "barrier to entry" arises where the new entrant must pay more to obtain capital to build a new plant than the incumbent must pay to replace the existing plant. That might be the case because banks or venture capitalists charge most new entrants a higher rate of interest (a "risk premium"), reflecting the fact that the entrant may not have the technical or managerial capacity to be successful, entry requires expensive price promotions to induce

---

6. *See, e.g.*, Dewey, Industrial Concentration and the Rate of Profit, 19 J. Law & Econ. 67 (1976).

consumers to try the new product, or simply because the new entrant or the new product lacks a record of success and achievement.[7] Suppose as a result of different costs of capital (and perhaps other factors), the new entrant's average costs of producing a product are $10.00, while the incumbents have average costs of only $8.00. The difference between the cost of the incumbents and the entrant is a more intractable barrier to entry—allowing the incumbents to charge more than their average cost without attracting new entry.

The principal barriers to entry that permit non-competitive pricing are slow speed of entry, cost and demand disadvantages, economies of scale, and sunk costs. These are discussed below.

1. **Slow Speed of Entry.** If entry takes a long time or if new producers are unable to gain sales rapidly after initially entering a market, the fear of potential entry provides less of a competitive check on that market. There are two reasons for this. First, if entry takes a long time, it may not be worthwhile for established firms to reduce their prices before entry actually occurs. In this case, only after actual entry occurred would prices fall back to the competitive level, as opposed to the fear of potential entry keeping prices at competitive levels before any entry occurred. Thus, consumers would pay higher prices in the interim until entry occurred. Second, if entry takes a long time, established firms have ample time to react to a planned entry (unless secrecy could be maintained by the entrant). Thus, the entrant would be unable to get a jump on the competition before it responds. This will deter entry. In short, if established firms do not fear the loss of significant sales to potential entrants, potential entry will not constrain them from raising prices.

2. **Cost and Demand Disadvantages.** If entrants face significant cost or demand disadvantages relative to established firms, potential entry will not constrain price increases, at least increases up to a level roughly equal to the cost or demand disadvantage. This is illustrated by the capital cost example discussed earlier. For example, if entrants' costs are 10% above the costs of established firms, or if later entrants must sell at a permanent 10% price discount below the prices of firms that entered earlier, they obviously would be unable to prevent established firms from raising prices by 5% above costs.

Significant cost disadvantages can arise when the established firms have patents or other legal licenses or when incumbents have superior access to scarce or low cost resources.

a. *Patents and Other Legal Licenses.* Entry might be impossible because a governmental unit has decided to franchise only one competitor—for example, a single cable TV outlet in a given city. In other industries regulated by federal or state bodies, entry is possible only after a license has been obtained. Similarly, we confer on inventors an exclusive right (usually for 20 years) in the form of patent protection. Common-law protection of trade secrets or know-how may also make it impossible for potential rivals to compete on equal terms in a given market.

The magnitude of the barrier will vary according to the circumstances. A true "monopoly" franchise means the incumbent need fear no competition for the duration of the legal privilege. The significance of patent protection as a barrier to entry varies according to the strength of the

---

7. Of course, if the "new entrant" is Procter & Gamble or General Electric initiating a new line, any risk premium is not likely to be as substantial. In contrast, if the expansion is internally financed, from retained earnings, management may tend to underestimate its own limitations, and include a smaller risk premium.

patent and scope of the invention. If a potential entrant can develop a comparable product that does not infringe on the patent, then the entry barrier—in the strict sense—is no greater than the costs of avoiding the patent. Similarly, trade information and know-how often can be purchased or developed independently; in either case, the barrier may only be the cost of acquiring the additional information and the cost may be comparable to the expenditure previously made by the incumbent.

Suppose there is extensive research and development activity continuously taking place in the drug industry, eventually leading to the securing of patents. Is the research and development activity itself a barrier to entry? In what sense?

b. *Scarce Resources.* Incumbents in a market can sometimes earn large profits because they control all or most of an essential raw material, a unique or superior locational advantage, or an existing distribution network that is impossible or extremely costly to duplicate. A classic example would be a situation in which a factory is located near an essential raw material or power source and other factories cannot be located nearby. If the resource is unique, entry is fully blockaded; this is a ''bottleneck'' case. Where it is not, the barrier—again in the strict sense—consists of the amount it would cost the entrant to obtain access to the resource in excess of the amount it costs the incumbent.

c. *Product Differentiation.* Particularly in consumer product markets, a potential entrant may find that the most serious barrier to entry is established consumer loyalty to an existing brand or brands. Thus, sellers with a high degree of product acceptance can charge considerably more than their costs—even including their cost of establishing consumer loyalty—confident that they will not quickly or easily lose sales to a newcomer.

Product loyalty can be based on a combination of several factors. It may reflect the cumulative impact of many years of successful and effective advertising. Studies show that any particular message—even an emphatic and repeated sales theme—will soon be forgotten by consumers, but the cumulative impression that a company makes reliable and reasonably priced products may persist. That impression may be reinforced by favorable experiences with its products (perhaps during an early period in which few or no other comparable products were on the market) and by special product characteristics.

A new entrant may find that it is necessary to charge a significantly lower price in order to overcome such established consumer loyalty, or it may have to spend greater sums in advertising and promotion than did the incumbent. The magnitude of those differences constitutes a barrier to entry in the strict sense described above.

On the other hand, promotional price discounts and temporary cost disadvantages may reflect necessary investments by all entrants, costs that the established firms also needed to bear when they entered. Competition must allow these costs to be recovered. Thus, if all firms must invest equal amounts and recover these costs on an equal basis after entry, a barrier is not created automatically. However, as discussed below, these costs also can have other effects: they increase effective scale economies and increase entrants' financial exposure. These effects of the entry costs and pricing discounts can serve to deter entry even if established firms had to bear similar costs when they entered.

3. **Economies of Scale.** If only large scale entry is possible or if entrants suffer significant cost disadvantages from small scale entry, established firms may be able to raise their prices above the competitive level without attracting entry. Minimum viable scale (MVS) is the smallest annual level of sales that an entrant must persistently achieve to make entry profitable.

If MVS is large, entry is less likely for two reasons. First, the entrant is less likely to achieve the MVS sales level, and so is less likely to enter. Second, when MVS is high, an entrant attempting to reach MVS is more likely to induce a competitive price reaction by incumbent firms, a price reaction that will reduce the profitability of the entry (*i.e.*, at a lower price MVS is higher).[8] Suppose, for example, there are five companies in an industry, each accounting for 20% of the market, and that a plant of a size efficient enough to produce at costs comparable to the incumbents must produce the equivalent of 20% of current sales. Since the incumbents have sufficient productive capacity to satisfy current demand, any effort to challenge them is likely to create significant excess capacity in the industry, leading to a price war and diminished profits for all. If no incumbent goes out of business, the industry will have so much capacity after the new entrant builds its plant to assure that all participants will find competition in that market less profitable. Since potential entrants will understand this, the incumbents will be able to charge a higher-than-competitive price without triggering entry, even if the entrants can produce as efficiently as incumbents.

Thus, the effect on consumers is ambiguous. Although *post-entry* competition increases the consumer benefits from *successful* entry, the fear of setting off a round of matching price reductions after entry may deter a potential entrant from attempting entry to begin with.

4. **Sunk Costs.** Successful entry is not a sure thing. Entry may fail because the entrant's costs are relatively high, its products prove to be unpopular, the economy enters a serious recession or the entry sets off a price war. Entry is a financially risky proposition to the extent that entry costs cannot be recovered if entry fails and the entrant must exit from the market. If entry costs are irreversible (or "sunk," in the jargon of economists), the entrant's financial exposure is greater and entry less likely to be attempted.

Some but not all capital costs are sunk. Promotional and design expenses usually cannot be used for other products if exit occurs. In addition, many new products must be sold at a loss until consumer goodwill is achieved. Because a significant portion of its capital costs of entry are sunk in the case of differentiated consumer products, the resulting lower likelihood of attempted entry permits established firms to earn monopoly profits without inducing entry.

It is by focusing only on costs that differentially affect new entrants, as opposed to established sellers, that some critics of antitrust policy have been led to argue that collusion will rarely be attempted and will frequently be unsuccessful. They conclude that anticompetitive effects are too infrequent and insignificant to justify a

---

8. MVS is a function of expected revenues and expected costs associated with entry, including an appropriate rate of return on invested capital. The appropriate rate of return, often called the "hurdle rate," depends on the degree of risk and the magnitude of sunk costs that would be lost if entry fails. For a further discussion of MVS, *see* U.S. Department of Justice and FTC Joint Horizontal Merger Guidelines, Chapter 9 *infra*.

costly antitrust enforcement program against price-fixing or other cartel activities. Consider the following questions in connection with that policy issue:

1. Are "strict" barriers to entry so unusual and insignificant as to justify a policy of indifference toward explicit or implicit cartels?

2. With respect to the broader definition of barriers to entry, will they protect cartel profits where the capital market does not operate perfectly or where a significant lag time will occur before effective new entry can make itself felt?

3. With respect to lag time, how long is it likely to be before fringe companies or outsiders detect the existence of persistent higher-than-competitive profits, assemble the staff and prepare plans for entry or expansion, obtain necessary capital, and construct and put into operation new production facilities? Might the incumbents use strategic ploys—for example, reducing their prices or threatening to reduce prices in the face of entry—to discourage new challengers? Might such conduct extend the lag time before entry sufficiently to give competitors an incentive to work out a price-fixing arrangement or settle into a price-leadership relationship?

4. What are the social costs of a vigorous anti-cartel policy that does not differentiate between various kinds of barriers to entry? How likely is it to deter efficient or otherwise desirable business conduct?

NOTE ON PRICE FIXING IN ACTION

1. **Auction Houses.** As indicated in Chapter 2, price-fixing conspiracies—domestic and increasingly international—have been a major concern of the antitrust enforcement agencies for many years. Criminal sanctions, imprisonment and heavy fines are usually imposed for hard-core price fixing. A sense of the new concern about international cartels is shown by the following comparison: for the five years from fiscal 1987 through 1991, the Antitrust Division brought only two cases against foreign corporations and no foreign individuals were charged; in fiscal 2001, however, about 70% of the companies prosecuted for price fixing by the Antitrust Division were foreign-based, and about 33% of the individual defendants were foreign citizens. The average prison sentence for foreign defendants in international price-fixing cases was 18 months in 2008. Foreign executives from, for example, Austria, Canada, Germany, Japan, Mexico, Norway, South Korean, Sweden, Switzerland, and the United Kingdom were recently convicted.

An auction house price-fixing scheme between Sotheby's and Christie's, the world's two dominant auction firms with more than 90% of the market, illustrates how modern price fixing may work in practice. For generations, Sotheby's and Christie's were known as archrivals and competed vigorously on commissions. But for much of the 1990's the most senior executives of the two firms colluded in order to take higher commissions from sellers of art, antiques, and other collectibles.

In the excerpt that follows, Diana D. Brooks, the CEO of Sotheby's, is testifying at the price-fixing trial of Alfred Taubman, the chairman of Sotheby's board during the conspiracy and the firm's dominant shareholder. Taubman was convicted in December 2001, and after an unsuccessful appeal, began serving a one-year prison term (at age 78) in 2002. Sotheby's was sentenced to pay a $45 million fine. Ms. Brooks was sentenced to three years of probation, including six months of home detention, and a $350,000 fine. The sentencing judge acknowledged her "substantial assistance in the investigation and prosecution of the price-fixing conspiracy," but concluded that she had "traded [her] title of CEO to be branded a thief," and blinded "by ambition, you substituted shame for fame." In private litigations, Sotheby's, Christie's, and Taubman reportedly paid over $500 million in settlements.

Q. While you were in London at the board meeting [in 1993], did you have a discussion with Alfred Taubman?

A. Brooks. Yes, I did.

Q. What did you say to him and what did he say to you at this meeting?

A. Mr. Taubman told me that he had just met with Sir Anthony Tennant, who was the chairman of Christie's, that they had had a very good meeting. . . . He told me that he and Mr. Tennant agreed that the business was—this is now in 1993, that we were both killing each other on the bottom line and that, you know, it was time to do something about it. He said that he and Mr. Tennant had gotten along very well and he could see working with him.

Q. Did Mr. Taubman show you anything?

A. Yes, he did. He showed me a piece of paper, a small piece of paper.

Q. What was on the paper?

A. There were a number of topics on the paper that started with pricing. . . .

Q. Would you tell the jury what Mr. Taubman told you with respect to the subjects on the paper and any other subjects that you mentioned?

A. Mr. Taubman told me that he and Mr. Tennant had agreed on a number of subjects and that they wanted Christopher Davidge [of Christie's] and I to meet and to go forward and implement them, some of the agreements that they had reached, and in some cases to actually work out the details.

He asked me not to talk to anyone else about this and it was left and I was to call Mr. Davidge. And on each of the topics, the first topic being pricing, Mr. Taubman told me that he and Mr. Tennant felt that it was time to increase pricing and he told me that he had told Mr. Tennant that it was their turn to go first. . . . He told me that they had agreed that we were no longer going to do interest free or single lot advances. He also told me that they had agreed that we were no longer going to let our people bad-mouth each other out in the public. . . .

And he told me that they had talked about not poaching each other's staff. They also had covered several other topics that they wanted us to work on, one being introductory commissions, which were commissions that were paid to third parties for delivering business, and the idea was that they were paying more and more out and they wanted us, Christopher Davidge and I, to work out an implementation of a maximum that we would pay, and they also had talked about charitable contributions that were more and more being used to obtain business. . . .

Q. After this did you in fact meet with Christopher Davidge?

A. Yes. I did. . . .

Q. You told Mr. Taubman beforehand?

A.   Yes, I did.

Q.   What did Mr. Taubman say about that?

A.   He was pleased that we were finally going to meet. . . .

Q.   [At the meeting, what] did Mr. Davidge say about . . . changing pricing?

A.   He said that his view was that we had to be careful as to when we did it because we had done the buyer's premium only a year before, which was the first time the buyer's premium had been changed in many, many years, the first time we had actually increased pricing. And that he wanted to work with me on coming up with what he thought would be the best way to change or increase pricing.

But all of us were concerned about the bottom line and the fact that we were killing each other and we were going to try to come up with a way that we were paid fairly for what we did and that we provided a decent return to our shareholders. . . .

Q.   Did you tell anybody about your conversation [on February 8, 1995] with Mr. Davidge at Kennedy Airport?

A.   Yes, I did.

Q.   Who did you tell?

A.   I told Mr. Taubman. . . .

Q.   This was a face-to-face meeting?

A.   Yes.

Q.   What did Mr. Taubman say to you?

A.   I don't remember what his words were. I think he was just pleased it was happening.

Q.   When did you first see Christie's March 9, 1995 price announcement?

A.   My first recollection of seeing this is on March 9, 1995.

Q.   What did you do when you saw the Christie's price announcement?

A.   I was thrilled. I was delighted that it actually had happened?

2.   **The Airlines.** In 1982, American Airlines and Braniff, two leading airlines serving the Dallas–Fort Worth airport, were engaged in a price war. The Department of Justice obtained a tape of a phone conversation between Robert L. Crandall, President of American Airlines, and Howard Putnam, President of Braniff. According to the Fifth Circuit of Appeals' opinion,[9] the following conversation occurred.

Crandall: I think it's dumb as hell for Christ's sake, all right, to sit here and pound the . . . out of each other and neither one of us making a . . . dime.

Putnam: Well—

---

9. United States v. American Airlines, 743 F.2d 1114 (5th Cir.1984), cert. dismissed, 474 U.S. 1001 (1985).

Crandall: I mean, you know, goddamn, what the . . . is the point of it?

Putnam: Nobody asked American to serve Harlingen. Nobody asked American to serve Kansas City, and there were low fares in there, you know, before. So—

Crandall: You better believe it, Howard. But, you, you, you know, the complex is here—ain't gonna change a goddamn thing, all right. We can, we can both live here and there ain't no room for Delta. But there's, ah, no reason that I can see, all right, to put both companies out of business.

Putnam: But if you're going to overlay every route of American's . . . on top of every route that Braniff has—I can't just sit here and allow you to bury us without giving our best effort.

Crandall: Oh sure, but Eastern and Delta do the same thing in Atlanta and have for years.

Putnam: Do you have a suggestion for me

Crandall: Yes. I have a suggestion for you. Raise your goddamn fares twenty percent. I'll raise mine the next morning

Putnam: Robert, we—

Crandall: You'll make more money and I will too.

Putnam: We can't talk about pricing.

Crandall: Oh Bull . . ., Howard. We can talk about any goddamn thing we want to talk about.

Putnam turned the tape recording of the conversation over to the Government. American Airlines and Crandall were proceeded against successfully by the Government, which charged an attempt to monopolize under Section 2 of the Sherman Act.

3. **Leniency Programs.** In the *Auction House* cases, Christie's had come forward to cooperate with the Antitrust Division in accordance with the Division's 1993 leniency program. Under this program, corporations and individuals will not be charged criminally if:

1. At the time the corporation comes forward to report the illegal activity, the Division has not received information about the illegal activity being reported from any other sources;

2. The corporation, upon its discovery of the illegal activity being reported, took prompt and effective action to terminate its part in the activity;

3. The corporation reports the wrongdoing with candor and completeness and provides full, continuing and complete cooperation with the Division throughout the investigation;

4. The confession of wrongdoing is truly a corporate act, as opposed to isolated confessions of individual executives or officials;

5. Where possible, the corporation makes restitution to injured parties; and

6. The corporation did not coerce another party to participate in the illegal activity and clearly was not the leader in, or originator of, the activity.[10]

A similar leniency program for individuals was put into effect in 1994. If a corporation (or individual) cannot meet all of the conditions set forth above, there are other ways (discretionary for the Antitrust Division) to qualify for leniency.

The leniency programs have been a great success. The Antitrust Division has received about 25 applications for immunity a year, in recent years, from what is considered the "Division's most effective generator of international cartel cases." Cases resulting from the programs have led to hundreds of convictions, billions in criminal fines, and the dismantling of many large international cartels.[11]

Leniency programs have become more common among foreign antitrust authorities as well. The EU adopted a revised leniency program in 2002, which "establishes a far more transparent and predictable policy than its predecessor and brings the EC's program closely in line with the Division's Corporate Leniency Policy."[12]

SECTION 2.   DEVELOPMENT OF THE *"PER SE"* RULE ON PRICE FIXING

United States v. Addyston Pipe & Steel Co.

Circuit Court of Appeals of the United States, Sixth Circuit, 1898.
85 F. 271, affirmed, 175 U.S. 211, 20 S.Ct. 96, 44 L.Ed. 136 (1899).

[Reprinted p. 40 *supra*].

Chicago Board of Trade v. United States

Supreme Court of the United States, 1918.
246 U.S. 231, 38 S.Ct. 242, 62 L.Ed. 683.

■ BRANDEIS, J. Chicago is the leading grain market in the world. Its Board of Trade is the commercial center through which most of the trading in grain is done. The character of the organization is described in Board of Trade v. Christie Grain & Stock Co., 198 U.S. 236. Its 1600 members include brokers, commission merchants, dealers, millers, maltsters, manufacturers of corn products and proprietors of elevators. Grains there dealt in are graded according to kind and quality and are sold usually "Chicago weight, inspection and delivery." The standard forms of trading are: (a) Spot sales; that is, sales of grain already in Chicago in railroad cars or elevators for

---

10. Antitrust Division, Corporate Leniency Policy (1993), at http://www.usdoj.gov/atr/public/guidelines/0091.htm

11. Hammond, An update of the Antitrust Division's Criminal Enforcement Program, 2005, at http://www.usdoj.gov/atr/public/speeches/213247.htm.

12. Griffin, The Modern Leniency Program After Ten Years ... (2003), at http://www.usdoj.gov/atr/public/speeches/201477.htm.

immediate delivery by order on carrier or transfer of warehouse receipt. (b) Future sales; that is, agreements for delivery later in the current or in some future month. (c) Sales "to arrive;" that is, agreements to deliver on arrival grain which is already in transit to Chicago or is to be shipped there within a time specified. On every business day sessions of the Board are held at which all bids and sales are publicly made. Spot sales and future sales are made at the regular sessions of the Board from 9:30 A.M. to 1:15 P.M., except on Saturdays, when the session closes at 12 P.M. Special sessions, termed the "Call," are held immediately after the close of the regular session, at which sales "to arrive" are made. These sessions are not limited as to duration, but last usually about half an hour. At all these sessions transactions are between members only; but they may trade either for themselves or on behalf of others. Members may also trade privately with one another at any place, either during the sessions or after, and they may trade with non-members at any time except on the premises occupied by the Board.

Purchases of grain "to arrive" are made largely from country dealers and farmers throughout the whole territory tributary to Chicago, which includes besides Illinois and Iowa, Indiana, Ohio, Wisconsin, Minnesota, Missouri, Kansas, Nebraska, and even South and North Dakota. The purchases are sometimes the result of bids to individual country dealers made by telegraph or telephone either during the sessions or after; but most purchases are made by the sending out from Chicago by the afternoon mails to hundreds of country dealers offers to buy, at the prices named, any number of carloads, subject to acceptance before 9:30 A.M. on the next business day.

In 1906 the Board adopted what is known as the "Call" rule. By it members were prohibited from purchasing or offering to purchase, during the period between the close of the Call and the opening of the session on the next business day, any wheat, corn, oats or rye "to arrive" at a price other than the closing bid at the Call. The Call was over, with rare exceptions, by two o'clock. The change effected was this: Before the adoption of the rule, members fixed their bids throughout the day at such prices as they respectively saw fit; after the adoption of the rule, the bids had to be fixed at the day's closing bid on the Call until the opening of the next session.

In 1913 the United States filed in the District Court for the Northern District of Illinois this suit against the Board and its executive officers and directors, to enjoin the enforcement of the Call rule, alleging it to be in violation of the Antitrust Law. The defendants admitted the adoption and enforcement of the Call rule, and averred that its purpose was not to prevent competition or to control prices, but to promote the convenience of members by restricting their hours of business and to break up a monopoly in that branch of the grain trade acquired by four or five warehousemen in Chicago. On motion of the Government the allegations concerning the purpose of establishing the regulation were stricken from the record. The case was then heard upon evidence; and a decree was entered which declared that defendants became parties to a combination or conspiracy to restrain interstate and foreign trade and commerce "by adopting, acting upon and enforcing" the Call rule; and enjoined them from acting upon the same or from adopting or acting upon any similar rule.

No opinion was delivered by the District Judge. The Government proved the existence of the rule and described its application and the change in business practice involved. It made no attempt to show that the rule was designed to or that it had the effect of limiting the amount of grain shipped to Chicago; or of retarding or accelerating shipment; or of raising or depressing prices; or of discriminating against any part of the public; or that it resulted in hardship to anyone. The case was rested upon the bald proposition, that a rule or agreement by which men occupying positions of strength in any branch of trade, fixed prices at which they would buy or sell during an important part of the business day, is an illegal restraint of trade under the Antitrust Law. But the legality of an agreement or regulation cannot be determined by so simple a test, as whether it restrains competition. Every agreement concerning trade, every regulation of trade, restrains. To bind, to restrain, is of their very essence. The true test of legality is whether the restraint imposed is such as merely regulates and perhaps thereby promotes competition or whether it is such as may suppress or even destroy competition. To determine that question the court must ordinarily consider the facts peculiar to the business to which the restraint is applied; its condition before and after the restraint was imposed; the nature of the restraint and its effect, actual or probable. The history of the restraint, the evil believed to exist, the reason for adopting the particular remedy, the purpose or end sought to be attained, are all relevant facts. This is not because a good intention will save an otherwise objectionable regulation or the reverse; but because knowledge of intent may help the court to interpret facts and to predict consequences. The District Court erred, therefore, in striking from the answer allegations concerning the history and purpose of the Call rule and in later excluding evidence on that subject. But the evidence admitted makes it clear that the rule was a reasonable regulation of business consistent with the provisions of the Antitrust Law.

First: The nature of the rule: The restriction was upon the period of price-making. It required members to desist from further price-making after the close of the Call until 9:30 A.M. the next business day: but there was no restriction upon the sending out of bids after close of the Call. Thus it required members who desired to buy grain "to arrive" to make up their minds before the close of the Call how much they were willing to pay during the interval before the next session of the Board. The rule made it to their interest to attend the Call; and if they did not fill their wants by purchases there, to make the final bid high enough to enable them to purchase from country dealers.

Second: The scope of the rule: It is restricted in operation to grain "to arrive." It applies only to a small part of the grain shipped from day to day to Chicago, and to an even smaller part of the day's sales; members were left free to purchase grain already in Chicago from anyone at any price throughout the day. It applies only during a small part of the business day; members were left free to purchase during the sessions of the Board grain "to arrive," at any price, from members anywhere and from nonmembers anywhere except on the premises of the Board. It applied only to grain shipped to Chicago: members were left free to purchase at any price throughout the day from either members or nonmembers, grain "to arrive" at any other market. Country dealers and farmers had available in practically every part of the territory called tributary to Chicago some other market for grain "to arrive." Thus Missouri, Kansas, Nebraska, and parts of Illinois are also tributary to St. Louis; Nebraska and Iowa, to Omaha; Minnesota, Iowa, South and North Dakota, to Minneapolis or Duluth; Wisconsin and parts of Iowa and of Illinois, to Milwaukee; Ohio, Indiana and parts of Illinois, to Cincinnati; Indiana and parts of Illinois, to Louisville.

Third: The effects of the rule: As it applies to only a small part of the grain shipped to Chicago and to that only during a part of the business day and does not apply at all to grain shipped to other markets, the rule had no appreciable effect on general market prices; nor did it materially affect the total volume of grain coming to Chicago. But within the narrow limits of its operation the rule helped to improve market conditions thus:

[margin note: 3) effects — none on prices, or volume of grain — good effects for mkt conditions]

(a) It created a public market for grain "to arrive." Before its adoption, bids were made privately. Men had to buy and sell without adequate knowledge of actual market conditions. This was disadvantageous to all concerned, but particularly so to country dealers and farmers.

(b) It brought into the regular market hours of the Board sessions more of the trading in grain "to arrive."

(c) It brought buyers and sellers into more direct relations; because on the Call they gathered together for a free and open interchange of bids and offers.

(d) It distributed the business in grain "to arrive" among a far larger number of Chicago receivers and commission merchants than had been the case there before.

(e) It increased the number of country dealers engaging in this branch of the business; supplied them more regularly with bids from Chicago; and also increased the number of bids received by them from competing markets.

(f) It eliminated risks necessarily incident to a private market, and thus enabled country dealers to do business on a smaller margin. In that way the rule made it possible for them to pay more to farmers without raising the price to consumers.

(g) It enabled country dealers to sell some grain to arrive which they would otherwise have been obliged either to ship to Chicago commission merchants or to sell for "future delivery."

(h) It enabled those grain merchants of Chicago who sell to millers and exporters to trade on a smaller margin and, by paying more for grain or selling it for less, to make the Chicago market more attractive for both shippers and buyers of grain.

(i) Incidentally it facilitated trading "to arrive" by enabling those engaged in these transactions to fulfill their contracts by tendering grain arriving at Chicago on any railroad, whereas formerly shipments had to be made over the particular railroad designated by the buyer.

The restraint imposed by the rule is less severe than that sustained in Anderson v. United States, 171 U.S. 604. Every board of trade and nearly every trade organization imposes some restraint upon the conduct of business by its members. Those relating to the hours in which business may be done are common; and they make a special appeal where, as here, they tend to shorten the working day or, at least, limit the period of most exacting activity. The decree of the District Court is reversed with directions to dismiss the bill.

■ McReynolds, J., took no part in the consideration or decision of this case.[13]

———

Appalachian Coals, Inc. v. United States, 288 U.S. 344, 53 S.Ct. 471, 77 L.Ed. 825 (1933). In 1932, Appalachian Coals, Inc., was organized as the exclusive selling agent for 137 producers of bituminous coal in the so-called Appalachian territory (*i.e.*, eight coal districts lying in Virginia, West Virginia, Kentucky and Tennessee). The company's capital stock was owned solely by the producers in proportion to their production.

For a commission of 10%, Appalachian Coals was to sell the entire production of its 137 shareholders. The coal was to be sold at prices to be fixed by the officers of the company. These were to be the best prices obtainable. It was insisted that the primary purpose of the formation of the selling agency was to increase the sale and production of Appalachian coal through better methods of distribution, intensive advertising and research, and the achievement of economies in marketing; the company was also to "eliminate abnormal deceptive and destructive trade practices."

The company was formed in response to depressed conditions in the coal industry. Circumstances during and after World War I had led to the development of over 700,000,000 tons capacity to meet a demand of less than 500,000,000 tons, which was being further eroded by oil, water power, and natural gas substitutes and the more efficient use of coal itself.

The unfavorable industry condition was further aggravated by alleged "destructive trade practices." "Distress coal," dumped on the market because a given buyer did not want certain grades or sizes and storage facilities were not available, pushed

---

13. Justice Brandeis' opinion was quoted by the Court in Continental T.V., Inc. v. GTE Sylvania, Inc., 433 U.S. 36 (1977), printed p. 655 *infra*. The views of Justice Brandeis on antitrust are discussed in Handler, Antitrust in Perspective 17 (1957); Comment, Mr. Justice Brandeis, Competition and Smallness: A Dilemma Reexamined, 66 Yale L.J. 69 (1956).

prices down. To make matters worse, producers often offered the same coal for sale through different agents, and this "pyramiding of coal" artificially inflated the supply and drove down prices as agents bid against each other.

In 1929, the 137 producers mined less than 12% of the bituminous coal east of the Mississippi River. But deducting the output of "captive" mines (those producing for the consumption of owners), the 137 producers mined 64% of the coal in the Appalachian territory and immediately surrounding area and 74.4% of coal in the Appalachian territory.

The serious economic condition of the industry led to discussions among coal operators and state and national officials. Finally, in December 1931, a meeting of producers, sales agents, and attorneys recommended the creation of Appalachian Coals.

The coal producers owned all of the voting stock in Appalachian Coals, divided among them in proportion to their production. Seventeen members owned the majority of the stock. The Company was by common agreement to serve as exclusive sales representative, selling all coal at the best price available, with prices tentatively set by the officers of the Company; if the entire production of members could not be sold, orders would be apportioned among members. The Company was paid a 10% commission on sales.

It was agreed that a minimum of 70% and a maximum of 80% of the commercial tonnage of a territory should be secured before the plan would become effective. Approximately 73% was actually obtained. The 80% maximum figure was adopted, according to the coal producers, because they felt that an organization with a greater percentage control of production would unduly restrict competition in the local markets. It was expected that similar agencies would be established in other districts, but the formation of Appalachian Coals was not dependent on that development.

The plan for Appalachian Coals was submitted to the Department of Justice for approval just prior to the commencement of operations. At the Government's request, a district court enjoined the plan under Section 1 of the Sherman Act because the concerted action would eliminate competition and would have a "tendency to stabilize prices and to raise prices to a higher level than would prevail under conditions of free competition."

The Supreme Court (per Hughes, C.J.) reversed, reasoning as follows:

The restrictions the Act imposes are not mechanical or artificial. Its general phrases, interpreted to attain its fundamental objects, set up the essential standard of reasonableness. They call for vigilance in the detection and frustration of all efforts unduly to restrain the free course of interstate commerce, but they do not seek to establish a mere delusive liberty either by making impossible the normal and fair expansion of that commerce or the adoption of reasonable measures to protect it from injurious and destructive practices and to promote competition upon a sound basis. . . .

In applying this test, a close and objective scrutiny of particular conditions and purposes is necessary in each case. Realities must dominate the judgment. The mere fact that the parties to an agreement eliminate competition between themselves is not enough to condemn it. . . . The question of the application of the statute is one of intent and effect, and is not to be determined by arbitrary assumptions. It is therefore necessary in this instance to consider the economic conditions peculiar to the coal

Consider:
- coal indus
- practices
- D's plan
    - reasoning
- consequences

industry, the practices which have obtained, the nature of defendants' plan of making sales, the reasons which led to its adoption, and the probable consequences of the carrying out of that plan in relation to market prices and other matters affecting the public interest in interstate commerce in bituminous coal.

With respect to defendants' purposes, we find no warrant for determining that they were other than those they declared. Good intentions will not save a plan otherwise objectionable, but knowledge of actual intent is an aid in the interpretation of facts and prediction of consequences. . . . The industry was in distress. It suffered from over-expansion and from a serious relative decline through the growing use of substitute fuels. It was afflicted by injurious practices within itself—practices which demanded correction. If evil conditions could not be entirely cured, they at least might be alleviated. The unfortunate state of the industry would not justify any attempt unduly to restrain competition or to monopolize, but the existing situation prompted defendants to make, and the statute did not preclude them from making, an honest effort to remove abuses, to make competition fairer, and thus to promote the essential interests of commerce. . . .

they were makig
attempt to
remove abuses,
not restrain
comp

The evidence as to the conditions of the production and distribution of bituminous coal, the available facilities for its transportation, the extent of developed mining capacity, and the vast potential undeveloped capacity, makes it impossible to conclude that defendants through the operation of their plan will be able to fix the price of coal in the consuming markets. . . . While conditions are more favorable to the position of defendants' group in some markets than in others, we think that the proof clearly shows that, wherever their selling agency operates, it will find itself confronted by effective competition backed by virtually inexhaustible sources of supply, and will also be compelled to cope with the organized buying power of large consumers. The plan cannot be said either to contemplate or to involve the fixing of market prices.

there's still
comp, they can't
really set price

The contention is, and the court below found, that while defendants could not fix market prices, the concerted action would "affect" them, that is, that it would have a tendency to stabilize market prices and to raise them to a higher level than would otherwise obtain. . . . A cooperative enterprise, otherwise free from objection, which carries with it no monopolistic menace, is not to be condemned as an undue restraint merely because it may effect a change in market conditions, where the change would be in mitigation of recognized evils and would not impair, but rather foster, fair competitive opportunities. Voluntary action to rescue and preserve these opportunities, and thus to aid in relieving a depressed industry and in reviving commerce by placing competition upon a sounder basis, may be more efficacious than an attempt to provide remedies through legal processes. . . . Defendants insist that on the evidence adduced as to their competitive position in the consuming markets, and in the absence of proof of actual operations showing an injurious effect upon competition, either through possession or abuse of power, no valid objection could have been interposed under the Sherman Act if the defendants had eliminated competition between themselves by a complete integration of their mining properties in a single ownership. United States v. U.S. Steel Corp., 251 U.S. 417. . . . We agree that there is no ground for holding defendants' plan illegal merely because they have not integrated their properties and have

coop enterprises
are not nec.
bad!!

chosen to maintain their independent plants, seeking not to limit but rather to facilitate production....

We think that the Government has failed to show adequate grounds for an injunction in this case. We recognize, however, that the case has been tried in advance of the operation of defendants' plan, and that it has been necessary to test that plan with reference to purposes and anticipated consequences without the advantage of the demonstrations of experience. If in actual operation it should prove to be an undue restraint upon interstate commerce, if it should appear that the plan is used to the impairment of fair competitive opportunities, the decision upon the present record should not preclude the Government from seeking the remedy which would be suited to such a state of facts....

[handwritten margin note: they haven't started operating yet – if they do & restrain trade then, gov't can go after then]

In appraising the effect of the *Appalachian Coals* case as a precedent, what weight should be given to the disorganized and distressed condition of the coal industry? Paragraph 3 of Article 81 (ex Article 85) of the Treaty of Rome, p. 13 *supra*, provides that the EU's prohibition against price fixing is "inapplicable" to agreements that contribute to "improving the production or distribution of goods or to promoting technical or economic progress, while allowing consumers a fair share of the resulting benefit." When, if at all, should this provision be read to protect price-fixing arrangements in distressed industries? *See* Comparative Note on Crisis Cartels, p. 303 *infra*. In *Appalachian Coals,* were there less onerous alternatives, from an antitrust standpoint, available to the coal producers? Could, for example, joint ventures as to storage facilities have mitigated the problem of "distress coal"? Chief Justice Hughes suggests that the 137 coal producers could have merged. That is doubtful under present law, as you will see when examining merger policy in Chapter 9 *infra*.[14]

United States v. Socony–Vacuum Oil Co.

Supreme Court of the United States, 1940.
310 U.S. 150, 60 S.Ct. 811, 84 L.Ed. 1129.

[Respondents were major oil companies operating in the Mid–Western States. They were integrated firms, engaged in every branch of the petroleum industry—owning and operating oil wells, pipelines, refineries, bulk storage plants and service stations—and they accounted for 83% of all gasoline sold in their market in 1935.

[handwritten margin note: oil co's 83% mkt power]

The course of conduct condemned in the indictment consisted of two concerted gasoline buying programs, one in the East Texas and the other in the Mid–Continent oil fields, for the purchase in spot transactions of large quantities of gasoline, in tank-car lots, by each respondent from independent refiners. This "distress" gasoline amounted to about 17% of the gasoline marketed in the territory but, as will be discussed below, the

---

14. For a discussion of distressed industries in the merger context, *see* FTC Staff, Anticipating the 21st Century: Competition Policy in the New High–Tech, Global Marketplace Ch. 3 (1996).

prices at which it was sold had an important effect on jobber and retail prices in the entire Mid–Western market. The purchases involved surplus gasoline that the independents could not dispose of except at distress prices.

All but one of the respondents sold large quantities of gasoline to jobbers in the Mid–Western area under long-term contracts, with the price to the jobbers in 80% of the agreements dependent, pursuant to a formula, on the spot market price. Jobbers in the area distributed about 50% of all gasoline sold to retail service stations. When respondents sold direct to retailers, they customarily sold at a standard margin of two cents a gallon above the jobber price. At the retail level a system of price leadership was customarily adhered to by both independent retailers and outlets owned or controlled by major companies. As thus formulated and executed, the alleged conspiracy enabled the major companies through the concerted purchase of a very small percentage of the total available gasoline to raise the spot market, tank-car price to artificial levels, and in turn indirectly to raise and maintain prices to jobbers and consumers throughout the Mid–Western area.

Certain market journals—including Chicago Journal of Commerce and Platt's Oilgram—were made defendants and charged with printing the prices which these buying programs effected, as though they were bona fide sales of gasoline by independent refiners in the two fields to their independent jobbers and consumers. The vulnerability of the spot market prices to manipulation was emphasized by the allegation that spot market prices published in the journals were the result of spot sales made chiefly by independent refiners of less than 5 per cent of the gasoline sold in the Mid–Western area. The prices paid by respondents themselves were not reported in the trade journals.

The history of depressed conditions in the petroleum industry, mainly relevant to certain defenses raised by respondents (including removal of competitive evils and acquiescence by the federal government), revealed a background of overproduction in the '20s and '30s, with prices often falling below costs of production. States had little success in enforcing proration laws aimed at limiting production. Unlawfully produced "hot oil" and "hot gasoline" were marketed for substantially lower prices than those posted for legal oil and gasoline. Moreover, as a result of inadequate storage facilities at the disposal of independent refiners, the market was further flooded with legally manufactured "distress" gasoline which had to be sold for whatever price it would bring.

As an outgrowth of the N.R.A., a Tank Car Stabilization Committee was established by respondents to consider methods of dealing with problems created by sale of distress gasoline. The Committee decided that the major companies would select one or more of the independent refiners having distress gasoline as its "dancing partner," and would assume responsibility for purchasing the distress supply. These were informal gentlemen's agreements lacking any specific coercive element. At monthly meetings each member indicated how much distress gasoline his company

[handwritten margin note: depressed oil mkt— "hot oil" sold cheaper surplus gas called "distress" gas]

would buy and from whom, relying on surveys and recommendations compiled by the Stabilization Committee. As contacts between respondent buyers and their dancing partners became well established, the buying program worked almost automatically.

Since the sale of gasoline to jobbers was for the most part computed pursuant to a formula dependent on the spot market price, the entire retail price structure throughout the Mid–Western area during the indictment period was based on the Mid–Continent spot market quotations.

The essence of the charge against respondents was that through regular purchases at the going market price they eliminated a part of the supply of distress gasoline which in the absence of the buying programs would have been a factor in determining prices of the spot market. Control over prices was not accomplished directly, but rather indirectly by maintaining a floor under the spot market through the removal of the depressing distress gasoline. It was not alleged that respondents concertedly bid up the spot market price in order to profit from the sale of their own products on the price chargeable under their jobbers' contracts. All purchases of distress gasoline were at prices determined by the forces of competition. Nevertheless, during the operation of the program, retail prices rose in close step with rising Mid–Continent spot market prices during 1935 and 1936. In March, 1935, before the buying program was instituted, the low Mid–Continent spot market price for regular gasoline was 4⅝ cents. In December, 1935, after the buying program, the price was 5⅜ cents. The retail price rose from 12.56 cents to 13.41 cents.]

■ DOUGLAS, J. . . . The court charged the jury that it was a violation of the Sherman Act for a group of individuals or corporations to act together to raise the prices to be charged for the commodity which they manufactured where they controlled a substantial part of the interstate trade and commerce in that commodity. The court stated that where the members of a combination had the power to raise prices and acted together for that purpose, the combination was illegal; and that it was immaterial how reasonable or unreasonable those prices were or to what extent they had been affected by the combination. It further charged that if such illegal combination existed, it did not matter that there may also have been other factors which contributed to the raising of the prices. In that connection, it referred specifically to the economic factors which we have previously discussed and which respondents contended were primarily responsible for the price rise and the spot markets' stability in 1935 and 1936, viz. control of production, the Connally Act, the price of crude oil, an increase in consumptive demand, control of inventories and manufacturing quotas, and improved business conditions. The court then charged that, unless the jury found beyond a reasonable doubt that the price rise and its continuance were "caused" by the combination and not caused by those other factors, verdicts of "not guilty" should be returned. It also charged that there was no evidence of governmental approval which would exempt the buying programs from the prohibitions of the Sherman Act; and that knowledge or acquiescence of officers of the government or the good intentions of the members of the combination would not give immunity from prosecution under that Act.

The Circuit Court of Appeals held this charge to be reversible error, since it was based upon the theory that such a combination was illegal *per se.* In its view respondents' activities were not unlawful unless they constituted an unreasonable restraint of trade. Hence, since that issue had not been submitted to the jury and since evidence bearing on it had been excluded, that court reversed and remanded for a new trial so that the character of those activities and their effect on competition could be determined. In answer to the government's petition respondents here contend that the judgment of the Circuit Court of Appeals was correct, since there was evidence that they had affected prices only in the sense that the removal of the competitive evil of distress gasoline by the buying programs had permitted prices to rise to a normal competitive level; that their activities promoted rather than impaired fair competitive opportunities; and therefore that their activities had not unduly or unreasonably restrained trade. And they also contend that certain evidence which was offered should have been admitted as bearing on the purpose and end sought to be attained, the evil believed to exist, and the nature of the restraint and its effect. By their cross-petition respondents contend that the record contains no substantial competent evidence that the combination, either in purpose or effect, unreasonably restrained trade within the meaning of the Sherman Act, and therefore that the Circuit Court of Appeals erred in holding that they were not entitled to directed verdicts of acquittal.

[The Court then reviews United States v. Trenton Potteries Co., 273 U.S. 392]. . . .

But respondents claim that other decisions of this Court afford them adequate defenses to the indictment. Among those on which they place reliance are Appalachian Coals, Inc. v. United States, 288 U.S. 344; Sugar Institute, Inc. v. United States, 297 U.S. 553; Maple Flooring Mfrs. Association v. United States, 268 U.S. 563; Cement Mfrs. Protective Association v. United States, 268 U.S. 588; Chicago Board of Trade v. United States, 246 U.S. 231; and the *American Tobacco* and *Standard Oil* cases [221 U.S. 1; 221 U.S. 106].

But we do not think that line of cases is apposite. As clearly indicated in the *Trenton Potteries* case, the *American Tobacco* and *Standard Oil* cases have no application to combinations operating directly on prices or price structures.

And we are of the opinion that Appalachian Coals, Inc. v. United States, *supra*, is not in point. . . .

Thus in reality the only essential thing in common between the instant case and the *Appalachian Coals* case is the presence in each of so-called demoralizing or injurious practices. The methods of dealing with them were quite divergent. In the instant case there were buying programs of distress gasoline which had as their direct purpose and aim the raising and maintenance of spot market prices and of prices to jobbers and consumers in the Mid–Western area, by the elimination of distress gasoline as a market factor. The increase in the spot market prices was to be accomplished by a well organized buying program on that market: regular ascertainment of the amounts of surplus gasoline; assignment of sellers among the buyers; regular purchases at prices which would place and keep a floor under the market. Unlike the plan in the instant case, the plan in the *Appalachian Coals* case was not designed to operate vis-à-vis the general consuming market and to fix the prices on that market. Furthermore, the effect, if any, of that plan on prices was not only wholly incidental but also highly conjectural. For the plan had not then been put into operation. Hence this Court expressly reserved jurisdiction in the District Court to take further proceedings if, inter alia, in "actual operation" the plan proved to be "an undue restraint upon interstate commerce." And as we have seen it would *per se* constitute such a restraint if price-fixing were involved. . . .

Nor can respondents find sanction in Chicago Board of Trade v. United States, *supra*, for the buying programs here under attack. That case involved a prohibition on the members of the Chicago Board of Trade from purchasing or offering to purchase between the closing of the session and its opening the next day grains (under a special class of contracts) at a price other than the closing bid. The rule was somewhat akin to rules of an exchange limiting the period of trading, for as stated by this Court the "restriction was upon the period of price-making" [246 U.S. 231, 239]. No attempt was made to show that the purpose or effect of the rule was to raise or depress prices. The rule affected only a small proportion of the commerce in question. And among its effects was the creation of a public market for grains under that special contract class, where prices were determined competitively and openly. Since it was not aimed at price manipulation or the control of the market prices and since it had "no appreciable effect on general market prices," the rule survived as a reasonable restraint of trade.

There was no deviation from the principle of the *Trenton Potteries* case in Sugar Institute, Inc. v. United States, *supra*. For in that case so-called competitive abuses were not permitted as defenses to violations of the Sherman Act bottomed on a trade association's efforts to create and maintain a uniform price structure.

Thus for over forty years this Court has consistently and without deviation adhered to the principle that price-fixing agreements are unlawful *per se* under the Sherman Act and that no showing of so-called competitive abuses or evils which those agreements were designed to eliminate or alleviate may be interposed as a defense. . . .

Therefore the sole remaining question on this phase of the case is the applicability of the rule of the *Trenton Potteries* case to these facts.

Respondents seek to distinguish the *Trenton Potteries* case from the instant one. They assert that in that case the parties substituted an agreed-on price for one determined by competition; that the defendants there had the power and purpose to suppress the play of competition in the determination of the market price; and therefore that the controlling factor in that decision was the destruction of market competition, not whether prices were higher or lower, reasonable or unreasonable. Respondents contend that in the instant case there was no elimination in the spot tank car market of competition which prevented the prices in that market from being made by the play of competition in sales between independent refiners and their jobber and consumer customers; that during the buying programs those prices were in fact determined by such competition; that the purchases under those programs were closely related to or dependent on the spot market prices; that there was no evidence that the purchases of distress gasoline under those programs had any effect on the competitive market price beyond that flowing from the removal of a competitive evil; and that if respondents had tried to do more than free competition from the effect of distress gasoline and to set an arbitrary non-competitive price through their purchases, they would have been without power to do so.

But we do not deem those distinctions material.

In the first place, there was abundant evidence that the combination had the purpose to raise prices. And likewise, there was ample evidence that the buying programs at least contributed to the price rise and the stability of the spot markets, and to increases in the price of gasoline sold in the Mid–Western area during the indictment period. That other factors also may have contributed to that rise and stability of the markets is immaterial. For in any such market movement, forces other than the purchasing power of the buyers normally would contribute to the price rise and the market stability. So far as cause and effect are concerned it is sufficient in this type of case if the buying programs of the combination resulted in a price rise and market stability which but for them would not have happened. For this reason the charge to the jury that the buying programs must have "caused" the price rise and its continuance was more favorable to respondents than they could have required. Proof that there was a conspiracy, that its purpose was to raise prices, and that it caused or contributed to a price rise is proof of the actual consummation or execution of a conspiracy under § 1 of the Sherman Act.

Secondly, the fact that sales on the spot markets were still governed by some competition is of no consequence. For it is indisputable that that competition was restricted through the removal by respondents of a part of the supply which but for the buying programs would have been a factor in determining the going prices on those markets. But the vice of the conspiracy was not merely the restriction of supply of gasoline by removal of a surplus. As we have said, this was a well organized program. The timing and strategic placement of the buying orders for distress gasoline played an important and significant role. Buying orders were carefully placed so as to remove the distress gasoline from weak hands. Purchases were timed. Sellers were assigned to the buyers so that regular outlets for distress gasoline would be available. The whole scheme was carefully planned and executed to the end that distress gasoline would not overhang the markets and depress them at any time. And as a result of the payment of fair going market prices a floor was placed and kept under the spot markets. Prices rose and jobbers and consumers in the Mid–Western area paid more for their gasoline than they would have paid but for the conspiracy. Competition was not eliminated from the markets; but it was clearly curtailed, since restriction of the supply of gasoline, the timing and placement of the purchases under the buying programs and the placing of a floor under the spot markets obviously reduced the play of the forces of supply and demand.

The elimination of so-called competitive evils is no legal justification for such buying programs. The elimination of such conditions was sought primarily for its effect on the price structures. Fairer competitive prices, it is claimed, resulted when distress gasoline was removed from the market. But such defense is typical of the protestations usually made in price-fixing cases. Ruinous competition, financial disaster, evils of price cutting and the like appear throughout our history as ostensible justifications for price-fixing. If the so-called competitive abuses were to be appraised here, the reasonableness of prices would necessarily become an issue in every price-fixing case. In that event the Sherman Act would soon be emasculated; its philosophy would be supplanted by one which is wholly alien to a system of free competition; it would not be the charter of freedom which its framers intended.

The reasonableness of prices has no constancy due to the dynamic quality of the business facts underlying price structures. Those who fixed reasonable prices today would perpetuate unreasonable prices tomorrow, since those prices would not be subject to continuous administrative supervision and readjustment in light of changed conditions. Those who controlled the prices would control or effectively dominate the market. And those who were in that strategic position would have it in their power to destroy or drastically impair the competitive system. But the thrust of the rule is deeper and reaches more than monopoly power. Any combination which tampers with price structures is engaged in an unlawful activity. Even though the members of the price-fixing group were in no position to control the market, to the extent that they raised, lowered, or stabilized prices they would be directly interfering with the free play of market forces. The Act places all such schemes beyond the pale and protects that vital part of our economy against any degree of interference. Congress has not left with us the determination of whether or not particular price-fixing schemes are wise or unwise, healthy or destructive. It has not permitted the age-old cry of ruinous competition and competitive evils to be a defense to price-fixing conspiracies. It has no more allowed genuine or fancied competitive abuses as a legal justification for such schemes than it has the good intentions of the members of the combination. If such a shift is to be made, it must be done by the Congress. Certainly Congress has not left us with any such choice. Nor has the Act created or authorized the creation of any special exception in favor of the oil industry. Whatever may be its peculiar problems and characteristics, the Sherman Act, so far as price-fixing agreements are concerned, establishes one uniform rule applicable to all industries alike. There was accordingly no error in the refusal to charge that in order to convict the jury must find that the resultant prices were raised and maintained at "high, arbitrary and non-competitive levels." The charge in the indictment to that effect was surplusage.

Nor is it important that the prices paid by the combination were not fixed in the sense that they were uniform and inflexible. Price-fixing as used in the *Trenton Potteries* case has no such limited meaning. An agreement to pay or charge rigid, uniform prices would be an illegal agreement under the Sherman Act. But so would agreements to raise or lower prices whatever machinery for price-fixing was used. That price-fixing includes more than the mere establishment of uniform prices is clearly evident from the *Trenton Potteries* case itself, where this Court noted with approval Swift & Co. v. United States, 196 U.S. 375, in which a decree was affirmed which restrained a combination from "raising or lowering prices or fixing uniform prices" at which meats will be sold. Hence prices are fixed within the meaning of the *Trenton Potteries* case if the range within which purchases or sales will be made is agreed upon, if the prices paid or charged are to be at a certain level or on ascending or descending scales, if they are to be uniform, or if by various formulae they are related to the market prices. They are fixed because they are agreed upon. And the fact that, as here, they are fixed at the fair going market price is immaterial. For purchases at or under the market are one species of price-fixing. In this case, the result was to place a floor under the market—a floor which served the function of increasing the stability and firmness of market prices. That was repeatedly characterized in this case as stabilization. But in terms of market operations stabilization is but one form of manipulation. And market manipulation in its various manifestations is implicitly an artificial stimulus applied to (or at times a brake on) market prices, a force which distorts those prices, a factor which prevents the determination of those prices by free competition alone. Respondents, however, argue that there was no correlation between the amount of gasoline which the major companies were buying and the trend of prices on the spot markets. They point to the fact that such purchasing was lightest during the period of the market rise in the spring of 1935, and heaviest in the summer and early fall of 1936 when the prices declined; and that it decreased later in 1936 when the prices rose. But those facts do not militate against the conclusion that these buying programs were a species of price-fixing or manipulation. Rather they are wholly consistent with the maintenance of a floor under the market or a stabilization operation of this type, since the need for purchases under such a program might well decrease as prices rose and increase as prices declined.

As we have indicated, the machinery employed by a combination for price-fixing is immaterial.

Under the Sherman Act a combination formed for the purpose and with the effect of raising, depressing, fixing, pegging, or stabilizing the price of a commodity in interstate or foreign commerce is illegal *per se*. Where the machinery for price-fixing is an agreement on the prices to be charged or paid for the commodity in the interstate or foreign channels of trade, the power to fix prices exists if the combination has control of a substantial part of the commerce in that commodity. Where the means for price-fixing are purchases or sales of the commodity in a market operation or, as here, purchases of a part of the supply of the commodity for the purpose of keeping it from having a depressive effect on the markets, such power may be found to exist though the combination does not control a substantial part of the commodity. In such a case that power may be established if as a result of market conditions, the resources available to the combinations, the timing and the strategic placement of orders and the like, effective means are at hand to accomplish the desired objective. But there may be effective influence over the market though the group in question does not control it. Price-fixing agreements may have utility to members of the group though the power possessed or exerted falls far short of domination and control. Monopoly power (United States v. Patten, 226 U.S. 525) is not the only power which the Act strikes down, as we have said. Proof that a combination was formed for the purpose of fixing prices and that it caused them to be fixed or contributed to that result is proof of the completion of a price-fixing conspiracy under § 1 of the Act.[15] The

---

15. [The following is the often-discussed footnote 59 to the Court's opinion—Ed.] Under this indictment proof that prices in the Mid–Western area were raised as a result of the activities of the combination was essential, since sales of gasoline by respondents at the increased prices in that area were necessary in order to establish jurisdiction in the Western District of Wisconsin. Hence we have necessarily treated the case as one where exertion of the power to fix prices (*i.e.*, the actual fixing of prices) was an ingredient of the offense. But that does not mean that both a purpose and a power to fix prices are necessary for the establishment of a conspiracy under § 1 of the Sherman Act. That would be true if power or ability to commit an offense was necessary in order to convict a person of conspiring to commit it. But it is well established that a person "may be guilty of conspiring, although incapable of committing the objective offense." United States v. Rabinowich, 238 U.S. 78, 86. And it is likewise well settled that conspiracies under the Sherman Act are not dependent on any overt act other than the act of conspiring. Nash v. United States, 229 U.S. 373, 378. It is the "contract, combination . . . or conspiracy in restraint of trade or commerce" which § 1 of the Act strikes down, whether the concerted activity be wholly nascent or abortive on the one hand, or successful on the other. See United States v. Trenton Potteries Co., 273 U.S. 392, 402. Cf. Retail Lumber Dealers' Ass'n v. State, 95 Miss. 337, 48 So. 1021. And the amount of interstate or foreign trade involved is not material (Montague & Co. v. Lowry, 193 U.S. 38), since § 1 of the Act brands as illegal the character of the restraint not the amount of commerce affected. In view of these considerations a conspiracy to fix prices violates § 1 of the Act though no overt act is shown, though it is not established that the conspirators had the means available for accomplishment of their objective, and though the conspiracy embraced but a part of the interstate or foreign commerce in the commodity. Whatever may have been the status of price-fixing agreements at common law (Allen, Criminal Conspiracies in Restraint of Trade at Common Law, 23 Harv.L.Rev. 531) the Sherman Act has a broader application to them than the common law prohibitions or sanctions. *See* United States v. Trans–Missouri Freight Ass'n, 166 U.S. 290, 328. Price-fixing agreements may or may not be aimed at complete elimination of price competition. The group making those agreements may or may not have power to control the market. But the fact that the group cannot control the market prices does not necessarily mean that the agreement as to prices has no utility to the members of the combination. The effectiveness of price-fixing agreements is dependent on many factors, such as competitive tactics, position in the industry, the formula underlying price policies. Whatever economic justification particular price-fixing agreements may be thought to have, the law does not permit an inquiry into their reasonableness. They are all indictment in this case charged that this combination had that purpose and effect. And there was abundant evidence to support it. Hence the existence of power on the part of members of the combination to fix prices was but a conclusion from the finding that the buying programs caused or contributed to the rise and stability of prices. . . .

Accordingly we conclude that the Circuit Court of Appeals erred in reversing the judgments on this ground. *A fortiori* the position taken by respondents in their cross petition that they were entitled to directed verdicts of acquittal is untenable. . . .[16]

NOTES AND QUESTIONS

1. Antitrust enforcement against agreements that affect price usually involve conspiracies among competitors to fix minimum prices on sales through channels of distribution toward consumers. For a recent case, *see* JTC Petroleum Co. v. Piasa Motor Fuels, Inc., 190 F.3d 775 (7th Cir. 1999).

But suppose the agreement among competitors relates to the purchase of products or of a raw material that is incorporated in products that they sell. In National Macaroni Manufacturers Association v. FTC, 345 F.2d 421 (7th Cir. 1965), the FTC charged that the Association and its members had entered into an agreement fixing the composition of macaroni products. Members of the Association constituted 84 of 125 commercially important domestic manufacturers of macaroni and macaroni products, accounting for about 70% of sales in the United States.

Macaroni products are manufactured from dough and flour mainly derived from "durum wheat" and farina flour which is a hard wheat other than durum. Durum wheat improves the quality of macaroni products, and products containing 100% durum enjoy the best consumer acceptance.

Early in 1961, it became apparent that there would be a short crop of durum wheat in the 1961–62 harvest year as a result of a drought. Association members saw as their alternatives continued production of 100% durum products which would gradually lead to the payment of "astronomical prices" to suppliers, discontinuance in the use of durum wheat with resulting sales loss because of consumer preferences, or an industry switch to 50–50 durum and non-durum wheat blends. Manufacturer-members of the Association adopted a resolution supporting the 50–50 blend alternative "to maintain the highest quality possible to best utilize the available supply of durum during the current crop year." Most manufacturers

---

banned because of their actual or potential threat to the central nervous system of the economy.

16. Hughes, C.J., and Murphy, J., did not participate. The dissenting opinion of Roberts, J., in which McReynolds, J., joined, is omitted.

Concerning the significance of the depressed status of an industry, compare *Socony–Vacuum* and Fashion Originators' Guild v. FTC, 312 U.S. 457, 467 (1941), with Appalachian Coals, Inc. v. United States, p. 192 *supra* and National Ass'n of Window Glass Mfrs. v. United States, 263 U.S. 403 (1923), p. 276 *infra*. See FTC Staff, Anticipating the 21st Century: Competition Policy in the New High–Tech, Global Marketplace Ch. 3 (1996); First, Structural Antitrust Rules and International Competition: The Case of Distressed Industries, 62 N.Y.U.L.Rev. 1054 (1987); Pitofsky, Antitrust and Problems of Adjustment in Distressed Industries, 55 Antitrust L.J. 21 (1986).

followed the course proposed in the resolution although a few did not, and sales of 100% durum products were negligible after the resolution was adopted.

The Commission found that "the agreement was intended to ward off price competition for durum wheat in short supply by lowering total industry demand to the level of available supply ... and concluded that 'where all or the dominant firms in the market combined to fix the composition of their product with the design and result of depressing the price of an essential raw material, they violate the rule against price fixing agreements....' " The Court of Appeals affirmed, noting that the Commission decision did not hold illegal all efforts at product standardization, or all buying agencies[17] or other cooperative agreements, or all attempts to cope with scarcity or other conditions of economic dislocation.

What kinds of agreements affecting components would be legal? For example, there is much evidence that children suffer serious health risks when they chew or swallow chipped paint containing lead. Would the same result follow if all manufacturers of toys agreed they would exclude paint containing lead from their toy products? Suppose the major automobile manufacturers agreed to add a special safety device on no more than one model per year for three years to test statistically the advantages and disadvantages of the new safety device?

2.   An agreement among competitors may relate to a term of sale only indirectly connected with price. In Catalano, Inc. v. Target Sales, Inc., 446 U.S. 643 (1980), a group of beer retailers charged that wholesalers had conspired to eliminate short-term credit in violation of Section 1 of the Sherman Act. The retailers alleged that prior to the agreement, the wholesalers had extended credit without interest up to the 30 and 42–day limits permitted by state law, and wholesalers had competed with each other in offering favorable credit terms. The District Court concluded that the allegations did not constitute a *per se* violation; the Court of Appeals affirmed, suggesting that the agreement might enhance competition by removing a barrier to entry to some sellers and by increasing visibility of price.

In a *per curiam* opinion, the Supreme Court reversed:

> It is virtually self-evident that extending interest-free credit for a period of time is equivalent to giving a discount equal to the value of the use of the purchase price for that period of time.... While it may be that the elimination of a practice of giving variable discounts will ultimately lead in a competitive market to corresponding decreases in the invoice price, that is surely not necessarily to be anticipated. It is more realistic to view an agreement to eliminate credit sales as extinguishing one form of competition among the sellers. In any event, when a particular concerted activity entails an obvious risk of anti-competitive impact with no apparent potentially redeeming value, the fact that a practice may turn out to be harmless in a particular set of circumstances will not prevent its being declared unlawful *per se*.

> The majority of the panel of the Court of Appeals suggested, however, that a horizontal agreement to eliminate credit sales may remove a barrier to other sellers who may wish to enter the market. But in any case in

---

17.   Ed. National Macaroni was distinguished by the First and Third Circuits as a case in which the buyer was "a 'sham' organization seeking only to combine otherwise independent buyers in order to suppress their otherwise competitive instinct to bid up price." Tennessean Truckstop, Inc. v. NTS, Inc., 875 F.2d 86, 89 (6th Cir. 1989), quoting Kartell v. Blue Shield of Mass., 749 F.2d 922, 925 (1st Cir. 1984). When would a buying agency pass antitrust muster? *See Northwest Wholesale*, p. 337 *infra*.

which competitors are able to increase the price level or to curtail production by agreement, it could be argued that the agreement has the effect of
making the market more attractive to potential new entrants. . . .

Nor can the informing function of the agreement, the increased price
visibility, justify its restraint on the individual wholesaler's freedom to
select his own prices and terms of sale. For, again, it is obvious that any
industrywide agreement on prices will result in a more accurate understanding of the terms offered by all parties to the agreement.

3. In Arizona v. Maricopa County Medical Society, 457 U.S. 332 (1982), the
Supreme Court considered whether Section 1 of the Sherman Act was violated by
an agreement among competing physicians that set, by majority vote, maximum
fees. The maximum fees were for health services provided to policyholders of
specified insurance plans. The Ninth Circuit had held that the issue could not be
decided without evaluating the purpose and effect of the agreement at a full trial.
Justice Stevens, writing for a 4–3 majority, concluded that the agreement constituted *per se* price fixing. The Supreme Court reasoned as follows:

Our decisions foreclose the argument that the agreements at issue
escape *per se* condemnation because they are horizontal and fix maximum
prices. . . . In this case the rule is violated by a price restraint that tends to
provide the same economic rewards to all practitioners regardless of their
skill, their experience, their training, or their willingness to employ innovative and difficult procedures in individual cases. Such a restraint also may
discourage entry into the market and may deter experimentation and new
developments by individual entrepreneurs. It may be a masquerade for an
agreement to fix uniform prices, or it may in the future take on that
character.

Nor does the fact that doctors—rather than nonprofessionals—are the
parties to the price fixing agreements support the respondents' position. In
Goldfarb v. Virginia State Bar, 421 U.S. 773, 788 n. 17 (1975), we stated
that the "public service aspect, and other features of the professions, may
require that a particular practice, which could properly be viewed as a
violation of the Sherman Act in another context, be treated differently."
See National Society of Professional Engineers v. United States, 435 U.S.
679, 696 (1978). The price fixing agreements in this case, however, are not
premised on public service or ethical norms. The respondents do not argue,
as did the defendants in *Goldfarb* and *Professional Engineers,* that the
quality of the professional service that their members provide is enhanced
by the price restraint. The respondents' claim for relief from the *per se* rule
is simply that the doctors' agreement not to charge certain insureds more
than a fixed price facilitates the successful marketing of an attractive
insurance plan. But the claim that the price restraint will make it easier
for customers to pay does not distinguish the medical profession from any
other provider of goods or services.

We are equally unpersuaded by the argument that we should not apply
the *per se* rule in this case because the judiciary has little antitrust
experience in the health care industry. The argument quite obviously is
inconsistent with *Socony–Vacuum.* In unequivocal terms, we stated that,
"[w]hatever may be its peculiar problems and characteristics, the Sherman
Act, so far as price-fixing agreements are concerned, establishes one
uniform rule applicable to all industries alike." 310 U.S., at 222. We also
stated that "[t]he elimination of so-called competitive evils [in an industry]

Sherman applies to all industries

is no legal justification" for price fixing agreements, id., at 220, yet the Court of Appeals refused to apply the *per se* rule in this case in part because the health care industry was so far removed from the competitive model. Consistent with our prediction in *Socony–Vacuum,* id., at 221, the result of this reasoning was the adoption by the Court of Appeals of a legal standard based on the reasonableness of the fixed prices, an inquiry we have so often condemned. Finally, the argument that the *per se* rule must be rejustified for every industry that has not been subject to significant antitrust litigation ignores the rationale for *per se* rules, which in part is to avoid "the necessity for an incredibly complicated and prolonged economic investigation into the entire history of the industry involved, as well as related industries, in an effort to determine at large whether a particular restraint has been unreasonable—an inquiry so often wholly fruitless when undertaken." Northern Pac. R. Co. v. United States.

The respondents' principal argument is that the *per se* rule is inapplicable because their agreements are alleged to have procompetitive justifications. The argument indicates a misunderstanding of the *per se* concept. The anticompetitive potential inherent in all price fixing agreements justifies their facial invalidation even if procompetitive justifications are offered for some. Those claims of enhanced competition are so unlikely to prove significant in any particular case that we adhere to the rule of law that is justified in its general application. Even when the respondents are given every benefit of the doubt, the limited record in this case is not inconsistent with the presumption that the respondents' agreements will not significantly enhance competition. . . .

   Even if a fee schedule is therefore desirable, it is not necessary that the doctors do the price fixing. The record indicates that the Arizona Comprehensive Medical/Dental Program for Foster Children is administered by the Maricopa foundation pursuant to a contract under which the maximum fee schedule is prescribed by a state agency rather than by the doctors. This program and the Blue Shield plan challenged in Group Life & Health Insurance Co. v. Royal Drug Co., 440 U.S. 205 (1979), indicate that insurers are capable not only of fixing maximum reimbursable prices but also of obtaining binding agreements with providers guaranteeing the insured full reimbursement of a participating provider's fee. In light of these examples, it is not surprising that nothing in the record even arguably supports the conclusion that this type of insurance program could not function if the fee schedules were set in a different way. . . .

   The foundations are not analogous to partnerships or other joint arrangements in which persons who would otherwise be competitors pool their capital and share the risks of loss as well as the opportunities for profit. In such joint ventures, the partnership is regarded as a single firm competing with other sellers in the market. The agreement under attack is an agreement among hundreds of competing doctors concerning the price at which each will offer his own services to a substantial number of consumers. It is true that some are surgeons, some anesthesiologists, and some psychiatrists, but the doctors do not sell a package of three kinds of services. If a clinic offered complete medical coverage for a flat fee, the cooperating doctors would have the type of partnership arrangement in which a price fixing agreement among the doctors would be perfectly proper. But the fee agreements disclosed by the record in this case are

[handwritten margin note: A per se— anti comp potential outweighs any pro effects of price fixing.]

among independent competing entrepreneurs. They fit squarely into the horizontal price fixing mold.

Did the doctors in *Maricopa* have a real incentive to achieve cost containment as they voted on prices? What if some of the doctors in *Maricopa* had negotiated as individuals—directly or through an organization—with health insurers to accept maximum fees? In Levine v. Central Florida Medical Affiliates, Inc., 72 F.3d 1538 (11th Cir. 1996), the Eleventh Circuit awarded summary judgment to defendant Healthchoice, Inc., a preferred provider organization, that negotiated "health care coverage [agreements] in which physicians agree to accept no more than a maximum allowable fee for services rendered to plan enrollees." The Court reasoned:

> Providers must either accept not more than the maximum reimbursement negotiated by Healthchoice with the payors and not charge the patient for any difference between their fee and the reimbursement, or else opt out of the plan. The result is that the providers' actual fees are not set. The only figure that is set is the maximum allowable fee that they will be reimbursed by Healthchoice. Nothing prevents the physician from dropping his fees even further in order to compete should he choose to do so.

> This method of negotiating fees, in which the payors decide the maximum amount they are willing to reimburse providers for medical services and providers decide whether they are willing to accept that limitation on the reimbursement they receive, is a kind of "price fixing," but it is a kind that the antitrust laws do not prohibit.... Dr. Levine's section 1 claim against these defendants, to the extent that it alleges illegal price fixing, fails.

> Our decision that Healthchoice's method of negotiating with payors the fees it pays providers does not violate the Sherman Act as a matter of law is supported by the Department of Justice and the Federal Trade Commission's recently issued "Statements of Enforcement Policy and Analytical Principles Relating to Health Care and Antitrust" ("DOJ Enforcement Policy" or "the policy"), available in WESTLAW, 1994 WL 642477 (F.T.C.). The DOJ Enforcement Policy separates those multiprovider networks wherein competitors agree with one another regarding prices or market allocation, from those networks wherein such decisions are handled unilaterally by each competitor or through a third party "messenger." The policy defines the "messenger model" as involving "an agent or third party conveying to purchasers information obtained individually from providers in the network about prices the network participants are willing to accept, and conveying to providers any contract offers made by purchasers." The latter will "rarely present substantial antitrust concerns." The policy states that "the critical antitrust issue is whether the arrangement creates or facilitates agreements that restrict price or other significant terms of competition among the provider members of the network." In this case, there is no evidence that the Healthchoice method of negotiating maximum fee reimbursement facilitates any agreements among its provider panel members to restrict price or any other forms of competition.

In North Texas Specialty Physicians v. FTC, 528 F.3d 346 (5th Cir. 2008), the Fifth Circuit affirmed an FTC decision that North Texas Specialty Physicians (NTSP) has engaged in horizontal price fixing in violation of § 5 of the FTC Act. The NTSP business model involved, among other concerns, the negotiation of fee contracts on behalf of its 575 doctor members with "payors" such as insurance companies. As part of this process, NTSP polled its physicians regarding the minimum fee each would accept. NTSP would not deliver a payor's offer to its physicians unless the offer was at least equal to the minimum fee determined (calculated through a formula) by the physicians' poll.

The Fifth Circuit upheld the FTC's "inherently suspect" analysis. The Court concluded that the "net anticompetitive effects of certain of NTSP's practices were obvious," such as its polling of physician approach. The decision confirmed FTC guidance that in a "messenger model," the messenger (*e.g.*, NTSP) can facilitate only "independent, unilateral decisions of network providers" and that it is unlawful to facilitate "collective decisions on pricing or price-related terms."

PROBLEM 2

PRICING PLAN OF THE SNORKA CAR DEALERS

Japan's popular front wheel drive compact car, the Snorka, sold in the San Francisco area last year for about $14,000. In that area, Snorka sales equalled 3% of all passenger car sales; 10% of all compact car sales; and 15% of all low-price compact car sales (sales at less than $15,000). All Snorka dealers in the area belong to the Snorka Car Dealers' Protective Association.

Intensive price competition among Snorka dealers last year led to public dissatisfaction with pricing practices. Each dealer posted the manufacturer's list price (about $13,500) on the car windows according to federal law but, because demand for the product exceeded supply, the dealers charged a "dealer's add-on" that ranged up to $1,000. Purchasers from one dealer complained bitterly when they discovered that lower "dealer add-ons" were being quoted by other dealers for the exact model they had just purchased. To overcome public animosity, the dealers agreed that henceforth the announced "dealer add-on" of a Snorka with standard accessories, prominently posted on the car window, would be $1,000, and that each dealer would make adjustments in individual cases by giving overly generous trade-in allowances and comparable discounts for "cash" (*i.e.*, non-trade-in transactions). Following the institution of this plan, vigorous competition continued; net prices remained in the vicinity of $14,000, no sales were recorded at the full list plus dealer add-on price, and competition from other car models forced downward revision, and ultimately abandonment, of the fixed "dealer add-on" price.

On an indictment for violation of the antitrust laws, the Snorka dealers moved to dismiss at the end of the government's case after the foregoing facts had been shown. What result?

SECTION 3.   CHARACTERIZATION QUESTIONS AND OTHER ISSUES

In its most sweeping formulation, *Socony–Vacuum* held that any combination which "tampers with price structures" is illegal *per se*. In effect, illegality would be determined without regard to the traditional criteria for ascertaining unreasonable restraints—market power of the parties to the agreement, purpose, anticompetitive effect, and consideration of justifications. (Note, however, that the arrangement in *Socony–Vacuum* systematically removed a portion of the supply of oil from the market, at least temporarily, and thus it can be said that it had the "necessary effect" of altering the forces of price-formation.)

This abbreviated approach to illegality stands in contrast to the "rule of reason," one formulation of which was announced by Justice Brandeis in *Chicago Board of Trade* (p. 188 *supra*). That approach calls for examination, analysis, and ultimately the balancing of a wide range of factors before any practice is condemned.

The rationale for a *per se* rule covering horizontal price fixing was touched upon in *Socony–Vacuum*, but has been formulated more explicitly in Supreme Court opinions that we will deal with later in the casebook. (*See* Northwest Wholesale Stationers, Inc. v. Pacific Stationery & Printing Co., 472 U.S. 284 (1985) and FTC v. Superior Court Trial Lawyers Association, 493 U.S. 411 (1990) in Chapter 5 and Continental TV, Inc. v. GTE Sylvania Inc., 433 U.S. 36 (1977) in Chapter 7.) Those decisions make it clear that where a practice usually results in significant adverse competitive effects, rarely is justified by significant redeeming virtues, and when there are often less restrictive alternatives available, there is no reason for an extended trial before such practices will be condemned.

The *per se* rule against outright horizontal price fixing satisfies those tests. Price-fixing cartels tend to misallocate society's resources, rarely achieve efficiencies that could not occur through less objectionable means, and seldom pass any benefits on to consumers. The *per se* rule itself is relatively clear and thus can be made effective through the self-policing of businessmen and their legal counselors. (In later chapters, we will see examples of *per se* rules, covering other sorts of practices, made less precise by exceptions which impair clarity and predictability.) Also, the alternative to a simple *per se* rule of illegality would involve continuing supervision of price by enforcement agencies and the judiciary—a "public utility" type rate regulation which is contrary to the central idea of a free-market economy and well beyond judicial competence. Note finally that defense of a *per se* rule does not require demonstrating that every transaction or form of conduct to which it applies is on balance anticompetitive. Rather, the point is that in the overwhelming majority of instances, full exploration or analysis of all relevant factors would show anticompetitive effects, and the few instances in which "errors" occur constitute a price worth paying to have an effective legal rule.

While a *per se* rule works well enough in simple price-fixing situations, there are many other arrangements that have some relatively less substantial effect on price—though they arguably "tamper" with price structure in some sense—or where efficiency claims are more plausible. In this situation, it is simply impossible to conclude without full analysis—or at least a fuller analysis than a *per se* rule would afford—that the type of restraint is socially undesirable. Actually, we have already seen examples of that in *Chicago Board of Trade*, and the multiprovider networks discussed after *Maricopa*. In *Chicago Board of Trade* the plausible argument was raised that the restrictions on the hours of bidding in effect "made a market," that is, facilitated effective competition during the hours in which the exchange operated. (Can you think of any less anticompetitive way in which that result could have been achieved?)

In this section, we will examine cases raising a series of "characterization" issues. In such cases, there is common ground that price fixing is illegal *per se,* but questions are raised as to what constitutes "price fixing" and how that determination is to be made. In the following cases, keep in mind how the courts deal, or fail to deal, with the following questions:

1. Is the conduct involved likely to have a substantial and direct effect on price; is that effect one which "necessarily" results from the arrangement?

2. Are there likely to be substantial redeeming virtues flowing from the practice or conduct?

3. Could the same or similar redeeming virtues be achieved through reasonably available and less harmful alternatives?

4. How difficult would it be to explore relevant considerations? In other words, what will the costs be in terms of transaction costs and future uncertainty with respect to the legality of certain categories of business behavior and thus the effectiveness of the rule?

Federal Trade Commission v. Superior Court Trial Lawyers Association

Supreme Court of the United States, 1990.
493 U.S. 411, 110 S.Ct. 768, 107 L.Ed.2d 851.

[Reprinted p. 355 *infra*].

NOTE ON REGULATION OF THE PROFESSIONS

1. National Society of Professional Engineers v. United States, 435 U.S. 679 (1978). The National Society of Professional Engineers ("Society") was an organization of 69,000 professional engineers who performed services in connection with the study, design, and construction of various kinds of improvements (buildings, bridges, factories, etc.) on real property. As a condition of membership, individual engineers were required to agree to refuse to negotiate or discuss the question of fees with a prospective client until the client had selected engineers for a particular project. This rule was embodied in Section 11(c) of the Society's Code of Ethics, which provided:

Section 11—The Engineer will not compete unfairly with another engineer by attempting to obtain employment or advancement or professional engagements by competitive bidding ...

(c) He shall not solicit or submit engineering proposals on the basis of competitive bidding. Competitive bidding for professional engineering services is defined as the formal or informal submission, or receipt, of verbal or written estimates of cost or proposals ... whereby the prospective client may compare engineering services on a price basis prior to the time that one engineer, or one engineering organization, has been selected for negotiations.... An Engineer requested to submit a proposal or bid prior to the selection of an engineer or firm subject to the negotiation of a satisfactory contract, shall attempt to have the procedure changed to conform to ethical practices, but if not successful he shall withdraw from consideration for the proposed work.

The United States challenged the Code on the ground that it constituted an agreement to suppress price competition and sought an injunction. The Society's principal defense was that competitive pressure to offer engineering services at low prices would be dangerous to the public health, safety, and welfare and therefore that the ethical provision was reasonable in the circumstances. The District Court rejected that defense, making no findings on the question of whether free competition would lead to inferior engineering, but concluded rather that any such inquiry was unnecessary. The Court of Appeals affirmed.

In the Supreme Court, the Society relied on Goldfarb v. Virginia State Bar, 421 U.S. 773 (1975), indicating that certain practices by members of a "learned profession" might be reasonable even though viewed as a violation in some other context. The rule of reason itself, the Court noted, can be traced to origins in the common law, and specifically to Mitchel v. Reynolds, 24 Eng.Rep. 347 (1711) (p. 23 *supra*). The Court described *Mitchel* as follows:

> *Mitchel* involved the enforceability of a promise by the seller of a bakery that he would not compete with the purchaser of his business. The covenant was for a limited time and applied only to the area in which the bakery had operated. It was therefore upheld as reasonable, even though it deprived the public of the benefit of potential competition. The long-run benefit of enhancing the marketability of the business itself—and thereby providing incentives to develop such an enterprise—outweighed the temporary and limited loss of competition.

The Court noted that subsequent rule of reason cases, such as *Standard Oil* and *Chicago Board of Trade,* developed the position that the inquiry mandated by the rule of reason is "whether the challenged agreement is one that promotes competition or one that suppresses competition":

> There are, thus, two complementary categories of antitrust analysis. In the first category are agreements whose nature and necessary effect are so plainly anticompetitive that no elaborate study of the industry is needed to establish their illegality—they are "illegal *per se*." In the second category are agreements whose competitive effect can only be evaluated by analyzing the facts peculiar to the business, the history of the restraint, and the reasons why it was imposed. In either event, the purpose of the analysis is to form a judgment about the competitive significance of the restraint; it is not to decide whether a policy of favoring competition is in the public interest ...

As to the ethical rule itself, the Court concluded that it should be judged as illegal on its face because it operated as an absolute ban on competitive bidding, applying with equal force to all kinds of transactions. The Society had argued that because the engineer and customer could bargain about price after selection of an engineer had occurred, the arrangement could be justified under *Chicago Board of Trade* as relating only to the timing of competition. The Court distinguished *Chicago Board of Trade* on two grounds; first, that negotiation between a single seller and single buyer is not the equivalent of competition among competing sellers, and second, because there was absent here any suggestion that the regulation of price information had "a positive effect on competition." The Sherman Act, the Court continued, reflects a legislative judgment that competition will produce not only lower prices but better goods and services, and any claim, with respect to particular products or markets, that competition will not produce such results should be addressed to the legislature.

As to the "learned profession" defense, the Court concluded:

> We adhere to the view expressed in *Goldfarb* that, by their nature, professional services may differ significantly from other business services, and accordingly, the nature of the competition in such services may vary.... But the Society's argument in this case is a far cry from such a position. We are faced with a contention that a total ban on competitive bidding is necessary because otherwise engineers will be tempted to submit deceptively low bids. Certainly, the problem of professional deception is a proper subject of an ethical canon. But once again, the equation of competition with deception, like the similar equation with safety hazards, is simply too broad; we may assume that competition is not entirely conducive to ethical behavior, but that is not a reason, cognizable under the Sherman Act, for doing away with competition.

> In sum, the Rule of Reason does not support a defense based on the assumption that competition is itself unreasonable.

Finally, the Court concluded that the injunction entered below, prohibiting the Society "from adopting any official opinion, policy statement or guideline stating or implying that competitive bidding is unethical" was not an abridgement of the Society's First Amendment rights but rather a reasonable method of eliminating the consequences of illegal conduct.

Blackmun, J., with whom Rehnquist, J., joined, concurred in the conclusion that the Society's ethical rules were overly broad in preventing any dissemination of competitive price information, but declined to concur in the conclusion that professional society rules "which have a more-than-*de minimis* anticompetitive effect" are illegal unless they produce the benefit of increased competition. The concurring Justices noted that it was necessary to leave "elbow room" for such regulations as a bar association restriction of "permissible forms of price advertising for non-routine legal services or a limitation of in-person solicitations...." Should there be special "elbow room" for noneconomic justifications of allegedly anticompetitive conduct by nonprofit institutions? *See* United States v. Brown University, 5 F.3d 658 (3d Cir. 1993), p. 246 *infra*.

Chief Justice Burger dissented from the portion of the opinion which prohibited the Society from stating in its Code the view that competitive bidding is unethical, regarding that as a right of expression protected by the First Amendment.

2.   American Medical Association v. FTC, 638 F.2d 443 (2d Cir. 1980), affirmed by an equally divided Court, 455 U.S. 676 (1982). The American Medical Association (AMA) is a not-for-profit corporation whose membership includes over 50% of all licensed physicians in the United States. Its legislative body is an elected House of Delegates which in 1957 approved some ethical canons called the "Principles of Medical Ethics." These principles in turn are interpreted by the Association's Judicial Council. In 1975 the FTC charged the AMA and its constituent state and local groups with restricting the ability of the members to advertise or solicit patients and with restricting their ability to engage in non-traditional forms of medical practice (*e.g.*, group practice) through interpretations and enforcement of its ethical canons.

The canons themselves were vague and sweeping; for example, Section 6 of the Principles provided that "a physician should not dispose of his services under terms or conditions which tend to interfere with or impair the free and complete exercise of his medical skill and judgment. . . ." The Commission found that, in the AMA's interpretations and enforcement actions, it restricted the ability of members to advertise (permitting only the furnishing of name, type of practice, location of office, and office hours) to "accepted local media" such as telephone listings, office signs, and professional cards. In effect, all price advertising, including the price of routine services such as a physical exam or blood test, was prevented in radio, newspapers, and other broadly disseminated publications. Similarly, ethical opinions of the AMA described as "unfair or unethical," among other practices, providing medical services at compensation so low as to make it impossible for competent service to be rendered, or underbidding by physicians in order to secure medical contracts.

The Federal Trade Commission rejected a *per se* approach to the AMA's restrictions—noting that regulation of professional services may justify differences in treatment under the antitrust laws—but found the arrangements illegal under a rule of reason. The Court of Appeals affirmed.

In its discussion of remedy, the FTC had noted that "the AMA has a valuable and unique role to play with respect to deceptive advertising and oppressive forms of solicitation by physicians." As a result, it incorporated in its Order the following paragraph:

> Nothing contained in this part shall prohibit respondents from . . . enforcing reasonable ethical guidelines governing the conduct of its members with respect to representations, including unsubstantiated representations, that would be false or deceptive within the meaning of § 5 of the Federal Trade Commission Act . . .

The Court of Appeals approved the proviso, adding however that AMA guidelines would not violate the order if "respondent reasonably believes" that any medical advertising or solicitation was false or deceptive.[18]

3. With respect to advertising rules, *see* California Dental Association v. Federal Trade Commission, 526 U.S. 756 (1999) p. 256 *infra*.

4. Vogel v. American Society of Appraisers, 744 F.2d 598 (7th Cir. 1984). Vogel, a gem appraiser, attempted to charge a flat 1% fee for his work, subject to a minimum fee of $10. As a result, he was expelled from the American Society of Appraisers on grounds that it was "unprofessional and unethical for [an] appraiser to do work for a fixed percentage of the amount of value . . . which he determines at the conclusion of his work." Vogel claimed he lost referrals from members of the society as a result of his expulsion.

On a request for a preliminary injunction, the Court of Appeals, per Posner, J., declined to treat the Association bylaw as either a boycott or price fixing that was illegal *per se*. Although in the broadest sense the bylaw may have had the effect of "tampering" with price, its purpose or likely effect was not to raise price above competitive levels. On the contrary, it seemed designed to outlaw a method of fee setting that could lead to fraud on customers; thus, the appraiser might have an incentive to over-appraise items in order to maximize his fee. Moreover, there was no evidence that the society's outlawing of fixed percentage of fees was designed as

---

18. Mansfield, J., dissented on grounds that the AMA had amended its ethical Principles and interpretations so as to eliminate any prior restraints that may have existed on advertising or solicitation.

a subterfuge to somehow maintain or stabilize cartel pricing. It remained open to Vogel, on a full trial and under a rule of reason, to demonstrate any anticompetitive purpose or effect of the society bylaw.

5. Regulation of competition within the professions, even when imposed as a result of state legislation, can be challenged under the First Amendment as well as the antitrust laws. For example, in Virginia State Board of Pharmacy v. Virginia Citizens Consumer Council, Inc., 425 U.S. 748 (1976), a Virginia statute providing that a licensed pharmacist was guilty of unprofessional conduct if he advertised or published price information about prescription drugs was struck down as a violation of the First Amendment. Similarly, in Bates v. State Bar of Arizona, 433 U.S. 350 (1977), state disciplinary rules prohibiting a lawyer from engaging in price advertising were condemned as violations of the First Amendment. These and similar cases are examined in Chapter 5 *infra* in connection with the "state action" doctrine.

Broadcast Music, Inc. v. Columbia Broadcasting System, Inc.

Supreme Court of the United States, 1979.
441 U.S. 1, 99 S.Ct. 1551, 60 L.Ed.2d 1.

■ WHITE, J. This case involves an action under the antitrust and copyright laws brought by respondent Columbia Broadcasting System, Inc. (CBS), against petitioners, American Society of Composers, Authors and Publishers (ASCAP) and Broadcast Music, Inc. (BMI), and their members and affiliates. The basic question presented is whether the issuance by ASCAP and BMI to CBS of blanket licenses to copyrighted musical compositions at fees negotiated by them is price fixing *per se* unlawful under the antitrust laws.

I

CBS operates one of three national commercial television networks, supplying programs to approximately 200 affiliated stations and telecasting approximately 7,500 network programs per year. Many, but not all, of these programs make use of copyrighted music recorded on the soundtrack. CBS also owns television and radio stations in various cities. It is "the giant of the world in the use of music rights," the "No. 1 outlet in the history of entertainment."

Since 1897 the copyright laws have vested in the owner of a copyrighted musical composition the exclusive right to perform the work publicly for profit, but the legal right is not self-enforcing. In 1914 Victor Herbert and a handful of other composers organized ASCAP because those who performed copyrighted music for profits were so numerous and widespread, and most performances so fleeting, that as a practical matter it was impossible for the many individual copyright owners to negotiate with and license the users and to detect unauthorized uses. "ASCAP was organized as a 'clearing-house' for copyright owners and users to solve these problems" associated with the licensing of music. CBS, Inc. v. ASCAP, 400 F.Supp. 737, 741 (S.D.N.Y.1975). As ASCAP operates today, its 22,000 members grant it nonexclusive rights to license nondramatic performances of their works, and ASCAP issues licenses and distributes royalties to copyright owners in accordance with a schedule reflecting the nature and amount of the use of their music and other factors.

BMI, a nonprofit corporation owned by members of the broadcasting industry, was organized in 1939, is affiliated with or represents some 10,000 publishing companies and 20,000 authors and composers, and operates in much the same manner as ASCAP. Almost every domestic copyrighted composition is in the repertory either of ASCAP, with a total of three million compositions, or of BMI, with one million.

Both organizations operate primarily through blanket licenses, which give the licensees the right to perform any and all of the compositions owned by the members or affiliates as often as the licensees desire for a stated term. Fees for blanket licenses are ordinarily a percentage of total revenues or a flat dollar amount, and do not directly depend on the amount or type of music used. Radio and television broadcasters are the largest users of music, and almost all of them hold blanket licenses from both ASCAP and BMI. Until this litigation, CBS held blanket licenses from both organizations for its television network on a continuous basis since the late 1940's and had never attempted to secure any other form of license from either ASCAP[19] or any of its members. 400 F.Supp., at 752–754.

The complaint filed by CBS charged various violations of the Sherman Act and the copyright laws.... After an eight-week trial, limited to the issue of liability, the court dismissed the complaint, rejecting ... the claim that the blanket license was price fixing and a *per se* violation of § 1 of the Sherman Act, and holding that since direct negotiation with individual copyright owners is available and feasible there is no undue restraint of trade, illegal tying, misuse of copyrights, or monopolization.

Though agreeing with the District Court's factfinding and not disturbing its legal conclusions on the other antitrust theories of liability,[20] the Court of Appeals held that the blanket license issued to television networks was a form of price fixing illegal *per se* under the Sherman Act. CBS, Inc. v. ASCAP, 562 F.2d 130, 140 (C.A.2 1977). This conclusion, without more, settled the issue of liability under the Sherman Act, ... and required reversal of the District Court's judgment, as well as a remand to consider the appropriate remedy.[21]

---

19.   Unless the context indicates otherwise, references to ASCAP alone in this opinion usually apply to BMI as well....

20.   The Court of Appeals affirmed the District Court's rejection of CBS's monopolization and tying contentions but did not rule on the District Court's conclusion that the blanket license was not an unreasonable restraint of trade.

21.   The Court of Appeals went on to suggest some guidelines as to remedy, indicating that despite its conclusion on liability the blanket license was not totally forbidden. The Court of Appeals said:

> "Normally, after a finding of price-fixing, the remedy is an injunction against the price-fixing—in this case, the blanket license. We think, however, that if on remand a remedy can be fashioned which will ensure that the blanket license will not affect the price or negotiations for direct licenses, the blanket license need not be prohibited in all

SC: NOT Per se illegal

... Because we disagree with the Court of Appeals' conclusions with respect to the *per se* illegality of the blanket license, we reverse its judgment and remand the cause for further appropriate proceedings.

II

... [The *per*] *se* rule is a valid and useful tool of antitrust policy and enforcement. And agreements among competitors to fix prices on their individual goods or services are among those concerted activities that the Court has held to be within the *per se* category. But easy labels do not always supply ready answers.

A

To the Court of Appeals and CBS, the blanket license involves "price fixing" in the literal sense: the composers and publishing houses have joined together into an organization that sets its price for the blanket license it sells. But this is not a question simply of determining whether two or more potential competitors have literally "fixed" a "price." As generally used in the antitrust field, "price fixing" is a shorthand way of describing certain categories of business behavior to which the *per se* rule has been held applicable. The Court of Appeals' literal approach does not alone establish that this particular practice is one of those types or that it is "plainly anticompetitive" and very likely without "redeeming virtue." Literalness is overly simplistic and often overbroad. When two partners set the price of their goods or services they are literally "price fixing," but they are not *per se* in violation of the Sherman Act. See United States v. Addyston Pipe & Steel Co., 85 F. 271, 280 (C.A.6 1898), aff'd, 175 U.S. 211 (1899). Thus, it is necessary to characterize the challenged conduct as falling within or without that category of behavior to which we apply the label "*per se* price fixing." That will often, but not always, be a simple matter.[22]

---

circumstances. The blanket license is not simply a "naked restraint" ineluctably doomed to extinction. There is not enough evidence in the present record to compel a finding that the blanket license does not serve a market need for those who wish full protection against infringement suits or who, for some other business reason, deem the blanket license desirable. The blanket license includes a practical covenant not to sue for infringement of any ASCAP copyright as well as an indemnification against suits by others.

"Our objection to the blanket license is that it reduces price competition among the members and provides a disinclination to compete. We think that these objections may be removed if ASCAP itself is required to provide some form of per use licensing which will ensure competition among the individual members with respect to those networks which wish to engage in per use licensing." 562 F.2d, at 140 (footnotes omitted).

22. Cf., *e.g.,* United States v. McKesson & Robbins, Inc., 351 U.S. 305 (1956) (manufacturer/wholesaler agreed with independent wholesalers on prices to be charged on products it manufactured); United States v. Socony–Vacuum Oil Co., 310 U.S. 150 (1940) (firms controlling a substantial part of an industry agreed to purchase "surplus" gasoline with the intent and necessary effect of increasing the price); United States v. Trenton Potteries Co., 273 U.S. 392 (1927) (manufacturers and distributors of 82% of certain vitreous pottery fixtures agreed to sell at uniform prices).

Consequently, as we recognized in United States v. Topco Associates, Inc., 405 U.S. 596, 607–608 (1972), "[i]t is only after considerable experience with certain business relationships that courts classify them as *per se* violations".... We have never examined a practice like this one before; indeed, the Court of Appeals recognized that "[i]n dealing with performing rights in the music industry we confront conditions both in copyright law and in antitrust law which are *sui generis*." And though there has been rather intensive antitrust scrutiny of ASCAP and its blanket licenses, that experience hardly counsels that we should outlaw the blanket license as a *per se* restraint of trade.

B

This litigation and other cases involving ASCAP and its licensing practices have arisen out of the efforts of the creators of copyrighted musical compositions to collect for the public performance of their works, as they are entitled to do under the Copyright Act. As already indicated, ASCAP and BMI originated to make possible and to facilitate dealings between copyright owners and those who desire to use their music. Both organizations plainly involve concerted action in a large and active line of commerce, and it is not surprising that, as the District Court found, "[n]either ASCAP nor BMI is a stranger to antitrust litigation."

The Department of Justice first investigated allegations of anticompetitive conduct by ASCAP over 50 years ago.... In separate complaints in 1941, the United States charged that the blanket license, which was then the only license offered by ASCAP and BMI, was an illegal restraint of trade and that arbitrary prices were being charged as the result of an illegal copyright pool. The Government sought to enjoin ASCAP's exclusive licensing powers and to require a different form of licensing by that organization. The case was settled by a consent decree that imposed tight restrictions on ASCAP's operations. Following complaints relating to the television industry, successful private litigation against ASCAP by movie theaters, and a Government challenge to ASCAP's arrangements with similar foreign organizations, the 1941 decree was reopened and extensively amended in 1950.[23]

Under the amended decree, which still substantially controls the activities of ASCAP, members may grant ASCAP only nonexclusive rights to license their works for public performance. Members, therefore, retain the rights individually to license public performances, along with the rights to license the use of their compositions for other purposes. ASCAP itself is forbidden to grant any license to perform one or more specified compositions in the ASCAP repertory unless both the user and the owner have requested it in writing to do so. ASCAP is required to grant to any user making written application a nonexclusive license to perform all ASCAP compositions either for a period of time or on a per program basis. ASCAP may not insist on the blanket license, and the fee for the per program license, which is to be based on the revenues for the program on which

---

23. United States v. ASCAP, 1950–1951 Trade Cas. ¶ 62,595 (S.D.N.Y.1950).

ASCAP music is played, must offer the applicant a genuine economic choice between the per program license and the more common blanket license. If ASCAP and a putative licensee are unable to agree on a fee within 60 days, the applicant may apply to the District Court for a determination of a reasonable fee, with ASCAP having the burden of proving reasonableness.[24]

The 1950 decree, as amended from time to time, continues in effect, and the blanket license continues to be the primary instrument through which ASCAP conducts its business under the decree. The courts have twice construed the decree not to require ASCAP to issue licenses for selected portions of its repertory. It also remains true that the decree guarantees the legal availability of direct licensing of performance rights by ASCAP members; and the District Court found, and in this respect the Court of Appeals agreed, that there are no practical impediments preventing direct dealing by the television networks if they so desire. Historically, they have not done so. Since 1946, CBS and other television networks have taken blanket licenses from ASCAP and BMI. It was not until this suit arose that the CBS network demanded any other kind of license.

Of course, a consent judgment, even one entered at the behest of the Antitrust Division, does not immunize the defendant from liability for actions, including those contemplated by the decree, that violate the rights of nonparties.... But it cannot be ignored that the Federal Executive and Judiciary have carefully scrutinized ASCAP and the challenged conduct, have imposed restrictions on various of ASCAP's practices, and, by the terms of the decree, stand ready to provide further consideration, supervision, and perhaps invalidation of asserted anticompetitive practices. In these circumstances, we have a unique indicator that the challenged practice may have redeeming competitive virtues and that the search for those values is not almost sure to be in vain.[25] Thus, although CBS is not bound by the Antitrust Division's actions, the decree is a fact of economic and legal life in this industry, and the Court of Appeals should not have ignored it completely in analyzing the practice. That fact alone might not remove a naked price-fixing scheme from the ambit of the *per se* rule, but, as discussed *infra*, Part III, here we are uncertain whether the practice on its face has the effect, or could have been spurred by the purpose, of restraining competition among the individual composers....

... [T]he United States disagrees with the Court of Appeals in this case and urges that the blanket licenses, which the consent decree authorizes ASCAP to issue to television networks, are not *per se* violations of the Sherman Act. It takes no position, however, on whether the practice is an unreasonable restraint of trade in the context of the network television industry.

---

24. BMI is in a similar situation....

25. Cf. Continental TV, Inc. v. GTE Sylvania Inc., 433 U.S. 36, 50 n. 16 (1977). Moreover, unthinking application of the *per se* rule might upset the balancing of economic power and of pro-and anticompetitive effects presumably worked out in the decree.

Finally, we note that Congress, in the new Copyright Act, has itself chosen to employ the blanket license and similar practices.... Though these provisions are not directly controlling, they do reflect an opinion that the blanket license, and ASCAP, are economically beneficial in at least some circumstances.

There have been District Court cases holding various ASCAP practices, including its licensing practices, to be violative of the Sherman Act,[26] but even so, there is no nearly universal view that either the blanket or the per-program licenses issued by ASCAP at prices negotiated by it are a form of price fixing subject to automatic condemnation under the Sherman Act, rather than to a careful assessment under the rule of reason.

III

Of course, we are no more bound than is CBS by the views of the Department of Justice, the results in the prior lower court cases, or the opinions of various experts about the merits of the blanket license. But while we must independently examine this practice, all those should caution us against too easily finding blanket licensing subject to *per se* invalidation.

A

As a preliminary matter, we are mindful that the Court of Appeals' holding would appear to be quite difficult to contain. If, as the court held, there is *per se* antitrust violation whenever ASCAP issues a blanket license to a television network for a single fee, why would it not also be automatically illegal for ASCAP to negotiate and issue blanket licenses to individual radio or television stations or to other users who perform copyrighted music for profit? Likewise, if the present network licenses issued through ASCAP on behalf of its members are *per se* violations, why would it not be equally illegal for the members to authorize ASCAP to issue licenses establishing various categories of uses that a network might have for copyrighted music and setting a standard fee for each described use?

Although the Court of Appeals apparently thought the blanket license could be saved in some or even many applications, it seems to us that the *per se* rule does not accommodate itself to such flexibility and that the observations of the Court of Appeals with respect to remedy tend to impeach the *per se* basis for the holding of liability.[27]

---

26. Those cases involved licenses sold to individual movie theaters to "perform" compositions already on the motion pictures' soundtracks. ASCAP had barred its members from assigning performing rights to movie producers at the same time recording rights were licensed, and the theaters were effectively unable to engage in direct transactions for performing rights with individual copyright owners.

27. The Court of Appeals would apparently not outlaw the blanket license across the board but would permit it in various circumstances where it is deemed necessary or sufficiently desirable. It did not even enjoin blanket licensing with the television networks, the relief it realized would normally follow a finding of *per se* illegality of the license in that context. Instead, as requested by CBS, it remanded to the District Court to require ASCAP to offer in addition to blanket licensing some competitive form of per-use licensing. But per-use licensing

CBS would prefer that ASCAP be authorized, indeed directed, to make all its compositions available at standard per-use rates within negotiated categories of use.[28] But if this in itself or in conjunction with blanket licensing constitutes illegal price fixing by copyright owners, CBS urges that an injunction issue forbidding ASCAP to issue any blanket license or to negotiate any fee except on behalf of an individual member for the use of his own copyrighted work or works. Thus, we are called upon to determine that blanket licensing is unlawful across the board. We are quite sure, however, that the *per se* rule does not require any such holding.

B

In the first place, the line of commerce allegedly being restrained, the performing rights to copyrighted music, exists at all only because of the copyright laws. Those who would use copyrighted music in public performances must secure consent from the copyright owner or be liable at least for the statutory damages for each infringement and, if the conduct is willful and for the purpose of financial gain, to criminal penalties. Furthermore, nothing in the Copyright Act of 1976 indicates in the slightest that Congress intended to weaken the rights of copyright owners to control the public performance of musical compositions. Quite the contrary is true. Although the copyright law confers no rights on copyright owners to fix prices among themselves or otherwise to violate the antitrust laws, we would not expect that any market arrangements reasonably necessary to effectuate the rights that are granted would be deemed a *per se* violation of the Sherman Act. Otherwise, the commerce anticipated by the Copyright Act and protected against restraint by the Sherman Act would not exist at all or would exist only as a pale reminder of what Congress envisioned.

C

More generally, in characterizing this conduct under the *per se* rule,[29] our inquiry must focus on whether the effect and, here because it tends to

---

by ASCAP, as recognized in the consent decrees, might be even more susceptible to the *per se* rule than blanket licensing.

The rationale for this unusual relief in a *per se* case was that "[t]he blanket license is not simply a 'naked restraint' ineluctably doomed for extinction." 562 F.2d, at 140. To the contrary, the Court of Appeals found that the blanket license might well "serve a market need" for some. Ibid. This, it seems to us is not the *per se* approach, which does not yield so readily to circumstances, but in effect is a rather bobtailed application of the rule of reason, bobtailed in the sense that it is unaccompanied by the necessary analysis demonstrating why the particular licensing system is an undue competitive restraint.

28. Surely, if ASCAP abandoned the issuance of all licenses and confined its activities to policing the market and suing infringers, it could hardly be said that member copyright owners would be in violation of the antitrust laws by not having a common agent issue per-use licenses. Under the copyright laws, those who publicly perform copyrighted music have the burden of obtaining prior consent. Cf. Zenith Radio Corp. v. Hazeltine Research, Inc., 395 U.S. 100, 139–140 (1969).

29. The scrutiny occasionally required must not merely subsume the burdensome analysis required under the rule of reason, see National Society of Professional Engineers v. United States, 435 U.S. 679 (1978), or else we should apply the rule of reason from the start.

show effect, see United States v. United States Gypsum Co., 438 U.S. 422, 436 n. 13 (1978), the purpose of the practice is to threaten the proper operation of our predominantly free market economy—that is, whether the practice facially appears to be one that would always or almost always tend to restrict competition and decrease output, and in what portion of the market, or instead one designed to "increase economic efficiency and render markets more rather than less competitive." Id., at 441 n. 16; see National Society of Professional Engineers v. United States, 435 U.S. 679, 688. . . .

The blanket license, as we see it, is not a "naked restraint of trade with no purpose except stifling of competition," White Motor Co. v. United States, 372 U.S. 253, 263 (1963), but rather accompanies the integration of sales, monitoring, and enforcement against unauthorized copyright use. See L. Sullivan, Antitrust, § 59, at 154 (1977). As we have already indicated, ASCAP and the blanket license developed together out of the practical situation in the market place: thousands of users, thousands of copyright owners, and millions of compositions. Most users want unplanned, rapid and indemnified access to any and all of the repertory of compositions, and the owners want a reliable method of collecting for the use of their copyrights. Individual sales transactions in this industry are quite expensive, as would be individual monitoring and enforcement, especially in light of the resources of single composers. Indeed, as both the Court of Appeals and CBS recognize, the costs are prohibitive for licenses with individual radio stations, night clubs, and restaurants, 562 F.2d, at 136–137, n. 26, and it was in that milieu that the blanket license arose.

A middleman with a blanket license was an obvious necessity if the thousands of individual negotiations, a virtual impossibility, were to be avoided. Also, individual fees for the use of individual compositions would presuppose an intricate schedule of fees and uses, as well as a difficult and expensive reporting problem for the user and policing task for the copyright owner. Historically, the market for public performance rights organized itself largely around the single-fee blanket license, which gave unlimited access to the repertory and reliable protection against infringement. When ASCAP's major and user-created competitor, BMI, came on the scene, it also turned to the blanket license.

With the advent of radio and television networks, market conditions changed, and the necessity for and advantages of a blanket license for those users may be far less obvious than is the case when the potential users are individual television or radio stations, or the thousands of other individuals and organizations performing copyrighted compositions in public.[30] But even for television network licenses, ASCAP reduces costs absolutely by creating a blanket license that is sold only a few, instead of thousands, of times, and that obviates the need for closely monitoring the networks to see

---

That is why the *per se* rule is not employed until after considerable experience with the type of challenged restraint.

30. And of course changes brought about by new technology or new marketing techniques might also undercut the justification for the practice.

that they do not use more than they pay for. ASCAP also provides the necessary resources for blanket sales and enforcement, resources unavailable to the vast majority of composers and publishing houses. Moreover, a bulk license of some type is a necessary consequence of the integration necessary to achieve these efficiencies, and a necessary consequence of an aggregate license is that its price must be established.

D

This substantial lowering of costs, which is of course potentially beneficial to both sellers and buyers, differentiates the blanket license from individual use licenses. The blanket license is composed of the individual compositions plus the aggregating service. Here, the whole is truly greater than the sum of its parts; it is, to some extent, a different product. The blanket license has certain unique characteristics: It allows the licensee immediate use of covered compositions, without the delay of prior individual negotiations and great flexibility in the choice of musical material. Many consumers clearly prefer the characteristics and cost advantages of this marketable package, and even small performing rights societies that have occasionally arisen to compete with ASCAP and BMI have offered blanket licenses. Thus, to the extent the blanket license is a different product, ASCAP is not really a joint sales agency offering the individual goods of many sellers, but is a separate seller offering its blanket license, of which the individual compositions are raw material.[31] ASCAP, in short, made a market in which individual composers are inherently unable to fully effectively compete.[32]

E

Finally, we have some doubt—enough to counsel against application of the *per se* rule—about the extent to which this practice threatens the "central nervous system of the economy," United States v. Socony–Vacuum Oil Co., 310 U.S. 150, 226 n. 59 (1940), that is, competitive pricing as the free market's means of allocating resources. Not all arrangements among actual or potential competitors that have an impact on price are *per se* violations of the Sherman Act or even unreasonable restraints. Mergers among competitors eliminate competition, including price competition, but they are not *per se* illegal and many of them withstand attack under any existing antitrust standard. Joint ventures and other cooperative arrange-

---

31. Moreover, because of the nature of the product—a composition can be simultaneously "consumed" by many users—composers have numerous markets and numerous incentives to produce, so the blanket license is unlikely to cause decreased output, one of the normal undesirable effects of a cartel. And since popular songs get an increased share of ASCAP's revenue distributions, composers compete even within the blanket license in terms of productivity and consumer satisfaction.

32. Cf. United States v. Socony–Vacuum Oil Co., 310 U.S. 150, 217 (1940) (distinguishing Chicago Bd. of Trade v. United States, 246 U.S. 231 (1918), on the ground that among the effects of the challenged rule there "was the creation of a public market"); United States v. Trenton Potteries Co., 273 U.S. 392, 401 (1927) (distinguishing Chicago Bd. of Trade on the ground that it did not involve "a price agreement among competitors in an open market").

ments are also not usually unlawful, at least not as price-fixing schemes, where the agreement on price is necessary to market the product at all.

Here, the blanket license fee is not set by competition among individual copyright owners, and it is a fee for the use of any of the compositions covered by the license. But the blanket license cannot be wholly equated with a simple horizontal arrangement among competitors. ASCAP does set the price for its blanket license, but that license is quite different from anything any individual owner could issue. The individual composers and authors have neither agreed not to sell individually in any other market nor use the blanket license to mask price fixing in such other markets.[33] Moreover, the substantial restraints placed on ASCAP and its members by the consent decree must not be ignored. The District Court found that there was no legal, practical, or conspiratorial impediment to CBS obtaining individual licenses; CBS, in short, had a real choice.

With this background in mind, which plainly enough indicates that over the years, and in the face of available alternatives, the blanket license has provided an acceptable mechanism for at least a large part of the market for the performing rights to copyrighted musical compositions, we cannot agree that it should automatically be declared illegal in all of its many manifestations. Rather, when attacked, it should be subjected to a more discriminating examination under the rule of reason. It may not ultimately survive that attack, but that is not the issue before us today.

IV

As we have noted, *supra*, the enigmatic remarks of the Court of Appeals with respect to remedy appear to have departed from the court's strict, *per se* approach and to have invited a more careful analysis. But this left the general import of its judgment that the licensing practices of ASCAP and BMI under the consent decree are *per se* violations of the Sherman Act. We reverse that judgment, and the copyright misuse judgment dependent upon it, and remand for further proceedings to consider any unresolved issues that CBS may have properly brought to the Court of Appeals.[34] Of course, this will include an assessment under the rule of reason of the blanket license as employed in the television industry, if that issue was preserved by CBS in the Court of Appeals.[35]

---

33. "CBS does not claim that the individual members and affiliates ('sellers') of ASCAP and BMI have agreed among themselves as to the prices to be charged for the particular 'products' (compositions) offered by each of them." 400 F. Supp. at 748.

34. It is argued that the judgment of the Court of Appeals should nevertheless be affirmed on the ground that the blanket license is a tying arrangement in violation of § 1 of the Sherman Act or on the ground that ASCAP and BMI have monopolized the relevant market contrary to § 2. The District Court and the Court of Appeals rejected both submissions, and we do not disturb the latter's judgment in these respects, particularly since CBS did not file its own petition for certiorari challenging the Court of Appeals' failure to sustain its tying and monopolization claims.

35. The Court of Appeals did not address the rule-of-reason issue, and BMI insists that CBS did not preserve the question in that court. In any event, if the issue is open in the Court of Appeals, we prefer that court first to address the matter. Because of the United States'

The judgment of the Court of Appeals is reversed and the case is remanded to that court for further proceedings consistent with this opinion.

■ STEVENS, J., dissenting. The Court holds that ASCAP's blanket license is not a species of price fixing categorically forbidden by the Sherman Act. I agree with that holding. The Court remands the case to the Court of Appeals, leaving open the question whether the blanket license as employed by ASCAP and BMI is unlawful under a rule of reason inquiry. I think that question is properly before us now and should be answered affirmatively. . . .

. . . It is the refusal to license anything less than the entire repertoire—rather than the decision to offer blanket licenses themselves—that raises the serious antitrust questions in this case. . . .

The market for music at issue here is wholly dominated by ASCAP-issued blanket licenses. Virtually every domestic copyrighted composition is in the repertoire of either ASCAP or BMI. And again, virtually without exception, the only means that has been used to secure authority to perform such compositions is the blanket license.

The blanket all-or-nothing license is patently discriminatory. The user purchases full access to ASCAP's entire repertoire, even though his needs could be satisfied by a far more limited selection. The price he pays for this access is unrelated either to the quantity or the quality of the music he actually uses, or, indeed to what he would probably use in a competitive system. Rather, in this unique all-or-nothing system, the price is based on a percentage of the user's advertising revenues, a measure that reflects the customer's ability to pay but is totally unrelated to factors—such as the cost, quality, or quantity of the product—that normally affect price in a competitive market. The ASCAP system requires users to buy more music than they want at a price which, while not beyond their ability to pay and perhaps not even beyond what is "reasonable" for the access they are getting, may well be far higher than what they would choose to spend for music in a competitive system. It is a classic example of economic discrimination.

The record plainly establishes that there is no price competition between separate musical compositions. Under a blanket license, it is no more expensive for a network to play the most popular current hit in prime time than it is to use an unknown composition as background music in a soap opera. Because the cost to the user is unaffected by the amount used on any program or on all programs, the user has no incentive to economize by, for example, substituting what would otherwise be less expensive songs for established favorites or by reducing the quantity of music used on a program. The blanket license thereby tends to encourage the use of more music, and also of a larger share of what is really more valuable music, than would be expected in a competitive system characterized by separate

---

interest in the enforcement of the consent decree, we assume it will continue to play a role in this litigation on remand.

licenses. And since revenues are passed on to composers on a basis reflecting the character and frequency of the use of their music, the tendency is to increase the rewards of the established composers at the expense of those less well known. Perhaps the prospect is in any event unlikely, but the blanket license does not present a new songwriter with any opportunity to try to break into the market by offering his product for sale at an unusually low price. The absence of that opportunity, however unlikely it may be, is characteristic of a cartelized rather than a competitive market.

The current state of the market cannot be explained on the ground that it could not operate competitively, or that issuance of more limited—and thus less restrictive—licenses by ASCAP is not feasible. The District Court's findings disclose no reason why music performing rights could not be negotiated on a per-composition or per-use basis, either with the composer or publisher directly or with an agent such as ASCAP. In fact, ASCAP now compensates composers and publishers on precisely those bases. If distributions of royalties can be calculated on a per-use and per-composition basis, it is difficult to see why royalties could not also be collected in the same way. Moreover, the record also shows that where ASCAP's blanket license scheme does not govern, competitive markets do. A competitive market for "synch rights" exists,[36] and after the use of blanket licenses in the motion picture industry was discontinued, such a market promptly developed in that industry. In sum, the record demonstrates that the market at issue here is one that could be highly competitive, but is not competitive at all.

Since the record describes a market that could be competitive and is not, and since that market is dominated by two firms engaged in a single, blanket method of dealing, it surely seems logical to conclude that trade has been restrained unreasonably. ASCAP argues, however, that at least as to CBS, there has been no restraint at all since the network is free to deal directly with copyright holders. . . .

. . . Despite its size, CBS itself may not obtain music on a competitive basis without incurring unprecedented costs and risks. The fear of unpredictable consequences, coupled with the certain and predictable costs and delays associated with a change in its method of purchasing music, unquestionably inhibits any CBS management decision to embark on a competitive crusade. Even if ASCAP offered CBS a special bargain to forestall any such crusade, that special arrangement would not cure the marketwide restraint. . . .

Antitrust policy requires that great aggregations of economic power be closely scrutinized. That duty is especially important when the aggregation is composed of statutory monopoly privileges. Our cases have repeatedly stressed the need to limit the privileges conferred by patent and copyright

---

36. The "synch" right is the right to record a copyrighted song in synchronization with the film or videotape, and is obtained separately from the right to perform the music. It is the latter which is controlled by ASCAP and BMI. See CBS, Inc. v. ASCAP, *supra*, 400 F.Supp., at 743.

strictly to the scope of the statutory grant. The record in this case plainly discloses that the limits have been exceeded and that ASCAP and BMI exercise monopoly powers that far exceed the sum of the privileges of the individual copyright holders. Indeed, ASCAP itself argues that its blanket license constitutes a product that is significantly different from the sum of its component parts. I agree with that premise, but I conclude that the aggregate is a monopolistic restraint of trade proscribed by the Sherman Act.

NOTES AND QUESTIONS

1. On remand in *BMI,* the Second Circuit affirmed the District Court decision, holding that its findings of fact "demonstrate that the blanket license has no anticompetitive effect at all," since CBS had always had a "realistic opportunity" to obtain performance rights from individual copyright holders, 620 F.2d 930 (2d Cir.1980), cert. denied, 450 U.S. 970 (1981). "An antitrust plaintiff is not obligated to pursue any imaginable alternative, regardless of cost or efficiency, before it can complain that a practice has restrained competition." But in this case, CBS had not even offered to buy from competing sellers, arguing that it had not done so because (1) there would have inevitably been a period of double payment—both to individual copyright owners and under the license, and (2) no machinery existed to handle the numerous individual negotiations. The Court of Appeals rejected these arguments: "CBS cannot expect the antitrust laws to assure it that a changeover to direct licensing can be accomplished instantly or at no expense."

2. In Buffalo Broadcasting Co. v. ASCAP, 744 F.2d 917, 924–32 (2d Cir.1984), cert. denied, 469 U.S. 1211 (1985), the Court of Appeals reversed a district court finding against BMI and ASCAP, concluding that even for small local TV stations, there were realistic alternative ways to obtain performance rights other than those being offered by the joint ventures.

3. Reconsider *Socony–Vacuum* in light of *BMI.* In *Socony–Vacuum,* the problem the major oil companies were trying to address was that independent refiners were producing more gasoline than the market could absorb, and these same independents had inadequate storage facilities. As a result, they occasionally flooded the market with "distress" gasoline which created "disorderly marketing conditions." Suppose that the majors, instead of the "dancing partner" scheme they adopted, set up an industry-wide joint venture for transportation and storage of gasoline with access available to all sellers, including the independents, on fair and reasonable terms. Suppose further that membership in the joint venture was voluntary for all parties, some efficiencies of scale from joint warehousing could be demonstrated, and that the warehousing plan did "stabilize" market conditions. Would that joint venture be legal under *BMI*? Why is it different from the dancing partner scheme which the court in *BMI* apparently assumed was properly declared illegal in *Socony–Vacuum*?

4. In United States v. United States Gypsum Co., 438 U.S. 422 (1978), six major manufacturers of gypsum board were indicted for engaging in a program of interseller price verification. Under the program, sellers telephoned competing producers to determine the price currently being offered on gypsum board to specific customers. Defendants claimed that the information was being exchanged

for the purpose of perfecting a "meeting competition" defense under Section 2(b) of the Robinson–Patman Act.

We will examine the Robinson–Patman Act in detail in Chapter 11. For the time being, simply note that the Act prohibits a seller from discriminating in price between competing customers where there is an injury to competition, but allows an absolute defense where the lower price is offered to a customer "in good faith to meet an equally low price of a competitor. . . ." The Supreme Court had concluded in FTC v. A.E. Staley Manufacturing Co., 324 U.S. 746 (1945), that the seller must "show the existence of facts which would lead a reasonable and prudent person to believe that the granting of a lower price would in fact meet the equally low price of a competitor." Thus, the gypsum manufacturers argued with some plausibility that *Staley* required that they not simply accept the word of their customers about receipt of lower prices, but rather that they investigate and verify these reports by checking with competing sellers.

The jury had returned criminal verdicts against defendants, but the Supreme Court reversed. It held that in criminal cases it was necessary for the government to prove both anticompetitive effect and intent (*i.e.,* "knowledge of . . . probable consequences" of an act), and that the requisite intent could not be inferred, as a matter of law, from a finding that the exchange of price information had an impact on prices:

> Although an effect on prices may well support an inference that the defendant had knowledge of the probability of such a consequence at the time he acted, the jury must remain free to consider additional evidence before accepting or rejecting the inference. Therefore, although it would be correct to instruct the jury that it may infer intent from an effect on prices, ultimately the decision on the issue of intent must be left to the trier of fact alone.

The conduct alleged in *Gypsum* was judged against a rule of reason. Would the "effects and intent" rule discussed above be applied in cases where *per se* violations are alleged? In *Gypsum,* the Supreme Court noted that its "knowledge of the probable consequences" intent formulation was not meant to "suggest that conduct undertaken with the purpose of producing anticompetitive effects would not also support criminal liability, even if such effects did not come to pass." *See, e.g.,* United States v. Alston, 974 F.2d 1206, 1212 (9th Cir. 1992) (the government need not prove specific intent to produce anticompetitive effects where a *per se* violation is alleged); United States v. Brown, 925 F.2d 1182, 1187 (9th Cir. 1991) (the intent requirement of *Gypsum* "does not apply to charges of *per se* violations"; a finding of intent to conspire to commit the offense is sufficient); United States v. Brighton Building and Maintenance Co., 598 F.2d 1101 (7th Cir. 1979) (only if the conduct "directly proved" is not illegal *per se* are defendants entitled to an instruction that the government must prove intent); United States v. Gillen, 599 F.2d 541 (3d Cir. 1979) (*Gypsum* directed at "borderline violations," not price-fixing conspiracies which are illegal *per se*). The *Gypsum* opinion will be examined in Chapter 11 in connection with consideration of policy questions in enforcement of the Robinson–Patman Act.

5.   In his memoirs, William S. Paley, founder and long-time Chairman of the Columbia Broadcasting System, reported that he had proposed to the presidents of NBC and ABC an arrangement whereby each network could broadcast cultural, educational, and high-quality programs without fear of adverse ratings. Paley said he proposed that "representatives of the three major networks meet to work out the feasibility and the details in setting aside a given period of time—say, two hours a

week in prime time—for special, high-quality programs that would appeal to educated, sophisticated tastes more than to the mass audience. Each network would take different nights of the week, thus offering the public six hours of high-quality programming each week." NBC and ABC were not interested. W. Paley, As It Happened 275–76 (1979).

Paley pointed out that no one network could schedule quality programs alone since it would not only derive small revenues from the hour devoted to quality broadcasting, but would forfeit revenues for the whole evening through the adverse effect on later scheduled programs. Should Paley's proposal be characterized as price fixing? If not, would its social and cultural virtues constitute a justification? Would such considerations be relevant under *Professional Engineers*? Consider these issues when reading United States v. Brown University, p. 246 *infra*.

Virginia Excelsior Mills, Inc. v. FTC, 256 F.2d 538 (4th Cir. 1958). Excelsior is a shredded wood product used principally to package fragile materials. A group of small producers in Northern Virginia found that competition among them was extremely keen and they therefore organized a corporate sales agency, Virginia Excelsior Mills, which they appointed as exclusive sales agent for each of them. Orders were to be allocated among producers on the basis of their relative productive capacity, and the producers agreed not to increase that capacity. The contracts also contemplated that prices would be established by the Board of Directors of the sales corporation elected by the producer members. Prices after establishment of the joint sales agency were uniform, and increased across the board in response to rising costs.

The Federal Trade Commission found the agreement illegal *per se* under § 1 of the Sherman Act, and the Court of Appeals affirmed:

> Price fixing through such an arrangement is a violation, *per se,* of § 1 of the Sherman Act. Though the needs and problems of the producers, which stimulated the creation of the arrangement, may have seemed pressing, they cannot lend a cloak of legality to conduct which, whatever the supposed justification, the Act condemns.... What contrary suggestion may be found in Appalachian Coals, Inc. v. United States, 288 U.S. 344, has not survived the strong and consistent course of subsequent decision....

In commenting on the Order entered by the FTC, the Court of Appeals noted that there would be nothing unlawful in an arrangement whereby each producer appoints a common sales agent, but reserves and exercises independence in pricing, acceptance of orders, production, and other similar decisions.

NOTE ON JOINT VENTURES

1. *Virginia Excelsior* is only one of many cases finding that price fixing occurring as a result of the activities of a joint sales agency can be illegal *per se. See, e.g.*, United States v. American Smelting and Refining Co., 182 F.Supp. 834 (S.D.N.Y.1960) (two competitors agree that one will serve as exclusive sales agent for the other in the eastern part of the United States, but that the agent would not sell on its own behalf in the western part of the United States); United States v. Columbia Pictures Industries, Inc., 507 F.Supp. 412 (S.D.N.Y.1980), affirmed without opinion, 659 F.2d 1063 (2d Cir. 1981) (joint venture to market films of various

production companies to cable TV systems). In most of these cases, the joint venture accounted for a substantial share of the market.

In another line of cases, joint buying and selling ventures, usually involving small companies joining together to reduce costs and compete more effectively with larger rivals, have been upheld under a rule of reason. *See, e.g.*, Webster County Memorial Hospital, Inc. v. United Mine Workers of America Welfare and Retirement Fund of 1950, 536 F.2d 419, 420 (D.C. Cir. 1976) (joint negotiation on behalf of fund beneficiaries with a hospital regarded as reasonable); Instant Delivery Corp. v. City Stores Co., 284 F.Supp. 941 (E.D. Pa. 1968) (joint purchasing arrangement designed to reduce costs found to be reasonable).

Is it a satisfactory resolution to declare joint buying and selling co-ops legal or illegal solely on grounds of the share of the market accounted for by the members of the co-op? Would *per se* treatment be avoided in a cartel which accounts for only a small share of the market? If not, why the difference here?

2.   As *Levine* and *North Texas Specialty Physicians,* pp. 208–09 *supra*, indicates joint ventures of various types have become particularly important in the fast-changing health care field. The Department of Justice and FTC "Statements of Enforcement Policy and Analytical Principles Relating to Health Care and Antitrust," cited in the *Levine* case, draws distinctions among ventures that should be treated as *per se,* scrutinized under a rule of reason, and treated as benign. Where would you draw the lines? These issues are raised continually in cases forthcoming in this chapter, again in Chapter 5, and still again in Chapter 9.

3.   For the Supreme Court's most recent decision on joint ventures, *see* Texaco v. Dagher, 547 U.S. 1 (2006), p. 271 *infra*. What factual differences could constitute the basis for applying a *per se* rule in some joint venture cases but a rule of reason in others?

National Collegiate Athletic Association v. Board of Regents of University of Oklahoma

Supreme Court of the United States, 1984.
468 U.S. 85, 104 S.Ct. 2948, 82 L.Ed.2d 70.

■ STEVENS, J. The University of Oklahoma and the University of Georgia contend that the National Collegiate Athletic Association has unreasonably restrained trade in the televising of college football games. After an extended trial, the District Court found that the NCAA had violated § 1 of the Sherman Act and granted injunctive relief. 546 F.Supp. 1276 (W.D.Okla.1982). The Court of Appeals agreed that the Statute had been violated but modified the remedy in some respects. 707 F.2d 1147 (C.A.10 1983). We granted certiorari, 464 U.S. 913 (1983), and now affirm.

I

The NCAA

Since its inception in 1905, the NCAA has played an important role in the regulation of amateur collegiate sports. It has adopted and promulgated playing rules, standards of amateurism, standards for academic eligibility, regulations concerning recruitment of athletes, and rules governing the size of athletic squads and coaching staffs. In some sports, such as baseball, swimming, basketball, wrestling and track, it has sponsored and conducted national tournaments. It has not done so in the sport of football, however. With the exception of football, the NCAA has not undertaken any regulation of the televising of athletic events.

The NCAA has approximately 850 voting members. The regular members are classified into separate divisions to reflect differences in size and scope of their athletic programs. Division I includes 276 colleges with major athletic programs; in this group only 187 play intercollegiate football. Divisions II and III include approximately 500 colleges with less extensive athletic programs. Division I has been subdivided into Divisions I–A and I–AA for football.

Some years ago, five major conferences together with major football-playing independent institutions organized the College Football Association (CFA). The original purpose of the CFA was to promote the interests of major football-playing schools within the NCAA structure. The Universities of Oklahoma and Georgia, respondents in this Court, are members of the CFA. . . .

The Current Plan

The plan adopted in 1981 for the 1982–1985 seasons is at issue in this case.[37] This plan, like each of its predecessors, recites that it is intended to reduce, insofar as possible, the adverse effects of live television upon football game attendance.[38] It provides that "all forms of television of the football games of NCAA member institutions during the Plan control periods shall be in accordance with this Plan." The plan recites that the television committee has awarded rights to negotiate and contract for the telecasting of college football games of members of the NCAA to two "carrying networks." In addition to the principal award of rights to the carrying networks, the plan also describes rights for a "supplementary series" that had been awarded for the 1982 and 1983 seasons,[39] as well as a procedure for permitting specific "exception telecasts."[40]

---

37. Because respondents sought and obtained only injunctive relief against future violations of § 1 in the District Court, we do not consider previous NCAA television plans except to the extent that they shed light on the purpose and effect of the current plan.

38. The purposes of this Plan shall be to reduce, insofar as possible, the adverse effects of live television upon football game attendance and, in turn, upon the athletic and related educational programs dependent upon the proceeds therefrom; to spread football television participation among as many colleges as practicable; to reflect properly the image of universities as educational institutions; to promote college football through the use of television, to advance the overall interests of intercollegiate athletics, and to provide college football television to the public to the extent compatible with these other objectives."

39. The supplementary series is described in a separate article of the plan. It is to consist of no more than 36 exposures in each of the first two years and no more than 40 exposures in the third and fourth years of the plan. Those exposures are to be scheduled on Saturday evenings or at other times that do not conflict with the principal football series that is scheduled for Saturday afternoons.

40. An "exception" telecast is permitted in the home team's market of games that are sold out and in the visiting team's market of games played more than 400 miles from the visiting team's campus, but in both cases only if the broadcast would not be shown in an area

In separate agreements with each of the carrying networks, ABC and the Columbia Broadcasting System (CBS), the NCAA granted each the right to telecast the 14 live "exposures" described in the plan, in accordance with the "ground rules" set forth therein.[41] Each of the networks agreed to pay a specified "minimum aggregate compensation to the participating NCAA member institutions" during the 4–year period in an amount that totaled $131,750,000. In essence the agreement authorized each network to negotiate directly with member schools for the right to televise their games. The agreement itself does not describe the method of computing the compensation for each game, but the practice that has developed over the years and that the District Court found would be followed under the current agreement involved the setting of a recommended fee by a representative of the NCAA for different types of telecasts, with national telecasts being the most valuable, regional telecasts being less valuable, and Division II or Division III games commanding a still lower price.[42] The aggregate of all these payments presumably equals the total minimum aggregate compensation set forth in the basic agreement. Except for differences in payment between national and regional telecasts, and with respect to Division II and Division III games, the amount that any team receives does not change with the size of the viewing audience, the number of markets in which the game is telecast, or the particular characteristic of the game or the participating teams. Instead, the "ground rules" provide that the carrying networks make alternate selections of those games they wish to televise, and thereby obtain the exclusive right to submit a bid at an essentially fixed price to the institutions involved.[43]

where another college football game is to be played. Also, Division II and Division III institutions are allowed complete freedom to televise their games, except that the games may not appear on a network of more than five stations without the permission of the NCAA.

41. In addition to its contracts with the carrying networks, the NCAA has contracted with Turner Broadcasting System, Inc. (TBS), for the exclusive right to cablecast NCAA football games. The minimum aggregate fee for the initial two-year period of the TBS contract is $17,696,000.

42. The football television committee's briefing book for 1981 recites that a fee of $600,000 was paid for each of the 12 national games telecast by ABC during the regular fall season and $426,779 was paid for each of the 46 regional telecasts in 1980. The report further recites that "Division I members received $27,842,185 from 1980 football television revenue, 89.8 percent of the total. Division II's share was $625,195 (2.0 percent), while Division III received $385,195 (1.3 percent) and the NCAA $2,147,425 (6.9 percent)."

43. The District Court explained how the agreement eliminates competition for broadcasting rights:

"First, the networks have no intention to engage in bidding. Second, once the network holding first choice for any given date has made its choice and agreed to a rights fee for that game with the two teams involved, the other network is then in a monopsony position. The schools cannot threaten to sell the broadcast rights to any other network. They cannot sell to NBC without committing a violation of NCAA rules. They cannot sell to the network which had first choice over that particular date because, again, they would be in violation of NCAA rules, and the network would be in violation of its agreement with NCAA. Thus, NCAA creates a single eligible buyer for the product of all but the two schools selected by the network having first choice. Free market competition is thus destroyed under the new plan."

The plan also contains "appearance requirements" and "appearance limitations" which pertain to each of the 2–year periods that the plan is in effect. The basic requirement imposed on each of the two networks is that it must schedule appearances for at least 82 different member institutions during each 2–year period. Under the appearance limitations no member institution is eligible to appear on television more than a total of six times and more than four times nationally, with the appearances to be divided equally between the two carrying networks. The number of exposures specified in the contracts also sets an absolute maximum on the number of games that can be broadcast.

Thus, although the current plan is more elaborate than any of its predecessors, it retains the essential features of each of them. It limits the total amount of televised intercollegiate football and the number of games that any one team may televise. No member is permitted to make any sale of television rights except in accordance with the basic plan.

Background of this Controversy

Beginning in 1979 CFA members began to advocate that colleges with major football programs should have a greater voice in the formulation of football television policy than they had in the NCAA. CFA therefore investigated the possibility of negotiating a television agreement of its own, developed an independent plan, and obtained a contract offer from the National Broadcasting Co. (NBC). This contract, which it signed in August 1981, would have allowed a more liberal number of appearances for each institution, and would have increased the overall revenues realized by CFA members.

In response the NCAA publicly announced that it would take disciplinary action against any CFA member that complied with the CFA–NBC contract. The NCAA made it clear that sanctions would not be limited to the football programs of CFA members, but would apply to other sports as well. On September 8, 1981, respondents commenced this action in the United States District Court for the Western District of Oklahoma and obtained a preliminary injunction preventing the NCAA from initiating disciplinary proceedings or otherwise interfering with CFA's efforts to perform its agreement with NBC. Notwithstanding the entry of the injunction, most CFA members were unwilling to commit themselves to the new contractual arrangement with NBC in the face of the threatened sanctions and therefore the agreement was never consummated.

[The District Court and the Court of Appeals found the *NCAA* television plan illegal *per se,* primarily on grounds that it constituted price fixing and a limitation on output. The Court of Appeals considered, but rejected on the facts, arguments by the NCAA that the plan promoted live attendance, and also rejected as illegitimate the NCAA's purpose of promoting an athletically balanced competition on grounds that such a consideration was inconsistent with the policy of the Sherman Act.]

II

There can be no doubt that the challenged practices of the NCAA constitute a "restraint of trade" in the sense that they limit members' freedom to negotiate and enter into their own television contracts. In that sense, however, every contract is a restraint of trade, and as we have repeatedly recognized, the Sherman Act was intended to prohibit only unreasonable restraints of trade.

It is also undeniable that these practices share characteristics of restraints we have previously held unreasonable. The NCAA is an association of schools which compete against each other to attract television revenues, not to mention fans and athletes. As the District Court found, the policies of the NCAA with respect to television rights are ultimately controlled by the vote of member institutions. By participating in an association which prevents member institutions from competing against each other on the basis of price or kind of television rights that can be offered to broadcasters, the NCAA member institutions have created a horizontal restraint—an agreement among competitors on the way in which they will compete with one another. A restraint of this type has often been held to be unreasonable as a matter of law. Because it places a ceiling on the number of games member institutions may televise, the horizontal agreement places an artificial limit on the quantity of televised football that is available to broadcasters and consumers. By restraining the quantity of television rights available for sale, the challenged practices create a limitation on output; our cases have held that such limitations are unreasonable restraints of trade.[44] Moreover, the District Court found that the minimum aggregate price in fact operates to preclude any price negotiation between broadcasters and institutions, thereby constituting horizontal price fixing, perhaps the paradigm of an unreasonable restraint of trade.[45]

Horizontal price-fixing and output limitation are ordinarily condemned as a matter of law under an "illegal *per se*" approach because the probability that these practices are anticompetitive is so high; a *per se* rule is applied when "the practice facially appears to be one that would always or almost always tend to restrict competition and decrease output." Broadcast Music, Inc. v. CBS, 441 U.S. 1, 19–20 (1979). In such circumstances a restraint is presumed unreasonable without inquiry into the particular market context in which it is found. Nevertheless, we have decided that it would be inappropriate to apply a *per se* rule to this case. This decision is not based on a lack of judicial experience with this type of arrangement,[46] on the fact

---

44. See, *e.g.*, United States v. Topco Associates, Inc., 405 U.S. 596, 608–609 (1972); United States v. Sealy, Inc., 388 U.S. 350 (1967); United States v. American Linseed Oil Co., 262 U.S. 371, 388–390 (1923); American Column & Lumber Co. v. United States, 257 U.S. 377, 410–412 (1921).

45. See, *e.g.*, Arizona v. Maricopa County Medical Society, 457 U.S. 332, 344–348 (1982); Catalano, Inc. v. Target Sales, Inc., 446 U.S. 643, 646–647 (1980) (per curiam); Kiefer–Stewart Co. v. Joseph E. Seagram & Sons, Inc., 340 U.S. 211, 213 (1951); United States v. Socony–Vacuum Oil Co., 310 U.S. 150, 212–214 (1940); United States v. Trenton Potteries Co., 273 U.S. 392, 396–398 (1927).

46. While judicial inexperience with a particular arrangement counsels against extending the reach of *per se* rules, see Broadcast Music, 441 U.S., at 9–10; United States v. Topco that the NCAA is organized as a nonprofit entity,[47] or on our respect for the NCAA's historic role in the preservation and encouragement of inter-collegiate amateur athletics.[48] Rather, what is critical is that this case involves an industry in which horizontal restraints on competition are essential if the product is to be available at all.

As Judge Bork has noted: "[S]ome activities can only be carried out jointly. Perhaps the leading example is league sports. When a league of professional lacrosse teams is formed, it would be pointless to declare their cooperation illegal on the ground that there are no other professional lacrosse teams." R. Bork, The Antitrust Paradox 278 (1978). What the NCAA and its member institutions market in this case is competition itself—contests between competing institutions. Of course, this would be completely ineffective if there were no rules on which the competitors agreed to create and define the competition to be marketed. A myriad of rules affecting such matters as the size of the field, the number of players on a team, and the extent to which physical violence is to be encouraged or proscribed, all must be agreed upon, and all restrain the manner in which institutions compete. Moreover, the NCAA seeks to market a particular brand of football—college football. The identification of this "product" with an academic tradition differentiates college football from and makes it more popular than professional sports to which it might otherwise be compara-ble, such as, for example, minor league baseball. In order to preserve the character and quality of the "product," athletes must not be paid, must be required to attend class, and the like. And the integrity of the "product" cannot be preserved except by mutual agreement; if an institution adopted such restrictions unilaterally, its effectiveness as a competitor on the playing field might soon be destroyed. Thus, the NCAA plays a vital role in

---

Associates, Inc., 405 U.S. 596, 607–608 (1972); White Motor Co. v. United States, 372 U.S. 253, 263 (1963); the likelihood that horizontal price and output restrictions are anticompetitive is generally sufficient to justify application of the *per se* rule without inquiry into the special characteristics of a particular industry. See Arizona v. Maricopa County Medical Society, 457 U.S. 332, 349–351 (1982); National Society of Professional Engineers v. United States, 435 U.S. 679, 689–690 (1978).

47.   There is no doubt that the sweeping language of § 1 applies to nonprofit entities, Goldfarb v. Virginia State Bar, 421 U.S. 773, 786–787 (1975), and in the past we have imposed antitrust liability on non-profit entities which have engaged in anticompetitive conduct, American Society of Mechanical Engineers, Inc. v. Hydrolevel Corp., 456 U.S. 556, 576 (1982). Moreover, the economic significance of the NCAA's nonprofit character is questionable at best. Since the District Court found that the NCAA and its member institutions are in fact organized to maximize revenues, see 546 F.Supp., at 1288–1289, it is unclear why petitioner is less likely to restrict output in order to raise revenues above those that could be realized in a competitive market than would be a for-profit entity. Petitioner does not rely on its nonprofit character as a basis for reversal.

48.   While as the guardian of an important American tradition, the NCAA's motives must be accorded a respectful presumption of validity, it is nevertheless well-settled that good motives will not validate an otherwise anticompetitive practice. See United States v. Griffith, 334 U.S. 100, 105–106 (1948); Associated Press v. United States, 326 U.S. 1, 16, n. 15 (1945); Chicago Board of Trade v. United States, 246 U.S. 231, 238 (1918); Standard Sanitary Manufacturing Co. v. United States, 226 U.S. 20, 49 (1912); United States v. Trans–Missouri Freight Assn., 166 U.S. 290, 342 (1897).

enabling college football to preserve its character, and as a result enables a product to be marketed which might otherwise be unavailable. In performing this role, its actions widen consumer choice—not only the choices available to sports fans but also those available to athletes—and hence can be viewed as procompetitive.

BMU

Broadcast Music squarely holds that a joint selling arrangement may be so efficient that it will increase sellers' aggregate output and thus be procompetitive. Similarly, as we indicated in Continental T.V., Inc. v. GTE Sylvania Inc., 433 U.S. 36, 51–57 (1977), a restraint in a limited aspect of a market may actually enhance marketwide competition. Respondents concede that the great majority of the NCAA's regulations enhance competition among member institutions. Thus, despite the fact that this case involves restraints on the ability of member institutions to compete in terms of price and output, a fair evaluation of their competitive character requires consideration of the NCAA's justifications for the restraints.

Our analysis of this case under the Rule of Reason, of course, does not change the ultimate focus of our inquiry. Both *per se* rules and the Rule of Reason are employed "to form a judgment about the competitive significance of the restraint." National Society of Professional Engineers v. United States, 435 U.S. 679, 692 (1978). A conclusion that a restraint of trade is unreasonable may be

> "based either (1) on the nature or character of the contracts, or (2) on surrounding circumstances giving rise to the inference or presumption that they were intended to restrain trade and enhance prices. Under either branch of the test, the inquiry is confined to a consideration of impact on competitive conditions."
> *Id.*, at 690 (footnotes omitted).

Per se rules are invoked when surrounding circumstances make the likelihood of anticompetitive conduct so great as to render unjustified further examination of the challenged conduct. But whether the ultimate finding is the product of a presumption or actual market analysis, the essential inquiry remains the same—whether or not the challenged restraint enhances competition.[49] Under the Sherman Act the criterion to be used in judging the validity of a restraint on trade is its impact on competition.

III

Because it restrains price and output, the NCAA's television plan has a significant potential for anticompetitive effects.[50] The findings of the Dis-

---

49.   Indeed, there is often no bright line separating *per se* from Rule of Reason analysis. *Per se* rules may require considerable inquiry into market conditions before the evidence justifies a presumption of anticompetitive conduct. For example, while the Court has spoken of a "per se" rule against tying arrangements, it has also recognized that tying may have procompetitive justifications that make it inappropriate to condemn without considerable market analysis. See Jefferson Parish Hosp. Dist. No. 2 v. Hyde, 466 U.S. 2, 16 (1984).

50.   In this connection, it is not without significance that Congress felt the need to grant professional sports an exemption from the antitrust laws for joint marketing of television trict Court indicate that this potential has been realized. The District Court found that if member institutions were free to sell television rights, many more games would be shown on television, and that the NCAA's output restriction has the effect of raising the price the networks pay for television rights.[51] Moreover, the court found that by fixing a price for television rights to all games, the NCAA creates a price structure that is unresponsive to viewer demand and unrelated to the prices that would prevail in a competitive market.[52] And, of course, since as a practical matter all member institutions need NCAA approval, members have no real choice but to adhere to the NCAA's television controls.[53]

---

rights. See 15 U.S.C. §§ 1291–1295. The legislative history of this exemption demonstrates Congress' recognition that agreements among league members to sell television rights in a cooperative fashion could run afoul of the Sherman Act, and in particular reflects its awareness of the decision in United States v. National Football League, 116 F.Supp. 319 (E.D. Pa.1953), which held that an agreement between the teams of the National Football League that each team would not permit stations within 75 miles of the home city of another team to telecast its games on a day when that team was playing at home violated § 1 of the Sherman Act. . . .

51. "It is clear from the evidence that were it not for the NCAA controls, many more college football games would be televised. This is particularly true at the local level. Because of NCAA controls, local stations are often unable to televise games which they would like to, even when the games are not being televised at the network level. The circumstances which would allow so-called exception telecasts arise infrequently for many schools, and the evidence is clear that local broadcasts of college football would occur far more frequently were it not for the NCAA controls. This is not a surprising result. Indeed, this horizontal agreement to limit the availability of games to potential broadcasters is the very essence of NCAA's agreements with the networks. The evidence establishes the fact that the networks are actually paying the large fees because the NCAA agrees to limit production. If the NCAA would not agree to limit production, the networks would not pay so large a fee. Because NCAA limits production, the networks need not fear that their broadcasts will have to compete head-to-head with other college football telecasts, either on the other networks or on various local stations. Therefore, the Court concludes that the membership of NCAA has agreed to limit production to a level far below that which would occur in a free market situation." 546 F.Supp., at 1294.

52. Turning to the price paid for the product, it is clear that the NCAA controls utterly destroy free market competition. NCAA has commandeered the rights of its members and sold those rights for a sum certain. In so doing, it has fixed the minimum, maximum and actual price which will be paid to the schools appearing on ABC, CBS and TBS. NCAA has created the mechanism which produces a uniform price for each national telecast, and a uniform price for each regional telecast. Because of the NCAA controls, the price which is paid for the right to televise any particular game is responsive neither to the relative quality of the teams playing the game nor to viewer preference.

"In a competitive market, each college fielding a football team would be free to sell the right to televise its games for whatever price it could get. The prices would vary for the games, with games between prominent schools drawing a larger price than games between less prominent schools. Games between the more prominent schools would draw a larger audience than other games. Advertisers would pay higher rates for commercial time because of the larger audience. The telecaster would then be willing to pay larger rights fees due to the increased prices paid by the advertisers. Thus, the price which the telecaster would pay for a particular game would be dependent on the expected size of the viewing audience. Clearly, the NCAA controls grossly distort the prices actually paid for an individual game from that to be expected in a free market." 546 F.Supp., at 1318.

53. Since, as the District Court found, NCAA approval is necessary for any institution that wishes to compete in intercollegiate sports, the NCAA has a potent tool at its disposal for

The anticompetitive consequences of this arrangement are apparent. Individual competitors lose their freedom to compete. Price is higher and output lower than they would otherwise be, and both are unresponsive to consumer preference.[54] This latter point is perhaps the most significant, since "Congress designed the Sherman Act as a 'consumer welfare prescription.'" Reiter v. Sonotone Corp., 442 U.S. 330, 343 (1979). A restraint that has the effect of reducing the importance of consumer preference in setting price and output is not consistent with this fundamental goal of antitrust law.[55] Restrictions on price and output are the paradigmatic examples of restraints of trade that the Sherman Act was intended to prohibit. See Standard Oil Co. v. United States, 221 U.S. 1, 52–60 (1911). At the same time, the television plan eliminates competitors from the market, since only those broadcasters able to bid on television rights covering the entire NCAA can compete.[56] Thus, as the District Court found, many telecasts that would occur in a competitive market are foreclosed by the NCAA's plan.

Petitioner argues, however, that its television plan can have no significant anticompetitive effect since the record indicates that it has no market power—no ability to alter the interaction of supply and demand in the

---

restraining institutions which require its approval. See Silver v. New York Stock Exchange, 373 U.S. 341, 347–349 and n. 5 (1963); Associated Press v. United States, 326 U.S. 1, 17–18 (1945).

54. In this case the rule is violated by a price restraint that tends to provide the same economic rewards to all practitioners regardless of their skill, their experience, their training, or their willingness to employ innovative and difficult procedures. Arizona v. Maricopa County Medical Society, 457 U.S. 332, 348 (1982). The District Court provided a vivid example of this system in practice:

> A clear example of the failure of the rights fees paid to respond to market forces occurred in the fall of 1981. On one weekend of that year, Oklahoma was scheduled to play a football game with the University of Southern California. Both Oklahoma and USC have long had outstanding football programs, and indeed, both teams were ranked among the top five teams in the country by the wire service polls. ABC chose to televise the game along with several others on a regional basis. A game between two schools which are not well-known for their football programs, Citadel and Appalachian State, was carried on four of ABC's local affiliated stations. The USC–Oklahoma contest was carried on over 200 stations. Yet, incredibly, all four of these teams received exactly the same amount of money for the right to televise their games." 546 F.Supp., at 1291.

55. As the District Court observed:

> "Perhaps the most pernicious aspect is that under the controls, the market is not responsive to viewer preference. Every witness who testified on the matter confirmed that the consumers, the viewers of college football television, receive absolutely no benefit from the controls. Many games for which there is a large viewer demand are kept from the viewers, and many games for which there is little if any demand are nonetheless televised." 546 F.Supp., at 1319.

56. The impact on competitors is thus analogous to the effect of block booking in the motion picture industry that we concluded violated the Sherman Act.

> "In the first place, they eliminate the possibility of bidding for films theater by theater. In that way they eliminate the opportunity for the small competitor to obtain the choice first runs, and put a premium on the size of the circuit." United States v. Paramount Pictures, Inc., 334 U.S. 131, 154 (1948).

market.[57] We must reject this argument for two reasons—one legal, one factual.

As a matter of law, the absence of proof of market power does not justify a naked restriction on price or output. To the contrary, when there is an agreement not to compete in terms of price or output, "no elaborate industry analysis is required to demonstrate the anticompetitive character of such an agreement." *Professional Engineers,* 435 U.S., at 692.[58] Petitioner does not quarrel with the District Court's finding that price and output are not responsive to demand. Thus the plan is inconsistent with the Sherman Act's command that price and supply be responsive to consumer preference.[59] We have never required proof of market power in such a case.[60] This naked restraint on price and output requires some competitive justification even in the absence of a detailed market analysis.[61]

(handwritten margin note: absence of mkt power doesn't matter)

---

57. Market power is the ability to raise prices above those that would be charged in a competitive market. Jefferson Parish Hosp. Dist. No. 2 v. Hyde, 466 U.S. 2, 27 n. 46 (1984); United States Steel Corp. v. Fortner Enterprises, 429 U.S. 610, 620 (1977); United States v. E.I. du Pont de Nemours & Co., 351 U.S. 377, 391 (1956).

58. "The fact that a practice is not categorically unlawful in all or most of its manifestations certainly does not mean that it is universally lawful. For example, joint buying or selling arrangements are not unlawful *per se*, but a court would not hesitate in enjoining a domestic selling arrangement by which, say, Ford and General Motors distributed their automobiles nationally through a single selling agent. Even without a trial, the judge will know that these two large firms are major factors in the automobile market, that such joint selling would eliminate important price competition between them, that they are quite substantial enough to distribute their products independently, and that one can hardly imagine a pro-competitive justification actually probable in fact or strong enough in principle to make this particular joint selling arrangement 'reasonable' under Sherman Act § 1. The essential point is that the rule of reason can sometimes be applied in the twinkling of an eye." P. Areeda, The "Rule of Reason" in Antitrust Analysis: General Issues 37–38 (Federal Judicial Center June 1981) (parenthetical omitted).

59. Moreover, because under the plan member institutions may not compete in terms of price and output, it is manifest that significant forms of competition are eliminated. See Catalano, Inc. v. Target Sales, Inc., 446 U.S. 643, 648–649 (1980) (per curiam); Professional Engineers, 435 U.S., at 692–695; Paramount Famous Lasky Corp. v. United States, 282 U.S. 30, 43–44 (1930).

60. See United States v. McKesson & Robbins, Inc., 351 U.S. 305, 309–310 (1956); United States v. Socony–Vacuum Oil Co., 310 U.S. 150, 221 (1940). See also Klor's, Inc. v. Broadway–Hale Stores, Inc., 359 U.S. 207, 213 (1959).

61. The Solicitor General correctly observes:

"There was no need for the respondents to establish monopoly power in any precisely defined market for television programming in order to prove the restraint unreasonable. Both lower courts found not only that NCAA has power over the market for intercollegiate sports, but also that in the market for television programming—no matter how broadly or narrowly the market is defined—the NCAA television restrictions have reduced output, subverted viewer choice, and distorted pricing. Consequently, unless the controls have some countervailing procompetitive justification, they should be deemed unlawful regardless of whether petitioner has substantial market power over advertising dollars. While the 'reasonableness' of a particular alleged restraint often depends on the market power of the parties involved, because a judgment about market power is the means by which the effects of the conduct on the market place can be assessed, market power is only one test of 'reasonableness.' And where the anticompetitive effects of conduct can be ascertained through means short of extensive market analysis, and where no countervail-

As a factual matter, it is evident that petitioner does possess market power. The District Court employed the correct test for determining whether college football broadcasts constitute a separate market—whether there are other products that are reasonably substitutable for televised NCAA football games.[62] Petitioner's argument that it cannot obtain *supra* competitive prices from broadcasters since advertisers, and hence broadcasters, can switch from college football to other types of programming simply ignores the findings of the District Court. It found that intercollegiate football telecasts generate an audience uniquely attractive to advertisers and that competitors are unable to offer programming that can attract a similar audience. These findings amply support its conclusion that the NCAA possesses market power. Indeed, the District Court's subsidiary finding that advertisers will pay a premium price per viewer to reach audiences watching college football because of their demographic characteristics is vivid evidence of the uniqueness of this product.[63] Moreover, the District Court's market analysis is firmly supported by our decision in International Boxing Club v. United States, 358 U.S. 242 (1959), that championship boxing events are uniquely attractive to fans[64] and hence constitute a market separate from that for non-championship events.[65] Thus, respondents have demonstrated that there is a separate market for telecasts of college football which "rest[s] on generic qualities differentiating" viewers. Times–Picayune Publishing Co. v. United States, 345 U.S. 594, 613 (1953). It inexorably follows that if college football broadcasts be defined as a separate market—and we are convinced they are—then the NCAA's complete control over those broadcasts provides a solid basis for the District Court's conclusion that the NCAA possesses market power with respect to those broadcasts. "When a product is controlled by one interest, without substitutes available in the market, there is monopoly power." United States v. E.I. du Pont de Nemours & Co., 351 U.S. 377, 394 (1956).

---

ing competitive virtues are evident, a lengthy analysis of market power is not necessary." Brief for United States as Amicus Curiae 19–20 (footnote and citation omitted).

62. See, *e.g.*, United States v. Grinnell Corp., 384 U.S. 563, 571 (1966); United States v. E.I. Du Pont de Nemours & Co., 351 U.S. 377, 394–395 (1956); Times–Picayune Publishing Co. v. United States, 345 U.S. 594, 612, n. 31 (1953).

63. As the District Court observed, 546 F.Supp., at 1297, the most analogous programming in terms of the demographic characteristics of its audience is professional football, and as a condition of its limited exemption from the antitrust laws the professional football leagues are prohibited from telecasting games at times that conflict with intercollegiate football. See 15 U.S.C. § 1293.

64. We approved of the District Court's reliance on the greater revenue-producing potential and higher television ratings of championship events as opposed to other events to support its market definition. See 358 U.S., at 250–251.

65. For the same reasons, it is also apparent that the unique appeal of NCAA football telecasts for viewers means that "from the standpoint of the consumer—whose interests the statute was especially intended to serve," Jefferson Parish Hosp. Dist. No. 2 v. Hyde, 466 U.S. 2, 15 (1984), there can be no doubt that college football constitutes a separate market for which there is no reasonable substitute. Thus we agree with the District Court that it makes no difference whether the market is defined from the standpoint of broadcasters, advertisers, or viewers.

Thus, the NCAA television plan on its face constitutes a restraint upon the operation of a free market, and the findings of the District Court establish that it has operated to raise price and reduce output. Under the Rule of Reason, these hallmarks of anticompetitive behavior place upon petitioner a heavy burden of establishing an affirmative defense which competitively justifies this apparent deviation from the operations of a free market. See *Professional Engineers,* 435 U.S., at 692–696. We turn now to the NCAA's proffered justifications.

IV

Relying on *Broadcast Music,* petitioner argues that its television plan constitutes a cooperative "joint venture" which assists in the marketing of broadcast rights and hence is procompetitive. While joint ventures have no immunity from the antitrust laws, as *Broadcast Music* indicates, a joint selling arrangement may "mak[e] possible a new product by reaping otherwise unattainable efficiencies." Arizona v. Maricopa County Medical Society, 457 U.S. 332, 365 (1982) (Powell, J., dissenting) (footnote omitted). The essential contribution made by the NCAA's arrangement is to define the number of games that may be televised, to establish the price for each exposure, and to define the basic terms of each contract between the network and a home team. The NCAA does not, however, act as a selling agent for any school or for any conference of schools. The selection of individual games, and the negotiation of particular agreements, is a matter left to the networks and the individual schools. Thus, the effect of the network plan is not to eliminate individual sales of broadcasts, since these still occur, albeit subject to fixed prices and output limitations. Unlike *Broadcast Music's* blanket license covering broadcast rights to a large number of individual compositions, here the same rights are still sold on an individual basis, only in a noncompetitive market.

The District Court did not find that the NCAA's television plan produced any procompetitive efficiencies which enhanced the competitiveness of college football television rights; to the contrary it concluded that NCAA football could be marketed just as effectively without the television plan. There is therefore no predicate in the findings for petitioner's efficiency justification. Indeed, petitioner's argument is refuted by the District Court's finding concerning price and output. If the NCAA's television plan produced procompetitive efficiencies, the plan would increase output and reduce the price of televised games. The District Court's contrary findings accordingly undermine petitioner's position. In light of these findings, it cannot be said that "the agreement on price is necessary to market the product at all." *Broadcast Music,* 441 U.S., at 23.[66] In

---

66. Compare 546 F.Supp., at 1307–1308 ("The colleges are clearly able to negotiate agreements with whatever broadcasters they choose. We are not dealing with tens of thousands of relatively brief musical works, but with three-hour football games played eleven times each year.") with Broadcast Music, 441 U.S., at 22–23 (footnotes omitted) ("[T]o the extent the blanket license is a different product, ASCAP is not really a joint sales agency offering the individual goods of many sellers, but is a separate seller offering its blanket

Broadcast Music, the availability of a package product that no individual could offer enhanced the total volume of music that was sold. Unlike this case, there was no limit of any kind placed on the volume that might be sold in the entire market and each individual remained free to sell his own music without restraint. Here production has been limited, not enhanced.[67] No individual school is free to televise its own games without restraint. The NCAA's efficiency justification is not supported by the record.

Neither is the NCAA's television plan necessary to enable the NCAA to penetrate the market through an attractive package sale. Since broadcasting rights to college football constitute a unique product for which there is no ready substitute, there is no need for collective action in order to enable the product to compete against its nonexistent competitors.[68] This is borne out by the District Court's finding that the NCAA's television plan *reduces* the volume of television rights sold.

V

Throughout the history of its regulation of intercollegiate football telecasts, the NCAA has indicated its concern with protecting live attendance. This concern, it should be noted, is not with protecting live attendance at games which *are* shown on television; that type of interest is not at issue in this case. Rather, the concern is that fan interest in a televised game may adversely affect ticket sales for games that will not appear on television.[69]

Although the NORC [National Opinion Research Center] studies in the 1950's provided some support for the thesis that live attendance would suffer if unlimited television were permitted,[70] the District Court found

license, of which the individual compositions are raw material. ASCAP, in short, made a market in which individual composers are inherently unable to compete fully effectively.'').

67. Ensuring that individual members of a joint venture are free to increase output has been viewed as central in evaluating the competitive character of joint ventures. See Brodley, Joint Ventures and Antitrust Policy, 95 Harv.L.Rev. 1523, 1550–1552, 1555–1560 (1982). See also Note, United Charities and the Sherman Act, 91 Yale L.J. 1593 (1982).

68. If the NCAA faced "interbrand" competition from available substitutes, then certain forms of collective action might be appropriate in order to enhance its ability to compete. See Continental T.V., Inc., 433 U.S., at 54–57. Our conclusion concerning the availability of substitutes in Part III, *supra,* forecloses such a justification in this case, however.

69. The NCAA's plan is not even arguably related to a desire to protect live attendance by ensuring that a game is not televised in the area where it is to be played. No cooperative action is necessary for that kind of "blackout." The home team can always refuse to sell the right to telecast its game to stations in the immediate area. The NCAA does not now and never has justified its television plan by an interest in assisting schools in "blacking out" their home games in the areas in which they are played.

70. During this period, the NCAA also expressed its concern to Congress in urging it to limit the antitrust exemption professional football obtained for telecasting its games to contests not held on Friday or Saturday when such telecasts might interfere with attendance at intercollegiate games. See H.R.Rep. No. 1178, 87th Cong., 1st Sess., 3–4 (1961); 107 Cong.Rec. 20060–20061 (1961) (remarks of Rep. Celler); id., at 20062; Hearings, *supra* n. 28, at 66–68 (statement of William R. Reed). The provision enacted as a result is now found in 15 U.S.C. § 1293.

that there was no evidence to support that theory in today's market. Moreover, as the District Court found, the television plan has evolved in a manner inconsistent with its original design to protect gate attendance. Under the current plan, games are shown on television during all hours that college football games are played. The plan simply does not protect live attendance by ensuring that games will not be shown on television at the same time as live events.[71]

There is, however, a more fundamental reason for rejecting this defense. The NCAA's argument that its television plan is necessary to protect live attendance is not based on a desire to maintain the integrity of college football as a distinct and attractive product, but rather on a fear that the product will not prove sufficiently attractive to draw live attendance when faced with competition from televised games. At bottom the NCAA's position is that ticket sales for most college games are unable to compete in a free market.[72] The television plan protects ticket sales by limiting output—just as any monopolist increases revenues by reducing output. By seeking to insulate live ticket sales from the full spectrum of competition because of its assumption that the product itself is insufficiently attractive to consumers, petitioner forwards a justification that is inconsistent with the basic policy of the Sherman Act. "[T]he Rule of Reason does not support a defense based on the assumption that competition itself is unreasonable." *Professional Engineers*, 435 U.S., at 696.

VI

Petitioner argues that the interest in maintaining a competitive balance among amateur athletic teams is legitimate and important and that it justifies the regulations challenged in this case. We agree with the first part of the argument but not the second.

Our decision not to apply a *per se* rule to this case rests in large part on our recognition that a certain degree of cooperation is necessary if the type of competition that petitioner and its member institutions seek to market is to be preserved. It is reasonable to assume that most of the regulatory controls of the NCAA are justifiable means of fostering competition among amateur athletic teams and therefore procompetitive because they enhance public interest in intercollegiate athletics. The specific restraints on football telecasts that are challenged in this case do not, however, fit into the same mold as do rules defining the conditions of the contest, the eligibility of

---

71. "[T]he greatest flaw in the NCAA's argument is that it is manifest that the new plan for football television does not limit televised football in order to protect gate attendance. The evidence shows that under the new plan, many areas of the country will have access to nine hours of college football television on several Saturdays in the coming season. Because the 'ground rules' eliminate head-to-head programming, a full nine hours of college football will have to be shown on television during a nine-to-twelve hour period on almost every Saturday of the football season in most of the major television markets in the country. It can hardly be said that such a plan is devised in order to protect gate attendance." 546 F.Supp., at 1296.

72. Ironically, to the extent that the NCAA's position has merit, it rests on the assumption that football telecasts are a unique product. If, as the NCAA argues, all television programming is essentially fungible, it would not be possible to protect attendance without banning all television during the hours at which intercollegiate football games are held.

participants, or the manner in which members of a joint enterprise shall share the responsibilities and the benefits of the total venture.

The NCAA does not claim that its television plan has equalized or is intended to equalize competition within any one league.[73] The plan is nationwide in scope and there is no single league or tournament in which all college football teams compete. There is no evidence of any intent to equalize the strength of teams in Division I–A with those in Division II or Division III, and not even a colorable basis for giving colleges that have no football program at all a voice in the management of the revenues generated by the football programs at other schools.[74] The interest in maintaining a competitive balance that is asserted by the NCAA as a justification for regulating all television of intercollegiate football is not related to any neutral standard or to any readily identifiable group of competitors.

The television plan is not even arguably tailored to serve such an interest. It does not regulate the amount of money that any college may spend on its football program, nor the way in which the colleges may use the revenues that are generated by their football programs, whether derived from the sale of television rights, the sale of tickets, or the sale of concessions or program advertising.[75] The plan simply imposes a restriction on one source of revenue that is more important to some colleges than to others. There is no evidence that this restriction produces any greater measure of equality throughout the NCAA than would a restriction on alumni donations, tuition rates, or any other revenue producing activity. At the same time, as the District Court found, the NCAA imposes a variety of other restrictions designed to preserve amateurism which are much better tailored to the goal of competitive balance than is the television plan, and which are "clearly sufficient" to preserve competitive balance to the extent it is within the NCAA's power to do so. And much more than speculation supported the District Court's findings on this score. No other NCAA sport employs a similar plan, and in particular the court found that in the most closely analogous sport, college basketball, competitive balance has been maintained without resort to a restrictive television plan.

Perhaps the most important reason for rejecting the argument that the interest in competitive balance is served by the television plan is the District Court's unambiguous and well supported finding that many more games would be televised in a free market than under the NCAA plan. The hypothesis that legitimates the maintenance of competitive balance as a

---

73. It seems unlikely, for example, that there would have been a greater disparity between the football prowess of Ohio State University and that of Northwestern University in recent years without the NCAA's television plan. The District Court found that in fact the NCAA has been strikingly unsuccessful if it has indeed attempted to prevent the emergence of a "power elite" in intercollegiate football. See 546 F.Supp., at 1310–1311. Moreover, the District Court's finding that there would be more local and regional telecasts without the NCAA controls means that Northwestern could well have generated more television income in a free market than was obtained under the NCAA regime.

74. Indeed, the District Court found that the basic reason the television plan has endured is that the NCAA is in effect controlled by schools that are not restrained by the plan.

75. Moreover, the District Court found that those schools which would realize increased revenues in a free market would not funnel those revenues into their football programs.

procompetitive justification under the Rule of Reason is that equal competition will maximize consumer demand for the product. The finding that consumption will materially increase if the controls are removed is a compelling demonstration that they do not in fact serve any such legitimate purpose.[76]

VII

The NCAA plays a critical role in the maintenance of a revered tradition of amateurism in college sports. There can be no question but that it needs ample latitude to play that role, or that the preservation of the student-athlete in higher education adds richness and diversity to intercollegiate athletics and is entirely consistent with the goals of the Sherman Act. But consistent with the Sherman Act, the role of the NCAA must be to *preserve* a tradition that might otherwise die; rules that restrict output are hardly consistent with this role. Today we hold only that the record supports the District Court's conclusion that by curtailing output and blunting the ability of member institutions to respond to consumer preference, the NCAA has restricted rather than enhanced the place of intercollegiate athletics in the Nation's life. Accordingly, the judgment of the Court of Appeals is affirmed.

■ WHITE, J., with whom REHNQUIST, J., joined, dissented. [The dissenters agreed with the majority that the NCAA television plan should be viewed under a rule of reason rather than a *per se* approach, emphasizing to a greater extent than the majority that the plan was "non-commercial" in character. They concluded, however, that the plan should have been declared legal under a rule of reason. They noted that there were many NCAA enforced rules limiting competition—for example, rules restricting compensation of student athletes, restricting the number of athletic scholarships that may be awarded, and establishing minimum academic standards—which would be condemned as anticompetitive in a more traditional business setting. The NCAA plan was reasonable in their view because (1) college football should be viewed as part of a broad entertainment market and hence collective action was an appropriate procompetitive response to existing competition, and (2) it was reasonably ancillary to the legitimate non-economic goal of fostering amateurism "by spreading revenues among various schools and reducing the financial incentives towards professionalism."]

NOTES AND QUESTIONS

1. Are the Supreme Court decisions in *BMI* and *NCAA* reconcilable? On what theory? Can the decisions be aligned on the basis of differences in market share,

---

76. This is true not only for television viewers, but also for athletes. The District Court's finding that the television exposure of all schools would increase in the absence of the NCAA's television plan means that smaller institutions appealing to essentially local or regional markets would get more exposure if the plan is enjoined, enhancing their ability to compete for student athletes.

nature and extent of efficiencies, or presence or absence of actual integration of resources? Are there other factors that the Court might have taken into account? How would you formulate the "*per se* rule" of *Socony Vacuum* in light of these more recent decisions?

2. What exactly was the role of the NCAA in negotiating with the networks on behalf of colleges? Did the NCAA negotiate actual fees with the various networks, or did it simply establish parameters within which the colleges and networks could bargain? If individual bargaining still had to occur, then what "efficiencies" were generated as a result of the NCAA contract?

United States v. Brown University

United States Court of Appeals, Third Circuit, 1993.
5 F.3d 658.

[In 1958, MIT and eight Ivy League schools formed the "Ivy Overlap Group" to collectively determine the amount of financial assistance to be awarded to students who had been admitted to more than one of the schools. The Overlap Group agreed that each school would award financial aid only on the basis of demonstrated need. To ensure that aid packages would be comparable, the Overlap Group agreed to share financial information concerning admitted students and to jointly develop and apply a "uniform needs analysis" for assessing family contributions.

Although each school employed the same analysis to compute need, "discrepancies" arose. To eliminate these discrepancies, Overlap Group members would meet in early April each year to jointly determine the amount of "family contribution" (*i.e.*, in determining need) for each commonly admitted student. In 1991, the Antitrust Division brought this civil action against MIT and the eight Ivy League schools.]

COWEN, J ... [The Antitrust Division] brought this civil suit alleging that the Ivy Overlap Group unlawfully conspired to restrain trade in violation of section one of the Sherman Act by (1) agreeing to award financial aid exclusively on the basis of need; (2) agreeing to utilize a common formula to calculate need; and (3) collectively setting, with only insignificant discrepancies, each commonly admitted students' family contribution toward the price of tuition. The Division sought only injunctive relief. All of the Ivy League institutions signed a consent decree with the United States, and only MIT proceeded to trial. After a ten-day bench trial, the district court held that the Ivy Overlap Group's conduct constituted "trade or commerce" under section one of the Sherman Act. Rejecting MIT's argument that financial aid is pure charity and thus exempt from the dictates of the Sherman Act, the district court characterized the Overlap Agreement as setting a selective discount off the price of educational services.

The district court found that the Overlap Agreement constituted price fixing. Due to the nonprofit status and educational mission of the alleged conspirators, however, the court declined to apply the *per se* rule of illegality that summarily invalidates most horizontal price fixing agreements. Because the conflicting and complex expert testimony left the court unsure that the economic effect of Overlap could be accurately measured, it assumed without deciding MIT's premise that the Overlap Agreement was revenue neutral, *i.e.*, did not increase or decrease the *average* tuition payment made by students. Nevertheless, the court was quick to point out that assuming the fact of revenue neutrality, without more, offers no insight into any alleged procompetitive virtue of a restraint. Hence, despite this assumption of revenue neutrality, the court found the Agreement plainly anticompetitive because it eliminated price competition for outstanding students among the participating schools. Because the harm was tampering with free market forces, the court deemed it irrelevant whether the total amount of tuition payments collected from all students increased, decreased or remained the same.

Faced with what it believed was a plainly anticompetitive agreement, the district court applied an abbreviated version of the rule of reason and took only a "quick look" to determine if MIT presented any plausible procompetitive affirmative defenses that justified the Overlap Agreement. MIT argued that Overlap widened the pool of applicants to Overlap institutions by providing needy students with the ability to enroll if accepted. This, MIT asserted, increased consumer choice and enhanced the quality of the education provided to all students by opening the doors of the most elite colleges in the nation to diversely gifted students of varied socio-economic backgrounds. The district court deemed these explanations to be social welfare justifications and flatly rejected the contention that the elimination of competition may be justified by non-economic considerations . . .

As a threshold matter, we must decide whether section one of the Sherman Act applies to the challenged conduct—MIT's agreement with the other Overlap institutions to award financial aid only to needy students and to set the amount of family contribution from commonly admitted students. Section one, by its terms, does not apply to all conspiracies, but only to those which restrain "trade or commerce." MIT characterizes its conduct as disbursing charitable funds to achieve the twin objectives of advancing equality of access to higher education and promoting socio-economic and racial diversity within the nation's most elite universities. This alleged pure charity, MIT argues, does not implicate trade or commerce, and is thus exempt from antitrust scrutiny.

It is axiomatic that section one of the Sherman Act regulates only transactions that are commercial in nature. Congress, however, intended this statute to embrace the widest array of conduct possible. Goldfarb v. Virginia State Bar, 421 U.S. 773, 787–88 (1975). Section one's scope thus reaches the activities of nonprofit organizations, including institutions of higher learning. NCAA v. Board of Regents of the Univ. of Oklahoma, 468 U.S. 85, 100 n. 22 (1984) ("There is no doubt that the sweeping language of § 1 applies to non-profit entities.") . . . .

Although nonprofit organizations are not entitled to a class exemption from the Sherman Act, when they perform acts that are the antithesis of commercial activity, they are immune from antitrust regulation. Cf. Apex

Hosiery Co. v. Leader, 310 U.S. 469 (1940) (labor union strike does not implicate commerce under Sherman Act); National Org. For Women, Inc. v. Scheidler, 968 F.2d 612 (7th Cir.1992) (violent pro-life protests that successfully closed abortion clinics do not implicate commerce), *cert. granted in part,* 113 S.Ct. 2958 (1993). This immunity, however, is narrowly circumscribed. It does not extend to commercial transactions with a "public-service aspect." *Goldfarb,* 421 U.S. at 787–88. Courts classify a transaction as commercial or noncommercial based on the nature of the conduct in light of the totality of surrounding circumstances.

The exchange of money for services, even by a nonprofit organization, is a quintessential commercial transaction. Therefore, the payment of tuition in return for educational services constitutes commerce. MIT concedes as much by acknowledging that its determination of the full tuition amount is a commercial decision.

We thus come to the crux of the issue—is providing financial assistance solely to needy students a selective reduction or "discount" from the full tuition amount, or a charitable gift? If this financial aid is a component of the process of setting tuition prices, it is commerce. See Catalano, Inc. v. Target Sales, Inc., 446 U.S. 643, 648 (1980) (agreement to eliminate discounts violates section one). If it is pure charity, it is not.[77]

When MIT admits an affluent student, that student must pay approximately $25,000 annually (tuition plus room, board, and incidental expenses) if he or she wishes to enroll at MIT. If MIT accepts a needy student and calculates that it will extend $10,000 in financial aid to that student, the student must pay approximately $15,000 to attend MIT. The student certainly is not free to take the $10,000 and apply it toward attendance at a different college. The assistance package is only available in conjunction with a complemented payment of approximately $15,000 to MIT. The amount of financial aid not only impacts, but directly determines the amount that a needy student must pay to receive an education at MIT. The financial aid, therefore, is part of the commercial process of setting tuition.

MIT suggests that providing aid exclusively to needy students and setting the amount of that aid is not commercial because the price needy students are charged is substantially below the marginal cost of supplying a year of education to an undergraduate student. Because profit maximizing companies would not engage in such economically abnormal behavior, MIT concludes that such activity must be noncommercial. MIT's concession, however, that setting the full tuition amount is a commercial decision subject to antitrust scrutiny undermines this argument. The full tuition figure, like the varying amounts charged to needy students, is significantly below MIT's marginal cost. Therefore, whether the price charged for educational services is below marginal cost is not probative of the commer-

---

77. The district court commenced its analysis by noting that MIT is a significant economic entity, controlling substantial assets and operating a billion dollar budget. We agree with MIT that the extent of its resources is not probative of whether its financial aid is commerce.

cial or noncommercial nature of the methodology utilized to determine financial aid packages.

The fact that MIT is not obligated to provide any financial aid does not transform that aid to charity. Similarly, discounting the price of educational services for needy students is not charity when a university receives tangible benefits in exchange. Regardless of whether MIT's motive is altruism, self-enhancement or a combination of the two,[78] MIT benefits from providing financial aid. MIT admits that it competes with other Overlap members for outstanding students. By distributing aid, MIT enables exceptional students to attend its school who otherwise could not afford to attend. The resulting expansion in MIT's pool of exceptional applicants increases the quality of MIT's student body. MIT then enjoys enhanced prestige by virtue of its ability to attract a greater portion of the "cream of the crop." The Supreme Court has recognized that nonprofit organizations derive significant benefit from increased prestige and influence. See American Society of Mechanical Engineers, Inc. v. Hydrolevel Corp., 456 U.S. 556, 576 (1982). Although MIT could fill its class with students able to pay the full tuition, the caliber of its student body, and consequently the institution's reputation, obviously would suffer. Overlap affords MIT the benefit of an overrepresentation of high caliber students, with the concomitant institutional prestige, without forcing MIT to be responsive to market forces in terms of its tuition costs. By immunizing itself through the Overlap from competition for students based on a price/quality ratio, MIT achieves certain institutional benefits at a bargain. . . .

We hold that financial assistance to students is part and parcel of the process of setting tuition and thus a commercial transaction. Although

---

78. The district court did not make a factual finding with respect to MIT's motivation for joining the Overlap Agreement. There is ample evidence that MIT's indirect objective was to promote equal access to higher education and diversity within the student body. We cannot overlook, however, that MIT also desired to attract the most talented students at the least expense to itself, a result which would also flow directly from the elimination of price competition among the Ivy Overlap member institutions. In fact, we could conjecture a number of self-serving reasons why MIT might have entered the Overlap Agreement, not the least of which might have been the market power which typically accompanies combinations. The higher than competitive tuition prices which MIT and the other Overlap members were able to charge, absent tuition competition, enhances "revenues," if not "profits," which can be allocated to any conceivable internal institutional purpose.

In any event, to determine whether trade or commerce is implicated, motive plays a much less important role when the nature of the activity, as here, is plainly commercial. An anticompetitive motive may trigger antitrust scrutiny of otherwise noncommercial conduct. See Marjorie Webster Junior College, Inc. v. Middle States Ass'n of Colleges and Secondary Schools, Inc., 432 F.2d 650, 654–55 (D.C.Cir.), cert. denied, 400 U.S. 965 (1970). The opposite, however, is not also true. A beneficent objective does not excuse commercial activities from compliance with the Sherman Act. In *Goldfarb*, the Supreme Court held that a minimum fee schedule for attorneys published by a county bar association violated section one of the Sherman Act. 421 U.S. at 781–87. The bar association argued that the goal of professions, in contrast to businesses, "is to provide services necessary to the community." The Supreme Court discounted the significance of this purported motive, finding that motive arguments lose force when used to justify an obviously commercial endeavor.

MIT's status as a nonprofit educational organization and its advancement of congressionally-recognized and important social welfare goals does not remove its conduct from the realm of trade or commerce, these factors will influence whether this conduct violates the Sherman Act....

In addition to the traditional rule of reason and the *per se* rule, courts sometimes apply what amounts to an abbreviated or "quick look" rule of reason analysis. The abbreviated rule of reason is an intermediate standard. It applies in cases where *per se* condemnation is inappropriate, but where "no elaborate industry analysis is required to demonstrate the anticompetitive character" of an inherently suspect restraint. See *NCAA,* 468 U.S. at 109 (quoting *Professional Engineers,* 435 U.S. at 692); *Indiana Dentists,* 476 U.S. at 459 (same). Because competitive harm is presumed, the defendant must promulgate "some competitive justification" for the restraint, "even in the absence of detailed market analysis" indicating actual profit maximization or increased costs to the consumer resulting from the restraint.... If the defendant offers sound procompetitive justifications, however, the court must proceed to weigh the overall reasonableness of the restraint using a full-scale rule of reason analysis.

In the present case, the district court applied the abbreviated rule of reason analysis. Emphasizing that its decision to apply this analysis did "not stem from a reluctance to characterize the Ivy Overlap process as the type of price fixing which is ordinarily *per se* unreasonable," the court nevertheless adopted the more cautious approach in deference to Supreme Court precedents counseling special scrutiny of restraints involving professional associations. Accordingly, rather than immediately condemning the Overlap because of its apparent quintessentially anticompetitive nature, the court afforded MIT an opportunity to proffer a procompetitive affirmative defense—an acknowledged "heavy burden."

MIT first claims that the district court erred by applying an abbreviated rather than a full-scale rule of reason analysis. The Division, on the other hand, argues that the district court erred by failing to declare Overlap illegal *per se.* In the alternative, the Division argues that if the *per se* rule is inapplicable, the district court correctly applied the abbreviated rule of reason....

[The Supreme] Court has been ... hesitant to condemn agreements by professional associations as unreasonable *per se,* or to apply a *per se* rejection to competitive restraints imposed in contexts where the economic impact of such practices is neither one with which the Court has dealt previously, nor immediately apparent. In *Indiana Dentists,* the Court once again reaffirmed *Goldfarb* and *Professional Engineers....*

As a qualified charitable organization under 26 U.S.C. § 501(c)(3), MIT deviates even further from the profit-maximizing prototype than do professional associations. While non-profit professional associations advance the commercial interests of their for-profit constituents, MIT is, as its § 501(c)(3) status suggests, an organization "operated exclusively for ... educational purposes ... no part of the net earnings of which inures to the benefit of any private shareholder or individual." This does not mean, of course, that MIT and other bona fide charitable organizations lack incentives to increase revenues. Nor does it necessarily mean that commercially motivated conduct of such organizations should be immune from *per se* treatment. Like the defendant associations in *Indiana Dentists* and *Professional Engineers,* however, MIT vigorously maintains that Overlap was the product of a concern for the public interest, here the undisputed public interest in equality of educational access and opportunity, and alleges the absence of any revenue maximizing purpose.

This alleged pure altruistic motive and alleged absence of a revenue maximizing purpose contribute to our uncertainty with regard to Overlap's anticompetitiveness, and thus prompts us to give careful scrutiny to the nature of Overlap, and to refrain from declaring Overlap *per se* unreasonable. We thus agree with the district court that Overlap must be judged under the rule of reason. . . .

MIT does not dispute that the stated purpose of Overlap is to eliminate price competition for talented students among member institutions. Indeed, the intent to eliminate price competition among the Overlap schools for commonly admitted students appears on the face of the Agreement itself. In addition to agreeing to offer financial aid solely on the basis of need and to develop a common system of needs analysis, the Overlap members agreed to meet each spring to compare data and to conform one another's aid packages to the greatest possible extent. Because the Overlap Agreement aims to restrain "competitive bidding" and deprive prospective students of "the ability to utilize and compare prices" in selecting among schools, it is anticompetitive "on its face." *Professional Engineers,* 435 U.S. at 693. Price is "the central nervous system of the economy," *Socony–Vacuum Oil,* 310 U.S. at 224 n. 59, and "[t]he heart of our national economic policy long has been faith in the value of competition," *Standard Oil Co. v. FTC,* 340 U.S. 231, 248 (1951). We therefore agree that Overlap initially "requires some competitive justification even in the absence of a detailed market analysis." *Indiana Dentists,* 476 U.S. at 460 (quoting *NCAA,* 468 U.S. at 109–10); see *Professional Engineers,* 435 U.S. at 695.

MIT's principal counterargument is that an abbreviated rule of reason analysis is appropriate only where economic harm to consumers may fairly be presumed; and such harm may be presumed only when evidence establishes that "the challenged practice, unlike Overlap, manifestly has an adverse effect on price, output, or quality." As the Division aptly points out, however, if an abbreviated rule of reason analysis always required a clear evidentiary showing of a detrimental effect on price, output, or quality, it would no longer be abbreviated. . . . This is because proof of actual adverse effects generally will require the elaborate, threshold industry analysis that an abbreviated inquiry is designed to obviate.

MIT's position also is contradicted by Supreme Court precedent. Without any mention of actual effects on price, output, or quality, the Court in *Professional Engineers* required the association of engineers to affirmatively defend an ethics rule prohibiting members from discussing fees with prospective customers prior to being selected for a project. 435 U.S. at 692–

96. The Court reasoned that the "anticompetitive character" of the agreement could be presumed because the ban on competitive bidding, like price fixing, "impede[d] the ordinary give and take of the market place."....

MIT claims that even if the district court properly decided to apply an abbreviated rule of reason analysis, the court applied it incorrectly by failing to adequately consider the economic and social welfare justifications proffered by MIT. We will address MIT's claims with respect to economic and social welfare justifications separately.

At trial, MIT maintained that Overlap had the following procompetitive effects: (1) it improved the quality of the educational program at the Overlap schools; (2) it increased consumer choice by making an Overlap education more accessible to a greater number of students; and (3) it promoted competition for students among Overlap schools in areas other than price. The district court rejected each of these alleged competitive virtues, summarily concluding that they amounted to no more than non-economic social welfare justifications....

MIT next claims that beyond ignoring the procompetitive effects of Overlap, the district court erroneously refused to consider compelling social welfare justifications. MIT argues that by enabling member schools to maintain a steadfast policy of need-blind admissions and full need-based aid, Overlap promoted the social ideal of equality of educational access and opportunity....

Both the public safety justification rejected by the Supreme Court in *Professional Engineers* and the public health justification rejected by the Court in *Indiana Dentists* were based on the defendants' faulty premise that consumer choices made under competitive market conditions are "unwise" or "dangerous." Here MIT argues that participation in the Overlap arrangement provided some consumers, the needy, with additional choices which an entirely free market would deny them. The facts and arguments before us may suggest some significant areas of distinction from those in *Professional Engineers* and *Indiana Dentists* in that MIT is asserting that Overlap not only serves a social benefit, but actually enhances consumer choice. Overlap is not an attempt to withhold a particular desirable service from customers, as was the professional combination in *Indiana Dentists,* but rather it purports only to seek to extend a service to qualified students who are financially "needy" and would not otherwise be able to afford the high cost of education at MIT. Further, while Overlap resembles the ban on competitive bidding at issue in *Professional Engineers,* MIT alleges that Overlap enhances competition by broadening the socio-economic sphere of its potential student body. Thus, rather than suppress competition, Overlap may in fact merely regulate competition in order to enhance it, while also deriving certain social benefits. If the rule of reason analysis leads to this conclusion, then indeed Overlap will be beyond the scope of the prohibitions of the Sherman Act.

We note the unfortunate fact that financial aid resources are limited even at the Ivy League schools. A trade-off may need to be made between providing some financial aid to a large number of the most needy students or allowing the free market to bestow the limited financial aid on the very few most talented who may not need financial aid to attain their academic goals. Under such circumstances, if this trade-off is proven to be worthy in terms of obtaining a more diverse student body (or other legitimate institutional goals), the limitations on the choices of the most talented students might not be so egregious as to trigger the obvious concerns which led the Court to reject the "public interest" justifications in *Professional Engineers* and *Indiana Dentists*. However, we leave it for the district court to decide whether full funding of need may be continued on an individual institutional basis, absent Overlap, whether tuition could be lowered as a way to compete for qualified "needy" students, or whether there are other imaginable creative alternatives to implement MIT's professed social welfare goal.

We note too, however, that another aspect of the agreements condemned in *Professional Engineers* and *Indiana Dentists* was that those agreements embodied a strong economic self-interest of the parties to them. In *Professional Engineers*, the undisputed objective of the ban on competitive bidding was to maintain higher prices for engineering services than a free competitive market would sustain. The engineers' public safety justification "rest[ed] on the assumption that the agreement [would] tend to maintain price level; if it had no such effect, it would not serve its intended purpose." *Id.* Likewise, the Court in *Indiana Dentists* characterized the dentists' agreement to withhold x-rays as an "attempt to thwart" the goal of "choosing the least expensive adequate course of dental treatment." *Indiana Dentists,* 476 U.S. at 461. Though not singled out by the Court in these two cases, the nature of the agreements made any public interest argument greatly suspect. To the extent that economic self-interest or revenue maximization is operative in Overlap, it too renders MIT's public interest justification suspect.

The role that economic self-interest plays in evaluating affirmative defenses to a Sherman Act claim was made clear by the Court in FTC v. Superior Court Trial Lawyers Ass'n, 493 U.S. 411 (1990), where the Court condemned as *per se* illegal the trial lawyers' concerted refusal to accept further assignments to defend indigents until they receive an increase in compensation. . . . In the case *sub judice,* the quest for economic self-interest is professed to be absent, as it is alleged that the Overlap agreement was intended, not to obtain an economic profit in the form of greater revenue for the participating schools, but rather to benefit talented but needy prospective students who otherwise could not attend the school of their choice.

The nature of higher education, and the asserted procompetitive and pro-consumer features of the Overlap, convince us that a full rule of reason analysis is in order here. It may be that institutions of higher education "require that a particular practice, which could properly be viewed as a violation of the Sherman Act in another context, be treated differently." Goldfarb v. Virginia, 421 U.S. 773, 788 n. 17 (1975). See also Klor's Inc. v. Broadway–Hale Stores, Inc., 359 U.S. 207, 213 n. 7 (1959) ("'[t]he Act is aimed primarily at combinations having commercial objectives and is applied only to a very limited extent to organizations ... which normally have other objectives").

It is most desirable that schools achieve equality of educational access and opportunity in order that more people enjoy the benefits of a worthy higher education. There is no doubt, too, that enhancing the quality of our educational system redounds to the general good. To the extent that higher education endeavors to foster vitality of the mind, to promote free exchange between bodies of thought and truths, and better communication among a broad spectrum of individuals, as well as prepares individuals for the intellectual demands of responsible citizenship, it is a common good that should be extended to as wide a range of individuals from as broad a range of socio-economic backgrounds as possible. It is with this in mind that the Overlap Agreement should be submitted to the rule of reason scrutiny under the Sherman Act.

We conclude that the district court was obliged to more fully investigate the procompetitive and noneconomic justifications proffered by MIT than it did when it performed the truncated rule of reason analysis. Accordingly, we will remand this case to the district court with instructions to evaluate Overlap using the full-scale rule of reason analysis outlined above.

The final step of the rule of reason involves determining whether the challenged agreement is necessary to achieve its purported goals. The district court alternatively rejected MIT's social welfare justifications because it "questioned" whether Overlap was necessary to achieve egalitarian educational access. Even if an anticompetitive restraint is intended to achieve a legitimate objective, the restraint only survives a rule of reason analysis if it is reasonably necessary to achieve the legitimate objectives proffered by the defendant.... To determine if a restraint is reasonably necessary, courts must examine first whether the restraint furthers the legitimate objectives, and then whether comparable benefits could be achieved through a substantially less restrictive alternative. 7 P. Areeda, *supra* ¶ 1505, at 388. Once a defendant demonstrates that its conduct promotes a legitimate goal, the plaintiff, in order to prevail, bears the burden of proving that there exists a viable less restrictive alternative....

The district court "questioned" whether the Overlap Agreement was "a necessary ingredient" to achieve the social welfare objectives offered by MIT. *Brown University*, 806 F.Supp. at 306. The district court implicitly concluded, and we agree, that to some extent the Overlap Agreement promoted equality of access to higher education and economic and cultural diversity. It thus turned directly to the second inquiry—whether a substantially less restrictive alternative, the free market coupled with MIT's institutional resolve, could achieve the same benefits. In a conclusory statement, the court found "no evidence supporting MIT's fatalistic prediction that the end of the Ivy Overlap Group necessarily would sound the death knell of need-blind admissions or need-based aid." Although the district court acknowledged that the end of Overlap could herald the end of full need-based aid at MIT, it also observed that this was not an inevitability if indeed MIT counted full need-based aid among its priority institutional goals.

On remand if the district court, under a full scale rule of reason analysis, finds that MIT has proffered a persuasive justification for the Overlap Agreement, then the Antitrust Division of the Justice Department, the plaintiff in this case, must prove that a reasonable less restrictive alternative exists. The district court should consider, if and when the issue arises, whether the Antitrust Division has shown, by a preponderance of the evidence, that another viable option, perhaps the free market, can achieve the same benefits as Overlap.

■ WEIS, J., dissenting. Although the century that has passed since the enactment of the Sherman Act may make reliance upon legislative history somewhat hazardous, it is a fair assumption that the drafters of the statute would have been quite astounded at the government's contention that the student aid program at issue here is covered by the antitrust laws. . . .

Glossing over the policy articulated in this bit of legislative history, the government has rushed into discussions of economic theory using pejorative terms such as "price fixing" and illegal "discounts." But before such considerations have any relevance, a formidable threshold must be crossed in this case—the applicability of the Sherman Act to agreements on need-blind admission policies and student aid. It is premature to analyze activities in the business world that violate antitrust law until it has been established that the Sherman Act does, in fact, govern the conduct in the circumstances present here.

The challenged practices, designed to provide high quality education to those who have demonstrated academic talent without regard to their financial status, do not instinctively conjure up images of reprehensible business dealings. Quite to the contrary, the initial reaction is to question why the heavy artillery of antitrust has been wheeled into position to shoot down practices that so obviously advance the public interest.

Practices that might be illegal in the commercial area do not transform a charitable activity into a business one. To the extent that the government pursues that course, its argument is simply a non sequitur. . . . My view that the antitrust laws do not apply to student aid activities in the circumstances of this case is not meant to convey any opinion on the desirability or necessity of all of the Overlap procedures. . . .

NOTES AND QUESTIONS

1. If MIT and the Ivy League schools had agreed on tuition, would the Third Circuit have applied the *per se* rule?

2. On December 22, 1993, MIT and the Department of Justice settled their litigation. The Department of Justice's press release said the following:

Under today's settlement, MIT acknowledges that it is obliged in its dealings with the Ivy League colleges to act in accordance with a 1991 consent decree in which Brown, Columbia, Cornell, Dartmouth, Harvard, Princeton, the University of Pennsylvania, and Yale agreed not to fix tuition, faculty salaries, or the payments needy students would be expected to make on their own.

MIT has further promised that in its dealings with other schools it will abide by standards of conduct, agreed upon today, that prohibit any discussion or agreement on the contribution expected to be made by students receiving financial aid. The standards also prohibit any discussion or agreement on the composition of financial aid packages. . . .

Under today's settlement, MIT may agree with other colleges on general principles for determining financial aid, to award aid solely on the basis of financial need, and to exchange limited data about applicants' financial profiles.

In order to do this, MIT and other participating schools must commit to need-blind admissions and to meet the full financial need of their undergraduate students. . . .

If you were in charge of the Antitrust Division, would you have agreed to the settlement? What is likely to have happened if the case had reached the Supreme Court?

3.   On June 27, 1995, the Antitrust Division and the ABA "resolved charges that the ABA process for accrediting law schools had been misused to inflate faculty salaries and benefits." The Department of Justice's press release indicated that the settlement (filed in the D.C. District Court) prohibited: (i) "fixing faculty salaries;" (ii) "refusing to accredit schools simply because they are for-profit;" and (iii) "refusing to allow ABA-approved law schools to accept credits for classes at schools that are state-accredited but not ABA-approved." The settlement also established "a special committee to determine if ABA accreditation requirements in six other areas should be revised—student to faculty ratios, teaching loads, sabbaticals, bar preparation courses, facilities, and other resources." The head of the Antitrust Division commented:

The powerful status of the ABA does not insulate it from the antitrust laws. The Antitrust Division has sued many professional trade associations, which, like the ABA, have violated the antitrust laws. Lawyers must keep their own house in order as well.

4.   In Dedication and Everlasting Love to Animals v. The Humane Society, 50 F.3d 710 (9th Cir. 1995), the Ninth Circuit held that the solicitation of donations by the Humane Society was not "trade or commerce" under the Sherman Act. Do you agree? *See* Hamilton Chapter of Alpha Delta Phi, Inc. v. Hamilton College, 128 F.3d 59 (2d Cir. 1997) (residency policy requiring all students to live in college housing and participate in meal plan was "trade or commerce").

California Dental Association v. Federal Trade Commission

Supreme Court of the United States, 1999.
526 U.S. 756, 119 S.Ct. 1604, 143 L.Ed.2d 935.

■ SOUTER, J. There are two issues in this case: whether the jurisdiction of the Federal Trade Commission extends to the California Dental Association

(CDA), a nonprofit professional association, and whether a "quick look" sufficed to justify finding that certain advertising restrictions adopted by the CDA violated the antitrust laws. We hold that the Commission's jurisdiction under the Federal Trade Commission Act (FTC Act) extends to an association that, like the CDA, provides substantial economic benefit to its for-profit members, but that where, as here, any anticompetitive effects of given restraints are far from intuitively obvious, the rule of reason demands a more thorough enquiry into the consequences of those restraints than the Court of Appeals performed.

I

The CDA is a voluntary nonprofit association of local dental societies to which some 19,000 dentists belong, including about three-quarters of those practicing in the State. In re California Dental Assn., 121 F.T.C. 190, 196–197 (1996). The CDA is exempt from federal income tax under 26 U.S.C. § 501(c)(6), covering "business leagues, chambers of commerce, real-estate boards, [and] boards of trade," although it has for-profit subsidiaries that give its members advantageous access to various sorts of insurance, including liability coverage, and to financing for their real estate, equipment, cars, and patients' bills. The CDA lobbies and litigates in its members' interests, and conducts marketing and public relations campaigns for their benefit.

The dentists who belong to the CDA through these associations agree to abide by a Code of Ethics (Code) including the following § 10:

"Although any dentist may advertise, no dentist shall advertise or solicit patients in any form of communication in a manner that is false or misleading in any material respect. In order to properly serve the public, dentists should represent themselves in a manner that contributes to the esteem of the public. Dentists should not misrepresent their training and competence in any way that would be false or misleading in any material respect."

The CDA has issued a number of advisory opinions interpreting this section, and through separate advertising guidelines intended to help members comply with the Code and with state law the CDA has advised its dentists of disclosures they must make under state law when engaging in discount advertising.[79]

Responsibility for enforcing the Code rests in the first instance with the local dental societies, to which applicants for CDA membership must

---

79. The disclosures include:

"1. The dollar amount of the nondiscounted fee for the service[.]

"2. Either the dollar amount of the discount fee or the percentage of the discount for the specific service[.]

"3. The length of time that the discount will be offered[.]

"4. Verifiable fees[.]

"5. [The identity of] [s]pecific groups who qualify for the discount or any other terms and conditions or restrictions for qualifying for the discount." Id., at 724.

submit copies of their own advertisements and those of their employers or referral services to assure compliance with the Code. The local societies also actively seek information about potential Code violations by applicants or CDA members. Applicants who refuse to withdraw or revise objectionable advertisements may be denied membership; and members who, after a hearing, remain similarly recalcitrant are subject to censure, suspension, or expulsion from the CDA.

The Commission brought a complaint against the CDA, alleging that it applied its guidelines so as to restrict truthful, nondeceptive advertising, and so violated § 5 of the FTC Act.[80] The complaint alleged that the CDA had unreasonably restricted two types of advertising: price advertising, particularly discounted fees, and advertising relating to the quality of dental services. An Administrative Law Judge (ALJ) held the Commission to have jurisdiction over the CDA, which, the ALJ noted, had itself "stated that a selection of its programs and services has a potential value to members of between $22,739 and $65,127," 121 F.T.C. at 207. He found that, although there had been no proof that the CDA exerted market power, no such proof was required to establish an antitrust violation under In re Mass. Bd. of Registration in Optometry, 110 F.T.C. 549 (1988), since the CDA had unreasonably prevented members and potential members from using truthful, nondeceptive advertising, all to the detriment of both dentists and consumers of dental services. He accordingly found a violation of § 5 of the FTC Act.

The Commission adopted the factual findings of the ALJ except for his conclusion that the CDA lacked market power, with which the Commission disagreed. The Commission treated the CDA's restrictions on discount advertising as illegal *per se*. In the alternative, the Commission held the price advertising (as well as the nonprice) restrictions to be violations of the Sherman and FTC Acts under an abbreviated rule-of-reason analysis. . . .

The Court of Appeals for the Ninth Circuit affirmed, sustaining the Commission's assertion of jurisdiction over the CDA and its ultimate conclusion on the merits. The court thought it error for the Commission to have applied *per se* analysis to the price advertising restrictions, finding analysis under the rule of reason required for all the restrictions. But the Court of Appeals went on to explain that the Commission had properly

> "applied an abbreviated, or 'quick look,' rule of reason analysis designed for restraints that are not *per se* unlawful but are sufficiently anticompetitive on their face that they do not require a full-blown rule of reason inquiry. See [National Collegiate Athletic Assn. v. Board of Regents of Univ. of Okla., 468 U.S. 85 and n. 39 (1984)] ('The essential point is that the rule of reason can sometimes be applied in the twinkling of an eye'). . . .

---

80. The FTC Act's prohibition of unfair competition and deceptive acts or practices overlaps the scope of § 1 of the Sherman Act, aimed at prohibiting restraint of trade, FTC v. Indiana Federation of Dentists, 476 U.S. 447, 454–455 (1986), and the Commission relied upon Sherman Act law in adjudicating this case.

The Court of Appeals thought truncated rule-of-reason analysis to be in order for several reasons. As for the restrictions on discount advertising, they "amounted in practice to a fairly 'naked' restraint on price competition itself. The CDA's procompetitive justification, that the restrictions encouraged disclosure and prevented false and misleading advertising, carried little weight because "it is simply infeasible to disclose all of the information that is required," id., at 728, and "the record provides no evidence that the rule has in fact led to increased disclosure and transparency of dental pricing," ibid. As to non-price advertising restrictions, the court said that

> "[t]hese restrictions are in effect a form of output limitation, as they restrict the supply of information about individual dentists' services.... The restrictions may also affect output more directly, as quality and comfort advertising may induce some customers to obtain nonemergency care when they might not otherwise do so.... Under these circumstances, we think that the restriction is a sufficiently naked restraint on output to justify quick look analysis." *Ibid.*

The Court of Appeals went on to hold that the Commission's findings with respect to the CDA's agreement and intent to restrain trade, as well as on the effect of the restrictions and the existence of market power, were all supported by substantial evidence. In dissent, Judge Real took the position that the Commission's jurisdiction did not cover the CDA as a nonprofit professional association engaging in no commercial operations. But even assuming jurisdiction, he argued, full-bore rule-of-reason analysis was called for, since the disclosure requirements were not naked restraints and neither fixed prices nor banned nondeceptive advertising.

We granted certiorari to resolve conflicts among the Circuits on the Commission's jurisdiction over a nonprofit professional association and the occasions for abbreviated rule-of-reason analysis. We now vacate the judgment of the Court of Appeals and remand.

II

The FTC Act gives the Commission authority over "persons, partnerships, or corporations," 15 U.S.C. § 45(a)(2), and defines "corporation" to include "any company ... or association, incorporated or unincorporated, without shares of capital or capital stock or certificates of interest, except partnerships, which is organized to carry on business for its own profit or that of its members," § 44. Although the Circuits have not agreed on the precise extent of this definition, the Commission has long held that some circumstances give it jurisdiction over an entity that seeks no profit for itself. While the Commission has claimed to have jurisdiction over a nonprofit entity if a substantial part of its total activities provide pecuniary benefits to its members, see In re American Medical Assn., 94 F.T.C. 701, 983–984 (1979), respondent now advances the slightly different formulation that the Commission has jurisdiction "over anticompetitive practices by nonprofit associations whose activities provide substantial economic benefits to their for-profit members' businesses."

Just as the FTC Act does not require that a supporting organization must devote itself entirely to its members' profits, neither does the Act say anything about how much of the entity's activities must go to raising the members' bottom lines. There is accordingly no apparent reason to let the statute's application turn on meeting some threshold percentage of activity for this purpose, or even satisfying a softer formulation calling for a substantial part of the nonprofit entity's total activities to be aimed at its members' pecuniary benefit. To be sure, proximate relation to lucre must appear; the FTC Act does not cover all membership organizations of profit-making corporations without more, and an organization devoted solely to professional education may lie outside the FTC Act's jurisdictional reach, even though the quality of professional services ultimately affects the profits of those who deliver them.

There is no line drawing exercise in this case, however, where the CDA's contributions to the profits of its individual members are proximate and apparent. Through for-profit subsidiaries, the CDA provides advantageous insurance and preferential financing arrangements for its members, and it engages in lobbying, litigation, marketing, and public relations for the benefit of its members' interests. This congeries of activities confers far more than de minimis or merely presumed economic benefits on CDA members; the economic benefits conferred upon the CDA's profit-seeking professionals plainly fall within the object of enhancing its members' "profit,"[81] which the FTC Act makes the jurisdictional touchstone. There is no difficulty in concluding that the Commission has jurisdiction over the CDA. . . .

III

The Court of Appeals treated as distinct questions the sufficiency of the analysis of anticompetitive effects and the substantiality of the evidence supporting the Commission's conclusions. Because we decide that the Court of Appeals erred when it held as a matter of law that quick-look analysis was appropriate (with the consequence that the Commission's abbreviated analysis and conclusion were sustainable), we do not reach the question of the substantiality of the evidence supporting the Commission's conclusion.[82]

---

81. . . . It should go without saying that the FTC Act does not require for Commission jurisdiction that members of an entity turn a profit on their membership, but only that the entity be organized to carry on business for members' profit. Nonetheless, we do not, and indeed, on the facts here, could not, decide today whether the Commission has jurisdiction over nonprofit organizations that do not confer profit on for-profit members but do, for example, show annual income surpluses, engage in significant commerce, or compete in relevant markets with for-profit players. We therefore do not foreclose the possibility that various paradigms of profit might fall within the ambit of the FTC Act. Nor do we decide whether a purpose of contributing to profit only in a presumed sense, as by enhancing professional educational efforts, would implicate the Commission's jurisdiction.

82. We leave to the Court of Appeals the question whether on remand it can effectively assess the Commission's decision for substantial evidence on the record, or whether it must

In National Collegiate Athletic Assn. v. Board of Regents of Univ. of Okla., 468 U.S. 85 (1984), we held that a "naked restraint on price and output requires some competitive justification even in the absence of a detailed market analysis." *Id.*, at 110. Elsewhere, we held that "no elaborate industry analysis is required "to demonstrate the anticompetitive character of "horizontal agreements among competitors to refuse to discuss prices," National Soc. of Professional Engineers v. United States, 435 U.S. 679, 692 (1978), or to withhold a particular desired service, FTC v. Indiana Federation of Dentists, 476 U.S. 447, 459, (1986). . . . In each of these cases, which have formed the basis for what has come to be called abbreviated or "quick-look" analysis under the rule of reason, an observer with even a rudimentary understanding of economics could conclude that the arrangements in question would have an anticompetitive effect on customers and markets. In National Collegiate Athletic Assn., the league's television plan expressly limited output (the number of games that could be televised) and fixed a minimum price. In National Soc. of Professional Engineers, the restraint was "an absolute ban on competitive bidding." In Indiana Federation of Dentists, the restraint was "a horizontal agreement among the participating dentists to withhold from their customers a particular service that they desire." As in such cases, quick-look analysis carries the day when the great likelihood of anticompetitive effects can easily be ascertained. See Law v. National Collegiate Athletic Assn., 134 F.3d 1010, 1020 (C.A.10 1998) (explaining that quick-look analysis applies "where a practice has obvious anticompetitive effects"); Chicago Professional Sports Limited Partnership v. National Basketball Assn., 961 F.2d 667, 674–676 (C.A.7 1992) (finding quick-look analysis adequate after assessing and rejecting logic of proffered procompetitive justifications); cf. United States v. Brown University, 5 F.3d 658, 677–678 (C.A.3 1993) (finding full rule-of-reason analysis required where universities sought to provide financial aid to needy students and noting by way of contrast that the agreements in *National Soc. of Professional Engineers* and *Indiana Federation of Dentists* "embodied a strong economic self-interest of the parties to them").

The case before us, however, fails to present a situation in which the likelihood of anticompetitive effects is comparably obvious. Even on JUSTICE BREYER's view that bars on truthful and verifiable price and quality advertising are prima facie anticompetitive, and place the burden of procompetitive justification on those who agree to adopt them, the very issue at the threshold of this case is whether professional price and quality advertising is sufficiently verifiable in theory and in fact to fall within such a general rule. Ultimately our disagreement with JUSTICE BREYER turns on our different responses to this issue. Whereas he accepts, as the Ninth Circuit seems to have done, that the restrictions here were like restrictions on advertisement of price and quality generally, it seems to us that the CDA's advertising restrictions might plausibly be thought to have a net procompetitive effect, or possibly no effect at all on competition. The

remand to the Commission for a more extensive rule-of-reason analysis on the basis of an enhanced record.

restrictions on both discount and nondiscount advertising are, at least on their face, designed to avoid false or deceptive advertising[83] in a market characterized by striking disparities between the information available to the professional and the patient.[84] Cf. Carr & Mathewson, The Economics of Law Firms: A Study in the Legal Organization of the Firm, 33 J. Law & Econ. 307, 309 (1990) (explaining that in a market for complex professional services, "inherent asymmetry of knowledge about the product" arises because "professionals supplying the good are knowledgeable [whereas] consumers demanding the good are uninformed"); Akerlof, The Market for 'Lemons': Quality Uncertainty and the Market Mechanism, 84 Q. J. Econ. 488 (1970) (pointing out quality problems in market characterized by asymmetrical information). In a market for professional services, in which advertising is relatively rare and the comparability of service packages not easily established, the difficulty for customers or potential competitors to get and verify information about the price and availability of services magnifies the dangers to competition associated with misleading advertising. What is more, the quality of professional services tends to resist either calibration or monitoring by individual patients or clients, partly because of the specialized knowledge required to evaluate the services, and partly because of the difficulty in determining whether, and the degree to which, an outcome is attributable to the quality of services (like a poor job of tooth-filling) or to something else (like a very tough walnut). . . . Patients' attachments to particular professionals, the rationality of which is difficult to assess, complicate the picture even further. Cf. Evans, Professionals and the Production Function: Can Competition Policy Improve Efficiency in the Licensed Professions?, in Occupational Licensure and Regulation 235–236 (S. Rottenberg ed. 1980) (describing long-term relationship between professional and client not as "a series of spot contracts" but rather as "a long-term agreement, often implicit, to deal with each other in a set of future unspecified or incompletely specified circumstances according to certain rules," and adding that "it is not clear how or if these [implicit contracts] can be reconciled with the promotion of effective price competition in individual spot markets for particular services"). The existence of such significant challenges to informed decisionmaking by the customer for professional services immediately suggests that advertising restrictions arguably protecting patients from misleading or irrelevant advertising call for more than cursory treatment as obviously comparable to classic horizontal agreements to limit output or price competition.

---

83. That false or misleading advertising has an anticompetitive effect, as that term is customarily used, has been long established. Cf. FTC v. Algoma Lumber Co., 291 U.S. 67, 79–80 (1934) (finding a false advertisement to be unfair competition).

84. "The fact that a restraint operates upon a profession as distinguished from a business is, of course, relevant in determining whether that particular restraint violates the Sherman Act. It would be unrealistic to view the practice of professions as interchangeable with other business activities, and automatically to apply to the professions antitrust concepts which originated in other areas. The public service aspect, and other features of the professions, may require that a particular practice, which could properly be viewed as a violation of the Sherman Act in another context, be treated differently." Goldfarb v. Virginia State Bar, 421 U.S. 773, 788–789 and n. 17 (1975).

The explanation proffered by the Court of Appeals for the likely anticompetitive effect of the CDA's restrictions on discount advertising began with the unexceptionable statements that "price advertising is fundamental to price competition," and that "restrictions on the ability to advertise prices normally make it more difficult for consumers to find a lower price and for dentists to compete on the basis of price," ibid. (citing Bates v. State Bar of Ariz., 433 U.S. 350, 364, (1977); Morales v. Trans World Airlines, Inc., 504 U.S. 374, 388 (1992)). The court then acknowledged that, according to the CDA, the restrictions nonetheless furthered the "legitimate, indeed procompetitive, goal of preventing false and misleading price advertising." 128 F.3d at 728. The Court of Appeals might, at this juncture, have recognized that the restrictions at issue here are very far from a total ban on price or discount advertising, and might have considered the possibility that the particular restrictions on professional advertising could have different effects from those "normally" found in the commercial world, even to the point of promoting competition by reducing the occurrence of unverifiable and misleading across-the-board discount advertising.[85] Instead, the Court of Appeals confined itself to the brief assertion that the "CDA's disclosure requirements appear to prohibit across-the-board discounts because it is simply infeasible to disclose all of the information that is required," followed by the observation that "the record provides no evidence that the rule has in fact led to increased disclosure and transparency of dental pricing," *ibid*.

But these observations brush over the professional context and describe no anticompetitive effects. Assuming that the record in fact supports the conclusion that the CDA disclosure rules essentially bar advertisement of across-the-board discounts, it does not obviously follow that such a ban would have a net anticompetitive effect here. Whether advertisements that announced discounts for, say, first-time customers, would be less effective at conveying information relevant to competition if they listed the original and discounted prices for checkups, X-rays, and fillings, than they would be if they simply specified a percentage discount across the board, seems to us a question susceptible to empirical but not a priori analysis. In a suspicious world, the discipline of specific example may well be a necessary condition of plausibility for professional claims that for all practical purposes defy comparison shopping. It is also possible in principle that, even if across-the-board discount advertisements were more effective in drawing customers in the short run, the recurrence of some measure of intentional or accidental misstatement due to the breadth of their claims might leak out over time to make potential patients skeptical of any such across-the-board advertising, so undercutting the method's effectiveness.... It might be, too, that across-the-board discount advertisements would continue to attract busi-

---

85. JUSTICE BREYER claims that "the Court of Appeals did consider the relevant differences." But the language he cites says nothing more than that *per se* analysis is inappropriate here and that "some caution" was appropriate where restrictions purported to restrict false advertising. Caution was of course appropriate, but this statement by the Court of Appeals does not constitute a consideration of the possible differences between these and other advertising restrictions.

ness indefinitely, but might work precisely because they were misleading customers, and thus just because their effect would be anticompetitive, not procompetitive. Put another way, the CDA's rule appears to reflect the prediction that any costs to competition associated with the elimination of across-the-board advertising will be outweighed by gains to consumer information (and hence competi) created by discount advertising that is exact, accurate, and more easily verifiable (at least by regulators). As a matter of economics this view may or may not be correct, but it is not implausible, and neither a court nor the Commission may initially dismiss it as presumptively wrong.[86]

In theory, it is true, the Court of Appeals neither ruled out the plausibility of some procompetitive support for the CDA's requirements nor foreclosed the utility of an evidentiary discussion on the point. The court indirectly acknowledged the plausibility of procompetitive justifications for the CDA's position when it stated that "the record provides no evidence that the rule has in fact led to increased disclosure and transparency of dental pricing." But because petitioner alone would have had the incentive to introduce such evidence, the statement sounds as though the Court of Appeals may have thought it was justified without further analysis to shift a burden to the CDA to adduce hard evidence of the procompetitive nature of its policy; the court's adversion to empirical evidence at the moment of this implicit burden-shifting underscores the leniency of its enquiry into evidence of the restrictions' anticompetitive effects.

The Court of Appeals was comparably tolerant in accepting the sufficiency of abbreviated rule-of-reason analysis as to the nonprice advertising restrictions. The court began with the argument that "[t]hese restrictions are in effect a form of output limitation, as they restrict the supply of information about individual dentists' services." Although this sentence does indeed appear as cited, it is puzzling, given that the relevant output for antitrust purposes here is presumably not information or advertising, but dental services themselves. The question is not whether the universe of possible advertisements has been limited (as assuredly it has), but whether the limitation on advertisements obviously tends to limit the total delivery of dental services. The court came closest to addressing this latter question when it went on to assert that limiting advertisements regarding quality and safety "prevents dentists from fully describing the package of services they offer," adding that "the restrictions may also affect output more

---

86. JUSTICE BREYER suggests that our analysis is "of limited relevance," because "the basic question is whether this ... theoretically redeeming virtue in fact offsets the restrictions' anticompetitive effects in this case." He thinks that the Commission and the Court of Appeals "adequately answered that question," but the absence of any empirical evidence on this point indicates that the question was not answered, merely avoided by implicit burden-shifting of the kind accepted by JUSTICE BREYER. The point is that before a theoretical claim of anticompetitive effects can justify shifting to a defendant the burden to show empirical evidence of procompetitive effects, as quick-look analysis in effect requires, there must be some indication that the court making the decision has properly identified the theoretical basis for the anticompetitive effects and considered whether the effects actually are anticompetitive. Where, as here, the circumstances of the restriction are somewhat complex, assumption alone will not do.

directly, as quality and comfort advertising may induce some customers to obtain nonemergency care when they might not otherwise do so," *ibid.* This suggestion about output is also puzzling. If quality advertising actually induces some patients to obtain more care than they would in its absence, then restricting such advertising would reduce the demand for dental services, not the supply; and it is of course the producers' supply of a good in relation to demand that is normally relevant in determining whether a producer-imposed output limitation has the anticompetitive effect of artificially raising prices,[87] see General Leaseways, Inc. v. National Truck Leasing Assn., 744 F.2d 588, 594–595 (C.A.7 1984) ("An agreement on output also equates to a price-fixing agreement. If firms raise price, the market's demand for their product will fall, so the amount supplied will fall too—in other words, output will be restricted. If instead the firms restrict output directly, price will as mentioned rise in order to limit demand to the reduced supply. Thus, with exceptions not relevant here, raising price, reducing output, and dividing markets have the same anticompetitive effects").

Although the Court of Appeals acknowledged the CDA's view that "claims about quality are inherently unverifiable and therefore misleading," 128 F.3d at 728, it responded that this concern "does not justify banning all quality claims without regard to whether they are, in fact, false or misleading," *ibid.* As a result, the court said, "the restriction is a sufficiently naked restraint on output to justify quick look analysis." *Ibid.* The court assumed, in these words, that some dental quality claims may escape justifiable censure, because they are both verifiable and true. But its implicit assumption fails to explain why it gave no weight to the countervailing, and at least equally plausible, suggestion that restricting difficult-to-verify claims about quality or patient comfort would have a procompetitive effect by preventing misleading or false claims that distort the market. It is, indeed, entirely possible to understand the CDA's restrictions on unverifiable quality and comfort advertising as nothing more than a procompetitive ban on puffery, cf. Bates, 433 U.S. at 366 (claims relating to the quality of legal services "probably are not susceptible of precise measurement or verification and, under some circumstances, might well be deceptive or misleading to the public, or even false"); *id.* at 383–384 ("[A]dvertising claims as to the quality of services . . . are not susceptible of measurement or verification; accordingly, such claims may be so likely to be misleading as to warrant restriction"), notwithstanding JUSTICE

---

87. JUSTICE BREYER wonders if we "mea[n] this statement as an argument against the anticompetitive tendencies that flow from an agreement not to advertise service quality." But as the preceding sentence shows, we intend simply to question the logic of the Court of Appeals's suggestion that the restrictions are anticompetitive because they somehow "affect output," 128 F.3d at 728, presumably with the intent to raise prices by limiting supply while demand remains constant. We do not mean to deny that an agreement not to advertise service quality might have anticompetitive effects. We merely mean that, absent further analysis of the kind JUSTICE BREYER undertakes, it is not possible to conclude that the net effect of this particular restriction is anticompetitive.

BREYER's citation (to a Commission discussion that never faces the issue of the unverifiability of professional quality claims, raised in Bates).[88]

The point is not that the CDA's restrictions necessarily have the procompetitive effect claimed by the CDA; it is possible that banning quality claims might have no effect at all on competitiveness if, for example, many dentists made very much the same sort of claims. And it is also of course possible that the restrictions might in the final analysis be anticompetitive. The point, rather, is that the plausibility of competing claims about the effects of the professional advertising restrictions rules out the indulgently abbreviated review to which the Commission's order was treated. The obvious anticompetitive effect that triggers abbreviated analysis has not been shown.

In light of our focus on the adequacy of the Court of Appeals's analysis, JUSTICE BREYER's thorough-going, *de novo* antitrust analysis contains much to impress on its own merits but little to demonstrate the sufficiency of the Court of Appeals's review. The obligation to give a more deliberate look than a quick one does not arise at the door of this Court and should not be satisfied here in the first instance. Had the Court of Appeals engaged in a painstaking discussion in a league with JUSTICE BREYER's (compare his 14 pages with the Ninth Circuit's 8), and had it confronted the comparability of these restrictions to bars on clearly verifiable advertising, its reasoning might have sufficed to justify its conclusion. Certainly JUSTICE BREYER's treatment of the antitrust issues here is no "quick look." Lingering is more like it, and indeed JUSTICE BREYER, not surprisingly, stops short of endorsing the Court of Appeals's discussion as adequate to the task at hand.

Saying here that the Court of Appeals's conclusion at least required a more extended examination of the possible factual underpinnings than it received is not, of course, necessarily to call for the fullest market analysis. Although we have said that a challenge to a "naked restraint on price and output" need not be supported by "a detailed market analysis" in order to "requir[e] some competitive justification," National Collegiate Athletic Assn., 468 U.S. at 110, it does not follow that every case attacking a less obviously anticompetitive restraint (like this one) is a candidate for plenary market examination. The truth is that our categories of analysis of anticompetitive effect are less fixed than terms like "*per se*," "quick look," and "rule of reason" tend to make them appear. We have recognized, for example, that "there is often no bright line separating *per se* from Rule of Reason analysis," since "considerable inquiry into market conditions" may be required before the application of any so-called "*per se*" condemnation is justified. *Id.*, at 104, n. 26. "[W]hether the ultimate finding is the product of a presumption or actual market analysis, the essential inquiry remains the same—whether or not the challenged restraint enhances competition."

---

88. The Commission said only that " 'mere puffing' deceives no one and has never been subject to regulation.' " 121 F.T.C. at 318. The question here, of course, is not whether puffery may be subject to governmental regulation, but whether a professional organization may ban it.

Id., at 104. Indeed, the scholar who enriched antitrust law with the metaphor of "the twinkling of an eye" for the most condensed rule-of-reason analysis himself cautioned against the risk of misleading even in speaking of a "spectrum" of adequate reasonableness analysis for passing upon antitrust claims:"There is always something of a sliding scale in appraising reasonableness, but the sliding scale formula deceptively suggests greater precision than we can hope for.... Nevertheless, the quality of proof required should vary with the circumstances." P. Areeda, Antitrust Law ¶ 1507, p. 402 (1986).[89] At the same time, Professor Areeda also emphasized the necessity, particularly great in the quasi-common law realm of antitrust, that courts explain the logic of their conclusions. "By exposing their reasoning, judges ... are subjected to others' critical analyses, which in turn can lead to better understanding for the future." *Id.* ¶ 1500, at 364. As the circumstances here demonstrate, there is generally no categorical line to be drawn between restraints that give rise to an intuitively obvious inference of anticompetitive effect and those that call for more detailed treatment. What is required, rather, is an enquiry meet for the case, looking to the circumstances, details, and logic of a restraint. The object is to see whether the experience of the market has been so clear, or necessarily will be, that a confident conclusion about the principal tendency of a restriction will follow from a quick (or at least quicker) look, in place of a more sedulous one. And of course what we see may vary over time, if rule-of-reason analyses in case after case reach identical conclusions. For now, at least, a less quick look was required for the initial assessment of the tendency of these professional advertising restrictions. Because the Court of Appeals did not scrutinize the assumption of relative anticompetitive tendencies, we vacate the judgment and remand the case for a fuller consideration of the issue.

■ BREYER, J., with whom STEVENS, KENNEDY, and GINSBURG, JJ., join, concurring in part and dissenting in part.

I agree with the Court that the Federal Trade Commission has jurisdiction over petitioner, and I join Parts I and II of its opinion. I also agree that in a "rule of reason" antitrust case "the quality of proof required should vary with the circumstances," that "[w]hat is required ... is an enquiry

---

89. Other commentators have expressed similar views. See, *e.g.*, Kolasky, Counterpoint: The Department of Justice's "Stepwise" Approach Imposes Too Heavy a Burden on Parties to Horizontal Agreements, Antitrust 41, 43 (Spring 1998) ("[I]n applying the rule of reason, the courts, as with any balancing test, use a sliding scale to determine how much proof to require"); Piraino, Making Sense of the Rule of Reason: A New Standard for Section 1 of the Sherman Act, 47 Vand. L. Rev. 1753, 1771 (1994) ("[C]ourts will have to undertake varying degrees of inquiry depending upon the type of restraint at issue. The legality of certain restraints will be easy to determine because their competitive effects are obvious. Other restrictions will require a more detailed analysis because their competitive impact is more ambiguous"). But see Klein, A "Stepwise" Approach for Analyzing Horizontal Agreements Will Provide a Much Needed Structure for Antitrust Review, Antitrust 41, 42 (Spring 1990) (examination of procompetitive justifications "is by no means a full scrutiny of the proffered efficiency justification. It is, rather, a hard look at the justification to determine if it meets the defendant's burden of coming forward with—but not establishing—a valid efficiency justification").

meet for the case," and that the object is a "confident conclusion about the principal tendency of a restriction." But I do not agree that the Court has properly applied those unobjectionable principles here. In my view, a traditional application of the rule of reason to the facts as found by the Commission requires affirming the Commission—just as the Court of Appeals did below.

I

The Commission's conclusion is lawful if its "factual findings," insofar as they are supported by "substantial evidence," "make out a violation of Sherman Act § 1." FTC v. Indiana Federation of Dentists, 476 U.S. 447, 454–455 (1986). To determine whether that is so, I would not simply ask whether the restraints at issue are anticompetitive overall. Rather, like the Court of Appeals (and the Commission), I would break that question down into four classical, subsidiary antitrust questions: (1) What is the specific restraint at issue? (2) What are its likely anticompetitive effects? (3) Are there offsetting procompetitive justifications? (4) Do the parties have sufficient market power to make a difference?

A

The most important question is the first: What are the specific restraints at issue? ... Those restraints do not include merely the agreement to which the California Dental Association's (Dental Association or Association) ethical rule literally refers, namely, a promise to refrain from advertising that is " 'false or misleading in any material respect.' " Instead, the Commission found a set of restraints arising out of the way the Dental Association implemented this innocent-sounding ethical rule in practice, through advisory opinions, guidelines, enforcement policies, and review of membership applications. As implemented, the ethical rule reached beyond its nominal target, to prevent truthful and nondeceptive advertising. In particular, the Commission determined that the rule, in practice:

(1) "precluded advertising that characterized a dentist's fees as being low, reasonable, or affordable,"

(2) "precluded advertising . . . of across the board discounts"; and

(3) "prohibited all quality claims."

[Justice Breyer then reviewed the evidence and concluded it was substantial]. Consequently, we must decide only the basic legal question whether the three restraints described above unreasonably restrict competition.

B

Do each of the three restrictions mentioned have "the potential for genuine adverse effects on competition"? Indiana Federation, 476 U.S. at 460; 7 P. Areeda, Antitrust Law ¶ 1503a, pp. 372–377 (1986) (hereinafter Areeda). I should have thought that the anticompetitive tendencies of the three restrictions were obvious. An agreement not to advertise that a fee is reasonable, that service is inexpensive, or that a customer will receive a discount makes it more difficult for a dentist to inform customers that he charges a lower price. If the customer does not know about a lower price, he will find it more difficult to buy lower price service. That fact, in turn, makes it less likely that a dentist will obtain more customers by offering lower prices. And that likelihood means that dentists will prove less likely to offer lower prices. . . .

Nor did the Commission rely solely on the unobjectionable proposition that a restriction on the ability of dentists to advertise on quality is likely to limit their incentive to compete on quality. Rather, the Commission pointed to record evidence affirmatively establishing that quality-based competition is important to dental consumers in California. Unsurprisingly, these consumers choose dental services based at least in part on "information about the type and quality of service." Similarly, as the Commission noted, the ALJ credited testimony to the effect that "advertising the comfort of services will 'absolutely' bring in more patients," and, conversely, that restraining the ability to advertise based on quality would decrease the number of patients that a dentist could attract. Finally, the Commission looked to the testimony of dentists who themselves had suffered adverse effects on their business when forced by petitioner to discontinue advertising quality of care.

The FTC found that the price advertising restrictions amounted to a "naked attempt to eliminate price competition." It found that the service quality advertising restrictions "deprive consumers of information they value and of healthy competition for their patronage." It added that the "anticompetitive nature of these restrictions" was "plain." The Court of Appeals agreed. I do not believe it possible to deny the anticompetitive tendencies I have mentioned.

C

We must also ask whether, despite their anticompetitive tendencies, these restrictions might be justified by other procompetitive tendencies or redeeming virtues. This is a closer question—at least in theory. The Dental Association argues that the three relevant restrictions are inextricably tied to a legitimate Association effort to restrict false or misleading advertising. The Association, the argument goes, had to prevent dentists from engaging in the kind of truthful, nondeceptive advertising that it banned in order effectively to stop dentists from making unverifiable claims about price or service quality, which claims would mislead the consumer.

The problem with this or any similar argument is an empirical one. Notwithstanding its theoretical plausibility, the record does not bear out such a claim. The Commission, which is expert in the area of false and misleading advertising, was uncertain whether petitioner had even *made* the claim. It characterized petitioner's efficiencies argument as rooted in the (unproven) factual assertion that its ethical rule "challenges *only* advertising that is false or misleading." Regardless, the Court of Appeals wrote, in respect to the price restrictions, that "the record provides no evidence that the rule has in fact led to increased disclosure and transparency of dental pricing." With respect to quality advertising, the Commission stressed that the Association "offered no convincing argument, let alone evidence, that consumers of dental services have been, or are likely to be, harmed by the broad categories of advertising it restricts." Nor did the Court of Appeals think that the Association's unsubstantiated contention that "claims about quality are inherently unverifiable and therefore misleading" could "justify banning all quality claims without regard to whether they are, in fact, false or misleading."

With one exception, my own review of the record reveals no significant evidentiary support for the proposition that the Association's members must agree to ban truthful price and quality advertising in order to stop untruthful claims. The one exception is the obvious fact that one can stop untruthful advertising if one prohibits all advertising. But since the Association made virtually no effort to sift the false from the true that fact does not make out a valid antitrust defense.

In the usual Sherman Act § 1 case, the defendant bears the burden of establishing a procompetitive justification.... And the Court of Appeals was correct when it concluded that no such justification had been established here. [Justice Breyer then concluded that the Association had enough market power to adversely affect competition.]

NOTES

1. In September 2000, after *California Dental* was remanded, the Ninth Circuit held that the FTC had failed to carry its burden of proving that the restrictions on price and quality advertising had a net anticompetitive effect. The FTC, according to the Ninth Circuit, made a tactical decision to try to win the case on a *per se* or abbreviated rule-of-reason theory, and under these circumstances, the CDA was found correct in arguing that "further factfinding would give the FTC an unwarranted second bite at the apple." California Dental Association v. FTC, 224 F.3d 942 (9th Cir. 2000).

2. Professor Timothy J. Muris provided the following conclusion with respect to *California Dental*:

Many antitrust lawyers read *CDA* without proper focus on its professional advertising context. Although new as an antitrust issue, for over two decades the Court has struggled with the extent to which the First Amendment protects professional advertising. *CDA*, like *WFI* [Florida Bar v. Went For It, 515 U.S. 618 (1995)] decided by the same Court four years before, is a victory for those who seek to restrict such advertising. The Court is closely divided, however, and resolution of this struggle is not in sight.

Thus, this article asserts that had some other group, such as car repairers, restrained advertising, the Court would have had little difficulty applying truncated analysis to condemn the restraint. Although defense lawyers would try to read *CDA* expansively, even a cautious judge should have little difficulty with the car repair case. *CDA* should be read to require all plaintiffs to have an empirical basis for why the restraint harms consumers, but not more. The literature discussed in ... this article provides such evidence regarding restraints on professional advertising. The few studies of advertising restraints among non-professionals are consistent with the studies of professionals. At a minimum, the existing evidence should establish the plaintiffs' *prima facie* case and force the defendants to produce evidence of their own about the positive benefits of restraining advertising. Muris, California Dental Association v. Federal Trade Commission: The Revenge of Footnote 17, 8 S.Ct. Econ. Rev. 265, 309–10 (2000).

3.   What does the Supreme Court mean when it seeks empirical evidence of effect in the marketplace? The record showed that virtually every dentist in California went along with the Dental Association's ban on price advertising. Is that the requisite effect? Or, must the plaintiff prove that the price of filling a cavity in Los Angeles is higher than in Oregon or Nevada, or higher than it otherwise would have been, but for the ban on price advertising? Is there non-price empirical evidence that could or should be considered?

4.   For recent applications of "quick look" analysis, *see* North Texas Specialty Physicians v. FTC, 528 F.3d 346 (5th Cir. 2008); Polygram Holding, Inc. v. FTC, 416 F.3d 29 (D.C. Cir. 2005).

Texaco Inc. v. Dagher

Supreme Court of the United States, 2006.
547 U.S. 1, 126 S.Ct. 1276, 164 L.Ed.2d 1.

■ THOMAS, J. From 1998 until 2002, petitioners Texaco Inc. and Shell Oil Co. collaborated in a joint venture, Equilon Enterprises, to refine and sell gasoline in the western United States under the original Texaco and Shell Oil brand names. Respondents, a class of Texaco and Shell Oil service station owners, allege that petitioners engaged in unlawful price fixing when Equilon set a single price for both Texaco and Shell Oil brand gasoline. We granted certiorari to determine whether it is *per se* illegal under § 1 of the Sherman Act for a lawful, economically integrated joint venture to set the prices at which the joint venture sells its products. We conclude that it is not, and accordingly we reverse the contrary judgment of the Court of Appeals.

Historically, Texaco and Shell Oil have competed with one another.... In 1998, Texaco and Shell Oil formed a joint venture, Equilon, to consolidate their operations in the western United States, thereby ending competition between the two companies in the domestic refining and marketing of gasoline. Under the joint venture agreement, Texaco and Shell Oil agreed to pool their resources and share the risks of and profits from Equilon's activities. Equilon's board of directors would comprise representatives of Texaco and Shell Oil, and Equilon gasoline would be sold to downstream purchasers under the original Texaco and Shell Oil brand names. The formation of Equilon was approved by consent decree, subject to certain divestments and other modifications, by the Federal Trade Commission, as well as by the state attorneys general of California, Hawaii, Oregon, and

Washington. Notably, the decrees imposed no restrictions on the pricing of Equilon gasoline.

After the joint venture began to operate, respondents brought suit in district court, alleging that, by unifying gasoline prices under the two brands, petitioners had violated the *per se* rule against price fixing that this Court has long recognized under § 1 of the Sherman Act. The District Court awarded summary judgment to Texaco and Shell Oil.... The Ninth Circuit reversed, characterizing petitioners' position as a request for an "exception to the *per se* prohibition on price fixing," and rejecting that request. We consolidated Texaco's and Shell Oil's separate petitions and granted certiorari to determine the extent to which the *per se* rule against price fixing applies to an important and increasingly popular form of business organization, the joint venture.

Price-fixing agreements between two or more competitors, otherwise known as horizontal price-fixing agreements, fall into the category of arrangements that are *per se* unlawful. These cases do not present such an agreement, however, because Texaco and Shell Oil did not compete with one another in the relevant market—namely, the sale of gasoline to service stations in the western United States—but instead participated in that market jointly through their investments in Equilon.[90] In other words, the pricing policy challenged here amounts to little more than price setting by a single entity—albeit within the context of a joint venture—and not a pricing agreement between competing entities with respect to their competing products. Throughout Equilon's existence, Texaco and Shell Oil shared in the profits of Equilon's activities in their role as investors, not competitors. When "persons who would otherwise be competitors pool their capital and share the risks of loss as well as the opportunities for profit ... such joint ventures [are] regarded as a single firm competing with other sellers in the market." *Arizona* v. *Maricopa County Medical Soc.* As such, though Equilon's pricing policy may be price fixing in a literal sense, it is not price fixing in the antitrust sense....

This conclusion is confirmed by respondents' apparent concession that there would be no *per se* liability had Equilon simply chosen to sell its gasoline under a single brand. We see no reason to treat Equilon differently just because it chose to sell gasoline under two distinct brands at a single price. As a single entity, a joint venture, like any other firm, must have the discretion to determine the prices of the products that it sells, including the

---

90. We presume for purposes of these cases that Equilon is a lawful joint venture. Its formation has been approved by federal and state regulators, and there is no contention here that it is a sham. As the court below noted: "There is a voluminous record documenting the economic justifications for creating the joint ventures. [T]he defendants concluded that numerous synergies and cost efficiencies would result" by creating Equilon as well as a parallel venture, Motiva Enterprises, in the eastern United States, and "that nationwide there would be up to $800 million in cost savings annually." Had respondents challenged Equilon itself, they would have been required to show that its creation was anticompetitive under the rule of reason.

discretion to sell a product under two different brands at a single, unified price. If Equilon's price unification policy is anticompetitive, then respondents should have challenged it pursuant to the rule of reason.[91] But it would be inconsistent with this Court's antitrust precedents to condemn the internal pricing decisions of a legitimate joint venture as *per se* unlawful.[92]

The court below reached the opposite conclusion by invoking the ancillary restraints doctrine. That doctrine governs the validity of restrictions imposed by a legitimate business collaboration, such as a business association or joint venture, on nonventure activities. See, *e.g.*, *National Collegiate Athletic Assn.* v. *Board of Regents of Univ. of Okla.*, 468 U. S. 85, 113–115 (1984). Under the doctrine, courts must determine whether the nonventure restriction is a naked restraint on trade, and thus invalid, or one that is ancillary to the legitimate and competitive purposes of the business association, and thus valid. We agree with petitioners that the ancillary restraints doctrine has no application here, where the business practice being challenged involves the core activity of the joint venture itself—namely, the pricing of the very goods produced and sold by Equilon. And even if we were to invoke the doctrine in these cases, Equilon's pricing policy is clearly ancillary to the sale of its own products. . . .

PROBLEM 3

SALES AGENCY FOR MONUMENTAL PICTURES

Monumental Pictures recently found itself in the following quandary: it had a substantial library of motion picture films suitable for showing on television; its market investigations revealed that the greatest return could be derived by releasing films in small packages for showing on individual stations throughout the country; but it had no sales organization adapted to such marketing and the cost of establishing such an organization would be high in relation to returns to be derived from Monumental's films alone.

At the same time, Zenith Epics was also having problems. It had embarked much earlier in distributing its feature films to television stations, using the method contemplated by Monumental; it had established a nationwide sales organization for the purpose; but now, having marketed many of its own films, it was having difficulty finding sufficient material to cover the overhead of its marketing organization.

Monumental's search for a distributor and Zenith's search for material led to an arrangement between the two companies under which:

---

91.   Respondents have not put forth a rule of reason claim. . . .

92.   Respondents alternatively contend that petitioners should be held liable under the quick look doctrine. To be sure, we have applied the quick look doctrine to business activities that are so plainly anticompetitive that courts need undertake only a cursory examination before imposing antitrust liability. See *California Dental Assn.* v. *FTC*, 526 U.S. 756, 770 (1999). But for the same reasons that *per se* liability is unwarranted here, we conclude that petitioners cannot be held liable under the quick look doctrine.

(a) Zenith agreed to distribute Monumental's films for a commission.

(b) Monumental gave Zenith complete freedom of action in establishing the terms and conditions of distribution of Monumental films, including the price to be charged, subject to the following limitations.

(c) Zenith agreed not to market Monumental films at less than their fair market value.

(d) Zenith was obligated not to discriminate against Monumental films; Monumental films were not to be released at rates less than the rates being charged contemporaneously for comparable Zenith films.

(e) For purposes of applying the anti-discrimination provision, and for dividing the proceeds of any sales of mixed packages of Zenith and Monumental films, individual films would be classified by a committee of Monumental and Zenith officials, and any disputes resolved by arbitration.

Pointing out that the arrangement would give Zenith control of 40% of all feature films in this country available for television, the Antitrust Division seeks to enjoin the arrangement. What result?

PROBLEM 4

PRICE ADVERTISING BY LAWYERS

A new private legal clinic opened recently in a large city. It ran a series of ads on radio and in local community newspapers, one of which was along the following lines:

> Marriage getting you down? More and more people are finding that divorce is cheaper and less of a hassle than they thought.

> We can handle your divorce for the lowest prices in town. As little as $10 down, $300 complete for an uncontested divorce. That's $100 less than any other clinic or firm in the area. We'll have you back in action, take care of any problems presented if there are children, and ensure no legal problems.

> Call the Modern Law Clinic today.

The local bar association petitioned the state court to commence disciplinary proceedings against lawyers working in Modern citing the state's Code of Professional Responsibility to the effect that information disclosed by a lawyer in any publication or broadcast may not be "false, fraudulent, or misleading," and must be "presented in a dignified manner." The bar noted that the ad (1) improperly and fraudulently understates the seriousness and complexity of divorce proceedings, and (2) implies that all legal services are comparable, regardless of the quality of work done. Modern says the bar is really up in arms because of low prices offered on divorces, which are 33% below the average in the community. It also claims that divorce work is simple and represents a high profit line of work for many specialty lawyers.

Modern's lawyers file suit in federal district court under the antitrust laws, alleging a price-fixing conspiracy, and seek an order enjoining the local bar from any further disciplinary proceedings, claiming the bar action violates Section 1 of the Sherman Act. The local bar association moves to dismiss the complaint. What result?

SECTION 4.   DIVISION OF TERRITORIES AND SOME OTHER HORIZONTAL RESTRAINTS

NOTE ON MARKET SHARING

Competitors, fearful of the consequences of unrestricted price competition and eager to establish competitive stability, may seek to accomplish their purpose by dividing markets rather than by resorting to direct price fixing. A division of the market may consist of allocating fixed percentages of the available business to each producer, dividing sales territory on a geographical basis or allotting customers to each seller. Techniques for market division vary; for example, by restricting the hours of plant operation, markets may be shared on the basis of productive capacity. Business may also be channeled through a common sales agency which may have the power either to impose production quotas on its members or apportion orders among them.

Though price fixing, of course, suppresses competition, such agreements do not of themselves guarantee that each competitor will receive a satisfactory share of the business. Especially when products are not fungible, as when they are built to specifications or possess brand names of differing attractiveness, price control alone may be insufficient and market division may be the only practicable means of "regulating" competition. Whether or not prices are fixed, each competitor will then receive his share of the business and no more. The policy is essentially one of "live and let live." The effect of any agreement for dividing the markets is manifestly to eliminate competition.

Even if not fixed by agreement, prices tend to be uniform when markets are divided, except as products differ or are marketed under conditions permitting differences in prices without disturbing the desired allocation of business. Flexibility and freedom in the response of prices to economic changes are lost. Markets may be divided at any level of prices and the tendency is for prices to be higher than when competition is left unrestrained.

Market division necessarily constricts firms capable of expansion and thus increases costs. The least efficient producers are often protected and the advantages of a less costly method of distribution and production are lost to the public.

The regulation of production may suppress competition as effectively as direct price fixing—or even more so—and may, in fact, be one of the methods by which prices are regulated. The essence of successful production control is the equation of industry supply with probable demand. As demand may vary with price, establishment of a definite price or price range reduces uncertainties as to probable demand and the production necessary to meet such demand. It is, therefore, not surprising that price-fixing agreements frequently accompany production controls.

Output control sometimes has for its object not the regulation of prices or the creation of artificial scarcity but the solution of problems created by excess capacity. Moreover, the regulation of output does not necessarily imply its curtailment. Production may be maintained at an agreed level or provision may even be made to increase production. Whatever the terms or object of the agreement, the evil of market division flows from its definite tendency to eliminate competition and to displace the normal operation of market forces by concerted and cooperative action of competitors.

National Association of Window Glass Manufacturers v. United States

Supreme Court of the United States, 1923.
263 U.S. 403, 44 S.Ct. 148, 68 L.Ed. 358.

■ Holmes, J. This is a proceeding brought by the United States . . . to prevent an alleged violation of section 1 [of the Sherman Act] which forbids combinations in restraint of trade among the States. The defendants are all the manufacturers of handblown window glass, with certain of their officers, and the National Window Glass Workers, a voluntary association, its officers and members, embracing all the labor to be had for this work in the United States. The defendants established a wage scale to be in effect from September 25, 1922, to January 27, 1923, and from January 29, 1923, to June 11, 1923; and the feature that is the object of the present attack is that this scale would be issued to one set of factories for the first period and to another for the second, but that no factory could get it for both, and without it they could not get labor and therefore must stop work. After a hearing a final decree was entered enjoining the defendants from carrying out the above or any similar agreements so far as they might limit and prescribe the time during which the defendant manufacturers should operate their factories for handblown window glass.

This agreement does not concern sales or distribution, it is directed only to the way in which union labor, the only labor obtainable it is true, shall be employed in production. If such an agreement can be within the Sherman Act at least it is not necessarily so. To determine its legality requires a consideration of the particular facts. Board of Trade of Chicago v. United States, 246 U.S. 231.

The dominant fact in this case is that in the last quarter of a century machines have been brought into use that dispense with the employment of the highly trained blowers . . . and in that and other ways have enabled the factories using machines to produce window glass at half the cost of the handmade. The price for the two kinds is the same. It has followed of course that the companies using machines fix the price, that they make much the greater part of the glass in the market, and probably, as was testified for the defendants, that the handmakers are able to keep on only by the sufferance of the others and by working longer hours. The defendants say, and it is altogether likely, that the conditions thus brought about and the nature of the work have driven many laborers away and made it impossible to get new ones. For the work is very trying, requires considerable training, and is always liable to a reduction of wages if the machine industry lowers the price. The only chance for the handworkers has been when and where they could get cheap fuel and therefore their tendency has been to follow the discoveries of natural gas. The defendants contend with a good deal of force that it is absurd to speak of their arrangements as possibly having any effect upon commerce among the States, when manufacturers of this kind obviously are not able to do more than struggle to survive a little longer before they disappear, as human effort always disappears when it is not needed to direct the force than can be got more cheaply from water or coal.

But that is not all of the defendants' case. There are not twenty-five hundred men at present in the industry. The Government says that this is the fault of the union; the defendants with much greater probability that it is the inevitable coming to pass. But wherever the fault, if there is any, that is the fact with which the defendants had to deal. There were not men enough to enable the factories to run continuously during the working season, leaving out the two or three summer months in which the heat makes it impossible to go on. To work undermanned costs the same in fuel and overhead expenses as to work fully manned, and therefore means a serious loss. On the other hand the men are less well off with the uncertainties that such a situation brings. The purpose of the arrangement is to secure employment for all the men during the whole of the two seasons, thus to give all the labor available to the factories, and to divide it equally among them. From the view that we take we think it unnecessary to explain how the present system sprang from experience during the war when the Government restricted production to one-half of what it had been and an accident was found to work well, or to do more than advert to the defendants' contention that with the means available the production is increased. It is enough that we see no combination in unreasonable restraint of trade in the arrangements made to meet the short supply of men.

Decree reversed. Petition dismissed.

NOTES AND QUESTIONS

1.   1 HOLMES–POLLOCK LETTERS 163 (1941); April 23, 1910: "I don't disguise my belief that the Sherman Act is a humbug based on economic ignorance and incompetence."

2.   The *Window Glass* facts are more elaborately set forth in the opinion of the lower court, 287 Fed. 228 (N.D. Ohio 1923). The district judge saw the arrangement as an attempt by the manufacturers to curtail production. The court points out that the arrangement favors the inefficient plants at the expense of the more efficient and suggests that the labor agreement was designed, not so much to spread employment, as to curb production. It is asserted that the members of the union, in August 1922, voted four to one in favor of abandoning the two period system of operation. The adverse effects of the plan upon the workers as well as the industry are stressed. Does Holmes or the district judge get the best of their debate?

3.   Local Union No. 189 v. Jewel Tea Co. 381 U.S. 676 (1965): "Judicial pronouncements regarding the reasonableness of restraints on hours of business are relatively few. Some cases appear to have viewed such restraints as tantamount to limits on hours of work and thus reasonable, even though contained in agreements

among competitors." Thus in Chicago Board of Trade v. United States, 246 U.S. 231 (1918), the Court upheld a rule of a grain exchange that had the form of a restriction on prices of transactions outside regular trading hours but was characterized by the Court as a rule designed to shift transactions to the regular trading period, *i.e.*, to limit hours of operation.... Other cases have upheld operating hours restraints in factual circumstances that make it seem likely that the agreement affected hours of operation and hours of work in equal measure but without stressing that fact.

"Kold Kist, Inc. v. Amalgamated Meat Cutters, Local No. 421, 99 Cal.App.2d 191, 221 P.2d 724 (1950), held unreasonable a union-employer agreement limiting night sales of frozen poultry, which had previously been obtained from the plaintiff-distributor. The plaintiff alleged, however, that he had been severely affected, since many stores had stopped carrying its products entirely due to the lack of storage facilities in which to keep the poultry during hours in which sale was prohibited, and such effects may be atypical. The decided cases thus do not appear to offer any easy answer to the question whether in a particular case an operating hours restraint is unreasonable." (White, J., 381 U.S. at 693–94 n. 6.)

"If ... employers alone agreed not to sell meat from 6 p.m. to 9 a.m., they would be guilty of an anticompetitive practice, barred by the antitrust laws." (Douglas, J., dissenting, 381 U.S. at 736.

4. Most restraints on hours today would arise in the context of labor negotiations and would be exempt from antitrust scrutiny under the statutory or nonstatutory labor exemptions. *See* p. 110 *supra*. *In re* Detroit Auto Dealers Ass'n., Inc. v. FTC, 955 F.2d 457 (6th Cir.1992), elaborates on the scope of the nonstatutory labor exemption and supports Justice Douglas's sense in *Jewel Tea* that restraints on hours, if not covered by the labor exemptions, can be vulnerable.

In 1984, the FTC challenged an agreement by 90 automobile dealers to keep their showrooms closed all day Saturdays and on three weekday evenings. The Sixth Circuit affirmed the FTC's finding of unreasonable restraint of trade, reasoning as follows:

> We adopted the standards set out in *Mackey* in analyzing ... [a] professional sport controversy between a hockey player and the National Hockey League. Those standards deemed to be proper in *Mackey* were reiterated in McCourt v. California Sports, Inc., 600 F.2d 1193 (6th Cir.1979):
>
> > First, the labor policy favoring collective bargaining may potentially be given preeminence over the antitrust laws where the restraint on trade primarily affects only the parties to the collective bargaining relationship. Second, federal labor policy is implicated sufficiently to prevail only where the agreement sought to be exempted concerns a mandatory subject of collective bargaining. Finally, the policy favoring collective bargaining is furthered to the degree necessary to override the antitrust laws only where the agreement sought to be exempted is the product of bona fide arm's-length bargaining....
>
> The FTC argues that because the agreement at issue was among dealers, not involving unions or employees, there was a direct antitrust violation through restraint of trade by means of closing of showrooms and foreclosing availability of new cars to the public. FTC adds that the purpose of the dealers' agreement was "to avoid collective bargaining and to obtain the benefits of reduced competition ... [and to avoid] arm's-

length good faith bargaining." Petitioners respond that they were forced, through union and collective salesperson pressure, to reach agreement on standardized and uniform—and limited—showroom hours. We must decide whether the agreement should be subject to the nonstatutory labor exemption and therefore be immunized from antitrust scrutiny....

The statutory labor exemption from antitrust laws specifically provides for labor unions and labor organizations. This exemption may only be asserted by a labor organization itself, not by employers.

The nonstatutory labor exemption is not so narrowly limited; it extends antitrust immunity to both labor unions, employees, and to non-labor parties; those who have engaged in bona fide labor negotiations....

We are ... satisfied that the Commission analyzed and set out in its opinion the legal precedent and rationale for its decision. We find no error in the following specific legal conclusions of the Commission:

1. To say that collective bargaining is at the heart of the [nonstatutory labor] exemption, however, is not to say that the exemption applies only to collective bargaining agreements.

2. [T]he cases also demonstrate that concerted conduct does not automatically qualify for the exemption simply because it is motivated by labor concerns ... motivation by labor concerns is only a necessary and not a sufficient condition for application of the nonstatutory exemption.

3. The vast majority of nonstatutory labor exemption cases involve some sort of concerted activity or agreement between a union and an employer.

4. [T]hose few cases [involving only employers] clearly show that the nonstatutory labor exemption protects employer agreements only when those agreements are part of the give-and-take of a negotiation process.

5. [T]he agreement ... was designed to *prevent* collective bargaining ... to *avoid* arm's-length negotiation.

6. The mere fact that sales employees benefit from the hours restraint also cannot justify granting an exemption ... since they have the same incentive to reduce competition as the dealers.

7. *Jewel Tea* [381 U.S. at 676] and the present case have superficial similarities. Both involve a restriction on marketing hours and efforts by labor unions to obtain shorter working hours. But in *Jewel Tea*, unlike the case before us, the agreement was one to which the employees and employers were parties. Moreover, there was no question in *Jewel Tea* that the restrictive agreement had been reached through bona fide, arm's-length bargaining.

8. Respondents [petitioners here as a group] have agreed among themselves, not with their employees....

We agree with the Commission that the process generally was not.... a direct product of employer collective bargaining, nor of arm's-length dealing with salespersons. 955 F.2d at 463–67.[93]

---

93. Ed. See Brown v. Pro Football, Inc., 518 U.S. 231 (1996), where the Supreme Court held that football club owners who had agreed among themselves—but not with the football

As to the reasonableness of the restraint, which the FTC viewed as "inherently suspect," the Sixth Circuit concluded:

> While we do not agree in all respects with the Commission's rationale, we find some legal basis and support for its conclusions in an area that is murky and unclear. Limitation of hours has been held to be an anticompetitive restraint although relief in that case was limited and the damages to users or customers was found to be "entirely speculative." Tennessee, ex rel. Leech v. Highland Memorial Cemetery, Inc., 489 F.Supp. 65, 68 (E.D. Tenn. 1980). We do not equate limitation of hours to price-fixing, but we do not find error in the Commission's conclusion that hours of operation in this business is a means of competition, and that such limitation may be an unreasonable restraint of trade.[94]

955 F.2d at 472.

---

players' union—to implement the terms of their last best bargaining offer (*i.e.*, a $1,000 weekly salary for "development squad" players) after an impasse in negotiations were protected by the nonstatutory labor exemption. Justice Breyer wrote for the Court:

> As a matter of logic, it would be difficult, if not impossible, to require groups of employers and employees to bargain together, but at the same time to forbid them to make among themselves or with each other any of the competition-restricting agreements potentially necessary to make the process work or its results mutually acceptable. Thus, the implicit exemption recognizes that, to give effect to federal labor laws and policies and to allow meaningful collective bargaining to take place, some restraints on competition imposed through the bargaining process must be shielded from antitrust sanctions. See *Connell* (federal labor law's "goals" could "never" be achieved if ordinary anticompetitive effects of collective bargaining were held to violate the antitrust laws); *Jewel Tea* (national labor law scheme would be "virtually destroyed" by the routine imposition of antitrust penalties upon parties engaged in collective bargaining); Pennington (implicit exemption necessary to harmonize Sherman Act with "national policy . . . of promoting 'the peaceful settlement of industrial disputes by subjecting labor-management controversies to the mediatory influence of negotiation' " . . .) Consequently, the question before us is one of determining the exemption's scope: Does it apply to an agreement among several employers bargaining together to implement after impasse the terms of their last best good-faith wage offer? We assume that such conduct, as practiced in this case, is unobjectionable as a matter of labor law and policy. On that assumption, we conclude that the exemption applies. . . .
>
> [W]e hold that the implicit ("nonstatutory") antitrust exemption applies to the employer conduct at issue here. That conduct took place during and immediately after a collective-bargaining negotiation. It grew out of, and was directly related to, the lawful operation of the bargaining process. It involved a matter that the parties were required to negotiate collectively. And it concerned only the parties to the collective-bargaining relationship.
>
> Our holding is not intended to insulate from antitrust review every joint imposition of terms by employers, for an agreement among employers could be sufficiently distant in time and in circumstances from the collective-bargaining process that a rule permitting antitrust intervention would not significantly interfere with that process. See, *e.g.*, 50 F.3d at 1057 (suggesting that exemption lasts until collapse of the collective-bargaining relationship, as evidenced by decertification of the union); El Cerrito Mill & Lumber Co., 316 N.L.R.B., at 1006–1007 (suggesting that "extremely long" impasse, accompanied by "instability" or "defunctness" of multiemployer unit, might justify union withdrawal from group bargaining). We need not decide in this case whether, or where, within these extreme outer boundaries to draw that line.

94. Neither do we necessarily agree that "the parties' focus on retail prices misses the point in this case." Under a Rule of Reason analysis, effect on prices, output and market forces in a competitive market of a particular practice is frequently relevant and may be determina-

5. Although restraints on hours may be analyzed as unreasonable, they clearly are not as competitively dangerous as horizontal agreements to fix prices, divide markets, and regulate production. Do horizontal agreements to fix prices, divide markets, and regulate production necessarily have the same effect upon competition? Are each of them pernicious enough to be declared illegal *per se?* Assuming that different types of market sharing arrangements and production regulations may have differing effects on competition, and may be adopted for different business reasons, does it follow that they should all be governed by different rules of law?

NOTE ON *TIMKEN, GENERAL MOTORS,* AND *SEALY*

1. Timken Roller Bearing Co. v. United States, 341 U.S. 593 (1951). In this civil action the government charged that Timken had combined, conspired and acted with British Timken, Ltd. and Societe Anonyme Francaise Timken (French Timken) to restrain interstate and foreign commerce in the manufacture and sale of antifriction bearings throughout the world in violation of §§ 1 and 3 of the Sherman Act.

In 1927, Timken and an English businessman, Dewar, purchased all the stock of British Timken. At the time of the suit, Timken controlled 30% of the outstanding stock and Dewar 24%. In 1928, Timken and Dewar organized French Timken; all of the stock was still owned by them when this action was commenced. Since 1928, the three companies had been parties to agreements regulating the manufacture and sale of antifriction bearings and providing for the use by the British and French corporations of the "Timken" trademark. "Under these agreements the contracting parties have (1) allocated trade territories among themselves; (2) fixed prices on products of one sold in the territory of the others; (3) cooperated to protect each other's markets and to eliminate outside competition; and (4) participated in cartels to restrict imports to, and exports from, the United States." Timken contended that the restraints were reasonable, and therefore, not in violation of the Sherman Act because they were ancillary to a joint venture between Timken and Dewar and to an exercise of Timken's right to license its trademark.

The Supreme Court held that, regardless of the purpose of the restrictive agreements, "agreements providing for an aggregation of trade restraints such as those existing in this case are illegal under the Act."

The Court also held that the restrictions went beyond the trademark's purpose of "merely afford[ing] protection to a name." A majority of the Court also rejected Timken's argument that tariffs, quotas and the like had made restrictive agreements necessary to sell products abroad.

Justice Jackson dissented and raised the question whether the antitrust laws should be interpreted with respect to foreign trade in the same way they are interpreted when applied to domestic transactions, thus raising in 1951 an issue that is hotly debated today.

2. United States v. General Motors Corp., 384 U.S. 127 (1966). Civil action by the Government for injunctive relief. General Motors distributes Chevrolets through independent franchised dealers. Although the franchise agreement contains

---

tive. The special factors noted in this case support the Commission's conclusion on restraint of trade despite lack of evidence of increased prices.

no limitations on the customers to whom or the territories in which the dealers may sell, it does contain a "location clause" which prohibits the dealer from moving to or establishing "a new or different location, branch sales office, branch service station, or place of business" without Chevrolet's consent. Starting in the late 1950's, discount houses began to sell Chevrolets at alleged bargain prices either by referral of the customer to a dealer (who sold at a lower than usual price, paying the discounter a commission) or by purchasing the car from the dealer at less than the retail price and reselling it to the customer. An association of dealers formally complained to General Motors, after which General Motors' personnel discussed the matter with every dealer in the area, eliciting a promise not to do business with discounters. Various associations policed the situation and, at General Motors' request, supplied it with information concerning dealers continuing to do business with discounters. *Held,* for plaintiff. "We do not decide whether the 'location clause' may be construed to prohibit a dealer, party to it, from selling through discounters, or whether General Motors could by unilateral action enforce the clause, so construed.[95] We have here a classic conspiracy in restraint of trade: joint, collaborative action by dealers, the appellee associations, and General Motors to eliminate a class of competitors by terminating business dealings between them and a minority of Chevrolet dealers and to deprive franchised dealers of their freedom to deal through discounters if they so choose.... Whatever General Motors might or might not lawfully have done to enforce individual Dealer Selling Agreements by action within the borders of those agreements and the relationship which each defines, is beside the point. And, because the action taken constitutes a combination or conspiracy, it is not necessary to consider what might be the legitimate interest of a dealer in securing compliance by others with the 'location clause,' or the lawfulness of action a dealer might individually take to vindicate this interest." (Fortas, J.)

3.   United States v. Sealy, Inc., 388 U.S. 350 (1967). Sealy licensed manufacturers of mattresses and bedding products to make and sell such products under the Sealy name and trademarks. Its 30 licensees owned substantially all of its stock. Each director was a stockholder or a stockholder-licensee's nominee. The Government charged that Sealy had violated Section 1 of the Sherman Act by conspiring with its licensees to fix prices at which the licensees' customers could resell bedding products bearing the Sealy name and to allocate exclusive territories among the manufacturers.

The district court's finding of price fixing was not appealed. The Supreme Court reversed the district court's holding that the territorial restraints had not been shown to be "unreasonable." The Court concluded that the "territorial arrangements must be regarded as the creature of horizontal action by the licensees. It would violate reality to treat them as equivalent to territorial limitations imposed by a manufacturer upon independent dealers as incident to the sale of a trademarked product. Sealy, Inc., is an instrumentality of the licensees for purposes of the horizontal territorial allocation. It is not the principal." The Court declared the territorial restraints unlawful, because "they gave to each licensee an enclave in which it could and did zealously and effectively maintain resale prices, free from the danger of outside incursions."

This "aggregation of trade restraints including unlawful price-fixing and policing" was "unlawful under Section 1 of the Sherman Act without the necessity for an inquiry in each particular case as to their business or economic justification, their impact in the marketplace, or their reasonableness." (Fortas, J.).

---

95. Ed. For a discussion of this point, *see* Chapter 7 *infra.*

United States v. Topco Associates, Inc.

Supreme Court of the United States, 1972.
405 U.S. 596, 92 S.Ct. 1126, 31 L.Ed.2d 515.

■ MARSHALL, J. The United States brought this action for injunctive relief against Topco Associates, Inc.'s (Topco) alleged violation of § 1 of the Sherman Act. Following a trial on the merits, the United States District Court for the Northern District of Illinois entered judgment for Topco.... We noted probable jurisdiction, and we now reverse the judgment of the District Court.

I

Topco is a cooperative association of approximately 25 small and medium-sized regional supermarket chains which operate stores in some 33 States. Each of the member chains operates independently; there is no pooling of earnings, profits, capital, management, or advertising resources. No grocery business is conducted under the Topco name. Its basic function is to serve as a purchasing agent for its members. In this capacity, it procures and distributes to the members more than 1,000 different food and related nonfood items, most of which are distributed under brand names owned by Topco. The association does not itself own any manufacturing, processing, or warehousing facilities, and the items that it procures for members are usually shipped directly from the packer or manufacturer to the members. Payment is made either to Topco or directly to the manufacturer at a cost that is virtually the same for the members as for Topco itself.

All of the stock in Topco is owned by the members, with the common stock, the only stock having voting rights, being equally distributed. The board of directors, which controls the operation of the association, is drawn from the members and is normally composed of high-ranking executive officers of member chains. It is the board that elects the association's officers and appoints committee members, and it is from the board that the principal executive officers of Topco must be drawn. Restrictions on the alienation of stock and the procedure for selecting all important officials of the association from within the ranks of its members give the members complete and unfettered control over the operations of the association.

Topco was founded in the 1940s by a group of small, local grocery chains, independently owned and operated, which desired to cooperate to obtain high quality merchandise under private labels in order to compete more effectively with larger national and regional chains.[96] With a line of

---

96. The founding members of Topco were having difficulty competing with larger chains. This difficulty was attributable in some degree to the fact that the larger chains were capable of developing their own private-label programs.

Private-label products differ from other brand-name products in that they are sold at a limited number of easily ascertainable stores. A & P, for example, was a pioneer in developing a series of products that were sold under an A & P label and that were only available in A & P stores. It is obvious that by using private-label products, a chain can achieve significant cost economies in purchasing, transportation, warehousing, promotion, and advertising. These canned, dairy, and other products, the association began. It added frozen foods in 1950, fresh produce in 1958, more general merchandise equipment and supplies in 1960, and a branded bacon and carcass beef selection program in 1966. By 1964, Topco's members had combined retail sales of more than $2 billion; by 1967, their sales totaled more than $2.3 billion, a figure exceeded by only three national grocery chains.

Members of the association vary in the degree of market share that they possess in their respective areas. The range is from 1.5% to 16%, with the average being approximately 6%. While it is more difficult to compare these figures with the market shares of larger regional and national chains because of the absence in the record of accurate statistics for these chains, there is much evidence in the record that Topco members are frequently in as strong a competitive position in their respective areas as any other chain. The strength of this competitive position is due, in some measure, to the success of Topco-brand products. Although only 10% of the total goods sold by Topco members bear the association's brand names, the profit on these goods is substantial and their very existence has improved the competitive potential of Topco members with respect to other large and powerful chains.

It is apparent that from meager beginnings approximately a quarter of a century ago, Topco has developed into a purchasing association wholly owned and operated by member chains, which possess much economic muscle, individually as well as cooperatively.

II

... The United States charged that, beginning at least as early as 1960 and continuing up to the time that the complaint was filed, Topco had combined and conspired with its members to violate § 1 in two respects. First, the Government alleged that there existed:

> "a continuing agreement, understanding and concert of action among the co-conspirator member firms acting through Topco, the substantial terms of which have been and are that each co-conspirator member firm will sell Topco-controlled brands only within the marketing territory allocated to it, and will refrain from selling Topco-controlled brands outside such marketing territory."

... Membership must first be approved by the board of directors, and thereafter by an affirmative vote of 75% of the association's members. If,

---

economies may afford the chain opportunities for offering private-label products at lower prices than other brand-name products. This, in turn, provides many advantages of which some of the more important are: a store can offer national-brand products at the same price as other stores, while simultaneously offering a desirable, lower priced alternative; or, if the profit margin is sufficiently high on private-brand goods, national-brand products may be sold at reduced price. Other advantages include: enabling a chain to bargain more favorably with national-brand manufacturers by creating a broader supply base of manufacturers, thereby decreasing dependence on a few, large national-brand manufacturers; enabling a chain to create a "price-mix" whereby prices on special items can be lowered to attract customers while profits are maintained on other items; and creating of general goodwill by offering lower priced, higher quality goods.

however, the member whose operations are closest to those of the applicant, or any member whose operations are located within 100 miles of the applicant, votes against approval, an affirmative vote of 85% of the members is required for approval. Bylaws, Art. I, § 5. Because, as indicated by the record, members cooperate in accommodating each other's wishes, the procedure for approval provides, in essence, that members have a veto of sorts over actual or potential competition in the territorial areas in which they are concerned.

Following approval, each new member signs an agreement with Topco designating the territory in which that member may sell Topco-brand products. No member may sell these products outside the territory in which it is licensed. Most licenses are exclusive, and even those denominated "coextensive" or "non-exclusive" prove to be *de facto* exclusive. Exclusive territorial areas are often allocated to members who do no actual business in those areas on the theory that they may wish to expand at some indefinite future time and that expansion would likely be in the direction of the allocated territory. When combined with each member's veto power over new members, provisions for exclusivity work effectively to insulate members from competition in Topco-brand goods. Should a member violate its license agreement and sell in areas other than those in which it is licensed, its membership can be terminated under Art. IV, §§ 2(a) and 2(b) of the bylaws. Once a territory is classified as exclusive, either formally or *de facto*, it is extremely unlikely that the classification will ever be changed. See Bylaws, Art. IX.

The Government maintains that this scheme of dividing markets violates the Sherman Act because it operates to prohibit competition in Topco-brand products among grocery chains engaged in retail operations. The Government also makes a subsidiary challenge to Topco's practices regarding licensing members to sell at wholesale. Under the bylaws, members are not permitted to sell any products supplied by the association at wholesale, whether trademarked or not, without first applying for and receiving special permission from the association to do so. Before permission is granted, other licensees (usually retailers), whose interests may potentially be affected by wholesale operations, are consulted as to their wishes in the matter. If permission is obtained, the member must agree to restrict the sale of Topco products to a specific geographic area and to sell under any conditions imposed by the association. Permission to wholesale has often been sought by members, only to be denied by the association. The Government contends that this amounts not only to a territorial restriction violative of the Sherman Act, but also to a restriction on customers which in itself is violative of the Act.

From the inception of this lawsuit, Topco accepted as true most of the Government's allegations regarding territorial divisions and restrictions on wholesaling, although it differed greatly with the Government on the conclusions, both factual and legal, to be drawn from these facts.

Topco's answer to the complaint is illustrative of its posture in the District Court and before this Court:

Topco

"Private label merchandising is a way of economic life in the food retailing industry, and exclusivity is the essence of a private label program; without exclusivity, a private label would not be private. Each national and large regional chain has its own exclusive private label products in addition to the nationally advertised brands which all chains sell. Each such chain relies upon the exclusivity of its own private label line to differentiate its private label products from those of its competitors and to attract and retain the repeat business and loyalty of consumers. Smaller retail grocery stores and chains are unable to compete effectively with the national and large regional chains without also offering their own exclusive private label products.

. . .

"The only feasible method by which Topco can procure private label products and assure the exclusivity thereof is through trademark licenses specifying the territory in which each member may sell such trademarked products."

needs divisions to compete w/ large chains

Topco essentially maintains that it needs territorial divisions to compete with larger chains; that the association could not exist if the territorial divisions were anything but exclusive; and that by restricting competition in the sale of Topco-brand goods, the association actually increases competition by enabling its members to compete successfully with larger regional and national chains.

The District Court, considering all these things relevant to its decision, agreed with Topco. It recognized that the panoply of restraints that Topco imposed on its members worked to prevent competition in Topco-brand products, but concluded that

"[w]hatever anti-competitive effect these practices may have on competition in the sale of Topco private label brands is far outweighed by the increased ability of Topco members to compete both with the national chains and other supermarkets operating in their respective territories." 319 F.Supp. 1031, 1043 (1970).

The court held that Topco's practices were pro-competitive and, therefore, consistent with the purposes of the antitrust laws. But we conclude that the District Court used an improper analysis in reaching its result.

. . . It is only after considerable experience with certain business relationships that courts classify them as *per se* violations of the Sherman Act. One of the classic examples of a *per se* violation of § 1 is an agreement between competitors at the same level of the market structure to allocate territories in order to minimize competition. Such concerted action is usually termed a "horizontal" restraint, in contradistinction to combinations of persons at different levels of the market structure, *e.g.*, manufacturers and distributors, which are termed "vertical" restraints. This Court has reiterated time and time again that "[h]orizontal territorial limitations . . . are naked restraints of trade with no purpose except stifling of competition." White Motor Co. v. United States, 372 U.S. 253, 263 (1963).

Such limitations are *per se* violations of the Sherman Act. See Addyston Pipe & Steel Co. v. United States, 175 U.S. 211 (1899), aff'g 85 F. 271 (C.A.6 1898) (Taft, J.); United States v. National Lead Co., 332 U.S. 319 (1947); Timken Roller Bearing Co. v. United States, 341 U.S. 593 (1951); Northern Pacific R. Co. v. United States, *supra*; Citizen Publishing Co. v. United States, 394 U.S. 131 (1969); United States v. Sealy, Inc., 388 U.S. 350 (1967); United States v. Arnold, Schwinn & Co., 388 U.S. 365, 390 (1967) (Stewart, J., concurring in part and dissenting in part); Serta Associates, Inc. v. United States, 393 U.S. 534 (1969), aff'g 296 F.Supp. 1121, 1128 (N.D.Ill.1968).

We think that it is clear that the restraint in this case is a horizontal one, and, therefore, a *per se* violation of § 1. The District Court failed to make any determination as to whether there were *per se* horizontal territorial restraints in this case and simply applied a rule of reason in reaching its conclusions that the restraints were not illegal. In so doing, the District Court erred. . . .

Whether or not we would decide this case the same way under the rule of reason used by the District Court is irrelevant to the issue before us. The fact is that courts are of limited utility in examining difficult economic problems.[97] Our inability to weigh, in any meaningful sense, destruction of competition in one sector of the economy against promotion of competition in another sector is one important reason we have formulated *per se* rules.

In applying these rigid rules, the Court has consistently rejected the notion that naked restraints of trade are to be tolerated because they are well intended or because they are allegedly developed to increase competition. . . .

Antitrust laws in general, and the Sherman Act in particular, are the Magna Carta of free enterprise. They are as important to the preservation of economic freedom and our free-enterprise system as the Bill of Rights is to the protection of our fundamental personal freedoms. And the freedom guaranteed each and every business, no matter how small, is the freedom to compete—to assert with vigor, imagination, devotion, and ingenuity whatever economic muscle it can muster. Implicit in such freedom is the notion that it cannot be foreclosed with respect to one sector of the economy because certain private citizens or groups believe that such foreclosure might promote greater competition in a more important sector of the economy. Cf. United States v. Philadelphia National Bank, 374 U.S. 321, 371 (1963).

The District Court determined that by limiting the freedom of its individual members to compete with each other, Topco was doing a greater good by fostering competition between members and other large supermar-

---

97. There has been much recent commentary on the wisdom of *per se* rules. . . . Without the *per se* rules, businessmen would be left with little to aid them in predicting in any particular case what courts will find to be legal and illegal under the Sherman Act. Should Congress ultimately determine that predictability is unimportant in this area of the law, it can, of course, make *per se* rules inapplicable in some or all cases, and leave courts free to ramble through the wilds of economic theory in order to maintain a flexible approach.

ket chains. But, the fallacy in this is that Topco has no authority under the Sherman Act to determine the respective values of competition in various sectors of the economy. On the contrary, the Sherman Act gives to each Topco member and to each prospective member the right to ascertain for itself whether or not competition with other supermarket chains is more desirable than competition in the sale of Topco-brand products. Without territorial restrictions, Topco members may indeed "[cut] each other's throats." Cf. *White Motor Co., supra*, at 278 (Clark, J., dissenting). But, we have never found this possibility sufficient to warrant condoning horizontal restraints of trade....

There have been tremendous departures from the notion of a free-enterprise system as it was originally conceived in this country. These departures have been the product of congressional action and the will of the people. If a decision is to be made to sacrifice competition in one portion of the economy for greater competition in another portion, this too is a decision that must be made by Congress and not by private forces or by the courts. Private forces are too keenly aware of their own interests in making such decisions and courts are ill-equipped and ill-situated for such decisionmaking. To analyze, interpret, and evaluate the myriad of competing interests and the endless data that would surely be brought to bear on such decisions, and to make the delicate judgment on the relative values to society of competitive areas of the economy, the judgment of the elected representatives of the people is required.

Just as the territorial restrictions on retailing Topco-brand products must fall, so must the territorial restrictions on wholesaling. The considerations are the same, and the Sherman Act requires identical results.

We also strike down Topco's other restrictions on the rights of its members to wholesale goods. These restrictions amount to regulation of the customers to whom members of Topco may sell Topco-brand goods. Like territorial restrictions, limitations on customers are intended to limit intra-brand competition and to promote inter-brand competition. For the reasons previously discussed, the arena in which Topco members compete must be left to their unfettered choice absent a contrary congressional determination.

We reverse the judgment of the District Court and remand the case for entry of an appropriate decree.

It is so ordered.

■ POWELL and REHNQUIST, JJ., took no part in the consideration or decision of this case.

■ BLACKMUN, J., concurring in the result.

The conclusion the Court reaches has its anomalous aspects for surely, as the District Court's findings make clear, today's decision in the Government's favor will tend to stultify Topco members' competition with the great and larger chains. The bigs, therefore, should find it easier to get bigger and, as a consequence, reality seems at odds with the public interest. The *per se* rule, however, now appears to be so firmly established by the

Court that, at this late date, I could not oppose it. Relief, if any is to be forthcoming, apparently must be by way of legislation.

■ BURGER, C.J., dissenting.

DISSENT

This case does not involve restraints on interbrand competition or an allocation of markets by an association with monopoly or near-monopoly control of the sources of supply of one or more varieties of staple goods. Rather, we have here an agreement among several small grocery chains to join in a cooperative endeavor which, in my view, has an unquestionably lawful principal purpose; in pursuit of that purpose they have mutually agreed to certain minimal ancillary restraints that are fully reasonable in view of the principal purpose and that have never before today been held by this Court to be *per se* violations of the Sherman Act.

In joining in this cooperative endeavor, these small chains did not agree to the restraints here at issue in order to make it possible for them to exploit an already established line of products through non-competitive pricing. There was no such thing as a Topco line of products until this cooperative was formed. The restraints to which the cooperative's members have agreed deal only with the marketing of the products in the Topco line, and the only function of those restraints is to permit each member chain to establish, within its own geographical area and through its own local advertising and marketing efforts, a local consumer awareness of the trademarked family of products as that member's "private label" line. The goal sought was the enhancement of the individual members' abilities to compete, albeit to a modest degree, with the large national chains which had been successfully marketing private-label lines for several years. The sole reason for a cooperative endeavor was to make economically feasible such things as quality control, large quantity purchases at bulk prices, the development of attractively printed labels, and the ability to offer a number of different lines of trademarked products. All these things, of course, are feasible for the large national chains operating individually, but they are beyond the reach of the small operators proceeding alone.[98]

After a careful review of the economic considerations bearing upon this case, the District Court determined that "the relief which the government here seeks would not increase competition in Topco private label brands"; on the contrary, such relief "would substantially diminish competition in the supermarket field." 319 F.Supp. 1031, 1043. This Court has not today determined, on the basis of an examination of the underlying economic realities, that the District Court's conclusions are incorrect. Rather, the majority holds that the District Court had no business examining Topco's practices under the "rule of reason"; it should not have sought to determine whether Topco's practices did in fact restrain trade or commerce within the meaning of § 1 of the Sherman Act; it should have found no

98. The District Court's findings of fact include the following:

"33. A competitively effective private label program to be independently undertaken by a single retailer or chain would require an annual sales volume of $250 million or more and in order to achieve optimum efficiency, the volume required would probably have to be twice that amount." 319 F.Supp. 1031, 1036.

more than that those practices involve a "horizontal division of markets" and are, by that very fact, *per se* violations of the Act.

I do not believe that our prior decisions justify the result reached by the majority. Nor do I believe that a new *per se* rule should be established in disposing of this case, for the judicial convenience and ready predictability that are made possible by *per se* rules are not such overriding considerations in antitrust law as to justify their promulgation without careful prior consideration of the relevant economic realities in the light of the basic policy and goals of the Sherman Act.

I

I deal first with the cases upon which the majority relies in stating that "[t]his Court has reiterated time and time again that '[h]orizontal territorial limitations ... are naked restraints of trade with no purpose except stifling of competition.' White Motor Co. v. United States, 372 U.S. 253, 263 (1963)." *White Motor,* of course, laid down no *per se* rule; nor were any horizontal territorial limitations involved in that case....

Having quoted this dictum from *White Motor,* the Court then cites eight cases for the proposition that horizontal territorial limitations are *per se* violations of the Sherman Act. One of these cases, Northern Pacific R. Co. v. United States, 356 U.S. 1 (1958), dealt exclusively with a prohibited tying arrangement and is improperly cited as a case concerned with a division of markets.[99] Of the remaining seven cases, four involved an aggregation of trade restraints that included price-fixing agreements. Timken Roller Bearing Co. v. United States, 341 U.S. 593 (1951); United States v. Sealy, Inc., 388 U.S. 350 (1967); Serta Associates, Inc. v. United States, 393 U.S. 534 (1969), aff'g 296 F.Supp. 1121 (N.D.Ill.1968). Price-fixing is, of course, not a factor in the instant case.

Another of the cases relied upon by the Court, United States v. National Lead Co., 332 U.S. 319 (1947), involved a worldwide arrangement for dividing territories, pooling patents, and exchanging technological information. The arrangement was found illegal by the District Court without any reliance on a *per se* rule; this Court, in affirming, was concerned almost exclusively with the remedies ordered by the District Court and made no attempt to declare a *per se* rule to govern the merits of the case.

In still another case on which the majority relies, United States v. Arnold, Schwinn & Co., 388 U.S. 365 (1967), the District Court had, indeed, held that the agreements between the manufacturer and certain of its distributors, providing the latter with exclusive territories, were horizontal in nature and that they were, as such, *per se* violations of the Act. 237 F.Supp. 323, 342–343. Since no appeal was taken from this part of the

---

99. There is dictum in the case to the effect that United States v. Addyston Pipe & Steel Co., 85 F. 271 (C.A.6 1898), aff'd, 175 U.S. 211 (1899), established a "division of markets" as unlawful in and of itself. 356 U.S., at 5. As I will show, however, Addyston Pipe established no such thing; it was primarily a price-fixing case.

District Court's order, that issue was not before this Court in its review of the case. . . .

Finally, there remains the eighth of the cases relied upon by the Court—actually, the first in its list of "authorities" for the purported *per se* rule. Circuit Judge (later Chief Justice) Taft's opinion for the court in United States v. Addyston Pipe & Steel Co., 85 F. 271 (C.A.6 1898), aff'd, 175 U.S. 211 (1899), has generally been recognized—and properly so—as a fully authoritative exposition of antitrust law. But neither he, nor this Court in affirming, made any pretense of establishing a *per se* rule against all agreements involving horizontal territorial limitations. . . . Although the case has frequently—and quite properly—been cited as a horizontal allocation-of-markets case, the sole purpose of the secret customer allocations was to enable the members of the association to fix prices charged to the public at non-competitive levels. Judge Taft rejected the defendants' argument that the prices actually charged were "reasonable"; he held that it was sufficient for a finding of a Sherman Act violation that the combination and agreement of the defendants gave them such monopoly power that they, rather than market forces, fixed the prices of all cast-iron pipe in three-fourths of the Nation's territory. The case unquestionably laid important groundwork for the subsequent establishment of *per se* rule against price fixing. It did not, however, establish that a horizontal division of markets is, without more, a *per se* violation of the Sherman Act.

II

The foregoing analysis of the cases relied upon by the majority indicates to me that the Court is not merely following prior holdings; on the contrary, it is establishing a new *per se* rule. In the face of the District Court's well supported findings that the effects of such a rule in this case will be adverse to the public welfare,[1] the Court lays down that rule without regard to the impact that the condemned practices may have on competition. In doing so, the Court virtually invites Congress to undertake to determine that impact. I question whether the Court is fulfilling the role assigned to it under the statute when it declines to make this determination; in any event, if the Court is unwilling on this record to assess the economic impact, it surely should not proceed to make a new rule to govern the economic activity. White Motor Co. v. United States, 372 U.S., at 263. . . .

---

1. Among the facts found by the District Court are the following: private label brand merchandising, which is beyond the reach of the small chains acting independently and which by definition depends upon local exclusivity, permits the merchandiser to offer the public "lower consumer prices on products of high quality" and "to bargain more favorably with national brand manufacturers"; such merchandising fosters "the establishment of a broader supply base of manufacturers, thereby decreasing dependence upon a relatively few, large national brand manufacturers"; it also enables "[s]maller manufacturers, the most common source of private label products, who are generally unable to develop national brand name recognition for their products, [to] benefit ... by the assurance of a substantial market for their products". . . . 319 F.Supp., at 1035.

In formulating a new *per se* rule today, the Court does not tell us what "pernicious effect on competition" the practices here outlawed are perceived to have; nor does it attempt to show that those practices "lack ... any redeeming virtue." Rather, it emphasizes only the importance of predictability, asserting that "courts are of limited utility in examining difficult economic problems" and have not yet been left free by Congress to "ramble through the wilds of economic theory in order to maintain a flexible approach."

With all respect, I believe that there are two basic fallacies in the Court's approach here. First, while I would not characterize our role under the Sherman Act as one of "rambl[ing] through the wilds," it is indeed one that requires our "examin[ation of] difficult economic problems." We can undoubtedly ease our task, but we should not abdicate that role by formulation of *per se* rules with no justification other than the enhancement of predictability and the reduction of judicial investigation. Second, from the general proposition that *per se* rules play a necessary role in antitrust law, it does not follow that the particular *per se* rule promulgated today is an appropriate one. Although it might well be desirable in a proper case for this Court to formulate a *per se* rule dealing with horizontal territorial limitations, it would not necessarily be appropriate for such a rule to amount to a blanket prohibition against all such limitations. More specifically, it is far from clear to me why such a rule should cover those division-of-market agreements which involve no price fixing and which are concerned only with trademarked products that are not in a monopoly or near-monopoly position with respect to competing brands. The instant case presents such an agreement; I would not decide it upon the basis of a *per se* rule.[2]

The District Court specifically found that the horizontal restraints involved here tend positively to promote competition in the supermarket field and to produce lower costs for the consumer. The Court seems implicitly to accept this determination, but says that the Sherman Act does not give Topco the authority to determine for itself "whether or not competition with other supermarket chains is more desirable than competition in the sale of Topco-brand products." But the majority overlooks a further specific determination of the District Court, namely, that the invalidation of the restraints here at issue "would not increase competition in Topco private label brands." Indeed, the District Court seemed to believe

---

2. The national chains market their own private-label products, and these products are available nowhere else than in the stores of those chains. The stores of any one chain, of course, do not engage in price competition with each other with respect to their chain's private-label brands, and no serious suggestion could be made that the Sherman Act requires otherwise. I fail to see any difference whatsoever in the economic effect of the Topco arrangement for the marketing of Topco-brand products and the methods used by the national chains in marketing their private-label brands. True, the Topco arrangement involves a "combination," while each of the national chains is a single integrated corporation. The controlling consideration, however, should be that in neither case is the policy of the Sherman Act offended, for the practices in both cases work to the benefit, and not to the detriment, of the consuming public.

that it would, on the contrary, lead to the likely demise of those brands in time. And the evidence before the District Court would appear to justify that conclusion.

There is no national demand for Topco brands, nor has there ever been any national advertising of those brands. It would be impracticable for Topco, with its limited financial resources, to convert itself into a national brand distributor in competition with distributors of existing national brands. Furthermore, without the right to grant exclusive licenses, it could not attract and hold new members as replacements for those of its present members who, following the pattern of the past, eventually grow sufficiently in size to be able to leave the cooperative organization and develop their own individual private-label brands. Moreover, Topco's present members, once today's decision has had its full impact over the course of time, will have no more reason to promote Topco products through local advertising and merchandising efforts than they will have such reason to promote any other generally available brands.

The issue presented by the antitrust cases reaching this Court are rarely simple to resolve under the rule of reason; they do indeed frequently require us to make difficult economic determinations. We should not for that reason alone, however, be overly zealous in formulating new *per se* rules, for an excess of zeal in that regard is both contrary to the policy of the Sherman Act and detrimental to the welfare of consumers generally. Indeed, the economic effect of the new rule laid down by the Court today seems clear: unless Congress intervenes, grocery staples marketed under private-label brands with their lower consumer prices will soon be available only to those who patronize the large national chains.

General Leaseways, Inc. v. National Truck Leasing Association

United States Court of Appeals, Seventh Circuit, 1984.
744 F.2d 588.

Defendant National Truck Leasing Association (NTLA) was a league of 130 companies that leased trucks to businesses, occasionally on a "full service" basis. Under those arrangements, the members of NTLA were responsible for maintaining the trucks and for repairing them at locations throughout the country. Members of the Association were small local companies, however, without nation-wide service facilities. The Association was created to establish a reciprocal service arrangement enabling each member to lease trucks on a full service basis and thus compete with national truck leasing companies which owned and operated service facilities throughout the United States. Each Association member was required to provide other members with prompt and efficient repair services.

As a condition of membership, each member accepted a franchise from NTLA designating a particular location at which it could conduct its business, and forbidding operations as a franchisee of NTLA at any other location. Members were also forbidden from affiliating with any other full service truck leasing enterprise such as Hertz or Avis. As a practical matter, lessees invariably dealt with firms having an outlet within a few miles of their place of business to insure the convenience of picking up trucks nearby and facilitating regular (as opposed to emergency repair) maintenance. The Association's policy was to space franchises at least 10 or 20 miles apart. Members of NTLA could open up outlets at unauthorized locations, but in those circumstances, the member would not be entitled to reciprocal service.

General Leaseways elected to defy the location and nonaffiliation restrictions and successfully obtained a preliminary injunction from the district court preventing it from being expelled from the Association pending trial on the merits. The Court of Appeals' discussion on appeal includes the following:

■ POSNER, J . . . . .

Until a few years ago it would have been possible to opine confidently . . . that when firms in the same line of business agree not to enter each other's territories they violate section 1 of the Sherman Act even if they might be able to show that dividing markets had yielded economic benefits greater than any plausible estimate of the costs in diminished competition; that, in short, horizontal market divisions are illegal *per se*. See, e.g., United States v. Topco Associates, Inc., 405 U.S. 596, 608; United States v. Sealy, Inc., 388 U.S. 350, 356–57; Timken Roller Bearing Co. v. United States, 341 U.S. 593, 598; United States v. Nationwide Trailer Rental System, Inc., 156 F.Supp. 800 (D.Kan.), aff'd without opinion, 355 U.S. 10.

In both *Sealy* and *Topco*, a group of small competitors had divided markets on geographic lines as an incident to the sharing of a trademark, and the group argued that its market share was too small to make cartelization a palpable danger to competition or a plausible explanation of what it was doing. Apparently each group was just trying to prevent members from taking a free ride on other members' efforts to promote the trademark. And yet in both cases the market division was held to be a *per se* violation of section 1. In *Sealy* (as in *Timken*) the division of markets was coupled with price fixing, against which antitrust law has long come down very hard—though, as we shall see, price fixing and division of markets have identical competitive effects. But *Topco* held that horizontal market division is illegal *per se* even if price fixing is not present.

This case is even stronger for condemnation, because the free-rider argument made by National Truck Leasing Association is much weaker than the free-rider arguments in *Sealy* and *Topco*. A member of the Sealy group who promoted the Sealy trademark in his sales area by extensive (and expensive) advertising could not recoup his expenses by charging the people who saw his ads for the privilege of seeing them; virtually no one will pay to consume advertising. He could recoup only by selling his mattresses at a price that covered those expenses along with all his other costs. It is this form of recoupment that the free rider—in *Sealy,* a manufacturer of mattresses under the same trademark who has not borne the expense of promoting the mark—thwarts by invading the territory of the advertising manufacturer: by seeking, in other words, to reap where he has not sown. But members of National Truck Leasing Association charge each other for emergency repair service.

The Association argues that they do not charge the full price: that is, do not charge the premium—indeed, the extortionate—price they could get in an unregulated market for providing the prompt service to which members of the Association are entitled by its rules. When a truck breaks down, the owner is pretty much at the mercy of the nearest repair service. Unless he owns the service or has a contract with the owner or the sort of reciprocal-service arrangement that the Association has created for its members, he will not have access to a competitive market in repairs. (The salvage of ships in distress involves surprisingly similar problems, on which see Gilmore & Black, The Law of Admiralty 578–81 (2d ed. 1975).) Therefore, if one member of the Association—General Leaseways, say— grew so large relative to the others that it was consistently demanding more repairs on its trucks than it was performing on its fellow members' trucks, it would be exploiting the "underpricing" of repair service by the other members.

This argument is terribly speculative, though. As a member of the Association grows, he puts himself in a position to expect more service calls on himself (because he is serving a larger area) as well as to demand more service from others. Moreover, there is no evidence that the Association seeks to limit the growth of its members so that all remain about the same size. Also the Association does not limit repair prices, and it has not explained why its members do not (has not even shown they do not) charge fully remunerative prices for the repair services they provide each other. Even if they do refrain from gouging one another, such forbearance would be a burden or cost of repairing a fellow member's truck only if that repair job made it impossible to do another repair job that would fetch a higher price. The Association put in no evidence that this has ever happened.

It is not repairs that sellers find hard to charge for directly. It is *information*— in the form of advertising, showroom display, sales demonstrations, courteous and informed salesmen, and other presale services— that free riders in previous cases were able to take advantage of because the information was being "given away" by a seller who could recover his cost only by selling the product to the consumer who used the information. Repairing is not informing. And National's franchisees do little advertising or other promotion of the NationaLease trademark. They are selling to businesses, not consumers, and advertising usually is less important in selling to businessmen than to consumers. But whatever the reason for the lack of promotional effort, the division of markets cannot (on this record) be justified as a measure for promoting the NationaLease mark....

Broadcast Music upheld the blanket licenses by which associations of composers sell musical performance rights to radio stations and other performance outlets. Since the blanket license gives the licensee, for a fixed fee, the right to play any composition in the association's library, it eliminates price competition among the composers belonging to the associa-

[margin note: DS argues BMI makes all reas cartel agreements ok. Posner says BMI not a cartel]

tion. Nevertheless the Supreme Court held that the blanket license was not a *per se* violation of section 1 of the Sherman Act. National Truck Leasing Association argues in effect that after *Broadcast Music* no reasonable cartel agreement can be a *per se* violation of section 1. We hesitate to read the decision so broadly. Access to a repertoire of thousands of songs is not something the individual composer can give, so what the performing-rights associations are engaged in is not (or not just) the suppression of price competition among composers. It is the provision of a distinctive product— access to a vast musical repertoire. Each association is the "producer," and is entitled to price its "product" as it wants as long as it does not collude with the other association. So viewed, *Broadcast Music* was not a cartel case.

There is nothing distinctive about the product involved in this case. Many firms offer full-service over-the-road commercial truck leasing; the Association merely makes it easier for small firms to offer it, by providing a reciprocal service arrangement that enables each member to provide his customers with emergency repair service anywhere in the nation. Unlike the composers' associations in the *Broadcast Music* case, this association sells nothing.

If this analysis is too formalistic—if *Broadcast Music* is more realistically described as a case where the Supreme Court, though aware that an exclusive sales agency normally is a method of cartelization ... upheld exclusive sales agencies of composers because of the enormous efficiency of selling musical performing rights jointly (see NCAA v. Board of Regents, *supra*, 104 S.Ct. at 2961, where *Broadcast Music* is so described)—National Truck Leasing Association still loses. ASCAP and BMI could not provide ready access to their entire repertoires if each radio station had to negotiate separately with each composer over the price of each song. But National's members could—were it not for the territorial restrictions— compete in each other's territories while continuing to provide each other emergency repair services of a specified quality at a specified price. Of course this would make the members each other's competitors in leasing and customers in repairs. But firms often have both a competitive and a supply relationship with one another. A manufacturer of aluminum might both sell aluminum to fabricators and do its own fabrication in competition with its customers. Airlines compete but also feed passengers to each other. Railroads compete but also join in offering through routes and joint rates. Oil companies compete in some markets and are joint venturers in others. It does not follow that because two firms sometimes have a cooperative relationship there are no competitive gains from forbidding them to cooperate in ways that yield no economies but simply limit competition....

[margin note: they could compete in same territory + still be + association]

After argument in this case, the Supreme Court decided the *NCAA* case, *supra*, and again refused to hold that an agreement between competitors not to compete was illegal *per se* under the Sherman Act. The agreement was among the college football teams that belong to the NCAA, and limited the number of football games that each team could license for television broadcast. The Supreme Court described this agreement as one to limit output. That is the equivalent of a division of markets. A firm that is free from effective competition will reduce its output below the competitive level (whether directly or, as we shall see in a moment, indirectly by raising price). Consumers will pay more when supply is scarcer, yet it will cost the firm less to produce a smaller supply—so the firm's profits will be greater at the reduced output. One way the firm can free itself from competition is by agreeing with sellers of the same product that they will not enter each other's markets; such an agreement will create a series of regional or local (sometimes, as in *Timken,* national) monopolies. An agreement on output also equates to a price-fixing agreement. If firms raise price, the market's demand for their product will fall, so the amount supplied will fall too—in other words, output will be restricted. If instead the firms restrict output directly, price will as mentioned rise in order to limit demand to the reduced supply. Thus, with exceptions not relevant here, raising price, reducing output, and dividing markets have the same anticompetitive effects.

The Court held nevertheless that the NCAA's agreement to limit output had to be tested under the Rule of Reason, because organized athletic competition is "an industry in which horizontal restraints on competition are essential if the product is to be available at all." The essence of successful league competition is maintaining a balance of power among the competitors—a goal antithetic to the goals of competition in a conventional economic market. *NCAA* may seem to go a step beyond *Broadcast Music* toward a regime in which only unreasonable horizontal restraints are illegal, because the Court in *NCAA* did not condition the applicability of the Rule of Reason on proof that the particular restriction that had been challenged was necessary if the product was to be brought to market at all. There was, however, a plausible connection between the specific restriction and the essential character of the product. Since the balance of power among the teams in the NCAA might be disturbed by disparities in team wealth, limiting the ability of the more popular teams to cash in on their popularity through unrestricted televising of their games might have promoted the NCAA's essential lawful objectives. It was arguable, in other words, that the television output restriction was "ancillary" to a lawful main purpose. See United States v. Addyston Pipe & Steel Co., 85 F. 271, 281–82 (6th Cir.1898), aff'd as modified, 175 U.S. 211, Bork, The Antitrust Paradox 29–30 (1978). But in this case the organic connection between the restraint and the cooperative needs of the enterprise that would allow us to call the restraint a merely ancillary one is missing. Although some degree of cooperation among members of National Truck Leasing Association in providing reciprocal services may well promote competition in the truck-leasing industry, no reason has been suggested why that cooperation requires that members be forbidden to compete with each other in leasing trucks.

The *per se* rule would collapse if every claim of economies from restricting competition, however implausible, could be used to move a horizontal agreement not to compete from the *per se* to the Rule of Reason category. We are told, therefore, to apply the *per se* rule when "the practice facially appears to be one that would always or almost always tend to restrict competition and decrease output." Broadcast Music.... In other words, if the elimination of competition is apparent on a quick look, without undertaking the kind of searching inquiry that would make the case a Rule of Reason case in fact if not in name, the practice is illegal *per se*.

Taking a quick look here, we conclude, on the basis of the record compiled in the preliminary-injunction hearing, that the division of markets among National Truck Leasing Association's members is a *per se* violation of section 1 of the Sherman Act. It is a horizontal market division that does not appear to be ancillary to the reciprocal provision of service or any other lawful activity....

[The Court went on to examine the arrangement under a rule of reason and concluded that, despite the modest market power of defendants, the arrangement was unreasonable largely because "the Association's attempted justification based on free-rider problems is unpersuasive." As a result, the district court's award of a preliminary injunction was affirmed.]

Palmer v. BRG of Georgia, Inc.

Supreme Court of the United States, 1990.
498 U.S. 46, 111 S.Ct. 401, 112 L.Ed.2d 349.

■ PER CURIAM.... HBJ began offering a Georgia bar review course on a limited basis in 1976, and was in direct, and often intense, competition with BRG during the period from 1977–1979. BRG and HBJ were two main providers of bar review courses in Georgia during this time period. In early 1980, they entered into an agreement that gave BRG an exclusive license to market HBJ's material in Georgia and to use its trade name "Bar/Bri." The parties agreed that HBJ would not compete with BRG in Georgia and that BRG would not compete with HBJ outside Georgia.[3] Under the agreement, HBJ received $100 per student enrolled by BRG and 40% of all revenues over $350. Immediately after the 1980 agreement, the price of BRG's course was increased from $150 to over $400.

On petitioners' motion for partial summary judgment as to the § 1 counts in the complaint and respondents' motion for summary judgment, the District Court held that the agreement was lawful. The United States Court of Appeals for the Eleventh Circuit, with one judge dissenting, agreed with the District Court that *per se* unlawful horizontal price fixing required an explicit agreement on prices to be charged or that one party have the right to be consulted about the other's prices. The Court of

---

3. The 1980 agreement contained two provisions, one called a "Covenant Not to Compete" and the other called "Other Ventures." The former required HBJ not to "directly or indirectly own, manage, operate, join, invest, control, or participate in or be connected as an officer, employee, partner, director, independent contractor or otherwise with any business which is operating or participating in the preparation of candidates for the Georgia State Bar Examination." The latter required BRG not to compete against HBJ in states in which HBJ currently operated outside the State of Georgia.

Appeals also agreed with the District Court that to prove a *per se* violation under a geographic market allocation theory, petitioners had to show that respondents had subdivided some relevant market in which they had previously competed. 874 F.2d 1417 (1989).[4] The Court of Appeals denied a petition for rehearing en banc that had been supported by the United States.

In United States v. Socony–Vacuum Oil Co., we held that an agreement among competitors to engage in a program of buying surplus gasoline on the spot market in order to prevent prices from falling sharply was unlawful, even though there was no direct agreement on the actual prices to be maintained. We explained that "under the Sherman Act a combination formed for the purpose and with the effect of raising, depressing, fixing, pegging, or stabilizing the price of a commodity in interstate or foreign commerce is illegal *per se.*" *Id.,* at 223. See also Catalano, Inc. v. Target Sales, Inc., 446 U.S. 643 (1980) (per curiam); National Society of Professional Engineers v. United States, 435 U.S. 679 (1978).

The revenue-sharing formula in the 1980 agreement between BRG and HBJ, coupled with the price increase that took place immediately after this agreement was "formed for the purpose and with the effect of raising" the price of the bar review course. It was, therefore, plainly incorrect for the District Court to enter summary judgment in respondents' favor. Moreover, it is equally clear that the District Court and the Court of Appeals erred when they assumed that an allocation of markets or submarkets by competitors is not unlawful unless the market in which the two previously competed is divided between them.

In *United States v. Topco Associates, Inc.*, we held that agreements between competitors to allocate territories to minimize competition are illegal:

> One of the classic examples of a *per se* violation of § 1 is an agreement between competitors at the same level of the market structure to allocate territories in order to minimize competition.... This Court has reiterated time and time again that "horizontal territorial limitations ... are naked restraints of trade with no purpose except stifling of competition." Such limitations are *per se* violations of the Sherman Act. (citations omitted).

The defendants in *Topco* had never competed in the same market, but had simply agreed to allocate markets. Here, HBJ and BRG had previously competed in the Georgia market; under their allocation agreement, BRG received that market, while HBJ received the remainder of the United States. Each agreed not to compete in the other's territories. Such agreements are anticompetitive regardless of whether the parties split a market

---

4. In dissent, Judge Clark explained that in his view HBJ and BRG were capable of engaging in *per se* horizontal restraints because they had competed against each other, and then had joined forces. He believed the District Court's analysis was flawed because it had failed to recognize that the agreements could be price-fixing agreements even without explicit reference to price and because it had failed to recognized the allocation, rather than subdivision, of markets could also constitute a *per se* antitrust violation.

per se unlawful — they split the mkts, the end of story

within which both do business or whether they merely reserve one market for one and another for the other. Thus, the 1980 agreement between HBJ and BRG was unlawful on its face.

The petition for writ of certiorari is granted, the judgment of the Court of Appeals is reversed, and the case is remanded for further proceedings consistent with this opinion.

NOTES AND QUESTIONS

1. Can you justify Justice Marshall's refusal in *Topco* to "ramble through the wilds of economic theory"? Would the Court's result have changed if a "reasonableness" analysis had been used?

2. Do you agree with Chief Justice Burger (who could cite many Supreme Court decisions which support his view) that a *per se* rule should be promulgated only when a practice has a "pernicious effect on competition" and lacks "any redeeming virtue"? When practices are likely to have a pernicious effect, how heavily should matters like (i) enforcement difficulties and limited resources, (ii) administrative and court time, and (iii) certainty weigh on the pro *per se* side of the scale?[5]

3. Chief Justice Burger's prediction, that "unless Congress intervenes ... private-label brands with their lower consumer prices will soon be available only to those who patronize the large national chains," should be evaluated in the context of the final judgment in *Topco* which was issued on remand below. The judgment contained provisions for both "areas of primary responsibility" (allowing for termination of those who did not adequately promote Topco's products) and "pass-overs." The "pass-over" clause would preclude "cream-skimming"—*i.e.*, selling in another's "primary area" absent the payment of a pro rata share for legitimate advertising and service expenditures. United States v. Topco Associates, 1973 Trade Cas. ¶ 74,485 (N.D.Ill.1973), affirmed per curiam, 414 U.S. 801 (1973). Arguably, these "less restrictive alternatives" indicate that Topco need not be seriously affected by the Supreme Court's adverse ruling. "Primary responsibility" and "pass-over" clauses are, of course, vulnerable to abuse; "pass-over" agreements, for example, may be set artificially high and thus create, in practice, an exclusive territory. Courts will closely scrutinize their use.[6]

4. Does anything in the Supreme Court's decision prevent Topco from acting as a "purchasing agent" or achieving cost economies related to transportation, warehousing, or promotion?

5. Judge Posner in *General Leaseways* suggests that arrangements designed to eliminate "free riders" reflect the kind of efficiencies that justify rule of reason

---

5. For commentaries on *per se* rules, *see* Goldschmid, Is Antitrust Antagonistic to American Competitiveness?, 93 Colum.L.Rev. 1572 (1993); Horizontal Territorial Restraints and the *per se* Rule, 28 Wash. & Lee L.Rev. 457 (1971); Elman, "Petrified Opinions" and Competitive Realities, 66 Colum.L.Rev. 625 (1966); Bork, The Rule of Reason and the *Per se* Concept: Price Fixing and Market Division, 74 Yale L.J. 775 (1965) and 75 Yale L.J. 373 (1966).

6. *See* Sherman v. British Leyland Motors Ltd., 601 F.2d 429, 449 (9th Cir.1979); Hobart Bros. Co. v. Gilliland, Inc., 471 F.2d 894, 900 (5th Cir.), cert. denied, 412 U.S. 923 (1973).

rather than *per se* treatment. If that is correct, does it follow that *Topco* and *Sealy* were wrongly decided, or at least decided on the basis of an incorrect theory?

Consider *General Leaseways* an introduction to the "free rider" debate. The issue usually arises in connection with vertical rather than horizontal arrangements, and its implications will be examined more extensively in Chapter 7 *infra*.

6. Can Justice Blackmun's "relief must come from the legislature" approach in *Topco* be reconciled with over 100 years of practice or the legislative history of the Sherman Act?

7. In Polk Brothers, Inc. v. Forest City Enterprises, Inc., 776 F.2d 185 (7th Cir. 1985), Polk Brothers, which sold appliances and home furnishings, and Forest City, which sold lumber, tools and building materials, entered into an agreement to own and operate their respective businesses out of a single building in Burbank, Illinois. Each party agreed, with minor exceptions, not to sell products which constituted the principal lines of the other. Seven years later, Forest City asked to be relieved of its covenant and, when Polk refused, advised Polk that it considered the covenant invalid; Polk responded by seeking an injunction.

The district court held the covenant invalid and the Seventh Circuit reversed. One theory of the Court of Appeals' opinion was that the parties would not have entered into the arrangement without assurances of noncompetition; hence, but for the covenant, there would not have been any joint arrangement. *Cf.* Broadcast Music Inc. v. CBS, p. 215 *supra*. A broader theme touched on by the Court distinguished between "naked" restraints, where a restraint on competition is unaccompanied by new production or products (and therefore a *per se* rule applies), and "ancillary" restraints which are part of a larger endeavor and deserve "rule of reason" treatment. That concept was related back to United States v. Addyston Pipe & Steel Co., p. 40 *supra*:

> A restraint is ancillary when it may contribute to the success of a cooperative venture that promises greater productivity and output. If the restraint, viewed at the time it was adopted, may promote the success of this more extensive cooperation, then the court must scrutinize things carefully under the Rule of Reason. Only when a quick look reveals that "the practice facially appears to be one that always or almost always tends to restrict competition and decrease output" should a court cut off further inquiry.

What are the limits of an "ancillary defense"? Suppose three companies in a distressed industry, all producing a long line of products, agreed that each would specialize in one-third of their previous product line. If that arrangement would allow each company to cut costs (by operating at higher levels of capacity on one-third of their line and dismantling the rest), lower prices, and increase output, would the arrangement be "ancillary" to an efficient, cooperative venture? Would that mean there is an efficiency defense to horizontal market division? Should there be?

8. If BRG and HBJ in *Palmer* could have shown that their 1980 agreement would achieve significant efficiencies, would the Supreme Court have considered the efficiencies an adequate justification? Would the Supreme Court have considered an efficiency justification to be relevant to the issues before it? Is the agreement in *Palmer* a horizontal price-fixing arrangement, a territorial division, or both? Does it matter?

NOTE ON AGREEMENTS BETWEEN HOLDERS OF PATENTED PHARMACEUTICAL PRODUCTS AND GENERIC CHALLENGERS

In recent years, a considerable number of cases have been brought by the Federal Trade Commission, private parties, and states challenging payments arising out of patent litigation between a pioneer (or "branded") patent holder of a drug and a challenging generic drug maker. The cases originally arose because of an extraordinarily complicated provision in the Hatch–Waxman Act[7] whereby generic drug companies were given incentives to try to enter a market prior to patent expiration, the brand name patent holder had the right to sue the generic for patent infringement, and the brand name drug producer paid the first generic to stay out of the market Some settlements achieved a further effect: if the "first-filed" generic stayed out of the market, it prevented any other generics from entering the market. If the generic could successfully challenge the legitimacy of the original patent, it would have the result of curtailing the period in which the original patent could be enforced.

The first round of cases reached inconsistent results. For example, in Cardizem CD Antitrust Litigation, 332 F.3d 896 (6th Cir. 2003), cert. denied, 543 U.S. 939 (2004), the payment to the generic for the generic's commitment to stay out of the market was found to be a division of markets and illegal *per se*. In a second case, Valley Drug Co. v. Geneva Pharmaceuticals, 344 F.3d 1294 (11th Cir. 2003), cert. denied, 543 U.S. 939 (2004), the Court of Appeals expressed skepticism about antitrust liability, but remanded the case to the district court, which condemned the settlement *per se*.

At first, many agency and court decisions went against the brand name patent holder, but in the last few years, courts of appeals have found in favor of the brand-name drug company. In Schering–Plough Corp. v. Federal Trade Commission, 402 F.3d 1056 (11th Cir. 2005), the Court of Appeals held that a payment to the generic drug challenger was consistent with rights accorded by patent, and that a contrary decision would undermine the useful procedure of negotiating patent settlements. In In re Tamoxifen Citrate Antitrust Litigation, 466 F.3d 187 (2d Cir. 2006), consumers and consumer groups filed some 30 lawsuits challenging the legality of a 1993 settlement between Zeneca, the holder of a patent on the most widely used cancer drug, and Barr Laboratories, a generic manufacturer who claimed that the Zeneca patent was invalid. The settlement occurred after the Zeneca patent was found by the district court to be invalid, and constituted a payment by Zeneca to Barr of $27 million on condition that Barr not introduce its low-price generic brand into the market. The Court of Appeals rejected a *per se* approach and concluded that the circumstances favored the defendants. In a two-to-one decision, it found that the Zeneca–Barr agreement was not an antitrust violation, largely on grounds that the agreement, unlike other branded drug-generic arrangements, did not bar other generic manufacturers from subsequently challenging Zeneca's patent in order to enter the market, and because, taking a broad variety of factors into account, the payment to Barr did not appear to be excessive.

The Supreme Court was asked to review the *Schering–Plough* and *Tamoxifen Citrate* decisions. Consistent with the recommendation of the Solicitor General's office, the Supreme Court rejected the Federal Trade Commission's request for review in *Schering–Plough*. In the *Tamoxifen Citrate* case, the Solicitor General's

---

7. Drug Price Competition and Patent Term Restoration Act, Pub. L. No. 98–417, 98 Stat. 1585 (1984). In 2003, the statute was amended in important respects. However, the basic public policy issue remains. *See* Pub. L. No. 108–173, 117 Stat. 2066 (2006).

office recommended that the Supreme Court decline review even though its brief noted: "The petition presents an important and difficult question, and the Court of Appeals adopted an incorrect standard. . . ." The standard adopted by the majority in the Second Circuit held that a settlement would be valid unless (1) the settlement extended the monopoly beyond the patent scope, (2) the settlement involved fraud, or (3) the underlying lawsuit was "objectively baseless in the sense that no reasonable litigant could realistically expect success on the merits." The Solicitor General's office thought a full rule-of-reason was a better approach, but recommended denial of review on grounds that the claims in the case appeared to be moot (the patent had expired), the factual setting was atypical and unlikely to recur, and subsequent regulatory changes may have undercut one of the theories of competitive harm advanced by petitioners. In June 2007, the Supreme Court denied certiorari.

The FTC and private litigants have continued bringing cases challenging patent holder payments. *See, e.g.*, Ciprofloxacin Hydrochloride Antitrust Litig., 544 F.3d 1323 (Fed. Cir. 2008) (antitrust claim rejected where $398 million payment to delay entry until patent expiration); Hemphill, An Aggregate Approach to Antitrust: Using New Data and Rulemaking to Preserve Drug Competition, 109 Colum. L. Rev. 629 (2009); Hemphill, Paying for Delay: Pharmaceutical Patent Settlement as a Regulatory Design Problem, 81 N.Y.U. L.Rev. 1553 (2006).

In July 2009, in Arkansas Carpenters Health and Welfare Fund v. Bayer AG, before the Second Circuit, the Antitrust Division (in an amicus brief) largely harmonized its litigation view with the FTC by proposing that reverse payment settlements be treated as "presumptively unlawful." Also, in July, Chairman Leibowitz of the FTC called on Congress to enact legislation banning reverse payments.[8] What do you think?

COMPARATIVE NOTE ON CRISIS CARTELS

As we have seen, the law in the United States has not always expressed as firm a prohibition against cartels as the Supreme Court articulated in *Socony–Vacuum*. Before that case, we saw *Appalachian Coals, supra* p. 192, and since then we have learned from *BMI*, that a sophisticated characterization process is necessary before something can be labeled a *per se* illegal cartel. It should not be surprising, therefore, to learn that differences of opinion exist from country to country about the advisability of making exceptions to the prohibition against cartels for industries facing structural crises or other severe adjustment problems. Indeed, one author in the United States has urged, using the tools of real options theory, that our own approach should be more accommodating. *See* Shubha Ghosh, Relaxing Antitrust During Economic Downturns: A Real Options Analysis of Appalachian Coals and the Failing Firm Defense, 68 Antitrust L.J. 111 (2000). The position of the United States, however, continues to be one of eschewing this approach to the economic crisis that began in 2008. *See, e.g.*, Varney, Vigorous Antitrust Enforcement in This Challenging Era, speech to the United States Chamber of Commerce, May 12, 2009, available at http://www.justice.gov/atr/public/speeches/245777.htm; *see also* Harkrider, Antitrust and the Economic Crisis: Lessons from the Great Depression, 23 Antitrust 6 (2009).

Two of the most important economies in the world, that of the European Union and that of Japan, provide for a safety valve in their competition laws. This is not

---

8. Leibowitz, Address at Center for American Progress (July 23, 2009).

inconsistent with the OECD's Recommendation Concerning Effective Action Against Hard Core Cartels, OECD Doc. C(98)35/Final (adopted by the Council on 25 March 1998), which carefully defines the term "hard core cartel" to exclude agreements "excluded directly or indirectly from the coverage of a Member country's own laws, or . . . authorized in accordance with those laws." *Id.* ¶ 2(b). The Recommendation merely calls for transparency for such exclusions and authorizations, and urges member states to consider eliminating or reducing them. *Id.* ¶ 3.

The Japanese Antimonopoly Law (AMA), Law No. 54, 1947, as amended through Law No. 63, 1977, contains a number of provisions that allow the Japanese Fair Trade Commission (JFTC) to authorize cartels. In addition (as is the case in virtually every other country as well, including the United States), other laws provide for exemptions from the general prohibitions of the AMA. Professor Mitsuo Matsushita, a leading expert on Japanese competition law, suggests that the following six exemptions are the most significant: (1) Article 24–3, which permits enterprises to obtain authorization from the JFTC for a "depression cartel," (2) specific laws, such as the Medium and Small Business Organizations Law, the Environmental Sanitation Law, and the Liquor Tax and Liquor Association Law, which permit joint activities for the purpose of "stabilizing operations," (3) the Medium and Small Business Cooperatives Law, which permits enterprises to associate in order to obtain countervailing power against larger suppliers or purchasers, (4) Article 24–4 of the AMA and certain other specific statutes that permit enterprises to agree on terms of business to promote "rationalization" of operations (*i.e.* standard-setting, specialization), (5) the Insurance Business Law, the Aviation Law, and the Marine Transportation Law, which permit associations to limit price and terms of business, and (6) the Export and Import Transactions Law, which authorizes agreements to implement voluntary export restraints. See Matsushita, Cartels Under the Japanese Antimonopoly Law, in Chih–Kang Wang et al. (eds.), International Harmonization of Competition Laws 65–66 (1995).

The European Community also has the legal authority to exempt companies from the cartel prohibitions of Article 81 of the Treaty, under strictly limited circumstances. *See generally* Andre Fiebig, Crisis Cartels and the Triumph of Industrial Policy Over Competition Law in Europe, 25 Brook. J. Int'l L. 607 (1999). For example, in the Synthetic Fibres decision, Commission decision 84/380, O.J. 207/17 (Aug. 2, 1984), the Commission approved a limited, short-term agreement to reduce excess capacity among the major European producers of synthetic fibers. The agreement was a narrow one; the Commission did not authorize the companies to agree on sensitive terms such as price, market sharing, or production or sales quotas. In its Twelfth Report on Competition Policy[9], the Commission had the following comment on structural adjustment arrangements:

> . . . within a given crisis-struck industry, economic circumstances do not necessarily guarantee a reduction of the least profitable surplus capacity. Undertakings which have failed to make the necessary adjustments may have their losses offset within their groups. . . . Against this background, and in order to combat the structural problems of individual sectors, the Commission may be able to condone agreements in restraint of competition which relate to a sector as a whole. . . .

---

9. Commission of the European Communities, Twelfth Report on Competition Policy 43 (1983). *See also* George and Jacquemin, Competition Policy in the European Community, in Comanor et al. (eds.), Competition Policy in Europe and North America: Economic Issues and Institutions 215–16 (1990).

The Commission has also exempted agreements designed to reduce overcapacity and to lower costs by increased specialization, in circumstances where the crisis element does not enter the picture.[10]

Do the Japanese and European systems introduce necessary flexibility into the general prohibition against cartels, or do they invite political undercutting of the market mechanism and industrial policy-style protectionism on behalf of unsuccessful companies or industries? Which provides the more reliable adjustment mechanism: administrative review of cartel arrangements, or market devices such as mergers, bankruptcies, and reorganizations?[11]

Whatever the correct answer may be for domestic antitrust policy, is there any justification for taking a different approach when we consider the role of international competition? Should cartels or mergers that would otherwise be unlawful under the U.S. antitrust laws be permitted as a way of helping U.S. companies compete globally?[12]

PROBLEM 5

THE TRANSOCEAN VENTURE FOR MARINE PAINT

Transocean was an organization created by agreement among 18 manufacturers of marine paint, each located in a different country. The parties agreed to develop, manufacture, and sell identical paint under an identical "Transocean" trademark. The "Transocean Venture," as it was called, spent large sums to develop a new and highly effective paint composition. In addition to economies in research, development, advertising, promotion, and service, the arrangement offered a special technical benefit in that paint applied over identical paint is more durable. Thus, a standardized paint available throughout the world was of particular value. The common trademark provided an efficient way to convey the idea that the paint offered by each member was identical.

The arrangement included prohibitions against establishing manufacturing facilities by a participant in the home territory of another. It also prohibited a member from selling in the home territory of another without its consent (supposedly routinely given), and then only on the payment of a commission in an unspecified amount. Alternatively, if an order were received by a member for sale outside its own country, it could turn that over to a local concern and a commission would be paid to the firm securing the order.

The arrangement has been in effect for about five years. During the first several years, members occasionally asked permission to make sales in the home territories of others and such requests were sometimes granted and sometimes denied. The United States member of the arrangement turned down three requests and granted two during the past two years. In general, in the great bulk of instances, members are content to accept a commission for referring sales.

---

10. *See, e.g.,* Enichem/ICI, Commission Decision 88/87, O.J. 50/18 (Feb. 24, 1988), described in the Seventeenth Report on Competition Policy 73 (1988).

11. *See* Pitofsky, Antitrust and Problems of Adjustment in Distressed Industries, 55 Antitrust L.J. 21 (1986).

12. *See, e.g.,* FTC Staff, Anticipating the 21st Century: Competition Policy in the New High–Tech, Global Marketplace (1996); Pitofsky, Proposals for Revised United States Merger Enforcement in a Global Economy, 81 Geo. L. J. 195 (1992); First, Structural Antitrust Rules and International Competition: The Case of Distressed Industries, 62 N.Y.U. L. Rev. 1054 (1987).

The Antitrust Division has initiated an investigation of the legality of the arrangement under Section 1. Is there a violation?

SELECTIVE BIBLIOGRAPHY

6–7 Areeda & Turner, Antitrust Law: An Analysis of Antitrust Principles and Their Application (2006 & 2009 Supplement).

Hovenkamp, Federal Antitrust Policy: The Law of Competition and Its Practice Chs. 4–5 (3d ed. 2005).

FTC Staff, Anticipating the 21st Century: Competition Policy in the New High–Tech, Global Marketplace Chs. 1, 3, 4, 9, and 10 (1996).

Scherer & Ross, Industrial Market Structure and Economic Performance Ch. 9 (3d ed. 1990).

Muris, California Dental Association v. Federal Trade Commission: The Revenge of Footnote 17, 8 S.Ct. Econ. Rev. 265 (2000).

Calkins, California Dental Association: Not a Quick Look But Not the Full Monty, 67 Antitrust L.J. 495 (2000).

Goldschmid, Horizontal Restraints in Antitrust: Current Treatment and Future Needs, 75 Cal.L.Rev. 925 (1987).

CHAPTER 5

GROUP REFUSALS TO DEAL AND JOINT VENTURES

INTRODUCTION

In Chapter 4, we began our consideration of agreements among competing firms. Despite the fact that one can find language in many opinions indicating that all such agreements are banned, the actual situation has always been far more complex. *BMI* was a case in which actual or potential competitors in the market for the sale of copyrighted music were permitted to band together and authorize a common selling agent to act for them. The Supreme Court recognized that the product made possible by this collaboration—the package license—would not have been possible in the absence of the agreement. Moreover, the collective product was better than the sum of its parts: it reduced costs for buyers and sellers alike, and it therefore enhanced output. In another case from Chapter 4, *NCAA*, the Court ultimately condemned the agreement among the competing colleges and universities before it. Nevertheless, it treated the NCAA as a joint venture and evaluated the television contract under the rule of reason. In the present chapter, we continue our consideration of collaborative arrangements among competitors. Which arrangements are legal? What ancillary restrictions on competition among the members will pass muster? How should actions that affect third parties, such as refusals to deal or group boycotts, be evaluated? Here as elsewhere, the trend has been toward increased use of the rule of reason and an increased need to consider the economic purpose and effect of the arrangement.

SECTION 1.   REFUSALS TO DEAL

Early Decisions

Two early cases illustrate the Court's group boycott doctrine prior to *FOGA*, *infra* p. 308, and the cases that followed. In W.W. Montague & Co. v. Lowry, 193 U.S. 38, 24 S.Ct. 307, 48 L.Ed. 608 (1904), the defendant was an association of wholesale dealers of tiles, mantels, and grates located in and around San Francisco; it also included manufacturers of such products located in other states who sold to dealer-members in the San Francisco area. Plaintiff Lowry was a dealer in tiles, mantels, and grates in San Francisco and a competitor of certain members of the association; Lowry itself was not a member. Prior to the formation of the association, Lowry had purchased tiles from manufacturers in eastern states, but afterwards, it was unable to purchase tiles from the same sources because those manufacturers had joined the association. Worse, Lowry found that it could obtain product from dealers in San Francisco only at the inflated "list prices" established by the association. Lowry challenged the unanimous voting and stock ownership rules for joining the association as violations of the Sherman Act.

The case went to trial before a jury, which returned a verdict for Lowry. The Supreme Court affirmed, finding that the association "constituted or amounted to an agreement or combination in restraint of trade" under the Sherman Act. The Court noted that any application was subject to arbitrary rejection by the association. It also noted that any application from Lowry would probably have been doomed because Lowry could not satisfy the essential eligibility condition (*i.e.*, maintenance of stock valued at $3,000). The Court concluded, therefore, that the association's agreement was an unlawful restraint of trade and that Lowry could not legally be required to conform to it as a condition of doing business with the members, as Lowry had done before the association's formation.

In Paramount Famous Lasky Corp. v. United States, 282 U.S. 30, 51 S.Ct. 42, 75 L.Ed. 145 (1930), members of the Motion Picture Producers and Distributors of America agreed that they would do business with some 25,000 theater owners and exhibitors for the display of films only through a standard contract requiring that exhibitors submit all disputes to arbitration or post $500 security with each distributor. An exhibitor's failure to comply with any lease provision or arbitration award would be grounds for all distributors to suspend all contracts with that exhibitor.

Noting that the arrangement was unusual at the time (consider how it would be regarded today, in light of the Supreme Court's far greater receptivity to arbitration) and tended to suppress normal competition, the Supreme Court concluded that it violated Section 1. The Court reasoned that it "may be that arbitration is well adapted to the needs of the motion picture industry; but when under the guise of arbitration parties enter into unusual arrangements which unreasonably suppress normal competition their action becomes illegal." The fact that the challenged arrangement did not suppress all competition between the parties was regarded as irrelevant.

Fashion Originators' Guild of America v. Federal Trade Commission

Supreme Court of the United States, 1941.
312 U.S. 457, 61 S.Ct. 703, 85 L.Ed. 949.

■ BLACK, J. The Circuit Court of Appeals, with modifications not here challenged, affirmed a Federal Trade Commission decree ordering petitioners to cease and desist from certain practices found to have been done in combination and to constitute "unfair methods of competition" tending to monopoly....

Some of the members of the combination design, manufacture, sell and distribute women's garments—chiefly dresses. Others are manufacturers, converters or dyers of textiles from which these garments are made.

Fashion Originators' Guild of America (FOGA), an organization controlled by these groups, is the instrument through which petitioners work to accomplish the purposes condemned by the Commission. The garment manufacturers claim to be creators of original and distinctive designs of fashionable clothes for women, and the textile manufacturers claim to be creators of similar original fabric designs. After these designs enter the channels of trade, other manufacturers systematically make and sell copies of them, the copies usually selling at prices lower than the garments copied. Petitioners call this practice of copying unethical and immoral, and give it the name of "style piracy." And although they admit that their "original creations" are neither copyrighted nor patented, and indeed assert that existing legislation affords them no protection against copyists, they nevertheless urge that sale of copied designs constitutes an unfair trade practice and a tortious invasion of their rights. Because of these alleged wrongs, petitioners, while continuing to compete with one another in many respects, combined among themselves to combat and, if possible, destroy all competition from the sale of garments which are copies of their "original creations." They admit that to destroy such competition they have in combination purposely boycotted and declined to sell their products to retailers who follow a policy of selling garments copied by other manufacturers from designs put out by Guild members. As a result of their efforts, approximately 12,000 retailers throughout the country have signed agreements to "cooperate" with the Guild's boycott program, but more than half of these signed the agreements only because constrained by threats that Guild members would not sell to retailers who failed to yield to their demands—threats that have been carried out by the Guild practice of placing on red cards the names of non-cooperators (to whom no sales are to be made), placing on white cards the names of cooperators (to whom sales are to be made), and then distributing both sets of cards to the manufacturers.

The one hundred and seventy-six manufacturers of women's garments who are members of the Guild occupy a commanding position in their line of business. In 1936, they sold in the United States more than 38% of all women's garments wholesaling at $6.75 and up, and more than 60% of those at $10.75 and above. The power of the combination is great; competition and the demand of the consuming public make it necessary for most retail dealers to stock some of the products of these manufacturers. And the power of the combination is made even greater by reason of the affiliation of some members of the National Federation of Textiles, Inc.— that being an organization composed of about one hundred textile manufacturers, converters, dyers and printers of silk and rayon used in making women's garments. Those members of the Federation who are affiliated with the Guild have agreed to sell their products only to those garment manufacturers who have in turn agreed to sell only to cooperating retailers.

The Guild maintains a Design Registration Bureau for garments, and the Textile Federation maintains a similar Bureau for textiles. The Guild employs "shoppers" to visit the stores of both cooperating and non-cooperating retailers, "for the purpose of examining their stocks, to determine and report as to whether they contain ... copies of registered designs...." An elaborate system of trial and appellate tribunals exists, for the determination of whether a given garment is in fact a copy of a Guild member's design. In order to assure the success of its plan of registration and restraint, and to ascertain whether Guild regulations are being violated, the Guild audits its members' books. And if violations of Guild requirements are discovered, as for example, sales to red-carded retailers, the violators are subject to heavy fines.

In addition to the elements of the agreement set out above, all of which relate more or less closely to competition by so-called style copyists, the Guild has undertaken to do many things apparently independent of and distinct from the fight against copying. Among them are the following: the combination prohibits its members from participating in retail advertising; regulates the discount they may allow; prohibits their selling at retail; cooperates with local guilds in regulating days upon which special sales shall be held; prohibits its members from selling women's garments to persons who conduct businesses in residences, residential quarters, hotels or apartment houses; and denies the benefits of membership to retailers who participate with dress manufacturers in promoting fashion shows unless the merchandise used is actually purchased and delivered.

other restrictions imposed on members

If the purpose and practice of the combination of garment manufacturers and their affiliates runs counter to the public policy declared in the Sherman and Clayton Acts, the Federal Trade Commission has the power to suppress it as an unfair method of competition. From its findings the Commission concluded that the petitioners, "pursuant to understandings, arrangements, agreements, combinations and conspiracies entered into jointly and severally," had prevented sales in interstate commerce, had "substantially lessened, hindered and suppressed" competition, and had tended "to create in themselves a monopoly." ... The relevance of ... section [3] of the Clayton Act to petitioners' scheme is shown by the fact that the scheme is bottomed upon a system of sale under which (1) textiles shall be sold to garment manufacturers only upon the condition and understanding that the buyers will not use or deal in textiles which are copied from the designs of textile manufacturing Guild members; (2) garment manufacturers shall sell to retailers only upon the condition and understanding that the retailers shall not use or deal in such copied designs. And the Federal Trade Commission concluded in the language of the Clayton Act that these understandings substantially lessened competition and tended to create a monopoly. We hold that the Commission, upon adequate and unchallenged findings, correctly concluded that this practice constituted an unfair method of competition.

Not only does the plan in the respects above discussed thus conflict with the principles of the Clayton Act; the findings of the Commission bring petitioners' combination in its entirety well within the inhibition of the policies declared by the Sherman Act itself.... Under the Sherman Act "competition, not combination, should be the law of trade." National Cotton Oil Co. v. Texas, 197 U.S. 115, 129. And among the many respects in which the Guild's plan runs contrary to the policy of the Sherman Act are these: it narrows the outlets to which garment and textile manufacturers can sell and the sources from which retailers can buy (Montague & Co. v. Lowry, 193 U.S. 38, 45; Standard Sanitary Manufacturing Co. v. United States, 226 U.S. 20, 48, 49); subjects all retailers and manufacturers who decline to comply with the Guild's program to an organized boycott (Eastern States Retail Lumber Dealers' Association v. United States, 234 U.S. 600, 609–611); takes away the freedom of action of members by requiring each to reveal to the Guild the intimate details of their individual affairs (United States v. American Linseed Oil Co., 262 U.S. 371, 389); and has both as its necessary tendency and as its purpose and effect the direct suppression of competition from the sale of unregistered textiles and copied designs (United States v. American Linseed Oil Co., *supra*, 262 U.S. at 389). In addition to all this, the combination is in reality an extra-governmental agency, which prescribes rules for the regulation and restraint of interstate commerce, and provides extra-judicial tribunals for determination and punishment of violations, and thus "trenches upon the power of the national legislature and violates the statute." Addyston Pipe & Steel Co. v. United States, 175 U.S. 211, 242.

Nor is it determinative in considering the policy of the Sherman Act that petitioners may not yet have achieved a complete monopoly. For "it is sufficient if it really tends to that end, and to deprive the public of the advantages which flow from free competition." United States v. E.C. Knight Co., 156 U.S. 1, 16; Addyston Pipe & Steel Co. v. United States, 175 U.S. 211, 237. It was, in fact, one of the hopes of those who sponsored the Federal Trade Commission Act that its effect might be prophylactic and that through it attempts to bring about complete monopolization of an industry might be stopped in their incipiency.

Petitioners, however, argue that the combination cannot be contrary to the policy of the Sherman and Clayton Acts, since the Federal Trade Commission did not find that the combination fixed or regulated prices, parceled out or limited production, or brought about a deterioration in quality. But action falling into these three categories does not exhaust the types of conduct banned by the Sherman and Clayton Acts. And as previously pointed out, it was the object of the Federal Trade Commission Act to reach not merely in their fruition but also in their incipiency combinations which could lead to these and other trade restraints and practices deemed undesirable. In this case, the Commission found that the combination exercised sufficient control and power in the women's garments and textile businesses "to exclude from the industry those manufacturers and distributors who do not conform to the rules and regulations of said respondents, and thus tend to create in themselves a monopoly in the said industries." While a conspiracy to fix prices is illegal, an intent to increase prices is not an ever-present essential of conduct amounting to a violation of the policy of the Sherman and Clayton Acts; a monopoly contrary to their policies can exist even though a combination may temporarily or even permanently reduce the price of the articles manufactured or sold. . . .

DS: policy reas
& nec to protect
against pirating

But petitioners further argue that their boycott and restraint of interstate trade is not within the ban of the policies of the Sherman and Clayton Acts because "the practices of FOGA were reasonable and necessary to protect the manufacturer, laborer, retailer and consumer against the devastating evils growing from the pirating of original designs and had in fact benefited all four." The Commission declined to hear much of the evidence that petitioners desired to offer on this subject. As we have pointed out, however, the aim of petitioners' combination was the intentional destruction of one type of manufacture and sale which competed with Guild members. The purpose and object of this combination, its potential power, its tendency to monopoly, the coercion it could and did practice upon a rival method of competition, all brought it within the policy of the prohibition declared by the Sherman and Clayton Acts. For this reason, the principles announced in Appalachian Coals, Inc. v. United States, 288 U.S. 344, and Sugar Institute v. United States, 297 U.S. 553, have no application here. Under these circumstances it was not error to refuse to hear the evidence offered, for the reasonableness of the methods pursued by the combination to accomplish its unlawful object is no more material than would be the reasonableness of the prices fixed by unlawful combination. Nor can the unlawful combination be justified upon the argument that systematic copying of dress designs is itself tortious, or should now be declared so by us. In the first place, whether or not given conduct is tortious is a question of state law, under our decision in Erie Railroad Co. v. Tompkins, 304 U.S. 64. In the second place, even if copying were an acknowledged tort under the law of every state, that situation would not justify petitioners in combining together to regulate and restrain interstate commerce in violation of federal law.... The decision below is accordingly

Affirmed.

NOTES AND QUESTIONS

1. *Reconciling* FOGA *with* BMI. Is *FOGA* still good law after *BMI?* Suppose the defendants in *FOGA* argued that it is very costly to prepare original designs for the fashion trade, and that design houses will eventually be driven out of business or at least severely hampered in their activities if they cannot control free riding "style pirates." Should a court today feel it had a responsibility under *BMI* to examine the merits of that contention before characterizing the arrangement as a boycott?

2. *Application of* FOGA *and* Paramount Famous Lasky. Would it be legal under *Paramount Famous Lasky* and *FOGA* for all insurance companies in a state to establish a committee to pass upon the creditworthiness of applicants for insurance pursuant to guidelines jointly established? Suppose that all the committee did was to establish criteria (*i.e.*, no coverage for environmental damage discovered more than 12 months after the termination date of the policy), but left it to each insurance company to implement the policy? Lastly, suppose the committee only recommended standards for acceptable insurance risks and then left it to each

insurance company to adopt or reject its proposals; suppose further that all insurance companies in the state can be shown to have adopted the proposal? What are the differences among these three fact situations?

3. *Intellectual property protection.* To what extent can the actions of the Guild members be explained as a private system for the protection of their intellectual property in their designs? Can this be done collectively, or must each holder of a trademarked or copyrighted design act individually? Companies might try to use intellectual property to obtain or extend market power, thereby attempting to reap monopoly profits beyond what the protected property itself would command. (Note that the soundness of this theory has been challenged; see the discussion of tying arrangements, at Chapter 8, Section 3.) But the question may be somewhat different if the degree of protection to which the intellectual property is entitled is less than complete. For example, companies today are testing the limits of patent law by obtaining broad "business method" patents. State Street Bank & Trust Co. v. Signature Financial Group, Inc., 149 F.3d 1368, 1375 (Fed. Cir. 1998) (squarely holding that there is no "business methods" exception to general rules of patentability, and upholding a patent for a data processing system).

Klor's, Inc. v. Broadway–Hale Stores, Inc.

Supreme Court of the United States, 1959.
359 U.S. 207, 79 S.Ct. 705, 3 L.Ed.2d 741.

■ BLACK, J. Klor's, Inc., operates a retail store on Mission Street, San Francisco, California; Broadway–Hale Stores, Inc., a chain of department stores, operates one of its stores next door. The two stores compete in the sale of radios, television sets, refrigerators and other household appliances. Claiming that Broadway–Hale and 10 national manufacturers and their distributors have conspired to restrain and monopolize commerce in violation of §§ 1 and 2 of the Sherman Act, 26 Stat. 209, as amended, 15 U.S.C. §§ 1, 2, Klor's brought this action for treble damages and injunction in the United States District Court.

In support of its claim Klor's made the following allegations: George Klor started an appliance store some years before 1952 and has operated it ever since either individually or as Klor's, Inc. Klor's is as well equipped as Broadway–Hale to handle all brands of appliances. Nevertheless, manufacturers and distributors of such well-known brands as General Electric, RCA, Admiral, Zenith, Emerson and others have conspired among themselves and with Broadway–Hale either not to sell to Klor's or to sell to it only at discriminatory prices and highly unfavorable terms. Broadway–Hale has used its "monopolistic" buying power to bring about this situation. The business of manufacturing, distributing and selling household appliances is in interstate commerce. The concerted refusal to deal with Klor's has seriously handicapped its ability to compete and has already caused it a great loss of profits, goodwill, reputation and prestige.

The defendants did not dispute these allegations, but sought summary judgment and dismissal of the complaint for failure to state a cause of action. They submitted unchallenged affidavits which showed that there were hundreds of other household appliance retailers, some within a few blocks of Klor's who sold many competing brands of appliances, including those the defendants refused to sell to Klor's. From the allegations of the complaint, and from the affidavits supporting the motion for summary judgment, the District Court concluded that the controversy was a "purely private quarrel" between Klor's and Broadway–Hale, which did not amount to a "public wrong proscribed by the [Sherman] Act." On this ground the complaint was dismissed and summary judgment was entered for the defendants. The Court of Appeals for the Ninth Circuit affirmed the summary judgment. 255 F.2d 214. It stated that "a violation of the Sherman Act requires conduct of defendants by which the public is or conceivably may be ultimately injured." 255 F.2d, at p. 233. It held that here the required public injury was missing since "there was no charge or proof that by any act of defendants the price, quantity, or quality offered the public was affected, nor that there was any intent or purpose to effect a change in, or an influence on, prices, quantity or quality." *Id.*, at page 230. The holding, if correct, means that unless the opportunities for customers to buy in a competitive market are reduced, a group of powerful business-men may act in concert to deprive a single merchant, like Klor, of the goods he needs to compete effectively. We granted certiorari to consider this important question in the administration of the Sherman Act. 358 U.S. 809.

We think Klor's allegations clearly show one type of trade restraint and public harm the Sherman Act forbids, and that defendants' affidavits provide no defense to the charges. Section 1 of the Sherman Act makes illegal any contract, combination or conspiracy in restraint of trade, and § 2 forbids any person or combination from monopolizing or attempting to monopolize any part of interstate commerce. In the landmark case of Standard Oil Co. of New Jersey v. United States, 221 U.S. 1, this Court read § 1 to prohibit those classes of contracts or acts which the common law had deemed to be undue restraints of trade and those which new times and economic conditions would make unreasonable. *Id.*, at 59–60. The Court construed § 2 as making "the prohibitions of the act all the more complete and perfect by embracing all attempts to reach the end prohibited by the 1st section, that is, restraints of trade, by any attempt to monopolize or monopolization thereof. . . ." *Id.*, at 61. The effect of both sections, the Court said, was to adopt the common-law proscription of all "contracts or acts which it was considered had a monopolistic tendency . . ." and which interfered with the "natural flow" of an appreciable amount of interstate commerce. *Id.*, at 57, 61; Eastern States Retail Lumber Dealers' Ass'n v. United States, 234 U.S. 600, 609. The Court recognized that there were some agreements whose validity depended on the surrounding circum-stances. It emphasized, however, that there were classes of restraints which from their "nature or character" were unduly restrictive, and hence forbidden by both the common law and the statute. 221 U.S. at 58, 65.[1] As

---

1.   See also United States v. American Tobacco Co., 221 U.S. 106, 179, where the Court noted that the statute forbade all "acts or contracts or agreements or combinations . . . which,

to these classes of restraints, the Court noted, Congress had determined its own criteria of public harm and it was not for the courts to decide whether in an individual case injury had actually occurred. *Id.*, at 63–68.[2]

Group boycotts, or concerted refusals by traders to deal with other traders, have long been held to be in the forbidden category.[3] They have not been saved by allegations that they were reasonable in the specific circumstances, nor by a failure to show that they "fixed or regulated prices, parcelled out or limited production, or brought about a deterioration in quality." Fashion Originators' Guild v. Federal Trade Commission, 312 U.S. 457, 466, 467–468. Cf. United States v. Trenton Potteries Co., 273 U.S. 392. Even when they operated to lower prices or temporarily to stimulate competition they were banned. For, as this Court said in Kiefer–Stewart Co. v. Joseph E. Seagram & Sons, 340 U.S. 211, 213, "such agreements, no less than those to fix minimum prices, cripple the freedom of traders and thereby restrain their ability to sell in accordance with their own judgment." Cf. United States v. Patten, 226 U.S. 525, 542.

Plainly the allegations of this complaint disclose such a boycott. This is not a case of a single trader refusing to deal with another,[4] nor even of a manufacturer and a dealer agreeing to an exclusive distributorship. Alleged in this complaint is a wide combination consisting of manufacturers, distributors and a retailer. This combination takes from Klor's its freedom to buy appliances in an open competitive market and drives it out of business as a dealer in the defendants' products. It deprives the manufacturers and distributors of their freedom to sell to Klor's at the same prices and conditions made available to Broadway–Hale and in some instances forbids them from selling to it on any terms whatsoever. It interferes with the natural flow of interstate commerce. It clearly has, by its "nature" and "character," a "monopolistic tendency." As such it is not to be tolerated merely because the victim is just one merchant whose business is so small that his destruction makes little difference to the economy.[5] Monopoly can

either because of their inherent nature or effect or because of the evident purpose of the acts, etc., injuriously restrained trade . . . ."

2. In this regard the Sherman Act should be contrasted with § 5 of the Federal Trade Commission Act, 38 Stat. 719, as amended, 15 U.S.C. § 45(b), which requires that the Commission find "that a proceeding by it . . . be to the interest of the public" before it issues a complaint for unfair competition.

3. See, *e.g.*, Eastern States Retail Lumber Dealers' Ass'n v. United States, 234 U.S. 600.

4. Compare United States v. Colgate & Co., 250 U.S. 300, with United States v. Schrader's Son, Inc., 252 U.S. 85; United States v. Bausch & Lomb Optical Co., 321 U.S. 707, 719–723; Lorain Journal Co. v. United States, 342 U.S. 143.

5. The court below relied heavily on Apex Hosiery Co. v. Leader, 310 U.S. 469, in reaching its conclusion. While some language in that case can be read as supporting the position that no restraint on trade is prohibited by § 1 of the Sherman Act unless it has or is intended to have an effect on market prices, such statements must be considered in the light of the fact that the defendant in that case was a labor union. The Court in Apex recognized that the Act is aimed primarily at combinations having commercial objectives and is applied only to a very limited extent to organizations, like labor unions, which normally have other objectives. See United States v. Hutcheson, 312 U.S. 219; Allen Bradley Co. v. Local Union No. 3, International Brotherhood of Electrical Workers, 325 U.S. 797. Moreover, cases subsequent as surely thrive by the elimination of such small businessmen, one at a time, as it can by driving them out in large groups. In recognition of this fact the Sherman Act has consistently been read to forbid all contracts and combinations "which 'tend to create a monopoly,' " whether "the tendency is a creeping one" or "one that proceeds at full gallop." International Salt Co. v. United States, 332 U.S. 392, 396.

The judgment of the Court of Appeals is reversed and the cause is remanded to the District Court for trial.

NYNEX Corp. v. Discon, Inc.

Supreme Court of the United States, 1998.
525 U.S. 128, 119 S.Ct. 493, 142 L.Ed.2d 510.

■ BREYER, J. In this case we ask whether the antitrust rule that group boycotts are illegal *per se* as set forth in Klor's, Inc. v. Broadway–Hale Stores, Inc., 359 U.S. 207, 212 (1959), applies to a buyer's decision to buy from one seller rather than another, when that decision cannot be justified in terms of ordinary competitive objectives. We hold that the *per se* group boycott rule does not apply.

I

Before 1984 American Telephone and Telegraph Company (AT&T) supplied most of the Nation's telephone service and, through wholly owned subsidiaries such as Western Electric, it also supplied much of the Nation's telephone equipment. In 1984 an antitrust consent decree took AT&T out of the local telephone service business and left AT&T a *long-distance* telephone service provider, competing with such firms as MCI and Sprint. See M. Kellogg, J. Thorne, & P. Huber, Federal Telecommunications Law § 4.6, p. 221 (1992). The decree transformed AT&T's formerly owned local telephone companies into independent firms. At the same time, the decree insisted that those local firms help assure competitive long-distance service by guaranteeing long-distance companies physical access to their systems and to their local customers. See *United States v. American Telephone & Telegraph Co.*, 552 F. Supp. 131, 225, 227 (D.D.C. 1982), *aff'd. sub nom. Maryland v. United States*, 460 U.S. 1001 (1983). To guarantee that physical access, some local telephone firms had to install new call-switching equipment; and to install new call-switching equipment, they often had to remove old call-switching equipment. This case involves the business of removing that old switching equipment (and other obsolete telephone equipment)—a business called *"removal services."*

Discon, Inc., the respondent, sold removal services used by New York Telephone Company, a firm supplying local telephone service in much of New York State and parts of Connecticut. New York Telephone is a subsidiary of NYNEX Corporation. NYNEX also owns Materiel Enterprises

---

to Apex have made clear that an effect on prices is not essential to a Sherman Act violation. *See, e.g.,* Fashion Originators' Guild v. Federal Trade Commission, 312 U.S. 457, 466.

Company, a purchasing entity that bought removal services for New York Telephone. Discon, in a lengthy detailed complaint, alleged that the NYNEX defendants (namely, NYNEX, New York Telephone, Materiel Enterprises, and several NYNEX related individuals) engaged in unfair, improper, and anticompetitive activities in order to hurt Discon and to benefit Discon's removal services competitor, AT&T Technologies, a lineal descendant of Western Electric. The Federal District Court dismissed Discon's complaint for failure to state a claim. The Court of Appeals for the Second Circuit affirmed that dismissal with an exception, and that exception is before us for consideration.

The Second Circuit focused on one of Discon's specific claims, a claim that Materiel Enterprises had switched its purchases from Discon to Discon's competitor, AT&T Technologies, as part of an attempt to defraud local telephone service customers by hoodwinking regulators. According to Discon, Materiel Enterprises would pay AT&T Technologies more than Discon would have charged for similar removal services. It did so because it could pass the higher prices on to New York Telephone, which in turn could pass those prices on to telephone consumers in the form of higher regulatory-agency-approved telephone service charges. At the end of the year, Materiel Enterprises would receive a special rebate from AT&T Technologies, which Materiel Enterprises would share with its parent, NYNEX. Discon added that it refused to participate in this fraudulent scheme, with the result that Materiel Enterprises would not buy from Discon, and Discon went out of business.

These allegations, the Second Circuit said, state a cause of action under § 1 of the Sherman Act, though under a "different legal theory" from the one articulated by Discon. The Second Circuit conceded that ordinarily "the decision to discriminate in favor of one supplier over another will have a pro-competitive intent and effect." But, it added, in this case, "no such pro-competitive rationale appears on the face of the complaint." Rather, the complaint alleges Materiel Enterprises' decision to buy from AT&T Technologies, rather than from Discon, was intended to be, and was, "anticompetitive." Hence, "Discon has alleged a cause of action under, at least, the rule of reason, and possibly under the *per se* rule applied to group boycotts in *Klor's*, if the restraint of trade 'has no purpose except stifling competition.' " ... For somewhat similar reasons the Second Circuit believed the complaint stated a valid claim of conspiracy to monopolize under § 2 of the Sherman Act. See 93 F.3d at 1061–1062.

The Second Circuit noted that the Courts of Appeals are uncertain as to whether, or when, the *per se* group boycott rule applies to a decision by a purchaser to favor one supplier over another (which the Second Circuit called a "two-firm group boycott").... We granted certiorari in order to consider the applicability of the *per se* group boycott rule where a single buyer favors one seller over another, albeit for an improper reason.

II

As this Court has made clear, the Sherman Act's prohibition of "[e]very" agreement in "restraint of trade," prohibits only agreements that *unreasonably* restrain trade. See *Business Electronics Corp. v. Sharp Electronics Corp.*, 485 U.S. 717, 723 (1988) (citing *National Collegiate Athletic Assn. v. Board of Regents of Univ. of Okla.*, 468 U.S. 85, 98 (1984)); *Standard Oil Co. of N. J. v. United States*, 221 U.S. 1, 59–62 (1911); 2 P. Areeda & H. Hovenkamp, Antitrust Law ¶ 320b, p. 49 (1995). Yet certain kinds of agreements will so often prove so harmful to competition and so rarely prove justified that the antitrust laws do not require proof that an agreement of that kind is, in fact, anticompetitive in the particular circumstances. See *State Oil Co. v. Khan*, 522 U.S. 3, 10 (1997); *Northwest Wholesale Stationers, Inc. v. Pacific Stationery & Printing Co.*, 472 U.S. 284, 289–290 (1985); *supra* 2 Areeda & Hovenkamp, ¶ 320b, at 49–52. An agreement of such a kind is unlawful *per se*. *See, e.g., United States v. Socony–Vacuum Oil Co.*, 310 U.S. 150, 218 (1940) (finding horizontal price-fixing agreement *per se* illegal); *Dr. Miles Medical Co. v. John D. Park & Sons Co.*, 220 U.S. 373, 408 (1911) (finding vertical price-fixing agreement *per se* illegal); *Palmer v. BRG of Ga., Inc.*, 498 U.S. 46, 49–50 (1990) (per curiam) (finding horizontal market division *per se* illegal).

The Court has found the *per se* rule applicable in certain group boycott cases. Thus, in *Fashion Originators' Guild of America, Inc. v. FTC*, 312 U.S. 457 (1941), this Court considered a group boycott created by an agreement among a group of clothing designers, manufacturers, suppliers, and retailers. The defendant designers, manufacturers, and suppliers had promised not to sell their clothes to retailers who bought clothes from competing manufacturers and suppliers. The defendants wanted to present evidence that would show their agreement was justified because the boycotted competitors used "pira[ted]" fashion designs. But the Court wrote that "it was not error to refuse to hear the evidence offered"—evidence that the agreement was reasonable and necessary to "protect . . . against the devastating evils" of design pirating—for that evidence "is no more material than would be the reasonableness of the prices fixed" by a price-fixing agreement.

In *Klor's* the Court also applied the *per se* rule. The Court considered a boycott created when a retail store, Broadway–Hale, and 10 household appliance manufacturers and their distributors agreed that the distributors would not sell, or would sell only at discriminatory prices, household appliances to Broadway–Hale's small, nearby competitor, namely, Klor's. 359 U.S. at 208–209. The defendants had submitted undisputed evidence that their agreement hurt only one competitor (Klor's) and that so many other nearby appliance-selling competitors remained that competition in the marketplace continued to thrive. *Id.* at 209–210. The Court held that this evidence was beside the point. The conspiracy was "not to be tolerated merely because the victim is just one merchant." The Court thereby inferred injury to the competitive process itself from the nature of the boycott agreement. And it forbade, as a matter of law, a defense based upon a claim that only one small firm, not competition itself, had suffered injury.

The case before us involves *Klor's*. The Second Circuit did not forbid the defendants to introduce evidence of "justification." To the contrary, it invited the defendants to do so, for it said that the *"per se rule"* would apply only if no "pro-competitive justification" were to be found. 93 F.3d at 1061; cf. 7 P. Areeda & H. Hovenkamp, Antitrust Law ¶ 1510, p. 416 (1986) ("Boycotts are said to be unlawful *per se* but justifications are routinely considered in defining the forbidden category"). Thus, the specific legal question before us is whether an antitrust court considering an agreement by a buyer to purchase goods or services from one supplier rather than another should (after examining the buyer's reasons or justifications) apply the *per se* rule if it finds no legitimate business reason for that purchasing decision. We conclude no boycott-related *per se* rule applies and that the plaintiff here must allege and prove harm, not just to a single competitor, but to the competitive process, *i.e.*, to competition itself.

Our conclusion rests in large part upon precedent, for precedent limits the *per se* rule in the boycott context to cases involving horizontal agreements among direct competitors. The agreement in *Fashion Originators' Guild* involved what may be called a group boycott in the strongest sense: A group of competitors threatened to withhold business from third parties unless those third parties would help them injure their directly competing rivals. Although *Klor's* involved a threat made by a *single* powerful firm, it also involved a horizontal agreement among those threatened, namely, the appliance suppliers, to hurt a competitor of the retailer who made the threat. See 359 U.S. at 208–209; see also P. Areeda & L. Kaplow, Antitrust Analysis: Problems, Text, and Cases 333 (5th ed. 1997) (defining paradigmatic boycott as "collective action among a group of competitors that may inhibit the competitive vitality of rivals"); 11 H. Hovenkamp, Antitrust Law ¶ 1901e, pp. 189–190 (1998). This Court emphasized in *Klor's* that the agreement at issue was

> "not a case of a single trader refusing to deal with another, nor even of a manufacturer and a dealer agreeing to an exclusive distributorship. Alleged in this complaint is a wide combination consisting of manufacturers, distributors and a retailer." 359 U.S. at 212–213 (footnote omitted).

This Court subsequently pointed out specifically that *Klor's* was a case involving not simply a "vertical" agreement between supplier and customer, but a case that also involved a "horizontal" agreement among competitors. See Business Electronics, 485 U.S. at 734. And in doing so, the Court held that a "vertical restraint is not illegal *per se* unless it includes some agreement on price or price levels." This precedent makes the *per se* rule inapplicable, for the case before us concerns only a vertical agreement and a vertical restraint, a restraint that takes the form of depriving a supplier of a potential customer. . . .

Nor have we found any special feature of this case that could distinguish it from the precedent we have just discussed. We concede Discon's claim that the petitioners' behavior hurt consumers by raising telephone service rates. But that consumer injury naturally flowed not so much from a less competitive market for removal services, as from the exercise of market power that is *lawfully* in the hands of a monopolist, namely, New

York Telephone, combined with a deception worked upon the regulatory agency that prevented the agency from controlling New York Telephone's exercise of its monopoly power.

To apply the *per se* rule here—where the buyer's decision, though not made for competitive reasons, composes part of a regulatory fraud—would transform cases involving business behavior that is improper for various reasons, say, cases involving nepotism or personal pique, into treble-damages antitrust cases. And that *per se* rule would discourage firms from changing suppliers—even where the competitive process itself does not suffer harm. . . .

The freedom to switch suppliers lies close to the heart of the competitive process that the antitrust laws seek to encourage. Cf. *Standard Oil*, 221 U.S., at 62 (noting "the freedom of the individual right to contract when not unduly or improperly exercised [is] the most efficient means for the prevention of monopoly"). At the same time, other laws, for example, "unfair competition" laws, business tort laws, or regulatory laws, provide remedies for various "competitive practices thought to be offensive to proper standards of business morality." 3 P. Areeda & H. Hovenkamp, Antitrust Law ¶ 651d, p. 78 (1996). Thus, this Court has refused to apply *per se* reasoning in cases involving that kind of activity. See *Brooke Group Ltd. v. Brown & Williamson Tobacco Corp.*, 509 U.S. 209, 225 (1993) ("Even an act of pure malice by one business competitor against another does not, without more, state a claim under the federal antitrust laws"); 3 Areeda & Hovenkamp, *supra*, ¶ 651d, at 80 ("[I]n the presence of substantial market power, some kinds of tortious behavior could anticompetitively create or sustain a monopoly, [but] it is wrong categorically to condemn such practices . . . or categorically to excuse them").

Discon points to another special feature of its complaint, namely, its claim that Materiel Enterprises hoped to drive Discon from the market lest Discon reveal its behavior to New York Telephone or to the relevant regulatory agency. That hope, says Discon, amounts to a special anticompetitive motive.

We do not see how the presence of this special motive, however, could make a significant difference. That motive does not turn Materiel Enterprises' actions into a "boycott" within the meaning of this Court's precedents. Nor, for that matter, do we understand how Discon believes the motive affected Materiel Enterprises' behavior. Why would Discon's demise have made Discon's employees less likely, rather than more likely, to report the overcharge/rebate scheme to telephone regulators? Regardless, a *per se* rule that would turn upon a showing that a defendant not only knew about but also hoped for a firm's demise would create a legal distinction—between corporate knowledge and corporate motive—that does not necessarily correspond to behavioral differences and which would be difficult to prove, making the resolution of already complex antitrust cases yet more difficult. We cannot find a convincing reason why the presence of this special motive should lead to the application of the *per se* rule.

Finally, we shall consider an argument that is related tangentially to Discon's *per se* claims. The complaint alleges that New York Telephone (through Materiel Enterprises) was the largest buyer of removal services in New York State, and that only AT&T Technologies competed for New York Telephone's business. We might ask whether these accompanying allegations are sufficient to warrant application of a *Klor's*-type presumption of consequent harm to the competitive process itself.

We believe that these allegations do not do so, for, as we have said, antitrust law does not permit the application of the *per se* rule in the boycott context in the absence of a horizontal agreement. (Though in other contexts, say, vertical price fixing, conduct may fall within the scope of a *per se* rule not at issue here. *See, e.g., Dr. Miles Medical Co.*, 220 U.S. at 408.) The complaint itself explains why any such presumption would be particularly inappropriate here, for it suggests the presence of other potential or actual competitors, which fact, in the circumstances, could argue against the likelihood of anticompetitive harm. The complaint says, for example, that New York Telephone itself was a potential competitor in that New York Telephone considered removing its equipment by itself, and in fact did perform a few jobs itself. The complaint also suggests that other nearby small local telephone companies needing removal services must have worked out some way to supply them. The complaint's description of the removal business suggests that entry was easy, perhaps to the point where other firms, employing workers who knew how to remove a switch and sell it for scrap, might have entered that business almost at will. To that extent, the complaint suggests other actual or potential competitors might have provided roughly similar checks upon "equipment removal" prices and services with or without Discon. At the least, the complaint provides no sound basis for assuming the contrary. Its simple allegation of harm to Discon does not automatically show injury to competition.

III

The Court of Appeals also upheld the complaint's charge of a conspiracy to monopolize in violation of § 2 of the Sherman Act. It did so, however, on the understanding that the conspiracy in question consisted of the very same purchasing practices that we have previously discussed. Unless those agreements harmed the competitive process, they did not amount to a conspiracy to monopolize. We do not see, on the basis of the facts alleged, how Discon could succeed on this claim without prevailing on its § 1 claim. . . . Given our conclusion that Discon has not alleged a § 1 *per se* violation, we think it prudent to vacate this portion of the Court of Appeals' decision and allow the court to reconsider its finding of a § 2 claim.

IV

Petitioners ask us to reach beyond the *"per se"* issues and to hold that Discon's complaint does not allege anywhere that their purchasing decisions harmed the competitive process itself and, for this reason, it should be dismissed. They note that Discon has not pointed to any paragraph of the complaint that alleges harm to the competitive process. This matter, however, lies outside the questions presented for certiorari. Those questions were limited to the application of the *per se* rule. For that reason, we believe petitioners cannot raise that argument in this Court.

V

For these reasons, the judgment of the Court of Appeals is vacated, and the case is remanded for further proceedings consistent with this opinion.

Toys "R" Us, Inc. v. Federal Trade Commission

United States Court of Appeals, Seventh Circuit, 2000.
221 F.3d 928.

[Reprinted p. 484, *infra*.]

NOTES AND QUESTIONS

1. *Categorizing group refusals.* Does *Klor's* recognize the possibility that some boycotts or group refusals to deal might not fall within the illegal *per se* approach taken in the opinion? Would different facts have compelled application of the rule of reason? What if the appliance manufacturers had a convincing rationale for refusing to deal with Klor's, such as a collective complaint that Klor's discount prices were undercutting Broadway–Hale's ability to maintain an extensive service department to the detriment of the manufacturers' reputations?

2. *Type of restrictive agreement.* Was the refusal to deal in *Klor's* horizontal, vertical, or both? If it was both, should that make a difference? Compare Business Electronics Corp. v. Sharp Electronics Corp., 485 U.S. 717 (1988), Chapter 7, *infra* p. 697. How does *NYNEX* affect your answer to this question?

3. *Procedural posture and market power.* Is it important that *Klor's* came up on a motion to dismiss, and hence that the allegations of the complaint—particularly that the refusal to sell was instigated by Broadway–Hale to impair Klor's ability to compete—were not disputed by defendants? Consider this question again after reading *Indiana Federation of Dentists*, p. 345, *infra*.

4. *Problems applying* Klor's. Between *Klor's* and *Northwest Stationers,* lower courts struggled mightily trying to decide what conduct to characterize as a "group boycott" and how far the *Klor's per se* ruling should extend. The problem they encountered was that the phrases "concerted refusal to deal" or "boycott" cover an extremely wide range of business behavior. Some courts simply applied a *per se* rule without extended discussion of its potential reach. *See, e.g.,* Com–Tel Inc. v. DuKane Corp., 669 F.2d 404 (6th Cir. 1982); Williams v. St. Joseph Hospital, 629 F.2d 448, 452 (7th Cir. 1980).

Other courts looked for alternative formulations. In Larry V. Muko, Inc. v. Southwestern Pennsylvania Bldg. & Constr. Trades Council, 670 F.2d 421, 429–31 (3d Cir. 1982), two groups of labor unions and the corporation that operated Long John Silver's fast-food restaurants were charged with conspiring to award construction contracts for new Silver's restaurants in the Pittsburgh area only to union contractors. Plaintiff, a general contractor, had built several restaurants for Silver's in the past and claimed that the arrangement was a boycott in violation of Section 1. The jury found, however, that the arrangement was not an unreasonable restraint of trade. Plaintiff appealed on grounds, *inter alia,* that a *per se* rule should have applied.

Relying on academic commentary and the Supreme Court's more recent decisions, the court affirmed the application of the rule of reason after it limited the boycotts that amounted to *per se* violations to a "core group." The core group included three situations: (1) horizontal combinations to exclude direct competitors, as in *Associated Press*; (2) vertical combinations, as in *Klor's*; and, (3) coercive combinations, as in *FOGA*. Noting that the claim did not fall comfortably into any of those core situations, the court concluded that a rule of reason applied. Silver's goal was not to affect Muko's business adversely, but rather to prevent labor strife; the labor organization wanted to ensure payment of the prevailing union wage to local construction workers. The Third Circuit concluded that the trial court correctly charged the jury under a rule of reason and that the jury was justified in finding no antitrust violation.

[handwritten margin note: 3 per se illegal can. refusals to deal]

5.   *Boycotts and Professional Sports.* Because professional sports leagues traditionally have been composed of a number of different entities, they often find their rules challenged under a group boycott theory. Their first line of defense typically has been to try to portray themselves as a single entity, rather than a group of competing firms, but those efforts have met with little success. *See* National Hockey League Players Ass'n v. Plymouth Whalers Hockey Club, 419 F.3d 462 (6th Cir. 2005); *compare* Chicago Prof'l Sports Ltd. v. National Basketball Ass'n, 95 F.3d 593 (7th Cir. 1996). The courts have recognized, however, that some collaboration must be accepted within leagues. The question is how much collaboration is too much. The Supreme Court's decision in *NCAA, supra,* Chapter 4, p. 230, makes it clear that at least some horizontal restraints on competition within sports leagues will not be treated under the *per se* rule.

Many associations of professional athletic teams use a standard player contract containing provisions that effectively prohibit a player from negotiating freely for his services with other teams in the league. Sometimes there is an absolute ban on negotiations without the consent of the team holding the contract; more frequently in recent years, the team that acquires the player's contract must "compensate" the original team for the loss of services. In addition, some of these associations use a player selection system, or "draft," in which negotiating rights to graduating college players are allocated among the clubs. Finally, most leagues have bylaws regulating movement of franchises from city to city, and controlling admission to the league of new franchises. Should professional athletes be deprived of the opportunity to take advantage of the kind of lively bidding for services that occurs with respect to outstanding scientists, film stars, or corporate vice-presidents? Should communities be denied the opportunity to compete for sports franchises, as they do for other industrial enterprises?

The attempt to describe what restrictions are reasonable under the special circumstances of sports competition has produced some perplexing questions and outcomes in the courts. In Mid–South Grizzlies v. National Football League, 720 F.2d 772 (3d Cir. 1983), a former member of the defunct World Football League (WFL) sued the National Football League (NFL) and its president for refusal to grant a franchise for a team in Memphis, Tennessee. The Grizzlies were rejected pursuant to a league rule, common in professional sports, that requires new franchises to be approved by at least three-fourths of existing members. Plaintiff charged that the exclusion was an illegal boycott under Section 1, motivated by a desire to punish the Grizzlies for participating in the WFL, which had challenged the NFL. The Third Circuit affirmed a grant of summary judgment, noting that an additional franchise would not enhance competition since the Memphis team would have a monopoly (and would compete with no other NFL team) in its home territory, and might actually diminish competition by depriving a future league that might challenge the NFL monopoly of an attractive site for a franchise.

In Los Angeles Mem'l Coliseum Comm'n v. NFL, 726 F.2d 1381 (9th Cir. 1984), a court of appeals was faced with another antitrust challenge to the three-fourths rule concerning franchise changes. The Oakland Raiders, an established franchise in the NFL, was denied permission by League members to move from Oakland to Los Angeles. The Los Angeles stadium sued, claiming that the League rule was a violation of Section 1 of the Sherman Act. The court of appeals sustained a jury verdict in favor of plaintiffs. It accepted at the outset the now-conventional approach that rule of reason treatment was justified because of the special economic and competitive attributes of league sports, but it then noted that the three-fourths rule had an anticompetitive effect insofar as it permitted the maintenance of local monopolies and prevented competition among stadia for tenants. In response to NFL arguments that the rule and the conditional exclusivity it provided helped induce teams to invest in football franchises, preserve traditional rivalries between cities, and satisfy TV viewers by ensuring a wide geographic dispersion of teams, the Ninth Circuit noted that the availability of less restrictive alternatives—for example, guidelines to NFL members about voting procedures and standards—may have led the jury justifiably to find a violation. Can you reconcile these two decisions? On what theory?

Other examples of cases involving application of the antitrust laws to sports competition include Law v. NCAA, 134 F.3d 1010 (10th Cir. 1998) (upholding summary judgment and an injunction against the NCAA's rule limiting compensation for certain Division I entry-level coaches to $16,000 per year; using "quick look" rule of reason analysis); Chicago Prof'l Sports, Ltd. P'ship v. National Basketball Ass'n, 961 F.2d 667 (7th Cir. 1992) (NBA's rule of limiting superstation broadcasts to no more than 20 per season held illegal under a rule of reason analysis); Brenner v. World Boxing Council, 675 F.2d 445 (2d Cir. 1982), *cert. denied*, 459 U.S. 835 (1982) (suspension of prize fight promoter not *per se* illegal); Smith v. Pro Football, Inc., 593 F.2d 1173, 1178 (D.C. Cir. 1978) (player draft system declared illegal under rule of reason); Mackey v. NFL, 543 F.2d 606, 618–20 (8th Cir. 1976), *cert. dismissed*, 434 U.S. 801 (1977) ("Rozelle Rule," which essentially provided that when a player's contract with a team expired and he signed with a different club the signing club must compensate that player's former team, held under a rule of reason analysis to be in violation of § 1 of the Sherman Act). See also Toscano v. Professional Golfers Ass'n, 258 F.3d 978 (9th Cir. 2001) (summary judgment affirmed based on failure to show that local sponsor contracts essentially prohibiting non-PGA tour play were a concerted restraint of trade between sponsors and PGA); United States Trotting Ass'n v. Chicago Downs Ass'n, 665 F.2d 781 (7th Cir. 1981) (en banc) (USTA rules disciplining members who race horses at non-Association meets upheld under rule of reason, because of "need for self-regulation of sporting activities" and as necessary to avoid "free ride" otherwise enjoyed by outsiders benefiting from Association's regulatory activities); North Am. Soccer League v. NFL, 670 F.2d 1249 (2d Cir. 1982) (proposed NFL by-law to prohibit club owners from acquiring any other professional sports league team unreasonable restraint, because it unnecessarily deprives NASL teams of access to "sports capital and skill," thus limiting their ability to compete with NFL teams for fans and TV revenue).

Has *Professional Engineers, supra* p. 211, made it more difficult to accord organized sports special antitrust treatment where the principal justification for the rule is noneconomic? *See Law v. NCAA, supra*; Neeld v. National Hockey League, 594 F.2d 1297, 1300 (9th Cir. 1979) (bylaw barring persons with one eye from playing professional hockey upheld on the basis of safety considerations).

6. *Baseball.* Baseball has always been different. *See* 15 U.S.C. § 26b (describing the application of the antitrust laws to professional major league baseball). The Supreme Court has adhered to a 1922 holding, despite all later developments in both antitrust and constitutional law, that baseball is not "trade or commerce" within the meaning of the Sherman Act. *See* Federal Baseball Club of Baltimore, Inc. v. National League of Prof'l Base Ball Clubs, 259 U.S. 200 (1922); Toolson v. New York Yankees, Inc., 346 U.S. 356 (1953); Flood v. Kuhn, 407 U.S. 258 (1972). Other sports do not benefit from any comparable "exemption" from the antitrust laws. *See* Radovich v. NFL, 352 U.S. 445 (1957). The scope of baseball's exemption is, however, unclear. *Compare* Major League Baseball v. Crist, 331 F.3d 1177, 1186–87 (11th Cir. 2003) (noting hesitancy to read the "business of baseball" exemption broadly, "especially since the Supreme Court has called the exemption an 'aberration'") *with* Charles O. Finley & Co. v. Kuhn, 569 F.2d 527, 541 (7th Cir. 1978) (the antitrust exemption extends to "the business of baseball, not any particular facet of that business").

7. *Non-commercial Boycotts.* The Supreme Court noted in *Klor's* that the Sherman Act "is aimed primarily at combinations having commercial objectives and is applied only to a very limited extent to organizations ... which normally have other objectives." The current status, scope, and application of this principle present difficult problems. In Marjorie Webster Junior College v. Middle States Ass'n of Colleges & Secondary Schools, 432 F.2d 650 (D.C. Cir. 1970), *cert. denied*, 400 U.S. 965, the D.C. Circuit noted that incidental restraints of trade in the noncommercial aspects of a profession are outside the scope of the antitrust laws. *Id.* at 654. *See also* NAACP v. Claiborne Hardware Co., 458 U.S. 886 (1982) (holding that NAACP could not be held liable for business losses that resulted from a boycott organized by the NAACP against white merchants, to the extent that the losses arose from nonviolent, protected expressive activity).

The Middle States Association, a nonprofit corporation whose principal business was accrediting member schools, refused to accredit Marjorie Webster since it considered only nonprofit institutions for accreditation, and Marjorie Webster was proprietary. The court held that the process of accreditation by a nonprofit educational corporation was an activity "distinct from the sphere of commerce"; instead it was one going to the "heart of the concept of education itself." The court tempered its finding that the antitrust laws are not applicable to noncommercial associations by noting that "the extent to which deference is due the professional judgment of the association will vary both with the subject matter at issue and with the degree of harm resulting from the association's action." *Id.* at 655–56. The court's conclusion that Middle States Association had not committed an antitrust violation rested in part on Marjorie Webster's ability to operate successfully for over 20 years without accreditation, and the possibility of setting up an accrediting association for proprietary schools. The court stressed that the situation is not analogous to that of an individual denied membership in or certification by a professional society, who might suffer greater injury, and who would lack the ability to set up an alternative group. *See* Massachusetts School of Law at Andover, Inc. v. American Bar Ass'n, 855 F.Supp. 108 (E.D. Pa. 1994); *compare* United States v. Brown Univ., 5 F.3d 658 (3d Cir. 1993), Chapter 4, *supra* p. 246.

8. *Commercial boycotts without clear commercial motive.* Some of the most difficult problems in the refusal-to-deal area arise where a commercial boycott is used to coerce or induce others to adopt certain lines of conduct for reasons that do not relate directly to commercial considerations. Consider whether a Section 1 violation should be found in the following situations, first under the rule announced in *Klor's,* and then under *NYNEX:*

(a) A union and its affiliates refuse to load ships trading with the Soviet Union as a means of discouraging such trade. See Allied Int'l, Inc. v. International Longshoremen's Ass'n, AFL–CIO, 640 F.2d 1368 (1st Cir. 1981);

(b) A patriotic organization attempts to persuade retail distributors not to handle publications that oppose specific aspects of American foreign policy. See Council of Def. of State of New Mexico v. International Magazine Co., 267 F. 390 (8th Cir. 1920);

(c) Organizations in a southern city agree that their members will not patronize stores within the city until the stores abandon policies of refusing to hire blacks. See Henry v. First Nat'l Bank of Clarksdale, 595 F.2d 291 (5th Cir. 1979), *cert. denied*, 444 U.S. 1074 (1980);

(d) A women's group urges organizations holding conventions to boycott states that have not ratified the Equal Rights Amendment. *See* Missouri v. National Org. for Women, 620 F.2d 1301 (8th Cir. 1980).

(e) Real estate brokers in all-white communities agree not to rent homes to blacks. *See* Bratcher v. Akron Area Board of Realtors, 381 F.2d 723 (6th Cir. 1967);

(f) A religious organization exhorts its members, under threat of punishment in an afterlife, to shun certain salacious books and movies. See Konecky v. Jewish Press, 288 F. 179 (8th Cir. 1923).

Can it be said that the activities described above are strictly noncommercial? May questions of economics be so inextricably interwoven with social justice as to make inadvisable any effort to restrict the group boycott rule to purely economic phenomena? Did Congress in 1890 have in mind that the Sherman Act might be applied in situations like those described above? Is that relevant? Of what relevance are First Amendment considerations? *See* NAACP v. Claiborne Hardware Co., 458 U.S. 886 (1982).

Consider Hamilton Chapter of Alpha Delta Phi, Inc. v. Hamilton College, 128 F.3d 59 (2d Cir. 1997). Four Hamilton College fraternities challenged the College's new policy forcing all students to live in college-owned housing for their entire time in college. The College's stated purpose for the policy was to eliminate the disparity in social opportunities created by fraternities, which in turn was allegedly causing the most talented prospective female students to seek education elsewhere. The fraternities alleged that the college was motivated by three commercial purposes: (1) forcing all students to purchase residential services from Hamilton; (2) allowing Hamilton to raise its prices for such services and (3) attempting to purchase the fraternity houses to below-market prices. The Second Circuit found that these allegations were enough to require further proceedings. It declined, however, to reach the question whether a failure to prove a commercial motive would be fatal to plaintiff's claim.

9. *Actual injury and proof of alternative.* In private antitrust suits, a plaintiff must prove actual injury in order to recover damages. In Malcolm v. Marathon Oil Co., 642 F.2d 845 (5th Cir. 1981), a discount gasoline retailer who went out of business after his supplies were cut off sued his suppliers alleging Section 1

violations. The lower court directed a verdict against Malcolm since he had not shown that his failure was caused by the refusal to deal. The defendants, Marathon and four other gasoline wholesalers, argued that since Malcolm had failed to contact all alternate suppliers, their refusal had not caused his demise. The court of appeals reversed the directed verdict, noting that lost business damages *should not* be recoverable for bypassing an "obviously adequate alternative supplier," but on the other hand holding that a plaintiff complaining about a refusal to deal was not required to demonstrate that no alternative supply was available. *Id.* at 863 (emphasis added). *But cf.* Elder–Beerman Stores Corp. v. Federated Dep't Stores, Inc., 459 F.2d 138 (6th Cir. 1972). In the latter case, after holding that Beerman's allegation of a conspiracy between his major competitor and several manufacturers to cut him off from several brand name products was not supported by the evidence, the Sixth Circuit noted that even if there was a conspiracy, Beerman was not entitled to damages because he had not shown the lack of "alternative comparable substitutes" for the defendants' products. *Id.* at 148.

10. *Unilateral versus group boycott.* Does *NYNEX* suggest that the rule respecting individual firm boycotts is analytically different from the group boycott rule, or is the Supreme Court developing a general jurisprudence with respect to this business practice? After *NYNEX*, can there ever be a *per se* illegal group boycott in the absence of a proven horizontal conspiracy at one of the relevant levels of the market?

11. *Anticompetitive element requirement?* A group refusal to deal, even if it is injurious to the plaintiff, may not be sufficient to sustain an antitrust claim. In Levine v. Central Florida Medical Affiliates, 72 F.3d 1538 (11th Cir. 1996), the court sustained summary judgment for the defendants. Although the plaintiff-physician's allegations were enough to create an issue of fact on the question whether a concerted refusal to deal had occurred, the district court ruled against the plaintiff "because he had failed to establish that his suspension resulted in any antitrust injury." The Eleventh Circuit affirmed, but not on antitrust injury grounds. It found that there was no threat to competition from the alleged refusal to deal, and thus that no violation of the antitrust laws could be proven. Is this result consistent with *Klor's*?

12. *Group standards and certification.* As we will see, the Supreme Court in 1985 and 1986 addressed the problem of general chaos in the lower courts in boycott decisions in its opinions in *Northwest Stationers* (*infra* p. 337) and *Indiana Federation of Dentists* (*infra* p. 345). Before turning to those two cases, we need to examine another line of "boycott" cases—those in which trade associations and other private groups establish standards or provide certification which may result directly or indirectly in the exclusion of competitors' products from the market. In Radiant Burners, Inc. v. Peoples Gas Light & Coke Co., 364 U.S. 656 (1961), the Court addressed Radiant Burners' challenge to an association of gas product manufacturers and utilities standard setting. Due to the association's members, Radiant Burners alleged that failure to receive the association's seal of approval effectively excluded their products from the market. The Court held that the alleged arbitrary standards and the exclusion from the market for failure to meet the standards sufficiently stated a Section 1 claim.

In the following case, by contrast, the D.C. Circuit reviewed an FTC finding that a computer hardware firm violated Sections 1 by its conduct in relation to the standard setting organization.

Rambus Inc. v. FTC

United States Court of Appeals for the District of Columbia, 2008.
522 F.3d 456.

■ WILLIAMS, SENIOR CIRCUIT JUDGE, Rambus Inc. develops computer memory technologies, secures intellectual property rights over them, and then licenses them to manufacturers in exchange for royalty payments. In 1990, Rambus's founders filed a patent application claiming the invention of a faster architecture for dynamic random access memory ("DRAM"). In recent years, Rambus has asserted that patents issued to protect its invention cover four technologies that a private standard-setting organization ("SSO") included in DRAM industry standards.

Before an SSO adopts a standard, there is often vigorous competition among different technologies for incorporation into that standard. After standardization, however, the dynamic typically shifts, as industry members begin adhering to the standard and the standardized features start to dominate. In this case, 90% of DRAM production is compliant with the standards at issue, and therefore the technologies adopted in those standards—including those over which Rambus claims patent rights—enjoy a similar level of dominance over their alternatives.

After lengthy proceedings, the Federal Trade Commission determined that Rambus, while participating in the standard-setting process, deceptively failed to disclose to the SSO the patent interests it held in four technologies that were standardized. Those interests ranged from issued patents, to pending patent applications, to plans to amend those patent applications to add new claims; Rambus's patent rights in all these interests are said to be sufficiently connected to the invention described in Rambus's original 1990 application that its rights would relate back to its date. Finding this conduct monopolistic and in violation of § 2 of the Sherman Act, 15 U.S.C. § 2, the Commission went on to hold that Rambus had engaged in an unfair method of competition and unfair or deceptive acts or practices prohibited by § 5(a) of the Federal Trade Commission Act ("FTC Act"), *id.* § 45(a).

Rambus petitions for review. We grant the petition, holding that the Commission failed to sustain its allegation of monopolization. Its factual conclusion was that Rambus's alleged deception enabled it *either* to acquire a monopoly through the standardization of its patented technologies rather than possible alternatives, *or* to avoid limits on its patent licensing fees that the SSO would have imposed as part of its normal process of standardizing patented technologies. But the latter—deceit merely enabling a monopolist to charge higher prices than it otherwise could have charged—would not in itself constitute monopolization. We also address whether there is substantial evidence that Rambus engaged in deceptive conduct at all, and express our serious concerns about the sufficiency of the evidence on two particular points.

* * *

During the early 1990s, the computer hardware industry faced a "memory bottleneck": the development of faster memory lagged behind the development of faster central processing units, and this risked limiting future gains in overall computer performance. To address this problem, Michael Farmwald and Mark Horowitz began collaborating during the late 1980s and invented a higher-performance DRAM architecture. Together, they founded Rambus in March 1990 and filed Patent Application No. 07/510,898 ("the '898 application") on April 18, 1990.

While Rambus was developing a patent portfolio based on its founders' inventions, the computer memory industry was at work standardizing DRAM technologies. The locus of those efforts was the Joint Electron Device Engineering Council ("JEDEC")—then an "activity" of what is now called the Electronics Industries Alliance ("EIA") and, since 2000, a trade association affiliated with EIA and known as the JEDEC Solid State Technology Association. Any company involved in the solid state products industry could join JEDEC by submitting an application and paying annual dues, and members could receive JEDEC mailings, participate in JEDEC committees, and vote on pending matters.

One JEDEC committee, JC 42.3, developed standards for computer memory products. Rambus attended its first JC 42.3 meeting as a guest in December 1991 and began formally participating when it joined JEDEC in February 1992. At the time, JC 42.3 was at work on what became JEDEC's synchronous DRAM ("SDRAM") standard. The committee voted to approve the completed standard in March 1993, and JEDEC's governing body gave its final approval on May 24, 1993. The SDRAM standard includes two of the four technologies over which Rambus asserts patent rights—programmable CAS latency and programmable burst length.

Despite SDRAM's standardization, its manufacture increased very slowly and asynchronous DRAM continued to dominate the computer memory market, so JC 42.3 began to consider a number of possible responses—among them specifications it could include in a next-generation SDRAM standard. As part of that process, JC 42.3 members received a survey ballot in October 1995 soliciting their opinions on features of an advanced SDRAM—which ultimately emerged as the double data rate ("DDR") SDRAM standard. Among the features voted on were the other two technologies at issue here: on-chip phase lock and delay lock loops ("on-chip PLL/DLL") and dual-edge clocking. The Committee tallied and discussed the survey results at its December 1995 meeting, which was Rambus's last as a JEDEC member. Rambus formally withdrew from JEDEC by letter dated June 17, 1996, saying (among other things) that the terms on which it proposed to license its proprietary technology "may not be consistent with the terms set by standards bodies, including JEDEC."

JC 42.3's work continued after Rambus's departure. In March 1998 the committee adopted the DDR SDRAM standard, and the JEDEC Board of Directors approved it in 1999. This standard retained SDRAM features including programmable CAS latency and programmable burst length, and it added on-chip PLL/DLL and dual-edge clocking; DDR SDRAM, therefore, included all four of the technologies at issue here.

Starting in 1999, Rambus informed major DRAM and chipset manufacturers that it held patent rights over technologies included in JEDEC's SDRAM and DDR SDRAM standards, and that the continued manufacture, sale, or use of products compliant with those standards infringed its rights. It invited the manufacturers to resolve the alleged infringement through licensing negotiations. A number of manufacturers agreed to licenses, see Opinion of the Commission ("Liability Op."); others did not, and litigation ensued.

On June 18, 2002, the Federal Trade Commission filed a complaint under § 5(b) of the FTC Act, 15 U.S.C. § 45(b), charging that Rambus engaged in unfair methods of competition and unfair or deceptive acts or practices in violation of the Act, see *id.* § 45(a). Specifically, the Commission alleged that Rambus breached JEDEC policies requiring it to disclose patent interests related to standardization efforts and that the disclosures it did make were misleading. By this deceptive conduct, it said, Rambus unlawfully monopolized four technology markets in which its patented technologies compete with alternative innovations to address technical issues relating to DRAM design-markets for latency, burst length, data acceleration, and clock synchronization technologies.

Proceedings began before an administrative law judge, who in due course dismissed the Complaint in its entirety. He concluded that Rambus did not impermissibly withhold material information about its intellectual property, and that, in any event, there was insufficient evidence that, if Rambus had disclosed all the information allegedly required of it, JEDEC would have standardized an alternative technology.

Complaint Counsel appealed the ALJ's Initial Decision to the Commission, which reopened the record to receive additional evidence and did its own plenary review. On July 31, 2006 the Commission vacated the ALJ's decision and set aside his findings of fact and conclusions of law. The Commission found that while JEDEC's patent disclosure policies were "not a model of clarity," members expected one another to disclose patents and patent applications that were relevant to technologies being considered for standardization, *plus* (though the Commission was far less clear on these latter items) planned amendments to pending applications or "anything they're working on that they potentially wanted to protect with patents down the road." Based on this interpretation of JEDEC's disclosure requirements, the Commission held that Rambus willfully and intentionally engaged in misrepresentations, omissions, and other practices that misled JEDEC members about intellectual property information "highly material" to the standard-setting process.

The Commission focused entirely on the allegation of monopolization. In particular, the Commission held that the evidence and inferences from Rambus's purpose demonstrated that "but for Rambus's deceptive course of conduct, JEDEC either would have excluded Rambus's patented technologies from the JEDEC DRAM standards, or would have demanded RAND assurances [*i.e.,* assurances of 'reasonable and nondiscriminatory' license fees], with an opportunity for *ex ante* licensing negotiations." [Liability Op.] at 74. Rejecting Rambus's argument that factors other than JEDEC's standards allowed Rambus's technologies to dominate their respective markets, the Commission concluded that Rambus's deception of JEDEC "significantly contributed to its acquisition of monopoly power," *id.* at 118.

After additional briefing by the parties, the Commission rendered a separate remedial opinion and final order. It held that it had the authority in principle to order compulsory licensing, but that remedies beyond injunctions against future anticompetitive conduct would require stronger proof that they were necessary to restore competitive conditions. Applying that more demanding burden to Complaint Counsel's claims for relief, the Commission refused to compel Rambus to license its relevant patents royalty-free because there was insufficient evidence that "absent Rambus's deception" JEDEC would have standardized non-proprietary technologies instead of Rambus's; thus, Complaint Counsel had failed to show that such a remedy was "necessary to restore competition that would have existed in the 'but for' world." Instead, the Commission decided to compel licensing at "reasonable royalty rates," which it calculated based on what it believed would have resulted from negotiations between Rambus and manufacturers before JEDEC committed to the standards. The Commission's order limits Rambus's royalties for three years to 0.25% for JEDEC-compliant SDRAM and 0.5% for JEDEC-compliant DDR SDRAM (with double those royalties for certain JEDEC-compliant, non-DRAM products); after those three years, it forbids any royalty collection.

Rambus moved for reconsideration, and the Commission denied the motion in relevant part on April 27, 2007. Rambus timely petitioned for our review of both the Commission's Final Order and its Denial of Reconsideration, see 15 U.S.C. § 45(c), and we consolidated those petitions.

Rambus challenges the Commission's determination that it engaged in unlawful monopolization—and thereby violated § 5 of the FTC Act—on a variety of grounds, of which two are most prominent. First, it argues that the Commission erred in finding that it violated any JEDEC patent disclosure rules and thus that it breached any antitrust duty to provide information to its rivals. Second, it asserts that even if its nondisclosure contravened JEDEC's policies, the Commission found the consequences of such nondisclosure only in the alternative: that it prevented JEDEC *either* from adopting a non-proprietary standard, *or* from extracting a RAND commitment from Rambus when standardizing its technology. As the latter would not involve an antitrust violation, says Rambus, there is an insufficient basis for liability.

We find the second of these arguments to be persuasive, and conclude that the Commission failed to demonstrate that Rambus's conduct was exclusionary under settled principles of antitrust law. Given that conclusion, we need not dwell very long on the substantiality of the evidence, which we address only to express our serious concerns about the breadth the Commission ascribed to JEDEC's disclosure policies and their relation to what Rambus did or did not disclose.

* * *

In this case under § 5 of the FTC Act, the Commission expressly limited its theory of liability to Rambus's unlawful monopolization of four markets in violation of § 2 of the Sherman Act . . .; see also *FTC v. Cement Inst.,* 333 U.S. 683, 694 (1948) (§ 5 reaches all conduct that violates § 2 of the Sherman Act). Therefore, we apply principles of antitrust law developed under the Sherman Act, and we review the Commission's construction and application of the antitrust laws *de novo. FTC v. Indiana Fed'n of Dentists,* 476 U.S. 447, 454 (1986).

It is settled law that the mere existence of a monopoly does not violate the Sherman Act. See *Verizon Commc'ns, Inc. v. Law Offices of Curtis V. Trinko, LLP,* 540 U.S. 398, 407 (2004); *United States v. Microsoft Corp.,* 253 F.3d 34, 58 (D.C. Cir. 2001) (en banc) (*per curiam*). In addition to "the possession of monopoly power in the relevant market," the offense of monopolization requires " 'the willful acquisition or maintenance of that power as distinguished from growth or development as a consequence of a superior product, business acumen, or historical accident.' " *Trinko,* 540 U.S. at 407 (quoting *United States v. Grinnell Corp.,* 384 U.S. 563, 570–71 (1966)); *Microsoft,* 253 F.3d at 50 (same). In this case, Rambus does not dispute the nature of the relevant markets or that its patent rights in the four relevant technologies give it monopoly power in each of those markets. The critical question is whether Rambus engaged in exclusionary conduct, and thereby acquired its monopoly power in the relevant markets unlawfully.

To answer that question, we adhere to two antitrust principles that guided us in *Microsoft.* First, "to be condemned as exclusionary, a monopolist's act must have 'anticompetitive effect.' That is, it must harm the competitive *process* and thereby harm consumers. In contrast, harm to one or more *competitors* will not suffice." *Microsoft,* 253 F.3d at 58; see also *Trinko,* 540 U.S. at 407; *Brooke Group Ltd. v. Brown & Williamson Tobacco Corp.,* 509 U.S. 209, 224 (1993); *Covad Commc'ns. Co. v. Bell Atlantic Corp.,* 398 F.3d 666, 672 (D.C. Cir. 2005). Second, it is the antitrust plaintiff—including the Government as plaintiff—that bears the burden of proving the anticompetitive effect of the monopolist's conduct. *Microsoft,* 253 F.3d at 58–59.

The Commission held that Rambus engaged in exclusionary conduct consisting of misrepresentations, omissions, and other practices that deceived JEDEC about the nature and scope of its patent interests while the organization standardized technologies covered by those interests. Had Rambus fully disclosed its intellectual property, "JEDEC either would have excluded Rambus's patented technologies from the JEDEC DRAM standards, or would have demanded RAND assurances, with an opportunity for *ex ante* licensing negotiations." Liability Op. at 74. But the Commission did not determine that one or the other of these two possible outcomes was the more likely. The Commission's conclusion that Rambus's conduct was exclusionary depends, therefore, on a syllogism: Rambus avoided one of two outcomes by not disclosing its patent interests; the avoidance of either of those outcomes was anticompetitive; therefore Rambus's nondisclosure was anticompetitive.

We assume without deciding that avoidance of the first of these possible outcomes was indeed anticompetitive; that is, that if Rambus's more complete disclosure would have caused JEDEC to adopt a different (open, non-proprietary) standard, then its failure to disclose harmed competition and would support a monopolization claim. But while we can assume that Rambus's nondisclosure made the adoption of its technologies somewhat more likely than broad disclosure would have, the Commission made clear in its remedial opinion that there was insufficient evidence that JEDEC would have standardized other technologies had it known the full scope of Rambus's intellectual property. Therefore, for the Commission's syllogism to survive—and for the Commission to have carried its burden of proving that Rambus's conduct had an anticompetitive effect—we must also be convinced that if Rambus's conduct merely enabled it to avoid the other possible outcome, namely JEDEC's obtaining assurances from Rambus of RAND licensing terms, such conduct, alone, could be said to harm competition. Cf. *Avins v. White,* 627 F.2d 637, 646 (3d Cir. 1980) ("Where . . . a general verdict may rest on either of two claims—one supported by the evidence and the other not—a judgment thereon must be reversed." (quoting *Albergo v. Reading Co.,* 372 F.2d 83, 86 (3d Cir. 1966))). We are not convinced.

Deceptive conduct—like any other kind—must have an anticompetitive effect in order to form the basis of a monopolization claim. "Even an act of pure malice by one business competitor against another does not, without more, state a claim under the federal antitrust laws," without proof of "a dangerous probability that [the defendant] would monopolize a particular market." *Brooke Group,* 509 U.S. at 225. Even if deception raises the price secured by a seller, but does so without harming competition, it is beyond the antitrust laws' reach. Cases that recognize deception as exclusionary hinge, therefore, on whether the conduct impaired rivals in a manner tending to bring about or protect a defendant's monopoly power. In *Microsoft,* for example, we found Microsoft engaged in anticompetitive conduct when it tricked independent software developers into believing that its software development tools could be used to design cross-platform Java applications when, in fact, they produced Windows-specific ones. The deceit had caused "developers who were opting for portability over performance . . . unwittingly [to write] Java applications that [ran] only on Windows." 253 F.3d at 76. The focus of our antitrust scrutiny, therefore, was properly placed on the resulting harms to competition rather than the deception itself.

Another case of deception with an anticompetitive dimension is *Conwood Co. v. U.S. Tobacco Co.,* 290 F.3d 768 (6th Cir. 2002), where the Sixth Circuit found that U.S. Tobacco's dominance of the moist snuff market caused retailers to rely on it as a "category manager" that would provide trusted guidance on the sales strategy and in-store display for all moist snuff products, *id.* at 773–78. Under those circumstances, the court held that its misrepresentations to retailers about the sales strength of its products versus its competitors' strength reduced competition in the monopolized market by increasing the display space devoted to U.S. Tobacco's products and decreasing that allotted to competing products. *Id.* at 783, 785–88, 790–91; see also *LePage's Inc. v. 3M,* 324 F.3d 141, 153 (3d Cir. 2003) (calling *Conwood* "a good illustration of the type of exclusionary conduct that will support a § 2 violation").

But an otherwise lawful monopolist's use of deception simply to obtain higher prices normally has no particular tendency to exclude rivals and thus to diminish competition. Consider, for example, *NYNEX Corp. v. Discon, Inc.,* 525 U.S. 128 (1998), in which the Court addressed the antitrust implications of allegations that NYNEX's subsidiary, New York Telephone Company, a lawful monopoly provider of local telephone services, charged its customers higher prices as result of fraudulent conduct in the market for the service of removing outdated telephone switching equipment (called "removal services"). Discon had alleged that New York Telephone (through its corporate affiliate, Materiel Enterprises) switched its purchases of removal services from Discon to a higher-priced independent firm (AT&T Technologies). Materiel Enterprises would pass the higher fees on to New York Telephone, which in turn passed them on to customers through higher rates approved by regulators. *Id.* at 131–32. The nub of the deception, Discon alleged, was that AT&T Technologies would provide Materiel Enterprises with a special rebate at year's end, which it would then share with NYNEX. *Id.* By thus hoodwinking the regulators, the scam raised prices for consumers; Discon, which refused to play the rebate game, was driven out of business. Discon alleged that this arrangement was anticompetitive and constituted both an agreement in restraint of trade in violation of § 1 of the Sherman Act and a conspiracy to monopolize the market for removal services in violation of § 2. *Id.* at 132.

As to Discon's § 1 claim, the Court held that where a single buyer favors one supplier over another for an improper reason, the plaintiff must "allege and prove harm, not just to a single competitor, but to the competitive process." *Id.* at 135. Nor, as Justice Breyer wrote for a unanimous Court, would harm to the consumers in the form of higher prices change the matter: "We concede Discon's claim that the [defendants'] behavior hurt consumers by raising telephone service rates. But that consumer injury naturally flowed not so much from a less competitive market for removal services, as from the exercise of market power that is *lawfully* in the hands of a monopolist, namely, New York Telephone, combined with a deception worked upon the regulatory agency that prevented the agency from controlling New York Telephone's exercise of its monopoly power." *Id.* at 136.

Because Discon based its § 2 claim on the very same allegations of fraud, the Court vacated the appellate court's decision to uphold that claim because "[u]nless those agreements harmed the competitive process, they did not amount to a conspiracy to monopolize." *Id.* at 139; see also *Forsyth v. Humana, Inc.,* 114 F.3d 1467, 1477–78 (9th Cir. 1997) (rejecting a claim that an insurance company's alleged kickback scheme caused antitrust injury to group health insurance customers where the evidence showed the scheme caused higher copayments and premium payments, but did "not explain how the scheme reduced competition in the relevant market"), *aff'd on other grounds,* 525 U.S. 299 (1999); *Schuylkill Energy Res., Inc. v. Penn. Power & Light Co.,* 113 F.3d 405, 414 (3d Cir. 1997) (finding conduct did not violate antitrust laws where absent that conduct consumers would still receive the same product and the same amount of competition).

While the Commission's brief doesn't mention *NYNEX,* much less try to distinguish it, it does cite *Broadcom Corp. v. Qualcomm Inc.,* 501 F.3d 297 (3d Cir. 2007), which in turn had cited the Commission's own "landmark" decision in the case under review here, *id.* at 311. There the court held that a patent holder's intentionally false promise to a standard-setting organization that it would license its technology on RAND terms, "coupled with [the organization's] reliance on that promise when including the technology in a standard," was anticompetitive conduct, on the ground that it increased "the likelihood that patent rights will confer monopoly power on the patent holder." *Id.* at 314; accord *id.* at 315–16. To the extent that the ruling (which simply reversed a grant of dismissal) rested on the argument that deceit lured the SSO away from non-proprietary technology, see *id.,* it cannot help the Commission in view of its inability to find that Rambus's behavior caused JEDEC's choice; to the extent that it may have rested on a supposition that there is a cognizable violation of the Sherman Act when a lawful monopolist's deceit has the effect of raising prices (without an effect on competitive structure), it conflicts with *NYNEX.*

Here, the Commission expressly left open the likelihood that JEDEC would have standardized Rambus's technologies *even if Rambus had disclosed* its intellectual property. Under this hypothesis, JEDEC lost only an opportunity to secure a RAND commitment from Rambus. But loss of such a commitment is not a harm to competition from alternative technologies in the relevant markets. See 2 Hovenkamp et al., IP & Antitrust § 35.5 at 35–45 (Supp.2008) [hereinafter "IP & Antitrust"] ("[A]n antitrust plaintiff must establish that the standard-setting organization would not have adopted the standard in question but for the misrepresentation or omission."). Indeed, had JEDEC limited Rambus to reasonable royalties and required it to provide licenses on a nondiscriminatory basis, we would expect *less* competition from alternative technologies, not more; high prices and constrained output tend to attract competitors, not to repel them.

Scholars in the field have urged that if nondisclosure to an SSO enables a participant to obtain higher royalties than would otherwise have been attainable, the "overcharge can properly constitute competitive harm attributable to the nondisclosure," as the overcharge "will distort competition in the downstream market." 2 IP & Antitrust § 35.5 at 35–47. The contention that price-raising deception has downstream effects is surely correct, but that consequence was equally surely true in *NYNEX* (though perhaps on a smaller scale) and equally obvious to the Court. The Commission makes the related contention that because the ability to profitably restrict output and set supracompetitive prices is the *sine qua non* of monopoly power, any conduct that permits a monopolist to avoid constraints on the exercise of that power must be anticompetitive. But again, as in *NYNEX,* an otherwise lawful monopolist's end-run around price constraints, even when deceptive or fraudulent, does not alone present a harm to competition in the monopolized market.

Thus, if JEDEC, in the world that would have existed but for Rambus's deception, would have standardized the very same technologies, Rambus's alleged deception cannot be said to have had an effect on competition in violation of the antitrust laws; JEDEC's loss of an opportunity to seek favorable licensing terms is not as such an antitrust harm. Yet the Commission did not reject this as being a possible—perhaps even the more probable—effect of Rambus's conduct. We hold, therefore, that the Commission failed to demonstrate that Rambus's conduct was exclusionary, and thus to establish its claim that Rambus unlawfully monopolized the relevant markets. . . .

We set aside the Commission's orders and remand for further proceedings consistent with this opinion.

So ordered.

NOTES AND QUESTIONS

1. *Nonarbitrary discriminatory standards—rule of reason.* Structural Laminates, Inc. v. Douglas Fir Plywood Ass'n, 261 F.Supp. 154 (D. Or. 1966), *aff'd,* 399 F.2d 155 (9th Cir. 1968). A plywood manufacturer brought a treble damage action against a trade association whose members accounted for 82 to 89 percent of the plywood produced in the United States, charging that defendant's quality control program blocked plaintiff's access to the market and, eventually, drove plaintiff out of business. After inspection and testing of members' products, the association permitted members whose products were approved to use its stamp and a certificate. Plywood not bearing a mark indicating conformity was more difficult to sell and brought a lower price.

The association played a dominant role in proposing standards and soliciting approval by members of this industry. One example was its 1948 standard (published by the Department of Commerce) that excluded plywood composed of relatively thick veneers, apparently because of bonding difficulties. Plaintiff believed that it had solved these technical problems and, after constructing a plywood mill in 1957, it sought a modification in this quality standard. Defendant conducted a series of tests over a substantial period of time and finally, in 1963, recommended that the quality standard be revised. In the meantime, plaintiff had gone out of business in November, 1960.

The district court found that "mere adoption of a standard which discriminates between products cannot be . . . a *per se* violation of the Sherman Act—particularly where, as here, the standard is the product of a Congressionally sanctioned scheme." The court went on to find that the plaintiff had failed to show that the quality standard that adversely affected plaintiff's business "was either unreasonable or done with an evil intent," although the court recognized that some of defendant's members were competitors of plaintiff and had "a real economic motive" in opposing widespread use of plaintiff's product.

The same result as in *Structural Laminates* was reached in Eliason Corp. v. National Sanitation Found., 614 F.2d 126 (6th Cir. 1980), where the independent, nonprofit, standard-setting organization (1) was not shown to have any relationship to the Department of Commerce or any governmental agency; (2) promulgated uniform health and product standards directly to local governments and buyers and encouraged their adoption; but (3) was not shown to be under the control of industry leaders or other competitors of plaintiff, or to discriminate against it in testing or applying standards.

The court held that, absent discrimination or "manifestly anticompetitive and unreasonable conduct," alleged boycotts arising from "standard-making or even industry self-regulation" did not give rise to Sherman Act problems. It noted that it did "not intend to foreclose the possibility that some standards may be so unreasonable in content that their net effect injures competition even though some policies of uniformity are served." Nationwide uniformity of standards, however, was seen to promote competition, enabling "manufacturers who elect to comply ... to be reasonably sure they will not have to modify their product in order to meet the different requirements of many jurisdictions."

Plaintiff had argued that the testing program gave large competitors an unfair competitive advantage over smaller manufacturers of functionally equivalent products and created barriers to entry for innovative manufacturers. One commentator speculates that the Foundation was "created and maintained by larger manufacturers ... to eliminate the need to innovate and to curtail competition by price-cutters ..." and that many states which adopted the uniform standards did so "only in response to the foundations' activities." J. Ponsoldt, *The Application of Sherman Act Antiboycott Law to Industry Self–Regulation*, 55 S. Cal. L. Rev. 1 (1981).

Can the theories of *Structural Laminates* and *Eliason* be reconciled with *FOGA* and *Radiant Burners*? Does *NYNEX* prove that these standard-setting cases were correctly decided, or is it unhelpful as an essentially vertical case?

2. *Concerns with standard-fixing agencies.* How real is the "barrier to entry" problem if standard-setting agencies win nationwide acceptance of their criteria or seal of approval? How would one prove that such an agency is (or is not) in fact totally independent and impartial? Would it be relevant that the agency is supported by industry members, perhaps proportionately to their volume of business, rather than exclusively by fees for testing and other services rendered? Should the agency, rather than the plaintiff, bear the burden of establishing that procedures it followed were adequate and standards it adopted were reasonable? *Cf. Allied Tube & Conduit Corp. v. Indian Head, infra* p. 401.

Northwest Wholesale Stationers, Inc. v. Pacific Stationery & Printing Co.

Supreme Court of the United States, 1985.
472 U.S. 284, 105 S.Ct. 2613, 86 L.Ed.2d 202.

■ BRENNAN, J. . . . This case requires that we decide whether a *per se* violation of § 1 of the Sherman Act, 15 U.S.C. § 1, occurs when a cooperative buying agency comprising various retailers expels a member without providing any procedural means for challenging the expulsion. This case also raises broader questions as to when *per se* antitrust analysis is appropriately applied to joint activity that is susceptible of being characterized as a concerted refusal to deal.

I

Because the District Court ruled on cross-motions for summary judgment after only limited discovery, this case comes to us on a sparse record. Certain background facts are undisputed. Petitioner Northwest Wholesale Stationers is a purchasing cooperative made up of approximately 100 office supply retailers in the Pacific Northwest States. The cooperative acts as the primary wholesaler for the retailers. Retailers that are not members of the cooperative can purchase wholesale supplies from Northwest at the same price as members. At the end of each year, however, Northwest distributes its profits to members in the form of a percentage rebate on purchases. Members therefore effectively purchase supplies at a price significantly lower than do nonmembers.[6] Northwest also provides certain warehousing facilities. The cooperative arrangement thus permits the participating retailers to achieve economies of scale in purchasing and warehousing that would otherwise be unavailable to them. In fiscal 1978 Northwest had $5.8 million in sales.

Respondent Pacific Stationery, Inc. sells office supplies at both the retail and wholesale levels. Its total sales in fiscal 1978 were approximately $7.6 million; the record does not indicate what percentage of revenue is attributable to retail and what percentage is attributable to wholesale. Pacific became a member of Northwest in 1958. In 1974 Northwest amended its bylaws to prohibit members from engaging in both retail and wholesale operations. A grandfather clause preserved Pacific's membership rights. In 1977 ownership of a controlling share of the stock of Pacific changed hands, and the new owners did not officially bring this change to the attention of the directors of Northwest. This failure to notify apparently violated another of Northwest's bylaws.

In 1978 the membership of Northwest voted to expel Pacific. Most factual matters relevant to the expulsion are in dispute. No explanation for the expulsion was advanced at the time and Pacific was given neither notice, a hearing, nor any other opportunity to challenge the decision. Pacific argues that the expulsion resulted from Pacific's decision to maintain a wholesale operation. Northwest contends that the expulsion resulted from Pacific's failure to notify the cooperative members of the change in

---

6. Although this patronage rebate policy is a form of price discrimination, § 4 of the Robinson–Patman Act specifically sanctions such activity by cooperatives.

> "Nothing in this Act shall prevent a cooperative association from returning to its members, producers, or consumers the whole, or any part of, the net earnings or surplus resulting from its trading operations, in proportion to their purchases or sales from, to, or through the association." 49 Stat. 1528, 15 U.S.C. § 13b. A relevant state-law provision provides analogous protection. Ore. Rev. Stat. 696.030 (1983).

stock ownership. The minutes of the meeting of Northwest's directors do not definitively indicate the motive for the expulsion. It is undisputed that Pacific received approximately $10,000 in rebates from Northwest in 1978, Pacific's last year of membership. Beyond a possible inference of loss from this fact, however, the record is devoid of allegations indicating the nature and extent of competitive injury the expulsion caused Pacific to suffer.

Pacific brought suit in 1980 in the United States District Court for the District of Oregon alleging a violation of § 1 of the Sherman Act. The gravamen of the action was that Northwest's expulsion of Pacific from the cooperative without procedural protections was a group boycott that limited Pacific's ability to compete and should be considered *per se* violative of § 1. On cross-motions for summary judgment the District Court rejected application of the *per se* rule and held instead that rule-of-reason analysis should govern the case. Finding no anticompetitive effect on the basis of the record as presented, the court granted summary judgment for Northwest.

The Court of Appeals for the Ninth Circuit reversed, holding "that the uncontroverted facts of this case support a finding of *per se* liability." 715 F.2d 1393, 1395 (1983). The court reasoned that the cooperative's expulsion of Pacific was an anticompetitive concerted refusal to deal with Pacific on equal footing, which would be a *per se* violation of § 1 in the absence of any specific legislative mandate for self-regulation sanctioning the expulsion. The court noted that § 4 of the Robinson–Patman Act, 15 U.S.C. § 13b, specifically approves the price discrimination occasioned by such expulsion and concluded that § 4 therefore provided a mandate for self-regulation. Such a legislative mandate, according to the court, would ordinarily result in evaluation of the challenged practice under the rule of reason. But, drawing on *Silver v. New York Stock Exchange*, 373 U.S. 341, 348–349 (1963), the court decided that rule-of-reason analysis was appropriate only on the condition that the cooperative had provided procedural safeguards sufficient to prevent arbitrary expulsion and to furnish a basis for judicial review. Because Northwest had not provided any procedural safeguards, the court held that the expulsion of Pacific was not shielded by Robinson–Patman immunity and therefore constituted a *per se* group boycott in violation of § 1 of the Sherman Act. 715 F.2d, at 1395–1398.

We granted certiorari to examine this application of *Silver v. New York Stock Exchange, supra*, in an area of antitrust law that has not been free of confusion. 469 U.S. 814 (1984). We reverse.

II

The decision of the cooperative members to expel Pacific was certainly a restraint of trade in the sense that every commercial agreement restrains trade. *Chicago Board of Trade v. United States*, 246 U.S. 231, 238 (1918). Whether this action violates § 1 of the Sherman Act depends on whether it is adjudged an unreasonable restraint. Rule-of-reason analysis guides the inquiry, see *Standard Oil Co. v. United States*, 221 U.S. 1 (1911), unless the challenged action falls into the category of "agreements or practices which because of their pernicious effect on competition and lack of any redeeming virtue are conclusively presumed to be unreasonable and therefore illegal without elaborate inquiry as to the precise harm they have caused or the business excuse for their use." *Northern Pacific R. Co. v. United States*, 356 U.S. 1, 5 (1958).

This *per se* approach permits categorical judgments with respect to certain business practices that have proved to be predominantly anticompetitive. Courts can thereby avoid the "significant costs" in "business certainty and litigation efficiency" that a full-fledged rule-of-reason inquiry entails. *Arizona v. Maricopa County Medical Society*, 457 U.S. 332, 343–344 (1982). See also *United States v. Topco Associates, Inc.*, 405 U.S. 596, 609–610 (1972). . . .

This Court has long held that certain concerted refusals to deal or group boycotts are so likely to restrict competition without any offsetting efficiency gains that they should be condemned as *per se* violations of § 1 of the Sherman Act. See *Klor's, Inc. v. Broadway–Hale Stores, Inc.*, 359 U.S. 207 (1959); *United States v. General Motors Corp.*, 384 U.S. 127 (1966); *Radiant Burners, Inc. v. Peoples Gas Light & Coke Co.*, 364 U.S. 656 (1961); *Associated Press v. United States*, 326 U.S. 1 (1945); *Fashion Originators' Guild of America, Inc. v. FTC*, 312 U.S. 457 (1941); *Eastern States Retail Lumber Dealers' Assn. v. United States*, 234 U.S. 600 (1914). The question presented in this case is whether Northwest's decision to expel Pacific should fall within this category of activity that is conclusively presumed to be anticompetitive. The Court of Appeals held that the exclusion of Pacific from the cooperative should conclusively be presumed unreasonable on the ground that Northwest provided no procedural protections to Pacific. Even if the lack of procedural protections does not justify a conclusive presumption of predominantly anticompetitive effect, the mere act of expulsion of a competitor from a wholesale cooperative might be argued to be sufficiently likely to have such effects under the present circumstances and therefore to justify application of the *per se* rule. These possibilities will be analyzed separately.

A

The Court of Appeals drew from *Silver v. New York Stock Exchange*, *supra*, a broad rule that the conduct of a cooperative venture—including a concerted refusal to deal—undertaken pursuant to a legislative mandate for self-regulation is immune from *per se* scrutiny and subject to rule of reason analysis only if adequate procedural safeguards accompany self-regulation. We disagree and conclude that the approach of the Court in *Silver* has no proper application to the present controversy.

The Court in *Silver* framed the issue as follows:

"[W]hether the New York Stock Exchange is to be held liable to a nonmember broker-dealer under the antitrust laws or regarded as impliedly immune therefrom when, pursuant to rules the Exchange has adopted under the Securities Exchange Act of 1934, it orders a number of its members to remove private direct telephone wire connections previously in operation between their offices and those of the nonmember, without giving the nonmember notice, assigning him any reason for the action, or affording him an opportunity to be heard." 373 U.S., at 343.

Because the New York Stock Exchange occupied such a dominant position in the securities trading markets that the boycott would devastate the nonmember, the Court concluded that the refusal to deal with the non-member would amount to a *per se* violation of § 1 unless the Securities Exchange Act provided an immunity. The question for the Court thus was whether effectuation of the policies of the Securities Exchange Act required partial repeal of the Sherman Act insofar as it proscribed this aspect of exchange self-regulation.

Finding exchange self-regulation—including the power to expel members and limit dealings with nonmembers—to be an essential policy of the Securities Exchange Act, the Court held that the Sherman Act should be construed as having been partially repealed to permit the type of exchange activity at issue. But the interpretive maxim disfavoring repeals by implication led the Court to narrow permissible self-policing to situations in which adequate procedural safeguards had been provided.

> "Congress . . . cannot be thought to have sanctioned and protected self-regulative activity when carried out in a fundamentally unfair manner. The point is not that the antitrust laws impose the requirement of notice and a hearing here, but rather that, in acting without according petitioners these safeguards in response to their request, the Exchange has plainly exceeded the scope of its authority under the Securities Exchange Act to engage in self-regulation."

Thus it was the specific need to accommodate the important national policy of promoting effective exchange self-regulation, tempered by the principle that the Sherman Act should be narrowed only to the extent necessary to effectuate that policy, that dictated the result in *Silver*.

Section 4 of the Robinson–Patman Act is not comparable to the self-policing provisions of the Securities Exchange Act. That section is no more than a narrow immunity from the price discrimination prohibitions of the Robinson–Patman Act itself. . . .

[T]here can be no argument that § 4 of the Robinson–Patman Act should be viewed as a broad mandate for industry self-regulation. No need exists, therefore, to narrow the Sherman Act in order to accommodate any competing congressional policy requiring discretionary self-policing. Indeed, Congress would appear to have taken some care to make clear that no constriction of the Sherman Act was intended. In any event, the absence of procedural safeguards can in no sense determine the anti-trust analysis. If the challenged concerted activity of Northwest's members would amount to a *per se* violation of § 1 of the Sherman Act, no amount of procedural protection would save it. If the challenged action would not amount to a violation of § 1, no lack of procedural protections would convert it into a

it's not ab procedural safeguards

per se violation because the antitrust laws do not themselves impose on joint ventures a requirement of process.

B

was expulsion a group boycott?

This case therefore turns not on the lack of procedural protections but on whether the decision to expel Pacific is properly viewed as a group boycott or concerted refusal to deal mandating *per se* invalidation. "Group boycotts" are often listed among the classes of economic activity that merit *per se* invalidation under § 1. See *Klor's, Inc. v. Broadway–Hale Stores, Inc.*, 359 U.S., at 212; *Northern Pacific Railway Co. v. United States*, 356 U.S., at 5; *Silver v. New York Stock Exchange*, 373 U.S., at 348; *White Motor Co. v. United States*, 372 U.S. 253, 259–260 (1963). Exactly what types of activity fall within the forbidden category is, however, far from certain. "[T]here is more confusion about the scope and operation of the *per se* rule against group boycotts than in reference to any other aspect of the *per se* doctrine." L. Sullivan, Law of Antitrust 229–230 (1977). Some care is therefore necessary in defining the category of concerted refusals to deal that mandate *per se* condemnation. . . .

per se cases have involved joint efforts to disadv comp

Cases to which this Court has applied the *per se* approach have generally involved joint efforts by a firm or firms to disadvantage competitors by "either directly denying or persuading or coercing suppliers or customers to deny relationships the competitors need in the competitive struggle." Sullivan, *supra*, at 261–262. See, *e.g.*, *Silver, supra* (denial of necessary access to exchange members); *Radiant Burners, Inc. v. Peoples Gas Light & Coke Co.*, 364 U.S. 656 (1961) (denial of necessary certification of product); *Associated Press v. United States*, 326 U.S. 1 (1945) (denial of important sources of news); *Klor's, Inc., supra* (denial of wholesale supplies). In these cases, the boycott often cut off access to a supply, facility, or market necessary to enable the boycotted firm to compete, *Silver, supra*; *Radiant Burners, Inc., supra*, and frequently the boycotting firms possessed a dominant position in the relevant market. *E.g.*, *Silver, supra*; *Associated Press, supra*; *Fashion Originators Guild of America, Inc. v. FTC*, 312 U.S. 457 (1941). . . . In addition, the practices were generally not justified by plausible arguments that they were intended to enhance overall efficiency and make markets more competitive. Under such circumstances the likelihood of anticompetitive effects is clear and the possibility of countervailing procompetitive effects is remote.

per se must have "predominantly anticompetitive consequences"

Although a concerted refusal to deal need not necessarily possess all of these traits to merit *per se* treatment, not every cooperative activity involving a restraint or exclusion will share with the *per se* forbidden boycotts the likelihood of predominantly anticompetitive consequences. For example, we recognized last Term in *National Collegiate Athletic Assn. v. Board of Regents of University of Oklahoma* that *per se* treatment of the NCAA's restrictions on the marketing of televised college football was inappropriate—despite the obvious restraint on output—because the "case involves an industry in which horizontal restraints on competition are essential if the product is to be available at all."

Wholesale purchasing cooperatives such as Northwest are not a form of concerted activity characteristically likely to result in predominantly anti-competitive effects. Rather, such cooperative arrangements would seem to be "designed to increase economic efficiency and render markets more, rather than less, competitive." *Broadcast Music, Inc. v. Columbia Broadcasting System, Inc.* [*supra*]. The arrangement permits the participating retailers to achieve economies of scale in both the purchase and warehousing of wholesale supplies, and also ensures ready access to a stock of goods that might otherwise be unavailable on short notice. The cost savings and order-filling guarantees enable smaller retailers to reduce prices and maintain their retail stock so as to compete more effectively with larger retailers.

Pacific, of course, does not object to the existence of the cooperative arrangement, but rather raises an antitrust challenge to Northwest's decision to bar Pacific from continued membership.[7] It is therefore the action of expulsion that must be evaluated to determine whether *per se* treatment is appropriate. The act of expulsion from a wholesale cooperative does not necessarily imply anticompetitive animus and thereby raise a probability of anticompetitive effect. See *Broadcast Music, Inc. v. Columbia Broadcasting System, Inc.* Wholesale purchasing cooperatives must establish and enforce reasonable rules in order to function effectively. Disclosure rules, such as the one on which Northwest relies, may well provide the cooperative with a needed means for monitoring the creditworthiness of its members.[8] Nor would the expulsion characteristically be likely to result in predominantly anticompetitive effects, at least in the type of situation this case presents. Unless the cooperative possesses market power or exclusive access to an element essential to effective competition, the conclusion that expulsion is virtually always likely to have an anticompetitive effect is not warranted.... Cf. *Jefferson Parish Hospital Dist. v. Hyde*, 466 U.S. 2, 12–15 (1984) (absent indication of market power, tying arrangement does not warrant *per se* invalidation). See generally *NCAA v. Board of Regents of University of Oklahoma*, 468 U.S., at 104, n. 26 ("*Per se* rules may require considerable inquiry into market conditions before the evidence justifies a

---

7. Because Pacific has not been wholly excluded from access to Northwest's wholesale operations, there is perhaps some question whether the challenged activity is properly characterized a concerted refusal to deal. To be precise, Northwest's activity is a concerted refusal to deal with Pacific on substantially equal terms. Such activity might justify *per se* invalidation if it placed a competing firm at a severe competitive disadvantage. See generally Brodley, Joint Ventures and Antitrust Policy, 95 Harv.L.Rev. 1521, 1532 (1982) ("Even if the joint venture does deal with outside firms, it may place them at a severe competitive disadvantage by treating them less favorably than it treats the [participants in the joint venture]").

8. Pacific argues, however, that this justification for expulsion was a pretext because the members of Northwest were fully aware of the change in ownership despite lack of formal notice. According to Pacific, Northwest's motive in the expulsion was to place Pacific at a competitive disadvantage to retaliate for Pacific's decision to engage in an independent wholesale operation. Such a motive might be more troubling. If Northwest's action were not substantially related to the efficiency-enhancing or procompetitive purposes that otherwise justify the cooperative's practices, an inference of anticompetitive animus might be appropriate. But such an argument is appropriately evaluated under the rule of reason analysis.

[handwritten margin note: wholesale coops aren't likely to be predominantly anticomp — designed for ec. efficiency]

no per se analysis

what you need for per se

remand for ROR analysis

presumption of anticompetitive conduct"). Absent such a showing with respect to a cooperative buying arrangement, courts should apply a rule-of-reason analysis. At no time has Pacific made a threshold showing that these structural characteristics are present in this case.[9]

The District Court appears to have followed the correct path of analysis—recognizing that not all concerted refusals to deal should be accorded *per se* treatment and deciding this one should not. The foregoing discussion suggests, however, that a satisfactory threshold determination whether anticompetitive effects would be likely might require a more detailed factual picture of market structure than the District Court had before it. Nonetheless, in our judgment the District Court's rejection of *per se* analysis in this case was correct. A plaintiff seeking application of the *per se* rule must present a threshold case that the challenged activity falls into a category likely to have predominantly anticompetitive effects. The mere allegation of a concerted refusal to deal does not suffice because not all concerted refusals to deal are predominantly anticompetitive. When the plaintiff challenges expulsion from a joint buying cooperative, some showing must be made that the cooperative possesses market power or unique access to a business element necessary for effective competition. Focusing on the argument that the lack of procedural safeguards required *per se* liability, Pacific did not allege any such facts. Because the Court of Appeals applied an erroneous *per se* analysis in this case, the court never evaluated the District Court's rule-of-reason analysis rejecting Pacific's claim. A remand is therefore appropriate for the limited purpose of permitting appellate review of that determination.

III

"The *per se* rule is a valid and useful tool of antitrust policy and enforcement." *Broadcast Music, Inc. v. Columbia Broadcasting System, Inc.*, 441 U.S., at 8. It does not denigrate the *per se* approach to suggest care in application. In this case, the Court of Appeals failed to exercise the requisite care and applied *per se* analysis inappropriately. The judgment of the Court of Appeals is therefore reversed, and the case is remanded for further proceedings consistent with this opinion.

■ MARSHALL, J., and POWELL, J., took no part in the decision of this case.

NOTES AND QUESTIONS

1. *Aftermath.* Can *Northwest Stationers* and *Klor's* be reconciled? What is the maximum and minimum reading that can be given to *Klor's* after *Northwest Stationers?*

---

9. Given the state of this record it is difficult to understand how the court of appeals could have concluded that Pacific "loses the ability to use Northwest's superior warehousing and expedited order-filling facilities, as well as any competitive advantages that may flow simply from being known in the industry as a member of an established cooperative." 715 F.2d 1393, 1395 (1983). The District Court had specifically found no anticompetitive effect....

2. Northwest Stationers' *standard*. What factors does *Northwest Stationers* require to be examined before one can conclude that a collaborative arrangement is a "boycott" meriting *per se* treatment? Are these the same factors that the Supreme Court examined in the "characterization" phase of *BMI?* Are they the same as the ones the Court consulted in *NYNEX?*

3. *Role of market power*. According to *Northwest Stationers,* is market power a precondition to application of *per se* rules in all boycott cases or only in buying and selling co-ops? If a precondition in all cases, what remains of *Klor's?* Consider the extent to which market power does, or does not, affect the application of the rule in the following case.

FTC v. Indiana Federation of Dentists

Supreme Court of the United States, 1986.
476 U.S. 447, 106 S.Ct. 2009, 90 L.Ed.2d 445.

■ WHITE, J. ... This case concerns commercial relations among certain Indiana dentists, their patients, and the patients' dental health care insurers. The question presented is whether the Federal Trade Commission correctly concluded that a conspiracy among dentists to refuse to submit x-rays to dental insurers for use in benefits determinations constituted an "unfair method of competition" in violation of § 5 of the Federal Trade Commission Act.

I

Since the 1970s, dental health insurers, responding to the demands of their policyholders, have attempted to contain the cost of dental treatment by, among other devices, limiting payment of benefits to the cost of the "least expensive yet adequate treatment" suitable to the needs of individual patients. Implementation of such cost-containment measures, known as "alternative benefits" plans, requires evaluation by the insurer of the diagnosis and recommendation of the treating dentist, either in advance of or following the provision of care. In order to carry out such evaluation, insurers frequently request dentists to submit, along with insurance claim forms requesting payment of benefits, any dental x-rays that have been used by the dentist in examining the patient as well as other information concerning their diagnoses and treatment recommendations. Typically, claim forms and accompanying x-rays are reviewed by lay claims examiners, who either approve payment of claims or, if the materials submitted raise a question whether the recommended course of treatment is in fact necessary, refer claims to dental consultants, who are licensed dentists, for further review. On the basis of the materials available, supplemented where appropriate by further diagnostic aids, the dental consultant may recommend that the insurer approve a claim, deny it, or pay only for a less expensive course of treatment.

Such review of diagnostic and treatment decisions has been viewed by some dentists as a threat to their professional independence and economic well-being. In the early 1970s, the Indiana Dental Association, a professional organization comprising some 85% of practicing dentists in the State of

Indiana, initiated an aggressive effort to hinder insurers' efforts to implement alternative benefits plans by enlisting member dentists to pledge not to submit x-rays in conjunction with claim forms.[10] The Association's efforts met considerable success: large numbers of dentists signed the pledge, and insurers operating in Indiana found it difficult to obtain compliance with their requests for x-rays and accordingly had to choose either to employ more expensive means of making alternative benefits determinations (for example, visiting the office of the treating dentist or conducting an independent oral examination) or to abandon such efforts altogether.

By the mid–1970s, fears of possible antitrust liability had dampened the Association's enthusiasm for opposing the submission of x-rays to insurers. In 1979, the Association and a number of its constituent societies consented to a Federal Trade Commission order requiring them to cease and desist from further efforts to prevent member dentists from submitting x-rays. *In re Indiana Dental Assn.*, 93 F.T.C. 392 (1979). Not all Indiana dentists were content to leave the matter of submitting x-rays to the individual dentist. In 1976, a group of such dentists formed the Indiana Federation of Dentists, respondent in this case, in order to continue to pursue the Association's policy of resisting insurers' requests for x-rays. The Federation, which styled itself a "union" in the belief that this label would stave off antitrust liability, immediately promulgated a "work rule" forbidding its members to submit x-rays to dental insurers in conjunction with claim forms. Although the Federation's membership was small, numbering less than 100, its members were highly concentrated in and around three Indiana communities: Anderson, Lafayette, and Fort Wayne. The Federation succeeded in enlisting nearly 100% of the dental specialists in the Anderson area, and approximately 67% of the dentists in and around Lafayette. In the areas of its strength, the Federation was successful in

---

10. A presentation made in 1974 by Dr. David McClure, an Association official and later one of the founders of respondent Indiana Federation of Dentists, is revealing as to the motives underlying the dentists' resistance to the provision of x-rays for use by insurers in making alternative benefits determinations:

The problems associated with third party programs are many, but I believe the "Indiana Plan" [*i.e.*, the policy of refusing to submit x-rays] to be sound and if we work together, we can win this battle. We are fighting an economic war where the very survival of our profession is at stake.

"How long can some of the leaders of dentistry in other states be so complacent and willing to fall into the trap that is being set for us. If only they would take the time, to see from whence come the arrows that are heading in our direction. The Delta Dental Plans have bedded down with the unions and have been a party to setting up the greatest controls that any profession has ever known in a free society. . . .

"The name of the game is money. The government and labor are determined to reduce the cost of the dental health dollar at the expense of the dentist. There is no way a dental service can be rendered cheaper when the third party has to have its share of the dollar.

"Already we are locked into a fee freeze that could completely control the quality of dental care, if left on long enough."

continuing to enforce the Association's prior policy of refusal to submit x-rays to dental insurers.

In 1978, the Federal Trade Commission issued a complaint against the Federation, alleging in substance that its efforts to prevent its members from complying with insurers' requests for x-rays constituted an unfair method of competition in violation of § 5 of the Federal Trade Commission Act. . . .

The Federation sought judicial review of the Commission's order in the United States Court of Appeals for the Seventh Circuit, which vacated the order on the ground that it was not supported by substantial evidence. Accepting the Federation's characterization of its rule against submission of x-rays as merely an ethical and moral policy designed to enhance the welfare of dental patients, the majority concluded that the Commission's findings that the policy was anticompetitive were erroneous. According to the majority, the evidence did not support the finding that in the absence of restraint dentists would compete for patients by offering cooperation with the requests of the patients' insurers, nor, even accepting that finding, was there evidence that the Federation's efforts had prevented such competition. Further, the court held that the Commission's findings were inadequate because of its failure both to offer a precise definition of the market in which the Federation was alleged to have restrained competition and to establish that the Federation had the power to restrain competition in that market. Finally, the majority faulted the Commission for not finding that the alleged restraint on competition among dentists had actually resulted in higher dental costs to patients and insurers. The third member of the Court of Appeals panel concurred in the judgment solely on the ground that there was insufficient proof that cooperation with insurers was an element of dental services as to which dentists would tend to compete. . . .

III

The relevant factual findings are that the members of the Federation conspired among themselves to withhold x-rays requested by dental insurers for use in evaluating claims for benefits, and that this conspiracy had the effect of suppressing competition among dentists with respect to cooperation with the requests of the insurance companies. As to the first of these findings there can be no serious dispute: abundant evidence in the record reveals that one of the primary reasons—if not the primary reason—for the Federation's existence was the promulgation and enforcement of the so-called "work rule" against submission of x-rays in conjunction with insurance claim forms.

As for the second crucial finding—that competition was actually suppressed—the Seventh Circuit held it to be unsupported by the evidence, on two theories. First, the court stated that the evidence did not establish that cooperation with requests for information by patients' insurance companies was an aspect of the provision of dental services with respect to which dentists would, in the absence of some restraint, compete. Second, the court found that even assuming that dentists would otherwise compete with respect to policies of cooperating or not cooperating with insurance companies, the Federation's policy did not impair that competition, for the member dentists continued to allow insurance companies to use other means of evaluating their diagnoses when reviewing claims for benefits: specifically, "the IFD member dentists allowed insurers to visit the dental office to review and examine the patient's x-rays along with all of the other diagnostic and clinical aids used in formulating a proper course of dental treatment."

Neither of these criticisms of the Commission's findings is well founded. The Commission's finding that "[i]n the absence of ... concerted behavior, individual dentists would have been subject to market forces of competition, creating incentives for them to ... comply with the requests of patients' third-party insurers," finds support not only in common sense and economic theory, upon both of which the FTC may reasonably rely, but also in record documents, including newsletters circulated among Indiana dentists, revealing that Indiana dentists themselves perceived that unrestrained competition tended to lead their colleagues to comply with insurers' requests for x-rays. Moreover, there was evidence that outside of Indiana, in States where dentists had not collectively refused to submit x-rays, insurance companies found little difficulty in obtaining compliance by dentists with their requests. A "reasonable mind" could conclude on the basis of this evidence that competition for patients, who have obvious incentives for seeking dentists who will cooperate with their insurers, would tend to lead dentists in Indiana (and elsewhere) to cooperate with requests for information by their patients' insurers.

The Commission's finding that such competition was actually diminished where the Federation held sway also finds adequate support in the record. The Commission found that in the areas where Federation membership among dentists was most significant (that is, in the vicinity of Anderson and Lafayette) insurance companies were unable to obtain compliance with their requests for submission of x-rays in conjunction with claim forms and were forced to resort to other, more costly, means of reviewing diagnoses for the purpose of benefit determination. Neither the opinion of the Court of Appeals nor the brief of respondent identifies any evidence suggesting that the Commission's finding that the Federation's policy had an actual impact on the ability of insurers to obtain the x-rays they requested was incorrect. The lower court's conclusion that this evidence is to be discounted because Federation members continued to cooperate with insurers by allowing them to use more costly—indeed, prohibitively costly—methods of reviewing treatment decisions is unpersuasive. The fact remains that the dentists' customers (that is, the patients and their insurers) sought a particular service: cooperation with the insurers' pretreatment review through the forwarding of x-rays in conjunction with claim forms. The Federation's collective activities resulted in the denial of the information the customers requested in the form that they requested it, and forced them to choose between acquiring that information in a more costly manner or forgoing it altogether. To this extent, at least, competition among dentists with respect to cooperation with the requests of insurers was restrained.

IV

The question remains whether these findings are legally sufficient to establish a violation of § 1 of the Sherman Act—that is, whether the Federation's collective refusal to cooperate with insurers' requests for x-rays constitutes an "unreasonable" restraint of trade. Under our precedents, a restraint may be adjudged unreasonable either because it fits within a class of restraints that has been held to be "*per se*" unreasonable, or because it violates what has come to be known as the "Rule of Reason," under which the "test of legality is whether the restraint imposed is such as merely regulates and perhaps thereby promotes competition or whether it is such as may suppress or even destroy competition." *Chicago Board of Trade v. United States*, 246 U.S., at 238.

are these findings enough for violation of Sherman ?

The policy of the Federation with respect to its members' dealings with third-party insurers resembles practices that have been labeled "group boycotts": the policy constitutes a concerted refusal to deal on particular terms with patients covered by group dental insurance.... Although this Court has in the past stated that group boycotts are unlawful *per se*, ... we decline to resolve this case by forcing the Federation's policy into the "boycott" pigeonhole and invoking the *per se* rule. As we observed last Term in *Northwest Wholesale Stationers, Inc. v. Pacific Stationery and Printing Co.*, 472 U.S. 284 (1985), the category of restraints classed as group boycotts is not to be expanded indiscriminately, and the *per se* approach has generally been limited to cases in which firms with market power boycott suppliers or customers in order to discourage them from doing business with a competitor—a situation obviously not present here. Moreover, we have been slow to condemn rules adopted by professional associations as unreasonable *per se*, see *National Society of Professional Engineers v. United States*, 435 U.S. 679 (1978), and, in general, to extend *per se* analysis to restraints imposed in the context of business relationships where the economic impact of certain practices is not immediately obvious, see *Broadcast Music, Inc. v. CBS*, 441 U.S. 1 (1979). Thus, as did the FTC, we evaluate the restraint at issue in this case under the Rule of Reason rather than a rule of *per se* illegality.

NOT using per se rule

ROR

Application of the Rule of Reason to these facts is not a matter of any great difficulty. The Federation's policy takes the form of a horizontal agreement among the participating dentists to withhold from their customers a particular service that they desire—the forwarding of x-rays to insurance companies along with claim forms. "While this is not price fixing as such, no elaborate industry analysis is required to demonstrate the anticompetitive character of such an agreement." *Society of Professional Engineers, supra*, 435 U.S. at 692. A refusal to compete with respect to the package of services offered to customers, no less than a refusal to compete with respect to the price term of an agreement, impairs the ability of the market to advance social welfare by ensuring the provision of desired goods and services to consumers at a price approximating the marginal cost of providing them. Absent some countervailing procompetitive virtue—such as, for example, the creation of efficiencies in the operation of a market or the provision of goods and services, see *Broadcast Music, Inc. v. CBS, supra; Chicago Board of Trade, supra;* cf. *NCAA v. Board of Regents of Univ. of Okla.,* 468 U.S. 85 (1984)—such an agreement limiting consumer choice by impeding the "ordinary give and take of the market place," *Society of Professional Engineers, supra,* 435 U.S. at 692, cannot be sustained under the Rule of Reason. No credible argument has been advanced for the proposition that making it more costly for the insurers and patients who are the dentists' customers to obtain information needed for evaluating the dentists' diagnoses has any such procompetitive effect.

The Federation advances three principal arguments for the proposition that, notwithstanding its lack of competitive virtue, the Federation's policy of withholding x-rays should not be deemed an unreasonable restraint of trade. First, as did the Court of Appeals, the Federation suggests that in the absence of specific findings by the Commission concerning the definition of the market in which the Federation allegedly restrained trade and the power of the Federation's members in that market, the conclusion that the Federation unreasonably restrained trade is erroneous as a matter of law, regardless of whether the challenged practices might be impermissibly anticompetitive if engaged in by persons who together possessed power in a specifically defined market. This contention, however, runs counter to the Court's holding in *NCAA v. Board of Regents, supra,* that "[a]s a matter of law, the absence of proof of market power does not justify a naked restriction on price or output," and that such a restriction "requires some competitive justification even in the absence of a detailed market analysis." 468 U.S., at 109–110. Moreover, even if the restriction imposed by the Federation is not sufficiently "naked" to call this principle into play, the Commission's failure to engage in detailed market analysis is not fatal to its finding of a violation of the Rule of Reason. The Commission found that in two localities in the State of Indiana (the Anderson and Lafayette areas), Federation dentists constituted heavy majorities of the practicing dentists and that as a result of the efforts of the Federation, insurers in those areas were, over a period of years, actually unable to obtain compliance with their requests for submission of x rays. Since the purpose of the inquiries into market definition and market power is to determine whether an arrangement has the potential for genuine adverse effects on competition, "proof of actual detrimental effects, such as a reduction of output" can obviate the need for an inquiry into market power, which is but a "surrogate for detrimental effects." ... In this case, we conclude that the finding of actual, sustained adverse effects on competition in those areas where IFD dentists predominated, viewed in light of the reality that markets for dental services tend to be relatively localized, is legally sufficient to support a finding that the challenged restraint was unreasonable even in the absence of elaborate market analysis.[11]

---

11. Because we find that the Commission's findings can be sustained on this basis, we do not address the Commission's contention that the Federation's activities can be condemned

2) no evidence of incr prices

Second, the Federation, again following the lead of the Court of Appeals, argues that a holding that its policy of withholding x-rays constituted an unreasonable restraint of trade is precluded by the Commission's failure to make any finding that the policy resulted in the provision of dental services that were more costly than those that the patients and their insurers would have chosen were they able to evaluate x-rays in conjunction with claim forms. This argument, too, is unpersuasive. Although it is true that the goal of the insurers in seeking submission of x-rays for use in their review of benefits claims was to minimize costs by choosing the least expensive adequate course of dental treatment, a showing that this goal was actually achieved through the means chosen is not an essential step in establishing that the dentists' attempt to thwart its achievement by collectively refusing to supply the requested information was an unreasonable restraint of trade. A concerted and effective effort to withhold (or make more costly) information desired by consumers for the purpose of determining whether a particular purchase is cost-justified is likely enough to disrupt the proper functioning of the price-setting mechanism of the market that it may be condemned even absent proof that it resulted in higher prices or, as here, the purchase of higher-priced services, than would occur in its absence. *Society of Professional Engineers, supra.* Moreover, even if the desired information were in fact completely useless to the insurers and their patients in making an informed choice regarding the least costly adequate course of treatment—or, to put it another way, if the costs of evaluating the information were far greater than the cost savings resulting from its use—the Federation would still not be justified in deciding on behalf of its members' customers that they did not need the information: presumably, if that were the case, the discipline of the market would itself soon result in the insurers' abandoning their requests for x-rays. The Federation is not entitled to pre-empt the working of the market by deciding for itself that its customers do not need that which they demand.

Third, the Federation complains that the Commission erred in failing to consider, as relevant to its Rule of Reason analysis, noncompetitive "quality of care" justifications for the prohibition on provision of x-rays to insurers in conjunction with claim forms. This claim reflects the Court of Appeals' repeated characterization of the Federation's policy as a "legal, moral, and ethical policy of quality dental care, requiring that insurers examine and review all diagnostic and clinical aids before formulating a proper course of dental treatment." The gist of the claim is that x-rays, standing alone, are not adequate bases for diagnosis of dental problems or for the formulation of an acceptable course of treatment. Accordingly, if insurance companies are permitted to determine whether they will pay a claim for dental treatment on the basis of x-rays as opposed to a full examination of all the diagnostic aids available to the examining dentist,

---

regardless of market power or actual effect merely because they constitute a continuation of the restraints formerly imposed by the Indiana Dental Association, which allegedly had market power throughout the State of Indiana.

there is a danger that they will erroneously decline to pay for treatment that is in fact in the interest of the patient, and that the patient will as a result be deprived of fully adequate care.

The Federation's argument is flawed both legally and factually. The premise of the argument is that, far from having no effect on the cost of dental services chosen by patients and their insurers, the provision of x-rays will have too great an impact: it will lead to the reduction of costs through the selection of inadequate treatment. Precisely such a justification for withholding information from customers was rejected as illegitimate in the *Society of Professional Engineers* case. The argument is, in essence, that an unrestrained market in which consumers are given access to the information they believe to be relevant to their choices will lead them to make unwise and even dangerous choices. Such an argument amounts to "nothing less than a frontal assault on the basic policy of the Sherman Act." *Society of Professional Engineers, supra*, 435 U.S. at 695. Moreover, there is no particular reason to believe that the provision of information will be more harmful to consumers in the market for dental services than in other markets. Insurers deciding what level of care to pay for are not themselves the recipients of those services, but it is by no means clear that they lack incentives to consider the welfare of the patient as well as the minimization of costs. They are themselves in competition for the patronage of the patients—or, in most cases, the unions or businesses that contract on their behalf for group insurance coverage—and must satisfy their potential customers not only that they will provide coverage at a reasonable cost, but also that that coverage will be adequate to meet their customers' dental needs. There is thus no more reason to expect dental insurance companies to sacrifice quality in return for cost savings than to believe this of consumers in, say, the market for engineering services. Accordingly, if noncompetitive quality-of-service justifications are inadmissible to justify the denial of information to consumers in the latter market, there is little reason to credit such justifications here.

In any event, the Commission did not, as the Federation suggests, refuse even to consider the quality of care justification for the withholding of x-rays. Rather, the Commission held that the Federation had failed to introduce sufficient evidence to establish such a justification: "IFD has not pointed to any evidence—or even argued—that any consumers have in fact been harmed by alternative benefits determinations, or that actual determinations have been medically erroneous." 101 F.T.C., at 177. The evidence before the Administrative Law Judge on this issue appears to have consisted entirely of expert opinion testimony, with the Federation's experts arguing that x-rays generally provide an insufficient basis, standing alone, for dental diagnosis, and the Commission's experts testifying that x-rays may be useful in assessing diagnosis of and appropriate treatment for a variety of dental complaints. *Id.*, 384 U.S. at 128–132. The Commission was amply justified in concluding on the basis of this conflicting evidence that even if concern for the quality of patient care could under some circumstances serve as a justification for a restraint of the sort imposed here, the evidence did not support a finding that the careful use of x-rays as a basis for evaluating insurance claims is in fact destructive of proper standards of dental care.

In addition to arguing that its conspiracy did not effect an unreasonable restraint of trade, the Federation appears to renew its argument, pressed before both the Commission and the Court of Appeals, that the conspiracy to withhold x-rays is immunized from antitrust scrutiny by virtue of a supposed policy of the State of Indiana against the evaluation of dental x-rays by lay employees of insurance companies. . . . Allegedly, such use of x-rays by insurance companies—even where no claim was actually denied without examination of an x-ray by a licensed dentist—would constitute unauthorized practice of dentistry by the insurance company and its employees. The Commission found that this claim had no basis in any authoritative source of Indiana law, and the Federation has not identified any adequate reason for rejecting the Commission's conclusion. Even if the Commission were incorrect in its reading of the law, however, the Federation's claim of immunity would fail. That a particular practice may be unlawful is not, in itself, a sufficient justification for collusion among competitors to prevent it. See *Fashion Originators' Guild of America, Inc. v. FTC*, 312 U.S. 457, 468 (1941). Anticompetitive collusion among private actors, even when its goal is consistent with state policy, acquires antitrust immunity only when it is actively supervised by the State. See *Southern Motor Carriers Rate Conference, Inc. v. United States*, 471 U.S. 48 (1985). There is no suggestion of "any" such active supervision here; accordingly, whether or not the policy that Federation has taken upon itself to advance is consistent with the policy of the State of Indiana, the Federation's activities are subject to Sherman Act condemnation. . . . Reversed.

NOTES AND QUESTIONS

1. *Effect of rule of reason rule*. What difference did it make in *Indiana Federation of Dentists* that the Court applied a "rule of reason" rather than a *per se* rule? What evidence did the Court take into account that would have been precluded a *per se* analysis?

2. *Market power in* Rothery. Rothery Storage and Van Co. v. Atlas Van Lines, 792 F.2d 210 (D.C. Cir. 1986), was decided before several of the Supreme Court cases we have considered, but Judge Bork's opinion was ahead of its time. In that case, defendant Atlas was a nationwide common carrier of household goods. Like most national moving companies, it employed independent moving companies throughout the country as its agents to find customers and handle packing, loading, hauling and storage. Atlas set the rates for shipment, chose routes, arranged backhauls, collected revenues, and paid the agents for their services. Atlas also conducted national advertising, established uniform rules for appearance and quality, maintained insurance and handled claims. In 1982, it announced that it would terminate agency arrangements with any affiliated company that handled interstate carriage on its own account as well as for Atlas. Agent carriers could compete in the interstate market by setting up separate corporations with new names, but they could not use the facilities or services of Atlas. Atlas stood sixth in 1981 national

market share for interstate van lines with 5.86%. The market itself was far from concentrated, with the top 15 firms accounting for less than 70%. Plaintiff carrier agents challenged the arrangement as a group boycott and illegal *per se.*

Writing a few months before *Indiana Federation of Dentists* was decided, Judge Bork upheld the arrangements on several grounds, including (1) that the challenged restraint was ancillary to the economic integration of the Atlas enterprise, (2) that the non-compete policy was a reasonable response to the problem of agent carriers taking a free ride on Atlas' name and investments, and (3) that Atlas' market share was far too small for the restraint to threaten competition.

On market power, the opinion had this to say:

> Analysis might begin and end with the observation that Atlas and its agents command between 5.1% and 6.0% of the relevant market, which is the interstate carriage of used household goods. It is impossible to believe that an agreement to eliminate competition within a group of that size can produce any of the evils of monopoly.... A monopolist (or those acting together to achieve monopoly results) enhances its revenues by raising the market price. It can do that only if its share of the market is so large that by reducing its output of goods and services the amount offered by the industry is substantially reduced so that the price is bid up. If a group of Atlas' size reduced its output of services, there would be no effect upon market price because firms making up the other 94% of the market would simply take over the abandoned business. The only effect would be a loss of revenues to Atlas. Indeed, so impotent to raise prices is a firm with a market share of 5% or 6% that any attempt by it to engage in monopolistic restriction of output would be little short of suicidal.

At a later point in the opinion, Judge Bork explicitly used market power as a screen for liability, despite the "boycott" label that had been used:

> We might well rest, therefore, upon the absence of market power as demonstrated both by Atlas' 6% national market share and by the structure of the market. If it is clear that Atlas and its agents by eliminating competition among themselves are not attempting to restrict industry output, then their agreement must be designed to make the conduct of their business more effective. No third possibility suggests itself.

Chief Judge Wald concurred in the result, largely on grounds that the challenged arrangements appeared to enhance efficiency of the van lines and clearly overbalanced any possible anticompetitive evils. On the question of market power, Judge Wald took a more restrained approach, commenting that there was not sufficient guidance from the Supreme Court to take the majority's rather myopic view anticompetitive behavior was not possible without sufficient market power.

3. *Evaluation of the market power test in* Rothery. Is it correct to argue (as the majority did in *Rothery*) that its market power test followed from Supreme Court decisions in *BMI, NCAA,* and *Northwest Wholesale Stationers?* If so, does it follow that *Topco* must have been overruled, *sub silentio,* by those three cases? Is the *Rothery* majority's view that a finding of substantial market power is a necessary prerequisite to any finding of an antitrust violation consistent with the Supreme Court's decision, handed down several months later, in *Indiana Federation of Dentists?* Should the Government ever bother to challenge practices by companies or groups of companies with modest market shares? Which ones (if any)? Why?

Federal Trade Commission v. Superior Court Trial Lawyers Association

Supreme Court of the United States, 1990.
493 U.S. 411, 110 S.Ct. 768, 107 L.Ed.2d 851.

[In 1983, a group of lawyers in the District of Columbia who were members of the Superior Court Trial Lawyers Association (SCTLA) agreed not to accept appointment under the District of Columbia Criminal Justice Act to represent indigent criminal defendants in the Superior Court unless the D.C. city government agreed to increase their compensation. There was widespread agreement that compensation to court-appointed lawyers was low, but the Mayor insisted that no money was available for a fee increase.

The lawyers' refusal to accept appointment was well publicized and garnered public support for a pay raise. Within ten days, city officials agreed to come to the bargaining table, and eventually the Mayor and the SCTLA lawyers negotiated and eventually agreed to a modest fee increase.

The FTC, however, proceeding under section 5 of the FTC Act, filed a complaint against SCTLA and four of its officers for conspiring to fix prices and to conduct a boycott. The Commission eventually found a *per se* violation. On appeal, the D.C. Circuit rejected SCTLA's argument that the boycott was justified because it was designed to improve the quality of representation for indigent defendants. The Court noted, however, that boycotts historically have been used as a dramatic means of expression and that the lawyers were conveying a political message deserving of some First Amendment protection. The Court concluded that such boycotts would not violate the antitrust laws unless there was a serious risk of competitive harm. That risk, in turn, could not be assessed without a determination whether respondents possessed "significant market power." Such a finding was impossible under a *per se* rule, and accordingly, the Court of Appeals remanded the case for further proceedings on that point.

The Supreme Court reinstated the Commission's finding of a violation. It concluded that the horizontal arrangement was a "naked restraint," constricting supply in order to raise price. It distinguished *Noerr* (*infra* p. 390) on the ground that in *Noerr* it was the desired legislation that would have created the restraint on competition, while in *SCTLA*, the *means* by which respondents sought favorable legislation was itself the source of the competitive injury.]

■ STEVENS, J. . . . The lawyers' association argues that if its conduct would otherwise be prohibited by the Sherman Act and the Federal Trade Act, it is nonetheless protected by the First Amendment rights recognized in *NAACP v. Claiborne Hardware*, 458 U.S. 886 (1982). That case arose after black citizens boycotted white merchants in Claiborne County, Miss. The white merchants sued under state law to recover losses from the boycott. We found that the "right of the States to regulate economic activity could not justify a complete prohibition against a nonviolent, politically motivated boycott designed to force governmental and economic change and to effectuate rights guaranteed by the Constitution itself." We accordingly held that "the nonviolent elements of petitioners' activities are entitled to the protection of the First Amendment."

The lawyers' association contends that because it, like the boycotters in *Claiborne Hardware,* sought to vindicate constitutional rights, it should enjoy a similar First Amendment protection. . . .

The activity that the FTC order prohibits is a concerted refusal by CJA lawyers to accept any further assignments until they receive an increase in their compensation; the undenied objective of their boycott was an economic advantage for those who agreed to participate. It is true that the *Claiborne Hardware* case also involved a boycott. That boycott, however, differs in a decisive respect. Those who joined the *Claiborne Hardware* boycott sought no special advantage for themselves. They were black citizens in Port Gibson, Mississippi, who had been the victims of political, social, and economic discrimination for many years. They sought only the equal respect and equal treatment to which they were constitutionally entitled. They struggled "to change a social order that had consistently treated them as second class citizens." 458 U.S., at 912. As we observed, the campaign was not intended "to destroy legitimate competition." *Id.,* at 914. Equality and freedom are preconditions of the free market, and not commodities to be haggled over within it.

The same cannot be said of attorney's fees. As we recently pointed out, our reasoning in *Claiborne Hardware* is not applicable to a boycott conducted by business competitors who "stand to profit financially from a lessening of competition in the boycotted market." *Allied Tube Corp. v. Indian Head.* . . .

The Court of Appeals, however, crafted a new exception to the *per se* rules, and it is this exception which provoked the FTC's petition to this Court. The Court of Appeals derived its exception from *United States v. O'Brien*, 391 U.S. 367 (1968). In that case O'Brien had burned his Selective Service registration certificate on the steps of the South Boston Courthouse. He did so before a sizable crowd and with the purpose of advocating his antiwar beliefs. We affirmed his conviction. We held that the governmental interest in regulating the "nonspeech element" of his conduct adequately justified the incidental restriction on First Amendment freedoms. Specifically, we concluded that the statute's incidental restriction on O'Brien's freedom of expression was no greater than necessary to further the Government's interest in requiring registrants to have valid certificates continually available.

However, the Court of Appeals held that, in light of *O'Brien,* the expressive component of respondents' boycott compelled courts to apply the antitrust laws "prudently and with sensitivity," 856 F.2d, at 233–234, with a "special solicitude for the First Amendment rights" of respondents. The Court of Appeals concluded that the governmental interest in prohibiting boycotts is not sufficient to justify a restriction on the communicative element of the boycott unless the FTC can prove, and not merely presume, that the boycotters have market power. Because the Court of Appeals imposed this special requirement upon the Government, it ruled that *per se* antitrust analysis was inapplicable to boycotts having an expressive component.

There are at least two critical flaws in the Court of Appeals' antitrust analysis: it exaggerates the significance of the expressive component in respondents' boycott and it denigrates the importance of the rule of law that respondents violated. Implicit in the conclusion of the Court of Appeals are unstated assumptions that most economic boycotts do not have an expressive component, and that the categorical prohibitions against price fixing and boycotts are merely rules of "administrative convenience" that do not serve any substantial governmental interest unless the price-fixing competitors actually possess market power.

It would not much matter to the outcome of this case if these flawed assumptions were sound. *O'Brien* would offer respondents no protection even if their boycott were uniquely expressive and even if the purpose of the *per se* rules were purely that of administrative efficiency. We have recognized that the Government's interest in adhering to a uniform rule may sometimes satisfy the *O'Brien* test even if making an exception to the rule in a particular case might cause no serious damage. *United States v. Albertini*, 472 U.S. 675, 688 (1985) ("The First Amendment does not bar application of a neutral regulation that incidentally burdens speech merely because a party contends that allowing an exception in the particular case will not threaten important government interests"). The administrative efficiency interests in antitrust regulation are unusually compelling. The *per se* rules avoid "the necessity for an incredibly complicated and prolonged economic investigation into the entire history of the industry involved, as well as related industries, in an effort to determine at large whether a particular restraint has been unreasonable." *Northern Pac. R. Co. v. United States*, 356 U.S. 1, 5 (1958). If small parties "were allowed to prove lack of market power, all parties would have that right, thus introducing the enormous complexities of market definition into every price-fixing case." R. Bork, The Antitrust Paradox 269 (1978). For these reasons, it is at least possible that the *Claiborne Hardware* doctrine, which itself rests in part upon *O'Brien,* exhausts *O'Brien's* application to the antitrust statutes.

In any event, however, we cannot accept the Court of Appeals' characterization of this boycott or the antitrust laws. Every concerted refusal to do business with a potential customer or supplier has an expressive component. At one level, the competitors must exchange their views about their objectives and the means of obtaining them. The most blatant, naked price-fixing agreement is a product of communication, but that is surely not a reason for viewing it with special solicitude. At another level, after the terms of the boycotters' demands have been agreed upon, they must be communicated to its target: "we will not do business until you do what we ask." That expressive component of the boycott conducted by these respondents is surely not unique. On the contrary, it is the hallmark of every effective boycott.

At a third level, the boycotters may communicate with third parties to enlist public support for their objectives; to the extent that the boycott is newsworthy, it will facilitate the expression of the boycotters' ideas. But this level of expression is not an element of the boycott. Publicity may be generated by any other activity that is sufficiently newsworthy. Some activities, including the boycott here, may be newsworthy precisely for the reasons that they are prohibited: the harms they produce are matters of public concern. Certainly that is no reason for removing the prohibition.

In sum, there is thus nothing unique about the "expressive component" of respondents' boycott. A rule that requires courts to apply the antitrust laws "prudently and with sensitivity" whenever an economic boycott has an "expressive component" would create a gaping hole in the fabric of those laws. Respondents' boycott thus has no special characteristics meriting an exemption from the *per se* rules of antitrust law.

Equally important is the second error implicit in respondents' claim to immunity from the *per se* rules. In its opinion, the Court of Appeals assumed that the antitrust laws permit, but do not require, the condemnation of price fixing and boycotts without proof of market power. The opinion further assumed that the *per se* rule prohibiting such activity "is only a rule of 'administrative convenience and efficiency,' not a statutory command." 856 F.2d, at 249. This statement contains two errors. The *per se* rules are, of course, the product of judicial interpretations of the Sherman Act, but the rules nevertheless have the same force and effect as any other statutory commands. Moreover, while the *per se* rule against price fixing and boycotts is indeed justified in part by "administrative convenience," the Court of Appeals erred in describing the prohibition as justified only by such concerns. The *per se* rules also reflect a long-standing judgment that the prohibited practices by their nature have "a substantial potential for impact on competition." *Jefferson Parish Hospital District,* 466 U.S., at 16....

The *per se* rules in antitrust law serve purposes analogous to *per se* restrictions upon, for example, stunt flying in congested areas or speeding. Laws prohibiting stunt flying or setting speed limits are justified by the State's interest in protecting human life and property. Perhaps most violations of such rules actually cause no harm. No doubt many experienced drivers and pilots can operate much more safely, even at prohibited speeds, than the average citizen.

If the especially skilled drivers and pilots were to paint messages on their cars, or attach streamers to their planes, their conduct would have an expressive component. High speeds and unusual maneuvers would help to draw attention to their messages. Yet the laws may nonetheless be enforced against these skilled persons without proof that their conduct was actually harmful or dangerous.

In part, the justification for these *per se* rules is rooted in administrative convenience. They are also supported, however, by the observation that every speeder and every stunt pilot poses some threat to the community. An unpredictable event may overwhelm the skills of the best driver or pilot, even if the proposed course of action was entirely prudent when initiated. A bad driver going slowly may be more dangerous than a good driver going quickly, but a good driver who obeys the law is safer still.

So it is with boycotts and price fixing. Every such horizontal arrangement among competitors poses some threat to the free market. A small participant in the market is, obviously, less likely to cause persistent damage than a large participant. Other participants in the market may act quickly and effectively to take the small participant's place. For reasons including market inertia and information failures, however, a small conspirator may be able to impede competition over some period of time. Given an appropriate set of circumstances and some luck, the period can be long enough to inflict real injury upon particular consumers or competitors. . . .

Of course, some boycotts and some price-fixing agreements are more pernicious than others; some are only partly successful, and some may only succeed when they are buttressed by other causative factors, such as political influence. But an assumption that, absent proof of market power, the boycott disclosed by this record was totally harmless—when overwhelming testimony demonstrated that it almost produced a crisis in the administration of criminal justice in the District and when it achieved its economic goal—is flatly inconsistent with the clear course of our antitrust jurisprudence. Conspirators need not achieve the dimensions of a monopoly, or even a degree of market power any greater than that already disclosed by this record, to warrant condemnation under the antitrust laws.

The judgment of the Court of Appeals is accordingly reversed insofar as that court held the *per se* rules inapplicable to the lawyers' boycott.[12] . . .

■ [BRENNAN, J., joined by BLACKMUN and MARSHALL, JJ., dissented on grounds that an expressive boycott—*i.e.*, one that appears to operate on a political rather than economic level—ought not to be condemned under a *per se* rule. Historically, such boycotts have been essential to the "poorly financed causes of little people," who often cannot use established organizational techniques to advance their political interests.]

NOTE ON HARTFORD FIRE INSURANCE CO. v. CALIFORNIA

In 1993, the Supreme Court decided Hartford Fire Insurance Co. v. California, 509 U.S. 764 (1993). Plaintiffs (for the most part, state attorneys general) alleged that certain domestic and foreign insurance companies and re-insurance companies had violated the Sherman Act by conspiring to change commercial general insurance policies from "occurrence based" policies to "claims-made" policies and to cease underwriting certain environmental risks. At the center of their claims was an

---

12. In response to [the dissent], and particularly to its observation that some concerted arrangements that might be characterized as "group boycotts" may not merit *per se* condemnation, we emphasize that this case involves not only a boycott but also a horizontal price-fixing arrangement—a type of conspiracy that has been consistently analyzed as a *per se* violation for many decades. . . .

allegation that the domestic insurers, acting with the foreign re-insurers, had agreed to boycott any company that did not abide by the new rules. Justice Scalia, writing for a five-person majority on this aspect of the case, concluded that the term "boycott" should not be so broadly construed. This was important because of the McCarran–Ferguson Act, 15 U.S.C. § 1011 *et seq.*, which exempts insurance companies from the antitrust laws to the extent that they are regulated by the states (and in this instance, arguably, by foreign governments). An exception to that exemption exists, under section 3(b) of the McCarran–Ferguson Act, 15 U.S.C. § 1013(b), for boycotts. Justice Scalia thought it important to distinguish between a "conditional boycott and a concerted agreement to seek particular terms in particular transactions." 509 U.S. at 801–02. Only the former qualified as a true boycott. Here, he wrote, it was "obviously not a 'boycott' for the reinsurers to 'refus[e] to reinsure coverages written on the ISO CGL forms until the desired changes were made,' . . . because the terms of the primary coverages are central elements of the reinsurance contract—they are *what* is reinsured." *Id.* at 806 (emphasis in original). Notwithstanding this narrow definition of boycott, the Court went on to find that there were sufficient allegations of a true conditional boycott in the complaints to survive a motion to dismiss. For example, there was an allegation that primary insurers who wrote insurance on disfavored forms would be refused all reinsurance, even for risks written on other forms. *Id.* at 810.

The dissenters, led by Justice Souter, believed that the majority had adopted an overly narrow definition of the term "boycott" as it was used in section 3(b) of the McCarran–Ferguson Act. They saw no reason to confine the concept of "boycott" to refusals to deal that are unrelated or collateral to the objective sought by those refusing to deal. Justice Souter also pointed out certain common ground between the majority and the dissenters: (1) only those refusals to deal involving the coordinated action of multiple actors fall within the scope of § 3(b); (2) a § 3(b) boycott need not involve an absolute refusal to deal; (3) such a boycott need not entail unequal treatment of the targets of the boycott and its instigators, and (4) concerted activity, while a necessary element of a § 3(b) boycott, is not by itself sufficient. The dissenters' view would have preserved far more of the complaint for further proceedings.

PROBLEM 6

INVESTIGATION AGENCY FOR KANSAS CITY BANKS

In Kansas City, all the local banks decided to eliminate duplication of effort and expense by setting up a common agency to investigate local applicants for loans to determine if they are creditworthy. Upon the request of a bank, the joint agency investigated any person or concern and circulated to all banks a resume of information supporting its conclusions as to whether the party involved was a good or bad risk under general criteria established by the local bankers' association.

The plaintiff owned a tavern in Kansas City and applied for a loan. The joint agency, however, determined that plaintiff should be disqualified because its tavern was located in a "crime-ridden" section of town and was therefore subject to constant risk of robbery. Plaintiff claimed that the refusal was racially motivated, since almost all of the establishments in the part of town designated as "crime-ridden" were patronized by African-Americans. Attempts to obtain loans from banks in nearby cities proved unavailing when the plaintiff explained why it had been refused by the Kansas City banks.

Plaintiff eventually received a loan from an out-of-state bank at higher interest rates than available earlier to businesses in Kansas City, and then sued the Kansas City banks and their common agency for treble damages under Section 1 of the Sherman Act. Should the plaintiff recover?

SECTION 2. JOINT VENTURES REVISITED: ISSUES OF MEMBERSHIP AND ACCESS

INTRODUCTION

1. *Joint ventures in antitrust context.* Almost any collaborative activity among business firms can be referred to as a joint venture, since the designation is not a technical "term of art" in antitrust law. In common usage, however, a joint venture carries the positive connotation of cooperation among firms, usually accompanied by some actual integration of managerial or production resources, to achieve some useful business objective more efficiently than either (or any) could alone. It is thus distinguished from a cartel or price-fixing arrangement, for example.

A joint venture often takes the form of a new jointly owned corporate subsidiary, in which case the asset and share transfers involved may invoke the antitrust law dealing with mergers, Section 7 of the Clayton Act. Thus, we will deal with joint ventures again in Chapter 9 *infra*.

But frequently joint ventures are contractual in form or a kind of partnership among firms for a limited purpose, and questions arise only under the Sherman Act. Since joint venture agreements may result in the exclusion of competitors from access to the jointly created new product, technology, or facility, thus placing the outsiders at a competitive disadvantage, the joint venture has some characteristics of a group boycott.

2. *The consumer welfare principle applied to joint ventures.* Joint ventures raise in a particularly significant way the question of the proper standard for evaluating injury under the antitrust laws. In a static sense, monopoly (or cartel) pricing has two effects. First, the monopoly overcharge transfers wealth from the consumer to the monopolist. Second, the higher price chokes off demand. Some consumers would be willing to buy the monopolist's product at a price less than the monopoly price but more than monopolist's cost of producing the product. The monopolist, assuming it cannot price discriminate, will not produce these units. (These points are explained more fully in the Economics Appendix.)

While everyone agrees that monopoly pricing has these effects, commentators disagree over whether both effects pose antitrust problems. Many commentators view the antitrust laws as consumer welfare statutes. They contend that the laws must be used to prevent both types of harm. Others insist that the antitrust laws are social welfare statutes. Those who take this view are indifferent to wealth transfers and focus solely on the deadweight loss.

To see why this disagreement becomes acute with joint ventures, consider an industry-wide joint venture that has two effects: (1) it creates production efficiencies that reduce costs and (2) it creates monopoly power by erecting barriers to entry and eliminating competition, allowing the participants to raise prices to the monopoly level. If the cost savings of the joint venture exceed the deadweight efficiency loss associated with the new monopoly pricing, should the antitrust laws applaud or condemn the arrangement?

The problem becomes even more complicated when posed in dynamic rather than static terms. The prospect of raising prices to the monopoly level gives firms incentives to expend resources to become monopolists. The way firms choose to expend these resources has important implications for social and consumer welfare.

Firms can attempt to create or maintain monopoly profits in a myriad of ways. They might attempt to deter rivals from entering their industries or to raise their rivals' costs. Economists refer to such behavior as "rent-seeking." It includes lobbying legislatures to create exclusionary regulations, licensing boards, or tariffs. According to some commentators, it includes hoarding scarce inputs in order to deny them to rivals. *See* Krattenmaker & Salop, *Anticompetitive Exclusion: Raising Rivals' Costs to Achieve Power Over Price*, 96 YALE L.J. 209 (1986). Whatever its form, rent-seeking behavior does not increase productive efficiency. On the other hand, firms might pursue monopoly profits through research and development. R & D might allow firms to reduce their costs of production or allow them to offer new and better products. R & D, although motivated by the same monopoly profits that drive rent-seeking, may benefit consumers.

Note, however, that a pure consumer welfare standard would find problematic a joint venture devoted to research and development. Suppose the industry-wide joint venture introduced above developed a production technology that reduced costs industry-wide. From the pure consumer welfare standpoint, such a combination would be unacceptable unless competition among the participating firms ensured that lower costs would be passed on to consumers in the form of lower prices.

Suppose the joint venture reduced production costs and created monopoly power. Suppose, also, that the post-development price was equal to (or less than) the pre-development price. Would the pure consumer welfare standard have a problem with this arrangement? Should it?

3. *Early Case*. United States v. Terminal Railroad Ass'n of St. Louis, 224 U.S. 383, 32 S.Ct. 507, 56 L.Ed. 810 (1912), is the seminal case involving an efficient joint venture and an inefficient refusal to deal. At the turn of the century, 24 railroads converged at the east and west banks of the Mississippi near St. Louis. About one half of the lines terminated (had their "termini") on the Illinois side of the river; others, coming from the west and north of St. Louis, terminated either in the city itself or on its northern edge. By 1890, in response to the growing demands of the railroads, bridges were built over the river to supplement the existing car ferry transfer system. Early on, three independent terminal companies operated the ferry and bridges for the railroad termini on each side of the Mississippi. This arrangement led to some duplication in services, but it also left open some opportunity for competition.

In 1899, 14 of the railroads, under the leadership of Jay Gould, formed the Terminal Railroad Association of St. Louis to acquire the terminal companies and operate them as a unified system. By their original agreement, the "proprietary companies" bound themselves to use the Association facilities exclusively. They required unanimous consent for the admission of new roads to the Association or use of the facility by non-member roads. The Court noted in its opinion that

> [t]he result of the geographical and topographical situation [was] that it [was], as a practical matter, impossible for any railroad company to pass through, or even enter St. Louis, so as to be within reach of its industries

or commerce, without using the facilities entirely controlled by the Terminal Company.

Id. at 397.

The Supreme Court concluded that the combination constituted a restraint of trade in violation of the Sherman Act and regarded it as no defense that the proprietary companies had not availed themselves of their power to impede free competition by excluding all non-proprietary companies or charging exorbitant rates. Justice Lurton, writing for the Court, noted that ordinarily, independent companies may combine for common, exclusive use because the alternative to onerous terms for admission or exclusion would be construction of another terminal. But, the Court noted, the St. Louis railroad junction was "most extraordinary," because of the physical and topographical characteristics of the area. Those traits both justified a unified system and demonstrated why such a system would restrain interstate commerce. The Court concluded that the unified system would not improperly restrain trade if it were an "impartial agent," but it pointed out several practices of the Terminal Company that did not meet that impartial agency standard.

The Court found that the effect of the "arbitrary discrimination" in rates was "obviously injurious to the commerce and manufacturers of St. Louis," and that the billing practices were justifiable only at a time when the eastern lines had no terminals in St. Louis. *Id.* at 408. The Court rejected the Government's petition for dissolution of the Association, and instead provided that the Association had to: (1) provide for admission to proprietary status or use of the terminal facilities by all railroads on reasonable and non-discriminatory terms; and (2) abolish the Company's discriminatory charges and billing practices.

4. *Next steps.* The rule established by *Terminal Railroad* was suitable only for a small subset of joint ventures: those in which the most efficient arrangement required near-universal access to the venture. In time, this came to be called the "essential facilities" doctrine. It was more than thirty years before the Supreme Court again confronted this kind of situation. Consider, as you read *Associated Press*, whether a different approach to the news-gathering joint venture would have been appropriate.

Associated Press v. United States

Supreme Court of the United States, 1945.
326 U.S. 1, 65 S.Ct. 1416, 89 L.Ed. 2013.

■ BLACK, J. The publishers of more than 1200 newspapers are members of the Associated Press (AP), a cooperative association incorporated under the Membership Corporations Law of the State of New York, Consol. Laws c. 35. Its business is the collection, assembly and distribution of news. The news it distributes is originally obtained by direct employees of the Association, employees of the member newspapers, and the employees of foreign independent news agencies with which AP has contractual relations, such as the Canadian Press. Distribution of the news is made through interstate channels of communication to the various newspaper members of the Association, who pay for it under an assessment plan which contemplates no profit to AP.

The United States filed a bill in a Federal District Court for an injunction against AP and other defendants charging that they had violated the Sherman Anti–Trust Act, 26 Stat. 209, 15 U.S.C.A. §§ 1–7, 15 note, in that their acts and conduct constituted (1) a combination and conspiracy in restraint of trade and commerce in news among the states, and (2) an attempt to monopolize a part of that trade.

The heart of the government's charge was that appellants had by concerted action set up a system of By–Laws which prohibited all AP members from selling news to non-members, and which granted each member powers to block its non-member competitors from membership. These By–Laws, to which all AP members had assented, were, in the context of the admitted facts, charged to be in violation of the Sherman Act.... The District Court, composed of three judges, held that the By–Laws unlawfully restricted admission to AP membership, and violated the Sherman Act insofar as the By–Laws' provisions clothed a member with powers to impose or dispense with conditions upon the admission of his business competitor. Continued observance of these By–Laws was enjoined.... The government's motion for summary judgment, under Rule 56 of the Rules of Civil Procedure, was granted and its prayer for relief was granted in part and denied in part. Both sides have brought the case to us on direct appeal....

To put the issue into proper focus, it becomes necessary at this juncture to examine the By–Laws.

All members must consent to be bound by them. They impose upon members certain duties and restrictions in the conduct of their separate businesses. For a violation of the By–Laws severe disciplinary action may be taken by the Association. The Board of Directors may impose a fine of $1000.00 or suspend a member and such "action ... shall be final and conclusive. No member shall have any right to question the same." ...

These By–Laws, for a violation of which members may be thus fined, suspended, or expelled, require that each newspaper member publish the AP news regularly in whole or in part, and that each shall "promptly furnish to the corporation, through its agents or employees, all the news of such member's district, the area of which shall be determined by the Board of Directors." All members are prohibited from selling or furnishing their spontaneous news to any agency or publisher except to AP. Other By–Laws require each newspaper member to conduct his or its business in such manner that the news furnished by the corporations shall not be made available to any non-member in advance of publication. The joint effect of these By–Laws is to block all newspaper non-members from any opportunity to buy news from AP or any of its publisher members. Admission to membership in AP thereby becomes a prerequisite to obtaining AP news or buying news from any one of its more than twelve hundred publishers. The erection of obstacles to the acquisition of membership consequently can make it difficult, if not impossible for non-members to get any of the news furnished by AP or any of the individual members of this combination of American newspaper publishers.[13] . . .

The District Court found that the By–Laws in and of themselves were contracts in restraint of commerce in that they contained provisions designed to stifle competition in the newspaper publishing field. The court also found that AP's restrictive By–Laws had hindered and impeded the growth of competing newspapers. This latter finding, as to the *past* effect of the restrictions, is challenged. We are inclined to think that it is supported by undisputed evidence, but we do not stop to labor the point. For the court below found, and we think correctly, that the By–Laws on their face, and without regard to their past effect, constitute restraints of trade. Combinations are no less unlawful because they have not as yet resulted in restraint. An agreement or combination to follow a course of conduct which will necessarily restrain or monopolize a part of trade or commerce may violate the Sherman Act, whether it be "wholly nascent or abortive on the one hand, or successful on the other." [United States v. Socony–Vacuum Oil Co., 310 U.S. 150, 225 (1940).] For these reasons the argument, repeated here in various forms, that AP had not yet achieved a complete monopoly is wholly irrelevant. Undisputed evidence did show, however, that its By–Laws had tied the hands of all of its numerous publishers, to the extent that they could not and did not sell any part of their news so that it could reach any of their non-member competitors. In this respect the Court did find, and that finding cannot possibly be challenged, that AP's By–Laws had hindered and restrained the sale of interstate news to non-members who competed with members. Inability to buy news from the largest news agency, or any one of its multitude of members, can have most serious effects on the publication of competitive newspapers, both those presently published and those which but for these restrictions, might be published in the future. This is illustrated by the District Court's finding that in 26 cities of the United States, existing newspapers already have contracts for AP news and the same newspapers have contracts with United Press and International News Service under which new newspapers would be required to pay the contract holders large sums to enter the field.[14] The net effect is seriously to limit the opportunity of any new paper to enter these cities. Trade restraints of this character, aimed at the destruction of competition, tend to block the initiative which brings newcomers into a field of business and to frustrate the free enterprise system which it was the purpose of the Sherman Act to protect. . . .

Nor can we treat this case as though it merely involved a reporter's contract to deliver his news reports exclusively to a single newspaper, or an exclusive agreement as to news between two newspapers in different cities.

---

13. The [District] Court found that out of the 1803 daily English language newspapers published in the United States, with a total circulation of 42,080,391, 1179 of them, with a circulation of 34,762,120, were under joint contractual obligations not to supply either AP or their own "spontaneous" news to any nonmember of AP.

14. INS and UP make so-called "asset value" contracts under which if another newspaper wishes to obtain their press services, the newcomer shall pay to the competitor holding the UP or INS contract the stipulated "asset value."

For such trade restraints might well be "reasonable," and therefore not in violation of the Sherman Act. Standard Oil Co. v. United States, 221 U.S. 1. But however innocent such agreements might be, standing alone, they would assume quite a different aspect if utilized as essential features of a program to hamper or destroy competition. It is in this light that we must view this case.

It has been argued that the restrictive By–Laws should be treated as beyond the prohibitions of the Sherman Act, since the owner of the property can choose his associates and can, as to that which he has produced by his own enterprise and sagacity, efforts or ingenuity, decide for himself whether and to whom to sell or not to sell. While it is true in a very general sense that one can dispose of his property as he pleases, he cannot "go beyond the exercise of this right, and by contracts or combinations, express or implied, unduly hinder or obstruct the free and natural flow of commerce in the channels of interstate trade." United States v. Bausch & Lomb Co., 321 U.S. 707, 722. The Sherman Act was specifically intended to prohibit independent businesses from becoming "associates" in a common plan which is bound to reduce their competitor's opportunity to buy or sell the things in which the groups compete. Victory of a member of such a combination over its business rivals achieved by such collective means cannot consistently with the Sherman Act or with practical, everyday knowledge be attributed to *individual* "enterprise and sagacity"; such hampering of business rivals can only be attributed to that which really makes it possible—the collective power of an unlawful combination. That the object of sale is the creation or product of a man's ingenuity does not alter this principle. Fashion Originators' Guild, Inc. v. Federal Trade Commission, 312 U.S. 457. It is obviously fallacious to view the By–Laws here in issue as instituting a program to encourage and permit full freedom of sale and disposal of property by its owners. Rather, these publishers have, by concerted arrangements, pooled their power to acquire, to purchase, and to dispose of news reports through the channels of commerce. They have also pooled their economic and news control power and, in exerting that power, have entered into agreements which the District Court found to be "plainly designed in the interest of preventing competition."[15]

It is further contended that since there are other news agencies which sell news, it is not a violation of the Act for an overwhelming majority of American publishers to combine to decline to sell their news to the minority. But the fact that an agreement to restrain trade does not inhibit competition in all of the objects of that trade cannot save it from the condemnation of the Sherman Act. It is apparent that the exclusive right to publish news in a given field, furnished by AP and all of its members gives

---

15. Even if additional purposes were involved, it would not justify the combination, since the Sherman Act cannot "be evaded by good motives. The law is its own measure of right and wrong, of what it permits, or forbids, and the judgment of the courts cannot be set up against it in a supposed accommodation of its policy with the good intention of parties, and, it may be, of some good results." Standard Sanitary Mfg. Co. v. United States, 226 U.S. 20, 49.

many newspapers a competitive advantage over their rivals.[16] Conversely, a newspaper without AP service is more than likely to be at a competitive disadvantage. The District Court stated that it was to secure this advantage over rivals that the By–Laws existed. It is true that the record shows that some competing papers have gotten along without AP news, but morning newspapers, which control 96% of the total circulation in the United States, have AP news service. And the District Court's unchallenged finding was that "AP is a vast, intricately reticulated organization, the largest of its kind, gathering news from all over the world, the chief single source of news for the American press, universally agreed to be of great consequence."

Nevertheless, we are asked to reverse these judgments on the ground that the evidence failed to show that AP reports, which might be attributable to their own "enterprise and sagacity," are clothed "in the robes of indispensability." The absence of "indispensability" is said to have been established under the following chain of reasoning: AP has made its news generally available to the people by supplying it to a limited and select group of publishers in the various cities; therefore, it is said, AP and its member publishers have not deprived the reading public of AP news; all local readers have an "adequate access" to AP news, since all they need do in any city to get it is to buy, on whatever terms they can in a protected market, the particular newspaper selected for the public by AP and its members. We reject these contentions. The proposed "indispensability" test would fly in the face of the language of the Sherman Act and all of our previous interpretations of it. Moreover, it would make that law a dead letter in all fields of business, a law which Congress has consistently maintained to be an essential safeguard to the kind of private competitive business economy this country has sought to maintain.

The restraints on trade in news here were no less than those held to fall within the ban of the Sherman Act with reference to combinations to restrain trade outlets in the sale of tiles, Montague & Co. v. Lowry, 193 U.S. 38.... By the restrictive By–Laws each of the publishers in the combination has, in effect, "surrendered himself completely to the control of the association," Anderson v. Shipowners' Ass'n, 272 U.S. 359, 362, in respect to the disposition of news in interstate commerce. Therefore this contractual restraint of interstate trade, "designed in the interest of preventing competition," cannot be one of the "normal and usual agreements in aid of trade and commerce which may be found not to be within the [Sherman] Act...." Eastern States Lumber Dealers' Ass'n v. United

16. The District Court pointed out that, "monopoly is a relative word. If one means by it the possession of something absolutely necessary to the conduct of an activity, there are few except the exclusive possession of some natural resource without which the activity is impossible. Most monopolies, like most patents, give control over only some means of production for which there is a substitute; the possessor enjoys an advantage over his competitors, but he can seldom shut them out altogether; his monopoly is measured by the handicap he can impose.... And yet that advantage alone may make a monopoly unlawful. It would be possible, for instance, to conduct some kind of a newspaper without any news service whatever; but nobody will maintain that, if AP were the only news service in existence, the members could keep it wholly to themselves and reduce all other papers to such news as they could gather by their own efforts." United States v. Associated Press, D.C., 52 F.Supp. 362, 371.

States, 234 U.S. 612, 613. It is further said that we reach our conclusion by application of the "public utility" concept to the newspaper business. This is not correct. We merely hold that arrangements or combinations designed to stifle competition cannot be immunized by adopting a membership device accomplishing that purpose. . . .

We now turn to the decree. Having adjudged the By–Laws imposing restrictions on applications for membership to be illegal, the court enjoined the defendants from observing them, or agreeing to observe any new or amended By–Law having a like purpose or effect. It further provided that nothing in the decree should prevent the adoption by the Associated Press of new or amended By–Laws "which will restrict admission, provided that members in the same city and in the same 'field' (morning, evening or Sunday), as an applicant published in a newspaper in the United States of America or its Territories, shall not have power to impose, or dispense with, any conditions upon his admission and that the By–Laws shall affirmatively declare that the effect of admission upon the ability of such applicant to compete with members in the same city and 'field' shall not be taken into consideration in passing upon its application." Some of appellants argue that this decree is vague and indefinite. They argue that it will be impossible for the Association to know whether or not its members took into consideration the competitive situation in passing upon applications for membership. We cannot agree that the decree is ambiguous. We assume, with the court below, that AP will faithfully carry out its purpose. Interpreting the decree to mean that AP news is to be furnished to competitors of old members without discrimination through By–Laws controlling membership, or otherwise, we approve it. . . .

The judgment in all three cases is affirmed.[17]

United States v. Visa U.S.A., Inc., et al.

United States Court of Appeals, Second Circuit, 2003.
344 F.3d 229.

■ LEVAL, CIRCUIT JUDGE. . . . The U.S. Department of Justice ("DOJ") brought this civil enforcement action challenging the organizational structure of two of the nation's four major payment card systems. The complaint charged that MasterCard and Visa U.S.A., which are organized as joint ventures owned by their member banking institutions, conspired to restrain trade in two ways: (1) By enacting rules permitting a member-owner of one to function as a director of the other (an arrangement the government described as "dual governance") (Count I); and (2) by enacting and enforcing "exclusionary rules," which prohibit their member banks from issuing American Express ("Amex") or Discover cards (Count II).

---

17. Ed. Jackson, J., did not participate in the decision. The concurring opinions of Douglas and Frankfurter, JJ., the dissenting opinion of Roberts, J., in which Stone, C.J., joined, and the dissenting opinion of Murphy, J., are omitted.

After a 34–day trial, the court, in a commendably comprehensive and careful opinion, ruled in the defendants' favor as to dual governance (Count I). As to Count II, however, the court held that Visa U.S.A. and MasterCard violated the Act by enforcing their respective versions of the exclusionary rule, barring their member banks from issuing Amex or Discover cards.... The court ordered the exclusionary rules revoked and permanently enjoined all three defendants from promulgating similar rules in the future. ...

The defendants brought this appeal. Visa U.S.A. and MasterCard argue that the district court erred in its conclusion that their respective exclusionary rules violate the Sherman Act. ...

For the reasons set forth below, we affirm the judgment.

BACKGROUND

I. Description of the General Purpose Payment Card Industry

A. The Structure of the Visa and MasterCard Networks

Visa U.S.A. and MasterCard are two of the United States's four major network systems in the payment card industry, the other two being Amex and Discover. Visa U.S.A. and MasterCard are organized as open joint ventures, owned by the numerous banking institutions that are members of the networks. (Because the vast majority of the members are banks, and because for purposes of this appeal nothing turns on whether members are banks or other types of financial institutions, we refer to the member institutions as "banks.") MasterCard is owned by its approximately 20,000 member banks; Visa U.S.A. is owned by its approximately 14,000 member banks. Because MasterCard allows its member banks to issue Visa cards, and Visa U.S.A. likewise allows its members to issue MasterCard cards, many of Visa U.S.A.'s 14,000 members are also members of the MasterCard network. The networks' operations are conducted primarily by their member banks. While the member banks engage in the card business for profit, MasterCard and Visa U.S.A. themselves operate as non-profit organizations and are largely funded through service and transaction fees paid by their members. Both make a "profit" on these fees, but their business model is not one that strives to maximize earnings at the "network" level. Rather, the two organizations' capital surpluses are held basically as security accounts, to pay merchants in the event a member bank defaults on a payment obligation.

The member banks of the MasterCard and Visa U.S.A. card networks may function either as "issuers" or "acquirers" or both. A member bank serving as an "issuer" issues cards to cardholders; it serves as the liaison between the network and the individual cardholder. A member bank serving as an "acquirer" acquires the card-paid transactions of a merchant; a particular acquiring bank acts as liaison between the network and those merchants accepting the network's payment cards with whom it has contracted.

When a consumer uses a Visa card or a MasterCard card to pay for goods or services, the accepting merchant relays the transaction information to the acquiring bank with whom it has contracted. The acquirer processes and packages that information and transmits it to the network (Visa U.S.A. or MasterCard). The network then relays the transaction information to the cardholder's issuing bank, which approves the transaction if the cardholder has a sufficient credit line. Approval is sent by the issuer to the acquirer, which relays it to the merchant.

Payment requests are sent by the merchant to the acquirer, which forwards the requests to the issuer. The issuer then pays the acquiring bank the amount requested, less what is called an "interchange fee"—typically 1.4%. The acquirer retains an additional fee—approximately .6%. Thus, the issuing bank and the acquirer withhold an aggregate of approximately 2% of the amount of the transaction from the merchant. This is known as the "merchant discount." For a $100 sale, the merchant typically will receive $98, the issuing bank retaining $1.40, while the acquiring bank retains 60 cents.

Both MasterCard and Visa are *open* joint ventures, meaning that there is no limit to the number of banks that may become members, either as issuers or as acquirers. Any member may serve as both an issuer and as an acquirer. Members agree to abide by their association's by-laws and other regulations.

A member of either the Visa U.S.A. or MasterCard network may also be a member of the other network. Thus a bank that is a member of Visa U.S.A.'s network and issues Visa cards may also be a member of the MasterCard and Visa U.S.A. have promulgated rules that prohibit their members from issuing American Express or Discover cards. Those rules—Visa's by-law 2.10(e) and MasterCard's Competitive Programs Policy ("CPP")[18]—are the focus of this action, and were held by the district court to violate the Sherman Act.

B.   The Structure of the American Express and Discover Networks

American Express and Discover, the other two major card systems in the United States, are quite differently organized. They are not joint venture membership associations. Rather, each is a vertically integrated entity, acting for profit, which combines issuing, acquiring, and network functions. (The parties and the District Court occasionally refer to this

---

18. Visa U.S.A's by-law 2.10(e), passed in 1991, states,

> The membership of any Member shall automatically terminate in the event it, or its parent, subsidiary or affiliate, issues, directly or indirectly, Discover Cards, or American Express Cards, or any other card deemed competitive by the Board of Directors....

MasterCard's CPP, passed in 1996, provide that

> With the exception of participation in Visa, which is essentially owned by same member entities, and several pre-existing programs to the extent individual members participate ... members of MasterCard may not participate either as issuers or acquirers in competitive general purpose careds....

structure as a "closed loop.") Amex and Discover deal directly with consumers (by issuing cards), and with merchants (by acquiring and processing transactions). When a consumer makes a purchase with an American Express card, for example, the merchant contacts Amex directly, and if the customer has sufficient credit available, Amex approves the sale. Amex then pays the merchant directly, retaining a percentage—usually 2.73%. (Discover is organized similarly to Amex. Its merchant discount is usually 1.5%.)

Since at least 1995, American Express has sought to change its structure by soliciting banks to issue American Express cards. This effort has been successful outside of the continental United States and abroad, where banks such as Puerto Rico's Banco Popular have begun issuing Amex-branded cards. In the continental United States, in contrast, Amex has been unsuccessful in its attempt to solicit outside issuers. Because of Visa U.S.A.'s and MasterCard's exclusionary rules, any bank that undertook to issue Amex-branded cards would be forced to give up issuing both Visa and MasterCard cards—a move no U.S. bank has been willing to make.

[Section C on the relationship between Visa International and Visa U.S.A. is omitted.]

II.   Competition in the General Purpose Payment Card Industry

Competition in the payment card industry takes place at the "network" level, as well as at the "issuing" and "acquiring" levels. At the network level, the four brands compete with one another to establish brand loyalty in favor of the Visa, MasterCard, Amex, or Discover card. At the issuing level, approximately twenty thousand banks that issue Visa and MasterCard cars to customers compete with one another and with Amex and Discover. Unlike the network service market, which has only four major participants, approximately 20,000 entities compete for customers in the issuing market, and no single participant is dominant. American Express is the largest single card issuer in the United States, as measured by transaction volume. By the same measure, Discover is the fifth largest issuer. The other large issuers are member banks in the Visa and Mastercard networks.

III.   The Challenged Regulations

This appeal concerns the propriety of Visa U.S.A.'s and MasterCard's so-called "exclusionary" or "exclusivity" rules, which prohibit members of their networks from issuing Amex and Discover cards. The district court concluded that these exclusivity rules are anticompetitive because they restrict the ability of American Express and Discover to compete with Visa and MasterCard in marketing their "network services" to banks. As a result of these exclusionary rules, American Express and Discover have been effectively foreclosed from the business of issuing cards through banks. By reason of the exclusivity rules, a bank choosing to issue Amex or Discover cards would be compelled to forego issuing Visa and MasterCard cards. No United States bank has been willing to give up its membership in the Visa U.S.A. and MasterCard networks in order to issue Amex or Discover cards.

DISCUSSION

... For over 100 years, the courts have understood the Sherman Act only to prohibit "unreasonable" restraints on trade. *See, e.g., Arizona v. Maricopa County Med. Soc'y.,* 457 U.S. 332, 342–43 (1982) (citing *United States v. Joint Traffic Ass'n.,* 171 U.S. 505 (1898)). Certain arrangements, such as price fixing and market division, are considered unreasonable *per se,* but most other restraints are evaluated case by case, under the "rule of reason." *See, e.g., Id.,* at 343–44. The principal question in a rule of reason case is often whether the anticompetitive effects of a restraint are outweighed by some procompetitive justification. *See, e.g., Clorox Co. v. Sterling Winthrop, Inc.,* 117 F.3d 50, 56 (2d Cir. 1997). The practices challenged in this case are properly analyzed under the rule of reason, as neither Visa U.S.A. nor MasterCard has restricted trade in a manner that constitutes a *per se* violation.

For the government to prevail in a rule of reason case under Section 1, the district court concluded, and the parties do not argue otherwise, that the following must be shown: As an initial matter, the government must demonstrate that the defendant conspirators have "market power" in a particular market for goods or services.[19] Next, the government must demonstrate that within the relevant market, the defendants' actions have had substantial adverse effects on competition, such as increases in price, or decreases in output or quality. *See, e.g., Atlantic Richfield Co. v. USA Petroleum Co.,* 495 U.S. 328 (1990). Once that initial burden is met, the burden of production shifts to the defendants, who must provide a procompetitive justification for the challenged restraint. *Capital Imaging Assocs., P.C. v. Mohawk Valley Medical Assocs.,* 996 F.2d 537, 543 (2d Cir. 1993). If the defendants do so, the government must prove either that the challenged restraint is not reasonably necessary to achieve the defendants' procompetitive justifications, or that those objectives may be achieved in a manner less restrictive of free competition. *Bhan v. NME Hosps., Inc.,* 929 F.2d 1404, 1413 (9th Cir. 1991)....

I. Relevant Markets and Market Power

The district court determined, and we agree, that this case involves two interrelated, but separate, product markets: (1) what the court called

---

19. Some authorities suggest that the market power requirement is unnecessary. *See, e.g., FTC v. Indiana Fed'n of Dentists,* 476 U.S. 447, 460 (1986) ("Since the purpose of the inquiries into market definition and market power is to determine whether an arrangement has the potential for genuine adverse effects on competition, proof of actual detrimental effects, such as a reduction of output, can obviate the need for an inquiry into market power, which is but a surrogate for detrimental effects." (internal quotation marks omitted)); *NCAA v. Bd. of Regents,* 468 U.S. 85, 110 n. 42, (similar); *KMB Warehouse Distribs. v. Walker Mfg. Co.,* 61 F.3d 123, 128–29 (2d Cir. 1995) ("This court has not made a showing of market power a prerequisite for recovery in all § 1 cases."). Whether market power is a necessary element is of no moment here; the district court found that the defendants had market power in the relevant markets, and as indicated below, we see no reason to question that finding.

the general purpose card market, consisting of the market for charge cards and credit cards, and (2) the network services market for general purpose cards.

A distinct product market comprises products that are considered by consumers to be "reasonabl[y] interchangeab[le]" with what the defendant sells. *Eastman Kodak Co. v. Image Tech'l Servs., Inc.,* 504 U.S. 451, 482 (1992); *United States v. E.I. du Pont de Nemours & Co.,* 351 U.S. 377, 404 (1956). After hearing substantial expert testimony, the district court found as a matter of fact that other forms of payment—such as cash, checks, debit cards, and proprietary cards (e.g. the Sears or Macy's cards)—are not considered by most consumers to be reasonable substitutes for general purpose credit or charge cards. As the government's expert witness explained, based on empirical analysis of consumer preferences, if prices for general purpose payment cards were to rise significantly, cardholders would likely pay the increased fees, rather than abandon their cards in favor of other forms of payment. Thus, general purpose payment cards constitute a distinct market, separate from the market for such other payment alternatives. We find no reason to doubt the court's conclusion.

Further, we agree with the district court that the four payment card networks compete with one another in a market for "network services." General purpose card networks, Judge Jones explained, "provide the infrastructure and mechanisms through which general purpose card transactions are conducted, including the authorization, settlement, and clearance of transactions." Whereas in the market for general purpose *cards,* the issuers are the sellers, and cardholders are the buyers, in the market for general purpose card *network services,* the four networks themselves are the sellers, and the issuers of cards and merchants are the buyers. Issuing banks purchase network services from MasterCard and/or Visa U.S.A., and those two brands compete with Amex and Discover for the banks' business. Networks also compete for merchants, because the price merchants pay for acceptance of payment cards (the merchant discount) is affected by the size of the interchange fee, which is set by the network.

The district court found, on the basis of expert testimony, that there are no products reasonably interchangeable, in the eyes of issuers or merchants, with the network services provided by the four major brands. This was a reasonable finding: (1) Network-level costs are so high that banks and merchants cannot provide these services for themselves, and (2) issuance and acceptance of credit and charge cards is so profitable (and network service fees so negligible in comparison) that even a large increase in network fees would not provide a rational financial incentive to abandon the business of issuing or accepting payment cards.

We agree with the district court's finding that Visa U.S.A. and Master-Card, jointly and separately, have power within the market for network services. Market power has been defined by the Supreme Court to mean the "power to control prices or exclude competition." *du Pont,* 351 U.S. at 391. *NCAA,* at 109 n. 38. Such power may be proven through evidence of specific conduct undertaken by the defendant that indicates he has the power to affect price or exclude competition. *KMB Warehouse Distribs., Inc. v. Walker Mfg. Co.,* 61 F.3d 123, 129 (2d Cir. 1995). Alternatively, market power may be presumed if the defendant controls a large enough share of the relevant market. *Id.* [The district court judge] based her finding of market power first on the fact that merchants testified that they could not refuse to accept payment by Visa or MasterCard, even if faced with significant price increases, because of customer preference. Indeed, despite recent increases in both networks' interchange fees, no merchant had discontinued acceptance of their cards. In addition, the court inferred market power from the defendants' large shares of a highly concentrated market: In 1999, Visa U.S.A. members accounted for approximately 47% of the dollar volume of credit and charge card transactions, while MasterCard members accounted for approximately 26%. (American Express accounted for 20%; Discover, for 6%.)

The evidence relied on by the district court was sufficient to sustain a finding of market power. In addition, Amex, despite repeated recent attempts, has been unable to persuade any issuing banks in the continental United States to utilize its network services because the exclusivity rule would require such issuing banks to give up membership in the Visa and MasterCard consortiums, and banks are unwilling to do so. In short, Visa U.S.A. and MasterCard have demonstrated their power in the network services market by effectively precluding their largest competitor from successfully soliciting any bank as a customer for its network services and brand.

II. Harms to Competition

As noted, to sustain a challenge under § 1 of the Sherman Act, the government must prove that the defendants' conduct has adversely affected competition. The district court found that Visa U.S.A. and MasterCard's exclusionary rules harm competition by "reducing overall card output and available card features," as well as by decreasing network services output and stunting price competition. We cannot say that these conclusions were erroneous.

The most persuasive evidence of harm to competition is the total exclusion of American Express and Discover from a segment of the market for network services. As noted, there are only four major payment card network providers in the United States. While competition among (and within) these networks is robust at the issuing level (where 20,000 separate issuers compete to provide products to consumers), at the network level (where four major networks seek to sell their technical, infrastructure, and financial services to issuer banks) competition has been seriously damaged by the defendants' exclusionary rules. As the district court noted, "[i]t is largely undisputed that the exclusionary rules have resulted in the failure of Visa and MasterCard member banks to become issuers of American Express and Discover-branded cards." [*Visa U.S.A.,* F. Supp. 2d,] at 383. The district court cited evidence that three major U.S. issuer banks—Banco Popular, Advanta, and Bank One—would have contracted with American

Express to issue Amex cards in the United States but for the exclusionary rules. In addition, Banco Popular has contracted with Amex to issue its cards in Puerto Rico, where no exclusionary rules apply.

As a result, then, of the challenged policies, only two rival networks are effectively able to compete for the business of issuer banks. Testimony at trial revealed that Visa U.S.A. and MasterCard "pay millions of dollars in incentive payments in the form of discounts from the price for network services to selected issuing banks to compete for their business and [that] the banks play Visa and MasterCard against [each] other to obtain lower net prices and higher value for card network services." *Id.* at 382. With only two viable competitors, however, such price and product competition is necessarily limited. Trial testimony strongly indicated that price competition and innovation in services would be enhanced if four competitors, rather than only two, were able to compete in this manner for issuing banks. Indeed, the district court found, based on testimony from Visa U.S.A. and MasterCard executives, that both defendants would "respond to . . . greater network competition by offering new and better products and services." *Id.* at 396. MasterCard's former CEO, for example, testified that MasterCard would be forced to "speed up" development of a premium card product were Amex cards issued through MasterCard member banks.

In foreign countries, where Visa International rather than Visa U.S.A. operates the Visa network, and no exclusionary rule applies, Amex has succeeded in convincing banks that issue Visa cards also to issue Amex cards. This has caused Visa International to "proactively strengthen" its product offerings to member banks abroad. In addition, an internal Visa International memorandum cautions that Visa U.S.A. would have to compete more vigorously for market share if Amex were permitted to partner with its member banks: "To date, AmEx has been precluded from partnering with U.S. banks, although that situation could change. Since bank partners could significantly increase [Amex's] acceptance and cards, Visa needs to monitor the situation and counter with competitive products that meet banks['] needs." *Id.* at 397.

The district court also found that product innovation and output has been stunted by the challenged policies. By excluding Amex and Discover from the market for outside card issuers, Visa U.S.A. and MasterCard effectively deny consumers access to products that could be offered only by a network in partnership with individual banks. Such products include cards that are able to link "to transaction accounts, to asset management accounts, to sale of mortgages or other financial products that [banks] offer[ ]." *Id.* at 396.

We find no error in the district court's finding that competition has been harmed by the defendants' exclusionary rules.

III.   The Defendants' Arguments

Defendants argue on appeal that the district court erred in two ways: (1) by finding that the exclusionary rules harm *competition,* when they in fact disadvantage only individual *competitors;* and (2) by failing to recognize that any adverse effects on competition are outweighed by the substantial procompetitive benefits of exclusivity.

A.   Harms to Competition

First, the defendants argue that the district court erred by mistaking harm to a *competitor* for harm to *competition*. They cite the familiar formula that the "antitrust laws protect competition, not competitors." *Clorox Co. v. Sterling Winthrop, Inc.*, 117 F.3d 50, 57 (2d Cir. 1997). Visa U.S.A. contends, for example, that "[t]he decision and remedy in this case will not benefit consumer welfare. Instead, virtually the sole beneficiary will be AmEx which hopes to gain not by offering lower prices or better products but largely by undermining its major brand competitors."

Defendants contend the exclusionary rules are akin to "exclusive distributorship" arrangements, which we have held are "presumptively legal." *Elec. Communications Corp. v. Toshiba Am. Consumer Prods., Inc.*, 129 F.3d 240, 245 (2d Cir. 1997) (citing *Oreck Corp. v. Whirlpool Corp.*, 579 F.2d 126, 131 (2d Cir. 1978) (in banc)). We find this argument unpersuasive.

Defendants are certainly correct that the proper inquiry is whether there has been an "*actual* adverse effect on competition as a whole in the relevant market." *KMB Warehouse*, 61 F.3d at 127 (citations and internal quotation marks omitted). We have held that competition is not adversely affected if, despite an exclusive dealership arrangement, "competitors can reach the ultimate consumer of the product by employing existing or potential alternative channels of distribution." *CDC Techs., Inc. v. IDEXX Labs., Inc.*, 186 F.3d 74, 80 (2d Cir. 1999) (citations and internal quotation marks omitted).

The defendants argue that the harms identified by the district court as stemming from their exclusionary rules—that the types of cards that consumers can get from their banks are limited and [that] banks are prevented from combining their particular issuing skills with the AmEx brand—are not harms to Amex's ability to compete as a network (or Discover's), but rather harms to its distributive capacity, in much the same way Pepsi–Cola's distributive capacity might be limited by an exclusive arrangement between Coca–Cola and its truckers. For an exclusive dealership arrangement to cause a harm to competition (and overcome the presumption of legality), it must prevent competitors from getting their products to consumers at all. *CDC Techs.*, 186 F.3d at 80 (citing *Gilbarco*, 127 F.3d at 1163). There is no question, the defendants argue, that Amex and Discover can get their products to consumers, as evidenced by the fact that they are respectively the largest and fifth largest issuers of payment cards in the United States.

The analogy to an exclusive arrangement between Coca–Cola and its truckers is not persuasive. The basic flaw in the analogy is that it depicts Visa U.S.A. (or MasterCard) as a single entity (like Coca–Cola) demanding a restrictive provision in its contract with a supplier of services to it. Visa U.S.A. and MasterCard, however, are not single entities; they are consortiums of competitors. They are owned and effectively operated by some 20,000 banks, which compete with one another in the issuance of payment cards and the acquiring of merchants' transactions. These 20,000 banks set the policies of Visa U.S.A. and MasterCard. These competitors have agreed to abide by a restrictive exclusivity provision to the effect that in order to share the benefits of their association by having the right to issue Visa or MasterCard cards, they must agree not to compete by issuing cards of Amex or Discover. The restrictive provision is a horizontal restraint adopted by 20,000 competitors.

The analogy proposed by the defendants would be more pertinent if Coca–Cola, Pepsi–Cola, and several other leading sellers of soft drinks joined together to form an association to contract for trucking services and exacted of contracting truckers a commitment not to carry for any soft drink maker that was not a part of the consortium. Even then the analogy would lack the feature here presented that the restraint imposed by the consortium members is on themselves. Each has agreed not to compete with the others in a manner which the consortium considers harmful to its combined interests. Far from being "presumptively legal," such arrangements are exemplars of the type of anticompetitive behavior prohibited by the Sherman Act. *See, e.g., NCAA v. Bd. of Regents,* 468 U.S. 85, 99 (1984) ("[M]ember institutions have created a horizontal restraint—an agreement among competitors on the way in which they will compete with one another."); *Fraser v. Major League Soccer, L.L.C.,* 284 F.3d 47, 57 (1st Cir. 2002) (league acting in a horizontal capacity when board acts to control competition among members); *Capital Imaging Assocs., P.C. v. Mohawk Valley Medical Assocs.,* 996 F.2d 537, 545 (2d Cir. 1993) (horizontal analysis when HMO board excluded radiology practice group to "insulate" HMO's member radiologists "from increased competition"); *Rothery Storage & Van Co. v. Atlas Van Lines, Inc.,* 792 F.2d 210, 214 (D.C. Cir. 1986) (horizontal restraint because "all of these legally separate corporations agreed to a policy that restricted competition"); *NASL v. NFL,* 670 F.2d 1249, 1252 (2d Cir. 1982) (NFL bylaw banning cross-ownership of other professional sports league teams is a horizontal restraint).

In the market for *network services,* where the four networks are sellers and issuing banks and merchants are buyers, the exclusionary rules enforced by Visa U.S.A. and MasterCard have absolutely prevented Amex and Discover from selling their products at all.

Without doubt the exclusionary rules in question harm competitors. The fact that they harm competitors does not, however, mean that they do not also harm competition. We find no fault with the district court's finding that the exclusion of Amex and Discover from the ability to market their cards and programs to banks has harmed competition in the market for network services, and that Visa U.S.A. and MasterCard would be impelled to design and market their products more competitively if the banks to which they sell their services were free to purchase network services from Amex and Discover. Nor do we fault the district court's determination that certain types of products combining unique features of cards offered by

Amex and Discover with the advantages of linkage to cardholders' bank accounts would likely become available. The district court was justified in finding harm to competition.

B. Procompetitive Justifications

The defendants argue that even if the exclusionary rules do harm competition, those harms are outweighed by the policies' substantial pro-competitive effects. The defendants assert that the principal benefit of the exclusionary rules is to promote "cohesion" within the MasterCard and Visa U.S.A. networks, so that those networks may compete effectively in the marketplace. Thus, the defendants argue, the exclusionary rules are ancillary to legitimate, procompetitive business strategies. The district court found that the exclusionary rules are not necessary to accomplish that goal, and that in any event the anticompetitive effects outweigh the procompetitive. We believe the court's finding was reasonable.

The district court found no evidence to suggest that allowing member banks to issue cards of rival networks would endanger cohesion in a manner adverse to the competitive process. MasterCard members have long been permitted to issue Visa cards, and vice versa, without such consequences. Moreover, as the district court noted, there is no evidence that the defendants' network cohesion has been harmed overseas, where, in the absence of exclusionary rules, Amex has contracted with Visa and Master-Card member banks to issue Amex-branded payment cards.

In sum, the defendants have failed to show that the anticompetitive effects of their exclusionary rules are outweighed by procompetitive benefits.

. . .

CONCLUSION

The judgment of the district court is AFFIRMED.

NOTES AND QUESTIONS

1. *Prior antitrust challenges to the Visa/Mastercard system.* Similar Visa/MasterCard exclusivity rules had previously been challenged under Section 1, but with the opposite result. The Tenth Circuit concluded that Visa USA's refusal to admit Sears to its membership did not violate Section 1. Sears introduced the Discover Card in 1985, intending that it compete with the other national proprietary cards available at the time: Visa, MasterCard, American Express, and Citibank's Diners' Club/Carte Blanche. As an umbrella organization, Visa USA provided technology to process credit card transactions and regulated and coordinated programs through rules and bylaws for its thousands of associates. In 1988, a Sears-owned Delaware bank, which issued Discover, applied to become a Visa USA member so that it could issue Visa cards. That application prompted Visa USA to adopt Bylaw 2.06, which directed the corporation to deny any applications for membership when the applicant (including its parent, subsidiaries or affiliates) issued Discover or American

Express cards. Two years later, Sears purchased the Visa USA membership among the other assets of a bankrupt thrift association in Utah. Sears then set off to introduce its own Prime Option Visa card by creating a new entity, SCFC ILC, Inc., doing business as MountainWest Financial. Visa USA tried to thwart Sears's plan by canceling the printing of the Prime Option cards pursuant to Bylaw 2.06. Sears, in turn, filed the antitrust suit in district court of Utah. The district court found that the exclusion inflicted antitrust injury and harmed competition.

Distinguishing the joint venture from mergers and cartels, the Tenth Circuit followed *BMI* and *Northwest Stationers* and applied a rule of reason approach. The first issue was whether Visa USA possessed sufficient market power in the relevant market. At the trial level, the parties stipulated that the issuer market—i.e. the financial institutions or banks issuing the credit cards—was the relevant market. In that market, the Tenth Circuit noted that the significant intrasystem competition among issuers with varying interest rates and terms negated the hypothesis of significant market concentration. Taking that evidence with the lack of evidence of higher prices or decreased output, the court of appeals concluded that there was insufficient evidence as a matter of law of Visa USA's market power. The second issue was the assessment of the efficiency justifications for Bylaw 2.06, for the purpose of determining whether the bylaw was anticompetitive. In that assessment, the court considered the free-riding and essential facility arguments brought up by the appellant and appellee, respectively. Visa USA argued that the bylaw prevented Sears from taking advantage of a brand it both did not develop and chose to compete against. Sears, by contrast, argued that the bylaw was simply a means to keep Sears out of the market, relying on *Terminal Railroad* and *Associated Press*. The court of appeals distinguished those two cases, noting that unlike the extraordinary market circumstances in those two cases, there was no evidence that the bylaw excluded Sears's access to the market. Similarly, there was no evidence of harm to consumers from the bylaw. The court stressed that the Sherman Act protects competition, not an individual competitor's goal of competing more effectively.

Can *MountainWest* and the Second Circuit's opinion in the government's Visa case be reconciled? How do the factual distinctions between the two cases affect the legal opinions that resulted?

In Worthen Bank and Trust Co. v. National BankAmericard, Inc., 485 F.2d 119 (8th Cir. 1973), *cert. denied*, 415 U.S. 918 (1974), plaintiff on behalf of itself and other small banks sued National BankAmericard (NBI), claiming that a bylaw precluding member banks in the NBI system from participating as credit card issuers in the Master Charge system constituted a group boycott in violation of Section 1. BankAmericard and Master Card were then the two principal nationwide bank credit cards, and each had numerous member banks. For purposes of summary judgment, Worthen Bank conceded that the bylaw promoted competition between the two national systems, and that absent the provision there would be a "substantial lessening of competition." The District Court found that the bylaw restricting membership in a competing credit card system was a group boycott and therefore illegal *per se*.

The Court of Appeals reversed. It noted that bylaw provisions in credit card systems involved questions of some novelty and importance, and that courts should be slow to apply *per se* rules in such situations. Moreover, Worthen had conceded that member banks, acting alone, could not issue and support a national credit card arrangement. The Court concluded that there was here an economic justification in terms of "productive capacity," whereas in *Klor's* and some other similar cases, the proscribed conduct had no redeeming virtue. It remanded the case, asking the district court to consider various proffered justifications for the rule.

Eventually, NBI (now Visa USA) amended its bylaw to allow member banks to issue the MasterCard.

What accounts for the different outcomes in *Visa* and *Worthen?* Did the *Worthen Bank* court err by characterizing the case as a group boycott? Did the *SCFC* court underestimate Visa USA's power to exclude Sears from the relevant market? Are there practices short of exclusion that would allow Visa USA to avoid the free riding problem? Should this have affected the *SCFC* court's analysis?

ESSENTIAL FACILITIES DOCTRINE: The Lingering Specter of *Terminal Railroad Ass'n*

1. *Scope.* It has been asserted that if joint ventures confer significant competitive advantages, those advantages must be made available to all on reasonable terms—a kind of public utility concept of antitrust. *See* Kaysen & Turner, Antitrust Policy 137 (1959). How far can this concept be carried? Would the American Medical Association be required to accept faith healers? *Cf.* American Medical Association v. United States, 317 U.S. 519 (1943).

2. *Joint venture versus single firm.* Is there any reason to treat a joint venture that dominates a relevant market differently under the antitrust laws from a single-firm monopoly? If not, does it follow that the limitations on permissible conduct by a single firm monopolist, set forth in *Alcoa* (p. 114 supra), apply equally to a dominant joint venture? Should even more stringent limitations apply in the joint venture situation? Note that in *Verizon Communications Inc. v. Law Offices of Curtis V. Trinko,* 540 U.S. 398 (2004), the Supreme Court signaled skepticism (or perhaps caution) about the concept of an essential facility. In rejecting a claim that a single firm had violated the antitrust laws through a refusal to deal with a competitor, the Court wrote "[w]e conclude that Verizon's alleged insufficient assistance in the provision of service to rivals is not a recognized antitrust claim under this Court's existing refusal-to-deal precedents. This conclusion would be unchanged even if we considered to be established law the 'essential facilities' doctrine crafted by some lower courts, under which the Court of Appeals concluded respondent's allegations might state a claim. . . . We have never recognized such a doctrine, . . . and we find no need either to recognize it or to repudiate it here. It suffices for present purposes to note that the indispensable requirement for invoking the doctrine is the unavailability of access to the 'essential facilities'; where access exists, the doctrine serves no purpose." *Id.* at 410–11.

3. *Role of essential facilities in antitrust analysis.* In Blue Cross & Blue Shield United of Wisconsin v. Marshfield Clinic, 65 F.3d 1406 (7th Cir. 1995), Blue Cross and its subsidiary health maintenance organization (HMO), Compcare, sued the Marshfield Clinic of north central Wisconsin and its subsidiary HMO, Security Health Plan. Compcare complained that the Marshfield Clinic maintained a monopoly in north Central Wisconsin, excluding Compcare from an alleged HMO market in the region. Blue Cross complained that the Marshfield clinic charged supracompetitive prices to patients covered by Blue Cross. A jury returned a verdict of $20 million against the defendants, after remittitur, trebling and attorney's fees.

The Seventh Circuit, in an opinion authored by Judge Posner, reversed Compcare's portion of the judgment. The court refused to find that HMOs always constitute a separate market. It explained that HMOs are simply one more means of pricing medical services. In the court's view, HMOs merely compete with other types of fee-for-service pricing mechanisms, including preferred provider plans. As for the market for all physicians' services in north central Wisconsin, the court declined to treat the Marshfield clinic as anything more than the alliance of 400 physicians. It noted that the 900 physicians who affiliated with Marshfield through Security did not have exclusive arrangements with either the clinic or its HMO. The court also pointed out that those physicians, on average, earned only 6% of their total income from their affiliation with Security. Based on the facts, the court found that Security, despite its membership base of 90% of all HMO subscribers in the region, was not a monopolist.

The court then addressed Compcare's argument that the Marshfield Clinic should be forced to contract with HMOs other than Security. Compcare argued, citing *Terminal Railroad Ass'n, supra* p. 362, that the clinic was an essential facility. Perhaps foreshadowing the Supreme Court's *Trinko* remarks, the court dismissed this argument, explaining:

> We are mindful that a concept of essential or bottleneck facilities has been used from time to time to require a natural monopolist to cooperate with would-be competitors.... The principal case remains the old St. Louis terminal case.... The decision, along with the rest of the decisions in the essential facilities line, has been criticized as having nothing to do with antitrust law.... Had the terminal facilities been owned by a firm unaffiliated with any railroad, the firm could have charged whatever prices it wanted, including prices that discriminated against some of the users (monopolists frequently price discriminate), because the antitrust laws do not regulate the prices of natural monopolists. A natural monopolist that acquired and maintained its monopoly without excluding competitors by improper means is not guilty of "monopolizing" in violation of the Sherman Act, ... for the antitrust laws are not a price-control statute or a public-utility or common-carrier rate-regulation statute.

> And the charging of a high price is, so far as potential competitors are concerned, an attracting rather than an excluding practice. Consumers are not better off if the natural monopolist is forced to share some of his profits with potential competitors, as required by *Terminal Railroad Ass'n*. Similarly, if the practice of medicine in some sparsely populated county of north central Wisconsin is a natural monopoly, consumers will not be helped by our forcing the handful of physicians there to affiliate with multiple HMOs. Those physicians will still charge fees reflecting their monopoly.

> We are not authorized to abrogate doctrines that have been endorsed and not yet rejected by the Supreme Court.... To be an essential facility, however, a facility must be essential. The terminal association controlled 100 percent of a market, assumed to be properly defined, consisting of terminal services at St. Louis. The Clinic does not control 100 percent—or even 50 percent—of any properly defined market.

Id. at 1412–13. The court thus rejected Compcare's essential facility argument.

The *Marshfield* opinion identified one factor as conclusive to its antitrust analysis: the lack of exclusive contracts between Security and the 900 physicians outside the clinic. The FTC and the Antitrust Division proposed a more flexible analysis in their Statement of Department of Justice and Federal Trade Commission Analytical Principles Relating to Multiprovider Networks. *See* Statements of Antitrust Enforcement Policy in Health Care (Aug. 28, 1996), 71 BNA ATRR 1777 (Sp. Supp. 8/29/96). The Guidelines suggest that exclusiveness would be looked at as one important factor among many. They also highlight economic integration among providers (sharing financial risk through shared capitation or through a bonus formula based on utilization review) as an important factor in assessing the legality of provider networks. Significant economic integration, they suggest, would bring joint pricing and service allocation by otherwise competing providers within rule of reason analysis.

4. *Remnants of impartial agency?* In United States v. Realty Multi–List Inc., 629 F.2d 1351 (5th Cir. 1980), the United States challenged certain bylaws of Realty Multi–List (RML) that controlled membership in the organization, on the ground that they constituted a boycott prohibited by Section 1 of the Sherman Act. A real estate multiple listing service is a joint venture in which members attempt to obtain from real estate sellers "exclusive" listings, which they then pool among other members. The system produces a variety of efficiencies: buyers have access to a broader range of listings; sellers have access to a wider range of potential buyers; and as a result price is more in line with supply and demand.

A key element of the RML arrangement provided that members may not allow non-members access to listing pool information. Membership criteria for RML included findings that the prospective member: (1) had a favorable credit report and business reputation; and (2) maintained a real estate office open during customary business hours. Also, each member was required to pay an initiation fee set by the RML Board of Directors. At the time of suit, RML was the sole multiple listing service in Muskogee County, Georgia, and its members comprised the majority of the active real estate brokers there.

The court of appeals rejected the United States's request for *per se* treatment of the multi-list system, noting that the arrangement arguably improved the efficient operation of the real estate market. The government had also argued that the specific bylaws arbitrarily excluded prospective members and therefore were "facially unreasonable"—an approach the court of appeals interpreted as a version of the rule of reason.

Under a rule of reason approach, the Fifth Circuit first concluded that RML had substantial market power and that membership was a competitive advantage and perhaps a competitive necessity. As a result, its membership regulations needed to be fair and reasonable, and they were not. With respect to the "favorable credit report and business reputation" requirement, the court noted that Georgia state law already regulated real estate brokers extensively. While such state regulation did not preclude self-regulation, the RML rule seemed unreasonable in the absence of a showing by RML that state regulation was inadequate. The rule was also objectionable because its "credit report" and "business reputation" criteria were unduly broad and vague. The court found the requirement that a member maintain an office during customary business hours similarly unreasonable. Although a prospective member might be required to be "actively engaged in the business," the hours requirement unreasonably discriminated against brokers who operated primarily on weekends or evenings, times particularly convenient for many customers. As to the third membership requirement—the membership fee—the court found that fees based on start-up costs and a pro-rata contribution toward maintenance and development of the list would be reasonable, but that a sizeable membership fee bearing no relationship to those cost factors created a strong inference of an anticompetitive intent. The case was remanded for further proceedings.

5. *Shopping center leases.* In shopping center leases, it is common for the developer to grant to major (or "anchor") tenants approval rights over admission to the shopping center of various other commercial enterprises. These lease provisions have been defended on grounds that the developer is unlikely to be able to secure

financing until long-term leases have been signed with anchor tenants (see The Antitrust Implications of Restrictive Covenants in Shopping Center Leases, 86 Harv. L. Rev. 1201 (1973)), and the anchor tenants have a legitimate interest in participating in the decision to include or exclude would-be entrants.

Could the series of agreements between the developer and major tenants be viewed as a joint venture? If the shopping center were in an isolated area or of unusual commercial prominence, might access constitute a significant competitive advantage under *Associated Press*? In Tyson's Corner Regional Shopping Center, FTC Docket 886, ATRR No. 722, p. E–1 (FTC 1975), the FTC declared illegal *per se* under Section 5 of the FTC Act lease clauses that gave to an anchor tenant a blanket veto over would-be entrants. It noted that such broad lease provisions would permit the anchor tenant to exclude later entrants because they were discounters or because they competed with the anchor tenant. The Commission went on to say that more carefully tailored provisions, such as those that would preclude subsequent entrants who were not financially sound or would require the developer to consider the objective of maintaining a balanced and diversified grouping of retail stores, would be permissible.

NOTE ON THE ASSESSMENT OF JOINT VENTURES' ACTIVITY

Evaluating the necessity of restrictions. If the joint venture involved in the *Associated Press* case were declared illegal today under the antitrust laws, could the substantial economies of scale and other beneficial results achieved by Associated Press and other cooperative news agencies be obtained by any alternative arrangement? Does it follow that joint ventures that produce economies that could not otherwise be achieved should be permitted under the antitrust laws, even where the joint venture has substantial market power?

The Supreme Court first seemed to answer this question with a qualified yes, even in price-fixing cases. Cf. Broadcast Music, Inc. v. Columbia Broadcasting System, Inc., 441 U.S. 1 (1979), *supra* p. 215 ("joint ventures and other cooperative arrangements are also not usually unlawful, at least not as price-fixing schemes, where the agreement on price is necessary to market the product at all"). Price-fixing in joint ventures was recently addressed by the Court in the following case. Where does the 8–0 decision in *Dagher* leave *per se* challenges to joint ventures under Section 1?

Texaco, Inc. v. Dagher

Supreme Court of the United States, 2006.
547 U.S. 1, 126 S.Ct. 1276, 164 L.Ed.2d 1.

[Reprinted p. 271 *supra*].

NOTE ON RESEARCH AND PRODUCTION JOINT VENTURES

In many high-tech industries, and increasingly in modern economies generally, successful innovation is the key to commercial success. Innovation may allow a company to cut cost or furnish a new and better product and thereby achieve greater market share, higher profits or both. Often, there are powerful reasons why research is best undertaken on a collaborative basis.

In 1984, responding to complaints by domestic companies that the antitrust laws were a threat to cooperative joint research, Congress enacted the National Cooperative Research Act, 15 U.S.C. §§ 4301 *et seq.* The NCRA provided that collaborative "joint research and development" activities, as defined in the NCRA, would be judged on the basis of a rule of reason. The NCRA also provided a limited "safe harbor" for joint R & D ventures. Under the NCRA, anyone filing a notification of the organization of a joint R & D venture with the Department of Justice and the FTC would limit their antitrust exposure to single damages and reasonable attorney's fees. Finally, the NCRA provided that defendants who prevail in a challenge to an R & D joint venture may recover costs and attorney's fees from the challenger if the claim or the claimant's conduct is found to be "frivolous, unreasonable, without foundation, or in bad faith."

The original NCRA defined "joint research and development" as:

[A]ny group of activities, including attempting to make, making or performing a contract, by two or more persons for the purpose of—

(A) theoretical analysis, experimentation, or systematic study of phenomena or observable facts,

(B) the development or testing of basic engineering techniques,

(C) the extension of investigative findings or theory of a scientific or technical nature into practical application for experimental and demonstration purposes, including the experimental production and testing of models, prototypes, equipment, materials, and processes,

(D) the collection, exchange and analysis of research information, or

(E) any combination of the purposes specified in subparagraphs (A), (B), (C), and (D),

and may include the establishment and operation of facilities for the conducting of research....

In 1993, Congress amended the meaning of "joint venture" to include joint production of a product, process, or service, and testing in conjunction with that production. Pub. L. No. 103–42, §§ 3(b), (c), June 10, 1993, 107 Stat. 117, 118. Later, in 2004 it amended the statute again to include standards development activity. Pub. L. No. 108–237, Title I, § 103, June 22, 2004, 118 Stat. 663. The term "standards development activity" is defined as "any action taken by a standards development organization for the purpose of developing, promulgating, revising, amending, reissuing, interpreting, or otherwise maintaining a voluntary consensus standard, or using such standard in conformity assessment activities, including actions relating to the intellectual property policies of the standards development organization." 43 U.S.C. § 4301(a)(7). It excludes activities that would raise serious antitrust concerns, such as exchanging information among competitors relating to cost, sales, prices, and the like, or entering into agreements that would allocate markets or set prices. *Id.* § 4301(c).

Similarly, joint research and development is defined to exclude activities like exchanging information relating to cost, sales, profitability, pricing, etc.; agreements relating to marketing; agreements relating to the sale, licensing or sharing of inventions; and agreements that restrict or require participation in other research and development activities, unless those restrictions are reasonably required to prevent misappropriation of proprietary information contributed by any person who is a party to such venture or the results of the venture. Conduct excluded from the protection of the NCRA is not necessarily unlawful; it is merely subject to a rule of reason.

Further guidance on the antitrust treatment of research and production joint ventures appears in the following Business Review Letter from the Antitrust Division of the Department of Justice. It concerns a possible patent pool in which the manufacturers of DVDs and DVD ROMs wished to participate, so that they could license all of the more than 100 patents required for these processes at once. The letter follows:

June 10, 1999

You have requested a statement of the Department of Justice's antitrust enforcement intentions with respect to a proposed arrangement pursuant to which Toshiba will assemble and offer a package license under the Licensors' patents that are "essential," as defined below, to manufacturing products in compliance with the DVD–ROM and DVD–Video formats and will distribute royalty income to the other Licensors.

A.   The patents to be licensed

The Licensors commit to license each other and third parties to make, use and sell DVD Products under their present and future patents that are "essential" to doing so. The Licensors agree to two separate means of carrying out this obligation. First, they agree to grant Toshiba the right to sublicense third parties under their present and future "essential" patents for these purposes, and Toshiba agrees in turn to sublicense those patents, along with its own such patents, in the DVD Patent Licenses. Second, each Licensor agrees to "offer to license its essential DVD patents on a non-exclusive basis to interested third-party licensees pursuant to separate negotiations on fair, reasonable and non-discriminatory terms, whether or not said third-party licensees intend to make, use and sell DVD products that are in conformity with the Specifications."

A Licensor's patent is "essential," and thus subject to the commitments in the MOU, if it is "necessarily infringed," or "there is no realistic alternative" to it, "in implementing the DVD Standard Specifications." Initially, each Licensor will identify its own "essential" patents in an attachment to its Authorization Agreement with Toshiba. Toshiba will then incorporate those patents in a list attached to the DVD Patent License. Shortly, however, an expert individual or panel, with "full and sufficient knowledge and skill in the relevant technology," will complete a review the patents each Licensor has designated as "essential" in order to determine whether they satisfy the MOU criteria. MOU, ¶ 8; Expert Agreement, preamble. At that time, any patent initially designated by a Licensor for inclusion in the DVD Patent License that the expert determines is not "essential" will be excluded from subsequent DVD Patent Licenses, although current licensees will have the option to retain it in their existing licenses.

B.   The joint licensing arrangement

In the Authorization Agreement, each Licensor grants Toshiba the non-exclusive right to grant: (1) sublicenses, "substantially on the terms contained in the form of the DVD Patent License," on its "essential" patents to third parties to "make, have made, use, sell or otherwise dispose of DVD Products"; and (2) releases to the same third parties from liability for pre-license infringement of the licensed patents. Toshiba assumes the obligation to grant such sublicenses and releases "to all interested third party licensees," to collect royalties from licensees, and to distribute royalty income to other Licensors.

Consistent with the MOU, the Authorization Agreement preserves the Licensors' right to license their "essential" patents independently for any application. While the Licensors agree to provide each other with notification of "infringement [of the portfolio patents] or other misuse or unauthorized use" and to cooperate "in taking such steps as may be reasonably necessary to prevent any such unauthorized uses," each Licensor remains "solely responsible" for enforcing its own patent rights against infringement.

III. Analysis

As with any aggregation of patent rights for the purpose of joint package licensing, commonly known as a patent pool, an antitrust analysis of this proposed licensing program must examine both the pool's expected competitive benefits and its potential restraints on competition. The potential benefit of a patent pool is that it "may provide competitive benefits by integrating complementary technologies, reducing transaction costs, clearing blocking positions, and avoiding costly infringement litigation." At the same time, "some patent pools can restrict competition, whether among intellectual property rights within the pool or downstream products incorporating the pooled patents or in innovation among parties to the pool." Accordingly, the following analysis addresses (1) whether the proposed licensing program here at issue is likely to integrate complementary patent rights and (2), if so, whether the resulting competitive benefits are likely to be outweighed by competitive harm posed by other aspects of the program.

A. Integration of Complementary Patent Rights

If the Licensors owned patent rights that could be licensed and used in competition with each other, they might have an economic incentive to utilize a patent pool to eliminate competition among them. A pool that served that purpose "would raise serious competitive concerns." In combining such substitute patents, the pool could serve as a price-fixing mechanism, ultimately raising the price of products and services that utilize the pooled patents. If, on the other hand, the pool were to bring together complementary patent rights, it could be "an efficient and procompetitive method of disseminating those rights to would-be users." By reducing what would otherwise be six licensing transactions to one, the pool would reduce transactions costs for Licensors and licensees alike. By ensuring that each Licensor's patents will not be blocked by those of the other five, the pool would enhance the value of all six Licensors' patents.

One way to ensure that the proposed pool will integrate only complementary patent rights is to limit the pool to patents that are essential to compliance with the Standard Specifications. Essential patents by definition have no substitutes; one needs licenses to each of them in order to comply with the standard. At the same time, they are complementary to each other; a license to one essential patent is more valuable if the licensee also has licenses to use other essential patents.

An inclusion criterion broader than "essentiality" carries with it two anticompetitive risks, both arising from the possibility that the pool might

include patents that are substitutes for one another and not just complements. Consider, for example, a situation in which there are several
patented methods for placing DVD–ROMs into packaging—each a useful
complement to DVD–ROM manufacturing technology, but not essential to
the standard. A DVD–ROM maker would need to license only one of them;
they would be substitutes for each other. Inclusion in the pool of two or
more such patents would risk turning the pool into a price-fixing mechanism. Inclusion in the pool of only one of the competing non-essential
patents, which the pool would convey along with the essential patents,
could in certain cases unreasonably foreclose the non-included competing
patents from use by manufacturers; because the manufacturers would
obtain a license to the one patent with the pool, they might choose not to
license any of the competing patents, even if they otherwise would regard
the competitive patents as superior. Limiting a pool to essential patents
ensures that neither of these concerns will arise; rivalry is foreclosed
neither among patents within the pool nor between patents in the pool and
patents outside it.

From the information you have provided us, it appears reasonably
likely that the pool will combine only complementary patents for which
there are no substitutes for the purpose of compliance with the Standard
Specifications. To be sure, the definition of "essential" contained in the
MOU and the Authorization Agreement introduces some uncertainty. By
asking the expert to identify not only those patents that are literally
essential to compliance with the DVD–ROM and DVD–Video standards, but
also those for which there is no "realistic" alternative, the definition
introduces a degree of subjectivity into the selection process. Based on your
representations, however, it appears that the expert will interpret "realistic" to mean economically feasible. So long as the patent expert applies this
criterion scrupulously and independently, it is reasonable to expect that the
Portfolio will combine only complementary patent rights, and not limit
competition between them and other patent rights for purposes of the
licensed applications. If, however, the expert over time interprets "realistic" more broadly, so as to include patents for which economically feasible
alternatives exist, there would be serious questions as to whether the pool
might injure competition by including such substitutes.

The retention of the expert by the Licensors creates some initial
concern about the expert's ability to apply the essentiality criterion entirely
independent of the Licensors. While the Licensors have agreed that the
expert must be free from any substantial business relationship with any
individual Licensor, the Licensors as a group, to which the expert answers,
have an economic incentive to do the opposite of what they have retained
the expert to do—to combine in the pool their competing DVD-related
patents and to foreclose others' competing patents. Without more, there
would be justifiable skepticism that the expert can be counted on to
undertake a disinterested review of the "essentiality" of the patent rights
put forward.

B. Foreclosure of Competition in Related Markets

As mentioned above, the Licensors are competitors in markets vertically related to the licensed technology—not only in "downstream" markets
such as the manufacture of DVD discs and players, but also in the creation
of content that is incorporated in DVD discs. Consequently, the question

arises whether the pool is likely to impede competition in any of those markets, not only between any Licensor and licensees or other third parties, but also among the Licensors themselves.

Based on what you have told us, the proposed licensing program does not appear to have any such anticompetitive potential in the markets in which the licensed technology will be used. First, the agreed royalty is sufficiently small relative to the total costs of manufacture that it is unlikely to enable collusion among sellers of DVD discs, decoders or players. Second, the proposed program should enhance rather than limit access to the Licensors' "essential" patents. Because Toshiba, the joint licensor, must license on a non-discriminatory basis to all interested parties, it cannot impose disadvantageous terms on competitors, let alone refuse to license to them altogether. Third, the extent of Toshiba's access to proprietary licensee information, either through information provided directly to its licensing employees or through audits conducted by independent accountants, is unlikely to afford it anticompetitive access to competitively sensitive proprietary information, such as cost data. The other Licensors' similarly limited right to an annual audit of Toshiba's conduct as joint licensor should not increase the likelihood of collusion. Nor does there seem to be any facet of the proposed program that would facilitate collusion or dampen competition among the Licensors in the creation of content for software.

C.   Effect on Innovation

The proposed licensing program would require Licensors and licensees alike to agree to license to each other not only their present "essential" patents, but also any ones they obtain in the future. The procompetitive benefits of such a requirement are clear. It ensures that no party to the pool will be able to benefit from the pool while blocking other parties from utilizing the Standard Specifications. Further, by bringing other "essential" patents into the portfolio, the requirement lowers licensees' costs in assembling the patent rights they need to comply with the Standard Specifications. And while it is unclear whether any future "essential" patent will emerge absent an amendment of the Standard Specifications, the requirement as to future patents reduces the possibility that a future patent will block licensees from practicing a technology in which they may already have invested in heavily. Reducing this uncertainty may be a significant benefit to licensees.

The question arises, nevertheless, whether these procompetitive benefits are likely to be outweighed by significant discouragement of research and development relating to the Standard Specifications. Licensors and licensees might have greater incentives to invest in research and development in the field were they free to refuse to license other users of the Standard Specifications under any patent that resulted.

IV.   Conclusion

For these reasons, the Department is not presently inclined to initiate antitrust enforcement action against the conduct you have described. This letter, however, expresses the Department's current enforcement intention. In accordance with our normal practices, the Department reserves the right to bring an enforcement action in the future if the actual operation of the proposed conduct proves to be anticompetitive in purpose or effect.

* * *

Comment: Compare the patent pool justifications accepted by the Justice Department in this letter with the justification accepted by the Court in Broadcast Music, Inc. v. Columbia Broadcasting System, Inc., *supra*, p. 215.

PROBLEM 7

JOINT RESEARCH AND PRODUCTION OF CHEMICAL RESEARCH ASSOCIATES

In order to counter the research laboratories of larger chemical companies, seven small manufacturers of industrial chemicals formed Chemical Research Associates, a partnership. Each of the seven manufacturers contributed $100,000 in cash and agreed to furnish up to $15,000 per year to meet the partnership's expenses. Chemical Research began by studying the techniques of the member corporations. After its study was complete, it took the following actions: (1) it recommended adoption of desirable techniques being used by some but not all of the seven constituent companies; (2) it recommended adoption of new techniques discovered by its own research, patenting them where appropriate and otherwise maintaining them as trade secrets; and (3) it licensed to members for a fee (and sometimes to non-members) major improvements which would not redound to the benefit of all constituent corporations equally. One such improvement, made available only to members, involved a secret manufacturing process that greatly reduced costs of a major product, Zap, produced by all the participating companies and most smaller producers.

Satisfied with Phase I of Chemical Research's work, the member companies met and decided that they would expand their cooperation to joint production of Zap. In order to organize the Zap production optimally, all the members agreed to produce Zap only through Chemical Research. They continued to compete as before on all other products that they manufactured, and each company marketed Zap independently.

There were four other small chemical manufacturers of about the same size as the seven above. One of these, Bluster, sought to participate in the Chemical Research venture and offered to pay its pro rata share of capital contribution and operating expenses. The offer was declined by Chemical Research and by its seven constituent members. They charged (a) that Bluster was a spy for the large chemical companies; (b) that Bluster was in poor condition financially and could not be relied on to meet its obligations under the arrangement; and (c) that some of Bluster's personnel were so untrustworthy that Chemical Research's trade secrets would not be safe with them. Bluster replied that the obvious reason for its exclusion was its record as a price-cutter. Furthermore, even though not admitted, Bluster sought a license at a reasonable royalty for the new secret process and admission to the joint production consortium.

Can Bluster obtain relief under the antitrust laws if the contentions of the Chemical Research group are accepted? What if Bluster is right as to the basis for exclusion?

SECTION 3.   GOVERNMENT ACTION

A.   EFFORTS TO INFLUENCE GOVERNMENT

Eastern Railroad Presidents Conference v. Noerr Motor Freight Inc.

Supreme Court of the United States, 1961.
365 U.S. 127, 81 S.Ct. 523, 5 L.Ed.2d 464.

■ BLACK, J. American railroads have always largely depended upon income from the long-distance transportation of heavy freight for economic survival. During the early years of their existence, they had virtually no competition in this aspect of their business, but, as early as the 1920s, the growth of the trucking industry in this country began to bring about changes in this situation. For the truckers found, just as the railroads had learned earlier, that a very profitable part of the transportation business was the long hauling of heavy freight. As the trucking industry became more and more powerful, the competition between it and the railroads for this business became increasingly intense until, during the period following the conclusion of World War II, at least the railroads, if not both of the competing groups, came to view the struggle as one of economic life or death for their method of transportation. The present litigation is an outgrowth of one part of that struggle.

The case was commenced by a complaint filed in the United States District Court in Pennsylvania on behalf of 41 Pennsylvania truck operators and their trade association, the Pennsylvania Motor Truck Association. This complaint, which named as defendants 24 Eastern railroads, an association of the presidents of those railroads known as the Eastern Railroad Presidents Conference, and a public relations firm, Carl Byoir & Associates, Inc., charged that the defendants had conspired to restrain trade in and monopolize the long-distance freight business in violation of §§ 1 and 2 of the Sherman Act. The gist of the conspiracy alleged was that the railroads had engaged Byoir to conduct a publicity campaign against the truckers designed to foster the adoption and retention of laws and law enforcement practices destructive of the trucking business, to create an atmosphere of distaste for the truckers among the general public, and to impair the relationships existing between the truckers and their customers. The campaign so conducted was described in the complaint as "vicious, corrupt, and fraudulent," first, in that the sole motivation behind it was the desire on the part of the railroads to injure the truckers and eventually to destroy them as competitors in the long-distance freight business, and, secondly, in that the defendants utilized the so-called third-party technique, that is, the publicity matter circulated in the campaign was made to appear as spontaneously expressed views of independent persons and civic groups when, in fact, it was largely prepared and produced by Byoir and paid for by the railroads. The complaint then went on to supplement these more or less general allegations with specific charges as to particular instances in which the railroads had attempted to influence legislation by means of their publicity campaign. One of several such charges was that the defendants had succeeded in persuading the Governor of Pennsylvania to veto a measure known as the "Fair Truck Bill," which would have permitted truckers to carry heavier loads over Pennsylvania roads.

The prayer of the complaint was for treble damages under § 4 of the Clayton Act and an injunction restraining the defendants from further acts in pursuance of the conspiracy. Insofar as the prayer for damages was concerned, a stipulation was entered that the only damages suffered by the individual truck operators was the loss of business that resulted from the veto of the "Fair Truck Bill" by the Governor of Pennsylvania, and accordingly the claim for damages was limited to an amount based upon the loss of profits as a result of this veto plus the expenses incurred by the truckers' trade association for the purpose of combatting the railroads' publicity campaign. The prayer for injunctive relief was much broader, however, asking that the defendants be restrained from disseminating any disparaging information about the truckers without disclosing railroad participation, from attempting to exert any pressure upon the legislature or Governor of Pennsylvania through the medium of front organizations, from paying any private or public organizations to propagate the arguments of the railroads against the truckers or their business, and from doing "any other act or thing to further . . . the objects and purposes" of the conspiracy.

In their answer to this complaint, the railroads admitted that they had conducted a publicity campaign designed to influence the passage of state laws relating to truck weight limits and tax rates on heavy trucks, and to encourage a more rigid enforcement of state laws penalizing trucks for overweight loads and other traffic violations, but they denied that their campaign was motivated either by a desire to destroy the trucking business as a competitor or to interfere with the relationships between the truckers and their customers. Rather, they insisted, the campaign was conducted in furtherance of their rights "to inform the public and the legislatures of the several states of the truth with regard to the enormous damage done to the roads by the operators of heavy and especially of overweight trucks, with regard to their repeated and deliberate violations of the law limiting the weight and speed of big trucks, with regard to their failure to pay their fair share of the cost of constructing, maintaining and repairing the roads, and with regard to the driving hazards they create. . . . Such a campaign, the defendants maintained, did not constitute a violation of the Sherman Act, presumably because that Act could not properly be interpreted to apply either to restraints of trade or monopolizations that result from the passage or enforcement of laws or to efforts of individuals to bring about the passage or enforcement of the laws."[22]

---

22. The answer to the truckers' complaint also interposed a number of other defenses, including the contention that the activities complained of were constitutionally protected

Subsequently, defendants broadened the scope of the litigation by filing a counterclaim in which they charged that the truckers had themselves violated §§ 1 and 2 of the Sherman Act by conspiring to destroy the railroads' competition in the long-distance freight business and to monopolize that business for heavy trucks. The means of the conspiracy alleged in the counterclaim were much the same as those with which the truckers had charged the railroads in the original complaint, including allegations of the conduct of a malicious publicity campaign designed to destroy the railroads' business by law, to create an atmosphere hostile to the railroads among the general public, and to interfere with relationships existing between the railroads and their customers. The prayer for relief of the counterclaim, like that of the truckers' original complaint, was for treble damages and an injunction restraining continuance of the allegedly unlawful practices. In their reply to this counterclaim, the truckers denied each of the allegations that charged a violation of the Sherman Act and, in addition, interposed a number of affirmative defenses, none of which are relevant here.

In this posture, the case went to trial. After hearings, the trial court entered a judgment, based upon extensive findings of fact and conclusions of law, that the railroads' publicity campaign had violated the Sherman Act while that of the truckers had not. In reaching this conclusion, the trial court expressly disclaimed any purpose to condemn as illegal mere efforts on the part of the railroads to influence the passage of new legislation or the enforcement of existing law. Instead, it rested its judgment upon findings, first, that the railroads' publicity campaign, insofar as it was actually directed at lawmaking and law enforcement authorities, was malicious and fraudulent—malicious in that its only purpose was to destroy the truckers as competitors, and fraudulent in that it was predicated upon the deceiving of those authorities through the use of the third-party technique; and, secondly, that the railroads' campaign also had as an important, if not overriding, purpose the destruction of the truckers' goodwill, among both the general public and the truckers' existing customers, and thus injured the truckers in ways unrelated to the passage or enforcement of law. In line with its theory that restraints of trade and monopolizations resulting from valid laws are not actionable under the Sherman Act, however, the trial court awarded only nominal damages to the individual truckers, holding that no damages were recoverable for loss of business due to the veto of the Pennsylvania "Fair Truck Bill." The judgment did, however, award substantial damages to the truckers' trade association as well as the broad injunction asked for in the complaint.[23]

---

under the First Amendment and the contention that the truckers were barred from prosecuting this suit by reason of the fact that they had themselves engaged in conduct identical to that about which they were complaining with regard to the railroads and were thus in pari delicto. Because of the view we take of the proper construction of the Sherman Act, we find it unnecessary to consider any of these other defenses.

23. If anything, the injunction was even broader than had been requested in the complaint for it effectively enjoined the defendants from any publicity activities against the truckers whether or not the third-party technique was used.

The conclusion that the truckers' publicity campaign had not violated the Sherman Act was reached despite findings that the truckers also had engaged in a publicity campaign designed to influence legislation, as charged in the counterclaim, and despite findings that the truckers had utilized the third-party technique in this campaign. Resting largely upon the fact that the efforts of the truckers were directed, at least for the most part, at trying to get legislation passed that was beneficial to them rather than harmful to the railroads, the trial court found that the truckers' campaign was purely defensive in purpose and concluded that the truckers' campaign differed from that of the railroads in that the truckers were not trying to destroy a competitor. Accordingly, it held that the truckers' campaign, though technically in restraint of trade, was well within the rule of reason which governs the interpretation of §§ 1 and 2 of the Sherman Act and consequently dismissed the counterclaim....

We accept, as the starting point for our consideration of the case, the same basic construction of the Sherman Act adopted ... below—that no violation of the Act can be predicated upon mere attempts to influence the passage or enforcement of laws. It has been recognized, at least since the landmark decision of this Court in Standard Oil Co. v. United States, that the Sherman Act forbids only those trade restraints and monopolizations that are created, or attempted, by the acts of "individuals or combinations of individuals or corporations." [221 U.S. 1, 57] Accordingly, it has been held that where a restraint upon trade or monopolization is the result of valid governmental action, as opposed to private action, no violation of the Act can be made out.[24] These decisions rest upon the fact that under our form of government the question whether a law of that kind should pass, or if passed be enforced, is the responsibility of the appropriate legislative or executive branch of government so long as the law itself does not violate some provision of the Constitution.

We think it equally clear that the Sherman Act does not prohibit two or more persons from associating together in an attempt to persuade the legislature or the executive to take particular action with respect to a law that would produce a restraint or a monopoly. Although such associations could perhaps, through a process of expansive construction, be brought within the general proscription of "combination[s] ... in restraint of trade," they bear very little if any resemblance to the combinations normally held violative of the Sherman Act, combinations ordinarily characterized by an express or implied agreement or understanding that the participants will jointly give up their trade freedom, or help one another to take away the trade freedom of others through the use of such devices as price-fixing agreements, boycotts, market-division agreements, and other similar arrangements.[25] This essential dissimilarity between an agreement jointly to seek legislation or law enforcement and the agreements traditionally condemned by § 1 of the Act, even if not itself conclusive on the question of the applicability of the Act, does constitute a warning against

---

24. United States v. Rock Royal Co-op., 307 U.S. 533; Parker v. Brown, 317 U.S. 341.

25. See Apex Hosiery Co. v. Leader, 310 U.S. 469, 491–493.

treating the defendants' conduct as though it amounted to a common-law trade restraint. And we do think that the question is conclusively settled, against the application of the Act, when this factor of essential dissimilarity is considered along with the other difficulties that would be presented by a holding that the Sherman Act forbids associations for the purpose of influencing the passage or enforcement of laws.

In the first place, such a holding would substantially impair the power of government to take actions through its legislature and executive that operate to restrain trade. In a representative democracy such as this, these branches of government act on behalf of the people and, to a very large extent, the whole concept of representation depends upon the ability of the people to make their wishes known to their representatives. To hold that the government retains the power to act in this representative capacity and yet hold, at the same time, that the people cannot freely inform the government of their wishes would impute to the Sherman Act a purpose to regulate, not business activity, but political activity, a purpose which would have no basis whatever in the legislative history of that Act. Secondly, and of at least equal significance, such a construction of the Sherman Act would raise important constitutional questions. The right of petition is one of the freedoms protected by the Bill of Rights, and we cannot, of course, lightly impute to Congress an intent to invade these freedoms. Indeed, such an imputation would be particularly unjustified in this case in view of all the countervailing considerations enumerated above. For these reasons, we think it clear that the Sherman Act does not apply to the activities of the railroads at least insofar as those activities comprised mere solicitation of governmental action with respect to the passage and enforcement of laws. We are thus called upon to consider whether the courts below were correct in holding that, notwithstanding this principle, the Act was violated here because of the presence in the railroads' publicity campaign of additional factors sufficient to take the case out of the area in which the principle is controlling.

The first such factor relied upon was the fact, established by the finding of the District Court, that the railroads' sole purpose in seeking to influence the passage and enforcement of laws was to destroy the truckers as competitors for the long-distance freight business. But we do not see how this fact, even if adequately supported in the record, could transform conduct otherwise lawful into a violation of the Sherman Act. All of the considerations that have led us to the conclusion that the Act does not apply to mere group solicitation of governmental action are equally applicable in spite of the addition of this factor. The right of the people to inform their representatives in government of their desires with respect to the passage or enforcement of laws cannot properly be made to depend upon their intent in doing so. It is neither unusual nor illegal for people to seek action on laws in the hope that they may bring about an advantage to themselves and a disadvantage to their competitors. This Court has expressly recognized this fact in its opinion in United States v. Rock Royal Co-op., where it was said: "If ulterior motives of corporate aggrandizement stimulated their activities, their efforts were not thereby rendered unlawful." If the Act and Order are otherwise valid, the fact that their effect would be to give cooperatives a monopoly of the market would not violate the Sherman Act. . . .[26] Indeed, it is quite probably people with just such a hope of personal advantage who provide much of the information upon which governments must act. A construction of the Sherman Act that would disqualify people from taking a public position on matters in which they are financially interested would thus deprive the government of a valuable source of information and, at the same time, deprive the people of their right to petition in the very instances in which that right may be of the most importance to them. We reject such a construction of the Act and hold that, at least insofar as the railroads' campaign was directed toward obtaining governmental action, its legality was not at all affected by any anticompetitive purpose it may have had.

The second factor relied upon by the courts below to justify the application of the Sherman Act to the railroads' publicity campaign was the use in the campaign of the so-called third-party technique. The theory under which this factor was related to the proscriptions of the Sherman Act, though not entirely clear from any of the opinions below, was apparently that it involved unethical business conduct on the part of the railroads. As pointed out above, the third-party technique, which was aptly characterized by the District Court as involving "deception of the public, manufacture of bogus sources of reference, [and] distortion of public sources of information," depends upon giving propaganda actually circulated by a party in interest the appearance of being spontaneous declarations of independent groups. We can certainly agree with the courts below that this technique, though in widespread use among practitioners of the art of public relations, is one which falls far short of the ethical standards generally approved in this country. It does not follow, however, that the use of the technique in a publicity campaign designed to influence governmental action constitutes a violation of the Sherman Act. Insofar as that Act sets up a code of ethics at all, it is a code that condemns trade restraints, not political activity, and, as we have already pointed out, a publicity campaign to influence governmental action falls clearly into the category of political activity. The proscriptions of the Act, tailored as they are for the business world, are not at all appropriate for application in the political arena. Congress has traditionally exercised extreme caution in legislating with respect to problems relating to the conduct of political activities, a caution which has been reflected in the decisions of this Court interpreting such legislation. All of this caution would go for naught if we permitted an extension of the Sherman Act to regulate activities of that nature simply because those activities have a commercial impact and involve conduct that can be termed unethical.

Moreover, we think the courts below themselves recognized this fact to some extent for their disposition of the case is inconsistent with the position that the use of the third-party technique alone could constitute a violation of the Sherman Act. This much is apparent from the fact that the

---

26. 307 U.S. 533, 560.

railroads' counterclaim against the truckers was not allowed. Since it is undisputed that the truckers were as guilty as the railroads of the use of the technique, this factor could not have been in any sense controlling of the holding against the railroads. Rather, it appears to have been relied upon primarily as an indication of the vicious nature of the campaign against the truckers. But whatever its purpose, we have come to the conclusion that the reliance of the lower courts upon this factor was misplaced and that the railroads' use of the third-party technique was, so far as the Sherman Act is concerned, legally irrelevant.

In addition to the foregoing factors, both of which relate to the intent and methods of the railroads in seeking governmental action, the courts below rested their holding that the Sherman Act had been violated upon a finding that the purpose of the railroads was "more than merely an attempt to obtain legislation. *It was the purpose and intent . . . to hurt the truckers in every way possible even though they secured no legislation.*" (Emphasis in original.) Specifically, the District Court found that the purpose of the railroads was to destroy the goodwill of the truckers among the public generally and among the truckers' customers particularly, in the hope that by doing so the over-all competitive position of the truckers would be weakened, and that the railroads were successful in these efforts to the extent that such injury was actually inflicted. The apparent effect of these findings is to take this case out of the category of those that involve restraints through governmental action and thus render inapplicable the principles announced above. But this effect is only apparent and cannot stand under close scrutiny. There are no specific findings that the railroads attempted directly to persuade anyone not to deal with the truckers. Moreover, all of the evidence in the record, both oral and documentary, deals with the railroads' efforts to influence the passage and enforcement of laws. Circulars, speeches, newspaper articles, editorials, magazine articles, memoranda and all other documents discuss in one way or another the railroads' charges that heavy trucks injure the roads, violate the laws and create traffic hazards, and urge that truckers should be forced to pay a fair share of the costs of rebuilding the roads, that they should be compelled to obey the laws, and that limits should be placed upon the weight of the loads they are permitted to carry. In the light of this, the findings of the District Court that the railroads' campaign was intended to and did in fact injure the truckers in their relationships with the public and with their customers can mean no more than that the truckers sustained some direct injury as an incidental effect of the railroads' campaign to influence governmental action and that the railroads were hopeful that this might happen.[27] Thus,

---

27. Here again, the petitioners have leveled a vigorous attack upon the trial court's findings. As a part of this attack, they urge that there is no basis in reason for the finding that some shippers quit doing business with the truckers as a result of the railroads' publicity campaign. Their contention is that since the theme of the campaign was that the truckers had an unfair competitive advantage and could consequently charge unfairly low prices, the campaign would have encouraged, rather than discouraged, shippers who availed themselves of the truckers' services. This argument has considerable appeal but, as before, we find it the issue presented by the lower courts' conclusion of a violation of the Sherman Act on the basis of this injury is no different than the issue presented by the factors already discussed. It is inevitable, whenever an attempt is made to influence legislation by a campaign of publicity, that an incidental effect of that campaign may be the infliction of some direct injury upon the interests of the party against whom the campaign is directed. And it seems equally inevitable that those conducting the campaign would be aware of, and possibly even pleased by, the prospect of such injury. To hold that the knowing infliction of such injury renders the campaign itself illegal would thus be tantamount to outlawing all such campaigns. We have already discussed the reasons which have led us to the conclusion that this has not been done by anything in the Sherman Act.

There may be situations in which a publicity campaign, ostensibly directed toward influencing governmental action, is a mere sham to cover what is actually nothing more than an attempt to interfere directly with the business relationships of a competitor and the application of the Sherman Act would be justified. But this certainly is not the case here. No one denies that the railroads were making a genuine effort to influence legislation and law enforcement practices. Indeed, if the version of the facts set forth in the truckers' complaint is fully credited, as it was by the courts below, that effort was not only genuine but also highly successful. Under these circumstances, we conclude that no attempt to interfere with business relationships in a manner proscribed by the Sherman Act is involved in this case.

In rejecting each of the grounds relied upon by the courts below to justify application of the Sherman Act to the campaign of the railroads, we have rejected the very grounds upon which those courts relied to distinguish the campaign conducted by the truckers. In doing so, we have restored what appears to be the true nature of the case—a "no-holds-barred fight" between two industries both of which are seeking control of a profitable source of income. Inherent in such fights, which are commonplace in the halls of legislative bodies, is the possibility, and in many instances even the probability, that one group or the other will get hurt by the arguments that are made. In this particular instance, each group appears to have utilized all the political powers it could muster in an attempt to bring about the passage of laws that would help it or injure the other. But the contest itself appears to have been conducted along lines normally accepted in our political system, except to the extent that each group has deliberately deceived the public and public officials. And that deception, reprehensible as it is, can be of no consequence so far as the Sherman Act is concerned. . . .

Reversed.

DEVELOPMENT OF NOERR–PENNINGTON AND THE SHAM EXCEPTION

United Mine Workers of America v. Pennington, 381 U.S. 657, 85 S. Ct. 1585, 14 L. Ed. 2d 626 (1965). In *Pennington*, small coal mine operators alleged that the

---

unnecessary to pass upon the validity of these findings for we think the conclusion must be the same whether they are allowed to stand or not.

United Mine Workers (UMW) and large coal mine employers attempted to drive small operations out of business by setting a higher minimum wage for coal miners whose companies sold to the Tennessee Valley Authority (TVA). Part of those efforts involved approaches to the Secretary of Labor and the TVA urging the establishment of a minimum wage in the Walsh–Healey Act. The Supreme Court addressed the effect of *Noerr* on this case. The lower courts had held that the UMW and employers were not exempt from Sherman Act liability under *Noerr* where, with anticompetitive objectives, they attempted to influence legislation with approaches to the public officials. The court of appeals concluded that *Noerr* applied only to approaches to public officials with good faith law enforcement or law modification—not anticompetitive—purposes. The Supreme Court reversed and reiterated the scope of *Noerr*'s holding: "Noerr shields from the Sherman Act a concerted effort to influence public officials regardless of intent of purpose." 381 U.S. at 670.

California Motor Transport Co. v. Trucking Unlimited, 404 U.S. 508, 92 S. Ct. 609, 30 L. Ed. 2d 642 (1972). A group of highway truckers sued another group of highway carriers seeking injunctive relief and damages, and charged that they had conspired to institute actions and federal agency proceedings to delay and defeat applications for operating rights. Defendants claimed that their resort to administrative agencies was protected by *Noerr*.

The Court began by observing that while *Noerr* involved attempts to influence passage of laws before the legislative branch and enforcement by the executive, "the same philosophy governs the approach of citizens or groups of them to administrative agencies ... and to courts ..." Emphasizing the "mere sham" exception in *Noerr,* however, the Court asserted that actions were not protected when designed "to harass and deter respondents in their use of administrative and judicial proceedings." Thus, defendants in this case were not seeking to influence public officials but rather "to bar their competitors from meaningful access to adjudicatory tribunals and to usurp that decision-making process."

After observing that the political campaign in *Noerr* employed deception and misrepresentation and used unethical tactics, the Court noted:

> Yet unethical conduct in the setting of the adjudicatory process often results in sanctions. Perjury of witnesses is one example. Use of a patent obtained by fraud to exclude a competitor from the market may involve a violation of the antitrust laws, as we held in Walker Process Equipment Inc. v. Food Machinery & Chemical Corp.... Conspiracy with a licensing authority to eliminate a competitor may also result in an antitrust transgression. Continental Ore Co. v. Union Carbide & Carbite Corp.... Similarly, bribery of a public purchasing agent may constitute a violation of Section 2(c) of the Clayton Act as amended by the Robinson–Patman Act....

> There are many other forms of illegal and reprehensible practices which may corrupt the administrative or judicial processes and which may result in antitrust violations. Misrepresentations, condoned in the political arena, are not immunized when used in the adjudicatory process. Opponents before agencies or courts often think poorly of the other's tactics, motions, or defenses and may readily call them baseless. One claim, which a court or agency may think baseless, may go unnoticed; but a pattern of baseless repetitive claims may emerge which leads the fact finder to conclude that the administrative and judicial processes have been abused.

404 U.S. at 512–13. The Court concluded that a combination "to harass and deter" competitors from access to agencies and courts could not be protected under the First Amendment.

NOTES AND QUESTIONS

1. *"Sham" exception.* What is the import of Justice Black's remarks in *Noerr* that the exemption from Sherman Act coverage will not apply if a campaign is a mere "sham" to cover an attempt "to interfere directly with the business relationships of a competitor...." Would the sham exception permit a court to take into account the very factors considered irrelevant in *Noerr*?

2. *Truthfulness of communications.* Assuming that the truth of information submitted is irrelevant in deciding whether the *Noerr* doctrine applies, should it follow that the means of communicating information is also irrelevant? Note that the "third-party technique" discussed in *Noerr* arguably serves only to confuse proper lines of communication between government officials and the public and yet the court in *Noerr* apparently did not regard that as important in reaching its decision.

3. *Which false communications?* In Woods Exploration and Producing Co. v. Aluminum Co. of America, 438 F.2d 1286 (5th Cir. 1971), the *Noerr* doctrine was held inapplicable where competitive injury occurred because of false production forecasts filed by defendants with the Texas Railroad Commission. The false forecasts allegedly led the Commission to reduce plaintiffs' allowable production. The earlier case of Okefenokee Rural Electric Membership Corp. v. Florida Power & Light Co., 214 F.2d 413 (5th Cir. 1954), was distinguished on grounds that the defendants there may have submitted exaggerated and misleading arguments to a state regulatory agency, but submitted no false factual data.

4. *Noncommercial activities.* In Missouri v. National Organization for Women, 620 F.2d 1301 (8th Cir.), cert. denied, 449 U.S. 842 (1980), the National Organization for Women (NOW) organized a convention boycott against all states that had not ratified the proposed Equal Rights Amendment (ERA). The state of Missouri sought an injunction claiming that its economy, and specifically Missouri motels and restaurants, were suffering revenue losses. The District Court denied relief and the Court of Appeals affirmed. Relying on *Noerr*, the Court noted that the boycott was an attempt to influence ratification by the Missouri legislature of the proposed ERA. With respect to the argument that the injury to economic interests in Missouri did not result from legislation, but rather as a direct consequence of the boycott designed to achieve that legislation, the Court concluded that was an incidental effect of NOW's campaign to influence government action. The Court appeared to be influenced by the fact that the legislation sought had social or political rather than commercial goals, and that the members of NOW were not competitors or potential competitors of the victims of the boycott.

5. *Scope of the "sham" exception. California Motor Transport's* approach to the *Noerr* doctrine's "sham" exception raises the question whether litigation must be repetitive before it becomes a "sham." Can a single lawsuit ever be a "sham?" *See* Vendo Co. v. Lektro–Vend Corp., 433 U.S. 623, 644 (1977) (Blackmun, J., concurring in result). *See also* Fischel, Antitrust Liability for Attempts to Influence Government Action: The Basis and Limits of the Noerr–Pennington Doctrine, 45 U. Chi. L. Rev. 80 (1977).

a. In Otter Tail Power Co. v. United States, 410 U.S. 366 (1973), *infra* p. 725, plaintiff alleged that Otter Tail, an electric utility company, had sponsored litigation against certain municipal electric systems, in part to hamper the marketing of necessary bonds to finance municipal systems. The Supreme Court remanded for consideration in light of *California Motor Transport,* and the District Court found that repetitive litigation was designed to prevent establishment of competitive systems and therefore fell within the "sham" exception. United States v. Otter Tail Power Co., 360 F. Supp. 451 (D. Minn. 1973), aff'd per curiam, 417 U.S. 901 (1974).

b. In MCI Communications Corp. v. AT&T Co., 708 F.2d 1081 (7th Cir.), cert. denied, 464 U.S. 891 (1983), the Seventh Circuit held that the filing of tariffs with numerous state utilities commissions, while defendant believed or knew that the state commissions lacked jurisdiction to approve them (by reason of exclusive FCC jurisdiction), provided a strong basis for a claim of "sham." The Court quoted with approval the view that "the requisite motive for the sham exception is the intent to harm one's competitors not by the *result* of the litigation, but by the simple fact of the *institution* of the litigation," citing Gainesville v. Florida Power & Light Co., 488 F. Supp. 1258 (S.D. Fla. 1980). AT&T's filings were found to have injured MCI by (1) imposing litigation costs in 49 different forums, (2) increasing the risk of disruption of MCI's plans if even only one commission were to take jurisdiction, and (3) adding additional months of costly delay in MCI's efforts to implement its plans.

c. In Clipper Exxpress v. Rocky Mountain Motor Tariff Bureau, Inc., 690 F.2d 1240 (9th Cir. 1982), cert. denied, 459 U.S. 1227 (1983), plaintiff alleged that defendant trucking companies violated the Sherman Act by conspiring to prosecute deliberate false protests before the ICC, against plaintiff's lower rate tariffs, to enforce and protect their illegal price fixing and customer allocations. The District Court granted summary judgment for defendants on grounds, among others, that the ICC protests were protected under *Noerr,* but the Ninth Circuit reversed. It held that there was no requirement in *California Motor Transport* that there be multiple suits or protests in order to support a claim of "sham"; in any event, defendants here had allegedly agreed to protest all plaintiff's tariff modifications without regard to their merit during the course of a single ICC proceeding. It concluded also that the abuse of administration process could injure competition by something less than complete blockage of access, for example, by delaying the effectiveness of new rates, imposing litigation costs, or injuring relationships with customers.

Is it sensible to subject parties seeking relief in court to antitrust liability (including possible treble damages) if it turns out that the lawsuit was lacking in merit? Is this an undue burden on the right to seek redress in court?

d. In re Burlington Northern Inc., 822 F.2d 518 (5th Cir. 1987), grew out of Energy Transportation System, Inc.'s unsuccessful attempt to build a coal slurry pipeline from Wyoming to Arkansas. ETSI claimed that a host of railroads conspired to prevent ETSI from completing the project, and it brought an antitrust claim against them. In particular, ETSI complained about two groups of lawsuits. The first group, the Andrews litigation, were brought by various railroads to void a contract between the United States Department of the Interior and ETSI for water for the pipeline. The second group, the Windows litigation, arose from ETSI's attempt to secure rights to cross the railroads' rights of way. ETSI wanted to show that both groups of lawsuits were shams, and it tried to obtain documents prepared in connection with the allegedly sham litigation. The district court allowed ETSI to proceed with its discovery.

The railroads petitioned the Fifth Circuit for mandamus to block the discovery. They claimed the protection of the Noerr–Pennington doctrine for their litigation efforts. They argued that a finding of sham was precluded because they had been partially successful in one lawsuit, the Andrews litigation, and defendants in the other, the Windows litigation. The Fifth Circuit rejected both arguments. It held that partial success on the merits is no substitute for the Noerr–Pennington inquiry into the antitrust defendant's reasons for bringing the underlying lawsuit. It also held that a defendant's conduct in a suit might be proved a sham for Noerr–Pennington purposes. The court, however, did find error in the district court's decision to allow discovery to proceed without first considering whether the railroads' litigation efforts had been driven by a genuine desire for judicial relief.

Allied Tube & Conduit Corp. v. Indian Head, Inc.

Supreme Court of the United States, 1988.
486 U.S. 492, 108 S.Ct. 1931, 100 L.Ed.2d 497.

■ BRENNAN, J. Petitioner contends that its efforts to affect the product standard-setting process of a private association are immune from antitrust liability under the *Noerr* doctrine primarily because the association's standards are widely adopted into law by state and local governments. *Eastern Railroad Presidents Conference v. Noerr Motor Freight, Inc.*, 365 U.S. 127 (1961). The United States Court of Appeals for the Second Circuit held that *Noerr* immunity did not apply. We affirm.

I

The National Fire Protection Association (Association) is a private, voluntary organization with more than 31,500 individual and group members representing industry, labor, academia, insurers, organized medicine, firefighters, and government. The Association, among other things, publishes product standards and codes related to fire protection through a process known as "consensus standard making." One of the codes it publishes is the National Electrical Code, which establishes product and performance requirements for the design and installation of electrical wiring systems. Revised every three years, the National Electric Code (Code) is the most influential electrical code in the nation. A substantial number of state and local governments routinely adopt the Code into law with little or no change; private certification laboratories, such as Underwriters Laboratories, normally will not list and label an electrical product that does not meet Code standards; many underwriters will refuse to insure structures that are not built in conformity with the Code; and many electrical inspectors, contractors, and distributors will not use a product that falls outside the Code.

Among the electrical products covered by the Code is electrical conduit, the hollow tubing used as a raceway to carry electrical wires through the walls and floors of buildings. Throughout the relevant period, the Code permitted using electrical conduit made of steel, and almost all conduit sold was in fact steel conduit. Starting in 1980, respondent began to offer plastic conduit made of polyvinyl chloride. Respondent claims its plastic conduit offers significant competitive advantages over steel conduit, including pliability, lower installed cost, and lower susceptibility to short circuiting. In 1980, however, there was also a scientific basis for concern that, during fires in high-rise buildings, polyvinyl chloride conduit might burn and emit toxic fumes.

Respondent initiated a proposal to include polyvinyl chloride conduit as an approved type of electrical conduit in the 1981 edition of the Code. Following approval by one of the Association's professional panels, this proposal was scheduled for consideration at the 1980 annual meeting, where it could be adopted or rejected by a simple majority of the members present. Alarmed that, if approved, respondent's product might pose a competitive threat to steel conduit, petitioner, the nation's largest producer of steel conduit, met to plan strategy with, among others, members of the steel industry, other steel conduit manufacturers, and its independent sales agents. They collectively agreed to exclude respondent's product from the 1981 Code by packing the upcoming annual meeting with new Association members whose only function would be to vote against the polyvinyl chloride proposal.

Combined, the steel interests recruited 230 persons to join the Association and to attend the annual meeting to vote against the proposal. Petitioner alone recruited 155 persons—including employees, executives, sales agents, the agents' employees, employees from two divisions that did not sell electrical products, and the wife of a national sales director. Petitioner and the other steel interests also paid over $100,000 for the membership, registration, and attendance expenses of these voters. At the annual meeting, the steel group voters were instructed where to sit and how and when to vote by group leaders who used walkie-talkies and hand signals to facilitate communication. Few of the steel group voters had any of the technical documentation necessary to follow the meeting. None of them spoke at the meeting to give their reasons for opposing the proposal to approve polyvinyl chloride conduit. Nonetheless, with their solid vote in opposition, the proposal was rejected and returned to committee by a vote of 394 to 390. Respondent appealed the membership's vote to the Association's Board of Directors, but the Board denied the appeal on the ground that, although the Association's rules had been circumvented, they had not been violated.[28]

In October 1981, respondent brought this suit in Federal District Court, alleging that petitioner and others had unreasonably restrained trade in the electrical conduit market in violation of § 1 of the Sherman Act. A bifurcated jury trial began in March 1985. Petitioner conceded that it had conspired with the other steel interests to exclude respondent's product from the Code and that it had a pecuniary interest to do so. The jury, instructed under the rule of reason that respondent carried the

---

28. Respondent also sought a tentative interim amendment to the Code, but that was denied on the ground that there was not sufficient exigency to merit an interim amendment. The Association subsequently approved use of polyvinyl chloride conduit for buildings of less than four stories in the 1984 Code, and for all buildings in the 1987 Code.

burden of showing that the anticompetitive effects of petitioner's actions outweighed any procompetitive benefits of standard setting, found petitioner liable. In answers to special interrogatories, the jury found that petitioner did not violate any rules of the Association and acted, at least in part, based on a genuine belief that plastic conduit was unsafe, but that petitioner nonetheless did "subvert" the consensus standard making process of the Association. The jury also made special findings that petitioner's actions had an adverse impact on competition, were not the least restrictive means of expressing petitioner's opposition to the use of polyvinyl chloride conduit in the marketplace, and unreasonably restrained trade in violation of the antitrust laws. The jury then awarded respondent damages, to be trebled, of $3.8 million for lost profits resulting from the effect that excluding polyvinyl chloride conduit from the 1981 Code had of its own force in the marketplace. No damages were awarded for injuries stemming from the adoption of the 1981 Code by governmental entities.[29]

The District Court then granted a judgment n.o.v. for petitioner, reasoning that *Noerr* immunity applied because the Association was "akin to a legislature" and because petitioner, "by the use of methods consistent with acceptable standards of political action, genuinely intended to influence the [Association] with respect to the National Electrical Code, and to thereby influence the various state and local legislative bodies which adopt the [Code]." The Court of Appeals reversed, rejecting both the argument that the Association should be treated as a "quasi-legislative" body because legislatures routinely adopt the Code and the argument that efforts to influence the Code were immune under *Noerr* as indirect attempts to influence state and local governments. 817 F.2d 938 (1987). We granted certiorari to address important issues regarding the application of *Noerr* immunity to private standard-setting associations.

II

Concerted efforts to restrain or monopolize trade by petitioning government officials are protected from antitrust liability under the doctrine established by *Noerr,* 365 U.S. 127 (1961); *Mine Workers v. Pennington,* 381 U.S. 657, 669–672 (1965); and *California Motor Transport Co. v. Trucking Unlimited,* 404 U.S. 508 (1972). The scope of this protection depends, however, on the source, context, and nature of the anticompetitive restraint at issue. "[W]here a restraint upon trade or monopolization is the result of valid governmental action, as opposed to private action," those urging the

---

29. Although the District Court was of the view that at trial respondent relied solely on the theory that its injury "flowed from legislative action," the Court of Appeals determined that respondent was awarded damages only on the theory "that the stigma of not obtaining [Code] approval of its products and [petitioner's] 'marketing' of that stigma caused independent marketplace harm to [respondent] in those jurisdictions *permitting* use of [polyvinyl chloride] conduit, as well as those which later adopted the 1984 [Code], which permitted use of [polyvinyl chloride] conduit in buildings less than three stories high. [Respondent] did *not* seek redress for any injury arising from the adopting of the [Code] by the various governments." 817 F.2d 938, 941, n. 3 (1987) (emphasis added). We decide the case as it was framed by the Court of Appeals.

governmental action enjoy absolute immunity from antitrust liability for the anticompetitive restraint. *Noerr*, 365 U.S., at 136; see also *Pennington, supra*, at 671. In addition, where, independent of any government action, the anticompetitive restraint results directly from private action, the restraint cannot form the basis for antitrust liability if it is "incidental" to a valid effort to influence governmental action. *Noerr, supra*, 365 U.S. at 143. The validity of such efforts, and thus the applicability of *Noerr* immunity, varies with the context and nature of the activity. A publicity campaign directed at the general public, seeking legislation or executive action, enjoys antitrust immunity even when the campaign employs unethical and deceptive methods. *Noerr, supra*, 365 U.S. at 140–41. But in less political arenas, unethical and deceptive practices can constitute abuses of administrative or judicial processes that may result in antitrust violations.[30] *California Motor Transport, supra*, 404 U.S. at 512–13.

In this case, the restraint of trade on which liability was predicated was the Association's exclusion of respondent's product from the Code, and no damages were imposed for the incorporation of that Code by any government. The relevant context is thus the standard-setting process of a private association. Typically, private standard-setting associations, like the Association in this case, include members having horizontal and vertical business relations. See generally 7 P. Areeda, Antitrust Law ¶ 1477, p. 343 (1986) (trade and standard-setting associations routinely treated as continuing conspiracies of their members). There is no doubt that the members of such associations often have economic incentives to restrain competition and that the product standards set by such associations have a serious potential for anticompetitive harm.[31] See *American Society of Mechanical Engineers, Inc. v. Hydrolevel Corp.*, 456 U.S. 556, 571 (1982). Agreement on a product standard is, after all, implicitly an agreement not to manufacture, distribute, or purchase certain types of products. Accordingly, private standard-setting associations have traditionally been objects of antitrust scrutiny. See, *e.g.*, *ibid.*; *Radiant Burners, Inc. v. Peoples Gas Light & Coke Co.*, 364 U.S. 656 (1961) (per curiam). See also *FTC v. Indiana Federation of Dentists*, 476 U.S. 447 (1986). When, however, private associations promulgate safety standards based on the merits of objective expert judgments and through procedures that prevent the standard-setting process from being biased by members with economic interests in stifling product competition, cf. *Hydrolevel, supra*, 456 U.S., at 570–573 (noting absence of "meaningful safeguards"), those private standards can have significant procompetitive advantages. It is this potential for procom-

---

30. Of course, in whatever forum, private action that is not genuinely aimed at procuring favorable government action is a mere sham that cannot be deemed a valid effort to influence government action. *Noerr*, 365 U.S., at 144; *California Motor Transport*, 404 U.S., at 511.

31. "Product standardization might impair competition in several ways.... [It] might deprive some consumers of a desired product, eliminate quality competition, exclude rival producers, or facilitate oligopolistic pricing by easing rivals' ability to monitor each other's prices." 7 P. Areeda, Antitrust Law ¶ 1503, p. 373 (1986).

petitive benefits that has led most lower courts to apply rule-of-reason analysis to product standard-setting by private associations.[32]

Given this context, petitioner does not enjoy the immunity accorded those who merely urge the government to restrain trade. We agree with the Court of Appeals that the Association cannot be treated as a "quasi-legislative" body simply because legislatures routinely adopt the Code the Association publishes. Whatever *de facto* authority the Association enjoys, no official authority has been conferred on it by any government, and the decisionmaking body of the Association is composed, at least in part, of persons with economic incentives to restrain trade. See *Continental Ore Co. v. Union Carbide & Carbon Corp.*, 370 U.S. 690, 707–708 (1962). See also *id.*, at 706–707; *Goldfarb v. Virginia State Bar*, 421 U.S. 773, 791–792 (1975). "We may presume, absent a showing to the contrary, that [a government] acts in the public interest. A private party, on the other hand, may be presumed to be acting primarily on his or its own behalf." *Hallie v. Eau Claire*, 471 U.S. 34, 45 (1985). The dividing line between restraints resulting from governmental action and those resulting from private action may not always be obvious.[33] But where, as here, the restraint is imposed by persons unaccountable to the public and without official authority, many of whom have personal financial interests in restraining competition, we have no difficulty concluding that the restraint has resulted from private action.

Noerr immunity might still apply, however, if, as petitioner argues, the exclusion of polyvinyl chloride conduit from the Code, and the effect that exclusion had of its own force in the marketplace, were incidental to a valid effort to influence governmental action. Petitioner notes that the lion's share of the anticompetitive effect in this case came from the predictable adoption of the Code into law by a large number of state and local governments. Indeed, petitioner argues that, because state and local governments rely so heavily on the Code and lack the resources or technical expertise to second-guess it, efforts to influence the Association's standard-setting process are the most effective means of influencing legislation regulating electrical conduit. This claim to *Noerr* immunity has some force. The effort to influence governmental action in this case certainly cannot be

---

32. See 2 J. von Kalinowski, Antitrust Laws and Trade Regulation §§ 6I.01[3], 6I.03, 6I.04, pp. 6I–6 to 6I–7, 6I–18 to 6I–29 (1981) (collecting cases). Concerted efforts to *enforce* (rather than just agree upon) private product standards face more rigorous antitrust scrutiny. See Radiant Burners, 364 U.S., at 659–660. See also Fashion Originators' Guild of America, Inc. v. FTC, 312 U.S. 457 (1941).

33. See, e.g., California Motor Transport, supra, 404 U.S., at 513 (stating in dicta that "[c]onspiracy with a licensing authority to eliminate a competitor" or "bribery of a public purchasing agent" may violate the antitrust laws); Mine Workers v. Pennington, 381 U.S. 657, 671, and n. 4 (1965) (holding that immunity applied but noting that the trade restraint at issue "was the act of a public official who is not claimed to be a co-conspirator" and contrasting Continental Ore); Continental Ore Co. v. Union Carbide & Carbon Corp., 370 U.S. 690, 707–708 (1962); 1 P. Areeda & D. Turner, Antitrust Law ¶ 206 (1978) (discussing the extent to which Noerr immunity should apply to commercial transactions involving the government). See also Goldfarb v. Virginia State Bar, 421 U.S. 773, 791–792 (1975); Continental Ore, supra, 370 U.S. at 706–707.

characterized as a sham given the actual adoption of the 1981 Code into a number of statutes and local ordinances. Nor can we quarrel with petitioner's contention that, given the widespread adoption of the Code into law, any effect the 1981 Code had in the marketplace of its own force was, in the main, incidental to petitioner's genuine effort to influence governmental action.[34] And, as petitioner persuasively argues, the claim of *Noerr* immunity cannot be dismissed on the ground that the conduct at issue involved no "direct" petitioning of government officials, for *Noerr* itself immunized a form of "indirect" petitioning. See *Noerr,* 365 U.S. 127 (1961) (immunizing a publicity campaign directed at the general public on the ground that it was part of an effort to influence legislative and executive action).

Nonetheless, the validity of petitioner's actions remains an issue. We cannot agree with petitioner's absolutist position that the *Noerr* doctrine immunizes every concerted effort that is genuinely intended to influence governmental action. If all such conduct were immunized then, for example, competitors would be free to enter into horizontal price agreements as long as they wished to propose that price as an appropriate level for governmental ratemaking or price supports. But see *Georgia v. Pennsylvania R. Co.,* 324 U.S. 439, 456–463 (1945). Horizontal conspiracies or boycotts designed to exact higher prices or other economic advantages from the government would be immunized on the ground that they are genuinely intended to influence the government to agree to the conspirators' terms. But see *Georgia v. Evans,* 316 U.S. 159 (1942). Firms could claim immunity for boycotts or horizontal output restrictions on the ground that they are intended to dramatize the plight of their industry and spur legislative action. Immunity might even be claimed for anticompetitive mergers on the theory that they give the merging corporations added political clout. Nor is it necessarily dispositive that packing the Association's meeting may have been the most effective means of securing government action, for one could imagine situations where the most effective means of influencing government officials is bribery, and we have never suggested that that kind of attempt to influence the government merits protection. We thus conclude that the *Noerr* immunity of anticompetitive activity intended to influence the government depends not only on its impact, but also on the context and nature of the activity.

Here petitioner's actions took place within the context of the standard-setting process of a private association. Having concluded that the Association is not a "quasi-legislative" body, we reject petitioner's argument that any efforts to influence the Association must be treated as efforts to influence a "quasi-legislature" and given the same wide berth accorded legislative lobbying. That rounding up supporters is an acceptable and

---

34. The effect, independent of government action, that the 1981 Code had in the marketplace may to some extent have been exacerbated by petitioner's efforts to "market" the stigma respondent's product suffered by being excluded from the Code. See 817 F.2d, at 941, n. 3. Given our disposition *infra,* we need not decide whether, or to what extent, these "marketing" efforts alter the incidental status of the resulting anticompetitive harm. See generally *Noerr,* 365 U.S., at 142 (noting that in that case there were "no specific findings that the railroads attempted directly to persuade anyone not to deal with the truckers").

constitutionally protected method of influencing elections does not mean that rounding up economically interested persons to set private standards must also be protected. Nor do we agree with petitioner's contention that, regardless of the Association's nonlegislative status, the effort to influence the Code should receive the same wide latitude given ethically dubious efforts to influence legislative action in the political arena, see *Noerr, supra*, at 365 U.S. at 140–141, simply because the ultimate aim of the effort to influence the private standard-setting process was (principally) legislative action. The ultimate aim is not dispositive. A misrepresentation to a court would not necessarily be entitled to the same antitrust immunity allowed deceptive practices in the political arena simply because the odds were very good that the court's decision would be codified—nor for that matter would misrepresentations made under oath at a legislative committee hearing in the hopes of spurring legislative action.

What distinguishes this case from *Noerr* and its progeny is that the context and nature of petitioner's activity make it the type of commercial activity that has traditionally had its validity determined by the antitrust laws themselves. True, in *Noerr* we immunized conduct that could be characterized as a conspiracy among railroads to destroy business relations between truckers and their customers. *Noerr, supra*, 365 U.S. at 142. But we noted there that:

> "There are no specific findings that the railroads attempted directly to persuade anyone not to deal with the truckers. Moreover, all the evidence in the record, both oral and documentary, deals with the railroads' efforts to influence the passage and enforcement of laws. Circulars, speeches, newspaper articles, editorials, magazine articles, memoranda and all other documents discuss in one way or another the railroads' charges that heavy trucks injure the roads, violate the laws and create traffic hazards, and urge that truckers should be forced to pay a fair share of the costs of rebuilding the roads, that they should be compelled to obey the laws, and that limits should be placed upon the weight of the loads they are permitted to carry." 365 U.S., at 142–143.

In light of those findings, we characterized the railroads' activity as a classic "attempt . . . to influence legislation by a campaign of publicity," an "inevitable" and "incidental" effect of which was "the infliction of some direct injury upon the interests of the party against whom the campaign is directed." *Id.*, at 143. The essential character of such a publicity campaign was, we concluded, political, and could not be segregated from the activity's impact on business. Rather, the plaintiff's cause of action simply embraced the inherent possibility in such political fights "that one group or the other will get hurt by the arguments that are made." As a political activity, special factors counseled against regulating the publicity campaign under the antitrust laws:

> "Insofar as [the Sherman] Act sets up a code of ethics at all, it is a code that condemns trade restraints, not political activity, and, as we have already pointed out, a publicity campaign to influence

governmental action falls clearly into the category of political activity. The proscriptions of the Act, tailored as they are for the business world, are not at all appropriate for application in the political arena. Congress has traditionally exercised extreme caution in legislating with respect to problems relating to the conduct of political activities, a caution which has been reflected in the decisions of this Court interpreting such legislation. All of this caution would go for naught if we permitted an extension of the Sherman Act to regulate activities of that nature simply because those activities have a commercial impact and involve conduct that can be termed unethical." *Id.*, 365 U.S., at 140–141 (footnote omitted).

In *Noerr,* then, the political context and nature of the activity precluded inquiry into its antitrust validity.[35]

Here the context and nature of the activity do not counsel against inquiry into its validity. Unlike the publicity campaign in *Noerr,* the activity at issue here did not take place in the open political arena, where partisanship is the hallmark of decisionmaking, but within the confines of a private standard-setting process. The validity of conduct within that process has long been defined and circumscribed by the antitrust laws without regard to whether the private standards are likely to be adopted into law. Indeed, because private standard-setting by associations comprising firms with horizontal and vertical business relations is permitted at all under the antitrust laws only on the understanding that it will be conducted in a nonpartisan manner offering procompetitive benefits, the standards of conduct in this context are, at least in some respects, more rigorous than the standards of conduct prevailing in the partisan political arena or in the adversarial process of adjudication. The activity at issue here thus cannot, as in *Noerr,* be characterized as an activity that has traditionally been regulated with extreme caution, see *Noerr,* or as an activity that "bear[s] little if any resemblance to the combinations normally held violative of the Sherman Act," 365 U.S., at 136. And petitioner did not confine itself to efforts to persuade an independent decisionmaker, cf. *id.,* at 138, 139 (describing the immunized conduct as "mere solicitation"); rather, it organized and orchestrated the actual exercise of the Association's decisionmaking authority in setting a standard. Nor can the setting of the Association's Code be characterized as merely an exercise of the power of persuasion, for it in part involves the exercise of market power. The Association's members, after all, include consumers, distributors, and manufacturers of electrical conduit, and any agreement to exclude polyvinyl chloride conduit from the Code is in part an implicit agreement not to trade in that type of electrical conduit. Although one could reason backwards from the legislative impact of the Code to the conclusion that the conduct at issue here is

---

35. Similarly in California Motor Transport any antitrust review of the validity of the activity at issue was limited and structured by the fact that there the antitrust defendants were "us[ing] the channels and procedures of state and federal agencies and courts." 404 U.S., at 511; see also id., at 512–513.

"political," we think that, given the context and nature of the conduct, it can more aptly be characterized as commercial activity with a political impact. Just as the antitrust laws should not regulate political activities "simply because those activities have a commercial impact," so the antitrust laws should not necessarily immunize what are in essence commercial activities simply because they have a political impact.[36]

NAACP v. Claiborne Hardware Co., 458 U.S. 886 (1982), is not to the contrary. In that case we held that the First Amendment protected the nonviolent elements of a boycott of white merchants organized by the National Association for the Advancement of Colored People and designed to make white government and business leaders comply with a list of demands for equality and racial justice. Although the boycotters intended to inflict economic injury on the merchants, the boycott was not motivated by any desire to lessen competition or to reap economic benefits but by the aim of vindicating rights of equality and freedom lying at the heart of the Constitution, and the boycotters were consumers who did not stand to profit financially from a lessening of competition in the boycotted market. Here, in contrast, petitioner was at least partially motivated by the desire to lessen competition, and, because of petitioner's line of business, stood to reap substantial economic benefits from making it difficult for respondent to compete.[37]

Thus in this case the context and nature of petitioner's efforts to influence the Code persuade us that the validity of those efforts must, despite their political impact, be evaluated under the standards of conduct set forth by the antitrust laws that govern the private standard-setting process. The antitrust validity of these efforts is not established, without more, by petitioner's literal compliance with the rules of the Association,

---

36. It is admittedly difficult to draw the precise lines separating anticompetitive political activity that is immunized despite its commercial impact from anticompetitive commercial activity that is unprotected despite its political impact, and this is itself a case close to the line. For that reason we caution that our decision today depends on the context and nature of the activity. Although criticizing the uncertainty of such a particularized inquiry, the dissent does not dispute that the types of activity we describe, could not be immune under Noerr and fails to offer an intelligible alternative for distinguishing those non-immune activities from the activity at issue in this case. Rather, the dissent states without elaboration that the sham exception "is enough to guard against flagrant abuse," apparently embracing the conclusion of the United States Court of Appeals for the Ninth Circuit that the sham exception covers the activity of a defendant who "genuinely seeks to achieve his governmental result, but does so *through improper means.*" Sessions Tank Liners, Inc. v. Joor Mfg., Inc., 827 F.2d 458, 465, n. 5 (1987) (emphasis in original). Such a use of the word "sham" distorts its meaning and bears little relation to the sham exception Noerr described to cover activity that was not genuinely intended to influence governmental action. 365 U.S., at 144....

37. Although the absence of such anticompetitive motives and incentives is relevant to determining whether petitioner's restraint of trade is protected under Claiborne Hardware, we do not suggest that the absence of anticompetitive purpose is necessary for Noerr immunity. As the dissent points out, in Noerr itself the major purpose of the activity at issue was anticompetitive. Our statement that the "ultimate aim" of petitioner "is not dispositive," stands only for the proposition that, at least outside the political context, the mere fact that an anticompetitive activity is also intended to influence governmental action is not alone *sufficient* to render that activity immune from antitrust liability.

for the hope of procompetitive benefits depends upon the existence of safeguards sufficient to prevent the standard-setting process from being biased by members with economic interests in restraining competition. An association cannot validate the anticompetitive activities of its members simply by adopting rules that fail to provide such safeguards.[38] The issue of immunity in this case thus collapses into the issue of antitrust liability. Although we do not here set forth the rules of antitrust liability governing the private standard-setting process, we hold that at least where, as here, an economically interested party exercises decisionmaking authority in formulating a product standard for a private association that comprises market participants, that party enjoys no *Noerr* immunity from any antitrust liability flowing from the effect the standard has of its own force in the marketplace.

This conclusion does not deprive state and local governments of input and information from interested individuals or organizations or leave petitioner without ample means to petition those governments. Cf. *Noerr, supra.* See also *California Motor Transport,* 404 U.S., at 510. Petitioner, and others concerned about the safety or competitive threat of polyvinyl chloride conduit, can, with full antitrust immunity, engage in concerted efforts to influence those governments through direct lobbying, publicity campaigns, and other traditional avenues of political expression. To the extent state and local governments are more difficult to persuade through these other avenues, that no doubt reflects their preference for and confidence in the nonpartisan consensus process that petitioner has undermined. Petitioner remains free to take advantage of the forum provided by the standard-setting process by presenting and vigorously arguing accurate scientific evidence before a nonpartisan private standard-setting body.[39] And petitioner can avoid the strictures of the private standard-setting process by attempting to influence legislatures through other forums. What petitioner may not do (without exposing itself to possible antitrust liability for direct injuries) is bias the process by, as in this case, stacking the private standard-setting body with decisionmakers sharing their economic interest in restraining competition.

The judgment of the Court of Appeals is *Affirmed.*

---

38. Even petitioner's counsel concedes, for example, that Noerr would not apply if the Association had a rule giving the steel conduit manufacturers a veto over changes in the Code. Tr. of Oral Arg. 41–42.

39. The dissent mistakenly asserts that we today hold that Noerr immunity does not apply to mere efforts to persuade others to exclude a competitor's product from a private code.... Our holding is expressly limited to cases where an "economically interested party exercises *decisionmaking* authority in formulating a product standard for a private association that comprises market participants." *Supra* [   ], at 509 (emphasis added); see also *supra*, at 506–507; (relying in part on the distinction between activity involving the exercise of decisionmaking authority and market power and activity involving mere attempts to persuade an independent decisionmaker). Cf. Noerr, 365 U.S., at 136. The dissent also mistakenly asserts that this description encompasses all private standard-setting associations. In fact, many such associations are composed of members with expertise but no economic interest in suppressing competition. See, e.g., Sessions, 827 F.2d, at 460, and n. 2.

■ JUSTICE WHITE, with whom JUSTICE O'CONNOR joins, dissenting.

Eastern Railroad Presidents Conference v. Noerr Motor Freight, Inc., 365 U.S. 127 (1961), held that the Sherman Act should not be construed to forbid joint efforts by railway companies seeking legislation that would disadvantage the trucking industry. These efforts for the most part involved a public relations campaign rather than direct lobbying of the lawmakers and were held not subject to antitrust challenge because of the fundamental importance of maintaining the free flow of information to the government and the right of the people to seek legislative relief, directly or indirectly. *Mine Workers v. Pennington,* 381 U.S. 657 (1965), and *California Motor Transport Co. v. Trucking Unlimited,* 404 U.S. 508 (1972), applied the rule to efforts to seek executive action and to administrative and adjudicative proceedings.

The Court now refuses to apply the rule of these cases to the participants in those private organizations, such as National Fire Protection Association (NFPA), that regularly propound and publish health and safety standards for a variety of products and industries and then present these codes to state and local authorities for the purpose of having them enacted into law. The NFPA and those participating in the code-writing process will now be subject to antitrust liability if their efforts have anti-competitive effects and do not withstand scrutiny under the rule of reason. Believing that this result is a misapplication of the *Noerr* decision and an improvident construction of the Sherman Act, I respectfully dissent.

This case presents an even stronger argument for immunity than did *Noerr* itself. That decision turned on whether the design or purpose of the conduct was to obtain or influence the passage or enforcement of laws. The Court concedes that petitioner's actions in this case constituted a "genuine effort to influence governmental action," and that this was its "ultimate aim." In *Noerr,* the publicity campaign was dispersed widely among the public in a broad but necessary diluted attempt to move public opinion in hopes that government officials would take note and respond accordingly. The campaign apparently had some influence on the passage of tax laws and other legislation favorable to the railroads in New Jersey, New York, and Ohio, and procured the governor's veto of a bill that had been passed in Pennsylvania. See 365 U.S., at 130; see also 155 F. Supp. 768, 777–801 (ED Pa.1957). Here, NFPA actually drafted proposed legislation in the form of the National Electrical Code (NEC) and presented it countrywide. Not only were petitioner's efforts in this case designed to influence the passage of state laws, but there was also a much greater likelihood that they would be successful than was the case in *Noerr.* This is germane because it establishes a much greater likelihood that the "purpose" and "design" of petitioner's actions in this case was the "solicitation of governmental action with respect to the passage and enforcement of laws," 365 U.S., at 138.

Rather than directly confronting the severe damage that today's decision does to the *Noerr* doctrine, the majority asserts that the "ultimate aim" of petitioner's efforts "is not dispositive." That statement cannot be reconciled with the statements quoted earlier from *Noerr,* where it was held that even if one of the major purposes, or even the *sole* purpose, of the publicity campaign was "to destroy the truckers as competitors," 365 U.S., at 138, those actions were immunized from antitrust liability because ultimately they were "directed toward obtaining governmental action," *id.*, at 140. The majority later doubles back on this statement, and suggests that it is important in this case that "petitioner was at least partially motivated by the desire to lessen competition, and . . . stood to reap substantial economic benefits from making it difficult for respondent to compete." It need hardly be said that all of this was also true in *Noerr*. Nobody condones fraud, bribery, or misrepresentation in any form, and other state and federal laws ensure that such conduct is punishable. But the point here is that conduct otherwise punishable under the antitrust laws either becomes immune from the operation of those laws when it is part of a larger design to influence the passage and enforcement of laws, or it does not. No workable boundaries to the *Noerr* doctrine are established by declaring, and then repeating at every turn, that everything depends on "the context and nature of" the activity, if we are unable to offer any further guidance about what this vague reference is supposed to mean, especially when the result here is so clearly wrong as long as *Noerr* itself is reputed to remain good law. One unfortunate consequence of today's decision, therefore, is that district courts and courts of appeals will be obliged to puzzle over claims raised under the doctrine without any intelligible guidance about when and why to apply it.

If there were no private code-writing organizations, and state legislatures themselves held the necessary hearing and wrote codes from scratch, then business concerns like Allied, together with their friends, could jointly testify with impunity about the safety of various products, even though they had anti-competitive motives in doing so. This much the majority concedes, as it does that the major purpose of the code-writing organizations is to influence legislative action. These days it is almost a foregone conclusion that the vast majority of the states will adopt these codes with little or no change. It is untenable to consider the code-writing process by such organizations as NFPA as too far removed from the legislative process to warrant application of the doctrine announced in *Noerr* and faithfully applied in other cases. This was the view of Judge Sneed and his colleagues on the Ninth Circuit in *Sessions Tank Liners, Inc. v. Joor Mfg., Inc.*, 827 F.2d 458 (1987), and the reasons they gave for applying *Noerr* in this context are much more persuasive than anything to the contrary the majority now has to offer.

The Court's decision is unfortunate for another reason. There are now over 400 private organizations preparing and publishing an enormous variety of codes and standards. State and local governments necessarily, and as a matter of course, turn to these proposed codes in the process of legislating to further the health and safety of their citizens. The code that is at issue in this case, for example, was adopted verbatim by 25 states and the District of Columbia; 19 others adopted it with only minor changes. It is the most widely disseminated and adopted model code in the world today. There is no doubt that the work of these private organizations contributes enormously to the public interest and that participation in their work by those who have the technical competence and experience to do so should not be discouraged.

The Court's decision today will surely do just that. It must inevitably be the case that codes such as NEC will set standards that some products cannot satisfy and hence in the name of health and safety will reduce or prevent competition, as was the case here. Yet, putative competitors of the producer of such products will now think twice before urging in the course of the code-making process that those products not be approved; for if they are successful (or even if they are not), they may well become antitrust defendants facing treble-damages liability unless they can prove to a court and a jury that they had no evil motives but were merely "presenting and vigorously arguing accurate scientific evidence before a nonpartisan private standard-setting body," *ante* at 15, (though with the knowing and inevitable result of eliminating competition). In this case, for example, even if Allied had not resorted to the tactics it employed, but had done no more than successfully argue in good faith the hazards of using respondent's products, it would have inflicted the same damage on respondent and would have risked facing the same antitrust suit, with a jury ultimately deciding the health and safety implications of the products at issue.

The Court's suggestion that its decision will not affect the ability of these organizations to assist state and local governments is surely wrong. The Court's holding is "that at least where, as here, an economically interested party exercises decisionmaking authority in formulating a product standard for a private association that comprises market participants, that party enjoys no *Noerr* immunity from any antitrust liability flowing from the effects the standard has of its own force in the marketplace." This description encompasses the structure and work of all such organizations as we now know them. The Court is saying, in effect, that where a private organization sets standards, the participants can be sued under the antitrust laws for *any* effects those standards have in the marketplace *other than* those flowing from their adoption into law. But the standards will have *some* effect in the marketplace even where they are also adopted into law, through publicity and other means, thus exposing the participants to liability. Henceforth, therefore, any private organization offers such standards at its peril, and without any of the breathing room enjoyed by other participants in the political process.

The alternative apparently envisioned by the Court is that an organization can gain the protection of the *Noerr* doctrine as long as nobody with any economic interest in the product is permitted to "exercis[e] decisionmaking authority" (*i.e.*, vote) on its recommendations as to particular product standards. Insisting that organizations like NFPA conduct themselves like courts of law will have perverse effects. Legislatures are willing to rely on such organizations precisely because their standards are being set by those who possess an expert understanding of the products and their uses, which are primarily if not entirely those who design, manufacture, sell, and distribute them. Sanitizing such bodies by discouraging the active participation of those with economic interests in the subject matter undermines their utility.

I fear that exposing organizations like NFPA to antitrust liability will impair their usefulness by inhibiting frank and open discussion of the health and safety characteristics of new or old products that will be affected by their codes. The Court focuses on the tactics of petitioner that are thought to have subverted the entire process. But it is not suggested that if there are abuses, they are anything more than occasional happenings. The Court does speculate about the terrible practices that applying *Noerr* in this context could lead us to condone in future cases, but these are no more than fantasies, since nothing of the sort occurred in the wake of *Noerr* itself. It seems to me that today's decision is therefore an unfortunate case of overkill.

Of course, the *Noerr* immunity is not unlimited and by its terms is unavailable where the alleged efforts to influence legislation are nothing but a sham. As the Ninth Circuit held, this limitation is enough to guard against flagrant abuse. In any event, occasional abuse is insufficient ground to render the entire process less useful and reliable. I would reverse the judgment below and remand for further proceedings.

NOTE

Public adoption of private codes. In Sessions Tank Liners, Inc. v. Joor Manufacturing Inc., 17 F.3d 295 (9th Cir. 1994), the president of Joor, a manufacturer of underground storage tanks, persuaded the Western Fire Chiefs Association to insert a provision into the Uniform Fire Code requiring the removal of leaking underground storage tanks. Sessions sued Joor for violating the antitrust laws. The Ninth Circuit ruled that Joor was shielded from antitrust liability by *Noerr–Pennington*. It distinguished *Allied Tube & Conduit,* pointing out that the plaintiff in *Allied* had been awarded damages on the theory that banishment from a uniform code had caused the product independent harm in the marketplace. Sessions, on the other hand, had suffered its injuries when municipal governments enacted the Uniform Fire Code

Massachusetts School of Law at Andover, Inc. v. American Bar Association

United States Court of Appeals, Third Circuit, 1997.
107 F.3d 1026.

■ GREENBERG, CIRCUIT JUDGE. This case is before this court on appeal from an order of the district court granting summary judgment on all counts to the appellees in this antitrust action brought against them by the Massachusetts School of Law at Andover, Inc. ("MSL").

I.   FACTUAL AND PROCEDURAL HISTORY

A.   The Parties

MSL has been operating a law school in Massachusetts since 1988. The Board of Regents of Massachusetts authorized MSL to grant the J.D.

degree in 1990. This authority allowed MSL's graduates to take several bar examinations, including that in Massachusetts. MSL has the stated policy of providing low-cost but high-quality legal education and attracting mid-life, working class, and minority students. MSL facilitates this policy with its admissions procedure and a tuition of $9,000 per year. Many of MSL's policies and practices conflict with American Bar Association ("ABA") accreditation standards, and MSL aggressively has sought changes in those standards.

The ABA, a national professional organization of attorneys whose membership is open to members of any bar in the United States, has been concerned with legal education and bar admissions throughout its history. In 1921, through its Section of Legal Education and Admissions to the Bar (the "Section"), the ABA first developed standards of accreditation for legal education programs. The ABA petitioned state supreme courts to rely on its accreditation decisions in connection with bar admission decisions. Now, all 50 states and the District of Columbia consider graduation from an ABA-accredited law school sufficient for the legal education requirement of bar admission. The United States Secretary of Education considers the Council of the Section to be the national agency for accreditation of professional schools of law and a reliable authority concerning the quality of legal education. The ABA informs the states of its accreditation decisions and annually sends them the Review of Legal Education in the United States, the ABA accreditation standards, and any proposed revisions of the standards. During the period at issue, there were 177 ABA-accredited law schools in the United States and over 50 unaccredited schools with some form of state approval such as MSL enjoys. The ABA consistently has opposed attempts to change or waive bar admission rules to allow graduates of schools not accredited by the ABA to take the bar examination.

Many states have methods of satisfying the legal education requirement other than graduation from an ABA-accredited school. These methods include legal apprenticeship, practice in another state, and graduation from a school approved by the American Association of Law Schools ("AALS") or a state agency. The AALS is an association of 160 law schools which serves as a learned society for law schools and legal faculty and as a representative of the law school community with the federal government and other education organizations. Furthermore, in every state, a bar applicant or law school can petition the bar admission authority for revision or waiver of the rules. MSL won a waiver of New Hampshire's rules to allow its graduates to take the bar in 1995, and has filed petitions seeking similar relief in Connecticut, Maine, New York, and Rhode Island. Maryland and Washington, D.C. have granted petitions of graduates of MSL to take the bar. MSL graduates can take the bar examination immediately after graduation in California, Massachusetts, New Hampshire, Vermont and West Virginia, and in 12 other states after practicing in another state first.

The ABA allows graduates of non-accredited schools to join the ABA once they are admitted to a bar and does not prohibit its members from hiring or otherwise dealing with graduates of such schools. The ABA does not prevent its members from teaching at non-ABA-accredited schools, but it does not allow its accredited schools to let students transfer credits from unaccredited schools or to accept graduates of unaccredited schools into graduate programs.

ABA accreditation is open to any law school that applies and meets the ABA standards. The ABA grants provisional accreditation to schools that substantially comply with its standards and promise to comply fully within three years. An Accreditation Committee makes an initial evaluation of a school for provisional accreditation and gives a recommendation to the Council of the Section. The Council then makes a recommendation to the ABA House of Delegates, which has the ultimate decisionmaking authority.

A law school must have been teaching students for five years and graduated three classes to be eligible for AALS membership. The AALS holds an annual meeting, professional conferences and workshops, and publishes the Journal of Legal Education. All of its current members are ABA-accredited, but accreditation is neither necessary nor sufficient for membership approval. The AALS accredits schools in the sense that it determines whether a school meets its membership requirements, but it has accreditation standards and procedures separate from those of the ABA. The AALS conducts a site visit, independently of the ABA, when a school applies for membership, and it conducts periodic visits after membership, usually jointly with the ABA if the school is ABA-accredited. The AALS is not involved with site inspections for provisional ABA accreditation, such as the one the ABA undertook at MSL.

The Law School Admissions Council, Inc. ("LSAC") is the successor organization to the Law School Admission Council and Law School Admission Services, Inc. The LSAC, as have its predecessors, administers the Law School Admissions Test ("LSAT"). The LSAC is not affiliated formally with either the ABA or the AALS and does not participate in the ABA accreditation process. Membership in the LSAC is open to any United States law school that (1) requires that "substantially all of its applicants for admission take the Law School Admission Test," and (2) is ABA-accredited or an AALS member. MSL does not require the LSAT, never has applied for AALS membership, and is not ABA-accredited, so thus is not eligible for LSAC membership.

In addition to administering the LSAT, the LSAC performs a number of other services. The Candidate Referral Service ("CRS") provides lists of names and addresses of people who have taken the LSAT. Use of the CRS is open to any school which has degree granting authority from a state, regardless of LSAC membership or ABA accreditation, and MSL has made use of this service. The Law School Data Assembly Service ("LSDAS") provides a summary of a law school applicant's college record and LSAT score. LSDAS is also open to all schools and has been used by MSL. The LSAC publishes a handbook, The Official Guide to U.S. Law Schools, with a two-page description of each United States LSAC member school, and two appendices with the names and addresses of Canadian LSAC members and unaccredited United States law schools, including MSL, known to the

LSAC. The LSAC also sponsors regional recruiting forums for law school applicants and conferences of pre-law advisors which are only open to LSAC members.

B.   The Complaint

MSL applied for provisional ABA accreditation during the fall of 1992 and early 1993. MSL never claimed it was or would be in compliance with ABA standards, but instead asked for a waiver under Standard 802 which allows the Council to grant variances from the standards. Following the established process, a seven-member site evaluation team appointed by and representing only the ABA visited MSL and then prepared a 76–page report which was sent to MSL. MSL sent a 90–page response to the site team report.

The Accreditation Committee, after reviewing the site report and the MSL materials, and hearing a presentation from six MSL representatives, recommended denial of MSL's accreditation application because it did not meet the ABA requirements. The Committee also recommended denial of the waiver request. In a letter to MSL explaining its denial recommendation, the Committee listed 11 areas where MSL failed to comply with ABA standards. These areas included the high student/faculty ratio, over reliance on part-time faculty, the heavy teaching load of full-time faculty, the lack of adequate sabbaticals for faculty, the use of a for-credit bar review class, the failure to limit the hours students may be employed, and the failure to use the LSAT or give evidence validating its own admission test. The body of the letter discussed the inadequacy of MSL's law library, but the letter did not cite that inadequacy as one of the reasons for the denial recommendation. The letter did not discuss the salaries of MSL's faculty. Invoking ABA procedures, MSL appealed but, after a full review at which MSL had the opportunity to make a presentation, the denial of accreditation was upheld on February 8, 1994.

MSL filed this action on November 23, 1993, alleging that the ABA, AALS, LSAC, and 22 individuals combined and conspired to organize and enforce a group boycott in violation of section 1 of the Sherman Act and conspired to monopolize legal education, law school accreditation, and the licensing of lawyers, in violation of section 2 of the Sherman Act. 15 U.S.C. §§ 1–2. The complaint basically alleged that the appellees conspired to enforce the ABA's anticompetitive accreditation standards by: (1) fixing the price of faculty salaries; (2) requiring reduced teaching hours and non-teaching duties; (3) requiring paid sabbaticals; (4) forcing the hiring of more professors in order to lower student/faculty ratios; (5) limiting the use of adjunct professors; (6) prohibiting the use of required or for-credit bar review courses; (7) forcing schools to limit the number of hours students could work; (8) prohibiting ABA-accredited schools from accepting credit transfers from unaccredited schools and from enrolling graduates of unaccredited schools in graduate programs; (9) requiring more expensive and elaborate physical and library facilities; and (10) requiring schools to use the LSAT. MSL alleged that enforcement of these anticompetitive criteria led to the denial of its application for provisional accreditation and caused MSL to suffer a "loss of prestige" and direct economic damage in the form of declining enrollments and tuition revenue. [Enrollments allegedly declined to 40% of the level they had attained prior to the denial of accreditation.]

After MSL filed its complaint, the Antitrust Division of the United States Department of Justice ("DOJ") began an investigation of the ABA's accreditation process and on June 27, 1995, filed suit against the ABA in the United States District Court for the District of Columbia alleging violations of section 1 of the Sherman Act. The ABA entered into a consent decree with the DOJ on June 25, 1996, settling that case.

[The District Court granted summary judgment for the appellees. MSL appealed from that order.]

II. DISCUSSION

. . .

C. Summary Judgment

MSL asserts three types of injury resulting from the ABA's allegedly anticompetitive conduct. The first is that MSL is at a competitive disadvantage in recruiting students because graduates of unaccredited schools cannot take the bar examination in most states. Second, MSL says that denial of accreditation creates a stigma, independent of the bar examination issue. Finally, MSL contends that the ABA's enforcement of its accreditation standards injures it directly by increasing the cost of faculty salaries and creating a boycott of unaccredited schools.

In granting summary judgment to the appellees, the district court held that they were not subject to antitrust liability for MSL's principal alleged injury, a competitive disadvantage in recruiting students, to the extent that the decisions of the individual states to prohibit graduates of unaccredited schools from taking their bar examinations caused the injury. The court based this holding on the principles of *Noerr*, 365 U.S. 127. MSL argues on appeal that the *Noerr* principles do not apply here because private anticompetitive conduct is immunized only where it is (1) clearly and affirmatively authorized by state policy, and (2) actively supervised by the state. *California Retail Liquor Dealers Ass'n v. Midcal Aluminum, Inc.*, 445 U.S. 97 (1980). See also *FTC v. Ticor Title Ins. Co.*, 504 U.S. 621 (1992); *Patrick v. Burget*, 486 U.S. 94 (1988).

In *Parker v. Brown* the Supreme Court held that the Sherman Act does not prohibit an anticompetitive restraint imposed by a state as an act of government. 317 U.S. 341, 352 (1943). The decision in *Noerr* reaffirmed the *Parker* doctrine in stating "where a restraint upon trade or monopolization is the result of valid governmental action, as opposed to private action, no violation of the Act can be made out." 365 U.S. at 136. *Noerr* went on to hold that any attempt to petition or influence the government to impose an anticompetitive restraint is immune from antitrust action. *Id.* Further, even if the anticompetitive restraint results directly from private action, it is still immune if it is an "incidental effect" of a legitimate attempt to influence governmental action. *Id.* at 143–44. As the Supreme Court put it, "*Parker* and *Noerr* are complementary expressions of the principle that the antitrust laws regulate business, not politics; the former decision protects the States' acts of governing, and the latter the citizens' participation in government." *City of Columbia v. Omni Outdoor Advertising, Inc.*, 499 U.S. 365, 383 (1991). Thus, the initial substantive issues on this appeal are whether state or private conduct caused the injury MSL alleges it suffered because its graduates could not take the bar examination in most states, and whether, if MSL suffered an injury as a result of the ABA's conduct, the injury was an incidental effect of the ABA's attempt to influence the states with respect to establishing criteria for bar admission. We will discuss each alleged injury separately.

1.   Injury from bar examination requirements

Each state retains the authority to decide what applicants may take its bar examination and may be admitted to the bar. Accordingly, MSL's argument that the ABA received "carte-blanche delegated authority to decide who can take bar exams," is simply wrong. Many, but not all, states consider the accreditation decisions of the ABA in their legal education requirement (one of many requirements) for taking the bar examination. Yet, every state retains the final authority to set all the bar admission rules, and individual applicants or law schools can petition the states for waivers or changes.

To the extent that MSL's alleged injury arises from the inability of its graduates to take the bar examination in most states, the injury is the result of state action and thus is immune from antitrust action under the doctrine of *Parker v. Brown*, 317 U.S. at 352. The ABA does not decide who can take the bar examinations. Rather, it makes an accreditation decision which it conveys to the states, but the states make the decisions as to bar admissions. Without state action, the ABA's accreditation decisions would not affect state bar admissions requirements. Because the states are sovereign in imposing the bar admission requirements, the clear articulation and active supervision requirements urged by MSL are inapplicable. In short, this case does not involve a delegation of state authority. To the contrary, the states use the ABA to assist them in their decision-making processes. Thus, we have here a government action case.

Our holding is consistent with current antitrust jurisprudence. The Supreme Court held in a challenge to Arizona's bar admissions policies that the conduct in question "was in reality that of the Arizona Supreme Court," and thus immune under *Parker*. *Hoover v. Ronwin*, 466 U.S. 558, 573–74 (1984). Further, the Supreme Court has held that when a state supreme court adopts a state bar rule banning legal advertising, and retains final enforcement authority over it, *Parker* immunity applies. *Bates v. State Bar of Arizona*, 433 U.S. 350, 361 (1977) ("The Arizona Supreme Court is the real party in interest; it adopted the rules, and it is the ultimate trier of fact and law in the enforcement process."). This case is entirely analogous. The states do not adopt the ABA's accreditation processes, but they do adopt and give effect to the results. Thus, the cases cited by MSL (*Midcal*, *Patrick*, and *Ticor*) are inapplicable because they dealt with situations where private parties were engaging in conduct, whether price-fixing (*Midcal* and *Ticor*) or denying hospital privileges (*Patrick*), which led directly to the alleged antitrust injury. Here, the state action setting the bar examination requirements led to the alleged injury.

[The court distinguished the Supreme Court's opinion in Allied Tube & Conduit Corp. v. Indian Head, Inc., 486 U.S. 492 (1988), because that case specifically did not reach the question of any injury caused by the adoption of the challenged standards by a governmental body. It then discussed several additional lower court decisions applying the principles of *Noerr* and rejected MSL's claim that the ABA's conduct injured it because its graduates could not take the bar examination in most states.]

2. Stigma Injury

MSL also alleges that independent of any bar examination requirements, it was injured by the stigmatic effect in the market place of the denial of accreditation. MSL claims that the ABA has conducted a campaign to convey the idea that ABA accreditation is the sine qua non of quality and that the ABA is the most, or only, competent organization to judge law schools. There is enough evidence to create a genuine dispute of material fact on this issue. Nevertheless, the district court ruled that this injury could not form the basis for antitrust liability because it was "incidental to the primary, protected injury," and thus immune under *Noerr*. MSL challenges this holding on the grounds that there was no petitioning of government here, and therefore *Noerr* does not apply. We hold that there was sufficient petitioning to invoke *Noerr* immunity.

MSL relies extensively on the Supreme Court's decision in *Allied Tube & Conduit Corp. v. Indian Head, Inc.*, 486 U.S. 492 (1988). [After further describing *Allied Tube*, the court applied it to MSL's claim.]

The conduct of which MSL complains here is basically the ABA's justification of its accreditation decisions and MSL is asserting a loss of prestige resulting from it. This conduct is neither normal commercial activity nor the type of restraint of trade involved in Allied Tube, and thus that case is not controlling. A loss of prestige resulting from a refusal to approve a product or service does not alone make out an antitrust claim.

Noerr immunity is proper in this case because the ABA engaged in petitioning activity, and the stigma injury which MSL suffered was incidental to that activity. [Citing *Omni Outdoor Advertising*, the court flatly rejected the concept of a "conspiracy" exception to either *Noerr* or *Parker* immunity] MSL admits that in the past, "from the 1920's to approximately the mid 1970's," the ABA petitioned the states in a campaign to prohibit graduates from unaccredited schools from taking bar examinations. This campaign was obviously successful as now most states require graduation from an ABA-accredited school for admission to the bar. The ABA's current conduct surely would be considered petitioning if it took place during the past campaign. The fact that the ABA was successful in lobbying the states does not weaken its position. The ABA continues to communicate its accreditation decisions to the states, and it desires that they continue to give them credence. Discussing the quality and competence of its decisions is a legitimate, although somewhat indirect, way of petitioning the states to continue to follow its guidance. Yet, such activity is no more indirect than the public relations campaign held to be petitioning in *Noerr*.

There is an exception to *Noerr* immunity that would apply if the ABA "attempted directly to persuade anyone not to deal with" MSL. There is no evidence that the ABA made such an attempt (there was such evidence in *Allied Tube*), nor is there any other evidence suggesting that *Noerr* immunity should not apply here. In a supplemental filing of information after oral argument, MSL produced two instances where it claims the ABA directly mentioned MSL. The first is a *Boston Globe* article about the denial of accreditation to MSL in which an ABA governor defended the ABA standards as providing "a minimum level of quality and consumer protection assurance to the public." The second proffered piece of evidence is a transcript of the ABA House of Delegates debate of MSL's accreditation application, where one member urged the denial of MSL's application and stated that the standards with which MSL did not comply "lie at the heart of a quality institution."

Both of these statements do nothing more than defend the ABA standards. As we discuss above, this is valid, if indirect, petitioning activity. The ABA is not saying directly that MSL is a bad institution, or that a particular student should not go there. MSL's attempts to characterize all the ABA's comments about the quality of its accreditation process as direct attacks on MSL does not make them direct attacks. We also point out that if a claim for stigma injury could be advanced in circumstances like those here, *Noerr* immunity would be confined severely; a petitioner for governmental action is likely to urge that the action is needed to ensure that standards are met, thereby suggesting that some entities do not meet appropriate standards.

3. Direct injury from ABA standards

MSL alleges a third injury which occurs directly from the ABA's enforcement of its standards, independent of both the bar examination and stigma issues. The challenged standards relate to faculty salaries (MSL charges price-fixing) and limitations on accredited schools accepting transfers or graduate students from unaccredited schools (MSL charges a boycott). Although the ABA is immune from liability attributable to the state action in requiring applicants for the bar examination to have graduated from an ABA-accredited law school and from any stigma injury resulting from the denial of accreditation under the *Noerr* petitioning doctrine, the ABA is not immune in the actual enforcement of its standards. The state action relates to the use of the results of the accreditation process, not the process itself. The process is entirely private conduct which has not been approved or supervised explicitly by any state. Thus, the ABA's enforcement of an anticompetitive standard which injures MSL would not be immune from possible antitrust liability. Extending *Noerr* immunity to this type of private activity would run counter to *Allied Tube*.

[MSL failed to show sufficient evidence that it was denied accreditation because it did not comply with the salary standard.]

MSL alleges that the faculty salary standards injured it in two ways. First, MSL asserts that it raised its salaries in an attempt to get accreditation. This claim is in direct conflict to its consistent assertion that it refused to comply with the ABA's anticompetitive standards and for that reason was denied accreditation. The claim also is remarkable because MSL made it clear that it would not comply with ABA standards to obtain certification. The only other related evidence shows that MSL acted independently to increase its salaries, and then later found that this action might help it get accreditation. . . . There has not been sufficient explanation of the contradiction to create a genuine issue of material fact and justify reversing the summary judgment.

MSL's second contention that the ABA's salary standards injured it is that the standards inflated the market cost of law professors, thereby increasing the salaries MSL must pay its faculty. This market price argument is equally unavailing. MSL's stated policy was to rely on adjunct faculty. MSL did not produce evidence that any of its faculty other than its dean ever had been employed at another law school. In effect, MSL was hiring faculty from a different market, one unaffected by the ABA's conduct, or at least a different provider in the same market (teachers who never taught at ABA-accredited schools). . . .

MSL also alleges a boycott in that the ABA prevented its accredited schools from accepting transfers or graduate students from unaccredited schools. The district court held that MSL had not produced any evidence that it was injured by either of these rules. This holding is correct. MSL has done nothing more than state the standards and allege that they injured MSL. There is no factual support for these allegations. Further, the evidence shows that MSL actively opposed its students transferring, both in policy and practice. MSL therefore cannot claim that the ABA's prohibition on transfers with credit injured it.

MSL also alleges that the AALS boycotted MSL by refusing membership and that the LSAC boycotted MSL by refusing to allow it to attend certain recruiting conferences. The allegations regarding the AALS are simply incorrect. AALS membership is independent of ABA accreditation, and MSL never has applied for such membership. Even though it is not a member, MSL can attend AALS conferences and has done so. Therefore MSL has not suffered any injury at the hands of the AALS.

The LSAC's failure to invite MSL to its conferences does not constitute a boycott. Under the fact-pattern here, to demonstrate a boycott MSL has to show that these conferences are an essential facility for recruiting students, as there is no other potential basis for the boycott claim. Such an essential facility or claim fails whenever a plaintiff (1) cannot show that the defendant has a monopoly over the alleged essential facility; (2) the facility cannot be duplicated in a reasonable manner; and (3) the plaintiff has been denied its use. *Ideal Dairy Farms, Inc. v. John Labatt, Ltd.,* 90 F.3d 737, 748 (3d Cir.1996). MSL has shown only that the LSAC denies it participation. There is no evidence suggesting that the LSAC has a monopoly over access to law students or pre-law advisors, or even over recruiting fairs. The LSAC does not hinder MSL's recruiting in any way, it just does not aid it by allowing MSL to attend its conferences. Such activity is not required by the antitrust laws, and its absence does not constitute antitrust injury.

Further, MSL has not shown that the LSAC injured it . . . .

III. CONCLUSION

The order of the district court entered August 29, 1996, granting the appellees summary judgment and the other orders on appeal will be affirmed.

Professional Real Estate Investors v. Columbia Pictures

Supreme Court of the United States, 1993.
508 U.S. 49, 113 S.Ct. 1920, 123 L.Ed.2d 611.

■ JUSTICE THOMAS delivered the opinion of the Court.

This case requires us to define the "sham" exception to the doctrine of antitrust immunity first identified in *Eastern Railroad Presidents Conference v. Noerr Motor Freight, Inc.,* 365 U.S. 127 (1961), as the doctrine applies in the litigation context. Under the sham exception, activity "ostensibly directed toward influencing governmental action" does not qualify for *Noerr* immunity if it "is a mere sham to cover . . . an attempt to interfere directly with the business relationships of a competitor." We hold that litigation cannot be deprived of immunity as a sham unless the litigation is objectively baseless. The Court of Appeals for the Ninth Circuit refused to characterize as sham a lawsuit that the antitrust defendant admittedly had probable cause to institute. We affirm.

I

Petitioners Professional Real Estate Investors, Inc., and Kenneth F. Irwin (collectively, PRE) operated La Mancha Private Club and Villas, a resort hotel in Palm Springs, California. Having installed videodisc players in the resort's hotel rooms and assembled a library of more than 200 motion picture titles, PRE rented videodiscs to guests for in-room viewing. PRE also sought to develop a market for the sale of videodisc players to other hotels wishing to offer in-room viewing of prerecorded material. Respondents, Columbia Pictures Industries, Inc., and seven other major motion picture studios (collectively, Columbia), held copyrights to the motion pictures recorded on the videodiscs that PRE purchased. Columbia also licensed the transmission of copyrighted motion pictures to hotel rooms through a wired cable system called Spectradyne. PRE therefore competed with Columbia not only for the viewing market at La Mancha but also for the broader market for in-room entertainment services in hotels.

In 1983, Columbia sued PRE for alleged copyright infringement through the rental of videodiscs for viewing in hotel rooms. PRE counter-claimed, charging Columbia with violations of §§ 1 and 2 of the Sherman Act and various state law infractions. In particular, PRE alleged that Columbia's copyright action was a mere sham that cloaked underlying acts of monopolization and conspiracy to restrain trade....

II

PRE contends that "the Ninth Circuit erred in holding that an antitrust plaintiff must, as a threshold prerequisite ..., establish that a sham lawsuit is baseless as a matter of law." It invites us to adopt an approach under which either "indifference to ... outcome," or failure to prove that a petition for redress of grievances "would ... have been brought but for [a] predatory motive," would expose a defendant to antitrust liability under the sham exception. We decline PRE's invitation....

In *California Motor Transport Co. v. Trucking Unlimited*, 404 U.S. 508 (1972), we elaborated on *Noerr* in two relevant respects. First, we extended *Noerr* to "the approach of citizens ... to administrative agencies ... and to courts." 404 U.S., at 510. Second, we held that the complaint showed a sham not entitled to immunity when it contained allegations that one group of highway carriers "sought to bar ... competitors from meaningful access to adjudicatory tribunals and so to usurp that decisionmaking process" by "institut[ing] ... proceedings and actions ... with or without probable cause, and regardless of the merits of the cases." *Id.*, at 512 (internal quotation marks omitted). We left unresolved the question presented by this case—whether litigation may be sham merely because a subjective expectation of success does not motivate the litigant. We now answer this question in the negative and hold that an objectively reasonable effort to litigate cannot be sham regardless of subjective intent.[40]

Our original formulation of antitrust petitioning immunity required that unprotected activity lack objective reasonableness. *Noerr* rejected the contention that an attempt "to influence the passage and enforcement of laws" might lose immunity merely because the lobbyists' "sole purpose ... was to destroy [their] competitors." 365 U.S., at 138. Nor were we persuaded by a showing that a publicity campaign "was intended to and did in fact injure [competitors] in their relationships with the public and with their

---

40. *California Motor Transportation* did refer to the antitrust defendants' "purpose to deprive ... competitors of meaningful access to the ... courts." 404 U.S., at 512. See also *id.*, at 515 (noting a "purpose to eliminate ... a competitor by denying him free and meaningful access to the agencies and courts"); *id.*, at 518 (Stewart, J., concurring in judgment) (agreeing that the antitrust laws could punish acts intended "to discourage and ultimately to prevent [a competitor] from invoking" administrative and judicial process). That a sham depends on the existence of anticompetitive intent, however, does not form the sham inquiry into a purely subjective investigation.

customers," since such "direct injury" was merely "an incidental effect of the ... campaign to influence governmental action." *Id.,* at 143. We reasoned that "[t]he right of the people to inform their representatives in government of their desires with respect to the passage or enforcement of laws cannot properly be made to depend upon their intent in doing so." *Id.,* at 139. In short, "*Noerr* shields from the Sherman Act a concerted effort to influence public officials regardless of intent or purpose." *Pennington,* 381 U.S. at 670.

Nothing in *California Motor Transport* retreated from these principles. Indeed, we recognized that recourse to agencies and courts should not be condemned as sham until a reviewing court has "discern[ed] and draw[n]" the "difficult line" separating objectively reasonable claims from "a pattern of baseless, repetitive claims ... which leads the factfinder to conclude that the administrative and judicial processes have been abused." 404 U.S., at 513. Our recognition of a sham in that case signifies that the institution of legal proceedings "without probable cause" will give rise to a sham if such activity effectively "bar[s] ... competitors from meaningful access to adjudicatory tribunals and so ... usurp[s] th[e] decisionmaking process." *Id.* at 512.

Since *California Motor Transport,* we have consistently assumed that the sham exception contains an indispensable objective component. We have described a sham as "evidenced by repetitive lawsuits carrying the hallmark of *insubstantial* claims." *Otter Tail Power Co. v. United States,* 410 U.S. 366, 380 (1973) (emphasis added). We regard as sham "private action that is not genuinely aimed at procuring favorable government action," as opposed to "a valid effort to influence government action." *Allied Tube & Conduit Corp. v. Indian Head, Inc.,* 486 U.S. 492, 500 n. 4 (1988). "And government action ... certainly cannot be characterized as a sham." *Id.,* at 502. See also *Vendo Co. v. Lektro–Vend Corp.,* 433 U.S. 623, 645 (1977) (Blackmun, J., concurring in result) (describing a successful lawsuit as a "genuine attemp[t] to use the ... adjudicative process legitimately" rather than "'a pattern of baseless, repetitive claims'"). Whether applying *Noerr* as an antitrust doctrine or invoking it in other contexts, we have repeatedly reaffirmed that evidence of anticompetitive intent or purpose alone cannot transform otherwise legitimate activity into a sham. See, *e.g., FTC v. Superior Court Trial Lawyers Assn.,* 493 U.S. 411, 424 (1990); *NAACP v. Claiborne Hardware Co.,* 458 U.S. 886, 913–914 (1982). Cf. *Vendo, supra,* at 635–636, n. 6, 639, n. 9 (plurality opinion of Rehnquist, J.); *id.,* at 644, n., 645 (Blackmun, J., concurring in result). Indeed, by analogy to *Noerr*'s sham exception, we held that even an "improperly motivated" lawsuit may not be enjoined under the National Labor Relations Act as an unfair labor practice unless such litigation is "baseless." *Bill Johnson's Restaurants, Inc. v. NLRB,* 461 U.S. 731, 743–744 (1983). Our decisions therefore establish that the legality of objectively reasonable petitioning "directed toward obtaining governmental action" is "not at all affected by an anticompetitive purpose [the actor] may have had." *Noerr,* 365 U.S., at 140, quoted in *Pennington, supra,* 381 U.S., at 669.

Our most recent applications of *Noerr* immunity further demonstrate that neither *Noerr* immunity nor its sham exception turns on subjective intent alone. In *Allied Tube,* 486 U.S., at 503, and *FTC v. Trial Lawyers, supra,* 493 U.S., at 424, 427, and n. 11, we refused to let antitrust defendants immunize otherwise unlawful restraints of trade by pleading a subjective intent to seek favorable legislation or to influence governmental action. Cf. *National Collegiate Athletic Assn. v. Board of Regents of Univ. of Okla.,* 468 U.S. 85, 101, n. 23 (1984) ("[G]ood motives will not validate an otherwise anticompetitive practice"). In *Columbia v. Omni Outdoor Advertising, Inc.,* 499 U.S. 365 (1991), we similarly held that challenges to allegedly sham petitioning activity must be resolved according to objective criteria. We dispelled the notion that an antitrust plaintiff could prove a sham merely by showing that its competitor's "purposes were to delay [the plaintiff's] entry into the market and even to deny it a meaningful access to the appropriate ... administrative and legislative fora." *Id.,* at 381. We reasoned that such inimical intent "may render the manner of lobbying improper or even unlawful, but does not necessarily render it a 'sham.' " *Ibid.*

In sum, fidelity to precedent compels us to reject a purely subjective definition of "sham." The sham exception so construed would undermine, if not vitiate, *Noerr.* And despite whatever "superficial certainty" it might provide, a subjective standard would utterly fail to supply "real 'intelligible guidance.' " *Allied Tube, supra,* at 508, n. 10.

III

We now outline a two-part definition of "sham" litigation. First, the lawsuit must be objectively baseless in the sense that no reasonable litigant could realistically expect success on the merits. If an objective litigant could conclude that the suit is reasonably calculated to elicit a favorable outcome, the suit is immunized under *Noerr,* and an antitrust claim premised on the sham exception must fail.[41] Only if challenged litigation is objectively meritless may a court examine the litigant's subjective motivation. Under this second part of our definition of sham, the court should focus on whether the baseless lawsuit conceals "an attempt to interfere *directly* with the business relationships of a competitor," *Noerr, supra,* at 144 (emphasis added), through the "use [of] the governmental *process*—as opposed to the *outcome* of that process—as an anticompetitive weapon," *Omni,* 499 U.S., at 380 (emphasis in original). This two-tiered process requires the plaintiff to disprove the challenged lawsuit's *legal* viability before the court will

---

41. A winning lawsuit is by definition a reasonable effort at petitioning for redress and therefore not a sham. On the other hand, when the antitrust defendant has lost the underlying litigation, a court must "resist the understandable temptation to engage in *post hoc* reasoning by concluding" that an ultimately unsuccessful "action must have been unreasonable or without foundation." *Christiansburg Garment Co. v. EEOC,* 434 U.S. 412, 421–422 (1978). Accord, *Hughes v. Rowe,* 449 U.S. 5, 114–15 (1980) (*per curiam*). The court must remember that "[e]ven when the law or the facts appear questionable or unfavorable at the outset, a party may have an entirely reasonable ground for bringing suit." *Christiansburg, supra,* at 422.

entertain evidence of the suit's *economic* viability. Of course, even a plaintiff who defeats the defendant's claim to *Noerr* immunity by demonstrating both the objective and the subjective components of a sham must still prove a substantive antitrust violation. Proof of a sham merely deprives the defendant of immunity; it does not relieve the plaintiff of the obligation to establish all other elements of his claim.

Some of the apparent confusion over the meaning of "sham" may stem from our use of the word "genuine" to denote the opposite of "sham." See *Omni, supra,* at 382; *Allied Tube, supra,* at 500, n. 4; *Noerr, supra,* at 144; *Vendo Co. v. Lektro–Vend Corp., supra* at 645 (Blackmun, J., concurring in result). The word "genuine" has both objective and subjective connotations. On one hand, "genuine" means "actually having the reputed or apparent qualities or character." Webster's Third New International Dictionary 948 (1986). "Genuine" in this sense governs Federal Rule of Civil Procedure 56, under which a "genuine issue" is one "that properly can be resolved only by a finder of fact because [it] may *reasonably* be resolved in favor of either party." *Anderson v. Liberty Lobby, Inc.,* 477 U.S. 242, 250 (1986) (emphasis added). On the other hand, "genuine" also means "sincerely and honestly felt or experienced." Webster's Dictionary, *supra,* at 948. To be sham, therefore, litigation must fail to be "genuine" in all senses of the word.[42]

IV

... The existence of probable cause to institute legal proceedings precludes a finding that an antitrust defendant has engaged in sham litigation. The notion of probable cause, as understood and applied in the common law tort of wrongful civil proceedings,[43] requires the plaintiff to prove that the defendant lacked probable cause to institute an unsuccessful civil lawsuit and that the defendant pressed the action for an improper, malicious purpose.... Because the absence of probable cause is an essential element of the tort, the existence of probable cause is an absolute defense.... Just as evidence of anticompetitive intent cannot affect the objective prong of *Noerr*'s sham exception, a showing of malice alone will

---

42. In surveying the "forms of illegal and reprehensible practice which may corrupt the administrative or judicial processes and which may result in antitrust violations," we have noted that "unethical conduct in the setting of the adjudicatory process often results in sanctions" and that "misrepresentations, condoned in the political arena, are not immunized when used in the adjudicatory process." *California Motor Transport,* 404 U.S., at 512–513. We need not decide here whether and, if so, to what extent *Noerr* permits the imposition of antitrust liability for a litigant's fraud or other misrepresentations. Cf. Fed.Rule Civ.Proc. 60(b)(3) (allowing a federal court to "relieve a party ... from a final judgment" for "fraud ..., misrepresentation, or other misconduct of an adverse party"); *Walker Process Equipment, Inc. v. Food Machinery & Chemical Corp.,* 382 U.S. 172, 176–177 (1965), *id.,* at 179–180 (Harlan, J., concurring).

43. This tort is frequently called "malicious prosecution," which (strictly speaking) governs the malicious pursuit of *criminal* proceedings without probable cause. See W. Keeton, D. Dobbs, R. Keeton, & D. Owen, Prosser and Keeton on Torts § 120, p. 892 (5th ed. 1984). The threshold for showing probable cause is no higher in the civil context than in the criminal. See Restatement (Second) of Torts § 674, Comment *e,* pp. 454–455 (1977).

neither entitle the wrongful civil proceedings plaintiff to prevail nor permit the factfinder to infer the absence of probable cause. *Stewart, supra,* at 194; *Wheeler, supra,* at 551; 2 C. Addison, Law of Torts § 1, ¶ 853, pp. 67–68 (1876); *T. Cooley, supra,* at 184. When a court has found that an antitrust defendant claiming *Noerr* immunity had probable cause to sue, that finding compels the conclusion that a reasonable litigant in the defendant's position could realistically expect success on the merits of the challenged lawsuit. Under our decision today, therefore, a proper probable cause determination irrefutably demonstrates that an antitrust plaintiff has not proved the objective prong of the sham exception and that the defendant is accordingly entitled to *Noerr* immunity.

The District Court and the Court of Appeals correctly found that Columbia had probable cause to sue PRE for copyright infringement....

■ JUSTICE STEVENS, with whom JUSTICE O'CONNOR joins, concurring in the judgment.

While I agree with the Court's disposition of this case and with its holding that an "objectively reasonable effort to litigate cannot be sham regardless of subjective intent," *ante,* at 7, I write separately to disassociate myself from some of the unnecessarily broad dicta in the Court's opinion. Specifically, I disagree with the Court's equation of "objectively baseless" with the answer to the question whether any "reasonable litigant could realistically expect success on the merits." There might well be lawsuits that fit the latter definition but can be shown to be objectively *unreasonable,* and thus shams. It might not be objectively reasonable to bring a lawsuit just because some form of success on the merits—no matter how insignificant—could be expected.[44] With that possibility in mind, the Court should avoid an unnecessarily broad holding that it might regret when confronted with a more complicated case.

As the Court recently explained, a "sham" is the use of "the governmental *process*—as opposed to the *outcome* of that process—as an anticompetitive weapon." *Columbia v. Omni Outdoor Advertising, Inc.,* 499 U.S. 365, 380 (1991). The distinction between abusing the judicial process to restrain competition, and prosecuting a lawsuit that, if successful, will restrain competition, must guide any court's decision whether a particular filing, or series of filings, is a sham. The label "sham" is appropriately applied to a case, or series of cases, in which the plaintiff is indifferent to the outcome of the litigation itself, but has nevertheless sought to impose a collateral harm on the defendant by, for example, impairing his credit, abusing the discovery process, or interfering with his access to governmental agencies. It might also apply to a plaintiff who had some reason to expect success on the merits but because of its tremendous cost would not bother to achieve that result without the benefit of collateral injuries imposed on its competitor by the legal process alone. Litigation filed or

---

44. The Court's recent decision in *Farrar v. Hobby,* 506 U.S. 103 (1992) makes me wonder whether "10 years of litigation and two trips to the Court of Appeals" to recover "one dollar from one defendant," (O'Connor, J., concurring), would qualify as a reasonable expectation of "favorable relief" under today's opinion.

pursued for such collateral purposes is fundamentally different from a case in which the relief sought in the litigation itself would give the plaintiff a competitive advantage or, perhaps, exclude a potential competitor from entering a market with a product that either infringes the plaintiff's patent or copyright or violates an exclusive franchise granted by a governmental body.

The case before us today is in the latter, obviously legitimate, category. There was no unethical or other improper use of the judicial system; instead, respondents invoked the federal court's jurisdiction to determine whether they could lawfully restrain competition with petitioners. The relief they sought in their original action, if granted, would have had the anticompetitive consequences authorized by federal copyright law. Given that the original copyright infringement action was objectively reasonable—and the District Court, the Court of Appeals, and this Court all agree that it was—neither the respondents' own measure of their chances of success nor an alleged goal of harming petitioners provides a sufficient basis for treating it as a sham. We may presume that every litigant intends harm to his adversary; moreover, uncertainty about the possible resolution of unsettled questions of law is characteristic of the adversary process. Access to the courts is far too precious a right for us to infer wrongdoing from nothing more than using the judicial process to seek a competitive advantage in a doubtful case. Thus, the Court's disposition in this case is unquestionably correct. . . .

NOTES AND QUESTIONS

1. *Sham standard after* PREI. Could an expensive lawsuit with very small potential damages and little chance of success be considered a sham? Might such a lawsuit be considered a sham under Justice Stevens's approach in his concurrence?

What is the difference (if any) among the following standards:

    a. "no reasonable litigant could realistically expect success on the merits";

    b. "an objective litigant could conclude that the suit is reasonably calculated to elicit a favorable outcome";

    c. "the existence of probable cause to institute legal proceedings"; and

    d. Fed. Rule Civ. Proc. 11.

Which standard does the Court adopt in *PREI*?

2. *Distinguishing standards.* How does Justice Stevens' objective standard of baselessness differ from the standard in the majority opinion? According to Justice Stevens, what must a "reasonable litigant" expect in addition to "success on the merits?"

3. *Antitrust implications of* PREI's *"sham" standard.* Would bringing a sham lawsuit against a competitor violate the antitrust laws, if the *ex ante* odds of winning were (a) 30%, (b) 15%, (c) 5%, or (d) so low that Rule 11 sanctions would be appropriate?

4. *Application to labor law.* In BE & K Const. Co. v. NLRB, 536 U.S. 516, 122 S.Ct. 2390 (2002), the Supreme Court considered the question whether a general contractor who had sued various unions, claiming that they had unlawfully attempted to delay work on the contractor's nonunion worksite, could be subjected to sanctions under § 8(a)(1) of the National Labor Relations Act, 29 U.S.C. § 158(a)(1). After the contractor lost its case, the unions had lodged complaints with the NLRB, and the Board found that the litigation itself had violated the labor laws. The Supreme Court reversed, relying heavily on *PREI*. As it saw the case, "a threshold question ... [was] whether the Board may declare that an unsuccessful retaliatory lawsuit violates the NLRA even if reasonably based." 536 U.S. at 529–30. It held that "unsuccessful but reasonably based suits advance some First Amendment interests," *id.* at 532, and that the Board went beyond the scope of the NLRA when it ruled that all reasonably based, unsuccessful suits prosecuted with a retaliatory motive were sanctionable. In a concurring opinion, Justice Scalia predicted that the Court would, in a later case, come to construe the NLRA in exactly the same way as the Sherman Act: "to prohibit only lawsuits that are *both* objectively baseless *and* subjectively intended to abuse process." *Id.* at 537.

PROBLEM 8

THE STRUGGLE FOR STONEFORD'S CABLE TV FRANCHISE

In 1988, Stone Cable Co. obtained from the City of Stoneford, Illinois, an exclusive ten-year franchise to install and operate a cable TV transmission system in that city. Illinois and federal law and regulations left cable TV franchising decisions to the discretion of local authorities, and the Stoneford city council recommended and the mayor approved grant of the franchise.

While Stone was undertaking studies and preparing to subcontract installation work, a regular city election was held, and the incumbent mayor and three of the five incumbent city council members were replaced. Prior to the election, the two principal shareholders of Stoneford's local regular television station, Able and Baker, and one of the successful city council candidates, Charlie, had formed CATV Stoneford, Inc., with the purpose of securing the exclusive franchise earlier issued to Stone. Able and Baker each made substantial campaign contributions to Charlie and other council candidates on the successful ticket. Stone alleges that their television station's coverage of the election was biased in favor of the same candidates.

After the election, CATV and its affiliated local TV station filed an unfair competition complaint in a state court in Stoneford alleging that Stone had within the previous year hired several employees from the affiliated local TV station to obtain trade secrets with respect to the Stoneford television advertising market. Plaintiffs claimed damages and sought an injunction prohibiting Stone from proceeding with any activity to carry out plans to implement its Stoneford cable TV franchise. Extensive discovery procedures failed to disclose facts sufficient to support the allegations and defendant's motion for summary judgment was eventually granted.

Shortly thereafter, at Charlie's behest, the city council invited Able and Baker to appear before it. They testified that Stone was both technically and financially unqualified to implement the franchise. After some discussion, but no public hearing or other opportunity for Stone to dispute the charges, the council exercised a revocation clause in the franchise agreement and transferred the exclusive franchise to CATV.

Stone charged a conspiracy in restraint of trade among Able, Baker, Charlie, and CATV. It alleged, *inter alia,* that CATV's lawsuit was brought in bad faith and for harassment, the statements of Able and Baker before the council were false and motivated solely by their interest in CATV's obtaining the franchise, and that the decision of the council was tainted as a result of Able and Baker's campaign contributions. Defendants moved to dismiss on the grounds that their conduct was protected under the *Noerr* doctrine. What result?

B. "STATE ACTION" AND TENSIONS WITH FEDERALISM

Parker v. Brown

Supreme Court of the United States, 1943.
317 U.S. 341, 63 S.Ct. 307, 87 L.Ed. 315.

[Action brought by a producer and packer of raisins to enjoin various state officials charged with the administration of a marketing program under the California Agricultural Prorate Act. In order to "prevent economic waste in the marketing of agricultural products," and to "conserve the agricultural wealth of the State" the Act authorized the establishment of marketing programs which would "restrict competition among the growers and maintain prices" of certain agricultural products. The Act further authorized the establishment of a Commission which was to hold public hearings and make findings to the effect that the institution of a program would "prevent agricultural waste ... without permitting unreasonable profits to producers." The Commission could then select a program committee principally from nominees chosen by producers in the area, and the program committee was required to formulate a marketing program which the Commission, after public hearings, was authorized to approve. The program would be instituted if consented to by 65 percent of the producers in the zone owning 5 percent of the acreage devoted to production of the particular crop.

The proration marketing program for raisins provided for classification of raisins as "standard," "substandard," and "inferior." Inferior raisins were unfit for human consumption and were to be disposed of by the committee for by-product and other diversion purposes. Substandard raisins and at least 20 percent of total standard and substandard raisins were to be placed in a "surplus pool" to be disposed of for by-product and other diversion purposes with the producers receiving from $25 to $27.50 per ton. Of the remainder of the raisin crop, 50 percent was to be placed in a "stabilization pool" and disposed of by the committee "in such manner as to obtain stability in the market" with the producers receiving from $50 to $55 per ton; the other 30 percent was denominated "free tonnage" and could be sold through ordinary commercial channels if the producer paid a fee of $2.50 per ton.

Plaintiff-producer had challenged the marketing program as invalid under both the "dormant" Commerce Clause of the Constitution and the Sherman Act.]

■ STONE, C.J. . . . We may assume for present purposes that the California prorate program would violate the Sherman Act if it were organized and made effective solely by virtue of a contract, combination or conspiracy of private persons, individual or corporate. We may assume also, without deciding, that Congress could, in the exercise of its commerce power, prohibit a state from maintaining a stabilization program like the present because of its effect on interstate commerce. . . .

But it is plain that the prorate program here was never intended to operate by force of individual agreement or combination. It derived its authority and its efficacy from the legislative command of the state and was not intended to operate or become effective without that command. We find nothing in the language of the Sherman Act or in its history which suggests that its purpose was to restrain a state or its officers or agents from activities directed by its legislature. In a dual system of government in which, under the Constitution, the states are sovereign, save only as Congress may constitutionally subtract from their authority, an unexpressed purpose to nullify a state's control over its officers and agents is not lightly to be attributed to Congress.

The Sherman Act makes no mention of the state as such, and gives no hint that it was intended to restrain state action or official action directed by a state. The Act is applicable to "persons" including corporations, and it authorizes suits under it by persons and corporations. A state may maintain a suit for damages under it, . . . but the United States may not—conclusions derived not from the literal meaning of the words "person" and "corporation" but from the purpose, the subject matter, the context and the legislative history of the statute.

There is no suggestion of a purpose to restrain state action in the Act's legislative history. The sponsor of the bill which was ultimately enacted as the Sherman Act declared that it prevented only "business combinations." 21 Cong.Rec. 2562, 2457; see also at 2459, 2461. That its purpose was to suppress combinations to restrain competition and attempts to monopolize by individuals and corporations, abundantly appears from its legislative history. See Apex Hosiery Co. v. Leader, 310 U.S. 469, 492, 493 and n. 15; United States v. Addyston Pipe & Steel Co., 85 F. 271, affirmed 175 U.S. 211; Standard Oil Co. v. United States, 221 U.S. 1, 54–58.

True, a state does not give immunity to those who violate the Sherman Act by authorizing them to violate it, or by declaring that their action is lawful, Northern Securities Co. v. United States, 193 U.S. 197, 332, 344–347; and we have no question of the state or its municipality becoming a participant in a private agreement or combination by others for restraint of trade, cf. Union Pacific R. Co. v. United States, 313 U.S. 450. Here the state command to the Commission and to the program committee of the California Prorate Act is not rendered unlawful by the Sherman Act since, in view of the latter's words and history, it must be taken to be a prohibition of individual and not state action. It is the state which has created the machinery for establishing the prorate program. Although the organization of a prorate zone is proposed by producers, and a prorate program, approved by the Commission, must also be approved by referendum of producers, it is the state, acting through the Commission, which adopts the program and which enforces it with penal sanctions, in the execution of a governmental policy. The prerequisite approval of the program upon referendum by a prescribed number of producers is not the imposition by them of their will upon the minority by force of agreement or combination which the Sherman Act prohibits. The state itself exercises its legislative authority in making the regulation and in prescribing the conditions of its application. The required vote on the referendum is one of these conditions. . . .

The state in adopting and enforcing the prorate program made no contract or agreement and entered into no conspiracy in restraint of trade or to establish monopoly but, as sovereign, imposed the restraint as an act of government which the Sherman Act did not undertake to prohibit. . . .

———

Goldfarb v. Virginia State Bar, 421 U.S. 773, 95 S.Ct. 2004, 44 L.Ed.2d 572 (1975). Chief Justice Burger rendered the following opinion on "state action" for a unanimous Court:[45]

In Parker v. Brown, 317 U.S. 341 (1943), the Court held that an anticompetitive marketing program which "derived its authority and its efficacy from the legislative command of the state" was not a violation of the Sherman Act because the Act was intended to regulate private practices and not to prohibit a State from imposing a restraint as an act of government. . . .

Through its legislature Virginia has authorized its highest court to regulate the practice of law. That court has adopted ethical codes which deal in part with fees, and far from exercising state power to authorize binding price fixing, explicitly directed lawyers not "to be controlled" by fee schedules.[46] The State Bar, a state agency by law, argues that in issuing

45. For a discussion of Chief Justice Burger's opinion, see p. 106, supra.

46. In 1938 the Supreme Court of Virginia adopted Rules for the Integration of the Virginia State Bar, and Rule II, § 12 dealt with the procedure for setting fees. Among six factors that court directed to be considered in setting a fee were "the customary charges of the Bar for similar services." The court also directed that

"[i]n determining the customary charges of the Bar for similar services, it is proper for a lawyer to consider a schedule of minimum fees adopted by a Bar Association, but *no lawyer should permit himself to be controlled* thereby or to follow it as his sole guide in determining the amount of his fee." Rules for Integration of the Virginia State Bar, 171 Va. xvii, xxiii. (Emphasis supplied.)

In 1970 the Virginia Supreme Court amended the 1938 rules in part, and adopted the Code of Professional Responsibility, effective January 1, 1971. 211 Va. 295 (1970). Certain of its provisions also dealt with the fee-setting procedure. In EC 2–18 lawyers were told again that fees vary according to many factors, but that "[s]uggested fee schedules and economic reports of state and local bar associations provide some guidance on the subject of reasonable fees." 211 Va., at 302. In DR 2–106(B), which detailed eight factors that should be considered in avoiding an excessive fee, one of the factors was "[t]he fee customarily charged in the locality for similar legal services." DR 2–106(B)(3). 211 Va., at 313.

fee schedule reports and ethical opinions dealing with fee schedules it was merely implementing the fee provisions of the ethical codes. The County Bar, although it is a voluntary association and not a state agency, claims that the ethical codes and the activities of the State Bar "prompted" it to issue fee schedules and thus its actions, too, are state action for Sherman Act purposes.

The threshold inquiry in determining if an anticompetitive activity is state action of the type the Sherman Act was not meant to proscribe is whether the activity is required by the State acting as sovereign. Parker v. Brown, 317 U.S., at 350–352; Continental Co. v. Union Carbide, 370 U.S. 690, 706–707 (1962). Here we need not inquire further into the state-action question because it cannot fairly be said that the State of Virginia through its Supreme Court Rules required the anticompetitive activities of either respondent. Respondents have pointed to no Virginia statute requiring their activities; state law simply does not refer to fees, leaving regulation of the profession to the Virginia Supreme Court; although the Supreme Court's ethical codes mention advisory fee schedules they do not direct either respondent to supply them, or require the type of price floor which arose from respondents' activities. Although the State Bar apparently has been granted the power to issue ethical opinions, there is no indication in this record that the Virginia Supreme Court approves the opinions. Respondents' arguments, at most, constitute the contention that their activities complemented the objective of the ethical codes. In our view that is not state action for Sherman Act purposes. It is not enough that, as the County Bar puts it, anticompetitive conduct is "prompted" by state action; rather, anticompetitive activities must be compelled by direction of the State acting as a sovereign.

The fact that the State Bar is a state agency for some limited purposes does not create an antitrust shield that allows it to foster anticompetitive practices for the benefit of its members. The State Bar, by providing that deviation from County Bar minimum fees may lead to disciplinary action, has voluntarily joined in what is essentially a private anticompetitive activity, and in that posture cannot claim it is beyond the reach of the Sherman Act. Parker v. Brown, *supra*. Its activities resulted in a rigid price floor from which petitioners, as consumers, could not escape if they wished to borrow money to buy a home.

We recognize that the States have a compelling interest in the practice of professions within their boundaries, and that as part of their power to protect the public health, safety, and other valid interests they have broad power to establish standards for licensing practitioners and regulating the practice of professions. We also recognize that in some instances the State may decide that "forms of competition usual in the business world may be demoralizing to the ethical standards of a profession." United States v. Oregon State Medical Society, 343 U.S. 326, 336 (1952). The interest of the States in regulating lawyers is especially great since lawyers are essential to the primary governmental function of administering justice, and have historically been "officers of the courts." ... In holding that certain anticompetitive conduct by lawyers is within the reach of the Sherman Act we intend no diminution of the authority of the State to regulate its professions.[47]

---

47. Ed. Since *Goldfarb* there has been considerable antitrust activity directed towards the professions. *See supra* Chapter 4, pp. 213–14.

NOTES AND QUESTIONS

1. *Federalism in* Parker. In *Parker,* the benefit to the participants was clear, but note also that 90% of all raisins were produced in California for export. This would give the State of California an additional reason to establish the cartel—its residents would benefit as producers very much more than they would pay as consumers. Check your Constitutional Law authorities to find out why the commerce clause wasn't offended by this apparent exploitation of out-of-state consumers in dealing with local resources. The answer may, in part, lie in the fact that Congress had affirmatively exercised its commerce power in general legislation supporting cartelization of agricultural products as national policy to combat the depression in the 1930s.

2. *Impact of state involvement on outcomes.* How important is the form and degree of state involvement in *Parker* and in *Goldfarb?*

3. *Role of Miller–Tydings.* For many years, there was a statute known as the Miller–Tydings Act, which immunized some forms of state "fair trade" laws from the Sherman Act (and the now-overruled *per se* rule against resale price maintenance that the decision in *Dr. Miles,* p. 610, infra, had established). That statute was passed before *Parker* was decided. Was it necessary, in retrospect, in light of *Parker?* Reconsider this after reading *California Retail Liquor Dealers Ass'n v. Midcal Aluminum, Inc.,* 445 U.S. 97, 100 S.Ct. 937, 63 L.Ed.2d 233 (1980), *infra* p. 438.

4. *Outstanding issues post-*Goldfarb. The *Goldfarb* formulation leaves open such questions as: (a) When does the state "act as sovereign," and through what instrumentalities may it act? (b) If action is through courts, regulatory agencies, or municipalities, must standards be set by the legislature? (c) Who may supervise? (d) Why is the "mandatory" nature of the state action crucial? These are but a few of the technical questions raised by the Court's approach, and the questions will be addressed, in large part, by later Supreme Court decisions in this Section. But what are the policy considerations motivating the Court? In this area in particular, understanding the underlying policy issues may be the only way to understand the Court's decisions.

"STATE ACTION" BETWEEN *GOLDFARB* AND *MIDCAL*

1. Cantor v. Detroit Edison Co., 428 U.S. 579, 96 S.Ct. 3110, 49 L.Ed. 2d 1141 (1976). Defendant Detroit Edison, an electric utility, distributed light bulbs to its residential customers without additional charge, including the cost in its state-regulated electricity rates. Cantor, a light bulb retailer, brought suit, claiming that the utility was using its monopoly power in the distribution of electricity to foreclose competition in the sale of light bulbs. The Court held that the utility could not immunize itself from an action challenging the tying arrangement under the "state action" doctrine by embodying the practice in a tariff routinely approved by the state public utility commission. Michigan had no independent regulatory interest in the market for light bulbs, and the light-bulb program was instigated by the utility. It was never independently considered by the commission.

2. Bates v. State Bar of Arizona, 433 U.S. 350, 97 S.Ct. 2691, 53 L.Ed.2d 810 (1977). Two Phoenix attorneys challenged disciplinary rules prohibiting a lawyer from publicizing himself or others in his firm through any form of advertising or "commercial publicity." The attorneys published a newspaper advertisement showing fees for the services of their "legal clinic," and for this, they were suspended

from practice for a short period after a disciplinary proceeding by the State Bar Association. The Supreme Court unanimously held the disciplinary rules immune from Sherman Act challenge:

> In *Parker v. Brown*, 317 U.S. 341 (1943), this Court held that the Sherman Act was not intended to apply against certain state action. . . . Appellee argues, and the Arizona Supreme Court held, that the *Parker* exemption also bars the instant Sherman Act claim. We agree. . . .

> In *Goldfarb* we held that § 1 of the Sherman Act was violated by the publication of a minimum-fee schedule by a county bar association and by its enforcement by the State Bar. The schedule and its enforcement mechanism operated to create a rigid price floor for services and thus constituted a classic example of price fixing. Both bar associations argued that their activity was shielded by the state-action exemption. This Court concluded that the action was not protected, emphasizing that "we need not inquire further into the state-action question because it cannot fairly be said that the State of Virginia through its Supreme Court Rules required the anticompetitive activities of either respondent." 421 U.S., at 790. In the instant case, by contrast, the challenged restraint is the affirmative command of the Arizona Supreme Court under its Rules 27(a) and 29(a) and its Disciplinary Rule 2–101(B). That court is the ultimate body wielding the State's power over the practice of law . . . and, thus, the restraint is "compelled by direction of the State acting as a sovereign." 421 U.S., at 791.[48]

> Appellants seek to draw solace from *Cantor*. . . . Since the disciplinary rule at issue here is derived from the Code of Professional Responsibility of the American Bar Association, appellants argue by analogy to *Cantor* that no immunity should result from the bar's success in having the Code adopted by the State. They also assert that the interest embodied in the Sherman Act must prevail over the state interest in regulating the bar. Particularly is this the case, they claim, because the advertising ban is not tailored so as to intrude upon the federal interest to the minimum extent necessary.

> We believe, however, that the context in which *Cantor* arose is critical. . . . [T]he Court emphasized in *Cantor* that the State had no independent regulatory interest in the market for light bulbs. . . . There was no suggestion that the bulb program was justified by flaws in the competitive market or was a response to health or safety concerns. And an exemption for the program was not essential to the State's regulation of electric utilities. In contrast, the regulation of the activities of the bar is at the core of the State's power to protect the public. Indeed, this Court in *Goldfarb* acknowledged that "[t]he interest of the States in regulating lawyers is especially great since lawyers are essential to the primary governmental function of administering justice, and have historically been 'officers of the courts.' " 421 U.S., at 792. . . . More specifically, controls over solicitation and advertising by attorneys have long been subject to the State's over-

---

48. We note, moreover, that the Court's opinion in Goldfarb concluded with the observation that "[i]n holding that certain anticompetitive conduct by lawyers is within the reach of the Sherman Act we intend no diminution of the authority of the State to regulate its professions." 421 U.S., at 793. Allowing the instant Sherman Act challenge to the disciplinary rule would have precisely that undesired effect.

sight.[49] Federal interference with a State's traditional regulation of a profession is entirely unlike the intrusion the Court sanctions in *Cantor*.[50]

Finally, the light-bulb program in *Cantor* was instigated by the utility with only the acquiescence of the state regulatory commission. The State's incorporation of the program into the tariff reflected its conclusion that the utility was authorized to employ the practice if it so desired. . . . The situation now before us is entirely different. The disciplinary rules reflect a clear articulation of the State's policy with regard to professional behavior. Moreover, as the instant case shows, the rules are subject to pointed re-examination by the policymaker—the Arizona Supreme Court—in enforcement proceedings. Our concern that federal policy is being unnecessarily and inappropriately subordinated to state policy is reduced in such a situation; we deem it significant that the state policy is so clearly and affirmatively expressed and that the State's supervision is so active.

Writing for a majority of five justices, Justice Blackmun then held that the First Amendment protects an attorney truthfully advertising the prices at which certain routine services may be performed. He reasoned that attorney advertising may be subject to some regulation but not blanket suppression, and, moreover, he suggested that the Court expected the bar would play a special role in assuring free but nondeceptive attorney advertising.

3. New Motor Vehicle Board of California v. Orrin W. Fox Co., 439 U.S. 96, 99 S.Ct. 403, 58 L.Ed.2d 361 (1978). Under the California Automobile Franchise Act a motor vehicle manufacturer was required to secure the approval of the New Motor Vehicle Board before opening a dealership within the market area of an existing franchisee. An auto manufacturer and two retail franchisees challenged the Act. A three-judge district court found the failure of the Act to provide a prior hearing to address the merits of an existing franchisee's protest was an unconstitutional violation of due process. The Supreme Court reversed, finding that the Act's scheme neither violated due process nor constituted an impermissible delegation of state power to the protesting citizens. The Court then addressed the appellees' argument that, under the Sherman Act, the delay that existing franchisees could through their protests illegally restrained trade under the Supreme Court's decision in *Schwegmann Bros. v. Calvert Distillers Corp.*, 341 U.S. 384 (1951). The Court addressed whether the "state action" doctrine put the scheme outside the reach of the antitrust laws. Concluding that the state action exemption did apply, the Court reasoned that the "Act's regulatory scheme is a system of regulation, clearly articulated and affirmatively expressed, designed to displace unfettered business freedom in the matter of the establishment and relocation of automobile dealerships." 439 U.S. at 109. The Court distinguished *Schwegmann*—where Louisiana had attempted (unsuccessfully) to authorize and immunize illegal price-fixing by private liquor distributors—noting that in this case the good faith protests and time involved in the subsequent Board action did not violate the Sherman Act.

---

49. The limitation on advertising by attorneys in Arizona seems to have commenced in 1919 with the incorporation by reference of the American Bar Association's 1908 Canons of Professional Ethics into Arizona's statutory law.

50. Indeed, our decision today on the Sherman Act issue was presaged in *Virginia Pharmacy Board v. Virginia Consumer Council*, 425 U.S. 748, 770 (1976). We noted there: "Virginia is free to require whatever professional standards it wishes of its pharmacists; it may subsidize them or protect them from competition in other ways. Cf. *Parker v. Brown*, 317 U.S. 341 (1943)."

California Retail Liquor Dealers Association v. Midcal Aluminum, Inc.

Supreme Court of the United States, 1980.
445 U.S. 97, 100 S.Ct. 937, 63 L.Ed.2d 233.

■ MR. JUSTICE POWELL delivered the opinion of the Court.... Under § 24866(b) of the California Business and Professions Code, all wine producers, wholesalers, and rectifiers must file fair trade contracts or price schedules with the State.[51] If a wine producer has not set prices through a fair trade contract, wholesalers must post a resale price schedule for that producer's brands. No state-licensed wine merchant may sell wine to a retailer at other than the price set "either in an effective price schedule or in an effective fair trade contract...."

The State is divided into three trading areas for administration of the wine pricing program. A single fair trade contract or schedule for each brand sets the terms for all wholesale transactions in that brand within a given trading area. Similarly, state regulations provide that the wine prices posted by a single wholesaler within a trading area bind all wholesalers in that area.... A licensee selling below the established prices faces fines, license suspension, or outright license revocation.[52] The State has no direct control over wine prices, and it does not review the reasonableness of the prices set by wine dealers.

Midcal Aluminum, Inc., is a wholesale distributor of wine in southern California. In July 1978, the Department of Alcoholic Beverage Control charged Midcal with selling 27 cases of wine for less than the prices set by the effective price schedule of the E. & J. Gallo Winery. The Department also alleged that Midcal sold wines for which no fair trade contract or schedule had been filed. Midcal stipulated that the allegations were true and that the State could fine it or suspend its license for those transgressions. Midcal then filed a writ of mandate in the California Court of Appeal for the Third Appellate District asking for an injunction against the State's wine pricing system.

The Court of Appeal ruled that the wine pricing scheme restrains trade in violation of the Sherman Act.... An appeal was brought by the California Retail Liquor Dealers Association, an intervenor.[53] The Califor-

---

51. The statute provides:

"Each wine grower, wholesaler licensed to sell wine, wine rectifier, and rectifier shall:

"(a) Post a schedule of selling prices of wine to retailers or consumers for which his resale price is not governed by a fair trade contract made by the person who owns or controls the brand.

"(b) Make and file a fair trade contract and file a schedule of resale prices, if he owns or controls a brand of wine resold to retailers or consumers." Cal.Bus. & Prof.Code Ann. § 24866 (West 1964).

52. Licensees that sell wine below the prices specified in fair trade contracts or schedules also may be subject to private damage suits for unfair competition.

53. The California Retail Liquor Dealers Association, a trade association of independent retail liquor dealers in California, claims over 3,000 members.

nia Supreme Court declined to hear the case, and the Dealers Association sought certiorari from this Court. We granted the writ, 444 U.S. 824 (1979), and now affirm the decision of the state court.

II

The threshold question is whether California's plan for wine pricing violates the Sherman Act. This Court has ruled consistently that resale price maintenance illegally restrains trade. In *Dr. Miles Medical Co. v. John D. Park & Sons Co.*, 220 U.S. 373, 407 (1911), the Court observed that such arrangements are "designed to maintain prices ..., and to prevent competition among those who trade in [competing goods]." For many years, however, the Miller–Tydings Act of 1937 permitted the States to authorize resale price maintenance. The goal of that statute was to allow the States to protect small retail establishments that Congress thought might otherwise be driven from the market place by large-volume discounters. But in 1975 that congressional permission was rescinded. The Consumer Goods Pricing Act of 1975, 89 Stat. 801, repealed the Miller–Tydings Act and related legislation. Consequently, the Sherman Act's ban on resale price maintenance now applies to fair trade contracts unless an industry or program enjoys a special antitrust immunity.

California's system for wine pricing plainly constitutes resale price maintenance in violation of the Sherman Act. The wine producer holds the power to prevent price competition by dictating the prices charged by wholesalers. As Mr. Justice Hughes pointed out in *Dr. Miles,* such vertical control destroys horizontal competition as effectively as if wholesalers "formed a combination and endeavored to establish the same restrictions ... by agreement with each other." 220 U.S., at 408. Moreover, there can be no claim that the California program is simply intrastate regulation beyond the reach of the Sherman Act. See *Schwegmann Bros. v. Calvert Corp., supra; Burke v. Ford,* 389 U.S. 320 (1967) (*per curiam*).

Thus, we must consider whether the State's involvement in the price-setting program is sufficient to establish antitrust immunity under *Parker v. Brown,* 317 U.S. 341 (1943). That immunity for state regulatory programs is grounded in our federal structure. "In a dual system of government in which, under the Constitution, the states are sovereign, save only as Congress may constitutionally subtract from their authority, an unexpressed purpose to nullify a state's control over its officers and agents is not lightly to be attributed to Congress." *Id.,* at 351. In *Parker v. Brown,* this Court found in the Sherman Act no purpose to nullify state powers. Because the Act is directed against "individual and not state action," the Court concluded that state regulatory programs could not violate it. *Id.,* at 352.

Under the program challenged in *Parker,* the State Agricultural Prorate Advisory Commission authorized the organization of local cooperatives to develop marketing policies for the raisin crop. The Court emphasized that the Advisory Commission, which was appointed by the Governor, had to approve cooperative policies following public hearings: "It is the state which has created the machinery for establishing the prorate program.... [I]t is the state, acting through the Commission, which adopts the program and enforces it...." *Ibid.* In view of this extensive official oversight, the Court wrote, the Sherman Act did not apply. Without such oversight, the result could have been different. The Court expressly noted that "a state does not give immunity to those who violate the Sherman Act by authorizing them to violate it, or by declaring that their action is lawful...." *Id.*, at 351.

Several recent decisions have applied *Parker*'s analysis....[54] These decisions establish two standards for antitrust immunity under *Parker v. Brown*. First, the challenged restraint must be "one clearly articulated and affirmatively expressed as state policy"; second, the policy must be "actively supervised" by the State itself. *City of Lafayette v. Louisiana Power & Light Co.*, 435 U.S. 389, 410 (1978) (opinion of Brennan, J.). The California system for wine pricing satisfies the first standard. The legislative policy is forthrightly stated and clear in its purpose to permit resale price maintenance. The program, however, does not meet the second requirement for *Parker* immunity. The State simply authorizes price-setting and enforces the prices established by private parties. The State neither establishes prices nor reviews the reasonableness of the price schedules; nor does it regulate the terms of fair trade contracts. The State does not monitor market conditions or engage in any "pointed reexamination" of the program. The national policy in favor of competition cannot be thwarted by casting such a gauzy cloak of state involvement over what is essentially a private price-fixing arrangement. As *Parker* teaches, "a state does not give immunity to those who violate the Sherman Act by authorizing them to violate it, or by declaring that their action is lawful...." 317 U.S., at 351.

NOTE: ELABORATIONS ON *MIDCAL*

1. Southern Motor Carriers Rate Conference v. United States, 471 U.S. 48 (1985). In this case, the United States brought an antitrust action against certain rate bureaus composed of private motor carriers operating in four southeastern states, each of which engaged in collective rate-setting for intrastate transactions (*i.e.*, price-fixing, in the Government's opinion). The respective states authorized, but did not compel, that activity. The rate bureaus, on behalf of their members, submitted joint rate proposals to the Public Service Commissions in each State for approval or rejection. This collective ratemaking was authorized, but not compelled, by the States in which the rate bureaus operate. The lower courts ruled against the rate bureaus, and the Supreme Court "granted certiorari to decide whether petitioners' collective ratemaking activities, though not compelled by the States in which they operate, are entitled to *Parker* immunity."

It decided that the answer to that question was yes. It began by noting that although *Parker* involved an action against a state official, the reasoning of that

---

54. Ed. The Court then discussed the *Goldfarb, Cantor,* and *New Motor Vehicle Board* cases.

case extended to suits against private parties. This was because *Parker* was premised on the assumption that Congress, in enacting the Sherman Act, did not intend to compromise the States' ability to regulate their domestic commerce. Later, in *Midcal,* the Court adopted the two-part test under which *Parker* immunity follows if (1) the restraint is one that is clearly articulated and affirmatively established as state policy, and (2) the policy is actively supervised by the state itself.

The first part of that test was at issue in *Southern Motor Carriers.* The Court rejected the Government's argument that only actual compulsion by the state would be sufficient to constitute "clear articulation" and "affirmative establishment" of the state policy. It explained that such analysis overlooked the importance of permissive state policies that allow a balance of collective ratemaking and individual submissions for lower rates by common carriers. The Court concluded that "[t]he federal antitrust laws do not forbid the States to adopt policies that permit, but do not compel, anticompetitive conduct by *regulated* private parties. As long as the State clearly articulates its intent to adopt a permissive policy, the first prong of the *Midcal* test is satisfied. . . ."

It explained its holding as follows:

> The *Parker* doctrine represents an attempt to resolve conflicts that may arise between principles of federalism and the goal of the antitrust laws, unfettered competition in the marketplace. A compulsion requirement is inconsistent with both values. It reduces the range of regulatory alternatives available to the State. At the same time, insofar as it encourages States to require, rather than merely permit, anticompetitive conduct, a compulsion requirement may result in *greater* restraints on trade. We do not believe that Congress intended to resolve conflicts between two competing interests by impairing both more than necessary.

> In summary, we hold *Midcal's* two-pronged test applicable to private parties' claims of state action immunity. Moreover, a state policy that expressly *permits,* but does not compel, anticompetitive conduct may be "clearly articulated" within the meaning of *Midcal.* Our holding today does not suggest, however, that compulsion is irrelevant. To the contrary, compulsion often is the best evidence that the State has a clearly articulated and affirmatively expressed policy to displace competition. See *Town of Hallie v. City of Eau Claire.* . . . Nevertheless, when other evidence conclusively shows that a State intends to adopt a permissive policy, the absence of compulsion should not prove fatal to a claim of *Parker* immunity. . . .

> Our holding that there is no inflexible "compulsion requirement" does not suggest necessarily that petitioners' collective ratemaking activities are shielded from the federal antitrust laws. A private party may claim state action immunity only if both prongs of the *Midcal* test are satisfied. Here the Court of Appeals found, and the Government concedes, that the State Public Service Commissions actively supervise the collective ratemaking activities of the rate bureaus. Therefore, the only issue left to resolve is whether the petitioners' challenged conduct was taken pursuant to a clearly articulated state policy. . . .

The Court found the latter requirement satisfied, and thus ruled for the petitioners.

2.   Town of Hallie v. City of Eau Claire, 471 U.S. 34 (1985). This case examined the other half of the *Midcal* test—what is enough to constitute active supervision—in the special context of municipal regulations. Specifically, it present-

ed the question whether a municipality's anticompetitive activities are protected by the state action exemption to the federal antitrust laws established by Parker v. Brown, 317 U.S. 341 (1943), when the activities are authorized, but not compelled, by the State, and the State does not actively supervise the anticompetitive conduct.

The plaintiffs were four unincorporated townships in Wisconsin who were suing the City of Eau Claire, alleging that the City violated the Sherman Act by acquiring a monopoly over the provision of sewage treatment services in Eau Claire and Chippewa Counties, and by tying the provision of such services to the provision of sewage collection and transportation services. Under the Federal Water Pollution Control Act, the City had obtained federal funds to help build a sewage treatment facility within the Eau Claire Service Area, that included the Towns; the facility was the only one in the market available to the Towns. The City had refused to supply sewage treatment services to the Towns, although it did supply the services to individual landowners located within the Towns if the people living in that area voted in favor of annexation by the City and use of its sewage collection and transportation services.

Alleging that they were potential competitors of the City in the collection and transportation of sewage, the Towns argued in the district court that the City used its monopoly over sewage treatment to gain an unlawful monopoly over the provision of sewage collection and transportation services, in violation of the Sherman Act. They also contended that the City's actions constituted an illegal tying arrangement and an unlawful refusal to deal with the Towns. Both the district court and the Court of Appeals for the Seventh Circuit ruled in favor of the City.

The Supreme Court began its discussion of the *Parker* doctrine by noting that municipalities are not "the state" for purposes of the antitrust laws, because they are not themselves sovereign, citing City of Lafayette v. Louisiana Power & Light Co., 435 U.S. 389 (1978). Rather, to obtain an exemption, municipalities (like the private parties in *Southern Motor Carriers*) must demonstrate that their anticompetitive activities were authorized by the State "pursuant to state policy to displace competition with regulation or monopoly public service." The Court then summarized the rule pertaining to municipalities:

> It is therefore clear from our cases that before a municipality will be entitled to the protection of the state action exemption from the antitrust laws, it must demonstrate that it is engaging in the challenged activity pursuant to a clearly expressed state policy. We have never fully considered, however, how clearly a state policy must be articulated for a municipality to be able to establish that its anticompetitive activity constitutes state action. Moreover, we have expressly left open the question whether action by a municipality—like action by a private party—must satisfy the "active state supervision" requirement. *City of Boulder*, *supra*. We consider both of those issues below.

After a detailed examination of the provisions of Wisconsin law that allegedly authorized the City's activities, the Court concluded that the statutes clearly contemplated that a city might engage in anticompetitive conduct. Such conduct is a foreseeable result of empowering the City to refuse to serve unannexed areas. It was not necessary for the state legislature to have stated explicitly that it expected the City to engage in conduct that would have anticompetitive effects. It was sufficient, instead, that the statutes authorized the City to provide sewage services and also to determine the areas to be served. The Court further rejected the Towns' argument that the statutes at issue were neutral on state policy, more like the Home Rule

Amendment involved in *City of Boulder*. "The Towns' argument amounts to a contention that to pass the 'clear articulation' test, a legislature must expressly state in a statute or its legislative history that it intends for the delegated action to have anticompetitive effects. This contention embodies an unrealistic view of how legislatures work and of how statutes are written. No legislature can be expected to catalog all of the anticipated effects of a statute of this kind."

In sum, said the Court, "we conclude that the Wisconsin statutes evidence a 'clearly articulated and affirmatively expressed' state policy to displace competition with regulation in the area of municipal provision of sewerage services. These statutory provisions plainly show that " 'the legislature contemplated the kind of action complained of.' " *City of Lafayette, supra*. This is sufficient to satisfy the clear articulation requirement of the state action test."

Finally, the Court held that the "active state supervision" requirement of the *Midcal* test should not be imposed in cases in which the actor is a municipality. That element served only an evidentiary function: it furnished one way of ensuring that the actor is engaging in the challenged conduct pursuant to state policy. The danger perceived in *Midcal* of a state's circumventing the Sherman Act's proscriptions "by casting ... a gauzy cloak of state involvement over what is essentially a private price-fixing arrangement," 445 U.S. at 10, might be a real one where a private party is engaging in the anticompetitive activity. "Where the actor is a municipality, there is little or no danger that it is involved in a *private* price-fixing arrangement. The only real danger is that it will seek to further purely parochial public interests at the expense of more overriding state goals. This danger is minimal, however, because of the requirement that the municipality act pursuant to a clearly articulated state policy. Once it is clear that state authorization exists, there is no need to require the State to supervise actively the municipality's execution of what is a properly delegated function."

3.   FTC v. Ticor Title Insurance Co., 504 U.S. 621 (1992). This was a case brought by the Federal Trade Commission against six of the nation's largest title insurance companies, alleging horizontal price fixing in their fees for title searches and title examinations. One company settled by consent decree, while five other firms continued to contest the matter. A key issue was whether *Parker* immunity protected them. The Commission thought not; the Court of Appeals for the Third Circuit disagreed and held that state-action immunity was available. The Supreme Court reversed and remanded the case to the Commission for further proceedings.

The title insurance companies performed a variety of services for their customers, including the insurance of real property titles, and searching the chain of title to alert the prospective buyer to any defects or risks. The insured is protected from some losses resulting from title defects not discoverable from a search of the public records, such as forgery, missing heirs, previous marriages, impersonation, or confusion in names. He or she is also protected against errors or mistakes in the search and examination. Negligence need not be proved in order to recover. Title insurance also includes the obligation to defend in the event that an insured is sued by reason of some defect within the scope of the policy's guarantee. The respondents accounted for 57 percent of the $1.35 billion in gross revenues that the industry had reaped in 1982. In 1985, the Commission issued an administrative complaint in which it charged classic horizontal price-fixing: "Respondents have agreed on the price to be charged for title search and examination services or settlement services through rating bureaus in various states...." The companies defended on several grounds: McCarran–Ferguson Act exemption, *Noerr–Penning-*

ton exemption, and state-action immunity. The ALJ rejected all three, and the Commission accepted his findings and conclusions.

Most importantly for the *Parker* argument, the Commission (and ALJ) found that the rating bureaus were not pooling risk information or otherwise setting insurance rates according to actuarial loss experience. Instead, they were looking simply at profitability studies. Each of the four States in question used what has come to be called a "negative option" system to approve rate filings by the bureaus. This meant in practice that the rating bureau filed rates for title searches and title examinations with the state insurance office, and the rates became effective unless the state rejected them within a specified period, such as 30 days. Although the negative option system provided a theoretical mechanism for substantive review, the ALJ determined that the rate filings were subject to minimal scrutiny by state regulators.

This was not enough, in the Commission's opinion, to rise to the level of "active supervision" for *Parker* and *Midcal* purposes. The court of appeals (agreeing here with the First Circuit's decision in New England Motor Rate Bureau, Inc. v. FTC, 908 F.2d 1064 (1st Cir. 1990)), held that it was enough if a state regulatory program existed, was staffed, funded, and empowered by law to supervise the private actions. The Supreme Court disagreed with that standard, with the following explanation:

> The principle of freedom of action for the States, adopted to foster and preserve the federal system, explains the later evolution and application of the *Parker* doctrine in our decisions in *Midcal, supra,* and *Patrick v. Burget*, 486 U.S. 94 (1988).... *Midcal* confirms that while a State may not confer antitrust immunity on private persons by fiat, it may displace competition with active state supervision if the displacement is both intended by the State and implemented in its specific details. Actual state involvement, not deference to private price-fixing arrangements under the general auspices of state law, is the precondition for immunity from federal law. Immunity is conferred out of respect for ongoing regulation by the State, not out of respect for the economics of price restraint. In *Midcal* we found that the intent to restrain prices was expressed with sufficient precision so that the first part of the test was met, but that the absence of state participation in the mechanics of the price posting was so apparent that the requirement of active supervision had not been met.

> The rationale was further elaborated in *Patrick v. Burget* [described p. 448, note 5]. Because the particular anticompetitive conduct at issue in *Patrick* had not been supervised by governmental actors, we decided that the actions of the peer review committee were not entitled to state-action immunity.

> Our decisions make clear that the purpose of the active supervision inquiry is not to determine whether the State has met some normative standard, such as efficiency, in its regulatory practices. Its purpose is to determine whether the State has exercised sufficient independent judgment and control so that the details of the rates or prices have been established as a product of deliberate state intervention, not simply by agreement among private parties. Much as in causation inquiries, the analysis asks whether the State has played a substantial role in determining the specifics of the economic policy. The question is not how well state regulation works but whether the anticompetitive scheme is the State's own.

Although the point bears but brief mention, we observe that our prior cases considered state-action immunity against actions brought under the Sherman Act, and this case arises under the Federal Trade Commission Act. The Commission has argued at other times that state-action immunity does not apply to Commission action under § 5 of the Federal Trade Commission Act.... We need not determine whether the antitrust statutes can be distinguished on this basis, because the Commission does not assert any superior pre-emption authority in the instant matter. We apply our prior cases to the one before us....

If the States must act in the shadow of state-action immunity whenever they enter the realm of economic regulation, then our doctrine will impede their freedom of action, not advance it. The fact of the matter is that the States regulate their economies in many ways not inconsistent with the antitrust laws. For example, Oregon may provide for peer review by its physicians without approving anticompetitive conduct by them.... Or Michigan may regulate its public utilities without authorizing monopolization in the market for electric light bulbs. See *Cantor v. Detroit Edison Co.*, 428 U.S. 579, 596 (1976). So we have held that state-action immunity is disfavored, much as are repeals by implication. *Lafayette v. Louisiana Power & Light Co.*, 435 U.S. 389, 398–399 (1978). By adhering in most cases to fundamental and accepted assumptions about the benefits of competition within the framework of the antitrust laws, we increase the States' regulatory flexibility....

The respondents contend that these concerns are better addressed by the requirement that the States articulate a clear policy to displace the antitrust laws with their own forms of economic regulation. This contention misapprehends the close relation between *Midcal*'s two elements. Both are directed at ensuring that particular anticompetitive mechanisms operate because of a deliberate and intended state policy. In the usual case, *Midcal*'s requirement that the State articulate a clear policy shows little more than that the State has not acted through inadvertence; it cannot alone ensure, as required by our precedents, that particular anticompetitive conduct has been approved by the State. It seems plain, moreover, in light of the *amici curiae* brief to which we have referred, that sole reliance on the requirement of clear articulation will not allow the regulatory flexibility that these States deem necessary. For States whose object it is to benefit their citizens through regulation, a broad doctrine of state-action immunity may serve as nothing more than an attractive nuisance in the economic sphere. To oppose these pressures, sole reliance on the requirement of clear articulation could become a rather meaningless formal constraint.

The Court found that the standard used by the courts of appeals, under which it was enough to have a program "in place, staffed, funded," under which the state officials had sufficient authority to regulate, was "insufficient to establish the requisite level of active supervision." Instead, the party claiming the immunity must show that state officials have undertaken the necessary steps to determine the specifics of the price-fixing or rate-setting scheme. The Court distinguished between the mere potential for state supervision and an actual decision by the State. Under those standards, it concluded that there was no active supervision in either Wisconsin or Montana:

This case involves horizontal price fixing under a vague imprimatur in form and agency inaction in fact. No antitrust offense is more pernicious than price fixing. *FTC v. Superior Court Trial Lawyers Assn.*, 493 U.S. 411, 434, n. 16 (1990). In this context, we decline to formulate a rule that would lead to a finding of active state supervision where in fact there was none. Our decision should be read in light of the gravity of the antitrust offense, the involvement of private actors throughout, and the clear absence of state supervision. We do not imply that some particular form of state or local regulation is required to achieve ends other than the establishment of uniform prices. Cf. *Columbia v. Omni Outdoor Advertising, Inc.*, 499 U.S. 365 (1991) (city billboard zoning ordinance entitled to state-action immunity). We do not have before us a case in which governmental actors made unilateral decisions without participation by private actors. Cf. *Fisher v. Berkeley*, 475 U.S. 260 (1986) (private actors not liable without private action). And we do not here call into question a regulatory regime in which sampling techniques or a specified rate of return allow state regulators to provide comprehensive supervision without complete control, or in which there was an infrequent lapse of state supervision. Cf. *324 Liquor Corp. v. Duffy*, 479 U.S. 335, 344, n. 6 (1987) (a statute specifying the margin between wholesale and retail prices may satisfy the active supervision requirement). In the circumstances of this case, however, we conclude that the acts of the respondents in the States of Montana and Wisconsin are not immune from antitrust liability.

The Court remanded for further findings on the actual extent of state supervision. Justice Scalia concurred, commenting that while the Court's standard was faithful to what prior cases had said about active supervision, it was troubling in its vagueness. He also noted that he was "skeptical about the *Parker v. Brown* exemption for state-programmed private collusion in the first place." Chief Justice Rehnquist (with Justices O'Connor and Thomas joining him) dissented, finding that the Court's standard was neither warranted by earlier cases nor sound as a matter of policy. He expressed concern about the way in which the courts were to decide whether a state had played a substantial enough role in determining the specifics of a policy to justify the immunity. Because, in the States at issue in the *Ticor* case itself, the particular conduct was approved by a state agency when it raised no objection, he would have found enough to satisfy the "active supervision" requirement.

NOTES AND QUESTIONS

1. *Clear articulation requirement.* After *Southern Motor Carriers,* how clearly and affirmatively must a state express a decision to replace competition with regulation? May any institution, agency, or part of state government, other than the legislature or the state's highest court, provide state authorization for regulation rather than competition? *See, e.g.,* Hoover v. Ronwin, 466 U.S. 558 (1984); Hardy v. City Optical Inc., 39 F.3d 765 (7th Cir. 1994); Hovenkamp, Federal Antitrust Policy: The Law of Competition and Its Practice 678–81 (1994). Why was the filing of tariffs in the *Ticor* case not considered petitioning protected by *Noerr*?

2. *State supervision.* Was there adequate state supervision in the *Parker* case? After *Ticor*, how far may (or must) federal courts now go in reviewing the effectiveness of state supervision? What if a state commission is tilted towards—or corrupted by—a regulated group? Against what policy objectives should active

supervision by the state be measured? Why do municipalities get a free pass, if they really are nothing more than corporate creations of the state?

3. *Supervision standard with different state actors.* What if, altering the facts of *Goldfarb,* the Supreme Court of Virginia, without specific legislative authority, had mandated minimum fee schedules and authorized each county bar to establish local levels of fees? Would complying associations, or their members, be subject to Sherman Act scrutiny? Would it make a difference if the Virginia Supreme Court reviewed each such schedule for reasonableness prior to its adoption?

What if the Virginia Supreme Court (or the legislature) actually set mandatory minimum fee schedules itself?

4. *Tacit supervision.* In 324 Liquor Corp. v. Duffy, 479 U.S. 335 (1987), the State of New York required retailers to charge at least 112 percent of the "posted" wholesale price for liquor, but permitted wholesalers to sell to retailers at less than the "posted" price. Justice Powell, writing for seven members of the Supreme Court, declared the legislation invalid and reasoned as follows:

> Section 101–bb directly restricts retail prices, and retailers are subject to penalties for failure to adhere to the resale price schedules. The New York statute, moreover, applies to *all* wholesalers and retailers of liquor. We have noted that industry wide resale price maintenance also may facilitate cartelization.... Mandatory industry wide resale price fixing is virtually certain to reduce interbrand competition as well as intrabrand competition, because it prevents manufacturers and wholesalers from allowing or requiring retail price competition. The New York statute specifically forbids retailers from reducing the minimum prices set by wholesalers....
>
> Our decisions have established a two-part test for determining immunity under *Parker v. Brown....* New York's liquor pricing system meets the first requirement. The state legislature clearly has adopted a policy of resale price maintenance. Just as clearly, however, New York's liquor pricing system is not actively supervised by the State. As in *Midcal,* the State "simply authorizes price setting and enforces the prices established by private parties."[55] New York "neither establishes prices nor reviews the reasonableness of the price schedules." New York "does not monitor

---

55. A simple "minimum markup" statute requiring retailers to charge 112 percent of their actual wholesale cost may satisfy the "active supervision" requirement, and so be exempt from the antitrust laws under Parker v. Brown, 317 U.S. 341 (1943). See Morgan v. Division of Liquor Control, 664 F.2d 353 (2d Cir. 1981) (upholding a simple markup statute). Section 101–bb, however, is not a simple minimum markup statute because it imposes a markup on the "posted bottle price," a price that may greatly exceed what the retailer actually paid for the liquor. As we have explained, Bulletin 471 permits wholesalers to reduce the case price—the price actually paid by most retailers—without reducing the bottle price. The New York Court of Appeals expressly held that Bulletin 471 "is consistent with Alcoholic Beverage Control Law § 101–b(3) which does not mandate any price ratio between scheduled case and bottle prices." ... We thus have no occasion to consider whether a simple minimum markup statute would be entitled to antitrust immunity under Parker v. Brown.

Some states completely control the distribution of liquor within their boundaries. *E.g.,* Va. Code §§ 4–15, 4–28 (1983). Such comprehensive regulation is immune under *Parker v. Brown* because the state substitutes its own power for "unfettered business freedom." See *New Motor Vehicle Bd. of Cal. v. Orrin W. Fox Co.,* 439 U.S. 96, 104 (1978).

market conditions or engage in any 'pointed reexamination' of the program." ...[56]

5. *Ultimate State control.* In Patrick v. Burget, 486 U.S. 94 (1988), an independent surgeon brought suit against medical practitioners who were partners in a private medical clinic in a small Oregon community. The partners made up a majority of the staff members of the only hospital in town. The plaintiff, who had declined membership in the clinic, complained that the clinic partners had initiated and participated in hospital peer-review proceedings designed to reduce competition by excluding him, in violation of the Sherman Act.

There was extensive evidence of other harassment by partners in the clinic after plaintiff had refused to become a member. That evidence doubtless played a role in the jury's substantial verdict and in the Court of Appeals' characterization of defendants' conduct as "shabby, unprincipled and unprofessional." The Court of Appeals nonetheless reversed the judgment for plaintiff and held that since Oregon had articulated a policy in favor of physician peer review and actively supervised the process, "state action" immunity was applicable. The Supreme Court, per Marshall, J., reversed and reasoned:

> In this case, we need not consider the "clear articulation" prong of the *Midcal* test, because the "active supervision" requirement is not satisfied.... The requirement is designed to ensure that the state action doctrine will shelter only the particular anticompetitive acts of private parties that, in the judgment of the State, actually further state regulatory policies. To accomplish this purpose, the active supervision requirement mandates that the State exercise ultimate control over the challenged anticompetitive conduct.... The mere presence of some state involvement or monitoring does not suffice.... The active supervision prong of the *Midcal* test requires that state officials have and exercise power to review particular anticompetitive acts of private parties and disapprove those that fail to accord with state policy. Absent such a program of supervision, there is no realistic assurance that a private party's anticompetitive conduct promotes state policy, rather than merely the party's individual interests.
>
> Respondents in this case contend that the State of Oregon actively supervises the peer-review process through the state Health Division, the [state Board of Medical Examiner (BOME)], and the state judicial system. The Court of Appeals, in finding the active supervision requirement satisfied, also relied primarily on the powers and responsibilities of these state actors. Neither the Court of Appeals nor respondents, however, have succeeded in showing that any of these actors review—or even could

---

56. In a concurring opinion, Judge Jasen argued that the State actively supervises the liquor pricing system.... Judge Jasen noted that the SLA can respond to market conditions by permitting individual wholesalers to depart from their posted prices, and by permitting individual retailers to sell below the statutory definition of "cost," ABC Law, § 101–bb(3), "for good cause shown." Bulletin 471 itself was issued by the SLA in response to market conditions. Moreover, the State Legislature frequently considers proposals to alter the liquor pricing system. Neither the "monitoring" by the SLA, nor the periodic reexaminations by the State Legislature, exerts any significant control over retail liquor prices or mark-ups. Thus, the State's involvement does not satisfy the second requirement of Midcal.

review—private decisions regarding hospital privileges to determine whether such decisions comport with state regulatory policy and to correct abuses.

[U]nder the statutory scheme, the Health Division has no power to review private peer-review decisions and overturn a decision that fails to accord with state policy. Thus, the activities of the Health Division under Oregon law cannot satisfy the active supervision requirement of the state action doctrine. Similarly, the BOME does not engage in active supervision over private peer-review decisions.... Certainly, respondents have not shown that the BOME in practice reviews privilege decisions or that it ever has asserted the authority to reverse them.

The only remaining alleged supervisory authority in this case is the state judiciary. Respondents claim, and the Court of Appeals agreed, that Oregon's courts directly review privilege-termination decisions and that this judicial review constitutes active state supervision. This Court has not previously considered whether state courts, acting in their judicial capacity, can adequately supervise private conduct for purposes of the state action doctrine. All of our prior cases concerning state supervision over private parties have involved administrative agencies, *see, e.g.,* [*Southern Motor Carriers*], or state supreme courts with agency-like responsibilities over the organized bar, see [*Bates*]. This case, however, does not require us to decide the broad question whether judicial review of private conduct ever can constitute active supervision, because judicial review of privilege-termination decisions in Oregon, if such review exists at all, falls far short of satisfying the active supervision requirement.

As an initial matter, it is not clear that Oregon law affords any direct judicial review of private peer-review decisions. Oregon has no statute expressly providing for judicial review of privilege terminations. Moreover, we are aware of no case in which an Oregon court has held that judicial review of peer-review decisions is available.

Moreover, the Oregon courts have indicated that even if they were to provide judicial review of hospital peer-review proceedings, the review would be of a very limited nature. The Oregon Supreme Court, in its most recent decision addressing this matter, stated that a court "should [not] decide the merits of plaintiff's dismissal" and that "[i]t would be unwise for a court to do more than to make sure that some sort of reasonable procedure was afforded and that there was evidence from which it could be found that plaintiff's conduct posed a threat to patient care." *Straube v. Emanuel Lutheran Charity Board, supra,* at 384, 600 P.2d, at 386. This kind of review would fail to satisfy the state action doctrine's requirement of active supervision. Under the standard suggested by the Oregon Supreme Court, a state court would not review the merits of a privilege-termination decision to determine whether it accorded with state regulatory policy. Such constricted review does not convert the action of a private party in terminating a physician's privileges into the action of the State for purposes of the state action doctrine. In so holding, we are not unmindful of the policy argument that respondents and their amici have advanced for reaching the opposite conclusion. They contend that effective peer review is essential to the provision of quality medical care and that any threat of antitrust liability will prevent physicians from participating openly and actively in peer-review proceedings. This argument, however, essentially challenges the wisdom of applying the antitrust laws to the sphere of medical care, and as such is properly directed to the legislative branch. To the extent that Congress has declined to exempt medical peer review from the reach of the antitrust laws, peer review is immune from antitrust scrutiny only if the State effectively has made this conduct its own. The State of Oregon has not done so.

6. *Clayton Act and § 5 suits.* Should the *Parker* exemption to the Sherman Act apply—or apply in precisely the same way—to violations of the Clayton Act? To proceedings brought by the Federal Trade Commission under § 5 of the FTC Act? Notice that the Supreme Court was able to avoid resolving this issue in *Ticor. See* p. 443 *supra.*

7. *Distinguishing "State" from local government action.* In City of Lafayette v. Louisiana Power & Light Co., 435 U.S. 389 (1978), discussed in *Town of Hallie,* two Louisiana cities sued several privately owned utilities, alleging that utility systems owned and operated by plaintiff cities had been injured as a result of defendants' conspiracy to restrain trade in the generation, transmission, and distribution of electric power in the region. Louisiana Power counterclaimed, alleging that, among other things, plaintiffs required that customers located outside city limits purchase electricity from their utilities as a condition of continued water and gas service, *i.e.,* employed tie-ins which deprived the private utilities of customers.

The Supreme Court rejected the cities' "state action" defense, noting in a plurality opinion: (1) that municipalities must be distinguished from the states from which they derive their existence; (2) that they did not "exercise the sovereign power of the state" for "state action" purposes, since their interests are necessarily more parochial than, and might even conflict with, the broader interest of the states recognized in the *Parker* case; (3) that redress through political action did not protect those injured by municipalities' conduct outside their borders; and (4) that if the "62,437 different units of local government in this country . . . were free to make economic choices without regard to anticompetitive effects" the national policy embodied in antitrust laws would be seriously subverted.

The plurality asserted that municipalities could claim "state action" exemption only "pursuant to state policy to displace competition with regulation or monopoly public service"; this need not be "a specific, detailed legislative authorization," but rather a sufficient basis for concluding that the legislature contemplated the kind of action complained of.

Applying the later *Town of Hallie* formulation, should the "state action" claim in the *Lafayette* case have been sustained? What further information would you need?

8. *Neutral or general articulation.* Community Communications Co. v. City of Boulder, 455 U.S. 40 (1982), also discussed in *Town of Hallie,* involved a claim that the City's "emergency" ordinance prohibiting plaintiff from expanding service under its cable TV franchise constituted an antitrust violation. The City of Boulder, organized as a "home rule" municipality under Colorado's state constitution, argued that this status entitled it to invoke the "state action" exemption.

The Supreme Court rejected this claim, stating that the general authority to act provided by "home rule" status was not sufficiently particularized to satisfy the requirement announced in *City of Lafayette.* The criterion of "clear articulation and affirmative expression is not satisfied when the State's position is one of mere *neutrality* respecting the municipal actions challenged as anticompetitive."

9. *Local Government Antitrust Act.* After the *City of Lafayette* and *City of Boulder* decisions, but before *Town of Hallie,* Congress responded to lower court treble damage awards against municipalities and municipal officials and a widespread fear of a deluge of such suits with the passage of the Local Government Antitrust Act of 1984.[57] The Act prohibits plaintiffs from recovering monetary damages "from any local government, or official or employee thereof acting in an official capacity." The Act also provides that no damages may be recovered from any person "based on any official action directed by a local government, or official or employee thereof acting in an official capacity."[58] The Act leaves intact the possibility of obtaining injunctive relief against local governments or other persons. In light of *Town of Hallie* and *Omni Outdoor* (p. 451 *infra*), should the Act now be repealed?

10. *Public entities/authorities.* School districts and "authorities" established by state law to operate highways, bridges, airports, seaports, stadiums, convention halls, and the like, sometimes compete with private business, and often enter into exclusive contracts or other arrangements which foreclose others from access to the facility or are otherwise anticompetitive. Such entities are usually created with explicit or implicit authority to enter into all necessary contracts. As *Town of Hallie* recognizes, at least for municipalities, "state action" requirements of clearly articulated policy to displace competition and continuing surveillance by the State are not entirely appropriate. Is this also the case as to special-purpose "authorities"? They are usually chartered as monopolies and they can hardly act as if they were operating in a competitive market. They also usually have no direct accountability to the electorate. Should they be subject to no greater requirement of surveillance than municipalities?

Columbia v. Omni Outdoor Advertising, Inc.

Supreme Court of the United States, 1991.
499 U.S. 365, 111 S.Ct. 1344, 113 L.Ed.2d 382.

■ SCALIA, J. This case requires us to clarify the application of the Sherman Act to municipal governments and to the citizens who seek action from them.

I

Petitioner Columbia Outdoor Advertising, Inc. (COA), a South Carolina corporation, entered the billboard business in the city of Columbia, South Carolina (also a petitioner here), in the 1940s. By 1981 it controlled more than 95% of what has been conceded to be the relevant market. COA was a local business owned by a family with deep roots in the community, and enjoyed close relations with the city's political leaders. The mayor and other members of the city council were personal friends of COA's majority

---

57. 15 U.S.C. §§ 34–36.

58. *See,* e.g., Cohn v. Wilkes General Hospital, 767 F.Supp. 111 (W.D.N.C.), aff'd sub. nom., Cohn v. Bond, 953 F.2d 154 (4th Cir. 1991), cert. denied, 505 U.S. 1230 (1992) (rejecting claim that the Act does not protect private physician defendants, at a municipal hospital, if they use their official capacity "as a cloak for advancing their private economic interests" because the Act does not require consideration of the actors' intentions but rather grants immunity for acts undertaken in an official capacity).

owner, and the company and its officers occasionally contributed funds and free billboard space to their campaigns. According to respondent, these beneficiaries were part of a "longstanding" "secret anticompetitive agreement" whereby "the City and COA would each use their [sic] respective power and resources to protect . . . COA's monopoly position," in return for which "City Council members received advantages made possible by COA's monopoly."

In 1981, respondent Omni Outdoor Advertising, Inc., a Georgia corporation, began erecting billboards in and around the city. COA responded to this competition in several ways. First, it redoubled its own billboard construction efforts and modernized its existing stock. Second—according to Omni—it took a number of anticompetitive private actions, such as offering artificially low rates, spreading untrue and malicious rumors about Omni, and attempting to induce Omni's customers to break their contracts. Finally (and this is what gives rise to the issue we address today), COA executives met with city officials to seek the enactment of zoning ordinances that would restrict billboard construction. COA was not alone in urging this course; a number of citizens concerned about the city's recent explosion of billboards advocated restrictions, including writers of articles and editorials in local newspapers.

In the spring of 1982, the city council passed an ordinance requiring the council's approval for every billboard constructed in downtown Columbia. This was later amended to impose a 180–day moratorium on the construction of billboards throughout the city, except as specifically authorized by the council. A state court invalidated this ordinance on the ground that its conferral of unconstrained discretion upon the city council violated both the South Carolina and Federal Constitutions. The city then requested the State's regional planning authority to conduct a comprehensive analysis of the local billboard situation as a basis for developing a final, constitutionally valid, ordinance. In September 1982, after a series of public hearings and numerous meetings involving city officials, Omni, and COA (in all of which, according to Omni, positions contrary to COA's were not genuinely considered), the city council passed a new ordinance restricting the size, location, and spacing of billboards. These restrictions, particularly those on spacing, obviously benefitted COA, which already had its billboards in place; they severely hindered Omni's ability to compete.

In November 1982, Omni filed suit against COA and the city in Federal District Court, charging that they had violated §§ 1 and 2 of the Sherman Act, as well as South Carolina's Unfair Trade Practices Act, S.C.Code § 39–5–140 (1976). Omni contended, in particular, that the city's billboard ordinances were the result of an anticompetitive conspiracy between city officials and COA that stripped both parties of any immunity they might otherwise enjoy from the federal antitrust laws. In January 1986, after more than two weeks of trial, a jury returned general verdicts against the city and COA on both the federal and state claims. It awarded damages, before trebling, of $600,000 on the § 1 Sherman Act claim, and $400,000 on the § 2 claim.[59] The jury also answered two special interrogatories, finding specifically that the city and COA had conspired both to restrain trade and to monopolize the market. Petitioners moved for judgment notwithstanding the verdict, contending among other things that their activities were outside the scope of the federal antitrust laws. In November 1988, the District Court granted the motion.

A divided panel of the United States Court of Appeals for the Fourth Circuit reversed the judgment of the District Court and reinstated the jury verdict on all counts. We granted certiorari.

II

In the landmark case of *Parker v. Brown*, 317 U.S. 341 (1943), we rejected the contention that a program restricting the marketing of privately produced raisins, adopted pursuant to California's Agricultural Prorate Act, violated the Sherman Act. Relying on principles of federalism and state sovereignty, we held that the Sherman Act did not apply to anticompetitive restraints imposed by the States "as an act of government."

Since *Parker* emphasized the role of sovereign States in a federal system, it was initially unclear whether the governmental actions of political subdivisions enjoyed similar protection. In recent years, we have held that *Parker* immunity does not apply directly to local governments, see *Hallie v. Eau Claire*, 471 U.S. 34, 38 (1985). We have recognized, however, that a municipality's restriction of competition may sometimes be an authorized implementation of state policy, and have accorded *Parker* immunity where that is the case.

The South Carolina statutes under which the city acted in the present case authorize municipalities to regulate the use of land and the construction of buildings and other structures within their boundaries.[60] It is undisputed that, as a matter of state law, these statutes authorize the city to regulate the size, location, and spacing of billboards. It could be argued, however, that a municipality acts beyond its delegated authority, for *Parker* purposes, whenever the nature of its regulation is substantively or even procedurally defective. On such an analysis it could be contended, for example, that the city's regulation in the present case was not "authorized" by S.C.Code Ann. § 5–23–10 (1976), if it was not, as that statute

---

59. The monetary damages in this case were assessed entirely against COA, the District Court having ruled that the city was immunized by the Local Government Antitrust Act of 1984, which exempts local governments from paying damages for violations of the federal antitrust laws. Although enacted in 1984, after the events at issue in this case, the Act specifically provides that it may be applied retroactively if "the defendant establishes and the court determines, in light of all the circumstances . . . that it would be inequitable not to apply this subsection to a pending case." 15 U.S.C. § 35(b). The District Court determined that it would be, and the Court of Appeals refused to disturb that judgment. Respondent has not challenged that determination in this Court, and we express no view on the matter.

60. S.C.Code § 5–23–10 (1976) ("Building and zoning regulations authorized") provides that "[f]or the purpose of promoting health, safety, morals or the general welfare of the community, the legislative body of cities and incorporated towns may by ordinance regulate and restrict the height, number of stories and size of buildings and other structures." . . .

requires, adopted "for the purpose of promoting health, safety, morals or the general welfare of the community." As scholarly commentary has noted, such an expansive interpretation of the *Parker*–defense authorization requirement would have unacceptable consequences.

> "To be sure, state law 'authorizes' only agency decisions that are substantively and procedurally correct. Errors of fact, law, or judgment by the agency are not 'authorized.' Erroneous acts or decisions are subject to reversal by superior tribunals because unauthorized. If the antitrust court demands unqualified 'authority' in this sense, it inevitably becomes the standard reviewer not only of federal agency activity but also of state and local activity whenever it is alleged that the governmental body, though possessing the power to engage in the challenged conduct, has actually exercised its power in a manner not authorized by state law. We should not lightly assume that *Lafayette*'s authorization requirement dictates transformation of state administrative review into a federal antitrust job. Yet that would be the consequence of making antitrust liability depend on an undiscriminating and mechanical demand for 'authority' in the full administrative law sense." P. Areeda & H. Hovenkamp, Antitrust Law ¶ 212.3b, p. 145 (Supp. 1989).

We agree with that assessment, and believe that in order to prevent *Parker* from undermining the very interests of federalism it is designed to protect, it is necessary to adopt a concept of authority broader than what is applied to determine the legality of the municipality's action under state law. We have adopted an approach that is similar in principle, though not necessarily in precise application, elsewhere. See *Stump v. Sparkman*, 435 U.S. 349 (1978). It suffices for the present to conclude that here no more is needed to establish, for *Parker* purposes, the city's authority to regulate than its unquestioned zoning power over the size, location, and spacing of billboards.

Besides authority to regulate, however, the *Parker* defense also requires authority to suppress competition—more specifically, "clear articulation of a state policy to authorize anticompetitive conduct" by the municipality in connection with its regulation. *Hallie,* 471 U.S., at 40 (internal quotation omitted). We have rejected the contention that this requirement can be met only if the delegating statute explicitly permits the displacement of competition. It is enough, we have held, if suppression of competition is the "foreseeable result" of what the statute authorizes, *id.,* at 42. That condition is amply met here. The very purpose of zoning regulation is to displace unfettered business freedom in a manner that regularly has the effect of preventing normal acts of competition, particularly on the part of new entrants. A municipal ordinance restricting the size, location, and spacing of billboards (surely a common form of zoning) necessarily protects existing billboards against some competition from newcomers.[61]

---

61. The dissent contends that, in order successfully to delegate its *Parker* immunity to a municipality, a State must expressly authorize the municipality to engage (1) in specifically

The Court of Appeals was therefore correct in its conclusion that the city's restriction of billboard construction was prima facie entitled to *Parker* immunity. The Court of Appeals upheld the jury verdict, however, by invoking a "conspiracy" exception to *Parker* that has been recognized by several Courts of Appeals. That exception is thought to be supported by two of our statements in *Parker:* "[W]e have no question of the state or its municipality becoming a *participant in a private agreement* or combination by others for restraint of trade." "The state in adopting and enforcing the prorate program made no contract or agreement *and entered into no conspiracy in restraint of trade or to establish monopoly* but, as sovereign, imposed the restraint as an act of government which the Sherman Act did not undertake to prohibit." *Id.*, at 352 (emphasis added). *Parker* does not apply, according to the Fourth Circuit, "where politicians or political entities are involved as conspirators" with private actors in the restraint of trade. 891 F.2d, at 1134.

There is no such conspiracy exception. The rationale of *Parker* was that, in light of our national commitment to federalism, the general language of the Sherman Act should not be interpreted to prohibit anticompetitive actions by the States in their governmental capacities as sovereign regulators. The sentences from the opinion quoted above simply clarify that this immunity does not necessarily obtain where the State acts not in a regulatory capacity but as a commercial participant in a given market.... These sentences should not be read to suggest the general proposition that even governmental *regulatory* action may be deemed private—and therefore subject to antitrust liability—when it is taken pursuant to a conspiracy with private parties. The impracticality of such a principle is evident if, for purposes of the exception, "conspiracy" means nothing more than an

---

"economic regulation," (2) of a specific industry. These dual specificities are without support in our precedents, for the good reason that they defy rational implementation.

If, by authority to engage in specifically "economic" regulation, the dissent means authority specifically to regulate competition, we squarely rejected that in *Hallie,* as discussed in text. Seemingly, however, the dissent means only that the State authorization must specify that sort of regulation whereunder *decisions* about prices and output are not made by individual firms, but rather by a public body. But why is not the restriction of billboards in a city a restriction on the "output" of the local billboard industry? It assuredly *is*—and that is indeed the very gravamen of Omni's complaint. It seems to us that the dissent's concession that "it is often difficult to differentiate economic regulation from municipal regulation of health, safety, and welfare" is a gross understatement. Loose talk about a "regulated industry" may suffice for what the dissent calls "antitrust parlance," but it is not a definition upon which the criminal liability of public officials ought to depend.

Under the dissent's second requirement for a valid delegation of *Parker* immunity—that the authorization to regulate pertain to a specific industry—the problem with the South Carolina statute is that it used the generic term "structures," instead of conferring its regulatory authority industry-by-industry (presumably "billboards," "movie houses," "mobile homes," "TV antennas," and every other conceivable object of zoning regulation that can be the subject of a relevant "market" for purposes of antitrust analysis). To describe this is to refute it. Our precedents not only fail to suggest but positively reject such an approach. "The municipality need not 'be able to point to a specific, detailed legislative authorization' in order to assert a successful *Parker* defense to an antitrust suit." *Hallie,* 471 U.S., at 39 (quoting *Lafayette,* 435 U.S., at 415).

agreement to impose the regulation in question. Since it is both inevitable and desirable that public officials often agree to do what one or another group of private citizens urge upon them, such an exception would virtually swallow up the *Parker* rule: All anticompetitive regulation would be vulnerable to a "conspiracy" charge. See Areeda & Hovenkamp, *supra*, ¶ 203.3b, at 34, and n. 1; *Elhauge,* The Scope of Antitrust Process, 104 Harv. L. Rev. 667, 704–705 (1991).[62]

Omni suggests, however, that "conspiracy" might be limited to instances of governmental "corruption," defined variously as "abandonment of public responsibilities to private interests," "corrupt or bad faith decisions," and "selfish or corrupt motives." Ultimately, Omni asks us not to define "corruption" at all, but simply to leave that task to the jury: "[a]t bottom, however, it was within the jury's province to determine what constituted corruption of the governmental process in their community." Omni's amicus eschews this emphasis on "corruption," instead urging us to define the conspiracy exception as encompassing any governmental act "not in the public interest."

A conspiracy exception narrowed along such vague lines is similarly impractical. Few governmental actions are immune from the charge that they are "not in the public interest" or in some sense "corrupt." The

---

62. The dissent is confident that a jury composed of citizens of the vicinage will be able to tell the difference between "independent municipal action and action taken for the sole purpose of carrying out an anticompetitive agreement for the private party." No doubt. But those are merely the polar extremes, which like the geographic poles will rarely be seen by jurors of the vicinage. Ordinarily the allegation will merely be (and the dissent says this is enough) that the municipal action was not prompted "*exclusively* by a concern for the general public interest" (emphasis added). Thus, the real question is whether a jury can tell the difference—whether Solomon can tell the difference—between municipal-action-not-entirely-independent-because-based-partly-on-agreement-with-private-parties

that is *lawful* and municipal-action-not-entirely-independent-because-based-partly-on-agreement-with-private-parties that is *unlawful*. The dissent does not tell us how to put this question coherently, much less how to answer it intelligently. "*Independent* municipal action" is unobjectionable, "action taken for the *sole* purpose of carrying out an anticompetitive agreement for the private party" is unlawful, and everything else (that is, the known world between the two poles) is unaddressed. . . .

The dissent contends, moreover, that "the instructions in this case, fairly read, told the jury that the plaintiff should not prevail *unless* the ordinance was enacted for the sole purpose of interfering with access to the market" (emphasis added). That is not so. The sum and substance of the jury's instructions here was that anticompetitive municipal action is not lawful when taken as part of a conspiracy, and that a conspiracy is "an agreement between two or more persons to violate the law, or to accomplish an otherwise lawful result in an unlawful manner." Although the District Court explained that "it is perfectly lawful for any and all persons to petition their government," the court immediately added, "but they may not do so as a part or as the object of a conspiracy." These instructions, then, are entirely circular: an anticompetitive agreement becomes unlawful if it is part of a conspiracy, and a conspiracy is an agreement to do something unlawful. The District Court's observation, upon which the dissent places so much weight, that "if by the evidence you find that [COA] procured and brought about the passage of ordinances solely for the purpose of hindering, delaying or otherwise interfering with the access of [Omni] to the marketing area involved in this case . . . and thereby conspired, then, of course, their conduct would not be excused under the antitrust laws" is in no way tantamount to an instruction that this was the only theory upon which the jury could find an immunity-destroying "conspiracy."

California marketing scheme at issue in *Parker* itself, for example, can readily be viewed as the result of a "conspiracy" to put the "private" interest of the State's raisin growers above the "public" interest of the State's consumers. The fact is that virtually all regulation benefits some segments of the society and harms others; and that it is not universally considered contrary to the public good if the net economic loss to the losers exceeds the net economic gain to the winners. *Parker* was not written in ignorance of the reality that determination of "the public interest" in the manifold areas of government regulation entails not merely economic and mathematical analysis but value judgment, and it was not meant to shift that judgment from elected officials to judges and juries. If the city of Columbia's decision to regulate what one local newspaper called "billboard jungles" is made subject to *ex post facto* judicial assessment of "the public interest," with personal liability of city officials a possible consequence, we will have gone far to "compromise the States' ability to regulate their domestic commerce," *Southern Motor Carriers Rate Conference, Inc. v. United States*, 471 U.S. 48, 56 (1985). The situation would not be better, but arguably even worse, if the courts were to apply a subjective test: not whether the action was in the public interest, but whether the officials involved thought it to be so. This would require the sort of deconstruction of the governmental process and probing of the official "intent" that we have consistently sought to avoid.[63] "[W]here the action complained of . . . was that of the State itself, the action is exempt from antitrust liability regardless of the State's motives in taking the action." *Hoover v. Ronwin*, 466 U.S. 558, 579–580 (1984).

The foregoing approach to establishing a "conspiracy" exception at least seeks (however impractically) to draw the line of impermissible action in a manner relevant to the purposes of the Sherman Act and of *Parker*: prohibiting the restriction of competition for private gain but permitting the restriction of competition in the public interest. Another approach is possible, which has the virtue of practicality but the vice of being unrelated to those purposes. That is the approach which would consider *Parker* inapplicable only if, in connection with the governmental action in question, bribery or some other violation of state or federal law has been established. Such unlawful activity has no necessary relationship to whether the governmental action is in the public interest. A mayor is guilty of accepting a bribe even if he would and should have taken, in the public interest, the same action for which the bribe was paid. (That is frequently the defense asserted to a criminal bribery charge—and though it is never valid in law, *see, e.g., United States v. Jannotti*, 673 F.2d 578, 601 (CA3) (en banc), cert. denied, 457 U.S. 1106 (1982), it is often plausible in fact.) When, moreover, the regulatory body is not a single individual but a state legislature or city council, there is even less reason to believe that violation

---

63. We have proceeded otherwise only in the "very limited and well-defined class of cases where the very nature of the constitutional question requires [this] inquiry." *United States v. O'Brien*, 391 U.S. 367, 383, n. 30 (1968) (bill of attainder). See also *Arlington Heights v. Metropolitan Housing Development Corp.*, 429 U.S. 252, 268, n. 18 (1977) (race-based motivation).

of the law (by bribing a minority of the decisionmakers) establishes that the regulation has no valid public purpose. To use unlawful political influence as the test of legality of state regulation undoubtedly vindicates (in a rather blunt way) principles of good government. But the statute we are construing is not directed to that end. Congress has passed other laws aimed at combatting corruption in state and local governments. "Insofar as [the Sherman Act] sets up a code of ethics at all, it is a code that condemns trade restraints, not political activity." *Eastern Railroad Presidents Conference v. Noerr Motor Freight, Inc.*, 365 U.S. 127, 140 (1961).

For these reasons, we reaffirm our rejection of any interpretation of the Sherman Act that would allow plaintiffs to look behind the actions of state sovereigns to base their claims on "perceived conspiracies to restrain trade," *Hoover*, 466 U.S., at 580. We reiterate that, with the possible market participant exception, any action that qualifies as state action is "*ipso facto* ... exempt from the operation of the antitrust laws," *id.*, at 568. This does not mean, of course, that the States may exempt private action from the scope of the Sherman Act; we in no way qualify the well established principle that "a state does not give immunity to those who violate the Sherman Act by authorizing them to violate it, or by declaring that their action is lawful." *Parker*, 317 U.S., at 351 (citing *Northern Securities Co. v. United States*, 193 U.S. 197, 332, 344–347 (1904)). See also *Schwegmann Brothers v. Calvert Distillers Corp.*, 341 U.S. 384 (1951).

III

While *Parker* recognized the States' freedom to engage in anticompetitive regulation, it did not purport to immunize from antitrust liability the private parties who urge them to engage in anticompetitive regulation. However, it is obviously peculiar in a democracy, and perhaps in derogation of the constitutional right "to petition the Government for a redress of grievances," U.S. Const., Amdt. 1, to establish a category of lawful state action that citizens are not permitted to urge. Thus, beginning with *Eastern Railroad Presidents Conference v. Noerr Motor Freight, Inc., supra*, we have developed a corollary to *Parker*: the federal antitrust laws also do not regulate the conduct of private individuals in seeking anticompetitive action from the government. This doctrine, like *Parker*, rests ultimately upon a recognition that the antitrust laws, "tailored as they are for the business world, are not at all appropriate for application in the political arena." *Noerr, supra*, at 141. That a private party's political motives are selfish is irrelevant: "*Noerr* shields from the Sherman Act a concerted effort to influence public officials regardless of intent or purpose." *United Mine Workers of America v. Pennington*, 381 U.S. 657, 670 (1965).

Noerr recognized, however, what has come to be known as the "sham" exception to its rule: "There may be situations in which a publicity campaign, ostensibly directed toward influencing governmental action, is a mere sham to cover what is actually nothing more than an attempt to interfere directly with the business relationships of a competitor and the application of the Sherman Act would be justified." 365 U.S., at 144. The

Court of Appeals concluded that the jury in this case could have found that COA's activities on behalf of the restrictive billboard ordinances fell within this exception. In our view that was error.

The "sham" exception to *Noerr* encompasses situations in which persons use the governmental *process*—as opposed to the *outcome* of that process—as an anticompetitive weapon. A classic example is the filing of frivolous objections to the license application of a competitor, with no expectation of achieving denial of the license but simply in order to impose expense and delay. See *California Motor Transport Co. v. Trucking Unlimited*, 404 U.S. 508 (1972). A "sham" situation involves a defendant whose activities are "not genuinely aimed at procuring favorable government action" at all, *Allied Tube & Conduit Corp. v. Indian Head, Inc.*, 486 U.S. 492, 500, n. 4 (1988), not one "who 'genuinely seeks to achieve his governmental result, but does so *through improper means*,'" *id.*, at 508, n. 10 (quoting *Sessions Tank Liners, Inc. v. Joor Mfg., Inc.*, 827 F.2d 458, 465, n. 5 (CA9 1987)).

Neither of the Court of Appeals' theories for application of the "sham" exception to the facts of the present case is sound. The court reasoned, first, that the jury could have concluded that COA's interaction with city officials "was 'actually nothing more than an attempt to interfere directly with the business relations [*sic*] of a competitor.'" 891 F.2d, at 1139 (quoting *Noerr, supra*, at 144). This analysis relies upon language from *Noerr,* but ignores the import of the critical word "directly." Although COA indisputably set out to disrupt Omni's business relationships, it sought to do so not through the very process of lobbying, or of causing the city council to consider zoning measures, but rather through the ultimate *product* of that lobbying and consideration, viz., the zoning ordinances. The Court of Appeals' second theory was that the jury could have found "that COA's purposes were to delay Omni's entry into the market and even to deny it a meaningful access to the appropriate city administrative and legislative fora." But the purpose of delaying a competitor's entry into the market does not render lobbying activity a "sham," unless (as no evidence suggested was true here) the delay is sought to be achieved only by the lobbying process itself, and not by the governmental action that the lobbying seeks. "If *Noerr* teaches anything it is that an intent to restrain trade as a result of government action sought ... does not foreclose protection." Sullivan, Developments in the Noerr Doctrine, 56 Antitrust L.J. 361, 362 (1987). As for "denying ... meaningful access to the appropriate city administrative and legislative fora," that may render the manner of lobbying improper or even unlawful, but does not necessarily render it a "sham." We did hold in *California Motor Transport, supra,* that a conspiracy among private parties to monopolize trade by excluding a competitor from participation in the regulatory process did not enjoy *Noerr* protection. But *California Motor Transport* involved a context in which the conspirators' participation in the governmental process was itself claimed to be a "sham," employed as a means of imposing cost and delay. ("It is alleged that petitioners 'instituted the proceedings and actions ... with or without probable cause, and regardless of the merits of the cases.'" 404 U.S., at

512.) The holding of the case is limited to that situation. To extend it to a context in which the regulatory process is being invoked genuinely, and not in a "sham" fashion, would produce precisely that conversion of antitrust law into regulation of the political process that we have sought to avoid. Any lobbyist or applicant, in addition to getting himself heard, seeks by procedural and other means to get his opponent ignored. Policing the legitimate boundaries of such defensive strategies, when they are conducted in the context of a genuine attempt to influence governmental action, is not the role of the Sherman Act. In the present case, of course, any denial to Omni of "meaningful access to the appropriate city administrative and legislative fora" was achieved by COA in the course of an attempt to influence governmental action that, far from being a "sham," was if anything more in earnest than it should have been. If the denial was wrongful there may be other remedies, but as for the Sherman Act, the *Noerr* exemption applies.

Omni urges that if, as we have concluded, the "sham" exception is inapplicable, we should use this case to recognize another exception to *Noerr* immunity—a "conspiracy" exception, which would apply when government officials conspire with a private party to employ government action as a means of stifling competition. We have left open the possibility of such an exception, see, *e.g., Allied Tube, supra*, at 502 n. 7, as have a number of Courts of Appeals. . . .

Giving full consideration to this matter for the first time, we conclude that a "conspiracy" exception to *Noerr* must be rejected. We need not describe our reasons at length, since they are largely the same as those set forth in Part II above for rejecting a "conspiracy" exception to *Parker*. As we have described, *Parker* and *Noerr* are complementary expressions of the principle that the antitrust laws regulate business, not politics; the former decision protects the States' acts of governing, and the latter the citizens' participation in government. Insofar as the identification of an immunity-destroying "conspiracy" is concerned, *Parker* and *Noerr* generally present two faces of the same coin. The *Noerr*-invalidating conspiracy alleged here is just the *Parker*-invalidating conspiracy viewed from the standpoint of the private-sector participants rather than the governmental participants. The same factors which, as we have described above, make it impracticable or beyond the purpose of the antitrust laws to identify and invalidate lawmaking that has been infected by selfishly motivated agreement with private interests likewise make it impracticable or beyond that scope to identify and invalidate lobbying that has produced selfishly motivated agreement with public officials. "It would be unlikely that any effort to influence legislative action could succeed unless one or more members of the legislative body became . . . 'coconspirators' " in some sense with the private party urging such action, *Metro Cable Co. v. CATV of Rockford, Inc.*, 516 F.2d 220, 230 (CA7 1975). And if the invalidating "conspiracy" is limited to one that involves some element of unlawfulness (beyond mere anticompetitive motivation), the invalidation would have nothing to do with the policies of the antitrust laws. In *Noerr* itself, where the private party "deliberately deceived the public and public officials" in its successful lobbying campaign, we said that "deception, reprehensible as it is, can be of no consequence so far as the Sherman Act is concerned." 365 U.S., at 145.

IV

Under *Parker* and *Noerr,* therefore, both the city and COA are entitled to immunity from the federal antitrust laws for their activities relating to enactment of the ordinances. This determination does not entirely resolve the dispute before us, since other activities are at issue in the case with respect to COA. Omni asserts that COA engaged in private anticompetitive actions such as trade libel, the setting of artificially low rates, and inducement to breach of contract. Thus, although the jury's general verdict against COA cannot be permitted to stand (since it was based on instructions that erroneously permitted liability for seeking the ordinances) if the evidence was sufficient to sustain a verdict on the basis of these other actions alone, and if this theory of liability has been properly preserved, Omni would be entitled to a new trial.

There also remains to be considered the effect of our judgment upon Omni's claim against COA under the South Carolina Unfair Trade Practices Act.... We leave these remaining questions for determination by the Court of Appeals on remand. The judgment of the Court of Appeals is reversed, and the case is remanded for further proceedings consistent with this opinion.

■ JUSTICE STEVENS, with whom JUSTICE WHITE and JUSTICE MARSHALL join, dissenting.... Today the Court adopts a significant enlargement of the state action exemption. The South Carolina statutes that confer zoning authority on municipalities in the State do not articulate any state policy to displace competition with economic regulation in any line of commerce or in any specific industry. As the Court notes, the state statutes were expressly adopted to promote the " 'health, safety, morals or the general welfare of the community.' " Like Colorado's grant of "home rule" powers to the city of Boulder, they are simply neutral on the question whether the municipality should displace competition with economic regulation in any industry. There is not even an arguable basis for concluding that the State authorized the city of Columbia to enter into exclusive agreements with any person, or to use the zoning power to protect favored citizens from competition. Nevertheless, under the guise of acting pursuant to a state legislative grant to regulate health, safety, and welfare, the city of Columbia in this case enacted an ordinance that amounted to economic regulation of the billboard market; as the Court recognizes, the ordinance "obviously benefitted COA, which already had its billboards in place ... [and] severely hindered Omni's ability to compete." ...

In this case, the jury found that the city's ordinance—ostensibly one promoting health, safety, and welfare—was in fact enacted pursuant to an agreement between city officials and a private party to restrict competition. In my opinion such a finding necessarily leads to the conclusion that the city's ordinance was fundamentally a form of economic regulation of the billboard market rather than a general welfare regulation having incidental anticompetitive effects. Because I believe our cases have wisely held that the decision to embark upon economic regulation is a nondelegable one that must expressly be made by the State in the context of a specific industry in order to qualify for state action immunity, I would hold that the city of Columbia's economic regulation of the billboard market pursuant to a general state grant of zoning power is not exempt from antitrust scrutiny. . . .

Just as I am convinced that municipal "lawmaking that has been infected by selfishly motivated agreement with private interests" is not authorized by a grant of zoning authority, and therefore not within the state action exemption, so am I persuaded that a private party's agreement with selfishly motivated public officials is sufficient to remove the antitrust immunity that protects private lobbying under *Eastern Railroad Presidents Conference v. Noerr Motor Freight, Inc.,* 365 U.S. 127 (1961), and *Mine Workers v. Pennington,* 381 U.S. 657 (1965). Although I agree that the "sham" exception to the *Noerr–Pennington* rule exempting lobbying activities from the antitrust laws does not apply to the private petitioner's conduct in this case for the reasons stated by the Court in Part III of its opinion, I am satisfied that the evidence in the record is sufficient to support the jury's finding that a conspiracy existed between the private party and the municipal officials in this case so as to remove the private petitioner's conduct from the scope of *Noerr–Pennington* antitrust immunity. Accordingly, I would affirm the judgment of the Court of Appeals as to both the city of Columbia and Columbia Outdoor Advertising.

NOTES AND QUESTIONS

1. *"Clearly articulated" requirement after* Omni. Is the *Omni* opinion consistent with—or does it significantly broaden—*Town of Hallie*'s "clearly articulated" test? After *Omni,* under what circumstances, if any, would bribing public officials be considered unprotected by the *Noerr–Pennington* doctrine? Is bribery really "petitioning"? If bribery is not protected by the First Amendment, should it be protected by *Noerr?* (Note that bribery of federal officials is a crime under 18 U.S.C. § 201, and bribery of state or local officials is normally caught by 18 U.S.C. § 666, which makes it a crime to give or take a bribe to anyone involved with a program that receives $5,000 or more in federal funds.) If a company is able to achieve monopoly power by means of bribery, is the "means" used irrelevant for Sherman Act purposes? Why not *presume* that the monopoly power improperly resulted from such unlawful conduct? Is private action entitled to *Noerr–Pennington* immunity when the defendants engage in anticompetitive conduct with the intent of achieving the ultimate end and of deterring competition through the process?

2. *Underlying principles and incentives. Parker* immunity rests on the principles of state sovereignty and government accountability. How do these concepts apply to the City of Columbia's action in this case? Would antitrust sanctions (*e.g.,* treble damages and attorney's fees) add to the deterrence of unlawful activity provided by state law? Would private parties have more incentive to bring actions if antitrust sanctions were available?

3. *Preemption by antitrust law.* In Fisher v. City of Berkeley, 475 U.S. 260 (1986), the Court considered yet another permutation of the immunity theme, when it decided whether a rent control ordinance enacted by the City of Berkeley, California, pursuant to popular initiative was unconstitutional because preempted by the Sherman Act. The Ordinance placed strict rent controls on all real property that "is being rented or is available for rent for residential use in whole or in part"; it made exceptions for government-owned units, transient units, cooperatives, hospitals, certain small owner-occupied buildings, and all newly constructed buildings. For the remaining units, numbering approximately 23,000, the Ordinance establishes a base rent ceiling reflecting the rents in effect at the end of May 1980 and made provisions for rent increases only upon the approval of a Rent Stabilization Board. Violators were subject to fines by the Board, suit by the tenants, rent withholding, and (for willful violations) criminal penalties.

This suit was brought in California Superior Court by a group of landlords owning rental property in Berkeley. They claimed that the Ordinance violated their rights under the Due Process and Equal Protection Clauses of the Fourteenth Amendment, and sought declaratory and injunctive relief. The Superior Court upheld the Ordinance on its face, but was reversed by the Court of Appeal. While that appeal was pending, the Supreme Court's decision in Community Communications Co. v. City of Boulder, 455 U.S. 40 (1982), raised the possibility of a federal preemption challenge to the ordinance. Although this had not been raised earlier, the California Supreme Court opted to consider the preemption claim along with the other properly preserved arguments. It found no conflict between the Rent Stabilization Ordinance and either § 1 or § 2 of the Sherman Act. The Supreme Court of the United States then noted probable jurisdiction limited to the antitrust preemption question. It affirmed the judgment of the California courts, but on different grounds, finding that "traditional antitrust analysis" was adequate to resolve the issue presented.

The problem for the Court was whether the regulatory scheme established by Berkeley conflicted with the Sherman Act and was therefore preempted. In *Rice v. Norman Williams Co.,* the Court had held that a "state statute is not pre-empted by the federal antitrust laws simply because the state scheme may have an anticompetitive effect," 458 U.S. 654, 659 (1982). See Exxon Corp. v. Governor of Maryland, 437 U.S. 117, 133 (1978). A state statute must be invalidated on preemption grounds "only if it mandates or authorizes conduct that necessarily constitutes a violation of the antitrust laws in all cases, or if it places irresistible pressure on a private party to violate the antitrust laws in order to comply with the statute." 458 U.S., at 661. The same rule, the Court observed, applied to municipal ordinances. Furthermore, legislation that would otherwise be preempted under *Rice* may nonetheless survive if it is found to be state action immune from antitrust scrutiny under Parker v. Brown, 317 U.S. 341 (1943). The ultimate source of that immunity can be only the State, not its subdivisions.

The Court agreed that if the owners of residential rental property in Berkeley had voluntarily banded together to stabilize rents in the city, their activities would not be saved from antitrust attack by claims that they had set reasonable prices out of solicitude for the welfare of their tenants. *See* National Society of Professional Engineers v. United States, 435 U.S., at 695; United States v. Trans–Missouri Freight Assn., 166 U.S. 290 (1897). It also conceded that the ordinance would affect the residential housing rental market in much the same way as would the philanthropic activities of this hypothetical trade association. What distinguished the operation of Berkeley's Ordinance from the activities of a benevolent landlords' cartel was not that the Ordinance will necessarily have a different economic effect, but that the rent ceilings imposed by the Ordinance and maintained by the Stabilization Board were unilaterally imposed by government upon landlords to the exclusion of private control.

As we have repeatedly seen, here too the distinction between unilateral and concerted action was critical. *See Copperweld,* Chapter 6, *infra* at p. 598. Applying that principle if the Berkeley Ordinance stabilized rents without the element of concerted action, the program it established by definition could not violate § 1. The Court rejected the landlords' argument that concerted action could be found in a combination between the City and its officials, on the one hand, and the property owners, on the other. This, it held, "misconstrue[d] the concerted action requirement of § 1. A restraint imposed unilaterally by government does not become concerted action within the meaning of the statute simply because it has a coercive effect upon parties who must obey the law. The ordinary relationship between the government and those who must obey its regulatory commands whether they wish to or not is not enough to establish a conspiracy. Similarly, the mere fact that all competing property owners must comply with the same provisions of the Ordinance is not enough to establish a conspiracy among landlords."

The Court then distinguished so-called hybrid restraints, in which private actors have some degree of private regulatory power, citing as examples Rice v. Norman Williams Co., 458 U.S., at 665 (Stevens, J., concurring in the judgment), Schwegmann Bros. v. Calvert Distillers Corp., 341 U.S. 384 (1951); and California Retail Liquor Dealers Ass'n v. Midcal Aluminum, Inc., 445 U.S. 97 (1980). It acknowledged that "[t]here may be cases in which what appears to be a state-or municipality-administered price stabilization scheme is really a private price-fixing conspiracy, concealed under a "gauzy cloak of state involvement," *Midcal, supra,* at 106. This might occur even where prices are ostensibly under the absolute control of government officials. The Berkeley ordinance did not present such case, however. The Court concluded:

> Because under settled principles of antitrust law, the rent controls established by Berkeley's Ordinance lack the element of concerted action needed before they can be characterized as a *per se* violation of § 1 of the Sherman Act, we cannot say that the Ordinance is facially inconsistent with the federal antitrust laws. See *Rice v. Norman Williams Co., supra,* 458 U.S., at 661. We therefore need not address whether, even if the controls were to mandate § 1 violations, they would be exempt under the state-action doctrine from antitrust scrutiny. See Town of Hallie v. City of Eau Claire, 471 U.S. 34 (1985).

Justice Powell concurred and argued that the Supreme Court should not have decided "a difficult pre-emption question," but instead should have found a state-action exemption. Justice Brennan dissented "because the Ordinance has the force of law" and compels "landlords to do what the Sherman Act plainly forbids—to fix prices for rental units in Berkeley." The Ordinance, Brennan continued, precluded the possibility that the city and the landlords were acting independently; the Ordinance eliminated "price competition more effectively than any private 'agreement' ever could, and is therefore pre-empted by the Sherman Act."

4. *Identifying the critical actor.* Is *Fisher* consistent with *Midcal?* Was there an "agreement" in *Midcal* between the producers and the retailers with respect to resale prices? After *Fisher,* how do you distinguish unilateral acts of government from concerted activities or "hybrid restraints"? If, for example, tenant representatives had sat on Berkeley's Rent Stabilization Board would this have changed the *Fisher* case? What if landlord representatives dominated the Rent Stabilization

Board? What if landlords had lobbied hard for what purported to be a rent stabilization program?

5. *Distinguishing* Fisher. In Hertz Corp. v. City of New York, 1 F.3d 121 (2d Cir. 1993), the City of New York passed a local law to prevent Hertz from charging higher rates to residents of different parts of the city. Hertz brought suit claiming that the law controlled an aspect of Hertz's pricing process and thus violated the Sherman Act. On the issue of whether the city ordinance was a "contract, combination, or conspiracy," the Second Circuit distinguished *Fisher* as follows:

> First, the law is not a "pure regulatory scheme," [citing *Fisher*] because it is not a "scheme" at all; the law is simply a directive for all rental-car companies doing business in New York City to remove one factor from their competitive-pricing structures. Second, the law lacks the independent, quasi-judicial board that in *Berkeley* could adjust rates and provide relief in individual circumstances. Finally, the City of Berkeley was operating in an area vital to its municipal authority—housing; less vital is the rental-car industry in New York City.

> Nor does the Hertz law easily fit the fact pattern of the cases held to involve "hybrid" restraints—those that restrain trade through some combination of governmental and private conduct. The three Supreme Court cases in this category involved the pricing of liquor [citing *324 Liquor, Midcal,* and *Schwegmann*]. Each involved classic price-setting that was delegated by statute or regulation to private industry but was left unsupervised by the state legislature. The Hertz law, in contrast, does not purport to authorize price-setting by private industry; it simply eliminates an element of price competition among industry members.

> We reject the city's suggestion to apply *Fisher* expansively so as to view Local Law No. 21 as a unilateral action that lacks the degree of private-governmental agreement required to be a contract, combination, or conspiracy in restraint of trade. To do so would remove from the reach of the antitrust laws all local governmental actions not fitting the precise fact pattern of the liquor cases. 1 F.3d at 127.

Regardless of the differences between the *Hertz* case and *324 Liquor, Midcal,* and *Schwegmann,* the Second Circuit concluded that the New York City law was best characterized as a "hybrid" situation, where the law called for "anticompetitive private conduct in setting rental rates and making rental decisions." Thus, it was a contract, combination, or conspiracy that would have to be evaluated—because no state action was found—under the Sherman Act. 1 F.3d at 127.

The Second Circuit remanded the *Hertz* case to the district court and asked it to conduct a broad rule of reason analysis (including consideration of such factors as the city's concern about not unfairly burdening "minorities and the working poor") of the restraint. *Cf. NCAA, supra* p. 230. The Second Circuit (quoting *City of Boulder*) noted that "*per se* treatment may not be well tailored to assessing municipal antitrust liability, and 'certain activities which might appear anticompetitive when engaged in by private parties, take on a different complexion when adopted by a local government.' " 1 F.3d at 129.

NOTE: STATE VIOLATION OF ANTITRUST LAWS

Whether a state's regulatory scheme is protected from a Sherman Act challenge was litigated in TFWS, Inc. v. Schaefer, 242 F.3d 198 (4th Cir. 2001). The Maryland state government instituted a number of restrictions on the liquor market. One of these restrictions was the post-and-hold system, which required the state's Comptroller and Administrator of the Alcohol and Tobacco Tax Unit to establish a price posting system. The price posting system required liquor manufacturers and wholesalers to file price schedules and proposed price changes. The price schedules and proposed price changes were then made available to competitors. Another restriction involved a prohibition on volume discounts. Liquor wholesalers were prohibited from offering any type of discount to its retailers. The purpose of the post-and-hold system and the volume discount ban was to foster and promote temperance by maintaining wholesale liquor prices at stable, higher levels.

The plaintiff, a liquor retailer, claimed that the post-and-hold system and the volume discount ban violated the Sherman Act because it restricted trade in two ways. First, it allowed wholesalers to match each other's prices at artificially high levels. Second, it allowed wholesalers to maintain those artificially higher prices. The Maryland Comptroller argued that the suit was barred by the state action doctrine.

The court articulated a three-step analysis to decide whether a state's liquor pricing regulations could be challenged under the antitrust laws. First, the court must decide whether the state's pricing regulations are violative of the Sherman Act. This requires the court to consider whether the pricing regulations were a unilateral or a hybrid restraint. A unilateral restraint is one that is undertaken solely by the state, whereas a hybrid restraint is one in which the government is enforcing private marketing decisions. If the regulations are a hybrid restraint, the court must then consider whether it involves a *per se* violation of section 1 of the Sherman Act. Second, the court must decide whether the regulations are shielded from the Sherman Act under the "state action" doctrine. Lastly, the court had to decide whether there was a constitutional provision (such as the 11th Amendment) that trumped the Sherman Act.

In finding that the state pricing regulations were illegal, the court stated:

> Again, Maryland's post-and-hold pricing scheme mandates the exchange of price information by wholesalers through public posting and dissemination, and it requires adherence to the publicly announced prices. The Maryland system thus mandates activity that is essentially a form of horizontal price fixing, which has been called "the paradigm of an unreasonable restraint of trade." *N.C.A.A. v. Board of Regents of the University of Oklahoma*, 468 U.S. 85, 100, 104 S.Ct. 2948, 82 L.Ed.2d 70 (1984). Maryland's post-and-hold regime is subject to § 1 as a hybrid restraint, and we hold that it is illegal *per se*.

The court also found that the volume discount ban was illegal *per se*, as other courts had held that the elimination of volume discounts is a *per se* violation of § 1 of the Sherman Act. In short, this case shows courts' unwillingness to accept state regulations that compel activity that is *per se* illegal.

PROBLEM 9

BOLDEN'S AIRPORT INDEPENDENT AUTHORITY

Kent's state constitution, like that of Colorado, provides for the "home rule" of cities of a certain size, delegating to them all powers of legislation, independent of the state legislature, in matters of primarily local concern. Kent's state legislature has adopted a general "Airport Independent Authorities" statute which provides for the incorporation of local "independent authorities" to build, own, and operate municipal airports after approval of plans by the appropriate municipal authorities. The first board of directors of each independent authority is selected by the state and municipal governments, and then becomes a self-perpetuating board with no governmental involvement in the selection of new board members.

The state Airport Independent authorities statute includes a provision which "authorizes and directs" any authority's board of directors "to enter into such contractual arrangements which in its judgment are necessary and proper to provide airport related commercial services." The statute also states that the board of directors "should act in the public interest by maximizing revenues and by providing the most cost-effective services to air travelers."

One year ago, the City Council of Bolden approved a plan for operating Bolden's new airport, which included a provision authorizing the Independent Authority's "board of directors to enter into commercial contracts of all types." Last month, the board of directors of Bolden's Independent Authority entered into two car rental contracts—one with Hurts, a national organization, and the other with Boldencars, a locally owned rental car company. Included in the contracts, which were exclusive and were to last for ten years, was a provision for setting rates by the Independent Authority on local rentals; the first rental rates set were at rates substantially in excess of the rates at other comparable airports. For car rentals that would not result in a car being returned in the Bolden area, Hurts (the sole supplier of such cars) was instructed to "charge what the market would bear." The Independent Authority will receive a percentage of Hurts' net revenues on such rentals.

Several excluded national and local car rental companies, and a local consumer group, have joined forces to seek to enjoin the implementation of the two rental contracts as violations of Sections 1 and 2 of the Sherman Act. They can prove that almost all airports of comparable size across the country provide four to six facilities for separate rental car companies, have much shorter contractual terms, and have no provision for the setting of rental rates.

How would the "state action" issues be argued and decided? Would it make any difference if plaintiffs could prove that Boldencars received its contract as a result of pressure placed on the Independent Authority by the president of the City Council of Bolden, who was "paying off" a political debt? In addition, would it make any difference if the rental rates that the Independent Authority set were based on intentionally erroneous projections of costs and revenues provided by Boldencars and Hurts? Finally, would it make any difference if plaintiffs could prove that the contract with Hurts (which at most would have been one of three national companies to receive a contract) resulted from bribes paid to the board members of the Independent Authority?

SELECTIVE BIBLIOGRAPHY

1. Group Boycotts and Refusals to Deal

Richman, The Antitrust of Reputation Mechanisms: Institutional Economics and Concerted Refusals To Deal, 95 Va. L. Rev. 325 (2009).

Rogers, Consumer Welfare and Group Boycott Law, 62 SMU L. Rev. 665 (2009).

Frischman & Waller, *Revitalizing Essential Facilities,* 75 Antitrust L.J. 1 (2008).

Lemley & Leslie, Categorical Analysis in Antitrust Jurisprudence, 93 Iowa L. Rev. 1207 (2008).

Anderson, Self–Regulation & League Rules under the Sherman Act, 30 Cap. U. L. Rev. 125 (2002).

Candeub, Trinko and Re–Grounding the Refusal To Deal Doctrine, 66 U. Pitt. L. Rev. 821 (2005).

Melamed, Exclusionary Conduct Under the Antitrust Laws: Balancing, Sacrifice, and Refusals To Deal, 20 Berkeley Tech. L. J. 1247 (2005).

Werden, The Law and Economics of the Essential Facility Doctrine, 32 St. Louis U. L. J. 433 (1987).

2. Joint Ventures

Piraino, The Antitrust Analysis of Joint Ventures after the Supreme Court's Dagher Decision, 57 Emory L. J. 735 (2008).

Carstensen, Using Dagher To Refine the Analysis of Mergers and Joint Ventures in Petroleum Industries and Beyond, 19 Loy. Consumer L. Rev. 447 (2007).

Farrell, Hayes, Shapiro & Sullivan, Standard–Setting, Patents, and Hold–Up, 74 Antitrust L. J. 603 (2007).

Semeraro, Credit Card Interchange Fees: Three Decades of Antitrust Uncertainty, 14 Geo. Mason L. Rev. 941 (2007).

Werden, Antitrust Analysis of Joint Ventures: An Overview, 66 Antitrust L. J. 701 (1998).

Hovenkamp, Exclusive Joint Ventures and Antitrust Policy, 1995 Colum. Bus. L. Rev. 1 (1995).

Makar, The Essential Facility Doctrine and the Health Care Industry, 21 Fla. St. U. L. Rev. 913 (1994).

Brodley, Joint Ventures and Antitrust Policy, 95 Harv. L. Rev. 1521 (1982).

Pitofsky, Joint Ventures under the Antitrust Laws: Some Reflections on the Significance of Penn–Olin, 82 Harv. L. Rev. 1007 (1969).

3. Noerr–Pennington and Parker Doctrines

Dogan & Lemley, Antitrust and Regulatory Gaming, 87 Tex. L. Rev. 685 (2009).

Squire, Antitrust and the Supremacy Clause, 59 Stanford L. Rev. 77 (2006).

Trujillo, State Action Antitrust Exemption Collides with Deregulation: Rehabilitating the Foreseeability Doctrine, 11 Fordham J. Corp. & Fin. L. 349 (2006).

Lao, Reforming the Noerr–Pennington Antitrust Immunity Doctrine, 55 Rutgers L. Rev. 965 (2003).

Lopatka & Page, State Action and the Meaning of Agreement under the Sherman Act: An Approach to Hybrid Restraints, 20 Yale L. J. on Reg. 269 (2003).

Wrona, A Clash of Titans: The First Amendment Right To Petition vs. The Antitrust Laws, 28 New Eng. L. Rev. 637 (1994).

Garland, Antitrust and State Action: Economic Efficiency and the Political Process, 96 Yale L. J. 486 (1987).

Page, Interest Groups, Antitrust, and State Regulation: Parker v. Brown in the Economic Theory of Legislation, 1987 Duke L. J. 618.

Fischel, Antitrust Immunity for Attempts To Influence Government Action: The Basis and Limits of the Noerr–Pennington Doctrine, 45 U. Chi. L. Rev. 80 (1977).

CHAPTER 6

MARKET CONCENTRATION, CONSPIRACY, AND THE ANTITRUST LAWS

SECTION 1. NOTE ON OLIGOPOLY

An oligopolistic market is one in which there is a small number of dominant sellers, each with a large market share.[1] A seller in such a market, unlike a monopolist, realizes that if it raises its price above the competitive level, its rivals will undercut its price.[2] In contrast to firms in a competitive market, however, the seller in an oligopolistic market realizes that initiating a round of price competition will make all rivals worse off.[3] This means that sellers in an oligopolistic market have an incentive to avoid rigorous competition and instead to collude with one another. The small number of firms in the market facilitates collusion, and in many instances, firms need not even reach express agreements with each other. The challenge for antitrust law lies in detecting tacit collusion and in improving the competitive structure of the market, so as to avoid such collusion.

Robert H. Lande and Howard P. Marvel write that there are three types of collusion: (1) collusion to raise prices, (2) collusion to disadvantage rivals, and (3) collusion to manipulate the rules under which competition takes place.[4] Firms in an oligopolistic market can collude to raise prices by either fixing prices directly, dividing the market into competition-free segments assigned to individual cartel members, or by bid rigging. The goal of the first type of collusion is to mimic the result that a monopolist could obtain in the marketplace. The second type of collusion consists of agreements to take action jointly to harm existing or potential rivals that are not party to the collusion. Colluding firms may attempt to harm rivals by boycotts, predatory pricing, or by raising their rivals' costs. These practices can cause rivals to exit the market or to compete less aggressively. The goal of the third type of collusion is to change the rules of competition so as to

---

1. Phil C. Neal, et al., *Report of the White House Task Force on Antitrust Policy* (1968), 2 Antitrust L. & Econ. Rev. 11, 22–30 (Winter 1968–69).

2. George A. Hay, *Oligopoly, Shared Monopoly, and Antitrust Law*, 67 Cornell L. Rev. 439 (1982).

3. *Id.*

4. Robert H. Lande and Howard P. Marvel, *The Three Types of Collusion: Fixing Prices, Rivals, and Rules*, 2000 Wis. L. Rev. 941 (2000).

decrease the price competition among members. Examples of this last type of collusion include restrictions on advertising, especially price advertising, restrictions on the information that can be made available to consumers, agreements to restrict affiliations, and agreements not to solicit customers of rivals. The third type of collusion often takes place within the context of a professional association. Many real world arrangements among firms will fit into more than one category of collusion.

Collusion is more likely to be successful in concentrated industries with homogenous, fungible products. When the product is homogenous or fungible, a consumer can easily purchase from different competitors; thus, with such products there is an incentive for competitors to collude to fix prices or reduce output. On the other hand, as F.M. Scherer writes:

> ... [C]ooperation to hold prices above the competitive level is less likely to be successful, the less concentrated an industry is; the larger the competitive fringe is, the more heterogeneous, complex, and changing the products supplied are; the higher the ratio of fixed or overhead to total costs is, the more depressed business conditions are; the more dependent the industry is on large, infrequent orders, the more opportunities there are for under-the-counter price shading, and the more relations among company executives are marred by distrust and animosity.[5]

None of these characteristics alone, however, unambiguously points to the existence of collusion among sellers. The difficulty for practitioners lies in determining which factors are probative in each situation. This is further complicated by the fact that a concentrated market structure will not automatically lead to a situation where prices are substantially above competitive levels for extended periods of time.[6]

Other challenges to antitrust practitioners lie in the changing global economy and the expansion of the high technology sector. Because U.S. companies must now compete with foreign firms, both domestically and abroad, competition increasingly occurs over more than just the selling price. Firms today also compete on the variety and speed of production, development, and innovation.[7] As an FTC staff report put it:

> ... [w]hen innovation is the mark of competition of the day, antitrust faces new challenges in analyzing the competitive effects of single and multi-firm transactions and strategies, as well as acting affirmatively while protecting incentives and the property of pioneers. The importance of these issues is only enhanced with the growth in communications networks and the increasing demand for compatibility among producers that are to present viable alternatives for consumers.

---

5. Frederic M. Scherer, Industrial Market Structure and Economics Performance 151, 227, 266 (2d. ed. 1980).

6. *Id.*

7. FTC Staff Report, *Anticipating the 21st Century: Competition Policy in the New High-Tech, Global Marketplace*, 70 Antitrust & Trade Reg. Rep. (BNA) 1765 (1996).

SECTION 2.   INTERFERENCE OF AGREEMENT AS A LEGAL BUILDING BLOCK

INTRODUCTORY NOTE

The Sherman Act, at least as interpreted and applied to date, has been inadequate to deal effectively with the oligopoly pricing or price leadership associated with concentrated industries. This is partly because of difficulties created by the Act's apparent "bi-polar" structure. Section 1 deals explicitly with conduct by more than a single firm, and it reaches only "contract, combination . . . or conspiracy." Section 2 deals with the single firm, but its proscriptions of "monopolization" and "attempts to monopolize" do not seem to encompass parallel conduct by firms of less than monopoly dimension. This produces the apparent paradox that joint action (not agreed upon) by an oligopoly group may legally achieve noncompetitive prices that would be illegal if set by a cartel enjoying the same or even a lesser degree of market dominance. If protecting consumers and others from market power is a central objective of antitrust, here is an obvious flaw.

Antitrust enforcers and others have argued occasionally that the antitrust laws are capable of reaching such oligopoly pricing. Legal building blocks to bring about this result would have to be found, of course, in the language of these laws and the cases interpreting them.

One approach would be to infer agreement from consciously parallel conduct. This step would enable action to be taken under Section 1 of the Sherman Act, which requires some kind of agreement, or the "conspiracy to monopolize" subpart of Section 2. For a variety of reasons that will be explored in this chapter, the courts have resisted that approach.

If conscious parallelism alone is not an appropriate basis for antitrust liability, what is? One possibility is to take a cumulative approach and look for "other circumstances"—or "plus factors"—which, if considered along with the consciously parallel conduct, add up to something from which agreement legitimately can be inferred. But on what principled basis does one determine what additional circumstances should produce this result? One suggestion is that when oligopolists independently engage in parallel practices that facilitate price uniformity—making it more likely, more complete, or more durable—the inference of conspiracy should be permissible. Short of that, perhaps such "facilitating practices" are properly characterized as an "unfair method of competition" under Section 5 of the Federal Trade Commission Act, which does not explicitly require direct or inferred agreement. Does or should Section 5 go beyond the Sherman and Clayton Acts to reach techniques to achieve oligopoly pricing?

Another approach, which has been taken in the European Union, is to entertain the possibility of shared monopoly (called "joint dominance" in EU terminology). If firms acting together as a group mimic the results that would be expected from a single dominant firm, then the EU has the legal tools with which to address the situation. Efforts in the United States to develop a shared monopoly doctrine have been notoriously unsuccessful, but the reasons for those failures help us to understand both the possibilities and the limits of antitrust law.

Finally, there was a time when it was thought that the necessary agreement for Section 1 liability could be found within a single firm (either a monopolist or one with less than monopoly power) through the so-called intra-enterprise conspiracy doctrine. That entailed treating the firm and (1) its officers or other employees, (2) its operating divisions, (3) its wholly-owned subsidiaries, or (4) controlled (but not wholly-owned) subsidiaries, as separate entities for purposes of agreement, conspiracy or combination, and through one of those devices attempting to satisfy Section 1's plurality requirement. Although that idea permitted review of pricing (and other competitive behavior) by large firms that had something less than monopoly power, it risked intrusive government regulation of virtually all internal company decisions. Recognizing the importance of the distinction between genuinely unilateral action and concerted action, in 1984 the Supreme Court rejected the intra-enterprise conspiracy doctrine as applied to firms and their wholly owned subsidiaries. We discuss in this chapter when, if ever, antitrust law might reach within a broader enterprise.

one firm cannot have a conspiracy

A closely related procedural problem is important: when should the ultimate questions of fact about "contract, combination or conspiracy" go to the jury, and when should the case be resolved by the court at or prior to trial? Is there a special rule for antitrust cases, or do they follow general rules with respect to devices such as summary judgment? Does antitrust policy dictate some degree of encouragement of private actions, or do the hazards of treble damages and class actions to sensible business decisionmaking suggest a restrained approach?

These are some of the major questions with which the remainder of this chapter deals.

Interstate Circuit v. United States

Supreme Court of the United States, 1939.
306 U.S. 208, 59 S.Ct. 467, 83 L.Ed. 610.

■ STONE, J. This case is here on appeal ... from a final decree of the District Court for Northern Texas restraining appellants from continuing in a combination and conspiracy condemned by the court as a violation of § 1 of the Sherman Antitrust Act ... and from enforcing or renewing certain contracts found by the court to have been entered into in pursuance of the conspiracy.... The case is now before us on findings of the District Court specifically stating that appellants did in fact agree with each other to enter into and carry out the contracts, which the court found to result in unreasonable and therefore unlawful restraints of interstate commerce.

Appellants comprise the two groups of defendants in the District Court.... The distributor appellants are engaged in the business of distributing in interstate commerce motion picture films, copyrights on which they own or control, for exhibition in theatres throughout the United States. They distribute about 75 per cent of all first-class feature films exhibited in the United States. They solicit from motion picture theatre owners and managers in Texas and other states applications for licenses to exhibit films, and forward the applications when received from such exhibitors, to their respective New York offices, where they are accepted or rejected. If the applications are accepted, the distributors ship the films from points outside the states of exhibition to their exchanges within those states, from which, pursuant to the license agreements, the films are delivered to the local theatres for exhibition. After exhibition the films are reshipped to the distributors at points outside the state.

The exhibitor group of appellants consists of Interstate Circuit, Inc., and Texas Consolidated Theatres, Inc., and Hoblitzelle and O'Donnell, who are respectively president and general manager of both and in active charge of their business operations. The two corporations are affiliated with each other and with Paramount Pictures Distributing Co., Inc., one of the distributor appellants.

Interstate operates forty-three first-run and second-run motion picture theatres, located in six Texas cities. It has a complete monopoly of first-run theatres in these cities, except for one in Houston operated by one distributor's Texas agent. In most of these theatres the admission price for adults for the better seats at night is 40 cents or more. Interstate also operates several subsequent-run theatres in each of these cities, twenty-two in all, but in all but Galveston there are other subsequent-run theatres which compete with both its first- and subsequent-run theatres in those cities.

Texas Consolidated operates sixty-six theatres, some first- and some subsequent-run houses, in various cities and towns in the Rio Grande Valley and elsewhere in Texas and in New Mexico. In some of these cities there are no competing theatres, and in six leading cities there are no competing first-run theatres. It has no theatres in the six Texas cities in which Interstate operates. That Interstate and Texas Consolidated dominate the motion picture business in the cities where their theatres are located is indicated by the fact that at the time of the contracts in question Interstate and Consolidated each contributed more than 74 per cent of all the license fees paid by the motion picture theatres in their respective territories to the distributor appellants.

On July 11, 1934, following a previous communication on the subject to the eight branch managers of the distributor appellants, O'Donnell, the manager of Interstate and Consolidated, sent to each of them a letter on the letterhead of Interstate, each letter naming all of them as addressees, in which he asked compliance with two demands as a condition of Interstate's continued exhibition of the distributors' films in its "A" or first-run theatres at a night admission of 40 cents or more. One demand was that the distributors "agree that in selling their product to subsequent runs, that this 'A' product will never be exhibited at any time or in any theatre at a smaller admission price than 25 [cents] for adults in the evening." The other was that "on 'A' pictures which are exhibited at a night admission of 40 [cents] or more—they shall never be exhibited in conjunction with another feature picture under the so-called policy of double features." The letter added that with respect to the "Rio Grande Valley situation," with which Consolidated alone was concerned, "We must insist that all pictures exhibited in our 'A' theatres at a maximum night admission price of 35 must also be restricted to subsequent runs in the Valley at 25 [cents]."

The admission price customarily charged for preferred seats at night in independently operated subsequent-run theatres in Texas at the time of these letters was less than 25 cents. In seventeen of the eighteen independent theatres of this kind whose operations were described by witnesses the admission price was less than 25 cents. In one only was it 25 cents. In most of them the admission was 15 cents or less. It was also the general practice in those theatres to provide double bills either on certain days of the week or with any feature picture which was weak in drawing power. The distributor appellants had generally provided in their license contracts for a minimum admission price of 10 or 15 cents, and three of them had included provisions restricting double-billing. But none was at any time previously subject to contractual compulsion to continue the restrictions. The trial court found that the proposed restrictions constituted an important departure from prior practice.

The local representatives of the distributors, having no authority to enter into the proposed agreements, communicated the proposal to their home offices. Conferences followed between Hoblitzelle and O'Donnell, acting for Interstate and Consolidated, and the representatives of the various distributors. In these conferences each distributor was represented by its local branch manager and by one or more superior officials from outside the state of Texas. In the course of them each distributor agreed with Interstate for the 1934–35 season to impose both the demanded restrictions upon their subsequent-run licensees in the six Texas cities served by Interstate, except Austin and Galveston. While only two of the distributors incorporated the agreement to impose the restrictions in their license contracts with Interstate, the evidence establishes, and it is not denied, that all joined in the agreement, four of them after some delay in negotiating terms other than the restrictions and not now material. These agreements for the restrictions—with the immaterial exceptions noted—were carried into effect by each of the distributors' imposing them on their subsequent-run licensees in the four Texas cities during the 1934–35 season. One agreement, that of Metro–Goldwyn–Mayer Distributing Corporation, was for three years. The others were renewed in the two following seasons and all were in force when the present suit was begun.

None of the distributors yielded to the demand that subsequent runs in towns in the Rio Grande Valley served by Consolidated should be restricted. One distributor, Paramount, which was affiliated with Consolidated, agreed to impose the restrictions in certain other Texas and New Mexico cities.

The trial court found that the distributor appellants agreed and conspired among themselves to take uniform action upon the proposals made by Interstate, and that they agreed and conspired with each other and with Interstate to impose the demanded restrictions upon all subsequent-run exhibitors in Dallas, Forth Worth, Houston and San Antonio; that they carried out the agreement by imposing the restrictions upon their subsequent-run licensees in those cities, causing some of them to increase their admission price to 25 cents, either generally or when restricted pictures were shown, and to abandon double-billing of all such pictures, and causing the other subsequent-run exhibitors, who were either unable or unwilling to accept the restrictions, to be deprived of any opportunity to exhibit the restricted pictures, which were the best and most popular of all new feature pictures; that the effect of the restrictions upon "low-income members of the community" patronizing the theatres of these exhibitors was to withhold from them altogether the "best entertainment furnished by the motion picture industry"; and that the restrictions operated to increase the income of the distributors and of Interstate and to deflect attendance from later-run exhibitors who yielded to the restrictions to the first-run theatres of Interstate.

The court concluded as matters of law that the agreement of the distributors with each other and those with Interstate to impose the restrictions upon subsequent-run exhibitors and the carrying of the agreements into effect, with the aid and participation of Hoblitzelle and O'Donnell, constituted a combination and conspiracy in restraint of interstate commerce in violation of the Sherman Act. It also concluded that each separate agreement between Interstate and a distributor that Interstate should subject itself to the restrictions in its subsequent-run theatres and that the distributors should impose the restrictions on all subsequent-run theatres in the Texas cities as a condition of supplying them with its feature pictures, was likewise a violation of the Act.

It accordingly enjoined the conspiracy and restrained the distributors from enforcing the restrictions in their license agreements with subsequent-run exhibitors and from enforcing the contracts or any of them. This included both the contracts of Interstate with the distributors and the contract between Consolidated and Paramount, whereby the latter agreed to impose the restrictions upon subsequent-run theatres in Texas and New Mexico served by it.

Appellants assail the decree of the District Court upon three principal grounds: (a) that the finding of agreement and conspiracy among the distributor appellants to impose the restrictions upon later-run exhibitors is not supported by the court's subsidiary findings or by the evidence; (b) that the several separate contracts entered into by Interstate with the distributors are within the protection of the Copyright Act and consequently are not violations of the Sherman Act; and (c) that the restrictions do not unreasonably restrain interstate commerce within the provisions of the Sherman Act.

Although the films were copyrighted, appellants do not deny that the conspiracy charge is established if the distributors agreed among themselves to impose the restrictions upon subsequent-run exhibitors. Straus v. American Publishers' Association, 231 U.S. 222; Paramount Famous Lasky Corp. v. United States, 282 U.S. 30. As is usual in cases of alleged unlawful agreements to restrain commerce, the government is without the aid of direct testimony that the distributors entered into any agreement with each other to impose the restrictions upon subsequent-run exhibitors. In order to establish agreement it is compelled to rely on inferences drawn from the course of conduct of the alleged conspirators.

The trial court drew the inference of agreement from the nature of the proposals made on behalf of Interstate and Consolidated; from the manner in which they were made; from the substantial unanimity of action taken upon them by the distributors; and from the fact that appellants did not call as witnesses any of the superior officials who negotiated the contracts with Interstate or any official who, in the normal course of business, would have had knowledge of the existence or non-existence of such an agreement among the distributors. This conclusion is challenged by appellants because not supported by subsidiary findings or by the evidence. We think this inference of the trial court was rightly drawn from the evidence. In the view we take of the legal effect of the cooperative action of the distributor appellants in carrying into effect the restrictions imposed upon subsequent-run theatres in the four Texas cities and of the legal effect of the separate agreements for the imposition of those restrictions entered into between Interstate and each of the distributors, it is unnecessary to discuss in great detail the evidence concerning this aspect of the case.

The O'Donnell letter named on its face as addressees the eight local representatives of the distributors, and so from the beginning each of the distributors knew that the proposals were under consideration by the others. Each was aware that all were in active competition and that without substantially unanimous action with respect to the restrictions for any given territory there was risk of a substantial loss of the business and good will of the subsequent-run and independent exhibitors, but that with it there was the prospect of increased profits. There was, therefore, strong motive for concerted action, full advantage of which was taken by Interstate and Consolidated in presenting their demands to all in a single document.

There was risk, too, that without agreement diversity of action would follow. Compliance with the proposals involved a radical departure from the previous business practices of the industry and a drastic increase in admission prices of most of the subsequent-run theatres. Acceptance of the proposals was discouraged by at least three of the distributors' local managers. Independent exhibitors met and organized a futile protest which they presented to the representatives of Interstate and Consolidated. While as a result of independent negotiations either of the two restrictions without the other could have been put into effect by any one or more of the distributors and in any one or more of the Texas cities served by Interstate, the negotiations which ensued and which in fact did result in modifications of the proposals resulted in substantially unanimous action of the distributors, both as to the terms of the restrictions and in the selection of the four cities where they were to operate. . . .

But we are unable to find in the record any persuasive explanation other than agreed concert of action, of the singular unanimity of action on the part of the distributors by which the proposals were carried into effect as written in four Texas cities but not in a fifth or in the Rio Grande Valley. Numerous variations in the form of the provisions in the distributors' license agreements and the fact that in later years two of them extended the restrictions into all six cities, do not weaken the significance or force of the nature of the response to the proposals made by all the distributor appellants. It taxes credulity to believe that the several distributors would, in the circumstances, have accepted and put into operation with substantial unanimity such far-reaching changes in their business methods without some understanding that all were to join, and we reject as beyond the range of probability that it was the result of mere chance.

it couldn't have just been chance that they all made these changes

Appellants present an elaborate argument, based on the minutiae of the evidence, that other inferences are to be drawn which explain, at least in some respects, the unanimity of action both in accepting the restrictions for some territories and rejecting them for others.... Taken together, the circumstances of the case which we have mentioned, when uncontradicted and with no more explanation than the record affords, justify the inference that the distributors acted in concert and in common agreement in imposing the restrictions upon their licensees in the four Texas cities.

This inference was supported and strengthened when the distributors, with like unanimity, failed to tender the testimony, at their command, of any officer or agent of a distributor who knew, or was in a position to know, whether in fact an agreement had been reached among them for concerted action.... The production of weak evidence when strong is available can lead only to the conclusion that the strong would have been adverse. Clifton v. United States, 4 How. 242, 247. Silence then becomes evidence of the most convincing character.

Ds offered no testimony from ppl who knew

While the District Court's finding of an agreement of the distributors among themselves is supported by the evidence, we think that in the circumstances of this case such agreement for the imposition of the restrictions upon subsequent-run exhibitors was not a prerequisite to an unlawful conspiracy. It was enough that, knowing that concerted action was contemplated and invited, the distributors gave their adherence to the scheme and participated in it. Each distributor was advised that the others were asked to participate; each knew that cooperation was essential to successful operation of the plan. They knew that the plan, if carried out, would result in a restraint of commerce, which ... was unreasonable within the meaning of the Sherman Act, and knowing it, all participated in the plan. The evidence is persuasive that each distributor early became aware that the others had joined. With that knowledge they renewed the arrangement and carried it into effect for the two successive years.

this is not a pre-reg to unlawful conspiracy – it IS the conspiracy

It is elementary that an unlawful conspiracy may be and often is formed without simultaneous action or agreement on the part of the conspirators.... Acceptance by competitors, without previous agreement, of an invitation to participate in a plan, the necessary consequence of which, if carried out, is restraint of interstate commerce, is sufficient to establish an unlawful conspiracy under the Sherman Act.[8] ...

* consp doesn't have to be simultaneous action

---

8. Ed. The omission is of the Court's discussion, and rejection, of the argument that the restrictions relating to admission prices and double billing were sheltered by the copyright laws and did not violate the Sherman Act.

We think the conclusion is unavoidable that the conspiracy and each contract between Interstate and the distributors by which those consequences were effected are violations of the Sherman Act and that the District Court rightly enjoined enforcement and renewal of these agreements, as well as of the conspiracy among the distributors.[9]

Affirmed.

NOTES

1. *Plus factors (not found):* In re Baby Food Antitrust Litigation, 166 F.3d 112 (3d Cir. 1999). In this case, plaintiffs were direct purchasers of baby food from the defendant manufacturers, including such well-known firms as Gerber, Heinz, and Beech–Nut. They claimed that the defendants were conspiring to create and maintain high prices for baby food in the United States. The district court granted summary judgment for the defendants, and the Court of Appeals for the Third Circuit affirmed. After it found no direct evidence of agreement, it discussed conscious parallelism and oligopoly pricing, with the following comments:

> Because the evidence of conscious parallelism is circumstantial in nature, courts are concerned that they do not punish unilateral, independent conduct of competitors. They therefore require that evidence of a defendant's parallel pricing be supplemented with "plus factors." The simple term "plus factors" refers to "the additional facts or factors required to be proved as a prerequisite to finding that parallel action amounts to a conspiracy." They are necessary conditions for the conspiracy inference.... The plus factors may include, and often do, evidence demonstrating that the defendants: (1) acted contrary to their economic interests, and (2) were motivated to enter into a price fixing conspiracy.

166 F.3d at 122. The court found that evidence showing (1) a pattern of parallel price increases during the certified time period, (2) documentary and testimonial evidence indicating that each company was deliberately matching the other's prices or pegging its prices to another competitor's level, (3) certain reciprocal exchanges of price information, and (4) evidence showing parallel list and transaction pricing, was insufficient to allow the agreement issue to reach the jury.

2. *Plus factors (found):* C–O–Two Fire Equipment Co. v. United States, 197 F.2d 489, 497 (9th Cir. 1952), *cert. denied*, 344 U.S. 892 (1952). In this case, the defendant-appellants were found guilty of violating Section 1 for anticompetitive behavior relating to the sale of portable carbon dioxide fire extinguishers in Southern California. Affirming the conviction, the Ninth Circuit highlighted several considerations in addition to parallel pricing to support its decision:

> Here, however, we have in addition to price uniformity, the other so-called plus factors hereinbefore treated. They include a background of illegal licensing agreements containing minimum price maintenance provisions, an artificial standardization of product, a raising of prices at a time when a surplus existed in the industry, and a policing of dealers to effectuate the maintenance of minimum price provisions in accordance with price lists

---

9. Ed. Frankfurter, J., did not participate. The dissenting opinion of Roberts, J., in which McReynolds and Butler, JJ., joined, is omitted.

published and distributed by the corporate defendants, including appellant, C–O–Two. Other factors which convinced the trial court, beyond a reasonable doubt, that the conspiracy did in fact exist, as charged, were the use of a delivered price system which resulted in price identity to the customer for the products sold, regardless of where they were manufactured, and the submitting of identical bids to public agencies. We think that the facts are not only consistent with the guilt of appellants, but also inconsistent with any other reasonable hypothesis.

3. *Susceptible to oligopolistic collusion.* Bailey v. Allgas, Inc., 284 F.3d 1237 (11th Cir. 2002), involved the Robinson–Patman Act, 15 U.S.C. § 13(a), but in the course of evaluating that claim, the court found it necessary to consider whether the seller had market power. This led it to discuss both the possibility of monopoly power and the possibility of an oligopoly. In the latter context, it remarked that "[t]he most reliable method of proving an oligopoly may be through extensive analysis of the historical price and output data for all the competitors within a relevant market. By examining such data, and even comparing data with similar retailers operating in non-oligopolistic markets, it may be possible to discern whether there is an interdependence in price and output between leading retailers in the market."

4. *To agree, or not to agree, that is the question.* In Esco Corp. v. United States, 340 F.2d 1000, 1007 (9th Cir. 1965), the court of appeals discussed the following hypothetical in an effort to illustrate the difficulties of this area:

> Let us suppose five competitors meet on several occasions, discuss their problems, and one finally states "I won't fix prices with any of you, but here is what I am going to do—put the price of my gidget at X dollars; now you all do what you want." He then leaves the meeting. Competitor number two says "I don't care whether number one does what he says he's going to do or not; nor do I care what the rest of you do, but I am going to price my gidget at X dollars." Number three makes a similar statement— "My price is X dollars." Number four says not one word. All leave and fix "their" prices at "X" dollars.

> We do not say the foregoing illustration compels an inference in this case that the competitors' conduct constituted a price-fixing conspiracy, including an agreement to so conspire, but neither can we say, as a matter of law, that an inference of no agreement is compelled. As in so many other instances, it remains a question for the trier of fact to consider and determine what inference appeals to it (the jury) as most logical and persuasive, after it has heard all the evidence as to what these competitors had done before such meeting, and what actions they took thereafter, or what actions they did not take.

Theatre Enterprises v. Paramount Film Distributing Corp.

Supreme Court of the United States, 1954.
346 U.S. 537, 74 S.Ct. 257, 98 L.Ed. 273.

■ CLARK, J. Petitioner brought this suit for treble damages and an injunction under §§ 4 and 16 of the Clayton Act, alleging that respondent motion picture producers and distributors had violated the antitrust laws by conspiring to restrict "first-run"[10] pictures to downtown Baltimore theatres, thus confining its suburban theatre to subsequent runs and unreasonable "clearances."[11] After hearing the evidence a jury returned a general verdict for respondents. The Court of Appeals for the Fourth Circuit affirmed the judgment based on the verdict. We granted certiorari.

Petitioner now urges, as it did in the Court of Appeals, that the trial judge should have directed a verdict in its favor and submitted to the jury only the question of the amount of damages. . . .

The opinion of the Court of Appeals contains a complete summary of the evidence presented to the jury. We need not recite that evidence again. It is sufficient to note that petitioner owns and operates the Crest Theatre, located in a neighborhood shopping district some six miles from the downtown shopping center in Baltimore, Maryland. The Crest, possessing the most modern improvements and appointments, opened on February 26, 1949. Before and after the opening, petitioner, through its president, repeatedly sought to obtain first-run features for the theatre. Petitioner approached each respondent separately, initially requesting exclusive first-runs, later asking for first-runs on a "day and date" basis.[12] But respondents uniformly rebuffed petitioner's efforts and adhered to an established policy of restricting first-runs in Baltimore to the eight downtown theatres. Admittedly there is no direct evidence of illegal agreement between the respondents and no conspiracy is charged as to the independent exhibitors in Baltimore, who account for 63% of first-run exhibitions. The various respondents advanced much the same reasons for denying petitioner's offers. Among other reasons they asserted that day and date first-runs are normally granted only to noncompeting theatres. Since the Crest is in "substantial competition" with the downtown theatres, a day and date arrangement would be economically unfeasible. And even if respondents wished to grant petitioner such a license, no downtown exhibitor would waive his clearance rights over the Crest and agree to a simultaneous showing. As a result, if petitioner were to receive first-runs, the license would have to be an exclusive one. However, an exclusive license would be economically unsound because the Crest is a suburban theatre, located in a small shopping center, and served by limited public transportation facilities; and, with a drawing area of less than one-tenth that of a downtown theatre, it cannot compare with those easily accessible theatres in the power to draw patrons. Hence the downtown theatres offer far greater opportunities for the widespread advertisement and exploitation of newly released features, which is thought necessary to maximize the overall

---

10. "Runs are successive exhibitions of a feature in a given area, first-run being the first exhibition in that area, second-run being the next subsequent, and so on. . . ." United States v. Paramount Pictures, Inc., 1948, 334 U.S. 131, 144–145, note 6.

11. "A clearance is the period of time, usually stipulated in license contracts, which must elapse between runs of the same feature within a particular area or in specified theatres." United States v. Paramount Pictures, Inc., 1948, 334 U.S. 131, 144, note 6.

12. A first-run "day-and-date" means that two theatres exhibit a first-run at the same time. Had petitioner's request for a day and date first-run been granted, the Crest and a downtown theatre would have exhibited the same features simultaneously.

return from subsequent runs as well as first-runs. The respondents, in the light of these conditions, attacked the guaranteed offers of petitioner, one of which occurred during the trial, as not being made in good faith. Respondents Loew's and Warner refused petitioner an exclusive license because they owned the three downtown theatres receiving their first-run product.

The crucial question is whether respondents' conduct toward petitioner stemmed from independent decision or from an agreement, tacit or express. To be sure, business behavior is admissible circumstantial evidence from which the fact finder may infer agreement. But this Court has never held that proof of parallel business behavior conclusively establishes agreement or, phrased differently, that such behavior itself constitutes a Sherman Act offense. Circumstantial evidence of consciously parallel behavior may have made heavy inroads into the traditional judicial attitude toward conspiracy; but "conscious parallelism" has not yet read conspiracy out of the Sherman Act entirely. Realizing this, petitioner attempts to bolster its argument for a directed verdict by urging that the conscious unanimity of action by respondents should be "measured against the background and findings in the Paramount case." In other words, since the same respondents had conspired in the Paramount case to impose a uniform system of runs and clearances without adequate explanation to sustain them as reasonable restraints of trade, use of the same device in the present case should be legally equated to conspiracy. But the Paramount decrees, even if admissible, were only prima facie evidence of a conspiracy covering the area and existing during the period there involved. Alone or in conjunction with the other proof of the petitioner, they would form no basis for a directed verdict. Here each of the respondents had denied the existence of any collaboration and in addition had introduced evidence of the local conditions surrounding the Crest operation which, they contended, precluded it from being a successful first-run house. They also attacked the good faith of the guaranteed offers of the petitioner for first-run pictures and attributed uniform action to individual business judgment motivated by the desire for maximum revenue. This evidence, together with other testimony of an explanatory nature, raised fact issues requiring the trial judge to submit the issue of conspiracy to the jury. . . .

Affirmed.[13]

NOTES AND QUESTIONS

1. *Oligopoly litigation under the antitrust laws.* Consider the interrelation between the oligopoly theory set forth in Section 1, *supra*, and the quality and quantum of evidence of conspiracy that one would expect to find in a case involving

---

13. Ed. Douglas, J., did not participate in the decision. Black, J., dissented in a memorandum stating that the charge to the jury as to the burden of proof resting on plaintiff (which is omitted here) deprived it of a large part of the benefits intended to be afforded by the prima facie evidence provision of § 5 of the Clayton Act.

a concentrated industry. What structural characteristics of a market are of any legal importance in an oligopoly case? Would conspirators in a concentrated or an unconcentrated industry be more likely to leave a well-marked trail? Should courts be more willing to sustain a jury's finding of conspiracy on limited evidence in a case involving a concentrated industry?

In Brooke Group v. Brown & Williamson Tobacco, 509 U.S. 209 (1993), *infra* Chapter 8, page 823, the Supreme Court had the occasion to comment on oligopolistic behavior. There, in the context of considering a claim that the respondent had engaged in predatory pricing, the Court said that "[e]ven in an oligopolistic market, when a firm drops its prices to a competitive level to demonstrate to a maverick the unprofitability of straying from the group, it would be illogical to condemn the price cut: The antitrust laws then would be an obstacle to the chain of events most conducive to a breakdown of oligopoly pricing and the onset of competition." Does this imply that the Court believes that oligopoly pricing issues are simply beyond the reach—and should be beyond the reach—of the antitrust laws?

2. *Parallel conduct and plus factors.* The Supreme Court's conclusion in *Theatre Enterprises* that "parallel business behavior" did not "conclusively" establish an agreement—*i.e.*, a contract, combination, or conspiracy under Section 1 of the Sherman Act—was unexceptional. This proposition was relatively well settled in the lower courts prior to *Theatre Enterprises* and has been uniformly acknowledged since 1954.[14]

A far more difficult issue was posed for the lower courts by the following question: Assuming uniformity of action, without any "plus" factor, is a court warranted in submitting the question of conspiracy to the jury? In general, the lower courts have concluded that consciously parallel business behavior cannot support a submission to the jury (or a conspiracy finding) unless the conduct is inconsistent with independent, non-concerted action. See InterVest, Inc. v. Bloomberg, L.P., 340 F.3d 144 (3d Cir. 2003) (summary judgment for defendant upheld where plaintiff financial services provider produced no evidence that defendant did *not* act independently with respect to alleged conspiracy with bond market broker-dealers to terminate contract with Bloomberg). See generally Bell Atlantic Corp. v. Twombly, 550 U.S. 544 (2007) (discussing standards for granting motion to dismiss antitrust conspiracy claims for failure to state a claim); Matsushita Elec. Indus. Co., Ltd. v. Zenith Radio Corp., 475 U.S. 574, 588 (1986) (discussing summary judgment standards in context of antitrust conspiracy allegations).

Of course, traditional evidence of conspiratorial activity—*e.g.*, clandestine meetings, secret exchanges of information—when combined with consciously parallel business conduct, will support a jury's finding of conspiracy. United States v. Andreas, 216 F.3d 645 (7th Cir. 2000), for example, involved an appeal from a criminal conviction for a conspiracy among top producers of lysine to fix the global price and allocate sales. Throughout the early 1990s, executives from American and foreign firms met to fix prices and allocate sales volume among themselves. In order to avoid liability for their actions, they created aliases and front organizations to hide their activities, hired prostitutes to gather information from competitors, lied, cheated, embezzled, extorted and obstructed justice.

3. *Acting against self-interest.* The most difficult cases after *Theatre Enterprises* have involved situations in which traditional conspiratorial conduct was not

---

14. *See, e.g.*, Bogosian v. Gulf Oil Corp., 561 F.2d 434 (3d Cir. 1977), *cert. denied*, 434 U.S. 1086 (1978); Modern Home Institute, Inc. v. Hartford Accident & Indemnity Co., 513 F.2d 102 (2d Cir. 1975).

shown, but defendants' "consciously parallel" conduct appeared to be inconsistent with each defendant's economic self-interest.

In Bogosian v. Gulf Oil Corp., 561 F.2d 434, 440, 445–46 (3d Cir. 1977), *cert. denied*, 434 U.S. 1086 (1978), operators of service stations brought antitrust class actions against major oil companies, alleging unlawful concerted action to tie the leasing of gas station sites to the purchase of gasoline supplied by each operator's lessor. Each defendant was alleged to have required its station lessees, through "a course of interdependent consciously parallel action" with other defendants, to handle its brand of gasoline exclusively. The district court granted motions for summary judgment made by all defendants with no business dealings with the named plaintiffs because "the allegation of 'interdependent consciously parallel action' in a complaint is an insufficient statement of the concerted action necessary to state a claim under § 1."

In a 2–1 decision, the Third Circuit reversed. The court first observed that plaintiffs' complaint alleged "an unlawful combination" and we "perceive no distinction between the terms combination and conspiracy.... Our reading of § 1 cases indicates that the two terms are used interchangeably."[15] The court then said:

> The law is settled that proof of consciously parallel business behavior is circumstantial evidence from which an agreement, tacit or express, can be inferred but that such evidence, without more, is insufficient unless the circumstances under which it occurred make the inference of rational, independent choice less attractive than that of concerted action.... We recently articulated those circumstances in Venzie Corp. v. United States Mineral Products Co., 521 F.2d 1309 (3d Cir. 1975);
>
> "(1) a showing of acts by defendants in contradiction of their own economic interests ..., and
>
> "(2) satisfactory demonstration of a motivation to enter an agreement ..."
>
> Plaintiffs argue that, given an opportunity to conduct discovery, they will prove that both of these circumstances are present. They contend that independent self-interest would indicate that each oil company seeks to market gasoline to their competitors' lessees, and that the failure to so compete can be explained only by a mutual understanding, tacit or expressed, that gasoline be marketed to lessee-dealers on an exclusive basis. The motivation to participate in such an agreement, of course, is the elimination of price competition among oil companies at the wholesale level.... We conclude that the ruling that the specific allegation of interdependent consciously parallel action made here fails to state a claim should be vacated....

Some years later, in Petruzzi's IGA Supermarkets, Inc. v. Darling–Delaware Company, Inc., 998 F.2d 1224 (3d Cir. 1993), the Third Circuit revisited this issue. In that case, a supermarket brought an action against fat and bone rendering companies for restraint of trade in violation of the Sherman Act. The defendants were alleged to have conspired to allocate existing accounts in parts of the Northeast. The court said:

> "To establish a conspiracy based on consciously parallel behavior, a plaintiff must show:
>
> that the defendants' behavior was parallel;

---

15. Ed. Compare the Supreme Court's analysis of "combination" and "conspiracy" *infra* at pp. 686–87.

that the defendants were conscious of each other's conduct and that this awareness was an element in their decision-making processes; and

certain "plus" factors . . .

. . . However, even without this evidence [the plus factors] purporting to show a traditional agreement, we have stated that a plaintiff can survive summary judgment if it shows that the defendants had a motive to conspire and acted contrary to their self-interest."

Under the Third Circuit's approach, if defendants' conduct is parallel, conscious, and interdependent, should a case go to the jury? Can a defendant's decision be "unilateral" and "interdependent" at the same time? What does the Third Circuit's focus on "motivation" and economic self-interest add to the "interdependence" analysis? Should a defendant's "motive" to profit from consciously parallel and interdependent activity provide a sufficient plus factor to permit a plaintiff to get to a jury? What does the Third Circuit mean by "contradiction of their own economic interests"? It is difficult to understand why a company would join in a decision against its economic interests. Furthermore, as we have already noted, it is in the oligopolist's independent interest to go along with pricing decisions its competitors have made. Do these words, as used by the Third Circuit, merely mean that a company should ignore the likely decisions of its competitors? Would ignoring the likely decisions of competitors (*e.g.*, refraining from marketing gasoline to their competitors' lessees or adopting a practice resulting in high entry barriers and high profits) truly be in furtherance of a company's "own economic interests"?

Toys "R" Us, Inc. v. F.T.C.

United States Court of Appeals, Seventh Circuit, 2000.
221 F.3d 928.

■ WOOD, CIRCUIT JUDGE. The antitrust laws, which aim to preserve and protect competition in economically sensible markets, have long drawn a sharp distinction between contractual restrictions that occur up and down a distribution chain—so-called vertical restraints—and restrictions that come about as a result of agreements among competitors, or horizontal restraints. Sometimes, however, it can be hard as a matter of fact to be sure what kind of agreement is at issue. This was the problem facing the Federal Trade Commission ("the Commission") when it brought under its antitrust microscope the large toy retailer Toys "R" Us ["TRU"]. . . .

The Commission concluded, upon an extensive administrative record, that TRU had acted as the coordinator of a horizontal agreement among a number of toy manufacturers. The agreements took the form of a network of vertical agreements between TRU and the individual manufacturers, in each of which the manufacturer promised to restrict the distribution of its products to low-priced warehouse club stores, on the condition that other manufacturers would do the same. This practice, the Commission found, violated § 5 of the Federal Trade Commission Act, 15 U.S.C. § 45. It also found that TRU had entered into a series of vertical agreements that flunked scrutiny under antitrust's rule of reason. TRU appealed that decision to us. It attacks both the sufficiency of the evidence supporting the Commission's conclusions and the scope of the Commission's remedial order. It is hard to prevail on either type of challenge: the former is fact-intensive and faces the hurdle of the substantial evidence standard of review, while the latter calls into question the Commission's exercise of its discretion to remedy an established violation of the law. We conclude that, while reasonable people could differ on the facts in this voluminous record, the Commission's decisions pass muster, and we therefore affirm.

I

TRU is a giant in the toy retailing industry. The Commission found that it sells approximately 20% of all the toys sold in the United States, and that in some metropolitan areas its share of toy sales ranges between 35% and 49%. The variety of toys it sells is staggering: over the course of a year, it offers about 11,000 individual toy items, far more than any of its competitors. As one might suspect from these figures alone, TRU is a critical outlet for toy manufacturers. It buys about 30% of the large, traditional toy companies' total output and it is usually their most important customer. According to evidence before the Commission's administrative law judge, or ALJ, even a company as large as Hasbro felt that it could not find other retailers to replace TRU—and Hasbro, along with Mattel, is one of the two largest toy manufacturers in the country, accounting for approximately 12% of the market for traditional toys and 10% of a market that includes video games. Similar opinions were offered by Mattel and smaller manufacturers.

Toys are sold in a number of different kinds of stores. At the high end are traditional toy stores and department stores, both of which typically sell toys for 40 to 50% above their cost. Next are the specialized discount stores—a category virtually monopolized by TRU today—that sell at an average 30% mark-up. General discounters like Wal–Mart, K–Mart, and Target are next, with a 22% mark-up, and last are the stores that are the focus of this case, the warehouse clubs like Costco and Pace. The clubs sell toys at a slender mark-up of 9% or so.

The toys customers seek in all these stores are highly differentiated products. The little girl who wants Malibu Barbie is not likely to be satisfied with My First Barbie, and she certainly does not want Ken or Skipper. The boy who has his heart set on a figure of Anakin Skywalker will be disappointed if he receives Jar–Jar Binks, or a truck, or a baseball bat instead. Toy retailers naturally want to have available for their customers the season's hottest items, because toys are also a very faddish product, as those old enough to recall the mania over Cabbage Patch Kids or Tickle Me Elmo dolls will attest.

What happened in this case, according to the Commission, was fairly simple. For a long time, TRU had enjoyed a strong position at the low price end for toy sales, because its only competition came from traditional toy stores who could not or did not wish to meet its prices, or from general discounters like Wal–Mart or K–Mart, which could not offer anything like the variety of items TRU had and whose prices were not too far off TRU's mark.

The advent of the warehouse clubs changed all that. They were a retail innovation of the late 1970s: the first one opened in 1976, and by 1992 there were some 600 individual club stores around the country. Rather than earning all of their money from their mark-up on products, the clubs sell only to their members, and they charge a modest annual membership fee, often about $30. As the word "warehouse" in the name suggests, the clubs emphasize price competition over service amenities. Nevertheless, the Commission found that the clubs seek to offer name-brand merchandise, including toys. During the late 1980s and early 1990s, warehouse clubs selected and purchased from the toy manufacturers' full array of products, just like everyone else. In some instances they bought specialized packs assembled for the "club" trade, but they normally preferred stocking conventional products so that their customers could readily compare the price of an item at the club against the price of the same item at a competing store.

To the extent this strategy was successful, however, TRU did not welcome it. By 1989, its senior executives were concerned that the clubs were a threat to TRU's low-price image and, more importantly, to its profits. A little legwork revealed that as of that year the clubs carried approximately 120–240 items in direct competition with TRU, priced as much as 25 to 30% below TRU's own price levels.

TRU put its President of Merchandising, a Mr. Goddu, to work to see what could be done. The response Goddu and other TRU executives formulated to beat back the challenge from the clubs began with TRU's decision to contact some of its suppliers, including toy manufacturing heavyweights Mattel, Hasbro, and Fisher Price. At the Toy Fair in 1992 (a major event at which the next Christmas season's orders are placed), Goddu informed the manufacturers of a new TRU policy, which was reflected in a memo of January 29, 1992. The policy set forth the following conditions and privileges for TRU:

- The clubs could have no new or promoted product unless they carried the entire line.
- All specials and exclusives to be sold to the clubs had to be shown first to TRU to see if TRU wanted the item.
- Old and basic product had to be in special packs.
- Clearance and closeout items were permissible provided that TRU was given the first opportunity to buy the product.
- There would be no discussion about prices.

TRU was careful to meet individually with each of its suppliers to explain its new policy. Afterwards, it then asked each one what it intended to do. Negotiations between TRU and the manufacturers followed, as a result of which each manufacturer eventually agreed that it would sell to the clubs only highly-differentiated products (either unique individual items or combo packs) that were not offered to anything but a club (and thus of course not to TRU). As the Commission put it, "through its announced policy and the related agreements discussed below, TRU sought to eliminate the competitive threat the clubs posed by denying them merchandise, forcing the clubs' customers to buy products they did not want, and frustrating customers' ability to make direct price comparisons of club prices and TRU prices."

The agreements between TRU and the various manufacturers were, of course, vertical agreements, because they ran individually from the supplier/manufacturer to the purchaser/retailer. The Commission found that TRU reached about 10 of these agreements. After the agreements were concluded, TRU then supervised and enforced each toy company's compliance with its commitment.

But TRU was not content to stop with vertical agreements. Instead, the Commission found, it decided to go further. It worked for over a year and a half to put the vertical agreements in place, but "the biggest hindrance TRU had to overcome was the major toy companies' reluctance to give up a new, fast-growing, and profitable channel of distribution." The manufacturers were also concerned that any of their rivals who broke ranks and sold to the clubs might gain sales at their expense, given the widespread and increasing popularity of the club format. To address this problem, the Commission found, TRU orchestrated a horizontal agreement among its key suppliers to boycott the clubs. The evidence on which the Commission relied showed that, at a minimum, Mattel, Hasbro, Fisher Price, Tyco, Little Tikes, Today's Kids, and Tiger Electronics agreed to join in the boycott "on the condition that their competitors would do the same."

The Commission first noted that internal documents from the manufacturers revealed that they were trying to expand, not to restrict, the number of their major retail outlets and to reduce their dependence on TRU. They were specifically interested in cultivating a relationship with the warehouse clubs and increasing sales there. Thus, the sudden adoption of measures under which they decreased sales to the clubs ran against their independent economic self-interest. Second, the Commission cited evidence that the manufacturers were unwilling to limit sales to the clubs without assurances that their competitors would do likewise. Goddu himself testified that TRU communicated the message "I'll stop if they stop" from manufacturer to competing manufacturer. He specifically mentioned having such conversations with Mattel and Hasbro, and he said more generally "We communicated to our vendors that we were communicating with all our key suppliers, and we did that I believe at Toy Fair 1992. We made a point to tell each of the vendors that we spoke to that we would be talking to our other key suppliers."

Evidence from the manufacturers corroborated Goddu's account. A Mattel executive said that it would not sell the clubs the same items it was selling to TRU, and that this decision was "based on the fact that competition would do the same." A Hasbro executive said much the same thing: "because our competitors had agreed not to sell loaded [that is, promoted] product to the clubs, that we would ... go along with this."

TRU went so far as to assure individual manufacturers that no one would be singled out.

Once the special warehouse club policy (or, in the Commission's more pejorative language, boycott) was underway, TRU served as the central clearinghouse for complaints about breaches in the agreement. The Commission gave numerous examples of this conduct in its opinion.

Last, the Commission found that TRU's policies had bite. In the year before the boycott began, the clubs' share of all toy sales in the United States grew from 1.5% in 1991 to 1.9% in 1992. After the boycott took hold, that percentage slipped back by 1995 to 1.4%. Local numbers were more impressive. Costco, for example, experienced overall growth on sales of all products during the period 1991 to 1993 of 25%. Its toy sales increased during [the] same period by 51%. But, after the boycott took hold in 1993, its toy sales decreased by 1.6% even while its overall sales were still growing by 19.5%. The evidence indicated that this was because TRU had succeeded in cutting off its access to the popular toys it needed. In 1989, over 90% of the Mattel toys Costco and other clubs purchased were regular (*i.e.* easily comparable) items, but by 1993 that percentage was zero. Once again, the Commission's opinion is chock full of similar statistics.

The Commission also considered the question whether TRU might have been trying to protect itself against free riding, at least with respect to its vertical agreements. It acknowledged that TRU provided several services that might be important to consumers, including "advertising, carrying an inventory of goods early in the year, and supporting a full line of products." Nevertheless, it found that the manufacturers compensated TRU directly for advertising toys, storing toys made early in the year, and stocking a broad line of each manufacturer's toys under one roof. A 1993 TRU memorandum confirms that advertising is manufacturer-funded and is "essentially free." In 1994, TRU's net cost of advertising was a tiny 0.02% of sales, or $750,000, out of a total of $199 million it spent on advertising that year. As the Commission saw it, "advertising . . . was a service the toy manufacturers provided for TRU and not the other way around." TRU records also showed that manufacturers routinely paid TRU credits for warehousing services, and that they compensated it for full line stocking. In short, the Commission found, there was no evidence that club competition without comparable services threatened to drive TRU services out of the market or to harm customers. Manufacturers paid each retailer directly for the services they wanted the retailer to furnish.

Based on this record, the Commission drew three central conclusions of law: (1) the TRU-led manufacturer boycott of the warehouse clubs was illegal *per se* under the rule enunciated in Northwest Wholesale Stationers, Inc. v. Pacific Stationery & Printing Co., 472 U.S. 284 (1985); (2) the boycott was illegal under a full rule of reason analysis because its anticompetitive effects "clearly outweighed any possible business justification"; and (3) the vertical agreements between TRU and the individual toy manufacturers, "entered into seriatim with clear anticompetitive effect, violate section 1 of the Sherman Act." These antitrust violations in turn were enough to prove a violation of FTC Act § 5, which for present purposes tracks the prohibitions of the Sherman and Clayton Acts. . . .

II

On appeal, TRU makes four principal arguments: (1) the Commission's finding of a horizontal conspiracy is contrary to the facts and impermissibly confuses the law of vertical restraints with the law of horizontal restraints; (2) whether the restrictions were vertical or horizontal, they were not unlawful because TRU has no market power, and thus the conduct can have no significant anticompetitive effect; (3) the TRU policy was a legitimate response to free riding; and (4) the relief ordered by the Commission goes too far. We review the Commission's legal conclusions *de novo*, but we must accept its findings of fact if they are supported by such relevant evidence as a reasonable mind might accept as adequate to support a conclusion. FTC v. Indiana Fed'n of Dentists, 476 U.S. 447, 454 (1986).

A.   Horizontal Conspiracy

As TRU correctly points out, the critical question here is whether substantial evidence supported the Commission's finding that there was a horizontal agreement among the toy manufacturers, with TRU in the center as the ringmaster, to boycott the warehouse clubs. It acknowledges that such an agreement may be proved by either direct or circumstantial evidence, under cases such as Matsushita Electric Indus. Co. v. Zenith Radio Corp., 475 U.S. 574 (1986) (horizontal agreements), Monsanto Co. v. Spray–Rite Service Corp., 465 U.S. 752 (1984) (vertical agreements), and Interstate Circuit, Inc. v. United States, 306 U.S. 208 (1939). When circumstantial evidence is used, there must be some evidence that "tends to exclude the possibility" that the alleged conspirators acted independently. *Monsanto*, 465 U.S. at 764, quoted in *Matsushita*, 475 U.S. at 588. This does not mean, however, that the Commission had to exclude all possibility that the manufacturers acted independently. As we pointed out in In re Brand Name Prescription Drugs Antitrust Litigation, 186 F.3d 781 (7th Cir. 1999), that would amount to an absurd and legally unfounded burden to prove with 100% certainty that an antitrust violation occurred. *Id.* at 787. The test states only that there must be some evidence which, if believed, would support a finding of concerted behavior. In the context of an appeal from the Commission, the question is whether substantial evidence supports its conclusion that it is more likely than not that the manufacturers acted collusively.

In TRU's opinion, this record shows nothing more than a series of separate, similar vertical agreements between itself and various toy manufacturers. It believes that each manufacturer in its independent self-interest had an incentive to limit sales to the clubs, because TRU's policy provided strong unilateral incentives for the manufacturer to reduce its sales to the clubs. Why gain a few sales at the clubs, it asks, when it would have much more to gain by maintaining a good relationship with the 100–pound gorilla of the industry, TRU, and make far more sales?

We do not disagree that there was some evidence in the record that would bear TRU's interpretation. But that is not the standard we apply when we review decisions of the Federal Trade Commission. Instead, we apply the substantial evidence test, which we described as follows in another case in which the Commission's decision to stop a hospital merger was at issue:

> Our only function is to determine whether the Commission's analysis of the probable effects of these acquisitions on hospital competition in Chattanooga is so implausible, so feebly supported by the record, that it flunks even the deferential test of substantial evidence.

Hospital Corp. of America v. F.T.C., 807 F.2d 1381, 1385 (7th Cir. 1986). There, as here, the Commission painstakingly explained in a long opinion exactly what evidence in the record supported its conclusion. We need only decide whether the inference the Commission drew of horizontal agreement was a permissible one from that evidence, not if it was the only possible one.

The Commission's theory, stripped to its essentials, is that this case is a modern equivalent of the old Interstate Circuit decision. That case too involved actors at two levels of the distribution chain, distributors of motion pictures and exhibitors. Interstate Circuit was one of the exhibitors; it had a stranglehold on the exhibition of movies in a number of Texas cities. The antitrust violation occurred when Interstate's manager, O'Donnell, sent an identical letter to the eight branch managers of the distributor companies, with each letter naming all eight as addressees, in which he asked them to comply with two demands: a minimum price for first-run theaters, and a policy against double features at night. The trial court there drew an inference of agreement from the nature of the proposals, from the manner in which they were made, from the substantial unanimity of action taken, and from the lack of evidence of a benign motive; the Supreme Court affirmed. The new policies represented a radical shift from the industry's prior business practices, and the Court rejected as beyond the range of probability that such unanimity of action was explainable only by chance.

The Commission is right. Indeed, as it argues in its brief, the TRU case if anything presents a more compelling case for inferring horizontal agreement than did *Interstate Circuit*, because not only was the manufacturers' decision to stop dealing with the warehouse clubs an abrupt shift from the past, and not only is it suspicious for a manufacturer to deprive itself of a profitable sales outlet, but the record here included the direct evidence of communications that was missing in *Interstate Circuit*. Just as in *Interstate Circuit*, TRU tries to avoid this result by hypothesizing independent motives. 306 U.S. at 223–24. If there were no evidence in the record tending to support concerted behavior, then we agree that *Matsushita* would require a ruling in TRU's favor. But there is. The evidence showed that the companies wanted to diversify from TRU, not to become more dependent upon it; it showed that each manufacturer was afraid to curb its sales to the warehouse clubs alone, because it was afraid its rivals would cheat and gain a special advantage in that popular new market niche. The Commission was not required to disbelieve the testimony of the different toy company executives and TRU itself to the effect that the only condition on which each toy manufacturer would agree to TRU's demands was if it could be sure its competitors were doing the same thing.

That is a horizontal agreement. As we explain further below in discussing TRU's free rider argument, it has nothing to do with enhancing efficiencies of distribution from the manufacturer's point of view. The typical story of a legitimate vertical transaction would have the manufacturer going to TRU and asking it to be the exclusive carrier of the manufacturer's goods; in exchange for that exclusivity, the manufacturer would hope to receive more effective promotion of its goods, and TRU would have a large enough profit margin to do the job well. But not all manufacturers think that exclusive dealing arrangements will maximize their profits. Some think, and are entitled to think, that using the greatest number of retailers possible is a better strategy. These manufacturers were in effect being asked by TRU to reduce their output (especially of the popular toys), and as is classically true in such cartels, they were willing to do so only if TRU could protect them against cheaters.

Northwest Stationers also demonstrates why the facts the Commission found support its conclusion that the essence of the agreement network TRU supervised was horizontal. There the Court described the cases that had condemned boycotts as "per se" illegal as those involving "joint efforts by a firm or firms to disadvantage competitors by either directly denying or persuading or coercing suppliers or customers to deny relationships the competitors need in the competitive struggle." 472 U.S. at 294 (internal citations omitted). The boycotters had to have some market power, though the Court did not suggest that the level had to be as high as it would require in a case under Sherman Act § 2. Here, TRU was trying to disadvantage the warehouse clubs, its competitors, by coercing suppliers to deny the clubs the products they needed. It accomplished this goal by inducing the suppliers to collude, rather than to compete independently for shelf space in the different toy retail stores. See also NYNEX Corp. v. Discon, Inc., 525 U.S. 128 (1998); Klor's, Inc. v. Broadway–Hale Stores, Inc., 359 U.S. 207 (1959).

B.   Degree of TRU's Market Power

TRU's efforts to deflate the Commission's finding of market power are pertinent only if we had agreed with its argument that the Commission's finding of a horizontal agreement was without support. Horizontal agreements among competitors, including group boycotts, remain illegal *per se* in the sense the Court used the term in *Northwest Stationers*. We have found that this case satisfies the criteria the Court used in *Northwest Stationers* for condemnation without an extensive inquiry into market power and economic pros and cons: (1) the boycotting firm has cut off access to a supply, facility or market necessary for the boycotted firm (*i.e.* the clubs) to compete; (2) the boycotting firm possesses a "dominant" position in the market (where "dominant" is an undefined term, but plainly chosen to stand for something different from antitrust's term of art "monopoly"); and (3) the boycott, as we explain further below, cannot be justified by plausible arguments that it was designed to enhance overall efficiency. 472 U.S. at 294. We address the market power point here, therefore, only in the alternative.

TRU seems to think that anticompetitive effects in a market cannot be shown unless the plaintiff, or here the Commission, first proves that it has a large market share. This, however, has things backwards. As we have explained elsewhere, the share a firm has in a properly defined relevant market is only a way of estimating market power, which is the ultimate consideration. Ball Memorial Hospital, Inc. v. Mutual Hospital Insurance, 784 F.2d 1325, 1336 (7th Cir. 1986). The Supreme Court has made it clear that there are two ways of proving market power. One is through direct evidence of anticompetitive effects. See FTC v. Indiana Fed'n of Dentists, 476 U.S. 447, 460–61 (1986) ("the finding of actual, sustained adverse effects on competition in those areas where IFD dentists predominated, viewed in light of the reality that markets for dental services tend to be relatively localized, is legally sufficient to support a finding that the challenged restraint was unreasonable even in the absence of elaborate market analysis."). The other, more conventional way, is by proving relevant product and geographic markets and by showing that the defendant's share exceeds whatever threshold is important for the practice in the case. See, *e.g.,* United States v. E.I. du Pont de Nemours & Co., 351 U.S. 377 (1956); United States v. Grinnell Corp., 384 U.S. 563 (1966); United States v. Aluminum Co. of America, 148 F.2d 416 (2d Cir. 1945) (suggesting that more than 90% is enough to constitute a monopoly for purposes of Sherman Act § 2 and 33% is not); Jefferson Parish Hospital Dist. No. 2 v. Hyde, 466 U.S. 2 (1984) (indicating that something more than 30% would be needed to show the kind of power over a tying product necessary for a violation of Sherman Act § 1).

The Commission found here that, however TRU's market power as a toy retailer was measured, it was clear that its boycott was having an effect in the market. It was remarkably successful in causing the 10 major toy manufacturers to reduce output of toys to the warehouse clubs, and that reduction in output protected TRU from having to lower its prices to meet the clubs' price levels. Price competition from conventional discounters like Wal–Mart and K–Mart, in contrast, imposed no such constraint on it, or so the Commission found. In addition, the Commission showed that the affected manufacturers accounted for some 40% of the traditional toy market, and that TRU had 20% of the national wholesale market and up to 49% of some local wholesale markets. Taking steps to prevent a price collapse through coordination of action among competitors has been illegal at least since United States v. Socony–Vacuum Oil Co., 310 U.S. 150 (1940). Proof that this is what TRU was doing is sufficient proof of actual anticompetitive effects that no more elaborate market analysis was necessary.

C.   Free Riding Explanation

TRU next urges that its policy was a legitimate business response to combat free riding by the warehouse clubs. We think, however, that it has fundamentally misunderstood the theory of free riding. Briefly, that theory is as follows. The manufacturer of a product, say widgets, has an incentive to distribute as many widgets as it can, while keeping its costs of distribution down as low as possible. In many instances, this means that the manufacturer will want to sell its widgets for a particular wholesale price and it will want its retailer to apply as low a mark-up as possible (*i.e.*, put the product on the market for as little extra expense as possible). Sometimes, however, the manufacturer will want the retailer to provide special services or amenities that cost money, such as attractive premises, trained salespeople, long business hours, full-line stocking, or fast warranty service. But the costs of providing some of those amenities (usually pre-sale services) are hard to pass on to customers unless some form of restricted distribution is available. What the manufacturer does not want is for the shopper to visit the attractive store with highly paid, intelligent sales help, learn all about the product, and then go home and order it from a discount warehouse or (today) on-line discounters. The shopper in that situation has taken a "free ride" on the retailer's efforts; the retailer never gets paid for them, and eventually it stops offering the services. If those services were genuinely useful, in the sense that the product plus service package resulted in greater sales for the manufacturer than the product alone would have enjoyed, there is a loss both for the manufacturer and the consumer. Hence, antitrust law permits nonprice vertical restraints that are designed to facilitate the provision of extra services, recognizing that a manufacturer in a competitive market who has guessed wrong will eventually be forced by the market to abandon the restrictions. See Business Electronics Corp. v. Sharp Electronics Corp., 485 U.S. 717, 724 (1988), quoting Continental T.V., Inc. v. GTE Sylvania Inc., 433 U.S. 36, 52 n. 19 (1977).

Here, the evidence shows that the free-riding story is inverted. The manufacturers wanted a business strategy under which they distributed their toys to as many different kinds of outlets as would accept them: exclusive toy shops, TRU, discount department stores, and warehouse clubs. Rightly or wrongly, this was the distribution strategy that each one believed would maximize its individual output and profits. The manufacturers did not think that the alleged "extra services" TRU might have been providing were necessary. This is crucial, because the most important insight behind the free rider concept is the fact that, with respect to the cost of distribution services, the interests of the manufacturer and the consumer are aligned, and are basically adverse to the interests of the retailer (who would presumably like to charge as much as possible for its part in the process). See Premier Electrical Construction Co. v. Nat'l Electrical Contractors Ass'n, 814 F.2d 358, 369–70 (7th Cir. 1987) ("[the rationale for permitting restricted distribution policies] depends on the alignment of interests between consumers and manufacturers. Destroy that alignment and you destroy the power of the argument.").

What TRU wanted or did not want is neither here nor there for purposes of the free rider argument. Its economic interest was in maximizing its own profits, not in keeping down its suppliers' cost of doing business. Furthermore, we note that the Commission made a plausible argument for the proposition that there was little or no opportunity to "free" ride on anything here in any event. The consumer is not taking a free ride if the cost of the service can be captured in the price of the item. As our earlier review of the facts demonstrated, the manufacturers were paying for the services TRU furnished, such as advertising, full-line product stocking, and extensive inventories. These expenses, we may assume, were folded into the price of the goods the manufacturers charged to TRU, and thus these services were not susceptible to free riding. On this record, in short, TRU cannot prevail on the basis that its practices were designed to combat free riding.

D.   Remedy

Last, we consider TRU's challenge to the remedial provisions the Commission ordered. TRU's basic point here is that the Commission has commanded it to do things that it would have been free to refuse, and conversely to refrain from actions it would have been free to take, in the absence of its violation of FTC Act § 5....

TRU makes a perfunctory, one-paragraph argument that paragraphs II(B), II(C), II(D), and II(E)(1) impose a "gag order" that contravenes the Supreme Court's recognition in Monsanto Co. v. Spray–Rite Corp., *supra*, that manufacturers and distributors have a legitimate need for a free flow of information between them. This order, they claim, will create an irrational dislocation in the market to the detriment of toy suppliers, retailers, and consumers. With respect to paragraph II(E)(2), it argues that the five-year restriction on refusals to deal impermissibly cabins its *Colgate* rights to choose the suppliers with which it wants to deal. In effect, it claims, the decree will force it to purchase all toys that are offered to anyone, unless it can somehow prove that its refusal was because of a safety defect or other similar flaw.

We consider first TRU's challenges to parts II(B) through II(D) of the order. (It has not mentioned II(A) in its brief, and thus it has waived any challenge to that part of the order.) In general, if a retailer had some kind of restricted distribution arrangement with a manufacturer, *Monsanto* holds that it is permissible for the retailer to urge the manufacturer to respect the limits of that agreement. The retailer may communicate complaints about the provision of product to discounters, if that runs afoul of the promises in the distribution agreement. *Colgate* indicates that the retailer would also be within its rights to tell the manufacturer that it will no longer stock the manufacturer's product, if it is unhappy with the company it is keeping (*i.e.*, if the manufacturer is sending too many goods to discounters, stores with a reputation for rude and sloppy service, or other undesirables).

Two facts distinguish these general rules from the situation in which TRU finds itself. First, unilateral actions of the sort protected by *Monsanto* and *Colgate* are not the same thing as a retailer's request to the manufacturer to change the latter's business practice. Under paragraph II(B) of the decree, TRU must not tell the manufacturer what to do; it is still permitted to decide which toys it wants to carry and which ones to drop, based on business considerations such as the expected popularity of the item. Second, to the extent paragraph II(B) might indirectly inhibit TRU from exercising its unilateral judgment, TRU must confront the fact that the FTC is not limited to restating the law in its remedial orders. Such orders can restrict the options for a company that has violated § 5, to ensure that the violation will cease and competition will be restored. See National Lead Co., *supra*, 352 U.S. at 430; FTC v. Cement Institute, 333 U.S. 683, 726–27 (1948); Corning Glass Works v. FTC, 509 F.2d 293, 303 (7th Cir. 1975). See also FTC v. Colgate–Palmolive Co., 380 U.S. 374, 392 (1965) (making the same point, in context of the Commission's deceptive practices authority).

The second point also applies to TRU's objections to paragraphs II(C) and II(D). In addition, we note that the retailer should not have any reason to obtain its suppliers' business records about shipments to the retailer's competitors. That is the supplier's concern. TRU is protected as long as it can ensure that it receives what was promised to it. Also, of course, the decree preserves TRU's right to enter into exclusive arrangements with respect to particular toys. In so doing, it also implicitly allows TRU to engage in communications that are necessary for the implementation and enforcement of such agreements. Paragraph II(D) directly addresses the Commission's finding of a horizontal agreement, and it orders TRU not to go out and create a new one. The Commission was certainly acting within the bounds of its discretion when it included these provisions.

Paragraph II(E) appears to be the one that causes the greatest concern to TRU. This strikes us as a closer call, but in this connection the standard of review becomes important. The Commission has represented in its brief to this court that the decree "leaves [TRU] free to make stocking decisions based on a wide range of business reasons; it must simply make those decisions—for a period of five years—independent of whether clubs or other discounters are carrying the same item." The attempt to use its market clout to harm the warehouse clubs lies at the heart of this case, and so it is easy to see why the Commission chose to prohibit reliance on the supplier's practices vis à vis the clubs as a reason for TRU's own purchasing decisions. At bottom, TRU is really just worried that it will be difficult to prove that any particular purchasing decision was free from the prohibited taint. It will be easy to refrain from announcements or communications about refusals to deal, which is what II(E)(1) prohibits. With respect to II(E)(2), if TRU implements adequate internal procedural safeguards, it should be possible to demonstrate that its buying decisions were not influenced by anything the manufacturers were doing with discounters like the clubs. These refusals to deal were the means TRU used to accomplish the unlawful result, and as such, they are subject to regulation by the Commission. See *National Lead*, 352 U.S. at 425. Under the abuse of discretion standard that governs our review of the Commission's choice of remedy, see Siegel Co. v. FTC, 327 U.S. 608, 612–13 (1946), this does not appear to be a remedy that "has no reasonable relation to the unlawful practices found to exist." We therefore have no warrant to set it aside. If, however, it becomes clear in practice that this provision is unworkable,

TRU is free to return to the Commission to petition for a modification of the order.

III

We conclude that the Commission's decision is supported by substantial evidence on the record, and that its remedial decree falls within the broad discretion it has been granted under the FTC Act.

The decision is hereby AFFIRMED.

NOTE ON BELL ATLANTIC CORP. v. TWOMBLY

The Supreme Court returned to the issue of parallel conduct in Bell Atlantic Corp. v. Twombly, 550 U.S. 544, 127 S.Ct. 1955, 167 L.Ed.2d 929 (2007). That case involved an alleged agreement among the so-called "incumbent local exchange carriers," or ILECs—essentially the local telecommunications companies that emerged after the break-up of the old AT&T firm—to restrain trade in two ways. Plaintiffs were two individuals seeking to represent a putative class consisting of all "subscribers of local telephone and/or high speed internet services ... from February 8, 1996 to present." Defendants were the four remaining ILECs in the market. Plaintiffs first alleged that the ILECs allegedly acted to impair access to their markets by rival firms, called "competitive local exchange carriers" or CLECs, through actions like provision of inferior connections, overcharges, and billing in ways designed to sabotage the CLECs' relations with their own customers. Second, the ILECs allegedly had agreements among themselves to refrain from competing in the markets of other ILECs. The district court dismissed the complaint for failure to state a claim, but the Second Circuit reversed, finding that it could imagine a set of facts that the plaintiff class could prove, consistent with the complaint, that would entitle the class to recover. In an opinion authored by Justice Souter, the Supreme Court reversed the Court of Appeals and reinstated the dismissal, finding that even under the notice pleading regime of Rule 8, an antitrust plaintiff in a Section 1 case must allege enough facts to show what agreement is being attacked and why that agreement (if proven) would be illegal.

Earlier decisions of the Supreme Court had focused on the level of proof necessary at the summary judgment stage (Matsushita Elec. Indus. Co. v. Zenith Radio Corp., 475 U.S. 574 (1986)), the directed verdict stage (Theatre Enterprises v. Paramount Film Distrib. Corp., 346 U.S. 537 (1954)), and the jury instruction stage (Monsanto Co. v. Spray–Rite Service Corp., 465 U.S. 752 (1984). This time, the Court addressed the threshold standard for pleading a complaint that can survive a motion to dismiss for failure to state a claim on which relief can be granted under Fed. R. Civ. P. 12(b)(6). In so doing, it expressed great concern about the potential expense and burden that an antitrust claim can place on a defendant:

> [I]t is one thing to be cautious before dismissing an antitrust complaint in advance of discovery, ... but quite another to forget that proceeding to antitrust discovery can be expensive. As we indicated over 20 years ago ... "a district court must retain the power to insist upon some specificity in pleading before allowing a potentially massive factual controversy to proceed." ... That potential expense is obvious enough in the present case: plaintiffs represent a putative class of at least 90 percent of all subscribers

to local telephone or high-speed Internet service in the continental United States, in an action against America's largest telecommunications firms (with many thousands of employees generating reams and gigabytes of business records) for unspecified (if any) instances of antitrust violations that allegedly occurred over a period of seven years.

It is no answer to say [as the dissent does] that a claim just shy of a plausible entitlement to relief can, if groundless, be weeded out early in the discovery process through "careful case management," ... given the common lament that the success of judicial supervision in checking discovery abuse has been on the modest side.... And it is self-evident that the problem of discovery abuse cannot be solved by "careful scrutiny of evidence at the summary judgment stage," much less "lucid instructions to juries," [quoting the dissent]; the threat of discovery expense will push cost-conscious defendants to settle even anemic cases before reaching those proceedings. Probably, then, it is only by taking care to require allegations that reach the level suggesting conspiracy that we can hope to avoid the potentially enormous expense of discovery in cases with no " 'reasonably founded hope that the [discovery] process will reveal relevant evidence' " to support a § 1 claim.

550 U.S. at 558–59. The Court's solution to this problem was to reject a broad reading of one of its oldest cases setting forth the rules for pleading under Fed. R. Civ. P. 8, Conley v. Gibson, 355 U.S. 41 (1957), and to hold that a Section 1 complaint must provide "more than labels and conclusions." Instead, the Court held,

> stating [a § 1] claim requires a complaint with enough factual matter (taken as true) to suggest that an agreement was made. Asking for plausible grounds to infer an agreement does not impose a probability requirement at the pleading stage; it simply calls for enough fact to raise a reasonable expectation that discovery will reveal evidence of illegal agreement. And, of course, a well-pleaded complaint may proceed even if it strikes a savvy judge that actual proof of those facts is improbable, and "that a recovery is very remote and unlikely." *Ibid.* In identifying facts that are suggestive enough to render a § 1 conspiracy plausible, we have the benefit of the prior rulings and considered views of leading commentators ... that lawful parallel conduct fails to bespeak unlawful agreement. It makes sense to say, therefore, that an allegation of parallel conduct and a bare assertion of conspiracy will not suffice. Without more, parallel conduct does not suggest conspiracy, and a conclusory allegation of agreement at some unidentified point does not supply facts adequate to show illegality. Hence, when allegations of parallel conduct are set out in order to make a § 1 claim, they must be placed in a context that raises a suggestion of a preceding agreement, not merely parallel conduct that could just as well be independent action.

Twombly pleading req: plausible not probable! [handwritten marginal note]

550 U.S. at 556–57.

From a substantive point of view, the Court reiterated its concern about the ambiguity of parallel or interdependent conduct, which it described as "consistent with conspiracy, but just as much in line with a wide swath of rational and competitive business strategy unilaterally prompted by common perceptions of the market." *Id.* at 554. The heart of its reasoning upholding the dismissal of the complaint is reflected in the following passage:

Ps alleged parallel conduct, not agreement - fails under plausibility std

When we look for plausibility in this complaint, we agree with the District Court that plaintiffs' claim of conspiracy in restraint of trade comes up short. To begin with, the complaint leaves no doubt that plaintiffs rest their § 1 claim on descriptions of parallel conduct and not on any independent allegation of actual agreement among the ILECs.... Although in form a few stray statements speak directly of agreement, on fair reading these are merely legal conclusions resting on the prior allegations. Thus, the complaint first takes account of the alleged "absence of any meaningful competition between [the ILECs] in one another's markets," "the parallel course of conduct that each [ILEC] engaged in to prevent competition from CLECs," "and the other facts and market circumstances alleged [earlier]"; "in light of" these, the complaint concludes "that [the ILECs] have entered into a contract, combination or conspiracy to prevent competitive entry into their ... markets and have agreed not to compete with one another." ... The nub of the complaint, then, is the ILECs' parallel behavior, consisting of steps to keep the CLECs out and manifest disinterest in becoming CLECs themselves, and its sufficiency turns on the suggestions raised by this conduct when viewed in light of common economic experience.

We think that nothing contained in the complaint invests either the action or inaction alleged with a plausible suggestion of conspiracy. As to the ILECs' supposed agreement to disobey the 1996 Act and thwart the CLECs' attempts to compete, we agree with the District Court that nothing in the complaint intimates that the resistance to the upstarts was anything more than the natural, unilateral reaction of each ILEC intent on keeping its regional dominance. The 1996 Act did more than just subject the ILECs to competition; it obliged them to subsidize their competitors with their own equipment at wholesale rates. The economic incentive to resist was powerful, but resisting competition is routine market conduct, and even if the ILECs flouted the 1996 Act in all the ways the plaintiffs allege, ... there is no reason to infer that the companies had agreed among themselves to do what was only natural anyway; so natural, in fact, that if alleging parallel decisions to resist competition were enough to imply an antitrust conspiracy, pleading a § 1 violation against almost any group of competing businesses would be a sure thing.

The complaint makes its closest pass at a predicate for conspiracy with the claim that collusion was necessary because success by even one CLEC in an ILEC's territory "would have revealed the degree to which competitive entry by CLECs would have been successful in the other territories." ... But, its logic aside, this general premise still fails to answer the point that there was just no need for joint encouragement to resist the 1996 Act; as the District Court said, "each ILEC has reason to want to avoid dealing with CLECs" and "each ILEC would attempt to keep CLECs out, regardless of the actions of the other ILECs." ...

Plaintiffs' second conspiracy theory rests on the competitive reticence among the ILECs themselves in the wake of the 1996 Act, which was supposedly passed in the " 'hop[e] that the large incumbent local monopoly companies ... might attack their neighbors' service areas, as they are the best situated to do so.' " ... Contrary to hope, the ILECs declined " 'to enter each other's service territories in any significant way,' " ..., and the local telephone and high speed Internet market remains highly compartmentalized geographically, with minimal competition. Based on this state of affairs, and perceiving the ILECs to be blessed with "especially attractive business opportunities" in surrounding markets dominated by other ILECs, the plaintiffs assert that the ILECs' parallel conduct was "strongly suggestive of conspiracy." . . .

But it was not suggestive of conspiracy, not if history teaches anything. In a traditionally unregulated industry with low barriers to entry, sparse competition among large firms dominating separate geographical segments of the market could very well signify illegal agreement, but here we have an obvious alternative explanation. In the decade preceding the 1996 Act and well before that, monopoly was the norm in telecommunications, not the exception. . . . The ILECs were born in that world, doubtless liked the world the way it was, and surely knew the adage about him who lives by the sword. Hence, a natural explanation for the noncompetition alleged is that the former Government-sanctioned monopolists were sitting tight, expecting their neighbors to do the same thing.

In fact, the complaint itself gives reasons to believe that the ILECs would see their best interests in keeping to their old turf. Although the complaint says generally that the ILECs passed up "especially attractive business opportunit[ies]" by declining to compete as CLECs against other ILECs, . . . it does not allege that competition as CLECs was potentially any more lucrative than other opportunities being pursued by the ILECs during the same period, and the complaint is replete with indications that any CLEC faced nearly insurmountable barriers to profitability owing to the ILECs' flagrant resistance to the network sharing requirements of the 1996 Act. . . . Not only that, but even without a monopolistic tradition and the peculiar difficulty of mandating shared networks, "[f]irms do not expand without limit and none of them enters every market that an outside observer might regard as profitable, or even a small portion of such markets." Areeda & Hovenkamp ¶ 307d, at 155 (Supp. 2006) (commenting on the case at bar). The upshot is that Congress may have expected some ILECs to become CLECs in the legacy territories of other ILECs, but the disappointment does not make conspiracy plausible. We agree with the District Court's assessment that antitrust conspiracy was not suggested by the facts adduced under either theory of the complaint, which thus fails to state a valid § 1 claim.

550 U.S. at 564–69. *Twombly* thus stands as a powerful reaffirmation of *Theatre Enterprises*, and a caution to future plaintiffs to provide the "who, what, when, where, and why" details of any alleged conspiracies, whether explicit or implicit, in their complaints.

NOTE ON SUMMARY DISPOSITION IN ANTITRUST CASES

As a practical matter, the likelihood that a plaintiff can prove "agreement" on the basis of conscious parallelism and other circumstantial evidence is affected by whether the decision is made by judge or jury. Especially where large corporate defendants are involved, the theory is that a jury is more likely to infer "agreement" from ambiguous evidence.

In the 1960s, many commentators and courts believed that summary disposition was particularly inappropriate in antitrust cases. To a large extent, the source of this view was some language in Poller v. Columbia Broadcasting System, 368 U.S. 464 (1962), where Justice Clark wrote:

... [s]ummary procedures should be used sparingly in complex antitrust litigation where motive and intent play leading roles, the proof is largely in the hands of the alleged conspirators, and hostile witnesses thicken the plot.... It is only when the witnesses are present and subject to cross-examination that their credibility and the weight to be given their testimony can be appraised. Trial by affidavit is no substitute for trial by jury which so long has been the hallmark of "even handed justice." 368 U.S. at 473.

Many commentators criticized the *Poller* language, and several studies showed that summary judgment or motions to dismiss were granted, if not as often, then *almost* as often in antitrust cases as in general civil litigation.[16] Moreover, there appeared to be a general trend toward granting summary disposition, especially to defendants, more frequently.

In 1986, the approach in *Poller* to the question of summary judgment in antitrust cases was changed dramatically in Matsushita Electric Industrial Co. v. Zenith Radio Corp., 475 U.S. 574 (1986). In *Matsushita*, the Court held that a group of Japanese television manufacturers were entitled to summary judgment in a case brought against them by their American rivals. The Court concluded that the plaintiffs' theory—which was that the Japanese companies had organized and maintained a two-decade-long conspiracy to charge predatorily low prices in the U.S. market and thereby to drive their U.S. rivals out of business—was so economically implausible that the case could not go forward based only on the evidence plaintiffs had presented. Some courts of appeals have interpreted Matsushita as effectively overruling that part of *Poller*. *See, e.g.*, Wallace v. SMC Pneumatics, Inc., 103 F.3d 1394, 1396 (7th Cir. 1997) ("[I]n antitrust law ... early decisions pronouncing it a field inapt for summary judgment were later repudiated"); Ideal Dairy Farms, Inc. v. John Labatt, Ltd., 90 F.3d 737, 747 (3d Cir. 1996) ("At one time, the Supreme Court endorsed a slightly stricter standard of review when a summary judgment order was challenged in an antitrust case.... However, that 'special standard' was abandoned in Eastman Kodak Co. v. Image Technical Servs., Inc., 504 U.S. 451, 468–69 (1992)...."). Other courts continue to cite *Poller*, even as they affirm grants of summary judgment for defendants. *See, e.g.*, Dickson v. Microsoft Corp., 309 F.3d 193, 212 (4th Cir. 2002); Toscano v. Professional Golfers Ass'n, 258 F.3d 978, 982–83 (9th Cir. 2001). Indeed, some courts thought that *Matsushita* imposed a special burden on plaintiffs to show that their claims made economic sense, but the Supreme Court rejected that theory in *Eastman Kodak*, 504 U.S. at 468–69....

In 1986, a comprehensive study of treble damage litigation—the *Georgetown Study of Private Antitrust Litigation*—included statistics on the likelihood that motions for summary disposition would be filed and what the rates of grants and denial were. The study found that motions for summary disposition were frequent in antitrust—perhaps because the financial stakes were so high. Nevertheless, plaintiffs rarely succeeded in obtaining summary judgment, even in relatively simple *per se* cases. Thus, summary judgment motions by plaintiff were successful in less than 1% of all cases filed during the period under review.

In contrast, the study found that defendants were more successful in winning summary judgments in the 1980's than previously. For example, defendants won

---

16. Commentary and statistics are gathered in Stephen Calkins, *Summary Judgment, Motions to Dismiss, and Other Examples of Equilibrating Tendencies in the Antitrust System*, 74 GEO. L.J. 1065, 1120–22 (1986).

summary disposition in about 6% of all antitrust cases in 1983 and 8.3% in 1984. This worked out to about a 50% success rate where summary disposition was sought. Presumably, the success rate will continue to climb as the effect of the *Matsushita* opinion is felt. Professor Stephen Calkins concluded his review of the data with the following comments:

> The most important finding in this article is that summary judgments and dismissals for failure to state a claim appear to be ordered as frequently in antitrust cases as in other cases, and they may be ordered even more frequently....

> This unexpected finding can be explained, at least in part, by the treble damages remedy. A number of courts recently have suggested that the *in terrorem* effect of the treble damages remedy makes summary procedures particularly appropriate in antitrust cases. The Supreme Court's [decision in *Matsushita* is] consistent with this suggestion. The empirical findings that use of summary procedures remains constant or rises with increasing damages requests, and is as great or greater in class action suits as in other ones, also supports this conclusion. Conventional wisdom would predict a decline with increasing complexity, and complexity should be associated with high damage requests and class status. Apparently, some courts want to prevent finders of fact from deciding high-stakes cases.

Donald F. Turner, The Definition of Agreement Under The Sherman Act[17]

75 Harv. L. Rev. 655, 663–66 (1962).

... [C]onscious parallelism is devoid of anything that might reasonably be called agreement when it involves simply the independent responses of a group of competitors to the same set of economic facts—independent in the sense that each would have made the same decision for himself even though his competitors decided otherwise. But the consciously parallel decisions of oligopolists in setting their basic prices, which are interdependent in that they depend on competitors setting the same price, are not nearly so easily disposed of on the ground that no agreement is involved.

One can pose an extreme hypothetical case in which it might be conceded that no element that could properly be called "agreement" is present. If there were an industry consisting of only two or three sellers, where the sellers were of identical size and had identical costs, where the products of the sellers were completely indistinguishable, where conditions of demand and supply were completely static, and where sellers and buyers were completely aware of all relevant facts—then the "best" price for each seller would be precisely the same, would be known to be the same by all, and would be charged without hesitation in absolute certainty that the others would price likewise. To be sure, the decisions would be interdependent in the sense that the best price for each depends on the others charging that same price, but this, under the assumed facts, would be so

17. Copyright © 1962 by the Harvard Law Review Association. Reprinted with permission.

completely certain that hardly a shade of even a "meeting of minds" could be said to be involved.[18]

But the hypothetical case has no counterpart in reality. There are indeed many cases of completely or almost completely standardized products; but sellers will always have some differences in cost structures, face somewhat different demand conditions, and be in ignorance of some relevant market facts. Moreover, conditions are not static, they change; and change breeds uncertainty. In short, in real life the "best" price for each seller in even the oligopolistic market will never be the same; and even if it were, individual calculations by each seller based on imperfect and usually different information would normally lead, in the absence of fully recognized interdependence, to different decisions as to price. For a pattern of noncompetitive pricing to emerge in such a situation requires something which we could, not unreasonably, call a "meeting of minds," or to use Professor Kaysen's phrase, an "agreement to agree...."[19]

Even if some explicit communication at some time was not involved, though in reality it probably always has been, explicit communication seems hardly a logically necessary ingredient of the kind of agreement that is an element in the legal concept of conspiracy. Considered purely as a problem in linguistic definition, there is no reason to exclude oligopolistic behavior from the scope of the term agreement simply because the circumstances make it possible to communicate without speech. It is not novel conspiracy doctrine to say that agreement can be signified by action as well as by words. And of course if there is agreement in the legal sense, the agreement seems inescapably an unlawful conspiracy in restraint of trade because a price-fixing agreement is unlawful *per se*.

Yet another look at the behavior involved points to a different conclusion. In a significant sense, the behavior of the rational oligopolist in setting his price is precisely the same as that of the rational seller in an industry consisting of a very large number of competitors. Both are pricing their product and determining their output so as to make the highest profit, or suffer the least loss, that can be obtained in the market conditions facing them. The rational oligopolist simply takes one more factor into account-the reactions of his competitors to any price change that he makes. He must take them into account because his competitors will inevitably react. They will inevitably react, for example, to a price cut on his part because otherwise the price cut will make a substantial inroad on their sales; if, for example, there are only three producers of equal size and a price cut by one doubles his sales, the sales of each of his two competitors will be cut in half. The rational seller in an industry with a very large number of competitors does not calculate their reactions to a price cut by him, because they are not likely to be sufficiently affected by the price cut

18. There is also no "agreement" in those cases of price leadership where the price leader is the dominant and the low-cost firm. See generally Markham, *The Nature and Significance of Price Leadership*, *in* Reading in Industrial Organization and Public Policy 176 (Heflebower & Stocking ed. 1958).

19. Kaysen, *Collusion Under the Sherman Act*, 65 Q.J. Econ. 263, 268 (1951).

to react; if, for example, there are one hundred producers of equal size, a doubling of sales by one, evenly drawn from his competitors, would cut their sales by only one ninety-ninth. To repeat, it can fairly be said that the rational oligopolist is behaving in exactly the same way as is the rational seller in a competitively structured industry; he is simply taking another factor into account, which he has to take into account because the situation in which he finds himself puts it there.

In this light, several comments may be made. First, there is fair ground for argument that oligopoly price behavior can be described as individual behavior-rational individual decision in the light of relevant economic facts-as well as it can be described as "agreement." It can readily be said that each seller in this situation, in refraining from price competition, is not agreeing with his competitors but simply throwing their probable decisions into his price calculus as impersonal market facts....

Second, it seems questionable to call the behavior of oligopolists in setting their prices unlawful when the behavior in essence is identical to that of sellers in a competitive industry. Particularly is this so when the behavior involved, setting the "profit-maximizing" price in light of all market facts, is not only legally acceptable but vitally necessary to make competitive markets function as they are supposed to function.

NOTES

1. *Rational competitive behavior.* After having served as Assistant Attorney General in charge of the Antitrust Division, Professor Turner wrote an article in which he modified his views concerning the applicability of the antitrust laws to oligopolies. *See* Donald Turner, *The Scope of Antitrust and Other Economic Regulatory Policies*, 82 Harv. L. Rev. 1207 (1969). As to individual monopolists, he concluded that Section 2 could be read to apply whenever significant monopoly power "has persisted over a long enough time to indicate relatively impervious barriers to entry, regardless of how it [the monopoly] was obtained or maintained, excepting only monopoly based on economies of scale or on the same unexpired patents that gave it birth."

Turner next focused on oligopolistic conduct, noting that an "attack on shared monopoly is a highly important aspect of any effective competition policy." He reasserted his position that consciously parallel non-competitive pricing by oligopolists could not reasonably be attacked as a conspiracy to fix prices, or as a conspiracy or combination to monopolize, but argued that other "exclusionary behavior without adequate business justification" by oligopolists could be deemed an unlawful attempt to monopolize under Section 2. Thus a lease-only policy, or packaging machines and service at a single price, was viewed as having a sufficiently substantial anticompetitive effect to justify a finding of illegality if each oligopolist engaged in similar conduct.

> ... I believe that the law on shared monopoly may be brought virtually in line with the law on individual monopoly, and divestiture where feasible invoked as a remedy, whenever it appears that injunctive relief would not adequate dissipate the power within a reasonable time.

Where oligopolists sharing monopoly power have engaged in restrictive conduct lacking any substantial justification, they may appropriately be said to have unlawfully attempted to monopolize. Where it appears that their decisions to carry on particular exclusionary practices are interdependent, where one would not have carried on the practice unless the others had gone along, they may also be charged with a conspiracy or combination to monopolize. Finally, where each of the companies effectively sharing monopoly power has engaged in possibly justifiable conduct that nevertheless has unnecessary exclusionary effects, it seems logical and appropriate to me to charge each with having individually "monopolized" in violation of Section 2. Each has obtained and maintained monopoly power—real, though shared—to which factors other than skill, foresight, industry, and the like have contributed.

The remaining question is whether one can fairly apply to shared monopoly power the prohibition of individual monopoly suggested by Alcoa that, barring economies of scale or power still based on the unexpired patents that created it, monopoly becomes subject to judicial relief when retained over a sufficient period of time to indicate that it is substantially impervious to erosion by market forces. I would conclude that it is appropriate to do so if one accepts the Alcoa principle in the first place, because there is not enough difference between individual and shared monopoly to warrant different treatment.

2. *Coordinated pricing conduct.* Professor Turner's view that consciously parallel pricing is nothing more than rational competitive behavior was challenged by many, including Professor (now Judge) Richard A. Posner, who argued that while noncompetitive pricing by oligopolists is made easier by market structure, it is not compelled. Structure may eliminate the need for explicit agreement, but coordinated pricing still requires action from which tacit agreement may be inferred. A showing of concentrated market structure and voluntary pricing conduct— such as signaling and response, systematic price discrimination, price leadership, or filing of identical sealed bids for sale of nonstandard items—could support an inference of tacit conspiracy. Other relevant factors would be oligopoly firms' refusal to offer discounts in the presence of prolonged excess capacity, market shares fixed over time, infrequent price changes, and abnormally high profits. Since Posner's emphasis is on conduct, he argues that injunctive relief can be effective in dealing with the problem of oligopoly pricing. Richard A. Posner, *Oligopoly and the Antitrust Laws: A Suggested Approach*, 21 Stan. L. Rev. 1562 (1969). *See also* Kauper, *New Approaches to the Old Problem*, 46 Antitrust L. J. 435 (1977).

3. *Weighing evidence of agreement at summary disposition.* Consider, in connection with the previous note, the Seventh Circuit's opinion in In re High Fructose Corn Syrup Antitrust Litigation, 295 F.3d 651 (7th Cir. 2002). There, writing for the court in a case charging that the principal manufacturers of high fructose corn syrup (HFCS) had unlawfully fixed prices, Judge Posner took the occasion to revisit the agreement requirement of Section 1, in the following passage:

> Section 1 of the Sherman Act forbids contracts, combinations, and conspiracies in restraint of trade. This statutory language is broad enough, as we noted in JTC Petroleum Co. v. Piasa Motor Fuels, Inc., 190 F.3d 775, 780 (7th Cir. 1999), to encompass a purely tacit agreement to fix prices, that is, an agreement made without any actual communication among the parties to the agreement. If a firm raises price in the expectation that its competitors will do likewise, and they do, the firm's behavior can be

conceptualized as the offer of a unilateral contract that the offerees accept by raising their prices. Or as the creation of a contract implied in fact. "Suppose a person walks into a store and takes a newspaper that is for sale there, intending to pay for it. The circumstances would create a contract implied in fact" even though there was no communication between the parties. A.E.I. Music Network, Inc. v. Business Computers, Inc., 290 F.3d 952, 956 (7th Cir. 1992). Nevertheless it is generally believed, and the plaintiffs implicitly accept, that an express, manifested agreement, and thus an agreement involving actual, verbalized communication, must be proved in order for a price-fixing conspiracy to be actionable under the Sherman Act.

295 F.3d at 654. Going on, Judge Posner discussed the kind of evidence that would permit an inference of agreement, assuming that the plaintiffs (as is usually the case) had no direct proof. The necessary evidence would be of two types, economic and non-economic. The economic evidence in turn typically takes two forms: evidence that the structure of the market was conducive to secret price-fixing, and evidence that the market was behaving in a non-competitive manner. *Id.* at 655. In weighing this economic evidence at the summary judgment stage, the court warned against falling into any of three possible traps. The first trap is the temptation to weigh conflicting economic testimony. The second is to assume that if no single item of evidence points unequivocally to conspiracy, then the plaintiffs must lose. The key word here is "unequivocally": the court stressed that most evidence is susceptible to competing interpretations, and that can be enough. Finally, the third trap is "failing to distinguish between the existence of a conspiracy and its efficacy." *Id.* at 656. In the case before it, after considering both the economic evidence and the non-economic evidence tending to show explicit agreement (party statements, damaging comments in documents, and the like), the court concluded that the district court should not have granted summary judgment for the defendants and it remanded the case for trial.

4. *"Collective dominance" in the European Union.* The concept of shared or collective dominance has received a warmer welcome in the competition law of the European Union. When such a position exists, the conduct of the companies is evaluated under Article 82 of the Treaty; similarly, the creation of a position of collective dominance is grounds for refusing to permit a merger. The first important case under Article 82 was the *Flat Glass* case, formally known as Società Italiano Vetro SpA (SIV) & Ors v. Commission of the European Communities (Joined Cases T–68/89, T–77/89 and T–78/89), CFI [1992] 2 CEC at 33 (CCH Europe). In that case, the Commission had proceeded against three Italian flat glass manufacturers under both Articles 81 and 82 of the Treaty of Rome. It found that the companies had infringed Article 81(1) through a number of agreements and arrangements affecting two markets: the automotive market and the non-automotive market. It also concluded that they abused their *collective* dominant position by depriving customers of the opportunity to get suppliers to compete on prices and terms of sales, and, by means of a quota system, limiting the outlets for glass. The Court of First Instance decided that there was "nothing, in principle, to prevent two or more independent economic entities from being, on a specific market, united by such economic links that, by virtue of that fact, together they hold a dominant position vis-à-vis the other operators on the same market." Opinion at ¶ 358. It cautioned, however, that the Commission could not simply "recycle" the facts of an alleged Article 81 violation through Article 82 and come up with a violation based on the joint dominance theory. It pointed out that Article 82 presupposes that a market has been defined, and that the firm or firms holds a dominant position in that

market—criteria that may not necessarily be present in an Article 81 case. Here the Commission failed, in the Court's view, to justify its position that there was a single market for flat glass for Article 82 purposes. Given the failure of proof, it annulled the Commission's finding of an Article 82 violation.

More recently, the European Court of Justice affirmed a decision of the Commission finding that the members of a liner conference that provided shipping services between two African countries and the North Sea area had violated Article 82. See Compagnie Maritime Belge Transports SA and others v. European Commission and others, ECJ (5th Chamber) [2000] All ER (EC) 385, 14 May, 29 Oct. 1998, 16 Mar. 2000. In the merger context, however, the Court of First Instance in 2002 reversed a decision by the Commission to prohibit a merger on the grounds of the creation of a situation of collective dominance among the remaining three providers of certain holiday packages. See Airtours PLC v. European Commission (Case T–342/99) CFI (5th Chamber) [2002] All ER (EC) 783, 11 Oct. 2001, 6 June 2002. The Court's decision was based on the Commission's failure to present sufficient evidence; it was not a rejection of the collective dominance idea in general.

As the 2007 *Football League* case (Piau v. Commission) described in Chapter 3 *supra* illustrates, the theory of shared or collective dominance seems clearly established as a matter of theory in Europe. Cases in which it is actually used either as a basis of liability under Article 82 or as a reason to block a merger exist, but they continue to be rare. Is the collective dominance, shared monopoly, or conscious parallelism problem a conundrum that antitrust law is simply incapable of solving, or do you see a place for enforcement against oligopoly?

PROBLEM 10

PROBLEM: AIRLINE PRICING

Seven airlines own the Airline Fare Finder Company (AFFC). AFFC is a database that collects and disseminates fare information for most of the domestic airlines in the United States. AFFC provides fare information to its subscribers, which include its seven owners, and to computer reservation systems.

Each airline supplies AFFC with fare information, including fare codes (*e.g.*, "F" is first class), fare amounts, restrictions, and routings. An airline can attach footnotes to any fare in the AFFC database. Footnotes can include information such as first and last ticket dates. The first ticket date is the future date at which a fare is supposed to become available for purchase by travelers. A last ticket date is the date at which a current fare ends.

Ameri–World Airlines (AWA) decided to offer discount fares between Dallas and San Francisco, two of its hubs, on a few flights. Gamma, through the AFFC database, observed the AWA-discounted fares and decided to offer the discount fare on all of its flights between the same cities. AWA responded by lowering its prices on flights between Gamma's hubs, Dallas and New York's Kennedy Airport, to the same fare level as the Dallas–San Francisco flights. AWA's Dallas–Kennedy fares on the AFFC system included the same footnote designator and last ticket date as the Dallas–San Francisco fares.

The Department of Justice believes that AFFC makes coordination more likely because it is effective and easy to punish deviations from coordinated fares. Can the government prove coordinated action? Would the system be any better, or any worse, if all first and last ticket dates were freely available over the Internet to users of on-line travel services?

SECTION 3.   DELIVERED PRICING SYSTEMS AND OTHER "FACILITATING PRACTICES"—USEFUL BUILDING BLOCKS?

NOTE ON PRICE COORDINATION AMONG OLIGOPOLISTS[20]

I.   The Difficulties of Price Coordination

In order to coordinate their prices successfully, oligopolists must (1) *agree* on the cooperative outcome, (2) *achieve* that outcome, and (3) *maintain* the outcome over time, in the face of changing conditions and incentives of the participants to deviate from the oligopolistic outcome. All three conditions are difficult to satisfy.

Firms will find it difficult to agree on a particular outcome because their interests are not perfectly aligned. To be sure, raising prices may increase joint profits among the participants in a cartel. But firms may not agree on how the oligopoly should distribute those joint profits. Some participants might prefer distribution based on market share in last period before the oligopoly was imposed. Others might favor distribution based on market share after the oligopoly has been formed. Still others might propose that distribution be tied to capital investment. Non-price variables complicate the matter even further. Oligopolists must coordinate product design, delivery schedules, transportation methods and customer service. The desire to indulge in price discrimination adds an additional layer of complexity. Also, to allow participants to respond to changing market conditions, any agreement must predict and plan for contingencies or allow the parties to renegotiate.

The difficulties are compounded because parties may not negotiate these agreements openly. They must signal their understandings through newspaper interviews and at meetings of trade associations, clearly enough to inform conspirators of their intentions yet subtly enough to avoid discovery. Once the parties have surmounted these hurdles, they must implement their agreements. While this is a simple matter for legal cartels, which can rely on courts to enforce their agreements, illegal cartels must devise self-enforcing agreements. Otherwise, the hoped-for gains will not materialize.

To see why this might be difficult, consider a two-firm industry composed of Bart Inc. and Homer Co. In each period, Bart and Homer independently set their price either "high" or "low." Each firm's profits are determined, in part, by the price the other has chosen. Profits are given by the following matrix with Homer's on the left and Bart's price on the right (the numbers are merely illustrative):

		Bart's Price	
		High	Low
Homer's Price	High	*(100, 100)*	*(–10, 140)*
	Low	*(140, –10)*	*(70, 70)*

---

20. Adapted from notes prepared by Steven C. Salop, professor of economics and law, Georgetown University Law Center.

Bart and Homer face a variant of the "prisoner's dilemma"—a situation where each actor's incentives cut against the interests of the whole group. (*See* Economics Appendix, section III on game theory.) Obviously, Bart and Homer would like to coordinate their behavior, pick the high price level and maximize joint profits. But, since combination is barred, it will be difficult for them to do so. If Bart implements the high price strategy and Homer does not, Bart's profits plunge to –10 while Homer's soar to 140. Both Bart and Homer, therefore, have an incentive to deviate from the joint profit maximizing outcome, keeping prices at the competitive (low/low) level. Their dilemma does not dissolve once they achieve the cooperative outcome. Even if they manage to coordinate their behavior in one period, they will face the same incentive to deviate from the cooperative outcome in the next period.

Bart and Homer may do better if they recognize that their long-term interests lie in cooperation. If they recognize that their "game" will be repeated in the future, they might be able to reach an equilibrium at the joint profit maximizing level by adopting a strategy where each threatens to match immediately a price cut by the other. In order for such a strategy to be effective, there must be almost no lag time between a price cut by one and a retaliatory cut by the other. If lag time is sufficiently long, both will have reason to cheat, making the cooperative outcome, even in a repeated game, unstable. Thus, Bart and Homer's likelihood of successfully imposing a cartel on their industry depends on: (i) the short-term benefits from cheating, relative to, (ii) the longer-term loss from not cooperating, and (iii) the detection lag, that is, the likelihood that cheating will be discovered and punished.

II. Structural Factors That Facilitate or Complicate Price Coordination

Certain structural factors in the market will make it easier for oligopolists to coordinate their behavior. These factors affect the relative payoffs from cooperating, cheating and competing. They also impede or facilitate the participants' ability to detect and to retaliate against cheating. Where these factors coincide, successful collusion (tacit or express) will be more likely.

1. *High Concentration.* When there are only a small number of competitors, coordination is more likely to succeed. An agreement is easier to reach because there are fewer firms that must agree. A few firms with large market shares also are more likely to recognize their interdependence. They have more to gain from collusion and more to lose from cheating because they will earn the higher collusive price on more sales.

2. *Barriers to Entry.* When barriers to entry are high, a cartel is more stable because it need not add new members to maintain control over the market. Coordinated pricing is more profitable and more likely to occur.

3. *Open Sales.* When sales are public and all market participants (buyers and sellers) know the prices, firms can detect cheating more easily. If cheating is easy to detect, an agreement or tacit understanding is easier to enforce, making such agreements more likely.

4. *Homogeneous Products.* When rivals sell identical products, the number of variables for which an agreement must account is reduced, again facilitating agreement and making cheating more difficult to hide.

5. *Lumpy Sales.* "Lumpy sales" occur in markets where large buyers or long term contracts account for a large share of sales (*e.g.*, the market for commercial airplanes). Lumpy sales increase the incentives for firms to cheat on the cartel, making collusion less likely in the first place.

6. *Excess Capacity*. Excess capacity cuts both ways. When firms have excess capacity, it is less costly for them to cheat. But, where demand is fixed or falling, firms have the incentive to collude to maintain higher profits.

7. *Static Demand*. When demand is fixed, rivals can detect cheating by looking at their own sales, making retaliation more likely.

8. *Similarity*. When rivals are similarly situated, they are more likely to have similar preferences regarding prices and output. Agreements are easier to negotiate and achieve than if firms have much different preferences.

III.   Facilitating Practices

Oligopolists also might adopt "facilitating practices" to increase the likelihood of successful collusion. "Facilitating practices," like structural conditions in the market, make collusion more likely by altering the incentives of market participants (*i.e.*, breaking the prisoner's dilemma). There are two distinct effects of facilitating practices—*information exchange* and *incentive management*. Although particular practices often combine elements of both, it is useful to distinguish between them. Because the information exchange effect is better understood, we will discuss it only briefly and focus on incentive management.

1. *Information exchange*. Information exchange facilitates both explicit and tacit coordination by eliminating uncertainty about rivals' actions. Classic examples of information exchanges are interseller verification of price quotations and advance notice of price changes. In each case, the exchange of information shortens or eliminates detection lags by competitors. By decreasing the transitional losses from price rises (*i.e.*, losses to the price leader before rivals follow) and the transitional gains from price discounts (gains to the initiator of the discount before rivals follow), incentives are altered in such a way as to make the joint profit outcome easier to achieve and maintain.

2. *Incentive management*. Facilitating practices affect incentive management by *directly* altering payoffs rather than working through the medium of information exchange. By restructuring payoffs, the incentives for a firm to offer price discounts or raise prices may be directly affected. Similarly, a firm may change its own incentives to match price changes initiated by its rivals, thereby affecting its rivals' incentives to initiate such price changes. In this way, adoption of facilitating practices can convert competitive oligopoly outcomes into cooperative ones.

Perhaps the purest example of an incentive management device is a monetary penalty on price discounts. For example, suppose in a two-firm industry, each seller agrees to pay a third party a monetary penalty equal to 50 percent of its price if either charges any of its customers a price below "list," and that price is not matched by the rival seller. Under those circumstances, price cuts by either seller become self-defeating, and a high oligopoly price is insured.

Incentive management devices can also be created by contractual arrangements between an oligopolist and its customers. Embedding an incentive management device in a sales contract has a number of advantages. First, use of a contract with a purchaser allows the oligopolist to make a binding commitment to transform its incentives. A court is likely to enforce the contract, so that the credibility of the promised behavior is increased. Moreover, the ability to collect damages gives the buyer an incentive to ensure performance and to bear the costs of enforcing the contract. If the buyer is better situated than rivals or third parties to detect price discounts, this can increase the efficiency of enforcement. More efficient enforcement increases the credibility of a promise.

3. *"Stampede" effect*. The obvious question is why rational buyers would be willing to act as accomplices in achieving this possibly anticompetitive conduct by their suppliers. To the extent that the contractual provision makes discounting less desirable or price increases less risky, it is difficult to see why buyers would agree to clauses that have such an effect. The answer lies in the possibility of designing contractual provisions that are valued by each buyer individually even as they create an external cost to all other buyers. If such clauses can be developed, they create a type of stampede. Each buyer willingly accepts (indeed, rushes to purchase) the clause. Yet the collective acceptance by all buyers eliminates the individual benefit by stabilizing the sellers' joint profit outcome.

We now turn to a number of examples of practices that can transform incentives so as to stabilize an agreement. It should be noted that these practices sometimes have procompetitive and efficiency benefits as well as potential anticompetitive effects, although in this note we focus on the latter.

4. *Most-favored-nation clauses*. A *most-favored-nation* (MFN) clause in a sales contract provides the buyer with insurance protection against the contingency that the seller offers a lower price to another customer. These clauses may prevent price discrimination when the seller offers a discount price to another buyer, either in the future (a "retroactive" MFN) or in the present (a "contemporaneous" MFN). Although all MFNs change the seller's incentives in the same general way, it is clearer to illustrate some issues with the case of a retroactive MFN and others with a contemporaneous MFN.

Consider an industry in which public utility customers contract for the purchase of custom-manufactured generators. Because delivery occurs many months after the contract is made, increased competition, reduced demand, or reduced costs during the intervening time period may reduce the average price paid by later buyers for comparable generators. By placing the following retroactive MFN clause in the sales agreement, early buyers may share that price decrease:

> If at any time before [buyer] takes delivery of said generator, [seller] offers a lower price for a comparable size and quality generator to any other purchaser, [seller] will also offer that lower price to [buyer].

That is, any future price decreases must be rebated to the buyer.[21] The MFN requires the seller to pay a monetary penalty if it lowers its price.[22] Because price decreases are penalized, they are discouraged. Thus, if all rivals provide all buyers with MFN protection, a high oligopoly price can be stabilized, once it is achieved.[23]

Provision of an MFN *by even just one rival* may be advantageous to all sellers, including the one that institutes the MFN. This may be surprising, because a seller's unilateral adoption of an MFN also places it at a competitive disadvantage—it is deterred from matching selective discounts offered by its rivals. However, this

---

21. Compare the GE/Westinghouse decree, discussed at p. 596 *infra*. Variants of this contract could provide for a rebate of price cuts made even after delivery is taken, or for a partial rather than a full rebate. The contract might also ease enforcement of the clause by providing the buyer with the right to inspect the seller's books.

22. The total penalty equals the price decrease times the number of outstanding orders. It is paid even if the discount is matched.

23. Of course, the MFN makes it more difficult to achieve a lower-price cooperative outcome, if changed conditions warrant a lower price. This is a cost to the oligopolists of adopting such a plan. In contrast, the penalty scheme discussed earlier does not share this problem because only *unmatched* price cuts are penalized.

competitive disadvantage may be more than offset by the effect of the clause in stabilizing a higher price.

Most-favored-nation clauses are also found in long-term requirements contracts governing the sale of repeatedly purchased industrial supplies. These clauses insure buyers against contemporaneous price discrimination in favor of other buyers who may or may not be rivals. Consider the following standard form:

> If [seller] should, during the term of this contract, offer or sell goods of equal quality and quantity to any other buyer at a price lower than that provided for herein, [buyer] shall receive the benefit of such lower price on all shipments made hereunder for which such lower price is effective.

This contemporaneous MFN clause differs somewhat from the retroactive MFN. Whereas the retroactive MFN penalizes all price decreases made after some date, this clause penalizes and deters only *selective discounts*, that is, price cuts that are restricted to a limited number of customers. General price cuts are not penalized or deterred. Thus, selective discounts are made relatively less profitable than general price cuts. In that oligopoly competition (*i.e.*, "cheating" on a cartel) usually takes the form of selective discounts, the MFN may serve to stabilize the cooperative outcome.

Since general price cuts are not penalized by a contemporaneous MFN, adjustments to a lower-price *cooperative* outcome are not deterred if they become necessary, for example, if costs fall. Similarly, the ability to retaliate with a general price reduction against rivals' secret discounts is not constrained. Only selective discounts are penalized.

Following this analysis, a contemporaneous MFN constrains the oligopolist's response in the same way as would its inability to identify the customers offered discounts. For example, suppose Company A offers a selective discount to a limited number of Company B's customers. Suppose Company B can identify these customers. However, because of the MFN, suppose Company B can feasibly respond only with a general price cut to all its customers. In this case, it will compare the profit reduction from the loss of these customers to the alternative of offering a general price cut to all its customers, including those not approached by Company A. The deeper Company A's discount is and the smaller the number of customers that it approaches, the relatively more costly is a matching response by Company B. In that case, it becomes more likely that Company B will accommodate the discounts rather than respond with a general price cut. In short, if Company A restricts its secret discounting, it is more profitable for Company B to accommodate rather than to touch off a price war.

In spite of this anticompetitive effect, buyers may be willing to "purchase" the "protection" of an MFN for two reasons. First, insurance protection against price reductions may have value to risk-averse buyers. The MFN provides this insurance. Of course, broad MFN protection reduces the probability that a lower price will ever materialize because it induces an adverse incentive in sellers who provide it. For any individual buyer, however, this effect may be small relative to the insurance benefit. Instead, the adverse incentive is mainly an "externality" that injures buyers other than the one that negotiates for the clause. The profit-maximizing purchaser does not reckon this external effect into its calculus. This creates the stampede mentality discussed earlier. In fact, the more buyers there are in the market, the more likely that the price stabilizing effect will be ignored by buyers.

Second, a buyer who does add this potential injury to other buyers into its profit calculus may count that injury as a benefit, not as a cost. If rival buyers are also his downstream product market competitors, then his profitability is enhanced when his rivals' costs rise. Looking at the problem in this way, a buyer even may be willing to pay more for an MFN, because the MFN acts as a type of bribe to the seller to forgo deeper discounts to rival buyers.

5. *Meeting competition clauses.* A *meeting competition* clause (MCC) in a long-term supply contract or advertisement provides the buyer with insurance protection against a lost opportunity in the event that the buyer is offered a lower price by some other seller. The economic effects of an MCC depend on the exact form the provision takes. One common variant is the *meet or release* (MOR) clause, as illustrated by the following example:

> If the [buyer] should be offered by a responsible manufacturer [product] of equal quality and in a quantity equivalent to or less than that remaining as a commitment hereunder, at a lower delivered cost to the [buyer], and [buyer] gives [seller] satisfactory evidence thereof before the date on which any shipment is required, [seller] shall either supply such quantity of [product] at the lower cost or permit [buyer] to purchase elsewhere. Any quantity so purchased shall be deducted from the quantity deliverable under this contract.

The MOR clause serves mainly as an information exchange device. If the buyer discovers a lower price elsewhere, it cannot escape its obligation to purchase from its original supplier without informing that supplier of the lower price. By requiring this flow of information, the clause eliminates any detection lag. Thus, the seller is protected against the possibility of losing sales to a rival offering an undetected discount to a current customer. In this way, an MOR facilitates selective matching of an otherwise secret discount.

It is unlikely that a seller would choose to *meet* rather than *release* in all cases. For example, if a rival offers a price below the seller's marginal cost, the seller has no obvious incentive to match. Likewise, the seller has no incentive to match a discount he suspects the buyer will reject. For example, if the rival's product is of lower quality or otherwise unsuitable, the buyer might be suspected of using the lower bid simply as a bluff in order to obtain a better deal.

In these cases, an MOR clause offers no protection to the buyer. The buyer prefers, all things being equal, a contractual provision that allows the seller no escape. This can be accomplished by deleting the *release* language from the provision. Of course, such a *no-release* MCC may lead to allocative inefficiencies if the seller, as a result of the clause, must provide units at a below-cost price. Nevertheless, if the seller's primary interest is in deterring rivals' discounts, the losses entailed by this inefficiency may be small relative to the anticompetitive benefit of the clause. For, by deleting the *release* option, the clause is made a more credible deterrent. Now the seller must meet all rivals' offers.

An MCC also facilitates successful *achievement* of the cooperative outcome. For example, a seller who provides a *no-release* MCC to current customers can raise price without losing any sales to a lower-pricing rival. Buyers are automatically given the rival's lower price until all firms raise their prices. This eliminates the transitional losses that might otherwise deter price rises. It also eliminates the rival's transitional gains and, with it, the incentive to delay a matching price increase. In this sense, when a duopoly seller who has an MCC raises his price, his rival is automatically transformed into a *de facto* price leader, with the ability to set prices for both firms.

6. *Entry deterrence.* To this point, the focus of this analysis has been oligopoly coordination. It has been assumed throughout that the industry is protected by insurmountable barriers to entry. As noted in the text, meeting competition clauses can also facilitate entry deterrence.

By providing a *no-release* MCC, an incumbent can add needed credibility to its threat to cut price in the event entry occurs. Even if the incumbent would otherwise prefer to accommodate a rational entrant, the MCC requires it to match the entrant's price. Similarly, even if below-cost pricing is unprofitable, it must be carried out. Knowing that the threat will be carried out, a rational entrant will be deterred. Although the exact effect of the MCC depends on the wording of the clause and the structure of the industry, the potential benefit of the MCC to the incumbent is clear. An MCC can deter entry by allowing the incumbent to make credible threats to lower its price in the event of entry, even to a below-cost, "predatory" level.

NOTE ON BOISE CASCADE CORP. v. FEDERAL TRADE COMMISSION

In Boise Cascade Corp. v. FTC, 637 F.2d 573 (9th Cir. 1980), first the Federal Trade Commission and then the Ninth Circuit considered the validity of a delivered price system that had been adopted by plywood manufacturers located in the southern United States. The FTC had found that the manufacturers violated § 5 of the FTC Act when they implemented a pricing system that used the computation of rail freight charges from the Pacific Northwest. *Boise Cascade Corp.*, 91 F.T.C. 1 (1978). The Ninth Circuit reversed.

The court's opinion began with a review of the history of the softwood plywood industry in the United States. Until 1947 the plywood came primarily from the Pacific Northwest, but by 1974 approximately 32% of all plywood and 46% of plywood sheathing was manufactured in the South. Some 50% of those southern manufacturers jointly implemented the delivered pricing system that the FTC attacked. The court acknowledged that competition in this industry takes place primarily on the basis of price. The delivered pricing system that the petitioners were using consisted of the mill price plus the amount for rail freight from the West Coast. During the early years, this practice reflected two facts: first, the western mills were still the dominant suppliers (and thus the southern companies had to match their prices); and second, southern plywood was considered to be slightly inferior. By the mid–1970s, however, these justifications had dissipated.

The court noted that "[t]he hallmark of delivered pricing systems has been the industry-wide use of an artificial freight factor as a 'freight equalizer.' " This practice, in turn, has the effect of eliminating any price-cutting based on locational advantages. The petitioners' West Coast freight rate, however, was not a true basing-point system, in the court's view. Nevertheless, it had the same "potential to stabilize prices as a basing-point system. When combined with the standardization of delivery methods, service extras, and discounts, any delivered price system can become a potent tool for assuring that competitors are able to match prices and avoid the rigors of price competition." Although the FTC has often challenged delivered price systems because of their tendency to dampen price competition, the court pointed out that "[t]he tension in the law of delivered pricing stems from the fact that, notwithstanding their potential for abuse as a price-fixing device, Congress has repeatedly refused to require the exclusive use of f.o.b. pricing or to prohibit freight equalization." Thus, the independent decision of "an individual seller to absorb freight in order to match a distant competitor's price is legal under the antitrust laws.''

Industry-wide use of such a system, the court acknowledged, is more problematic, at least when there is no evidence of actual collusion. Since 1948, the FTC had taken the view that consciously parallel use of this device could be enough, even without evidence of a traditional Sherman Act conspiracy, to support a finding that § 5 of the FTC Act was violated. This position, however, was met with considerable opposition. The court concluded, therefore, that "the weight of the case law and the Commission's own policy statement make it clear that we are looking for at least tacit agreement to use a formula which has the effect of fixing prices." This meant, the court said, that the Commission had the burden of demonstrating that the system "has actually had the effect of fixing or stabilizing prices. Without such effect, a mere showing of parallel action will not establish a section 5 violation."

In the remainder of the opinion, the court examined the evidence to see if the Commission had met this burden. It acknowledged that the system used by the petitioners bore some resemblance to classic basing-point cases, in that the following factors were present: industry concentration; importance of freight as a component of price; widespread use of the basing-point system; common use of a formula to calculate shipping weights; and common reliance on commercial price reporters. On the other hand, there was no finding that the system "was used with the price-stabilizing purpose and effect of a classic basing-point system": there was no overt collusion; there was no finding that any of the practices had resulted in "exactly matching price offers to any customers"; and there was evidence that price variations were significant enough that buyers invested time and effort in shopping around. Price movements appeared to reflect broader market conditions.

The Commission, relying on circumstantial evidence, had operated under the theory that the system had nonetheless reduced the range of prices and stabilized them at a supra-competitive level. It had concluded that this evidence was sufficient to shift the burden of proof to the petitioners to show that any anticompetitive effects had been dissipated. The petitioners, on the other hand, emphasized that "the evidence of competition in the index price of plywood, price fluctuations over time, and the consistently lower price of southern plywood" rebutted any inference that the delivered-price system had any stabilizing effect on prices. Petitioners also argued that the evidence revealed that buyers preferred the delivered price quotations.

The court concluded that Commission had failed in its burden to show that substantial evidence in the record supported its conclusion. "In truth," it said, "the Commission has provided us with little more than a theory of the likely effect of the challenged pricing practices." It then pointed to the following flaws in the Commission's case: (1) there was no meaningful evidence substantiating a finding that price levels for southern plywood reflected any anticompetitive effect; (2) there was no evidence that the narrow range of prices for plywood was attributable in any way to the use of West Coast freight charges, as opposed to being the natural pattern of pricing for a standardized commodity; (3) the evidence showed, contrary to the Commission's theory, that substantial bargaining in the base price of plywood existed, which the court saw as supporting "at least a prima facie inference that competition has not been affected by the use of West Coast freight"; (4) there was a complete lack of testimony from buyers objecting to the practice—indeed, to the contrary, buyers indicated that they preferred this system; and (5) the record data on costs and profits did not lend any support to the Commission's thesis.

Finally, the court flatly rejected any effort to shift the burden of proof to the petitioners, or to adopt something less than the substantial evidence standard. It "decline[d] to follow the Commission's suggestion that industry-wide adoption of an artificial method of price-quoting should be deemed a *per se* violation of Section by analogy to section 1 price-tampering cases." It concluded with the following observations:

> The Commission asks us to find that the industry-wide use of West Coast freight constitutes a form of private control over the pricing process equivalent to conspiracy for purposes of *per se* analysis under section 5. We believe, however, that parallel behavior, without more, does not trigger the *per se* treatment which is given to overt agreement. Under our antitrust laws, we begin with the assumption that decisions are made independently and competitively. The debate over conscious parallelism comes down to whether it is ever appropriate for evidence of the anticompetitive effect of certain types of parallel conduct to serve as a substitute for the Sherman Act requirement of agreement. Without reaching that broader issue, we believe that to apply *per se* analysis to these facts would be to assume what must be proven, namely, that the use of West Coast freight by southern plywood producers is not a natural competitive response to buyer preference for traditional forms of price quotation, but rather is a deliberate restraint on competition. Without proof that the practice exerts an anticompetitive effect on the price of plywood, we have no reason to make such an assumption. . . .

> Second, we are not persuaded that a different result is warranted by the unique features of the FTCA. It is often repeated that the Commission was set up as an expert body with power "to restrain practices . . . which, although not yet having grown into Sherman Act dimensions, would most likely do so if left unrestrained." The policies calling for deference to the Commission are, of course, in tension with the acknowledged responsibility of the courts to interpret section 5. Moreover, the law of delivered pricing is well forged, having been developed by the Commission and courts over years of litigation. As we concluded in part II, the weight of the case law, as well as the practices and statements of the Commission, establish the rule that the Commission must find either collusion or actual effect on competition to make out a section 5 violation for use of delivered pricing. In this setting at least, where the parties agree that the practice was a natural and competitive development in the emergence of the southern plywood industry, and where there is a complete absence of evidence implying overt conspiracy, to allow a finding of a section 5 violation on the theory that the mere widespread use of the practice makes it an incipient threat to competition would be to blur the distinction between guilty and innocent commercial behavior. Since we have found that there is not substantial evidence in the record to support the Commission's finding of anticompetitive effect, it follows that the Commission's order may not be enforced.

NOTES AND QUESTIONS

1. After *Boise Cascade*, several classes of plywood purchasers and users succeeded in private damage actions based on the same underlying facts. Plaintiffs in those cases, however, introduced direct evidence of conspiracy, as well as expert testimony on injury caused plaintiffs by "phantom freight" and other practices. On

appeal, the Fifth Circuit held that there was plainly enough evidence to permit the jury finding of collusion. In re Plywood Antitrust Litigation, 655 F.2d 627, 636 (5th Cir. 1981), *cert. granted sub nom.*, Weyerhaeuser Co. v. Lyman Lamb Co., 456 U.S. 971 (1982), *later dismissed* (after settlement), 462 U.S. 1125 (1983). Was the Fifth Circuit's result correct?

2.   Consider carefully the facts in *Cement Institute*, summarized *infra* p. 585. Why was the basing point system in *Cement* more anticompetitive than the delivered price system in *Boise*?

Ethyl Corp. v. FTC

United States Circuit Court of Appeals, Second Circuit, 1984.
729 F.2d 128.

■ MANSFIELD, CIRCUIT JUDGE. . . . From the 1920s until 1948, Ethyl was the sole domestic producer of antiknock compounds. Demand for the compounds increased with the increase in gasoline use, however, and in 1948 Du Pont entered the industry and captured a substantial market share. In 1961 PPG (then known as Houston Chemical Company) began to manufacture and sell the compounds; and in 1964 Nalco followed suit. By 1974, Du Pont had 38.4% of the market; Ethyl 33.5%; PPG 16.2%; and Nalco 11.8%. During 1974–1979, the period of the alleged violations, these were the only four domestic producers and sellers of the compounds. No other firm has ever made or sold the compounds in this country. Thus the industry has always been highly concentrated. However, there are no technological or financial barriers to new entries.

The only purchasers of lead antiknocks are the gasoline refining companies which are large, aggressive and sophisticated buyers. Indeed, several are among the largest industrial corporations in the world. If prospective profits from the sale of antiknock compounds were sufficiently attractive, nothing would prevent them from integrating backwards into the antiknock industry. Of the 154 refiners who purchase the product, the ten largest buy about 30% of the total amount produced in this country.

The steady increase in demand for antiknock compounds during the 1960s allowed PPG and Nalco to enter the market. From August 1971 to January 1974, however, federal controls froze the price of the compounds and beginning in 1973 the federal government initiated steps that were to lead to a drastic reduction in demand. At that time the Environmental Protection Agency ("EPA") required that all automobiles made in the United States, beginning in 1975, be equipped with catalytic converters; since the lead in antiknock compounds fouls such converters, almost all new cars produced since 1975 require unleaded gasoline. At about the same time, in order to reduce the amount of lead in the atmosphere the EPA imposed severe limitations on the amount of lead that could be used in gasoline. As a result of these two measures the use of lead antiknock compounds sharply declined from more than one billion pounds in 1974 to approximately 400 million pounds in 1980, leaving manufacturers with excess capacity. Additional EPA regulations are likely to cause a further decline in the use of the product from an estimated 260 million pounds in 1985 to an estimated 90 million pounds in 1990.

Thus, even though there are no technological or financial constraints barring new entries into the industry and there were two new entrants during the 1960s, the cost of staying in production in a dying industry has made it unlikely that there will be new entrants in the future. The problem confronted by existing producers is the same as that faced by potentially new entrants. Indeed, PPG has recently ceased production of lead anti-knock compounds, leaving only three manufacturers in this evaporating line of business. . . .

. . .

These characteristics of the industry—high concentration, small likelihood of new entries because of a sharply declining market, inelastic demand, and homogeneity of product—led to a natural oligopoly with a high degree of pricing interdependence in which there was far less incentive to engage in price competition than if there had been many sellers in an expanding market. . . . [D]uring the 1970s, profits in the industry—particularly Du Pont's and Ethyl's—were substantially greater than what is described as the benchmark in the chemical industry, which in this case is 150% of the average rate of return in that industry. During the 1974–1979 period under investigation by the FTC, the returns of Ethyl and Du Pont on investment substantially exceeded the 150% benchmark in each year; although PPG's and Nalco's returns on investment also exceeded the 150% benchmark in four of the five years, PPG operated at a loss in 1979 and in 1983 ceased production.

Notwithstanding the highly concentrated structure of the industry, there was substantial price and non-price competition during the 1974–1979 period that is the subject of the complaint. More than 80% of Nalco's sales during that period were at discounts off its list price, and more than one-third of PPG's sales during the same period were at discounts, rising to 58% of its sales in 1979. Despite the fact that the compounds were sold by all four firms on a delivered price basis, the record reveals that, because of the variations in secret discounts granted by Nalco to its customers, the other 3 producers were uncertain as to Nalco's strategy and the net prices actually received by it. Du Pont, for example, was unclear whether Nalco always followed price increases or even had a price list. Ethyl was unsure whether Nalco sometimes sold to certain customers on an f.o.b. basis. . . .

Ethyl and Du Pont, apparently recognizing the futility of meeting price discounts in an inelastic, declining market, each individually chose to meet this price competition on the part of PPG and Nalco not by price discounts but by various forms of non-price competition. These included late billing and "advance buying," the latter of which permitted customers to order extra volume at the old price before a price increase went into effect. Du Pont and Ethyl also provided valuable "free" services, including (1) provision of free equipment, (2) education on how to use the product more efficiently, (3) assistance in building and monitoring facilities for the storage and blending of antiknock compounds, (4) computer programming assistance, (5) training of refiners' employees, (6) payment for consultant services, and (7) favorable credit terms. These competitive practices, according to the ALJ, "played a significant role in the competitive rivalry between the antiknock suppliers" and were responsible for a 35% increase in sales by one respondent to 10 sizeable customers in 1975 over the previous year. . . .

On May 30, 1979, the FTC filed a complaint against the four manufacturers, alleging that each of the companies had engaged in "unfair methods of competition" and "unfair acts and practices" in violation of § 5 of the Act. The complaint attacked the following non-collusive practices: (1) the sale of lead antiknock additives by each respondent only on the basis of a delivered price that included the cost of transportation; (2) the use by Du Pont and Ethyl of "most favored nation" clauses in their standard form sales contracts and the use of such clauses by Nalco in a substantial number of its sales contracts; (3) the use by each company of contract clauses requiring at least 30 days advance notice to customers of changes in price; and (4) providing advance notice of price increases to the press. The complaint did not claim that the practices were the result of any agreement, express or tacit, among the manufacturers or that the practices had been undertaken for other than legitimate business purposes. It simply alleged that the practices "individually and in combination had the effect of reducing uncertainty about competitors' prices of lead-based antiknock compounds," and that such reduced uncertainty "unfairly facilitated the maintenance of substantial, uniform price levels and the reduction or elimination of price competition in the lead-based antiknock market."

Each of the challenged practices was initiated by Ethyl during the period prior to 1948 when it was the sole producer in the industry. There is no suggestion that the practices constituted unfair methods of competition at that time. For example, Ethyl began quoting prices on a delivered basis in 1937 in response to customer demand. Each of the three subsequent manufacturers, upon entry into the market, followed that practice. There is no evidence that the practice was adopted by any of the respondents for other than legitimate business reasons, the principal of which were tradition and customer demand. Customers demanded a delivered price because it would require the manufacturers to retain title to and responsibility for the dangerously volatile compounds during transit to the refiner's plant and in at least some cases would result in savings on state transportation and inventory taxes which the customer would pay if title passed prior to delivery. It is undisputed that, as the ALJ found, the delivery charge is a very small factor in relation to the sales price of the compounds. In 1979, for instance, average delivery costs to respondents' customers amounted to $1.53 cents per pound or less than 2% of list price, hardly a substantial competitive factor.

At trial the FTC offered no expert freight witnesses or other proof regarding the effect of delivered pricing on price competition. Du Pont's expert witness, who had extensive experience in f.o.b. pricing and who was the only witness to testify on the subject, stated that even without uniform delivered pricing (i.e., if antiknocks were sold f.o.b.) published freight tariffs would allow each manufacturer easily to determine any other manufacturer's freight prices to each customer and to match those prices to the penny.

Similarly, Ethyl adopted the "most favored nation" contractual clause more than fifty years ago when it was the sole producer of antiknocks as a guarantee against price discrimination between its own customers who competed against each other in the sale of gasoline containing antiknock compounds. The clause assured the smaller refiners that they would not be placed at a competitive disadvantage on account of price discounts to giants such as Standard Oil, Texaco and Gulf. For the same legitimate business reason Du Pont adopted the same contractual clause when it later entered the industry. Even though such clauses arguably reduce price discounting, they comport with the requirements of the Robinson–Patman Act, which prohibits price discrimination between customers. There is no evidence that Ethyl or Du Pont adopted or continued to use the most favored nation clause for the purpose of influencing the price discounting policies of other producers or of facilitating their adoption of or adherence to uniform prices. Indeed, PPG did not include the clause in its standard contract with customers and the complaint did not charge it with engaging in this practice. Nalco made only limited use of the clause.

Finally, the issuance of advance notice of price increases both to buyers and to the press, a common practice in the chemical industry, was initiated by Ethyl, well before the entry of Du Pont or the other two manufacturers into the market, as a means of aiding buyers in their financial and purchase planning. The contract clause used by two producers (Ethyl and Nalco) required them to give 30 days notice to the customer of price changes, while the clause used by the others (Du Pont and PPG) was limited to price increases. Du Pont and Ethyl gave customers a few days additional notice of their price increases (sometimes called a "grace period") but Nalco did not do so and PPG did not do so in any price increase that it initiated. Although the advance noticing had the indirect effect of informing competitors as to the producer's price increases, the record, not surprisingly, contains considerable proof that in such a small industry manufacturers quickly learn of competitors' price changes, usually within hours, regardless of the advance public notice. Typically, when one producer changed its price and communicated that change to its buyers, those buyers would immediately call the other producers to secure the best price. Moreover, the giving of 30 or more days advance notice of a price increase did not preclude the initiator, upon finding that competitors did not follow, from rescinding or modifying the increase or extending its effective date at any time prior to the end of the 30–day period.[24]

· · ·

---

24. An example was Du Pont's giving of a 30–day notice of a price increase in August 1977 without any additional advance, or grace period, notice. When Ethyl thereafter undercut

The Commission concluded from its examination of the record that the structure of the antiknock industry—high concentration, high barriers to entry, a homogeneous product, and inelastic demand—rendered it susceptible to unilateral but interdependent conduct which lessened competition. The Commission further decided that the record contained substantial evidence of noncompetitive performance in the industry: highly uniform prices and price changes, limited price discounting, stable market shares, relatively high profits, prices in excess of marginal cost, and rising prices despite excess capacity and sluggish demand. On such a record, the FTC held that unilateral but interdependent practices engaged in by the petitioners constituted an unfair method of competition in violation of § 5. . . .

The essential question is whether, given the characteristics of the antiknock industry, the Commission erred in holding that the challenged business practices constitute "unfair methods of competition" in violation of § 5 simply because they "facilitate" consciously parallel pricing at identical levels. . . .

   . . . .

The Commission here asks us . . . to hold that the "unfair methods of competition" provision of § 5 can be violated by non-collusive, non-predatory and independent conduct of a non-artificial nature, at least when it results in a substantial lessening of competition. We recognize that § 5 invests the Commission with broad powers designed to enable it to cope with new threats to competition as they arise. . . . However, . . . appropriate standards must be adopted and applied to protect a respondent against abuse of power. As the Commission moves away from attacking conduct that is either a violation of the antitrust laws or collusive, coercive, predatory, restrictive or deceitful, and seeks to break new ground by enjoining otherwise legitimate practices, the closer must be our scrutiny upon judicial review. A test based solely upon restraint of competition, even if qualified by the requirement that the conduct be "analogous" to an antitrust violation, is so vague as to permit arbitrary or undue government interference with the reasonable freedom of action that has marked our country's competitive system.

The term "unfair" is an elusive concept, often dependent upon the eye of the beholder.[25] A line must therefore be drawn between conduct that is anticompetitive and legitimate conduct that has an impact on competition.

Du Pont's increased by adopting a lesser increase Du Pont rolled back its increase to the lesser competitive amount rather than sell at its proposed higher price.

25. Two decisions heavily relied on by the Commission, *Triangle Conduit & Cable Co. v. FTC*, 168 F.2d 175 (7th Cir. 1948), *aff'd by an equally divided court sub nom.*, *Clayton Mark & Co. v. FTC*, 336 U.S. 956 (1949), and *Boise Cascade Corp. v. FTC*, 637 F.2d 573 (9th Cir. 1980), are not of assistance in resolving the issue before us. In *Triangle Conduit* the FTC had found that the use of a mathematical formula by members of a trade association to compute delivered price amounted to both a conspiracy to fix prices and an unfair method of competition in violation of § 5. Upon appeal the Seventh Circuit held that the conspiracy had been proved by circumstantial evidence. 168 F.2d at 180. Although it went on to state in reliance on *FTC v. Cement Institute*, *supra*, that it could not "say the Commission was wrong in concluding that the individual use of the basing point method . . . does constitute an unfair method of competition," *id.* at 181, the finding of a conspiracy sheds doubt on the significance

Lessening of competition is not the substantial equivalent of "unfair methods" of competition. Section 5 is aimed at conduct, not at the result of such conduct, even though the latter is usually a relevant factor in determining whether the challenged conduct is "unfair." Nor does the statute obligate a business to engage in competition; if that were the case, many acceptable pricing and market decisions would be barred. A manufacturer, for instance, would be prevented from making a concededly lawful change in its distribution system, designed to increase sales efficiency, by unilaterally reducing the number of its wholesalers, since the effect would be to diminish substantial competition at the wholesaler level. Similarly, if anticompetitive impact were the sole test, the admittedly lawful unilateral closing of a plant or refusal to expand capacity could be found to be "unfair." The holder of a valid product patent could be prevented from exercising its lawful monopoly to charge whatever the traffic would bear, even though "a monopolist, as long as he has no purpose to restrain competition or to enhance or expand his monopoly, and does not act coercively, retains [the right to trade with whom he wishes]." *Official Airline Guides, Inc. v. FTC*, 630 F.2d 920, 927–28 (2d Cir. 1980), *cert. denied*, 450 U.S. 917 (1981); *see United States v. Colgate & Co.*, 250 U.S. 300, 307 (1919).

    . . . The mere existence of an oligopolistic market structure in which a small group of manufacturers engage in consciously parallel pricing of an

---

of the latter statement. Indeed, a majority of the Commission took the view that *Cement Institute* and *Triangle Conduit* apply only to "conspiracy situations." Interim Report on the Study of the Federal Trade Commission Pricing Policies, S.Doc. No. 27, 81st Cong., 1st Sess. 62–63 (1949). The Commission's failure thereafter for over 30 years to seek to apply § 5 to consciously parallel behavior not involving collusion, coercion or restrictive conduct indicates that it believed it has no power to curb otherwise legitimate behavior allegedly facilitating conscious price parallelism.

Boise Cascade Corp. is at best ambiguous. . . . The FTC argued that even though there was no agreement, there was liability because of the anticompetitive effect [from adopting the West Coast freight factor in southern plywood manufacturers' pricing scheme, Ed.]. The Ninth Circuit set aside the FTC order, finding no anticompetitive effect. The FTC in the instant case relies upon the following statement by the court:

> "We thus hold that in the absence of evidence of overt agreement to utilize a pricing system to avoid price competition, the Commission must demonstrate that the challenged pricing system has actually had the effect of fixing or stabilizing prices. Without such effect, a mere showing of parallel action will not establish a section 5 violation." 637 F.2d at 577.

Standing alone, the statement tends to support the Commission's position here, particularly since a finding of price conspiracy would obviate the necessity of proving that it had the effect of fixing or stabilizing prices. But earlier in the same paragraph the court stated:

> "It is important to stress that the weight of the case law and the Commission's own policy statement make it clear that we are looking for at least tacit agreement to use a formula which has the effect of fixing prices. Indeed, none of the delivered pricing cases support a finding of a section 5 violation for the bare existence of an industry-wide artificial freight factor. In each case, the system had been utilized, tacitly or overtly, to match prices and avoid price competition." *Id.* at 576–77.

In view of this statement we cannot place much reliance on *Boise Cascade* as support for the Commission's position here.

identical product does not violate the antitrust laws. *Theatre Enterprises, Inc. v. Paramount Film Distributing Corp.*, 346 U.S. 537 (1954). It represents a condition, not a "method;" indeed it could be consistent with intense competition. Labeling one producer's price change in such a market as a "signal," parallel price changes as "lock-step," or prices as "supracompetitive," hardly converts its pricing into an "unfair" method of competition. To so hold would be to condemn any such price increase or moves, however independent; yet the FTC has not suggested that § 5 authorizes it to ban all price increases in an oligopolistic market. On the contrary, it states that "Section 5 should not prohibit oligopolistic *pricing* alone, even supracompetitive parallel prices, in the absence of specific conduct which promotes such a result." (Emphasis in original). This fine distinction creates doubt as to the types of otherwise legitimate conduct that are lawful and those that are not. The doubt is increased by the Commission's concession that price uniformity is normal in a market with few sellers and homogeneous products, such as that in the antiknock compound industry.

In view of this patent uncertainty the Commission owes a duty to define the conditions under which conduct claimed to facilitate price uniformity would be unfair so that businesses will have an inkling as to what they can lawfully do rather than be left in a state of complete unpredictability. The Commission's decision in the present case does not provide any guidelines; it would require each producer not only to assess the general conduct of the antiknock business but also that of each of its competitors and the reaction of each to the other, which would be virtually impossible. Some idea of the fickleness and uncertainty of the FTC's position in the present case can be gathered from its ambivalent view towards some of the practices which it attacks. Certain otherwise-legitimate practices were declared unlawful only when used cumulatively with other practices. Others were found unfair when used by certain producers (Du Pont and Ethyl) but not when used by others (PPG and Nalco). Press announcements of price increases and contractual 30–day price increase notice requirements were held permissible but giving buyers a few days additional notice was found to be unfair even though there was no proof that the extra days made any competitive difference. Indeed, with or without the additional days' notice the initiator of a price increase was not precluded from withdrawing or modifying it within the 30–day period or from extending the 30–day notice period itself. Thus the FTC's rulings and order appear to represent uncertain guesswork rather than workable rules of law.

In our view, before business conduct in an oligopolistic industry may be labeled "unfair" within the meaning of § 5 a minimum standard demands that, absent a tacit agreement, at least some indicia of oppressiveness must exist such as (1) evidence of anticompetitive intent or purpose on the part of the producer charged, or (2) the absence of an independent legitimate business reason for its conduct.[26] If, for instance, a seller's

---

26. The requirement is comparable to the principle that there must be a "plus factor" before conscious parallelism may be found to be conspiratorial in violation of the Sherman Act.

conduct, even absent identical behavior on the part of its competitors, is contrary to its independent self-interest, that circumstance would indicate that the business practice is "unfair" within the meaning of § 5. In short, in the absence of proof of a violation of the antitrust laws or evidence of collusive, coercive, predatory, or exclusionary conduct, business practices are not "unfair" in violation of § 5 unless those practices either have an anticompetitive purpose or cannot be supported by an independent legitimate reason. To suggest, as does the Commission in its opinion, that the defendant can escape violating § 5 only by showing that there are "countervailing procompetitive justifications" for the challenged business practices goes too far. . . .

The tenuousness of the Commission's finding that the challenged practices are "unfair" is illustrated by the fact that it does not tell us when the practices became unlawful: at the time of their original adoption by Ethyl when it was the sole manufacturer of antiknock compounds, when Du Pont entered the market in 1948, when PPG entered in 1961, when Nalco appeared on the scene in 1964, or at some other time. . . .

In the first place, price uniformity and parallelism was much more limited than the FTC would have it. During the relevant period (1974–1979) Nalco extended price discounts on more than 80% of its sales and PPG on more than one-third of its sales, the latter increasing to 58% of its sales in 1979 as the sellers competed for fewer buyers in a diminishing market. Although there was for the most part price parallelism on the part of Du Pont and Ethyl, they effectively met the price discounts of the other two producers by providing competition in the form of extensive services which had the effect of retaining old customers or luring away new ones. Thus the total package, including free valuable services and discounts, presents a picture of a competitive market in which large, sophisticated and aggressive buyers were making demands and were satisfied with the results. To the extent that there was price uniformity, that condition is as consistent with competitive as with anticompetitive behavior.

See, e.g., Naumkeag Theatres Co. v. New England Theatres, Inc., 345 F.2d 910, 911–12 (1st Cir.), *cert. denied*, 382 U.S. 906 (1965) (parallel clearances and run schedules by motion picture distributors); *Modern Home Inst. Inc. v. Hartford Accident & Indemn. Co.*, 513 F.2d 102 (2d Cir. 1975) (defendant insurers had independent reasons for refusing to buy plaintiff's list of customers). The "plus factor" may be conduct that is contrary to the defendants' independent self-interest, *Morton Salt Co. v. United States*, 235 F.2d 573, 578–79 (10th Cir. 1956), the presence or absence of a strong motive on a defendants' part to enter an alleged conspiracy, *First National Bank of Arizona v. Cities Service Co.*, 391 U.S. 253, 286–88 (1968); *Interstate Circuit, Inc. v. United States*, 306 U.S. 208, 222–23 (1939), or the artificial standardization of products, *C–O–Two Fire Equip. Co. v. United States*, 197 F.2d 489, 493 (9th Cir.), *cert. denied*, 344 U.S. 892 (1952). In *United States v. General Electric Co.*, et al., 565 F.2d 208 [1977–2] Trade Cas. & 61,659, at 72,715 (E.D. Pa. 1977), for instance, General Electric in addition to announcing that it would adhere to its published prices and grant no discounts, adopted a "price-protection" policy under which, if it offered a discount to a customer, it obligated itself to give the same discount retroactively to all other customers who had bought the product within the previous six months, thus voluntarily penalizing itself for price-discounting.

The problems faced by anyone thinking of entering the market were not "barriers" in the usual sense used by economists, such as requirements for high capital investment or advanced technological know-how. The main problem has been that market demand, due to factors uncontrolled by petitioners, is sharply declining. A dying market, which will soon dry up altogether, does not attract new entries. Absent some reasonable prospect that a price reduction would increase demand—and there is none—it is not surprising that existing producers have not engaged in as much price competition as might exist under other conditions. To suggest that industry-wide use of delivered instead of f.o.b. pricing restrained price competition in such a market ignores the de minimis part freight charges played in the price paid by customers. It also overlooks the fact that f.o.b. pricing is not necessarily more competitive than delivered pricing.

In short, we do not find substantial evidence in this record as a whole that the challenged practices significantly lessened competition in the antiknock industry or that the elimination of those practices would improve competition.

The FTC's order is vacated.

[Judge Lumbard concurred in the conclusion of the majority that the "record does not support the FTC's finding of substantial [anticompetitive] effect," but stated that it was unnecessary to reach the "broader question" of whether "§ 5 is limited to conduct that is either *per se* pernicious (*i.e.*, collusive, coercive, predatory, or exclusionary) or could not have been adopted for other than pernicious reasons; or whether, as the FTC now argues, it extends also to conduct that may be acceptable in some situations but not in others, in light of poor industry structure and performance, substantial anticompetitive effects, and lack of offsetting procompetitive justification."]

NOTE ON GE/WESTINGHOUSE

A number of electrical equipment manufacturers and many of their employees were indicted in 1960 for a conspiracy to fix prices and allocate business in various heavy electrical equipment product lines. Most of the defendants pleaded guilty and some individuals went to jail, substantial fines were paid, an order was entered against the manufacturers and some 1,800 private treble damage lawsuits were filed. In many respects, it was the biggest cartel "bust" in the history of Sherman Act enforcement.

For a time, vigorous competition flourished, but eventually only GE and Westinghouse remained as active competitors in the market for sale of large turbine generators. In 1972, the government undertook an investigation and concluded that beginning in 1963, price competition between the two had been eliminated. As we noted in Chapter 4, the government contended that this had been accomplished in the following ways: (1) each company published a similar and unusually extensive price book which would allow the other to predict the price each would bid on a particular type and size of machine; (2) both companies adopted a "price protection plan" whereby if the manufacturer lowered a price to a customer, any other customer purchasing within the previous six-month period would be given an identical retroactive discount; and (3) each company published a list of outstanding bids whenever there was a price change, so that customers (and the other seller) would not be confused as to who was entitled to a particular price.

The government did not claim any of these practices were adopted by agreement, but rather that these consciously parallel policies had led to identical prices.

GE and Westinghouse denied that any violation had occurred, but agreed to a modification in the order that had been entered after the 1960 price-fixing conspiracy was uncovered. As a result of the order, the two companies were enjoined, among other things, from: (1) "offering a price protection policy or entering into any agreement whereby the price of a large turbine-generator to any customer would be retroactively reduced ..." and (2) publishing any price book or price list relating to large turbine-generators, except one "based on the defendant's own individually determined criteria and costs...."

Consider the following questions with respect to GE/Westinghouse:

1. Can you reconcile the government's view in GE/Westinghouse that consciously parallel adoption of price protection plans was illegal with the Second Circuit's conclusion in *Ethyl* that the most favored customer clauses adopted by several of the lead additive manufacturers created no antitrust problems? In that connection, *see* note 31 of the Second Circuit's opinion, where the Court attempts to distinguish the GE/Westinghouse arrangement. Did the Second Circuit adequately consider the type of economic concerns raised by Professor Salop?

2. Suppose two competing department stores announce publicly that each will not be undersold by the other on any item carried in both stores. Each tells customers that if they will bring in an ad or sales slip from the other store showing a lower price, each will meet that price. Is that different from the price protection plan? Should it be illegal?

3. Suppose members of a trade association agree that trade association dues and support for the association's public welfare activities would be computed according to the number of successful bids by each member; can you imagine a set of circumstances in which that might be regarded as a "facilitating practice"?

Todd v. Exxon Corporation

United States Court of Appeals, Second Circuit, 2001.
275 F.3d 191.

■ SOTOMAYOR, CIRCUIT JUDGE: Plaintiff-appellant Roberta Todd appeals from an order ... granting defendants-appellees' motion to dismiss the complaint for failure to state a claim pursuant to Fed. R. Civ. P. 12(b)(6). We hold that plaintiff adequately alleges a § 1 Sherman Act violation for an unlawful information exchange. Plaintiff's complaint alleges a plausible product market, a market structure that is susceptible to collusive activity, a data exchange with anticompetitive potential, and antitrust injury. We therefore vacate and remand.

Background

Plaintiff brought this action against fourteen major companies in the integrated oil and petrochemical industry, collectively accounting for 80–

90% of the industry's revenues and employing approximately the same percentage of the industry's workforce. On behalf of herself and all other similarly situated current and former Exxon employees (the putative class), plaintiff alleges that defendants violated § 1 of the Sherman Act by regularly sharing detailed information regarding compensation paid to nonunion managerial, professional, and technical ("MPT") employees and using this information in setting the salaries of these employees at artificially low levels. Plaintiff seeks money damages and equitable relief pursuant to § 1 of the Sherman Act.

Accepting the allegations in the complaint as true, as we must on this motion to dismiss, the facts of this case are as follows. Defendants instituted a system whereby they periodically conducted surveys comparing past and current MPT salary information and participated in regular meetings at which current and future salary budgets were discussed. The data exchanges were also accompanied by assurances that the information would be used in setting the salaries of MPT employees. Defendants' "Job Match Survey" created a common denominator to facilitate the comparison of MPT salaries. The survey used certain jobs at defendant Chevron as benchmarks. The other defendants would submit detailed information regarding the jobs at their companies that were most comparable to the Chevron benchmark jobs so that they could be matched. The survey compared the responsibilities and compensation packages offered by defendants for certain jobs and job types against those of the benchmark positions at Chevron. This survey was coordinated by defendants Unocal and Chevron. Chevron and Unocal each would meet with half of the other companies involved to develop matches to the benchmarks, and then would gather the information before submitting it to a third-party consultant, Towers Perrin. Towers Perrin compiled the information, then analyzed, refined, and distributed it to the defendants on diskettes and in the form of hard copies. Since not all jobs could be matched precisely, defendants agreed upon certain percentage "offsets" to facilitate the comparison. The Job Match Survey was performed every two years and was supplemented in the "off years" by the "Grade Average Update," which would calculate the change in grade average salaries since the last Job Match Survey and then adjust the salary level from the previous year's survey by the amount of the change.

Defendants' "Job Family Survey" provided the most current account of the compensation being paid in the industry. Each company submitted information on salaries actually paid in thirty different categories of jobs, or "job families," classified according to the nature of the work. The information exchanged for each family was broken down by the job level classification, experience level, and academic background of the MPT employee. This survey was coordinated by Exxon, and again the information was submitted to and compiled by Towers Perrin. Each participating company received the information from Towers Perrin in hard copy and disk form. The information gathered in the survey was updated and distributed to the participants several times per year.

Furthermore, each company was entitled to receive subsets of Job Family Survey data, consisting of salary information from as few as three companies at a time. Plaintiff alleges that Exxon used these subsets to compare its own salaries with those of six particular competitors, referred to as the "Six Majors." These periodically updated data sets were used by each defendant to determine whether the announced budgets of its competitors had been implemented so that each could consider what adjustments should be made to coordinate salary levels.

Although these were the primary forms of salary information exchange, defendants supplemented this information with data from other sources. Defendants' "Advancement Guides" established requirements for advancement within a given salary grade of employee. These guides were used by defendants to slow the rates of advancement for MPT employees in defendants' companies. The "ABC," "B–1" and "B–2" surveys collected additional data regarding bonuses and other non-standard payments above base compensation that were not captured in the Job Match and Job Family Surveys. The "Long–Term Incentive Survey" refined the comparison further by accounting for the economic value of certain non-cash benefits paid to MPT employees. The "Starting Salary Survey," in which only the Six Majors apparently participated, measured starting salaries of college graduates entering MPT positions. In addition to the data exchange surveys, human resource personnel at defendant companies held regular meetings—at least three times per year—to discuss and exchange salary and salary-related information. These meetings included discussions of individual defendants' current and future salary budgets for MPT employees.

Plaintiff contends that defendants' arrangement violated § 1 of the Sherman Act. According to the complaint, these violations had the purpose and effect of depressing MPT salaries paid by defendants. The arrangement reduced the incentive for defendants to bid up salaries in order to attract experienced MPT employees or to retain employees who might be lured to other firms. As a result, the plaintiffs in the putative class received compensation that was materially lower than what they would have received but for defendants' anticompetitive practices.

Plaintiff alleges that Exxon, in particular, used this data to maintain a market position slightly above the so-called "Six Majors" and below three higher-paying competitors referred to as the "High Three." Exxon capitalized on the shared data to decrease its "competitive factor"—the percentage by which Exxon would have to adjust its salary levels in order to maintain alignment with the salaries offered by its competitors. Exxon's competitive factor dropped from 6.5% in 1991 to 0% in 1995, and its salaries decreased 4.1% between 1987 and 1994 in comparison to the Six Majors. The various information exchanges also allowed Exxon to reduce its overall salary index versus the competition from 110.7% in 1987 to 107.0% in 1993.

The district court granted defendants' motion to dismiss the complaint for failure to state a claim pursuant to Fed. R. Civ. P. 12(b)(6). The court held that (1) plaintiff failed to plead a plausible product market, undermining the claim that defendants control 80–90% of the relevant market; (2) even if the alleged market were plausible, plaintiff failed to allege that the market structure is susceptible to collusive activity; (3) plaintiff failed to allege facts supporting an agreement to fix salary levels; and (4) plaintiff failed to show detrimental effects on competition. Plaintiff appeals the dismissal.

Discussion

I. [In this section, the court noted that its standard of review was *de novo*; that the complaint would be reviewed in the light most favorable to the plaintiff; and that there is no heightened pleading requirement applicable to antitrust cases.]

II.   The Rule of Reason

Section 1 of the Sherman Act prohibits "every contract, combination in the form of trust or otherwise, or conspiracy, in restraint of trade or commerce among the several States, or with foreign nations." 15 U.S.C. § 1. Traditional "hard-core" price fixing remains *per se* unlawful under the seminal case *United States v. Socony–Vacuum Oil Co.*, 310 U.S. 150, 212–24 (1940), and its progeny. If the plaintiff in this case could allege that defendants actually formed an agreement to fix MPT salaries, this *per se* rule would likely apply. Furthermore, even in the absence of direct "smoking gun" evidence, a horizontal price-fixing agreement may be inferred on the basis of conscious parallelism, when such interdependent conduct is accompanied by circumstantial evidence and plus factors such as defendants' use of facilitating practices. *See, e.g., Interstate Circuit, Inc. v. United States*, 306 U.S. 208, 226–27 (1939); *Ambook Enters. v. Time Inc.*, 612 F.2d 604, 614–18 (2d Cir. 1979). Information exchange is an example of a facilitating practice that can help support an inference of a price-fixing agreement.

There is a closely related but analytically distinct type of claim, also based on § 1 of the Sherman Act, where the violation lies in the information exchange itself—as opposed to merely using the information exchange as evidence upon which to infer a price-fixing agreement. This exchange of information is not illegal *per se*, but can be found unlawful under a rule of reason analysis. . . . The state of the law on this issue was not always so clear. . . . In *United States v. Container Corp. of America*, the Supreme Court held that information exchange itself could constitute a § 1 violation, upholding the sufficiency of a complaint charging "an exchange of price information but no agreement to adhere to a price schedule." 393 U.S. 333, 334 (1969). The Court found that under the market conditions present in that case, and in light of the nature of the information disseminated, the data exchange caused a stabilization of prices and thus had an anticompetitive effect on the market for corrugated containers. *See id.* 393 U.S. at 337. Unclear in the wake of *Container Corp.* was whether such exchanges were *per se* unlawful or subject to a rule of reason. The Court used some of the language of the Court's *per se* jurisprudence, yet conducted a market analysis that suggested a rule of reason. *See id.* 393 U.S. at 336–38.

The Supreme Court resolved the confusion in *United States v. Citizens & Southern National Bank*, clarifying that "the dissemination of price information is not itself a *per se* violation of the Sherman Act." 422 U.S. 86 (1975). In *United States v. United States Gypsum Co.*, the Court explained its reasoning: "The exchange of price data and other information among competitors does not invariably have anticompctitive effects; indeed such practices can in certain circumstances increase economic efficiency and render markets more, rather than less, competitive." 438 U.S. 422, 441 n. 16 (1978). The Court then set out the basic framework for the rule of reason inquiry in this context: "A number of factors including most prominently the structure of the industry involved and the nature of the information exchanged are generally considered in divining the procompetitive or anticompetitive effects of this type of interseller communication." *Id.*

As plaintiff does not allege an actual agreement among defendants to fix salaries, we analyze plaintiff's complaint solely as to whether it alleges unlawful information exchange pursuant to this rule of reason.

III. Market Power

A. The Relevant Market

... Plaintiff argues that the relevant market in this case is the market for "the services of experienced, salaried, non-union, managerial, professional and technical (MPT) employees in the oil and petrochemical industry, in the continental United States and various submarkets thereof." If the market is defined in this way, defendants would have a substantial market share of 80–90%. If the market cannot be limited in this way, defendants' percentage market share would drop substantially....

[The district court rejected the plaintiff's proposed market, on the grounds that it was both over-inclusive (because it had failed to explain why a variety of professional jobs in the oil industry were interchangeable with one another) and under-inclusive (because it was skeptical about the existence of industry-specific expertise). The court of appeals disagreed on both counts. It agreed with plaintiffs that the proper focus was on the commonality and interchangeability of the buyers, not the sellers, and that employees indeed did acquire industry-specific expertise.]

In sum, plaintiff's complaint alleges a plausible product market. The district court erred by requiring that the different MPT jobs be interchangeable with one another, by rejecting plaintiff's allegation about industry-specific experience on a Rule 12(b)(6) motion to dismiss, and by failing to consider allegations about industry recognition.

B. Anticompetitive Effect As an Indication of Market Power

Plaintiff's alleged product market would support the 80–90% market share figure for defendants. Market power defined as a percentage market share, however, is not the only way to demonstrate defendants' ability to depress salaries. If a plaintiff can show that a defendant's conduct exerted an actual adverse effect on competition, this is a strong indicator of market power. In fact, this arguably is more direct evidence of market power than calculations of elusive market share figures.

In this Circuit, a threshold showing of market share is not a prerequisite for bringing a § 1 claim. If, for example, the plaintiff in this case could prove that (1) defendants engaged in information exchanges that would be deemed anticompetitive under *Gypsum* and (2) such activities did in fact have an anticompetitive effect on the market for MPT labor in the oil and petrochemical industry, we would not deny relief on the basis of market share figures. On remand, therefore, the court should consider whether plaintiff has demonstrated anticompetitive effects as part of the court's assessment of defendants' market power.

Defendants mistake this approach for the "quick look" or "truncated" rule of reason inquiry that the Supreme Court has endorsed in certain contexts. Defendants are correct to assert that in *California Dental Ass'n v. FTC* the Supreme Court limited the use of the "quick look" to cases in which the probable anticompetitive effects of the alleged conduct would be "intuitively obvious" and "easily . . . ascertained" with "even a rudimentary understanding of economics." 526 U.S. 756, 759, 770 (1999). . . . The alleged conduct in this case—the exchange of information—is not so inherently or intuitively anticompetitive. The Supreme Court has said as much and specifically prescribed a full rule of reason. *See Gypsum*, 438 U.S. at 441 n. 16. . . . We do not suggest that the district court can avoid conducting a full analysis of the pro- and anticompetitive characteristics of the arrangement in this case.

The use of anticompetitive effects to demonstrate market power, however, is not limited to "quick look" or "truncated" rule of reason cases. This Court's precedents discussed above were not "quick look" cases; they merely accepted alternative ways of demonstrating market power. The question of whether plaintiff has alleged adverse effects on competition and antitrust injury sufficient to survive a Rule 12(b)(6) motion is addressed *infra* Part VI.

IV.   Susceptibility of the Market

The Supreme Court in *Gypsum* explained that one of the two "most prominent[]" factors in the rule of reason analysis of a data exchange is "the structure of the industry involved." 438 U.S. at 441 n. 16. Therefore, once the relevant market is defined, a court must analyze the structure of that market to determine whether it is "susceptible to the exercise of market power through tacit coordination." As the district court explained, "susceptible markets tend to be highly concentrated—that is, oligopolistic—and to have fungible products subject to inelastic demand." These factors are addressed in turn.

A. Concentration

Generally speaking, the possibility of anticompetitive collusive practices is most realistic in concentrated industries. If the relevant market in this case is defined as the plaintiff contends, the defendants would control collectively a 80–90% market share. While this is an extremely high market share by any measure, the district court contends that the alleged market "is not, as plaintiff contends, so clearly oligopolistic." The district court points out that there are fourteen defendants in this case, and that this is not a concentrated market under the Department of Justice Merger Guidelines. That the market would not be deemed highly concentrated by this measure, however, does not preclude the possibility of collusive activity. . . .

The Supreme Court has found that data exchange can be unlawful despite a relatively large number of sellers. In *Container Corp.*, the Court used the oft-cited language that the industry was "dominated by relatively few sellers." 393 U.S. at 337. But in fact, the defendants in *Container Corp.* were eighteen firms controlling 90% of the market, defined as the sale of cardboard cartons in the Southeast. *Id.* 393 U.S. at 342 (Marshall, J., dissenting). The Court nonetheless found the market sufficiently concentrated to support the finding of a violation. *Id.* 393 U.S. at 334–38. It is fairly clear that the reason the Court reached its holding despite the multiplicity of sellers was the specific anticompetitive characteristics of the information exchange. Given that the market concentration in this case is not radically different from that in *Container Corp.*, and given that concentration is part of a rule of reason inquiry that also emphasizes the nature of the information exchanged, we do not think that fourteen companies sharing an 80–90% market share is so unconcentrated as to warrant a Rule 12(b)(6) dismissal where the nature of the exchanges appears anticompetitive. We also find it unsurprising that data exchange cases may involve a number of participants that begins to push the boundaries of oligopoly. These players are most in need of such data exchange arrangements in order to facilitate price coordination; a very small handful of firms in a more highly concentrated market may be less likely to require the kind of sophisticated data dissemination alleged in this case.

B. Fungibility

The district court also asserted that "even if the proposed market were oligopolistic, plaintiff still could not establish its susceptibility to the exercise of market power through tacit coordination. The 'products' in her proposed market are, as discussed above, far from fungible." The district court apparently refers to its previous discussion of interchangeability, wherein it argued that the various types of jobs included in the MPT category are vastly different from one other.

It is important to bear in mind the context in which the fungibility question arises. The inquiry is one part of the question of whether the market is susceptible to the exercise of market power though tacit coordination. Fungibility is relevant on this point because it is less realistic for a cartel to establish and police a price conspiracy where it is difficult to compare the products being sold. In contrast, "fungible products facilitate coordination of pricing in a concentrated industry because it is easier to determine and monitor a consensus on some competitive variable." Therefore, fungibility plays a significant role in evaluating the anticompetitive potential of an information exchange.

The question in this case is whether jobs at the various oil and petrochemical companies were comparable, or fungible enough so that the defendants could have used the exchanged information as part of a tacit conspiracy to depress salaries....

As an initial matter, the district court's discussion about the clear differences among the various types of MPT jobs is inapposite. Plaintiff alleges that the information exchanged by defendants related to specific job categories—not to MPT employment in general. Therefore, the fact that a job as an attorney and one as a geologist are not comparable does not bear on the ability of defendants to coordinate salaries. Rather, the relevant question is whether jobs *within* each category are fungible enough across the oil and petrochemical industry to allow for such coordination.

One might argue that the jobs still are not fungible—even within each category of MPT employee. Varied jobs in a complex industry are far less fungible than, say, a product such as corrugated containers. Services generally tend not to be fungible or susceptible to standardization, and it is unlikely that these fourteen different companies would have positions with job descriptions that precisely match one another. Even this argument, however, is complicated by the specific facts of this case, coupled with the policy rationale behind the fungibility inquiry.

Plaintiff's complaint alleges in detail the sophisticated techniques defendants used to "achieve a common denominator" with respect to the compensation paid to their MPT employees. Defendants developed the Job Match Survey because they "realized it was not functionally efficient simply to know what each others' employees were being paid unless they were able to horizontally match the various job classifications." The survey revolved around certain benchmark jobs provided by Chevron. The defendants would submit detailed information relating to the jobs most nearly comparable to the benchmark jobs so that they could be matched. "A 'match' is defined as a similar job in a similar organization whose combined reporting functions and scope adjustments are not more than two survey salary grades above or below the benchmarked job." Plaintiff alleges that, during the relevant time period, Exxon was able to match 70–80% of its jobs to the 155 Chevron benchmark positions. Furthermore, because not all jobs could be matched precisely, the defendants agreed upon certain "offsets" reflecting the specific differences between jobs as a percentage figure. For purposes of the survey, each grade level was assumed to have a salary difference of 14% at its midpoint. The offset factor assigned to each job was thus stated as a fraction of 14%—a positive fraction for jobs with greater responsibilities than the Chevron benchmark job and a negative fraction for jobs with lesser responsibilities. Defendants even devised a formula to enhance the comparability of non-cash benefits afforded to MPT employees in their Long Term Incentive Survey.

Plaintiff is thus on solid ground when she argues that defendants "made their own employees' positions 'fungible' for comparison purposes with those of their competitors." The jobs in question may not be inherently fungible, but since the purpose of the fungibility inquiry is to test whether defendants would be able to compare the positions for coordination purposes, the sophisticated techniques employed by defendants to account for the differences among jobs are extremely telling.

C. Inelastic Demand

Concluding its discussion of the susceptibility of the market to tacit coordination, the district court stated that "plaintiff has pleaded no facts tending to establish that the demand for these 'products' is inelastic." We disagree. This part of the inquiry, easily confused with the cross-elasticity and interchangeability analysis that is used to define the relevant market, traditionally asks whether demand is inelastic because "buyers place orders only for immediate, short-run needs." In other words, the question is whether it is economically feasible for buyers to abstain from purchasing the product for some period of time.

Here again, we reverse the equation in the context of an oligopsony. Where market power is exercised by buyers, it is the elasticity of the sellers' *supply* that is at issue. Sellers' supply could be elastic if, for example, they have "the option of withholding some output from the market in hopes of higher prices in future years." If, however, the goods are perishable, short-run supply may be quite inelastic. In this case, the supply at issue is the labor of the MPT employees. "Labor is an extremely perishable commodity—an hour not worked today can never be recovered." As a result, "collusion among employers can drive the wage down to the individual's reservation wage." As labor is a classic example of inelastic supply flow, it is unclear what additional facts plaintiffs would have to allege with regard to this aspect of the inquiry.

In sum, the pleadings support the contention that the market was susceptible to tacit coordination by the defendant companies: The market is sufficiently concentrated under *Container Corp.*; the defendants have in effect manufactured a form of fungibility through sophisticated comparison techniques; and the supply of labor has an inherently inelastic quality.

V. The Nature of the Information Exchanged

Alongside the "structure of the industry involved," the other major factor for courts to consider in a data exchange case is the "nature of the information exchanged." There are certain well-established criteria used to help ascertain the anticompetitive potential of information exchanges. As part of the analysis, a court should consider, "broadly speaking, whether it was of the sort in *American Column & Lumber Co. v. United States* . . . or of that in *Maple Flooring Manufacturers Ass'n v. United States*." Applying the relevant criteria reveals anticompetitive potential in this case.

The first factor to consider is the time frame of the data. The Supreme Court has made clear that "exchanges of current price information, of course, have the greatest potential for generating anti-competitive effects and although not *per se* unlawful have consistently been held to violate the Sherman Act." The exchange of past price data is greatly preferred because current data have greater potential to affect future prices and facilitate price conspiracies. By the same reasoning, exchanges of future price information are considered especially anticompetitive.

Plaintiff's complaint alleges that defendants exchanged past and current salary information, as well as future salary budget information. It claims that there has been an:

> exchange among Defendants of massive amounts of extremely detailed information concerning job classifications, salaries, bonuses, and benefits paid, or to be paid, to categories of employees within the different job classifications; starting salaries of new employees; "signing bonuses"; relocation expenses, stock options; and related information.... Updated information on salaries is exchanged in oral and written communications throughout the year.

Most prominently, the Job Family Survey coordinated by Exxon gathered information regarding the salaries paid for specific types of work to employees with particular experience levels and academic backgrounds. This survey sought and obtained current data on the actual compensation paid by defendants to employees in various "job families." The information gathered was distributed to the survey participants several times a year. Meanwhile, the Starting Salary Survey gathered information from the Six Majors measuring starting salaries of college graduates entering MPT positions. Defendants also attended meetings at least three times per year at which various types of salary information were discussed. "Among the information exchanged at these meetings [were] current and future increases in Defendants' salary budgets."

In addition to the time frame, another factor courts look to is the specificity of the information. Price exchanges that identify particular parties, transactions, and prices are seen as potentially anticompetitive because they may be used to police a secret or tacit conspiracy to stabilize prices. Courts prefer that information be aggregated in the form of industry averages, thus avoiding transactional specificity.

Two aspects of the information exchange at issue are problematic in this regard. First, although the salary information was aggregated and distributed by a third-party consulting firm, companies participating in the Job Family Survey received compensation data broken down to subsets consisting of as few as three competitors. Plaintiff alleges that these periodically updated data sets were used by each defendant to determine whether the announced budgets of its competitors had in fact been implemented so that each could consider what adjustments should be made to coordinate salaries.... This practice, plaintiff argues on appeal, made deviations from previously announced salary levels easily and quickly detectable. Second, at their meetings defendants discussed current and future salary budgets, including "company-specific" information, such that all participants learn where each other participant is going with its salary budget for the upcoming year or, if a participant's salary year had only recently begun, for that new year.

Another important factor to consider in evaluating an information exchange is whether the data are made publicly available. Public dissemination is a primary way for data exchange to realize its procompetitive potential. For example, in the traditional oligopoly (seller-side) context, access to information may better equip buyers to compare products, rendering the market more efficient while diminishing the anticompetitive effects of the exchange. A court is therefore more likely to approve a data exchange where the information is made public.

In the instant case, dissemination of the information to the employees could have helped mitigate any anticompetitive effects of the exchange and possibly enhanced market efficiency by making employees more sensitive to salary increases. No such dissemination occurred, however. The information was not disclosed to the public nor to the employees whose salaries were the subject of the exchange. Plaintiff alleges that the confidential treatment of the information exchanged impedes the ability of employees to bargain intelligently and competitively with the members of the information exchange.

A final troubling aspect of the arrangement at issue is the fact that the defendants allegedly participated in frequent meetings to discuss the salary information, accompanied by assurances that the participants would primarily use the exchanged data in setting their MPT salaries. Meetings, of course, are not inherently unlawful but in this context they have the potential to enhance the anticompetitive effects and "likelihood of . . . uniformity" caused by information exchange. Meanwhile, the frequency of the meetings is itself problematic for the same reason that the exchange of current price data is suspect: It tends to facilitate the policing of price conspiracies.

In sum, the "nature of the information exchanged" weighs against the motion to dismiss. The characteristics of the data exchange in this case are precisely those that arouse suspicion of anticompetitive activity under the rule of reason.

VI.   Effect on Competition and Antitrust Injury

An antitrust plaintiff must allege not only cognizable harm to herself, but an adverse effect on competition market-wide. In the traditional oligopoly case, horizontal coordination may inflate prices to supracompetitive levels. In an oligopsony, the risk is that buyers will collude to depress prices, causing harm to sellers. However, information exchange is not always anticompetitive and can enhance competition by making competitors more sensitive to each other's price changes, enhancing rivalry among them.

The complaint in this case, however, points to anticompetitive effects the exchanges have had on MPT salaries market-wide, most particularly with respect to Exxon. Plaintiff specifically alleges that salary levels across the integrated oil and petrochemical industry have been artificially depressed because the information exchange has reduced competitive incentives. Moreover, Exxon has supposedly used the information to reduce its competitive factor from 6.5% in 1991 to 0% in 1995, to reduce its salaries 4.1% between 1987 and 1994 in comparison to the Six Majors, and to reduce its salary index in relation to the competition from 110.7% in 1987 to 107.0% in 1993. In her claim for relief, plaintiff again alleges that she received compensation "materially below" what she would have received in an "uncontaminated marketplace."

The district court found that the pleadings support, if anything, an inference that "each defendant oil company used the information exchanged to stake out an optimal competitive level for its MPT salaries." The district court interprets the decrease in the competitive factor as "indicating that Exxon was *raising* its salaries to meet the competition." *Id.* The court concludes that "raising salary levels to meet the competition and attract highly qualified employees is certainly not evidence of a conspiracy to restrain trade." *Id.* We read the complaint differently. The fact that Exxon increased its salaries each year would not defeat an allegation that those increases were lower than they would have been but for a conspiracy to stabilize prices. We understand the complaint as alleging a market where Exxon's salaries and those of the Six Majors continue to increase, but where the difference grows gradually smaller—a portrait of market stabilization.

Plaintiff further claims that information exchanged at the meetings among defendants and in the "Advancement Guides" created by defendants were used by Exxon "to 'slow down' its employee advancement rates, reduce the payments made to the uppermost members of some of its employee classifications, and lower the top classification levels for most of its job families." According to the complaint, "the result has slowed the advancement rate at Exxon by two to eight years."

In all, plaintiff alleges that with Exxon's total salary budget at $800 million, the conduct described in the complaint had the effect of lowering Exxon's MPT salaries by a total of $20 million per year. Whether this is so is a question of fact that cannot be resolved on this Rule 12(b)(6) motion. Plaintiff will have to make a substantial presentation of evidence to support her claim that salaries would have been higher without the information exchange. Furthermore, we agree with plaintiff that the economic effects of the arrangement with respect to the other defendants is an appropriate matter for discovery.

CONCLUSION

For the reasons stated, we vacate the district court's grant of defendants' Rule 12(b)(6) motion to dismiss and remand for proceedings consistent with this opinion.

Blomkest Fertilizer, Inc. v. Potash Corp. of Sask., Inc.

United States Court of Appeals, Eighth Circuit (en banc), 2000.
203 F.3d 1028.

■ BEAM, CIRCUIT JUDGE. A certified class of potash consumers appeals the district court's grant of summary judgment in favor of defendants (collectively "the producers") in this action for conspiracy in restraint of trade under section 1 of the Sherman Act. We affirm.

I.   BACKGROUND

This case involves the production and sale of potash, a mineral essential to plant growth and therefore used in fertilizer. The certified class includes all of those persons who directly purchased potash from one of the producers between April 1987 and July 1994. The class named six Canadian potash companies and two American companies.

Both parties agree that the North American potash industry is an oligopoly.... The Canadian province of Saskatchewan is the source of most potash consumed in the United States. The province founded defendant Potash Corporation of Saskatchewan (PCS), which holds thirty-eight percent of the North American potash production capacity. As a governmental company, PCS had no mandate to maximize profits and was not accountable to private owners. Instead, the company was primarily concerned with maintaining employment and generating money for the local economy. Not surprisingly, PCS suffered huge losses as it mined potash in quantities that far outstripped global demand. These policies impacted the entire potash industry: during the 1980s, the price of potash fell to an historic low. In 1986, Saskatchewan voters elected a provincial government which had promised to privatize PCS. New management was appointed to PCS after the elections. Thereafter, PCS significantly reduced its output and raised its price.

Also in 1986, New Mexico Potash Corporation (NMPC) and another American potash producer (who is not a named defendant) filed a complaint with the United States Department of Commerce. Frustrated with low potash prices, the petitioners alleged that Canadian producers had been dumping their product in the United States at prices below fair market value. In 1987, the Department issued a preliminary determination that the Canadian producers were dumping potash and ordered the companies to post bonds on all exports to the United States. These bonds were set according to each firm's calculated "dumping margin." Eventually, the Department negotiated a Suspension Agreement with each of the Canadian producers. The agreement raised the price of Canadian potash in the United States by setting a minimum price at which each Canadian producer could sell in the United States. That agreement remains in effect today. When the Canadian producers entered into the Suspension Agreement, PCS announced that it was raising its prices by eighteen dollars per ton. Other producers quickly followed suit. The price of potash has remained markedly higher after the Suspension Agreement, although prices have slowly but steadily declined for the most part since the agreement was signed by the producers on January 8, 1988.

The class alleges that between April 1987 and July 1994 the producers colluded to increase the price of potash. The producers, in turn, maintain that the price increase was the product of the interdependent nature of the industry and its reaction to the privatization of PCS and the Suspension Agreement. The district court granted the producers' motions for summary judgment and the class appeals.

II. DISCUSSION

The class asserts that if we affirm the district court, we will "stand alone in holding that circumstantial evidence, even if overwhelming, cannot be used to defeat a summary judgment motion in anti-trust cases." We make no such legal history here, however, because the class's proffered evidence, far from overwhelming, fails to establish the elements of a prima facie case.

[The court reviewed the familiar test for finding an agreement covered by section 1, stating that the "plaintiffs must present evidence that 'tends to exclude the possibility of independent action' by the defendants."] Applied in this case, the standard requires that if it is as reasonable to infer from the evidence a price-fixing conspiracy as it is to infer permissible activity, then the plaintiffs' claim, without more, fails on summary judgment.

The class's price-fixing claim is based on a theory of conscious parallelism. Conscious parallelism is the process "not in itself unlawful, by which firms in a concentrated market might in effect share monopoly power, setting their prices at a profit-maximizing, supracompetitive level by recognizing their shared economic interests." *Brooke Group Ltd. v. Brown & Williamson Tobacco Corp.*, 509 U.S. 209 (1993). The class points out that the producers' prices were roughly equivalent during the alleged conspiracy, despite differing production costs. It further points out that price changes by one producer were quickly met by the others. This establishes only that the producers consciously paralleled each other's prices.

Evidence that a business consciously met the pricing of its competitors does not prove a violation of the antitrust laws. *See Theatre Enter., Inc. v. Paramount Film Distrib. Corp.*, 346 U.S. 537, 540–41 (1954). Particularly when the product in question is fungible, as potash is, courts have noted that parallel pricing lacks probative significance. An agreement is properly inferred from conscious parallelism only when certain "plus factors" exist. A plus factor refers to " 'the additional facts or factors required to be proved as a prerequisite to finding that parallel [price] action amounts to a conspiracy.' "

A plaintiff has the burden to present evidence of consciously paralleled pricing *supplemented with* one or more plus factors. However, even if a plaintiff carries its initial burden, a court must still find, based upon all the evidence before it, that the plaintiff's evidence tends to exclude the possibility of independent action. As noted, the class identified parallel pricing. The class also asserts that it has established the existence of three plus factors: (1) interfirm communications between the producers; (2) the producers's acts against self-interest; and (3) econometric models which purport to prove that the price of potash would have been substantially lower in the absence of collusion. The evidence underlying these assertions, however, does not bear the weight the class places upon it.

A.   Interfirm Communications

The class alleges a high level of interfirm communications between the producers and complains most vociferously about price verification information. Courts have held that a high level of communications among competitors can constitute a plus factor which, when combined with parallel behavior, supports an inference of conspiracy.... However, the evidence presented by the class here is far too ambiguous to support such an inference. Considering the proof as a whole, the evidence of interfirm communications does not tend to exclude the possibility of independent action, as required under *Monsanto* and *Matsushita*, since other significant events strongly suggest independent behavior. The fundamental difficulty with the class's argument regarding price verifications is that it assumes a conspiracy first, and then sets out to "prove" it. However, a litigant may not proceed by first assuming a conspiracy and then explaining the evidence accordingly.

The class's evidence shows that the communications include meetings at trade shows and conventions, price verification calls, discussions regarding a Canadian potash export association, and the like. Taking the class's evidence as true, roughly three dozen price verifications occurred between employees, including high-level sales employees, of different companies, over at least a seven-year period. In large part, these contacts involved the verification of prices the companies had already charged on particular sales. The impotence of this circumstantial evidence is that it bears no relationship to the price increases most in question because it lacks the logical link necessary to infer such a relationship.

The class alleges that the price-fixing conspiracy began at least as early as April, 1987. In 1987, the price for potash was at historically low levels, such that producers were losing millions of dollars. Then, a sudden and dramatic increase in price by PCS occurred on September 4, 1987, and approximately a week later the remaining producers followed suit. The class argues that the large and parallel price increases together with nearly simultaneous price verifications create an inference sufficient to survive summary judgment.

The problem with this theory, as indicated, is that the price verification communications only concerned charges on particular completed sales, not future market prices. There is no evidence to support the inference that the verifications had an impact on price increases. The only evidence is that prices were possibly cut as a result. "To survive summary judgment, there must be evidence that the exchanges of information had an impact on pricing decisions." *In re Baby Food*, 166 F.3d at 125. There is no evidence here that price increases resulted from any price verification or any specific communication of any kind. *Subsequent* price verification evidence on particular sales cannot support a conspiracy for the setting of a broad market price on September 4, 1987.

Even if we were to find the price verification evidence relevant, when considered with all the facts, it does not tend to exclude the possibility of independent action. To the contrary, there is strong evidence of independent action. Just before and concurrent with the suspect price increases, the following occurred: the price of potash was at historic lows and the producers were losing millions; potash companies in the United States complained to the United States Department of Commerce that the Canadian producers were dumping potash at well-below market value; the Department of Commerce made a preliminary determination that the Canadian producers were dumping and required expensive bonds for all imports; the industry leader, the government-founded PCS, hired new management and began privatization with the goal of becoming profitable; legislation was passed in the province of Saskatchewan—the source of nearly all United States potash—that provided for the setting and prorating of potash production; potash producers reached a Suspension Agreement with the Department of Commerce that set price floors for potash; and PCS was finally privatized and significantly reduced its output. In the face of these circumstances and with the price leadership of PCS in this oligopolistic industry, it would have been ridiculous for the remaining companies to not also raise their prices in a parallel fashion. Thus, we find the class's weak circumstantial evidence that the dramatic increases were the result of a price-fixing agreement is not sufficient to survive summary judgment.

This leaves only the question whether there is sufficient evidence to support an agreement to stabilize and maintain prices in violation of section 1 of the Sherman Act. The class's evidence of an agreement to maintain the price of potash at an artificially high level after the initial price increases is again the parallel pricing and price verifications. Parallel pricing has been conceded, leaving the burden once again on the verifications. Common sense dictates that a conspiracy to fix a price would involve one company communicating with another company *before* the price quotation to the customer. Here, however, the class's evidence consists solely of communications to verify a price on a *completed* sale. The price verifications relied upon were sporadic and testimony suggests that price verifications were not always given. The fact that there were several dozen communications is not so significant considering the communications occurred over at least a seven-year period in which there would have been tens of thousands of transactions. Furthermore, one would expect companies to verify prices considering that this is an oligopolistic industry and accounts are often very large. We find the evidence falls far short of excluding the possibility of independent action.

In re Baby Food, 166 F.3d 112, aptly illustrates why the communications complained about here are inadequate to exclude the possibility of independent action by the producers. The defendants, nationally prominent corporations with ninety-eight percent of the baby food business, were Gerber, H.J. Heinz, and Beech–Nut. It is true that the numerous intercompany pricing communications found by the Third Circuit to be *insufficient* to support a section 1 violation were characterized in one part of the opinion as price discussions among low-level employees. However, deposition testimony in that case revealed that district sales employees and district sales managers of Heinz were required to submit competitive activity reports to their superiors concerning baby food sales from information they picked up from competitor sales representatives. This same line of testimony revealed that supervising managers for Heinz informed district managers "on a regular basis before any announcement to the trade as to when Heinz's competitors were going to increase [their] wholesale list prices." The president of Beech–Nut "testified that it was [Beech–Nut's] policy for sales representatives to gather *and report* pricing information of [Beech–Nut's] competitors." Indeed, the *In re Baby Food* case is replete with evidence that pricing information was systematically obtained and directed to high-level executives of Gerber (including Gerber's vice president of sales), Beech–Nut and Heinz, the principal national competitors in the baby food industry.

The evidence in the case shows that a carefully conceived and effective system of price information gathering for the benefit of corporate executives was at all relevant times alive and well in the baby food industry. Notwithstanding communications that far surpassed any information exchanges established in this case, the Third Circuit applied *Matsushita* and granted summary judgment to the defendants, in large part because there was no evidence that the exchanges of information had an impact on pricing decisions. As earlier stated, there likewise is absolutely no such evidence in this litigation, only speculation.

The class directs our attention to *In re Brand Name Prescription Drugs Antitrust Litigation*, 123 F.3d 599, 614 (7th Cir.), *cert. denied*, 522 U.S. 1153 (1998), in which the plaintiffs, like the class, searched through an enormous quantity of discovery material and culled out a number of suspicious interfirm communications. The court in *Brand Name* described these documents produced as "smoking guns." By contrast, the communications here are facially innocent contacts which are, at most, ambiguous on the question of whether the producers schemed to set prices.

The class argues that a memorandum issued by Canpotex, a lawful Canadian cartel that sets prices for potash sold outside of the United States, is the class's "smoking gun." This memorandum, dated January 8, 1988, and directed to its "agents and offices" reads in pertinent part:

> FYI Canadian potash producers have reached agreement with the United States Department of Commerce and all dumping action has been suspended for minimum 5 years. It is rumoured that the USD 35.00 per metric ton increase posted by Canadian producers in 1987 to cover possible tariff payments to the U.S. Govt will be

refunded in full or part. In the meantime new price lists are being issued on Monday Jan. 11 at:

Standard Grade	USD 80.00
Coarse Grade	USD 84.00
Granular Grade	USD 86.00

The class asserts that this memorandum establishes an agreement to fix prices. The class argues that the people who received the January 8, 1988, memorandum were all high-ranking officials in the producers' companies who were on the Board of Directors of Canpotex, and therefore, the memorandum is evidence that tends to exclude an inference that the producers acted independently.

The magistrate judge disagreed that this memorandum was sufficient evidence to exclude the possibility that the producers acted independently. The magistrate judge first noted that PCS had also announced the same prices in a telex to its customers on January 8, 1988, and thus the possibility that Canpotex learned of the price list from a customer of PCS could not be excluded. Further, the magistrate judge discovered that while most of the Canadian defendants had matched the prices in the memorandum by January 22, 1988, they did not uniformly issue price lists matching those prices on January 11, 1988, and one producer, Kalium, did not match those prices at all. However, as the magistrate judge pointed out, "evidence that the alleged conspirators were aware of each other's prices, before announcing their own prices, 'is nothing more than a restatement of conscious parallelism, 'which is not enough to show an antitrust conspiracy.' "

We agree with the magistrate judge's finding that this document was not sufficient evidence to exclude an inference that the producers acted independently. First, the memorandum was written by R.J. Ford and directed to "agents and offices." It is not at all clear who this memorandum was sent to or received by.... Dozens of these high-ranking officials were deposed during pretrial discovery, and according to the documents submitted by the class in its joint appendix, only one person, Dave Benusa, was asked if he received "any document dated the 8th of January 1988 concerning pricing." Benusa was manager of marketing for Cominco American in 1988. Benusa stated in his deposition that he did not receive any document dated January 8, 1988, concerning pricing. The class apparently did not depose the author of the memorandum, R.J. Ford, nor did they make any further attempt that we can find to identify who received this "smoking gun" piece of evidence. Another document produced by Canpotex, an inter-office memorandum dated September 8, 1993, is actually directed to "Members of the Board of Directors of Canpotex Limited." We assume that had the January 8, 1988, memorandum been intended for the members of the board of directors, it likewise would have so stated.

Furthermore, even if, as the class asserts, the memorandum had been received by high-ranking officials in the producers' companies, we agree with the magistrate judge's reasoning that the memorandum does not assist the class in proving the existence of a conspiracy. As the magistrate judge pointed out, the producers did not uniformly increase prices to match the memorandum on January 11, 1988, and furthermore, one producer, Kalium, did not match the memorandum price at all. The fact that most of the producers did increase prices to match the PCS price increase of January 11, 1988, is not surprising in a market where conscious parallelism is the norm. Despite submitting a five-volume joint appendix, the class has failed to present evidence about this memorandum which tends to exclude the possibility of independent action by the producers. As it turns out, the "smoke" from this gun is barely, if at all, discernible.

Finally, the class asserts that the producers signaled pricing intentions to each other through advance price announcements and price lists. The Supreme Court has held, however, that "the dissemination of price information is not itself a *per se* violation of the Sherman Act." *United States v. Citizens & S. Nat'l Bank*, 422 U.S. 86, 113 (1975).

As we noted at the outset, the class may not proceed by first assuming a conspiracy and then setting out to prove it. If the class were to present independent evidence tending to exclude an inference that the producers acted independently, then, and only then, could it use these communications for whatever additional evidence of conspiracy they may provide. As the record stands, we find these contacts far too ambiguous to defeat summary judgment.

B.   Actions Against Self-interest

Evidence that defendants have acted against their economic interest can also constitute a plus factor. However, where there is an independent business justification for the defendants' behavior, no inference of conspiracy can be drawn. See *Todorov v. DCH Healthcare Auth.*, 921 F.2d 1438, 1456–57 (11th Cir. 1991).

The only evidence of actions against interest that the class has identified is the producers' uniform participation in the Suspension Agreement. The class argues that those producers with low dumping margins could have undercut other producers' prices and gained market share while still maintaining prices at profitable levels. Instead, the low tariff producers joined the Suspension Agreement. The class further posits that NMPC's failure to object to the agreement was an action against self-interest.

In response, the producers point out that Department of Commerce investigations are unpredictable, and participation in the agreement reduced uncertainty. Furthermore, without the Suspension Agreement, even low tariff producers would have been required to post substantial bonds which would have caused considerable capital drain on corporate coffers. Like the Canadian producers, NMPC was uncertain about the ultimate outcome of the Department of Commerce's investigation. Under the Suspension Agreement, NMPC obtained certainty and a higher price for potash sold in the American market. This is the relief NMPC initially sought, and it is unsurprising that NMPC would not oppose such an outcome.

The class has thus failed to carry its burden to rebut the producers' independent business justification for their actions. There is nothing in this record that contradicts the conclusion that ending the dumping investigation with a settlement that required unreasonably low potash prices to rise was a legitimate business decision for the low tariff producers. They benefited from increased revenues, while avoiding the cost of litigation and the risk of penalties. This cannot be construed as an act against self-interest.

C.   Expert Testimony

Finally, the class argues that its expert's econometric model provided crucial confirmation that the prevailing potash prices during the alleged conspiracy were above those expected in the absence of collusion. While their expert concedes that the prices have primarily steadily decreased since January 8, 1988, he asserts that prices would have been much lower absent an agreement to fix prices. We need not decide whether such evidence, in a proper case, could constitute a plus factor, because we find the report in this case is not probative of collusion.

[The court concluded the class's expert's economic model failed to evidence collusion because the model: (1) did not take events of 1986 into consideration and (2) leaned heavily on unreliable facts.]

III.   CONCLUSION

We have carefully considered each of the class's other arguments and find them to be without merit. The class has failed to present evidence of collusion sufficient to create a genuine issue of material fact. The producers are therefore entitled to summary judgment. For the foregoing reasons, the decision of the district court is affirmed.

■ JOHN R. GIBSON, CIRCUIT JUDGE, dissenting, with whom HEANEY, MCMILLIAN, RICHARD S. ARNOLD, and MURPHY, CIRCUIT JUDGES, join.

I dissent.

The Court today rejects circumstantial evidence of conspiracy and requires direct evidence to withstand summary judgment in an antitrust case. The court's requirement of direct evidence is contrary to *Monsanto v. Spray–Rite Service Corp.*, 465 U.S. 752, 768 (1984), which only required "direct or circumstantial evidence that reasonably tends to prove ... a conscious commitment to a common scheme designed to achieve an unlawful objective." Because conspirators cannot be relied upon either to confess or to preserve signed agreements memorializing their conspiracies, the court's requirement for direct evidence will substantially eliminate antitrust conspiracy as a ground for recovery in our circuit.

The potash industry is an oligopoly in which the producers ended a price war and raised prices dramatically. The question is whether the class has shown that the new prices resulted from an agreement among the producers to raise and stabilize prices, rather than from independent reactions to market conditions combined with actions of the United States and Canadian governments. I believe that the class has satisfied the existing standards for circumstantial proof that the prices resulted from collusion.

The market for potash in the United States is dominated by Canadian firms. In 1986, 84.3 per cent of the potash consumed in the United States was imported from Canada. The principal Canadian potash producers are defendants in this case: Potash Corporation of Saskatchewan Incorporated (PCS); Potash Corporation of America (PCA); IMC Fertilizer Group, Inc.; Kalium; Noranda Minerals, Inc.; and Cominco. These Canadian firms are allied in Canpotex, a cartel that exists to sell potash outside the United States.

Potash is a mineral that is an essential ingredient in fertilizer. Because potash is an essential ingredient, the demand for potash is "inelastic," meaning that people will continue to buy it even if the price goes up, and they will not buy much more, even if the price goes down. The effect of this inelastic demand is that low prices are bad for the producers because the low price does not result in greater sales, except insofar as one producer can take sales away from other producers. Conversely, producers benefit from high prices, because they can sell about as much potash and keep the extra money. Newcomers cannot enter the market without first gaining control of a potash mine, which is a significant entry barrier preventing new sellers from entering the market.

The biggest of the Canadian producers, PCS, was originally owned by the province of Saskatchewan and was run as a governmental company for the avowed purposes of providing jobs and promoting the local Saskatchewan economy. Unfortunately for the potash industry, due to a slump in agriculture, potash demand fell tremendously in the 1980s, resulting in oversupply. The effect of the oversupply was a potash price war, with prices bottoming in 1986 when PCS charged C$45.36 per ton FOB mine. The industry was in crisis. PCS alone lost $103 million in 1986. The president of PCS Sales wrote in an internal memorandum that the industry would not be able to end the price war without "joint action":

> It is not possible for a single producer to affect [sic] a turn-around; however, joint action by a group of producers or governments could achieve this.

> Given the competitive nature of the business, joint action in North America is not possible except through a vehicle such as Canpotex.

> Canpotex by itself cannot achieve the objectives unless there is tacit approval and support on the part of other potash exporters. The danger inherent in multilateral decisions by Canpotex (or PCS Sales) is that the world will again see us as a residual supplier.... PCS Sales' past support of price with a view to achieve stability is proof of the fallacy of such attempts.

In fact, Noranda, Kalium, PCA, and PCS had each tried to increase prices unilaterally during 1986 and were forced to rescind the increases when the other producers undercut them.

In 1986, the province of Saskatchewan elected a government which promised to privatize PCS. In preparation for privatizing the company, PCS replaced its management with Charles Childers, CEO, and William Doyle, sales chief, who came to PCS from rival company IMC. Childers was quoted in a trade publication as saying that it was incumbent on PCS "to lead" in order to "straighten out our own company and hopefully give some strength to the potash industry as a whole."

Also in 1986, two American producers filed a complaint with the United States Department of Commerce alleging that the Canadian companies were dumping potash in the United States at less than fair value (which can mean below prices charged for exports to a third country, below domestic prices in the country where the product is produced, or below a reconstructed cost of production). The Department investigated the claim and in August 1987 issued a preliminary determination that the Canadian producers were dumping potash. The Department ordered the Canadian companies to post bonds on all exports to the United States, which would be payable to the United States as a duty if there were a final determination of dumping and injury to American producers. The amount of the bond varied for each firm according to the firm's "dumping margin," that is, the average amount by which the firm's United States sale price fell below the foreign market value in the cases examined by the Department. The dumping margins varied wildly, from 9.14 percent for IMC up to a crippling 85.2 percent for Noranda.

The Saskatchewan government responded to the United States action by adopting legislation which would give the province the power to limit and prorate production among Saskatchewan producers. Within days of the introduction of the Saskatchewan legislation, on September 4, 1987, PCS announced that it would increase its prices by $35 per ton (from $58 to $93 per short ton for coarse grade FOB mine) to account for the bond expense. PCS's dumping margin was set at 51.9 per cent. PCS chose to raise its price only by $35, the amount necessary to pay duties on the industry average dumping margin of 36.62 per cent, rather than by the amount necessary to pay its own duty of 51.9 percent. It is undisputed that PCS chose the industry average figure in an attempt to pick a figure that other producers would follow. On September 11, 1987, the other Canadian producer defendants all announced either a $35 price increase or a new price of $93, rather than simply increasing the price by the amount necessary to cover their individual duty costs.

On January 8, 1988, the Canadian producers reached an agreement with the Department of Commerce, suspending the earlier order. The suspension agreement imposed a minimum price on Canadian producers selling in the United States market, but oddly, the minimum price chosen was still less than the "foreign market value": the Canadians were only forbidden from undercutting "foreign market value" by more than fifteen percent of the producer's dumping margin. The literal terms of the suspension agreement made each producer's minimum price vary with its own foreign market value (which was arrived at by different methodologies for different firms) and with its own dumping margin; as the producers' expert William Barringer opined, the "uncertainties" in such a calculation make it impossible to predict with accuracy what price for any particular transaction would be in compliance with the agreement. However, correspondence from the Department of Commerce, which had responsibility for monitoring compliance with the suspension agreement, indicates that the Department used an industry average figure in assessing compliance.

As soon as the suspension agreement was in place, PCS again led the way in determining industry pricing, announcing it would rebate the earlier $35 surcharge, and on January 11, 1988, publishing its new price list at $86 per ton for granular grade, a net increase of $28 over the $58 it charged before the Department of Commerce imposed the bond requirement. The other Canadian producers matched PCS's increase within 11 days, and Kalium raised its price to $87. The Department of Commerce, in monitoring compliance with the agreement, noted that the agreement imposed an average floor price of $60.67, and that in the five months following the agreement the average price charged was $79.28.

The class's expert, Professor Gordon Rausser, opined and presented data purporting to show that the industry average prices for potash were higher than would be expected based on market factors during the 1988–1993 period (*i.e.*, prices were "supra-competitive"). Perhaps more to the point, prices remained significantly higher than the minimum prices imposed by the suspension agreement from 1988 to 1992, with the exception of a short period in 1990 after PCS cut its prices drastically (and temporarily) for the avowed purpose of stabilizing prices within the industry. Only in January and February 1990, in the wake of this "market correction," did prices briefly dip below the suspension agreement price floor.

I.

This is a circumstantial evidence case based on parallel pricing, an example of the economic phenomenon called "conscious parallelism," in which competitors act alike. Conscious parallelism is never meaningful by itself, but always assumes whatever significance it might have from additional facts. The threshold question in deciding whether parallelism could be evidence of an agreement is whether the parallelism is "interdependent," meaning that the sellers would only take the course of action they took if they expected the others to behave the same way. In this case interdependence is obvious; no producer would have been able to raise prices and keep them high unless the others did.

According to accepted economic theory, oligopolies are characterized by interdependent behavior because each seller is a big enough player to affect the market by price cuts; as a result, in raising or lowering prices or output, each seller must take into account his competitors' responses to his action. In an oligopoly, price rises are not sustainable as long as one major seller continues to undercut the price leader and steal his customers. When one seller raises his price, no buyers will buy his product unless the other sellers follow the price leader and raise their prices. The other oligopolists know that if they keep their prices low, the brave price leader will simply cut his prices and the battle will resume. On the other hand, if they raise their prices in turn, all sellers will receive higher prices and end up with more money in their pockets. The loser will be the consumer, who benefits from competition, not peaceful coexistence between suppliers.

Even though oligopoly pricing harms the consumer in the same way monopoly does, interdependent pricing that occurs with no actual agreement does not violate the Sherman Act, for the very good reason that we cannot order sellers to make their decisions without taking into account the reactions of their competitors. As then-Judge Breyer explained:

> Courts have noted that the Sherman Act prohibits agreements, and they have almost uniformly held, at least in the pricing area, that such individual pricing decisions (even when each firm rests its own decision upon its belief that competitors will do the same) do not constitute an unlawful agreement under section 1 of the Sherman Act. That is not because such pricing is desirable (it is not), but because it is close to impossible to devise a judicially enforceable remedy for "interdependent" pricing. How does one order a firm to set its prices without regard to the likely reactions of its competitors?

Clamp–All, 851 F.2d at 484 (citations omitted).

Although interdependent pricing tends to happen naturally in an oligopoly, there are good reasons for competitors to enter into an actual agreement to fix prices. First, successful price coordination requires accurate predictions about what other competitors will do; it is easier to predict what people mean to do if they tell you. In the absence of express agreements, oligopolists

> must rely on uncertain and ambiguous signals to achieve concerted action. The signals are subject to misinterpretation and are a blunt and imprecise means of ensuring smooth cooperation, especially in the context of changing or unprecedented market circumstances. This anticompetitive minuet is most difficult to compose and to perform, even for a disciplined oligopoly.

Brooke Group Ltd. v. Brown & Williamson Tobacco Corp., 509 U.S. 209, 227–28 (1993). Second, competitors may have different preferences on decisions such as pricing and therefore may not be willing just to follow a leader's decision; words (or word substitutes) may be necessary to negotiate a common course of action. Third, some oligopoly markets are more conducive than others to supra-competitive pricing. Market traits that make oligopoly pricing more likely to succeed include a standardized product and publicly announced prices, which make it easier for sellers to keep track of each others' prices. Actual agreement allows competitors to modify their market to facilitate collusion, particularly by setting up procedures for detecting and punishing price-cutting.

While the oligopoly market structure naturally facilitates supra-competitive pricing, that same market structure also makes cooperative arrangements unstable, for this reason: It is in the best interest of each individual competitor for his competitors to charge high prices, while he charges somewhat less when that will help him steal customers from his competitors. The temptation to shade prices secretly is just as inherent in the oligopoly market structure as the temptation to collude to raise prices. Of course, if the competitors know about the undercutting, they will match it. Therefore, price-shading and secrecy must go hand in hand. While publicly announced prices discourage the sellers from cutting prices because they know that their price cuts will be matched, thus eliminating any competitive advantage, conversely, secretly negotiated discounts encourage price-cutting, since each seller hopes to steal customers without suffering retaliation from its competitors. As a result, a cartel can only succeed for any period of time if it has the ability to detect cheating and punish it effectively.

If the oligopolists agree, either tacitly or expressly, to coordinate price increases, they have committed a *per se* violation of section 1 of the Sherman Act. From the outside, however, the conspirators' actions may look the same as innocent oligopoly pricing. Although parallel pricing evidence is consistent with illegal conduct, it is equally consistent with lawful conduct, and thus does not tend to exclude the possibility of independent action, as required by *Monsanto*. Therefore, parallel pricing in a concentrated market cannot make a submissible section one case, although it may set the groundwork for such a case.

In a rather primitive way, the "plus factors" test incorporates the economic principles outlined above as a way to distinguish between innocent interdependence and illegal conspiracy. Under this test, plaintiffs can establish a prima facie case of conspiracy by showing parallel prices together with "plus factors" that increase the likelihood that the parallel prices resulted from conspiracy.

We must, of course, take care to interpret the "plus factors" test in a way that is consistent with *Monsanto*. With *Monsanto* in mind, it is useful to distinguish between "plus factors" that establish a background making conspiracy likely and "plus factors" that tend to exclude the possibility that the defendants acted without agreement. For instance, "motive to conspire" and "high level of interfirm communications," are often cited as "plus factors" because they make conspiracy possible. Background facts showing a situation conducive to collusion do not tend to exclude the possibility of independent action, but they nevertheless form an essential foundation for a circumstantial case. In *Matsushita Electric Industrial Co. v. Zenith Radio Corp.*, 475 U.S. 574, 593–98 (1986), the Supreme Court held that a conspiracy case based on circumstantial evidence must be economically plausible. The background "plus factors" of market structure, motivation and opportunity play an important role in establishing such plausibility. Generally, these background "plus factors" are necessary but not sufficient to prove conspiracy.

On the other hand, acts that would be irrational or contrary to the defendant's economic interest if no conspiracy existed, but which would be rational if the alleged agreement existed, do tend to exclude the possibility of innocence.

A.

Of the "plus factors" that merely make conspiracy possible, such as motive and opportunity to conspire, the class has adduced abundant evidence. Within this category some "plus factors" are purely situational, involving no action on the part of the defendant, and some are volitional; while the former are important, the latter begin to make the required showing of collusion.

The purely situational factors in this case are the market structure and the crisis in the potash industry. The structure of the potash market was conducive to collusion, featuring an oligopoly, barriers to new sellers entering the market, inelastic demand, and a standardized product. However, there was excess production capacity, which spurs competition, and a price war, which shows the producers had not been able to achieve a stable interdependent equilibrium. Individual attempts in 1986 by Noranda, Kalium, PCA, and PCS to initiate a price rise had failed. The producers were losing millions of dollars. The producers had good reason to wish for a truce.

The volitional background "plus factors" are also very strong in this case. At least one of the defendants actively considered the possibility of joint action, as is stated in the PCS "Corporate Plan" document dated September 25, 1986: "It is not possible for a single producer to affect [sic] a turn-around; however, joint action by a group of producers or governments could achieve this." Then there was a break in pattern, as the market went from price-war to profitability.

The class has introduced significant evidence of solicitations to enter a price-fixing agreement. Most, but not all, of the solicitations were by PCS. For instance, PCS freely complained to Kalium about Kalium's failure to adhere to pricing cut-offs. It was the custom in the industry to give lower prices at times of year when there was no immediate need for fertilizer, but to raise prices during high-use periods. Kalium published price lists announcing the pricing cut-off pattern, but in fact often shipped at the lower price after the cut-off date when it did not get orders filled before the cut-off date. PCS sales chief William Doyle repeatedly upbraided Kalium's vice president Robert Turner for shipping at the lower price after the cut-off date. Turner responded "something to the effect" that he would run his own business. Another time, Doyle called Turner and advised him that neither PCS, IMC, nor Cominco planned to accede to a certain customer's request to delay filling an order-that is, to ship at the old price after the cut-off. Turner answered that Kalium would try to ship by a certain date, as it had already said it would do in a letter to its customers. In the same vein, Doyle approached Turner about a certain bid and told Turner that Kalium's action was "wrong." John Ripperger, vice president of PCA, also testified that Doyle asked him if PCA was going to institute a price increase and not carry over product at the old price; Ripperger interpreted this question to mean that Doyle "would prefer that we don't make sales at the old price." Also, Doyle complained to Ripperger that PCA's pricing was undermining prices in Florida. Ripperger reported a conversation in which Gary Snyder of PCS asked a PCA salesman if he had sold at a certain price, and then said, "We [PCS] will take it [price] down and bury you [PCA] if that's what you want."

In 1988, after the sale of Kalium, Charles Childers, the CEO of PCS, called on Jay Proops, one of Kalium's new owners, armed with a chart showing that PCS was losing market share and that Kalium and other producers were gaining. Childers said Kalium was undercutting the price. Proops did some research and concluded that the chart had incorrect information and that Kalium was not undercutting. Therefore, Proops took no action in response to Childers's visit. In August 1990, Childers telephoned Joseph Sullivan, the other owner of Kalium. Childers told Sullivan that PCS's "price leadership was not working, despite major efforts" and that Childers "wanted to discuss this issue" with Sullivan. Sullivan declined to discuss prices.

Another time, a PCS employee took advantage of a trade meeting to apologize to Kalium's Turner about a low bid PCS had made by mistake. The PCS employee testified that he explained the mistake to Turner because he had "some concern that [the low price] may spread in the marketplace," and that he "was hopeful that it wouldn't go any darn further." Turner testified that Kalium matched the bid, but the reaction was "pretty much confined to that account. It did not go beyond that."

Though PCS made most of these overtures, on isolated occasions others did the same. Kalium's Turner called Ripperger of PCA to complain about a salesman who was cutting prices in Wisconsin. Similarly, Kip Williams of IMC complained to Ripperger about price-cutting in Florida.

Despite evidence that various defendants invited others to join in stabilizing prices, the class was not able to adduce direct evidence that the people on the receiving end of these solicitations accepted them and formed a deal. The evidence of solicitation is relevant, however, because it shows conspiratorial state of mind on the part of the solicitor and may also indicate that the solicitor was acting upon an earlier agreement.

B.

The stage was clearly set for conspiracy in this case. The question is whether the additional evidence tends to exclude the possibility that the producers acted independently. I believe that it does.

First, the class has produced evidence that the producers cooperated in disclosing prices they had charged on particular sales. The industry practice was that each producer published a price list stating its price, the dates for which that price would be available, and any discounts that the producer would extend. The price lists were widely distributed to customers and certainly were no secret. However, actual prices sometimes deviated from the lists. When Childers and Doyle came to PCS, a key aspect of their program to raise industry prices was to insist on the list price. Doyle stated in an industry publication: "When I first came on board in the spring of 1987, the first word I put out to our sales force was that the price list was our price, stick to that price and no bending. Anybody who bends was out of here." Despite published price lists with the high follow-the-leader price, the producers continued to undercut each other in privately negotiated deals. When word of the discounting got around to PCS, PCS executives, particularly sales chief Doyle, were quite active in contacting the discounter and asking for verification of the rumored price. Significantly, Doyle testified that he never made any such price verification calls before 1987. The number of these verification communications is difficult to pin down, but Doyle estimated he initiated or received three to four calls per year with PCA, five to six per year with IMC, three to four per year with Cominco, five to six total with Kalium, "a few" with NMPC, and one to two total with Noranda. Doyle was by no means the only person making such calls on behalf of PCS, and there is evidence that the other defendants called each other as well (except that there is no evidence of others calling Noranda).

These exchanges were often between high-level executives who were responsible for pricing decisions for their companies or who conveyed the price information to those who did set prices. For instance, Dale Massie, vice president of marketing for Cominco, testified that he had price verification communications with Doyle, head of sales at PCS. Massie testified that he made up the Cominco price lists, and the evidence shows that Doyle had a key role in determining PCS pricing policy. Charles Hoffman at IMC reported price information from Doyle to his superiors to inform them that "we would have to meet" PCS's price. Similarly, John Ripperger, vice president of PCA, had price verification discussions with Doyle, and Doyle said he had obtained price information from John Huber, Kalium's vice president of sales.

Price verification communications can either violate section 1 directly or they can be evidence of a violation. An agreement to exchange such communications can constitute an unreasonable restraint of trade under the rule of reason if the anticompetitive effect of the agreement outweighs its beneficial effects. In price fixing cases, the exchange of sensitive price information can sometimes be circumstantial evidence of the existence of a *per se* violation. It is this second theory that the class pursues in this case.

Again, acts that would be contrary to the actor's self-interest in the absence of a conspiracy, but which make economic sense as part of a conspiracy, provide the crucial type of "plus factor" evidence necessary to exclude the possibility of independent action. The class contends that "the price verification calls were inconsistent with the 'pricing secrecy' sought by participants in oligopolistic industries because in such industries 'each producer would like to secretly "shade" prices, thereby gaining sales and avoiding retaliation.'" The class's argument finds support in the reasoning of *United States v. United States Gypsum Co.*, 438 U.S. 422 (1978), which stated:

> Price concessions by oligopolists generally yield competitive advantages only if secrecy can be maintained; when the terms of the concession are made publicly known, other competitors are likely to follow and any advantage to the initiator is lost in the process. Thus, if one seller offers a price concession for the purpose of winning over one of his competitor's customers, it is unlikely that the same seller will freely inform its competitor of the details of the concession so that it can be promptly matched and diffused.

Id. at 456 (citations omitted). Therefore, if there were no reciprocal agreement to share prices (and the producers certainly do not argue that there was), an individual seller who revealed to his competitors the amount of his privately negotiated discounts would have been shooting himself in the foot. On the other hand, if there were a cartel, it would be crucial for the cartel members to cooperate in telling each other about actual prices charged in order to prevent the sort of widespread discounting that would eventually sink the cartel.

Nor is there any legitimate business purpose which would make it desirable for the producers to reveal their pricing concessions notwithstanding the disadvantage of helping their competitors compete more effectively. These private communications between competitors had no redeeming effect of informing customers of prices ... To the contrary, the prices stated here were discounts from the published price lists that reflected the prices the producers wanted to charge. The producers had no interest in publicizing these discounts to the market as a whole. Nor is there any evidence of special necessity for horizontal price communications, such as the customer fraud which justified the producers' practices in *Cement Manufacturers Protective Ass'n v. United States*, 268 U.S. 588, 595–96 (1925). The price communications in this case are more like those in *In re Coordinated Pretrial Proceedings*, 906 F.2d at 448, which served "little purpose" other than facilitating price coordination.

The Court today concludes that voluntarily revealing secret price-cutting to one's competitors is not probative of conspiracy, for three reasons, each of which is unsound. First, the price verification communications involved completed sales, not future sales. The Court states: "Common sense dictates that a conspiracy to fix a price would involve one company communicating with another company before the price quotation to the customer." This misconceives the purpose for which the price communications are being offered. The communications are not supposed to be direct evidence of a one-time mini-conspiracy to fix the price on one sale. Rather, they are circumstantial evidence of a type of behavior one would not expect in the absence of an agreement to cooperate. If no cartel was in place, each competitor would seek to benefit from high prices generally, while secretly shading prices when it would gain a customer without provoking retaliation. Confessing price-cutting when one needn't do so would only invite retaliation and guarantee that one's competitors could match the discounted price exactly next time. This is contrary to self-interest. On the other hand, if the producers were cooperating in a cartel, a necessary feature of their arrangement would be some way to determine who was discounting. Thus, confessing price-cutting to competitors makes no economic sense for independent actors, but makes perfect economic sense for cartel members. The Court has rejected circumstantial evidence of an agreement because it is not direct evidence.

The Court's second reason for dismissing the price verification evidence is that "there is no evidence to support the inference that the verifications had an impact on price increases." The class points to the price verifications as circumstantial evidence of a broader conspiracy. Parallel price increases are the starting point for the class's case, so that if the conspiracy is proved, effect on prices has been proved at the first step. The Court argues that prices eventually went down, but this glosses over the fact that they first rose dramatically, then remained above both the forecasted price based on market factors and the suspension agreement price until 1992 (with the exception of the two-month dip caused by the PCS "market correction program"). If, to prove collusion, a plaintiff has to prove that there was no cheating, thus no downward pressure on prices, cartels will be quite safe from the Sherman Act.

To support its proposition that there is nothing suspicious about oligopolists exchanging non-public price information, the Court relies on *In re Baby Food Antitrust Litigation*, where the Third Circuit stated: "No evidence ... shows that any executive of any defendant exchanged price or market information with any other executive." 166 F.3d at 135. The court held that price discussions among low level employees did not show a conspiracy. *Id.* at 137. This reasoning implies that if high-level executives had been involved, it would have constituted evidence of conspiracy (if, indeed, the plaintiffs had been able to prove parallel pricing, which they did not in *In re Baby Food*, 166 F.3d at 128–32). In our case there is a wealth of evidence that high level executives, who were in a position to respond to what they learned, were directly involved in exchanging secret price information. Citing *In re Baby Food* in a case with this kind of evidence vitiates the distinction on which the Third Circuit relied.

The Court ignores the Third Circuit's articulated rationale in *In re Baby Food* because the Court thinks the rationale is belied by facts in that case showing that high level executives used information gathered by low-level employees. The Third Circuit apparently saw a crucial difference between gathering information to use to one's own advantage and giving out information for one's competitors to use to their advantage (and one's own detriment). However gladly the baby food executives used information relayed to them, the facts of *In re Baby Food* recited by the Third Circuit do not show that the executives were giving away their firms' secrets. The Third Circuit expressly stated that Anderson, a salesman who testified that he gathered information for his superiors, was not instructed to go around giving out advance pricing information about his own company. In this case, it is the potash producers' pattern of giving their competitors valuable information that we identify as an act contrary to the producers' self-interest unless there was an agreement.

The Court's third reason for dismissing the price verifications is that the verifications were "sporadic." The evidence indicates that the producers called each other when they had reason to think their competitors were cutting prices, and that they responded to each other's inquiries. The total number of such inquiries is difficult to set, but the defendants characterize it as "no more than several dozen"—surely more than a scintilla.

This "sporadic" argument seems to be directed to the quantum of proof, rather than the quality of it. In other words, it is an argument that more proof should exist, rather than an argument that the existing proof is not probative. If the plaintiff adduces evidence of the kind that tends to prove the existence of a conspiracy, I do not believe that *Monsanto* and *Matsushita* give a justification for rejecting it. *Monsanto* and *Matsushita* lay out a test for the kind of proof necessary in antitrust cases, not the quantity of it. There is no heightened "clear and convincing" standard of proof in civil antitrust conspiracy cases, requiring a greater quantum of proof than the ordinary "preponderance of the evidence" standard. The plaintiff's evidence must amount to more than a scintilla, but the plaintiff does not have to outweigh the defendant's evidence item by item.

The Ninth Circuit, in its recent decision of *In re Citric Acid Litigation*, dismissed evidence of price discussions as "sporadic," but it is not clear whether the court rejected the evidence qualitatively under *Monsanto* or because it was not quantitatively sufficient to create a material issue of fact. In *Citric Acid* the existence of a price-fixing conspiracy was conceded, but the question remained whether one defendant, Cargill, had been a party to the conspiracy. *See* 191 F.3d at 1093. Cargill received summary judgment despite testimony that a competitor had discussions regarding the bidding price of citric acid with someone from Cargill. The Ninth Circuit cited *In re Baby Foods* and dismissed the evidence as "sporadic price discussions with one individual at Cargill." The testimony in question was vague, with no specific evidence of what was said, and there were other qualitative reasons for rejecting it, including the fact that the timing of the alleged discussions was inconsistent with the plaintiff's theory of the case. The court also concluded the case by saying that there was no more than a scintilla of evidence that Cargill participated in the conspiracy. *In re Citric Acid* is therefore consistent with the ordinary summary judgment standard in cases requiring a preponderance of evidence, and it does not stand for the proposition that a heightened quantum of proof is necessary to survive summary judgment in antitrust cases.

The Court states in this case that the fact that there were "several dozen communications" among competitors is not "significant." I would hold that evidence of several dozen communications of the type that tends to prove conspiracy creates a genuine issue of material fact.

In addition to the price verification practices, evidence concerning PCS's "market correction program" in December 1989 also tends to exclude the hypothesis of independent action. On December 18, 1989, PCS cut its prices by $18 a ton for five days. PCS's Carlos Smith stated that the purpose (and effect) of the program was to stabilize prices in the industry:

> Q. Was it an attempt to stabilize prices?
>
> A. Yes....
>
> Q. And did it work?
>
> A. It leveled them.

A high-level Kalium executive, John Huber, wrote the following notes: "Program was a market correction. Weren't trying to teach other people— only got tired of people who kept chipping away. Program was reasonable one—checked with people.... People started cheating.... We wanted to get their attention. Program to be short, very specific." Huber said he did not recall to whom he had been talking when he made these notes, but the use of the phrase, "We wanted to get their attention," suggests he was taking dictation from someone at PCS.

The wording of Huber's notes implies that the "market correction" program was a way of disciplining producers who had breached an earlier agreement. In plain English, the use of the word "cheating" denotes the breach of an agreement or convention, not independent action. Without an agreement, price cutting would be called "competing," not "cheating."

Moreover, the Huber notes suggest PCS's action was not lonely price leadership, but rather that PCS "checked with people" before cutting prices. Apparently, PCS did not want to risk sparking another price war by letting other producers misunderstand the intent behind the "market correction program." These notes illustrate a situation in which smoke signals were just too ambiguous and dangerous to be trusted, so that competitors had to resort to explicit communications to coordinate prices. The notes, taken together with the successful "market correction" program, tend to exclude the possibility of independent action.

The class also points to another piece of evidence that tends to exclude the hypothesis of independent action. This is the Canpotex memorandum of Friday, January 8, 1988, which stated:

> FYI Canadian potash producers have reached agreement with the United States Department of Commerce and all dumping action has been suspended for a minimum of 5 years. It is rumored that the USD per metric ton increase posted by Canadian producers in 1987 to cover possible tariff payments to the U.S. Govt will be refunded in full or part. *In the meantime new price lists are being issued on Monday Jan. 11 at: Standard Grade USD 80.00; Coarse Grade USD 84.00; Granular Grade USD 86.00.*

(emphasis added). Canpotex is the Canadian producers' cartel organized for sales outside the United States.

Again, the Court misconceives the import of this evidence, rejecting it as direct evidence of an attempt to reach an agreement, when the class offers it as circumstantial evidence of an agreement that already existed. The Court considers it crucial to establish who received the Canpotex memorandum, apparently reasoning that if the memorandum was meant to negotiate an agreement, only people who got the memorandum could respond to it. Instead, the class offers this memorandum as circumstantial evidence tending to show that Canpotex knew on Friday, January 8, of an existing agreement to raise prices. The prophecy by Canpotex that its members would issue new "price lists" with particular prices does indeed tend to show the price increase was coordinated, because otherwise it would have been impossible to know in advance what the individual producers would do.

In sum, the class has adduced evidence of a market structure ripe for collusion, a sudden change from price war to supra-competitive pricing, price-fixing overtures from one competitor to another, voluntary disclosure of secret price concessions, an explicitly discussed cheater punishment program, and advance knowledge of other producers' price moves. Taken together, this list of "plus factors" adds up to evidence that satisfies the *Monsanto* standard.

II.

As I understand our previous cases, it is still necessary to take into account the producers' explanation of their conduct in order to ascertain whether their theory deprives the plaintiffs' case of its probative value. In this case, the producers' theory is that the price rises are explained entirely by the suspension agreement and the spectre of Saskatchewan prorationing legislation. In light of the evidence adduced by Professor Rausser and the Commerce Department correspondence indicating that the industry price far exceeded the price floors set by the suspension agreement, I cannot see that the producers' explanation deflates the class's price-fixing theory. I fully understand that the producers dispute Rausser's understanding of the suspension agreement price levels. Moreover, there is absolutely no dispute that prices had to rise above the price-war levels to comply with the suspension agreement. However, the producers make no attempt to identify a price floor required by the suspension agreement or to show that the producers actually set their prices, for instance the January 11 price of $86.00 for granular grade, by reference to the suspension agreement floor. Indeed, their expert William Barringer argued that it was actually impossible to ascertain whether a given price would satisfy the agreement. Instead, the producers' expert Andrew Rosenfield opined that the defendants needed only to set their prices "well above" suspension agreement floor prices. Under these experts' testimony, the suspension agreement did not dictate the actual prices charged; therefore, the existence of the suspension agreement does not explain away the facts supporting the class's theory that the actual prices were set by illegal collusion.

Not only were the January 1988 prices higher than the prices required by the suspension agreement, but there is evidence tending to prove that the producers felt free to dip below the suspension agreement prices when it served their purposes. Professor Rausser's price chart shows that during PCS's "market correction" program in January and February 1990, prices dipped below the suspension agreement floor. Deliberately taking prices below the suspension agreement floor to punish price-cutters is not a convincing sign of industry devotion to the suspension agreement, and the fact that it happened discredits the producers' argument that their prices were compelled by the suspension agreement.

The producers have not made a showing that the governmental intervention so explains their actual behavior as to take away the probative power of the class's case. This case should therefore proceed to trial. Accordingly, I dissent.

COMMENT

Lest you think, after reading *Boise Cascade, Ethyl,* and *Blomkest Fertilizer,* that the courts have ceased to find antitrust violations based on concerted practices, consider the following opinion from the Seventh Circuit:

In re High Fructose Corn Syrup Antitrust Litigation

United States Court of Appeals, Seventh Circuit, 2002.
295 F.3d 651.

■ POSNER, CIRCUIT JUDGE. The plaintiffs appeal from the grant of summary judgment for the defendants in an antitrust class action charging price fixing in violation of section 1 of the Sherman Act, 15 U.S.C. § 1. 156 F. Supp. 2d 1017 (C.D. Ill. 2001). The defendants are the principal manufacturers of high fructose corn syrup (HFCS)–Archer Daniels Midland (ADM), A.E. Staley, Cargill, American Maize–Products, and CPC International (which has settled with the plaintiffs, however, and thus is no longer a party). The plaintiffs represent a certified class consisting of direct purchasers from the defendants.

HFCS is a sweetener manufactured from corn and used in soft drinks and other food products. There are two grades, HFCS 42 and HFCS 55, the numbers referring to the percentage of fructose. HFCS 55, which constitutes about 60 percent of total sales of HFCS, is bought mostly by producers of soft drinks, with Coca–Cola and Pepsi–Cola between them accounting for about half the purchases. But many purchasers, of both grades of HFCS, are small. Industry sales exceeded $1 billion a year during the relevant period.

The plaintiffs claim that in 1988 the defendants secretly agreed to raise the prices of HFCS, that the conspiracy was implemented the following year, and that it continued until mid–1995 when the FBI raided ADM in search of evidence of another price-fixing conspiracy. Billions of dollars in treble damages are sought; we do not know whether the plaintiffs are also seeking injunctive relief, whether against renewal of the conspiracy, specific practices left in its wake (such as the 90 percent rule, of which more shortly), or both. The suit was brought in 1995 and though an enormous amount of evidence was amassed in pretrial discovery, the district judge concluded that "no reasonable jury could find in [the plaintiffs'] favor on the record presented in this case without resorting to pure speculation or conjecture." The soundness of this conclusion is the basic issue presented by the appeal.

Section 1 of the Sherman Act forbids contracts, combinations, and conspiracies in restraint of trade. This statutory language is broad enough, as we noted in *JTC Petroleum Co. v. Piasa Motor Fuels, Inc.,* 190 F.3d 775, 780 (7th Cir. 1999), to encompass a purely tacit agreement to fix prices, that is, an agreement made without any actual communication among the parties to the agreement. If a firm raises price in the expectation that its competitors will do likewise, and they do, the firm's behavior can be conceptualized as the offer of a unilateral contract that the offerees accept by raising their prices. Or as the creation of a contract implied in fact. "Suppose a person walks into a store and takes a newspaper that is for sale there, intending to pay for it. The circumstances would create a contract implied in fact" even though there was no communication between the parties. *A.E.I. Music Network, Inc. v. Business Computers, Inc.,* 290 F.3d 952, 956 (7th Cir. 2002). Nevertheless it is generally believed, and the plaintiffs implicitly accept, that an express, manifested agreement, and thus an agreement involving actual, verbalized communication, must be proved in order for a price-fixing conspiracy to be actionable under the Sherman Act. . . .

Because price fixing is a per se violation of the Sherman Act, an admission by the defendants that they agreed to fix their prices is all the proof a plaintiff needs. In the absence of such an admission, the plaintiff must present evidence from which the existence of such an agreement can be inferred–and remember that the plaintiffs in this case concede that it must be an explicit, manifested agreement rather than a purely tacit meeting of the minds. The evidence upon which a plaintiff will rely will usually be and in this case is of two types–economic evidence suggesting that the defendants were not in fact competing, and noneconomic evidence suggesting that they were not competing because they had agreed not to compete. The economic evidence will in turn generally be of two types, and is in this case: evidence that the structure of the market was such as to make secret price fixing feasible (almost any market can be cartelized if the law permits sellers to establish formal, overt mechanisms for colluding, such as exclusive sales agencies); and evidence that the market behaved in a noncompetitive manner. Neither form of economic evidence is strictly necessary, see *United States v. Andreas,* 216 F.3d 645, 666 (7th Cir. 2000), since price-fixing agreements are illegal even if the parties were completely unrealistic in supposing they could influence the market price. But economic evidence is important in a case such as this in which, although there is noneconomic evidence, that evidence is suggestive rather than conclusive.

In deciding whether there is enough evidence of price fixing to create a jury issue, a court asked to dismiss a price-fixing suit on summary judgment must be careful to avoid three traps that the defendants in this case have cleverly laid in their brief. The first is to weigh conflicting evidence (the job of the jury), and is illustrated by a dispute between the parties over testimony by an executive of A.E. Staley that Coca–Cola, a major customer, suggested that the prices of HFCS 42 and HFCS 55 be fixed in a ratio of 9 to 10. The fact that the defendants all adopted this ratio is part of the plaintiffs' evidence of conspiracy, and the inference of conspiracy would be weakened if the initiative for the adoption had come from a customer. The defendants treat the Staley testimony as uncontradicted because Coca–Cola's witness did not deny having suggested the 9:10 ratio but instead testified that he didn't recall having suggested it and was not aware of his company's ever having such a preference. The absence of a flat denial by Coca–Cola's witness of the Staley testimony would not as the defendants contend require a reasonable jury to accept that testimony, which is self-serving, uncorroborated, implausible (because the defendants achieved the ratio by raising the price of HFCS 42 rather than by lowering the price of HFCS 55, so Coca–Cola could not have benefited unless it just bought 55 and a competitor 42, which is not suggested), and inconsistent with the overall evidence of conspiracy, which as we shall see was abundant although not conclusive. A plaintiff cannot make his case just by asking the jury to disbelieve the defendant's witnesses, but there is much more here. The defendants' handling of the 90 percent issue illustrates how the statement of facts in the defendants' brief combines a recital of the facts favorable to the defendants with an interpretation favorable to them of the remaining evidence; and that is the character of a trial brief rather than of a brief defending a grant of summary judgment.

The second trap to be avoided in evaluating evidence of an antitrust conspiracy for purposes of ruling on the defendants' motion for summary judgment is to suppose that if no single item of evidence presented by the plaintiff points unequivocally to conspiracy, the evidence as a whole cannot defeat summary judgment. It is true that zero plus zero equals zero. But evidence can be susceptible of different interpretations, only one of which supports the party sponsoring it, without being wholly devoid of probative value for that party. Otherwise what need would there ever be for a trial? The question for the jury in a case such as this would simply be whether, when the evidence was considered as a whole, it was more likely that the defendants had conspired to fix prices than that they had not conspired to fix prices. *E.g.*, *In re Brand Name Prescription Drugs Antitrust Litigation*, 186 F.3d 781, 787 (7th Cir. 1999).

The third trap is failing to distinguish between the existence of a conspiracy and its efficacy. The defendants point out that many of the actual sales of HFCS during the period of the alleged conspiracy were made at prices below the defendants' list prices, and they intimate, without quite saying outright, that therefore even a bald-faced agreement to fix list prices would not be illegal in this industry. (Their brief states, for example, that "list prices are irrelevant here because the vast majority of HFCS sales were *not* made at list price" (emphasis in original).) That is wrong. An agreement to fix list prices is, as the defendants' able counsel reluctantly conceded at the argument of the appeal, a *per se* violation of the Sherman Act even if most or for that matter all transactions occur at lower prices. Anyway sellers would not bother to fix list prices if they thought there would be no effect on transaction prices. Many sellers are blessed with customers who are "sleepers," that is, customers who don't shop around for the best buy; and even for those who do bargain for a lower price, the list price is usually the starting point for the bargaining and the higher it is (within reason) the higher the ultimately bargained price is likely to be. The defendants acknowledge that their "price lists served a useful purpose." The only useful purpose they might serve is as a guide to likely transaction prices. What is true is that if many sales are made at prices below the list price, the fact that the sellers' list prices are the same is not compelling proof of collusion. See *Reserve Supply Corp. v. Owens–Corning Fiberglas Corp., supra,* 971 F.2d at 53–54. But it wouldn't be anyway, since identical list prices might be adopted by imitation rather than by explicit agreement.

Let us turn to the evidence that the HFCS market is one in which secret price fixing might actually have an effect on price and thus be worth attempting. The fact that price fixing has to be kept secret in order to avoid immediate detection followed promptly by punishment tends to rule out price fixing in markets that have many sellers selling a product heterogeneous with regard to quality and specifications and having good substitutes in production or consumption; that are concentrated on the buying side, enabling the buyers to tempt sellers to shade any agreed-upon price in order to obtain a big bloc of business; and that have other characteristics, unnecessary to detail here, that make it irrational to run the legal and business risks of fixing prices.

The plaintiffs' economic expert opined in his report and the defendants pretty much concede that the structure of the HFCS market, far from being inimical to secret price fixing, is favorable to it. We need not go into great detail on the point as it is not seriously contested. There are few sellers of HFCS. The five original defendants (recall that one has now settled with the plaintiffs) accounted during the period of the alleged conspiracy for 90 percent of the sales of the product. Therefore elaborate communications, quick to be detected, would not have been necessary to enable pricing to be coordinated. And if one seller broke ranks, the others would quickly discover the fact, and so the seller would have gained little from cheating on his coconspirators; the threat of such discovery tends to shore up a cartel. In addition, the product, HFCS, is highly standardized. Remember that there are only two grades, 42 and 55; and both are uniform. So colluding sellers would not have to agree not only on price but also on quality, design, post-sale services, and the like. This is another reason why a successful conspiracy would not require such frequent communications as to make prompt detection likely. There also are no close substitutes for HFCS. Not that there aren't plenty of other sweeteners, such as sugar; but apparently they are not perceived as close substitutes by soft-drink manufacturers and other purchasers of HFCS. An attempt to raise price above cost would not be likely to come to grief by causing a hemorrhage of business to sellers in other markets.

And the defendants had a lot of excess capacity, a condition that makes price competition more than usually risky and collusion more than usually attractive. When a market's productive capacity exceeds the demand for the market's product, a very low price will cover the incremental cost of additional output because capacity will not have to be expanded in order to enable additional production. Competition will tend to drive price down to that level because any price above it will make some contribution to the seller's fixed costs (the costs that do not vary with output, such as the cost of building the seller's plant). But it will not be remunerative pricing, because it will not cover those costs in full. A seller might have a huge debt (a fixed cost, because owed regardless of how much the seller produces) because of its huge underutilized plant and yet find it impossible to service the debt because competition from other firms also cursed with excess capacity and so also desperate to find buyers who will pay a price that makes *some* contribution to their heavy fixed costs had driven its price down to, or very near, the incremental cost of its output. Suppose for example that the average total cost of some quantity X of HFCS is $10, but the incremental cost required to sell X more of HFCS is only $5. Then at any price above $5, even if it is below $10, a sale will make some contribution to covering the seller's fixed costs. If several sellers with similar cost structures are competing, the tendency will be to drive the market price all the way down to $5, which will prevent the sellers from covering their total costs and thus confront them with the risk of bankruptcy. Conversely, precisely because of the discrepancy between total and variable cost, an agreement among the sellers that eliminates price competition will generate revenues enormously in excess of variable cost and so go far to stave off the threat of bankruptcy. And so the sellers will have a big incentive to fix prices.

As our numerical example suggests, the significance of excess capacity depends on the ratio of fixed to variable costs. If it is very low, the impact on the firms' solvency of competition that forces price down to variable costs may be slight. This is so far an unexplored issue in the litigation.

The defendants continued to add to their capacity during the period of the alleged conspiracy. This behavior does not disprove the existence of the conspiracy, as the defendants argue. Maintenance of excess capacity discourages new entry, which supracompetitive prices would otherwise attract, and also shores up a cartel by increasing the risk that its collapse will lead to a devastating price war ending in the bankruptcy of some or all of the former cartelists.

The principal features of the HFCS market that might seem to bear against an inference that secret price fixing was feasible and attractive during the period of the alleged conspiracy are, first, that HFCS is sold under two different types of contract: straight sale, and what are called "tolling agreements." Under the latter, the customer buys the corn and hires one of the sellers of HFCS to manufacture it into HFCS. That sounds like something that would greatly complicate an HFCS price-fixing conspiracy, but there is evidence that it did not. It seems that the only practical difference between the two forms of sale is that the tolling agreement shifts the risk of a change in the raw-material cost (the cost of the corn) from seller to buyer. Prices under the two arrangements are highly correlated and the price of the HFCS net of the cost of the corn is easily determined, so that sellers could not easily cheat on a price-fixing agreement by reducing the price of their tolling contracts.

Second, there are some very large buyers of HFCS, notably Coca–Cola and Pepsi–Cola, and, as theory predicts, they drove hard bargains and obtained large discounts from the list price of HFCS 55. But it does not follow that the defendants could not and did not fix the price of HFCS 55. There is a difference between a market in which all or virtually all the buyers are large and one in which there are some large and some small buyers. Suppose the buying side of the HFCS market were as concentrated as the selling side, meaning that five firms bought 90 percent of all the HFCS sold. They would be able to whipsaw the sellers into granting large discounts, and probably therefore any effort at fixing prices would quickly collapse. When instead there are some large and some small buyers, which is the situation here, this need not prevent price fixing; it may simply cause the price fixers to engage in price discrimination, giving large discounts to the big buyers and no (or small) discounts to the small ones.

Market-wide price discrimination is a symptom of price fixing when, as in this case, the product sold by the market is uniform. *In re Brand Name Prescription Drugs Antitrust Litigation*, 288 F.3d 1028, 1030–31 (7th Cir. 2002). If the product is differentiated and as a result each seller has a little pocket of monopoly power, enabling it to charge some of its customers a price above cost without their switching to its competitors, no inference of collusion can be drawn from the fact that the sellers are all discriminating. *Id.* In this case, however, the product is uniform (a "commodity"), so that competition would be expected to prevent any one seller from raising his price to any of his customers above his cost. If sellers are competing in the sale of an identical product which costs each of them $1 to produce (including in cost the market return on equity capital, "profit" in a financial but not in an economic sense), so that the competitive price, which is the market price because the sellers are competing, is $1, no one of them can sell his product to some of his customers for $2, for they can buy from his competitors for $1–unless the sellers collude, and agree not to cut price to the disfavored buyers. This is a highly simplified example, obviously. It ignores and the parties do not discuss the possible erosion of price discrimination by arbitrage, that is, by the favored buyers' buying more than they need and reselling the excess to the disfavored, a process that may continue until all buyers obtain the seller's product at the same price. *Id.* But the example does illustrate an economic logic that favors the plaintiffs.

We turn now to the evidence of noncompetitive behavior, as distinct from evidence that the structure of the market was conducive to such behavior. Early in 1988, which is to say at the outset of the alleged conspiracy, ADM announced that it was raising its price for HFCS 42 to 90 percent of the price of HFCS 55, and the other defendants quickly followed suit. The defendants offer various explanations, of which the most plausible is that HFCS 42 is 90 percent as sweet as HFCS 55. Even if this is correct (there is evidence that the true percentage is only 71 percent), it does not counter an inference of price fixing. In a competitive market, price is based on cost rather than on value. Therefore the fact that buyers of HFCS are willing to pay more for HFCS 55 than for HFCS 42 because it is sweeter just shows that a monopolist or cartel could charge more for the higher grade whereas competition would bid price down to cost. (That was our $1–$2 example; the fact that some customers would pay $2 did not make that a competitive price.) Under competition, if the cost of the lower grade were, say, half the cost of the higher, so would the price be. There is no evidence that HFCS 42 costs 90 percent as much to produce as HFCS 55. Nor is there any evidence that industry-wide adoption of the 90 percent rule followed or anticipated a change in relative costs. In fact, the evidence suggests that it costs only 65 percent as much to manufacture HFCS 42, implying that under competition its price would be 65 percent–not 90 percent-of the price of HFCS 55.

A few months after the adoption of the 90 percent rule, the defendants switched from making contracts with their customers that specified the contract price for an entire year to contracts in which price was negotiated quarterly. They did this although virtually all their customers preferred the former system in order to minimize risk. In other words, the defendants shifted risk to their customers (the sort of thing the tolling agreements did for customers who bought under those agreements) at the same time that, according to evidence discussed below, the defendants were raising their prices net of cost, rather than lowering them to compensate the customers for assuming additional risk. That is not competitive behavior.

There is evidence that defendants bought HFCS from one another even when the defendant doing the buying could have produced the amount bought at a lower cost than the purchase price. There is nothing suspicious about a firm's occasionally buying from a competitor to supply a customer whom the firm for one reason or another can't at the moment supply. The firm would rather buy from a competitor to supply its customer than tell the customer to buy from the competitor, lest the customer never return. But if the firm *could* supply its customer (remember there was a lot of excess capacity in the HFCS industry during the period of the alleged conspiracy) *and* at a lower cost than its competitor would charge, why would it buy from the competitor rather than expanding its own production? The possibility that springs immediately to mind is that this is a way of shoring up a sellers' cartel by protecting the market share of each seller. A seller who experiences a surge in demand, but meets the surge by buying what it needs from another seller rather than by expanding its own production, protects the other firm's market share and so preserves peace among the cartelists. It is pertinent to note that these inter-competitor transactions ended with the end of the alleged conspiracy.

In part because of those transactions the market shares of the defendants changed very little during the period of the alleged conspiracy, which is just what one would expect of a group of sellers who are all charging the same prices for a uniform product and trying to keep everyone happy by maintaining the relative sales positions of the group's members. This evidence probably does not deserve as much weight as the plaintiffs give it. They don't point us to any evidence of how market shares fluctuated before or after the period of the alleged conspiracy; and without such evidence there is no benchmark against which to assess the stability of the defendants' market shares during that period. But it is something, the evidence of stable market shares, for two reasons. First, had they gyrated wildly, this would be some evidence of active competition. The defendants argue that they did gyrate wildly, but their evidence involves comparing pre-conspiracy (1988) market shares with market shares during the period of the alleged conspiracy (the district court followed them in this mistake). If, consistent with that evidence, the gyrations moderated during the period of the alleged conspiracy, this would be evidence for the plaintiffs.

Second and much more important, the output of HFCS grew during this period and one might expect that growth to have brought about changes in market shares; for it would be unlikely that all the sellers had the same ability to exploit the new sales opportunities opened by the growing demand. This is why a growth in demand usually makes it more difficult for a cartel to hold together than if demand is steady. If demand is growing it is difficult for a seller to determine whether a decline in its market share is due to cheating by another member of the cartel or just to the superior ability of some other member or members of the cartel to attract new business without cutting price. The defendants emphasize *that* point but fail to acknowledge that the fact that market shares did not fluctuate significantly during the period of the alleged HFCS conspiracy may indicate that the sellers had agreed tacitly or otherwise to share the sales opportunities created by the growth in demand. This is conjecture, but conjecture has its place in building a case out of circumstantial evidence.

The plaintiffs' economic expert witness conducted a regression analysis that found, after correcting for other factors likely to influence prices of HFCS, that those prices were higher during the period of the alleged conspiracy than they were before or after.... The judge deemed the analysis admissible as evidence, thus certifying it as the responsible though of course not necessarily correct work of a qualified professional.... The defendants presented a competing regression analysis done by one of their economic experts, who added a couple of variables to the analysis of the plaintiffs' expert and, presto, the [plaintiffs'] variable ceased to be statistically significant. The plaintiffs rebutted with still another expert, who pointed out correctly that adding variables that are correlated with the variable of interest can make the effect of the latter disappear–to which the defendants reply, also correctly, that there are statistical methods for solving this problem (the problem of multicollinearity, as it is called by statisticians). They argue that their expert solved it and the plaintiffs argue that he did not and also that there was no statistical rationale for adding those other variables in the first place. Resolving this dispute requires a knowledge of statistical inference that judges do not possess. Later we'll suggest a method for resolving it. But in the present state of the record we must accept that the plaintiffs have presented some admissible evidence that higher prices during the period of the alleged conspiracy cannot be fully explained by causes consistent with active competition, such as changes in the price of corn. . . .

To summarize the discussion to this point, there is evidence both that the HFCS market has a structure that is auspicious for price fixing and that during the period of the alleged conspiracy the defendants avoided or at least limited price competition. But as the defendants point out (when they are not arguing, inconsistently, that the industry was in fact fiercely competitive), all of this evidence is consistent with the hypothesis that they had a merely tacit agreement, which at least for purposes of this appeal the plaintiffs concede is not actionable under section 1 of the Sherman Act. The question then becomes whether there is enough evidence for a reasonable jury to find that there was an explicit agreement, not merely a tacit one. To repeat, there is evidence that the defendants were not competing; we might go so far as to say they had tacitly agreed not to compete, or at least to compete as little as possible; but the plaintiffs must prove that there was an actual, manifest agreement not to compete. Another and equivalent way to put this is that they must present evidence that would enable a reasonable jury to reject the hypothesis that the defendants foreswore price competition without actually agreeing to do so. See, e.g., *Matsushita Electric Industrial Co. v. Zenith Radio Corp.,* 475 U.S. 574, 588 (1986).

More evidence is required the less plausible the charge of collusive conduct. In *Matsushita,* for example, the charge was that the defendants had conspired to lower prices below cost in order to drive out competitors, and then to raise prices to monopoly levels. This was implausible for a variety of reasons, such as that it would mean that losses would be incurred in the near term in exchange for the speculative possibility of more than making them up in the uncertain and perhaps remote future—when, moreover, the competitors might come right back into the market as soon as (or shortly after) prices rose above cost, thus thwarting the conspirators' effort at recouping their losses with a commensurate profit. But the charge in this case involves no implausibility. The charge is of a garden-variety price-fixing conspiracy orchestrated by a firm, ADM, conceded to have fixed prices on related products (lysine and citric acid) during a period over-lapping the period of the alleged conspiracy to fix the prices of HFCS. . . .

We shall now summarize the evidence of explicit agreement, first noting however that the district judge refused to consider any of this evidence because he thought its character was such as to "require that a substantial inference be drawn in order to have evidentiary significance." This is correct in the sense that no single piece of the evidence that we're about to summarize is sufficient in itself to prove a price-fixing conspiracy. But that is not the question. The question is simply whether this evidence, considered as a whole and in combination with the economic evidence, is sufficient to defeat summary judgment. The judge may have been confused by the language found in cases such as *In re Baby Food Antitrust Litigation*, 166 F.3d 112, 118 (3d Cir. 1999), that "direct evidence in a Section 1 conspiracy must be evidence that is explicit and requires no inferences to establish the proposition or conclusion being asserted." We tried in *Troupe v. May Department Stores Co.*, 20 F.3d 734, 736–37 (7th Cir. 1994), to straighten out the confusing (and, as it seems to us, largely if not entirely superfluous) distinction between direct and circumstantial evidence. The former is evidence tantamount to an acknowledgment of guilt; the latter is everything else *including* ambiguous statements. These are not to be disregarded because of their ambiguity; most cases are constructed out of a tissue of such statements and other circumstantial evidence, since an outright confession will ordinarily obviate the need for a trial.

Here at any rate is the plaintiffs' evidence, which the district judge should not have disregarded, that there was an explicit agreement to fix prices: One of Staley's HFCS plant managers was heard to say: "We have an understanding within the industry not to undercut each other's prices." ... A Staley document states that Staley will "support efforts to limit [HFCS] pricing to a quarterly basis." Presumably the reference is to efforts by its competitors. The president of ADM stated that "our competitors are our friends. Our customers are the enemy." This sentiment, which will win no friends for capitalism, was echoed by a director of Staley's parent company who said in a memo to Staley executives that "competitors['] happiness is at least as important as customers['] happiness." A director of Staley was reported to have said that "*every* business I'm in is an organization" (emphasis added)–which sounds innocuous enough, but he said it in reference to the conspiracy to fix the price of lysine ("lysine is an organization") and so in context it appears that "organization" meant price-fixing conspiracy. Michael Andreas, the vice chairman and executive vice president of ADM, said: "What are you gonna tell [Keough, the recently retired president of Coca–Cola], that we gotta [*i.e.*, have a] deal with ... our two biggest competitors to f*** ya over[?]" Andreas, a principal figure in the lysine and citric-acid price-fixing conspiracies, also referred to Cargill's president as a "friendly competitor" and mentioned an "understanding between the companies that ... causes us not to ... make irrational decisions." In a discussion with a Japanese businessman indicted along with Andreas for fixing the price of lysine, Andreas compared the relations between ADM and Cargill to those between Mitsubishi and Mitsui, two Japanese conglomerates widely believed to fix prices and allocate markets. . . .

A handwritten Cargill document refers under the heading "competitors" to "entry of new entrants (barriers) and will they play by the rules (discipline)." A price-fixing conspiracy increases the attractiveness of entry into a market by creating a wedge between price and cost. And so conspirators will naturally worry whether, if there is entry, the new entrant will join rather than compete with the conspiracy and, if he refuses to join, whether the conspirators can punish him in some way. This is not the only possible interpretation of the document, but it is a plausible one.

Shortly after the FBI raided ADM's headquarters seeking evidence of the company's involvement in the lysine and citric-acid conspiracies, Terrence Wilson, the head of ADM's corn processing division–the division responsible for HFCS as well as for the other two products–said he didn't know "what other companies [the FBI] hit. . . . I don't know . . . if they hit Staley or not." Since Staley did not manufacture lysine or citric acid, but did of course manufacture HFCS, Wilson may have been expressing a concern that the FBI would uncover evidence of an HFCS price-fixing conspiracy as well. It is further worth noting that the alleged HFCS conspiracy began shortly after Wilson became head of ADM's corn products division—which raises the question why, if as the defendants argue the 90 percent rule and the other parallel behavior that is the plaintiffs' evidence of a lack of price competition in the HFCS market were just the natural expression of the oligopolistic structure of the market, this behavior should have begun when Wilson, later to be imprisoned for price fixing, took charge of ADM's HFCS operations. There may be an answer (pure coincidence, perhaps, or a change in the structure of the HFCS industry that suddenly made tacit collusion more attractive)—a point with general application to our review of the evidence that favors the plaintiffs—but its adequacy presents a genuine issue of material fact and therefore cannot be determined on summary judgment. And in a civil case price fixing need be proved only by a preponderance of the evidence.

There is some more evidence of the kind we've just been discussing, that is, evidence of explicit agreement, and other economic evidence as well that bolsters the plaintiffs' case, evidence for example that ADM had significant ownership interests in two of the other defendants. But we can stop here because the evidence that we have summarized would have been enough to enable a reasonable jury to infer that the agreement to fix prices was express rather than tacit. The evidence is not conclusive by any means—there are alternative interpretations of every bit of it—but it is highly suggestive of the existence of an explicit though of course covert agreement to fix prices.

But there is one more piece of evidence that we do have to discuss because it was the subject of an evidentiary ruling that the plaintiffs challenge. After Andreas and Wilson were convicted and sent to prison for fixing the price of lysine, the plaintiffs deposed them and asked them whether they had fixed prices of HFCS as well. They (along with a third executive of ADM) refused to answer, on the ground that their answers might incriminate them. The general rule is that an adverse inference may be drawn from such a refusal in a civil case, . . . though of course the district judge retains his general power under Fed.R.Evid. 403 to exclude relevant evidence if its probative value is clearly outweighed by (so far as relevant here) its capacity to confuse the jury. Without referring to the rule, the district judge ruled the evidence of the deponents' silence inadmissible because the three had refused to answer *any* substantive question, so that, the judge reasoned, no inference could be drawn from their refusal to answer questions about the alleged HFCS price-fixing conspiracy, at least in the absence of other evidence of such a conspiracy. But there *was* other evidence, as we have just seen.

The deeper problem with the judge's ruling is that it assumes that a person has carte blanche by virtue of the Fifth Amendment's self-incrimination clause to refuse to answer questions. The assumption is incorrect. To be privileged by the Fifth Amendment to refuse to answer a question, the answer one would give if one did answer it (and answer it truthfully) must have *some* tendency to subject the person being asked the question to criminal liability. . . . The fact that Andreas and Wilson were in prison for having fixed prices for lysine would not have authorized them to invoke the Fifth Amendment if asked whether they had helped Richard III kill the little princes and bury them in the Tower of London. Andreas and Wilson had been convicted and sentenced for their role in the other price-fixing conspiracies and had exhausted their appellate remedies. They faced no further jeopardy—unless truthful answers to questions about the HFCS conspiracy would have tended to show that ADM had conspired to fix the price of that product as well. That would justify and explain their taking the Fifth and it would also entitle a jury to treat their refusal to answer as evidence that there indeed was such a conspiracy.

The judge was correct that their refusal to answer could not be "imputed" to ADM, but imputation is not the issue. The issue is whether there was a conspiracy, and Andreas's and Wilson's refusal to answer the plaintiffs' questions was one more piece of evidence that there was and that it involved their former employer, ADM, one of the defendants in this case. So it was admissible against ADM though not against the other defendants despite the coconspirator exception to the hearsay rule. Fed.R.Evid. 801(d)(2)(E). The rule is applicable only to statements in furtherance of the conspiracy, and when Andreas and Wilson refused to speak the conspiracy was long over. Even if they were trying to conceal the conspiracy, this would not make their silence in furtherance of it, because efforts at concealing a conspiracy are not themselves part of the conspiracy. . . .

In affirming Andreas's conviction for his role in the lysine price-fixing conspiracy, this court remarked "an inexplicable lack of business ethics and an atmosphere of general lawlessness that infected the very heart of" ADM, whose senior executives "lied, cheated, embezzled, extorted and obstructed justice." United States v. Andreas, *supra*, 216 F.3d at 650. Since evidence of past crimes, or of other bad acts committed in the past, is inadmissible to prove that the defendant probably is guilty of whatever he is now being charged with, merely because he has demonstrated a propensity to violate the law, Fed.R.Evid. 404(b), ADM's previous misconduct cannot be used as evidence that it participated in a conspiracy to fix the price of HFCS. But neither can it be used, as the defendants wish to use it in this case, to show that because the Justice Department has not moved against the alleged HFCS price-fixing conspiracy, there must not have been one. . . . It may also have felt that the antitrust class action bar had both the desire and the resources to prosecute such a suit vigorously, as indeed it has done. The evidence of the defendants' guilt is weaker in this case than in the lysine and citric-acid conspiracy cases, but not so weak as to justify summary judgment in their favor.

[In the remainder of the opinion, the court commented on the best way to manage a trial in which so much highly statistical material is proffered by both sides. It observed that "[s]o far as the nonstatistical evidence is concerned, it is remarkable how little is in dispute. Most of the facts that we have recited in this opinion are not denied by the defendants; their quarrel with the plaintiffs is merely over the inferences to be drawn both from individual pieces of evidence and from the evidence considered as a whole." It also recommended such devices as stipulations by the parties and the use of a court-appointed expert.]

We do not mean to prejudge the outcome of the trial. We have construed the evidence as favorably to the plaintiffs as the record permits because that is how a grant of summary judgment in favor of defendants is reviewed. Maybe the defendants could convince a jury that the spin that their brief puts on the evidence is the correct one. We hold only that there is sufficient admissible evidence in support of the hypothesis of a price-fixing conspiracy to prevent the grant of summary judgment to the defendants. We trust that guided by this opinion the parties will make every effort to settle the case in advance of trial. And finally, although constrained to disagree with the district judge's decision to grant summary judgment, we commend him for his painstaking analysis of the record and for his patient shepherding of this formidable litigation.

Reversed and Remanded.

NOTE: THE EUROPEAN APPROACH TO THE OLIGOPOLY PROBLEM

As noted in Chapter 1, Article 81 of the Treaty establishing the European Community prohibits "all agreements between undertakings, decisions by associations of undertakings and concerted practices which may affect trade between Member States, and which have as their object or effect the prevention, restriction, or distortion of competition within the common market...." Article 82 prohibits "abuse by one or more undertakings of a dominant position."

Although the language of the EC Treaty is similar to the language of the first two sections of the Sherman Act, the European Commission's approach to the problem of tacit collusion differs from that of the American antitrust enforcement agencies and courts. In contrast to the law in the United States, the European regime is more concerned with the ability of dominant firms to exert market power than with the possibility of market-wide collusion. The law is violated whenever such an exertion of market power amounts to an "abuse of a dominant position." As a result of its somewhat different focus, the Commission's analysis tends to emphasize the impact of the merger on competitors. Kauper, Merger Control in the United States and the European Union: Some Observations, 74 St. John's L. Rev. 305, 346 (2000). Some criticize the European antitrust regulators' emphasis on "abuse of a dominant position." The critics believe that the abuse concept may serve to control "excesses and concentration" in oligopolistic markets, but that it is ineffective in dealing with issues such as conscious parallelism. Raffaelli, Oligopolies and Antitrust Law, 19 Fordham Int'l L.J. 915, 932 (1996). In large part, just as in the United States, the difficulty in tackling conscious parallelism is attributable to the fact that European law also requires, at least for Article 81 cases, a finding of concerted practices.

Though analogous to the American theory of conscious parallelism, the theory of concerted practices is not the same. In the *Wood Pulp* decision, an Article 81 case, the Commission challenged the practices of 40 wood pulp producers from the United States, Canada, and Finland and three of their trade associations. The European Court of Justice held that the practice of issuing quarterly price announcements in dollar terms did not infringe Article 81(1). It also analyzed whether the price announcements constituted evidence of "concertation." The Court held that "parallel conduct cannot be regarded as furnishing proof of concertation unless concertation constituted the only plausible explanation for such conduct." The Court found that the system of price announcements, the simultaneity of the price announcements, and the parallelism of the announced prices could be explained by reasons other than consciously coordinated behavior, such as common business practices, rapid means of communication, and the transparency of the market. *A. Ahlstrom Osakeyhtio v. Commission*, Cases C–89, 104, 114, 116–117, 125–129/85 (1992) ECR I–1307; Rodger, The Oligopoly Problem and the Concept of Collective Dominance, 2 Colum. J. Euro. L. 25, 38–39 (Winter 1996). In the *Italian Flat Glass* decision, 1989 O.J. (L 33), 1990 C.M.L.R. 535, *supra*, the Court of First Instance included some *dicta* to the effect that abuse of a dominant position through concerted practices could be established only by the presence of "economic links" between the dominant parties. *Id.* at 45.

> As Raffaelli puts it:
>
> Based on this case law, a concerted practice exists when the following conditions are met: (1) there must be a form of coordination or practical cooperation between undertakings that replaces their independent action; (2) this coordination needs to be achieved through direct or indirect contact; and (3) the aim must be to remove, in advance, any uncertainty as to the future conduct of their competitors. On the other hand, conscious parallelism results from undertakings' experience in an oligopolistic market, which by its very nature restricts competition, especially with respect to price. The comparison of concerted practices to conscious parallelism is problematic because it may lead to the repression of individual conduct by oligopolistic undertakings, such as the decision to make one's prices uniform with the others. Furthermore, this repression may occur even in the absence of the abuses that trigger the application of antitrust provisions against a monopolistic or dominant undertaking.

Raffaelli, *supra*, 19 Fordham Int'l L.J. at 932. In contrast to the conscious parallelism theory, the "concertation" theory places a higher burden of proof on the antitrust plaintiff, whether a governmental authority or otherwise.

PROBLEM 11

PRICING PRACTICES OF GLUCOSE MANUFACTURERS

Glucose is manufactured in 50 mills in the United States, owned by 30 different companies. About half of the productive capacity is owned by 6 companies. Relatively little glucose is imported.

Over at least the last ten years, prices for glucose have followed this pattern: X Company, the largest in the industry, would announce a change in "base price," to take effect in 48 hours; all other companies would then make similar announcements within 48 hours, and by the time X Company's price change went into effect identical price changes had been made by all other producers. The price to glucose purchasers was a "delivered price"—the "base price" plus the cost of rail shipment to the station nearest the point of use. If the price was quoted by the nearest mill, the rail shipment costs equaled the freight actually paid; if the price was quoted by a more distant mill, the rail shipment costs added were the expenses incurred by the *nearest* glucose producer (*i.e.*, the additional freight costs were absorbed by the more distant seller). As a result, a purchaser at any point would receive, from every glucose manufacturer solicited, identical delivered prices to the nearest railroad station. Discounts for cash, sales warranties, and other terms of sale were the same for all manufacturers. Glucose producers also uniformly refused to quote prices on other than a delivered basis or to use other than rail transportation. The Government has been unable to show that the glucose manufacturers have ever conferred about price or any of these sales practices.

Have the glucose manufacturers engaged in any "contract, combination or conspiracy" to restrain trade? Has any of them engaged in an "unfair method of competition"?

SECTION 4. THE ROLE OF TRADE ASSOCIATIONS AND INFORMATION DISSEMINATION

NOTE

"People of the same trade seldom meet together, even for merriment and diversion, but the conversation ends in a conspiracy against the public, or in some contrivance to raise prices. It is impossible indeed to prevent such meetings, by any law which either could be executed, or would be consistent with liberty and justice. But though the law cannot hinder people of the same trade from sometimes assembling together, it ought to do nothing to facilitate such assemblies, much less to render them necessary." Adam Smith, The Wealth of Nations, Bk. I, Ch. X (1776).

INTRODUCTION

Trade associations engage in a broad variety of activities, many of which are beneficial from a commercial point of view and raise little or no threat of anticompetitive effects. Such activities include joint insurance arrangements, arbitration services to consumers, lobbying activities and publication of journals relating to the businesses of its members.

Another function performed by a trade association for the benefit of its members is dissemination of information about price, terms of sale, output, and other industrial statistics. Such exchanges characteristically occur pursuant to agreement (often in the bylaws of the trade association), and questions may arise whether the data exchanged in a particular market setting will have an anticompetitive effect.

In one sense, information can be procompetitive in assisting enterprises to know at what levels they must price in order to compete effectively. Arguably a stock exchange is an example of perfect data dissemination in that each seller and each buyer knows almost instantaneously the price and quantity of each previous transaction. On the other hand, where sellers and buyers are fewer in number, too much information or the wrong kind of information may impair the operation of an effective competitive market. In the following line of cases, the courts addressed the question of what kinds of information exchanges may demonstrate a purpose or effect of restraining competition.

American Column & Lumber Co. v. United States

Supreme Court of the United States, 1921.
257 U.S. 377, 42 S.Ct. 114, 66 L.Ed. 284.

■ CLARKE, J. The unincorporated "American Hardwood Manufacturers' Association" was formed in December, 1918, by the consolidation of two similar associations, from one of which it took over a department of activity designated the "Open Competition Plan," and hereinafter referred to as the "Plan."

Participation in the Plan was optional with the members of the Association, but, at the time this suit was commenced, of its 400 members, 365, operating 465 mills, were members of the Plan. The importance and strength of the Association are shown by the admission in the joint answer that while the defendants operated only five per cent of the number of mills engaged in hardwood manufacture in the country, they produced one-third of the total production of the United States. The places of business of the corporations and partnerships, members of the Plan, were located in many States from New York to Texas, but chiefly in the hardwood producing territory of the Southwest. The defendants are the members of the Plan, their personal representatives, and F.R. Gadd, its "Manager of Statistics."

The bill alleged, in substance, that the Plan constituted a combination and conspiracy to restrain interstate commerce in hardwood lumber by restricting competition and maintaining and increasing prices, in violation of the Antitrust Act of 1890 (26 Stat. 209).

The answer denied that the Plan had any such purpose and effect as charged, and averred that it promoted competition, especially among its own members.

A temporary injunction, granted by the District Court, restricting the activities of the "Plan" in specified respects, by consent of the parties was made permanent and a direct appeal brings the case here for review.

The activities which we shall see were comprehended within the "Open Competition Plan" (which is sometimes called "The New Competition") have come to be widely adopted in our country, and as this is the first time their legality has been before this Court for decision, some detail of statement with respect to them is necessary.

There is very little dispute as to the facts. The testimony of the Government consists of various documents and excerpts from others, obtained from the files of the Plan, and the testimony of the defendants consists of like documents and excerpts from other documents, also from the same files, supplemented by affidavits of a number of persons, members and non-members, chiefly to the point that the confessedly great increases of prices during 1919 were due to natural trade and weather conditions and not to the influence of the Plan.

The record shows that the Plan was evolved by a committee, which, in recommending its adoption, said:

> "The purpose of this plan is to disseminate among members accurate knowledge of production and market conditions so that each member may gauge the market intelligently instead of guessing at it; to make competition open and above board instead of secret and concealed; to substitute, in estimated market conditions, frank and full statements of our competitors for the frequently misleading and colored statements of the buyer." ...

... [A] further explanation of the objects and purposes of the Plan was made in an appeal to members to join it, in which it is said:

> "The theoretical proposition at the basis of the Open Competition plan is that,
>
> "*Knowledge regarding prices actually made is all that is necessary to keep prices at reasonably stable and normal levels.*
>
> "The Open Competition plan is a central clearing house for information on prices, trade statistics and practices. By keeping all members fully and quickly informed of what the others have done, the work of the plan results in *a certain uniformity of trade practice*. There is no agreement to follow the practice of others, *although members do naturally follow their most intelligent competitors*, if they know what these competitors have been actually doing.
>
> "The monthly meetings held in various sections of the country each month have improved the human relations existing between the members before the organization of this Plan." ...

Thus, the Plan proposed a system of cooperation among the members, consisting of the interchange of reports of sales, prices, production and practices, and in meetings of the members for discussion, for the avowed purpose of substituting "co-operative competition" for ["]cutthroat competition," of keeping "prices at reasonably stable and normal levels," and of improving the "human relations" among the members. But the purpose to agree upon prices or production was always disclaimed.

Coming now to the fully worked out paper plan as adopted.

It required each member to make six reports to the secretary, viz.:

> 1. A *daily* report of all sales actually made, with the name and address of the purchaser, the kind, grade and quality of lumber sold and all special agreements of every kind, verbal or

written with respect thereto. "These reports are to be exact copies of orders taken."

2. A *daily* shipping report, with exact copies of the invoices, all special agreements as to terms, grade, etc. The classification shall be the same as with sales.

3. A *monthly* production report, showing the production of the member reporting during the previous month, with the grades and thickness classified as prescribed in the "Plan."

4. A *monthly* stock report by each member, showing the stock on hand on the first day of the month, sold and unsold, green and dry, with the total of each kind, grade and thickness.

5. Price-lists. Members must file at the beginning of each month price lists showing prices f.o.b. shipping point, which shall be stated. New prices must be filed with the association as soon as made.

6. Inspection reports. These reports are to be made to the association by a service of its own, established for the purpose of checking up grades of the various members and the Plan provides for a chief inspector and sufficient assistants to inspect the stocks of all members from time to time.

The declared purpose of the inspection service is not to change any member's grading except with his consent, but to furnish each member a basis on which he can compare his prices with those of other members, thereby making all members' reports more intelligible and accurate.

All of these reports by members are subject to complete audit by representatives of the association. Any member who fails to report *shall not receive the reports* of the secretary, and failure to report for twelve days in six months shall cause the member failing to be dropped from membership. . . .

But, since such voluminous disclosures to the secretary would be valueless unless communicated to the members in a condensed and interpreted form, provision is made for this, as follows:

The secretary is required to send to each member:

1. A *monthly* summary showing the production of each member for the previous month, "subdivided as to grade, kind, thickness," etc.

2. A *weekly* report, not later than Saturday, of all sales, to and including the preceding Tuesday, giving each sale and the price, and the name of the purchaser.

3. On Tuesday of each week the secretary must send to each member a report of each shipment by each member, complete up to the evening of the preceding Thursday.

4. He must send a *monthly* report, showing the individual stock on hand of each member and a summary of all stocks, green

and dry, sold and unsold. This report is very aptly referred to by the managing statistician as a monthly inventory of the stock of each member.

5. Not later than the 10th of each month the secretary shall send a summary of the price lists furnished by members, showing the prices asked by each, and any changes made therein must be immediately transmitted to all the members.

6. A market report letter shall be sent to each member of the association (whether participating in the Plan or not) pointing "out changes in conditions both in the producing and consuming sections, giving a comparison of production and sales and in general an analysis of the market conditions."

7. Meetings shall be held once a month at Cincinnati "or at points to be agreed upon by the members." "It is intended that the regular meetings shall afford opportunity for the discussion of all subjects of interest to the members."

"The Plan also requires the selection of a man to take charge of the gathering and dissemination of data, with necessary assistants," and the defendant F.R. Gadd was selected and given the title of "Manager of Statistics." . . .

Such, in outline, was the paper plan adopted by the association, but elaborate though it was, in practice three important additions were made to it.

First of all, the southwestern territory for meeting purposes was divided into four districts, and instead of the monthly meeting provided for in the Plan, "in order that members could more conveniently attend," the record shows that forty-nine of these meetings were held between January 31, 1919, and February 19, 1920—approximately one for each week, in some part of the territory.

Second. Before each of these meetings a questionnaire was sent out to the members, and from the replies received, supplementing the other reports, the statistician compiled an estimate of the condition of the market, actual and prospective, which was distributed to the members attending each meeting, and was mailed to those not present. There were eleven questions on this list of which the most important were:

"(4) What was your total production of hardwoods during the last month? What do you estimate your production will probably be for the next two months?"

"(10) Do you expect to shut down within the next few months on account of shortage of logs or for any other reason? If so, please state how long mill will be idle."

"(11) What is your view of market conditions for the next few months? What is the general outlook for business? State all reasons for your conclusion."

The Plan on paper provided only for reports of past transactions and much is made of this in the record and in argument—that reporting to one another past transactions cannot fix prices for the future. But each of these three questions plainly invited an estimate and discussion of future market conditions by each member, and a coordination of them by an expert analyst could readily evolve an attractive basis for cooperative, even if unexpressed, "harmony" with respect to future prices.

Third. The Plan provided for a monthly "market report letter" to go to all members of the association. In practice this market report letter was prepared by F.R. Gadd, Manager of Statistics, but his review of the market and forecast for the future were contained, almost from the beginning, not only in these market letters but also in the weekly sales reports, so that they were sent out to all of the members nineteen times between February 1 and December 6, 1919, and they were discussed at all but one or two of the forty-nine meetings which were held. All the activities of the Plan plainly culminated in the counsels contained in these letters and reports.

This elaborate plan for the interchange of reports does not simply supply to each member the amount of stock held, the sales made and the prices received, by every other member of the group, thereby furnishing the data for judging the market, on the basis of supply and demand and current prices. It goes much farther. It not only furnishes such information, with respect to stock, sales and prices, but also reports, giving the views of each member as to "market conditions for the next few months," what the production of each will be for the next "two months;" frequent analyses of the reports by an expert, with, we shall see, significant suggestions as to both future prices and production; and opportunities for future meetings for the interchange of views, which the record shows were very important. It is plain that the only element lacking in this scheme to make it a familiar type of the competition suppressing organization is a definite agreement as to production and prices. But this is supplied: By the disposition of men "to follow their most intelligent competitors," especially when powerful; by the inherent disposition to make all the money possible, joined with the steady cultivation of the value of "harmony" of action; and by the system of reports, which makes the discovery of price reductions inevitable and immediate. The sanctions of the plan obviously are, financial interest, intimate personal contact, and business honor, all operating under the restraint of exposure of what would be deemed bad faith and of trade punishment by powerful rivals. . . .

Obviously the organization of the defendants constitutes a combination and confessedly they are engaged in a large way in the transportation and sale of lumber in interstate commerce so that there remains for decision only the question whether the system of doing business adopted resulted in that direct and undue restraint of interstate commerce which is condemned by this Antitrust statute.

It has been repeatedly held by this court that the purpose of the statute is to maintain free competition in interstate commerce and that any concerted action by any combination of men or corporations to cause, or which in fact does cause, direct and undue restraint of competition in such commerce falls within the condemnation of the act and is unlawful. . . .

With this rule of law and the details of the Plan in mind, we come to consider what the record shows as to the purpose of this combination and as to its effect upon interstate commerce. . . .

The record shows that the lumber market was inactive in the months of January and February and the first part of March of 1919. It grew better late in March and progressively stronger until in July, when it became very active, with prices high, and so continued until the end of the year we are considering.

In the first quarter of the year the problem was to maintain the war prices then prevailing rather than to advance them, and although the minutes of the various meetings were kept in barest outline, we find that, beginning within a month of the consolidation of the two associations, the members of the Plan began actively to co-operate, through the meetings, to suppress competition by restricting production. This is very clearly shown by the excerpts following from the minutes of meetings and from the market letters and sales reports distributed at them.

Thus, at the meeting held at Cincinnati, on January 21, 1919, in the discussion of business conditions, the chairman said:

> "If there is *no increase in production*, particularly in oak, there is going to be good business. . . . *No man is safe in increasing production*. If he does, he will be in bad shape, as the demand won't come." . . .

Again, a week later, at a meeting at Shreveport, Louisiana, in the discussion of market conditions, one of the members declared: that in his opinion it was "*suicidal to run mills night and day*; that the pine mills had done it, but he hoped they [we] would profit by their past experience and not do it this year."

Much more of like purport appears in the minutes of the meetings throughout the year, but this is sufficient to convincingly show that one of the prime purposes of the meetings, held in every part of the lumber district, and of the various reports, was to induce members to cooperate in restricting production, thereby keeping the supply low and the prices high, and that whenever there was any suggestion of running the mills to an extent which would bring up the supply to a point which might affect prices, the advice against operations which might lead to such result was put in the strongest possible terms. The cooperation is palpable and avowed, its purpose is clear, and we shall see that it was completely realized.

Next, the record shows clearly that the members of the combination were not satisfied to secure, each for himself, the price which might be obtainable even as the result of cooperative restriction of production, but that throughout the year they assiduously cultivated, through the letters of Gadd, speaking for them all, and through the discussions at the meetings, the general conviction that higher and higher prices were obtainable and a disposition on the part of all to demand them. . . .

To this we must add that constantly throughout the minutes of the various meetings there is shown discussion of the stock and production reports in which the shortage of supply was continually emphasized, with the implication, not disguised, that higher prices must result. Men in general are so easily persuaded to do that which will obviously prove profitable that this reiterated opinion from the analyst of their association, with all obtainable data before him, that higher prices were justified and could easily be obtained must, inevitably, have resulted, as it did result, in concert of action in demanding them.

But not only does the record thus show a persistent purpose to encourage members to unite in pressing for higher and higher prices without regard to cost, but there are many admissions by members, not only that this was the purpose of the Plan, but that it was fully realized. . . .

As to the price conditions during the year. Without going into detail the record shows that the prices of the grades of hardwood in most general use were increased to an unprecedented extent during the year. Thus, the increases in prices of varieties of oak, range from 33.3 per cent to 296 per cent during the year; of gum, 60 per cent to 343 per cent, and of ash, from 55 per cent to 181 per cent. While it is true that 1919 was a year of high and increasing prices generally and that wet weather may have restricted production to some extent, we cannot but agree with the members of the Plan themselves, as we have quoted them, and with the District Court in the conclusion that the united action of this large and influential membership of dealers contributed greatly to this extraordinary price increase.

Such close co-operation, between many persons, firms, and corporations controlling a large volume of interstate commerce, as is provided for in this Plan, is plainly in theory, as it proved to be in fact, inconsistent with that free and unrestricted trade which the statute contemplates shall be maintained. . . .

To call the activities of the defendants, as they are proved in this record, an "Open Competition Plan" of action is plainly a misleading misnomer.

Genuine competitors do not make daily, weekly and monthly reports of the minutest details of their business to their rivals, as the defendants did; they do not contract, as was done here, to submit their books to the discretionary audit and their stocks to the discretionary inspection of their rivals for the purpose of successfully competing with them; and they do not submit the details of their business to the analysis of an expert, jointly employed, and obtain from him a "harmonized" estimate of the market as it is and as, in his specially and confidentially informed judgment, it promises to be. This is not the conduct of competitors but is so clearly that of men united in an agreement, express or implied, to act together and pursue a common purpose under a common guide that, if it did not stand confessed a combination to restrict production and increase prices in interstate commerce and as, therefore, a direct restraint upon that commerce as we have seen that it is, that conclusion must inevitably have been inferred from the facts which were proved. To pronounce such abnormal conduct on the part of 365 natural competitors, controlling one-third of the trade of the country in an article of prime necessity, a "new form of competition" and not an old form of combination in restraint of trade, as it so plainly is, would be for this Court to confess itself blinded by words and forms to realities which men in general very plainly see and understand and condemn as an old evil in a new dress and with a new name.

The Plan is, essentially, simply an expansion of the gentlemen's agreement of former days, skillfully devised to evade the law. To call it open competition because the meetings were nominally open to the public, or because some voluminous reports were transmitted to the Department of Justice, or because no specific agreement to restrict trade or fix prices is proved, cannot conceal the fact that the fundamental purpose of the Plan was to procure "harmonious" individual action among a large number of naturally competing dealers with respect to the volume of production and prices, without having any specific agreement with respect to them, and to rely for maintenance of concerted action in both respects, not upon fines and forfeitures as in earlier days, but upon what experience has shown to be the more potent and dependable restraints, of business honor and social penalties—cautiously reinforced by many and elaborate reports, which would promptly expose to his associates any disposition in any member to deviate from the tacit understanding that all were to act together under the subtle direction of a single interpreter of their common purposes, as evidenced in the minute reports of what they had done and in their expressed purposes as to what they intended to do.

In the presence of this record it is futile to argue that the purpose of the Plan was simply to furnish those engaged in this industry, with widely scattered units, the equivalent of such information as is contained in the newspaper and government publications with respect to the market for commodities sold on boards of trade or stock exchanges. One distinguishing and sufficient difference is that the published reports go to both seller and buyer, but these reports go to the seller only; and another is that there is no skilled interpreter of the published reports, such as we have in this case, to insistently recommend harmony of action likely to prove profitable in proportion as it is unitedly pursued.

Convinced, as we are, that the purpose and effect of the activities of the Open Competition Plan, here under discussion, were to restrict competition and thereby restrain interstate commerce in the manufacture and sale of hardwood lumber by concerted action in curtailing production and in increasing prices, we agree with the District Court that it constituted a combination and conspiracy in restraint of interstate commerce within the meaning of the Antitrust Act of 1890 (26 Stat. 209) and the decree of that court must be

Affirmed.

■ MR. JUSTICE HOLMES, dissenting.

When there are competing sellers of a class of goods, knowledge of the total stock on hand, of the probable total demand, and of the prices paid, of course will tend to equalize the prices asked. But I should have supposed that the Sherman Act did not set itself against knowledge—did not aim at a transitory cheapness unprofitable to the community as a whole because not corresponding to the actual conditions of the country. I should have thought that the ideal of commerce was an intelligent interchange made with full knowledge of the facts as a basis for a forecast of the future on both sides. A combination to get and distribute such knowledge, notwithstanding its tendency to equalize, not necessarily to raise, prices, is very far from a combination in unreasonable restraint of trade. It is true that it is a combination of sellers only, but the knowledge acquired is not secret, it is public, and the buyers, I think I may assume, are not less active in their efforts to know the facts. A combination in unreasonable restraint of trade imports an attempt to override normal market conditions. An attempt to conform to them seems to me the most reasonable thing in the world. I see nothing in the conduct of the appellants that binds the members even by merely social sanctions to anything that would not be practised, if we could imagine it, by an allwise socialistic government acting for the benefit of the community as a whole. The parties to the combination are free to do as they will.

I must add that the decree as it stands seems to me surprising in a country of free speech that affects to regard education and knowledge as desirable. It prohibits the distribution of stock, production, or sales reports, the discussion of prices at association meetings, and the exchange of predictions of high prices. It is true that these acts are the main evidence of the supposed conspiracy, but that to my mind only shows the weakness of the Government's case. I cannot believe that the fact, if it be assumed, that the acts have been done with a sinister purpose, justifies excluding mills in the backwoods from information, in order to enable centralized purchasers to take advantage of their ignorance of the facts. I agree with the more elaborate discussion of the case by my Brother BRANDEIS.

■ MR. JUSTICE BRANDEIS, dissenting, with whom MR. JUSTICE MCKENNA, concurs.

. . . Restraint of trade may be exerted upon rivals; upon buyers or upon sellers; upon employers or upon employed. Restraint may be exerted through force or fraud or agreement. It may be exerted through moral or through legal obligations; through fear or through hope. It may exist although it is not manifested in any overt act and even though there is no intent to restrain. Words of advice seemingly innocent and perhaps benevolent, may restrain, when uttered under circumstances that make advice equivalent to command. For the essence of restraint is powers; and power may arise merely out of position. Wherever a dominant position has been attained, restraint necessarily arises. And when dominance is attained, or is sought, through combination—however good the motives or the manners of those participating—the Sherman Law is violated; provided, of course, that the restraint be what is called unreasonable.

In the case before us there was clearly no coercion. There is no claim that a monopoly was sought or created. There is no claim that a division of territory was planned or secured. There is no claim that uniform prices were established or desired. There is no claim that by agreement, force, or fraud, any producer, dealer or consumer was to be or has in fact been controlled or coerced. The Plan is a voluntary system for collecting from these independent concerns detailed information concerning the business operations of each, and its opinions as to trade conditions, prospects and policy; and of collating, interpreting, and distributing the data so received among the members of the association and others. No information gathered under the Plan was kept secret from any producer, any buyer or the public. . . .

It is claimed that the purpose of the Open Competition Plan was to lessen competition. Competition among members was contemplated and was in vigorous operation. The Sherman Law does not prohibit every lessening of competition; and it certainly does not command that competition shall be pursued blindly, that business rivals shall remain ignorant of trade facts or be denied aid in weighing their significance. It is lawful to regulate competition in some degree. Chicago Board of Trade v. United States, 246 U.S. 231. But it was neither the aim of the plan, nor the practice under it, to regulate competition in any way. Its purpose was to make rational competition possible by supplying data not otherwise available and without which most of those engaged in the trade would be unable to trade intelligently.

The hardwood lumber mills are widely scattered. The principal area of production is the Southern States. But there are mills in Minnesota, New York, New England and the Middle States. Most plants are located near the sources of supply; isolated, remote from the larger cities and from the principal markets. No official, or other public, means have been established for collecting from these mills and from dealers data as to current production, stocks on hand and market prices. Concerning grain, cotton, coal and oil, the Government collects and publishes regularly, at frequent intervals, current information on production, consumption and stocks on hand; and boards of trade furnish freely to the public details of current market prices of those commodities, the volume of sales, and even individual sales, as recorded in daily transactions. Persons interested in such commodities are enabled through this information to deal with one another on an equal footing. The absence of such information in the hardwood lumber trade enables dealers in the large centers more readily to secure advantage over the isolated producer. And the large concerns, which are able to establish their own bureaus of statistics, secure an advantage over smaller concerns. Surely it is not against the public interest to distribute knowledge of trade facts, however detailed. Nor are the other features of the Plan—the market letters and the regional conferences, an unreasonable interference with freedom in trade. Intelligent conduct of business implies not only knowledge of trade facts, but an understanding of them. To this understanding editorial comment and free discussion by those engaged in the business and by others interested are aids. Opinions expressed may be unsound; predictions may be unfounded; but there is nothing in the Sherman Law which should limit freedom of discussion, even among traders.

. . . The illegality of a combination under the Sherman Law lies not in its effect upon the price level, but in the coercion thereby effected. It is the limitation of freedom, by agreements which narrow a market, as in Addyston Pipe & Steel Co. v. United States, 175 U.S. 211, and Montague & Co. v. Lowry, 193 U.S. 38, or by organized boycott, as in Loewe v. Lawlor, 208 U.S. 274, and Eastern States Retail Lumber Dealers' Association v. United States, 234 U.S. 600, or by the coercive power of rebates, as in Thomsen v. Cayser, 243 U.S. 66, which constitutes the unlawful restraint.

The co-operation which is incident to this Plan does not suppress competition. On the contrary it tends to promote all in competition which is desirable. By substituting knowledge for ignorance, rumor, guess and suspicion, it tends also to substitute research and reasoning for gambling and piracy, without closing the door to adventure or lessening the value of prophetic wisdom. In making such knowledge available to the smallest concern it creates among producers equality of opportunity. In making it available also to purchasers and the general public it does all that can actually be done to protect the community from extortion. If, as is alleged, the Plan tends to substitute stability in prices for violent fluctuations, its influence, in this respect, is not against the public interest. The evidence in this case, far from establishing an illegal restraint of trade, presents, in my opinion, an instance of commendable effort by concerns engaged in a chaotic industry to make possible its intelligent conduct under competitive conditions.

The refusal to permit a multitude of small rivals to co-operate, as they have done here, in order to protect themselves and the public from the chaos and havoc wrought in their trade by ignorance, may result in suppressing competition in the hardwood industry. These keen business rivals, who sought through cooperative exchange of trade information to create conditions under which alone rational competition is possible, produce in the aggregate about one-third of the hardwood lumber of the country. This Court held in United States v. United States Steel Corporation, 251 U.S. 417, that it was not unlawful to vest in a single corporation control of 50 per cent of the steel industry of the country; and in United States v. United Shoe Machinery Co., 247 U.S. 32, the Court held that it was not unlawful to vest in a single corporation control of practically the whole shoe machinery industry. May not these hardwood lumber concerns, frustrated in their efforts to rationalize competition, be led to enter the inviting field of consolidation? And if they do, may not another huge trust with highly centralized control over vast resources, natural, manufacturing and financial, become so powerful as to dominate competitors, wholesalers, retailers, consumers, employees and, in large measure, the community?[27]

NOTES

1. *Permissible exchange of price information.*

a. *Later hardwood litigation:* Maple Flooring Mfrs' Ass'n v. United States, 268 U.S. 563 (1925). The Maple Flooring Manufacturers' Association consisted of producers of rough lumber and manufacturers of finished flooring. While the manufacturing capacity of the defendants was much less than that of non-members, their output was about 70 percent of the total production of the types of flooring produced by them. The association engaged in many activities which were not questioned by the Government, such as cooperative advertising, and standardization and improvement of their products. The Government complained of the following activities: (1) the computation and distribution of the average cost of all grades and dimensions of flooring to members; (2) the compilation and distribution of a freight book showing rates from Cadillac, Michigan, to about 6,000 points in the United States; (3) the gathering of information by the association as to prices, stocks on hand and the kind and quantity of flooring sold by members, which was summarized and circulated in tabular form without disclosing the identity of the members regarding the information summarized; and (4) the meetings held to discuss the conditions of the industry. There was no proof nor was it alleged that any agreements had been made affecting prices or production. In preparing the cost data, the association statisticians made use of various arbitrary cost accounting conventions as, for example, in allocating the costs of the rough lumber to the various grades and types of flooring which were produced. Since prices were determined on a delivered basis, it was imperative for the sellers to have ready access to information revealing the pertinent freight rates. The rates from Cadillac to most places of shipment approximated that from the various places of manufacture of the association members and the freight book was compiled for purposes of convenience. The Government contended the association had under a previous plan used the freight book as a cloak for price-fixing activities and that the present plan was used for the same purpose. Under the earlier plan, the association fixed a minimum price consisting of cost plus 10 percent profit, to which the arbitrary freight rate was added. It was contended that under the present plan, price uniformity could be attained by adding the freight rates to the average costs as determined by the secretary from the data submitted by members. The earlier plan had been abandoned after the failure of the association to obtain the approval of the FTC and defendants denied that the present plan was being used to fix prices. The Court sustained the contention of the defendants, pointing out, however, that the Sherman Act forbade price fixing and that if defendants used the cost and price data plus an arbitrary percentage of profit as the basis of fixing prices, the statute would be violated.

---

27. Ed. On the dissemination of statistics, *see* George P. Lamb & Carrington Shields, Trade Association Law and Practice Ch. 3 (1971).

The trade statistics related to past and closed transactions and the association before suit had abandoned the practice of identifying the information of members in its reports to them. The data compiled by the association were submitted to the Department of Commerce and the Federal Reserve Board. The statistics did not include present price quotations or details as to new or unfilled orders. There was no discussion of prices at the meetings of the association. The district court granted an injunction at the request of the Government. This was reversed by the Supreme Court. The Court pointed out that defendants had not attempted to monopolize their industry and that they had not limited by agreement their freedom of action regarding prices and production. The Sherman Act, it said, did not inhibit the intelligent conduct of business operations. Justice Stone, writing for the Court, reasoned that under the Sherman Act parties may gather to disseminate production and pricing information without unlawfully conspiring to constrain trade, even if the ultimate result stabilizes prices or limits production. The Court distinguished *American Column & Lumber Co.* by noting the absence of any evidence of any concerted action or agreement by the association members to use the information to restrain trade in this case. Concluding that the association did not violate the Sherman Act, the Court held that it is not an unreasonable restraint of trade for the members to meet, discuss, and disseminate production and pricing information so long as there is no attempt to agree or agreement or concerted action to fix prices or restrict production or competition.[28]

b.   Cement Manufacturers' Protective Ass'n v. United States, 268 U.S. 588 (1925). Following its decision in the companion case of the *Maple Flooring Association*, the Court, per Justice Stone, denied the Government's prayer for an injunction preventing the association from engaging in certain activities. The Government made no charge that the association had placed any limitations upon prices or production. Prices of cement were found in fact to have advanced less than in other fields. The Government challenged the statistical and credit activities of the association. Members submitted to the association a monthly statement of their production, shipments and stocks on hand, and semi-monthly statements of their shipments. These were distributed to members without change or comment, each member thus receiving full information as to the available supply of cement and by whom it was held. It is customary in this industry for manufacturers to make specific job contracts whereby cement is sold for future delivery for use in specific construction jobs. The contract is really an option which does not bind the purchaser but insures him of necessary supplies for the particular construction project. In a rising market, purchasers entered into numerous contracts with manufacturers for the same construction project and thus were able to obtain cement much in excess of their requirements for that job. As they were not bound themselves, they could refuse to accept delivery if the market fell and obtain more than they were entitled to receive when prices rose. To avoid the abuses that had occurred, the manufacturers exchanged detailed information as to all their specific job contracts and employed checkers to inspect and ascertain the exact amounts of cement required on specific jobs. The buyers were thus prevented from obtaining greater supplies than they were entitled to receive under these one-sided agreements. Extensive credit information, including detailed reports concerning delinquent accounts, was also exchanged. "The evidence falls far short of establishing any understanding . . . or that any cooperation resulted . . . or that there were any

---

28.   Taft, C.J., and Sanford, and McReynolds, JJ., dissented. *See* Almarin Phillips, MARKET STRUCTURE, ORGANIZATION AND PERFORMANCE Ch. VII (1962) (discussing the *Hardwood* litigation). *See also* Wire Mesh Products, Inc. v. Wire Belting Ass'n, 520 F. Supp. 1004 (E.D. Pa. 1981).

consequences ... other than such as would naturally ensue from the exercise of the individual judgment of manufacturers in determining, on the basis of available information, whether to extend credit or to require cash or security from any given customer." 268 U.S. at 600. A freight book, involving a basing point system, was distributed by the association to its members. Periodic meetings were held at which minor subjects, such as return of bags, bag reports, and trade acceptances were discussed, but not current or future prices, or production or market conditions. There was no proof that these meetings resulted in any agreement or in any uniformity of trade practice. Chief Justice Taft, and Sanford and McReynolds, JJ., dissented. See L.C.L. Theatres, Inc. v. Columbia Pictures Inc., 421 F.Supp. 1090 (N.D. Tex. 1976), reversed on other grounds, 566 F.2d 494 (5th Cir. 1978) (no violation where exchange of information designed to prevent fraudulent reporting).

2. *Prohibition of secret discounts.* Sugar Institute v. United States, 297 U.S. 553 (1936). The defendant sugar refining companies, which supplied 70 to 80 percent of the sugar consumed in the United States, organized The Sugar Institute in 1927 to cope with the widespread practice of giving largely arbitrary secret price concessions. The members of the Institute agreed in its "Code of Ethics" to sell only upon prices and terms openly announced. The trade practice was to sell on "moves," *i.e.*, price changes were publicly announced in advance and buyers, according to the long-standing custom, were permitted a grace period in which to purchase at a lower price. The Institute replaced an uncertain period of grace with a definite one. There was no agreement to maintain prices or to follow an advance in price, no comment on circulated price changes, and no discussions of prices at meetings.

"The distinctive feature of the 'basic agreement' was not the advance announcements of prices, or a concert to maintain any particular basis price for any period, but a requirement of adherence, without deviation, to the prices and terms publicly announced." 297 U.S. at 583. Among the practices designed to support the basic agreement were preventing the combination of distribution functions by brokers and warehousemen; concertedly maintaining a system of delivered, rather than f.o.b. refinery, prices; concertedly reducing consignment points from which sugar was distributed; concertedly prohibiting long-term contracts; concertedly refusing to grant quantity discounts, though cost justified. The members also agreed to disseminate statistics—which were withheld from purchasers—relating to production and deliveries of individual refiners, to deliveries by states, to deliveries by states by important differential routes, and to consigned and in-transit stocks by states, while other statistics on total production and deliveries were also supplied to purchasers. Chief Justice Hughes, writing for the Court, held:

> The restraints, found to be unreasonable, were the offspring of the basic agreement. The vice in that agreement was not in the mere open announcement of prices and terms in accordance with the custom of the trade. That practice which had grown out of the special character of the industry did not restrain competition.... The unreasonable restraints which defendants imposed lay not in advance announcements, but in the steps taken to secure adherence, without deviation, to prices and terms thus announced. It was that concerted undertaking which cut off opportunities for variation in the course of competition however fair and appropri-

ate they might be. But, in ending that restraint, the beneficial and curative agency of publicity should not be unnecessarily hampered. The trial court left defendants free to provide for immediate publicity as to prices and terms in all closed transactions. We think that a limitation to that sort of publicity fails to take proper account of the practice of the trade in selling on "moves," as already described, a practice in accordance with which the court found that "the great bulk of sugar always was and is purchased." That custom involves advance announcements, and it does not appear that arrangements merely to circulate or relay such announcements threaten competitive opportunities. On the other hand, such provision for publicity may be helpful in promoting fair competition. If the requirement that there must be adherence to prices and terms openly announced in advance is abrogated and the restraints which followed that requirement are removed, the just interests of competition will be safeguarded and the trade will still be left with whatever advantage may be incidental to its established practice.

Id. at 601–02.

The defendants were also ordered to make statistical information relating to production, sales, deliveries, stocks on hand, on consignment or in transit, transportation, and new business, fully and fairly available to the purchasing and distributing trade, as well as to refiners. (Sutherland and Stone, JJ., not participating).

3. *Price reporting plan comparison.* Compare the legality of the following price reporting plans:

I	**II**	**III**
1. Detailed reports to Association of all closed transactions.	1. Filing current and future prices.	1. Detailed reports of all closed transactions and filing current and future prices.
2. Circulation of abstract, statistical summaries.	2. Circulation of prices of individual sellers.	2. Circulation of abstract, statistical summaries.
3. Availability of reports to customers and the public.	3. Non-disclosure of reports to customers and the public.	3. Availability of reports to customers and the public.
4. No agreement affecting freedom of price action.	4. Agreement not to deviate from filed prices without notice to Association.	4. No agreement affecting freedom of price action.
	5. Immediate report to the Association of all price changes.	5. Use of impartial statistical agency.
	6. Waiting period.	6. No waiting period.
	7. Circulation of interpretative comments.	7. No interpretative comments.
	8. Penalties for noncompliance with plan.	8. Penalties for not furnishing accurate information.

Would the validity of Plan I be affected by the full disclosure of all the terms of sale, including the names of buyers and sellers? Would the validity of Plan II be affected by the use of an impartial statistical agency and the disclosure of statistical reports to customers and the public? How much would the validity of each plan be affected by a finding that the companies involved were in a highly or moderately concentrated market?[29]

United States v. Container Corporation of America

Supreme Court of the United States, 1969.
393 U.S. 333, 89 S.Ct. 510, 21 L.Ed.2d 526.

■ DOUGLAS, J. This is a civil antitrust action charging a price-fixing agreement in violation of § 1 of the Sherman Act. The District Court dismissed the complaint. . . .

The case as proved is unlike any other price decisions we have rendered. There was here an exchange of price information but no agreement to adhere to a price schedule as in Sugar Institute v. United States, 297 U.S. 553, or United States v. Socony–Vacuum Oil Co., 310 U.S. 150. There was here an exchange of information concerning specific sales to identified customers, not a statistical report on the average cost to all members, without identifying the parties to specific transactions, as in Maple Flooring Mfrs. Assn. v. United States, 268 U.S. 563. While there was present here, as in Cement Mfrs. Protective Assn. v. United States, 268 U.S. 588, an exchange of prices to specific customers, there was absent the controlling circumstances, *viz.*, that cement manufacturers, to protect themselves from delivering to contractors more cement than was needed for a specific job and thus receiving a lower price, exchanged price information as a means of protecting their legal rights from fraudulent inducements to deliver more cement than needed for a specific job.

Here all that was present was a request by each defendant of its competitor for information as to the most recent price charged or quoted, whenever it needed such information and whenever it was not available from another source. Each defendant on receiving that request usually furnished the data with the expectation that he would be furnished reciprocal information when he wanted it.[30] That concerted action is of

---

29. *See* Lawrence Anthony Sullivan, Handbook of the Law of Antitrust 265–73 (1977). Lamb & Shields, Trade Association Law and Practice, *supra* note 32, Pt. I (1971), presents a most helpful summary and analysis of the antitrust laws as they affect trade association activities, and ABA Antitrust Section, Antitrust Law Developments 35–36; 92–99 (6th ed. 2007), contains a useful summary of recent cases. *See also* Symposium on Trade Associations, 27 ABA Antitrust Section 127 (1965); 1955 Att'y Gen. Rep. 17; Trenam Kemker, *Legality of Trade Association Statistical Reporting under the Antitrust Laws*, 11 Vand. L. Rev. 361 (1958); Kern, *Price Reporting by Trade Associations*, 6 ABA Antitrust Section 62 (1955); Jacobs, *Statistical Standardization and Research Activities*, 6 ABA Antitrust Section 80 (1955).

30. This is obviously quite different from the parallel business behavior condoned in Theatre Enterprises, Inc. v. Paramount Film Distributing Corp., 346 U.S. 537.

course sufficient to establish the combination or conspiracy, the initial ingredient of a violation of § 1 of the Sherman Act.

There was of course freedom to withdraw from the agreement. But the fact remains that when a defendant requested and received price information, it was affirming its willingness to furnish such information in return.

There was to be sure an infrequency and irregularity of price exchanges between the defendants; and often the data was available from the records of the defendants or from the customers themselves. Yet the essence of the agreement was to furnish price information whenever requested.

Moreover, although the most recent price charged or quoted was sometimes fragmentary, each defendant had the manuals with which it could compute the price charged by a competitor on a specific order to a specific customer.

Further, the price quoted was the current price which a customer would need to pay in order to obtain products from the defendant furnishing the data.

The defendants account for about 90% of the shipment of corrugated containers from plants in the southeastern United States. While containers vary as to dimensions, weight, color, and so on, they are substantially identical, no matter who produces them, when made to particular specifications. The prices paid depend on price alternatives. Suppliers when seeking new or additional business or keeping old customers, do not exceed a competitor's price. It is common for purchasers to buy from two or more suppliers concurrently. A defendant supplying a customer with containers would usually quote the same price on additional orders, unless costs had changed. Yet where a competitor was charging a particular price, a defendant would normally quote the same price or even a lower price.

The exchange of price information seemed to have the effect of keeping prices within a fairly narrow ambit. Capacity has exceeded the demand from 1955 to 1963, the period covered by the complaint, and the trend of corrugated container prices has been downward. Yet despite this excess capacity and the downward trend of prices, the industry has expanded in the Southeast from 30 manufacturers with 49 plants to 51 manufacturers with 98 plants. An abundance of raw materials and machinery makes entry into the industry easy with an investment of $50,000 to $75,000.

The result of this reciprocal exchange of prices was to stabilize prices though at a downward level. Knowledge of a competitor's price usually meant matching that price. The continuation of some price competition is not fatal to the Government's case. The limitation or reduction of price competition brings the case within the ban, for as we held in United States v. Socony–Vacuum Oil Co., *supra*, 310 U.S. at 224, n. 59, interference with the setting of price by free market forces is unlawful *per se*. Price information exchanged in some markets may have no effect on a truly competitive price. But the corrugated container industry is dominated by relatively few sellers. The product is fungible and the competition for sales is price. The demand is inelastic, as buyers place orders only for immediate, short-run needs. The exchange of price data tends toward price uniformity. For a lower price does not mean a larger share of the available business but a sharing of the existing business at a lower return. Stabilizing prices as well as raising them is within the ban of § 1 of the Sherman Act. As we said in United States v. Socony–Vacuum Oil Co., "in terms of market operations, stabilization is but one form of manipulation." The inferences are irresistible that the exchange of price information has had an anticompetitive effect in the industry, chilling the vigor of price competition. The agreement in the present case, though somewhat casual, is analogous to American Column & Lumber Co. v. United States, 257 U.S. 377; United States v. American Linseed Oil Co., 262 U.S. 371.[31]

Price is too critical, too sensitive a control to allow it to be used even in an informal manner to restrain competition.[32]

Reversed.

■ FORTAS, J., concurring. I join in the judgment and opinion of the Court. I do not understand the Court's opinion to hold that the exchange of specific information among sellers as to price charged to individual customers, pursuant to mutual arrangement, is a *per se* violation of the Sherman Act.

Absent *per se* violation, proof is essential that the practice resulted in an unreasonable restraint of trade. There is no single test to determine when the record adequately shows an "unreasonable restraint of trade"; but a practice such as that here involved, which is adopted for the purpose of arriving at determination of prices to be quoted to individual customers, inevitably suggests the probability that it so materially interfered with the operation of the price mechanism of the marketplace as to bring it within the condemnation of this Court's decisions. [Citing cases]

Theoretical probability, however, is not enough unless we are to regard mere exchange of current price information as so akin to price fixing by

---

31. The *American Column* case was a sophisticated and well supervised plan for the exchange of price information between competitors with the idea of keeping prices reasonably stable and of putting an end to cutthroat competition. There were no sanctions except financial interest and business honor. But the purpose of the plan being to increase prices, it was held to fall within the ban of the Sherman Act.

Another elaborate plan for the exchange of price data among competitors was involved in *American Linseed Oil;* and informal sanctions were used to establish "modern cooperative business methods." The arrangement was declared illegal because its "necessary tendency" was to suppress competition. 262 U.S. at 389.

32. Thorstein Veblen in The Theory of Business Enterprise (1904) makes clear how the overabundance of a commodity creates a business appetite to regulate or control prices or output or both. Measures short of monopoly may have "a salutary effect," as for example a degree of control or supervision over prices not obtainable while the parties "stood on their old footing of severalty." But that relief is apt to be "only transient," for as the costs of production decline and growth of the industry "catches up with the gain in economy," the need for further controls or restraints increase. And so the restless, never-ending search for price control and other types of restraint.

We held in United States v. Socony–Vacuum Oil Co., 310 U.S. 150, that all forms of price fixing are *per se* violations of the Sherman Act....

combination or conspiracy as to deserve the *per se* classification. I am not prepared to do this, nor is it necessary here. In this case, the probability that the exchange of specific price information led to an unlawful effect upon prices is adequately buttressed by evidence in the record. This evidence, although not overwhelming, is sufficient in the special circumstances of this case to show an actual effect on pricing and to compel us to hold that the court below erred in dismissing the Government's complaint.

In summary, the record shows that the defendants sought and obtained from competitors who were part of the arrangement information about the competitors' prices to specific customers. "[I]n the majority of instances," the District Court found, once a defendant had this information he quoted substantially the same price as the competitor, although a higher or lower price would "occasionally" be quoted. Thus the exchange of prices made it possible for individual defendants confidently to name a price equal to that which their competitors were asking. The obvious effect was to "stabilize" prices by joint arrangement—at least to limit any price cuts to the minimum necessary to meet competition. In addition, there was evidence that, in some instances, during periods when various defendants ceased exchanging prices exceptionally sharp and vigorous price reductions resulted.

On this record, taking into account the specially sensitive function of the price term in the antitrust equation, I cannot see that we would be justified in reaching any conclusion other than that defendants' tacit agreement to exchange information about current prices to specific customers did in fact substantially limit the amount of price competition in the industry. That being so, there is no need to consider the possibility of a *per se* violation.

■ MARSHALL, J., with whom HARLAN, J., and STEWART, J., join, dissenting.

I agree with the Court's holding that there existed an agreement among the defendants to exchange price information whenever requested. However, I cannot agree that that agreement should be condemned, either as illegal *per se*, or as having had the purpose or effect of restricting price competition in the corrugated container industry in the Southeastern United States.

Under the antitrust laws, numerous practices have been held to be illegal *per se* without regard to their precise purpose or harm.... This Court has refused to apply a *per se* rule to exchanges of price and market information in the past.... I believe we should follow the same course in the present case.

Per se rules always contain a degree of arbitrariness. They are justified on the assumption that the gains from imposition of the rule will far outweigh the losses and that significant administrative advantages will result. In other words, the potential competitive harm plus the administrative costs of determining in what particular situations the practice may be harmful must far outweigh the benefits that may result. If the potential *doesn't think per se should've been applied*

benefits in the aggregate are outweighed to this degree, then they are simply not worth identifying in individual cases.

I do not believe that the agreement in the present case is so devoid of potential benefit or so inherently harmful that we are justified in condemning it without proof that it was entered into for the purpose of restraining price competition or that it actually had that effect. . . .

Complete market knowledge is certainly not an evil in perfectly competitive markets. This is not, however, such a market, and there is admittedly some danger that price information will be used for anticompetitive purposes, particularly the maintenance of prices at a high level. If the danger that price information will be so used is particularly high in a given situation, then perhaps exchange of information should be condemned.

I do not think the danger is sufficiently high in the present case. Defendants are only 18 of the 51 producers of corrugated containers in the Southeastern United States. Together, they do make up 90% of the market and the six largest defendants do control 60% of the market. But entry is easy; an investment of $50,000 to $75,000 is ordinarily all that is necessary. In fact, the number of sellers has increased from 30 to the present 51 in the eight-year period covered by the complaint. The size of the market has almost doubled because of increased demand for corrugated containers. Nevertheless, some excess capacity is present. The products produced by defendants are undifferentiated. Industry demand is inelastic, so that price changes will not, up to a certain point, affect the total amount purchased. The only effect of price changes will to be to reallocate market shares among sellers.

In a competitive situation, each seller will cut his price in order to increase his share of the market, and prices will ultimately stabilize at a competitive level—*i.e.*, price will equal cost, including a reasonable return on capital. Obviously, it would be to everyone's benefit to avoid such price competition and maintain prices at a higher level, with a corresponding increase in profit. In a market with very few sellers, and detailed knowledge of each other's price, such action is possible. However, I do not think it can be concluded that this particular market is sufficiently oligopolistic, especially in light of the ease of entry, to justify the inference that price information will necessarily be used to stabilize prices. Nor do I think that the danger of such a result is sufficiently high to justify imposing a *per se* rule without actual proof.

In this market, we have a few sellers presently controlling a substantial share of the market. We have a large number competing for the remainder of the market, also quite substantial. And total demand is increasing. In such a case, I think it just as logical to assume that the sellers, especially the smaller and newer ones will desire to capture a larger market share by cutting prices as it is that they will acquiesce in oligopolistic behavior. The likelihood that prices will be cut and that those lower prices will have to be met acts as a deterrent to setting prices at an artificially high level in the first place. Given the uncertainty about the probable effect of an exchange of price information in this context, I would require that the Government prove that the exchange was entered into for the purpose of or that it had the effect of restraining price competition.

I do not find the inference that the exchange of price information has had an anticompetitive effect as "irresistible" as does the Court. Like my Brother Fortas, I would prefer that a finding of anticompetitive effect be supported by "evidence in the record." I cannot agree that the evidence in this case was sufficient to prove such an effect. The Government has simply not proved its case.

The Court does not hold that the agreement in the present case was a purposeful attempt to stabilize prices. The evidence in the case, largely the result of stipulation, would not support such a holding. The Government points to a few isolated statements found in the depositions of industry witnesses, but I find these few fragmentary references totally insufficient. The weight of the evidence in the present case indicates that the price information was employed by each defendant on an individual basis, and was used by the defendant to set his prices for a specific customer; ultimately each seller wanted to obtain all or part of that customer's business at the expense of a competitor. The District Court found that there was no explicit agreement among defendants to stabilize prices and I do not believe that the desire of a few industry witnesses to use the information to minimize price cuts supports the conclusion that such an agreement was implicit. On the contrary, the evidence establishes that the information was used by defendants as each pleased and was actually employed for the purpose of engaging in active price competition.

Nor do I believe that the Government has proved that the exchange of price information has in this case had the necessary effect of restraining price competition.[33] In its brief before this Court, the Government relies very largely on one finding of the District Court and upon economic theory. The Government has presented a convincing argument in theoretical terms. However, the evidence simply does not square with that theory. And, this is not a case in which it would be unduly difficult to demonstrate anticompetitive effects.

The record indicates that defendants have offered voluminous evidence concerning price trends and competitive behavior in the corrugated container market. Their exhibits indicate a downward trend in prices, with substantial price variations among defendants and among their different plants. There was also a great deal of shifting of accounts. The District Court specifically found that the corrugated container market was highly competitive and that each defendant engaged in active price competition. The Government would have us ignore this evidence and these findings, and assume that because we are dealing with an industry with overcapacity and yet continued entry, the new entrants must have been attracted by high profits. The Government then argues that high profits can only result

---

33. Here, it is relevant to note again that the evidence was largely the result of stipulation, with the Government admittedly introducing very little evidence on the actual effect of the allegedly illegal practice.

from stabilization of prices at an unduly high level. Yet the Government did not introduce any evidence about the level of profits in this industry, and no evidence about price levels. Not one customer was called, although the Government surely had ample access to defendants' customers. The Government admits that the price trend was down, but asks the Court to assume that the trend would have been accelerated with less informed, and hence more vigorous, price competition.[34] In the absence of any proof whatsoever, I cannot make such an assumption. It is just as likely that price competition was furthered by the exchange as is it that it was depressed.

Finally, the Government focuses on the finding of the District Court that in a majority of instances a defendant, when it received what it considered reliable price information, would quote or charge substantially the same price.[35] The Court and my Brother Fortas also focus on this finding. Such an approach ignores, however, the remainder of the District Court's findings. The trial judge found that price decisions were individual decisions, and that defendants frequently did cut prices in order to obtain a particular order. And, the absence of any price parallelism or price uniformity and the downward trend in the industry undercuts the conclusion that price information was used to stabilize prices.

The Government is ultimately forced to fall back on the theoretical argument that prices would have been more unstable and would have fallen faster without price information. As I said earlier, I cannot make this assumption on the basis of the evidence in this record.... Rather the record indicates that, while each defendant occasionally received price information from a competitor, that information was used in the same manner as other reliable market information—*i.e.*, to reach an individual price decision based upon all available information. The District Court's findings that this was a competitive industry, lacking any price parallelism or uniformity, effectively refute the Government's assertion that the result of those decisions was to maintain or tend to maintain prices at other than a competitive level. Accordingly, I would affirm the decision of the court below.

NOTE ON UNITED STATES v. UNITED STATES GYPSUM CO.

In a footnote that was omitted from the *Gypsum* opinion, as noted at p. 227 *supra*, the Supreme Court said:

---

34. There was no effort to demonstrate that the price behavior of those manufacturers who didn't exchange price information, if any, varied significantly from the price behavior of those who did. In fact, several of the District Court's findings indicate that when certain defendants stopped exchanging price information, their price behavior remained essentially the same, and, in some cases, prices actually increased.

35. It should be noted that, in most cases, this information was obtained from a customer rather than a competitor, a practice the Government does not condemn.

The exchange of price data and other information among competitors does not invariably have anti-competitive effects; indeed such practices can in certain circumstances increase economic efficiency and render markets more rather than less competitive. For this reason, we have held that such exchanges of information do not constitute a *per se* violation of the Sherman Act. See, *e.g.*, *United States v. Citizens & Southern National Bank*, 422 U.S. 86, 113; *United States v. Container Corp.*, 393 U.S. 333, 338 (Fortas, J., concurring). A number of factors including most prominently the structure of the industry involved and the nature of the information exchanged are generally considered in divining the procompetitive or anticompetitive effects of this type of interseller communication. See *United States v. Container Corp.*, *supra*. See generally L. Sullivan, Law of Antitrust, 265–274 (1977). Exchanges of current price information, of course, have the greatest potential for generating anti-competitive effects and although not *per se* unlawful have consistently been held to violate the Sherman Act. See *American Column & Lumber Co. v. United States*, 257 U.S. 377 (1921); *United States v. American Linseed Oil Co.*, 262 U.S. 371 (1923); *United States v. Container Corp.*, *supra*.

NOTE ON INFORMATION DISSEMINATION

1. *Evidentiary limits for price exchange agreement.* Richard A. Posner, in *Information and Antitrust: Reflections on the* Gypsum *and* Engineers *Decisions*, 67 Geo. L. J. 1187, 1197, 1199 (1979), proposes the following with respect to exchanges of price data and other information:

> I want to suggest an approach that would dispel this uncertainty in a manner consistent with the fundamental spirit, if not the specific results and narrow holdings, of the series of price exchange cases from *Hardwood* [*i.e.*, *American Column & Lumber*, p. 573] to *Gypsum*. The heart of my proposal is that an agreement simply to exchange price information should not be regarded as a violation of the antitrust laws. Such an agreement should only be admissible as evidence of an agreement to fix prices, which would be, in my view, unlawful whether express or tacit. If the trier of fact is satisfied that a group of firms has agreed to exchange price information but has not directly or indirectly, tacitly or explicitly, formally or informally, agreed to fix prices, there should be no finding of a Sherman Act violation.... If the only thing that a group of competitors does is exchange price information—no matter how detailed the information is, how frequently it is exchanged, or whether it pertains to past or current prices— the price level will be unaffected. Some firms will discover that their prices are too high, others that their prices are too low, but the average price should be unchanged. Narrowing the dispersion of prices will have none of the bad effects associated with monopoly or price fixing; on the contrary, it will bring the pricing in the market more closely in line with the conditions that would prevail under perfect competition.... A pure agreement to exchange price information should always be considered lawful. Market structure becomes relevant only when the Government or a private plaintiff argues, as it is always free to do, that the existence of the agreement to exchange information provides circumstantial evidence of an underlying agreement to fix prices. Suppose, for example, that there were only two firms in a market, selling a completely homogeneous product to knowledgeable buyers, and that the two firms agreed on a very detailed exchange of

current and future prices.... There would thus be a strong basis for an inference that the agreement was a mask for something more sinister....

What are the advantages, if any, of forcing the Government or a private plaintiff to prove a conspiracy to fix prices rather than treating an agreement to exchange information as a contract, combination, or conspiracy that may be an unreasonable restraint of trade? What are the disadvantages? Why not allow the Government or a private plaintiff to use the exchange of information to prove either a conspiracy to fix prices or an unreasonable restraint of trade? Are the *Container* and *Gypsum* decisions consistent or inconsistent with Posner's view?

2. *Limiting information sharing in highly concentrated markets.* A consent decree between the Government and GE and Westinghouse[36] summarized at pp. 524–525 *supra*, addressed the situation postulated by Posner as to two firms in a market. As noted earlier, the consent decree prohibited GE and Westinghouse, producers of large turbine generators, from: (i) disseminating price lists or price-related information from which a general pricing policy can be inferred; (ii) using or retaining "price books" of the other; (iii) publicly announcing price changes or examining the bid that the other manufacturer had made to a customer; and (iv) granting retroactive price cuts on previously concluded transactions. GE had previously announced a retroactive discount program that guaranteed that if GE cut a price it would pay a retroactive discount to all customers who had purchased similar equipment in a prior period. Assistant Attorney General Donald I. Baker explained:

> Essentially, the Government's allegations were that GE and Westinghouse engaged in indirect price communication and signaling. Information was communicated, in public, which established a body of public data sufficient to identify the appropriate price of a given turbine generator. At the same time certain policy positions were adopted which had the effect, and we contend the purpose, of assuring each seller that the other would adhere to a formula price based on the book. Rather than simply a case of unavoidable conscious parallelism, the Government views this as a case of "avoidable cooperation."

> We drafted relief designed to eliminate those artificially-created conditions which made it possible for two companies jointly to control prices and market conditions—to create certainty where uncertainty should have existed.... Some of the specific provisions will illustrate our efforts to ensure independent pricing in the future. For example ... by limiting the distribution of such individually prepared price books, and prohibiting the companies from announcing their pricing policies, we hope to have broken the parallel pricing pattern of the past thirteen years. In the event the companies rely upon formulas, multipliers or pricing policies internally, they may not communicate such formulas or policies outside the company. The publication of such factors facilitates the communication of prices and changes in prices.[37]

3. *FTC Guidelines for health care information sharing.* The federal government has taken a similar position with regard to the sharing of information in the health care industry. Three of the nine statements released by the FTC and the

---

36.   United States v. General Electric Co., 1977–2 Trade Cases ¶ 72,717 (E.D. Pa. 1977).

37.   Donald I. Baker, Assistant Attorney General, 1976–77, Antitrust Division, U.S. Department of Justice, Monopoly: Problems & Progress, Address at the Association of the Bar of the City of New York (Jan. 18, 1977)

Antitrust Division in September 1994 on antitrust and the health care industry deal with information sharing and gathering by competing providers. All three of the statements related to information recognize that information sharing among providers provides some benefit to consumers. The Guidelines suggest that allowing providers to collect and to share information with health care purchasers (particularly third-party payers) should help consumers decide what procedures to cover and how much to pay and that allowing providers to participate in market surveys of current and past fees, reimbursement and costs should help individual providers to set prices more competitively. To ensure that the sharing of fee information does not diminish competition, the Guidelines establish an antitrust safety zone. Three conditions must be met to remain within the safety zone: (i) a third party (*e.g.*, the government, a purchaser, a consultant or an academic institution) must collect the information; (ii) the information available to competing providers (but not to consumers) must be more than three months old; and (iii) at least five providers must supply information, with no individual provider's data representing more than 25% of a given statistic on a weighted basis. The sharing of information about prospective fees is outside the safety zone. According to the Guidelines, prospective fee information poses a more significant risk to competition. As a result, the Guidelines provide that any agreement to share information about future fees will be evaluated on a case-by-case basis.

NOTE ON TRADE MEETINGS

Should a trade association be liable when its members use its meetings as the planning grounds for the conspiracy? In one case, two metal building insulation suppliers faced with an increase in the price of fiberglass, a major metal building insulation component, adopted uniform pricing policies. The purpose of the uniform price was to ensure that neither company would quote or sell under the other's prices. At a laminators' trade association meeting, the two suppliers discussed the plan to adopt uniform prices with other members, and solicited additional competitors to participate in the conspiracy. The two suppliers were successful in their recruitment scheme, and at the criminal appeal, a representative from another supplier testified that he agreed to the proposal to fix prices and to publish a common or substantially identical price list. United States v. Maloof, 205 F.3d 819 (5th Cir. 2000). In this case, the trade association's liability was not litigated, implying that the trade association must take affirmative action in order to be liable under the antitrust laws.

PROBLEM 12

STATISTICAL REPORTING OF TAG MFRS. INSTITUTE

The Tag Manufacturers Institute is a trade association of the producers of 95 percent of the tag products sold in the United States; the four largest manufacturers share 55 percent of the business. The Institute engages in the collection and dissemination of statistics; the participation of members is defined in the Institute's bylaws and reinforced by provisions for liquidated damages in the event members are derelict in performing their duties.

Members provide the Institute with a complete list of their products, including specifications, and with a complete list of prices, including terms of sale. By the close of business on the day following the event, members are obliged to sell to the Institute complete details concerning: (1) changes in their price lists or specifications; (2) sales at other than list prices, which the members retain complete freedom to make; and (3) sales at list prices. The Institute then sends to its members, within a few days and without commentary, (1) revisions in the Institute's compilation of the price lists of all members, (2) complete details concerning off-list sales (except for the identity of the buyer), and (3) summaries of volume and value of list-price sales of various categories of tags, without indicating either seller or buyer identity. These materials are available to members of the public desiring to pay the expense of the service; there is but one such subscriber. The materials are also examined occasionally by members of the public at the Institute's offices in New York City.

No fixed patterns have emerged with respect to pricing policies under the Institute's arrangements. Some 25 percent of sales are made at off-list prices, scattered without regard to size or location of buyer or seller. Prices on some products are more uniform than on others, but no increase or decrease in price uniformity is discernible since the beginning of the Institute's operations. Off-list prices consist largely of responses by other members to non-uniform competitive offers by two or three members of the Institute.

Do any of the Institute's activities violate the antitrust laws?

PROBLEM 13

INFORMATION ON THE INTERNET

A trade association maintains a website that serves as a discussion board for its members. Mindful of the antitrust case law, the trade association clearly states that its members must neither explicitly nor implicitly agree to fix prices, boycott suppliers or customers, or violate the laws against collusion in any other manner. The members, ably aided by antitrust counsel, restrict their discussions to matters of technical import.

One of the member companies, Company A, lays off its Marketing and Business Development Manager. The Manager, in a fit of anger, posts his company's price list, including current prices and expected price changes. Shortly thereafter, the other member companies begin to raise their prices to match those of Company A. Their prices do not rise above the level charged by Company A, and Company A does not lower its price levels in an attempt to attract more customers.

Are the member companies liable under the antitrust laws?

SECTION 5. INTRA-ENTERPRISE CONSPIRACY

In Copperweld Corp. v. Independence Tube Corp., 467 U.S. 752 (1984), the Supreme Court swept aside the largely lamented intra-enterprise conspiracy doctrine. Prior to *Copperweld*, plaintiffs could pursue § 1 Sherman Act claims against companies and their wholly-owned subsidiaries because, according to United States v. Yellow Cab Co., 332 U.S. 218 (1947), "common ownership and control ... are impotent to liberate [an] alleged combination and conspiracy from the impact of the Act." *Id.* at 227. In *Copperweld*, the Court reexamined the intra-enterprise conspiracy doctrine started by Yellow Cab and found it wanting. The Court explained that the unity of purpose between parent and subsidiary makes conspiracy for § 1 purposes impossible. It held that "the coordinated conduct of a parent and its wholly owned subsidiary must be viewed as that of a single enterprise for purposes of § 1 of the Sherman Act." 467 U.S. at 772. *Copperweld* has spawned nearly as many questions as it answered. *See* Stephen Calkins, Copperweld *in the Courts: The Road to* Caribe, 63 Antitrust L.J. 345 (1995).

1. *Partial ownership issues.* While the Supreme Court rejected the intra-enterprise conspiracy doctrine for parents and their wholly-owned subsidiaries, it carefully left open the question at what point below full ownership such protection would cease. Courts agree that *de minimis* departures from 100 percent ownership fall within the rule. But once that threshold is crossed courts are all over the map. *Copperweld* has been applied where the parent held 91.9, 85, 82, 80, and 51 percent of its subsidiary's stock but not to holdings of 79, 74, and 54 percent. For a sense of the confusion, *compare* Viacom International, Inc. v. Time, Inc., 785 F. Supp. 371 (S.D.N.Y. 1992) (sufficient unity of interest with 82 percent of the stock and 93 percent of the voting power) *with* Aspen Title & Escrow, Inc. v. Jeld–Wen, Inc., 677 F. Supp. 1477 (D. Or. 1987) (75 percent insufficient to fall within *Copperweld*).

On this issue, there is also a split of authority in agencies and in the academy. The Justice Department has advocated at least two different positions. The Solicitor General, in his brief to the Supreme Court in *Copperweld*, suggested that ownership levels between 50 percent and 100 percent should create a presumption that two companies are insufficiently independent to conspire. However, in the 1988 International Guidelines, the Antitrust Division adopted a majority-stockholding test. The Division dropped this test from the most recent revision of the International Guidelines. As for the academy, Professor (now Judge) Diane Wood suggested that courts should extend *Copperweld* to reach 51–99 percent subsidiaries, because they do not pose a risk to competition. Diane Wood (Hutchinson), *Antitrust 1984: Five Decisions in Search of a Theory*, 1984 Sup. Ct. Rev. 69, 96. Other commentators have suggested that partially owned subsidiaries and affiliates should be distinguished from their wholly-owned cousins. Jennifer Stewart, Comment, *The Intra–Enterprise Conspiracy Doctrine After* Copperweld Corp. v. Independence Tube Corp., 86 Colum. L. Rev.198 (1986).

2. *Intra-enterprise immunity and mergers. Copperweld* problems arise when companies (and shareholders) have contemplated but not consummated a merger (or a transfer of a controlling interest). Should intra-enterprise immunity apply once two companies have agreed to merge? If so, at what point in the merger negotiations should the suitors be outside § 1? The Eighth Circuit has concluded that once a merger agreement has been announced, the parties to the agreement are beyond the reach of § 1. International Travel Arrangers v. NWA, Inc., 991 F.2d 1389, 1398 (8th Cir.), *cert. denied*, 510 U.S. 932 (1993). Do you agree? Consider the planned 1996 merger of two large drugstore chains, Rite Aid and Revco. The FTC opposed the deal, and, eventually, it collapsed. Should the companies be beyond the reach of § 1 for any joint decision made during their engage-

ment? Until the merger is completed, aren't companies distinct enough to have divergent economic interests?

3. *Common owners.* Another variant of this problem arises when companies have common owners. The Fifth Circuit rejected a § 1 claim against two companies that were owned in common by three people, two of whom each owned 30% and the other 40% of both companies. Century Oil Tool, Inc. v. Production Specialties, Inc., 737 F.2d 1316 (5th Cir. 1984). Should this rule apply when ownership groups only partially overlap or when the interests are not identical? Is there a sufficient "unity of purpose" among the two companies? What if the companies had been integrated in the past? What if control was all in the family, such that a mother controlled one company and her daughter the other? In Fishman v. Estate of Wirtz, 807 F.2d 520, 542 n.19 (7th Cir. 1986), the Seventh Circuit suggested that control, even if all in the family, would not create the "complete unity of interest" necessary to fall within *Copperweld*. Judge Easterbrook, dissenting, disagreed. He emphasized that the two companies allegedly conspiring—the company that owned the Chicago Stadium and a group of investors put together to buy the Chicago Bulls, which included the stadium owner's son—had never operated independently. 807 F.2d at 576–77.

4. *Agency rule. Copperweld* also crops up when antitrust conspiracies are alleged between a corporation and its agents. Even before *Copperweld*, courts had recognized that agents ordinarily cannot conspire with their principals for § 1 purposes. Courts had created, as the Supreme Court recognized in *Copperweld*, an exception to this general rule "for corporate officers acting on their own behalf." 467 U.S. at 770 n.15. Courts have stated (and restated) this exception in different ways. In Siegel Transfer, Inc. v. Carrier Express, Inc., 54 F.3d 1125, 1136–37 (3d Cir. 1995), the court explained it as follows:

> [F]or the concept of a conspiracy between a principal and an agent to apply in the antitrust context, the exception to the general rule should arise only where an agent acts to further his own economic interest in a marketplace actor which benefits from the alleged restraint, and cause his principal to take the anticompetitive actions about which the plaintiff complains. In this way, the exception captures agreements that bring together the economic power of actors which were previously pursuing divergent interests and goals, the type of activity that § 1 was intended to overcome.

a. While other courts have put a different spin on the exception, the trick is not in reconciling competing verbal formulae but in deciding whether an agent has an interest independent of its principal sufficiently related to the alleged conspiracy. In St. Joseph's Hosp. v. Hospital Corp. of America, 795 F.2d 948 (11th Cir. 1986), St. Joseph's sought approval from a state regulatory body to provide cardiac surgery. A competing hospital managed by a wholly-owned subsidiary of HCA asked the state to deny the request. When the state did, St. Joseph's sued HCA and the hospital, alleging that they had conspired to prevent St. Joseph's from competing in the cardiac surgery market. The district court granted HCA's motion to dismiss the complaint on the ground that HCA and the hospital were incapable of conspiring with one another for § 1 purposes.

The Eleventh Circuit reversed. It explained that HCA's relationship with the hospital was more complicated than the usual employee/employer relationship. It noted that HCA and the hospital were separate corporate entities and that HCA, because it owned and managed hundreds of hospitals around the country, could have its own reasons for opposing St. Joseph's expansion. The court pointed out, however, that St. Joseph's had not alleged facts to support an inference that HCA had any reason, independent of its employee relationship with the hospital, to oppose St. Joseph's petition. The court remanded the case to the district court to give St. Joseph's the opportunity to allege the missing facts.

b.   The issue of independent interest frequently arises when hospitals deny (or revoke) admitting privileges to physicians. As traditionally organized, hospitals grant certain doctors the right to admit patients to their facilities based on the recommendations of "staff physicians" (*i.e.*, the physicians that already have admitting privileges). The doctors market their practices independently of the hospitals but draw on the resources of the hospital to care for their patients. Physicians denied admitting privileges or whose privileges the hospital has revoked often sue the hospital and the staff physicians, alleging violations of § 1 of the Sherman Act. *See generally*, Havighurst, Doctors and Hospitals: An Antitrust Perspective on Traditional Relationships, 1984 Duke L.J. 1071.

Post *Copperweld*, courts have tread an uncertain path in deciding whether these decisions can be challenged under § 1. In Oksanen v. Page Memorial Hosp., 945 F.2d 696, 703 (4th Cir. 1991) (en banc), *cert. denied*, 502 U.S. 1074 (1992), the court, after examining the relationship between the staff and the hospital, concluded that "[f]ar from being a competitor with the hospital, the medical staff was in fact a natural component of the hospital's management structure." It explained that the hospital's bylaws left it in complete control over the peer review process and that this control would enable it to bend the process to its, rather than its staff's, interest. The court held that intra-corporate immunity shields a hospital and its medical staff from antitrust liability for decisions made by the staff in the peer review process. However, in Bolt v. Halifax Hospital Medical Center, 851 F.2d 1273, 1280 (11th Cir. 1988), *cert. denied*, 495 U.S. 924 (1990), the court "perceive[d] no basis . . . for holding that the members of a medical staff are legally incapable of conspiring with one another" or the hospital. It explained that "each [physician] is a separate economic entity potentially in competition with other physicians." *Id.* It likewise found the hospital distinct from the staff, declining to draw an analogy to the company/officer cases.

5.   *Franchises*. Other "untraditional" business relationships also raise the unity of economic purpose issue. In Williams v. I.B. Fischer Nevada, 999 F.2d 445 (9th Cir. 1993) (*per curiam*), the manager of a Jack-in-the-Box fast food restaurant in Las Vegas, Nevada, sued the owner of his franchise,

Fischbein, and several others when Fischbein refused to grant him permission to manage a Jack-in-the-Box opening up in Bullhead City, Nevada. The manager alleged that a provision in the contract between the franchisor and the franchisees violated § 1. The provision at issue required him to get the permission of the owner of one franchise in order to take a job at another franchise. The district court found that the franchisor and franchisee shared such a unity of economic purpose that they could not conspire within the meaning of § 1. The court noted, among other things: that all franchises serve the same food; that all share the same logo; that all benefit from advertising created and approved by the franchisor; that employees of every franchise wear the same uniform; and that every contract provides for an exclusive geographic area. The court also noted that franchisors strive to prevent competition among franchises. The Ninth Circuit affirmed.

Are you persuaded? Do any of the facts noted by the district court justify treating a franchisor and a franchisee the same for § 1 purposes as a parent and its wholly-owned subsidiary? Can you think of any relevant differences overlooked by the district court? If this contractual relationship is immune from § 1 scrutiny, should all contractual relationships be similarly immune as long as the alleged conspiracy falls within the ambit of the contract? *See generally* Oliver E. Williamson, Markets and Hierarchies: Analysis and Antitrust Implications (1975); Harvey Leibenstein, Inside The Firm: The inefficiencies of Hierarchy (1988). Wouldn't that practically read § 1 out of the statute?

6. *Joint ventures.* Joint ventures also pose *Copperweld* problems. The latest one to reach the Supreme Court arose in the context of a professional sports league—in particular, the National Football League. *See* American Needle Inc. v. National Football League, 538 F.3d 736 (7th Cir. 2008), *cert. granted*, 129 S.Ct. 2859 (2009) (No. 08–661). (Recall the discussion of professional sports leagues in Chapter 5, *supra,* in which you saw that professional sports leagues have often argued, usually unsuccessfully, that they should be treated as single economic units for the purposes of § 1.) American Needle involved a separate corporate entity, known as NFL Properties, that was created by the 32 teams that make up the NFL. NFL Properties was responsible for the development, licensing, and marketing of the intellectual property (logos, trademarks, and the like) owned by each member team. Plaintiff American Needle had held a license to manufacture headware, but NFL Properties decided in 2000 to solicit bids for an exclusive license, which it then awarded to a competitor firm. American Needle responded with an antitrust action against the NFL as a whole, each member NFL team, NFL Properties, and the successful bidder. The first argument that the NFL defendants made was that they were a single entity, as *Copperweld* uses that term, and thus that they were immune from liability under § 1.

The court of appeals commented that "We have yet to render a definitive opinion as to whether the teams of a professional sports league can be considered a single entity in light of Copperweld. The characteristics that sports leagues generally exhibit make the determination difficult; in some contexts, a league seems more aptly described as a single entity immune from antitrust scrutiny, while in others a league appears to be a joint venture between independently owned teams that is subject to review under § 1." 538 F.3d at 741. In light of that complexity, the court "compartmentalized" Copperweld and ruled that "the question of whether a professional sports league is a single entity should be addressed not only one league at a time, but also one facet of a league at a time. . . . Thus, in reviewing the district court's decision, we will limit our review to (1) the actions of the NFL, its members teams, and NFL Properties; and (2) the actions of the NFL and its member teams as they pertain to the teams' agreement to license their intellectual property collectively via NFL Properties." *Id.* at 742. With that said, the court concluded that the central activity before it was the promotion of NFL football as a whole, and for that purpose, the teams' collective efforts to license and market their intellectual property did not "deprive[] the market of independent sources of economic power. . . ." *Id.* at 743. In the final analysis, the court concluded that "nothing in § 1 prohibits the NFL teams from cooperating so the league can compete against other entertainment providers." *Id.* at 744. And once the court took this approach, it followed that American Needle's claim under Sherman Act § 2 was also doomed.

As noted, the Supreme Court has granted *certiorari* in American Needle, see 129 S.Ct. 2859 (2009) (No. 08–661), and so we are likely soon to learn more about the extent of *Copperweld*. Up until now, however, sports teams have tried hard to fit within *Copperweld*'s safe harbor. Major League Soccer, for example, was designed at least in part with antitrust concerns in mind. In the MLS, the league owns all the teams while individual investors, in addition to owning shares in the league, own the rights to operate the teams. The league's backers hoped that this structure would allow them to avoid the antitrust problems that have plagued the NBA and NFL. Were they well advised? Given the Supreme Court's decision in *Brown v. Pro Football, Inc., supra* p. 279 n. 93, should future sports leagues choose a similar ownership structure?

At least one admitted joint venture has been held to be a single economic unit for § 1 purposes. In City of Mt. Pleasant, Iowa v. Associated Elec. Co-op., 838 F.2d 268 (8th Cir. 1988), the City sued a three-tier rural electrical cooperative, alleging a "price-squeeze" (*i.e.*, that the organization's prices left the city with little room to buy or resell power). At the top of the pyramid sat the Associated Electric Cooperative. The Cooperative owned the organization's transmission grid and most of its electrical generating capacity. It controlled the production and distribution of electricity for the organization. Beneath the Cooperative stood six generation-and-transmission cooperatives (G & Ts). The G & Ts owned a small portion of the transmission grid (mostly smaller lines) and were responsible for selling and transporting power to the next tier, 43 local distribution companies. The 43 distribution companies sold power to 425,000 retail customers. Each customer owned a share of its distribution company, which owned a share of its G & T, which owned the Cooperative. The

Eighth Circuit found that the organization was a "single enterprise pursuing a common goal—the provision of low-cost electricity to its rural consumer-members." 838 F.2d at 276. The court found "no evidence that any defendant ever pursued interests antithetical to those of the cooperative as a whole." *Id.* It held that the organization was shielded from § 1 liability by *Copperweld*.

Do you agree that the entire organization was a "single enterprise?" If not, could the organization be structured differently and yet still be owned by the retail consumers (and so retain eligibility for financial assistance from the federal government through the Rural Electrification Administration)? Can this organization be distinguished from other joint ventures, particularly production joint ventures?

SELECTIVE BIBLIOGRAPHY

1. **General**

Posner, *Antitrust Law: An Economic Perspective* (2d ed. 2001).

Baumol, Panzar & Willig, *Contestable Markets and the Theory of Industry Structure* (1988 ed.).

Bork, *The Antitrust Paradox* 163–97 (1978).

Goldschmid, Mann & Weston (eds.), *Industrial Concentration: The New Learning* (1974).

Goldman, *Trouble for Private Enforcement of the Sherman Act:* Twombly, *Pleading Standards, and the Oligopoly Problem,* 2008 B. Y. U. L. Rev. 1057 (2008).

Raffaelli, *Oligopolies and Antitrust Law,* 19 Fordham Int'l L. J. 915 (1996).

Calkins, Copperweld *in the Courts: The Road to Caribe,* 63 Antitrust L. J. 345 (1995).

Hay, *Oligopoly, Shared Monopoly, and Antitrust Law,* 67 Cornell L. Rev. 439 (1982).

Turner, *The Scope of Antitrust and Other Economic Regulatory Policies,* 82 Harv. L. Rev. 1207 (1969).

2. **The Problem of Oligopoly**

Vives, *Oligopoly Pricing: Old Ideas and New Tools* (Sept. 2001).

Chamberlin, *The Theory of Monopolistic Competition* (8th ed. 1962).

Sagi, *The Oligopolistic Pricing Problem: A Suggested Price Freeze Remedy,* 2008 Colum. Bus. L. Rev. 269 (2008).

Page, *Communication and Concerted Action,* 38 Loy. U. Chi. L. J. 405 (2007).

Levin, *The Nomos and Narrative of* Matsushita, 73 Fordham L. Rev. 1627 (2005).

Manne & Williamson, *Hot Docs Vs. Cold Economics: The Use and Misuse of Business Documents in Antitrust Enforcement and Adjudication,* 47 Ariz. L. Rev. 609 (2005).

Skocilich, *Narrower Is Better—The Third Circuit's Latest Word on Conscious Parallelism and the Problem of Plus Factors:* In re Flat Glass, 50 Vill. L. Rev. 1309 (2005).

Leslie, *Trust, Distrust, and Antitrust,* 82 Tex. L. Rev. 515 (2004).

Piraino, *Regulating Oligopoly Conduct under the Antitrust Laws,* 89 Minn. L. Rev. 9 (2004).

Salop, *Strategic Entry Deterrence,* 69 Am Economic Rev. 335 (1979).

3. Facilitating Mechanisms

Schinkel, *Forensic Economics in Competition Law Enforcement,* 4 J. Comp. L. & Econ. 1 (2008).

Werden, *Economic Evidence on the Existence of Collusion: Reconciling Antitrust Law with Oligopoly Theory,* 71 Antitrust L. J. 719 (2004).

Shulman, *Proof of Conspiracy in Antitrust Cases & The Oligopoly Problem,* 4 Sedona Conf. J. 1 (2003).

Gavil, *Defining Reliable Forensic Economics in the Post-Daubert/Kumho Tire Era: Case Studies from Antitrust,* 57 Wash. & Lee L. Rev. 831 (2000).

Crocker, *What Do "Facilitating Practices" Facilitate? An Empirical Investigation of Most–Favored–Nation Clauses in Natural Gas Contracts,* 37 J. L. & Econ. 297 (1994).

Kattan, *Beyond Facilitating Practices: Price Signaling and Price Protection Clauses in the New Antitrust Environment,* 63 Antitrust L. J. 133 (1994).

Havighurst, *Doctors and Hospitals: An Antitrust Perspective on Traditional Relationships,* 1984 Duke L.J. 1071.

Carlton, *A Reexamination of Delivered Pricing Systems,* 26 J. L. & Econ. 51 (1983).

Willis & Pitofsky, *Antitrust Consequences of Using Corporate Subsidiaries,* 43 N.Y.U. L. Rev. 20 (1968).

Turner, *The Definition of Agreement under the Sherman Act: Conscious Parallelism and Refusals To Deal,* 75 Harv. L. Rev. 655 (1962).

4. Trade Associations

Goldman, *Trade Associations: Toeing the Line between Antitrust Concerns and Protected Speech,* 16 Geo. Mason U. Civ. Rts. L. J. 393 (2006).

Aviram & Tor, *Overcoming Impediments to Information Sharing,* 55 Ala. L. Rev. 231 (2004).

Lande & Marvel, *The Three Types of Collusion: Fixing Prices, Rivals, and Rules,* 2000 Wisc. L. Rev. 941 (2000).

CHAPTER 7

VERTICAL RESTRAINTS ON COMPETITION

SECTION 1. THE ECONOMICS OF VERTICAL RESTRAINTS

INTRODUCTORY NOTE ON VERTICAL RESTRAINTS

Manufacturers usually decide to develop a network of independent intermediate distributors and retail outlets, rather than to sell products to consumers directly or through agents. When their product is a trademarked commodity or line of goods, they frequently enter into continuing contractual relations, sometimes designating the distributors as "franchisees." They may find it in their interests to limit the degree and nature of competition among their dealers or classes of dealers. Such so-called "vertical" restraints on competition in distribution produce a host of anti-trust problems.

As this chapter explores, the most important vertical restraints relate to the prices at which distributors sell, the geographic territories or classes of customers to which they sell, or the degree of exclusivity the manufacturer or the distributor can count on from the other.

Vertical *price fixing* can involve the fixing of either maximum or minimum prices at which dealers can resell. Effects on price can also be achieved indirectly through lesser restraints—for example, an agreement between the supplier and intermediate dealers that does not limit the price at which they sell, but provides that they will not do business with "known discounters."

Vertical *market allocation* usually establishes the territories in which dealers may sell or the classes of customers to whom they may sell. Territorial restraints may be "air-tight" in the sense that each dealer has an exclusive territory, or they may create a system in which several dealers service the same geographic area but are bound not to sell outside it. An example of customer allocation would be a distribution system in which one set of dealers agrees to service only wholesalers or industrial users, and another set of dealers agrees to service only retailers.

Less pronounced market allocation effects can be achieved in other ways. A "location clause," for example, specifies the site of a distributor's place of business and may provide that the distributor cannot sell the manufacturer's product (without permission) from any other location. Unlike "air-tight" territorial alloca-tion, however, a location clause permits the distributor to sell to any customer whose business it can obtain wherever the customer is located. A "primary responsibility" clause entails an agreement by a distributor to use its best effort to achieve an agreed-upon sales target within a specified geographic area or to a specified class of customers. After it has achieved that target (for example, a sales quota of at least 75% of the previous year's annual sales), it is free to sell anywhere or to any class of customers it chooses. A "profit passover" clause provides that the

606

distributor may sell into territories or to classes of customers not assigned to it, provided that it pays over a portion of the profit attributable to such sales to the distributor whose assigned territory or class of customers is "invaded." The amount of profit "passed over" is often designed to compensate the recipient for past expenses incurred in advertising or pre-sale marketing efforts that may have been instrumental in the sale.

A third general class of vertical restrictions involves *exclusive dealership* agreements, in which the manufacturer itself agrees not to sell in competition with the dealer and not to establish another dealership in the assigned area. The legality of exclusive dealerships will be examined in Chapter 8. They need to be mentioned here, however, because of the way they relate to vertical territorial and customer restraints. Promises of air-tight exclusivity by a manufacturer can usually be made effective only if territorial or customer restraints, location clauses, or other vertical restrictions effectively prevent the manufacturer's other distributors from intruding. In effect, exclusive distribution systems require that each dealer accept at least some limitations on its own freedom to compete in favor of others.

exclusive dealing

Arguments with respect to the pro- and anticompetitive effects of vertical price fixing and vertical territorial and customer allocation are similar but not identical. We will examine first arguments concerning the effects of minimum vertical price fixing.

1. Anticompetitive Effect of Vertical Price Fixing

The essential argument supporting antitrust illegality of vertical minimum price fixing—or "resale price maintenance" ("RPM")—is that such agreements may produce the same effects as horizontal price fixing among dealers. The argument posits that a manufacturer may be induced to act as organizer of a dealers' cartel by the dealers' threat to turn elsewhere or because it expects in return some "payment" from the dealers in terms of preferred treatment (such as shelf space), or more aggressive marketing of the manufacturer's product.

Another possible anticompetitive effect of RPM is that it tends to stabilize prices at the manufacturers' level. Cartels, as we have learned, are often unstable because of the tendency of members to "cheat." Manufacturers in a cartel—especially one that generates high monopoly profits by sharply curtailing output—will be tempted to offer price concessions to some buyers to increase their volume at least in part at the expense of fellow cartel members. If RPM eliminates distributor price-cutting, one important pressure for manufacturer price concessions is diminished and the manufacturers' cartel is stabilized. Detection of "cheating" at the manufacturer level is also more readily accomplished where resale prices are generally maintained. This does not mean that there can be no price competition among manufacturers where there is industry-wide resale price maintenance. Manufacturers still might offer lower prices to compete for dealers, as opposed to seeking additional sales volume by competing through dealers for a larger share of purchases by consumers. But RPM does change and arguably diminishes the incentives to cut price at the manufacturers' level, and in that sense may be viewed as a "facilitating device" for a manufacturers' cartel.

2. Possible Justifications

Despite the plausibility of the argument that vertical price fixing may have horizontal effects at either the dealer or the manufacturer level, it does not follow that it has the *same* anticompetitive impact as horizontal price fixing and should therefore, by analogy, be treated as illegal *per se*. Set out below are some of the arguments that have been advanced to distinguish vertical from horizontal price fixing, and some questions with respect to each. To a large extent, the answer to the policy questions about how to treat vertical price fixing and other vertical restraints under the antitrust laws depends on the relative weight that you attach to these contentions.

a. *Differing Incentives*

Once a manufacturer has sold a product to one of its dealers, it has extracted all the profit it can take from that particular sale. If the dealer raises or lowers the resale price, that action will raise or lower the dealer's profit margin, but it will have no effect on the manufacturer's profit on that particular item. On the other hand, generally higher dealer markups, with resulting higher prices to consumers, will (all other things being equal) tend to lower sales volume.

Thus if the manufacturer is acting to further its own interests—*i.e.*, if it is not simply acting on behalf of a dealer cartel—the resale price it establishes is almost certain to be different from the resale price that would be set by a dealer cartel. The main argument against treating vertical price fixing as the equivalent of horizontal price fixing (and thus as illegal per se) is that the manufacturer, concerned about higher sales volume to prevail in interbrand competition, can be depended upon to set the minimum resale price at a reasonable (or "efficient") level.

Will the manufacturer act as an effective surrogate for consumers' interests? Suppose the manufacturer has a relatively high market share or its products can successfully be differentiated from those of interbrand rivals by advertising. Or suppose the rivals also engage in RPM. In those circumstances is interbrand competition enough to assure that appropriate competitive prices will be charged? Also, is it an accurate reflection of actual markets to depict the manufacturer as either fully controlling distributional processes for its own interests, on the one hand, or simply serving as an agent for its dealers, on the other? Are there plausible intermediate relationships between those two extremes? For example, might the manufacturers and dealers sometimes best be viewed as joint venturers, seeking over the long run to achieve higher prices and greater profits for all at the expense of consumers?

b. *Attracting Dealers*

Resale price maintenance may assure substantial distributor profits and thereby induce dealers to stock and promote the supplier's brand. This might be particularly important where taking on a new brand requires a substantial investment. But is this defense consistent with the argument that vertical price fixing is different from horizontal price fixing because of the manufacturer's interest in maintaining a high-volume, low-markup sales policy? Are there ways to secure and hold dealers that do not risk the adverse competitive impact of RPM?

c. *Inducing Desired Services*

A manufacturer may independently conclude that a particular mix of price and service competition will be the optimum strategy for selling its product in competition with other brands. For example, suppose marketing studies show that point of sale advertising, elaborate dealer demonstrations and post-sale warranty programs are highly prized by consumers and will help to sell the manufacturer's product. Distributors may not respond to these competitive incentives on their own because of so-called "free rider" and "cream-skimming" problems. Thus, dealers will hesitate to make investments in those kinds of services if other dealers, without being burdened by comparable costs, can offer the same product at lower prices.

As an example of a "free ride," consider the situation in which one dealer maintains an attractive showroom and provides salesperson demonstrations of complicated products while a dealer across the street or on the Internet sells the same product in a no-frills discount operation. Customers may take advantage of the free demonstrations and then buy from the second dealer at a lower price. The free-rider argument posits that unless the manufacturer can prevent the latter type of operation, retailer services essential to its competitive success will be provided by no one. Similarly, other distributors might seek out only low-cost repeat or high volume business, "skimming the cream" from a market and leaving the less profitable, more difficult sales to the regular outlet.

Is this a persuasive justification for RPM? If higher markups are assured to dealers, does it follow that they will undertake outlays on non-price competition up to the level of extra profits made available through the vertical restriction? If competition is less than perfect, will not the dealers pocket at least a part of the additional profit? Also, if some purchasers truly want service competition, why can the market not be depended upon to solve this problem by producing some outlets that sell the product at a low price without services and other outlets that charge a higher price but provide more advertising, explanations, and post-sale guarantees? Is there no less anticompetitive way in which any "market failure" can be remedied? Is RPM the only or even the most likely technique a manufacturer would use to deliver these services to consumers? Why cannot the manufacturer deliver the services itself or separately contract with the dealer to pay all or part of the costs of the services that are desired? Can you think of any services that can be provided only through vertical price fixing?

d. *Product Image and "Loss Leaders"*

In an earlier day, advocates of vertical price fixing relied heavily on the argument that it was unfair to force the manufacturer to allow its dealers to sell its product, against the manufacturer's wishes, at discount prices. The argument is most persuasive when a manufacturer invests resources to create a product image of "quality" or luxury, so that price reductions may actually reduce sales volume. Some manufacturers dislike seeing their product used as a "loss leader"—i.e. a product sold at or below cost—to induce customers to come into a store and stay to buy other products.

Is it frequently the case that a manufacturer's prospects for profits will be injured by a dealer's offering its product at an extremely low price? Are there some limits on how low that price can be?

e. *Preservation of Small Business*

At various times intense political pressure has been exercised to legalize or even mandate vertical price fixing (*see infra* pp. 647–649). In many states, statutes have been enacted declaring "sales below cost" illegal. Most of the political pressure has been generated by the small business community, apparently because many have been apprehensive that aggressive national chains or discount operations would eventually drive small or local merchants out of business. Associations of retail druggists and grocers have been most active historically in advocating RPM.

In the long run, is RPM likely to enable an otherwise inefficient retailer to stay in business? Are such attitudes favoring "soft competition" defensible in the public interest?

3. Vertical Restraints Induced by a Policy of Refusals To Deal

The restraints discussed in this section can be implemented either by agreements (express or tacit) between a manufacturer and individual distributors, or by a manufacturer's refusal to deal with distributors who do not comply with suggested prices or other distributional restraints. Agreements fall within the scope of § 1 of the Sherman Act, although the extent to which they may be justified has changed over time. To what extent can or should the antitrust laws reach a manufacturer's individual refusal to deal? In terms of economic effect, are there any reasons why the two should be treated differently?

SECTION 2. THE INTERPLAY OF COMMON LAW AND ANTITRUST LAWS

A. VERTICAL PRICE FIXING

INTRODUCTION

For almost a century, Dr. Miles Medical Co. v. John D. Park & Sons Co., 220 U.S. 373 (1911), served as the bedrock for vertical price fixing decisions. Plaintiff Dr. Miles used "secret formulas" to manufacture proprietary medicines and sold its products at the wholesale and retail level through dealers. Dr. Miles developed a system to fix the minimum resale prices which would apply down the distribution chain. The system involved two types of restrictive agreements: "Consignment Contract—Wholesale" and "Retail Agency Contract." John D. Park & Sons Co. was a wholesale drug concern that had refused to enter into the restrictive agreements; instead, Park had allegedly purchased Dr. Miles' medicines at "cut prices" by inducing dealers who had made the agreements to violate the price restrictions. Seeking to stop this practice, Dr. Miles sued Park for equitable relief. The district court dismissed Dr. Miles's suit on a demurrer for want of equity, and the Sixth Circuit affirmed. The Supreme Court then accepted the case for review.

The Court first addressed the validity of Dr. Miles' restrictive agreements, and then turned to the question whether Dr. Miles had the right to restrict the prices at which its dealers could sell its proprietary medicines.

Dr. Miles had attempted to structure its contracts with its dealers as consignment agreements. It argued that these contracts created an agency relationship between the wholesalers and itself, and that Park had induced a breach of trust by Dr. Miles's agents. The Court was unpersuaded that this was a true consignment; like the district court, it thought that this was just an effort to disguise the wholesalers "in the mask of agency" in an attempt to restrict the alleged agent's sale prices. The Supreme Court found that the practice between Dr. Miles and its wholesalers contradicted the agency theory, concluding that "the tenor of the agreement as set forth must be taken to override the inconsistent general allegations to which we have referred...." Because Dr. Miles had failed to establish the agency relationship, the Court rejected the claim that Park had induced an agent's breach of trust. Second, the Court dismissed the "retail agents" argument, which it said was "clearly an agreement looking to sale and not to agency."

Recognizing that the resale price restrictions eliminated competition between retailers, the Court turned to the question whether eliminating competition "with 'most of the jobbers and wholesale druggists and a majority of the retail druggists of the country' " was invalid either at common law or under the Sherman Act. Dr. Miles argued that the Court should analogize the secret processes used to manufacture its medicines to patent rights. Had the Court chosen to follow an earlier patent case [E. Bement v. National Harrow Co., 186 U.S. 70 (1902)], it would have permitted Dr. Miles to fix the resale prices. But the Court rejected the analogy. It noted that not only was Dr. Miles's process unpatented, but, moreover, the issue at hand did not concern the rights in the process, but rather the final product. It explained that:

> [Dr. Miles's argument] implies that, if for any reason monopoly of production exists, it carries with it the right to control the entire trade of the produced article and to prevent any competition that otherwise might arise between wholesale and retail dealers. The principle would not be limited to secret processes, but would extend to goods manufactured by anyone who secured control of the source of supply of a necessary raw material or ingredient. But, because there is monopoly of production, it certainly cannot be said that there is no public interest in maintaining freedom of trade with respect to future sales after the article has been placed on the market and the producer has parted with his title.... The fact that the market may not be supplied with the particular article, unless he produces it, is a practical consequence which does not enlarge his right of property in what he does produce.

The second avenue Dr. Miles pursued attempted to justify its price controls on the basis of its proprietary interest in its own products. The argument relied on both property and contract rights by suggesting that as a producer/owner of the medicines, Dr. Miles was entitled to add conditions to the resale of its medicines by virtue of its right to dispose of its property as it pleased. Unpersuaded, the Court reasoned that:

> ... because a manufacturer is not bound to make or sell, it does not follow in case of sales actually made he may impose upon purchasers every sort of restriction. Thus a general restraint upon alienation is ordinarily invalid. "The right of alienation is one of the essential incidents of a right of general property in movables, and restraints upon alienation have been generally regarded as obnoxious to public policy, which is best subserved by great freedom of traffic in such things as pass from hand to hand. General restraint in the alienation of articles, things, chattels, except when a very special kind of property is involved, such as a slave or an heirloom, have been generally held void. 'If a man,' says Lord Coke, in Coke on Littleton, section 360, 'be possessed of a horse or any other chattel, real or personal, and give his whole interest or property therein, upon condition that the donee or vendee shall not alien the same, the same is void, because his whole interest and property is out of him, so as he hath no possibility of reverter; and it is against trade and traffic and bargaining and contracting between man and man.' " John D. Park & Sons v. Hartman, supra. See also Gray on Restraints on Alienation, §§ 27, 28.

> Nor can the manufacturer by rule and notice, in the absence of contract or statutory right, even though the restriction be known to purchasers, fix prices for future sales. It has been held by this court that no such privilege exists under the copyright statutes, although the owner of the copyright has the sole right to vend copies of the copyrighted production. Bobbs–Merrill Co. v. Straus, 210 U.S. 339. It will hardly be contended, with respect to such a matter, that the manufacturer of an article of commerce, not protected by any statutory grant is in any better case. Whatever right

the manufacturer may have to project his control beyond his own sales must depend not upon an inherent power incident to production and original ownership, but upon agreement.

With respect to contracts in restraint of trade, the earlier doctrine of the common law has been substantially modified in adaptation to modern conditions. But the public interest is still the first consideration. To sustain the restraint, it must be found to be reasonable both with respect to the public and to the parties and that it is limited to what is fairly necessary, in the circumstances of the particular case, for the protection of the convenantee. Otherwise restraints of trade are void as against public policy. . . .

Dr. Miles asserted that the restraints were important to protect against the damage and confusion that would be caused by lower prices. The Court, however, recognized that argument as primarily a concern for dealers; it construed Dr. Miles's injury as an inability to allow its favored dealers to realize increased profits brought about by the price restraints. It concluded:

> . . . If there be an advantage to a manufacturer in the maintenance of fixed retail prices, the question remains whether it is one which he is entitled to secure by agreements restricting the freedom of trade on the part of dealers who own what they sell. As to this, the complainant can fare no better with its plan of identical contracts than could the dealers themselves if they formed a combination and endeavored to establish the same restrictions, and thus to achieve the same result, by agreement with each other. If the immediate advantage they would thus obtain would not be sufficient to sustain such a direct agreement, the asserted ulterior benefit to the complainant cannot be regarded as sufficient to support its system.

> But agreements or combinations between dealers, having for their sole purpose the destruction of competition and the fixing of prices, are injurious to the public interest and void. They are not saved by the advantages which the participants expect to derive from the enhanced price to the consumer.

The judgment was affirmed. Justice Holmes dissented, primarily because he considered price competition to be less important to the public than the competition of conflicting desires for products in the marketplace. For almost hundred years after the *Dr. Miles* decision, the Court consistently read it as establishing the rule that minimum resale price agreements are *per se* illegal under Section 1.

NOTES AND QUESTIONS

1. *Divisibility theory.* Dr. Miles's initial argument was that the price restrictions were valid because they related to proprietary medicines manufactured under a secret process. Since no one else could manufacture them, Dr. Miles had the legal right to keep them from reaching the market; price restrictions in licenses, it was argued, are less restrictive than no distribution at all. If the more restrictive course of conduct is protected, the less restrictive cannot logically be illegal. This kind of argument—sometimes called the "inherency" or "divisibility theory"[1]—had been successful for patent owners engaging in resale price maintenance. *See* E. Bement & Sons v. National Harrow Co., 186 U.S. 70 (1902). Dr. Miles unsuccessfully urged

---

1. *See* Martin J. Adelman and Friedrich K. Juenger, *Patent–Antitrust: Patent Dynamics and Field of Use Licensing*, 50 N.Y.U. L. REV. 273 (1975); Richard M. Buxbaum, *Restrictions Inherent in the Patent Monopoly: A Comparative Critique*, 113 U. PA. L. REV. 633 (1965).

that the owner of a secret process be accorded the same treatment. What is wrong with this line of argument? The *Bement* case is no longer good law and price maintenance of a patented[2] or copyrighted[3] article is no more (or less) protected than price maintenance of any other. Is this the correct rule for any kind of product protected by intellectual property?

2. *Restraints on alienation rule.* How essential to the outcome and opinion is the Court's reliance on the common law rule against general restraints on the alienability of chattels, for which Coke on Littleton is cited? What was the policy underlying that rule? What relevance does it have to maintaining resale prices? Were such restraints on alienability always unlawful at common law, or only when unreasonable?

3. *Vertical/Horizontal intersection.* What does it mean to say that vertical price fixing "falls within the same principle which condemns" horizontal price fixing? Would an Interstate Circuit type of inference of agreement among the retailers be supportable? When retailers go along with a RPM scheme, is their conduct, according to Professor Turner's analysis (*see supra* p. 501, independent or interdependent?

4. *Who have a greater incentive to maintain resale prices?* Are manufacturers or their distributors more likely to initiate RPM programs? Consider the following in light of *Dr. Miles*:

> ... [R]esale price maintenance is a method used by organized dealers to force unwilling manufacturers to work for them to protect dealer profit margins. This is a simple, plausible explanation of resale price maintenance, and probably explains much of its recent as well as its early use. This explanation is supported by the very high proportion of "fair-trade" cases involving products the dealers of which have been organized in effective trade associations, for example, drugs, cosmetics and liquor.

Ward Bowman, *The Prerequisites and Effect of Resale Price Maintenance*, 22 U. CHI. L. REV. 825, 830–31 (1955).

In litigation, is it likely that dealer-initiated RPM will be exposed? Cf. United States v. General Motors Corp., 323 U.S. 373 (1945) (finding that GM and Chevrolet dealers' associations conspired to exclude discounters from market for new Chevrolet sales in the Los Angeles area, thereby reversing the district court).

5. *Impact on retail prices.* Studies by the Antitrust Division of the Department of Justice and others indicate that RPM does result in increased retail prices. For example, see Fair Trade Laws: Hearings on S. 408 Before the Subcomm. on Antitrust and Monopoly of the Senate Judiciary Comm., 94th Cong., 1st Sess., 174 (1975). That should not be surprising, however, since the arguments in favor of RPM assume that it is imposed in order to generate high profit margins that in turn will be used to subsidize pre-sale and post-sale services. How would you devise a study to see whether consumers were getting a better package of product plus service under RPM?

6. *RPM via consignment agreements redux.* In Simpson v. Union Oil Co., 377 U.S. 13 (1964), the Supreme Court extended the prohibition on RPM to strike down

---

2. *See* United States v. Univis Lens Co., 316 U.S. 241 (1942); Ethyl Gasoline Corp. v. United States, 309 U.S. 436 (1940); Straus v. Victor Talking Mach. Co., 243 U.S. 490 (1917); Boston Store v. American Graphophone Co., 246 U.S. 8 (1918); Bauer & Cie. v. O'Donnell, 229 U.S. 1 (1913).

3. *See* Bobbs–Merrill Co. v. Straus, 210 U.S. 339 (1908).

a retail-dealer consignment agreement. Under the terms of the agreement struck down in *Simpson*, Union Oil set the retail price of gasoline and retained "title" to the gasoline until it passed into the consumer's tanks. While Union Oil paid property taxes on the gasoline consigned to its dealers, the dealers were liable for any gasoline lost, except for losses caused by certain acts of God. Simpson received a commission on each sale. The Court described Union Oil's consignment agreement as a "clever" attempt to avoid "the end result of United States v. Socony–Vacuum Co." *Id.* at 21–22. It held "that resale price maintenance through the present, coercive type of 'consignment' agreement is illegal under the antitrust laws." *Id.* at 24.

Justice Stewart dissented. He explained:

> I think upon remand there should a full trial of all the issues in this litigation, because I completely disagree with the Court that whenever a bona fide consignor, employing numerous agents, sets the price at which his property is to be sold "the antitrust laws prevent calling the 'consignment' an agency," and transform the consignment into a sale. In the present posture of this case, such a determination, overruling as it does a doctrine which has stood unquestioned for almost 40 years, is unwarranted, unnecessary and premature.

Id. at 26.

7. *Reconciling principle with precedent.* In Morrison v. Murray Biscuit Co., 797 F.2d 1430 (7th Cir. 1986), Morrison, a wholesale distributor of cookies and crackers, sued the Murray Biscuit Co. on grounds that Murray had agreed with Feldman, a competitor of Morrison, to terminate Morrison because it had ignored certain supplier-imposed restrictions on customers to whom it could sell. One defense was that Murray Biscuit and Feldman could not conspire because Feldman was a broker/agent and therefore had no discretion in the sales policies it followed.

Feldman took orders from grocery stores and forwarded them to Murray Biscuit, which then shipped the goods directly to the stores. It maintained no inventory. Murray Biscuit set the price and after it received payment, remitted to Feldman 5 percent as compensation. In analyzing whether the arrangement was a legitimate "agency" or "consignment" under the antitrust laws, the Seventh Circuit (Posner, J.) wrote the following:

> The challenge is to reconcile *Simpson* with the proposition that a homeowner does not violate section 1 of the Sherman Act when he tells his broker at what price to sell his home. The courts' travails in meeting this challenge, well discussed in 7 Areeda, Antitrust Law ¶ 1473 (1986), included such ingenious metaphoric flights as asking whether the agent and his principal constitute "a unified economic consciousness incapable of conspiring with itself." Pink Supply Corp. v. Hiebert, Inc., 788 F.2d 1313, 1317 (8th Cir. 1986). We think the key to reconciliation is to be found by asking whether the agency relationship has a function other than to circumvent the rule against price fixing. The consignment arrangement in *Simpson* was described by the Court as "a so-called retail dealer 'consignment' agreement," a "clever manipulation of words," a "wooden formula for administering prices on a vast scale," an "easy manipulation," and a product of "clever draftsmanship." There is no suggestion that the brokerage arrangement between Murray Biscuit and Feldman is artificial or unnatural. Feldman really is just an order taker for Murray Biscuit and

other suppliers. He has no interest in or capacity for setting the retail prices of the goods he brokers.

To answer a question about antitrust as about any other field of law it is always helpful and often essential to consider what the purpose of the law is. The purpose of antitrust law, at least as articulated in the modern cases, is to protect the competitive process as a means of promoting economic efficiency. . . . Efficiency would not be promoted by a rule that forbade principals to tell their agents at what price to sell the principal's product unless the agent was an employee. Principals would either convert their sales agents from independent contractors to employees or give their sales agents a discretion over price that the agents, for lack of information and expertise, would not be in a position to exercise intelligently. . . . Brokerage is no more a device for evading the Sherman Act than is telling one's sales clerk what price to mark on a bag of sugar rather than letting him decide for himself.

8. *RPM regulation rollercoaster*. Largely because of academic criticism (mostly from the economic wing of the profession) of the *Dr. Miles* rule making minimum RPM *per se* illegal, enforcement at the federal level was non-existent in the 1980s. A few tentative enforcement efforts were launched during the first Bush Administration, and federal enforcement was substantially restored during the Clinton Administration, but mostly in complaints issued by the Federal Trade Commission. All complaints were settled with entry of consent orders.

An interesting case involved a variation on outright RPM—Minimum Advertised Price policies ("MAP")—adopted by the Big Five prerecorded music distributors (Warner, Universal, EMI, Sony and Bertelsmann). These five firms collectively accounted for about 85 percent of the market for prerecorded music. Retail margins of 40 percent were common in the 1980s, but were slashed in the 1990s as a result of a retail price war largely initiated by new entrants such as Best Buy and Circuit City.

Over a period of eleven months in 1995 and 1996, the majors adopted seriatum nearly identical policies providing that minimum prices be identified in all advertising, including ads funded solely by the retailer, as a prerequisite for obtaining any cooperative advertising funds from each music company. The policy also applied to all in-store advertising other than non-promotional stickers on the product (*i.e.*, small and not brightly colored). Severe penalties were imposed for violations, usually involving the loss of all promotional support for six to nine months.

The Federal Trade Commission issued complaints challenging MAP as a "facilitating practice" supporting horizontal price fixing (see discussion in Chapter 6, Section 2, *supra*), and accusing each defendant of imposing vertical minimum price restraints. The vertical cases were based on a rule of reason rather than the *Dr. Miles per se* rule, because the Commission's experience with programs like MAP was limited. Supporting the rule of reason challenge were the following factors: sizable market shares, high barriers to entry, and evidence that services provided by the price cutters were as good or better than services provided by smaller stores (*i.e.*, no significant free rider problem). In addition, the Commission's complaint indicated it was prepared to prove that MAP was adopted not only to preserve retail profit margins, but because it was becoming increasingly clear to the music companies that if the price war was not stopped, wholesale margins would eventually be affected. Consider the last allegation in light of the argument that the upstream seller, once it has sold a product to a dealer, has no incentive other than to insure that dealer mark-ups are at the appropriate level (see discussion of "differing incentives" at *supra* p. 608.

The case was resolved with a consent order that imposed the standard cease and desist provisions, with the unusual addition that the companies were denied their Colgate right, see *infra* p. 681 for a period of five years to facilitate the restoration of competition in the industry. (FTC file No. 971 0070 (May 10, 2000)).

State Oil Co. v. Khan

Supreme Court of the United States, 1997.
522 U.S. 3, 118 S.Ct. 275, 139 L.Ed.2d 199.

■ O'CONNOR, J., delivered the opinion for a unanimous Court. Under § 1 of the Sherman Act, "[e]very contract, combination ..., or conspiracy, in restraint of trade" is illegal. In Albrecht v. Herald Co., 390 U.S. 145, 88 S.Ct. 869, 19 L.Ed.2d 998 (1968), this Court held that vertical maximum price fixing is a *per se* violation of that statute. In this case, we are asked to reconsider that decision in light of subsequent decisions of this Court. We conclude that *Albrecht* should be overruled.

I

Respondents, Barkat U. Khan and his corporation, entered into an agreement with petitioner, State Oil Company, to lease and operate a gas station and convenience store owned by State Oil. The agreement provided that respondents would obtain the station's gasoline supply from State Oil at a price equal to a suggested retail price set by State Oil, less a margin of 3.25 cents per gallon. Under the agreement, respondents could charge any amount for gasoline sold to the station's customers, but if the price charged was higher than State Oil's suggested retail price, the excess was to be rebated to State Oil. Respondents could sell gasoline for less than State Oil's suggested retail price, but any such decrease would reduce their 3.25 cents-per-gallon margin.

About a year after respondents began operating the gas station, they fell behind in lease payments. State Oil then gave notice of its intent to terminate the agreement and commenced a state court proceeding to evict respondents. At State Oil's request, the state court appointed a receiver to operate the gas station. The receiver operated the station for several months without being subject to the price restraints in respondents' agreement with State Oil. According to respondents, the receiver obtained an overall profit margin in excess of 3.25 cents per gallon by lowering the price of regular-grade gasoline and raising the price of premium grades.

Respondents sued State Oil in the United States District Court for the Northern District of Illinois, alleging in part that State Oil had engaged in price fixing in violation of § 1 of the Sherman Act by preventing respondents from raising or lowering retail gas prices. According to the complaint, but for the agreement with State Oil, respondents could have charged different prices based on the grades of gasoline, in the same way that the receiver had, thereby achieving increased sales and profits. State Oil responded that the agreement did not actually prevent respondents from setting gasoline prices, and that, in substance, respondents did not allege a violation of antitrust laws by their claim that State Oil's suggested retail price was not optimal.

The District Court found that the allegations in the complaint did not state a *per se* violation of the Sherman Act because they did not establish the sort of "manifestly anticompetitive implications or pernicious effect on competition" that would justify *per se* prohibition of State Oil's conduct. Subsequently, in ruling on cross-motions for summary judgment, the District Court concluded that respondents had failed to demonstrate antitrust injury or harm to competition. The District Court held that respondents had not shown that a difference in gasoline pricing would have increased the station's sales; nor had they shown that State Oil had market power or that its pricing provisions affected competition in a relevant market. Accordingly, the District Court entered summary judgment for State Oil on respondents' Sherman Act claim.

The Court of Appeals for the Seventh Circuit reversed. The court first noted that the agreement between respondents and State Oil did indeed fix maximum gasoline prices by making it "worthless" for respondents to exceed the suggested retail prices. After reviewing legal and economic aspects of price fixing, the court concluded that State Oil's pricing scheme was a *per se* antitrust violation under Albrecht v. Herald Co., *supra*. Although the Court of Appeals characterized *Albrecht* as "unsound when decided" and "inconsistent with later decisions" of this Court, it felt constrained to follow that decision. In light of *Albrecht* and Atlantic Richfield Co. v. USA Petroleum Co., 495 U.S. 328 (1990) (ARCO), the court found that respondents could have suffered antitrust injury from not being able to adjust gasoline prices.

We granted certiorari to consider two questions, whether State Oil's conduct constitutes a per se violation of the Sherman Act and whether respondents are entitled to recover damages based on that conduct.

II

A

Although the Sherman Act, by its terms, prohibits every agreement "in restraint of trade," this Court has long recognized that Congress intended to outlaw only unreasonable restraints. See, *e.g.*, Arizona v. Maricopa County Medical Soc., 457 U.S. 332, 342–343 (1982) (citing United States v. Joint Traffic Assn., 171 U.S. 505 (1898)). As a consequence, most antitrust claims are analyzed under a "rule of reason," according to which the finder of fact must decide whether the questioned practice imposes an unreasonable restraint on competition, taking into account a variety of factors, including specific information about the relevant business, its condition before and after the restraint was imposed, and the restraint's history, nature, and effect. 457 U.S., at 343, and n. 13 (citing Board of Trade of Chicago v. United States, 246 U.S. 231, 238 (1918)).

Some types of restraints, however, have such predictable and pernicious anticompetitive effect, and such limited potential for procompetitive benefit, that they are deemed unlawful *per se*. Northern Pacific R. Co. v. United States, 356 U.S. 1, 5 (1958). Per se treatment is appropriate "[o]nce experience with a particular kind of restraint enables the Court to predict with confidence that the rule of reason will condemn it." Maricopa County, *supra*, at 344; see also Broadcast Music, Inc. v. Columbia Broadcasting System, Inc., 441 U.S. 1, 19, n. 33 (1979). Thus, we have expressed reluctance to adopt per se rules with regard to "restraints imposed in the context of business relationships where the economic impact of certain practices is not immediately obvious." FTC v. Indiana Federation of Dentists, 476 U.S. 447, 458–459 (1986).

A review of this Court's decisions leading up to and beyond *Albrecht* is relevant to our assessment of the continuing validity of the *per se* rule established in *Albrecht*. Beginning with Dr. Miles Medical Co. v. John D. Park & Sons Co., 220 U.S. 373 (1911), the Court recognized the illegality of agreements under which manufacturers or suppliers set the minimum resale prices to be charged by their distributors. By 1940, the Court broadly declared all business combinations "formed for the purpose and with the effect of raising, depressing, fixing, pegging, or stabilizing the price of a commodity in interstate or foreign commerce" illegal *per se*. United States v. Socony–Vacuum Oil Co., 310 U.S. 150, 223 (1940). Accordingly, the Court condemned an agreement between two affiliated liquor distillers to limit the maximum price charged by retailers in Kiefer–Stewart Co. v. Joseph E. Seagram & Sons, Inc., 340 U.S. 211 (1951), noting that agreements to fix maximum prices, "no less than those to fix minimum prices, cripple the freedom of traders and thereby restrain their ability to sell in accordance with their own judgment." *Id.*, at 213.

In subsequent cases, the Court's attention turned to arrangements through which suppliers imposed restrictions on dealers with respect to matters other than resale price. In White Motor Co. v. United States, 372 U.S. 253 (1963), the Court considered the validity of a manufacturer's assignment of exclusive territories to its distributors and dealers. The Court determined that too little was known about the competitive impact of such vertical limitations to warrant treating them as *per se* unlawful. *Id.*, at 263. Four years later, in United States v. Arnold, Schwinn & Co., 388 U.S. 365 (1967), the Court reconsidered the status of exclusive dealer territories and held that, upon the transfer of title to goods to a distributor, a supplier's imposition of territorial restrictions on the distributor was "so obviously destructive of competition" as to constitute a *per se* violation of the Sherman Act. *Id.*, at 379. In *Schwinn*, the Court acknowledged that some vertical restrictions, such as the conferral of territorial rights or franchises, could have procompetitive benefits by allowing smaller enterprises to compete, and that such restrictions might avert vertical integration in the distribution process. *Id.*, at 379–380. The Court drew the line, however, at permitting manufacturers to control product marketing once dominion over the goods had passed to dealers. *Id.*, at 380.

Albrecht, decided the following Term, involved a newspaper publisher who had granted exclusive territories to independent carriers subject to their adherence to a maximum price on resale of the newspapers to the public. Influenced by its decisions in *Socony–Vacuum, Kiefer–Stewart,* and *Schwinn*, the Court concluded that it was per se unlawful for the publisher to fix the maximum resale price of its newspapers. 390 U.S., at 152–154. The Court acknowledged that "[m]aximum and minimum price fixing may have different consequences in many situations," but nonetheless condemned maximum price fixing for "substituting the perhaps erroneous judgment of a seller for the forces of the competitive market." *Id.*, at 152.

Albrecht was animated in part by the fear that vertical maximum price fixing could allow suppliers to discriminate against certain dealers, restrict the services that dealers could afford to offer customers, or disguise minimum price fixing schemes. *Id.*, at 152–153. The Court rejected the notion (both on the record of that case and in the abstract) that, because the newspaper publisher "granted exclusive territories, a price ceiling was necessary to protect the public from price gouging by dealers who had monopoly power in their own territories." *Id.*, at 153.

In a vigorous dissent, Justice Harlan asserted that the majority had erred in equating the effects of maximum and minimum price fixing. *Id.*, at 156–168 (Harlan, J., dissenting). Justice Harlan pointed out that, because the majority was establishing a *per se* rule, the proper inquiry was "not whether dictation of maximum prices is ever illegal, but whether it is always illegal." *Id.*, at 165–166. He also faulted the majority for conclusively listing "certain unfortunate consequences that maximum price dictation might have in other cases," even as it rejected evidence that the publisher's practice of fixing maximum prices counteracted potentially anticompetitive actions by its distributors. *Id.*, at 165. Justice Stewart also dissented, asserting that the publisher's maximum price fixing scheme should be properly viewed as promoting competition, because it protected consumers from dealers such as Albrecht, who, as "the only person who could sell for home delivery the city's only daily morning newspaper," was "a monopolist within his own territory." *Id.*, at 168 (Stewart, J., dissenting).

Nine years later, in Continental T.V., Inc. v. GTE Sylvania Inc., 433 U.S. 36 (1977), the Court overruled *Schwinn*, thereby rejecting application of a *per se* rule in the context of vertical nonprice restrictions. The Court acknowledged the principle of *stare decisis*, but explained that the need for clarification in the law justified reconsideration of *Schwinn*:

> "Since its announcement, *Schwinn* has been the subject of continuing controversy and confusion, both in the scholarly journals and in the federal courts. The great weight of scholarly opinion has been critical of the decision, and a number of the federal courts confronted with analogous vertical restrictions have sought to limit its reach. In our view, the experience of the past 10 years should be brought to bear on this subject of considerable commercial importance." 433 U.S., at 47–49 (footnotes omitted).

The Court considered the historical context of *Schwinn*, noting that *Schwinn*'s per se rule against vertical nonprice restrictions came only four years after the Court had refused to endorse a similar rule in White Motor Co., and that the decision neither explained the "sudden change in position," nor referred to the accepted requirements for *per se* violations set forth in Northern Pacific R. Co., 433 U.S., at 51–52. The Court then reviewed scholarly works supporting the economic utility of vertical nonprice restraints. See *id.*, at 54–57 (citing, *e.g.*, Posner, Antitrust Policy and the Supreme Court: An Analysis of the Restricted Distribution, Horizontal Merger and Potential Competition Decisions, 75 Colum.L.Rev. 282 (1975); Preston, Restrictive Distribution Arrangements: Economic Analysis and Public Policy Standards, 30 Law & Contemp. Prob. 506 (1965)). The Court concluded that, because "departure from the rule of reason standard must be based upon demonstrable economic effect rather than as in Schwinn upon formalistic line drawing," the appropriate course would be "to return to the rule of reason that governed vertical restrictions prior to Schwinn." *GTE Sylvania, supra*, at 58–59.

In *GTE Sylvania*, the Court declined to comment on *Albrecht*'s *per se* treatment of vertical maximum price restrictions, noting that the issue "involve[d] significantly different questions of analysis and policy." 433 U.S., at 51, n. 18. Subsequent decisions of the Court, however, have hinted that the analytical underpinnings of *Albrecht* were substantially weakened by *GTE Sylvania*. We noted in *Maricopa County* that vertical restraints are generally more defensible than horizontal restraints. See 457 U.S., at 348, n. 18. And we explained in 324 Liquor Corp. v. Duffy, 479 U.S. 335, 341–342 (1987), that decisions such as *GTE Sylvania* "recognize the possibility that a vertical restraint imposed by a single manufacturer or wholesaler may stimulate interbrand competition even as it reduces intrabrand competition."

Most recently, in *ARCO*, 495 U.S. 328 (1990), although *Albrecht*'s continuing validity was not squarely before the Court, ... we specifically acknowledged that vertical maximum price fixing "may have procompetitive interbrand effects," and pointed out that, in the wake of *GTE Sylvania*, "[t]he procompetitive potential of a vertical maximum price restraint is more evident ... than it was when *Albrecht* was decided, because exclusive territorial arrangements and other nonprice restrictions were unlawful *per se* in 1968." 495 U.S., at 344, n. 13 (citing several commentators identifying procompetitive effects of vertical maximum price fixing, including, *e.g.*, P. Areeda & H. Hovenkamp, Antitrust Law ¶ 340.30b, p. 378, n. 24 (1988 Supp.); Blair & Harrison, Rethinking Antitrust Injury, 42 Vand. L.Rev. 1539, 1553 (1989); Easterbrook, Maximum Price Fixing, 48 U. Chi. L.Rev. 886, 887–890 (1981)).

B

Thus, our reconsideration of *Albrecht*'s continuing validity is informed by several of our decisions, as well as a considerable body of scholarship discussing the effects of vertical restraints. Our analysis is also guided by our general view that the primary purpose of the antitrust laws is to protect interbrand competition. See, *e.g.*, Business Electronics Corp. v. Sharp Electronics Corp., 485 U.S. 717, 726 (1988). "Low prices," we have explained, "benefit consumers regardless of how those prices are set, and so long as they are above predatory levels, they do not threaten competition." *ARCO, supra*, at 340. Our interpretation of the Sherman Act also incorporates the notion that condemnation of practices resulting in lower prices to consumers is "especially costly" because "cutting prices in order to increase business often is the very essence of competition." Matsushita Elec. Industrial Co. v. Zenith Radio Corp., 475 U.S. 574, 594 (1986).

So informed, we find it difficult to maintain that vertically-imposed maximum prices could harm consumers or competition to the extent necessary to justify their *per se* invalidation. As Chief Judge Posner wrote for the Court of Appeals in this case:

> "As for maximum resale price fixing, unless the supplier is a monopsonist he cannot squeeze his dealers' margins below a competitive level; the attempt to do so would just drive the dealers into the arms of a competing supplier. A supplier might, however, fix a maximum resale price in order to prevent his dealers from exploiting a monopoly position.... [S]uppose that State Oil, perhaps to encourage ... dealer services ... has spaced its dealers sufficiently far apart to limit competition among them (or even given each of them an exclusive territory); and suppose further that Union 76 is a sufficiently distinctive and popular brand to give the dealers in it at least a modicum of monopoly power. Then State Oil might want to place a ceiling on the dealers' resale prices in order to prevent them from exploiting that monopoly power fully. It would do this not out of disinterested malice, but in its commercial self-interest. The higher the price at which gasoline is resold, the smaller the volume sold, and so the lower the profit to the supplier if the higher profit per gallon at the higher price is being snared by the dealer." 93 F.3d, at 1362.

See also R. Bork, The Antitrust Paradox 281–282 (1978) ("There could, of course, be no anticonsumer effect from [the type of price fixing considered in Albrecht], and one suspects that the paper has a legitimate interest in keeping subscriber prices down in order to increase circulation and maximize revenues from advertising").

We recognize that the *Albrecht* decision presented a number of theoretical justifications for a *per se* rule against vertical maximum price fixing. But criticism of those premises abounds. The *Albrecht* decision was grounded in the fear that maximum price fixing by suppliers could interfere with dealer freedom. 390 U.S., at 152. In response, as one commentator has pointed out, "the ban on maximum resale price limitations declared in *Albrecht* in the name of 'dealer freedom' has actually prompted many suppliers to integrate forward into distribution, thus eliminating the very independent trader for whom *Albrecht* professed solicitude." 7 P. Areeda, Antitrust Law, ¶ 1635, p. 395 (1989). For example, integration in the newspaper industry since *Albrecht* has given rise to litigation between independent distributors and publishers. See P. Areeda & H. Hovenkamp, Antitrust Law ¶ 729.7, pp. 599–614 (1996 Supp.).

The *Albrecht* Court also expressed the concern that maximum prices may be set too low for dealers to offer consumers essential or desired services. 390 U.S., at 152–153. But such conduct, by driving away customers, would seem likely to harm manufacturers as well as dealers and consumers, making it unlikely that a supplier would set such a price as a matter of business judgment. See, *e.g.*, Lopatka, Stephen Breyer and Modern Antitrust: A Snug Fit, 40 Antitrust Bull. 1, 60 (1995); Blair & Lang, Albrecht After ARCO: Maximum Resale Price Fixing Moves Toward the Rule of Reason, 44 Vand. L.Rev. 1007, 1034 (1991). In addition, Albrecht noted that vertical maximum price fixing could effectively channel distribution through large or specially-advantaged dealers. 390 U.S., at 153. It is unclear, however, that a supplier would profit from limiting its market by excluding potential dealers. See, *e.g.*, Easterbrook, *supra*, at 905–908. Further, although vertical maximum price fixing might limit the viability of inefficient dealers, that consequence is not necessarily harmful to competition and consumers. See, *e.g.*, *id.*, *supra*, at 907; Lopatka, *supra*, at 60.

Finally, *Albrecht* reflected the Court's fear that maximum price fixing could be used to disguise arrangements to fix minimum prices, 390 U.S. at 153, which remain illegal *per se*. Although we have acknowledged the possibility that maximum pricing might mask minimum pricing, see *Maricopa County*, 457 U.S., at 348, we believe that such conduct as with the other concerns articulated in *Albrecht* can be appropriately recognized and punished under the rule of reason. See, *e.g.*, Easterbrook, at 901–904; see also Pitofsky, In Defense of Discounters: The No–Frills Case for a Per Se Rule Against Vertical Price Fixing, 71 Geo. L.J. 1487, 1490, n. 17 (1983).

Not only are the potential injuries cited in *Albrecht* less serious than the Court imagined, the *per se* rule established therein could in fact exacerbate problems related to the unrestrained exercise of market power by monopolist-dealers. Indeed, both courts and antitrust scholars have noted that *Albrecht*'s rule may actually harm consumers and manufacturers. See, *e.g.*, Caribe BMW, Inc. v. Bayerische Motoren Werke Aktiengesellschaft, 19 F.3d 745, 753 (C.A.1 1994) (Breyer, C.J.); Areeda, ¶ 1636a, at 395; G. Mathewson & R. Winter, Competition Policy and Vertical Exchange 13–14 (1985). Other commentators have also explained that *Albrecht*'s *per se* rule has even more potential for deleterious effect on competition after our decision in GTE Sylvania, because, now that vertical nonprice restrictions are not unlawful *per se*, the likelihood of dealer monopoly power is increased. See, *e.g.*, Easterbrook, *supra*, at 890, n. 20; see also ARCO, 495 U.S., at 343, n. 13. We do not intend to suggest that dealers generally possess sufficient market power to exploit a monopoly situation. Such retail market power may in fact be uncommon. See, *e.g.*, *Business Electronics*, 485 U.S., at 727, n. 2; *GTE Sylvania*, 433 U.S. at 54. Nor do we hold that a ban on vertical maximum price fixing inevitably has anticompetitive consequences in the exclusive dealer context.

After reconsidering *Albrecht*'s rationale and the substantial criticism the decision has received, however, we conclude that there is insufficient economic justification for *per se* invalidation of vertical maximum price fixing. That is so not only because it is difficult to accept the assumptions underlying *Albrecht*, but also because *Albrecht* has little or no relevance to ongoing enforcement of the Sherman Act. See Copperweld Corp. v. Independence Tube Corp., 467 U.S. 752, 777, and n. 25 (1984). Moreover, neither the parties nor any of the amici curiae have called our attention to any cases in which enforcement efforts have been directed solely against the conduct encompassed by *Albrecht's per se* rule.

Respondents argue that reconsideration of *Albrecht* should require "persuasive, expert testimony establishing that the *per se* rule has distorted the market." Their reasoning ignores the fact that *Albrecht* itself relied solely upon hypothetical effects of vertical maximum price fixing. Further, *Albrecht*'s dire predictions have not been borne out, even though manufacturers and suppliers appear to have fashioned schemes to get around the *per se* rule against vertical maximum price fixing. In these circumstances, it is the retention of the rule of *Albrecht*, and not, as respondents would have it, the rule's elimination, that lacks adequate justification. See, *e.g.*, *GTE Sylvania, supra*, at 58–59.

Respondents' reliance on Toolson v. New York Yankees, Inc., 346 U.S. 356 (1953) (*per curiam*), and Flood v. Kuhn, 407 U.S. 258 (1972), is similarly misplaced, because those decisions are clearly inapposite, having to do with the antitrust exemption for professional baseball, which this Court has described as "an aberration . . . rest[ing] on a recognition and an acceptance of baseball's unique characteristics and needs," *id.*, at 282. In the context of this case, we infer little meaning from the fact that Congress has not reacted legislatively to *Albrecht*. In any event, the history of various legislative proposals regarding price fixing seems neither clearly to support nor to denounce the *per se* rule of *Albrecht*. Respondents are of course free to seek legislative protection from gasoline suppliers of the sort embodied in the Petroleum Marketing Practices Act, 92 Stat. 322, 15 U.S.C. § 2801 *et seq.* For the reasons we have noted, however, the remedy for respondents' dispute with State Oil should not come in the form of a *per se* rule affecting the conduct of the entire marketplace.

C

Despite what Chief Judge Posner aptly described as *Albrecht*'s "infirmities, [and] its increasingly wobbly, moth-eaten foundations," there remains the question whether *Albrecht* deserves continuing respect under the doctrine of *stare decisis*. The Court of Appeals was correct in applying that principle despite disagreement with *Albrecht*, for it is this Court's prerogative alone to overrule one of its precedents.

We approach the reconsideration of decisions of this Court with the utmost caution. *Stare decisis* reflects "a policy judgment that 'in most matters it is more important that the applicable rule of law be settled than that it be settled right.'" Agostini v. Felton, 521 U.S. 203, 235 (1997) (quoting Burnet v. Coronado Oil & Gas Co., 285 U.S. 393, 406 (1932) (Brandeis, J., dissenting)). It "is the preferred course because it promotes the evenhanded, predictable, and consistent development of legal principles, fosters reliance on judicial decisions, and contributes to the actual and perceived integrity of the judicial process." Payne v. Tennessee, 501 U.S. 808, 827 (1991). This Court has expressed its reluctance to overrule decisions involving statutory interpretation, and has acknowledged that *stare decisis* concerns are at their acme in cases involving property and contract rights, see, *e.g.*, *Payne*, 501 U.S., at 828. Both of those concerns are arguably relevant in this case.

But *"[s]tare decisis* is not an inexorable command." *Ibid*. In the area of antitrust law, there is a competing interest, well-represented in this Court's decisions, in recognizing and adapting to changed circumstances and the lessons of accumulated experience. Thus, the general presumption that legislative changes should be left to Congress has less force with respect to the Sherman Act in light of the accepted view that Congress "expected the courts to give shape to the statute's broad mandate by drawing on common-law tradition." National Soc. of Professional Engineers v. United States, 435 U.S. 679, 688 (1978). As we have explained, the term "restraint of trade," as used in § 1, also "invokes the common law itself, and not merely the static content that the common law had assigned to the term in 1890." *Business Electronics*, 485 U.S., at 732; see also GTE Sylvania, 433 U.S., at 53, n. 21; McNally v. United States, 483 U.S. 350, 372–373 (1987) (Stevens, J., dissenting). Accordingly, this Court has reconsidered its decisions construing the Sherman Act when the theoretical underpinnings of those decisions are called into serious question. See, *e.g., Copperweld Corp., supra*, at 777; *GTE Sylvania, supra*, at 47–49; Tigner v. Texas, 310 U.S. 141, 147 (1940).

Although we do not "lightly assume that the economic realities underlying earlier decisions have changed, or that earlier judicial perceptions of those realities were in error," we have noted that "different sorts of agreements" may amount to restraints of trade "in varying times and circumstances," and "[i]t would make no sense to create out of the single term 'restraint of trade' a chronologically schizoid statute, in which a 'rule of reason' evolves with new circumstances and new wisdom, but a line of *per se* illegality remains forever fixed where it was." *Business Electronics, supra*, at 731–732. Just as *Schwinn* was "the subject of continuing controversy and confusion" under the "great weight" of scholarly criticism, *GTE Sylvania, supra*, at 47–48, *Albrecht* has been widely criticized since its inception. With the views underlying *Albrecht* eroded by this Court's precedent, there is not much of that decision to salvage.

Although the rule of *Albrecht* has been in effect for some time, the inquiry we must undertake requires considering " 'the effect of the antitrust laws upon vertical distributional restraints in the American economy today.' " *GTE Sylvania, supra*, at 53, n. 21, (quoting *Schwinn*, 388 U.S., at 392 (Stewart, J., concurring in part and dissenting in part)). As the Court noted in *ARCO*, 495 U.S., at 336, n. 6, there has not been another case since *Albrecht* in which this Court has "confronted an unadulterated vertical, maximum-price-fixing arrangement." Now that we confront *Albrecht* directly, we find its conceptual foundations gravely weakened.

In overruling *Albrecht*, we of course do not hold that all vertical maximum price fixing is *per se* lawful. Instead, vertical maximum price fixing, like the majority of commercial arrangements subject to the antitrust laws, should be evaluated under the rule of reason. In our view, rule-of-reason analysis will effectively identify those situations in which vertical maximum price fixing amounts to anticompetitive conduct.

There remains the question whether respondents are entitled to recover damages based on State Oil's conduct. Although the Court of Appeals noted that "the district judge was right to conclude that if the rule of reason is applicable, Khan loses," 93 F.3d, at 1362, its consideration of this case was necessarily premised on *Albrecht*'s *per se* rule. Under the circumstances, the matter should be reviewed by the Court of Appeals in the first instance. We therefore vacate the judgment of the Court of Appeals and remand the case for further proceedings consistent with this opinion.

It is so ordered.

Leegin Creative Leather Products, Inc. v. PSKS, Inc.

Supreme Court of the United States, 2007.
551 U.S. 877, 127 S.Ct. 2705, 168 L.Ed.2d 623.

■ KENNEDY, J. In Dr. Miles Medical Co. v. John D. Park & Sons Co., 220 U.S. 373 (1911), the Court established the rule that it is *per se* illegal under § 1 of the Sherman Act . . . for a manufacturer to agree with its distributor to set the minimum price the distributor can charge for the manufacturer's goods. The question presented by the instant case is whether the Court should overrule the *per se* rule and allow resale price maintenance agreements to be judged by the rule of reason, the usual standard applied to determine if there is a violation of § 1. The Court has abandoned the rule of *per se* illegality for other vertical restraints a manufacturer imposes on its distributors. Respected economic analysts, furthermore, conclude that vertical price restraints can have procompetitive effects. We now hold that *Dr. Miles* should be overruled and that vertical price restraints are to be judged by the rule of reason.

I

Petitioner, Leegin Creative Leather Products, Inc. (Leegin), designs, manufactures, and distributes leather goods and accessories. In 1991, Leegin began to sell belts under the brand name "Brighton." The Brighton brand has now expanded into a variety of women's fashion accessories. It is sold across the United States in over 5,000 retail establishments, for the most part independent, small boutiques and specialty stores. Leegin's president, Jerry Kohl, also has an interest in about 70 stores that sell Brighton products. Leegin asserts that, at least for its products, small retailers treat customers better, provide customers more services, and make their shopping experience more satisfactory than do larger, often impersonal retailers. Kohl explained: "[W]e want the consumers to get a different experience than they get in Sam's Club or in Wal–Mart. And you can't get that kind of experience or support or customer service from a store like Wal–Mart."

Respondent, PSKS, Inc. (PSKS), operates Kay's Kloset, a women's apparel store in Lewisville, Texas. Kay's Kloset buys from about 75 different manufacturers and at one time sold the Brighton brand. It first started purchasing Brighton goods from Leegin in 1995. Once it began selling the brand, the store promoted Brighton. For example, it ran Brighton advertisements and had Brighton days in the store. Kay's Kloset became the destination retailer in the area to buy Brighton products. Brighton was the store's most important brand and once accounted for 40 to 50 percent of its profits.

In 1997, Leegin instituted the "Brighton Retail Pricing and Promotion Policy." Following the policy, Leegin refused to sell to retailers that discounted Brighton goods below suggested prices. The policy contained an exception for products not selling well that the retailer did not plan on reordering.... Leegin adopted the policy to give its retailers sufficient margins to provide customers the service central to its distribution strategy. It also expressed concern that discounting harmed Brighton's brand image and reputation.... [Leegin also instituted a complementary program under which retailers could become "Heart Stores." Kay's Kloset had that status for a time, but it later lost it.]

In December 2002, Leegin discovered Kay's Kloset had been marking down Brighton's entire line by 20 percent. Kay's Kloset contended it placed Brighton products on sale to compete with nearby retailers who also were undercutting Leegin's suggested prices. Leegin, nonetheless, requested that Kay's Kloset cease discounting. Its request refused, Leegin stopped selling to the store. The loss of the Brighton brand had a considerable negative impact on the store's revenue from sales.

PSKS sued Leegin in the United States District Court for the Eastern District of Texas. It alleged, among other claims, that Leegin had violated the antitrust laws by "enter[ing] into agreements with retailers to charge only those prices fixed by Leegin." *Id.*, at 1236. Leegin planned to introduce expert testimony describing the procompetitive effects of its pricing policy. The District Court excluded the testimony, relying on the *per se* rule established by *Dr. Miles*. At trial PSKS argued that the Heart Store program, among other things, demonstrated Leegin and its retailers had agreed to fix prices. Leegin responded that it had established a unilateral pricing policy lawful under § 1, which applies only to concerted action. See United States v. Colgate & Co., 250 U.S. 300 (1919). The jury agreed with PSKS and awarded it $1.2 million....

The Court of Appeals for the Fifth Circuit affirmed (*per curiam*). On appeal Leegin did not dispute that it had entered into vertical price-fixing agreements with its retailers. Rather, it contended that the rule of reason should have applied to those agreements. The Court of Appeals rejected this argument. *Id.*, at 466–467. It was correct to explain that it remained bound by *Dr. Miles* "[b]ecause [the Supreme] Court has consistently applied the *per se* rule to [vertical minimum price-fixing] agreements." On this premise the Court of Appeals held that the District Court did not abuse its discretion in excluding the testimony of Leegin's economic expert, for the *per se* rule rendered irrelevant any procompetitive justifications for Leegin's pricing policy. *Id.*, at 467. We granted certiorari to determine whether vertical minimum resale price maintenance agreements should continue to be treated as *per se* unlawful.

[handwritten margin note: 5th Cir: per se rule made any pro-competitive justifications irrelevant]

II

. . .

The rule of reason is the accepted standard for testing whether a practice restrains trade in violation of § 1. See *Texaco, supra*. . . . "Under this rule, the factfinder weighs all of the circumstances of a case in deciding whether a restrictive practice should be prohibited as imposing an unreasonable restraint on competition." Continental T. V., Inc. v. GTE Sylvania Inc., 433 U.S. 36, 49 (1977). Appropriate factors to take into account include "specific information about the relevant business" and "the restraint's history, nature, and effect." Khan, supra. . . . Whether the businesses involved have market power is a further, significant consideration. . . . In its design and function the rule distinguishes between restraints with anticompetitive effect that are harmful to the consumer and restraints stimulating competition that are in the consumer's best interest.

[handwritten margin note: explaining ROR]

The rule of reason does not govern all restraints. Some types "are deemed unlawful *per se*." . . . The *per se* rule, treating categories of restraints as necessarily illegal, eliminates the need to study the reasonableness of an individual restraint in light of the real market forces at work, . . . and, it must be acknowledged, the *per se* rule can give clear guidance for certain conduct. Restraints that are *per se* unlawful include horizontal agreements among competitors to fix prices. . . .

Resort to *per se* rules is confined to restraints, like those mentioned, "that would always or almost always tend to restrict competition and decrease output." *Business Electronics, supra*, at 723 (internal quotation marks omitted). To justify a *per se* prohibition a restraint must have "manifestly anticompetitive" effects, *GTE Sylvania, supra*, at 50, and "lack . . . any redeeming virtue," Northwest Wholesale Stationers, Inc. v. Pacific Stationery & Printing Co., 472 U.S. 284, 289 (1985) (internal quotation marks omitted).

[handwritten margin note: per se]

As a consequence, the *per se* rule is appropriate only after courts have had considerable experience with the type of restraint at issue, see Broadcast Music, Inc. v. Columbia Broadcasting System, Inc., 441 U.S. 1, 9 (1979), and only if courts can predict with confidence that it would be invalidated in all or almost all instances under the rule of reason, see Arizona v. Maricopa County Medical Soc., 457 U.S. 332, 344 (1982). It should come as no surprise, then, that "we have expressed reluctance to adopt *per se* rules with regard to restraints imposed in the context of business relationships where the economic impact of certain practices is not immediately obvious." *Khan, supra,* at 10, (internal quotation marks omitted).... And, as we have stated, a "departure from the rule-of-reason standard must be based upon demonstrable economic effect rather than ... upon formalistic line drawing." *GTE Sylvania, supra,* at 58–59.

III

The Court has interpreted Dr. Miles Medical Co. v. John D. Park & Sons Co., 220 U.S. 373 (1911), as establishing a *per se* rule against a vertical agreement between a manufacturer and its distributor to set minimum resale prices. See, *e.g.,* Monsanto Co. v. Spray–Rite Service Corp., 465 U.S. 752, 761 (1984). In *Dr. Miles* the plaintiff, a manufacturer of medicines, sold its products only to distributors who agreed to resell them at set prices. The Court found the manufacturer's control of resale prices to be unlawful. It relied on the common-law rule that "a general restraint upon alienation is ordinarily invalid." 220 U.S., at 404–405. The Court then explained that the agreements would advantage the distributors, not the manufacturer, and were analogous to a combination among competing distributors, which the law treated as void. *Id.,* at 407–408.

The reasoning of the Court's more recent jurisprudence has rejected the rationales on which *Dr. Miles* was based. By relying on the common-law rule against restraints on alienation, *id.,* at 404–405, the Court justified its decision based on "formalistic" legal doctrine rather than "demonstrable economic effect," *GTE Sylvania, supra,* at 58–59. The Court in *Dr. Miles* relied on a treatise published in 1628, but failed to discuss in detail the business reasons that would motivate a manufacturer situated in 1911 to make use of vertical price restraints. Yet the Sherman Act's use of "restraint of trade" "invokes the common law itself, ... not merely the static content that the common law had assigned to the term in 1890." *Business Electronics, supra,* at 732. The general restraint on alienation, especially in the age when then-Justice Hughes used the term, tended to evoke policy concerns extraneous to the question that controls here. Usually associated with land, not chattels, the rule arose from restrictions removing real property from the stream of commerce for generations. The Court should be cautious about putting dispositive weight on doctrines from antiquity but of slight relevance. We reaffirm that "the state of the common law 400 or even 100 years ago is irrelevant to the issue before us: the effect of the antitrust laws upon vertical distributional restraints in the American economy today." *GTE Sylvania,* 433 U.S., at 53, n. 21 (internal quotation marks omitted).

Dr. Miles, furthermore, treated vertical agreements a manufacturer makes with its distributors as analogous to a horizontal combination among competing distributors.... In later cases, however, the Court rejected the approach of reliance on rules governing horizontal restraints when defining rules applicable to vertical ones. See, *e.g., Business Electronics, supra,* at 734 (disclaiming the "notion of equivalence between the scope of horizontal *per se* illegality and that of vertical *per se* illegality"); *Maricopa*

County, supra, at 348, n. 18 (noting that "horizontal restraints are generally less defensible than vertical restraints"). Our recent cases formulate antitrust principles in accordance with the appreciated differences in economic effect between vertical and horizontal agreements, differences the *Dr. Miles* Court failed to consider.

The reasons upon which *Dr. Miles* relied do not justify a *per se* rule. As a consequence, it is necessary to examine, in the first instance, the economic effects of vertical agreements to fix minimum resale prices, and to determine whether the *per se* rule is nonetheless appropriate. . . .

A

Though each side of the debate can find sources to support its position, it suffices to say here that economics literature is replete with procompetitive justifications for a manufacturer's use of resale price maintenance. . . . Even those more skeptical of resale price maintenance acknowledge it can have procompetitive effects. See, *e.g.*, Brief for William S. Comanor et al. as *Amici Curiae* 3 ("[G]iven [the] diversity of effects [of resale price maintenance], one could reasonably take the position that a rule of reason rather than a *per se* approach is warranted"); F.M. Scherer & D. Ross, Industrial Market Structure and Economic Performance 558 (3d ed. 1990) (hereinafter Scherer & Ross) ("The overall balance between benefits and costs [of resale price maintenance] is probably close").

The few recent studies documenting the competitive effects of resale price maintenance also cast doubt on the conclusion that the practice meets the criteria for a *per se* rule. See T. Overstreet, Resale Price Maintenance: Economic Theories and Empirical Evidence 170 (1983) (hereinafter Overstreet) (noting that "[e]fficient uses of [resale price maintenance] are evidently not unusual or rare"); see also Ippolito, Resale Price Maintenance: Empirical Evidence From Litigation, 34 J. Law & Econ. 263, 292–293 (1991) (hereinafter Ippolito).

The justifications for vertical price restraints are similar to those for other vertical restraints. . . . Minimum resale price maintenance can stimulate interbrand competition—the competition among manufacturers selling different brands of the same type of product—by reducing intrabrand competition—the competition among retailers selling the same brand. The promotion of interbrand competition is important because "the primary purpose of the antitrust laws is to protect [this type of] competition." *Khan*, 522 U.S., at 15. A single manufacturer's use of vertical price restraints tends to eliminate intrabrand price competition; this in turn encourages retailers to invest in tangible or intangible services or promotional efforts that aid the manufacturer's position as against rival manufacturers. Resale price maintenance also has the potential to give consumers more options so that they can choose among low-price, low-service brands; high-price, high-service brands; and brands that fall in between.

Absent vertical price restraints, the retail services that enhance interbrand competition might be underprovided. This is because discounting retailers can free ride on retailers who furnish services and then capture some of the increased demand those services generate.... Consumers might learn, for example, about the benefits of a manufacturer's product from a retailer that invests in fine showrooms, offers product demonstrations, or hires and trains knowledgeable employees. R. Posner, Antitrust Law 172–173 (2d ed. 2001) (hereinafter Posner). Or consumers might decide to buy the product because they see it in a retail establishment that has a reputation for selling high-quality merchandise. Marvel & McCafferty, Resale Price Maintenance and Quality Certification, 15 Rand J. Econ. 346, 347–349 (1984) (hereinafter Marvel & McCafferty). If the consumer can then buy the product from a retailer that discounts because it has not spent capital providing services or developing a quality reputation, the high-service retailer will lose sales to the discounter, forcing it to cut back its services to a level lower than consumers would otherwise prefer. Minimum resale price maintenance alleviates the problem because it prevents the discounter from undercutting the service provider. With price competition decreased, the manufacturer's retailers compete among themselves over services.

Resale price maintenance, in addition, can increase interbrand competition by facilitating market entry for new firms and brands. "[N]ew manufacturers and manufacturers entering new markets can use the restrictions in order to induce competent and aggressive retailers to make the kind of investment of capital and labor that is often required in the distribution of products unknown to the consumer." *GTE Sylvania, supra,* at 55; see Marvel & McCafferty 349 (noting that reliance on a retailer's reputation "will decline as the manufacturer's brand becomes better known, so that [resale price maintenance] may be particularly important as a competitive device for new entrants"). New products and new brands are essential to a dynamic economy, and if markets can be penetrated by using resale price maintenance there is a procompetitive effect.

Resale price maintenance can also increase interbrand competition by encouraging retailer services that would not be provided even absent free riding. It may be difficult and inefficient for a manufacturer to make and enforce a contract with a retailer specifying the different services the retailer must perform. Offering the retailer a guaranteed margin and threatening termination if it does not live up to expectations may be the most efficient way to expand the manufacturer's market share by inducing the retailer's performance and allowing it to use its own initiative and experience in providing valuable services....

B

While vertical agreements setting minimum resale prices can have procompetitive justifications, they may have anticompetitive effects in other cases; and unlawful price fixing, designed solely to obtain monopoly profits, is an ever present temptation. Resale price maintenance may, for example, facilitate a manufacturer cartel.... An unlawful cartel will seek to discover if some manufacturers are undercutting the cartel's fixed prices.

Resale price maintenance could assist the cartel in identifying price-cutting manufacturers who benefit from the lower prices they offer. Resale price maintenance, furthermore, could discourage a manufacturer from cutting prices to retailers with the concomitant benefit of cheaper prices to consumers. . . .

Vertical price restraints also "might be used to organize cartels at the retailer level.". . . . A group of retailers might collude to fix prices to consumers and then compel a manufacturer to aid the unlawful arrangement with resale price maintenance. In that instance the manufacturer does not establish the practice to stimulate services or to promote its brand but to give inefficient retailers higher profits. Retailers with better distribution systems and lower cost structures would be prevented from charging lower prices by the agreement. . . . Historical examples suggest this possibility is a legitimate concern. . . .

retail cartels

A horizontal cartel among competing manufacturers or competing retailers that decreases output or reduces competition in order to increase price is, and ought to be, *per se* unlawful. See *Texaco*, 547 U.S., at 5; *GTE Sylvania*, 433 U.S., at 58, n. 28. To the extent a vertical agreement setting minimum resale prices is entered upon to facilitate either type of cartel, it, too, would need to be held unlawful under the rule of reason. This type of agreement may also be useful evidence for a plaintiff attempting to prove the existence of a horizontal cartel.

Resale price maintenance, furthermore, can be abused by a powerful manufacturer or retailer. A dominant retailer, for example, might request resale price maintenance to forestall innovation in distribution that decreases costs. A manufacturer might consider it has little choice but to accommodate the retailer's demands for vertical price restraints if the manufacturer believes it needs access to the retailer's distribution network. See Overstreet 31; 8 P. Areeda & H. Hovenkamp, Antitrust Law 47 (2d ed. 2004) (hereinafter Areeda & Hovenkamp); cf. Toys "R" Us, Inc. v. FTC, 221 F.3d 928, 937–938 (C.A.7 2000). A manufacturer with market power, by comparison, might use resale price maintenance to give retailers an incentive not to sell the products of smaller rivals or new entrants. . . . As should be evident, the potential anticompetitive consequences of vertical price restraints must not be ignored or underestimated.

potential for abuse

C

Notwithstanding the risks of unlawful conduct, it cannot be stated with any degree of confidence that resale price maintenance "always or almost always tend[s] to restrict competition and decrease output." . . . Vertical agreements establishing minimum resale prices can have either procompetitive or anticompetitive effects, depending upon the circumstances in which they are formed. And although the empirical evidence on the topic is limited, it does not suggest efficient uses of the agreements are infrequent or hypothetical. . . . As the rule would proscribe a significant amount of procompetitive conduct, these agreements appear ill suited for *per se* condemnation.

Respondent contends, nonetheless, that vertical price restraints should be *per se* unlawful because of the administrative convenience of *per se* rules. See, *e.g., GTE Sylvania, supra*, at 50, n. 16 (noting "*per se* rules tend to provide guidance to the business community and to minimize the burdens on litigants and the judicial system"). That argument suggests *per se* illegality is the rule rather than the exception. This misinterprets our antitrust law. *Per se* rules may decrease administrative costs, but that is only part of the equation. Those rules can be counterproductive. They can increase the total cost of the antitrust system by prohibiting procompetitive conduct the antitrust laws should encourage. See Easterbrook, Vertical Arrangements and the Rule of Reason, 53 Antitrust L.J. 135, 158 (1984) (hereinafter Easterbrook). They also may increase litigation costs by promoting frivolous suits against legitimate practices. The Court has thus explained that administrative "advantages are not sufficient in themselves to justify the creation of *per se* rules," *GTE Sylvania*, 433 U.S., at 50, n. 16, and has relegated their use to restraints that are "manifestly anticompetitive," *id.*, at 49–50. Were the Court now to conclude that vertical price restraints should be *per se* illegal based on administrative costs, we would undermine, if not overrule, the traditional "demanding standards" for adopting *per se* rules. *Id.*, at 50. Any possible reduction in administrative costs cannot alone justify the *Dr. Miles* rule.

Respondent also argues the *per se* rule is justified because a vertical price restraint can lead to higher prices for the manufacturer's goods.... For, as has been indicated already, the antitrust laws are designed primarily to protect interbrand competition, from which lower prices can later result.... The Court, moreover, has evaluated other vertical restraints under the rule of reason even though prices can be increased in the course of promoting procompetitive effects.... And resale price maintenance may reduce prices if manufacturers have resorted to costlier alternatives of controlling resale prices that are not *per se* unlawful.

Respondent's argument, furthermore, overlooks that, in general, the interests of manufacturers and consumers are aligned with respect to retailer profit margins. The difference between the price a manufacturer charges retailers and the price retailers charge consumers represents part of the manufacturer's cost of distribution, which, like any other cost, the manufacturer usually desires to minimize.... A manufacturer has no incentive to overcompensate retailers with unjustified margins. The retailers, not the manufacturer, gain from higher retail prices. The manufacturer often loses; interbrand competition reduces its competitiveness and market share because consumers will "substitute a different brand of the same product." ... As a general matter, therefore, a single manufacturer will desire to set minimum resale prices only if the "increase in demand resulting from enhanced service ... will more than offset a negative impact on demand of a higher retail price." ...

The implications of respondent's position are far reaching. Many decisions a manufacturer makes and carries out through concerted action can lead to higher prices. A manufacturer might, for example, contract with different suppliers to obtain better inputs that improve product quality. Or it might hire an advertising agency to promote awareness of its goods. Yet no one would think these actions violate the Sherman Act because they lead to higher prices. The antitrust laws do not require manufacturers to produce generic goods that consumers do not know about or want. The manufacturer strives to improve its product quality or to promote its brand because it believes this conduct will lead to increased demand despite higher prices. The same can hold true for resale price maintenance.

ROR Factors

Resale price maintenance, it is true, does have economic dangers. If the rule of reason were to apply to vertical price restraints, courts would have to be diligent in eliminating their anticompetitive uses from the market. This is a realistic objective, and certain factors are relevant to the inquiry. For example, the number of manufacturers that make use of the practice in a given industry can provide important instruction. When only a few manufacturers lacking market power adopt the practice, there is little likelihood it is facilitating a manufacturer cartel, for a cartel then can be undercut by rival manufacturers. . . . Likewise, a retailer cartel is unlikely when only a single manufacturer in a competitive market uses resale price maintenance. Interbrand competition would divert consumers to lower priced substitutes and eliminate any gains to retailers from their price-fixing agreement over a single brand. . . . Resale price maintenance should be subject to more careful scrutiny, by contrast, if many competing manufacturers adopt the practice. . . .

1

The source of the restraint may also be an important consideration. If there is evidence retailers were the impetus for a vertical price restraint, there is a greater likelihood that the restraint facilitates a retailer cartel or supports a dominant, inefficient retailer. . . . If, by contrast, a manufacturer adopted the policy independent of retailer pressure, the restraint is less likely to promote anticompetitive conduct. . . . A manufacturer also has an incentive to protest inefficient retailer-induced price restraints because they can harm its competitive position.

2

As a final matter, that a dominant manufacturer or retailer can abuse resale price maintenance for anticompetitive purposes may not be a serious concern unless the relevant entity has market power. If a retailer lacks market power, manufacturers likely can sell their goods through rival retailers. . . . And if a manufacturer lacks market power, there is less likelihood it can use the practice to keep competitors away from distribution outlets.

3

The rule of reason is designed and used to eliminate anticompetitive transactions from the market. This standard principle applies to vertical price restraints. A party alleging injury from a vertical agreement setting minimum resale prices will have, as a general matter, the information and resources available to show the existence of the agreement and its scope of operation. As courts gain experience considering the effects of these restraints by applying the rule of reason over the course of decisions, they can establish the litigation structure to ensure the rule operates to eliminate anticompetitive restraints from the market and to provide more guidance to businesses. Courts can, for example, devise rules over time for offering proof, or even presumptions where justified, to make the rule of reason a fair and efficient way to prohibit anticompetitive restraints and to promote procompetitive ones.

For all of the foregoing reasons, we think that were the Court considering the issue as an original matter, the rule of reason, not a *per se* rule of unlawfulness, would be the appropriate standard to judge vertical price restraints.

IV

We do not write on a clean slate, for the decision in *Dr. Miles* is almost a century old. So there is an argument for its retention on the basis of *stare decisis* alone. Even if Dr. Miles established an erroneous rule, *"[s]tare decisis* reflects a policy judgment that in most matters it is more important that the applicable rule of law be settled than that it be settled right." *Khan*, 522 U.S., at 20 (internal quotation marks omitted). And concerns about maintaining settled law are strong when the question is one of statutory interpretation. . . .

Stare decisis is not as significant in this case, however, because the issue before us is the scope of the Sherman Act. . . . From the beginning the Court has treated the Sherman Act as a common-law statute. See National Soc. of Professional Engineers v. United States, 435 U.S. 679, 688 (1978); see also Northwest Airlines, Inc. v. Transport Workers, 451 U.S. 77, 98, n. 42 (1981) ("In antitrust, the federal courts . . . act more as common-law courts than in other areas governed by federal statute"). Just as the common law adapts to modern understanding and greater experience, so too does the Sherman Act's prohibition on "restraint[s] of trade" evolve to meet the dynamics of present economic conditions. The case-by-case adjudication contemplated by the rule of reason has implemented this common-law approach. . . . Likewise, the boundaries of the doctrine of *per se* illegality should not be immovable. For "[i]t would make no sense to create out of the single term 'restraint of trade' a chronologically schizoid statute, in which a 'rule of reason' evolves with new circumstance and new wisdom, but a line of *per se* illegality remains forever fixed where it was." *Business Electronics*, 485 U.S., at 732.

A

Stare decisis, we conclude, does not compel our continued adherence to the *per se* rule against vertical price restraints. As discussed earlier, respected authorities in the economics literature suggest the *per se* rule is inappropriate, and there is now widespread agreement that resale price maintenance can have procompetitive effects. See, *e.g.*, Brief for Economists as *Amici Curiae* 16. It is also significant that both the Department of Justice and the Federal Trade Commission—the antitrust enforcement agencies with the ability to assess the long-term impacts of resale price maintenance—have recommended that this Court replace the *per se* rule with the traditional rule of reason. See Brief for United States as *Amicus*

Curiae 6. In the antitrust context the fact that a decision has been "called into serious question" justifies our reevaluation of it. . . .

Other considerations reinforce the conclusion that *Dr. Miles* should be overturned. Of most relevance, "we have overruled our precedents when subsequent cases have undermined their doctrinal underpinnings." Dickerson v. United States, 530 U.S. 428, 443 (2000). The Court's treatment of vertical restraints has progressed away from *Dr. Miles'* strict approach. We have distanced ourselves from the opinion's rationales. . . . This is unsurprising, for the case was decided not long after enactment of the Sherman Act when the Court had little experience with antitrust analysis. Only eight years after *Dr. Miles*, moreover, the Court reined in the decision by holding that a manufacturer can announce suggested resale prices and refuse to deal with distributors who do not follow them. *Colgate*, 250 U.S., at 307–308.

In more recent cases the Court, following a common-law approach, has continued to temper, limit, or overrule once strict prohibitions on vertical restraints. In 1977, the Court overturned the *per se* rule for vertical nonprice restraints, adopting the rule of reason in its stead. *GTE Sylvania*, 433 U.S., at 57–59 (overruling United States v. Arnold, Schwinn & Co., 388 U.S. 365 (1967)); see also 433 U.S., at 58, n. 29 (noting "that the advantages of vertical restrictions should not be limited to the categories of new entrants and failing firms"). While the Court in a footnote in *GTE Sylvania* suggested that differences between vertical price and nonprice restraints could support different legal treatment, see 433 U.S., at 51, n. 18, the central part of the opinion relied on authorities and arguments that find unequal treatment "difficult to justify," *id.*, at 69–70 (White, J., concurring in judgment).

Continuing in this direction, in two cases in the 1980's the Court defined legal rules to limit the reach of *Dr. Miles* and to accommodate the doctrines enunciated in *GTE Sylvania* and *Colgate*. See *Business Electronics, supra*, at 726–728, *Monsanto*, 465 U.S., at 763–764. In *Monsanto*, the Court required that antitrust plaintiffs alleging a § 1 price-fixing conspiracy must present evidence tending to exclude the possibility a manufacturer and its distributors acted in an independent manner. *Id.*, at 764. Unlike Justice Brennan's concurrence, which rejected arguments that *Dr. Miles* should be overruled, see 465 U.S., at 769, the Court "decline[d] to reach the question" whether vertical agreements fixing resale prices always should be unlawful because neither party suggested otherwise, *id.*, at 761–762, n. 7. In *Business Electronics* the Court further narrowed the scope of *Dr. Miles*. It held that the *per se* rule applied only to specific agreements over price levels and not to an agreement between a manufacturer and a distributor to terminate a price-cutting distributor. 485 U.S., at 726–727, 735–736.

Most recently, in 1997, after examining the issue of vertical maximum price-fixing agreements in light of commentary and real experience, the Court overruled a 29–year–old precedent treating those agreements as *per se* illegal. *Khan*, 522 U.S., at 22 (overruling Albrecht v. Herald Co., 390 U.S. 145 (1968)). It held instead that they should be evaluated under the traditional rule of reason. 522 U.S., at 22. Our continued limiting of the reach of the decision in *Dr. Miles* and our recent treatment of other vertical restraints justify the conclusion that *Dr. Miles* should not be retained.

The *Dr. Miles* rule is also inconsistent with a principled framework, for it makes little economic sense when analyzed with our other cases on vertical restraints. If we were to decide the procompetitive effects of resale price maintenance were insufficient to overrule *Dr. Miles*, then cases such as *Colgate* and *GTE Sylvania* themselves would be called into question. These later decisions, while they may result in less intrabrand competition, can be justified because they permit manufacturers to secure the procompetitive benefits associated with vertical price restraints through other methods. The other methods, however, could be less efficient for a particular manufacturer to establish and sustain. The end result hinders competition and consumer welfare because manufacturers are forced to engage in second-best alternatives and because consumers are required to shoulder the increased expense of the inferior practices.

The manufacturer has a number of legitimate options to achieve benefits similar to those provided by vertical price restraints. A manufacturer can exercise its *Colgate* right to refuse to deal with retailers that do not follow its suggested prices.... The economic effects of unilateral and concerted price setting are in general the same.... The problem for the manufacturer is that a jury might conclude its unilateral policy was really a vertical agreement, subjecting it to treble damages and potential criminal liability.... Even with the stringent standards in *Monsanto* and *Business Electronics*, this danger can lead, and has led, rational manufacturers to take wasteful measures.... A manufacturer might refuse to discuss its pricing policy with its distributors except through counsel knowledgeable of the subtle intricacies of the law. Or it might terminate longstanding distributors for minor violations without seeking an explanation.... The increased costs these burdensome measures generate flow to consumers in the form of higher prices.

Furthermore, depending on the type of product it sells, a manufacturer might be able to achieve the procompetitive benefits of resale price maintenance by integrating downstream and selling its products directly to consumers. *Dr. Miles* tilts the relative costs of vertical integration and vertical agreement by making the former more attractive based on the *per se* rule, not on real market conditions. See *Business Electronics, supra*, at 725; see generally Coase, The Nature of the Firm, 4 Economica, New Series 386 (1937). This distortion might lead to inefficient integration that would not otherwise take place, so that consumers must again suffer the consequences of the suboptimal distribution strategy. And integration, unlike vertical price restraints, eliminates all intrabrand competition....

There is yet another consideration. A manufacturer can impose territorial restrictions on distributors and allow only one distributor to sell its goods in a given region. Our cases have recognized, and the economics literature confirms, that these vertical nonprice restraints have impacts similar to those of vertical price restraints; both reduce intrabrand competition and can stimulate retailer services.... The same legal standard (*per se* unlawfulness) applies to horizontal market division and horizontal price fixing because both have similar economic effect. There is likewise little economic justification for the current differential treatment of vertical price and nonprice restraints. Furthermore, vertical nonprice restraints may prove less efficient for inducing desired services, and they reduce intra-brand competition more than vertical price restraints by eliminating both price and service competition

In sum, it is a flawed antitrust doctrine that serves the interests of lawyers—by creating legal distinctions that operate as traps for the unwary—more than the interests of consumers—by requiring manufacturers to choose second-best options to achieve sound business objectives.

B

Respondent's arguments for reaffirming *Dr. Miles* on the basis of *stare decisis* do not require a different result. Respondent looks to congressional action concerning vertical price restraints. In 1937, Congress passed the Miller–Tydings Fair Trade Act, 50 Stat. 693, which made vertical price restraints legal if authorized by a fair trade law enacted by a State. Fifteen years later, Congress expanded the exemption to permit vertical price-setting agreements between a manufacturer and a distributor to be enforced against other distributors not involved in the agreement. McGuire Act, 66 Stat. 632. In 1975, however, Congress repealed both Acts. Consumer Goods Pricing Act, 89 Stat. 801. That the *Dr. Miles* rule applied to vertical price restraints in 1975, according to respondent, shows Congress ratified the rule.

This is not so. The text of the Consumer Goods Pricing Act did not codify the rule of *per se* illegality for vertical price restraints. It rescinded statutory provisions that made them *per se* legal. Congress once again placed these restraints within the ambit of § 1 of the Sherman Act. And, as has been discussed, Congress intended § 1 to give courts the ability "to develop governing principles of law" in the common-law tradition.... Congress could have set the *Dr. Miles* rule in stone, but it chose a more flexible option. We respect its decision by analyzing vertical price restraints, like all restraints, in conformance with traditional § 1 principles, including the principle that our antitrust doctrines "evolv[e] with new circumstances and new wisdom." *Business Electronics, supra*, at 732....

The rule of reason, furthermore, is not inconsistent with the Consumer Goods Pricing Act. Unlike the earlier congressional exemption, it does not treat vertical price restraints as *per se* legal. In this respect, the justifications for the prior exemption are illuminating. Its goal "was to allow the States to protect small retail establishments that Congress thought might otherwise be driven from the marketplace by large-volume discounters." California Retail Liquor Dealers Assn. v. Midcal Aluminum, Inc., 445 U.S. 97, 102 (1980). The state fair trade laws also appear to have been justified on similar grounds. See Areeda & Hovenkamp 298. The rationales for these provisions are foreign to the Sherman Act. Divorced from competition and consumer welfare, they were designed to save inefficient small retailers from their inability to compete. The purpose of the antitrust laws, by contrast, is "the protection of *competition*, not *competitors*." Atlantic Richfield Co. v. USA Petroleum Co., 495 U.S. 328, 338 (1990) (internal quotation marks omitted). To the extent Congress repealed the exemption for some vertical price restraints to end its prior practice of encouraging anticompetitive conduct, the rule of reason promotes the same objective.

Respondent also relies on several congressional appropriations in the mid–1980's in which Congress did not permit the Department of Justice or the Federal Trade Commission to use funds to advocate overturning *Dr. Miles*. . . . We need not pause long in addressing this argument. The conditions on funding are no longer in place, . . . and they were ambiguous at best. As much as they might show congressional approval for *Dr. Miles*, they might demonstrate a different proposition: that Congress could not pass legislation codifying the rule and reached a short-term compromise instead.

Reliance interests do not require us to reaffirm *Dr. Miles*. . . . The reliance interests here, however, like the reliance interests in *Khan*, cannot justify an inefficient rule, especially because the narrowness of the rule has allowed manufacturers to set minimum resale prices in other ways. And while the *Dr. Miles* rule is longstanding, resale price maintenance was legal under fair trade laws in a majority of States for a large part of the past century up until 1975.

It is also of note that during this time "when the legal environment in the [United States] was most favorable for [resale price maintenance], no more than a tiny fraction of manufacturers ever employed [resale price maintenance] contracts." Overstreet 6; see also *id.*, at 169 (noting that "no more than one percent of manufacturers, accounting for no more than ten percent of consumer goods purchases, ever employed [resale price maintenance] in any single year in the [United States]"); Scherer & Ross 549 (noting that "[t]he fraction of U.S. retail sales covered by [resale price maintenance] in its heyday has been variously estimated at from 4 to 10 percent"). To the extent consumers demand cheap goods, judging vertical price restraints under the rule of reason will not prevent the market from providing them. *Cf.* Easterbrook 152–153 (noting that "S.S. Kresge (the old K–Mart) flourished during the days of manufacturers' greatest freedom" because "discount stores offer a combination of price and service that many customers value" and that "[n]othing in restricted dealing threatens the ability of consumers to find low prices"); Scherer & Ross 557 (noting that "for the most part, the effects of the [Consumer Goods Pricing Act] were imperceptible because the forces of competition had already repealed the [previous antitrust exemption] in their own quiet way").

For these reasons the Court's decision in Dr. Miles Medical Co. v. John D. Park & Sons Co., 220 U.S. 373 (1911), is now overruled. Vertical price restraints are to be judged according to the rule of reason.

V

. . .

The judgment of the Court of Appeals is reversed, and the case is remanded for proceedings consistent with this opinion.

■ BREYER, J., with whom STEVENS, SOUTER, and GINSBURG, JJ., join, dissenting. In Dr. Miles Medical Co. v. John D. Park & Sons Co., 220 U.S. 373, 394, 408–409 (1911), this Court held that an agreement between a manufacturer of proprietary medicines and its dealers to fix the minimum price at which its medicines could be sold was "invalid . . . under the [Sherman Act, 15 U.S.C. § 1]." This Court has consistently read *Dr. Miles* as establishing a bright-line rule that agreements fixing minimum resale prices are *per se* illegal. See, *e.g.*, United States v. Trenton Potteries Co., 273 U.S. 392, 399–401 (1927); NYNEX Corp. v. Discon, Inc., 525 U.S. 128, 133 (1998). That *per se* rule is one upon which the legal profession, business, and the public have relied for close to a century. Today the Court holds that courts must determine the lawfulness of minimum resale price maintenance by applying, not a bright-line *per se* rule, but a circumstance-specific "rule of reason." And in doing so it overturns *Dr. Miles*.

The Court justifies its departure from ordinary considerations of *stare decisis* by pointing to a set of arguments well known in the antitrust literature for close to half a century. Congress has repeatedly found in these arguments insufficient grounds for overturning the *per se* rule. . . . And, in my view, they do not warrant the Court's now overturning so well-established a legal precedent.

I

The Sherman Act seeks to maintain a marketplace free of anticompetitive practices, in particular those enforced by agreement among private firms. The law assumes that such a marketplace, free of private restrictions, will tend to bring about the lower prices, better products, and more efficient production processes that consumers typically desire. In determining the lawfulness of particular practices, courts often apply a "rule of reason." They examine both a practice's likely anticompetitive effects and its beneficial business justifications. See, *e.g.*, National Collegiate Athletic Assn. v. Board of Regents of Univ. of Okla., 468 U.S. 85, 109–110, and n. 39 (1984). . . .

Nonetheless, sometimes the likely anticompetitive consequences of a particular practice are so serious and the potential justifications so few (or, *e.g.*, so difficult to prove) that courts have departed from a pure "rule of reason" approach. And sometimes this Court has imposed a rule of *per se* unlawfulness—a rule that instructs courts to find the practice unlawful all (or nearly all) the time. See, *e.g.*, NYNEX, *supra*, at 133; Arizona v. Maricopa County Medical Soc., 457 U.S. 332, 343–344, and n. 16 (1982); Continental T. V., Inc. v. GTE Sylvania Inc., 433 U.S. 36, 50, n. 16 (1977); United States v. Topco Associates, Inc., 405 U.S. 596, 609–611 (1972);

United States v. Socony–Vacuum Oil Co., 310 U.S. 150, 213–214 (1940) (citing and quoting *Trenton Potteries, supra*, at 397–398).

The case before us asks which kind of approach the courts should follow where minimum resale price maintenance is at issue. Should they apply a *per se* rule (or a variation) that would make minimum resale price maintenance always (or almost always) unlawful? Should they apply a "rule of reason"? Were the Court writing on a blank slate, I would find these questions difficult. But, of course, the Court is not writing on a blank slate, and that fact makes a considerable legal difference.

To best explain why the question would be difficult were we deciding it afresh, I briefly summarize several classical arguments for and against the use of a *per se* rule. The arguments focus on three sets of considerations, those involving: (1) potential anticompetitive effects, (2) potential benefits, and (3) administration. The difficulty arises out of the fact that the different sets of considerations point in different directions....

On the one hand, agreements setting minimum resale prices may have serious anticompetitive consequences. *In respect to dealers*: Resale price maintenance agreements, rather like horizontal price agreements, can diminish or eliminate price competition among dealers of a single brand or (if practiced generally by manufacturers) among multibrand dealers. In doing so, they can prevent dealers from offering customers the lower prices that many customers prefer; they can prevent dealers from responding to changes in demand, say falling demand, by cutting prices; they can encourage dealers to substitute service, for price, competition, thereby threatening wastefully to attract too many resources into that portion of the industry; they can inhibit expansion by more efficient dealers whose lower prices might otherwise attract more customers, stifling the development of new, more efficient modes of retailing; and so forth....

In respect to producers: Resale price maintenance agreements can help to reinforce the competition-inhibiting behavior of firms in concentrated industries. In such industries firms may tacitly collude, *i.e.*, observe each other's pricing behavior, each understanding that price cutting by one firm is likely to trigger price competition by all.... *Cf.* United States v. Container Corp. of America, 393 U.S. 333 (1969).... Where that is so, resale price maintenance can make it easier for each producer to identify (by observing retail markets) when a competitor has begun to cut prices. And a producer who cuts wholesale prices without lowering the minimum resale price will stand to gain little, if anything, in increased profits, because the dealer will be unable to stimulate increased consumer demand by passing along the producer's price cut to consumers. In either case, resale price maintenance agreements will tend to prevent price competition from "breaking out"; and they will thereby tend to stabilize producer prices. See Pitofsky 1490–1491. *Cf., e.g.*, Container Corp., supra, at 336–337.

Those who express concern about the potential anticompetitive effects find empirical support in the behavior of prices before, and then after, Congress in 1975 repealed the Miller–Tydings Fair Trade Act, 50 Stat. 693, and the McGuire Act, 66 Stat. 631. Those Acts had permitted (but not required) individual States to enact "fair trade" laws authorizing minimum resale price maintenance. At the time of repeal minimum resale price maintenance was lawful in 36 States; it was unlawful in 14 States.... Comparing prices in the former States with prices in the latter States, the Department of Justice argued that minimum resale price maintenance had raised prices by 19% to 27%....

After repeal, minimum resale price maintenance agreements were unlawful *per se* in every State. The Federal Trade Commission (FTC) staff, after studying numerous price surveys, wrote that collectively the surveys "indicate[d] that [resale price maintenance] in most cases increased the prices of products sold with [resale price maintenance]." Bureau of Economics Staff Report to the FTC, T. Overstreet, Resale Price Maintenance: Economic Theories and Empirical Evidence, 160 (1983) (hereinafter Overstreet). Most economists today agree that, in the words of a prominent antitrust treatise, "resale price maintenance tends to produce higher consumer prices than would otherwise be the case." 8 Areeda & Hovenkamp ¶ 1604b, at 40....

On the other hand, those favoring resale price maintenance have long argued that resale price maintenance agreements can provide important consumer benefits. The majority lists two: First, such agreements can facilitate new entry.... For example, a newly entering producer wishing to build a product name might be able to convince dealers to help it do so—if, but only if, the producer can assure those dealers that they will later recoup their investment. Without resale price maintenance, late-entering dealers might take advantage of the earlier investment and, through price competition, drive prices down to the point where the early dealers cannot recover what they spent. By assuring the initial dealers that such later price competition will not occur, resale price maintenance can encourage them to carry the new product, thereby helping the new producer succeed. See 8 Areeda & Hovenkamp ¶¶ 1617a, 1631b, at 193–196, 308. The result might be increased competition at the producer level, *i.e.*, greater interbrand competition, that brings with it net consumer benefits.

Second, without resale price maintenance a producer might find its efforts to sell a product undermined by what resale price maintenance advocates call "free riding." ... Suppose a producer concludes that it can succeed only if dealers provide certain services, say, product demonstrations, high quality shops, advertising that creates a certain product image, and so forth. Without resale price maintenance, some dealers might take a "free ride" on the investment that others make in providing those services. Such a dealer would save money by not paying for those services and could consequently cut its own price and increase its own sales. Under these circumstances, dealers might prove unwilling to invest in the provision of necessary services....

Moreover, where a producer and not a group of dealers seeks a resale price maintenance agreement, there is a special reason to believe some such benefits exist. That is because, other things being equal, producers should want to encourage price competition among their dealers. By doing so they will often increase profits by selling more of their product. . . . And that is so, even if the producer possesses sufficient market power to earn a supernormal profit. That is to say, other things being equal, the producer will benefit by charging his dealers a competitive (or even a higher-than-competitive) wholesale price while encouraging price competition among them. Hence, if the producer is the moving force, the producer must have some special reason for wanting resale price maintenance; and in the absence of, say, concentrated producer markets (where that special reason might consist of a desire to stabilize wholesale prices), that special reason may well reflect the special circumstances just described: new entry, "free riding," or variations on those themes. . . .

Economic discussion, such as the studies the Court relies upon, can help provide answers to these questions, and in doing so, economics can, and should, inform antitrust law. But antitrust law cannot, and should not, precisely replicate economists' (sometimes conflicting) views. That is because law, unlike economics, is an administrative system the effects of which depend upon the content of rules and precedents only as they are applied by judges and juries in courts and by lawyers advising their clients. And that fact means that courts will often bring their own administrative judgment to bear, sometimes applying rules of *per se* unlawfulness to business practices even when those practices sometimes produce benefits. . . .

I have already described studies and analyses that suggest (though they cannot prove) that resale price maintenance can cause harms with some regularity—and certainly when dealers are the driving force. But what about benefits? How often, for example, will the benefits to which the Court points occur in practice? I can find no economic consensus on this point. There is a consensus in the literature that "free riding" takes place. But "free riding" often takes place in the economy without any legal effort to stop it. . . .

To be more specific, one can easily *imagine* a dealer who refuses to provide important presale services, say a detailed explanation of how a product works (or who fails to provide a proper atmosphere in which to sell expensive perfume or alligator billfolds), lest customers use that "free" service (or enjoy the psychological benefit arising when a high-priced retailer stocks a particular brand of billfold or handbag) and then buy from another dealer at a lower price. Sometimes this must happen in reality. But does it happen often? We do, after all, live in an economy where firms, despite *Dr. Miles' per se* rule, still sell complex technical equipment (as well as expensive perfume and alligator billfolds) to consumers.

All this is to say that the ultimate question is not whether, but *how much*, "free riding" of this sort takes place. . . .

How easily can courts identify instances in which the benefits are likely to outweigh potential harms? My own answer is, *not very easily*. For one thing, it is often difficult to identify who—producer or dealer—is the moving force behind any given resale price maintenance agreement. Suppose, for example, several large multibrand retailers all sell resale-price-maintained products. Suppose further that small producers set retail prices because they fear that, otherwise, the large retailers will favor (say, by allocating better shelf-space) the goods of other producers who practice resale price maintenance. Who "initiated" this practice, the retailers hoping for considerable insulation from retail competition, or the producers, who simply seek to deal best with the circumstances they find? For another thing, as I just said, it is difficult to determine just when, and where, the "free riding" problem is serious enough to warrant legal protection.

I recognize that scholars have sought to develop check lists and sets of questions that will help courts separate instances where anticompetitive harms are more likely from instances where only benefits are likely to be found. . . . But applying these criteria in court is often easier said than done. The Court's invitation to consider the existence of "market power," for example, . . . invites lengthy time-consuming argument among competing experts, as they seek to apply abstract, highly technical, criteria to often ill-defined markets. And resale price maintenance cases, unlike a major merger or monopoly case, are likely to prove numerous and involve only private parties. One cannot fairly expect judges and juries in such cases to apply complex economic criteria without making a considerable number of mistakes, which themselves may impose serious costs. . . .

Are there special advantages to a bright-line rule? Without such a rule, it is often unfair, and consequently impractical, for enforcement officials to bring criminal proceedings. And since enforcement resources are limited, that loss may tempt some producers or dealers to enter into agreements that are, on balance, anticompetitive.

Given the uncertainties that surround key items in the overall balance sheet, particularly in respect to the "administrative" questions, I can concede to the majority that the problem is difficult. And, if forced to decide now, at most I might agree that the *per se* rule should be slightly modified to allow an exception for the more easily identifiable and temporary condition of "new entry." See Pitofsky 1495. But I am not now forced to decide this question. The question before us is not what should be the rule, starting from scratch. We here must decide whether to change a clear and simple price-related antitrust rule that the courts have applied for nearly a century.

II

We write, not on a blank slate, but on a slate that begins with *Dr. Miles* and goes on to list a century's worth of similar cases, massive amounts of advice that lawyers have provided their clients, and untold numbers of business decisions those clients have taken in reliance upon that advice. . . . Indeed a Westlaw search shows that *Dr. Miles* itself has been cited dozens of times in this Court and hundreds of times in lower courts. Those who wish this Court to change so well-established a legal precedent bear a heavy burden of proof. See Illinois Brick Co. v. Illinois, 431 U.S. 720, 736 (1977) (noting, in declining to overrule an earlier case interpreting § 4 of the Clayton Act, that "considerations of *stare decisis* weigh heavily in the area of statutory construction, where Congress is free to change this Court's interpretation of its legislation"). I am not aware of any case in which this Court has overturned so well-established a statutory precedent. Regardless, I do not see how the Court can claim that ordinary criteria for over-ruling an earlier case have been met. . . .

A

I can find no change in circumstances in the past several decades that helps the majority's position. In fact, there has been one important change that argues strongly to the contrary. In 1975, Congress repealed the McGuire and Miller–Tydings Acts. See Consumer Goods Pricing Act of 1975, 89 Stat. 801. And it thereby consciously extended *Dr. Miles'* per se rule. Indeed, at that time the Department of Justice and the FTC, then urging application of the *per se* rule, discussed virtually every argument presented now to this Court as well as others not here presented. And they explained to Congress why Congress should reject them. . . . Congress fully understood, and consequently intended, that the result of its repeal of McGuire and Miller–Tydings would be to make minimum resale price maintenance *per se* unlawful. . . .

Congress did not prohibit this Court from reconsidering the *per se* rule. But enacting major legislation premised upon the existence of that rule constitutes important public reliance upon that rule. And doing so aware of the relevant arguments constitutes even stronger reliance upon the Court's keeping the rule, at least in the absence of some significant change in respect to those arguments.

Have there been any such changes? There have been a few economic studies, described in some of the briefs, that argue, contrary to the testimony of the Justice Department and FTC to Congress in 1975, that resale price maintenance is not harmful. One study, relying on an analysis of litigated resale price maintenance cases from 1975 to 1982, concludes that resale price maintenance does not ordinarily involve producer or dealer collusion. See Ippolito, Resale Price Maintenance: Empirical Evidence from Litigation, 34 J. Law & Econ. 263, 281–282, 292 (1991). But this study equates the failure of plaintiffs to *allege* collusion with the *absence* of collusion—an equation that overlooks the superfluous nature of allegations of horizontal collusion in a resale price maintenance case and the tacit form that such collusion might take. . . .

The other study provides a theoretical basis for concluding that resale price maintenance "need not lead to higher retail prices." Marvel & McCafferty, The Political Economy of Resale Price Maintenance, 94 J. Pol. Econ. 1074, 1075 (1986). But this study develops a theoretical model "under the assumption that [resale price maintenance] is efficiency-enhancing." *Ibid.* Its only empirical support is a 1940 study that the authors acknowledge is much criticized. See *id.*, at 1091. And many other economists take a different view. . . .

Regardless, taken together, these studies ... cannot constitute a major change in circumstances.

Petitioner and some *amici* have also presented us with newer studies that show that resale price maintenance sometimes brings consumer benefits. Overstreet 119–129 (describing numerous case studies). But the proponents of a *per se* rule have always conceded as much. What is remarkable about the majority's arguments is that *nothing* in this respect is new.... The only new feature of these arguments lies in the fact that the most current advocates of overruling *Dr. Miles* have abandoned a host of other not-very-persuasive arguments upon which prior resale price maintenance proponents used to rely....

The one arguable exception consists of the majority's claim that "even absent free riding," resale price maintenance "may be the most efficient way to expand the manufacturer's market share by inducing the retailer's performance and allowing it to use its own initiative and experience in providing valuable services." ... I cannot count this as an exception, however, because I do not understand how, in the absence of free-riding (and assuming competitiveness), an established producer would need resale price maintenance. Why, on these assumptions, would a dealer not "expand" its "market share" as best that dealer sees fit, obtaining appropriate payment from consumers in the process? There may be an answer to this question. But I have not seen it. And I do not think that we should place significant weight upon justifications that the parties do not explain with sufficient clarity for a generalist judge to understand.

No one claims that the American economy has changed in ways that might support the majority. Concentration in retailing has increased.... That change, other things being equal, may enable (and motivate) more retailers, accounting for a greater percentage of total retail sales volume, to seek resale price maintenance, thereby making it more difficult for price-cutting competitors (perhaps internet retailers) to obtain market share.

Nor has anyone argued that concentration among manufacturers that might use resale price maintenance has diminished significantly. And as far as I can tell, it has not. Consider household electrical appliances, which a study from the late 1950's suggests constituted a significant portion of those products subject to resale price maintenance at that time. See Hollander, United States of America, in Resale Price Maintenance 67, 80–81 (B. Yamey ed. 1966). Although it is somewhat difficult to compare census data from 2002 with that from several decades ago (because of changes in the classification system), it is clear that at least some subsets of the household electrical appliance industry are *more* concentrated, in terms of manufacturer market power, now than they were then. For instance, the top eight domestic manufacturers of household cooking appliances accounted for 68% of the domestic market (measured by value of shipments) in 1963 (the earliest date for which I was able to find data), compared with 77% in 2002.... The top eight domestic manufacturers of household laundry equipment accounted for 95% of the domestic market in 1963 (90% in 1958), compared with 99% in 2002.... And the top eight domestic manufacturers of household refrigerators and freezers accounted for 91% of the domestic market in 1963, compared with 95% in 2002.... Increased concentration among manufacturers increases the likelihood that producer-originated resale price maintenance will prove more prevalent today than in years past, and more harmful. At the very least, the majority has not explained how these, or other changes in the economy could help support its position.

In sum, there is no relevant change. And without some such change, there is no ground for abandoning a well-established antitrust rule.

B

With the preceding discussion in mind, I would consult the list of factors that our case law indicates are relevant when we consider overruling an earlier case. Justice Scalia, writing separately in another of our cases this Term, well summarizes that law. See Wisconsin Right to Life, Inc., ante ... (opinion concurring in part and concurring in judgment). And every relevant factor he mentions argues against overruling *Dr. Miles* here.

[Justice Breyer here discusses six factors that are relevant when deciding whether to overrule a prior decision. First, he notes that prior Court decisions applied *stare decisis* more rigidly in statutory—rather than constitutional—cases. Second, citing a concurrence from Justice Scalia, he observes that the Court is more likely to overrule a "wrongly" decided case if it is recent. Third, overruling a decision is more palatable if that decision creates an "unworkable" legal regime. Fourth, a decision that "unsettles" the law favors overruling. Fifth, overruling is disfavored if it will adversely affect the reliance interests present in property rights and contract rights. Sixth, overruling is disfavored if the rule of law is "embedded" in the "national culture." After considering each factor in light of precedents, the amicus briefs, and industry statistics, Justice Breyer concludes that each one cuts against overruling *Dr. Miles*.]

The only contrary *stare decisis* factor that the majority mentions consists of its claim that this Court has "[f]rom the beginning ... treated the Sherman Act as a common-law statute," and has previously overruled antitrust precedent. *Ante*, at 20, 21–22. It points in support to State Oil Co. v. Khan, 522 U.S. 3 (1997), overruling Albrecht v. Herald Co., 390 U.S. 145 (1968), in which this Court had held that maximum resale price agreements were unlawful *per se*, and to *Sylvania*, overruling United States v. Arnold, Schwinn & Co., 388 U.S. 365 (1967), in which this Court had held that producer-imposed territorial limits were unlawful *per se*.

The Court decided *Khan*, however, 29 years after *Albrecht*—still a significant period, but nowhere close to the century *Dr. Miles* has stood. The Court specifically noted the lack of any significant reliance upon *Albrecht*. 522 U.S., at 18–19 (*Albrecht* has had "little or no relevance to ongoing enforcement of the Sherman Act"). *Albrecht* had far less support in traditional antitrust principles than did *Dr. Miles*.... And Congress had nowhere expressed support for *Albrecht*'s rule. *Khan, supra*....

In *Sylvania*, the Court, in overruling *Schwinn*, explicitly distinguished *Dr. Miles* on the ground that while Congress had "recently ... expressed its approval of a *per se* analysis of vertical price restrictions" by repealing the Miller–Tydings and McGuire Acts, "[n]o similar expression of congressional intent exists for nonprice restrictions." 433 U.S., at 51, n. 18. Moreover, the Court decided *Sylvania* only a decade after *Schwinn*. And it based its overruling on a generally perceived need to avoid "confusion" in the law, 433 U.S., at 47–49, a factor totally absent here.

The Court suggests that it is following "the common-law tradition."... But the common law would not have permitted overruling *Dr. Miles* in these circumstances. Common-law courts rarely overruled well-established earlier rules outright. Rather, they would over time issue decisions that gradually eroded the scope and effect of the rule in question, which might eventually lead the courts to put the rule to rest. One can argue that modifying the *per se* rule to make an exception, say, for new entry, see Pitofsky 1495, could prove consistent with this approach. To swallow up a century-old precedent, potentially affecting many billions of dollars of sales, is not. The reader should compare today's "common-law" decision with Justice Cardozo's decision in Allegheny College v. National Chautauqua Cty. Bank of Jamestown, 159 N.E. 173 (1927), and note a gradualism that does not characterize today's decision.

Moreover, a Court that rests its decision upon economists' views of the economic merits should also take account of legal scholars' views about common-law overruling. Professors Hart and Sacks list 12 factors (similar to those I have mentioned) that support judicial "adherence to prior holdings." They all support adherence to *Dr. Miles* here. See H. Hart & A. Sacks, The Legal Process 568–569 (W. Eskridge & P. Frickey eds.1994). Karl Llewellyn has written that the common-law judge's "conscious reshaping" of prior law "must so move as to hold the degree of movement down to the degree to which need truly presses." The Bramble Bush 156 (1960). Where here is the pressing need? The Court notes that the FTC argues here in favor of a rule of reason.... But both Congress and the FTC, unlike courts, are well-equipped to gather empirical evidence outside the context of a single case. As neither has done so, we cannot conclude with confidence that the gains from eliminating the *per se* rule will outweigh the costs....

* * *

The only safe predictions to make about today's decision are that it will likely raise the price of goods at retail and that it will create considerable legal turbulence as lower courts seek to develop workable principles. I do not believe that the majority has shown new or changed conditions sufficient to warrant overruling a decision of such long standing. All ordinary *stare decisis* considerations indicate the contrary. For these reasons, with respect, I dissent.

NOTE ON RESALE PRICE MAINTENANCE

Resale price maintenance was not a substantial problem until the post–1890 development of complex distributional systems.[4] Although the Supreme Court in *Dr. Miles* did not explicitly state that vertical price-fixing agreements are *per se*

---

4. The English cases upheld such agreements. E.T. Grether, Resale Price Maintenance In Great Britain (1935). *See* Dunlop Pneumatic Tyre Co. v. New Garage & Motor Co., [1915] illegal under the Sherman Act, its reasoning supports that conclusion. As Justice Breyer emphasizes in his *Leegin* dissent, for nearly a century the Court took the view that minimum vertical price fixing contravenes the Sherman Act regardless of the nature of the commodity involved[5] and regardless of the market position of the seller.[6] Resale price maintenance has also been held to be an unfair method of competition within the meaning of the Federal Trade Commission Act.[7] *Dr. Miles* was repeatedly reaffirmed in the 1980's before being overruled in *Leegin*.[8]

In response to the condemnation of vertical price fixing in *Dr. Miles*, wholesaler and retailer groups lobbied to secure state and Federal "fair trade" laws.[9] In 1937, the Sherman Act was amended by the Miller–Tydings Act to exempt "agreements prescribing minimum prices for the resale of a [branded or trademarked] commodity which . . . is in free and open competition with commodities of the same general class produced or distributed by others" where such agreements were lawful in the state of resale. Most states passed "fair trade" laws making such agreements lawful.[10] Still, many retailers preferred not to sign "fair trade" agreements, relying on a higher volume of (discount) sales to generate profits. To compel all retailers to comply with manufacturers' minimum prices, most states added "non-signer" provisions to their "fair trade" laws. "Non-signer" statutes made it "unfair competition" for any merchant to sell a "fair traded" product at less than the established price whether or not he had so agreed with the manufacturer. However, in Schwegmann Brothers v. Calvert Distillers Corp., 341 U.S. 384 (1951), the Supreme Court interpreted the Miller–Tydings exemption not to extend to "non-signer" statutes. Enforcement of "fair trade" statutes thus became virtually impossible, since non-signers could not be bound by established minimum prices. In 1952, Congress acted to strengthen state "fair trade" policies by passing the McGuire Act (66 Stat. 632, 15 U.S.C.A. § 45) which in effect overruled *Schwegmann* and sanctioned state laws' non-signer provisions.

A.C. 79; Dunlop Pneumatic Tyre Co. v. Selfridge & Co., [1915] A.C. 847; *cf.* Chloride Elec. Storage Co. v. Silvia Wireless Stores, (1931) 48 R.P.C. 468. *See also* 44 L. Q. Rev. 278 (1928);3 Cambridge L.J. 434 (1929).

5. *See* United States v. Line Material Co., 333 U.S. 287, 307 (1948); United States v. Bausch & Lomb Optical Co., 321 U.S. 707 (1944); United States v. Univis Lens Co., 316 U.S. 241 (1942); Ethyl Gasoline Corp. v. United States, 309 U.S. 436 (1940); Straus v. Victor Talking Mach. Co., 243 U.S. 490 (1917). *Cf.* Purity Stores, Inc. v. Blue Chip Stamp Co., 1963 Trade Cas. ¶ 70,895 (N.D. Cal. 1963).

6. *See* United States v. McKesson & Robbins, Inc., 351 U.S. 305 (1956); United States v. Bausch & Lomb Optical Co., 321 U.S. 707, 721 (1944).

7. *See* FTC v. Beech–Nut Packing Co., 257 U.S. 441 (1922).

8. *See, e.g.,* Business Elecs. Corp. v. Sharp Elecs. Corp., *infra* p. 697; 324 Liquor Corp. v. Duffy, 479 U.S. 335 (1987); California Retail Liquor Dealers Ass'n v. Midcal Aluminum, Inc., *supra* p. 438.

9. "Fair trade" laws provided that a contract may specify the resale price of a trademarked or similarly identified commodity, and that willfully and knowingly advertising or selling such commodity at less than the specified price constituted unfair competition permitting suit by any injured party.

10. By 1941, every state but Texas, Missouri, and Vermont, had enacted its own statute authorizing "fair trade."

SECTION 2 COMMON LAW AND ANTITRUST LAWS **649**

"Fair trade" still did not flourish. A number of state courts struck down non-signer provisions, often as unconstitutional delegations of state legislative power. Shoppers in "fair trade" states could order by mail or otherwise arrange major purchases in "non-fair trade" states, where prices were lower. Manufacturers who also engaged in distribution could not under Fair Trade fix the resale prices of distributors with whom they competed.[11] As "discount house" merchandising grew more substantial, many manufacturers grew unenthusiastic about devoting substantial resources, or any at all, to the extensive litigation against violators necessary to make the "fair trade" system function.

Finally, after abortive efforts by retreating "fair traders" to get a mandatory federal "fair trade" law, the Ford Administration, as part of a "free market" anti-inflation program, proposed repeal of the McGuire Act. Congress responded promptly and the Consumer Goods Pricing Act of 1975 was enacted,[12] restoring the supremacy of the Sherman Act.

PROBLEM 14

SOUSCHEF PURSUES THE AFFLUENT HOME CHEF

For some time, SousChef has manufactured and sold a mixer to restaurants and caterers. The SousChef mixer is generally recognized as the best in the field. Its stylish design—white or black enamel with chrome highlights and a stainless steel bowl—and powerful motor have made it one of the more successful commercial kitchen products of all time. In 1995, sensing that Americans, particularly affluent Americans, have less time to cook but more money to spend on kitchen gadgets, SousChef decided to create a mixer designed for the home cook. After designing the home mixer—a slightly smaller version of the original but now available in five colors, the original black and white plus blue, green and red—but before marketing it, SousChef conducted some market research. The market research suggested that, in order for the product to succeed, SousChef had to build an upscale "brand image." Marketing consultants recommended that SousChef limit distribution to high-end specialty stores and sell the mixer at a price between $150 and $200 for five years. The consultants projected that SousChef would then be able to expand its distribution network to include traditional department stores and, possibly, consumer appliance stores. SousChef followed these recommendations and solicited information from kitchen appliance stores around the country. One month ago, SousChef signed contracts with 10 up-scale retail chains. In the contracts, the retailers agreed not to sell the SousChef home mixer for less than $150 but got the option to sell the mixers back to SousChef after six months for $110 (the wholesale price plus $5). SousChef began shipping the mixer to the authorized dealers two weeks ago. Last week, it learned that one of its retailers has violated the agreement by reselling the mixer to Electric Brands, a national consumer appliance store, which plans to sell it for $120. What can SousChef do?

COMPARATIVE NOTE ON RESALE PRICE MAINTENANCE

Most other countries with competition laws continue to prohibit resale price maintenance, without regard to the existence of possible efficiencies in a particular case. In that sense, the holding of *Leegin* was unusual. Thus, for example, in the

---

11. United States v. McKesson & Robbins, 351 U.S. 305 (1956).

12. Consumer Goods Pricing Act of 1975, Pub. L. No. 94–145, 89 Stat. 801 (codified as amended in 15 U.S.C. §§ 1, 45(a) (2006)).

European Union, Article 81(1)(a) of the Treaty expressly prohibits agreements that "directly or indirectly fix purchase or selling prices or any other trading conditions." Nonetheless, the Commission has refined its views with respect to vertical restrictions, including vertical price arrangements, over the years. During the summer of 2009, it accepted comments relating to its review of the competition rules applicable to vertical restraints, with an eye to deciding how it might wish to revise its block exemption that is scheduled to expire in May 2010. It has also issued Draft Guidelines on Vertical Restraints, available at http://ec.europa.eu/competition/consultations/2009_vertical_agreements/draft_notice_en.pdf. Traditionally, the Commission has construed the Treaty language broadly to cover not only retail price fixing, but also the setting of minimum profit margins, maximum discounts, or minimum wholesale price fixing. *See, e.g.*, GERO–Fabriek, Com. Dec., 1977 O.J. L 16/8, 11 (Dec. 11, 1976); Centraal Bureau voor de Rijwielhandel, Com. Dec., 1978 O.J. L 20/18, 24 (Dec. 2, 1977); Flemish Travel Agents, ECJ Oct. 10, 1987, 1987 ECR 3801, 3827–28, 1989–4 CMLR 213, 234 (¶ 17).

The Draft Guidelines, and the Draft Regulation that accompanies them, continue to treat resale price maintenance as a "hardcore" restriction that will lead to the exclusion of the whole vertical agreement from the scope of application of the block exemption regulation. Interestingly, the Guidelines refer to a "fixed or minimum resale price," and thus may exclude maximum resale price fixing, unless it is a disguised form of minimum RPM. Some European countries have permitted RPM under national laws, either in general or for particular sectors, although to the extent that the Member States have over the years adopted competition laws that mirror Articles 81 and 82, that trend may be disappearing. The Commission will respect the national laws if there is no effect on trade between Member States. Furthermore, as is the case with all restrictions under Article 81, one must bear in mind that parties to the agreement can always try to obtain an exemption under Article 81(3), if the efficiency case is strong enough. Finally, through the Commission's Notice on Agreements of Minor Importance, Official Journal C 368, 22.12.2001, pages 13–15, whose restrictions are mirrored in the Draft Guidelines and Regulation, the Commission has effectively exempted from Article 81 agreements between enterprises that do not represent more than 10 or 15% (depending on whether the agreements are concluded among competitors or not) of the total market for the goods or services in question. The Notice, in addition, provides that small or medium-size enterprises (enterprises having fewer than 250 employees and either an annual turnover not exceeding EUR 40 million or an annual balance sheet total not exceeding EUR 27 million) are rarely capable of appreciably affecting trade between Member States. In U.S. terms, this would be the equivalent of a minimum market power threshold for the RPM prohibition.

Most of the most important trading partners of the United States continue to prohibit RPM as a matter of national law. Canada, for example, has long had a strict prohibition against RPM, which now appears in the Competition Act 1986, § 61. One of the most important differences between the Canadian prohibition and U.S. law, as it now stands, is the lack of any agreement requirement under the Canadian law. The language of the Canadian law is also more sweeping than the U.S. prohibition: § 61(a) prohibits any person from directly or indirectly "by agreement, threat, promise or any like means, attempt[ing] to influence upward, or to discourage the reduction of, the price at which any other person engaged in a business in Canada supplies or offers to supply or advertises a product within Canada. . . ." Section 61(b) prohibits refusing to deal or discriminating against anyone because of the latter's low pricing policy.

The United Kingdom, which modernized its competition law in 1998, now follows rules comparable to those used by the EU. See Competition Act 1998, Ch. 1, sec. 2(2) (prohibiting agreements that directly or indirectly fix purchase or selling prices or any other trading conditions; this includes RPM). (See generally the Website of the Office of Fair Trading, http://www.oft.gov.uk.) In France, under the 1986 Competition Law (Ordonnance No. 86–1243 du 1er decembre, 1986, relative à la liberté des prix et de la concurrence), resale price maintenance is prohibited *per se.* Enforcement of the prohibition, interestingly, takes place in the regular courts, rather than before the Conseil de la Concurrence, which handles cartel and abuse of dominance cases, or before the Economics Ministry, which handles merger cases (referring them when appropriate to the Conseil for a recommendation). In Germany, section 15 of the Act against Restraints on Competition (1957), as amended, makes RPM agreements imposed by producers on wholesalers and retailers null and void. This section applies to both legal and economic restraints, such as those where a dealer receives a smaller rebate if her price system departs from the producer's suggested prices.

In light of the extensive economic literature suggesting that RPM may not invariably be anticompetitive, and in fact may enhance efficient distribution in some circumstances, the Mexican Federal Economic Competition Law is especially interesting. This law was passed in December 1992 and became effective in June 1993 at a time when Mexico was engaged in a comprehensive program of economic reforms. Ley Federal de Competencia Económica, D.O. Dec. 24, 1992 at 9 (LFCE). It distinguishes between "absolute monopolistic practices," which have no legitimate procompetitive purpose and are illegal *per se,* and "relative monopolistic practices," which are subject to a rule of reason-type analysis. Resale price maintenance, along with all other vertical restraints, appears only in the relative monopolistic practices section, LFCE art. 10. According to LFCE art. 11, before a relative monopolistic practice can be considered a violation of the law, the Federal Competition Commission must prove that the actor has "substantial power" in the relevant market, and that market power is being exercised with respect to the practices in question. The LFCE is being studied carefully by a number of other Latin American countries interested in strengthening their own competition laws, or in adopting such a law for the first time.

In the European Union important developments have occurred recently with respect to the law of vertical restraints. The current reform is part of the wider review undertaken by the Commission to simplify the rules and reduce the regulatory burden for companies (especially for small and medium-size enterprises), while ensuring a more effective control of restraints implemented by companies holding significant market power. The reforms will allow the Commission to concentrate on important cases. Member States will play an increased role in the application of Community competition rules.

The current competition rules concerning vertical arrangements have as a central focus the block exemption regulation[13] that entered into force in the year 2000; it is scheduled to expire in May 2010, and the Commission has been studying how best to replace it. There is also a set of Guidelines on Vertical Restraints[14] that implements the block exemption; here, too, the Commission has published draft replacement guidelines. Replacing three previous block exemption regulations appli-

---

13. Regulation (EC) No. 2790/1999 of 22 December 1999 on the Application of Article 81(3) (ex Article 85(3)) of the Treaty to categories of vertical agreements and market practices. See OJ L 336, 29.12.1999, p. 21.

14. *See* Official Journal C 291 of 13.10.2000, page 1.

cable to exclusive distribution, exclusive purchasing and franchising agreements, the 2000 Regulation and Guidelines together form the basis for a new competition policy towards vertical agreements. The texts of the block exemption and of the Guidelines are available through the Commission's website.[15]

The block exemption defines vertical agreements in Article 2(1) as "agreements or concerted practices entered into between two or more undertakings each of which operates, for the purposes of the agreement, at a different level of the production or distribution chain, and relating to the conditions under which the parties may purchase, sell or resell certain goods or services." The regulation allows companies whose market share is below 30% to benefit from a safe harbor, provided their vertical arrangements are in accordance with the other provisions of the block exemption. *See* Article 3.

Perhaps the most important change the 2000 block exemption made, in comparison with the EU's earlier law, was in its explicitly economic approach to the analysis of this type of restriction. Paragraph 7 of the Guidelines puts the point as follows:

> The protection of competition is the primary objective of EC competition policy, as this enhances consumer welfare and creates an efficient allocation of resources. In applying the EC competition rules, the Commission will adopt an economic approach which is based on the effects on the market; vertical agreements have to be analysed in their legal and economic context. However, in the case of restrictions by object as listed in Article 4 of the [block exemption regulation], the Commission is not required to assess the actual effects on the market. Market integration is an additional goal of EC competition policy. Market integration enhances competition in the Community. Companies should not be allowed to recreate private barriers between Member States where State barriers have been successfully abolished.

The "restrictions by object" in Article 4 to which this refers are the blacklisted clauses that will lead the entire agreement to be excluded from the scope of the block exemption. The Commission further warns that individual exemption of such agreements is also unlikely (although it is legally possible). The prohibited clauses include things like the fixing of minimum resale prices, either directly or indirectly, and agreements that have as their direct or indirect object the restriction of sales by the buyer, insofar as those restrictions relate to the territory in which the customers are located (maintaining the Community's traditional distinction between active and passive sales for this purpose).

The Commission does not, however, apply these rules to arrangements that will have a *de minimis* effect in the Community. It defines that term for vertical agreements to include those "agreements entered into by undertakings whose market share on the relevant market does not exceed 10%." See Guidelines on Vertical Restraints, Part II.1, ¶ 8 (2000/C 291/01, Oct. 13, 2000). The Commission reserves the right to apply Article 81(1) to the "hardcore" restrictions of firms below that 10% threshold, if the arrangement nonetheless has an appreciable effect on trade between Member States and on competition. It also indicates that agreements between small and medium-sized enterprises will rarely be of concern.

The last point to make about the 2000 block exemption regulation is that it is more comprehensive than its predecessors that applied to vertical restraints.

---

15. *See*   http://eur-lex.europa.eu/LexUriServ/LexUriServ.do?uri=OJ:L:1999:336:0021:0025:EN:PDF.

Instead of treating separately the question of vertical restraints in intellectual property licenses, franchises, distribution agreements, etc., the Commission has put forth a single block exemption that applies across-the-board. Having said that, however, it is important to note that specific block exemptions continue to exist in certain areas, including technology transfer, car distribution, and certain vertical agreements concluded in connection with horizontal agreements.

B.   CUSTOMER AND TERRITORIAL RESTRAINTS

SCOPE NOTE

The rules for non-price vertical restraints have followed a somewhat different path than those for price restrictions, even though, with the Court's decision in *Leegin*, the two areas have converged. What follows is a brief review of the development of the law governing vertical territorial and customer restraints.

1.   White Motor Co. v. United States, 372 U.S. 253, 83 S.Ct. 696, 9 L.Ed.2d 738 (1963). White Motor manufactured trucks and truck components. It sold directly to large users and dealers, and through distributors to dealers and individual users. Its contracts limited distributors to developing an assigned territory and to selling only to dealers and users there. These contracts also prohibited distributors and their dealers from making sales to federal or state governmental units.

The district court, in granting summary judgment, held these territorial and customer restrictions to be *per se* violations of the Sherman Act. The Supreme Court (per Douglas, J.) reversed, and reasoned:

> We are asked to extend the holding in Timken Roller Bearing Co. v. United States, (which banned *horizontal* arrangements among competitors to divide territory), to a *vertical* arrangement by one manufacturer restricting the territory of his distributors or dealers. We intimate no view one way or the other on the legality of such an arrangement, for we believe that the applicable rule of law should be designed after a trial.

> This is the first case involving a territorial restriction in a vertical arrangement; and we know too little of the actual impact of both that restriction and the one respecting customers to reach a conclusion on the bare bones of the documentary evidence before us....

> Horizontal territorial limitations ... are naked restraints of trade with no purpose except stifling of competition. A vertical territorial limitation may or may not have that purpose or effect. We do not know enough of the economic and business stuff out of which these arrangements emerge to be certain. They may be too dangerous to sanction or they may be allowable protections against aggressive competitors or the only practicable means a small company has for breaking into or staying in business and within the "rule of reason." We need to know more than we do about the actual impact of these arrangements on competition to decide whether they ... should be classified as *per se* violations of the Sherman Act.

Justice Clark (joined by Warren and Black, JJ.) dissented, stating that White Motor's distribution system was "one of the most brazen violations of the Sherman Act that I have experienced in a quarter of a century." White, J., did not participate.

Shortly after remand for development of a trial record in *White Motor*, the defendant agreed to a consent decree, and the Department of Justice discontinued the action. Trade Reg. Rep., 1964 Trade Cas., ¶ 79,762 (N.D. Ohio). The decree enjoined White Motor from agreeing with any distributor, dealer, or any other person to limit, allocate or restrict the territories in which, or the persons or classes of persons to whom, any distributor, dealer or other person may sell trucks.

2. United States v. Arnold, Schwinn & Co., 388 U.S. 365 (1967). The facts are set forth in *GTE Sylvania, infra* p. 655. The majority distinguished *White Motor*, holding that vertical customer and territorial restraints after sale of a product to a wholesaler or retailer were illegal *per se*: "... Such restraints are so obviously destructive of competition that their mere existence is enough." Similar restraints imposed on *bona fide* agents or consignees, however, were held subject to a rule of reason, and were upheld as reasonable.

As to the latter the Court noted:

> ... [A]s indicated in *White Motor*, we are not prepared to introduce the inflexibility which a *per se* rule might bring if it were applied to prohibit all vertical restrictions of territory and all franchising, in the sense of designating specified distributors and retailers as the chosen instruments through which the manufacturer, retaining ownership of the goods, will distribute them to the public. Such a rule might severely hamper smaller enterprises resorting to reasonable methods of meeting the competition of giants and of merchandising through independent dealers, and it might sharply accelerate the trend towards vertical integration of the distribution process. But to allow this freedom where the manufacturer has parted with dominion over the goods—the usual marketing situation—would violate the ancient rule against restraints on alienation and open the door to exclusivity of outlets and limitation of territory further than prudence permits.

> The Government does not here contend for a *per se* rule as to agency, consignment, or Schwinn Plan transactions even though these may be used—as they are here—to implement a scheme of confining distribution outlets as in this case. Where the manufacturer retains title, dominion, and risk with respect to the product and the position and function of the dealer in question is, in fact, indistinguishable from that of an agent or salesman of the manufacturer, it is only if the impact of the confinement is "unreasonably" restrictive of competition that a violation of § 1 results from such confinement, unencumbered by culpable price fixing. Simpson v. Union Oil Co., 377 U.S. 13 (1964). As the District Court found, Schwinn adopted the challenged distribution programs in a competitive situation dominated by mass merchandisers which command access to large-scale advertising and promotion, choice of retail outlets, both owned and franchised, and adequate sources of supply. It is not claimed that Schwinn's practices or other circumstances resulted in an inadequate competitive situation with respect to the bicycle market; and there is nothing in this record—after elimination of the price-fixing issue—to lead us to conclude that Schwinn's program exceeded the limits reasonably necessary to meet the competitive problems posed by its more powerful competitors. In these circumstances, the rule of reason is satisfied.

> We do not suggest that the unilateral adoption by a single manufacturer of an agency or consignment pattern and the Schwinn type of restrictive distribution system would be justified in any and all circumstances by the

presence of the competition of mass merchandisers and by the demonstrated need of the franchise system to meet that competition. . . .

. . . [C]ritical in this respect are the facts: (1) that other competitive bicycles are available to distributors and retailers in the marketplace, and there is no showing that they are not in all respects reasonably interchangeable as articles of competitive commerce with the Schwinn product; (2) that Schwinn distributors and retailers handle other brands of bicycles as well as Schwinn's; (3) in the present posture of the case we cannot rule that the vertical restraints are unreasonable because of their intermixture with price fixing; and (4) we cannot disagree with the findings of the trial court that competition made necessary the challenged program; that it was justified by, and went no further than required by, competitive pressures; and that its net effect is to preserve and not to damage competition in the bicycle market. Application of the rule of reason here cannot be confined to intrabrand competition. When we look to the product market as a whole, we cannot conclude that Schwinn's franchise system with respect to products as to which it retains ownership and risk constitutes an unreasonable restraint of trade.

3. The third Supreme Court decision is Continental T.V., Inc. v. GTE Sylvania Inc., on which the *Leegin* majority relied so heavily:

Continental T.V., Inc. v. GTE Sylvania Inc.

Supreme Court of the United States, 1977.
433 U.S. 36, 97 S.Ct. 2549, 53 L.Ed.2d 568.

■ POWELL, J. Franchise agreements between manufacturers and retailers frequently include provisions barring the retailers from selling franchised products from locations other than those specified in the agreements. This case presents important questions concerning the appropriate antitrust analysis of these restrictions under § 1 of the Sherman Act, 15 U.S.C.A. § 1, and the Court's decision in United States v. Arnold, Schwinn & Co., 388 U.S. 365 (1967).

I.

Respondent GTE Sylvania Inc. (Sylvania) manufactures and sells television sets through its Home Entertainment Products Division. Prior to 1962, like most other television manufacturers, Sylvania sold its televisions to independent or company-owned distributors who in turn resold to a large and diverse group of retailers. Prompted by a decline in its market share to a relatively insignificant 1% to 2% of national television sales,[16] . . . [In 1962,] Sylvania phased out its wholesale distributors and began to sell its televisions directly to a smaller and more select group of franchised retailers. An acknowledged purpose of the change was to decrease the number of competing Sylvania retailers in the hope of attracting the more aggressive and competent retailers thought necessary to the improvement

---

16. RCA at that time was the dominant firm with as much as 60% to 70% of national television sales in an industry with more than 100 manufacturers.

of the company's market position.[17] To this end, Sylvania limited the number of franchises granted for any given area and required each franchisee to sell his Sylvania products only from the location or locations at which he was franchised.[18] A franchise did not constitute an exclusive territory, and Sylvania retained sole discretion to increase the number of retailers in an area in light of the success or failure of existing retailers in developing their market. The revised marketing strategy appears to have been successful during the period at issue here, for by 1965 Sylvania's share of national television sales had increased to approximately 5%, and the company ranked as the Nation's eighth largest manufacturer of color television sets.

This suit is the result of the rupture of a franchisor-franchisee relationship that had previously prospered under the revised Sylvania plan. Dissatisfied with its sales in the city of San Francisco,[19] Sylvania decided in the spring of 1965 to franchise Young Brothers, an established San Francisco retailer of televisions, as an additional San Francisco retailer. The proposed location of the new franchise was approximately a mile from a retail outlet operated by petitioner Continental T.V., Inc. (Continental), one of the most successful Sylvania franchisees. Continental protested that the location of the new franchise violated Sylvania's marketing policy, but Sylvania persisted in its plans. Continental then cancelled a large Sylvania order and placed a large order with Phillips, one of Sylvania's competitors.

During this same period, Continental expressed a desire to open a store in Sacramento, Cal., a desire Sylvania attributed at least in part to Continental's displeasure over the Young Brothers decision. Sylvania believed that the Sacramento market was adequately served by the existing Sylvania retailers and denied the request.[20] In the face of this denial, Continental advised Sylvania in early September 1965, that it was in the process of moving Sylvania merchandise from its San Jose, Cal., warehouse to a new retail location that it had leased in Sacramento. Two weeks later, allegedly for unrelated reasons, Sylvania's credit department reduced Continental's credit line from $300,000 to $50,000.[21] In response to the reduction in credit and the generally deteriorating relations with Sylvania, Continental withheld all payments owed to John P. Maguire & Co., Inc.

---

17. The number of retailers selling Sylvania products declined significantly as a result of the change, but in 1965 there were at least two franchised Sylvania retailers in each metropolitan center of more than 100,000 population.

18. Sylvania imposed no restrictions on the right of the franchisee to sell the products of competing manufacturers.

19. Sylvania's market share in San Francisco was approximately 2.5%—half its national and Northern California average.

20. Sylvania had achieved exceptional results in Sacramento, where its market share exceeded 15 percent in 1965.

21. In its findings of fact made in conjunction with Continental's plea for injunctive relief, the District Court rejected Sylvania's claim that its actions were prompted by independent concerns over Continental's credit. The jury's verdict is ambiguous on this point. In any event, we do not consider it relevant to the issue before us.

(Maguire), the finance company that handled the credit arrangements between Sylvania and its retailers. Shortly thereafter, Sylvania terminated Continental's franchises, and Maguire filed this diversity action in the United States District Court for the Northern District of California seeking recovery of money owed and of secured merchandise held by Continental.

The antitrust issues before us originated in cross-claims brought by Continental against Sylvania and Maguire. Most important for our purposes was the claim that Sylvania had violated § 1 of the Sherman Act by entering into and enforcing franchise agreements that prohibited the sale of Sylvania products other than from specified locations.[22] At the close of evidence in the jury trial of Continental's claims, Sylvania requested the District Court to instruct the jury that its location restriction was illegal only if it unreasonably restrained or suppressed competition.... Relying on this Court's decision in United States v. Arnold, Schwinn & Co., supra, the District Court rejected the proffered instruction in favor of the following one:

> "Therefore, if you find by a preponderance of the evidence that Sylvania entered into a contract, combination or conspiracy with one or more of its dealers pursuant to which Sylvania exercised dominion or control over the products sold to the dealer, after having parted with title and risk to the products, you must find any effort thereafter to restrict outlets or store locations from which its dealers resold the merchandise which they had purchased from Sylvania to be a violation of Section 1 of the Sherman Act, regardless of the reasonableness of the location restrictions."

In answers to special interrogatories, the jury found that Sylvania had engaged "in a contract, combination or conspiracy in restraint of trade in violation of the antitrust laws with respect to location restrictions alone," and assessed Continental's damages at $591,505, which was trebled....

On appeal, the Court of Appeals for the Ninth Circuit, sitting en banc, reversed by a divided vote.... The court acknowledged that there is language in *Schwinn* that could be read to support the District Court's instruction but concluded that *Schwinn* was distinguishable on several grounds. Contrasting the nature of the restrictions, their competitive impact, and the market shares of the franchisors in the two cases, the court concluded that Sylvania's location restriction had less potential for competitive harm than the restrictions invalidated in *Schwinn* and thus should be judged under the "rule of reason" rather than the *per se* rule stated in *Schwinn*. The court found support for its position in the policies of the Sherman Act and in the decisions of other federal courts involving nonprice vertical restrictions.

---

22. Although Sylvania contended in the District Court that its policy was unilaterally enforced, it now concedes that its location restriction involved understandings or agreements with the retailers.

II.

A.

We turn first to Continental's contention that Sylvania's restriction on retail locations is a *per se* violation of § 1 of the Sherman Act as interpreted in *Schwinn*. The restrictions at issue in *Schwinn* were part of a three-tier distribution system comprising, in addition to Arnold, Schwinn & Co. (Schwinn), 22 intermediate distributors and a network of franchised retailers. Each distributor had a defined geographic area in which it had the exclusive right to supply franchised retailers. Sales to the public were made only through franchised retailers, who were authorized to sell Schwinn bicycles only from specified locations. In support of this limitation, Schwinn prohibited both distributors and retailers from selling Schwinn bicycles to non-franchised retailers. At the retail level, therefore, Schwinn was able to control the number of retailers of its bicycles in any given area according to its view of the needs of that market.

As of 1967 approximately 75% of Schwinn's total sales were made under the "Schwinn Plan." Acting essentially as a manufacturer's representative or sales agent, a distributor participating in this plan forwarded orders from retailers to the factory. Schwinn then shipped the ordered bicycles directly to the retailer, billed the retailer, bore the credit risk, and paid the distributor a commission on the sale. Under the Schwinn Plan, the distributor never had title to or possession of the bicycles. The remainder of the bicycles moved to the retailers through the hands of the distributors. For the most part, the distributors functioned as traditional wholesalers with respect to these sales, stocking an inventory of bicycles owned by them to supply retailers with emergency and "fill-in" requirements. A smaller part of the bicycles that were physically distributed by the distributors were covered by consignment and agency arrangements that had been developed to deal with particular problems of certain distributors. Distributors acquired title only to those bicycles that they purchased as wholesalers; retailers, of course, acquired title to all of the bicycles sold by them.

In the District Court, the United States charged a continuing conspiracy by Schwinn and other alleged co-conspirators to fix prices, allocate exclusive territories to distributors, and confine Schwinn bicycles to franchised retailers. [T]he Government argued that the non-price restrictions were *per se* illegal as part of a scheme for fixing the retail prices of Schwinn bicycles. The District Court rejected the price-fixing allegation because of a failure of proof and held that Schwinn's limitation of retail bicycle sales to franchised retailers was permissible under § 1. The court found a § 1 violation, however, in "a conspiracy to divide certain borderline or overlapping counties in the territories served by four Midwestern cycle distributors." . . . The court described the violation as a "division of territory by agreement between the distributors . . . horizontal in nature," and held that Schwinn's participation did not change that basic characteristic. . . . The District Court limited its injunction to apply only to the territorial restrictions on the resale of bicycles purchased by the distributors in their roles as wholesalers. . . .

Schwinn came to this Court on appeal by the United States from the District Court's decision. Abandoning its *per se* theories, the Government argued that Schwinn's prohibition against distributors and retailers selling Schwinn bicycles to nonfranchised retailers was unreasonable under § 1 and that the District Court's injunction against exclusive distributor territories should extend to all such restrictions regardless of the form of the transaction. The Government did not challenge the District Court's decision on price-fixing, and Schwinn did not challenge the decision on exclusive distributor territories.

The Court acknowledged the Government's abandonment of its *per se* theories and stated that the resolution of the case would require an examination of "the specifics of the challenged practices and their impact upon the marketplace in order to make a judgment as to whether the restraint is or is not 'reasonable' in the special sense in which § 1 of the Sherman Act must be read for purposes of this type of inquiry." . . . Despite this description of its task, the Court proceeded to articulate the following "bright line" *per se* rule of illegality for vertical restrictions: "Under the Sherman Act, it is unreasonable without more for a manufacturer to seek to restrict and confine areas or persons with whom an article may be traded after the manufacturer has parted with dominion over it." . . . But the Court expressly stated that the rule of reason governs when "the manufacturer retains title, dominion, and risk with respect to the product and the position and function of the dealer in question are, in fact, indistinguishable from those of an agent or salesman of the manufacturer." . . .

Application of these principles to the facts of *Schwinn* produced sharply contrasting results depending upon the role played by the distributor in the distribution system. With respect to that portion of Schwinn's sales for which the distributors acted as ordinary wholesalers, buying and reselling Schwinn bicycles, the Court held that the territorial and customer restrictions challenged by the Government were *per se* illegal. But, with respect to that larger portion of Schwinn's sales in which the distributors functioned under the Schwinn Plan and under the less common consignment and agency arrangements, the Court held that the same restrictions should be judged under the rule of reason. The only retail restriction challenged by the Government prevented franchised retailers from supplying nonfranchised retailers. . . . The Court apparently perceived no material distinction between the restrictions on distributors and retailers, for it held that:

> "The principle is, of course, equally applicable to sales to retailers, and the decree should similarly enjoin the making of any sales to retailers upon any condition, agreement or understanding limiting the retailer's freedom as to where and to whom it will resell the products." . . .

Applying the rule of reason to the restrictions that were not imposed in conjunction with the sale of bicycles, the Court had little difficulty finding them all reasonable in light of the competitive situation in "the product market as a whole." . . .

B.

In the present case, it is undisputed that title to the televisions passed from Sylvania to Continental. Thus, the *Schwinn per se* rule applies unless Sylvania's restriction on locations falls outside *Schwinn*'s prohibition against a manufacturer attempting to restrict a "retailer's freedom as to where and to whom it will resell the products." . . . As the Court of Appeals conceded, the language of *Schwinn* is clearly broad enough to apply to the present case. Unlike the Court of Appeals, however, we are unable to find a principled basis for distinguishing *Schwinn* from the case now before us.

Both Schwinn and Sylvania sought to reduce but not to eliminate competition among their respective retailers through the adoption of a franchise system. Although it was not one of the issues addressed by the District Court or presented on appeal by the Government, the Schwinn franchise plan included a location restriction similar to the one challenged here. These restrictions allowed Schwinn and Sylvania to regulate the amount of competition among their retailers by preventing a franchisee from selling franchised products from outlets other than the one covered by the franchise agreement. To exactly the same end, the Schwinn franchise plan included a companion restriction, apparently not found in the Sylvania plan, that prohibited franchised retailers from selling Schwinn products to nonfranchised retailers. In *Schwinn* the Court expressly held that this restriction was impermissible under the broad principle stated there. In intent and competitive impact, the retail customer restriction in *Schwinn* is indistinguishable from the location restriction in the present case. In both cases the restrictions limited the freedom of the retailer to dispose of the purchased products as he desired. The fact that one restriction was addressed to territory and the other to customers is irrelevant to functional antitrust analysis and, indeed, to the language and broad thrust of the opinion in *Schwinn*.[23] . . .

---

23. The distinctions drawn by the Court of Appeals and endorsed in Mr. Justice White's separate opinion have no basis in *Schwinn*. The intrabrand competitive impact of the restrictions at issue in *Schwinn* ranged from complete elimination to mere reduction; yet, the Court did not even hint at any distinction on this ground. Similarly, there is no suggestion that the *per se* rule was applied because of Schwinn's prominent position in its industry. That position was the same whether the bicycles were sold or consigned, but the Court's analysis was quite different. In light of Mr. Justice White's emphasis on the "superior consumer acceptance" enjoyed by the Schwinn brand name, . . . we note that the Court rejected precisely that premise in *Schwinn*. Applying the rule of reason to the restrictions imposed in nonsale transactions, the Court stressed that there was "no showing that [competitive bicycles were] not in all respects reasonably interchangeable as articles of competitive commerce with the Schwinn product" and that it did "not regard Schwinn's claim of product excellence as establishing the contrary." . . . Although *Schwinn* did hint at preferential treatment for new entrants and failing firms, the District Court below did not even submit Sylvania's claim that it was failing to the jury. Accordingly, Mr. Justice White's position appears to reflect an extension of *Schwinn* in this regard. Having crossed the "failing firm" line, Mr. Justice White neither attempts to draw a new one nor to explain why one should be drawn at all.

III.

Sylvania argues that if *Schwinn* cannot be distinguished, it should be reconsidered. Although *Schwinn* is supported by the principle of *stare decisis*, Illinois Brick Co. v. Illinois, . . . we are convinced that the need for clarification of the law in this area justifies reconsideration. *Schwinn* itself was an abrupt and largely unexplained departure from White Motor Co. v. United States, 372 U.S. 253 (1963), where only four years earlier the Court had refused to endorse a *per se* rule for vertical restrictions. Since its announcement, *Schwinn* has been the subject of continuing controversy and confusion, both in the scholarly journals and in the federal courts. The great weight of scholarly opinion has been critical of the decision, and a number of the federal courts confronted with analogous vertical restrictions have sought to limit its reach. In our view, the experience of the past 10 years should be brought to bear on this subject of considerable commercial importance.

. . . Since the early years of this century a judicial gloss on [Section 1] has established the "rule of reason" as the prevailing standard of analysis. Standard Oil Co. v. United States, 221 U.S. 1 (1911). Under this rule, the factfinder weighs all of the circumstances of a case in deciding whether a restrictive practice should be prohibited as imposing an unreasonable restraint on competition.[24] *Per se* rules of illegality are appropriate only when they relate to conduct that is manifestly anti-competitive. As the Court explained in Northern Pac. R. Co. v. United States, 356 U.S. 1, 5 (1958), "there are certain agreements or practices which because of their pernicious effect on competition and lack of any redeeming virtue are conclusively presumed to be unreasonable and therefore illegal without elaborate inquiry as to the precise harm they have caused or the business excuse for their use."[25]

---

24. One of the most frequently cited statements of the rule of reason is that of Justice Brandeis in *Chicago Board of Trade v. United States*, 246 U.S. 231, 238 (1918):

> "The true test of legality is whether the restraint imposed is such as merely regulates and perhaps thereby promotes competition or whether it is such as may suppress or even destroy competition. To determine that question the court must ordinarily consider the facts peculiar to the business to which the restraint is applied; its condition before and after the restraint was imposed; the nature of the restraint and its effect, actual or probable. The history of the restraint, the evil believed to exist, the reason for adopting the particular remedy, the purpose or end sought to be attained, are all relevant facts. This is not because a good intention will save an otherwise objectionable regulation or the reverse; but because knowledge of the intent may help the court to interpret facts and to predict consequences."

25. *Per se* rules thus require the Court to make broad generalizations about the social utility of particular commercial practices. The probability that anticompetitive consequences will result from a practice and the severity of those consequences must be balanced against its procompetitive consequences. Cases that do not fit the generalization may arise, but a *per se* rule reflects the judgment that such cases are not sufficiently common or important to justify the time and expense necessary to identify them. Once established, *per se* rules tend to provide guidance to the business community and to minimize the burdens on litigants and the judicial system of the more complex rule of reason trials, see *Northern Pac. R. Co. v. United States*, 356 U.S. 1, 5 (1958); *United States v. Topco Associates*, 405 U.S. 596, 609–610 (1972), but those advantages are not sufficient in themselves to justify the creation of *per se* rules. If it

In essence, the issue before us is whether *Schwinn*'s *per se* rule can be justified under the demanding standards of *Northern Pac. R. Co.* The Court's refusal to endorse a *per se* rule in *White Motor Co.* was based on its uncertainty as to whether vertical restrictions satisfied those standards. . . .

Only four years later the Court in *Schwinn* announced its sweeping *per se* rule without even a reference to *Northern Pac. R. Co.* and with no explanation of its sudden change in position. We turn now to consider *Schwinn* in light of *Northern Pac. R. Co.*

The market impact of vertical restrictions[26] is complex because of their potential for a simultaneous reduction of intrabrand competition and stimulation of interbrand competition.[27] Significantly, the Court in Schwinn did not distinguish among the challenged restrictions on the basis of their individual potential for intrabrand harm or interbrand benefit. Restrictions that completely eliminated intrabrand competition among Schwinn distributors were analyzed no differently than those that merely moderated intrabrand competition among retailers. The pivotal factor was the passage of title: All restrictions were held to be *per se* illegal where title had passed, and all were evaluated and sustained under the rule of reason where it had not. The location restriction at issue here would be subject to the same pattern of analysis under *Schwinn.*

---

were otherwise, all of antitrust law would be reduced to *per se* rules, thus introducing an unintended and undesirable rigidity in the law.

26. As in *Schwinn,* we are concerned here only with nonprice vertical restrictions. The *per se* illegality of price restrictions has been established firmly for many years and involves significantly different questions of analysis and policy. As Mr. Justice White notes, some commentators have argued that the manufacturer's motivation for imposing vertical price restrictions may be the same as for non-price restrictions. There are, however, significant differences that could easily justify different treatment. In his concurring opinion in *White Motor Co.,* Mr. Justice Brennan noted that, unlike nonprice restrictions, "[r]esale price maintenance is not designed to, but almost invariably does in fact, reduce price competition not only among sellers of the affected product, but quite as much between that product and competing brands." 372 U.S., at 268. Judge Posner also recognized that "industry-wide resale price maintenance might facilitate cartelizing." Posner, *supra,* n. 22, at 294 (footnote omitted); see Posner, Antitrust: Cases, Economic Notes and Other Materials 134 (1974); Gellhorn, Antitrust Law and Economics 252 (1976); Note, 10 Colum.J.L. & Soc.Prob., *supra,* n. 22, at 498 n. 12. Furthermore, Congress recently has expressed its approval of a *per se* analysis of vertical price restrictions by repealing those provisions of the Miller–Tydings and McGuire Acts allowing fair trade pricing at the option of the individual States. . . . No similar expression of congressional intent exists for nonprice restrictions.

27. Interbrand competition is the competition among the manufacturers of the same generic product—television sets in this case—and is the primary concern of antitrust law. The extreme example of a deficiency of interbrand competition is monopoly, where there is only one manufacturer. In contrast, intrabrand competition is the competition between the distributors—wholesale or retail—of the product of a particular manufacturer.

The degree of intrabrand competition is wholly independent of the level of interbrand competition confronting the manufacturer. Thus, there may be fierce intrabrand competition among the distributors of a product produced by a monopolist and no intrabrand competition among the distributors of a product produced by a firm in a highly competitive industry. But when interbrand competition exists, as it does among television manufacturers, it provides a significant check on the exploitation of intrabrand market power because of the ability of consumers to substitute a different brand of the same product.

It appears that this distinction between sale and nonsale transactions resulted from the Court's effort to accommodate the perceived intrabrand harm and interbrand benefit of vertical restrictions. The *per se* rule for sale transactions reflected the view that vertical restrictions are "so obviously destructive" of intrabrand competition[28] that their use would "open the door to exclusivity of outlets and limitation of territory further than prudence permits." . . .[29] Conversely, the continued adherence to the traditional rule of reason for nonsale transactions reflected the view that the restrictions have too great a potential for the promotion of interbrand competition to justify complete prohibition.[30] The Court's opinion provides no analytical support for these contrasting positions. Nor is there even an assertion in the opinion that the competitive impact of vertical restrictions is significantly affected by the form of the transaction. Nonsale transactions appear to be excluded from the *per se* rule, not because of a greater danger of intrabrand harm or a greater promise of interbrand benefit, but

---

28. The Court did not specifically refer to intrabrand competition, but this meaning is clear from the context.

29. The Court also stated that to impose vertical restrictions in sale transactions would "violate the ancient rule against restraints on alienation." 388 U.S., at 380. This isolated reference has provoked sharp criticism from virtually all of the commentators on the decision, most of whom have regarded the Court's apparent reliance on the "ancient rule" as both a misreading of legal history and a perversion of antitrust analysis. See, e.g., *Handler, supra,* n. 22, at 1684–1686; *Posner, supra,* n. 22, at 295–296; *Robinson, supra,* n. 22, at 270–271; but see *Louis, supra,* n. 22, at 276 n. 6. We quite agree with Mr. Justice Stewart's dissenting comment in *Schwinn* that "the state of the common law 400 or even 100 years ago is irrelevant to the issue before us: the effect of the antitrust laws upon vertical distributional restraints in the American economy today." 388 U.S., at 392.

We are similarly unable to accept Judge Browning's interpretation of *Schwinn.* In his dissent below he argued that the decision reflects the view that the Sherman Act was intended to prohibit restrictions on the autonomy of independent businessmen even though they have no impact on "price, quality, and quantity of goods and services,". . . . This view is certainly not explicit in *Schwinn,* which purports to be based on an examination of the "impact [of the restrictions] upon the marketplace." . . . Competitive economies have social and political as well as economic advantages, see, e.g., *Northern Pac. R. Co. v. United States,* 356 U.S., at 4, but an antitrust policy divorced from market considerations would lack any objective benchmarks. As Justice Brandeis reminded us, "Every agreement concerning trade, every regulation of trade, restrains. To bind, to restrain is of their very essence." *Chicago Board of Trade v. United States,* 246 U.S., at 238. Although Mr. Justice White's opinion endorses Judge Browning's interpretation, it purports to distinguish *Schwinn* on grounds inconsistent with that interpretation.

30. In that regard, the Court specifically stated that a more complete prohibition "might severely hamper smaller enterprises resorting to reasonable methods of meeting the competition of giants and of merchandising through independent dealers." . . . The Court also broadly hinted that it would recognize additional exceptions to the *per se* rule for new entrants in an industry and for failing firms, both of which were mentioned in *White Motor* as candidates for such exceptions. . . . The Court might have limited the exceptions to the *per se* rule to these situations, which present the strongest arguments for the sacrifice of intrabrand competition for interbrand competition. Significantly, it chose instead to create the more extensive exception for nonsale transactions which is available to all businesses, regardless of their size, financial health, or market share. This broader exception demonstrates even more clearly the Court's awareness of the "redeeming virtues" of vertical restrictions.

rather because of the Court's unexplained belief that a complete *per se* prohibition would be too "inflexible." . . .

Vertical restrictions reduce intrabrand competition by limiting the number of sellers of a particular product competing for the business of a given group of buyers. Location restrictions have this effect because of practical constraints on the effective marketing area of retail outlets. Although intrabrand competition may be reduced, the ability of retailers to exploit the resulting market may be limited both by the ability of consumers to travel to other franchised locations and, perhaps more importantly, to purchase the competing products of other manufacturers. None of these key variables, however, is affected by the form of the transaction by which a manufacturer conveys his products to the retailers.

Vertical restrictions promote interbrand competition by allowing the manufacturer to achieve certain efficiencies in the distribution of his products. These "redeeming virtues" are implicit in every decision sustaining vertical restrictions under the rule of reason. Economists have identified a number of ways in which manufacturers can use such restrictions to compete more effectively against other manufacturers. . . . For example, new manufacturers and manufacturers entering new markets can use the restrictions in order to induce competent and aggressive retailers to make the kind of investment of capital and labor that is often required in the distribution of products unknown to the consumer. Established manufacturers can use them to induce retailers to engage in promotional activities or to provide service and repair facilities necessary to the efficient marketing of their products. Service and repair are vital for many products, such as automobiles and major household appliances. The availability and quality of such services affect a manufacturer's goodwill and the competitiveness of his product. Because of market imperfections such as the so-called "free rider" effect, these services might not be provided by retailers in a purely competitive situation, despite the fact that each retailer's benefit would be greater if all provided the services than if none did. Posner, *supra*, n. 22, at 285; *cf.* P. Samuelson, Economics 506–507 (10th ed. 1976).

Economists also have argued that manufacturers have an economic interest in maintaining as much intrabrand competition as is consistent with the efficient distribution of their products. Bork, The Rule of Reason and the Per se Concept: Price Fixing and Market Division II, 75 Yale L.J. 373, 403 (1966); Posner, *supra*, n. 22, at 283, 287–288.[31] Although the view that the manufacturer's interest necessarily corresponds with that of the public is not universally shared, even the leading critic of vertical restrictions concedes that *Schwinn*'s distinction between sale and nonsale transactions is essentially unrelated to any relevant economic impact. Comanor,

---

31. "Generally a manufacturer would prefer the lowest retail price possible, once its price to dealers has been set, because a lower retail price means increased sales and higher manufacturer revenues." Note, 88 Harv. L. Rev. 636, 641 (1975). In this context, a manufacturer is likely to view the difference between the price at which it sells to its retailers and their price to the consumer as his "cost of distribution," which it would prefer to minimize. Posner, *supra*, n. 22, at 283.

Vertical Territorial and Customer Restrictions: White Motor and Its After-math, 81 Harv. L. Rev. 1419, 1422 (1968).[32] Indeed, to the extent that the form of the transaction is related to interbrand benefits, the Court's distinction is inconsistent with its articulated concern for the ability of smaller firms to compete effectively with larger ones. Capital requirements and administrative expenses may prevent smaller firms from using the exception for nonsale transactions....[33]

We conclude that the distinction drawn in *Schwinn* between sale and nonsale transactions is not sufficient to justify the application of a *per se* rule in one situation and a rule of reason in the other. The question remains whether the *per se* rule stated in *Schwinn* should be expanded to include nonsale transactions or abandoned in favor of a return to the rule of reason. We have found no persuasive support for expanding the rule. As noted above, the *Schwinn* Court recognized the undesirability of "prohib-it[ing] all vertical restrictions of territory and all franchising...."[34] And even Continental does not urge us to hold that all such restrictions are *per se* illegal.

We revert to the standard articulated in *Northern Pac. R. Co.*, and reiterated in *White Motor*, for determining whether vertical restrictions must be "conclusively presumed to be unreasonable and therefore illegal without elaborate inquiry as to the precise harm they have caused or the business excuse for their use." Such restrictions, in varying forms, are widely used in our free market economy. As indicated above, there is substantial scholarly and judicial authority supporting their economic utili-ty. There is relatively little authority to the contrary.[35] Certainly, there has been no showing in this case, either generally or with respect to Sylvania's agreements, that vertical restrictions have or are likely to have a "perni-cious effect on competition" or that they "lack ... any redeeming virtue."

---

32. Professor Comanor argues that the promotional activities encouraged by vertical restrictions result in product differentiation and, therefore, a decrease in interbrand competi-tion. This argument is flawed by its necessary assumption that a large part of the promotional efforts resulting from vertical restrictions will not convey socially desirable information about product availability, price, quality and services. Nor is it clear that a *per se* rule would result in anything more than a shift to less efficient methods of obtaining the same promotional effects.

33. We also note that *per se* rules in this area may work to the ultimate detriment of the small businessmen who operate as franchisees. To the extent that a *per se* rule prevents a firm from using the franchise system to achieve efficiencies that it perceives as important to its successful operation, the rule creates an incentive for vertical integration into the distribution system, thereby eliminating to that extent the role of independent businessmen. See, e.g., Keck, The *Schwinn* case, 23 Bus.Law. 669 (1968); Pollock, *supra*, n. 22, at 608–610.

34. Continental's contention that balancing intrabrand and interbrand competitive effects of vertical restrictions is not a "proper part of the judicial function," is refuted by Schwinn itself. *United States v. Topco Associates, Inc.*, 405 U.S. 596 (1972), is not to the contrary, for it involved a horizontal restriction among ostensible competitors. 405 U.S., at 608.

35. There may be occasional problems in differentiating vertical restrictions from horizontal restrictions originating in agreements among the retailers. There is no doubt that restrictions in the latter category would be illegal *per se*, see, e.g., *United States v. General Motors Corp.*, 384 U.S. 127 (1966); *United States v. Topco Associates, Inc.*, *supra*, but we do not regard the problems of proof as sufficiently great to justify a *per se* rule.

Ibid.[36] Accordingly, we conclude that the *per se* rule stated in *Schwinn* must be overruled. In so holding we do not foreclose the possibility that particular applications of vertical restrictions might justify *per se* prohibition under *Northern Pac. R. Co.* But we do make clear that departure from the rule of reason standard must be based upon demonstrable economic effect rather than—as in *Schwinn*—upon formalistic line drawing.

In sum, we conclude that the appropriate decision is to return to the rule of reason that governed vertical restrictions prior to *Schwinn*. When anticompetitive effects are shown to result from particular vertical restrictions they can be adequately policed under the rule of reason, the standard traditionally applied for the majority of anticompetitive practices challenged under § 1 of the Act. Accordingly, the decision of the Court of Appeals is affirmed.

■ REHNQUIST, J., took no part in the consideration or decision of this case.

■ WHITE, J., concurring. Although I agree with the majority that the location clause at issue in this case is not a *per se* violation of the Sherman Act and should be judged under the rule of reason, I cannot agree that this result requires the overruling of United States v. Arnold, Schwinn & Co., 388 U.S. 365 (1967). In my view this case is distinguishable from *Schwinn* because there is less potential for restraint of intrabrand competition and more potential for stimulating interbrand competition. As to intrabrand competition, Sylvania, unlike Schwinn, did not restrict the customers to whom or the territories where its purchasers could sell. As to interbrand competition, Sylvania, unlike Schwinn, had an insignificant market share at the time it adopted its challenged distribution practice and enjoyed no consumer preference that would allow its retailers to charge a premium over other brands. In two short paragraphs, the majority disposes of the view, adopted after careful analysis by the Ninth Circuit en banc below, that these differences provide a "principled basis for distinguishing *Schwinn*," . . . despite holdings by three Courts of Appeals and the District Court on remand in *Schwinn* that the *per se* rule established in that case does not apply to location clauses such as Sylvania's. To reach out to overrule one of this Court's recent interpretations of the Sherman Act, after such a cursory examination of the necessity for doing so, is surely an affront to the principle that considerations of *stare decisis* are to be given particularly strong weight in the area of statutory construction. Illinois

---

36. The location restriction used by Sylvania was neither the least nor the most restrictive provision that it could have used. . . . But we agree with the implicit judgment in *Schwinn* that a *per se* rule based on the nature of the restriction is, in general, undesirable. Although distinctions can be drawn among the frequently used restrictions, we are inclined to view them as differences of degree and form. See Robinson, *supra*, n. 22, at 279–280; *Averill, Sealy, Schwinn* and Sherman One: An Analysis and Prognosis, 15 N.Y.L.F. 39, 65 (1969). We are unable to perceive significant social gain from channeling transactions into one form or another. Finally, we agree with the Court in *Schwinn* that the advantages of vertical restrictions should not be limited to the categories of new entrants and failing firms. Sylvania was faltering, if not failing and we think it would be unduly artificial to deny it the use of valuable competitive tools.

Brick Co. v. Illinois, 431 U.S. 720 (1977); Runyon v. McCrary, 427 U.S. 160, 175 (1976); Edelman v. Jordan, 415 U.S. 651, 671 (1974).

One element of the system of interrelated vertical restraints invalidated in *Schwinn* was a retail customer restriction prohibiting franchised retailers from selling *Schwinn* products to nonfranchised retailers. The Court rests its inability to distinguish Schwinn entirely on this retail customer restriction, finding it "[i]n intent and competitive impact . . . indistinguishable from the location restriction in the present case," because "[i]n both cases the restrictions limited the freedom of the retailer to dispose of the purchased products as he desired." . . . The customer restriction may well have, however, a very different "intent and competitive impact" than the location restriction: it prevents discount stores from getting the manufacturer's product and thus prevents intrabrand price competition. Suppose, for example, that interbrand competition is sufficiently weak that the franchised retailers are able to charge a price substantially above wholesale. Under a location restriction, these franchisers are free to sell to discount stores seeking to exploit the potential for sales at prices below the prevailing retail level. One of the franchised retailers may be tempted to lower its price and act in effect as a wholesaler for the discount house in order to share in the profits to be had from lowering prices and expanding volume.[37]

Under a retail customer restriction, on the other hand, the franchised dealers cannot sell to discounters, who are cut off altogether from the manufacturer's product and the opportunity for intrabrand price competition. This was precisely the theory on which the Government successfully challenged Schwinn's customer restrictions in this Court. The District Court in that case found that "[e]ach one of [Schwinn's franchised retailers] knows also that he is not a wholesaler and that he cannot sell as a wholesaler or act as an agent for some other unfranchised dealer, such as a discount house retailer who has not been franchised as a dealer by Schwinn." . . . The Government argued on appeal, with extensive citations to the record, that the effect of this restriction was "to keep Schwinn products out of the hands of discount houses and other price cutters so as to discourage price competition in retailing. . . ."[38]

It is true that as the majority states, Sylvania's location restriction inhibited to some degree "the freedom of the retailer to dispose of the purchased products" by requiring the retailer to sell from one particular place of business. But the retailer is still free to sell to any type of

---

37. The franchised retailers would be prevented from engaging in discounting themselves if, under the *Colgate* doctrine, . . . the manufacturer could lawfully terminate dealers who did not adhere to its suggested retail price.

38. Given the Government's emphasis on the inhibiting effect of the *Schwinn* restrictions on discounting activities, the Court may well have been referring to this effect when it condemned the restrictions as "obviously destructive of competition." . . . But the Court was also heavily influenced by its concern for the freedom of dealers to control the disposition of products they purchased from Schwinn. . . . In any event, the record in *Schwinn* illustrates the potentially greater threat to intrabrand competition posed by customer as opposed to location restrictions.

customer—including discounters and other unfranchised dealers—from any area. I think this freedom implies a significant difference for the effect of a location clause on intrabrand competition....

An additional basis for finding less restraint of intrabrand competition in this case, emphasized by the Ninth Circuit en banc, is that *Schwinn* involved restrictions on competition among distributors at the wholesale level. [Schwinn had created air-tight exclusive geographical sales territories and had required its dealers to sell only within their own territory.] Moreover, like its franchised retailers, Schwinn's distributors were absolutely barred from selling to nonfranchised retailers, further limiting the possibilities of intrabrand price competition.

The majority apparently gives no weight to the Court of Appeals' reliance on the difference between the competitive effects of Sylvania's location clause and Schwinn's interlocking "system of vertical restraints affecting both wholesale and retail distribution." ... It also ignores post-*Schwinn* decisions of the Third and Tenth Circuits upholding the validity of location clauses similar to Sylvania's here. Salco Corp. v. General Motors Corp., Buick Motor Division, 517 F.2d 567 (C.A.10 1975); Kaiser v. General Motors Corp., 530 F.2d 964 (C.A.3 1976), aff'g 396 F. Supp. 33 (E.D. Pa. 1975). Finally, many of the scholarly authorities the majority cites in support of its overruling of Schwinn have not had to strain to distinguish location clauses from the restrictions invalidated there. E.g., Robinson, Recent Antitrust Developments: 1974, 75 Colum. L. Rev. 243, 278 (1975) (outcome in *Sylvania* not preordained by *Schwinn* because of marked differences in the vertical restraints in the two cases)' ...".

Just as there are significant differences between *Schwinn* and this case with respect to intrabrand competition, there are also significant differences with respect to interbrand competition. Unlike Schwinn, Sylvania clearly had no economic power in the generic product market. At the time they instituted their respective distribution policies, Schwinn was "the leading bicycle producer in the Nation," with a national market share of 22.5%, ... whereas Sylvania was a "faltering, if not failing" producer of television sets, with "a relatively insignificant 1% to 2%".... Moreover, the Schwinn brand name enjoyed superior consumer acceptance and commanded a premium price as, in the District Court's words, "the Cadillac of the bicycle industry." ... This premium gave Schwinn dealers a margin of protection from interbrand competition and created the possibilities for price cutting by discounters that the Government argued were forestalled by Schwinn's customer restrictions. Thus, judged by the criteria economists use to measure market power—product differentiation and market share[39]—Schwinn enjoyed a substantially stronger position in the bicycle market than did Sylvania in the television market. This Court relied on Schwinn's market position as one reason not to apply the rule of reason to the vertical restraints challenged there...." And the Court of Appeals below found "another significant distinction between our case and *Schwinn*" in Sylva-

---

39. See, e.g., Scherer, Industrial Market Structure and Economic Performance 10–11 (1970); Samuelson, Economics 485–491 (10th ed. 1976).

nia's "precarious market share," which "was so small when it adopted its locations practice that it was threatened with expulsion from the television market." . . . [40]

In my view there are at least two considerations, both relied upon by the majority to justify overruling *Schwinn*, that would provide a "principled basis" for instead refusing to extend *Schwinn* to a vertical restraint that is imposed by a "faltering" manufacturer with a "precarious" position in a generic product market dominated by another firm. The first is that, as the majority puts it, "when interbrand competition exists, as it does among television manufacturers, it provides a significant check on the exploitation of intrabrand market power because of the ability of consumers to substitute a different brand of the same product." . . . Second is the view, argued forcefully in the economic literature cited by the majority, that the potential benefits of vertical restraints in promoting interbrand competition are particularly strong where the manufacturer imposing the restraints is seeking to enter a new market or to expand a small market share.[41] The majority even recognizes that *Schwinn* "hinted" at an exception for new entrants and failing firms from its *per se* rule. . . .

In other areas of the antitrust law, this Court has not hesitated to base its rules of *per se* illegality in part on the defendant's market power. Indeed, in the very case from which the majority draws its standard for *per se* rules, Northern Pac. R. Co. v. United States, 356 U.S. 1, 5 (1958), the Court stated the reach of the *per se* rule against tie-ins under § 1 of the Sherman Act as extending to all defendants with "sufficient economic power with respect to the tying product to appreciably restrain free competition in the market for the tied product. . . ." And the Court subsequently approved an exception to this *per se* rule for "infant industries" marketing a new product. United States v. Jerrold Electronics Corp., 187 F. Supp. 545 (E.D. Pa. 1960), aff'd per curiam, 365 U.S. 567 (1961). See also United States v. Philadelphia National Bank, 374 U.S. 321, 363 (1963), where the Court held presumptively illegal a merger "which produces a firm controlling an undue percentage share of the relevant market. . . ." I see no doctrinal obstacle to excluding firms with such minimal market power as Sylvania's from the reach of the *Schwinn* rule.

I have, moreover, substantial misgivings about the approach the majority takes to overruling *Schwinn*. The reason for the distinction in Schwinn between sale and nonsale transactions was not as the majority would have

---

40. Schwinn's national market share declined to 12.8% in the 10 years following the institution of its distribution program, at which time it ranked second behind a firm with a 22.8% share. . . . In the three years following the adoption of its locations practice, Sylvania's national market share increased to 5%, placing it eighth among manufacturers of color television sets. . . . At this time Sylvania's shares of the San Francisco, Sacramento, and Northern California markets were respectively 2.5%, 15%, and 5%. . . . The District Court made no findings as to Schwinn's shares of local bicycle markets.

41. Preston, Restrictive Distribution Arrangements: Economic Analysis and Public Policy Standards, 30 Law & Contemp. Prob. 506, 511 (1965); Posner, Antitrust Policy and the Supreme Court: An Analysis of the Restricted Distribution, Horizontal Merger, and Potential Competition Decisions, 75 Colum. L. Rev. 282, 293 (1975); Scherer, *supra*, at 510.

it, "the Court's effort to accommodate the perceived intrabrand harm and interbrand benefit of vertical restrictions," . . . the reason was rather, as Judge Browning argued in dissent below, the notion in many of our cases involving vertical restraints that independent businessmen should have the freedom to dispose of the goods they own as they see fit. Thus the first case cited by the Court in *Schwinn* for the proposition that "restraints upon alienation . . . are beyond the power of the manufacturer to impose upon its vendees and . . . are violations of § 1 of the Sherman Act," 388 U.S., at 377, was this Court's seminal decision holding a series of resale price-maintenance agreements *per se* illegal, Dr. Miles Medical Co. v. John D. Park & Sons Co., 220 U.S. 373 (1911). In *Dr. Miles* the Court stated that "a general restraint on alienation is ordinarily invalid," citing Coke on Little-ton, and emphasized that the case involved "agreements restricting the freedom of trade on the part of dealers who own what they sell." . . . Mr. Justice Holmes stated in dissent, "If [the manufacturer] should make the retail dealers agent in law as well as in name and retain the title until the goods left their hands I cannot conceive that even the present enthusiasm for regulating the prices to be charged by other people would deny that the owner was acting within his rights." . . .

After summarily rejecting this concern, reflected in our interpretations of the Sherman Act, for "the autonomy of independent businessmen," . . . the majority not surprisingly finds "no justification" for *Schwinn*'s distinc-tion between sale and nonsale transactions because the distinction is "essentially unrelated to any relevant economic impact." . . . But while according some weight to the businessman's interest in controlling the terms on which he trades in his own goods may be anathema to those who view the Sherman Act as directed solely to economic efficiency,[42] this principle is without question more deeply embedded in our cases than the notions of "free rider" effects and distributional efficiencies borrowed by the majority from the "new economics of vertical relationships." . . . Perhaps the Court is right in partially abandoning this principle and in judging the instant nonprice vertical restraints solely by their "relevant economic impact"; but the precedents which reflect this principle should not be so lightly rejected by the Court. The rationale of *Schwinn* is no doubt difficult to discern from the opinion, and it may be wrong; it is not, however, the aberration the majority makes it out to be here.

I have a further reservation about the majority's reliance on "relevant economic impact" as the test for retaining *per se* rules regarding vertical restraints. It is common ground among the leading advocates of a purely economic approach to the question of distribution restraints that the economic arguments in favor of allowing vertical nonprice restraints gener-ally apply to vertical price restraints as well.[43] Although the majority

---

42. E.g., Bork, Legislative Intent and the Policy of the Sherman Act, 9 J.Law & Econ. 7 (1966); Bork, The Rule of Reason and the *per se* Concept: Price Fixing and Market Division I, 74 Yale L.J. 775 (1965).

43. Professor Posner writes, for example,

asserts that "the *per se* illegality of price restrictions ... involves significantly different questions of analysis and policy," ... I suspect this purported distinction may be as difficult to justify as that of *Schwinn* under the terms of the majority's analysis. Thus Professor Posner, in an article cited five times by the majority, concludes, "I believe the law should treat price and nonprice restrictions the same and that it should make no distinction between the imposition of restrictions in a sale contract and their imposition in an agency contract." Antitrust Policy and the Supreme Court: An Analysis of the Restricted Distribution, Horizontal Merger and Potential Competition Decisions, 75 Colum. L. Rev. 282, 298 (1975). Indeed, the Court has already recognized that resale price maintenance may increase output by inducing "demand-creating activity" by dealers (such as additional retail outlets, advertising and promotion, and product servicing) that outweighs the additional sales that would result from lower prices brought about by dealer price competition. Albrecht v. Herald Co., 390 U.S. 145, 151 n. 7 (1968). These same output-enhancing possibilities of nonprice vertical restraints are relied upon by the majority as evidence of their "social utility and economic soundness," and as a justification for judging them under the rule of reason. The effect, if not the intention, of the Court's opinion is necessarily to call into question the firmly established *per se* rule against price restraints.... In order to decide this case, the Court need only hold that a location clause imposed by a manufacturer with negligible economic power in the product market has a competitive impact sufficiently less restrictive than the *Schwinn* restraints to justify a rule of reason standard, even if the same weight is given here as in *Schwinn* to dealer autonomy. I therefore concur in the judgment.

■ BRENNAN, J., with whom MARSHALL, J., joins, dissenting. I would not overrule the *per se* rule stated in United States v. Arnold, Schwinn & Co., 388 U.S. 365 (1967), and would therefore reverse the decision of the Court of Appeals for the Ninth Circuit.

NOTES AND QUESTIONS

1. *Burden of proof for location clause challenge.* On remand, the Ninth Circuit Court of Appeals affirmed a grant of summary judgment for Sylvania. It started out by noting that the burden of proof was on Continental T.V. to prove that the location clause arrangement was unreasonable, and then noted the following points in concluding that it had not discharged that burden:

> "There is no basis for choosing between [price fixing and market division] on social grounds. If resale price maintenance is like dealer price fixing, and therefore bad, a manufacturer's assignment of exclusive territories is like market division, and therefore bad too....
>
> "[If helping new entrants break into a market] is a good justification for exclusive territories, it is an equally good justification for resale price maintenance, which as we have seen is simply another method of dealing with the free rider problem.... In fact, *any* argument that can be made on behalf of exclusive territories can be made on behalf of resale price maintenance." Posner, *supra*, at 292–293. (Footnote omitted.) ...

a. The distribution arrangement was adopted unilaterally by Sylvania, with no indication that any distributor had influenced that judgment;

b. A location clause (unlike more extreme distribution arrangements like airtight territorial restrictions) has only a modest impact on intrabrand competition; and

c. At the interbrand level, there were many competitors of Sylvania who could have supplied Continental if it sought to open an outlet in a location not acceptable to Sylvania. Continental T.V., Inc. v. GTE Sylvania, Inc., 694 F.2d 1132 (9th Cir. 1982).

2. *Distinguishing vertical distribution techniques.* Note how difficult it is to distinguish the competitive effect of minimum resale price fixing, on the one hand, from territorial and customer allocation, on the other, where a "free rider" justification is advanced. In both instances, the supplier claims that it terminated, or otherwise restricted the freedom of, a "price cutter" in order to ensure the availability of services in the market. Are these vertical distribution techniques only different ways of achieving the same result? If you had to make the legal rules consistent, would you make both *per se* illegal, both subject to the rule of reason (as the Supreme Court eventually did), or both *per se* legal?

In footnote 30 of *Sylvania*, the Supreme Court distinguishes price from non-price restrictions on two grounds: (1) that resale price maintenance "almost invariably" has an effect on interbrand competition among suppliers while nonprice vertical restrictions do not, and (2) that Congress in repealing fair trade in 1975 should be understood as expressing "its approval of a *per se* analysis of vertical price restrictions...." Why exactly is the interbrand effect at the manufacturer's level different with respect to price and nonprice restrictions? Was the majority in *Leegin* correct to reject any inference about the *per se* rule against minimum resale price maintenance from Congress' repeal of fair trade, or does Justice Breyer have the better of the argument?

3. *Evaluating restraints.* In adopting a rule of reason approach for nonprice vertical restrictions, the principal guidance the Court offered in *Sylvania* was a reference to the famous statement of Justice Brandeis in Chicago Board of Trade v. United States:

> The true test of legality is whether the restraint imposed is such as merely regulates and perhaps thereby promotes competition or whether it is such as may suppress or even destroy competition. To determine that question, the Court must ordinarily consider the facts peculiar to the business to which the restraint is applied; its condition before and after the restraint was imposed; the nature of the restraint and its effect, actual or probable. The history of the restraint, the evil believed to exist, the reason for adopting the particular remedy, the purpose or end sought to be attained, are all relevant facts. 246 U.S. 231, 238 (1918).

Is this a helpful guideline for deciding cases? What priority and relative weight does the Court expect will be accorded to each factor? Note the odd fact that market share, usually regarded as critical in a rule of reason analysis, is not listed among this array of factors.

Several courts and commentators have summarized the rule of reason approach by asking three questions: (1) what are the anticompetitive effects of the arrangement, (2) what are its beneficial purposes and effects, and (3) is the restraint reasonably necessary for the achievement of the legitimate objective? *See, e.g.*, Care Heating & Cooling, Inc. v. American Standard, Inc., 427 F.3d 1008, 1012 (6th Cir.

2005); Eiberger v. Sony Corp. of Am., 622 F.2d 1068, 1076 (2d Cir. 1980);; P. Areeda, Antitrust Law 371 (1986).

Does this formulation capture the relevant issues? Who should have the burden of proof on each of these elements?

4. *Distinguishing horizontal from vertical territorial allocation.* It is logical to infer from Sylvania that vertical territorial allocation in some circumstances is justifiable as an effort to curtail the activities of "free riders." But, as we have seen, participants in a horizontal market division scheme similarly could argue that they adopted the arrangement to prevent free riding. Is the anticompetitive effect or business justification of vertical territorial allocation different from a horizontal territorial allocation? In United States v. Topco Associates, Inc., 405 U.S. 596 (1972), the Court held that regional restrictions imposed by a supermarket buying association on its members—for wholesale of association products—constituted a horizontal restraint and *per se* violation of Section 1. Despite the approving reference to *Topco*, in notes 34 and 35 of *Sylvania*, can it be argued that *Sylvania* overruled *Topco*? Compare Toys "R" Us v. FTC, 221 F.3d 928 (7th Cir. 2000), *supra* p. 484.

5. *Territorial restrictions: in form or in substance?* Before *Leegin*, manufacturers went to some lengths to avoid having their vertical restrictions characterized as price restraints. For example, in Eastern Scientific Co. v. Wild Heerbrugg Instruments Inc., 572 F.2d 883 (1st Cir.), cert. denied, 439 U.S. 833 (1978), plaintiff, Eastern, distributed the products of defendant Wild, an importer and distributor of scientific equipment. Eastern agreed not to sell Wild's products outside its assigned area of Rhode Island at less than list price. Within Rhode Island, Wild imposed no price restrictions upon Eastern. In upholding the price restraint under the rule of reason, the Court of Appeals admitted that the defendant's policies "appear[ed] in form to resemble price maintenance agreements," but it found that the competitive effect was no different from "a pure policy of territorial restrictions." It concluded that "the resale price restriction in the present case produces the same anti-competitive effect as pure territorial restrictions but to a lesser degree. If the Supreme Court holds that pure territorial restrictions should be analyzed under the rule of reason, we can see no reason based on substantive economic effect why a similar but less anti-competitive scheme should be treated differently."

6. *Reasonably necessary restraints.* In Eiberger v. Sony Corp. of America, 459 F. Supp. 1276 (S.D.N.Y. 1978), rev'd in part, 622 F.2d 1068 (2d Cir. 1980), Sony Corporation of America (Sonam) sold dictation equipment through a network of authorized Sony retail dealerships, franchised in various locations. Prior to 1975, its agreements with dealers provided that each would "primarily devote and otherwise concentrate its operations in the retail sale" of Sony products in the dealer's area. Each dealer was responsible for providing warranty service on all Sony machines sold by the dealer. The agreement stated, however, that it was not intended to restrict dealers to sales within their territories which were "non-exclusive." Dealers who sold outside their territories could retain warranty responsibility or transfer it to the dealer in whose territory the machine was sold by paying a fee according to a schedule devised by Sonam.

In 1974, ABP, a wholly owned subsidiary of Eiberger, began selling outside its territory "wholesale quantities" of Sony machines to a former business associate in Florida who sold them at retail and performed the warranty services for ABP. After complaints by Florida authorized dealers, Sonam changed its warranty system. Dealers who sold outside their territory were now required to pay a warranty fee to Sonam, which in turn would credit the account of the authorized dealer in that territory. Sonam began to keep written records of the serial numbers of its dictation machines and relied upon authorized dealers to discover and report unauthorized sales. Sonam would compare serial numbers to determine which dealer had sold each reported machine and automatically debit its account for the warranty fees and credit the account of the reporting dealer.

The new warranty fee was charged whether or not the machine required service, even while the machine was still in the hands of an "unauthorized dealer." The fee approximated the dealer's average profit on a machine.

The trial court held that, under rule of reason analysis, the new warranty system was a vertical restraint of trade in violation of Section 1 of the Sherman Act. The court stated that the adverse effect upon intrabrand competition outweighed the slight benefits to interbrand competition, and that the object of the conspiracy was eliminating unauthorized dealers of Sony dictation equipment from the market. 459 F. Supp. at 1282.The court concluded that a violation of Section 1 existed without analyzing the relevant market or the effect of the restraint in that market.

On appeal, Sonam argued that ABP should have been required to show that Sonam's anticompetitive activities had some impact on interbrand competition in the dictation machine market. But the Second Circuit rejected the argument, affirming the trial court's analysis, noting: "[T]he warranty fees were such as to eliminate any profit.... [T]he system had the effect of stifling intrabrand competition...." 622 F.2d at 1075. "Unless we are to conclude that an anticompetitive impact on intrabrand competition cannot alone support a finding that Section 1 has been violated ... we must conclude that ABP has proven such a violation here." *Id.* at 1081.

The Second Circuit noted that the legitimate purpose of ensuring that users receive needed warranty service "could have been achieved with but a slight change in the pre–1975 system: the introduction of a requirement that a selling dealer pay a non-selling dealer for warranty services actually performed...." *Id.* at 1076 n.11. *See also* Ohio–Sealy Mattress Manufacturing Co. v. Sealy, 585 F.2d 821 (7th Cir. 1978), cert. denied, 440 U.S. 930 (1979) (jury may find that payover requirement of 3.2% to 12% of revenues on out-of-territory sales to "reimburse" for cost of servicing goods unreasonable where service seldom required and usually performed by seller); Response of Carolina v. Leasco Response, 537 F.2d 1307 (5th Cir. 1976) (jury question whether provision that franchisee pay 15% royalty on sales within its area of primary responsibility but 70% on sales outside constitutes an illegal territorial restriction).

Eiberger is one of the very few instances since *Sylvania* in which a plaintiff prevailed in challenging a nonprice vertical restriction. Another instance was Graphic Products Distributors v. ITEK Corp., 717 F.2d 1560 (11th Cir. 1983). In scores of other cases, however, the defendant has prevailed since a rule of reason analysis was introduced.

7. *Market power matters.* One reason plaintiffs find successful challenges to nonprice vertical restrictions so difficult is the development of the rule—later ratified in *Leegin*—that "whether the businesses involved have market power is a ... significant consideration." *See, e.g.*, Assam Drug Co. v. Miller Brewing Co., 624 F. Supp. 411 (D.S.D. 1985), aff'd, 798 F.2d 311 (8th Cir. 1986) (19% market share not enough to avoid summary judgment); JBL Enterprises Inc. v. Jhirmack Enterprises, Inc., 698 F.2d 1011 (9th Cir. 1983) (4.2% share in the market for beauty products was insufficient to enable a customer restriction to affect interbrand competition substantially); Donald B. Rice Tire Co. v. Michelin Tire Corp., 483 F.

Supp. 750 (D. Md. 1980), aff'd, 638 F.2d 15 (4th Cir.), cert. denied, 454 U.S. 864 (1981) (market shares of 7.9% of passenger radial tire market and 20–25% of the truck radial tire market not sufficient to demonstrate anticompetitive effect); cf. Valley Liquors, Inc. v. Renfield Importers, Ltd., 678 F.2d 742 (7th Cir. 1982) (noting that lack of significant market power favors defendant). Should market power be a "screening device" in the area of vertical nonprice restrictions? Would your analysis be different if other manufacturers in the same market adopted the same or similar distributional restraints?

8. *Necessity of Restrictions.* The question whether a nonprice restraint was more restrictive than necessary to achieve legitimate business purposes was addressed in American Motor Inns, Inc. v. Holiday Inns, Inc., 521 F.2d 1230 (3d Cir. 1975). American Motor Inns, Inc. (AMI), the largest franchisee of Holiday Inns, Inc. (HI), sought a license from HI to open a Holiday Inn on property it had purchased for this purpose. HI rejected the application. Pursuant to the terms of HI's standard licensing agreement, AMI was foreclosed from building any other hotel on the property, since under the "Non–Holiday Inns" clause, each franchisee agreed not to own, directly or indirectly, any hotel, motel, or motor inn which was not a Holiday Inn. An antitrust action was brought by AMI, which claimed *inter alia* that the non-Holiday Inns franchising practice was an exclusive dealing arrangement that violated Section 3 of the Clayton Act and Section 1 of the Sherman Act.

HI claimed that the clause permitted it to enforce another franchise requirement that licensees refer their customers only to other Holiday Inns if possible—a practice which, facilitated by a computerized national reservation system, contributed to the commercial success of the Holiday Inn System.

The trial court found that the effect of the non-Holiday Inns clauses was "the intended one of reducing and preventing competition among Holiday Inn franchisees." Protection of the reservation-referral system "was and is available through other provisions of its contract . . . , and through less restrictive provisions of the type utilized by other national hostelers." The court concluded that the non-Holiday Inns clause was an unreasonable restraint of trade.

The Court of Appeals for the Third Circuit reversed, notably distinguishing the district court's "least restrictive means" approach—to protect the referral system—from *Chicago Board of Trade*'s "fairly necessary" standard for a Section 1 claim. The Third Circuit considered the least restrictive means unduly burdensome on businesses like HI, and was concerned that the standard would improperly require the courts to second-guess business judgments at a granular level. In so ruling, the court rejected cases from other circuits using a "least restrictive alternative" analysis, distinguishing them on the basis that the restraints involved were *per se* unlawful. Siegel v. Chicken Delight, Inc., 448 F.2d 43, 51 (9th Cir. 1971), cert. denied, 405 U.S. 955 (1972); Copper Liquor, Inc. v. Adolph Coors Co., 506 F.2d 934, 942–43 (5th Cir. 1975).

Would the *Eiberger* court have decided *American Motor Inns* differently? Vice versa? Is the Third Circuit's concern about "second-guessing" a disabling problem when, as in *Eiberger*, the defendant itself grew and flourished under a less restrictive arrangement? Or where successful competitors do so?

9. *Trademark soft drink exemption.* In 1978, the FTC concluded that agreements between Coca–Cola and its bottlers that the bottlers would not sell outside assigned territories was an unreasonable restraint. The bottlers then turned to Congress for relief. In the Soft Drink Interbrand Competition Act of 1980, 15 U.S.C. §§ 3501 *et seq.*, Congress created an exemption from the antitrust laws covering a

"trademark soft drink" license granting a manufacturing licensee "the sole and exclusive right to manufacture, distribute and sell . . . in a defined geographic area" or permitting such a licensee to sell "only for ultimate resale to consumers within a defined geographic area." The exemption applies only to a soft drink that is "in substantial and effective competition with other products of the same general class in the relevant market or markets." Other industries, notably the beer bottlers, have sought similar legislation, but so far have not succeeded in their efforts.

10. *The future of vertical restraints.* Taking *Sylvania* and *Leegin* together, there is now a unified rule for all vertical restraints: the rule of reason. This raises two questions: first, now that it has become so central, is there a way to clarify what will and will not pass muster under the rule of reason; and second, is the next step *per se* legality for some or all vertical restraints? Professor (now Judge) Richard A. Posner and others have argued for the latter result. They assert that unilateral vertical restraints that divert dealers' efforts from price competition to service competition "are usually and perhaps always procompetitive and thus should be *per se* legal."[44] Resulting higher prices for the product will be kept in bounds by the competition of interbrand substitutes. They advanced the argument, later accepted by the Supreme Court, that vertically imposed price restraints do not have the same economic effect as horizontal price-fixing among dealers. Instead, they say, the manufacturer's self-interest acts as a "surrogate" for consumers' interests, since the manufacturer is unlikely to set the same resale price (or markup) as would dealers acting collusively. It will instead attempt to set a price or impose non-price restraints that will result in the optimum price/service mix in response to consumer preferences. If consumers like the package, the manufacturer will succeed in the market and output will rise; if they do not, it will lose business and its interbrand rivals will prosper.[45]

Does Judge Posner's output rule protect the interests of those consumers who are interested in a no-frills product at the lowest possible price? Is output a reliable indicator of the purpose and effect of an arrangement? Might not output increase for reasons unrelated to the distributional restraint, such as product improvement or changes in consumer taste?

11. *Exclusive dealerships.* An "exclusive dealership" involves a promise by a manufacturer that it will not sell or authorize others to sell the product in an assigned territory. This was not the arrangement in either Schwinn or Sylvania, but suppliers sometimes use it (frequently in the form of a "franchise") in distribution systems.

To implement the promise of complete exclusivity, the supplier arguably must impose territorial restraints on others in order to insure the promised exclusivity.

Cases dealing with exclusive dealerships will be examined in Chapter 8, *infra* pp. 919–963 For now, it is enough to note that even during the *Schwinn* era, courts almost uniformly held that exclusive dealership arrangements were governed by a rule of reason. Absent evidence of horizontal collusion or an exceptionally large market share on the part of the supplier granting the exclusive, and assuming the duration is reasonable, it will frequently be upheld.

Does it follow that a rule of *per se* illegality for "air-tight" territorial exclusivity cannot be maintained in the face of a rule that treats exclusive dealerships in many

---

44. Richard A. Posner, *The Rule of Reason and the Economic Approach: Reflections on the* Sylvania *Decision*, 45 U. Chi. L. Rev. 1, 17–19 (1977).

45. Richard A. Posner, *The Next Step in the Antitrust Treatment of Restricted Distribution:* per se *Legality*, 48 U. Chi. L.Rev. 6, 9 (1981).

circumstances as legal? Perhaps the most a supplier ought to be able to promise is that it will not compete with its own distributor and won't appoint another distributor in the same area.

PROBLEM 15

DISTRIBUTION OF BRECHT BEER

Brecht is the third largest of six U.S. brewers with national distribution. Bosch and Muller stand first and second with a combined market share in the U.S. of over 60%. Brecht accounts for 12% of the U.S. market and its share has been declining.

Prior to Sylvania, all brewers either made no effort to control areas in which customers sold or imposed primary responsibility obligations which were often unenforced. In California, wholesale beer prices varied as much as 10% in different parts of the state because of the location of breweries, distribution patterns, and consumer preferences. As a result, wholesale distributors, especially when they had excess capacity, would ship to retailers in other parts of the state to take advantage of temporarily attractive price conditions.

A few years after Sylvania was decided, Bosch and later Muller changed their distribution systems, established franchises for their wholesalers, and required each to sell within a designated territory (usually, in California, the size of a county or two). Brecht wholesalers soon began clamoring for a similar arrangement, and two or three of its most efficient distributors threatened to switch and become distributors for the market leaders. Brecht had about 20 independent distributors in California (some were the only distributor in an area and others had non-exclusive franchises), and decided to introduce into its revised distributor agreement the following provision:

> Distributor will serve as Brecht's distributor within the described geographic area. Distributor may not sell or supply Brecht's products to any retail location in an area assigned to another Brecht distributor without prior written approval by Brecht, nor sell to any person the distributor has reason to believe will sell or supply to a retail location in another dealer's territory.

Documents in Brecht's files show that the provision was introduced for the following reasons: (1) to insure that able distributors would not switch to another brand of beer; (2) to eliminate the "chaotic conditions" in which distributors were shipping to all parts of the state; and (3) because Brecht felt that a requirement that distributors concentrate on a local territory would make the distributors more aggressive in marketing and promotional efforts, including sponsorship of local clubs and sporting events and attentiveness to quality control such as removal from retailer shelves of "stale beer."

Last year, Brecht became aware that one of its wholesale dealers, without asking permission, was selling in vast quantities to a retailer which in turn was shipping its beer throughout the state. At first it ignored the practice, but after several other wholesalers brought the matter to its attention, it terminated the offending wholesaler. Has Brecht violated the antitrust laws?

COMPARATIVE NOTE ON EXCLUSIVE TERRITORIAL ARRANGEMENTS

An overriding objective of the Treaty of Rome, which established the European Economic Community, was to eliminate the divisive economic effects of tariffs, quotas, and other attributes that flowed from the national boundary lines of the Member States. Horizontal agreements dividing territories among competitors, the EU's founders believed, could result in similar insulation of geographic markets. They therefore included the competition articles of the treaty, in particular Article 81 of the Treaty, to eliminate such horizontal restraints, as well as other restrictive practices cartels frequently seek to implement. The Commission's enforcement activities have reflected that goal.

Vertical agreements establishing exclusive territories may have similar effects on competition. Thus the Commission from its earliest days has devoted substantial efforts to formulating procedures and rules to deal with territorial exclusives, particularly where their limits coincide with national boundaries. The Commission's regulations and decisions treat "exclusive dealing agreements" as a generic term, with subcategories (1) territorial restrictions—limiting in geographic terms a purchaser's freedom to resell; (2) exclusive supply arrangements—limiting the supplier's freedom to sell, such as by creating an exclusive dealer or franchise in a designated territory; (3) exclusive dealing—agreement by a distributor to purchase largely or exclusively from one supplier (dealt with in Chapter 8 *infra*); and (4) customer restrictions—limiting a purchaser's freedom to resell to designated classes of customers, frequently other resellers or large users reserved to the producer of the product.

The EC competition rules were first defined in connection with exclusive dealerships, in part because of the large number that were notified when Regulation 17, which established and defined powers of the Commission in the competition field, first went into effect. The first test of the law in the European Court of Justice, *Consten & Grundig v. Commission*, Comm. Mkt. Rep. (CCH) ¶ 8046 (ECCJ 1966), also involved an exclusive dealership. A year later the Commission issued Regulation 67/67, which granted a block exemption to certain classes of such agreements. This Regulation has been replaced by the 2000 Block Exemption Regulation and the Guidelines on Vertical Restraints, and Regulation 17 became obsolete as of May 2004, when it was replaced by Council Regulation (EC) No. 1/2003 of Dec. 16, 2002, OJ L1, 04.01.2003, p. 1–25.

In the *Consten–Grundig* case, the Court of Justice affirmed the Commission's determination that an exclusive distributorship agreement between Grundig, a German manufacturer of radio, television and electronic office equipment, and Consten, a French wholesaler, violated Article 81(1) of the Treaty of Rome. In 1957 Grundig made Consten its exclusive distributor for France. Consten agreed to advertise Grundig's products, to maintain a repair service and a stock of spare parts, to carry out repairs required by sales warranties, and not to sell competing product lines. There was a secondary agreement which entitled Consten to use and enforce Grundig's "GINT" trademark which had been devised by Grundig to enable its foreign distributors to register a trademark in their respective countries while permitting Grundig to retain exclusive control over its own trademark. The distributors were thus able to maintain trademark infringement suits against nonauthorized importers of Grundig products. Grundig agreed not to allow any of its other distributors to deliver to retailers in France, and Consten agreed not to make any direct or indirect deliveries outside of France.

The Commission had found that intrabrand competition, *i.e.*, competition between wholesalers or distributors of a manufacturer's product, was of crucial importance in the case. Without such competition, consumers and retailers in an area would be forced to buy the brand product at an excessive mark-up because no competition would exist in the distribution of the product.

The Court of Justice concurred in the Commission's emphasis on *intra*brand competition and rejected Grundig's argument that the agreement was valid because it increased *inter*brand competition even though *intra*brand competition might have been impaired:

> The principle of freedom of competition applies to all economic levels and all aspects of competition. Competition between producers is generally more apparent than competition between distributors of the same brand. This does not, however, mean that an agreement that restricts competition between distributors should escape the prohibition of Article 85, paragraph 1, because it might strengthen competition between producers.

The Court found that Grundig, by agreeing not to permit its other distributors to deliver Grundig products to France and by prohibiting Consten from re-exporting Grundig products to other countries, had established absolute territorial protection for Consten. The Court held that these provisions, including the provision providing for Consten's registration of the "GINT" trademark, which enabled Consten to eliminate parallel imports, violated Article 85(1) of the Treaty:

> The situation found to exist . . . results in isolating the French market and makes it possible to apply to the products in question prices in which there is no effective competition. Furthermore, competition between producers generally loses its effectiveness as producers become more successful in their efforts to clearly differentiate their brands from other brands. Because distribution costs account for a substantial part of the total cost price, it appears important that competition between dealers should also be promoted. . . .

Grundig's argument that the agreement came within the exemption of Article 81(3) was rejected by the Commission. There was no indication from the evidence that consumers would "share in an equitable part of the profit." In fact, the Commission found that wholesale prices for Grundig products in France ranged between 23 and 44 percent higher than those in Germany, net of customs duties and taxes and after taking discounts into consideration. As far as any "improvement in . . . production or distribution" was concerned, the Commission noted that Consten's advertising and repair facility costs constituted approximately two percent of the 53 to 89 percent mark-ups that Consten received. The Commission stated further that even if some improvement in distribution were to exist, absolute territorial protection was not "indispensable" to the improvement; these functions could be suitably performed even though other French wholesalers were permitted to buy Grundig products elsewhere.

The Court agreed with the Commission's rejection of Grundig's contention that the agreement came within the exemption provided by Article 81(3).

As to Grundig's argument that the reputation of its products depended on the proper performance of warranty and repair service, the Court said:

> . . . [A] buyer can ordinarily claim his right to such a guarantee only from his supplier and then only under the conditions agreed upon. . . . The fears concerning any possible harm to the reputation of Grundig products due to insufficient guarantee service do not, in these circumstances, appear to be justified. In fact, the UNEF company, Consten's chief competitor, which started selling Grundig products in France more recently than Consten and had to incur fairly substantial risks nevertheless furnishes free guarantee and paid after-sale services under conditions that on the whole do not appear to have harmed the reputation of the Grundig brand. Furthermore,

there is nothing to prevent the plaintiffs from informing consumers, through suitable advertising, of the services and the other advantages that may be offered by the official distribution network for Grundig products. It is therefore not true that the advertising done by Consten would be of equal benefit to parallel importers.

Before its block exemptions and vertical guidelines became so well developed, the Commission often granted individual exemptions to distribution arrangements containing dealer location clauses, on grounds that they improve distribution by "consolidating sales efforts." Goodyear Italiana S.A., Comm.Mkt.Rep. (CCH) ¶ 9708 (Comm'n 1974); Gebruder Junghans GmbH, Comm.Mkt.Rep. (CCH) ¶ 9912 (Comm'n 1976); SABA, Comm.Mkt.Rep. (CCH) ¶ 9802 (Comm'n 1975), aff'd sub nom. Metro SB–Grossmarkte GmbH & Co. v. Comm'n, Comm.Mkt.Rep. (CCH) ¶ 8435 (ECCJ 1977). "Area of primary responsibility" clauses have also been present in exempted arrangements. Bayerische Motoren Werke (BMW) AG, Comm. Mkt.Rep. (CCH) ¶ 9701 (Comm'n 1974).[46]

Although the Commission has taken important steps to incorporate economic analysis into its assessment of nonprice vertical restraints, such restraints continue to be regulated more closely in Europe than they are in the United States. In order to accomplish this task within the resources it has, the Commission relies heavily on the block exemption regulation that entered into force in the year 2000. As noted above, this regulation, complemented by a set of Guidelines on Vertical Restraints, replaces three old block exemption regulations that were respectively applicable to exclusive distribution, exclusive purchasing and franchising agreements. The current regulation, and its planned 2010 successor, apply more generally to all categories of vertical agreements and concerted practices. The block exemption regulation establishes definitional criteria, coverage criteria, and specifies particular clauses that are permissible and particular clauses that may not be included in the agreement, if one wants the benefit of the block exemption. (Note, importantly, that a firm would still have the option of trying to persuade either the Commission or a national authority that such a restriction fell within the scope of Article 81(3) in that particular case.)

The prohibitions are interesting for what they reveal about the Commission's vertical restraints policy. The block exemption regulation excludes reciprocal exclusive distribution arrangements between competitors; it excludes even non-reciprocal exclusive distribution agreements between competitors unless (a) the buyer has a total annual turnover not exceeding EUR 100 million, or (b) the supplier is a manufacturer and a distributor of goods, while the buyer is a distributor not manufacturing goods competing with the contract goods, or (c) the supplier is a provider of services at several levels of trade, while the buyer does not provide competing services at the level of trade where it purchases the contract services. In addition, following *Consten & Grundig*, it prohibits clauses restricting the territory into which the buyer may sell, except for the restriction of active sales, where such a restriction does not limit sales by the customers of the buyer. Subject to a limited number of permissible exceptions, the Regulation also excludes clauses that restrict the customers to whom the buyer may sell.

---

46. While the Commission in general has been more inclined in recent years to treat vertical restrictions under a flexible rule of reason, it appears not to have abandoned its position to treat more severely those territorial restrictions that result in preventing dealers from selling into non-authorized territories. *See, e.g.*, Pronuptia de Paris GmbH v. Irmgard Schillgallis, Case 161/84, 1986 ERC 353, Comm.Mkt.Rep. (CCH) ¶ 14,245.

The Commission also uses a concept called "selective distribution," which refers to a distribution network in which only selected dealers have the right to distribute a certain brand, and those dealers are prohibited from reselling to dealers outside the system. The selection criteria must be objective, such as technical qualifications or expertise of the reseller's staff, particularly where high quality or complex consumer durable goods are being distributed. *Metro SB–Grossmarkte GmbH & Co. (SABA) v. Commission*, Comm.Mkt.Rep. (CCH) ¶ 8435 (ECJ 1977). In that case, the Court noted the importance of strengthening competition in factors other than price in a selective distribution system. It also approved prohibitions against wholesalers' reselling to large institutional customers. Here, as with other vertical arrangements, all of the European authorities are particularly sensitive to arrangements that tend to wall off one Member State from another. The courts and the Commission also carefully monitor the strength of intra-brand competition both within and across national boundaries. The exemptions apply so long as the market share held by the supplier does not exceed 30 percent.

C.   VERTICAL RESTRAINTS AND REFUSAL TO DEAL

United States v. Colgate & Co.

Supreme Court of the United States, 1919.
250 U.S. 300, 39 S.Ct. 465, 63 L.Ed. 992.

■ MCREYNOLDS, J. [The Court explained that, on writs of error challenging a district court's decision to quash an indictment, it was bound to accept the district court's interpretation of the indictment and could review only the lower court's interpretation of the statute.]

We are confronted by an uncertain interpretation of an indictment itself couched in rather vague and general language. Counsel differ radically concerning the meaning of the opinion below and there is much room for the controversy between them.

The indictment runs only against Colgate & Co., a corporation engaged in manufacturing soap and toilet articles and selling them throughout the Union. It makes no reference to monopoly, and proceeds solely upon the theory of an unlawful combination. After setting out defendant's organization, place and character of business, and general methods of selling and distributing products through wholesale and retail merchants, it alleges:

> "During the aforesaid period of time, within the said Eastern district of Virginia and throughout the United States, the defendant knowingly and unlawfully created and engaged in a combination with said wholesale and retail dealers, in the Eastern district of Virginia and throughout the United States, for the purpose and with the effect of procuring adherence on the part of such dealers (in reselling such products sold to them aforesaid) to resale prices fixed by the defendant, and of preventing such dealers from reselling such products at lower prices, thus suppressing competition amongst such wholesale dealers, and amongst such retail dealers, in restraint of the aforesaid trade and commerce among the several States, in violation of the act entitled 'an act to protect

trade and commerce against unlawful restraints and monopolies,' approved July 2, 1890.''

Following this is a summary of things done to carry out the purposes of the combination: Distribution among dealers of letters, telegrams, circulars and lists showing uniform prices to be charged; urging them to adhere to such prices and notices, stating that no sales would be made to those who did not; requests, often complied with, for information concerning dealers who had departed from specified prices; investigation and discovery of those not adhering thereto and placing their names upon ''suspended lists;'' requests to offending dealers for assurances and promises of future adherence to prices, which were often given; uniform refusals to sell to any who failed to give the same; sales to those who did; similar assurances and promises required of, and given by, other dealers followed by sales to them; unrestricted sales to dealers with established accounts who had observed specified prices, etc.

Immediately thereafter comes this paragraph:

> ''By reason of the foregoing, wholesale dealers in the aforesaid products of the defendant in the Eastern district of Virginia and throughout the United States, with few exceptions, resold, at uniform prices fixed by the defendant, the aforesaid products, sold to them by the defendant, and refused to resell such products at lower prices to retail dealers in the state where the respective wholesale dealers did business and in other states. For the same reason retail dealers in the aforesaid products of the defendant in the Eastern district of Virginia and throughout the United States resold, at uniform prices fixed by the defendant, the aforesaid products, sold to them by the defendant and by the aforesaid wholesale dealers, and refused to sell such products at lower prices to the consuming public in the states where the respective retail dealers did business and in other states. Thus competition in the sale of such products, by wholesale dealers to retail dealers, and by retail dealers to the consuming public, was suppressed, and the prices of such products to the retail dealers and to the consuming public in the Eastern district of Virginia and throughout the United States were maintained and enhanced.''

In the course of its opinion the trial court said:

> ''No charge is made that any contract was entered into by and on the part of the defendant, and any of its retail customers, in restraint of interstate trade and commerce, the averment being, in effect, that it knowingly and unlawfully created and engaged in a combination with certain of its wholesale and retail customers, to procure adherence on their part, in the sale of its products sold to them, to resale prices fixed by the defendant, and that, in connection therewith, such wholesale and retail customers gave assurances and promises, which resulted in the enhancement and maintenance of such prices, and in the suppression of competition

by wholesale dealers and retail dealers, and by the latter to the consuming public.

* * *

"In the view taken by the court, the indictment here fairly presents the question of whether a manufacturer of products shipped in interstate trade, is subject to criminal prosecution under the Sherman Act, for entering into a combination in restraint of such trade and commerce, because he agrees with his wholesale and retail customers, upon prices claimed by them to be fair and reasonable, at which the same may be resold, and declines to sell his products to those who will not thus stipulate as to prices. This, at the threshold, presents for the determination of the court, how far one may control and dispose of his own property; that is to say, whether there is any limitation thereon, if he proceeds in respect thereto in a lawful and bona fide manner. That he may not do so, fraudulently, collusively, and in unlawful combination with others, may be conceded. Eastern States Retail Lumber Dealers' Association v. United States, 234 U.S. 600, 614. But it by no means follows that being a manufacturer of a given article, he may not, without incurring any criminal liability, refuse absolutely to sell the same at any price, or to sell at a named sum to a customer, with the understanding that such customer will resell only at an agreed price between them, and should the customer not observe the understanding as to retail prices, exercise his undoubted right to decline further to deal with such person. * * *

"The pregnant fact should never be lost sight of that no averment is made of any contract or agreement having been entered into whereby the defendant, the manufacturer, and his customers, bound themselves to enhance and maintain prices, further than is involved in the circumstances that the manufacturer, the defendant here, refused to sell to persons who would not resell at indicated prices, and that certain retailers made purchases on this condition, whereas, inferentially, others declined so to do. No suggestion is made that the defendant, the manufacturer, attempted to reserve or retain any interest in the goods sold, or to restrain the vendee in his right to barter and sell the same without restriction. The retailer, after buying, could, if he chose, give away his purchase or sell it at any price he saw fit, or not sell it at all, his course in these respects being affected only by the fact that he might by his action incur the displeasure of the manufacturer who could refuse to make further sales to him, as he had the undoubted right to do. There is no charge that the retailers themselves entered into any combination or agreement with each other, or that the defendant acted other than with his customers individually."

Our problem is to ascertain, as accurately as may be, what interpretation the trial court placed upon the indictment—not to interpret it ourselves; and then to determine whether, so construed, it fairly charges violation of the Sherman Act. Counsel for the government maintain, in effect, that, as so interpreted, the indictment adequately charges an unlawful combination (within the doctrine of Dr. Miles Medical Co. v. Park & Sons Co., 220 U.S. 373) resulting from restrictive agreements between defendant and sundry dealers whereby the latter obligated themselves not to resell except at agreed prices, and to support this position they specifically rely upon the above-quoted sentence in the opinion which begins, "In the view taken by the court," etc. On the other hand, defendant maintains that looking at the whole opinion it plainly construes the indictment as alleging only recognition of the manufacturer's undoubted right to specify resale prices and refuse to deal with any one who failed to maintain the same.

Considering all said in the opinion (notwithstanding some serious doubts) we are unable to accept the construction placed upon it by the government. We cannot, *e.g.*, wholly disregard the statement that—

"The retailer, after buying, could, if he chose, give away his purchase or sell it at any price he saw fit, or not sell it at all, his course in these respects being affected only by the fact that he might by his action incur the displeasure of the manufacturer who could refuse to make further sales to him, as he had the undoubted right to do."

And we must conclude that, as interpreted below, the indictment does not charge Colgate & Co. with selling its products to dealers under agreements which obligated the latter not to resell except at prices fixed by the company.

The position of the defendant is more nearly in accord with the whole opinion and must be accepted. And as counsel for the Government were careful to state on the argument that this conclusion would require affirmation of the judgment below, an extended discussion of the principles involved is unnecessary.

The purpose of the Sherman Act is to prohibit monopolies, contracts and combinations which probably would unduly interfere with the free exercise of their rights by those engaged, or who wish to engage, in trade and commerce—in a word to preserve the right of freedom to trade. In the absence of any purpose to create or maintain a monopoly, the act does not restrict the long recognized right of trader or manufacturer engaged in an entirely private business, freely to exercise his own independent discretion as to parties with whom he will deal; and, of course, he may announce in advance the circumstances under which he will refuse to sell. "The trader or manufacturer, on the other hand, carries on an entirely private business, and can sell to whom he pleases." United States v. Trans–Missouri Freight Association, 166 U.S. 290, 320. "A retail dealer has the unquestioned right to stop dealing with a wholesaler for reasons sufficient to himself, and may do so because he thinks such dealer is acting unfairly in trying to undermine his trade." Eastern States Retail Lumber Dealers' Association v. United States, 234 U.S. 600, 614.... In Dr. Miles Medical Co. v. Park &

Sons Co., supra, the unlawful combination was effected through contracts which undertook to prevent dealers from freely exercising the right to sell.

The judgment of the District Court must be Affirmed.

NOTES AND QUESTIONS

1. United States v. Parke, Davis & Co., 362 U.S. 29, 80 S.Ct. 503, 4 L.Ed.2d 505 (1960). In this case, the Government sought an injunction against the drug manufacturer Parke, Davis & Company on complaint. It claimed that Parke, Davis had conspired with retail and wholesale druggists to maintain wholesale and retail prices of its pharmaceutical products. The U.S. District Court entered a judgment dismissing the complaint. The Supreme Court reversed. It recognized that Parke, Davis was trying to implement a program to promote general compliance with its suggested retail prices. Nevertheless, the company had not contented itself with merely announcing a policy of refusing to do business with any retailers who disregarded its pricing policy, but instead it went further and refused to deal with wholesalers in order to elicit their willingness to deny its products to retailers. Furthermore, retailers who disregarded the price policy were promptly cut off when Parke, Davis supplied wholesalers with their names. The net result was that Parke, Davis was the organizer of a retail price maintenance conspiracy in violation of Sherman Act. The Court did not repudiate the rule that a simple refusal to sell to customers who will not resell at prices suggested by seller is permissible under the *Colgate* doctrine. When the manufacturer's actions go beyond mere announcement of its policy and a simple refusal to deal with retailers, however, it becomes guilty of participating in a combination in violation of the Sherman Act. In his dissent, Justice Harlan asserted that "scrutiny of the [majority] opinion will reveal that the Court has done no less than send to its demise the *Colgate* doctrine which has been a basic part of antitrust law concepts since it was first announced in 1919...."[47]

2. Dart Drug Corp. v. Parke, Davis & Co., 221 F. Supp. 948 (D.D.C. 1963), aff'd, 344 F.2d 173 (D.C. Cir. 1965). Upon learning that Dart Drug was selling at prices considerably below manufacturer's list price, Parke, Davis informed the retail drug chain that it no longer wished to have any further business relations with Dart Drug and that "effective immediately" it was "permanently" closing Dart Drug's account. Parke, Davis made no attempt to prevent wholesalers or distributors from selling Parke, Davis' products to Dart Drug, and Dart Drug in fact was still able to buy these products from such distributors, though at a higher price than from Parke, Davis directly. Dart Drug thereupon brought a treble damage action. On cross-motions for summary judgment, the district court granted summary judgment for Parke, Davis.

Judge Holtzoff stated that Parke, Davis' action was but "a simple refusal on the part of the manufacturer to sell his goods to a specific retailer. No effort is being made to cut off other sources of supply to the retailer." 221 F. Supp. at 950. The Supreme Court's view in the *Parke, Davis* case that "the *Colgate* doctrine still applied ... to a simple refusal to sell to a customer who will not resell at prices

---

47. The decision is discussed in 1 Milton Handler, TWENTY-FIVE YEARS OF ANTITRUST 444–48 (1973); Kenneth W. Dam and Robert Pitofsky, *Debate: Is the Colgate Doctrine Dead?* 37 ABA ANTITRUST L.J. 772 (1968); Edward H. Levi, *The Parke Davis–Colgate Doctrine: The Ban on Resale Price Maintenance*, 1960 SUP. CT. REV. 258 (1960).

suggested by the seller," established the principle that "a simple refusal to sell to an individual customer for any purpose or for any reason is permissible, provided there is no attempt to induce others to follow that course." *Id.*

3. *Identifying an agreement.* If a supplier says to its distributor "sell at not less than $1.00 or I will cut you off," and the dealer then sells at $1.00, in what sense is that, or is it not, an "agreement?" Should it matter that the dealer would be happy to adopt the $1.00 price for reasons of its own, unrelated to the threat? Compare Restatement (Second) of Contracts, §§ 19(2), (3); 32; 50 (all recognizing acceptance of contract by performance). If each of several dealers goes along with the $1.00 price as a result of the threat, knowing that a similar threat had been made to other competing dealers, might that be viewed as a horizontal agreement among the dealers? In that respect, reconsider the question of "agreement" in the horizontal line where a group of dealers, knowing that concerted action was invited, uniformly adhere to a scheme. *See Interstate Circuit, supra*, at p. 472.

Whatever the theoretical merits of the debate about "agreement" in the vertical line, the Supreme Court, when dealing with the problem in the 1960's and 1970's, chose not to overrule *Colgate*, but it did create exceptions that made it extremely difficult for suppliers to rely on *Colgate* to impose vertical restrictions. Where a supplier set up a policing mechanism to discover violators, it was said to lose its *Colgate* defense. If the supplier distributed through both wholesalers and retailers, and somehow drew the wholesalers into assisting in the policing of its vertical price arrangements, the *Parke, Davis* decision indicated that *Colgate* protection would be lost. It was even suggested that if a supplier solicited reports from retailers about pricing policies of other retailers with whom they competed, that could move the supplier outside the protective confines of *Colgate. See* Girardi v. Gates Rubber Co. Sales Div., Inc., 325 F.2d 196 (9th Cir. 1963); *but see* Klein v. American Luggage Works, Inc., 323 F.2d 787 (3d Cir. 1963). In 1960, one circuit court summarized the situation as follows:

> [t]he Supreme Court has left a narrow channel through which a manufacturer may pass even though the facts would have to be of such Doric simplicity as to be somewhat rare in this day of complex business enterprise.[48]

4. Albrecht v. Herald Co., 390 U.S. 145 (1968) (overruled with respect to maximum resale price maintenance by State Oil v. Khan, *supra* p. 616), probably represents the high point of Supreme Court hostility to *Colgate*. In that case, Herald Co., publisher of the St. Louis Globe–Democrat, told independent distributors, each with an exclusive territory, that they would be terminated if their delivered prices for the paper exceeded a suggested maximum. When Albrecht nevertheless exceeded the maximum price, Herald informed subscribers that it would provide the paper at a lower price itself. Milne was hired to solicit readers for the newspaper and about 25 percent of Albrecht's customers switched to direct delivery; Kroner, another carrier, was induced to take over Albrecht's route "knowing that respondent would not tolerate over-charging and understanding that he might have to return the route if [Albrecht] discontinued his pricing practice."

The Supreme Court considered two issues: (1) was there a "combination or conspiracy" in restraint of trade; and (2) does a *per se* rule apply to vertical maximum resale price maintenance?

---

48. George W. Warner & Co. v. Black & Decker Mfg. Co., 277 F.2d 787, 790 (2d Cir. 1960).

On the first question, the Court wrote:

> If a combination arose when Parke, Davis threatened its wholesalers with termination unless they put pressure on their retail customers, then there can be no doubt that a combination arose between respondent, Milne and Kroner to force petitioners to conform to the advertised retail price.

In a footnote, the court offered the following comments about the ways in which an "illegal combination" could arise under Section 1 of the Sherman Act:

> ... Under *Parke, Davis*, petitioner could have claimed a combination between respondent and himself, at least as of the day he unwillingly complied with respondent's advertised price. Likewise he might successfully have claimed that respondent had combined with other carriers because the firmly enforced price policy applied to all carriers, most of whom acquiesced in it....
>
> Petitioner's amended complaint did allege a combination between respondent and petitioner's customers. Because of our disposition of this case it is unnecessary to pass on this claim. It was not, however, a frivolous contention.

Later decisions of the Supreme Court, especially Monsanto Co. v. Spray–Rite Corp., *infra* p. 688, take a far narrower approach to the agreement issue. As for the second question—whether maximum resale price maintenance should continue to be treated as illegal *per se*—the *Albrecht* Court decided that the rules should be the same for maximum and minimum resale price fixing. Justice Harlan dissented on that point. As we have seen, he was later vindicated in *State Oil*.

5. *Failed challenge to Colgate*. Part of the reason for confusion in the *Colgate* area is that neither the government nor any private party ever asked the Supreme Court to overrule *Colgate*; rather, in each case, the anti-*Colgate* party pointed to facts which would lead the Court to conclude that the *Colgate* doctrine had been overstepped, and therefore waived. The Federal Trade Commission attempted to remedy the situation by directly challenging the validity of the *Colgate* doctrine in Russell Stover Candies, Inc. v. FTC, 718 F.2d 256 (8th Cir. 1983).

Russell Stover was one of at least seven major manufacturers of boxed chocolates and candies in the United States selling through over 18,000 retailers. It designated minimum resale prices for all of its products and ceased selling to retailers when they sold its products at less than designated prices. A survey showed that 97.4% of Stover's products were sold at or above the designated resale price, and it was stipulated that certain retailers would have sold for less except for fear of termination. A Commission majority held that Stover had illegally combined with those retailers who "unwillingly complied" with designated resale prices, interpreting *Colgate* to protect only a manufacturer's right to initially select customers.

The Eighth Circuit reversed:

> The Commission notes that in vertical restraint cases, courts continue to require the existence of "plus factors" to take the case beyond *Colgate*. The Commission believes, however, that the search for "plus factors" is illogical and in fact unnecessary. The Commission's view finds support in commentary critical of *Colgate*. Professor Sullivan has stated:
>
> > "Like the *Colgate* doctrine itself, the cases drawing these laborious distinctions between their own facts and those of *Colgate* are infused with anomaly; many of them require nothing which in any realistic sense can be said to enhance the degree of concert involved in the price

maintenance; yet, because of some added fact which is logically unrelated to whether or not an agreement is being reached, they hold that
the manufacturer has exceeded the scope of the *Colgate* defense."

... It may be that ... *Albrecht* foreshadows the Supreme Court's
overruling of *Colgate* or it may be, as the Commission suggests, that the
Court has already confined *Colgate* to willing compliance with suggested
prices and to initial customer selection. However, courts continue to cite
Colgate. As was stated by the Second Circuit in 1960 and applicable today,
" '[w]hen a leading case is beset by qualifications and then atrophied by
lack of use, its final demise may be difficult to detect. Perhaps the *Colgate*
case is dead, despite frequent citation.' " ... In this case, the Commission
has presented ... a case of "Doric simplicity." There are no "plus factors"
to take the case beyond *Colgate....* If *Colgate* no longer stands for the
proposition that a "simple refusal to sell to customers who will not sell at
prices suggested by the seller is permissible under the Sherman Act,"
United States v. Parke, Davis & Co., 362 U.S. at 43, it is for the Supreme
Court, not this court, to so declare.

Any thought that the Supreme Court might have an opportunity in reviewing
Russell Stover to clarify the standing of the *Colgate* doctrine was abandoned when,
after a change of Administrations, a new FTC elected not to seek Supreme Court
review of the Eighth Circuit decision. In light of the Supreme Court's decision in
Copperweld Corp. v. Independence Tube Corp., 467 U.S. 752 (1984), p. 598 *supra*, is
the *Colgate* doctrine at present unassailable?

Monsanto Co. v. Spray–Rite Service Corp.

Supreme Court of the United States, 1984.
465 U.S. 752, 104 S.Ct. 1464, 79 L.Ed.2d 775.

■ POWELL, J. ... This case presents a question as to the standard of proof
required to find a vertical price-fixing conspiracy in violation of Section 1 of
the Sherman Act.

I

Petitioner Monsanto Company manufactures chemical products, including agricultural herbicides. By the late 1960's, the time at issue in this
case, its sales accounted for approximately 15% of the corn herbicide
market and 3% of the soybean herbicide market. In the corn herbicide
market, the market leader commanded a 70% share. In the soybean
herbicide market, two other competitors each had between 30% and 40% of
the market. Respondent Spray–Rite Service Corp. was engaged in the
wholesale distribution of agricultural chemicals from 1955 to 1972. Spray–
Rite was essentially a family business, whose owner and president, Donald
Yapp, was also its sole salaried salesman. Spray–Rite was a discount
operation, buying in large quantities and selling at a low margin.

Spray–Rite was an authorized distributor of Monsanto herbicides from
1957 to 1968. In October 1967, Monsanto announced that it would appoint
distributors for one-year terms, and that it would renew distributorships
according to several new criteria. Among the criteria were: (i) whether the
distributor's primary activity was soliciting sales to retail dealers; (ii)

whether the distributor employed trained salesmen capable of educating its customers on the technical aspects of Monsanto's herbicides; and (iii) whether the distributor could be expected "to exploit fully" the market in its geographical area of primary responsibility. Shortly thereafter, Monsanto also introduced a number of incentive programs, such as making cash payments to distributors that sent salesmen to training classes, and providing free deliveries of products to customers within a distributor's area of primary responsibility.[49]

In October 1968, Monsanto declined to renew Spray–Rite's distributorship. At that time, Spray–Rite was the tenth largest out of approximately 100 distributors of Monsanto's primary corn herbicide. Ninety percent of Spray–Rite's sales volume was devoted to herbicides sales, and 16% of its sales were of Monsanto's products. After Monsanto's termination, Spray–Rite continued as a herbicide dealer until 1972. It was able to purchase some of Monsanto's products from other distributors, but not as much as it desired or as early in the season as it needed. Monsanto introduced a new corn herbicide in 1969. By 1972, its share of the corn herbicide market had increased to approximately 28%. Its share of the soybean herbicide market had grown to approximately 19%.

Spray–Rite brought this action under Section 1 of the Sherman Act. It alleged that Monsanto and some of its distributors conspired to fix the resale prices of Monsanto herbicides. Its complaint further alleged that Monsanto terminated Spray–Rite's distributorship, adopted compensation programs and shipping policies, and encouraged distributors to boycott Spray–Rite in furtherance of this conspiracy. Monsanto denied the allegations of conspiracy, and asserted that Spray–Rite's distributorship had been terminated because of its failure to hire trained salesmen and promote sales to dealers adequately.

The case was tried to a jury. The District Court instructed the jury that Monsanto's conduct was *per se* unlawful if it was in furtherance of a conspiracy to fix prices. In answers to special interrogatories, the jury found that (i) the termination of Spray–Rite was pursuant to a conspiracy between Monsanto and one or more of its distributors to set resale prices, (ii) the compensation programs, areas of primary responsibility, and/or shipping policies were created by Monsanto pursuant to such a conspiracy, and (iii) Monsanto conspired with one or more distributors to limit Spray–Rite's access to Monsanto herbicides after 1968.[50] The jury awarded $3.5

---

49. These areas of primary responsibility were not exclusive territorial restrictions. Approximately ten to twenty distributors were assigned to each area, and distributors were permitted to sell outside their assigned area.

50. The three special interrogatories were as follows:

"1. Was the decision by Monsanto not to offer a new contract to plaintiff for 1969 made by Monsanto pursuant to conspiracy or combination with one or more of its distributors to fix, maintain or stabilize resale prices of Monsanto herbicides?"

"2. Were the compensation programs and/or areas of primary responsibility, and/or shipping policy created by Monsanto pursuant to a conspiracy to fix, maintain or stabilize resale prices of Monsanto herbicides?"

million in damages, which was trebled to $10.5 million. Only the first of the jury's findings is before us today.[51]

The Court of Appeals for the Seventh Circuit affirmed. It held that there was sufficient evidence to satisfy Spray–Rite's burden of proving a conspiracy to set resale prices. The court stated that "proof of termination following competitor complaints is sufficient to support an inference of concerted action." *Id.*, at 1238.[52] Canvassing the testimony and exhibits that were before the jury, the court found evidence of numerous complaints from competing Monsanto distributors about Spray–Rite's price-cutting practices. It also noted that there was testimony that a Monsanto official had said that Spray–Rite was terminated because of the price complaints.

In substance, the Court of Appeals held that an antitrust plaintiff can survive a motion for a directed verdict if it shows that a manufacturer terminated a price-cutting distributor in response to or following complaints by other distributors. This view brought the Seventh Circuit into direct conflict with a number of other Courts of Appeals.[53] We granted certiorari to resolve the conflict. We reject the statement by the Court of Appeals for the Seventh Circuit of the standard of proof required to submit a case to the jury in distributor-termination litigation, but affirm the judgment under the standard we announce today.[54]

"3. Did Monsanto conspire or combine with one or more of its distributors so that one or more of those distributors would limit plaintiff's access to Monsanto herbicides after?"

The jury answered "Yes" to each of the interrogatories.

51. See note 54, *infra.*

52. The court later in the same paragraph restated the standard of sufficiency as follows: "Proof of distributorship termination *in response to* competing distributors' complaints about the terminated distributor's pricing policies is sufficient to raise an inference of concerted action." 684 F.2d, at 1239 (emphasis added). It may be argued that this standard is different from the one quoted in text in that this one requires a showing of a minimal causal connection between the complaints and the termination of the plaintiff, while the textual standard requires only that the one "follow" the other. As we explain *infra*, the difference is not ultimately significant in our analysis.

53. The court below recognized that its standard was in conflict with that articulated in *Edward J. Sweeney & Sons, Inc. v. Texaco, Inc.*, 637 F.2d 105, 110–111 (CA3 1980), cert. denied, 451 U.S. 911 (1981). Other circuit courts also have rejected the standard adopted by the Court of Appeals for the Seventh Circuit. . . .

54. Monsanto also challenges another part of the Court of Appeals' opinion. It argues that the court held that the nonprice restrictions in the case—the compensation and shipping policies—would be judged under a rule of reason rather than a *per se* rule "only if there is no allegation that the [nonprice] restrictions are part of a conspiracy to fix prices." Monsanto asserts that under this holding a mere allegation that nonprice restrictions were part of a price conspiracy would subject them to *per se* treatment. Monsanto contends that this view undermines our decision in *Continental T.V., Inc. v. GTE Sylvania Inc.*, 433 U.S. 36 (1977), that such restrictions are subject to the rule of reason.

If this were what the Court of Appeals held, it would present an arguable conflict. We think, however, that Monsanto misreads the court's opinion. Read in context, the court's somewhat broad language fairly may be read to say that a plaintiff must prove, as well as allege, that the nonprice restrictions were in fact a part of a price conspiracy. Thus, later in its opinion the court notes that the District Court properly instructed the jury "that Monsanto's

II

This Court had drawn two important distinctions that are at the center of this and any other distributor-termination case. First, there is the basic distinction between concerted and independent action—a distinction not always clearly drawn by parties and courts. Section 1 of the Sherman Act requires that there be a "contract, combination . . . or conspiracy" between the manufacturer and other distributors in order to establish a violation. Independent action is not proscribed. A manufacturer of course generally has a right to deal, or refuse to deal, with whomever it likes, as long as it does so independently. United States v. Colgate & Co., 250 U.S. 300, 307 (1919); cf. United States v. Parke, Davis & Co., 362 U.S. 29 (1960). Under *Colgate*, the manufacturer can announce its resale prices in advance and refuse to deal with those who fail to comply. And a distributor is free to acquiesce in the manufacturer's demand in order to avoid termination.

The second important distinction in distributor-termination cases is that between concerted action to set prices and concerted action on non-price restrictions. The former have been *per se* illegal since the early years of national antitrust enforcement. See Dr. Miles Medical Co. v. John D. Park & Sons Co., 220 U.S. 373, 404–409 (1911). The latter are judged under the rule of reason, which requires a weighing of the relevant circumstances of a case to decide whether a restrictive practice constitutes an unreasonable restraint on competition. See Continental T.V., Inc. v. GTE Sylvania Inc., 433 U.S. 36 (1977).[55]

While these distinctions in theory are reasonably clear, often they are difficult to apply in practice. In *Sylvania* we emphasized that the legality of arguably anticompetitive conduct should be judged primarily by its "mar-

---

otherwise lawful compensation programs and shipping policies were *per se* unlawful *if undertaken as part of an illegal scheme to fix prices.*" (emphasis added). The court cited *White Motor Co. v. United States*, 372 U.S. 253, 260 (1963), in which this Court wrote that restrictive practices ancillary to a price-fixing agreement would be restrained only if there was a finding that the two were sufficiently linked. And the Court of Appeals elsewhere noted the jury's finding that the nonprice practices here were "created by Monsanto pursuant to a conspiracy to fix . . . resale prices."

Monsanto does not dispute Spray–Rite's view that if the nonprice practices were proven to have been instituted as part of a price-fixing conspiracy, they would be subject to *per se* treatment. Instead, Monsanto argues that there was insufficient evidence to support the jury's finding that the nonprice practices were "created by Monsanto pursuant" to a price-fixing conspiracy. Monsanto failed to make its sufficiency-of-the-evidence argument in the Court of Appeals with respect to this finding, and the court did not address the point. We therefore decline to reach it. *See, e.g., Adickes v. S.H. Kress & Co.*, 398 U.S. 144, 147, n. 2 (1970); *Duignan v. United States*, 274 U.S. 195, 200 (1927).

In view of Monsanto's concession that a proper finding that nonprice practices were part of a price-fixing conspiracy would suffice to subject the entire conspiracy to *per se* treatment, *Sylvania* is not applicable to this case. In that case only a nonprice restriction was challenged. See 433 U.S., at 51, n. 18. Nothing in our decision today undercuts the holding of *Sylvania* that nonprice restrictions are to be judged under the rule of reason. In fact, the need to ensure the viability of *Sylvania* is an important consideration in our rejection of the Court of Appeals' standard of sufficiency of the evidence.

55. [In this footnote, the Court declined to take a position on the continued validity of *Dr. Miles.*]

ket impact." But the economic effect of all of the conduct described above—unilateral and concerted vertical price setting, agreements on price and nonprice restrictions—is in many, but not all, cases similar or identical. See, *e.g.*, Parke, Davis, supra. And judged from a distance, the conduct of the parties in the various situations can be indistinguishable. For example, the fact that a manufacturer and its distributors are in constant communication about prices and marketing strategy does not alone show that the distributors are not making independent pricing decisions. A manufacturer and its distributors have legitimate reasons to exchange information about the prices and the reception of their products in the market. Moreover, it is precisely in cases in which the manufacturer attempts to further a particular marketing strategy by means of agreements on often costly nonprice restrictions that it will have the most interest in the distributors' resale prices. The manufacturer often will want to ensure that its distributors earn sufficient profit to pay for programs such as hiring and training additional salesmen or demonstrating the technical features of the product, and will want to see that "free-riders" do not interfere. See *Sylvania*, supra. Thus, the manufacturer's strongly felt concern about resale prices does not necessarily mean that it has done more than the *Colgate* doctrine allows.

Nevertheless, it is of considerable importance that the independent action by the manufacturer, and concerted action on nonprice restrictions, be distinguished from price-fixing agreements, since under present law the latter are subject to *per se* treatment and treble damages. On a claim of concerted price-fixing, the antitrust plaintiff must present evidence sufficient to carry its burden of proving that there was such an agreement. If an inference of such an agreement may be drawn from highly ambiguous evidence, there is a considerable danger that the doctrines enunciated in *Sylvania*, and *Colgate* will be seriously eroded.

The flaw in the evidentiary standard adopted by the Court of Appeals in this case is that it disregards this danger. Permitting an agreement to be inferred merely from the existence of complaints, or even from the fact that termination came about "in response to" complaints, could deter or penalize perfectly legitimate conduct. As Monsanto points out, complaints about price-cutters "are natural—and from the manufacturer's perspective, unavoidable—reactions by distributors to the activities of their rivals." Such complaints, particularly where the manufacturer has imposed a costly set of nonprice restrictions, "arise in the normal course of business and do not indicate illegal concerted action." Roesch, Inc. v. Star Cooler Corp., 671 F.2d 1168, 1172 (CA8 1982), on rehearing en banc, 712 F.2d 1235 (CA8 1983) (affirming District Court judgment by an equally divided court). Moreover, distributors are an important source of information for manufacturers. In order to assure an efficient distribution system, manufacturers and distributors constantly must coordinate their activities to assure their product will reach the consumer persuasively and efficiently. To bar a manufacturer from acting solely because the information upon which it acts originated as a price complaint would create an irrational dislocation in the market. See F. Warren–Boulton, Vertical Control of Markets 13, 164

(1978). In sum, "[t]o permit the inference of concerted action on the basis of receiving complaints alone and thus to expose the defendant to treble damage liability would both inhibit management's exercise of independent business judgment and emasculate the terms of the statute." Edward J. Sweeney & Sons, Inc. v. Texaco, Inc., 637 F.2d 105, 111, n. 2 (CA3 1980), cert. denied, 451 U.S. 911 (1981).[56]

Thus, something more than evidence of complaints is needed. There must be evidence that tends to exclude the possibility that the manufacturer and nonterminated distributors were acting independently. As Judge Aldisert has written, the antitrust plaintiff should present direct or circumstantial evidence that reasonably tends to prove that the manufacturer and others "had a conscious commitment to a common scheme designed to achieve an unlawful objective." Edward J. Sweeney & Sons, supra, at 111; accord, H.L. Moore Drug Exchange v. Eli Lilly & Co., 662 F.2d 935, 941 (CA2 1981), cert. denied, 459 U.S. 880 (1982); cf. American Tobacco Co. v. United States, 328 U.S. 781, 810 (1946) (Circumstances must reveal "a unity of purpose or a common design and understanding, or a meeting of minds in an unlawful arrangement").[57]

III

A

Applying this standard to the facts of this case we believe there was sufficient evidence for the jury reasonably to have concluded that Monsanto and some of its distributors were parties to an "agreement" or "conspiracy" to maintain resale prices and terminate price-cutters. In fact there was substantial direct evidence of agreements to maintain prices. There was testimony from a Monsanto district manager, for example, that Monsanto on at least two occasions in early 1969, about five months after Spray–Rite was terminated, approached price-cutting distributors and advised that if they did not maintain the suggested resale price, they would not receive adequate supplies of Monsanto's new corn herbicide. When one of the distributors did not assent, this information was referred to the Monsanto regional office, and it complained to the distributor's parent company. There was evidence that the parent instructed its subsidiary to comply, and the distributor informed Monsanto that it would charge the suggested price. Evidence of this kind plainly is relevant and persuasive as to a meeting of minds.[58]

---

56. We do not suggest that evidence of complaints has no probative value at all, but only that the burden remains on the antitrust plaintiff to introduce additional evidence sufficient to support a finding of an unlawful contract, combination, or conspiracy.

57. The concept of "a meeting of the minds" or "a common scheme" in a distributor-termination case includes more than a showing that the distributor conformed to the suggested price. It means as well that evidence must be presented both that the distributor communicated its acquiescence or agreement, and that this was sought by the manufacturer.

58. In addition, there was circumstantial evidence that Monsanto sought agreement from the distributor to conform to the resale price. The threat to cut off the distributor's supply came during Monsanto's "shipping season" when herbicide was in short supply. The

An arguably more ambiguous example is a newsletter from one of the distributors to his dealer-customers. The newsletter is dated October 1, 1968, just four weeks before Spray–Rite was terminated. It was written after a meeting between the author and several Monsanto officials, and discusses Monsanto's efforts to "ge[t] the 'market place in order.'" The newsletter reviews some of Monsanto's incentive and shipping policies, and then states that in addition "every effort will be made to maintain a minimum market price level." The newsletter relates these efforts as follows:

> "In other words, we are assured that Monsanto's company-owned outlets will not retail at less than their suggested retail price to the trade as a whole. Furthermore, those of us on the distributor level are not likely to deviate downward on price to anyone as the idea is implied that doing this possibly could discolor the outlook for continuity as one of the approved distributors during the future upcoming seasons. So, none interested in the retention of this arrangement is likely to risk being deleted from this customer service opportunity. Also, so far as the national accounts are concerned, they are sure to recognize the desirability of retaining Monsanto's favor on a continuing basis by respecting the wisdom of participating in the suggested program in a manner assuring order on the retail level 'playground' throughout the entire country. It is elementary that harmony can only come from following the rules of the game and that in case of dispute, the decision of the umpire is final."

It is reasonable to interpret this newsletter as referring to an agreement or understanding that distributors and retailers would maintain prices, and Monsanto would not undercut those prices on the retail level and would terminate competitors who sold at prices below those of complying distributors; these were "the rules of the game."[59]

B

If, as the courts below reasonably could have found, there was evidence of an agreement with one or more distributors to maintain prices, the remaining question is whether the termination of Spray–Rite was part of or pursuant to that agreement. It would be reasonable to find that it was, since it is necessary for competing distributors contemplating compliance with suggested prices to know that those who do not comply will be terminated. Moreover, there is some circumstantial evidence of such a link.

---

jury could have concluded that Monsanto sought this agreement at a time when it was able to use supply as a lever to force compliance.

59. The newsletter also is subject to the interpretation that the distributor was merely describing the likely reaction to unilateral Monsanto pronouncements. But Monsanto itself appears to have construed the flyer as reporting a price-fixing understanding. Six weeks after the newsletter was written, a Monsanto official wrote its author a letter urging him to "correct immediately any misconceptions about Monsanto's marketing policies." The letter disavowed any intent to enter into an agreement on resale prices. The interpretation of these documents and the testimony surrounding them properly was left to the jury.

Following the termination, there was a meeting between Spray–Rite's president and a Monsanto official. There was testimony that the first thing the official mentioned was the many complaints Monsanto had received about Spray–Rite's prices.[60] In addition, there was reliable testimony that Monsanto never discussed with Spray–Rite prior to the termination the distributorship criteria that were the alleged basis for the action. By contrast, a former Monsanto salesman for Spray–Rite's area testified that Monsanto representatives on several occasions in 1965–1966 approached Spray–Rite, informed the distributor of complaints from other distributors—including one major and influential one, and requested that prices be maintained. Later that same year, Spray–Rite's president testified, Monsanto officials made explicit threats to terminate Spray–Rite unless it raised its prices.[61]

IV

We conclude that the Court of Appeals applied an incorrect standard to the evidence in this case. The correct standard is that there must be evidence that tends to exclude the possibility of independent action by the manufacturer and distributor. That is, there must be direct or circumstantial evidence that reasonably tends to prove that the manufacturer and others had a conscious commitment to a common scheme designed to achieve an unlawful objective. Under this standard, the evidence in this case created a jury issue as to whether Spray–Rite was terminated pursuant to a price-fixing conspiracy between Monsanto and its distributors.[62] The judgment of the court below is affirmed.

■ WHITE, J. took no part in the consideration or decision of this case.

■ BRENNAN, J. concurring. As the Court notes, the Solicitor General has filed a brief in this Court as *amicus curiae* urging us to overrule the Court's

60. Monsanto argues that the reference could have been to complaints by Monsanto employees rather than distributors, suggesting that the price controls were merely unilateral action, rather than accession to the demands of the distributors. The choice between two reasonable interpretations of the testimony properly was left for the jury.

61. The existence of the illegal joint boycott after Spray–Rite's termination, a finding that the Court of Appeals affirmed and that is not before us, is further evidence that Monsanto and its distributors had an understanding that prices would be maintained, and that price-cutters would be terminated. This last, however, is also consistent with termination for other reasons, and is probative only of the ability of Monsanto and its distributors to act in concert.

62. Monsanto's contrary evidence has force, but we agree with the courts below that it was insufficient to take the issue from the jury. It is true that there was no testimony of any complaints about Spray–Rite's pricing for the fifteen months prior to termination. But it was permissible for the jury to conclude that there were complaints during that period from the evidence that they were mentioned at Spray–Rite's post-termination meeting with Monsanto. There is also evidence that resale prices in fact did not stabilize after 1968. On the other hand, the former Monsanto salesman testified that prices were more stable in 1969–1970 than in his earlier stint in 1965–1966. And, given the evidence that Monsanto took active measures to stabilize prices, it may be that distributors did not assent in sufficient numbers, or broke their promises. In any event, we cannot say that the courts below erred in finding that Spray–Rite produced substantial evidence of the concerted action required by Section 1 of Sherman Act, and that—despite the sharp conflict in evidence—the case properly was submitted to the jury.

decision in Dr. Miles Medical Co. v. John D. Park & Sons Co., 220 U.S. 373 (1911). That decision has stood for 73 years, and Congress has certainly been aware of its existence throughout that time. Yet Congress has never enacted legislation to overrule the interpretation of the Sherman Act adopted in that case. Under these circumstances, I see no reason for us to depart from our longstanding interpretation of the Act. Because the Court adheres to that rule and, in my view, properly applies *Dr. Miles* to this case, I join the opinion and judgment of the Court.

NOTES AND QUESTIONS

1. Garment District, Inc. v. Belk Stores Services, Inc., 799 F.2d 905 (4th Cir. 1986). Plaintiff Garment District was a single outlet discounter in Gastonia, North Carolina, which sold a full line of Jantzen clothing at a markup of about 30–35% over the wholesale price. It was the only discounter of Jantzen clothing in Gastonia. Belk operated 400 stores in the Southeastern United States and also carried a full line of Jantzen clothing in its Gastonia store, commonly selling at a 100% markup.

Belk pressured Jantzen to stop supplying Garment District, and at one point, placed its Jantzen line in the "budget basement" and sold the product at discount prices. After meetings with Belk officials, Jantzen terminated Garment District on what the District Court found was the "pretext" that the store did not present a suitable image for a Jantzen retailer. In fact, the relationship was terminated because of the pressure exerted by Belk to stop Garment District's price cutting. After termination, Jantzen wrote to Belk stating that "the situation that exists in Gastonia is a mistake on our part and ... we intend to rectify this situation. Thank you for bringing this problem to my attention."

The District Court entered a directed verdict against Garment District and the Court of Appeals affirmed. It concluded that Jantzen terminated the single outlet Garment District to retain the vastly more valuable business of Belk, and the fact that it did so after complaints and coercion by Belk did not satisfy the *Monsanto* requirement that there "must be evidence that tends to exclude the possibility that the manufacturer and non-terminated distributors were acting independently."

Is *Belk* a fair interpretation of *Monsanto*? If it is, how will a plaintiff ever get to a jury with a claim that it was terminated as a result of an agreement between a complaining competitor and the supplier?

2. *Free rider rationale for vertical distribution restraints. Monsanto* confirms *Sylvania*'s reliance on a "free rider" explanation for some vertical distribution restraints. But the free-rider explanation may not account for many vertical distribution restraints. For example, in the years when fair trade was legal, products that tended frequently to be "fair traded" were over-the-counter drugs (*e.g.*, toothpaste, mouthwash, shaving cream), and cosmetics (cold cream, underarm deodorant). *See* Thomas R. Overstreet, Jr., Resale Price Maintenance: Economic Theories and Empirical Evidence, Bureau of Economics Staff report, Federal Trade Commission 177–98 (1983). What are the services that are so essential to the manufacturer in the retail sale of those products? Similarly, products involved in cases in which the FTC attacked resale price maintenance agreements—*e.g.*, blue jeans, pet food, ammunition, boxed candy, and men's underwear—are not typically "service-added" retail items. What were the services the manufacturer was con-

cerned about in insisting on resale price maintenance for blue jeans and men's underwear?

3. *Applications of* Colgate *and* Monsanto. Would the *Monsanto* court have found a violation on the facts in *Beech–Nut, Parke, Davis,* and *Albrecht*? If the *Colgate* doctrine was almost dead before *Monsanto,* that obviously is no longer the case. *See* Copperweld Corp. v. Independence Tube Corp., 467 U.S. 752 (1984), stressing the importance of distinguishing between single-firm behavior and agreements between independent entities. What are the limits now on a manufacturer setting resale prices by the *Colgate* technique?

4. *Evidentiary weight of termination. Monsanto* makes clear that termination following complaints, without more, is not enough to get to a jury on the question of "agreement." That is correct, is it not, since the complaints may have been nothing more than a source of information which then led the manufacturer to take a step entirely in its own interest. Suppose the rule were that termination following complaints is enough to get to a jury if the complaints constitute "the major contributing cause of such termination or refusal to supply." That was the approach of several bills in Congress including The Consumer Protection against Price Fixing Act of 1989, S. 865, 101st Cong. (1989), seeking to "clarify" *Monsanto.* Is that what the Supreme Court had in mind in *Monsanto*? Would it change the result in a case like *Belk*? Is it a workable standard? None of those bills ever passed, and it appears that the momentum behind them has largely faded away.

5. The next case, Business Electronics Corp. v. Sharp Electronics Corp., 485 U.S. 717 (1988), focuses primarily on the proper dividing line between price and non-price vertical restraints. Is that line still important, after *Leegin*? Is it possible that the evaluation of a manufacturer's practices under the rule of reason might need to take into account the question whether the vertical restriction is a direct one on price, or one imposed on a non-price element of competition?

Business Electronics Corp. v. Sharp Electronics Corp.

Supreme Court of the United States, 1988.
485 U.S. 717, 108 S.Ct. 1515, 99 L.Ed.2d 808.

■ SCALIA, J. Petitioner Business Electronics Corporation seeks review of a decision of the United States Court of Appeals for the Fifth Circuit holding that a vertical restraint is *per se* illegal under § 1 of the Sherman Act, only if there is an express or implied agreement to set resale prices at some level. We granted certiorari to resolve a conflict in the Courts of Appeals regarding the proper dividing line between the rule that vertical price restraints are illegal *per se* and the rule that vertical nonprice restraints are to be judged under the rule of reason.

I

In 1968, petitioner became the exclusive retailer in the Houston, Texas area of electronic calculators manufactured by respondent Sharp Electronics Corporation. In 1972, respondent appointed Gilbert Hartwell as a second retailer in the Houston area. During the relevant period, electronic calculators were primarily sold to business customers for prices up to $1,000. While much of the evidence in this case was conflicting—in particular, concerning whether petitioner was "free riding" on Hartwell's provision of presale educational and promotional services by providing inadequate services itself—a few facts are undisputed. Respondent published a list of suggested minimum retail prices, but its written dealership agreements with petitioner and Hartwell did not obligate either to observe them, or to charge any other specific price. Petitioner's retail prices were often below respondent's suggested retail prices and generally below Hartwell's retail prices, even though Hartwell too sometimes priced below respondent's suggested retail prices. Hartwell complained to respondent on a number of occasions about petitioner's prices. In June 1973, Hartwell gave respondent the ultimatum that Hartwell would terminate his dealership unless respondent ended its relationship with petitioner within 30 days. Respondent terminated petitioner's dealership in July 1973.

Petitioner brought suit in the United States District Court for the Southern District of Texas, alleging that respondent and Hartwell had conspired to terminate petitioner and that such conspiracy was illegal *per se* under § 1 of the Sherman Act. The case was tried to a jury. The District Court submitted a liability interrogatory to the jury that asked whether "there was an agreement or understanding between Sharp Electronics Corporation and Hartwell to terminate Business Electronics as a Sharp dealer because of Business Electronics' price cutting." The District Court instructed the jury at length about this question:

> "The Sherman Act is violated when a seller enters into an agreement or understanding with one of its dealers to terminate another dealer because of the other dealer's price cutting. Plaintiff contends that Sharp terminated Business Electronics in furtherance of Hartwell's desire to eliminate Business Electronics as a price-cutting rival.

> "If you find that there was an agreement between Sharp and Hartwell to terminate Business Electronics because of Business Electronics' price cutting, you should answer yes to Question Number 1.

>   . . .

> "A combination, agreement or understanding to terminate a dealer because of his price cutting unreasonably restrains trade and cannot be justified for any reason. Therefore, even though the combination, agreement or understanding may have been formed or engaged in . . . to eliminate any alleged evils of price cutting, it is still unlawful. . . .

> "If a dealer demands that a manufacturer terminate a price cutting dealer, and the manufacturer agrees to do so, the agreement is illegal if the manufacturer's purpose is to eliminate the price cutting."

The jury answered Question 1 affirmatively and awarded $600,000 in damages. The District Court . . . entered judgment for petitioner for treble damages plus attorney's fees.

The Fifth Circuit reversed, holding that the jury interrogatory and instructions were erroneous, and remanded for a new trial. It held that, to render illegal *per se* a vertical agreement between a manufacturer and a dealer to terminate a second dealer, the first dealer "must expressly or impliedly agree to set its prices at some level, though not a specific one. The distributor cannot retain complete freedom to set whatever price it chooses."

II

A

. . .

[The Court began by reviewing the *Dr. Miles* rule and by emphasizing that "the scope of *per se* illegality should be narrow in the context of vertical restraints." Citing Continental T.V., Inc. v. GTE Sylvania Inc., it acknowledged the use of the rule of reason for vertical nonprice restraints and cautioned that "especially in the vertical restraint context 'departure from the rule-of-reason standard must be based on demonstrable economic effect rather than . . . upon formalistic line drawing.'" It then reiterated the importance of distinguishing between intrabrand competition and interbrand competition and emphasized that the antitrust laws are primarily concerned with the latter. "[S]o long as interbrand competition existed," it wrote, "that would provide a 'significant check' on any attempt to exploit intrabrand market power. In fact, in order to meet that interbrand competition, a manufacturer's dominant incentive is to lower resale prices." It also predicted that "the *per se* illegality of vertical restraints would create a perverse incentive for manufacturers to integrate vertically into distribution, an outcome hardly conducive to fostering the creation and maintenance of small businesses." Last, it recalled that the opinion in *GTE Sylvania* "noted a significant distinction between vertical nonprice and vertical price restraints. That is, there was support for the proposition that vertical price restraints reduce *inter* brand price competition because they "'facilitate cartelizing.'" The authorities cited by the Court suggested how vertical price agreements might assist horizontal price fixing at the manufacturer level (by reducing the manufacturer's incentive to cheat on a cartel, since its retailers could not pass on lower prices to consumers) or might be used to organize cartels at the retailer level. . . . Similar support for the cartel-facilitating effect of vertical nonprice restraints was and remains lacking." At that point it turned to the heart of the opinion, which was devoted to drawing the line between price and non-price restraints.]

We have been solicitous to assure that the market-freeing effect of our decision in *GTE Sylvania* is not frustrated by related legal rules. In Monsanto Co. v. Spray–Rite Service Corp., which addressed the evidentiary showing necessary to establish vertical concerted action, we expressed concern that "[i]f an inference of such an agreement may be drawn from highly ambiguous evidence, there is considerable danger that the doctrin[e] enunciated in *Sylvania* . . . will be seriously eroded." We eschewed adoption of an evidentiary standard that "could deter or penalize perfectly legitimate conduct" or "would create an irrational dislocation in the market" by preventing legitimate communication between a manufacturer and its distributors.

Our approach to the question presented in the present case is guided by the premises of *GTE Sylvania* and *Monsanto*: that there is a presumption in favor of a rule-of-reason standard; that departure from that standard must be justified by demonstrable economic effect, such as the facilitation of cartelizing, rather than formalistic distinctions; that interbrand competition is the primary concern of the antitrust laws; and that rules in this area should be formulated with a view towards protecting the doctrine of *GTE Sylvania*. These premises lead us to conclude that the line drawn by the Fifth Circuit is the most appropriate one.

There has been no showing here that an agreement between a manufacturer and a dealer to terminate a "price cutter," without a further agreement on the price or price levels to be charged by the remaining dealer, almost always tends to restrict competition and reduce output. Any assistance to cartelizing that such an agreement might provide cannot be distinguished from the sort of minimal assistance that might be provided by vertical nonprice agreements like the exclusive territory agreement in *GTE Sylvania*, and is insufficient to justify a *per se* rule. Cartels are neither easy to form nor easy to maintain. Uncertainty over the terms of the cartel, particularly the prices to be charged in the future, obstructs both formation and adherence by making cheating easier. . . . Without an agreement with the remaining dealer on price, the manufacturer both retains its incentive to cheat on any manufacturer-level cartel (since lower prices can still be passed on to consumers) and cannot as easily be used to organize and hold together a retailer-level cartel.[63]

The District Court's rule on the scope of *per se* illegality for vertical restraints would threaten to dismantle the doctrine of *GTE Sylvania*. Any agreement between a manufacturer and a dealer to terminate another dealer who happens to have charged lower prices can be alleged to have been directed against the terminated dealer's "price cutting." In the vast majority of cases, it will be extremely difficult for the manufacturer to convince a jury that its motivation was to ensure adequate services, since price cutting and some measure of service cutting usually go hand in hand. Accordingly, a manufacturer that agrees to give one dealer an exclusive territory and terminates another dealer pursuant to that agreement, or even a manufacturer that agrees with one dealer to terminate another for failure to provide contractually-obligated services, exposes itself to the highly plausible claim that its real motivation was to terminate a price

---

63. The dissent's principal fear appears to be not cartelization at either level, but Hartwell's assertion of dominant retail power. This fear does not possibly justify adopting a rule of *per se* illegality. Retail market power is rare, because of the usual presence of interbrand competition and other dealers, see *Continental T.V., Inc. v. GTE Sylvania Inc.*, 433 U.S. 36, 54 (1977), and it should therefore not be assumed but rather must be proved. Cf. Baxter, The Viability of Vertical Restraints Doctrine, 75 Calif. L. Rev. 933, 948–949 (1987). Of course this case was not prosecuted on the theory, and therefore the jury was not asked to find, that Hartwell possessed such market power.

cutter. Moreover, even vertical restraints that do not result in dealer termination, such as the initial granting of an exclusive territory or the requirement that certain services be provided, can be attacked as designed to allow existing dealers to charge higher prices. Manufacturers would be likely to forgo legitimate and competitively useful conduct rather than risk treble damages and perhaps even criminal penalties.

We cannot avoid this difficulty by invalidating as illegal *per se* only those agreements imposing vertical restraints that contain the word "price," or that affect the "prices" charged by dealers. Such formalism was explicitly rejected in *GTE Sylvania*. As the above discussion indicates, all vertical restraints, including the exclusive territory agreement held not to be *per se* illegal in *GTE Sylvania*, have the potential to allow dealers to increase "prices" and can be characterized as intended to achieve just that. In fact, vertical nonprice restraints only accomplish the benefits identified in *GTE Sylvania* because they reduce intrabrand price competition to the point where the dealer's profit margin permits provision of the desired services. As we described it in *Monsanto*: "The manufacturer often will want to ensure that its distributors earn sufficient profit to pay for programs such as hiring and training additional salesmen or demonstrating the technical features of the product, and will want to see that 'free-riders' do not interfere." See also *GTE Sylvania*, 433 U.S., at 55.

The dissent erects a much more complex analytic structure, which ultimately rests, however, upon the same discredited premise that the only function this nonprice vertical restriction can serve is restraint of dealer-level competition. Specifically, the dissent's reasoning hinges upon its perception that the agreement between Sharp and Hartwell was a "naked" restraint—that is, it was not "ancillary" to any other agreement between Sharp and Hartwell. But that is not true, unless one assumes, contrary to *GTE Sylvania* and *Monsanto*, and contrary to our earlier discussion, that it is not a quite plausible purpose of the restriction to enable Hartwell to provide better services under the sales franchise agreement.[64] From its faulty conclusion that what we have before us is a "naked" restraint, the dissent proceeds, by reasoning we do not entirely follow, to the further conclusion that it is therefore a horizontal rather than a vertical restraint. We pause over this only to note that in addition to producing what we think the wrong result in the present case, it introduces needless confusion into antitrust terminology. Restraints imposed by agreement between com-

---

64. The conclusion of "naked" restraint could also be sustained on another assumption, namely that an agreement is not "ancillary" unless it is designed to enforce a contractual obligation of one of the parties to the contract. The dissent appears to accept this assumption. It is plainly wrong. The classic "ancillary" restraint is an agreement by the seller of a business not to compete within the market. See *Mitchel v. Reynolds*, 1 P.Wms. 181, 24 Eng.Rep. 347 (1711); Restatement (Second) of Contracts § 188(2)(a) (1981). That is not ancillary to any other contractual obligation, but, like the restraint here, merely enhances the value of the contract, or permits the "enjoyment of [its] fruits." *United States v. Addyston Pipe & Steel Co.*, 85 F. 271, 282 (CA6 1898), aff'd, 175 U.S. 211 (1899); cf. Restatement (Second) of Contracts §§ 187, 188 (1981) (restraint may be ancillary to a "transaction or relationship") (emphasis added); R. Bork, The Antitrust Paradox 29 (1978) (hereinafter Bork) (vertical arrangements are ancillary to the "transaction of supplying and purchasing")....

petitors have traditionally been denominated as horizontal restraints, and those imposed by agreement between firms at different levels of distribution as vertical restraints.[65]

Finally, we do not agree with petitioner's contention that an agreement on the remaining dealer's price or price levels will so often follow from terminating another dealer "because of [its] price cutting" that prophylaxis against resale price maintenance warrants the District Court's *per se* rule. Petitioner has provided no support for the proposition that vertical price agreements generally underlie agreements to terminate a price cutter. That proposition is simply incompatible with the conclusion of *GTE Sylvania* and *Monsanto* that manufacturers are often motivated by a legitimate desire to have dealers provide services, combined with the reality that price cutting is frequently made possible by "free riding" on the services provided by other dealers. The District Court's *per se* rule would therefore discourage conduct recognized by *GTE Sylvania* and *Monsanto* as beneficial to consumers.

B

In resting our decision upon the foregoing economic analysis, we do not ignore common-law precedent concerning what constituted "restraint of trade" at the time the Sherman Act was adopted. But neither do we give that pre–1890 precedent the dispositive effect some would. The term "restraint of trade" in the statute, like the term at common law, refers not to a particular list of agreements, but to a particular economic consequence, which may be produced by quite different sorts of agreements in varying times and circumstances. The changing content of the term "restraint of trade" was well recognized at the time the Sherman Act was enacted....

The Sherman Act adopted the term "restraint of trade" along with its dynamic potential. It invokes the common law itself, and not merely the static content that the common law had assigned to the term in 1890.... If it were otherwise, not only would the line of *per se* illegality have to be drawn today precisely where it was in 1890, but also case-by-case evaluation of legality (conducted where *per se* rules do not apply) would have to be governed by 19th–century notions of reasonableness. It would make no sense to create out of the single term "restraint of trade" a chronologically schizoid statute, in which a "rule of reason" evolves with new circumstances and new wisdom, but a line of *per se* illegality remains forever fixed where it was.

Of course the common law, both in general and as embodied in the Sherman Act, does not lightly assume that the economic realities underlying earlier decisions have changed, or that earlier judicial perceptions of those realities were in error. It is relevant, therefore, whether the common

---

65. The dissent apparently believes that whether a restraint is horizontal depends upon whether its anticompetitive effects are horizontal, and not upon whether it is the product of a horizontal agreement. That is of course a conceivable way of talking, but if it were the language of antitrust analysis there would be no such thing as an unlawful vertical restraint, since all anticompetitive effects are by definition horizontal effects....

law of restraint of trade ever prohibited as illegal *per se* an agreement of the sort made here, and whether our decisions under § 1 of the Sherman Act have ever expressed or necessarily implied such a prohibition.

. . .

Petitioner's principal contention has been that the District Court's rule on *per se* illegality is compelled not by the old common law, but by our more recent Sherman Act precedents. First, petitioner contends that since certain horizontal agreements have been held to constitute price fixing (and thus to be *per se* illegal) though they did not set prices or price levels, see, *e.g.*, Catalano, Inc. v. Target Sales, Inc., 446 U.S. 643, 647–650 (1980) (*per curiam*), it is improper to require that a vertical agreement set prices or price levels before it can suffer the same fate. This notion of equivalence between the scope of horizontal *per se* illegality and that of vertical *per se* illegality was explicitly rejected in GTE Sylvania, supra, 433 U.S., at 57, n. 27—as it had to be, since a horizontal agreement to divide territories is *per se* illegal, see United States v. Topco Associates., Inc., 405 U.S. 596, 608 (1972), while *GTE Sylvania* held that a vertical agreement to do so is not. . . .

Second, petitioner contends that *per se* illegality here follows from our two cases holding *per se* illegal a group boycott of a dealer because of its price cutting. See United States v. General Motors Corp., 384 U.S. 127 (1966); Klor's, Inc. v. Broadway–Hale Stores, Inc., 359 U.S. 207 (1959). This second contention is merely a restatement of the first, since both cases involved horizontal combinations—*General Motors*, supra, 384 U.S., at 140, 143–145, at the dealer level,[66] and *Klor's*, supra, 359 U.S., at 213, at the manufacturer and wholesaler levels. . . .

[The Court then rejected petitioner's arguments based on Albrecht v. Herald Co., 390 U.S. 145 (1968), later overruled in State Oil Co. v. Khan, 522 U.S. 3 (1997), and United States v. Parke, Davis & Co., 362 U.S. 29 (1960). In *Albrecht*, the maker of the product formed a combination to force a retailer to charge the maker's advertised retail price. That combination had two aspects: the hiring of a third party to solicit customers away from the noncomplying retailer, and the engagement of another retailer who undertook to deliver the products at the suggested price to the noncomplying retailer's customers obtained by the solicitor. It was that combination that led to the illegality. As the Court said, "[i]t is plain that the combination involved both an explicit agreement on resale price and an agreement to force another to adhere to the specified price." It distinguished *Parke, Davis* by noting that the manufacturer there combined first with wholesalers and then with retailers in order to gain "the retailers' adherence to its suggested minimum retail prices." The manufacturer also brokered an agreement among its retailers not to advertise prices below its suggested

---

66. Contrary to the dissent, *General Motors* does not differ from the present case merely in that it involved a three-party rather than a two-party agreement. The agreement was among competitors in *General Motors;* it was between noncompetitors here. Cf. Bork 330 (defining "boycotts" as "agreements among competitors to refuse to deal").

retail prices, which agreement was held to be part of the *per se* illegal combination. The holding, the Court concluded, did not support a rule that an agreement on price or price level is not required for a vertical restraint to be *per se* illegal. First, the agreement in *Parke, Davis* not to advertise prices was part and parcel of the combination that contained the price agreement, and second because the agreement among retailers that the manufacturer organized was a horizontal conspiracy among competitors.]

In sum, economic analysis supports the view, and no precedent opposes it, that a vertical restraint is not illegal *per se* unless it includes some agreement on price or price levels. Accordingly, the judgment of the Fifth Circuit is Affirmed.

■ KENNEDY, J., took no part in the consideration or decision of this case.

■ STEVENS, J., with whom WHITE, J., joins, dissenting.

In its opinion the majority assumes, without analysis, that the question presented by this case concerns the legality of a "vertical nonprice restraint." As I shall demonstrate, the restraint that results when one or more dealers threatens to boycott a manufacturer unless it terminates its relationship with a price-cutting retailer is more properly viewed as a "horizontal restraint." Moreover, an agreement to terminate a dealer because of its price cutting is most certainly not a "nonprice restraint." The distinction between "vertical nonprice restraints" and "vertical price restraints," on which the majority focuses its attention, is therefore quite irrelevant to the outcome of this case. Of much greater importance is the distinction between "naked restraints" and "ancillary restraints" that has been a part of our law since the landmark opinion written by Judge (later Chief Justice) Taft in United States v. Addyston Pipe & Steel Co., 85 F. 271 (CA6 1898), aff'd, 175 U.S. 211 (1899)....

* * *

It may be helpful to begin by explaining why the agreement in this case does not fit into certain categories of agreement that are frequently found in antitrust litigation. First, despite the contrary implications in the majority opinion, this is not a case in which the manufacturer is alleged to have imposed any vertical nonprice restraints on any of its dealers. The term "vertical nonprice restraint," as used in Continental T.V., Inc. v. GTE Sylvania, Inc., 433 U.S. 36 (1977), and similar cases, refers to a contractual term that a dealer must accept in order to qualify for a franchise. Typically, the dealer must agree to meet certain standards in its advertising, promotion, product display, and provision of repair and maintenance services in order to protect the goodwill of the manufacturer's product. Sometimes a dealer must agree to sell only to certain classes of customers—for example, wholesalers generally may only sell to retailers and may be required not to sell directly to consumers. In *Sylvania*, to take another example, we examined agreements between a manufacturer and its dealers that included "provisions barring the retailers from selling franchised products from locations other than those specified in agreements." *Id.*, 433 U.S., at 37. Restrictions of that kind, which are a part of, or ancillary to, the basic franchise agreement, are perfectly lawful unless the "rule of reason" is violated. Although vertical nonprice restraints may have some adverse effect on competition, as long as they serve the main purpose of a procompetitive distribution agreement, the ancillary restraints may be defended under the rule of reason. And, of course, a dealer who violates such a restraint may properly be terminated by the manufacturer.

In this case, it does not appear that respondent imposed any vertical nonprice restraints upon either petitioner or Hartwell. Specifically, respondent did not enter into any "exclusive" agreement, as did the defendant in *Sylvania*. It is true that before Hartwell was appointed and after petitioner was terminated, the manufacturer was represented by only one retailer in the Houston market, but there is no evidence that respondent ever made any contractual commitment to give either of them any exclusive rights. This therefore is not a case in which a manufacturer's right to grant exclusive territories, or to change the identity of the dealer in an established exclusive territory, is implicated. The case is one in which one of two competing dealers entered into an agreement with the manufacturer to terminate a particular competitor without making any promise to provide better or more efficient services and without receiving any guarantee of exclusivity in the future. The contractual relationship between respondent and Hartwell was exactly the same after petitioner's termination as it had been before that termination.

Second, this case does not involve a typical vertical price restraint. As the Court of Appeals noted, there is some evidence in the record that may support the conclusion that respondent and Hartwell implicitly agreed that Hartwell's prices would be maintained at a level somewhat higher than petitioner had been charging before petitioner was terminated. The illegality of the agreement found by the jury does not, however, depend on such evidence. For purposes of analysis, we should assume that no such agreement existed and that respondent was perfectly willing to allow its dealers to set prices at levels that would maximize their profits. That seems to have been the situation during the period when petitioner was the only dealer in Houston. Moreover, after respondent appointed Hartwell as its second dealer, it was Hartwell, rather than respondent, who objected to petitioner's pricing policies.

Third, this is not a case in which the manufacturer acted independently. Indeed, given the jury's verdict, it is not even a case in which the termination can be explained as having been based on the violation of any distribution policy adopted by respondent. The termination was motivated by the ultimatum that respondent received from Hartwell and that ultimatum, in turn, was the culmination of Hartwell's complaints about petitioner's competitive price cutting. The termination was plainly the product of coercion by the stronger of two dealers rather than an attempt to maintain an orderly and efficient system of distribution.[67]

---

67. "When a manufacturer acts on its own, in pursuing its own market strategy, it is seeking to compete with other manufacturers by imposing what may be defended as reasonable vertical restraints. This would appear to be the rationale of the *GTE Sylvania* decision.

In sum, this case does not involve the reasonableness of any vertical restraint imposed on one or more dealers by a manufacturer in its basic franchise agreement. What the jury found was a simple and naked " 'agreement between Sharp and Hartwell to terminate Business Electronics because of Business Electronics' price cutting.' "

III

Because naked agreements to restrain the trade of third parties are seldom identified with such stark clarity as in this case, there appears to be no exact precedent that determines the outcome here. There are, however, perfectly clear rules that would be decisive if the facts were changed only slightly.

Thus, on the one hand, if it were clear that respondent had acted independently and decided to terminate petitioner because respondent, for reasons of its own, objected to petitioner's pricing policies, the termination would be lawful. See United States v. Parke, Davis & Co., 362 U.S. 29, 43–45 (1960). On the other hand, it is equally clear that if respondent had been represented by three dealers in the Houston market instead of only two, and if two of them had threatened to terminate their dealerships "unless respondent ended its relationship with petitioner within 30 days," an agreement to comply with the ultimatum would be an obvious violation of the Sherman Act. See, *e.g.*, United States v. General Motors Corp., 384 U.S. 127 (1966); Klor's, Inc. v. Broadway–Hale Stores, Inc., 359 U.S. 207 (1959). The question then is whether the two-party agreement involved in this case is more like an illegal three-party agreement or a legal independent decision. For me, the answer is plain.

The distinction between independent action and joint action is fundamental in antitrust jurisprudence.[68] Any attempt to define the boundaries of *per se* illegality by the number of parties to different agreements with the same anticompetitive consequences can only breed uncertainty in the law and confusion for the businessman.

More importantly, if instead of speculating about irrelevant vertical nonprice restraints, we focus on the precise character of the agreement before us, we can readily identify its anticompetitive nature. Before the agreement was made, there was price competition in the Houston retail market for respondent's products. The stronger of the two competitors was unhappy about that competition; it wanted to have the power to set the price level in the market and therefore it "complained to respondent on a

---

However, if the action of a manufacturer or other supplier is taken at the direction of its customer, the restraint becomes primarily horizontal in nature in that one customer is seeking to suppress its competition by utilizing the power of a common supplier. Therefore, although the termination in such a situation is, itself, a vertical restraint, the desired impact is horizontal and on the dealer, not the manufacturer, level." *Cernuto, Inc. v. United Cabinet Corp.*, 595 F.2d 164, 168 (CA3 1979).

68. See *United States v. Colgate & Co.*, 250 U.S. 300, 307–308 (1919). In *Monsanto Co. v. Spray–Rite Service Corp.*, 465 U.S. 752, 761 (1984), we noted that "the basic distinction between concerted and independent action" was "not always clearly drawn by parties and courts." In its opinion today the majority virtually ignores that basic distinction .....

number of occasions about petitioner's prices." Quite obviously, if petitioner had agreed with either Hartwell or respondent to discontinue its competitive pricing, there would have been no ultimatum from Hartwell and no termination by respondent. It is equally obvious that either of those agreements would have been illegal *per se*. Moreover, it is also reasonable to assume that if respondent were to replace petitioner with another price-cutting dealer, there would soon be more complaints and another ultimatum from Hartwell. Although respondent has not granted Hartwell an exclusive dealership—it retains the right to appoint multiple dealers—its agreement has protected Hartwell from price competition. Indeed, given the jury's finding and the evidence in the record, that is the *sole function* of the agreement found by the jury in this case. It therefore fits squarely within the category of "naked restraints of trade with no purpose except stifling of competition." White Motor Co. v. United States, 372 U.S. 253, 263 (1963)....

Indeed, since the economic consequences of Hartwell's ultimatum to respondent are identical to those that would result from a comparable ultimatum by two of three dealers in a market—and since a two-party price-fixing agreement is just as unlawful as a three-party price-fixing agreement—it is appropriate to employ the term "boycott" to characterize this agreement. In my judgment the case is therefore controlled by our decision in United States v. General Motors Corp., 384 U.S. 127 (1966).

The majority disposes quickly of both *General Motors* and Klor's Inc. v. Broadway–Hale Stores, Inc., 359 U.S. 207 (1959), by concluding that "both cases involved horizontal combinations." But this distinction plainly will not suffice. In *General Motors*, a group of Chevrolet dealers conspired with General Motors to eliminate sales from the manufacturer to discounting dealers. We held that "[e]limination, by joint collaborative action, of discounters from access to the market is a *per se* violation of the Act," 384 U.S., at 145, and explained that "inherent in the success of the combination in this case was a substantial restraint upon price competition—a goal unlawful *per se* when sought to be effected by combination or conspiracy." *Id.*, at 147. Precisely the same goal was sought and effected in this case—the elimination of price competition at the dealer level. Moreover, the method of achieving that goal was precisely the same in both cases—the manufacturer's refusal to sell to discounting dealers. The difference between the two cases is not a difference between horizontal and vertical agreements—in both cases the critical agreement was between market actors at the retail level on the one hand and the manufacturer level on the other. Rather, the difference is simply a difference in the number of conspirators....

* * *

What is most troubling about the majority's opinion is its failure to attach any weight to the value of intrabrand competition. In Continental T.V., Inc. v. GTE Sylvania Inc., 433 U.S. 36 (1977), we correctly held that a demonstrable benefit to interbrand competition will outweigh the harm to intrabrand competition that is caused by the imposition of vertical nonprice restrictions on dealers. But we also expressly reaffirmed earlier cases in which the illegal conspiracy affected only intrabrand competition.[69] Not a word in the *Sylvania* opinion implied that the elimination of intrabrand competition could be justified as reasonable without any evidence of a purpose to improve interbrand competition.

In the case before us today, the relevant economic market was the sale at retail in the Houston area of calculators manufactured by respondent.[70] There is no dispute that an agreement to fix prices in that market, either horizontally between petitioner and Hartwell or vertically between respondent and either or both of the two dealers, would violate the Sherman Act. The "quite plausible" assumption . . . that such an agreement might enable the retailers to provide better services to their customers would not have avoided the strict rule against price fixing that this Court has consistently enforced in the past.

Under petitioner's theory of the case, an agreement between respondent and Hartwell to terminate petitioner because of its price cutting was just as indefensible as any of those price-fixing agreements. At trial the jury found the existence of such an agreement to eliminate petitioner's price competition. Respondent had denied that any agreement had been made and asked the jury to find that it had independently decided to terminate

---

69. *See* 433 U.S., at 58, n. 28 (citing *United States v. General Motors Corp.*, 384 U.S. 127 (1966), and *United States v. Topco Associates, Inc.*, 405 U.S. 596 (1972)).

70. It might be helpful to note at this point that although the majority mentions only the reduction of inter brand competition as a justification for a *per se* rule against vertical price restraints, our opinion in *Sylvania* was quite different. As we stated then:

"The market impact of vertical restrictions is complex because of their potential for a simultaneous reduction of intrabrand competition and stimulation of interbrand competition. Significantly, the Court in *Schwinn* did not distinguish among the challenged restrictions on the basis of their individual potential for intrabrand harm or interbrand benefit. Restrictions that completely eliminated intrabrand competition among Schwinn distributors were analyzed no differently from those that merely moderated intrabrand competition among retailers." . . .

In the following pages, we pointed out that because vertical nonprice restrictions imposed by manufacturers may serve to advance interbrand competition, the restriction on intrabrand competition should be subject only to a rule of reason analysis. Along these same lines, we explained that "[e]conomists also have argued that manufacturers have an economic interest in maintaining as much intrabrand competition as is consistent with the efficient distribution of their products." . . . Thus, although the majority neglects to mention it, fostering intrabrand competition has been recognized as an important goal of antitrust law, and although a manufacturer's efficiency-enhancing vertical nonprice restraints may subject a reduction of intrabrand competition only to a rule of reason analysis, a similar reduction without the procompetitive "redeeming virtues" of manufacturer-imposed vertical nonprice restraints, . . . causes nothing but economic harm. As one commentator has recently stated:

"Intrabrand competition can benefit the consumer, and it is therefore important to insure that a manufacturer's motive for a vertical restriction is not simply to acquiesce in his distributors' desires to limit competition among themselves. The Supreme Court has recognized that restrictions on intrabrand competition can only be tolerated because of the countervailing positive impact on interbrand competition." Piraino, The Case for Presuming the Legality of Quality Motivated Restrictions on Distribution, 63 Notre Dame L.Rev. 1, 17 (1988) (footnotes omitted).

petitioner because of its poor sales performance, but after hearing several days of testimony, the jury concluded that this defense was pretextual.

Neither the Court of Appeals nor the majority questions the accuracy of the jury's resolution of the factual issues in this case. Nevertheless, the rule the majority fashions today is based largely on its concern that in other cases juries will be unable to tell the difference between truthful and pretextual defenses. . . .

The majority fails to consider that manufacturers such as respondent will only be held liable in the rare case in which the following can be proved: First, the terminated dealer must overcome the high hurdle of Monsanto Co. v. Spray–Rite Service Corp., 465 U.S. 752 (1984). A terminated dealer must introduce "evidence that tends to exclude the possibility that the manufacturer and nonterminated distributors were acting independently." Requiring judges to adhere to the strict test for agreement laid down in *Monsanto*, in their jury instructions or own findings of fact, goes a long way toward ensuring that many legitimate dealer termination decisions do not succumb improperly to antitrust liability.[71]

Second, the terminated dealer must prove that the agreement was based on a purpose to terminate it because of its price cutting. Proof of motivation is another commonplace in antitrust litigation of which the majority appears apprehensive, but as we have explained or demonstrated many times . . . in antitrust, as in many other areas of the law, motivation matters and factfinders are able to distinguish bad from good intent.

Third, the manufacturer may rebut the evidence tending to prove that the sole purpose of the agreement was to eliminate a price cutter by offering evidence that it entered the agreement for legitimate, nonprice-related reasons.

Although in this case the jury found a naked agreement to terminate a dealer because of its price cutting, the majority boldly characterizes the same agreement as "this nonprice vertical restriction." That characterization is surely an oxymoron when applied to the agreement the jury actually found. Nevertheless, the majority proceeds to justify it as "ancillary" to a "quite plausible purpose . . . to enable Hartwell to provide better services

---

71. Although at trial respondent had asked the jury to find that it had acted independently, respondent has not disputed, either in the Court of Appeals or here, the jury's finding of an agreement. (Respondent has, of course, contended that no agreement was reached requiring some level of resale price maintenance. As I have argued, though, such an agreement is not needed to invoke the *per se* rule in a case such as this.) Respondent did argue before the District Court for an instruction explaining that "it must be shown that the manufacturer agreed with the complaining dealer to terminate the existing dealer and that, in so agreeing, the manufacturer shared with the complaining dealer the same desire of eliminating price competition for the complaining dealer." Respondent later objected to the court's decision not to give this instruction, but the court in fact had quite carefully explained to the jury that "[w]hat a preponderance . . . of the evidence in the case must show in order to establish the existence of the required combination, agreement, or understanding is that Sharp and Hartwell knowingly came to a common and mutual understanding to accomplish or to attempt to accomplish an unlawful purpose." *Id.*, at 1584–1585.

under the sales franchise agreement." There are two significant reasons why that justification is unacceptable.

First, it is not supported by the jury's verdict. Although it did not do so with precision, the District Court did instruct the jury that in order to hold respondent liable it had to find that the agreement's purpose was to eliminate petitioner because of its price cutting and that no valid vertical nonprice restriction existed to which the motivation to eliminate price competition at the dealership level was merely ancillary.

Second, the "quite plausible purpose" the majority hypothesizes as salvation for the otherwise anticompetitive elimination of price competition—"to enable Hartwell to provide better services under the sales franchise agreement,"—is simply not the type of concern we sought to protect in Continental T.V. Inc. v. GTE Sylvania Inc., 433 U.S. 36 (1977). I have emphasized in this dissent the difference between restrictions imposed in pursuit of a manufacturer's structuring of its product distribution, and those imposed at the behest of retailers who care less about the general efficiency of a product's promotion than their own profit margins. *Sylvania* stressed the importance of the former, not the latter; we referred to the use that *manufacturers* can make of vertical nonprice restraints, see *id.*, at 54–57, and nowhere did we discuss the benefits of permitting dealers to structure intrabrand competition at the retail level by coercing manufacturers into essentially anticompetitive agreements. Thus, while Hartwell may indeed be able to provide better services under the sales franchise agreement with petitioner out of the way, one would not have thought, until today, that the mere possibility of such a result—at the expense of the elimination of price competition and absent the salutary overlay of a manufacturer's distribution decision with the entire product line in mind—would be sufficient to legitimate an otherwise purely anticompetitive restraint. In fact, given the majority's total reliance on "economic analysis," it is hard to understand why, if such a purpose were sufficient to avoid the application of a *per se* rule in this context, the same purpose should not also be sufficient to trump the *per se* rule in all other price-fixing cases that arguably permit cartel members to "provide better services." . . .

NOTES AND QUESTIONS

1. *Free rider factor.* As the dissent in *Sharp* points out, there was no evidence that Sharp ever sought or that Business Electronics ever failed to provide relevant services. In effect, does the majority presume that the termination occurred because Sharp was a free rider? Is there any justification for such a presumption in this case? Generally, in distribution situations?

2. *Alternate discounter-termination scenario.* Did those who opposed the *Dr. Miles* rule succeed in part by implying that *all* discounters are "free riders," calling forth images of a lazy cheat who takes advantage of honest businessmen by selling at low prices without accompanying services? Consider a different model. Assume ten dealers of the same branded product, nine of whom are selling at roughly the

same high price. The tenth dealer works longer and harder, is more aggressive, handles purchasing, inventory and sales more efficiently—and seeks to pass those efficiencies on to consumers in the form of lower prices in order to expand its sales. Under the analysis of the majority in *Sharp*, would a termination of the price cutter in that situation be permissible—assuming the other nine dealers separately complained, but the manufacturer and the dealers never agreed as to a specific resale price? How would that case be analyzed under *Leegin*'s rule of reason?

Although cases in which vertical price-fixing claims are recognized are relatively rare, consider the following decision from the Third Circuit. Do you think it is consistent with *Business Electronics* and *Monsanto*? Does the result survive *Leegin*?

Pace Electronics, Inc. v. Canon Computer Systems, Inc.

United States Court of Appeals, Third Circuit, 2000.
213 F.3d 118.

■ ROSENN, CIRCUIT JUDGE. The issue in this appeal is whether the termination of a wholesale dealer's contract for its refusal to acquiesce in an alleged vertical minimum price fixing conspiracy constitutes an antitrust injury that will support an action for damages under section 4 of the Clayton Act. The United States District Court for the District of New Jersey reasoned that a dealer terminated under these circumstances does not suffer an antitrust injury unless it can demonstrate that its termination had an actual, adverse economic effect on a relevant market. After concluding that the plaintiff's complaint in the instant case failed to allege such an effect, the District Court dismissed the complaint for failure to state a claim upon which relief may be granted. Because we believe the court misconstrued the antitrust injury requirement, we will reverse.

I.

The plaintiff, Pace Electronics, Inc. ("Pace"), a New Jersey corporation, is engaged in the business of distributing various electronic products, including computer printers and related accessories. Pace purchases these products from manufacturers and wholesale distributors and then resells them to smaller retailers, who operate in the New Jersey and New York region.

In April of 1996, Pace entered into a nonexclusive dealer agreement with defendant Canon Computer Systems, Inc. ("Canon"), a California corporation. Under this agreement, Pace obtained the right to purchase Canon-brand ink-jet printers and related accessories from Canon at "dealer prices." In consideration for the right to purchase these products at "dealer prices," Pace agreed to purchase certain minimum quantities of the products.

The dealer agreement between Pace and Canon remained in effect for approximately one year and three months. Thereafter, on July 1, 1997, Canon terminated the agreement with Pace on the stated ground that Pace failed to purchase the minimum quantities of Canon-brand products required of it under the dealer agreement. Although Pace concedes that it did not purchase the amount of Canon-brand products called for under the dealer agreement, Pace contends that it was unable to do so because Canon ignored its purchase orders. Pace further contends that Canon ignored its purchase orders because Pace refused to acquiesce in a vertical minimum price fixing agreement designed and implemented by Canon and defendant Laguna Corporation ("Laguna"), Pace's direct competitor in the New Jersey and New York region.

In this connection, Pace alleges that, prior to the time it entered its dealer agreement with Canon, Laguna had entered into a similar dealer agreement with Canon. Additionally, Pace alleges that the agreement between Canon and Laguna contemplated the maintenance of a minimum resale price below which Laguna would not sell Canon-brand ink-jet printers. In support of its allegation, Pace asserts that after it entered into its dealer agreement with Canon, the president of Canon repeatedly instructed Pace's president not to sell to past or existing customers of Laguna and not to sell Canon brand ink-jet printers at prices less than those at which Laguna was selling its products.

Pace alleges that it has suffered financial losses as a result of its termination as an authorized Canon-brand dealer. Specifically, Pace avers that "[a]s a direct and proximate result of the actions of Defendants ... Pace has suffered significant financial detriment, consisting of, but not necessarily limited to, lost profits. Pace's losses result directly and proximately from the efforts of Canon and Laguna to limit price competition in the market ... for which both Laguna and Pace were competing." ... Although these allegations of loss appear somewhat vague and conclusory, we accept them as true, as we must, for the purposes of this appeal.

Pace also alleges that its termination as an authorized dealer of Canon-brand products has harmed competition in two respects. First, it contends that its termination as a dealer has reduced price competition in the wholesale market for Canon-brand ink-jet printers (an intrabrand market) because Laguna no longer faces price competition from Pace in selling these products to smaller retailers. Second, Pace asserts that its termination as a dealer has reduced price competition in the wholesale market for all brands of ink-jet printers (an interbrand market). In this connection, Pace alleges that: (1) Canon-brand ink-jet printers enjoy an inherent competitive price advantage over the ink-jet printers of other manufacturers; (2) until Canon permits its distributors to take advantage of this price advantage, other manufacturers will not attempt to reduce their production costs; and, (3) until an unrestrained free competitive market requires other manufacturers to reduce their production costs, the price of all brands of ink-jet printers will remain at an artificially high level.

II.

To state a claim for damages under section 4 of the Clayton Act, 15 U.S.C. § 15, a plaintiff must allege more than that it has suffered an injury causally linked to a violation of the antitrust laws. See Brunswick Corp. v. Pueblo Bowl–O–Mat, Inc., 429 U.S. 477, 489 (1977). In addition, it must allege antitrust injury, "which is to say injury of the type the antitrust laws were intended to prevent and that flows from that which makes defendants' acts unlawful." *Id.* This is so even where, as in the instant case, the alleged acts of the defendants constitute a *per se* violation of the antitrust laws. See also Atlantic Richfield Co. v. USA Petroleum Co., 495 U.S. 328, 341 (1990). In applying the antitrust injury requirement, the Supreme Court has inquired whether the injury alleged by the plaintiff "resembles any of the potential dangers" which led the Court to label the defendants' alleged conduct violative of the antitrust laws in the first instance. *Id.* at 336. . . .

For example, in *Atlantic Richfield*, the plaintiff, an independent retail marketer of gasoline, brought suit against ARCO, an integrated oil company which sold gasoline to consumers through its own stations and indirectly through ARCO-brand dealers, claiming that ARCO violated section 1 of the Sherman Act by conspiring with its dealers to fix the maximum resale price of gasoline at an artificially low level. *Id.* at 331. Although the plaintiff conceded that the fixed prices were not predatory, it nevertheless maintained that it suffered antitrust injury, in the form of lost profits, as a result of the vertical maximum price fixing agreement between ARCO and its dealers. See *id.* at 334–35. The Supreme Court disagreed, noting that the plaintiff's alleged injury did not resemble any of the dangers which caused the Court to label vertical maximum price fixing *per se* illegal in Albrecht v. Herald Co., 390 U.S. 145 (1968).[72] See *id.* at 336.

[The court then reviewed the reasons why *Albrecht* had condemned vertical maximum price arrangements: replacement of the manufacturer's judgment of market conditions with that of the dealer; prices too low for essential services; limitation on non-price competition; and transformation of a fixed maximum price into a fixed minimum.]

Having identified the potential dangers which led it to condemn categorically vertical maximum price fixing agreements, the Supreme Court had little difficulty determining that the plaintiff in *Atlantic Richfield* had not suffered an antitrust injury. The Court noted that the dangers identified in the *Albrecht* decision focused on the potential adverse effects of vertical maximum price fixing agreements on *dealers and consumers*, not competitors of dealers subject to such agreements. See *id.* The Court explained: "[i]ndeed, the gravamen of [the plaintiff's] complaint—that the price fixing scheme between[the defendant] and its dealers enabled those dealers to increase their sales—amounts to an assertion that the dangers with which we were concerned in *Albrecht* have not materialized in the instant case." *Id.* at 337. In sum, the Court concluded that the plaintiff had

---

72. *Albrecht*'s specific holding—that vertical maximum price fixing is *per se* illegal—has since been overruled. *See State Oil Co. v. Khan,* 522 U.S. 3, 7 (1997). However, *Atlantic Richfield*'s approach—*i.e.,* discerning the reasons that led the Supreme Court to label certain conduct a *per se* violation, and determining whether the harm suffered by the plaintiff is consistent with the rationale for labeling the defendant's conduct *per se* illegitimate—remains valid and is clearly applicable to the case before us.

not suffered antitrust injury because its losses did not flow from those aspects of vertical maximum pricing that rendered it illegal. *Id*. at 337.

Turning now to the instant case, we think it appropriate to ask whether Pace's alleged injury resembles any of the dangers which have led the Supreme Court to condemn vertical minimum price fixing agreements under the antitrust laws. Pace alleges that it has suffered antitrust injury because it was terminated as a wholesale dealer after it sold Canon-brand products at prices below the minimum resale price allegedly fixed by Canon and Laguna. Pace further alleges that its termination as a wholesale dealer has caused it to suffer lost profits because it may no longer obtain profits from selling Canon-brand products at "dealer prices." Under the Supreme Court's jurisprudence, these allegations suffice to establish antitrust injury.

On this point, Simpson v. Union Oil, 377 U.S. 13 (1964) is instructive. In *Simpson*, the plaintiff entered into a year-to-year "consignment" agreement with Union Oil. See *id*. at 14. Under the agreement, which was terminable by either party at the end of any one-year term, Union Oil required the plaintiff to charge a minimum retail price for gasoline. See *id*. Contrary to the terms of the agreement with Union Oil, the plaintiff sold gasoline below the minimum retail price. See *id*. at 15. Because he did so, Union Oil terminated its "consignment" agreement with the plaintiff at the end of the first one-year term. See *id*.

Sometime thereafter, the plaintiff brought suit against Union Oil seeking damages under section 4 of the Clayton Act. See *id*. After two pretrial hearings, the District Court granted summary judgment in favor of Union Oil, holding that the plaintiff failed to establish a violation of section 1 of the Sherman Act and that, even assuming the plaintiff had established a violation, the plaintiff suffered no actionable damage. See *id*. at 15–16. The Court of Appeals affirmed on the ground that the plaintiff suffered no actionable wrong or damage. See *id*. at 16. The Supreme Court granted certiorari and reversed.

In reversing, the Court placed primary focus on the consignment agreement's restriction on the ability of dealers such as the plaintiff to make independent, competitive pricing decisions. For example, the Court explained:

> We disagree with the Court of Appeals that there is no actionable wrong or damage if a Sherman Act violation is assumed. If the "consignment" agreement achieves resale price maintenance in violation of the Sherman Act, it and the lease are being used to injure interstate commerce *by depriving independent dealers of the exercise of free judgment* whether to become consignees at all, or remain consignees, and, in any event, to sell at competitive prices. *Id*. (emphasis added).

The Court also stated:

> Dealers, like [the plaintiff], are independent businessmen; and they have all or most of the indicia of entrepreneurs, except for price fixing. . . . Their return is affected by the rise and fall

in the market price, their commissions declining as retail prices drop. *Practically the only power they have to be wholly independent businessmen, whose service depends on their own initiative and enterprise, is taken from them by the proviso that they must sell their gasoline at prices fixed by Union Oil....* The evil of the resale price maintenance program ... is its inexorable potentiality for and even certainty in destroying competition in retail sales of gasoline by these nominal 'consignees' who are in reality small struggling competitors seeking retail gas customers.

Id. at 21 (emphasis added) (footnote and citations omitted).

Thus, the Supreme Court considered a restriction on dealer independence with respect to pricing decisions to be an anticompetitive aspect of vertical minimum price fixing agreements, and one that the antitrust laws have an interest in forestalling.... Accordingly, we think that a maverick dealer, such as Pace, which is terminated for charging prices less than those set under a vertical minimum price fixing agreement, suffers the type of injury which the antitrust laws are designed to prevent and may recover damages, such as lost profits, which flow from that termination....

Naturally, the defendants argue that the above analysis misses the mark. In essence, they contend that *Simpson* is no longer good law in light of the Supreme Court's decision in *Atlantic Richfield*. Furthermore, they urge, and the district court agreed, that a terminated dealer seeking to establish that it has suffered antitrust injury must allege facts demonstrating that its termination as an authorized dealer resulted in an actual, adverse economic effect on competition in a relevant interbrand market. In support of their position, the defendants primarily rely on the Supreme Court's statement in *Atlantic Richfield* that a plaintiff can recover damages under section 4 of the Clayton Act "only if [its] loss[es] stem[ ] from a competition-reducing aspect or effect of the defendant's behavior." *Atlantic Richfield*, 495 U.S. at 344. On the basis of this brief statement, the defendants then argue that to be "competition-reducing" a defendant's challenged conduct must have had an actual adverse effect on a relevant interbrand market. Although the defendants' syllogism may have some allure, we decline to construe the antitrust injury requirement as suggested by the defendants for the following reasons.

First, we believe that requiring a plaintiff to demonstrate that an injury stemming from a *per se* violation of the antitrust laws caused an actual, adverse effect on a relevant market in order to satisfy the antitrust injury requirement comes dangerously close to transforming a *per se* violation into a case to be judged under the rule of reason. The *per se* standard is reserved for certain categories of conduct which experience has shown to be "manifestly anticompetitive." Continental T.V., Inc. v. GTE Sylvania Inc., 433 U.S. 36, 39 (1977). That standard, which is based on considerations of "business certainty and litigation efficiency," Arizona v. Maricopa County Med. Society, 457 U.S. 332, 344 (1982), allows a court to presume that certain limited classes of conduct have an anticompetitive effect without engaging in the type of involved, market-specific analysis ordinarily necessary to reach such a conclusion. See Business Electronics Corp. v. Sharp Electronics Corp., 485 U.S. 717, 723 (1988) ("Certain categories of agreements, however, have been held to be *per se* illegal, dispensing with the need for case-by-case evaluation."). Were we to accept the defendants' construction of the antitrust injury requirement, we would, in substance, be removing the presumption of anticompetitive effect implicit in the *per se* standard under the guise of the antitrust injury requirement.[73]

Second, we do not believe that the Supreme Court's statement in *Atlantic Richfield* that a plaintiff can recover for losses only if they stem "from a competition-reducing aspect or effect of the defendant's behavior," *Atlantic Richfield*, 495 U.S. at 344, when viewed in the context of the Court's entire opinion, can be fairly read to require a terminated dealer to prove that its termination caused an actual, adverse economic effect on a relevant market. In this connection, we note that in determining that the plaintiff in *Atlantic Richfield* failed to satisfy the antitrust injury requirement, the Supreme Court simply did not focus on whether the challenged conduct of the defendant had an actual, adverse economic effect on a relevant market. Rather, as outlined above, the Court focused on whether the plaintiff's injury stemmed from any of the potential anticompetitive dangers which led the Court to label vertical maximum price fixing unlawful in the first instance. Implicit in the Court's approach is that a plaintiff who had suffered loss as a result of an anticompetitive aspect of a *per se* restraint of trade agreement would have suffered antitrust injury, without demonstrating that the challenged practice had an actual, adverse economic effect on a relevant market.... The issue, thus, is not whether the plaintiff's alleged injury produced an anticompetitive result, but, rather, whether the injury claimed resulted from the anticompetitive aspect of the challenged conduct.

Finally, we point out that our holding—that a dealer terminated for its refusal to abide by a vertical minimum price fixing agreement suffers antitrust injury and may recover losses flowing from that termination—is consistent with the decisions of those courts which have explored the issue thus far. See, *e.g.*, Sterling Interiors Group, Inc. v. Haworth, Inc., No. 94–9216, 1996 WL 426379 at *18–*19 (S.D.N.Y. July 30, 1996) ("The anticompetitive dangers of minimum price arrangements flow to both customers who purchase at prices set higher than competitive levels, and to dealers who are effectively foreclosed from competing in the marketplace.").

---

73. We recognize that various scholars have taken issue with the Supreme Court's *per se* treatment of vertical minimum price fixing agreements and argued that these agreements may have significant, procompetitive attributes. *See, e.g., Antitrust Policy*, 75 Colum. L.Rev. at 283. But, academic commentary, even if persuasive, does not permit us to expand the antitrust injury requirement to a point which undermines the Court's categorical disapproval of vertical minimum price fixing.

III.

For the reasons set forth above, the district court's order dismissing Pace's complaint will be reversed and the case remanded to the district court for further proceedings consistent with this opinion. Costs taxed against the appellees.

NOTES AND QUESTIONS

1. *Antitrust injury doctrine.* The court in *Pace* approaches the vertical restraint before it—an alleged minimum price-fixing conspiracy—through the lens of the "antitrust injury" doctrine, aspects of which are discussed in Chapter 2, *supra,* pp. 83–91, and in Chapter 9, *infra,* pp. 1020–21. This brings to mind the famous observation of the English legal scholar Henry Sumner Maine, who wrote that "substantive law has at first the look of being gradually secreted in the interstices of procedure." Henry Sumner Maine, Dissertations on Early Law and Custom 389 (Arno Press 1975) (1886). Much of antitrust law has also been secreted in the interstices of procedure: the antitrust standing doctrines, the antitrust injury idea, summary judgment rules, and the like. The district court here found that the allegations of a vertical price-fixing conspiracy failed to describe "antitrust injury," which as the court says is "injury of the type the antitrust laws were intended to prevent and that flows from that which makes the defendants' acts unlawful." Brunswick Corp. v. Pueblo Bowl–O–Mat, Inc., 429 U.S. 477, 489 (1977). The court of appeals, of course, disagreed. The important point for present purposes is that the court of appeals thought that the theory the plaintiff was presenting, which we have been exploring in this section, was plausible enough as an antitrust violation that the plaintiff was entitled to have a decision on the merits. In reaching that decision, the court was necessarily making substantive choices about how far the antitrust laws go in regulating vertical arrangements. Compare this to Cargill, Inc. v. Monfort of Colorado, Inc., 479 U.S. 104 (1986), Chapter 9, *infra,* p. 1021, which also made important contributions to the substantive law of merger regulation under the guise of deciding whether the plaintiff had suffered antitrust injury.

2. *Interbrand competition concern.* Note the comment in the majority opinion in *Business Electronics* that "interbrand competition is the primary concern of the antitrust laws," *supra* p. 700. Is such a principle fairly deduced from the Court's analysis of non-price vertical restrictions in *Sylvania* and other cases? If that dictum is the law, does it follow that *Topco* has been overruled? Note, however, that the majority opinion in *Sharp* cited *Topco* favorably. *See supra* p. 703.

3. *Retailer market power.* The dissenters in *Business Electronics* raised the concern that the dominant dealer in the market had coerced Sharp into terminating the other dealer in order to consolidate market power. The majority dismissed this concern, remarking that dominant retailer power is unlikely to occur and that the plaintiff did not allege it. While the majority may have been right with respect to the record before it, its suggestion that competition in the retail market will prevent dominant retailers from wielding market power is far less certain. To be sure, most of the cases in this chapter (and the next) arose as small retailers challenged the policies imposed on them by manufacturers. While these cases sometimes explore whether the challenged policies were forged by the manufacturer or produced by horizontal agreements of various dealers, they operate from the general assumption that manufacturers have more power than retailers. Is this still a valid premise? In

the past 10 years, retailing in America has changed dramatically. Over the span of just a few years, super-sized retail chains, such as Wal–Mart, Home Depot and Toys "R" Us, have grown up to dominate the industry in a way never before seen. Might the volume of sales these chains control enable them to wring special concessions or contract terms from manufacturers and might some of these contract terms be open to attack as "vertical restraints on competition"?

With this in mind, reconsider *Toys "R" Us, supra* p. 484. Recall that the Commission condemned the arrangement both under the horizontal and vertical theories. Some critics derided the FTC for overreaching since Toys "R" Us controls only 20% of the retail market. Skipping over the market power question, isn't the FTC's real problem distinguishing these special arrangements from volume discounts? Is the FTC's action justified as a way to get manufacturers and retailers to compete on price? Along these lines, see also the opinion of the court-appointed expert in State of New York v. Kraft General Foods, expressing concerns about the emphasis on non-price competition in the ready-to-eat cereal industry. 926 F. Supp. 321, 351, 1995–1 Trade Cases (CCH) ¶ 70,911 (S.D.N.Y. 1995).

PROBLEM 16

DISTRIBUTION ARRANGEMENTS FOR GLORY HAIR RINSE

Glory Hair Rinse is one of the ten leading preparations in the United States for tinting hair; there are no others of consequence. Glory accounts for about 15% of the U.S. market.

The product is marketed primarily through wholesalers who sell to retail druggists. Each wholesaler buys the product for $5.60 per bottle. Glory suggests a wholesale price of $7.00 and a retail price of $9.50. Glory advertises heavily in fashion magazines and other media, aiming to create the image of a prestige product. Consistent with that advertising campaign, it asks its wholesalers not to sell to discount druggists and other discount outlets.

To assure that its recommended prices are followed, Glory has notified all retailers of its product as follows:

> If you are disturbed by retail sales by others of Glory Hair Rinse at less than the suggested retail price, you should notify your wholesaler of the facts surrounding the cut-rate sales.

Wholesalers have been informed that:

> It is Glory's policy to maintain suggested retail prices. However, you must not under any circumstances consult with retailers selling at less than the suggested price. Action speaks louder than words.

Wholesalers are expected to warehouse and deliver the product promptly to retailers on order. Retailers are asked but not required to display Glory's product prominently. No other services are required or requested.

A pattern has developed whereby, if a retailer sells Glory products at less than the suggested resale price, the wholesaler fills the particular order but refuses to honor future orders. The wholesaler also refuses to discuss the matter with the retailer that has been cut off. At some later date, usually after a year or 18 months, the wholesaler may offer to fill orders of the retailer; the wholesaler will again refuse to discuss the retailer's practices. Where wholesalers have not followed this practice promptly upon receiving complaints of cut-rate sales, Glory has cut off the wholesaler and performed its own wholesaling function, including the temporary suspension of sales to price-cutting retailers. Six of the other nine hair rinse manufacturers follow similar distribution practices. Their prices to wholesalers are identical with Glory's and they suggest the same wholesale and retail price. The other three manufacturers aggressively market their products to all outlets.

Last year, Able Drug complained to its wholesaler and Glory that Baker Drug, a direct rival, was purchasing Glory Hair Rinse in vast quantities, not for sale to customers, but for transshipment to discount drug stores in the area. After investigating the matter, the wholesaler cut off Baker without ever discussing the matter with Glory. Has Glory violated the antitrust laws?

SELECTIVE BIBLIOGRAPHY

1. Resale Price Maintenance

Arthur, The Core of Antitrust and the Slow Death of Dr. Miles, 62 SMU L. Rev. 437 (2009).

Lambert, Dr. Miles Is Dead. Now What?: Structuring a Rule of Reason for Evaluating Minimum Resale Price Maintenance, 50 Wm. & Mary L. Rev. 1937 (2009).

Bauer, Whither Dr. Miles? 20 Loy. Consumer L. Rev. 1 (2007).

Harbour, A Tale of Two Marks, and Other Antitrust Concerns, 20 Loy. Consumer L. Rev. 32 (2007).

Pitofsky, Are Retailers Who Offer Discounts Really "Knaves"? The Coming Challenge to the Dr. Miles Rule, 21–SPG Antitrust 61 (2007).

Blair, Herndon & Lopatka, Resale Price Maintenance and the Private Antitrust Plaintiff, 83 Wash. U. L. Q. 657 (2005).

Blair & Lopatka, The Albrecht Rule after Khan: Death Becomes Her, 74 Notre Dame L. Rev. 123 (1998).

Grimes, The Seven Myths of Vertical Price Fixing: The Politics and Economics of a Century–Long Debate, 21 Sw. U. L. Rev. 1285 (1992).

Comanor, Vertical Price Fixing, Vertical Market Restrictions, and the New Antitrust Policy, 98 Harv. L. Rev. 983 (1985).

Easterbrook, Vertical Arrangements and the Rule of Reason, 53 Antitrust L. J. 135 (1984).

Pitofsky, In Defense of Discounters: The No–Frills Case for a *per se* Rule against Vertical Price Fixing, 71 Geo. L. J. 1487 (1983).

Telser, Why Should Manufacturers Want Fair Trade? 3 J. L. & Econ. 86 (1960).

2. Other Vertical and Distributional Restraints

Olszewski, Overruling a Nearly Century–Old Precedent: Why Leegin Got It Right, 94 Iowa L. Rev. 375 (2008).

Gevurtz, Vertical Restraints on Competition, 54 Am. J. Comp. L. 357 (2006).

Grimes, The Future of Distribution Restraints Law: Will the New Learning Take Hold? 2006 Utah L. Rev. 885 (2006).

Shores, Economic Formalism in Antitrust Decisionmaking, 68 Alb. L. Rev. 1053 (2005).

Meurer, Vertical Restraints and Intellectual Property Law: Beyond Antitrust, 87 Minn. L. Rev. 1871 (2003).

Baxter, The Viability of Vertical Restraints Doctrine, 75 Cal. L. Rev. 933 (1987).

Bork, Vertical Restraints: Schwinn Overruled, 1977 Sup. Ct. Rev. 171 (1977).

Posner, The Next Step in the Antitrust Treatment of Restricted Distribution: *per se* Legality, 48 U. Chi. L. Rev. 6 (1980).

3. Inferring Combination and Conspiracy

Page, Twombly and Communication: The Emerging Definition of Concerted Action under the New Pleading Standards, 5 J. Comp. L. & Econ. 439 (2009).

Fitzsimons, The Injustice of Notice & Heightened Pleading Standards for Antitrust Conspiracy Claims: It Is Time To Balance the Scale for Plaintiffs, Defendants, and Society, 39 Rutgers L.J. 199 (2007).

4. Comparative Material

Commission of the European Union, Competition Directorate, Guidelines on Vertical Restraints, 2000/C 291/01, available at http://eur-lex.europa.eu/Lex UriServ/LexUriServ.do?uri=CELEX:32000Y1013% 2801% 29:EN:NOT.

Cooper et al., A Comparative Study of United States and European Union Approaches to Vertical Policy, 13 Geo. Mason L. Rev. 289 (2005).

Verouden, Vertical Agreements and Article 81(1) EC: The Evolving Role of Economic Analysis, 71 Antitrust L. J. 525 (2003).

Van Fleet, Mexico's Federal Economic Competition Law: The Dawn of a New Antitrust Era, 64 Antitrust L. J. 183 (1995).

Pigassou, Oligopoly and Antitrust Law: A Comparison of United States, European Community, West German, and French Law, 19 Geo. Wash. J. Int'l L. & Econ. 633 (1985).

CHAPTER 8

ADDITIONAL LIMITATIONS ON A SINGLE FIRM EXERCISING MARKET POWER

INTRODUCTORY NOTE

As we first noted in Chapter 3, much of the law limiting conduct by single firms exercising market power has developed around the words "exclusionary" and "predatory." Chapter 8 will now deal with a wide range of possible predatory and exclusionary strategies, which may, for example, involve blocking entry or expansion, "disciplining" competitors, diminishing a rival's revenues, or adding more to a competitor's costs than to the costs of a dominant firm. In each of the cases reviewed in this Chapter, the basic need is to separate those acts to be condemned from legitimate competitive conduct. Throughout the Chapter, please keep a careful eye on how the courts define "predatory" and "exclusionary," and how they distinguish legitimate competition from anticompetitive activity.

Illegal predatory or exclusionary conduct by a firm will arise most dramatically under Section 2 of the Sherman Act (where this Chapter begins), but such conduct can arise in a number of other contexts. It can involve: an "agreement" in violation of Section 1 of the Sherman Act; a substantial lessening of competition under Section 3 of the Clayton Act; an "unfair method of competition" under Section 5 of the FTC Act; or an element of an illegal price discrimination in violation of the Robinson–Patman Act.

The D. C. Circuit's *Microsoft* decision (p. 767 *infra*) is a landmark because of Microsoft's economic importance and the Circuit's Section 2 analysis. But the decision also covers Section 1 issues and Clayton Act Section 3 issues like tying and exclusive dealing. While the major part of the *Microsoft* decision is set forth in Section 1 of this Chapter—"Section 2 Revisited"—its non-Section 2 implications are cross-referenced and discussed throughout Chapter 8.

SECTION 1.   SECTION 2 REVISITED: SPECIAL LIMITS ON SINGLE FIRM MARKET POWER BY MONOPOLISTS AND WOULD-BE MONOPOLISTS

A.   MONOPOLY CONDUCT REVISITED

United States v. Aluminum Co. of America

United States Circuit Court of Appeals, Second Circuit, 1945.
148 F.2d 416.

[Reprinted p. 114 *supra*]

United States v. Grinnell Corp.

Supreme Court of the United States, 1966.
384 U.S. 563, 86 S.Ct. 1698, 16 L.Ed.2d 778.

[Reprinted p. 152 *supra*]

NOTE ON TELEX

During the late 1960's and early 1970's, IBM was the world's largest supplier of computers. Organizationally, the center of a computer system is referred to as the central processing unit ("CPU"); other hardware in the system is called "peripheral equipment." This includes memory or storage units, tape drives, disks, printers, etc. and, during the relevant years, constituted 50% to 75% of the total price of a hardware system.

Telex was principally in the business of selling peripheral equipment to owners or lessees of IBM CPUs, and, in the period prior to 1970, was able to offer prices or rentals lower than those offered by IBM. Telex along with its fellow peripheral manufacturers, had, for example, managed to cut IBM's share of the disk market by about 32%. An IBM Management Committee studying the "market erosion" problem estimated that IBM could lose "over one-half of its lease base in the disk drive market and could lose up to 20% of its tape lease business to its competitors." 510 F.2d at 903.

Telex peripheral equipment was compatible with IBM's CPUs, but because of relatively slight differences in design, usually was not compatible with the CPUs of other manufacturers. Similarly, the relatively few peripherals manufactured by Telex and its fellow peripheral manufacturers for interconnection with the systems of full-line companies other than IBM were not compatible for immediate connection with IBM systems.

During the period 1968–71, IBM reacted to the substantial business inroads by Telex and the other peripheral manufacturers. First, it cut its price on certain disk units to a level below that being offered by Telex and other peripheral manufacturers. There was some evidence that at the time IBM cut rates on peripherals, it raised its rates on CPUs in order to recoup lost profits. IBM's prices were not below its own costs, however, and in fact, IBM earned a 20% pretax margin at the lower prices. Telex and the other peripheral manufacturers responded by cutting their own prices below the new IBM levels. Second, IBM offered a series of "long-term" lease plans (for one or two years) which gave customers substantial direct and indirect price concessions, with stiff termination charges to customers who canceled before the end of a lease. Telex and the other peripheral manufacturers had similar lease plans, but at IBM's lowered rental rates they lost considerable business to IBM. Finally, IBM countered increasing competition for "memory" peripherals by integrating the previously separate memory component into the IBM CPU, and by lowering the price of other memory units. IBM justified these actions on grounds that the integrated memory was a technological improvement and that the lowered prices on the memory units still returned to IBM a 20% profit margin.

The parties agreed that the relevant geographic market was the United States. The trial court ruled that the relevant product market was "peripheral equipment plug-compatible to IBM CPUs" and subcategories (*e.g.*, printers, disks, tape drives) of this peripheral equipment.[1] Since IBM manufactured most of the peripheral equipment used in its own systems, this market definition produced market shares for IBM in the 80%–90% range. Relying on *Alcoa* and *Grinnell*, the district court found a violation of Section 2 because IBM had raised prices on CPUs and lowered prices on peripheral products where competition was more intense, and because of the long-term leases with punitive termination provisions which cut into new order rates of plug-compatible competitors. IBM was ordered to pay $259.5 million in treble damages, and a variety of injunctive provisions were imposed, including a requirement that IBM enter into no lease agreement longer than 90 days that included a penalty clause.

The Court of Appeals reversed. As to the relevant market, it pointed out that some peripheral equipment not plug-compatible with IBM equipment could easily and cheaply be modified for interconnection. IBM had claimed that the cost of such modification amounted to less than 1% of the product's purchase price. The Court also noted that Telex had in fact modified a peripheral unit designed for interconnection with IBM equipment when a marketing opportunity arose for connection with some RCA CPUs.

The Tenth Circuit held:

> [R]easonable interchangeability is proven in the case at bar and hence the market should include not only peripheral products plug compatible with IBM CPUs, but all peripheral products, those compatible not only with IBM CPUs but those compatible with non-IBM systems. This is wholly justifiable because the record shows that these products, although not fungible, are fully interchangeable and may be interchanged with minimal financial outlay, and so cross-elasticity exists within meaning of the *DuPont* decision. 510 F.2d at 919.

Insofar as the Tenth Circuit included in the relevant product market peripheral products plug-compatible with systems other than IBM whose interfaces could not easily and cheaply be modified, it apparently did so because IBM's discretion over price was limited by the fact that peripheral equipment comprised the costliest part of a computer hardware system (50% to 75%) and IBM faced competition from its

---

1. Telex Corp. v. IBM, 367 F.Supp. 258 (N.D.Okl.1973), reversed per curiam, 510 F.2d 894 (10th Cir.), cert. dism'd, 423 U.S. 802 (1975)

full-line competitors on a system-by-system basis. Compare the Supreme Court's subsequent switching costs discussion in *Kodak*, p. 885 *infra*.

The Court of Appeals also rejected the trial court's finding that IBM's business conduct represented monopolizing behavior. Citing *Alcoa* and *Grinnell,* the court below had indicated that the applicable rule was that a company with monopoly power violates Section 2 where there is:

> willful acquisition or maintenance of ... [monopoly] power with intent to monopolize, which intent need not be evidenced by predatory practices but which is not to be gathered merely from growth or development as a consequence of a superior product. 510 F.2d at 925.

The Tenth Circuit found that this test was inappropriately applied in that the district court failed to take into account two relevant factors—(i) whether or not the acts were ordinary business practices typical of those used in a competitive market; and (ii) whether or not the acts derive from *use* by a monopolist of its power or size. Making the "monopoly thrust upon" defense available only to involuntary conduct would deny to a company achieving monopoly power legally—for example, by research and technological innovations—the ability to defend its market share against inroads by those who market copies of its products. The Court indicated that a more expansive view of the "monopoly thrust upon" exception, and the requirement that illegal behavior reflect a "use" of monopoly power, is particularly appropriate where the alleged monopolist has achieved its market position legally, and the charge is that it is maintaining that position by illegal means.

As to IBM's direct and indirect price cuts (including the lease terms), the court noted that these were ordinary business practices and were not exclusively available to IBM because of its monopoly position. The price cuts resulted in prices which were "reasonable in that they yielded a reasonable profit" and at no time were they below IBM's costs. Thus, each of IBM's products stood on its own base and did not rely for marketing on IBM's financial reserves. Finally, the conclusion of the court below that IBM's various marketing maneuvers were "predatory" in that they were specifically aimed at particular challengers was rejected as inconsistent with the record. Apparently because of this finding that IBM's activities were not predatory but simply the actions of a vigorous, aggressive competitor, the Tenth Circuit rejected without discussion the lower court finding of an attempt to monopolize.

In a portion of the opinion not involving antitrust claims, the Court of Appeals affirmed the trial court's award to IBM of damages against Telex for misappropriation of trade secrets, though it reduced the damage award on the counterclaim from almost $22 million to $17.5 million. It also affirmed the award of $1 million as punitive damages.

Telex petitioned the Supreme Court for certiorari, but shortly before the decision on certiorari was to be announced, Telex and IBM settled the case. In return for Telex abandoning its antitrust charges, it was released from any obligation to pay damages under IBM's unfair competition counterclaim.

a. Is the Tenth Circuit's gloss in *Telex* on the definition of monopolizing conduct consistent with the tests in *Grinnell* and *Alcoa?* For example, under the *Telex* approach, would a lease-only policy by a company with monopoly power be legal under Section 2 as long as small companies in the same market followed that practice? Compare the conduct discussions in the *Aspen Skiing* (p. 726 *infra*) and *Kodak* (p. 791 and p. 885 *infra*) cases.

b. In United States v. Standard Oil Co. of California, 362 F.Supp. 1331 (N.D.Cal.1972), affirmed, 412 U.S. 924 (1973), a conspiracy to monopolize in violation of Section 2 was found where a dominant company entered into long-term supply contracts with key customers which operated to preclude entry by potential rivals. Socal was "virtually the only supplier and distributor of petroleum products in the territory of American Samoa," selling diesel fuel, aviation gasoline and jet fuel, gasoline, and other petroleum products. It entered into 10–year requirements contracts with certain large customers, including the two largest tuna canners and processors in Samoa, calling for delivery of from 60% to 100% of operational requirements of petroleum products. As a result, it supplied 100% of the fuel for all tuna fleets operating in the area, preventing competitors from obtaining a commercial foothold in the market. The requirements contracts were found to be illegal under Section 3 and to be part of a conspiracy to monopolize distribution and sale of petroleum products in American Samoa. Why were IBM's long-term lease plans, with their stiff termination charges, less vulnerable than the Socal supply contracts?

c. In *Alcoa*, p. 114 *supra*, Judge Hand justified a tough antimonopoly rule for political as well as economic reasons. He wrote:

> [Congress] did not condone "good trusts" and condemn "bad" ones; it forbad all. Moreover, in so doing it was not necessarily actuated by economic motives alone. It is possible, because of its indirect social or moral effect, to prefer a system of small producers, each dependent for his success upon his own skill and character, to one in which the great mass of those engaged must accept the direction of a few.

Most monopoly opinions, like the Tenth Circuit's *Telex* opinion, address Section 2 issues exclusively in economic terms. If you wanted to introduce considerations like those described by Judge Hand into the question of defining predation or exclusionary behavior, how would you do it? Is it true, as economically oriented critics often charge, that the *Alcoa* language reflects nothing more than a political prejudice against big business?

————

Otter Tail Power Co. v. United States, 410 U.S. 366, 93 S.Ct. 1022, 35 L.Ed.2d 359 (1973). In an action under § 2 of the Sherman Act against Otter Tail Power Company, the following facts were shown:

Otter Tail sold electric power at retail in 465 towns in Minnesota, North Dakota and South Dakota. There also were 45 towns in its territory served by municipal systems. Where Otter Tail provided service, it did so pursuant to municipally granted franchises, which were limited to from 10 to 20 years. When such franchises expired in various towns served by Otter Tail, proposals sometimes were made to supplant Otter Tail with municipal systems. However, the municipal systems required a source of power and, when requested to sell power at wholesale to municipal systems, Otter Tail refused. Otter Tail also refused to transfer power to the municipalities from other wholesaler suppliers over its lines. The results were as follows: Colman and Aurora, two towns in South Dakota, had access to transmission facilities not controlled by Otter Tail and were able to proceed despite Otter Tail's actions. Elbow Lake, Minnesota, constructed its own generating plant. But Hankinson, North Dakota, without access to other transmission facilities, renewed Otter Tail's retail franchise.

Each town in Otter Tail's territory generally could accommodate only one distribution system, making each such town a "natural monopoly" market for the sale and distribution of electric power at retail. Competition for the right to serve an entire retail market within the limits of a particular town generally was between Otter Tail and a prospective or existing municipal system. Between 1947 and 1970, Otter Tail acquired six municipal systems. In 12 towns, including the four mentioned above, there were contests between Otter Tail and a proposed municipal system, and in only three of these—Aurora, Elbow Lake, and Colman—were municipal systems established. In many areas of its territory, the only transmission lines available were those of Otter Tail, and the latter refused to sell or transfer power to municipal systems despite the absence of engineering or capacity obstacles to such sale or transfer. Otter Tail's position was that development of municipal systems would so erode the earnings it derived from selling electric power at retail that the viability of its total operation would be jeopardized.

Otter Tail obtained some of its power from the Bureau of Reclamation. When towns such as Elbow Lake and Hankinson requested the Bureau of Reclamation and various electric cooperatives to furnish them with wholesale power, the latter were willing to supply it; but Otter Tail refused to "wheel" the power, relying on provisions in its contracts which barred the use of its lines for wheeling power to towns which it served at retail.

The Supreme Court held that Otter Tail's conduct violated § 2 of the Sherman Act, and was not immunized from antitrust prosecution by the regulatory provisions of the Federal Power Act.

... The District Court determined that Otter Tail has "a strategic dominance in the transmission of power in most of its service area" and that it used this dominance to foreclose potential entrants into the retail arena from obtaining electric power from outside sources of supply.... Use of monopoly power "to destroy threatened competition" is a violation of the "attempt to monopolize" clause of § 2 of the Sherman Act.... There were no engineering factors that prevented Otter Tail from selling power at wholesale to those towns that wanted municipal plants nor wheeling the power. The District Court found—and its findings are supported—that Otter Tail's refusals to sell at wholesale or to wheel were solely to prevent municipal power systems from eroding its monopolistic position.

Otter Tail's wheeling contracts with the Bureau of Reclamation were held unlawful as "territorial allocation schemes," denying defendant's competitors access to fenced-off markets. Otter Tail's argument that its overall system would go downhill if more and more municipalities turned to public power was rejected; the Sherman Act "assumes that an enterprise will protect itself against loss by operating with superior service, lower costs, and improved efficiency. Otter Tail's theory collides with the Sherman Act as it sought to substitute for competition anticompetitive uses of its dominant economic power." However, the Court also observed that Otter Tail's pessimistic "erosion study" was not supported by the record, and that Bureau of Reclamation power was not a serious threat to Otter Tail.

Aspen Skiing Co. v. Aspen Highlands Skiing Corp.

Supreme Court of the United States, 1985.
472 U.S. 585, 105 S.Ct. 2847, 86 L.Ed.2d 467.

■ STEVENS, J.... In a private treble damages action, the jury found that petitioner Aspen Skiing Company (Ski Co.) had monopolized the market for downhill skiing services in Aspen, Colorado. The question presented is whether that finding is erroneous as a matter of law because it rests on an assumption that a firm with monopoly power has a duty to cooperate with its smaller rivals in a marketing arrangement in order to avoid violating § 2 of the Sherman Act.

I

Aspen is a destination ski resort with a reputation for "super powder," "a wide range of runs," and an "active night life," including "some of the best restaurants in North America." Between 1945 and 1960, private investors independently developed three major facilities for downhill skiing: Aspen Mountain (Ajax), Aspen Highlands (Highlands), and Buttermilk. A fourth mountain, Snowmass, opened in 1967.

The development of any major additional facilities is hindered by practical considerations and regulatory obstacles. The identification of appropriate topographical conditions for a new site and substantial financing are both essential. Most of the terrain in the vicinity of Aspen that is suitable for downhill skiing cannot be used for that purpose without the approval of the United States Forest Service. That approval is contingent, in part, on environmental concerns. Moreover, the county government must also approve the project, and in recent years it has followed a policy of limiting growth.

Between 1958 and 1964, three independent companies operated Ajax, Highlands, and Buttermilk. In the early years, each company offered its own day or half-day tickets for use of its mountain. In 1962, however, the three competitors also introduced an interchangeable ticket.[2] The 6–day, all-Aspen ticket provided convenience to the vast majority of skiers who visited the resort for weekly periods, but preferred to remain flexible about what mountain they might ski each day during the visit. It also emphasized the unusual variety in ski mountains available in Aspen.

As initially designed, the all-Aspen ticket program consisted of booklets containing six coupons, each redeemable for a daily lift ticket at Ajax, Highlands, or Buttermilk. The price of the booklet was often discounted from the price of six daily tickets, but all six coupons had to be used within a limited period of time—seven days, for example. The revenues from the sale of the 3area coupon books were distributed in accordance with the number of coupons collected at each mountain.

In 1964, Buttermilk was purchased by Ski Co., but the interchangeable ticket program continued. In most seasons after it acquired Buttermilk, Ski Co. offered 2–area, 6– or 7–day tickets featuring Ajax and Buttermilk in competition with the 3–area, 6–coupon booklet. Although it sold briskly,

---

2. Friedl Pfeiffer, one of the developers of Buttermilk, initiated the idea of an all-Aspen ticket at a luncheon with the owner of Highlands and the President of Ski Co. Pfeiffer, a native of Austria, informed his competitors that " '[i]n St. Anton, we have a mountain that has three different lift companies—lifts owned by three different lift companies . . . We sell a ticket that is interchangeable.' It was good on any of those lifts; and he said, 'I think we should do the same thing here.' " *Id.*, at 153.

the all-Aspen ticket did not sell as well as Ski Co.'s multi-area ticket until Ski Co. opened Snowmass in 1967. Thereafter, the all-Aspen coupon booklet began to outsell Ski Co.'s ticket featuring only its mountains.

In the 1971–1972 season, the coupon booklets were discontinued and an "around the neck" all-Aspen ticket was developed. This refinement on the interchangeable ticket was advantageous to the skier, who no longer found it necessary to visit the ticket window every morning before gaining access to the slopes. Lift operators at Highlands monitored usage of the ticket in the 1971–1972 season by recording the ticket numbers of persons going onto the slopes of that mountain. Highlands officials periodically met with Ski Co. officials to review the figures recorded at Highlands, and to distribute revenues based on that count.

There was some concern that usage of the all-Aspen ticket should be monitored by a more scientific method than the one used in the 1971–1972 season. After a one-season absence, the 4–area ticket returned in the 1973–1974 season with a new method of allocating revenues based on usage. Like the 1971–1972 ticket, the 1973–1974 4–area ticket consisted of a badge worn around the skier's neck. Lift operators punched the ticket when the skier first sought access to the mountain each day. A random-sample survey was commissioned to determine how many skiers with the 4–area ticket used each mountain, and the parties allocated revenues from the ticket sales in accordance with the survey's results.

In the next four seasons, Ski Co. and Highlands used such surveys to allocate the revenues from the 4–area, 6–day ticket. Highlands' share of the revenues from the ticket was 17.5% in 1973–1974, 18.5% in 1974–1975, 16.8% in 1975–1976, and 13.2% in 1976–1977.[3] During these four seasons, Ski Co. did not offer its own 3–area, multi-day ticket in competition with the all-Aspen ticket.[4] By 1977, multi-area tickets accounted for nearly 35% of the total market. Holders of multi-area passes also accounted for additional daily ticket sales to persons skiing with them.

Between 1962 and 1977, Ski Co. and Highlands had independently offered various mixes of 1–day, 3–day and 6–day passes at their own mountains.[5] In every season except one, however, they had also offered some form of all-Aspen, 6–day ticket, and divided the revenues from those sales on the basis of usage. Nevertheless, for the 1977–1978 season, Ski Co.

---

3. Highlands' share of the total market during those seasons, as measured in skier visits was 15.8% in 1973–1974, 17.1% in 1974–1975, 17.4% in 1975–1976, and 20.5% in 1976–1977.

4. In 1975, the Colorado Attorney General filed a complaint against Ski Co. and Highlands alleging, in part, that the negotiations over the 4–area ticket had provided them with a forum for price-fixing in violation of § 1 of the Sherman Act and that they had attempted to monopolize the market for downhill skiing services in Aspen in violation of § 2. Record Ex. X. In 1977, the case was settled by a consent decree that permitted the parties to continue to offer the 4–area ticket provided that they set their own ticket prices unilaterally before negotiating its terms. Tr. 229–231.

5. About 15–20% of each company's ticket revenues were derived from sales to tour operators at a wholesale discount of 10–15%, while 80–85% of the ticket revenues were derived from sales to skiers in Aspen.

offered to continue the all-Aspen ticket only if Highlands would accept a 13.2% fixed share of the ticket's revenues.

Although that had been Highlands' share of the ticket revenues in 1976–1977, Highlands contended that that season was an inaccurate measure of its market performance since it had been marked by unfavorable weather and an unusually low number of visiting skiers. Moreover, Highlands wanted to continue to divide revenues on the basis of actual usage, as that method of distribution allowed it to compete for the daily loyalties of the skiers who had purchased the tickets. Fearing that the alternative might be no interchangeable ticket at all, and hoping to persuade Ski Co. to reinstate the usage division of revenues, Highlands eventually accepted a fixed percentage of 15% for the 1977–1978 season. No survey was made during that season of actual usage of the 4–area ticket at the two competitors' mountains.

In the 1970s the management of Ski Co. increasingly expressed their dislike for the all-Aspen ticket. They complained that a coupon method of monitoring usage was administratively cumbersome. They doubted the accuracy of the survey and decried the "appearance, deportment, [and] attitude" of the college students who were conducting it. In addition, Ski Co.'s President had expressed the view that the 4–area ticket was siphoning off revenues that could be recaptured by Ski Co. if the ticket was discontinued. In fact, Ski Co. had reinstated its 3–area, 6–day ticket during the 1977–1978 season, but that ticket had been outsold by the 4–area, 6–day ticket nearly two to one.

In March 1978, the Ski Co. management recommended to the Board of Directors that the 4–area ticket be discontinued for the 1978–1979 season. The Board decided to offer Highlands a 4–area ticket provided that Highlands would agree to receive a 12.5% fixed percentage of the revenue—considerably below Highlands' historical average based on usage. Later in the 1978–1979 season, a member of Ski Co.'s Board of Directors candidly informed a Highlands official that he had advocated making Highlands "an offer that [it] could not accept."

Finding the proposal unacceptable, Highlands suggested a distribution of the revenues based on usage to be monitored by coupons, electronic counting or random sample surveys. If Ski Co. was concerned about who was to conduct the survey, Highlands proposed to hire disinterested ticket counters at its own expense-"somebody like Price Waterhouse"—to count or survey usage of the 4–area ticket at Highlands. Ski Co. refused to consider any counterproposals, and Highlands finally rejected the offer of the fixed percentage.

As far as Ski Co. was concerned, the all-Aspen ticket was dead. In its place Ski Co. offered the 3–area, 6–day ticket featuring only its mountains. In an effort to promote this ticket, Ski Co. embarked on a national advertising campaign that strongly implied to people who were unfamiliar with Aspen that Ajax, Buttermilk, and Snowmass were the only ski mountains in the area. For example, Ski Co. had a sign changed in the Aspen Airways waiting room at Stapleton Airport in Denver. The old sign had a picture of the four mountains in Aspen touting "Four Big Mountains" whereas the new sign retained the picture but referred only to three.

Ski Co. took additional actions that made it extremely difficult for Highlands to market its own multi-area package to replace the joint offering. Ski Co. discontinued the 3–day, 3–area pass for the 1978–1979 season,[6] and also refused to sell Highlands any lift tickets, either at the tour operator's discount or at retail.[7] Highlands finally developed an alternative product, the "Adventure Pack," which consisted of a 3–day pass at Highlands and three vouchers, each equal to the price of a daily lift ticket at a Ski Co. mountain. The vouchers were guaranteed by funds on deposit in an Aspen bank, and were redeemed by Aspen merchants at full value. Ski Co., however, refused to accept them.

Later, Highlands redesigned the Adventure Pack to contain American Express Traveler's checks or money orders instead of vouchers. Ski Co. eventually accepted these negotiable instruments in exchange for daily lift tickets.[8] Despite some strengths of the product, the Adventure Pack met considerable resistance from tour operators and consumers who had grown accustomed to the convenience and flexibility provided by the all-Aspen ticket.

Without a convenient all-Aspen ticket, Highlands basically "becomes a day ski area in a destination resort." Highlands' share of the market for downhill skiing services in Aspen declined steadily after the 4–area ticket based on usage was abolished in 1977: from 20.5% in 1976–1977, to 15.7% in 1977–1978, to 13.1% in 1978–1979, to 12.5% in 1979–1980, to 11% in 1980–1981.[9] Highlands' revenues from associated skiing services like the ski school, ski rentals, amateur racing events, and restaurant facilities declined sharply as well.

---

6. Highlands' owner explained that there was a key difference between the 3–day, 3–area ticket and the 6–day, 3–area ticket: "with the three day ticket, a person could ski on the . . . Aspen Skiing Corporation mountains for three days and then there would be three days in which he could ski on our mountain; but with the six-day ticket, we are absolutely locked out of those people." As a result of "tremendous consumer demand" for a 3–day ticket, Ski Co. reinstated it late in the 1978–1979 season, but without publicity or a discount off the daily rate. *Id.*, at 622.

7. In the 1977–1978 negotiations, Ski Co. previously had refused to consider the sale of any tickets to Highlands noting that it was "obviously not interested in helping sell" a package competitive with the 3–area ticket. Later, in the 1978–1979 negotiations, Ski Co.'s Vice President of Finance told a Highlands official that "We will not have anything to do with a four-area ticket sponsored by the Aspen Highlands Skiing Corporation." When the Highlands official inquired why Ski Co. was taking this position considering that Highlands was willing to pay full retail value for the daily lift tickets, the Ski Co. official answered tersely: "we will not support our competition."

8. Of course, there was nothing to identify Highlands as the source of these instruments, unless someone saw the skier "taking it out of an Adventure Pack envelope." *Id.*, at 505. For the 1981–1982 season, Ski Co. set its single ticket price at $22 and discounted the 3–area, 6–day ticket to $114. According to Highlands, this price structure made the Adventure Pack unprofitable.

9. In these seasons, Buttermilk Mountain, in particular, substantially increased its market share at the expense of Highlands.

II

In 1979, Highlands filed a complaint in the United States District Court for the District of Colorado naming Ski Co. as a defendant. Among various claims, the complaint alleged that Ski Co. had monopolized the market for downhill skiing services at Aspen in violation of § 2 of the Sherman Act, and prayed for treble damages. The case was tried to a jury which rendered a verdict finding Ski Co. guilty of the § 2 violation and calculating Highlands' actual damages at $2.5 million.

In her instructions to the jury, the District Judge explained that the offense of monopolization under § 2 of the Sherman Act has two elements: (1) the possession of monopoly power in a relevant market, and (2) the willful acquisition, maintenance, or use of that power by anticompetitive or exclusionary means or for anticompetitive or exclusionary purposes.[10] Although the first element was vigorously disputed at the trial and in the Court of Appeals, in this Court Ski Co. does not challenge the jury's special verdict finding that it possessed monopoly power.[11] Nor does Ski Co. criticize the trial court's instructions to the jury concerning the second element of the § 2 offense.

On this element, the jury was instructed that it had to consider whether "Aspen Skiing Corporation willfully acquired, maintained, or used that power by anti-competitive or exclusionary means or for anti-competitive or exclusionary purposes." The instructions elaborated:

> "In considering whether the means or purposes were anti-competitive or exclusionary, you must draw a distinction here between practices which tend to exclude or restrict competition on the one hand and the success of a business which reflects only a superior product, a well-run business, or luck, on the other. The line between legitimately gained monopoly, its proper use and maintenance, and improper conduct has been described in various ways. It has been said that obtaining or maintaining monopoly power cannot represent monopolization if the power was gained and maintained by conduct that was honestly industrial. Or it is said that monopoly power which is thrust upon a firm due to its superior business ability and efficiency does not constitute monopolization.
>
> "For example, a firm that has lawfully acquired a monopoly position is not barred from taking advantage of scale economies by constructing a large and efficient factory. These benefits are a

---

10. In United States v. Grinnell Corp., 384 U.S. 563, 570–571 (1966), we explained:

"The offense of monopoly under § 2 of the Sherman Act has two elements: (1) the possession of monopoly power in the relevant market and (2) the willful acquisition or maintenance of that power as distinguished from growth or development as a consequence of a superior product, business acumen, or historic accident."

11. The jury found that the relevant product market was "[d]ownhill skiing at destination ski resorts," that the "Aspen area" was a relevant geographic submarket, and that during the years 1977–1981, Ski Co. possessed monopoly power, defined as the power to control prices in the relevant market or to exclude competitors.

consequence of size and not an exercise of monopoly power. Nor is a corporation which possesses monopoly power in a relevant market, has not violated the law. We are concerned with conduct which unnecessarily excludes or handicaps competitors. This is conduct which does not benefit consumers by making a better product or service available—or in other ways—and instead has the effect of impairing competition.

"To sum up, you must determine whether Aspen Skiing Corporation gained, maintained, or used monopoly power in a relevant market by arrangements and policies which rather than being a consequence of a superior product, superior business sense, or historic element, were designed primarily to further any domination of the relevant market or sub-market." *Id.*, at 181–182.

The jury answered a specific interrogatory finding the second element of the offense as defined in these instructions.

Ski Co. filed a motion for judgment notwithstanding the verdict, contending that the evidence was insufficient to support a § 2 violation as a matter of law. In support of that motion, Ski Co. incorporated the arguments that it had advanced in support of its motion for a directed verdict, at which time it had primarily contested the sufficiency of the evidence on the issue of monopoly power. Counsel had, however, in the course of the argument at that time, stated: "Now, we also think, Judge, that there clearly cannot be a requirement of cooperation between competitors." The District Court denied Ski Co.'s motion and entered a judgment awarding Highlands treble damages of $7,500,000, costs and attorney's fees.[12]

The Court of Appeals affirmed in all respects. 738 F.2d 1509 (C.A.10 1984). The court advanced two reasons for rejecting Ski Co.'s argument that " 'there was insufficient evidence to present a jury issue of monopolization because, as a matter of law, the conduct at issue was pro-competitive conduct that a monopolist could lawfully engage in.' " First, relying on United States v. Terminal Railroad Assn. of St. Louis, 224 U.S. 383 (1912), the Court of Appeals held that the multi-day, multi-area ticket could be characterized as an "essential facility" that Ski Co. had a duty to market jointly with Highlands. Second, it held that there was sufficient evidence to support a finding that Ski Co.'s intent in refusing to market the 4–area ticket, "considered together with its other conduct," was to create or maintain a monopoly. *Id.*, at 1522.

In its review of the evidence on the question of intent, the Court of Appeals considered the record "as a whole" and concluded that it was not necessary for Highlands to prove that each allegedly anticompetitive act

---

12. The District Court also entered an injunction requiring the parties to offer jointly a 4–area, 6–out-of-7 day coupon booklet substantially identical to the "Ski the Summit" booklet accepted by Ski Co. at its Breckenridge resort in Summit County, Colorado. The injunction was initially for a 30–year period, but was later extended through the 1984–1985 season by stipulation of the parties. Highlands represents that "it will not seek an extension of the injunction." No question is raised concerning the character of the injunctive relief ordered by the District Court.

was itself sufficient to demonstrate an abuse of monopoly power. The court noted that by "refusing to cooperate" with Highlands, Ski Co. "became the only business in Aspen that could offer a multi-day multi-mountain skiing experience;" that the refusal to offer a 4–mountain ticket resulted in "skiers' frustration over its unavailability;" that there was apparently no valid business reason for refusing to accept the coupons in Highlands' Adventure Pack; and that after Highlands had modified its Adventure Pack to meet Ski Co.'s objections, Ski Co. had increased its single ticket price to $22 "thereby making it unprofitable . . . to market [the] Adventure Pack." *Id.*, at 1522. In reviewing Ski Co.'s argument that it was entitled to a directed verdict, the Court of Appeals assumed that the jury had resolved all contested questions of fact in Highlands' favor.

III

In this Court, Ski Co. contends that even a firm with monopoly power has no duty to engage in joint marketing with a competitor, that a violation of § 2 cannot be established without evidence of substantial exclusionary conduct, and that none of its activities can be characterized as exclusionary. It also contends that the Court of Appeals incorrectly relied on the "essential facilities" doctrine and that an "anticompetitive intent" does not transform nonexclusionary conduct into monopolization. In response, Highlands submits that, given the evidence in the record, it is not necessary to rely on the "essential facilities" doctrine in order to affirm the judgment.

"The central message of the Sherman Act is that a business entity must find new customers and higher profits through internal expansion— that is, by competing successfully rather than by arranging treaties with its competitors." United States v. Citizens & Southern National Bank, 422 U.S. 86, 116 (1975). Ski Co., therefore, is surely correct in submitting that even a firm with monopoly power has no general duty to engage in a joint marketing program with a competitor. Ski Co. is quite wrong, however, in suggesting that the judgment in this case rests on any such proposition of law. For the trial court unambiguously instructed the jury that a firm possessing monopoly power has no duty to cooperate with its business rivals.

The absence of an unqualified duty to cooperate does not mean that every time a firm declines to participate in a particular cooperative venture, that decision may not have evidentiary significance, or that it may not give rise to liability in certain circumstances. The absence of a duty to transact business with another firm is, in some respects, merely the counterpart of the independent businessman's cherished right to select his customers and his associates. The high value that we have placed on the right to refuse to deal with other firms does not mean that the right is unqualified.[13]

---

13. Under § 1 of the Sherman Act, a business "generally has a right to deal, or refuse to deal, with whomever it likes, as long as it does so independently." Monsanto Co. v. Spray–Rite Service Corp., 465 U.S. 752, 761 (1984); United States v. Colgate & Co., 250 U.S. 300, 307 (1919).

In Lorain Journal v. United States, 342 U.S. 143 (1951), we squarely held that this right was not unqualified. Between 1933 and 1948 the publisher of the Lorain Journal, a newspaper, was the only local business disseminating news and advertising in that Ohio town. In 1948, a small radio station was established in a nearby community. In an effort to destroy its small competitor, and thereby regain its "pre–1948 substantial monopoly over the mass dissemination of all news and advertising," the Journal refused to sell advertising to persons that patronized the radio station.

In holding that this conduct violated § 2 of the Sherman Act, the Court dispatched the same argument raised by the monopolist here:

> "The publisher claims a right as a private business concern to select its customers and to refuse to accept advertisements from whomever it pleases. We do not dispute that general right. 'But the word 'right' is one of the most deceptive of pitfalls; it is so easy to slip from a qualified meaning in the premise to an unqualified one in the conclusion. Most rights are qualified.' American Bank & Trust Co. v. Federal Bank, 256 U.S. 350, 358. The right claimed by the publisher is neither absolute nor exempt from regulation. Its exercise as a purposeful means of monopolizing interstate commerce is prohibited by the Sherman Act. The operator of the radio station, equally with the publisher of the newspaper, is entitled to the protection of that Act. '*In the absence of any purpose to create or maintain a monopoly,* the act does not restrict the long recognized right of trader or manufacturer engaged in an entirely private business, freely to exercise his own independent discretion as to parties with whom he will deal.' (Emphasis supplied.) United States v. Colgate & Co., 250 U.S. 300, 307. See Associated Press v. United States, 326 U.S. 1, 15; United States v. Bausch & Lomb Co., 321 U.S. 707, 721–723." 342 U.S., at 155.

The Court approved the entry of an injunction ordering the Journal to print the advertisements of the customers of its small competitor.

In *Lorain Journal,* the violation of § 2 was an "attempt to monopolize," rather than monopolization, but the question of intent is relevant to both offenses. In the former case it is necessary to prove a "specific intent" to accomplish the forbidden objective—as Judge Hand explained, "an intent which goes beyond the mere intent to do the act." United States v. Aluminum Co. of America, 148 F.2d 416, 432 (C.A.2 1945). In the latter case evidence of intent is merely relevant to the question whether the challenged conduct is fairly characterized as "exclusionary" or "anticompetitive"—to use the words in the trial court's instructions—or "predatory," to use a word that scholars seem to favor. Whichever label is used, there is agreement on the proposition that "no monopolist monopolizes unconscious of what he is doing."[14] As Judge Bork stated more recently:

---

14. "In order to fall within § 2, the monopolist must have both the power to monopolize, and the intent to monopolize. To read the passage as demanding any 'specific' intent, makes

"Improper exclusion (exclusion not the result of superior efficiency) is always deliberately intended."[15]

The qualification on the right of a monopolist to deal with whom he pleases is not so narrow that it encompasses no more than the circumstances of *Lorain Journal*. In the actual case that we must decide, the monopolist did not merely reject a novel offer to participate in a cooperative venture that had been proposed by a competitor. Rather, the monopolist elected to make an important change in a pattern of distribution that had originated in a competitive market and had persisted for several years. The all-Aspen, 6–day ticket with revenues allocated on the basis of usage was first developed when three independent companies operated three different ski mountains in the Aspen area. It continued to provide a desirable option for skiers when the market was enlarged to include four mountains, and when the character of the market was changed by Ski Co.'s acquisition of monopoly power. Moreover, since the record discloses that interchangeable tickets are used in other multi-mountain areas which apparently are competitive, it seems appropriate to infer that such tickets satisfy consumer demand in free competitive markets.

Ski Co.'s decision to terminate the all-Aspen ticket was thus a decision by a monopolist to make an important change in the character of the market.[16] Such a decision is not necessarily anticompetitive, and Ski Co. contends that neither its decision, nor the conduct in which it engaged to implement that decision, can fairly be characterized as exclusionary in this case. It recognizes, however, that as the case is presented to us, we must interpret the entire record in the light most favorable to Highlands and give to it the benefit of all inferences which the evidence fairly supports, even though contrary inferences might reasonably be drawn.

Moreover, we must assume that the jury followed the court's instructions. The jury must, therefore, have drawn a distinction "between practices which tend to exclude or restrict competition on the one hand, and the success of a business which reflects only a superior product, a well-run business, or luck, on the other." Since the jury was unambiguously instructed that Ski Co.'s refusal to deal with Highlands "does not violate § 2

nonsense of it, for no monopolist monopolizes unconscious of what he is doing. So here, 'Alcoa' meant to keep, and did keep, that complete and exclusive hold upon the ingot market with which it started. That was to 'monopolize' that market, however innocently it otherwise proceeded." United States v. Aluminum Co. of America, 148 F.2d at 432.

15. R. Bork, The Antitrust Paradox 160 (1978) (hereinafter Bork).

16. "In any business, patterns of distribution develop over time; these may reasonably be thought to be more efficient than alternative patterns of distribution that do not develop. The patterns that do develop and persist we may call the optimal patterns. By disturbing optimal distribution patterns one rival can impose costs upon another, that is, force the other to accept higher costs." Bork 156.

In § 1 cases where this Court has applied the *per se* approach to invalidity to concerted refusals to deal, "the boycott often cut off access to a supply, facility or market necessary to enable the boycotted firm to compete, ... and frequently the boycotting firms possessed a dominant position in the relevant market." Northwest Wholesale Stationers, Inc. v. Pacific Stationery & Printing Co.

if valid business reasons exist for that refusal," we must assume that the jury concluded that there were no valid business reasons for the refusal. The question then is whether that conclusion finds support in the record.

IV

The question whether Ski Co.'s conduct may properly be characterized as exclusionary cannot be answered by simply considering its effect on Highlands. In addition, it is relevant to consider its impact on consumers and whether it has impaired competition in an unnecessarily restrictive way.[17] If a firm has been "attempting to exclude rivals on some basis other than efficiency," it is fair to characterize its behavior as predatory. It is, accordingly, appropriate to examine the effect of the challenged pattern of conduct on consumers, on Ski Co.'s smaller rival, and on Ski Co. itself.

Superior Quality of the All–Aspen Ticket

The average Aspen visitor "is a well-educated, relatively affluent, experienced skier who has skied a number of times in the past.... Over 80% of the skiers visiting the resort each year have been there before—40% of these repeat visitors have skied Aspen at least five times. Over the years, they developed a strong demand for the 6–day, all-Aspen ticket in its various refinements. Most experienced skiers quite logically prefer to purchase their tickets at once for the whole period that they will spend at the resort; they can then spend more time on the slopes and enjoying apres-ski amenities and less time standing in ticket lines. The 4–area attribute of the ticket allowed the skier to purchase his 6–day ticket in advance while reserving the right to decide in his own time and for his own reasons which mountain he would ski on each day. It provided convenience and flexibility, and expanded the vistas and the number of challenging runs available to him during the week's vacation.

While the 3–area, 6–day ticket offered by Ski Co. possessed some of these attributes, the evidence supports a conclusion that consumers were adversely affected by the elimination of the 4–area ticket. In the first place, the actual record of competition between a 3–area ticket and the all-Aspen ticket in the years after 1967 indicated that skiers demonstrably preferred four mountains to three. Highlands' expert marketing witness testified that many of the skiers who come to Aspen want to ski the four mountains, and the abolition of the 4–area pass made it more difficult to satisfy that ambition. A consumer survey undertaken in the 1979–1980 season indicated that 53.7% of the respondents wanted to ski Highlands, but would not; 39.9% said that they would not be skiing at the mountain of their choice because their ticket would not permit it.

Expert testimony and anecdotal evidence supported these statistical measures of consumer preference. A major wholesale tour operator asserted

---

17. "Thus, 'exclusionary' comprehends at the most behavior that not only (1) tends to impair the opportunities of rivals, but also (2) either does not further competition on the merits or does so in an unnecessarily restrictive way." 3 P. Areeda & D. Turner, Antitrust Law 78 (1978).

that he would not even consider marketing a 3–area ticket if a 4–area ticket were available. During the 1977–1978 and 1978–1979 seasons, people with Ski Co.'s 3–area ticket came to Highlands "on a very regular basis" and attempted to board the lifts or join the ski school. Highlands officials were left to explain to angry skiers that they could only ski at Highlands or join its ski school by paying for a 1–day lift ticket. Even for the affluent, this was an irritating situation because it left the skier the option of either wasting one day of the 6–day, 3–area pass or obtaining a refund which could take all morning and entailed the forfeit of the 6–day discount. An active officer in the Atlanta Ski Club testified that the elimination of the 4–area pass "infuriated" him.

Highlands' Ability to Compete

The adverse impact of Ski Co.'s pattern of conduct on Highlands is not disputed in this Court. Expert testimony described the extent of its pecuniary injury. The evidence concerning its attempt to develop a substitute product either by buying Ski Co.'s daily tickets in bulk, or by marketing its own Adventure Pack, demonstrates that it tried to protect itself from the loss of its share of the patrons of the all-Aspen ticket. The development of a new distribution system for providing the experience that skiers had learned to expect in Aspen proved to be prohibitively expensive. As a result, Highlands' share of the relevant market steadily declined after the 4–area ticket was terminated. The size of the damages award also confirms the substantial character of the effect of Ski Co.'s conduct upon Highlands.[18]

Ski Co.'s Business Justification

Perhaps most significant, however, is the evidence relating to Ski Co. itself, for Ski Co. did not persuade the jury that its conduct was justified by any normal business purpose. Ski Co. was apparently willing to forgo daily ticket sales both to skiers who sought to exchange the coupons contained in Highlands' Adventure Pack, and to those who would have purchased Ski Co. daily lift tickets from Highlands if Highlands had been permitted to purchase them in bulk. The jury may well have concluded that Ski Co. elected to forgo these short run benefits because it was more interested in reducing competition in the Aspen market over the long run by harming its smaller competitor.

That conclusion is strongly supported by Ski Co.'s failure to offer any efficiency justification whatever for its pattern of conduct.[19] In defending

---

18. In considering the competitive effect of Ski Co.'s refusal to deal or cooperate with Highlands, it is not irrelevant to note that similar conduct carried out by the concerted action of three independent rivals with a similar share of the market would constitute a *per se* violation of § 1 of the Sherman Act. See Northwest Wholesale Stationers, Inc. v. Pacific Stationery & Printing Co. Cf. Lorain Journal Co. v. United States, 342 U.S. 143, 154 (1951).

19. "The law can usefully attack this form of predation only when there is evidence of specific intent to drive others from the market by means other than superior efficiency and when the predator has overwhelming market size, perhaps 80 or 90 percent. Proof of specific intent to engage in predation may be in the form of statements made by the officers or agents of the company, evidence that the conduct was used threateningly and did not continue when the decision to terminate the jointly offered ticket, Ski Co. claimed that usage could not be properly monitored. The evidence, however, established that Ski Co. itself monitored the use of the 3–area passes based on a count taken by lift operators, and distributed the revenues among its mountains on that basis.[20] Ski Co. contended that coupons were administratively cumbersome, and that the survey takers had been disruptive and their work inaccurate. Coupons, however, were no more burdensome than the credit cards accepted at Ski Co. ticket windows. Moreover, in other markets Ski Co. itself participated in interchangeable lift tickets using coupons. As for the survey, its own manager testified that the problems were much overemphasized by Ski Co. officials, and were mostly resolved as they arose. Ski Co.'s explanation for the rejection of Highlands' offer to hire—at its own expense—a reputable national accounting firm to audit usage of the 4–area tickets at Highlands' mountain, was that there was no way to "control" the audit.

In the end, Ski Co. was pressed to justify its pattern of conduct on a desire to disassociate itself from—what it considered—the inferior skiing services offered at Highlands. The all-Aspen ticket based on usage, however, allowed consumers to make their own choice on these matters of quality. Ski Co.'s purported concern for the relative quality of Highlands' product was supported in the record by little more than vague insinuations, and was sharply contested by numerous witnesses. Moreover, Ski Co. admitted that it was willing to associate with what it considered to be inferior products in other markets.

Although Ski Co.'s pattern of conduct may not have been as " 'bold, relentless, and predatory' " as the publisher's actions in *Lorain Journal,* the record in this case comfortably supports an inference that the monopolist made a deliberate effort to discourage its customers from doing business with its smaller rival. The sale of its 3–area, 6–day ticket, particularly when it was discounted below the daily ticket price, deterred the ticket holders from skiing at Highlands.[21] The refusal to accept the Adventure

---

a rival capitulated, or *evidence that the conduct was not related to any apparent efficiency.* These matters are not so difficult of proof as to render the test overly hard to meet." Bork 157 (emphasis added).

20.   Under the Ski Co. system, each skier's ticket, whether a daily or weekly ticket, is punched before he goes out on the slopes for the day. Revenues are distributed between the mountains on the basis of this count. Ski Co.'s Vice President for Finance testified that Ski Co. "would never consider" a system like that for monitoring usage on a 4–area ticket: "it's fine to approximate within your own company." The U.S. Forest Service, however, required the submission of financial information on a mountain-by-mountain basis as a condition of the permits issued for each mountain. A lift operator at Ajax conceded that the survey count during the years of the 4–area ticket was "generally pretty close" to the count made by Ski Co.'s staff.

21.   "[W]hy didn't they buy an individual daily lift ticket at Aspen Highlands? ... For those who had bought six-day tickets, I think despite the fact that they are all relatively affluent—a lot of them are relatively affluent when they go to Aspen—they are all sort of managerial types and they seem to be pretty cautious. Certainly the comments that I have had from individual skiers and from the tour operators, club people that I have talked to—they are pretty careful with their money and they would feel—these are the people who will buy the

Pack coupons in exchange for daily tickets was apparently motivated entirely by a decision to avoid providing any benefit to Highlands even though accepting the coupons would have entailed no cost to Ski Co. itself, would have provided it with immediate benefits, and would have satisfied its potential customers. Thus the evidence supports an inference that Ski Co. was not motivated by efficiency concerns and that it was willing to sacrifice short-run benefits and consumer good will in exchange for a perceived long-run impact on its smaller rival.[22]

Because we are satisfied that the evidence in the record,[23] construed most favorably in support of Highlands' position, is adequate to support the verdict under the instructions given by the trial court, the judgment of the Court of Appeals is

■ Affirmed.

■ WHITE, J., took no part in the decision of this case.

Eastman Kodak Co. v. Image Technical Services, Inc.

Supreme Court of the United States, 1992.
504 U.S. 451, 112 S.Ct. 2072, 119 L.Ed.2d 265.

[Reprinted p. 885 *infra*]

Verizon Communications v. Law Offices of Curtis V. Trinko

Supreme Court of the United States, 2004.
540 U.S. 398, 124 S.Ct. 872, 157 L.Ed.2d 823.

■ SCALIA, J. The Telecommunications Act of 1996, Pub. L. 104–104, 110 Stat. 56, imposes certain duties upon incumbent local telephone companies in order to facilitate market entry by competitors, and establishes a complex regime for monitoring and enforcement. In this case we consider whether a complaint alleging breach of the incumbent's duty under the 1996 Act to share its network with competitors states a claim under § 2 of the Sherman Act.

I

Petitioner Verizon Communications Inc. is the incumbent local exchange carrier (LEC) serving New York State. Before the 1996 Act,

---

six-day, three-area ticket that giving up one of those days and going over to ski at Aspen Highlands would mean spending extra money."

22. The Ski Co. advertising that conveyed the impression that there were only three skiing mountains in Aspen is consistent with this conclusion, even though this evidence would not be sufficient in itself to sustain the judgment.

23. Given our conclusion that the evidence amply supports the verdict under the instructions as given by the trial court, we find it unnecessary to consider the possible relevance of the "essential facilities" doctrine, or the somewhat hypothetical question whether nonexclusionary conduct could ever constitute an abuse of monopoly power if motivated by an anticompetitive purpose. If, as we have assumed, no monopolist monopolizes unconscious of what he is doing, that case is unlikely to arise.

Verizon, like other incumbent LECs, enjoyed an exclusive franchise within its local service area. The 1996 Act sought to "uproo[t]" the incumbent LECs' monopoly and to introduce competition in its place. *Verizon Communications Inc.* v. *FCC*, 535 U.S. 467, 488 (2002). Central to the scheme of the Act is the incumbent LEC's obligation under 47 U.S.C. § 251(c) to share its network with competitors, see *AT & T Corp.* v. *Iowa Utilities Bd.*, 525 U.S. 366, 371 (1999), including provision of access to individual elements of the network on an "unbundled" basis. § 251(c)(3). New entrants, so-called competitive LECs, resell these unbundled network elements (UNEs), recombined with each other or with elements belonging to the LECs.

Verizon, like other incumbent LECs, has taken two significant steps within the Act's framework in the direction of increased competition. First, Verizon has signed interconnection agreements with rivals such as AT & T, as it is obliged to do under § 252, detailing the terms on which it will make its network elements available. (Because Verizon and AT & T could not agree upon terms, the open issues were subjected to compulsory arbitration under §§ 252(b) and (c).) In 1997, the state regulator, New York's Public Service Commission (PSC), approved Verizon's interconnection agreement with AT & T.

Second, Verizon has taken advantage of the opportunity provided by the 1996 Act for incumbent LECs to enter the long-distance market (from which they had long been excluded). That required Verizon to satisfy, among other things, a 14–item checklist of statutory requirements, which includes compliance with the Act's network-sharing duties. §§ 271(d)(3)(A) and (c)(2)(B). Checklist item two, for example, includes "nondiscriminatory access to network elements in accordance with the requirements" of § 251(c)(3). § 271(c)(2)(B)(ii). Whereas the state regulator approves an interconnection agreement, for long-distance approval the incumbent LEC applies to the Federal Communications Commission (FCC). In December 1999, the FCC approved Verizon's § 271 application for New York.

Part of Verizon's UNE obligation under § 251(c)(3) is the provision of access to operations support systems (OSS), a set of systems used by incumbent LECs to provide services to customers and ensure quality. Verizon's interconnection agreement and long-distance authorization each specified the mechanics by which its OSS obligation would be met. As relevant here, a competitive LEC sends orders for service through an electronic interface with Verizon's ordering system, and as Verizon completes certain steps in filling the order, it sends confirmation back through the same interface. Without OSS access a rival cannot fill its customers' orders.

In late 1999, competitive LECs complained to regulators that many orders were going unfilled, in violation of Verizon's obligation to provide access to OSS functions. The PSC and FCC opened parallel investigations, which led to a series of orders by the PSC and a consent decree with the FCC. Under the FCC consent decree, Verizon undertook to make a "voluntary contribution" to the U.S. Treasury in the amount of $3 million; under the PSC orders, Verizon incurred liability to the competitive LECs in the amount of $10 million. Under the consent decree and orders, Verizon was subjected to new performance measurements and new reporting requirements to the FCC and PSC, with additional penalties for continued noncompliance. In June 2000, the FCC terminated the consent decree.... The next month the PSC relieved Verizon of the heightened reporting requirement.

Respondent Law Offices of *Curtis V. Trinko, LLP*, a New York City law firm, was a local telephone service customer of AT & T. The day after Verizon entered its consent decree with the FCC, respondent filed a complaint in the District Court for the Southern District of New York, on behalf of itself and a class of similarly situated customers. The complaint, as later amended, alleged that Verizon had filled rivals' orders on a discriminatory basis as part of an anticompetitive scheme to discourage customers from becoming or remaining customers of competitive LECs, thus impeding the competitive LECs' ability to enter and compete in the market for local telephone service. According to the complaint, Verizon "has filled orders of [competitive LEC] customers after filling those for its own local phone service, has failed to fill in a timely manner, or not at all, a substantial number of orders for [competitive LEC] customers ..., and has systematically failed to inform [competitive LECs] of the status of their customers' orders." The complaint set forth a single example of the alleged "failure to provide adequate access to [competitive LECs]," namely the OSS failure that resulted in the FCC consent decree and PSC orders. It asserted that the result of Verizon's improper "behavior with respect to providing access to its local loop" was to "deter potential customers [of rivals] from switching." The complaint sought damages and injunctive relief for violation of § 2 of the Sherman Act, 15 U.S.C. § 2, pursuant to the remedy provisions of §§ 4 and 16 of the Clayton Act.

The District Court dismissed the complaint in its entirety. As to the antitrust portion, it concluded that respondent's allegations of deficient assistance to rivals failed to satisfy the requirements of § 2. The Court of Appeals for the Second Circuit reinstated the complaint in part, including the antitrust claim. 305 F. 3d 89, 113 (2002). We granted certiorari, limited to the question whether the Court of Appeals erred in reversing the District Court's dismissal of respondent's antitrust claims.

II

To decide this case, we must first determine what effect (if any) the 1996 Act has upon the application of traditional antitrust principles. The Act imposes a large number of duties upon incumbent LECs—above and beyond those basic responsibilities it imposes upon all carriers, such as assuring number portability and providing access to rights-of-way. Under the sharing duties of § 251(c), incumbent LECs are required to offer three kinds of access. Already noted, and perhaps most intrusive, is the duty to offer access to UNEs on "just, reasonable, and nondiscriminatory" terms, § 251(c)(3), a phrase that the FCC has interpreted, to mean a price reflecting long-run incremental cost. A rival can interconnect its own facilities with those of the incumbent LEC, or it can simply purchase services at wholesale from the incumbent and resell them to consumers. The Act also imposes upon incumbents the duty to allow physical "colloca-tion"—that is, to permit a competitor to locate and install its equipment on the incumbent's premises—which makes feasible interconnection and ac-cess to UNEs.

That Congress created these duties, however, does not automatically lead to the conclusion that they can be enforced by means of an antitrust claim. Indeed, a detailed regulatory scheme such as that created by the 1996 Act ordinarily raises the question whether the regulated entities are not shielded from antitrust scrutiny altogether by the doctrine of implied immunity....

Congress, however, precluded that interpretation. Section 601(b)(*l*) of the 1996 Act is an antitrust-specific saving clause providing that "nothing in this Act or the amendments made by this Act shall be construed to modify, impair, or supersede the applicability of any of the antitrust laws." This bars a finding of implied immunity. As the FCC has put the point, the saving clause preserves those "claims that satisfy established antitrust standards."....

But just as the 1996 Act preserves claims that satisfy existing antitrust standards, it does not create new claims that go beyond existing antitrust standards; that would be equally inconsistent with the saving clause's mandate that nothing in the Act "modify, impair, or supersede the applica-bility" of the antitrust laws. We turn, then, to whether the activity of which respondent complains violates preexisting antitrust standards.

III

The complaint alleges that Verizon denied interconnection services to rivals in order to limit entry. If that allegation states an antitrust claim at all, it does so under § 2 of the Sherman Act, which declares that a firm shall not "monopolize" or "attempt to monopolize." It is settled law that this offense requires, in addition to the possession of monopoly power in the relevant market, "the willful acquisition or maintenance of that power as distinguished from growth or development as a consequence of a superior product, business acumen, or historic accident." *United States* v. *Grinnell Corp.*, 384 U.S 563, 570–571 (1966). The mere possession of monopoly power, and the concomitant charging of monopoly prices, is not only not unlawful; it is an important element of the free-market system. The opportunity to charge monopoly prices—at least for a short period—is what attracts "business acumen" in the first place; it induces risk taking that produces innovation and economic growth. To safeguard the incentive to innovate, the possession of monopoly power will not be found unlawful unless it is accompanied by an element of anticompetitive *conduct*.

Firms may acquire monopoly power by establishing an infrastructure that renders them uniquely suited to serve their customers. Compelling such firms to share the source of their advantage is in some tension with the underlying purpose of antitrust law, since it may lessen the incentive for the monopolist, the rival, or both to invest in those economically beneficial facilities. Enforced sharing also requires antitrust courts to act as central planners, identifying the proper price, quantity, and other terms of dealing—a role for which they are ill-suited. Moreover, compelling negotiation between competitors may facilitate the supreme evil of antitrust: collusion. Thus, as a general matter, the Sherman Act "does not restrict the long recognized right of [a] trader or manufacturer engaged in an entirely private business, freely to exercise his own independent discretion as to parties with whom he will deal." *United States* v. *Colgate & Co.,* 250 U.S. 300, 307 (1919).

However, "[t]he high value that we have placed on the right to refuse to deal with other firms does not mean that the right is unqualified." *Aspen Skiing Co.* v. *Aspen Highlands Skiing Corp.,* 472 U.S. 585, 601 (1985). Under certain circumstances, a refusal to cooperate with rivals can constitute anticompetitive conduct and violate § 2. We have been very cautious in recognizing such exceptions, because of the uncertain virtue of forced sharing and the difficulty of identifying and remedying anticompetitive conduct by a single firm. The question before us today is whether the allegations of respondent's complaint fit within existing exceptions or provide a basis, under traditional antitrust principles, for recognizing a new one.

The leading case for § 2 liability based on refusal to cooperate with a rival, and the case upon which respondent understandably places greatest reliance, is *Aspen Skiing.* The Aspen ski area consisted of four mountain areas. The defendant, who owned three of those areas, and the plaintiff, who owned the fourth, had cooperated for years in the issuance of a joint, multiple-day, all-area ski ticket. After repeatedly demanding an increased share of the proceeds, the defendant canceled the joint ticket. The plaintiff, concerned that skiers would bypass its mountain without some joint offering, tried a variety of increasingly desperate measures to re-create the joint ticket, even to the point of in effect offering to buy the defendant's tickets at retail price. The defendant refused even that. We upheld a jury verdict for the plaintiff, reasoning that "[t]he jury may well have concluded that [the defendant] elected to forgo these short-run benefits because it was more interested in reducing competition ... over the long run by harming its smaller competitor."

Aspen Skiing is at or near the outer boundary of § 2 liability. The Court there found significance in the defendant's decision to cease participation in a cooperative venture. The unilateral termination of a voluntary *(and thus presumably profitable)* course of dealing suggested a willingness to forsake short-term profits to achieve an anticompetitive end. Similarly, the defendant's unwillingness to renew the ticket *even if compensated at retail price* revealed a distinctly anticompetitive bent.

The refusal to deal alleged in the present case does not fit within the limited exception recognized in *Aspen Skiing.* The complaint does not allege that Verizon voluntarily engaged in a course of dealing with its rivals, or would ever have done so absent statutory compulsion. Here, therefore, the defendant's prior conduct sheds no light upon the motivation of its refusal to deal—upon whether its regulatory lapses were prompted not by competitive zeal but by anticompetitive malice. The contrast between the cases is heightened by the difference in pricing behavior. In *Aspen Skiing,* the defendant turned down a proposal to sell at its own retail price, suggesting a calculation that its future monopoly retail price would be higher. Verizon's reluctance to interconnect at the cost-based rate of compensation available under § 251(c)(3) tells us nothing about dreams of monopoly.

The specific nature of what the 1996 Act compels makes this case different from *Aspen Skiing* in a more fundamental way. In *Aspen Skiing,* what the defendant refused to provide to its competitor was a product that it already sold at retail—to oversimplify slightly, lift tickets representing a bundle of services to skiers. Similarly, in *Otter Tail Power Co. v. United States,* 410 U.S. 366 (1973), another case relied upon by respondent, the defendant was already in the business of providing a service to certain customers (power transmission over its network), and refused to provide the same service to certain other customers. In the present case, by contrast, the services allegedly withheld are not otherwise marketed or available to the public. The sharing obligation imposed by the 1996 Act created "something brand new"—"the wholesale market for leasing network elements." The unbundled elements offered pursuant to § 251(c)(3) exist only deep within the bowels of Verizon; they are brought out on compulsion of the 1996 Act and offered not to consumers but to rivals, and at considerable expense and effort. New systems must be designed and implemented simply to make that access possible—indeed, it is the failure of one of those systems that prompted the present complaint.[24]

We conclude that Verizon's alleged insufficient assistance in the provision of service to rivals is not a recognized antitrust claim under this Court's existing refusal-to-deal precedents. This conclusion would be unchanged even if we considered to be established law the "essential facilities" doctrine crafted by some lower courts, under which the Court of Appeals concluded respondent's allegations might state a claim. See generally Areeda, Essential Facilities: An Epithet in Need of Limiting Principles, 58 Antitrust L. J. 841 (1989). We have never recognized such a doctrine, see *Aspen Skiing Co.,* 472 U.S., at 611, n. 44; *AT & T Corp. v. Iowa Utilities Bd.,* 525 U.S., at 428 (opinion of BREYER, J.), and we find no need either to recognize it or to repudiate it here. It suffices for present purposes to note that the indispensable requirement for invoking the doctrine is the unavailability of access to the "essential facilities"; where access exists, the doctrine serves no purpose. Thus, it is said that "essential facility claims

24. Respondent also relies upon *United States v. Terminal Railroad Assn. of St. Louis,* 224 U.S. 383 (1912), and *Associated Press v. United States,* 326 U.S. 1 (1945). These cases involved *concerted* action, which presents greater anticompetitive concerns and is amenable to a remedy that does not require judicial estimation of free-market forces: simply requiring that the outsider be granted nondiscriminatory admission to the club.

should ... be denied where a state or federal agency has effective power to compel sharing and to regulate its scope and terms." P. Areeda & H. Hovenkamp, Antitrust Law, p. 150, ¶ 773e (2003 Supp,). Respondent believes that the existence of sharing duties under the 1996 Act supports its case. We think the opposite: The 1996 Act's extensive provision for access makes it unnecessary to impose a judicial doctrine of forced access. To the extent respondent's "essential facilities" argument is distinct from its general § 2 argument, we reject it.

IV

Finally, we do not believe that traditional antitrust principles justify adding the present case to the few existing exceptions from the proposition that there is no duty to aid competitors. Antitrust analysis must always be attuned to the particular structure and circumstances of the industry at issue. Part of that attention to economic context is an awareness of the significance of regulation....

One factor of particular importance is the existence of a regulatory structure designed to deter and remedy anticompetitive harm. Where such a structure exists, the additional benefit to competition provided by antitrust enforcement will tend to be small, and it will be less plausible that the antitrust laws contemplate such additional scrutiny. Where, by contrast, "[t]here is nothing built into the regulatory scheme which performs the antitrust function," *Silver* v. *New York Stock Exchange,* 373 U.S. 341, 358 (1963), the benefits of antitrust are worth its sometimes considerable disadvantages. Just as regulatory context may in other cases serve as a basis for implied immunity, see, *e.g., United States* v. *National Assn. of Securities Dealers, Inc.,* 422 U.S., at 730–735, it may also be a consideration in deciding whether to recognize an expansion of the contours of § 2.

The regulatory framework that exists in this case demonstrates how, in certain circumstances, "regulation significantly diminishes the likelihood of major antitrust harm." *Concord* v. *Boston Edison Co., supra,* at 25....

The regulatory response to the OSS failure complained of in respondent's suit provides a vivid example of how the regulatory regime operates. When several competitive LECs complained about deficiencies in Verizon's servicing of orders, the FCC and PSC responded. The FCC soon concluded that Verizon was in breach of its sharing duties under § 251(c), imposed a substantial fine, and set up sophisticated measurements to gauge remediation, with weekly reporting requirements and specific penalties for failure. The PSC found Verizon in violation of the PAP even earlier, and imposed additional financial penalties and measurements with *daily* reporting requirements. In short, the regime was an effective steward of the antitrust function.

Against the slight benefits of antitrust intervention here, we must weigh a realistic assessment of its costs. Under the best of circumstances, applying the requirements of § 2 "can be difficult" because "the means of illicit exclusion, like the means of legitimate competition, are myriad." *United States* v. *Microsoft Corp.,* 253 F. 3d 34, 58 (CADC 2001) (en banc) *(per curiam)*. Mistaken inferences and the resulting false condemnations "are especially costly, because they chill the very conduct the antitrust laws are designed to protect." *Matsushita Elec. Industrial Co. v. Zenith Radio Corp.*, 475 U.S. 574, 594 (1986). The cost of false positives counsels against an undue expansion of § 2 liability. One false-positive risk is that an incumbent LEC's failure to provide a service with sufficient alacrity might have nothing to do with exclusion. Allegations of violations of § 251(c)(3) duties are difficult for antitrust courts to evaluate, not only because they are highly technical, but, also because they are likely to be extremely numerous, given the incessant, complex, and constantly changing interaction of competitive and incumbent LECs implementing the sharing and interconnection obligations. *Amici* States have filed a brief asserting that competitive LECs are threatened with "death by a thousand cuts." Brief for New York et al. as *Amici Curiae* 10 (internal quotation marks omitted)—the identification of which would surely be a daunting task for a generalist antitrust court. Judicial oversight under the Sherman Act would seem destined to distort investment and lead to a new layer of interminable litigation, atop the variety of litigation routes already available to and actively pursued by competitive LECs.

Even if the problem of false positives did not exist, conduct consisting of anticompetitive violations of § 251 may be, as we have concluded with respect to above-cost predatory pricing schemes, "beyond the practical ability of a judicial tribunal to control." *Brooke Group Ltd.* v. *Brown & Williamson Tobacco Corp.*, 509 U.S. 209, 223 (1993). Effective remediation of violations of regulatory sharing requirements will ordinarily require continuing supervision of a highly detailed decree. We think that Professor Areeda got it exactly right: "No court should impose a duty to deal that it cannot explain or adequately and reasonably supervise. The problem should be deemed irremedia[ble] by antitrust law when compulsory access requires the court to assume the day-to-day controls characteristic of a regulatory agency." Areeda, 58 Antitrust L.J., at 853. In this case, respondent has requested an equitable decree to "[p]reliminarily and permanently enjoi[n] [Verizon] from providing access to the local loop market ... to [rivals] on terms and conditions that are not as favorable" as those that Verizon enjoys. An antitrust court is unlikely to be an effective day-to-day enforcer of these detailed sharing obligations.[25]

The 1996 Act is in an important respect much more ambitious than the antitrust laws. It attempts *"to eliminate the monopolies* enjoyed by the inheritors of AT & T's local franchises." *Verizon Communications Inc.* v. *FCC*, 535 U.S., at 476 (emphasis added). Section 2 of the Sherman Act, by contrast, seeks merely to prevent *unlawful monopolization*. It would be a serious mistake to conflate the two goals. The Sherman Act is indeed the

---

25. The Court of Appeals also thought that respondent's complaint might state a claim under a 'monopoly leveraging' theory (a theory barely discussed by respondent.) We disagree. To the extent the Court of Appeals dispensed with a requirement that there be a "dangerous probability of success" in monopolizing a second market, it erred, *Spectrum Sports, Inc.* v. *McQuillan*, 506 U.S. 447, 459 (1993). In any event, leveraging presupposes anticompetitive conduct, which in this case could only be the refusal-to-deal claim we have rejected.

"Magna Carta of free enterprise," *United States* v. *Topco Associates, Inc.,* 405 U.S. 596, 610 (1972), but it does not give judges *carte blanche* to insist that a monopolist alter its way of doing business whenever some other approach might yield greater competition. We conclude that respondent's complaint fails to state a claim under the Sherman Act.[26]

Accordingly, the judgment of the Court of Appeals is reversed, and the case is remanded for further proceedings consistent with this opinion.

Pacific Bell Telephone v. Linkline Communication, Inc.

Supreme Court of the United States, 2009.
___ U.S. ___, 129 S.Ct. 1109, 172 L.Ed.2d 836.

■ ROBERTS, C. J., The plaintiffs in this case, respondents here, allege that a competitor subjected them to a "price squeeze" in violation of § 2 of the Sherman Act. They assert that such a claim can arise when a vertically integrated firm sells inputs at wholesale and also sells finished goods or services at retail. If that firm has power in the wholesale market, it can simultaneously raise the wholesale price of inputs and cut the retail price of the finished good. This will have the effect of "squeezing" the profit margins of any competitors in the retail market. Those firms will have to pay more for the inputs they need; at the same time, they will have to cut their retail prices to match the other firm's prices. The question before us is whether such a price-squeeze claim may be brought under § 2 of the Sherman Act when the defendant is under no antitrust obligation to sell the inputs to the plaintiff in the first place. We hold that no such claim may be brought.

This case involves the market for digital subscriber line (DSL) service, which is a method of connecting to the Internet at high speeds over telephone lines. AT&T owns much of the infrastructure and facilities needed to provide DSL service in California. In particular, AT&T controls most of what is known as the "last mile"—the lines that connect homes and businesses to the telephone network. Competing DSL providers must generally obtain access to AT&T's facilities in order to serve their customers.

Until recently, the Federal Communications Commission (FCC) required incumbent phone companies such as AT&T to sell transmission service to independent DSL providers, under the theory that this would spur competition. In 2005, the Commission largely abandoned this forced-sharing requirement in light of the emergence of a competitive market beyond DSL for high-speed Internet service; DSL now faces robust competition from cable companies and wireless and satellite services. As a condition for a recent merger, however, AT&T remains bound by the mandatory interconnection requirements, and is obligated to provide wholesale "DSL

---

26. Our disposition makes it unnecessary to consider petitioner's alternative contention that respondent lacks antitrust standing.

transport" service to independent firms at a price no greater than the retail price of AT&T's DSL service.

The plaintiffs are four independent Internet service providers (ISPs) that compete with AT&T in the retail DSL market. Plaintiffs do not own all the facilities needed to supply their customers with this service. They instead lease DSL transport service from AT&T pursuant to the merger conditions described above. AT&T thus participates in the DSL market at both the wholesale and retail levels; it provides plaintiffs and other independent ISPs with wholesale DSL transport service, and it also sells DSL service directly to consumers at retail.

In July 2003, the plaintiffs brought suit in District Court, alleging that AT&T violated § 2 of the Sherman Act by monopolizing the DSL market in California. The complaint alleges that AT&T refused to deal with the plaintiffs, denied the plaintiffs access to essential facilities, and engaged in a "price squeeze." Specifically, plaintiffs contend that AT&T squeezed their profit margins by setting a high wholesale price for DSL transport and a low retail price for DSL Internet service. This maneuver allegedly "exclude[d] and unreasonably impede[d] competition," thus allowing AT&T to "preserve and maintain its monopoly control of DSL access to the Internet."

[In *Trinko,*] we held that a firm with no antitrust duty to deal with its rivals at all is under no obligation to provide those rivals with a "sufficient" level of service. Shortly after we issued that decision, AT&T moved for judgment on the pleadings, arguing that the plaintiffs' claims in this case were foreclosed by *Trinko*. The District Court held that AT&T had no antitrust duty to deal with the plaintiffs, but it denied the motion to dismiss with respect to the price-squeeze claims. The court acknowledged that AT&T's argument "has a certain logic to it," but held that *Trinko* "simply does not involve price-squeeze claims." The District Court also noted that price-squeeze claims have been recognized by several Circuits and "are cognizable under existing antitrust standards...."

On interlocutory appeal, the Court of Appeals for the Ninth Circuit affirmed the District Court's denial of AT&T's motion for judgment on the pleadings on the price-squeeze claims. The court emphasized that "*Trinko* did not involve a price squeezing theory." Because "a price squeeze theory formed part of the fabric of traditional antitrust law prior to *Trinko*," the Court of Appeals concluded that "those claims should remain viable notwithstanding either the telecommunications statutes or *Trinko.*" Based on the record before it, the court held that plaintiffs' original complaint stated a potentially valid claim under § 2 of the Sherman Act.

Judge Gould dissented, noting that "the notion of a 'price squeeze' is itself in a squeeze between two recent Supreme Court precedents." A price-squeeze claim involves allegations of both a high wholesale price and a low retail price, so Judge Gould analyzed each component separately. He concluded that "*Trinko* insulates from antitrust review the setting of the upstream price." With respect to the downstream price, he argued that "the retail side of a price squeeze cannot be considered to create an antitrust violation if the retail pricing does not satisfy the requirements of *Brooke Group*, [*see* p. 823 *infra* which set unmistakable limits on what can be considered to be predatory within the meaning of the antitrust laws." Judge Gould concluded that the plaintiffs' complaint did not satisfy these requirements because it contained no allegations that the retail price was set below cost and that those losses could later be recouped. Judge Gould would have allowed the plaintiffs to amend their complaint if they could, in good faith, raise predatory pricing claims meeting the *Brooke Group* requirements.

We granted certiorari, to resolve a conflict over whether a plaintiff can bring price-squeeze claims under § 2 of the Sherman Act when the defendant has no antitrust duty to deal with the plaintiff. We reverse.

This case has assumed an unusual posture. The plaintiffs now assert that they agree with Judge Gould's dissenting position that price-squeeze claims must meet the *Brooke Group* requirements for predatory pricing. They ask us to vacate the decision below in their favor and remand with instructions that they be given leave to amend their complaint to allege a *Brooke Group* claim. In other words, plaintiffs are no longer pleased with their initial theory. . . .

Section 2 of the Sherman Act makes it unlawful to "monopolize, or attempt to monopolize, or combine or conspire with any other person or persons, to monopolize any part of the trade or commerce among the several States, or with foreign nations." Simply possessing monopoly power and charging monopoly prices does not violate § 2; rather, the statute targets "the willful acquisition or maintenance of that power as distinguished from growth or development as a consequence of a superior product, business acumen, or historic accident." *United States v. Grinnell Corp., 384 U.S. 563, 570–571 (1966).*

As a general rule, businesses are free to choose the parties with whom they will deal, as well as the prices, terms, and conditions of that dealing. See *United States v. Colgate & Co., 250 U.S. 300, 307 (1919).* But there are rare instances in which a dominant firm may incur antitrust liability for purely unilateral conduct. For example, we have ruled that firms may not charge "predatory" prices—below-cost prices that drive rivals out of the market and allow the monopolist to raise its prices later and recoup its losses. *Brooke Group.* Here, however, the complaint at issue does not contain allegations meeting those requirements.

There *are* also limited circumstances in which a firm's unilateral refusal to deal with its rivals can give rise to antitrust liability. See *Aspen Skiing Co.* Here, however, the District Court held that AT&T had no such antitrust duty to deal with its competitors, and this holding was not challenged on appeal.[27]

---

27. The Court of Appeals assumed that any duty to deal arose only from FCC regulations, and the question on which we granted certiorari made the same assumption. Even aside from the District Court's reasoning, it seems quite unlikely that AT&T would have an antitrust duty to deal with the plaintiffs. Such a duty requires a showing of monopoly power,

The challenge here focuses on retail prices—where there is no predatory pricing—and the terms of dealing—where there is no duty to deal. Plaintiffs' price-squeeze claims challenge a different type of unilateral conduct in which a firm "squeezes" the profit margins of its competitors. This requires the defendant to be operating in two markets, a wholesale ("upstream") market and a retail ("downstream") market. A firm with market power in the upstream market can squeeze its downstream competitors by raising the wholesale price of inputs while cutting its own retail prices. This will raise competitors' costs (because they will have to pay more for their inputs) and lower their revenues (because they will have to match the dominant firm's low retail price). Price-squeeze plaintiffs assert that defendants must leave them a "fair" or "adequate" margin between the wholesale price and the retail price. In this case, we consider whether a plaintiff can state a price-squeeze claim when the defendant has no obligation under the antitrust laws to deal with the plaintiff at wholesale.

1. A straightforward application of our recent decision in *Trinko* forecloses any challenge to AT&T's *wholesale* prices. In *Trinko*, Verizon was required by statute to lease its network elements to competing firms at wholesale rates. The plaintiff—a customer of one of Verizon's rivals—asserted that Verizon denied its competitors access to interconnection support services, making it difficult for those competitors to fill their customers' orders. The complaint alleged that this conduct in the upstream market violated § 2 of the Sherman Act by impeding the ability of independent carriers to compete in the downstream market for local telephone service.

We held that the plaintiff's claims were not actionable under § 2. Given that Verizon had no antitrust duty to deal with its rivals at all, we concluded that "Verizon's alleged insufficient assistance in the provision of service to rivals" did not violate the Sherman Act. *Trinko* thus makes clear that if a firm has no antitrust duty to deal with its competitors at wholesale, it certainly has no duty to deal under terms and conditions that the rivals find commercially advantageous.

In this case, as in *Trinko*, the defendant has no antitrust duty to deal with its rivals at wholesale; any such duty arises only from FCC regulations, not from the Sherman Act. There is no meaningful distinction between the "insufficient assistance" claims we rejected in *Trinko* and the plaintiffs' price-squeeze claims in the instant case. The *Trinko* plaintiffs challenged the quality of Verizon's interconnection service, while this case involves a challenge to AT&T's pricing structure. But for antitrust purposes, there is no reason to distinguish between price and nonprice components of a transaction. . . . The nub of the complaint in both *Trinko* and this case is identical—the plaintiffs alleged that the defendants (upstream monopolists) abused their power in the wholesale market to prevent rival firms from competing effectively in the retail market. *Trinko* holds that

_____

but—as the FCC has recognized—the market for high-speed Internet service is now quite competitive; DSL providers face stiff competition from cable companies and wireless and satellite providers.

such claims are not cognizable under the Sherman Act in the absence of an antitrust duty to deal.

The District Court and the Court of Appeals did not regard *Trinko* as controlling because that case did not directly address price-squeeze claims. This is technically true, but the reasoning of *Trinko* applies with equal force to price-squeeze claims. AT&T could have squeezed its competitors' profits just as effectively by providing poor-quality interconnection service to the plaintiffs, as Verizon allegedly did in *Trinko*. But a firm with no duty to deal in the wholesale market has no obligation to deal under terms and conditions favorable to its competitors. If AT&T had simply stopped providing DSL transport service to the plaintiffs, it would not have run afoul of the Sherman Act. Under these circumstances, AT&T was not required to offer this service at the wholesale prices the plaintiffs would have preferred.

2.   The other component of a price-squeeze claim is the assertion that the defendant's *retail* prices are "too low." Here too plaintiffs' claims find no support in our existing antitrust doctrine.

"[C]utting prices in order to increase business often is the very essence of competition." *Matsushita Elec.* In cases seeking to impose antitrust liability for prices that are too low, mistaken inferences are "especially costly, because they chill the very conduct the antitrust laws are designed to protect." To avoid chilling aggressive price competition, we have carefully limited the circumstances under which plaintiffs can state a Sherman Act claim by alleging that prices are too low. Specifically, to prevail on a predatory pricing claim, a plaintiff must demonstrate that: (1) "the prices complained of are below an appropriate measure of its rival's costs"; and (2) there is a "dangerous probability" that the defendant will be able to recoup its "investment" in below-cost prices. *Brooke Group*....

In the complaint at issue in this interlocutory appeal, there is no allegation that AT&T's conduct met either of the *Brooke Group* requirements. Recognizing a price-squeeze claim where the defendant's retail price remains above cost would invite the precise harm we sought to avoid in *Brooke Group*: Firms might raise their retail prices or refrain from aggressive price competition to avoid potential antitrust liability....

3.   Plaintiffs' price-squeeze claim, looking to the relation between retail and wholesale prices, is thus nothing more than an amalgamation of a meritless claim at the retail level and a meritless claim at the wholesale level. If there is no duty to deal at the wholesale level and no predatory pricing at the retail level, then a firm is certainly not required to price *both* of these services in a manner that preserves its rivals' profit margins.[28]

---

28.   Like the Court of Appeals, amici argue that price-squeeze claims have been recognized by Circuit Courts for many years, beginning with Judge Hand's opinion in *United States v. Aluminum Co. of America, 148 F.2d 416 (CA2 1945) (Alcoa)*. In that case, the Government alleged that Alcoa was using its monopoly power in the upstream aluminum ingot market to squeeze the profits of downstream aluminum sheet fabricators. The court concluded: "That it was unlawful to set the price of 'sheet' so low and hold the price of ingot so high, seems to us unquestionable, provided, as we have held, that on this record the price of ingot must be regarded as higher than a 'fair price.' " Given developments in economic theory and antitrust

Institutional concerns also counsel against recognition of such claims. We have repeatedly emphasized the importance of clear rules in antitrust law. Courts are ill suited "to act as central planners, identifying the proper price, quantity, and other terms of dealing." *Trinko.* " 'No court should impose a duty to deal that it cannot explain or adequately and reasonably supervise. The problem should be deemed irremedia[ble] by antitrust law when compulsory access requires the court to assume the day-to-day controls characteristic of a regulatory agency.' " See also *Town of Concord v. Boston Edison Co., 915 F.2d 17, 25 (CA1 1990)* (Breyer, C. J.) ("[A]ntitrust courts normally avoid direct price administration, relying on rules and remedies . . . that are easier to administer").

It is difficult enough for courts to identify and remedy an alleged anticompetitive practice at one level, such as predatory pricing in retail markets or a violation of the duty-to-deal doctrine at the wholesale level. . . . Recognizing price-squeeze claims would require courts simultaneously to police both the wholesale and retail prices to ensure that rival firms are not being squeezed. And courts would be aiming at a moving target, since it is the *interaction* between these two prices that may result in a squeeze.

Perhaps most troubling, firms that seek to avoid price-squeeze liability will have no safe harbor for their pricing practices. See *Town of Concord, supra, at 22* (antitrust rules "must be clear enough for lawyers to explain them to clients"). At least in the predatory pricing context, firms know they will not incur liability as long as their retail prices are above cost. No such guidance is available for price-squeeze claims. . . .

The most commonly articulated standard for price squeezes is that the defendant must leave its rivals a "fair" or "adequate" margin between the wholesale price and the retail price. One of our colleagues has highlighted the flaws of this test in Socratic fashion:

> "[H]ow is a judge or jury to determine a 'fair price?' Is it the price charged by other suppliers of the primary product? None exist. Is it the price that competition 'would have set' were the primary level not monopolized? How can the court determine this price without examining costs and demands, indeed without acting like a rate-setting regulatory agency, the rate-setting proceedings of which often last for several years? Further, how is the court to decide the proper size of the price 'gap?' Must it be large enough for all independent competing firms to make a 'living profit,' no matter how inefficient they may be? . . . And how should the court respond when costs or demands change over time, as they inevitably will?" *Town of Concord.*

Some amici respond to these concerns by proposing a "transfer price test" for identifying an unlawful price squeeze: A price squeeze should be presumed if the upstream monopolist could not have made a profit by

---

jurisprudence since *Alcoa,* we find our recent decisions in *Trinko* and *Brooke Group* more pertinent to the question before us.

selling at its retail rates if it purchased inputs at its own wholesale rates. Whether or not that test is administrable, it lacks any grounding in our antitrust jurisprudence. An upstream monopolist with no duty to deal is free to charge whatever wholesale price it would like; antitrust law does not forbid lawfully obtained monopolies from charging monopoly prices. *Trinko.* ("The mere possession of monopoly power, and the concomitant charging of monopoly prices, is not only not unlawful; it is an important element of the free-market system"). Similarly, the Sherman Act does not forbid—indeed, it *encourages*—aggressive price competition at the retail level, as long as the prices being charged are not predatory. If both the wholesale price and the retail price are independently lawful, there is no basis for imposing antitrust liability simply because a vertically integrated firm's wholesale price happens to be greater than or equal to its retail price.

Amici assert that there are circumstances in which price squeezes may harm competition. For example, they assert that price squeezes may raise entry barriers that fortify the upstream monopolist's position; they also contend that price squeezes may impair nonprice competition and innovation in the downstream market by driving independent firms out of business.

The problem, however, is that amici have not identified any independent competitive harm caused by price squeezes above and beyond the harm that would result from a duty-to-deal violation at the wholesale level or predatory pricing at the retail level.... To the extent a monopolist violates one of these doctrines, the plaintiffs have a remedy under existing law. We do not need to endorse a new theory of liability to prevent such harm.

Lastly, as mentioned above, plaintiffs have asked us for leave to amend their complaint to bring a *Brooke Group* predatory pricing claim. We need not decide whether leave to amend should be granted. Our grant of certiorari was limited to the question whether price-squeeze claims are cognizable in the absence of an antitrust duty to deal. The Court of Appeals addressed only AT&T's motion for judgment on the pleadings on the plaintiffs' *original* complaint. For the reasons stated, we hold that the price-squeeze claims set forth in that complaint are not cognizable under the Sherman Act....

It is for the District Court on remand to consider whether the amended complaint states a claim upon which relief may be granted in light of the new pleading standard we articulated in *Twombly*, whether plaintiffs should be given leave to amend their complaint to bring a claim under *Brooke Group*, and such other matters properly before it. Even if the amended complaint is further amended to add a *Brooke Group* claim, it may not survive a motion to dismiss. For if AT&T can bankrupt the plaintiffs by refusing to deal altogether, the plaintiffs must demonstrate why the law prevents AT&T from putting them out of business by pricing them out of the market. Nevertheless, such questions are for the District Court to decide in the first instance....

In this case, plaintiffs have not stated a duty-to-deal claim under *Trinko* and have not stated a predatory pricing claim under *Brooke Group*. They have nonetheless tried to join a wholesale claim that cannot succeed with a retail claim that cannot succeed, and alchemize them into a new form of antitrust liability never before recognized by this Court. We decline the invitation to recognize such claims. Two wrong claims do not make one that is right.

■ BREYER, J. with whom STEVENS, SOUTER, and GINSBURG, JJ., join, concurring in the judgment.

I would accept respondents' concession that the Ninth Circuit majority's "price squeeze" holding is wrong, I would vacate the Circuit's decision, and I would remand the case in order to allow the District Court to determine whether respondents may proceed with their "predatory pricing" claim as set forth in Judge Gould's dissenting Ninth Circuit opinion.

A "price squeeze" claim finds its natural home in a Sherman Act *§ 2* monopolization case where the Government as plaintiff seeks to show that a defendant's monopoly power rests, not upon "skill, foresight and industry," *United States v. Aluminum Co. of America, 148 F.2d 416, 430 (CA2 1945) (Alcoa)*, but upon exclusionary conduct. As this Court pointed out in [*Trinko*] the " 'means of illicit exclusion, like the means of legitimate competition, are myriad.' " They may involve a "course of dealing" that, even if profitable, indicates a "willingness to forsake short-term profits to achieve an anticompetitive end." *Trinko*. See, *e.g., Aspen Skiing Co.;* Complaint in *United States* v. *International Business Machines Corp.*, Civil Action No. 69 Civ. 200 (SDNY, filed Jan. 17, 1969). And, as Judge Hand wrote many years ago, a "price squeeze" may fall within that latter category. As a matter of logic, it may be that a particular price squeeze can only be exclusionary if a refusal by the monopolist to sell to the "squeezed customer" would also be exclusionary. But a court, faced with a price squeeze rather than a refusal to deal, is unlikely to find the latter (hypothetical) question any easier to answer than the former.

I would try neither to answer these hypothetical questions here nor to foreshadow their answer. We have before us a regulated firm. During the time covered by the complaint, petitioners were required to provide wholesale digital subscriber line (DSL) transport service as a common carrier, charging "just and reasonable" rates that were not "unreasonabl[y] discriminat[ory]." And, in my view, a purchaser from a regulated firm (which, if a natural monopolist, is lawfully such) cannot win an antitrust case simply by showing that it is "squeezed" between the regulated firm's wholesale price (to the plaintiff) and its retail price (to customers for whose business both firms compete). When a regulatory structure exists to deter and remedy anticompetitive harm, the costs of antitrust enforcement are likely to be greater than the benefits. . . .

Unlike *Town of Concord,* the regulators here controlled prices only at the wholesale level. But respondents do not claim that that regulatory fact makes any difference; and rightly so, for as far as I can tell, respondents could have gone to the regulators and asked for petitioners' wholesale prices to be lowered in light of the alleged price squeeze.

Respondents now seek to show only that the defendant engaged in predatory pricing, within the terms of this Court's decision in *Brooke Group Ltd.* The District Court can determine whether there is anything in the procedural history of this case that bars respondents from asserting their predatory pricing claim. And if not, it can decide the merits of that claim. As I said, I would remand the case so that it can do so.

NOTES AND QUESTIONS

1. *Aspen Skiing* was the first significant monopolization case to be decided by the Supreme Court since *Grinnell* (p. 152 *supra*) in 1966. One way of looking at the case is to analyze Ski Co.'s conduct as involving the strategic raising of a rival's cost. As Professors Krattenmaker, Lande and Salop put it:

> A single firm or group of firms that is not constrained by competition from a sufficient number of equally efficient existing and potential competitors can profitably raise price or prevent price from falling in two ways.

> First, the firm or group of firms may raise or maintain price above the competitive level directly by restraining its own output ("control price"). The power to control price by restraining one's own output is the usual focus of Chicago School antitrust analysts. . . .

> Second, the firm or group of firms may raise price above the competitive level or prevent it from falling to a lower competitive level by raising its rivals' costs and thereby causing them to restrain their output ("exclude competition"). Such allegations are at the bottom of most antitrust cases in which one firm or group of firms is claimed to have harmed competition by foreclosing or excluding its competitors.[29]

Ski Co.'s decision to terminate the all-Aspen ticket may have disadvantaged Ski Co., but may have been even more costly to Highlands. Should such "strategic behavior" violate the conduct requirement of Section 2? Notice that consumer welfare losses result from "controlling price" and from "excluding competition" by "strategic behavior." In both situations, output will be restrained below the efficient competitive level and consumers will be denied products they value. In addition, excluding competition by strategic behavior reduces production efficiency. What if the firm with monopoly power helps induce costly new regulatory requirements or, if it is capital intensive as compared to rivals, agrees to costly labor settlements?

2. Are Justice Scalia (in *Trinko)* and Chief Justice Roberts (in *Linkline)* overly cautious about use of Section 2 of the Sherman Act and overly concerned about "false positives"? According to one recent commentator, who agreed both cases were correctly decided, *dictum* in each "seriously undermines the traditional policy underpinnings of Section 2." He provided the following critique of *Trinko*:

---

29. Krattenmaker, Lande & Salop, Monopoly Power and Market Power in Antitrust Law, 76 Geo.L.J. 241, 249 (1987).

Justice Scalia, wearing rose-colored glasses, asserts that the "mere possession of monopoly power, and the concomitant charging of monopoly prices, is not only not unlawful; it is an important element of the free-market system. The opportunity to charge monopoly prices ... is what attracts 'business acumen' in the first place." Scalia is correct that charging monopoly prices would be lawful under the *Grinnell* test so long as unreasonably exclusionary or predatory conduct is not found. Moreover, the prospect of monopoly profits could certainly spur the efforts of rational business executives. But monopoly power and profits exact large costs. Nowhere in Scalia's opinion is there an expression of concern about the traditional evils of dominance or monopoly power—excessive price, misallocation of resources, and loss of dynamic efficiency. Indeed, Scalia suggests that dominance is benign or beneficial because it "induces risk taking that produces innovation and economic growth."

Scalia and others in the Chicago School would argue that concern about the "traditional evils" of monopoly power resulted in the *Alcoa* test requiring harmful passivity. I agree that *Alcoa's* conduct test was too restrictive, but the *Grinnell* and *Aspen Skiing* formulations—and the focus on unreasonably exclusionary conduct—provided the necessary corrective. Under these formulations, there is plenty of room for efficient, dynamic, innovative conduct.[30]

The Obama Administration's new chief of the Antitrust Division recently "withdrew" a Bush Administration Section 2 Report because:

The Report's adoption of the disproportionality test [*i.e.,* anticompetitive harm must substantially outweigh precompetitive benefits] reflects an excessive concern with the risks of over-deterrence and a resulting preference for an overly lenient approach to enforcement. The failing of this approach is that it effectively straightjackets antitrust enforcers and courts from redressing monopolistic abuses, thereby allowing all but the most bold and predatory conduct to go unpunished and undeterred.[31]

3. In *Linkline*, Chief Justice Roberts carefully observed that "AT&T had no ... antitrust duty to deal with its competitors, and this holding was not challenged on appeal." What analysis and result if an antitrust obligation to sell to plaintiff had been a serious, unresolved issue in the case?

4. In Data General Corp. v. Grumman Systems Support Corp., 36 F.3d 1147, 1183 (1st Cir.1994), the First Circuit analyzed the *Aspen Skiing* and *Kodak* cases as follows:

[A] monopolist's unilateral refusal to deal with its competitors (as long as the refusal harms the competitive process) may constitute prima facie evidence of exclusionary conduct in the context of a Section 2 claim. See *Kodak* (citing Aspen Skiing Co. v. Aspen Highlands Skiing Corp., 472 U.S. 585, 602–05 (1985)). A monopolist may nevertheless rebut such evidence by establishing a valid business justification for its conduct. See *Kodak* (suggesting that monopolist may rebut an inference of exclusionary conduct by establishing "legitimate competitive reasons for the refusal"); *Aspen Ski-*

---

30. Goldschmid, Comment on ... the Dominant Firm, in Pitofsky (ed.), How the Chicago School Overshot the Mark 125 (2008).

31. Varney, Vigorous Antitrust Enforcement in this Challenging Era, http://www.usdoj.gov/atr/public/speeches/245711.htm (May 11, 2009).

ing (suggesting that sufficient evidence of harm to consumers and competitors triggers further inquiry as to whether the monopolist has "persuaded the jury that its [harmful] conduct was justified by [a] normal business purpose"). In general, a business justification is valid if it relates directly or indirectly to the enhancement of consumer welfare. Thus, pursuit of efficiency and quality control might be legitimate competitive reasons for an otherwise exclusionary refusal to deal, while the desire to maintain a monopoly market share or thwart the entry of competitors would not.... In essence, a unilateral refusal to deal is prima facie exclusionary if there is evidence of harm to the competitive process; a valid business justification requires proof of countervailing benefits to the competitive process.

The First Circuit went on to conclude that Data General's refusal to license copyrighted material (a sophisticated computer program) was not a Section 2 violation because "an author's desire to exclude others from use of its copyrighted work is a presumptively valid business justification for any immediate harm to consumers." The Court noted: "Wary of undermining the Sherman Act ... we do not hold that an antitrust plaintiff can never rebut this presumption, for there may be rare cases in which imposing liability is unlikely to frustrate the objectives of the Copyright Act." *Compare* the First circuit's approach *with* the Ninth Circuit's *Kodak* opinion p. 791 *infra*.

5.   In *Aspen Skiing* (p. 726 *supra*) the Supreme Court found it "unnecessary to consider the possible relevance of the 'essential facilities' doctrine," and in *Trinko* (p. 739 *supra*) indicated that we "have never recognized such a doctrine ... and we find no need either to recognize it or to repudiate it here." Do you see any need for the development of an essential facilities doctrine?

6.   In Olympia Equipment Leasing Co. v. Western Union Telegraph Co., 797 F.2d 370, 376–78 (7th Cir.1986), Western Union was found guilty of monopolization under Section 2 because it abruptly stopped assisting some customers that it had helped to enter the telex service business. The Seventh Circuit distinguished *Aspen Skiing* and found a business justification for Western Union's conduct in the following discussion:

> If a monopolist does extend a helping hand, though not required to do so, and later withdraws it as happened in this case, does he incur antitrust liability? We think not.... Since Western Union had no duty to encourage the entry of new firms into the equipment market, the law would be perverse if it made Western Union's encouraging gestures the fulcrum of an antitrust violation. Then no firm would dare to attempt a graceful exit from a market in which it was a major seller. We can imagine, though with difficulty, an argument that a monopolist might decide to entice new firms into its market only to destroy them and so deter other firms from trying to enter. But no such diabolical scheme is ascribed to Western Union, which undoubtedly was sincere in inviting new vendors into the market and in wanting to leave the market as soon as it liquidated its inventory of terminals bought from Teletype Corporation and leased to its subscribers.

> Some cases hold, however, that a firm which controls a facility essential to its competitors may be guilty of monopolization if it refuses to allow them access to the facility. We accept the authority of these cases absolutely. They are well illustrated by Otter Tail Power Co. v. United States, 410 U.S. 366 (1973), where a wholesale supplier of electricity refused to supply electric power to a power system that competed with it in the retail

electrical power market and had no other source of supply. It might seem that if a monopolist's refusal to sell his products or services to a competitor can thus be actionable under antitrust law, it must mean that monopolists sometimes do have a duty to help their competitors and that the cases which deny this proposition are wrong. But the monopolistic-refusal-to-deal cases qualify rather than refute the no-duty-to-help-competitors cases. . . .

The present case would be an essential-facility case if Western Union had refused to supply telex service to a customer who got his terminal equipment from Olympia rather than from it, or if Olympia were a competing supplier of telex service who, like the specialized common carriers in the long-distance telephone market, depended on the owner of the local exchanges (here Western Union) to complete its service. Neither condition is satisfied. The essential feature of the refusal-to-deal cases—a monopoly supplier's discriminating against a customer because the customer has decided to compete with it—is missing here. . . .

Aspen Skiing Co. v. Aspen Highlands Skiing Corp., supra, goes the furthest of any case we know toward imposing (more precisely, allowing a jury to impose) a duty under antitrust law to help a competitor; and as a recent decision by the Supreme Court it requires our most careful and respectful consideration. . . . *Aspen Highlands* is not a conventional monopoly refusal-to-deal case like *Otter Tail* because Aspen Highlands was never a customer of Aspen Skiing Company; the skiers are the customers. But it is like the essential-facility cases in that the plaintiff could not compete with the defendant without being able to offer its customers access to the defendant's larger facilities.

Olympia analogizes access to all the major mountains at Aspen to Western Union's vendor list, and argues that just as Aspen Highlands could not survive without access to the mountains so Olympia could not survive without the list. The analogy lacks not only plausibility but also evidentiary support. . . .

Aspen Highlands could not acquire three more mountains in the Aspen area in order to be able to compete more effectively with the Aspen Skiing Company but Olympia could and did hire salesmen to substitute for the Western Union sales force that had been helping it. If Western Union had tried to prevent Olympia from making the substitution it would have been guilty of exclusionary conduct. But Olympia had no right under antitrust law to take a free ride on its competitor's sales force. You cannot conscript your competitor's salesmen to sell your product even if the competitor has monopoly power and you are a struggling new entrant. . . .

Olympia cites *Aspen Highlands* for the proposition that if a firm with monopoly power cannot give a good business justification for not cooperating with a competitor, its refusal to cooperate violates antitrust law. Conjoined with other evidence, lack of business justification may indicate probable anticompetitive effect. But there is a clear business justification in this case: Western Union wanted to liquidate its supply of telex terminals faster, so it stopped promoting a competitor's supply. . . .

In the *Olympia* case, the Seventh Circuit appeared to accept a narrow version of the essential facilities doctrine. A critical commentary[32] on the doctrine sets forth the following analysis:

---

32. Boudin, Antitrust Doctrine and the Sway of Metaphor, 75 Geo.L.J. 395, 397–401 (1986).

The bottleneck doctrine, a supposed rule expressed as a metaphor, is also described more plainly as the "essential facilities" doctrine. A recent and fairly typical formulation appears in *United States v. AT&T*,[33] where Judge Greene stated:

> It may be helpful at the outset to state the applicable legal standard. Any company which controls an "essential facility" or a "strategic bottleneck" in the market violates the antitrust laws if it fails to make access to that facility available to its competitors on fair and reasonable terms that do not disadvantage them.

The opinion cited a number of Supreme Court and lower court decisions for this proposition.[34]

This bottleneck doctrine, couched in similar terms by other courts of appeals and district courts, is not an idle fancy but is intended as a rule of decision. Among other applications, it has been employed against a football team with an exclusive lease on a Washington stadium,[35] petroleum storage facilities in American Samoa,[36] a gas pipeline,[37] an electric power grid,[38] a distribution system for newspapers,[39] a realty listing service,[40] and a Colorado ski resort.[41] Courts often state the doctrine in the confident and unqualified terms used by Judge Greene. The bottleneck doctrine is also a favorite in pleadings filed by the Justice Department's Antitrust Division with courts and administrative agencies, usually accompanied by a reference to *United States v. Terminal Railroad Association* and *Associated Press v. United States* . . . .

Yet when one examines the Supreme Court decisions commonly cited for the doctrine by lower courts, they do not offer much support. . . .

A lack of Supreme Court support for the bottleneck doctrine is only the first warning signal. Doubts multiply as one ponders the implications of a general obligation for a monopolist to "share" its essential facility with its competitors. Is it truly the case that the dominant producer in an industry, having skillfully designed a plant of unique efficiency, has to let

---

33. 524 F.Supp. 1336 (D.D.C.1981).

34. Judge Greene cited United States v. Terminal R.R. Ass'n, 224 U.S. 383 (1912), and Otter Tail Power Co. v. United States, 410 U.S. 366 (1973). Although these are the Supreme Court decisions most commonly cited, Associated Press v. United States, 326 U.S. 1 (1945), and United States v. Griffith, 334 U.S. 100 (1948), are, among others, invoked by lower courts in support of the doctrine from time to time.

35. Hecht v. Pro–Football, Inc., 570 F.2d 982 (D.C.Cir.1977), cert. denied, 436 U.S. 956 (1978).

36. United States v. Standard Oil Co., 362 F.Supp. 1331, 1341 (N.D.Cal.1972), aff'd mem., 412 U.S. 924 (1973).

37. Venture Technology, Inc. v. National Fuel Gas Distribution Corp., 1980–81 Trade Cas. (CCH) ¶ 63,780, at 78,169 (W.D.N.Y.1981), rev'd on other grounds, 685 F.2d 41 (2d Cir.), cert. denied, 459 U.S. 1007 (1982).

38. United States v. Otter Tail Power Co., 331 F.Supp. 54 (D.Minn.1971), aff'd in pertinent part, 410 U.S. 366 (1973).

39. Byars v. Bluff City News Co., 609 F.2d 843 (6th Cir.1979).

40. United States v. Realty Multi–List, 629 F.2d 1351 (5th Cir.1980).

41. Aspen Highlands Skiing Corp. v. Aspen Skiing Co., 738 F.2d 1509 (10th Cir.1984), aff'd on other grounds, 472 U.S. 585 (1985).

competitors use its factory at night so that they too can enjoy the benefits of this "essential facility"? If a soft drink company supplies most of the market because its secret formula produces a widely liked beverage, does section 2 require it to supply distributors even though it wishes to do all its own wholesale distribution? As the permutations pass in review, it is apparent that there are no easy answers to the problem of a monopolist dealing or refusing to deal with competitors.

Indeed, the "problem" itself is not unitary. The source of the monopoly power varies, from a natural monopoly due to economies of scale, or acquired by skill and foresight, to one granted by government franchise or patent, to one illegally acquired. The conduct may be a refusal to provide facilities, services, or supplies to a competitor or merely a discrimination in supply, price, or information. The competitor may be trying to compete in the monopolized market, a geographically adjacent one, or one vertically related. Within each class of cases, facts vary as to intent, administrative regulation, feasibility of remedies, and the economic (or other) justifications offered for denying access, refusing to deal, or discrimination. It would be amazing if this collection of concerns and variables could all be reduced to order by a one-sentence doctrine asserting that a monopolist controlling an essential facility has a duty to deal with competitors.

7. Judge Boudin's reservations (in note 6) about the validity and scope of the essential facilities doctrine characterize much of the academic literature on the subject. If U.S. scholarship were the last word, one would expect that the essential facilities would be circumscribed narrowly or even fully abandoned. *See, e.g.*, 3A Areeda & Hovenkamp, Antitrust Law ¶ 771c (2d ed. 2002); Areeda, Essential Facilities: An Epithet in Need of Limiting Principles, 58 Antitrust L.J. 841, 852 (1989).

While acknowledging Judge Boudin's point that the essential facilities doctrine needs to be limited in application, a recent commentary on the doctrine treats it more sympathetically. *See* Pitofsky, Patterson & Hooks, The Essential Facilities Doctrine Under U.S. Antitrust Law, 70 Antitrust L.J. 443 (2002). The authors note that the essential facilities doctrine has a long and respected history, tracing back at the Supreme Court level to United States v. Terminal Railroad Ass'n, 224 U.S. 383 (1912) and Associated Press v. United States, 326 U.S. 1 (1945). *See* p. 362 and p. 363 *supra*. Interestingly, there are literally scores of lower court cases acknowledging the legitimacy of the doctrine and occasionally mandating access, generally reflecting a view that if the facility is truly essential and controlled by a monopolist, mandated access is necessary if competition is ever to flourish. The authors note with approval cases that have established stringent conditions before the doctrine may apply. These conditions include: (1) control of the essential facility must be by a monopolist; (2) a competitor would not be able practically or reasonably to duplicate the essential facility; (3) access to the facility was denied to a competitor; and (4) it would have been feasible to provide the facility to competitors. *See* MCI Communications v. AT&T, 708 F.2d 1081, 1132–33 (7th Cir.1983). Among many cases adopting similar limits, *see* City of Chanute v. Williams Natural Gas Co., 955 F.2d 641 (10th Cir.1992). The last factor has occasionally been expanded into a broad business justification, allowing a monopolist to deny access if there is a legitimate business or technological justification. City of Anaheim v. Southern Cal. Edison Co., 955 F.2d 1373, 1380 (9th Cir.1992).

One reason courts are cautious in mandating access even to an essential facility controlled by a monopolist is that the court's obligation does not stop with a simple order. To make access a reality, the court must also specify the price of access (*i.e.*, reasonable royalty), priority, and other relevant terms. That kind of continuing supervision is difficult for courts to manage (as opposed to regulatory agencies that have an ongoing mandate) with the result that mandated access is usually a last resort, imposed when the facility is truly essential and when there is no other way to preserve or restore competition.

What difference, if any, would there be between a claim that a monopolist violated Section 2 because it refused to deal without legitimate competitive reasons for the refusal (*e.g.* under *Aspen Skiing* and *Kodak*), and an essential facilities claim? Would the business justification need to be more compelling if an essential facility were being denied?

How should an "essential facility" be defined? In general, probably the clearest case for application of the essential facilities doctrine is where the essential facility is owned or subsidized by government or is a public utility with an exclusive right created by government. Should the doctrine be applied to any natural monopoly cutting a competitor or potential competitor off from customers? Where else should the doctrine apply? *See* Lao, Networks, Access, and "Essential Facilities": From Terminal Railroad to Microsoft, 62 SMU L.Rev. 557 (2009). What role should intent play?

8. In Official Airline Guides, Inc. v. FTC, 630 F.2d 920 (2d Cir.1980), cert. denied, 450 U.S. 917 (1981), the Second Circuit considered whether a "monopolist publisher of flight schedules not itself an air carrier" had a duty under Section 5 of the FTC Act not to discriminate unjustifiably between certified air carriers and commuter airlines so as to place the latter at a significant competitive disadvantage. The Court of Appeals concluded:

> Conceding in effect that there is no case precisely in point, the Commission suggested in oral argument that it was but a "small step" that we would be taking were we to uphold their decision. Of course we are reminded by the line of cases including FTC v. Cement Institute, 333 U.S. 683, 692–93 (1948) and Atlantic Refining Co. v. FTC, 381 U.S. 357, 367–68 (1965), that "[w]hile the final word is left to the courts, necessarily 'we give great weight to the Commission's conclusion' " ... as to what is an "unfair method of competition" or "an unfair act or practice" within the meaning of section 5 of the FTC Act. We note that the FTC with some justification states that the arbitrary refusal of a monopolist to deal leaves the disadvantaged competitor, even though in another field, with no recourse to overcome the disadvantage, and the Commission wants us to take the "small step" in terms of "the fundamental goals of antitrust." Reuben H. Donnelley Corp., [1980] 3 Trade Reg.Rep. (CCH) ¶ 21,650, at 21,818.

> But we think enforcement of the FTC's order here would give the FTC too much power to substitute its own business judgment for that of the monopolist in any decision that arguably affects competition in another industry. Such a decision would permit the FTC to delve into, as the Commission itself put the extreme case, "social, political, or personal reasons" for a monopolist's refusal to deal. Professors Areeda and Turner give examples of a monopolist theater which refuses to admit men with long hair or a monopolist newspaper which refuses to publish advertising from cigarette manufacturers. 3 P. Areeda & D. Turner, *supra*, at 270–71. The Commission says that neither of these examples would trigger anti-trust scrutiny because there is no competition among persons who attend

movies, and refusing to publish advertisements for all cigarette companies would not place any of them at a disadvantage *vis-a-vis* a competitor. Nevertheless, the Commission's own example in footnote 38 of its opinion of a monopolist newspaper refusing to take advertisements from a particular cigarette company because of the style of prior advertisements or the political views of its president shows just how far the Commission's opinion could lead us. What we are doing, as the Commission itself recognized, is weighing benefits to competition in the other field against the detrimental effect of allowing the Commission to pass judgment on many business decisions of the monopolist that arguably discriminate among customers in some way. Thus, if the only supermarket in town decides to stock Birdseye vegetables but not Green Giant vegetables, the FTC would be able to require it to stock Green Giant vegetables if it were to find Green Giant competitively disadvantaged.

> We do not think that the *Colgate* doctrine is as dead as the Commission would have it. . . . We think that even a monopolist, as long as he has no purpose to restrain competition or to enhance or expand his monopoly, and does not act coercively, retains this right. Absent enlightenment from above, or clarification from Congress, this is our decision on the merits.

Section 5 of the FTC Act might be given a broader sweep than Section 2 of the Sherman Act because it is prospective only, has no criminal enforcement potential, and cannot be the basis of a private action. Should this have made a difference in the *Official Airline Guides* case? What if, making the Second Circuit's illustration more appropriate, there was only one supermarket chain in the nation, it decided to stock Birdseye vegetables and not Green Giant, and it offered no plausible justifications?

9. In Conwood Co. v. United States Tobacco Co., 290 F.3d 768 (6th Cir. 2002), a seller of moist snuff with about a 13% national market share sued United States Tobacco ("U.S.T."), the dominant firm in the field with 77% of the market (down from 97% since the 1980s) for violations of Section 2 of the Sherman Act. Moist snuff is a finely chopped smokeless tobacco. The Sixth Circuit Court of Appeals affirmed a jury verdict that resulted in a damage award of $1.05 billion, the largest award in the history of antitrust.

The case revolved around the growing marketing arrangement called "category management" in which suppliers of products compete for assignment as the category captain. In that role, the category captain supplies data to the retailer about which brand, including its own, should be given advantageous shelf space and advertising prominence, and sometimes designs and services the product rack or shelf space area. Conwood alleged that U.S.T bid for and often won the category captain position (Conwood itself did not compete), and then provided false information that induced some retailers to prefer U.S.T. and removed Conwood's display racks and advertising without retailer consent. Final decisions on shelf space and display remain with the retailer, but there was extensive evidence that U.S.T.'s purpose and effect in becoming category captain was to take advantage of negligent retail employees and to eliminate or control the display of competitive products including particularly cut rate or discount offerings.

U.S.T.'s principal defenses were that its behavior amounted at worst to sporatic business torts and should not qualify as exclusionary behavior under *Aspen Skiing*, and that its behavior could not have resulted in substantial market foreclosure since the collective market share of its competitors nearly doubled during the period of the alleged violation. The Court of Appeals concluded that while business torts should not casually be treated as exclusionary conduct under Section 2, U.S.T.'s orchestrated campaign to use its category manager position to disadvantage competitors, which the chairman of U.S.T. testified should not have happened and caused him some embarrassment, was exclusionary conduct lacking any business justification. As to the growth of U.S.T.'s competitors during the period of alleged violation, the Sixth Circuit simply concluded that they might have grown even more but for U.S.T.'s anticompetitive conduct.

If the antitrust laws regard business torts by a monopolist as exclusionary conduct, may that have the result of discouraging aggressive competitive programs? On the other hand, when a monopolist succeeds in becoming category manager, should it have an obligation to treat competitors and potential competitors in a particularly fair and scrupulous manner?

10. In Alaska Airlines, Inc. v. United Airlines, Inc., 948 F.2d 536 (9th Cir.1991), the Ninth Circuit examined both leveraging and essential facilities as forms of exclusionary conduct under Section 2 of the Sherman Act. In *Alaska Airlines,* the defendant airlines established computerized reservations systems ("CRS") which provide flight information to travel agents who subscribe to their systems. American Airlines and United Airlines established the SABRE and Apollo systems, respectively. Airlines generally subscribe to every CRS because CRSs charge airlines per booking, generally $1.75 per booking. The plaintiff airlines brought suit against American and United Airlines, contending that each had violated Section 2 of the Sherman Act by: (1) denying plaintiffs reasonable access to the CRS services which were allegedly "essential facilities"; and (2) "leveraging" their dominance over CRS services to gain a competitive edge in the downstream air transportation market. The district court granted summary judgment for the defendants on both claims.

The Ninth Circuit stated that the "essential facilities doctrine imposes liability when one firm, which controls an essential facility, denies a second firm reasonable access to a product or service that the second firm must obtain in order to compete with the first." The Court of Appeals then observed:

> *Otter Tail,* the foundation of the essential facilities doctrine in the single firm context, was an extreme case. Otter Tail Power, an "upstream" monopolist, baldly refused to deal with its potential "downstream" competitors. Given the difficulty of duplicating Otter Tail's facilities, this refusal did more than merely impose some handicap on potential competitors; it eliminated all possibility of competition in the downstream market. As the Supreme Court indicated, Otter Tail Power had both attempted to monopolize and had succeeded in monopolizing the downstream market for "retail" electric services. . . .

> *Weider* [2d Cir.], *Olympia* and *MCI* [7th Cir.] share a concern that transcends their fact-based differences. A facility that is controlled by a single firm will be considered "essential" only if control of the facility carries with it the power to *eliminate* competition in the downstream market.

As to the essential facilities doctrine, the Ninth Circuit concluded:

> In the instant case, it is clear that defendants' control of their CRSs did not give them power to eliminate competition in the downstream air transportation market. Basic economic theory tells us that plaintiffs will withdraw from SABRE or Apollo if the cost of using either CRS causes the cost to the airline of providing a flight booked on a CRS to exceed the

revenue that the airline gains by providing the flight. It is difficult to imagine that a travel agent would subscribe to a CRS if it only contained information about 12–14% of available flights. Because the parties agree that neither United nor American controlled more than 12–14% of the air transportation market, SABRE and Apollo would contain information concerning approximately 12–14% of available flights if competitors withdrew from either SABRE or Apollo. Thus, the ability of United or American to abuse their downstream competitors by manipulating their CRSs is severely limited.

Moreover, United and American have never refused any of the plaintiffs access to their respective CRSs. *See Otter Tail,* 410 U.S. at 378 (outright refusal); *MCI,* 708 F.2d at 1132 (same). Rather, United and American have always given all of their competitors in the air transportation market such access for a fee. Neither United nor American have ever set this fee at a level that would drive their competitors away. As noted above, it is unlikely that defendants would set their fee at such a level, for if they did, they would destroy their CRSs rather than their competition.

Plaintiffs claim that each defendant's CRS was an "essential" facility because each defendant's control of its CRS gave it power to redistribute a portion of its rivals' revenues to itself. Plaintiffs make this claim even though they concede that each defendant's control of its CRS did not create a dangerous probability of monopolization in the downstream air transportation market. Although each defendant may have gained some leverage over its competitors through control of its CRS, each defendant's power fell far short of the power to *eliminate* competition seen in *Otter Tail* and *MCI.* At most, defendants gained a monetary profit at their rivals' expense. The exercise of this limited power is not actionable under Section 2.

Our view of the essential facilities doctrine does not render the doctrine superfluous or otherwise inappropriately curtail its reach. When a firm's power to exclude rivals from a facility gives the firm the power to *eliminate* competition in a market downstream from the facility, and the firm excludes at least some of its competitors, the danger that the firm will monopolize the downstream market is clear. In this circumstance, a finding of monopolization, or at least attempted monopolization, is appropriate, and there is little need to engage in the usual lengthy analysis of factors such as intent. We hold that neither defendant denied plaintiffs an "essential" facility in violation of the antitrust laws.

As to "monopoly leveraging," the Ninth Circuit concluded:

Plaintiffs next allege that each defendant violated Section 2 by "leveraging" its monopoly power over its competitors in the CRS market to gain a competitive advantage over these airlines in the downstream air transportation market. Plaintiffs admit that, because there was no dangerous probability that either defendant would monopolize the downstream air transportation market, they have no claim under the traditional Section 2 doctrine of attempted monopolization. This circuit expressly declined to decide whether "monopoly leveraging is a distinct Section 2 violation" in Catlin v. Washington Energy Co., 791 F.2d 1343, 1348 (9th Cir.1986).

The origin of the notion that a single firm may be liable for "monopoly leveraging," even in the absence of a threat that the "leveraged" market will be monopolized, is Berkey Photo, Inc. v. Eastman Kodak Co., 603 F.2d

263 (2d Cir.1979), *cert. denied* 444 U.S. 1093 (1980). In *Berkey Photo,* Kodak possessed a monopoly in the film and camera markets. Berkey Photo argued that Kodak had "leveraged" its dominant position in these areas to gain a "competitive advantage" in the photofinishing equipment and services markets. Berkey Photo conceded that there was no dangerous probability that Kodak could monopolize either of these markets.

The *Berkey Photo* court announced and applied the rule that "a firm violates § 2 by using its monopoly power in one market to gain a competitive advantage in another, albeit without an attempt to monopolize the second market." *Id.* In contrast to the traditional actions for monopoly and attempted monopoly, *Berkey Photo's* "monopoly leveraging" doctrine has only two rather loose elements: 1) there must be monopoly power in some market, and 2) such power must be "exercised ... to the detriment of competition" in another market....

We now reject *Berkey's* monopoly leveraging doctrine as an independent theory of liability under Section 2. Even in the two-market situation, a plaintiff cannot establish a violation of Section 2 without proving that the defendant used its monopoly power in one market to obtain, or attempt to attain, a monopoly in the downstream, or leveraged, market. We believe that *Berkey Photo* misapplied the elements to Section 2 by concluding that a firm violates Section 2 merely by obtaining a competitive advantage in the second market, even in the absence of an attempt to monopolize the leveraged market.... The anticompetitive dangers that implicate the Sherman Act are not present when a monopolist had a lawful monopoly in one market and uses its power to gain a competitive advantage in the second market. By definition, the monopolist has failed to gain, or attempt to gain, a monopoly in the second market. Thus, such activity fails to meet the second element necessary to establish a violation of Section 2. Unless the monopolist uses its power in the first market to acquire and maintain a monopoly in the second market, or to attempt to do so, there is no Section 2 violation.

For a discussion of attempt to monopolize, *see* Section B *infra.*

11.   In *Trinko,* Justice Scalia commented that "a detailed regulatory scheme such as that created by the 1996 Act ordinarily raises the question whether the regulated entities are not shielded from antitrust scrutiny altogether by the doctrine of implied immunity." The question in *Trinko* was answered by the 1996 Act's specific antitrust savings clause.

In June 2007, in *Credit Suisse Securities (USA) LLC v. Billing,* 551 U.S. 264 (2007), the Supreme Court addressed the issue of implied antitrust immunity. A group of buyers of newly issued securities had filed antitrust claims against underwriters that distributed so-called IPOs. The buyers alleged tying arrangements (*i.e.,* forcing IPO buyers to commit to purchasing less attractive securities) and other potential antitrust violations.

The Supreme Court, reversing the Second Circuit, dismissed the antitrust claims because in this context there was "a 'clear repugnancy' between the securities law and the antitrust complaint." The Court reasoned:

> This Court's prior decisions.... have treated the following factors as critical: (1) the existence of regulatory authority under the securities law to supervise the activities in question; (2) evidence that the responsible regulatory entities exercise that authority; and (3) a resulting risk that the

securities and antitrust laws, if both applicable, would produce conflicting guidance, requirements, duties, privileges, or standards of conduct. We also note (4) that in *Gordon* and *NASD* the possible conflict affected practices that lie squarely within an area of financial market activity that the securities law seeks to regulate. . . .

We believe it fair to conclude that, where conduct at the core of the marketing of new securities is at issue; where securities regulators proceed with great care to distinguish the encouraged and permissible from the forbidden; where the threat of antitrust lawsuits, through error and disincentive, could seriously alter underwriter conduct in undesirable ways, to allow an antitrust lawsuit would threaten serious harm to the efficient functioning of the securities markets.

Second, any enforcement-related need for an antitrust lawsuit is unusually small. For one thing, the SEC actively enforces the rules and regulations that forbid the conduct in question. For another, as we have said, investors harmed by underwriters' unlawful practices may bring lawsuits and obtain damages under the securities law. Finally, the SEC is itself required to take account of competitive considerations when it creates securities-related policy and embodies it in rules and regulations. And that fact makes it somewhat less necessary to rely upon antitrust actions to address anticompetitive behavior.

12. Compare the European approach to essential facilities with *Trinko's* hesitancy to adopt such a doctrine. On April 29, 2004, the European Court of Justice issued its ruling in *IMS Health GmbH & Co. OHG v. NDC Health GmbH & Co. KG*, Case C–418/01, OJ C 118.30.04.2004, p. 14. The opinion provides clarification of the EU's application of the "essential facilities" doctrine.

Citing an earlier decision, the Court of Justice held that "to determine whether a product or service is indispensable . . . it must be determined whether there are products or services which constitute alternative solutions . . . even if less advantageous . . . and whether there are technical, legal or economic obstacles . . . making it impossible or at least unreasonably difficult . . . to create . . . alternative products or services. The Court concluded that a refusal to grant access to a copyright that meets this test would violate EU competition law when the refusal "prevent[s] the emergence of a new product for which there is potential consumer demand, [the refusal] is unjustified and . . . exclude[s] any competition on a secondary market." The Court emphasized that these conditions are *cumulative*, which resolved an earlier debate about whether all three were necessary.

At this point, the Court of Justice's concept of indispensability closely resembles the U.S. lower court definition of "essential." The European court has moved from an emphasis on the dominant position of the supplier to a position that rejects the idea that dominance alone demonstrates that the service or product is indispensable. *See* Sebastien J. Evrard, *Essential Facilitates in the European Union: Bronner and Beyond*, 10 Colum. J. Eur. L. 491, 509 (2004). U.S. courts have likewise refused to apply the doctrine where the plaintiff had a clear opportunity to use a substitute input, such as a sales force. *See Olympia Equipment*, p. 757 *supra*. Difficult questions remain, however. Commentators have criticized the lack of guidance with respect to the question whether a refusal to license hinders the development of a new product. For example, the Court did not say whether the new product could exist on the same market as the original product in question and what attributes made it "new." Donna M. Gitter, *Strong Medicine for Competition Ills: The Judgment of the European Court of Justice in the IMS Health Action and*

Its Implications for Microsoft Corporation, 15 Duke J. Comp. & Int'l L. 153, 185 (2004) *citing* Estelle Derclaye, *The IMS Health Decision: A Triple Victory,* 27 World Competition 397, 404 (2004).

The Court of Justice, like the U.S. courts, rejected in *IMS Health* the notion that the essential facilities doctrine contains an explicit requirement of two existing, vertically integrated markets. The Court held that the only requirement was to identify "a potential or even hypothetical market." C–418/01 at para. 44 of Court's Reply. Thus, as long as "two different stages of production may be identified and are interconnected, the upstream product is indispensable." *Id.* at para. 44. *Compare* Pitofsky, Patterson & Hooks, The Essential Facilities Doctrine under U.S. Antitrust Law, 70 Antitrust L.J. 443, 458 (2002).

The requirement in *IMS Health* that there be a risk of all competition being eliminated underscores a lingering ambiguity in the application of the doctrine in the United States. The European Court of Justice left it to the national court to decide whether IMS's refusal to grant a license for its copyrighted "brick structure" (used for providing sales data for pharmaceutical products) would result in the elimination of all competition on the secondary market. This aspect of the opinion calls to mind two conflicting interpretations of the essential facilities doctrine: under one, the facility is essential only if control carries with it the power utterly to eliminate competition, and under the other, something less than the ability to achieve total annihilation will suffice. On balance, the *IMS Health* decision appears to have moved the European Union toward the position that the lower courts have maintained in the United States. But, as *Trinko* illustrates, the situation in the United States is a moving target. At present, this is another area in which important, though nuanced, differences remain between these two major systems of competition law.

United States v. Microsoft Corp.

United States Court of Appeals, District of Columbia Circuit, 2001.
253 F.3d 34.

■ Before: EDWARDS, CHIEF JUDGE, WILLIAMS, GINSBURG, SENTELLE, RANDOLPH, ROGERS, and TATEL, CIRCUIT JUDGES.

■ PER CURIAM. Microsoft Corporation appeals from judgments of the District Court finding the company in violation of §§ 1 and 2 of the Sherman Act and ordering various remedies.

The action against Microsoft arose pursuant to a complaint filed by the United States and separate complaints filed by individual States. The District Court determined that Microsoft had maintained a monopoly in the market for Intel-compatible PC operating systems in violation of § 2; attempted to gain a monopoly in the market for internet browsers in violation of § 2; and illegally tied two purportedly separate products, Windows and Internet Explorer ("IE"), in violation of § 1. *United States v. Microsoft Corp.,* 87 F. Supp. 2d 30 (D.D.C. 2000). The District Court then found that the same facts that established liability under §§ 1 and 2 of the Sherman Act mandated findings of liability under analogous state law antitrust provisions. *Id.* To remedy the Sherman Act violations, the District Court issued a Final Judgment requiring Microsoft to submit a proposed plan of divestiture, with the company to be split into an operating systems business and an applications business. The District Court's remedial order also contains a number of interim restrictions on Microsoft's conduct.

microsoft argues

Microsoft's appeal contests both the legal conclusions and the resulting remedial order. There are three principal aspects of this appeal. First, Microsoft challenges the District Court's legal conclusions as to all three alleged antitrust violations and also a number of the procedural and factual foundations on which they rest. Second, Microsoft argues that the remedial order must be set aside, because the District Court failed to afford the company an evidentiary hearing on disputed facts and, also, because the substantive provisions of the order are flawed. Finally, Microsoft asserts that the trial judge committed ethical violations by engaging in impermissible ex parte contacts and making inappropriate public comments on the merits of the case while it was pending. Microsoft argues that these ethical violations compromised the District Judge's appearance of impartiality, thereby necessitating his disqualification and vacatur of his Findings of Fact, Conclusions of Law, and Final Judgment.

After carefully considering the voluminous record on appeal—including the District Court's Findings of Fact and Conclusions of Law, the testimony and exhibits submitted at trial, the parties' briefs, and the oral arguments before this court—we find that some but not all of Microsoft's liability challenges have merit. Accordingly, we affirm in part and reverse in part the District Court's judgment that Microsoft violated § 2 of the Sherman Act by employing anticompetitive means to maintain a monopoly in the operating system market; we reverse the District Court's determination that Microsoft violated § 2 of the Sherman Act by illegally attempting to monopolize the internet browser market; and we remand the District Court's finding that Microsoft violated § 1 of the Sherman Act by unlawfully tying its browser to its operating system. Our judgment extends to the District Court's findings with respect to the state law counterparts of the plaintiffs' Sherman Act claims.

We also find merit in Microsoft's challenge to the Final Judgment embracing the District Court's remedial order. There are several reasons supporting this conclusion. First, the District Court's Final Judgment rests on a number of liability determinations that do not survive appellate review; therefore, the remedial order as currently fashioned cannot stand. Furthermore, we would vacate and remand the remedial order even were we to uphold the District Court's liability determinations in their entirety, because the District Court failed to hold an evidentiary hearing to address remedies-specific factual disputes....

I.   INTRODUCTION

A.   Background

... On May 18, 1998, ... the United States and a group of State plaintiffs filed separate (and soon thereafter consolidated) complaints, asserting antitrust violations by Microsoft and seeking preliminary and permanent injunctions against the company's allegedly unlawful conduct.... The District Court scheduled the case on a "fast track." The hearing on the preliminary injunction and the trial on the merits were consolidated pursuant to FED. R. CIV. P. 65(a)(2). The trial was then scheduled to commence on September 8, 1998, less than four months after the complaints had been filed. In a series of pretrial orders, the District Court limited each side to a maximum of 12 trial witnesses plus two rebuttal witnesses. It required that all trial witnesses' direct testimony be submitted to the court in the form of written declarations. The District Court also made allowances for the use of deposition testimony at trial to prove subordinate or predicate issues. Following the grant of three brief continuances, the trial started on October 19, 1998.

After a 76–day bench trial, the District Court issued its Findings of Fact. This triggered two independent courses of action. First, the District Court established a schedule for briefing on possible legal conclusions, inviting Professor Lawrence Lessig to participate as amicus curiae. Second, the District Court referred the case to mediation to afford the parties an opportunity to settle their differences. The Honorable Richard A. Posner, Chief Judge of the United States Court of Appeals for the Seventh Circuit, was appointed to serve as mediator. The parties concurred in the referral to mediation and in the choice of mediator.

Mediation failed after nearly four months of settlement talks between the parties. On April 3, 2000, with the parties' briefs having been submitted and considered, the District Court issued its conclusions of law....

B. Overview

Before turning to the merits of Microsoft's various arguments, we pause to reflect briefly on two matters of note, one practical and one theoretical.

The practical matter relates to the temporal dimension of this case. The litigation timeline in this case is hardly problematic. Indeed, it is noteworthy that a case of this magnitude and complexity has proceeded from the filing of complaints through trial to appellate decision in a mere three years....

What is somewhat problematic, however, is that just over six years have passed since Microsoft engaged in the first conduct plaintiffs allege to be anticompetitive. As the record in this case indicates, six years seems like an eternity in the computer industry. By the time a court can assess liability, firms, products, and the marketplace are likely to have changed dramatically. This, in turn, threatens enormous practical difficulties for courts considering the appropriate measure of relief in equitable enforcement actions, both in crafting injunctive remedies in the first instance and reviewing those remedies in the second. Conduct remedies may be unavailing in such cases, because innovation to a large degree has already rendered the anticompetitive conduct obsolete (although by no means harmless). And broader structural remedies present their own set of problems, including how a court goes about restoring competition to a dramatically changed, and constantly changing, marketplace. That is just one reason why we find the District Court's refusal in the present case to

[handwritten margin note: Posner was mediator?? Mediation failed.]

hold an evidentiary hearing on remedies—to update and flesh out the available information before seriously entertaining the possibility of dramatic structural relief—so problematic.

We do not mean to say that enforcement actions will no longer play an important role in curbing infringements of the antitrust laws in technologically dynamic markets, nor do we assume this in assessing the merits of this case. Even in those cases where forward-looking remedies appear limited, the Government will continue to have an interest in defining the contours of the antitrust laws so that law-abiding firms will have a clear sense of what is permissible and what is not. And the threat of private damage actions will remain to deter those firms inclined to test the limits of the law.

The second matter of note is more theoretical in nature. We decide this case against a backdrop of significant debate amongst academics and practitioners over the extent to which "old economy" § 2 monopolization doctrines should apply to firms competing in dynamic technological markets characterized by network effects. In markets characterized by network effects, one product or standard tends towards dominance, because "the utility that a user derives from consumption of the good increases with the number of other agents consuming the good." Michael L. Katz & Carl Shapiro, Network Externalities, Competition, and Compatibility, 75 AM. ECON. REV. 424, 424 (1985). For example, "an individual consumer's demand to use (and hence her benefit from) the telephone network ... increases with the number of other users on the network whom she can call or from whom she can receive calls." Once a product or standard achieves wide acceptance, it becomes more or less entrenched. Competition in such industries is "for the field" rather than "within the field." See Harold Demsetz, Why Regulate Utilities?, 11 J.L. & ECON. 55, 57 & n.7 (1968) (emphasis omitted).

In technologically dynamic markets, however, such entrenchment may be temporary, because innovation may alter the field altogether. See JOSEPH A. SCHUMPETER, CAPITALISM, SOCIALISM AND DEMOCRACY 81–90 (Harper Perennial 1976) (1942). Rapid technological change leads to markets in which "firms compete through innovation for temporary market dominance, from which they may be displaced by the next wave of product advancements." ... Microsoft argues that the operating system market is just such a market.

Whether or not Microsoft's characterization of the operating system market is correct does not appreciably alter our mission in assessing the alleged antitrust violations in the present case. As an initial matter, we note that there is no consensus among commentators on the question of whether, and to what extent, current monopolization doctrine should be amended to account for competition in technologically dynamic markets characterized by network effects. Compare Steven C. Salop & R. Craig Romaine, Preserving Monopoly: Economic Analysis, Legal Standards, and Microsoft, 7 GEO. MASON L. REV. 617, 654–55, 663–64 (1999) (arguing that exclusionary conduct in high-tech networked industries deserves heightened antitrust scrutiny in part because it may threaten to deter innovation), with Ronald A. Cass & Keith N. Hylton, Preserving Competition: Economic Analysis, Legal Standards and Microsoft, 8 GEO. MASON L. REV. 1, 36–39 (1999) (equivocating on the antitrust implications of network effects and noting that the presence of network externalities may actually encourage innovation by guaranteeing more durable monopolies to innovating winners). Indeed, there is some suggestion that the economic consequences of network effects and technological dynamism act to offset one another, thereby making it difficult to formulate categorical antitrust rules absent a particularized analysis of a given market. . . .

Moreover, it should be clear that Microsoft makes no claim that anticompetitive conduct should be assessed differently in technologically dynamic markets. It claims only that the measure of monopoly power should be different. For reasons fully discussed below, we reject Microsoft's monopoly power argument. *See infra* Section II.A.

With this backdrop in mind, we turn to the specific challenges raised in Microsoft's appeal.

II. MONOPOLIZATION

. . . We begin by considering whether Microsoft possesses monopoly power, and finding that it does, we turn to the question whether it maintained this power through anticompetitive means. Agreeing with the District Court that the company behaved anticompetitively, and that these actions contributed to the maintenance of its monopoly power, we affirm the court's finding of liability for monopolization.

A. Monopoly Power

While merely possessing monopoly power is not itself an antitrust violation, it is a necessary element of a monopolization charge, *see Grinnell.* The Supreme Court defines monopoly power as "the power to control prices or exclude competition." *United States v. E.I. du Pont de Nemours & Co., 351 U.S. 377, 391 (1956).* More precisely, a firm is a monopolist if it can profitably raise prices substantially above the competitive level. . . . Where evidence indicates that a firm has in fact profitably done so, the existence of monopoly power is clear. *See Rebel Oil Co. v. Atl. Richfield Co., 51 F.3d 1421, 1434 (9th Cir.1995); see also FTC v. Indiana Fed'n of Dentists, 476 U.S. 447 (1986)* (using direct proof to show market power in Sherman Act § 1 unreasonable restraint of trade action). Because such direct proof is only rarely available, courts more typically examine market structure in search of circumstantial evidence of monopoly power. Under this structural approach, monopoly power may be inferred from a firm's possession of a dominant share of a relevant market that is protected by entry barriers. "Entry barriers" are factors (such as certain regulatory requirements) that prevent new rivals from timely responding to an increase in price above the competitive level.

The District Court considered these structural factors and concluded that Microsoft possesses monopoly power in a relevant market. Defining the market as Intel-compatible PC operating systems, the District Court found that Microsoft has a greater than 95% share. It also found the company's market position protected by a substantial entry barrier.

Microsoft argues that the District Court incorrectly defined the relevant market. It also claims that there is no barrier to entry in that market. Alternatively, Microsoft argues that because the software industry is uniquely dynamic, direct proof, rather than circumstantial evidence, more appropriately indicates whether it possesses monopoly power. Rejecting each argument, we uphold the District Court's finding of monopoly power in its entirety. . . .

[The D.C. Circuit's analysis of market structure is set forth in Chapter 3, p. 147 *supra*. As indicated, the Court of Appeals affirmed the finding of an "Intel-compatible PC operating systems" market.]

b. Market power

Having thus properly defined the relevant market, the District Court found that Windows accounts for a greater than 95% share. The court also found that even if Mac OS were included, Microsoft's share would exceed 80%. Microsoft challenges neither finding, nor does it argue that such a market share is not predominant.

Instead, Microsoft claims that even a predominant market share does not by itself indicate monopoly power. Although the "existence of [monopoly] power ordinarily may be inferred from the predominant share of the market," *Grinnell,* we agree with Microsoft that because of the possibility of competition from new entrants, looking to current market share alone can be "misleading." In this case, however, the District Court was not misled. Considering the possibility of new rivals, the court focused not only on Microsoft's present market share, but also on the structural barrier that protects the company's future position. That barrier—the "applications barrier to entry"—stems from two characteristics of the software market: (1) most consumers prefer operating systems for which a large number of applications have already been written; and (2) most developers prefer to write for operating systems that already have a substantial consumer base. This "chicken-and-egg" situation ensures that applications will continue to be written for the already dominant Windows, which in turn ensures that consumers will continue to prefer it over other operating systems. . . .

Having sustained the District Court's conclusion that circumstantial evidence proves that Microsoft possesses monopoly power, we turn to Microsoft's alternative argument that it does not behave like a monopolist. . . . [The Court then rejected Microsoft's argument that monopoly power, in this uniquely dynamic market, should require direct proof of actual behavior.]

B. Anticompetitive Conduct

As discussed above, having a monopoly does not by itself violate § 2. A firm violates § 2 only when it acquires or maintains, or attempts to acquire or maintain, a monopoly by engaging in exclusionary conduct "as distinguished from growth or development as a consequence of a superior product, business acumen, or historic accident." *Grinnell.*

In this case, after concluding that Microsoft had monopoly power, the District Court held that Microsoft had violated § 2 by engaging in a variety of exclusionary acts (not including predatory pricing), to maintain its monopoly by preventing the effective distribution and use of products that might threaten that monopoly. Specifically, the District Court held Microsoft liable for: (1) the way in which it integrated IE into Windows; (2) its various dealings with Original Equipment Manufacturers ("OEMs"), Internet Access Providers ("IAPs"), Internet Content Providers ("ICPs"), Independent Software Vendors ("ISVs"), and Apple Computer; (3) its efforts to contain and to subvert Java technologies; and (4) its course of conduct as a whole. Upon appeal, Microsoft argues that it did not engage in any exclusionary conduct.

Whether any particular act of a monopolist is exclusionary, rather than merely a form of vigorous competition, can be difficult to discern: the means of illicit exclusion, like the means of legitimate competition, are myriad. The challenge for an antitrust court lies in stating a general rule for distinguishing between exclusionary acts, which reduce social welfare, and competitive acts, which increase it.

From a century of case law on monopolization under § 2, however, several principles do emerge. First, to be condemned as exclusionary, a monopolist's act must have an "anticompetitive effect." That is, it must harm the competitive process and thereby harm consumers. In contrast, harm to one or more competitors will not suffice. "The [Sherman Act] directs itself not against conduct which is competitive, even severely so, but against conduct which unfairly tends to destroy competition itself." *Spectrum Sports, Inc. v. McQuillan, 506 U.S. 447 (1993); see also Brooke Group Ltd. v. Brown & Williamson Tobacco Corp., 509 U.S. 209, 225 (1993)* ("Even an act of pure malice by one business competitor against another does not, without more, state a claim under the federal antitrust laws....").

Second, the plaintiff, on whom the burden of proof of course rests, must demonstrate that the monopolist's conduct indeed has the requisite anticompetitive effect. In a case brought by a private plaintiff, the plaintiff must show that its injury is "of 'the type that the statute was intended to forestall,'" *Brunswick Corp. v. Pueblo Bowl–O–Mat, Inc., 429 U.S. 477, 487–88 (1977)*; no less in a case brought by the Government, it must demonstrate that the monopolist's conduct harmed competition, not just a competitor.

Third, if a plaintiff successfully establishes a prima facie case under § 2 by demonstrating anticompetitive effect, then the monopolist may proffer a "procompetitive justification" for its conduct. *See Eastman Kodak.* If the monopolist asserts a procompetitive justification—a nonpretextual claim that its conduct is indeed a form of competition on the merits because it involves, for example, greater efficiency or enhanced consumer appeal—then the burden shifts back to the plaintiff to rebut that claim.

[handwritten marginalia:]

monopolization:

1. anti comp effect

2. P has burden to show conduct has that effect

3. D can offer pro-comp just.

[handwritten margin note: 4. P must show harm > benefit]

Fourth, if the monopolist's procompetitive justification stands unrebutted, then the plaintiff must demonstrate that the anticompetitive harm of the conduct outweighs the procompetitive benefit. In cases arising under § 1 of the Sherman Act, the courts routinely apply a similar balancing approach under the rubric of the "rule of reason." The source of the rule of reason is *Standard Oil Co. v. United States, 221 U.S. 1 (1911),* in which the Supreme Court used that term to describe the proper inquiry under both sections of the Act. . . .

[handwritten margin note: 5. Intent doesn't matter, only effects]

Finally, in considering whether the monopolist's conduct on balance harms competition and is therefore condemned as exclusionary for purposes of § 2, our focus is upon the effect of that conduct, not upon the intent behind it. Evidence of the intent behind the conduct of a monopolist is relevant only to the extent it helps us understand the likely effect of the monopolist's conduct. *See, e.g., Chicago Bd. of Trade v. United States, 246 U.S. 231, 238 (1918)* ("knowledge of intent may help the court to interpret facts and to predict consequences"); *Aspen Skiing.*

With these principles in mind, we now consider Microsoft's objections to the District Court's holding that Microsoft violated § 2 of the Sherman Act in a variety of ways.

1.   Licenses Issued to Original Equipment Manufacturers

The District Court condemned a number of provisions in Microsoft's agreements licensing Windows to OEMs, because it found that Microsoft's imposition of those provisions (like many of Microsoft's other actions at issue in this case) serves to reduce usage share of Netscape's browser and, hence, protect Microsoft's operating system monopoly. The reason market share in the browser market affects market power in the operating system market is complex, and warrants some explanation.

Microsoft's efforts to gain market share in one market (browsers) served to meet the threat to Microsoft's monopoly in another market (operating systems) by keeping rival browsers from gaining the critical mass of users necessary to attract developer attention away from Windows as the platform for software development. Plaintiffs also argue that Microsoft's actions injured competition in the browser market—an argument we will examine below in relation to their specific claims that Microsoft attempted to monopolize the browser market and unlawfully tied its browser to its operating system so as to foreclose competition in the browser market. In evaluating the § 2 monopoly maintenance claim, however, our immediate concern is with the anticompetitive effect of Microsoft's conduct in preserving its monopoly in the operating system market.

In evaluating the restrictions in Microsoft's agreements licensing Windows to OEMs, we first consider whether plaintiffs have made out a prima facie case by demonstrating that the restrictions have an anticompetitive effect. In the next subsection, we conclude that plaintiffs have met this burden as to all the restrictions. We then consider Microsoft's proffered justifications for the restrictions and, for the most part, hold those justifications insufficient.

a.   Anticompetitive effect of the license restrictions

The restrictions Microsoft places upon Original Equipment Manufacturers are of particular importance in determining browser usage share because having an OEM pre-install a browser on a computer is one of the two most cost-effective methods by far of distributing browsing software. (The other is bundling the browser with internet access software distributed by an IAP.) [The Circuit Court then upheld the district court's findings that various restrictions Microsoft imposed in licensing Windows to OEMs prevented many OEMs from distributing browsers other than IE. In particular, the Court found anticompetitive effects in license provisions prohibiting the OEMs from: (1) removing any desktop icons, folders, or "Start" menu entries; (2) altering the initial boot sequence; and (3) otherwise altering the appearance of the Windows desktop.] . . . .

b.   Microsoft's justifications for the license restrictions

Microsoft argues that the license restrictions are legally justified because, in imposing them, Microsoft is simply "exercising its rights as the holder of valid copyrights." Microsoft also argues that the licenses "do not unduly restrict the opportunities of Netscape to distribute Navigator in any event."

Microsoft's primary copyright argument borders upon the frivolous. The company claims an absolute and unfettered right to use its intellectual property as it wishes: "If intellectual property rights have been lawfully acquired," it says, then "their subsequent exercise cannot give rise to antitrust liability. That is no more correct than the proposition that use of one's personal property, such as a baseball bat, cannot give rise to tort liability. As the Federal Circuit succinctly stated: "Intellectual property rights do not confer a privilege to violate the antitrust laws." *In re Indep. Serv. Orgs. Antitrust Litig.,* 203 F.3d 1322, 1325 (Fed.Cir.2000). . . .

The only license restriction Microsoft seriously defends as necessary to prevent a "substantial alteration" of its copyrighted work is the prohibition on OEMs automatically launching a substitute user interface upon completion of the boot process. ("[A] few large OEMs developed programs that ran automatically at the conclusion of a new PC system's first boot sequence. These programs replaced the Windows desktop either with a user interface designed by the OEM or with Navigator's user interface."). We agree that a shell that automatically prevents the Windows desktop from ever being seen by the user is a drastic alteration of Microsoft's copyrighted work, and outweighs the marginal anticompetitive effect of prohibiting the OEMs from substituting a different interface automatically upon completion of the initial boot process. We therefore hold that this particular restriction is not an exclusionary practice that violates § 2 of the Sherman Act.

In a second variation upon its copyright defense, Microsoft argues that the license restrictions merely prevent OEMs from taking actions that would reduce substantially the value of Microsoft's copyrighted work: that is, Microsoft claims each license restriction in question is necessary to prevent OEMs from so altering Windows as to undermine "the principal value of Windows as a stable and consistent platform that supports a broad range of applications and that is familiar to users." Microsoft, however, never substantiates this claim, and, because an OEM's altering the appearance of the desktop or promoting programs in the boot sequence does not affect the code already in the product, the practice does not self-evidently affect either the "stability" or the "consistency" of the platform....

Apart from copyright, Microsoft raises one other defense of the OEM license agreements: It argues that, despite the restrictions in the OEM license, Netscape is not completely blocked from distributing its product. That claim is insufficient to shield Microsoft from liability for those restrictions because, although Microsoft did not bar its rivals from all means of distribution, it did bar them from the cost-efficient ones.

In sum, we hold that with the exception of the one restriction prohibiting, all the OEM license restrictions at issue represent uses of Microsoft's market power to protect its monopoly, unredeemed by any legitimate justification. The restrictions therefore violate § 2 of the Sherman Act.

2. Integration of IE and Windows

Although Microsoft's license restrictions have a significant effect in closing rival browsers out of one of the two primary channels of distribution, the District Court found that "Microsoft's executives believed ... its contractual restrictions placed on OEMs would not be sufficient in themselves to reverse the direction of Navigator's usage share. Consequently, in late 1995 or early 1996, Microsoft set out to bind [IE] more tightly to Windows 95 as a technical matter."

Technologically binding IE to Windows, the District Court found, both prevented OEMs from pre-installing other browsers and deterred consumers from using them. In particular, having the IE software code as an irremovable part of Windows meant that pre-installing a second browser would "increase an OEM's product testing costs," because an OEM must test and train its support staff to answer calls related to every software product preinstalled on the machine; moreover, pre-installing a browser in addition to IE would to many OEMs be "a questionable use of the scarce and valuable space on a PC's hard drive."

Although the District Court, in its Conclusions of Law, broadly condemned Microsoft's decision to bind "Internet Explorer to Windows with ... technological shackles," its findings of fact in support of that conclusion center upon three specific actions Microsoft took to weld IE to Windows: excluding IE from the "Add/Remove Programs" utility; designing Windows so as in certain circumstances to override the user's choice of a default browser other than IE; and commingling code related to browsing and other code in the same files, so that any attempt to delete the files containing IE would, at the same time, cripple the operating system....
[The Court then discussed at some length the anticompetitive effect of these practices. It rejected most justifications, accepting only Microsoft's claim that valid technological reasons explained its designing Windows so

as to override the user's choice of a default browser in certain circumstances.]

    3.   Agreements with Internet Access Providers

    ... We turn now to Microsoft's deals with IAPs concerning desktop placement. Microsoft concluded these exclusive agreements with all "the leading IAPs," including the major OLSs. The most significant of the OLS deals is with AOL, which, when the deal was reached, "accounted for a substantial portion of all existing Internet access subscriptions and ... attracted a very large percentage of new IAP subscribers." Under that agreement Microsoft puts the AOL icon in the OLS folder on the Windows desktop and AOL does not promote any non-Microsoft browser, nor provide software using any non-Microsoft browser except at the customer's request, and even then AOL will not supply more than 15% of its subscribers with a browser other than IE....

    Following Tampa Electric, [a 1961 Supreme Court case on exclusive dealing, *see* p. 927 *infra*], courts considering antitrust challenges to exclusive contracts have taken care to identify the share of the market foreclosed. Some courts have indicated that § 3 of the Clayton Act and § 1 of the Sherman Act require an equal degree of foreclosure before prohibiting exclusive contracts. *See, e.g., Roland Mach. Co. v. Dresser Indus., Inc., 749 F.2d 380, 393 (7th Cir.1984)* (Posner, J.). Other courts, however, have held that a higher market share must be foreclosed in order to establish a violation of the Sherman Act as compared to the Clayton Act.

    Though what is "significant" may vary depending upon the antitrust provision under which an exclusive deal is challenged, it is clear that in all cases the plaintiff must both define the relevant market and prove the degree of foreclosure. This is a prudential requirement; exclusivity provisions in contracts may serve many useful purposes....

    In this case, plaintiffs challenged Microsoft's exclusive dealing arrangements with the IAPs under both §§ 1 and 2 of the Sherman Act. The District Court, in analyzing the § 1 claim, stated, "unless the evidence demonstrates that Microsoft's agreements excluded Netscape altogether from access to roughly forty percent of the browser market, the Court should decline to find such agreements in violation of § 1." The court recognized that Microsoft had substantially excluded Netscape from "the most efficient channels for Navigator to achieve browser usage share"...., and had relegated it to more costly and less effective methods (such as mass mailing its browser on a disk or offering it for download over the internet); but because Microsoft has not "completely excluded Netscape" from reaching any potential user by some means of distribution, however ineffective, the court concluded the agreements do not violate § 1. Plaintiffs did not cross-appeal this holding.

    Turning to § 2, the court stated: "the fact that Microsoft's arrangements with various [IAPs and other] firms did not foreclose enough of the relevant market to constitute a § 1 violation in no way detracts from the Court's assignment of liability for the same arrangements under § 2....

All of Microsoft's agreements, including the non-exclusive ones, severely restricted Netscape's access to those distribution channels leading most efficiently to the acquisition of browser usage share.''

On appeal Microsoft argues that "courts have applied the same standard to alleged exclusive dealing agreements under both Section 1 and Section 2," and it argues that the District Court's holding of no liability under § 1 necessarily precludes holding it liable under § 2. The District Court appears to have based its holding with respect to § 1 upon a "total exclusion test" rather than the 40% standard drawn from the caselaw. Even assuming the holding is correct, however, we nonetheless reject Microsoft's contention.

The basic prudential concerns relevant to §§ 1 and 2 are admittedly the same: exclusive contracts are commonplace-particularly in the field of distribution—in our competitive, market economy, and imposing upon a firm with market power the risk of an antitrust suit every time it enters into such a contract, no matter how small the effect, would create an unacceptable and unjustified burden upon any such firm. At the same time, however, we agree with plaintiffs that a monopolist's use of exclusive contracts, in certain circumstances, may give rise to a § 2 violation even though the contracts foreclose less than the roughly 40% or 50% share usually required in order to establish a § 1 violation. *See generally* Dennis W. Carlton, A General Analysis of Exclusionary Conduct and Refusal to Deal—Why Aspen and Kodak Are Misguided, *68 ANTITRUST L.J. 659 (2001)* (explaining various scenarios under which exclusive dealing, particularly by a dominant firm, may raise legitimate concerns about harm to competition).

In this case, plaintiffs allege that, by closing to rivals a substantial percentage of the available opportunities for browser distribution, Microsoft managed to preserve its monopoly in the market for operating systems. The IAPs constitute one of the two major channels by which browsers can be distributed. Microsoft has exclusive deals with "fourteen of the top fifteen access providers in North America[, which] account for a large majority of all Internet access subscriptions in this part of the world." By ensuring that the "majority" of all IAP subscribers are offered IE either as the default browser or as the only browser, Microsoft's deals with the IAPs clearly have a significant effect in preserving its monopoly; they help keep usage of Navigator below the critical level necessary for Navigator or any other rival to pose a real threat to Microsoft's monopoly.

Plaintiffs having demonstrated a harm to competition, the burden falls upon Microsoft to defend its exclusive dealing contracts with IAPs by providing a procompetitive justification for them. Significantly, Microsoft's only explanation for its exclusive dealing is that it wants to keep developers focused upon its APIs—which is to say, it wants to preserve its power in the operating system market. That is not an unlawful end, but neither is it a procompetitive justification for the specific means here in question, namely exclusive dealing contracts with IAPs. Accordingly, we affirm the

District Court's decision holding that Microsoft's exclusive contracts with IAPs are exclusionary devices, in violation of § 2 of the Sherman Act.

4. Dealings with Internet Content Providers, Independent Software Vendors, and Apple Computer

The District Court held that Microsoft engages in exclusionary conduct in its dealings with ICPs, which develop websites; ISVs, which develop software; and Apple, which is both an OEM and a software developer.... [The Circuit Court upheld these finding with respect to various "exclusivity provisions," but reversed as to ICPs because plaintiffs had failed to prove that Microsoft's promotional restrictions actually had a "substantial, deleterious impact on Navigator's usage share."]

5. Java

Java, a set of technologies developed by Sun Microsystems, is another type of middleware posing a potential threat to Windows' position as the ubiquitous platform for software development. The Java technologies include: (1) a programming language; (2) a set of programs written in that language, called the "Java class libraries," which expose APIs; (3) a compiler, which translates code written by a developer into "bytecode"; and (4) a Java Virtual Machine ("JVM"), which translates bytecode into instructions to the operating system. Programs calling upon the Java APIs will run on any machine with a "Java runtime environment," that is, Java class libraries and a JVM.

In May 1995 Netscape agreed with Sun to distribute a copy of the Java runtime environment with every copy of Navigator, and "Navigator quickly became the principal vehicle by which Sun placed copies of its Java runtime environment on the PC systems of Windows users." Microsoft, too, agreed to promote the Java technologies—or so it seemed. For at the same time, Microsoft took steps "to maximize the difficulty with which applications written in Java could be ported from Windows to other platforms, and vice versa." Specifically, the District Court found that Microsoft took four steps to exclude Java from developing as a viable cross-platform threat: (a) designing a JVM incompatible with the one developed by Sun; (b) entering into contracts, the so-called "First Wave Agreements," requiring major ISVs to promote Microsoft's JVM exclusively; (c) deceiving Java developers about the Windows-specific nature of the tools it distributed to them; and (d) coercing Intel to stop aiding Sun in improving the Java technologies.

a. The incompatible JVM

The District Court held that Microsoft engaged in exclusionary conduct by developing and promoting its own JVM. Sun had already developed a JVM for the Windows operating system when Microsoft began work on its version. The JVM developed by Microsoft allows Java applications to run faster on Windows than does Sun's JVM, but a Java application designed to work with Microsoft's JVM does not work with Sun's JVM and vice versa. The District Court found that Microsoft "made a large investment of engineering resources to develop a high-performance Windows JVM," and, "by bundling its ... JVM with every copy of [IE] ... Microsoft endowed its

Java runtime environment with the unique attribute of guaranteed, enduring ubiquity across the enormous Windows installed base." As explained above, however, a monopolist does not violate the antitrust laws simply by developing a product that is incompatible with those of its rivals. In order to violate the antitrust laws, the incompatible product must have an anticompetitive effect that outweighs any procompetitive justification for the design. Microsoft's JVM is not only incompatible with Sun's, it allows Java applications to run faster on Windows than does Sun's JVM. Microsoft's faster JVM lured Java developers into using Microsoft's developer tools, and Microsoft offered those tools deceptively, as we discuss below. The JVM, however, does allow applications to run more swiftly and does not itself have any anticompetitive effect. Therefore, we reverse the District Court's imposition of liability for Microsoft's development and promotion of its JVM.

b. The First Wave Agreements

The District Court also found that Microsoft entered into First Wave Agreements with dozens of ISVs to use Microsoft's JVM. ("In exchange for costly technical support and other blandishments, Microsoft induced dozens of important ISVs to make their Java applications reliant on Windows-specific technologies and to refrain from distributing to Windows users JVMs that complied with Sun's standards."). Again, we reject the District Court's condemnation of low but non-predatory pricing by Microsoft.

To the extent Microsoft's First Wave Agreements with the ISVs conditioned receipt of Windows technical information upon the ISVs' agreement to promote Microsoft's JVM exclusively, they raise a different competitive concern. The District Court found that, although not literally exclusive, the deals were exclusive in practice because they required developers to make Microsoft's JVM the default in the software they developed.

While the District Court did not enter precise findings as to the effect of the First Wave Agreements upon the overall distribution of rival JVMs, the record indicates that Microsoft's deals with the major ISVs had a significant effect upon JVM promotion. As discussed above, the products of First Wave ISVs reached millions of consumers.... Moreover, Microsoft's exclusive deals with the leading ISVs took place against a backdrop of foreclosure: the District Court found that "when Netscape announced in May 1995 [prior to Microsoft's execution of the First Wave Agreements] that it would include with every copy of Navigator a copy of a Windows JVM that complied with Sun's standards, it appeared that Sun's Java implementation would achieve the necessary ubiquity on Windows." As discussed above, however, Microsoft undertook a number of anticompetitive actions that seriously reduced the distribution of Navigator, and the District Court found that those actions thereby seriously impeded distribution of Sun's JVM. Because Microsoft's agreements foreclosed a substantial portion of the field for JVM distribution and because, in so doing, they protected Microsoft's monopoly from a middleware threat, they are anticompetitive.

Microsoft offered no procompetitive justification for the default clause that made the First Wave Agreements exclusive as a practical matter. Because the cumulative effect of the deals is anticompetitive and because Microsoft has no procompetitive justification for them, we hold that the provisions in the First Wave Agreements requiring use of Microsoft's JVM as the default are exclusionary, in violation of the Sherman Act.

c.   Deception of Java developers

Microsoft's "Java implementation" included, in addition to a JVM, a set of software development tools it created to assist ISVs in designing Java applications. The District Court found that, not only were these tools incompatible with Sun's cross-platform aspirations for Java—no violation, to be sure-but Microsoft deceived Java developers regarding the Windows-specific nature of the tools. Microsoft's tools included "certain 'keywords' and 'compiler directives' that could only be executed properly by Microsoft's version of the Java runtime environment for Windows." As a result, even Java "developers who were opting for portability over performance ... unwittingly [wrote] Java applications that [ran] only on Windows." That is, developers who relied upon Microsoft's public commitment to cooperate with Sun and who used Microsoft's tools to develop what Microsoft led them to believe were [cross-platform] applications ended up producing applications that would run only on the Windows operating system....

Finally, other Microsoft documents confirm that Microsoft intended to deceive Java developers, and predicted that the effect of its actions would be to generate Windows-dependent Java applications that their developers believed would be cross-platform; these documents also indicate that Microsoft's ultimate objective was to thwart Java's threat to Microsoft's monopoly in the market for operating systems. One Microsoft document, for example, states as a strategic goal: "Kill cross-platform Java by growing the polluted Java market."

Microsoft's conduct related to its Java developer tools served to protect its monopoly of the operating system in a manner not attributable either to the superiority of the operating system or to the acumen of its makers, and therefore was anticompetitive. Unsurprisingly, Microsoft offers no procompetitive explanation for its campaign to deceive developers. Accordingly, we conclude this conduct is exclusionary, in violation of § 2 of the Sherman Act.

d.   The threat to Intel

The District Court held that Microsoft also acted unlawfully with respect to Java by using its "monopoly power to prevent firms such as Intel from aiding in the creation of cross-platform interfaces." In 1995 Intel was in the process of developing a high performance, Windows-compatible JVM. Microsoft wanted Intel to abandon that effort because a fast, cross-platform JVM would threaten Microsoft's monopoly in the operating system market. At an August 1995 meeting, Microsoft's Gates told Intel that its "cooperation with Sun and Netscape to develop a Java runtime environment ... was one of the issues threatening to undermine cooperation between Intel and Microsoft." Three months later, "Microsoft's Paul Maritz told a senior Intel executive that Intel's [adaptation of its multimedia software to comply with] Sun's Java standards was as inimical to Microsoft as Microsoft's support for non-Intel microprocessors would be to Intel."

Intel nonetheless continued to undertake initiatives related to Java. By 1996 "Intel had developed a JVM designed to run well ... while complying with Sun's cross-platform standards." In April of that year, Microsoft again urged Intel not to help Sun by distributing Intel's fast, Suncompliant JVM. *Id*. And Microsoft threatened Intel that if it did not stop aiding Sun on the multimedia front, then Microsoft would refuse to distribute Intel technologies bundled with Windows.

Intel finally capitulated in 1997, after Microsoft delivered the coup de grace.

One of Intel's competitors, called AMD, solicited support from Microsoft for its "3DX" technology.... Microsoft's Allchin asked Gates whether Microsoft should support 3DX, despite the fact that Intel would oppose it. Gates responded: "If Intel has a real problem with us supporting this then they will have to stop supporting Java Multimedia the way they are. I would gladly give up supporting this if they would back off from their work on JAVA."

Microsoft's internal documents and deposition testimony confirm both the anticompetitive effect and intent of its actions.... Microsoft does not deny the facts found by the District Court, nor does it offer any procompetitive justification for pressuring Intel not to support cross-platform Java. Microsoft lamely characterizes its threat to Intel as "advice." The District Court, however, found that Microsoft's "advice" to Intel to stop aiding cross-platform Java was backed by the threat of retaliation, and this conclusion is supported by the evidence cited above. Therefore we affirm the conclusion that Microsoft's threats to Intel were exclusionary, in violation of § 2 of the Sherman Act....

C.   Causation

As a final parry, Microsoft urges this court to reverse on the monopoly maintenance claim, because plaintiffs never established a causal link between Microsoft's anticompetitive conduct, in particular its foreclosure of Netscape's and Java's distribution channels, and the maintenance of Microsoft's operating system monopoly. ("There is insufficient evidence to find that, absent Microsoft's actions, Navigator and Java already would have ignited genuine competition in the market for Intel-compatible PC operating systems."). This is the flip side of Microsoft's earlier argument that the District Court should have included middleware in the relevant market. According to Microsoft, the District Court cannot simultaneously find that middleware is not a reasonable substitute and that Microsoft's exclusionary conduct contributed to the maintenance of monopoly power in the operating system market. Microsoft claims that the first finding depended on the court's view that middleware does not pose a serious threat to Windows, while the second finding required the court to find that Navigator and Java would have developed into serious enough cross-platform threats to erode the applications barrier to entry. We disagree.

Microsoft points to no case, and we can find none, standing for the proposition that, as to § 2 liability in an equitable enforcement action, plaintiffs must present direct proof that a defendant's continued monopoly power is precisely attributable to its anticompetitive conduct.... To require that § 2 liability turn on a plaintiff's ability or inability to reconstruct the hypothetical marketplace absent a defendant's anticompetitive conduct would only encourage monopolists to take more and earlier anticompetitive action.

We may infer causation when exclusionary conduct is aimed at producers of nascent competitive technologies as well as when it is aimed at producers of established substitutes. Admittedly, in the former case there is added uncertainty, inasmuch as nascent threats are merely potential substitutes. But the underlying proof problem is the same—neither plaintiffs nor the court can confidently reconstruct a product's hypothetical technological development in a world absent the defendant's exclusionary conduct. To some degree, "the defendant is made to suffer the uncertain consequences of its own undesirable conduct." 3 AREEDA & HOVENKAMP, ANTITRUST LAW ¶ 651c, at 78.

Given this rather edentulous test for causation, the question in this case is not whether Java or Navigator would actually have developed into viable platform substitutes, but (1) whether as a general matter the exclusion of nascent threats is the type of conduct that is reasonably capable of contributing significantly to a defendant's continued monopoly power and (2) whether Java and Navigator reasonably constituted nascent threats at the time Microsoft engaged in the anticompetitive conduct at issue. As to the first, suffice it to say that it would be inimical to the purpose of the Sherman Act to allow monopolists free reign to squash nascent, albeit unproven, competitors at will—particularly in industries marked by rapid technological advance and frequent paradigm shifts. As to the second, the District Court made ample findings that both Navigator and Java showed potential as middleware platform threats....

Microsoft's concerns over causation have more purchase in connection with the appropriate remedy issue, *i.e.*, whether the court should impose a structural remedy or merely enjoin the offensive conduct at issue. As we point out later in this opinion, divestiture is a remedy that is imposed only with great caution, in part because its long-term efficacy is rarely certain. Absent some measure of confidence that there has been an actual loss to competition that needs to be restored, wisdom counsels against adopting radical structural relief. *See* 3 AREEDA & HOVENKAMP, ANTITRUST LAW p. 653b, at 91–92 ("More extensive equitable relief, particularly remedies such as divestiture designed to eliminate the monopoly altogether, raise more serious questions and require a clearer indication of a significant causal connection between the conduct and creation or maintenance of the market power."). But these queries go to questions of remedy, not liability. In short, causation affords Microsoft no defense to liability for its unlawful actions undertaken to maintain its monopoly in the operating system market....

[In Section III, the Circuit Court considered plaintiffs' attempt to monopolize claims. The district court had found an illegal attempt to amass monopoly power in the "browser market." The Circuit Court reversed, concluding that plaintiffs had neither carried their burden to prove the relevant market (*i.e.,* "defining what a browser is or what products might constitute substitutes") nor to "demonstrate that substantial barriers to entry protect that market." For a discussion of attempt to monopolize, *see* p. 810 *infra.*

In Section IV, the D.C. Circuit considered plaintiffs' tying claims. This part of the opinion is found at p. 906 *infra* with other tying materials.]

V. TRIAL PROCEEDINGS AND REMEDY

Microsoft additionally challenges the District Court's procedural rulings on two fronts. First, with respect to the trial phase, Microsoft proposes that the court mismanaged its docket by adopting an expedited trial schedule and receiving evidence through summary witnesses. Second, with respect to the remedies decree, Microsoft argues that the court improperly ordered that it be divided into two separate companies. Only the latter claim will long detain us. The District Court's trial-phase procedures were comfortably within the bounds of its broad discretion to conduct trials as it sees fit. We conclude, however, that the District Court's remedies decree must be vacated for three independent reasons: (1) the court failed to hold a remedies-specific evidentiary hearing when there were disputed facts; (2) the court failed to provide adequate reasons for its decreed remedies; and (3) this Court has revised the scope of Microsoft's liability and it is impossible to determine to what extent that should affect the remedies provisions....

Microsoft's first contention—that the District Court erred by adopting an expedited trial schedule and receiving evidence through summary witnesses—is easily disposed of. Trial courts have extraordinarily broad discretion to determine the manner in which they will conduct trials.... Although the company claims that setting an early trial date inhibited its ability to conduct discovery, it never identified a specific deposition or document it was unable to obtain. And while Microsoft now argues that the use of summary witnesses made inevitable the improper introduction of hearsay evidence, the company actually agreed to the District Court's proposal to limit each side to 12 summary witnesses.... Even absent Microsoft's agreement, the company's challenge fails to show that this use of summary witnesses falls outside the trial court's wide latitude to receive evidence as it sees fit....

The District Court's remedies-phase proceedings are a different matter. It is a cardinal principle of our system of justice that factual disputes must be heard in open court and resolved through trial-like evidentiary proceedings. Any other course would be contrary "to the spirit which imbues our judicial tribunals prohibiting decision without hearing." *Sims v. Greene, 161 F.2d 87, 88 (3d Cir.1947)*.

A party has the right to judicial resolution of disputed facts not just as to the liability phase, but also as to appropriate relief. "Normally, an evidentiary hearing is required before an injunction may be granted." *United States v. McGee, 714 F.2d 607, 613 (6th Cir.1983)*. . . . Other than a temporary restraining order, no injunctive relief may be entered without a hearing. See generally FED. R. CIV. P. 65. A hearing on the merits—*i.e.*, a trial on liability—does not substitute for a relief-specific evidentiary hearing unless the matter of relief was part of the trial on liability, or unless there are no disputed factual issues regarding the matter of relief. . . .

Despite plaintiffs' protestations, there can be no serious doubt that the parties disputed a number of facts during the remedies phase. In two separate offers of proof, Microsoft identified 23 witnesses who, had they been permitted to testify, would have challenged a wide range of plaintiffs' factual representations, including the feasibility of dividing Microsoft, the likely impact on consumers, and the effect of divestiture on shareholders. To take but two examples, where plaintiffs' economists testified that splitting Microsoft in two would be socially beneficial, the company offered to prove that the proposed remedy would "cause substantial social harm by raising software prices, lowering rates of innovation and disrupting the evolution of Windows as a software development platform." And where plaintiffs' investment banking experts proposed that divestiture might actually increase shareholder value, Microsoft proffered evidence that structural relief "would inevitably result in a significant loss of shareholder value," a loss that could reach "tens—possibly hundreds—of billions of dollars." . . .

We vacate the District Court's remedies decree for the additional reason that the court has failed to provide an adequate explanation for the relief it ordered. The Supreme Court has explained that a remedies decree in an antitrust case must seek to "unfetter a market from anticompetitive conduct," *Ford Motor Co., 405 U.S. at 577,* to "terminate the illegal monopoly, deny to the defendant the fruits of its statutory violation, and ensure that there remain no practices likely to result in monopolization in the future," *United States v. United Shoe Mach. Corp., 391 U.S. 244, 250 (1968); see also United States v. Grinnell Corp., 384 U.S. 563, 577 (1966).*

The District Court has not explained how its remedies decree would accomplish those objectives. Indeed, the court devoted a mere four paragraphs of its order to explaining its reasons for the remedy. They are: (1) Microsoft "does not yet concede that any of its business practices violated the Sherman Act"; (2) Microsoft "continues to do business as it has in the past"; (3) Microsoft "has proved untrustworthy in the past"; and (4) the Government, whose officials "are by reason of office obliged and expected to consider—and to act in—the public interest," won the case, "and for that reason alone have some entitlement to a remedy of their choice.". Nowhere did the District Court discuss the objectives the Supreme Court deems relevant. . . .

[We must also vacate the remedies decree because this] court has drastically altered the District Court's conclusions on liability. On remand, the District Court, after affording the parties a proper opportunity to be heard, can fashion an appropriate remedy for Microsoft's antitrust violations. In particular, the court should consider which of the decree's conduct restrictions remain viable in light of our modification of the original liability decision. While the task of drafting the remedies decree is for the District Court in the first instance, because of the unusually convoluted nature of the proceedings thus far, and a desire to advance the ultimate resolution of this important controversy, we offer some further guidance for the exercise of that discretion.

As a general matter, a district court is afforded broad discretion to enter that relief it calculates will best remedy the conduct it has found to be unlawful.... And divestiture is a common form of relief in successful antitrust prosecutions: it is indeed "the most important of antitrust remedies." *See, e.g., United States v. E.I. du Pont de Nemours & Co., 366 U.S. 316, 331 (1961).*

On remand, the District Court must reconsider whether the use of the structural remedy of divestiture is appropriate with respect to Microsoft, which argues that it is a unitary company. By and large, cases upon which plaintiffs rely in arguing for the split of Microsoft have involved the dissolution of entities formed by mergers and acquisitions. On the contrary, the Supreme Court has clarified that divestiture "has traditionally been the remedy for Sherman Act violations whose heart is intercorporate combination and control," *du Pont*, and that "complete divestiture is particularly appropriate where asset or stock acquisitions violate the antitrust laws," *Ford Motor Co., 405 U.S. at 573.*

One apparent reason why courts have not ordered the dissolution of unitary companies is logistical difficulty. As the court explained in *United States v. ALCOA, 91 F. Supp. 333, 416 (S.D.N.Y.1950)*, a "corporation, designed to operate effectively as a single entity, cannot readily be dismembered of parts of its various operations without a marked loss of efficiency." A corporation that has expanded by acquiring its competitors often has preexisting internal lines of division along which it may more easily be split than a corporation that has expanded from natural growth. Although time and corporate modifications and developments may eventually fade those lines, at least the identifiable entities preexisted to create a template for such division as the court might later decree. With reference to those corporations that are not acquired by merger and acquisition, Judge Wyzanski accurately opined in United Shoe:

> United conducts all machine manufacture at one plant in Beverly, with one set of jigs and tools, one foundry, one laboratory for machinery problems, one managerial staff, and one labor force. It takes no Solomon to see that this organism cannot be cut into three equal and viable parts.

United States v. United Shoe Machine Co., 110 F. Supp. 295, 348 (D.Mass. 1953).

Depending upon the evidence, the District Court may find in a remedies proceeding that it would be no easier to split Microsoft in two than United Shoe in three. Microsoft's Offer of Proof in response to the court's denial of an evidentiary hearing included proffered testimony from its President and CEO Steve Ballmer that the company "is, and always has been, a unified company without free-standing business units. Microsoft is not the result of mergers or acquisitions." Microsoft further offered evidence that it is "not organized along product lines," but rather is housed in a single corporate headquarters and that it has

> only one sales and marketing organization which is responsible for selling all of the company's products, one basic research organization, one product support organization, one operations department, one information technology department, one facilities department, one purchasing department, one human resources department, one finance department, one legal department and one public relations department.

If indeed Microsoft is a unitary company, division might very well require Microsoft to reproduce each of these departments in each new entity rather than simply allocate the differing departments among them.

In devising an appropriate remedy, the District Court also should consider whether plaintiffs have established a sufficient causal connection between Microsoft's anticompetitive conduct and its dominant position in the OS market. "Mere existence of an exclusionary act does not itself justify full feasible relief against the monopolist to create maximum competition." 3 AREEDA & HOVENKAMP, ANTITRUST LAW p. 650a, at 67. Rather, structural relief, which is "designed to eliminate the monopoly altogether ... requires a clearer indication of a significant causal connection between the conduct and creation or maintenance of the market power." (emphasis added). Absent such causation, the antitrust defendant's unlawful behavior should be remedied by "an injunction against continuation of that conduct." *Id*. p. 650a, at 67.

As noted above, we have found a causal connection between Microsoft's exclusionary conduct and its continuing position in the operating systems market only through inference. *See* 3 AREEDA & HOVENKAMP, ANTITRUST LAW p. 653(b), at 91–92 (suggesting that "more extensive equitable relief, particularly remedies such as divestiture designed to eliminate the monopoly altogether, ... require a clearer indication of significant causal connection between the conduct and creation or maintenance of the market power"). Indeed, the District Court expressly did not adopt the position that Microsoft would have lost its position in the OS market but for its anticompetitive behavior.... If the court on remand is unconvinced of the causal connection between Microsoft's exclusionary conduct and the company's position in the OS market, it may well conclude that divestiture is not an appropriate remedy.

While we do not undertake to dictate to the District Court the precise form that relief should take on remand, we note again that it should be tailored to fit the wrong creating the occasion for the remedy....

NOTES AND QUESTIONS

1. Both the government and Microsoft claimed victory after the D.C. Circuit rendered its decision. Which side was closer to correct?

2. Compare the D.C. Circuit's rejection, as bordering "upon the frivolous," of Microsoft's claim that it has "an absolute and unfettered right to use its intellectual property as it wishes" with the Federal Circuit's *Xerox* opinion, p. 801 *infra*. The D.C. Circuit acknowledged that in technologically dynamic markets conduct remedies may be unavailing "because innovation to a large degree has already rendered the anticompetitive conduct obsolete (although by no means harmless)." What should be the standard for the awarding of structural relief in such a situation? On remand, the government and various states settled with Microsoft for conduct relief (*i.e.*, injunctive provisions). A lively debate continues as to whether these injunctive provisions provided effective—or even meaningful—relief.

NOTE ON THE EU *MICROSOFT* DECISION

In 2004, the European Commission (the executive arm of the European Union) issued a far-reaching decision against Microsoft, finding that the software company violated European competition rules by abusing its dominant position in the market for personal computer operating systems (OS). *Sun Microsystems* v. *Microsoft Corp.*, EC Comm 1 (Comp/C–3/37.792) (March 24, 2004) ("European Commission Decision"), *online at* http://europa.eu.int/comm/competition/antitrust/cases/decisions/ 37792/en.pdf. Specifically, the Commission found that Microsoft illegally leveraged its dominant position in the OS market into two adjacent markets: (1) the market for work group server (WGS) operating systems, and (2) the market for media players.

In the server market, Microsoft had refused to disclose documentation that would allow its competitors to create server software that is fully compatible with PCs that use the popular Microsoft Windows OS. The Commission held that this nondisclosure put competitors at an unfair disadvantage and risked eliminating competition in the WGS market. It held that Microsoft's actions created a significant risk of eliminating competition in the WGS market and that this violated Article 82(b) of the EU Treaty, which forbids a company from abusing its dominant position by "limiting production, markets or technical development to the prejudice of consumers." The Commission ordered Microsoft to disclose the relevant information within 120 days of the decision, but it allowed Microsoft to receive reasonable compensation to the extent that the information being disclosed was entitled to protection as intellectual property.

The Commission also found that Microsoft abused its dominant position by tying its Windows Media Player (WMP) with the Windows OS by technically integrating WMP software into Windows, a charge similar to the one the company faced in the United States relating to its web browser software. By bundling its media software with Windows, Microsoft unfairly placed its competitors in that market at a competitive disadvantage and reduced consumer choice in violation of Article 82. The Commission ordered Microsoft to offer two versions of the Windows OS without the WMP to its customers within 90 days of its decision.

The Commission concluded that Microsoft's violations were severe enough to warrant drastic penalties:

Microsoft's anti-competitive behaviour weakens effective competition on the markets for work group server operating systems and media players in an appreciable way. Microsoft's refusal to supply interface information brings about a risk of elimination of competition on the world-wide market for work group server operating systems. Microsoft's tying of WMP with Windows risks impairing the effective structure of competition in the world-wide market for media players. European Commission Decision at para. 992.

In addition to enjoining Microsoft from continuing its abusive activity, the Commission levied a record fine of over €497 million (about $603 million) in the hopes of deterring Microsoft or others from engaging in similar conduct.

Microsoft's initial reaction to the decision was twofold: first, it announced that it would comply, but second, it stated that it intended to appeal the decision to the European Court of First Instance. In the meantime, the Commission became concerned that Microsoft was not complying properly with the terms of the 2004 decision. On October 4, 2005, the Commission and Microsoft agreed on the appointment of Professor Neil Barrett to be the Monitoring Trustee for compliance. Later, two advisors were appointed to assist the Trustee.

By mid–2006, the Trustee had concluded that the disclosures Microsoft had made could not be used to develop an interoperable work group server operating system. Microsoft, of course, contested that finding, but the Commission was persuaded that the Trustee had the better of the argument. It concluded, that "Microsoft has not complied with its obligations to make Interoperability Information available to interested undertakings. . . ." In order to assure Microsoft's future compliance, the Commission decided to impose additional fines on Microsoft, based on its turnover of US $39.7 billion in the last year available (2004–05) and its average daily turnover of US $109 million. A July 12, 2006 Commission decision fixed the "definitive" amount of the periodic payment Microsoft owed for failing to comply with its obligations at €280.5 million (or $357 million) for the period from December 16, 2005 to June 20, 2006 inclusive. From July 31 forward, the penalty was fixed at €3 million per day. Microsoft, while still defending the legality of its actions, filed revised documents with the Commission in late November 2006, hoping to avoid the rapidly increasing fines.

This ongoing saga is a sobering reminder of the differences in perspective and approach that continue to exist between the European Union and the United States on the topic of abuses of a dominant position (or monopolization). The parallel action that went forward in the United States has resulted in court supervision, to be sure, but the remedies look nothing like the disclosure obligations and supporting fines that Microsoft is facing in the EU. In the fall of 2007, the Court of First Instance rejected Microsoft's underlying appeal on the merits. In 2009, the Commission and Microsoft informally resolved their litigation on the issue of non-disclosure of interoperability information whereby Microsoft is publishing an improved version of the undertaking consistent with the terms disclosed above.

NOTE ON ISSUES AT THE INTERSECTION OF ANTITRUST AND INTELLECTUAL PROPERTY

An emerging area of interest in recent years concerns issues that arise at the intersection of intellectual property rights (mainly patent and copyright) and antitrust. Values underlying the two systems can be reconciled: IP rights subsidize investments in innovation by conferring time-limited market power on the innovator; antitrust seeks to ensure that markets remain open and firms compete to find new paths to innovation. But there are times when the systems are in conflict—for example, patents can be enforced so as to create market power outside the legitimate scope of the patent—and reconciliation in a way that rewards, but does not over-reward, incentives to innovate can be difficult.

These issues are particularly important because products that are the embodiment of ideas, and therefore candidates for intellectual property protection, are found in the most dynamic and fastest growing sectors of the U.S. economy, including computer software, internet services, biotechnology, new forms of communications, and others. Some have suggested that IP is just another form of property and deserves no special treatment under the antitrust laws. The United States Department of Justice and FTC Antitrust Guidelines for the Licensing of Intellectual Property 1995 says as much at § 2.1, but the Guidelines later go on to identify characteristics, such as ease of misappropriation, that distinguish IP from any other forms of property. Others have suggested that sectors of the economy characterized by IP are so dynamic that antitrust has little or no useful role to play. *See* Teece & Coleman, The Meaning of Monopoly: Antitrust Analysis in High–Technology Industries, 43 Antitrust Bull. 801, 843, 846 (1998). Are there differences between IP and other forms of property? Several, although not uniquely limited to IP, are noteworthy:

1. Differences in Fundamental Economics

Products and services based on IP are more often characterized by large initial investments ("fixed costs") and low cost to produce individual items ("variable costs"). For example, compare the cost of developing a new line of computer code with duplicating the code and making it available to others. As a result, producers at least in the short run tend to expand sales rapidly to maximize market share and therefore prices in early stages often decline.

Moreover, there is a tendency for IP markets to drift towards single-firm dominance and even monopoly. Market power can be protected by patent or copyright law. Most IP does not confer a monopoly—there are substitute products outside the scope of the IP—but it often confers significant market power. Also, some IP products and services exhibit "network effects," *i.e.*, each individual's demand for a particular company's product or service is positively related to its wide-spread use by others. Examples include fax machines and email which become more valuable to users as more people use the service. There also can be indirect network effects such as where producers of complementary goods design and manufacture complements to work with the goods of a single dominant firm. In sum, the economics of IP can both enhance and restrain innovation and competition.

2. Importance of Innovation in a Dynamic Economy

In a dynamic economy, the major concern need not be with ensuring maximum output and minimum consumer cost but rather with protecting incentives to innovate. On the other hand, as the *Microsoft* case demonstrates, it is important not to allow abusive market behavior which impairs the ability of other firms to challenge the technology incumbent, and to promote both price and innovation competition.

3. Uncertain Durability of Market Power

The most frequently cited reason for treating IP products and services more leniently under the antitrust laws is that those markets are characterized by an increased rate of innovation, relative ease of entry, and instability of market shares. As a result, it is argued that cartels and monopoly power in IP markets will necessarily be short-lived and, in any event, will be defeated more quickly and efficiently by market forces such as new entry and innovation than by government enforcement. *See* Shapiro & Varian, Information Rules 305 (1999) ("Certain high-tech industries are highly dynamic, making any monopoly power transitory"). While conceding that market power on average is less durable with respect to some sectors of the economy characterized by IP, it has also been noted that some IP giants (think of Microsoft and Intel) have retained their dominant position for substantial periods of time. That would suggest that the question whether market power is durable or ephemeral is fact specific and needs to be addressed on a market-by-market and product-by-product basis.

The following two cases, which reviewed very similar conduct but reached substantially different results, nicely frame the antitrust-IP controversy. Before turning to the two cases, you might reread the "Overview" section of the unanimous Court of Appeals decision in *Microsoft* about whether " 'old economy' Section 2 monopolization doctrines should apply to firms competing in dynamic technology markets...." *see* p. 769 *supra*. The D.C. Circuit concluded that the dynamic aspect of the market in which Microsoft operates "does not appreciably alter our mission." *See* pp. 770–71 *supra*. Note also the Court's treatment of Microsoft's argument that its challenged license restrictions were legally justified because it was simply "exercising its rights as the holder of valid copyrights." The Court concluded that the claim that the company has an unfettered right to use its intellectual property as it wishes "borders upon the frivolous." *See* p. 775 *supra*.

Oddly, the *Eastman Kodak* case that is printed below is a remand from a Supreme Court decision that is set out in Section 3 of this Chapter. When the case was first in the Supreme Court, the plaintiffs' principal charges related to alleged tie-in sales and other forms of leverage. The plaintiffs won and the case was remanded for trial. At the trial, the plaintiffs withdrew their tie-in claims and focused on their attempted monopolization and monopolization charges based on refusals to deal, and were met with a defense that the refusal related to patented and copyrighted materials and therefore was legitimate. The plaintiffs won again at the trial level, and we turn now to the Ninth Circuit's review of that decision.

After a brief discussion of monopoly leveraging and essential facilities theory (*see* note pp. 757–67 *supra*), the Ninth Circuit turns to a defense based on intellectual property.

Image Technical Services, Inc. v. Eastman Kodak Co.

United States Court of Appeals, Ninth Circuit, 1997.
125 F.3d 1195.

■ BEEZER, J. Plaintiffs–Appellees Image Technical Services, and ten other independent service organizations ("ISOs") that service Kodak photocopiers and micrographic equipment sued the Eastman Kodak Co. ("Kodak") for violations of the Sherman Act. The ISOs alleged that Kodak used its monopoly in the market for Kodak photocopier and micrographic parts to create a second monopoly in the equipment service markets. A jury verdict awarded treble damages totaling $71.8 million. The district court denied Kodak's post trial motions and entered a ten-year permanent injunction requiring Kodak to sell "all parts" to ISOs....

This appeal raises questions relating to the application of antitrust principles upon a finding that a monopolist unilaterally refused to deal with competitors. We also address overlapping patent and copyright issues and their significance in the antitrust context. . . .

I

Kodak manufactures, sells and services high volume photocopiers and micrographic (or microfilm) equipment. Competition in these markets is strong. In the photocopier market Kodak's competitors include Xerox, IBM and Canon. Kodak's competitors in the micrographics market include Minolta, Bell & Howell and 3M. Despite comparable products in these markets, Kodak's equipment is distinctive. Although Kodak equipment may perform similar functions to that of its competitors, Kodak's parts are not interchangeable with parts used in other manufacturers' equipment.

Kodak sells and installs replacement parts for its equipment. Kodak competes with ISOs in these markets. Kodak has ready access to all parts necessary for repair services because it manufactures many of the parts used in its equipment and purchases the remaining necessary parts from independent original-equipment manufacturers. ISOs began servicing Kodak equipment in the early 1980s, and have provided cheaper and better service at times, according to some customers. ISOs obtain parts for repair service from a variety of sources, including, at one time, Kodak.

As ISOs grew more competitive, Kodak began restricting access to its photocopiers and micrographic parts. In 1985, Kodak stopped selling copier parts to ISOs and in 1986, Kodak halted sales of micrographic parts to ISOs. Additionally, Kodak secured agreements from their contracted original-equipment manufacturers not to sell parts to ISOs. These parts restrictions limited the ISOs' ability to compete in the service market for Kodak machines. Competition in the service market requires that service providers have ready access to all parts.

Kodak offers annual or multi-year service contracts to its customers. Service providers generally contract with equipment owners through multi-year service contracts. ISOs claim that they were unable to provide similar contracts because they lack a reliable supply of parts. Some ISOs content that the parts shortage forced them out of business. . . .

After remand [from the Supreme Court], the case proceeded to trial in the district court. Before closing arguments, the ISOs withdrew their § 1 tying and conspiracy claims. The remaining § 2 attempted monopolization and monopolization claims were submitted to the jury. A unanimous verdict awarded damages to the ISOs totaling $71.8 million after trebling. Ten ISOs were awarded damages covering lost service profits in the amount of $12,172,900 (before trebling) and six ISOs were awarded damages covering lost profits for used equipment sales totaling $11,775,40 (before trebling).

After accepting the verdict, the district court crafted a ten year injunction requiring Kodak to sell all parts to ISOs on "reasonable and nondiscriminatory terms and prices. . . ."

II

Section 2 of the Sherman Act prohibits monopolies, attempts to form monopolies, as well as combinations and conspiracies to do so. The ISOs presented evidence in support of two § 2 theories: attempted monopolization and monopolization. They alleged, and the jury concluded, that Kodak used its monopoly over Kodak photocopier and micrographic parts to attempt to create and actually create a second monopoly over the service markets. . . .

Kodak primarily attacks the ISOs' monopoly claim because success would likely upset the "attempt" verdict as well. We now address Kodak's appeal against the background of the Supreme Court's opinion in *Kodak* and the extensive record developed at trial. . . .

[The Ninth Circuit concluded that Kodak had monopoly power in "all Kodak parts" markets for photocopiers and micrographics equipment.]

The second element of a § 2 monopoly claim, the "conduct" element, is the use of monopoly power "to foreclose competition, to gain a competitive advantage, or to destroy a competitor." *Kodak*. The ISOs proceeded under a "monopoly leveraging" theory, alleging that Kodak used its monopoly over Kodak parts to gain or attempt to gain a monopoly over the service of Kodak equipment. The Supreme Court endorsed this theory in *Kodak* noting: "If Kodak adopted its parts and service policies as part of a scheme of willful acquisition or maintenance of monopoly power, it will have violated § 2." "Willful acquisition" or "maintenance of monopoly power" involves "exclusionary conduct," not power gained "from growth or development as a consequence of a superior product, business acumen, or historic accident." *Grinnell*.

Kodak attacks the district court's monopoly conduct jury instructions as well as the ISOs' evidence establishing Kodak's exclusionary conduct. A challenge to a jury instruction on the grounds that it misstates the relevant elements is a question of law reviewed de novo. As noted, the jury's verdict will stand if supported by substantial evidence.

1. Kodak's chief complaint with the monopoly power jury instructions lies with Jury Instruction No. 29. That Instruction, entitled "Monopolization–Monopoly Conduct," states in relevant part:

> [a] company with monopoly power in a relevant market has no general duty to cooperate with its business rivals and may refuse to deal with them or with their customers if valid business reasons exist for such refusal. It is unlawful, however, for a monopolist to engage in conduct, including refusals to deal, that unnecessarily excludes or handicaps competitors in order to maintain a monopoly.

Kodak argues that this instruction lacks objective standards and improperly includes within the prohibited activities a lawful monopolist's "aggressive" competition.

Specifically, Kodak challenges Instruction No. 29's "unnecessarily excludes or handicaps competitors" language. Kodak says that this language is based on a form of "monopoly leveraging" that we previously rejected in *Alaska Airlines*. In *Alaska Airlines* we did reject the Second Circuit's holding in *Berkey Photo*. *Berkey Photo* recognized liability under § 2 of the Sherman Act on a theory of monopoly leveraging involving a firm which used "its monopoly power in one market to gain a competitive advantage in another, albeit without an attempt to monopolize the second market." In *Alaska Airlines*, we held that "monopoly leveraging" could not exist as a basis for § 2 liability in the absence of the defendant using its monopoly in one market to monopolize or attempt to monopolize the downstream market. We characterized Berkey Photo's downstream monopoly requirement—"to gain a competitive advantage"—as too "loose."

Kodak accuses the district court of incorporating Berkey Photo's repudiated language into the court's instructions. We disagree. Instruction No. 29 required the jury to find that Kodak's monopoly conduct be undertaken "in order to maintain a monopoly" in the downstream market. Berkey Photo's watered-down standard does not go this far. Instruction No. 29 makes clear that the monopolies at issue are Kodak's alleged service monopolies and the Instruction required the jury to find that Kodak acted in furtherance of maintaining its service monopolies. Instruction No. 29's "unnecessarily excludes or handicaps competitors" language does not come from *Berkey Photo*, but from the jury instruction endorsed by the Supreme Court in *Aspen Skiing*.

2. Kodak also objects to the attempted monopolization and monopolization jury instructions on the grounds that they fail to describe adequately the "essential facilities" doctrine, which Kodak contends is the controlling law in unilateral refusal to deal cases. Kodak asserts that this doctrine is the sole legal theory which could require Kodak to sell "all parts." Kodak argues that the essential facilities doctrine required the jury to find that Kodak's parts monopoly carries "the power to eliminate competition."

Kodak's challenge raises a novel issue: whether a monopolist is liable under § 2 of the Sherman Act for an anticompetitive refusal to deal only under an "essential facilities" theory, that is, only when the refusal involves something "essential" to the survival of competitors. As noted, Kodak would answer affirmatively; we reject this theory. Instead, relying on *Kodak and Aspen Skiing*, we endorse the ISOs' theory that § 2 of the Sherman Act prohibits a monopolist from refusing to deal in order to create or maintain a monopoly absent a legitimate business justification. We need not apply the essential facilities doctrine....

III

Our conclusion that the ISOs have shown that Kodak has both attained monopoly power and exercised exclusionary conduct does not end our inquiry. Kodak's conduct may not be actionable if supported by a legitimate business justification. When a legitimate business justification supports a monopolist's exclusionary conduct, that conduct does not violate

§ 2 of the Sherman Act. *See Kodak*. A plaintiff may rebut an asserted business justification by demonstrating either that the justification does not legitimately promote competition or that the justification is pretextual. Kodak asserts that the protection of its patented and copyrighted parts is a valid business justification for its anticompetitive conduct and argues that the district court's erroneous jury instructions made it impossible for the jury to properly consider this justification. Kodak attacks the district court's failure both to provide a "less restrictive alternatives" instruction, and to instruct as to Kodak's intellectual property rights. . . .

A. Least Restrictive Alternatives

Kodak argues that the district court erred by failing to instruct the jury that it was not to consider whether Kodak could have accomplished its business objectives through less restrictive alternatives. Kodak also questions the sufficiency of the ISOs' pretext evidence. . . .

Kodak argues that monopolization, unlike tying, does not require considerations of whether the defendant could have achieved its aims through less restrictive alternatives. Kodak, however, cites no authority mandating an instruction requirement that the jury not consider "less restrictive alternatives." Kodak's argument rests on the combination of the district court's refusal to use Kodak's requested language and Kodak's disagreement with the "unnecessarily excludes or handicaps competitors" language of Jury Instructions Nos. 29 and 34. As a result of this combination, Kodak argues, the ISOs were able to argue a "necessity" standard and ask the jury to weigh what Kodak did "against the alternatives."

As discussed above, the "unnecessarily excluded or handicaps" language was permissible under *Aspen Skiing*. Moreover, the district court's instruction here was very similar to both the language proposed by Kodak and the language endorsed by the Supreme Court in *Aspen Skiing*. Jury Instruction No. 28 defines "exclusionary conduct" as impairing "the efforts of others to compete for customers in an unnecessarily restrictive way." The district court also instructed that: (1) Kodak could refuse to deal if valid business reasons existed and (2) the jury could not "second guess whether Kodak's business judgment was wise or correct in retrospect." Under these instructions the jury could not consider "less restrictive alternatives" without "second guessing" Kodak and thus violating the jury instructions. We presume that the jury followed the court's instructions.

Kodak next argues that the ISOs' primary arguments refuting Kodak's business justifications were "less restrictive alternative" arguments. Kodak focuses on the ISOs' attack on Kodak's quality control justification as one such "less restrictive alternative" argument. Kodak argues that because "the legitimacy of quality control is beyond reproach," the ISOs were forced to establish this justification, and others, were pretextual. The ISOs did establish pretext: they attacked Kodak's quality control justification on the grounds that it was pretextual, not because it was the least restrictive alternative. Counsel for the ISOs argued that Kodak's quality control justification was "a joke" because ISOs do not interfere with the quality of

Kodak's service. We hold that the district court did not err in its instructions.

... The ISOs' evidence suffices to support the jury's rejection of Kodak's business justifications, as the record reflects evidence of pretext. The ISOs presented evidence that: (1) Kodak adopted its parts policy only after an ISO won a contract with the State of California; (2) Kodak allowed its own customers to service their machines; (3) Kodak customers could distinguish breakdowns due to poor service from breakdowns due to parts; and (4) many customers preferred ISO service.

B.   Intellectual Property Rights

Kodak also attacks the district court's business justifications instructions for their failure to properly detail Kodak's intellectual property rights. Kodak argues that the court failed to instruct the jury that Kodak's numerous patents and copyrights provide a legitimate business justification for Kodak alleged exclusionary conduct. Kodak holds 220 valid United States patents covering 65 parts for its high volume photocopiers and micrographics equipment, and all Kodak diagnostic software and service software are copyrighted. The jury instructions do not afford Kodak any "rights" or "privileges" based on its patents and copyrights: all parts are treated the same. In Jury Instruction No. 37, the court told the jury:

> if you find that Kodak engaged in monopolization or attempted monopolization by misuse of its alleged parts monopoly ... then the fact that some of the replacement parts are patented or copyrighted does not provide Kodak with a defense against any of those antitrust claims.

In Jury Instruction No. 28, the court stated, over Kodak's objection, that:

> such [exclusionary] conduct does not refer to ordinary means of competition, like offering better products or services, exercising superior skills or business judgment, utilizing more efficient technology, or exercising natural competitive advantages.

Kodak proposed to include "exercising lawful patents and copyrights" amongst the list of non-exclusionary conduct in Instruction No. 28, but the district court rejected that language.

Kodak's challenge raises unresolved questions concerning the relationship between federal antitrust, copyright and patent laws. In particular we must determine the significance of a monopolist's unilateral refusal to sell or license a patented or copyrighted product in the context of a § 2 monopolization claim based upon monopoly leveraging. This is a question of first impression.

1.   We first identify the general principles of antitrust, copyright and patent law as we must ultimately harmonize these statutory schemes in responding to Kodak's challenge.

Antitrust law seeks to promote and protect a competitive marketplace for the benefit of the public. The Sherman Act, the relevant antitrust law here, prohibits efforts both to restrain trade by combination or conspiracy and the acquisition or maintenance of a monopoly by exclusionary conduct.

Patent law seeks to protect inventions, while inducing their introduction into the market for public benefit. Patent laws "reward the inventor with the power to exclude others from making, using or selling [a patented] invention through the United States." Meanwhile, the public benefits both from the faster introduction of inventions, and the resulting increase in market competition. Legally, a patent amounts to a permissible monopoly over the protected work. *See* Zenith Radio Corp. v. Hazeltine Research, Inc., 395 U.S. 100 (1969). Patent laws "are in pari materia with the antitrust laws and modify them pro tanto (as far as the patent laws go)." Simpson v. Union Oil Co., 377 U.S. 13, 24 (1964).

Federal copyright laws "secures a fair return for an author's creative labor" in the short run, while ultimately seeking "to stimulate artistic creativity for the general public good." Twentieth Century Music Corp. v. Aiken 422 U.S. 151, 156 (1975). The Copyright Act grants to the copyright owner the exclusive right to distribute the protected work. This right encompasses the right to "refrain from vending or licensing," as the owner may "content [itself] with simply exercising the right to exclude others from using [its] property."

Clearly the antitrust, copyright and patent laws both overlap and, in certain situations, seem to conflict. This is not a new revelation. We have previously noted the "obvious tension" between the patent and antitrust laws: "one body of law creates and protects monopoly power while the other seeks to proscribe it." United States v. Westinghouse Electric Corp., 648 F.2d 642, 646 (9th Cir.1981) (citations omitted). Similarly, tension exists between the antitrust and copyright laws. *See* Data General, 36 F.3d at 1187.

Two principles have emerged regarding the interplay between these laws: (1) neither patent nor copyright holders are immune from antitrust liability, and (2) patent and copyright holders may refuse to sell or license protected work. First, as to antitrust liability, case law supports the proposition that a holder of a patent or copyright violates the antitrust laws by "concerted and contractual behavior that threatens competition." *Id.* at 1185 n. 63 (citation omitted). In *Kodak*, the Supreme Court noted:

> [we have] held many times that power gained through some natural advantage such as a patent, copyright, or business acumen can give rise to liability if "a seller exploits his dominant position in one market to expand his empire into the next."

Case law also supports the right of a patent or copyright holder to refuse to sell or license protected work. In United States v. Westinghouse Electric Corp., we held that "the right to license [a] patent, exclusively or otherwise, or to refuse to license at all, is the 'untrammeled right' of the patentee."

2. Next we lay out the problem presented here. The Supreme Court touched on this question in *Kodak*, *i.e.*, the effect to be given a monopolist's

unilateral refusal to sell or license a patented or copyrighted product in the context of a § 2 monopoly leveraging claim.... [T]he Supreme Court in *Kodak* refutes the argument that the possession by a manufacturer of "inherent power" in the market for its parts "should immunize [that manufacturer] from the antitrust laws in another market." 504 U.S. at 480 n. 29. The Court stated that a monopolist who acquires a dominant position in one market through patents and copyrights may violate § 2 if the monopolist exploits that dominant position to enhance a monopoly in another market. Although footnote 29 appears in the Court's discussion of the § 1 tying claims, the § 2 discussion frequently refers back to the § 1 discussion, and the Court's statement that "exploiting [a] dominant position in one market to expand [the] empire into the next" is broad enough to cover monopoly leveraging under § 2. By responding in this fashion, the Court in *Kodak* supposed that intellectual property rights do not confer an absolute immunity from antitrust claims.

The *Kodak* Court, however, did not specifically address the question of antitrust liability based upon a unilateral refusal to deal in a patented or copyrighted product. Kodak and its amicus correctly indicate that the right of exclusive dealing is reserved from antitrust liability. We find no reported case in which a court has imposed antitrust liability for a unilateral refusal to sell or license a patent or copyright. Courts do not generally view a monopolist's unilateral refusal to license a patent as "exclusionary conduct." *See* Data General, 36 F.3d at 1186 (citing Miller Insituform, Inc. v. Insituform of North America, 830 F.2d 606, 609 (6th Cir.1987) ("A patent holder who lawfully acquires a patent cannot be held liable under Section 2 of the Sherman Act for maintaining the monopoly power he lawfully acquired by refusing to license the patent to others.")); Westinghouse, 648 F.2d at 647 (finding no antitrust violation because "Westinghouse has done no more than to license some of its patents and refuse to license other"); SCM Corp., 645 F.2d at 1206 ("where a patent has been lawfully acquired, subsequent conduct permissible under the patent laws cannot trigger any liability under the antitrust laws.").

This basic right of exclusion does have limits. For example, a patent offers no protection if it was unlawfully acquired. *Data General*. Nor does the right of exclusion protect an attempt to extend a lawful monopoly beyond the grant of a patent. Section 2 of the Sherman Act condemns exclusionary conduct that extend natural monopolies into separate markets. Much depends, therefore, on the definition of the patent grant and the relevant market.

The relevant market for determining the patent or copyright grant is determined under patent or copyright law. The relevant markets for antitrust purposes are determined by examining economic conditions. *See Kodak*.

Parts and service here have been proven separate markets in the antitrust context, but this does not resolve the question whether the service market falls "reasonably within the patent [or copyright] grant" for the purpose of determining the extent of the exclusive rights conveyed.

Mallinckrodt, Inc. v. Medipart, Inc., 976 F.2d 700, 708–09 (Fed.Cir.1992). These are separate questions, which may result in contrary answers. At the border of intellectual property monopolies and antitrust markets lies a field of dissonance yet to be harmonized by statute or the Supreme Court.

When an owner of intellectual property takes concerted action in violation of § 1, this dissonance does not threaten his core right of exclusion. Contrary to the ISOs' arguments, there is an important difference between § 1 tying and § 2 monopoly leveraging: the limiting principles of § 1 restrain those claims from making the impact on intellectual property rights threatened by § 2 monopoly leveraging claims. Where, as here, the claim involves a failure to act that is at the heart of the property right, liability depends largely on market definition and lacks the limiting principles of § 1. Under § 2, "behavior that might otherwise not be of concern to the antitrust laws—or that might even be viewed as procompetitive—can take on exclusionary connotations when practiced by a monopolist." Kodak, 504 U.S. at 488 (Scalia, J. dissenting) (citing 3 Areeda & Turner, Par. 813, at 300–302); see also Greyhound Computer v. International Business Machines, 559 F.2d 488, 498 (9th Cir.1977) (otherwise lawful conduct may be exclusionary when practiced by a monopolist). Harmonizing antitrust monopoly theory with the monopolies granted by intellectual property law requires that some weight be given to the intellectual property rights of the monopolist.

The effect of claims based upon unilateral conduct on the value of intellectual property rights is a cause for serious concern. Unilateral conduct is the most common conduct in the economy. After Kodak, unilateral conduct by a manufacturer in its own aftermarkets may give rise to liability and, in one-brand markets, monopoly power created by patents and copyrights will frequently be found. Under current law the defense of monopolization claims will rest largely on the legitimacy of the asserted business justifications, as evidenced by the jury instructions approved in Aspen Skiing....

3. We now resolve the question detailed above. Under the fact-based approaches of Aspen Skiing and Kodak, some measure must guarantee that the jury account for the procompetitive effects and statutory rights extended by the intellectual property laws. To assure such consideration, we adopt a modified version of the rebuttable presumption created by the First Circuit in Data General, and hold that "while exclusionary conduct can include a monopolist's unilateral refusal to license a [patent or] copyright," or to sell its patented or copyrighted work, a monopolist's "desire to exclude others from its [protected] work is a presumptively valid business justification for any immediate harm to consumers." Data General, 36 F.3d at 1187.

This presumption does not "rest on formalistic distinctions" which "are generally disfavored in antitrust laws;" rather it is based on "actual market realities." Kodak, 504 U.S. at 466–67. This presumption harmonizes the goals of the relevant statutes and takes into account the long term effects of regulation on these purposes. The presumption should act to focus the factfinder on the primary interest of both intellectual property and antitrust laws: public interest. Mercoid, 320 U.S. at 665 (citation omitted) ("It is the public interest which is dominant in the patent system."); Standard Oil, 221 U.S. at 58 (antitrust laws serve the public interest by encouraging effective competition).

Given this presumption, the district court's failure to give any weight to Kodak's intellectual property rights in the jury instructions constitutes an abuse of discretion. This error was, however, harmless. The ISOs maintain that Kodak argued protection of intellectual property as a business justification to the jury, which rejected this justification as pretextual. An error in instructing the jury in a civil case does not require reversal if it is more probably than not harmless. Jenkins v. Union Pacific R. Co., 22 F.3d 206, 210 (9th Cir.1994). . . .

Phrased in these broad terms, Kodak's argument repeats the "free-riding" justification rejected, as a matter of law, by the Supreme Court. *Kodak*, 504 U.S. at 485. The Supreme Court held that preventing the ISOs from "exploiting the investment Kodak has made in product development, manufacturing and equipment sales" does not suffice as a business justification. *Id*. ("This understanding of free-riding has no support in our case law.").

Given the interplay of the antitrust and intellectual property laws discussed above, Kodak's contention that its refusal to sell its parts to ISOs was based on its reluctance to sell its patented or copyrighted parts was a presumptively legitimate business justification. *See* Data General, 36 F.3d at 1187. Kodak may assert that its desire to profit from its intellectual property rights justifies its conduct, and the jury should presume that this justification is legitimately procompetitive.

Nevertheless, this presumption is rebuttable. In *Data General*, the First Circuit reasoned that the plaintiff did not rebut the presumption by drawing an analogy to *Aspen Skiing*, where a monopolist made an important change in its practices, which had both originated in a competitive market and persisted for several years. Because competitive conditions had never prevailed in the service market, the First Circuit concluded that it would be inappropriate to infer "from [defendant's] change of heart that its former policies 'satisfy consumer demand in free competitive markets.'" As in Data General, we are not faced here with a simple comparison between the monopolist's market and the established competitive market found in *Aspen Skiing*.

The *Data General* court noted that the presumption of legitimacy can be rebutted by evidence that the monopolist acquired the protection of the intellectual property laws in an unlawful manner. The presumption may also be rebutted by evidence of pretext. Neither the aims of intellectual property law, nor the antitrust laws justify allowing a monopolist to rely upon a pretextual business justification to mask anticompetitive conduct. *See Kodak*. (Because "Kodak's willingness to allow self-service casts doubt on its quality claim ... a reasonable tier of fact could conclude that [this justification] is pretextual.")

Kodak defends its intellectual property rights "justification" against claims of pretext. Kodak argues that its subjective motivation is irrelevant. Kodak also contends, citing *Olympia Equipment*, [p. 757 *supra*], that a desire to best the competition does not prove pretext, nor does hostility to competitors. Kodak's argument and its accompanying authority stands for nothing more than the proposition that a desire to compete does not demonstrate pretext.

Evidence regarding the state of mind of Kodak employees may show pretext, when such evidence suggests that the proffered business justification played no part in the decision to act. Kodak's parts manager testified that patents "did not cross [his] mind" at the time Kodak began the parts policy. Further, no distinction was made by Kodak between "proprietary" parts covered by tooling or engineering clauses and patented or copyrighted products. In denying Kodak's motion for a new trial, the district court commented that Kodak was not actually motivated by protecting its intellectual property rights. Kodak argues that the district court should have allowed the jury to reach this conclusion.

Kodak photocopy and micrographics equipment requires thousands of parts, of which only 65 were patented. Unlike the other cases involving refusals to license patents, this case concerns a blanket refusal that included protected and unprotected products. From this evidence, it is more probably than not that the jury would have found Kodak's presumptively valid business justification rebutted on the grounds of pretext.

Kodak argues that the existence of some patented and copyrighted products undermines ISOs "all parts" theory. To the contrary, as discussed above, the "all parts market" reflect the "commercial realities" of the marketplace and the lack of identifiable separate markets for individual parts. The fact that Kodak did not differentiate between patented and nonpatented parts lends further support to the existence of these commercial realities. The jury accepted the "all parts" theory and found a scheme of monopolize the service market through Kodak's conduct. We hold that the district court's failure to instruct on Kodak's intellectual property rights was harmless....[42]

In re Independent Service Organizations Antitrust Litigation v. Xerox Corp.

United States Court of Appeals, Federal Circuit, 2000.
203 F.3d 1322.

■ MAYER, J. CSU appeals the judgment of the United States District Court for the District of Kansas, dismissing on summary judgment CSU's claims that Xerox's refusal to sell patented parts and copyrighted manuals and to license copyrighted software violate the antitrust laws.... Because we agree with the district court that CSU has not raised a genuine issue as to

---

42. The Court then affirmed the findings below on all liability issues, revised and remanded specific damage awards, and affirmed various damage awards.

any material fact and that Xerox is entitled to judgment as a matter of law, we affirm.

Background

Xerox manufactures, sells, and services high-volume copiers. Beginning in 1984, it established a policy of not selling parts unique to its series 10 copiers to independent service organizations ("ISOs"), including CSU, unless they were also end-users of the copiers. In 1987, the policy was expanded to include all new products as well as existing series 9 copiers. Enforcement of this policy was tightened in 1989, and Xerox cut off CSU's direct purchase of restricted parts. Xerox also implemented an "on-site end-user verification" procedure to confirm that the parts ordered by certain ISOs or their customers were actually for their end-user use. Initially this procedure applied to only the six most successful ISOs, which included CSU.

To maintain its existing business of servicing Xerox equipment, CSU used parts cannibalized from used Xerox equipment, parts obtained from other ISOs, and parts purchased through a limited number of its customers. For approximately one year, CSU also obtained parts from Rank Xerox, a majority-owed European affiliate of Xerox, until Xerox forced Rank Xerox to stop selling parts to CSU and other ISOs. In 1994, Xerox settled an antitrust lawsuit with a class of ISOs by which it agreed to suspend its restrictive parts policy for six and one-half years and to license its diagnostic software for four and one-half years. CSU opted out of that settlement filed this suit alleging that Xerox violated the Sherman Act by setting the prices on its patented parts much higher for ISOs than for end-users to force ISOs to raise their prices. This would eliminate ISOs in general and CSU in particular as competitors in the relevant service markets for high speed copiers and printers.

Xerox counterclaimed for patent and copyright infringement and contested CSU's antitrust claims as relying on injury solely caused by Xerox's lawful refusal to sell or license patented parts and copyrighted software. Xerox also claimed that CSU could not assert a patent or copyright misuse defense to Xerox's infringement counterclaims based on Xerox's refusal to deal.

The district court granted summary judgment to Xerox dismissing CSU's antitrust claims and holding that if a patent or copyright is lawfully acquired, the patent or copyright holder's unilateral refusal to sell or license its patented invention or copyrighted expression is not unlawful exclusionary conduct under the antitrust laws, even if the refusal to deal impacts competition in more than one market. The court also held, in both the patent and copyright contexts, that the right holder's intent in refusing to deal and any other alleged exclusionary acts committed by the right holder are irrelevant to antitrust law. This appeal followed.

Discussion

... As a general proposition, when reviewing a district court's judgment involving federal antitrust law, we are guided by the law of the regional circuit in which that district court sits, in this case the Tenth Circuit. We apply our own law, not regional circuit law, to resolve issues that clearly involve our exclusive jurisdiction. "Whether conduct in procuring or enforcing a patent is sufficient to strip a patentee of its immunity for the antitrust laws is to be decided as a question of Federal Circuit law." ... The district court's grant of summary judgment as to CSU's antitrust claims arising from Xerox's refusal to sell its patented parts is therefore reviewed as a matter of Federal Circuit law, while consideration of the antitrust claim based on Xerox's refusal to sell or license its copyrighted manuals and software is under Tenth Circuit law.

A.

Intellectual property rights do not confer a privilege to violate the antitrust laws. *See* Intergraph Corp. v. Intel Corp., 195 F.3d 1346, 1362 (Fed.Cir.1999). "But it is also correct that the antitrust laws do not negate the patentee's right to exclude others from patent property." *Id.* "The commercial advantage gained by new technology and its statutory protection by patent do not convert the possessor thereof into a prohibited monopolist." Abbott Lab. v. Brennan, 952 F.2d 1346, 1354 (Fed.Cir.1991). "The patent right must be 'coupled with violations of § 2,' and the elements of violation of § 2 must be met." *Id.* "Determination of whether the patentee meets the Sherman Act elements of monopolization or attempt to monopolize is governed by the rules of application of the antitrust laws to market participants, with due consideration to the exclusivity that inheres in the patent grant." *Id.* at 1354–55.

A patent alone does not demonstrate market power. The United States Department of Justice and Federal Trade Commission have issued guidance that, even where it exists, such "market power does not 'impose on the intellectual property owner an obligation to license the use of that property to others.' " *Intergraph*, 195 F.3d at 1362 (citing United States Department of Justice and Federal Trade Comm'n Antitrust Guidelines for the Licensing of Intellectual Property 4 (1995)). There is "no reported case in which a court has imposed antitrust liability for a unilateral refusal to sell or license a patent...." *Id.* The patentee's right to exclude is further supported by section 271(d) of the Patent Act which states, in pertinent part, that "no patent owner otherwise entitled to relief ... shall be denied relief or deemed guilty of misuse or illegal extension of the patent right by reason of his having ... (4) refused to license or use any rights to the patent ..." 35 U.S.C. § 271(d) (1999).

The patentee's right to exclude, however, is not without limit. As we recently observed in Glass Equipment Development Inc. v. Besten, Inc., a patent owner who brings suit to enforce the statutory right to exclude others from making, using, or selling the claimed invention is exempt from the antitrust laws, even though such a suit may have an anticompetitive effect, unless the infringement defendant proves one of two conditions. First, he may prove that the asserted patent was obtained through knowing and willful fraud within the meaning of Walker Process Equipment, Inc. v. Food Machinery & Chemical Corp., 382 U.S. 172, 177 (1965). Or he may demonstrate that the infringement suit was a mere sham to cover what is actually no more than an attempt to interfere directly with the business relationships of a competitor. Here, CSU makes no claim that Xerox obtained its patents through fraud in the Patent and Trademark Office; the *Walker Process* analysis is not implicated.

"Irrespective of the patent applicant's conduct before the [Patent and Trademark Office], an antitrust claim can also be based on [an] allegation that a suit is baseless; in order to prove that a suit was within *Noerr's* 'sham' exception to immunity, an antitrust plaintiff must prove that the suit was both objectively baseless and subjectively motivated by a desire to impose collateral, anti-competitive injury rather than to obtain a justifiable legal remedy." *Nobelpharma*, 141 F.3d at 1071. "Accordingly, if a suit is not objectively baseless, an antitrust defendant's subjective motivation is immaterial." CSU has alleged that Xerox misused its patents but has not claimed that Xerox's patent infringement counterclaims were shams.

To support its argument that Xerox illegally sought to leverage its presumably legitimate dominance in the equipment and parts market into dominance in the service market, CSU relies on a footnote in *Kodak* that "the Court has held many times that power gained through some natural and legal advantage such as a patent, . . . can give rise to liability if 'a seller exploits his dominant position in one market to expand his empire into the next.'" Notably, *Kodak* was a tying case when it came before the Supreme Court, and no patents had been asserted in defense of the antitrust claims against Kodak. Conversely, there are no claims in this case of illegally tying the sale of Xerox's patented parts to unpatented products. Therefore, the issue was not resolved by the *Kodak* language cited by CSU. Properly viewed within the framework of a tying case, the footnote can be interpreted as restating the undisputed premise that the patent holder cannot use his statutory right to refuse to sell patented parts to gain a monopoly in a market beyond the scope of the patent. . . .

The cited language from *Kodak* does nothing to limit the right of the patentee to refuse to sell or license in markets within the scope of the statutory patent grant. In fact, we have expressly held that, absent exceptional circumstances, a patent may confer the right to exclude competition altogether in more than one antitrust market. *See B.* Braun Med., Inc. v. Abbott Lab., 124 F.3d 1419, 1427 n. 4 (Fed.Cir.1997) (patentee had right to exclude competition in both the market for patented valves and the market for extension sets incorporating patented valves).

CSU further relies on the Ninth Circuit's holding on remand in *Image Technical Services* that "while exclusionary conduct can include a monopolist's unilateral refusal to license a [patent] or to sell its patented . . . work, a monopolist's 'desire to exclude others from its [protected] work is a presumptively valid business justification for any immediate harm to consumers.'" By that case, the Ninth Circuit adopted a rebuttable presumption that the exercise of the statutory right to exclude provides a valid business justification for consumer harm, but then excused as harmless the district court's error in failing to give any instruction on the effect of intellectual property rights on the application of the antitrust laws. It concluded that the jury must have rejected the presumptively valid business justification as pretextual. This logic requires an evaluation of the patentee's subjective motivation for refusing to sell or license its patented products for pretext. We decline to follow *Image Technical Services*.

We have held that "if a [patent infringement] suit is not objectively baseless, an antitrust defendant's subjective motivation is immaterial." *Nobelpharma*, 141 F.3d at 1072. We see no more reason to inquire into the subjective motivation of *Xerox* in refusing to sell or license its patented works than we found in evaluating the subjective motivation of a patentee in bringing suit to enforce that same right. In the absence of any indication of illegal tying, fraud in the Patent and Trademark Office, or sham litigation, the patent holder may enforce the statutory right to exclude others from making using, or selling the claimed invention free from liability under the antitrust laws. We therefore will not inquire into his subjective motivation for exerting his statutory rights, even though his refusal to sell or license his patented invention may have an anticompetitive effect, so long as that anticompetitive effect is not illegally extended beyond the statutory patent grant. It is the infringement defendant and not the patentee that bears the burden to show that one of these exceptional situations exists and, in the absence of such proof, we will not inquire into the patentee's motivations for asserting his statutory right to exclude. Even in cases where the infringement defendant has met this burden, which CSU has not, he must then also prove the elements of the Sherman Act violation.

We answer the threshold question of whether Xerox's refusal to sell its patented parts exceeds the scope of the patent grant in the negative.[43] Therefore, our inquiry is at an end. Xerox was under no obligation to sell or license its patented parts and did not violate the antitrust laws by refusing to do so.

B.

The Copyright Act expressly grants a copyright owner the exclusive right to distribute the protected work by "transfer of ownership, or by rental, lease, or lending." 17 U.S.C. § 106(3) (1996). "The owner of the copyright, if [it] pleases, may refrain from vending or licensing and content [itself] with simply exercising the right to exclude others from using [its] property." *Data General*, 36 F.3d at 1186.

The Supreme Court has made clear that the property right granted by copyright law cannot be used with impunity to extend power in the marketplace beyond what Congress intended. *See* United States v. Loew's, Inc., 371 U.S. 38, 47–48 (1962) (block booking of copyrighted motion pictures is illegal tying in violation of the Sherman Act). The Court has not, however, directly addressed the antitrust implications of a unilateral refusal to sell or license copyrighted expression.

---

43. Having concluded that Xerox's actions fell within the statutory patent grant, we need not separately consider CSU's allegations of patent misuse and they are rejected.

The Tenth Circuit has not addressed in any published opinion the extent to which the unilateral refusal to sell or license copyrighted expression can form the basis of a violation of the Sherman Act. We are therefore left to determine how that circuit would likely resolve the issue; the precedent of other circuits is instructive in that consideration. The Fourth Circuit has rejected a claim of illegal tying, supported only by evidence of a unilateral decision to license copyrighted diagnostic software to some but not to others. *See* Service & Training, Inc. v. Data General Corp., 963 F.2d 680, 686, 23 (4th Cir.1992). In reaching this conclusion, the court recognized the copyright owner's exclusive right to "sell, rent, lease, lend, or otherwise distribute copies of a copyrighted work," *id*. and concluded that "Section 1 of the Sherman Act does not entitle 'a purchaser ... to buy a product that the seller does not wish to offer for sale.' " *Id*.

Perhaps the most extensive analysis of the effect of a unilateral refusal to license copyrighted expression was conducted by the First Circuit in Data General Corp. v. Grumman Systems Support Corp., 36 F.3d 1147. There, the court noted that the limited copyright monopoly is based on Congress' empirical assumption that the right to "exclude others from using their works creates a system of incentives that promotes consumder welfare in the long term by encouraging investment in the creation of desirable artistic and functional works of expression.... We cannot require antitrust defendants to prove and reprove the merits of this legislative assumption in every case where a refusal to license a copyrighted work comes under attack." The court went on to establish as a legal standard that "while exclusionary conduct can include a monopolist's unilateral refusal to license a copyright, an author's desire to exclude others from use of its copyrighted work is a presumptively valid business justification for any immediate harm to consumers." The burden to overcome this presumption was firmly placed on the antitrust plaintiff. The court gave no weight to evidence showing knowledge that developing a proprietary position would help to maintain a monopoly in the service market in the face of contrary evidence of the defendant's desire to develop state-of-the-art diagnostic software to enhance its service and consumer benefit.

As discussed above, the Ninth Circuit adopted a modified version of this *Data General* standard. Both courts agreed that the presumption could be rebutted by evidence that "the monopolist acquired the protection of the intellectual property laws in an unlawful manner." Image Technical Servs., 125 F.3d at 1219. The Ninth Circuit, however, extended the possible means of rebutting the presumption to include evidence that the defense and exploitation of the copyright grant was merely a pretextual business justification to mask anticompetitive conduct. The hazards of this approach are evidence in both the path taken and the outcome reached. The jury in that case was instructed to examine each proffered business justification for pretext, and no weight was given to the intellectual property rights in the instructions. This permitted the jury to second guess the subjective motivation of the copyright holder in asserting its statutory rights to exclude under the copyright laws without properly weighing the presumption of legitimacy in asserting its rights under the copyright laws. While concluding that the failure to weigh the intellectual property rights was an abuse of discretion, the Ninth Circuit nevertheless held the error harmless because it thought the jury must have rejected the presumptive validity of asserting the copyrights as pretextual. This is in reality a significant departure from the First Circuit's central premise that rebutting the presumption would be an uphill battle and would only be appropriate in those rare cases in which imposing antitrust liability is unlikely to frustrate the objectives of the Copyright Act.

We believe the First Circuit's approach is more consistent with both the antitrust and the copyright laws and is the standard that would most likely be followed by the Tenth Circuit in considering the effects of Xerox's unilateral right to refuse to license or sell copyrighted manuals and diagnostic software on liability under the antitrust laws. We therefore reject CSU's invitation to examine Xerox's subjective motivation in asserting its right to exclude under the copyright laws for pretext, in the absence of any evidence that the copyrights were obtained by unlawful means or were used to gain monopoly power beyond the statutory copyright granted by Congress. In the absence of such definitive rebuttal evidence, Xerox's refusal to sell or license its copyrighted works was squarely within the rights granted by Congress to the copyright holder and did not constitute a violation of the antitrust laws.

NOTES AND QUESTIONS

1. Can the *Kodak* and *Xerox* opinions be reconciled? If not, which is right? Should the existence of an antitrust violation turn on the alleged violator's state of mind as appeared to be the case in *Kodak*? How would the "sham exception" work in *Xerox*?

2. The law is reasonably clear that a party owning intellectual property—even a monopolist—is not required to license that property in the first instance, regardless of intent or effect on competition, *see* SCM Corp. v. Xerox Corp., 645 F.2d 1195, 1204 (2d Cir.), cert. denied, 455 U.S. 1016 (1982). Problems arise, however, as to how antitrust should treat situations where the legitimate holder of a patent or copyright conditions its license on what would be an antitrust violation if intellectual property were not involved. In the *Xerox* case, the Federal Circuit appeared to conclude that any conditioning of a license is exempt from the antitrust laws unless the IP was obtained by fraud, the infringement claim is a sham to cover an attempt to injure a competitor, or the refusal is part of a tie-in sales strategy. Does that mean it would be acceptable to license a patent on condition that the licensee agrees not to deal with a competitor of the licensor? That would be illegal if non-IP were involved. *See* Lorain Journal Co. v. United States, p. 811 *infra*. Is there reason to believe that more lenient treatment of IP in that context would have a positive effect on incentives to innovate? What about the incentives of the rival of the patent holder who is precluded from dealing with the licensee?

3. *See* Townshend v. Rockwell Int'l Corp., 2000 WL 433505 (N.D. Cal. 2000) illustrating how some lower courts are interpreting the Federal Circuit's *Xerox* opinion. In that case, the owner of basic patents underlying the 56K modem

technology sued for patent infringement. The co-defendant, Rockwell, asserted antitrust counterclaims alleging that the patents on which the suit was based were invalid, the technology covered by the patents had been adopted as part of an industry standard through fraud, and the patents were made available to competitors only on the condition that they cross-license their technology to the patent holder. The district court dismissed all antitrust counterclaims. "Because a patent owner has the legal right to refuse to license his or her patent on any terms, the existence of a predicate condition to a license agreement cannot state the antitrust violation." Does this mean that the undeniable premise that an intellectual property holder generally does not have to license anyone in the first instance leads to a conclusion that it can select among licensees or condition a license in any way it chooses to achieve an anticompetitive effect?

4. Does the Federal Circuit's decision cast doubt on the FTC's complaint against Intel, subsequently settled by consent order, that it is an antitrust violation for a monopolist to deny copyrighted technical information and advance samples to those customers and competitors who sue the monopolist for infringing on their intellectual property? *See* pp. 128–29 *supra.*

5. The D.C. Court of Appeals in *Microsoft* addressed the question of whether antitrust analysis must be modified when antitrust rules are applied to high-tech industries. For relevant comments in the *Microsoft* case, *see* pp. 769–71 *supra.*

6. Consider the wisdom—or lack thereof—of the following recent commentary by Professor Goldschmid:

> . . . No agreement is required for a Section 2 violation. Why not easily condemn the dominant manufacturer that uses a refusal-to-deal threat to significantly inhibit or retard the distribution of products made by its small competitors? Indeed, given the "evils" of monopoly power, why not condemn with rigor significant entry blocking or expansion retarding exclusive dealing—in a dominance context—as did the D.C. Circuit in *Microsoft* and the Third Circuit in *Dentsply*? [*See* p. 949 *infra.*]
>
> Similarly, it seems to me that the Ninth Circuit was correct in condemning Kodak's use of monopoly power in the parts market (for its photocopiers and micrographic equipment) in order to harm or destroy independent service organizations ("ISOs") by refusing to sell parts to them. Hovenkamp cites *Kodak* (where the unilateral refusal to deal included the refusal to license parts that were patented) as a case that was "almost certainly wrong" because the court's conduct test "either misread or ignored existing law."[44] But assume that the Ninth Circuit's and Supreme Court's market definition, of "locked-in" consumers in aftermarkets for parts and services, was correct. Why should dominant Kodak—with monopoly power in parts—be permitted to refuse to deal with competitor ISOs in the service markets? . . . .
>
> [I]n the Ninth Circuit, Kodak acknowledged that it supplied parts to buyers who were doing repairs themselves. There appeared to be no realistic quality control justification for Kodak's refusal to deal with ISOs. Without a plausible business justification, was not Kodak's refusal to deal an unreasonable exclusionary activity?[45] In my view, sharing may be forced

---

44. Herbert Hovenkamp, *The Harvard and Chicago Schools and the Dominant Firm, supra.*

45. It is true, as Hovenkamp indicates, that the "Federal Circuit promptly took issue with the Ninth Circuit's *Kodak* decision," but one can legitimately ask whether decisions of under Section 2 when a dominant firm misuses its monopoly power by, for example, creating the exclusive dealing blockages found in *Dentsply* or by leveraging, without business justification, its power in one market to dominate another as in *Kodak*. In addition, sharing should be forced when (1) a dominant firm controls an "essential facility" that cannot reasonably be duplicated by a present or potential competitor; (2) it is practical for the dominant firm to share the facility; and (3) on balance, forcing the sharing of the facility (which, of course, can be compensated) must be both (a) fair and (b) not counterproductive in terms of efficiency incentives.[46]

Under this formulation, it would be easiest to require the sharing of a unique natural resource or a leased municipal stadium, where the dominant firm had invested relatively little and could be adequately compensated. It would be much harder to order the sharing of a patented pharmaceutical, which had been developed at considerable cost and over a period of many years. Of course, this formulation relies on reasoned, balanced decisionmaking by our federal courts; it would create some uncertainty. But the formulation would only be used after monopoly power is found, and factors (1)–(3) above would not create an easy road for claimants to travel in litigation.[47]

PROBLEM 17

THE BATTLE FOR SAWVILLE: ROUND 2

Referring to the facts of Problem 1 (p. 171 *supra*), assume that the product market is exhibition of films in "art houses" and the geographic market is Sawville.

After being rebuffed in previous efforts to enter the market, Read Theaters, the largest chain of art houses on the East Coast, purchased the Bramble Bush, one of the three motion picture theaters previously devoted to "regular" films, and converted it to art films. Since the Bramble Bush was uniquely well-located, Read was willing to take the risk that it could challenge the entrenched Frolic.

The new Bramble Bush, ultramodern in decor and comfort, has been operating for two years. Read used its extensive bargaining power, partly derived from the fact that it is the only art house in some of the towns in which it operates, to bring the best art films to Sawville simultaneously with their New York City runs. The films were made available to Read on an exclusive basis, and could not be shown elsewhere until 90 days after they stopped being shown by Read. Furthermore, it reduced admission charges from the $12.00 level formerly set by the Frolic, requiring the Frolic to lower prices as well. It also engaged in extensive and costly promotion and advertising—tripling its newspaper ad budget. The net result was that the Bramble Bush, unlike any of Read's other art houses, operated at a net loss during its first two years as an art house. However, because many expenses of a movie theater are fixed rather than variable, it managed to stay barely above average variable costs.

---

the Federal Circuit, with that Circuit's focus on patent and intellectual property issues, have not tilted the playing field heavily against key Section 2 values.

46. *See* Pitofsky, Patterson, & Hooks, *The Essential Facilities Doctrine Under U.S. Antitrust Law,* 70 ANTITRUST L.J. 443 (2002).

47. Goldschmid, Comment on … the Dominant Firm, in Pitofsky (ed.), How the Chicago School Overshot the Mark 126–27 (2008).

At the end of the first year, the Bramble Bush had won a large share of the Frolic's clientele, causing the Frolic to suffer losses for the first time in its history. At the end of the second year, it had achieved near full-capacity attendance and was comfortably in the black. The Frolic then went out of business. As soon as that happened, the Bramble Bush raised its prices to $14.00, $2.00 more than the Frolic had charged before the Bramble Bush entered the market.

Is Read a monopolist and has it violated Section 2? If so, what remedy would you impose?

B. ATTEMPT TO MONOPOLIZE

INTRODUCTORY NOTE

In attempt to monopolize cases under Section 2 of the Sherman Act the courts have generally examined three elements: (1) intent; (2) the nature of the conduct; and (3) a dangerous probability that, if the conduct that constitutes the attempt is allowed to proceed unchecked, it will result in monopoly power. The classic statement of the "attempt" rule is by Justice Holmes in Swift & Co. v. United States, 196 U.S. 375, 396 (1905):

> Where acts are not sufficient in themselves to produce a result which the law seeks to prevent—for instance, the monopoly—but require further acts in addition to the mere forces of nature to bring that result to pass, an intent to bring it to pass is necessary in order to produce a dangerous probability that it will happen.... But when that intent and the consequent dangerous probability exists, this statute, like many others and like the common law in some cases, directs itself against that dangerous probability as well as against the completed result.

The conduct challenged in attempt cases ranges across a broad spectrum of allegedly anticompetitive behavior; indeed, an attempt count often parallels and duplicates monopolization or restraint of trade charges in a complaint. In recent years, questions about the proper scope of the attempt to monopolize provision have been coming up frequently in the lower federal courts, particularly in private treble damage actions, and there is a good deal of confusion as to what the law is and what it ought to be. To some extent, the debate reflects the pros and cons of filling a gap in antitrust coverage. We have already seen that violations of Section 1 require more than one party. Violations of the monopolization provision of Section 2 can be charged against single-firm conduct, but the firm must be found to have monopoly power in a properly defined relevant market. However, anticompetitive market behavior—that is, conduct that has severe anticompetitive consequences and no significant economic or social redeeming virtues—can be engaged in by single firms with relatively little market power.

In part, the debate over what sort of intent, conduct, or dangerous probability needs to be proved concerns the issue of how important it is to fill the gap between Section 1 and the monopolization provisions of Section 2. In the *Spectrum Sports* case,[48] the Supreme Court made clear that proof of dangerous probability—*i.e.*, the "realistic probability that the defendants could achieve monopoly power" in a market—is a prerequisite to finding a violation in an attempt to monopolize case.

---

48. *See* p. 814 *infra.*

Lorain Journal Co. v. United States

Supreme Court of the United States, 1951.
342 U.S. 143, 72 S.Ct. 181, 96 L.Ed. 162.

■ BURTON, J. The principal question here is whether a newspaper publisher's conduct constituted an attempt to monopolize interstate commerce, justifying the injunction issued against it under §§ 2 and 4 of the Sherman Antitrust Act. For the reasons hereafter stated, we hold that the injunction was justified.

This is a civil action, instituted by the United States in the District Court for the Northern District of Ohio, against The Lorain Journal Company, an Ohio corporation, publishing, daily except Sunday, in the City of Lorain, Ohio, a newspaper here called the Journal.... The District Court declined to issue a temporary injunction but, after trial, found that the parties were engaging in an attempt to monopolize as charged. Confining itself to that issue, the court enjoined them from continuing the attempt. 92 F.Supp. 794....

The appellant corporation, here called the publisher, has published the Journal in the City of Lorain since before 1932. In that year it, with others, purchased the Times–Herald which was the only competing daily paper published in that city. Later, without success, it sought a license to establish and operate a radio broadcasting station in Lorain....

The court below describes the position of the Journal, since 1933, as "a commanding and an overpowering one. It has a daily circulation in Lorain of over 13,000 copies and it reaches ninety-nine per cent of the families in the city." 92 F.Supp. at 796. Lorain is an industrial city on Lake Erie with a population of about 52,000 occupying 11,325 dwelling units. The Sunday News, appearing only on Sundays, is the only other newspaper published there....

From 1933 to 1948 the publisher enjoyed a substantial monopoly in Lorain of the mass dissemination of news and advertising, both of a local and national character. However, in 1948 the Elyria–Lorain Broadcasting Company, a corporation independent of the publisher, was licensed by the Federal Communications Commission to establish and operate in Elyria, Ohio, eight miles south of Lorain, a radio station whose call letters, WEOL, stand for Elyria, Oberlin and Lorain. Since then it has operated its principal studio in Elyria and a branch studio in Lorain. Lorain has about twice the population as Elyria and is by far the largest community in the station's immediate area. Oberlin is much smaller than Elyria and eight miles south of it....

The court below found that appellants knew that a substantial number of Journal advertisers wished to use the facilities of the radio station as well. For some of them it found that advertising in the Journal was essential for the promotion of their sales in Lorain County. It found that at all times since WEOL commenced broadcasting, appellants had executed a plan conceived to eliminate the threat of competition from the station. Under this plan the publisher refused to accept local advertisements in the

Journal from any Lorain County advertiser who advertised or who appellants believed to be about to advertise over WEOL. The court found expressly that the purpose and intent of this procedure was to destroy the broadcasting company.

The court characterized all this as "bold, relentless, and predatory commercial behavior." 92 F.Supp. at 796. To carry out appellants' plan, the publisher monitored WEOL programs to determine the identity of the station's local Lorain advertisers. Those using the station's facilities had their contracts with the publisher terminated and were able to renew them only after ceasing to advertise through WEOL. The program was effective. Numerous Lorain County merchants testified that as a result of the publisher's policy, they either ceased or abandoned their plans to advertise over WEOL. . . .

1.   *The conduct complained of was an attempt to monopolize interstate commerce.* It consisted of the publisher's practice of refusing to accept local Lorain advertising from parties using WEOL for local advertising. Because of the Journal's complete daily newspaper monopoly of local advertising in Lorain and its practically indispensable coverage of 99% of the Lorain families, this practice forced numerous advertisers to refrain from using WEOL for local advertising. That result not only reduced the number of customers available to WEOL in the field of local Lorain advertising and strengthened the Journal's monopoly in that field, but more significantly tended to destroy and eliminate WEOL altogether. Attainment of that sought-for elimination would automatically restore to the publisher of the Journal its substantial monopoly in Lorain of the mass dissemination of all news and advertising, interstate and national, as well as local. It would deprive not merely Lorain but Elyria and all surrounding communities of their only nearby radio station. . . .

2.   *The publisher's attempt to regain its monopoly of interstate commerce by forcing advertisers to boycott a competing radio station violated § 2.* The findings and opinion of the trial court describe the conduct of the publisher upon which the Government relies. The surrounding circumstances are important. The most illuminating of these is the substantial monopoly which was enjoyed in Lorain by the publisher from 1933 to 1948, together with a 99% coverage of Lorain families. Those factors made the Journal an indispensable medium of advertising for many Lorain concerns. Accordingly, its publisher's refusals to print Lorain advertising for those using WEOL for like advertising often amounted to an effective prohibition of the use of WEOL for that purpose. Numerous Lorain advertisers wished to supplement their local newspaper advertising with local radio advertising but could not afford to discontinue their newspaper advertising in order to use the radio.

WEOL's greatest potential source of income was local Lorain advertising. Loss of that was a major threat to its existence. The court below found unequivocally that appellants' conduct amounted to an attempt by the publisher to destroy WEOL and, at the same time, to regain the publisher's pre–1948 substantial monopoly over the mass dissemination of all news and advertising. . . .

Assuming the interstate character of the commerce involved, it seems clear that if all the newspapers in a city, in order to monopolize the dissemination of news and advertising by eliminating a competing radio station, conspired to accept no advertisements from anyone who advertised over that station, they would violate §§ 1 and 2 of the Sherman Act. It is consistent with that result to hold here that a single newspaper, already enjoying a substantial monopoly in its area, violates the "attempt to monopolize" clause of § 2 when it uses its monopoly to destroy threatened competition.[49]

The publisher claims a right as a private business concern to select its customers and to refuse to accept advertisements from whomever it pleases. We do not dispute that general right. "But the word 'right' is one of the most deceptive of pitfalls; it is so easy to slip from a qualified meaning in the premise to an unqualified one in the conclusion. Most rights are qualified." American Bank & Trust Co. v. Federal Reserve Bank, 256 U.S. 350, 358. The right claimed by the publisher is neither absolute nor exempt from regulation. Its exercise of a purposeful means of monopolizing interstate commerce is prohibited by the Sherman Act. The operator of the radio station, equally with the publisher of the newspaper, is entitled to the protection of that Act. "*In the absence of any purpose to create or maintain a monopoly,* the act does not restrict the long recognized right of trader or manufacturer engaged in an entirely private business, freely to exercise his own independent discretion as to parties with whom he will deal." (Emphasis supplied.) United States v. Colgate & Co., 250 U.S. 300, 307.

Affirmed.[50]

NOTES AND QUESTIONS

1. Federal Trade Commission v. Raymond Bros.–Clark Co., 263 U.S. 565 (1924). Raymond was a grocery wholesaler who purchased from Snider at the wholesale price. Basket Stores was a wholesaler competitor of Raymond (doing about 10% of its business this way) who also operated a chain of retail stores.

---

49. Appellants have sought to justify their conduct on the ground that it was part of the publisher's program for the protection of the Lorain market from outside competition. The publisher claimed to have refused advertising from Elyria or other out-of-town advertisers for the reason that such advertisers might compete with Lorain concerns. The publisher then classified WEOL as the publisher's own competitor from Elyria and asked its Lorain advertisers to refuse to employ WEOL as an advertising medium in competition with the Journal. We find no principle of law which required Lorain advertisers thus to boycott an Elyria advertising medium merely because the publisher of a Lorain advertising medium had chosen to boycott some Elyria advertisers who might compete for business in the Lorain market. Nor do we find any principle of law which permitted this publisher to dictate to prospective advertisers that they might advertise either by newspaper or by radio but that they might not use both facilities.

50. Clark and Minton, JJ., did not participate.

Raymond protested "against the sale direct to Basket Stores" by Snider and asked "for the allowance of a jobber's profit on such sale." When Snider refused to raise prices to Basket Stores or to grant a jobber's profit to Raymond, Raymond discontinued purchases. The FTC found that Raymond had engaged in an unfair method of competition and ordered it to cease attempting to influence selection of customers or direct dealing between manufacturers and purchasers of groceries.

The Supreme Court reversed, noting that Raymond had acted unilaterally. In threatening to withdraw and then withdrawing its trade from Snider, Raymond was exercising its lawful right to deal with whomever it chose—leaving it to the manufacturer to decide which customer it desired to retain. How would you distinguish *Raymond Bros.–Clark* from *Lorain Journal?* Are you helped by the Supreme Court's observation that Raymond did not have monopoly power?

2.   A.H. Cox & Co. v. Star Machinery Co., 653 F.2d 1302 (9th Cir. 1981). Plaintiff Cox had been the sole distributor of heavy equipment, including truck mounted hydraulic cranes, for R.O. Products, Inc., one of four domestic manufacturers of the product line. Star succeeded in persuading R.O. Products to allow Star to carry its line exclusively instead of Cox; as a result, Cox was driven into bankruptcy and sued, charging a concerted refusal to deal in violation of Section 1 and an attempt to monopolize in violation of Section 2 of the Sherman Act.

The Ninth Circuit affirmed summary judgment against Cox. As to the alleged concerted refusal to deal, it noted that there was no horizontality at the manufacturer level since R.O. Products, in deciding to switch from Cox to Star, engaged in no concerted action with the other manufacturers. As to the attempt charge, the Court found no anticompetitive intent or effect since the result of the behavior challenged by Cox was simply to replace one distributor with another in marketing a particular manufacturer's line of products.

> Where each distributor has only one line, it is particularly appropriate to recognize the right of a distributor to initiate changes; otherwise, a weak distributor could continue ineffective promotion of a good brand, while a strong distributor could be forced to continue representing a manufacturer with whom it has poor relations. 653 F.2d at 1307.

3.   Discussion of attempt to monopolize in the *Microsoft* case is found at p. 784 *supra*.

Spectrum Sports, Inc. v. McQuillan

Supreme Court of the United States, 1993.
506 U.S. 447, 113 S.Ct. 884, 122 L.Ed.2d 247.

■ WHITE, J. Section 2 of the Sherman Act makes it an offense for any person to "monopolize, or attempt to monopolize, or combine or conspire with any other person or persons, to monopolize any part of the trade or commerce among the several States." The jury in this case returned a verdict finding that petitioners had monopolized, attempted to monopolize, and/or conspired to monopolize. The District Court entered a judgment ruling that petitioners had violated § 2, and the Court of Appeals affirmed on the ground that petitioners had attempted to monopolize. The issue we have before us is whether the District Court and the Court of Appeals correctly defined the elements of that offense.

I

Sorbothane is a patented elastic polymer whose shock-absorbing characteristics make it useful in a variety of medical, athletic, and equestrian products. BTR, Inc. (BTR), owns the patent rights to sorbothane, and its wholly owned subsidiaries manufacture the product in the United States and Britain. Hamilton–Kent Manufacturing Company (Hamilton–Kent) and Sorbothane, Inc. (S. I.) were at all relevant times owned by BTR. S. I. was formed in 1982 to take over Hamilton–Kent's sorbothane business. Respondents Shirley and Larry McQuillan, doing business as Sorboturf Enterprises, were regional distributors of sorbothane products from 1981 to 1983. Petitioner Spectrum Sports, Inc. (Spectrum), was also a distributor of sorbothane products. Petitioner Kenneth B. Leighton, Jr., is a co-owner of Spectrum. Kenneth Leighton, Jr., is the son of Kenneth Leighton, Sr., the president of Hamilton–Kent and S. I. at all relevant times.

In 1980, respondents Shirley and Larry McQuillan signed a letter of intent with Hamilton–Kent, which then owned all manufacturing and distribution rights to sorbothane. The letter of intent granted the McQuillans exclusive rights to purchase sorbothane for use in equestrian products. Respondents were designing a horseshoe pad using sorbothane.

In 1981, Hamilton–Kent decided to establish five regional distributorships for sorbothane. Respondents were selected to be distributors of all sorbothane products, including medical products and shoe inserts, in the Southwest. Spectrum was selected as distributor for another region.

In January 1982, Hamilton–Kent shifted responsibility for selling medical products from five regional distributors to a single national distributor. In April 1982, Hamilton–Kent told respondents that it wanted them to relinquish their athletic shoe distributorship as a condition for retaining the right to develop and distribute equestrian products. As of May 1982, BTR had moved the sorbothane business from Hamilton–Kent to S. I. In May, the marketing manager of S. I. again made clear that respondents had to sell their athletic distributorship to keep their equestrian distribution rights. At a meeting scheduled to discuss the sale of respondents' athletic distributorship to petitioner Leighton, Jr., Leighton, Jr., informed Shirley McQuillan that if she did not come to agreement with him she would be " 'looking for work.' " Respondents refused to sell and continued to distribute athletic shoe inserts.

In the fall of 1982, Leighton, Sr., informed respondents that another concern had been appointed as the national equestrian distributor, and that they were "no longer involved in equestrian products." In January 1983, S. I. began marketing through a national distributor a sorbothane horseshoe pad allegedly indistinguishable from the one designed by respondents. In August 1983, S. I. informed respondents that it would no longer accept their orders. Spectrum thereupon became national distributor of sorbothane athletic shoe inserts. Respondents sought to obtain sorbothane from the BTR's British subsidiary, but were informed by that subsidiary that it would not sell sorbothane in the United States. Respondents' business failed. . . .

The case was tried to a jury, which returned a verdict against one or more of the defendants on each of the 11 alleged violations on which it was to return a verdict. All of the defendants were found to have violated § 2 by, in the words of the verdict sheet, "monopolizing, attempting to monopolize, and/or conspiring to monopolize." Petitioners were also found to have violated civil RICO and the California unfair practices law, but not § 1 of the Sherman Act. The jury awarded $1,743,000 in compensatory damages on each of the violations found to have occurred. This amount was trebled under § 4 of the Clayton Act. The District Court also awarded nearly $1 million in attorneys' fees and denied motions for judgment notwithstanding the verdict and for a new trial.

The Court of Appeals for the Ninth Circuit affirmed the judgment in an unpublished opinion.... The court went on to conclude that a case of attempted monopolization had been established. The court rejected petitioners' argument that attempted monopolization had not been established because respondents had failed to prove that petitioners had a specific intent to monopolize a relevant market. The court also held that in order to show that respondents' attempt to monopolize was likely to succeed it was not necessary to present evidence of the relevant market or of the defendants' market power. In so doing, the Ninth Circuit relied on Lessig v. Tidewater Oil Co., 327 F.2d 459 (CA9), cert. denied, 377 U.S. 993 (1964), and its progeny. The Court of Appeals noted that these cases, in dealing with attempt to monopolize claims, had ruled that "if evidence of unfair or predatory conduct is presented, it may satisfy both the specific intent and dangerous probability elements of the offense, without any proof of relevant market or the defendant's marketpower [*sic*]." If, however, there is insufficient evidence of unfair or predatory conduct, there must be a showing of "relevant market or the defendant's marketpower [*sic*]." The court went on to find:

> "There is sufficient evidence from which the jury could conclude that the S. I. Group and Spectrum Group engaged in unfair or predatory conduct and thus inferred that they had the specific intent and the dangerous probability of success and, therefore, McQuillan did not have to prove relevant market or the defendant's marketing power."

The decision below, and the *Lessig* line of decisions on which it relies, conflicts with holdings of courts in other Circuits. Every other Court of Appeals has indicated that proving an attempt to monopolize requires proof of a dangerous probability of monopolization of a relevant market. We granted certiorari to resolve this conflict among the Circuits. We reverse.

II

While § 1 of the Sherman Act forbids contracts or conspiracies in restraint of trade or commerce, § 2 addresses the actions of single firms that monopolize or attempt to monopolize, as well as conspiracies and combinations to monopolize. Section 2 does not define the elements of the offense of attempted monopolization. Nor is there much guidance to be had in the scant legislative history of that provision, which was added late in the legislative process. . . .

This Court first addressed the meaning of attempt to monopolize under § 2 in Swift & Co. v. United States, 196 U.S. 375 (1905). . . . The Court went on to explain . . . that not every act done with intent to produce an unlawful result constitutes an attempt. "It is a question of proximity and degree." *Swift* thus indicated that intent is necessary, but alone is not sufficient, to establish the dangerous probability of success that is the object of § 2's prohibition of attempts.

The Court's decisions since *Swift* have reflected the view that the plaintiff charging attempted monopolization must prove a dangerous probability of actual monopolization, which has generally required a definition of the relevant market and examination of market power. In Walker Process Equipment, Inc. v. Food Machinery & Chemical Corp., 382 U.S. 172, 177 (1965), we found that enforcement of a fraudulently obtained patent claim could violate the Sherman Act. We stated that, to establish monopolization or attempt to monopolize under § 2 of the Sherman Act, it would be necessary to appraise the exclusionary power of the illegal patent claim in terms of the relevant market for the product involved. The reason was that "without a definition of that market there is no way to measure [the defendant's] ability to lessen or destroy competition." *Ibid.*

Similarly, this Court reaffirmed in Copperweld Corp. v. Independence Tube Corp., 467 U.S. 752 (1984), that "Congress authorized Sherman Act scrutiny of single firms only when they pose a danger of monopolization. Judging unilateral conduct in this manner reduces the risk that the antitrust laws will dampen the competitive zeal of a single aggressive entrepreneur." Thus, the conduct of a single firm, governed by § 2, "is unlawful only when it threatens actual monopolization." *Id.,* at 767. See also Lorain Journal Co. v. United States. . . .

The Courts of Appeals other than the Ninth Circuit have followed this approach. Consistent with our cases, it is generally required that to demonstrate attempted monopolization a plaintiff must prove (1) that the defendant has engaged in predatory or anticompetitive conduct with (2) a specific intent to monopolize and (3) a dangerous probability of achieving monopoly power. In order to determine whether there is a dangerous probability of monopolization, courts have found it necessary to consider the relevant market and the defendant's ability to lessen or destroy competition in that market.

Notwithstanding the array of authority contrary to *Lessig,* the Court of Appeals in this case reaffirmed its prior holdings; indeed, it did not mention either this Court's decisions discussed above or the many decisions of other Courts of Appeals reaching contrary results. Respondents urge us to affirm the decision below. We are not at all inclined, however, to embrace *Lessig's* interpretation of § 2, for there is little if any support for it in the statute or the case law, and the notion that proof of unfair or predatory conduct alone is sufficient to make out the offense of attempted monopolization is contrary to the purpose and policy of the Sherman Act.

The *Lessig* opinion claimed support from the language of § 2, which prohibits attempts to monopolize "any part" of commerce, and therefore forbids attempts to monopolize any appreciable segment of interstate sales of the relevant product. The "any part" clause, however, applies to charges of monopolization as well as to attempts to monopolize, and it is beyond doubt that the former requires proof of market power in a relevant market.

In support of its determination that an inference of dangerous probability was permissible from a showing of intent, the *Lessig* opinion cited, and added emphasis to, this Court's reference in its opinion in *Swift* to "intent and the *consequent* dangerous probability." But any question whether dangerous probability of success requires proof of more than intent alone should have been removed by the subsequent passage in *Swift* which stated that "not every act that may be done with an intent to produce an unlawful result ... constitutes an attempt. It is a question of proximity and degree...."

It is also our view that *Lessig* and later Ninth Circuit decisions refining and applying it are inconsistent with the policy of the Sherman Act. The purpose of the Act is not to protect businesses from the working of the market; it is to protect the public from the failure of the market. The law directs itself not against conduct which is competitive, even severely so, but against conduct which unfairly tends to destroy competition itself. It does so not out of solicitude for private concerns but out of concern for the public interest. Thus, this Court and other courts have been careful to avoid constructions of § 2 which might chill competition, rather than foster it. It is sometimes difficult to distinguish robust competition from conduct with long-term anticompetitive effects; moreover, single-firm activity is unlike concerted activity covered by § 1, which "inherently is fraught with anticompetitive risk." *Copperweld,* 467 U.S., at 767–769. For these reasons, § 2 makes the conduct of a single firm unlawful only when it actually monopolizes or dangerously threatens to do so. The concern that § 2 might be applied so as to further anticompetitive ends is plainly not met by inquiring only whether the defendant has engaged in "unfair" or "predatory" tactics. Such conduct may be sufficient to prove the necessary intent to monopolize, which is something more than an intent to compete vigorously, but demonstrating the dangerous probability of monopolization in an attempt case also requires inquiry into the relevant product and geographic market and the defendant's economic power in that market.

We hold that petitioners may not be liable for attempted monopolization under § 2 of the Sherman Act absent proof of a dangerous probability that they would monopolize a particular market and specific intent to monopolize. In this case, the trial instructions allowed the jury to infer specific intent and dangerous probability of success from the defendants' predatory conduct, without any proof of the relevant market or of a realistic probability that the defendants could achieve monopoly power in that market. In this respect, the instructions misconstrued § 2, as did the

Court of Appeals in affirming the judgment of the District Court. Since the affirmance of the § 2 judgment against petitioners rested solely on the legally erroneous conclusion that petitioners had attempted to monopolize in violation of § 2 and since the jury's verdict did not negate the possibility that the § 2 verdict rested on the attempt to monopolize ground alone, the judgment of the Court of Appeals is reversed, and the case is remanded for further proceedings consistent with this opinion.

NOTES AND QUESTIONS

1.   Does the Supreme Court in *Spectrum Sports* give any indication as to how much market power is required for there to be a dangerous probability of successful monopolization? After *Spectrum Sports,* what is the difference between monopolization and attempted monopolization?

2.   After *Spectrum Sports,* may the Ninth Circuit still use "unfair or predatory conduct" as a factor in proving dangerous probability of success, as long as some evidence of the defendant's market power is also considered?

3.   United States v. Empire Gas Corp., 537 F.2d 296 (8th Cir.1976), cert. denied, 429 U.S. 1122 (1977). Empire was a large wholesaler and retailer of liquified petroleum (LP), a generic term for gas fuels such as propane and butane sold to consumers for heating and cooking. Empire operated in twenty-four states, but the competitive behavior challenged by the government largely had occurred in connection with retail sales of LP in areas surrounding Lebanon and Wheaton, Missouri.

On several occasions, Empire had invited competitors to raise retail prices to higher levels, equal to prices charged by an Empire subsidiary. If the competitor refused, Empire threatened to price the company out of business; if it still refused, Empire began selling gas in the rival's territory at drastically lowered prices. Salesmen solicitors of Empire told customers that the rival company was going out of business. In these price wars, Empire occasionally acquired the source of supply of gas of a competitor, and then raised the price at which it sold LP at wholesale so that the competitor could not retail the product at a price equal to Empire and still make a profit. In one such competitive episode, Empire also limited the credit of a retailer competitor to two loads of gas and then failed to mail invoices to the competitor. As a result, the competitor could not pay previous bills and on that pretense, Empire refused to sell needed supplies. In at least one instance in the record, a coerced competitor of Empire capitulated to its pressure and a compromise was worked out whereby Empire and the competitor sold at retail at a uniform higher price.

The Court of Appeals recited the familiar rule with respect to attempts to monopolize: proof is required of "specific intent" and "dangerous probability of success." The Court further found that Empire's price cuts and threats to price cut established a specific intent to monopolize. On the second element, the Court accepted plaintiff's contentions that the product market was LP gas, and that the geographic markets were Lebanon and Wheaton, Missouri, where the Court assumed (despite doubt about the government's proof) that Empire had 50 percent and 47 percent respectively, and some 11 other local marketing areas. The Eighth Circuit found no attempt to monopolize in Lebanon and Wheaton because in those areas there was no evidence that competitors of Empire raised or fixed prices because of Empire's threats or pricing actions. Presumably in other market areas where Empire's conduct had an effect on its competitors, Empire's market share was too small, and thus the company was too remote from monopoly power, to indicate any dangerous probability of achieving monopoly power. Finally, the Eighth Circuit found that the prices of LP gas in market areas spotlighted by the government were only slightly higher than in other areas, and in any event, the reasons for the difference were a matter of speculation, and that Empire's profits, averaging 11.1 percent from 1963 to 1973, were not so high as to require a conclusion that Empire was successful in controlling prices or competition in the relevant market areas. Accordingly, the Court of Appeals affirmed the district court's decision in favor of Empire. Was *Empire Gas* correctly decided?

4. In International Distribution Centers, Inc. v. Walsh Trucking Co., Inc., 812 F.2d 786, 791–93 (2d Cir.), cert. denied, 482 U.S. 915 (1987), the Second Circuit rejected removal of the "dangerous probability" element and provided the following reasoning:

> Eliminating the dangerous probability element from attempted monopolization would have the effect of extending the coverage of section 2 of the Sherman Act to similar behavior already covered by state and federal law. The Federal Trade Commission Act § 5, regulatory statutes and state business tort law all reach anticompetitive behavior by firms that lack market power. Civil RICO may have also expanded into this area.... There is no unmet need calling for judicial expansion of section 2 to reach similar behavior.

> Furthermore, any significant reduction in the antitrust plaintiff's burden of proving that the defendant has a dangerous probability of monopolizing the market might discourage the healthy competition that section 2 is intended to nurture and deter businesses from aggressively expanding into new markets. Existing firms that lost market share to a newcomer could seize upon some hiring or marketing tactic, label it "anticompetitive" and then recover treble damages and attorneys' fees. *See, e.g.*, Gerber Products Co. v. Beech–Nut Life Savers, 160 F.Supp. 916, 918 (S.D.N.Y.1958) (plaintiff with 73% share of relevant market for baby food sued defendant with 4.3% share for attempted monopolization, alleging that "puffing" of baby food in glass jars and price reduction to meet plaintiff's price were anticompetitive acts). Surely the potential liability from such a suit would cast a long shadow over business planning.

> We, therefore, adhere to the traditional rule that an action under section 2 of the Sherman Act for attempting to monopolize a market will lie only where there is anticompetitive conduct, a specific intent to monopolize *and* a dangerous probability that monopoly will be achieved. A dangerous probability of monopoly may exist where the defendant firm possesses a significant market share when it undertakes the challenged anticompetitive conduct.

> We note that market share analysis, while essential, is not necessarily determinative in the calculation of monopoly power under this standard. Other market characteristics must also be considered in determining whether a given firm has monopoly power or has a dangerous probability of acquiring monopoly power.... Among these characteristics are the strength of the competition, the probable development of the industry, the barriers to entry, the nature of the anticompetitive conduct and the elasticity of consumer demand....

Applying this standard, NRT was entitled to a judgment notwithstanding the verdict.... One year after entering the market, NRT had no more than a seventeen percent share of the carriage of garments on hangers in the Pennsylvania Corridor. Even if NRT drove IDC out of business and took over *all* of IDC's accounts, NRT would still have a market share of no more than fifty percent. It is unlikely that even with a fifty percent market share NRT could raise prices without losing business to the several other trucking firms that had been unaffected by NRT's employee raids or alleged predatory pricing. The evidence at trial indicated that NRT's 1983 tariffs were already above those of at least three of its other competitors in the Pennsylvania Corridor.

Assuming *arguendo* that NRT could have cannibalized IDC, appropriated *all* of its customers and obtained sufficient power to raise prices in the market temporarily, the competitors from outside the market could easily have surmounted any barriers to entry and competed with NRT for business in the Pennsylvania Corridor....

Under the conditions in the market for the carriage of garments on hangers in the Pennsylvania Corridor, therefore, NRT's market share was not sufficiently significant to give rise to a dangerous probability that it would monopolize the market even when its anticompetitive conduct is taken into account. A jury could not reasonably find that such a probability existed without engaging in speculation concerning matters not in evidence.

Thus, we conclude that IDC failed as a matter of law to establish that NRT, which had at most a seventeen percent market share one year after it entered an intensely competitive market with low entry barriers, had a dangerous probability of successfully monopolizing that market. Our conclusion is supported by the majority of cases with similar facts finding no dangerous probability of a monopoly. Lektro–Vend Corp. v. Vendo Co., 660 F.2d 255, 270–71 (7th Cir. 1981) (30% market share, no significant barriers to entry), cert. denied, 455 U.S. 921 (1982); Nifty Foods Corp. v. Great Atlantic & Pacific Tea Co., 614 F.2d 832, 841 (2d Cir. 1980) (33% market share, defendant's share continuously declining); Yoder Brothers, Inc. v. California–Florida Plant Corp., 537 F.2d 1347, 1368–69 (5th Cir.1976) (20% market share in highly competitive market with low barriers to entry), cert. denied, 429 U.S. 1094 (1977); Hiland Dairy, Inc. v. Kroger Co., 402 F.2d 968, 971–72, 974–75 (8th Cir.1968) (20% market share in highly competitive market)....

5. Could the legitimate concern with chilling aggressive competitive behavior be dealt with by some sort of sliding scale? Thus, in situations where conduct was particularly anticompetitive and lacking in redeeming virtues, a finding of less significant market power might suffice. Would such an approach be consistent with *Spectrum Sports*? A National Commission for Review of Antitrust Laws and Procedures recommended the following:

RECOMMENDATION 1: The "dangerous probability of success" necessary to establish an attempt to monopolize under Section 2 of the Sherman Act should not be interpreted as requiring proof of a high probability of actual monopoly, but rather a determination of whether the defendant has significantly threatened competition. Such determination should be based on the weighing of various factors including the defendant's intent, market power, and conduct.

National Commission, Report to the President and the Attorney General vii–viii (1979).

6. The conduct element in many attempt cases involves business torts of the sort traditionally covered by state law—for example, false advertising, tortious interference with contract relations, and misappropriation of trade secrets. Is that kind of conduct a serious threat to the competitive process, as opposed to the victim of the business tort? While such conduct often lacks business justification, would it often contribute significantly to the establishment of a monopoly position? Is it wise, as the Second Circuit suggests in *Walsh Trucking* (note 4 *supra*), to depend on state business tort law or civil RICO to remedy anticompetitive conduct? The best vehicle for dealing with predatory single-firm conduct (other than Section 2) may be Section 5 of the Federal Trade Commission Act, outlawing unfair methods of competition, since there is no criminal exposure or potential for private treble damage action. Or should the law simply leave the victim of this conduct to its common-law and other non-antitrust remedies? Would that unduly weaken deterrence?

PROBLEM 18

PASTA SUPREME TAKES ON A NEWCOMER

National Foods sells Pasta Supreme, the leading prepared spaghetti sauce in the United States, with 40% of annual sales. It distributes nationally along with its two principal competitors; they account for 12% and 10% of sales respectively, while the rest of the market consists of sales by a large number of regional manufacturers and private-label sales by large supermarket chains. There has been no new entry by companies selling on a national basis for many years.

About a year ago, Lunt–Dresson, an established packaged food producer with no previous presence in the spaghetti sauce market, introduced Prima Sauce, a thicker and spicier spaghetti sauce differentiated from existing products by additional and expensive processing. It announced plans to introduce its new product in several test markets (the New York metropolitan area, Syracuse, Buffalo, and Cincinnati–Dayton) with vigorous local advertising campaigns, low introductory prices, and special discounts to supermarkets. It also initiated market studies to see what kind of advertising was effective, and whether the product was perceived by consumers as different and better than existing spaghetti sauces.

Two months later, National Foods introduced Pasta Premium, a spaghetti sauce described on the label as "Extra Thick and Zesty," which also was different because of additional processing. It immediately introduced the product in six test markets (including the New York metropolitan area, Syracuse, and Cincinnati–Dayton). It offered special discounts to retailers in all test markets (though not so great as to drive the price below average variable cost) on condition that it was granted preferred shelf space in the stores.

Lunt–Dresson claimed that National Foods' business behavior amounted to an attempt to monopolize. It alleges that Pasta Premium was introduced "precipitously" before the product had been fully tested within the company. The name of the new product and the label design allegedly were meant to confuse people as to the source of this new kind of spaghetti sauce, and the special discounts were intended to deny Prima Sauce access to shelf space. Since supermarkets rarely carry more than two brands of spaghetti sauce, the aggressive sales in test markets by National Foods had two effects. It denied Prima Sauce access to markets and kept its sales volume low, and interfered with Lunt–Dresson's efforts to run a test program to determine whether the product and its marketing were effective. The choice by National Foods of test markets which largely duplicated the major test markets of Lunt–Dresson was cited as evidence of exclusionary intent.

Lunt–Dresson sued, charging an attempt to monopolize under Section 2, and National Foods moved to dismiss on grounds that the plaintiff had failed to state a cause of action. What result? Would the result be different if a memorandum were introduced in evidence in which a mid-level marketing executive for National Foods reported to a Vice President of the company that aggressive marketing of the new thick and zesty sauce had "stopped Lunt–Dresson in its tracks?" Would it make a difference if an important reason for the absence of large-scale entry was that successful national distribution required extensive advertising in national media?

SECTION 2.   PREDATORY PRICE CUTTING

Characterizing a price cut as predatory or nonpredatory in a particular case is often not easy. The same observable conduct—reducing the price of a product to consumers—may be either a necessary and desirable response to competitive forces or undesirable conduct which injures competition. Furthermore, "intent" is an uncertain indicator in these cases since the price cut is motivated in all instances by the same immediate objective— winning sales from competitors and occupying a larger share of the market—even though this may make it unprofitable for one or more competitors to remain in the market. Finding workable criteria to identify predatory pricing and other forms of predatory conduct thus becomes critical.

Brooke Group v. Brown & Williamson Tobacco

Liggett

Supreme Court of the United States, 1993.
509 U.S. 209, 113 S.Ct. 2578, 125 L.Ed.2d 168.

■ KENNEDY, J. This case stems from a market struggle that erupted in the domestic cigarette industry in the mid–1980s. Petitioner Brooke Group, Inc., whom we, like the parties to the case, refer to as Liggett because of its former corporate name, charges that to counter its innovative development of generic cigarettes, respondent Brown & Williamson Tobacco Corporation introduced its own line of generic cigarettes in an unlawful effort to stifle price competition in the economy segment of the national cigarette market. Liggett contends that Brown & Williamson cut prices on generic cigarettes below cost and offered discriminatory volume rebates to wholesalers to force Liggett to raise its own generic cigarette prices and introduce oligopoly pricing in the economy segment. We hold that Brown & Williamson is entitled to judgment as a matter of law.

I

In 1980, Liggett pioneered the development of the economy segment of the national cigarette market by introducing a line of "black and white" generic cigarettes. The economy segment of the market, sometimes called the generic segment, is characterized by its bargain prices and comprises a variety of different products: black and whites, which are true generics sold in plain white packages with simple black lettering describing their contents; private label generics, which carry the trade dress of a specific purchaser, usually a retail chain; branded generics, which carry a brand name but which, like black and whites and private label generics, are sold at a deep discount and with little or no advertising; and "Value–25s," packages of 25 cigarettes that are sold to the consumer some 12.5% below the cost of a normal 20–cigarette pack. By 1984, when Brown & Williamson entered the generic segment and set in motion the series of events giving rise to this suit, Liggett's black and whites represented 97% of the generic segment, which in turn accounted for a little more than 4% of domestic cigarette sales. Prior to Liggett's introduction of black and whites in 1980, sales of generic cigarettes amounted to less than 1% of the domestic cigarette market.

Because of the procedural posture of this case, we view the evidence in the light most favorable to Liggett. The parties are in basic agreement, however, regarding the central, historical facts. Cigarette manufacturing has long been one of America's most concentrated industries, see F. Scherer & D. Ross, Industrial Market Structure and Economic Performance 250 (3d ed. 1990) (hereinafter Scherer & Ross), and for decades, production has been dominated by six firms: R.J. Reynolds, Philip Morris, American Brands, Lorillard, and the two litigants involved here, Liggett and Brown & Williamson. R.J. Reynolds and Philip Morris, the two industry leaders, enjoyed respective market shares of about 28% and 40% at the time of trial. Brown & Williamson ran a distant third, its market share never exceeding 12% at any time relevant to this dispute. Liggett's share of the market was even less, from a low of just over 2% in 1980 to a high of just over 5% in 1984.

The cigarette industry also has long been one of America's most profitable, in part because for many years there was no significant price competition among the rival firms. List prices for cigarettes increased in lock-step, twice a year, for a number of years, irrespective of the rate of inflation, changes in the costs of production, or shifts in consumer demand. Substantial evidence suggests that in recent decades, the industry reaped the benefits of prices above a competitive level, though not through unlawful conduct of the type that once characterized the industry. See Tennant, *supra*, at 275, 342; cf. American Tobacco Co. v. United States, 328 U.S. 781 (1946); United States v. American Tobacco Co., 221 U.S. 106 (1911); Scherer & Ross 451.

By 1980, however, broad market trends were working against the industry. Overall demand for cigarettes in the United States was declining, and no immediate prospect of recovery existed. As industry volume shrank, all firms developed substantial excess capacity. This decline in demand, coupled with the effects of nonprice competition, had a severe negative impact on Liggett. Once a major force in the industry, with market shares in excess of 20%, Liggett's market share had declined by 1980 to a little over 2%. With this meager share of the market, Liggett was on the verge of going out of business.

At the urging of a distributor, Liggett took an unusual step to revive its prospects: It developed a line of black and white generic cigarettes. When introduced in 1980, black and whites were offered to consumers at a list price roughly 30% lower than the list price of full-priced, branded cigarettes. They were also promoted at the wholesale level by means of rebates that increased with the volume of cigarettes ordered. Black and white cigarettes thus represented a new marketing category. The category's principal competitive characteristic was low price. Liggett's black and whites were an immediate and considerable success, growing from a fraction of a percent of the market at their introduction to over 4% of the total cigarette market by early 1984.

As the market for Liggett's generic cigarettes expanded, the other cigarette companies found themselves unable to ignore the economy segment. In general, the growth of generics came at the expense of the other firms' profitable sales of branded cigarettes. Brown & Williamson was hardest hit, because many of Brown & Williamson's brands were favored by consumers who were sensitive to changes in cigarette prices. Although Brown & Williamson sold only 11.4% of the market's branded cigarettes, 20% of the converts to Liggett's black and whites had switched from a Brown & Williamson brand. Losing volume and profits in its branded products, Brown & Williamson determined to enter the generic segment of the cigarette market. In July 1983, Brown & Williamson had begun selling Value–25s, and in the spring of 1984, it introduced its own black and white cigarette.

Brown & Williamson was neither the first nor the only cigarette company to recognize the threat posed by Liggett's black and whites and to respond in the economy segment. R.J. Reynolds had also introduced a Value–25 in 1983. And before Brown & Williamson introduced its own black and whites, R.J. Reynolds had repriced its "Doral" branded cigarette at generic levels. To compete with Liggett's black and whites, R.J. Reynolds dropped its list price on Doral about 30% and used volume rebates to wholesalers as an incentive to spur orders. Doral was the first competition at Liggett's price level.

Brown & Williamson's entry was an even graver threat to Liggett's dominance of the generic category. Unlike R.J. Reynolds' Doral, Brown & Williamson's product was also a black and white and so would be in direct competition with Liggett's product at the wholesale level and on the retail shelf. Because Liggett's and Brown & Williamson's black and whites were more or less fungible, wholesalers had little incentive to carry more than one line. And unlike R.J. Reynolds, Brown & Williamson not only matched Liggett's prices but beat them. At the retail level, the suggested list price of Brown & Williamson's black and whites was the same as Liggett's, but Brown & Williamson's volume discounts to wholesalers were larger. Brown & Williamson's rebate structure also encompassed a greater number of volume categories than Liggett's, with the highest categories carrying special rebates for orders of very substantial size. Brown & Williamson marketed its black and whites to Liggett's existing distributors as well as to its own full list of buyers, which included a thousand wholesalers who had not yet carried any generic products.

Liggett responded to Brown & Williamson's introduction of black and whites in two ways. First, Liggett increased its own wholesale rebates. This precipitated a price war at the wholesale level, in which Liggett five times attempted to beat the rebates offered by Brown & Williamson. At the end of each round, Brown & Williamson maintained a real advantage over Liggett's prices. Although it is undisputed that Brown & Williamson's original net price for its black and whites was above its costs, Liggett contends that by the end of the rebate war, Brown & Williamson was selling its black and whites at a loss. This rebate war occurred before Brown & Williamson had sold a single black and white cigarette.

Liggett's second response was to file a lawsuit.... These claims were either dismissed on summary judgment or rejected by the jury. They were not appealed.

Liggett also amended its complaint to add a second Robinson–Patman Act claim, which is the subject of the present controversy. Liggett alleged that Brown & Williamson's volume rebates to wholesalers amounted to price discrimination that had a reasonable possibility of injuring competition, in violation of § 2(a) [of the Robinson–Patman Act]. Liggett claimed that Brown & Williamson's discriminatory volume rebates were integral to a scheme of predatory pricing, in which Brown & Williamson reduced its net prices for generic cigarettes below average variable costs. According to Liggett, these below-cost prices were not promotional but were intended to pressure it to raise its list prices on generic cigarettes, so that the percentage price difference between generic and branded cigarettes would narrow. Liggett explained that it would have been unable to reduce its wholesale rebates without losing substantial market share to Brown & Williamson; its only choice, if it wished to avoid prolonged losses on its principal product line, was to raise retail prices. The resulting reduction in the list price gap, it was said, would restrain the growth of the economy segment and preserve Brown & Williamson's supracompetitive profits on its branded cigarettes.

The trial began in the fall of 1989. By that time, all six cigarette companies had entered the economy segment. The economy segment was the fastest growing segment of the cigarette market, having increased from about 4% of the market in 1984, when the rebate war in generics began, to about 15% in 1989. Black and white generics had declined as a force in the economy segment as consumer interest shifted toward branded generics, but Liggett's overall volume had increased steadily to 9 billion generic cigarettes sold. Overall, the 2.8 billion generic cigarettes sold in 1981 had become 80 billion by 1989.

The consumer price of generics had increased along with output. For a year, the list prices for generic cigarettes established at the end of the rebate war remained stable. But in June of 1985, Liggett raised its list price, and the other firms followed several months later. The precise effect of the list price increase is difficult to assess, because all of the cigarette firms offered a variety of discounts, coupons, and other promotions directly to consumers on both generic and branded cigarettes. Nonetheless, at least some portion of the list price increase was reflected in a higher net price to the consumer.

In December 1985, Brown & Williamson attempted to increase its list prices, but retracted the announced increase when the other firms adhered to their existing prices. Thus, after Liggett's June 1985 increase, list prices on generics did not change again until the summer of 1986, when a pattern of twice yearly increases in tandem with the full-priced branded cigarettes was established. The dollar amount of these increases was the same for generic and full-priced cigarettes, which resulted in a greater percentage price increase in the less expensive generic cigarettes and a narrowing of the percentage gap between the list price of branded and black and white cigarettes, from approximately 38% at the time Brown & Williamson entered the segment, to approximately 27% at the time of trial. Also by the time of trial, five of the six manufacturers, including Liggett, had introduced so-called "subgenerics," a category of branded generic cigarette that sold at a discount of 50% or more off the list price of full-priced branded cigarettes.

After a 115–day trial involving almost 3,000 exhibits and over a score of witnesses, the jury returned a verdict in favor of Liggett, finding on the special verdict form that Brown & Williamson had engaged in price discrimination that had a reasonable possibility of injuring competition in the domestic cigarette market as a whole. The jury awarded Liggett $49.6 million in damages, which the District Court trebled to $148.8 million. After reviewing the record, however, the District Court held that Brown & Williamson was entitled to judgment as a matter of law on three separate grounds: lack of injury to competition, lack of antitrust injury to Liggett, and lack of a causal link between the discriminatory rebates and Liggett's alleged injury. Liggett Group, Inc. v. Brown & Williamson Tobacco Corp., 748 F.Supp. 344 (M.D.N.C.1990). With respect to the first issue, which is the only one before us, the District Court found that no slowing of the growth rate of generics, and thus no injury to competition, was possible unless there had been tacit coordination of prices in the economy segment of the cigarette market by the various manufacturers. The District Court held that a reasonable jury could come to but one conclusion about the existence of such coordination among the firms contending for shares of the economy segment: it did not exist, and Brown & Williamson therefore had no reasonable possibility of limiting the growth of the segment.

The United States Court of Appeals for the Fourth Circuit affirmed. Liggett Group, Inc. v. Brown & Williamson Tobacco Corp., 964 F.2d 335 (1992). The Court of Appeals held that the dynamic of conscious parallelism among oligopolists could not produce competitive injury in a predatory pricing setting, which necessarily involves a price cut by one of the oligopolists. In the Court of Appeals' view, "[t]o rely on the characteristics of an oligopoly to assure recoupment of losses from a predatory pricing scheme after one oligopolist has made a competitive move is ... economically irrational."

II

A

Price discrimination is made unlawful by § 2(a) of the Clayton Act, as amended by the Robinson–Patman Act....

Although we have reiterated that " 'a price discrimination within the meaning of [this] provision is merely a price difference,' " Texaco Inc. v. Hasbrouck, 496 U.S. 543, 558 (1990) (quoting FTC v. Anheuser–Busch, Inc., 363 U.S. 536, 549 (1960)), the statute as a practical matter could not, and does not, ban all price differences charged to "different purchasers of commodities of like grade and quality." Instead, the statute contains a number of important limitations, one of which is central to evaluating Liggett's claim: By its terms, the Robinson–Patman Act condemns price discrimination only to the extent that it threatens to injure competition. The availability of statutory defenses permitting price discrimination when it is based on differences in costs, § 13(a), "changing conditions affecting the market for or the marketability of the goods concerned," *ibid.,* or conduct undertaken "in good faith to meet an equally low price of a competitor," § 13(b); Standard Oil Co. v. FTC, 340 U.S. 231, 250 (1951), confirms that Congress did not intend to outlaw price differences that result from or further the forces of competition. Thus, "the Robinson–Patman Act should be construed consistently with broader policies of the antitrust laws." Great Atlantic & Pacific Tea Co., Inc. v. FTC, 440 U.S. 69, 80, n. 13 (1979).

Liggett contends that Brown & Williamson's discriminatory volume rebates to wholesalers threatened substantial competitive injury by furthering a predatory pricing scheme designed to purge competition from the economy segment of the cigarette market. This type of injury, which harms direct competitors of the discriminating seller, is known as primary-line injury. See FTC v. Anheuser–Busch, Inc., *supra*, at 538. We last addressed primary line injury over 25 years ago, in Utah Pie Co. v. Continental Baking Co., 386 U.S. 685 (1967). In *Utah Pie,* we reviewed the sufficiency of the evidence supporting jury verdicts against three national pie companies that had engaged in a variety of predatory practices in the market for frozen pies in Salt Lake City, with the intent to drive a local pie manufacturer out of business. We reversed the Court of Appeals and held that the evidence presented was adequate to permit a jury to find a likelihood of injury to competition.

Utah Pie has often been interpreted to permit liability for primary-line price discrimination on a mere showing that the defendant intended to harm competition or produced a declining price structure. The case has been criticized on the grounds that such low standards of competitive injury are at odds with the antitrust laws' traditional concern for consumer welfare and price competition.... We do not regard the *Utah Pie* case itself as having the full significance attributed to it by its detractors. *Utah Pie* was an early judicial inquiry in this area and did not purport to set forth explicit, general standards for establishing a violation of the Robinson–Patman Act. As the law has been explored since *Utah Pie,* it has become evident that primary-line competitive injury under the Robinson–Patman Act is of the same general character as the injury inflicted by predatory pricing schemes actionable under § 2 of the Sherman Act.... There are, to be sure, differences between the two statutes. For example, we interpret § 2 of the Sherman Act to condemn predatory pricing when it poses "a dangerous probability of actual monopolization," Spectrum Sports, Inc. v. McQuillan, 506 U.S. 447, 455 (1993), whereas the Robinson–Patman Act requires only that there be "a reasonable possibility" of substantial injury to competition before its protections are triggered. Falls City Industries, Inc. v. Vanco Beverage, Inc., 460 U.S. 428, 434 (1983). But whatever additional flexibility the Robinson–Patman Act standard may imply, the essence of the claim under either statute is the same: A business rival has priced its products in an unfair manner with an object to eliminate or retard competition and thereby gain and exercise control over prices in the relevant market.

Accordingly, whether the claim alleges predatory pricing under § 2 of the Sherman Act or primary-line price discrimination under the Robinson–Patman Act, the two prerequisites to recovery remain the same. First, a plaintiff seeking to establish competitive injury resulting from a rival's low prices must prove that the prices complained of are below an appropriate measure of its rival's costs.[51] See, *e.g., Cargill, Inc. v. Monfort of Colorado, Inc.,* 479 U.S. 104, 117 (1986); Matsushita Electric Industrial Co. v. Zenith Radio Corp., 475 U.S. 574, 585, n. 8 (1986); Utah Pie, 386 U.S., at 698, 701, 702–703, n. 14. Although *Cargill* and *Matsushita* reserved as a formal matter the question " 'whether recovery should *ever* be available ... when the pricing in question is above some measure of incremental cost,' " the reasoning in both opinions suggests that only below-cost prices should suffice, and we have rejected elsewhere the notion that above-cost prices that are below general market levels or the costs of a firm's competitors inflict injury to competition cognizable under the antitrust laws. See Atlantic Richfield Co. v. USA Petroleum Co., 495 U.S. 328, 340 (1990). "Low prices benefit consumers regardless of how those prices are set, and so long as they are above predatory levels, they do not threaten competition.... We have adhered to this principle regardless of the type of antitrust claim involved." As a general rule, the exclusionary effect of prices above a relevant measure of cost either reflects the lower cost structure of the alleged predator, and so represents competition on the merits, or is beyond the practical ability of a judicial tribunal to control without courting intolerable risks of chilling legitimate price-cutting. See Areeda & Hovenkamp ¶¶ 714.2, 714.3. "To hold that the antitrust laws

---

51. Because the parties in this case agree that the relevant measure of cost is average variable cost, however, we again decline to resolve the conflict among the lower courts over the appropriate measure of cost. See *Cargill, supra,* at 117–118, n. 12; *Matsushita, supra,* at 585, n. 8.

protect competitors from the loss of profits due to such price competition would, in effect, render illegal any decision by a firm to cut prices in order to increase market share. The antitrust laws require no such perverse result." *Cargill, supra,* at 116.

Even in an oligopolistic market, when a firm drops its prices to a competitive level to demonstrate to a maverick the unprofitability of straying from the group, it would be illogical to condemn the price cut: The antitrust laws then would be an obstacle to the chain of events most conducive to a breakdown of oligopoly pricing and the onset of competition. Even if the ultimate effect of the cut is to induce or reestablish supracompetitive pricing, discouraging a price cut and forcing firms to maintain supracompetitive prices, thus depriving consumers of the benefits of lower prices in the interim, does not constitute sound antitrust policy.

The second prerequisite to holding a competitor liable under the antitrust laws for charging low prices is a demonstration that the competitor had a reasonable prospect, or, under § 2 of the Sherman Act, a dangerous probability, of recouping its investment in below-cost prices. See *Matsushita, supra,* at 589; *Cargill, supra,* at 119, n. 15. "For the investment to be rational, the [predator] must have a reasonable expectation of recovering, in the form of later monopoly profits, more than the losses suffered." *Matsushita, supra,* at 588–589. Recoupment is the ultimate object of an unlawful predatory pricing scheme; it is the means by which a predator profits from predation. Without it, predatory pricing produces lower aggregate prices in the market, and consumer welfare is enhanced. Although unsuccessful predatory pricing may encourage some inefficient substitution toward the product being sold at less than its cost, unsuccessful predation is in general a boon to consumers.

That below-cost pricing may impose painful losses on its target is of no moment to the antitrust laws if competition is not injured: It is axiomatic that the antitrust laws were passed for "the protection of *competition,* not *competitors.*" Brown Shoe Co. v. United States, 370 U.S. 294, 320 (1962). Earlier this Term, we held in the Sherman Act § 2 context that it was not enough to inquire "whether the defendant has engaged in 'unfair' or 'predatory' tactics"; rather, we insisted that the plaintiff prove "a dangerous probability that [the defendant] would monopolize a particular market." *Spectrum Sports.* Even an act of pure malice by one business competitor against another does not, without more, state a claim under the federal antitrust laws; those laws do not create a federal law of unfair competition or "purport to afford remedies for all torts committed by or against persons engaged in interstate commerce." Hunt v. Crumboch, 325 U.S. 821, 826 (1945).

For recoupment to occur, below-cost pricing must be capable, as a threshold matter, of producing the intended effects on the firm's rivals, whether driving them from the market, or, as was alleged to be the goal here, causing them to raise their prices to supracompetitive levels within a disciplined oligopoly. This requires an understanding of the extent and duration of the alleged predation, the relative financial strength of the predator and its intended victim, and their respective incentives and will. The inquiry is whether, given the aggregate losses caused by the below-cost pricing, the intended target would likely succumb.

If circumstances indicate that below-cost pricing could likely produce its intended effect on the target, there is still the further question whether it would likely injure competition in the relevant market. The plaintiff must demonstrate that there is a likelihood that the predatory scheme alleged would cause a rise in prices above a competitive level that would be sufficient to compensate for the amounts expended on the predation, including the time value of the money invested in it. As we have observed on a prior occasion, "[i]n order to recoup their losses, [predators] must obtain enough market power to set higher than competitive prices, and then must sustain those prices long enough to earn in excess profits what they earlier gave up in below-cost prices." *Matsushita*, 475 U.S., at 590–591.

Evidence of below-cost pricing is not alone sufficient to permit an inference of probable recoupment and injury to competition. Determining whether recoupment of predatory losses is likely requires an estimate of the cost of the alleged predation and a close analysis of both the scheme alleged by the plaintiff and the structure and conditions of the relevant market. Cf. *e.g.*, Elzinga & Mills, Testing for Predation: Is Recoupment Feasible?, 34 Antitrust Bull. 869 (1989) (constructing one possible model for evaluating recoupment). If market circumstances or deficiencies in proof would bar a reasonable jury from finding that the scheme alleged would likely result in sustained *supra*competitive pricing, the plaintiff's case has failed. In certain situations—for example, where the market is highly diffuse and competitive, or where new entry is easy, or the defendant lacks adequate excess capacity to absorb the market shares of his rivals and cannot quickly create or purchase new capacity—summary disposition of the case is appropriate. See, *e.g., Cargill*, 479 U.S., at 119–120, n. 15.

These prerequisites to recovery are not easy to establish, but they are not artificial obstacles to recovery; rather, they are essential components of real market injury. As we have said in the Sherman Act context, "predatory pricing schemes are rarely tried, and even more rarely successful," *Matsushita, supra*, at 589, and the costs of an erroneous finding of liability are high. "[T]he mechanism by which a firm engages in predatory pricing—lowering prices—is the same mechanism by which a firm stimulates competition; because 'cutting prices in order to increase business often is the very essence of competition . . . [;] mistaken inferences . . . are especially costly, because they chill the very conduct the antitrust laws are designed to protect.'" *Cargill, supra*, at 122, n. 17 (quoting *Matsushita, supra*, at 594). It would be ironic indeed if the standards for predatory pricing liability were so low that antitrust suits themselves became a tool for keeping prices high.

B

Liggett does not allege that Brown & Williamson sought to drive it from the market but that Brown & Williamson sought to preserve supracompetitive profits on branded cigarettes by pressuring Liggett to raise its generic cigarette prices through a process of tacit collusion with the other cigarette companies. Tacit collusion, sometimes called oligopolistic price coordination or conscious parallelism, describes the process, not in itself unlawful, by which firms in a concentrated market might in effect share monopoly power, setting their prices at a profit-maximizing, supracompetitive level by recognizing their shared economic interests and their interdependence with respect to price and output decisions. See 2 Areeda & Turner ¶ 404; Scherer & Ross 199–208.

In *Matsushita,* we remarked upon the general implausibility of predatory pricing. See 475 U.S., at 588–590. *Matsushita* observed that such schemes are even more improbable when they require coordinated action among several firms. *Matsushita* involved an allegation of an express conspiracy to engage in predatory pricing. The Court noted that in addition to the usual difficulties that face a single firm attempting to recoup predatory losses, other problems render a conspiracy "incalculably more difficult to execute." *Ibid.* In order to succeed, the conspirators must agree on how to allocate present losses and future gains among the firms involved, and each firm must resist powerful incentives to cheat on whatever agreement is reached. *Ibid.*

However unlikely predatory pricing by multiple firms may be when they conspire, it is even less likely when, as here, there is no express coordination. Firms that seek to recoup predatory losses through the conscious parallelism of oligopoly must rely on uncertain and ambiguous signals to achieve concerted action. The signals are subject to misinterpretation and are a blunt and imprecise means of ensuring smooth cooperation, especially in the context of changing or unprecedented market circumstances. This anticompetitive minuet is most difficult to compose and to perform, even for a disciplined oligopoly.

From one standpoint, recoupment through oligopolistic price coordination could be thought more feasible than recoupment through monopoly: In the oligopoly setting, the victim itself has an economic incentive to acquiesce in the scheme. If forced to choose between cutting prices and sustaining losses, maintaining prices and losing market share, or raising prices and enjoying a share of supracompetitive profits, a firm may yield to the last alternative. Yet on the whole, tacit cooperation among oligopolists must be considered the least likely means of recouping predatory losses. In addition to the difficulty of achieving effective tacit coordination and the high likelihood that any attempt to discipline will produce an outbreak of competition, the predator's present losses in a case like this fall on it alone, while the later supracompetitive profits must be shared with every other oligopolist in proportion to its market share, including the intended victim. In this case, for example, Brown & Williamson, with its 11–12% share of the cigarette market, would have had to generate around $9 in supracompetitive profits for each $1 invested in predation; the remaining $8 would belong to its competitors, who had taken no risk. . . .

To the extent that the Court of Appeals may have held that the interdependent pricing of an oligopoly may never provide a means for achieving recoupment and so may not form the basis of a primary-line injury claim, we disagree. A predatory pricing scheme designed to preserve or create a stable oligopoly, if successful, can injure consumers in the same way, and to the same extent, as one designed to bring about a monopoly. However unlikely that possibility may be as a general matter, when the realities of the market and the record facts indicate that it has occurred and was likely to have succeeded, theory will not stand in the way of liability. See Eastman Kodak Co. v. Image Technical Services, Inc., 504 U.S. 451 (1992).

The Robinson–Patman Act, which amended § 2 of the original Clayton Act, suggests no exclusion from coverage when primary-line injury occurs in an oligopoly setting. Unlike the provisions of the Sherman Act, which speak only of various forms of express agreement and monopoly, the Robinson–Patman Act is phrased in broader, disjunctive terms, prohibiting price discrimination "where the effect of such discrimination may be substantially to lessen competition or tend to create a monopoly." 15 U.S.C. § 13(a). For all the words of the Act to carry adequate meaning, competitive injury under the Act must extend beyond the monopoly setting. Cf. Reiter v. Sonotone Corp., 442 U.S. 330, 339 (1979) ("Canons of construction ordinarily suggest that terms connected by a disjunctive be given separate meanings, unless the context dictates otherwise."). The language referring to a substantial lessening of competition was part of the original Clayton Act § 2 and the same phrasing appears in § 7 of that Act. In the § 7 context, it has long been settled that excessive concentration, and the oligopolistic price coordination it portends, may be the injury to competition the Act prohibits. See, *e.g.,* United States v. Philadelphia National Bank, 374 U.S. 321 (1963). We adhere to "the normal rule of statutory construction that identical words used in different parts of the same act are intended to have the same meaning." We decline to create a *per se* rule of nonliability for predatory price discrimination when recoupment is alleged to take place through supracompetitive oligopoly pricing. Cf. *Cargill,* 479 U.S., at 121.

III

Although Liggett's theory of liability, as an abstract matter, is within the reach of the statute, we agree with the Court of Appeals and the District Court that Liggett was not entitled to submit its case to the jury. It is not customary for this Court to review the sufficiency of the evidence, but we will do so when the issue is properly before us and the benefits of providing guidance concerning the proper application of a legal standard and avoiding the systemic costs associated with further proceedings justify the required expenditure of judicial resources. The record in this case demonstrates that the anticompetitive scheme Liggett alleged, when judged against the realities of the market, does not provide an adequate basis for a finding of liability.

A

Liggett's theory of competitive injury through oligopolistic price coordination depends upon a complex chain of cause and effect: Brown & Williamson would enter the generic segment with list prices matching Liggett's but with massive, discriminatory volume rebates directed at Liggett's biggest wholesalers; as a result, the net price of Brown & Williamson's generics would be below its costs; Liggett would suffer losses trying to defend its market share and wholesale customer base by matching Brown & Williamson's rebates; to avoid further losses, Liggett would raise its list prices on generics or acquiesce in price leadership by Brown & Williamson; higher list prices to consumers would shrink the percentage gap in retail price between generic and branded cigarettes; and this narrowing of the gap would make generics less appealing to the consumer, thus slowing the growth of the economy segment and reducing cannibalization of branded sales and their associated supracompetitive profits.

Although Brown & Williamson's entry into the generic segment could be regarded as procompetitive in intent as well as effect, the record contains sufficient evidence from which a reasonable jury could conclude that Brown & Williamson envisioned or intended this anticompetitive course of events. There is also sufficient evidence in the record from which a reasonable jury could conclude that for a period of approximately 18 months, Brown & Williamson's prices on its generic cigarettes were below its costs, and that this below-cost pricing imposed losses on Liggett that Liggett was unwilling to sustain, given its corporate parent's effort to locate a buyer for the company. Liggett has failed to demonstrate competitive injury as a matter of law, however, because its proof is flawed in a critical respect: The evidence is inadequate to show that in pursuing this scheme, Brown & Williamson had a reasonable prospect of recovering its losses from below-cost pricing through slowing the growth of generics. As we have noted, "[t]he success of any predatory scheme depends on maintaining monopoly power for long enough both to recoup the predator's losses and to harvest some additional gain." *Matsushita,* 475 U.S., at 589 (emphasis omitted).

No inference of recoupment is sustainable on this record, because no evidence suggests that Brown & Williamson—whatever its intent in introducing black and whites may have been—was likely to obtain the power to raise the prices for generic cigarettes above a competitive level. Recoupment through supracompetitive pricing in the economy segment of the cigarette market is an indispensable aspect of Liggett's own proffered theory, because a slowing of growth in the economy segment, even if it results from an increase in generic prices, is not itself anticompetitive. Only if those higher prices are a product of nonmarket forces has competition suffered. If prices rise in response to an excess of demand over supply, or segment growth slows as patterns of consumer preference become stable, the market is functioning in a competitive manner. Consumers are not injured from the perspective of the antitrust laws by the price increases; they are in fact causing them. Thus, the linchpin of the predatory scheme alleged by Liggett is Brown & Williamson's ability, with the other oligopolists, to raise prices above a competitive level in the generic segment of the market. Because relying on tacit coordination among oligopolists as a means of recouping losses from predatory pricing is "highly speculative," Areeda & Hovenkamp ¶ 711.2c, at 647, competent evidence is necessary to allow a reasonable inference that it poses an authentic threat to competition. The evidence in this case is insufficient to demonstrate the danger of Brown & Williamson's alleged scheme.

B

Based on Liggett's theory of the case and the record it created, there are two means by which one might infer that Brown & Williamson had a reasonable prospect of producing sustained supracompetitive pricing in the generic segment adequate to recoup its predatory losses: first, if generic output or price information indicates that oligopolistic price coordination in fact produced supracompetitive prices in the generic segment; or second, if evidence about the market and Brown & Williamson's conduct indicate that the alleged scheme was likely to have brought about tacit coordination and oligopoly pricing in the generic segment, even if it did not actually do so.

In this case, the price and output data do not support a reasonable inference that Brown & Williamson and the other cigarette companies elevated prices above a competitive level for generic cigarettes. Supracompetitive pricing entails a restriction in output. In the present setting, in which output expanded at a rapid rate following Brown & Williamson's alleged predation, output in the generic segment can only have been restricted in the sense that it expanded at a slower rate than it would have absent Brown & Williamson's intervention. Such a counterfactual proposition is difficult to prove in the best of circumstances; here, the record evidence does not permit a reasonable inference that output would have been greater without Brown & Williamson's entry into the generic segment.

Following Brown & Williamson's entry, the rate at which generic cigarettes were capturing market share did not slow; indeed, the average rate of growth doubled. During the four years from 1980 to 1984 in which Liggett was alone in the generic segment, the segment gained market share at an average rate of 1% of the overall market per year, from .4% in 1980 to slightly more than 4% of the cigarette market in 1984. In the next five years, following the alleged predation, the generic segment expanded from 4% to more than 15% of the domestic cigarette market, or greater than 2% per year.

While this evidence tends to show that Brown & Williamson's participation in the economy segment did not restrict output, it is not dispositive. One could speculate, for example, that the rate of segment growth would have tripled, instead of doubled, without Brown & Williamson's alleged predation. But there is no concrete evidence of this. Indeed, the only industry projection in the record estimating what the segment's growth would have been without Brown & Williamson's entry supports the opposite inference. In 1984, Brown & Williamson forecast in an important planning document that the economy segment would account for 10% of the total cigarette market by 1988 if it did not enter the segment. In fact, in 1988, after what Liggett alleges was a sustained and dangerous anticompetitive campaign by Brown & Williamson, the generic segment accounted for over 12% of the total market. Thus the segment's output expanded more robustly than Brown & Williamson had estimated it would had Brown & Williamson never entered.

Brown & Williamson did note in 1985, a year after introducing its black and whites, that its presence within the generic segment "appears to have resulted in . . . a slowing in the segment's growth rate." *Id.,* at 257. But this statement was made in early 1985, when Liggett itself contends the below-cost pricing was still in effect and before any anticompetitive contraction in output is alleged to have occurred. Whatever it may mean,[52] this statement has little value in evaluating the competitive implications of Brown & Williamson's later conduct, which was alleged to provide the basis for recouping predatory losses.

In arguing that Brown & Williamson was able to exert market power and raise generic prices above a competitive level in the generic category through tacit price coordination with the other cigarette manufacturers, Liggett places its principal reliance on direct evidence of price behavior. This evidence demonstrates that the list prices on all cigarettes, generic and branded alike, rose to a significant degree during the late 1980s. From 1986 to 1989, list prices on both generic and branded cigarettes increased twice a year by similar amounts. Liggett's economic expert testified that these price increases outpaced increases in costs, taxes, and promotional expenditures. The list prices of generics, moreover, rose at a faster rate than the prices of branded cigarettes, thus narrowing the list price differential between branded and generic products. Liggett argues that this would permit a reasonable jury to find that Brown & Williamson succeeded in bringing about oligopolistic price coordination and supracompetitive prices in the generic category sufficient to slow its growth, thereby preserving supracompetitive branded profits and recouping its predatory losses.

A reasonable jury, however, could not have drawn the inferences Liggett proposes. All of Liggett's data is based upon the list prices of various categories of cigarettes. Yet the jury had before it undisputed evidence that during the period in question, list prices were not the actual prices paid by consumers. As the market became unsettled in the mid–1980s, the cigarette companies invested substantial sums in promotional schemes, including coupons, stickers, and giveaways, that reduced the actual cost of cigarettes to consumers below list prices. This promotional

---

52. This statement could well have referred to the rate at which the segment was growing relative to prior years' generic volume; this "internal" rate of growth would inevitably slow as the base volume against which it was measured grew.

activity accelerated as the decade progressed. Many wholesalers also passed portions of their volume rebates on to the consumer, which had the effect of further undermining the significance of the retail list prices. Especially in an oligopoly setting, in which price competition is most likely to take place through less observable and less regulatable means than list prices, it would be unreasonable to draw conclusions about the existence of tacit coordination or supracompetitive pricing from data that reflects only list prices.

Even on its own terms, the list price data relied upon by Liggett to demonstrate a narrowing of the price differential between generic and full-priced branded cigarettes could not support the conclusion that supracompetitive pricing had been introduced into the generic segment. Liggett's gap data ignores the effect of "subgeneric" cigarettes, which were priced at discounts of 50% or more from the list prices of normal branded cigarettes. Liggett itself, while supposedly under the sway of oligopoly power, pioneered this development in 1988 with the introduction of its "Pyramid" brand. By the time of trial, five of the six major manufacturers offered a cigarette in this category at a discount from the full list price of at least 50%. Thus, the priced difference between the highest priced branded cigarette and the lowest price cigarettes in the economy segment, instead of narrowing over the course of the period of alleged predation as Liggett would argue, grew to a substantial extent. In June 1984, before Brown & Williamson entered the generic segment, a consumer could obtain a carton of black and white generic cigarettes from Liggett at a 38% discount from the list price of a leading brand; after the conduct Liggett complains of, consumers could obtain a branded generic from Liggett for 52% off the list price of a leading brand.

It may be that a reasonable jury could conclude that the cumulative discounts attributable to subgenerics and the various consumer promotions did not cancel out the full effect of the increases in list prices, and that actual prices to the consumer did indeed rise, but rising prices do not themselves permit an inference of a collusive market dynamic. Even in a concentrated market, the occurrence of a price increase does not in itself permit a rational inference of conscious parallelism or supracompetitive pricing. Where, as here, output is expanding at the same time prices are increasing, rising prices are equally consistent with growing product demand. Under these conditions, a jury may not infer competitive injury from price and output data absent some evidence that tends to prove that output was restricted or prices were above a competitive level. Cf. *Monsanto,* 465 U.S., at 763.

Quite apart from the absence of any evidence of that sort, an inference of supracompetitive pricing would be particularly anomalous in this case, as the very party alleged to have been coerced into pricing through oligopolistic coordination denied that such coordination existed: Liggett's own officers and directors consistently denied that they or other firms in the industry priced their cigarettes through tacit collusion or reaped supracompetitive profits. Liggett seeks to explain away this testimony by arguing that its officers and directors are businesspeople who do not ascribe the same meaning to words like "competitive" and "collusion" that an economist would. This explanation is entitled to little, if any, weight. As the District Court found:

> "This argument was considered at the summary judgment stage since these executives gave basically the same testimony at their depositions. The court allowed the case to go to trial in part because the Liggett executives were not economists and in part because of affidavits from the Liggett executives stating that they were confused by the questions asked by B[rown] & W[illiamson] lawyers' and did not mean to contradict the testimony of [their economic expert] Burnett. However, at trial, despite having consulted extensively with Burnett and having had adequate time to familiarize themselves with concepts such as tacit collusion, oligopoly, and monopoly profits, these Liggett executives again contradicted Burnett's theory." 748 F.Supp., at 356.

Not only does the evidence fail to show actual supracompetitive pricing in the generic segment, it also does not demonstrate its likelihood. At the time Brown & Williamson entered the generic segment, the cigarette industry as a whole faced declining demand and possessed substantial excess capacity. These circumstances tend to break down patterns of oligopoly pricing and produce price competition. See Scherer & Ross 294, 315; 2 Areeda & Turner ¶ 404b2, at 275–276; 6 P. Areeda, Antitrust Law ¶ 1430e, at 181 (1986). The only means by which Brown & Williamson is alleged to have established oligopoly pricing in the face of these unusual competitive pressures is through tacit price coordination with the other cigarette firms.

Yet the situation facing the cigarette companies in the 1980's would have made such tacit coordination unmanageable. Tacit coordination is facilitated by a stable market environment, fungible products, and a small number of variables upon which the firms seeking to coordinate their pricing may focus. Uncertainty is an oligopoly's greatest enemy. By 1984, however, the cigarette market was in an obvious state of flux. The introduction of generic cigarettes in 1980 represented the first serious price competition in the cigarette market since the 1930's. See Scherer & Ross 250–251. This development was bound to unsettle previous expectations and patterns of market conduct and to reduce the cigarette firms' ability to predict each other's behavior.

The larger number of product types and pricing variables also decreased the probability of effective parallel pricing. . . . In addition, R.J. Reynolds had incentives that, in some respects, ran counter to those of the other cigarette companies. It is implausible that without a shared interest in retarding the growth of the economy segment, Brown & Williamson and its fellow oligopolists could have engaged in parallel pricing and raised generic prices above a competitive level. "[C]oordination will not be possible when any significant firm chooses, for any reason, to 'go it alone.'" 2 Areeda and Turner ¶ 404b2, at 276. It is undisputed—indeed it was conceded by Liggett's expert—that R.J. Reynolds acted without regard to the supposed benefits of oligopolistic coordination when it repriced Doral at generic levels in the spring of 1984 and that the natural and probable consequence of its entry into the generic segment was procompetitive. Indeed, Reynolds' apparent objective in entering the segment was to capture a significant amount of volume in order to regain its number one sales position in the cigarette industry from Philip Morris. There is no evidence that R.J. Reynolds accomplished this goal during the period relevant to this case, or that its commitment to achieving that goal changed. Indeed, R.J. Reynolds refused to follow Brown & Williamson's attempt to raise generic prices in June 1985. The jury thus had before it undisputed evidence that contradicts the suggestion that the major cigarette companies shared a goal of limiting the growth of the economy segment; one of the industry's two major players concededly entered the segment to expand volume and compete.

Even if all the cigarette companies were willing to participate in a scheme to restrain the growth of the generic segment, they would not have been able to coordinate their actions and raise prices above a competitive level unless they understood that Brown & Williamson's entry into the segment was not a genuine effort to compete with Liggett. If even one other firm misinterpreted Brown & Williamson's entry as an effort to expand market share, a chain reaction of competitive responses would almost certainly have resulted, and oligopoly discipline would have broken down, perhaps irretrievably. "[O]nce the trust among rivals breaks down, it is as hard to put back together again as was Humpty–Dumpty, and non-collusive behavior is likely to take over." Samuelson & Nordhaus, Economics, at 534.

Liggett argues that the means by which Brown & Williamson signaled its anticompetitive intent to its rivals was through its pricing structure. According to Liggett, maintaining existing list prices while offering substantial rebates to wholesalers was a signal to the other cigarette firms that Brown & Williamson did not intend to attract additional smokers to the generic segment by its entry. But a reasonable jury could not conclude that this pricing structure eliminated or rendered insignificant the risk that the other firms might misunderstand Brown & Williamson's entry as a competitive move. The likelihood that Brown & Williamson's rivals would have regarded its pricing structure as an important signal is low, given that Liggett itself, the purported target of the predation, was already using similar rebates, as was R.J. Reynolds in marketing its Doral branded generic. A Reynolds executive responsible for Doral testified that given its and Liggett's use of wholesaler rebates, Brown & Williamson could not have competed effectively without them. And despite extensive discovery of the corporate records of R.J. Reynolds and Philip Morris, no documents appeared that indicated any awareness of Brown & Williamson's supposed signal by its principal rivals. Without effective signaling, it is difficult to see how the alleged predation could have had a reasonable chance of success through oligopoly pricing.

Finally, although some of Brown & Williamson's corporate planning documents speak of a desire to slow the growth of the segment, no objective evidence of its conduct permits a reasonable inference that it had any real prospect of doing so through anticompetitive means. It is undisputed that when Brown & Williamson introduced its generic cigarettes, it offered them to a thousand wholesalers who had never before purchased generic cigarettes. The inevitable effect of this marketing effort was to expand the segment, as the new wholesalers recruited retail outlets to carry generic cigarettes. Even with respect to wholesalers already carrying generics, Brown & Williamson's unprecedented volume rebates had a similar expansionary effect. Unlike many branded cigarettes, generics came with no sales guarantee to the wholesaler; any unsold stock represented pure loss to the wholesaler. By providing substantial incentives for wholesalers to place large orders, Brown & Williamson created strong pressure for them to sell more generic cigarettes. In addition, as we have already observed, many wholesalers passed portions of the rebates about which Liggett complains on to consumers, thus dropping the retail price of generics and further stimulating demand. Brown & Williamson provided a further, direct stimulus, through some $10 million it spent during the period of alleged predation placing discount stickers on its generic cartons to reduce prices to the ultimate consumer. In light of these uncontested facts about Brown & Williamson's conduct, it is not reasonable to conclude that Brown & Williamson threatened in a serious way to restrict output, raise prices above a competitive level, and artificially slow the growth of the economy segment of the national cigarette market.

To be sure, Liggett's economic expert explained Liggett's theory of predatory price discrimination and testified that he believed it created a reasonable possibility that Brown & Williamson could injure competition in the United States cigarette market as a whole. But this does not alter our analysis. When an expert opinion is not supported by sufficient facts to validate it in the eyes of the law, or when indisputable record facts contradict or otherwise render the opinion unreasonable, it cannot support a jury's verdict. . . .

IV

We understand that the chain of reasoning by which we have concluded that Brown & Williamson is entitled to judgment as a matter of law is demanding. But a reasonable jury is presumed to know and understand the law, the facts of the case, and the realities of the market. We hold that the evidence cannot support a finding that Brown & Williamson's alleged scheme was likely to result in oligopolistic price coordination and sustained supracompetitive pricing in the generic segment of the national cigarette market. Without this, Brown & Williamson had no reasonable prospect of recouping its predatory losses and could not inflict the injury to competition the antitrust laws prohibit. The judgment of the Court of Appeals is affirmed.

■ STEVENS J., with whom WHITE and BLACKMAN, JJ., joined, dissented. [The dissenters divided the period under review into three phases: *phase 1,* prior to July 1984, when it was generally agreed that cigarette prices increased in lock step and produced unusually large industry profits; *phase 2,* during the period July 1984 to the end of 1985, when Brown & Williamson (B & W) initiated a price war that clearly put its prices below its average variable cost; and *phase 3,* covering the period after the price war, when prices of generic brands and black and whites increased so as to narrow the profit between products in the economy market and branded cigarettes. Thereafter, the prices of all cigarettes—branded and unbranded—increased in lock step as they had prior to the price war.

The dissent emphasized that the Robinson–Patman Act required only a "reasonable probability" of harm and cited documents that clearly would have indicated to a jury that B & W's intention was to "manage up the prices of branded generics" and "manage down generic volume." In their view, it was reasonable for the jury to assume that B & W had embarked on a strategy with a reasonable probability of success and, to the extent cooperation from other cigarette companies was necessary, B & W could signal its intention and goals to the other companies and expect them to respond cooperatively.

With respect to the majority's dismissal of evidence that prices in the post-price war period were supracompetitive because list prices were not an accurate indicator of competitive conditions without taking promotional activities into account, the dissent noted that the promotions related primarily to branded cigarettes, and accordingly, did not reduce the consumer price of black and whites. The dissent suggested that the majority's conclusion was speculative in light of record evidence that semiannual list price increases offset consumer promotions. Justice Stevens concluded:]

As a matter of economics, the Court reminds us that price-cutting is generally pro-competitive, and hence a "boon to consumers." This is true, however, only so long as reduced prices do not fall below cost, as the cases cited by the majority make clear. When a predator deliberately engages in below-cost pricing targeted at a particular competitor over a sustained period of time, then price-cutting raises a credible inference that harm to competition is likely to ensue. None of our cases disputes that proposition.

Also as a matter of economics, the Court insists that a predatory pricing program in an oligopoly is unlikely to succeed absent actual conspiracy. Though it has rejected a somewhat stronger version of this proposition as a rule of decision, the Court comes back to the same economic theory, relying on the supposition that an "anticompetitive minuet is most difficult to compose and to perform, even for a disciplined oligopoly" (implausibility of tacit coordination among cigarette oligopolists in 1980's). I would suppose, however, that the professional performers who had danced the minuet for 40 to 50 years would be better able to predict whether their favorite partners would follow them in the future than would an outsider, who might not know the difference between Haydn and Mozart. In any event, the jury was surely entitled to infer that at the time of the price war itself, B & W reasonably believed that it could signal its intentions to its fellow oligopolists assuring their continued cooperation.

Perhaps the Court's most significant error is the assumption that seems to pervade much of the final sections of its opinion: that Liggett had the burden of proving either the actuality of supracompetitive pricing, or the actuality of tacit collusion.... In my opinion, the jury was entitled to infer from the succession of price increases after 1985—when the prices for branded and generic cigarettes increased every six months from $33.15 and $19.75, respectively, to $46.15 and $33.75—that B & W's below-cost pricing actually produced supracompetitive prices, with the help of tacit collusion among the players. But even if that were not so clear, the jury would surely be entitled to infer that B & W's predatory plan, in which it invested millions of dollars for the purpose of achieving an admittedly anticompetitive result, carried a "reasonable possibility" of injuring competition.

NOTES AND QUESTIONS

1. What is the difference between a primary line competitive injury case under the Robinson–Patman Act and a predatory pricing scheme under Section 2 of the Sherman Act? In what respect, if any, would it be easier for the plaintiff to win under the Robinson–Patman Act?

2. Is the idea that predatory pricing by a firm could lead to tacit collusion or "conscious parallelism" economically irrational? In emphasizing that prices declined and output increased during the price war, was the majority in the *Brooke Group* case confusing the first phase of a predatory strategy with the entire game plan? Is it not usually the case that prices will decline and output increase during the first phase of a predatory scheme?

3. Prior to the Supreme Court's decision in *Brooke Group*, much of the debate regarding predatory pricing revolved around the issue of the measure of cost to be used in judging whether a defendant's price was predatory. In *Brooke Group*, as it had done in two earlier cases (*i.e.*, *Cargill* and *Matsushita*), the Supreme Court deferred consideration of the measure of cost issue until another day. *See* p. 829 n. 51 *supra*. Nevertheless, the issue remains of great consequence. The writings of Professors Areeda and Turner have been particularly prominent in measure of cost debates. They developed a series of cost-based rules to distinguish legal from illegal pricing. They defined "alternative measures of cost" in the following way:

The economic costs facing a firm differ in an important respect: some are "fixed," and others are "variable." *Fixed costs* are costs that do not vary with changes in output. They typically include some management expenses, interest on bonded debt, depreciation (to the extent that equipment is not consumed by using it), property taxes, and other irreducible overhead. And though not an accounting cost, fixed costs should be deemed to include the return on investment that would currently be necessary to attract capital to the firm—what the economist refers to as the *opportunity cost* to the owners of the firm. In short, it is reasonably accurate to say that fixed costs are costs that would continue even if the firm produced no output at all.

Variable costs, as the name implies, are costs that vary with changes in output. They typically include such items as materials, fuel, labor directly used to produce the product, indirect labor such as foremen, clerks, and custodial help, use-depreciation, repair and maintenance, and per unit royalties and license fees. The average variable cost is the sum of all variable costs divided by output.

Marginal cost is the increment to total cost that results from producing an additional increment of output. It is a function solely of variable costs, since fixed costs, by definition, are costs unaffected by changes in output. Marginal cost usually decreases over low levels of output and increases as production approaches plant capacity.

Total cost is the sum of fixed cost and total variable cost. That total divided by output is *average cost* or, to use the layman's synonym, *full cost.* It is, by definition, higher than average variable cost at all outputs, but will typically be below marginal cost at very high levels of output, when the plant is strained beyond efficient operating capacity.

Which costs are fixed and which are variable (and hence marginal) is a function of both (1) the magnitude of the contemplated change in output, and (2) time. Virtually all costs are variable when a firm, operating at capacity, plans to double its output by constructing new plants and purchasing new equipment. Moreover, more costs become variable as the time period increases. The variable costs described above are those incurred in what is usually termed the "short run," namely, the period in which the firm cannot replace or increase plant or equipment. Conversely, in the "long run" the firm can vary quantities of *all* inputs (plant and equipment as well as short run variable inputs); thus, all costs are variable over the long run. Accordingly, *long-run marginal cost* approximates anticipated average total cost (full cost) for various levels of output.

In order to determine which of these various costs is relevant to predatory, "below-cost" selling, we must first ask what costs are relevant to the firm which is seeking to maximize profits or minimize losses, since a firm which seeks to do so is normally responding to acceptable economic incentives and thus is not engaging in predatory behavior. The profit-maximizing or loss-minimizing output for any firm, whether competitive or monopolistic, is that where any increase in output would add more to costs than to revenues and any decrease in output would reduce revenues more than costs. In short, in deciding whether it would increase or decrease output, the firm looks to the *incremental* effects on revenues and costs. Thus, the relevant cost is marginal cost.

Although Areeda and Turner believed "marginal-cost pricing is the economically sound division between acceptable, competitive behavior and 'below-cost' predation," they concluded that "average variable cost" is a reasonable proxy for marginal cost and more satisfactory as a test because of the extreme difficulty of ascertaining marginal cost. For prices below average variable cost a "presumption of illegality" exists and this presumption will usually prove conclusive. Conversely, prices above average variable cost are "presumptively lawful" and this presumption will usually prove conclusive. Areeda and Turner also pointed out that the legality of price levels should be based on "reasonably anticipated" costs, so that prices may be cut without antitrust consequences in anticipation of lower costs in the future. 3 Areeda & Turner, Antitrust Law ¶¶ 712–15 (1978); *see* 3 Areeda & Hovenkamp, Antitrust Law ¶¶ 722–24, 735–41 (2d ed. 2002).

4. The Areeda and Turner proposals have not lacked critics. A number of alternative approaches have been offered (mostly by economists):

(a) *Scherer.* Professor Frederic M. Scherer was an early critic of the Areeda and Turner proposals, arguing that rigid cost-based rules were simplistic and overly generous to predators and would-be monopolists. He urged that the focus be on "long-term economic welfare," which involved a determination of:

> [T]he relative cost positions of the monopolist and fringe firms, the scale of entry required to secure minimum costs, whether fringe firms are driven out entirely or merely suppressed, whether the monopolist expands its output to replace the output of excluded rivals or restricts supply again when the rivals withdraw, and whether any long-run compensatory expansion by the monopolist entails investment in scale economy-embodying new plant.

Scherer, Predatory Pricing and the Sherman Act: A Comment, 89 Harv.L.Rev. 869, 890 (1976). Are the factors cited by Scherer relevant after *Brooke Group*? Is his approach administratively feasible?

(b) *Baumol.* A recurrent criticism of Areeda and Turner is that their cost-based rules failed to take "timing" into account. Professor William J. Baumol has suggested that a seller be permitted to reduce its price to whatever level it chooses, but it would then be prevented for a period of time from raising its price unless it could show necessity as a result of marketplace cost changes. Baumol, Quasi–Permanence of Price Reductions: A Policy for Prevention of Predatory Pricing, 89 Yale L.J. 1 (1979).

(c) *Posner.* Viewing the Areeda and Turner rule as somewhat too permissive, Chief Judge Richard A. Posner defined the level of predatory pricing as the "level calculated to exclude from the market an equally or more efficient competitor." He suggests that predatory pricing occurs not only on sales below average variable costs but also, at least presumptively, where there are sales at less than long-run marginal costs (ordinarily higher than short-run marginal costs) accompanied by intent to exclude an equally or more efficient competitor. This approach recognizes that new entrants may have short-run costs—such as expenditures to build "image" or create research capacity—which have long since become fixed costs to the established firm. Posner, Antitrust Law 215 (2d ed. 2001).

(d) *Joskow & Klevorick.* In an effort to simplify predatory pricing litigation (with similarities to the approach later used in *Brooke Group*), Professors Paul Joskow and Richard A. Klevorick proposed a "two-tier" approach. In a preliminary inquiry, courts would determine whether the market in question was conducive to predation; if so, behavioral considerations would then be examined. The central inquiries of a first-tier analysis would look to number and size distribution of firms, entry barriers, and profit levels of the alleged predator. In a second stage inquiry, prices below average variable cost would establish predation while prices above average total cost would be presumed legal unless withdrawn within two years. In that event, the burden of proof would shift to the dominant firm to show that the increase was justified (*i.e.*, the Baumol proposal). Prices between average variable cost and average total cost would be presumed predatory unless the dominant firm could show that the strategy was justified because it maximized short-run profits (essentially, that substantial excess capacity was unused by the price cutter). Finally, documentary evidence about "intent" would also be admissible. Joskow & Klevorick, A Framework For Analyzing Predatory Pricing Policy, 89 Yale L.J. 213 (1979).

(e) *Bolton, Brodley, and Riordan*. Recent criticism of the Areeda & Turner rule focuses on its static as opposed to dynamic approach to predatory pricing issues, and specifically on its assumption that predatory pricing is rare and usually does not have severe market consequences. More recent literature asserts that when strategic considerations are incorporated, and particularly in light of modern game theory, predatory pricing is a rational and often-used strategy.

In connection with easing various elements that plaintiff must prove to establish predatory pricing, the authors offer several examples of low pricing that would be rational if strategic factors were taken into account. These include: (1) *Financial Market Predation*. Low prices by a dominant incumbent can cut off access to financial markets for its victim by undermining the relationship between the victim and its investors. Given that new ventures will often offer disappointing initial results, a predator may use cost-cutting to make initial performance poor and thus cut off a competitor's access to capital. (2) *Signaling Strategies*. A predator may cut costs in one market to establish a reputation as a price-cutter in other markets where new entry is threatened. (A "reputation for predation" issue is presented by the Department of Justice's recent complaint against American Airlines, *see* p. 849 *infra*.) (3) *Test Market Predation*. The predator may cut prices in a potential entrant's test market to skew results as to demand for new products. The victim, lacking knowledge and experience in the market, is prevented from discovering whether demand is sufficiently strong to justify entry or continued presence in the test market. (4) *Cost Signalling*. A predator attempts to establish a reputation for low cost by cutting its price below its short-run profit-maximizing level. The target of the cost-cutting, particularly when it is a company considering entry, is persuaded to seek some other market which seems more likely to be profitable and less threatening. Bolton, Brodley & Riordan, Predatory Pricing: Strategic Theory and Legal Policy, 88 Geo. L.J. 2239 (2000); *see* Elzinga & Mills, Predatory Pricing and Strategic Theory, 89 Geo. L.J. 2475 (2001); Bolton, Brodley & Riordan, Predatory Pricing: Response to Critique and Further Elaboration, 89 Geo. L.J. 2495 (2001).

5.   In the courts, the Areeda and Turner cost proposals have had a mixed reception. In McGahee v. Northern Propane Gas Co., 858 F.2d 1487 (11th Cir.1988), cert. denied, 490 U.S. 1084 (1989), for example, the Eleventh Circuit concluded:

> The Areeda and Turner test is like the Venus de Milo: it is much admired and often discussed, but rarely embraced. Perhaps this reluctance to embrace is due to the substance from which it is formed. The Areeda and Turner test is carved from economic assumptions, not from antitrust statutes and judicial precedents. Perhaps this reluctance is due to attacks upon it. The Areeda and Turner test has been criticized for being impractical, for using static short-run analysis, and for being too permissive of predatory activity; these criticisms break any notion that economists agree that the Areeda and Turner test is best. We ... decline to embrace the Areeda and Turner test.

A commentary[53] concluded that the circuits "applying the anticipated average variable cost standard (or a substantially equivalent formulation) include the First, Second, Fifth, and Eighth." The commentary went on to observe:

> In various circuits, courts have held, as *Brooke Group* suggested, that prices above average total cost are *per se* lawful. These courts have also held that prices below average total cost may be unlawful, placing different burdens on plaintiff and defendant when the price is above average variable cost but below average total cost. Such circuits include the Sixth, Eighth, Ninth, Tenth, and Eleventh. Moreover, the Fifth Circuit permits evidence of pricing above average variable cost in some cases when entry barriers are high and where the defendant has charged a price below its short-run, profit-maximizing price.... Circuits that have not articulated a cost standard for determining predatory pricing include the Third, Fourth, Seventh, and the District of Columbia.

To date, the Supreme Court has permitted the measure of cost debate to rage in the lower courts and has kept its options open. *See Brooke Group,* and *Weyerhaeuser* (p. 851 *infra*). If you were on the Supreme Court, how would you cast your vote?

6. Judgments about the formulation of legal rules for predatory pricing turn largely on estimates as to three uncertain factual matters: first, how often does predatory pricing actually occur and how likely is it to be destructive of competition absent legal intervention; second, the degree of difficulty courts will have in administering cost-based rules; and third, the capacity of courts to distinguish accurately between—and the utility of distinguishing—long-term and short-term costs and fixed and variable costs.

With respect to the first issue, there is much theoretical justification (although not much empirical proof) for concluding that predatory pricing may be more prevalent than the Supreme Court majority in *Brooke Group* seemed to suggest. In addition to Bolton, Brodley and Riordan (note 4(e) *supra*), Jonathan Baker[54] provided the following hypothetical example of how multimarket recoupment might work:

> Suppose a chain store faces a non-chain rival in each of a large number of towns. The chain cuts its prices drastically in a few towns. When the chain's rivals in those towns either exit or begin to compete less aggressively with the chain, the price war ends and high prices are restored. In addition, the chain store's rivals in all the other towns, in which the chain did not cut prices, also respond by avoiding aggressive competition with the chain. As a result, prices also increase in the towns in which predation did not occur.

> In this hypothetical example of price predation with multimarket recoupment, the firm developed a reputation as a predator by reducing price in a small number of markets.[55] It in effect engaged in selective predation. The rivals in the markets in which predation occurred may have

53. Denger & Herfort, Predatory Pricing Claims After *Brooke Group,* 62 Antitrust L.J. 541, 548–50 (1994).

54. Baker, Predatory Pricing After *Brooke Group:* An Economic Perspective, 62 Antitrust L.J. 585, 590–91 (1994).

55. In the example, the other markets involved different geographic areas; a similar story could be told involving different product markets.

ended up crippled or destroyed, as the traditional predatory pricing story would have it. But rivals competing against the predator in markets in which predation did not occur were not injured directly. Most of the victimized rivals never experienced a price war but were merely intimidated by the threat of a price war into engaging in less aggressive behavior than they would otherwise have found most profitable.[56]

The hypothetical demonstrates that a dynamic analysis—taking into account possible strategic uses of predatory behavior—indicates that predatory pricing may be more prevalent than had earlier been believed.

Some of the difficulties courts have in administering cost-based rules—and the problem of distinguishing between fixed and variable costs—are illustrated by the Second Circuit's opinion in Kelco Disposal, Inc. v. Browning–Ferris Industries of Vermont, Inc., 845 F.2d 404 (2d Cir.1988). The Second Circuit, in affirming the award of damages for predatory pricing,[57] dealt with fixed and variable cost distinctions as follows:

> Kelco claims that defendants' anticompetitive or exclusionary conduct consisted of predatory pricing, and introduced evidence that defendants' price of $65 per roll-off haul was below its average variable cost of roughly $104 per haul. Defendants argue that Kelco's $104 figure was inflated because Kelco's expert witness mistakenly characterized certain fixed costs as variable in making his computations. Asserting that depreciation of equipment, selling and administrative costs, and national overhead should have been considered fixed costs, defendants contend that their true average variable cost was less than $50 per haul, well below their $65 haul charge. . . .

> Prices that are below reasonably anticipated marginal cost, and its surrogate, reasonably anticipated average variable cost, see *Northeastern Telephone,* 651 F.2d at 88, are presumed predatory. *Id.* By definition variable costs are dependent on the firm's output, while fixed costs are not. The characterization of certain costs as either variable or fixed frequently becomes a battleground where the plaintiff proceeds on a predatory pricing theory. The reason is obvious: the higher a party's average variable cost, the more likely it is that the party has priced below that cost.

> Defendants argue that equipment depreciation should have been considered a fixed cost because defendants' accountants have always treated it so. Passing, for the moment, the bootstrap feature of this argument, the general legal rule is that depreciation caused by use is a variable cost, while depreciation through obsolescence is a fixed cost. See *id.* The characterization of legitimately disputed costs is a question of fact for the jury. The jury may consider, but obviously cannot be bound by, a party's characterization of its own costs.

> In this case, we conclude that the jury could have reasonably characterized equipment depreciation as a variable cost. The waste disposal

---

56. In the hypothetical example, these firms refrained from cutting price below the price the predator preferred, and they refrained from taking a larger market share than the predator permitted them to have. In other cases, the indirectly victimized rivals might refrain from soliciting the predator's customers, not expand into other markets, or agree to be acquired at a low price.

57. The predatory pricing was found to be an attempt to monopolize under Section 2 of the Sherman Act. For a discussion of attempt to monopolize, *see* Section 1B *supra.*

industry makes intensive use of heavy equipment. There was no evidence presented that defendants' trucks, compactors, or containers became obsolete; rather, the picture painted was one of constant wear, tear, and damage due to use.

Defendants do not challenge the characterization of disposal fees and drivers' salaries as variable costs. Adding equipment depreciation costs to these other costs yields an average variable cost of roughly $81 per haul, well above defendants' $65 fee. Based on these figures alone, we conclude that the jury could have found that defendants engaged in predatory pricing.

7. Must market power and specific intent (*i.e.*, in an attempt to monopolize case) be shown in predatory pricing cases under Section 2 of the Sherman Act? *See, e.g.,* Rebel Oil Co. v. Atlantic Richfield Co., 51 F.3d 1421 (9th Cir.), cert. denied, 516 U.S. 987 (1995) (plaintiff failed to establish a "genuine issue of material fact on market power"); Advo, Inc. v. Philadelphia Newspapers, Inc., 51 F.3d 1191 (3d Cir.1995) (summary judgment where no specific intent in an attempt to monopolize case); United States Anchor Manufacturing v. Rule Industries, 7 F.3d 986 (11th Cir.1993), cert. denied, 512 U.S. 1221 (1994); Chapter 8, Section 1B, *supra*. Would market power or specific intent have to be shown in a Robinson–Patman case? *See* Chapter 11 *infra*.

8. One commentary concluded:

Brooke Group unquestionably sends a chilling message to potential predatory pricing plaintiffs. The recoupment standard is rigorous and, as explained by the Court, invites lower courts to scrutinize the record before trial to find facts that mitigate against a likelihood of effective *supra*competitive pricing or output restriction. This "screen," as well as the Court's list of factors warranting "summary disposition," doubtless will be used to strengthen pretrial summary judgment motions. In non-Robinson–Patman Act cases, focus on the defendant's market share alone—as in the Eleventh Circuit's decision in *U.S. Anchor* may also serve as a filtering mechanism.[58]

Is this analysis consistent with your reading of *Brooke Group?* Does it apply equally to single firm monopoly situations and to concentrated industries? Please note that since *Brooke Group* was decided, no plaintiff has succeeded on the merits of a predatory pricing claim in federal court. Professor Goldschmid recently provided the following critique of predatory pricing law:

In a market with entry barriers, predation to prevent entry, or to discipline competitors, may be perfectly rational. Predatory pricing in a concentrated market by an oligopolistic group may be difficult, but dominant firm predation can be easily accomplished and economically sensible. Indeed, in a dominant firm context, I would interpret *Brooke Group* and *Weyerhaeuser* [*see* p. 851 *infra*] to mean that where recoupment (including the rewards stemming from the disciplining of rivals) is probable, a presumption should exist that any price below average total cost is predatory. In this area, skepticism about feasibility and naiveté have led to law that is much too permissive.[59]

---

58. Denger & Herfort, Predatory Pricing Claims After *Brooke Group,* 62 Antitrust L.J. 541, 556–57 (1994).

59. Goldschmid, Comment on ... the Dominant Firm, in Pitofsky (ed.), How the Chicago School Overshot the Mark 127–28 (2008).

United States v. AMR Corp., American Airlines Inc.

United States Court of Appeals, Tenth Circuit, 2003.
335 F.3d 1109.

■ LUCERO, J. This case involves the nature of permissible competitive practices in the airline industry under the antitrust laws of this country, centered around the hub-and-spoke system of American Airlines. The United States brought this suit against AMR Corporation, American Airlines, Inc., and American Eagle Holding Corporation ("American'), alleging monopolization and attempted monopolization through predatory pricing in violation of § 2 of the Sherman Act. In essence, the government alleges that American engaged in multiple episodes of price predation in four city-pair airline markets, all connected to American's hub at Dallas/Fort Worth International Airport ("DFW"), with the ultimate purpose of using the reputation for predatory pricing it earned in those four markets to defend a monopoly at its DFW hub. At its root, the government's complaint alleges that American: (1) priced its product on the routes in question below cost; and (2) intended to recoup these losses by charging supracompetitive prices either on the four core routes themselves, or on those routes where it stands to exclude competition by means of its "reputation for predation." Finding that the government failed to demonstrate the existence of a genuine issue of material fact as to either of these allegations, the district court granted summary judgment in favor of American, from which the government now appeals. Because we agree that the record is void of evidence that rises to the level of a material conflict, we affirm. . . .

Both American and Delta Airlines ("Delta") maintain hubs at DFW, though Delta's presence is considerably smaller than American's. As of May 2000, American's share of passengers boarded at DFW was 70.2%, Delta's share was roughly 18%, and LCC [i.e., low cost carriers] share was 2.4%. As of mid–2000, there were seven low-cost airlines serving DFW. . . .

American responded to lower LCC fares on [four] routes with changes in: (1) pricing (matching LCC prices); (2) capacity (adding flights or switching to larger planes); and (3) yield management (making more seats available at the new, lower prices). By increasing capacity, American overrode its own internal capacity-planning models for each route, which had previously indicated that such increases would be unprofitable. In each instance, American's response produced the same result: the competing LCC failed to establish a presence, moved its operations, American generally resumed its prior marketing strategy, reducing flights and raising prices to levels roughly comparable to those prior to the period of low-fare competition. Capacity was reduced after LCC exit, but usually remained higher than prior to the alleged episode of predatory activity. . . .

In the instant case, the anticompetitive conduct at issue is predatory pricing. The crux of the government's argument is that the "incremental" revenues and costs specifically associated with American" capacity additions show a loss. Because American spent more to add capacity than the revenues generated by the capacity additions, such capacity additions made no economic sense unless American intended to drive LCCs out of the market. Under the government" theory, American attempted to monopo-lize the four city-pair routes in question in order to develop a reputation as an exceedingly aggressive competitor and set an example to all potential competitors. Fearing American's predatory response, the theory goes, fu-ture potential competitors will decline to enter other DFW market routes and compete. If American succeeds in preventing or at least forestalling the formation of an LCC hub at DFW, it will then be able to charge higher prices on other DFW routes and thereby recoup the losses it incurred from its "capacity dumping" on the four core routes.

Scholars from the Chicago School of economic thought have long labeled predatory pricing as implausible and irrational.... Post–Chicago economists have theorized that price predation is not only plausible, but profitable, especially in a multi-market context where predation can occur in one market and recoupment can occur rapidly in other markets. Al-though this court approaches the matter with caution, we do not do so with the incredulity that once prevailed....

... The Supreme Court has declined to state which of the various cost measures is definitive. In *Brooke Group*, the Court accepted for the pur-poses of the case the parties' agreement that the appropriate measure of cost was AVC, but declined to "resolve the conflict among the lower courts over the appropriate measure of cost." In this circuit, we have spoken of both AVC and other marginal cost measures as relevant.... Because there may be times when courts need the flexibility to examine both AVC as well as other proxies for marginal cost in order to evaluate an alleged predatory pricing scheme, we again decline to dictate a definitive cost measure for all cases. Sole reliance on AVC as the appropriate measure of cost may obscure the nature of a particular predatory scheme and, thus, contrary to what is suggested by the district court, we do not favor AVC to the exclusion of other proxies for marginal cost. Whatever the proxy used to measure marginal cost, it must be accurate and reliable in the specific circumstances of the case at bar.

Conceding that AVC is a good proxy for marginal cost in most cases, the government nevertheless argues that there may be times when looking only to a market-wide AVC test will disguise the nature of the predatory conduct at issue. Where there is a challenge to well-defined incremental conduct, and where incremental costs may be directly and confidently measured utilizing alternative proxies to AVC, argues the government, the market-wide AVC test is inappropriate.

Considering this to be the situation in the instant case, the govern-ment proffers four tests that purport to measure reliably incremental costs—the price costs associated with the capacity additions at issue.... [The Court then analyzed and rejected all four tests proposed by the government. It observed the following about the government's forth test:]

Because the cost component of Test Four includes arbitrarily allocated variable costs, it does not compare incremental revenue to average avoid-able cost. Instead, it compares incremental revenue to a measure of both average variable cost and average avoidable cost. Therefore, Test Four does not measure only the avoidable or incremental cost of the capacity additions and cannot be used to satisfy the government's burden in this case. We conclude that all four proxies are invalid as a matter of law, fatally flawed in their application, and fundamentally unreliable.[60] Because it is uncontested that American did not price below AVC for any route as a whole, we agree with the district court's conclusion that the government has not succeeded in establishing the first element of *Brooke Group*, pricing below an appropriate measure of cost. Our conclusion that the government has not succeeded in establishing a genuine issue of material fact as to the first prong of *Brooke Group*, pricing below an appropriate measure of cost, renders an examination of whether the government has succeeded in creating a genuine issue of material fact as to the second prong of *Brooke Group*, dangerous probability of recoupment, unnecessary. Given the exceedingly thin line between vigorous price competition and predatory pricing, the balance the Supreme Court has struck in *Brooke Group*, and the fatally flawed nature of the alternative pricing proxies proffered by the government, we conclude that the summary judgment in favor of American was appropriate.

NOTE AND QUESTIONS

1. If the government's allegations are correct about ICCs leaving the four markets, and thereafter, American raising prices to recoup, why affirm summary judgment because "American did not price below AVC for any route as a whole"? What if the cost of adding capacity and lowering price resulted in a net loss with respect to each new passenger added? What other alternative to AVC on the "route as a whole" would you consider?

2. If American Airlines had sufficient advantages (*e.g.*, name recognition, reputation) to meet lower prices and force new or smaller carriers from the field, will customers truly be better off in the long run? What about the antitrust policy to protect public welfare? What impact, if any, should the government's "reputation for predation" claim have had? What if the Antitrust Division could have proven that equally efficient rivals of American had, in fact, been deterred from competing because of American's reputation?

Weyerhaeuser Co. v. Ross–Simmons Hardwood Lumber Co.

Supreme Court of the United States, 2007.
549 U.S. 312, 127 S.Ct. 1069, 166 L.Ed.2d 911.

■ THOMAS, J. Respondent Ross–Simmons, a sawmill, sued petitioner Weyerhaeuser, alleging that Weyerhaeuser drove it out of business by bidding up

60. The government's four proxies are, in effect, an illustration of the long-recognized fact that "the true marginal costs of production are difficult to generate." *Stearns*, 170 F.3d at 532. The difficulty inherent in isolating the precise costs associated with production increases is precisely why most courts attempt to "estimate [marginal cost] by using average variable costs."

the price of sawlogs to a level that prevented Ross–Simmons from being profitable. A jury returned a verdict in favor of Ross–Simmons on its monopolization claim, and the Ninth Circuit affirmed. We granted certiorari to decide whether the test we applied to claims of predatory pricing in *Brooke Group* also applies to claims of predatory bidding. We hold that it does. Accordingly, we vacate the judgment of the Court of Appeals.

I

This antitrust case concerns the acquisition of red alder sawlogs by the mills that process those logs in the Pacific Northwest. These hardwood-lumber mills usually acquire logs in one of three ways. Some logs are purchased on the open bidding market. Some come to the mill through standing short-and long-term agreements with timberland owners. And others are harvested from timberland owned by the sawmills themselves. The allegations relevant to our decision in this case relate to the bidding market.

Ross–Simmons began operating a hardwood-lumber sawmill in Longview, Washington, in 1962. Weyerhaeuser entered the Northwestern hardwood-lumber market in 1980 by acquiring an existing lumber company. Weyerhaeuser gradually increased the scope of its hardwood-lumber operation, and it now owns six hardwood sawmills in the region. By 2001, Weyerhaeuser's mills were acquiring approximately 65 percent of the alder logs available for sale in the region.

From 1990 to 2000, Weyerhaeuser made more than $75 million in capital investments in its hardwood mills in the Pacific Northwest. During this period, production increased at every Northwestern hardwood mill that Weyerhaeuser owned. In addition to increasing production, Weyerhaeuser used "state-of-the-art technology," including sawing equipment, to increase the amount of lumber recovered from every log. By contrast, Ross–Simmons appears to have engaged in little efficiency-enhancing investment.

Logs represent up to 75 percent of a sawmill's total costs. And from 1998 to 2001, the price of alder sawlogs increased while prices for finished hardwood lumber fell. These divergent trends in input and output prices cut into the mills' profit margins, and Ross–Simmons suffered heavy losses during this time. Saddled with several million dollars in debt, Ross–Simmons shut down its mill completely in May 2001.

Ross–Simmons blamed Weyerhaeuser for driving it out of business by bidding up input costs, and it filed an antitrust suit against Weyerhaeuser for monopolization and attempted monopolization under § 2 of the Sherman Act. Ross–Simmons alleged that, among other anticompetitive acts, Weyerhaeuser had used "its dominant position in the alder sawlog market to drive up the prices for alder sawlogs to levels that severely reduced or eliminated the profit margins of Weyerhaeuser's alder sawmill competition." Proceeding in part on this "predatory-bidding" theory, Ross–Simmons argued that Weyerhaeuser had overpaid for alder sawlogs to cause sawlog prices to rise to artificially high levels as part of a plan to drive Ross–Simmons out of business. As proof that this practice had occurred,

Ross–Simmons pointed to Weyerhaeuser's large share of the alder purchasing market, rising alder sawlog prices during the alleged predation period, and Weyerhaeuser's declining profits during that same period.

Prior to trial, Weyerhaeuser moved for summary judgment on Ross–Simmons' predatory-bidding theory. The District Court denied the motion. At the close of the 9–day trial, Weyerhaeuser moved for judgment as a matter of law, or alternatively, for a new trial. The motions were based in part on Weyerhaeuser's argument that Ross–Simmons had not satisfied the standard this Court set forth in *Brooke Group*. The District Court denied Weyerhaeuser's motion. The District Court also rejected proposed predatory-bidding jury instructions that incorporated elements of the *Brooke Group* test. Ultimately, the District Court instructed the jury that Ross–Simmons could prove that Weyerhaeuser's bidding practices were anticompetitive acts if the jury concluded that Weyerhaeuser "purchased more logs than it needed, or paid a higher price for logs than necessary, in order to prevent [Ross–Simmons] from obtaining the logs they needed at a fair price." Finding that Ross–Simmons had proved its claim for monopolization, the jury returned a $26 million verdict against Weyerhaeuser. The verdict was trebled to approximately $79 million.

Weyerhaeuser appealed to the Court of Appeals for the Ninth Circuit. There, Weyerhaeuser argued that *Brooke Group*'s standard for claims of predatory pricing should also apply to claims of predatory bidding. The Ninth Circuit disagreed and affirmed the verdict against Weyerhaeuser.

The Court of Appeals reasoned that "buy-side predatory bidding" and "sell-side predatory pricing," though similar, are materially different in that predatory bidding does not necessarily benefit consumers or stimulate competition in the way that predatory pricing does. Concluding that "the concerns that led the *Brooke Group* Court to establish a high standard of liability in the predatory-pricing context do not carry over to this predatory bidding context with the same force," the Court of Appeals declined to apply *Brooke Group* to Ross–Simmons' claims of predatory bidding. The Court of Appeals went on to conclude that substantial evidence supported a finding of liability on the predatory-bidding theory. We granted certiorari to decide whether *Brooke Group* applies to claims of predatory bidding. We hold that it does, and we vacate the Court of Appeals' judgment.

II

In *Brooke Group*, we considered what a plaintiff must show in order to succeed on a claim of predatory pricing under § 2 of the Sherman Act. In a typical predatory-pricing scheme, the predator reduces the sale price of its product (its output) to below cost, hoping to drive competitors out of business. Then, with competition vanquished, the predator raises output prices to a supracompetitive level. For the scheme to make economic sense, the losses suffered from pricing goods below cost must be recouped (with interest) during the supracompetitive-pricing stage of the scheme. . . .

III

Predatory bidding, which Ross–Simmons alleges in this case, involves the exercise of market power on the buy side or input side of a market. In a predatory-bidding scheme, a purchaser of inputs "bids up the market price of a critical input to such high levels that rival buyers cannot survive (or compete as vigorously) and, as a result, the predating buyer acquires (or maintains or increases its) monopsony power. . . ."

A predatory bidder ultimately aims to exercise the monopsony power gained from bidding up input prices. To that end, once the predatory bidder has caused competing buyers to exit the market for purchasing inputs, it will seek to "restrict its input purchases below the competitive level," thus "reducing the unit price for the remaining inputs it purchases." Salop, Anticompetitive Overbuying by Power Buyers, *72 Antitrust L. J. 669, 672 (2005)* (hereinafter Salop). The reduction in input prices will lead to "a significant cost saving that more than offsets the profits that would have been earned on the output." If all goes as planned, the predatory bidder will reap monopsonistic profits that will offset any losses suffered in bidding up input prices.[61] (In this case, the plaintiff was the defendant's competitor in the input-purchasing market. Thus, this case does not present a situation of suppliers suing a monopsonist buyer under *§ 2* of the Sherman Act, nor does it present a risk of significantly increased concentration in the market in which the monopsonist sells, *i.e.*, the market for finished lumber.)

IV

A

Predatory-pricing and predatory-bidding claims are analytically similar. See Hovenkamp, The Law of Exclusionary Pricing, 2 Competition Policy Int'l, No. 1, pp. 21, 35 (Spring 2006). . . . The kinship between monopoly and monopsony suggests that similar legal standards should apply to claims of monopolization and to claims of monopsonization.

Tracking the economic similarity between monopoly and monopsony, predatory-pricing plaintiffs and predatory-bidding plaintiffs make strikingly similar allegations. A predatory-pricing plaintiff alleges that a predator cut prices to drive the plaintiff out of business and, thereby, to reap monopoly profits from the output market. In parallel fashion, a predatory-bidding plaintiff alleges that a predator raised prices for a key input to drive the plaintiff out of business and, thereby, to reap monopsony profits in the input market. Both claims involve the deliberate use of unilateral pricing measures for anticompetitive purposes.[62] And both claims logically require

---

61. If the predatory firm's competitors in the input market and the output market are the same, then predatory bidding can also lead to the bidder's acquisition of monopoly power in the output market. In that case, which does not appear to be present here, the monopsonist could, under certain market conditions, also recoup its losses by raising output prices to monopolistic levels. See Salop 679–682 (describing a monopsonist's predatory strategy that depends upon raising prices in the output market).

62. Predatory bidding on inputs is not analytically different from predatory overbuying of inputs. Both practices fall under the rubric of monopsony predation and involve an input

firms to incur short-term losses on the chance that they might reap
supracompetitive profits in the future.

B

More importantly, predatory bidding mirrors predatory pricing in
respects that we deemed significant to our analysis in *Brooke Group*. In
Brooke Group, we noted that "predatory pricing schemes are rarely tried,
and even more rarely successful." Predatory pricing requires a firm to
suffer certain losses in the short term on the chance of reaping supracompetitive profits in the future. A rational business will rarely make this
sacrifice. The same reasoning applies to predatory bidding. A predatory-
bidding scheme requires a buyer of inputs to suffer losses today on the
chance that it will reap supracompetitive profits in the future. For this
reason, "successful monopsony predation is probably as unlikely as successful monopoly predation." R. Blair & J. Harrison, Monopsony 66 (1993).

And like the predatory conduct alleged in *Brooke Group*, actions taken
in a predatory-bidding scheme are often "the very essence of competition."
Just as sellers use output prices to compete for purchasers, buyers use bid
prices to compete for scarce inputs. There are myriad legitimate reasons—
ranging from benign to affirmatively procompetitive—why a buyer might
bid up input prices. A firm might bid up inputs as a result of miscalculation
of its input needs or as a response to increased consumer demand for its
outputs. A more efficient firm might bid up input prices to acquire more
inputs as a part of a procompetitive strategy to gain market share in the
output market. A firm that has adopted an input-intensive production
process might bid up inputs to acquire the inputs necessary for its process.
Or a firm might bid up input prices to acquire excess inputs as a hedge
against the risk of future rises in input costs or future input shortages.
There is nothing illicit about these bidding decisions. Indeed, this sort of
high bidding is essential to competition and innovation on the buy side of
the market.[63]

Brooke Group also noted that a failed predatory-pricing scheme may
benefit consumers. The potential benefit results from the difficulty an
aspiring predator faces in recouping losses suffered from below-cost pricing.
Without successful recoupment, "predatory pricing produces lower aggregate prices in the market, and consumer welfare is enhanced." Failed
predatory-bidding schemes can also, but will not necessarily, benefit consumers. In the first stage of a predatory-bidding scheme, the predator's
high bidding will likely lead to its acquisition of more inputs. Usually, the

---

purchaser's use of input prices in an attempt to exclude rival input purchasers. The economic
effect of the practices is identical: input prices rise. In a predatory-bidding scheme, the
purchaser causes prices to rise by offering to pay more for inputs. In a predatory-overbuying
scheme, the purchaser causes prices to rise by demanding more of the input. Either way, input
prices increase. Our use of the term "predatory bidding" is not meant to suggest that different
legal treatment is appropriate for the economically identical practice of "predatory overbuying."

63.   Higher prices for inputs obviously benefit existing sellers of inputs and encourage
new firms to enter the market for input sales as well.

acquisition of more inputs leads to the manufacture of more outputs. And increases in output generally result in lower prices to consumers.[64] Thus, a failed predatory-bidding scheme can be a "boon to consumers" in the same way that we considered a predatory-pricing scheme to be. See *Brooke Group*.

In addition, predatory bidding presents less of a direct threat of consumer harm than predatory pricing. A predatory-pricing scheme ultimately achieves success by charging higher prices to consumers. By contrast, a predatory-bidding scheme could succeed with little or no effect on consumer prices because a predatory bidder does not necessarily rely on raising prices in the output market to recoup its losses. Even if output prices remain constant, a predatory bidder can use its power as the predominant buyer of inputs to force down input prices and capture monopsony profits.

C

The general theoretical similarities of monopoly and monopsony combined with the theoretical and practical similarities of predatory pricing and predatory bidding convince us that our two-pronged *Brooke Group* test should apply to predatory-bidding claims.

The first prong of *Brooke Group*'s test requires little adaptation for the predatory-bidding context. A plaintiff must prove that the alleged predatory bidding led to below-cost pricing of the predator's outputs. That is, the predator's bidding on the buy side must have caused the cost of the relevant output to rise above the revenues generated in the sale of those outputs. As with predatory pricing, the exclusionary effect of higher bidding that does not result in below-cost output pricing "is beyond the practical ability of a judicial tribunal to control without courting intolerable risks of chilling legitimate" procompetitive conduct. Given the multitude of procompetitive ends served by higher bidding for inputs, the risk of chilling procompetitive behavior with too lax a liability standard is as serious here as it was in *Brooke Group*. Consequently, only higher bidding that leads to below-cost pricing in the relevant output market will suffice as a basis for liability for predatory bidding.

A predatory-bidding plaintiff also must prove that the defendant has a dangerous probability of recouping the losses incurred in bidding up input prices through the exercise of monopsony power. Absent proof of likely recoupment, a strategy of predatory bidding makes no economic sense because it would involve short-term losses with no likelihood of offsetting long-term gains. As with predatory pricing, making a showing on the recoupment prong will require "a close analysis of both the scheme alleged by the plaintiff and the structure and conditions of the relevant market."

---

64. Consumer benefit does not necessarily result at the first stage because the predator might not use its excess inputs to manufacture additional outputs. It might instead destroy the excess inputs. See Salop 677, n. 22. Also, if the same firms compete in the input and output markets, any increase in outputs by the predator could be offset by decreases in outputs from the predator's struggling competitors.

Ross–Simmons has conceded that it has not satisfied the *Brooke Group* standard. Therefore, its predatory-bidding theory of liability cannot support the jury's verdict.

QUESTIONS

1. In general, is probability for recoupment as unlikely for a monopolist or monopsonist as for an oligopolist group?

2. What theoretical or empirical basis does the Court provide for its skepticism about Weyerhaeuser's ability to recoup? What basis does Justice Thomas provide for rejecting the jury's finding that Weyerhaeuser's bidding practices were anticompetitive and aimed at driving Ross–Simmons out of business?

COMPARATIVE NOTE: PREDATORY PRICING IN THE EUROPEAN UNION

EU competition law takes a somewhat more critical view of predatory pricing than its American counterpart now does. In AKZO Chemie BV v. Commission, Case C–62/86, [1991] ECR I–3359, the Court of Justice had before it a case in which Akzo, a large Dutch multinational firm, was accused of holding a dominant position in benzoyl peroxide, which is used as a bleaching agent for flour and as a catalyst in the production of certain plastics. One of Akzo's tactics involved the alleged use of predatory pricing. In that connection, the Court of Justice said that "[p]rices below average variable costs (that is to say, those which vary depending on the quantities produced) by means of which a dominant undertaking seeks to eliminate a competitor must be regarded as abusive." *Id.*, ¶ 71. The Court focused there on the intent of the dominant firm to eliminate a competitor by means of such pricing. In a later decision given by the Court of First Instance in Tetra Pak International SA v. Commission, Case T–83/91, [1994] ECR II–755, the CFI held that the intent to eliminate a competitor was crucial, but it implied that prices would be predatory only if recoupment could occur. The Court of Justice disagreed with the CFI on this point. It described the rules for predatory pricing as follows:

> In *Akzo* this court did indeed sanction the existence of two different methods of analysis for determining whether an undertaking has practised predatory pricing. First, prices below average variable costs must always be considered abusive.... Secondly, prices below total costs but above average variable costs are only to be considered abusive if an intention to eliminate can be shown.
>
> ... Furthermore, it would not be appropriate, in the circumstances of the present case, to require in addition proof that Tetra Pak had a realistic chance of recouping its losses. It must be possible to penalise predatory pricing whenever there is a risk that competitors will be eliminated.

Case C–333/94P, [1996] ECR I–5951, ¶¶ 41, 44.

In 2009, the Court of Justice upheld a decision by the Commission (which had also been confirmed by the Court of First Instance) in which it had found that Wanadoo Interactive S.A., at the relevant time a subsidiary of France Telecom, had abused a dominant position in the market for high-speed internet access by engaging in predatory pricing. In sharp contrast to the Supreme Court's *Brooke*

Group decision, the ECJ ruled that the Commission was not required to prove that Wanadoo had the possibility of recouping its losses. Instead, consistently with the *Akzo* decision, the Court said that recoupment was merely one factor that the Commission might take into account in assessing whether the practice was abusive. *See* France Télécom SA v. Commission, Case C–202/07 (April 2, 2009). It is plain, therefore, that the United States and Europe continue to have different views on the type of pricing that should be condemned as "predatory" and hence abusive. *See also* "North Atlantic Competition Policy: Converging Toward What?", Address by William J. Kolasky, Deputy Assistant Attorney General, Antitrust Division, U.S. Dept. of Justice, Before the BIICL Second Annual Int'l and Comp. Law Conference, London, May 17, 2002, at http://www.usdoj.gov/atr/public/speeches/ 11153.htm.

PROBLEM 19

AMERICAN FOODS EXPANDS ITS MARKET SHARE

American Foods is one of the largest manufacturers and distributors of household products in the United States. Its sales last year were in excess of $5 billion and its profits were $500 million. It is the third largest general advertiser and second largest TV advertiser in the United States.

One of its relatively minor product lines is potato chips. Last year it accounted for 28% of sales and stood first in the market, but it has been losing market share. Its high water mark occurred five years ago when it accounted for 39% of sales, which contributed about $10 million to the company's profits. Two other diversified national food companies—Jones & Turner and National Mills—stand second and third respectively with 18% and 15%; and their market shares have also been down in the last five years. All other potato chip sales are by regional and local companies or are accounted for by private label sales. Several regional companies have enjoyed great success in recent years and have cut into the market leaders' market shares.

An American Foods strategic planning task force reported that American's potato chip plants were obsolete and that an aggressive expansion program would require modernization of existing plants and construction of two new plants on the east and west coasts. Despite the decline in the company's market share, its total volume of potato chip sales had fallen only slightly in the last five years so that there was little unused capacity in the American Foods system.

To justify a modernization and expansion program, the strategic planning group proposed and implemented a three-pronged promotional program to expand the company's sales base and respond to the effective competition of the regionals. The advertising budget, currently the largest in the potato chip industry, was doubled with emphasis on national spot TV. New types and brands were introduced (*i.e.*, Bar–B–Que chips, low calorie chips), as well as more package sizes. Finally, selective wholesale price cuts were offered in major cities where regional companies had made their most extensive in-roads. The combination of advertising expenditures and price cuts has placed American Foods' national average price well below average total cost, but about 4% above average variable cost. In eight key cities, price was above but within 1% of average variable cost and in a ninth city— Rochester, New York—American Foods' price last year was below average variable cost. This occurred because of a delivery strike which cut sales for the year below anticipated volume. The wholesale price in other cities would have been below average variable cost if advertising expenditures had been expensed in the year in which they were made. American Foods follows an allocation program, however, which treats advertising in part as current expense and in part as a future "investment," and allocates only 60% in the year in which the ads are run, 30% the following year, and 10% the third year. This accounting formula was adopted by American Foods two years before implementation of the expansion program.

American Foods' market share is up to 41% this year and it anticipates that it will be 45% next year if it continues its marketing program. The two other national firms have met American Foods' price cuts and maintained their market shares, but several regionals are losing money and either have been or will be driven out of business unless American Foods' promotional program is discontinued.

The Federal Trade Commission has challenged the program, charging an attempt to monopolize under Section 2 and an unfair method of competition under Section 5. What result? If the Commission prevails in court, what remedy should be imposed?

SECTION 3.   TYING ARRANGEMENTS

Clayton Act, Section 3[65]

That it shall be unlawful for any person engaged in commerce, in the course of such commerce, to lease or make a sale or contract for sale of goods, wares, merchandise, machinery, supplies or other commodities, whether patented or unpatented, for use, consumption or resale within the United States or any Territory thereof or the District of Columbia or any insular possession or other place under the jurisdiction of the United States, or fix a price charged therefor or discount from or rebate upon, such price, on the condition, agreement or understanding that the lessee or purchaser thereof shall not use or deal in the goods, wares, merchandise, machinery, supplies, or other commodities of a competitor or competitors of the lessor or seller, where the effect of such lease, sale, or contract for sale or such condition, agreement or understanding may be to substantially lessen competition or tend to create a monopoly in any line of commerce.

United Shoe Machinery Corp. v. United States, 258 U.S. 451 (1922). This was a suit to enjoin the defendants from making leases containing clauses and conditions alleged to violate Section 3 of the Clayton Act. The United Shoe Machinery Corporation controlled more than ninety-five percent of the shoe machinery business in this country. Its machines were protected by patents. The district court had enjoined the use of

---

65. 38 Stat. 731 (1914), 15 U.S.C. § 14.

(1) the restricted use clause, which provides that the leased machinery shall not ... be used upon shoes, etc., or portions thereof, upon which certain other operations have not been performed on other machines of the defendants; (2) the exclusive use clause, which provides that if the lessee fails to use exclusively machinery of certain kinds made by the lessor, the lessor shall have the right to cancel the right to use all such machinery so leased; (3) the supplies clause, which provides that the lessee shall purchase supplies exclusively from the lessor; (4) the patent insole clause, which provides that the lessee shall only use machinery leased on shoes which have had certain other operations performed upon them by the defendant's machines; (5) the additional machinery clause, which provides that the lessee shall take all additional machinery for certain kinds of work from the lessor or lose his right to retain the machines which he has already leased; (6) the factory output clause, which requires the payment of a royalty on shoes operated upon by machines made by competitors; (7) the discriminatory royalty clause, providing lower royalty for lessees who agree not to use certain machinery on shoes lasted on machines other than those leased from the lessor. The defendant's restrictive form of lease embraces the right of the lessor to cancel a lease for the breach of a provision in such lease, or in any other lease or license agreement between the lessor and the lessee. The lessor in such case is given the right, by notice in writing to the lessee, to terminate any and all leases or licenses then in force to use the machinery and this notwithstanding previous breaches or defaults may have been unnoticed, waived, or condoned by or on behalf of the lessor.

The Supreme Court (Day, J.) affirmed:

While the clauses enjoined do not contain specific agreements not to use the machinery of a competitor of the lessor, the practical effect of these drastic provisions is to prevent such use. We can entertain no doubt that such provisions as were enjoined are embraced in the broad terms of the Clayton Act which cover all conditions, agreements, or understandings of this nature. That such restrictive and tying agreements must necessarily lessen competition and tend to monopoly is, we believe, equally apparent. When it is considered that the United Company occupies a dominating position in supplying shoe machinery of the classes involved, these covenants signed by the lessee and binding upon him effectually prevent him from acquiring the machinery of a competitor of the lessor except at the risk of forfeiting the right to use the machines furnished by the United Company which may be absolutely essential to the prosecution and success of his business.

This system of "tying" restrictions is quite as effective as express covenants could be and practically compels the use of the machinery of the lessor except upon risks which manufacturers will not willingly incur. It is true that the record discloses that in many instances these provisions were not enforced.... The fact that the lessor in many instances forbore to enforce these provisions does not make them any the less agreements within the condemnation of the Clayton Act.

It is contended that the decree in favor of the defendants affirmed in the former suit [brought by] the Government under the Sherman Act ... is res judicata [as to] the present issues....

The Sherman Act suit had for its object the dissolution of the United Company, which had been formed by the union of other shoe machinery companies. It also attacked and sought to enjoin the use of the restrictive and tying clauses contained in the leases as being in themselves contracts in violation of the Sherman Act. The Sherman Act and the Clayton Act provide different tests of liability.

The previous litigation merely concerned the validity of the leases under the Sherman law. The restrictions in the defendant's leases are specifically forbidden by the Clayton Act.

International Salt Co. v. United States

Supreme Court of the United States, 1947.
332 U.S. 392, 68 S.Ct. 12, 92 L.Ed. 20.

■ JACKSON, J. The Government brought this civil action to enjoin the International Salt Company, appellant here, from carrying out provisions of the leases of its patented machines to the effect that lessees would use therein only International's salt products. The restriction is alleged to violate § 1 of the Sherman Act, and § 3 of the Clayton Act. Upon appellant's answer and admissions of fact, the Government moved for summary judgment under Rule 56 of the Rules of Civil Procedure, upon the ground that no issue as to a material fact was presented and that, on the admissions, judgment followed as a matter of law. Neither party submitted affidavits. Judgment was granted and appeal was taken directly to this Court.

It was established by pleadings or admissions that the International Salt Company is engaged in interstate commerce in salt, of which it is the country's largest producer for industrial uses. It also owns patents on two machines for utilization of salt products. One, the "Lixator," dissolves rock salt into a brine used in various industrial processes. The other, the "Saltomat," injects salt, in tablet form, into canned products during the canning process. The principal distribution of each of these machines is under leases which, among other things, require the lessees to purchase from appellant all unpatented salt and salt tablets consumed in the leased machines.

Appellant had outstanding 790 leases of an equal number of "Lixators," all of which leases were on appellant's standard form containing the tying clause and other standard provisions; of 50 other leases which somewhat varied the terms, all but 4 contained the tying clause. It also had in effect 73 leases of 96 "Saltomats," all containing the restrictive clause. In 1944, appellant sold approximately 119,000 tons of salt, for about $500,000, for use in these machines.

The appellant's patents confer a limited monopoly of the invention they reward. From them appellant derives a right to restrain others from making, vending or using the patented machines. But the patents confer no right to restrain use of, or trade in, unpatented salt. By contracting to close this market for salt against competition, International has engaged in a restraint of trade for which its patents afford no immunity from the antitrust laws. [Citing cases.]

Int'l Salt arg 1

Appellant contends, however, that summary judgment was unauthorized because it precluded trial of alleged issues of fact as to whether the restraint was unreasonable within the Sherman Act or substantially lessened competition or tended to create a monopoly in salt within the Clayton Act. We think the admitted facts left no genuine issue. Not only is price-fixing unreasonable, *per se*, United States v. Socony–Vacuum Oil Co., 310 U.S. 150; United States v. Trenton Potteries Co., 273 U.S. 392, but also it is unreasonable, *per se*, to foreclose competitors from any substantial market. *Fashion Originators' Guild.* The volume of business affected by these contracts cannot be said to be insignificant or insubstantial and the tendency of the arrangement to accomplishment of monopoly seems obvious. Under the law, agreements are forbidden which "tend to create a monopoly," and it is immaterial that the tendency is a creeping one rather than one that proceeds at full gallop; nor does the law await arrival at the goal before condemning the direction of the movement.

Arg 2: leases provided that IS would meet comp prices on salt

Appellant contends, however, that the "Lixator" contracts are saved from unreasonableness and from the tendency to monopoly because they provided that if any competitor offered salt of equal grade at a lower price, the lessee should be free to buy in the open market, unless appellant would furnish the salt at an equal price; and the "Saltomat" agreements provided that the lessee was entitled to the benefit of any general price reduction in lessor's salt tablets. The "Lixator" provision does, of course, afford a measure of protection to the lessee, but it does not avoid the stifling effect of the agreement on competition. The appellant had at all times a priority on the business at equal prices. A competitor would have to undercut appellant's price to have any hope of capturing the market, while appellant could hold that market by merely meeting competition. We do not think this concession relieves the contract of being a restraint of trade, albeit a less harsh one than would result in the absence of such a provision. The "Saltomat" provision obviously has no effect of legal significance since it gives the lessee nothing more than a right to buy appellant's salt tablets at appellant's going price. All purchases must in any event be of appellant's product.

Arg 3: high qual salt nec for machines

Appellant also urges that since under the leases it remained under an obligation to repair and maintain the machines, it was reasonable to confine their use to its own salt because its high quality assured satisfactory functioning and low maintenance cost. The appellant's rock salt is alleged to have an average sodium chloride content of 98.2%. Rock salt of other producers, it is said, "does not run consistent in sodium chloride content and in many instances runs as low as 95% of sodium chloride." This greater percentage of insoluble impurities allegedly disturbs the functioning of the "Lixator" machine. A somewhat similar claim is pleaded as to the "Saltomat."

Of course, a lessor may impose on a lessee reasonable restrictions designed in good faith to minimize maintenance burdens and to assure satisfactory operation. We may assume, as matter of argument, that if the "Lixator" functions best on rock salt of average sodium chloride content of

98.2%, the lessee might be required to use only salt meeting such a specification of quality. But it is not pleaded, nor is it argued, that the machine is allergic to salt of equal quality produced by anyone except International. If others cannot produce salt equal to reasonable specifications for machine use, it is one thing; but it is admitted that, at times, at least, competitors do offer such a product. They are, however, shut out of the market by a provision that limits it, not in terms of quality, but in terms of a particular vendor. Rules for use of leased machinery must not be disguised restraints of free competition, though they may set reasonable standards which all suppliers must meet. *Cf.* International Business Machines Corporation v. United States, 298 U.S. 131....

Judgment affirmed.

NOTES AND QUESTIONS

International Salt suggests that antitrust enforcement against tie-in sales rests on the assumption that firms with market power with respect to a tying product will distort competition as to a second or tied product by insisting that the two products be purchased jointly. A question to keep in mind in thinking about *International Salt* and the following tie-in cases is what kind of incentives— legitimate or illegitimate—lead the seller to insist on a tie-in arrangement. Consider the following questions when reviewing the cases and materials in the remainder of this section.

1.   Suppose the seller has no discernable market power with respect to the tying product, but nevertheless offers that product for sale only if purchased in conjunction with a second independent product. Why would any seller follow such a marketing strategy? Would it be likely to succeed?

2.   At the other extreme, consider a situation in which a seller has an absolute monopoly of a tying product and offers it for sale only in conjunction with purchase of a second, independent product. What are the possible incentives for tie-in sales in that situation? Will a tie-in strategy succeed, or are there limits on its effectiveness? Is it necessarily the case that the seller will earn greater profits from this linked sale of the tying and tied products than it could earn by selling the monopolized tying product at the highest possible price and reducing the price on the tied product or giving the tied product away?

3.   Suppose instead of an outright tie-in, the seller offers the tying product with or without the tied product, but offers the two products at a lower combined price than could be obtained if they were purchased separately. That situation is covered by Section 3 which deals not only with a "lease or ... sale" of a commodity but also with a "discount from or rebate upon" a sales price. Is that kind of offer significantly less anticompetitive than an outright tie-in sale? What is the difference in competitive effect?

4.   Are there explanations for tie-in sales other than an intention on the part of the seller to increase sales and thereby profits on the tied product? What are these other possible justifications and do they reflect legitimate business considerations?

5. In Times–Picayune Publishing Co. v. United States, 345 U.S. 594 (1953), the Supreme Court considered the legality of a plan under which a company that owned the sole morning newspaper in New Orleans and one of two afternoon papers required advertisers to buy space in both, if they wanted to advertise in either. The Court found that this so-called "unit plan" did not violate Section 1 of the Sherman Act. Before a tying arrangement would violate Section 1, the government would have had to prove (1) that the seller enjoyed a monopolistic position in the market for the tying product, and (2) that a substantial volume of commerce in the tied product was restrained. (Either one of those showings, the Court said, would have been enough to make out a violation of Section 3 of the Clayton Act.) The government's proof failed on both counts: the paper had only about 40% of the market for advertising sales, and the unit plan did not have a substantial adverse effect on competition.

———————

Northern Pacific Railway v. United States, 356 U.S. 1 (1958). In 1864 and 1870, Congress granted the predecessor of the Northern Pacific Railway Company approximately 40 million acres of land in several Northwestern States and Territories to facilitate its construction of a railroad from Lake Superior to Puget Sound. By 1949, the Northern Pacific had sold about 37 million acres of its holdings. In a large number of its sales contracts and most of its lease agreements Northern Pacific had inserted "preferential routing" clauses which compelled the transferee to ship over Northern Pacific lines all commodities produced or manufactured on the land, provided that its rates (and in some instances its services) were equal to those of competing carriers. There were alternative means of transportation available, including two major railroad systems.

The government, in a suit alleging violations of Section 1 of the Sherman Act, moved for summary judgment which was granted by the district court. In affirming the grant of summary judgment, the Supreme Court, per Black, J., wrote:

> For our purposes a tying arrangement may be defined as an agreement by a party to sell one product but only on the condition that the buyer also purchases a different (or tied) product, or at least agrees that he will not purchase that product from any other supplier.[66] Where such conditions are successfully exacted competition on the merits with respect to the tied product is inevitably curbed. Indeed "tying agreements serve hardly any purpose beyond the suppression of competition." . . . They deny competitors free access to the market for the tied product, not because the party imposing the tying requirements has a better product or a lower price but because of his power or leverage in another market. At the same time buyers are forced to forego their free choice between competing products. For these reasons "tying agreements fare harshly under the laws forbidding restraints of trade." Times–Picayune Publishing Co. v. United States. They are unreasonable in and of themselves whenever a party has sufficient economic power with respect to the tying product to appreciably restrain free competition in the market for the tied product and a "not insubstantial" amount of interstate commerce is affected. International Salt Co. v. United States. . . . Of course where the seller has no control or

———————

66. Of course, when the buyer is free to take either product by itself, there is no tying problem even though the seller may also offer the two items as a unit at a single price.

dominance over the tying product so that it does not represent an effectual weapon to pressure buyers into taking the tied item any restraint of trade attributable to such tying arrangements would obviously be insignificant at most. As a simple example, if one of a dozen food stores in a community were to refuse to sell flour unless the buyer also took sugar it would hardly tend to restrain competition in sugar if its competitors were ready and able to sell flour by itself.

The Court explained that requisite market power in the tying "product" was clearly present.

> We wholly agree that the undisputed facts established beyond any genuine question that the defendant possessed substantial economic power by virtue of its extensive landholdings which it used as leverage to induce large numbers of purchasers and lessees to give it preference, to the exclusion of its competitors, in carrying goods or produce from the land transferred to them.... This land was strategically located ... amid private holdings and within economic distance of transportation facilities.... [C]ommon sense makes it evident that this particular land was often prized by those who purchased or leased it and was frequently essential to their business activities.

The Court went on to explain:

> The very existence of this host of tying arrangements is itself compelling evidence of the defendant's great power, at least where, as here, no other explanation has been offered for the existence of these restraints.

The Court conceded that there was language in *Times–Picayune* which referred to "monopoly power" or "dominance" over the tying product as being a precondition for application of the *per se* rule to tying arrangements, but declined to construe the requirement as anything more than "sufficient economic power to impose an appreciable restraint on free competition in the tied product (assuming all the time, of course, that a 'not insubstantial' amount of interstate commerce is affected)."

NOTES CONCERNING TYING LAW PRIOR TO THE JEFFERSON PARISH CASE AND QUESTIONS

1. The Supreme Court in *Northern Pacific* came down heavily on the point that the tying arrangements were suspect because of the failure of the defendant to offer any legitimate business justification for their existence. On the question of possible justifications, consider the following excerpt from Scherer, Industrial Market Structure and Economic Performance 582–83 (2d ed. 1980):

> Businesses have diverse reasons for attempting to tie the sale of one product to that of another. First, a firm may have monopoly power over one product by virtue of patent protection, strong product differentiation, or scale economies; and it may try to exploit this leverage in a second market where, without the tie, it could earn no more than a normal return. Thus, it adds to its monopoly profits in the tying good market the profits it can realize by exercising power over price in at least part of the tied good market. The economics of such ties are similar to those of downstream integration by a firm to obtain control over the purchase of inputs complementary in production to the input on which the firm enjoys monopoly power. Second and closely related, the profits attainable from coordinated monopoly pricing of two goods which, for example, are comple-

ments in use, will generally be higher than those realized by setting a monopoly price for each commodity separately. This is so because, by ignoring interdependence between the demand functions of complementary products, a producer in effect fails to adjust for all the variables affecting its profit maximum, just as oligopolists producing the same product maximize joint profits only when they take into account fully the interdependence of their demand functions. Third, tying is sometimes a convenient way of discriminating in price according to intensity of demand. Suppose, for instance, that one copying machine user makes 3,000 copies per month, while another makes 10,000 copies per month. It would be difficult for a company selling only copying machines to price its machines in such a way as to extract more revenue from the more intensive user. But if the machine maker can tie the purchase of special copying paper to the purchase of its machine, and if it can wield sufficient leverage in the paper market to realize a supranormal profit margin there, it will be able to secure additional profits from the high-volume user. An analogous but more complex variant occurs when firms sell related but separable products only at a single package or bundled price. Fourth, the producer of a technically complex machine may engage in tying to control the quality of materials and supplies used with its machine, so that the reputation of its product is not sullied by breakdowns caused through the use of faulty supplies. Fifth, certain economies may be realized by producing or distributing the tied and tying goods together. For example, supplies of special copying machine paper or ink may be delivered by maintenance personnel in the course of routine service visits, saving separate delivery costs. It is doubtful, however, whether the savings realized in this way could be very substantial. Finally, tying contracts may be employed to evade governmental price controls—*e.g.*, when a firm supplying some commodity such as gas or telephone service whose price is regulated requires customers to buy from it fixtures and attachments whose prices are not effectively controlled.

In studying the remaining cases in this section, you should consider whether any of these explanations for tying are applicable. Which, if any, explanations should be treated as a legitimate defense?

2.   In United States v. Loew's Inc., 371 U.S. 38, 45–47 (1962), the Supreme Court concluded that even "absent a showing of market dominance, the crucial economic power may be inferred from the tying product's desirability to consumers or from uniqueness in its attributes."

3.   In Fortner Enterprises, Inc. v. United States Steel Corp., 394 U.S. 495 (1969) (*Fortner I*) and 429 U.S. 610 (1977) (*Fortner II*), cases discussed at some length in *Jefferson Parish infra*, the Court spoke in terms of "appreciable economic power."

4.   It was commonly said that tie-in sales are illegal *per se* if certain preconditions are satisfied (*e.g.*, sufficient or appreciable economic power with respect to the tying product, not insubstantial amount of commerce in the tied product, etc.). Consider the following cases in light of this qualified *per se* rule covering tie-in sales:

(a) United States v. Jerrold Electronics Corp., 187 F.Supp. 545 (E.D.Pa.1960), affirmed per curiam, 365 U.S. 567 (1961). Defendant, which had pioneered the community television antenna industry, sold various items of equipment, including cable, amplifiers, converters and electronic units only as components of a single system, and also required purchasers to secure servicing solely from Jerrold. The arrangement was attacked as a Sherman Act violation. Finding that the scheme constituted a tie-in, the court nevertheless upheld the arrangement as justified during the development period of this new industry. At least at that time, the arrangement assured Jerrold's profits, reputation, and future, upon which the success and orderly growth of the industry depended.

> Unrestricted sales would have resulted in much of this equipment going into systems where prospects of success were at best extremely doubtful. Jerrold's short and long-term well-being depended on the success of these first systems. It could not afford to permit some of its limited equipment to be used in such a way that it would work against its interest. A wave of system failures at the start would have greatly retarded, if not destroyed, this new industry.... [But] as the industry took root and grew, the reasons for the blanket insistence on a service contract disappeared.... [A]t some time during its use, Jerrold's tie-in of services to equipment became unreasonable.

(b) Dehydrating Process Co. v. A.O. Smith Corp., 292 F.2d 653 (1st Cir.), cert. denied, 368 U.S. 931 (1961). Defendant was a manufacturer of patented glass-lined silos used for the storage of fish meal and also of a patented unloading device installed in the bottom of the silo for the unloading of the meal. Defendant had originally sold the two products separately. Many buyers of unloaders who did not use its silos complained about the performance of the unloader. Eighteen customers made claims against A.O. Smith, and six unloaders were taken back for refunds. As a result, defendant adopted a policy of selling unloaders only to those purchasing or already owning the silos. Plaintiff argued that the sales policy established a tying arrangement that violated Section 3 of the Clayton Act. The First Circuit upheld a directed verdict for defendant. Although finding the products separable, the Court found that "a proper business reason may justify what might otherwise be an unlawful tie-in." Since about half of the persons who had bought the unloaders separately had been dissatisfied, the "tie-in" was justified.

Jefferson Parish Hospital District No. 2 v. Hyde

Supreme Court of the United States, 1984.
466 U.S. 2, 104 S.Ct. 1551, 80 L.Ed.2d 2.

■ STEVENS, J.... At issue in this case is the validity of an exclusive contract between a hospital and a firm of anesthesiologists. We must decide whether the contract gives rise to a *per se* violation of § 1 of the Sherman Act because every patient undergoing surgery at the hospital must use the services of one firm of anesthesiologists, and, if not, whether the contract is nevertheless illegal because it unreasonably restrains competition among anesthesiologists.

In July 1977, respondent Edwin G. Hyde, a board certified anesthesiologist, applied for admission to the medical staff of East Jefferson Hospital. The credentials committee and the medical staff executive committee recommended approval, but the hospital board denied the application because the hospital was a party to a contract providing that all anesthesiological services required by the hospital's patients would be performed by Roux & Associates, a professional medical corporation. Respondent then commenced this action seeking a declaratory judgment that the contract is unlawful and an injunction ordering petitioners to appoint him to the hospital staff. After trial, the District Court denied relief, finding that the anticompetitive consequences of the Roux contract were minimal and outweighed by benefits in the form of improved patient care. 513 F.Supp. 532 (E.D.La.1981). The Court of Appeals reversed because it was persuaded that the contract was illegal "per se." 686 F.2d 286 (5th Cir.1982). We granted certiorari, 460 U.S. 1021, and now reverse.

I

In February 1971, shortly before East Jefferson Hospital opened, it entered into an "Anesthesiology Agreement" with Roux & Associates ("Roux"), a firm that had recently been organized by Dr. Kermit Roux. The contract provided that any anesthesiologist designated by Roux would be admitted to the hospital's medical staff. The hospital agreed to provide the space, equipment, maintenance, and other supporting services necessary to operate the anesthesiology department. It also agreed to purchase all necessary drugs and other supplies. All nursing personnel required by the anesthesia department were to be supplied by the hospital, but Roux had the right to approve their selection and retention.[67] The hospital agreed to "restrict the use of its anesthesia department to Roux & Associates and [that] no other persons, parties or entities shall perform such services within the Hospital for the term of this contract."[68]

The 1971 contract provided for a one-year term automatically renewable for successive one-year periods unless either party elected to terminate. In 1976, a second written contract was executed containing most of the provisions of the 1971 agreement. Its term was five years and the clause excluding other anesthesiologists from the hospital was deleted;[69] the hospital nevertheless continued to regard itself as committed to a closed anesthesiology department. Only Roux was permitted to practice anesthesiology at the hospital. At the time of trial the department included four anesthesiologists. The hospital usually employed 13 or 14 certified registered nurse anesthetists.[70]

The exclusive contract had an impact on two different segments of the economy: consumers of medical services, and providers of anesthesiological

---

67. The contract required all of the physicians employed by Roux to confine their practice of anesthesiology to East Jefferson.

68. Originally Roux agreed to provide at least two full time anesthesiologists acceptable to the hospital's credentials committee. Roux agreed to furnish additional anesthesiologists as necessary. The contract also provided that Roux would designate one of its qualified anesthesiologists to serve as the head of the hospital's department of anesthesia.

69. "Roux testified that he requested the omission of the exclusive language in his 1976 contract because he believes a surgeon or patient is entitled to the services of the anesthesiologist of his choice. He admitted that he and others in his group did work outside East Jefferson following the 1976 contract but felt he was not in violation of the contract in light of the changes made in it." 513 F.Supp., at 537.

70. Approximately 875 operations are performed at the hospital each month; as many as 12 or 13 operating rooms may be in use at one time.

services. Any consumer of medical services who elects to have an operation performed at East Jefferson Hospital may not employ any anesthesiologist not associated with Roux. No anesthesiologists except those employed by Roux may practice at East Jefferson.

There are at least 20 hospitals in the New Orleans metropolitan area and about 70 percent of the patients living in Jefferson Parish go to hospitals other than East Jefferson. Because it regarded the entire New Orleans metropolitan area as the relevant geographic market in which hospitals compete, this evidence convinced the District Court that East Jefferson does not possess any significant "market power"; therefore it concluded that petitioners could not use the Roux contract to anticompetitive ends. The same evidence led the Court of Appeals to draw a different conclusion. Noting that 30 percent of the residents of the Parish go to East Jefferson Hospital, and that in fact "patients tend to choose hospitals by location rather than price or quality," the Court of Appeals concluded that the relevant geographic market was the East Bank of Jefferson Parish. The conclusion that East Jefferson Hospital possessed market power in that area was buttressed by the facts that the prevalence of health insurance eliminates a patient's incentive to compare costs, that the patient is not sufficiently informed to compare quality, and that family convenience tends to magnify the importance of location.

The Court of Appeals held that the case involves a "tying arrangement" because the "users of the hospital's operating rooms (the tying product) are also compelled to purchase the hospital's chosen anesthesia service (the tied product)." 686 F.2d at 289. Having defined the relevant geographic market for the tying product as the East Bank of Jefferson Parish, the court held that the hospital possessed "sufficient market power in the tying market to coerce purchasers of the tied product." 686 F.2d, at 291. Since the purchase of the tied product constituted a "not insubstantial amount of interstate commerce," under the Court of Appeals' reading of our decision in Northern Pac. R. Co. v. United States, 356 U.S. 1, 11 (1958), the tying arrangement was therefore illegal "*per se.*"[71]

II

... It is far too late in the history of our antitrust jurisprudence to question the proposition that certain tying arrangements pose an unacceptable risk of stifling competition and therefore are unreasonable "*per se.*" The rule was first enunciated in International Salt Co. v. United States, 332 U.S. 392, 396 (1947), and has been endorsed by this Court many times since. The rule also reflects congressional policies underlying the antitrust laws. In enacting § 3 of the Clayton Act, Congress expressed great concern about the anticompetitive character of tying arrangements. While this case does not arise under the Clayton Act, the congressional finding made therein concerning the competitive consequences of tying is illuminating, and must be respected.

---

71. The Court of Appeals rejected as "clearly erroneous" the District Court's finding that the exclusive contract was justified by quality considerations.

decision to sell 2 in 1 isn't unreas restraint when competitors still sell them sep.

It is clear, however, that every refusal to sell two products separately cannot be said to restrain competition. If each of the products may be purchased separately in a competitive market, one seller's decision to sell the two in a single package imposes no unreasonable restraint on either market, particularly if competing suppliers are free to sell either the entire package or its several parts.[72] For example, we have written that "if one of a dozen food stores in a community were to refuse to sell flour unless the buyer also took sugar it would hardly tend to restrain competition if its competitors were ready and able to sell flour by itself." Northern Pac. R. Co. v. United States, 356 U.S. 1, 7 (1958).[73] Buyers often find package sales attractive; a seller's decision to offer such packages can merely be an attempt to compete effectively—conduct that is entirely consistent with the Sherman Act. See Fortner Enterprises v. United States Steel Corp. (*Fortner I*), 394 U.S. 495, 517–518 (1969) (White, J., dissenting); *id.* at 524–525 (Fortas, J., dissenting).

unlawful tying arr - "forcing"

Our cases have concluded that the essential characteristic of an invalid tying arrangement lies in the seller's exploitation of its control over the tying product to force the buyer into the purchase of a tied product that the buyer either did not want at all, or might have preferred to purchase elsewhere on different terms. When such "forcing" is present, competition on the merits in the market for the tied item is restrained and the Sherman Act is violated.

"Basic to the faith that a free economy best promotes the public weal is that goods must stand the cold test of competition; that the public, acting through the market's impersonal judgment, shall allocate the Nation's resources and thus direct the course its economic development will take.... By conditioning his sale of one commodity on the purchase of another, a seller coerces the abdication of buyers' independent judgment as to the 'tied' product's merits and insulates it from the competitive stresses of the open market. But any intrinsic superiority of the 'tied' product would convince freely choosing buyers to select it over others anyway." Times–Picayune Publishing Co. v. United States, 345 U.S. 594, 605 (1953) (footnote omitted).

using mkt pwr to force buyer to do something he wouldn't do in comp. mkt

Accordingly, we have condemned tying arrangements when the seller has some special ability—usually called "market power"—to force a purchaser to do something that he would not do in a competitive market.... When "forcing" occurs, our cases have found the tying arrangement to be unlawful.

---

72. "Of course where the buyer is free to take either product by itself there is no tying problem even though the seller may also offer the two items as a unit at a single price." Northern Pac. R. Co. v. United States, 356 U.S. 1, 6, n. 4 (1958).

73. Thus, we have held that a seller who ties the sale of houses to the provision of credit simply as a way of effectively competing in a competitive market does not violate the antitrust laws. "The unusual credit bargain offered to Fortner proves nothing more than a willingness to provide cheap financing to sell expensive houses." United States Steel Corp. v. Fortner Enterprises, 429 U.S. 610, 622 (1977) (footnote omitted).

Thus, the law draws a distinction between the exploitation of market power by merely enhancing the price of the tying product, on the one hand, and by attempting to impose restraints on competition in the market for a tied product, on the other. When the seller's power is just used to maximize its return in the tying product market, where presumably its product enjoys some justifiable advantage over its competitors, the competitive ideal of the Sherman Act is not necessarily compromised. But if that power is used to impair competition on the merits in another market, a potentially inferior product may be insulated from competitive pressures. This impairment could either harm existing competitors or create barriers to entry of new competitors in the market for the tied product, *Fortner I*, 394 U.S., at 509, and can increase the social costs of market power by facilitating price discrimination, thereby increasing monopoly profits over what they would be absent the tie, *Fortner II*, 429 U.S., at 617.[74] And from the standpoint of the consumer—whose interests the statute was especially intended to serve—the freedom to select the best bargain in the second market is impaired by his need to purchase the tying product, and perhaps by an inability to evaluate the true cost of either product when they are available only as a package.[75] In sum, to permit restraint of competition on the merits through tying arrangements would be, as we observed in *Fortner II*, to condone "the existence of power that a free market would not tolerate." 429 U.S., at 617 (footnote omitted).

Per se condemnation—condemnation without inquiry into actual market conditions—is only appropriate if the existence of forcing is probable.[76] Thus, application of the *per se* rule focuses on the probability of anticompetitive consequences. Of course, as a threshold matter there must be a substantial potential for impact on competition in order to justify *per se* condemnation. If only a single purchaser were "forced" with respect to the purchase of a tied item, the resultant impact on competition would not be sufficient to warrant the concern of antitrust law. It is for this reason that we have refused to condemn tying arrangements unless a substantial volume of commerce is foreclosed thereby. See *Fortner I*, ... *International Salt*, 332 U.S., at 396. Similarly, when a purchaser is "forced" to buy a product he would not have otherwise bought even from another seller in the tied product market, there can be no adverse impact on competition because no portion of the market which would otherwise have been available to other sellers has been foreclosed.

---

74. Sales of the tied item can be used to measure demand for the tying item; purchasers with greater needs for the tied item make larger purchases and in effect must pay a higher price to obtain the tying item....

75. Especially where market imperfections exist, purchasers may not be fully sensitive to the price or quality implications of a tying arrangement, and hence it may impede competition on the merits.

76. The rationale for *per se* rules in part is to avoid a burdensome inquiry into actual market conditions in situations where the likelihood of anticompetitive conduct is so great as to render unjustified the costs of determining whether the particular case at bar involves anticompetitive conduct. *See, e.g.*, Arizona v. Maricopa County Medical Society, 457 U.S. 332, 350–351 (1982).

Once this threshold is surmounted, *per se* prohibition is appropriate if anticompetitive forcing is likely. For example, if the government has granted the seller a patent or similar monopoly over a product, it is fair to presume that the inability to buy the product elsewhere gives the seller market power. . . . Any effort to enlarge the scope of the patent monopoly by using the market power it confers to restrain competition in the market for a second product will undermine competition on the merits in that second market. Thus, the sale or lease of a patented item on condition that the buyer make all his purchases of a separate tied product from the patentee is unlawful. . . .

(handwritten: high mkt share / unique product lend to mkt power abuse / per se treatment)

The same strict rule is appropriate in other situations in which the existence of market power is probable. When the seller's share of the market is high, see Times–Picayune Publishing Co. v. United States, 345 U.S. 594, 611–613 (1953), or when the seller offers a unique product that competitors are not able to offer, see *Fortner I*, the Court has held that the likelihood that market power exists and is being used to restrain competition in a separate market is sufficient to make *per se* condemnation appropriate. Thus, in Northern Pac. R. Co. v. United States, 356 U.S. 1 (1958), we held that the railroad's control over vast tracts of western real estate, although not itself unlawful, gave the railroad a unique kind of bargaining power that enabled it to tie the sales of that land to exclusive, long term commitments that fenced out competition in the transportation market over a protracted period. When, however, the seller does not have either the degree or the kind of market power that enables him to force customers to purchase a second, unwanted product in order to obtain the tying product, an antitrust violation can be established only by evidence of an unreasonable restraint on competition in the relevant market. See *Fortner I*, 394 U.S., at 499–500; Times–Picayune Publishing Co. v. United States, 345 U.S. 594, 614–615 (1953).

(handwritten: w/o mkt power, must show actual unreas restraint on comp.)

In sum, any inquiry into the validity of a tying arrangement must focus on the market or markets in which the two products are sold, for that is where the anticompetitive forcing has its impact. Thus, in this case our analysis of the tying issue must focus on the hospital's sale of services to its patients, rather than its contractual arrangements with the providers of anesthesiological services. In making that analysis, we must consider whether petitioners are selling two separate products that may be tied together, and, if so, whether they have used their market power to force their patients to accept the tying arrangement.

III

The hospital has provided its patients with a package that includes the range of facilities and services required for a variety of surgical operations.[77] At East Jefferson Hospital the package includes the services of the

---

77. The physical facilities include the operating room, the recovery room, and the hospital room where the patient stays before and after the operation. The services include those provided by staff physicians, such as radiologists or pathologists, and interns, nurses, dietitians, pharmacists and laboratory technicians.

anesthesiologist.[78] Petitioners argue that the package does not involve a tying arrangement at all—they are merely providing a functionally integrated package of services. Therefore, petitioners contend that it is inappropriate to apply principles concerning tying arrangements to this case.

Our cases indicate, however, that the answer to the question whether one or two products are involved turns not on the functional relation between them, but rather on the character of the demand for the two items.[79] In Times–Picayune Publishing Co. v. United States, 345 U.S. 594 (1953), the Court held that a tying arrangement was not present because the arrangement did not link two distinct markets for products that were distinguishable in the eyes of buyers. In *Fortner I*, the Court concluded that a sale involving two independent transactions, separately priced and purchased from the buyer's perspective, was a tying arrangement. These cases make it clear that a tying arrangement cannot exist unless two separate product markets have been linked.

The requirement that two distinguishable product markets be involved follows from the underlying rationale of the rule against tying. The definitional question depends on whether the arrangement may have the type of competitive consequences addressed by the rule.[80] The answer to the question whether petitioners have utilized a tying arrangement must be based on whether there is a possibility that the economic effect of the arrangement is that condemned by the rule against tying that petitioners have foreclosed competition on the merits in a product market distinct

[handwritten: demand for the 2 items det. whether they are tied]

---

78. It is essential to differentiate between the Roux contract and the legality of the contract between the hospital and its patients. The Roux contract is nothing more than an arrangement whereby Roux supplies all of the hospital's needs for anesthesiological services. That contract raised only an exclusive dealing question. The issue here is whether the hospital's insistence that its patients purchase anesthesiological services from Roux creates a tying arrangement.

79. The fact that anesthesiological services are functionally linked to the other services provided by the hospital is not in itself sufficient to remove the Roux contract from the realm of tying arrangements. We have often found arrangements involving functionally linked products at least one of which is useless without the other to be prohibited tying devices.... In fact, in some situations the functional link between the two items may enable the seller to maximize its monopoly return on the tying item as a means of charging a higher rent or purchase price to a larger user of the tying item.

80. Professor Dam has pointed out that the *per se* rule against tying can be coherent only if tying is defined by reference to the economic effect of the arrangement.

"[T]he definitional question is hard to separate from the question when tie-ins are harmful. Yet the decisions, in adopting the *per se* rule, have been attempting to flee from that economic question by ruling that tying arrangements are presumptively harmful, at least whenever certain nominal threshold standards on power and foreclosure are met. The weakness of the *per se* methodology is that it places crucial importance on the definition of the practice. Once an arrangement falls within the defined limits, no justification will be heard. But the *per se* rule gives no economic standards for defining the practice. To treat the definitional question as an abstract inquiry into whether one or two products is involved is thus to compound the weakness of the *per se* approach." Dam, [Fortner Enterprises v. United States Steel: "Neither a Borrower Nor a Lender Be," 1969 Sup.Ct.Rev. 19].

from the market for the tying item.[81] Thus, in this case no tying arrangement can exist unless there is a sufficient demand for the purchase of anesthesiological services separate from hospital services to identify a distinct product market in which it is efficient to offer anesthesiological services separately from hospital services.

Unquestionably, the anesthesiological component of the package offered by the hospital could be provided separately and could be selected either by the individual patient or by one of the patient's doctors if the hospital did not insist on including anesthesiological services in the package it offers to its customers. As a matter of actual practice, anesthesiological services are billed separately from the hospital services petitioners provide. There was ample and uncontroverted testimony that patients or surgeons often request specific anesthesiologists to come to a hospital and provide anesthesia, and that the choice of an individual anesthesiologist separate from the choice of a hospital is particularly frequent in respondent's specialty, obstetric anesthesiology. The District Court found that "[t]he provision of anesthesia services is a medical service separate from the other services provided by the hospital." 513 F.Supp., at 540. The Court of Appeals agreed with this finding, and went on to observe that "an anesthesiologist is normally selected by the surgeon, rather than the patient, based on familiarity gained through a working relationship. Obviously, the surgeons who practice at East Jefferson Hospital do not gain familiarity with any anesthesiologists other than Roux and Associates." 686 F.2d, at 291. The record amply supports the conclusion that consumers differentiate between anesthesiological services and other hospital services provided by petitioners.[82]

---

81. Of course, the Sherman Act does not prohibit "tying," it prohibits "contracts . . . in restraint of trade." Thus, in a sense the question whether this case involves "tying" is beside the point. The legality of petitioners' conduct depends on its competitive consequences, not whether it can be labeled "tying." If the competitive consequences of this arrangement are not those to which the *per se* rule is addressed, then it should not be condemned irrespective of its label.

82. One of the most frequently cited statements on this subject was made by Judge Van Dusen in United States v. Jerrold Electronics Corp., 187 F.Supp. 545 (E.D.Pa.1960), affirmed, 365 U.S. 567 (1961) (per curiam). While this statement was specifically made with respect to § 3 of the Clayton Act, its analysis is also applicable to § 1 of the Sherman Act, since with respect to the definition of tying the standards used by the two statutes are the same. See Times–Picayune, 345 U.S., at 608–609.

> "There are several facts presented in this record which tend to show that a community television antenna system cannot properly be characterized as a single product. Others who entered the community antenna field offered all the equipment necessary for a complete system, but none of them sold their gear exclusively as a single package as did Jerrold. The record also establishes that the number of pieces in each system varied considerably so that hardly any two versions of the alleged product were the same. Furthermore, the customer was charged for each item of equipment and not a lump sum for total payment. Finally, while Jerrold had cable and antennas to sell which were manufactured by other concerns, it required that the electronic equipment in the system be bought from it." 187 F.Supp., at 559.

The record here shows that other hospitals often permit anesthesiological services to be purchased separately, that anesthesiologists are not fungible in that the services provided by

Thus, the hospital's requirement that its patients obtain necessary anesthesiological services from Roux combined the purchase of two distinguishable services in a single transaction.[83] Nevertheless, the fact that this case involved a required purchase of two services that would otherwise be purchased separately does not make the Roux contract illegal. As noted above, there is nothing inherently anticompetitive about packaged sales. Only if patients are forced to purchase Roux's services as a result of the hospital's market power would the arrangement have anticompetitive consequences. If no forcing is present, patients are free to enter a competing hospital and to use another anesthesiologist instead of Roux.[84] The fact that petitioners' patients are required to purchase two separate items is only the beginning of the appropriate inquiry.[85]

[handwritten margin note: Consumers are req. to purchase 2 sep items, but it's only unreas if Jeff is abusing mkt power to force them to do so]

---

each are not precisely the same, that anesthesiological services are billed separately, and that the hospital required purchases from Roux even though other anesthesiologists were available and Roux had no objection to their receiving staff privileges at East Jefferson. Therefore, the *Jerrold* analysis indicates that there was a tying arrangement here. *Jerrold* also indicates that tying may be permissible when necessary to enable a new business to break into the market. See *id.*, at 555–558. Assuming this defense exists, and assuming it justified the 1971 Roux contract in order to give Roux an incentive to go to work at a new hospital with an uncertain future, that justification is inapplicable to the 1976 contract, since by then Roux was willing to continue to service the hospital without a tying arrangement.

83. This is not to say that § 1 of the Sherman Act gives a purchaser the right to buy a product that the seller does not wish to offer for sale. A grocer may decide to carry four brands of cookies and no more. If the customer wants a fifth brand, he may go elsewhere but he cannot sue the grocer even if there is no other in town. However, in such a case the customer is free to purchase no cookies at all, while buying other needed food. If the grocer required the customer to buy an unwanted brand of cookies in order to buy other items which the customer needs and cannot readily obtain elsewhere, then a tying question arises. Cf. Northern Pac. R. Co. v. United States, 356 U.S. 1, 7 (1958) (grocer selling flour can require customers to also buy sugar only "if its competitors were ready and able to sell flour by itself"). Here, the question is whether patients are forced to use an unwanted anesthesiologist in order to obtain needed hospital services.

84. An examination of the reason or reasons why petitioners denied respondent staff privileges will not provide the answer to the question whether the package of services they offered to their patients is an illegal tying arrangement. As a matter of antitrust law, petitioners may give their anesthesiology business to Roux because he is the best doctor available, because he is willing to work long hours, or because he is the son-in-law of the hospital administrator without violating the *per se* rule against tying. Without evidence that petitioners are using market power to force Roux upon patients there is no basis to view the arrangement as unreasonably restraining competition whatever the reasons for its creation. Conversely, with such evidence, the *per se* rule against tying may apply. Thus, we reject the view of the District Court that the legality of an arrangement of this kind turns on whether it was adopted for the purpose of improving patient care.

85. Petitioners argue and the District Court found that the exclusive contract had what it characterized as procompetitive justifications in that an exclusive contract ensures 24–hour anesthesiology coverage, enables flexible scheduling, and facilitates work routine, professional standards and maintenance of equipment. The Court of Appeals held these findings to be clearly erroneous since the exclusive contract was not necessary to achieve these ends. Roux was willing to provide 24–hour coverage even without an exclusive contract and the credentials committee of the hospital could impose standards for staff privileges that would ensure staff would comply with the demands of scheduling, maintenance, and professional standards. 686 F.2d, at 292. In the past, we have refused to tolerate manifestly anticompetitive conduct simply because the health care industry is involved. See Arizona v. Maricopa Medical Society,

IV

The question remains whether this arrangement involves the use of market power to force patients to buy services they would not otherwise purchase. Respondent's only basis for invoking the *per se* rule against tying and thereby avoiding analysis of actual market conditions is by relying on the preference of persons residing in Jefferson Parish to go to East Jefferson, the closest hospital. A preference of this kind, however, is not necessarily probative of significant market power.

Seventy per cent of the patients residing in Jefferson Parish enter hospitals other than East Jefferson. 513 F.Supp., at 539. Thus East Jefferson's "dominance" over persons residing in Jefferson Parish is far from overwhelming.[86] The fact that a substantial majority of the parish's residents elect not to enter East Jefferson means that the geographic data does not establish the kind of dominant market position that obviates the need for further inquiry into actual competitive conditions. The Court of Appeals acknowledged as much; it recognized that East Jefferson's market share alone was insufficient as a basis to infer market power, and buttressed its conclusion by relying on "market imperfections" that permit petitioners to charge noncompetitive prices for hospital services: the prevalence of third party payment for health care costs reduces price competition, and a lack of adequate information renders consumers unable to evaluate the quality of the medical care provided by competing hospitals. 686 F.2d, at 290. While these factors may generate "market power" in some abstract sense,[87] they do not generate the kind of market power that justifies condemnation of tying.

Tying arrangements need only be condemned if they restrain competition on the merits by forcing purchases that would not otherwise be made. A lack of price or quality competition does not create this type of forcing. If consumers lack price consciousness, that fact will not force them to take an anesthesiologist whose services they do not want—their indifference to price will have no impact on their willingness or ability to go to another hospital where they can utilize the services of the anesthesiologist of their

---

457 U.S. 332, 348–351 (1982); National Gerimedical Hospital v. Blue Cross, 452 U.S. 378 (1981); American Medical Assn. v. United States, 317 U.S. 519, 528–529 (1943). Petitioners seek no special solicitude. We have also uniformly rejected similar "goodwill" defenses for tying arrangements, finding that the use of contractual quality specifications are generally sufficient to protect quality without the use of a tying arrangement.... Since the District Court made no finding as to why contractual quality specifications would not protect the hospital, there is no basis for departing from our prior cases here.

86.   In fact its position in this market is not dissimilar from the market share at issue in *Times–Picayune*, which the Court found insufficient as a basis for inferring market power. See 345 U.S., at 611–613. Moreover, in other antitrust contexts this Court has found that market shares comparable to that present here do not create an unacceptable likelihood of anticompetitive conduct. See United States v. Connecticut National Bank, 418 U.S. 656 (1974); United States v. Du Pont & Co., 351 U.S. 377 (1956).

87.   As an economic matter, market power exists whenever prices can be raised above the levels that would be charged in a competitive market. See *Fortner II*, 429 U.S., at 620; *Fortner I*, 394 U.S., at 503–504.

choice. Similarly, if consumers cannot evaluate the quality of anesthesiolog-ical services, it follows that they are indifferent between certified anesthesi-ologists even in the absence of a tying arrangement—such an arrangement cannot be said to have foreclosed a choice that would have otherwise been made "on the merits."

Thus, neither of the "market imperfections" relied upon by the Court of Appeals forces consumers to take anesthesiological services they would not select in the absence of a tie. It is safe to assume that every patient undergoing a surgical operation needs the services of an anesthesiologist; at least this record contains no evidence that the hospital "forced" any such services on unwilling patients.[88] The record therefore does not provide a basis for applying the *per se* rule against tying to this arrangement.

V

In order to prevail in the absence of *per se* liability, respondent has the burden of proving that the Roux contract violated the Sherman Act because it unreasonably restrained competition. That burden necessarily involves an inquiry into the actual effect of the exclusive contract on competition among anesthesiologists. This competition takes place in offering services to patients; it may encompass competition among anesthesiologists for exclusive contracts such as the Roux contract and might be statewide or merely local.[89] There is, however, insufficient evidence in this record to

---

88. Nor is there an indication in the record that respondents' practices have increased the social costs of its market power. Since patients' anesthesiological needs are fixed by medical judgment, respondent does not argue that the tying arrangement facilitates price discrimination. Where variable-quantity purchasing is unavailable as a means to enable price discrimination, commentators have seen less justification for condemning tying. See Dam, *supra*, at 15–17; Turner, *supra*, at 67–72. While tying arrangements like the one at issue here are unlikely to be used to facilitate price discrimination, they could have the similar effect of enabling hospitals "to evade price control in the tying product through clandestine transfer of the profit to the tied product...." *Fortner I*, 394 U.S., at 513 (White, J., dissenting). Insurance companies are the principal source of price restraint in the hospital industry; they place some limitations on the ability of hospitals to exploit their market power. Through this arrangement, petitioners may be able to evade the restraint by obtaining a portion of the anesthesiologists' fees and therefore realize a greater return than they could in the absence of the arrangement. This could also have an adverse effect on the anesthesiology market since it is possible that only less able anesthesiologists would be willing to give up part of their fees in return for the security of an exclusive contract. However, there are no findings of either the District Court or the Court of Appeals which indicate that this type of exploitation of market power has occurred here. The Court of Appeals found only that Roux's use of nurse anesthetists increased its and the hospital's profits, but there was no finding that nurse anesthetists might not be used with equal frequency absent the exclusive contract. Indeed, the District Court found that nurse anesthetists are utilized in all hospitals in the area. 513 F.Supp., at 537, 543. Moreover, there is nothing in the record which details whether this arrangement has enhanced the value of East Jefferson's market power or harmed quality competition in the anesthesiology market.

89. While there was some rather impressionistic testimony that the prevalence of exclusive contracts tended to discourage young doctors from entering the market, the evidence was equivocal and neither the District Court nor the Court of Appeals made any findings concerning the contract's effect on entry barriers. Respondent does not press the point before this Court. It is possible that under some circumstances an exclusive contract could raise entry *no evidence of effect on comp*

provide a basis for finding that the Roux contract, as it actually operates in the market, has unreasonably restrained competition. The record sheds little light on how this arrangement affected consumer demand for separate arrangements with a specific anesthesiologist. The evidence indicates that some surgeons and patients preferred respondent's services to those of Roux, but there is no evidence that any patient who was sophisticated enough to know the difference between two anesthesiologists was not also able to go to a hospital that would provide him with the anesthesiologist of his choice.[90]

In sum, all that the record establishes is that the choice of anesthesiologists at East Jefferson has been limited to one of the four doctors who are associated with Roux and therefore have staff privileges.[91] Even if Roux did not have an exclusive contract, the range of alternatives open to the patient would be severely limited by the nature of the transaction and the hospital's unquestioned right to exercise some control over the identity and the number of doctors to whom it accords staff privileges. If respondent is admitted to the staff of East Jefferson, the range of choice will be enlarged from four to five doctors, but the most significant restraints on the patient's freedom to select a specific anesthesiologist will nevertheless remain.[92] Without a showing of actual adverse effect on competition, respondent cannot make out a case under the antitrust laws, and no such showing has been made.

VI

Petitioners' closed policy may raise questions of medical ethics, and may have inconvenienced some patients who would prefer to have their

---

barriers since anesthesiologists could not compete for the contract without raising the capital necessary to run a hospital-wide operation. However, since the hospital has provided most of the capital for the exclusive contractor in this case, that problem does not appear to be present.

90. If, as is likely, it is the patient's doctor and not the patient who selects an anesthesiologist, the doctor can simply take the patient elsewhere if he is dissatisfied with Roux. The District Court found that most doctors in the area have staff privileges at more than one hospital. 513 F.Supp., at 541.

91. The effect of the contract has, of course, been to remove the East Jefferson Hospital from the market open to Roux's competitors. Like any exclusive requirements contract, this contract could be unlawful if it foreclosed so much of the market from penetration by Roux's competitors as to unreasonably restrain competition in the affected market, the market for anesthesiological services. See generally Tampa Electric Co. v. Nashville Coal Co., 365 U.S. 320 (1961); United States v. Standard Oil Co., 337 U.S. 293 (1949). However, respondent has not attempted to make this showing.

92. The record simply tells us little if anything about the effect of this arrangement on price or quality of anesthesiological services. As to price, the arrangement did not lead to an increase in the price charged to the patient. 686 F.2d, at 291. As to quality, the record indicates little more than that there have never been any complaints about the quality of Roux's services, and no contention that his services are in any respect inferior to those of respondent. Moreover, the self interest of the hospital, as well as the ethical and professional norms under which it operates, presumably protects the quality of anesthesiological services. See Joint Commission on Accreditation of Hospitals, Accreditation Manual for Hospitals 3–10, 151–154 (1983).

anesthesia administered by someone other than a member of Roux & Associates, but it does not have the obviously unreasonable impact on purchasers that has characterized the tying arrangements that this Court has branded unlawful. There is no evidence that the price, the quality, or the supply or demand for either the "tying product" or the "tied product" involved in this case has been adversely affected by the exclusive contract between Roux and the hospital. It may well be true that the contract made it necessary for Dr. Hyde and others to practice elsewhere, rather than at East Jefferson. But there has been no showing that the market as a whole has been affected at all by the contract. Indeed, as we previously noted, the record tells us very little about the market for the services of anesthesiologists. Yet that is the market in which the exclusive contract has had its principal impact. There is simply no showing here of the kind of restraint on competition that is prohibited by the Sherman Act. Accordingly, the judgment of the Court of Appeals is reversed and the case is remanded to that court for further proceedings consistent with this opinion.

■ BRENNAN, J., with whom MARSHALL, J., joins, concurring. As the opinion for the Court demonstrates, we have long held that tying arrangements are subject to evaluation for *per se* illegality under § 1 of the Sherman Act. Whatever merit the policy arguments against this longstanding construction of the Act might have, Congress, presumably aware of our decision, has never changed the rule by amending the Act. In such circumstances, our practice usually has been to stand by a settled statutory interpretation and leave the task of modifying the statute's reach to Congress. . . . I see no reason to depart from the principle in this case and therefore join the opinion and judgment of the Court.

■ O'CONNOR, J., with whom BURGER, J., POWELL, J., and REHNQUIST, J., join, concurring in the judgment. . . . Under the usual logic of the *per se* rule, a restraint on trade that rarely serves any purposes other than to restrain competition is illegal without proof of market power or anticompetitive effect. . . . Some of our earlier cases did indeed declare that tying arrangements serve "hardly any purpose beyond the suppression of competition." Standard Oil Co. of California v. United States, 337 U.S. 293, 305–306 (1949) (dictum). However, this declaration was not taken literally even by the cases that purported to rely upon it. In practice, a tie has been illegal only if the seller is shown to have "sufficient economic power with respect to the tying product to appreciably restrain free competition in the market for the tied product. . . ." *Northern Pacific R. Co., supra.* Without "control or dominance over the tying product" the seller could not use the tying product as "an effectual weapon to pressure buyers into taking the tied item," so that any restraint of trade would be "insignificant." Ibid. The Court has never been willing to say of tying arrangements, as it has of price-fixing, division of markets and other agreements subject to *per se* analysis, that they are always illegal, without proof of market power or anticompetitive effect.

The *"per se"* doctrine in tying cases has thus always required an elaborate inquiry into the economic effects of the tying arrangement.[93] As a result, tying doctrine incurs the costs of a rule of reason approach without achieving its benefits: the doctrine calls for the extensive and time-consuming economic analysis characteristic of the rule of reason, but then may be interpreted to prohibit arrangements that economic analysis would show to be beneficial. Moreover, the *per se* label in the tying context has generated more confusion than coherent law because it appears to invite lower courts to omit the analysis of economic circumstances of the tie that has always been a necessary element of tying analysis.

The time has therefore come to abandon the *"per se"* label and refocus the inquiry on the adverse economic effects, and the potential economic benefits, that the tie may have. The law of tie-ins will thus be brought into accord with the law applicable to all other allegedly anticompetitive economic arrangements, except those few horizontal or quasi-horizontal restraints that can be said to have no economic justification whatsoever.[94] This change will rationalize rather than abandon tie-in doctrine as it is already applied.

Our prior opinions indicate that the purpose of tying law has been to identify and control those tie-ins that have a demonstrably exclusionary impact in the tied product market, see Times–Picayune Publishing Co. v. United States, 345 U.S. 594, 605 (1953), or that abet the harmful exercise of market power that the seller possesses in the tying product market. Under the rule of reason tying arrangements should be disapproved only in such instances.

Market power in the tying product may be acquired legitimately (*e.g.*, through the grant of a patent) or illegitimately (*e.g.*, as a result of unlawful monopolization). In either event, exploitation of consumers in the market for the tying product is a possibility that exists and that may be regulated under § 2 of the Sherman Act without reference to any tying arrangements that the seller may have developed. The existence of a tied product normally does not increase the profit that the seller with market power can extract from sales of the *tying* product. A seller with a monopoly on flour, for example, cannot increase the profit it can extract from flour consumers simply by forcing them to buy sugar along with their flour. Counterintui-

---

93. This inquiry has been required in analyzing both the prima facie case and affirmative defenses. Most notably, United States v. Jerrold Electronics Corp., 187 F.Supp. 545, 599–560 (E.D.Pa.1960), affirmed per curiam 365 U.S. 567 (1961), upheld a requirement that buyers of television systems purchase the complete system, as well as installation and repair service, on the grounds that the tie assured that the systems would operate and thereby protected the seller's business reputation.

94. Tying law is particularly anomalous in this respect because arrangements largely indistinguishable from tie-ins are generally analyzed under the rule of reason. For example, the *"per se"* analysis of tie-ins subjects restrictions on a franchisee's freedom to purchase supplies to a more searching scrutiny than restrictions on his freedom to sell his products. Compare, *e.g.*, Siegel v. Chicken Delight, Inc., 448 F.2d 43 (C.A.9 1971), cert. denied, 405 U.S. 955 (1972), with Continental T.V., Inc. v. GTE Sylvania Inc., 433 U.S. 36 (1977). And exclusive contracts, that, like tie-ins, require the buyer to purchase a product from one seller, are subject only to the rule of reason.

tive though that assertion may seem, it is easily demonstrated and widely accepted. *See, e.g.,* R. Bork, The Antitrust Paradox 372–374 (1978); P. Areeda, Antitrust Analysis 735 (3d ed. 1981).

Tying may be economically harmful primarily in the rare cases where power in the market for the tying product is used to create *additional* market power in the market for the *tied* product.[95] The antitrust law is properly concerned with tying when, for example, the flour monopolist threatens to use its market power to acquire additional power in the sugar market, perhaps by driving out competing sellers of sugar, or by making it more difficult for new sellers to enter the sugar market. . . .

These three conditions—market power in the tying product, a substantial threat of market power in the tied product, and a coherent economic basis for treating the products as distinct—are only threshold requirements. Under the Rule of Reason a tie-in may prove acceptable even when all three are met. Tie-ins may entail economic benefits as well as economic harms, and if the threshold requirements are met these benefits should enter the Rule of Reason balance.

> "Tie-ins . . . may facilitate new entry into fields where established sellers have wedded their customers to them by ties of habit and custom. Brown Shoe Co. v. United States, 370 U.S. 294, 330 (1962). . . . They may permit clandestine price cutting in products which otherwise would have no price competition at all because of fear of retaliation from the few other producers dealing in the market. They may protect the reputation of the tying product if failure to use the tied product in conjunction with it may cause it to misfunction: [citing Pick Mfg. Co. v. General Motors Corp., 80 F.2d 641 (C.A.7 1935), affirmed 299 U.S. 3 (1936)]. . . . And, if the tied and tying products are functionally related, they may reduce costs through economies of joint production and distribution." *Fortner I*, 394 U.S., at 514 n. 9 (WHITE, J., dissenting).

The ultimate decision whether a tie-in is illegal under the antitrust laws should depend upon the demonstrated economic effects of the challenged agreement. It may, for example, be entirely innocuous that the seller

---

95. Tying might be undesirable in two other instances, but the Hospital–Roux arrangement involves neither one.

In a regulated industry a firm with market power may be unable to extract a supercompetitive profit because it lacks control over the prices it charges for regulated products or services. Tying may then be used to extract that profit from sale of the unregulated, tied products or services. See Fortner Enterprises, Inc. v. United States Steel Corp., 394 U.S. 495, 513 (1969) (White, J., dissenting).

Tying may also help the seller engage in price discrimination by "metering" the buyer's use of the tying product. . . . Price discrimination may be independently unlawful, see 15 U.S.C. § 13. Price discrimination may, however, *decrease* rather than increase the economic costs of a seller's market power. . . . [*Fortner II*] did not hold that price discrimination in the form of a tie-in is always economically harmful; that case indicated only that price discrimination may indicate market power in the tying product market. But there is no need in this case to address the problem of price discrimination facilitated by tying. The discussion herein is aimed only at tying arrangements as to which no price discrimination is alleged.

exploits its control over the tying product to "force" the buyer to purchase the tied product. For when the seller exerts market power only in the tying product market, it makes no difference to him or his customers whether he exploits that power by raising the price of the tying product or by "forcing" customers to buy a tied product.... On the other hand, tying may make the provision of packages of goods and services more efficient. A tie-in should be condemned only when its anticompetitive impact outweighs its contribution to efficiency.

Application of these criteria to the case at hand is straightforward.

Although the issue is in doubt, we may assume that the Hospital does have market power in the provision of hospital services in its area....

Second, in light of the Hospital's presumed market power, we may also assume that there is a substantial threat that East Jefferson will acquire market power over the provision of anesthesiological services in its market. By tying the sale of anesthesia to the sale of other hospital services the Hospital can drive out other sellers of those services who might otherwise operate in the local market. The Hospital may thus gain local market power in the provision of anesthesiology: anesthesiological services offered in the Hospital's market, narrowly defined, will be purchased only from Roux, under the Hospital's auspices.

But the third threshold condition for giving closer scrutiny to a tying arrangement is not satisfied here: there is no sound economic reason for treating surgery and anesthesia as separate services. Patients are interested in purchasing anesthesia only in conjunction with hospital services, so the Hospital can acquire no *additional* market power by selling the two services together. Accordingly, the link between the Hospital's services and anesthesia administered by Roux will affect neither the amount of anesthesia provided nor the combined price of anesthesia and surgery for those who choose to become the Hospital's patients. In these circumstances, anesthesia and surgical services should probably not be characterized as distinct products for tying purposes.

Even if they are, the tying should not be considered a violation of § 1 of the Sherman Act because tying here cannot increase the seller's already absolute power over the volume of production of the tied product, which is an inevitable consequence of the fact that very few patients will choose to undergo surgery without receiving anesthesia. The Hospital–Roux contract therefore has little potential to harm the patients. On the other side of the balance, the District Court found, and the Court of Appeals did not dispute, that the tie-in conferred significant benefits upon the hospital and the patients that it served.

The tie-in improves patient care and permits more efficient hospital operation in a number of ways. From the viewpoint of hospital management, the tie-in ensures 24 hour anesthesiology coverage, aids in standardization of procedures and efficient use of equipment, facilitates flexible scheduling of operations, and permits the hospital more effectively to monitor the quality of anesthesiological services. Further, the tying arrangement is advantageous to patients because, as the District Court found, the closed anesthesiology department places upon the hospital, rather than the individual patient, responsibility to select the physician who is to provide anesthesiological services. The hospital also assumes the responsibility that the anesthesiologist will be available, will be acceptable to the surgeon, and will provide suitable care to the patient. In assuming these responsibilities—responsibilities that a seriously ill patient frequently may be unable to discharge—the hospital provides a valuable service to its patients. And there is no indication that patients were dissatisfied with the quality of anesthesiology that was provided at the hospital or that patients wished to enjoy the services of anesthesiologists other than those that the hospital employed. Given this evidence of the advantages and effectiveness of the closed anesthesiology department, it is not surprising that, as the District Court found, such arrangements are accepted practice in the majority of hospitals of New Orleans and in the health care industry generally. Such an arrangement, that has little anti-competitive effect and achieves substantial benefits in the provision of care to patients, is hardly one that the antitrust law should condemn. This conclusion reaffirms our threshold determination that the joint provision of hospital services and anesthesiology should not be viewed as involving a tie between distinct products, and therefore should require no additional scrutiny under the antitrust law.

Whether or not the Hospital–Roux contract is characterized as a tie between distinct products, the contract unquestionably does constitute exclusive dealing.... The Hospital–Roux arrangement could conceivably have an adverse effect on horizontal competition among anesthesiologists, or among hospitals. Dr. Hyde, who competes with the Roux anesthesiologists, and other hospitals in the area, who compete with East Jefferson, may have grounds to complain that the exclusive contract stifles horizontal competition and therefore has an adverse, albeit indirect, impact on consumer welfare even if it is not a tie....

At issue here is an exclusive dealing arrangement between a firm of four anesthesiologists and one relatively small hospital. There is no suggestion that East Jefferson Hospital is likely to create a "bottleneck" in the availability of anesthesiologists that might deprive other hospitals of access to needed anesthesiological services, or that the Roux associates have unreasonably narrowed the range of choices available to other anesthesiologists in search of a hospital or patients that will buy their services. Contrast Associated Press v. United States, 326 U.S. 1 (1945). A firm of four anesthesiologists represents only a very small fraction of the total number of anesthesiologists whose services are available for hire by other hospitals, and East Jefferson is one among numerous hospitals buying such services. Even without engaging in a detailed analysis of the size of the relevant markets we may readily conclude that there is no likelihood that the exclusive dealing arrangement challenged here will either unreasonably enhance the Hospital's market position relative to other hospitals, or unreasonably permit Roux to acquire power relative to other anesthesiologists. Accordingly, this exclusive dealing arrangement must be sustained under the Rule of Reason. . . .

NOTE

In *Jefferson Parish*, Justice Stevens suggested that market power could be presumed from a "patent or similar monopoly over a product." Recently, however, in Illinois Tool Works Inc. v. Independent Ink, Inc., 547 U.S. 28 (2006), he delivered a contrary opinion for a unanimous Supreme Court.

Tridant, a subsidiary of Illinois Tool Works, held a patent on print-head technology to manufacture printers, usually used to place barcodes on cartons. Tridant also manufactured and sold ink, and its standard contract provided that it would license its ink-printing device only if used in connection with ink supplied by Tridant. Independent Ink, a competitor of Tridant in the ink market, challenged the licensing arrangement as a tie-in sale under Section 1 and monopolization under Section 2.

With respect to the tie-in sale, Independent Ink did not prove that the patent on print-head technology conferred significant economic power but rather relied on the "presumption" in *Jefferson Parish*. Justice Stevens rejected the presumption of market power, with the following reasoning:

> Over the years, however, this Court's strong disapproval of tying arrangements has substantially diminished. Rather than relying on assumptions, in its more recent opinions the Court has required a showing of market power in the tying product. . . .

> It is no doubt the virtual consensus among economists that has persuaded the enforcement agencies to reject the position that the Government took when it supported the *per se* rule that the Court adopted in the 1940's. In antitrust guidelines issued jointly by the Department of Justice and the Federal Trade Commission in 1995, the enforcement agencies stated that in the exercise of their prosecutorial discretion they "will not presume that a patent, copyright, or trade secret necessarily confers market power upon its owner." U. S. Dept. of Justice and FTC, Antitrust Guidelines for the Licensing of Intellectual Property § 2.2 (Apr. 6, 1995), available at http://www.usdoj.gov/atr/public/guidelines/0558.pdf. . . . While that choice is not binding on the Court, it would be unusual for the Judiciary to replace the normal rule of lenity that is applied in criminal cases with a rule of severity for a special category of antitrust cases.

> Congress, the antitrust enforcement agencies, and most economists have all reached the conclusion that a patent does not necessarily confer market power upon the patentee. Today, we reach the same conclusion, and therefore hold that, in all cases involving a tying arrangement, the plaintiff must prove that the defendant has market power in the tying product.

> In this case, respondent reasonably relied on our prior opinions in moving for summary judgment without offering evidence defining the relevant market or proving that petitioners possess power within it. When the case returns to the District Court, respondent should therefore be

given a fair opportunity to develop and introduce evidence on that issue, as well as any other issues that are relevant to its remaining § 1 claims.

Eastman Kodak Co. v. Image Technical Services, Inc.

Supreme Court of the United States, 1992.
504 U.S. 451, 112 S.Ct. 2072, 119 L.Ed.2d 265.

■ BLACKMUN, J. This is yet another case that concerns the standard for summary judgment in an antitrust controversy. The principal issue here is whether a defendant's lack of market power in the primary equipment market precludes—as a matter of law—the possibility of market power in derivative aftermarkets.

Petitioner Eastman Kodak Company manufactures and sells photocopiers and micrographic equipment. Kodak also sells service and replacement parts for its equipment. Respondents are 18 independent service organizations (ISOs) that in the early 1980s began servicing Kodak copying and micrographic equipment. Kodak subsequently adopted policies to limit the availability of parts to ISOs and to make it more difficult for ISOs to compete with Kodak in servicing Kodak equipment.

Respondents instituted this action in the United States District Court for the Northern District of California alleging that Kodak's policies were unlawful under both 1 and 2 of the Sherman Act. After truncated discovery, the District Court granted summary judgment for Kodak. The Court of Appeals for the Ninth Circuit reversed. The appellate court found that respondents had presented sufficient evidence to raise a genuine issue concerning Kodak's market power in the service and parts markets. It rejected Kodak's contention that lack of market power in service and parts must be assumed when such power is absent in the equipment market. Because of the importance of the issue, we granted certiorari.

I

A

Because this case comes to us on petitioner Kodak's motion for summary judgment, "the evidence of [respondents] is to be believed, and all justifiable inferences are to be drawn in [their] favor. . . ." Kodak manufactures and sells complex business machines—as relevant here, high-volume photocopier and micrographic equipment.[96] Kodak equipment is unique; micrographic software programs that operate on Kodak machines, for example, are not compatible with competitors' machines. Kodak parts are

---

96. Kodak's micrographic equipment includes four different product areas. The first is capture products such as microfilmers and electronic scanners, which compact an image and capture it on microfilm. The second is equipment such as microfilm viewers and viewer/printers. This equipment is used to retrieve the images. The third is Computer Output Microform (COM) recorders, which are data-processing peripherals that record computer-generated data onto microfilm. The fourth is Computer Assisted Retrieval (CAR) systems, which utilize computers to locate and retrieve micrographic images.

not compatible with other manufacturers' equipment, and vice versa. Kodak equipment, although expensive when new, has little resale value.

Kodak provides service and parts for its machines to its customers. It produces some of the parts itself; the rest are made to order for Kodak by independent original-equipment manufacturers (OEMs). Kodak does not sell a complete system of original equipment, lifetime service, and lifetime parts for a single price. Instead, Kodak provides service after the initial warranty period either through annual service contracts, which include all necessary parts, or on a per-call basis. It charges, through negotiations and bidding, different prices for equipment, service, and parts for different customers. Kodak provides 80% to 95% of the service for Kodak machines.

Beginning in the early 1980s, ISOs began repairing and servicing Kodak equipment. They also sold parts and reconditioned and sold used Kodak equipment. Their customers were federal, state, and local government agencies, banks, insurance companies, industrial enterprises, and providers of specialized copy and microfilming services. ISOs provide service at a price substantially lower than Kodak does. Some customers found that the ISO service was of higher quality.

Some of the ISOs' customers purchase their own parts and hire ISOs only for service. Others choose ISOs to supply both service and parts. ISOs keep an inventory of parts, purchased from Kodak or other sources, primarily the OEMs.[97]

In 1985 and 1986, Kodak implemented a policy of selling replacement parts for micrographic and copying machines only to buyers of Kodak equipment who use Kodak service or repair their own machines. As part of the same policy, Kodak sought to limit ISO access to other sources of Kodak parts. Kodak and the OEMs agreed that the OEMs would not sell parts that fit Kodak equipment to anyone other than Kodak. Kodak also pressured Kodak equipment owners and independent parts distributors not to sell Kodak parts to ISOs. In addition, Kodak took steps to restrict the availability of used machines.

Kodak intended, through these policies, to make it more difficult for ISOs to sell service for Kodak machines. It succeeded. ISOs were unable to obtain parts from reliable sources, and many were forced out of business, while others lost substantial revenue. Customers were forced to switch to Kodak service even though they preferred ISO service.

B

In 1987, the ISOs filed the present action in the District Court, alleging, *inter alia*, that Kodak had unlawfully tied the sale of service for Kodak machines to the sale of parts, in violation of § 1 of the Sherman Act,

---

97. In addition to the OEMs, other sources of Kodak parts include (1) brokers who would buy parts from Kodak, or strip used Kodak equipment to obtain the useful parts and resell them, (2) customers who buy parts from Kodak and make them available to ISOs, and (3) used equipment to be stripped for parts.

and had unlawfully monopolized and attempted to monopolize the sale of service for Kodak machines, in violation of § 2 of that Act.

Kodak filed a motion for summary judgment before respondents had initiated discovery. The District Court permitted respondents to file one set of interrogatories and one set of requests for production of documents, and to take six depositions. Without a hearing, the District Court granted summary judgment in favor of Kodak.... The Court of Appeals for the Ninth Circuit, by a divided vote, reversed. 903 F.2d 612 (1990)....

II

A tying arrangement is "an agreement by a party to sell one product but only on the condition that the buyer also purchases a different (or tied) product, or at least agrees that he will not purchase that product from any other supplier." Northern Pacific R. Co. v. United States, 356 U.S. 1, 5–6 (1958). Such an arrangement violates § 1 of the Sherman Act if the seller has "appreciable economic power" in the tying product market and if the arrangement affects a substantial volume of commerce in the tied market. Fortner Enterprises, Inc. v. United States Steel Corp., 394 U.S. 495, 503 (1969).

Kodak did not dispute that its arrangement affects a substantial volume of interstate commerce. It, however, did challenge whether its activities constituted a "tying arrangement" and whether Kodak exercised "appreciable economic power" in the tying market. We consider these issues in turn.

A

For the respondents to defeat a motion for summary judgment on their claim of a tying arrangement, a reasonable trier of fact must be able to find, first, that service and parts are two distinct products, and, second, that Kodak has tied the sale of the two products.

For service and parts to be considered two distinct products, there must be sufficient consumer demand so that it is efficient for a firm to provide service separately from parts. Jefferson Parish Hospital Dist. No. 2 v. Hyde, 466 U.S. 2, 21–22 (1984). Evidence in the record indicates that service and parts have been sold separately in the past and still are sold separately to self-service equipment owners.[98] Indeed, the development of the entire high-technology service industry is evidence of the efficiency of a separate market for service.

Kodak insists that because there is no demand for parts separate from service, there cannot be separate markets for service and parts. By that logic, we would be forced to conclude that there can never be separate markets, for example, for cameras and film, computers and software, or automobiles and tires. That is an assumption we are unwilling to make.

---

98. The Court of Appeals found: "Kodak's policy of allowing customers to purchase parts on condition that they agree to service their own machines suggests that the demand for parts can be separated from the demand for service."

"We have often found arrangements involving functionally linked products at least one of which is useless without the other to be prohibited tying devices." *Jefferson Parish*, 466 U.S., at 19, n. 30.

Kodak's assertion also appears to be incorrect as a factual matter. At least some consumers would purchase service without parts, because some service does not require parts, and some consumers, those who self-service for example, would purchase parts without service.[99] Enough doubt is cast on Kodak's claim of a unified market that it should be resolved by the trier of fact.

Finally, respondents have presented sufficient evidence of a tie between service and parts. The record indicates that Kodak would sell parts to third parties only if they agreed not to buy service from ISOs.[1]

B

Having found sufficient evidence of a tying arrangement, we consider the other necessary feature of an illegal tying arrangement: appreciable economic power in the tying market. Market power is the power "to force a purchaser to do something that he would not do in a competitive market." *Jefferson Parish*, 466 U.S., at 14. It has been defined as "the ability of a single seller to raise price and restrict output." *Fortner*, 394 U.S., at 503. The existence of such power ordinarily is inferred from the seller's possession of a predominant share of the market. *Jefferson Parish*, 466 U.S., at 17; United States v. Grinnell Corp., 384 U.S. 563, 571 (1966); Times–Picayune Publishing Co. v. United States, 345 U.S. 594, 611–613 (1953).

1

Respondents contend that Kodak has more than sufficient power in the parts market to force unwanted purchases of the tied market service. Respondents provide evidence that certain parts are available exclusively through Kodak. Respondents also assert that Kodak has control over the availability of parts it does not manufacture. According to respondents' evidence, Kodak has prohibited independent manufacturers from selling Kodak parts to ISOs, pressured Kodak equipment owners and independent parts distributors to deny ISOs the purchase of Kodak parts, and taken steps to restrict the availability of used machines.

Respondents also allege that Kodak's control over the parts market has excluded service competition, boosted service prices, and forced unwilling

99. The dissent suggests that parts and service are not separate products for tying purposes because all service may involve installation of parts. Because the record does not support this factual assertion, under the approach of both the Court and the concurrence in Jefferson Parish Hospital Dist. No. 2 v. Hyde, 466 U.S. 2 (1984), Kodak is not entitled to summary judgment on whether parts and service are distinct markets.

1. In a footnote, Kodak contends that this practice is only a unilateral refusal to deal, which does not violate the antitrust laws. Assuming, *arguendo*, that Kodak's refusal to sell parts to any company providing service can be characterized as a unilateral refusal to deal, its alleged sale of parts to third parties on condition that they buy service from Kodak is not. See 903 F.2d at 619.

consumption of Kodak service. Respondents offer evidence that consumers have switched to Kodak service even though they preferred ISO service, that Kodak service was of higher price and lower quality than the preferred ISO service, and that ISOs were driven out of business by Kodak's policies. Under our prior precedents, this evidence would be sufficient to entitle respondents to a trial on their claim of market power.

2

Kodak counters that even if it concedes monopoly share of the relevant parts market, it cannot actually exercise the necessary market power for a Sherman Act violation. This is so, according to Kodak, because competition exists in the equipment market.[2] Kodak argues that it could not have the ability to raise prices of service and parts above the level that would be charged in a competitive market because any increase in profits from a higher price in the aftermarkets at least would be offset by a corresponding loss in profits from lower equipment sales as consumers began purchasing equipment with more attractive service costs.

Kodak does not present any actual data on the equipment, service, or parts markets. Instead, it urges the adoption of a substantive legal rule that "equipment competition precludes any finding of monopoly power in derivative aftermarkets." Kodak argues that such a rule would satisfy its burden as the moving party of showing "that there is no genuine issue as to any material fact" on the market power issue.[3]

Legal presumptions that rest on formalistic distinctions rather than actual market realities are generally disfavored in antitrust law. This Court has preferred to resolve antitrust claims on a case-by-case basis, focusing on the "particular facts disclosed by the record." In determining the existence of market power, and specifically the "responsiveness of the sales of one product to price changes of the other," *du Pont*, 351 U.S., at 400, this Court has examined closely the economic reality of the market at issue.[4]

Kodak contends that there is no need to examine the facts when the issue is market power in the aftermarkets. A legal presumption against a finding of market power is warranted in this situation, according to Kodak, because the existence of market power in the service and parts markets absent power in the equipment market "simply makes no economic sense,"

---

2. In their brief and at oral argument, respondents argued that Kodak's market share figures for high-volume copy machines, computer-assisted retrieval systems, and micrographic-capture equipment demonstrate Kodak's market power in the equipment market.

3. Kodak argues that such a rule would be *per se*, with no opportunity for respondents to rebut the conclusion that market power is lacking in the parts market. . . .

4. See, *e.g., Jefferson Parish*, 466 U.S., at 26–29; United States v. Connecticut National Bank, 418 U.S. 656, 661–666 (1974); United States v. Grinnell Corp., 384 U.S. 563, 571–576 (1966); International Boxing Club of New York, Inc. v. United States, 358 U.S. 242, 250–251 (1959); see also *Jefferson Parish*, 466 U.S., at 37, n. 6 (O'Connor, J., concurring) (citing cases and describing the careful consideration the Court gives to the particular facts when determining market power).

and the absence of a legal presumption would deter procompetitive behavior.

Kodak analogizes this case to *Matsushita* where a group of American corporations that manufactured or sold consumer electronic products alleged that their 21 Japanese counterparts were engaging in a 20–year conspiracy to price below cost in the United States in the hope of expanding their market share sometime in the future. After several years of detailed discovery, the defendants moved for summary judgment. Because the defendants had every incentive not to engage in the alleged conduct which required them to sustain losses for decades with no foreseeable profits, the Court found an "absence of any rational motive to conspire." In that context, the Court determined that the plaintiffs' theory of predatory pricing makes no practical sense, was "speculative" and was not "reasonable." Accordingly, the Court held that a reasonable jury could not return a verdict for the plaintiffs and that summary judgment would be appropriate against them unless they came forward with more persuasive evidence to support their theory.

The Court's requirement in *Matsushita* that the plaintiffs' claims make economic sense did not introduce a special burden on plaintiffs facing summary judgment in antitrust cases. The Court did not hold that if the moving party enunciates any economic theory supporting its behavior, regardless of its accuracy in reflecting the actual market, it is entitled to summary judgment. *Matsushita* demands only that the nonmoving party's inferences be reasonable in order to reach the jury, a requirement that was not invented, but merely articulated, in that decision. If the plaintiff's theory is economically senseless, no reasonable jury could find in its favor, and summary judgment should be granted.

Kodak, then, bears a substantial burden in showing that it is entitled to summary judgment. It must show that despite evidence of increased prices and excluded competition, an inference of market power is unreasonable. To determine whether Kodak has met that burden, we must unravel the factual assumptions underlying its proposed rule that lack of power in the equipment market necessarily precludes power in the aftermarkets.

The extent to which one market prevents exploitation of another market depends on the extent to which consumers will change their consumption of one product in response to a price change in another, *i.e.*, the "cross-elasticity of demand." See *du Pont*, 351 U.S., at 400; P. Areeda & L. Kaplow, Antitrust Analysis 342(c) (4th ed. 1988).[5] Kodak's proposed

---

5. Courts usually have considered the relationship between price in one market and demand in another in defining the relevant market. Because market power is often inferred from market share, market definition generally determines the result of the case. Pitofsky, New Definitions of Relevant Market and the Assault on Antitrust, 90 Colum.L.Rev. 1805, 1806–1813 (1990). Kodak chose to focus on market power directly rather than arguing that the relationship between equipment and service and parts is such that the three should be included in the same market definition. Whether considered in the conceptual category of "market definition" or "market power," the ultimate inquiry is the same—whether competi-rule rests on a factual assumption about the cross-elasticity of demand in the equipment and aftermarkets: "If Kodak raised its parts or service prices above competitive levels, potential customers would simply stop buying Kodak equipment. Perhaps Kodak would be able to increase short term profits through such a strategy, but at a devastating cost to its long term interests."[6] Kodak argues that the Court should accept, as a matter of law, this "basic economic realit[y]" that competition in the equipment market necessarily prevents market power in the aftermarkets.[7]

Even if Kodak could not raise the price of service and parts one cent without losing equipment sales, that fact would not disprove market power in the aftermarkets. The sales of even a monopolist are reduced when it sells goods at a monopoly price, but the higher price more than compensates for the loss in sales. Areeda & Kaplow, at ¶¶ 112 and 340(a). Kodak's claim that charging more for service and parts would be a "short-run game" is based on the false dichotomy that there are only two prices that can be charged—a competitive price or a ruinous one. But there could easily be a middle, optimum price at which the increased revenues from the higher-priced sales of service and parts would more than compensate for the lower revenues from lost equipment sales. The fact that the equipment market imposes a restraint on prices in the aftermarkets by no means disproves the existence of power in those markets. See Areeda & Kaplow, at ¶ 340(b) ("[T]he existence of significant substitution in the event of *further* price increases or even at the *current* price does not tell us whether the defendant *already* exercises significant market power") (emphasis in original). Thus, contrary to Kodak's assertion, there is no immutable physical law—no "basic economic reality"—insisting that competition in the equipment market cannot coexist with market power in the aftermarkets.

We next consider the more narrowly drawn question: Does Kodak's theory describe actual market behavior so accurately that respondents' assertion of Kodak market power in the aftermarkets, if not impossible, is at least unreasonable?[8]

---

tion in the equipment market will significantly restrain power in the service and parts markets.

6. The United States as Amicus Curiae in support of Kodak echoes this argument: "The ISOs' claims are implausible because Kodak lacks market power in the markets for its copier and micrographic equipment. Buyers of such equipment regard an increase in the price of parts or service as an increase in the price of the equipment, and sellers recognize that the revenues from sales of parts and service are attributable to sales of the equipment. In such circumstances, it is not apparent how an equipment manufacturer such as Kodak could exercise power in the aftermarkets for parts and service."

7. It is clearly true, as the United States claims, that Kodak "cannot set service or parts prices without regard to the impact on the market for equipment." The fact that the cross-elasticity of demand is not zero proves nothing; the disputed issue is how much of an impact an increase in parts and service prices has on equipment sales and on Kodak's profits.

8. Although Kodak repeatedly relies on *Continental T.V.* as support for its factual assertion that the equipment market will prevent exploitation of the service and parts markets, the case is inapposite. In *Continental T.V.*, the Court found that a manufacturer's policy restricting the number of retailers that were permitted to sell its product could have a procompetitive effect. The Court also noted that any negative effect of exploitation of the

To review Kodak's theory, it contends that higher service prices will lead to a disastrous drop in equipment sales. Presumably, the theory's corollary is to the effect that low service prices lead to a dramatic increase in equipment sales. According to the theory, one would have expected Kodak to take advantage of lower-priced ISO service as an opportunity to expand equipment sales. Instead, Kodak adopted a restrictive sales policy consciously designed to eliminate the lower-priced ISO service, an act that would be expected to devastate either Kodak's equipment sales or Kodak's faith in its theory. Yet, according to the record, it has done neither. Service prices have risen for Kodak customers, but there is no evidence or assertion that Kodak equipment sales have dropped.

Kodak and the United States attempt to reconcile Kodak's theory with the contrary actual results by describing a "marketing strategy of spreading over time the total cost to the buyer of Kodak equipment." In other words, Kodak could charge subcompetitive prices for equipment and make up the difference with supracompetitive prices for service, resulting in an overall competitive price. This pricing strategy would provide an explanation for the theory's descriptive failings—if Kodak in fact had adopted it. But Kodak never has asserted that it prices its equipment or parts subcompetitively and recoups its profits through service. Instead, it claims that it prices its equipment comparably to its competitors, and intends that both its equipment sales and service divisions be profitable. Moreover, this hypothetical pricing strategy is inconsistent with Kodak's policy toward its self-service customers. If Kodak were underpricing its equipment, hoping to lock in customers and recover its losses in the service market, it could not afford to sell customers parts without service. In sum, Kodak's theory does not explain the actual market behavior revealed in the record.

Respondents offer a forceful reason why Kodak's theory, although perhaps intuitively appealing, may not accurately explain the behavior of the primary and derivative markets for complex durable goods: the existence of significant information and switching costs. These costs could create a less responsive connection between service and parts prices and equipment sales.

For the service-market price to affect equipment demand, consumers must inform themselves of the total cost of the "package"—equipment, service and parts—at the time of purchase; that is, consumers must engage in accurate lifecycle pricing.[9] Lifecycle pricing of complex, durable equip-

intrabrand market (the competition between retailers of the same product) would be checked by competition in the interbrand market (competition over the same generic product) because consumers would substitute a different brand of the same product. Unlike *Continental T.V.*, this case does not concern vertical relationships between parties on different levels of the same distribution chain. In the relevant market, service, Kodak and the ISOs are direct competitors; their relationship is horizontal. The interbrand competition at issue here is competition over the provision of service. Despite petitioner's best effort, repeating the mantra "interbrand competition" does not transform this case into one over an agreement the manufacturer has with its dealers that would fall under the rubric of *Continental T.V.*

9. See Craswell, Tying Requirements in Competitive Markets: The Consumer Protection Issues, 62 B.U.L.Rev. 661, 676 (1982); Beales, Craswell, & Salop, The Efficient Regulation of ment is difficult and costly. In order to arrive at an accurate price, a consumer must acquire a substantial amount of raw data and undertake sophisticated analysis. The necessary information would include data on price, quality, and availability of products needed to operate, upgrade, or enhance the initial equipment, as well as service and repair costs, including estimates of breakdown frequency, nature of repairs, price of service and parts, length of "down-time" and losses incurred from down-time.[10]

Much of this information is difficult—some of it impossible—to acquire at the time of purchase. During the life of a product, companies may change the service and parts prices, and develop products with more advanced features, a decreased need for repair, or new warranties. In addition, the information is likely to be customer-specific: lifecycle costs will vary from customer to customer with the type of equipment, degrees of equipment use, and costs of down-time.

Kodak acknowledges the cost of information, but suggests, again without evidentiary support, that customer information needs will be satisfied by competitors in the equipment markets. It is a question of fact, however, whether competitors would provide the necessary information. A competitor in the equipment market may not have reliable information about the lifecycle costs of complex equipment it does not service or the needs of customers it does not serve. Even if competitors had the relevant information, it is not clear that their interests would be advanced by providing such information to consumers. See 2 P. Areeda & D. Turner, Antitrust Law, ¶ 404b1 (1978).[11]

Moreover, even if consumers were capable of acquiring and processing the complex body of information, they may choose not to do so. Acquiring the information is expensive. If the costs of service are small relative to the equipment price, or if consumers are more concerned about equipment capabilities than service costs, they may not find it cost-efficient to compile the information. Similarly, some consumers, such as the Federal Government, have purchasing systems that make it difficult to consider the complete cost of the "package" at the time of purchase. State and local

---

Consumer Information, 24 J.Law & Econ. 491, 509–511 (1981); *Jefferson Parish*, 466 U.S., at 15.

10. In addition, of course, in order to price accurately the equipment, a consumer would need initial purchase information such as prices, features, quality, and available warranties, for different machinery with different capabilities, and residual value information such as the longevity of product use and its potential resale or trade-in value.

11. To inform consumers about Kodak, the competitor must be willing to forgo the opportunity to reap supra*competitive prices in its own service and parts markets. The competitor may anticipate that charging lower service and parts prices and informing consumers about Kodak in the hopes of gaining future equipment sales will cause Kodak to lower the price on its service and parts, canceling any gains in equipment sales to the competitor and leaving both worse off. Thus, in an equipment market with relatively few sellers, competitors may find it more profitable to adopt Kodak's service and parts policy than to inform the consumers. See 2 P. Areeda & D. Turner, Antitrust Law ¶ 404b1 (1978); App. 177 (Kodak, Xerox, and IBM together have nearly 100% of relevant market). Even in a market with many sellers, any one competitor may not have sufficient incentive to inform consumers because the increased patronage attributable to the corrected consumer beliefs will be governments often treat service as an operating expense and equipment as a capital expense, delegating each to a different department. These governmental entities do not lifecycle price, but rather choose the lowest price in each market.

As Kodak notes, there likely will be some large-volume, sophisticated purchasers who will undertake the comparative studies and insist, in return for their patronage, that Kodak charge them competitive lifecycle prices. Kodak contends that these knowledgeable customers will hold down the package price for all other customers. There are reasons, however, to doubt that sophisticated purchasers will ensure that competitive prices are charged to unsophisticated purchasers, too. As an initial matter, if the number of sophisticated customers is relatively small, the amount of profits to be gained by supracompetitive pricing in the service market could make it profitable to let the knowledgeable consumers take their business elsewhere. More importantly, if a company is able to price-discriminate between sophisticated and unsophisticated consumers, the sophisticated will be unable to prevent the exploitation of the uninformed. A seller could easily price-discriminate by varying the equipment/parts/service package, developing different warranties, or offering price discounts on different components.

Given the potentially high cost of information and the possibility a seller may be able to price-discriminate between knowledgeable and unsophisticated consumers, it makes little sense to assume, in the absence of any evidentiary support, that equipment-purchasing decisions are based on an accurate assessment of the total cost of equipment, service, and parts over the lifetime of the machine.

Indeed, respondents have presented evidence that Kodak practices price-discrimination by selling parts to customers who service their own equipment, but refusing to sell parts to customers who hire third-party service companies. Companies that have their own service staff are likely to be high-volume users, the same companies for whom it is most likely to be economically worthwhile to acquire the complex information needed for comparative lifecycle pricing.

A second factor undermining Kodak's claim that supracompetitive prices in the service market lead to ruinous losses in equipment sales is the cost to current owners of switching to a different product. See Areeda & Turner, at ¶ 519a.[12] If the cost of switching is high, consumers who already have purchased the equipment, and are thus "locked-in," will tolerate some level of service-price increases before changing equipment brands. Under this scenario, a seller profitably could maintain supracompetitive prices in the aftermarket if the switching costs were high relative to the increase in service prices, and the number of locked-in customers were high relative to the number of new purchasers.

12. A firm can exact leverage whenever other equipment is not a ready substitute. F.M. Scherer & D. Ross, Industrial Market Structure and Economic Performance 16–17 (3d ed. 1990).

Moreover, if the seller can price-discriminate between its locked-in customers and potential new customers, this strategy is even more likely to prove profitable. The seller could simply charge new customers below-marginal cost on the equipment and recoup the charges in service, or offer packages with lifetime warranties or long-term service agreements that are not available to locked-in customers.

Respondents have offered evidence that the heavy initial outlay for Kodak equipment, combined with the required support material that works only with Kodak equipment, makes switching costs very high for existing Kodak customers. And Kodak's own evidence confirms that it varies the package price of equipment/parts/service for different customers.

In sum, there is a question of fact whether information costs and switching costs foil the simple assumption that the equipment and service markets act as pure complements to one another.[13]

We conclude, then, that Kodak has failed to demonstrate that respondents' inference of market power in the service and parts markets is unreasonable, and that, consequently, Kodak is entitled to summary judgment. It is clearly reasonable to infer that Kodak has market power to raise prices and drive out competition in the aftermarkets, since respondents offer direct evidence that Kodak did so. It is also plausible, as discussed above, to infer that Kodak chose to gain immediate profits by exerting that market power where locked-in customers, high information costs, and discriminatory pricing limited and perhaps eliminated any long-term loss. Viewing the evidence in the light most favorable to respondents, their allegations of market power "make ... economic sense." Cf. *Matsushita*, 475 U.S., at 587.

Nor are we persuaded by Kodak's contention that it is entitled to a legal presumption on the lack of market power because, as in *Matsushita*, there is a significant risk of deterring procompetitive conduct. Plaintiffs in *Matsushita* attempted to prove the antitrust conspiracy "through evidence of rebates and other price-cutting activities." Because cutting prices to increase business is "the very essence of competition," the Court was concerned that mistaken inferences would be "especially costly," and would "chill the very conduct the antitrust laws are designed to protect." *Id.*, at 594. See also Monsanto Co. v. Spray–Rite Service Corp., 465 U.S. 752, 763 (1984) (permitting inference of concerted action would "deter or penalize perfectly legitimate conduct"). But the facts in this case are just the opposite. The alleged conduct—higher service prices and market foreclo-

---

13. The dissent disagrees based on its hypothetical case of a tie between equipment and service. "The only thing lacking" to bring this case within the hypothetical case, states the dissent, "is concrete evidence that the restrictive parts policy was ... generally known." But the dissent's "only thing lacking" is the crucial thing lacking—evidence. Whether a tie between parts and service should be treated identically to a tie between equipment and service, as the dissent and Kodak argue, depends on whether the equipment market prevents the exertion of market power in the parts market. Far from being "anomalous," requiring Kodak to provide evidence on this factual question is completely consistent with our prior precedent.

"facially anticompetitive"

sure—is facially anticompetitive and exactly the harm that antitrust laws aim to prevent. In this situation, *Matsushita* does not create any presumption in favor of summary judgment for the defendant.

Kodak contends that, despite the appearance of anticompetitiveness, its behavior actually favors competition because its ability to pursue innovative marketing plans will allow it to compete more effectively in the equipment market. A pricing strategy based on lower equipment prices and higher aftermarket prices could enhance equipment sales by making it easier for the buyer to finance the initial purchase.[14] It is undisputed that competition is enhanced when a firm is able to offer various marketing options, including bundling of support and maintenance service with the sale of equipment. Nor do such actions run afoul of the antitrust laws.[15] But the procompetitive effect of the specific conduct challenged here, eliminating all consumer parts and service options, is far less clear.

We need not decide whether Kodak's behavior has any procompetitive effects and, if so, whether they outweigh the anticompetitive effects. We note only that Kodak's service and parts policy is simply not one that appears always or almost always to enhance competition, and therefore to warrant a legal presumption without any evidence of its actual economic impact. In this case, when we weigh the risk of deterring procompetitive behavior by proceeding to trial against the risk that illegal behavior go unpunished, the balance tips against summary judgment.

For the foregoing reasons, we hold that Kodak has not met the requirements of Fed.Rule Civ.Proc. 56(c). We therefore affirm the denial of summary judgment on respondents' § 1 claim.[16]

---

14. It bears repeating that in this case Kodak has never claimed that it is in fact pursuing such a pricing strategy.

15. See *Jefferson Parish*, 466 U.S., at 12 ("Buyers often find package sales attractive; a seller's decision to offer such packages can merely be an attempt to compete effectively—conduct that is entirely consistent with the Sherman Act"). See also Yates & DiResta, Software Support and Hardware, Maintenance Practices: Tying Considerations, 8 The Computer Lawyer 17 (1991) (describing various service and parts policies that enhance quality and sales but do not violate the antitrust laws).

16. The dissent urges a radical departure in this Court's antitrust law. It argues that because Kodak has only an "inherent" monopoly in parts for its equipment the antitrust laws do not apply to its efforts to expand that power into other markets. The dissent's proposal to grant *per se* immunity to manufacturers competing in the service market would exempt a vast and growing sector of the economy from antitrust laws. Leaving aside the question whether the Court has the authority to make such a policy decision, there is no support for it in our jurisprudence or the evidence in this case.

Even assuming, despite the absence of any proof from the dissent, that all manufacturers possess some inherent market power in the parts market, it is not clear why that should immunize them from the antitrust laws in another market. The Court has held many times that power gained through some natural and legal advantage such as a patent, copyright, or business acumen can give rise to liability if "a seller exploits his dominant position in one market to expand his empire into the next." Times–Picayune Publishing Co. v. United States, 345 U.S. 594, 611 (1953); *see, e.g.*, Northern Pacific R. Co. v. United States, 356 U.S. 1 (1958). Moreover, on the occasions when the Court has considered tying in derivative aftermarkets by manufacturers, it has not adopted any exception to the usual antitrust analysis, treating derivative aftermarkets as it has every other separate market. See International Salt Co. v.

III

Respondents also claim that they have presented genuine issues for trial as to whether Kodak has monopolized or attempted to monopolize the service and parts markets in violation of § 2 of the Sherman Act. "The offense of monopoly under § 2 of the Sherman Act has two elements: (1) the possession of monopoly power in the relevant market and (2) the willful acquisition or maintenance of that power as distinguished from growth or development as a consequence of a superior product, business acumen, or historic accident." United States v. Grinnell Corp., 384 U.S., at 570–571.

§ 2: monopolize

A

The existence of the first element, possession of monopoly power, is easily resolved. As has been noted, respondents have presented a triable claim that service and parts are separate markets, and that Kodak has the "power to control prices or exclude competition" in service and parts. *du Pont*, 351 U.S., at 391. Monopoly power under § 2 requires, of course, something greater than market power under § 1. See Fortner, 394 U.S., at 502. Respondents' evidence that Kodak controls nearly 100% of the parts market and 80% to 95% of the service market, with no readily available substitutes, is, however, sufficient to survive summary judgment under the more stringent monopoly standard of § 2. . . .

this is a monopoly

Kodak also contends that, as a matter of law, a single brand of a product or service can never be a relevant market under the Sherman Act. We disagree. The relevant market for antitrust purposes is determined by the choices available to Kodak equipment owners. See *Jefferson Parish*, 466 U.S., at 19. Because service and parts for Kodak equipment are not interchangeable with other manufacturers' service and parts, the relevant market from the Kodak-equipment owner's perspective is composed of only those companies that service Kodak machines. See *du Pont*, 351 U.S., at 404 (the "market is composed of products that have reasonable inter-

---

United States, 332 U.S. 392 (1947); International Business Machines Corp. v. United States, 298 U.S. 131 (1936); United Shoe Machinery Co. v. United States, 258 U.S. 451 (1922). Our past decisions are reason enough to reject the dissent's proposal. . . .

Nor does the record in this case support the dissent's proposed exemption for aftermarkets. The dissent urges its exemption because the tie here "does not permit the manufacturer to project power over a class of consumers distinct from that which it is already able to exploit (and fully) without the inconvenience of the tie." Beyond the dissent's obvious difficulty in explaining why Kodak would adopt this expensive tying policy if it could achieve the same profits more conveniently through some other means, respondents offer an alternative theory, supported by the record, that suggests Kodak is able to exploit some customers who in the absence of the tie would be protected from increases in parts prices by knowledgeable customers.

At bottom, whatever the ultimate merits of the dissent's theory, at this point it is mere conjecture. Neither Kodak nor the dissent have provided any evidence refuting respondents' theory of forced unwanted purchases at higher prices and price discrimination. While it may be, as the dissent predicts, that the equipment market will prevent any harms to consumers in the aftermarkets, the dissent never makes plain why the Court should accept that theory on faith rather than requiring the usual evidence needed to win a summary judgment motion.

changeability").[17] This Court's prior cases support the proposition that in some instances one brand of a product can constitute a separate market. See National Collegiate Athletic Assn., 468 U.S., at 101–102, 111–112 (1984); International Boxing Club of New York, Inc. v. United States, 358 U.S. 242, 249–252 (1959); International Business Machines Corp. v. United States, 298 U.S. 131 (1936).[18] The proper market definition in this case can be determined only after a factual inquiry into the "commercial realities" faced by consumers. United States v. Grinnell Corp., 384 U.S., at 572.

B

The second element of a § 2 claim is the use of monopoly power "to foreclose competition, to gain a competitive advantage, or to destroy a competitor." United States v. Griffith, 334 U.S. 100, 107 (1948). If Kodak adopted its parts and service policies as part of a scheme of willful acquisition or maintenance of monopoly power, it will have violated § 2. Grinnell Corp., 384 U.S., at 570–571; United States v. Aluminum Co. of America, 148 F.2d 416, 432 (C.A.2 1945); Aspen Skiing Co. v. Aspen Highlands Skiing Corp., 472 U.S. 585, 600–605 (1985).[19]

As recounted at length above, respondents have presented evidence that Kodak took exclusionary action to maintain its parts monopoly and used its control over parts to strengthen its monopoly share of the Kodak service market. Liability turns, then, on whether "valid business reasons" can explain Kodak's actions. Aspen Skiing Co., 472 U.S., at 605; United States v. Aluminum Co. of America, 148 F.2d, at 432. Kodak contends that it has three valid business justifications for its actions: "(1) to promote interbrand equipment competition by allowing Kodak to stress the quality of its service; (2) to improve asset management by reducing Kodak's inventory costs; and (3) to prevent ISOs from free riding on Kodak's capital investment in equipment, parts and service." Factual questions exist, however, about the validity and sufficiency of each claimed justification, making summary judgment inappropriate.

Kodak first asserts that by preventing customers from using ISOs, "it [can] best maintain high quality service for its sophisticated equipment"

---

17. Kodak erroneously contends that this Court in *du Pont* rejected the notion that a relevant market could be limited to one brand. The Court simply held in *du Pont* that one brand does not necessarily constitute a relevant market if substitutes are available. 351 U.S., at 393. See also *Boxing Club, 358* U.S., at 249–250. Here respondents contend there are no substitutes.

18. Other courts have limited the market to parts for a particular brand of equipment. See *e.g.*, International Logistics Group, Ltd. v. Chrysler Corp., 884 F.2d 904, 905, 908 (C.A.6 1989) (parts for Chrysler cars is the relevant market), cert. denied, 494 U.S. 1066 (1990); Dimidowich v. Bell & Howell, 803 F.2d 1473, 1480–1481, n. 3 (C.A.9 1986), modified, 810 F.2d 1517 (1987) (service for Bell & Howell equipment is the relevant market); In re General Motors Corp., 99 F.T.C. 464, 554, 584 (1982) (crash parts for General Motors cars is the relevant market); Heatransfer Corp. v. Volkswagenwerk A.G., 553 F.2d 964 (CAS 1977), cert. denied, 434 U.S. 1087 (1978) (air conditioners for Volkswagens is the relevant market).

19. It is true that as a general matter a firm can refuse to deal with its competitors. But such a right is not absolute; it exists only if there are legitimate competitive reasons for the refusal. See Aspen Skiing Co. v. Aspen Highlands Skiing Corp., 472 U.S. 585, 602–605 (1985).

and avoid being "blamed for an equipment malfunction, even if the problem is the result of improper diagnosis, maintenance or repair by an ISO." Respondents have offered evidence that ISOs provide quality service and are preferred by some Kodak equipment owners. This is sufficient to raise a genuine issue of fact. See International Business Machines Corp. v. United States, 298 U.S., at 139–140 (rejecting IBM's claim that it had to control the cards used in its machines to avoid "injury to the reputation of the machines and the good will of" IBM in the absence of proof that other companies could not make quality cards); International Salt Co. v. United States, 332 U.S. 392, 397–398 (1947) (rejecting International Salt's claim that it had to control the supply of salt to protect its leased machines in the absence of proof that competitors could not supply salt of equal quality).

Moreover, there are other reasons to question Kodak's proffered motive of commitment to quality service; its quality justification appears inconsistent with its thesis that consumers are knowledgeable enough to lifecycle price, and its self-service policy. Kodak claims the exclusive-service contract is warranted because customers would otherwise blame Kodak equipment for breakdowns resulting from inferior ISO service. Thus, Kodak simultaneously claims that its customers are sophisticated enough to make complex and subtle lifecycle-pricing decisions, and yet too obtuse to distinguish which breakdowns are due to bad equipment and which are due to bad service. Kodak has failed to offer any reason why informational sophistication should be present in one circumstance and absent in the other. In addition, because self-service customers are just as likely as others to blame Kodak equipment for breakdowns resulting from (their own) inferior service, Kodak's willingness to allow self-service casts doubt on its quality claim. In sum, we agree with the Court of Appeals that respondents "have presented evidence from which a reasonable trier of fact could conclude that Kodak's first reason is pretextual." 903 F.2d, at 618.

There is also a triable issue of fact on Kodak's second justification—controlling inventory costs. As respondents argue, Kodak's actions appear inconsistent with any need to control inventory costs. Presumably, the inventory of parts needed to repair Kodak machines turns only on breakdown rates, and those rates should be the same whether Kodak or ISOs perform the repair. More importantly, the justification fails to explain respondents' evidence that Kodak forced OEMs, equipment owners, and parts brokers not to sell parts to ISOs, actions that would have no effect on Kodak's inventory costs.

Nor does Kodak's final justification entitle it to summary judgment on respondents' § 2 claim. Kodak claims that its policies prevent ISOs from "exploit[ing] the investment Kodak has made in product development, manufacturing and equipment sales in order to take away Kodak's service revenues." Kodak does not dispute that respondents invest substantially in the service market, with training of repair workers and investment in parts inventory. Instead, according to Kodak, the ISOs are free-riding because they have failed to enter the equipment and parts markets. This understanding of free-riding has no support in our case law.[20] To the contrary, as the Court of Appeals noted, one of the evils proscribed by the antitrust laws is the creation of entry barriers to potential competitors by requiring them to enter two markets simultaneously. *Jefferson Parish*, 466 U.S., at 14; *Fortner*, 394 U.S., at 509.

None of Kodak's asserted business justifications, then, are sufficient to prove that Kodak is "entitled to a judgment as a matter of law" on respondents' § 2 claim. Fed.Rule.Civ.Proc. 56(c).

justifications are not enough for SJ

IV

In the end, of course, Kodak's arguments may prove to be correct. It may be that its parts, service, and equipment are components of one unified market, or that the equipment market does discipline the aftermarkets so that all three are priced competitively overall, or that any anticompetitive effects of Kodak's behavior are outweighed by its competitive effects. But we cannot reach these conclusions as a matter of law on a record this sparse. Accordingly, the judgment of the Court of Appeals denying summary judgment is affirmed.

■ SCALIA, J., with whom O'CONNOR and THOMAS, JJ., join, dissenting. This is not, as the Court describes it, just "another case that concerns the standard for summary judgment in an antitrust controversy." Rather, the case presents a very narrow—but extremely important—question of substantive antitrust law: Whether, for purposes of applying our *per se* rule condemning "ties," and for purposes of applying our exacting rules governing the behavior of would-be monopolists, a manufacturer's conceded lack of power in the interbrand market for its equipment is somehow consistent with its possession of "market," or even "monopoly," power in wholly derivative aftermarkets for that equipment. In my view, the Court supplies an erroneous answer to this question, and I dissent.

Per se rules of antitrust illegality are reserved for those situations where logic and experience show that the risk of injury to compensation from the defendant's behavior is so pronounced that it is needless and wasteful to conduct the usual judicial inquiry into the balance between the behavior's procompetitive benefits and its anticompetitive costs.... The *per se* rule against tying is just such a rule: Where the conditions precedent to application of the rule are met, *i.e.*, where the tying arrangement is backed up by the defendant's market power in the "tying" product, the arrangement is adjudged in violation of § 1 of the Sherman Act without

---

20. Kodak claims that both *Continental T.V.* and *Monsanto* support its free-rider argument. Neither is applicable. In both *Continental T.V.*, 433 U.S., at 55, and *Monsanto*, 465 U.S., at 762–763, the Court accepted free-riding as a justification because without restrictions a manufacturer would not be able to induce competent and aggressive retailers to make the kind of investment of capital and labor necessary to distribute the product. In *Continental T.V.* the relevant market level was retail sale of televisions and in *Monsanto* retail sales of herbicides. Some retailers were investing in those markets; others were not, relying, instead, on the investment of the other retailers. To be applicable to this case, the ISOs would have to be relying on Kodak's investment in the service market; that, however, is not Kodak's argument.

any inquiry into the practice's actual effect on competition and consumer welfare. But see United States v. Jerrold Electronics Corp., 187 F.Supp. 545, 560 (E.D.Pa.1960), aff'd *per curiam*, 365 U.S. 567 (1961) (accepting affirmative defense to *per se* tying allegation).

Despite intense criticism of the tying doctrine in academic circles, see, *e.g.*, R. Bork, The Antitrust Paradox 365–381 (1978), the stated rationale for our *per se* rule has varied little over the years. When the defendant has genuine "market power" in the tying product—the power to raise price by reducing output—the tie potentially enables him to extend that power into a second distinct market, enhancing barriers to entry in each. . . .

Our Section 2 monopolization doctrines are similarly directed to discrete situations in which a defendant's possession of substantial market power, combined with his exclusionary or anticompetitive behavior, threatens to defeat or forestall the corrective forces of competition and thereby sustain or extend the defendant's agglomeration of power. See United States v. Grinnell Corp., 384 U.S. 563, 570–571 (1966). Where a defendant maintains substantial market power, his activities are examined through a special lens: Behavior that might otherwise not be of concern to the antitrust laws—or that might even be viewed as procompetitive—can take on exclusionary connotations when practiced by a monopolist. 3 P. Areeda & D. Turner, Antitrust Law ¶ 813, pp. 300–302 (1978) (hereinafter 3 Areeda & Turner).

The concerns, however, that have led the courts to heightened scrutiny both of the "exclusionary conduct" practiced by a monopolist and of tying arrangements subject to *per se* prohibition, are completely without force when the participants lack market power. . . . The Court today finds in the typical manufacturer's inherent power over its own brand of equipment—over the sale of distinctive repair parts for that equipment, for example—the sort of "monopoly power" sufficient to bring the sledgehammer of § 2 into play. And, not surprisingly in light of that insight, it readily labels single-brand power over aftermarket products "market power" sufficient to permit an antitrust plaintiff to invoke the *per se* rule against tying. In my opinion, this makes no economic sense. The holding that market power can be found on the present record causes these venerable rules of selective proscription to extend well beyond the point where the reasoning that supports them leaves off. Moreover, because the sort of power condemned by the Court today is possessed by every manufacturer of durable goods with distinctive parts, the Court's opinion threatens to release a torrent of litigation and a flood of commercial intimidation that will do much more harm than good to enforcement of the antitrust laws and to genuine competition. . . .

[Justice Scalia, in Parts II and III of his dissent, explained at length how "neither logic nor experience" warranted application of "the *per se* tying prohibition and the monopolization doctrine" to Kodak's behavior in its single-branded aftermarket, "when the seller is without power at the interbrand level."]

NOTES AND QUESTIONS

1. Note that both the majority and the dissent in *Kodak* appeared to discuss tying arrangements under a *per se* rule. What does that suggest about the staying power of Justice O'Connor's concurrence in *Jefferson Parish*? Contrast the treatment of tying in United States v. Microsoft Corp., p. 906 *infra*. Would the *per se* treatment have been different if the *Kodak* case had not been before the Court on summary judgment?

2. With respect to the analysis of market power, carefully note the majority's insistence in *Kodak* on examining "economic reality" (including information costs and switching costs), and its unwillingness to rely on theoretical economic arguments about why Kodak could not have market power in the aftermarkets when there is interbrand competition in the equipment market.

3. Does *Kodak* mean that virtually every manufacturer has monopoly power in parts and service aftermarkets? Is Justice Scalia correct in arguing that the majority decision "threatens to release a torrent of litigation?" On remand of the *Kodak* case, a jury returned a verdict against *Kodak* and awarded treble damages totaling $71.8 million; the district court issued an injunction which included a broad compulsory licensing provision. The Ninth Circuit affirmed. *See* Image Technical Services, Inc. v. Eastman Kodak Co., p. 791 *supra*; *see also* Note on Issues at the Intersection of Antitrust and Intellectual Property, p. 789 *supra*. The Ninth Circuit agreed that the ISOs had satisfactorily demonstrated both that Kodak had attained monopoly power in a market for Kodak photocopiers and micrographic parts and that it had engaged in exclusionary conduct to gain or attempt to gain a monopoly over the servicing of Kodak equipment. The Court rejected Kodak's asserted business justifications for its conduct, which centered principally on its alleged right to protect its patented and copyrighted parts. The Court of Appeals for the Federal Circuit issued an opinion in substantial tension with the Ninth Circuit's decision on remand in *Kodak*, in In re Independent Service Organizations Antitrust Litigation (Xerox), p. 801 *supra*.

4. In Mozart Co. v. Mercedes–Benz of North America, Inc., 833 F.2d 1342 (9th Cir.1987), cert. denied, 488 U.S. 870 (1988), the Ninth Circuit accepted a district court's finding that Mercedes passenger cars and their replacement parts are separate products. Similarly, in Multistate Legal Studies, Inc. v. Harcourt Brace Jovanovich Legal and Professional Publications, Inc., 63 F.3d 1540 (10th Cir.1995), cert. denied, 516 U.S. 1044 (1996), the Court had to decide whether a bar examination course focused on the Multistate Bar Exam (MBE) was the same product as a "full-service course," which prepared students for all components of Colorado's bar examination. The Tenth Circuit concluded that two products were involved and reasoned as follows:

> The elements, then, of a *per se* violation, are (1) two separate products, (2) a tie—or conditioning of the sale of one product on the purchase of another, (3) sufficient economic power in the tying product market, and (4) substantial volume of commerce affected in the tied product market.... [Defendants] argue that their actions involved nothing more than the improvement of a single product—their full-service course. PMBR argues on appeal that the district court failed to apply the proper test to determine whether two products exist. We agree. The court focused on PMBR's stipulation that the purpose of a full-service course includes preparing bar applicants for the MBE as well as for the other parts of the bar exam. From this, the court appears to have concluded that any effort to improve the full-service course by adding elements to it could not possibly constitute

the bundling of a second product, at least where those added elements related to the MBE. In this the court erred.

The Supreme Court has made clear that the test for determining whether two components are separate products turns not on their function, but on the nature of any consumer demand for them. For two items at issue to be considered distinct products, "there must be sufficient consumer demand so that it is efficient for a firm to provide [one] separate from [the other]." *Kodak. . . . Jefferson Parish. . . . See also* Service & Training, Inc. v. Data Gen. Corp., 963 F.2d 680, 684–85 (4th Cir.1992) (district court erred in reasoning that since customers' only legitimate purpose for using defendant's diagnostic software was to repair computers, defendant was providing only a single integrated product of computer servicing, rather than a package of service and diagnostic software). . . .

PMBR maintains that by incorporating BAR/BRI and Gilbert into a package, the Defendants have "linked two distinct markets for products that were distinguishable in the eyes of buyers." Jefferson Parish, 466 U.S. at 19.

PMBR's evidence includes the following: . . .

Defendants have marketed their full-service course and their supplemental workshop as separate products, for separate fees, for over a decade and still offer Gilbert separately.

In Kansas, Ohio and Hawaii, HBJL and/or its licensees still offer the full-service course unbundled from Gilbert.

Prior to Defendants' bundling, not every full-service course customer chose to purchase a supplemental workshop; in Colorado, only one-third to one-half did so.

In the past, HBJL officials worked to keep their external Gilbert workshop separate and distinct in customers' minds from the HarBrace workshop within the full-service course, because many customers preferred to buy from two different companies to get multiple providers' perspectives on the MBE.

Defendants have not consolidated the operation of the full-service and supplemental courses; Gilbert continues to be administered and marketed separately. . . .

Other bar review industry participants view full-service and supplemental MBE courses as separate products.

This evidence is sufficient to create a material factual dispute over whether there is enough consumer demand in Colorado for full-service courses without supplemental MBE workshops to make it efficient to sell the two separately. If there is, then the BAR/BRI–Gilbert package should be viewed as two products.

Does the Tenth Circuit's opinion suggest that new, improved product development—*i.e.*, when two products are combined—may be vulnerable? Should the nature and efficiency of the product integration matter? How would you formulate a rule for distinguishing one product from two separate products for purposes of the tying doctrine? Should courts give weight, as a number have, to the fact that at times selling what are two products together results in manufacturing savings or other cost savings? Should this tip a close case to a single-product conclusion, or is it better to recognize both the reality of two products and the cost savings by encouraging manufacturers to sell the two products together at a cost-justified lower price?

5. Is it likely that the usual franchisor will be found to have sufficient or appreciable economic power in the tying product? In Grappone, Inc. v. Subaru of New England, Inc., 858 F.2d 792 (1st Cir. 1988), the First Circuit dealt with the "market power" concept as follows:

> The majority and concurrence [in *Jefferson Parish*] recognized that a Seller, possessing significant market power with respect to Product A, may cause anticompetitive harm by tying as follows: by reducing the price of Product A slightly (or by otherwise not fully exploiting its power with respect to Product A), the Seller may induce the Buyer to accept the tie; by doing so, the Seller may build a strong market position in Product B; and *that position* in Product B, in turn, may increase its power to charge high prices in respect to Product A. If a monopolist of patented can-closing machinery, for example, insists, as a condition of selling his machines, that its purchasers buy his cans, he will likely soon have a monopoly in cans as well as machines. And, that fact—the fact that he controls *both* cans and machines—may make his monopoly safer from competitive attack when his patent on the can-closing machinery expires. A new competitor would then have to enter *both* levels of the business (cans and machines) to deprive him of monopoly profits. And, this added security may enable the machinery monopolist to charge higher prices. The tie, by permitting the Seller to extend its market power from one level to two, may thereby raise entry barriers, providing security that helps a monopolist-seller further harm the consumer....

> [Plaintiffs, however, were not able to meet the "market power" requirement of *Jefferson Parish* because they] have not provided evidence that SNE could raise prices significantly above the competitive level; in fact, the evidence in the record indicates the contrary. For one thing, Subaru's market share, whether measured in terms of sales of all autos or of imports or in any other reasonable way, is miniscule.... National sales of Subarus during the relevant years (as suggested by the import figures in the record) were likely about a fraction of 1 percent of all autos sold. Subaru at most accounted for 3.4 percent of auto imports sold in New Hampshire in 1974.... The record shows that Subaru was but one of many automobile franchisors, and that Grappone itself held not only Subaru, but also AMC, Pontiac, Jeep, Toyota, and Peugeot franchises....

> Finally, plaintiff has made no showing that Subarus had any special or unique features, such as patents or copyrights, that might demonstrate market power. See Digidyne Corp. v. Data General Corp., 734 F.2d 1336, 1341–42 (9th Cir.1984), cert. denied, 473 U.S. 908 (1985); cf. Jefferson Parish, 466 U.S. at 16–17. The most one can say is that Subaru has a brand name and sells through "authorized" Subaru dealers. But, we find no Supreme Court case law suggesting that such features by themselves are sufficient to show "market power." They do not automatically demonstrate any "economic" or "cost advantage" or any other advantage "not shared by ... competitors," *Fortner II*, 429 U.S. at 620–21 (quoting in part *Fortner I*, 394 U.S. at 505 n. 2), particularly in an industry where many larger competing firms all do business in this way. *Will*, 776 F.2d at 672 (no uniqueness argument unless plaintiff shows barrier preventing rivals from offering same package at same cost); cf. Ungar v. Dunkin' Donuts of

America, Inc., 531 F.2d 1211, 1224–25 (3d Cir.1976) (proof of coercion needed, otherwise factors "inherent" in voluntary franchise agreement would suffice to show tie), cert. denied, 429 U.S. 823 (1976). Grappone points to *Digidyne, supra,* as contrary authority, but in that case the Ninth Circuit found a tying product, a computer operating system, "unique" because (1) it was copyrighted, and (2) many of its buyers had previously invested millions of dollars in software design that worked only with that system. We find no directly analogous circumstances here. Grappone does not offer similar evidence of such large dealer investments in Subaru dealerships by those who protested the tie; Grappone's multiple brand representation suggests the contrary, at least for some significant number of franchisees. . . .

For discussions of market power in other lower court cases, *see, e.g.,* Allen–Myland, Inc. v. IBM, 33 F.3d 194 (3d Cir.), cert. denied, 513 U.S. 1066 (1994) (vacating a district court finding that IBM lacked sufficient market power in large-scale mainframe computers); Breaux Bros. Farms, Inc. v. Teche Sugar Co., 21 F.3d 83 (5th Cir. 1994), cert. denied, 513 U.S. 963 (1994); (manufacturer of sugar held at most 17.5% of the tying market, and thus lacked sufficient market power).

6. Did the majority opinions in *Jefferson Parish* and *Kodak* bless a "business justification" defense? If so, what is the breadth of the defense? If a broad business justification defense exists, would it leave any substance in the *per se* tying rule? How would you narrowly define business justifications?

7. Plaintiffs have challenged so-called "technological ties"—that is, situations in which a seller is alleged to have designed a product so as to integrate it, or make it compatible, with a second product which it exclusively sells. For example, in Telex Corp. v. IBM, 367 F.Supp. 258 (N.D.Okl.1973), reversed on other grounds, 510 F.2d 894 (10th Cir.), cert. dismissed, 423 U.S. 802 (1975), a manufacturer of "memory units" sued IBM on grounds, among others, that it had contrived to integrate "memory capacity" into its central processing units (CPUs) so as to preclude effective competition from competitors offering compatible memory units. Computers consisted of a group of electronically interconnected "boxes" (called "hardware") operating under the control of a set of electronic instructions (called "software"). Organizationally, the center of a hardware system was the CPU and the rest of the hardware in the system (such as memory units, printers, tape drives, etc.) was called peripheral equipment. By putting memory units into the CPU "box," purchasers desiring to purchase IBM CPUs, in effect, were denied a choice as to the source of memory equipment. The district court found that IBM's main incentive in integrating memory into CPUs was to reduce costs and improve performance, and that competitors of IBM accept increasing integration as an objective of good engineering design. The court indicated that it was influenced in its determination that no violation had occurred by a recognition that a finding of a tie-in under the antitrust laws could "preclude or discourage the utilization of advancing technology. . . ." 367 F.Supp. at 306. How would you distinguish the *Telex* case from the Tenth Circuit's *Multistate Legal Studies* case discussed in Note 4 *supra*?

8. Price discrimination is a very controversial issue in antitrust. Courts and commentators disagree over whether or not it usually harms consumers. It is easy to construct examples where price discrimination either raises or lowers total output. Notice the concern about "metering" and other forms of price discrimination indicated in the majority opinions in *Jefferson Parish* and *Kodak,* and the more ambiguous attitude of Justice O'Connor in her *Jefferson Parish* concurrence.

United States v. Microsoft Corp.

United States Court of Appeals, District of Columbia Circuit, 2001.
253 F.3d 34, cert. denied, 534 U.S. 952.

[Among other contributions it made to antitrust law, the decision of the D.C. Court of Appeals with respect to the government's allegations of illegal tying raised an important issue with respect to the tying doctrine. The tie-in portion of the opinion is printed below.]

TYING

Microsoft also contests the District Court's determination of liability under § 1 of the Sherman Act. The District Court concluded that Microsoft's contractual and technological bundling of the IE web browser (the "tied" product) with its Windows operating system ("OS") (the "tying" product) resulted in a tying arrangement that was *per se* unlawful. We hold that the rule of reason, rather than *per se* analysis, should govern the legality of tying arrangements involving platform software products. The Supreme Court has warned that " 'it is only after considerable experience with certain business relationships that courts classify them as *per se* violations....' " *Broad.Music.* While every "business relationship" will in some sense have unique features, some represent entire, novel categories of dealings. As we shall explain, the arrangement before us is an example of the latter, offering the first up-close look at the technological integration of added functionality into software that serves as a platform for third-party applications. There being no close parallel in prior antitrust cases, simplistic application of *per se* tying rules carries a serious risk of harm. Accordingly, we vacate the District Court's finding of a *per se* tying violation and remand the case. Plaintiffs may on remand pursue their tying claim under the rule of reason.

The facts underlying the tying allegation substantially overlap with those set forth in connection with the § 2 monopoly maintenance claim. The key District Court findings are that (1) Microsoft required licensees of Windows 95 and 98 also to license IE as a bundle at a single price; (2) Microsoft refused to allow OEMs to uninstall or remove IE from the Windows desktop; (3) Microsoft designed Windows 98 in a way that withheld from consumers the ability to remove IE by use of the Add/Remove Programs utility; and (4) Microsoft designed Windows 98 to override the user's choice of default web browser in certain circumstance. The court found that these acts constituted *per se* tying violation. Although the District Court also found that Microsoft commingled operating system-only and browser-only routines in the same library files, it did not include this as a basis for tying liability despite plaintiffs' request that it do so.

There are four elements to a *per se* tying violation: (1) the tying and tied goods are two separate products; (2) the defendant has market power in the tying product market; (3) the defendant affords consumers no choice but to purchase the tied product from it; and (4) the tying arrangement forecloses a substantial volume of commerce.

Microsoft does not dispute that it bound Windows and IE in the four ways the District Court cited. Instead it argues that Windows (the tying good) and IE browsers (the tied good) are not "separate products," and that it did not substantially foreclose competing browsers from the tied product market. (Microsoft also contends that it does not have monopoly power in the tying product market, but we uphold the District Court's finding to the contrary.)

We first address the separate-products inquiry, a source of much argument between the parties and of confusion in the cases. Our purpose is to highlight the poor fit between the separate-products test and the facts of this case. We then offer further reasons for carving an exception to the *per se* rule when the tying product is platform software. In the final section we discuss the District Court's inquiry if plaintiffs pursue a rule of reason claim on remand.

A. Separate–Products Inquiry Under the *per se* Test

The requirement that a practice involve two separate products before being condemned as an illegal tie started as a purely linguistic requirement: unless products are separate, one cannot be "tied" to the other. Indeed, the nature of the products involved in early tying cases—intuitively distinct items such as a movie projector and a film, Motion Picture Patents Co. v. Universal Film Mfg. Co., 243 U.S. 502 (1917)—courts either to disregard the separate-products question.... It was not until Times–Picayune Publishing Co. v. United States, 345 U.S. 594 (1953), that the separate-products issue became a distinct element of the test for an illegal tie. Even that case engaged in a rather cursory inquiry into whether ads sold in the morning edition of a paper were a separate product from ads sold in the evening edition.

The first case to give content to the separate-products test was *Jefferson Parish*. That case addressed a tying arrangement in which a hospital conditioned surgical care at its facility on the purchase of anesthesiological services from an affiliated medical group. The facts were a challenge for casual separate-products analysis because the tied service—anesthesia—was neither intuitively distinct from nor intuitively contained within the tying service—surgical care. A further complication was that, soon after the Court enunciated the *per se* rule for tying liability in International Salt Co. v. United States, 332 U.S. 392, 396 (1947), new economic research began to cast doubt on the assumption, voiced by the Court when it established the rule, that "tying agreements serve hardly any purpose beyond the suppression of competition...."

The *Jefferson Parish* Court resolved the matter in two steps. First, it clarified that "the answer to the question whether one or two products are involved" does not turn "on the functional relation between them...." *Jefferson Parish*. In other words, the mere fact that two items are complements, that "one ... is useless without the other," does not make them a single "product" for purposes of tying law. Second, reasoning that the "definitional question [whether two distinguishable products are involved] depends on whether the arrangement may have the type of competitive *separate markets are rec*

Jeff Parish = consumer demand test

consequences addressed by the rule [against tying]," the Court decreed that "no tying arrangement can exist unless there is a sufficient demand for the purchase of anesthesiological services separate from hospital services to identify a distinct product market in which it is efficient to offer anesthesiological services separately from hospital service."

To understand the logic behind the Court's consumer demand test, consider first the postulated harms from tying. The core concern is that tying prevents goods from competing directly for consumer choice on their merits, *i. e.,* being selected as a result of "buyers' independent judgment." With a tie, a buyer's "freedom to select the best bargain in the second market [could be] impaired by his need to purchase the tying product, and perhaps by an inability to evaluate the true cost of either product..." Direct competition on the merits of the tied product is foreclosed when the tying product either is sold only in a bundle with the tied product or, though offered separately, is sold at a bundled price, so that the buyer pays the same price whether he takes the tied product or not. In both cases, a consumer buying the tying product becomes entitled to the tied product; he will therefore likely be unwilling to buy a competitor's version of the tied product even if, making his own price/quality assessment, that is what he would prefer.

But not all ties are bad. Bundling obviously saves distribution and consumer transaction costs. This is likely to be true, to take some examples from the computer industry, with the integration of math coprocessors and memory into microprocessor chips and the inclusion of spell checkers in word processors.... Bundling can also capitalize on certain economies of scope. A possible example is the "shared" library files that perform OS and browser functions with the very same lines of code and thus may save drive space from the clutter of redundant routines and memory when consumers use both the OS and browser simultaneously.... Indeed, if there were no efficiencies from a tie (including economizing on consumer transaction costs such as the time and effort involved in choice), we would expect distinct consumer demand for each individual component of every good. In a competitive market with zero transaction costs, the computers on which this opinion was written would only be sold piecemeal-keyboard, monitor, mouse, central processing unit, disk drive, and memory all sold in separate transactions and likely by different manufacturers.

Recognizing the potential benefits from tying, the Court in *Jefferson Parish* forged a separate-products test that, like those of market power and substantial foreclosure, attempts to screen out false positives under *per se* analysis. The consumer demand test is a rough proxy for whether a tying arrangement may, on balance, be welfare-enhancing, and unsuited to *per se* condemnation. In the abstract, of course, there is always direct separate demand for products: assuming choice is available at zero cost, consumers will prefer it to no choice. Only when the efficiencies from bundling are dominated by the benefits to choice for enough consumers, however, will we actually observe consumers making independent purchases. In other words, perceptible separate demand is inversely proportional to net efficiencies. On the supply side, firms without market power will bundle two goods only when the cost savings from joint sale outweigh the value consumers place on separate choice. So bundling by all competitive firms implies strong net efficiencies. If a court finds either that there is no noticeable separate demand for the tied product or, there being no convincing direct evidence of separate demand that the entire "competitive fringe" engages in the same behavior as the defendant, tied products should be declared one product and *per se* liability should be rejected.

Before concluding our exegesis of *Jefferson Parish's* separate-products test, we should clarify two things. First, *Jefferson Parish* does not endorse a direct inquiry into the efficiencies of a bundle. Rather, it proposes easy-to-administer proxies for net efficiency. In describing the separate-products test we discuss efficiencies only to explain the rationale behind the consumer demand inquiry. To allow the separate-products test to become a detailed inquiry into possible welfare consequences would turn a screening test into the very process it is expected to render unnecessary.

Second, the separate-products test is not a one-sided inquiry into the cost savings from a bundle. Although *Jefferson Parish* acknowledged that prior lower court cases looked at cost-savings to decide separate products, the Court conspicuously did not adopt that approach in its disposition of tying arrangement before it. Instead it chose proxies that balance costs savings against reduction in consumer choice.

With this background, we now turn to the separate products inquiry before us. The District Court found that many consumers, if given the option, would choose their browser separately from the OS. Turning to industry custom, the court found that, although all major OS vendors bundled browsers with their OSs, these companies either sold versions without a browser, or allowed OEMs or end-users either not to install the bundled browser or in any event to "uninstall" The court did not discuss the record evidence as to whether OS vendors other than Microsoft sold at a bundled price, with no discount for a browserless OS, perhaps because the record evidence on the issue was in conflict.

Microsoft does not dispute that many consumers demand alternative browsers. But on industry custom Microsoft contends that no other firm requires non-removal because no other firm has invested the resources to integrate web browsing as deeply into its OS as Microsoft has. . . . Microsoft contends not only that its integration of IE into Windows is innovative and beneficial but also that it requires non-removal of IE. In our discussion of monopoly maintenance we find that these claims fail the efficiency balancing applicable in that context. But the separate-products analysis is supposed to perform its function as a proxy without embarking on any direct analysis of efficiency. Accordingly, Microsoft's implicit argument—that in this case looking to a competitive fringe is inadequate to evaluate fully its potentially innovative technological integration, that such a comparison is between apples and oranges—poses a legitimate objection to the operation of *Jefferson Parish's* separate-products test for the *per se* rule.

In fact there is merit to Microsoft's broader argument that *Jefferson Parish's* consumer demand test would "chill innovation to the detriment of consumers by preventing firms from integrating into their products new functionality previously provided by standalone products—and hence, by definition, subject to separate consumer demand." The *per se* rule's direct consumer demand and indirect industry custom inquiries are, as a general matter, backward-looking and therefore systematically poor proxies for overall efficiency in the presence of new and innovative integration. The direct consumer demand test focuses on historic consumer behavior, likely before integration, and the indirect industry custom test looks at firms that, unlike the defendant, may not have integrated the tying and tied goods. Both tests compare incomparables—the defendant's decision to bundle in the presence of integration, on the one hand, and consumer and competitor calculations in its absence, on the other. If integration has efficiency benefits, these may be ignored by the *Jefferson Parish* proxies. Because one cannot be sure beneficial integration will be protected by the other elements of the *per se* rule, simple application of that rule's separate-products test may make consumers worse off.

In light of the monopoly maintenance section, obviously, we do not find that Microsoft's integration is welfare-enhancing or that it should be absolved of tying liability. Rather, we heed Microsoft's warning that the separate-products element of the *per se* rule may not give newly integrated products a fair shake.

B.   *Per se* Analysis Inappropriate for this Case.

We now address directly the larger question as we see it: whether standard *per se* analysis should be applied "off the shelf" to evaluate the defendant's tying arrangement, one which involves software that serves as a platform for third party applications. There is no doubt that "it is far too late in the history of our antitrust jurisprudence to question the proposition that certain tying arrangements pose an unacceptable risk of stifling competition and therefore are unreasonable 'per se.' " *Jefferson Parish.* But there are strong reasons to doubt that the integration of additional software functionality into an as falls among these arrangements. Applying *per se* analysis to such an amalgamation creates undue risks of error and of deterring welfare-enhancing innovation. . . .

In none of these [Supreme Court] cases was the tied good physically and technologically integrated with the tying good. Nor did the defendants ever argue that their tie improved the value of the tying product to users and to makers of complementary goods. In those cases where the defendant claimed that use of the tied good made the tying good more valuable to users, the Court ruled that the same result could be achieved via quality standards for substitutes of the tied good. *See, e.g., Int'l Salt; IBM.* Here Microsoft argues that IE and Windows are an integrated physical product and that the bundling of IE APIs with Windows makes the latter a better applications platform for third-party software. It is unclear how the benefits from IE APIs could be achieved by quality standards for different browser manufacturers. We do not pass judgment on Microsoft's claims regarding the benefits from integration of its APIs. We merely note that these and other novel, purported efficiencies suggest that judicial "experience" provides little basis for believing that, "because of their pernicious effect on competition and lack of any redeeming virtue," a software firm's decisions to sell multiple functionalities as a package should be "conclusively presumed to be unreasonable and therefore illegal without elaborate inquiry as to the precise harm they have caused or the business excuse for their use." *N. Pac. Ry.* Nor have we found much insight into software integration among the decisions of lower federal courts....

While the paucity of cases examining software bundling suggests a high risk that *per se* analysis may produce inaccurate results, the nature of the platform software market affirmatively suggests that *per se* rules might stunt valuable innovation. We have in mind two reasons.

First, as we explained in the previous section, the separate products test is a poor proxy for net efficiency from newly integrated products. Under *per se* analysis the first firm to merge previously distinct functionalities *(e.g.,* the inclusion of starter motors in automobiles) or to eliminate entirely the need for a second function *(e.g.,* the invention of the stain resistant carpet) risks being condemned as having tied two separate products because at the moment of integration there will appear to be a robust "distinct" market for the tied product. Rule of reason analysis, however, affords the first mover an opportunity to demonstrate that an efficiency gain from its "tie" adequately offsets any distortion of consumer choice....

The failure of the separate-products test to screen out certain cases of productive integration is particularly troubling in platform software markets such as that in which the defendant competes. Not only is integration common in such markets, but it is common among firms without market power. We have already reviewed evidence that nearly all competitive as vendors also bundle browsers. Moreover, plaintiffs do not dispute that as vendors can and do incorporate basic internet plumbing and other useful functionality into their OSs.... Firms without market power have no incentive to package different pieces of software together unless there are efficiency gains from doing so. The ubiquity of bundling in competitive platform software markets should give courts reason to pause before condemning such behavior in less competitive markets.

Second, because of the pervasively innovative character of platform software markets, tying in such markets may produce efficiencies that courts have not previously encountered and thus the Supreme Court had not factored into the *per se* rule as originally conceived. For example, the bundling of a browser with OSs enables an independent software developer to count on the presence of the browser's APIs, if any, on consumers' machines and thus to omit them from its own package.... It is true that software developers can bundle the browser APIs they need with their own products, but that may force consumers to pay twice for the same API if it is bundled with two different software programs. It is also true that OEMs can include APIs with the computers they sell, but diffusion of uniform APIs by that route may be inferior. . . .

These arguments all point to one conclusion: we cannot comfortably say that bundling in platform software markets has so little "redeeming virtue, and that there would be so "very little loss to society" from its ban, that "an inquiry into its costs in the individual case [can be] considered [ ] unnecessary." We do not have enough empirical evidence regarding the effect of Microsoft's practice on the amount of consumer surplus created or consumer choice foreclosed by the integration of added functionality into platform software to exercise sensible judgment regarding that entire class of behavior. (For some issues we have no data.) "We need to know more than we do about the actual impact of these arrangements on competition to decide whether they . . . should be classified as *per se* violations of the Sherman Act. Until then, we will heed the wisdom that "easy labels do not always supply ready answers," *Broad. Music,* and vacate the District Court's finding of *per se* tying liability under Sherman Act § 1. We remand the case for evaluation of Microsoft's tying arrangements under the rule of reason. . . .

Our judgment regarding the comparative merits of the *per se* rule and the rule of reason is confined to the tying arrangement before us, where the tying product is software whose major purpose is to serve as a platform for third-party applications and the tied product is complementary software functionality. While our reasoning may at times appear to have broader force, we do not have the confidence to speak to facts outside the record, which contains scant discussion of software integration generally. Microsoft's primary justification for bundling IE APIs is that their inclusion with Windows increases the value of third-party software (and Windows) to consumers. Because this claim applies with distinct force when the tying product is platform software, we have no present basis for finding the *per se* rule inapplicable to software markets generally. Nor should we be interpreted as setting a precedent for switching to the rule of reason every time a court identifies an efficiency justification for a tying arrangement. Our reading of the record suggests merely that integration of new functionality into platform software is a common practice and that wooden application of *per se* rules in this litigation may cast a cloud over platform innovation in the market for PCs, network computers and information appliances. . . .

NOTES AND QUESTIONS

1.   Did the D.C. Circuit go too far in this case when it decided to apply the rule of reason to the tying arrangements before it? How can you reconcile this step with the fact that the majority in *Jefferson Parish* expressly refused to take it, over the explicit invitation of Justice O'Connor's concurring opinion. Could the D.C. Circuit have avoided fashioning a special rule of reason when the "tying product is platform software" by focusing its analysis on the special "one product" or "two product"

issue? Would there be any antitrust problem to selling two products together at a lower price than would be the case when each is purchased separately if the lower price were the result of efficiency gains from bundling the two together? How can you explain the fact that the Supreme Court denied certiorari in *Microsoft*, apart from the usual fact that a denial of review carries no substantive implications one way or the other?

2. With respect to the Court's comments on price bundling, *see* the Note on Package Discounts, *infra*.

3. Do you agree that *Jefferson Parish* adopted consumer demand as the sole determinant of whether one is faced with one product (or service) or two? Has the Supreme Court directly addressed the issue of efficient product intergration? How would you deal with the efficient product integration issue?

4. In April 2007, the Antitrust Division and the FTC issued a joint report on "Antitrust Enforcement and Intellectual Property Rights." With respect to tying they concluded:

> Legal and policy analysis of intellectual property bundling has evolved over time. Older case law, with its *per se* rule and presumption of market power, contends with the current analysis of the Agencies and some more recent lower court decisions that embody, in essence, a rule of reason approach. Moreover, the Supreme Court recently eliminated its rule presuming market power based on intellectual property. Panelists noted that, although intellectual property bundling may have anticompetitive potential in certain circumstances, there may also be significant efficiency justifications for such bundling in some cases. Thus, as a matter of their prosecutorial discretion, the Agencies will apply the rule of reason when evaluating intellectual property tying and bundling agreements. Given the ubiquitous use of these arrangements by businesses lacking in market power and the efficiencies that such arrangements can often entail, these practices usually are not anticompetitive. When the Agencies do identify anticompetitive situations, however, they will pursue them.

Should antitrust officials in the new Obama Administration revise this policy?

NOTE ON PACKAGE DISCOUNTS

An increasingly popular marketing approach (and frequent subject of private litigation in the lower courts) is the offer of a package of two or more products at a discount. The offer does not represent a tie-in sale because each product is available separately at a specified price. If the buyer takes all items in the package, however, the combined price is lower than the total of prices if all items were purchased separately.

Some have suggested that package discounts can never be illegal, citing a footnote in *Northern Pacific* stating that: "Of course, when the buyer is free to take either product by itself, there is no tying problem even though the seller may also offer the two items as a unit at a single price." The Supreme Court probably only meant to suggest by that footnote that the harsh rules against tie-in sales—in *Northern Pacific* a rule of *per se* illegality was adopted—might be relaxed with respect to package discounts. In support of that view, note that a rule of complete immunity would mean that the seller could charge a very high price for the tying product and a trivial price for the tied product and, as a result of that strategy, induce purchase of the tied product and yet avoid any challenge under traditional tie-in restrictions. At the other extreme, others have argued that package discounts are the equivalent of outright tie-in sales because consumers are "coerced" into taking the various items in the package if offered at a substantial discount. *See* Advance Business Systems & Supply Co. v. SCM Corp., 415 F.2d 55 (4th Cir.1969), cert. denied, 397 U.S. 920 (1970) declaring illegal a plan to rent machines, supplies and service in a single package because it effectively deprived customers of freedom of choice. These extreme positions are summarized and criticized in 10 Areeda, Elhauge & Hovenkamp, Antitrust Law: An Analysis of Antitrust Principles and Their Application, 341–43 (1996).

In seeking a more nuanced approach, courts have recognized that package discounts are a way of waging competition and usually result in lower prices to purchasers. Also, the seller's goal might be to increase total sales through a promotional discount, and then pass the efficiencies on to consumers in the form of lower prices. Finally, a rule that discourages package pricing might discourage aggressive competition by efficient firms and hold a price umbrella over their less efficient rivals. On the other hand, there can be circumstances in which package discounts can be anticompetitive. Two sorts of challenges have emerged in the cases: (1) charges that one or more of the items in the package, as a result of the discount, are sold at "predatory prices" (*see* section 2 of this chapter) or (2) that the exclusionary effect of the package discount is much the same as a conventional tie-in sale.

With respect to predatory pricing, we have already seen that price on a product can only be "predatory" if it is below some appropriate measure of cost, *see Brooke Group*, p. ___ *supra* regarded in the lower courts and in treatises as below average variable cost. In that connection, consider a marketing plan in which ten items are included in a package. Each item can be purchased separately but, if a customer takes the entire package, it receives a three percent discount on each of the ten items. Assuming each product in the package is purchased in equal quantities, the competitor on item ten might complain that in effect it must lower its price by 30% to induce the customer to buy its product in place of packaged item 10. In effect, the complainant would be asking that the entire value of the discount be allocated to each of the products in the package. *See* Ortho Diagnostic Systems v. Abbott Laboratories, 926 F.Supp. 371 (S.D.N.Y.1996) (accepting the concept of allocating the entire discount to each product but finding no predation on the record before it). In Cascade Health Solutions v. PeaceHealth, 502 F.3d 895 (9th Cir. 2007), the Ninth Circuit concluded that a bundle of discounts on separate services offered by a hospital to insurers is not illegal under Section 2, even when the entire collection of discounts is allocated to a particular competitive service provided by a competitor so long as the collection of discounts is above average variable cost (*i.e.*, not predatory). The *PeaceHealth* approach has not attracted much support in subsequent case law.

An alternative to allocating the entire discount to one product would be to require that the price of the entire package remain above the standard for predatory pricing. Note that if the approach of allocating the discount to each product were adopted, many package discounts, especially with a considerable number of items in the package, would be illegal. Perhaps it would even be illegal to add an eleventh item to the package without increasing the price of the package—essentially an offer of a free good—as a reward or bonus for taking the first ten items.

The second line of attack on package discounts is the charge that they often are identical in effect to outright tie-in sales. Thus a package discount could be illegal if the package price is so attractive that all or nearly all customers would accept it because it would be economically irrational to pay the higher price for the separate products. *See* T. Harris Young & Assoc. v. Marquette Electr., Inc., 931 F.2d 816, 822 (11th Cir.1991). With regard to that charge, the lower courts appear to be moving generally in the direction of a common rule of law—*i.e.*, that no antitrust violation can be found where a significant number of purchasers offered the package decline the offer and buy the product separately. *See* Nobel Scientific Indus. v. Beckman Instruments, 670 F.Supp. 1313, 1324 (D.Md.1986) (no *de facto* tie because 50–55% of the tied product sales were separate); Ways & Means v. IVAC Corp., 506 F.Supp. 697, 701 (N.D.Cal.1979), affirmed, 638 F.2d 143 (9th Cir.1981) (no *de facto* tie because 25% of the time product sales were separate). *But see* LaPage's Inc. v. 3M, 324 F.3d 141 (3d Cir.2003) where the Third Circuit, in an *en banc* opinion, found that 3M, the leading supplier of transparent tape in the United States through its Scotch Tape brand, offered rebates to a number of its customers on condition that they purchase unrelated 3M product lines; the Court affirmed a monopolization judgment against 3M and did not examine whether all or most customers that were offered rebates accepted the deal.

Should the law be less or more concerned about package discounts than outright ties? Are any of the defenses that have progressively developed in the area of tie-in sales irrelevant or inappropriate to package ties? Should we be concerned about the plight of the rival on product ten—a single item manufacturer—losing out to the diversified company even though its product is of equal or better quality and price?

PROBLEM 20

SERVICE CONTRACTS FOR BURGLAR ALARM SYSTEMS

In 2000, Berger Co. invented a new and highly complicated electronic burglar alarm system. Included in the system is a device containing a new, secret conductive alloy which makes for more reliable performance. Because of dissatisfaction with existing systems, Berger had no difficulty in selling its product to numerous industrial and commercial establishments throughout the country. From a negligible share of burglar systems installed in 2000, Berger installed 2% in 2001, 8% in 2002, 43% in 2004, and 78% in 2005. A competitive system went on the market at the end of 2005, and in 2006 reduced Berger's share to 66% of new installations. During these same years, Berger accounted for the following shares of systems in use: 2001, 0.5%; 2002, 2%; 2004, 12%; 2005, 21%; and 2006, 29%.

Throughout the period 2000–2006, Berger refused to sell its system except on the condition that the system be serviced exclusively by Berger's technicians. Among other reasons, Berger does not want repairmen not in its employ to have access to the secret feature of its system. In the first two years, while the system was relatively unknown and unused, any notoriety about failures of the system would have been disastrous to Berger. On the other hand, Berger's services have always been expensive and it is conceded that, without the compulsory service contract, many purchasers of the system would have made other servicing arrangements.

Has Berger violated the antitrust laws?

NOTE ON RECIPROCITY

A variation on the characteristic tie-in occurs when firm A (producing Product A) agrees with firm B (producing Product B) that it will buy Product B only on condition that firm B buys Product A. Arguably, one or both companies are using their purchasing power with respect to one product to "distort competition on the merits" with respect to sale of another product.

Reciprocity antitrust problems can arise in two ways. First, there can be formal or informal agreements, consensual or coerced, which lead to reciprocal dealings. Second, a merger can be challenged on grounds that it puts the combined company in a position to exercise reciprocity pressures, when the combined firm both buys from and sells to intermediate enterprises. The company is thus in a position to suggest that it will initiate or continue purchases only if the supplier agrees to buy from its newly acquired subsidiary. During the 1960s, there was much discussion of reciprocity. *See* Handler, Emerging Antitrust Issues: Reciprocity, Diversification and Joint Ventures, 49 Va.L.Rev. 433 (1963); Hausman, Reciprocal Dealing and the Antitrust Laws, 77 Harv.L.Rev. 873 (1964). In United States v. General Dynamics Corp., Trade Reg.Rep. (CCH) ¶ 71,870 (S.D.N.Y. 1966), a merger was found invalid under Section 7 of the Clayton Act because actual and potential resort to reciprocity pressures, made possible by the merger, led to a substantial lessening of competition. In general, there has been little further litigation involving reciprocity; the issue has been raised in a few merger cases, and we will deal with reciprocity issues again, in the merger context in Chapter 9.

Betaseed, Inc. v. U & I Inc., 681 F.2d 1203 (9th Cir.1982) is a rare exception to the paucity of caselaw in the reciprocity area. Betaseed, which sold seeds to sugarbeet farmers, alleged that U & I, a company which competed in the sale of seeds and also purchased sugarbeets for processing sugar, used its purchasing power with respect to sugarbeets to induce growers to buy its seeds. U & I had considerable purchasing power as the only processor of sugarbeets in the relevant geographic area. Beginning in 1975, U & I included a clause in its sugarbeet purchase contracts providing that it would be obligated to buy beets only from those purchasers who accepted its seeds or "such other seed as has been established by tests satisfactory to the COMPANY to produce beets having substantially the same characteristics...."

Betaseed claimed that the equivalency clause was a sham in that U & I never established objective standards to determine when seeds possessed "substantially the same characteristics," and in fact, never accepted as a satisfactory substitute any seeds offered by other sellers.

Betaseed alleged, among other antitrust claims, that the contractual arrangement and the course of dealing constituted coercive reciprocal dealing in violation of Section 1 of the Sherman Act. The Court of Appeals reversed a grant of summary judgment for U & I, concluding that the cause of action was valid and that there were legitimate issues of fact that needed to be tried.

After a review of the history of reciprocity enforcement, the Court of Appeals concluded that coercive reciprocity should be treated as illegal *per se*, but under the same kind of modified *per se* approach applied in tie-in cases. Specifically, the Court noted that there needed to be two distinct products or services, some "modicum of coercion," sufficient economic power in the market for the tying product to impose significant restrictions in the tied market, and a not insubstantial amount of commerce:

> "In our view, the malevolent economic results of market foreclosure and raising of artificial entry barriers in a market tinged with coercive reciprocity evinces the anticompetitive and predatory nature of the practice. The similarity between coercive reciprocity and tying arrangements, both in form and in anticompetitive consequences, leads to the conclusion

that the two practices should be judged by similar standards. Coercive reciprocity, in our view, is a form of tying and hence 'fits' this category."

The Court noted that there was no serious dispute about the fact that U & I had significant economic power and that a not insubstantial amount of commerce was affected. As to whether coercion had occurred, that was an issue of fact turning on whether an appreciable number of buyers had been induced not to purchase Betaseed's products because of U & I's contractual provision conditioning its purchase of sugarbeets on its sale of sugarbeet seeds.

Finally, the Court of Appeals noted that even if the U & I contractual arrangement did not deserve *per se* treatment, it might nevertheless be illegal under a rule of reason analysis. In either event a full trial would be necessary to explore those issues and therefore the grant of summary judgment was improper.

It is interesting to speculate why there have been so few reciprocity cases since the 1960s. One explanation is that the antitrust enforcement agencies have come to doubt that reciprocity is as anticompetitive as earlier thought. Can you think of any "business justifications" for coercive reciprocity? What if the reciprocity comes about because of non-coercive voluntary purchasing? Should the antitrust laws be concerned about non-coercive, consensual reciprocity?

COMPARATIVE NOTE: TYING IN THE EUROPEAN UNION

As discussed in Chapter 3, Article 82 of the Rome Treaty prohibits abuses of a dominant position.[21] The Article provides a non-exclusive list of what may constitute such an abuse. The list includes, in paragraph (d), "making the conclusion of contracts subject to acceptance by the other parties of supplementary obligations which, by their nature or according to commercial usage, have no connection with the subject of such contracts."

A company with market power may resort to tying in order to identify and extract a higher price from those who put the tying product to heavier use and therefore are able and willing to pay more. By putting a premium on the tied product, the seller is able to charge more to heavy users and less to light users. *See* Hilti v. Commission, Case C–53/92, [1994] ECR I–667. Companies with market power in the tying product may also use tying to strengthen their position in the market for the tied product. One of the leading tying cases in the European Union is Tetra Pak International S.A. v. Commission.[22] The case involves what is called the problem of "associated product markets" in the European Union and "monopoly leveraging" in the United States. While reading the following case summary, watch out for the differences in approach on the two sides of the Atlantic.

Tetra Pak was a Swiss-based group that made packaging machines and containers for liquid and semi-liquid food, especially for milk. It operated in the aseptic, as well as in the non-aseptic sector. It accounted for 78% of both sectors combined, which was seven times more than the market share of its leading competitor. The structure of the market for aseptic packaging was quasi-monopolistic, with Tetra Pak holding 90% to 95% of the Community market. In the non-aseptic sector, the market was oligopolistic. Tetra Pak held 50% to 55% and the Norwegian group Elopak held 27%. The third largest player on the market was PKL with 11%. Non-

---

21. *Id.*

22. *See* Case T–83/91, [1994] ECR II–755, aff'd, Case C–333/94P, [1996] ECR I–5951.

aseptic packaging requires less sterility and less sophisticated equipment than aseptic packaging.

The Commission charged Tetra Pak with both tying and predatory practices. The Commission distinguished between four different markets: aseptic cartons, aseptic filling machines, non-aseptic cartons and non-aseptic filling machines. In terms of tying, the Commission found that Tetra Pak had a dominant position on the aseptic markets and abused its dominance by requiring buyers of its non-aseptic machines to use Tetra Pak cartons for the non-aseptic machines in the UK. The Court of First Instance (CFI) upheld the Commission decision.

Tetra Pak argued that the marketing of complete packaging systems was objectively justified by public health concerns, as well as its reputation through exclusive control of the entire packaging process. The CFI, however, found these points unpersuasive. Citing to Hilti v. EC Commission, it noted that it was "clearly not the task of an undertaking in a dominant position to take steps on its own initiative to eliminate products which, rightly or wrongly, it regards as dangerous or at least as inferior in quality to its own products." The CFI found that compliance with standards of hygiene could be ensured by requiring the users of Tetra Pak machines to adhere to all the technical specifications concerning the cartons to be used on those systems. Under those circumstances, the court thought it was clear that the tied-sale clauses went beyond their purpose and were intended to strengthen Tetra Pak's dominant position by reinforcing its customers' economic dependence on it.

On appeal to the European Court of Justice (ECJ), Tetra Pak argued that Article 82 was inapplicable because the tie-in neither strengthened its dominant position in the tying market, nor threatened to create a new dominant position in the market of the tied product. The ECJ, referring extensively to the judgment of the CFI, rejected Tetra Pak's arguments. The ECJ acknowledged that "Article [82] presupposes a link between the dominant position and the alleged abusive conduct, which is normally not present where conduct on the market distinct from the dominated market produces effects on the distinct market." The Court went on to say that "[i]n the case of distinct, but associated markets, as in the present case, application of art. [82] to conduct found on the associated, non-dominated market can only be justified by special circumstances." The Court then reviewed the circumstances of the case and concluded that such special circumstances did, in fact, exist.

Following a summary of the findings of the CFI regarding markets shares, the Court emphasized that application of Article 82 was justified by the situation on the different markets and the close associative links between them. The Court stated that "[t]he fact that the various materials involved are used for packaging the same basic liquid products shows that Tetra Pak's customers in one sector are also potential customers in the other.... Given its almost complete domination of the aseptic markets, Tetra Pak could also count on favored status on the non-aseptic markets.... The circumstances thus ... justified the Court of First Instance, without any need to show that the undertaking was dominant on the non-aseptic markets, in finding that Tetra Pak enjoyed freedom of conduct compared with other economic operators on those markets." Accordingly, the Court concluded that "the Court of First Instance was right to accept the application of [Article 82] of the Treaty in this case, given that the quasi-monopoly enjoyed by Tetra Pak on the aseptic markets, and its leading position on the distinct, though closely associated, non-aseptic markets placed it in a situation comparable to that of holding a dominant position on the markets in question as a whole."

In his Address before the BIICL Second Annual International and Comparative Law Conference in London, on May 17, 2002, William J. Kolasky, then Deputy Assistant Attorney General, Antitrust Division, U.S. Department of Justice, compared the U.S. and EU approaches on monopoly leveraging as follows:[23]

> The final area of divergence is what we call monopoly leveraging in the United States—that is, using a dominant position in one market to gain a competitive advantage in another. Most U.S. courts have held that it is not unlawful for a firm with a monopoly in one market to use its monopoly power in that market to gain a competitive advantage in neighboring markets, unless by so doing it serves either to maintain its existing monopoly or to create a dangerous probability of gaining a monopoly in the adjacent market as well.[24] My understanding is that under EU law, by contrast, it is an abuse of dominance for a firm that is dominant in one market to use that position to gain a competitive advantage in a neighboring market in which it is not dominant even if the conduct is not shown to be likely to create a dominant position in the second market unless the dominant firm can show a legitimate business justification for its conduct.[25]

> Our view, by contrast, is that, "so long as we allow a firm to compete in several markets, we must expect it to seek the competitive advantages of its broad-based activity—more efficient production, greater ability to develop complementary products, reduced transactions costs, and so forth,"[26] and that allowing it to do so ultimately benefits consumers. Again, this is an area that would benefit from a constructive transatlantic dialog over our differing approaches.

SECTION 4. PARTIAL VERTICAL INTEGRATION BY CONTRACT: EXCLUSIVE SELLING AND EXCLUSIVE DEALING ARRANGEMENTS

A. EXCLUSIVE SELLING

INTRODUCTORY NOTE

An "exclusive selling arrangement," also termed an "exclusive dealership" and a "sole outlet," usually comes about through a contractual arrangement under which all but one seller is eliminated or, in a start-up context, only one seller is appointed. Typically, the supplier of the product agrees not to appoint another seller and to do all its business through the single outlet. The basic antitrust issue raised by exclusive selling is whether the agreement—which by definition precludes other sellers from entering the market—may violate Section 1 of the Sherman Act and, if

23. *See* North Atlantic Competition Policy: Converging Toward What? Address by William J. Kolasky, Deputy Assistant Attorney General, Antitrust Division, U.S. Department of Justice Before the BIICL Second Annual International and Comparative Law Conference, London, England on May 17, 2002, retrieved from http://www.usdoj.gov/atr/public/speeches/11153.htm

24. *See* ABA Section of Antitrust Law, I Antitrust Developments 282–85 (4th ed. 1997).

25. *See, e.g.*, Tetra Pack Rausing SA v. Comm'n, C–333/94P, [1996] ECR I–5951 (1996).

26. Berkey Photo v. Eastman Kodak Co., 603 F.2d 263 (2d Cir.1979).

so, under what circumstances? Since the manufacturer is agreeing to restrict its own freedom, and in a pure case, not limiting the seller, Section 3 of the Clayton Act is not applicable.

In general, courts have been quite permissive in dealing with exclusive selling arrangements. For example, in Packard Motor Car Co. v. Webster Motor Car Co., 243 F.2d 418, 420–21 (D.C.Cir.1957), the Court of Appeals quoted with approval the following language: "When an exclusive dealership 'is not part and parcel of a scheme to monopolize, and effective competition exists at both the seller and buyer levels, the arrangement has invariably been upheld as a reasonable restraint of trade.' " In the *Packard* case, the Court of Appeals overturned a jury award for Webster Motor, one of three dealers in Packard cars in Baltimore. Packard terminated Webster Motor because Zell Motor, Packard's largest dealer in Baltimore, demanded an exclusive contract.

The Court rejected Webster Motor's claim under Section 2 of the Sherman Act because there were many other cars "reasonably interchangeable" with Packard cars and therefore "an exclusive contract for marketing Packards does not create a monopoly." As to Section 1, the Court, quoting language indicating "the rule was virtually one of *per se* legality," brushed aside the "fact that Zell asked for the arrangement," since "the immediate object of an exclusive dealership is to protect the dealer from competition in the manufacturer's product, it is likely to be the dealer who asks for it."

Packard was a small manufacturer. The Court observed that it would be "advantageous [for Packard] to retain its largest dealer in Baltimore," and to "penalize the small manufacturer for competing in this way not only fails to promote the policy of the antitrust laws but defeats it."

In evaluating exclusive selling arrangements, please note that many of the efficiency incentives, for both manufacturer and dealer, discussed in Chapter 7 are applicable. Are such arrangements as "dangerous" to competition, intrabrand and interbrand, as some of the arrangements (*e.g.*, resale price maintenance, airtight territorial arrangements) considered in Chapter 7? Are they likely to be "harmless" in all circumstances? What if the manufacturer was dominant? What if the surviving dealer was also the sole outlet for all or most other manufacturers selling in the area?

Also, as the *Renfield* case (*infra*) indicates, often at issue in these cases is whether the exclusive or semi-exclusive selling arrangement comes about because of a horizontal conspiracy to set price or a vertical resale price maintenance agreement. Please review Chapters 4 and 7 as to these aspects of the *Renfield* case, and ask yourself whether Judge Posner's reasoning is consistent with the cases in those Chapters.

Valley Liquors, Inc. v. Renfield Importers, Ltd.

United States Court of Appeals, Seventh Circuit, 1982.
678 F.2d 742.

■ POSNER, J. Valley Liquors, Inc., is a wholesale wine and liquor distributor in northern Illinois, and Renfield Importers, Ltd., is one of its suppliers. Effective November 1, 1981, Renfield terminated Valley as a distributor of Renfield products (which include such popular brands as Gordon's and Martini & Rossi) in two counties, McHenry and Du Page (and part of a third, which we shall ignore to simplify this opinion). Valley sued, charging that Renfield had violated section 1 of the Sherman Act. . . .

Until November 1, Renfield generally sold its products to several wholesalers in the same county. But its sales had not been growing as rapidly in Illinois as in the rest of the country, and it decided to adopt a system of restricted distribution whereby it would sell to one, or at most two, wholesalers in each county. (In some instances, however, the plan resulted in an increase in the number of wholesalers from one to two.) Although Valley was Renfield's largest wholesaler in McHenry and Du Page Counties, accounting for some 50 percent of Renfield's total sales there, the new plan terminated Valley and all of Renfield's other distributors in the two counties except Continental and Romano; they were, however, terminated in some other areas. There is unrebutted evidence that Valley had been selling Renfield products at prices five percent below those charged by Renfield's other distributors in McHenry and Du Page Counties and that Valley's termination followed discussions between Renfield and Continental and between Renfield and Romano in which Continental and Romano had expressed unhappiness of Renfield's terminating them in other areas. There is virtually no evidence concerning Renfield's motivation for the adoption of a more restricted distribution system and the concomitant realignment of wholesaler territories, except that it was a reaction to Renfield's disappointing sales in Illinois.

Valley contends that two distinct restraints of trade can be inferred from these facts. The first is a conspiracy among Renfield, Continental, and Romano to increase the wholesale prices of Renfield products in McHenry and Du Page Counties by cutting off Valley—Valley's termination being a concession demanded by Continental and Romano in exchange for consenting to the proposed realignment, under which they lost some of their territories. This is alleged to be a "horizontal" conspiracy, unlawful without more ("*per se*") under section 1 of the Sherman Act. The second alleged restraint of trade is the exclusion of Valley, pursuant to its distribution agreement with Renfield, from McHenry and Du Page Counties. Valley argues that this "vertical" restriction is unreasonable and hence unlawful under section 1's "Rule of Reason."

The district judge denied a preliminary injunction against Renfield's termination of Valley because he did not think that Valley had demonstrated that it was likely to win the case if tried in full. If the judge was right in his estimation of Valley's chances of success, he was right to deny a preliminary injunction, regardless of other considerations relevant to the exercise of his equitable powers.

If Continental and Romano had agreed to raise the prices of Renfield products in McHenry and Du Page Counties and to that end had persuaded Renfield (perhaps by threatening to discontinue carrying its products if it did not cooperate with them) to terminate Valley, their pesky low-price competitor, then they and their cat's paw Renfield would be guilty of a *per se* unlawful restraint of trade. Although there was no direct evidence of such a chain of events—in particular no evidence that Continental and

Romano ever communicated with each other about Valley—we are asked to infer from the fact that Continental and Romano (separately) expressed unhappiness at being terminated in some of their sales areas that they demanded and received, as a quid pro quo, the termination of their major competitor in the two counties, Valley. However, this hypothesis is too speculative to compel a trier of fact to infer conspiracy, at least if Renfield may have had independent reasons for wanting to terminate Valley. We are asked to exclude that possibility because Valley was Renfield's largest and lowest-priced wholesaler in McHenry and Du Page Counties, and therefore its best. We follow the argument until "therefore." If Renfield had been content with a policy of maximizing wholesaler price competition, it would not have changed to a system of exclusive and dual wholesalers; it would have thought that the more competing wholesalers it had the better off it was. The adoption of a restricted distribution system implies a decision to emphasize nonprice competition over price competition, which such a system tends to suppress. This does not make restricted distribution good, or even lawful; we shall get to that question in a moment. Right now we are just concerned with whether Renfield may have had reasons for terminating Valley that were independent of the desires of Continental and Romano to be rid of the competition of a price cutter. It may have. That possibility is enough to rebut an inference of collusion with those distributors based solely on the termination of Valley. . . .

There is, we admit, a certain unreality in the careful parsing of motives that *Cernuto* [595 F.2d 164 (3d Cir.1979)] seems to require. If a supplier wants his distributors to emphasize nonprice rather than price competition, which as we said is the usual reason why he would restrict his distribution, he will be hostile to price cutters because they will make it harder for his other distributors to recoup the expenditures that he wants them to make on pre-sale services to consumers and on other forms of nonprice competition, and of course the undersold distributors will be equally or more hostile. The motive of supplier and distributors alike could thus be described as wanting to eliminate price cutters yet there would be no *per se* illegality so long as the supplier was not just knuckling under to the distributors' desire for less competition. It is difficult to see how a court could distinguish empirically between such a case and the pure antipathy to price competition envisaged by *Cernuto*. But the unraveling of this skein can be left for another occasion. It is enough that in this case the plaintiff did not prove an improper motive by its supplier.

We turn to the vertical aspect of the case. If we accept, as on the state of the record we must, that Valley sold at lower prices than the other distributors in McHenry and Du Page Counties, then the territorial restriction pursuant to which it was terminated in those two counties has reduced price competition among wholesalers of the brands supplied by Renfield ("intrabrand price competition"). Valley contends that this reduction establishes a prima facie case of unreasonable restraint of trade which shifts to Renfield the burden of showing an offsetting increase in competition between brands supplied by Renfield on the one hand and brands supplied by other importers or national distributors of alcoholic beverages on the other hand ("interbrand competition").

We reject the casual equation of intrabrand price competition with interbrand competition. The elimination of a price cutter who is taking a free ride on the promotional efforts of competing distributors will tend to stimulate nonprice competition among the distributors at the same time that it dampens price competition among them, so that the net effect on intrabrand competition need not be negative. In any event, the suggestion that proof of a reduction in intrabrand competition creates a presumption of illegality is inconsistent with the test that the courts apply in restricted distribution cases. Building from a suggestive footnote in Continental T.V., Inc. v. GTE Sylvania Inc., 433 U.S. 36, 57 n. 27 (1976), the courts have held that the effects on intrabrand and on interbrand competition must be balanced in deciding whether a challenged restriction on distribution is unreasonable. And it is not generally true of balancing tests that the plaintiff, in order to make out a prima facie case, has only to show that if you put something on his side of the empty balance the balance will tilt his way. The plaintiff in a restricted distribution case must show that the restriction he is complaining of was unreasonable because, weighing effects on both intrabrand and interbrand competition, it made consumers worse off.

Admittedly, this test of illegality is easier to state than to apply, the effects to be weighed being so difficult to measure or even estimate by the methods of litigation. The courts have therefore looked for shortcuts. A popular one is to say that the balance tips in the defendant's favor if the plaintiff fails to show that the defendant has significant market power (that is, power to raise prices significantly above the competitive level without losing all of one's business).... A firm that has no market power is unlikely to adopt policies that disserve its consumers; it cannot afford to. And if it blunders and does adopt such a policy, market retribution will be swift. Thus its mistakes do not seriously threaten consumer welfare, which is the objective that we are told should guide us in interpreting the Sherman Act. Even if there is some possibility that the distribution practices of a powerless firm will have a substantial anticompetitive effect, it is too small a possibility to warrant trundling out the great machinery of antitrust enforcement.

Since market power can rarely be measured directly by the methods of litigation, it is normally inferred from possession of a substantial percentage of the sales in a market carefully defined in terms of both product and geography. In this case no evidence of market share was presented. In fact, no market was defined, either in product or in geographical terms, so that we do not have even a rough idea whether Renfield was a big firm in its market or a small firm. Nor did Valley seek to establish Renfield's market power by some alternative route, not involving proof of relevant market and market share.

On this as on all the other issues in this case our comments on the weight of the evidence have reference only to the evidence introduced in support of and in opposition to Valley's motion for a preliminary injunction. We are not prejudging Valley's right to a permanent injunction at the end of the trial. That right depends on the evidence introduced at trial, which for all we know may cure the deficiencies in Valley's proof that require us to order that the denial of its motion for a preliminary injunction be, and it hereby is, affirmed.[27]

B. EXCLUSIVE DEALING

Clayton Act, Section 3

[Reprinted p. 859 *supra*]

Standard Fashion Co. v. Magrane–Houston Co.

Supreme Court of the United States, 1922.
258 U.S. 346, 42 S.Ct. 360, 66 L.Ed. 653.

■ DAY, J. Petitioner brought suit in the United States District Court for the District of Massachusetts to restrain the respondent from violating a certain contract concerning the sale of patterns for garments worn by women and children, called Standard Patterns. The bill was dismissed by the District Court and its decree was affirmed by the Circuit Court of Appeals.

Petitioner is a New York corporation engaged in the manufacture and distribution of patterns. Respondent conducted a retail dry goods business at the corner of Washington Street and Temple Place in the City of Boston. On November 25, 1914, the parties entered into a contract by which the petitioner granted to the respondent an agency for the sale of Standard Patterns at respondent's store, for a term of two years from the date of the contract, and from term to term thereafter until the agreement should be terminated as thereinafter provided.... Respondent agreed not to assign or transfer the agency, or to remove it from its original location without the written consent of the petitioner, and not to sell or permit to be sold on its premises during the term of the contract any other make of patterns, and not to sell Standard Patterns except at labeled prices....

The contract contains an agreement that the respondent shall not sell or permit to be sold on its premises during the term of the contract any other make of patterns. It is shown that on or about July 1, 1917, the respondent discontinued the sale of the petitioner's patterns and placed on sale in its store patterns of a rival company known as the McCall Company....

---

27. On remand, the district court granted summary judgment for defendant Renfield and the Seventh Circuit affirmed. 822 F.2d 656 (7th Cir.1987).

The contract required the purchaser not to deal in goods of competitors of the seller. It is idle to say that the covenant was limited to the premises of the purchaser, and that sales might be made by it elsewhere. The contract should have a reasonable construction. The purchaser kept a retail store in Boston. It was not contemplated that it would make sales elsewhere. The covenant, read in the light of the circumstances in which it was made, is one by which the purchaser agreed not to sell any other make of patterns while the contract was in force. The real question is: Does the contract of sale come within the third section of the Clayton Act because the covenant not to sell the patterns of others "may be to substantially lessen competition or tend to create a monopoly." . . .

The Clayton Act sought to reach the agreements embraced within its sphere in their incipiency, and in the section under consideration to determine their legality by specific tests of its own which declared illegal contracts of sale made upon the agreement or understanding that the purchaser shall not deal in the goods of a competitor or competitors of the seller, which may "substantially lessen competition or tend to create a monopoly."

Much is said in the briefs concerning the Reports of Committees concerned with the enactment of this legislation, but the words of the act are plain and their meaning is apparent without the necessity of resorting to the extraneous statements and often unsatisfactory aid of such reports. . . .

Section 3 condemns sales or agreements where the effect of such sale or contract of sale "may" be to substantially lessen competition or tend to create monopoly. It thus deals with consequences to follow the making of the restrictive covenant limiting the right of the purchaser to deal in the goods of the seller only. But we do not think that the purpose in using the word "may" was to prohibit the mere possibility of the consequences described. It was intended to prevent such agreements as would under the circumstances disclosed probably lessen competition, or create an actual tendency to monopoly. That it was not intended to reach every remote lessening of competition is shown in the requirement that such lessening must be substantial.

Both courts below found that the contract interpreted in the light of the circumstances surrounding the making of it was within the provisions of the Clayton Act as one which substantially lessened competition and tended to create monopoly. These courts put special stress upon the fact found that, of 52,000 so-called pattern agencies in the entire country, the petitioner, or a holding company controlling it and two other pattern companies, approximately controlled two-fifths of such agencies. As the Circuit Court of Appeals summarizing the matter pertinently observed:

> The restriction of each merchant to one pattern manufacturer must in hundreds, perhaps in thousands of small communities amount to giving such single pattern manufacturer a monopoly of the business in such community. Even in the larger cities, to limit to a single pattern maker the pattern business of dealers most

resorted to by customers whose purchases tend to give fashions their vogue, may tend to facilitate further combinations; so that the plaintiff, or some other aggressive concern, instead of controlling two-fifths, will shortly have almost, if not quite, all the pattern business.

We agree with these conclusions, and have no doubt that the contract, properly interpreted, with its restrictive covenant, brings it fairly within the section of the Clayton Act under consideration.

Affirmed.

NOTES

1. Standard Oil Co. of California v. United States, 337 U.S. 293 (1949). Standard Oil Company of California and its wholly owned subsidiary, Standard Stations, Inc., entered into exclusive supply contracts with independent service stations. Standard Oil was the largest seller of gasoline in the market with 23% of the total taxable gallonage. Sales by company-owned service stations constituted 6.8% of the total, and sales under exclusive dealing contracts with independent service stations constituted 6.7%. Standard Oil had entered into exclusive supply contracts with about 16% of the independent service stations in the market. Justice Frankfurter, writing for the Court, trying to narrow the scope of the inquiry under Section 3 of the Clayton Act, held:

> We conclude, therefore, that the qualifying clause of § 3 is satisfied by proof that competition has been foreclosed in a substantial share of the line of commerce affected. It cannot be gainsaid that observance by a dealer of his requirements contract with Standard does effectively foreclose whatever opportunity there might be for competing suppliers to attract his patronage, and it is clear that the affected proportion of retail sales of petroleum products is substantial. In view of the widespread adoption of such contracts by Standard's competitors and the availability of alternative ways of obtaining an assured market, evidence that competitive activity has not actually declined is inconclusive. Standard's use of the contracts creates just such a potential clog on competition as it was the purpose of § 3 to remove wherever, were it to become actual, it would impede a substantial amount of competitive activity.[28]

2. Federal Trade Commission v. Motion Picture Advertising Service Co., 344 U.S. 392, 73 S.Ct. 361, 97 L.Ed. 426 (1953). Motion Picture Advertising's exclusive contracts were alleged to be an "unfair method of competition" in violation of § 5 of the Federal Trade Commission Act. Respondent produced and distributed advertising motion pictures which depict commodities offered for sale by commercial establishments. Its contracts with theatre owners for the display of such films provide that the theatre owner will display only advertising films supplied by the respondent, with certain exceptions. These contracts run for terms up to five years, although most are for one or two years. They covered almost forty percent of the theatres in the 27–state area in which it operated. Motion Picture and three other firms (against which proceedings were also brought) together had exclusive arrange-

---

28. 337 U.S. at 314.

ments with approximately three-fourths of the total number of theatres in the United States showing such films.

The Court of Appeals reversed the Commission's holding that the exclusive contracts were unduly restrictive of competition when they extended for periods in excess of one year.

The Supreme Court upheld the Commission:

> This is not a situation where by the nature of the market there is room for newcomers, irrespective of the existing restrictive practices. The number of outlets for the films is quite limited. And due to the exclusive contracts, respondent and the three other major companies have foreclosed to competitors 75 percent of all available outlets for this business throughout the United States. It is, we think, plain ... that a device which has sewed up a market so tightly for the benefit of a few falls within the prohibitions of the Sherman Act and is therefore an "unfair method of competition" within the meaning of § 5(a) of the Federal Trade Commission Act.

The Court noted that "unfair methods of competition" were not confined to those condemned by the Sherman Act or illegal at common law. The Court also affirmed the Commission's finding that, in light of the compelling business reasons for some exclusive arrangement, exclusive contracts limited to one year would not unduly restrain competition:

> The precise impact of a particular practice on the trade is for the Commission, not the courts, to determine. The point where a method of competition becomes "unfair" within the meaning of the Act will often turn on the exigencies of a particular situation, trade practices, or the practical requirements of the business in question.

Tampa Electric Co. v. Nashville Coal Co.

Supreme Court of the United States, 1961.
365 U.S. 320, 81 S.Ct. 623, 5 L.Ed.2d 580.

■ CLARK, J. We granted certiorari to review a declaratory judgment holding illegal under § 3 of the Clayton Act a requirements contract between the parties providing for the purchase by petitioner of all the coal it would require as boiler fuel at its Gannon Station in Tampa, Florida, over a 20–year period. Both the District Court and the Court of Appeals, Judge Weick dissenting, agreed with respondents that the contract fell within the proscription of § 3 and therefore was illegal and unenforceable. We cannot agree that the contract suffers the claimed antitrust illegality and, therefore, do not find it necessary to consider respondents' additional argument that such illegality is a defense to the action and a bar to enforceability.

Petitioner Tampa Electric Company is a public utility located in Tampa, Florida. It produces and sells electric energy to a service area, including the city, extending from Tampa Bay eastward 60 miles to the center of the State, and some 30 miles in width. As of 1954 petitioner operated two electrical generating plants comprising a total of 11 individual generating units, all of which consumed oil in their burners. In 1955 Tampa Electric decided to expand its facilities by the construction of an additional generating plant to be comprised ultimately of six generating units, and to be known as the "Francis J. Gannon Station." Although every electrical generating plant in peninsular Florida burned oil at that time, Tampa Electric decided to try coal as boiler fuel in the first two units constructed at the Gannon Station. Accordingly, it contracted with the respondents to furnish the expected coal requirements for the units. The agreement, dated May 23, 1955, embraced Tampa Electric's "total requirements of fuel ... for the operation of its first two units to be installed at the Gannon Station ... not less than 225,000 tons of coal per unit per year," for a period of 20 years. The contract further provided that "if during the first 10 years of the term ... the Buyer constructs additional units [at Gannon] in which coal is used as the fuel, it shall give the Seller notice thereof two years prior to the completion of such unit or units and upon completion of same the fuel requirements thereof shall be added to this contract." It was understood and agreed, however, that "the Buyer has the option to be exercised two years prior to completion of said unit or units of determining whether coal or some other fuel shall be used in same." Tampa Electric had the further option of reducing, up to 15%, the amount of its coal purchases covered by the contract after giving six months' notice of an intention to use as fuel a by-product of any of its local customers. The minimum price was set at $6.40 per ton delivered, subject to an escalation clause based on labor cost and other factors. Deliveries were originally expected to begin in March 1957, for the first unit, and for the second unit at the completion of its construction.

In April 1957, soon before the first coal was actually to be delivered and after Tampa Electric, in order to equip its first two Gannon units for the use of coal, had expended some $3,000,000 more than the cost of constructing oil-burning units, and after respondents had expended approximately $7,500,000 readying themselves to perform the contract, the latter advised petitioner that the contract was illegal under the antitrust laws, would therefore not be performed, and no coal would be delivered. This turn of events required Tampa Electric to look elsewhere for its coal requirements. The first unit at Gannon began operating August 1, 1957, using coal purchased on a temporary basis, but on December 23, 1957, a purchase order contract for the total coal requirements of the Gannon Station was made with Love and Amos Coal Company. It was for an indefinite period cancellable on 12 months' notice by either party, or immediately upon tender of performance by respondents under the contract sued upon here. The maximum price was $8.80 per ton, depending upon the freight rate. In its purchase order to the Love and Amos Company, Tampa estimated that its requirements at the Gannon Station would be 350,000 tons in 1958; 700,000 tons in 1959 and 1960; 1,000,000 tons in 1961; and would increase thereafter, as required, to "about 2,250,000 tons per year." The second unit at Gannon Station commenced operation 14 months after the first, *i.e.*, October 1958. Construction of a third unit, the coal for which was to have been provided under the original contract, was also begun.

The record indicates that the total consumption of coal in peninsular Florida, as of 1958, aside from Gannon Station, was approximately 700,000 tons annually. It further shows that there were some 700 coal suppliers in the producing area where respondents operated, and that Tampa Electric's anticipated maximum requirements at Gannon Station, *i.e.*, 2,250,000 tons annually, would approximate 1% of the total coal of the same type produced and marketed from respondents' producing area.

Petitioner brought this suit in the District Court for a declaration that its contract with respondents was valid, and for enforcement according to its terms.... The District Court ... granted respondents' motion for summary judgment on the sole ground that the undisputed facts, recited above, showed the contract to be a violation of § 3 of the Clayton Act. The Court of Appeals agreed....

Both courts admitted that the contract "does not expressly contain the 'condition'" that Tampa Electric would not use or deal in the coal of respondents' competitors. Nonetheless, they reasoned, the "total requirements" provision had the same practical effect, for it prevented Tampa Electric for a period of 20 years from buying coal from any other source for use at that station. Each court cast aside as "irrelevant" arguments citing the use of oil as boiler fuel by Tampa Electric at its other stations, and by other utilities in peninsular Florida, because oil was not in fact used at Gannon Station, and the possibility of exercise by Tampa Electric of the option reserved to it to build oil-burning units at Gannon was too remote. Found to be equally remote was the possibility of Tampa's conversion of existing oil-burning units at its other stations to the use of coal which would not be covered by the contract with respondents. It followed, both courts found, that the "line of commerce" on which the restraint was to be tested was coal—not boiler fuels. Both courts compared the estimated coal tonnage as to which the contract pre-empted competition for 20 years, namely, 1,000,000 tons a year by 1961, with the previous annual consumption of peninsular Florida, 700,000 tons. Emphasizing that fact as well as the contract value of the coal covered by the 20–year term, *i.e.*, $128,000,000, they held that such volume was not "insignificant or insubstantial" and that the effect of the contract would "be to substantially lessen competition," in violation of the Act. Both courts were of the opinion that in view of the executory nature of the contract, judicial enforcement of any portion of it could not be granted without directing a violation of the Act itself, and enforcement was, therefore, denied....

... Following the guidelines of earlier decisions, certain considerations must be taken. *First,* the line of commerce, *i.e.*, the type of goods, wares, or merchandise, etc., involved must be determined, where it is in controversy, on the basis of the facts peculiar to the case. *Second,* the area of effective competition in the known line of commerce must be charted by careful selection of the market area in which the seller operates, and to which the purchaser can practically turn for supplies. In short, the threatened foreclosure of competition must be in relation to the market affected....

... In [*Standard Oil*], the area of effective competition—the relevant market—was found to be where the seller and some 75 of its competitors sold petroleum products. Conveniently identified as the Western Area, it included Arizona, California, Idaho, Nevada, Oregon, Utah and Washington.

Third, and last, the competition foreclosed by the contract must be found to constitute a substantial share of the relevant market. That is to say, the opportunities for other traders to enter into or remain in that market must be significantly limited as was pointed out in *Standard Oil.* There the impact of the requirements contracts was studied in the setting of the large number of gasoline stations—5,937 or 16% of the retail outlets in the relevant market—and the large number of contracts, over 8,000, together with the great volume of products involved. This combination dictated a finding that "Standard's use of the contracts [created] just such a potential clog on competition as it was the purpose of § 3 to remove" where, as there, the affected proportion of retail sales was substantial.

To determine substantiality in a given case, it is necessary to weigh the probable effect of the contract on the relevant area of effective competition, taking into account the relative strength of the parties, the proportionate volume of commerce involved in relation to the total volume of commerce in the relevant market area, and the probable immediate and future effects which pre-emption of that share of the market might have on effective competition therein. It follows that a mere showing that the contract itself involves a substantial number of dollars is ordinarily of little consequence.

In applying these considerations to the facts of the case before us, it appears clear that both the Court of Appeals and the District Court have not given the required effect to a controlling factor in the case—the relevant competitive market area. This omission, by itself, requires reversal, for, as we have pointed out, the relevant market is the prime factor in relation to which the ultimate question, whether the contract forecloses competition in a substantial share of the line of commerce involved, must be decided. For the purposes of this case, therefore, we need not decide two threshold questions pressed by Tampa Electric. They are whether the contract in fact satisfies the initial requirement of § 3, *i.e.*, whether it is truly an exclusive-dealing one, and, secondly, whether the line of commerce is boiler fuels, including coal, oil and gas, rather than coal alone. We, therefore, for the purposes of this case, assume, but do not decide, that the contract is an exclusive-dealing arrangement within the compass of § 3, and that the line of commerce is bituminous coal.

Neither the Court of Appeals nor the District Court considered in detail the question of the relevant market. They do seem, however, to have been satisfied with inquiring only as to competition within "Peninsular Florida." It was noted that the total consumption of peninsular Florida was 700,000 tons of coal per year, about equal to the estimated 1959 requirements of Tampa Electric. It was also pointed out that coal accounted for less than 6% of the fuel consumed in the entire State. The District Court concluded that though the respondents were only one of 700 coal producers who could serve the same market, peninsular Florida, the contract for a period of 20 years excluded competitors from a substantial amount of trade. Respondents contend that the coal tonnage covered by the contract must be weighed against either the total consumption of coal in peninsular Florida, or all of Florida, or the Bituminous Coal Act area comprising peninsular Florida and the Georgia "finger," or, at most, all of Florida and Georgia. If the latter area were considered the relevant market, Tampa Electric's proposed requirements would be 18% of the tonnage sold therein. Tampa Electric says that both courts and respondents are in error, because the "700 coal producers who could serve" it, as recognized by the trial court and admitted by respondents, operated in the Appalachian coal area and that its contract requirements were less than 1% of the total marketed production of these producers; that the relevant effective area of competition was the area in which these producers operated, and in which they were willing to compete for the consumer potential.

We are persuaded that on the record in this case, neither peninsular Florida, nor the entire State of Florida, nor Florida and Georgia combined constituted the relevant market of effective competition. We do not believe that the pie will slice so thinly. By far the bulk of the overwhelming tonnage marketed from the same producing area as serves Tampa is sold outside of Georgia and Florida, and the producers were "eager" to sell more coal in those States. While the relevant competitive market is not ordinarily susceptible to a "metes and bounds" definition, it is of course the area in which respondents and the other 700 producers effectively compete. *Standard Oil*. The record shows that, like the respondents, they sold bituminous coal "suitable for [Tampa's] requirements," mined in parts of Pennsylvania, Virginia, West Virginia, Kentucky, Tennessee, Alabama, Ohio and Illinois. We take notice of the fact that the approximate total bituminous coal (and lignite) product in the year 1954 from the districts in which these 700 producers are located was 359,289,000 tons, of which some 290,567,000 tons were sold on the open market. Of the latter amount some 78,716,000 tons were sold to electric utilities. We also note that in 1954 Florida and Georgia combined consumed at least 2,304,000 tons, 1,100,000 of which were used by electric utilities, and the sources of which were mines located in no less than seven States. We take further notice that the production and marketing of bituminous coal (and lignite) from the same districts, and assumedly equally available to Tampa on a commercially feasible basis, is currently on a par with prior years. In point of statistical fact, coal consumption in the combined Florida–Georgia area has increased significantly since 1954. In 1959 more than 3,775,000 tons were there consumed, 2,913,000 being used by electric utilities including, presumably, the coal used by the petitioner.

The coal continued to come from at least seven States. From these statistics it clearly appears that the proportionate volume of the total relevant coal product as to which the challenged contract pre-empted competition, less than 1%, is, conservatively speaking, quite insubstantial. A more accurate figure, even assuming pre-emption to the extent of the maximum anticipated total requirements, 2,250,000 tons a year, would be .77%.

It may well be that in the context of antitrust legislation protracted requirements contracts are suspect, but they have not been declared illegal *per se.* Even though a single contract between single traders may fall within the initial broad proscription of the section, it must also suffer the qualifying disability, tendency to work a substantial—not remote—lessening of competition in the relevant competitive market. It is urged that the present contract pre-empts competition to the extent of purchases worth perhaps $128,000,000, and that this "is, of course, not insignificant or insubstantial." While $128,000,000 is a considerable sum of money, even in these days, the dollar volume, by itself, is not the test, as we have already pointed out.

The remaining determination, therefore, is whether the pre-emption of competition to the extent of the tonnage involved tends to substantially foreclose competition in the relevant coal market. We think not. That market sees an annual trade in excess of 250,000,000 tons of coal and over a billion dollars—multiplied by 20 years it runs into astronomical figures. There is here neither a seller with a dominant position in the market as in *Standard Fashions, supra*; nor myriad outlets with substantial sales volume, coupled with an industry-wide practice of relying upon exclusive contracts, as in *Standard Oil, supra*; nor a plainly restrictive tying arrangement as in *International Salt, supra*. On the contrary, we seem to have only that type of contract which "may well be of economic advantage to buyers as well as to sellers." Standard Oil v. United States, *supra*, 337 U.S. at 306. In the case of the buyer it "may assure supply," while on the part of the seller it "may make possible the substantial reduction of selling expenses, give protection against price fluctuations, and . . . offer the possibility of a predictable market." *Id.*, 337 U.S. at 306–307. The 20–year period of the contract is singled out as the principal vice, but at least in the case of public utilities the assurance of a steady and ample supply of fuel is necessary in the public interest. Otherwise consumers are left unprotected against service failures owing to shutdowns; and increasingly unjustified costs might result in more burdensome rate structures eventually to be reflected in the consumer's bill. The compelling validity of such considerations has been recognized fully in the natural gas public utility field. This is not to say that utilities are immunized from Clayton Act proscriptions, but merely that, in judging the term of a requirements contract in relation to the substantiality of the foreclosure of competition, particularized considerations of the parties' operations are not irrelevant. In weighing the various factors, we have decided that in the competitive bituminous coal marketing area involved here the contract sued upon does not tend to foreclose a substantial volume of competition. . . .

The judgment is reversed and the case remanded to the District Court for further proceedings not inconsistent with this opinion.

NOTES AND QUESTIONS

1. *Curly's Dairy, Inc. v. Dairy Cooperative Association,* 202 F.Supp. 481 (D.Or.1962), was a private action for damages and an injunction brought against a wholesaler of dairy products by a competing wholesaler. Plaintiff has alleged that defendant granted loans to retail stores and restaurants on condition that the borrower agree to purchase its complete dairy requirements from defendant as long as the debt remained outstanding. After defining the relevant market for sale of dairy products at wholesale to include most of the states of Washington and Oregon, the district court concluded that the challenged agreements covered less than 1% of sales in that market, and dismissed the complaint under authority of *Tampa Electric.* With respect to the *Standard Oil* decision, the court wrote:

> The Court in *Tampa* made it perfectly clear that neither comparative quantitative substantiality (*i.e.,* the market share foreclosed) nor absolute quantitative substantiality (*i.e.,* the dollar volume foreclosed) (as defined in *Standard*) should be the controlling factor. 202 F.Supp. at 484–85.

2. How greatly do the approaches in *Tampa Electric* and *Standard Oil* (p. 926 *supra*) differ? Is the more complex economic analysis suggested by *Tampa Electric* likely to provide enhanced accuracy in gauging anticompetitive effect? Will it increase certainty or be easily administrable in courts? What factors beyond market power, extent of foreclosure, ease of replicating the distribution scheme, and duration should be considered in determining whether there has been a substantial lessening of competition? How about the level of, and trends with respect to, concentration and the use of exclusive dealing arrangements by other competitors? Barriers to entry and history of entry? Justifications for the exclusive dealing arrangement? Which of these, and other factors you might think of, are likely to be truly important in a given case?

3. As the *Jefferson Parish* case (p. 867 *supra*) demonstrates, the Supreme Court is now approaching tying more cautiously, and this may have implications for exclusive dealing too. Indeed, one commentary concluded:

> *Jefferson Parish Hospital District No. 2 v. Hyde* teetered on the brink between characterization as a tying case and characterization as an exclusive dealing case, as evidenced by the four-vote concurring opinion which would have treated the arrangement as exclusive dealing. Because of this, the decision is important to the law of exclusive dealing as well as to the law of tying. Justice O'Connor wrote:
>
>> A firm of four anesthesiologists represents only a very small fraction of the total number of anesthesiologists whose services are available for hire by other hospitals, and East Jefferson is one among numerous hospitals buying such services. Even without engaging in a detailed analysis of the size of the relevant markets we may readily conclude that there is no likelihood that the exclusive dealing arrangement challenged here will either unreasonably enhance the hospital's market position relative to other hospitals, or unreasonably permit Roux [the holder of the exclusive contract] to acquire power relative to other anesthesiologists. Accordingly, this exclusive dealing arrangement must be sustained under the rule of reason.
>
> Justice O'Connor was correct, of course, in pointing out that the defendant hospital was only one of many hospitals admitting patients in New Orleans, so the foreclosure effect on other anesthesiologists was limited. At the same time, however, that hospital did account for fully

thirty percent of the patients in the area. If a thirty percent foreclosure is not significant, we now know considerably more about where to draw the line than we did after *Tampa Electric* (the Supreme Court's last statement on exclusive dealing), where less than one percent of the market was foreclosed.[29]

Review Justice Stevens' majority opinion in *Jefferson Parish* and Justice O'Connor's concurrence; is it true that thirty percent of the market for anesthesiological services was foreclosed? For exclusive dealing purposes, what is the relevance of the fact that thirty percent of the patients living in Jefferson Parish went to East Jefferson Hospital and seventy percent went elsewhere—most to the "at least 20 hospitals in the New Orleans metropolitan area"?

4. In Roland Machinery Co. v. Dresser Industries, Inc., 749 F.2d 380 (7th Cir.1984), Judge Posner, in reversing the grant of a preliminary injunction, set forth his view of the state of exclusive dealing law:

[Defendant Dresser signed a dealership agreement with Roland, a dealer in construction equipment and related items.] The agreement provided that it could be terminated by either party, without cause, on 90 days' notice. It did not contain an exclusive-dealing clause (that is, a clause forbidding the dealer to sell any competing manufacturer's construction equipment). Eight months after signing the agreement Roland signed a similar agreement with Komatsu, a Japanese manufacturer of construction equipment. Several months after discovering that Roland had done this, Dresser gave notice that it would exercise its contract right to terminate its dealership agreement with Roland without cause. Roland brought this suit shortly before the end of the 90-day notice period, charging that Dresser had violated section 3 of the Clayton Act and other provisions of federal and state law. The district judge granted Roland a preliminary injunction based solely on the section 3 charges, and Dresser has appealed....

In order to prevail on its section 3 claim, Roland will have to show both that there was an agreement, though not necessarily an explicit agreement (see Tire Sales Corp. v. Cities Service Oil Co., 637 F.2d 467, 474 (7th Cir.1980); McElhenney Co. v. Western Auto Supply Co., 269 F.2d 332, 338 (4th Cir.1959)), between it and Dresser that it not carry a line of construction equipment competitive with Dresser's, and that the agreement was likely to have a substantial though not necessarily an immediate anticompetitive effect. Regarding the first of these required showings, the record of the preliminary-injunction proceeding contains no evidence that either Roland or any other Dresser dealer agreed with Dresser not to carry a competing manufacturer's line. Nothing in the dealership agreement even hints at a requirement of exclusive dealing, and the fact that after signing the agreement with Dresser, Roland applied for a Komatsu dealership is evidence that Roland itself did not think it had made an implied commitment to exclusive dealing. True, Dresser prefers exclusive dealers—so much so as to be willing to terminate its only dealer in a large marketing area. The district judge believed that evidence of this preference, coupled with the absence of any reason for Dresser's having terminated Roland other than Roland's having taken on an additional line of construction equipment, established a prima facie case of agreement. But an

29. Steuer, Exclusive Dealing After Jefferson Parish, 54 Antitrust L.J. 1229, 1232 (1985).

agreement requires a meeting of minds, and there is no evidence that Roland ever thought itself bound to carry only the Dresser line. Indeed, at argument Roland disclaimed any knowledge of what it describes as the implied exclusive-dealing term in the contract; it called it a "secret" term, echoing the district judge's description of exclusive dealing as something "in the mind of" Dresser. One mind is not enough for a meeting of minds. The fact that Dresser was hostile to dealers who would not live and die by its product (as the district judge put it), and acted on its hostility by canceling a dealer who did the thing to which it was hostile, does not establish an agreement, but if anything the opposite: a failure to agree on a point critical to one of the parties.

Actually, it is not important whether Dresser's antipathy to nonexclusive dealing was secret. Assume that Dresser made clear to Roland and its other dealers that it wanted only exclusive dealers and would exercise its contract right to terminate, immediately and without cause, any dealer who took on a competing line. The mere announcement of such a policy, and the carrying out of it by canceling Roland or any other noncomplying dealer, would not establish an agreement. It would be a classic example of the conduct permitted by United States v. Colgate & Co., 250 U.S. 300 (1919). . . . True, there is some evidence that Dresser, fearing the competition of Komatsu, made efforts to discover which of its dealers were considering dealing with Komatsu. Surveillance could in some circumstances intimidate—could be the stick that forced dealers into a tacit understanding not to handle a competitor's goods. See Yentsch v. Texaco, Inc., 630 F.2d 46, 54 (2d Cir.1980). But there is no evidence that it was such here, when Roland within months after signing a dealership agreement with Dresser went and signed another one with Komatsu. The district judge did not rely on evidence of surveillance in concluding that there was an implicit exclusive-dealing agreement.

Dresser's preference for exclusive dealers, its efforts to find out whether its dealers were exclusive dealers, and its terminating Roland when it found out that Roland no longer was its exclusive dealer do not support an inference "both that the distributor communicated its acquiescence or agreement" to exclusive dealing "and that this was sought by the manufacturer." Monsanto Co. v. Spray–Rite. But even if Roland can prove at trial that there was an exclusive-dealing agreement, it will have grave difficulty—we infer from this record—in proving that the agreement is anticompetitive. The objection to exclusive-dealing agreements is that they deny outlets to a competitor during the term of the agreement. At one time it was thought that this effect alone would condemn exclusive-dealing agreements under section 3 of the Clayton Act, provided that the agreements covered a large fraction of the market. See *Standard Stations*. Although the Supreme Court has not decided an exclusive-dealing case in many years, it now appears most unlikely that such agreements, whether challenged under section 3 of the Clayton Act or section 1 of the Sherman Act, will be judged by the simple and strict test of *Standard Stations*. They will be judged under the Rule of Reason, and thus condemned only if found to restrain trade unreasonably.

The exclusion of competitors is cause for antitrust concern only if it impairs the health of the competitive process itself. Hence a plaintiff must prove two things to show that an exclusive-dealing agreement is unreasonable. First, he must prove that it is likely to keep at least one significant

to prove exclusive dealing unreas:
1) likely to keep at least 1 competitor of D from doing business
2) probable effect will be to raise prices or otherwise injure comp -

competitor of the defendant from doing business in a relevant market. If there is no exclusion of a significant competitor, the agreement cannot possibly harm competition. Second, he must prove that the probable (not certain) effect of the exclusion will be to raise prices above (and therefore reduce output below) the competitive level, or otherwise injure competition; he must show in other words that the anticompetitive effects (if any) of the exclusion outweigh any benefits to competition from it. Roland has as yet made very little effort to establish either of these two things.

5. The 90–days' notice provision—exercisable by either party—in *Roland* helped greatly in the defense of the implied exclusive dealing arrangement. But does either *Tampa Electric* or *Jefferson Parish* stand for the proposition that a plaintiff "must prove that ... [the exclusive dealing arrangement] is likely to keep at least one significant competitor ... from doing business in a relevant market" *and* that price will probably rise above "the competitive level"? Has not the Supreme Court since *Standard Fashion* (p. 924 *supra*) spoken in terms of "probability" and "incipiency" in this area?

The willingness of courts to imply an exclusive dealing arrangement—as Judge Posner was willing to do in *Roland* if proper evidence had been presented—varies. *Compare* Alles Corp. v. Senco Products, Inc., 329 F.2d 567 (6th Cir.1964) (exclusive dealing arrangements can be "implied," in part, from a refusal to deal with a distributor who handles competitors' products) *with* Nelson Radio and Supply Co. v. Motorola, Inc., 200 F.2d 911 (5th Cir.1952), cert. denied, 345 U.S. 925 (1953) ("there is nothing whatever in [Section 3] to suggest that it covers a situation where the manufacturer refuses to make a sale or enter into a contract.... There is a real difference between the act of refusing to deal and the execution of a contract which prevents a person from dealing with another").

Although Dresser's distributors were free to switch to another supplier on 90–days' notice, they apparently could not carry two lines of construction equipment from different manufacturers simultaneously. Might that arrangement have anti-competitive effects?

6. Should vertical integration by exclusive dealing contracts be treated in the same way—or more permissively or more harshly—as vertical integration by merger? In which circumstance would the foreclosure be more permanent and complete? *See* Chapter 9, Section 4, *infra*.

Federal Trade Commission v. Brown Shoe Co.

Supreme Court of the United States, 1966.
384 U.S. 316, 86 S.Ct. 1501, 16 L.Ed.2d 587.

■ Black, J. Section 5(a)(6) of the Federal Trade Commission Act empowers and directs the Commission "to prevent persons, partnerships, or corporations ... from using unfair methods of competition in commerce and unfair or deceptive acts or practices in commerce." Proceeding under the authority of § 5, the Federal Trade Commission filed a complaint against the Brown Shoe Co., Inc., one of the world's largest manufacturers of shoes with total sales of $236,946,078 for the year ending October 31, 1957. The unfair practices charged against Brown revolve around the "Brown Franchise Stores' Program" through which Brown sells its shoes to some 650 retail stores. The complaint alleged that under this plan Brown, a corporation engaged in interstate commerce, had "entered into contracts or franchises with a substantial number of its independent retail shoe store operator customers which require said customers to restrict their purchases of shoes for resale to the Brown lines and which prohibit them from purchasing, stocking or reselling shoes manufactured by competitors of Brown." Brown's customers who entered into these restrictive franchise agreements, so the complaint charged, were given in return special treatment and valuable benefits which were not granted to Brown's customers who did not enter into the agreements. In its answer to the Commission's complaint Brown admitted that approximately 259 of its retail customers had executed written franchise agreements and that over 400 others had entered into its franchise program without execution of the franchise agreement. Also in its answer Brown attached as an exhibit an unexecuted copy of the "Franchise Agreement" which, when executed by Brown's representative and a retail shoe dealer, obligates Brown to give to the dealer but not to other customers certain valuable services, including among others, architectural plans, costly merchandising records, services of a Brown field representative, and a right to participate in group insurance at lower rates than the dealer could obtain individually. In return, according to the franchise agreement set out in Brown's answer, the retailer must make this promise:

> "In return I will:

> "1. Concentrate my business within the grades and price lines of shoes representing Brown Shoe Company Franchises of the Brown Division and will have no lines conflicting with Brown Division Brands of the Brown Shoe Company."

Brown's answer further admitted that the operators of "such Brown Franchise Stores in individually varying degrees accept the benefits and perform the obligations contained in such franchise agreements or implicit in such Program," and that Brown refuses to grant these benefits "to dealers who are dropped or voluntarily withdraw from the Brown Franchise Program...." The foregoing admissions of Brown as to the existence and operation of the franchise program were buttressed by many separate detailed fact findings of a trial examiner, one of which findings was that the franchise program effectively foreclosed Brown's competitors from selling to a substantial number of retail shoe dealers.[30] Based on these findings and on Brown's admissions the Commission concluded that the restrictive contract program was an unfair method of competition within the meaning of § 5 and ordered Brown to cease and desist from its use.

---

30. In its opinion the Commission found that the services provided by Brown in its franchise program were the "prime motivation" for dealers to join and remain in the program; that the program resulted in franchised stores purchasing 75% of their total shoe requirements from Brown—the remainder being for the most part shoes which were not "conflicting" lines, as provided by the agreement; that the effect of the plan was to foreclose retail outlets to Brown's competitors, particularly small manufacturers; and that enforcement of the plan was effected by teams of field men who called upon the shoe stores, urged the elimination of other manufacturers' conflicting lines and reported deviations to Brown who then cancelled under a provision of the agreement. Compare Brown Shoe Co. v. United States, 370 U.S. 294, 296.

On review the Court of Appeals set aside the Commission's order. In doing so the court said:

> "By passage of the Federal Trade Commission Act, particularly § 5 thereof, we do not believe that Congress meant to prohibit or limit sales programs such as Brown Shoe engaged in in this case.... The custom of giving free service to those who will buy their shoes is widespread, and we cannot agree with the Commission that it is an unfair method of competition in commerce." 339 F.2d 45, 56.

In addition the Court of Appeals held that there was a "complete failure to prove an exclusive dealing agreement which might be held violative of Section 5 of the Act." We are asked to treat this general conclusionary statement as though the court intended it to be a rejection of the Commission's findings of fact. We cannot do this. Neither this statement of the court nor any other statement in the opinion indicates a purpose to hold that the evidence failed to show an agreement between Brown and more than 650 franchise dealers which restrained the dealers from buying competing lines of shoes from Brown's competitors. Indeed, in view of the crucial admissions in Brown's formal answer to the complaint we cannot attribute to the Court of Appeals a purpose to set aside the Commission's findings that these restrictive agreements existed and that Brown and most of the franchised dealers in varying degrees lived up to their obligations. Thus the question we have for decision is whether the Federal Trade Commission can declare it to be an unfair practice for Brown, the second largest manufacturer of shoes in the Nation, to pay a valuable consideration to hundreds of retail shoe purchasers in order to secure a contractual promise from them that they will deal primarily with Brown and will not purchase conflicting lines of shoes from Brown's competitors. We hold that the Commission has power to find, on the record here, such an anticompetitive practice unfair, subject of course to judicial review.

In holding that the Federal Trade Commission lacked the power to declare Brown's program to be unfair the Court of Appeals was much influenced by and quoted at length from this Court's opinion in Federal Trade Comm'n v. Gratz, 253 U.S. 421. That case, decided shortly after the Federal Trade Commission Act was passed, construed the Act over a strong dissent by Mr. Justice Brandeis as giving the Commission very little power to declare any trade practice unfair. Later cases of this Court, however, have rejected the *Gratz* view and it is now recognized in line with the dissent of Mr. Justice Brandeis in *Gratz* that the Commission has broad powers to declare trade practices unfair. This broad power of the Commission is particularly well established with regard to trade practices which conflict with the basic policies of the Sherman and Clayton Acts even though such practices may not actually violate these laws. The record in this case shows beyond doubt that Brown, the country's second largest manufacturer of shoes, has a program, which requires shoe retailers, unless faithless to their contractual obligations with Brown, substantially to limit their trade with Brown's competitors. This program obviously conflicts with the central policy of both § 1 of the Sherman Act and § 3 of the Clayton Act against contracts which take away freedom of purchasers to buy in an open market. Brown nevertheless contends that the Commission had no power to declare the franchise program unfair without proof that its effect "may be to substantially lessen competition or tend to create a monopoly" which of course would have to be proved if the Government were proceeding against Brown under § 3 of the Clayton Act rather than § 5 of the Federal Trade Commission Act. We reject the argument that proof of this § 3 element must be made for as we pointed out above our cases hold that the Commission has power under § 5 to arrest trade restraints in their incipiency without proof that they amount to an outright violation of § 3 of the Clayton Act or other provisions of the antitrust laws. This power of the Commission was emphatically stated in F.T.C. v. Motion Picture Adv. Co., 344 U.S. 392, at 394–395:

> "It is ... clear that the Federal Trade Commission Act was designed to supplement and bolster the Sherman Act and the Clayton Act ... to stop in their incipiency acts and practices which, when full blown, would violate those Acts ... as well as to condemn as 'unfair methods of competition' existing violations of them."

We hold that the Commission acted well within its authority in declaring the Brown franchise program unfair whether it was completely full blown or not.

Reversed.

NOTES AND QUESTIONS

1. Note 30 in the Supreme Court's *Brown Shoe* opinion indicates that if Brown Shoe's franchised outlets did not abide by the terms of the agreement, they were cancelled as franchisees. In the Commission opinion, it is clear that many of the franchise arrangements were oral and terminable at any time, and written franchise contracts contained a clause saying the dealer could terminate at will. Brown Shoe Co., 62 F.T.C. 679 (1963). Given those facts, what was the duration and consequent anticompetitive effect of the franchise agreements? What sort of competitor of Brown Shoe would be disadvantaged by the franchise arrangements? Is *Brown Shoe* really a tying case in which availability of services is conditioned upon acceptance of shoes? There is a suggestion to that effect in the Commission opinion, 62 F.T.C. at 715, but it was not picked up by the Supreme Court. Would the arrangement be illegal under *Jefferson Parish, Kodak,* and other tying cases?

2. Characterization questions about what constitutes an "exclusive dealing contract" occasionally arise. For example, in Magnus Petroleum Co. v. Skelly Oil Co., 599 F.2d 196 (7th Cir.), cert. denied, 444 U.S. 916 (1979) the Seventh Circuit reversed jury verdicts for plaintiff based on findings of violation of Section 1 of the Sherman Act and Section 3 of the Clayton Act. Magnus Petroleum was a wholesaler and retailer of gasoline and fuel oil in Sheboygan, Wisconsin. It entered into a series of franchise sales agreements and lease agreements with Skelly Oil calling for Skelly

to sell and Magnus to buy specified quantities of gasoline each year. The agreements were terminable by either party on 60 days' notice at the end of a five-year "primary term" and year to year thereafter. Plaintiff charged that the contracts in effect made it impossible for it to distribute branded products of other oil companies and thus were illegal exclusive dealing contracts.

The Court of Appeals reversed on two grounds. First, it noted that the specified quantity (for example, 810,000 gallons in 1976) amounted to less than 60%–80% of plaintiff's total requirements and that plaintiff regularly purchased the remainder of its requirements from competitors of Skelly. The Seventh Circuit concluded that there was no "exclusive dealing" or "total requirements" contract. Second, even if the franchise sales agreements amounted to exclusive dealing contracts, the Court noted that Magnus accounted for less than 1% of all purchases of gasoline in the 13 county area surrounding Sheboygan which it regarded as the relevant geographic market.

Compare United States v. Richfield Oil Corp., 99 F.Supp. 280 (S.D.Cal.1951), affirmed per curiam, 343 U.S. 922 (1952), where the government charged that Richfield's contracts with leased and owned retail gasoline stations amounted to exclusive dealing contracts violative of Section 1 of the Sherman Act and Section 3 of the Clayton Act. Richfield had entered into a sales contract with all its gas stations calling for purchase of specified quantities of gasoline, lubricating oil and greases per month which were intended to cover 80% of each station's estimated requirements. If lessees failed to achieve the indicated quotas, their lease could be terminated on as little as 24 hours' notice. As to owned stations, Richfield entered into "painting agreements" whereby Richfield agreed to paint the station in its own colors and insignia. If those station owners failed to purchase and sell specified quotas, the agreement was breached and the dealer became liable to Richfield for the cost of painting. In addition, Richfield sales representatives urged all dealers to sell Richfield products exclusively, terminated dealers who located competitive pumps on their station property ("split-pump operators"), and ceased dealing with those stations who showed signs advertising competitive products. The court found that the intent of the arrangements was to exclude *all* competition, that the stations in fact sold only Richfield products, and that the dealings constituted *de facto* exclusive dealing contracts.

3. Please note that the opinion in *Brown Shoe* is the most explicit authority we have seen for the proposition that the Commission's authority under Section 5 to prevent unfair methods of competition extends beyond the reach of the Sherman and Clayton Acts. Questions arise as to what the Supreme Court intended to cover under "trade practices which conflict with the basic policies of the Sherman and Clayton Acts, even though such practices may not actually violate these laws." One set of applications would involve practices which slip through the relatively intricate language of the Clayton Act, and particularly the Robinson–Patman amendments to that statute, which are indistinguishable in purpose and effect from practices which are clearly covered. That coverage is relatively non-controversial, and we will see some examples when we take up the Robinson–Patman Act in Chapter 11. The opinion in *Brown Shoe* seems to go further, however, and may be understood to interpret Section 5 to reach practices which lack anticompetitive effects necessary to make out violations of the Sherman and Clayton Acts. By definition, those practices do not violate the basic antitrust laws; when that is the case, what standards are available to define this Commission authority?

There is no criminal exposure under Section 5, and the statute cannot be used as a basis for private treble damage actions. Do these differences indicate any guidelines for limiting the reach of Section 5? Could Section 5 be used successfully by the Commission to challenge monopolies without evidence of illegal conduct (*i.e.,* the no-fault monopoly concept, *see* p. 164 *supra*), or to declare consciously parallel pricing illegal? (*see* p. 516 *supra*.) Is it likely that Congress intended to place such a broad grant of authority with respect to major policy questions in the hands of a regulatory agency? Or is the development of new law at the frontiers of antitrust— without criminal sanctions or treble damage exposure—a role Congress had in mind when it created a second agency to enforce the antitrust laws?

United States Healthcare, Inc. v. Healthsource, Inc.

United States Court of Appeals, First Circuit, 1993.
986 F.2d 589.

■ BOUDIN, J. U.S. Healthcare and two related companies (collectively "U.S. Healthcare") brought this antitrust case in the district court against Healthsource, Inc., its founder and one of its subsidiaries. Both sides are engaged in providing medical services through health maintenance organizations ("HMOs") in New Hampshire. In its suit U.S. Healthcare challenged an exclusive dealing clause in the contracts between the Healthsource HMO and doctors who provide primary care for it in New Hampshire. After a trial in district court, the magistrate judge found no violation, and U.S. Healthcare appealed. We affirm.

I. BACKGROUND

Healthsource New Hampshire is an HMO founded in 1985 by Dr. Norman Payson and a group of doctors in Concord, N.H. Its parent company, Healthsource, Inc., is headed by Dr. Payson, and it manages or has interests in HMOs in a number of states. We refer to both the parent company and its New Hampshire HMO as "Healthsource."

In simpler days, health care comprised a doctor, a patient and sometimes a hospital, but the Norman Rockwell era of medicine has given way to a new world of diverse and complex insurance and provider arrangements. One of the more successful innovations is the HMO, which acts both as a health insurer and provider, charging employers a fixed premium for each employee who subscribes. To provide medical care to subscribers, an HMO of Healthsource's type—sometimes called an individual practice association or "IPA" model HMO—contracts with independent doctors. These doctors continue to treat other patients, in contrast to a "staff" model HMO whose doctors would normally be full-time employees of the HMO.

HMOs often can provide health care at lower cost by stressing preventative care, controlling costs, and driving hard bargains with doctors or hospitals (who thereby obtain more patients in exchange for a reduced charge). Healthsource, like other HMOs, uses primary care physicians— usually internists but sometimes pediatricians or others—as "gatekeepers" who direct the patients to specialists only when necessary and who monitor hospital stays. Typically, the contracting primary care physicians do not charge by the visit but are paid "capitations" by the HMO, a fixed amount per month for each patient who selects the doctor as the patient's primary care physician. Unlike a patient with ordinary health insurance, the HMO patient is limited to the panel of doctors who have contracted with the HMO.

There are familiar alternatives to HMOs. At the "financing" end, these include traditional insurance company policies that reimburse patients for doctor or hospital bills without limiting the patient's choice of doctor, as well as Blue Cross/Blue Shield plans of various types and Medicare and Medicaid programs. At the "provider" end, there is also diversity. Doctors may now form so-called preferred provider organizations, which may include peer review and other joint activities, and contract together to provide medical services to large buyers like Blue Cross or to "network" model HMOs. There are also ordinary group medical practices. And, of course, there are still doctors engaged solely in independent practice on a fee-for-service basis.

Healthsource's HMO operations in New Hampshire were a success. At the time of suit, Healthsource was the only non-staff HMO in the state with 47,000 patients (some in nearby areas of Massachusetts), representing about 5 percent of New Hampshire's population. Stringent controls gave it low costs, including a low hospital utilization rate; and it sought and obtained favorable rates from hospitals and specialists. Giving doctors a further stake in Healthsource's success and incentive to contain costs, Dr. Payson apparently encouraged doctors to become stockholders as well, and at least 400 did so. By 1989 Dr. Payson was proposing to make Healthsource a publicly traded company, in part to permit greater liquidity for its doctor shareholders.

U.S. Healthcare is also in the business of operating HMOs. U.S. Healthcare, Inc., the parent of the other two plaintiff companies—U.S. Healthcare, Inc. (Massachusetts) and U.S. Healthcare of New Hampshire, Inc.—may be the largest publicly held provider of HMO services in the country, serving over one million patients and having total 1990 revenues of well over a billion dollars.... In 1989, U.S. Healthcare had a substantial interest in expanding into New Hampshire.

Dr. Payson was aware in the fall of 1989 that HMOs operating in other states were thinking about offering their services in New Hampshire. He was also concerned that, when Healthsource went public, many of its doctor-shareholders would sell their stock, decreasing their interest in Healthsource and their incentive to control its costs. After considering alternative incentives, Dr. Payson and the HMO's chief operating officer conceived the exclusivity clause that has prompted this litigation. Shortly after the Healthsource public offering in November 1989, Healthsource notified its panel doctors that they would receive greater compensation if they agreed not to serve any other HMO.

The new contract term, effective January 26, 1990, provided for an increase in the standard monthly capitation paid to each primary care physician, for each Healthsource HMO patient cared for by that doctor, if the doctor agreed to the following *optional* paragraph in the basic doctor-Healthsource agreement:

> 11.01 *Exclusive Services of Physicians.* Physician agrees during the term of this Agreement not to serve as a participating physician for any other HMO plan; this shall not, however, preclude Physician from providing professional courtesy coverage arrangements for brief periods of time or emergency services to members of other HMO plans.

A doctor who adopted the option remained free to serve non-HMO patients under ordinary indemnity insurance policies, under Blue Cross/Blue Shield plans, or under preferred provider arrangements. A doctor who accepted the option could also return to non-exclusive status by giving notice.[31]

Although Healthsource capitation amounts varied, a doctor who accepted the exclusivity option generally increased his or her capitation payments by a little more than $1 per patient per month; the magistrate judge put the amount at $1.16 and said that it represented an average increase of about 14 percent as compared with non-exclusive status. The dollar benefit of exclusivity for an individual doctor obviously varies with the number of HMO patients handled by the doctor. Many of the doctors had less than 100 Healthsource patients while about 50 of them had 200 or more. About 250 doctors, or 87 percent of Healthsource's primary care physicians, opted for exclusivity. . . .

II. DISCUSSION

In this court, U.S. Healthcare attacks the exclusivity clause primarily as a *per se* or near *per se* violation of section 1; accordingly we begin by examining the case through the *per se* or "quick look" lenses urged by U.S. Healthcare. We then consider the claim recast in the more conventional framework of Tampa Electric Co. v. Nashville Coal Co., the Supreme Court's latest word on exclusivity contracts, appraising them under section 1's rule of reason. Finally, we address U.S. Healthcare's claims of section 2 violation and its attacks on the market-definition findings of the magistrate judge.

The per se *and "Quick Look" Claims.* U.S. Healthcare's challenge to the exclusivity clause, calling it first a *per se* violation and later a monopolization offense, invokes a signal aspect of antitrust analysis: the same competitive practice may be reviewed under several different rubrics and a plaintiff may prevail by establishing a claim under any one of them. Thus, while an exclusivity arrangement is often considered under section 1's rule of reason, it might in theory play a role in a *per se* violation of section 1 or as an element in attempted or actual monopolization, United States v. United Shoe Machinery Corp., 110 F.Supp. 295 (D.Mass.1953), *aff'd per*

---

31. The original notice period was 180 days. This was reduced to 30 days in March or April 1991. It appears, at least in practice, that a doctor could switch to non-exclusive status more rapidly by returning some of the extra compensation previously paid.

curiam, 347 U.S. 521 (1954). But each rubric has its own conditions and requirements of proof.

We begin, as U.S. Healthcare does, with the *per se* rules of section 1 of the Sherman Act. It is a familiar story that Congress left the development of the Sherman Act largely to the courts and they in turn responded by classifying certain practices as *per se* violations under section 1. Today, the only serious candidates for this label are price (or output) fixing agreements and *certain* group boycotts or concerted refusals to deal.[32] The advantage to a plaintiff is that given a *per se* violation, proof of the defendant's power, of illicit purpose and of anticompetitive effect are all said to be irrelevant, *see* United States v. Socony–Vacuum Oil Co., 310 U.S. 150 (1940); the disadvantage is the difficulty of squeezing a practice into the ever narrowing *per se* niche.

U.S. Healthcare's main argument for *per se* treatment is to describe the exclusivity clause as a group boycott. To understand why the claim ultimately fails one must begin by recognizing that *per se* condemnation is not visited on every arrangement that might, as a matter of language, be called a group boycott or concerted refusal to deal. Rather, today that designation is principally reserved for cases in which competitors agree with each other not to deal with a supplier or distributor if it continues to serve a competitor whom they seek to injure. . . .

We doubt that the modern Supreme Court would use the boycott label to describe, or the rubric to condemn, a joint venture among competitors in which participation was allowed to some but not all, *compare* Northwest Wholesale Stationers, Inc. v. Pacific Stationery & Printing Co., 472 U.S. 284 (1985), *with* Associated Press v. United States, 326 U.S. 1 (1945), although such a restriction might well fall after a more complete analysis under the rule of reason. What is even more clear is that a purely vertical arrangement, by which (for example) a supplier or dealer makes an agreement exclusively to supply or serve a manufacturer, is not a group boycott. Were the law otherwise, every distributor or retailer who agreed with a manufacturer to handle only one brand of television or bicycle would be engaged in a group boycott of other manufacturers.

There are multiple reasons why the law permits (or, more accurately, does not condemn *per se*) vertical exclusivity; it is enough to say here that the incentives for and effects of such arrangements are usually more benign than a horizontal arrangement among competitors that none of them will supply a company that deals with one of their competitors. No one would think twice about a doctor agreeing to work full time for a staff HMO, an extreme case of vertical exclusivity. Imagine, by contrast, the motives and effects of a horizontal agreement by all of the doctors in a town not to work at a hospital that serves a staff HMO which competes with the doctors.

---

32. Tying is sometimes also described as a *per se* offense but, since some element of power must be shown and defenses are effectively available, "quasi" *per se* might be a better label. *See Kodak.*

In this case, the exclusivity arrangements challenged by U.S. Healthcare are vertical in form, that is, they comprise individual promises to Healthsource made by each doctor selecting the option not to offer his or her services to another HMO. The closest that U.S. Healthcare gets to a possible horizontal case is this: it suggests that the exclusivity clause in question, although vertical in form, is in substance an implicit horizontal agreement by the doctors involved. U.S. Healthcare appears to argue that stockholder-doctors dominate Healthsource and, in order to protect their individual interests (as stockholders in Healthsource), they agreed (in their capacity as doctors) not to deal with any other HMO that might compete with Healthsource. We agree that such a horizontal arrangement, if devoid of joint venture efficiencies, might warrant *per se* condemnation.

The difficulty is that there is no evidence of such a horizontal agreement in this case. Although U.S. Healthcare notes that doctor-stockholders predominate on the Healthsource board that adopted the option, there is nothing to show that the clause was devised or encouraged by the panel doctors. On the contrary, the record indicates that Dr. Payson and Healthsource's chief operating officer developed the option to serve Healthsource's own interests. Formally vertical arrangements used to disguise horizontal ones are not unknown, *see* Interstate Circuit, Inc. v. United States, 306 U.S. 208 (1939), but U.S. Healthcare has supplied us with no evidence of such a masquerade in this case.

There is less to be said for U.S. Healthcare's alternative argument that, if *per se* treatment is not proper, then at least the exclusivity clause can be condemned almost as swiftly based on "a quick look." Citing FTC v. Indiana Federation of Dentists, 476 U.S. 447 (1986), and NCAA v. Board of Regents, 468 U.S. 85 (1984), U.S. Healthcare argues that the exclusivity clause is so patently bad that even a brief glance at its impact, lack of business benefit and anticompetitive intent suffice to condemn it. The cases relied on provide little help to U.S. Healthcare and, even on its own version of those cases, the facts would not conceivably justify a "quick look" condemnation of the clause.

In the cited cases, the Supreme Court actually contracted the *per se* rule by refusing to apply it to horizontal agreements that involved price and output fixing (television rights by NCAA members) or the setting of other terms of trade (refusal of dentists by agreement to provide x-rays to insurers). Given the unusual contexts (an interdependent sports league in one case; medical care in the other), the Court declined to condemn the arrangements *per se*, without at least weighing the alleged justifications. At the same time it required only the briefest inspection (the cited "quick look") for the Court to reject the excuses and strike down the agreements. *Accord*, National Society of Professional Engineers v. United States, 435 U.S. 679 (1978).

In any event, no "quick look" would ever suffice to condemn the exclusivity clause at issue in this case. Exclusive dealing arrangements come with the imprimatur of two leading Supreme Court decisions describing the potential virtues of such arrangements. *Tampa; Standard Oil*. To condemn such arrangements after *Tampa* requires a detailed depiction of circumstances and the most careful weighing of alleged dangers and potential benefits, which is to say the normal treatment afforded by the rule of reason. To that subject we now turn.

Rule of Reason. Exclusive dealing arrangements, like information exchanges or standard settings, come in a variety of forms and serve a range of objectives. Many of the purposes are benign, such as assurance of supply or outlets, enhanced ability to plan, reduced transaction costs, creation of dealer loyalty, and the like. *See Standard Stations.* But there is one common danger for competition: an exclusive arrangement may "foreclose" so much of the available supply or outlet capacity that existing competitors or new entrants may be limited or excluded and, under certain circumstances, this may reinforce market power and raise prices for consumers.

Although the Supreme Court once said that a "substantial" percentage foreclosure of suppliers or outlets would violate section 1, *Standard Stations,* the Court's *Tampa* decision effectively replaced any such quantitative test by an open-ended inquiry into competitive impact. What is required under *Tampa* is to determine "the probable effect of the [exclusive] contract on the relevant area of effective competition, taking into account ... [various factors including] the probable immediate and future effects which pre-emption of that share of the market might have on effective competition therein." The lower courts have followed *Tampa* and under this standard judgments for plaintiffs are not easily obtained.

On this appeal we are handicapped in appraising the extent and impact of the foreclosure wrought by Healthsource because U.S. Healthcare has not chosen to present its argument in these traditional terms. *Tampa* is not even cited in the opening or reply briefs. Some useful facts pertaining to the extent of the foreclosure are adverted to in U.S. Healthcare's opening "statement of the case" but never seriously developed in the argument section of its brief. Since the brief itself also describes countervailing evidence of Healthsource, something more is assuredly needed. In the two paragraphs of its "quick look" formulation addressed to "anticompetitive impact," U.S. Healthcare simply asserts that competitive impact has already been discussed and that the exclusivity clause has completely foreclosed U.S. Healthcare and any other non-staff HMO from operation in New Hampshire.

This is not a persuasive treatment of a difficult issue or, rather, a host of issues. First, the extent to which the clause operated economically to restrict doctors is a serious question.[33] True, most doctors signed up for it; but who would not take the extra compensation when no competing non-staff HMO was yet operating? The extent of the financial incentive to

---

33. Even with no notice period, Healthsource's differential pricing policy—paying more to those who exclusively serve Healthsource—would disadvantage competing HMOs. Some courts hesitate to apply the exclusivity label to such arrangements because there is no continuing promise not to deal, but the differential pricing plan is unquestionably part of a contract and so subject to section 1, whatever label may be applied.

remain in an exclusive status is unclear, since it varies with patient load, and the least loaded (and thus least constrained by the clause) doctors would normally be the best candidates for a competing HMO. Healthsource suggests that by relatively modest amounts, U.S. Healthcare could offset the exclusivity bonus for a substantial number of Healthsource doctors. U.S. Healthcare's reply brief offers no response.

Second, along with the economic inducement is the issue of duration. Normally an exclusivity clause terminable on 30 days' notice would be close to a *de minimus* constraint (*Tampa* involved a 20–year contract, and one year is sometimes taken as the trigger for close scrutiny). On the other hand, it may be that the original 180–day clause did frustrate U.S. Healthcare's initial efforts to enlist panel doctors, without whom it would be hard to sign up employers. Perhaps even a 30–day clause would have this effect, especially if a reimbursement penalty were visited on doctors switching back to non-exclusive status. Once again, U.S. Healthcare's brief offers conclusions and a few record references, but neither the precise operation of the clause nor its effects on individual doctors are clearly settled.

Third, even assuming that the financial incentive and duration of the exclusivity clause did remove many of the Healthsource doctors from the reach of new HMOs, it is unclear how much this foreclosure impairs the ability of new HMOs to operate. Certainly the number of primary care physicians tied to Healthsource was significant—one figure suggested is 25 percent or more of all such primary care physicians in New Hampshire—but this still leaves a much larger number not tied to Healthsource. It may be, as U.S. Healthcare urges, that many of the remaining "available" doctors cannot fairly be counted (*e.g.,* those employed full time elsewhere, or reaching retirement, or unwilling to serve HMOs at all). But the dimensions of this limitation were disputed and, by the same token, new doctors are constantly entering the market with an immediate need for patients.

U.S. Healthcare lays great stress upon claims, supported by some meeting notes of Healthsource staff members, that the latter was aware of new HMO entry and conscious that new HMOs like U.S. Healthcare could be adversely affected by the exclusivity clause.[34] Healthsource in turn says that these were notes made in the absence of policy-making officers and that its real motivation for the clause was to bolster loyalty and cost-cutting incentives. Motive can, of course, be a guide to expected effects, but effects are still the central concern of the antitrust laws, and motive is mainly a clue, *see* Barry Wright Corp. v. ITT Grinnell Corp., 724 F.2d 227 (1st Cir.1983). This case itself suggests how far motives in business arrangement may be mixed, ambiguous, and subject to dispute. In any

34. Two examples of these staff notes give their flavor: "Looking at '90 rates—and a deterent [sic] to joining other HMOs (like Healthcare)"; and "amend contract (sending this or next week) based on exclusivity. HMOs only (careful about restraint of trade) will be sent to even those in Healthcare already...."

event, under *Tampa* the ultimate issue in exclusivity cases remains the issue of foreclosure and its consequences.

Absent a compelling showing of foreclosure of substantial dimensions, we think there is no need for us to pursue any inquiry into Healthsource's precise motives for the clause, the existence and measure of any claimed benefits from exclusivity, the balance between harms and benefits, or the possible existence and relevance of any less restrictive means of achieving the benefits. We are similarly spared the difficulty of assessing the fact that the clause is limited to HMOs, a fact from which more than one inference may be drawn. The point is that proof of substantial foreclosure and of "probable immediate and future effects" is the essential basis under *Tampa* for an attack on an exclusivity clause. U.S. Healthcare has not supplied that basis. . . .

United States v. Microsoft Corp.

United States Court of Appeals, District of Columbia Circuit, 2001.
253 F.3d 34.

[The extensive discussion of exclusive dealing contracts in general, and then legality of such contracts when the seller has monopoly power, can be found at pp. 777–79, *supra.*]

NOTE

1. In Concord Boat Corp. v. Brunswick Co., 207 F.3d 1039 (8th Cir.2000), Brunswick Corporation, accounting for 75% or more of the stern drive boat engine market, offered an array of discounts to certain boat builders for committing to its engines. These discounts included a market share discount (*e.g.*, 3% off if the builder bought 80% of its engines from Brunswick), and quantity discounts depending on the quantity of engines purchased.

The Eighth Circuit summarized modern exclusive dealing law by stating that antitrust analysis proceeds through a rule of reason, and requires proof of a substantial portion of the market foreclosed (including definition of relevant product and geographic market), barriers to entry, and evidence that the contracts persisted for a substantial period of time. Even if those elements were demonstrated, defendants could still avoid liability by showing good business reasons that motivated the arrangements. The court found that the discount program lacked duration because buyers were free to accept or reject the various discounts and switch at any time to Brunswick's rivals and there were few if any barriers to entry. Finally, the court saw the aggressive pricing by Brunswick as a way of waging competition:

> Because cutting prices in order to increase business often is the very essence of competition, which antitrust laws were designed to encourage, it "is beyond the practical ability of a judicial tribunal to control [above cost discounting] without courting intolerable risks of chilling legitimate price cutting."

United States v. Dentsply International, Inc.

United States Court of Appeals, Third Circuit, 2005.
399 F.3d 181.

■ WEIS, J. In this antitrust case we conclude that an exclusivity policy imposed by a manufacturer on its dealers violates Section 2 of the Sherman Act. We come to that position because of the nature of the relevant market and the established effectiveness of the restraint despite the lack of long term contracts between the manufacturer and its dealers. Accordingly, we will reverse the judgment of the District Court in favor of the defendant and remand with directions to grant the Government's request for injunctive relief.

The Government alleged that Defendant, Dentsply International, Inc., acted unlawfully to maintain a monopoly in violation of Section 2 of the Sherman Act; entered into illegal restrictive dealing agreements prohibited by Section 3 of the Clayton Act; and used unlawful agreements in restraint of interstate trade in violation of Section 1 of the Sherman Act. After a bench trial, the District Court denied the injunctive relief sought by the Government and entered judgment for defendant.

In its comprehensive opinion, the District Court found the following facts. Dentsply International, Inc. is a Delaware Corporation with its principal place of business in York Pennsylvania. It manufactures artificial teeth for use in dentures and other restorative appliances and sells them to dental products dealers. The dealers, in turn, supply the teeth and various other materials to dental laboratories, which fabricate dentures for sale to dentists.

The relevant market is the sale of prefabricated artificial teeth in the United States. Because of advances in dental medicine, artificial tooth manufacturing is marked by a low or no-growth potential. Dentsply has long dominated the industry consisting of 12–13 manufacturers and enjoys a 75%—80% market share on a revenue basis, 67% on a unit basis, and is about 15 times larger than its next closest competitor. The other significant manufacturers and their market shares are:

5%	Ivoclar Vivadent, Inc.
3%	Vita Zahnfabrik
3%	Myerson LLC
2%	[35]American Tooth Industries
1%–2%	Universal Dental Company
1%	Heraeus Kulzer GmbH
1%	Davis, Schottlander & Davis, Ltd.

Dealers sell to dental laboratories a full range of metals, porcelains, acrylics, waxes, and other materials required to fabricate fixed or removal restorations. Dealers maintain large inventories of artificial teeth and carry thousands of products, other than teeth, made by hundreds of different

---

35. These companies sell directly to dental laboratories as well as to dealers.

manufacturers. Dentsply supplies $400 million of products other than teeth to its network of 23 dealers.

There are hundreds of dealers who compete on the basis of price and service among themselves, as well as with manufacturers who sell directly to laboratories. The dealer field has experienced significant consolidation with several large national and regional firms emerging. For more than fifteen years, Dentsply has operated under a policy that discouraged its dealers from adding competitors' teeth to their lines of products. In 1993, Dentsply adopted "Dealer Criterion 6." It provides that in order to effectively promote Dentsply–York products, authorized dealers "may not add further tooth lines to their product offering." Dentsply operates on a purchase order basis with its distributors and, therefore, the relationship is essentially terminable at will. Dealer Criterion 6 was enforced against dealers with the exception of those who had carried competing products before 1993 and were "grandfathered" for sales of those products. Dentsply rebuffed attempts by those particular distributors to expand their lines of competing products beyond the grandfathered ones.

Dentsply's five top dealers sell competing grandfathered brands of teeth. In 2001, their share of Dentsply's overall sales were

Zahn	39%
Patterson	28%
Darby	8%
Benco	4%
DLDS	<4%
TOTAL....	83%

16,000 dental laboratories fabricate restorations and a subset of 7,000 provide dentures. The laboratories compete with each other on the basis of price and service. Patients and dentists value fast service, particularly in the case of lost or damaged dentures. When laboratories' inventories cannot supply the necessary teeth, dealers may fill orders for walk-ins or use overnight express mail as does Dentsply, which dropped-shipped some 60% of orders from dealers.

Dealers have been dissatisfied with Dealer Criterion 6, but, at least in the recent past, none of them have given up the popular Dentsply teeth to take on a competitive line. Dentsply at one time considered selling directly to the laboratories, but abandoned the concept because of fear that dealers would retaliate by refusing to buy its other dental products.

In the 1990's Dentsply implemented aggressive sales campaigns, including efforts to promote its teeth in dental schools, providing rebates for laboratories' increased usage, and deploying a sales force dedicated to teeth, rather than the entire product mix. Its chief competitors did not as actively promote their products. Foreign manufacturers were slow to alter their designs to cope with American preferences, and, in at least one instance, pursued sales of porcelain products rather than plastic teeth.

Dentsply has had a reputation for aggressive price increases in the market and has created a high price umbrella. Its artificial tooth business is characterized as a "cash cow" whose profits are diverted to other operations of the company. A report in 1996 stated its profits from teeth since 1990 had increased 32% from $16.8 million to $22.2 million.

The District Court found that Dentsply's business justification for Dealer Criterion 6 was pretextual and designed expressly to exclude its rivals from access to dealers. The Court however concluded that other dealers were available and direct sales to laboratories was a viable method of doing business. Moreover, it concluded that Dentsply had not created a market with supra competitive pricing, dealers were free to leave the network at any time, and the Government failed to prove that Dentsply's actions "have been or could be successful in preventing 'new or potential competitors from gaining a foothold in the market.' " Accordingly, the Court concluded that the Government had failed to establish violations of Section 3 of the Clayton Act and Sections 1 or 2 of the Sherman Act.

The Government appealed, contending that a monopolist that prevents rivals from distributing through established dealers has maintained its monopoly by acting with predatory intent and violates Section 2. Additionally, the Government asserts that the maintenance of a 75%—80% market share, establishment of a price umbrella, repeated aggressive price increases and exclusion of competitors from a major source of distribution, show that Dentsply possesses monopoly power, despite the fact that rivals are not entirely excluded from the market and some of their prices are higher. The Government did not appeal the rulings under Section 1 of the Sherman Act or Section 3 of the Clayton Act.

Dentsply argues that rivals had obtained a share of the relevant market, that there are no artificially high prices and that competitors have access to all laboratories through existing or readily convertible systems. In addition, Dentsply asserts that its success is due to its leadership in promotion and marketing and not the imposition of Dealer Criterion 6.

I. STANDARD OF REVIEW

We exercise *de novo* review over the District Court's conclusions of law. However, we will not disturb its findings of fact unless they are clearly erroneous.

II. APPLICABLE LEGAL PRINCIPLES

. . . A violation of Section 2 consists of two elements: (1) possession of monopoly power and (2) ". . . maintenance of that power as distinguished from growth or development as a consequence of a superior product, business acumen, or historic accident." "Monopoly power under § 2 requires . . . something greater than market power under § 1" *Kodak*.

To run afoul of Section 2, a defendant must be guilty of illegal conduct "to foreclose competition, gain a competitive advantage, or to destroy a competitor." Behavior that otherwise might comply with antitrust law may be impermissibly exclusionary when practiced by a monopolist. As we said in LePage's, Inc. v. 3M, 324 F.3d 141, 151–52 (3d Cir.2003), "a monopolist is not free to take certain actions that a company in a competitive (or even oligopolistic) market may take, because there is no market constraint on a monopolist's behavior."

Although not illegal in themselves, exclusive dealing arrangements can be an improper means of maintaining a monopoly. *Grinnell*; *LePage's*, 324 F.3d at 157. A prerequisite for such a violation is a finding that monopoly power exists. In addition, the exclusionary conduct must have an anti-competitive effect. If those elements are established, the monopolist still retains a defense of business justification.

Unlawful maintenance of a monopoly is demonstrated by proof that a defendant has engaged in anti-competitive conduct that reasonably appears to be a significant contribution to maintaining monopoly power. *Microsoft;* 3 Phillip E. Areeda & Herbert Hovenkamp, *Antitrust Law,* ¶ 651c at 78 (1996). Predatory or exclusionary practices in themselves are not sufficient. There must be proof that competition, not merely competitors, has been harmed.

III. MONOPOLY POWER

... [T]he existence of monopoly power may be inferred from a predominant share of the market, *Grinnell*, and the size of that portion is a primary factor in determining whether power exists.

A less than predominant share of the market combined with other relevant factors may suffice to demonstrate monopoly power. Absent other pertinent factors, a share significantly larger than 55% has been required to established prima facie market power. Other germane factors include the size and strength of competing firms, freedom of entry, pricing trends and practices in the industry, ability of consumers to substitute comparable goods, and consumer demand.

A. The Relevant Market

Defining the relevant market is an important part of the analysis. The District Court found the market to be "the sale of prefabricated artificial teeth in the United States." Further, the Court found that "[t]he manufacturers participating in the United States artificial tooth market historically have distributed their teeth into the market in one of three ways: (1) directly to dental labs; (2) through dental dealers; or (3) through a hybrid system combining manufacturer direct sales and dental dealers." The Court also found that the "labs are the relevant consumers for prefabricated artificial teeth."

There is no dispute that the laboratories are the ultimate consumers because they buy the teeth at the point in the process where they are incorporated into another product. Dentsply points out that its representatives concentrate their efforts at the laboratories as well as at dental schools and dentists.

During oral argument, Dentsply's counsel said, "the dealers are not the market ... [t]he market is the dental labs that consume the product." Emphasizing the importance of end users, Dentsply argues that the District Court understood the relevant market to be the sales of artificial teeth to dental laboratories in the United States. Although the Court used the word "market" in a number of differing contexts, the findings demonstrate that the relevant market is not as narrow as Dentsply would have it. The Court said that Dentsply "has had a persistently high market share between 75% and 80% on a revenue basis, in the artificial tooth market." Dentsply sells only to dealers and the narrow definition of market that it urges upon us would be completely inconsistent with that finding of the District Court.

The Court went on to find that Ivoclar "has the second-highest share of the market, at approximately 5%." Ivoclar sells directly to the laboratories. Therefore, these two findings establish that the relevant market in this case includes sales to dealers and direct sales to the laboratories. Other findings on Dentsply's "market share" are consistent with this understanding.

These findings are persuasive that the District Court understood, as do we, the relevant market to be the total sales of artificial teeth to the laboratories and the dealers combined.

Dentsply's apparent belief that a relevant market cannot include sales both to the final consumer and a middleman is refuted in the closely analogous case of Allen–Myland, Inc. v. IBM Corp., 33 F.3d 194 (3d Cir.1994). In that case, IBM sold mainframe computers directly to the ultimate consumers and also sold to companies that leased computers to ultimate users. We concluded that the relevant market encompassed the sales directly to consumers as well as those to leasing companies. "... to the extent that leasing companies deal in used, non-IBM mainframes that have not already been counted in the sales market, these machines belong in the relevant market for large-scale mainframe computers."

To resolve any doubt, therefore, we hold that the relevant market here is the sale of artificial teeth in the United States both to laboratories and to the dental dealers.

B. *Power to Exclude*

Dentsply's share of the market is more than adequate to establish a prima facie case of power. In addition, Dentsply has held its dominant share for more than ten years and has fought aggressively to maintain that imbalance. One court has commented that, "[i]n evaluating monopoly power, it is not market share that counts, but the ability to *maintain* market share." United States v. Syufy Enters., 903 F.2d 659, 665–66 (9th Cir. 1990).

The District Court found that it could infer monopoly power because of the predominant market share, but despite that factor, concluded that Dentsply's tactics did not preclude competition from marketing their products directly to the dental laboratories. "Dentsply does not have the power to exclude competitors from the ultimate consumer."

Moreover, the Court determined that failure of Dentsply's two main rivals, Vident and Ivoclar, to obtain significant market shares resulted from their own business decisions to concentrate on other product lines, rather than implement active sales efforts for teeth.

The District Court's evaluation of Ivoclar and Vident business practices as a cause of their failure to secure more of the market is not persuasive. The reality is that over a period of years, because of Dentsply's domination of dealers, direct sales have not been a practical alternative for most manufacturers. It has not been so much the competitors' less than enthusiastic efforts at competition that produced paltry results, as it is the blocking of access to the key dealers. This is the part of the real market that is denied to the rivals.

The apparent lack of aggressiveness by competitors is not a matter of apathy, but a reflection of the effectiveness of Dentsply's exclusionary policy. Although its rivals could theoretically convince a dealer to buy their products and drop Dentsply's line, that has not occurred. In United States v. Visa U.S.A., 344 F.3d at 229, 240 (2d Cir. 2003), the Court of Appeals held that similar evidence indicated that defendants had excluded their rivals from the marketplace and thus demonstrated monopoly power.

The Supreme Court on more than one occasion has emphasized that economic realities rather than a formalistic approach must govern review of antitrust activity. "Legal presumptions that rest on formalistic distinctions rather than actual market realities are generally disfavored in antitrust law . . . in determining the existence of market power . . . this Court has examined closely the economic reality of the market at issue."

The realities of the artificial tooth market were candidly expressed by two former managerial employees of Dentsply when they explained their rules of engagement. One testified that Dealer Criterion 6 was designed to "block competitive distribution points." He continued, "Do not allow competition to achieve toeholds in dealers; tie up dealers; do not 'free up' key players."

Another former manager said:

> You don't want your competition with your distributors, you don't want to give the distributors an opportunity to sell a competitive product. And you don't want to give your end user, the customer, meaning a laboratory and/or a dentist, a choice. He has to buy Dentsply teeth. That's the only thing that's available. The only place you can get it is through the distributor and the only one that the distributor is selling is Dentsply teeth. That's your objective.

These are clear expressions of a plan to maintain monopolistic power.

The District Court detailed some ten separate incidents in which Dentsply required agreement by new as well as long-standing dealers not to handle competitors' teeth. For example, when the DLDS firm considered adding two other tooth lines because of customers' demand, Dentsply threatened to sever access not only to its teeth, but to other dental products as well. DLDS yielded to that pressure. The termination of Trinity Dental, which had previously sold Dentsply products other than teeth, was a similar instance. When Trinity wanted to add teeth to its line for the first time and chose a competitor, Dentsply refused to supply other dental products.

Dentsply also pressured Atlanta Dental, Marcus Dental, Thompson Dental, Patterson Dental and Pearson Dental Supply when they carried or considered adding competitive lines. In another incident, Dentsply recognized DTS as a dealer so as to "fully eliminate the competitive threat that [DTS locations] pose by representing Vita and Ivoclar in three of four regions." The evidence demonstrated conclusively that Dentsply had supremacy over the dealer network and it was at that crucial point in the distribution chain that monopoly power over the market for artificial teeth was established. The reality in this case is that the firm that ties up the key dealers rules the market.

In concluding that Dentsply lacked the power to exclude competitors from the laboratories, "the ultimate consumers," the District Court overlooked the point that the relevant market was the "sale" of artificial teeth to both dealers and laboratories. Although some sales were made by manufacturers to the laboratories, overwhelming numbers were made to dealers. Thus, the Court's scrutiny should have been applied not to the "ultimate consumers" who used the teeth, but to the "customers" who purchased the teeth, the relevant category which included dealers as well as laboratories. This mis-focus led the District Court into clear error.

The factual pattern here is quite similar to that in *LePage's*. There, a manufacturer of transparent tape locked up high volume distribution channels by means of substantial discounts on a range of its other products. We concluded that the use of exclusive dealing and bundled rebates to the detriment of the rival manufacturer violated Section 2. Similarly, in *Microsoft,* the Court of Appeals for the D.C. Circuit concluded that, through the use of exclusive contracts with key dealers, a manufacturer foreclosed competitors from a substantial percentage of the available opportunities for product distribution.

The evidence in this case demonstrates that for a considerable time, through the use of Dealer Criterion 6 Dentsply has been able to exclude competitors from the dealers' network, a narrow, but heavily traveled channel to the dental laboratories.

C. Pricing

An increase in pricing is another factor used in evaluating existence of market power. Although in this case the evidence of exclusion is stronger than that of Dentsply's control of prices, testimony about suspect pricing is also found in this record.

The District Court found that Dentsply had a reputation for aggressive price increases in the market. It is noteworthy that experts for both parties testified that were Dealer Criterion 6 abolished, prices would fall. A former sales manager for Dentsply agreed that the company's share of the market would diminish should Dealer Criterion 6 no longer be in effect. In 1993, Dentsply's regional sales manager complained, "[w]e need to moderate our increases—twice a year for the last few years was not good." Large scale distributors observed that Dentsply's policy created a high price umbrella.

Although Dentsply's prices fall between those of Ivoclar and Vita's premium tooth lines, Dentsply did not reduce its prices when competitors elected not to follow its increases. Dentsply's profit margins have been growing over the years. The picture is one of a manufacturer that sets prices with little concern for its competitors, "something a firm without a monopoly would have been unable to do." *Microsoft*. The results have been favorable to Dentsply, but of no benefit to consumers.

Moreover, even "if monopoly power has been acquired or maintained through improper means, the fact that the power has not been used to extract [a monopoly price] provides no succor to the monopolist." *Microsoft*, 253 F.3d at 57 (quoting *Berkey Photo, Inc. v. Eastman Kodak, Co.*, 603 F.2d 263, 274 (2d Cir.1979)). The record of long duration of the exclusionary tactics and anecdotal evidence of their efficacy make it clear that power existed and was used effectively. The District Court erred in concluding that Dentsply lacked market power.

IV. ANTI–COMPETITIVE EFFECTS

Having demonstrated that Dentsply possessed market power, the Government must also establish the second element of a Section 2 claim, that the power was used "to foreclose competition." Assessing anti-competitive effect is important in evaluating a challenge to a violation of Section 2. Under that Section of the Sherman Act, it is not necessary that all competition be removed from the market. The test is not total foreclosure, but whether the challenged practices bar a substantial number of rivals or severely restrict the market's ambit. *LePage's*, 324 F.3d at 159–60; *Microsoft*. A leading treatise explains,

> A set of strategically planned exclusive dealing contracts may slow the rival's expansion by requiring it to develop alternative outlets for its products or rely at least temporarily on inferior or more expensive outlets. Consumer injury results from the delay that the dominant firm imposes on the smaller rival's growth. Herbert Hovenkamp, *Antitrust Law* ¶ 1802c, at 64 (2d ed.2002).

By ensuring that the key dealers offer Dentsply teeth either as the only or dominant choice, Dealer Criterion 6 has a significant effect in preserving Dentsply's monopoly. It helps keep sales of competing teeth below the critical level necessary for any rival to pose a real threat to Dentsply's market share. As such, Dealer Criterion 6 is a solid pillar of harm to competition. . . .

A. *Benefits of Dealers*

Dentsply has always sold its teeth through dealers. Vita sells through Vident, its exclusive distributor and domestic affiliate, but has a mere 3% of the market. Ivoclar had some relationship with dealers in the past, but its direct relationship with laboratories yields only a 5% share.

A number of factors are at work here. For a great number of dental laboratories, the dealer is the preferred source for artificial teeth. Although the District Court observed that "labs prefer to buy direct because of potential cost savings attributable to the elimination of the dealer middleman [,]" in fact, laboratories are driven by the realities of the marketplace to buy far more heavily from dealers than manufacturers. This may be largely attributed to the beneficial services, credit function, economies of scale and convenience that dealers provide to laboratories, benefits which are otherwise unavailable to them when they buy direct.

The record is replete with evidence of benefits provided by dealers. For example, they provide laboratories the benefit of "one stop-shopping" and extensive credit services. Because dealers typically carry the products of multiple manufacturers, a laboratory can order, with a single phone call to a dealer, products from multiple sources. Without dealers, in most instances laboratories would have to place individual calls to each manufacturer, expend the time, and pay multiple shipping charges to fill the same orders.

The dealer-provided reduction in transaction costs and time represents a substantial benefit, one that the District Court minimized when it characterized "one stop shopping" as merely the ability to order from a single manufacturer all the materials necessary for crown, bridge and denture construction. Although a laboratory can call a manufacturer directly and purchase any product made by it, the laboratory is unable to procure from that source products made by its competitors. Thus, purchasing through dealers, which as a class traditionally carries the products of multiple vendors, surmounts this shortcoming, as well as offers other advantages.

Buying through dealers also enables laboratories to take advantage of obtaining discounts. Because they engage in price competition to gain laboratories' business, dealers often discount manufacturers' suggested laboratory price for artificial teeth. There is no finding on this record that manufacturers offer similar discounts.

Another service dealers perform is taking back tooth returns. Artificial teeth and denture returns are quite common in dentistry. Approximately 30% of all laboratory tooth purchases are returned for exchange or credit. The District Court disregarded this benefit on the ground that all manufacturers except Vita accept tooth returns. However, in equating dealer and manufacturer returns, the District Court overlooked the fact that using dealers, rather than manufacturers, enables laboratories to consolidate their returns. In a single shipment to a dealer, a laboratory can return the products of a number of manufacturers, and so economize on shipping, time, and transaction costs.

Conversely, when returning products directly to manufacturers, a laboratory must ship each vendor's product separately and must track each exchange individually. Consolidating returns yields savings of time, effort, and costs.

Dealers also provide benefits to manufacturers, perhaps the most obvious of which is efficiency of scale. Using select high-volume dealers, as opposed to directly selling to hundreds if not thousands of laboratories, greatly reduces the manufacturer's distribution costs and credit risks. Dentsply, for example, currently sells to twenty three dealers. If it were instead to sell directly to individual laboratories, Dentsply would incur significantly higher transaction costs, extension of credit burdens, and credit risks.

Although a laboratory that buys directly from a manufacturer may be able to avoid the marginal costs associated with "middleman" dealers, any savings must be weighed against the benefits, savings, and convenience offered by dealers.

In addition, dealers provide manufacturers more marketplace exposure and sales representative coverage than manufacturers are able to generate on their own. Increased exposure and sales coverage traditionally lead to greater sales.

B.   "Viability" of Direct Sales

The benefits that dealers provide manufacturers help make dealers the preferred distribution channels—in effect, the "gateways"—to the artificial teeth market. Nonetheless, the District Court found that selling direct is a "viable" method of distributing artificial teeth. But we are convinced that it is "viable" only in the sense that it is "possible," not that it is practical or feasible in the market as it exists and functions. The District Court's conclusion of "viability" runs counter to the facts and is clearly erroneous. On the entire evidence, we are "left with the definite and firm conviction that a mistake has been committed."

It is true that Dentsply's competitors can sell directly to the dental laboratories and an insignificant number do. The undeniable reality, however, is that dealers have a controlling degree of access to the laboratories. The long-entrenched Dentsply dealer network with its ties to the laboratories makes it impracticable for a manufacturer to rely on direct distribution to the laboratories in any significant amount.

That some manufacturers resort to direct sales and are even able to stay in business by selling directly is insufficient proof that direct selling is an effective means of competition. The proper inquiry is not whether direct sales enable a competitor to "survive" but rather whether direct selling "poses a real threat" to defendant's monopoly. See *Microsoft*. The minuscule 5% and 3% market shares eked out by direct-selling manufacturers Ivoclar and Vita, Dentsply's "primary competitors," reveal that direct selling poses little threat to Dentsply.

C.   *Efficacy of Dealer Criterion 6*

Although the parties to the sales transactions consider the exclusionary arrangements to be agreements, they are technically only a series of independent sales. Dentsply sells teeth to the dealers on an individual transaction basis and essentially the arrangement is "at-will." Nevertheless, the economic elements involved—the large share of the market held by Dentsply and its conduct excluding competing manufacturers—realistically make the arrangements here as effective as those in written contracts. See Monsanto Co. v. Spray–Rite Serv. Corp., 465 U.S. 752, 764 n. 9 (1984).

Given the circumstances present in this case, there is no ground to doubt the effectiveness of the exclusive dealing arrangement. In *LePage's*, 324 F.3d at 162, we concluded that 3M's aggressive rebate program damaged LePage's ability to compete and thereby harmed competition itself. LePage's simply could not match the discounts that 3M provided. Similarly, in this case, in spite of the legal ease with which the relationship can be terminated, the dealers have a strong economic incentive to continue carrying Dentsply's teeth. Dealer Criterion 6 is not edentulous.[36]

D.   *Limitation of Choice*

An additional anti-competitive effect is seen in the exclusionary practice here that limits the choices of products open to dental laboratories, the ultimate users. A dealer locked into the Dentsply line is unable to heed a request for a different manufacturers' product and, from the standpoint of convenience, that inability to some extent impairs the laboratory's choice in the marketplace.

As an example, current and potential customers requested Atlanta Dental to carry Vita teeth. Although these customers could have ordered the Vita teeth from Vident in California, Atlanta Dental's tooth department manager believed that they were interested in a local source. Atlanta Dental chose not to add the Vita line after being advised that doing so would cut off access to Dentsply teeth, which constituted over 90% of its tooth sales revenue.

Similarly, DLDS added Universal and Vita teeth to meet customers' requests, but dropped them after Dentsply threatened to stop supplying its product. Marcus Dental began selling another brand of teeth at one point because of customer demand in response to supply problems with Dentsply.

---

36. In some cases which we find distinguishable, courts have indicated that exclusive dealing contracts of short duration are not violations of the antitrust laws. See, e.g., CDC Techs., Inc. v. IDEXX Labs., Inc., 186 F.3d 74, 81 (2d Cir.1999) ("distributors" only provided sales leads and sales increased after competitor imposed exclusive dealing arrangements); Omega Envtl., Inc. v. Gilbarco, Inc., 127 F.3d 1157, 1163 (9th Cir.1997) (manufacturer with 55% market share sold both to consumers and distributors, market showed decreasing prices and fluctuating shares); Ryko Mfg., Co. v. Eden Servs., 823 F.2d 1215 (8th Cir.1987) (manufacturer sold its products through direct sales and distributors); Roland Mach. Co. v. Dresser Indus., Inc., 749 F.2d 380 (7th Cir.1984) (contract between dealer and manufacturer did not contain exclusive dealing provision).

After Dentsply threatened to enforce Dealer Criterion 6, Marcus dropped the other line.

E.   Barriers to Entry

Entrants into the marketplace must confront Dentsply's power over the dealers. The District Court's theory that any new or existing manufacturer may "steal" a Dentsply dealer by offering a superior product at a lower price simply has not proved to be realistic. To the contrary, purloining efforts have been thwarted by Dentsply's longtime, vigorous and successful enforcement actions. The paltry penetration in the market by competitors over the years has been a refutation of theory by tangible and measurable results in the real world.

The levels of sales that competitors could project in wooing dealers were minuscule compared to Dentsply's, whose long-standing relationships with these dealers included sales of other dental products. For example, Dentsply threatened Zahn with termination if it started selling Ivoclar teeth. At the time, Ivoclar's projected $1.2 million in sales were 85% lower than Zahn's $8 million in Dentsply's sales.

When approached by Leach & Dillon and Heraeus Kulzer, Zahn's sales of Dentsply teeth had increased to $22–$23 million per year. In comparison, the president of Zahn expected that Leach & Dillon would add up to $200,000 (or less than 1% of its Dentsply's sales) and Heraeus Kulzer would contribute "maybe hundreds of thousands." Similarly, Vident's $1 million in projected sales amounted to 5.5% of its $18 million in annual Dentsply's sales.

The dominant position of Dentsply dealers as a gateway to the laboratories was confirmed by potential entrants to the market. The president of Ivoclar testified that his company was unsuccessful in its approach to the two large national dealers and other regional dealers. He pointed out that it is more efficient to sell through dealers and, in addition, they offered an entre to future customers by promotions in the dental schools.

Further evidence was provided by a Vident executive, who testified about failed attempts to distribute teeth through ten identified dealers. He attributed the lack of success to their fear of losing the right to sell Dentsply teeth.

Another witness, the president of Dillon Company, advised Davis, Schottlander & Davis, a tooth manufacturer, "to go through the dealer network because anything else is futile.... Dealers control the tooth industry. If you don't have distribution with the dealer network, you don't have distribution." Some idea of the comparative size of the dealer network was illustrated by the Dillon testimony: "Zahn does $2 billion, I do a million-seven. Patterson does over a billion dollars, I do a million-seven. I have ten employees, they have 6,000."

Dealer Criterion 6 created a strong economic incentive for dealers to reject competing lines in favor of Dentsply's teeth. As in *LePage*'s, the rivals simply could not provide dealers with a comparable economic incentive to switch. Moreover, the record demonstrates that Dentsply added Darby as a dealer "to block Vita from a key competitive distribution point." According to a Dentsply executive, the "key issue" was "Vita's potential distribution system." He explained that Vita was "having a tough time getting teeth out to customers. One of their key weaknesses is their distribution system."

Teeth are an important part of a denture, but they are but one component. The dealers are dependent on serving all of the laboratories' needs and must carry as many components as practicable. The artificial teeth business cannot realistically be evaluated in isolation from the rest of the dental fabrication industry.

A leading treatise provides a helpful analogy to this situation:

> [S]uppose that mens's bow ties cannot efficiently be sold in stores that deal exclusively in bow ties or even ties generally; rather, they must be sold in department stores where clerics can spread their efforts over numerous products and the ties can be sold in conjunction with shirts and suits. Suppose further that a dominant bow tie manufacturer should impose exclusive dealing on a town's only three department stores. In this case the rival bow tie maker cannot easily enter. Setting up another department store is an unneeded and a very large investment in proportion to its own production, which we assume is only bow ties, but any store that offers less will be an inefficient and costly seller of bow ties. As a result, such exclusive dealing could either exclude the nondominant bow tie maker or else raise its costs in comparison to the costs of the dominant firm. While the department stores might prefer to sell the ties of multiple manufacturers, if faced with an "all-or-nothing" choice they may accede to the dominant firm's wish for exclusive dealing. Herbert Hovenkamp, *Antitrust Law* ¶ 1802e3, at 78–79 (2d ed.2002).

Criterion 6 imposes an "all-or-nothing" choice on the dealers. The fact that dealers have chosen not to drop Dentsply teeth in favor of a rival's brand demonstrates that they have acceded to heavy economic pressure.

This case does not involve a dynamic, volatile market like that in *Microsoft* or a proven alternative distribution channel. The mere existence of other avenues of distribution is insufficient without an assessment of their overall significance to the market. The economic impact of an exclusive dealing arrangement is amplified in the stagnant, no growth context of the artificial tooth field.

Dentsply's authorized dealers are analogous to the high volume retailers at issue in *LePage's*. Although the dealers are distributors and the stores in *LePage's*, such as K–Mart and Staples, are retailers, this is a distinction in name without a substantive difference. *LePage's*, 324 F.3d at 144. Selling to a few prominent retailers provided "substantially reduced distribution costs" and "cheap, high volume supply lines." The manufacturer sold to a few high volume businesses and benefitted from the widespread locations and strong customer goodwill that prominent retailers provided as opposed to selling directly to end-user consumers or to a multitude of smaller retailers. There are other ways across the "river" to consumers, but high volume retailers provided the most effective bridge.

The same is true here. The dealers provide the same advantages to Dentsply, widespread locations and long-standing relationships with dental labs, that the high volume retailers provided to 3M. Even orders that are drop-shipped directly from Dentsply to a dental lab originate through the dealers. This underscores that Dentsply's dealers provide a critical link to end-users.

Although the District Court attributed some of the lack of competition to Ivoclar's and Vident's bad business decisions, that weakness was not ascribed to other manufacturers. Logically, Dealer Criterion 6 cannot be both a cause of the competitors' lower promotional expenditures which hurt their market positions, and at the same time, be unrelated to their exclusion from the marketplace. Moreover, in *Microsoft,* in spite of the competitors' self-imposed problems, the Court of Appeals held that Microsoft possessed monopoly power because it benefitted from a significant barrier to entry.

Dentsply's grip on its 23 authorized dealers effectively choked off the market for artificial teeth, leaving only a small sliver for competitors. The District Court erred when it minimized that situation and focused on a theoretical feasibility of success through direct access to the dental labs. While we may assume that Dentsply won its preeminent position by fair competition, that fact does not permit maintenance of its monopoly by unfair practices. We conclude that on this record, the Government established that Dentsply's exclusionary policies and particularly Dealer Criterion 6 violated Section 2.

V.   BUSINESS JUSTIFICATION

As noted earlier, even if a company exerts monopoly power, it may defend its practices by establishing a business justification. The Government, having demonstrated harm to competition, the burden shifts to Dentsply to show that Dealer Criterion 6 promotes a sufficiently pro-competitive objective. United States v. Brown Univ., 5 F.3d 658, 669 (3d Cir.1993). Significantly, Dentsply has not done so. The District Court found that "Dentsply's asserted justifications for its exclusionary policies are inconsistent with its announced reason for the exclusionary policies, its conduct enforcing the policy, its rival suppliers' actions, and dealers' behavior in the marketplace."

Some of the dealers opposed Dentsply's policy as exerting too much control over the products they may sell, but the grandfathered dealers were no less efficient than the exclusive ones, nor was there any difference in promotional support. Nor was there any evidence of existence of any substantial variation in the level of service provided by exclusive and grandfathered dealers to the laboratories.

The record amply supports the District Court's conclusion that Dentsply's alleged justification was pretextual and did not excuse its exclusionary practices.

VI.   AVAILABILITY OF SHERMAN ACT SECTION 2 RELIEF

One point remains. Relying on *dicta* in *Tampa Electric Co. v. Nashville Coal Co.*, 365 U.S. 320 (1961), the District Court said that because it had found no liability under the stricter standards of Section 3 of the Clayton Act, it followed that there was no violation of Section 2 of the Sherman Act. However, as we explained in *LePage's* v. 3M, a finding in favor of the defendant under Section 1 of the Sherman Act and Section 3 of the Clayton Act, did not "preclude the application of evidence of . . . exclusive dealing to support the [Section 2] claim." All of the evidence in the record here applies to the Section 2 claim and, as in *LePage's*, a finding of liability under Section 2 supports a judgment against defendant. . . . Here, the Government can obtain all the relief to which it is entitled under Section 2 and has chosen to follow that path without reference to Section 1 of the Sherman Act or Section 3 of the Clayton Act. We find no obstacle to that procedure.

PROBLEM 21

GILBERT'S ARRANGEMENTS WITH GAS PUMP DISTRIBUTORS

Gilbert is the largest of five U.S. manufacturers of petroleum dispensing equipment (*i.e.*, gas pumps) accounting for 55% of U.S. sales. U.S. manufacturers sell directly to major oil companies, but sell through distributors to regional oil companies, independent retail stations, and convenience store chains. Although the major oil companies buy direct from the five manufacturers, smaller companies buy through some 500 authorized dealers—each restricted to selling only one manufacturer's equipment. Competition at the dealer level is intense.

Gilbert follows the trend of most of its competitors and sells one-third of its equipment direct and two-thirds through dealers. Gilbert has signed up 220 dealers as exclusive distributors of its equipment. Each initial agreement is for a three-year term, and thereafter agreements can be cancelled without cause and without penalty on 90–days' notice. The other four manufacturers insist on the same terms with respect to exclusivity and duration. Sigma attempted to enter the petroleum dispensing equipment market, initially by purchasing six of Gilbert's largest dealers. Its business plan was to offer to sell all manufacturers' products and related equipment (credit card readers, underground tanks, etc.) as a form of one-stop shopping. Gilbert learned of the business plan and, after 60–days' notice, terminated the Sigma dealers as distributors of Gilbert products.

Occasionally companies that service dispensing equipment, of which there are thousands, go into the business of selling equipment, but because of inadequate finances, lack of sales ability or absence of existing customer relations, they are not as effective as authorized dealers. Only 40 of the 500 existing dealers migrated from the service company sector of the market.

Sigma sues under Sections 1 and 2 of the Sherman Act and Section 3 of the Clayton Act, claiming it was foreclosed from the ability to compete in the relevant market. It is prepared to prove at trial that two foreign manufacturers of petroleum dispensing equipment made initial efforts to enter the U.S. market, but were discouraged and eventually withdrew because of what they regarded as the absence of distribution opportunities.

SELECTIVE BIBLIOGRAPHY

1. General

Pitofsky (ed.), How the Chicago School Overshot the Mark Ch. 3 (2008).

3, 3A Areeda & Hovenkamp, Antitrust Law: An Analysis of Antitrust Principles and Their Application (2006 & 2009 Supplement).

Hovenkamp, Federal Antitrust Policy: The Law of Competition and Its Practice (3d ed. 2005).

Posner, Antitrust Law (2d ed. 2001).

FTC Staff, Anticipating the 21st Century: Competition Policy in the New High–Tech, Global Marketplace (1996).

2. Predatory Pricing And Attempts To Monopolize

3 Areeda & Hovenkamp, Antitrust Law: An Analysis of Antitrust Principles and Their Application ¶¶ 722–24, 735–41 (2006 & 2009 Supplement).

Hovenkamp, Federal Antitrust Policy: The Law of Competition and Its Practice Chs. 6–8 (3d ed. 2005).

Posner, Antitrust Law 215 (2d ed. 2001).

Scherer & Ross, Industrial Market Structure and Economic Performance Ch. 12 (3d ed. 1990).

Edlin, Stopping Above–Cost Predatory Pricing, 111 Yale L.J. 941 (2002).

Bolton, Brodley & Riordan, Predatory Pricing: Strategic Theory and Legal Policy, 88 Geo.L.J. 2239 (2000).

Krattenmaker, Lande & Salop, Monopoly Power and Market Power in Antitrust Law, 76 Geo.L.J. 241 (1987).

Krattenmaker & Salop, Anticompetitive Exclusion: Raising Rivals' Costs to Achieve Power Over Price, 96 Yale L.J. 209 (1986).

Handler & Steuer, Attempts to Monopolize and No–Fault Monopolization, 129 U.Pa.L.Rev. 125 (1980).

Areeda & Turner, Predatory Pricing and Related Practices under Section 2 of the Sherman Act, 88 Harv.L.Rev. 697 (1975).

3. Tie–In Sales

Sullivan & Grimes, The Law of Antitrust: An Integrated Handbook (2d ed. 2006).

Hovenkamp, Federal Antitrust Policy: The Law of Competition and Its Practice Ch. 10 (3d ed. 2005).

Hylton & Salinger, Tying Law and Policy: A Decision–Theoretic Approach, 69 Antitrust L.J. 469 (2001).

Feldman, Defensive Leveraging in Antitrust, 87 Georgetown L.J. 2079 (1999).

[Materials relating to monopolization are found in the Selective Bibliography following Chapter 3, and materials relating to discriminatory pricing will be found in the Selective Bibliography following Chapter 11.]

CHAPTER 9

MERGERS

SECTION 1. BACKGROUND ON EARLY MERGER LAW AND THE AMENDMENT OF SECTION 7 OF THE CLAYTON ACT IN 1950

Chapters 1 (*see* pp. 1–53, and 6 (*see* pp. 469–605), discussed the ebb and flow of merger enforcement during the first fifty years of this century and, in many instances, the discussions of "market power" throughout the casebook illustrate the negative consequences of periods of lax or permissive merger enforcement. Where a market has grown concentrated, for example, there is reason to monitor more closely the conduct of firms in that market. Although, as Chapter 6 indicates, prices above competitive levels do not automatically result from a concentrated market structure, one must be concerned about interdependent pricing and other parallel anticompetitive practices. Even those in the Chicago School recognize that concentrated markets facilitate collusion.

In the United States, the basic alternative to intensive governmental monitoring or regulation has been an effective merger policy. The goal is both to maintain efficiency and to keep market structures fragmented enough to allow competitive pressures to work. As Professor F.M. Scherer put it,

> Unless one believes that noncompetitive conduct is naturally rare and fleeting in duration, [effective merger policy] is the less interventionist of the alternatives, since minimal monitoring is required and, if intervention proves warranted, it can be episodic. It is not too far fetched to say that merger policy is to price conduct policy as surgery is to continuing drug therapy.[1]

United States v. Columbia Steel Co., 334 U.S. 495 (1948), provides an excellent illustration of the type of case which concerned Congress when it enacted the Celler–Kefauver Act of 1950, amending Section 7 of the Clayton Act. In *Columbia Steel*, the government sued under Sections 1 and 2 of the Sherman Act to enjoin the acquisition by United States Steel Company of Consolidated Steel, a West Coast manufacturer of fabricated steel plates and shapes (*e.g.*, building framework, bridges, tanks, welded pipe). The acquisition was to be accomplished through United States Steel's wholly owned subsidiary, Columbia Steel.

Rolled steel products, made from ingots at rolling mills, consist of plates, shapes, bars and other unfinished steel products, which in turn are used in various types of steel fabrication. United States Steel was the

---

1. Scherer, Merger Policy in the 1970s and 1980s 1 (1988).

largest producer of rolled steel products in the United States, accounting for about one-third of the market with annual sales of about $1 billion. Columbia Steel was the largest producer of rolled steel on the Pacific Coast, and also acted as sales agent for two other subsidiaries of United States Steel that were engaged in structural fabrication. In addition, United States Steel had acquired after World War II a government-owned rolled steel plant at Geneva, Utah; this occurred after the War Assets Administration had received an opinion from the Attorney General that the sale of the Geneva facilities to United States Steel would not violate the antitrust laws.

The government challenged the acquisition of Consolidated principally on the grounds that: (1) it would lessen actual and potential horizontal competition between Consolidated and United States Steel in the sale of structural fabricated products, and (2) it would exclude all sellers except United States Steel from supplying Consolidated's requirements of rolled steel.

As to the charge of lessening competition in sales of rolled steel, the government contended that the relevant market included the purchase of all rolled steel in the eleven western states in which Consolidated marketed (Consolidated accounting for about 3% in that market), and that it could be further refined to include the consumption in that area of rolled steel only by structural and plate fabricators (in which case, Consolidated would account for about 13%).

The Supreme Court majority adopted as the relevant market "total demand for rolled steel products in the eleven-state area." The government argued that because vertical integration excludes other producers of rolled steel from the opportunity to sell to the acquired company, any vertical integration involving an appreciable amount of interstate commerce should be illegal *per se*. Justice Reed responded:

> The legality of the acquisition by United States Steel of a market outlet for its rolled steel through the purchase of the manufacturing facilities of Consolidated depends not merely upon the fact of that acquired control but also upon many other factors. Exclusive dealings for rolled steel between Consolidated and United States Steel, brought about by vertical integration or otherwise, are not illegal, at any rate until the effect of such control is to unreasonably restrict the opportunities of competitors to market their product....
>
> It seems clear to us that vertical integration, as such without more, cannot be held violative of the Sherman Act. It is an indefinite term without explicit meaning. Even in the iron industry, where could a line be drawn—at the end of mining the ore, the production of the pig-iron or steel ingots, when the rolling mill operation is completed, fabrication on order or at some stage of manufacture into standard merchandise? No answer would be possible and therefore the extent of permissible integration must

be governed, as other factors in Sherman Act violations, by the other circumstances of individual cases.

As to the alleged lessening of horizontal competition, the majority concluded that while United States Steel accounted for 13% of the fabricating business in the eleven-state area and Consolidated for 11%, the merger did not violate Section 1—principally because the relevant geographic market was viewed as nationwide. In addition, the Court took account of developments then taking place in the western steel industry and concluded that it was unlikely that the companies would continue to account for 11% and 13%, even if the geographic market were more narrowly defined.

The Court held that the same tests were to be applied in judging the legality of both vertical and horizontal integration. The approach for measuring the legality of a corporate fusion under the Sherman Act was described as follows:

> It is first necessary to delimit the market in which the concerns compete and then determine the extent to which the concerns are in competition in that market. If such acquisition results in or is aimed at unreasonable restraint, then the purchase is forbidden by the Sherman Act. In determining what constitutes unreasonable restraint, we do not think the dollar volume is in itself of compelling significance; we look rather to the percentage of business controlled, the strength of the remaining competition, whether the action springs from business requirements or purpose to monopolize, the probable development of the industry, consumer demands, and other characteristics of the market.

Douglas, J., with whom Black, Murphy and Rutledge, JJ., joined, dissented. He stated that the majority had failed to heed the lesson about, as Brandeis put it, the "curse of bigness." The lesson, in Douglas' opinion, was forgotten by the Supreme Court in the United States Steel and similar cases; the vice of the majority opinion was that it was in the tradition of discredited precedents.

Congress had been holding hearings throughout most of the 1940's on proposals for stricter merger laws. The Columbia Steel decision provided fuel for those efforts. Another problem to be addressed was the fact that the original version of Section 7 of the Clayton Act, as enacted in 1914, contained some gaping loopholes. Thus, the original Clayton Act[2] applied to stock but not asset acquisitions. It was of little significance to the acquiring company, however, whether it obtained stock or assets, and the result was increasing numbers of merger transactions were accomplished through asset acquisitions to avoid application of the statute. A second loophole in the statute arose because of language which required that the anticompeti-

---

2. The original version of Section 7 provided: "That no corporation engaged in commerce shall acquire, directly or indirectly, the whole or any part of the stock or other share capital of another corporation engaged also in commerce, where the effect of such acquisition may be to substantially lessen competition between the corporation whose stock is so acquired and the corporation making the acquisition, or to restrain such commerce in any section or community, or tend to create a monopoly of any line of commerce . . ."

tive effect be between the acquiring and the acquired company. Since the effect of a vertical merger is not on the merging parties, but on a third party foreclosed or otherwise injured as a result of the merger, several courts interpreted the statute as not covering vertical mergers. The result was a significantly amended Section 7, enacted in 1950.

Brown Shoe Co. v. United States, 370 U.S. 294, 315–23 (1962) was the first merger case that came before the Supreme Court after Section 7 was amended in 1950. The opinion is a good indication of how Congress and the Court thought about merger issues in the several decades after the Act was revised. The case involved alleged anticompetitive effects in both the horizontal and vertical lines, and its discussion on the merits will be examined at pages 1143 to 1148, *infra*. We set out here the Court's review of the legislative history of the Celler–Kefauver Act:

> The dominant theme pervading congressional consideration of the 1950 amendments was a fear of what was considered to be a rising tide of economic concentration in the American economy. Apprehension in this regard was bolstered by the publication in 1948 of the Federal Trade Commission's study on corporate mergers. Statistics from this and other current studies were cited as evidence of the danger to the American economy in unchecked corporate expansions through mergers. Other considerations cited in support of the bill were the desirability of retaining "local control" over industry and the protection of small businesses. Throughout the recorded discussion may be found examples of Congress' fear not only of accelerated concentration of economic power on economic grounds, but also of the threat to other values a trend toward concentration was thought to pose.
>
> What were some of the factors, relevant to a judgment as to the validity of a given merger, specifically discussed by Congress in redrafting § 7?
>
> First, there is no doubt that Congress did wish to "plug the loophole" and to include within the coverage of the Act the acquisition of assets no less than the acquisition of stock.[3]
>
> Second, by the deletion of the "acquiring-acquired" language in the original text, it hoped to make plain that § 7 applied not only to mergers between actual competitors, but also to vertical and conglomerate mergers whose effect may tend to lessen competition in any line of commerce in any section of the country.
>
> Third, it is apparent that a keystone in the erection of a barrier to what Congress saw was the rising tide of economic concentration was its provision of authority for arresting mergers at a time when the trend to a lessening of competition in a line of commerce was still in its incipiency. Congress saw the process of concentration in American business as a dynamic force; it sought

---

3. Virtually every member of Congress who spoke in support of the amendments indicated that this aspect of the legislation was its salient characteristic....

to assure the Federal Trade Commission and the courts the power
to brake this force at its outset and before it gathered momentum.[4]

Fourth, and closely related to the third, Congress rejected, as
inappropriate to the problem it sought to remedy, the application
to § 7 cases of the standards for judging the legality of business
combinations adopted by the courts in dealing with cases arising
under the Sherman Act, and which may have been applied to some
early cases arising under original § 7.[5]

Fifth, at the same time that it sought to create an effective
tool for preventing all mergers having demonstrable anticompetitive effects, Congress recognized the stimulation to competition
that might flow from particular mergers. When concern as to the
Act's breadth was expressed, supporters of the amendments indicated that it would not impede, for example, a merger between two
small companies to enable the combination to compete more
effectively with larger corporations dominating the relevant market, nor a merger between a corporation which is financially
healthy and a failing one which no longer can be a vital competitive factor in the market. The deletion of the word "community"
in the original Act's description of the relevant geographic market

---

4. That § 7 of the Clayton Act was intended to reach incipient monopolies and trade
restraints outside the scope of the Sherman Act was explicitly stated in the Senate Report on
the original Act. S.Rep. No. 698, 63d Cong., 2d Sess. 1. See United States v. E.I. du Pont de
Nemours & Co., 353 U.S. 586, 589. This theme was reiterated in congressional consideration
of the amendments adopted in 1950, and found expression in the final House and Senate
Reports on the measure. H.R.Rep. No. 1191, 81st Cong., 1st Sess. 8 ("Acquisitions of stock or
assets have a cumulative effect, and control of the market . . . may be achieved not in a single
acquisition but as the result of a series of acquisitions. The bill is intended to permit
intervention in such a cumulative process when the effect of an acquisition may be a
significant reduction in the vigor of competition."); S.Rep. No. 1775, 81st Cong., 2d Sess. 4–5,
U.S.Code Cong. and Adm.News, 1950, p. 4296 ("The intent here . . . is to cope with
monopolistic tendencies in their incipiency and well before they have attained such effects as
would justify a Sherman Act proceeding."). And see F.T.C., The Merger Movement: A
Summary Report 6–7.

5. The Report of the House Judiciary Committee on H.R. 515 recommended the adoption
of tests more stringent than those in the Sherman Act. 15 U.S.C.A. §§ 1–7, 15 note H.R.Rep.
No. 596, 80th Cong., 1st Sess. 7. A vigorous minority thought no new legislation was needed.
Between the issuance of this Report and the Committee's subsequent consideration of H.R.
2734, this Court had decided United States v. Columbia Steel Co., 334 U.S. 495, which some
understood to indicate that existing law might be inadequate to prevent mergers that had
substantially lessened competition in a section of the country, but which, nevertheless, had not
risen to the level of those restraints of trade or monopoly prohibited by the Sherman Act. See
96 Cong.Rec. 16502 (remarks of Senator Kefauver); Numerous other statements by Congressmen and Senators and by representatives of the Federal Trade Commission, the Department
of Justice and the President's Council of Economic Advisors were made to the Congress
suggesting that a standard of illegality stricter than that imposed by the Sherman Act was
needed. The House Judiciary Committee's 1949 Report supported this concept unanimously
although five of the nine members who had dissented two years earlier in H.R.Rep. No. 596
were still serving on the Committee. The Senate Report was explicit: "The committee wish to
make it clear that the bill is not intended to revert to the Sherman Act test. The intent here
. . . is to cope with monopolistic tendencies in their incipiency and well before they have
attained such effects as would justify a Sherman Act proceeding. . . ."

is another illustration of Congress' desire to indicate that its concern was with the adverse effects of a given merger on competition only in an economically significant "section" of the country.[6] Taken as a whole, the legislative history illuminates congressional concern with the protection of competition, not competitors, and its desire to restrain mergers only to the extent that such combinations may tend to lessen competition.

Sixth, Congress neither adopted nor rejected specifically any particular tests for measuring the relevant markets, either as defined in terms of product or in terms of geographic locus of competition, within which the anticompetitive effects of a merger were to be judged. Nor did it adopt a definition of the word "substantially," whether in quantitative terms of sales or assets or market shares or in designated qualitative terms, by which a merger's effects on competition were to be measured.[7]

Seventh, while providing no definite quantitative or qualitative tests by which enforcement agencies could gauge the effects of a given merger to determine whether it may "substantially" lessen competition or tend toward monopoly, Congress indicated plainly that a merger had to be functionally viewed, in the context of its

---

6. The Federal Trade Commission's amendment, included the phrase "where ... in any section, community, or trade area, there is reasonable probability that the effect of such acquisition may be to substantially lessen competition." Congressman Kefauver urged deletion of the word "community" on the ground that it might suggest, for example, that a merger between two small filling stations in a section of a city was proscribed. The fear of literal prohibition of all but de minimis mergers through the use of the word "community" was also cited by the Senate Report as the basis for its retention solely of the word "section." S.Rep. No. 1775, 81st Cong., 2d Sess. 4. The reference to "trade area" was deleted as redundant, when it became clear that the "section" of the country to which the Act was to apply, referred not to a definite geographic area of the country, but rather the geographic area of effective competition in the relevant line of commerce ... The Senate Report cited with approval the definition of the market employed by the Court in Standard Oil Co. of California v. United States, 337 U.S. 293, 299 n. 5 (1949).

7. The House Report on H.R. 2734 stated that two tests of illegality were included in the proposed Act: whether the merger substantially lessened competition or tended to create a monopoly. It stated that such effects could be perceived through findings, for example, that a whole or material part of the competitive activity of an enterprise, which had been a substantial factor in competition, had been eliminated; that the relative size of the acquiring corporation had increased to such a point that its advantage over competitors threatened to be "decisive"; that an "undue" number of competing enterprises had been eliminated; or that buyers and sellers in the relevant market had established relationships depriving their rivals of a fair opportunity to compete. H.R.Rep. No. 1191, 81st Cong., 1st Sess. 8. Each of these standards, couched in general language, reflects a conscious avoidance of exclusively mathematical tests even though the case of Standard Oil Co. of California v. United States, 337 U.S. 293 (1949), said to have created a "quantitative substantiality" test for suits arising under § 3 of the Clayton Act, was decided while Congress was considering H.R. 2734. Some discussion of the applicability of this test to § 7 cases ensued, but this aspect of the *Standard Oil* decision was neither specifically endorsed nor impugned by the bill's supporters. However, the House Judiciary Committee's Report, issued two months after *Standard Oil* had been decided, remarked that the tests of illegality under the new Act were intended to be "similar to those which the courts have applied in interpreting the same language as used in other sections of the Clayton Act." H.R.Rep. No. 1191, 81st Cong., 1st Sess. 8.

particular industry.[8] That is, whether the consolidation was to take place in an industry that was fragmented rather than concentrated, that had seen a recent trend toward domination by a few leaders or had remained fairly consistent in its distribution of market shares among the participating companies, that had experienced easy access to markets by suppliers and easy access to suppliers by buyers or had witnessed foreclosure of business, that had witnessed the ready entry of new competition or the erection of barriers to prospective entrants, all were aspects, varying in importance with the merger under consideration, which would properly be taken into account.

Eighth, Congress used the words "may be substantially to lessen competition" (emphasis supplied), to indicate that its concern was with probabilities, not certainties.[9] Statutes existed for dealing with clear-cut menaces to competition; no statute was sought for dealing with ephemeral possibilities. Mergers with a probable anticompetitive effect were to be proscribed by this Act.

Clayton Act, Section 7

> **That no person engaged in commerce or in any activity affecting commerce shall acquire, directly or indirectly, the whole or any part of the stock or other share capital and no person subject to the jurisdiction of the Federal Trade Commission shall acquire the whole or any part of the assets of another person engaged also in commerce or in any activity affecting commerce, where in any line of**

---

8. A number of the supporters of the amendments voiced their concern that passage of the bill would amount to locking the barn door after most of the horses had been stolen, but urged approval of the measure to prevent the theft of those still in the barn. Which was to say that, if particular industries had not yet been subject to the congressionally perceived trend toward concentration, adoption of the amendments was urged as a way of preventing the trend from reaching those industries as yet unaffected. . . .

9. In the course of both the Committee hearings and floor debate, attention was occasionally focused on the issue of whether "possible," "probable" or "certain" anticompetitive effects of a proposed merger would have to be proven to establish a violation of the Act. Language was quoted from prior decisions of the Court in antitrust cases in which each of these interpretations of the word "may" was suggested as appropriate. The final Senate Report on the question was explicit on the point:

> "The use of these words ["may be"] means that the bill, if enacted, would not apply to the mere possibility but only to the reasonable probability of the prescribed [sic] effect. . . . The words 'may be' have been in section 7 of the Clayton Act since 1914. The concept of reasonable probability conveyed by these words is a necessary element in any statute which seeks to arrest restraints of trade in their incipiency and before they develop into full-fledged restraints violative of the Sherman Act. A requirement of certainty and actuality of injury to competition is incompatible with any effort to supplement the Sherman Act by reaching incipient restraints." S.Rep. No. 1775, 81st Cong., 2d Sess. 6. . . .

commerce or in any activity affecting commerce in any section of the country, the effect of such acquisition may be substantially to lessen competition, or to tend to create monopoly....

This section shall not apply to persons purchasing such stock solely for investment and not using the same by voting or otherwise to bring about, or in attempting to bring about, the substantial lessening of competition. Nor shall anything contained in this section prevent a corporation engaged in commerce or in any activity affecting commerce from causing the formation of subsidiary corporations for the actual carrying on of their immediate lawful business, or the natural and legitimate branches or extensions thereof, or from owning and holding all or a part of the stock of such subsidiary corporations, when the effect of such formation is not to substantially lessen competition....

SECTION 2.   PROSCRIBED EFFECT IN HORIZONTAL MERGERS

F.M. Scherer & D. Ross, Industrial Market Structure and Economic Performance

159–67 (3d ed. 1990).

The Motives for Merger

Mergers occur for a myriad of reasons, and in any given case, several different motives may simultaneously influence the merging parties' behavior. Still it is useful to attempt a preliminary sorting-out of the diverse motivating forces.

The Monopoly Motive

In horizontal mergers, and especially in the massive consolidations that took place around the turn of the century, the desire to achieve or strengthen monopoly power played a prominent role. Some 1887–1904 consolidations gained monopoly power by creating firms that dominated their industries. Others fell short of dominance, but transformed market structures sufficiently to curb the tendencies toward price competition toward which sellers gravitated in the rapidly changing market conditions of the time. As Thomas Edison remarked to a reporter concerning reasons for the formation of the General Electric Company in 1892:

"Recently there has been sharp rivalry between [Thomson–Houston and Edison General Electric], and prices have been cut so that there has been little profit in the manufacture of electrical machinery for anybody. The consolidation of the companies ... will do away with a competition which has become so sharp that the product of the factories has been worth little more than ordinary hardware...."[10]

Those were days when businesspeople were not yet intimidated by the wrath of trustbusters or public opinion. Now they are more circumspect, and evidence of monopoly-creating intent is harder to find....

Speculative Motives

Monopoly and speculative motives interacted to propel the great merger wave of 1887–1904. The value of a company's common stock depends upon investor expectations regarding future profits. If competition can be eliminated or reduced through merger, profits will presumably rise, making the new consolidated firm's shares worth more than the sum of the previously competing companies' share values. Entrepreneurs sought to achieve such capital value transformations by arranging competition-reducing mergers. However, many went farther. Because investors were captivated by the prospect of pursuing this road to fortune, and because there were no effective controls on the quality of information disseminated in connection with new stock flotations, promoters arranged mergers with little chance of securing appreciable monopoly power, but simultaneously issued prospectuses, planted rumors, and primed the market to convince investors otherwise. By exciting false expectations, the promoters were able to sell the stocks of newly consolidated firms at prices far exceeding their true economic value—a practice known at the time as stock watering. As in honestly monopolistic consolidations, the promoters were paid in newly issued stock for their contribution. Only in this case, the merger makers hastened to sell their shares to unwary outsiders before the bubble burst....

Alarm over such abuses led to passage of the Securities Act of 1933 and the Securities Exchange Act of 1934, establishing federal regulation of securities issue information and other promotional practices. They and the antitrust laws made it difficult for promoters to repeat the experiences of the 1890s and 1920s....

Normal Business Motives

Any explanation of mergers that ignores such speculative inducements is likely to miss the mark. Yet it must be recognized that there are many normal, wholesome business motives for merger. These compel careful examination.

It is widely believed that mergers serve as an efficient, humane escape route for companies that are otherwise about to fail. This is true, but not very important quantitatively. As a rule, merger makers seek healthy acquisition targets, not basket cases. Among 698 sizable manufacturing companies acquired between 1948 and 1968, only 4.8 percent had negative

---

10. *New York Times,* February 21, 1892, p. 2, cited in H.C. Passer, *The Electrical Manufacturers: 1875–1900* (Cambridge: Harvard University Press, 1953), p. 326. See also p. 54 of Passer on the motives for several earlier Thomson–Houston mergers.

profits in the year before acquisition occurred.[11] In a 634 company sample including a cross section of both small and large acquisition targets, 5.8 percent had negative operating income (before deduction of interest charges) in the year before acquisition.[12]

Small companies are often acquired because their owner-managers are aging or weary of business pressures and lack heirs or other successors to take their place. Interacting with this motive is the desire of family company owners to diversify their investment portfolios, thereby reducing their risk exposure, and to raise funds for paying the sometimes substantial estate taxes levied when an owner-manager dies.

Tax considerations also affect the urge to merge in a variety of more complex ways. When an acquisition premium is paid above the values at which a company's depreciable assets are recorded in tax accounts, the acquired assets can under U.S. law be stepped up and subjected to higher depreciation charges, shielding the acquirer from tax liabilities. Until reforms were enacted in 1986, acquiring companies making such step-ups could normally escape immediate capital gains taxation. Such tax advantages appear to have been an important consideration in many merger decisions, but not critical enough to determine whether merger would or would not occur.[13] Under the structure of U.S. and many other nations' tax laws, corporate profits are taxed directly when realized by the corporation and again at the personal level when they are distributed as dividends to individual (but not institutional) stockholders. To avoid this double taxation, corporations are tempted to reinvest their profits in merger-making rather than paying them out as dividends. When capital gains are taxed more lightly than dividend income, as was true in the United States until 1989, successful reinvestment increased the value of the company's stock, permitting shareholders to sell some of their shares and realize their gains under the more lightly-taxed capital gains provisions. Expanding upon this theme, Oliver Williamson argued that conglomerate firms achieved efficiencies by reinvesting earnings in internal capital markets better able than external markets to assimilate information on investment opportunities.[14] However, intracompany capital markets are often highly bureaucratic and politicized, and it is unclear whether they actually do a better job allocating

---

11. Stanley E. Boyle, "Pre–Merger Growth and Profit Characteristics of Large Conglomerate Mergers in the United States, 1948–1968," *St. John's Law Review,* vol. 44 (Spring 1970, special edition), pp. 152–170.

12. Ravenscraft and Scherer, *Mergers*, p. 60.

13. *See* Ronald J. Gilson, Myron S. Scholes, and Mark A. Wolfson, "Taxation and the Dynamics of Corporate Control," in John C. Coffee, Louis Lowenstein, and Susan Rose–Ackerman, eds., *Knights, Raiders, and Targets: The Impact of the Hostile Takeover* (New York: Oxford University Press, 1988), pp. 271–299.

14. Oliver E. Williamson, *Corporate Control and Business Behavior* (Englewood Cliffs, NJ: Prentice–Hall, 1970), pp. 121–130, 163–164, and 176–177.

capital than is achieved in the give-and-take between a firm and its outside investors....[15]

Other merger-based economies of scale are even more difficult to evaluate. Distinctions must be made inter alia between horizontal mergers, in which the merging firms produce and sell similar products, and conglomerates, in which the product lines differ, perhaps greatly.

Economies of scale in production are much more likely to be achieved following horizontal (or perhaps vertical) mergers than when unrelated operations are combined. Even then, problems arise.

When firms that make the same products merge, their plants are already built; not much can be done in the short run to unbuild them and achieve the principal plant-specific economies of scale. Exceptions are most likely to be found in declining or severely depressed industries. When multiple plants are combined, the least efficient units can be shut down and the most efficient units retained or even expanded....

Mergers may also confer advantages in marketing—for example, through the pooling and streamlining of field sales forces, the ability to offer distributors a broader product line, the use of common advertising themes, and (to the extent they exist) the sharing of advertising media quantity discounts. In a survey of sixty-nine U.S. acquisitions, mostly conglomerate, John Kitching found marketing complementarities to be much more important than production economies, and second only in importance to capital-cost economies.[16] However, conflicting evidence emerged from analyses by the Federal Trade Commission, the Economic Council of Canada, and (for the United Kingdom) Gerald Newbould, all of whom found post-merger marketing economies to be relatively unimportant.[17] The Canadian study showed marketing economies to emerge even less frequently than production economies, which were reported in 6.5 percent of the 1,826 surveyed acquisitions and 15.2 percent of the horizontal manufacturing industry mergers.

Complementarities also exist in research and development. One firm may have two or three unusually creative engineers but lack the distribution network needed to derive full commercial benefit from the new products they turn out. Another may have superb marketing channels but find its laboratories populated by unimaginative clods. Together they can make beautiful music. Ideas and money can also be brought together through merger. There is reason to believe that such motives have influenced an appreciable number of mergers, especially those in which small

---

15. Ravenscraft and Scherer, *Mergers,* pp. 213–214; and Joseph L. Bower, *Managing the Resource Allocation Process* (Boston: Harvard Business School Division of Research, 1970), especially Chapter 9.

16. John Kitching, "Why Do Mergers Miscarry?" *Harvard Business Review,* vol. 45 (November–December 1967), pp. 87–90.

17. Gerald D. Newbould, *Management and Merger Activity* (Liverpool: Guthstead, 1970), p. 178; Eonomic Council of Canada, *Interim Report on Competition Policy* (Ottawa: Queen's Printer, July 1969), pp. 213–218; and Federal Trade Commission staff report, *Conglomerate Merger Performance: An Empirical Analysis of Nine Corporations* (Washington: Government Printing Office, 1972), pp. 37, 41, and 47–49.

research-based enterprises were acquired.[18] Once such creative individuals are ensconced in the larger, more bureaucratic R & D organizations of large acquirers, however, they often become frustrated. A study by super-computer specialist Control Data Corporation revealed that fewer than 15 percent of the innovative engineers and scientists recruited through acquisitions over a period of twenty-two years remained with the company.[19] More generally, a statistical analysis covering 2,955 lines of business showed that having all of a line's assets stemming from conglomerate mergers was associated with R & D/sales ratios 18 percent lower on average than those prevailing generally in the industry in which the unit operated.[20]

Finally, there is the possibility that mergers infuse superior new management into companies suffering from talent or motivational deficiencies. Or they may permit managerial overhead streamlining.

U.S. Department of Justice and Federal Trade Commission Horizontal Merger Guidelines, 1992

[Ed. The reasons for concern about anticompetitive effects of mergers and the structure of the analysis under which they are reviewed are summarized in the introduction to the joint Department of Justice–FTC merger guidelines.]

1.   Purpose and Underlying Policy Assumptions of the Guidelines

Mergers are motivated by the prospect of financial gains. The possible sources of the financial gains from mergers are many, and the Guidelines do not attempt to identify all possible sources of gain in every merger. Instead, the Guidelines focus on the one potential source of gain that is of concern under the antitrust laws: market power.

The unifying theme of the Guidelines is that mergers should not be permitted to create or enhance market power or to facilitate its exercise. Market power to a seller is the ability profitably to maintain prices above competitive levels for a significant period of time.[21] In some circumstances, a sole seller (a "monopolist") of a product with no good substitutes can maintain a selling price that is above the level that would prevail if the market were competitive. Similarly, in some circumstances, where only a

---

18. *See* Murray N. Friedman, *The Research and Development Factor in Mergers and Acquisitions,* Study No. 16, U.S. Senate Committee on the Judiciary; Subcommittee on Patents, Trademarks, and Copyrights (Washington: USGPO, 1958). In a survey of venture capital institutions, Robert Premus found that approximately 42 percent of the new high-technology companies in which the funds invested were expected to "go public" with their own stock exchange listings, 26 percent would merge with larger firms, 19 percent would "just survive," and 13 percent would fail outright. *Venture Capital and Innovation,* study prepared for the Joint Economic Committee, U.S. Congress (Washington: USGPO, 1985), p. 35. Premus' percentages for three size categories were weighted to yield the overall averages reported here.

19. William C. Norris, "The Social Costs of Takeovers," *Corporate Report,* September 1983, p. 47.

20. Ravenscraft and Scherer, *Mergers,* pp. 120–121.

21. Sellers with market power also may lessen competition on dimensions other than price, such as product quality, service, or innovation.

few firms account for most of the sales of a product, those firms can exercise market power, perhaps even approximating the performance of a monopolist, by either explicitly or implicitly coordinating their actions. Circumstances also may permit a single firm, not a monopolist, to exercise market power through unilateral or non-coordinated conduct—conduct the success of which does not rely on the concurrence of other firms in the market or on coordinated responses by those firms. In any case, the result of the exercise of market power is a transfer of wealth from buyers to sellers or a misallocation of resources.

Market power also encompasses the ability of a single buyer (a "monopsonist"), a coordinating group of buyers, or a single buyer, not a monopsonist, to depress the price paid for a product to a level that is below the competitive price and thereby depress output. The exercise of market power by buyers ("monopsony power") has adverse effects comparable to those associated with the exercise of market power by sellers. In order to assess potential monopsony concerns, the Agency will apply an analytical framework analogous to the framework of these Guidelines.

While challenging competitively harmful mergers, the Agency seeks to avoid unnecessary interference with the larger universe of mergers that are either competitively beneficial or neutral. In implementing this objective, however, the Guidelines reflect the congressional intent that merger enforcement should interdict competitive problems in their incipiency.

2.   Overview

The Guidelines describe the analytical process that the Agency will employ in determining whether to challenge a horizontal merger. First, the Agency assesses whether the merger would significantly increase concentration and result in a concentrated market, properly defined and measured. Second, the Agency assesses whether the merger, in light of market concentration and other factors that characterize the market, raises concern about potential adverse competitive effects. Third, the Agency assesses whether entry would be timely, likely and sufficient either to deter or to counteract the competitive effects of concern. Fourth, the Agency assesses any efficiency gains that reasonably cannot be achieved by the parties through other means. Finally the Agency assesses whether, but for the merger, either party to the transaction would be likely to fail, causing its assets to exit the market. The process of assessing market concentration, potential adverse competitive effects, entry, efficiency and failure is a tool that allows the Agency to answer the ultimate inquiry in merger analysis: whether the merger is likely to create or enhance market power or to facilitate its exercise.

NOTES

1. As Chapter 6 indicates, the state of economic knowledge about the consequences of industrial concentration is still relatively rudimentary, subject to sub-

stantial debate, and somewhat in flux. Traditional economic theory emphasizes that the "fewness" of firms in a market is a "necessary" but not "sufficient" prerequisite to higher prices and profits, lower output, and generally poor performance. During the past three decades in particular, however, "revisionist" economists have argued that high concentration most often results from efficiency considerations and that concentrated markets often work well.

This led Professors Scherer and Ross to conclude:

> Economists have developed literally dozens of oligopoly pricing theories—some simple, some marvels of mathematical complexity. Recognizing the wide range of behavioral and theoretical predictions, some economists have asserted that the oligopoly problem is indeterminate. This is correct in the narrow sense that one cannot forge unique and compelling mechanistic links from cost and demand conditions to price equilibria. But a more constructive interpretation is this: To make workable predictions, we need a theory much richer than the received theories of pure competition and monopoly—a theory that includes variables irrelevant to these polar cases. We must not expect too much, however. The most that can be hoped for is a kind of soft determinism: an understanding of broad tendencies and predictions correct on the average, but subject to occasional substantial errors.[22]

Some economic studies have found that high market shares of the leading firm or the two leading firms in a market are a more significant determinant of excessive profitability than concentration.[23] The reasons for the reported significance of high market share are still being debated. But there appears to be no doubt that many firms are acting on the assumption that high market share will, at least in the long run, lead to high profitability.

2. Largely influenced by economic analysis, there is an increased level of skepticism that mergers that leave a significant number of firms in the market—for example, that reduce the number of significant firms to seven or eight—have much of an impact on competition. Also, there is an increasing awareness that some mergers might be competitively beneficial, at least as long as the number of firms did not become too few. *Cf.* Weiss, "The Structure–Conduct—Performance Paradigm and Antitrust," 127 U.Pa. L.Rev. 1104, 1119 (1979).

As you read the cases set out in Section 2 of this Chapter, consider what effect, if any, these continuing dialogues among industrial organization economists should have on horizontal merger policy. Given the limits as to what economists now know or can agree upon, should we be cautious about erring on the side of a permissive horizontal merger policy? What are the costs of a relatively restrictive merger policy? If major markets become too concentrated and this results in poor economic performance, do we have the "tools" to undo the harm?

3. Recent economic studies also have emphasized the existence of barriers to entry as a crucial determinant of noncompetitive pricing and performance. As you read the cases in Section 2, consider whether courts have paid sufficient attention or excessive attention to barriers to entry.

---

22. Scherer & Ross, Industrial Market Structure and Economic Performance 199–200 (3d ed. 1990).

23. *See, e.g.*, Kwoka & Ravenscraft, Collusion vs. Rivalry: Price–Cost Margins by Line of Business, 53 Economica 642 (1986); Kwoka, Does the Choice of Concentration Measure Really Matter?, 29 J. Industrial Economics 445 (1981).

United States v. Philadelphia National Bank

Supreme Court of the United States, 1963.
374 U.S. 321, 83 S.Ct. 1715, 10 L.Ed.2d 915.

■ BRENNAN, J. The United States, appellant here, brought this civil action . . . to enjoin a proposed merger of The Philadelphia National Bank (PNB) and Girard Trust Corn Exchange Bank (Girard), appellees here. . . . We reverse the judgment of the District Court [upholding the merger]. We hold that the merger of appellees is forbidden by § 7 of the Clayton Act and so must be enjoined. . . .

I.   The Facts and Proceedings Below

A.   *The Background: Commercial Banking in the United States*

Because this is the first case which has required this Court to consider the application of the antitrust laws to the commercial banking industry, and because aspects of the industry and of the degree of governmental regulation of it will recur throughout our discussion, we deem it appropriate to begin with a brief background description.

Commercial banking in this country is primarily unit banking. That is, control of commercial banking is diffused throughout a very large number of independent, local banks—13,460 of them in 1960—rather than concentrated in a handful of nationwide banks, as, for example, in England and Germany. There are, to be sure, in addition to the independent banks, some 10,000 branch banks; but branching, which is controlled largely by state law—and prohibited altogether by some States—enables a bank to extend itself only to state lines and often not that far. It is also the case, of course, that many banks place loans and solicit deposits outside their home area. But with these qualifications, it remains true that ours is essentially a decentralized system of community banks. Recent years, however, have witnessed a definite trend toward concentration. Thus, during the decade ending in 1960 the number of commercial banks in the United States declined by 714, despite the chartering of 887 new banks and a very substantial increase in the Nation's credit needs during the period. Of the 1,601 independent banks which thus disappeared, 1,503, with combined total resources of well over $25,000,000,000, disappeared as the result of mergers. . . .

Banking operations are varied and complex; "commercial banking" describes a congeries of services and credit devices.[24] But among them the

---

    24. The principal banking "products" are of course various types of credit, for example: unsecured personal and business loans, mortgage loans, loans secured by securities or accounts receivable, automobile installment and consumer goods installment loans, tuition financing, bank credit cards, revolving credit funds. Banking services include: acceptance of demand deposits from individuals, corporations, governmental agencies, and other banks; acceptance of time and savings deposits; estate and trust planning and trusteeship services; lock boxes and safety deposit boxes; account reconciliation services; foreign department services (acceptances and letters of credit); correspondent services; investment advice. It should be noted that many other institutions are in the business of supplying credit, and so more or less in competition with commercial banks . . ., for example: mutual savings banks, creation of additional money and credit, the management of the checking-account system, and the furnishing of short-term business loans, would appear to be the most important. For the proper discharge of these functions is indispensable to a healthy national economy, as the role of bank failures in depression periods attests. It is therefore not surprising that commercial banking in the United States is subject to a variety of governmental controls, state and federal.

Federal supervision of banking has been called "[p]robably the outstanding example in the federal government of regulation of an entire industry through methods of supervision. . . . The system may be one of the most successful [systems of economic regulation], if not the most successful." . . . To the efficacy of this system we may owe, in part, the virtual disappearance of bank failures from the American economic scene.

B. *The Proposed Merger of PNB and Girard*

The Philadelphia National Bank and Girard Trust Corn Exchange Bank are, respectively, the second and third largest of the 42 commercial banks with head offices in the Philadelphia metropolitan area, which consists of the City of Philadelphia and its three contiguous counties in Pennsylvania. The home county of both banks is the city itself; Pennsylvania law, however, permits branching into the counties contiguous to the home county, Pa.Stat.Ann. (1961 Supp.), Tit. 7, §§ 819–204.1, and both banks have offices throughout the four-county area. PNB, a national bank, has assets of over $1,000,000,000, making it (as of 1959) the twenty-first largest bank in the Nation. Girard, a state bank, is a member of the FRS and is insured by the FDIC; it has assets of about $750,000,000. Were the proposed merger to be consummated, the resulting bank would be the largest in the four-county area, with (approximately) 36% of the area banks' total assets, 36% of deposits, and 34% of net loans. It and the second largest (First Pennsylvania Bank and Trust Company, now the largest) would have between them 59% of the total assets, 58% of deposits, and 58% of the net loans, while after the merger the four largest banks in the area would have 78% of total assets, 77% of deposits, and 78% of net loans.

The present size of both PNB and Girard is in part the result of mergers. Indeed, the trend toward concentration is noticeable in the Philadelphia area generally, in which the number of commercial banks has declined from 108 in 1947 to the present 42. Since 1950, PNB has acquired nine formerly independent banks and Girard six; and these acquisitions have accounted for 59% and 85% of the respective banks' asset growth during the period, 63% and 91% of their deposit growth, and 12% and 37% of their loan growth. During this period, the seven largest banks in the area increased their combined share of the area's total commercial bank resources from about 61% to about 90%. . . .

---

savings and loan associations, credit unions, personal-finance companies, sales-finance companies, private businessmen (through the furnishing of trade credit), factors, direct-lending government agencies, the Post Office, Small Business Investment Corporations, life insurance companies.

C. *The Trial and the District Court's Decision*

The Government's case in the District Court relied chiefly on statistical evidence bearing upon market structure and on testimony by economists and bankers to the effect that, notwithstanding the intensive governmental regulation of banking, there was a substantial area for the free play of competitive forces; that concentration of commercial banking, which the proposed merger would increase was inimical to that free play; that the principal anticompetitive effect of the merger would be felt in the area in which the banks had their offices, thus making the four-county metropolitan area the relevant geographical market; and that commercial banking was the relevant product market. The defendants, in addition to offering contrary evidence on these points, attempted to show business justifications for the merger. They conceded that both banks were economically strong and had sound management, but offered the testimony of bankers to show that the resulting bank, with its greater prestige and increased lending limit,[25] would be better able to compete with large out-of-state (particularly New York) banks, would attract new business to Philadelphia, and in general would promote the economic development of the metropolitan area. ... [The Court next explained its reasons for (1) affirming the district court's holding that the passage of the Bank Merger Act of 1960 did not repeal by implication the antitrust laws insofar as they might apply to bank mergers, and (2) reversing the district court's holding that § 7 of the Clayton Act is inapplicable to bank mergers.]

III.   The Lawfulness of the Proposed Merger Under Section 7

The statutory test is whether the effect of the merger "may be substantially to lessen competition" "in any line of commerce in any section of the country." We analyzed the test in detail in *Brown Shoe Co. v. United States*, 370 U.S. 294, and that analysis need not be repeated or extended here, for the instant case presents only a straightforward problem of application to particular facts.

We have no difficulty in determining the "line of commerce" (relevant product or services market) and "section of the country" (relevant geographical market) in which to appraise the probable competitive effects of appellees' proposed merger. We agree with the District Court that the cluster of products (various kinds of credit) and services (such as checking accounts and trust administration) denoted by the term "commercial banking," see note [24 at 979], *supra*, composes a distinct line of commerce. Some commercial banking products or services are so distinctive that they are entirely free of effective competition from products or services of other financial institutions; the checking account is in this category. Others enjoy such cost advantages as to be insulated within a broad range from substitutes furnished by other institutions. For example, commercial banks compete with small-loan companies in the personal-loan market; but the

---

25. See 12 U.S.C.A § 84. The resulting bank would have a lending limit of $15,000,000, of which $1,000,000 would not be attributable to the merger but to unrelated accounting factors.

small-loan companies' rates are invariably much higher than the banks', in part, it seems, because the companies' working capital consists in substantial part of bank loans. Finally, there are banking facilities which, although in terms of cost and price they are freely competitive with the facilities provided by other financial institutions, nevertheless enjoy a settled consumer preference, insulating them, to a marked degree, from competition; this seems to be the case with savings deposits.[26] In sum, it is clear that commercial banking is a market "sufficiently inclusive to be meaningful in terms of trade realities."

We part company with the District Court on the determination of the appropriate "section of the country." The proper question to be asked in this case is not where the parties to the merger do business or even where they compete, but where, within the area of competitive overlap, the effect of the merger on competition will be direct and immediate. See Bock, Mergers and Markets (1960), 42. This depends upon "the geographic structure of supplier-customer relations." Kaysen and Turner, Antitrust Policy (1959), 102. In banking, as in most service industries, convenience of location is essential to effective competition. Individuals and corporations typically confer the bulk of their patronage on banks in their local community; they find it impractical to conduct their banking business at a distance.[27] See *Transamerica Corp. v. Board of Govs. of Fed.Res.Sys.*, 206 F.2d 163, 169 (C.A.3d Cir., 1953). The factor of inconvenience localizes banking competition as effectively as high transportation costs in other industries. See, *e.g.*, *American Crystal Sugar Co. v. Cuban–American Sugar Co.*, 152 F.Supp. 387, 398 (S.D.N.Y.1957), affirmed, 259 F.2d 524 (C.A.2d Cir., 1958). Therefore, since as we recently said in a related context the "area of effective competition in the known line of commerce must be charted by careful selection of the market area in which the seller operates, and to which the purchaser can practically turn for supplies," *Tampa Elec.*

---

26. As one witness for the defendants testified:

"We have had in Philadelphia for 50 years or more the mutual savings banks offering ½ per cent and in some instances more than ½ per cent higher interest than the commercial banks. Nevertheless, the rate of increase in savings accounts in commercial banks has kept pace with and in many of the banks exceeded the rate of increase of the mutual banks paying 3½ per cent. . . .

"I have made some inquiries. There are four banks on the corner of Broad and Chestnut. Three of them are commercial banks all offering 3 per cent, and one is a mutual savings bank offering 3½. As far as I have been able to discover, there isn't anybody in Philadelphia who will take the trouble to walk across Broad Street to get ½ of 1 percent more interest. If you ask me why, I will say I do not know. Habit, custom, personal relationships, convenience, doing all your banking under one roof appear to be factors superior to changes in the interest rate level." (R. 1388–1389.)

27. As far as the customer for a bank loan is concerned, "the size of his market is somewhat dependent upon his own size, how well he is known, and so on. For example, for small business concerns known primarily locally, they may consider that their market is a strictly local one, and they may be forced by circumstances to do business with banks in a nearby geographic relationship to them. On the other hand, as businesses increase in size, the scope of their business activities, their national reputation, the alternatives, they have available to them will be spread again over a very large area, possibly as large as the entire United States." (R. 1372.) (Defendants' testimony on direct examination.)

Co. v. Nashville Coal Co., 365 U.S. 320, 327 (emphasis supplied); see *Standard Oil Co. v. United States*, 337 U.S. 293, 299 and 300, n. 5, the four-county area in which appellees' offices are located would seem to be the relevant geographical market. Cf. *Brown Shoe Co., supra*, 370 U.S. at 338–339. In fact, the vast bulk of appellees' business originates in the four-county area. Theoretically, we should be concerned with the possibility that bank offices on the perimeter of the area may be in effective competition with bank offices within; actually, this seems to be a factor of little significance.[28]

We recognize that the area in which appellees have their offices does not delineate with perfect accuracy an appropriate "section of the country" in which to appraise the effect of the merger upon competition. Large borrowers and large depositors, the record shows, may find it practical to do a large part of their banking business outside their home community; very small borrowers and depositors may, as a practical matter, be confined to bank offices in their immediate neighborhood; and customers of intermediate size, it would appear, deal with banks within an area intermediate between these extremes. So also, some banking services are evidently more local in nature than others. But that in banking the relevant geographical market is a function of each separate customer's economic scale means simply that a workable compromise must be found: some fair intermediate delineation which avoids the indefensible extremes of drawing the market either so expansively as to make the effect of the merger upon competition seem insignificant, because only the very largest bank customers are taken into account in defining the market, or so narrowly as to place appellees in different markets, because only the smallest customers are considered. We think that the four-county Philadelphia metropolitan area, which state law apparently recognizes as a meaningful banking community in allowing Philadelphia banks to branch within it, and which would seem roughly to delineate the area in which bank customers that are neither very large nor very small find it practical to do their banking business, is a more appropriate "section of the country" in which to appraise the instant

---

28. Appellees suggest not that bank offices skirting the four-county area provide meaningful alternatives to bank customers within the area, but that such alternatives are provided by large banks, from New York and elsewhere, which solicit business in the Philadelphia area. There is no evidence of the amount of business done in the area by banks with offices outside the area; it may be that such figures are unobtainable. In any event, it would seem from the local orientation of banking insofar as smaller customers are concerned, that competition from outside the area would only be important to the larger borrowers and depositors. If so, the four-county area remains a valid geographical market in which to assess the anticompetitive effect of the proposed merger upon the banking facilities available to the smaller customer—a perfectly good "line of commerce," in light of Congress' evident concern, in enacting the 1950 amendments to § 7, with preserving small business. See Brown Shoe Co., *supra*, 370 U.S., at 315–316. As a practical matter the small businessman can only satisfy his credit needs at local banks. To be sure, there is still some artificiality in deeming the four-county area the relevant "section of the country" so far as businessmen located near the perimeter are concerned. But such fuzziness would seem inherent in any attempt to delineate relevant geographical market. Note, 52 Colum.L.Rev. 766, 778–779, n. 77 (1952). And it is notable that outside the four-county area, appellees' business rapidly thins out....

merger than any larger or smaller or different area. Cf. Hale and Hale, Market Power: Size and Shape Under the Sherman Act (1958), 119. . . .

Having determined the relevant market, we come to the ultimate question under § 7: whether the effect of the merger "may be substantially to lessen competition" in the relevant market. Clearly, this is not the kind of question which is susceptible of a ready and precise answer in most cases. It requires not merely an appraisal of the immediate impact of the merger upon competition, but a prediction of its impact upon competitive conditions in the future; this is what is meant when it is said that the amended § 7 was intended to arrest anticompetitive tendencies in their "incipiency." See *Brown Shoe Co.*, *supra*, 370 U.S., at 317, 322. Such a prediction is sound only if it is based upon a firm understanding of the structure of the relevant market; yet the relevant economic data are both complex and elusive. See generally Bok, Section 7 of the Clayton Act and the Merging of Law and Economics, 74 Harv.L.Rev. 226 (1960). And unless businessmen can assess the legal consequences of a merger with some confidence, sound business planning is retarded. . . . So also, we must be alert to the danger of subverting congressional intent by permitting a too-broad economic investigation. *Standard Oil Co. of Cal. v. United States*, 337 U.S. 293. And so in any case in which it is possible, without doing violence to the congressional objective embodied in § 7, to simplify the test of illegality, the courts ought to do so in the interest of sound and practical judicial administration. . . . This is such a case.

We noted in *Brown Shoe Co.*, *supra*, that "[t]he dominant theme pervading congressional consideration of the 1950 amendments [to § 7] was a fear of what was considered to be a rising tide of economic concentration in the American economy." This intense congressional concern with the trend toward concentration warrants dispensing, in certain cases, with elaborate proof of market structure, market behavior, or probable anticompetitive effects. Specifically, we think that a merger which produces a firm controlling an undue percentage share of the relevant market, and results in a significant increase in the concentration of firms in that market is so inherently likely to lessen competition substantially that it must be enjoined in the absence of evidence clearly showing that the merger is not likely to have such anticompetitive effects. . . .

Such a test lightens the burden of proving illegality only with respect to mergers whose size makes them inherently suspect in light of Congress' design in § 7 to prevent undue concentration. Furthermore, the test is fully consonant with economic theory.[29] That "[c]ompetition is likely to be greatest when there are many sellers, none of which has any significant market share," is common ground among most economists, and was undoubtedly a premise of congressional reasoning about the antimerger statute.

---

29. See Kaysen and Turner, Antitrust Policy (1959), 133; Stigler, Mergers and Preventive Antitrust Policy, 104 U. of Pa.L.Rev. 176, 182 (1955); Bok, *supra*, at 308–316, 328. Cf. Markham, Merger Policy Under the New Section 7: A Six–Year Appraisal, 43 Va.L.Rev. 489, 521–522 (1957).

The merger of appellees will result in a single bank's controlling at least 30% of the commercial banking business in the four-county Philadelphia metropolitan area. Without attempting to specify the smallest market share which would still be considered to threaten undue concentration, we are clear that 30% presents that threat.[30] Further, whereas presently the two largest banks in the area (First Pennsylvania and PNB) control between them approximately 44% of the area's commercial banking business, the two largest after the merger (PNB–Girard and First Pennsylvania) will control 59%. Plainly, we think, this increase of more than 33% in concentration must be regarded as significant.[31]

Our conclusion that these percentages raise an inference that the effect of the contemplated merger of appellees may be substantially to lessen competition is not an arbitrary one, although neither the terms of § 7 nor the legislative history suggests that any particular percentage share was deemed critical. The House Report states that the tests of illegality under amended § 7 "are intended to be similar to those which the courts have applied in interpreting the same language as used in other sections of the Clayton Act." H.R.Rep. No. 1191, 81st Cong., 1st Sess. 8. Accordingly, we have relied upon decisions under these other sections in applying § 7. See *Brown Shoe Co., supra, passim;* cf. *United States v. E.I. Du Pont De Nemours & Co.,* 353 U.S. 586, 595, and n. 15. In *Standard Oil Co. of Cal. v. United States,* 337 U.S. 293, cited in S.Rep. No. 1775, 81st Cong., 2d Sess. 6, this Court held violative of § 3 of the Clayton Act exclusive contracts whereby the defendant company, which accounted for 23% of the sales in the relevant market and, together with six other firms, accounted for 65% of such sales, maintained control over outlets through which approximately 7% of the sales were made. In *Federal Trade Comm'n v. Motion Picture Adv. Serv. Co.,* 344 U.S. 392, we held unlawful, under § 1 of the Sherman Act and § 5 of the Federal Trade Commission Act, rather than under § 3 of the Clayton Act, exclusive arrangements whereby the four major firms in the industry had foreclosed 75% of the relevant market; the respondent's market share, evidently, was 20%. Kessler and Stern, Competition, Contract, and Vertical Integration, 69 Yale L.J. 1, 53 n. 231 (1959). In the

---

30. Kaysen and Turner, *supra*, note [29], suggest that 20% should be the line of prima facie unlawfulness; Stigler suggests that any acquisition by a firm controlling 20% of the market after the merger is presumptively unlawful; Markham mentions 25%. Bok's principal test is increase in market concentration, and he suggests a figure of 7% or 8%. [And consider the *Columbia Steel* case, a prime target of the amendment of § 7, which in its horizontal aspect resulted in the creation of a firm with 24% of the market.] We intimate no view on the validity of such tests for we have no need to consider percentages smaller than those in the case at bar, but we note that such tests are more rigorous than is required to dispose of the instant case. Needless to say, the fact that a merger results in a less-than-30% market share, or in a less substantial increase in concentration than in the instant case, does not raise an inference that the merger is *not* violative of § 7.

31. It is no answer that, among the three presently largest firms (First Pennsylvania, PNB, and Girard), there will be no increase in concentration. If this argument were valid, then once a market had become unduly concentrated, further concentration would be legally privileged. On the contrary, if concentration is already great, the importance of preventing even slight increases in concentration and so preserving the possibility of eventual deconcentration is correspondingly great....

instant case, by way of comparison, the four largest banks after the merger will foreclose 78% of the relevant market.... And in *Standard Fashion Co. v. Magrane–Houston Co.*, 258 U.S. 346, the Court held violative of § 3 a series of exclusive contracts whereby a single manufacturer controlled 40% of the industry's retail outlets. Doubtless these cases turned to some extent upon whether "by the nature of the market there is room for newcomers." *Federal Trade Com'n v. Motion Picture Adv. Serv. Co., supra*, 344 U.S., at 395. But they remain highly suggestive in the present context, for as we noted in *Brown Shoe Co., supra*, integration by merger is more suspect than integration by contract, because of the greater permanence of the former. The market share and market concentration figures in the contract-integration cases, taken together with scholarly opinion, ... support, we believe, the inference we draw in the instant case from the figure disclosed by the record....[32]

We turn now to three affirmative justifications which appellees offer for the proposed merger. The first is that only through mergers can banks follow their customers to the suburbs and retain their business. This justification does not seem particularly related to the instant merger, but in any event it has no merit. There is an alternative to the merger route: the opening of new branches in the areas to which the customers have moved— so-called de novo branching. Appellees do not contend that they are unable to expand thus, by opening new offices rather than acquiring existing ones, and surely one premise of an antimerger statute such as § 7 is that corporate growth by internal expansion is socially preferable to growth by acquisition.

Second, it is suggested that the increased lending limit of the resulting bank will enable it to compete with the large out-of-state bank, particularly the New York banks, for very large loans. We reject this application of the concept of "countervailing power." Cf. *Kiefer–Stewart Co. v. Joseph E. Seagram & Sons*, 340 U.S. 211. If anticompetitive effects in one market could be justified by procompetitive consequences in another, the logical upshot would be that every firm in an industry could, without violating § 7, embark on a series of mergers that would make it in the end as large as the industry leader. For if all the commercial banks in the Philadelphia area merged into one, it would be smaller than the largest bank in New York City. This is not a case, plainly, where two small firms in a market propose to merge in order to be able to compete more successfully with the leading firms in that market. Nor is it a case in which lack of adequate banking facilities is causing hardships to individuals or businesses in the community. The present two largest banks in Philadelphia have lending limits of $8,000,000 each. The only businesses located in the Philadelphia area which find such limits inadequate are large enough readily to obtain bank credit in other cities.

---

32. "[C]ongressional concern [was] with the protection of *competition,* not *competitors.*" Brown Shoe Co., *supra*, 370 U.S. at 320. In an oligopolistic market, small companies may be perfectly content to follow the high prices set by the dominant firms, yet the market may be profoundly anticompetitive.

This brings us to appellees' final contention, that Philadelphia needs a bank larger than it now has in order to bring business to the area and stimulate its economic development.... We are clear, however, that a merger the effect of which "may be substantially to lessen competition" is not saved because, on some ultimate reckoning of social or economic debits and credits, it may be deemed beneficial. A value choice of such magnitude is beyond the ordinary limits of judicial competence, and in any event has been made for us already, by Congress when it enacted the amended § 7. Congress determined to preserve our traditionally competitive economy. It therefore proscribed anticompetitive mergers, the benign and the malignant alike, fully aware, we must assume, that some price might have to be paid.

In holding as we do that the merger of appellees would violate § 7 and must therefore be enjoined, we reject appellees' pervasive suggestion that application of the procompetitive policy of § 7 to the banking industry will have dire, although unspecified, consequences for the national economy. Concededly, PNB and Girard are healthy and strong; they are not undercapitalized or overloaned; they have no management problems; the Philadelphia area is not overbanked; ruinous competition is not in the offing. Section 7 does not mandate cutthroat competition in the banking industry, and does not exclude defenses based on dangers to liquidity or solvency, if to avert them a merger is necessary.[33] It does require, however, that the forces of competition be allowed to operate within the broad framework of governmental regulation of the industry....

Reversed and remanded with direction.[34]

NOTE ON MERGER CASES DURING THE 1960S

After *Philadelphia National Bank*, a relatively large number of merger cases reached the Supreme Court during the 1960s. The Court's decisions almost always favored those opposing a merger. Critics of the Court's decisions pointed to lack of precision in its analysis, alleged "gerrymandering" of market definitions to produce results favorable to the government, overly aggressive use of the "incipiency" concept, and inadequate concern for the efficiency-enhancing aspects of proposed mergers. As Justice Stewart put it in dissenting in *Von's Grocery* (p. 989 *infra*): "The Court has substituted bare conjecture for the statutory standard of a reasonable probability that competition may be lessened.... The sole consistency that I can find [in the Court's decisions] is that in litigation under § 7, the Government always wins." The following cases—some easier to defend than others—are representative of the Court's merger jurisprudence during the 1960s.

---

33. Thus, arguably, the so-called failing-company defense, see *International Shoe Co. v. Federal Trade Comm'n*, 280 U.S. 291, 299–303, might have somewhat larger contours as applied to bank mergers because of the greater public impact of a bank failure compared with ordinary business failures. But the question what defenses in § 7 actions must be allowed in order to avert unsound banking conditions is not before us, and we intimate no view upon it.

34. White, J., did not participate in the decision of this case. The dissenting opinion of Harlan, J., in which Stewart, J., joined, is omitted.

1.   United States v. Aluminum Co. of America, 377 U.S. 271, 84 S.Ct. 1283, 12 L.Ed.2d, 314 (1964). There is a long history of the enforcement agencies and the courts taking into account whether one of the parties to a merger, usually the acquired firm, is a "maverick"—*i.e.*, a firm that, as a result of aggressive pricing or innovation, makes it difficult for other firms in the market to achieve coordinated results. *See* J. Baker, "Mavericks, Mergers and Exclusion: Providing Coordinated Competitive Effects Under the Antitrust Laws," 77 NYU L.Rev. 135 (2002). An extreme example involved a successful challenge to Alcoa, the leading producer in several lines of aluminum wire and cable, when it attempted in 1964 to acquire Rome Cable, a company principally in the cooper wire and cable line, but with some production in aluminum wire and cable. Rome Cable was a small company that added little to Alcoa's existing market share; Rome accounted for 0.3% of total industry production of bare aluminum conductor, 4.7% of insulated aluminum conductor, and 1.3% of the broader aluminum conductor line.

The Supreme Court acknowledged that acquisition of a company with such small market shares would rarely result in a finding of a violation, but observed that Rome was an aggressive, independent competitor that had been a pioneer in aluminum insulation and continued to have an active and efficient research and sales organization; and Rome had a broad line of quality cooper wire and cable products and special aptitudes and skill in insulation. The Court concluded: "Preservation of Rome, rather than its absorption by one of the giants, will keep it as an 'important competitive factor.' ... Rome seems to us the prototype of the small independent that Congress aimed to preserve by § 7."

2.   United States v. Pabst Brewing Co., 384 U.S. 546, 86 S.Ct. 1665, 16 L.Ed.2d 765 (1966). In 1958, the Pabst Brewing Co., the nation's tenth largest brewer, acquired the Blatz Brewing Company, the eighteenth largest. The two companies competed against each other in 40 states, and in 1957, had combined sales of 23.95% of beer sales in Wisconsin, 11.32% of sales in the three-state area of Wisconsin, Illinois and Michigan, and 4.49% of sales throughout the country. By 1961, three years after the merger, Pabst had increased its share of the national beer market to 5.83% and ranked third in the country. The district court dismissed the government's complaint, holding that it failed to show that Wisconsin or the three-state area were proper relevant geographic markets, and had not shown substantial anticompetitive effects in a national market. The Supreme Court reversed. On the relevant geographic market question, Justice Black wrote:

> Apparently the District Court thought that in order to show a violation of § 7 it was essential for the Government to show a "relevant geographic market" in the same way the corpus delicti must be proved to establish a crime. But when the Government brings an action under § 7 it must, according to the language of the statute, prove no more than that there has been a merger between two corporations engaged in commerce and that the effect of the merger may be substantially to lessen competition or tend to create a monopoly in any line of commerce "in any section of the country." (Emphasis supplied.) The language of this section requires merely that the Government prove the merger has a substantial anti-competitive effect somewhere in the United States—"in any section" of the United States. This phrase does not call for the delineation of a "section of the country" by metes and bounds as a surveyor would lay off a plot of ground. The Government may introduce evidence which shows that as a result of a merger competition may be substantially lessened throughout the country, or on the other hand it may prove that competition may be substantially lessened only in one or more sections of the country. In either event a

violation of § 7 would be proved. Certainly the failure of the Government to prove by an army of expert witnesses what constitutes a relevant "economic" or "geographic" market is not an adequate ground on which to dismiss a § 7 case....

On the question of anticompetitive effect, the majority opinion noted that the number of breweries in the United States had declined from 714 in 1934 to 229 in 1961, and the total number of different competitors had fallen from 206 in 1957 to 162 in 1961. There had also been a sharp rise in the percentage share of the market controlled by the leading brewers. Viewing the respective market shares of Pabst and Blatz against that background, the majority found a proscribed effect on competition in Wisconsin, the three-state area, and the nation.

Justice Fortas concurred in the result, noting his view, contrary to statements in the majority opinion, that it continues to be the government's duty to prove the relevant market or "section of the country" in which the alleged anticompetitive effect had occurred.

Harlan and Stewart, JJ., concurred in the result, expressing similar misgivings about that part of the majority opinion which "appears to emasculate the statutory phrase 'in any section of the country.'"

3. United States v. Von's Grocery Co., 384 U.S. 270, 86 S.Ct. 1478, 16 L.Ed.2d 555 (1966). In 1960, Von's—ranked third in retail grocery sales in the Los Angeles area—acquired Shopping Bag Food stores, sixth in rank, to make them, combined, the second largest chain in the area. Before the merger, in 1958, the largest firm had 8% of sales; in that same year, Von's had 4.7% and Shopping Bag had 4.2%. In 1958, the top four firms had accounted for 24.4%, the top eight for 40.9%, and the top twelve for 48.8% of the Los Angeles retail grocery market. Ten years earlier, the four-firm share was 25.9%, the eight-firm share was 33.7%, and the twelve-firm share was 38.8%. During those ten years, the top ten firms had gained market share, and remained quite stable in identity. Both Von's and Shopping Bag had increased market share. After the merger, their combined share of the market was 7.5%.

The Supreme Court reversed the district court's judgment for defendants and ordered prompt divestiture. The majority pointed to the fact that the number of owners operating a single store had "decreased from 5,365 in 1950 to 3,818 in 1961," while the number and size of chains was increasing, largely as a result of "absorptions." The Court held that "these facts alone are enough to cause us to conclude ... that the ... merger did violate § 7." Justice Black's review of the legislative history of the 1950 amendments that "revitalized § 7" led him to conclude that the Von's Grocery facts "present exactly the threatening trend toward concentration which Congress wanted to halt."

Fortas, J., did not participate, while White, J., concurred on the basis of the market share data. Justice White observed that after the "merger the four largest firms had 28.8%, the eight largest had 44%, and the twelve largest had 50%. The merger not only disposed of a substantial competitor but increased the concentration in the leading firms." Justice White noted that he did not read the Court's opinion to declare illegal every merger where the resulting firm had 7.5% of the market even "in any industry exhibiting a decided trend toward concentration."

Stewart, J., and Harlan, J., in dissent, anticipated the strong criticisms which would be leveled at the majority opinion and termed the Court's ruling "a startling *per se* rule based not on analysis of market concentration or effect on competition but a simple exercise in sums." They questioned whether a decline in the total number of sellers in the market was relevant for purposes of antitrust enforcement (as opposed to concentration among the largest sellers), and noted that a nationwide "supermarket revolution" had been taking place, adding to the intensity of competition in Los Angeles, as well as elsewhere, by replacing stodgy "mom and pop" stores with more efficient chains. They also pointed out that ease of entry with "modest initial investment" assured that vigorous competition would continue.

4. In *Philadelphia National Bank*, the Supreme Court rejected as justification for anticompetitive effects in a "local" market that the "increased lending limit of the resulting bank will enable it to compete with the large out-of-state bank." Would this rejection of "countervailing power" be as persuasive if the claim related to the need to compete in a global market with foreign companies? The Court also dismissed the allegation that the resulting bank would contribute to the economic development of Philadelphia by observing that Congress "proscribed anticompetitive mergers, the benign and malignant alike" and by noting that a "value choice" of this type "is beyond the ordinary limits of judicial competence." Do you agree with the Court's reasoning? With the rejection of this claim on the facts of the *Philadelphia National Bank* case?

5. It was against the background of very aggressive enforcement, supported consistently by the Supreme Court, that the government in 1974 finally lost a merger case in the Supreme Court. In *General Dynamics*, set out below, the Court not only rejected the government's contentions in that particular case, but signaled the beginning of a significant change in attitude toward antitrust limits on mergers.

United States v. General Dynamics Corp.

Supreme Court of the United States, 1974.
415 U.S. 486, 94 S.Ct. 1186, 39 L.Ed.2d 530.

■ STEWART, J. On September 22, 1967, the Government commenced this suit in the United States District Court for the Northern District of Illinois, challenging as violative of § 7 of the Clayton Act, 15 U.S.C. 18, the acquisition of the stock of United Electric Coal Companies by Material Service Corp. and its successor, General Dynamics Corp. After lengthy discovery proceedings, a trial was held from March 30 to April 22, 1970, and on April 13, 1972, the District Court issued an opinion and judgment finding no violation of the Clayton Act. . . .

I

At the time of the acquisition involved here, Material Service Corp. was a large midwest producer and supplier of building materials, concrete, limestone, and coal. All of its coal production was from deep-shaft mines operated by it or its affiliate, appellee Freeman Coal Mining Corp., and production from these operations amounted to 6.9 million tons of coal in 1959 and 8.4 million tons in 1967. In 1954, Material Service began to acquire the stock of United Electric Coal Companies. United Electric at all relevant times operated only strip or open pit mines in Illinois and Kentucky; at the time of trial in 1970 a number of its mines had closed and its operations had been reduced to four mines in Illinois and none in Kentucky. In 1959, it produced 3.6 million tons of coal, and by 1967, it had increased this output to 5.7 million tons. Material Service's purchase of

United Electric stock continued until 1959. At this point Material's holdings amounted to more than 34% of United Electric's outstanding shares and—all parties are now agreed on this point—Material had effective control of United Electric. The president of Freeman was elected chairman of United Electric's Executive Committee, and other changes in the corporate structure of United Electric were made at the behest of Material Service.

Some months after this takeover, Material Service was itself acquired by the appellee General Dynamics Corp. General Dynamics is a large diversified corporation, much of its revenues coming from sales of aircraft, communications, and marine products to government agencies. The trial court found that its purchase of Material Service was part of a broad diversification program aimed at expanding General Dynamics into commercial nondefense business. As a result of the purchase of Material Service, and through it, of Freeman and United Electric, General Dynamics became the Nation's fifth largest commercial coal producer. During the early 1960s General Dynamics increased its equity in United Electric by direct purchases of United Electric stock, and by 1966 it held or controlled 66.15% of United Electric's outstanding shares. In September 1966 the Board of Directors of General Dynamics authorized a tender offer to holders of the remaining United Electric stock. This offer was successful, and United Electric shortly thereafter became a wholly-owned subsidiary of General Dynamics.

The thrust of the Government's complaint was that the acquisition of United Electric by Freeman and Material Service in 1959 violated § 7 of the Clayton Act because the takeover substantially lessened competition in the production and sale of coal in either or both of two geographical markets. It contended that a relevant "section of the country" within the meaning of § 7 was, alternatively, the State of Illinois or the Eastern Interior Coal Province Sales Area, the latter being one of four major coal distribution areas recognized by the coal industry and comprising Illinois and Indiana, and parts of Kentucky, Tennessee, Iowa, Minnesota, Wisconsin, and Missouri.[35]

At trial controversy focused on three basic issues: the propriety of coal as a "line of commerce," the definition of Illinois or the Eastern Interior Coal Province Sales Area as a relevant "section of the country," and the probability of a lessening of competition within these or any other product and geographic markets resulting from the acquisition. The District Court decided against the Government on each of these issues.

---

35. Testimony at trial indicated that the Eastern Interior Coal Province—the area of coal production upon which the Eastern Coal Province Sales Area was based—was originally named by United States Geological Survey maps of the coalfields in the United States and described one portion of a sequence of coal-bearing rock formations known geologically as the Pennsylvania System. The Sales Area of the Eastern Interior Coal Province was derived from the assumption, acknowledged in the trial court's opinion, that the high costs of transporting coal—which may amount to 40% of the price of delivered coal—will inevitably give producers of coal a clear competitive advantage in sales in the immediate areas of the mines.

As to the relevant product market, the court found that coal faced strong and direct competition from other sources of energy such as oil, natural gas, nuclear energy, and geothermal power which created a cross-elasticity of demand among those various fuels. As a result, it concluded that coal, by itself, was not a permissible product market and that the "energy market" was the sole "line of commerce" in which anticompetitive effects could properly be canvassed.

Similarly, the District Court rejected the Government's proposed geographic markets on the ground that they were "based essentially on past and present production statistics and do not relate to actual coal consumption patterns." The court found that a realistic geographic market should be defined in terms of transportation arteries and freight charges that determined the cost of delivered coal to purchasers and thus the competitive position of various coal producers. In particular, it found that Freight Rate Districts, designated by the Interstate Commerce Commission for determining rail transportation rates, of which there were four in the area served by the respondent companies, were the prime determinants for the geographic competitive patterns among coal producers. In addition, the court concluded that two large and specialized coal consumption units were sufficiently differentiable in their coal use patterns to be included as relevant geographic areas.[36] In lieu of the State of Illinois or the Eastern Interior Coal Province Sales Area, the court accordingly found the relevant geographic market to be 10 smaller areas, comprising the two unique consumers together with four utility sales areas and four non-utility sales areas based on the ICC freight rate districts.

Finally, and, for purposes of this appeal most significantly, the District Court found that the evidence did not support the Government's contention that the 1959 acquisition of United Electric substantially lessened competition in any product or geographic market. This conclusion was based on four determinations made in the court's opinion. First, the court noted that while the number of coal producers in the Eastern Interior Coal Province declined from 144 to 39 during the period of 1957–1967, this reduction "occurred not because small producers have been acquired by others, but as the inevitable result of the change in the nature of demand for coal." Consequently, the court found, "this litigation presents a very different situation from that in such cases as *United States v. Philadelphia National Bank*, 374 U.S. 321 (1963), and *United States v. Von's Grocery Co.*, 384 U.S. 270 (1966) where the Supreme Court was concerned with

---

36. The trial court found that Commonwealth Edison, a large private electric utility with generation facilities in many parts of Illinois, and the Metropolitan Chicago Interstate Air Quality Control Region constituted separate and unique geographic regions. Commonwealth Edison was found to have unique attributes because of the great size of its coal consumption requirements, its distinctive distribution patterns, and its extensive commitment to air pollution programs and the development of nuclear energy. The Chicago Control Region, a congressionally designated area consisting of six counties in Illinois and two in Indiana, was distinguished from other geographic markets because of the impact of existing and anticipated air pollution regulations which would create special problems in the competition for coal sales contracts.

'preventing even slight increases in concentration.' " Second, the court noted that United Electric and Freeman were "predominantly complementary in nature" since "United Electric is a strip mining company with no experience in deep mining nor likelihood of acquiring it [and] Freeman is a deep mining company with no experience or expertise in strip mining." *Ibid.* Third, the court found that if Commonwealth Edison, a large investor-owned public utility, were excluded, "none of the sales by United Electric in the period 1965 to 1967, the years chosen by the Government for analysis, would have or could have been competitive with Freeman, had the two companies been independent," because of relative distances from potential consumers and the resultant impact on relative competitive position. *Ibid.* Finally, the court found that United Electric's coal reserves were so low that its potential to compete with other coal producers in the future was far weaker than the aggregate production statistics relied on by the Government might otherwise have indicated. In particular, the court found that virtually all of United Electric's proven coal reserves were either depleted or already committed by long-term contracts with large customers, and that United Electric's power to affect the price of coal was thus severely limited and steadily diminishing. On the basis of these considerations, the court concluded: "Under these circumstances, continuation of the affiliation between United Electric and Freeman is not adverse to competition, nor would divestiture benefit competition even were this court to accept the Government's unrealistic product and geographic market definitions." *Id.*, at 560.

II

The Government sought to prove a violation of § 7 of the Clayton Act principally through statistics showing that within certain geographic markets the coal industry was concentrated among a small number of large producers; that this concentration was increasing; and that the acquisition of United Electric would materially enlarge the market share of the acquiring company and thereby contribute to the trend toward concentration.

The concentration of the coal market in Illinois and, alternatively, in the Eastern Interior Coal Province was demonstrated by a table of the shares of the largest two, four, and 10 coal producing firms in each of these areas and for both 1957 and 1967 that revealed the following:[37]

	Eastern Interior Coal Province		Illinois	
	1957	1967	1957	1967
Top 2 firms	29.6	48.6	37.8	52.9
Top 4 firms	43.0	62.9	54.5	75.2
Top 10 firms	65.5	91.4	84.0	98.0

---

37. The figures for 1967 reflect the impact on market concentration of the acquisition involved here.

These statistics, the Government argued, showed not only that the coal industry was concentrated among a small number of leading producers, but that the trend had been toward increasing concentration.[38] Furthermore, the undisputed fact that the number of coal-producing firms in Illinois decreased almost 73% during the period of 1957 to 1967 from 144 to 39 was claimed to be indicative of the same trend. The acquisition of United Electric by Freeman resulted in increased concentration of coal sales among the leading producers in the areas chosen by the Government, as shown by the following table:[39]

	1959			1967		
	Share of top 2 but for merger	Share of top 2 given merger	Percent increase	Share of top 2 but for merger	Share of top 2 given merger	Percent increase
Province	33.1	37.9	14.5	45.0	48.6	8.0
Illinois	36.6	44.3	22.4	44.0	52.9	20.2

Finally, the Government's statistics indicated that the acquisition increased the share of the merged company in the Illinois and Eastern Interior Coal Province coal markets by significant degrees:[40]

	Province		Illinois	
	Rank	Share (percent)	Rank	Share (percent)
1959				
Freeman		7.6		15.1
United Electric ...		4.8		8.1

38. The figures demonstrating the degree of concentration in the two coal markets chosen by the Government were roughly comparable to those in United States v. Von's Grocery Co., 384 U.S. 270, where the top four firms in the market controlled 24.4% of the sales, the top eight 40.9%, and the top 12, 48.8%. See, id., at 281 (White, J., concurring). See also United States v. Pabst Brewing Co., 384 U.S. 546, 551, where the top four producers of beer in Wisconsin were found to control 47.74% of the market, and the top 10 in the Nation and the local three-state area to control 45.06% and 58.93%, respectively. The statistics in the present case appear to represent a less advanced state of concentration than those involved in United States v. Aluminum Co. of America, 377 U.S. 271, 279, where the two largest firms held 50% of the market, and the top five and the top nine controlled, respectively, 76% and 95.7%; and in United States v. Philadelphia National Bank, 374 U.S. 321, 363, where the two largest banks controlled 44% of the pre-merger market.

39. The percentage increase in concentration asserted here was thus analogous to that found in Von's Grocery, supra, where the concentration among the top four, eight, and 12 firms was increased, respectively, by 18.0%, 7.6%, and 2.5% as a result of the merger invalidated there. In Philadelphia Bank, supra, the 34% increase in concentration in the two largest firms from 44% to 59% was found to be clearly significant. 374 U.S., at 365.

40. The 1959 Illinois figure of 23.2% was asserted by the Government to be comparable to the 23.94% share of the Wisconsin beer market found to be significant in Pabst, supra, and the 25% share controlled by the merged company in United States v. Continental Can Co., 378 U.S. 441, 461. The Province figure of 12.4% was compared with the shares held by the merged companies in Von's Grocery (7.5%), and in the Pabst national (4.49%) and three-state (11.32%) markets.

Combined	12.4	23.2
1967		
Freeman	6.5	12.9
United Electric ...	4.4	8.9
Combined	10.9	21.8

In prior decisions involving horizontal mergers between competitors, this Court has found prima facie violations of § 7 of the Clayton Act from aggregate statistics of the sort relied on by the United States in this case. In *Brown Shoe Co. v. United States*, 370 U.S. 294, the Court reviewed the legislative history of the most recent amendments to the Act and found that "[t]he dominant theme pervading congressional consideration of the 1950 amendment was a fear of what was considered to be a rising tide of economic concentration in the American economy." *Id.*, at 315. A year later, in *United States v. Philadelphia National Bank*, 374 U.S. 321, the Court clarified the relevance of a statistical demonstration of concentration in a particular industry and of the effects thereupon of a merger or acquisition with the following language:

> This intense congressional concern with the trend toward concentration warrants dispensing, in certain cases, with elaborate proof of market structure, market behavior, or probable anticompetitive effects. Specifically, we think that a merger which produces a firm controlling an undue percentage share of the relevant market, and results in a significant increase in the concentration of firms in that market, is so inherently likely to lessen competition substantially that it must be enjoined in the absence of evidence clearly showing that the merger is not likely to have such anticompetitive effects. *Id.*, at 363.

See also *United States v. Continental Can Co.*, 378 U.S. 441, 458; *United States v. Von's Grocery Co.*, 384 U.S. 270, 277; *United States v. Pabst Brewing Co.*, 384 U.S. 546, 550–552.

The effect of adopting this approach to a determination of a "substantial" lessening of competition is to allow the Government to rest its case on a showing of even small increases of market share or market concentration in those industries or markets where concentration is already great or has been recently increasing, since "if concentration is already great, the importance of preventing even slight increases in concentration and so preserving the possibility of eventual deconcentration is correspondingly great." *United States v. Aluminum Co. of America*, 377 U.S. 271, 279, *citing United States v. Philadelphia National Bank, supra*, 374 U.S., at 365, n. 42.

While the statistical showing proffered by the Government in this case, the accuracy of which was not discredited by the District Court or contested by the respondents, would under this approach have sufficed to support a finding of "undue concentration" in the absence of other considerations, the question before us is whether the District Court was justified in finding that other pertinent factors affecting the coal industry and the business of the respondents mandated a conclusion that no substantial lessening of competition occurred or was threatened by the acquisition of United Electric. We are satisfied that the court's ultimate finding was not in error.

In *Brown Shoe v. United States, supra*, we cautioned that statistics concerning market share and concentration, while of great significance, were not conclusive indicators of anticompetitive effects:

"Congress indicated plainly that a merger had to be functionally viewed, in the context of its particular industry. 370 U.S., at 321–322."

"Statistics reflecting the shares of the market controlled by the industry leaders and the parties to the merger are, of course, the primary index of market power; but only a further examination of the particular market—its structure, history and probable future—can provide the appropriate setting for judging the probable anticompetitive effect of the merger. *Id.*, at 322 n. 38."

See also *United States v. Continental Can Co., supra*, 378 U.S. at 458. In this case, the District Court assessed the evidence of the "structure, history and probable future" of the coal industry, and on the basis of this assessment found no substantial probability of anticompetitive effects from the merger.

Much of the District Court's opinion was devoted to a description of the changes that have affected the coal industry since World War II. On the basis of more than three weeks of testimony and a voluminous record, the court discerned a number of clear and significant developments in the industry. First, it found that coal had become increasingly less able to compete with other sources of energy in many segments of the energy market. Following the War the industry entirely lost its largest single purchaser of coal—the railroads—and faced increasingly stiffer competition from oil and natural gas as sources of energy for industrial and residential uses. Because of these changes in consumption patterns, coal's share of the energy resources consumed in this country fell from 78.4% in 1920 to 21.4% in 1968. The court reviewed evidence attributing this decline not only to the changing relative economics of alternative fuels and to new distribution and consumption patterns, but also to more recent concern with the effect of coal use on the environment and consequent regulation of the extent and means of much coal consumption.

Second, the court found that to a growing extent since 1954, the electric utility industry has become the mainstay of coal consumption. While electric utilities consumed only 15.76% of the coal produced nationally in 1947, their share of total consumption increased every year thereafter, and in 1968 amounted to more than 59% of all the coal consumed throughout the Nation.[41]

Third, and most significantly, the court found that to an increasing degree, nearly all coal sold to utilities is transferred under long-term

---

41. In 1968, electric utilities accounted for 59.09% of United States coal consumption, coke plants 18.20%, cement mills 1.88%, other manufacturing (including steel and rolling mills) 17.70%, and retail and miscellaneous consumers 3.14%.

requirements contracts, under which coal producers promise to meet utilities' coal consumption requirements for a fixed period of time, and at predetermined prices.... These developments in the patterns of coal distribution and consumption, the District Court found, have limited the amounts of coal immediately available for "spot" purchases on the open market, since "[t]he growing practice by coal producers of expanding mine capacity only to meet long-term contractual commitments and the gradual disappearance of the small truck mines has tended to limit the production capacity available for spot sales." *Ibid*.

Because of these fundamental changes in the structure of the market for coal, the District Court was justified in viewing the statistics relied on by the Government as insufficient to sustain its case. Evidence of past production does not, as a matter of logic, necessarily give a proper picture of a company's future ability to compete. In most situations, of course, the unstated assumption is that a company that has maintained a certain share of a market in the recent past will be in a position to do so in the immediate future. Thus, companies that have controlled sufficiently large shares of a concentrated market are barred from merger by § 7 not because of their past acts, but because their past performances imply an ability to continue to dominate with at least equal vigor. In markets involving groceries or beer, as in *Von's Market, supra*, and *Pabst, supra*, statistics involving annual sales naturally indicate the power of each company to compete in the future. Evidence of the amount of annual sales is relevant as a prediction of future competitive strength, since in most markets distribution systems and brand recognition are such significant factors that one may reasonably suppose that a company which has attracted a given number of sales will retain that competitive strength.

In the coal market, as analyzed by the District Court, however, statistical evidence of coal production was of considerably less significance. The bulk of the coal produced is delivered under long-term requirements contracts, and such sales thus do not represent the exercise of competitive power but rather the obligation to fulfill previously negotiated contracts at a previously fixed price. The focus of competition in a given time-frame is not on the disposition of coal already produced but on the procurement of new long-term supply contracts. In this situation, a company's past ability to produce is of limited significance, since it is in a position to offer for sale neither its past production nor the bulk of the coal it is presently capable of producing, which is typically already committed under a long-term supply contract. A more significant indicator of a company's power effectively to compete with other companies lies in the state of a company's uncommitted reserves of recoverable coal. A company with relatively large supplies of coal which are not already under contract to a consumer will have a more important influence upon competition in the contemporaneous negotiation of supply contracts than a firm with small reserves, even though the latter may presently produce a greater tonnage of coal. In a market where the availability and price for coal are set by long-term contracts rather than immediate or short-term purchases and sales, reserves rather than past production are the best measure of a company's ability to compete.

The testimony and exhibits in the District Court revealed that United Electric's coal reserve prospects were "unpromising." United's relative position of strength in reserves was considerably weaker than its past and current ability to produce. While United ranked fifth among Illinois coal producers in terms of annual production, it was 10th in reserve holdings, and controlled less than 1% of the reserves held by coal producers in Illinois, Indiana, and western Kentucky. Many of the reserves held by United had already been depleted, at the time of trial, forcing the closing of some of United's midwest mines.[42] Even more significantly, the District Court found that of the 52,033,304 tons of currently mineable reserves in Illinois, Indiana, and Kentucky controlled by United, only four million tons had not already been committed under long-term contracts. United was found to be facing the future with relatively depleted resources at its disposal, and with the vast majority of those resources already committed under contracts allowing no further adjustment in price. In addition, the District Court found that "United Electric has neither the possibility of acquiring more [reserves] nor the ability to develop deep coal reserves," and thus was not in a position to increase its reserves to replace those already depleted or committed. *Id.*, at 560.

Viewed in terms of present and future reserve prospects—and thus in terms of probable future ability to compete—rather than in terms of past production, the District Court held that United Electric was a far less significant factor in the coal market than the Government contended or the production statistics seemed to indicate. While the company had been and remained a "highly profitable" and efficient producer of relatively large amounts of coal, its current and future power to compete for subsequent long-term contracts was severely limited by its scarce uncommitted resources.[43] Irrespective of the company's size when viewed as a producer, its weakness as a competitor was properly analyzed by the District Court and fully substantiated that court's conclusion that its acquisition by Material Service would not "substantially ... lessen competition...." The validity of this conclusion is not undermined, we think, by the three-faceted attack made upon it by the Government in this Court—to which we now turn.

III

First, the Government urges that the court committed legal error by giving undue consideration to facts occurring after the effective acquisition

---

42. The District Court found that while United Electric held six mines operating in the midwest in 1948, it had opened only three new ones since then and four had closed because of exhaustion of reserves. The court found that the evidence showed that reserves in two other mines would soon be depleted, and the respondents inform us in their briefs that these events have already occurred.

43. As an example of the impact of depleted or committed reserves on a company's ability to compete for long-term contracts, the District Court noted that a number of requirements contracts signed by United Electric to supply coal to electric utilities were backed up by reserves belonging to Freeman and *"could not have been obtained without that guarantee"* because of the utilities' fear that the contract obligation could not otherwise be fulfilled. 341 F.Supp. at 599 (emphasis in original).

in 1959.[44] In *FTC v. Consolidated Foods Corp.*, 380 U.S. 592, 598, this Court stated that post-acquisition evidence tending to diminish the probability or impact of anticompetitive effects might be considered in a § 7 case. See also *United States v. E.I. du Pont de Nemours & Co.*, 353 U.S. 586, 597 *et seq.*, 602 *et seq.* But in *Consolidated Foods and in United States v. Continental Can Co.*, 378 U.S. 441, 463, the probative value of such evidence was found to be extremely limited, and judgments against the Government were in each instance reversed in part because "too much weight" had been given to post-acquisition events. The need for such a limitation is obvious. If a demonstration that no anticompetitive effects had occurred at the time of trial or of judgment constituted a permissible defense to a § 7 divestiture suit, violators could stave off such actions merely by refraining from aggressive or anticompetitive behavior when such a suit was threatened or pending.[45]

Furthermore, the fact that no concrete anticompetitive symptoms have occurred does not itself imply that competition has not already been affected, "for once the two companies are united no one knows what the fate of the acquired company and its competitors would have been but for the merger." *FTC v. Consolidated Foods, supra*, 380 U.S. 592, 598. And, most significantly, § 7 deals in "probabilities, not certainties," *Brown Shoe v. United States, supra*, 370 U.S., at 323, and the mere nonoccurrence of a substantial lessening of competition in the interval between acquisition and trial does not mean that no substantial lessening will develop thereafter; the essential question remains whether the probability of such future impact exists at the time of trial.

In this case, the District Court relied on evidence relating to changes in the patterns and structure of the coal industry and in United Electric's coal reserve situation after the time of acquisition in 1959. Such evidence could

---

44. The court's reliance on such facts and the absence of specific findings of fact concerning the competitive situation in 1959, at which point both sides now agree the acquisition took place, may have been engendered by the Government's apparent inconsistency in its position concerning the critical date. Certain of the respondents' proposed findings of fact concerning its resources in 1959 and its attempts to increase its depleted holdings were termed "irrelevant" by the Government at the trial.

45. The mere nonoccurrence of anticompetitive effects from a merger would, of course, merely postpone rather than preclude a divestiture suit. This Court indicated in *United States v. E.I. du Pont de Nemours & Co.*, 353 U.S. 586, 597, that a merger may be attacked *ab initio* long after its culmination if effect on competition not apparent immediately after the merger subsequently appears, since § 7 was designed to arrest the creation of monopolies "in their incipiency" and " 'incipiency' ... denotes not the time the stock was acquired but any time when the acquisition threatens to ripen into a prohibited effect...." See also *FTC v. Consolidated Foods Corp.*, 380 U.S. 592, 598. The scope this "time of suit" concept gives to the Government in attacking mergers under § 7 is discussed in Orrick, The Clayton Act: Then and Now, 24 ABA Antitrust Section 44 (1964); Subcommittee on Section 7, The Backward Sweep Theory and the Oligopoly Problem, 32 ABA Antitrust L.J. 306 (1966). In the context of the present case, the "time of suit" rule coupled with the limited weight given to post-merger evidence of no anticompetitive impact tends to give the Government a "Heads–I–win, Tails-you-lose" advantage over a § 7 defendant: post-merger evidence showing a lessening of competition may constitute an "incipiency" on which to base a divestiture suit, but evidence showing that such lessening has not, in fact, occurred cannot be accorded "too much weight."

not reflect a positive decision on the part of the merged companies to deliberately but temporarily refrain from anticompetitive actions, nor could it reasonably be thought to reflect less active competition than that which might have occurred had there not been an acquisition in 1959. As the District Court convincingly found, the trend toward increased dependence on utilities as consumers of coal and toward the near-exclusive use of long-term contracts were the products of inevitable pressures on the coal industry in all parts of the country. And unlike evidence showing only that no lessening of competition has yet occurred, the demonstration of weak coal resources necessarily and logically implied that United Electric was not merely disinclined but unable to compete effectively for future contracts. Such evidence went directly to the question of whether future lessening of competition was probable, and the District Court was fully justified in using it.

Second, the Government contends that reliance on depleted and committed resources is essentially a failing company defense which must meet the strict limits placed on that defense by this Court's decisions in *United States v. Third National Bank of Nashville*, 390 U.S. 171; *Citizen Publishing Co. v. United States*, 394 U.S. 131; and *United States v. Greater Buffalo Press, Inc.*, 402 U.S. 549. The failing company doctrine, recognized as a valid defense to a § 7 suit in *Brown Shoe, supra*, 370 U.S., at 346, was first announced by this Court in *International Shoe Co. v. FTC*, 280 U.S. 291, and was preserved by explicit references in the legislative history of the modern amendments to § 7. H.R.Rep. No. 1191, 81st Cong., 1st Sess., 6 (1949); S.Rep. No. 1775, 81st Cong., 2d Sess., 7 (1950). A company invoking the defense has the burden[46] of showing that its "resources [were] so depleted and the prospect of rehabilitation so remote that it faced the grave probability of a business failure ...," *International Shoe, supra*, 280 U.S., at 302, and further that it tried and failed to merge with a company other than the acquiring one, *Citizen Publishing Co., supra*, 394 U.S., at 138; *Greater Buffalo Press, supra*, 402 U.S., at 555.

The Government asserts that United Electric was a healthy and thriving company at the time of the acquisition and could not be considered on the brink of failure, and also that the respondents have not shown that Material Service was the only available acquiring company. These considerations would be significant if the District Court had found no violation of § 7 by reason of United Electric's being a failing company, but the District Court's conclusion was not, as the Government suggests, identical with or even analogous to such a finding. The failing company defense presupposes that the effect on competition and the "loss to [the company's] stockholders and injury to the communities where its plants were operated," International Shoe, *supra*, 280 U.S., at 302, will be less if a company continues to exist even as a party to a merger than if it disappears entirely from the market. It is, in a sense, a "lesser of two evils" approach, in which the

46. In *Citizen Publishing Co. v. United States*, 394 U.S. 131, 138–139, "[t]he burden of proving that the conditions of the failing company doctrine have been satisfied" was found to be "on those who seek refuge under it."

possible threat to competition resulting from an acquisition is deemed preferable to the adverse impact on competition and other losses if the company goes out of business. The respondents' demonstration of United's weak reserves position, however, proved an entirely different point. Rather than showing that United would have gone out of business but for the merger with Material Service, the finding of inadequate reserves went to the heart of the Government's statistical prima facie case based on production figures and substantiated the District Court's conclusion that United Electric, even if it remained on the market, did not have sufficient reserves to compete effectively for long-term contracts. The failing company defense is simply inapposite to this finding and the failure of the respondents to meet the prerequisites of that doctrine did not detract from the validity of the court's analysis.

Finally, the Government contends that the factual underpinning of the District Court's opinion was not supported by the evidence contained in the record, and should be reevaluated by this Court.... Suffice it to say that we find the controlling findings and conclusions contained in the District Court's careful and lengthy opinion to be supported by the evidence in the record and not clearly erroneous.

One factual claim by the Government, however, goes to the heart of the reasoning of the District Court and thus is worthy of explicit note here. The Government asserts that the paucity of United Electric's coal reserves could not have the significance perceived by the District Court, since all companies engaged in extracting minerals at some point deplete their reserves and then acquire new reserves or the new technology required to extract more minerals from their existing holdings. United Electric, the Government suggests, could at any point either purchase new strip reserves or acquire the expertise to recover currently held deep reserves.

But the District Court specifically found new strip reserves not to be available: "Evidence was presented at trial by experts, by state officials, by industry witnesses and by the Government itself indicating that economically mineable strip reserves that would permit United Electric to continue operations beyond the life of its present mines are not available. The Government failed to come forward with any evidence that such reserves are presently available." In addition, there was considerable testimony at trial, apparently credited by the District Court, indicating that United Electric and others had tried to find additional strip reserves not already held for coal production, and had been largely unable to do so.

Moreover, the hypothetical possibility that United Electric might in the future acquire the expertise to mine deep reserves proves nothing—or too much. As the Government pointed out in its brief and at oral argument, in recent years a number of companies with no prior experience in extracting coal have purchased coal reserves and entered the coal production business in order to diversify and complement their current operations. The mere possibility that United Electric, in common with all other companies with the inclination and the corporate treasury to do so, could someday expand into an essentially new line of business does not depreciate the validity of the conclusion that United Electric at the time of the trial did not have the power to compete on a significant scale for the procurement of future long-term contracts, nor does it vest in the production statistics relied on by the Government more significance than ascribed to them by the District Court.

IV

In addition to contending that the District Court erred in finding that the acquisition of United Electric would not substantially lessen competition, the Government urges us to review the court's determinations of the proper product and geographic markets. The Government suggests that while the "energy market" might have been an appropriate "line of commerce," coal also had sufficient "practical indicia" as a separate "line of commerce" to qualify as an independent and consistent submarket. Cf. *United States v. Continental Can Co.*, 378 U.S. 441, 456–457. It also suggests that irrespective of the validity of the criteria adopted by the District Court in selecting its 10 geographic markets, competition between United Electric and Material Service within the larger alternative geographic markets claimed by the Government established those areas as a permissible "section of the country" within the meaning of § 7.

While under normal circumstances a delineation of proper geographic and product markets is a necessary precondition to assessment of the probabilities of a substantial effect on competition within them, in this case we nevertheless affirm the District Court's judgment without reaching these questions. By determining that the amount and availability of usable reserves, and not the past annual production figures relied on by the Government, were the proper indicators of future ability to compete, the District Court wholly rejected the Government's *prima facie* case. Irrespective of the markets within which the acquiring and the acquired company might be viewed as competitors for purposes of this § 7 suit, the Government's statistical presentation simply did not establish that a substantial lessening of competition was likely to occur in any market. By concluding that "divestiture [would not] benefit competition even were this court to accept the Government's unrealistic product and geographic market definitions," 341 F.Supp., at 560, the District Court rendered superfluous its further determinations that the Government also erred in its choice of relevant markets. Since we agree with the District Court that the Government's reliance on production statistics in the context of this case was insufficient, it follows that the judgment before us may be affirmed without reaching the issues of geographic and product markets.

The judgment of the District Court is affirmed.

■ Douglas, J., with whom Brennan, White, and Marshall, JJ., concur, dissenting.

In this case the United States appeals from a district court decision upholding the acquisition of stock in United Electric Coal Companies by Material Service Corporation and its successor, General Dynamics Corporation, against a challenge that the acquisition violated § 7 of the Clayton Act. The United States instituted this civil antitrust action on the claim that the acquisition may substantially lessen competition in the Illinois and Eastern Interior Coal Province sales area coal markets. After trial on the merits the District Court rejected the Government's proposed product and geographic markets and dismissed the action, concluding that the Government had failed to show a substantial lessening of competition in the markets the court deemed relevant.

I

The combination here challenged is the union of two major Illinois coal producers—Freeman Coal Mining Corporation and United Electric Coal Companies—under the ultimate corporate control of General Dynamics Corporation.

[Ed. In Sections II and III, the dissenting justices argued against the district court's findings that the relevant product market was all energy and the relevant geographic market was ICC Freight Rate Districts, localized producing areas grouped for ICC ratemaking purposes.

On the product market question, the dissenters argued that coal should be a relevant submarket, relying on its substantial price advantages over other energy sources and operational disadvantages for certain purposes, *i.e.*, the virtual requirement of liquid fuel for highway and air transportation. As a result of these factors, the market for coal had become limited for the most part to large industrial energy consumers such as electric utilities and certain manufacturers. For example, in the years under review coal accounted for over 90% of energy consumed by steam electric utility plants. Finally, since coal using facilities are not easily adaptable to alternative energy sources, there was little inter-fuel price sensitivity.

As to the narrow geographic market categories—which had the effect of putting Freeman and United Electric in different markets—the dissenters argued that they did not correspond to "commercial realities," noting in that connection, that Freeman and United Electric sold one half of their output to the same customers at the same facilities.]

IV

The court further found that United Electric, standing alone, would not contribute meaningfully to further competition since virtually all its economically mineable strip reserves were committed under long-term contracts and it possessed neither the capability to obtain more strip reserves nor the expertise to develop its deep reserves. Although the doctrine was not invoked by name, this appears to be an application of the "failing company" defense. See *Citizen Publishing Co. v. United States*, 394 U.S. 131 (1969). If it is, the court proceeded on an analysis made at the wrong point in time and failed to discuss the legal standards employed in finding the defense to be established. The finding that 48 of United's 52 million tons of strip reserves were committed related to the time of trial. But, since the rationale of the failing company defense is the lack of anticompetitive consequence if one of the combining companies was about to disappear from the market at any rate, the viability of the "failing company" must be assessed as of the time of the merger. *United States v. Greater Buffalo Press, Inc.*, 402 U.S. 549, 555 (1971); *Citizen Publishing Co. v. United States*, *supra*, at 138.

The Court urges that United's weak reserve position, rather than establishing a failing company defense "went to the heart of the Government's prima facie case based on production figures." Under this view United's weak reserve position at the time of trial constitutes postacquisition evidence which diminishes the possibility of anticompetitive impact and thus directly affects the strength of time-of-acquisition findings. The problem with this analysis is that the District Court made no time-of-acquisition findings which such postacquisition evidence could affect. The majority concedes the obvious need for a limitation on the weight given postacquisition evidence and notes that we have reversed cases where "too much weight" has been given. Here the postacquisition events were given all the weight because all the District Court's findings were made as of the time of the trial. While findings made as of the time of the merger could concededly be tempered to a limited degree by postacquisition events, no such findings were ever made.

Many of the commitments here which reduced United's available reserves occurred after the acquisition; 21 million tons for example were committed in 1968. Similarly, though the District Court found further mineable strip reserves unavailable at the time of trial, there is no finding that they were unavailable in 1959 or 1967. To the contrary, the record demonstrates that other coal producers did acquire new strip reserves during the 1960s. United's 1959 viability is further supported by the fact that it possessed 27 million tons of deep reserves. While we do not know if all these reserves were economically mineable at the time of the acquisition, there was no finding that they would not become so in the near future with advances in technology or changes in the price structure of the coal market.[47] Further there was no contention nor finding that further deep reserves were not available for acquisition.[48] The District Court merely concluded that United had no "ability to develop deep coal reserves."[49]

---

47. Research into new methods of extraction or a rise in the price of coal could make reserves which are uneconomical to mine at any given point in time economically mineable in the future.

48. To the contrary, United Electric acquired substantial new deep reserves since the time of the acquisition since it now owns about 44 million tons of deep reserves and controls by location another 40 to 50 million tons. Reserves are controlled by location if, in order to be mined at all, they must be mined by those who control, by ownership, lease or option, the contiguous reserves.

49. If that conclusion is to lend support to the combination on the ground that United "standing alone, cannot contribute meaningfully to competition," it must be made in light of the stringent standards applicable to the failing company defense. In *Citizen Publishing Co. v. United States*, 394 U.S. 131, 139, we said that defense is one of "narrow scope" and that the burden of proving the defense is "on those who seek refuge under it." We also stated that the prospects of continued independent existence must be "dim or nonexistent" and that it must be established that the acquiring company is the only available purchaser. See also *United*

While it is true that United is a strip mining company which has not extracted deep reserves since 1954, this does not mean that United would not develop deep mining expertise if deep reserves were all it had left or that it could not sell the reserves to some company which poses less of a threat to increased concentration in the coal market than does Freeman. United Electric was not, as the Court suggests, merely one of many companies with the possible "inclination and corporate treasury" to allow expansion into "an essentially new line of business." United was a coal company with a thriving coal marketing structure. At the time of the merger it had access to at least 27 million tons of deep reserves and it had operated a deep mine only five years previously. While deep coal mining may have been an essentially new line of business for many, it was for United merely a matter of regaining the expertise it once had to extract reserves it already owned for sale in a market where it already had a good name.

V

Thus, from product and geographic markets to market share and industry concentration analysis to the failing company defense, the findings below are based on legal standards which are either incorrect or not disclosed. While the court did gratuitously state that no § 7 violation would be found "even were this court to accept the Government's unrealistic product and market definitions," this conclusory statement is supported by no analysis sufficient to allow review in this Court. The majority notes that production figures are of limited significance because they include deliveries under long-term contracts entered into in prior years. It is true that uncommitted reserves or sales of previously uncommitted coal would be preferable indicia of competitive strength, but the District Court made no findings as to United's or Freeman's respective market shares at the time of the acquisition under either of these standards.[50]

On the basis of a record so devoid of findings based on correct legal standards, the judgment may not be affirmed except on a deep-seated judicial bias against § 7 of the Clayton Act. We should remand the case to the District Court with directions to assess the impact of the Freeman–United Electric combination on the Illinois and Eastern Interior Coal Province sales area coal markets as of 1959.[51] We should direct the court to

---

States v. Greater Buffalo Press, Inc., 402 U.S. 549, 555–556 (1971), and *United States v. Third National Bank of Nashville*, 390 U.S. 171, 189 (1968).

50. The District Court did find that, as of 1968, Freeman controlled 6.5% of the total coal reserves dedicated to existing mines in the EICP. At the same point in time, United Electric controlled 2.5% of that total, but almost all of this was contractually committed. If market shares are to be determined by percentage of total reserves, what is necessary is a finding as to each company's 1959 share of uncommitted Illinois and EICP reserves—including reserves which were economically mineable or which might have become so in the reasonably near future and further including an estimate as to uncontrolled reserves which might have been acquired by either company in the reasonably near future.

51. Common control of the two companies was achieved in 1959 and the combination was completed in 1967; at oral argument both parties conceded that the merger "took place" in 1959.

make findings of respective market shares, and further to evaluate United Electric's viability as an independent producer or as the possible "acquiree" of a company other than General Dynamics as of 1959, in light of the strict standards applicable to the failing company defense. Since we abdicate our duty for responsible review and accept the mere conclusion that no § 7 violation is established on the basis of a record with none of these necessary findings, I dissent from the affirmance of the District Court's judgment.

————

Citizen Publishing Co. v. United States, 394 U.S. 131, 89 S.Ct. 927, 22 L.Ed.2d 148 (1969). The Star and the Citizen were the only two daily newspapers of general circulation in Tucson, Arizona. Prior to 1940, they competed vigorously and while their circulation was equal, the Star sold 50% more advertising space than the Citizen and operated at a slight profit while the Citizen sustained losses. The Citizen was not about to go out of business, however, nor had its owners sought to sell the paper to others.

In 1940, a joint operating agreement was negotiated providing for the establishment of a 50–50 joint venture which would manage all departments of the newspapers' business except news and editorial policy. Subscription and advertising rates were set jointly, profits were pooled and distributed to the Star and Citizen pursuant to an agreed ratio, and it was further agreed that neither the Star nor the Citizen nor any of its stockholders, officers and executives would engage in any other business in metropolitan Tucson in conflict with the agreement.

The government challenged the joint venture agreement under Sections 1 and 2 of the Sherman Act on grounds that it involved price fixing and division of markets, and under Section 7 of the Clayton Act on the ground that the joint venture constituted an illegal acquisition.

The Supreme Court affirmed the district court's holding for the government, noting that the newspapers' only real defense depended upon the "failing company" doctrine—a judicially created defense (*see* International Shoe Co. v. FTC, 280 U.S. 291 (1930)), referred to with approval in the legislative history of the 1950 amendments to Section 7 of the Clayton Act.

The Court gave a narrow scope to the failing company defense, emphasizing that *International Shoe* was a case where the evidence showed that the resources of the acquired company were so depleted and its prospects for rehabilitation so remote that "it faced the grave probability of a business failure," and that there was no other prospective purchaser available. The failing company defense on behalf of the Citizen was rejected because there was no evidence that "the joint operating agreement was the last straw" nor that the acquiring company was "the only available purchaser." The Court also noted: ". . . no effort was made to sell the Citizen; its properties and franchise were not put in the hands of a broker; and the record is silent on what the market, if any, for the Citizen might have been." The burden of proof to demonstrate a failing company defense was placed on defendants, and the Court concluded they had not satisfied that burden. Justice Stewart, who later wrote the majority opinion in *General Dynamics* touching on failing company considerations, dissented.

NOTE ON FAILING COMPANIES, FLAILING COMPANIES, AND DISTRESSED INDUSTRIES

The legislative history of revised Section 7 does not squarely address a failing company defense for mergers but rather refers in approving language to an older case—International Shoe Co. v. FTC, 280 U.S. 291 (1930). That decision arguably justifies only a very limited failing company exception since the evidence there showed that the resources of the acquired company were so depleted and its prospects for rehabilitation so remote that "it faced the grave probability of a business failure" and there were no other prospective purchasers available.

By addressing the failing company issue simply by an approving reference to an old case, the legislation provides little guidance as to what constitutes a "failing company," whether the defense is absolute or qualified, or the reasons underlying the exemption. Derek Bok, in his 1960 article, Section 7 of the Clayton Act and the Merging of Law and Economics, 74 Harv.L.Rev. 226, 339–47 (1960), cites three possible sets of considerations that might have motivated Congress: (1) efficiency considerations, since a failing company might be improved by a change in management (regarded as unlikely in light of Congress' general lack of concern in the legislative debates and reports with efficiency considerations); (2) a view that the disappearance from competitive markets of the failing company would not lessen competition; and (3) legislative concern with the interests of creditors, owners, and employees who would be interested in avoiding a total collapse and realizing the highest selling price possible.

The second argument—disappearance of a failing firm cannot affect competition in a significant way—is weak. A failing firm's assets could be of immense competitive significance since the ability of a large firm to extract higher than competitive profits can be augmented by acquisition of those assets. To take an obvious example, the failing firm may be a more aggressive price-cutting competitor or a more innovative designer than its rivals, and its disruptive influence may be extinguished if a large competitor acquires its assets.

But what of the other factors? Might some sort of antitrust approach to failing firms be grounded on the theory that a merger might produce a more efficient firm, or help pay off creditors, owners or employees?

United States antitrust law and policy with respect to failing firms and distressed industries falls into three categories:

1.   *Failing Firm/Absolute Defense.* If a company (or one of its divisions) is truly failing, it may be sold to any purchaser without any antitrust consequence. We have already noted, however, that "failing firm" is defined narrowly and in effect, firms must be virtually on the steps of a bankruptcy court before they can assert a failing firm or failing division defense, and a few courts seem to have insisted on present insolvency before they would permit the defense. *See* United States v. Pabst Brewing Co., 296 F.Supp. 994, 1000–01 (E.D.Wis.1969); United States v. Reed Roller Bit Co., 274 F.Supp. 573, 584 (W.D.Okl.1967). For a recent example of a successful failing firm defense, *see* California v. Sutter Health System, aff'd 217 F.3d 846 (9th Cir. 2000). Also, there must be no other prospective purchaser available that poses a less severe danger to competition than does the proposed merger. *Citizen Publishing Co. v. United States*, p. 1006 *supra.*

The 1992 DOJ/FTC Horizontal Merger Guidelines adopt this restrictive approach to the defense and in addition provide that it is available only if the allegedly failing firm would not be able to reorganize successfully through bankruptcy proceedings, and only if, absent the merger, the assets of the failing firm would exit from the market. *See* Merger Guidelines, p. 976 *infra*.

One reason for a rigorous approach to a failing firm exemption involves the difficulty of determining if a business failure really is imminent. Is the company unalterably in decline? Are its problems permanent or temporary (for example, where a decline in demand is cyclical)? Could efficiency be restored by the sale or elimination of excess capacity? It is partly because of a lack of confidence in judges' ability to weigh such factors accurately, and fairly balance private and public (*i.e.*, competitive) interests that American law insists that this absolute defense be available only where the qualifying conditions are demonstrated by clear proof.

There is, however, one important exception to the rule that firms must be in a condition of actual failure rather than likely failure to take advantage of the defense. In 1970, Congress passed the Newspaper Preservation Act, 15 U.S.C.A. 1801–04, which eased the law with respect to joint publishing ventures involving one or more failing newspapers, allowing them to merge their business functions if they kept their editorial functions separate. The Act defined a failing newspaper as a newspaper that, regardless of its ownership or affiliations, was in "probable danger of financial failure." 15 U.S.C.A. 1802(5). The standard providing that one of the two newspapers in the joint agreement need only be suffering losses that probably could not be reversed was sustained by an equally divided Supreme Court in Michigan Citizens for an Independent Press v. Thornburgh, 493 U.S. 38 (1989).

Why not adopt the Newspaper Preservation Act across the board? Admittedly, it is easier to ascertain that a firm is presently insolvent than that it will become insolvent as a result of prevailing conditions. But if uncertainty of proof is the concern, why not simply require clear proof of probable failure, rather than waiting until actual failure (and its attendant waste and dislocations) occurs?

2. *Flailing Firm/Qualified Defense.* Even if a firm is not on the brink of bankruptcy, its financial position may be so weak or its capacity to compete so diminished (for example, because of depleted financial resources, lack of access to an essential raw material, or weakened distribution) that its market share measured by percentage of past sales may overstate its competitive significance. In United States v. International Harvester Co., 564 F.2d 769, 773 (7th Cir.1977), the Seventh Circuit appeared to accept a "weak competitor" defense when it stated:

> This showing, which has been called the "General Dynamics defense," establishes that the Government's past market statistics are really insufficient to constitute a prima facie case because Steiger's weak financial reserves (like United Electric's weak coal reserves in General Dynamics) would not allow it to be as strong a competitor as the bald statistical projections indicate.[52]

Professors Areeda and Turner offered the following critique of International Harvester and similar "weak competitor" cases:

> We conclude that financial difficulties should be disregarded unless it is reasonably clear that (1) if unresolved, they would cause the firm's market share to decline to a level that would make the merger permissible, and (2) there is no competitively preferable alternative for resolving them.

---

52. *See, e.g.*, FTC v. University Health Inc., 938 F.2d 1206, 1221 (11th Cir.1991) (financial weakness just one factor among many); Lektro–Vend Corp. v. Vendo Co., 660 F.2d 255, 277 n. 22 (7th Cir.1981).

Such a showing is likely to be rare, at least in other than marginal cases. Financial difficulties peculiar to one of the merging firms would normally have already been reflected in declining market shares, which would be taken into account without regard to specific cause. Indeed, the cause-and-effect relationship would usually run the other way-low or declining sales causing the financial difficulties, rather than vice versa. And even if it were established that financial difficulties would cause the requisite further sales decline—as, for example, inability to obtain capital for expansion in a growing market—it would be a rare case where there would be no competitively preferable alternative solutions....

All that we have said concerning financial difficulties applies to claims of management weaknesses, and more. Any inability to revamp management would in all likelihood simply be a derivative of financial difficulties. Moreover, it seems highly implausible that a presumptively unlawful merger would be the only suitable avenue for replacing poor management.[53]

In Kaiser Aluminum & Chemical Corp. v. FTC, 652 F.2d 1324 (7th Cir.1981), the Seventh Circuit explained its present position:

It should be emphasized that *International Harvester* does not rely solely on the acquired firm's weak financial condition as a defense to § 7. The case instead considers the firm's weak condition as one relevant economic factor among many. It is therefore a mischaracterization to view *International Harvester* as adopting a weakened company doctrine as a *per se* defense to § 7 liability.... Financial weakness, while perhaps relevant in some cases, is probably the weakest ground of all for justifying a merger. The acquisition of a financially weak company in effect hands over its customers to the financially strong, thereby deterring competition by preventing others from acquiring those customers, making entry into the market more difficult. Moreover, a weak company defense would extend the failing company doctrine, a defense which the Supreme Court in *General Dynamics* observed has strict limits.[54]

If courts permit "weak financial condition" (or similar factors that are easily manipulatable and correctable) to override market share statistics, how much will be left of Section 7?

3. *Distressed Industries*. There is nothing in Section 7, its legislative history, or the case law that would modify antitrust enforcement when all or most firms in an industry are barely breaking even (though not in imminent danger of failure) and long-term excess capacity is growing worse. The fact that an industry is under economic siege because of chronic excess capacity and too high unit costs is irrelevant.

We saw earlier that the Supreme Court did take distressed industry conditions into account in the 1930s when much of the American economy was made up of "distressed industries." In Appalachian Coals v. United States, *supra*, a joint sales venture of producers of bituminous coal was upheld, in part because of distressed conditions in the production and distribution of coal. *Appalachian Coals* was more of a cartel than a merger and put together firms with a very large market share, so

---

53. 4 Areeda & Turner, Antitrust Law: An Analysis of Antitrust Principles and Their Application 141–42 (1980).

54. 652 F.2d at 1339.

that its lenient approach might not have been justified. In any event, after World War II when prosperity followed, the concept of distressed industry was discarded by the enforcement agencies and the courts.

To date, the problem of distressed industries has been left for the market to solve—a "survival of the fittest" approach. The orthodox economic view is if there is capacity underutilization combined with financial problems and declining demand, eventually the appropriate number of firms will exit from the market—presumably the least efficient—and in that way capacity will be brought in line with demand. Exit can occur abruptly through bankruptcy or more slowly through downsizing of facilities and staff.

But is it always predictable that the less efficient firms are most likely to leave the market? Conceivably, the more efficient firm will exit first and the less efficient firm with better access to capital will remain.

Presumably, special treatment for firms in a distressed industry would only occur in moderately concentrated markets where the merger is borderline in terms of illegality. But who is to say that after the merger, the lower costs or higher profits resulting from the merger will be devoted to addressing problems of chronic structural weakness? How might a "distressed industry" be defined so as to avoid a gaping hole in antitrust enforcement?

Hospital Corporation of America v. FTC

United States Court of Appeals, Seventh Circuit, 1986.
807 F.2d 1381.

■ POSNER, J. Hospital Corporation of America, the largest proprietary hospital chain in the United States, asks us to set aside the decision by the Federal Trade Commission that it violated section 7 of the Clayton Act by the acquisition in 1981 and 1982 of two corporations, Hospital Affiliates International, Inc. and Health Care Corporation. Before these acquisitions (which cost Hospital Corporation almost $700 million), Hospital Corporation had owned one hospital in Chattanooga, Tennessee. The acquisitions gave it ownership of two more. In addition, pursuant to the terms of the acquisitions it assumed contracts, both with four-year terms, that Hospital Affiliates International had made to manage two other Chattanooga-area hospitals. So after the acquisitions Hospital Corporation owned or managed 5 of the 11 hospitals in the area. Later one of the management contracts was cancelled; and one of the lesser issues raised by Hospital Corporation, which we might as well dispose of right now, is whether the Commission should have disregarded the assumption of that contract. We agree with the Commission that it was not required to take account of a post-acquisition transaction that may have been made to improve Hospital Corporation's litigating position. The contract was cancelled after the Commission began investigating Hospital Corporation's acquisition of Hospital Affiliates, and while the initiative in cancelling was taken by the managed hospital, Hospital Corporation reacted with unaccustomed mildness by allowing the hospital to withdraw from the contract. For it had sued three other hospitals that tried to get out of their management contracts with Hospital Affiliates when Hospital Corporation assumed the contracts—only none of these hospitals was in a market where Hospital Corporation's acquisition of Hospital Affiliates was likely to be challenged. Post-acquisition evidence that is subject to manipulation by the party seeking to use it is entitled to little or no weight. *Cf. Lektro–Vend Corp. v. Vendo Co.*, 660 F.2d 255, 276 (7th Cir.1981). The Commission was entitled to give it no weight in this case, both to simplify the adjudication of merger cases generally and because excluding this one hospital would not have altered the market share figures significantly.

If all the hospitals brought under common ownership or control by the two challenged acquisitions are treated as a single entity, the acquisitions raised Hospital Corporation's market share in the Chattanooga area from 14 percent to 26 percent. This made it the second largest provider of hospital services in a highly concentrated market where the four largest firms together had a 91 percent market share compared to 79 percent before the acquisitions. These are the FTC's figures, and Hospital Corporation thinks they are slightly too high (quite apart from the question what to do with either or both management contracts); but the discrepancy is too slight to make a legal difference. Nor would expressing the market shares in terms of the Herfindahl index alter the impression of a highly concentrated market. . . .

The Clayton Act allows Hospital Corporation to seek judicial review of the Commission's order in any circuit in which it does business and for unexplained reasons it has chosen this circuit. It makes three arguments to us: there is no reasonable probability that its acquisitions in Chattanooga will lessen competition substantially; anyway the Federal Trade Commission has no constitutional power to bring an enforcement action, because the members of the Commission do not serve at the pleasure of the President; failing all else, Hospital Corporation should at least not be required to give the Commission advance notice of all future acquisitions. . . .

The Commission's detailed analysis of [the] effects [of the acquisitions] fills most of a 117–page opinion that, whatever its substantive merits or demerits, is a model of lucidity. The Commission may have made its task harder (and opinion longer) than strictly necessary, however, by studiously avoiding reliance on any of the Supreme Court's section 7 decisions from the 1960s except *United States v. Philadelphia Nat'l Bank*, 374 U.S. 321, 83 S.Ct. 1715, 10 L.Ed.2d 915 (1963), which took an explicitly economic approach to the interpretation of the statute. The other decisions in that decade—in particular *Brown Shoe Co. v. United States*, 370 U.S. 294, 82 S.Ct. 1502, 8 L.Ed.2d 510 (1962); *United States v. Aluminum Co. of America*, 377 U.S. 271, 84 S.Ct. 1283, 12 L.Ed.2d 314 (1964); *United States v. Von's Grocery Co.*, 384 U.S. 270, 86 S.Ct. 1478, 16 L.Ed.2d 555 (1966), and *United States v. Pabst Brewing Co.*, 384 U.S. 546, 86 S.Ct. 1665, 16 L.Ed.2d 765 (1966)—seemed, taken as a group, to establish the illegality of any nontrivial acquisition of a competitor, whether or not the acquisition was likely either to bring about or shore up collusive or oligopoly pricing. The elimination of a significant rival was thought by itself to infringe the complex of social and economic values conceived by a majority of the Court to inform the statutory words "may ... substantially ... lessen competition."

None of these decisions has been overruled. Although both *United States v. General Dynamics Corp.*, 415 U.S. 486 (1974), and *United States v. Citizens & Southern Nat'l Bank*, 422 U.S. 86 (1975) refused to equate the possession of a significant market share with a significant threat to competition, these cases involved highly unusual facts, having no counterpart in this case, that required discounting large market shares. In General Dynamics the shares were of current sales (of coal) made pursuant to long-term contracts entered into a long time ago; future sales would depend on uncommitted reserves, and one of the acquired firms had no uncommitted reserves. In *Citizens & Southern* the acquired banks were already under the effective control of the acquirer (they were its "*de facto* branches"), so that the formal merger had little competitive significance.

These cases show that market share figures are not always decisive in a section 7 case, but it can be argued that the cases themselves carve only limited exceptions to the broad holdings of some of the merger decisions of the 1960s. General Dynamics was like a failing-company case; in *Citizens & Southern* the merger was a mere formality—like a marriage ceremony between common law spouses. The most important developments that cast doubt on the continued vitality of such cases as *Brown Shoe* and *Von's* are found in other cases, where the Supreme Court, echoed by the lower courts, has said repeatedly that the economic concept of competition, rather than any desire to preserve rivals as such, is the lodestar that shall guide the contemporary application of the antitrust laws, not excluding the Clayton Act.... Applied to cases brought under section 7, this principle requires the district court (in this case, the Commission) to make a judgment whether the challenged acquisition is likely to hurt consumers, as by making it easier for the firms in the market to collude, expressly or tacitly, and thereby force price above or farther above the competitive level. So it was prudent for the Commission, rather than resting on the very strict merger decisions of the 1960s, to inquire into the probability of harm to consumers. In any event, even if we thought those decisions still authoritative, we could not uphold the Commission's decision on a rationale different from its own.

When an economic approach is taken in a section 7 case, the ultimate issue is whether the challenged acquisition is likely to facilitate collusion. In this perspective the acquisition of a competitor has no economic significance in itself; the worry is that it may enable the acquiring firm to cooperate (or cooperate better) with other leading competitors on reducing or limiting output, thereby pushing up the market price. Hospital Corporation calls the issue whether an acquisition is likely to have such an effect "economic," which of course it is. But for purposes of judicial review, as we have said, it is a factual issue subject to the substantial evidence rule, not a legal issue on which review usually is plenary and invariably is much less deferential than is the review of findings of fact. One of the main reasons for creating the Federal Trade Commission and giving it concurrent jurisdiction to enforce the Clayton Act was that Congress distrusted judicial determination of antitrust questions. It thought the assistance of an administrative body would be helpful in resolving such questions and indeed expected the FTC to take the leading role in enforcing the Clayton Act, which was passed at the same time as the statute creating the Commission. See Henderson, The Federal Trade Commission, ch. 1 (1924). In the present case the underlying facts are, as Hospital Corporation asserts, largely undisputed. The dispute is over the inferences of competitive consequence to be drawn from them. But the drawing of those inferences is a matter within the Commission's primary responsibility too. There is plenty of evidence to support the Commission's prediction of adverse competitive effect in this case; whether we might have come up with a different prediction on our own is irrelevant.

The acquisitions reduced the number of competing hospitals in the Chattanooga market from 11 to 7. True, this calculation assumes that the hospitals that came under the management although not ownership of Hospital Corporation should be considered allies rather than competitors of Hospital Corporation; but the Commission was entitled to so conclude. The manager (Hospital Corporation) sets the prices charged by the managed hospitals, just as it sets its own prices. Although the pricing and other decisions that it makes in its management role are subject to the ultimate control of the board of directors of the managed hospital, there is substantial evidence that the board usually defers to the manager's decisions. If it were not inclined to defer, it would not have a management contract; it would do its own managing, through officers hired by it. A hospital managed by Hospital Corporation is therefore unlikely to engage in vigorous or perhaps in any price competition with Hospital Corporation—or so at least the Commission was entitled to conclude.

The reduction in the number of competitors is significant in assessing the competitive vitality of the Chattanooga hospital market. The fewer competitors there are in a market, the easier it is for them to coordinate their pricing without committing detectable violations of section 1 of the Sherman Act, which forbids price fixing. This would not be very important if the four competitors eliminated by the acquisitions in this case had been insignificant, but they were not; they accounted in the aggregate for 12 percent of the sales of the market. As a result of the acquisitions the four largest firms came to control virtually the whole market, and the problem of coordination was therefore reduced to one of coordination among these four.

Moreover, both the ability of the remaining firms to expand their output should the big four reduce their own output in order to raise the market price (and, by expanding, to offset the leading firms' restriction of their own output), and the ability of outsiders to come in and build completely new hospitals, are reduced by Tennessee's certificate-of-need law. Any addition to hospital capacity must be approved by a state agency. The parties disagree over whether this law, as actually enforced, inhibits the expansion of hospital capacity. The law may indeed be laxly enforced. Not only is there little evidence that it has ever prevented a hospital in Chattanooga from making a capacity addition it wanted to make, but empirical studies of certificate of need regulation nationwide have found little effect on hospital expenditures. See Joskow, Controlling Hospital Costs: The Role of Government Regulation, ch. 7 (1981). Yet the Tennessee law might have some effect under the conditions that would obtain if the challenged acquisitions enabled collusive pricing of hospital services. Should the leading hospitals in Chattanooga collude, a natural consequence would be the creation of excess hospital capacity, for the higher prices resulting from collusion would drive some patients to shorten their hospital stays and others to postpone or reject elective surgery. If a noncolluding hospital wanted to expand its capacity so that it could serve patients driven off by the high prices charged by the colluding hospitals, the colluders would have not only a strong incentive to oppose the grant of a certificate of need but also substantial evidence with which to oppose it—the excess capacity (in the market considered as a whole) created by their own collusive efforts. At least the certificate of need law would enable them to delay any competitive sally by a noncolluding competitor. Or so the Commission could conclude (a refrain we shall now stop repeating). We add that at the very least a certificate of need law forces hospitals to give public notice, well in advance, of any plans to add capacity. The requirement of notice makes it harder for the member of a hospital cartel to "cheat" on the cartel by adding capacity in advance of other members; its attempt to cheat will be known in advance, and countermeasures taken.

All this would be of little moment if, in the event that hospital prices in Chattanooga rose above the competitive level, persons desiring hospital services in Chattanooga would switch to hospitals in other cities, or to nonhospital providers of medical care. But this would mean that the Chattanooga hospital market, which is to say the set of hospital-services providers to which consumers in Chattanooga can feasibly turn, see *United States v. Philadelphia Nat'l Bank, supra,* 374 U.S. at 358–61; *Tampa Elec. Co. v. Nashville Coal Co.,* 365 U.S. 320 (1961), includes hospitals in other cities plus non-hospital providers both in Chattanooga and elsewhere; and we do not understand Hospital Corporation to be challenging the Commission's market definition, which is limited to hospital providers in Chattanooga. Anyway, these competitive alternatives are not important enough to deprive the market shares statistics of competitive significance. Going to another city is out of the question in medical emergencies; and even when an operation or some other hospital service can be deferred, the patient's doctor will not (at least not for reasons of price) send the patient to another city, where the doctor is unlikely to have hospital privileges. Finally, although hospitals increasingly are providing services on an out-patient basis, thus competing with nonhospital providers of the same services (tests, minor surgical procedures, etc.), most hospital services cannot be provided by nonhospital providers; as to these, hospitals have no competition from other providers of medical care.

In showing that the challenged acquisitions gave four firms control over an entire market so that they would have little reason to fear a competitive reaction if they raised prices above the competitive level, the Commission went far to justify its prediction of probable anticompetitive effects. Maybe it need have gone no further. See *United States v. Philadelphia Nat'l Bank, supra*, 374 U.S. at 362–63; *Monfort of Colorado, Inc. v. Cargill, Inc.*, 761 F.2d 570, 580 (10th Cir.1985), rev'd on other grounds, 479 U.S. 104 (1986). But it did. First it pointed out that the demand for hospital services by patients and their doctors is highly inelastic under competitive conditions. This is not only because people place a high value on their safety and comfort and because many of their treatment decisions are made for them by their doctor, who doesn't pay their hospital bills; it is also because most hospital bills are paid largely by insurance companies or the federal government rather than by the patient. The less elastic the demand for a good or service is, the greater are the profits that providers can make by raising price through collusion. A low elasticity of demand means that raising price will cause a relatively slight fall in demand, with the result that total revenues will rise sharply. For example, if the price elasticity of demand throughout the relevant portion of the demand curve is -.2, meaning that within that area every 1 percent increase in price will result in a two-tenths of 1 percent decrease in the quantity demanded, then a 10 percent increase in price will cause only a 2 percent reduction in quantity sold, and hence an almost 8 percent increase in total revenue. And since less is being produced, costs will fall at the same time that revenue is rising, resulting in an even greater percentage increase in profit than in revenue.

Second, there is a tradition, well documented in the Commission's opinion, of cooperation between competing hospitals in Chattanooga. Of course, not all forms of cooperation between competitors are bad. See, *e.g., Broadcast Music, Inc. v. Columbia Broadcasting System, Inc.*, 441 U.S. 1 (1979). But a market in which competitors are unusually disposed to cooperate is a market prone to collusion. The history of successful cooperation establishes a precondition to effective collusion-mutual trust and forbearance, without which an informal collusive arrangement is unlikely to overcome the temptation to steal a march on a fellow colluder by undercutting him slightly. That temptation is great. A seller who makes a profit of $10 on each sale at the cartel price, and then cuts price by $1 and thereby (let us suppose) doubles his output, will increase his total profits by 180 percent.

The management contracts between Hospital Affiliates (itself an owner as well as manager of hospitals) and two other hospitals in Chattanooga— contracts that when taken over by Hospital Corporation gave it virtual control over the pricing and other decisions of two of its competitors, at least for a time—illustrate the unusual degree of cooperation in this industry; imagine Ford's signing a management contract with General Motors whereby General Motors installed one of its officers (who would remain an officer of GM) as Ford's manager. Hospitals routinely exchange intimate information on prices and costs in connection with making joint applications to insurers for higher reimbursement schedules. Such cooperation may be salutary but it facilitates collusion and therefore entitles the Commission to worry even more about large horizontal acquisitions in this industry than in industries where competitors deal with each other at arm's length.

Third, hospitals are under great pressure from the federal government and the insurance companies to cut costs. One way of resisting this pressure is by presenting a united front in negotiations with the third-party payors—which indeed, as we have just said, hospitals in Chattanooga have done. See also *United States v. North Dakota Hospital Ass'n,* 640 F.Supp. 1028 (D.N.D.1986). The fewer the independent competitors in a hospital market, the easier they will find it, by presenting an unbroken phalanx of representations and requests, to frustrate efforts to control hospital costs. This too is a form of collusion that the antitrust laws seek to discourage, though within the limitations of the Noerr–Pennington doctrine, which insulates some cooperative efforts to obtain government benefits from attack under antitrust law. Not all third-party payors, however, are governmental; not all cooperative efforts to influence government are immunized by the doctrine, see, *e.g., California Motor Transport Co. v. Trucking Unlimited,* 404 U.S. 508 (1972); most important, the doctrine does not forbid enforcement efforts designed to make such efforts less effective by preserving a substantial number of competitors.

All these considerations, taken together, supported—we do not say they compelled—the Commission's conclusion that the challenged acquisitions are likely to foster collusive practices, harmful to consumers, in the Chattanooga hospital market. Section 7 does not require proof that a merger or other acquisition has caused higher prices in the affected market. All that is necessary is that the merger create an appreciable danger of such consequences in the future. A predictive judgment, necessarily probabilistic and judgmental rather than demonstrable (see *United States v. Philadelphia Nat'l Bank, supra,* 374 U.S. at 362 is called for. Considering the concentration of the market, the absence of competitive alternatives, the regulatory barrier to entry (the certificate of need law), the low elasticity of demand, the exceptionally severe cost pressures under which American hospitals labor today, the history of collusion in the industry, and the sharp reduction in the number of substantial competitors in this market brought about by the acquisition of four hospitals in a city with only eleven (one already owned by Hospital Corporation), we cannot say that the Commission's prediction is not supported by substantial evidence.

But of course we cannot just consider the evidence that supports the Commission's prediction. We must consider all the evidence in the record. We must therefore consider the significance of the facts, pressed on us by Hospital Corporation, that hospital services are complex and heterogeneous, that the sellers in this market are themselves heterogeneous because of differences in the services provided by the different hospitals and differences in the corporate character of the hospitals (some are publicly owned, some are proprietary, and some are private but nonprofit), that the hospital industry is undergoing rapid technological and economic change, that the payors for most hospital services (Blue Cross and other insurance companies, and the federal government) are large and knowledgeable, and that the FTC's investigation which led to this proceeding was touched off by a complaint from a competitor of Hospital Corporation. Most of these facts do detract from a conclusion that collusion in this market is a serious danger, but it was for the Commission—it is not for us—to determine their weight.

The first fact is the least impressive. It is true that hospitals provide a variety of different services many of which are "customized" for the individual patient, but the degree to which this is true seems no greater than in other markets. Although collusion is more difficult the more heterogeneous the output of the colluding firms, there is no established threshold of complexity beyond which it is infeasible and Hospital Corporation made no serious effort to show that hospital services are more complex than products and services in other markets, such as steel, building materials, and transportation, where collusion has been frequent.

The heterogeneity of the sellers has two aspects: the hospitals in Chattanooga offer different mixtures of services; and they have different types of ownership—private for-profit ("proprietary"), private not-for-profit, public. The significance of these features is unclear. Concerning the first, if one assumes that collusion is practiced on a service-by-service basis, the fact that hospitals provide different mixtures of service seems irrelevant to the feasibility of collusion. True, since different types of service may not be substitutable—open-heart surgery is not a substitute for setting a broken leg—specialized hospitals might not compete with one another. But that is not Hospital Corporation's argument. Its argument is that the different mixture of services in the different hospitals would make it difficult for their owners to fix prices of competing services, and this we don't understand.

Different ownership structures might reduce the likelihood of collusion but this possibility is conjectural and the Commission was not required to give it conclusive weight. The adoption of the nonprofit form does not change human nature, see Clark, *Does the Nonprofit Form Fit the Hospital Industry?*, 93 Harv.L.Rev. 1416, 1447, 1465 (1980), as the courts have recognized in rejecting an implicit antitrust exemption for nonprofit enterprises. *National Collegiate Athletic Ass'n v. Board of Regents*, 468 U.S. 85, 100 n. 22, 104 S.Ct. 2948, 2960 n. 22, 82 L.Ed.2d 70 (1984). (There is a possible gap in the FTC's jurisdiction over acquisitions involving nonprofit corporations, but it doesn't affect this case, since the acquired and acquiring firms are all proprietary.) Nonprofit status affects the method of financing the enterprise (substituting a combination of gift and debt financing for equity and debt financing) and the form in which profits (in the sense of the difference between revenue and costs) are distributed, and it may make management somewhat less beady-eyed in trying to control costs, see Clarkson, *Some Implications of Property Rights in Hospital Management*, 15 J. Law & Econ. 363 (1972). But no one has shown that it makes the enterprise unwilling to cooperate in reducing competition (some contrary evidence is presented in Hersch, Competition and the Performance of Hospital Markets, 1 Rev.Ind.Org. 324 (1984))—which most enterprises dislike and which nonprofit enterprises may dislike on ideological as well as selfish grounds. "Nonprofit hospitals, in fact, make rather sizable profits and these profits have been growing over time." True, nonprofit hospitals, private and public, harbor considerable antipathy toward proprietary hospitals, regarding them as "cream skimmers" who lure away the affluent patients that nonproprietary hospitals need to defray the costs of serving the less affluent. This antipathy may retard the emergence of the mutual trust and forbearance that informal collusive schemes depend on for their effectiveness. But the other side of this coin is that the nonproprietaries fear the competition of the proprietaries (that is the source, or a source, of their antipathy to them)—and what better foundation for a collusive arrangement than fear of competition?

Political pressures might inhibit publicly owned hospitals from raising prices. But similar pressures might inhibit them from expanding capacity to take on additional patients attracted by lower prices. A seller's refusal to join a cartel is significant only insofar as the seller can expand output if and when the cartel, by raising prices, drives consumers to search for sellers who are not part of the cartel and are willing to undersell it. A public hospital that in order to expand its capacity must seek governmental appropriations is in a poor position to take advantage of the competitive opportunities created by the presence of a cartel in its market. Moreover, compelled as they are to treat charity cases while minimizing the cost to the taxpayers of supporting the hospital, public hospitals are under added pressure to charge high prices to their paying (or insured) patients, which may make collusion particularly attractive to these hospitals.

The economic and technological ferment in the hospital industry may make collusion more difficult, but also more urgent, since risk-averse managers may be strongly inclined to stabilize, if necessary through collusion, whatever features of an uncertain environment they are able to bring under their control. Regarding the weighing of such imponderables as this, much must be left to the judgment of the Commission.

The concentration of the buying side of a market does inhibit collusion. The bigger a buyer is, the more easily and lucratively a member of the cartel can cheat on his fellows; for with a single transaction, he may be able to increase his sales and hence profits dramatically. But with all the members thus vying for the large orders of big buyers, the cartel will erode. See Stigler, *A Theory of Oligopoly*, in Stigler, The Organization of Industry 39, 43–44 (1968). Hospital Corporation argues that the effective buyers of most hospital services are large and knowledgeable institutions rather than the patients who are the nominal buyers. But the role of the third-party payor is not quite that of a large buyer. The explicit contract between the insurance companies and their patients, and the statutory and regulatory obligations of government to Medicare and Medicaid recipients, require reimbursing patients for hospital services. Of course the insurer is not required to, and no insurer does, reimburse the insured for whatever services are consumed, regardless of price. But as a practical matter Blue Cross could not tell its subscribers in Chattanooga that it will not reimburse them for any hospital services there because prices are too high. As a practical matter it could not, if the four major hospital owners in the city, controlling more than 90 percent of the city's hospital capacity, raised their prices, tell its subscribers that they must use the remaining hospitals— whose aggregate capacity would be completely inadequate and, for reasons discussed earlier, could not readily, or at least rapidly, be expanded—if they want to be reimbursed. The insurers are in a better position to detect violations of the Sherman Act than the patients are but if the challenged acquisitions enable the major hospital owners in Chattanooga to collude without violating the Sherman Act, that is, collude tacitly rather than expressly, there would be no violations to detect and report.

Hospital Corporation's most telling point is that the impetus for the Commission's complaint came from a competitor—a large nonprofit hospital in Chattanooga. A rational competitor would not complain just because it thought that Hospital Corporation's acquisitions would facilitate collusion. Whether the competitor chose to join a cartel or stay out of it, it would be better off if the cartel were formed than if it were not formed. For the cartel would enable this seller to raise its price, whether or not to the cartel level. By staying out of the cartel and by pricing just below the cartel price, the competitor might, as we noted earlier, do even better than by joining the cartel.

The hospital that complained to the Commission must have thought that the acquisitions would lead to lower rather than high prices—which would benefit consumers, and hence, under contemporary principles of antitrust law, would support the view that the acquisitions were lawful. But this is just one firm's opinion. It was not binding on the Commission, which having weighed all the relevant facts concluded that the acquisitions had made collusion in this market significantly more likely than before. Since, moreover, the complainant was a nonprofit hospital, in attributing the complaint to fear of lower prices Hospital Corporation is contradicting its argument that the non-profit sector of the hospital industry does not obey the laws of economic self-interest.

[In the remaining portions of its opinion, the Court found unpersuasive the argument that the Federal Trade Commission was unconstitutional because it exercised executive (*i.e.*, prosecutorial) authority and yet the members could not be removed by the President except for cause. It also rejected a challenge to that portion of the Commission's order requiring that Hospital Corporation of America provide the Commission with advance notification of future acquisitions, noting earlier decisions to the effect that the Commission operated like a court of equity and had broad discretion to fence in respondents found guilty of violating the law.]

The Commission's order is affirmed and enforced.

NOTE ON "ANTITRUST INJURY," PRIVATE ENFORCEMENT, AND REMEDIES UNDER SECTION 7

1. *Brunswick Corp. v. Pueblo Bowl–O–Mat, Inc.*, 429 U.S. 477 (1977). Defendant Brunswick was one of the two largest manufacturers of bowling equipment in the United States. Plaintiffs were three bowling centers. Beginning in 1965, Brunswick had acquired and operated a large number of bowling centers. It had done so because most of its sales of bowling equipment had been on credit, and when the bowling industry went into sharp decline in the early 1960s, attempts to sell or lease repossessed equipment from delinquent purchasers met with only limited success. The acquisitions made Brunswick by far the largest operator of bowling centers in the United States, but it controlled only 2% of the national total.

Plaintiffs contended that Brunswick's acquisitions in three local markets violated Section 7 of the Clayton Act. They attempted to establish damages by showing that if Brunswick had allowed certain defaulting centers to close, plaintiffs' profits would have increased. A jury returned a verdict of $2,358,030 for plaintiffs and, with some modification, this figure was trebled.

The Court of Appeals for the Third Circuit found that a properly instructed jury could have concluded that Brunswick was a "giant" whose entry into a "market of pygmies" might lessen horizontal retail competition. The Court also said that there was sufficient evidence to permit a jury to find that but for Brunswick's actions the acquired centers would have gone out of business, and if such a finding were made, plaintiffs would be entitled to treble damages. After reviewing the trial judge's instructions, however, the Court decided that the jury had been improperly charged. The Third Circuit reversed the judgment and remanded for a new trial.

The Supreme Court granted defendant judgment notwithstanding the verdict and reasoned:

> Every merger of two existing entities into one, whether lawful or unlawful, has the potential for producing economic readjustments that adversely affect some persons. But Congress has not condemned mergers on that account; it has condemned them only when they may produce anticompetitive effects. Yet under the Court of Appeals' holding, once a merger is found to violate § 7, all dislocations caused by the merger are actionable, regardless of whether those dislocations have anything to do with the reason the merger was condemned. This holding would make § 4 recovery entirely fortuitous, and would authorize damages for losses which are of no concern to the antitrust laws.

> Both of these consequences are well illustrated by the facts of this case. If the acquisitions here were unlawful, it is because they brought a "deep pocket" parent into a market of "pygmies." Yet respondents' injury—the loss of income that would have accrued had the acquired centers gone bankrupt—bears no relationship to the size of either the acquiring company or its competitors. Respondents would have suffered the identical "loss"—but no compensable injury—had the acquired centers instead obtained refinancing or been purchased by "shallow pocket" parents as the Court of Appeals itself acknowledged, 523 F.2d at 279. Thus, respondents' injury was not of "the type that the statute was intended to forestall," *Wyandotte Co. v. United States*, 389 U.S. 191, 202 (1967).

> But the antitrust laws are not merely indifferent to the injury claimed here. At base, respondents complain that by acquiring the failing centers petitioner preserved competition, thereby depriving respondents of the

benefits of increased concentration. The damages respondents obtained are designed to provide them with the profits they would have realized had competition been reduced. The antitrust laws, however, were enacted for "the protection of *competition* not *competitors*," *Brown Shoe Co. v. United States*, 370 U.S. 294, 320 (1962). It is inimical to the purposes of these laws to award damages for the type of injury claimed here. . . .

We therefore hold that for the plaintiffs to recover treble damages on account of § 7 violations, they must prove more than injury causally linked to an illegal presence in the market. Plaintiffs must prove *antitrust* injury, which is to say injury of the type the antitrust laws were intended to prevent and that flows from that which makes defendants' acts unlawful. The injury should reflect the anticompetitive effect either of the violation or of anticompetitive acts made possible by the violation. It should, in short, be "the type of loss that the claimed violations . . . would be likely to cause." *Zenith Radio Corp. v. Hazeltine Research, Inc., supra*, 395 U.S., at 125.

Some courts are very grudging in allowing "no antitrust injury" defenses, others exceptionally lenient, and the cases are at times difficult to reconcile. For recent cases taking different policy positions on the question of antitrust injury *compare* Geneva Pharmaceuticals Technology Corp. v. Barr Laboratories, 386 F.3d 485 (2nd Cir. 2004), concluding there could be no injury to competition where merging firms already had a monopoly on the product because the merger would have no effect on competition *with* Theme Promotions v. News America Marketing, FSI, 546 F.3d 991 (9th Cir. 2008), upholding a jury verdict that antitrust injury had occurred where plaintiff claimed it could not place ads with defendant's lower price competitors because defendant had extracted right of first refusal agreements from plaintiffs customers.

See Chapter 2 (pp. 92–93 *supra*) for a discussion of how lower courts have, at times, wrenched the "antitrust injury" concept free of these sensible Section 7 moorings.

2.   Cargill, Inc. v. Monfort of Colorado, Inc., 479 U.S. 104 (1986). Monfort, the nation's fifth largest beef packer, brought an action under the Clayton Act to enjoin a merger between the second and third largest beef packers. After a trial, a district court enjoined the proposed merger, and held that Monfort's allegation of a "price-cost squeeze" that would severely narrow its profit margins constituted an allegation of antitrust injury. The Tenth Circuit affirmed. Justice Brennan, writing for six members of the Supreme Court, reversed and reasoned as follows:

This case requires us to decide, at the outset, a question we have not previously addressed: whether a private plaintiff seeking an injunction under § 16 of the Clayton Act must show a threat of antitrust injury. To decide the question, we must look first to the source of the antitrust injury requirement, which lies in a related provision of the Clayton Act, § 4. . . . In *Brunswick Corp. v. Pueblo Bowl–O–Mat, Inc., supra*, we held that plaintiffs seeking treble damages under § 4 must show more than simply an "injury causally linked" to a particular merger; instead, "plaintiffs must prove antitrust injury, which is to say injury of the type the antitrust laws were intended to prevent and that flows from that which makes the defendants' acts unlawful." . . .

Section 16 of the Clayton Act provides in part that "[a]ny person, firm, corporation, or association shall be entitled to sue for and have injunctive relief . . . against threatened loss or damage by a violation of the antitrust laws. . . ." 15 U.S.C. § 26. It is plain that § 16 and § 4 do differ in various ways. For example, § 4 requires a plaintiff to show actual injury, but § 16 requires a showing only of "threatened" loss or damage; similarly, § 4 requires a showing of injury to "business or property," *cf. Hawaii v. Standard Oil Co.*, 405 U.S. 251 (1972), while § 16 contains no such limitation.[55] Although these differences do affect the nature of the injury cognizable under each section, the lower courts, including the courts below, have found that under both § 16 and § 4 the plaintiff must still allege an injury of the type the antitrust laws were designed to prevent. We agree.

The wording concerning the relationship of the injury to the violation of the antitrust laws in each section is comparable. Section 4 requires proof of injury "by reason of anything forbidden in the antitrust laws"; § 16 requires proof of "threatened loss or damage by a violation of the antitrust laws." It would be anomalous, we think, to read the Clayton Act to authorize a private plaintiff to secure an injunction against a threatened injury for which he would not be entitled to compensation if the injury actually occurred. . . .

Sections 4 and 16 are thus best understood as providing complementary remedies for a single set of injuries. Accordingly, we conclude that in order to seek injunctive relief under § 16, a private plaintiff must allege threatened loss or damage "of the type the antitrust laws were designed to prevent and that flows from that which makes defendants' acts unlawful." Brunswick, 429 U.S., at 489. We therefore turn to the question of whether the proposed merger in this case threatened respondent with antitrust injury. . . .

Monfort's first claim is that after the merger, Excel would lower its prices to some level at or slightly above its costs in order to compete with other packers for market share. Excel would be in a position to do this because of the multiplant efficiencies its acquisition of Spencer would provide. To remain competitive, Monfort would have to lower its prices; as a result, Monfort would suffer a loss in profitability, but would not be driven out of business. The question is whether Monfort's loss of profits in such circumstances constitutes antitrust injury. . . .

---

55. Standing analysis under § 16 will not always be identical to standing analysis under § 4. For example, the difference in the remedy each section provides means that certain considerations relevant to a determination of standing under § 4 are not relevant under § 16. The treble-damage remedy, if afforded to "every person tangentially affected by an antitrust violation," *McCready*, 457 U.S., at 476–477, or for "all injuries that might conceivably be traced to an antitrust violation," Hawaii v. Standard Oil Co., 405 U.S., at 263, n. 14 would "open the door to duplicative recoveries," and to multiple lawsuits. In order to protect against multiple lawsuits and duplicative recoveries, courts should examine other factors in addition to antitrust injury, such as the potential for duplicative recovery, the complexity of apportioning damages, and the existence of other parties that have been more directly harmed, to determine whether a party is a proper plaintiff under § 4. See *Associated General Contractors, supra*, at 544–545; Illinois Brick Co. v. Illinois, 431 U.S. 720 (1977). Conversely, under § 16, the only remedy available is equitable in nature, and, as we recognized in *Hawaii v. Standard Oil Co.*, "the fact is that one injunction is as effective as 100, and concomitantly, that 100 injunctions are no more effective than one." 405 U.S., at 261 (1972). Thus, because standing under § 16 raises no threat of multiple lawsuits or duplicative recoveries, some of the factors other than antitrust injury that are appropriate to a determination of standing under § 4 are not relevant under § 16.

We find respondent's proposed construction of § 7 too broad, for reasons that *Brunswick* illustrates. *Brunswick* holds that the antitrust laws do not require the courts to protect small businesses from the loss of profits due to continued competition, but only against the loss of profits from practices forbidden by the antitrust laws. The kind of competition that Monfort alleges here, competition for increased market share, is not activity forbidden by the antitrust laws. It is simply, as petitioners claim, vigorous competition. To hold that the antitrust laws protect competitors from the loss of profits due to such price competition would, in effect, render illegal any decision by a firm to cut prices in order to increase market share. The antitrust laws require no such perverse result, for "[i]t is in the interest of competition to permit dominant firms to engage in vigorous competition, including price competition." . . . The logic of *Brunswick* compels the conclusion that the threat of loss of profits due to possible price competition following a merger does not constitute a threat of antitrust injury.

The second theory of injury argued here is that after the merger Excel would attempt to drive Monfort out of business by engaging in sustained predatory pricing. Predatory pricing may be defined as pricing below an appropriate measure of cost for the purpose of eliminating competitors in the short run and reducing competition in the long run. It is a practice that harms both competitors and competition. In contrast to price cutting aimed simply at increasing market share, predatory pricing has as its aim the elimination of competition. Predatory pricing is thus a practice "inimical to the purposes of [the antitrust] laws," *Brunswick*, 429 U.S., at 488, and one capable of inflicting antitrust injury. . . .

[T]he Court of Appeals can be understood to mean that Monfort had shown a credible threat of injury from below-cost pricing. To the extent the judgment rests on this ground, however, it must also be reversed, because Monfort did not allege injury from below-cost pricing before the District Court. . . .

In its *amicus* brief, the United States argues that the "danger of allowing a competitor to challenge an acquisition on the basis of necessarily speculative claims of post-acquisition predatory pricing far outweighs the danger that any anticompetitive merger will go unchallenged." Brief for United States as *Amicus Curiae* 25. On this basis, the United States invites the Court to adopt in effect a *per se* rule "denying competitors standing to challenge acquisitions on the basis of predatory pricing theories."

We decline the invitation. As the foregoing discussion makes plain, predatory pricing is an anticompetitive practice forbidden by the antitrust laws. While firms may engage in the practice only infrequently, there is ample evidence suggesting that the practice does occur. It would be novel indeed for a court to deny standing to a party seeking an injunction against threatened injury merely because such injuries rarely occur. In any case, nothing in the language or legislative history of the Clayton Act suggests that Congress intended this Court to ignore injuries caused by such anticompetitive practices as predatory pricing. . . .

In dissent, Justice Stevens, joined by Justice White, argued as follows:

In Brunswick, we began our analysis by acknowledging the difficulty of meshing § 7, "a statutory prohibition against acts that have a potential to cause certain harms," with § 4, a "damages action intended to remedy those harms." We concluded that a plaintiff must prove more than a violation of § 7 to recover damages, "since such proof establishes only that injury may result." Beyond the special nature of an action for treble damages, § 16 differs from § 4 because by its terms it requires only that the antitrust violation threaten that a competitor of the merging firms will suffer some corresponding harm in due course. In my opinion, that reasonable probability gives the competitor an interest in the proceeding adequate to confer standing to challenge the merger. To hold otherwise is to frustrate § 7 and to read § 16 far too restrictively.

It would be a strange antitrust statute indeed which defined a violation enforceable by no private party. Effective enforcement of the antitrust laws has always depended largely on the work of private attorney generals, for whom Congress made special provision in the Clayton Act itself. As recently as 1976, Congress specifically indicated its intent to encourage private enforcement of § 16 by authorizing recovery of a reasonable attorney's fee by a plaintiff in an action for injunctive relief. The Hart–Scott–Rodino Antitrust Improvements Act of 1976.

The Court misunderstands the message that Congress conveyed in 1914 and emphasized in 1950. If, as the District Court and the Court of Appeals held, the merger is illegal, it should be set aside.

3. The 1980s was a period of minimal enforcement of the anti-merger laws by the federal enforcement agencies. Until the Supreme Court's decision in *Cargill*, private plaintiffs had enjoyed significant success in obtaining preliminary injunctive relief against proposed transactions.[56] Many of the acquisitions found to be likely to violate Section 7 by the courts had been "cleared" by the Department of Justice or the FTC.

Although there was great fear in 1986 that *Cargill* would sharply curtail—or eliminate—private actions in the merger area, this appears to be much less the case than originally feared.

For example, in R.C. Bigelow, Inc. v. Unilever N.V., 867 F.2d 102 (2d Cir. 1989), *cert. denied*, 493 U.S. 815 (1989), the FTC had "cleared" a merger between two herbal tea manufacturers that would have given the merger combination 84 percent of the national herbal tea market. The FTC apparently thought the relevant market included, at least, "all tea" and that entry was easy. The Second Circuit, on the assumption that the relevant market was in fact limited to herbal teas, reversed a district court's grant of summary judgment for defendants and concluded:

> Although we must be wary of competitors attempting to obtain antitrust standing based upon prospective loss or damage due to competition for increased market share, *cf. Cargill*, 479 U.S. at 116 & 122, we have little doubt that antitrust injury to a competitor can be found when the market share of the merging firms threatens to be decisive.

Similarly, in Consolidated Gold Fields PLC v. Minorco, S.A., 871 F.2d 252 (2d Cir.1989), the FTC had "cleared" a hostile tender offer by foreign gold-mining interests seeking to acquire a foreign corporation with gold-mining interests in the United States. Consummation of the transaction would have given the combined

---

56. *See, e.g.*, Christian Schmidt Brewing Co. v. G. Heileman Brewing Co., 600 F.Supp. 1326 (E.D.Mich.), aff'd, 753 F.2d 1354 (6th Cir.1985); Cia. Petrolera Caribe, Inc. v. Arco Caribbean, Inc., 754 F.2d 404 (1st Cir.1985).

entity 32 percent of the market. Although several courts and commentators have argued that a "target company" has no standing because after the takeover it would benefit from a "super-competitive advantage,"[57] the Second Circuit rejected this analysis:

> This Circuit has previously upheld target standing to challenge takeovers alleged to violate section 7, and we reaffirm that position today. In our view, Gold Fields has demonstrated a threat of "antitrust injury." If the acquisition is permitted to go forward, Gold Fields will lose its ability to compete independently in the gold production market. Its wholly owned United States mining subsidiary, GFMC, is threatened with curtailment of its production, much like Newmont. Surely Gold Fields' loss of independence is causally linked to the injury occurring in the marketplace, where the acquisition threatens to diminish competitive forces. Though what happens to Gold Fields and what happens to competition may not be precisely the same type of injury, there is a common element in that the independent existence of a major competitor is being eliminated. It is not a sufficient answer to say that even though competition is diminished, Gold Fields is not injured because of its absorption into the Minorco group. The enlarged entity that emerges from the takeover may benefit from the acquisition, but Gold Fields will have lost one of the vital components of competition—the power of independent decision-making as to price and output. It is hard to imagine an injury to competition more clearly "of the type the antitrust laws were intended to prevent," *Brunswick Corp. v. Pueblo Bowl–O–Mat, Inc., supra* 429 U.S. at 489, than the elimination of a major competitor's power to determine its prices and output. It is precisely the loss of this power that makes a section 1 conspiracy so pernicious. For this reason, a member of a section 1 conspiracy has standing to challenge the restraint upon its freedom to compete, even though, in the long run, it may enjoy the benefits of the cartel....
>
> It is possible, of course, that Gold Fields, if it remains a distinct corporation within the enlarged Minorco combination, will ultimately derive some economic benefit from the enhanced power of its corporate parent. But Gold Fields is entitled to prefer to take its chances on its capacity to prosper as an independent entity. Whether in the long run more profits will enter its corporate treasury as an independent company than as a subsidiary of Minorco is a speculative matter that need not concern us. The antitrust laws ensure the right to compete. That is what Gold Fields wishes to do, and that is what it will not be able to do if the threatened takeover succeeds.

The Second Circuit then asserted that the Supreme Court decision in *Cargill* did not require a different result since in that case the Supreme Court held only that a claim by a competitor that it would be hurt by *increased* competition resulting from the acquisition did not constitute "antitrust injury." Here, the injury alleged would result from the new parent's decision to *reduce* competition by eliminating the target as a competitor.

The Second Circuit also upheld the district court's findings: (1) that the 32 percent market share which would result from the takeover triggered a presumption of Section 7 illegality under *Philadelphia Bank*; (2) that eastern bloc gold

---

57. *See, e.g.*, Central Nat'l Bank v. Rainbolt, 720 F.2d 1183 (10th Cir.1983); *but see* Marathon Oil Co. v. Mobil Corp., 669 F.2d 378 (6th Cir.1981).

sources were properly excluded from the market definition, since there was evidence that sales of eastern bloc gold did not increase when the price of western gold rose over substantial periods; and (3) that a preliminary injunction was appropriate relief.

During the period 1988 to 2000, federal enforcement of antimerger legislation increased substantially and, as a consequence, challenges by state attorneys general and private parties declined. Nevertheless, there are still occasional instances when the federal agencies clear a transaction that is subsequently challenged. *See State of New York v. Kraft General Foods, Inc.*, 926 F.Supp. 321 (S.D.N.Y.1995), where a district court found that the acquisition by Kraft (owner of Post cereals with 11.7% of sales in the ready-to-eat cereal market) of Nabisco (with 2.8% of sales—primarily of shredded wheat cereals), previously cleared by the Federal Trade Commission, did not violate Section 7 of the antitrust laws.

4. Problems related to designing appropriate remedies are often of central importance to the effective enforcement of Section 7. The guiding principle is that equitable decrees should restore effective competition. United States v. Crescent Amusement Co., 323 U.S. 173 (1944); *see* Chapter 2, p. 93 *supra*. In the remedy phase of the *du Pont–GM* case, the Supreme Court noted that equitable relief may not go beyond what is necessary to restore effective competition. But possible economic hardship, however severe, is relevant only if a court has a choice between two effective remedies; an effective remedy cannot be defeated because it would entail harsh consequences. The Court concluded: "... complete divestiture is particularly appropriate in cases of stock acquisitions which violate Section 7.... It is simple, relatively easy to administer and sure. It should always be in the forefront of a Court's mind when a violation of Section 7 has been found." 366 U.S. at 331.

5. A dispute arose in lower federal courts as to the availability of divestiture as a remedy in private actions under the Sherman and Clayton Acts. In ITT v. General Telephone & Electronics Corp., 518 F.2d 913 (9th Cir.1975), the Court of Appeals heard GTE's appeal from a district court's ruling that "equitable remedies are available to private plaintiffs under Section 16." 351 F.Supp. at 1207. The district court had held that GTE's acquisition of telephone operating companies had foreclosed manufacturing competitors of GTE from selling equipment and supplies to the operating companies in violation of Sections 1 and 2 of the Sherman Act and Section 7 of the Clayton Act.

The Ninth Circuit held that the remedy of divestiture was not available in private actions. The Court noted that the reference in Section 16 of the Clayton Act to "injunctive relief" is ambiguous; "while some courts have viewed divestiture as a subspecies of 'injunctive relief,' others have held that injunctive remedies and divestiture are distinct categories of equitable relief" and that Section 16 "is not broad enough to include divestiture." 518 F.2d at 921. After a review of the Clayton Act's legislative history, the Court concluded that Congressional intent precluded the use of divestiture as a remedy in private cases. Injunctive relief was chosen as a substitute for divestiture, the Court suggested, because the latter was too harsh and potent a remedy to be entrusted to private hands. The Court reasoned:

> In holding that the remedy of divestiture is not available we do not jeopardize the district court's ability to restrain GTE effectively from violating the antitrust laws. Injunctive remedies under § 16 may be as broad as necessary to ensure that "threatened loss or damage" does not materialize or that prior violations do not recur.

518 F.2d at 924–25, *see, e.g.,* Calnetics Corp. v. Volkswagen of America, Inc., 532 F.2d 674 (9th Cir.), *cert. denied,* 429 U.S. 940 (1976); Venner v. Pennsylvania Steel Co., 250 F. 292 (D.N.J.1918).

A contrary view was taken by the Court of Appeals for the Third Circuit in *NBO Industries Treadway Co. v. Brunswick Corp.,* 523 F.2d 262 (3d Cir.1975), cert. denied on this issue, 429 U.S. 1090 (1977). In *dictum,* the Third Circuit questioned the Ninth Circuit's legislative history and perceived:

> danger in permitting the pronouncements of statesmen long deceased to control the contemporary meaning of statutes which are almost an economic constitution for our complex national economy. 523 F.2d at 279.[58]

In 1990, the Supreme Court resolved the conflict in the circuits in *California v. American Stores Co.*[59] The Court held that divestiture is a form of injunctive relief within the meaning of Section 16 of the Clayton Act.

The history of the *American Stores* case provides important insights into the usefulness of private actions—or state attorneys general acting in an analogous capacity—under Section 7. The FTC had challenged the merger but settled for a consent decree that California's Attorney General found inadequate, and he challenged the acquisition on behalf of himself and as *parens patriae* for consumers in California.

The district court, using the geographic market defined by American Stores, found American Stores' average post-merger share of the market to be 24 percent, with a range from 15 to 38 percent in individual areas. After considering concentration ratios and entry barriers, the Ninth Circuit concluded that "the district court's holding that American Stores did not satisfy its burden of rebutting California's prima facie showing of a violation of Section 7 was not an abuse of discretion." The Ninth Circuit, however, modified the district judge's grant of relief because "divestiture, whether direct or indirect, is not an available form of relief under Section 16...."[60]

Justice Stevens, writing for a unanimous Supreme Court, reversed the Ninth Circuit and reasoned:

> If we assume that the merger violated the antitrust laws, and if we agree with the District Court's finding that the conduct of the merged enterprise threatens economic harm to California consumers, the literal text of § 16 is plainly sufficient to authorize injunctive relief, including an order of divestiture, that will prohibit that conduct from causing that harm. This interpretation is consistent with our precedents, which have upheld injunctions issued pursuant to § 16 regardless of whether they were mandatory or prohibitory in character.... We have recognized when construing § 16 that it was enacted "not merely to provide private relief, but ... to serve as well the high purpose of enforcing the antitrust laws." *Zenith Radio Corp.,* 395 U.S., at 130–131. We have accordingly applied the section "with this purpose in mind, and with the knowledge that the remedy it affords, like other equitable remedies, is flexible and capable of nice 'adjustment and reconciliation between the public interest and private

58. *See, e.g.,* Cia. Petrolera Caribe, Inc. v. Arco Caribbean, Inc., 754 F.2d 404 (1st Cir.1985); Julius Nasso Concrete Corp. v. DIC Concrete Corp., 467 F.Supp. 1016 (S.D.N.Y. 1979).

59. 495 U.S. 271 (1990).

60. 872 F.2d 837 (9th Cir.1989).

needs as well as between competing private claims.' " *Ibid.*, quoting *Hecht Co. v. Bowles*, 321 U.S. 321, 329–330 (1944).

Finally, by construing § 16 to encompass divestiture decrees we are better able than is American to harmonize the section with its statutory context. The Act's other provisions manifest a clear intent to encourage vigorous private litigation against anticompetitive mergers. Section 7 itself creates a relatively expansive definition of antitrust liability: to show that a merger is unlawful, a plaintiff need only prove that its effect *"may be substantially to lessen competition."* Clayton Act § 7, 38 Stat. 731, 15 U.S.C. § 18 (emphasis supplied). See *Brown Shoe Co. v. United States*, 370 U.S. 294, 323 (1962). In addition, § 5 of the Act provided that during the pendency of a government action, the statute of limitations for private actions would be tolled. The section also permitted plaintiffs to use the final judgment in a government antitrust suit as prima facie evidence of liability in a later civil suit. Private enforcement of the Act was in no sense an afterthought; it was an integral part of the congressional plan for protecting competition. See *Minnesota Mining & Mfg. Co. v. New Jersey Wood Finishing Co.*, 381 U.S. 311, 318 (1965). Congress also made express its view that divestiture was the most suitable remedy in a suit for relief from a § 7 violation: in § 11 of the Act, Congress directed the Federal Trade Commission to issue orders requiring that a violator of § 7 "cease and desist from the violation," and, specifically, that the violator "divest itself of the stock held" in violation of the Act. Section 16, construed to authorize a private divestiture remedy when appropriate in light of equitable principles, fits well in a statutory scheme that favors private enforcement, subjects mergers to searching scrutiny, and regards divestiture as the remedy best suited to redress the ills of an anticompetitive merger. . . .

[I]n *Weinberger v. Romero–Barcelo*, 456 U.S. 305, 313 (1982), we observed that when Congress endows the federal courts with equitable jurisdiction, Congress acts aware of this longstanding tradition of flexibility. " 'Unless a statute in so many words, or by a necessary and inescapable inference, restricts the court's jurisdiction in equity, the full scope of that jurisdiction is to be recognized and applied.' " *Id.*, quoting *Porter v. Warner Holding Co.*, 328 U.S. 395, 398 (1946). These principles unquestionably support a construction of the statute that will enable a chancellor to impose the most effective, usual and straightforward remedy to rescind an unlawful purchase of stock or assets. The fact that the term "divestiture" is used to describe what is typically nothing more than the familiar remedy of rescission does not place the remedy beyond the normal reach of the chancellor.

Our conclusion that a district court has the power to order divestiture in appropriate cases brought under § 16 of the Clayton Act does not, of course, mean that such power should be exercised in every situation in which the Government would be entitled to such relief under § 15. In a Government case the proof of the violation of law may itself establish sufficient public injury to warrant relief. See *Du Pont*, 366 U.S., at 319–321; see also *Virginian R. Co. v. Railway Employees*, 300 U.S. 515, 552 (1937) ("Courts of equity may, and frequently do, go much farther both to give and withhold relief in furtherance of the public interest than they are accustomed to go when only private interests are involved"); *United States v. San Francisco*, 310 U.S. 16, 30–31 (1940) (authorizing issuance of injunction at Government's request without balancing of the equities). A private litigant, however, must have standing—in the words of § 16, he must prove "threatened loss or damage" to his own interests in order to obtain relief. See *Cargill, Inc. v. Monfort of Colorado, Inc.*, 479 U.S. 104 (1986). Moreover, equitable defenses such as laches, or perhaps "unclean hands," may protect consummated transactions from belated attacks by private parties when it would not be too late for the Government to vindicate the public interest.

Such questions, however, are not presented in this case. We are merely confronted with the naked question whether the District Court had the power to divest American of any part of its ownership interests in the acquired Lucky Stores, either by forbidding the exercise of the owner's normal right to integrate the operations of the two previously separate companies, or by requiring it to sell certain assets located in California. We hold that such a remedy is a form of "injunctive relief" within the meaning of § 16 of the Clayton Act. Accordingly, the judgment of the Court of Appeals is reversed and the case is remanded for further proceedings consistent with this opinion.[61]

U.S. Department of Justice and FTC Joint Horizontal Merger Guidelines, 1992

[Introduction. Federal merger enforcement has largely become a matter of administrative action.

If the government elects not to sue, the transaction usually goes forward. It is relatively rare that private parties or state attorneys general will elect to challenge. If the government believes the transaction violates Section 7, the parties often attempt to negotiate a settlement (frequently spinning off a portion of the acquired assets in order to allow the rest of the deal to go through), or they abandon the deal. There was a slight uptick in government merger litigation in the mid-1990s—see *FTC v. Staples*, *infra*, p. 1062, and *FTC v. Beechnut–Heinz*, *infra*, p. 1059, but throughout the period litigation was very much the exception to the rule of administrative treatment.

In order to advise businesses of enforcement intentions, the Justice Department issued merger guidelines in 1968, 1982 and 1984. In 1992, the Federal Trade Commission and the Department of Justice issued joint horizontal merger guidelines, amended in 1997 to introduce an expanded section 4 dealing with claims of efficiency. Vertical and conglomerate mergers continue to be examined under the now rather dated and not very influential 1984 guidelines.

In general, the guidelines have tended to become more lenient with each iteration and also more detailed, specific, and economically sophisticated.

---

61. 495 U.S. 271, 283–85, 295–96 (1990).

These guidelines are designed to help people predict the enforcement intentions of the federal agencies. They have no binding effect on courts, although a few courts have taken the guidelines and their analytical approaches into account. Although not binding, the guidelines have had an enormous impact on merger policy in the United States. Particularly because the Supreme Court has not accepted review of the merits of a merger since its General Dynamics opinion in 1974, the guidelines have been the principal source of new thinking about merger policy.

The joint FTC–DOJ 1992 horizontal merger guidelines (including the 1997 revisions) are set out below and the 1984 vertical and conglomerate guidelines in subsequent sections of this chapter.]

1. MARKET DEFINITION, MEASUREMENT AND CONCENTRATION

1.0 Overview

A merger is unlikely to create or enhance market power or to facilitate its exercise unless it significantly increases concentration and results in a concentrated market, properly defined and measured. Mergers that either do not significantly increase concentration or do not result in a concentrated market ordinarily require no further analysis.

The analytic process described in this section ensures that the Agency evaluates the likely competitive impact of a merger within the context of economically meaningful markets—*i.e.,* markets that could be subject to the exercise of market power. Accordingly, for each product or service (hereafter "product") of each merging firm, the Agency seeks to define a market in which firms could effectively exercise market power if they were able to coordinate their actions.

Market definition focuses solely on demand substitution factors—*i.e.,* possible consumer responses. Supply substitution factors—*i.e.,* possible production responses—are considered elsewhere in the Guidelines in the identification of firms that participate in the relevant market and the analysis of entry. *See* Sections 1.3 and 3. A market is defined as a product or group of products and a geographic area in which it is produced or sold such that a hypothetical profit-maximizing firm, not subject to price regulation, that was the only present and future producer or seller of those products in that area likely would impose at least a "small but significant and nontransitory" increase in price, assuming the terms of sale of all other products are held constant. A relevant market is a group of products and a geographic area that is no bigger than necessary to satisfy this test. The "small but significant and nontransitory" increase in price is employed solely as a methodological tool for the analysis of mergers: it is not a tolerance level for price increases.

Absent price discrimination, a relevant market is described by a product or group of products and a geographic area. In determining whether a hypothetical monopolist would be in a position to exercise market power, it is necessary to evaluate the likely demand responses of consumers to a price increase. A price increase could be made unprofitable by consumers either switching to other products or switching to the same product produced by firms at other locations. The nature and magnitude of these two types of demand responses respectively determine the scope of the product market and the geographic market.

In contrast, where a hypothetical monopolist likely would discriminate in prices charged to different groups of buyers, distinguished, for example, by their uses or locations, the Agency may delineate different relevant markets corresponding to each such buyer group. Competition for sales to each such group may be affected differently by a particular merger and markets are delineated by evaluating the demand response of each such buyer group. A relevant market of this kind is described by a collection of products for sale to a given group of buyers.

Once defined, a relevant market must be measured in terms of its participants and concentration. Participants include firms currently producing or selling the market's products in the market's geographic area. In addition, participants may include other firms depending on their likely supply responses to a "small but significant and nontransitory" price increase. A firm is viewed as a participant if, in response to a "small but significant and nontransitory" price increase, it likely would enter rapidly into production or sale of a market product in the market's area, without incurring significant sunk costs of entry and exit. Firms likely to make any of these supply responses are considered to be "uncommitted" entrants because their supply response would create new production or sale in the relevant market and because that production or sale could be quickly terminated without significant loss.[62] Uncommitted entrants are capable of making such quick and uncommitted supply responses that they likely influenced the market pre-merger, would influence it post-merger, and accordingly are considered as market participants at both times. This analysis of market definition and market measurement applies equally to foreign and domestic firms.

If the process of market definition and market measurement identifies one or more relevant markets in which the merging firms are both participants, then the merger is considered to be horizontal. Sections 1.1 through 1.5 describe in greater detail how product and geographic markets will be defined, how market shares will be calculated and how market concentration will be assessed.

1.1   Product Market Definition

The Agency will first define the relevant product market with respect to each of the products of each of the merging firms.[63]

---

62. Probable supply responses that require the entrant to incur significant sunk costs of entry and exit are not part of market measurement, but are included in the analysis of the significance of entry. See Section 3. Entrants that must commit substantial sunk costs are regarded as "committed" entrants because those sunk costs make entry irreversible in the short term without foregoing that investment; thus the likelihood of their entry must be evaluated with regard to their long-term profitability.

63. Although discussed separately, product market definition and geographic market definition are interrelated. In particular, the extent to which buyers of a particular product

1.11 General Standards

Absent price discrimination, the Agency will delineate the product market to be a product or group of products such that a hypothetical profit-maximizing firm that was the only present and future seller of those products ("monopolist") likely would impose at least a "small but significant and nontransitory" increase in price. That is, assuming that buyers likely would respond to an increase in price for a tentatively identified product group only by shifting to other products, what would happen? If the alternatives were, in the aggregate, sufficiently attractive at their existing terms of sale, an attempt to raise prices would result in a reduction of sales large enough that the price increase would not prove profitable, and the tentatively identified product group would prove to be too narrow.

Specifically, the Agency will begin with each product (narrowly defined) produced or sold by each merging firm and ask what would happen if a hypothetical monopolist of that product imposed at least a "small but significant and nontransitory" increase in price, but the terms of sale of all other products remained constant. If, in response to the price increase, the reduction in sales of the product would be large enough that a hypothetical monopolist would not find it profitable to impose such an increase in price, then the Agency will add to the product group the product that is the next best substitute for the merging firm's product.[64]

In considering the likely reaction of buyers to a price increase, the Agency will take into account all relevant evidence, including, but not limited to, the following:

(1) evidence that buyers have shifted or have considered shifting purchases between products in response to relative changes in price or other competitive variables;

(2) evidence that sellers base business decisions on the prospect of buyer substitution between products in response to relative changes in price or other competitive variables;

(3) the influence of downstream competition faced by buyers in their output markets; and

(4) the timing and costs of switching products.

The price increase question is then asked for a hypothetical monopolist controlling the expanded product group. In performing successive iterations of the price increase test, the hypothetical monopolist will be assumed to pursue maximum profits in deciding whether to raise the prices of any or all of the additional products under its control. This process will continue until a group of products is identified such that a hypothetical monopolist

---

would shift to other products in the event of a "small but significant and nontransitory" increase in price must be evaluated in the context of the relevant geographic market.

64. Throughout the Guidelines, the term "next best substitute" refers to the alternative which, if available in unlimited quantities at constant prices, would account for the greatest value of diversion of demand in response to a "small but significant and nontransitory" price increase.

over that group of products would profitably impose at least a "small but significant and nontransitory" increase, including the price of a product of one of the merging firms. The Agency generally will consider the relevant product market to be the smallest group of products that satisfies this test.

In the above analysis, the Agency will use prevailing prices of the products of the merging firms and possible substitutes for such products, unless premerger circumstances are strongly suggestive of coordinated interaction, in which case the Agency will use a price more reflective of the competitive price.[65] However, the Agency may use likely future prices, absent the merger, when changes in the prevailing prices can be predicted with reasonable reliability. Changes in price may be predicted on the basis of, for example, changes in regulation which affect price either directly or indirectly by affecting costs or demand.

In general, the price for which an increase will be postulated will be whatever is considered to be the price of the product at the stage of the industry being examined.[66] In attempting to determine objectively the effect of a "small but significant and nontransitory" increase in price, the Agency, in most contexts, will use a price increase of five percent lasting for the foreseeable future. However, what constitutes a "small but significant and nontransitory" increase in price will depend on the nature of the industry, and the Agency at times may use a price increase that is larger or smaller than five percent.

1.12   Product Market Definition in the Presence of Price Discrimination

The analysis of product market definition to this point has assumed that price discrimination—charging different buyers different prices for the same product, for example—would not be profitable for a hypothetical monopolist. A different analysis applies where price discrimination would be profitable for a hypothetical monopolist.

Existing buyers sometimes will differ significantly in their likelihood of switching to other products in response to a "small but significant and nontransitory" price increase. If a hypothetical monopolist can identify and price differently to those buyers ("targeted buyers") who would not defeat the targeted price increase by substituting to other products in response to a "small but significant and nontransitory" price increase for the relevant product, and if other buyers likely would not purchase the relevant product and resell to targeted buyers, then a hypothetical monopolist would profitably impose a discriminatory price increase on sales to targeted buyers. This is true regardless of whether a general increase in price would cause such significant substitution that the price increase would not be profitable.

---

65.   The terms of sale of all other products are held constant in order to focus market definition on the behavior of consumers. Movements in the terms of sale for other products, as may result from the behavior of producers of those products, are accounted for in the analysis of competitive effects and entry. See Sections 2 and 3.

66.   For example, in a merger between retailers, the relevant price would be the retail price of a product to consumers. In the case of a merger among oil pipelines, the relevant price would be the tariff—the price of the transportation service.

The Agency will consider additional relevant product markets consisting of a particular use or uses by groups of buyers of the product for which a hypothetical monopolist would profitably and separately impose at least a "small but significant and nontransitory" increase in price.

1.2 Geographic Market Definition

For each product market in which both merging firms participate, the Agency will determine the geographic market or markets in which the firms produce or sell. A single firm may operate in a number of different geographic markets.

1.21 General Standards

Absent price discrimination, the Agency will delineate the geographic market to be a region such that a hypothetical monopolist that was the only present or future producer of the relevant product at locations in that region would profitably impose at least a "small but significant and nontransitory" increase in price, holding constant the terms of sale for all products produced elsewhere. That is, assuming that buyers likely would respond to a price increase on products produced within the tentatively identified region only by shifting to products produced at locations of production outside the region, what would happen? If those locations of production outside the region were, in the aggregate, sufficiently attractive at their existing terms of sale, an attempt to raise price would result in a reduction in sales large enough that the price increase would not prove profitable, and the tentatively identified geographic area would prove to be too narrow.

In defining the geographic market or markets affected by a merger, the Agency will begin with the location of each merging firm (or each plant of a multiplant firm) and ask what would happen if a hypothetical monopolist of the relevant product at that point imposed at least a "small but significant and nontransitory" increase in price, but the terms of sale at all other locations remained constant. If, in response to the price increase, the reduction in sales of the product at that location would be large enough that a hypothetical monopolist producing or selling the relevant product at the merging firm's location would not find it profitable to impose such an increase in price, then the Agency will add the location from which production is the next-best substitute for production at the merging firm's location.

In considering the likely reaction of buyers to a price increase, the Agency will take into account all relevant evidence, including, but not limited to, the following:

(1) evidence that buyers have shifted or have considered shifting purchases between different geographic locations in response to relative changes in price or other competitive variables;

(2) evidence that sellers base business decisions on the prospect of buyer substitution between geographic locations in response to relative changes in price or other competitive variables;

(3) the influence of downstream competition faced by buyers in their output markets; and

(4) the timing and costs of switching suppliers.

The price increase question is then asked for a hypothetical monopolist controlling the expanded group of locations. In performing successive iterations of the price increase test, the hypothetical monopolist will be assumed to pursue maximum profits in deciding whether to raise the price at any or all of the additional locations under its control. This process will continue until a group of locations is identified such that a hypothetical monopolist over that group of locations would profitably impose at least a "small but significant and nontransitory" increase, including the price charged at a location of one of the merging firms.

The "smallest market" principle will be applied as it is in product market definition. The price for which an increase will be postulated, what constitutes a "small but significant and nontransitory" increase in price, and the substitution decisions of consumers all will be determined in the same way in which they are determined in product market definition.

1.22 Geographic Market Definition in the Presence of Price Discrimination

The analysis of geographic market definition to this point has assumed that geographic price discrimination—charging different prices net of transportation costs for the same product to buyers in different areas, for example—would not be profitable for a hypothetical monopolist. However, if a hypothetical monopolist can identify and price differently to buyers in certain areas ("targeted buyers") who would not defeat the targeted price increase by substituting to more distant sellers in response to a "small but significant and nontransitory" price increase for the relevant product, and if other buyers likely would not purchase the relevant product and resell to targeted buyers,[67] then a hypothetical monopolist would profitably impose a discriminatory price increase. This is true even where a general price increase would cause such significant substitution that the price increase would not be profitable. The Agency will consider additional geographic markets consisting of particular locations of buyers for which a hypothetical monopolist would profitably and separately impose at least a "small but significant and nontransitory" increase in price.

1.3 Identification of Firms That Participate in the Relevant Market

1.31 Current Producers or Sellers

The Agency's identification of firms that participate in the relevant market begins with all firms that currently produce or sell in the relevant market. This includes vertically integrated firms to the extent that such inclusion accurately reflects their competitive significance in the relevant

---

67. This arbitrage is inherently impossible for many services and is particularly difficult where the product is sold on a delivered basis and where transportation costs are a significant percentage of the final cost.

market prior to the merger. To the extent that the analysis under Section 1.1 indicates that used, reconditioned or recycled goods are included in the relevant market, market participants will include firms that produce or sell such goods and that likely would offer those goods in competition with other relevant products.

1.32   Firms That Participate Through Supply Response

In addition, the Agency will identify other firms not currently producing or selling the relevant product in the relevant area as participating in the relevant market if their inclusion would more accurately reflect probable supply responses. These firms are termed "uncommitted." These supply responses must be likely to occur within one year and without the expenditure of significant sunk costs of entry and exit, in response to a "small but significant and nontransitory" price increase. If a firm has the technological capability to achieve such an uncommitted supply response, but likely would not (*e.g.*, because difficulties in achieving product acceptance, distribution, or production would render such a response unprofitable), that firm will not be considered to be a market participant. The competitive significance of supply responses that require more time or that require firms to incur significant sunk costs of entry and exit will be considered in entry analysis. *See* Section 3.[68]

Sunk costs are the acquisition costs of tangible and intangible assets that cannot be recovered through the redeployment of these assets outside the relevant market, *i.e.*, costs uniquely incurred to supply the relevant product and geographic market. Examples of sunk costs may include market-specific investments in production facilities, technologies, marketing (including product acceptance), research and development, regulatory approvals, and testing. A significant sunk cost is one which would not be recouped within one year of the commencement of the supply response, assuming a "small but significant and nontransitory" price increase in the relevant market. In this context, a "small but significant and nontransitory" price increase will be determined in the same way in which it is determined in product market definition, except the price increase will be assumed to last one year. In some instances, it may be difficult to calculate sunk costs with precision. Accordingly, when necessary, the Agency will make an overall assessment of the extent of sunk costs for firms likely to participate through supply responses.

These supply responses may give rise to new production of products in the relevant product market or new sources of supply in the relevant geographic market. Alternatively, where price discrimination is likely so that the relevant market is defined in terms of a targeted group of buyers, these supply responses serve to identify new sellers to the targeted buyers. Uncommitted supply responses may occur in several different ways: by the

---

68.   If uncommitted entrants likely would also remain in the market and would meet the entry tests of timeliness, likelihood and sufficiency, and thus would likely deter anticompetitive mergers or deter or counteract the competitive effects of concern (see Section 3, *infra*), the Agency will consider the impact of those firms in the entry analysis.

switching or extension of existing assets to production or sale in the relevant market; or by the construction or acquisition of assets that enable production or sale in the relevant market.

1.321 Production Substitution and Extension: The Switching or Extension of Existing Assets to Production or Sale in the Relevant Market

The productive and distributive assets of a firm sometimes can be used to produce and sell either the relevant products or products that buyers do not regard as good substitutes. Production substitution refers to the shift by a firm in the use of assets from producing and selling one product to producing and selling another. Production extension refers to the use of those assets, for example, existing brand names and reputation, both for their current production and for production of the relevant product. Depending upon the speed of that shift and the extent of sunk costs incurred in the shift or extension, the potential for production substitution or extension may necessitate treating as market participants firms that do not currently produce the relevant product.[69]

If a firm has existing assets that likely would be shifted or extended into production and sale of the relevant product within one year, and without incurring significant sunk costs of entry and exit, in response to a "small but significant and nontransitory" increase in price for only the relevant product, the Agency will treat that firm as a market participant. In assessing whether a firm is such a market participant, the Agency will take into account the costs of substitution or extension relative to the profitability of sales at the elevated price, and whether the firm's capacity is elsewhere committed or elsewhere so profitably employed that such capacity likely would not be available to respond to an increase in price in the market.

1.322 Obtaining New Assets for Production or Sale of the Relevant Product

A firm may also be able to enter into production or sale in the relevant market within one year and without the expenditure of significant sunk costs of entry and exit, in response to a "small but significant and nontransitory" increase in price for only the relevant product, even if the firm is newly organized or is an existing firm without products or productive assets closely related to the relevant market. If new firms, or existing firms without closely related products or productive assets, likely would enter into production or sale in the relevant market within one year

---

69. Under other analytical approaches, production substitution sometimes has been reflected in the description of the product market. For example, the product market for stamped metal products such as automobile hub caps might be described as "light metal stamping," a production process rather than a product. The Agency believes that the approach described in the text provides a more clearly focused method of incorporating this factor in merger analysis. If production substitution among a group of products is nearly universal along the firms selling one or more of those products, however, the Agency may use an aggregate description of those markets as a matter of convenience.

without the expenditure of significant sunk costs of entry and exit, the Agency will treat those firms as market participants.

1.4 Calculating Market Shares

1.41 General Approach

The Agency normally will calculate market shares for all firms (or plants) identified as market participants in Section 1.3 based on the total sales or capacity currently devoted to the relevant market together with that which likely would be devoted to the relevant market in response to a "small but significant and nontransitory" price increase. Market shares can be expressed either in dollar terms through measurement of sales, shipments, or production, or in physical terms through measurement of sales, shipments, production, capacity, or reserves.

Market shares will be calculated using the best indicator of firms' future competitive significance. Dollar sales or shipments generally will be used if firms are distinguished primarily by differentiation of their products. Unit sales generally will be used if firms are distinguished primarily on the basis of their relative advantages in serving different buyers or groups of buyers. Physical capacity or reserves generally will be used if it is these measures that most effectively distinguish firms.[70] Typically, annual data are used, but where individual sales are large and infrequent so that annual data may be unrepresentative, the Agency may measure market shares over a longer period of time.

In measuring a firm's market share, the Agency will not include its sales or capacity to the extent that the firm's capacity is committed or so profitably employed outside the relevant market that it would not be able to increase price in the market.

1.42 Price Discrimination Markets

When markets are defined on the basis of price discrimination (Sections 1.12 and 1.22), the Agency will include only sales likely to be made into, or capacity likely to be used to supply, the relevant market in response to a "small but significant and nontransitory" price increase.

1.43 Special Factors Affecting Foreign Firms

Market shares will be assigned to foreign competitors in the same way in which they are assigned to domestic competitors. However, if exchange rates fluctuate significantly, so that comparable dollar calculations on an annual basis may be unrepresentative, the Agency may measure market shares over a period longer than one year.

If shipments from a particular country to the United States are subject to a quota, the market shares assigned to firms in that country will not exceed the amount of shipments by such firms allowed under the quota.[71]

---

70. Where all firms have, on a forward-looking basis, an equal likelihood of securing sales, the Agency will assign firms equal shares.

71. The constraining effect of the quota on the importer's ability to expand sales is relevant to the evaluation of potential adverse competitive effects. See Section 2.

In the case of restraints that limit imports to some percentage of the total amount of the product sold in the United States (*i.e.*, percentage quotas), a domestic price increase that reduced domestic consumption also would reduce the volume of imports into the United States. Accordingly, actual import sales and capacity data will be reduced for purposes of calculating market shares. Finally, a single market share may be assigned to a country or group of countries if firms in that country or group of countries act in coordination.

1.5   Concentration and Market Shares

Market concentration is a function of the number of firms in a market and their respective market shares. As an aid to the interpretation of market data, the Agency will use the Herfindahl–Hirschman Index ("HHI") of market concentration. The HHI is calculated by summing the squares of the individual market shares of all the participants.[72] Unlike the four-firm concentration ratio, the HHI reflects both the distribution of the market shares of the top four firms and the composition of the market outside the top four firms. It also gives proportionately greater weight to the market shares of the larger firms, in accord with their relative importance in competitive interactions.

The Agency divides the spectrum of market concentration as measured by the HHI into three regions that can be broadly characterized as unconcentrated (HHI below 1000), moderately concentrated (HHI between 1000 and 1800), and highly concentrated (HHI above 1800). Although the resulting regions provide a useful framework for merger analysis, the numerical divisions suggest greater precision than is possible with the available economic tools and information. Other things being equal, cases falling just above and just below a threshold present comparable competitive issues.

1.51   General Standards

In evaluating horizontal mergers, the Agency will consider both the post-merger market concentration and the increase in concentration resulting from the merger.[73] Market concentration is a useful indicator of the

---

72. For example, a market consisting of four firms with market shares of 30 percent, 30 percent, 20 percent and 20 percent has an HHI of 2600 ($30^2 + 30^2 + 20^2 + 20^2 = 2600$). The HHI ranges from 10,000 (in the case of a pure monopoly) to a number approaching zero (in the case of an atomistic market). Although it is desirable to include all firms in the calculation, lack of information about small firms is not critical because such firms do not affect the HHI significantly.

73. The increase in concentration as measured by the HHI can be calculated independently of the overall market concentration by doubling the product of the market shares of the merging firms. For example, the merger of firms with shares of 5 percent and 10 percent of the market would increase the HHI by 100 ($5 \times 10 \times 2 = 100$). The explanation for this technique is as follows: In calculating the HHI before the merger, the market shares of the merging firms are squared individually: $(a)^2 + (b)^2$. After the merger, the sum of those shares would be squared: $(a + b)^2$, which equals $a^2 + 2ab + b^2$. The increase in the HHI therefore is represented by $2ab$.

likely potential competitive effect of a merger. The general standards for horizontal mergers are as follows:

a) Post–Merger HHI Below 1000. The Agency regards markets in this region to be unconcentrated. Mergers resulting in unconcentrated markets are unlikely to have adverse competitive effects and ordinarily require no further analysis.

b) Post–Merger HHI Between 1000 and 1800. The Agency regards markets in this region to be moderately concentrated. Mergers producing an increase in the HHI of less than 100 points in moderately concentrated markets post-merger are unlikely to have adverse competitive consequences and ordinarily require no further analysis. Mergers producing an increase in the HHI of more than 100 points in moderately concentrated markets postmerger potentially raise significant competitive concerns depending on the factors set forth in Sections 2–5 of the Guidelines.

c) Post–Merger HHI Above 1800. The Agency regards markets in this region to be highly concentrated. Mergers producing an increase in the HHI of less than 50 points, even in highly concentrated markets post-merger, are unlikely to have adverse competitive consequences and ordinarily require no further analysis. Mergers producing an increase in the HHI of more than 50 points in highly concentrated markets post-merger potentially raise significant competitive concerns, depending on the factors set forth in Sections 2–5 of the Guidelines. Where the post-merger HHI exceeds 1800, it will be presumed that mergers producing an increase in the HHI of more than 100 points are likely to create or enhance market power or facilitate its exercise. The presumption may be overcome by a showing that factors set forth in Sections 2–5 of the Guidelines make it unlikely that the merger will create or enhance market power or facilitate its exercise, in light of market concentration and market shares.

1.52   Factors Affecting the Significance of Market Shares and Concentration

The post-merger level of market concentration and the change in concentration resulting from a merger affect the degree to which a merger raises competitive concerns. However, in some situations, market share and market concentration data may either understate or overstate the likely future competitive significance of a firm or firms in the market or the impact of a merger. The following are examples of such situations.

1.521   Changing Market Conditions

Market concentration and market share data of necessity are based on historical evidence. However, recent or ongoing changes in the market may indicate that the current market share of a particular firm either understates or overstates the firm's future competitive significance. For example, if a new technology that is important to long-term competitive viability is available to other firms in the market, but is not available to a particular firm, the Agency may conclude that the historical market share of that firm overstates its future competitive significance. The Agency will consider reasonably predictable effects of recent or ongoing changes in market conditions in interpreting market concentration and market share data.

1.522   Degree of Difference Between the Products and Locations in the Market and Substitutes Outside the Market

All else equal, the magnitude of potential competitive harm from a merger is greater if a hypothetical monopolist would raise price within the relevant market by substantially more than a "small but significant and nontransitory" amount. This may occur when the demand substitutes outside the relevant market, as a group, are not close substitutes for the products and locations within the relevant market. There thus may be a wide gap in the chain of demand substitutes at the edge of the product and geographic market. Under such circumstances, more market power is at stake in the relevant market than in a market in which a hypothetical monopolist would raise price by exactly five percent.

2.   THE POTENTIAL ADVERSE COMPETITIVE EFFECTS OF MERGERS

2.0   Overview

Other things being equal, market concentration affects the likelihood that one firm, or a small group of firms, could successfully exercise market power. The smaller the percentage of total supply that a firm controls, the more severely it must restrict its own output in order to produce a given price increase, and the less likely it is that an output restriction will be profitable. If collective action is necessary for the exercise of market power, as the number of firms necessary to control a given percentage of total supply decreases, the difficulties and costs of reaching and enforcing an understanding with respect to the control of that supply might be reduced. However, market share and concentration data provide only the starting point for analyzing the competitive impact of a merger. Before determining whether to challenge a merger, the Agency also will assess the other market factors that pertain to competitive effects, as well as entry, efficiencies and failure.

This section considers some of the potential adverse competitive effects of mergers and the factors in addition to market concentration relevant to each. Because an individual merger may threaten to harm competition through more than one of these effects, mergers will be analyzed in terms of as many potential adverse competitive effects as are appropriate. Entry, efficiencies, and failure are treated in Sections 3–5.

2.1   Lessening of Competition Through Coordinated Interaction

A merger may diminish competition by enabling the firms selling in the relevant market more likely, more successfully, or more completely to engage in coordinated interaction that harms consumers. Coordinated interaction is comprised of actions by a group of firms that are profitable for each of them only as a result of the accommodating reactions of the others. This behavior includes tacit or express collusion, and may or may not be lawful in and of itself.

Successful coordinated interaction entails reaching terms of coordination that are profitable to the firms involved and an ability to detect and punish deviations that would undermine the coordinated interaction. Detection and punishment of deviations ensure that coordinating firms will find it more profitable to adhere to the terms of coordination than to pursue short-term profits from deviating, given the costs of reprisal. In this phase of the analysis, the Agency will examine the extent to which post-merger market conditions are conducive to reaching terms of coordination, detecting deviations from those terms, and punishing such deviations. Depending upon the circumstances, the following market factors, among others, may be relevant: the availability of key information concerning market conditions, transactions and individual competitors; the extent of firm and product heterogeneity; pricing or marketing practices typically employed by firms in the market; the characteristics of buyers and sellers; and the characteristics of typical transactions.

Certain market conditions that are conducive to reaching terms of coordination also may be conducive to detecting or punishing deviations from those terms. For example, the extent of information available to firms in the market, or the extent of homogeneity, may be relevant to both the ability to reach terms of coordination and to detect or punish deviations from those terms. The extent to which any specific market condition will be relevant to one or more of the conditions necessary for coordinated interaction will depend on the circumstances of the particular case.

It is likely that market conditions are conducive to coordinated interaction when the firms in the market previously have engaged in express collusion and when the salient characteristics of the market have not changed appreciably the most recent such incident. Previous express collusion in another geographic market will have the same weight when the salient characteristics of that other market at the time of the collusion are comparable to those in the relevant market.

In analyzing the effect of a particular merger on coordinated interaction, the Agency is mindful of the difficulties of predicting likely future behavior based on the types of incomplete and sometimes contradictory information typically generated in merger investigations. Whether a merger is likely to diminish competition by enabling firms more likely, more successfully or more completely to engage in coordinated interaction depends on whether market conditions, on the whole, are conducive to reaching terms of coordination and detecting and punishing deviations from those terms.

2.11 Conditions Conducive to Reaching Terms of Coordination

Firms coordinating their interactions need not reach complex terms concerning the allocation of the market output across firms or the level of the market prices but may, instead, follow simple terms such as a common price, fixed price differentials, stable market shares, or customer or territorial restrictions. Terms of coordination need not perfectly achieve the monopoly outcome in order to be harmful to consumers. Instead, the terms of coordination may be imperfect and incomplete—inasmuch as they omit some market participants, omit some dimensions of competition, omit some customers, yield elevated prices short of monopoly levels, or lapse into episodic price wars—and still result in significant competitive harm. At some point, however, imperfections cause the profitability of abiding by the terms of coordination to decrease and, depending on their extent, may make coordinated interaction unlikely in the first instance.

Market conditions may be conducive to or hinder reaching terms of coordination. For example, reaching terms of coordination may be facilitated by product or firm homogeneity and by existing practices among firms, practices not necessarily themselves antitrust violations, such as standardization of pricing or product variables on which firms could compete. Key information about rival firms and the market may also facilitate reaching terms of coordination. Conversely, reaching terms of coordination may be limited or impeded by product heterogeneity or by firms having substantially incomplete information about the conditions and prospects of their rivals' businesses, perhaps because of important differences among their current business operations. In addition, reaching terms of coordination may be limited or impeded by firm heterogeneity, for example, differences in vertical integration or the production of another product that tends to be used together with the relevant product.

2.12   Conditions Conducive to Detecting and Punishing Deviations

Where market conditions are conducive to timely detection and punishment of significant deviations, a firm will find it more profitable to abide by the terms of coordination than to deviate from them. Deviation from the terms of coordination will be deterred where the threat of punishment is credible. Credible punishment, however, may not need to be any more complex than temporary abandonment of the terms of coordination by other firms in the market.

Where detection and punishment likely would be rapid, incentives to deviate are diminished and coordination is likely to be successful. The detection and punishment of deviations may be facilitated by existing practices among firms, themselves not necessarily antitrust violations, and by the characteristics of typical transactions. For example, if key information about specific transactions or individual price or output levels is available routinely to competitors, it may be difficult for a firm to deviate secretly. If orders for the relevant product are frequent, regular and small relative to the total output of a firm in a market, it may be difficult for the firm to deviate in a substantial way without the knowledge of rivals and without the opportunity for rivals to react. If demand or cost fluctuations are relatively infrequent and small, deviations may be relatively easy to deter.

By contrast, where detection or punishment is likely to be slow, incentives to deviate are enhanced and coordinated interaction is unlikely to be successful. If demand or cost fluctuations are relatively frequent and large, deviations may be relatively difficult to distinguish from these other sources of market price fluctuations, and, in consequence, deviations may be relatively difficult to deter.

In certain circumstances, buyer characteristics and the nature of the procurement process may affect the incentives to deviate from terms of coordination. Buyer size alone is not the determining characteristic. Where large buyers likely would engage in long-term contracting, so that the sales covered by such contracts can be large relative to the total output of a firm in the market, firms may have the incentive to deviate. However, this only can be accomplished where the duration, volume and profitability of the business covered by such contracts are sufficiently large as to make deviation more profitable in the long term than honoring the terms of coordination, and buyers likely would switch suppliers.

In some circumstances, coordinated interaction can be effectively prevented or limited by maverick firms—firms that have a greater economic incentive to deviate from the terms of coordination than do most of their rivals (*e.g.*, firms that are unusually disruptive and competitive influences in the market). Consequently, acquisition of a maverick firm is one way in which a merger may make coordinated interaction more likely, more successful, or more complete. For example, in a market where capacity constraints are significant for many competitors, a firm is more likely to be a maverick the greater its excess or divertable capacity in relation to its sales or its total capacity, and the lower its direct and opportunity costs are of expanding sales in the relevant market.[74] This is so because a firm's incentive to deviate from price-elevating and output-limiting terms of coordination is greater the more the firm is able profitably to expand its output as a proportion of the sales it would obtain if it adhered to the terms of coordination and the smaller is the base of sales on which it enjoys elevated profits prior to the price cutting deviation.[75] A firm also may be a maverick if it has an unusual ability secretly to expand its sales in relation to the sales it would obtain if it adhered to the terms of coordination. This ability might arise from opportunities to expand captive production for a downstream affiliate.

2.2   Lessening of Competition Through Unilateral Effects

A merger may diminish competition even if it does not lead to increased likelihood of successful coordinated interaction, because merging firms may find it profitable to alter their behavior unilaterally following the acquisition by elevating price and suppressing output. Unilateral competitive effects can arise in a variety of different settings. In each setting,

---

74. But excess capacity in the hands of non-maverick firms may be a potent weapon with which to punish deviations from the terms of coordination.

75. Similarly, in a market where product design or quality is significant, a firm is more likely to be an effective maverick the greater the sales potential of its products are among customers of its rivals, in relation to the sales it would obtain if it adhered to the terms of coordination. The likelihood of expansion responses by a maverick will be analyzed in the same fashion as uncommitted entry or committed entry (see Sections 1.3 and 3) depending on the significance of the sunk costs entailed in expansion.

particular other factors describing the relevant market affect the likelihood of unilateral competitive effects. The settings differ by the primary characteristics that distinguish firms and shape the nature of their competition.

2.21   Firms Distinguished Primarily by Differentiated Products

In some markets the products are differentiated, so that products sold by different participants in the market are not perfect substitutes for one another. Moreover, different products in the market may vary in the degree of their substitutability for one another. In this setting, competition may be non-uniform (*i.e.*, localized), so that individual sellers compete more directly with those rivals selling closer substitutes.[76]

A merger between firms in a market for differentiated products may diminish competition by enabling the merged firm to profit by unilaterally raising the price of one or both products above the premerger level. Some of the sales loss due to the price rise merely will be diverted to the product of the merger partner and, depending on relative margins, capturing such sales loss through merger may make the price increase profitable even though it would not have been profitable premerger. Substantial unilateral price elevation in a market for differentiated products requires that there be a significant share of sales in the market accounted for by consumers who regard the products of the merging firms as their first and second choices, and that repositioning of the non-parties' product lines to replace the localized competition lost through the merger be unlikely. The price rise will be greater the closer substitutes are to the products of the merging firms, *i.e.*, the more the buyers of one product consider the other product to be their next choice.

2.211   Closeness of the Products of the Merging Firms

The market concentration measures articulated in Section 1 may help assess the extent of the likely competitive effect from a unilateral price elevation by the merged firm notwithstanding the fact that the affected products are differentiated. The market concentration measures provide a measure of this effect if each product's market share is reflective of not only its relative appeal as a first choice to consumers of the merging firms' products but also its relative appeal as a second choice, and hence as a competitive constraint to the first choice.[77] Where this circumstance holds,

---

76. Similarly, in some markets sellers are primarily distinguished by their relative advantages in serving different buyers or groups of buyers, and buyers negotiate individually with sellers. Here, for example, sellers may formally bid against one another for the business of a buyer, or each buyer may elicit individual price quotes from multiple sellers. A seller may find it relatively inexpensive to meet the demands of particular buyers or types of buyers, and relatively expensive to meet others' demands. Competition, again, may be localized: sellers compete more directly with those rivals having similar relative advantages in serving particular buyers or groups of buyers. For example, in open outcry auctions, price is determined by the cost of the second lowest-cost seller. A merger involving the first and second lowest-cost sellers could cause prices to rise to the constraining level of the next lowest-cost seller.

77. Information about consumers' actual first and second product choices may be provided by marketing surveys, information from bidding structures, or normal course of business documents from industry participants.

market concentration data fall outside the safeharbor regions of Section 1.5, and the merging firms have a combined market share of at least thirty-five percent, the Agency will presume that a significant share of sales in the market are accounted for by consumers who regard the products of the merging firms as their first and second choices.

Purchasers of one of the merging firms' products may be more or less likely to make the other their second choice than market shares alone would indicate. The market shares of the merging firms' products may understate the competitive effect of concern, when, for example, the products of the merging firms are relatively more similar in their various attributes to one another than to other products in the relevant market. On the other hand, the market shares alone may overstate the competitive effects of concern when, for example, the relevant products are less similar in their attributes to one another than to other products in the relevant market.

Where market concentration data fall outside the safeharbor regions of Section 1.5, the merging firms have a combined market share of at least thirty-five percent, and where data on product attributes and relative product appeal show that a significant share of purchasers of one merging firm's product regard the other as their second choice, then market share data may be relied upon to demonstrate that there is a significant share of sales in the market accounted for by consumers who would be adversely affected by the merger.

2.212 Ability of Rival Sellers to Replace Lost Competition

A merger is not likely to lead to unilateral elevation of prices of differentiated products if, in response to such an effect, rival sellers likely would replace any localized competition lost through the merger by repositioning their product lines.[78]

In markets where it is costly for buyers to evaluate product quality, buyers who consider purchasing from both merging parties may limit the total number of sellers they consider. If either of the merging firms would be replaced in such buyers' consideration by an equally competitive seller not formerly considered, then the merger is not likely to lead to a unilateral elevation of prices.

2.22 Firms Distinguished Primarily by Their Capacities

Where products are relatively undifferentiated and capacity primarily distinguishes firms and shapes the nature of their competition, the merged firm may find it profitable unilaterally to raise price and suppress output. The merger provides the merged firm a larger base of sales on which to enjoy the resulting price rise and also eliminates a competitor to which customers otherwise would have diverted their sales. Where the merging

---

78. The timeliness and likelihood of repositioning responses will be analyzed using the same methodology as used in analyzing uncommitted entry or committed entry (see Sections 1.3 and 3), depending on the significance of the sunk costs entailed in repositioning.

firms have a combined market share of at least thirty-five percent, merged firms may find it profitable to raise price and reduce joint output below the sum of their premerger outputs because the lost markups on the foregone sales may be outweighed by the resulting price increase on the merged base of sales.

This unilateral effect is unlikely unless a sufficiently large number of the merged firm's customers would not be able to find economical alternative sources of supply, *i.e.,* competitors of the merged firm likely would not respond to the price increase and output reduction by the merged firm with increases in their own outputs sufficient in the aggregate to make the unilateral action of the merged firm unprofitable. Such non-party expansion is unlikely if those firms face binding capacity constraints that could not be economically relaxed within two years or if existing excess capacity is significantly more costly to operate than capacity currently in use.[79]

3.   ENTRY ANALYSIS

3.0   Overview

A merger is not likely to create or enhance market power or to facilitate its exercise, if entry into the market is so easy that market participants, after the merger, either collectively or unilaterally could not profitably maintain a price increase above premerger levels. Such entry likely will deter an anticompetitive merger in its incipiency, or deter or counteract the competitive effects of concern.

Entry is that easy if entry would be timely, likely, and sufficient in its magnitude, character and scope to deter or counteract the competitive effects of concern. In markets where entry is that easy (*i.e.,* where entry passes these tests of timeliness, likelihood, and sufficiency), the merger raises no antitrust concern and ordinarily requires no further analysis.

The committed entry treated in this Section is defined as new competition that requires expenditure of significant sunk costs of entry and exit.[80] The Agency employs a three step methodology to assess whether committed entry would deter or counteract a competitive effect of concern.

The first step assesses whether entry can achieve significant market impact within a timely period. If significant market impact would require a longer period, entry will not deter or counteract the competitive effect of concern.

The second step assesses whether committed entry would be a profitable and, hence, a likely response to a merger having competitive effects of concern. Firms considering entry that requires significant sunk costs must evaluate the profitability of the entry on the basis of long term participation in the market, because the underlying assets will be committed to

---

79. The timeliness and likelihood of non-party expansion will be analyzed using the same methodology as used in analyzing uncommitted or committed entry (see Sections 1.3 and 3) depending on the significance of the sunk costs entailed in expansion.

80. Supply responses that require less than one year and insignificant sunk costs to effectuate are analyzed as uncommitted entry in Section 1.3.

the market until they are economically depreciated. Entry that is sufficient to counteract the competitive effects of concern will cause prices to fall to their premerger levels or lower. Thus, the profitability of such committed entry must be determined on the basis of premerger market prices over the long-term.

A merger having anticompetitive effects can attract committed entry, profitable at premerger prices, that would not have occurred premerger at these same prices. But following the merger, the reduction in industry output and increase in prices associated with the competitive effect of concern may allow the same entry to occur without driving market prices below premerger levels. After a merger that results in decreased output and increased prices, the likely sales opportunities available to entrants at premerger prices will be larger than they were premerger, larger by the output reduction caused by the merger. If entry could be profitable at premerger prices without exceeding the likely sales opportunities—opportunities that include pre-existing pertinent factors as well as the merger-induced output reduction—then such entry is likely in response to the merger.

The third step assesses whether timely and likely entry would be sufficient to return market prices to their premerger levels. This end may be accomplished either through multiple entry or individual entry at a sufficient scale. Entry may not be sufficient, even though timely and likely, where the constraints on availability of essential assets, due to incumbent control, make it impossible for entry profitably to achieve the necessary level of sales. Also, the character and scope of entrants' products might not be fully responsive to the localized sales opportunities created by the removal of direct competition among sellers of differentiated products. In assessing whether entry will be timely, likely, and sufficient, the Agency recognizes that precise and detailed information may be difficult or impossible to obtain. In such instances, the Agency will rely on all available evidence bearing on whether entry will satisfy the conditions of timeliness, likelihood, and sufficiency.

3.1 Entry Alternatives

The Agency will examine the timeliness, likelihood, and sufficiency of the means of entry (entry alternatives) a potential entrant might practically employ, without attempting to identify who might be potential entrants. An entry alternative is defined by the actions the firm must take in order to produce and sell in the market. All phases of the entry effort will be considered, including, where relevant, planning, design, and management; permitting, licensing, and other approvals; construction, debugging, and operation of production facilities; and promotion (including necessary introductory discounts), marketing, distribution, and satisfaction of customer testing and qualification requirements.[81] Recent examples of entry, whether successful or unsuccessful, may provide a useful starting point for identify-

---

81. Many of these phases may be undertaken simultaneously.

ing the necessary actions, time requirements, and characteristics of possible entry alternatives.

3.2 Timeliness of Entry

In order to deter or counteract the competitive effects of concern, entrants quickly must achieve a significant impact on price in the relevant market. The Agency generally will consider timely only those committed entry alternatives that can be achieved within two years from initial planning to significant market impact.[82] Where the relevant product is a durable good, consumers, in response to a significant commitment to entry, may defer purchases by making additional investments to extend the useful life of previously purchased goods and in this way deter or counteract for a time the competitive effects of concern. In these circumstances, if entry only can occur outside of the two year period, the Agency will consider entry to be timely so long as it would deter or counteract the competitive effects of concern within the two year period and subsequently.

3.3 Likelihood of Entry

An entry alternative is likely if it would be profitable at premerger prices, and if such prices could be secured by the entrant.[83] The committed entrant will be unable to secure prices at premerger levels if its output is too large for the market to absorb without depressing prices further. Thus, entry is unlikely if the minimum viable scale is larger than the likely sales opportunity available to entrants.

Minimum viable scale is the smallest average annual level of sales that the committed entrant must persistently achieve for profitability at premerger prices.[84] Minimum viable scale is a function of expected revenues, based upon premerger prices,[85] and all categories of costs associated with the entry alternative, including an appropriate rate of return on invested capital given that entry could fail and sunk costs, if any, will be lost.[86]

Sources of sales opportunities available to entrants include: (a) the

---

82. Firms which have committed to entering the market prior to the merger generally will be included in the measurement of the market. Only committed entry or adjustments to pre-existing entry plans that are induced by the merger will be considered as possibly deterring or counteracting the competitive effects of concern.

83. Where conditions indicate that entry may be profitable at prices below premerger levels, the Agency will assess the likelihood of entry at the lowest price at which such entry would be profitable.

84. The concept of minimum viable scale ("MVS") differs from the concept of minimum efficient scale ("MES"). While MES is the smallest scale at which average costs are minimized, MVS is the smallest scale at which average costs equal the premerger price.

85. The expected path of future prices, absent the merger, may be used if future price changes can be predicted with reasonable reliability.

86. The minimum viable scale of an entry alternative will be relatively large when the fixed costs of entry are large, when the fixed costs of entry are largely sunk, when the marginal costs of production are high at low levels of output, and when a plant is underutilized for a long time because of delays in achieving market acceptance.

output reduction associated with the competitive effect of concern,[87] (b) entrants' ability to capture a share of reasonably expected growth in market demand,[88] (c) entrants' ability securely to divert sales from incumbents, for example, through vertical integration or through forward contracting, and (d) any additional anticipated contraction in incumbents' output in response to entry.[89] Factors that reduce the sales opportunities available to entrants include: (a) the prospect that an entrant will share in a reasonably expected decline in market demand, (b) the exclusion of an entrant from a portion of the market over the long term because of vertical integration or forward contracting by incumbents, and (c) any anticipated sales expansion by incumbents in reaction to entry, either generalized or targeted at customers approached by the entrant, that utilizes prior irreversible investments in excess production capacity. Demand growth or decline will be viewed as relevant only if total market demand is projected to experience long-lasting change during at least the two year period following the competitive effect of concern.

3.4   Sufficiency of Entry

Inasmuch as multiple entry generally is possible and individual entrants may flexibly choose their scale, committed entry generally will be sufficient to deter or counteract the competitive effects of concern whenever entry is likely under the analysis of Section 3.3. However, entry, although likely, will not be sufficient if, as a result of incumbent control, the tangible and intangible assets required for entry are not adequately available for entrants to respond fully to their opportunities. In addition, where the competitive effect of concern is not uniform across the relevant market, in order for entry to be sufficient, the character and scope of entrants' products must be responsive to the localized sales opportunities that include the output reduction associated with the competitive effect of concern. For example, where the concern is unilateral price elevation as a result of a merger between producers of differentiated products, entry, in order to be sufficient, must involve a product so close to the products of the merging firms that the merged firm will be unable to internalize enough of the sales loss due to the price rise, rendering the price increase unprofitable.

4.   EFFICIENCIES

Competition usually spurs firms to achieve efficiencies internally. Nevertheless, mergers have the potential to generate significant efficiencies by permitting a better utilization of existing assets, enabling the combined

---

87. Five percent of total market sales typically is used because where a monopolist profitably would raise price by five percent or more across the entire relevant market, it is likely that the accompanying reduction in sales would be no less than five percent.

88. Entrants' anticipated share of growth in demand depends on incumbents' capacity constraints and irreversible investments in capacity expansion, as well as on the relative appeal, acceptability and reputation of incumbents' and entrants' products to the new demand.

89. For example, in a bidding market where all bidders are on equal footing, the market share of incumbents will contract as a result of entry.

firm to achieve lower costs in producing a given quantity and quality than either firm could have achieved without the proposed transaction. Indeed, the primary benefit of mergers to the economy is their potential to generate such efficiencies.

Efficiencies generated through merger can enhance the merged firm's ability and incentive to compete, which may result in lower prices, improved quality, enhanced service, or new products. For example, merger-generated efficiencies may enhance competition by permitting two ineffective (*e.g.*, high cost) competitors to become one effective (*e.g.*, lower cost) competitor. In a coordinated interaction context (see Section 2.1), marginal cost reductions may make coordination less likely or effective by enhancing the incentive of a maverick to lower price or by creating a new maverick firm. In a unilateral effects context (see Section 2.2), marginal cost reductions may reduce the merged firm's incentive to elevate price. Efficiencies also may result in benefits in the form of new or improved products, and efficiencies may result in benefits even when price is not immediately and directly affected. Even when efficiencies generated through merger enhance a firm's ability to compete, however, a merger may have other effects that may lessen competition and ultimately may make the merger anticompetitive.

The Agency will consider only those efficiencies likely to be accomplished with the proposed merger and unlikely to be accomplished in the absence of either the proposed merger or another means having comparable anticompetitive effects. These are termed merger-specific efficiencies.[90] Only alternatives that are practical in the business situation faced by the merging firms will be considered in making this determination; the Agency will not insist upon a less restrictive alternative that is merely theoretical.

Efficiencies are difficult to verify and quantify, in part because much of the information relating to efficiencies is uniquely in the possession of the merging firms. Moreover, efficiencies projected reasonably and in good faith by the merging firms may not be realized. Therefore, the merging firms must substantiate efficiency claims so that the Agency can verify by reasonable means the likelihood and magnitude of each asserted efficiency, how and when each would be achieved (and any costs of doing so), how each would enhance the merged firm's ability and incentive to compete, and why each would be merger-specific. Efficiency claims will not be considered if they are vague or speculative or otherwise cannot be verified by reasonable means.

Cognizable efficiencies are merger-specific efficiencies that have been verified and do not arise from anticompetitive reductions in output or service. Cognizable efficiencies are assessed net of costs produced by the merger or incurred in achieving those efficiencies.

The Agency will not challenge a merger if cognizable efficiencies are of a character and magnitude such that the merger is not likely to be

---

90. The Agency will not deem efficiencies to be merger-specific if they could be preserved by practical alternatives that mitigate competitive concerns, such as divestiture or licensing. If a merger affects not whether but only when an efficiency would be achieved, only the timing advantage is a merger-specific efficiency.

anticompetitive in any relevant market.[91] To make the requisite determination, the Agency considers whether cognizable efficiencies likely would be sufficient to reverse the merger's potential to harm consumers in the relevant market, *e.g.*, by preventing price increases in that market. In conducting this analysis,[92] the Agency will not simply compare the magnitude of the cognizable efficiencies with the magnitude of the likely harm to competition absent the efficiencies. The greater the potential adverse competitive effect of a merger—as indicated by the increase in the HHI and post-merger HHI from Section 1, the analysis of potential adverse competitive effects from Section 2, and the timeliness, likelihood, and sufficiency of entry from Section 3—the greater must be cognizable efficiencies in order for the Agency to conclude that the merger will not have an anticompetitive effect in the relevant market. When the potential adverse competitive effect of a merger is likely to be particularly large, extraordinarily great cognizable efficiencies would be necessary to prevent the merger from being anticompetitive.

In the Agency's experience, efficiencies are most likely to make a difference in merger analysis when the likely adverse competitive effects, absent the efficiencies, are not great. Efficiencies almost never justify a merger to monopoly or near-monopoly.

The Agency has found that certain types of efficiencies are more likely to be cognizable and substantial than others. For example, efficiencies resulting from shifting production among facilities formerly owned separately, which enable the merging firms to reduce the marginal cost of production, are more likely to be susceptible to verification, merger-specific, and substantial, and are less likely to result from anticompetitive reductions in output. Other efficiencies, such as those relating to research and development, are potentially substantial but are generally less susceptible to verification and may be the result of anticompetitive output reductions. Yet others, such as those relating to procurement, management, or capital cost are less likely to be merger-specific or substantial, or may not be cognizable for other reasons.

---

91. Section 7 of the Clayton Act prohibits mergers that may substantially lessen competition "in any line of commerce ... in any section of the country." Accordingly, the Agency normally assesses competition in each relevant market affected by a merger independently and normally will challenge the merger if it is likely to be anticompetitive in any relevant market. In some cases, however, the Agency in its prosecutorial discretion will consider efficiencies not strictly in the relevant market, but so inextricably linked with it that a partial divestiture or other remedy could not feasibly eliminate the anticompetitive effect in the relevant market without remedy could not feasibly eliminate the anticompetitive effect in the relevant market without sacrificing the efficiencies in the other market(s). Inextricably linked efficiencies rarely are a significant factor in the Agency's determination not to challenge a merger. They are most likely to make a difference when they are great and the likely anticompetitive effect in the relevant market(s) is small.

92. The result of this analysis over the short term will determine the Agency's enforcement decision in most cases. The Agency also will consider the effects of cognizable efficiencies with no short-term, direct effect on prices in the relevant market. Delayed benefits from efficiencies (due to delay in the achievement of, or the realization of consumer benefits from the efficiencies) will be given less weight because they are less proximate and more difficult to predict.

5. FAILURE AND EXITING ASSETS

5.0 Overview

Notwithstanding the analysis of Sections 1–4 of the Guidelines, a merger is not likely to create or enhance market power or to facilitate its exercise, if imminent failure, as defined below, of one of the merging firms would cause the assets of that firm to exit the relevant market. In such circumstances, post-merger performance in the relevant market may be no worse than market performance had the merger been blocked and the assets left the market.

5.1 Failing Firm

A merger is not likely to create or enhance market power or facilitate its exercise if the following circumstances are met: 1) the allegedly failing firm would be unable to meet its financial obligations in the near future; 2) it would not be able to reorganize successfully under Chapter 11 of the Bankruptcy Act;[93] 3) it has made unsuccessful good-faith efforts to elicit reasonable alternative offers of acquisition of the assets of the failing firm[94] that would both keep its tangible and intangible assets in the relevant market and pose a less severe danger to competition than does the proposed merger; and 4) absent the acquisition, the assets of the failing firm would exit the relevant market.

5.2 Failing Division

A similar argument can be made for "failing" divisions as for failing firms. First, upon applying appropriate cost allocation rules, the division must have a negative cash flow on an operating basis. Second, absent the acquisition, it must be that the assets of the division would exit the relevant market in the near future if not sold. Due to the ability of the parent firm to allocate costs, revenues, and intracompany transactions among itself and its subsidiaries and divisions, the Agency will require evidence, not based solely on management plans that could be prepared solely for the purpose of demonstrating negative cash flow or the prospect of exit from the relevant market. Third, the owner of the failing division also must have complied with the competitively-preferable purchaser requirement of Section 5.1.

NOTES

1. The introduction to the Guidelines indicated that the "Department hopes to reduce uncertainty associated with enforcement of the antitrust laws in this

---

93. 11 U.S.C. §§ 1101–1174 (1988).

94. Any offer to purchase the assets of the failing firm for a price above the liquidation value of those assets—the highest valued use outside the relevant market or equivalent offer to purchase the stock of the failing firm—will be regarded as a reasonable alternative offer.

area." Are the Guidelines likely to reduce uncertainty? Are the various "what if" hypotheticals (*e.g.*, the 5% test) likely to enhance predictability?

2. What are the advantages and disadvantages of the Herfindahl–Hirschman Index (HHI)? Is, for example, the extra emphasis that the HHI will put on dominant firms (*i.e.*, as opposed to four-firm and eight-firm concentration ratios) helpful? Donald I. Baker, a former chief of the Antitrust Division, prepared the following chart to indicate the impact of the HHI on some leading horizontal merger cases:

CASE	MARKET SHARES		TOTAL*	HHI INCREASE
U.S. v. Bethlehem Steel (1957)	16.3% +	4.6%	1,429	150
U.S. v. Philadelphia National Bank (1963)	21.3% +	14.5%	1,337	618
U.S. v. ALCOA–Rome (1964)	27.8% +	1.3%	2,354	72
U.S. v. Continental Can (1964)	21.9% +	3.1%	1,494	136
U.S. v. Pabst (1966): Wisconsin	10.7% +	13.0%	N.A.	275
Three States	5.5% +	5.6%	N.A.	64
National	2.7% +	2.0%	N.A. <	11
U.S. v. Von's Grocery Co. (1966)	4.7% +	4.2%	257	39

* In various instances, this is understated because of incomplete data. (The understatement may be as much as 150 in some cases).[95]

3. Note that the Guidelines appear studiously to avoid reference to "trend towards concentration" as a factor in the evaluation of mergers. How would you explain this neglect of a factor that played a large role in the enactment of the Celler–Kefauver amendments to Section 7 in 1950 and weighed heavily in many key cases? Might the answer be that a trend to concentration indicates no more than that a particular line of mergers makes sense to participants in the industry, probably because there are substantial efficiencies to be achieved by the mergers? Even if that generalization were true, is that an interpretation that properly should be made only by Congress? Similarly, the Guidelines state that a merger in a market falling below 1,000 on the HHI will not be challenged "except in extraordinary circumstances." Should mergers in markets below 1,000 on the HHI be in a "safe harbor"? How would you deal with a merger between two firms with 14% and 15% of a market where all of the other competitors were minnows too small to count in terms of HHI?

4. The 1992 Guidelines preserve the generally successful analytical approach to relevant market definition of the earlier guidelines. In particular, they preserve the government's hostility to the use of submarkets. This hostility is not consistent with Supreme Court analyses in United States v. Philadelphia National Bank (p. 980 *supra*), and United States v. Pabst Brewing Co. (p. 988 *supra*). As a matter of policy, is the free and easy use of submarket analysis best discarded?

5. In the 1980s, challenges to mergers were often defeated even where post-merger market shares were 40% or more on grounds that if the parties tried to raise price after the merger, they would be swamped by new entry. For example, *see* United States v. Waste Management Inc., 743 F.2d 976 (2d Cir.1984); United States

---

95. Baker, Justice Dept. Merger Guidelines Contribute a Dose of Rationality, National L.J., June 28, 1982, at 16. Mr. Baker's chart was addressed to the original 1982 version of the Guidelines, but the analysis would not change under the 1992 Guidelines.

v. Calmar Inc., 612 F.Supp. 1298 (D.N.J.1985). Many of these cases treated entry as relevant if a firm *could* enter a market (*i.e.*, there were no insurmountable or even serious barriers to entry), apparently on the theory that firms that *could* enter *would* do so if profitable opportunities were created by price increases after the merger. Section 3 of the 1992 Guidelines ("Entry Analysis") takes a much tougher stand on the question of entry, noting that entry is easy only if it "would be timely, likely and sufficient in its magnitude, character and scope to deter or counteract the competitive acts of concern."

Consider the various policy reasons that argue in favor of a restrictive or a permissive standard on the question of entry.

6. Do the Guidelines deal adequately with foreign competition? In recent years, increasing attention has been paid to the question of whether there can or should be international or global markets in antitrust enforcement. Economists, members of the business community, and others have raised the question whether competition limited to a national market is realistic in many industries (*e.g.*, automobiles, steel and textiles). *See* 2 Areeda & Turner, Antitrust Law 362–63 (1978). Of course, even if a market is defined as national, current imports (along with domestic production) would be taken into account. But should not a defendant in a merger case be permitted to prove, for example, that production by a foreign company that sells to the United States, when that production is currently sold to purchasers abroad, is relevant in determining the probable consequences of a merger? In effect, the argument would be that production already committed to export by the foreign firm could easily and quickly be diverted to the U.S. if post-merger prices increased. When should such foreign production not be taken into account?

7. A new and complicated concept introduced in these guidelines relates to "sunk costs"—*i.e.* the acquisition costs of tangible and intangible assets incurred in order to participate in a relevant product and geographic market. Certain firms will be regarded as "in the market" if through supply responses or geographic diversion, they can switch production and sales into a market. Firms that will be so regarded are called "uncommitted entrants," designated as those firms that do not have significant sunk costs. A firm has no significant sunk costs and therefore is an "uncommitted entrant" if there are no such investments or if they are sufficiently modest that they can be recouped within one year. If a firm has sunk costs, and therefore is a "committed" entrant, its competitive potential will only be taken into account if it satisfies the requirements of "new entry."

As a practical matter, will firms often have no significant sunk costs in order to be characterized as "uncommitted" entrants? How often will a firm enter a market with no costs, or make sufficient money in the first year to recoup its entire investment? The people who drafted the new guidelines obviously believe that concepts of supply substitution, geographic diversion and new entry were too lax under the former guidelines—but have they tightened up too much?

8. The 1992 guidelines retain the market concentration analysis and use of the Herfindahl–Hirschman index of concentration. In some respects however, treatment varies from the earlier guidelines:

a. Mergers resulting in concentrations below 1,000 on the HHI scale are still in a "safe harbor."

b. In the HHI zone between 1,000 and 1,800, the 1984 guidelines indicated that the Department was "likely to challenge" if there was an increase of 100 points. Now the guidelines only say that in that concentration zone, mergers "potentially raise significant competitive concerns" and will be analyzed in terms of other factors. In fact, the Department of Justice and FTC brought almost no cases in the 1,000–1,800 range in the period from 1981 to 2000. Cases that were brought in the below 1800 range were invariably challenges to mergers where anticompetitive effects occurred in a number of different markets. Some markets were above 1800 and others below that mark. For example, in oil industry mergers such as the combination of Exxon and Mobil and British Petroleum's acquisition of Amoco, the parties were required to sell off company-owned stations in concentrated local markets, including some local markets where the HHI numbers were well below 1800. Might the explanation be that gasoline sold at retail is a largely homogeneous product, and price increases and decreases at retail are public and therefore prices often tend to be identical?

c.   In the over 1,800 HHI range, the earlier guidelines indicated that the government was likely to challenge mergers if they added 50 points on the Herfindahl scale, and would challenge mergers that added 100 points except in "extraordinary circumstances." The 1992 guidelines establish a presumption that mergers that result in an HHI of over 1,800 will only be challenged if there is an increase of more than 100 points, and indicate that even that presumption can be overcome by a showing based on other factors. The indication that a failure to sue in the over 1,800 zone would only occur in "extraordinary circumstances" is dropped.

9.   Most of the attention in the 1992 Guidelines, and most of the cases challenging horizontal mergers in the several decades after Section 7 was revised in 1950, were concerned with lessening of competition through coordinate interaction. When the merger involved companies producing differentiated products, however, the typical merger analysis is not to look for coordinated effects, but rather to examine whether there were anticompetitive "unilateral effects" (see Guideline provisions 2.2 through 2.22). Suppose that two merging parties are the closest substitute for each other. If one of the merging parties raised its price significantly, it would ordinarily be concerned about losing business to competitors. But if the acquisition involves a second party that sells the closest substitute, either can raise its price and not worry as much about the loss of output to competitors. For example, suppose A and B are the closest substitutes and A raises its price 10%; as a result it may lose 20% of its business, but 15% of the 20% loss will be captured by B. In those circumstances, the merger partners will have increased incentives to raise price and to lead anticompetitive effects.

To reach a conclusion on anticompetitive unilateral effects, one must take into account a variety of factors: (1) how much business is likely to be captured by the merging partner; (2) can companies that do not offer the closest substitutes reposition to take advantage of the business loss as a result of A's price increase; (3) can a new entry entrant pick up or at least compete for A's loss of business; and (4) might there be efficiencies to the merger transaction that more than compensate for the price increase.

As a result of analytical work by economists and lawyers in recent decades, the enforcement agencies have become much more adept in demonstrating anticompetitive unilateral effects, and enforcement actions based on such theories are more frequent.

10.   The Guidelines add a new qualification to the failing company defense. Aside from the preconditions that previously had to be satisfied, the Guidelines add that the firm claiming a failing company status must demonstrate that its assets,

but for the merger, would probably leave the market. Why tighten up on the failing company defense?

11. Section 4 of the Guidelines, revised in 1997, opened the door to an efficiency defense and reflects a remarkable turnaround in United States antitrust law. In *United States v. Brown Shoe*, the first Supreme Court case to interpret revised Section 7, the Court held efficiencies against the legality of the merger. In that portion of the opinion that addressed the competitive effect of vertical integration between a shoe manufacturer and retail shoe outlets, the Court concluded as follows:

> [Another] significant aspect of this merger is that it creates a large national chain which is integrated with a manufacturing operation. The retail outlets of integrated companies, by eliminating wholesalers and by increasing the volume of purchases from the manufacturing division of the enterprise, can market their own brands at prices below those of competing independent retailers. Of course, some of the results of large integrated or chain operations are beneficial to consumers.... But, we cannot fail to recognize Congress' desire to promote competition through the protection of viable, small, locally owned business. Congress appreciated that occasionally higher costs and prices might result from the maintenance of fragmented industries and markets.

The Supreme Court soon retreated from the position that efficiencies were anticompetitive and moved on to the view that they were not a defense, but were essentially neutral, in evaluating the competitive effects of the merger. *See FTC v. Procter & Gamble Co.*, p. 69, *infra.* To the extent that earlier Merger Guidelines mentioned efficiency claims, they were addressed to prosecutorial discretion.

The 1997 revisions allow efficiency claims addressed to prosecutorial discretion *and* in courts. Note that the efficiency defense in the Guidelines is circumscribed in various ways, and some have criticized Section 4 on grounds that the defense is unduly narrow and grudging. The efficiencies must be merger specific (*i.e.*, they could not be achieved in some less anticompetitive way), substantial, verifiable, and will almost never justify mergers to monopoly or near monopoly. In addition, a successful efficiency defense requires proof that the claimed efficiency likely would be sufficient to reverse the merger's potential to harm consumers in the relevant market. So far, no party has successfully asserted an efficiency defense in court, but it is said that mergers that might otherwise have been challenged were allowed to proceed as a matter of prosecutorial discretion because of the presence of significant efficiencies.

Finally recall that in *Philadelphia National Bank* (*supra*, p. 980, the Supreme Court concluded it was not permissible to justify anticompetitive effects in one market by pointing to redeeming virtues in another market. Note at p. 1052 of the 1997 Guideline revision recognizes that precedent, but goes on to say that the enforcement agencies, as a matter of prosecutorial discretion, will consider efficiencies in a different market if they are "inextricably linked." Can you imagine a set of facts that would satisfy the "inextricably linked" standard?

MERGER ACTIVITY AND ENFORCEMENT SINCE 1990

The decade of the 1990s witnessed probably the greatest merger wave in the history of the country—certainly the greatest since the end of the 19th Century. The number of mergers filed with the government under the Hart–Scott–Rodino

Act, the statute requiring that mergers and joint ventures with acquired assets valued at more than $15 million be prefiled with the government, increased from 1529 filings in 1991 to 4642 in 1999.[96] Total assets acquired by merger increased from $169 billion in 1991 to almost $2 trillion in 1999—about an 11–fold increase.

About 97% of mergers that were large enough to require filing were neither challenged nor extensively investigated, roughly the same percentage as in the 1980s. The difference, however, was that of the 3% investigated, over 60% resulted in enforcement actions. Some very large mergers were restructured and then allowed to proceed. These included Exxon–Mobil, British Petroleum–Amoco, Bell Atlantic–Nynex (now "Verizon"), AT&T–Media One, Ciba Geigy–Sandoz, and two of the largest mergers of the decade—Time Warner–Turner and then AOL–Time Warner. There were substantially more government challenges than in the 1980s. Most resulted in the deals being abandoned or restructured, but a few government challenges were litigated. Important aspects of merger analysis during the decade are illustrated in the following two court opinions, *Staples* and *Heinz*.

Federal Trade Commission v. Staples, Inc., 970 F.Supp. 1066 (D.D.C.1997), Staples, the second largest office supply superstore in the United States with 550 retail stores, sought to acquire Office Depot, the largest office supply superstore chain, with over 500 outlets. The office supply superstore market was defined to include superstores selling "consumable" office products—*e.g.,* paper, pens, file folders, computer discs and toner cartridges, but "consumable" did not include capital goods such as computers and office furniture. Defendants argued that the proper product market was all outlets selling office supply products, and in any such market, Staples and Office Depot accounted for only 5.5 percent of total North American sales. They also argued that the efficiencies of the transaction would lead to lower consumer prices and outweigh any possible anticompetitive effect. In that connection the parties emphasized a long record of office supply superstores cutting prices in order to increase market share, and claimed that track record showed that efficiencies would be passed along to consumers.

The proposed merger was the last of a series that had reduced the superstore category from 23 to 3. Office Max was third after Staples and Office Depot. Efforts by chains selling other products to expand into office supplies had not been successful.

The key question was whether office supply superstores constituted, as alleged by the government, an appropriate market or submarket, since functionally interchangeable products could be purchased at many outlets, including chains that did not emphasize office supplies but carried some items, and also at small stationery stores.

In seeking a preliminary injunction, the FTC had offered econometric evidence—more extensive than in previous cases—about prices in cities where a company owned the only superstore in town compared to cities where there were two or three competing superstores. In all cities reviewed, non-superstore outlets were present. The court summarized the Commission's approach as follows:

> First, the FTC presented evidence comparing Staples' prices in geographic markets where Staples is the only office superstore, to markets where Staples competes with Office Depot or Office Max, or both. Based on the FTC's calculations, in markets where Staples faces no office superstore competition at all, something which was termed a one-firm market during

---

96. R. Parker, Report from the Bureau of Competition (April 7, 2000); http://www.FTC.gov/os.

the hearing, prices are 13% higher than in three firm markets where it competes with both Office Depot and Office Max.

* * *

The evidence all suggests that office superstore prices are affected primarily by other office superstores and not by non-superstore competitors such as mass merchandisers like Wal–Mart, K–Mart or Target, wholesale clubs such as BJ's, Sam's and Price Costco, computer or electronic stores such as Computer City and Best Buy, independent retail office supply stores, mail-order firms like Quill and Viking, and contract stationers.

Staples' and Office Depot's internal documents confirmed the differences in price in one, two, and three superstore cities. In addition, upon request, District Judge Hogan visited and viewed many of the different types of retail formats and found that office superstores were very different in appearance, physical size, format, the number and variety of products offered, and the type of customers targeted and served than other sellers of office supplies.

Assuming an office supply superstore market, concentration statistics showed the merged company would have a dominant market share in 42 geographic markets across the country, with 100 percent in 15 metropolitan areas. In 27 other areas, post-merger market share would range from 45 percent to 94 percent. The average increase in HHI caused by the merger would be 2,715 points.

With respect to efficiency claims in defense of the merger, the court acknowledged that the government had changed its merger guidelines to allow the offer of an efficiency defense, but also noted that the Supreme Court, in *Procter & Gamble* (*see, p. 1101 infra,*), concluded that "possible economies cannot be used as a defense to illegality in Section 7 merger cases." Despite the *Procter & Gamble* language, the district court assumed that efficiencies could be offered as a viable defense. Nevertheless, the court rejected the efficiency claims on grounds that those proffered were speculative and conjectural. The court noted the defendant claims of $5 billion dollar cost savings over 5 years, but observed that most of these alleged savings were undocumented, lacking backup sources and calculations. It further noted that the $5 billion figure exceeded by almost 500 percent the figures presented to the boards of directors of the companies when they were asked to approve the transaction, and were substantially greater than claims in the joint proxy statement/prospectus which was said to reflect the best currently available estimate of savings by management and was submitted to the Securities and Exchange Commission.

The court concluded that the Commission had shown a likelihood it would succeed after a full administrative trial and granted a preliminary injunction.

Federal Trade Commission v. H.J. Heinz Co.

United States Court of Appeals, D.C. Circuit 2001.
246 F.3d 708.

■ HENDERSON, J. On February 28, 2000 H.J. Heinz Company (Heinz) and Milnot Holding Corporation (Beech–Nut) entered into a merger agreement. The Federal Trade Commission (Commission or FTC) sought a preliminary injunction pursuant to section 13(b) of the Federal Trade Commission Act, to enjoin the consummation of the merger.... The district court denied the preliminary injunction and the FTC appealed to this court. For the reasons set forth below, we reverse the district court and remand for entry of a preliminary injunction against Heinz and Beech–Nut.

I. Background

Four million infants in the United States consume 80 million cases of jarred baby food annually, representing a domestic market of $865 million to $1 billion. The baby food market is dominated by three firms, Gerber Products Company (Gerber), Heinz and Beech–Nut. Gerber, the industry leader, enjoys a 65 per cent market share while Heinz and Beech–Nut come in second and third, with a 17.4 per cent and a 15.4 per cent share respectively. The district court found that Gerber enjoys unparalleled brand recognition with a brand loyalty greater than any other product sold in the United States. Gerber's products are found in over 90 per cent of all American supermarkets.[97]

By contrast, Heinz is sold in approximately 40 per cent of all supermarkets. Its sales are nationwide but concentrated in northern New England, the Southeast and Deep South and the Midwest. Despite its second-place domestic market share, Heinz is the largest producer of baby food in the world with $1 billion in sales worldwide. Its domestic baby food products with annual net sales of $103 million are manufactured at its Pittsburgh, Pennsylvania plant, which was updated in 1991 at a cost of $120 million. The plant operates at 40 per cent of its production capacity and produces 12 million cases of baby food annually. Its baby food line includes about 130 SKUs (stock keeping units), that is, product varieties (*e.g.*, strained carrots, apple sauce, etc.). Heinz lacks Gerber's brand recognition; it markets itself as a "value brand" with a shelf price several cents below Gerber's.

Beech–Nut has a market share (15.4%) comparable to that of Heinz (17.4%), with $138.7 million in annual sales of baby food, of which 72 per cent is jarred baby food. Its jarred baby food line consists of 128 SKUs. Beech–Nut manufactures all of its baby food in Canajoharie, New York at a manufacturing plant that was built in 1907 and began manufacturing baby food in 1931. Beech–Nut maintains price parity with Gerber, selling at about one penny less. It markets its product as a premium brand. Consumers generally view its product as comparable in quality to Gerber's. Beech–Nut is carried in approximately 45 per cent of all grocery stores. Although its sales are nationwide, they are concentrated in New York, New Jersey, California and Florida.[98]

---

97. Product volume in retail stores throughout the country is measured by the product's All Commodity Volume (ACV). Gerber's near 100 per cent ACV is impressive because virtually all supermarkets stock at most two brands of baby food. In at least one area of the country as many as 80 per cent of supermarket retailers stock only Gerber.

98. Although Heinz and Beech–Nut introduced evidence showing that in areas that account for 80% of Beech–Nut sales, Heinz has a market share of about 2% and in areas that account for about 72% of Heinz sales, Beech–Nut's share is about 4%, the FTC introduced evidence that Heinz and Beech–Nut are locked in an intense battle at the wholesale level to gain (and maintain) position as the second brand on retail shelves.

At the wholesale level Heinz and Beech–Nut both make lump-sum payments called "fixed trade spending" (also known as "slotting fees" or "pay-to-stay" arrangements) to grocery stores to obtain shelf placement. Gerber, with its strong name recognition and brand loyalty, does not make such pay-to-stay payments. The other type of wholesale trade spending is "variable trade spending," which typically consists of manufacturers' discounts and allowances to supermarkets to create retail price differentials that entice the consumer to purchase their product instead of a competitor's.

Under the terms of their merger agreement, Heinz would acquire 100 per cent of Beech–Nut's voting securities for $185 million....

II. Analysis

A. Standard of Review

We review a district court order denying preliminary injunctive relief for abuse of discretion, *National Wildlife Fed'n v. Burford*, 835 F.2d 305, 319 (D.C.Cir.1987), and will set aside the court's factual findings only if they are "clearly erroneous." ....

B. Section 7 of the Clayton Act

... "Merger enforcement, like other areas of antitrust, is directed at market power. It shares with the law of monopolization a degree of schizophrenia: an aversion to potent power that heightens risk of abuse; and tolerance of that degree of power required to attain economic benefits." Lawrence A. Sullivan & Warren S. Grimes, The Law of Antitrust § 9.1, at 511 (2000). The Congress has empowered the FTC, inter alia, to weed out those mergers whose effect "may be substantially to lessen competition" from those that enhance competition. In section 13(b) of the FTCA, the Congress provided a mechanism whereby the FTC may seek preliminary injunctive relief preventing the merging parties from consummating the merger until the Commission has had an opportunity to investigate and, if necessary, adjudicate the matter.

C. Section 13(b) of the Federal Trade Commission Act

"Whenever the Commission has reason to believe that a corporation is violating, or is about to violate, Section 7 of the Clayton Act, the FTC may seek a preliminary injunction to prevent a merger pending the Commission's administrative adjudication of the merger's legality." *FTC v. Staples, Inc.*, 970 F. Supp. 1066, 1070 (D.D.C.1997)....

1. Likelihood of Success

To determine likelihood of success on the merits we measure the probability that, after an administrative hearing on the merits, the Commission will succeed in proving that the effect of the Heinz/Beech–Nut merger "may be substantially to lessen competition, or to tend to create a monopoly" in violation of section 7 of the Clayton Act. This court and others have suggested that the standard for likelihood of success on the merits is met if the FTC "has raised questions going to the merits so serious, substantial, difficult and doubtful as to make them fair ground for thorough investigation, study, deliberation and determination by the FTC in the first instance and ultimately by the Court of Appeals."....

In *United States v. Baker Hughes Inc.*, 908 F.2d 981, 982–83 (D.C.Cir. 1990), we explained the analytical approach by which the government establishes a section 7 violation. First the government must show that the merger would produce "a firm controlling an undue percentage share of the relevant market, and [would] result in a significant increase in the concentration of firms in that market." *Philadelphia Nat'l Bank*, 374 U.S. at 363. Such a showing establishes a "presumption" that the merger will substantially lessen competition. To rebut the presumption, the defendants must produce evidence that "shows that the market-share statistics [give] an inaccurate account of the [merger's] probable effects on competition" in the relevant market. *United States v. Citizens & S. Nat'l Bank*, 422 U.S. 86, 120 (1975).[99] "If the defendant successfully rebuts the presumption [of illegality], the burden of producing additional evidence of anticompetitive effect shifts to the government, and merges with the ultimate burden of persuasion, which remains with the government at all times." *Baker Hughes Inc.*, 908 F.2d at 983; *see also Kaiser Aluminum & Chemical Corp. v. FTC*, 652 F.2d 1324 at 1340 & n. 12. Although *Baker Hughes* was decided at the merits stage as opposed to the preliminary injunctive relief stage, we can nonetheless use its analytical approach in evaluating the Commission's showing of likelihood of success. Accordingly, we look at the FTC's *prima facie* case and the defendants' rebuttal evidence.

a. Prima Facie Case

Merger law "rests upon the theory that, where rivals are few, firms will be able to coordinate their behavior, either by overt collusion or implicit understanding, in order to restrict output and achieve profits above competitive levels." FTC v. PPG Indus., 798 F.2d 1500, 1503 (D.C.Cir. 1986). Increases in concentration above certain levels are thought to "raise a likelihood of 'interdependent anticompetitive conduct.'" Id. (quoting General Dynamics, 415 U.S. at 497); see FTC v. Elders Grain, 868 F.2d 901, 905 (7th Cir.1989). Market concentration, or the lack thereof, is often measured by the Herfindahl–Hirschmann Index (HHI).[1]

Sufficiently large HHI figures establish the FTC's prima facie case that a merger is anti-competitive. The district court found that the pre-merger

---

99. To rebut the defendants may rely on "nonstatistical evidence which casts doubt on the persuasive quality of the statistics to predict future anticompetitive consequences" such as "ease of entry into the market, the trend of the market either toward or away from concentration, and the continuation of active price competition." Kaiser Aluminum & Chem. Corp. v. FTC, 652 F.2d 1324, 1341 (7th Cir.1981). In addition, the defendants may demonstrate unique economic circumstances that undermine the predictive value of the government's statistics. See United States v. General Dynamics Corp., 415 U.S. 486, 506–10 (1974) (fundamental changes in structure of coal market made market concentration statistics inaccurate predictors of anticompetitive effect); see also University Health, 938 F.2d at 1218.

1. The FTC and the Department of Justice, as well as most economists, consider the measure superior to such cruder measures as the four-or eight-firm concentration ratios which merely sum up the market shares of the largest four or eight firms. PPG, 798 F.2d at 1503. The Department of Justice and the FTC rely on the HHI in evaluating proposed horizontal

HHI "score for the baby food industry is 4775"—indicative of a highly concentrated industry.[2] The merger of Heinz and Beech–Nut will increase the HHI by 510 points. This creates, by a wide margin, a presumption that the merger will lessen competition in the domestic jarred baby food market. See Horizontal Merger Guidelines, *supra*, § 1.51 (stating that HHI increase of more than 100 points, where post-merger HHI exceeds 1800, is "presumed ... likely to create or enhance market power or facilitate its exercise"); *see also Baker Hughes*, 908 F.2d at 982–83 & n.3; PPG, 798 F.2d at 1503.[3] Here, the FTC's market concentration statistics[4] are bolstered by the indisputable fact that the merger will eliminate competition between the two merging parties at the wholesale level, where they are currently the only competitors for what the district court described as the "second position on the supermarket shelves." Heinz's own documents recognize the wholesale competition and anticipate that the merger will end it. Indeed, those documents disclose that Heinz considered three options to end the vigorous wholesale competition with Beech–Nut: two involved innovative measures while the third entailed the acquisition of Beech–Nut. Heinz chose the third, and least pro-competitive, of the options.

Finally, the anticompetitive effect of the merger is further enhanced by high barriers to market entry.[5] The district court found that there had

---

mergers. See United States Dep't of Justice & Federal Trade Comm'n, Horizontal Merger Guidelines §§ 1.5, 1.51 (1992), as revised (1997). Although the Merger Guidelines are not binding on the court, they provide "a useful illustration of the application of the HHI." PPG, 798 F.2d at 1503 n.4.

2. To determine the HHI score the district court first had to define the relevant market. The court defined the product market as jarred baby food and the geographic market as the United States. H.J. Heinz, 116 F. Supp. 2d at 195. The parties do not challenge the court's definition.

3. The FTC argues that this finding alone—that it is certain to establish a prima facie case—entitles it to preliminary injunctive relief under PPG. We disagree with the Commission's reading of PPG. In PPG, the Commission appealed the district court's denial of its request for a preliminary injunction to prevent PPG Industries, the world's largest producer of glass aircraft transparencies, from acquiring Swedlow, Inc., the world's largest manufacturer of acrylic aircraft transparencies. 798 F.2d at 1502. After defining the relevant market and determining market share, the district court found that the merger would significantly increase the concentration in an already highly concentrated market. It also "found high market-entry barriers that would prolong high market concentration." *Id.* at 1503. On appeal, this court stated: "There is no doubt that the pre- and post-acquisition HHI's and market shares found in this case entitle the Commission to some preliminary relief." *Id.* This statement came, however, in the context of a case in which the appellants offered no rebuttal (other than the observation of rapid and continuing technological changes in the industry) to the presumption generated by the market concentration data on which the FTC based its prima facie showing. *Id.* at 1506. The court then noted the rule established in Weyerhaeuser that the FTC is entitled to a "presumption in favor of a preliminary injunction when [it] establishes a strong likelihood of success on the merits." *Id.* at 1507.

4. The Supreme Court has cautioned that statistics reflecting market share and concentration, while of great significance, are not conclusive indicators of anticompetitive effects. *See* General Dynamics, 415 U.S. at 498.

5. Barriers to entry are important in evaluating whether market concentration statistics accurately reflect the pre-and likely post-merger competitive picture. *Cf.* Baker Hughes, 908 been no significant entries in the baby food market in decades and that new entry was "difficult and improbable." This finding largely eliminates the possibility that the reduced competition caused by the merger will be ameliorated by new competition from outsiders and further strengthens the FTC's case.

As far as we can determine, no court has ever approved a merger to duopoly under similar circumstances.

b. Rebuttal Arguments

In response to the FTC's prima facie showing, the appellees make three rebuttal arguments, which the district court accepted in reaching its conclusion that the merger was not likely to lessen competition substantially. For the reasons discussed below, these arguments fail and thus were not a proper basis for denying the FTC injunctive relief.

1. Extent of Pre–Merger Competition

The appellees first contend, and the district court agreed, that Heinz and Beech–Nut do not really compete against each other at the retail level. Consumers do not regard the products of the two companies as substitutes, the appellees claim, and generally only one of the two brands is available on any given store's shelves. Hence, they argue, there is little competitive loss from the merger.

This argument has a number of flaws that render clearly erroneous the court's finding that Heinz and Beech–Nut have not engaged in significant pre-merger competition. First, in accepting the appellees' argument that Heinz and Beech–Nut do not compete, the district court failed to address the record evidence that the two do in fact price against each other, and that, where both are present in the same areas,[6] they depress each other's prices as well as those of Gerber even though they are virtually never all found in the same store. This evidence undermines the district court's factual finding.

F.2d at 987. If entry barriers are low, the threat of outside entry can significantly alter the anticompetitive effects of the merger by deterring the remaining entities from colluding or exercising market power. *See* United States v. Falstaff Brewing Corp., 410 U.S. 526, 532–33 (1973); Baker Hughes, 908 F.2d at 987 ("In the absence of significant barriers, a company probably cannot maintain supracompetitive pricing for any length of time."); Horizontal Merger Guidelines, *supra*, § 3.0 ("A merger is not likely to create or enhance market power or to facilitate its exercise, if entry into the market is so easy that market participants, after the merger, either collectively or unilaterally could not profitably maintain a price increase above premerger levels."). Low barriers to entry enable a potential competitor to deter anticompetitive behavior by firms within the market simply by its ability to enter the market. FTC v. Procter & Gamble Co., 386 U.S. 568, 581 (1967) ("It is clear that the existence of Procter at the edge of the industry exerted considerable influence on the market."). Existing firms know that if they collude or exercise market power to charge supracompetitive prices, entry by firms currently not competing in the market becomes likely, thereby increasing the pressure on them to act competitively. *See* Baker Hughes, 908 F.2d at 988; Byars v. Bluff City News Co., 609 F.2d 843, 851 n. 19 (6th Cir.1979).

6. There are at least ten metropolitan areas in which Heinz and Beech–Nut both have more than a 10 per cent market share and their combined share exceeds 35 per cent. PX 781 at Ex. 1B.

Second, the district court's finding is inconsistent with its conclusion that there is a single, national market for jarred baby food in the United States. The Supreme Court has explained that "the outer boundaries of a product market are determined by the reasonable interchangeability of use [by consumers] or the cross-elasticity of demand between the product itself and substitutes for it." *Brown Shoe*, 370 U.S. at 325; *see also United States v. E.I. du Pont de Nemours & Co.*, 351 U.S. 377, 395 (1956).[7] The definition of product market thus "focuses solely on demand substitution factors," *i.e.*, that consumers regard the products as substitutes. *Horizontal Merger Guidelines, supra*, § 1.0; *Sullivan & Grimes, supra*, § 11.2b1, at 579. By defining the relevant product market generically as jarred baby food, the district court concluded that in areas where Heinz's and Beech–Nut's products are both sold, consumers will switch between them in response to a "small but significant and nontransitory increase in price (SSNIP)." *Horizontal Merger Guidelines, supra*, § 1.11. The district court never explained this inherent inconsistency in its logic nor could counsel for the appellees explain it at oral argument.

Third, and perhaps most important, the court's conclusion concerning pre-merger competition does not take into account the indisputable fact that the merger will eliminate competition at the wholesale level between the only two competitors for the "second shelf" position. Competition between Heinz and Beech–Nut to gain accounts at the wholesale level is fierce with each contest concluding in a winner-take-all result. The district court regarded this loss of competition as irrelevant because the FTC did not establish to its satisfaction that wholesale competition ultimately benefited consumers through lower retail prices. The district court concluded that fixed trade spending did not affect consumer prices and that "the FTC's assertion that the proposed merger will affect variable trade spending levels and consumer prices is ... at best, inconclusive."[8] *H.J. Heinz*, 116 F. Supp. 2d at 197. Although the court noted the FTC's examples of consumer benefit through couponing initiatives, the court held that it was "impossible to conclude with any certainty that the consumer benefit from such couponing initiatives would be lost in the merger." *Id.*

In rejecting the FTC's argument regarding the loss of wholesale competition, the court committed two legal errors. First, as the appellees conceded at oral argument, no court has ever held that a reduction in competition for wholesale purchasers is not relevant unless the plaintiff can prove impact at the consumer level. *See Hospital Corp. of Am. v. FTC*, 807 F.2d 1381, 1389 (7th Cir.1986) ("Section 7 does not require proof that a merger or other acquisition has caused higher prices in the affected market.

---

7. Interchangeability of use and cross-elasticity of demand look to the availability of products that are similar in nature or use and the degree to which buyers are willing to substitute those similar products for one another. See E.I. du Pont de Nemours, 351 U.S. at 393.

8. Fixed trade spending consists of "slotting fees," "pay-to-stay" arrangements, new store allowances and other payments to retailers in exchange for shelf space and desired product display. Variable trade spending includes payments to retailers tied to sales volume and intended to insure a specific sales volume and lower shelf price.

All that is necessary is that the merger create an appreciable danger of [collusive practices] in the future. A predictive judgment, necessarily probabilistic and judgmental rather than demonstrable, is called for.") Second, it is, in any event, not the FTC's burden to prove such an impact with "certainty." To the contrary, the antitrust laws assume that a retailer faced with an increase in the cost of one of its inventory items "will try so far as competition allows to pass that cost on to its customers in the form of a higher price for its product." *In re Brand Name Prescription Drugs Antitrust Litig.*, 123 F.3d 599, 605 (7th Cir.1997). Section 7 is, after all, concerned with probabilities, not certainties. *United States v. El Paso Natural Gas Co.*, 376 U.S. 651, 658 (1964); *Brown Shoe*, 370 U.S. at 323; *Baker Hughes*, 908 F.2d at 984.[9]

2.   Post–Merger Efficiencies

The appellees' second attempt to rebut the FTC's prima facie showing is their contention that the anticompetitive effects of the merger will be offset by efficiencies resulting from the union of the two companies, efficiencies which they assert will be used to compete more effectively against Gerber. It is true that a merger's primary benefit to the economy is its potential to generate efficiencies. *See generally* 4A Phillip E. Areeda, Herbert Hovenkamp & John L. Solow, Antitrust Law p. 970 at 22–25 (1998). As the Merger Guidelines now recognize, efficiencies "can enhance the merged firm's ability and incentive to compete, which may result in lower prices, improved quality, or new products." Horizontal Merger Guidelines, *supra*, § 4.

Although the Supreme Court has not sanctioned the use of the efficiencies defense in a section 7 case, *see Procter & Gamble Co.*, 386 U.S. at 580,[10]

---

9.   Although the merger's effects on the wholesale market for baby food are important to a determination of whether the merger is likely to reduce competition in the baby food market overall, we reject the FTC's argument here that the "wholesale competition" between Heinz and Beech–Nut is an entirely distinct "line of commerce" within the meaning of section 7 of the Clayton Act such that it must be analyzed independently from "retail competition." The Congress amended section 7 in 1950 "to make the measure of anticompetitive acquisitions the extent to which they lessened competition 'in any line of commerce,' rather than the extent to which they lessened competition 'between' the two companies." *Citizen Publishing Co. v. United States*, 394 U.S. 131, 137 n. 3 (1969). Courts interpret "line of commerce" as synonymous with the relevant product market. See *General Dynamics, 415 U.S. at 510; Falstaff Brewing*, 410 U.S. at 531–32. The district court defined only one market—jarred baby food sold throughout the line of commerce in the United States. Thus, the proper "line of commerce" for analysis in this case is the overall market for jarred baby food, which includes both retail and wholesale levels. At this point in the proceedings, the wholesale market cannot be separated out for analysis without regard to the merger's effect on other levels of competition.

10.   In Procter & Gamble Co., 386 U.S. at 580, the Supreme Court stated that "possible economies cannot be used as a defense to illegality" in section 7 merger cases. The issue is, however, not a closed book. See Staples, 970 F. Supp. at 1088. Areeda and Turner explain that "in interpreting the Clorox language, moreover, observe that the court referred only to 'possible' economies and to economies that 'may' result from mergers that lessen competition. To reject an economies defense based on mere possibilities does not mean that one should reject such a defense based on more convincing proof." 4 Phillip Areeda & Donald Turner, the trend among lower courts is to recognize the defense. *See, e.g., FTC v. Tenet Health Care Corp.*, 186 F.3d 1045, 1054 (8th Cir.1999); *University Health*, 938 F.2d at 1222; *FTC v. Cardinal Health, Inc.*, 12 F. Supp. 2d 34, 61 (D.D.C.1998); *Staples,* 970 F. Supp. at 1088–89; *see also* ABA Antitrust Section, Mergers and Acquisitions: Understanding the Antitrust Issues 152 (2000) ("The majority of courts have considered efficiencies as a means to rebut the government's prima facie case that a merger will lead to restricted output or increased prices. These courts, however, generally have found inadequate proof of efficiencies to sustain a rebuttal of the government's case."). In 1997 the Department of Justice and the FTC revised their Horizontal Merger Guidelines to recognize that "mergers have the potential to generate significant efficiencies by permitting a better utilization of existing assets, enabling the combined firm to achieve lower costs in producing a given quantity and quality than either firm could have achieved without the proposed transaction." Horizontal Merger Guidelines, *supra*, § 4.

Nevertheless, the high market concentration levels present in this case require, in rebuttal, proof of extraordinary efficiencies, which the appellees failed to supply. *See University Health*, 938 F.2d at 1223 ("[A] defendant who seeks to overcome a presumption that a proposed acquisition would substantially lessen competition must demonstrate that the intended acquisition would result in significant economies and that these economies ultimately would benefit competition and, hence, consumers."); Horizontal Merger Guidelines, *supra*, § 4 (stating that "efficiencies almost never justify a merger to monopoly or near-monopoly"); 4A Areeda, et al., Antitrust Law p. 971f, at 44 (requiring "extraordinary" efficiencies where the "HHI is well above 1800 and the HHI increase is well above 100"). Moreover, given the high concentration levels, the court must undertake a rigorous analysis of the kinds of efficiencies being urged by the parties in order to ensure that those "efficiencies" represent more than mere speculation and promises about post-merger behavior. The district court did not undertake that analysis here.

In support of its conclusion that post-merger efficiencies will outweigh the merger's anticompetitive effects, the district court found that the consolidation of baby food production in Heinz's under-utilized Pittsburgh plant "will achieve substantial cost savings in salaries and operating costs." The court also credited the appellees' promise of improved product quality as a result of recipe consolidation.[11] The only cost reduction the court

---

Antitrust Law p 941b, at 154 (1980). They conclude that "the Court's brief and unelaborated language [in Clorox] cannot reasonably be taken as a definitive disposition of so important and complex an issue as the role of economies in analyzing legality of a merger." *Id.*

11. In addition, the district court described Heinz's distribution network as much more efficient than Beech–Nut's. It failed to find, however, a significant diseconomy of scale in distribution from which either Heinz or Beech–Nut suffers. 4A Areeda, et al., *supra*, p. 975e1, at 73. In other words, although Beech–Nut has an inefficient distribution system, it can make that system more efficient without merger. Heinz's own efficient distribution network illustrates that a firm the size of Beech–Nut does not need to merge in order to attain an efficient distribution system.

quantified as a percentage of pre-merger costs, however, was the so-called "variable conversion cost": the cost of processing the volume of baby food now processed by Beech–Nut. The court accepted the appellees' claim that this cost would be reduced by 43% if the Beech–Nut production were shifted to Heinz's plant, a reduction the appellees' expert characterized as "extraordinary."

The district court's analysis falls short of the findings necessary for a successful efficiencies defense in the circumstances of this case. We mention only three of the most important deficiencies here. First, "variable conversion cost" is only a percentage of the total variable manufacturing cost. A large percentage reduction in only a small portion of the company's overall variable manufacturing cost does not necessarily translate into a significant cost advantage to the merger. Thus, for cost reduction to be relevant, we must at least consider the percentage of Beech–Nut's total variable manufacturing cost that would be reduced as a consequence of the merger. At oral argument, the appellees' counsel agreed. This correction immediately cuts the asserted efficiency gain in half since, according to the appellees' evidence, using total variable manufacturing cost as the measure cuts the cost savings from 43% to 22.3%.

Second, the percentage reduction in Beech–Nut's cost is still not the relevant figure. After the merger, the two entities will be combined, and to determine whether the merged entity will be a significantly more efficient competitor, cost reductions must be measured across the new entity's combined production—not just across the pre-merger output of Beech–Nut. The district court, however, did not consider the cost reduction over the merged firm's combined output. At oral argument the appellees' counsel was unable to suggest a formula that could be used for determining that cost reduction.

Finally, and as the district court recognized, the asserted efficiencies must be "merger-specific" to be cognizable as a defense. That is, they must be efficiencies that cannot be achieved by either company alone because, if they can, the merger's asserted benefits can be achieved without the concomitant loss of a competitor. *See generally* 4A Areeda, et al., *supra*, p. 973. Yet the district court never explained why Heinz could not achieve the kind of efficiencies urged without merger. As noted, the principal merger benefit asserted for Heinz is the acquisition of Beech–Nut's better recipes, which will allegedly make its product more attractive and permit expanded sales at prices lower than those charged by Beech–Nut, which produces at an inefficient plant. Yet, neither the district court nor the appellees addressed the question whether Heinz could obtain the benefit of better recipes by investing more money in product development and promotion— say, by an amount less than the amount Heinz would spend to acquire Beech–Nut. At oral argument, Heinz's counsel agreed that the taste of Heinz's products was not so bad that no amount of money could improve the brand's consumer appeal. That being the case, the question is how much Heinz would have to spend to make its product equivalent to the Beech–Nut product and hence whether Heinz could achieve the efficiencies of merger without eliminating Beech–Nut as a competitor. The district court, however, undertook no inquiry in this regard. In short, the district court failed to make the kind of factual determinations necessary to render the appellees' efficiency defense sufficiently concrete to offset the FTC's prima facie showing.

3. Innovation

The appellees claim next that the merger is required to enable Heinz to innovate, and thus to improve its competitive position against Gerber. Heinz and Beech–Nut asserted, and the district court found, that without the merger the two firms are unable to launch new products to compete with Gerber because they lack a sufficient shelf presence or ACV. This kind of defense is often a speculative proposition. See 4A Areeda, et al., *supra*, p. 975g (noting "truly formidable" proof problems in determining innovation economies). In this case, given the old-economy nature of the industry as well as Heinz's position as the world's largest baby food manufacturer, it is a particularly difficult defense to prove. The court below accepted the appellees' argument principally on the basis of their expert's testimony that new product launches are cost-effective only when a firm's ACV is 70% or greater (Heinz's is presently 40%; Beech–Nut's is 45%). That testimony, in turn, was based on a graph that plotted revenue against ACV. According to the expert, the graph showed that only four out of 27 new products launched in 1995 had been successful—all for companies with an ACV of 70% or greater.

The chart, however, does not establish this proposition and the court's consequent finding that the merger is necessary for innovation is thus unsupported and clearly erroneous. All the chart plotted was revenue against ACV and hence all it showed was the unsurprising fact that the greater a company's ACV, the greater the revenue it received. Because the graph did not plot the profitability (or any measure of "cost-effectiveness"), there is no way to know whether the expert's claim—that a 70% ACV is required for a launch to be "successful" in an economic sense—is true.[12] Moreover, the number of data points on the chart were few; they were limited to launches in a single year; and they involved launches of all new grocery products rather than of baby food alone. Assessing such data's statistical significance in establishing the proposition at issue, *i.e.*, the necessity of 70% ACV penetration, is thus highly speculative. The district court did not even address the question of the data's statistical significance and the appellees' counsel could offer no help at oral argument. ("I'm not aware of the statistical significance of the underlying study.").[13] In the

---

12. For example, a 5 cent piece of bubble gum introduced with a 90 ACV could appear as a failure on the graph because of low revenue but nonetheless be profitable. On the other hand, a high priced grocery product introduced with the same ACV could generate a lot of revenue (and thus appear as a "success" on the graph) yet be unprofitable.

13. The graph evidence is also not useful unless we know the "sunk" costs in bringing the product to market and the manufacturer's fixed and variable costs in producing the product. Sunk costs are costs that have already been incurred such as research and development and promotional expenses, including brand name development. *See* Henry N. Butler, absence of reliable and significant evidence that the merger will permit innovation that otherwise could not be accomplished, the district court had no basis to conclude that the FTC's showing was rebutted by an innovation defense. . . .

4.   Structural Barriers to Collusion

In a footnote the district court dismissed the likelihood of collusion derived from the FTC's market concentration data. "Structural market barriers to collusion" in the retail market for jarred baby food, the court said, rebut the normal presumption that increases in concentration will increase the likelihood of tacit collusion. The court's sole citation, however, was to testimony by the appellees' expert, Jonathan B. Baker, a former Director of the Bureau of Economics at the FTC, who testified that in order to coordinate successfully, firms must solve "cartel problems" such as reaching a consensus on price and market share and deterring each other from deviating from that consensus by either lowering price or increasing production. He opined that after the merger the merged entity would want to expand its market share at Gerber's expense, thereby decreasing the likelihood of consensus on price and market share. In his report, Baker elaborated on his theory, explaining that the efficiencies created by the merger will give the merged firm the ability and incentive to take on Gerber in price and product improvements. He also predicted that policing and monitoring of any agreement would be more difficult than it is now, due in part to a time lag in the ability of one firm to detect price cuts by another. But the district court made no finding that any of these "cartel problems" are so much greater in the baby food industry than in other industries that they rebut the normal presumption. In fact, Baker's testimony about "time lag" is refuted by the record that reflects that supermarket prices are available from industry-wide scanner data within 4–8 weeks. His testimony is further undermined by the record evidence of past price leadership in the baby food industry.[14]

The combination of a concentrated market and barriers to entry is a recipe for price coordination. *See University Health*, 938 F.2d at 1218 n.24 ("Significant market concentration makes it 'easier for firms in the market to collude, expressly or tacitly, and thereby force price above or farther above the competitive level.' " (citation omitted)). "Where rivals are few, firms will be able to coordinate their behavior, either by overt collusion or implicit understanding, in order to restrict output and achieve profits above

---

Economic Analysis for Lawyers 935 (1998). Fixed costs refer to those expenses that do not vary with output and will be incurred as long as the firm continues in business. Variable costs are those that change with the rate of output such as wages paid to workers and payments for raw materials. *See id.* at 920, 936; E. Thomas Sullivan & Jeffrey L. Harrison, *Understanding Antitrust and its Economic Implications* 19–21 (3d ed. 1998).

14. In an oligopolistic market characterized by few producers, price leadership occurs when firms engage in interdependent pricing, setting their prices at a profit-maximizing, supracompetitive level by recognizing their shared economic interests with respect to price and output decisions. *See* Brooke Group Ltd. v. Brown & Williamson Tobacco Corp., 509 U.S. 209, 227 (1993).

competitive levels." PPG, 798 F.2d at 1503. The creation of a durable duopoly affords both the opportunity and incentive for both firms to coordinate to increase prices. The district court recognized this when it questioned Baker on whether the merged entity will, up to a point, expand its market share but "then [with Gerber will] find a nice equilibrium and they'll all get along together." 9/8/2000 Tr. 1014. Tacit coordination

> is feared by antitrust policy even more than express collusion, for tacit coordination, even when observed, cannot easily be controlled directly by the antitrust laws. It is a central object of merger policy to obstruct the creation or reinforcement by merger of such oligopolistic market structures in which tacit coordination can occur.

4 Phillip E. Areeda, Herbert Hovenkamp & John L. Solow, Antitrust Law p. 901b2, at 9 (rev. ed. 1998). Because the district court failed to specify any "structural market barriers to collusion" that are unique to the baby food industry, its conclusion that the ordinary presumption of collusion in a merger to duopoly was rebutted is clearly erroneous.

* * *

Although we recognize that, post-hearing, the FTC may accept the rebuttal arguments proffered by the appellees, including their efficiencies defense, and permit the merger to proceed, we conclude that the FTC succeeded in "raising questions going to the merits so serious, substantial, difficult and doubtful as to make them fair ground for thorough investigation, study, deliberation and determination by the FTC." *Warner Communications*, 742 F.2d at 1162. The FTC demonstrated that the merger to duopoly will increase the concentration in an already highly concentrated market; that entry barriers in the market make it unlikely that any anticompetitive effects will be avoided; that pre-merger competition is vigorous at the wholesale level nationwide and present at the retail level in some metropolitan areas; and that post-merger competition may be lessened substantially. These substantial questions have not been sufficiently answered by the appellees. As we said in *Baker Hughes,* "the more compelling the prima facie case, the more evidence the defendant must present to rebut it successfully." 908 F.2d at 991. In concluding that the FTC failed to make the requisite showing, the district court erred in a number of respects. Regarding the contention of lack of pre-merger competition, it made a clearly erroneous factual finding and misunderstood the law with respect to the import of competition at the wholesale level. Regarding the proffered efficiencies defense, the court failed to make the kind of factual findings required to render that defense sufficiently concrete to rebut the government's prima facie showing. Finally, as to the contention that the merger is necessary for innovation, the court clearly erred in relying on evidence that does not support its conclusion. Because the district court incorrectly assessed the merits of the appellees' rebuttal arguments, it improperly discounted the FTC's showing of likelihood of success. . . .

[In a concluding section, the Court of Appeals "weighed the equities." On the government's side, it cited legislative history and prior cases to the effect that denial of an injunction might prevent the government from ever undoing the anticompetitive effects of the merger. It assumed that the Beech–Nut manufacturing facility would be closed and its distribution channels closed. On the defendants' side, it recognized that the parties might abandon the proposed merger if they had to await full administrative litigation before the FTC and a possible appeal. The D.C. Circuit came down in favor of the government, noting that the alleged efficiencies would still be available after litigation.]

III. Conclusion

It is important to emphasize the posture of this case. We do not decide whether the FTC will ultimately prove its case or whether the defendants' claimed efficiencies will carry the day[15] Our task is to review the district court's order to determine whether, under section 13(b), preliminary injunctive relief would be in the public interest. We have considered the FTC's likelihood of success on the merits. We have weighed the equities. We conclude that the FTC has raised serious and substantial questions. We also conclude that the public equities weigh in favor of preliminary injunctive relief and therefore that a preliminary injunction would be in the public interest. Accordingly, we reverse the district court's denial of preliminary injunctive relief and remand the case for entry of a preliminary injunction pursuant to section 13(b) of the Federal Trade Commission Act.[16]

NOTE ON HOSPITAL MERGERS

During the 1990s, the Department of Justice and the Federal Trade Commission had a remarkable string of successes in challenging proposed mergers in court. An exception to that general level of success related to hospital mergers. In that sector of the economy, the contrast was striking with the federal enforcement agencies losing most of the merger challenges that were mounted.

An example of judicial reaction to government enforcement in this area is Federal Trade Commission v. Tenet Health Care, 186 F.3d 1045 (8th Cir.1999) where the Commission challenged the acquisition by Tenet of the only other acute care hospital in Popular Bluff, Missouri. Hospital customers, including health insurance providers such as employers, health plans and network providers, unanimously opposed the merger, arguing that they had played the two hospitals—Lucy Lee and Doctors' Regional—against each other and obtained significant discounts. The controlling issue related to definition of relevant geographic market. The

---

15. "The most difficult mergers to assess may be those that combine both negative and positive effects: creating market power that increases the risk of oligopolistic pricing while at the same time creating efficiencies that reduce production or marketing costs." Sullivan & Grimes, *supra*, § 9.1, at 511.

16. Ed. The parties abandoned the merger shortly after the D.C. Circuit's decision was issued.

Commission alleged that the market was the city of Popular Bluff and eight surrounding counties, an area covering approximately a 50–mile radius. Other hospitals in that area were small rural operations. The Commission charged that the Lucy Lee and Doctors' Regional between them drew 90% of their patients from zip codes within the 50–mile radius and accounted for a post-merger market share of 84%. The hospitals responded that the relevant market should be slightly larger—roughly an area with a radius of 65 miles from Popular Bluff (thereby including additional hospitals), and, more important, that many patients living at the outer edges of the proposed geographic market already traveled to hospitals outside the radius. In a "critical loss" analysis—*i.e.*, an investigation of whether enough patients would abandon the Popular Bluff hospitals if prices were increased so as to defeat that increase—defendants contended that even with respect to services offered at the Popular Bluff hospitals, 22% to 70% of potential patients were already dealing with hospitals outside the proposed geographic area.

The Court of Appeals reversed a District Court decision to issue an injunction blocking the merger, finding that the Commission had failed to discharge its burden of establishing a plausible relevant geographic market. It appeared also to be influenced by the claims of the sponsors of the merger that the combined hospitals would result in enhanced efficiency, and that it might be that Popular Bluff was such a small market as not to be able to sustain two high quality hospitals.

NOTE

United States v. Oracle Corp., 331 F. Supp. 2d 1098 (D.C. Cal. 2004). In 2004, the Department of Justice and 10 states sought a preliminary injunction to block Oracle Corporation from acquiring People Soft, Inc., two companies that manufactured and sold a type of application software that automated business data processing ("EAS"). Programs that provide EAS functions include human relations management ("HRM"), financial management systems ("FMS"), customer relations management, supply chain management, product life cycle management, and business intelligence, among many others. The government claimed that the combination of the HRM and FMS functions, and then only at the high end of those two application systems, constituted a relevant market. One other large company— SAP—(like Oracle and People Soft) offered a comprehensive set of software, and many other companies offered specific sets of software to the market.

The case depended largely on relevant product market definition, and that issue in turn depended upon what various witnesses testified about the ability of the combined firms to raise price after the proposed merger.

In support of their proposed product market definition, the government presented at trial or through depositions 10 customer witnesses, five industry witnesses, two systems integration witnesses, three expert witnesses, and a few others who according to the court appeared mostly to fill a gap or two in the evidence or to supply "spice" for the record. Typically, competitor testimony has been regarded as suspect because rivals may be comfortable with the idea of a merger that leads to higher prices, which would lead to higher profits for all competitors in the market. On the other hand, customer evidence had in the past been regarded as fairly persuasive. The District Court, in denying a preliminary injunction, took a different view of the customer evidence in this particular case.

[After reviewing the customer witness testimony in detail, the court concluded as follows:]

In the main, and contrary to the characterization of plaintiffs' counsel before trial, the court found the testimony of the customer witnesses largely unhelpful to plaintiffs' effort to define a narrow market of high function FMS and HRM. Each of these witnesses had an impressive background in the field of information technology. They appeared knowledgeable and well informed about their employers' ERP needs and resources. And the court does not doubt the sincerity of these witnesses' beliefs in the testimony that they gave. What the court questions is the grounds upon which these witnesses offered their opinions on the definition of the product market and competition within that market.

The test of market definition turns on reasonable substitutability. *E. I. du Pont,* 351 U.S. 377, 76 S.Ct. 994, 100 L.Ed. 1264. This requires the court to determine whether or not products have "reasonable interchangeability" based upon "price, use and qualities * * *." What, instead, these witnesses testified to was, largely, their preferences.

Customer preferences towards one product over another do not negate interchangeability. See *R R Donnelley & Sons Co.,* 120 FTC 36, 54 n. 65 (1995) (citing Robert Pitofsky, *New Definitions of the Relevant Market and the Assault on Antitrust,* 90 Colum. L. Rev. 1805, 1816 (1990) ("There will almost always be classes of customers with strong preferences * * * but to reason from the existence of such classes to a conclusion that each is entitled to * * * a separate narrow market definition grossly overstates the market power of the sellers.")). The preferences of these customer witnesses for the functional features of PeopleSoft or Oracle products was evident. But the issue is not what solutions the customers would *like* or *prefer* for their data processing needs; the issue is what they *could* do in the event of an anticompetitive price increase by a post-merger Oracle. Although these witnesses speculated on that subject, their speculation was not backed up by serious analysis that they had themselves performed or evidence they presented. There was little, if any, testimony by these witnesses about what they would or could do or not do to avoid a price increase from a post-merger Oracle. To be sure, each testified, with a kind of rote, that they would have no choice but to accept a ten percent price increase by a merged Oracle/PeopleSoft. But none gave testimony about the cost of alternatives to the hypothetical price increase a post-merger Oracle would charge: *e.g.,* how much outsourcing would actually cost, or how much it would cost to adapt other vendors' products to the same functionality that the Oracle and PeopleSoft products afford.

If backed by credible and convincing testimony of this kind or testimony presented by economic experts, customer testimony of the kind plaintiffs offered can put a human perspective or face on the injury to competition that plaintiffs allege. But unsubstantiated customer apprehensions do not substitute for hard evidence.

While listening to the testimony of these customer witnesses, it became clear to the court that these witnesses represent a group of extremely sophisticated buyers and users of information technology; they have decades of experience in negotiating in this field. This made more evident the failure of these witnesses to present cost/benefit analyses of the type that surely they employ and would employ in assessing an ERP purchase. The evidence at trial established that ERP customers have choices outside the integrated suites of Oracle, PeopleSoft and SAP. Indeed, Glover's testimony showed that—as Oracle contends—customers have some leverage by virtue of their existing installed base "to do nothing" and thereby resist anticompetitive price increases by ERP vendors. Although the court is not convinced that this is a long-term option due to the ever changing business and legal environment in which enterprises operate, this option does afford ERP customers some limited protection and leverage. At any rate, plaintiffs' customer witnesses did not, in their testimony, provide the court with data from actual or probable ERP purchases and installations to demonstrate that the witnesses' employers would have had no choice but to submit to a SSNIP imposed by a post-merger Oracle.

The court, therefore, finds that these witnesses did not establish by a preponderance of the evidence that the products offered by Oracle, PeopleSoft and SAP are in a distinct line of commerce or product market from those offered by other ERP vendors. The court finds that these witnesses did not establish that it was more likely than not that customers of a post-merger Oracle would have no choice but to submit to a small but significant non-transitory price increase by the merged entity. These findings do not rest alone on the court's skepticism about the testimony of plaintiffs' customer witnesses.

* * *

In the concluding sections of the opinion, the Court turned to questions of likely anticompetitive effects as the result of collusive behavior or unilateral effects. Largely on the basis of the government's failure to establish relevant product market on the basis of consumer testimony or otherwise, the government's request for an injunction was denied.

HORIZONTAL MERGER ENFORCEMENT SINCE 2000

Merger activity and enforcement at the federal level were very different in the last decade of the 20th century compared to the first decade of the 21st. Premerger notification filings generally decreased in the decade beginning in 2000, second requests (*i.e.*, formal requests from the government for additional information about the transaction) declined and challenges leading to consent orders or litigated cases declined even more rapidly. There were fewer government challenges to horizontal mergers than in previous decades and no enforcement at all against vertical or conglomerate mergers during the Bush Administrations. These declines were more pronounced at the Antitrust Division of Department of Justice than at the Federal Trade Commission.[17]

A strong indication of the direction of future government merger enforcement can be found in the 2006 decision of the senior management of the Antitrust Division not to challenge the proposed merger of WhirlPool and Maytag, even though the staff strongly advocated a challenge.

The two companies were very large in their own markets. WhirlPool's share of unit shipments in the U.S. was 51% and Maytag's share was 20%; GE was a distant third with 17% and Electrolux fourth with 9%. Using those figures, even though the HHI would increase about 2,000 point—far beyond the cutoff points in the Horizontal Merger Guidelines—challenge was not deemed necessary because two small

---

17. Feinstein, "Recent Trends in U.S. Merger Enforcement: Down But Not Out," pp. 74–76, Antitrust Magazine (Summer 2007).

foreign companies were on the edge of initiating sales in the United States, there were substantial efficiencies as a result of the merger, and the typical customers were "Big Buyers." In many ways the decision, at least in the period of the Bush Administration, signaled the demise of anything approaching a structural presumption.[18]

One reason the government may have become more cautious in merger enforcement is that it lost several merger challenges early in the decade, often because of very stringent standards of illegality imposed by the courts, and therefore, became more cautious in its challenges.

For example, in FTC v. Arch Coal Inc., 329 F.Supp. 2d 109 (D.D.C. 2004), the FTC and six states sought to enjoin a merger between two 'companies that owned a total of four mines in the Southern Powder River Basin of Wyoming (an area that produces one-third of coal produced annual in the United States). Arch indicated an intention to sell one of the acquired mines upon completion of transaction. The court applied a fairly rigid in its interpretation of "sufficiently probable and imminent" effects and dismissed the challenge.

Two other decisions were notable after 2000: first, because they were among the relatively few cases filed by the federal government; second, because they established some law) (*Oracle see* p. 1073 *supra*); and, finally, because there were exploration of new approaches to relevant market and anticompetitive effect (Whole Foods) discussed immediately below. Whole Foods was eventually dropped by the parties so there is no final opinion, but some of the discussion in earlier stages of the proceeding could prove interesting in future merger analysis.

Federal Trade Commission v. Whole Foods Market, Inc.

United States Court of Appeals for the District of Columbia, 2008.
548 F.3d 1028.

■ BROWN, J. [The FTC unsuccessfully sought a preliminary injunction to block the merger of Whole Foods and Wild Oats in the district court; the Court of Appeals reversed. The key issue was definition of relevant product market and the D.C. Circuit concluded the district court underestimated the FTC's likelihood of success on the merits and should have granted the injunction.]

Whole Foods Market, Inc. ("Whole Foods") and Wild Oats Markets, Inc. ("Wild Oats") operate 194 and 110 grocery stores, respectively, primarily in the United States. In February 2007, they announced that Whole Foods would acquire Wild Oats....

[In seeking a preliminary injunction,] [t]he FTC contended Whole Foods and Wild Oats are the two largest operators of what it called premium, natural, and organic supermarkets ("PNOS"). Such stores "focus on high-quality perishables, specialty and natural organic produce, prepared foods, meat, fish[,] and bakery goods; generally have high levels of customer services; generally target affluent and well educated customers [and] ... are mission driven with an emphasis on social and environmental

18. Baker & Shapiro, Reinvigorating Horizontal Merger Enforcement, 235 249, Chapter 6, in Pitofsky (ed.), How the Chicago School Overshot the Mark (2008).

responsibility." *FTC v. Whole Foods Market, Inc.*, 502 F. Supp. 2d 1, 28 (D.D.C. 2007). In eighteen cities, asserted the FTC, the merger would create monopolies because Whole Foods and Wild Oats are the only PNOS. To support this claim, the FTC relied on emails Whole Foods's CEO John Mackey sent to other Whole Foods executives and directors suggesting the purpose of the merger was to eliminate a competitor. In addition the FTC produced pseudonymous blog postings in which Mr. Mackey touted Whole Foods and denigrated other supermarkets as unable to compete. The FTC's expert economist, Dr. Kevin Murphy, analyzed sales data from the companies to show how entry by various supermarkets into a local market affected sales at a Whole Foods or Wild Oats store.

On the other hand, the defendants' expert, Dr. David Scheffman, focused on whether a hypothetical monopolist owning both Whole Foods and Wild Oats would actually have power over a distinct market. He used various third-party market studies to predict that such an owner could not raise prices without driving customers to other supermarkets. In addition, deposition testimony from other supermarkets indicated they regarded Whole Foods and Wild Oats as critical competition. Internal documents from the two defendants reflected their extensive monitoring of other supermarkets' prices as well as each other's.

The district court concluded that PNOS was not a distinct market and that Whole Foods and Wild Oats compete within the broader market of grocery stores and supermarkets. Believing such a basic failure doomed any chance of the FTC's success, the court denied the preliminary injunction without considering the balance of the equities.

On August 17, the FTC filed an emergency motion for an injunction pending appeal, which this court denied on August 23. . . .

[Before turning to the merits of the district court decision, the Court of Appeals was asked to address two preliminary points. First, Whole Foods contended that the injunction issue was moot because, after the district court denied a preliminary injunction, some stores were closed and others sold. The argument was rejected on grounds that the FTC has broad equity powers and could improve the competitive situation, for example, by requiring divestiture of some stores that had not been closed or sold (*i.e.*, there was the possibility of a partial remedy).

Second, the Court of Appeals addressed the question whether the district court denied a preliminary injunction on correct legal grounds. "Correct grounds" consists of serving the public interest by examining the likelihood of success of the FTC and weighing competing equities in blocking or allowing the merger. The Court of Appeals concluded that the district court must have thought the agency had virtually no likelihood of success since it never attempted to weigh the equities. The Court then turned to the merits of the likelihood of success.]

. . . The FTC contends the district court abused its discretion in two ways: first, by treating market definition as a threshold issue; and second, by ignoring the FTC's main evidence. We conclude the district court acted reasonably in focusing on the market definition, but it analyzed the product market incorrectly.

First, the FTC complains the district court improperly focused on whether Whole Foods and Wild Oats operate within a PNOS market. However, this was not an abuse of discretion given that the district court was simply following the FTC's outline of the case.

Inexplicably, the FTC now asserts a market definition is not necessary in a § 7 case, in contravention of the statute itself, (barring an acquisition "where in any line of commerce . . . the effect of such acquisition may be substantially to lessen competition"); *see also Brown Shoe Co.* v. *United States,* 370 U.S. 294, 324 (1962) (interpreting "any line of commerce" to require a "determination of the relevant market" to find "a violation of the Clayton Act"). The FTC suggests "market definition . . . is a means to an end—to enable some measurement of market power—not an end in itself." But measuring market power is not the only purpose of a market definition; only "examination of the particular market-its structure, history, and probable future-can provide the appropriate setting for judging the probable anticompetitive effect of the merger." *Brown Shoe,* 370 U.S. at 322 n.38. . . .

In this case, however, the FTC itself made market definition key. It claimed "[t]he operation of premium natural and organic supermarkets is a distinct 'line of commerce' within the meaning of Section 7," and its theory of anticompetitive effect was that the merger would "substantially increase concentration in the operation of [PNOS]." Throughout its briefs, the FTC presented a straightforward § 7 case in which "whether the transaction creates an appreciable danger of anticompetitive effects . . . depends upon . . . [the] relevant product . . . [and] geographic market . . . and the transaction's probable effect on competition in the product and geographic markets." It purported to show "undue concentration in the relevant market," as the mainstay of its case. Because of the concentration in the supposed PNOS market, the FTC urged the district court to hold the merger "presumptively unlawful," and this was its sole reason for blocking the merger. . . .

Thus, the FTC assumed the burden of raising some question of whether PNOS is a well-defined market. As the FTC presented its case, success turned on whether there exist core customers, committed to PNOS, for whom one should consider PNOS a relevant market. The district court assumed "the 'marginal' consumer, not the so-called 'core' or 'committed' consumer, must be the focus of any analysis." To the contrary, core consumers can, in appropriate circumstances, be worthy of antitrust protection. *See* Horizontal Merger Guidelines § 1.12 (explaining the possibility of price discrimination for "targeted buyers"). The district court's error of law led it to ignore FTC evidence that strongly suggested Whole Foods and Wild Oats compete for core consumers within a PNOS market, even if they also compete on individual products for marginal consumers in the broader market

A market "must include all products reasonably interchangeable by consumers for the same purposes." *Microsoft,* 253 F.3d at 52. Whether one product is reasonably interchangeable for another depends not only on the ease and speed with which customers can substitute it and the desirability of doing so, but also on the cost of substitution, which depends most sensitively on the price of the products. A broad market may also contain relevant submarkets which themselves "constitute product markets for antitrust purposes." *Brown Shoe.* "The boundaries of such a submarket may be determined by examining such practical indicia as industry or public recognition of the submarket as a separate economic entity, the product's peculiar characteristics and uses, unique production facilities, distinct customers, distinct prices, sensitivity to price changes, and specialized vendors."

To facilitate this analysis, the Department of Justice and the FTC developed a technique called the SSNIP ("small but significant non-transitory increase in price") test, which both Dr. Murphy and Dr. Scheffman used. In the SSNIP method, one asks whether a hypothetical monopolist controlling all suppliers in the proposed market could profit from a small price increase. Horizontal Merger Guidelines § 1.11. If a small price increase would drive consumers to an alternative product, then that product must be reasonably substitutable for those in the proposed market and must therefore be part of the market, properly defined.

Experts for the two sides disagreed about how to do the SSNIP of the proposed PNOS market. Dr. Scheffman used a method called critical loss analysis, in which he predicted the loss that would result when marginal customers shifted purchases to conventional supermarkets in response to a SSNIP.[19] He concluded a hypothetical monopolist could not profit from a SSNIP, so that conventional supermarkets must be within the same market as PNOS. In contrast, Dr. Murphy disapproved of critical loss analysis generally, preferring a method called critical diversion that asked how many customers would be diverted to Whole Foods and how many to conventional supermarkets if a nearby Wild Oats closed. Whole Foods's internal planning documents indicated at least a majority of these customers would switch to Whole Foods, thus making the closure profitable for a hypothetical PNOS monopolist. One crucial difference between these approaches was that Dr. Scheffman's analysis depended only on the *marginal* loss of sales, while Dr. Murphy's used the *average* loss of customers. Dr. Murphy explained that focusing on the average behavior of customers was appropriate because a core of committed customers would continue to shop at PNOS stores despite a SSNIP.

In appropriate circumstances, core customers can be a proper subject of antitrust concern. In particular, when one or a few firms differentiate themselves by offering a particular package of goods or services, it is quite possible for there to be a central group of customers for whom "only [that

---

19. Dr. Scheman did not actually calculate the amount of this loss. He simply predicted that because many Whole Foods and Wild Oats customers also shop at conventional supermarkets, the loss would at any rate be too large.

package] will do." *United States* v. *Grinnell Corp.,* 384 U.S. 563, 574 (1966); *see also United States* v. *Phillipsburg Nat'l Bank & Trust Co.,* 399 U.S. 350, 360 (1970)....

Such customers may be captive to the sole supplier, which can then, by means of price discrimination, extract monopoly profits from them while competing for the business of marginal customers. Not that prices that segregate core from marginal consumers are in themselves anticompetitive; such pricing simply indicates the existence of a submarket of core customers, operating in parallel with the broader market but featuring a different demand curve. *See United States* v. *Rockford Mem'l Corp.,* 898 F.2d 1278, 1284 (7th Cir. 1990). Sometimes, for some customers a package provides "access to certain products or services that would otherwise be unavailable to them." Because the core customers require the whole package, they respond differently to price increases from marginal customers who may obtain portions of the package elsewhere. Of course, core customers may constitute a submarket even without such an extreme difference in demand elasticity. After all, market definition focuses on what products are *reasonably* substitutable; what is reasonable must ultimately be determined by "settled consumer preference." *Phila. Nat'l Bank.*

In short, a core group of particularly dedicated, "distinct customers," paying "distinct prices," may constitute a recognizable submarket, *Brown Shoe,* whether they are dedicated because they need a complete "cluster of products," *Phila. Nat'l Bank,* because their particular circumstances dictate that a product "is the only realistic choice," *SuperTurf, Inc.* v. *Monsanto Co.,* or because they find a particular product "uniquely attractive," *Nat'l Collegiate Athletic Ass'n* v. *Bd. of Regents of the Univ. of Okla.* For example, the existence of core customers dedicated to office supply superstores, with their "unique combination of size, selection, depth[,] and breadth of inventory," was an important factor distinguishing that submarket. *FTC* v. *Staples, Inc.,* 970 F. Supp. 1066, 1078–79 (D.D.C. 1997). As always in defining a market, we must "take into account the realities of competition." *Weiss* v. *York Hosp.,* 745 F.2d 786, 826 (3d Cir. 1984). We look to the *Brown Shoe* indicia, among which the economic criteria are primary.

The FTC's evidence delineated a PNOS submarket catering to a core group of customers who "have decided that natural and organic is important, lifestyle of health and ecological sustainability is important." *Whole Foods,* 502 F. Supp. at 223, It was undisputed that Whole Foods and Wild Oats provide higher levels of customer service than conventional supermarkets, a "unique environment," and a particular focus on the "core values" these customers espoused. The FTC connected these intangible properties with concrete aspects of the PNOS model, such as a much larger selection of natural and organic products, FTC's Proposed Findings of Fact (noting Earth Fare, a PNOS, carries "more than 45,000 natural and organic SKUs") and a much greater concentration of perishables than conventional supermarkets, ("Over 60% of Wild Oats' revenues" and "[n]early 70% of Whole Foods sales are natural or organic perishables."). *See also Whole*

Foods, 502 F. Supp. 2d at 22–23 (citing defendants' depositions as evidence of Whole Foods's and Wild Oats's focus on "high-quality perishables" and a large variety of products).

Further, the FTC documented exactly the kind of price discrimination that enables a firm to profit from core customers for whom it is the sole supplier. Dr. Murphy compared the margins of Whole Foods stores in cities where they competed with Wild Oats. He found the presence of a Wild Oats depressed Whole Foods's margins significantly. Notably, while there was no effect on Whole Foods's margins in the product category of "groceries," where Whole Foods and Wild Oats compete on the margins with conventional supermarkets, the effect on margins for perishables was substantial. Confirming this price discrimination, Whole Foods's documents indicated that when it price-checked conventional supermarkets, the focus was overwhelmingly on "dry grocery," rather than on the perishables that were 70% of Whole Foods's business. Thus, in the high-quality perishables on which both Whole Foods and Wild Oats made most of their money, they competed directly with each other, and they competed with supermarkets only on the dry grocery items that were the fringes of their business.

Additionally, the FTC provided direct evidence that PNOS competition had a greater effect than conventional supermarkets on PNOS prices. Dr. Murphy showed the opening of a new Whole Foods in the vicinity of a Wild Oats caused Wild Oats's prices to drop, while entry by non-PNOS stores had no such effect. Similarly, the opening of Earth Fare stores (another PNOS) near Whole Foods stores caused Whole Foods's prices to drop immediately. The price effect continued, while decreasing, until the Earth Fare stores were forced to close.

Finally, evidence of consumer behavior supported the conclusion that PNOS serve a core consumer base. Whole Foods's internal projections, based on market experience, suggested that if a Wild Oats near a Whole Foods were to close, the majority (in some cases nearly all) of its customers would switch to the Whole Foods rather than to conventional supermarkets, Since Whole Foods's prices for perishables are higher than those of conventional supermarkets, such customers must not find shopping at the latter interchangeable with PNOS shopping. They are the core customers. Moreover, market research, including Dr. Scheffman's own studies, indicated 68% of Whole Foods customers are core customers who share the Whole Foods "core values."

Against this conclusion the defendants posed evidence that customers "cross-shop" between PNOS and other stores and that Whole Foods and Wild Oats check the prices of conventional supermarkets. But the fact that PNOS and ordinary supermarkets "are direct competitors in some submarkets ... is not the end of the inquiry," *United States v. Conn. Nat'l Bank.* Of course customers cross-shop; PNOS carry comprehensive inventories. The fact that a customer might buy a stick of gum at a supermarket or at a convenience store does not mean there is no definable groceries market. Here, cross-shopping is entirely consistent with the existence of a core group of PNOS customers. Indeed, Dr. Murphy explained that Whole

Foods competes actively with conventional supermarkets for dry groceries sales, even though it ignores their prices for high-quality perishables.

In addition, the defendants relied on Dr. Scheffman's conclusion that there is no "clearly definable" core customer. However, this conclusion was inconsistent with Dr. Scheffman's own report and testimony. Market research had found that customers who shop at Whole Foods because they share the core values it champions constituted at least a majority of its customers. Moreover, Dr. Scheffman acknowledged "there are core shoppers [who] will only buy organic and natural" and for that reason go to Whole Foods or Wild Oats. Re contended they could be ignored because the numbers are not "substantial." Again, Dr. Scheffman's own market data undermined this assertion.

In sum, the district court believed the antitrust laws are addressed only to marginal consumers. This was an error of law, because in some situations core consumers, demanding exclusively a particular product or package of products, distinguish a submarket. The FTC described the core PNOS customers, explained how PNOS cater to these customers, and showed these customers provided the bulk of PNOS's business. The FTC put forward economic evidence-which the district court ignored-showing directly how PNOS discriminate on price between their core and marginal customers, thus treating the former as a distinct market. Therefore, we cannot agree with the district court that the FTC would never be able to prove a PNOS submarket. We do not say the FTC has in fact proved such a market, which is not necessary at this point. To obtain a preliminary injunction under § 53(b), the FTC need only show a likelihood of success sufficient, using the sliding scale, to balance any equities that might weigh against the injunction.

It remains to address the equities, which the district court did not reach, and see whether for some reason there is a balance against the FTC that would require a greater likelihood of success. The FTC urges us to carry out the rest of this determination, but "[w]e believe the proper course of action at this point is to remand to the district court. . . .

■ TATEL, J. concurring: I agree with my colleagues that the district court produced a thoughtful opinion under incredibly difficult circumstances, that this case presents a live controversy, and that the district court generally applied the correct standard in reviewing the Federal Trade Commission's request for a preliminary injunction. I also agree with Judge Brown that the district court nonetheless erred in concluding that the FTC failed to "raise[] questions going to the merits so serious, substantial, difficult and doubtful as to make them fair ground for thorough investigation, study, deliberation and determination by the FTC in the first instance and ultimately by the Court of Appeals." *FTC v. H.J. Heinz Co.,* 246 F.3d 708 (D.C. Cir. 2001). I write separately because although I agree with Judge Brown that the district court erred in focusing only on marginal customers, I believe the district court also overlooked or mistakenly rejected evidence supporting the FTC's view that Whole Foods and Wild Oats occupy a separate market of "premium natural and organic supermarkets." . . . .

. . . Following the FTC's lead, the court focused on defining the product market in which Whole Foods and Wild Oats operate, saying:

> [I]f the relevant product market is, as the FTC alleges, a product market of "premium natural and organic supermarkets" . . . , there can be little doubt that the acquisition of the second largest firm in the market by the largest firm in the market will tend to harm competition in that market. If, on the other hand, the defendants are merely differentiated firms operating within the larger relevant product market of "supermarkets," the proposed merger will not tend to harm competition.

Thus, the " 'case hinge[d]'-almost entirely-'on the proper definition of the relevant product market.' " And after reviewing the evidence, the district court concluded that "[t]here is no substantial likelihood that the FTC can prove its asserted product market and thus no likelihood that it can prove that the proposed merger may substantially lessen competition or tend to create a monopoly."

I agree with the district court that this " 'case hinges'—almost entirely—'on the proper definition of the relevant product market,' " for if a separate natural and organic market exists, "there can be little doubt that the acquisition of the second largest firm in the market by the largest firm in the market will tend to harm competition in that market." But I respectfully part ways with the district court when it comes to assessing the FTC's evidence in support of its contention that Whole Foods and Wild Oats occupy a distinct market. . . . In this case the FTC presented a great deal of credible evidence—either unmentioned or rejected by the district court—suggesting that Whole Foods and Wild Oats are not "reasonabl[y] interchangeab[le]" with conventional supermarkets and do not compete directly with them.

To begin with, the FTC's expert prepared a study showing that when a Whole Foods opened near an existing Wild Oats it reduced sales at the Wild Oats store dramatically. By contrast, when a conventional supermarket opened near a Wild Oats store, Wild Oats's sales were virtually unaffected. This strongly suggests that although Wild Oats customers consider Whole Foods an adequate substitute, they do not feel the same way about conventional supermarkets. Rejecting this study, the district court explained that it was "unwilling to accept the assumption that the effects on Wild Oats from Whole Foods' entries provide a mirror from which predictions can reliably be made about the effects on Whole Foods from Wild Oats' future exits if this transaction occurs." But even if exit and entry events differ, this evidence suggests that consumers do not consider Whole Foods and Wild Oats "reasonabl[y] interchangeab[le]" with conventional supermarkets. *Brown Shoe.*

The FTC also highlighted Whole Foods's own study-called "Project Goldmine" showing what Wild Oats customers would likely do after the proposed merger in cities where Whole Foods planned to close Wild Oats stores. According to the study, the average Whole Foods store would capture most of the revenue from the closed Wild Oats store, even though virtually every city contained multiple conventional retailers closer to the shuttered Wild Oats store. This high diversion ratio further suggests that many consumers consider conventional supermarkets inadequate substitutes for Wild Oats and Whole Foods. The district court cited the Project Goldmine study for the opposite conclusion, pointing only to cities in which Whole Foods expected to receive a low percentage of Wild Oats business. These examples, however, do not undermine the study's broader conclusion that Whole Foods would capture most of the revenue from the closed Wild Oats, and the district court never mentioned the FTC expert's testimony that the diversion ratio estimated here "is at least {**Sealed**} *times* the diversion ratio needed to make a price increase of 5% profitable for a joint owner of the two stores." The dissent also ignores this testimony, saying incorrectly that the Project Goldmine study "says nothing about whether Whole Foods could impose a five percent or more price increase". . . .

In addition to direct evidence that Whole Foods and Wild Oats occupy a separate market from conventional supermarkets, the FTC presented an enormous amount of evidence of "industry or public recognition" of the natural and organic market "as a separate economic entity"—one of the "practical indicia" the Supreme Court has said can be used to determine the boundaries of a distinct market. *Brown Shoe.* For example, dozens of record studies about the grocery store industry-including many prepared for Whole Foods or Wild Oats—distinguish between "traditional" or "conventional" grocery stores on the one hand and "natural food" or "organic" stores on the other. *See, e.g.,* FOOD MKTG. INST., U.S. GROCERY SHOPPER TRENDS 2007, at 20–22 (2007). Moreover, record evidence indicates that the Whole Foods and Wild Oats CEOs both believed that their companies occupied a market separate from the conventional grocery store industry. In an email to his company's board, Whole Foods CEO John Mackey explained that "[Wild Oats] is the only existing company that has the brand and number of stores to be a meaningful springboard for another player to get into this space. Eliminating them means eliminating this threat forever, or almost forever." Echoing this point, former Wild Oats CEO Perry Odak said that "there's really only two players of any substance in the organic and all natural [market], and that's Whole Foods and Wild Oats. . . . [T]here's really nobody else in that particular space." Executives from several conventional retailers agreed.

. . . As Judge Bork explained, this evidence of " 'industry or public recognition of the submarket as a separate economic' unit matters because we assume that economic actors usually have accurate perceptions of economic realities." *Rothery Storage & Van Co. v. Atlas Van Lines, Inc.*

The FTC also presented strong evidence that Whole Foods and Wild Oats have "peculiar characteristics" distinguishing them from traditional supermarkets, another of the "practical indicia" the Supreme Court has said can be used to determine the boundaries of a distinct market. *Brown*

Shoe, 370 U.S. at 325. Most important, unlike traditional grocery stores, both Whole Foods and Wild Oats carry only natural or organic products. Glossing over this distinction, the dissent says "the dividing line between 'organic' and conventional supermarkets has been blurred" because "[m]ost products that Whole Foods sells are not organic" while "conventional supermarkets" have e un selling more organic products. But the FTC never proposed market as "organic supermarkets," it defined it as "premium natural and organic supermarkets." And everything Whole Foods sells is natural and/or organic, while many of the things sold by traditional grocery stores are not...

Insisting that all this evidence of a separate market is irrelevant, Whole Foods and the dissent argue that the FTC's case must fail because the record contains no evidence that Whole Foods or Wild Oats charged higher prices in cities where the other was absent—i.e., where one had a local monopoly on the asserted natural and organic market—than they did in cities where the other was present. This argument is both legally and factually incorrect.

As a legal matter, although evidence that a company charges more when other companies in the alleged market are absent certainly indicates that the companies operate in a distinct market, *see, e.g., Staples* [p. 1062 *supra*] that is not the *only* way to prove a separate market. Indeed, *Brown Shoe* lists "distinct prices" as only one of a non exhaustive list of seven "practical indicia" that may be examined to determine whether a separate market exists. Furthermore, even if the FTC could *prove* a section 7 violation only by showing evidence of higher prices in areas where a company had a local monopoly in an alleged market, the FTC need not *prove* a section 7 violation to obtain a preliminary injunction; rather, it need only raise "serious, substantial" questions as to the mergers legality. *Heinz.* Thus, the dissent misses the mark when it cites the FTC's Horizontal Merger Guidelines to assert that the Commission may obtain a preliminary injunction only by presenting "solid evidence that the post-merger company could profitably impose a significant nontransitory price increase of 5% or more." Such evidence in a case like this, which turns entirely on market definition, would be enough *to prove* a section 7 violation in the FTC's administrative proceeding. *See Hosp. Corp.,* [p. 1010 supra] (stating that "[a]ll that is necessary" to prove a section 7 case "is that the merger create an appreciable danger of [higher prices] in the future"). Yet our precedent dearly holds that to obtain a preliminary injunction "[t]he FTC is not required to *establish* that the proposed merger would in fact violate section 7 of the Clayton Act." *Heinz,* [p. 1059 *supra*]. Moreover, the Merger Guidelines—which "are by no means to be considered binding on the court," *FTC v. PPG Indus., Inc.,* 798 F.2d 1500, 1503 n.4 (D.C. Cir. 1986) specify how the FTC decides which cases to bring, *"not* ... how the Agency will conduct the litigation of cases to bring, "not ... how the Agency will conduct the litigation of cases that it decides to bring, "Horizontal Merger Guidelines § 0.1....

In any event, the FTC did present evidence indicating that Whole Foods' and Wild Oats charged more when they were the only natural and organic supermarket present. The FTC's expert looked at prices Whole Foods charged in several of its North Carolina stores before and after entry of a regional natural food chain called Earth Fare. Before any Earth Fare stores opened, Whole Foods charged essentially the same prices at its five North Carolina stores, but when an Earth Fare opened near the Whole Foods in Chapel Hill, that store's prices dropped 5% below those at the other North Carolina Whole Foods. Prices at that store remained lower than at the other Whole Foods in North Carolina. . . .

The FTC's expert presented similar evidence regarding Whole Foods store opening near a Wild Oats caused immediate and lasting reductions in prices at the Wild Oats store compared to prices at other Wild Oats stores. In addition to this quantitative evidence, the FTC pointed to Whole Foods CEO John Mackey's statement explaining to the company's board why the merger made sense: "By buying [Wild Oats] we will . . . avoid nasty price wars in [several cities where both companies have stores]". . . .

The district court next emphasized that when a new Whole Foods store opens, it takes business from conventional grocery stores, and even when an existing Wild Oats is nearby, most of the new Whole Foods store's revenue comes from customers who previously shopped at conventional stores. According to the district court, this led "to the inevitable conclusion that Whole Foods' and Wild Oats' main competitors are other supermarkets, not just each other." As the FTC points out, however, "an innovative [product] can create a new product market for antitrust purposes" by "satisfy[ing] a previously-unsatisfied Consumer demand." To use the Commission's example, when the automobile was first invented, competing auto manufacturers obviously took customers primarily from companies selling horses and buggies, not from other auto manufacturers, but that hardly shows that cars and horse-drawn carriages should be treated as the same product market. That Whole Foods and Wild Oats have attracted many customers away from conventional grocery stores by offering extensive selections of natural and organic products thus tells us nothing about whether Whole Foods and Wild Oats should be treated as operating in the same market as conventional grocery stores. Indeed, courts have often found that sufficiently innovative retailers can constitute a distinct product market even when they take customers from existing retailers. *See, e.g., Photovest Corp. v. Fotomat Corp.*, 606 F.2d 704, 712–14 (7th Cir. 1979) (finding a distinct market of drive-up photo-processing companies even though such companies took photo-processing customers from drugstores, camera stores, and supermarkets); *Staples* (finding a distinct market of office supply superstores even though such stores took sales primarily from mail-order catalogues and stores carrying a broader range of merchandise).

The district court also cited evidence that Whole Foods compares its prices to those at conventional stores, not just natural foods stores. But nearly all of the items on which Whole Foods checks prices are dry grocery items, even though nearly 70% of Whole Foods's revenue comes from perishables. As the majority opinion explains, this suggests that any competition between Whole Foods and conventional retailers may be limited to a narrow range of products that play a minor role in Whole Foods's profitability.

Finally, the district court observed that more and more conventional stores are carrying natural and organic products, and that consumers who shop at Whole Foods and Wild Oats also shop at conventional stores. But as noted above, other record evidence suggests that although some conventional retailers are beginning to offer a limited range of popular organic products, they have difficulty competing with Whole Foods and Wild Oats. . . .

Because we have decided that the FTC showed the requisite likelihood of success by raising serious and substantial questions about the merger's legality, all that remains is to "weigh the equities in order to decide whether enjoining the merger would be in the public interest." Although in some cases we have conducted this weighing ourselves, three factors lead me to agree with Judge Brown that the better course here is to remand to the district court for it to undertake this task. First, in cases in which we have weighed the equities, the district court had already done so, giving us the benefit of its factfinding and reasoning. Here, by contrast, the district court never reached the equities and the parties have not briefed the issue, leaving us without the evidence needed to decide this question. Second, this case stands in a unique posture, for in cases where we reversed a district court's denial of a section 13(b) injunction either the district court or this court had enjoined the merger pending appeal. *See Heinz.* Here, by contrast, the companies have already merged, and although this doesn't moot the case, it may well affect the balance of the equities, likely requiring the district court to take additional evidence. Finally, given this case's unique posture, the usual remedy in section 13(b) cases—blocking the merger—is no longer an option. Therefore, if the district court concludes that the equities tilt in the FTC's favor, it will need to craft an alternative, factbound remedy sufficient to achieve section 13(b)'s purpose, namely allowing the FTC to review the transaction in an administrative proceeding and reestablish the premerger status quo if it finds a section 7 violation. To accomplish this, the district court could choose anything from issuing a hold separate order, *see FTC* v. *Weyerhaeuser Co.,* 665 F.2d 1072, 1083–84 (D.C. Cir. 1981), to enjoining further integration of the companies, to ordering the transaction partially or entirely rescinded, *see FTC* v. *Elders Grain,* 868 F.2d 901, 907–08 (7th Cir. 1989) (Posner, J.). Without more facts, however, we are in no position to suggest which remedy is most appropriate. . . .

Kavanaugh, J. dissented, agreeing with the district court that the market was all supermarkets, primarily because Whole Food's prices did not differ based on the presence or absence of Wild Oats in the market, but that conventional supermarkets place a limit on Whole Food's prices.

PROBLEM 22

MERGERS AT CEDAR LAKE

Cedar Lake, Colorado is the site of a major winter sports resort, similar but 100 miles distant from Aspen, Colorado. Its main attraction lies in downhill skiing offered on the high slopes of Mount Cedar. Five companies run the major ski operations, each offering daily and weekly lift tickets. The companies and their ticket revenues for last season were as follows: Colorado Ski Resorts, $30 million; Mount Cedar Ski, $30 million; Big Sky, $20 million; High Sky, $8 million; and Ski America, $5 million.

Cedar Lake is one of three major destination ski resorts in Colorado (a destination ski resort is one where most of the patrons come from elsewhere; in the case of Cedar Lake, 80% come from distant locations and 20% are local residents). Two other ski areas, totaling $4 million in revenues, are located 10 to 15 miles south of the town of Cedar Lake. These are primarily used by local residents, although they could be expanded to offer more destination resort competition with the Cedar Lake group. Expansion could occur within one year and would allow ski slopes in these adjacent areas to double the number of skiers they could handle. Constructing a hotel at the base of the slope would increase the potential of these areas even more, though hotel construction would take at least three years.

Ski America and High Sky, located adjacent to each other on the southern slopes of Mount Cedar, have proposed a merger. All three other Mount Cedar ski operations are on the northern slope. Skiers using the southern slope find it convenient if they are staying at one of the hotels nearby at the base of the mountain. About 50% of skiers on Ski America and High Sky use only the southern slopes, while the rest occasionally migrate to the northern side during an average stay.

Until three or four years ago, Ski America and High Sky offered a weekly joint ticket that allowed the skier to use the slopes of either company, but that joint ticket was eliminated following a series of squabbles between the two companies over the proper division of revenues. The companies anticipate a number of benefits from the merger, including new and better trails that combine the two facilities and can be developed at a lower cost, a better and more highly utilized ski school, and the ability to offer a joint weekly ticket as well as to offer package tours in conjunction with the hotels on the southern slope.

New ski resorts could be opened in Colorado, Utah, and Wyoming. The cost of laying out slopes and constructing lifts amounts to approximately $4 million, and the cost of land can range from $5 million to $15 million. Additional operations could be profitably constructed if new operations could achieve the equivalent of 10% of current total Cedar Lake ski revenues. It would take about three years to complete a new operation.

All of the ski operations at Cedar Lake except High Sky have been exceptionally profitable. High Sky is saddled with obsolete equipment and has shown small deficits in four of the last five years. As a result, High Sky is the least aggressive of the five in offering discounts on bulk sales of lift tickets or in creating package tours. Before closing the deal, the owners of High Sky made a conscientious effort to find a purchaser completely outside its ski area. It received an offer from Aspen Ski at a price 30% below the amount offered by Ski America, but well above scrap value. Because of the special expertise necessary in running a ski operation, other business enterprises shied away from the investment.

Would the proposed merger violate the antitrust laws?

SECTION 3.   JOINT VENTURES, POTENTIAL COMPETITION, AND CONGLOMERATE MERGERS

United States v. El Paso Natural Gas Co., 376 U.S. 651, 84 S.Ct. 1044, 12 L.Ed.2d 12 (1964). Suit by the government for violation of Section 7 by reason of the acquisition of the stock and assets of Pacific Northwest Pipeline Corp. by El Paso Natural Gas Co. El Paso was the "sole out of state supplier" of natural gas in California, with a pre-acquisition share exceeding 50%. Pacific Northwest was "the only other important interstate pipeline west of the Rocky Mountains." Although Pacific, prior to the acquisition, sold no gas in California, it had "proximity to the California market" by virtue of its facilities and "enormous reserves" in surrounding areas. In addition, it had "adequate ... managerial skill" and "was so strong and militant that it was viewed with concern, and coveted, by El Paso." Pacific's pre-acquisition attempts to sell natural gas in California had been unsuccessful. Its efforts to obtain a contract from a large California utility were fought "to the last ditch" by El Paso, which ultimately closed the deal, only after reducing its original offer from 40¢ per million cubic feet to 30¢. Moreover, the Federal Power Commission rejected Pacific's proposal to pipe gas into that state and refused to issue the necessary certification. Held, for the government. Pacific Northwest was a "substantial factor in the California market at the time it was acquired by El Paso." The Court viewed the merger in the context of a regulated industry, rather than in a "field where merchants are in a continuous daily struggle to hold old customers and to win new ones over from their rivals." Competition in natural gas "is for the new increments of demand that may emerge with an expanding population and with an expanding industrial or household use of gas." Accordingly, in the natural gas field, the merger foreclosed Pacific from competing for new contracts for the incremental gas demand. (Douglas, J.)

United States v. Penn–Olin Chemical Co.

Supreme Court of the United States, 1964.
378 U.S. 158, 84 S.Ct. 1710, 12 L.Ed.2d 775.

■ CLARK, J. Pennsalt Chemicals Corporation and Olin Mathieson Chemical Corporation jointly formed Penn–Olin Chemical Company to produce and sell sodium chlorate in the southeastern United States. The Government seeks to dissolve this joint venture as violative of both § 7 of the Clayton Act and § 1 of the Sherman Act....

Pennsalt is engaged solely in the production and sale of chemicals and chemical products throughout the United States. Its assets are around a hundred million dollars and its sales are about the same amount. Its sodium chlorate production is located at Portland, Oregon, with a capacity of some 15,000 tons as of 1959. It occupied 57.8% of the market west of the Rocky Mountains. It has marketed sodium chlorate in the southeastern United States to some extent since 1957. Its shipments into that territory in 1960 were 4,186 tons of which Olin sold 3,202 tons on its sales agency contract.

Olin is a large diversified corporation, the result of a merger of Olin Industries, Inc., and Mathieson Chemical Corporation in 1954. One of its seven divisions operates plants in 15 States and produces a wide range of chemicals and chemical products accounting for about 30% of Olin's revenues. Olin's sales in 1960 grossed some $690,000,000 and its total assets were $860,000,000.

Penn–Olin was organized in 1960 as a joint venture of Olin and Pennsalt. Each owns 50% of its stock and the officers and directors are divided equally between the parents. Its plant at Calvert City, Kentucky, was built by equal contribution of the two parents and cost $6,500,000. It has a capacity to produce 26,500 tons of sodium chlorate annually and began operations in 1961. Pennsalt operates the plant and Olin handles the sales. Penn–Olin deals in no other chemicals.

Prior to 1961 the sodium chlorate industry in the United States was made up of three producing companies. The largest producer, Hooker Chemical Corporation, entered the industry in 1956 when it acquired Oldbury Electro Chemical Company, which had been producing sodium chlorate for over half a century. Hooker now has two plants, one in the relevant marketing area at Columbus, Mississippi, which originally had a capacity of 16,000 tons but which was doubled in 1962. The other plant is at Niagara Falls, New York, with a capacity of 18,000 tons. Hooker has assets of almost $200,000,000. American Potash & Chemical Corporation entered the industry in 1955 by the acquisition of Western Electro Chemical Company. American Potash also has two plants, one located at Henderson, Nevada, with a 27,000–ton capacity and the other at Aberdeen, Mississippi (built in 1957), the capacity of which was 15,000 tons. Its assets are almost $100,000,000. The trial court found that these two corporations "had a virtual monopoly" in the relevant southeast market, holding over 90% of the market.

A third company in the industry was Pennsalt which had a 15,392–ton plant at Portland, Oregon. It entered seriously into the relevant marketing area through a sales arrangement with Olin dated December 1957 and finalized in 1958, which was aimed at testing the availability of the southeastern market. Olin as an exclusive seller was to undertake the sale of 2,000 tons of sodium chlorate per year to pulp and paper mills in the southeast (except for Buckeye Cellulose Co., at Foley, Florida, which Pennsalt reserved to serve directly). In 1960, 4,186 tons of sodium chlorate were marketed in the relevant market with the aid of this agreement. This accounted for 8.9% of the sales in that market.

During the previous decade no new firms had entered the sodium chlorate industry, and little effort had been made by existing companies to expand their facilities prior to 1957. In 1953 Olin had made available to

Pennsalt its Mathieson patented process for bleaching pulp with chlorine dioxide and the latter had installed it 100% in all of the western paper mills. This process uses sodium chlorate. At about the same time the process was likewise made available, royalty free, to the entire pulp and paper industry. By 1960 most of the chlorine dioxide generated by paper manufacturers was being produced under the Olin controlled process. This created an expanding demand for sodium chlorate and by 1960 the heaviest concentration of purchasers was located in the relevant southeastern territory. By 1957 Hooker began increasing the capacity of its Columbus plant and by 1960 it had been almost doubled. American Potash sensed the need of a plant in Mississippi to compete with Hooker and began its Aberdeen plant in 1957. It was completed to a 15,000–ton capacity in 1959, and this capacity was expanded 50% by 1961.

The sales arrangement between Pennsalt and Olin, previously mentioned, was superseded by the joint venture agreement on February 11, 1960, and the Penn–Olin plant operations at Calvert City, Kentucky, began in 1961. In the same year Pittsburgh Plate Glass Company announced that it would build a plant at Lake Charles, Louisiana, with a capacity of 15,000 tons. Pittsburgh Plate Glass had operated a sodium chlorate plant in Canada.

As a result of these expansions and new entries into the southeastern market, the projected production of sodium chlorate there more than doubled. By 1962 Hooker had 32,000 tons; American Potash, 22,500 tons; Penn–Olin, 26,500 tons; and Pittsburgh Glass, 15,000 tons—a total of 96,000 tons as contrasted to 41,150 in 1959. Penn–Olin's share of the expanded relevant market was about 27.6%....

As early as 1951 Pennsalt had considered building a plant at Calvert City and starting in 1955 it initiated several cost and market studies for a sodium chlorate plant in the southeast. Three different proposals from within its own organization were rejected prior to 1957, apparently because the rate of return was so unattractive that "the expense of refining these figures further would be unwarranted." When Hooker announced in December 1956 that it was going to increase the capacity of its Columbus plant, the interest of Pennsalt management was reactivated. It appointed a "task force" to evaluate the company's future in the eastern market; it retained management consultants to study that market and its chief engineer prepared cost estimates. However, in December 1957 the management decided that the estimated rate of return was unattractive and considered it "unlikely" that Pennsalt would go it alone. It was suggested that Olin would be a "logical partner" in a joint venture and might in the interim be interested in distributing in the East 2,000 tons of the Portland sodium chlorate production. The sales agreement with Olin, heretofore mentioned, was eventually made. In the final draft the parties agreed that "neither ... should move in the chlorate or perchlorate field without keeping the other party informed ..." and that one would "bring to the attention of the other any unusual aspects of this business which might make it desirable to proceed further with production plans." Pennsalt claims that it finally decided, prior to this agreement, that it should not build a plant itself and that this decision was never reconsidered or changed. But the District Court found to the contrary.

During this same period—beginning slightly earlier—Olin began investigating the possibility of entering the sodium chlorate industry. It had never produced sodium chlorate commercially, although its predecessor had done so years before. However, the electrolytic process used in making sodium chlorate is intimately related to other operations of Olin and required the same general knowledge. Olin also possessed extensive experience in the technical aspects of bleaching pulp and paper and was intimate with the pulp and paper mills of the southeast. In April 1958 Olin's chemical division wrote and circulated to the management a "Whither Report" which stated in part:

> We have an unparalleled opportunity to move sodium chlorate into the paper industry as the result of our work on the installation of chlorine dioxide generators. We have a captive consumption for sodium chlorate.

And Olin's engineering supervisor concluded that entry into sodium chlorate production was "an attractive venture" since it "represents a logical expansion of the product line of the Industrial Chemicals Division ..." with respect to "one of the major markets, pulp and paper bleaching, [with which] we have a favorable marketing position, particularly in the southeast."

The staff, however, did not agree with the engineering supervisor or the "Whither Report" and concluded "that they didn't feel that this particular project showed any merit worthy of serious consideration by the corporation at that time." They were dubious of the cost estimates and felt the need to temper their scientists' enthusiasm for new products with the uncertainties of plant construction and operation. But, as the trial court found, the testimony indicated that Olin's decision to enter the joint venture was made without determining that Olin could not or would not be an independent competitor. That question, "never reached the point of final decision."

This led the District Court to find that the president of Penn–Olin testified, "[t]he possibility of individual entry into the southeastern market had not been completely rejected by either Pennsalt or Olin before they decided upon the joint venture."

Appellees argue that § 7 applies only where the acquired company is "engaged" in commerce and that it would not apply to a newly formed corporation, such as Penn–Olin. The test, they say, is whether the enterprise to be acquired is engaged in commerce—not whether a corporation formed as the instrumentality for the acquisition is itself engaged in commerce at the moment of its formation. We believe that this logic fails in the light of the wording of the section and its legislative background. The test of the section is the effect of the acquisition. Certainly the formation of a joint venture and purchase by the organizers of its stock would substantially lessen competition—indeed foreclose it—as between them, both being engaged in commerce. This would be true whether they were in actual or potential competition with each other and even though the new corporation was formed to create a wholly new enterprise. Realistically, the parents would not compete with their progeny. Moreover, in this case the progeny was organized to further the business of its parents, already in commerce, and the fact that it was organized specifically to engage in commerce should bring it within the coverage of § 7. In addition, long prior to trial Penn–Olin was actually engaged in commerce. To hold that it was not "would be illogical and disrespectful of the plain congressional purpose in amending § 7 ... [for] it would create a large loophole in a statute designed to close a loophole." *United States v. Philadelphia National Bank,* 374 U.S. 321, 343 (1963). In any event, Penn–Olin was engaged in commerce at the time of suit and the economic effects of an acquisition are to be measured at that point rather than at the time of acquisition. *United States v. E.I. du Pont de Nemours & Co.,* 353 U.S. 586, 607 (1957). The technicality could, therefore, be averted by merely refiling an amended complaint at the time of trial. This would be a useless requirement.

This is the first case reaching this Court and on which we have written that directly involves the validity under § 7 of the joint participation of two corporations in the creation of a third as a new domestic producing organization. We are, therefore, plowing new ground. It is true, however, that some aspects of the problem might be found in *United States v. Terminal R. Assn.,* 224 U.S. 383 (1912), and *Associated Press v. United States,* 326 U.S. 1 (1945), where joint ventures with great market power were subjected to control, even prior to the amendment to § 7....

The District Court found that "Pennsalt and Olin each possessed the resources and general capability needed to build its own plant in the southeast and to compete with Hooker and [American Potash] in that market. Each could have done so if it had wished." 217 F.Supp. 110, 129.[20] In addition, the District Court found that, contrary to the position of the management of Olin and Pennsalt, "the forecasts of each company indicated that a plant could be operated with profit."

The District Court held, however, that these considerations had no controlling significance, except "as a factor in determining whether as a matter of probability both companies would have entered the market as individual competitors if Penn–Olin had not been formed. Only in this

---

20. The court explained further: "At the time when the joint venture was agreed upon Pennsalt and Olin each had an extensive background in sodium chlorate. Pennsalt had years of experience in manufacturing and selling it. Although Olin had never been a commercial manufacturer, it possessed a substantially developed manufacturing technique of its own, and also had available to it a process developed by Vickers–Krebs with whom it had been negotiating to construct a plant. Olin had contacts among the southeastern pulp and paper mills which Pennsalt lacked, but Pennsalt's own estimates indicate that in a reasonable time it would develop adequate business to support a plant if it decided to build. A suitable location for a plant was available to each company—Calvert City, Kentucky for Pennsalt, and the TVA area around Chattanooga, Tennessee for Olin. The financing required would not have been a problem for either company." *Ibid.*

event would potential competition between the two companies have been foreclosed by the joint venture." *Id.*, at 130. In this regard the court found it "impossible to conclude that as a matter of reasonable probability both Pennsalt and Olin would have built plants in the southeast if Penn–Olin had not been created." *Ibid.* The court made no decision concerning the probability that one would have built "while the other continued to ponder." It found that this "hypothesized situation affords no basis for concluding that Penn–Olin had the effect of substantially lessening competition." *Ibid.* That would depend, the court said, "upon the competitive impact which Penn–Olin will have as against that which might have resulted if Pennsalt or Olin had been an individual market entrant." *Ibid.* The court found that this impact could not be determined from the record in this case. "Solely as a matter of theory," it said, ". . . no reason exists to suppose that Penn–Olin will be a less effective competitor than Pennsalt or Olin would have been. The contrary conclusion is the more reasonable." *Id.*, at 131.

We believe that the court erred in this regard. Certainly the sole test would not be the probability that both companies would have entered the market. Nor would the consideration be limited to the probability that one entered alone. There still remained for consideration the fact that Penn–Olin eliminated the potential competition of the corporation that might have remained at the edge of the market, continually threatening to enter. Just as a merger eliminates actual competition, this joint venture may well foreclose any prospect of competition between Olin and Pennsalt in the relevant sodium chlorate market. The difference, of course, is that the merger's foreclosure is present while the joint venture's is prospective. Nevertheless, "[p]otential competition . . . as a substitute for . . . [actual competition] may restrain producers from overcharging those to whom they sell or underpaying those from whom they buy. . . . Potential competition, insofar as the threat survives [as it would have here in the absence of Penn–Olin], may compensate in part for the imperfection characteristic of actual competition in the great majority of competitive markets." Wilcox, Competition and Monopoly in American Industry, TNEC Monograph No. 21 (1940) 7–8. Potential competition cannot be put to a subjective test. It is not "susceptible of a ready and precise answer." As we found in *United States v. El Paso Natural Gas Co.*, *supra*, 376 U.S. at 660, the "effect on competition . . . is determined by the nature or extent of that market and by the nearness of the absorbed company to it, that company's eagerness to enter that market, its resourcefulness, and so on." The position of a company "as a competitive factor . . . was not disproved by the fact that it had never sold . . . there. . . . [I]t is irrelevant in a market . . . where incremental needs are booming." The existence of an aggressive, well equipped and well financed corporation engaged in the same or related lines of commerce waiting anxiously to enter an oligopolistic market would be a substantial incentive to competition which cannot be underestimated. Witness the expansion undertaken by Hooker and American Potash as soon as they heard of the interest of Olin Mathieson and of Pennsalt in southeast territory. This same situation might well have come about had either Olin or Pennsalt entered the relevant market alone and the other remained aloof watching developments.

Here the evidence shows beyond question that the industry was rapidly expanding; the relevant southeast market was requiring about one-half of the national production of sodium chlorate; few corporations had the inclination, resources and know-how to enter this market; both parent corporations of Penn–Olin had great resources; each had long been identified with the industry, one owning valuable patent rights while the other had engaged in sodium chlorate production for years; each had other chemicals, the production of which required the use of sodium chlorate; right up to the creation of Penn–Olin, each had evidenced a long-sustained and strong interest in entering the relevant market area; each enjoyed good reputation and business connections with the major consumers of sodium chlorate in the relevant market, *i.e.*, the pulp and paper mills; and, finally, each had the know-how and the capacity to enter that market and could have done so individually at a reasonable profit. Moreover, each company had compelling reasons for entering the southeast market. Pennsalt needed to expand its sales to the southeast, which it could not do economically without a plant in that area. Olin was motivated by "the fact that [it was] already buying and using a fair quantity [of sodium chlorate] for the production of sodium chlorite and that [it was] promoting the Mathieson process of the generation of chlorine dioxide which uses sodium chlorate." Unless we are going to require subjective evidence, this array of probability certainly reaches the prima facie stage. As we have indicated, to require more would be to read the statutory requirement of reasonable probability into a requirement of certainty. This we will not do.

However, despite these strong circumstances, we are not disposed to disturb the court's finding that there was not a reasonable probability that both Pennsalt and Olin would have built a plant in the relevant market area. But we have concluded that a finding should have been made as to the reasonable probability that either one of the corporations would have entered the market by building a plant, while the other would have remained a significant potential competitor....

We note generally the following criteria which the trial court might take into account in assessing the probability of a substantial lessening of competition: the number and power of the competitors in the relevant market; the background of their growth; the power of the joint venturers; the relationship of their lines of commerce; the competition existing between them and the power of each in dealing with the competitors of the other; the setting in which the joint venture was created; the reasons and necessities for its existence; the joint venture's line of commerce and the relationship thereof to that of its parents; the adaptability of its line of commerce to non-competitive practices; the potential power of the joint venture in the relevant market; an appraisal of what the competition in the relevant market would have been if one of the joint venturers had entered it alone instead of through Penn–Olin; the effect, in the event of this occurrence, of the other joint venturer's potential competition; and such other factors as might indicate potential risk to competition in the relevant market. In weighing these factors the court should remember that the mandate of the Congress is in terms of the probability of a lessening of substantial competition, not in terms of tangible present restraint....

Vacated and remanded.[21]

Texaco Inc. v. Dagher

Supreme Court Of The United States, 2006.
547 U.S. 1, 126 S.Ct. 1276, 164 L.Ed.2d 1.

[Reprinted p. 271 *supra*]

NOTES AND QUESTIONS

1. On remand, the district court in *Penn–Olin* took additional evidence and then entered a finding that neither Pennsalt nor Olin Mathieson would have entered the southeastern market on its own. On the basis of that finding, it dismissed the government's action, 246 F.Supp. 917 (D.Del.1965). The Supreme Court affirmed *per curiam* by an equally divided court, 389 U.S. 308 (1967). Does it necessarily follow that where none of the parents of a joint venture would have entered the market on its own, the formation of the joint venture cannot violate Section 7? Even if none of the joint venture parents would have entered alone, might not the venture constitute a dangerous aggregation of market power?

2. General Motors Corp., 103 FTC 374 (1984). A majority of the Federal Trade Commission approved, as modified pursuant to Commission order, a joint venture between GM and Toyota to manufacture subcompact cars in the United States. Plans for the design of the car were contributed by Toyota and construction would occur at an underutilized GM plant in California. Ownership of the joint venture was on a 50–50 basis, with Toyota's representative serving as chief of management.

At the time of the venture, GM stood first in automobile sales in the U.S. market with 44% and Toyota stood fourth; in the subcompact portion of the U.S. market, Ford stood first with over 19%, Toyota second with a little over 16% and GM third with 14.4%. The duration of the joint venture was 12 years, with a maximum production per year of 250,000 cars. Distribution of the new car was to be handled entirely by GM in the United States, with Toyota and GM free to compete in all respects with the joint venture. A key provision of the arrangement related to the price charged GM by the joint venture. This was to be determined and then adjusted according to a complicated formula which took into account market prices of ten other best selling models in the U.S., with special weight given to the wholesale price of Toyota's Corolla model. In effect, the joint venture car price would rise or fall depending on price changes on the ten leading subcompact cars in the previous model year, weighting the Corolla at 30% of the total market price.

The Commission majority saw three significant procompetitive effects resulting from the joint venture: (1) it would allow introduction into the U.S. of a new small

---

21. White, J. dissented. The dissenting opinion of Douglas, J., with whom Black, J., agreed, and the dissenting opinion of Harlan, J., are omitted.

car, an addition to competition that was unlikely to be achieved by Toyota alone because Voluntary Restrictive Agreements instituted by the Japanese government put a ceiling on the number of imports per year from Japan to the U.S.; (2) the joint venture car could be produced efficiently and therefore would cost consumers less; and (3) the joint venture offered an opportunity for GM to learn about more efficient Japanese manufacturing and management techniques.

Two dissenting Commissioners concluded that these advantages could have been achieved through less restrictive alternatives than a joint venture between two of the largest automobile companies in the world, and noted that there were two important anticompetitive aspects to the joint venture. First, the dissenters argued that the pricing formula for sale of joint venture cars to GM, an average of the price of many cars but based heavily on the sales prices of Toyota's Corolla, would have a market-wide impact on price. Toyota might be induced to raise the price on its Corolla model, knowing this would inevitably lead to price increases on the joint venture model and give it greater profits; also, GM would be led to raise the prices on its more expensive cars to maintain margins between the joint venture subcompact and the rest of the GM line. The majority regarded these pricing effects as speculative and uncertain. Second, the dissenters were concerned that the inevitable exchange of information between GM and Toyota, in the operation of the joint venture, would lead to anticompetitive effects in other portions of the GM/Toyota line. The majority noted that the Commission staff had required modifications in the original joint venture arrangement prohibiting the exchange of information with respect to future prices, and requiring that extensive records be maintained on all other sensitive competitive information that was exchanged.

Is it troublesome that the wholesale price of the joint venture car was influenced to a great extent by the price of cars sold by Toyota? Chrysler intervened in the proceeding and argued that any pricing formula should be triggered "by a cost index which is not under Toyota's control yet is highly correlated to Toyota's costs" and urged that the inclusion of Corolla prices in the equation was grounds to strike down the entire joint venture. Do you find convincing GM's claim that the joint venture was competitively valuable as a device to help GM learn about highly successful Japanese manufacturing and marketing techniques? Would Toyota be likely to sell that kind of information and experience to a competitor like GM, without an equity arrangement that allowed it to share in profits? Is that kind of learning advantage a factor the antitrust laws should take into account?

3. Suppose two or more parents of a joint venture were about to enter a market separately, but agreed to join forces in a joint undertaking on the eve of entry. Are there any circumstances in which such a joint venture should survive a challenge under Section 7? Suppose the parents are already in the market and then join forces to market a new improved or modified product to compete with products sold by each of the parents. Was not that the situation with respect to G.M. and Toyota? Did the Commission correctly measure the procompetitive and anticompetitive aspects of that deal?

4. Should joint research and joint exploration ventures be treated differently than joint sales agencies with respect to legality under Section 7? Why? In this connection, *see* Chapter 5, p. 380 *supra*; Pitofsky, A Framework for Antitrust Analysis of Joint Ventures, 74 Geo.L.J. 1605 (1986).

5. Penn–Olin recognized that a joint venture that precludes future market entry can be the basis of a violation of Section 7. It examined only in a very general way what the necessary elements would be to prove future entry. Subsequent case law indicates that the essential elements are capacity, interest, and economic

incentive. *See, e.g., Yamaha Motor Co. v. FTC*, 657 F.2d 971 (8th Cir.1981). A determination of what a company would have done had it not entered the joint venture—would it have proceeded alone or jointly in a less anticompetitive partnership—has proven to be an extremely difficult piece of analysis. *See* Brodley, Potential Competition Mergers: A Structural Synthesis, 87 Yale L.J. 1 (1977). Even if entry by one or both members of a joint venture is likely, should not the government still have to prove a probable substantial lessening of competition as a result of the venture? How would you make that showing?

6. In 1986, Professor Pitofsky commented on developments in the law since the Penn–Olin case:

> The likelihood of a successful antitrust challenge in the "one-in, one-out" situation has declined radically in the 20 years since Penn–Olin was decided because of the array of conditions that the courts require to be satisfied before an "in the wings" competitive effect can be shown. Assuming it is clear that the first parent was either in the market or had the capacity, interest, and economic incentive to enter, the plaintiff must further show the following: (1) the market in which the joint venture would operate is not competitive, so that an "in the wings" entrant could have some significant effects on levels of competition (generally requiring proof of high levels of concentration and of substantial barriers to entry); (2) other competitors in the market served by the joint venture would have perceived the nonentering parent as a likely potential entrant; (3) the nonentering parent was one of a few (probably two or three) most likely potential entrants so that the loss of in the wings potential competition was a substantial loss; and (4) the in the wings entrant would have a substantial likely procompetitive effect on the market. It is possible to challenge a joint venture on the basis of loss of potential competition, but the plaintiff's burden is a formidable one. Where it is clear that only one parent was in the market or would have entered and that substantial efficiencies are really generated by the joint arrangement, it would be an exceptional case in which the joint venture could be struck down because of the loss of potential competition. As a result, the central question in joint venture analysis has become whether both parents were in the market or about to enter. Without that preliminary finding, the likelihood that a violation will be found on the basis of a loss of potential competition declines sharply.[22]

PROBLEM 23

THE BZT THREE–WAY VENTURE

General Circuits Co. and Electro, Inc. have dominated the United States electrical industry for decades. Each has been independently working on the development of a new kind of circuit breaker for high voltage power. This device would use a vacuum to interrupt electric power instead of conventional systems based on use of oil, compressed air, or inert gas. A vacuum circuit breaker would produce extremely rapid cut-off of power, have less risk of fire, and dramatically increase the durability of working parts. Both General Circuits and Electro have perfected small-sized vacuum circuit breakers, but neither has been able to solve a number of difficult problems in applying that technology to high voltages. The same is true for Brits, Ltd., a British company, ZAF, a German company, and Toyo, Inc.,

---

22. Pitofsky, A Framework for Antitrust Analysis of Joint Ventures, 74 Geo.L.J. 1605, 1609–10 (1986).

a Japanese company, all of which manufacture circuit breakers and are the world's only other significant electrical concerns. If a vacuum circuit breaker for high voltage power is developed, the market would be very sizeable.

Breakers, Inc., a United States company, is a very small but highly successful, aggressive, technology-oriented firm in the electrical industry. Rather than offering a full range of electrical products, Breakers sells only a few products which it can produce at lower prices or which are technologically superior to those produced by the industry giants. Breakers is the only other United States manufacturer of circuit breakers using conventional technology and is interested in producing high voltage vacuum circuit breakers.

Breakers is about to enter a "research joint venture" with ZAF and Toyo. BZT, Inc. will be formed, in a three-way venture, to conduct research on and develop a high voltage vacuum circuit breaker. The terms of the joint venture provide that: (1) each of the three venturers will receive equal access to the research; (2) profits will be shared equally; (3) sale of high voltage vacuum circuit breakers in the United States will be made only by Breakers; (4) sale of high voltage vacuum breakers in Germany will be made only by ZAF and in Japan only by Toyo; and (5) all other world-wide sales of high voltage vacuum breakers will be made only by BZT.

Breakers' president has explained the venture as follows:

> Although ZAF and Toyo have been working on similar ideas, we are well ahead of them. Indeed, in the absence of the joint venture, it is almost certain that Toyo would have given up on its vacuum circuit breaker research and possible that ZAF also would have done so. But the resource supplementation (particularly by ZAF) and the manufacturing and distribution skills of Toyo will cut several years off the time it would otherwise take us to get the high voltage vacuum breakers to the market. ZAF and Toyo now have about 4% of the United States market for conventional circuit breakers (Breakers has 3%) and have competition only from General Circuits and Electro in their own countries. This will be a wonderful relationship for all concerned. Our attorneys have advised that "any antitrust challenge to the venture stands near zero chance of success."

Do you agree with the legal advice provided by Breakers' attorneys? If you have problems, can you suggest more viable alternatives?

INTRODUCTION TO QUESTIONS RELATING TO CONGLOMERATE MERGERS

Section 7 covers some mergers that do not involve firms in either a horizontal or vertical relationship. If the firms don't compete, and don't buy or sell to each other, what is the problem?

The legislative history of Section 7 establishes that Congress intended to cover "conglomerate" mergers as well as horizontal and vertical mergers, but said almost nothing about possible theories. Several have been developed by the courts. We saw in *Penn–Olin,* a joint venture case but in many ways related to conglomerate theory, that a firm that enters a market by acquisition is no longer "in the wings" and threatening to enter, and the elimination of that perceived threat may substantially lessen competition by relieving incumbents of the need to keep prices low or the quality of service high to deter entry. The theory can easily be applied to mergers as well as joint ventures. A related but more straightforward theory concerns the firm that enters the market by acquisition, but was reasonably likely to enter by internal expansion (so called "actual potential entry"), or by acquisition of a much smaller firm and expansion from the smaller base (so called "toe hold" acquisition)—with the result that the path it did take may substantially lessen competition. Beyond these "potential competition" theories, questions have been raised as a result of "bigness" and "diversification"—how might the concentration of industrial assets by merger produce anticompetitive effects (or even political or social effects) that are undesirable and deserve to be blocked.

One such theory is that a large firm with "deep pockets" can focus its aggressive actions on a smaller local rival and put that rival out of business, or persuade the rival to be a docile follower, without any danger of retaliation by the smaller rival against the extensive resources of the larger corporation. An increase in size can also produce "opportunities for self-sufficiency." *See* G Stocking, Comment on C. Edwards "Conglomerate Bigness as a Source of Power" Business Concentration and Price Policy, 353–57 (1957). The large firm can effectively bargain with its suppliers and customers by threatening to integrate into their line of business. Also, large diversified conglomerate firms that meet each other in many product and geographic markets may engage in "mutual forbearance"—that is one conglomerate will not compete as aggressively in a particular market for fear that a rival conglomerate will respond aggressively in a different market. Some studies suggest that prices and profits are higher where conglomerate firms have high levels of multimarket contacts. *See* Scott, Multimarket Contact and Economic Performance, 64 Rev. Econ. Stat. 368–75 (1982) and Feinberg, "Sales at Risk": A Test of the Mutual Forbearance Theory of Conglomerate Behavior, 58 J. Bus. 225–41 (1985). Lastly, it has been suggested that heavy advertising is a characteristic marketing approach of very large firms, and that advertising expenditures raise barriers to entry by new but smaller competitors.

Beyond traditional competition theory, it has been argued that there are some political consequences to high levels of concentration of market power. For example, it has been suggested that firms with scores of production facilities and distributors in different states and congressional districts will have more clout in the federal legislature than smaller rivals. One response might be that associations of small businesses (gasoline dealers, funeral directors, even doctors and lawyers) have demonstrated time and again their ability to influence the political process. Another "political" theory is that firms may become "too big to fail"—that is the consequences on employees, suppliers and the economy in general may be so disastrous that federal or state legislatures will bail the firm out rather than allow it to proceed into bankruptcy. After a long period during which large firm bailouts did not occur, they were frequently resorted to during the economic crisis of 2008–9. Many in positions of authority in the country registered their distaste for bailouts, particularly where part of the company's financial problems traced to management errors, but indicated that the consequences of letting the company fail would be worse than the bailout. Should the "too big to fail" problem be taken into account in future conglomerate merger enforcement, particularly with respect to prosecutorial discretion?

Balanced against these concerns is the fact that many conglomerate mergers are extremely efficient, placing resources in the hands of experienced and capable management or integrating related economic functions in a single corporate institution. How should claims of efficiency be treated in the context of conglomerate mergers? Recall the 1997 amendments to the FTC horizontal merger guidelines, expressly providing that the government "will not challenge a merger if efficiencies are of a character and magnitude such that the merger is not likely to be anticompetitive." Is there any reason to treat efficiencies in the conglomerate context any different than in the horizontal merger context?

We begin with the Supreme Court's 1967 decision in *Procter & Gamble,* addressing many of the issues that have arisen in connection with conglomerate acquisitions.

Federal Trade Commission v. Procter & Gamble Co.

Supreme Court of the United States, 1967.
386 U.S. 568, 87 S.Ct. 1224, 18 L.Ed.2d 303.

■ DOUGLAS, J. This is a proceeding initiated by the Federal Trade Commission charging that respondent, Procter & Gamble Co., had acquired the assets of Clorox Chemical Co. in violation of § 7 of the Clayton Act. . . . The charge was that Procter's acquisition of Clorox may substantially lessen competition or tend to create a monopoly in the production and sale of household liquid bleaches.

. . .

As indicated by the Commission in its painstaking and illuminating report, it does not particularly aid analysis to talk of this merger in conventional terms, namely, horizontal or vertical or conglomerate. This merger may most appropriately be described as a "product-extension merger," as the Commission stated. The facts are not disputed, and a summary will demonstrate the correctness of the Commission's decision.

At the time of the merger, Clorox was the leading manufacturer in the heavily concentrated household liquid bleach industry. It is agreed that household liquid bleach is the relevant line of commerce. The product is used in the home as a germicide and disinfectant, and, more importantly, as a whitening agent in washing clothes and fabrics. It is a distinctive product with no close substitutes. Liquid bleach is a low-price, high-turnover consumer product sold mainly through grocery stores and supermarkets. The relevant geographical market is the Nation and a series of regional markets. Because of high shipping costs and low sales price, it is not feasible to ship the product more than 300 miles from its point of manufacture. Most manufacturers are limited to competition within a single region since they have but one plant. Clorox is the only firm selling nationally; it has 13 plants distributed throughout the Nation. Purex, Clorox's closest competitor in size, does not distribute its bleach in the northeast or middle-Atlantic States; in 1957, Purex's bleach was available in less than 50% of the national market.

At the time of the acquisition, Clorox was the leading manufacturer of household liquid bleach, with 48.8% of the national sales—annual sales of slightly less than $40,000,000. Its market share had been steadily increasing for the five years prior to the merger. Its nearest rival was Purex, which manufactures a number of products other than household liquid bleaches, including abrasive cleaners, toilet soap, and detergents. Purex accounted for 15.7% of the household liquid bleach market. The industry is highly concentrated; in 1957, Clorox and Purex accounted for almost 65% of the Nation's household liquid bleach sales, and, together with four other firms, for almost 80%. The remaining 20% was divided among over 200 small producers. Clorox had total assets of $12,000,000; only eight producers had assets in excess of $1,000,000 and very few had assets of more than $75,000.

In light of the territorial limitations on distribution, national figures do not give an accurate picture of Clorox's dominance in the various regions. Thus, Clorox's seven principal competitors did no business in New England, the mid-Atlantic States, or metropolitan New York. Clorox's share of the sales in those areas was 56%, 72%, and 64% respectively. Even in regions where its principal competitors were active, Clorox maintained a dominant position. Except in metropolitan Chicago and the west-central States Clorox accounted for at least 39%, and often a much higher percentage, of liquid bleach sales.

Since all liquid bleach is chemically identical, advertising and sales promotion is vital. In 1957 Clorox spent almost $3,700,000 on advertising, imprinting the value of its bleach in the mind of the consumer. In addition, it spent $1,700,000 for other promotional activities. The Commission found that these heavy expenditures went far to explain why Clorox maintained so high a market share despite the fact that its brand, though chemically indistinguishable from rival brands, retailed for a price equal to or, in many instances, higher than its competitors.

Procter is a large, diversified manufacturer of low-price, high-turnover household products sold through grocery, drug, and department stores. Prior to its acquisition of Clorox, it did not produce household liquid bleach. Its 1957 sales were in excess of $1,100,000,000 from which it realized profits of more than $67,000,000; its assets were over $500,000,000. Procter has been marked by rapid growth and diversification. It has successfully developed and introduced a number of new products. Its primary activity is in the general area of soaps, detergents, and cleansers; in 1957, of total domestic sales, more than one-half (over $500,000,000) were in this field. Procter was the dominant factor in this area. It accounted for 54.4% of all packaged detergent sales. The industry is heavily concentrated—Procter and its nearest competitors, Colgate–Palmolive and Lever Brothers, account for 80% of the market.

In the marketing of soaps, detergents, and cleansers, as in the marketing of household liquid bleach, advertising and sales promotion are vital. In 1957, Procter was the Nation's largest advertiser, spending more than $80,000,000 on advertising and an additional $47,000,000 on sales promotion. Due to its tremendous volume, Procter receives substantial discounts from the media. As a multi-product producer Procter enjoys substantial advantages in advertising and sales promotion. Thus, it can and does feature several products in its promotions, reducing the printing, mailing, and other costs for each product. It also purchases network programs on behalf of several products, enabling it to give each product network exposure at a fraction of the cost per product that a firm with only one product to advertise would incur.

Prior to the acquisition, Procter was in the course of diversifying into product lines related to its basic detergent-soap-cleanser business. Liquid bleach was a distinct possibility since packaged detergents—Procter's primary product line—and liquid bleach are used complementarily in washing clothes and fabrics, and in general household clothing. . . .

. . . .

The decision to acquire Clorox was the result of a study conducted by Procter's promotion department designed to determine the advisability of entering the liquid bleach industry. The initial report noted the ascendancy of liquid bleach in the large and expanding household bleach market, and recommended that Procter purchase Clorox rather than enter independently. Since a large investment would be needed to obtain a satisfactory market share, acquisition of the industry's leading firm was attractive. "Taking over the Clorox business . . . could be a way of achieving a dominant position in the liquid bleach market quickly, which would pay out reasonably well." The initial report predicted that Procter's "sales, distribution and manufacturing setup" could increase Clorox's share of the markets in areas where it was low. The final report confirmed the conclusions of the initial report and emphasized that Procter could make more effective use of Clorox's advertising budget and that the merger would facilitate advertising economies. A few months later, Procter acquired the assets of Clorox in the name of a wholly owned subsidiary, the Clorox Company, in exchange for Procter stock.

. . . The Commission found that the substitution of Procter with its huge assets and advertising advantages for the already dominant Clorox would dissuade new entrants and discourage active competition from the firms already in the industry due to fear of retaliation by Procter. The Commission thought it relevant that retailers might be induced to give Clorox preferred shelf space since it would be manufactured by Procter, which also produced a number of other products marketed by the retailers. There was also the danger that Procter might underprice Clorox in order to drive out competition, and subsidize the underpricing with revenue from other products. The Commission carefully reviewed the effect of the acquisition on the structure of the industry, noting that "the practical tendency of the . . . merger . . . is to transform the liquid bleach industry into an arena of big business competition only, with the few small firms falling by the wayside, unable to compete with their giant rivals." Further, the merger would seriously diminish potential competition by eliminating Procter as a potential entrant into the industry. Prior to the merger, the Commission found that Procter was the most likely prospective entrant, and absent the merger would have remained on the periphery, restraining Clorox from exercising its market power. If Procter had actually entered, Clorox's dominant position would have been eroded and the concentration of the industry reduced. The Commission stated that it had not placed reliance on post-acquisition evidence in holding the merger unlawful.

. . .

The anticompetitive effects with which this product-extension merger is fraught can easily be seen: (1) the substitution of the powerful acquiring firm for the smaller, but already dominant, firm may substantially reduce the competitive structure of the industry by raising entry barriers, and by dissuading the smaller firms from aggressively competing; (2) the acquisition eliminates the potential competition of the acquiring firm.

The liquid bleach industry was already oligopolistic before the acquisition, and price competition was certainly not as vigorous as it would have been if the industry were competitive. Clorox enjoyed a dominant position nationally, and its position approached monopoly proportions in certain areas. The existence of some 200 fringe firms certainly does not belie that fact. Nor does the fact, relied upon by the court below, that after the merger, producers other than Clorox "were selling more bleach for more money than ever before." 358 F.2d at 80. In the same period, Clorox increased its share from 48.8% to 52%. The interjection of Procter into the market considerably changed the situation. There is every reason to assume that the smaller firms would become more cautious in competing due to their fear of retaliation by Procter. It is probable that Procter would become the price leader and that oligopoly would become more rigid.

The acquisition may also have the tendency of raising the barriers to new entry. The major competitive weapon in the successful marketing of bleach is advertising. Clorox was limited in this area by its relatively small budget and its inability to obtain substantial discounts. By contrast, Procter's budget was much larger; and, although it would not devote its entire budget to advertising Clorox, it could divert a large portion to meet the short-term threat of a new entrant. Procter would be able to use its volume discounts to advantage in advertising Clorox. Thus, a new entrant would be much more reluctant to face the giant Procter than it would have been to face the smaller Clorox.[23]

---

23.   The barriers to entry have been raised both for entry by new firms and for entry into new geographical markets by established firms. The latter aspect is demonstrated by Purex's lesson in Erie, Pennsylvania. In October 1957, Purex selected Erie, Pennsylvania—where it had not sold previously—as an area in which to test the salability, under competitive conditions, of a new bleach. The leading brands in Erie were Clorox, with 52%, and the "101" brand, sold by Gardner Manufacturing Company, with 29% of the market. Purex launched an advertising and promotional campaign to obtain a broad distribution in a short time, and, in five months captured 33% of the Erie market. Clorox's share dropped to 35% and 101's to 17%. Clorox responded by offering its bleach at reduced prices, and then added an offer of a $1–value ironing board cover for 50 cents with each purchase of Clorox at the reduced price. It also increased its advertising with television spots. The result was to restore Clorox's lost market share and, indeed, to increase it slightly. Purex's share fell to 7%.

Since the merger Purex has acquired the fourth largest producer of bleach, John Paul Products Company, which owned and marketed "Fleecy White" brand in geographic markets which Purex was anxious to enter. One of the reasons for this acquisition, according to Purex's president, was that:

Possible economies cannot be used as a defense to illegality. Congress was aware that some mergers which lessen competition may also result in economies but it struck the balance in favor of protecting competition. *See Brown Shoe Co. v. United States*, 370 U.S. at 344.

The Commission also found that the acquisition of Clorox by Procter eliminated Procter as a potential competitor. The Court of Appeals declared that this finding was not supported by evidence because there was no evidence that Procter's management had ever intended to enter the industry independently and that Procter had never attempted to enter. The evidence, however, clearly shows that Procter was the most likely entrant. Procter had recently launched a new abrasive cleaner in an industry similar to the liquid bleach industry, and had wrested leadership from a brand that had enjoyed even a larger market share than had Clorox. Procter was engaged in a vigorous program of diversifying into product lines closely related to its basic products. Liquid bleach was a natural avenue of diversification since it is complementary to Procter's products, is sold to the same customers through the same channels, and is advertised and merchandised in the same manner. Procter had substantial advantages in advertising and sales promotions, which, as we have seen, are vital to the success of liquid bleach. No manufacturer had a patent on the product or its manufacture, necessary information relating to manufacturing methods and processes was readily available, there was no shortage of raw material, and the machinery and equipment required for a plant of efficient capacity were available at reasonable cost. Procter's management was experienced in producing and marketing goods similar to liquid bleach. Procter had considered the possibility of independently entering but decided against it because the acquisition of Clorox would enable Procter to capture a more commanding share of the market.

It is clear that the existence of Procter at the edge of the industry exerted considerable influence on the market. First, the market behavior of the liquid bleach industry was influenced by each firm's predictions of the market behavior of its competitors, actual and potential. Second, the barriers to entry by a firm of Procter's size and with its advantages were not significant. There is no indication that the barriers were so high that the price Procter would have to charge would be above the price that would maximize the profits of the existing firms. Third, the number of potential entrants was not so large that the elimination of one would be insignificant. Few firms would have the temerity to challenge a firm as solidly entrenched as Clorox. Fourth, Procter was found by the Commission to be the most likely entrant. These findings of the Commission were amply supported by the evidence.

■ STEWART, J., and FORTAS, J., took no part in the consideration or decision of this case.

"Purex had been unsuccessful in expanding its market position geographically on Purex liquid bleach. The economics of the bleach business, and the strong competitive factors as illustrated by our experience in Erie, Pennsylvania, make it impossible, in our judgment for us to expand our market on liquid bleach."

■ HARLAN, J., concurring. I agree that the Commission's order should be sustained, but I do not share the majority opinion's view that a mere "summary will demonstrate the correctness of the Commission's decision" nor that "[t]he anticompetitive effects with which this product-extension merger is fraught can easily be seen." I consider the case difficult within its own four corners, and beyond that, its portents for future administrative and judicial application of § 7 of the Clayton Act to this kind of merger important and far reaching. . . .

Deciding that § 7 inquiry in conglomerate or product-extension merger cases should be directed toward reasonably probable changes in market structure does not, however, decide how that inquiry should be narrowed and focused. The Commission and the Court isolate two separate structural elements, the degree of concentration in the existing market and the "condition of entry." The interplay of these two factors is said to determine the existence and extent of market power, since the "condition of entry" determines the limits potential competition places on the existing market. It must be noted, however, that economic theory teaches that potential competition will have no effect on the market behavior of existing firms unless present market power is sufficient to drive the market price to the point where entry would become a real possibility. So long as existing competition is sufficient to keep the market price below that point, potential competition is of marginal significance as a market regulator. Thus in a conglomerate or product-extension case, where the effects on market structure which are easiest to discover are generally effects on the "condition of entry," an understanding of the workings of the premerger market cannot be ignored, and, indeed, is critical to a determination whether the visible effects on "condition of entry" have any competitive significance.

The Commission pinned its analysis of the premerger market exclusively on its concentration, the large market share enjoyed by the leading firms. In so doing the Commission was following the path taken by this Court in judging more conventional merger cases, *e.g., United States v. Philadelphia Nat'l Bank, supra*, and taking the position favored by the great weight of economic authority. See, *e.g.*, Bain, Industrial Organization. The Sixth Circuit discounted the Commission's analysis because of the presence of some 200 small competitors in the market. The Court bases its agreement with the Commission and its rejection of the Court of Appeals' position on Clorox's alleged domination of the market. But domination is an elusive term, for dominance in terms of percentage of sales is not the equivalent of dominance in terms of control over price or other aspects of market behavior. Just as the total number of sellers in the market is not determinative of its operation, the percentage of sales made by any group of sellers is similarly not conclusive. The determinative issue is, instead, how the sellers interact and establish the pattern of market behavior. The significance of concentration analysis is that it allows measurement of one easily determined variable to serve as an opening key to the pattern of market behavior.

I think that the Commission, on this record, was entitled to regard the market as "oligopolistic" and that it could properly ignore the impact of the smaller firms. I hasten to add, however, that there are significant "economic dissents" from oligopoly analysis in general and stronger arguments that if its principles are justified in some cases, they are not justified in all cases.... Brodley, *supra*. In adjudicating § 7 questions in a conglomerate or product-extension merger context where the pattern of behavior in the existing market is apt to be crucial, I would, therefore, allow the introduction by a defendant of evidence designed to show that the actual operation of the market did not accord with oligopoly theory, or whatever other theory the Commission desires to apply. In other words, I believe that defendants in § 7 proceedings are entitled, in the case of conglomerate or product-extension mergers, to build their own economic case for the proposition that the merger will not substantially impair competition.

For example, had Procter desired to go beyond demonstrating the mere presence of small competitors and attempted to show that the prices of unadvertised bleaches which were cost-determined set an effective ceiling on market price through the mechanism of an acceptable differential, I think that the Commission would have been obliged to receive and evaluate the proof. But to challenge effectively the presumption which the Commission is entitled to draw from general economic theory, a defendant must present, in my opinion, not only contradictory facts but a more cogent explanation of the pattern of market behavior.

If the proof as a whole establishes that pricing power may be exercised by a firm or firms in the market—that prices may be raised in the long run over competitive prices—then the Commission may legitimately focus on the role of potential competition and the "condition of entry." See Bain, Barriers to New Competition 5, 27. In so doing, however, a new difficulty is encountered. The threat of potential competition merely affects the range over which price power extends. Potential competition does not compel more vigorous striving in the market, nor advance any other social goal which Congress might be said to have favored in passing § 7.[24] Thus it may legitimately be questioned whether even a substantial increase in entry barriers creates a substantial lessening of competition or tendency to monopoly as required by § 7.

Two justifications for the use of entry barriers as a determinant under § 7 can be given. The first is that an increased range over which pricing power may be exercised is contrary to the mandate of § 7 because Congress' use of the word "competition" was a shorthand for the invocation of the benefits of a competitive market, one of which is a price close to average cost. Such an approach leads also to the conclusion that economic

---

24. Potential entry does not keep "a large number of small competitors in business," United States v. Von's Grocery Co., 384 U.S. 270, 275, even if that goal could be considered desirable. In fact, by placing a ceiling market price it may serve to drive out small competitors who may be relatively inefficient producers. Potential entry does not control the market share of dominant firms or prevent them from expanding their power to force others to accede to their practices.

efficiencies produced by the merger must be weighed against anticompetitive consequences in the final determination whether the net effect on competition is substantially adverse. See Bork & Bowman, The Crisis in Antitrust, 65 Col.L.Rev. 363. The second justification is found in the tendency to monopoly clause of § 7. Certainly the clearest evil of monopoly is the excessive power the monopolist has over price. Since "antitrust operates to forestall concentrations of economic power which, if allowed to develop unhindered, would call for much more intrusive government supervision of the economy," Blake & Jones, In Defense of Antitrust, 65 Col.L.Rev. 377, 383, increased power over price should be attackable under § 7. Cf. S.Rep. No. 1775, 81st Cong., 2d Sess., 4–5. For these reasons I conclude that the Commission may properly find a conglomerate or product-extension merger illegal under § 7 because it substantially increases pricing power in the relevant market.

    . . .

    To summarize then, four important guides to the adjudication of conglomerate or product-extension mergers under § 7 seem to come forward. First, the decision can rest on analysis of market structure without resort to evidence of post-merger anticompetitive behavior. Second, the operation of the premerger market must be understood as the foundation of successful analysis. The responsible agency may presume that the market operates in accord with generally accepted principles of economic theory, but the presumption must be open to the challenge of alternative operational formulations. Third, if it is reasonably probable that there will be a change in market structure which will allow the exercise of substantially greater market power, then a *prima facie* case has been made out under § 7. Fourth, where the case against the merger rests on the probability of increased market power, the merging companies may attempt to prove that there are countervailing economies reasonably probable which should be weighed against the adverse effects.

    The Commission's decision did, I think, conform to this analysis. . . . To hold the merger unlawful, the Commission relied on five factors which taken together convinced it that "substantial" anticompetitive consequences could be expected. A "substantial" impact was said to be "significant and real, and discernible not merely to theorists or scholars but to practical hard-headed businessmen." The relevant factors were (1) the excessive concentration in the industry at the time of the merger and the commanding market position of Clorox, (2) the relative disparity in size and strength as between Procter and the firms in the liquid bleach industry, (3) the position of Procter in other markets, (4) the elimination of Procter as a potential competitor, and (5) the nature of the "economies" expected from the merger. The net of these factors was to establish a substantial effect on the market structure variable involved, condition of entry.

    . . .

    I do not think . . . that on the record presented Procter has shown any true efficiencies in advertising. Procter has merely shown that it is able to command equivalent resources at a lower dollar cost than other bleach producers. No peculiarly efficient marketing techniques have been demonstrated, nor does the record show that a smaller net advertising expenditure could be expected. Economies cannot be premised solely on dollar figures, lest accounting controversies dominate § 7 proceedings. Economies employed in defense of a merger must be shown in what economists label "real" terms, that is in terms of resources applied to the accomplishment of the objective. For this reason, the Commission, I think, was justified in discounting Procter's efficiency defense. . . .

NOTES AND QUESTIONS

1.   In *Procter & Gamble*, the majority relied in part on a finding that the combined firm could drive smaller liquid bleach rivals out of the market, or render those firms more cautious because of fear of retaliation through predatory or otherwise low pricing. But a strategy of predation or even aggressively low pricing does not follow inevitably from the entry by merger of a large firm into a market populated by smaller rivals. Was there evidence cited by the majority or concurring justice that Procter would follow a predatory strategy or was it simply assumed from the size of the combined parties?

2.   A second theory in *Procter* was that the merger raised barriers to entry by making available to the combined company volume discounts in advertising previously only available to Procter with its enormous advertising budget. Suppose the efficiencies did not relate to advertising—for, example, suppose the merger lowered distribution costs for two non-competing products sold to the same outlets. Would that be a reason for blocking the merger? In effect, would that amount to holding efficiencies against the legality of the transaction? Is it likely that the Department of Justice or the FTC would challenge a conglomerate merger on any such theory, given the amendments in 1997 which clarify and allow more scope to efficiencies claims?

3.   It has been suggested that advertising efficiencies be treated differently from other forms of efficiencies because they are characteristically a marketing tool of very large companies, quantity discounts are not available to smaller firms, and high levels of advertising appear to be associated systematically with high levels of concentration and high barriers to entry. *See* Turner, Advertising and Competition, speech delivered in Washington, D.C. before the briefing Conference on Federal Controls of Advertising and Promotion (June 2, 1966). Even severe critics of advertising acknowledge that it can serve a pro-competitive purpose by making potential customers aware of new, improved or superior products. On the other hand, extremely heavy advertising may create consumer preferences that cannot be broken down except by comparable counter-advertising, but is often wasteful in a sense that it does not provide information that consumers can use to make sensible choices between products. Does hostility to advertising makes sense in competitive terms, or is it just an anti-Madison Avenue reaction?

4.   In *Procter*, and more clearly in the *Falstaff* opinion summarized immediately following, we begin to see a difference between the two forms of lessening of potential competition. If the anticompetitive effect of the merger is the elimination of a perceived potential entrant ("in the wings"), the analysis focuses on the

question of whether that elimination would make a competitive difference. If the theory is that the consequence of the merger is that the acquiring firm would have entered the market if the acquisition were blocked ("actual potential entry") and by that entry improved competition, that could be seen as an argument that competition was not necessarily lessened, but rather that it was not improved as much as it would have been through entry by internal expansion. Can you argue that a failure to improve competition is a violation of Section 7? Consider whether that question is the reason why the Supreme Court in *Falstaff* and elsewhere has left open the question of whether the elimination of actual potential entry is a legitimate theory under Section 7.

United States v. Falstaff Brewing Corp., 410 U.S. 526, 93 S.Ct. 1096, 35 L.Ed.2d 475 (1973). The government charged that the 1965 acquisition of Narragansett Brewing Co. by Falstaff Brewing Corp. violated Section 7. The district court held that there was no violation. The Supreme Court reversed and remanded the proceeding for further consideration by the district court.

The parties stipulated that the relevant product market was the production and sale of beer, and that the relevant geographic market was the six New England states. Within this market, the eight largest sellers accounted for 81.2% of sales in 1965, up from 74% in 1960; the four largest accounted for 61.3% in 1965, up from 50% in 1960; Narragansett, the largest seller in 1965, accounted for approximately 20% of sales. The number of brewers operating plants in New England declined from 11 in 1957 to 6 in 1964.

Falstaff was the fourth largest producer of beer in the United States with 5.9% of national production. However, Falstaff did not distribute beer nationally, and, of the nation's ten largest brewers, Falstaff was the largest of three that did not sell beer in New England. In relation to the New England market, Falstaff's sales in western Ohio and in Washington, D.C., were the closest of these three firms. Falstaff had been interested in entering the New England market for some time, had made public statements to that effect, and had commissioned studies on the subject. "National brewers possess competitive advantages since they are able to advertise on a nationwide basis, their beers have greater prestige than regional or local beers, and they are less affected by the weather or labor problems in a particular region." Thus, Falstaff wished to move from regional to national status. A 1958 study recommended entry de novo into the New England market rather than entry by acquisition. However, Falstaff decided to enter by acquisition because such an approach would be more profitable and would provide an existing distributorship arrangement which Falstaff considered essential to successful entry. After negotiations with other firms, the acquisition of Narragansett was consummated. Falstaff's management maintained that they would not enter the New England market by any means other than the acquisition of Narragansett. The government contended that entry by Falstaff would be both feasible and profitable if Falstaff entered de novo or made a "toehold acquisition" of one of the small brewers in the New England market.

The district court accepted the position of Falstaff and held that, since Falstaff would not have entered the New England market by any means other than the acquisition of Narragansett, such acquisition did not have an anticompetitive effect. Competition in the market was found to be vigorous at the time of the acquisition and not to have diminished subsequent to the acquisition. Narragansett's market share dropped from 21.5% in 1964 to 15.5% in 1969, while the shares of the two leading national brewers increased from 16.5% to 35.8%.

The Supreme Court reversed, writing four separate opinions. The opinion of the Court, by Justice White, in which Chief Justice Burger and Justice Blackmun concurred in full, and Justice Douglas concurred in part, held that the district court erred in assuming "that because Falstaff, as a matter of fact, would never have entered the market de novo, it could in no sense be considered a potential competitor. More specifically, the district court failed to give separate consideration to whether Falstaff was a potential competitor in the sense that it was so positioned on the edge of the market that it exerted beneficial influence on competitive conditions in that market." The Court continued:

> The specific question with respect to this phase of the case is not what Falstaff's internal company decisions were but whether, given its financial capabilities and conditions in the New England market, it would be reasonable to consider it a potential entrant into that market. Surely, it could not be said on this record that Falstaff's general interest in the New England market was unknown; and if it would appear to rational beer merchants in New England that Falstaff might well build a new brewery to supply the northeastern market then its entry by merger becomes suspect under § 7. The District Court should therefore have appraised the economic facts about Falstaff and the New England market in order to determine whether in any realistic sense Falstaff could be said to be a potential competitor on the fringe of the market with likely influence on existing competition. This does not mean that the testimony of company officials about actual intentions of the company is irrelevant or is to be looked upon with suspicion; but it does mean that theirs is not necessarily the last word in arriving at a conclusion about how Falstaff should be considered in terms of its status as a potential entrant into the market in issue.

> Since it appears that the District Court entertained too narrow a view of Falstaff as a potential competitor and since it appears that the District Court's conclusion that the merger posed no probable threat to competition followed automatically from the finding that Falstaff had no intent to enter de novo, we remand this case for the District Court to make the proper assessment of Falstaff as a potential competitor....

> Because we remand for proper assessment of Falstaff as an on-the-fringe potential competitor, it is not necessary to reach the question of whether § 7 bars a market-extension merger by a company whose entry into the market would have no influence whatsoever on the present state of competition in the market—that is, the entrant will not be a dominant force in the market and has no current influence in the marketplace. We leave for another day the question of the applicability of § 7 to a merger that will leave competition in the marketplace exactly as it was, neither hurt nor helped, and that is challengeable under § 7 only on grounds that the company could, but did not, enter de novo or through "toe-hold" acquisition and that there is less competition than there would have been had entry been in such a manner. There are traces of this view in our cases, see Ford Motor Co. v. United States, 405 U.S. 562, 567 (1972); id., at 587 (Burger, C.J., concurring in part and dissenting in part); FTC v. Procter & Gamble Co., 386 U.S., at 580; id., at 586 (Harlan, J., concurring); United States v. Penn–Olin Chemical Co., 378 U.S., at 173, but the Court has not squarely faced the question, if for no other reason than because

there has been no necessity to consider it. *See* Ford Motor Co. v. United States, *supra*; FTC v. Procter & Gamble Co., *supra*; United States v. Penn–Olin Chemical Co., *supra*; United States v. El Paso Natural Gas Co., 376 U.S. 651 (1964).

Justices Brennan and Powell did not participate in the decision. Justice Douglas concurred for the most part in the Court's opinion, but inclined to the view that the question left open should be resolved in favor of the government.

Justice Marshall disagreed with the basis of the Court's remand because the government had not claimed that Falstaff was exerting a present pro-competitive influence and had introduced no evidence to support this view; Justices Rehnquist and Stewart dissented.

On remand, the district court found that Falstaff had not been perceived as a potential competitor. It dismissed the complaint and the government did not appeal. *See* United States v. Falstaff Brewing Corp., 383 F.Supp. 1020 (D.R.I.1974).

———

BOC International, Ltd. v. FTC, 557 F.2d 24 (2d Cir.1977). British Oxygen, the world's second largest producer of industrial gases, acquired a controlling interest in Airco, the third largest industrial gas producer in the United States with approximately 16% of the national market. British Oxygen had never sold industrial gases in the United States.

The FTC found that the acquisition constituted a violation of Section 7 under the "actual potential entrant" theory—that is, if the acquisition were blocked, British Oxygen would have entered the market de novo or by a toe-hold acquisition and such entry would have had pro-competitive effects. The Commission specifically found that there was no evidence that British Oxygen, prior to the acquisition, exerted any "in the wings" pro-competitive effect. As a result, the legal issue presented was one the Supreme Court had twice declined to pass upon: Whether the "actual potential entrant" doctrine was a valid form of Section 7 enforcement?

As to the likelihood of independent entry but for the acquisition, the FTC found:

> [A]s of December 1973, there was a "reasonable probability" that [British Oxygen] would have eventually entered the U.S. industrial gases market by internal expansion, or its equivalent, but for the acquisition of Airco. . . .

The Second Circuit approved the Commission's adoption of a "reasonable probability" test, but set aside the Commission order finding a violation because the Commission's reference to "eventual entry" makes the overall FTC test one based largely on "ephemeral possibilities." At oral argument, Commission counsel had conceded that the "eventually" standard contained no time estimate or time limitation whatsoever, but rather involved "long-range considerations" that might take decades to come to pass. The Court of Appeals reacted as follows:

> We hold that such uncabined speculation cannot be the basis of a finding that Section 7 has been violated. . . . While it is not clear—and we need not decide—whether the probable entry of the acquiring firm must be "imminent" in an actual potential entrant situation, it seems necessary under Section 7 that the finding of probable entry at least contain some reasonable temporal estimate relating to the near future, with "near" defined in

terms of the entry barriers and lead time necessary for entry in the particular industry, and that the finding be supported by substantial evidence in the record.

We emphasize that we are not requiring any exact, precisely calibrated assessment of time of entry. . . . But here there was no finding regarding a reasonable probability of entry in the near future, nor is there any evidence in the record on which such a finding might be based.

The Court of Appeals declined to pass upon, and like the Supreme Court decided to "leave for another day," the issue of the basic validity of the "actual potential entrant" doctrine.

––––––

FTC v. Consolidated Foods Corp., 380 U.S. 592, 85 S.Ct. 1220, 14 L.Ed.2d 95 (1965), raises in the merger context "reciprocity" issues examined in Chapter 8. Consolidated Foods Corporation owned "food processing plants and a network of wholesale and retail food stores." In 1951 it acquired Gentry, Inc., a manufacturer of dehydrated onion and garlic. The FTC found this to be a violation of Section 7 because it gave Consolidated the opportunity for reciprocal dealing as well as "the power to foreclose competition from a substantial share of the markets for dehydrated onion and garlic." The Court of Appeals for the Seventh Circuit set aside the Commission's order of divestiture, relying on post-acquisition experience to conclude that the Commission had failed to prove a probability that the acquisition would substantially lessen competition. Consolidated Foods Corp. v. FTC, 329 F.2d 623 (7th Cir.1964). The Supreme Court reversed in an opinion written by Justice Douglas.

As a wholesaler and retailer Consolidated purchased goods from food processors. As a manufacturer, Gentry sold its products to many of these same food processors and could potentially sell to still more. There was evidence presented that the food processors who sold to Consolidated "would give their onion and garlic business to Gentry for reciprocity reasons if it could meet the price and quality of its competitors' products."

The dehydrated onion and garlic industry was highly concentrated at the time of the merger, with Gentry and Basic, its principal competitor, accounting for about 90% of sales. The Commission found:

If it is desirable to prevent a trend toward oligopoly it is a fortiori desirable to remove, so far as possible, obstacles to the creation of genuinely competitive conditions in an oligopolistic industry. Respondent's reciprocal buying power, obtained through acquisition of Gentry, is just such an anticompetitive obstacle. 380 U.S. at 597.

The Supreme Court accepted the Commission's findings. It disagreed with the analysis made by the Court of Appeals of post-acquisition evidence. Justice Douglas found that "the post-acquisition evidence ... tended to confirm rather than cast doubt upon, the probable anticompetitive effect which the Commission found the merger would have." He concluded:

We do not go so far as to say that any acquisition, no matter how small, violates § 7 if there is a probability of reciprocal buying. Some situations may amount only to de minimis. But where, as here, the acquisition is of a company that commands a substantial share of a market, a finding of probability of reciprocal buying by the Commission, whose expertise the Congress trusts, should be honored, if there is substantial evidence to support it. 380 U.S. at 600.[25]

In considering the implications of this decision, note the following questions:

1. If Consolidated Foods did attempt to pressure food processors into buying from Gentry, and those processors found it disadvantageous to purchase from Gentry (because Gentry could not compete as to price, quality, or service), why would not the processors simply shift their purchases to Basic or some other supplier and shift their sales to a competitor of Consolidated Foods?

2. Is it likely that Consolidated Foods, owner of a network of wholesale and retail food outlets, would be willing to forego handling a brand with established consumer acceptance solely because the seller of that brand would not purchase from Gentry? At a minimum, would not Consolidated Foods have to balance the loss of profit resulting from discontinuance of the national brand against possible profits that might be earned by Gentry if it succeeded in selling to the coerced food processor? Would food processors realize this and therefore assume they could buy or refrain from buying from Gentry without any threat to continued sales relations with Consolidated Foods?

NOTE ANALYZING ENFORCEMENT AGAINST CONGLOMERATE MERGERS SINCE *PROCTER & GAMBLE* AND THE ECONOMIC IMPACT OF A VERY PERMISSIVE PERIOD

The United States witnessed a great surge of conglomerate merger activity from 1965 through 1968.[26] Although during this period the Supreme Court and FTC decided a number of cases in which conglomerate mergers were declared illegal under Section 7 (*see Consolidated Foods*, p. 1113 *supra*), the conglomerate merger movement continued to accelerate.

In the late 1970s, a new and even more dramatic conglomerate merger wave took shape. This time, as opposed to the 1960s where most significant acquisitions were by "glamour" firms using highly leveraged stock, the acquiring firms included the nation's largest and most established corporations (*e.g.*, American Express, Exxon, GE, Grace, Kraft, Mobil, RCA, R.J. Reynolds, and United Technologies). A prominent characteristic of the new conglomerate merger wave was the increase in very large acquisitions. For example, the number of acquisitions valued at $100 million or more rose from forty-one in 1977, to eighty in 1978, to eighty-three in 1979, and to ninety-four in 1980.[27]

This conglomerate merger activity may have been stimulated, in part, by the permissive approach taken to conglomerate acquisitions (*i.e.*, certainly as compared to the relatively strict approach taken to horizontal mergers) in the courts. To

---

25. Ed. After *Consolidated Foods,* the courts struggled with reciprocity problems in several merger cases, including Allis–Chalmers Manufacturing Co. v. White Consolidated Industries Inc., 414 F.2d 506 (3d Cir.1969), cert. denied, 396 U.S. 1009 (1970); United States v. International Telephone & Telegraph Corp., 306 F.Supp. 766 (D.Conn.1969), appeal dismissed, 404 U.S. 801 (1971); United States v. Northwest Industries, Inc., 301 F.Supp. 1066 (N.D.Ill. 1969). Since 1970, there have been no federal challenges based on a reciprocity theory.

26. FTC Bureau of Economics, Current Trends in Merger Activity, 1971, Table 6 (1972).

27. *See* Davidson, Looking at the Strategic Impacts of Mergers, 2 J. of Business Strategy 13, 18 (1981).

paraphrase Justice Stewart's dissent in the *Von's Grocery* case, the only consistency in conglomerate merger litigation since the late 1960s has been that the government almost never wins. The *Falstaff* case, p. 1110 *supra*, stands for this proposition and a number of lower court decisions may also be cited.[28]

Two Court of Appeals cases,[29] offer evidence that the government must travel a very rough road in potential competition cases in the courts. In the *Yamaha Motor* case, Brunswick, a diversified manufacturer, was the second largest seller of outboard motors in the United States and had somewhere between 19.8% and 26% of a highly concentrated market. Brunswick entered into a joint venture with Yamaha, a Japanese corporation which manufactured outboard motors but did not sell them in the United States, to produce outboard motors. The Eighth Circuit, after evaluating both objective and subjective evidence, affirmed the FTC's finding of a violation of Section 7 and reasoned:

> The Commission's first ground [for finding a Section 7 violation] involves application of a theory known as the "actual potential entrant doctrine." In essence the doctrine, under the circumstances of this case, would bar under § 7 acquisitions by a large firm in an oligopolistic market, if the acquisition eliminated the acquired firm as a potential competitor, and if the acquired firm would otherwise have been expected to enter the relevant market de novo. To put the question in terms applicable to the present case, would Yamaha, absent the joint venture, probably have entered the U.S. outboard-motor market independently, and would this new entry probably have increased competition more than the joint venture did? We stress the word "probably" in this formulation of the issue, because the question under Section 7 is not whether competition was actually lessened, but whether it "may be" lessened substantially. The question arises here, of course, not in the perhaps more common context of an outright acquisition of a competitor that might otherwise have entered, but in the form of acquisition of stock in a jointly owned company, an acquisition that necessarily foreclosed (for the duration of the joint venture) the independent entry of Yamaha, the other joint venturer.

> Although the Supreme Court has yet to rule specifically on the validity of the actual-potential-entrant doctrine, it has delineated two pre-conditions that must be present, prior to any resolution of the issue. First, it must be shown that the alleged potential entrant had "available feasible means" for entering the relevant market, and second, "that those means offer[ed] a substantial likelihood of ultimately producing deconcentration of that market or other significant procompetitive effects." *United States v. Marine Bancorporation*, *supra*, 418 U.S. at 633. On this basis the Commission's decision is amply supported by the evidence.[30]

In the *Tenneco* case, the Second Circuit held the FTC to a very high standard of proof of potential entry. In a 2–1 decision, the Court placed heavy emphasis on a lack of evidence of Tenneco's subjective intent to enter the market, in the near

28. *See, e.g.*, Tenneco, Inc. v. FTC, 689 F.2d 346 (2d Cir.1982), United States v. Siemens Corp., 621 F.2d 499 (2d Cir.1980); BOC Int'l Ltd. v. FTC, *supra*; FTC v. Atlantic Richfield Co., 549 F.2d 289 (4th Cir.1977). *But see* Yamaha Motor Co. v. FTC, 657 F.2d 971 (8th Cir.1981).

29. Yamaha Motor Co. v. FTC, 657 F.2d 971 (8th Cir.1981), cert. denied, 456 U.S. 915 (1982), and Tenneco, Inc. v. FTC, 689 F.2d 346 (2d Cir.1982).

30. 657 F.2d at 977–78.

future, either de novo or through a toehold acquisition; the Court set aside the FTC's order reasoning as follows:

> Even though the market was oligopolistic] we reject the Commission's finding that Tenneco was an actual potential entrant likely to increase competition in the market for replacement shock absorbers....
>
> The record contains abundant evidence that Tenneco had both the interest and the incentive to enter the market for replacement shock absorbers.... In addition, uncontradicted evidence revealed that Tenneco had negotiated with major European shock absorber manufacturers regarding possible acquisitions or license arrangements and had actually acquired a small manufacturing company that held a patent on a new shock absorber design. The record strongly supports the conclusion that Tenneco was actively considering entry into the market and was pursuing all leads to that end at least since the late 1960s or early 1970s. Moreover, Tenneco clearly possessed adequate financial resources to make the large initial investment needed to attempt to penetrate the market. The record, however, is deficient in evidence that there were viable toehold options available to Tenneco or that Tenneco would have entered the market *de novo*.
>
> The Commission conceded in its opinion that Tenneco never expressed any interest in entering the market for replacement shock absorbers "on a completely *de novo* basis." However, the Commission found that Tenneco had expressed interest in entering the market essentially *de novo*, building the required production facilities from scratch and acquiring the necessary technology via a license from an established foreign shock absorber producer. The Commission concluded that Tenneco would likely have done so absent its acquisition of Monroe.
>
> The Commission's reasoning is flawed. It ignores Tenneco's decision not to enter the market during the 1960s and early 1970s, a period of high profitability for shock absorber manufacturers, because of anticipated inadequate earnings during early years. The record is devoid of evidentiary support for the Commission's assertion that in the period relevant to this case, when industry earnings were in decline, Tenneco would have been willing to suffer the "cost disadvantage" inherent in the building of an efficient scale plant that would remain underutilized "for a number of years." The Commission's conclusion that Tenneco would have entered the market *de novo* with the aid of a license absent its acquisition of Monroe is based on the kind of unsupported speculation that the Supreme Court condemned when it warned that we should "remember that § 7 deals in 'probabilities,' not 'ephemeral possibilities.' " *Marine Bancorporation*....
>
> The Commission's conclusion that Tenneco would likely have entered the replacement shock absorber market through toehold acquisition is similarly flawed....
>
> We also conclude that the record contains inadequate evidence to support the Commission's conclusion that Tenneco's acquisition of Monroe violated section 7 by eliminating Tenneco as a perceived potential competitor in the market for replacement shock absorbers.[31]

---

31. 689 F.2d at 353–55.

Judge Mansfield dissented and noted that the majority opinion "flies in the face of the record" and "violates well-established rules" of judicial review of administrative proceedings.

Partly because of generally relaxed attitudes towards antitrust enforcement in the 1980s, but also because of widespread doubts about the validity of theories used earlier to attack conglomerate mergers, there was virtually no conglomerate merger enforcement in the 1980s and little in the 1990s. In the few cases in which government challenges were mounted, the parties either settled with the government or abandoned the transaction. The only conglomerate merger case brought in court during the period of the Clinton Administration was an FTC challenge to an acquisition in the natural gas pipeline industry, *FTC v. Questar*, file no. 961 001 (D.Utah 1995). After suit was filed, the parties abandoned the transaction.

There has been no enforcement against conglomerate mergers at the federal level since 1995. Note also that in the 1984 Department of Justice merger guidelines, the controversial theories underlying decisions like *Procter & Gamble* and *Consolidated Foods* were simply ignored, and the only theories supporting challenge to conglomerate mergers were based on elimination of perceived or actual potential competition.

The 1980s and particularly the 1990s were periods of manic merger and acquisition activity. In 1980, as noted earlier, the total reported value of U.S. corporate acquisitions and takeovers was $33 billion; by 1986 that figure had risen to $190 billion. ATRR No. 1305, p. 451 (1987). The level of merger activity was still modest when compared to the merger wave that swamped the country in the 1990s. Much of that merger activity was conglomerate. Although precise data for measurement are not yet available, it appears that the impact of the merger wave on the conglomerate area has been mixed.

Some huge conglomerate mergers, with significant potential competition attributes (*e.g.*, GE and RCA, BellAtlantic–Nynex), were consummated, but many of the acquisitions have, in fact, been correcting the excesses of the 1960s and 1970s. The so-called "bust up" takeover (or corporate restructuring done under takeover threat) often has reflected a widely shared view in the 1980s and 1990s that the conglomerate merger waves of the 1960s and 1970s had, on balance, efficiency-reducing effects. After the most comprehensive study to date, Professors Ravenscraft and Scherer[32] reached the following conclusions:

> . . . How successful have manufacturing mergers of the 1960s and early 1970s been? Did they serve the economy well by increasing the efficiency of resource allocation and utilization? . . .

> One important insight is that corporate acquirers of the 1960s and 1970s began by selecting good material. They sought promising, well-managed acquisition targets, and on average, they succeeded in finding them. The typical acquired company reported operating returns on assets well above the norms for all manufacturing industry in the last year before surrendering its independence. The typical acquiree was also small, and the target selection process had a size bias: the smaller the target, the more its profitability tended to surpass peer industry norms. Yet even the larger acquired firms had good records. . . .

> After merger, the acquired entities sooner or later divided into two groups—the sell-offs and the survivors. . . .

---

32. Ravenscraft & Scherer, Mergers, Sell–Offs and Economic Efficiency 192–227 (1987).

[R]oughly a third of all acquisitions were eventually divested, with an average lag of nearly ten years.

For the divested entities, the story from an efficiency perspective is overwhelmingly one of failure. Operating income fell, turning negative on average in the year preceding divestiture. The reasons for this decline are not rooted simply in industry-specific problems.... Our case studies illuminate the reasons. The targets were often acquired at or near a profit peak, and some subsequent disappointment was virtually inevitable. Bad luck struck frequently. But the fault was not only in the stars. The acquired entities often coped poorly with adversity because the new and more complex organizational structures imposed upon them slowed corrective responses and sapped motivation. Crises aggravated the organizational mismatch between parent and subsidiary and impaired constructive problem-solving. [T]he evidence points strongly toward a conclusion that the loss of control was worse under merger than it would have been in the simpler organizational structure of an independent entity. And in a smaller set of cases, organizational complexity and incentive breakdowns actively precipitated new problems, rather than merely impeding the solution of exogenously generated problems.

For the more numerous acquisitions that were survivors, the evidence on efficiency effects ... suggests a post-merger profitability decline of roughly one-half percentage point per year.... Although some of the decline is attributable to the unsustainably high level of pre-merger profits, an appreciable fraction appears to be a scaled-down manifestation of the control loss problems that led to sell-off in more extreme cases. Not surprisingly, the problems were most serious following pure conglomerate acquisitions, in which the parent's managerial experience was least well-suited to crisis problem-solving. Even for the "related business" and horizontal acquisitions, however, post-acquisition profitability was depressed relative to the levels identified in our pre-merger analysis ...

There are surely more opinions on why mergers are made than there are economists who have written on the subject. This may be inevitable, since merger motives are complex, and multiple motives may be at work in any given decision. Despite the difficulties, it is useful to see what light our research sheds on the question. Among other things, we must attempt to explain what motives led companies to make so many acquisitions that on average yielded such modest returns.

There are many broad (but not necessarily mutually exclusive) theories of merger motivation. The efficiency theory says that mergers occur because they improve the combined firms' operations—for example, by letting superior managers assume control, by exploiting cost-reducing "synergies" or complementarities in the partners' operations, or by taking fuller advantage of scale economies and risk-spreading opportunities, among other things in securing capital. The monopoly theory stresses the price-raising opportunities arising from consolidated market control, especially following horizontal mergers, or the possibility of buying inputs more cheaply owing to enhanced monopsony power. Undervalued-assets and bargain theories point to the opportunity for perceived mutual gain when a potential acquirer values a company's anticipated earnings stream more highly than current shareholders do. Empire-building theories propose that managers make acquisitions because they seek the power, prestige, and perquisites of controlling a large organization, even if shareholders' wealth is reduced in the process. Mergers can also be effected to secure tax advantages or to avoid investment strategy constraints imposed by the tax laws. And to round out what must necessarily be an incomplete list, we include the speculative or "bubble" theories, which imply that firms can persuade investors to support intensive merger activity through accounting manipulations, clever public relations, and the like.

None of these theories can be rejected flatly on the basis of our evidence. The most we can do is suggest degrees of plausibility and importance.... Our finding that, on average, profitability declined and efficiency losses resulted from mergers of the 1960s and early 1970s casts doubt on the widespread applicability of an efficiency theory of merger motives....

Pure conglomerate acquisitions were the least successful members of our sample, in terms of both subsequent sell-off rates and the profitability of the survivors. The movement away from such acquisitions is, as indicated already, a good sign. Our sample included 96 tender offer acquisitions or their "white knight" alternatives, so unless managers have become considerably more adept at making hostile unions turn out favorably, our findings continue to have relevance....

Our historical research suggests a skeptical public policy stance toward mergers. This is not to say that all mergers are bad, which is most assuredly not true. Some mergers are clearly efficiency-increasing.

If the conclusions of Professors Ravenscraft and Scherer are assumed to be correct, what impact, if any, should they have on the judicial treatment of conglomerate mergers? Should courts, for example, be more cautious and less permissive when considering a potential competition case? If you assume that the odds were less than even that the merger would be efficiency enhancing, which way would you vote in the *Falstaff*, *BOC International*, and *Tenneco* cases?

Department of Justice Merger Guidelines, 1984[33]

4. HORIZONTAL EFFECT FROM NON–HORIZONTAL MERGERS

4.0 By definition, non-horizontal mergers involve firms that do not operate in the same market. It necessarily follows that such mergers produce no immediate change in the level of concentration in any relevant market as defined in Section 2 of these Guidelines. Although non-horizontal mergers are less likely than horizontal mergers to create competitive problems, they are not invariably innocuous. This section describes the principal theories under which the Department is likely to challenge non-horizontal mergers.

4.1 Elimination of Specific Potential Entrants

4.11 The Theory of Potential Competition

---

33. *See* pp. 976 *supra*. As noted earlier, these Guidelines were not modified in 1992, when new horizontal merger guidelines were published, nor in 1997 when the horizontal merger guidelines were revised.

In some circumstances, the non-horizontal merger[34] of a firm already in a market (the "acquired firm") with a potential entrant to that market (the "acquiring firm")[35] may adversely affect competition in the market. If the merger effectively removes the acquiring firm from the edge of the market, it could have either of the following effects:

4.111   Harm to "Perceived Potential Competition"

By eliminating a significant present competitive threat that constrains the behavior of the firms already in the market, the merger could result in an immediate deterioration in market performance. The economic theory of limit pricing suggests that monopolists and groups of colluding firms may find it profitable to restrain their pricing in order to deter new entry that is likely to push prices even lower by adding capacity to the market. If the acquiring firm had unique advantages in entering the market, the firms in the market might be able to set a new and higher price after the threat of entry by the acquiring firm was eliminated by the merger.

4.112   Harm to "Actual Potential Competition"

By eliminating the possibility of entry by the acquiring firm in a more procompetitive manner, the merger could result in a lost opportunity for improvement in market performance resulting from the addition of a significant competitor. The more procompetitive alternatives include both new entry and entry through a "toehold" acquisition of a present small competitor.

4.12   Relation Between Perceived and Actual Competition

If it were always profit-maximizing for incumbent firms to set price in such a way that all entry was deterred and if information and coordination were sufficient to implement this strategy, harm to perceived potential competition would be the only competitive problem to address. In practice, however, actual potential competition has independent importance. Firms already in the market may not find it optimal to set price low enough to deter all entry; moreover, those firms may misjudge the entry advantages of a particular firm and, therefore, the price necessary to deter its entry.[36]

4.13   Enforcement Standards

Because of the close relationship between perceived potential competition and actual potential competition, the Department will evaluate mergers that raise either type of potential competition concern under a single structural analysis analogous to that applied to horizontal mergers. The Department first will consider a set of objective factors designed to identify cases in which harmful effects are plausible. In such cases, the Department then will conduct a more focused inquiry to determine whether the likeli-

34. Under traditional usage, such a merger could be characterized as either "vertical" or "conglomerate," but the label adds nothing to the analysis.

35. The terms "acquired" and "acquiring" refer to the relationship of the firms to the market of interest, not to the way the particular transaction is formally structured.

36. When collusion is only tacit, the problem of arriving at and enforcing the correct limit price is likely to be particularly difficult.

hood and magnitude of the possible harm justify a challenge to the merger. In this context, the Department will consider any specific evidence presented by the merging parties to show that the inferences of competitive harm drawn from the objective factors are unreliable.

The factors that the Department will consider are as follows:

4.131 Market Concentration

Barriers to entry are unlikely to affect market performance if the structure of the market is otherwise not conducive to monopolization or collusion. Adverse competitive effects are likely only if overall concentration, or the largest firm's market share, is high. The Department is unlikely to challenge a potential competition merger unless overall concentration of the acquired firm's market is above 1800 HHI (a somewhat lower concentration will suffice if one or more of the factors discussed in Section 3.4 indicate that effective collusion in the market is particularly likely). Other things being equal, the Department is increasingly likely to challenge a merger as this threshold is exceeded.

4.132 Conditions of Entry Generally

If entry to the market is generally easy, the fact that entry is marginally easier for one or more firms is unlikely to affect the behavior of the firms in the market. The Department is unlikely to challenge a potential competition merger when new entry into the acquired firm's market can be accomplished by firms without any specific entry advantages under the conditions stated in Section 3.3. Other things being equal, the Department is increasingly likely to challenge a merger as the difficulty of entry increases above that threshold.

4.133 The Acquiring Firm's Entry Advantage

If more than a few firms have the same or a comparable advantage in entering the acquired firm's market, the elimination of one firm is unlikely to have any adverse competitive effect. The other similarly situated firm(s) would continue to exert a present restraining influence, or, if entry would be profitable, would recognize the opportunity and enter. The Department is unlikely to challenge a potential competition merger if the entry advantage ascribed to the acquiring firm (or another advantage of comparable importance) is also possessed by three or more other firms. Other things being equal, the Department is increasingly likely to challenge a merger as the number of other similarly situated firms decreases below three and as the extent of the entry advantage over non-advantaged firms increases.

If the evidence of likely actual entry by the acquiring firm is particularly strong,[37] however, the Department may challenge a potential competition merger, notwithstanding the presence of three or more firms that are objectively similarly situated. In such cases, the Department will determine the likely scale of entry, using either the firm's own documents or the minimum efficient scale in the industry. The Department will then evalu-

---

37. For example, the firm already may have moved beyond the stage of consideration and have made significant investments demonstrating an actual decision to enter.

ate the merger much as it would a horizontal merger between a firm the size of the likely scale of entry and the acquired firm.

4.134 The Market Share of the Acquired Firm

Entry through the acquisition of a relatively small firm in the market may have a competitive effect comparable to new entry. Small firms frequently play peripheral roles in collusive interactions, and the particular advantages of the acquiring firm may convert a fringe firm into a significant factor in the market.[38] The Department is unlikely to challenge a potential competition merger when the acquired firm has a market share of five percent or less. Other things being equal, the Department is increasingly likely to challenge a merger as the market share of the acquired firm increases above that threshold. The Department is likely to challenge any merger satisfying the other conditions in which the acquired firm has a market share of 20 percent or more.

4.135 Efficiencies

As in the case of horizontal mergers, the Department will consider expected efficiencies in determining whether to challenge a potential competition merger. See Section 3.5 (Efficiencies).

PROBLEM 24

MERGER OF NATIONAL FOODS WITH PERFECT PAPER

National Foods, with annual sales of $3 billion, manufactures a wide variety of food products, and is the country's largest producer of packaged food. Competitive conditions in the various product markets in which National competes vary, but those markets generally exhibit a high degree of price rigidity and fairly high profit margins. National is one of the country's largest advertisers, with an annual advertising budget of $445 million. The company takes advantage of the maximum bulk rate discounts offered by the various media to large advertisers. This merger will constitute its second recent entry into a non-food market. The merger represents an early fruit of a diversification program under which National "is entering a number of new markets either through acquisitions or by de novo expansion."

Perfect Paper Products manufactures paper napkins and other household paper products, but does not produce containers. It also owns large tracts of timber in Canada, and mills and other facilities for the conversion of this timber into paper. It produces considerably more paper than it uses for the manufacture of paper products, and sells the rest to fabricators. Perfect is the second largest competitor in the household paper products market, which is dominated by four large producers having 80% of the market among them, but which also contains about ten smaller firms.

For the four large producers, the household paper products market is extremely profitable. The ten smaller firms are not, however, very profitable, and entry and exit for the smaller firms appears relatively easy; four smaller firms have entered and six have departed from the market in the past five years. No paper products

---

38. Although a similar effect is possible with the acquisition of larger firms, there is an increased danger that the acquiring firm will choose to acquiesce in monopolization or collusion because of the enhanced profits that would result from its own disappearance from the edge of the market.

company spends more than $30 million per year in advertising, with Perfect spending about $29 million.

The paper and cardboard container industry consists of five large, integrated firms, each owning its own timberland, paper mills, etc., and over thirty smaller, non-integrated firms. These latter firms must purchase their raw paper from other companies. The integrated and non-integrated firms each account for about 50% of the market.

National has never been a purchaser of paper napkins or other household paper products, but is a large purchaser of paper and cardboard containers, accounting for 6% of the industrial market. Presently, it buys half of its requirements from integrated and half from non-integrated companies.

The merger of National and Perfect will result in cost savings in the distribution and promotion of paper products of about 3%, about half of which will come from savings in advertising costs directly related to Perfect's newly created ability to take advantage of the bulk rate discounts presently allowed by the media to National.

Another cost saving will result from the fact that Perfect will be able to participate in the sponsorship of the "National Food Hour," a popular network television program. (It is generally considered that the sponsorship of a network program is a more efficient utilization of advertising dollars for those who are able to afford it than the purchase of "spot" time. Companies spending less than $34 million per year on advertising cannot generally become sponsors.) Other less important efficiency savings will arise in the warehousing and distribution of Perfect's products through National channels. In connection with the proposed merger, the president of Perfect publicly stated the following:

> We thought that any one of four other companies might enter the household paper products market, but we never thought National would want to come in. Nevertheless, National made a very tempting offer and we are all delighted with the serendipitous result.

Does this proposed merger violate Section 7?

COMPARATIVE NOTES ON CONGLOMERATE MERGERS, PORTFOLIO EFFECTS, AND OTHER DIFFERENCES BETWEEN US AND EC MERGER ENFORCEMENT

1. *Introduction to the theory of portfolio effects.* The term "portfolio effects" or "range effects" refers to the potential anticompetitive effects of conglomerate mergers between manufacturers of complementary products. In such mergers some have argued that there may be a potential threat that an already dominant firm may extend power from one product market to another complementary product market. This is, in part, explained by the tendency of purchasers to prefer buying a full line of complementary products from a single supplier, instead of purchasing each product separately from different suppliers who do not offer a full line of products. Therefore, if a company with market power acquires a fuller line, the idea is that the acquisition may enable the firm to foreclose market access to firms that do not offer a full line.

2. *Approach to portfolio theory in the United States.* As noted above, during the ten-year period from 1965 to 1975, the United States experienced a wave of conglomerate mergers. During this period, the courts and the antitrust agencies

experimented with a number of theories of competitive harm from conglomerate mergers, including the entrenchment theory, which bears some similarity to the "portfolio effects" or "range effects" theories. Under the entrenchment doctrine, as embodied in the *Procter & Gamble* case, mergers could be prohibited if they strengthened an already dominant firm through greater efficiencies or gave the acquired firm access to a broader line of products or greater financial resources, thereby as a practical matter foreclosing participation in the market by smaller rivals. Although the Supreme Court has never taken the occasion to revisit its *Procter & Gamble* entrenchment theory, the U.S. antitrust agencies eliminated entrenchment as a basis for challenging non-horizontal mergers in 1982 when the Department issued its new Merger Guidelines and the Federal Trade Commission issued its Statement on Horizontal Mergers. According to the approach used since 1982 by both federal authorities, a close scrutiny of conglomerate mergers on the basis of portfolio effects would place the interests of competitors ahead of those of consumers and would run the risk of blocking or deterring pro-competitive, efficiency-enhancing mergers. Because efficiencies are likely to benefit consumers, such mergers are actually to be encouraged, even if they may strengthen a particular firm at the expense of its competitors.

3. *European approach to portfolio theory.* Once again, the emphasis is different in Europe. There, at least until the middle of 2002, the Commission was willing to undertake much more severe scrutiny of conglomerate mergers. A series of recent decisions of the Court of First Instance, however, have rejected decisions of the Commission that were based on portfolio effects, and thus it is possible that an approach that gives greater weight to the positive effects of efficiencies and less to the harm to competitors—in short, a less interventionist approach—might be the future trend in Europe as well.

The term "portfolio effects" came into use in Europe in connection with the merger of the hard liquor subsidiaries of Guinness and Grand Metropolitan,[39] although the concept itself had been used in earlier cases, including in *de Havilland* and in *Boeing*.[40]

In *Guinness*, the Commission found that there were some product and geographic markets in Europe in which the merging firms had direct horizontal overlaps. In the Greek market, however, the problem was different. There was no competitive overlap, but the merged firm would have had the advantages of a full portfolio. The Commission accepted the merger, but set conditions to address both the problems of horizontal overlap and the portfolio problem. Among other things, the Commission ordered spin-offs of competing brands and termination of certain distribution agreements. The Commission justified the relief relating to the non-overlapping markets on the grounds that a wide portfolio of leading brands "confers considerable price flexibility and marketing opportunities" and gives the merged firm "the possibility of bundling sales or increasing the sales volume of one category by tying it to the sale of another category."

In the *Boeing/McDonnell–Douglas* merger, the Commission again predicted that there was a substantial chance that the merger would result in enhanced dominance by the merged firm: "Where a large fleet in service is combined with a

39. *See* Guinness/Grand Metropolitan, Commission Decision, Case IV/M. 938, O.J. L 288/24 (Oct. 27, 1998).

40. *See* Aerospatiale–Alenia/de Havilland, Commission Decision 91/619, O.J. L 334/42 (Dec. 5, 1991) and Boeing/McDonell Douglas, Commission Decision, Case IV/M877, O.J. L. 336/16 (Dec. 8, 1997).

broad product range, the existing fleet in service can be a key factor which may often determine decisions of airlines on fleet planning or acquisitions. Cost savings arising from commonality benefits, such as engineering, spares, inventory and flight crew qualifications, are very influential in an airline's decision-making process for aircraft type selections and may frequently lead to the acquisition of a certain type of aircraft even if the price of competing products is lower."

In addition, the Commission feared that the sheer size and scope of the merged firm would lead to a strengthening of Boeing's dominant position in commercial airframe manufacture: "The doubling of governmental-funded military R & D and the tripling of Boeing's general revenues generated in the defense and space sector will increase the scope of cross-subsidization of Boeing's sales in commercial aircraft in cases where Boeing wants to meet specific competition.... It is clear that, as already stated, the addition of products from McDonnell–Douglas (in particular the small-segment MD–95) and the large increase in its overall resources would enhance Boeing's opportunities to engage in such pricing practices, especially in view of its strong, and increasingly strengthening, cash-flow position as outlined above." The net result was that, as in *Guinness*, it cleared the merger (after substantial trans-Atlantic consultations), but only on certain conditions.

4. *General Electric/Honeywell, Commission Decision.*[41] The case that brought the most attention to portfolio effects, and that continues to cast a shadow, is the Commission's decision to block the merger of General Electric and Honeywell. The proposed takeover of Honeywell by the U.S. conglomerate General Electric became the focus for intensifying trade antagonisms between the European Union and the United States.

General Electric, one of the world's largest companies, is also the world's largest maker of jet engines. Honeywell manufactures products for the aerospace industry, in particular industrial automation and control systems, and it is also a supplier to the automotive sector. General Electric and Honeywell agreed to GE's planned takeover of Honeywell in October 2000; the acquisition would at the time have been the largest in industrial history, increasing GE's size by nearly a third. The U.S. Department of Justice Antitrust Division indicated that it would not seek to stop the GE/Honeywell deal in May 2001, on the minor condition that the merged group had to sell off a helicopter engine business. The European Commission, however, blocked the merger in July of the same year, on the stated ground that the integration of Honeywell's avionics and GE's strength in jet engines might lead to dominance of the market. The theory on which the Commission relied was fundamentally different from anything in the U.S. authorities' own merger guidelines. Moreover, this was the first time that a proposed merger between two U.S. companies was vetoed solely by European regulators. It is instructive to use the *GE/Honeywell* matter as a case study on portfolio effects, because the two antitrust agencies reached fundamentally different conclusions despite analyzing the identical product and geographic markets, considering the same theories of competitive harm, and largely having access to the same set of facts.

In adopting its decision, the Commission concluded that the merger would create or strengthen dominant positions on several markets and that the remedies proposed by GE were insufficient to resolve the competitive concerns. The Commission's investigation concluded that GE alone already had a dominant position in the markets for jet engines for large commercial and large regional aircraft. Its strong

41. *See* General Electric/Honeywell, Case COMP/M.2220, Commission Decision of July 3, 2001, app. to Court of First Instance pending.

market position combined with its financial strength and vertical integration into aircraft leasing was a key reason for the finding of GE's dominance in these markets. The investigation also showed that Honeywell was the leading supplier of avionics and non-avionics products, as well as of engines for corporate jets and of engine starters (which are a key input in the manufacturing of engines).

According to the Commission's findings, the combination of the two companies' activities would have resulted in the creation of dominant positions in the markets for the supply of avionics, non-avionics and corporate jet engines, as well as to the strengthening of GE's existing dominant positions in jet engines for large commercial and large regional jets. The dominance would have been strengthened as a result of horizontal overlaps in some markets as well as through the extension of GE's financial power and vertical integration to Honeywell's activities and of the combination of their respective complementary products. Such integration would enable the merged entity to leverage the respective market power of the two companies into the products of one another. This would have the effect of foreclosing competitors, thereby eliminating competition in these markets, ultimately affecting adversely product quality, service and increasing prices.

More specifically, the Commission's decision focused on the following anticompetitive effects: (i) that the merger would create opportunities for the merged firm to offer low-priced bundles of aircraft engines and systems to which narrow-line competitors would be unable to respond effectively; (ii) that GE would leverage its existing dominance in aircraft engines into avionics and non-avionics systems markets by, among other things, bringing its "enormous financial means" to bear; (iii) that GE's aircraft leasing arm (GECAS) would buy only (or at least would heavily favor) Honeywell products, which would lead airframe manufacturers to prefer Honeywell products in the hope that this would induce GE to buy their airframes, and thus would help create a dominant position for the merged firm in avionics and non-avionics systems markets in which Honeywell is currently active. The Commission concluded that as result of these actions, revenue streams for GE and Honeywell competitors in both engines and avionics/non-avionics systems markets would shrink, leading to a reduction in their future investment and their competitiveness.

Working with largely the same facts and analyzing identical problems, the Antitrust Division of the U.S. Department of Justice came to a different conclusion. First, in terms of GE's market power, it concluded that while GE currently enjoys a large market share, the market for large aircraft engines is a bid market with three strong competitors—GE, Rolls Royce, and Pratt & Whitney. In such a market, historic market shares are only weakly indicative of future success, as illustrated by the fact that recent contract awards have been quite evenly divided among the three firms, with GE winning 42%, Pratt & Whitney 32%, and Rolls Royce 27%. The Antitrust Division therefore saw no basis for finding that GE would be able to impose restrictions on its engines customers (for example, by tying Honeywell avionics to its engine sales) without disadvantaging itself in its battle against Pratt & Whitney and Rolls Royce to have its engines selected on future platforms.

The Antitrust Division was also unpersuaded that GE would be able to leverage its strong position in engines to gain a decisive competitive advantage in the markets for avionics and non-avionics systems through either mixed bundling or technological tying. The mixed bundling theory of competitive harm used the so-called "Cournot effect" to predict that the merged firm would lower the price of complementary goods because it would internalize the external effects of its prices on sales of the complementary goods it now controls. That is, the firm adjusts its pricing to reflect the fact that if it lowers the price of its product A, it will stimulate sales of product B, if B is a complement of A. The agency pointed out that this theory predicts that the merged firm's prices will go down post-merger, at least in the short run. Harm occurs only if competitors lose profits *and* are forced to withdraw from the market. Thus, while the benefits are certain and immediate, the predicted harm is much more distant and speculative.

The Antitrust Division also examined the claim that GE had used its aircraft leasing arm, GE Capital Aviation Services ("GECAS"), to gain an advantage in engine competitions and would be likely, post-merger, to use GECAS similarly to expand Honeywell's market share for avionics and non-avionics systems. The Antitrust Division concluded that GECAS's share of aircraft purchases—less than 10% of all planes worldwide—was too small to give rise to a significant foreclosure effect. To the extent GECAS was offering more attractive financing terms than its competitors, GE was simply discounting its engines.

In summary, the Antitrust Division found no factual support for any of the key elements of portfolio effects theory, even assuming that in principle the theory was a sound one. To the contrary, it concluded that to the extent those elements were based on the argument that the merged firm would have the ability and incentive to offer customers lower prices and better products, and that this meant that the merger would benefit customers both directly—through the lower prices and better products offered by the merged firm—and indirectly—by inducing rivals to respond with their own lower prices and product improvements. In other words, in the U.S. view, there were good reasons to welcome the merger, not to condemn it.

General Electric and Honeywell appealed to the Court of First Instance, but they were unsuccessful. See Honeywell v. Comm'n and General Electric v. Comm'n, Cases T–209/01 and T–210/01, decided Dec. 14, 2005. In its decision, the CFI ruled that the Commission had committed errors in its analysis of conglomerate effects, but that the fact that the proposed transaction would have either created or strengthened GE's dominant position in three markets (jet engines for large regional aircraft, engines for corporate jet aircraft, and small marine gas turbines) was enough to uphold the result. One might say that it was a Pyrrhic victory for GE and Honeywell insofar as they were arguing agains the conglomerate effects theory. The Court ruled that the Commission had failed to establish that the merged entity would have extended GE's economic power to Honeywell's avionics and non-avionics products, nor that competitive harm would result from bundling.

The CFI's ruling in *GE/Honeywell* was not as much of a surprise as it might have been before the following three decisions of the European courts were handed down. In light of all four cases, what future do you see for the theory of portfolio effects in Europe?

5. *Airtours v. Commission.* In June 2002, the European Court of First Instance reversed the Commission's decision to stop travel group AirTours from buying rival First Choice. According to the Commission decision, the merger would have created a collective dominant position, as a result of which effective competition would have been significantly impeded. The court held that the conditions for collective dominance have not been met.

The merger was between two of the four largest tour operators in the United Kingdom. The relevant market was the so-called "short-haul" package holidays from the UK; the market shares of the four largest tour operators were as follows: Thomson 27%, Airtours 21%, Thomas Cook 20% and First Choice 11%. All other operators had less than 5%. So far the Commission and the court agreed. The

Commission found that the merger would create a collective dominant position in which the three leading tour operators would restrict capacity, that is, would reduce the numbers of holidays they sold. This would lead to a tightening of the market with a corresponding increase in prices and profits.

Collective dominance, as we have noted earlier, arises where the structure of the market is such that the few players may tacitly adopt a common policy and can act independently of competitors, without having to enter into an agreement or resort to a concerted practice.[42] Characteristics of the market include, most importantly, market concentration, transparency and product homogeneity. Assuming that there is a market structure conducive to collective dominance, what other conditions need to be met before antitrust law enforcement can step in and prohibit a merger? The Commission and the court agreed that the three key elements of collective dominance are transparency, deterrence, and the reaction of customers and competitors. Transparency refers to the requirement that each member of the group in question must have a means of knowing whether the other operators are adopting the same strategy and whether they are maintaining it. The deterrence requirement requires the Commission to ensure that adequate measures are in place to ensure that each participant has a long-term incentive not to depart from the common policy. Third, the Commission must establish that the foreseeable reaction of current and potential competitors, as well as of consumers, would not jeopardize the results expected from the common policy.

The Commission had found that the market showed a high degree of transparency: (i) tour operators planned the next year's holidays by simply adjusting capacity by a fixed percentage from the year before, (ii) major tour operators used the same hotels, and (iii) capacity expansions could not be kept secret (because of the need to charter new planes). The court, in contrast, found that (i) capacity decisions were taken on a package-by-package basis; (ii) the major tour operators did not in general use the same hotels, and (iii) decisions about airline seats were taken after the capacity planning stage and so would not increase transparency. The court found that the Commission had wrongly concluded that the high degree of transparency made the market conducive to collective dominance.

As far as deterrence is concerned, although the court did not suggest that a specific punishment mechanism was required, it is clear from the judgment that the court will insist upon an effective deterrent. The court rejected the mechanisms proposed by the Commissions as insufficient. The mere threat of returning to a situation of oversupply was insufficient.

With respect to the third element of collective dominance, the court found that the Commission should also have established that the foreseeable reactions of current and future competitors and consumers would not jeopardize the results expected from the large tour operators' common policy. Although in this case all fringe competitors were small, the court held that this did not mean that they were powerless to affect competition. To the contrary, it found that small competitors could nevertheless counteract the creation of collective dominance. The court also found that foreign tour operators could enter the UK market if capacity was artificially reduced. The same point was made with respect to customers: although individual customers have no buying power, the question was whether customers would be able to react to the price increases caused by the oligopoly's restriction of capacity. The Commission, therefore, in the opinion of the court, had underestimat-

---

42. *See* Gencor Ltd. v. Commission, Case T–102/96, [1999] ECR II–753, p. 970, 988.

ed the reaction of competitors and consumers as a countervailing force capable of counteracting the effects of collective dominance.

Although the case involves a horizontal rather than a conglomerate merger and did not implicate the "portfolio effects" theory, it was a landmark in the development of the role of judicial review in EU merger control: *Airtours* is the first case in which the Court of First Instance overturned a Commission decision to block a major merger.

6.   *Schneider Electric SA v. Commission.* Within just a couple of months of the *Airtours* decision, the European Court of First Instance overturned yet another European Commission decision to block a merger. The court annulled the Commission's prohibition on essentially two grounds: (i) substantial errors in the economic analysis and (ii) failure to respect the rights of defense. The case, once again, confirms the increased importance of judicial review in the European Union.

In October 2001, the Commission prohibited a merger between Schneider Electric and Legrand, two French-based electrical equipment manufacturers, on the ground that it would considerably weaken competition on a large number of electrical equipment markets both at a wholesale and retail level.

The court's main criticism has been that after the Commission had cited the purely national dimensions of the various electrical product markets, it proceeded to take into account the European and global positions of the merging parties without demonstrating their relevance to competition at the national level. The court was of the view that this led the Commission to overestimate the power of the merged entity on each of the national markets. In addition, the court rejected the conclusion that the merged entity would have power because of portfolio effects, on grounds that the facts did not support such an assertion. Finally, the court found fault with the Commission's estimates of market shares of competitors (which had not included internal sales by certain suppliers to their specialized subsidiaries) and concluded that there were further mistakes arising out of its analysis of the figures and data on the Italian and Danish markets.

The court accepted that in relation to the various product markets in France where the two companies had considerable market shares, there was an elimination of competition. The court took the view, however, that the Commission violated the parties' rights of defense (essentially because the decision was based on reasoning not previously presented to the parties in the earlier statements of objections to the merger) and so, even with respect of the French markets, the decision could not be upheld.

Observers of the EU believe that the *Schneider/Legrand* decision supports renewed criticism of the Commission's performance in investigating mergers. At the same time, Commission officials have argued that the court's more active approach demonstrates that there is indeed an effective judicial review procedure attached to the EC's regulation of mergers. It is notable in that connection that Schneider successfully appealed to the court using the court's new "fast track procedure" that allows urgent cases to be dealt with on an accelerated basis. As a result, the Court of First Instance reached a judgment after only twelve months (as opposed to two or three years—*see Airtours*, for example). By way of comparison, this is roughly the same amount of time it would take for a U.S. trial court to pass on a government request to block a merger with a preliminary injunction.

7.   *Tetra Laval BV v. Commission.*[43] The *Schneider/Legrand* decision was followed by yet another defeat for the Commission in the Court of First Instance in

---

43.   Tetra Laval BV v. Commission, cases T–5/02 and T–80/02, Judgments of the Court of First Instance of 25 October 2002.

a merger case. *Tetra Laval* marks the third consecutive time in the year 2002 that the court reversed a Commission decision blocking a merger. In March 2001, Tetra Laval SA (part of the group including Tetra Pak, the world leader in liquid food carton packaging) made an unconditional bid (as required under French law) for Sidel SA (active in producing a particular form of plastic bottles ("PETs") and filling machines). Despite Tetra's offering two separate sets of undertakings to remedy competition problems, the Commission prohibited the transaction on 30 October 2001. The Commission based its prohibition on three kinds of anti-competitive effects: horizontal (overlaps in the relevant markets), vertical (the creation of a vertically integrated structure as a result of the merger) and conglomerate (the ability of the merged party to leverage its position into related markets, eliminate potential competition and strengthen its overall position).

Looking first at the horizontal overlaps, the court noted that in markets where the merged company would combine the businesses of both Tetra and Sidel, the resulting firm's market share would be between 0% and 20%. Following by then well-established caselaw, the court found that this would be extremely unlikely to indicate a dominant position. In one market the court pointed out that the Commission referred to Sidel's market share as between 60% and 70%, although this figure actually referred to the combined market shares of both Tetra and Sidel; moreover, the Commission failed to take account of the fact that Tetra undertook to divest itself of its business altogether, thereby eliminating any horizontal overlap. With respect to the alleged vertical issues, the court held that Tetra's undertakings would be sufficient to ensure that the market remained highly competitive.

The court accepted the Commission's view that conglomerate mergers could properly be prohibited under the merger regulation, but it made a number of critical observations. The court stated: "... the Commission's analysis of a merger producing a conglomerate effect is conditioned by requirements similar to those defined by the court with regard to the creation of a situation of collective dominance. Thus the Commission's analysis of a merger transaction which is expected to have an anti-competitive conglomerate effect calls for a particularly close examination of the circumstances which are relevant for an assessment of that effect on the conditions of competition in the reference market." On the facts, the court found that carton users would switch to PET products only in response to a price rise of 20% or more and that competition on the aseptic carton market was driven mainly by consumer-led innovation and not PET products. The court also held that the Commission had grossly overestimated future growth trends in the relevant markets and the potential convergence between aseptic cartons and PETs. Therefore, it concluded that, in relation to its competitors, Tetra's position on the aseptic carton market would not be strengthened by purchasing Sidel.

When one couples the results in these three cases to the one in *GE/Honeywell*, one thing is certain: the Court of First Instance has unequivocally signaled just how closely it will now scrutinize the Commission's rationale for its decision—both from the standpoint of economic analysis and from the standpoint of other factual support. Indeed, in the wake of these decisions, the Competition Directorate at the Commission added, effective September 1, 2003, a new high-level position of Chief Competition Economist. *See generally* Röller and Buigues, The Office of the Chief Competition Economist at the European Commission, at http://ec.europa.eu/dgs/competition/officechiefecon_ec.pdf.

From a theoretical standpoint, however, the court has not signaled a retreat from the more distinctly European theories. In *GE/Honeywell*, after all, it affirmed the result that the Commission had reached, if not one of the Commission's important theories. In *Tetra Pak,* it approved the application of the "associative links" theory to merger decisions, even though it held at the same time that the theory was not relevant to the case. "Associative links" first arose in a case against Tetra Pak for an abuse of a dominant position under Article 82 of the EC Treaty where it was held that its conduct (tying and predatory pricing) on the non-aseptic carton market (where Tetra was not dominant) constituted an abuse of its dominant position on the aseptic market since the two were closely associated and it was placed in a situation comparable to that of holding a dominant position on the markets in question as a whole.

In its analysis, the court distinguished between a situation where the conglomerate effect immediately changes the conditions of competition on the market to result in the creation or strengthening of a dominant position and that where such creation or strengthening will occur only after a certain time and as a result of the future conduct of the merged entity. The court held that in the second category the Commission may take account of incentives for the merged party to engage in future conduct which would, in itself, be anticompetitive (and separately prohibited by Articles 81 and/or 82 EC), but held that the Commission: "must also consider the extent to which those incentives would be reduced, or even eliminated owing to the illegality of the conduct in question, the likelihood of its detection, action taken by the competent authorities, both at Community and national level, and the financial penalties which could ensue." In the present case, the court held that because the MTF had not undertaken such assessment, it could only take into account future behavior, which "at least probably" did not constitute an abuse of Tetra's dominant position.

SECTION 4. INTEGRATION THROUGH VERTICAL MERGER

Robert H. Bork, The Antitrust Paradox: A Policy at War with Itself

225–233 (1978).

Vertical Mergers

Antitrust has been concerned about the effects of vertical mergers upon competition for over sixty years, but it has never evolved a satisfactory theory of the ways in which such integration could be harmful. The predominant fear has been that the acquisition of a customer or supplier would "foreclose" a market or source of supply to rivals and thereby fence out competition. That theory appeared in the 1911 *American Tobacco* decision, which supposed that the acquisition of suppliers was a means of gaining or maintaining monopoly in tobacco manufacture....

Antitrust's concern with vertical mergers is mistaken. Vertical mergers are means of creating efficiency, not of injuring competition. There is a faint theoretical case, hardly worth mentioning, that vertical mergers can be used by very large firms for purposes of predation under exceptional circumstances, but it is highly doubtful that that narrow possibility has any application to reality. In any event, the vertical mergers attacked by the law do not contain even that possibility. The vertical mergers the law currently outlaws have no effect other than the creation of efficiency.

It is conventional and useful to say, as Morris Adelman does, that vertical integration exists when a firm "transmits from one of its departments to another a good or service which could, without major adaptation, be sold in a market." This definition calls attention to the choice of the firm to bypass a market transaction in favor of internal control. But the definition may lead us to overlook the ubiquity of such integration in our economy. Often there is no outside market for a good or service transmitted within a firm precisely because the efficiencies of vertical integration are so great that no firm would think of selling or buying at that stage. Every firm in the economy is vertically integrated in the sense that goods and services are transmitted within it and not offered on any market. This fact is important because it shows the vertical integration is indispensable to the realization of productive efficiencies. One can imagine the chaos and costs that would arise if the law were logically to extend its aversion to vertical integration by requiring, for example, an open market transaction every time goods moved from one worker or department to another or, indeed, by forbidding individuals to perform more than one task in the productive chain before selling. This is entirely fanciful, of course, but it is worth stressing that all economic activity displays vertical integration, because that tends to remove some of the sinister coloration this essential form of integration has undeservedly acquired.

The word "integration" means only that administrative direction rather than a market transaction organizes the cooperation of two or more persons engaged in a productive or distributive activity. The firm chooses between modes of organization according to their relative costs. On this basis, it chooses to perform particular tasks itself, to subtract them to others, or to sell a finished or semifinished product to other firms which perform further functions in bringing a finished product to the final market. The firm itself is best defined for purposes of economic analysis as the area of operations within which administration, rather than market processes, coordinates work.

What antitrust law perceives as vertical merger, and therefore as a suspect and probably traumatic event, is merely an instance of replacing a market transaction with administrative direction because the latter is believed to be a more efficient method of coordination. Vertical mergers may cut sales and distribution costs, facilitate the flow of information between levels of the industry (for example, marketing possibilities may be transmitted more effectively from the retail to the manufacturing level, new product possibilities may be transmitted in the other direction, better inventory control may be attained, and better planning of production runs may be achieved), create economies of scale in management, and so on. When such possibilities become apparent throughout an industry, a trend toward vertical integration will develop, as it did in shoe manufacturing and retailing, and as it has done in many other industries. Such trends are merely the responses of businessmen to changing circumstances. They are essentially no different from, and certainly no more cause for alarm than, countless other trends in product styles, types of outlets, automation, prices, and the like. What is incipient in any such trend is not the lessening of competition but the attainment of new efficiency, and it is the latter result at which amended Section 7 of the Clayton Act is actually striking in vertical merger cases.

It is thoroughly naive of the law to suppose that vertical merger affects resource allocation adversely while vertical growth affects it not at all. The only difference between vertical merger and vertical growth is that in a specific situation at a particular moment one or the other will be the lower-cost way of achieving the efficiencies of integration. In fact, the sole difference between vertical merger and existing vertical integration within all firms is historical. In the latter case the efficiencies of integration have been present, recognized, and realized in firm structures for some time, while in the case of merger the efficiencies are either just becoming possible or are just being recognized, and firms are seeking to realize them through structural change.

Vertical integration is often believed somehow to cause or permit a firm to behave differently than it would in the absence of integration. Aside from the efficiency effect, however, it is clear that vertical integration does not affect the firm's pricing and output policies. If, for example, a firm operates at both the manufacturing and retailing levels of an industry, it maximizes overall profit by setting the output at each level as though the units were independent of one another. The firm will not, as is frequently suggested, sell to its own retail subsidiary for less than it sells to outsiders, unless the efficiencies of integration lower the cost of selling to its own retail unit.

The reasons for this are obvious. It is impossible for a firm actually to sell to itself for less than it sells to outside firms because the real cost of any transfer from the manufacturing unit to the retailing unit includes the return that could have been made on a sale to an outsider. No matter what the bookkeeper writes down as the transfer price, the real cost is always the opportunity foregone. (If a garment manufacturer spends $50 to make a dress, could sell it for $100, but chooses to give it to his wife, the cost to him is $100, not $50, and the fact cannot be altered by any number he chooses to put in his books.) Nor would there be any point in the firm's subsidizing its retail level by transfers at artificially low prices. Such a policy would merely entail the sacrifice of return at the manufacturing level, and the self-deception as to true costs would cause the retailing subsidiary to operate at an uneconomical rate. If the marginal costs of retailing are rising—as they certainly are, unless the retailer is a natural monopolist—the artificially low price would result in an increased output at higher costs. The integrated firm would be paying more for the performance of the retailing function than it would if it recognized real costs and operated at a smaller scale on the retail level.

These principles may usefully be applied to varying industry structures. Where the firm is competitive at both levels, it maximizes by equating marginal cost and price at each level, and each level makes a competitive rate of return. Should the firm enjoy a monopoly at the manufacturing level but face competition in retailing, it will of course exact a monopoly profit in manufacturing; but, for the reasons discussed, it will sell to the retail level at the same monopoly price it asks of independent retailers.

If the integrated firm has monopoly positions in both manufacturing and retailing, however, the levels will not maximize independently. This is true because vertically related monopolies can take only one monopoly profit. If each level tries to maximize by restricting output, the result will be a price higher than the monopoly price and an output smaller, the result being less than a full monopoly return. The reason for this is easily seen. Suppose the firm starts as a manufacturing monopoly selling to a competitive retail level. The manufacturer would set his output and price so that the appropriate monopoly price would be charged consumers after retailers had added their costs, including a competitive return. The monopolist must allow the retailers a competitive return, and he will not want to allow them more than that. If he allowed them less, the level of investment and operation in retailing would decline to the manufacturer's detriment. If he allowed them more, the level of investment and operation would rise above the optimal, and the manufacturer would be paying for retailing services he did not want.

We may suppose that the manufacturer purchases all of the retailers, converting that level of the industry to a second monopoly held by him. This will not change his price and output decisions at all. Though he now holds both manufacturing and retailing, the monopolist is still facing the same consumer demand and the same costs at both levels. The maximizing price to consumers, therefore, remains the same. The new retail subsidiary will not be permitted to act independently and restrict output further than the manufacturing level had already restricted it, since that would result in an output lower and a price higher than the maximizing level.

The case under discussion is, in any event, a very rare one: the acquisition by a monopolist of a second vertically-related monopoly. Much of the theoretical case against vertical integration begins by trying to establish some possibility of competitive hard from the joining of two vertically related monopolies, and then proceeds on the unstated assumption that a case has been made which is applicable to all vertical mergers. The point here is that no case has been made against the vertical acquisition by a monopolist of a second monopoly; moreover, even if such a case could be made, it would be largely an academic exercise and would have no force in the broader context of the vertical mergers the law is actually preventing.

The argument so far holds, of course, whether vertical integration is created by growth or merger. Vertical merger does not create or increase the firm's power to restrict output. The ability to restrict output depends upon the share of the market occupied by the firm. Horizontal mergers increase market share, but vertical mergers do not.

These observations indicate that vertical mergers are merely one means of creating a valuable form of integration and that there is no reason for the law to oppose such mergers. Adherence to an economic fallacy almost as old as antitrust policy, however, has caused the law to take an entirely different course.

"Foreclosure": The Law's Objection to Vertical Merger

The law developed under amended Section 7 of the Clayton Act assumes that vertical mergers may sometimes be beneficial or neutral but that their dominant effect is so heavily deleterious as to merit the prohibition of almost all such integrations. The law's current theory of the way in which vertical mergers injure competition is contained in the concept of "foreclosure." It is supposed that, for instance, a manufacturer may acquire a retailer, force the retail subsidiary to sell the manufacturer parent's products, and thus "foreclose" rival manufacturers from the market represented by the captive retailer. This thought to be a means by which the competitive process may be injured.

In analyzing the *Brown Shoe* case we have seen the extremes to which this theory can be carried, but once an erroneous idea is let loose in antitrust it tends to run riot. Even before *Brown Shoe* the Federal Trade Commission had ingeniously devised what was, apparently, a doctrine of reciprocal foreclosure. This theory, whose sole merit is that it establishes a new high in preposterousness, is illustrated by the Commission's refusal to permit the acquisition by A.G. Spalding & Bros. of another full-line sporting goods company, Rawling Manufacturing Co. The case was decided primarily as a horizontal merger, but the Commission objected to possible vertical foreclosure as well.

A fair sample of the *Spalding* opinion's foreclosure reasoning runs this way: before the merger Spalding did not manufacture baseball gloves but bought its requirements from others. Rawlings, on the other hand, made gloves and sold them to others. The merger might therefore wreak havoc on competition at both manufacturing and selling levels, for as the Commission saw it "by acquiring Rawlings, Spalding can not only prevent competitors from purchasing [baseball gloves] from Rawlings but can also foreclose manufacturers of [gloves] from access to Spalding as a purchaser thereof."

A two-edge sword indeed! The Commission's opinion does not inform us why the people who formerly made gloves for Spalding could not sell them to the people who formerly bought gloves from Rawlings. Instead, we are left to imagine eager suppliers and hungry customers, unable to find each other, forever foreclosed and left to languish. It would appear the Commission could have cured this aspect of the situation by throwing an industry social mixer.

M.H. Riordan & S.C. Salop, Evaluating Vertical Mergers: A Post–Chicago Approach

63 Antitrust L.J. 516–19 (1995).

THE POST–CHICAGO ANALYSIS OF VERTICAL MERGERS

The permissive policy toward vertical mergers, derived from the Chicago School, is premised on a simple economic model. In contrast, the post-

Chicago approach relies on more realistic and complex economic analysis that facilitates the identification of anticompetitive concerns that have less importance in the Chicago School approach.

A. The Chicago School Critique of 1960s Vertical Merger Law

The Chicago School critique . . . is based on two main tenets. First, the mere fact that a vertical merger forecloses rival firms' access to the supply of inputs produced by one input supplier does not mean that the net supply of inputs available to those rival firms has been reduced. When the rivals lose access to the input supplies produced by one firm, they are likely to gain access to the input suppliers that previously supplied the merging supplier's downstream merger partner. In that case, according to Chicago School theory, the vertical merger does not reduce the net supply available to rivals. Instead, it merely realigns purchase patterns among competing firms.[44]

Second, the Chicago School utilizes an oversimplified microeconomic model to conclude that vertical mergers carried out by a monopolist cannot enhance monopoly power. The idea is that there is only a "single monopoly profit" that can be earned by the monopolist, whether or not the monopolist is vertically integrated.[45] Instead of enhancing monopoly power, the only economic motive for vertical merger is to reduce costs by achieving synergies.

Post–Chicago industrial organization economics accepts, as a starting point, these criticisms of pre-Chicago foreclosure theory. However, it has extended the economic models to more realistic assumptions that reach a more refined understanding of foreclosure. The modern industrial organization literature has formulated models of vertical integration in which vertical mergers lead to real foreclosure in which the net supply of inputs available to rivals is decreased. Models have been formulated in which monopoly power may be created or enhanced—and monopoly profits thereby increased—by vertical mergers that have little or no efficiency benefits. In these post-Chicago models, some vertical mergers can be anticompetitive, although others are procompetitive.

Post–Chicago analysis also relaxes the restrictive assumptions upon which the single monopoly profit theory is based. In particular, the single monopoly profit theory relies on the following four assumptions:[46]

(1) there is a monopoly input supplier, whose monopoly is protected by prohibitive barriers to entry;

---

44. As Bork points out, the cure for such naive allegations of foreclosure could be "an industry social mixer" to facilitate the realignment, *see* p. 1135 *supra*.

45. Ed. The "single monopoly profit" theory traces most notably to the scholarship of Robert Bork: ". . . vertically related monopolies can take only one monopoly profit. . . ."

46. An analogous version would center the monopoly in the output market and perfect competition in the input market. Relaxing those assumptions alters the results analogously to the results discussed in the text below.

(2) the monopoly is unregulated;

(3) there is perfect competition in the downstream output market; and

(4) the technology for producing output involves usage of all inputs in fixed proportions.

In the absence of these four assumptions, the single monopoly profit result no longer holds. Instead, vertical mergers may be motivated by either monopoly power, economic efficiency concerns, or both.

When the input market is not a monopoly, the analysis of vertical mergers is altered. Vertical mergers in these circumstances can have anticompetitive or procompetitive effects through a number of mechanisms. A vertical merger can create barriers to entry or expansion by foreclosing or disadvantaging unintegrated rivals. A vertical merger also can facilitate tacit or express pricing coordination among the competing input suppliers. In either case, a vertical merger may lead to a reduction in net input supply to rivals, not just a supply realignment.

Further, even if there is an input monopolist but that monopolist's price is regulated, a vertical merger can be used to evade price control regulations. A vertical merger also can be used to facilitate price discrimination, where price discrimination by an unintegrated monopolist would be constrained by regulation or a competitive output market.

By contrast, when there is not perfect competition in the output market, a vertical merger has the potential to reduce costs and increase efficiency by eliminating a double monopoly markup on input costs. When the output technology is not in fixed proportions, a vertical merger also has the potential to reduce costs by eliminating distortions in efficient input usage that arise from noncompetitive input prices.

Although the original Chicago School commentators focused primarily on the efficiency benefits of vertical mergers, they did identify some competitive concerns. For example, they paid close attention to the potential for collusion and recognized evasion of regulation as a potential concern. Nevertheless, the original Chicago School approach placed little credence in the harm from foreclosure. This rejection of foreclosure as a competitive concern has two sources in addition to those identified earlier. First, the Chicago School approach is based on an assumption that barriers to entry generally are low. Second, the Chicago approach pre-dated the recent interest among economists in game theory and strategic behavior. Along with other advances in economic theory, the game theoretic analysis of strategic behavior forms the core of what has been termed the post-Chicago approach.[47] The strategic behavior models study the decisions of firms that take rivals' likely reactions to their conduct into account when making their decisions. These involve models of strategic oligopoly conduct

---

47. *See* Oliver Williamson, Antitrust Enforcement: Where It's Been, Where It's Going, 27 St. Louis U.L.J. 289 (1983); Herbert Hovenkamp, Antitrust Policy After Chicago, 84 Mich.L.Rev. 213, 274–80 (1985); Carl Shapiro, The Theory of Business Strategy, 20 Rand J.Econ. 125 (1989).

rather than the models of simple monopoly and perfect competition that form the foundations of the traditional Chicago School approach.[48]

These more realistic models of competitive behavior form the basis for a richer analysis of vertical mergers and their potential anticompetitive or procompetitive effects. In such a light, vertical mergers should be neither universally condemned nor universally applauded.

United States v. E.I. du Pont de Nemours & Co.

Supreme Court of the United States, 1957.
353 U.S. 586, 77 S.Ct. 872, 1 L.Ed.2d 1057.

■ BRENNAN, J. This is a direct appeal under § 2 of the Expediting Act from a judgment of the District Court for the Northern District of Illinois, dismissing the Government's action brought in 1949 under § 15 of the Clayton Act. The complaint alleged a violation of § 7 of the Act[49] resulting from the purchase by E.I. du Pont de Nemours and Company in 1917–1919 of a 23% stock interest in General Motors Corporation. This appeal is from the dismissal of the action as to du Pont, General Motors and the corporate holders of large amounts of du Pont stock, Christiana Securities Corporation and Delaware Realty & Investment Company.[50]

The primary issue is whether du Pont's commanding position as General Motors' supplier of automotive finishes and fabrics was achieved on competitive merit alone, or because its acquisition of the General Motors' stock, and the consequent close intercompany relationship, led to the insulation of most of the General Motors' market from free competition, with the resultant likelihood, at the time of suit, of the creation of a monopoly of a line of commerce. . . .

Section 7 is designed to arrest in its incipiency not only the substantial lessening of competition from the acquisition by one corporation of the whole or any part of the stock of a competing corporation, but also to arrest in their incipiency restraints or monopolies in a relevant market which, as a reasonable probability, appear at the time of suit likely to result from the acquisition by one corporation of all or any part of the stock of any other corporation. The section is violated whether or not actual restraints or monopolies, or the substantial lessening of competition, have occurred or

48. Chicago School economist George Stigler was a pioneer in the modern analysis of oligopoly theory. George J. Stigler, A Theory of Oligopoly, 72 J.Pol.Econ. 44 (1964). However, that work had little impact on the Chicago School approach to monopoly conduct or vertical relationships. Cf. Carl Shapiro & David J. Teece, Systems Competition and Aftermarkets: An Economic Analysis of Kodak, 39 Antitrust Bull. 135 (1994).

49. This action is governed by the Clayton Act as it was before the 1950 amendments, which by their terms are inapplicable to acquisitions prior to 1950. 64 Stat. 1125, 15 U.S.C. § 18, 15 U.S.C.A. § 18.

50. The amended complaint also alleged violation of §§ 1 and 2 of the Sherman Act, 26 Stat. 209, as amended, 50 Stat. 693, 15 U.S.C. §§ 1, 2. In view of our determination of the case, we are not deciding the Government's appeal from the dismissal of the action under the Sherman Act.

are intended. Acquisitions solely for investment are excepted, but only if, and so long as, the stock is not used by voting or otherwise to bring about, or in attempting to bring about, the substantial lessening of competition.

We are met at the threshold with the argument that § 7 before its amendment applied only to an acquisition of the stock of a competing corporation, and not to an acquisition by a supplier corporation of the stock of a customer corporation—in other words, that the statute applied only to horizontal and not to vertical acquisitions. . . .

We hold that any acquisition by one corporation of all or any part of the stock of another corporation, competitor or not, is within the reach of the section whenever the reasonable likelihood appears that the acquisition will result in a restraint of commerce or in the creation of a monopoly of any line of commerce. Thus, although du Pont and General Motors are not competitors, a violation of the section has occurred if, as a result of the acquisition, there was at the time of suit a reasonable likelihood of a monopoly of any line of commerce. . . .

Appellees argue that there exists no basis for a finding of a probable restraint or monopoly within the meaning of § 7 because the total General Motors market for finishes and fabrics constituted only a negligible percentage of the total market for these materials for all uses, including automotive uses. It is stated in the General Motors brief that in 1947 du Pont's finish sales to General Motors constituted 3.5% of all sales of finishes to industrial users, and that its fabrics sales to General Motors comprised 1.6% of the total market for the type of fabric used by the automobile industry.

Determination of the relevant market is a necessary predicate to a finding of a violation of the Clayton Act because the threatened monopoly must be one which will substantially lessen competition "within the area of effective competition."[51] Substantiality can be determined only in terms of the market affected. The record shows that automobile finishes and fabrics have sufficient peculiar characteristics and uses to constitute them products sufficiently distinct from all other finishes and fabrics to make them a "line of commerce" within the meaning of the Clayton Act. Cf. *Van Camp & Sons Co. v. American Can Co.*, 278 U.S. 245.[52] Thus, the bounds of the relevant market for the purposes of this case are not coextensive with the total market for finishes and fabrics, but are coextensive with the automobile industry, the relevant market for automotive finishes and fabrics.

The market affected must be substantial. *Standard Fashion Co. v. Magrane–Houston Co.*, 258 U.S. 346, 357. Moreover, in order to establish a

---

51. Standard Oil Co. of California v. United States, 337 U.S. 293, 299, note 5. Section 3 of the Act, with which the Court was concerned in *Standard Oil*, makes unlawful certain agreements ". . . where the effect . . . may be to substantially lessen competition or tend to create a monopoly *in any line of commerce*." 38 Stat. 731, 15 U.S.C. (1946 ed.) § 14, 15 U.S.C.A. § 14. (Emphasis added.)

52. "The phrase ['in any line of commerce'] is comprehensive and means that if the forbidden effect or tendency is produced in *one* out of *all* the various lines of commerce, the words 'in *any* line of commerce' literally are satisfied." 278 U.S. at 253.

violation of § 7 the Government must prove a likelihood that competition may be "foreclosed in a substantial share of ... [that market]."[53] Both requirements are satisfied in this case. The substantiality of a relevant market comprising the automobile industry is undisputed. The substantiality of General Motors' share of that market is fully established in the evidence.

General Motors is the colossus of the giant automobile industry. It accounts annually for upwards of two fifths of the total sales of automotive vehicles in the nation. In 1955 General Motors ranked first in sales and second in assets among all United States industrial corporations and became the first corporation to earn over a billion dollars in annual net income. In 1947 General Motors' total purchases of all products from du Pont were $26,628,274, of which $18,938,229 (71%) represented purchases from du Pont's Finishes Division. Of the latter amount purchases of "Duco"[54] and the thinner used to apply "Duco" totaled $12,224,798 (65%), and "Dulux"[55] purchases totaled $3,179,225. Purchases by General Motors of du Pont fabrics in 1948 amounted to $3,700,000, making it the largest account of du Pont's Fabrics Division. Expressed in percentages, du Pont supplied 67% of General Motors' requirements for finishes in 1946 and 68% in 1947. In fabrics du Pont supplied 52.3% of requirements in 1946, and 38.5% in 1947. Because General Motors accounts for almost one-half of the automobile industry's annual sales, its requirements for automotive finishes and fabrics must represent approximately one-half of the relevant market for these materials. Because the record clearly shows that quantitatively and percentagewise du Pont supplies the largest part of General Motors' requirements, we must conclude that du Pont has a substantial share of the relevant market.

The appellees argue that the Government could not maintain this action in 1949 because § 7 is applicable only to the acquisition of stock and not to the holding or subsequent use of the stock. This argument misconceives the objective toward which § 7 is directed. The Clayton Act was intended to supplement the Sherman Act. Its aim was primarily to arrest apprehended consequences of inter-corporate relationships before those relationships could work their evil, which may be at or any time after the acquisition, depending upon the circumstances of the particular case. The Senate declared the objective of the Clayton Act to be as follows:

> ... Broadly stated, the bill, in its treatment of unlawful restraints and monopolies, seeks to prohibit and make unlawful certain trade practices which, as a rule, singly and in themselves, are not covered by the Act of July 2, 1890 [the Sherman Act], or other existing antitrust acts, and thus, by making these practices illegal, to arrest the creation of trusts, conspiracies, and monopo-

---

53. Standard Oil Co. of California v. United States, 337 U.S. 293, at 314.

54. A finish developed specially by du Pont and General Motors for use as an automotive finish.

55. A synthetic enamel developed by du Pont which is used on refrigerators, also manufactured by General Motors.

lies *in their incipiency and before consummatio....* S.Rep. No.
698, 63d Cong., 2d Sess. 1. (Emphasis added.)

"Incipiency" in this context denotes not the time the stock was
acquired, but any time when the acquisition threatens to ripen into a
prohibited effect. See *Transamerica Corp. v. Board of Governors*, 3 Cir., 206
F.2d 163, 166. To accomplish the congressional aim, the Government may
proceed at any time that an acquisition may be said with reasonable
probability to contain a threat that it may lead to a restraint of commerce
or tend to create a monopoly of a line of commerce. Even when the
purchase is solely for investment, the plain language of § 7 contemplates
an action at any time the stock is used to bring about or in attempting to
bring about the substantial lessening of competition....

Related to this argument is the District Court's conclusion that 30
years of nonrestraint negated "any reasonable probability of such a restraint" at the time of the suit. While it is, of course, true that proof of a
mere possibility of a prohibited restraint or tendency to monopoly will not
establish the statutory requirement that the effect of an acquisition "may
be" such restraint or tendency, the basic facts found by the District Court
demonstrate the error of its conclusion.[56]

The du Pont Company's commanding position as a General Motors
supplier was not achieved until shortly after its purchase of a sizeable block
of General Motors stock in 1917. At that time its production for the
automobile industry and its sales to General Motors were relatively insignificant. General Motors then produced only about 11% of the total
automobile production and its requirements, while relatively substantial,
were far short of the proportions they assumed as it forged ahead to its
present place in the industry....

This background of the acquisition, particularly the plain implications
of the contemporaneous documents, destroys any basis for a conclusion
that the purchase was made "solely for investment." Moreover, immediately after the acquisition, du Pont's influence growing out of it was brought
to bear within General Motors to achieve primacy for du Pont as General
Motors' supplier of automotive fabrics and finishes....

The fact that sticks out in this voluminous record is that the bulk of du
Pont's production has always supplied the largest part of the requirements
of the one customer in the automobile industry connected to du Pont by a
stock interest. The inference is overwhelming that du Pont's commanding
position was promoted by its stock interest and was not gained solely on
competitive merit.

We agree with the trial court that considerations of price, quality and
service were not overlooked by either du Pont or General Motors. Pride in
its product and its high financial stake in General Motors' success would
naturally lead du Pont to try to supply the best. But the wisdom of this

---

56. There is no significant dispute as to the basic facts pertinent to the decision. We are
thus not confronted here with the provision of Fed.Rules Civ.Proc. 52(a), 28 U.S.C.A., that
findings of fact shall not be set aside unless clearly erroneous.

business judgment cannot obscure the fact, plainly revealed by the record, that du Pont purposely employed its stock to pry open the General Motors market to entrench itself as the primary supplier of General Motors' requirements for automotive finishes and fabrics.

Similarly, the fact that all concerned in high executive posts in both companies acted honorably and fairly, each in the honest conviction that his actions were in the best interests of his own company and without any design to overreach anyone, including du Pont's competitors, does not defeat the Government's right to relief. It is not requisite to the proof of a violation of § 7 to show that restraint or monopoly was intended.

The statutory policy of fostering free competition is obviously furthered when no supplier has an advantage over his competitors from an acquisition of his customer's stock likely to have the effects condemned by the statute. We repeat, that the test of a violation of § 7 is whether at the time of suit there is a reasonable probability that the acquisition is likely to result in the condemned restraints. The conclusion upon this record is inescapable that such likelihood was proved as to this acquisition. The fire that was kindled in 1917 continues to smolder. It burned briskly to forge the ties that bind the General Motors market to du Pont, and if it has quieted down, it remains hot, and, from past performance, is likely at any time to blaze and make the fusion complete.[57]

The judgment must therefore be reversed and the cause remanded to the District Court for a determination after further hearing of the equitable relief necessary and appropriate in the public interest to eliminate the effects of the acquisition offensive to the statute. The District Courts, in the framing of equitable decrees, are clothed "with large discretion to model their judgments to fit the exigencies of the particular case." *International Salt Co. v. United States*, 332 U.S. 392, 400–401 . . . .[58]

NOTE AND QUESTIONS

In considering the majority's decision in the *du Pont–GM* case to analyze legality under Section 7 as of the time of trial—rather than as of the time of the acquisition—determine the probable outcome of the following hypothetical suits instituted in 2009. Assume in each case that company A is the leading producer of goods used by company B, the leading customer for those goods.

(a) In 1920, A purchases all the assets of B. A becomes exclusive supplier of B, but both are newcomers to the field. As B grows, however, A—as exclusive supplier—grows with it so that both are dominant in their fields at the time of suit.

---

57. The potency of the influence of du Pont's 23% stock interest is greater today because of the diffusion of the remaining shares which, in 1947, were held by 436,510 stockholders; 92% owned no more than 100 shares each, and 60% owned no more than 25 shares each. 126 F.Supp. at page 244.

58. Clark, Harlan and Whittaker, JJ., did not participate. The dissenting opinion of Burton, J., with whom Frankfurter, J., concurred, is omitted.

(b) In 1920, A purchases a controlling stock interest in B. A produces goods that are wholly unrelated to B's needs, but in 1940, A begins producing a line of goods used by B and gradually thereafter becomes B's exclusive supplier.

Notice that the *du Pont–GM* case, if broadly read, would appear to give the government power under existing law to radically restructure large parts of the nation's industry. What would prevent the Antitrust Division, for example, from challenging the asset acquisition in "(a)" above under Section 1 of the Sherman Act? *See, e.g.*, United States v. First National Bank & Trust Co. of Lexington, 376 U.S. 665 (1964), citing with approval the rigorous merger standard set forth by the Supreme Court in four (pre–1914) railroad consolidation cases.

Why not challenge mergers consummated before and after 1914 under either Section 7 of the Clayton Act and/or Section 1 of the Sherman Act? Many of the mergers that occurred at the turn of the century and in the second great merger wave in the 1920s would violate current antitrust standards.

Obviously, one must consider arguments about whether it is fair to challenge half century old transactions, legal when originally consummated, on the basis of anticompetitive consequences that probably could not have been foreseen at the time. Also, many have argued that no such radical restructuring should occur—certainly not on the basis of imprecise language in judicial opinions unconcerned with broad policy questions—without authorization from Congress in the form of a specific deconcentration statute.

Brown Shoe Co. v. United States

Supreme Court of the United States, 1962.
370 U.S. 294, 82 S.Ct. 1502, 8 L.Ed.2d 510.

[In 1955, the government brought suit to enjoin the acquisition by Brown Shoe, the nation's third largest seller of shoes, of G.R. Kinney Company, Inc. ("Kinney"), the eighth largest seller. The district court enjoined the merger and the Supreme Court affirmed.[59] Kinney's 350 retail outlets accounted for less than 2% of the nation's retail sales, but it was the largest distributor to handle brands other than its own. Brown Shoe distributed its own brands through an even larger retail network consisting of 1,230 outlets (470 were owned by Brown Shoe and 760 were "controlled," franchised independents). Prior to the merger, Brown Shoe manufactured about 4% of the nation's shoes, and after the merger, the 24 largest manufacturers produced approximately 35% of the nation's shoes, with the top 4 (including Brown Shoe) producing 23%.

The public purchased shoes through about 70,000 retail outlets, but only 22,000 of these derived 50% of their gross receipts from the sale of shoes and were classified as "shoe stores." The district court had "found a 'definite trend' among shoe manufacturers to acquire retail outlets." Between "1950 and 1956 nine independent shoe store chains, operating 1,114 retail shoe stores, were found to have become subsidiaries of these large firms and to have ceased their independent operations." The district court

---

59. The merger had several horizontal aspects, which have been deleted from the case by the editors. Chief Justice Warren's important and illuminating discussion of the Celler–Kefauver amendments is set forth at pp. 968–971 *supra*.

also "found there was a 'definite trend' for the parent-manufacturers to supply an ever increasing percentage of the retail outlets' needs thereby foreclosing other manufacturers from effectively competing for the retail accounts. Manufacturer-dominated stores were found to be 'drying up' the available outlets for independent producers."]

■ WARREN, C.J. . . . [T]he Clayton Act does not render unlawful all . . . vertical arrangements, but forbids only those whose effect "may be substantially to lessen competition, or to tend to create a monopoly" "in any line of commerce in any section of the country." Thus, as we have previously noted,

> [d]etermination of the relevant market is a necessary predicate to a finding of a violation of the Clayton Act because the threatened monopoly must be one which will substantially lessen competition "within the area of effective competition." Substantiality can be determined only in terms of the market affected.[60]

The "area of effective competition" must be determined by reference to a product market (the "line of commerce") and a geographic market (the "section of the country").

The outer boundaries of a product market are determined by the reasonable interchangeability of use or the cross-elasticity of demand between the product itself and substitutes for it.[61]

However, within this broad market, well-defined submarkets may exist which, in themselves, constitute product markets for antitrust purposes. *United States v. E.I. du Pont de Nemours & Co.*, 353 U.S. 586, 593–595. The boundaries of such a submarket may be determined by examining such practical indicia as industry or public recognition of the submarket as a separate economic entity, the product's peculiar characteristics and uses, unique production facilities, distinct customers, distinct prices, sensitivity to price changes, and specialized vendors. Because § 7 of the Clayton Act prohibits any merger which may substantially lessen competition "in *any* line of commerce" (emphasis supplied), it is necessary to examine the effects of a merger in each such economically significant submarket to determine if there is a reasonable probability that the merger will substantially lessen competition. If such a probability is found to exist, the merger is proscribed.

Applying these considerations to the present case, we conclude that the record supports the District Court's finding that the relevant lines of commerce are men's, women's, and children's shoes. These product lines

---

60. United States v. E.I. du Pont de Nemours & Co., 353 U.S. 586, 593

61. The cross-elasticity of production facilities may also be an important factor in defining a product market within which a vertical merger is to be viewed. Cf. United States v. Columbia Steel Co., 334 U.S. 495; United States v. Bethlehem Steel Corp., 168 F.Supp. 576, 592 (S.D.N.Y.). However, the District Court made but limited findings concerning the feasibility of interchanging equipment in the manufacture of nonrubber footwear. At the same time, the record supports the court's conclusion that individual plants generally produced shoes in only one of the product lines the court found relevant.

are recognized by the public; each line is manufactured in separate plants; each has characteristics peculiar to itself rendering it generally noncompetitive with the others; and each is, of course, directed toward a distinct class of customers. . . .

This is not to say, however, that "price/quality" differences, where they exist, are unimportant in analyzing a merger; they may be of importance in determining the likely effect of a merger. But the boundaries of the relevant market must be drawn with sufficient breadth to include the competing products of each of the merging companies and to recognize competition where, in fact, competition exists. Thus we agree with the District Court that in this case a further division of product lines based on "price/quality" differences would be "unrealistic." . . . .

We agree with the parties and the District Court that insofar as the vertical aspect of this merger is concerned, the relevant geographic market is the entire Nation. The relationships of product value, bulk, weight and consumer demand enable manufacturers to distribute their shoes on a nationwide basis, as Brown and Kinney, in fact, do. The anticompetitive effects of the merger are to be measured within this range of distribution. . . .

Once the area of the effective competition affected by a vertical arrangement has been defined, an analysis must be made to determine if the effect of the arrangement "may be substantially to lessen competition, or to tend to create a monopoly" in this market.

Since the diminution of the vigor of competition which may stem from a vertical arrangement results primarily from a foreclosure of a share of the market otherwise open to competitors, an important consideration in determining whether the effect of a vertical arrangement "may be substantially to lessen competition, or to tend to create a monopoly" is the size of the share of the market foreclosed. However, this factor will seldom be determinative. If the share of the market foreclosed is so large that it approaches monopoly proportions, the Clayton Act will, of course, have been violated; but the arrangement will also have run afoul of the Sherman Act. And the legislative history of § 7 indicates clearly that the tests for measuring the legality of any particular economic arrangement under the Clayton Act are to be less stringent than those used in applying the Sherman Act. On the other hand, foreclosure of a *de minimis* share of the market will not tend "substantially to lessen competition."

Between these extremes, in cases such as the one before us, in which the foreclosure is neither of monopoly nor *de minimis* proportions, the percentage of the market foreclosed by the vertical arrangement cannot itself be decisive. In such cases, it becomes necessary to undertake an examination of various economic and historical factors in order to determine whether the arrangement under review is of the type Congress sought to proscribe.

A most important such factor to examine is the very nature and purpose of the arrangement.[62] Congress not only indicated that "the tests of illegality [under § 7] are intended to be similar to those which the courts have applied in interpreting the same language as used in other sections of the Clayton Act," but also chose for § 7 language virtually identical to that of § 3 of the Clayton Act, which had been interpreted by this Court to require an examination of the interdependence of the market share foreclosed by, and the economic purpose of, the vertical arrangement. Thus, for example, if a particular vertical arrangement, considered under § 3, appears to be a limited term exclusive-dealing contract, the market foreclosure must generally be significantly greater than if the arrangement is a tying contract before the arrangement will be held to have violated the Act....

The importance which Congress attached to economic purpose is further demonstrated by the Senate and House Reports on H.R. 2734, which evince an intention to preserve the "failing company" doctrine of *International Shoe Co. v. Federal Trade Comm.*, 280 U.S. 291. Similarly, Congress foresaw that the merger of two large companies or a large and a small company might violate the Clayton Act while the merger of two small companies might not, although the share of the market foreclosed be identical, if the purpose of the small companies is to enable them in combination to compete with larger corporations dominating the market.

The present merger involved neither small companies nor failing companies.... [I]n this industry, no merger between a manufacturer and an independent retailer could involve a larger potential market foreclosure. Moreover, it is apparent both from past behavior of Brown and from the testimony of Brown's President, that Brown would use its ownership of Kinney to force Brown shoes into Kinney stores. Thus, in operation this vertical arrangement would be quite analogous to one involving a tying clause.[63]

Another important factor to consider is the trend toward concentration in the industry. It is true, of course, that the statute prohibits a given merger only if the effect of that merger may be substantially to lessen competition. But the very wording of § 7 requires a prognosis of the probable future effect of the merger.

The existence of a trend toward vertical integration, which the District Court found, is well substantiated by the record. Moreover, the court found a tendency of the acquiring manufacturers to become increasingly important sources of supply for their acquired outlets. The necessary corollary of

---

62. Although it is "unnecessary for the Government to speculate as to what is in the 'back of the minds' of those who promote a merger," H.R.Rep. No. 1191, 81st Cong., 1st Sess. 8, evidence indicating the purpose of the merging parties, where available, is an aid in predicting the probable future conduct of the parties and thus the probable effects of the merger....

63. Moreover, ownership integration is a more permanent and irreversible tie than is contract integration. See Kessler and Stern, Competition, Contract, and Vertical Integration, 69 Yale L.J. 1, 78 (1959).

these trends is the foreclosure of independent manufacturers from markets otherwise open to them. And because these trends are not the product of accident but are rather the result of deliberate policies of Brown and other leading shoe manufacturers, account must be taken of these facts in order to predict the probable future consequences of this merger. It is against this background of continuing concentration that the present merger must be viewed.

Brown argues, however, that the shoe industry is at present composed of a large number of manufacturers and retailers, and that the industry is dynamically competitive. But remaining vigor cannot immunize a merger if the trend in that industry is toward oligopoly. See *Pillsbury Mills, Inc.*, 50 F.T.C. 555, 573. It is the probable effect of the merger upon the future as well as the present which the Clayton Act commands the courts and the Commission to examine.

Moreover, as we have remarked above, not only must we consider the probable effects of the merger upon the economics of the particular markets affected but also we must consider its probable effects upon the economic way of life sought to be preserved by Congress. Congress was desirous of preventing the formation of future oligopolies with their attendant adverse effects upon local control of industry and upon small business. Where an industry was composed of numerous units, Congress appeared anxious to preserve this structure. . . .

The District Court's findings, and the record facts, . . . convince us that the shoe industry is being subjected to . . . a cumulative series of vertical mergers which, if left unchecked, will be likely "substantially to lessen competition."

We reach this conclusion because the trend toward vertical integration in the shoe industry, when combined with Brown's avowed policy of forcing its own shoes upon its retail subsidiaries, may foreclose competition from a substantial share of the markets for men's, women's, and children's shoes, without producing any countervailing competitive, economic, or social advantages. . . .

[Another] significant aspect of this merger is that it creates a large national chain which is integrated with a manufacturing operation. The retail outlets of integrated companies, by eliminating wholesalers and by increasing the volume of purchases from the manufacturing division of the enterprise, can market their own brands at prices below those of competing independent retailers. Of course, some of the results of large integrated or chain operations are beneficial to consumers. Their expansion is not rendered unlawful by the mere fact that small independent stores may be adversely affected. It is competition, not competitors, which the Act protects. But we cannot fail to recognize Congress' desire to promote competition through the protection of viable, small, locally-owned businesses. Congress appreciated that occasional higher costs and prices might result from the maintenance of fragmented industries and markets. It resolved these competing considerations in favor of decentralization. We must give effect to that decision.[64]

NOTES AND QUESTIONS

1.   Most of the shoe stores attributed to Brown Shoe for purposes of computing its market share in the retail sale of shoes were owned by others. In assigning these shoe stores to Brown Shoe's control, Chief Justice Warren referred, *inter alia*, to the fact that Brown Shoe provided substantial assistance in the form of merchandising and advertising aids, granted loans, and sold to the stores under short-term franchise agreements. Also, Brown Shoe required retailers to deal "almost exclusively" in its products. In that connection, consider the facts and discussion in *FTC v. Brown Shoe*, p. 1143 *supra*, where the Commission successfully challenged these arrangements under Section 5 of the FTC Act. Does the relationship between Brown Shoe and these retailers, as described in the Supreme Court opinions in the two Brown Shoe cases, persuasively demonstrate that the outlets were subject to Brown Shoe's "control"? What standard of "control" ought to apply for purposes of measuring market shares under Section 7?

2.   In his concurring opinion, Justice Harlan noted the following facts with respect to the effects of the Brown Shoe–Kinney merger in the vertical line:

> . . . While Kinney was making only about 1.2% of the total retail dollar sales in the United States in 1955, that percentage can hardly be deemed an accurate reflection of its proportion of nationwide shoe *purchases* by retailers since the retail sales figure is based on a computation that includes all retail stores, whether or not they were vertically integrated or otherwise affiliated. In terms of available markets for independent shoe manufacturers, the percentage of Kinney's purchases must have been substantially larger—though the precise figure is unavailable on the record before us.

The implication of these remarks seems to be that for purposes of computing market shares foreclosed by the merger, captive sales in the industry ought to be excluded. Does this make sense since shoe manufacturers that had supplied Kinney and were displaced by the merger could not turn to captive outlets of other shoe manufacturers and expect to compete on an equal footing? On the other hand, recall Section 1.31 of the DOJ–FTC Horizontal Merger Guidelines which proposes to include in the market the production of "vertically integrated firms to the extent that such inclusion accurately reflects their competitive significance in the relevant market prior to the merger." That suggests that captive production is in the market unless there is a special reason (for example, commitment of capacity under long-term supply contracts) why the captive production could not flow into the market in response to a post-merger price increase. That formulation seems to buy into the Bork notion that an upstream firm is likely to abandon its downstream subsidiary

---

64.   Frankfurter, J., took no part in the decision of the case and White, J., took no part in the consideration or decision of the case. The concurring opinion of Clark, J., is omitted, as is the opinion of Harlan, J., dissenting in part and concurring in part.

and sell in the open market (unless prevented by contract or some other reason) if it can obtain a better price in the open market. Which approach seems more realistic?

3. According to the majority opinion, Brown Shoe, by 1957, supplied 7.9 percent of Kinney's shoe needs, and Kinney accounted for 1.6 percent of national pairage of non-rubber shoes. Does this mean that the Supreme Court found a violation of Section 7 where a merger resulted in the foreclosure of 7.9 percent of 1.6 percent?

4. Also, the Court concluded that a principal purpose of the merger was to "force Brown Shoes into Kinney stores." How could Brown Shoe profit from forcing Kinney to purchase its shoes? Would advantages to Brown Shoe be offset by equivalent disadvantages to Kinney?

5. After the merger, it will almost certainly be true that Brown Shoe will continue to supply independent, unintegrated shoe stores that compete with Kinney. To what extent is it predictable that Brown Shoe will discriminate in favor of Kinney as opposed to the unaffiliated outlets? In price? Quality? Reliability of service? Should the fact that a vertically integrated firm is likely to follow a preferential policy in favor of itself be a major consideration in developing standards to test the legality of vertical mergers under Section 7? Or would it be wiser to wait until some sort of "price squeeze" or "discrimination" results in injury to competition before intervention under the antitrust laws is attempted?

6. Professors Blake and Jones defended the Supreme Court's decision in the *Brown Shoe* case by spotlighting the remarkable trend toward vertical integration between major shoe manufacturers and large chain operations (for example, of 3534 stores in large chain operations, 1114 had become subsidiaries of the major shoe manufacturers), and the fact that the "incipiency" aspect of Section 7 justified government intervention at an early point when there was a marked trend toward concentration. Blake & Jones, Towards a Three–Dimensional Antitrust Policy, 65 Colum. L.Rev. 422, 453–57 (1965). Again, recall that the DOJ–FTC Horizontal Merger Guidelines omit any mention of industry trend as a factor in analyzing mergers even though it was so clearly a part of Congress' thinking when it revised Section 7 in 1950 (*see* note 4, p. 969 *supra*).

7. Professors Areeda and Turner reached the following conclusion about the *Brown Shoe* case:

> Both the reasoning and the result in *Brown Shoe* seem indefensible. As a Supreme Court precedent never subsequently repudiated, the decision was undoubtedly responsible in large part for those subsequent court and Federal Trade Commission decisions invalidating vertical mergers involving relatively small "foreclosures" and no substantial threats to competition. Accordingly, those subsequent decisions do not "add" to the weight of precedent or impose any significant obstacle to those courts willing to think hard about the competitive implications of vertical mergers while confining *Brown Shoe* to its particular facts as perceived by the 1962 Court.

4 Areeda & Turner, Antitrust Law 314 (1980).

Do you agree with Areeda and Turner? How much weight would you put on the trend towards vertical integration described by Professors Blake and Jones? Although the Supreme Court's decision points in both directions, would your view of the *Brown Shoe* case be influenced by solid evidence that the merger had no "countervailing competitive, economic, or social advantages"? Do you think the *Ford Motor* case (discussed in note 9 below) falls into the Areeda and Turner category of "vertical mergers involving relatively small 'foreclosures' and no substantial threats to competition"?

8. The indicia for defining "submarkets" set forth in *Brown Shoe supra* have been criticized as unduly generous in allowing easy definition of submarkets, and therefore responsible to a large extent for the result in years following *Brown Shoe* that in merger cases before the Supreme Court the government always wins. Note that in the FTC–DOJ Merger Guidelines, submarkets can only be drawn if the seller can successfully discriminate in price among different sets of buyers. (*See* 1.12 of the Merger Guidelines, p. 1033 *supra*, a much narrower interpretation of the submarket concept.) Is that a sensible interpretation of relevant market principles in the context of merger law.

9. Ford Motor Co. v. United States, 405 U.S. 562, 92 S.Ct. 1142, 31 L.Ed.2d 492 (1972). Ford Motor Company, the nation's second largest producer of automobiles, in 1961 acquired from Electric Autolite Co. the following assets: the Autolite trade name, Autolite's only spark plug plant in this country (located in New Fostoria, Ohio), a battery plant, and extensive rights to Autolite's nationwide distribution organization for spark plugs and batteries. Electric Autolite continued in business, and in 1962 began manufacturing spark plugs under the brand name Prestolite, capturing 1.6% of the market by 1964. The district court ruled that Ford's acquisition of the Autolite assets violated Section 7 of the Clayton Act, and the Supreme Court affirmed, the issues on appeal being limited to the spark plug business.

The three leading automobile manufacturers, General Motors, Ford and Chrysler (accounting for 90% of the nation's automobile production), were matched by three leading spark plug manufacturers. General Motors manufactured spark plugs under its AC brand for its own automobiles; Ford purchased spark plugs from Champion for its automobiles; and Chrysler purchased spark plugs from Autolite for its automobiles. By custom in the repair trade, mechanics used the same plugs as the original equipment. This "OE tie" was of significance, leading Champion and Autolite to sell spark plugs at less than cost to Ford and Chrysler in order to assure their participation in the profitable "aftermarket." In 1961, Autolite's share of the spark plug market was 15%, Champion's share was 50%, and AC's share was 30%. Subsequently, Champion's share declined to 33%. Other small manufacturers of spark plugs had no important share of the market. Ford was interested in participating in the profitable spark plug aftermarket, and, in order to avoid the 5–to–8–year delay that would be incident to internal expansion, it acquired the designated assets of Autolite.

The merger was held to be unlawful on two grounds. First, Ford was a potential entrant into the spark plug industry and exerted a moderating influence on Champion and the other spark plug companies, because it was both a prime candidate for entry and because it was a major customer of Champion. Also, Ford might someday have entered by internal expansion and set the stage for noticeable deconcentration. Second, the acquisition of the Autolite assets resulted in the foreclosure of Ford as a purchaser of about 10% of spark plug output. Considered with the General Motors ownership of AC, the acquisition tended to transmit to the spark plug industry the rigidity of the automobile industry, reducing the chances for future deconcentration of the spark plug industry and raising barriers to entry.

The Court rejected as not material the argument that the acquisition would make Autolite a more vigorous and effective competitor against Champion and AC than Autolite had been as an independent. Ford was seeking a foothold in the aftermarket. Once established, it would have every incentive to perpetuate the "OE tie" and thus maintain the virtually insurmountable barriers to entry to the aftermarket. The major possibility for deconcentration of the aftermarket was the development of private brands by mass merchandisers. To the extent that spark plug manufacturers were not owned by the auto makers, they would be more favorably disposed toward private-brand sales and would compete more vigorously for such sales. It would be in the interest of OE plug manufacturers to discourage private-brand sales and to encourage the "OE tie."

In addition to ordering divestiture, the district court's decree:

(1) enjoined Ford for 10 years from manufacturing spark plugs,

(2) ordered Ford for five years to purchase one-half of its total annual requirements of spark plugs from the divested plant under the "Autolite" name,

(3) prohibited Ford for the same period from using its own trade names on spark plugs, and

(4) required Ford for 10 years to continue its policy of selling spark plugs to its dealers at prices no less than its prevailing minimum suggested jobbers' selling price.

The latter provision, designed to assemble an adequate distribution system for the aftermarket by permitting service stations and independent jobbers to compete with franchised car dealers, was not challenged before the Supreme Court. The first three provisions were challenged but were sustained by a divided Court. The majority opinion reasoned: "The ancillary measures ordered by the District Court are designed to allow Autolite to re-establish itself in the OE and replacement markets and to maintain it as a viable competitor until such time as forces within the market place weaken the OE tie." Ford argued that the 10–year prohibition on its manufacture of spark plugs would lessen competition because it would remove a potential competitor from the marketplace. Recalling the 5–to–8 years estimated as required for Ford to establish a spark plug division internally, the Court observed:

> The five-year prohibition on the use of its own name and the 10–year limitation on its own manufacturing mesh neatly to allow Ford to establish itself in the aftermarket prior to becoming a manufacturer.... Thus, the District Court's decree delays for only two to five years the date on which Ford may become a manufacturer with an established share of the aftermarket. Given the normal five-to-eight year lead time on entry through internal expansion, the District Court's decree does not significantly lessen Ford's moderating influence as a potential entrant on the edge of the market.

Justices Powell and Rehnquist did not participate in the decision. Justice Stewart concurred in the result in a separate opinion not markedly different from the majority opinion. Chief Justice Burger and Justice Blackmun dissented on the ancillary injunctive provisions.

Fruehauf Corp. v. FTC

United States Court of Appeals, Second Circuit, 1979.
603 F.2d 345.

[Fruehauf, the nation's largest manufacturer of truck trailers, acquired Kelsey, which made heavy duty wheels ("HDW"), an "essential component" of truck trailers. It was "undisputed" that the relevant geographic market in which to judge the acquisition was the United States and that the product markets were truck trailers and HDW.[65] The total value of truck trailer shipments in the United States was approximately $1 billion per year. Fruehauf accounted for about 25% of sales; the top four firms accounted for about 49% and the top eight firms for about 64%. In the HDW market, Kelsey accounted for 15% of the market sales. The top four HDW producers accounted for between 65% and 71% of the market and the top eight firms had 93% to 95% of the market. HDW were used for either trucks (or similar vehicles) or truck trailers.

The FTC found a violation of Section 7 of the Clayton Act. The Second Circuit reversed and denied enforcement.]

■ MANSFIELD, J. . . . .

As the Supreme Court recognized in *Brown Shoe, supra*, the fountainhead of § 7 analysis of vertical mergers, the competitive significance of a vertical merger results primarily from the degree, if any, to which it may increase barriers to entry into the market or reduce competition by (1) foreclosing competitors of the purchasing firm in the merger from access to a potential source of supply, or from access on competitive terms, (2) by foreclosing competitors of the selling firm (in this case other HDW . . . manufacturers) from access to the market or a substantial portion of it, or (3) by forcing actual or potential competitors to enter or continue in the market only on a vertically integrated basis because of advantages unrelated to economies attributable solely to integration. The ultimate objective, however, is to determine whether and how the particular merger in issue may lessen competition, *i.e.*, what its anticompetitive effect on the market, if any, is likely to be . . . .

In *Brown Shoe* the Court described some of the factors to be considered in "predicting the probable future conduct of the parties and thus the probable effects of the merger." Most important among the factors are the nature and economic purpose of the arrangement, the likelihood and size of any market foreclosure, the extent of concentration of sellers and buyers in the industry, the capital cost required to enter the market, the market share needed by a buyer or seller to achieve a profitable level of production (sometimes referred to as "scale economy"), the existence of a trend toward vertical concentration or oligopoly in the industry, and whether the merger will eliminate potential competition by one of the merging parties. To these factors may be added the degree of market power that would be possessed by the merged enterprise and the number and strength of competing suppliers and purchasers, which might indicate whether the merger would

---

65. Ed. Kelsey also made antiskid brake devices ("ASBD") and accounted for 32% of sales by unit and 28.6% of sales by dollar volume in this market. Fruehauf's purchases amounted to 4.7% of the market. But the ASBD were purchased only to satisfy certain government regulations which had been withdrawn as to truck trailers. Therefore, Fruehauf was unlikely to purchase a significant volume of these devices in the future, and the Second Circuit set aside the FTC's conclusions "without prejudice to its right to renew its proceeding if future developments should prove that the predicted demise of the ASBD market is greatly exaggerated." 603 F.2d at 356.

increase the risk that prices or terms would cease to be competitive. This list, with some variations, has been the standard framework for analysis of the legality of a vertical merger. . . . Application of these factors may reveal that a vertical merger poses no threat to competition at all, resulting merely in a realignment of sales as a result of "in-house" transactions within the merged enterprise but leaving the number of competing sellers and their market shares unchanged, or that it poses a threatened lessening of competition that may be *de minimis*, may be of monopoly proportions, or may lie somewhere in between the two, 370 U.S. at 328–29.

As the Supreme Court made clear in *Brown Shoe*, there are no precise formulas for determining whether a vertical merger may probably lessen competition. Rather, the objective of discerning what, if any, anticompetitive effects the merger may have can be achieved only by examining the foregoing market factors as they exist for the particular merger in issue. It is true that the Department of Justice has for many years issued "Merger Guidelines" for the purpose of indicating to the business community, legal profession and the public generally when the Department may question the legality of a merger. See U.S. Dept. of Justice Merger Guidelines, 1 Trade Reg.Rep. (CCH) ¶ 4510.[66] But just as these guidelines do not preclude governmental challenge to a merger which does not fall within all the terms of the guidelines, see *Atlantic Richfield*, *supra*, 297 F.Supp. at 1073, so the guidelines do not establish the illegality of a merger which does fit the criteria used by the Justice Department in deciding whether to challenge a merger. The guidelines, therefore, simply reflect the considered view of the Justice Department as to which mergers are most likely to create a reasonable probability of substantially lessening competition and which may therefore warrant the institution of legal action. See Guidelines ¶ 1, *supra*, at 6882. Accordingly, whether or not the degree of market concentration, the height of entry barriers, the size of the merging firms, and the extent of foreclosure match or exceed the benchmarks incorporated into the Justice Department's guidelines, the Commission still bears the burden of showing the likelihood that the future effect of "*that* merger [of Kelsey and Fruehauf] may be substantially to lessen competition." *Brown Shoe*, *supra*, 370 U.S. at 332 (emphasis in original).

With these basic principles in mind we proceed to review the Commission's findings and conclusions with respect to the Fruehauf–Kelsey merger.

The Truck Trailer Market

The Commission concluded that the merger violated § 7 with respect to the truck trailer market solely on the theory that in the event of a shortage of HDWs Kelsey would give Fruehauf a substantial competitive

---

66. The Guidelines [of 1968] state that the Department may be expected to challenge "a merger or series of mergers between a supplying firm, accounting for approximately 10% or more of the sales in its market, and one or more purchasing firms, accounting *in toto* for approximately 6% or more of the total purchases in that market, unless it clearly appears that there are no significant barriers to entry into the business of the purchasing firm or firms." Guidelines ¶ 12.

advantage over other trailer manufacturers by diverting to Fruehauf wheels that would otherwise go to Kelsey's other customers, some of which are trailer manufacturers.[67] This conclusion rests upon several assumptions, having no appreciable evidentiary support. One assumption is that Kelsey is a significant and substantial supplier of HDWs to Fruehauf's competitors. The record reveals that, on the contrary, trailer manufacturers have in the past purchased almost all of their HDWs from other suppliers, with Kelsey's sales of wheels to trailer manufacturers other than Fruehauf amounting to approximately $1.4 million per year out of total average annual HDW market sales amounting to $200 million per year during the three-year period prior to the merger. In the years 1970–72, sales to trailer manufacturers, including Fruehauf, accounted for only about 7% of Kelsey's HDW output. Thus Kelsey, while a large manufacturer of HDWs, has hardly been a substantial supplier of HDWs to trailer manufacturers.

The second unsupported assumption is that Kelsey would, in the event of an HDW shortage, divert to Fruehauf HDW sales that would otherwise be made to other customers. There is no evidence, and it is not alleged, that Fruehauf contemplated such a stratagem when it entered the merger with Kelsey. More important, there is no credible evidence that another shortage is reasonably foreseeable. Even if it were, the evidence that Kelsey would give priority to Fruehauf's needs is insubstantial. As to the likelihood of a shortage, the record indicates that the combined capacity of wheel producers was considerably expanded after the 1973–74 shortage and that, even when conservatively estimated, this capacity exceeds a liberal estimate of anticipated demand during the next five or ten years.

During past shortages Kelsey, like other wheel producers, has allocated its production pro rata among its customers in accordance with their regular volume of purchases. Appellant insists that Kelsey will follow this precedent in the future, notwithstanding Fruehauf's ownership of the company. The Commission cites no evidence shedding doubt upon this representation. On the contrary a spokesman from Trailmobile Corp., Fruehauf largest competitor, testified that his company believed that the merger would not affect Kelsey's policy in favor of pro rata distribution in the event of a shortage.

One might reasonably question the weight to be given to appellant's self-serving assurances that Kelsey would allocate pro rata if the need arose, as well as the significance of Kelsey's pro rata distribution of wheels during the 1973–74 shortage, which took place after the merger but at a time when appellant could have anticipated a challenge to its legality. However Kelsey's policy in favor of pro rata allocation need not rest upon some philosophical commitment to egalitarianism since it could also make

---

67. Fruehauf would enjoy an unfair advantage over its competitors if Kelsey diverted sales to Fruehauf from customers who do not build trailers, but the relative advantage would not be as great. Moreover, Kelsey's non-trailer customers, including Ford and General Motors, exercise the greatest leverage over Kelsey with the threat of retaliatory withdrawal of patronage.

sound business sense. If Kelsey deprived its regular customers of a proportionate share of HDWs in times of shortage it would risk their retaliating by shifting to competing suppliers not only their purchases of HDWs but of other products presently bought from Kelsey, which could cause it greater economic harm. In addition, by granting priority to Fruehauf over other trailer manufacturers who purchase wheels from Kelsey, Kelsey would invite antitrust damage actions against it by these trailer firms. Under the circumstances, it appears highly unlikely that Kelsey would take such risks.

Thus the Commission's finding that the merger violates § 7 with respect to the truck trailer market is based on speculation rather than fact. It assumes in the face of contrary evidence that a shortage will recur in the reasonably proximate future. Upon this unsupported basis it infers that in the event of a shortage Kelsey would give priority to Fruehauf to the detriment of its competitors. Although neither of these assumptions is by any means beyond the realm of the possible, here they run counter to the actual evidence in the record. We cannot therefore say that they add up to a reasonable probability that the merger will substantially lessen competition. Accordingly, the finding of a § 7 violation based upon the effect of the merger on the truck trailer market must be set aside as unsupported by substantial evidence. . . .

We accept at the outset the Commission's findings that the HDW market is significantly concentrated, based on evidence that the top four producers account for 65–71% of the market, the top eight for 93–95%, and Kelsey, the third largest producer, 15%. Moreover, the Commission's determination that barriers to entry into HDW production are substantial is supported by evidence that the initial capital outlay required to enter production at an efficient level is $10–$20 million. . . .

There is, therefore, substantial evidence, albeit not uncontroverted, supporting the Commission's conclusion that the capital cost barrier is substantial and significant, whatever the minimum level of efficient production might be. For this reason we do not reject the Commission's decision on this issue.

The Commission further concluded that the amount of market foreclosure likely to result from the merger would range from "a weak 3.9" [actually 3.3%] to a "strong 5.8" of the market production of HDWs, depending upon whether one limits the calculation of Fruehauf's purchases of cast spoke HDWs, which are made by Kelsey and accounted for 3.3% of the market during the three-year premerger period, or also includes Fruehauf's purchases of heavy duty disc wheels, not presently manufactured by Kelsey, which accounted for 2.5% of the total HDW market during the same period. Since Kelsey does make discs for light-weight trucks and could produce heavy duty discs, the Commission was entitled to infer that Fruehauf, with its tradition of in-house purchasing, could expand Kelsey's disc wheel facilities to furnish at least the major part of Fruehauf's disc needs except possibly for nonintegral hubs. However, there is no evidence that competing purchasers of these products would be foreclosed from continuing to obtain all or part of their cast spoke needs from Kelsey or its competitors at competitive prices. Nor was there proof that removal from the market of up to 5.8% of its HDW sales would preclude any existing competitor from continuing to operate economically or any potential competitor from entering the market.

The Commission further found that there had been periodic HDW shortages within the 12 years prior to the merger (*i.e.*, in 1966, 1968–69, 1973–74) and that, although Fruehauf was not itself a potential competitor in the production of HDWs prior to the merger, it had engaged in certain pro-competitive activities, consisting of experiments with new types of fabricated aluminum and steel wheels and encouragement of one foundry, McConway and Torley, to produce cast spoke wheels.

From the foregoing the Commission concluded that the merger

"runs afoul of Section 7 by foreclosing Fruehauf as a source of patronage of heavy duty wheels in a market setting in which such foreclosure is likely to increase barriers to entry, make new entry more difficult and less likely, and thereby enhance the market power conferred by a highly concentrated market structure into which entry was previously difficult to begin with. Additionally we believe that the merger is likely to lessen competition substantially by foreclosing Kelsey–Hayes as a source of supply to truck trailer manufacturers should shortages of supply recur." 91 F.T.C. at 236.

With due respect for the Commission's expertise, we fail to find any logical basis in the evidence for this conclusion, even when the record is viewed most favorably to the Commission. Not only is the conclusion a *non sequitur* but it flies in the face of undisputed contrary evidence.

There is no evidence in the record that existing barriers to entry into the HDW market or the existing concentration of producers in it, both admittedly substantial, have been or would be increased by the merger. There is no reason to believe that the merger will adversely affect scale economies for HDW production, thereby increasing the cost of entry. Nor does the Commission suggest that as a result of the merger a firm could successfully enter the HDW or the trailer market only by simultaneously entering at both levels. As to the effect of the merger on the concentration of the HDW industry, since Fruehauf's principal supplier of spoke wheels has been Dayton?Walther, the largest producers of spokes and second largest wheel producer, any shifting of patronage from Dayton to Kelsey will tend to even out the market shares of the three largest sellers of HDWs, but not increase their aggregate market share. The ALJ expressly refused to find that the merger would entrench Kelsey as a producer, stating "I cannot conclude that Kelsey–Hayes has been 'entrenched' as that term has heretofore been used in Section 7 cases."

Moreover, there is no allegation that the merger of Fruehauf and Kelsey is part of an existing or prospective trend toward vertical integration, such as existed in *Brown Shoe, supra*, and in other cases.[68] There is no suggestion, much less evidence, that the merger was motivated by a desire to restrain competition. On the contrary, the evidence is undisputed

---

68. See Brown Shoe, *supra*, 370 U.S. at 332–33, 334; United States Steel Corp. v. FTC, 426 F.2d 592, 603 (6th Cir.1970); United States v. Ford Motor Co., 315 F.Supp. 372, 375

that Kelsey, whose stock was selling substantially below book value, sought out Fruehauf in order to avoid takeover efforts on the part of others. Nor is there any evidence that the merger might impair competition by conferring upon one of the merging partners a "deep pocket" or financial clout not enjoyed by its rivals. It is true that some market foreclosure may ensue from the merger, but not one that deprives rivals from major channels of distribution, much less one that excludes them from the market altogether. Even if Fruehauf were to switch its purchase of its entire HDW wheel needs, amounting to 5.8% of the market, from others to Kelsey (which would require Kelsey to enter heavy duty disc production), there would merely be a realignment of existing market sales without any likelihood of a diminution in competition.

The only theory suggested by the Commission as to how the merger might impair competition in the HDW market is that, assuming Kelsey supplied all of Fruehauf's HDW needs, amounting to 5.8% of the market or slightly less than the minimum Department of Justice Guideline figure, this foreclosure would be sufficient alone in such a setting to significantly lessen the likelihood that a new firm would enter this market or, what amounts to the same thing for our purposes, to lessen the chance that an existing small competitor would substantially increase its capacity and compete on a wider scale. According to the Commission, although it found that Fruehauf itself was not a potential entrant into the HDW market, Fruehauf had a pro-competitive effect on the market through its collaborative efforts to develop new types of heavy duty wheels and by virtue of its ability to draw new entrants into production of conventional wheels by offering to deliver its patronage.[69]

In light of the record evidence, this theory is too ephemeral to sustain the Commission's decision. Although Fruehauf did experiment in the

---

(E.D.Mich.1970), aff'd, 405 U.S. 562 (1972); United States v. Kennecott Copper Corp., 231 F.Supp. 95, 103–05 (S.D.N.Y.1964), aff'd per curiam, 381 U.S. 414 (1965); Ash Grove Cement Co., 85 F.T.C. 1123, 1165–66 (1975), aff'd, 577 F.2d 1368 (9th Cir.1978).

69. In the late 1960s and early 1970s Fruehauf experimented with a fabricated aluminum wheel and a fabricated steel wheel for production in Fruehauf's own facilities. Fruehauf abandoned the steel wheel project in early 1970 in order to concentrate its efforts on the aluminum wheel, which seemed more promising. This project was abandoned in 1971 when Fruehauf determined that under existing market conditions production of fabricated aluminum wheels was not economically feasible. Following the termination of these efforts to develop a wheel for in-house production, Fruehauf explored with U.S. Steel the development of a fabricated steel wheel to be designed by an outside engineering firm and produced by U.S. Steel. The prototype turned out to be unacceptable for commercial use, and the project ended in September 1973.

In 1967–68, when a strike halted wheel production at Dayton–Walther, the leading producer of cast spoke wheels and Fruehauf's traditional principal supplier, Fruehauf favorably responded to an inquiry from McConway and Torley, a leading producer of cast steel components used by the railroad industry, about the possibility of it producing wheels for Fruehauf. Eager to cultivate an alternate source of supply, Fruehauf provided McConway with necessary drawings and helped finance the purchase of patterns and equipment. For a few years, McConway sold cast spokes to Fruehauf. Fruehauf stopped buying from McConway in late 1973, and shortly thereafter McConway, which had experienced greater than anticipated production problems, exited from the market....

development of new kinds of wheels and assisted one foundry in temporary production of HDWs, both adventures proved to be complete failures and there is no evidence that, if the merger were disapproved, Fruehauf would engage in similar activities. Moreover, the Commission has presented no evidence suggesting that Fruehauf was unique in its ability to elicit new competition, and there is no reason to believe that other firms patronizing the HDW market, particularly the automotive and trucking giants, will not encourage firms in the wings to enter that market, should they be dissatisfied with the quality of the existing competition.

NOTES AND QUESTIONS

1. Is the *Fruehauf* case consistent with *Brown Shoe* in approach? In level of concern about the dangers of vertical integration? If, for example, you were a manufacturer of truck trailers (or another purchaser of HDW) would you feel more vulnerable after the Fruehauf–Kelsey acquisition? How could you protect yourself in terms of supply and price?

2. In its *Fruehauf* opinion, the Second Circuit states that the merger was not motivated by "a desire to restrain competition" but rather Kelsey sought out Fruehauf "in order to avoid takeover efforts on the part of others." In this regard, a report by the Congressional Research Service concluded:

> In the current hostile atmosphere, few companies faced with an unsolicited tender offer survive as independent companies even though companies are employing a variety of defensive tactics to thwart raiders. Often the only possibility is to secure the protection of a "white knight," a company willing to purchase the target on terms arguably more favorable to it and usually with a provision to retain existing management.... But the spectacle of large Fortune 500 companies attacking each other, counter-attacking and maneuvering as if engaged in war games has raised public policy questions which go beyond the traditional antitrust and economic concentration questions raised in prior merger periods.

> In a somewhat skewed notion of the survival of the fittest, it is the well-managed firms which are frequently the targets. At a time of concern over the competitive position and the rate of investment of U.S. industry, some cash-rich firms are moving to acquire in order to avoid being acquired.[70]

When a vertical (or other) merger comes about in this "war games" atmosphere, is it as likely to be efficiency enhancing? Should such a consideration be relevant to the analysis of mergers under Section 7?

3. The reference in the *Fruehauf* case to Department of Justice Merger Guidelines is to a set of guidelines issued in 1968. As you know, the latest version of the Guidelines covering vertical mergers was issued in 1984, and that portion of the Guidelines is printed directly below. Do you agree with the Second Circuit's treatment of the legal effect of the old guidelines? Are the 1984 Guidelines consistent with *Brown Shoe*? With *Fruehauf*? With sound public policy?

---

70. Congressional Research Service, Merger Tactics and Public Policy 24–25 (March 1982).

Department of Justice Merger Guidelines, 1984

June 14, 1984.

4.2   Competitive Problems from Vertical Mergers

4.21   Barriers to Entry from Vertical Mergers

In certain circumstances, the vertical integration resulting from vertical mergers could create competitively objectionable barriers to entry. Stated generally, three conditions are necessary (but not sufficient) for this problem to exist. First, the degree of vertical integration between the two markets must be so extensive that entrants to one market (the "primary market") also would have to enter the other market (the "secondary market")[71] simultaneously. Second, the requirement of entry at the secondary level must make entry at the primary level significantly more difficult and less likely to occur. Finally, the structure and other characteristics of the primary market must be otherwise so conducive to non-competitive performance that the increased difficulty of entry is likely to affect its performance. The following standards state the criteria by which the Department will determine whether these conditions are satisfied.

4.211   Need for Two–Level Entry

If there is sufficient unintegrated capacity[72] in the secondary market, new entrants to the primary market would not have to enter both markets simultaneously. The Department is unlikely to challenge a merger on this ground where post-merger sales (purchases) by unintegrated firms in the secondary market would be sufficient to service two minimum-efficient-scale plants in the primary market. When the other conditions are satisfied, the Department is increasingly likely to challenge a merger as the unintegrated capacity declines below this level.

4.212   Increased Difficulty of Simultaneous Entry to Both Markets

The relevant question is whether the need for simultaneous entry to the secondary market gives rise to a substantial incremental difficulty as

---

71. This competitive problem could result from either upstream or downstream integration, and could affect competition in either the upstream market or the downstream market. In the text, the term "primary market" refers to the market in which the competitive concerns are being considered, and the term "secondary market" refers to the adjacent market.

72. Ownership integration does not necessarily mandate two-level entry by new entrants to the primary market. Such entry is most likely to be necessary where the primary and secondary markets are completely integrated by ownership and each firm in the primary market uses all of the capacity of its associated firm in the secondary market. In many cases of ownership integration, however, the functional fit between vertically integrated firms is not perfect, and an outside market exists for the sales (purchases) of the firms in the secondary market. If that market is sufficiently large and diverse, new entrants to the primary market may be able to participate without simultaneous entry to the secondary market. In considering the adequacy of this alternative, the Department will consider the likelihood of predatory price or supply "squeezes" by the integrated firms against their unintegrated rivals.

compared to entry into the primary market alone. If entry at the secondary level is easy in absolute terms, the requirement of simultaneous entry to that market is unlikely adversely to affect entry to the primary market. Whatever the difficulties of entry into the primary market may be, the Department is unlikely to challenge a merger on this ground if new entry into the secondary market can be accomplished under the conditions stated in Section 3.3.[73] When entry is not possible under those conditions, the Department is increasingly concerned about vertical mergers as the difficulty of entering the secondary market increases. The Department, however, will invoke this theory only where the need for secondary market entry significantly increases the costs (which may take the form of risks) of primary market entry.

More capital is necessary to enter two markets than to enter one. Standing alone, however, this additional capital requirement does not constitute a barrier to entry to the primary market. If the necessary funds were available at a cost commensurate with the level of risk in the secondary market, there would be no adverse effect. In some cases, however, lenders may doubt that would-be entrants to the primary market have the necessary skills and knowledge to succeed in the secondary market and, therefore, in the primary market. In order to compensate for this risk of failure, lenders might charge a higher rate for the necessary capital. This problem becomes increasingly significant as a higher percentage of the capital assets in the secondary market are long-lived and specialized to that market and, therefore, difficult to recover in the event of failure. In evaluating the likelihood of increased barriers to entry resulting from increased cost of capital, therefore, the Department will consider both the degree of similarity in the essential skills in the primary and secondary markets and the economic life and degree of specialization of the capital assets in the secondary market.

Economies of scale in the secondary market may constitute an additional barrier to entry to the primary market in some situations requiring two-level entry. The problem could arise if the capacities of minimum-efficient-scale plants in the primary and secondary markets differ significantly. For example, if the capacity of a minimum-efficient-scale plant in the secondary market were significantly greater than the needs of a minimum-efficient-scale plant in the primary market, entrants would have to choose between inefficient operation at the secondary level (because of operating an efficient plant at an inefficient output or because of operating an inefficiently small plant) or a larger than necessary scale at the primary level. Either of these effects could cause a significant increase in the operating costs of the entering firm.[74]

---

73. Entry into the secondary market may be greatly facilitated in that an assured supplier (customer) is provided by the primary market entry.

74. It is important to note, however, that this problem would not exist if a significant outside market exists at the secondary level. In that case, entrants could enter with the appropriately scaled plants at both levels, and sell or buy in the market as necessary.

4.213 Structure and Performance of the Primary Market

Barriers to entry are unlikely to affect performance if the structure of the primary market is otherwise not conducive to monopolization or collusion. The Department is unlikely to challenge a merger on this ground unless overall concentration of the primary market is above 1800 HHI (a somewhat lower concentration will suffice if one or more of the factors discussed in Section 3.4 indicate that effective collusion is particularly likely). Above that threshold, the Department is increasingly likely to challenge a merger that meets the other criteria set forth above as the concentration increases.

4.22 Facilitating Collusion Through Vertical Mergers

4.221 Vertical Integration to the Retail Level

A high level of vertical integration by upstream firms into the associated retail market may facilitate collusion in the upstream market by making it easier to monitor price. Retail prices are generally more visible than prices in upstream markets, and vertical mergers may increase the level of vertical integration to the point at which the monitoring effect becomes significant. Adverse competitive consequences are unlikely unless the upstream market is generally conducive to collusion and a large percentage of the products produced there are sold through vertically integrated retail outlets.

The Department is unlikely to challenge a merger on this ground unless 1) overall concentration of the upstream market is above 1800 HHI (a somewhat lower concentration will suffice if one or more of the factors discussed in Section 3.4 indicate that effective collusion is particularly likely), and 2) a large percentage of the upstream product would be sold through vertically integrated retail outlets after the merger. Where the stated thresholds are met or exceeded, the Department's decision whether to challenge a merger on this ground will depend upon an individual evaluation of its likely competitive effect.

4.222 Elimination of a Disruptive Buyer

The elimination by vertical merger of a particularly disruptive buyer in a downstream market may facilitate collusion in the upstream market. If upstream firms view sales to a particular buyer as sufficiently important, they may deviate from the terms of a collusive agreement in an effort to secure that business, thereby disrupting the operation of the agreement. The merger of such a buyer with an upstream firm may eliminate that rivalry, making it easier for the upstream firms to collude effectively. Adverse competitive consequences are unlikely unless the upstream market is generally conducive to collusion and the disruptive firm is significantly more attractive to sellers than the other firms in its market.

The Department is unlikely to challenge a merger on this ground unless 1) overall concentration of the upstream market is 1800 HHI or above (a somewhat lower concentration will suffice if one or more of the factors discussed in Section 3.4 indicate that effective collusion is particularly likely), and 2) the allegedly disruptive firm differs substantially in volume of purchases or other relevant characteristics from the other firms in its market. Where the stated thresholds are met or exceeded, the Department's decision whether to challenge a merger on this ground will depend upon an individual evaluation of its likely competitive effect.

4.23 Evasion of Rate Regulation

Non-horizontal mergers may be used by monopoly public utilities subject to rate regulation as a tool for circumventing that regulation. The clearest example is the acquisition by a regulated utility of a supplier of its fixed or variable inputs. After the merger, the utility would be selling to itself and might be able arbitrarily to inflate the prices of internal transactions. Regulators may have great difficulty in policing these practices, particularly if there is no independent market for the product (or service) purchased from the affiliate. As a result, inflated prices could be passed along to consumers as "legitimate" costs. In extreme cases, the regulated firm may effectively preempt the adjacent market, perhaps for the purpose of suppressing observable market transactions, and may distort resource allocation in that adjacent market as well as in the regulated market. In such cases, however, the Department recognizes that genuine economies of integration may be involved. The Department will consider challenging mergers that create substantial opportunities for such abuses.

4.24 Efficiencies

As in the case of horizontal mergers, the Department will consider expected efficiencies in determining whether to challenge a vertical merger. *See* Section 3.5 (Efficiencies) [ed: now Section 4]. An extensive pattern of vertical integration may constitute evidence that substantial economies are afforded by vertical integration. Therefore, the Department will give relatively more weight to expected efficiencies in determining whether to challenge a vertical merger than in determining whether to challenge a horizontal merger.

NOTES AND QUESTIONS

1. The Department of Justice Vertical Merger Guidelines were adopted in 1982 and revised in 1984; arguably they still represent Department of Justice views on the subject. In neither instance did the Federal Trade Commission join in adoption of the Guidelines.

2. The Vertical Merger Guidelines, which purport to introduce new economic learning into conventional antitrust enforcement, have been controversial. Note that they do not mention the concept of "foreclosure" as a relevant competitive effect. Rather they suggest that the only challenges the Department of Justice would support involve vertical mergers that have horizontal effects—either by raising barriers to entry at the primary or secondary level, or by contributing to the feasibility of collusion. Does that mean the Department of Justice, at least in the 1980s, believed that *Ford–Autolite* was wrongly decided?

Federal Enforcement Against Vertical Mergers in the 1990s

During the 1980s and early 1990s, influenced by conservative scholarship like the excerpt from Robert Bork (p. 1010, *supra*) and the permissive 1984 Department of Justice Merger Guidelines, there was no enforcement against vertical mergers at the federal level. In addition, there was widespread rejection of the views expressed by the Supreme Court in *Brown Shoe* that made vertical mergers between relatively small firms, with low barriers to entry, a violation of revised Section 7. The enforcement situation changed in the 1990s when a series of vertical mergers were either blocked or substantially restructured as a condition of government approval. Enforcement activity that was exclusively or primarily addressed to vertical aspects of a merger occurred for the most part at the Federal Trade Commission. Three examples of vertical challenges are described below:

1. *In re Silicon Graphics, Inc.*, 120 FTC 928 (1995). (5 Trade Reg. Rep. ¶ 23,838 (1995)). Silicon Graphics ("SGI") was the dominant provider of entertainment graphics workstations with a 90% market share, and proposed to acquire Alias and Wavefront, two of the three dominant developers of entertainment graphics and animation software. The workstation and software created 3–D computer graphics special effects used in film and video, television and interactive computer games. The Commission indicated concern about vertical foreclosure in both directions. Workstation manufacturers that were rivals to SGI would not be able to compete effectively if Alias and Wavefront were to design their software to be compatible only with SGI, and at the same time rival graphic software manufacturers would be foreclosed from 90% of the market if SGI were to close its previously open software interface so that only Alias and Wavefront would be able to design compatible software. On the other hand, there were very strong indications that the combination of SGI, Alias and Wavefront's complementary capacities was efficient and would lead to important innovation. To allow the merger to proceed, SGI signed a consent order providing that SGI would use best efforts to ensure optimal interoperation of Alias' leading software programs with competitor workstations, and that SGI would maintain an open architecture and publish its application programming interface for its workstations so that it did not discriminate against software rivals of Alias and Wavefront.

2. In *Time Warner–Turner*, 5 Trade Reg. Rep. ¶ 24,104 (1996), the Commission examined the potential competitive effects of a merger of Time Warner, a dominant programmer in movies, magazines, music, and network broadcasting (and also the second largest cable company in the U.S.) with Turner, another major television programmer. Concern was expressed both with respect to upstream and downstream foreclosure effects. Programming competitors of Turner feared that they would be denied equal access to Time Warner cable as a result of the merger, and competitors of Time Warner cable (including particularly companies delivering programming through satellite systems) feared that they would be denied equal

access to Turner's valuable news, sports and movie programming. The merger was allowed to proceed pursuant to a consent order that imposed an elaborate set of restrictions on the complying companies preserving access to competitors and banning unjustified discrimination.

The blockbuster sequel to *Time Warner–Turner* was *AOL–Time Warner*, a merger that involved both horizontal and vertical effects. Again, the merger was allowed to proceed, but only after acceptance of some unusually regulatory provisions designed to keep access open to new broadband technology and thereby allow programming competitors of Time Warner and internet service provider competitors of AOL to compete effectively after the merger.

3. *Barnes & Noble–Ingram.* In 1999, Barnes & Noble, the largest retail bookseller in the United States with 34% of national sales, proposed to acquire Ingram, the largest book wholesaler in the United States with 23% of national sales. The Commission investigated primarily on the theory that smaller bookstores competing with Barnes & Noble, after the merger, would not receive from the Ingram subsidiary comparable discounts, terms of sale, delivery dates, or marketing specials since their source of supply would be owned by a direct competitor. Another theory, explored but not emphasized, is that new entrants who wanted to come into the market for sale of books on the internet (and compete with such powerful early entrants as Amazon and Barnes & Noble's electronic subsidiary) would be denied a source of supply and arguably would have to enter not just internet retailing but become their own wholesaler. After the Commission staff indicated its intention to propose challenging the deal, the merger was abandoned. See Labaton, "Book Chain Gives In; Barnes and Noble Won't Seek $600 Million Deal," N.Y. Times, June 3, 1999.

4. Consider whether any or all of these transactions could be successfully challenged under the 1984 Department of Justice Merger Guidelines.

5. There has been no vertical merger enforcement at the federal level since 1999.

PROBLEM 25

PHILIPS PAPER ACQUIRES SOME PULP SOURCES

Five years ago, Philips Paper was the third largest manufacturer in the United States of paper products including toilet tissue, facial tissue, paper napkins, paper towels, and a full line of other specialty items. Philips sells directly to retail stores, grocery chains and supermarkets, and to wholesalers for distribution to industrial plants, offices, and hotels. Before the mergers here challenged, it accounted for 8% of total sales; National was first with 28% of sales, Wells second with 11%, and six other full-line companies averaged about 5% each. The remainder of the market was accounted for by about 30 small companies, each specializing in some particular paper product. Entry barriers into the business are moderate for full-line companies, involving a minimum investment of about $50 million, but low for specialty outlets.

Traditionally all full-line companies owned some timberland and paper pulp mills, but none was fully integrated. On the average, these companies including

Philips supplied about 50% of their own needs; the captive share of the market was stable, however, and there had been no sizable vertical mergers in recent years. After several years of careful study, Philips decided to make itself independent of pulp suppliers and converters by acquiring three companies, each of which had extensive timber holdings and pulp converting facilities. The three together accounted for only about 2½% of all pulp sold, but 13% of the type of semi-processed materials suitable for conversion into Philips products. The acquisition involved an enormous outlay of cash and securities by Philips, since the acquired companies were valued at nearly $500 million. As a result of the acquisitions, Philips could not only satisfy all of its own needs but became a seller of semi-processed pulp to some of the specialty companies in the business. Soon after this acquisition, Philips embarked on a program of replacement or improvement of pulp conversion equipment in the acquired companies. The improvement program and full integration have led to substantial efficiencies of operation, with the result that Philips has become an aggressive competitor on sales of semi-processed pulp to specialty paper producers and on sales of its own finished paper products to retail and industrial users. With respect to the latter, Philips now accounts for 12% of total sales of paper products, is second in the industry, and continues to grow. Several news and business magazines have done feature stories on the remarkable recent success engineered by Philips' management, and its stock is highly prized by institutional investors.

Early last year, labor troubles led to a temporary period of short supply of pulp suitable for conversion to products other than newsprint. Philips used its supply of processed pulp to keep its own conversion operation going and delayed deliveries to independent converters. As soon as the shortages eased, Philips went back to supplying the independents at better prices than anyone else in the industry. Too late, however, because the independents had already complained to the FTC, and, as a result, a complaint will soon be filed.

Has Philips violated the antitrust laws?

NOTE ON FOREIGN MERGER REGULATION

Since the early 1970s, there has been a virtual explosion of merger regulation legislation around the world. One convenient place to place the beginning is in 1973, which was when merger control provisions were added to the German Law Against Restraints of Competition. In that same year, the Commission of the European Community first began serious discussions of its proposal for a new Council Regulation on the subject of mergers—a discussion that did not culminate in the enactment of the Merger Regulation until December 21, 1989, when the Council adopted Regulation 4064/89, O.J. L 395/1 (Dec. 30, 1989), corrected, O.J. L 257/14 (Sept. 21, 1990), with an effective date of September 21, 1990. (The current Merger Regulation is Council Regulation (EC) No. 139/2004 of Jan. 20, 2004, OJ L 24, 29.01.2004, p. 1–22.) In the United Kingdom, the Secretary of State for Trade and Industry was given the discretionary power to refer certain mergers to the Monopolies and Mergers Commission (MMC) under the Fair Trading Act 1973, for the MMC to investigate their effect on "the public interest." Merger regulation in its current form became part of the French and Canadian competition laws in 1986. *See generally* Kekelekis, EC Merger Control Regulation: Rights of Defence (2006).

Perhaps because few subjects in antitrust law cut more closely at the basic industrial or economic policy of a country, there is considerable variation in the substantive standards of the different merger regimes. In the United States, of course, mergers and acquisitions can be enjoined only if their effect would be substantially to lessen competition in a particular, defined market. The European Merger Regulation also uses criteria derived from competition law, as opposed to other fields of economic or social policy. Article 2(1) of the Regulation instructs the Commission to take into account "the need to maintain and develop effective competition within the common market," and familiar factors such as the market position of the companies, alternatives available to suppliers and users, their access to supplies or markets, barriers to entry, supply and demand trends, and "the development of technical and economic progress provided that it is to consumers' advantage and does not form an obstacle to competition." Article 2(2) provides that "a concentration which would not significantly impede effective competition in the common market or in a substantial part, in particular as a result of the creation or strengthening of a dominant position, shall be declared compatible with the common market." Article 2(3) states the converse: if the concentration "would significantly impede effective competition, in the common market or in a substantial part of it, in particular as a result of the creation or strengthening of a dominant position, shall be declared incompatible with the common market." Through this language, the Council has attempted to tie the Merger Regulation to the language of the Treaty, while at the same time emphasizing the need to show that a substantial effect on competition is likely before condemning a merger.

Some merger laws are based on competition criteria, but they contain a political safety valve for the extraordinary case. The German law is a good case in point. The Federal Cartel Office reviews mergers for compliance with the German competition law, but its decisions are subject to review by the Economics and Technology Minister, who can override a decision to prohibit a merger for compelling reasons of public policy. Grounds for giving ministerial authorization can include rationalization advantages, the wish to preserve jobs or secure the supply of energy or raw materials. Merger review is organized in two stages: the Federal Cartel Office is exclusively responsible for review of the merger from the perspective of competition law. Any political grounds for the justification of the merger can be taken into account only in the second stage, in the form of a ministerial authorization. This power is exercised quite rarely: over one 20–year period, a ministerial authorization was granted in only 6 cases.[75]

The same possibility also appears to exist in the French system under the merger control rules that came into effect in the spring of 2002. As in Germany, the French merger control procedure comprises two phases. In the first phase, the Minister for Economy, acting through the Director General for Competition, Consumer Protection, and Repression of Fraud (DGCCRF), decides whether the transaction should be approved (possibly subject to conditions), or whether the transaction is likely to harm competition so as to trigger the second phase of the procedure. If the Minister decides to enter into phase II, he must request a formal opinion from the Competition Council (Conseil de la Concurrence). If a transaction has been brought before the Council, the Council must examine whether it is likely to jeopardize competition, particularly by creating or strengthening a dominant position or by creating or strengthening buying power that places suppliers in a state of economic dependence. It must also assess whether the operation makes a great enough contribution to economic progress that the damage to competition will be offset. The Council is obliged to take into account the competitiveness of the undertaking in question with respect to international competition.[76] Following

---

75. *See generally* http://www.internationalcompetitionnetwork.org/.

76. *See generally* Article L430–6 of the French Commercial Code.

receipt of the Council's opinion, the Minister of Economy may either prohibit or approve the transaction, with or without conditions. The Minister is not bound by the opinions of the Competition Council. Although in a majority of cases the final decision of the Minister essentially reiterates the Council's formal opinion, there are cases in which the Minister did not follow the analysis or the solutions suggested by the Council.[77]

At the other extreme is the United Kingdom's "public interest" standard that, up until the time the U.K. adopted its present law, was applicable. Although some governments have chosen to interpret the public interest as referring exclusively, or almost exclusively, to competition criteria, nothing in the statutes requires this kind of self-restraint. Like France or Germany, the U.K. operated under a system of divided powers for mergers. Indeed, it still does: the Office of Fair Trading (OFT) begins the process by obtaining and reviewing information relating to mergers. (There is no formal requirement of pre-merger notification, but companies often prefer the legal certainty that a notification can give.) If OFT believes that the proposed transaction may lead to a substantial lessening of competition, it must then refer the case to the Competition Commission. *See generally* Merger Assessment Guidelines (A joint publication of the Competition Commission and the Office of Fair Trading, Consultation Document, April 2009), at http://www.oft.gov.uk/ shared_oft/consultations/OFT1078con.pdf. recommends The Secretary of State for Business, Enterprise and Regulatory Reform continues to have the power to intervene if he or she believes that a public interest consideration may be relevant to the evaluation of the merger. In such cases, however, the Secretary must accept the decisions of OFT and the CC with respect to jurisdiction and the likelihood of an anticompetitive outcome. The statute identifies three public interest factors (national security, the media, and the stability of the U.K. financial system), and permits the Secretary either to add to the list or to remove or amend an existing criterion. Any undertakings required following an adverse report by the CC are negotiated by the OFT.

Systems vary almost as much procedurally as they do substantively. Some countries and regions, such as the United States, Canada, the EU, Mexico, Japan, Germany, (more recently) France and others, have a system of mandatory pre-merger notification in place. These systems usually rely on quantitative criteria to establish who must notify. In the EU, the Merger Regulation itself applies only to very large transactions, where the combined aggregate worldwide turnover of all the undertakings concerned is more than EUR 5 billion (more than $5 billion), and where the aggregate Community-wide turnover of each of at least two of the undertakings concerned is more than EUR 250 million, unless each of the undertakings concerned achieves more than two-thirds of its turnover in one and the same Member State. In the United States, in contrast, notification under the Hart–Scott–Rodino Antitrust Improvements Act of 1976, 15 U.S.C. § 18a, must normally take place if one party has total assets or net annual sales of $200 million or more (a number that is now indexed), or if one party has $10 million and the other $100 million (also indexed numbers). (As of 2009, the first threshold had increased to $260.7 million; the $10 million/$100 million figures had gone up to $19 million and $130.3 million. *See* http://www.ftc.gov/os/fedreg/2009/january/090113section7aclay tonact.pdf.) Timetables are also different, ranging from the EU's currently rigid maximum of five months, if the case must be studied beyond the "first stage" one-month period, to the U.S. open-ended period that depends on a party's compliance with requests for information from the government, to an utterly open-ended time to study the deal in some countries.

---

77. *See* the DGCCRF website at http://www.finances.gouv.fr/DGCCRF/concurrence/ index.html, and the links to the applicable part of the French Commercial Code.

As multinational activities increase, difficulties for firms can also increase if their mergers are subject to review in more than one country. The problems are well illustrated by the first case in which the EC blocked a merger, Aerospatiale–Alenia/de Havilland, Com.Dec. 91/619, O.J. L 334/42 (Dec. 5, 1991). The case arose when the United States aircraft manufacturer, Boeing, decided to sell its Canadian aircraft subsidiary, de Havilland, to a joint venture called ATR, which had been formed by two European firms, Aerospatiale (France) and Alenia e Selenia (Italy). ATR was the world's leading manufacturer of commuter aircraft, and de Havilland was the number two firm. Boeing's decision to sell de Havilland meant that it was exiting this market. Few other competitors existed: British Aerospace and Fokker in Europe were smaller factors in the market; Indonesian and East European companies were unable to compete effectively due to a combination of financial and quality problems. From the Canadian perspective, however, de Havilland was a "failing firm," and the Canadians therefore affirmatively wanted the deal to go through. The Commission concluded that the proposed concentration would create a dominant position that was incompatible with the common market. The GE/Honeywell case, discussed above in connection with portfolio effects is another, more recent example of the problems that may arise in a global economy with multiple and conflicting notifications systems.

More commonly, the Commission, like other authorities with responsibility for mergers, imposes conditions on mergers that appear troublesome but allows the overall transaction to be completed. The business community has begun to express concern that conflicting conditions from a variety of merger authorities may (at best) impose unwarranted transaction costs on them, or (at worst) subject them to conflicting legal requirements. In any event, many concede that consistency in enforcement policy in different jurisdictions and elimination of unnecessary or duplicative procedural burdens would benefit consumers and businesses around the globe. *See* the Report of the Special Committee on International Antitrust of the American Bar Association Section of Antitrust Law, September 1, 1991. *See also* OECD, Merger Cases in the Real World: A Study of Merger Control Procedures (1994). Is there a need for harmonized procedural rules for mergers? What about harmonized substantive standards? Can or should merger rules be the same regardless of the size of national markets? Would you expect merger standards to be the same between the EC and Brazil, or between the United States and Mexico? Why or why not? How can jurisdiction best be allocated among countries when a transnational merger is simultaneously being considered by as many as 10 or 15 or even more authorities?

Although "hard" harmonization may not be on the agenda of the day (except, notably, in regional arrangements such as within the European Union), there are a growing number of initiatives for soft harmonization, including an increasing number of global fora for discussions. The OECD Competition Committee has for decades been a leading forum for regular policy dialogue among the world's leading competition officials. The Competition Committee has also identified voluntary "best practices" and created substantial analytical convergence.[78] The OECD has sponsored a "Global Forum on Competition." This Forum comprises an expanded network of high-level officials from 55 or more economies who meet regularly (in principle twice a year) to share experiences on competition issues.

---

78. *See, e.g.,* documents entitled Portfolio Effects in Conglomerate Mergers; Airline Mergers and Alliances; Efficiency Claims in Mergers and Other Horizontal Agreements; Failing Firm Defense. Long extracts of these documents are available on-line at OECD's website at http://www.oecd.org.

Other initiatives are also underway. The one that has brought the greatest number of actors under the same roof is the International Competition Network (ICN). ICN has been working to provide antitrust agencies from both developed and developing countries with a network for addressing practical antitrust enforcement and policy issues of common concern. Its stated aim is to facilitate procedural and substantive convergence in antitrust enforcement. By enhancing convergence and cooperation, ICN hopes to promote more efficient, effective antitrust enforcement worldwide. ICN's work products[79] include the "Guiding Principles for Merger Notification and Review." as well as "Recommended Practices for Merger Notification Procedures."

In addition, the European Commission, the Department of Justice and the Federal Trade Commission, the competition authorities of the world's two most significant antitrust regulatory systems, have been cooperating closely for decades in an attempt to minimize the risk of divergent outcomes in cases that involve both jurisdictions. The initial basis for the cooperation was the conclusion of the EU–US Agreement on the Application of their Competition Laws Competition Laws in 1991. In October, 2002, the EU and the US jointly issued a set of best practices for cooperation in reviewing mergers that require approval on both sides of the Atlantic. The best practices recognize that cooperation is most effective when the investigation timetables of the reviewing agencies run in parallel. Merging companies will therefore be offered the possibility of meeting at an early stage with the agencies to discuss timing issues. Companies are also encouraged to permit the agencies to exchange information, which they have submitted and, where appropriate, to allow joint EU/US interviews of the companies concerned. The practices also designate key points in the investigations when it may be appropriate for direct contacts to occur between senior officials on both sides.

Clayton Act, Section 8

No person at the same time shall be a director in any two or more corporations, any one of which has capital, surplus, and undivided profits aggregating more than $10,000,000, engaged in whole or in part in commerce, ... if such corporations are or shall have been theretofore, by virtue of their business and location of operation, competitors, so that the elimination of competition by agreement between them would constitute a violation of any of the provisions of any of the antitrust laws....

NOTES AND QUESTIONS

1. United States v. Sears, Roebuck & Co., 111 F.Supp. 614 (S.D.N.Y.1953). Motion for summary judgment by the government in an action seeking the resigna-

---

79. Available at the ICN website at http://www.internationalcompetitionnetwork.org.

tion of Sidney J. Weinberg as a director of Sears, Roebuck & Co. or The B.F. Goodrich Co. because of an alleged violation of Section 8 of the Clayton Act. Defendants admit that the corporations are of the required size; that Weinberg is a director of both corporations; that each corporation is engaged in commerce; and that they compete in the sale of seven categories of items at retail in commerce. They also admit that Sears and Goodrich compete in the sale of these items in 97 communities, in 31 states, and that Sears' sales of these items in such communities exceeded $65 million and Goodrich's exceeded $16 million. Held, for the government. Defendants argue that Section 8 does not prohibit Weinberg's directorship on both Boards, absent a showing that the effect of an assumed consolidation of Sears and Goodrich would be to violate Section 7 of the Clayton Act. The vital distinction between Section 7 and Section 8, however, is that Section 8 promulgates its own substantiality standard in the form of the $1 million size requirement. Were the defendants' construction to be adopted, it would require the application of a test which Congress appears deliberately to have omitted. Further, defendants' construction would denude of meaning the phrase "any of the provisions of any of the antitrust laws." There is no logical basis upon which to infer that this all-inclusive language was intended to exclude methods other than merger or acquisition from the reach of Section 8. "Since Sears and Goodrich are competitors, since a price fixing or division of territory agreement would eliminate competition between them, and since such an agreement would *per se* violate at least one 'of the provisions of ... the antitrust laws,' namely § 1 of the Sherman Act, it follows that § 8 forbids defendant Weinberg to be a director of both corporations." (Weinfeld, J.).[80]

2.   In 1990, Congress amended Section 8 to raise the threshold level from $1 million to $10 million dollars each in capital surplus and undivided profits. The same 1990 amendments provided for certain safe harbors even when the $10 million dollar minimum was met. These exceptions applied where the sales of either corporation in competition with the other were less than $1 million dollars, where the sales of either corporation in competition with the other were less than 2% of that corporation's total sales, or where sales of each corporation in competition with the other were less than 4% of that corporation's sales.

The statute is not enforced aggressively or systematically. In those rare instances where an illegal interlocking arrangement is found, the remedy is for the director to resign from one board or the other.

SELECTIVE BIBLIOGRAPHY

1.   Horizontal and Conglomerate Mergers

Baker & Shapiro, Reinvigorating Horizontal Merger Enforcement.

Pitofsky (ed.), How the Chicago School Overshot the Mark, Ch. 6, 235 (2008).

---

80.   *See* United States v. Sears, Roebuck & Co., 165 F.Supp. 356 (S.D.N.Y.1958), holding that the decree barred Weinberg from serving as a trustee of the Sears Savings and Profit Sharing Pension Fund, which held 26% of the total Sears shares outstanding, while he continued as a director of Goodrich.

In United States v. W.T. Grant Co., 345 U.S. 629 (1953), the Court noted, in passing, that Section 8 has not been systematically enforced and held that the director's resignation from the board of one of the competing corporations rendered injunctive relief unnecessary. *See also* Paramount Pictures Corp. v. Baldwin–Montrose Chemical Co., 1966 Trade Cas. (CCH) ¶ 71,678 (S.D.N.Y. 1966), holding that: (1) Section 8 does not apply to: (1) vertical relationships, or (2) *de minimis* competition.

Hovenkamp, Federal Antitrust Policy: The Law of Competition and Its Practice 9, 12, and 13 (3d ed. 2005).

Sullivan & Grimes, The Law of Antitrust: An Integrated Handbook (2d ed. 2006), Ch. IX

4–5 Areeda & Hovenkamp, Antitrust Law: An Analysis of Antitrust Principles and Their Application Chs. 9–11 (2006 & 2009 Supplement).

FTC Staff, Anticipating the 21st Century: Competition Policy in the New High–Tech, Global Marketplace (1996).

Gellhorn & Kovacic, Antitrust Law and Economics in a Nutshell (4th ed. 1994).

Scherer, Industrial Market Structure and Economic Performance Chs. 12 and 20 (3d ed. 1990).

Kwoka & White (ed.), The Antitrust Revolution 1–119 (1989).

Bork, The Antitrust Paradox 217–24, 246–62 (1978).

Kaysen & Turner, Antitrust Policy Ch. 3 (1959).

Baker, Mavericks, Mergers and Exclusion: Proving Coordinated Competitive Effects Under the Antitrust Laws, 77 NYU L.Rev. 135, 177–88 (2002).

R. Epstein & Lee Rubinfeld, Merger Simulation: A Simplified Approach with New Application, 69 Antitrust L.J. 883 (2002).

Patterson & Shapiro, Transatlantic Divergence in GE/Honeywell: Causes and Lessons, 16 Antitrust 18 (Fall 2001).

Pitofsky, Proposals for Revised United States Merger Enforcement in a Global Economy, 81 Geo.L.J. 195 (1992).

Cirace, The Horizontal Merger Guidelines of the Department of Justice and the National Association of Attorneys General Compared, 33 Vill.L.Rev. 281 (1988).

Krattenmaker & Pitofsky, Antitrust Merger Policy and the Reagan Administration, 33 Antitrust Bull. 211 (1988).

Calkins, Developments in Merger Litigation: The Government Doesn't Always Win, 56 Antitrust L.J. 855 (1987).

Fisher, Lande & Vandaele, Efficiency Considerations in Merger Enforcement 71 Cal.L.Rev. 1580 (1983).

Landes & Posner, Market Power in Antitrust Cases, 94 Harv.L.Rev. 937 (1981).

Weiss, The Structure–Conduct–Performance Paradigm and Antitrust, 127 U.Pa.L.Rev. 1104 (1979).

Brodley, Potential Competition Mergers: A Structural Synthesis, 87 Yale L.J. 1 (1977).

Bok, Section 7 of the Clayton Act and the Merging of Law and Economics, 74 Harv.L.Rev. 226 (1960).

2. Joint Ventures

Pitofsky, A Framework for Antitrust Analysis of Joint Ventures, 74 Geo.L.J. 1605 (1986).

Brodley, Potential Competition Mergers: A Structural Synthesis, 87 Yale L.J. 1 (1977).

Pitofsky, Joint Ventures Under the Antitrust Laws: Some Reflections on the Significance of Penn–Olin, 82 Harv.L.Rev. 1007 (1969).

3. Vertical Mergers

4 Areeda & Hovenkamp, Antitrust Law: An Analysis of Antitrust Principles and Their Application Ch. 10 (2006 & Supp. 2009).

Sullivan & Grimes, Hornbook on the Law of Antitrust (2d ed. 2006).

Posner, Antitrust Law: An Economic Perspective 223–229 (2d ed. 2001).

Scherer & Ross, Industrial Market Structure and Economic Performance Ch. 5 (3d ed. 1990).

Bork, The Antitrust Paradox 225–45 (1978).

Bain, Industrial Organization 360–62 (2d ed. 1968).

Kaysen & Turner, Antitrust Policy 130–33 (1959).

Kirkwood, Buyer Power and Exclusionary Conduct, 72 Antitrust L.J. 625 (2005).

Riordan & Salop, Evaluating Vertical Mergers: A Post–Chicago Approach, 63 Antitrust L.J. 513 (1995).

Posner, The Chicago School of Antitrust Analysis, 127 U.Pa.L.Rev. 925 (1979).

Bork & Bowman, The Crisis in Antitrust, 65 Colum.L.Rev. 363 (1965).

Blake & Jones, Toward a Three–Dimensional Antitrust Policy, 65 Colum.L.Rev. 422 (1965); In Defense of Antitrust, 65 Colum.L.Rev. 377 (1965).

Bork, Contrasts in Antitrust Theory: I, 65 Colum.L.Rev. 401 (1965).

Bowman, Contrasts in Antitrust Theory: II, 65 Colum.L.Rev. 417 (1965).

4. Comparative Materials

Fox, Monopolization, Abuse of Dominance And the Indeterminacy of Economics: The US/EU Divide, 2006 Utah L. Rev. 725 (2006).

Antitrust Division Submission for OECD Roundtable on portfolio effects in Conglomerate Mergers, Range Effects: the United States Perspective (10/12/01) available at http://www.usdoj.gov/atr/public/international/9550.htm.

Reynolds and Ordover, Archimedean Leveraging and the GE/Honeywell Transaction, 70 Antitrust L.J. 171 (2002).

C H A P T E R   10

FOREIGN COMMERCE AND THE U.S. ANTITRUST LAWS

SCOPE NOTE

From the day the Sherman Act was passed to the present time, it has been clear that the U.S. antitrust laws have some application to foreign trade and commerce. Sections 1 and 2 of the Sherman Act both refer explicitly to restraints or monopolization of "trade or commerce among the several States, or with foreign nations...." On the other hand, it is equally clear that the United States did not, and cannot, legislate rules of market organization or behavior for the entire world. The questions of how far the U.S. antitrust laws reach beyond our borders, and how they interact with the competition laws that exist today in almost every other commercially significant country in the world, is one of increasing importance.

The expansion of global commerce, particularly since the end of World War II, is an economic development of surpassing importance not only for U.S. business, but also for consumers and producers around the world. As of the end of FY 2008, the U.S. Department of Commerce reported that the U.S. gross domestic product (GDP) was a seasonally adjusted $14,441.4 billion; of that figure, exports contributed $1,831.1 billion, and imports $2,538.9 billion.[1] Taken together, international trade in goods amounted to about 23% of U.S. GDP;[2] the Commerce Department reported that international trade in services for 2008 was just over 30% of total exports, and on the import side trade in services was about 15% of the total.[3] The world-wide figures are even more impressive: the World Trade Organization estimates that the value of global trade in 2008 was $16,070 billion in merchandise exports, and $16,422 billion in merchandise imports.[4] Finally, more and more companies are "multi-national enterprises," with affiliates, subsidiaries, plants, and customers in two or more countries around the world. When we couple these facts with the reality that more than 100 countries now have antitrust laws, the risk of conflict and the possibilities of cooperation among antitrust authorities become plain.

---

1. U.S. Dept. of Commerce, Bureau of Economic Analysis, *Nat'l Income & Accounts Table 1.1.5. Gross Domestic Product*, http://bea.gov/national/nipaweb/index.asp (follow "All NIPA Tables" hyperlink, then follow "Table 1.1.5. Gross Domestic Product (A) (Q)" hyperlink).

2. According to the Bureau of Economic Analysis, in 2008, trade in goods totaled $3,393.3 billion—$1,266.9 billion in exports, and $2,126.4 billion in imports. *Id.*

3. Total seasonally adjusted exports for 2008 were $1,831.1 billion, as noted; exports of services were $564.2 billion (about 30.81%). Total seasonally adjusted imports were $2,538.9 billion, of which $412.4 billion were services (about 16.24%). *Id.*

4. Statistics are available on the WTO's International Trade and Tariff Data Statistics Database, http://www.wto.org/english/res_e/statis_e/statis_e.htm (follow "Time Series on international trade" hyperlink).

The materials that follow provide an introduction to the doctrines that address the twin problems of complex international commercial activity and multiplicity of regulating sovereigns. We begin with the scope of legislative jurisdiction under U.S. antitrust law to reach conduct that is in whole or in part located abroad—often referred to as the "extraterritoriality" question. In a more forward-looking sense we then consider some of the international agreements that address comity and cooperation issues more directly. Finally, we turn to some of the special considerations that are present when foreign sovereigns have acted, including the doctrine of foreign sovereign immunity, the act of state doctrine, and the concept of foreign sovereign compulsion.

SECTION 1.   JURISDICTION OVER FOREIGN COMMERCE

The question of how far the U.S. antitrust laws may extend to regulate people, companies, and transactions whose actions affect U.S. markets has been both legally and politically sensitive. We begin here with the earliest case to give the question significant attention, with an opinion by Justice Holmes. The Justice, who was at best skeptical about the value of the antitrust laws (note his dissenting opinion in *Dr. Miles, supra* Ch. 7, p. 610 took a narrow approach both to the jurisdictional reach of the statute and to the related question of how much deference was due to the acts of a foreign authority.

A.   FOREIGN COMMERCE BEFORE 1982

American Banana Co. v. United Fruit Co.

Supreme Court of the United States, 1909.
213 U.S. 347, 29 S.Ct. 511, 53 L.Ed. 826.

■ HOLMES, J. This is an action brought to recover threefold damages under the [Sherman Act]. The Circuit Court dismissed the complaint upon motion, as not setting forth a cause of action. This judgment was affirmed by the Circuit Court of Appeals....

The allegations of the complaint may be summed up as follows: The plaintiff is an Alabama corporation, organized in 1904. The defendant is a New Jersey corporation, organized in 1899. Long before the plaintiff was formed, the defendant, with intent to prevent competition and to control and monopolize the banana trade, bought the property and business of several of its previous competitors, with provision against their resuming the trade, made contracts with others, including a majority of the most important, regulating the quantity to be purchased and the price to be paid, and acquired a controlling amount of stock in still others. For the same purpose it organized a selling company, of which it held the stock, that by agreement sold at fixed prices all the bananas of the combining parties. By this and other means it did monopolize and restrain the trade and maintained unreasonable prices. The defendant being in this ominous attitude, one McConnell in 1903 started a banana plantation in Panama, then part of the United States of Colombia, and began to build a railway (which would afford his only means of export), both in accordance with the laws of the United States of Colombia. He was notified by the defendant that he must either combine or stop. Two months later, it is believed at the defendant's instigation, the governor of Panama recommended to his national government that Costa Rica be allowed to administer the territory through which the railroad was to run, and this although that territory had been awarded to Colombia under an arbitration agreed to by treaty. The defendant, and afterwards, in September, the government of Costa Rica, it is believed by the inducement of the defendant, interfered with McConnell. In November, 1903, Panama revolted and became an independent republic, declaring its boundary to be that settled by the award. In June, 1904, the plaintiff bought out McConnell and went on with the work, as it had a right to do under the laws of Panama. But in July, Costa Rican soldiers and officials, instigated by the defendant, seized a part of the plantation and a cargo of supplies and have held them ever since, and stopped the construction and operation of the plantation and railway. In August one Astua, by ex parte proceedings, got a judgment from a Costa Rican court, declaring the plantation to be his, although, it is alleged, the proceedings were not within the jurisdiction of Costa Rica, and were contrary to its laws and void. Agents of the defendant then bought the lands from Astua. The plaintiff has tried to induce the government of Costa Rica to withdraw its soldiers, and also has tried to persuade the United States to interfere, but has been thwarted in both by the defendant and has failed. The government of Costa Rica remained in possession down to the bringing of the suit.

As a result of the defendant's acts the plaintiff has been deprived of the use of the plantation, and the railway, the plantation and supplies have been injured. The defendant also, by outbidding, has driven purchasers out of the market and has compelled producers to come to its terms, and it has prevented the plaintiff from buying for export and sale. This is the substantial damage alleged. There is thrown in a further allegation that the defendant has "sought to injure" the plaintiff's business by offering positions to its employees, and by discharging and threatening to discharge persons in its own employ who were stockholders of the plaintiff. But no particular point is made of this. It is contended, however, that, even if the main argument fails and the defendant is held not to be answerable for acts depending on the cooperation of the government of Costa Rica for their effect, a wrongful conspiracy resulting in driving the plaintiff out of business is to be gathered from the complaint and that it was entitled to go to trial upon that.

It is obvious that, however stated, the plaintiff's case depends on several rather startling propositions. In the first place the acts causing the damage were done, so far as appears, outside the jurisdiction of the United States and within that of other states. It is surprising to hear it argued that they were governed by the act of Congress.

No doubt in regions subject to no sovereign, like the high seas, or to no law that civilized countries would recognize as adequate, such countries may treat some relations between their citizens as governed by their own law, and keep, to some extent, the old notion of personal sovereignty alive. See The Hamilton (Old Dominion S. S. Co. v. Gilmore), 207 U.S. 398, 403; Hart v. Gumpach, L.R., 4 P.C. 439, 463, 464; British South Africa Co. v. Companhia de Mocambique [1893] A.C. 602. They go further, at times, and declare that they will punish any one, subject or not, who shall do certain things, if they can catch him, as in the case of pirates on the high seas. In cases immediately affecting national interests they may go further still and may make, and, if they get the chance, execute, similar threats as to acts done within another recognized jurisdiction. . . . But the general and almost universal rule is that the character of an act as lawful or unlawful must be determined wholly by the law of the country where the act is done. . . . For another jurisdiction, if it should happen to lay hold of the actor, to treat him according to its own notions rather than those of the place where he did the acts, not only would be unjust, but would be an interference with the authority of another sovereign, contrary to the comity of nations, which the other state concerned justly might resent. . . .

The foregoing considerations would lead in case of doubt to a construction of any statute as intended to be confined in its operation and effect to the territorial limits over which the lawmaker has general and legitimate power. "All legislation is *prima facie* territorial." . . . Words having universal scope, such as "Every contract in restraint of trade," "Every person who shall monopolize," etc., will be taken as a matter of course to mean only everyone subject to such legislation, not all that the legislator subsequently may be able to catch. In the case of the present statute the improbability of the United States attempting to make acts done in Panama or Costa Rica criminal is obvious, yet the law begins by making criminal the acts for which it gives a right to sue. We think it entirely plain that what the defendant did in Panama or Costa Rica is not within the scope of the statute so far as the present suit is concerned. . . .

For again, not only were the acts of the defendant in Panama or Costa Rica not within the Sherman Act, but they were not torts by the law of the place and therefore were not torts at all, however contrary to the ethical and economic postulates of that statute. The substance of the complaint is that, the plantation being within the *de facto* jurisdiction of Costa Rica, that state took and keeps possession of it by virtue of its sovereign power. But a seizure by a state is not a thing that can be complained of elsewhere in the courts. Underhill v. Hernandez, 168 U.S. 250. The fact, if it be one, that *de jure* the estate is in Panama does not matter in the least; sovereignty is pure fact. The fact has been recognized by the United States, and, by the implications of the bill is assented to by Panama.

The fundamental reason why persuading a sovereign power to do this or that cannot be a tort is not that the sovereign cannot be joined as a defendant or because it must be assumed to be acting lawfully. . . . The fundamental reason is that it is a contradiction in terms to say that within its jurisdiction, it is unlawful to persuade a sovereign power to bring about a result that it declares by its conduct to be desirable and proper. It does not, and foreign courts cannot, admit that the influences were improper or the results bad. It makes the persuasion lawful by its own act. The very meaning of sovereignty is that the decree of the sovereign makes law. See Kawananakoa v. Polyblank, 205 U.S. 349, 353. In the case of private persons it consistently may assert the freedom of the immediate parties to an injury and yet declare that certain persuasions addressed to them are wrong. . . .

The plaintiff relied a good deal on Rafael v. Verelst, 2 W. Bl. 983, 1055. But in that case, although the nabob who imprisoned the plaintiff was called a sovereign for certain purposes, he was found to be the mere tool of the defendant, an English Governor. That hardly could be listened to concerning a really independent state. But of course it is not alleged that Costa Rica stands in that relation to the United Fruit Company.

The acts of the soldiers and officials of Costa Rica are not alleged to have been without the consent of the government and must be taken to have been done by its order. It ratified them, at all events, and adopted and keeps the possession taken by them. . . . The injuries to the plantation and supplies seem to have been the direct effect of the acts of the Costa Rican government which is holding them under an adverse claim of right. The claim for them must fall with the claim for being deprived of the use and profits of the place. As to the buying at a high price, etc., it is enough to say that we have no ground for supposing that it was unlawful in the countries where the purchases were made. Giving to this complaint every reasonable latitude of interpretation we are of opinion that it alleges no case under the act of Congress and discloses nothing that we can suppose to have been a tort where it was done. A conspiracy in this country to do acts in another jurisdiction does not draw to itself those acts and make them unlawful, if they are permitted by the local law. . . .

Judgment affirmed.

■ HARLAN, J., concurred in the result.

NOTES AND QUESTIONS

1. United States v. American Tobacco Co., 221 U.S. 106 (1911). Two years after *American Banana*, the Supreme Court found jurisdiction in a foreign commerce cases notwithstanding the holding in *American Banana*. In *American Tobacco* the Supreme Court asserted subject matter jurisdiction without even discussing this issue in any detail and held that an anticompetitive conspiracy to monopolize the tobacco industry violated the Sherman Act, despite the fact that some of the contracts leading to the violation were executed in England. *American Banana*'s strict territorial doctrine was further eroded in a series of subsequent cases.

2. *Principals' activities.* In United States v. Pacific & Arctic Ry., 228 U.S. 87 (1913), the Supreme Court upheld a criminal indictment charging American and Canadian corporations with conspiring to set discriminatory rates on shipping between points in the United States and Canada. The conspiracy was effectuated by control of certain wharves in American territory. This was enough, in the Supreme

Court's view, to justify applying the Sherman Act both to the U.S. side of the conspiracy and to activity taking place partially in Canada. In his opinion, Justice McKenna said that American antitrust law applied to foreign "citizens and corporations operating in our territory."

3. *Agents' activities.* In Thomsen v. Cayser, 243 U.S. 66 (1917), the Supreme Court applied the Sherman Act to a combination affecting foreign commerce that was put into operation in the United States. The Court awarded treble damages in a suit against the agents of foreign shipping lines for charging discriminatory rates on shipments between New York and South Africa, pursuant to an agreement made in London; the Court held that the agents' activities within the United States were a sufficient basis for liability. The mere fact that a combination in restraint of trade was formed in a foreign country, the Court said, did not exempt it from American law so long as it "affected the foreign commerce of this country and was put into operation here." The laws were found applicable, therefore, based on the idea that an antitrust conspiracy is subject to U.S. law even if some of the actions took place outside the country, so long as some activity also occurred within. As in the *Sisal* case which we discuss next, the Court was willing to expand, but not to entirely dispense with, the strict territorial approach.

4. *Distinguishing* American Banana. In United States v. Sisal Sales Corp., 274 U.S. 268 (1927), a conspiracy to control the American market for sisal—an agave rope-making fiber—entered into and partially carried out in the United States and implemented by legislation secured in Mexico to regulate the sources of supply was held to violate the U.S. antitrust laws. The Supreme Court once again upheld the extraterritorial application of the Sherman Act to the conspiracy between U.S. and Mexican firms. The Court distinguished *American Banana* by noting that a few of the agreements in that conspiracy were reached in the United States and that the conspiracy was funded by U.S. banks. The Court also distinguished *American Banana* as a case involving an alleged conspiracy in the United States "to do acts in another jurisdiction." Such a conspiracy, Justice McReynolds said, does not violate the Sherman Act. In *Sisal*, by contrast, the conspiracy in question was "entered into by parties within the United States," and it was "made effective by acts done therein." Do you find these distinctions satisfactory?

These decisions lead us to the famous *Alcoa* decision of the Second Circuit, other parts of which you saw in Chapter 3, *supra* p. 114. *Alcoa* was a final, unappealable judgment even though it was not before the United States Supreme Court. Because a quorum of the Supreme Court could not be assembled, the case was certified to the Court of Appeals for the Second Circuit, which sat in place of the Supreme Court.

United States v. Aluminum Co. of America

United States Court of Appeals, Second Circuit, 1945.
148 F.2d 416.

[As the excerpt from *Alcoa supra* p. 114, sets forth, this case involved Alcoa's alleged monopolization of the market for virgin aluminum ingot in violation of Sherman Act § 2. The government also claimed that Alcoa had entered into a conspiracy in restraint of commerce in aluminum, including in foreign commerce. Because much of the conduct took place outside the United States, and was undertaken by foreign companies, the Court had to consider whether the Sherman Act even applied. Judge Hand's discussion of that issue remains, more than sixty years later, a leading formulation of the jurisdictional reach of the U.S. antitrust laws.

The Second Circuit divided the classes of defendants into four groups, of which the most important for present purposes were Alcoa itself, with its wholly-owned subsidiaries, directors, officers and shareholders, and Aluminum Limited (Alcoa's Canadian subsidiary) ("Limited"), with its directors, officers and shareholders. The discussion that follows was the third part of the court's opinion, in which it discussed whether Limited and Alcoa were in an unlawful conspiracy, and whether, if not, Limited was guilty of a conspiracy with foreign producers.]

■ L. HAND, CIRCUIT JUDGE.

* * *

III.   Limited.

Limited was incorporated in Canada on May 31, 1928, to take over those properties of Alcoa which were outside the United States. Only two were excepted: a Dutch company which owned bauxite deposits in Dutch Guiana; and a Canadian power transmission company, which supplied Alcoa's Massena plant. . . . At first there remained some officers common to both companies; but by the middle of 1931, this had ceased, and, formally at any rate, the separation between the two companies was complete. At the conclusion of the transfers a majority, though only a bare majority, of the common shares of Alcoa was in the hands of three persons: Andrew W. Mellon, Richard B. Mellon, his brother, and Arthur V. Davis. Richard Mellon died in 1933, and Andrew in 1937, and their shares passed to their families; but in January, 1939, the Davises, the officers and directors of Alcoa and the Mellon families—eleven individuals in all—collectively still held 48.9 per cent of Alcoa's shares, and 48.5 per cent of Limited's and Arthur V. Davis was then the largest shareholder in both companies.

The companies had a number of transactions with each other, upon which the plaintiff relies to prove that they did not deal at arms length, but that Limited was organized only as a creature of Alcoa. . . . Alcoa also did some fabrication for Limited from Limited's own aluminum, and did it at only mill cost without overhead. That substantially ended by 1931; but, while it lasted, it was confessedly a favor, and indeed for a short season Alcoa undoubtedly did cast a kindly eye upon its "fledgling," as Arthur V. Davis called it. . . .

There was also some evidence that Alcoa took part in the formation of the Alliance, a foreign "cartel" which we shall describe later. This consists very largely of declarations of Arthur V. Davis, put in his mouth by other witnesses; of a cable of Edward K. Davis to one of Limited's other officers; and of the improbability that the Alliance should have been set up without the active cooperation of Arthur V. Davis, especially as he was concededly in Europe and in communication with some foreign producers at about the time that the Alliance was first bruited. Edward K. Davis was the originator of the Alliance; he gave as his reason for it that he feared that the other foreign producers who had already joined in a "cartel," would shut him out. When these producers came to Canada in 1931 to arrange for the Alliance, they visited Arthur V. Davis and made an extended visit to Alcoa's plants in the East. As anticipatory confirmation that Alcoa had had a share in forming the Alliance, the plaintiff also introduced evidence to show that before 1928 Alcoa had already had an understanding with foreigners as to prices. This consisted largely of the statements of what others had said about an agreement to keep their prices the same as Alcoa's. The plaintiff rested particularly upon the testimony of Haskell, (who testified, not only upon this point, but more generally), because, when Haskell testified, although he had been one of the important figures in the Baush company, he had made his peace with Alcoa which had employed him in some advisory capacity. It must be remembered, however, that he had already testified in the action of the Baush company against Alcoa, and that he could scarcely have repudiated what he then said.

The Davises in answer to all this evidence swore that Limited had been organized for three reasons, quite different from controlling prices in the United States. First, there was at that time a growing nationalism in the British Empire—where Alcoa sold most of its foreign aluminum—which manifested itself in the slogan: "Buy British," and which would be better satisfied, if the properties were owned by a Canadian corporation, even though its shareholders were American. Next, Alcoa had neglected its foreign properties—relatively—and they would better prosper under a management, singly devoted to them. Finally, the time was coming when Arthur V. Davis wished to take a less active part in affairs; and there would be embarrassment in choosing between Hunt and Edward K. Davis, as his successor. Both said that the separation between the companies had been actually as complete as it was in form. Arthur said that, although while in Europe shortly before the Alliance was formed, foreign producers had spoken to him, he had then and always referred all their inquiries to his brother. He had discussed little with Edward any questions of policy about Limited; they had talked for the most part only about the history, development and future of the properties. He had indeed seen a preliminary draft of the agreement, forming the Alliance, but not its final form until the time of the trial; and he had had nothing whatever to do with its formation. As for the trip of the foreign producers in the United States, it was purely social; a "good-will" excursion, so to say, in which the relations of Alcoa and foreign production was not discussed.

Upon the whole evidence the judge found that by 1935 Limited had become altogether free from any connection with Alcoa, and that Alcoa had had no part in forming the Alliance, or in any effort at any time to limit imports, to fix their price, or to intervene in price fixing "cartels" in Europe—except the early ones. In short, he again felt persuaded by the testimony against any inferences to be drawn from the conceded facts, and from the declarations put in the mouths of the Davises. As before, to do otherwise he would have had to find that both these men had deliberately perjured themselves; and we cannot see that these findings present us with anything different in substance from those on which we have already passed. Considering the interests in Limited which Arthur V. Davis and both the Mellons had, it would perhaps have taxed our credulity to the breaking point to believe that they knew nothing about the formation of the Alliance. Arthur V. Davis did not go as far as that; and that he and the Mellons should have put into the hands of Edward K. Davis the whole management of Limited, does not appear to us to pass the bounds of reasonable entertainment. Alcoa had had collisions in plenty with the plaintiff and others before 1931; the first Baush action, which challenged the "price squeeze," had been filed in April, 1928, and the second in July, 1931. It was not unreasonable to believe that Arthur V. Davis and the Mellons, seeing that some kind of "cartel" might be an inescapable incident to continuing business abroad, wished in 1931 to keep Alcoa as far removed from it as possible.

[The Court then concluded that Alcoa could not be held responsible for the Alliance's actions solely by virtue of the fact that a majority (or controlling group) of Alcoa's shareholders were also a majority (or controlling group) of Limited's shareholders.] For these reasons we conclude that Alcoa was not a party to the Alliance, and did not join in any violation of Sec. 1 of the Act, so far as concerned foreign commerce.

Whether Limited itself violated that section depends upon the character of the Alliance. It was a Swiss corporation, created in pursuance of an agreement entered into on July 3, 1931, the signatories to which were a French corporation, two German, one Swiss, a British, and Limited. The original agreement, or "cartel," provided for the formation of a corporation in Switzerland which should issue shares, to be taken up by the signatories. This corporation was from time to time to fix a quota of production for each share, and each shareholder was to be limited to the quantity measured by the number of shares it held, but was free to sell at any price it chose. The corporation fixed a price every year at which it would take off any shareholder's hands any part of its quota which it did not sell. No shareholder was to "buy, borrow, fabricate or sell" aluminum produced by anyone not a shareholder except with the consent of the board of governors, but that must not be "unreasonably withheld." Nothing was said as to whether the arrangement extended to sales in the United States; but Article X, known as the "Conversion Clause," provided that any shareholder might exceed his quota to the extent that he converted into aluminum in the United States or Canada any ores delivered to him in either of those countries by persons situated in the United States. This was confessedly put in to allow Limited to receive bauxite or alumina from Alcoa, to smelt it into aluminum and to deliver the aluminum to Alcoa.

Edward K. Davis gave as an explanation of this that Limited needed some protection against Alcoa's possible refusal to convey Alcoa Power Company, which Alcoa had never actually bound itself to transfer. Although in 1931 Alcoa had all the producing capacity which it seemed likely to need (and so the event proved, for the clause was never invoked), Davis said that he did not know whether in the future the demand might not outrun that capacity, and whether Alcoa might not therefore be tempted to hold onto the Lower Development, unless Limited would smelt its alumina.

That does indeed seem a somewhat farfetched reason; but on the other hand it is hard to suppose that Alcoa really feared that it could not meet its future needs and meant to lean upon Limited. The incident may be thought to have a bearing on Alcoa's implication in the Alliance; but its only substantial importance, so far as we can see, is as showing whether the 1931 agreement was intended to cover the United States. That question arose very shortly after the agreement was made, and Edward K. Davis took the position that the United States was included, relying upon absence of any exception in the general language. His interpretation would seem to have been plainly right, not only for the reason he gave, but because otherwise there would have been no occasion for the "Conversion Clause." However, the other shareholders overruled him, and until 1936, when the new arrangement was made, imports into the United States were not included in the quotas. The issue turned out to be unimportant anyway, for the annual average of imports during the five years was in the neighborhood of only fifteen million pounds.

The agreement of 1936 abandoned the system of unconditional quotas, and substituted a system of royalties. Each shareholder was to have a fixed free quota for every share it held, but as its production exceeded the sum of its quotas, it was to pay a royalty, graduated progressively in proportion to the excess; and these royalties the Alliance divided among the shareholders in proportion to their shares. This agreement—unlike the first—did not contain an express promise that the Alliance would buy any undisposed of stocks at a fixed price, although perhaps § 3 of Subdivision A, of Part X may have impliedly recognized such an obligation. Probably, during the two years in which the shareholders operated under this agreement, that question did not arise for the demand for aluminum was very active. Nevertheless, we understand from Limited's answer to an interrogatory that the last price fixed under the agreement of 1931 was understood to remain in force. Although this agreement, like its predecessor, was silent as to imports into the United States, when that question arose during its preparation, as it did, all the shareholders agreed that such imports should be included in the quotas. The German companies were exempted from royalties—for obvious reasons—and that, it would seem, for practical purposes put them out of the "cartel" for the future, for it was scarcely possible that a German producer would be unable to dispose of all its production, at least within any future period that would be provided for. The shareholders continued this agreement unchanged until the end of March, 1938, by which time it had become plain that, at least for the time being, it was no longer of service to anyone. Nothing was, however, done to end it, although the German shareholders of course became enemies of the French, British and Canadian shareholders in 1939. The Alliance itself has apparently never been dissolved; and indeed it appeared on the "Proclaimed List of Blocked Nationals" of September 13, 1944.

Did either the agreement of 1931 or that of 1936 violate § 1 of the Act? The answer does not depend upon whether we shall recognize as a source of liability a liability imposed by another state. On the contrary we are concerned only with whether Congress chose to attach liability to the conduct outside the United States of persons not in allegiance to it. That being so, the only question open is whether Congress intended to impose the liability, and whether our own Constitution permitted it to do so: as a court of the United States, we cannot look beyond our own law. Nevertheless, it is quite true that we are not to read general words, such as those in this Act, without regard to the limitations customarily observed by nations upon the exercise of their powers; limitations which generally correspond to those fixed by the "Conflict of Laws." We should not impute to Congress an intent to punish all whom its courts can catch, for conduct which has no consequences within the United States. American Banana Co. v. United Fruit Co., 213 U.S. 347, 357; United States v. Bowman, 260 U.S. 94, 98; Blackmer v. United States, 284 U.S. 421, 437. On the other hand, it is settled law—as Limited itself agrees—that any state may impose liabilities, even upon persons not within its allegiance, for conduct outside its borders that has consequences within its borders which the state reprehends; and these liabilities other states will ordinarily recognize. Strassheim v. Daily, 221 U.S. 280, 284, 285; Lamar v. United States, 240 U.S. 60, 65, 66; Ford v. United States, 273 U.S. 593, 620, 621; Restatement of Conflict of Laws § 65.

It may be argued that this Act extends further. Two situations are possible. There may be agreements made beyond our borders not intended to affect imports, which do affect them, or which affect exports. Almost any limitation of the supply of goods in Europe, for example, or in South America, may have repercussions in the United States if there is trade between the two. Yet when one considers the international complications likely to arise from an effort in this country to treat such agreements as unlawful, it is safe to assume that Congress certainly did not intend the Act to cover them. Such agreements may on the other hand intend to include imports into the United States, and yet it may appear that they had no effect upon them. That situation might be thought to fall within the doctrine that intent may be a substitute for performance in the case of a contract made within the United States; or it might be thought to fall within the doctrine that a statute should not be interpreted to cover acts abroad which have no consequence here. We shall not choose between these alternatives; but for argument we shall assume that the Act does not cover agreements, even though intended to affect imports or exports, unless its performance is shown actually to have had some effect upon them. Where both conditions are satisfied, the situation certainly falls within such decisions as United States v. Pacific & Arctic R. & Navigation Co., 228 U.S. 87; Thomsen v. Cayser, 243 U.S. 66; and United States v. Sisal Sales Corporation, 274 U.S. 268. . . . It is true that in those cases the persons held liable had sent agents into the United States to perform part of the agreement; but an agent is merely an animate means of executing his principal's purposes, and, for the purposes of this case, he does not differ from an inanimate means; besides, only human agents can import and sell ingot.

Both agreements would clearly have been unlawful, had they been made within the United States; and it follows from what we have just said that both were unlawful, though made abroad, if they were intended to affect imports and did affect them. Since the shareholders almost at once agreed that the agreement of 1931 should not cover imports, we may ignore it and confine our discussion to that of 1936: indeed that we should have to do anyway, since it superseded the earlier agreement. The judge found that it was not the purpose of the agreement to "suppress or restrain the exportation of aluminum to the United States for sale in competition with Alcoa." By that we understand that he meant that the agreement was not specifically directed to Alcoa, because it only applied generally to the production of the shareholders. If he meant that it was not expected that the general restriction upon production would have an effect upon imports, we cannot agree, for the change made in 1936 was deliberate and was expressly made to accomplish just that. It would have been an idle gesture, unless the shareholders had supposed that it would, or at least might, have that effect. The first of the conditions which we mentioned was therefore satisfied; the intent was to set up a quota system for imports.

The judge also found that the 1936 agreement did not "materially affect the . . . foreign trade or commerce of the United States"; apparently because the imported ingot was greater in 1936 and 1937 than in earlier years. We cannot accept this finding, based as it was upon the fact that, in 1936, 1937 and the first quarter of 1938, the gross imports of ingot increased. It by no means follows from such an increase that the agreement did not restrict imports; and incidentally it so happens that in those years such inference as is possible at all, leads to the opposite conclusion. It is true that the average imports—including Alcoa's—for the years 1932–1935 inclusive were about 15 million pounds, and that for 1936, 1937 and one-fourth of 1938 they were about 33 million pounds; but the average domestic ingot manufacture in the first period was about 96 million and in the second about 262 million; so that the proportion of imports to domestic ingot was about 15.6 per cent for the first period and about 12.6 per cent for the second. We do not mean to infer from this that the quota system of 1936 did in fact restrain imports, as these figures might suggest; but we do mean that nothing is to be inferred from the gross increase of imports. We shall dispose of the matter therefore upon the assumption that, although the shareholders intended to restrict imports, it does not appear whether in fact they did so. Upon our hypothesis the plaintiff would therefore fail, if it carried the burden of proof upon this issue as upon others. We think, however, that, after the intent to affect imports was proved, the burden of proof shifted to Limited. In the first place a depressant upon production which applies generally may be assumed, *ceteris paribus*, to distribute its effect evenly upon all markets. Again, when the parties took the trouble specifically to make the depressant apply to a given market, there is reason to suppose that they expected that it would have some effect, which it could have only by lessening what would otherwise have been imported. If the motive they introduced was over-balanced in all instances by motives which induced the shareholders to import, if the United States market became so attractive that the royalties did not count at all and their expectations were in fact defeated, they to whom the facts were more accessible than to the plaintiff ought to prove it, for a prima facie case had been made. Moreover, there is an especial propriety in demanding this of Limited, because it was

Limited which procured the inclusion in the agreement of 1936 of imports in the quotas.

There remains only the question whether this assumed restriction had any influence upon prices, Apex Hosiery Co. v. Leader, *supra*, 310 U.S. 469. To that Socony–Vacuum Oil Co. v. United States, *supra*, 310 U.S. 150, is an entire answer. It will be remembered that, when the defendants in that case protested that the prosecution had not proved that the "distress" gasoline had affected prices, the court answered that that was not necessary, because an agreement to withdraw any substantial part of the supply from a market would, if carried out, have some effect upon prices, and was as unlawful as an agreement expressly to fix prices. The underlying doctrine was that all factors which contribute to determine prices, must be kept free to operate unhampered by agreements. For these reasons we think that the agreement of 1936 violated Sec. 1 of the Act. . . .

NOTES AND QUESTIONS

1. *Sherman Act vis-à-vis public international law.* Justice Holmes considered the plaintiff's claim that the Sherman Act covered the foreign conduct in question in *American Banana* at least "surprising," if not "startling," while Judge Hand thought it equally clear that "any state may impose liabilities, even upon persons not within its allegiance, for conduct outside its borders that has consequences within its borders which the state reprehends." Does this reflect a difference in views about the content of international law limitations on State prescriptive jurisdiction? See generally ALI, Restatement (Third) of the Foreign Relations Law of the United States §§ 401–03 (1987). Does it suggest that international law itself had evolved between the opening years of the 20th century and the time immediately after World War II? To what extent, if at all, should or must the Sherman Act be construed to conform to norms of public international law? *See* The Paquete Habana, 175 U.S. 677 (1900); *see also* Hartford Fire Ins. Co. v. California, 509 U.S. 764 (1993) (dissenting opinion of Justice Scalia), *infra* p. 1198.

2. *Conflicts of law analogy. Alcoa* is usually cited for the proposition that the Sherman Act (as it then read) reaches the conduct of foreigners undertaken solely in their own countries, if the necessary actual and intended effects on U.S. commerce can be detected. If this is true, then where does U.S. jurisdiction stop? Judge Hand thought that principles borrowed from the field of conflicts of law would be adequate to prevent excessive assertions of U.S. jurisdiction. But given the ease with which actual effects can be proven under *Socony*, was he right? Suppose one of the foreign countries in question had an express policy that encouraged membership in the international aluminum cartel. If the company were then found guilty of an offense under U.S. law, or in private litigation it was subject to treble damages, whose law should prevail?

Continental Ore Co. v. Union Carbide and Carbon Corp.

Supreme Court of the United States, 1962.
370 U.S. 690, 82 S.Ct. 1404, 8 L.Ed.2d 777.

■ WHITE, J. This is a private treble damage action under the anti-trust laws. Continental Ore Company, a partnership, and its individual partners, who were plaintiffs in the trial court, are petitioners here. Henry J. Leir, the principal party in Continental, had engaged in the buying and selling of metals, including vanadium products, in Europe prior to 1938, in which year he immigrated to the United States. This case concerns his subsequent efforts in this country to build a successful business in the production and sale of vanadium.

Vanadium is a metal obtained from certain ores which, in this country, are mined principally on the Colorado plateau. The ore is processed at mills near the mines into a substance commonly known as vanadium oxide. The oxide is then transported to the East and converted into ferrovanadium, which is purchased chiefly by steel companies for use as an alloy in hardening steels.

The defendants named in the complaint were Vanadium Corporation of America (VCA), a fully integrated miner and manufacturer of vanadium products, Union Carbide and Carbon Corporation (Carbide), and the following four wholly owned subsidiary corporations of the latter company: United States Vanadium Corporation (USV), engaged in mining vanadium ore and processing vanadium oxide; Electro Metallurgical Company (Electro Met), engaged in making ferrovanadium; Electro Metallurgical Sales Corporation (Electro Met Sales), engaged in the sale of vanadium oxide and ferrovanadium; and Electro Metallurgical Company of Canada, Ltd. (Electro Met of Canada), engaged in selling vanadium products in Canada....

The complaint alleged that, beginning in about 1933, the defendants and others acting in concert with them violated §§ 1 and 2 of the Sherman Act by conspiring to restrain, by monopolizing, and by attempting and conspiring to monopolize, trade and commerce in ferrovanadium and vanadium oxide. The defendants were charged with purchasing and acquiring control over substantially all accessible vanadium-bearing ore deposits in the United States and substantially all vanadium oxide produced by others in the United States, with refusing to sell vanadium oxide to other potential producers of ferrovanadium, including Continental and its associates, with apportioning and dividing sales of ferrovanadium and vanadium oxide among themselves in certain proportions, with fixing identical prices for the sale of ferrovanadium and vanadium oxide and for the purchase of ore, and with making certain mutual arrangements whereby one or more Carbide subsidiaries supplied VCA with substantial quantities of vanadium oxide at preferential prices to VCA. The complaint stated that between 1933 and 1949 the defendants produced over 99% of all ferrovanadium and over 90% of all vanadium oxide produced in the United States and that during the same period the defendants sold over 99% of the ferrovanadium and vanadium oxide sold in this country.[5]

---

5. The complaint alleged that VCA sold approximately two-thirds of all ferrovanadium and vanadium oxide sold by defendants (which was said to amount to approximately 99% of all ferrovanadium and vanadium oxide sold and consumed in the United States), while Electro Met Sales (a Carbide subsidiary) sold approximately one-third. According to petitioners' evidence, the Carbide group produced approximately 77% of domestic vanadium oxide, while VCA produced about 65% of ferrovanadium.

According to the complaint, as a proximate consequence of defendants' monopolistic and restrictive practices, independent producers and distributors of ferrovanadium and vanadium oxide, including Continental, were eliminated from the business. Specifically, the complaint detailed several efforts which Continental made to enter and maintain itself in the vanadium business, all of which were allegedly frustrated by defendants' Sherman Act violations: (1) In 1938, Continental negotiated a contract with Apex Smelting Company of Chicago whereby Apex was to build and operate a plant for the conversion of oxide to ferrovanadium by use of the alumino-thermic process. Continental and Apex were to share the profits of this venture. On its part, Continental agreed to obtain raw materials for Apex and to sell the finished product. Operations under this contract began in the spring of 1940, but Apex terminated the agreement in 1942 allegedly because the illegal activities of defendants prevented the obtaining of a sufficient supply of vanadium oxide. (2) Meanwhile, Continental itself had begun to produce a compound called "Van–Ex," composed of vanadium oxide and other materials, which was designed for direct introduction into the steel-making process without prior conversion to ferrovanadium. This venture was allegedly terminated in 1944 because of the difficulty of securing raw materials caused by defendants' unlawful practices, including the efforts of defendants to obtain ownership or control of the mines and mills of Continental's suppliers. (3) Continental had developed a business with a Canadian customer during 1942. When Electro Met Sales of Canada was appointed by the Canadian Government as the exclusive wartime agent to purchase and allocate vanadium for Canadian industries, that company, it is alleged, acting under the control and direction of its parent, Carbide, eliminated Continental entirely from the Canadian market and divided Continental's business solely between defendants. (4) Defendants in 1943, by open threats of reprisals, allegedly frustrated certain arrangements which Continental had with the Climax Molybdenum Corporation for the manufacture of ferrovanadium. (5) In January 1944, Continental contracted with Imperial Paper & Color Corporation for the processing by the latter of vanadium oxide and ferrovanadium. Continental agreed to act as sales agent for the output. The complaint charged that Imperial abandoned the contract at the end of 1944 because of the inability to secure raw materials and that Continental then left the vanadium business altogether, all as a result of the restrictive and monopolistic practices of the defendants.

[The Court next reviewed the evidence presented or offered by plaintiff relating to allegations other than those with respect to the Canadian market, holding that the trial court had erred in excluding certain items and that the court of appeals had erred in its affirmance on grounds that there was insufficient evidence to go to the jury.]

Continental's alleged elimination from the Canadian market raises different issues. At the trial Continental introduced evidence to show that beginning in March 1942, it had shipped Van–Ex to a Canadian customer each month during the remainder of that year. There was then received in evidence a letter dated January 19, 1943, from Continental to Electro Met in New York City reciting that the new allocation system in Canada[6] had eliminated Continental from the Canadian market in January, that Continental had inquired about the matter from the Metals Controller for the Canadian Government and that the latter had referred Continental to Electro Met. The court then struck this letter from the record and rejected petitioners' offer to prove that Continental was excluded from the Canadian market by Electro Met of Canada, a wholly owned subsidiary corporation of Carbide, acting as exclusive purchasing agent for the Metals Controller but allegedly operating in this connection under the control and direction of Carbide for the purpose of carrying out the overall conspiracy to restrain and monopolize the vanadium industry. To that end, Continental offered to prove that its former share of the Canadian market was divided between Carbide and VCA. Continental offered various correspondence with Electro Met of Canada and a memorandum and proposed testimony by Continental's vice president concerning his conversations with an employee of Electro Met who had communicated with Continental in response to Continental's letter of January 19, 1943, to Electro Met. The court denied the entire offer of proof "for the reason that this is a transaction wholly in the hands of the Canadian Government and that whether or not this plaintiff was permitted to sell his material to a customer in Canada was a matter wholly within the control of the Canadian Government."

The Court of Appeals agreed with the trial court and concluded that Continental was not legally entitled to recover from respondents for the destruction of its Canadian business. The court said that no vanadium oxide could be imported into Canada by anyone other than the Canadian Government's agent, Electro Met of Canada, which refused to purchase from the petitioners. Thus, according to the court, "even if we assume that Electro Metallurgical Company of Canada, Ltd. acted for the purpose of entrenching the monopoly position of the defendants in the United States, it was acting as an arm of the Canadian Government, and we do not see how such efforts as appellants claim defendants took to persuade and influence the Canadian Government through its agent are within the purview of the Sherman Act." . . . This ruling was erroneous and we hold that Continental's offer of proof was relevant evidence of a violation of the Sherman Act . . . and was not inadmissible. . . .

Respondents say that American Banana Co. v. United Fruit Co., 213 U.S. 347, shields them from liability. This Court there held that an

---

6. Canada's entry into World War II prompted the Canadian Government to take extraordinary measures to assure optimum availability of strategic materials to Canadian private industries engaged in the war effort. Pursuant to these measures, the Office of Metals Controller was established and given broad powers to regulate the procurement of the materials and to allocate them to industrial users. See Order of the Governor General in Council, P.C. 3187, July 15, 1940. The Metals Controller enlisted the aid of Electro Met of Canada in early 1943, delegating to it the discretionary agency power to purchase and allocate to Canadian industries all vanadium products required by them. The validity of these wartime measures and delegations under Canadian law is not here contested. Cf. Reference Re Regulations (Chemicals) Under War Measures Act, 1 D.L.R. [1943] 248.

antitrust plaintiff could not collect damages from a defendant who had allegedly influenced a foreign government to seize plaintiff's properties. But in the light of later cases in this Court respondents' reliance upon *American Banana* is misplaced. A conspiracy to monopolize or restrain the domestic or foreign commerce of the United States is not outside the reach of the Sherman Act just because part of the conduct complained of occurs in foreign countries. United States v. American Tobacco Co., 221 U.S. 106; United States v. Pacific & Arctic R. & Navigation Co., 228 U.S. 87; Thomsen v. Cayser, 243 U.S. 66; United States v. Sisal Sales Corp., 274 U.S. 268. Cf. Steele v. Bulova Watch Co., 344 U.S. 280; Branch v. Federal Trade Comm'n, 141 F.2d 31 (7th Cir.). See United States v. Aluminum Co. of America, 148 F.2d 416 (2d Cir.); United States v. National Lead Co., 63 F. Supp. 513 (D.C.S.D.N.Y.), aff'd 332 U.S. 319.

Furthermore, in the *Sisal* case, *supra*, a combination entered into within the United States to monopolize an article of commerce produced abroad was held to violate the Sherman Act even though the defendants' control of that production was aided by discriminatory legislation of the foreign country which established an official agency as the sole buyer of the product from the producers and even though one of the defendants became the exclusive selling agent of that governmental authority. Since the activities of the defendants had an impact within the United States and upon its foreign trade, *American Banana* was expressly held not to be controlling.[7]

Olsen v. Smith, 195 U.S. 332; United States v. Rock Royal Co-op, 307 U.S. 533; and Parker v. Brown, 317 U.S. 341, do not help respondents. These decisions, each of which sustained the validity of mandatory state or federal governmental regulations against a claim of antitrust illegality, are wide of the mark. In the present case petitioners do not question the validity of any action taken by the Canadian Government or of its Metals Controller. Nor is there left in the case any question of the liability of the Canadian Government's agent for Electro Met of Canada was not served. What the petitioners here contend is that the respondents are liable for actions which they themselves jointly took, as part of their unlawful conspiracy, to influence or to direct the elimination of Continental from the Canadian market. As in *Sisal*, the conspiracy was laid in the United States, was effectuated both here and abroad, and respondents are not insulated by

---

7. "The circumstances of the present controversy are radically different from those presented in American Banana Co. v. United Fruit Co., *supra*, and the doctrine there approved is not controlling here. . . .

[In *Sisal*], we had "a contract, combination and conspiracy entered into by parties within the United States and made effective by acts done therein. The fundamental object was control of both importation and sales of sisal and complete monopoly of both internal and external trade and commerce therein. The United States complain of a violation of their laws within their own territory by parties subject to their jurisdiction, not merely of something done by another government at the instigation of private parties. True, the conspirators were aided by discriminating legislation, but by their own deliberate acts, here and elsewhere, they brought about forbidden results within the United States. They are within the jurisdiction of our courts and may be punished for offenses against our laws." 274 U.S., at 275–276.

the fact that their conspiracy involved some acts by the agent of a foreign government.

From the evidence which petitioners offered it appears that Continental complained to the Canadian Metals Controller that Continental had lost its Canadian business. The Controller referred Continental to one of the respondents. But there is no indication that the Controller or any other official within the structure of the Canadian Government approved or would have approved of joint efforts to monopolize the production and sale of vanadium or directed that purchases from Continental be stopped. The exclusion, Continental claims, resulted from the action of Electro Met of Canada, taken within the area of its discretionary powers granted by the Metals Controller and in concert with or under the direction of the respondents. The offer of proof at least presented an issue for the jury's resolution as to whether the loss of Continental's Canadian business was occasioned by respondents' activities. Respondents are afforded no defense from the fact that Electro Met of Canada, in carrying out the bare act of purchasing vanadium from respondents rather than Continental, was acting in a manner permitted by Canadian law. There is nothing to indicate that such law in any way compelled discriminatory purchasing, and it is well settled that acts which are in themselves legal lose that character when they become constituent elements of an unlawful scheme.…

The case of Eastern Railroad Presidents Conf. v. Noerr Motor Freight, Inc., 365 U.S. 127, cited by the court below and much relied upon by respondents here, is plainly inapposite. The Court there held not cognizable under the Sherman Act a complaint charging, in essence, that the defendants had engaged in a concerted publicity campaign to foster the adoption of laws and law enforcement practices inimical to plaintiffs' business. Finding no basis for imputing to the Sherman Act a purpose to regulate political activity, a purpose which would have encountered serious constitutional barriers, the Court ruled the defendants' activities to be outside the ban of the Act "at least insofar as those activities comprised mere solicitation of governmental action with respect to the passage and enforcement of laws." 365 U.S., at 138. In this case, respondents' conduct is wholly dissimilar to that of the defendants in *Noerr*. Respondents were engaged in private commercial activity, no element of which involved seeking to procure the passage or enforcement of laws. To subject them to liability under the Sherman Act for eliminating a competitor from the Canadian market by exercise of the discretionary power conferred upon Electro Met of Canada by the Canadian Government would effectuate the purposes of the Sherman Act and would not remotely infringe upon any of the constitutionally protected freedoms spoken of in *Noerr*.

Since our decision concerning the alleged loss of Continental's Canadian business will in any event require a new trial of the entire case in view of the close interconnection between the Canadian and domestic issues, we shall remand the case to the District Court for further proceedings.…

Judgment of Court of Appeals vacated and case remanded.

■ FRANKFURTER, J., took no part in the consideration or decision of this case.

NOTES AND QUESTIONS

1. *Status of foreign states.* In Pfizer, Inc. v. Government of India, 434 U.S. 308 (1978), the Court held that "a foreign nation otherwise entitled to sue in our courts is entitled to sue for treble damages under the antitrust laws to the same extent as any other plaintiff." The Court noted that the phrase "any person" in the Sherman Act did not exclude a foreign sovereign. The governments of several foreign countries, as purchasers of antibiotics, had brought antitrust treble damage suits against major pharmaceutical firms in the United States. The Court was asked to decide whether a foreign sovereign was a "person" within the meaning of Section 4 of the Clayton Act. The Court reasoned that since "the antitrust laws extend to trade 'with foreign nations as well as among the several States of the Union' . . . Congress did not intend to make the treble damage remedy available only to consumers in our own country." The Court relied on its decision in Georgia v. Evans, 316 U.S. 159 (1942), which held that a state could sue for treble damages, to reject "the proposition that the word 'person' as used in the antitrust laws excludes all sovereign states." It also noted that depriving foreign sovereigns of standing to sue would, in some circumstances, greatly diminish the deterrent effect of the statutory treble damage provisions. A foreign sovereign remains a "person" under Section 4 of the Clayton Act, pursuant to the Antitrust Reciprocity Amendment Act of 1982, Pub. L. No. 97–393, 96 Stat. 1964 (1982), but pursuant to 15 U.S.C. § 15(b) it may recover only actual damages.

2. *State action in extraterritorial jurisdiction cases.* Note that *Parker v. Brown*, the leading "state action" case, *supra* p. 431, is cited in *Continental Ore*. How was it used by counsel, and how was it distinguished by the Court? Should "state action" cases be persuasive in deciding cases implicating actions by foreign governments?

3. *Imports versus exports.* Do you see any difference, for purposes of determining extraterritorial coverage, between cases alleging restrictions on U.S. import commerce, such as *Alcoa*, and cases alleging restrictions on exports from the United States, such as *Continental Ore*? This distinction moved to the forefront in the late 1980s, as a result of 1982 legislation and several rounds of guidelines from the U.S. Department of Justice and the Federal Trade Commission. *See* Antitrust Enforcement Guidelines for International Operations, available at http://www.justice.gov/atr/public/guidelines/internat.htm. The *Canadian Radio Patent Pool* case summarized in note 4 illustrates a time when the Supreme Court was relatively unaware of the international sensitivities that might be offended by exercises of jurisdiction in export cases. *Compare* F. Hoffmann–LaRoche, Ltd. v. Empagran S.A., 542 U.S. 155 (2004), *infra* p. 1216.

4. Zenith Radio Corp. v. Hazeltine Research, Inc., 395 U.S. 100 (1969). Zenith was a Delaware corporation that manufactured radio and television sets for sale in the United States and abroad. Hazeltine and its subsidiary HRI had the right to a number of foreign and U.S. patents that Zenith needed in its business. For a time, it licensed a package of patents from Hazeltine, but in 1959 it decided that it did not need to renew its package license. Litigation ensued in which Hazeltine tried to enforce its patent rights and Zenith resisted, eventually filing an antitrust counterclaim against Hazeltine. The district court found that Hazeltine had violated the antitrust laws, but the court of appeals reversed, principally on the ground that the U.S. courts had no jurisdiction over Hazeltine. The Supreme Court then reversed the court of appeals, finding that there was enough evidence in the record to support the district court's finding of injury to Zenith's export business from the way in which Hazeltine used its Canadian patents.

The holder of the patents in question was a patent pool in Canada (Canadian Radio Patents, Ltd., or CRPL), which had been formed in 1926 by the Canadian subsidiaries of two U.S. companies, General Electric and Westinghouse. The Supreme Court noted that:

> The pool was made up largely of Canadian manufacturers, most of which were subsidiaries of American companies. The pool for many years had the exclusive right to sublicense the patents of its member companies and also those of Hazeltine and a number of other foreign concerns. About 5,000 patents were available to the pool for licensing, and only package licenses were granted, covering all patents in the pool and strictly limited to manufacture in Canada. No license to importers was available. The chief purpose of the pool was to protect the manufacturing members and licensees from competition by American and other foreign companies seeking to export their products into Canada.

> CRPL's efforts to prevent importation of radio and television sets from the United States were highly organized and effective.

Zenith tried to establish itself in Canada without obtaining a license from the pool, but it was unsuccessful. It then brought an antitrust suit against several individual pool members and settled the suit in a way that gave it worldwide licenses on patents owned by the named defendants. Armed with these and other licenses, Zenith in 1958 began exporting radio and television products to Canada. CRPL immediately took steps to enforce its Canadian rights, informing Zenith that it had to sign CRPL's standard license, which did not permit importation, and that to sell in Canada it must manufacture there. Zenith refused, and this lawsuit was the result. Without so much as a nod to the fact that it was dealing with an arrangement that blocked U.S. exports into a foreign country, or any indication of concern about the legality of the arrangement in Canada, the Supreme Court found that:

> The evidence was quite sufficient to sustain a finding that competing business concerns and patentees joined together to pool their Canadian patents, granting only package licenses and refusing to license imported goods. Their clear purpose was to exclude concerns like Zenith from the Canadian market unless willing to manufacture there. Zenith, consequently, was never able to obtain a license. This fact and the pool's vigorous campaign to discourage importers, distributors, dealers, and consumers from selling, handling, or using unlicensed foreign merchandise effectively prevented Zenith from making any headway in the Canadian market until after the 1957 settlement with RCA and its codefendants. And even in 1958, when Zenith undertook in earnest to establish its distribution system in Canada and to market its merchandise, Zenith was met with further pool advertisements threatening action against imported goods and further notifications, continuing past May 22, 1959, that its products were infringing pool patents and that no license was available unless Zenith manufactured in Canada.

It was enough, in the Court's view, that "Zenith was denied a valuable license and submitted testimony that without the license it had encountered distribution difficulties which prevented its securing a share of the market comparable to that which it enjoyed in the United States, and which its business proficiency, demonstrated in the United States, dictated it should have obtained in Canada." It concluded that the district court's injunction was proper, with the following statements:

The findings of the District Court were that HRI and CRPL were conspiring to exclude Zenith and others from the Canadian market; there was nothing indicating that this clear violation of the antitrust laws had terminated or that the threat to Zenith inherent in the conduct would cease in the foreseeable future. Neither the relative quiescence of the pool during the litigation nor claims that objectionable conduct would cease with the judgment negated the threat to Zenith's foreign trade. That threat was too clear for argument, and injunctive relief against HRI with respect to the Canadian market was wholly proper.

The Court reinstated the injunction barring HRI from conspiring with others to restrict or to prevent Zenith's entry into other foreign markets, particularly noting findings of HRI's participation in similar pools in the Australia and British markets. Quoting NLRB v. Express Publishing Co., 312 U.S. 426, 435 (1941), the Court explained that federal courts have broad equitable jurisdiction to restrain acts of the same type or class the court has found it has committed or may be fairly anticipated to commit in the future unless enjoined.

5. *Reining in extraterritorial antitrust laws.* Cases like *Continental Ore* and *Canadian Patent Pools* represented a high-water mark for the extraterritorial application of the U.S. antitrust laws. Several developments coincided to rein in these ambitious positions: objections from foreign governments; the development of an abstention-like doctrine of comity by the federal courts; and the enactment of legislation by Congress. We look at the comity issue in Section 2 of this chapter; here, we continue the story with the statute that currently regulates most assertions of jurisdiction in foreign commerce cases: section 6a of the Sherman Act (and its FTC Act analog), which was enacted in 1982 as the Foreign Trade Antitrust Improvements Act ("FTAIA").

B. THE FOREIGN TRADE ANTITRUST IMPROVEMENTS ACT

The FTAIA amended both the Sherman Act and the Federal Trade Commission Act to clarify the meaning of the phrase "conduct involving trade or commerce with foreign nations" in the two statutes. Because there is no pertinent difference in the amendments of the two statutes, only the Sherman Act language is reproduced here:

> Sections 1 to 7 of this title [Title 15, U.S.C.] shall not apply to conduct involving trade or commerce (other than import trade or import commerce) with foreign nations unless—
>
> > (1) such conduct has a direct, substantial, and reasonably foreseeable effect—
> >
> > > (A) on trade or commerce which is not trade or commerce with foreign nations, or on import trade or import commerce with foreign nations; or
> > >
> > > (B) on export trade or export commerce with foreign nations, of a person engaged in such trade or commerce in the United States; and
> >
> > (2) such effect gives rise to a claim under the provisions of sections 1 to 7 of this title, other than this section.

If sections 1 to 7 of this title apply to such conduct only because of the operation of paragraph (1)(B), then sections 1 to 7 of this title shall apply to such conduct only for injury to export business in the United States.

Although the statute may not be destined for inclusion in a manual of style, it essentially creates two categories of "foreign commerce" cases: those in which the effects of the conduct in question are felt in domestic or import commerce, and those in which the effects of the conduct are felt in the export trade of U.S. exporters.

NOTES AND QUESTIONS

1. *The FTAIA limit on jurisdiction.* The extent to which this statute governs applications of the U.S. antitrust laws to foreign commerce cases has not been as clear as the drafters might have hoped. Nor is it clear whether the statute creates a limitation on the subject matter jurisdiction of the federal courts, in the same way that 28 U.S.C. § 1332 allows assertions of jurisdiction only when there is "complete" diversity, or whether it addresses jurisdiction in the broader sense of international prescriptive jurisdiction or legislative jurisdiction. Which do you think it is, and why? *See* United Phosphurs, Ltd. v. Angus Chem. Co., 322 F.3d 942 (7th Cir. 2003) (en banc), in which the court held by a 5–4 vote that the statute creates the former type of limitation on the subject matter jurisdiction of the federal courts.

2. *Import commerce cases.* Why do you think Congress so explicitly excluded import commerce from the statute? Is the formula "direct, substantial, and reasonably foreseeable effects" an appropriate one for import commerce cases, or should the courts use something more like the test in Summit Health, Ltd. v. Pinhas, 500 U.S. 322 (1991), which governs conventional jurisdictional analysis under the Sherman Act? Is there any reason to treat criminal cases differently? *See* United States v. Nippon Paper Indus., 109 F.3d 1 (1st Cir. 1997), *infra* p. 1203.

3. *International "comity."* Congress specified when it passed the FTAIA that it was not taking a position one way or the other on the question whether the exercise of judicial power should also be tempered by "comity." *See* Timberlane Lumber Co. v. Bank of America, N.T. & S.A., 549 F.2d 597 (9th Cir. 1976), *cert. denied,* 472 U.S. 1032, *infra* p. 1235. How should the "comity" considerations of *Timberlane* interact with the statutory test established by the FTAIA?

4. After passage of the FTAIA, a number of district courts began to dismiss cases on the grounds that the jurisdictional allegations were insufficient. *See, e.g.,* Eurim–Pharm GmbH v. Pfizer Inc., 593 F. Supp. 1102 (S.D.N.Y. 1984); Liamuiga Tours v. Travel Impressions, Ltd., 617 F. Supp. 920 (E.D.N.Y. 1985); The In Porters, S.A. v. Hanes Printables, Inc., 663 F. Supp. 494 (M.D.N.C. 1987); Optimum, S.A. v. Legent Corp., 926 F. Supp. 530 (W.D. Pa. 1996). Occasionally, however, jurisdiction succeeds. *See, e.g.,* Coors Brewing Co. v. Miller Brewing Co., 889 F. Supp. 1394 (D. Colo. 1995).

5. *Post-FTAIA decisions.* The next case, *Hartford Fire,* arose out of an elaborate alleged conspiracy in international insurance markets that limited policies written in the United States. Which theory of jurisdiction did the majority adopt? Which did the dissent advocate?

Hartford Fire Insurance Co. v. California

Supreme Court of the United States, 1993.
509 U.S. 764, 113 S.Ct. 2891, 125 L.Ed.2d 612.

[Nineteen states and many private plaintiffs sued domestic insurance companies and domestic and foreign reinsurers alleging a conspiracy to restrict the coverage of commercial general liability (CGL) insurance available in the United States. Plaintiffs alleged conspiracies to curtail insurance coverage in several respects, the most important limiting the insurer's responsibility so that it must pay only for claims made during the policy period on accidents occurring during the time period the policy was in effect, rather than for insurable events that occurred during the policy period, no matter when the claim was filed. Other conspiracies allegedly made pollution coverage unavailable or practically unavailable in the plaintiffs' states.

The Supreme Court's review of dismissal of the complaints focused on two issues: whether the alleged conduct was immune from the antitrust laws because it constituted "the business of insurance" within the meaning of the McCarran–Ferguson Act, and whether the action against several of the foreign defendants should be dismissed because the Sherman Act should not apply to the foreign conduct at issue.

The Court found that the McCarran–Ferguson Act was no bar to Sherman Act enforcement and then turned for the first time in many years to the question of the extraterritorial reach of the Sherman Act. The majority opinion of Justice Souter and the dissenting opinion of Justice Scalia follow.]

■ SOUTER, J.... Finally, we take up the question ... whether certain claims against the London reinsurers should have been dismissed as improper applications of the Sherman Act to foreign conduct. The Fifth Claim for Relief of the California Complaint alleges a violation of § 1 of the Sherman Act by certain London reinsurers who conspired to coerce primary insurers in the United States to offer CGL coverage on a claims-made basis, thereby making "occurrence CGL coverage ... unavailable in the State of California for many risks." The Sixth Claim for Relief of the California Complaint alleges that the London reinsurers violated § 1 by a conspiracy to limit coverage of pollution risks in North America, thereby rendering "pollution liability coverage ... almost entirely unavailable for the vast majority of casualty insurance purchasers in the State of California."

At the outset, we note that the District Court undoubtedly had jurisdiction of these Sherman Act claims, as the London reinsurers apparently concede. ("Our position is not that the Sherman Act does not apply in the sense that a minimal basis for the exercise of jurisdiction doesn't exist here. Our position is that there are certain circumstances, and that this is one of them, in which the interests of another State are sufficient that the exercise of that jurisdiction should be restrained").[8] Although the proposition was perhaps not always free from doubt, see *American Banana Co. v. United Fruit Co.*, 213 U.S. 347 (1909), it is well established by now that the Sherman Act applies to foreign conduct that was meant to produce and did in fact produce some substantial effect in the United States. See *Matsushita Elec. Industrial Co. v. Zenith Radio Corp.*, 475 U.S. 574, 582, n. 6 (1986); *United States v. Aluminum Co. of America*, 148 F.2d 416, 444 (CA2 1945) (L. Hand, J.); Restatement (Third) of Foreign Relations Law of the United States § 415, and Reporters' Note 3 (1987) (hereinafter Restatement (Third) Foreign Relations Law)....[9] Such is the conduct alleged here: that the London reinsurers engaged in unlawful conspiracies to affect the market for insurance in the United States and that their conduct in fact produced substantial effect.[10]

According to the London reinsurers, the District Court should have declined to exercise such jurisdiction under the principle of international comity.[11] The Court of Appeals agreed that courts should look to that

8. One of the London reinsurers, Sturge Reinsurance Syndicate Management Limited, argues that the Sherman Act does not apply to its conduct in attending a single meeting at which it allegedly agreed to exclude all pollution coverage from its reinsurance contracts. Brief for Petitioner Sturge Reinsurance Syndicate Management Limited in No. 91–1128, p. 22. Sturge may have attended only one meeting, but the allegations, which we are bound to credit, remain that it participated in conduct that was intended to and did in fact produce a substantial effect on the American insurance market.

9. Justice Scalia believes that what is at issue in this case is prescriptive, as opposed to subject-matter, jurisdiction. The parties do not question prescriptive jurisdiction, however, and for good reason: it is well established that Congress had exercised such jurisdiction under the Sherman Act....

10. Under [the FTAIA], the Sherman Act does not apply to conduct involving foreign trade or commerce, other than import trade or import commerce, unless "such conduct has a direct, substantial, and reasonably foreseeable effect" on domestic or import commerce. 15 U.S.C. § 6a(1)(A). The FTAIA was intended to exempt from the Sherman Act export transactions that did not injure the United States economy, *see* H.R.Rep. No. 97–686, pp. 2–3, 9–10 (1982); P. Areeda & H. Hovenkamp, Antitrust Law ¶ 236'a, pp. 296–297 (Supp.1992), and it is unclear how it might apply to the conduct alleged here. Also unclear is whether the Act's "direct, substantial, and reasonably foreseeable effect" standard amends existing law or merely codifies it. See *id.*, ¶ 236'a, p. 297. We need not address these questions here. Assuming that the FTAIA's standard affects this case, and assuming further that the standard differs from the prior law, the conduct alleged plainly meets its requirements.

11. Justice Scalia contends that comity concerns figure into the prior analysis whether jurisdiction exists under the Sherman Act. This contention is inconsistent with the general understanding that the Sherman Act covers foreign conduct producing a substantial intended effect in the United States, and that concerns of comity come into play, if at all, only after a court has determined that the acts complained of are subject to Sherman Act jurisdiction. See *United States v. Aluminum Co. of America*, 148 F.2d 416, 444 (CA2 1945) ("it follows from what we have ... said that [the agreements at issue] were unlawful [under the Sherman Act], though made abroad, if they were intended to affect imports and did affect them"); *Mannington Mills, Inc. v. Congoleum Corp.*, 595 F.2d 1287, 1294 (CA3 1979) (once court determines that jurisdiction exists under the Sherman Act, question remains whether comity precludes its exercise); H.R.Rep. No. 97–686, p. 13 (1982). But cf. *Timberlane Lumber Co. v. Bank of America, N.T. & S.A.*, 549 F.2d 597, 613 (CA9 1976); 1 J. Atwood & K. Brewster, Antitrust and American Business Abroad 166 (1981). In any event, the parties conceded jurisdiction at oral argument, and we see no need to address this contention here.

principle in deciding whether to exercise jurisdiction under the Sherman Act. This availed the London reinsurers nothing, however. To be sure, the Court of Appeals believed that "application of [American] antitrust laws to the London reinsurance market 'would lead to significant conflict with English law and policy,' " and that "such a conflict, unless outweighed by other factors, would by itself be reason to decline exercise of jurisdiction." But other factors, in the court's view, including the London reinsurers' express purpose to affect United States commerce and the substantial nature of the effect produced, outweighed the supposed conflict and require the exercise of jurisdiction in this case.

When it enacted the [FTAIA], Congress expressed no view on the question whether a court with Sherman Act jurisdiction should ever decline to exercise such jurisdiction on grounds of international comity. See H.R.Rep. No. 97–686, p. 13 (1982) ("If a court determines that the requirements for subject matter jurisdiction are met, [the FTAIA] would have no effect on the court['s] ability to employ notions of comity ... or otherwise to take account of the international character of the transaction") (citing *Timberlane*). We need not decide that question here, however, for even assuming that in a proper case a court may decline to exercise Sherman Act jurisdiction over foreign conduct (or, as Justice Scalia would put it, may conclude by the employment of comity analysis in the first instance that there is no jurisdiction), international comity would not counsel against exercising jurisdiction in the circumstances alleged here.

The only substantial question in this case is whether "there is in fact a true conflict between domestic and foreign law." *Societe Nationale Industrielle Aerospatiale v. United States District Court*, 482 U.S. 522, 555 (1987) (Blackmun, J., concurring in part and dissenting in part). The London reinsurers contend that applying the Act to their conduct would conflict significantly with British law, and the British Government, appearing before us as amicus curiae, concurs. They assert that Parliament has established a comprehensive regulatory regime over the London reinsurance market and that the conduct alleged here was perfectly consistent with British law and policy. But this is not to state a conflict. "[T]he fact that conduct is lawful in the state in which it took place will not, of itself, bar application of the United States antitrust laws," even where the foreign state has a strong policy to permit or encourage such conduct. Restatement (Third) Foreign Relations Law § 415, Comment j; see *Continental Ore Co.*, *supra*, at 706–707. No conflict exists, for these purposes, "where a person subject to regulation by two states can comply with the laws of both." Restatement (Third) Foreign Relations Law § 403, Comment e.[12] Since the London reinsurers do not argue that British law requires them to act in some fashion prohibited by the law of the United States, or claim that their compliance with the laws of both countries is otherwise impossible, we see no conflict with British law. See Restatement (Third) Foreign Relations

---

12. Justice Scalia says that we put the cart before the horse in citing this authority, for he argues it may be apposite only after a determination that jurisdiction over the foreign acts is reasonable. But whatever the order of cart and horse, conflict in this sense is the only substantial issue before the Court.

Law § 403, Comment e, § 415, Comment j. We have no need in this case to address other considerations that might inform a decision to refrain from the exercise of jurisdiction on grounds of international comity.

■ SCALIA, J., dissenting [in part].... The petitioners, ... various British corporations and other British subjects, argue that certain of the claims against them constitute an inappropriate extraterritorial application of the Sherman Act. It is important to distinguish two distinct questions raised by this petition: whether the District Court had jurisdiction, and whether the Sherman Act reaches the extraterritorial conduct alleged here. On the first question, I believe that the District Court had subject-matter jurisdiction over the Sherman Act claims against all the defendants (personal jurisdiction is not contested). The respondents asserted nonfrivolous claims under the Sherman Act, and 28 U.S.C. § 1331 vests district courts with subject-matter jurisdiction over cases "arising under" federal statutes. As precedents such as *Lauritzen v. Larsen*, 345 U.S. 571 (1953), make clear, that is sufficient to establish the District Court's jurisdiction over these claims. *Lauritzen* involved a Jones Act claim brought by a foreign sailor against a foreign shipowner. The shipowner contested the District Court's jurisdiction apparently on the grounds that the Jones Act did not govern the dispute between the foreign parties to the action. Though ultimately agreeing with the shipowner that the Jones Act did not apply, see discussion infra, the Court held that the District Court had jurisdiction.

> "As frequently happens, a contention that there is some barrier to granting plaintiff's claim is cast in terms of an exception to jurisdiction of subject matter. A cause of action under our law was asserted here, and the court had power to determine whether it was or was not founded in law and in fact." 345 U.S., at 575....

The second question—the extraterritorial reach of the Sherman Act—has nothing to do with the jurisdiction of the courts. It is a question of substantive law turning on whether, in enacting the Sherman Act, Congress asserted regulatory power over the challenged conduct. See *EEOC v. Arabian American Oil Co.*, 499 U.S. 244 (1991) ("It is our task to determine whether Congress intended the protections of Title VII to apply to United States citizens employed by American employers outside of the United States"). If a plaintiff fails to prevail on this issue, the court does not dismiss the claim for want of subject-matter jurisdiction—want of power to adjudicate; rather, it decides the claim, ruling on the merits that the plaintiff has failed to state a cause of action under the relevant statute. See *Romero, supra*, at 384 (holding no claim available under the Jones Act); *American Banana Co. v. United Fruit Co.*, 213 U.S. 347, 359 (1909) (holding that complaint based upon foreign conduct "alleges no case under the [Sherman Act]").

There is, however, a type of "jurisdiction" relevant to determining the extraterritorial reach of a statute; it is known as "legislative jurisdiction," *Aramco, supra* at 253, Restatement (First) Conflict of Laws § 60 (1934), or "jurisdiction to prescribe," 1 Restatement (Third) of Foreign Relations Law of the United States 235 (1987) (hereinafter Restatement (Third)). This refers to "the authority of a state to make its law applicable to persons or activities," and is quite a separate matter from "jurisdiction to adjudicate." There is no doubt, of course, that Congress possesses legislative jurisdiction over the acts alleged in this complaint: Congress has broad power under Article I, § 8, cl. 3 "[t]o regulate Commerce with foreign Nations," and this Court has repeatedly upheld its power to make laws applicable to persons or activities beyond our territorial boundaries where United States interests are affected. See *Ford v. United States*, 273 U.S. 593, 621–623 (1927); *United States v. Bowman*, 260 U.S. 94, 98–99 (1922); *American Banana*, *supra*, at 356. But the question in this case is whether, and to what extent, Congress has exercised that undoubted legislative jurisdiction in enacting the Sherman Act.

Two canons of statutory construction are relevant in this inquiry. The first is the "long-standing principle of American law 'that legislation of Congress, unless a contrary intent appears, is meant to apply only within the territorial jurisdiction of the United States.'" *Aramco, supra*.... Applying that canon in *Aramco*, we held that the version of Title VII of the Civil Rights Act of 1964 then in force, 42 U.S.C. §§ 2000e–2000e–17 (1988 ed.), did not extend outside the territory of the United States even though the statute contained broad provisions extending its prohibitions to, for example, "'any activity, business, or industry in commerce.'" We held such "boilerplate language" to be an insufficient indication to override the presumption against extraterritoriality. The Sherman Act contains similar "boilerplate language," and if the question were not governed by precedent, it would be worth considering whether that presumption controls the outcome here. We have, however, found the presumption to be overcome with respect to our antitrust laws; it is now well established that the Sherman Act applies extraterritorially. See *Matsushita Elec. Industrial Co. v. Zenith Radio Corp.*, 475 U.S. 574, 582 n. 6 (1986); *Continental Ore Co. v. Union Carbide & Carbon Corp.*, 370 U.S. 690, 704 (1962); see also *United States v. Aluminum Co. of America*, 148 F.2d 416 (CA2 1945).

But if the presumption against extraterritoriality has been overcome or is otherwise inapplicable, a second canon of statutory construction becomes relevant: "[A]n act of congress ought never to be construed to violate the law of nations if any other possible construction remains." *Murray v. Schooner Charming Betsy*, 6 U.S. 64 (1804) (Marshall, C.J.). This canon is "wholly independent" of the presumption against extraterritoriality. [citation omitted] It is relevant to determining the substantive reach of a statute because "the law of nations," or customary international law, includes limitations on a nation's exercise of its jurisdiction to prescribe. See Restatement (Third) §§ 401–416. Though it clearly has constitutional authority to do so, Congress is generally presumed not to have exceeded those customary international-law limits on jurisdiction to prescribe.

Consistent with that presumption, this and other courts have frequently recognized that, even where the presumption against extraterritoriality does not apply, statutes should not be interpreted to regulate foreign persons or conduct if that regulation would conflict with principles of international law. For example, in *Romero v. International Terminal Operating Co.*, 358 U.S. 354 (1959), the plaintiff, a Spanish sailor who had been injured while working aboard a Spanish-flag and Spanish-owned vessel, filed a Jones Act claim against his Spanish employer. The presumption against extraterritorial application of federal statutes was inapplicable to the case, as the actionable tort had occurred in American waters. See *id.*, at 383. The Court nonetheless stated that, "in the absence of contrary congressional direction," it would apply "principles of choice of law that are consonant with the needs of a general federal maritime law and with due recognition of our self-regarding respect for the relevant interests of foreign nations in the regulation of maritime commerce as part of the legitimate concern of the international community." *Id.*, at 382–383. "The controlling considerations" in this choice-of-law analysis were "the interacting interests of the United States and of foreign countries." *Id.*, at 383.

Romero referred to, and followed, the choice-of-law analysis set forth in *Lauritzen v. Larsen*, 345 U.S. 571 (1953). As previously mentioned, *Lauritzen* also involved a Jones Act claim brought by a foreign sailor against a foreign employer. The *Lauritzen* Court recognized the basic problem: "If [the Jones Act were] read literally, Congress has conferred an American right of action which requires nothing more than that plaintiff be 'any seaman who shall suffer personal injury in the course of his employment.'" *Id.*, at 576. The solution it adopted was to construe the statute "to apply only to areas and transactions in which *American law would be considered operative under prevalent doctrines of international law.*" *Id.*, at 577 (emphasis added). To support application of international law to limit the facial breadth of the statute, the Court relied upon—of course—Chief Justice Marshall's statement in *Schooner Charming Betsy* quoted *supra*, at 16. It then set forth "several factors which, alone or in combination, are generally conceded to influence choice of law to govern a tort claim." [citations omitted.]

Lauritzen, Romero, and *McCulloch* were maritime cases, but we have recognized the principle that the scope of generally worded statutes must be construed in light of international law in other areas as well. See, *e.g., Sale v. Haitian Centers Council, Inc.*, 509 U.S. 155, 178, n. 35 (1993); *Weinberger v. Rossi*, 456 U.S. 25, 32, 71 L.Ed.2d 715 102 S.Ct. 1510 (1982). More specifically, the principle was expressed in United States v. Aluminum Co. of America, 148 F.2d 416 (C.A.2 1945), the decision that established the extraterritorial reach of the Sherman Act. In his opinion for the court, Judge Learned Hand cautioned "we are not to read general words, such as those in [the Sherman] Act, without regard to the limitations customarily observed by nations upon the exercise of their powers; limitations which generally correspond to those fixed by the 'Conflict of Laws.'" *Id.*, at 443.

More recent lower court precedent has also tempered the extraterritorial application of the Sherman Act with considerations of "international comity." See *Timberlane Lumber Co. v. Bank of America, N.T. & S.A.*, 549 F.2d 597, 608–615 (CA9 1976); *Mannington Mills, Inc. v. Congoleum Corp.*,

595 F.2d 1287, 1294–1298 (CA3 1979); *Montreal Trading Ltd. v. Amax Inc.,* 661 F.2d 864, 869–871 (CA10 1981); *Laker Airways v. Sabena, Belgian World Airlines,* 235 U.S.App.D.C. 207, 236, 731 F.2d 909, and n. 109, 731 F.2d 909, 938, and n. 109 (1984); see also *Pacific Seafarers, Inc. v. Pacific Far East Line, Inc.,* 404 F.2d 804, 814, and n. 31 (1968). The "comity" they refer to is not the comity of courts, whereby judges decline to exercise jurisdiction over matters more appropriately adjudged elsewhere, but rather what might be termed "prescriptive comity": the respect sovereign nations afford each other by limiting the reach of their laws. That comity is exercised by legislatures when they enact laws, and courts assume it has been exercised when they come to interpreting the scope of laws their legislatures have enacted. It is a traditional component of choice-of-law theory. See J. Story, Commentaries on the Conflict of Laws § 38 (1834) (distinguishing between the "comity of the courts" and the "comity of nations," and defining the latter as "the true foundation and extent of the obligation of the laws of one nation within the territories of another"). Comity in this sense includes the choice-of-law principles that, "in the absence of contrary congressional direction," are assumed to be incorporated into our substantive laws having extraterritorial reach. *Romero, supra,* at 382–383; see also *Lauritzen, supra,* at 578–579; *Hilton v. Guyot,* 159 U.S. 113, 162–166 (1895). Considering comity in this way is just part of determining whether the Sherman Act prohibits the conduct at issue.[13]

In sum, the practice of using international law to limit the extraterritorial reach of statutes is firmly established in our jurisprudence. In proceeding to apply that practice to the present case, I shall rely on the Restatement (Third) of Foreign Relations Law for the relevant principles of international law. Its standards appear fairly supported in the decisions of this Court construing international choice-of-law principles (*Lauritzen, Romero,* and *McCulloch*) and in the decisions of other federal courts, especially *Timberlane.* Whether the Restatement precisely reflects international law in every detail matters little here, as I believe this case would be resolved the same way under virtually any conceivable test that takes account of foreign regulatory interests.

Under the Restatement, a nation having some "basis" for jurisdiction to prescribe law should nonetheless refrain from exercising that jurisdiction "with respect to a person or activity having connections with another state when the exercise of such jurisdiction is unreasonable." Restatement (Third) § 403(1). The "reasonableness" inquiry turns on a number of factors including, but not limited to: "the extent to which the activity takes place within the territory [of the regulating state]," *id.,* § 403(2)(a); "the

---

13. Some antitrust courts, including the Court of Appeals in the present case, have mistaken the comity at issue for the "comity of courts," which has led them to characterize the question presented as one of "abstention," that is, whether they should "exercise or decline jurisdiction." *Mannington Mills, Inc. v. Congoleum Corp.,* 595 F.2d 1287, 1294, 1296 (CA3 1979); see also *In re Insurance Antitrust Litigation,* 938 F.2d 919, 932 (CA9 1991). As I shall discuss, that seems to be the error the Court has fallen into today. Because courts are generally reluctant to refuse the exercise of conferred jurisdiction, confusion on this seemingly theoretical point can have the very practical consequence of greatly expanding the extraterritorial reach of the Sherman Act.

connections, such as nationality, residence, or economic activity, between the regulating state and the person principally responsible for the activity to be regulated," *id.*, § 403(2)(b); "the character of the activity to be regulated, the importance of regulation to the regulating state, the extent to which other states regulate such activities, and the degree to which the desirability of such regulation is generally accepted," *id.*, § 403(2)(c); "the extent to which another state may have an interest in regulating the activity," *id.*, § 403(2)(g); and "the likelihood of conflict with regulation by another state," *id.*, § 403(2)(h). Rarely would these factors point more clearly against application of United States law. The activity relevant to the counts at issue here took place primarily in the United Kingdom, and the defendants in these counts are British corporations and British subjects having their principal place of business or residence outside the United States.[14] Great Britain has established a comprehensive regulatory scheme governing the London reinsurance markets, and clearly has a heavy "interest in regulating the activity," *id.*, § 403(2)(g). See 935 F.2d, at 932–933; *In re Insurance Antitrust Litigation*, 723 F.Supp. 464, 487–488 (N.D.Cal.1989); see also J. Butler & R. Merkin, Reinsurance Law A.1.1–02 (1992). Finally, § 2(b) of the McCarran–Ferguson Act allows state regulatory statutes to override the Sherman Act in the insurance field, subject only to the narrow "boycott" exception set forth in § 3(b)—suggesting that "the importance of regulation to the [United States]," *id.*, § 403(2)(c), is slight. Considering these factors, I think it unimaginable that an assertion of legislative jurisdiction by the United States would be considered reasonable, and therefore it is inappropriate to assume, in the absence of statutory indication to the contrary, that Congress had made such an assertion.

It is evident from what I have said that the Court's comity analysis, which proceeds as though the issue is whether the courts should "decline to exercise . . . jurisdiction," rather than whether the Sherman Act covers this conduct, is simply misdirected. I do not at all agree, moreover, with the Court's conclusion that the issue of the substantive scope of the Sherman Act is not in the case. To be sure, the parties did not make a clear distinction between adjudicative jurisdiction and the scope of the statute. Parties often do not, as we have observed (and have declined to punish with procedural default) before. See the excerpt from *Lauritzen* quoted *supra*, at 14; see also *Romero*, 358 U.S. 359. It is not realistic, and also not helpful, to pretend that the only really relevant issue in this case is not before us. In any event, if one erroneously chooses, as the Court does, to make adjudicative jurisdiction (or more precisely, abstention) the vehicle for taking account of the needs of prescriptive comity, the Court still gets it wrong. It concludes that no "true conflict" counseling nonapplication of United States law (or rather, as it thinks, United States judicial jurisdiction) exists unless compliance with United States law would constitute a violation of another country's law. That breathtakingly broad proposition, which contradicts the many cases discussed earlier, will bring the Sherman Act and

---

14. Some of the British corporations are subsidiaries of American corporations, and the Court of Appeals held that "[t]he interests of Britain are at least diminished where the parties are subsidiaries of American corporations." 938 F.2d, at 933. In effect, the Court of Appeals pierced the corporate veil in weighing the interests at stake. I do not think that was proper.

other laws into sharp and unnecessary conflict with the legitimate interests of other countries—particularly our closest trading partners.

In the sense in which the term "conflic[t]" was used in *Lauritzen*, 345 U.S., at 582, 592, and is generally understood in the field of conflicts of laws, there is clearly a conflict in this case. The petitioners here, like the defendant in *Lauritzen*, were not compelled by any foreign law to take their allegedly wrongful actions, but that no more precludes a conflict-of-laws analysis here than it did there. See *id.*, at 575–576 (detailing the differences between foreign and United States law). Where applicable foreign and domestic law provide different substantive rules of decision to govern the parties' dispute, a conflict-of-laws analysis is necessary. *See generally* R. Weintraub, Commentary on Conflict of Laws 2–3 (1980); Restatement (First) of Conflict of Laws § 1, Comment c and Illustrations (1934).

Literally the only support that the Court adduces for its position is § 403 of the Restatement (Third) of Foreign Relations Law—or more precisely Comment e to that provision, which states:

"Subsection (3) [which says that a state should defer to another state if that state's interest is clearly greater] applies only when one state requires what another prohibits, or where compliance with the regulations of two states exercising jurisdiction consistently with this section is otherwise impossible. It does not apply where a person subject to regulation by two states can comply with the laws of both. . . ."

The Court has completely misinterpreted this provision. Subsection (3) of § 403 (requiring one State to defer to another in the limited circumstances just described) comes into play only after subsection (1) of § 403 has been complied with—*i.e.*, after it has been determined that the exercise of jurisdiction by both of the two states is not "unreasonable." That prior question is answered by applying the factors (inter alia) set forth in subsection (2) of § 403, that is, precisely the factors that I have discussed in text and that the Court rejects.[15]

I would reverse the judgment of the Court of Appeals on this issue, and remand to the District Court with instructions to dismiss for failure to state a claim on the three counts at issue in No. 91–1128.

United States v. Nippon Paper Indus. Co.

United States Court of Appeals, First Circuit, 1997.
109 F.3d 1.

■ SELYA, CIRCUIT JUDGE. This case raises an important, hitherto unanswered question. In it, the United States attempts to convict a foreign corporation

---

15. The Court skips directly to subsection (3) of § 403, apparently on the authority of Comment j to § 415 of the Restatement (Third). But the preceding commentary to § 415 makes clear that "any exercise of [legislative] jurisdiction under this section is subject to [a] the requirement of reasonableness" set forth in § 403(2). Restatement (Third) § 415, Comment a. Comment j refers back to the conflict analysis set forth in § 403(3) which, as noted above, comes after the reasonableness analysis of § 403(2).

under the Sherman Act, a federal antitrust statute, alleging that price-fixing activities which took place entirely in Japan are prosecutable because they were intended to have, and did in fact have, substantial effects in this country. The district court, declaring that a criminal antitrust prosecution could not be based on wholly extraterritorial conduct, dismissed the indictment. We reverse.

I.   JUST THE FAX

Since the district court granted the defendant's motion to dismiss for failure to state a prosecutable offense, we draw our account of the pertinent events from the well-pleaded facts in the indictment itself. . . .

In 1995, a federal grand jury handed up an indictment naming as a defendant Nippon Paper Industries Co., Ltd. (NPI), a Japanese manufacturer of facsimile paper. The indictment alleges that in 1990 NPI and certain unnamed coconspirators held a number of meetings in Japan which culminated in an agreement to fix the price of thermal fax paper throughout North America. NPI and other manufacturers who were privy to the scheme purportedly accomplished their objective by selling the paper in Japan to unaffiliated trading houses on condition that the latter charge specified (inflated) prices for the paper when they resold it in North America. The trading houses then shipped and sold the paper to their subsidiaries in the United States who in turn sold it to American consumers at swollen prices. The indictment further relates that, in 1990 alone, NPI sold thermal fax paper worth approximately $6,100,000 for eventual import into the United States; and that in order to ensure the success of the venture, NPI monitored the paper trail and confirmed that the prices charged to end users were those that it had arranged. These activities, the indictment posits, had a substantial adverse effect on commerce in the United States and unreasonably restrained trade in violation of Section One of the Sherman Act, 15 U.S.C. § 1 (1994).

NPI moved to dismiss because, *inter alia*, if the conduct attributed to NPI occurred at all, it took place entirely in Japan, and, thus, the indictment failed to limn an offense under Section One of the Sherman Act. The government opposed this initiative on two grounds. First, it claimed that the law deserved a less grudging reading and that, properly read, Section One of the Sherman Act applied criminally to wholly foreign conduct as long as that conduct produced substantial and intended effects within the United States. Second, it claimed that the indictment, too, deserved a less grudging reading and that, properly read, the bill alleged a vertical conspiracy in restraint of trade that involved overt acts by certain coconspirators within the United States. Accepting a restrictive reading of both the statute and the indictment, the district court dismissed the case. This appeal followed.

II.   ANALYSIS

We begin—and end—with the overriding legal question. Because this question is one of statutory construction, we review de novo the holding that Section One of the Sherman Act does not cover wholly extraterritorial conduct in the criminal context. . . .

Our analysis proceeds in moieties. We first present the historical context in which this important question arises. We move next to the specifics of the case.

A. *An Historical Perspective.*

Our law has long presumed that "legislation of Congress, unless a contrary intent appears, is meant to apply only within the territorial jurisdiction of the United States." *EEOC v. Arabian American Oil Co.*, 499 U.S. 244 (1991) (citation omitted). In this context, the Supreme Court has charged inquiring courts with determining whether Congress has clearly expressed an affirmative desire to apply particular laws to conduct that occurs beyond the borders of the United States. *See id.*

The earliest Supreme Court case which undertook a comparable task in respect to Section One of the Sherman Act determined that the presumption against extraterritoriality had not been overcome. In *American Banana Co. v. United Fruit Co.*, 213 U.S. 347 (1909), the Court considered the application of the Sherman Act in a civil action concerning conduct which occurred entirely in Central America and which had no discernible effect on imports to the United States. Starting with what Justice Holmes termed "the general and almost universal rule" holding "that the character of an act as lawful or unlawful must be determined wholly by the law of the country where the act is done," *id.* at 356, and the ancillary proposition that, in cases of doubt, a statute should be "confined in its operation and effect to the territorial limits over which the lawmaker has general and legitimate power," *id.* at 357, the Court held that the defendant's actions abroad were not proscribed by the Sherman Act.

Our jurisprudence is precedent-based, but it is not static. By 1945, a different court saw a very similar problem in a somewhat softer light. In *United States v. Aluminum Co. of Am.*, 148 F.2d 416 (2d Cir.1945) (*Alcoa*), the Second Circuit, sitting as a court of last resort, see 15 U.S.C. § 29 (authorizing designation of a court of appeals as a court of last resort for certain antitrust cases), mulled a civil action brought under Section One against a Canadian corporation for acts committed entirely abroad which, the government averred, had produced substantial anticompetitive effects within the United States. The *Alcoa* court read *American Banana* narrowly; that case, Judge Learned Hand wrote, stood only for the principle that "[w]e should not impute to Congress an intent to punish all whom its courts can catch, for conduct which has no consequences within the United States." *Id.* at 443. But a sovereign ordinarily can impose liability for conduct outside its borders that produces consequences within them, and while considerations of comity argue against applying Section One to situations in which no effect within the United States has been shown—the *American Banana* scenario—the statute, properly interpreted, does proscribe extraterritorial acts which were "intended to affect imports [to the United States] and did affect them." *Id.* at 444. On the facts of *Alcoa*, therefore, the presumption against extraterritoriality had been overcome, and the Sherman Act had been violated. . . .

Any perceived tension between *American Banana* and *Alcoa* was eased by the Supreme Court's most recent exploration of the Sherman Act's extraterritorial reach. In *Hartford Fire Ins. Co. v. California*, 509 U.S. 764 (1993), the Justices endorsed *Alcoa*'s core holding, permitting civil antitrust claims under Section One to go forward despite the fact that the actions which allegedly violated Section One occurred entirely on British soil. While noting *American Banana*'s initial disagreement with this proposition, the *Hartford Fire* Court deemed it "well established by now that the Sherman Act applies to foreign conduct that was meant to produce and did in fact produce some substantial effect in the United States." *Id.* at 796. The conduct alleged, a London-based conspiracy to alter the American insurance market, met that benchmark. *See id.*

To sum up, the case law now conclusively establishes that civil antitrust actions predicated on wholly foreign conduct which has an intended and substantial effect in the United States come within Section One's jurisdictional reach. In arriving at this conclusion, we take no view of the government's asseveration that the [FTAIA], 15 U.S.C. § 6a (1994), makes manifest Congress' intent to apply the Sherman Act extraterritorially. The FTAIA is inelegantly phrased and the court in *Hartford Fire* declined to place any weight on it. *See Hartford Fire*, 509 U.S. at 796 n. 23. We emulate this example and do not rest our ultimate conclusion about Section One's scope upon the FTAIA.

B.   *The Merits.*

Were this a civil case, our journey would be complete. But here the United States essays a criminal prosecution for solely extraterritorial conduct rather than a civil action. This is largely uncharted terrain; we are aware of no authority directly on point, and the parties have cited none.

Be that as it may, one datum sticks out like a sore thumb: in both criminal and civil cases, the claim that Section One applies extraterritorially is based on the same language in the same section of the same statute: "Every contract, combination in the form of trust or otherwise, or conspiracy, in restraint of trade or commerce among the several States, or with foreign nations, is declared to be illegal." 15 U.S.C. § 1. Words may sometimes be chameleons, possessing different shades of meaning in different contexts, . . . but common sense suggests that courts should interpret the same language in the same section of the same statute uniformly, regardless of whether the impetus for interpretation is criminal or civil.

Common sense is usually a good barometer of statutory meaning. Here, however, we need not rely on common sense alone; accepted canons of statutory construction point in the same direction. It is a fundamental interpretive principle that identical words or terms used in different parts of the same act are intended to have the same meaning. . . . This principle—which the Court recently called "the basic canon of statutory construction," . . . operates not only when particular phrases appear in different sections of the same act, but also when they appear in different paragraphs or sentences of a single section. *See Russo v. Texaco, Inc.*, 808 F.2d 221, 227 (2d Cir.1986) ("It is a settled principle of statutory construction that [w]hen the same word or phrase is used in the same section of an act more than once, and the meaning is clear as used in one place, it will be construed to have the same meaning in the next place.") (citations and internal quotation marks omitted).... It follows, therefore, that if the language upon which the indictment rests were the same as the language upon which civil liability rests but appeared in a different section of the Sherman Act, or in a different part of the same section, we would be under great pressure to follow the lead of the *Hartford Fire* Court and construe the two iterations of the language identically. Where, as here, the tie binds more tightly—that is, the text under consideration is not merely a duplicate appearing somewhere else in the statute, but is the original phrase in the original setting—the pressure escalates and the case for reading the language in a manner consonant with a prior Supreme Court interpretation is irresistible. *See United States v. Thompson/Center Arms Co.*, 504 U.S. 505, 518 n. 10 (1992) (plurality op.) (flatly rejecting the idea, while construing language from a statute with both civil and criminal implications, that a court should "refrain in criminal cases from applying statutory language that would have been held to apply if challenged in civil litigation").

[The court here discussed the Supreme Court's opinion in *Ratzlaf v. United States*, 510 U.S. 135 (1994), and its own opinions in *Strickland v. Commissioner, Me. Dep't of Human Servs.*, 48 F.3d 12, 21 (1st Cir.), *cert. denied*, 516 U.S. 850 (1995), and *Strickland v. Commissioner, Me. Dep't of Human Servs.*, 96 F.3d 542, 547 (1st Cir. 1996). All three supported the proposition that the same phrase, appearing in the same portion of the same statute, cannot bear divergent interpretations in different litigation contexts.]

The shared rationale of the *Ratzlaf* and *Strickland* cases reinforces the basic canon of construction and gives us confidence that we should follow the canon here. The words of Section One have not changed since the *Hartford Fire* Court found that they clearly evince Congress' intent to apply the Sherman Act extraterritorially in civil actions, and it would be disingenuous for us to pretend that the words had lost their clarity simply because this is a criminal proceeding. Thus, unless some special circumstance obtains in this case, there is no principled way in which we can uphold the order of dismissal.

NPI and its amicus, the Government of Japan, urge that special reasons exist for measuring Section One's reach differently in a criminal context. We have reviewed their exhortations and found them hollow. We discuss the five most promising theses below. The rest do not require comment.

1. *Lack of Precedent.* NPI and its amicus make much of the fact that this appears to be the first criminal case in which the United States endeavors to extend Section One to wholly foreign conduct. We are not impressed. There is a first time for everything, and the absence of earlier

criminal actions is probably more a demonstration of the increasingly global nature of our economy than proof that Section One cannot cover wholly foreign conduct in the criminal milieu.

Moreover, this argument overstates the lack of precedent. There is, for example, solid authority for applying a state's criminal statute to conduct occurring entirely outside the state's borders. *See Strassheim v. Daily*, 221 U.S. 280 (1911) (Holmes, J.) ("Acts done outside a jurisdiction, but intended to produce and producing detrimental effects within it, justify a State in punishing the cause of the harm as if he had been present at the effect, if the State should succeed in getting him within its power."). It is not much of a stretch to apply this same principle internationally, especially in a shrinking world. *See, e.g., Chua Han Mow v. United States*, 730 F.2d 1308, 1311–12 (9th Cir.1984) (applying *Strassheim* principle to conduct in Malaysia involving drugs intended for distribution in the United States), *cert. denied*, 470 U.S. 1031 (1985); ... *cf.* John Donne, Devotions Upon Emergent Occasions, no. 17 (1624) (warning that "no man is an island, entire of itself; every man is a piece of the continent, a part of the main").

2. *Difference in Strength of Presumption.* The lower court and NPI both cite *United States v. Bowman*, 260 U.S. 94 (1922), for the proposition that the presumption against extraterritoriality operates with greater force in the criminal arena than in civil litigation. This misreads the opinion. To be sure, the *Bowman* Court, dealing with a charged conspiracy to defraud, warned that if the criminal law "is to be extended to include those [crimes] committed outside of the strict territorial jurisdiction, it is natural for Congress to say so in the statute, and failure to do so will negative the purpose of Congress in this regard." *Id.* at 98. But this pronouncement merely restated the presumption against extraterritoriality previously established in civil cases like *American Banana*, 213 U.S. at 357. The *Bowman* Court nowhere suggested that a different, more resilient presumption arises in criminal cases.

Nor does *United States v. United States Gypsum Co.*, 438 U.S. 422 (1978), offer aid and succor to NPI. Recognizing that "the behavior proscribed by the [Sherman] Act is often difficult to distinguish from the gray zone of socially acceptable and economically justifiable business conduct," *id.* at 440–41, the *Gypsum* Court held that criminal intent generally is required to convict under the Act. *See id.* at 443. Although this distinguishes some civil antitrust cases (in which intent need not be proven) from their criminal counterparts, the *Gypsum* Court made it plain that intent need not be shown to prosecute criminally "conduct regarded as *per se* illegal because of its unquestionably anticompetitive effects." *Id.* at 440. This means, of course, that defendants can be convicted of participation in price-fixing conspiracies without any demonstration of a specific criminal intent to violate the antitrust laws. *See, e.g., United States v. Brown*, 936 F.2d 1042, 1046 (9th Cir.1991); *United States v. Society of Indep. Gas. Marketers*, 624 F.2d 461, 465 (4th Cir.1980), *cert. denied*, 449 U.S. 1078 (1981); *United States v. Gillen*, 599 F.2d 541, 544–45 (3d Cir.), *cert. denied*,

444 U.S. 866 (1979). Because the instant case falls within that rubric, *Gypsum* does not help NPI.

We add that even if *Gypsum* had differentiated between civil and criminal price-fixing cases, NPI's reliance on it would still be problematic. Reduced to bare essence, *Gypsum* focuses on mens rea, noting that centuries of Anglo–American legal tradition instruct that criminal liability ordinarily should be premised on malevolent intent, *see id.* at 436–37, whereas civil liability, to which less stigma and milder consequences commonly attach, often requires a lesser showing of intent. There is simply no comparable tradition or rationale for drawing a criminal/civil distinction with regard to extraterritoriality, and neither NPI nor its amicus have alluded to any case which does so.

3. *The Restatement.* NPI and the district court, both sing the praises of the Restatement (Third) of Foreign Relations Law (1987), claiming that it supports a distinction between civil and criminal cases on the issue of extraterritoriality. The passage to which they pin their hopes states:

> [I]n the case of regulatory statutes that may give rise to both civil and criminal liability, such as the United States antitrust and securities laws, the presence of substantial foreign elements will ordinarily weigh against application of criminal law. In such cases, legislative intent to subject conduct outside the state's territory to its criminal law should be found only on the basis of express statement or clear implication.

Id. at § 403 cmt. f. We believe that this statement merely reaffirms the classic presumption against extraterritoriality—no more, no less. After all, nothing in the text of the Restatement proper contradicts the government's interpretation of Section One. *See, e.g., id.* at § 402(1)(c) (explaining that, subject only to a general requirement of reasonableness, a state has jurisdiction to proscribe "conduct outside its territory that has or is intended to have substantial effect within its territory"); *id.* at § 415(2) ("Any agreement in restraint of United States trade that is made outside of the United States ... [is] subject to the jurisdiction to prescribe of the United States, if a principal purpose of the conduct or agreement is to interfere with the commerce of the United States, and the agreement or conduct has some effect on that commerce."). What is more, other comments indicate that a country's decision to prosecute wholly foreign conduct is discretionary. *See, e.g., id.* at § 403 rep. n. 8.

4. *The Rule of Lenity.* The next arrow which NPI yanks from its quiver is the rule of lenity. The rule itself is venerable; it provides that, in the course of interpreting statutes in criminal cases, a reviewing court should resolve ambiguities affecting a statute's scope in the defendant's favor.... But the rule of lenity is inapposite unless a statutory ambiguity looms, and a statute is not ambiguous for this purpose simply because some courts or commentators have questioned its proper interpretation.... Rather, "[t]he rule of lenity applies only if, after seizing everything from which aid can be derived, [a court] can make no more than a guess as to what Congress intended." *Reno [v. Koray]*, 515 U.S. [50, 64–65], (citations,

internal quotation marks, and certain brackets omitted); *accord United States v. O'Neil*, 11 F.3d 292, 301 n. 10 (1st Cir.1993) (describing the rule of lenity as "a background principle that properly comes into play when, at the end of a thorough inquiry, the meaning of a criminal statute remains obscure"). Put bluntly, the rule of lenity cannot be used to create ambiguity when the meaning of a law, even if not readily apparent, is, upon inquiry, reasonably clear.

That ends the matter of lenity. In view of the fact that the Supreme Court deems it "well established" that Section One of the Sherman Act applies to wholly foreign conduct, *Hartford Fire*, 509 U.S. at 796, we effectively are foreclosed from trying to tease an ambiguity out of Section One relative to its extraterritorial application. Accordingly, the rule of lenity plays no part in the instant case.

5.   *Comity.* International comity is a doctrine that counsels voluntary forbearance when a sovereign which has a legitimate claim to jurisdiction concludes that a second sovereign also has a legitimate claim to jurisdiction under principles of international law. *See Harold G. Maier, Extraterritorial Jurisdiction at a Crossroads: An Intersection Between Public and Private International Law*, 76 A.J. Int'l L. 280, 281 n. 1 (1982). Comity is more an aspiration than a fixed rule, more a matter of grace than a matter of obligation. In all events, its growth in the antitrust sphere has been stunted by *Hartford Fire*, in which the Court suggested that comity concerns would operate to defeat the exercise of jurisdiction only in those few cases in which the law of the foreign sovereign required a defendant to act in a manner incompatible with the Sherman Act or in which full compliance with both statutory schemes was impossible. *See Hartford Fire*, 509 U.S. at 798–99; *see also* Kenneth W. Dam, *Extraterritoriality in an Age of Globalization: The Hartford Fire Case*, 1993 Sup. Ct. Rev. 289, 306–07 (1993). Accordingly, the *Hartford Fire* Court gave short shrift to the defendants' entreaty that the conduct leading to antitrust liability was perfectly legal in the United Kingdom. *See Hartford Fire*, 509 U.S. at 798–99.

In this case the defendant's comity-based argument is even more attenuated. The conduct with which NPI is charged is illegal under both Japanese and American laws, thereby alleviating any founded concern about NPI being whipsawed between separate sovereigns. And, moreover, to the extent that comity is informed by general principles of reasonableness, see Restatement (Third) of Foreign Relations Law § 403, the indictment lodged against NPI is well within the pale. In it, the government charges that the defendant orchestrated a conspiracy with the object of rigging prices in the United States. If the government can prove these charges, we see no tenable reason why principles of comity should shield NPI from prosecution. We live in an age of international commerce, where decisions reached in one corner of the world can reverberate around the globe in less time than it takes to tell the tale. Thus, a ruling in NPI's favor would create perverse incentives for those who would use nefarious means to influence markets in the United States, rewarding them for erecting as many territorial firewalls as possible between cause and effect.

We need go no further. *Hartford Fire* definitively establishes that Section One of the Sherman Act applies to wholly foreign conduct which has an intended and substantial effect in the United States. We are bound to accept that holding. Under settled principles of statutory construction, we also are bound to apply it by interpreting Section One the same way in a criminal case. The combined force of these commitments requires that we accept the government's cardinal argument, reverse the order of the district court, reinstate the indictment, and remand for further proceedings.

Reversed and remanded.

■ LYNCH, CIRCUIT JUDGE (concurring).

The question presented in this case is whether Section One of the Sherman Act authorizes criminal prosecutions of defendants for their actions committed entirely outside the United States. Judicial precedents, culminating with the Supreme Court's decision in *Hartford Fire Insurance Co. v. California*, 509 U.S. 764 (1993), conclusively establish that Section One's jurisdictional reach extends, in civil actions, to foreign conduct that is meant to produce, and does in fact produce, substantial effects in the United States. The next question to be asked is whether there is any persuasive reason to believe that, with regard to wholly foreign conduct, Section One in the criminal context is not co-extensive with Section One in the civil context.

In answering this second question, courts must be careful to determine whether this construction of Section One's criminal reach conforms with principles of international law. "It has been a maxim of statutory construction since the decision in *Murray v. The Charming Betsy,* 2 Cranch 64, 118 (1804), that 'an act of congress ought never to be construed to violate the law of nations, if any other possible construction remains.' " *Weinberger v. Rossi,* 456 U.S. 25, 32 (1982). In the *Alcoa* case, Judge Learned Hand found this canon of construction relevant to determining the substantive reach of the Sherman Act, observing that "we are not to read general words [*i.e.,* Section One] . . . without regard to the limitations customarily observed by nations upon the exercise of their powers." *United States v. Aluminum Co. of Am.,* 148 F.2d 416, 443 (2d Cir.1945); *see also Hartford Fire,* 509 U.S. at 814–15 (Scalia, J., dissenting).

The task of construing Section One in this context is not the usual one of determining congressional intent by parsing the language or legislative history of the statute. The broad, general language of the federal antitrust laws and their unilluminating legislative history place a special interpretive responsibility upon the judiciary. The Supreme Court has called the Sherman Act a "charter of freedom" for the courts, with "a generality and adaptability comparable to that found . . . in constitutional provisions." *Appalachian Coals, Inc. v. United States*, 288 U.S. 344, 359–60 (1933). As Professors Areeda and Turner have said, the federal courts have been invested "with a jurisdiction to create and develop an 'antitrust law' in the manner of the common law courts." I Areeda & Turner, Antitrust Law ¶ 106, at 15 (1978). The courts are aided in this task by canons of statutory construction, such as the presumption against violating international law, which serve as both guides and limits in the absence of more explicit indicia of congressional intent.

Here, we are asked to determine the substantive content of Section One's inexact jurisdictional provision, "commerce ... with foreign nations." 15 U.S.C. § 1. Because of the "compunctions against the creation of crimes by judges rather than by legislators," II Areeda & Hovenkamp, Antitrust Law ¶ 311b, at 33 (1995 rev. ed.), the constitution-like aspects of the antitrust laws must be handled particularly carefully in criminal prosecutions.

As the antitrust laws give the federal enforcement agencies a relatively blank check, the development of antitrust law has been largely shaped by the cases that the executive branch chooses—or does not choose—to bring. Accordingly it has been said that:

> novel interpretations or great departures have seldom, if ever, occurred in criminal cases, which prosecutors have usually reserved for defendants whose knowing behavior would be generally recognized as appropriate for criminal sanctions.

Id. at 34. This case does present a new interpretation. We are told this is the first instance in which the executive branch has chosen to interpret the criminal provisions of the Sherman Act as reaching conduct wholly committed outside of this country's borders.

Changing economic conditions, as well as different political agendas, mean that antitrust policies may change from administration to administration. The present administration has promulgated new Antitrust Enforcement Guidelines for International Operations which "focus primarily on situations in which the Sherman Act will grant jurisdiction and when the United States will exercise that jurisdiction" internationally. Brockbank, The 1995 International Antitrust Guidelines: The Reach of U.S. Antitrust Law Continues to Expand, 2 J. Int'l Legal Stud. 1, *22 (1996). The new Guidelines reflect a stronger enforcement stance than earlier versions of the Guidelines, and have been described as a "warning to foreign governments and enterprises that the [antitrust enforcement] Agencies intend to actively pursue restraints on trade occurring abroad that adversely affect American markets or damage American exporting opportunities." *Id.* at *21. The instant case is likely a result of this policy.

It is with this context in mind that we must determine if the exercise of jurisdiction occasioned by the decision of the executive branch of the United States is proper in this case. While courts, including this one, speak of determining congressional intent when interpreting statutes, the meaning of the antitrust laws has emerged through the relationship among all three branches of government. In this criminal case, it is our responsibility to ensure that the executive's interpretation of the Sherman Act does not conflict with other legal principles, including principles of international law.

That question requires examination beyond the language of Section One of the Sherman Act. It is, of course, generally true that, as a principle of statutory interpretation, the same language should be read the same way in all contexts to which the language applies. But this is not invariably true. New content is sometimes ascribed to statutory terms depending upon context.... As NPI and the Government of Japan point out, the Supreme Court has held that Section One of the Sherman Act, which defines both criminal and civil violations with one general phrase, "should be construed as including intent as an element" of a criminal violation. *United States v. United States Gypsum Co.*, 438 U.S. 422, 443 (1978). Where Congress intends that our laws conform with international law, and where international law suggests that criminal enforcement and civil enforcement be viewed differently, it is at least conceivable that different content could be ascribed to the same language depending on whether the context is civil or criminal. It is then worth asking about the effect of the international law which Congress presumably also meant to respect.

The content of international law is determined "by reference 'to the customs and usages of civilized nations, and, as evidence of these, to the works of jurists and commentators.'" *Hilao v. Estate of Marcos*, 103 F.3d 789, 794 (9th Cir.1996) (quoting *The Paquete Habana*, 175 U.S. 677, 700 (1900)); *see also Kadic v. Karadzic*, 70 F.3d 232 (2d Cir.1995). The Restatement (Third) of the Foreign Relations Law of the United States restates international law, as derived from customary international law and from international agreements to which the United States is a party, as it applies to the United States. [Judge Lynch then concluded that the Restatement served "as a useful guide to evaluating the international interests at stake."] ...

Restatement Section 402(1)(c) states that "Subject to § 403," a state has jurisdiction to prescribe law to "conduct outside its territory that has or is intended to have substantial effect within its territory." *Id.* § 402(1)(c). Section 403(1) states that, even when Section 402 has been satisfied, jurisdiction may not be exercised if it is "unreasonable." *Id.* § 403(1). Section 403(2) lists factors to be evaluated in determining if jurisdiction is reasonable:

(a) the link of the activity to the territory of the regulating state, *i.e.*, the extent to which the activity takes place within the territory, or has substantial, direct, and foreseeable effect upon or in the territory;

(b) the connections, such as nationality, residence, or economic activity, between the regulating state and the person principally responsible for the activity to be regulated, or between that state and those whom the regulation is designed to protect;

(c) the character of the activity to be regulated, the importance of regulation to the regulating state, the extent to which other states regulate such activities, and the degree to which the desirability of such regulation is generally accepted;

(d) the existence of justified expectations that might be protected or hurt by the regulation;

(e) the importance of the regulation to the international political, legal, or economic system;

(f) the extent to which the regulation is consistent with the traditions of the international system;

(g) the extent to which another state may have an interest in regulating the activity; and

(h) the likelihood of conflict with regulation by another state.

Id. § 403(2).

Comment f to Section 403 states that the principles of Sections 402 and 403 "apply to criminal as well as to civil regulation." *Id.* § 403 cmt. f. But, specifically naming the United States antitrust laws, the comment also says that for statutes that give rise to both types of liability, "the presence of substantial foreign elements will ordinarily weigh against application of criminal law." *Id.* The comment argues that legislative intent to apply these laws criminally should only be found on the basis of "express statement or clear implication." *Id.*

While the majority opinion accurately states that this comment is an expression of the clear statement rule, the comment also implies that there are special concerns associated with the imposition of criminal sanctions on foreign conduct. *See also id.* § 403 n. 8 ("In applying the principle of reasonableness, the exercise of criminal (as distinguished from civil) jurisdiction in relation to acts committed in another state may be perceived as particularly intrusive."). Indeed, most people recognize a distinction between civil and criminal liability; that the law of nations should do so as well is not surprising. And while *Hartford Fire* and earlier judicial decisions have found that the antitrust laws do apply, in the civil context, to foreign conduct, this antitrust common law is not the express statement of legislative intent that the Restatement suggests may be appropriate in the criminal context.

Also relevant to the present inquiry is section 415(2), which states that:

> Any agreement in restraint of United States trade that is made outside of the United States, and any conduct or agreement in restraint of such trade that is carried out predominantly outside of the United States, are subject to the jurisdiction to prescribe of the United States, if a principal purpose of the conduct or agreement is to interfere with the commerce of the United States and the agreement or conduct has some effect on that commerce.

Restatement § 415(2). Comment a to Section 415 states that the reasonableness principles articulated in Section 403 must still be satisfied. *See id* cmt. a.

Application of these principles to the indictment at issue here leads to the conclusion that the exercise of jurisdiction is reasonable in this case. Here, raising prices in the United States and Canada was not only a purpose of the alleged conspiracy, it was *the* purpose, thus satisfying Section 415's "principal purpose" requirement. Moreover, Section 415's requirement of "some effect" on United States markets is amply met here. The indictment alleges that NPI sold $6.1 million of fax paper into the United States during 1990, approximately the period covered by the charged conspiracy. In 1990, total sales of fax paper in North America were approximately $100 million. NPI's price increases thus affected a not insignificant share of the United States market.

These same factors weigh heavily in the Section 403 reasonableness analysis. Because only North American markets were targeted, the United States' interest in combatting this activity appears to be greater than the Japanese interest, which may only be the general interest of a state in having its industries comport with foreign legal norms. Japan has no interest in protecting Japanese consumers in this case as they were unaffected by the alleged conspiracy.... In another case, where the consumers of the situs nation were injured as well, that state's interest in regulating anticompetitive conduct might be stronger than it is here.

... The Government of Japan acknowledges that antitrust regulation is part of the international legal system, and NPI does not really assert that it has justified expectations that were hurt by the regulation. The only factor counseling against finding that the United States' antitrust laws apply to this conduct is the fact that the situs of the conduct was Japan and that the principals were Japanese corporations. This consideration is inherent in the nature of jurisdiction based on effects of conduct, where the situs of the conduct is, by definition, always a foreign country. This alone does not tip the balance against jurisdiction.

For these reasons, I agree with the majority that the district court erred in dismissing the indictment.

NOTES AND QUESTIONS

1. *Interpreting "comity."* Does "comity" have any role to play after *Hartford Fire*? Does the Supreme Court regard the term "comity" as a synonym for conflict (or lack thereof) with foreign laws? Compare *Timberlane, infra* p. 1235.

2. *Indirect conflict or tensions between U.S. and foreign law.* In *Hartford Fire*, as in *Continental Ore*, the Court faced a situation where the foreign law was arguably more lenient from an antitrust point of view than the U.S. law. Thus, it was possible to say that the companies in question could comply with both by simply complying with the U.S. law. As we will see below, if the companies had faced directly conflicting commands from two sovereigns, they might have been able to take advantage of the foreign sovereign compulsion defense. Given that fact, how much content is there to this notion of conflict? More seriously, does the Court's approach give proper deference to countries that have decided to adopt a deregula-

tory, laissez-faire system for certain sectors of their economies? In *Hartford Fire,* it was impossible for the insurance companies both to benefit from the freedom of action the U.K. wanted to extend to them and to comply with the antitrust rules in force in the United States. What happens when the United States is the country with the more permissive rule? *Compare* General Electric Co. v. Commission of the European Communities, Case T–210/01, Court of First Instance 14 Dec. 2005. How would the U.S. enforcers or courts react if they were faced with a case in which a U.S. company's non-price vertical restrictions (*e.g.*, territorial divisions), which were perfectly legal under U.S. antitrust law, were attacked in Europe as violations of Article 85, and the company had no practical way of complying with the order of the European Commission without modifying its international distributional scheme as a whole?

3. *Statutory or "jurisdictional" approach?* How did each of the First Circuit judges in *Nippon Paper* approach the question of extraterritorial jurisdiction: as a "jurisdictional" matter, or as a question of the statutory coverage of the Sherman Act, as Justice Scalia argued in *Hartford Fire*?

Should U.S. courts resort to general principles of international law when they confront questions of extraterritorial jurisdiction, as Judge Lynch did in her concurring opinion in *Nippon Paper*, or is it enough to look to conventional principles of statutory construction, as the majority did?

4. *Per se rules in foreign commerce cases.* The subject of foreign commerce enforcement took a somewhat different twist in the Ninth Circuit's decision in Metro Industries, Inc. v. Sammi Corp., 82 F.3d 839 (9th Cir. 1996). Metro, an importer and wholesaler of kitchenware, sued Sammi, a South Korean exporting company, and two of its U.S. subsidiaries, claiming that a Korean design registration system—which gave Korean holloware producers the exclusive right to export a particular design for three years—constituted an unlawful market division that was a *per se* violation of Sherman Act § 1. The Court of Appeals, in a broadly worded opinion, held that the *per se* rule can never apply to foreign conduct, because it is always necessary in a foreign commerce case to examine the impact of the practice on commerce in the United States. The opinion also suggests, however, that the registration system was not the kind of thing that would ordinarily receive *per se* treatment. Do you agree that the substantive rules of antitrust should be different in foreign commerce cases? Why or why not? Is the necessity of examining the links to U.S. foreign commerce any different from the need to examine the interstate commerce nexus in ordinary antitrust cases? If so, what distinguishes the two? If not, then what does that imply for the *per se* rule any time the interstate or foreign commerce element is disputed?

5. *Which effects count?* One important question remained unanswered in the FTAIA: what kind of effects count to support a finding that the statute covers the conduct in question? The circuits were split on this question until the Supreme Court decided the next case.

F. Hoffman–La Roche, Ltd. v. Empagran S.A.

Supreme Court of the United States, 2004.
542 U.S. 155, 124 S.Ct. 2359, 159 L.Ed.2d 226.

■ BREYER, J., The Foreign Trade Antitrust Improvements Act of 1982 (FTAIA) excludes from the Sherman Act's reach much anticompetitive conduct that causes only foreign injury. It does so by setting forth a general rule stating that the Sherman Act "shall not apply to conduct involving trade or commerce ... with foreign nations." It then creates exceptions to the general rule, applicable where (roughly speaking) that conduct significantly harms imports, domestic commerce, or American exporters.

We here focus upon anticompetitive price-fixing activity that is in significant part foreign, that causes some domestic antitrust injury, and that independently causes separate foreign injury. We ask two questions about the price-fixing conduct and the foreign injury that it causes. First, does that conduct fall within the FTAIA's general rule excluding the Sherman Act's application? That is to say, does the price-fixing activity constitute "conduct involving trade or commerce ... with foreign nations"? We conclude that it does.

Second, we ask whether the conduct nonetheless falls within a domestic-injury exception to the general rule, an exception that applies (and makes the Sherman Act nonetheless applicable) where the conduct (1) has a "direct, substantial, and reasonably foreseeable effect" on domestic commerce, and (2) "such effect gives rise to a [Sherman Act] claim." §§ 6a(1)(A), (2). We conclude that the exception does not apply where the plaintiff's claim rests solely on the independent foreign harm.

To clarify: The issue before us concerns (1) significant foreign anticompetitive conduct with (2) an adverse domestic effect and (3) an independent foreign effect giving rise to the claim. In more concrete terms, this case involves vitamin sellers around the world that agreed to fix prices, leading to higher vitamin prices in the United States and independently leading to higher vitamin prices in other countries such as Ecuador. We conclude that, in this scenario, a purchaser in the United States could bring a Sherman Act claim under FTAIA based on domestic injury, but a purchaser in Ecuador could not bring a Sherman Act claim based on foreign harm.

The plaintiffs in this case originally filed a class-action suit on behalf of foreign and domestic purchasers of vitamins under, *inter alia*, § 1 of the Sherman Act ... and §§ 4 and 16 of the Clayton Act.... Their complaint alleged that petitioners, foreign and domestic vitamin manufacturers and distributors, had engaged in a price-fixing conspiracy, raising the price of vitamin products to customers in the United States and to customers in foreign countries.

As relevant there, petitioners moved to dismiss the suit as to the *foreign* purchasers (the respondents here), five foreign vitamin distributors located in Ukraine, Australia, Ecuador, and Panama, each of which bought vitamins from petitioners for delivery outside the United States describing the relevant transactions as "wholly foreign"). Respondents have never asserted that they purchased any vitamins in the United States or in transactions in United States commerce, and the question presented assumes that the relevant "transactions occurr[ed] entirely outside U.S. commerce." The District Court dismissed their claims. It applied the FTAIA and found none of the exceptions applicable. Thereafter, the domestic purchasers transferred their claims to another pending suit and did not take part in the subsequent appeal.

A divided panel of the Court of Appeals reversed. The panel concluded that the FTAIA's general exclusionary rule applied to the case, but that its domestic-injury exception also applied. It basically read the plaintiffs' complaint to allege that the vitamin manufacturers' price-fixing conspiracy (1) had "a direct, substantial, and reasonably foreseeable effect" on ordinary domestic trade or commerce, i.e., the conspiracy brought about higher domestic vitamin prices, and (2) "such effect" gave "rise to a [Sherman Act] claim," i.e., an injured domestic customer could have brought a Sherman Act suit, 15 U.S.C. §§ 6a(1), (2). Those allegations, the court held, are sufficient to meet the exception's requirements.

The court assumed that the foreign effect, i.e., higher prices in Ukraine, Panama, Australia, and Ecuador, was independent of the domestic effect, i.e., higher domestic prices. But it concluded that, in light of the FTAIA's text, legislative history, and the policy goal of deterring harmful price-fixing activity, this lack of connection does not matter. . . .

We granted certiorari to resolve a split among the Courts of Appeals about the exception's application. Compare *Den Norske Stats Oljeselskap As* v. *HeereMac Vof*, 241 F. 3d 420, 427 (C.A.5 2001) (exception does not apply where foreign injury independent of domestic harm), with *Kruman* v. *Christie's Int'l PLC*, 284 F. 3d 384, 400 (C.A.2 2002) (exception does apply even where foreign injury independent); 315 F. 3d, at 341 (similar).

The FTAIA seeks to make clear to American exporters (and to firms doing business abroad) that the Sherman Act does not prevent them from entering into business arrangements (say, joint-selling arrangements), however anticompetitive, as long as those arrangements adversely affect only foreign markets. See H. R. Rep. No. 97–686, pp. 1–3, 9–10 (1982) (hereinafter House Report). It does so by removing from the Sherman Act's reach, (1) export activities and (2) other commercial activities taking place abroad, unless those activities adversely affect domestic commerce, imports to the United States, or exporting activities of one engaged in such activities within the United States.

[At this point the Court set out the text of the FTAIA; *see supra* p. 1193.]

This technical language initially lays down a general rule placing *all* (non-import) activity involving foreign commerce outside the Sherman Act's reach. It then brings such conduct back within the Sherman Act's reach *provided that* the conduct *both* (1) sufficiently affects American commerce, i.e., it has a "direct, substantial, and reasonably foreseeable effect" on American domestic, import, or (certain) export commerce, and (2) has an effect of a kind that antitrust law considers harmful, i.e., the "effect" must "giv[e] rise to a [Sherman Act] claim." §§ 6a(1), (2).

We ask here how this language applies to price-fixing activity that is in significant part foreign, that has the requisite domestic effect, and that also has independent foreign effects giving rise to the plaintiffs claim.

Respondents make a threshold argument. They say that the transactions here at issue fall outside the FTAIA because the FTAIA's general exclusionary rule applies only to conduct involving exports. The rule says that the Sherman Act "shall not apply to conduct involving trade or commerce (other than import trade or import commerce) *with* foreign nations." § 6a (emphasis added). The word "with" means *between* the United States and foreign nations. And, they contend, commerce between the United States and foreign nations that is not import commerce must consist of export commerce—a kind of commerce irrelevant to the case at hand.

The difficulty with respondents' argument is that the FTAIA originated in a bill that initially referred only to "export trade or export commerce." H.R. 5235, 97th Cong., 1st Sess., § 1 (1981). But the House Judiciary Committee subsequently changed that language to "trade or commerce (other than import trade or import commerce)." 15 U.S.C. § 6a. And it did so deliberately to include commerce that did not involve American exports but which was wholly foreign.

The House Report says in relevant part:

> "The Subcommittee's 'export' commerce limitation appeared to make the amendments inapplicable to transactions that were neither import nor export, i.e., transactions within, between, or among other nations.... Such foreign transactions should, for the purposes of this legislation, be treated in the same manner as export transactions—that is, there should be no American antitrust jurisdiction absent a direct, substantial and reasonably foreseeable effect on domestic commerce or a domestic competitor. The Committee Amendment therefore deletes references to 'export' trade, and substitutes phrases such as 'other than import' trade. It is thus clear that wholly foreign transactions as well as export transactions are covered by the amendment, but that import transactions are not." House Report 9–10 (emphases added).

For those who find legislative history useful, the House Report's account should end the matter. Others, by considering carefully the amendment itself and the lack of any other plausible purpose, may reach the same conclusion, namely that the FTAIA's general rule applies where the anticompetitive conduct at issue is foreign.

We turn now to the basic question presented, that of the exception's application. Because the underlying antitrust action is complex, potentially raising questions not directly at issue here, we reemphasize that we base our decision upon the following: The price-fixing conduct significantly and adversely affects both customers outside the United States and customers within the United States, but the adverse foreign effect is independent of any adverse domestic effect. In these circumstances, we find that the FTAIA exception does not apply (and thus the Sherman Act does not apply) for two main reasons.

First, this Court ordinarily construes ambiguous statutes to avoid unreasonable interference with the sovereign authority of other nations.

See, *e.g., McCulloch* v. *Sociedad Nacional de Marineros de Honduras*, 372 U.S. 10, 20–22 (1963) (application of National Labor Relations Act to foreign-flag vessels); *Romero* v. *International Terminal Operating Co.*, 358 U.S. 354, 382–383 (1959) (application of Jones Act in maritime case); *Lauritzen* v. *Larsen*, 345 U.S. 571, 578 (1953) (same). This rule of construction reflects principles of customary international law—law that (we must assume) Congress ordinarily seeks to follow. See Restatement (Third) of Foreign Relations Law of the United States §§ 403(1), 403(2) (1986) (hereinafter Restatement) (limiting the unreasonable exercise of prescriptive jurisdiction with respect to a person or activity having connections with another State); *Murray* v. *Schooner Charming Betsy*, 2 Cranch 64, 118 (1804) ("[A]n act of Congress ought never to be construed to violate the law of nations if any other possible construction remains"); *Hartford Fire Insurance Co.* v. *California*, 509 U.S. 764, 817 (1993) (Scalia, J., dissenting) (identifying rule of construction as derived from the principle of "prescriptive comity").

This rule of statutory construction cautions courts to assume that legislators take account of the legitimate sovereign interests of other nations when they write American laws. It thereby helps the potentially conflicting laws of different nations work together in harmony—a harmony particularly needed in today's highly interdependent commercial world.

No one denies that America's antitrust laws, when applied to foreign conduct, can interfere with a foreign nation's ability independently to regulate its own commercial affairs. But our courts have long held that application of our antitrust laws to foreign anticompetitive conduct is nonetheless reasonable, and hence consistent with principles of prescriptive comity, insofar as they reflect a legislative effort to redress domestic antitrust injury that foreign anticompetitive conduct has caused. See *United States* v. *Aluminum Co. of America*, 148 F. 2d 416, 443–444 (C.A.2 1945) (L. Hand, J.); 1 P. Areeda & D. Turner, Antitrust Law ¶ 236 (1978).

But why is it reasonable to apply those laws to foreign conduct *insofar as that conduct causes independent foreign harm and that foreign harm alone gives rise to the plaintiff's claim?* Like the former case, application of those laws creates a serious risk of interference with a foreign nation's ability independently to regulate its own commercial affairs. But, unlike the former case, the justification for that interference seems insubstantial. See Restatement § 403(2) (determining reasonableness on basis of such factors as connections with regulating nation, harm to that nation's interests, extent to which other nations regulate, and the potential for conflict). Why should American law supplant, for example, Canada's or Great Britain's or Japan's own determination about how best to protect Canadian or British or Japanese customers from anticompetitive conduct engaged in significant part by Canadian or British or Japanese or other foreign companies?

We recognize that principles of comity provide Congress greater leeway when it seeks to control through legislation the actions of *American* companies, see Restatement § 402; and some of the anticompetitive price-fixing conduct alleged here took place in *America*. But the higher foreign prices of which the foreign plaintiffs here complain are not the consequence of any domestic anti-competitive conduct *that Congress sought to forbid*, for Congress did not seek to forbid any such conduct insofar as it is here relevant, i.e., insofar as it is intertwined with foreign conduct that causes independent foreign harm. Rather Congress sought to release domestic (and foreign) anticompetitive conduct from Sherman Act constraints when that conduct causes foreign harm. Congress, of course, did make an exception where that conduct also causes domestic harm. See House Report 13 (concerns about American firms' participation in international cartels addressed through "domestic injury" exception). But any independent domestic harm the foreign conduct causes here has, by definition, little or nothing to do with the matter.

We thus repeat the basic question: Why is it reasonable to apply this law to conduct that is significantly foreign *insofar as that conduct causes independent foreign harm and that foreign harm alone gives rise to the plaintiff's claim*? We can find no good answer to the question.

The Areeda and Hovenkamp treatise notes that under the Court of Appeals' interpretation of the statute

> "a Malaysian customer could ... maintain an action under United States law in a United States court against its own Malaysian supplier, another cartel member, simply by noting that unnamed third parties injured [in the United States] by the American [cartel member's] conduct would also have a cause of action.

> Effectively, the United States courts would provide worldwide subject matter jurisdiction to any foreign suitor wishing to sue its own local supplier, but unhappy with its own sovereign's provisions for private antitrust enforcement, provided that a different plaintiff had a cause of action against a different firm for injuries that were within U.S. [other-than-import] commerce. It does not seem excessively rigid to infer that Congress would not have intended that result." P. Areeda & H. Hovenkamp, Antitrust Law ¶ 273, pp. 51–52 (Supp. 2003).

We agree with the comment. We can find no convincing justification for the extension of the Sherman Act's scope that it describes.

Respondents reply that many nations have adopted antitrust laws similar to our own, to the point where the practical likelihood of interference with the relevant interests of other nations is minimal. Leaving price fixing to the side, however, this Court has found to the contrary. See, *e.g.*, *Hartford Fire*, 509 U.S. at 797–799 (noting that the alleged conduct in the London reinsurance market, while illegal under United States antitrust laws, was assumed to be perfectly consistent with British law and policy); see also, *e.g.*, 2 W. Fugate, Foreign Commerce and the Antitrust Laws § 16.6 (5th ed. 1996) (noting differences between European Union and United States law on vertical restraints).

Regardless, even where nations agree about primary conduct, say price fixing, they disagree dramatically about appropriate remedies. The application, for example, of American private treble-damages remedies to anticompetitive conduct taking place abroad has generated considerable controversy.... And several foreign nations have filed briefs here arguing that to apply our remedies would unjustifiably permit their citizens to bypass their own less generous remedial schemes, thereby upsetting a balance of competing considerations that their own domestic antitrust laws embody. [Citing amicus briefs from the governments of Germany, Canada, and Japan, respectively.]

These briefs add that a decision permitting independently injured foreign plaintiffs to pursue private treble-damages remedies would undermine foreign nations' own antitrust enforcement policies by diminishing foreign firms' incentive to cooperate with antitrust authorities in return for prosecutorial amnesty. [Citing amicus briefs from the governments of Germany, Canada, and the United States, respectively.]

Respondents alternatively argue that comity does not demand an interpretation of the FTAIA that would exclude independent foreign injury cases across the board. Rather, courts can take (and sometimes have taken) account of comity considerations case by case, abstaining where comity considerations so dictate. Cf., *e.g., Hartford Fire, supra*, at 797, n. 24; *United States* v. *Nippon Paper Industries Co.*, 109 F. 3d 1, 8 (C.A.1 1997); *Mannington Mills, Inc.* v. *Congoleum Corp.*, 595 F. 2d 1287, 1294–1295 (C.A.3 1979).

In our view, however, this approach is too complex to prove workable. The Sherman Act covers many different kinds of anticompetitive agreements. Courts would have to examine how foreign law, compared with American law, treats not only price fixing but also, say, information-sharing agreements, patent-licensing price conditions, territorial product resale limitations, and various forms of joint venture, in respect to both primary conduct and remedy. The legally and economically technical nature of that enterprise means lengthier proceedings, appeals, and more proceedings—to the point where procedural costs and delays could themselves threaten interference with a foreign nation's ability to maintain the integrity of its own antitrust enforcement system. Even in this relatively simple price-fixing case, for example, competing briefs tell us (1) that potential treble-damage liability would help enforce widespread anti-price-fixing norms (through added deterrence) and (2) the opposite, namely that such liability would hinder antitrust enforcement (by reducing incentives to enter amnesty programs).... How could a court seriously interested in resolving so empirical a matter—a matter potentially related to impact on foreign interests—do so simply and expeditiously?

We conclude that principles of prescriptive comity counsel against the Court of Appeals' interpretation of the FTAIA. Where foreign anticompetitive conduct plays a significant role and where foreign injury is independent of domestic effects, Congress might have hoped that America's antitrust laws, so fundamental a component of our own economic system, would commend themselves to other nations as well. But, if America's antitrust policies could not win their own way in the international market-place for such ideas, Congress, we must assume, would not have tried to impose them, in an act of legal imperialism, through legislative fiat.

Second, the FTAIA's language and history suggest that Congress designed the FTAIA to clarify, perhaps to limit, but not to *expand* in any significant way, the Sherman Act's scope as applied, to foreign commerce. See House Report 2–3. And we have found no significant indication that at the time Congress wrote this statute courts would have thought the Sherman Act applicable in these circumstances.

The Solicitor General and petitioners tell us that they have found no case in which any court applied the Sherman Act to redress foreign injury in such circumstances. . . . [S]ee also [*Den Norske Stats Oljeselskap As v. HeereMac Vof*, 241 F. 3d 420, 429 (5th Cir. 2001)] ("[W]e have found no case in which jurisdiction was found in a case like this—where a foreign plaintiff is injured in a foreign market with no injuries arising from the anticompetitive effect on a United States market"). And respondents themselves apparently conceded as much at a May 23, 2001, hearing before the District Court below.

Nevertheless, respondents now have called to our attention six cases, three decided by this Court and three decided by lower courts. In the first three cases the defendants included both American companies and foreign companies jointly engaged in anticompetitive behavior having both foreign and domestic effects. See *Timken Roller Bearing Co.* v. *United States*, 341 U.S. 593, 595 (1951) (agreements among American, British, and French corporations to eliminate competition in the manufacture and sale of anti-friction bearings in world, including United States, markets); *United States* v. *National Lead Co.*, 332 U.S. 319, 325–328 (1947) (international cartels with American and foreign members, restraining international commerce, including United States commerce, in titanium pigments); *United States* v. *American Tobacco Co.*, 221 U.S. 106, 171–172 (1911) (American tobacco corporations agreed in England with British company to divide world markets). In all three cases the plaintiff sought relief, including relief that might have helped to protect those injured abroad.

In all three cases, however, the plaintiff was the Government of the United States. A Government plaintiff, unlike a private plaintiff, must seek to obtain the relief necessary to protect the public from further anticompet-itive conduct and to redress anticompetitive harm. And a Government plaintiff has legal authority broad enough to allow it to carry out this mission. 15 U.S.C. § 25; see also, *e.g., United States* v. *E. I. du Pont de Nemours & Co.*, 366 U.S. 316, 334 (1961) ("[I]t is well settled that once the Government has successfully borne the considerable burden of establishing a violation of law, all doubts as to the remedy are to be resolved in its favor"). Private plaintiffs, by way of contrast, are far less likely to be able to secure broad relief. See *California* v. *American Stores Co.*, 495 U.S. 271, 295 (1990) ("Our conclusion that a district court has the power to order divestiture in appropriate cases brought [by private plaintiffs] does not, of course, mean that such power should be exercised in every situation in which the Government would be entitled to such relief"); 2 P. Areeda & H. Hovenkamp, Antitrust Law §§ 303d–303e, pp. 40–45 (2d ed. 2000) (distinguishing between private and government suits in terms of availability, public interest motives, and remedial scope); Griffin, Extraterritoriality in U.S. and EU Antitrust Enforcement, 67 Antitrust L. J. 159, 194 (1999) ("[P]rivate plaintiffs often are unwilling to exercise the degree of self-restraint and consideration of foreign governmental sensibilities generally exercised by the U.S. Government"). This difference means that the Government's ability, in these three cases, to obtain relief helpful to those injured abroad tells us little or nothing about whether this Court would have awarded similar relief at the request of private plaintiffs.

Neither did the Court focus explicitly in its opinions on a claim that the remedies sought to cure only independently caused foreign harm. Thus the three cases tell us even less about whether this Court then thought that foreign private plaintiffs could have obtained foreign relief based solely upon such independently caused foreign injury.

Respondents also refer to three lower court cases brought by private plaintiffs. In the first, *Industria Siciliana Asfalti, Bitumi, S. p. A. v. Exxon Research & Engineering Co.*, 1977 WL 1353 (S.D.N.Y., Jan. 18, 1977), a District Court permitted an Italian firm to proceed against an American firm with a Sherman Act claim based upon a purely foreign injury, *i.e.*, an injury suffered in Italy. The court made clear, however, that the foreign injury was *"inextricably bound up with ... domestic restraints of trade,"* and that the plaintiff *"was injured ... by reason of an alleged restraint of our domestic trade,"* id., at *11, *12 (emphasis added), *i.e.*, the foreign injury was dependent upon, *not independent of*, domestic harm. See Part VI, *infra*.

In the second case, *Dominicus Americana Bohio v. Gulf & Western Industries, Inc.*, 473 F. Supp. 680 (S.D.N.Y.1979), a District Court permitted Dominican and American firms to proceed against a competing American firm and the Dominican Tourist Information Center with a Sherman Act claim based upon injury apparently suffered in the Dominican Republic. The court, in finding the Sherman Act applicable, weighed several different factors, including the participation of American firms in the unlawful conduct, the partly domestic nature of both conduct and harm (to American tourists, a kind of "export"), and the fact that the domestic harm depended in part upon the foreign injury. *Id.*, at 688. The court did not separately analyze the legal problem before it in terms of independently caused foreign injury. Its opinion simply does not discuss the matter. It consequently cannot be taken as significant support for application of the Sherman Act here.

The third case, *Hunt* v. *Mobil Oil Corp.*, 550 F. 2d 68, 72 (C.A.2 1977), involved a claim by Hunt, an independent oil producer with reserves in Libya, that other major oil producers in Libya and the Persian Gulf (the "seven majors") had conspired in New York and elsewhere to make it more difficult for Hunt to reach agreement with the Libyan government on production terms and thereby eliminate him as a competitor. The case can be seen as involving a primarily foreign conspiracy designed to bring about foreign injury in Libya. But, as in *Dominicus*, the court nowhere considered the problem of independently caused foreign harm. Rather, the case was about the "act of state" doctrine, and the sole discussion of Sherman Act applicability—one brief paragraph—refers to other matters. 550 F. 2d, at 72, and n. 2. We do not see how Congress could have taken this case as significant support for the proposition that the Sherman Act applies in present circumstances.

The upshot is that no pre–1982 case provides significant authority for application of the Sherman Act in the circumstances we here assume. Indeed, a leading contemporaneous lower court case contains language suggesting the contrary. See *Timberlane Lumber Co.* v. *Bank of America*, 549 F. 2d 597, 613 (C.A.9 1976) (insisting that the foreign conduct's domestic effect be "sufficiently large to present a cognizable injury to the plaintiffs" (emphasis added)).

Taken together, these two sets of considerations, the one derived from comity and the other reflecting history, convince us that Congress would not have intended the FTAIA's exception to bring independently caused foreign injury within the Sherman Act's reach.

V

Respondents point to several considerations that point the other way. For one thing, the FTAIA's language speaks in terms of the Sherman Act's *applicability* to certain kinds of *conduct*. The FTAIA says that the Sherman Act applies to foreign "conduct" with a certain kind of harmful domestic effect. Why isn't that the end of the matter? How can the Sherman Act both *apply to the conduct* when one person sues but *not apply to the same conduct* when another person sues? The question of who can or cannot sue is a matter for other statutes (namely, the Clayton Act) to determine.

Moreover, the exception says that it applies if the conduct's domestic effect gives rise to "a claim," not to "*the plaintiff's claim*" or "*the claim at issue.*" 15 U.S.C. § 6a(2) (emphasis added). The alleged conduct here did have domestic effects, and those effects were harmful enough to give rise to "a" claim. Respondents concede that this claim is not their own claim; it is someone else's claim. But, linguistically speaking, they say, that is beside the point. Nor did Congress place the relevant words "gives rise to a claim" in the FTAIA to suggest any geographical limitation; rather it did so for a more neutral reason, namely, in order to make clear that the domestic effect must be an adverse (as opposed to a beneficial) effect. See House Report 11 (citing *National Bank of Canada* v. *Interbank Card Assn.*, 666 F. 2d 6, 8 (C.A.2 1981)).

Despite their linguistic logic, these arguments are not convincing. Linguistically speaking, a statute can apply and not apply to the same conduct, depending upon other circumstances; and those other circumstances may include the nature of the lawsuit (or of the related underlying harm). It also makes linguistic sense to read the words "a claim" as if they refer to the "plaintiffs claim" or "the claim at issue."

At most, respondents' linguistic arguments might show that respondents' reading is the more natural reading of the statutory language. But those arguments do not show that we *must* accept that reading. And that is the critical point. The considerations previously mentioned—those of comity and history—make clear that the respondents' reading is not consistent with the FTAIA's basic intent. If the statute's language reasonably permits an interpretation consistent with that intent, we should adopt it. And, for the reasons stated, we believe that the statute's language permits the reading that we give it.

Finally, respondents point to policy considerations that we have previously discussed, *supra* . . . namely, that application of the Sherman Act in present circumstances will (through increased deterrence) help protect Americans against foreign-caused anticompetitive injury. As we have explained, however, the plaintiffs and supporting enforcement-agency *amici* have made important experience-backed arguments (based upon amnesty-seeking incentives) to the contrary. We cannot say whether, on balance, respondents' side of this empirically based argument or the enforcement agencies' side is correct. But we can say that the answer to the dispute is neither clear enough, nor of such likely empirical significance, that it could overcome the considerations we have previously discussed and change our conclusion.

For these reasons, we conclude that petitioners' reading of the statute's language is correct. That reading furthers the statute's basic purposes, it properly reflects considerations of comity, and it is consistent with Sherman Act history.

VI

We have assumed that the anticompetitive conduct here independently caused foreign injury; that is, the conduct's domestic effects did not help to bring about that foreign injury. Respondents argue, in the alternative, that the foreign injury was not independent. Rather, they say, the anticompetitive conduct's domestic effects were linked to that foreign harm. Respondents contend that, because vitamins are fungible and readily transportable, without an adverse domestic effect (*i.e.*, higher prices in the United States), the sellers could not have maintained their international price-fixing arrangement and respondents would not have suffered their foreign injury. They add that this "but for" condition is sufficient to bring the price-fixing conduct within the scope of the FTAIA's exception.

The Court of Appeals, however, did not address this argument, . . . and, for that reason, neither shall we. Respondents remain free to ask the Court of Appeals to consider the claim. The Court of Appeals may determine whether respondents properly preserved the argument, and, if so, it may consider it and decide the related claim.

For these reasons, the judgment of the Court of Appeals is vacated, and the case is remanded for further proceedings consistent with this opinion.

■ O'CONNER, J. took no part in the consideration or decision of this case.

■ SCALIA, J., with whom THOMAS, J., joins, concurring in the judgment.

I concur in the judgment of the Court because the language of the statute is readily susceptible of the interpretation the Court provides and because only that interpretation is consistent with the principle that statutes should be read in accord with the customary deference to the application of foreign countries' laws within their own territories.

Empagran S.A. v. F. Hoffmann–LaRoche, Ltd.

United States Court of Appeals, D.C. Circuit, 2005.
417 F.3d 1267.

■ HENDERSON, CIRCUIT JUDGE. The appellants, foreign corporations that purchased vitamin products outside of the United States for distribution in foreign countries from the appellee foreign manufacturers, brought this action asserting, *inter alia,* price fixing in violation of the Sherman Act.... The United States Supreme Court granted *certiorari* and vacated this court's decision concluding that under the FTAIA the Sherman Act does not apply where "price-fixing conduct significantly and adversely affects both customers outside the United States and customers within the United States, but the adverse foreign effect is independent of any adverse domestic effect." *F. Hoffmann–La Roche, Ltd. v. Empagran S.A.,* 124 S.Ct. 2359, 2366 (2004). The Supreme Court remanded to this court, however, to assess the appellants' alternate theory for Sherman Act liability, namely, that "because vitamins are fungible and readily transportable, without an adverse domestic effect (*i.e.,* higher prices in the United States), the sellers could not have maintained their international price-fixing arrangement and respondents would not have suffered their foreign injury." ... We reject the appellants' alternate theory and conclude that we are without subject-matter jurisdiction under the FTAIA.

While the FTAIA excludes from the Sherman Act's reach most anti-competitive conduct that causes only foreign injury, it creates exceptions for conduct that "significantly harms imports, domestic commerce, or American exporters." ... At issue is the "domestic-injury exception" of section 6a(2), which we conclude, as counsel for the United States argued, applies in only limited circumstances.

The appellees suggest that the exception applies only to injuries that arise in U.S. commerce, thus describing its reach by the situs of the transaction and resulting injuries rather than by the situs of the effects of the allegedly anti-competitive conduct giving rise to the appellants' claims. This interpretation has no support from the text of the statute, which expressly covers conduct involving "trade or commerce with foreign nations." In addition, the legislative history makes clear that the FTAIA's "domestic effects" requirement "does not exclude all persons injured abroad from recovering under the antitrust laws of the United States." The appellants need only demonstrate therefore that the U.S. effects of the appellees' allegedly anti-competitive conduct "g[a]ve rise to" their claims.

During oral argument, counsel for the United States identified three decisions with factual scenarios that, in its view, satisfy the narrow "domestic-injury exception": *Pfizer, Inc. v. Gov't of India,* 434 U.S. 308 (1978); *Industria Siciliana Asfalti, Bitumi, S.p.A. v. Exxon Research & Eng'g Co.,* 1977 WL 1353 (S.D.N.Y.1977); and *Caribbean Broad. Sys. v. Cable & Wireless PLC,* 148 F.3d 1080 (D.C.Cir.1998). Counsel nonetheless argued, and we agree, that each of these cases is distinguishable. For example, in *Pfizer,* which involved a conspiracy that operated both domestically and internationally, the Supreme Court held "only that a foreign nation otherwise entitled to sue in our courts is entitled to sue for treble damages under the antitrust laws to the same extent as any other plaintiff," without addressing the requisite causal relationship between domestic effect and foreign injury. In *Industria,* the foreign injury was "inextricably bound up with the domestic restraints of trade," because a reciprocal tying agreement effected the exclusion of the American rival of one defendant, resulting in higher consumer prices. Finally, in *Caribbean* this court expressly found the FTAIA permitted a Sherman Act claim that involved solely foreign injury. There the plaintiff broadcaster, Caribbean, which operated an FM radio station based in the British Virgin Islands, filed an antitrust action against a competing FM radio station and its joint venturer, alleging that the defendants had violated the Sherman Act by preserving the defendant station's radio broadcast monopoly in the eastern Caribbean region through, *inter alia,* misrepresentations to its advertisers regarding the station's broadcasting reach. While the court expressly addressed only how Caribbean's allegations satisfied subsection 1 of the FTAIA (finding the requisite effect of the defendants' conduct on domestic trade or commerce), it is clear from the court's opinion that Caribbean's allegations satisfied subsection 2 as well. The domestic effect the court found was that U.S. advertisers paid the defendant station excessive prices for advertising. It was this effect of the defendants' monopolizing conduct—forcing U.S. businesses to pay for advertising on the defendant station—that caused Caribbean to lose revenue because it was unable to sell advertising to the same U.S. businesses. *See* 148 F.3d at 1087.

The appellants' theory in a nutshell is as follows:

> Because the appellees' product (vitamins) was fungible and globally marketed, they were able to sustain super-competitive prices abroad only by maintaining super-competitive prices in the United States as well.[16] Otherwise, overseas purchasers would have purchased bulk vitamins at lower prices either directly from U.S.

---

16. The appellants assert the appellees accomplished this equipoise both by fixing a single global price for the vitamins and by creating barriers to international vitamin commerce in the form of market division agreements that prevented bulk vitamins from being traded between North America and other regions.

sellers or from arbitrageurs selling vitamins imported from the United States, thereby preventing the appellees from selling abroad at the inflated prices. Thus, the super-competitive pricing in the United States "gives rise to" the foreign super-competitive prices from which the appellants claim injury.

The appellants paint a plausible scenario under which maintaining super-competitive prices in the United States might well have been a "but-for" cause of the appellants' foreign injury. As the appellants acknowledged at oral argument, however, "but-for" causation between the domestic effects and the foreign injury claim is simply not sufficient to bring anti-competitive conduct within the FTAIA exception. The statutory language—"gives rise to"—indicates a direct causal relationship, that is, proximate causation, and is not satisfied by the mere but-for "nexus" the appellants advanced in their brief. . . . This interpretation of the statutory language accords with principles of "prescriptive comity"—"the respect sovereign nations afford each other by limiting the reach of their laws," *Hartford Fire Ins. Co. v. California,* 509 U.S. 764, 817 (1993) (Scalia, J., dissenting)— which require that we "ordinarily construe[ ] ambiguous statutes to avoid unreasonable interference with the sovereign authority of other nations." *F. Hoffmann–La Roche, Ltd.,* 124 S.Ct. at 2366. To read the FTAIA broadly to permit a more flexible, less direct standard than proximate cause would open the door to just such interference with other nations' prerogative to safeguard their own citizens from anti-competitive activity within their own borders. *See id.* at 2367 ("Why should American law supplant, for example, Canada's or Great Britain's or Japan's own determination about how best to protect Canadian or British or Japanese customers from anticompetitive conduct engaged in [in] significant part by Canadian or British or Japanese or other foreign companies?").

Applying the proximate cause standard, we conclude the domestic effects the appellants cite did not give rise to their claimed injuries so as to bring their Sherman Act claim within the FTAIA exception. While maintaining super-competitive prices in the United States may have facilitated the appellees' scheme to charge comparable prices abroad, this fact demonstrates at most but-for causation. It does not establish, as in the cases the United States cites, that the U.S. effects of the appellees' conduct—i.e., increased prices in the United States—proximately caused the foreign appellants' injuries. Nor do the appellants otherwise identify the kind of direct tie to U.S. commerce found in the cited cases. Although the appellants argue that the vitamin market is a single, global market facilitated by market division agreements so that their injuries arose from the higher prices charged by the global conspiracy (rather than from super-competitive prices in one particular market), they still must satisfy the FTAIA's requirement that the U.S. effects of the conduct give rise to their claims. The but-for causation the appellants proffer establishes only an indirect connection between the U.S. prices and the prices they paid when they purchased vitamins abroad. *Cf. Sniado v. Bank Austria AG,* 378 F.3d 210, 213 (2d. Cir.2004). Under the appellants' theory, it was the foreign effects of price-fixing outside of the United States that directly caused, or "g[a]ve rise to," their losses when they purchased vitamins abroad at super-competitive prices. That the appellees knew or could foresee the effect of their allegedly anti-competitive activities in the United States on the appellants' injuries abroad or had as a purpose to manipulate United States trade does not establish that "U.S. effects" proximately caused the appellants' harm. The foreign injury caused by the appellees' conduct, then, was not "inextricably bound up with . . . domestic restraints of trade," as in *Industria* and *Caribbean Broadcasting. See Empagran,* 124 S.Ct. at 2370. It was the foreign effects of price-fixing outside of the United States that directly caused or "g[a]ve rise to" the appellants' losses when they purchased vitamins abroad at super-competitive prices.

For the foregoing reasons, the judgment of the district court is affirmed.

NOTE

The Supreme Court's *Empagran* decision left one significant issue unresolved: whether the foreign injuries alleged were independent of the domestic effects of the conduct at issue. A high threshold for proving linkage would be consistent with the Court's general message of restraint in the remainder of the *Empagran* decision; conversely, if linkage could be proven easily, because of factors like fungibility, ease of transport, and world-market pricing, then this final point in the opinion might have taken away with the left hand much of what the right hand gave. In the years following *Empagran,* the lower courts have adopted the former approach, generally imposing a stringent test for plaintiffs who are trying to bring foreign conduct within the reach of the U.S. antitrust laws.

The Second Circuit was the first to address the issue, in a case involving a conspiracy by foreign banks to fix the exchange rates for the Euro. Sniado v. Bank Austria, 378 F.3d 210 (2d Cir. 2004). There, the plaintiff alleged in his complaint that the "domestic component of the conspiracy was necessary . . . for the conspiracy's overall success." *Sniado,* 378 F.3d at 213. Notably, the plaintiff refrained from asserting "that currency exchange fees in the United States reached supra-competitive levels, [or] that but for the European conspiracy's effect on United States commerce, he would not have been injured in Europe." The Second Circuit concluded that the allegation of a "necessary" link was too conclusory, and thus found that the conduct was outside the reach of the U.S. antitrust laws. *Id.* at 213.

When *Empagran* returned to the D.C. Circuit on remand, *see* decision *supra,* the court found, as a preliminary matter, that "the statutory language— "gives rise to" —indicates a direct causal relationship, that is, proximate causation, and is not satisfied by the mere but-for 'nexus' the appellants advanced. . . ." Empagran S.A. v. F. Hoffmann–La Roche, Ltd., 417 F.3d 1267, 1271 (D.C. Cir. 2005). The appellants countered that because the product (vitamins) was fungible and marketed globally, the only way to sustain supra-competitive prices outside the United States was to maintain such prices within the United States, to the detriment of U.S. consumers. Otherwise, they continued, foreign high prices would collapse as a result of arbitrage. The D.C. Circuit was unpersuaded, noting that this theory "demonstrates at most but-for causation." *Id.* at 1271. In general, later courts have followed this approach.

Prior to the D.C. Circuit's decision on remand, a district court in Minnesota had refused to dismiss the claims of a foreign plaintiff in an international MSG price-fixing case. In re Monosodium Glutamate Antitrust Litigation, No. 00–MDL–1328, 2005 WL 1080790 (D. Minn. May 2, 2005). The court declared that "[i]n *Empagran*, the Supreme Court recognized that a claim based on foreign injury that depends on the domestic effect of the defendant's anti-competitive conduct involves but-for causation." *Id.* at *3. The court went on to find that the plaintiffs had successfully pleaded the alternative theory presented in *Empagran*. *Id.* at *8. Upon reconsideration, however, the court dismissed the case, explicitly following the D.C. Circuit's reasoning. In re Monosodium Glutamatc, No. 00 MDL 1328, 2005 WL 2810682, at *3 (D. Minn. Oct. 26, 2005).

The global marketplace theory also failed in three other cases involving fungible commodities. In a magnesium oxide case, the court declared that allowing the theory would "effectively nullify the Supreme Court's ruling in *Empagran*." eMAG Solutions LLC v. Toda Kogyo Corp., No. C 02–1611 PJH, 2005 WL 1712084, at *8 (N.D. Cal. July 20, 2005). Plaintiffs claiming that the adverse effects on U.S. commerce were "necessary for the success of [a food additive price-fixing] conspiracy" were told that their theory had been "explicitly rejected in *Sniado*." Latino Quimica–Amtex v. Akzo Nobel Chemicals B.V., No. 03–Civ–10312 (HBDF), 2005 WL 2207017, at *11 (S.D.N.Y. Sept. 8, 2005). Finally, in a case alleging global price fixing of DRAM chips, the court dismissed the claims, stating "[t]here is simply no persuasive authority that plaintiff can muster to support an argument that . . . [a] global price-fixing conspiracy sufficiently alleges causation . . . post *Empagran I* and *II*." In re Dynamic Random Access Memory Antitrust Litig., Nos. C 02–1486 PJH & C 05–3026 PJH, 2006 WL 515629, at *5 (N.D. Cal. March 1, 2006.)

One case stands out from this trend: MM Global Servs. v. Dow Chem. Co., 329 F. Supp. 2d 337 (D. Conn. 2004). There, the plaintiff foreign distributors alleged that they had been forced to participate in a resale-price-maintenance conspiracy. That conspiracy, they claimed, decreased competition in the primary sales market and directly injured plaintiffs when they purchased the products for resale. *MM Global*, 329 F. Supp. 2d at 342. The court held that there was a sufficient causal link between this domestic effect and the plaintiff's injury. *Id.* at 342. The decision was not changed after *Empagran*, but the fact that it involved a vertical arrangement makes it distinguishable from the other cases.

Empagran has not yet affected the general tendency of courts to speak of the FTAIA rule as one concerning subject matter jurisdiction, rather than coverage of the statute, despite the fact that Justice Breyer's opinion (without discussing the point) takes the latter approach. This question may return, however, given the fact that the Supreme Court continues to caution against confusing a missing element of a claim with a jurisdictional defect. Arbaugh v. Y & H Corp., 546 U.S. 500 (2006). In that decision, the Court emphasized that judges should not presume that a limitation on a statute's scope is jurisdictional unless Congress clearly indicates that this is what it meant. *Id.* at 1245.

Some post-*Empagran* decisions have used the language of subject matter jurisdiction with little analysis. Thus, the Second Circuit's *Sniado* decision affirmed a dismissal for lack of subject matter jurisdiction "[i]n light of the Supreme Court's decision in *Empagran*" without any subsequent commentary. *Sniado, supra,* 378 F.3d 210. The *MM Global Services* court adopted a similar approach in addressing a defendant's motion under Fed. R. Civ. P. 12(b)(1). *MM Global Services, supra,* 329 F. Supp. 2d at 342. Finally, when the district court in Minnesota dismissed the *MSG* case, it did so with scant analysis of the jurisdictional question. *In re*

Monosodium Glutamate, supra, 2005 WL 2810682. The court used jurisdictional terminology in the body of its opinion, *see id.* at *2, but (confusingly) concluded finally that "Plaintiffs cannot state a claim under the Sherman Act." *Id.* at *3.

Other courts have simply followed pre-*Empagran* decisions that characterize the FTAIA as a rule of subject-matter jurisdiction, without considering whether *Empagran* itself or *Arbaugh* requires another look at the question. The district court in New Jersey cited cases from the Seventh, Ninth and Third Circuits as authority for the proposition that "the FTAIA establishes *jurisdictional* prerequisites for foreign antitrust claims, and does not merely impose additional substantive elements." *CSR Limited v. CIGNA Corporation,* 405 F. Supp. 2d 526 (D.N.J. 2005). The Southern District of New York likewise held that any claim that could not allege proximate causation failed on its face to allege subject-matter jurisdiction. *Latino Quimica,* 2005 WL 2207017 at *13. Additionally, the court in *EMAG Solutions* agreed with the defendants that the Supreme Court's admonition to keep the test simple meant to keep the *jurisdictional* test simple. *EMAG Solutions,* 2005 WL 1712084 at *8. The court dismissed the claims under Fed. R. Civ. P. 12(b)(1) and found it unnecessary to address the defendant's motion to dismiss for lack of antitrust standing. *Id.* at *12.

NOTES AND QUESTIONS

1. *Effects debate.* Kruman v. Christie's Intern. PLC, 284 F.3d 384 (2d Cir. 2002), was a class action in which the plaintiffs claimed that the two largest auction houses in the world had entered into an agreement to fix the prices they charged their clients for auction services. Both defendants were based outside the United States. The court found that the FTAIA applied. With respect to the "effects" debate, it stated that "[w]e find that an interpretation [of the FTAIA] centered on whether the plaintiff has suffered domestic injury cannot be squared with the text of the FTAIA." *Id.* at 396. How should this case be decided today if (a) the plaintiff is a U.S. customer, or if (b) the plaintiff is a foreign customer?

2. *Geographic factors. Empagran* may not resolve all issues in this area. In Turicentro, S.A. v. American Airlines Inc., 303 F.3d 293 (3d Cir. 2002), the court considered the question whether an alleged conspiracy among four domestic U.S. airlines and their trade association to fix the commissions paid to foreign travel agents, operating outside the United States, fell within the scope of U.S. law. The court concluded that it did not. The key, in its view, was the geographic target of the alleged conspiracy; there was no allegation that this one caused any injury felt in the United States or any impact on the U.S. economy.

The Fourth Circuit, in Dee–K Enterprises, Inc. v. Heveafil Sdn. Bhd., 299 F.3d 281 (4th Cir. 2002), confronted a suit brought by U.S. purchasers of a type of rubber thread made by South East Asian producers. After a jury trial, the jury found that the plaintiffs had failed to prove sufficient effects on U.S. markets, and the district court entered judgment for the defendants. The court of appeals affirmed. It found that the FTAIA did not apply directly, because the commerce in question related to imports. It therefore turned to the older line of cases for guidance. Ultimately it adopted a test under which it asked if the "participants, acts, targets, and effects [challenged in the suit] are primarily foreign or primarily domestic." 299 F.3d at 294. Finding that the jury reasonably could have concluded that these factors were primarily foreign, it concluded that there was no "jurisdiction" under the Sherman Act.

3. *Eschewing FTAIA?* Finally, there is Carpet Group Int'l v. Oriental Rug Importers Ass'n, Inc., 227 F.3d 62 (3d Cir. 2000), in which the court considered whether the FTAIA divested the district court of jurisdiction over a case alleging a conspiracy to monopolize the U.S. market for oriental rugs. The plaintiffs were Virginia entities selling oriental rugs to U.S. consumers; the defendants were an association of importers and wholesalers of the rugs (Oriental Rug Importers Association, Inc., or ORIA), several member companies, and some individual officers and directors of the association. The district court had found that there was no jurisdiction, but the court of appeals reversed. It noted that the defendants were claiming that the facts did not support the court's "subject matter jurisdiction," and thus that the court would need to consider the evidence supporting its power to hear the case. The complaint detailed various alleged restraints, including threats not to purchase rugs from manufacturers that participated in the plaintiffs' trade shows and other boycott-like activity, retaliatory threats, and efforts to induce export groups not to participate in the plaintiffs' trade shows.

The court of appeals concluded that ordinary Sherman Act principles applied to the case, because it involved import commerce, and import commerce is expressly excluded from the coverage of the FTAIA. The lower courts had erred, it held, when they found that the FTAIA applied. That error came about because the lower courts were looking at the brokerage function the plaintiffs played, rather than at the defendants' conduct. As for that, the court said that "the defendants intended their alleged conduct to subvert commercial activities that solely impacted domestic commerce," and that they took steps "designed to ensure that only United States importers, and not United States retailers, could bring oriental rugs manufactured abroad into the stream of American commerce." It went on to hold that jurisdiction existed and was not barred by FTAIA. Evidence supporting its conclusion included the defendants' efforts to:

(1) prevent foreign manufacturers from selling to United States retailers, (2) prevent at least one American retailer from purchasing rugs directly from foreign manufacturers, (3) prevent foreign governments and trade associations from sponsoring trade fairs at which retailers could purchase directly from foreign manufacturers, and (4) prevent an American rug retailers' trade association from sponsoring the trade fairs.

The plaintiff's evidence, moreover, sufficiently supported the defendants' alleged anticompetitive intent. The court concluded that "the activities of the wholesale importers were intended to and adversely did impact on domestic commerce by engaging in a course of anticompetitive conduct to ensure that only they, the importers, could bring oriental rugs manufactured abroad into the United States for distribution." Thus, the court held that subject matter jurisdiction existed under the Sherman Act, and the plaintiffs had antitrust standing.

In your opinion, does *Empagran* cast any doubt on the correctness of the court's ruling?

NOTE ON JURISDICTION IN EXPORT CASES

As you can see from Zenith Radio v. Hazeltine, 395 U.S. 100 (1969), *supra* p. 1191, the U.S. courts from time to time have entertained cases in which the alleged restriction on U.S. commerce focused on outbound trade to other countries. This became one of the most sensitive issues in the eyes of other countries, who regarded it as an impermissible extension of extraterritorial jurisdiction into their own markets. Why, for example, should the Canadian government not be the one to decide whether the patent pool at issue in *Zenith* was consistent with its own competition policy? Why should it matter if a U.S. firm is denied access to one foreign market, if the markets of the other 190–some countries in the world are open to it? If we think the antitrust laws are principally designed to protect U.S. consumer welfare, what justifies this "market access" branch of jurisdiction? On the other hand, is subsection (1)(B) of the FTAIA a plain indication from Congress that it regards market access cases as something that may fall within the antitrust laws?

This area had never been the central point of U.S. enforcement activity, but there had been a steady stream of cases over the years nonetheless. For example, in United States v. C. Itoh & Co., 1982–83 Trade Cas. (CCH) ¶ 65,010 (W.D. Wash. 1982), the U.S. Department of Justice obtained a consent decree against an alleged monopsonistic cartel of Japanese fish importers, who had agreed to depress the price they were willing to pay Alaskan fishermen for certain products. However, the Reagan Administration's Department of Justice announced in its 1988 Antitrust Enforcement Guidelines for International Operations, at footnote 159, that it would no longer bring export cases unless harm to U.S. consumers was also present. This position met with criticism both from Congress, which believed that its six-year old statute was being flouted, and from U.S. exporters anxious to be able to bring antitrust actions when anticompetitive behavior was barring access to foreign markets. Four years later, in 1992, footnote 159 was withdrawn by the first Bush Administration. *See* U.S. Department of Justice Press Release dated April 3, 1992. A diplomatic firestorm ensued. Claiming that the withdrawal of footnote 159 was a signal that antitrust had become just another retaliatory weapon for international trade problems, foreign governments argued strongly that market access cases violated international law.

Notwithstanding the controversial nature of market access jurisdiction abroad, the 1995 International Guidelines make it clear that this is one ground of jurisdiction that falls within the Agencies' competence. *See* 1995 Guidelines, § 3.122 and Illustrative Examples D and E. *See also* United States v. Pilkington, 1994–2 Trade Cas. (CCH) ¶ 70,842 (D. Ariz. 1994) (dismantling restrictions on exports of glass-making technology from the United States to other countries). Which position, in your view, is more consistent with the FTAIA? With international law? With a wise use of prosecutorial resources? It is worth noting that the increase in the number of cooperation agreements and the spread of antitrust to the majority of countries around the world has had the effect of diminishing the importance of direct enforcement designed to protect export markets. This is because the countries to which the goods or services are sent now enforce their own laws against foreign-based restraints that harm their consumers (either on their own initiative or because of a "positive comity" request from the exporting nation).

NOTE ON THE EXPORT TRADING COMPANY ACT OF 1982

Congress enacted the Export Trading Company Act of 1982, Pub.L. No. 97–290, 96 Stat. 1233 (1982), to stimulate the export trade of United States businesses by encouraging the establishment of export trading companies ("ETCs"), and by modifying the jurisdictional reach of the Sherman Act.

With respect to ETCs, the statute provides:

> The term "export trading company" means a company which does business under the laws of the United States or any state, which is exclusively engaged in activities related to international trade, and which is

organized and operated principally for purposes of exporting goods or services in the United States or for purposes of facilitating the exportation of goods or services produced in the United States by unaffiliated persons by providing one or more export trade services.

The Act encourages the formation of ETCs in three ways. First, it gives ETCs greater access to financing and financial expertise by permitting bank holding companies and certain other financial institutions to invest in ETCs. Bank holding companies may invest up to 5% of their consolidated capital and surplus in the ownership of ETCs. An investor may extend credit to an affiliated ETC, but the outstanding credit may not exceed 10% of the investor's consolidated capital and surplus. The Act also reduces limitations on export trade financing by financial institutions.

Second, the Act establishes an office in the Department of Commerce to promote the formation of ETCs and to serve as a clearing house of information for ETCs and producers of goods and services that could be exported.

Finally, and most important for our purposes, the Act provides ETCs with certain exemptions from the antitrust laws. It provides for issuance by the Secretary of Commerce of certificates that specifically exempt from antitrust scrutiny particular export activities by any person who acquires a certificate.

Certificate-holders are protected from the trebling of damages for any injury arising from, and from criminal liability for, conduct that is specified in, and that complies with, the terms of a certificate. For this purpose antitrust laws are defined as the Sherman Act (15 U.S.C.A. §§ 1–7), the Wilson Tariff Act (15 U.S.C.A. §§ 8–11), the Clayton Act (15 U.S.C.A. §§ 10, 13, 14–21, and 22–27), and all state antitrust and unfair competition laws. Notwithstanding this protection, there are three ways in which certificate-holders may be subject to actions for conduct subject to antitrust laws:

1. A person who is injured by the conduct of a certificate-holder who is protected from antitrust liability still may obtain injunctive relief and actual damages for violation by the certificate-holder of the standards of § 303(a) of the Act.

2. The Attorney General may bring an action under § 15 of the Clayton Act, 15 U.S.C. § 25, to enjoin conduct that threatens clear and irreparable harm to the national interest.

3. Certificate-holders are protected from liability only to the extent they have complied with their certificates. Conduct that is not specified in a certificate therefore is fully subject to all antitrust laws, as is the conduct of any person who does not hold a valid certificate.

SECTION 2. COMITY AND COOPERATION

A. COMITY IN THE COURTS

Timberlane Lumber Co. v. Bank of America, N.T. & S.A.

United States Court of Appeals, Ninth Circuit, 1976.
549 F.2d 597, *cert. denied*, 472 U.S. 1032, 105 S.Ct. 3514, 87 L.Ed.2d 643.

[Timberlane Lumber Co., an Oregon partnership engaged in the purchase, importation, and distribution of lumber in the U.S., formed two

Honduran corporations to acquire forest properties and operate a lumber mill in that country. Timberlane, through one of these subsidiaries, sought to acquire the Lima family mill, which had been in competition with the two largest lumber companies in Honduras, both defendants in the suit. Defendant Bank of America's Tegucigalpa branch held significant financial interests in each. The Lima mill had passed into the hands of creditors, including one of the defendant firms and certain unpaid employees, who under Honduras law had priority. From the latter Timberlane purchased the controlling assets and reactivated the Lima mill. It also sought to acquire the remaining interests in the Lima assets, to clear title, but was refused. Allegedly conspiring to eliminate plaintiff's competition, defendants placed their claims in the hands of an agent who took them to court for enforcement. The agent obtained court orders of attachment ("embargos") and appointment of a judicial officer ("interventor"), alleged to be on the payroll of the Bank, who caused guards and "troops" to cripple and partially shut down Timberlane's milling operations. The conspirators also allegedly caused defamatory articles regarding Timberlane to be published in the press and the false arrest and imprisonment of the manager of Timberlane's operations. Plaintiffs alleged damages in excess of $5 million and a "direct and substantial" effect on U.S. foreign commerce, intended by defendants.]

■ CHOY, CIRCUIT JUDGE.... This action raises important questions concerning the application of American antitrust laws to activities in another country, including actions of foreign government officials. The district court dismissed the Timberlane action under the act of state doctrine and for lack of subject matter jurisdiction....

I.   The Timberlane Action

The basic allegation of the Timberlane plaintiffs is that officials of the Bank of America and others located in both the United States and Honduras conspired to prevent Timberlane, through its Honduras subsidiaries, from milling lumber in Honduras and exporting it to the United States, thus maintaining control of the Honduran lumber export business in the hands of a few select individuals financed and controlled by the Bank. The intent and result of the conspiracy, they contend, was to interfere with the exportation to the United States, including Puerto Rico, of Honduran lumber for sale or use there by the plaintiffs, thus directly and substantially affecting the foreign commerce of the United States....

... The court gave as its reason [for dismissal] "that it is prohibited under the act of state doctrine from examining the acts of a foreign sovereign state; and in any event, that there is no direct and substantial effect on United States foreign commerce," the latter apparently being deemed a prerequisite for jurisdiction. No specific findings of fact were announced, nor were any more extensive conclusions of law stated.

It is unclear whether the decision was a dismissal for lack of subject matter jurisdiction or for failure to state a claim, F.R.Civ.P. 12(b)(1) & (6), or a summary judgment under F.R.Civ.P. 56....

We will ... review the judgment ... treating it as a Rule 12(b)(6) dismissal. Accordingly, we assume the allegations of the Timberlane plaintiffs to be true....

* * *

The classic enunciation of the act of state doctrine is found in *Underhill v. Hernandez*, 168 U.S. 250, 252 (1897):

> Every sovereign State is bound to respect the independence of every other sovereign State, and the courts of one country will not sit in judgment on the acts of the government of another done within its own territory.

From the beginning, this principle has been applied in foreign trade antitrust cases. In *American Banana Co. v. United Fruit Co.*, 213 U.S. 347 (1909), the first such case of significance, the American owner of a banana plantation caught in a border dispute between Panama and Costa Rica claimed that a competitor violated the Sherman Act by persuading the Costa Rican government to seize his lands. The act complained of would have required an adjudication of the legality of the Costa Rican seizure, an action which the Supreme Court said our courts could not challenge....

The defendants argue—as the district court apparently held—that the injuries allegedly suffered by Timberlane resulted from acts of the Honduran government, principally in connection with the enforcement of the security interests in the ... plant, which American courts cannot review. Such an application of the act of state doctrine seems to us to be erroneous. Even if the *coup de grace* to Timberlane's enterprise in Honduras was applied by official authorities, we do not agree that the doctrine necessarily shelters these defendants or requires dismissal of the Timberlane action.

The leading modern statement of the act of state doctrine appears in *Banco Nacional de Cuba v. Sabbatino*, 376 U.S. 398 (1964). Despite contrary implications in *Underhill* and *American Banana*, the Court concluded that the doctrine was not compelled by the nature of sovereignty, by international law, or by the text of the Constitution. 376 U.S. at 421–23. Rather, it derives from the judiciary's concern for its possible interference with the conduct of foreign affairs by the political branches of the government:

> The doctrine as formulated in past decisions expresses the strong sense of the Judicial Branch that its engagement in the task of passing on the validity of foreign acts of state may hinder rather than further this country's pursuit of goals both for itself and for the community of nations as a whole in the international sphere.

Id. at 423. The Court recognized that not every case is identical in its potential impact on our relations with other nations. For instance:

> [S]ome aspects of international law touch much more sharply on national nerves than do others; the less important the implications of an issue are for our foreign relations, the weaker the justification for exclusivity in the political branches.

Id. at 428. Thus the Court explicitly rejected "laying down or reaffirming an inflexible and all-encompassing rule." *Id.* Whether forbearance by an American court in a given situation is advisable or appropriate depends upon the "balance of relevant considerations." *Id.*

It is apparent that the doctrine does not bestow a blank-check immunity upon all conduct blessed with some imprimatur of a foreign government. In *Continental Ore Co. v. Union Carbide & Carbon Corp.*, 370 U.S. 690 (1962), the Canadian government had made a private corporation its exclusive agent for the purchase of vanadium, a material used in steel production. The Canadian corporation, acting in concert with an affiliated American company, used its position to exclude a competitor of the American affiliate from the Canadian market. The Court held that the Canadian corporation's activity was not entitled to immunity, carefully noting that the plaintiff did not question the validity of any action taken by the Canadian government and that there was no indication that any Canadian government official "approved or would have approved" of the monopolizing efforts. *Id.* at 706.

In *Alfred Dunhill of London, Inc. v. The Republic of Cuba*, 425 U.S. 682 (1976), interventors appointed by the Cuban government to take possession of and operate nationalized Cuban cigar manufacturers had been paid large sums by importers in the United States and elsewhere for pre-nationalization shipments. These payments were found to have been made in error, since they should have been made to the prior owners of the cigar firms. The importers sought to recover the money. Counsel for the Cuban government and the interventors argued that the interventors' refusal to repay the pre-intervention sums represented a sovereign repudiation of any obligation to refund the amounts and as such an act of state not subject to challenge in American courts. The Court disagreed, refusing to conclude that "the conduct in question was the public act of those with authority to exercise sovereign authority and was entitled to respect in our courts." *Id.* at 694. There was no proof that the failure of the interventors to repay the money reached the level of an "act of state," a sovereign assertion of the Cuban government:

> No statute, decree, order or resolution of the Cuban government itself was offered in evidence indicating that Cuba had repudiated her obligations in general or any class thereof or that she had as a sovereign matter determined to confiscate the amounts due three foreign importers.

Id.

A corollary to the act of state doctrine in the foreign trade antitrust field is the often-recognized principle that corporate conduct which is compelled by a foreign sovereign is also protected from antitrust liability, as if it were an act of the state itself. Thus, in *Interamerican Refining Corp. v. Texaco Maracaibo, Inc.*, 307 F.Supp. 1291 (D.Del.1970), a refusal by defendants to sell Venezuelan crude oil to plaintiff was held not to be an illegal restraint of trade because it was a complete defense that the Venezuelan government had imposed a boycott forbidding such sales. The court there observed that "[w]hen a nation compels a trade practice, firms there have no choice but to obey. Acts of business become effectively acts of the sovereign." *Id.* at 1298.

On the other hand, mere governmental approval or foreign governmental involvement which the defendants had arranged does not necessarily provide a defense. In *United States v. Sisal Sales Corp.*, 274 U.S. 268 (1927), the defendants were accused of conspiring to monopolize sales of sisal, a material used in making rope, from Mexico to the United States by inducing Mexican officials to recognize the conspirators as the exclusive traders and to impose discriminatory taxes on rival sellers. The Court rejected the defendants' claim to act of state protection, ruling that a conspiracy formed in the United States for the purpose of monopolizing sales to the United States was not protected simply because one element of the conspiracy involved securing favorable action by foreign officials. In *Continental Ore*, the Court indicated that it continued to accept the *Sisal* reasoning. See 370 U.S. at 705.

The distinction was recognized and relied upon in *United States v. The Watchmakers of Switzerland Information Center, Inc.*, 1963 Trade Cases ¶ 70,600 (S.D.N.Y.1962), order modified, 1965 Trade Cases ¶ 70,352 (S.D.N.Y.1965), the *"Swiss Watch"* case:

> If, of course, the defendants' activities had been required by Swiss law, this court could indeed do nothing. An American court would have under such circumstances no right to condemn the governmental activity of another sovereign nation. In the present case, however, the defendants' activities were not required by the laws of Switzerland. They were agreements formulated privately without compulsion on the part of the Swiss Government. It is clear that these private agreements were then recognized as facts of economic and industrial life by that nation's government. Nonetheless, the fact that the Swiss Government may, as a practical matter, approve of the effects of this private activity cannot convert what is essentially a vulnerable private conspiracy into an unassailable system resulting from foreign governmental mandate. . . .

The touchstone of *Sabbatino*—the potential for interference with our foreign relations—is the crucial element in determining whether deference should be accorded in any given case. We wish to avoid "passing on the validity" of foreign acts. *Sabbatino*, 376 U.S. at 423. Similarly, we do not wish to challenge the sovereignty of another nation, the wisdom of its policy, or the integrity and motivation of its action. On the other hand, repeating the terms of *Sabbatino, id.* at 428, "the less important the implications of an issue are for our foreign relations, the weaker the justification for exclusivity in the political branches."

While we do not wish to impugn or question the nobility of a foreign nation's motivation, we are necessarily interested in the depth and nature of its interest. The Restatement (Second) of Foreign Relations Law of the

United States § 41 (1965) makes an important distinction on this basis in limiting the deference of American courts:

> [A] court in the United States ... will refrain from examining the validity of an act of a foreign state by which that state has exercised its jurisdiction to *give effect to its public interests.* [Emphasis added.]

The "public interest" qualification is intentional and significant in the context of Timberlane's action, as a comment to § 41 makes plain:

> *Comment d. Nature of act of state.* An "act of state" as the term is used in this Title involves the public interests of a state as a state, as distinct from its interest in providing the means of adjudicating disputes or claims that arise within its territory.... A judgment of a court may be an act of state. Usually it is not, because it involves the interests of private litigants or because court adjudication is not the usual way in which the state exercises its jurisdiction to give effect to public interests.

Id. at 127.

... The actions of the Honduran government that are involved here—including the application by its courts and their agents of the Honduran laws concerning security interests and the protection of the underlying property against diminution are clearly distinguishable from the sovereign decree ... at issue in *Occidental Petroleum*.... Here, the allegedly "sovereign" acts of Honduras consisted of judicial proceedings which were initiated by ... one of the alleged co-conspirators, not by the Honduran government itself.... Timberlane does not seek to name Honduras or any Honduran officer as a defendant or co-conspirator, nor does it challenge Honduran policy or sovereignty in any fashion that appears on its face to hold any threat to relations between Honduras and the United States. In fact, there is no indication that the actions of the Honduran court and authorities reflected a sovereign decision that Timberlane's efforts should be crippled or that trade with the United States should be restrained....

Under these circumstances, it is clear that the "act of state" doctrine does not require dismissal of the Timberlane action.

Extraterritorial Reach of the United States Antitrust Laws

There is no doubt that American antitrust laws extend over some conduct in other nations.[17] There was language in the first Supreme Court

---

17. The subject of extraterritorial jurisdiction of American antitrust laws is one about which there has been a great deal of discussion. The commentaries cited in this opinion represent only a fraction of those discussing the subject. Worthy of special comment are K. Brewster, Antitrust and American Business Abroad (1958), and W. Fugate, Foreign Commerce and the Antitrust Laws (2d ed. 1973). There has, however, been much less action. In actual litigation, jurisdiction has not often been found lacking. Up to May 1973, the Department of Justice filed some 248 foreign trade antitrust cases; not one was lost for want of jurisdiction over the activities claimed to violate the law. W. Fugate, Foreign Commerce and the Antitrust Laws, App. B. at 498 (2d ed. 1973). The instant case is, of course, a private action, but reported dismissals of such cases also appear to be infrequent. The only case lost on appeal on case in point, *American Banana Co. v. United Fruit Co.*, 213 U.S. 347 (1909), casting doubt on the extension of the Sherman Act to acts outside United States territory. But subsequent cases have limited *American Banana* to its particular facts, and the Sherman Act—and with it other antitrust laws—has been applied to extraterritorial conduct. *See, e.g., Continental Ore Co. v. Union Carbide & Carbon Corp.*, 370 U.S. 690 (1962); *United States v. Sisal Sales Corp.*, 274 U.S. 268 (1927); *United States v. Aluminum Co. of America*, 148 F.2d 416 (2d Cir.1945) (the *"Alcoa"* case). The act may encompass the foreign activities of aliens as well as American citizens. . . .

That American law covers some conduct beyond this nation's borders does not mean that it embraces all, however. Extraterritorial application is understandably a matter of concern for the other countries involved. Those nations have sometimes resented and protested, as excessive intrusions into their own spheres, broad assertions of authority by American courts. . . . Our courts have recognized this concern and have, at times, responded to it, even if not always enough to satisfy all the foreign critics. . . . In any event, it is evident that at some point the interests of the United States are too weak and the foreign harmony incentive for restraint too strong to justify an extraterritorial assertion of jurisdiction.

What that point is or how it is determined is not defined by international law. . . . Nor does the Sherman Act limit itself. In the domestic field the Sherman Act extends to the full reach of the commerce power. *United States v. South–Eastern Underwriters Assn.*, 322 U.S. 533, 558 (1944). To define it somewhat more modestly in the foreign commerce area courts have generally, and logically, fallen back on a narrower construction of congressional intent, such as expressed in Judge Learned Hand's oft-cited opinion in *Alcoa*, 148 F.2d at 443:

> [T]he only question open is whether Congress intended to impose the liability and whether our own Constitution permitted it to do so: as a court of the United States we cannot look beyond our own law. Nevertheless, it is quite true that we are not to read general words, such as those in this Act, without regard to the limitations customarily observed by nations upon the exercise of their powers; limitations which generally correspond to those fixed by the "Conflict of Laws." We should not impute to Congress an intent to punish all whom its courts can catch, for conduct which has no consequences within the United States.

It is the effect on American foreign commerce which is usually cited to support extraterritorial jurisdiction. *Alcoa* set the course, when Judge Hand declared, *id.*:

> [I]t is settled law . . . that any state may impose liabilities, even upon persons not within its allegiance, for conduct outside its

---

this ground was *American Banana Co. v. United Fruit Co.*, 213 U.S. 347 (1909), a decision which is today considered largely obsolete. Rahl, Foreign Commerce Jurisdiction of the American Antitrust Laws, 43 Antitrust L.J. 521 (1974).

borders that has consequences within its borders which the state reprehends; and these liabilities other states will ordinarily recognize.

Despite its description as "settled law," *Alcoa*'s assertion has been roundly disputed by many foreign commentators as being in conflict with international law, comity, and good judgment. Nonetheless, American courts have firmly concluded that there is some extraterritorial jurisdiction under the Sherman Act.

Even among American courts and commentators, however, there is no consensus on how far the jurisdiction should extend. The district court here concluded that a "direct and substantial effect" on United States foreign commerce was a prerequisite, without stating whether other factors were relevant or considered.... Restatement (Second) of Foreign Relations Law of the United States § 18.[18]

Other courts have used different expressions, however. *See e.g., Thomsen v. Cayser*, 243 U.S. 66, 88 (1917) ("the combination affected the foreign commerce of this country"); *Alcoa*, 148 F.2d at 444 ("intended to affect imports and exports [and] . . . is shown actually to have had some effect on them");[19] *United States v. Imperial Chemical Industries, Ltd.*, 100 F.Supp. 504, 592 (S.D.N.Y.1951) ("a conspiracy . . . which affects American commerce"); *United States v. Timken Roller Bearing Co.*, 83 F.Supp. 284, 309 (N.D.Ohio 1949), *modified and affirmed*, 341 U.S. 593 (1951) ("a direct and influencing effect on trade")....

Few cases have discussed the nature of the effect required for jurisdiction, perhaps because most of the litigated cases have involved relatively obvious offenses and rather significant and apparent effects on competition within the United States. It is probably in part because the standard has not often been put to a real test that it seems so poorly defined.... What the threshold of significance is, however, has not been identified. Nor is it quite clear what the "direct-indirect" distinction is supposed to mean....

---

18.   Restatement § 18 reads:

A state has jurisdiction to prescribe a rule of law attaching legal consequences to conduct that occurs outside its territory and causes an effect within its territory, if either

(a) the conduct and its effect are generally recognized as constituent elements of a crime or tort under the law of states that have reasonably developed legal systems, or

(b)(i) the conduct and its effect are constituent elements of activity to which the rule applies; (ii) the effect within the territory is substantial; (iii) it occurs as a direct and foreseeable result of the conduct outside the territory; and (iv) the rule is not inconsistent with the principles of justice generally recognized by states that have reasonably developed legal systems.

The "direct" and "substantial" requirements come from (b)(ii) and (iii). Comment a to this section specifically indicates, however, that this rule applies only to aliens, since United States citizens may be bound by nationality, and govern only where there has been no significant conduct within the United States, since otherwise territorial jurisdiction could be asserted.

19.   This portion of *Alcoa* referred only to a combination of foreigners, specifically for whom the intent requirement may have been imposed, not American citizens or corporations. Further, Judge Hand's opinion noted that either intent or effect individually might suffice, but that both were present in that case, so that the question did not have to be faced.

The effects test by itself is incomplete because it fails to consider other nations' interests. Nor does it expressly take into account the full nature of the relationship between the actors and this country. Whether the alleged offender is an American citizen, for instance, may make a big difference; applying American laws to American citizens raises fewer problems than application to foreigners. As was observed in *Pacific Seafarers, Inc. v. Pacific Far East Line, Inc.*, 404 F.2d 804, 815 (1968), *cert. denied*, 393 U.S. 1093 (1969):

> If . . . [American antitrust] policy cannot extend to the full sweep of American foreign commerce because of the international complications involved, then surely the test which determines whether United States law is applicable must focus on the nexus between the parties and their practices and the United States, not on the mechanical circumstances of effect on commodity exports or imports.

American courts have, in fact, often displayed a regard for comity and the prerogatives of other nations and considered their interests as well as other parts of the factual circumstances, even when professing to apply an effects test. To some degree, the requirement for a "substantial" effect may silently incorporate these additional considerations, with "substantial" as a flexible standard that varies with other factors. The intent requirement suggested by *Alcoa*, 148 F.2d at 443–44, is one example of an attempt to broaden the court's perspective, as is drawing a distinction between American citizens and non-citizens.

The failure to articulate these other elements in addition to the standard effects analysis is costly, however, for it is more likely that they will be overlooked or slighted in interpreting past decisions and reaching new ones. Placing emphasis on the qualification that effects be "substantial" is also risky, for the term has a meaning in the interstate antitrust context which does not encompass all the factors relevant to the foreign trade case.

Indeed, that "substantial effects" element of interstate antitrust analysis may well be responsible for the use of an effects test for foreign commerce. The Sherman Act reaches restraints directly intended to limit the flow of interstate trade or whose sole impact is on interstate commerce, but it also reaches "wholly local business restraints" if the particular restraint "substantially and adversely affects interstate commerce." *Hospital Building*, 425 U.S. at 743; *Gulf Oil Corp. v. Copp Paving Co.*, 419 U.S. 186, 195 (1974); *United States v. Employing Plasterers Assn.*, 347 U.S. 186, 189 (1954). Such a test is necessary in the interstate context to separate the restraints which fall within the federal ambit under the interstate commerce clause from those which, as purely intrastate burdens, remain the province of the states. . . . Since, however, no comparable constitutional problem exists in defining the scope of congressional power to regulate foreign commerce, it may be unwise blindly to apply the "substantiality" test to the international setting. . . . Only respect for the role of the executive and for international notions of comity and fairness limit that constitutional grant.

A tripartite analysis seems to be indicated. As acknowledged above, the antitrust laws require in the first instance that there be some effect—actual or intended—on American foreign commerce before the federal courts may legitimately exercise subject matter jurisdiction under those statutes. Second, a greater showing of burden or restraint may be necessary to demonstrate that the effect is sufficiently large to present a cognizable injury to the plaintiffs and, therefore, a civil violation of the antitrust laws.... Third, there is the additional question which is unique to the international setting of whether the interests of, and links to, the United States—including the magnitude of the effect on American foreign commerce—are sufficiently strong, vis-à-vis those of other nations, to justify an assertion of extraterritorial authority.

It is this final issue which is both obscured by undue reliance on the "substantiality" test and complicated to resolve. An effect on United States commerce, although necessary to the exercise of jurisdiction under the antitrust laws, is alone not a sufficient basis on which to determine whether American authority should be asserted in a given case as a matter of international comity and fairness.... A more comprehensive inquiry [than the direct and substantial test] is necessary. We believe that the field of conflict of laws presents the proper approach, as was suggested, if not specifically employed, in *Alcoa* in expressing the basic limitation on application of American laws:

> [W]e are not to read general words, such as those in this Act, without regard to the limitations customarily observed by nations upon the exercise of their powers; limitations which generally correspond to those fixed by the "Conflict of Laws."

148 F.2d at 443. The same idea is reflected in Restatement (Second) of Foreign Relations Law of the United States § 40:

> Where two states have jurisdiction to prescribe and enforce rules of law and the rules they may prescribe require inconsistent conduct upon the part of a person, each state is required by international law to consider, in good faith, moderating the exercise of its enforcement jurisdiction....

The act of state doctrine discussed earlier demonstrates that the judiciary is sometimes cognizant of the possible foreign implications of its action. Similar awareness should be extended to the general problems of extraterritoriality. Such acuity is especially required in private suits, like this one, for in these cases there is no opportunity for the executive branch to weigh the foreign relations impact, nor any statement implicit in the filing of the suit that that consideration has been outweighed.

What we prefer is an evaluation and balancing of the relevant considerations in each case—in the words of Kingman Brewster, a "jurisdictional rule of reason." Balancing of the foreign interests involved was the approach taken by the Supreme Court in *Continental Ore Co. v. Union*

Carbide & Carbon Corp., 370 U.S. 690 (1962), where the involvement of the Canadian government in the alleged monopolization was held not to require dismissal. The Court stressed that there was no indication that the Canadian authorities approved or would have approved of the monopolization, meaning that the Canadian interest, if any, was slight and was outweighed by the American interest in condemning the restraint. . . .

The elements to be weighed include the degree of conflict with foreign law or policy, the nationality or allegiance of the parties and the locations or principal places of business of corporations, the extent to which enforcement by either state can be expected to achieve compliance, the relative significance of effects on the United States as compared with those elsewhere, the extent to which there is explicit purpose to harm or affect American commerce, the foreseeability of such effect, and the relative importance to the violations charged of conduct within the United States as compared with conduct abroad.[20] A court evaluating these factors should identify the potential degree of conflict if American authority is asserted. A difference in law or policy is one likely sore spot, though one which may not always be present. Nationality is another; though foreign governments may have some concern for the treatment of American citizens and business residing there, they primarily care about their own nationals. Having assessed the conflict, the court should then determine whether in the face of it the contacts and interests of the United States are sufficient to support the exercise of extraterritorial jurisdiction.

We conclude, then, that the problem should be approached in three parts: Does the alleged restraint affect, or was it intended to affect, the foreign commerce of the United States? Is it of such a type and magnitude so as to be cognizable as a violation of the Sherman Act? As a matter of international comity and fairness, should the extraterritorial jurisdiction of

---

20. Restatement (Second) of Foreign Relations Law of the United States § 40 states that a court should act in the light of such factors as

(a) vital national interests of each of the states,

(b) the extent and the nature of the hardship that inconsistent enforcement actions would impose upon the person,

(c) the extent to which the required conduct is to take place in the territory of the other state,

(d) the nationality of the person, and

(e) the extent to which enforcement by action of either state can reasonably be expected to achieve compliance with the rule prescribed by that state.

President (then Professor) Brewster lists these variables:

(a) the relative significance to the violations charged of conduct within the United States as compared with conduct abroad; (b) the extent to which there is explicit purpose to harm or affect American consumers or Americans' business opportunities; (c) the relative seriousness of effects on the United States compared with those abroad; (d) the nationality or allegiance of the parties or in the case of business associations, their corporate location, and the fairness of applying our law to them; (e) the degree of conflict with foreign laws and policies, and (f) the extent to which conflict can be avoided without serious impairment of the interests of the United States or the foreign country.

K. Brewster, *supra* at 446.

the United States be asserted to cover it? The district court's judgment found only that the restraint involved in the instant suit did not produce a direct and substantial effect on American foreign commerce. That holding does not satisfy any of these inquiries.

The Sherman Act is not limited to trade restraints which have both a direct and substantial effect on our foreign commerce. Timberlane has alleged that the complained of activities were intended to, and did, affect the export of lumber from Honduras to the United States—the flow of United States foreign commerce, and as such they are within the jurisdiction of the federal courts under the Sherman Act. Moreover, the magnitude of the effect alleged would appear to be sufficient to state a claim.[21]

The comity question is more complicated. From Timberlane's complaint it is evident that there are grounds for concern as to at least a few of the defendants, for some are identified as foreign citizens: Laureano Gutierrez Falla, Michael Casanova and the Casanova firms, of Honduras, and Patrick Byrne, of Canada. Moreover, it is clear that most of the activity took place in Honduras, though the conspiracy may have been directed from San Francisco, and that the most direct economic effect was probably on Honduras. However, there has been no indication of any conflict with the law or policy of the Honduran government, nor any comprehensive analysis of the relative connections and interests of Honduras and the United States. Under these circumstances, the dismissal by the district court cannot be sustained on jurisdictional grounds.

We, therefore, vacate the dismissal and remand the Timberlane action.

NOTES AND QUESTIONS

1. *Interest analysis.* What foreign interests can you identify in the facts of *Timberlane*? The mere fact that the conduct in question was occurring in another country? The fact that the foreign sovereign in question had taken some positive action, if only a fairly routine court order? Is this case more or less likely to interfere with legitimate foreign regulatory interests than *Continental Ore* or *Canadian Radio Patent Pool*?

---

21. Our separation in the foreign commerce context between the degree of restraint necessary for establishing subject matter jurisdiction as opposed to that required to state a claim is, of course, not duplicated in the interstate setting, for there a "substantial" restraint is in any event necessary for the establishment of jurisdiction itself. Nevertheless, since the interstate cases provide a standard for both jurisdiction and the statement of a claim, *Hospital Building Co. v. Trustees of the Rex Hospital*, 425 U.S. 738, 742, n. 1 (1976), they thus offer some guidance for determining the degree of restraint necessary to support a claim for relief in the foreign commerce context as well.... Although the decision whether the restraint alleged in the instant case qualifies to state a claim is for the district court in the first instance, we note that the quantitative test of substantiality is a "practical, case-by-case economic judgment," not one based on "abstract or mechanistic formulae," *Rasmussen v. American Dairy Ass'n*, 472 F.2d 517, 523 (9th Cir.1972), *cert. denied* 412 U.S. 950 (1973), and that the barrier raised is not very high. *See, e.g., Hospital Building*, 425 U.S. at 743–47; *United States v. Employing Plasterers Ass'n*, 347 U.S. 186, 189 (1954).

2. *Addressing international "intrusion."* *Timberlane's* "balancing" test was in part a response to long-standing criticism of *Alcoa's* test as insular and overly intrusive into conduct mainly of interest to other nations. One foreign observer, expressing a typical sentiment, hailed Judge Choy's approach as one that eliminated "an affront to international law occasioned by the present exercise of American antitrust jurisdiction purely on the basis of 'effects' upon American commerce." G. Taylor, *The Extraterritoriality of Australian Antitrust Law*, 13 J. Int'l L. & Econ. 273, 300 (1979).

3. *Defining jurisdictional limits.* The balancing test has come in for criticism as well as praise. Although at first blush it is hard to imagine defending the right to make unreasonable assertions of jurisdiction, the real question is whether jurisdictional limitations are best defined through complex balancing tests like the one adopted in *Timberlane*, or if it is better to try to confine the initial scope of jurisdiction through a clear threshold rule.

(a) The history of *Timberlane* itself casts some doubt on the efficiency and utility of the jurisdictional rule of reason. Recall that the case was filed around 1974 in the district court in California, after some years of litigation in both Honduras and in California state courts. The Ninth Circuit announced its path-breaking test in 1976. On remand, the district court (with the help of a master) allowed the parties to conduct extensive discovery, so that it would be able to evaluate the relevant factors appropriately. In 1983, the district court once again dismissed the case for lack of jurisdiction, hinting broadly that it would also have dismissed on the merits if jurisdiction were proper. 574 F. Supp. 1453 (N.D. Cal. 1983). Up again on appeal to the Ninth Circuit, the court decided that it was not fully satisfied with the district court's application of the balancing test, and it therefore conducted yet another full-blown analysis of the factors. Finally, it concluded that jurisdiction was indeed lacking, just as the district court had initially decided nearly a decade earlier. 749 F.2d 1378 (9th Cir. 1984). Ten years is a long time to spend on a "preliminary" matter like jurisdiction.

(b) Some argue that the balancing test presses judges well beyond any special competence, and perhaps authority, of the judiciary to evaluate the foreign relations policies of the United States and foreign governments. Under what circumstances do you think a court would be entitled to refuse to enforce the U.S. antitrust laws where it concluded that the parties were predominantly foreign and the greater weight of the effects was felt in foreign countries, if you also assume that direct and intended effects existed in the United States and U.S. consumers were affected? Does the answer to this question depend on whether the plaintiff is a private party, the Department of Justice, or the Federal Trade Commission? What weight, if any, should the court give to a communication from the U.S. Department of State to the effect that entertaining a particular antitrust suit would have an adverse effect on U.S. foreign relations with an affected country?

(c) Whenever multiple-factor tests like the *Timberlane* balancing approach exist, the point can be made that the test creates the appearance, but not the reality, of structure. The factors do not have weights attached to them; they are not capable of any kind of measurement; and there is no way to tell which ones should be able to offset which other ones. In short, virtually any result can be justified under the balancing test, no matter what facts are in the record, unless the case has such an obvious outcome that the test was unnecessary to begin with. One can always add more factors as well, as the Third Circuit did in Mannington Mills, Inc. v. Congoleum Corp., 595 F.2d 1287, 1297–98 (3d Cir. 1979), where it took *Timberlane* one step further and created a ten-factor test.

4. *Need to characterize "jurisdiction."* Is the *Timberlane* balancing test part of the jurisdictional inquiry, or is it more properly viewed as something like abstention? If it is the former, then what kind of "jurisdiction" are we talking about: federal court subject matter jurisdiction, in the sense of Fed. R. Civ. P. 12(b)(1), or legislative jurisdiction, which is better addressed under Fed. R. Civ. P. 12(b)(6)? What difference does this make as a practical matter?

5. *British–U.S. judicial power struggle.* In a case involving substantial interest to U.S. consumers, Laker Airways Ltd. v. Sabena, 731 F.2d 909 (D.C. Cir. 1984), Judge Wilkey rejected the balancing approach and found in favor of U.S. jurisdiction. The liquidators of Freddie Laker's no-frills airline, Laker Airways, sued U.S. and foreign airlines, all of which were members of the International Air Transport Association, a treaty-based international group of air carriers. The IATA member collectively set fares that were then approved by the appropriate national authorities. Laker alleged a predatory cartel that drove his airline company out of business. At the instance of British defendants, a British court ordered Laker not to proceed against the British defendants in the U.S. courts. British Airways Bd. v. Laker Airways Ltd., [1984] 1 Q.B. 142. The injunction was later dissolved by the British House of Lords, which observed that the U.S. court was the only forum in which Laker could seek relief, British Airways Bd. v. Laker Airways Ltd., [1985] A.C. 58 (H.L.). But before the latter decision, Laker brought a motion in the U.S. district court to enjoin defendants Sabena, the Belgian airline, and KLM, the Dutch airline, from trying to bring themselves under the protection of the British court's injunction. Judge Greene granted Laker's motion, holding that the district court clearly had prescriptive jurisdiction and ought to exercise it. *See Laker Airways v. Pan American World Airways*, 577 F. Supp. 348 (D.D.C. 1983). The case then took a bizarre turn when, after that ruling, the plaintiffs sought an injunction that would have restrained the British airlines from petitioning Parliament for relief. After rejecting the proposition that he had no *power* to grant such an injunction, Judge Greene ultimately refused to issue it on the ground that international comity required the court to respect political processes in the U.K., and in turn required Parliament to respect the lawful jurisdiction of the U.S. court. Laker Airways v. Pan Am. World Airways, 604 F. Supp. 280 (D.D.C. 1984).

6. *Department of Justice/Federal Trade Commission International Guidelines.* The subjects of jurisdiction and international comity are treated extensively in the 1995 Antitrust Enforcement Guidelines for International Operations, jointly issued by the U.S. Department of Justice and the Federal Trade Commission. The Guidelines are intended to inform businesses with international operations about the Agencies' international antitrust enforcement policy. Topics covered include subject matter jurisdiction, comity, mutual assistance in international antitrust enforcement, and the effects of foreign state action on private entities' antitrust liability. The full text is available at http://www.justice.gov/atr/public/guidelines/internat.htm.

B. ANTITRUST COOPERATION AGREEMENTS

Perhaps the most important modern development in the area of international comity has been the expansion of the cooperation agreements that exist among some of the major antitrust enforcement authorities of the world. The United States is now party to a number of such agreements.[22] In one, the Treaty with Canada on Mutual Legal Assistance in

---

22. *See* Agreement Relating to Mutual Cooperation Regarding Restrictive Business Practices, June 23, 1976, U.S.–Federal Republic of Germany, 27 U.S.T. 1956, T.I.S. No. 8291,

Criminal Matters (MLAT), S. Treaty Doc. No. 28, 100th Cong., 2d Sess. (1988), the U.S. Department of Justice and the Canadian Bureau of Competition Policy are empowered actually to conduct joint investigations, including the sharing of confidential information. This has been done successfully in a number of cases. The practical result of these cooperation agreements has been to reduce tensions over extraterritoriality, for the simple reason that agencies now feel free to call upon one another's resources rather than to try to act unilaterally. On November 2, 1994, the President signed the International Antitrust Enforcement Assistance Act (IAEAA), Pub.L. No. 103–438, 108 Stat. 4597 (1994), which authorizes the U.S. antitrust agencies to enter into antitrust mutual assistance agreements along the lines of the U.S.–Canada MLAT. The Antitrust Division of the U.S. Department of Justice, as of late 2009, reports that it has cooperation agreements with the following countries or areas: Australia, Brazil, Canada, Germany, the European Communities, Israel, Japan, and Mexico. *See* http://www.justice.gov/atr/public/international/int_arrange ments.htm.

Most of the more recent cooperation agreements, such as the U.S.–EC agreements and the 1995 U.S.–Canada agreement, emphasize both traditional comity and so-called positive comity. The U.S. authorities promise, in those agreements, to take into account the interests of the foreign country in the course of their enforcement activities. In the 1995 International Guidelines, § 3.2, the Agencies list eight non-exclusive factors that they consider:

(1) the relative significance to the alleged violation of conduct within the United States, as compared to conduct abroad;

(2) the nationality of the persons involved in or affected by the conduct;

(3) the presence or absence of a purpose to affect U.S. consumers, markets, or exporters;

(4) the relative significance and foreseeability of the effects of the conduct on the United States as compared to the effects abroad;

(5) the existence of reasonable expectations that would be furthered or defeated by the action;

(6) the degree of conflict with foreign law or articulated foreign economic policies;

---

reprinted in 4 Trade Reg.Rep. (CCH) ¶ 13,501; Agreement Between the Government of the United States and the Government of Australia Relating to Cooperation on Antitrust Matters, June 29, 1982, U.S.–Australia, T.I.A.S. No. 10365, reprinted in 4 Trade Reg.Rep. (CCH) ¶ 13,502; the Agreement Between the Government of The United States of America and The Government of Canada Regarding the Application of Their Competition and Deceptive Marketing Practices Laws, U.S.–Canada, reprinted in 4 Trade Reg.Rep. (CCH) ¶ 13,503; and the Agreement Between the Government of the United States of America and the Council of the European Communities Regarding the Application of Their Competition Laws, Sept. 23, 1991, 30 I.L.M. 1491 (Nov. 1991), reprinted in 4 Trade Reg.Rep. (CCH) ¶ 13,504, as amended in 1998.

(7) the extent to which the enforcement activities of another country with respect to the same persons, including remedies resulting from those activities, may be affected; and

(8) the effectiveness of foreign enforcement as compared to U.S. enforcement action.

The concept of positive comity builds on the last two factors. Briefly, it allows the enforcement agency to seek action from the foreign authority in whose territory the alleged anticompetitive conduct is taking place, if that conduct would also violate the foreign country's law. In its present form, positive comity has not been made mandatory either for the requesting agency or for the requested agency. Instead, it is an option that is encouraged under the cooperation agreements.

On April 17, 1997, the U.S. Department of Justice and the Federal Trade Commission announced the conclusion of the first International Antitrust Assistance Agreement made possible by the IAEAA which was concluded with Australia. After publication in the Federal Register and a lengthy period of consideration, the agreement formally entered into force on April 27, 1999.[23]

Although the United States and the European Community have yet to conclude an agreement for direct enforcement cooperation under the auspices of the IAEAA, they have nonetheless managed to move forward under more conventional agreements. On June 4, 1998, representatives of the U.S. government and the European Community signed an Agreement between the Government of the United States of America and the European Communities on the Application of Positive Comity Principles in the Enforcement of Their Competition Laws.[24] It commits both parties to greater use of the positive comity principle, under which one party may request another to take enforcement action against anticompetitive activities occurring within its territory in violation of its law, when those activities also have an effect on the other party.

Is positive comity the answer to the problem of extraterritorial jurisdiction, or is more necessary? In other areas of international law, notably the law of diplomatic protection, a State will not espouse the claim of its national unless the national has either exhausted local remedies or it can show that application of the exhaustion requirement would be futile in the circumstances. *See generally* ALI Restatement of the Law of Foreign Relations, § 703, comment d, § 713, comments b and f, and § 902(2) and comment k. Should the antitrust enforcement agencies adopt an analogous exhaustion requirement, under which they would consider bringing a market access case pursuant to § 6(1)(B)? What advantages or disadvantages would you foresee in such an approach?

* * *

---

23. The full text can be found at http://www.justice.gov/atr/public/international/docs/usaus7.htm.

24. The full text of the agreement can be found, at http://www.ftc.gov/bc/us-ec-pc.Shtm.

PROBLEM 26

JEANS AROUND THE WORLD

In 2005, the United States, Italy, and China were among the top ten countries for both imports and exports of denim fabric. That year, the worldwide exports of denim fabric exceeded US$4 billion. The major denim fabric manufacturers generate significant business by selling the "raw" fabric to purchasers. Those purchasers then use the fabric for a litany of products, but particularly jeans brands, which is a billion dollar business in its own right. Veil's, Inc. (U.S.), False Idol Apparel (U.S.), Houston's Brand (U.K.), Adriano Auro (Italy), Conception Jeans (France), and Black Pony, Ltd. (China) are major manufacturers of designer jeans (collectively "denim purchasers"). A single pair of these jeans can range anywhere from US$30 to over US$400. Profits in the designer jeans market has dwarfed the rather moderate growth of denim fabric sales.

Denim manufacturers and denim purchasers require the distributors with which they deal to use an expensive treatment apparatus to ensure the integrity of the denim. Ott Wanda Lay Industries, Inc. (OWL) is the biggest player in the global denim distribution market, both on the import and export side. OWL is incorporated in Delaware, and it has over twenty offices and distribution centers worldwide. There are two major denim distributors in addition to OWL: Rock Solid, Ltd. (Rock), a U.K. company operating worldwide, and Honest Al Co. (HAC), which is based in Maine. All three distributors maintain strong ties with the major denim manufacturers in the United States, Italy, and China, and competition among them is intense, yielding slim profit margins and relatively equal market shares.

In 2008, as the world economies sank into recession, sales for designer jeans remained strong. After reviewing their dwindling profit margins in the face of eight-figure profits by the downstream jeans manufacturers, OWL, Rock, and HAC decide that they have been letting others' pockets get too deep at their expense. At a meeting held in the Cayman Islands, executives from the three companies decide that they will each impose a minimum resale price on the denim fabric they sell to the manufacturers, and that this price will be at a level that assures their financial health. Most of the transactions that followed between the distributors and the denim purchasers occurred entirely outside the United States.

Six months later, the designer jeans manufacturers listed above sue OWL, Rock, and HAC in the United States District Court for the District of Delaware, under Section 1 of the Sherman Act and Section 4 of the Clayton Act, claiming that the distributors engaged in a price-fixing conspiracy. The distributors move to dismiss the claims brought by the foreign denim purchasers. Should the district court grant the motion? If so, on what grounds? Under the FTAIA, which plaintiffs and defendants, if any, should remain in the suit? What result should follow from the distributors' motion to dismiss the foreign purchasers, if the distributors' price maintenance restrained trade in the United States and the foreign purchasers were then injured in their home countries? What additional facts about the resale price maintenance and the subsequent transactions would support denying the motion to dismiss?

SECTION 3. THE EFFECT OF FOREIGN SOVEREIGN INVOLVEMENT

A number of doctrines apply when a foreign sovereign has taken some affirmative action that relates to the conduct being examined in a U.S.

antitrust case. We have already seen examples of this in *American Banana*, *Continental Ore*, and *Timberlane*. This section briefly considers the three most important of these doctrines: foreign sovereign immunity, the act of state doctrine, and the defense of foreign sovereign compulsion. For a comprehensive examination of these and other special defenses, see ABA Antitrust Section, Monograph No. 20, Special Defenses in International Antitrust Litigation (1995).

A.   FOREIGN SOVEREIGN IMMUNITY

Since 1976, this area has been governed by the Foreign Sovereign Immunities Act, 28 U.S.C. §§ 1330, 1602 et seq. (FSIA). The FSIA adopts what is known as the "restrictive" theory of sovereign immunity, under which "states are not immune from the jurisdiction of foreign courts insofar as their commercial activities are concerned...." 28 U.S.C. § 1602. Of importance for antitrust litigation is the breadth of the definition of the term "foreign state" in the statute. According to 28 U.S.C. § 1603(a), a foreign state includes not only the state itself, but also its political subdivisions and its agencies or instrumentalities. If the foreign state owns a majority of the shares of a corporation, that corporation is an "instrumentality" of the state for FSIA purposes. 28 U.S.C. § 1603(b)(1), (2).

An interesting sub-issue with significant practical implications involves the question of "tiering". The issue is whether, in a tiered corporate structure, indirect subsidiaries of a foreign state or political subdivision can also qualify as state instrumentalities, or if instead the statute confers "foreign state" status only on entities directly owned by the state itself. The circuits were split on that issue, but the Supreme Court resolved it in Dole Food Co. v. Patrickson, 538 U.S. 468 (2003). The *Dole Food* case was brought by banana workers from various countries against Dole Food, among others, seeking damages for injuries. The defendants impleaded two Israeli chemical companies, which removed the case to federal court claiming that they were "foreign states" for purposes of the FSIA. Whether they satisfied the statutory definitions or not depended on whether the FSIA contemplated "tiering." The State of Israel owned a majority of the shares of another corporation, which in turn owned a majority of the shares of the impleaded companies.

The Supreme Court decided that the FSIA extends only to instrumentalities or subsidiaries whose shares are held directly by the foreign state itself, thus rejecting the "tiering" theory. It relied on general principles of corporate law and the fact that the FSIA itself makes no mention of indirect ownership. The net result, of course, will be to restrict the applicability of the FSIA to a smaller number of entities in which foreign states have an ultimate interest.

The FSIA confers significant protections on foreign states, agencies or instrumentalities of foreign states, and companies in which foreign states hold a majority share of the ownership. Under the statute, a foreign state is presumed to be immune from suit unless one of the exceptions set forth in § 1605 applies. Some of the exceptions are unlikely to be of interest in an antitrust case, including explicit waiver (§ 1605(a)(1)), expropriations in violation of international law (§ 1605(a)(3)), disputes over gifts or succession rights (§ 1605(a)(4)), and torts committed by the foreign state or its agents in the course of their employment (§ 1605(a)(5), a rough equivalent to the Federal Tort Claims Act). The exception that is of intense interest to antitrust practitioners is the so-called commercial activity exception, found in § 1605(a)(2):

> [A foreign state shall not be immune from the jurisdiction of courts of the United States or of the States in any case—]
>
> (2) in which the action is based upon a commercial activity carried on in the United States by the foreign state; or upon an act performed in the United States in connection with a commercial activity of the foreign state elsewhere; or upon an act outside the territory of the United States in connection with a commercial activity of the foreign state elsewhere and that act causes a direct effect in the United States.

The statute instructs that whether or not something is a "commercial activity" must be determined "by reference to the nature of the course of conduct or particular transaction or act, rather than by reference to its purpose." § 1603(d). In the legislative history of the Act, Congress explained that a regular course of commercial conduct would include "the carrying on of a commercial enterprise such as a mineral extraction company, an airline or a state trading corporation.... [I]f an activity is customarily carried on for profit, its commercial nature could readily be assumed." H.Rep. No. 94–1487, 94th Cong., 2d Sess. (1976).

In Republic of Argentina v. Weltover, Inc., 504 U.S. 607 (1992), the Supreme Court gave a broad interpretation to § 1605(a)(2)'s requirement of a "direct effect" in the United States. There the Court rejected the argument that the effect had to be substantial and foreseeable, although it admitted that the effect should be more than *de minimis*. It defined a "direct effect" as one that follows "as an immediate consequence of the defendant's ... activity." 504 U.S. at 618. Note that this places the courts in the difficult position of applying three distinct tests for the degree of contact a foreign sovereign's instrumentality has with the United States: the "direct, substantial, and reasonably foreseeable" test of the FTAIA for antitrust jurisdiction; the "minimum contacts" test usually applied to questions of personal jurisdiction, and the "direct effect" test for assessing whether an exception to sovereign immunity exists. Are these tests really different, or do they merge in practice? Do the purposes of the three separate inquiries (reach of the antitrust laws, connections to the forum, and sovereign immunity) justify the separate formulations?

NOTE ON THE APPLICATION OF THE FOREIGN SOVEREIGN IMMUNITY DOCTRINE IN ANTITRUST CASES

1. Before the passage of the FSIA, U.S. courts had occasionally faced the question whether foreign sovereign immunity would apply. In United States v.

Deutsches Kalisyndikat Gesellschaft, 31 F.2d 199 (S.D.N.Y.1929), the government charged members of a European potash cartel with conspiring to monopolize the importation of potash into the United States. The French Ambassador intervened in the suit, claiming that the French defendant, a corporation in which the French government owned an 11/15ths interest, was an instrumentality of the Republic of France and that the suit was, in effect, an impermissible action against the French sovereign.

The court held that the French corporation could be sued despite the plea of sovereign immunity, because a private corporation was an "entity distinct from its stockholders," and cannot claim immunity "on the ground that it and the government of France are identical in any respect." The court noted that the company's French charter explicitly provided that it, like any private corporation, could be sued, and that French courts did not extend immunity to commercial enterprises owned or controlled by a sovereign state. The court added that:

> A foreign sovereign cannot authorize his agents to violate the law in a foreign jurisdiction, or to perform any sovereign or governmental functions within the domain of another sovereign, without his consent. He, therefore, cannot claim as a matter of comity or otherwise that the act of the alleged agent in such case is the act of the sovereign, and that the suit against the agent is in fact a suit against the sovereign. *Id.* at 203.

2. In the 1953 grand jury investigation of the oil cartels, In re Investigation of World Arrangements, 13 F.R.D. 280 (D.D.C.1952), Anglo–Iranian Oil Company, Ltd., a corporation controlled by the British government, moved to quash a subpoena on the ground that the company was an instrumentality of the British crown. Although the corporation's counsel claimed only that the company could not produce the necessary documents as a result of an order of the British government, the trial court held that the corporation itself was immune from the grand jury proceedings. It distinguished the Deutsches Kalisyndikat case, relying on the fact that Anglo–Iranian performed a vital government function in supplying oil for the British navy.

Would the same justification be available today under §§ 1603(d) and 1605(a)(2)?

3. Before the collapse of most of the Communist regimes, the courts occasionally faced questions about state trading organizations from those countries. In Outboard Marine Corp. v. Pezetel, 461 F. Supp. 384 (D.Del.1978), the Polish government tried to assert a sovereign immunity defense in a case brought by Outboard Marine claiming that the Polish company was attempting to monopolize the U.S. market for electric golf carts by means of sales in violation of the antidumping laws. The court was unpersuaded, finding that the type of market activity in which Pezetel was engaged (competing through low-priced sales) was subject to the jurisdiction of the U.S. courts under the commercial activity exception.

4. The most complex cases have arisen where foreign governments, either singly or in combination with other governments, have regulated the extraction, processing, and sale of natural resources. The leading case remains International Association of Machinists v. Organization of Petroleum Exporting Countries, 477 F. Supp. 553 (C.D.Cal.1979), *aff'd* on other grounds, 649 F.2d 1354 (9th Cir.1981), *cert. denied*, 454 U.S. 1163 (1982). At a time when gasoline pump prices were soaring in the United States due to the OPEC cartel, the Machinists' Union sued OPEC itself in federal district court in California, claiming a classic violation of Sherman Act

§ 1. The district court dismissed on the ground that OPEC's actions in controlling oil production were sovereign, not commercial, and that OPEC's price-fixing activities were merely incidental to its regulatory acts. As is noted in Section 2 below, the Ninth Circuit was uncomfortable with this analysis, because of the distinction drawn in the FSIA between the nature of a course of conduct and its purpose. It therefore did not rely on foreign sovereign immunity in disposing of the case, but instead it affirmed on the basis of the act of state doctrine.

Does a case like *OPEC* belong in the federal courts of the United States? Should the Executive Branch have any role in advising the court of the foreign policy implications of such litigation? Note that the government never intervened in any capacity, either formally or as amicus, to express views in the OPEC case. For contrasting views on the OPEC litigation, *see* Hovenkamp, Can a Foreign Sovereign Be an Antitrust Defendant? 32 Syracuse L.Rev. 879 (1981), and de Kieffer, The Foreign Sovereign Immunities Act and Antitrust: A Hollow Promise, 7 Syracuse J. Int'l L. & Com. 37 (1979).

B. THE ACT OF STATE DOCTRINE

Timberlane contains a brief introduction to the act of state doctrine. This section adds only a few additional notes about the doctrine and its application in antitrust cases. In order to place it in perspective, it may be useful to note that there have actually been two strands of act of state cases: one in which the action of the foreign government allegedly violates international law, such as the *Sabbatino* and *Dunhill* cases discussed in *Timberlane*, and the other in which the action of the foreign government allegedly violates either its own law or U.S. law. As Justice White's dissenting opinion in Sabbatino implies, the justification for abstaining from decision when an international law violation is alleged (such as an expropriation of property without the payment of prompt, adequate, and effective compensation) is harder to find than when the problem is essentially one of choice of law.

In *W.S. Kirkpatrick & Co. v. Environmental Tectonics Corp.*, 493 U.S. 400 (1990), the Supreme Court considered the application of the act of state doctrine in a case arising under RICO and the anti-bribery provisions of the Robinson–Patman Act. The chief executive officer of Kirkpatrick & Co. had arranged with a Nigerian official to pay a bribe to other officials of the Nigerian government in order to obtain a contract for some construction work at an air force base in Nigeria. Environmental Tectonics, the unsuccessful bidder allegedly ousted from the work because of the bribes, complained to the U.S. government. After an investigation, both Kirkpatrick & Co. and its CEO pleaded guilty to violations of the Foreign Corrupt Practices Act. Tectonics then brought a civil action for damages against the company, the CEO, and the Nigerian agent.

The district court granted summary judgment against Tectonics on the ground that the claim required an inquiry into "the motivations of a sovereign act which would result in embarrassment to the sovereign or constitute interference in the conduct of foreign policy in the United States." The Third Circuit reversed, relying to a great extent on a letter from the Legal Adviser to the U.S. Department of State stating that the judicial inquiry would not produce "unique embarrassment" to the foreign policy of the United States. (Indeed, the opposite might have been true, although this does not appear on the record. The State Department had been trying for years to strengthen international rules against bribery and corrupt practices, and it may have welcomed this kind of case.)

The Supreme Court affirmed the Third Circuit's view. It noted that the "act of state" doctrine only comes into play where the relief sought or the defense interposed requires a U.S. court to declare invalid the official act of a foreign sovereign performed within its territory. Thus, the issue in this litigation was not whether the award of the contract was valid but whether, valid or not, it was secured by illegal acts of the defendants. The Supreme Court concluded:

> The Act of State doctrine does not establish an exception for cases and controversies that may embarrass foreign governments, but merely requires that in the process of deciding, the acts of foreign sovereigns taken within their own jurisdictions shall be deemed valid. That doctrine has no application to the present case because the validity of no foreign sovereign act is at issue.

If the Nigerian government's award of the contract to Kirkpatrick must be deemed valid, has Tectonics stated a claim upon which relief can be granted? What damages would be available to Tectonics if it were entitled to base liability on actions of Kirkpatrick (*e.g.*, in offering the bribes), if the court cannot look behind the government's action?

NOTES AND QUESTIONS

1.   The defense of "act of state" was sufficient to defeat an antitrust claim in Occidental Petroleum Corp. v. Buttes Gas and Oil Co., 331 F. Supp. 92 (C.D. Cal. 1971), *aff'd*, 461 F.2d 1261 (9th Cir.), *cert. denied*, 409 U.S. 950 (1972). There the sheik supported by the British as Ruler of Sharjah was charged with conspiring with U.S. oil companies to deprive plaintiff of the value of oil concessions granted to it by a neighboring sheikdom. This injury was caused by the Ruler's decree asserting his proprietary claim, as sovereign, to land and oil under coast waters located in an area between the two mainlands. Since few things are more traditional acts of sovereignty than defining and defending boundaries, it was not surprising that the U.S. antitrust court, even though accepting extraterritorial jurisdiction, refused to decide the issue on "act of state" grounds.

2.   Hunt v. Mobil Oil Corp., 550 F.2d 68 (2d Cir. 1977), *cert. denied*, 434 U.S. 984 (1977), involved Nelson Bunker Hunt's claim that defendant major oil companies' conspiracy caused the government of Libya to nationalize Hunt's oil production rights. The District Court had noted that this would require it to explore the sovereign's motives for the expropriation. The Second Circuit agreed that the "act of state" doctrine prohibited such judicial intrusions into sovereign decision-making. Note that Hunt's lawyers carefully did not charge Libya as a co-conspirator; on the contrary, plaintiff's position was that the oil companies' alleged conspiracy was at the expense of both Libya and Hunt. Why did they have reason to hope that this would improve their client's case?

Hunt was criticized by a divided Fifth Circuit in Industrial Investment Development Corp. v. Mitsui & Co., Ltd., 594 F.2d 48 (5th Cir. 1979), *cert. denied*, 445 U.S. 903 (1980), which involved an allegation that defendants had procured the Indonesian government's cancellation of plaintiff's timber concession in an effort to monopolize the regional timber market. The majority criticized *Hunt* as encouraging the use of the "act of state" doctrine as a shield by private conspirators who are able to include some foreign governmental act in their anticompetitive scheme. The Fifth Circuit advanced a "two-step" inquiry to determine whether the alleged conspiracy afforded an independent basis for liability, and concluded that defendants' acts in the case before it were divisible from the ultimate denial of the concession by Indonesia.

3. International Association of Machinists v. Organization of Petroleum Exporting Countries, 649 F.2d 1354 (9th Cir. 1981), *cert. denied*, 454 U.S. 1163 (1982). A labor union sued OPEC and its member nations for allegedly fixing oil prices, resulting in reduced economic activity and fewer and less well-paid jobs for the union's members. No defendant appeared, but the trial court held a full hearing as required by the Foreign Sovereign Immunities Act, then held the member states protected by it. The Ninth Circuit, however, held that the OPEC cartel fell within the Act's "commercial activity" exemption, Judge Choy again writing the opinion. Congress intended the commercial exception to be broadly read, and the trial court's characterization of defendant's acts as "the establishment by a sovereign state of the terms and conditions for the removal of a prime natural resource" contravenes the Act by looking to the "purpose" rather than the nature of the conduct, price-fixing.

However, Congress did not intend to limit the "act of state" defense:

> While the [Act] ignores the underlying purpose of a state's action, the act of state doctrine does not. This court has stated that the motivations of the sovereign must be examined for a public interest basis. [Citing *Timberlane*.] ... Because the act of state doctrine and the doctrine of sovereign immunity address different concerns and apply in different circumstances, we find that the act of state doctrine remains available when ... caution is appropriate, regardless of any commercial component of the activity involved.

Id. at 1360. The District Court's dismissal was affirmed on that ground.

Note that under this approach, which seems likely to prevail, the absolute bar to jurisdiction arising from sovereign immunity is present only in cases of purely governmental conduct. The act of state doctrine assures that non-immune conduct may also be privileged where intervention by U.S. courts would endanger foreign relations interests. Perhaps where private parties claim act of state through sovereign compulsion, fairness will also be taken into account.

C. FOREIGN SOVEREIGN COMPULSION

Although the defense of foreign sovereign compulsion is rarely raised, and even more rarely succeeds, in litigated cases, it is nonetheless an important concept for international antitrust. If, in a case brought in a U.S. court, a defendant can show that its actions were compelled by a foreign sovereign, it may be relieved of liability. This is so both because it is inherently unfair to force a defendant to violate the law of one country or another, with no "legal" middle road, and because considerations of international comity sometimes require this kind of deference to the foreign country's laws.

The defense applies only when the foreign government has actually compelled the conduct in question. In the 1995 International Guidelines, the Agencies explain that "compulsion" exists "under circumstances in which a refusal to comply with the foreign government's command would give rise to the imposition of penal or other severe sanctions." 1995 Guidelines, § 3.32. Thus, encouragement, toleration, administrative guidance, or similar practices will not suffice. The defense also does not apply to procedural matters, such as a foreign government's command that documents located within its territory are not to be produced in response to an order of a U.S. court. In the latter cases, a more complex balancing process (ultimately informed by due process) governs how much weight the foreign government's order will be given.

There is also a territorial component to the defense, for the obvious reason that there would be no need to defer if the government of Country X told its company "we are hereby ordering you to violate the antitrust laws of Country A in your business there." From the standpoint of comity, the need to apply the defense is strongest when the actor is abiding by compulsory orders of its own government (*e.g.*, applying mandatory product standards, belonging to a compulsory association, etc.) that might raise antitrust problems elsewhere.

Remarkably, it appears that only one court has applied the foreign sovereign compulsion defense in circumstances that were dispositive: the district court in Interamerican Refining Corp. v. Texaco Maracaibo, Inc., 307 F. Supp. 1291 (D.Del.1970). Interamerican, the plaintiff, was a company owned by Venezuelan nationals that planned to process low-cost Venezuelan crude oil in a bonded refinery off the coast of New Jersey, and to export the product to New York. This tactic would have enabled it to avoid certain tariffs and import quotas. It took steps to implement the plan, but it found itself thwarted when its supplier of the Venezuelan crude (Amoco, and ultimately Texaco Maracaibo) refused to continue selling to it. The reason was that the Venezuelan government had flatly forbidden further sales of oil that either directly or indirectly would end up in Interamerican's hands. No other seller in Venezuela was willing to supply oil without the express permission of the government, which was not forthcoming.

When Interamerican sued Texaco Maracaibo and others under Sherman Act §§ 1 and 2, claiming an unlawful group boycott or concerted refusal to deal, the defendants moved for summary judgment on the ground that their actions were compelled by the Venezuelan government. The district court agreed, and dismissed the case. It noted first that "sovereignty includes the right to regulate commerce within the nation. When a nation compels a trade practice, firms there have no choice but to obey...." *Id.* at 1298. It then observed:

> Anticompetitive practices compelled by foreign nations are not restrains of commerce, as commerce is understood in the Sherman Act, because refusal to comply would put an end to commerce....

Commerce may exist at the will of the [foreign] government, and to impose liability for obedience to that will would eliminate for many companies the ability to transact business in foreign lands. Were compulsion not a defense, American firms abroad faced with a government order would have to choose one country or the other in which to do business. The Sherman Act does not go so far. *Id.* at 1297.

Why, if there is so little law, has the foreign sovereign compulsion defense remained as important as it has? The answer lies not in antitrust law, but in international trade law. From time to time, either at the request of the U.S. government or on their own, foreign governments have imposed "voluntary restraints" on the export of products to the United States. In order to be effective, those restraints normally must be controlled by the foreign government just as any output-restricting cartel is controlled: an overall quantity must be set, and shares of the market must be parceled out somehow to the companies involved. This is, more or less, what happened when the Japanese government imposed a series of voluntary restraints on the export of automobiles to the U.S. market. Nervous about the antitrust consequences of the arrangement, the Government of Japan asked whether liability would result from these actions. The U.S. government advised it, on a number of occasions, that as long as the Government of Japan was actually compelling its companies to take the specified measures and otherwise conformed to the requirements of the foreign sovereign compulsion defense, it believed that a U.S. court would dismiss any action that was brought. (Interestingly, no direct attack was brought during the many years the auto restraints were in place. *Compare Hammons v. Alcan Aluminum Corp.*, (No. 96–CV–319) 1996 WL 438605 (C.D.Cal. July 1, 1996), a case in which plaintiffs attempted to sue an alleged international aluminum cartel formed under the cover of an intergovernmental agreement regarding trade in aluminum, part of which involved restrictions on exports from the Russian market. The district court dismissed one defendant for want of personal jurisdiction and granted summary judgment on behalf of the remaining defendants.) These trade measures, with their obvious effect on competition in U.S. markets, are possible under existing U.S. antitrust laws largely because of the foreign sovereign compulsion defense.

SELECTIVE BIBLIOGRAPHY

Born and Rutledge, International Civil Litigation in United States Courts (4th ed. 2006).

Joelson, An International Antitrust Primer: A Guide to the Operation of United States, European Union and Other Key Competition Laws in the Global Economy (3d ed. 2006).

Fugate and Simowitz, Foreign Commerce and the Antitrust Laws (5th ed. 2005) (2 vol.).

Foster, While America Slept: the Harmonization of Competition Laws Based upon the European Union Model (2001).

Atwood, Brewster & Waller, Antitrust and American Business Abroad (3d ed. 1997).

Scherer, Competition Policies for an Integrated World Economy (1994).

Neale & Stephens, International Business and National Jurisdiction (1988).

ABA Section of Antitrust Law, Special Defenses in International Antitrust Litigation, Monograph 20 (1995).

U.S. Department of Justice and the Federal Trade Commission, Antitrust Enforcement Guidelines for International Operations (1995).

ABA Section of Antitrust Law, Report of the Special Committee on International Antitrust (Sept. 1, 1991) (2 vol.).

Hawk, International Antitrust Law and Policy: Fordham Competition Law [Annual Series].

Sokol, Monopolists Without Borders: the Institutional Challenge of International Antitrust in a Global Gilded Age, 4 Berkeley Bus. L. J. 37 (2007).

Stephen, Global Governance, Antitrust, and the Limits of International Cooperation, 30 Cornell Int'l L.J. 172 (2005).

Guzman, The Case for International Antitrust, 22 Berkeley J. Int'l L. 355 (2004).

Wood, International Harmonization of Antitrust Law: the Tortoise or the Hare?, 3 Chi. J. Int'l L. 391 (Fall 2002).

Kennedy, Global Trade Issues in the New Millennium: Foreign Direct Investment and Competition Policy at the World Trade Organization (2001).

Lowenstein, The Foreign Sovereign Immunities Act and Corporate Subsidiaries of Agencies or Instrumentalities of Foreign States, 19 Berkeley J. Int'l L. 350, 379 (2001).

Fox, Antitrust and Regulatory Federalism: Races Up, Down, and Sideways, 75 N.Y.U. L. Rev. 1781 (2000).

Fox, National Law, Global Markets, and Hartford: Eyes Wide Shut, 68 Antitrust L. J. 73 (2000).

Klein, EC Merger Control 10th Anniversary Conference, Time for a Global Competition Initiative? (Sept 14, 2000), http://www.justice.gov/atr/public/speeches/6486.htm.

Griffin, Extraterritoriality in U.S. and E.U. Antitrust Enforcement, 67 Antitrust L. J. 159 (1999).

Gifford, The Draft International Antitrust Code proposed at Munich: Good Intentions Gone Awry, 6 Minn. J. Global Trade 1 (1997).

Shank, The Justice Department's Recent Antitrust Enforcement Policy: Toward a "Positive Comity" Solution to International Competition Problems?, Vanderbilt J. Transnat'l L. 155 (1996).

Kramer, Note: Extraterritorial Application of American Law After the Insurance Antitrust Case: A Reply to Professors Lowenfeld and Trimble, 89 Am. J. Int'l L. 750 (1995).

Lowenfeld, Conflict, Balancing of Interests, and the Exercise of Jurisdiction to Prescribe: Reflections on the Insurance Antitrust Case, 89 Am. J. Int'l L. 42 (1995).

Trimble, The Supreme Court and International Law: The Demise of Restatement Section 403, 89 Am. J. Int'l L. 53 (1995).

Dam, Extraterritoriality in an Age of Globalization: The Hartford Fire Case, 1993 Sup. Ct. Rev. 289.

Wood, The Impossible Dream: Real International Antitrust, 1992 U. Chi. Legal Forum 277.

International Competition Network website at http://www.international competitionnetwork.org.

Website of the Organization for Economic Co-operation and Development (OECD), http://www.oecd.com.

CHAPTER 11

Price Discrimination and the Robinson–Patman Act

Section 1.   The Economics and Politics of Price Discrimination Legislation

Few things are more attractive to a seller with some degree of market power, even when no more than that conferred by a brand name, than to be able to structure a marketing operation in which he or she can engage in price discrimination. There is no more profitable way to sell a product than to charge each purchaser exactly that price which reflects the value of the product to him or her. (Indeed, if the product is consumed in quantity, the monopolist would like to be able to charge a different price for each unit sold even to the same buyer, to reflect the normal "diminishing incremental utility" of successive units.)

To be most profitable, the discrimination must be "systematic"—that is, not simply a "one-shot" concession, but a continuing differential reflecting different elasticities of demand for the good on the part of different users or different classes of users. The problem, in most cases, is that if a price discrimination is continuing, the buyer paying the higher price will find a way to get his supply from someone who buys at a lower price. In other words, arbitrage eliminates the differential since the different markets cannot be kept separate. With services, as opposed to discrete products, arbitrage is usually no problem—a doctor can charge each patient whatever he is thought to be willing to pay for his appendectomy, and Grinnell presumably worked out individual contracts with major users of its burglar alarm service. *See* United States v. Grinnell, p. 152 *supra*. Television networks or stations, newspapers, periodicals and other media can discriminate between large and small advertisers. Sylvania attempted to separate markets by a direct "customer restriction" on its dealers specifying locations from which they might sell. *See* Continental T.V., Inc. v. GTE Sylvania Inc., p. 655 *supra*. One way to succeed is to acquire by merger (or effectively to control through less formal means of vertical integration) the "low price, high elasticity" users, if they are not too great in number, so that the price to other "low elasticity" users may be increased, *i.e.*, to discriminate in favor of a vertically integrated subsidiary which can be prevented from engaging in arbitrage. Often this is feasible, however, only if one's rivals share the burden, *i.e.*, if the entire industry integrates vertically into the offending submarket.

If a cartel or oligopoly works well enough to enable the members of the group to develop parallel marketing structures and methods, as for example in the vertical integration example just discussed, the rewards of price discrimination may be even greater or the costs of policing the marketing structure reduced for each individual firm.

Many tying arrangements may be explained, in part or in whole, as "metering" devices that enable lessors to engage in price discrimination between high intensity and low intensity users, as in package licensing situations designed as devices to allow a single "package" price to effectuate profitable discriminations in the prices of unit components.

Finally, discrimination in price or through refusal to deal may be an inexpensive and potent weapon for use in protecting an existing market position or in expanding into a vertically related field.

None of these cases arose under the Robinson–Patman Act. Indeed, as we will note, if that Act is interpreted restrictively, *i.e.*, as limited to "purchasers" as opposed to lessees or consignees, and to discrete, physical "commodities," as opposed to services or goods more broadly defined, it will not apply to just those cases in which systematic price discrimination is most likely to exist and to have potent economic effects. Price discrimination, in an economic sense, pervades the marketing practices to which the Sherman Act and Clayton Act in general apply. So it is inaccurate to call the Robinson–Patman Act *the* price discrimination law. It is only one somewhat specialized aspect of the concern of antitrust law with the economic problems that arise from discriminatory treatment of suppliers or purchasers.

Section 2 of the original Clayton Act, as enacted in 1914, made it illegal "to discriminate in price between different purchasers of commodities . . . , where the effect of such discrimination may be to substantially lessen competition or tend to create a monopoly in any line of commerce. . . ." However, this prohibition was qualified to allow discrimination "on account of differences in the . . . quantity of the commodity sold . . . or discrimination in price . . . made in good faith to meet competition. . . ."

Large-scale buyers often negotiated for discounts without regard to sellers' costs, using their large orders as a bargaining weapon. They sought not only quantity discounts and special advertising and promotional allowances but to capture for themselves the brokerage commissions which had characterized traditional distributional methods. The severe economic depression of the 1930's accentuated the problems of the many small local merchants who could neither buy in large enough quantities to claim real cost savings nor exert much economic muscle in the interests of getting favored treatment. The local retailer, however, was not without political influence. Forming alliances with the wholesalers and distributors whose prosperity depended on his survival, he was able to bring pressure to bear on local and state legislative bodies.

Further relief was found in the short-lived National Industrial Recovery Act's industry-devised manufacturing, wholesaling, and retailing codes which barred or severely limited discounts and allowances to mass buyers. But even before the *Schechter* decision struck down the NIRA, the U.S. Wholesale Grocers' Association was preparing legislation that was to become the Robinson–Patman Act. Within two weeks after that decision, on June 11, 1935, Representative Wright Patman introduced a bill which drastically limited mass buyers by prohibiting all price differentials other than those based on the seller's cost savings or the distributional activities of the buyer, without regard to whether the discrimination had an adverse effect on competition. Furthermore, the cost justification proviso was extremely narrow.

The legislative history of the original bill reflects the multiple conflicts of different policy and group interests. Those legislators who envisioned a statute extending the existing antitrust laws scored an early victory in both the Senate and House committees. They succeeded in limiting the discriminations interdicted by the bill to those whose effect "may be to substantially lessen competition or tend to create a monopoly." However, a further amendment proscribed discrimination if its effect might be "to injure competition with any person who receives or grants the benefit of the discrimination, or with customers of either of them." This was a victory for those whose interest was to protect individual competitors rather than concern for the health of competition in a broader sense. The Section 2 defense that the differential was granted "in good faith to meet an equally low price of a competitor" was continued.

A second bill was pending before the Senate committee during the Robinson–Patman debate. The Borah–Van Nuys bill was not, however, an amendment to the Clayton Act, but was intended as an alternative to the Robinson–Patman bill, providing criminal penalties for the granting or receiving of any discriminatory "discount, rebate, allowance, or advertising service charge . . . [on] a sale of goods of like grade, quality, and quantity." The same penalties were to attach to geographical price discriminations or the sale of goods at "unreasonably low prices . . . for the purpose of destroying competition or eliminating a competitor." The Borah–Van Nuys bill was killed in committee, but was later tacked on to the Robinson–Patman bill as a floor amendment and now survives as Section 3 of the Act. The bill finally went to the Conference Committee with an additional amendment that made it unlawful for a buyer to "knowingly . . . induce or receive" a prohibited seller's price discrimination.

Few significant changes were made by the committee. The conferees apparently failed to reach a consensus on the basic issue of whether the new law should be primarily an extension of the antitrust law or a measure for the protection of traditional distributional arrangements. The House discussion prior to the adoption of the Conference Committee report indicates that the conferees took the pragmatic position of compromise rather than agreement on basic policy.

Robinson–Patman Act[1]

Section 2. (a) That it shall be unlawful for any person engaged in commerce, in the course of such commerce, either directly or indirectly, to discriminate in price between different purchasers of commodities of like grade and quality, where either or any of the purchases involved in such discrimination are in commerce, where such commodities are sold for use, consumption, or resale within the United States or any Territory thereof or the District of Columbia or any insular possession or other place under the jurisdiction of the United States, and where the effect of such discrimination may be substantially to lessen competition or tend to create a monopoly in any line of commerce, or to injure, destroy, or prevent competition with any person who either grants or knowingly receives the benefit of such discrimination, or with customers of either of them: *Provided,* That nothing herein contained shall prevent differentials which make only due allowance for differences in the cost of manufacture, sale, or delivery resulting from the differing methods or quantities in which such commodities are to such purchasers sold or delivered: *Provided, however,* That the Federal Trade Commission may, after due investigation and hearing to all interested parties, fix and establish quantity limits, and revise the same as it finds necessary, as to particular commodities or classes of commodities, where it finds that available purchasers in greater quantities are so few as to render differentials on account thereof unjustly discriminatory or promotive of monopoly in any line of commerce; and the foregoing shall then not be construed to permit differentials based on differences in quantities greater than those so fixed and established: *And provided further,* That nothing herein contained shall prevent persons engaged in selling goods, wares, or merchandise in commerce from selecting their own customers in bona fide transactions and not in restraint of trade: *And provided further,* That nothing herein contained shall prevent price changes from time to time where in response to changing conditions affecting the market for or the marketability of the goods concerned, such as but not limited to actual or imminent deterioration of perishable goods, obsolescence of seasonal goods, distress sales under court process, or sales in good faith in discontinuance of business in the goods concerned.

---

1. Section 2 of the Robinson–Patman Act is Section 2 of the Clayton Act, as amended, 49 Stat. 1526 (1936), 15 U.S.C. § 13. Section 3 of the Act is 49 Stat. 1528 (1936), 15 U.S.C. § 13a.

(b) Upon proof being made, at any hearing on a complaint under this section, that there has been discrimination in price or services or facilities furnished, the burden of rebutting the prima-facie case thus made by showing justification shall be upon the person charged with a violation of this section, and unless justification shall be affirmatively shown, the Commission is authorized to issue an order terminating the discrimination: *Provided, however,* That nothing herein contained shall prevent a seller rebutting the prima-facie case thus made by showing that his lower price or the furnishing of services or facilities to any purchaser or purchasers was made in good faith to meet an equally low price of a competitor, or the services or facilities furnished by a competitor.

(c) That it shall be unlawful for any person engaged in commerce, in the course of such commerce to pay or grant, or to receive or accept, anything of value as a commission, brokerage, or other compensation, or any allowance or discount in lieu thereof, except for services rendered in connection with the sale or purchase of goods, wares, or merchandise, either to the other party to such transaction or to an agent, representative or other intermediary therein where such intermediary is acting in fact for or in behalf, or is subject to the direct or indirect control, of any party to such transaction other than the person by whom such compensation is so granted or paid.

(d) That it shall be unlawful for any person engaged in commerce to pay or contract for the payment of anything of value to or for the benefit of a customer of such person in the course of such commerce as compensation or in consideration for any services or facilities furnished by or through such customer in connection with the processing, handling, sale, or offering for sale of any products or commodities manufactured, sold, or offered for sale by such person, unless such payment or consideration is available on proportionally equal terms to all other customers competing in the distribution of such products or commodities.

(e) That it shall be unlawful for any person to discriminate in favor of one purchaser against another purchaser or purchasers of a commodity bought for resale, with or without processing, by contracting to furnish or furnishing, or by contributing to the furnishing of, any services or facilities connected with the processing, handling, sale, or offering for sale of such commodity so purchased upon terms not accorded to all purchasers on proportionally equal terms.

(f) That it shall be unlawful for any person engaged in commerce, in the course of such commerce, knowingly to induce or receive a discrimination in price which is prohibited by this section.

Section 3. It shall be unlawful for any person engaged in commerce, in the course of such commerce, to be a party to, or assist in, any transaction of sale, or contract to sell, which discriminates to his knowledge against competitors of the purchaser, in that, any discount, rebate, allowance, or advertising service charge is granted to the purchaser over and above any discount, rebate, allowance, or advertising service charge available at the time of such transaction to said competitors in respect of a sale of goods of like grade, quality, and quantity; to sell, or contract to sell, goods in any part of the United States at prices lower than those exacted by said person elsewhere in the United States for the purpose of destroying competition, or eliminating a competitor in such part of the United States; or, to sell, or contract to sell, goods at unreasonably low prices for the purpose of destroying competition or eliminating a competitor.

Any person violating any of the provisions of this section shall, upon conviction thereof, be fined not more than $5,000 or imprisoned not more than one year, or both.

SECTION 2. SOME JURISDICTIONAL PROBLEMS AND ISSUES OF LANGUAGE

The Act starts with a series of jurisdictional provisions that a plaintiff must satisfy before moving on to the question of whether there has been an unjustified injury to competition. Many of these raise difficult issues because, as the Supreme Court observed in the *Automatic Canteen* case, "precision of expression is not an outstanding characteristic of the Robinson–Patman Act..."[2]

Current law on these jurisdictional requirements is summarized below:

1. *Interstate Commerce.* Section 2(a) prevents persons "engaged in commerce" from discriminating "in the course of such commerce" where either of the purchases involved in the discrimination is "in commerce." In practice, if the third element is proven, it has been found that the other two elements must necessarily be present.[3] But one of the sales—either the high price sale or the low price sale—must cross a state line.

---

2. Automatic Canteen Co. v. FTC, 346 U.S. 61, 65 (1953).

3. See, e.g., McCallum v. City of Athens, Ga., 976 F.2d 649 (11th Cir.1992) (discussing strict interstate commerce requirement under Robinson–Patman Act). See *also*, Chawla v. Shell Oil Co., 75 F.Supp.2d 626 (S.D.Tex.1999) (rejecting plaintiff's reliance on defendant's

In Gulf Oil Corp. v. Copp Paving Co., 419 U.S. 186 (1974), plaintiffs were concrete processors who sold paving materials to California contractors engaged in building interstate highways. Plaintiffs charged that the defendant oil companies had engaged in price discrimination in sales of "asphaltic oil" produced and sold in California. Copp argued that there was a "nexus" between the sales and interstate commerce, and that Congress intended the "in commerce" language of the Robinson–Patman Act to be construed to include the full scope of Congress' commerce power. The Supreme Court rejected those arguments, noting that the distinct "in commerce" language of the Robinson–Patman Act requires that at least one of the two transactions must cross a state line. There is authority that only a small volume of sales crossing a state line is necessary to satisfy a jurisdictional requirement.[4]

Section 2(a) does not apply at all to sales for export since the provision includes the phrase "sold for use, consumption or resale within the United States ... or other place under the jurisdiction of the United States."

2. *The Requirement of Discrimination.* The term "discrimination" as used in the Robinson–Patman Act presupposes that there is a difference in price charged by a seller to two different purchasers.[5] In computing what constitutes price, the various components of price—including discounts, surcharges, credit terms—are taken into account, and a substantial difference in these terms can produce a price difference.[6]

The majority view appears to be that where nondiscriminatory prices are *made available* to competing purchasers, any buyers paying a higher price are not victims of price discrimination.[7] Of course, the lower price must be realistically available to all customers. If a small buyer cannot take advantage of the lower price (for example, because minimum quantity purchases are required and smaller companies do not have adequate storage facilities), availability will not constitute a defense.

3. *Sales to Two Different Purchasers.* The Robinson–Patman Act only applies where goods have been sold to two different purchasers. Thus, a very early interpretation of the Act concluded that it does not apply where the seller "discriminates" by selling to one customer and refusing to sell to

---

interstate advertising activities and use of additives transported from out of state to refine gasoline to establish "in commerce" requirement.)

4. William Inglis & Sons Baking Co. v. ITT Continental Baking Co., 668 F.2d 1014, 1044 (9th Cir.), cert. denied, 459 U.S. 825 (1982).

5. *See* FTC v. Anheuser–Busch Inc., 363 U.S. 536, 549 (1960); Hoover Color Corp. v. Bayer Corp., 199 F.3d 160, 163 (4th Cir.1999).

6. *See* Rose Confections, Inc. v. Ambrosia Choc. Co., 816 F.2d 381 (8th Cir.1987); O'Connell v. Citrus Bowl Inc., 99 F.R.D. 117, 121–22 (E.D.N.Y.1983) (discounts for prompt payment and access to preferable distribution centers).

7. *See, e.g.,* Metro Ford Truck Sales v. Ford Motor Co., 145 F.3d 320, 326 (5th Cir.1998) ("A price discount equally available to all purchasers for the same customer and product is not price discrimination"); Caribe BMW, Inc. v. Bayerische Motoren Werke, 19 F.3d 745, 751 (1st Cir.1994) ("[I]f a seller makes its favorable prices and terms available to an otherwise disfavored customer, that customer has no legal right to complain").

another.[8] Similarly, a sale at one price and nothing more than an offer to sell at a different price would not satisfy the "two purchaser requirement."[9]

Similarly, the Act does not apply to certain "non-sale transactions." For example, it has been held inapplicable to software and movie licenses[10] and product swaps among oil companies.[11]

Some difference of view has arisen where purported sales occur between different affiliates or subsidiaries within the same corporate family. Most courts would conclude that where a wholly owned subsidiary receives a low price, especially when fully controlled by the parent, that is not a reviewable sale that may be compared to purchases by outsiders at a higher price.

Problems arise when supplier sells directly to retailers, and indirectly by selling to wholesalers who in turn sell to retailers. If the sale to the direct-buying retailers and to the wholesalers is at the same price, there are no two buyers paying different prices, and therefore there is no discrimination cognizable under the statute. Assuming the retailer who buys indirectly (*i.e.*, through wholesale channels) will end up paying more than the direct-buying retail competitor, the retailer can only obtain relief if it can somehow "attribute" the wholesale price to the manufacturer so that there are sales at two difference prices. Such attribution can only occur if the intermediary is owned or controlled by the manufacturer. *See* National Lead Co. v. FTC, 227 F.2d 825 (7th Cir.1955), rev'd on other grounds, 352 U.S. 419 (1957); Purolator Products Inc. v. FTC, 352 F.2d 874 (7th Cir.1965).

Finally, there is a statutory exemption to the Robinson–Patman Act that provides that it does not apply to non-profit institutions.[12]

4. *The Requirement of "Commodity."* Section 2(a) prohibits discrimination in price between different purchasers of "commodities," a condition also described in Section 2(a), apparently interchangeably, as the sale of "goods, wares or merchandise."[13] In general, the term "commodity" has been limited to tangible products and, as a result, the Act has been held not to apply to newspaper advertising,[14] services and trades on a stock ex-

---

8. In the Matter of Bird & Son, Inc., 25 F.T.C. 548 (1937).

9. Crossroads Cogeneration Corp. v. Orange & Rockland Util., Inc., 159 F.3d 129, 142 (3d Cir.1998) (offer to sell insufficient).

10. Microsoft Corp. v. BEC Computer Co., 818 F.Supp. 1313 (C.D.Cal.1992) (computer software licenses are not sales to different purchasers); County Theatre Co. v. Paramount Film Distributing Corp., 146 F.Supp. 933 (E.D.Pa.1956) (movie licenses).

11. Rebel Oil Co. v. Atlantic Richfield Co., 146 F.3d 1088 (9th Cir.), cert. denied, 525 U.S. 1017 (1998) (swap transactions not subject to statute); American Oil Co. v. McMullin, 508 F.2d 1345, 1353 (10th Cir.1975).

12. 52 Stat. 446 (1938), 15 U.S.C. § 13C (1980).

13. 15 U.S.C. § 13(a) (1962).

14. Ambook Enterprises v. Time, Inc., 612 F.2d 604 (2d Cir.1979), cert. dismissed, 448 U.S. 914 (1980).

change,[15] sales of telephone pole space for cable television,[16] or the loan of money at interest[17] nor medical services.[18]

In Columbia Broadcasting System v. Amana Refrigeration, Inc.,[19] Amana charged that CBS violated Section 2(a) by granting greater discounts on the basis of quantity to sponsors of evening hour programs, including competitors of Amana. The court concluded that the transaction between CBS and advertisers was not accurately characterized as a "sale" of television "time," but rather involved the purchase by Amana of the privilege of having itself identified as sponsor of a program broadcast. The court concluded that the word "commodity" in context applies to tangible products, not the privilege of sponsorship identification involved in TV broadcasting.[20]

5. *Like Grade and Quality.* Violation of Section 2(a) occurs only if the discrimination occurs with respect to commodities "of like grade and quality."

One set of questions involves application of the statute to products that are comparable in the eyes of consumers but not identical. In Atalanta Trading Corp. v. FTC,[21] a Court of Appeals rejected a Commission conclusion that canned hams, pork shoulders and precooked Canadian bacon were of like grade and quality because, as the Commission put it, "ham is ham...."The court concluded that because various products are derived from a common source, it does not follow that they all need to be marketed in an identical fashion. Other cases have concluded some "more than insubstantial" difference is required to trigger the statute.[22]

It has been urged that the question of fungibility be analyzed in terms of consumer reaction. If buyers would be equally happy with one product or the other for the same amount of money, they should be determined "of like grade and quality" for purposes of the statute.[23] Manufacturing costs have occasionally been looked to as an aid in deciding "like grade and

---

15.   Gordon v. New York Stock Exchange, 366 F.Supp. 1261 (S.D.N.Y.1973).

16.   T.V. Signal Co. v. American Tel. & Tel. Co., 462 F.2d 1256 (8th Cir.1972).

17.   Bichel Optical Laboratories, Inc. v. Marquette National Bank, 336 F.Supp. 1368 (D.Minn.1971). Recent cases addressing what is covered by "commodity" have held cellular phone services and telecommunications services are not "commodities" under the Robinson–Patman Act. Metro Comm. Co. v. Ameritech Mobile Comm., Inc., 984 F.2d 739 (6th Cir.1993) (cellular telephone services); National Comm. Ass'n v. AT&T, 808 F.Supp. 1131 (S.D.N.Y. 1992) (long distance voice telecommunications).

18.   Ball Memorial Hospital v. Mutual Hospital Ins., 784 F.2d 1325, 1340 (7th Cir.1986).

19.   295 F.2d 375 (7th Cir.1961), cert. denied, 369 U.S. 812 (1962).

20.   *See* Blake & Blum, Network Television Rate Practices: A Case Study in the Failure of Social Control of Price Discrimination, 74 Yale L.J. 1339 (1965).

21.   258 F.2d 365 (2d Cir.1958).

22.   William Inglis & Sons Baking Co. v. ITT Continental Baking Co., 461 F.Supp. 410, 421 (N.D.Cal.1978), aff'd in part and reversed in part on other grounds, 668 F.2d 1014 (9th Cir.), cert. denied, 459 U.S. 825 (1982); *but see* A.A. Poultry Farms v. Rose Acre Farms, 881 F.2d 1396, 1407 (7th Cir.1989), cert. denied, 494 U.S. 1019 (1990).

23.   F. Rowe, Price Discrimination Under the Robinson–Patman Act, 74–76 (1962).

quality" questions. Where manufacturing costs are the same, that can contribute to a finding of fungibility;[24] on the other hand, if there are substantial physical differences in products which affect consumer preference or marketability, similar products will not be found to be of like grade and quality just because manufacturing costs are the same.[25]

More vexing questions arise where products are chemically identical but, because of national advertising or trade names, can be sold at different prices. In FTC v. Borden Co.,[26] Borden produced and sold evaporated milk under the Borden name as a nationally advertised, premium brand. It also marketed evaporated milk under various private brands owned by its customers. The private label milk was physically and chemically identical with the Borden brand milk, but the former was sold at both wholesale and retail levels at prices regularly below those obtained for the premium brand. The Supreme Court, in a 7–2 decision, held that Borden brand milk and the private label were of "like grade and quality" within the meaning of Section 2(a) of the Robinson–Patman Act. The majority was reluctant to read out of the reach of the statute on a jurisdictional basis price discrimination between chemically identical products, preferring to preserve for the Commission an opportunity to examine under the more flexible standards of cost justification and injury to competition whether a violation had occurred. On remand, the Court of Appeals, noting evidence of a strong consumer preference for the premium brand, concluded there had been no violation because of no injury to competition.[27]

Finally, there is a time dimension to the issue of like grade and quality. For example, in Atalanta Trading Corp. v. FTC, 258 F.2d 365 (2d Cir.1958), a court regarded the failure to provide a promotional allowance more than five months after the original transaction as not relating to a reasonably contemporaneous transaction, and hence not an actionable discrimination. It noted that a contrary determination would require sellers to hold open promotional arrangements to prospective purchasers for extended periods of time or to refuse to deal with them altogether. The nature of the product or special market conditions may affect the question of what constitutes reasonably contemporaneous sales. For example, later sales of perishable products at lower prices may not be treated as being of like grade and quality because perishable foods may become less valuable after a short period of time.[28]

6. *Proof of Damages.* In government cases where the relief sought is an injunction, the standard for proof of damages is not very demanding.

---

24. *See* Quaker Oats Co., FTC Docket 8112, 66 F.T.C. 1190, 1192 (1964).

25. Universal–Rundle Corp., FTC Docket 8070, 65 F.T.C. 924, 955 (1964).

26. 383 U.S. 637 (1966).

27. To the same effect, see Texaco Inc. v. Hasbrouck, 496 U.S. 543, 556 (1990); International Tel. & Tel. Corp., 3 Trade Reg.Rep. (CCH) ¶ 22,188 (FTC 1984).

28. Dyno Nobel, Inc. v. Amotech Corp., 63 F.Supp.2d 140, 147 (D.P.R.1999) (old blasting caps that were obsolete or approaching end of their shelf lives differed in grade and quality from new blasting caps; an essential feature of a blasting capability is to set off explosives with exact timing and as product ages, ability to do so deteriorates).

The statute itself talks about situations where the effect of a discrimination "may be substantially to lessen competition," and usually proof of a substantial discrimination in a market in which there is keen competition will be adequate to establish a base for a remedy.

Where a private party sues for damages, it must proceed under Section 4 of the Clayton Act which provides such damages to "any person who *shall be injured* in his business or property by reason of anything forbidden in the antitrust laws ..." (emphasis added).[29] Prior to 1981, there was a division in the lower courts on what a plaintiff needed to prove. Some courts followed the "automatic damage theory" which allowed an inference of an injury from a showing of a substantial price discrimination,[30] while other courts insisted on evidence that the private injury complained of was directly attributable to something outlawed by the antitrust laws.[31]

The issue is important because, given the difficulty of proving the particular effect of a price discrimination, a demanding standard of evidence will restrict opportunities for private plaintiffs to bring treble damage actions under the Robinson–Patman Act.

7. *Criminal Provisions.* Section 3 of the Robinson–Patman Act makes it criminal to sell goods at "unreasonably low prices for the purpose of destroying competition or eliminating a competitor." The provision can be enforced by the government but not by private parties.[32]

In United States v. National Dairy Products Corp., 372 U.S. 29 (1963), the Supreme Court sustained the statute against a claim by defendants that the phrase "unreasonably low prices" was unconstitutionally vague. The Court concluded that the Act fairly applied to sales below cost (although it did not attempt to specify what elements of cost, such as direct and indirect, needed to be taken into account), and emphasized that the additional element of predatory intent alleged in the indictment provided adequate definition of the prohibited conduct. The Court did not attempt to specify whether the intent or conduct necessary to make out a civil violation of Section 2(a) of the Act would automatically also violate Section 3, although the tenor of the opinion and its emphasis on intent would appear to indicate that a higher standard of proof would be required before a Section 3 criminal violation would be found.

Criminal enforcement of the Robinson–Patman Act has rarely been undertaken, and not at all in over 40 years.

8. *Enforcement Since 1980.* Although the target of widespread and constant criticism, the Robinson–Patman Act has been neither repealed nor significantly amended.

---

29. 15 U.S.C. § 15 (Supp.1982).

30. Fowler Manufacturing Co. v. Gorlick, 415 F.2d 1248 (9th Cir.1969), cert. denied, 396 U.S. 1012 (1970); Elizabeth Arden Sales Corp. v. Gus Blass Co., 150 F.2d 988 (8th Cir.), cert. denied, 326 U.S. 773 (1945).

31. *See* Enterprise Industries Inc. v. Texas Co., 240 F.2d 457 (2d Cir.), cert. denied, 353 U.S. 965 (1957); Edward J. Sweeney & Sons v. Texaco, Inc., 637 F.2d 105 (3d Cir.1980).

32. Nashville Milk Co. v. Carnation Co., 355 U.S. 373 (1958).

Largely as a result of doubts about the Act's utility, it has been virtually unenforced at the federal level in recent years. The Antitrust Division of the Department of Justice has never enforced the statute. The Federal Trade Commission brought scores of Robinson–Patman cases each year in the 1940s and the 1950s, but that situation has changed. Since 1980, the Commission has enforced the Act only twice. It sued six major U.S. book publishers for price and service discrimination, but later abandoned the actions. In 2000, the Commission brought an action against McCormick & Co. and later settled the case. For a description of the case *see* p. 1290, *infra*.

Robinson–Patman Act enforcement continues to be a favorite of the private bar; many treble damage actions are brought each year by private plaintiffs, but their chances of prevailing have declined substantially. One reason is the widespread skepticism within the judiciary that price discrimination often leads to serious injuries to competition (as opposed to individual competitors). Another reason is the development of a rule of damages, requiring proof of actual injury "attributable to something the antitrust law was designed to prevent." *See* J. Truett Payne v. Chrysler Motors Corp., 451 U.S. 557 (1981). Since it is difficult to prove that a particular price or service discrimination led to injury to competition, the rule has significantly deterred private plaintiffs from even initiating actions.

NOTE ON INTERNATIONAL PRICE DISCRIMINATION

As noted above, the Robinson–Patman Act does not apply to sales for export, nor does it apply when one sale is made in a foreign country and the other sale is in the United States. A different body of laws does apply to such sales, however: the antidumping provisions of the laws regulating international trade. Dumping, in its simplest form, is international price discrimination. It occurs when a company sells merchandise in its home country at a higher price than it sells the same merchandise in a foreign market (the importing country). The difference between the home market price and the foreign price is known as the "margin of dumping," and the sales made in the importing country are sometimes referred to as the "less than fair value" sales.

U.S. law on dumping today implements the international agreement known as the General Agreement on Tariffs and Trade (GATT), which in turn is now administered by the World Trade Organization. Article VI of the GATT 1947 recognizes dumping as an unfair trade practice, and it permits countries to impose an "antidumping" duty on goods that have been dumped, if the practice causes injury to the affected industry in the importing country. Although it is far beyond the scope of this book to provide a comprehensive discussion of antidumping law, the differences between the treatment of international price discrimination and its domestic counterpart are stark enough that a brief look is warranted.

The Tariff Act of 1930, as amended, is the principal U.S. antidumping statute today. *See* 19 U.S.C. §§ 1673 *et seq.*; 1677 *et seq.* Two different agencies administer the laws. It is the responsibility of the Department of Commerce's International

Trade Administration (ITA) to determine, upon a proper petition, whether the merchandise in question is being sold at "less than fair value," or LTFV, and if so, to calculate the margin of dumping. An independent agency, the International Trade Commission, is charged with deciding whether the dumped merchandise is materially injuring, or threatening to inflict material injury, or materially retarding the establishment of, a U.S. industry. If both determinations are affirmative, the Department of Commerce issues an antidumping order requiring the collection of a duty, which must be equal to the dumping margin (regardless of whether or not the injury would be redressed with a smaller duty). The U.S. Customs Service actually collects the duty, on a company-specific basis. Both the need for duties and their amounts can be reviewed on an annual basis.

The salient differences between the dumping laws and the Robinson–Patman Act and other U.S. antitrust laws include the following. First, in an ordinary dumping case it does not matter whether the LTFV sales are made below cost or at a fully remunerative price. It is enough to show that there is a difference, and that the cheaper price (adjusted to show ex-factory equivalents for both sales being compared) is in the United States. Second, the dumping laws have no defenses analogous to the meeting competition defense or the cost-justification defense recognized under the Robinson–Patman Act. *See* Section 4 *infra*. Third, in some antidumping cases, where the ITA either has insufficient home market sales from which to derive a price, or it believes that the home market sales themselves were below the cost of production or otherwise not cost-based (as in nonmarket economy countries), it may "construct" a value. To construct a value, the ITA adds up (1) the costs of materials and fabrication, using whatever data it can gather from the country or an appropriate surrogate, (2) an amount for general expenses based on actual financial performance, which *cannot* be less than 10% of materials and fabrication, (3) an amount for profits, based on actual performance, but which *cannot* be less than 8% of the sum of (1) and (2), and (4) the costs of containers, coverings, and packing. Throughout this process, if companies in the exporting country do not wish to turn over proprietary financial information to the U.S. Department of Commerce, the ITA is entitled to rely on the "best information available," which usually comes from the complaining U.S. company or industry. These rules mean, in effect, that dumping will be found when sales below "total cost" are occurring, even though for antitrust purposes this would not suffice to show predatory pricing. *See* Chapter 8, Section 2 *supra*. Finally, the rules for injury in an antidumping cases require only a form of "but-for causation"—but for the dumped imports, prices and profits would have been higher, ergo injury exists. *See* Wood, "Unfair" Trade Injury: A Competition–Based Approach, 41 Stanford L.Rev. 1153 (1989). This is in marked contrast to the rules for antitrust injury that have evolved since Brunswick v. Pueblo Bowl–O–Mat, 429 U.S. 477 (1977).

Since the conclusion of the Uruguay Round of Multilateral Trade Negotiations, which led to the agreements establishing the WTO, more people have begun to call for greater harmonization of antitrust law at a global level. Some believe that it will be enough to put mechanisms in place that will facilitate enforcement cooperation at the national level, and others urge the drafting and adoption of a WTO agreement on competition law. If discussions for such an agreement are launched, the antidumping laws could be part of the agenda. Within NAFTA, working groups are already considering the question whether antitrust law in the three countries can replace dumping laws within the free trade area, and if so, what aspects of both laws the new regime should retain. If and when international competition policy moves to the forefront of the economic agenda, we may find concepts from the Robinson–Patman Act playing a part in the debate. As you consider the materials that follow, you should therefore ask yourself how they might operate if the rules were expanded to cover international cases, either in lieu of today's antidumping laws or in addition to them.

SECTION 3.   THE ANTICOMPETITIVE EFFECTS OF PRICE DISCRIMINATION

A.   "PRIMARY-LINE" EFFECTS

Utah Pie Co. v. Continental Baking Co.

Supreme Court of the United States, 1967.
386 U.S. 685, 87 S.Ct. 1326, 18 L.Ed.2d 406.

[Utah Pie was a small family-owned company that baked frozen dessert pies—apple, cherry, boysenberry, peach, pumpkin and mince—in Salt Lake City and sold in Utah and surrounding states. Defendants were Continental Baking, Carnation Company and Pet Milk—each a large company selling frozen dessert pies in one or more regions of the country. None of the defendants had a plant in Utah and for the most part supplied the Salt Lake City market from California bakeries.

During the period covered by the suit—1958, 1959, 1960 and the first 8 months of 1961—Utah Pie's share of the market was 66.5%, 34.3%, 45.5% and 45.3%, respectively. The frozen pie market itself was a rapidly expanding one and Utah Pie's sales volume steadily increased over the 4 years. Its total sales more than doubled during the period under review, although its net income remained very low, in the neighborhood of $7,000 to $12,000 per year.

For most of the period under review, Utah Pie's prices were the lowest in Salt Lake City. Price competition was extremely aggressive among the four companies, however, and there was evidence that each company in the course of a price war sold frozen pies in the Salt Lake City market at prices lower than they sold pies of like grade and quality in other markets closer to their bakeries.

Each of the defendants charged very low prices, but it is not clear from the opinion what standard the court applied to measure whether prices were "below cost." Thus, the court said with respect to Continental that its price in Salt Lake City was "less than its direct cost plus an allocation for overhead" and described Carnation's prices as "well below its costs." Pet was described as having suffered "substantial losses, greater than those incurred elsewhere." In addition, the court cited evidence from which the jury could have concluded that some of the discriminatory pricing was aimed at Utah Pie and predatory in its intent.

Pet's own management, as early as 1959, identified Utah Pie as an "unfavorable factor," one which "dug holes in our operation" and posed a constant "check" on Pet's performance in the Salt Lake

City market. Moreover, Pet candidly admitted that during the period when it was establishing its relationship with Safeway, it sent into Utah Pie's plant an industrial spy to seek information that would be of use to Pet in convincing Safeway that Utah Pie was not worthy of its custom?

386 U.S. 685, 697, 87 S.Ct. 1326, 1333. A jury found for Utah Pie on price discrimination charges, a court of appeals reversed on grounds that the evidence was not sufficient to support a finding of probable injury to competition, and the Supreme Court reinstated the jury verdict.]

■ WHITE, J.

Section 2(a) does not forbid price competition that will probably injure or lessen competition by eliminating competitors, discouraging entry into the market or enhancing the market shares of the dominant sellers. But Congress has established some ground rules for the game. Sellers may not sell like goods to different purchasers at different prices if the result may be to injure competition in either the sellers' or the buyers' market unless such discriminations are justified as permitted by the Act. This case concerns the sellers' market. In this context, the Court of Appeals placed heavy emphasis on the fact that Utah Pie constantly increased its sales volume and continued to make a profit. But we disagree with its apparent view that there is no reasonably possible injury to competition as long as the volume of sales in a particular market is expanding and at least some of the competitors in the market continue to operate at a profit. Nor do we think that the Act only comes into play to regulate the conduct of price discriminators when their discriminatory prices consistently undercut other competitors. It is true that many of the primary line cases that have reached the courts have involved blatant predatory price discriminations employed with the hope of immediate destruction of a particular competitor. On the question of injury to competition such cases present courts with no difficulty, for such pricing is clearly within the heart of the proscription of the Act. Courts and commentators alike have noted that the existence of predatory intent might bear on the likelihood of injury to competition. In this case there was some evidence of predatory intent with respect to each of these respondents.[33] There was also other evidence upon which the jury could rationally find the requisite injury to competition. The frozen pie market in Salt Lake City was highly competitive. At times Utah Pie was a

---

33. It might be argued that the respondents' conduct displayed only fierce competitive instincts. Actual intent to injure another competitor does not, however, fall into that category, and neither, when viewed in the context of the Robinson–Patman Act, do persistent sales below cost and radical price cuts themselves discriminatory. Nor does the fact that a local competitor has a major share of the market make him fair game for discriminatory price cutting free of Robinson–Patman Act proscriptions. "The Clayton Act proscription as to discrimination in price is not nullified merely because of a showing that the existing competition in a particular market had a major share of the sales of the product involved." Maryland Baking Co., 52 F.T.C. 1679, aff'd, 243 F.2d 716. In that case the local competitor's share of the market when price discrimination began was 91.3%, yet the Federal Trade Commission was not impressed by the argument that the effect of the discrimination had been to terminate a monopoly and to create a competitive market.

leader in moving the general level of prices down, and at other times each of the respondents also bore responsibility for the downward pressure on the price structure. We believe that the Act reaches price discrimination that erodes competition as much as it does price discrimination that is intended to have immediate destructive impact. In this case, the evidence shows a drastically declining price structure which the jury could rationally attribute to continued or sporadic price discrimination. The jury was entitled to conclude that "the effect of such discrimination," by each of these respondents, "may be substantially to lessen competition ... or to injure, destroy, or prevent competition with any person who either grants or knowingly receives the benefit of such discrimination...." The statutory test is one that necessarily looks forward on the basis of proven conduct in the past. Proper application of that standard here requires reversal of the judgment of the Court of Appeals.[34]

■ WARREN, C.J., took no part in the decision of this case.

■ STEWART, J., with whom HARLAN, J., joins, dissenting.

I would affirm the judgment, agreeing substantially with the reasoning of the Court of Appeals....

There is only one issue in this case in its present posture: ... did the respondents' actions have the anticompetitive effect required by the statute as an element of a cause of action?

The Court's own description of the Salt Lake City frozen pie market from 1958 through 1961 shows that the answer to that question must be no. In 1958 Utah Pie had a quasi-monopolistic 66.5% of the market. In 1961—after the alleged predations of the respondents—Utah Pie still had a commanding 45.3%, Pet had 29.4%, and the remainder of the market was divided almost equally between Continental, Carnation, and other small local bakers. Unless we disregard the lessons so laboriously learned in scores of Sherman and Clayton Act cases, the 1961 situation has to be considered more competitive than that of 1958. Thus, if we assume that the

---

34. Each respondent argues here that prior price discrimination cases in the courts and before the Federal Trade Commission, in which no primary line injury to competition was found, establish a standard which compels affirmance of the Court of Appeals' holding. But the cases upon which the respondents rely are readily distinguishable. In Anheuser–Busch, Inc. v. FTC, 289 F.2d 835, 839, there was no general decline in price structure attributable to the defendant's price discrimination, nor was there any evidence that the price discriminations were "a single lethal weapon aimed at a victim for predatory purposes." Id., at 842. In Borden Co. v. FTC, 339 F.2d 953, the court reversed the Commission's decision on price discrimination in one market for want of sufficient interstate connection, and the Commission's charge regarding the other market failed to show any lasting impact upon prices caused by the single, isolated incident of price discrimination proved. Absence of proof that the alleged injury was due to challenged price discriminations was determinative in International Milling Co., Trade Reg.Rep.Transfer Binder, 1963–1965, ¶¶ 16,494, 16,648. In Uarco, Inc., Trade Reg.Rep.Transfer Binder, 1963–1965, ¶ 16,807, there was no evidence from which predatory intent could be inferred and no evidence of a long-term market price decline. Similar failure of proof and absence of sales below cost were evident in Quaker Oats Co., Trade Reg.Rep.Transfer Binder, 1963–1965, ¶ 17,134. Dean Milk Co., 3 Trade Reg.Rep. ¶ 17,357, is not to the contrary. There in the one market where the Commission found no primary line injury there was no evidence of a generally declining price structure.

price discrimination proven against the respondents had any effect on competition, that effect must have been beneficent.

That the Court has fallen into the error of reading the Robinson–Patman Act as protecting competitors, instead of competition, can be seen from its unsuccessful attempt to distinguish cases relied upon by the respondents. Those cases are said to be inapposite because they involved "no general decline in price structure," and no "lasting impact upon prices." But lower prices are the hallmark of intensified competition.

The Court of Appeals squarely identified the fallacy which the Court today embraces:

> ... a contention that Utah Pie was entitled to hold the extraordinary market share percentage of 66.5, attained in 1958, falls of its own dead weight. To approve such a contention would be to hold that Utah Pie was entitled to maintain a position which approached, if it did not in fact amount to a monopoly, and could not exist in the face of proper and healthy competition.

349 F.2d 122, 155.

I cannot hold that Utah Pie's monopolistic position was protected by the federal antitrust laws from effective price competition, and I therefore respectfully dissent.

Anheuser–Busch, Inc. v. FTC

United States Court of Appeals, Seventh Circuit, 1961.
289 F.2d 835.

[The Seventh Circuit previously had held that certain pricing practices by Anheuser–Busch, described below, did not constitute price discrimination and the Supreme Court reversed and remanded, 363 U.S. 536 (1960).

The statement of facts in the Supreme Court included the following. Anheuser–Busch (AB) ranked first or second nationally in brewing, and sold its Budweiser label at prices higher than beers of regional and local breweries in most markets. Prices and price differentials between beers varied a good deal from market to market. In the St. Louis area, AB's principal competitors were Falstaff Brewing Corp., Griesedieck Western Brewing Co. (GW), and Griesedieck Bros. Brewery Co. (GB). In line with the prevailing price structure, these competitors normally sold their product at a price substantially lower than AB.

In late 1953, most breweries in the country introduced a price increase following renegotiation of an employee wage contract, but AB and its competitors in the St. Louis market maintained their previous prices. Thereafter, the following price moves occurred. In January 1954, AB cut its price on Budweiser in St. Louis by 25 cents per case, thereby reducing the previous differential between Budweiser and the local beers from 58 to 33 cents. In June, 1954, AB again cut its prices so as to be exactly equal to the prices of its St. Louis competitors. In March 1955, AB increased its price in

St. Louis by 45 cents per case, and its competitors raised their prices by 15 cents per case which reestablished a substantial price differential. Prior to the 1954 price cut and during the period of the price war, AB prices on Budweiser were lower in the St. Louis market than in other markets around the country.

The Commission had originally held that these price cuts constituted a discrimination in that they diverted business to AB from its St. Louis competitors. In its first decision, the Court of Appeals reversed on grounds that there could be no "price discrimination" under 2(a) unless different competing purchasers bought at different prices; here all competing purchasers bought at the same price. The Supreme Court reversed and remanded, and the Court of Appeals' second opinion picks up at that point:]

■ SCHNAKENBERG, J. . . . The gains and losses in the shares of the St. Louis packaged beer market commencing before and ending after AB's price reductions of January 4, and June 21, 1954, expressed in percentages of sales as divided among AB, Griesedieck Brothers (GB), Falstaff, Griesedieck Western (GW) and "All Others," are set forth in the following tabulation:

	Dec. 31 1953	June 30 1954*	March 1 1955	July 31 1955	Jan. 31 1956[35]
AB	12.5	16.55	39.3	21.03	17.5
GB	14.4	12.58	4.8	7.36	6.2
Falstaff	29.4	32.05	29.1	36.62	43.2
GW	38.9	33.00	23.1	27.78	27.3
All Others	4.8	5.82	3.94	7.21	5.8

* The entire packaged beer sales in the St. Louis market during the six months ending June 30, 1954 increased 2.7% over the same period for 1953.

This tabulation shows that AB's overall market increase in the St. Louis market area from December 31, 1953 to February 1, 1956 was 5% of the said market, while Falstaff's was 13.8% thereof.

In 1953 AB stood in fourth place in the St. Louis market and in 1956 it was in third place, having displaced GB.[36] While GW at all dates shown in the table led AB in the St. Louis market, with the exception of March 1,

---

35. The trial examiner found that regardless of the cut-off date used, July 31, 1955 or January 31, 1956, competition was lessened or injured. In order to determine the actual effect on competition, a statistical period must extend a reasonable time beyond the alleged illegal price reduction in order that all factors affecting the market may come into play. The tabulation becomes more comprehensive.

36. The hearing examiner's finding reveals: GB's sales were progressively declining in the St. Louis market from a share thereof in 1950 of 18% to 14.4% in 1953. In 1953 it replaced the beer it had theretofore been selling with an entirely new product which was badly named, poorly merchandised, bitter in taste and "wild"—that is with unstabilized air content. AB offered the testimony of eleven saloonkeepers and storekeepers that this new beer was disliked by the consumer with the result that consumer sales thereof dropped sharply during the latter part of 1954.

1955, its relatively low rating of 23.1% at that date is explainable by unique circumstances.[37]

At the hearing before the examiner, counsel for the Commission made it clear that no claim was made that the statutory effect on competition resulted from the January 4, 1954 drop in price by AB.

Outside of St. Louis, Falstaff had eight different breweries and grew from sixth to fourth largest brewer in the United States from 1954 to 1955; its beer was sold in 26 states in the West, Midwest, South and Southeast. GB was sold in 13 states, and, indeed, as was true with each of the other beers, it was found that more than three-quarters of its sales were outside St. Louis. GW was sold in 20 states.

While AB sells its Budweiser beer throughout the United States and has ranked first or second in national sales, it has never accounted for more than about 7% of such sales and is not first in any major market in the United States. Rather, competitors such as Falstaff, GW and GB dominate most markets, just as they dominated St. Louis with 82.7% of sales.

Although the hearing examiner found that AB's position in the St. Louis market had increased from sixth to fourth from 1945 to 1953, the fact is that at all these times AB was in *last* place in St. Louis, the number of brewers having decreased from six to four by reason of mergers, none of which involved AB.

In the fall of 1953, after an increase in costs due to a new wage contract, AB increased the price of Budweiser .15¢ a case in all markets except those in Missouri and Wisconsin. In many areas this small increase was multiplied by wholesalers' and retailers' markups to $1.20 a case at the retail level.

Despite similar cost increases due to the same new wage contracts, a number of brewers, including Falstaff and AB's other St. Louis competitors, chose to absorb the increased costs, and did not raise prices in any market in which they did business. Their right to do so is not challenged. However, as a consequence, there was a spread between the price of Budweiser and the price of other beers in markets other than in Missouri and Wisconsin. In some cases this spread was created by this increase, but in most cases a preexisting spread was increased. As a result, in November and December 1953, AB began to suffer severe sales losses in the Midwest sales area, supplied by its St. Louis brewery—losses as high as 73% in Nebraska, 53% in Oklahoma, 58% in Texas, etc. In some states AB's sales were down as much as 83% below the previous year; and while industry sales were down only 8%, AB's sales were more than 35% below the previous year.

---

37. GW had been progressively losing sales in the St. Louis market prior to 1954. Its management had been maintaining a highly liquid cash position at the expense of renewal or replacement of productive facilities. In October 1954, GW was sold to Carling Brewing Company (a subsidiary of Canadian Brewers, Ltd., which owned 18 breweries throughout the United States and Canada), at a price which reflected the good will to be about one-fifth of realizable net worth.

AB contends that it was obvious that something had to be done to correct the situation. The question was *what* should be done.

AB tried to roll back its price increase in one area, Ohio. but found, as it had anticipated, that the retailers and wholesalers were unwilling to give up their total additional markup of $1.20 per case merely because AB reduced its price 15¢ per case.

The first price reduction in St. Louis went into effect on January 4, 1954 and amounted to $25 per case. This still left the price of Budweiser $33 higher than the prices of its three principal competitors in St. Louis. All St. Louis brewers sold directly to retailers, and there were no wholesalers' markups to concern them. Furthermore, AB's home office was in St. Louis, and by a direct effort it was able to convince 85% of the retailers there to pass on the price reduction to consumers. Thus the problem of wholesalers' and retailers' markups was not present in St. Louis as it was elsewhere. Moreover, from a freight standpoint, AB was one of the few brewers who attempted to sell throughout the United States from one or two brewing sites. For example, in the area served by AB's single St. Louis brewery, Falstaff had seven breweries and intensely cultivated the area within about 300 miles of each of those seven, resulting in an estimated annual saving of $1,000,000. If AB reduced its price in an area where it had no plant, it would have to pay high freight costs from St. Louis and compete with the regional brewery getting its products from a local plant. Accordingly, all four named brewers there had at least one local plant so that none of them was faced with a freight disadvantage.

While the January 4, 1954 new price was in effect, AB also increased its advertising expenditures in St. Louis, which theretofore had been a fraction of its competitors' advertising. AB also changed its method of solicitation and delivery of orders to the system used by all of its St. Louis competitors and changed the organization of its sales force.

Despite all these changes, AB's national sales continued to decline. Then, on June 21, 1954, the second price reduction of Budweiser in St. Louis was made, the new price being the same as its three competitors had been, and were then, charging for their beers, or, as the complaint states, the price of beer "exactly matched the established price charged for beer" by the St. Louis competitors. In addition AB continued its efforts to solve its sales problem. Early in 1954, it considered proposals for reducing the capacity of its containers. On March 1, 1955, it marketed a new brand of beer to be priced competitively with its dominant competitors in the various markets, but this beer proved to be a failure. It then raised the price of Budweiser 45¢ per case and the St. Louis competitors raised their price by 15¢ a case, making Budweiser 30¢ higher-priced than its competitors. The record fails to reveal the fate of a different and cheaper beer introduced by AB in August, 1955.

While it is true that AB's sales increased in St. Louis during the period of the price reductions,[38] a fact which alone surely cannot constitute a

---

38. As indicated, ... AB's sales increase was equal to 5% of the St. Louis market between Dec. 31, 1953 and Feb. 1, 1956.

violation of § 2(a), nevertheless AB's competitors still controlled more than three-fourths of market sales in the twelve months after the price of Budweiser was voluntarily increased in St. Louis in March, 1955. While Budweiser and other premium beers were selling at the same price in St. Louis, buyers had a greater freedom of choice at the same price level and thus the contest for beer sales was intensified.

During the 1954–1955 price reductions, AB's St. Louis competitors continued to sell in St. Louis at the same price at which they had previously sold. None of them lost retail customers; each continued to sell to the same retailers to whom it had always sold; and each continued to sell at the same prices at which it had previously sold. Each continued to make profits—Falstaff, for example, earned almost $7,000,000 in 1954. Each continued to vary its competitive activities, *e.g.*, changing the formula of its products, changing its labels, varying its advertising, offering special price promotions, entering new markets, etc.

The record reveals only a temporary shift in volume of business among the competitors in the St. Louis market. Although AB did attain a monthly average of 36.6% of sales during the eight months of the second price reduction, nevertheless this was not as great a share of the market as its leading competitors obtained before or after the price reduction. Whatever position AB obtained was temporary; by 1956 its sales had receded to 17.5% of the market, whereas Falstaff at that time had increased to 43% of the market from the 29.4% it had enjoyed before the price reductions.

The examiner expressly found that there was no proof that AB used income or profit from the rest of its business to stabilize losses in St. Louis, or indeed, that there were any losses by AB in St. Louis during the period of the price reductions.

AB's two price reductions were parts of an experimental program of sales promotion in the St. Louis market and the reductions were temporary and made necessary by competitive conditions. A primary result of AB's price reductions was that the consumers of beer in St. Louis enjoyed a lower price on Budweiser, since the price reductions were passed on to them by the retailers.

While AB's two price reductions undoubtedly contributed to moderate changes in the division of the beer sales in the St. Louis market, there was also a causal connection between those changes and (a) GW's and GB's special problems, ... (b) Falstaff's gain of 13.8% of the market and (c) a 1% gain by "All Others."

Considering that the Commission relied on a percentage test, no one is able to determine from this record how much of the losses of AB's competitors were attributable to these special facts as compared to any losses resulting solely from AB's price reductions.

From these undisputed facts we find that the Commission failed to prove that AB's price reductions in 1954 caused any present, actual injury to competition. . . .

... [We now] consider the Commission's reliance on Corn Products Refining Co. v. Federal Trade Commission, 1945, 324 U.S. 726. In that case, 324 U.S. at page 738 the Court pointed out:

> ... § 2(a) does not require a finding that the discriminations in price have in fact had an adverse effect on competition.... It is enough that they "may" have the proscribed effect.... The use of the word "may" was not to prohibit discriminations having "the mere possibility" of those consequences, but to reach those which would probably have the defined effect on competition.

... [W]e find that, there being no showing that AB had aid from its other markets and despite a decrease in its national sales,[39] AB forthrightly met its robust competition in the St. Louis market by a multiple-pronged program, which included but was not limited to a two-step reduction in its price to exactly meet that of its competitors. The record affirmatively shows that AB used restraint in its competitive efforts. Its conduct was in conformity with the principle that competition is the decisive force in the market place. That conduct is the antithesis of the predatory misconduct condemned in ... territorial pricing cases relied on by the Commission. In each of those cases the motive for the price cut was vindictive and the effect was punitive. There was not even a pretense that the price change was incident to a general intensification of the sales effort, as in the case at bar. It was a single lethal weapon aimed at a victim for a predatory purpose.

The Commission relies heavily upon finding 26 in the initial decision of the examiner, which includes the following statements:

> ... we are here concerned not only with actual injury but with potential injury as well, and there is nothing in this record to show that what A.B. did in the St. Louis market could not or would not be done by it, in the future, in other markets as well.... A.B. has total assets of more than twice those of its three St. Louis brewery competitors, and, selling nation-wide as it does, is able, *although there is no proof that it did,* to use income or profit from the rest of its business to stabilize losses, if any, incurred in such a price raid. I repeat, there is *no showing that it did, but* the record shows *it could*—the potentiality is there.... (Italics supplied.)

It is true that the effects of AB's acts on competition might have been different from what they actually were and that nevertheless it could be held to account under § 2(a) for what actually happened as well as the reasonably possible effects thereof. But, to prove the *acts* themselves, the Commission was required to adduce evidence of what AB *did* and a finding of a violation cannot rest upon a conjecture as to what it *might do.* Potentiality to commit an act cannot be used as a substitute for proof of the act itself. While it has been said that every person has a little larceny in his

---

39. Its total sales were off more than 1,000,000 cases in May and 1,500,000 cases in June 1954. These followed successive declines in national sales for each preceding month in 1954 and for November and December 1953.

heart, not even a cynic would attempt to procure a conviction on that ground alone. Nor are we convinced that guilt of an alleged malefactor can be proved by only its bigness.[40] The Commission's argument that the "over-all size of the interstate enterprise" of AB "is significant, for it enables a seller to engage in area price discriminations without fear of severe monetary loss to itself", is met by the examiner's finding that there was no proof that AB had employed its size to support its price reductions.

. . . [T]he findings of the Commission cannot, on the consideration of the whole record, be deemed to be supported by substantial evidence.

Brooke Group v. Brown & Williamson Tobacco

Supreme Court of the United States, 1993.
509 U.S. 209, 113 S.Ct. 2578, 125 L.Ed.2d 168.

[Reprinted p. 823 *supra*]

NOTE

In recent years, particularly since the Supreme Court decision in *Brooke Group*, there is a tendency to define predatory pricing under the Sherman Act the same as injury to competition in primary line cases—*i.e.*, the challenged price in each situation must be "below cost." For an early indication of this change in direction, *see* International Air Industries Inc. v. American Excelsior Co., 517 F.2d 714 (5th Cir.1975); cert. denied, 424 U.S. 943 (1976).

Should the analysis under the Sherman Act and the Robinson–Patman Act be identical, given the "reasonable probability" standard of the Robinson–Patman Act?

PROBLEM 27

BARRY'S DAIRY v. BARDEN FARMS

Barden Farms manufactures and sells ice cream and other dairy products in California and nearby western states. In Los Angeles, it is in competition with three national producers and three local competitors, one of which is Barry's Dairy. Barry's specializes in making ice cream.

Barden's three national dairy competitors have been steadily increasing their share of the Los Angeles market, primarily by marketing aggressively to the larger chain food stores. Barden's share in the Los Angeles market had fallen from 23% in 1999 to 18% in 2002. During that same stretch, Barry's share had held steady at 2.5%.

At the end of 2002, Barden made a 15% discount available to all purchasers in the Los Angeles market, but did not grant any comparable discount to purchasers in other cities in California or nearby states. Barden's national competitors responded

---

40. If bigness be a disqualification for a firm to compete, interesting collateral questions arise, such as, how small does a company have to be before it has the right to enter into price competition with its competitors? And how large does it have to be before it must stop competing in price?

by offering the same localized price cut in Los Angeles. As a result of the discount, Barden was close to but slightly above short-run average variable cost. Barden's share of the Los Angeles market promptly rose to 20%. Shortly thereafter, one of Barden's competitors cut price again and, when Barden met that price, it was below its average variable cost. As a result of this "price war," Barry's lost several of its largest customers, two of them to Barden, and was forced to go out of business. The two other local competitors also encountered hard times and quit the market. Thereafter, Barden raised the prices, the national competition followed, and dairy product prices in Los Angeles were restored to levels that were maintained before the initial Barden price reduction.

Has Barry's a cause of action against Barden under the Robinson–Patman Act?

B.   "SECONDARY-LINE" EFFECTS

Federal Trade Commission v. Morton Salt Co.

Supreme Court of the United States, 1948.
334 U.S. 37, 68 S.Ct. 822, 92 L.Ed. 1196.

■ BLACK, J. The Federal Trade Commission, after a hearing, found that the respondent, which manufactures and sells table salt in interstate commerce, had discriminated in price between different purchasers of like grades and qualities, and concluded that such discriminations were in violation of § 2 of the Clayton Act, as amended by the Robinson–Patman Act. Upon petition of the respondent the Circuit Court of Appeals, with one judge dissenting, set aside the Commission's findings and order, directed the Commission to dismiss its complaint against respondent, and denied a cross petition of the Commission for enforcement of its order.

Respondent manufactures several different brands of table salt and sells them directly to (1) wholesalers or jobbers, who in turn resell to the retail trade, and (2) large retailers, including chain store retailers. Respondent sells its finest brand of table salt, known as Blue Label, on what it terms a standard quantity discount system available to all customers. Under this system the purchasers pay a delivered price and the cost to both wholesale and retail purchasers of this brand differs according to the quantities bought. These prices are as follows, after making allowance for rebates and discounts:

	Per case
Less-than-carload purchases	$1.60
Carload purchases	1.50
5,000–case purchases in any consecutive 12 months	1.40
50,000–case purchases in any consecutive 12 months . . .	1.35

Only five companies have ever bought sufficient quantities of respondent's salt to obtain the $1.35 per case price. These companies could buy in such quantities because they operate large chains of retail stores in various parts of the country. As a result of this low price these five companies have been able to sell Blue Label salt at retail cheaper than wholesale purchasers from respondent could reasonably sell the same brand of salt to independently operated retail stores, many of whom competed with the local outlets of the five chain stores.

Respondent's table salts, other than Blue Label, are also sold under a quantity discount system differing slightly from that used in selling Blue Label. Sales of these other brands in less-than-carload lots are made at list price plus freight from plant to destination. Carload purchasers are granted approximately a 5 per cent discount; approximately a 10 per cent discount is granted to purchasers who buy as much as $50,000 worth of all brands of salt in any consecutive twelve-month period. Respondent's quantity discounts on Blue Label and on other table salts were enjoyed by certain wholesalers and retailers who competed with other wholesalers and retailers to whom these discounts were refused.

In addition to these standard quantity discounts, special allowances were granted certain favored customers who competed with other customers to whom they were denied.

First. Respondent's basic contention, which it argues this case hinges upon, is that its "standard quantity discounts, available to all on equal terms, as contrasted for example, to hidden or special rebates, allowances, prices or discounts, are not discriminatory, within the meaning of the Robinson–Patman Act." Theoretically, these discounts are equally available to all, but functionally they are not. For as the record indicates (if reference to it on this point were necessary) no single independent retail grocery store, and probably no single wholesaler, bought as many as 50,000 cases or as much as $50,000 worth of table salt in one year. Furthermore, the record shows that, while certain purchasers were enjoying one or more of respondent's standard quantity discounts, some of their competitors made purchases in such small quantities that they could not qualify for any of respondent's discounts, even those based on carload shipments. The legislative history of the Robinson–Patman Act makes it abundantly clear that Congress considered it to be an evil that a large buyer could secure a competitive advantage over a small buyer solely because of the large buyer's quantity purchasing ability. The Robinson–Patman Act was passed to deprive a large buyer of such advantages except to the extent that a lower price could be justified by reason of a seller's diminished costs due to quantity manufacture, delivery or sale, or by reason of the seller's good faith effort to meet a competitor's equally low price.

The foregoing references, without regard to others that could be mentioned, establish that respondent's standard quantity discounts are discriminatory within the meaning of the Act, and are prohibited by it whenever they have the defined effect on competition. See Federal Trade Comm. v. Staley Co., 324 U.S. 746, 751.

Second. The Government interprets the opinion of the Circuit Court of Appeals as having held that in order to establish "discrimination in price" under the Act the burden rested on the Commission to prove that respondent's quantity discount differentials were not justified by its cost savings. Respondent does not so understand the Court of Appeals decision, and furthermore admits that no such burden rests on the Commission. We agree that it does not. First, the general rule of statutory construction that the burden of proving justification or exemption under a special exception to the prohibitions of a statute generally rests on one who claims its benefits, requires that respondent undertake this proof under the proviso of § 2(a). Secondly, § 2(b) of the Act specifically imposes the burden of showing justification upon one who is shown to have discriminated in prices. And the Senate committee report on the bill explained that the provisos of § 2(a) throw "upon any who claims the benefit of those exceptions the burden of showing that their case falls within them." We think that the language of the Act, and the legislative history just cited, show that Congress meant by using the words "discrimination in price" in § 2 that in a case involving competitive injury between a seller's customers the Commission need only prove that a seller had charged one purchaser a higher price for like goods than he had charged one or more of the purchaser's competitors. . . .

Third. It is argued that the findings fail to show that respondent's discriminatory discounts had in fact caused injury to competition. There are specific findings that such injuries had resulted from respondent's discounts although the statute does not require the Commission to find that injury has actually resulted. The statute requires no more than that the effect of the prohibited price discriminations "may be substantially to lessen competition . . . or to injure, destroy, or prevent competition." After a careful consideration of this provision of the Robinson–Patman Act, we have said that "the statute does not require that the discriminations must in fact have harmed competition, but only that there is a reasonable possibility that they 'may' have such an effect." Corn Products Co. v. Federal Trade Comm., 324 U.S. 726, 742. Here the Commission found what would appear to be obvious, that the competitive opportunities of certain merchants were injured when they had to pay respondent substantially more for their goods than their competitors had to pay. The findings are adequate.

Fourth. It is urged that the evidence is inadequate to support the Commission's findings of injury to competition. As we have pointed out, however, the Commission is authorized by the Act to bar discriminatory prices upon the "reasonable possibility" that different prices for like goods to competing purchasers may have the defined effect on competition. That respondent's quantity discounts did result in price differentials between competing purchasers sufficient in amount to influence their resale price of salt was shown by evidence. This showing in itself is adequate to support the Commission's appropriate findings. . . .

The adequacy of the evidence to support the Commission's findings of reasonably possible injury to competition from respondent's price differentials between competing carload and less-than-carload purchasers is singled out for special attacks here. It is suggested that in considering the adequacy of the evidence to show injury to competition respondent's carload discounts and its other quantity discounts should not be treated alike. The argument is that there is an obvious saving to a seller who delivers goods in carload lots. Assuming this to be true, that fact would not tend to disprove injury to the merchant compelled to pay the less-than-carload price. For a ten-cent carload price differential against a merchant would injure him competitively just as much as a ten-cent differential under any other name. However relevant the separate carload argument might be to the question of justifying a differential by cost savings, it has no relevancy in determining whether the differential works an injury to a competitor. Since Congress has not seen fit to give carload discounts any favored classification we cannot do so. Such discounts, like all others, can be justified by a seller who proves that the full amount of the discount is based on his actual savings in cost. The trouble with this phase of respondent's case is that it has thus far failed to make such proof.

It is also argued that respondent's less-than-carload sales are very small in comparison with the total volume of its business and for that reason we should reject the Commission's finding that the effect of the carload discrimination may substantially lessen competition and may injure competition between purchasers who are granted and those who are denied this discriminatory discount. To support this argument, reference is made to the fact that salt is a small item in most wholesale and retail businesses and in consumers' budgets. For several reasons we cannot accept this contention.

There are many articles in a grocery store that, considered separately, are comparatively small parts of a merchant's stock. Congress intended to protect a merchant from competitive injury attributable to discriminatory prices on any or all goods sold in interstate commerce, whether the particular goods constituted a major or minor portion of his stock. Since a grocery store consists of many comparatively small articles, there is no possible way effectively to protect a grocer from discriminatory prices except by applying the prohibitions of the Act to each individual article in the store.

Furthermore, in enacting the Robinson–Patman Act Congress was especially concerned with protecting small businesses that were unable to buy in quantities, such as the merchants here who purchased in less-than-carload lots. To this end it undertook to strengthen this very phase of the old Clayton Act. The committee reports on the Robinson–Patman Act emphasized a belief that § 2 of the Clayton Act had "been too restrictive in requiring a showing of general injury to competitive conditions...." The new provision, here controlling, was intended to justify a finding of injury to competition by a showing of "injury to the competitor victimized by the discrimination." Since there was evidence sufficient to show that the less-than-carload purchasers might have been handicapped in competing with the more favored carload purchasers by the differential in price established by respondent, the Commission was justified in finding that competition might have thereby been substantially lessened or have been injured within the meaning of the Act.

Apprehension is expressed in this Court that enforcement of the Commission's order against respondent's continued violations of the Robinson–Patman Act might lead respondent to raise table salt prices to its carload purchasers. Such a conceivable, though, we think, highly improbable, contingency could afford us no reason for upsetting the Commission's findings and declining to direct compliance with a statute passed by Congress.

The Commission here went much further in receiving evidence than the statute requires. It heard testimony from many witnesses in various parts of the country to show that they had suffered actual financial losses on account of respondent's discriminatory prices. Experts were offered to prove the tendency of injury from such prices. The evidence covers about two thousand pages, largely devoted to this single issue—injury to competition. It would greatly handicap effective enforcement of the Act to require testimony to show that which we believe to be self-evident, namely, that there is a "reasonable possibility" that competition may be adversely affected by a practice under which manufacturers and producers sell their goods to some customers substantially cheaper than they sell like goods to the competitors of these customers. This showing in itself is sufficient to justify our conclusion that the Commission's findings of injury to competition were adequately supported by evidence. . . .

The judgment of the Circuit Court of Appeals is reversed and the proceedings are remanded to that court to be disposed of in conformity with this opinion.[41]

————

Coastal Fuels of Puerto Rico v. Caribbean Petroleum Corp., 79 F.3d 182 (1st Cir. 1996). Carribean owned and operated a refinery in Puerto Rico and sold fuel products to resellers, including "bunker fuel" used by cruise ships and other ocean going vehicles. Coastal was a reseller and claimed a violation of Section 2(a) of the Robinson–Patman Act on grounds that Caribbean sold to two other competing resellers in San Juan harbor at a substantially lower price than to Coastal. A jury found for Coastal and assessed damages of $1.5 million, trebled to $4.5 million under the statute.

On appeal, Caribbean challenged the finding of a secondary line price discrimination on, among other grounds, an absence of competitive injury. Caribbean recognized that the *Morton Salt* rule, providing that injury to competition is established *prima facie* by proof of a substantial price discrimination between competing purchasers over time, supported Coastal's position. It asked the Court of Appeals to treat *Morton Salt* as no longer good law as a result of the Supreme Court's 1993 decision in *Brooke Group* (*see* p. 1284, *supra*). It described *Brooke Group* as concluding that in primary line Robinson–Patman cases, courts must reconcile the goals of the Robinson–Patman and Sherman Acts, and that both statutes were designed to protect competition and not competitors, and argued that this same reasoning should apply in secondary line cases.

The First Circuit Court of Appeals joined two other circuits in rejecting the claim that *Morton Salt* had been overruled. The Court concluded from legislative history and the statutory language of the Robinson–Patman Act that Congress' intent in 1936 was to protect small retailers from being driven out of business by

———

41. The opinion of Jackson, J., with whom Frankfurter, J., joined, dissenting in part, is omitted.

large retail chains' ability to secure discriminatory discounts. The economic evil Congress intended to address did not necessarily relate to "consumer welfare *per se*" alone, but had an element of protecting small business. Noting that the *Brooke Group* opinion expressly applied only to primary line cases, the Court concluded that "given the legislative history and statutory language distinctions, we will not presume, without more guidance, that the Supreme Court intended in *Brooke Group* to alter the well established rule that it had adopted in *Morton Salt*".

In the Matter of McCormick & Co. In 2000, the Federal Trade Commission added another twist to the interpretation of *Morton Salt*. McCormick was the world's largest manufacturer and distributor of spice products sold through supermarkets and other grocery outlets, and offered substantial discounts to some large supermarket chains but not to competing stores. Typically, McCormick's discounts were in the form of upfront cash payments that resembled the payments sometimes called slotting allowances in the supermarket industry. The payments commonly required that the customer allocate to Mccormick a large portion, often as much as 90%, of the shelf space devoted to spice products.

The Commission's complaint alleged that each instance of discrimination involved a substantial price difference, over a substantial period of time, between competing purchasers in markets where profit margins were low and competition was keen—circumstances that give rise to an inference of competitive harm within the meaning of *Morton Salt*. The Commission did not rest entirely on *Morton Salt*, however, but looked at a range of other factors to examine whether there was actual injury to competition. In its Analysis to Aid Public Comment, the Commission explained:

> While [*Morton Salt*] inference may not be sufficient by itself in some circumstances to warrant bringing a case, in this instance, the inference is strengthened by McCormick's position as the largest supplier of spice and seasoning products in the United States and by the fact that McCormick typically demanded that customers allocate to McCormick the large majority of the space devoted to spice products. . . .

As alleged in the Complaint, disfavored purchasers consequently had few, if any, alternative sources from which to purchase comparable goods at prices and terms equivalent to those which McCormick provided to the favored purchasers.

. . .

NOTE

Volvo Trucks North American v. Reeder–Simco, 546 U.S. 164 (2006). Reeder–Simco was one of many franchised dealers selling new and used heavy-duty Volvo trucks to government and industrial purchasers. The sales process involved competitive bidding. The customer described its product specifications and invited bids from particular dealers based on existing relationships with the dealer, the dealers' reputation, geographic location and other factors. When a dealer received an invitation to bid, it turned to Volvo and requested a discount on the wholesale price, and that discount affected the dealer's bid to the customer.

With two exceptions, Reeder–Simco never bid for a sale to a particular customer against another Volvo dealer. It learned, however, that Volvo had granted greater concessions to other Volvo dealers competing for sales to other customers greater than the concessions granted to Reeder–Simco. A jury found discrimination that violated the Robinson–Patman Act and the Court of Appeals affirmed, concluding that Reeder–Simco and the favored dealers were competing purchasers at the "same functional level."

The Supreme Court reversed, concluding that the Robinson–Patman Act only applied to discrimination between dealers competing to sell products to the same customer at about the same time. When the allegedly favored dealer received a better concession to sell to a different purchaser, it was rarely a "competitor" of Reeder–Simco at the same time. As to the two instances where Reeder–Simco did compete head-to-head with another Volvo dealer, the majority found that the discrimination had not been shown to be substantial.

In a concluding statement of policy, Justice Ginsburg offered the following:

"Even if the Act's text could be construed in the manner urged by Reeder and embraced by the Court of Appeals, we would resist an interpretation geared more to the protection of existing *competitors* than to the stimulation of *competition*.... By declining to extend Robinson–Patman's governance [to cases like this], we continue to construe the Act 'consistently with broader policies of the antitrust laws.' ... See *Automatic Canteen Co. of America* v. *FTC* (cautioning against Robinson–Patman constructions that 'extend beyond the prohibitions of the Act and, in doing so, help give rise to a price uniformity and rigidity in open conflict with the purposes of other antitrust legislation')."

Justices Stevens and Thomas dissented.

C.   More Remote Effects

Perkins v. Standard Oil Co. of California, 395 U.S. 642, 89 S.Ct. 1871, 23 L.Ed.2d 599 (1969). Perkins, a large independent gasoline wholesaler and retailer in Washington and Oregon, sued for treble damages under §§ 2(a), (d), and (e) of the Robinson–Patman Act alleging that Standard of California had discriminated between it and Signal Oil.

Standard sold gasoline to the motoring public through its own retail stations, to independent dealers handling Standard brands ("branded dealers"), to re-brand jobbers (including Perkins) and to other integrated oil companies like Signal. Perkins purchased from Standard virtually all the gas which it distributed through numerous retail service stations and bulk storage plants. Signal also purchased from Standard, allegedly at discriminatorily low prices and at other favorable terms of sale, and in turn sold Standard gasoline to Western Highway, a corporation of which it was 60% owner, the other 40% being owned by Signal's officers. Western in turn sold to Regal, an operator of stations which competed with Perkins' stations; Western owned a 55% stock interest in Regal.

Perkins won a jury verdict of about $1.3 million based on injury to competition both with Regal stations and with Standard's branded dealers. The Court of Appeals reversed, primarily because the jury award included damages for injury to Perkins resulting from discrimination not only in favor of Standard's branded dealers but also because of competition from Regal retail stations. Noting that the statute makes liable the seller who offers discriminatorily lower prices that affect competition "with any person who ... knowingly receives the benefit of such discrimination or with customers of either of them ...," it found that Regal operated in a market "four levels removed" from that in which the discriminatory price was charged. Since Regal purchased from Western, which in turn purchased from Signal, the court concluded that damages in such remote markets were not contemplated under the statute.

The Supreme Court reversed. In an opinion by Black, J., the Court observed:

> ... We find no basis in the language or purpose of the Act for immunizing Standard's price discriminations simply because the product in question passed through an additional formal exchange before reaching the level of Perkins' actual competitor. From Perkins' point of view, the competitive harm done him by Standard is certainly no less because of the presence of an additional link in this particular distribution chain from the producer to the retailer. Here Standard discriminated in price between Perkins and Signal, and there was evidence from which the jury could conclude that Perkins was harmed competitively when Signal's price advantage was passed on to Perkins' retail competitor Regal. These facts are sufficient to give rise to recoverable damages under the Robinson–Patman Act.

>   Before an injured party can recover damages under the Act, he must, of course, be able to show a causal connection between the price discrimination in violation of the Act and the injury suffered. This is true regardless of the "level" in the chain of distribution on which the injury occurs. The court below held that as a matter of law, "Section 2(a) does not recognize a causal connection, essential to liability, between a supplier's price discrimination and the trade practices of a customer as far removed on the distribution ladder as Regal was from Standard." As we have noted above, we do not accept such an artificial limitation. If there is sufficient evidence in the record to support an inference of causation, the ultimate conclusion as to what that evidence proves is for the jury.

Marshall, J., concurred in part and dissented in part, in an opinion in which Stewart, J. joined. They went along with the majority on the competitive injury point because the case involved a chain of majority-owned subsidiaries and they therefore treated Signal, the beneficiary of the discriminatory price, as if it were directly competing with Perkins. They expressly left open the question what the result would be if wholly independent firms had intervened in the distribution chain.

SECTION 4.   DEFENSES

A.   COST JUSTIFICATION

United States v. Borden Co.

Supreme Court of the United States, 1962.
370 U.S. 460, 82 S.Ct. 1309, 8 L.Ed.2d 627.

■ CLARK, J. This is a direct appeal from a judgment dismissing the Government's Section 2(a) Clayton Act suit in which is sought an injunction against the selling of fluid milk products by the appellees, The Borden Company and Bowman Dairy Company, at prices which discriminate between independently owned grocery stores and grocery store chains. The District Court in an unreported decision found the pricing plan of each dairy to be a prima facie violation of § 2(a) but concluded that these discriminatory prices were legalized by the cost justification proviso of § 2(a), which permits price differentials as long as they "make only due allowance for differences in the cost of manufacture, sale, or delivery resulting from the differing methods or quantities in which such commodities are to such purchasers sold or delivered." To review the Government's contention that the District Court had improperly permitted cost justifications based on the *average* cost of dealing with broad groups of customers unrelated in cost-saving factors, we noted probable jurisdiction, 368 U.S. 924, and directed the parties to brief and argue the case separately as to each appellee, 368 U.S. 963. However, finding the same problem at the root of the cost justifications of each appellee, we have dealt with both in this single opinion. We have concluded that the class cost justifications submitted to the District Court by the appellees did not satisfy their burden of showing that their respective discriminatory pricing plans reflected only a "due allowance" for cost differences.

[The Court summarized the background of litigation between the parties which began in 1951, concluding that the sole question in the instant case was whether the differences in price reflected permissible allowances for variances in cost.]

In view of our disposition, we need not relate the facts in detail. Both appellees are major distributors of fluid milk products in metropolitan Chicago. The sales of both dairies to retail stores during the period in question were handled under plans which gave most of their customers— the independently owned stores—percentage discounts off list price which increased with the volume of their purchases to a specified maximum while granting a few customers—the grocery store chains—a flat discount without reference to volume and substantially greater than the maximum discount available under the volume plan offered independent stores. These discounts were made effective through schedules which appeared to cover all stores; however, the schedules were modified by private letters to the grocery chains confirming their higher discounts.[42] Although the two sets of

---

42. Borden in June of 1954 issued the following discount schedule to "be applied to all purchases of Borden's fresh milk":

Average converted points per day:<	Percent of discounts
0–24	0
25–74	2
75–149	3
150 and over	4

At this same time, letters were sent to The Great Atlantic and Pacific Tea Company and The Jewel Food Stores granting them flat 8½% discounts. A few of the larger independents by special arrangement were given an additional 1½% discount thereby raising their total discount to 5½%.

discounts were never officially labeled "independent" and "chain" prices, they were treated, called, and regarded as such throughout the record.

To support their defense that the disparities in price between independents and chains were attributable to differences in the cost of dealing with the two types of customers, the appellees introduced cost studies which will be described separately because of their differing content and analytical approach.

The Borden pricing system produced two classes of customers. The two chains, A & P and Jewel, with their combined total of 254 stores constituted one class. The 1,322 independent stores, grouped in four brackets based on the volume of their purchases, made up the other. Borden's cost justification was built on comparisons of its average cost per $100 of sales to the chains in relation to the average cost of similar sales to each of the four groups of independents. The costs considered were personnel (including routemen, clerical and sales employees), truck expenses, and losses on bad debts and returned milk. Various methods of cost allocation were utilized: drivers' time spent at each store was charged directly to that store; certain clerical expenses were allocated between the two general classes; costs not susceptible of either of the foregoing were charged to the various stores on a per stop, per store, or volume basis.

Bowman's cost justification was based on differences in volume and methods of delivery. It relied heavily upon a study of the cost per minute of

---

In September 1955, Borden discontinued the above discount system and utilized a net price scheme which resulted in even greater disparities between chains and independents.

Bowman in June of 1954 operated under the following "Resale Store Discount Schedule":

This schedule was modified in August by the addition of the following discounts:

Average converted points per day	*Percent of discounts*
0 to 10	3.0 to 3.4
10 to 20	3.4 to 3.8
20 to 30	3.8 to 4.2
30 to 40	4.2 to 4.6
40 to 50	4.6 to 5.0
50 to 60	5.0 to 5.2
60 to 70	5.2 to 5.4
70 to 80	5.4 to 5.6
80 to 90	5.6 to 5.8
90 to 100	5.8 to 6.0
100 to 110	6.0 to 6.2
110 to 120	6.2 to 6.4
120 to 130	6.4 to 6.6
130 to 140	6.6 to 6.8
140 to 150	6.8 to 7.0
150 to 200	7.0 to 8.0
Over 200	8.0

During this same period Bowman by letter granted The Great Atlantic and Pacific Tea Company and the Kroger Company flat 11% discounts. Goldblatt Bros., also a multi-store operation, was granted a flat 8½%.

In 1955 and again in 1956 Bowman modified the brackets and percentages of its discount schedules, but not in a manner which reduced the disparity between independents and chains.

its routemen's time. It determined that substantial portions of this time were devoted to three operations, none of which was ever performed for the 163 stores operated by its two major chain customers. These added work steps arose from the method of collection, *i.e.*, cash on delivery and the delayed collections connected therewith, and the performance of "optional customer services." The customer services, performed with varying frequency depending upon the circumstances, included "services that the driver may be requested to do, such as deliver the order inside, place the containers in a refrigerator, rearrange containers so that any product remaining unsold from yesterday will be sold first today, leave cases of products at different spots in the store, etc." The experts conducting the study calculated as to these elements a "standard" cost per unit of product delivered: the aggregate time required to perform the services, as determined by sample time studies, was divided by the total number of units of product delivered. In essence, the Bowman justification was merely a comparison of the cost of these services in relation to the disparity between the chain and independent prices. Although it was shown that the five sample independents in the Government's prima facie case received the added services, it was not shown or found that all 2,500 independents supplied by Bowman partook of them. On the basis of its studies Bowman estimated that about two-thirds of the independent stores received the "optional customer services" on a daily basis and that "most store customers pay the driver in cash daily."

On these facts, stated here in rather summary fashion, the trial court held that appellees had met the requirements of the proviso of § 2(a) on the theory that the general cost differences between chain stores as a class and independents as a class justified the disparities in price reflected in appellees' schedules. In so doing the trial court itself found "the studies ... imperfect in some respects...." It noted the "seemingly arbitrary" nature of a classification resulting "in percentage discounts which do not bear a direct ratio to differences in volume of sales." But it found "this mode of classification is *not* wholly arbitrary—after all, most chain stores do purchase larger volumes of milk than do most independent stores."[43] We believe it was erroneous for the trial court to permit cost justifications based upon such classifications.

The burden, of course, was upon the appellees to prove that the illegal price discrimination, which the Government claimed and the trial court found present, was immunized by the cost justification proviso of § 2(a). Such is the mandate of § 2(b) as interpreted by this Court in Federal Trade Comm'n v. Morton Salt Co., 334 U.S. 37, 44–45 (1948). There can be no doubt that the § 2(a) proviso as amended by the Robinson–Patman Act contemplates, both in express wording and legislative history, a showing of

---

43. Even the trial court was unwilling to give its "stamp of approval to all pricing policies and practices revealed by the evidence." But it concluded that to enjoin such practices would lead to regulation and would require the court continually "to pass judgment on the pricing practices of these defendants," a matter which might better be handled by proceedings before the Federal Trade Commission.

actual cost differences resulting from the differing methods or quantities in which the commodities in question are sold or delivered. The only question before us is how accurate this showing must be in relation to each particular purchaser.

Although the language of the proviso, with some support in the legislative history, is literally susceptible of a construction which would require any discrepancy in price between any two purchasers to be individually justified, the proviso has not been so construed by those charged with its enforcement. The Government candidly recognizes in its briefs filed in the instant case that "[a]s a matter of practical necessity . . . when a seller deals with a very large number of customers, he cannot be required to establish different cost-reflecting prices for each customer." In this same vein, the practice of grouping customers for pricing purposes has long had the approval of the Federal Trade Commission. We ourselves have noted the "elusiveness of cost data" in a Robinson–Patman Act proceeding. Automatic Canteen Co. v. Federal Trade Comm'n, 346 U.S. 61, 68 (1953). In short, to completely renounce class pricing as justified by class accounting would be to eliminate in practical effect the cost justification proviso as to sellers having a large number of purchasers, thereby preventing such sellers from passing on economies to their customers. It seems hardly necessary to say that such a result is at war with Congress' language and purpose.

But this is not to say that price differentials can be justified on the basis of arbitrary classifications or even classifications which are representative of a numerical majority of the individual members. At some point practical considerations shade into a circumvention of the proviso. A balance is struck by the use of classes for cost justification which are composed of members of such selfsameness as to make the averaging of the cost of dealing with the group a valid and reasonable indicium of the cost of dealing with any specific group member. High on the list of "musts" in the use of the average cost of customer groupings under the proviso of § 2(a) is a close resemblance of the individual members of each group on the essential point or points which determine the costs considered.

In this regard we do not find the classifications submitted by the appellees to have been shown to be of sufficient homogeneity. Certainly, the cost factors considered were not necessarily encompassed within the manner in which a customer is owned. Turning first to Borden's justification, we note that it not only failed to show that the economies relied upon were isolated within the favored class but affirmatively revealed that members of the classes utilized were substantially unlike in the cost saving aspects considered. For instance, the favorable cost comparisons between the chains and the larger independents were for the greater part controlled by the higher average volume of the chain stores in comparison to the average volume of the 80–member class to which these independents were relegated. The District Court allowed this manner of justification because "most chain stores do purchase larger volumes of milk than do most independent stores." However, such a grouping for cost justification purposes, composed as it is of some independents having volumes comparable to, and in some cases larger than, that of the chain stores, created artificial disparities between the larger independents and the chain stores. It is like averaging one horse and one rabbit. As the Federal Trade Commission said in In the Matter of Champion Spark Plug Co., 50 F.T.C. 30, 43 (1953): "A cost justification based on the difference between an estimated average cost of selling to one or two large customers and an average cost of selling to all other customers cannot be accepted as a defense to a charge of price discrimination." This volume gap between the larger independents and the chain stores was further widened by grouping together the two chains, thereby raising the average volume of the stores of the smaller of the two chains in relation to the larger independents. Nor is the vice in the Borden class justification solely in the paper volumes relied upon, for it attributed to many independents cost factors which were not true indicia of the cost of dealing with those particular consumers. To illustrate, each independent was assigned a portion of the total expenses involved in daily cash collections, although it was not shown that all independents paid cash and in fact Borden admitted that only a "large majority" did so.

Likewise the details of Bowman's cost study show a failure in classification. Only one additional point need be made. Its justification emphasized its costs for "optional customer service" and daily cash collection with the resulting "delay to collect." As shown by its study these elements were crucial to Bowman's cost justification. In the study the experts charged all independents and no chain store with these costs. Yet, it was not shown that all independents received these services daily or even on some lesser basis. Bowman's studies indicated only that a large majority of independents took these services on a daily basis. Under such circumstances the use of these cost factors across the board in calculating independent store costs is not a permissible justification for it possibly allocates costs to some independents whose mode of purchasing does not give rise to them. The burden was upon the profferer of the classification to negate this possibility and this burden has not been met here. If these factors control the cost of dealing, then their presence or absence might with more justification be the password for admission into the various price categories.[44]

The appellees argue in the alternative that their cost justifications can be sufficiently unscrambled to remove any taint the Court may find in them and still show a cost gap sufficient to justify the price disparity between the chains and any independent. This mass of underlying statistical data not considered by the trial court and now tied together by untried theories can best be evaluated on remand, and we therefore do not consider its sufficiency here.

In sum, the record here shows that price discriminations have been permitted on the basis of cost differences between broad customer group-

---

44. Another suspect feature is that classifications based on services received by independents were apparently frozen—making it impossible for them to obtain larger discounts by electing not to receive the cost-determinative services—with no justifiable business reason offered in support of the practice.

ings, apparently based on the nature of ownership but in any event not shown to be so homogeneous as to permit the joining together of these purchasers for cost allocations purposes. If this is the only justification for appellees' pricing schemes, they are illegal. We do not believe that an appropriate decree would require the trial court continuously to "pass judgment on the pricing practices of these defendants." As to the issuance of an injunction, however, the case is now 11 years old and we have no way of knowing whether equitable relief is in order. Certainly a relevant factor in such consideration would be whether the practices described above are still being followed in any form. This the record here does not show. Such matters can only be ascertained upon the presently existing facts and the careful application of the principles we have enunciated. For that purpose the case is reversed and remanded.

Reversed and remanded.[45]

B.   GOOD FAITH MEETING OF COMPETITION

Interpretation of the meeting competition defense has varied over the years, particularly on the issues of the degree of certainty required for a seller to satisfy the defense, and the related question of how to define the defense to best reconcile the goals of the Sherman Act and the Robinson–Patman Act.

The Supreme Court in the following two decisions has done much to clarify the scope of the defense and reconcile prior conflicting doctrine.

United States v. United States Gypsum Co.

Supreme Court of the United States, 1978.
438 U.S. 422, 98 S.Ct. 2864, 57 L.Ed.2d 854.

[The *Gypsum* opinion, setting forth the consequences of an exchange of current price information, and determining that "intent" is an element of a criminal antitrust offense, is summarized at p. 227 *supra*. In Part III of the Supreme Court's opinion, printed below, Chief Justice Burger attempted to reconcile the proscriptions of the Sherman Act with those of Section 2(b) of the Robinson–Patman Act.]

III

Our construction of the Sherman Act to require proof of intent as an element of a criminal antitrust violation leaves unresolved the question upon which the Court of Appeals focused, whether verification of price concessions with competitors for the sole purpose of taking advantage of the § 2(b) meeting competition defense of the Robinson–Patman Act should

---

45. Frankfurter, J., took no part in the consideration or decision of the case. A concurring opinion by Douglas, J., and a dissenting opinion by Harlan, J., are omitted.

Defendants have rarely succeeded in establishing a cost justification defense.

be treated as a "controlling circumstance" precluding liability under § 1 of the Sherman Act. We now turn to that question.[46]

A

In Cement Mfgrs. Protective Assn. v. United States, 268 U.S. 588, the Court held exempt from Sherman § 1 liability an exchange of price information among competitors because the exchange of information was necessary to protect the cement manufacturers from fraudulent behavior by contractors.[47] Over 40 years later, in United States v. Container Corp., 393 U.S. 333, 335, Mr. Justice Douglas characterized the *Cement* holding in the following terms:

> While there was present here, as in Cement Mfrs. Protective Association v. United States, 268 U.S. 588, an exchange of prices to specific customers, there was absent the controlling circumstances, viz., that cement manufacturers, to protect themselves from delivering to contractors more cement than was needed for a specific job and thus receiving a lower price, exchanged price information as a means of protecting their legal rights from fraudulent inducements to deliver more cement than needed for a specific job.

The use of the phrase "controlling circumstance" in *Container* implied that the exception from Sherman Act liability recognized in *Cement Mfgrs.* was not necessarily limited to special circumstances of that case, although the exact scope of the exception remained largely undefined.

Since *Container,* several courts have read the controlling circumstance exception as encompassing exchanges of price information when undertaken for the purpose of compliance with § 2(b) of the Robinson–Patman Act.... The Court of Appeals in the instant case essentially adopted the same tack—albeit with some additional limitations—finding such a step necessary to eliminate a perceived conflict between the Sherman Act's proscriptions regarding the exchange of price information among competitors and the claimed necessity of such exchanges to perfect the § 2(b) defense of the Robinson–Patman Act....

---

46. This question was not resolved by the prior discussion because a purpose of complying with the Robinson–Patman Act by exchanging price information is not inconsistent with knowledge that such exchanges of information will have the probable effect of fixing or stabilizing prices. Since we hold knowledge of the probable consequences of conduct to be the requisite mental state in a criminal prosecution like the instant one where an effect on prices is also alleged, a defendant's purpose in engaging in the proscribed conduct will not insulate him from liability unless it is deemed of sufficient merit to justify a general exception to the Sherman Act's proscriptions. Cf. Cement Mfrs. Protective Assn. v. United States, 268 U.S. 588.

47. Respondents maintain that their verification practices not only were for the purpose of complying with the Robinson–Patman Act, but also served to protect them from fraud on the part of their customers, and thus fall squarely within the *Cement* exception. The Court of Appeals rejected this claim, 550 F.2d, at 123 n. 9, and we find no reason to upset this determination.

B

Section 2(a) of the Robinson–Patman Act, 15 U.S.C.A. § 13(a), embodies a general prohibition of price discrimination between buyers when an injury to competition is the consequence. The primary exception to the § 2(a) bar is the meeting-competition defense....

In FTC v. A.E. Staley Manufacturing Co., 324 U.S. 746 (1945), the Court provided the first and still the most complete explanation of the kind of showing which a seller must make in order to satisfy the good-faith requirement of the § 2(b) defense:

> Section 2(b) does not require the seller to justify price discriminations by showing that in fact they met a competitor's price. But it does place on the seller the burden of showing that the price was made in good faith to meet a competitor's.... We agree with the Commission that the statute at least requires the seller, who has knowingly discriminated in price, to show the existence of facts which would lead a reasonable and prudent person to believe that the granting of a lower price would in fact meet the equally low price of a competitor.

324 U.S., at 759–760.

Application of these standards to the facts in *Staley* led to the conclusion that the § 2(b) defense had not been made out. The record revealed that the lower price had been based simply on reports of salesmen, brokers, or purchasers with no efforts having been made by the seller "to investigate or verify" the reports or the character and reliability of the informants. Id., at 758. Similarly, in Corn Products v. FTC, 324 U.S. 726 (1945), decided the same day, the § 2(b) defense was not allowed because "the only evidence said to rebut the *prima facie* case ... of the price discriminations was given by witnesses who had no personal knowledge of the transactions, and was limited to statements of each witness's assumption or conclusion that the price discriminations were justified by competition." Id., at 741.

Staley's "investigate or verify" language coupled with the *Corn Products'* focus on "personal knowledge of the transactions" have apparently suggested to a number of courts that, at least in certain circumstances, direct verification of discounts between competitors may be necessary to meet the burden of proof requirements of the § 2(b) defense.... The Court of Appeals critically and perceptively analyzed these cases and concluded that only a very narrow exception to Sherman Act liability should be recognized; that exception would cover the relatively few situations where the veracity of the buyer seeking the matching discount was legitimately in doubt, other reasonable means of corroboration were unavailable to the seller, and the interseller communication was for the sole purpose of complying with the Robinson–Patman Act. Despite the court's efforts to circumscribe the scope of the exception it was constrained to recognize, we find its analysis unacceptable.

C

A good-faith belief, rather than absolute certainty, that a price concession is being offered to meet an equally low price offered by a competitor is sufficient to satisfy the Robinson–Patman's § 2(b) defense. While casual reliance on uncorroborated reports of buyers or sales representatives without further investigation may not, as we noted earlier, be sufficient to make the requisite showing of good faith, nothing in the language of § 2(b) or the gloss on that language in *Staley* and *Corn Products* indicates that direct discussions of price between competitors are required. Nor has any court, so far as we are aware, ever imposed such a requirement.[48] ... On the contrary, the § 2(b) defense has been successfully invoked in the absence of interseller verification on numerous occasions,.... And in Kroger Co. v. FTC, 438 F.2d 1372, 1376–1377 (C.A.6 1971), aff'g Beatrice Foods Co., 76 F.T.C. 719, the defense was recognized despite the fact that the price concession was ultimately found to have undercut that of the competition and thus technically to have fallen outside the "meet not beat" strictures of the defense. As these cases indicate, and as the Federal Trade Commission observed, it is the concept of good faith which lies at the core of the meeting-competition defense and good faith

> "is a flexible and pragmatic, not technical or doctrinaire, concept.... Rigid rules and inflexible absolutes are especially inappropriate in dealing with the § 2(b) defense; the facts and circumstances of the particular case, not abstract theories or remote conjectures, should govern its interpretation and application."

Continental Baking Co., 63 F.T.C. 2071, 2163 (1963).

The so-called problem of the untruthful buyer which concerned the Court of Appeals does not in our view call for a different approach to the § 2(b) defense. The good-faith standard remains the benchmark against which the seller's conduct is to be evaluated, and we agree with the government and the FTC that this standard can be satisfied by efforts falling short of interseller verification in most circumstances where the seller has only vague, generalized doubts about the reliability of its commercial adversary—the buyer.[49] Given the fact specific nature of the

---

48. In Viviano Macaroni Co. v. FTC, 411 F.2d 255 (C.A.3 1969), the § 2(b) defense was not recognized because the seller had relied solely on the report of its customer regarding other competitive offers without undertaking any investigation to corroborate the offer or the reliability of the customer. The Court of Appeals in the instant case read *Viviano* as at least suggesting, if not requiring, interseller verification when the veracity of the buyer was in doubt. As we read that case, however, it simply reaffirms the teaching of *Staley,* and does not compel the further conclusion that only interseller verification will satisfy the good-faith requirement, even in the particular circumstances identified by the Court of Appeals. See 550 F.2d, at 135 (Weis, J., dissenting).

49. "Although a seller may take advantage of the meeting competition defense only if it has a commercially reasonable belief that its price concession is necessary to meet an equally low price of a competitor, a seller may acquire this belief, and hence perfect its defense, by doing everything reasonably feasible—short of violating some other statute, such as the Sherman Act—to determine the veracity of a customer's statement that he has been offered a lower price. If, after making reasonable, lawful, inquiries, the seller cannot ascertain that the inquiry, it is difficult to predict all the factors the FTC or a court would consider in appraising a seller's good faith in matching a competing offer in these circumstances. Certainly, evidence that a seller had received reports of similar discounts from other customers, cf. Jones v. Borden Co., [430 F.2d 568, 572–573 (5th Cir.1970)]; or was threatened with a termination of purchases if the discount were not met, cf. International Air Industries, Inc. v. American Excelsior Co., [517 F.2d 714, 726 (5th Cir.1975)], Cadigan v. Texaco, Inc., [492 F.2d 383, 386 (9th Cir.1974)], would be relevant in this regard. Efforts to corroborate the reported discount by seeking documentary evidence or by appraising its reasonableness in terms of available market data would also be probative as would the seller's past experience with the particular buyer in question.[50]

There remains the possibility that in a limited number of situations a seller may have substantial reasons to doubt the accuracy of reports of a competing offer and may be unable to corroborate such reports in any of the generally accepted ways. Thus the defense may be rendered unavailable since unanswered questions about the reliability of a buyer's representations may well be inconsistent with a good-faith belief that a competing offer had in fact been made.[51] As an abstract proposition, resort to interseller verification as a means of checking the buyer's reliability seems a possible solution to the seller's plight, but careful examination reveals serious problems with the practice.

Both economic theory and common human experience suggest that interseller verification—if undertaken on an isolated and infrequent basis with no provision for reciprocity or cooperation—will not serve its putative function of corroborating the representations of unreliable buyers regarding the existence of competing offers. Price concessions by oligopolists generally yield competitive advantages only if secrecy can be maintained; when the terms of the concession are made publicly known, other competitors are likely to follow and any advantage to the initiator is lost in the

buyer is lying, the seller is entitled to make the sale. There is no need for a seller to discuss price with his competitors to take advantage of the meeting competition defense." (Citations omitted.) Brief of Petitioner, 86–87, and n. 78. See also Pet.App., 97a–99a.

50. It may also turn out that sustained enforcement of § 2(f) of the Robinson–Patman Act, which imposes liability on buyers for inducing illegal price discounts, will serve to bolster the credibility of buyer's representations and render reliance thereon by sellers a more reasonable and secure predicate for a finding of good faith under § 2(b). See generally Note, Meeting Competition Under the Robinson–Patman Act, 90 Harv.L.Rev. 1476, 1495–1496 (1977). In both Great Atlantic & Pacific Tea Co. v. FTC, 557 F.2d 971 (C.A.2 1977), and Kroger v. FTC, *supra*, buyers have been held liable under § 2(f) despite the fact that the sellers were either found not to have violated the Robinson–Patman Act (Kroger) or were not charged with such a violation (A & P). Certiorari has been granted in *Great Atlantic & Pacific Tea Co.* to consider the permissibility of enforcing the Robinson–Patman Act in this manner. 435 U.S. 922 (1978).

51. We need not and do not decide that in all such circumstances the defense would be unavailable. The case by case interpretation and elaboration of the § 2(b) defense is properly left to the other federal courts and the FTC in the context of concrete fact situations. We note also that our conclusion regarding the proper interpretation of § 2(f) of the Robinson–Patman Act, see n. 66 *supra*, may well affect subsequent application of the § 2(b) defense.

process.... Thus, if one seller offers a price concession for the purpose of winning over one of his competitor's customers, it is unlikely that the same seller will freely inform its competitor of the details of the concession so that it can be promptly matched and diffused. Instead, such a seller would appear to have at least as great an incentive to misrepresent the existence or size of the discount as would the buyer who received it. Thus verification, if undertaken on a one shot basis for the sole purpose of complying with the § 2(b) defense, does not hold out much promise as a means of shoring up buyers' representations.

The other variety of interseller verification is, like the conduct charged in the instant case, undertaken pursuant to an agreement, either tacit or express, providing for reciprocity among competitors in the exchange of price information. Such an agreement would make little economic sense, in our view, if its sole purpose were to guarantee all participants the opportunity to match the secret price concessions of other participants under § 2(b) of the Robinson–Patman Act. For in such circumstances, each seller would know that his price concession could not be kept from his competitors and no seller participating in the information exchange arrangement would, therefore, have any incentive for deviating from the prevailing price level in the industry. See United States v. Container Corp., 393 U.S., at 336–337. Regardless of its putative purpose, the most likely consequence of any such agreement to exchange price information would be the stabilization of industry prices.... Instead of facilitating use of the § 2(b) defense, such an agreement would have the effect of eliminating the very price concessions which provide the main element of competition in oligopolistic industries and the primary occasion for resort to the meeting competition defense.

Especially in oligopolistic industries such as the gypsum board industry, the exchange of price information among competitors carries with it the added potential for the development of concerted price-fixing arrangements which lie at the core of the Sherman Act's prohibitions. The Department of Justice's 1977 Report on the Robinson–Patman Act focused on the growing use of the Act as a cover for price fixing; former Antitrust Division Assistant Attorney General Kauper discussed the mechanics of the process:

> And thus you find in some industries relatively extensive exchanges of price information for the purpose, at least the stated purpose, of complying with the Robinson–Patman Act....
>
> Now, the mere exchange of price information itself may tend to stabilize prices. But I think it is also relatively common that once the exchange process begins, certain understandings go along with it—that we will exchange prices, but it will be understood, for example, you will not undercut my prices.
>
> And from there it is a rather easy step into a full-fledged price-fixing agreement. I think we have seen that from time to time, and I suspect we will continue to see it as long as there

continues to be a need to justify particular price discriminations in the terms of the Robinson–Patman Act.

United States Department of Justice, Report on the Robinson–Patman Act 58–61 (1977).

We are left, therefore, on the one hand, with doubts about both the need for and the efficacy of interseller verification as a means of facilitating compliance with § 2(b) of the Robinson–Patman Act, and, on the other, with recognition of the tendency for price discussions between competitors to contribute to the stability of oligopolistic prices and open the way for the growth of prohibited anticompetitive activity. To recognize even a limited "controlling circumstance" exception for interseller verification in such circumstances would be to remove from scrutiny under the Sherman Act conduct falling near its core with no assurance, and indeed with serious doubts, that competing antitrust policies would be served thereby. In Automatic Canteen v. FTC, 346 U.S. 61, 74 (1953), the Court suggested that as a general rule the Robinson–Patman Act should be construed so as to insure its coherence with "the broader antitrust policies that have been laid down by Congress"; that observation buttresses our conclusion that exchanges of price information—even when putatively for purposes of Robinson–Patman Act compliance—must remain subject to close scrutiny under the Sherman Act.[52]

Falls City Industries v. Vanco Beverage

Supreme Court of the United States, 1983.
460 U.S. 428, 103 S.Ct. 1282, 75 L.Ed.2d 174.

[Falls City sold beer to wholesalers in Indiana, Kentucky and eleven other states. Vanco was its sole wholesale distributor in Evansville, Indiana and Dawson Springs was its sole wholesale distributor in nearby Henderson, Kentucky. Because of state regulations, neither wholesaler could sell to retailers in the state served by the other, but consumers frequently crossed state lines to buy beer from retailers offering the lowest prices. Vanco sued Falls City under Section 2(a) of the Robinson–Patman Act charging that the defendant had charged 10–30% higher prices in Indiana than it charged in Kentucky. It claimed it was injured because Dawson Springs passed on the lower prices to retailers in Kentucky, and

---

52. That the § 2(b) defense may not be available in every situation where a competing offer has in fact been made is not, in our view, a meaningful objection to our holding. The good-faith requirement of the § 2(b) defense implicitly suggests a somewhat imperfect matching between competing offers actually made and those allowed to be met. Unless this requirement is to be abandoned, it seems clear that inadequate information will in a limited number of cases, deny the defense to some who, if all the facts had been known, would have been entitled to invoke it. For reasons already discussed, interseller verification does not provide a satisfactory solution to this seemingly inevitable problem of inadequate information. Moreover, § 2(b) affords only a defense to liability and not an affirmative right under the Act. While sellers are of course entitled to take advantage of the defense when they can satisfy its requirements, efforts to increase its availability at the expense of broader, affirmative antitrust policies must be rejected.

that many consumers purchased in Kentucky to obtain lower prices, thus reducing Vanco's total sales.

Justice Blackmun, writing for a unanimous Court, noted that the Robinson–Patman Act is not limited in coverage to injuries to competition between the favored and disfavored purchaser, but also applies to injuries in competition between their customers. The Court then turned to Falls City's defense that its price structure was justified because it was meeting equally low prices in Kentucky.]

. . .

III

When proved, the meeting-competition defense of § 2(b) exonerates a seller from Robinson–Patman Act liability. Standard Oil Co. v. FTC, 340 U.S. 231, 246–247 (1951). This Court consistently has held that the meeting-competition defense " 'at least requires the seller, who has knowingly discriminated in price, to show the existence of facts which would lead a reasonable and prudent person to believe that the granting of a lower price would in fact meet the equally low price of a competitor.' " United States v. United States Gypsum Co., 438 U.S. 422, 451 (1978), quoting FTC v. A.E. Staley Mfg. Co., 324 U.S. 746, 759–760 (1945); see Great A & p. Tea Co. v. FTC, 440 U.S. 69, 82 (1979). The seller must show that under the circumstances it was reasonable to believe that the quoted price or a lower one was available to the favored purchaser or purchasers from the seller's competitors. See *United States Gypsum Co.,* 438 U.S., at 451. Neither the District Court nor the Court of Appeals addressed the question whether Falls City had shown information that would have led a reasonable and prudent person to believe that its lower Kentucky price would meet competitors' equally low prices there; indeed, no findings whatever were made regarding competitors' Kentucky prices, or the information available to Falls City about its competitors' Kentucky prices.

Instead, the Court of Appeals reasoned that Falls City had otherwise failed to show that its pricing "was a good faith effort" to meet competition. The Court of Appeals considered it sufficient to defeat the defense that the price difference "resulted from price increases in Indiana, not price decreases in Kentucky," and that the higher Indiana price was the result of Falls City's policy of following the Indiana prices of its larger competitors in order to enhance its profits. The Court of Appeals also suggested that Falls City's defense failed because it adopted a "general system of competition," rather than responding to "individual situations." The court believed that FTC v. A.E. Staley Mfg. Co., *supra,* supported this holding. 654 F.2d, at 1230.

A

On its face, § 2(b) requires more than a showing of facts that would have led a reasonable person to believe that a lower price was available to the favored purchaser from a competitor. The showing required is that the "lower price ... *was made* in good faith *to meet*" the competitor's low price. 15 U.S.C. § 13(b) (emphasis added). Thus, the defense requires that the seller offer the lower price in good faith *for the purpose* of meeting the competitor's price, that is, the lower price must actually have been a good-faith response to that competing low price. See Rowe, at 234–235. See generally Kuenzel & Schiffres, Making Sense of Robinson–Patman: The Need to Revitalize Its Affirmative Defenses, 62 Va.L.Rev. 1211, 1237–1255 (1976). In most situations, a showing of facts giving rise to a reasonable belief that equally low prices were available to the favored purchaser from a competitor will be sufficient to establish that the seller's lower price was offered in good faith to meet that price. In others, however, despite the availability from other sellers of a low price, it may be apparent that the defendant's low offer was not a good-faith response.

In *Staley,* this Court applied that principle. The Federal Trade Commission (FTC) had proceeded against Staley and six competing manufacturers of glucose, all of whom adhered to the same Chicago basing-point pricing system. Like its competitors, Staley, whose plant was located in Decatur, Ill., sold glucose to candy and syrup manufacturers at a delivered price that included the freight rate from Chicago to the point of delivery. Purchasers nearer Decatur thus were charged an element of "phantom" freight, while Staley "absorbed" an element of freight in sales to buyers nearer Chicago. Customers located near Staley's Decatur plant were harmed because, despite being located closer to the plant, they were forced to pay more for glucose than did their Chicago area competitors.

The FTC eventually charged all seven manufacturers individually with price discrimination and jointly under the Federal Trade Commission Act with price fixing. See Corn Products Refining Co., 47 F.T.C. 587 (1950). At the time of the *Staley* decision, both the FTC and this Court had determined that use of the pricing system by Staley's competitors was illegal under § 2(a). See Corn Products Refining Co. v. FTC, 324 U.S., at 732, 737–739. And, although neither the FTC nor this Court directly relied on the fact in finding price discrimination, Staley itself had been found to be a party to an interseller conspiracy aimed at maintaining "oppressive and uniform net delivered prices" throughout the country. See A.E. Staley Mfg. Co. v. FTC, 4 F.T.C. Stat. & Dec. 795, 805 (1943).

The Court observed that § 2(b) could exonerate Staley only if that section permitted a seller to establish "an otherwise unlawful system of discriminatory prices" in order to benefit from "a like unlawful system maintained by his competitors." Staley could not claim that its low Chicago prices were set for the purpose of meeting the equally low prices of competitors there; the Chicago prices could be seen only as part of a collusive pricing system designed to exact artificially high prices throughout the country. Since the low prices were set "in order to establish elsewhere the artificially high prices whose discriminatory effect permeates respondents' entire pricing system," the Court sustained the FTC's finding "that respondents' price discriminations were not made to meet a 'lower' price and consequently were not in good faith," *id.,* at 758.

Thus, even had Staley been able to show that its prices throughout the country did not undercut those of its competitors, its lower price in the Chicago area was not a good-faith response to the lower prices there. Staley had not priced in response to competitors' discrete pricing decisions, but from the outset had followed an industrywide practice of setting its prices according to a single, arbitrary scheme that by its nature *precluded* independent pricing in response to normal competitive forces.

B

Almost 20 years ago, the FTC set forth the standard that governs the requirement of a "good-faith response":

"At the heart of Section 2(b) is the concept of 'good faith'. This is a flexible and pragmatic, not a technical or doctrinaire, concept. The standard of good faith is simply the standard of the prudent businessman responding fairly to what he reasonably believes is a situation of competitive necessity." Continental Baking Co., 63 F.T.C. 2071, 2163 (1963).

Whether this standard is met depends on " 'the facts and circumstances of the particular case, not abstract theories or remote conjectures.' " United States v. United States Gypsum Co., 438 U.S., at 454, quoting Continental Baking Co., 63 F.T.C., at 2163.

The "facts and circumstances" present in *Staley* differ markedly from those present here. Although the District Court characterized the Indiana prices charged by Falls City and its competitors as "artificially high," there is no evidence that Falls City's lower prices in Kentucky were set as part of a plan to obtain artificially high profits in Indiana rather than in response to competitive conditions in Kentucky. Falls City did not adopt an illegal system of prices maintained by its competitors.[53] The District Court found that Falls City's prices rose in Indiana in response to competitors' price increases there; it did not address the crucial question whether Falls City's Kentucky prices remained lower in response to competitors' prices in that State.

Vanco attempts to liken this case to *Staley* by arguing that the existence of industrywide price discrimination within the single geographic retail market itself indicates "tacit or explicit collusion, or ... market power" inconsistent with a good-faith response. By its terms, however, the meeting-competition defense requires a seller to justify only its *lower* price. See *Staley,* 324 U.S., at 753. Thus, although the Sherman Act would provide a remedy if Falls City's higher Indiana price were set collusively, collusion is relevant to Vanco's Robinson–Patman Act claim only if it affected Falls City's lower Kentucky price. If Falls City set its lower price in

---

53. Except through its rejected Sherman Act claim, Vanco has never attempted to prove that the competing prices Falls City claims to have met were themselves illegal, or that Falls City met those prices knowing them to be unlawful. The plaintiff bears the burden of proving that the prices met were actually illegal. Cadigan v. Texaco, Inc., 492 F.2d 383, 387 (C.A.9 1974); National Dairy Products Corp. v. FTC, 395 F.2d 517, 524 (CA7), cert. denied, 393 U.S. 977 (1968); see Standard Oil Co. v. Brown, 238 F.2d 54, 58, and n. 7 (C.A.5 1956).

good faith to meet an equally low price of a competitor, it did not violate the Robinson–Patman Act.

Moreover, the collusion argument founders on a complete lack of proof. Persistent, industrywide price discrimination within a geographic market should certainly alert a court to a substantial possibility of collusion.[54] See Posner, Oligopoly and the Antitrust Laws: A Suggested Approach, 21 Stan.L.Rev. 1562, 1578–1579 (1969). Here, however, the persistent interstate price difference could well have been attributable, not to Falls City, but to extensive state regulation of the sale of beer. Indiana required each brewer to charge a single price for its beer throughout the State, and barred direct competition between Indiana and Kentucky distributors for sales to retailers. In these unusual circumstances, the prices charged to Vanco and other wholesalers in Vanderburgh County may have been influenced more by market conditions in distant Gary and Fort Wayne than by conditions in nearby Henderson County, Ky. Moreover, wholesalers in Henderson County competed directly, and attempted to price competitively, with wholesalers in neighboring Kentucky counties. A separate pricing structure might well have evolved in the two States without collusion, notwithstanding the existence of a common retail market along the border. Thus, the sustained price discrimination does not itself demonstrate that Falls City's Kentucky prices were not a good-faith response to competitors' prices there.

C

The Court of Appeals explicitly relied on two other factors in rejecting Falls City's meeting-competition defense: the price discrimination was created by raising rather than lowering prices, and Falls City raised its prices in order to increase its profits. Neither of these factors is controlling. Nothing in § 2(b) requires a seller to *lower* its price in order to meet competition. On the contrary, § 2(b) requires the defendant to show only that its "lower price ... was made in good faith to meet an equally low price of a competitor." A seller is required to justify a price difference by showing that it reasonably believed that an equally low price was available to the purchaser and that it offered the lower price for that reason; the

---

54. Indeed, in some circumstances there may be no other plausible explanation for persistent "economic" price discrimination. Cf. FTC v. Cement Institute, 333 U.S. 683, 715 (1948) ("the multiple basing point system of delivered prices as employed by respondents contravened accepted economic principles and could only have been maintained through collusion"); *Staley,* 324 U.S., at 756 (it "seems inescapable" that basing point system was adopted not to meet equally low prices of competitors, but to establish artificially high prices elsewhere).

"Economic" price discrimination consists in selling a product to different customers at prices that bear different ratios to the marginal costs of sales to those customers, for example, charging the same price to two customers despite the fact that the seller incurs higher costs to serve one than the other, or charging different prices to two customers despite the fact that the seller's costs of service are the same. Price discrimination under the Robinson–Patman Act, however, "is merely a price difference." FTC v. Anheuser–Busch, Inc., 363 U.S. 536, 549 (1960).

seller is not required to show that the difference resulted from subtraction rather than addition.

A different rule would not only be contrary to the language of the statute, but also might stifle the only kind of legitimate price competition reasonably available in particular industries. In a period of generally rising prices, vigorous price competition for a particular customer or customers may take the form of smaller price increases rather than price cuts. Thus, a price discrimination created by selective price increases can result from a good-faith effort to meet a competitor's low price.

Nor is the good faith with which the lower price is offered impugned if the prices raised, like those kept lower, respond to competitors' prices and are set with the goal of increasing the seller's profits. A seller need not choose between "ruinously cutting its prices to all its customers to match the price offered to one, [and] refusing to meet the competition and then ruinously raising its prices to its remaining customers to cover increased unit costs." Standard Oil Co. v. FTC, 340 U.S., at 250. Nor need a seller choose between keeping all its prices ruinously low to meet the price offered to one, and ruinously raising its prices to all customers to a level significantly above that charged by its competitors. A seller is permitted "to retain a customer by realistically meeting in good faith the price offered to that customer, without necessarily changing the seller's price to its other customers." Ibid. The plain language of § 2(b) also permits a seller to retain a customer by realistically meeting in good faith the price offered to that customer, without necessarily freezing his price to his other customers.

Section 2(b) does not require a seller, meeting in good faith a competitor's lower price to certain customers, to forgo the profits that otherwise would be available in sales to its remaining customers. The very purpose of the defense is to permit a seller to treat different competitive situations differently. The prudent businessman responding fairly to what he believes in good faith is a situation of competitive necessity might well raise his prices to some customers to increase his profits, while meeting competitors' prices by keeping his prices to other customers low.

The Court in *Staley* said that the meeting-competition defense "presupposes that the person charged with violating the Act would, by his normal, non-discriminatory pricing methods, have reached a price so high that he could reduce it in order to meet the competitor's equally low price." In that case, however, the Court was not dealing with a seller whose "normal, non-discriminatory pricing methods" called for a price increase but who wished to exempt certain customers from the increase in order to meet prices, lower than the increased price, available to those customers from competitors. Of course, a seller could accomplish the same result within the guidelines the Court of Appeals would impose by instituting across-the-board price increases followed by selective reductions. But far from being flexible and pragmatic, a rule requiring such costly behavior would be nonsensical.[55]

D

Vanco also contends that Falls City did not satisfy § 2(b) because its price discrimination "was not a *defensive* response to competition." Brief for Respondent 47 (emphasis supplied). According to Vanco, the Robinson–Patman Act permits price discrimination only if its purpose is to retain a customer. We agree that a seller's response must be defensive, in the sense that the lower price must be calculated and offered in good faith to "meet not beat" the competitor's low price. See *United States Gypsum Co.,* 438 U.S., at 454. Section 2(b), however, does not distinguish between one who meets a competitor's lower price to retain an old customer and one who meets a competitor's lower price in an attempt to gain new customers.[56] See Stevens, Defense of Meeting the Lower Price of a Competitor in Summer Institute on International and Comparative Law, University of Michigan Law School, Lectures on Federal Antitrust Laws 129, 135–136 (1953). Such a distinction would be inconsistent with that section's language and logic, see Sunshine Biscuits, Inc. v. FTC, 306 F.2d 48, 51–52 (C.A.7 1962), "would not be in keeping with elementary principles of competition, and would in fact foster tight and rigid commercial relationships by insulating them from market forces." 1955 Report, at 184; see 1977 Report, at 26, 265.[57]

IV

The Court of Appeals also relied on *Staley* for the proposition that the meeting-competition defense " 'places emphasis on individual [competitive] situations, rather than upon a general system of competition' " (quoting *Staley,* 324 U.S., at 753), and "does not justify the maintenance of discriminatory pricing among classes of customers that results merely from the adoption of a competitor's discriminatory pricing structure." The Court of Appeals was apparently invoking the District Court's findings that Falls City set prices statewide rather than on a "customer to customer basis," and the District Court's conclusion that this practice disqualified Falls City from asserting the meeting-competition defense. 1980–2 Trade Cases, at

---

55. "Section 2(b) should not require proof that the seller departed from a previously uniform price schedule. Such *previous* pricing is not relevant to evaluation of genuine responses to a *current* competitive situation." Report of the Attorney General's National Committee to Study the Antitrust Laws 182 (1955 Report) (emphasis in original).

56. At least three Courts of Appeals have held that the defense is not limited to attempts to retain customers. Cadigan v. Texaco, Inc., 492 F.2d, at 387, and n. 3; Hanson v. Pittsburgh Plate Glass Industries, Inc., 482 F.2d 220, 226–227 (C.A.5 1973), cert. denied, 414 U.S. 1136 (1974); Sunshine Biscuits, Inc. v. FTC, 306 F.2d 48, 51–52 (C.A.7 1962). But see Standard Motor Products, Inc. v. FTC, 265 F.2d 674, 677 (CA2) (defense available only if lower price responds to individual competitive demand).

57. Standard Oil Co. v. FTC, 340 U.S. 231 (1951) is not to the contrary. The Court there referred to the defense's being available to a seller seeking to "retain" customers, id., at 242, 249, 250, simply because the petitioner had so framed its defense in that particular case. Id., at 234, 236; see 1955 Report, at 184; Kuenzel & Schiffres, Making Sense of Robinson–Patman: The Need to Revitalize its Affirmative Defenses, 62 Va.L.Rev. 1211, 1253–1254 (1976).

75,817. At least two other Courts of Appeals have read *Staley* to hold that the defense is unavailable to sellers pricing on other than a customer-by-customer basis, while two Courts of Appeals have held that a customer-by-customer response is not required.[58] . . .

Section 2(b) specifically allows a "lower price . . . to any purchaser or purchasers" made in good faith to meet a competitor's equally low price. A single low price surely may be extended to numerous purchasers if the seller has a reasonable basis for believing that the competitor's lower price is available to them.[59] Beyond the requirement that the lower price be reasonably calculated to "meet not beat" the competition, Congress intended to leave it a "question of fact . . . whether the way in which the competition was met lies within the latitude allowed." 80 Cong.Rec. 9418 (1936) (remarks of Rep. Utterback). Once again, this inquiry is guided by the standard of the prudent businessman responding fairly to what he reasonably believes are the competitive necessities.

A seller may have good reason to believe that a competitor or competitors are charging lower prices throughout a particular region. See William Inglis & Sons Baking Co. v. ITT Continental Baking Co., 668 F.2d 1014, 1046 (C.A.9 1981), cert. denied, 459 U.S. 825 (1982); Balian Ice Cream Co. v. Arden Farms Co., 231 F.2d 356, 366 (C.A.9 1955), cert. denied, 350 U.S. 991 (1956); Rowe, at 235–236. In such circumstances, customer-by-customer negotiations would be unlikely to result in prices different from those set according to information relating to competitors' territorial prices. A customer-by-customer requirement might also make meaningful price competition unrealistically expensive for smaller firms such as Falls City, which was attempting to compete with larger national breweries in 13 separate States. Cf. Callaway Mills Co. v. FTC, 362 F.2d 435, 442 (C.A.5 1966) (in some circumstances, requirement of customer-by-customer pricing "would be burdensome, unreasonable, and practically unfeasible").

In *Staley,* 324 U.S., at 753, as in each of the later cases in which this Court has contrasted a "general system of competition" with "individual competitive situations," see, *e.g.,* FTC v. National Lead Co., 352 U.S. 419, 431 (1957); FTC v. Cement Institute, 333 U.S. 683, 708 (1948), the seller's lower price was quoted not *"because* of lower prices by a competitor," but

---

58. Compare Exquisite Form Brassiere, Inc. v. FTC, 360 F.2d 492, 493 (1965) (customer-by-customer response required), cert. denied, 384 U.S. 959 (1966), and Standard Motor Products, Inc. v. FTC, 265 F.2d, at 677 (same), with William Inglis & Sons Baking Co. v. ITT Continental Baking Co., 668 F.2d 1014, 1046 (C.A.9 1981) (customer-by-customer response not necessarily required), cert. denied, 459 U.S. 825 (1982), Callaway Mills Co. v. FTC, 362 F.2d 435, 442 (C.A.5 1966) (same), and Balian Ice Cream Co. v. Arden Farms Co., 231 F.2d 356, 366 (C.A.9 1955) (same), cert. denied, 350 U.S. 991 (1956).

59. See also Standard Oil Co. v. FTC, 340 U.S., at 247, n. 13, quoting statement of Herbert A. Bergson, Assistant Attorney General, at Hearings on S. 236 before a Subcommittee of the Senate Committee on Interstate and Foreign Commerce, 81st Cong., 1st Sess., 77 (1949) (" 'The section presently permits sellers to justify otherwise forbidden price discriminations on the ground that the lower prices to one set of buyers were made in good faith to meet the equally low prices of a competitor' ").

"because of a preconceived pricing scale which [was] operative regardless of variations in competitor's prices." Rowe, at 234 (emphasis in original). In those cases, the contested lower prices were not truly *"responsive* to rivals' competitive prices," ibid. (emphasis in original), and therefore were not genuinely made to meet competitors' lower prices. Territorial pricing, however, can be a perfectly reasonable method—sometimes the most reasonable method—of responding to rivals' low prices.[60] We choose not to read into § 2(b) a restriction that would deny the meeting-competition defense to one whose areawide price is a well-tailored response to competitors' low prices.

Of course, a seller must limit its lower price to that group of customers reasonably believed to have the lower price available to it from competitors. A response that is not reasonably tailored to the competitive situation as known to the seller, or one that is based on inadequate verification, would not meet the standard of good faith. Similarly, the response may continue only as long as the competitive circumstances justifying it, as reasonably known by the seller, persist.[61] One choosing to price on a territorial basis, rather than on a customer-by-customer basis, must show that this decision was a genuine, reasonable response to prevailing competitive circumstances. See International Air Industries, Inc. v. American Excelsior Co., 517 F.2d 714, 725–726 (C.A.5 1975), cert. denied, 424 U.S. 943 (1976); Callaway Mills Co. v. FTC, 362 F.2d, at 441–442. See generally 1977 Report, at 265. Unless the circumstances call into question the seller's good faith, this burden will be discharged by showing that a reasonable and prudent businessman would believe that the lower price he charged was generally available from his competitors throughout the territory and throughout the period in which he made the lower price available. See William Inglis & Sons Baking Co. v. ITT Continental Baking Co., 668 F.2d, at 1045–1046.

V

[The case was remanded to give Falls City an opportunity to prove that its prices were equal to those offered by competitors in the relevant territory and throughout the period during which lower prices were offered.]

---

60. See Rowe, at 240 ("a seller's area-wide and blanket lower price, if made in good faith to meet competitors' lower prices, may be justified ... as responsive to an 'individual competitive situation' "). Cf. Maryland Baking Co. v. FTC, 243 F.2d 716, 719 (C.A.4 1957) (FTC permits competitive area price variations to avert placing "prices in a straightjacket throughout the country"); Anheuser–Busch, Inc., 54 F.T.C. 277, 301 (1957) (suggesting that offer of lower price throughout particular area might be responsive to "individual competitive situation"); C.E. Niehoff & Co., 51 F.T.C. 1114, 1130, 1146 (1955) (rejecting position that "showing that the seller's discriminations were temporary and localized in area is an indispensable prerequisite" to defense).

61. See Klein, Meeting Competition by Price Systems Under § 2(b) of the Robinson–Patman Act: Problems and Prospects, 16 Antitrust Bull. 213, 233–234, 238 (1971); Kuenzel & Schiffres, 62 Va.L.Rev., at 1244–1249.

SECTION 5.   BROKERAGE, AD ALLOWANCES AND SERVICES

Congress recognized that the provisions of Section 2(a) of the Robinson–Patman Act, forbidding discrimination in price to favored buyers, might be circumvented by indirect forms of discrimination. It therefore set out to outlaw payments of "brokerage" in 2(c) of the Act, payments to customers as compensation for the customer providing services or facilities (for example, sales people who demonstrated a product), in 2(d) of the Act, or by direct contribution of services or facilities (such as storage or display units) in Section 2(e) of the Act.[62]

During the 1940's and 1950's, government enforcement of the provisions of 2(c), 2(d) and 2(e) represented a substantial portion of all Robinson Patman enforcement. In the past two decades, the level of enforcement actions under these sections has subsided. Nevertheless, precedent remains on the books—often quite restrictive and demanding—and most companies try to comply with the provisions of these portions of the Act even though it is burdensome and expensive and even though there have been signals in Supreme Court and lower court cases that some of the more rigid aspects of those provisions would not be enforced in the courts today.

A.   Allowances or Services.

Section 2(d) covers a supplier's payment for services or facilities and provides as follows:

> "That it shall be unlawful for any person engaged in commerce to pay or contract for the payment of anything of value to or for the benefit of a customer of such person in the course of such commerce as compensation or in consideration for any services or facilities furnished by or through such customer in connection with the processing, handling, sale or offering for sale of any products or commodities manufactured, sold, or offered for sale by such person, unless such payment or consideration is available on proportionally equal terms to all other customers competing in the distribution of such products or commodities."

Section 2(e) of the Act covers a supplier's furnishing of services or facilities to the customer and provides:

> "That it shall be unlawful for any person to discriminate in favor of one purchaser against another purchaser or purchasers of a commodity bought for resale, with or without processing, by contracting to furnish or furnishing, or by contributing to the furnishing of, any services or facilities connected with the processing, handling, sale, or offering for sale of such commodity so purchased

---

62.   For Sections 2(c), 2(d) and 2(f) of the Robinson–Patman Act, *see* pp. 1282–1283, *supra.*

upon terms not accorded to all purchasers on proportionally equal terms."[63]

In guidelines published by the Federal Trade Commission in 1969 and amended in 1972, the following were listed as examples of services for which sellers frequently pay the buyer: any kind of advertising including cooperative advertising, hand bills, window and floor displays and demonstrators and demonstrations. As examples of services or facilities frequently furnished to customers, the guidelines list the following: any kind of advertising, catalogs, demonstrators, display and storage cabinets, display materials, special packaging, accepting returns for credit, or prizes or merchandise for conducting promotional contests.

Although the language of the two sections is not identical, the case law interpreting the provisions has worked out a reconciliation so that the same statutory requirements and defenses apply to both sections.[64] As will be discussed below, the real problem is that the coverage and interpretation of 2(d) and 2(e) is sharply different from the coverage and interpretation of 2(a) of the Robinson–Patman Act.

1.   Definition of allowance or service.

In general, a payment in connection with the original sale of a product to a distributor is covered under 2(a) of the Robinson–Patman Act, while a payment or provision of services in connection with resale of the product is covered by 2(d) or 2(e) of the Act.[65] Thus if a supplier simply pays money to a distributor for the distributor's account, that would be covered under 2(a) of the Act, but if it pays money for a joint program in connection with the resale of the supplier's product, that would be covered under Section 2(d).

2.   Available and unavailable defenses.

2(d) and 2(e) come into play only if the seller discriminates between competing buyers[66] and there is also available a meeting competition defense. For a time, the commission argued that the meeting competition defense was unavailable under Section 2(d) because the language of Section 2(b) referred only to "services or facilities" and not to allowances for services or facilities, but the court in *Exquisite Form Brassiere* rejected that interpretation.[67]

On the other hand, Sections 2(d) and 2(e) have an almost *per se* quality in the sense that allowances or services cannot be defended as "cost justified" and, more importantly, there is no requirement of a showing of competitive injury in order to establish a violation. Thus a direct and unjustified payment to a customer may be defended on grounds that the

---

63.   15 U.S.C. §§ 13(d), 13(e) (1936).

64.   *See* Rowe, Price Discrimination Under the Robinson–Patman Act 390 (1962).

65.   Herbert R. Gibson, Sr., 95 F.T.C. 553, 725 (1980), aff'd, 682 F.2d 554 (5th Cir.1982).

66.   *See* Exquisite Form Brassiere v. FTC, 301 F.2d 499 (D.C.Cir.1961), cert. denied, 369 U.S. 888 (1962).

67.   Exquisite Form Brassiere note 5 *supra*, at 502.

payment was not sufficiently significant to cause competitive injury, but a payment in the same amount for a service or facility would be illegal. In FTC v. Simplicity Pattern Co.,[68] the Supreme Court justified different treatment on the grounds that Congress' purpose was to deter difficult to detect payments for services or the providing of services, and force such discrimination into the form of a direct discount. Why direct discounts (pocketed by the buyer) would be easier to detect than discriminatory payments for services by the buyer was not made clear in the opinion.

3. Available on proportionally equal terms.

The text of both sections requires that services and facilities, or payments for services and facilities, be made available "on proportionally equal terms." The first requirement is that the plan be "functionally available." In Guide 9 of the FTC's 1972 guideline amendments, the Commission advised:

> "The plan should be such that all types of competing customers may participate. It should not be tailored to favor or discriminate against a particular customer or class of customers, but should in its terms be usable in a practical business sense by all competing customers. This may require offering all such customers more than one way to participate in the plan ... if [the seller] offers alternative plans, all the plans offered should provide the same proportionate equality and the seller should inform competing customers of the various alternative plans...."

As interpreted, "functional availability" means that the allowance or service must realistically be useful to all customers, regardless of their size, location, or way of doing business.[69] Thus, all dealers must legitimately be on notice that certain services or payments are available.[70] And if the particular service provided or subsidized is not appropriate for a class of customers, the seller must offer a subsidy for alternative marketing efforts. For example, a facility that requires substantial floor space at the retail outlet would not be "functionally available" to small dealers and some sort of alternative marketing support would have to be offered. Thus the Commission guidelines provide: "This may require offering all such customers more than one way to participate in the plan or offering alternative terms and conditions to customers for whom the basic plan is not usable and suitable."[71]

Even greater complications emerge out of the provision that payments and services must be made available on "proportionally equal terms." In Guide 7 of its 1979 guidelines, the Commission explained:

> "This means that payments or services shall be proportionalized on some basis that is fair to all customers who compete in the

68. 360 U.S. 55 (1959).

69. 16 C.F.R. § 240.9(a) (1982).

70. *See* Vanity Fair Paper Mills v. FTC, 311 F.2d 480 (2d Cir.1962).

71. 16 C.F.R. § 240.9(a) (1982).

resale of the sellers' products. No single way to proportionalize is prescribed by law. Any method that treats competing customers on proportionally equal terms may be used. Generally this can best be done by basing the payments made or the services furnished on the dollar volume or on the quantity of the goods purchased during a specified period. Other methods which are fair to all competing customers are also acceptable.''

If all distributors buy approximately in the same amounts, no problem arises since they can all be accorded the same payments or services. But where large and small dealers are involved, questions of proportionality are perplexing. The fact that a display in the front of a store in a mall is of much greater marketing impact—*i.e.*, the value to the seller is great—does not justify a larger payment than to an isolated store in an untravelled part of town. Plans which grant allowances or services based on the dollar amount or quantity of purchases have usually been approved, but other plans keyed to market impact—for example, payments depending on how much business increased in a period of time or the number of transactions in the store—have been rejected.[72]

The result of the Commission's interpretation is that sellers often find themselves in a position where they must subsidize forms of market support that are not especially efficient or cost effective or be willing to give up the form of merchandising support entirely. Also, administrative expenses in seeing to it that plans and alternatives are made available to competing customers can undermine the effectiveness of the whole marketing program. In a 1966 dissent, Commissioner Elman summarized the ways in which interpretations of 2(d) and 2(e) have placed burdens on sellers:

> "He must disregard his own promotional needs and set up an intricate 'promotional program' designed to satisfy the desires of all his customers. He may be compelled to pay for 'promotional activity' which is of no benefit to him whatsoever and which indeed is wasteful as well as not beneficial . . .
>
> "I do not believe that Section 2(d) was intended to have this result. As I read the Act, it provides that a seller may choose those promotional and advertising services for which he will compensate his customers; if he gives a payment to one customer who renders such services, he must give proportionally equal payments to all other customers who are ready, able and willing to provide him with the same services.''[73]

4.   Direct and indirect sales to dealers: The problem of *Fred Meyer*.

Often suppliers will sell directly to some distributors (often large outlets or chains who can afford to do their own wholesaling) and indirectly (*i.e.*, through wholesalers) to smaller retailers. In *Fred Meyer*[74], several

---

72.   Amstar Corp., 78 F.T.C. 536 (1971).

73.   House of Lords, Inc., 69 F.T.C. 44 (1966).

74.   FTC v. Fred Meyer, 390 U.S. 341 (1968).

suppliers made allowances available to a direct purchasing retailer but did not make comparable allowances available to small retailers who competed with the direct buyer. The suppliers defended on grounds that the statute only requires payment of allowances or provision of services to customers, and the indirect purchasing retailers were not "customers" of the suppliers but only of the wholesalers. The Supreme Court rejected that interpretation, noting that it would lead to the anomalous result that smaller retailers who can only afford to purchase through wholesalers would be left unprotected against discriminatory promotional allowances to the direct buyers. Incidentally, the court found that the suppliers did not have to provide comparable payments or services to the wholesalers and the direct buying retailers because they did not compete at the same functional level.

In response to the argument that suppliers may not always find it feasible to seek out and compensate retailers with whom they have no direct dealings, the Court noted that the supplier could simply compensate the wholesalers and then ensure that the wholesalers distribute payments or administer programs to the indirect buyers.

In dissent, Justice Harlan noted that compensating retailers with whom the supplier had no business relationship will be "no simple matter." In fact, that has clearly turned out to be the case. For example, it has been held that the intermediate wholesalers need only compensate those retailers who compete with the favored direct-buying retailer. *See* Motive Parts Warehouse v. Facet Enterprises, 774 F.2d 380 (10th Cir.1985). However, wholesalers may be ill-equipped to determine which of their retailers compete with the favored buyer and which do not. Furthermore, assuming the supplier must make available some allowances to some of its direct buying purchasers, it then must determine whether it has to make comparable allowances to all of its indirect buying retailers or at least those who compete with each other. Again, the administrative burdens of making "proportionally equal" services and allowances available to retailers who buy directly or indirectly through various channels of distribution may be so great as to undermine the effectiveness of the entire program.

SECTION 6.   BUYER'S LIABILITY FOR INDUCING OR RECEIVING DISCRIMINATIONS IN PRICE[75]

Great Atlantic & Pacific Tea Co. v. Federal Trade Commission

Supreme Court of the United States, 1979.
440 U.S. 69, 99 S.Ct. 925, 59 L.Ed.2d 153.

■ STEWART, J. The question presented in this case is whether the petitioner, the Great Atlantic & Pacific Tea Company (A & P), violated § 2(f) of the

---

75. For Section 2(f) of the Robinson–Patman Act, *see* p. 1267 *supra*.

Robinson–Patman Act, as amended, 15 U.S.C.A. § 13(f), by knowingly inducing or receiving illegal price discriminations from the Borden Company (Borden).

The alleged violation was reflected in a 1965 agreement between A & P and Borden under which Borden undertook to supply "private label" milk to more than 200 A & P stores in a Chicago area that included portions of Illinois and Indiana. This agreement resulted from an effort by A & P to achieve cost savings by switching from the sale of "brand label" milk (milk sold under the brand name of the supplying dairy) to the sale of "private label" milk (milk sold under the A & P label).

To implement this plan, A & P asked Borden, its longtime supplier, to submit an offer to supply under private label certain of A & P's milk and other dairy product requirements. After prolonged negotiations, Borden offered to grant A & P a discount for switching to private label milk provided A & would accept limited delivery service. Borden claimed that this offer would save A & P $410,000 a year compared to what it had been paying for its dairy products. A & P, however, was not satisfied with this offer and solicited offers from other dairies. A competitor of Borden, Bowman Dairy, then submitted an offer which was lower than Borden's.[76]

·   At this point, A & P's Chicago buyer contacted Borden's chain store sales manager and stated, "I have a bid in my pocket. You [Borden] people are so far out of line it is not even funny. You are not even in the ball park." When the Borden representative asked for more details, he was told nothing except that a $50,000 improvement in Borden's bid "would not be a drop in the bucket."

Borden was thus faced with the problem of deciding whether to rebid. A & P at the time was one of Borden's largest customers in the Chicago area. Moreover, Borden had just invested more than five million dollars in a new dairy facility in Illinois. The loss of the A & P account would result in underutilization of this new plant. Under these circumstances, Borden decided to submit a new bid which doubled the estimated annual savings to A & P, from $410,000 to $820,000. In presenting its offer, Borden emphasized to A & P that it needed to keep A & P's business and was making the new offer in order to meet Bowman's bid. A & P then accepted Borden's bid after concluding that it was substantially better than Bowman's.

I

Based on these facts, the Federal Trade Commission filed a ... complaint against A & P Count I charged that A & P had violated § 5 of the Federal Trade Commission Act by misleading Borden in the course of negotiations for the private label contract, in that A & P had failed to inform Borden that its second offer was better than the Bowman bid. Count II involving the same conduct, charged that A & P had violated

---

76. The Bowman bid would have produced estimated annual savings of approximately $737,000 for A & P as compared with the first Borden bid, which would have produced estimated annual savings of $410,000.

§ 2(f) of the Robinson–Patman Act by knowingly inducing or receiving price discriminations from Borden. . . .

An Administrative Law Judge found, after extended discovery and a hearing that lasted over 110 days, that A & P had acted unfairly and deceptively in accepting the second offer from Borden and had therefore violated § 5 of the Federal Trade Commission Act as charged in Count I. The Administrative Law Judge similarly found that this same conduct had violated § 2(f) of the Robinson–Patman Act. . . .

On review, the Commission reversed the Administrative Law Judge's finding as to Count I. Pointing out that the question at issue was what amount of disclosure is required of the buyer during contract negotiations, the Commission held that the imposition of a duty of affirmative disclosure would be "contrary to normal business practice and we think, contrary to the public interest." Despite this ruling, however, the Commission held as to Count II that the identical conduct on the part of A & P had violated § 2(f) of the Robinson–Patman Act, finding that Borden had discriminated in price between A & P and its competitors, that the discrimination had been injurious to competition, and that A & P had known or should have known that it was the beneficiary of unlawful price discrimination. The Commission rejected A & P's defenses that the Borden bid had been made to meet competition and was cost justified.[77]

A & P filed a petition for review of the Commission's order in the Court of Appeals for the Second Circuit. The court held that substantial evidence supported the findings of the Commission, and that as a matter of law A & P could not successfully assert a meeting competition defense because it, unlike Borden, had known that Borden's offer was better than Bowman's.[78] Finally, the court held that the Commission had correctly determined that A & P had no cost justification defense.

II

The Robinson–Patman Act was passed in response to the problem perceived in the increased market power and coercive practices of chain stores and other big buyers that threatened the existence of small indepen-

---

77. With respect to the meeting competition defense, the Commission stated that even though Borden as the seller might have had a meeting competition defense, A & P as the buyer did not have such a defense because it knew that the bid offered was, in fact, better than the Bowman bid. With respect to the cost justification defense, the Commission found that Commission counsel had met the initial burden of going forward as required by this Court's decision in Automatic Canteen Co. of America v. FTC, 346 U.S. 61, and that A & P had not then satisfied its burden of showing that the prices were cost justified, or that it did not know that they were not. . . .

78. The Court of Appeals, like the Commission, relied on Kroger Co. v. FTC, 438 F.2d 1372 ([6th Cir.] 1971), for the proposition that a buyer can be liable under § 2(f) of the Act even if the seller has a meeting competition defense. The Kroger case involved a buyer who had made deliberate misrepresentations to a seller in order to induce price concessions. While the Court of Appeals in this case did not find that A & P had made any affirmative misrepresentations, it viewed the distinction between a "lying buyer" and a buyer who knowingly accepts the lower of two bids as without legal significance. See n. 82, infra.

dent retailers. Notwithstanding this concern with buyers, however, the emphasis of the Act is in § 2(a), which prohibits price discrimination by sellers. Indeed, the original Patman Bill as reported by Committees of both Houses prohibited only seller activity, with no mention of buyer liability. Section 2(f) of the Act, making buyers liable for inducing or receiving price discriminations by sellers, was the product of a belated floor amendment near the conclusion of the Senate debates.[79]

As finally enacted, § 2(f) provides:

"That it shall be unlawful for any person engaged in commerce, in the course of such commerce, knowingly to induce or receive a discrimination in price *which is prohibited by this section*." (Emphasis added.)

Liability under § 2(f) thus is limited to situations where the price discrimination is one "which is prohibited by this section." While the phrase "this section" refers to the entire § 2 of the Act, only subsections (a) and (b) dealing with seller liability involve discriminations in price. Under the plain meaning of § 2(f), therefore, a buyer cannot be liable if a prima facie case could not be established against a seller or if the seller has an affirmative defense. In either situation, there is no price discrimination "prohibited by this section." The legislative history of § 2(f) fully confirms the conclusion that buyer liability under § 2(f) is dependent on seller liability under § 2(a).

The derivative nature of liability under § 2(f) was recognized by this Court in Automatic Canteen Co. of America v. FTC, 346 U.S. 61. In that case, the Court stated that even if the Commission has established a prima facie case of price discrimination, a buyer does not violate § 2(f) if the lower prices received are either within one of the seller's defenses or not known by him not to be within one of those defenses.... The Court thus explicitly recognized that a buyer cannot be held liable under § 2(f) if the lower prices received are justified by reason of one of the seller's affirmative defenses.

III

The petitioner, relying on this plain meaning of § 2(f) and the teaching of the *Automatic Canteen* case, argues that it cannot be liable under § 2(f) if Borden had a valid meeting competition defense. The respondent, on the other hand, argues that the petitioner may be liable even assuming that Borden had such a defense. The meeting competition defense, the respondent contends, must in these circumstances be judged from the point of view of the buyer. Since A & P knew for a fact that the final Borden bid beat the Bowman bid, it was not entitled to assert the meeting competition defense even though Borden may have honestly believed that it was simply meeting competition. Recognition of a meeting competition defense for the

---

79. F. Rowe, Price Discrimination Under the Robinson Patman Act 423 (1962). Section 2(f) has been described by commentators as an "afterthought." *Id.*, at 421; J. McCord, Commentaries on the Robinson–Patman Act 96 (1969).

buyer in this situation, the respondent argues, would be contrary to the basic purpose of the Robinson–Patman Act to curtail abuses by large buyers.

A

The short answer to these contentions of the respondent is that Congress did not provide in § 2(f) that a buyer can be liable even if the seller has a valid defense. The clear language of § 2(f) states that a buyer can be liable only if he receives a price discrimination "prohibited by this section." If a seller has a valid meeting competition defense, there is simply no prohibited price discrimination. . . .

B

In the *Automatic Canteen* case, the Court warned against interpretations of the Robinson–Patman Act which "extend beyond the prohibitions of the Act and, in so doing, help give rise to a price uniformity and rigidity in open conflict with the purposes of other antitrust legislation." 346 U.S., at 63. Imposition of § 2(f) liability on the petitioner in this case would lead to just such price uniformity and rigidity[80]

In a competitive market, uncertainty among sellers will cause them to compete for business by offering buyers lower prices. Because of the evils of collusive action, the Court has held that the exchange of price information by competitors violates the Sherman Act. United States v. Container Corp., 393 U.S. 333. Under the view advanced by the respondent, however, a buyer, to avoid liability, must either refuse a seller's bid or at least inform him that his bid has beaten competition. Such a duty of affirmative disclosure would almost inevitably frustrate competitive bidding and, by reducing uncertainty, lead to price matching and anticompetitive cooperation among sellers.[81]

Ironically, the Commission itself, in dismissing the charge under § 5 of the Federal Trade Commission Act in this case, recognized the dangers inherent in a duty of affirmative disclosure:

> The imposition of a duty of affirmative disclosure, applicable to a buyer whenever a seller states that his offer is intended to meet competition, is contrary to normal business practice and, we think, contrary to the public interest.
>
> . . .
>
> We fear a scenario where the seller automatically attaches a meeting competition caveat to every bid. The buyer would then state whether such bid meets, beats, or loses to another bid. The

---

80. More than once the Court has stated that the Robinson–Patman Act should be construed consistently with broader policies of the antitrust laws. United States v. United States Gypsum Co., 438 U.S. 422; Automatic Canteen Co. v. FTC, *supra*, 346 U.S., at 74.

81. A duty of affirmative disclosure might also be difficult to enforce. In cases where a seller offers differing quantities or a different quality product, or offers to serve the buyer in a different manner, it might be difficult for the buyer to determine when disclosure is required.

seller would then submit a second, a third, and perhaps a fourth
bid until finally he is able to ascertain his competitor's bid.

The effect of the finding that the same conduct of the petitioner violated
§ 2(f), however, is to impose the same duty of affirmative disclosure which
the Commission condemned as anticompetitive, "contrary to the public
interest," and "contrary to normal business practice," in dismissing the
charge under § 5 of the Federal Trade Commission Act. Neither the
Commission nor the Court of Appeals offered any explanation for this
apparent anomaly.

As in the *Automatic Canteen* case, we decline to adopt a construction of
§ 2(f) that is contrary to its plain meaning and would lead to anticompetitive results. Accordingly, we hold that a buyer who has done no more than
accept the lower of two prices competitively offered does not violate § 2(f)
provided the seller has a meeting competition defense.[82]

IV

Because both the Commission and the Court of Appeals proceeded on
the assumption that a buyer who accepts the lower of two competitive bids
can be liable under § 2(f) even if the seller has a meeting competition
defense, there was not a specific finding that Borden did in fact have such a
defense. But it quite clearly did.

A

The test for determining when a seller has a valid meeting competition
defense is whether a seller can "show the existence of facts which would
lead a reasonable and prudent person to believe that the granting of a
lower price would in fact meet the equally low price of a competitor." FTC

---

82. In Kroger Co. v. FTC, *supra*, the Court of Appeals for the Sixth Circuit held that a
buyer who induced price concessions by a seller by making deliberate misrepresentations could
be liable under § 2(f) even if the seller has a meeting competition defense.

This case does not involve a "lying buyer" situation. The complaint issued by the FTC
alleged that "A & P accepted Borden's offer knowing that Borden had granted a substantially
lower price than the only other competitive bidder without notifying Borden of this fact." The
complaint did not allege that Borden's second bid was induced by any misrepresentation. The
Court of Appeals recognized that the *Kroger* case involved a "lying buyer," but stated that
there was no meaningful distinction between the situation where "the buyer lies or merely
keeps quiet about the nature of the competing bid." 557 F.2d 971, 983.

Despite this background, the respondent argues that A & P did engage in misrepresentations and therefore can be found liable as a "lying buyer" under the rationale of the *Kroger*
case. The misrepresentation relied upon by the respondent is a statement allegedly made by a
representative of A & P to Borden after Borden made its second bid which would have resulted
in annual savings to A & P of $820,000. The A & P representative allegedly told Borden to
"sharpen your pencil a little bit because you are not quite there." But the Commission itself
referred to this comment only to note its irrelevance, and neither the Commission nor the
Court of Appeals mentioned it in considering the § 2(f) charge against A & P This is quite
understandable, since the comment was allegedly made *after* Borden made its second bid and
therefore cannot be said to have induced the bid as in the *Kroger* case.

Because A & P was not a "lying buyer," we need not decide whether such a buyer could
be liable under § 2(f) even if the seller has a meeting competition defense.

v. A.E. Staley Manufacturing Co., 324 U.S. 746. "A good faith belief, rather than absolute certainty, that a price concession is being offered to meet an equally low price offered by a competitor is sufficient to satisfy the Robinson–Patman's § 2(b) defense." United States v. United States Gypsum Co., 438 U.S. 422.[83] Since good faith, rather than absolute certainty, is the touchstone of the meeting competition defense, a seller can assert the defense even if it has unknowingly made a bid that in fact not only met but beat his competition. Id., at 453–55.

B

Under the circumstances of this case, Borden did act reasonably and in good faith when it made its second bid. The petitioner, despite its long-standing relationship with Borden, was dissatisfied with Borden's first bid and solicited offers from other dairies. The subsequent events are aptly described in the opinion of the Commission:

> Thereafter, on August 31, 1965, A & P received an offer from Bowman Dairy that was lower than Borden's August 13 offer. On or about September 1, 1965, Elmer Schmidt, A & P's Chicago unit buyer, telephoned Gordon Tarr, Borden's Chicago chain store sales manager, and stated, "I have a bid in my pocket. You [Borden] people are so far out of line it is not even funny. You are not even in the ball park." Although Tarr asked Schmidt for some details, Schmidt said that he could not tell Tarr anything except that a $50,000 improvement in Borden's bid "would not be a drop in the [bucket]." Contrary to its usual practice, A & P then offered Borden the opportunity to submit another bid. (Footnotes and record citations omitted.)

Thus Borden was informed by the petitioner that it was in danger of losing it's A & P business in the Chicago area unless it came up with a better offer. It was told that its first offer was "not even in the ball park" and that a $50,000 improvement "would not be a drop in the bucket." In light of Borden's established business relationship with the petitioner, Borden could justifiably conclude that A & P's statements were reliable and that it was necessary to make another bid offering substantial concessions to avoid losing its account with the petitioner.

Borden was unable to ascertain the details of the Bowman bid. It requested more information about the bid from the petitioner, but this request was refused. It could not then attempt to verify the existence and

---

83. Recognition of the right of a seller to meet a lower competitive price in good faith may be the primary means of reconciling the Robinson–Patman Act with the more general purposes of the antitrust laws of encouraging competition between sellers. As the Court stated in Standard Oil Co. v. FTC, 340 U.S. 231, 249:

> "We need not now reconcile, in its entirety, the economic theory which underlies the Robinson–Patman Act with that of the Sherman and Clayton Acts. It is enough to say that Congress did not seek by the Robinson–Patman Act either to abolish competition or so radically to curtail it that a seller would have no substantial right of self-defense against a price raid by a competitor."

terms of the competing offer from Bowman without risking Sherman Act liability. United States v. United States Gypsum Co., *supra*. Faced with a substantial loss of business and unable to find out the precise details of the competing bid, Borden made another offer stating that it was doing so in order to meet competition. Under these circumstances, the conclusion is virtually inescapable that in making that offer Borden acted in a reasonable and good-faith effort to meet its competition, and therefore was entitled to a meeting competition defense.[84]

Since Borden had a meeting competition defense and thus could not be liable under § 2(b) the petitioner who did no more than accept that offer cannot be liable under § 2(f).[85]

Accordingly, the judgment is reversed.

■ STEVENS, J., took no part in the consideration or decision of this case.

■ WHITE, J., concurring in part and dissenting in part.

I concur in Parts I, II, and III of the Court's opinion but dissent from Part IV. Because it was thought the issue was irrelevant where the buyer knows that the price offered is lower than necessary to meet competition, neither the Commission nor the Court of Appeals decided whether Borden itself would have had a valid meeting-competition defense. The Court should not decide this question here but should remand to the Commission whose job it is initially to consider such matters.

For the reason stated by the Commission and the Court of Appeals, I am also convinced that the United States made a sufficient, unrebutted showing that Borden would not have a cost-justification defense to a Robinson–Patman Act charge.

NOTE

Sections 2(d) and 2(e) of the Robinson–Patman Act cover allowances and services made available by sellers, but those two provisions do not address the question of buyer liability. In *Grand Union Co. v. FTC*, 300 F.2d 92 (2d Cir.1962),

---

84. The facts of this case are thus readily distinguishable from Corn Products v. FTC, 324 U.S. 726, and FTC v. A.E. Staley Manufacturing Co., 324 U.S. 746, in both of which the Court held that a seller had failed to establish a meeting competition defense. In the *Corn Products* case, the only evidence to rebut the prima facie case of price discrimination was testimony by witnesses who had no personal knowledge of the transactions in question. Similarly, in the *Staley Manufacturing Co.* case, unsupported testimony from informants of uncertain character and reliability was insufficient to establish the defense. In the present case, by contrast, the source of the information was a person whose reliability was not questioned and who had personal knowledge of the competing bid. Moreover, Borden attempted to investigate by asking A & P for more information about the competing bid. Finally, Borden was faced with a credible threat of a termination of purchases by A & P if it did not make a second offer. All of these factors serve to show that Borden did have a valid meeting competition defense. See United States v. United States Gypsum Co., *supra*.

85. Because we hold that the petitioner is not liable under § 2(f), we do not reach the question whether Borden might also have had a cost justification defense under § 2(a).

the Court of Appeals sustained a Commission finding that knowing receipt of an illegal allowance could constitute an unfair method of competition under Section 5 of the Federal Trade Commission Act. This expansive interpretation of Section 5 appears to have been limited by the Court to situations in which an omission in the antitrust laws by Congress appeared to be inadvertent, and the coverage of the transaction under Section 5 was consistent with the overall purposes of the particular antitrust provision. *Compare FTC v. Brown Shoe Co.*, page 968, *supra.*

SELECTIVE BIBLIOGRAPHY

Sullivan & Grimes, Hornbook on The Law of Antitrust (2d ed. 2006).

Hovenkamp, Federal Antitrust Policy Ch. 14 (3d ed. 2005).

Shniderman, Price Discrimination in Perspective (2d ed. 1987).

ABA Antitrust Section, The Robinson–Patman Act: Policy and Law (2 vol. 1980).

Posner, The Robinson–Patman Act (1976).

Rowe, Price Discrimination Under the Robinson–Patman Act (1962 & Supp. 1964).

Antitrust Modernization Commission Report 311–32 (2007).

United States Department of Justice, Report on the Robinson–Patman Act (1977).

Report of the White House Task Force on Antitrust Policy, 2 Antitrust Law & Econ.Rev. 11, 17–18 (Winter 1968–69).

Celnicker & Seaman, Functional Discounts, Trade Discounts, Economic Price Discrimination and the Robinson–Patman Act, 1989 Utah L.Rev. 813 (1989).

Kintner & Bauer, The Robinson–Patman Act: A Look Backward, A View Forward, 31 Antitrust Bull. 571 (1986).

Rill, Availability and Functional Discounts Justifying Discriminatory Pricing, 56 Antitrust L.J. 929 (1985).

Calvani, Government Enforcement of the Robinson–Patman Act, 53 Antitrust L.J. 921 (1985).

APPENDIX

BASIC ECONOMICS FOR ANTITRUST

NIRIT SANDMAN ERIKSSON

I. Levels of Competition

The economy comprises a multitude of interrelated markets, each with its own idiosyncrasies. Because a primary concern of antitrust laws is the preservation of competition, however, it is helpful to organize a study of markets by focusing on several idealized models of markets exhibiting different levels of competition. As we will see, the level of competition can affect prices charged, amount produced, social welfare, and wealth distribution between producers and consumers. We will first discuss the defining characteristics of each model of competition, addressing later the economic implications flowing from each.

A. Perfect Competition

In a perfectly competitive market, there are many sellers, each selling an essentially identical product, and entry into the market is easy. The output of each seller is very small in relation to the total output of the market. As a result, an individual seller can increase or decrease output without measurably affecting the scarcity of the product in the market; thus, the seller can choose any level of output (and will be able to sell whatever amount he produces), but that choice will not affect the prevailing price of the product. For this reason, sellers in perfectly competitive markets are often referred to as "price takers." At equilibrium, firms in perfect competition earn no greater profits than the normal rate of return on invested capital; if conditions change such that firms in perfect competition start earning a profit beyond this level, new firms would promptly enter the market and dissipate the prior profit margin.

B. Monopoly

If perfect competition is one extreme on a continuum of competition, monopoly lies at the other extreme. In a completely monopolized market, one seller supplies all products of a given type. The monopolist therefore has substantial control over the price of the product. The ability to characterize a firm as a monopolist depends heavily on how narrowly one defines the market. For example, if it is impractical to transport a product across distances and consumers are unlikely to travel to acquire it, a firm may have a monopoly if it is the only seller of that product in a certain geographic region. Instead of with respect to geographic layout of the sellers, a market may be defined broadly or narrowly with respect to the characteristics of the product itself. While there are a number of firms making cola soft drinks, due to a well-kept trade secret there is only one firm making a cola with Coca–Cola's exact formula and flavor, and that firm is of course the Coca–Cola Company. However, the characteristics that distinguish Coca–Cola from other colas may be very important to some consumers and irrelevant to others. Thus, monopoly power is really a matter of degree and depends upon the suitability of potential substitutes.

C. Monopolistic Competition

The model of monopolistic competition attempts to capture a more commonplace type of market, exhibiting some of the attributes of both perfect competition and monopoly. In this model, as in perfect competition, there are many sellers of a product and each firm's output is small in relation to the market as a whole. However, the products are not identical. Sellers are able to distinguish their product in the minds of consumers through distinct product attributes, quality level, service, and branding. Thus, although products in such a market may compete with close substitutes, each firm does possess a limited degree of monopoly power.

D. Oligopoly

An oligopoly is a market in which a small number of large firms together satisfy a very large share of the market demand. It figures prominently in antitrust enforcement because such a market structure is conducive to explicit or tacit collusion among the firms to raise prices and restrict output in order to extract supracompetitive profits (also called economic profits, meaning profit above the normal rate of return on invested capital).

A number of criteria influence the firms' likelihood of forming and preserving a successful cartel. Doing so is a challenge because the firms must agree not only on price but on how to divide up the profits, given that member firms possess diffcrent market shares and different costs of production. The cartel must employ enforcement mechanisms to curtail cheating by member firms through secret price cuts aimed at expanding the firm's market share. In addition, agreements must be revised if economic conditions change, for example if a decline in costs warrants a new price.

Thus, factors favoring cartelization of the industry include: a small number of firms (to minimize dissent and defection), very similar products (to reduce the need to accommodate differences when agreeing on essential terms), publicly available pricing data (to create transparency and reduce risk of price cuts), smooth stream of small transactions rather than large, infrequent transactions (to reduce incentive to issue isolated discounts), and constancy of economic conditions (to reduce need to revise agreements).

E.   Dominant Firm and Competitive Fringe

The last model of competition we will address consists of one large firm with substantial market share (or a cartel behaving as one firm with less than 100% of the market share) and many small firms each of which produce a very small share of the industry's output. The large firm is large enough to be able to set the price of the product, and the small firms (also called the competitive fringe) are price takers in much the same way as would happen under perfect competition. This market structure differs from a monopoly because although the dominant firm has some monopoly power, the market share covered by the fringe is substantial enough to figure into the dominant firm's economic decision-making, discussed further below. At the same time, it differs from an oligopoly because the large number of other firms makes it impracticable for the dominant firm to collude with them in the setting of price and output so as to mimic a pure monopolist.

II.   Economic Fundamentals

Now that we have a basic familiarity with the defining characteristics of different market structures, we can investigate the economic consequences flowing from each structure. Along the way, we will develop some necessary economic concepts, such as downward-sloping demand, elasticity, measures of cost, and the universal short-term profit-maximization formula. We will finish up with an introductory discussion of game theory and its growing role in modern antitrust analysis, with several examples illustrating game theory's power to explain some strategic behavior while at the same time undermining prior assumptions and understandings.

A. Demand Curve Faced by an Industry

An essential tool for understanding the behavior of a given product market is a good grasp of the demand schedule (also called demand curve) for that product. A demand schedule simply shows, for each hypothetical price of the product, the total number of units consumers would be willing to purchase. Aside from an exceptional class of goods which we need not discuss here, demand for a product is inversely related to price; that is, the higher the price, the fewer number of units sold, and the lower the price, the greater number of units sold. When the relationship is presented graphically, with quantity along the horizontal axis and price along the vertical axis, the demand curve has a negative, or downward, slope.

The reason for this relationship has to do with the related notions of substitution and intensity of preference. As the price of a product increases (relative to the price of all other goods, which are assumed to hold constant), some consumers will purchase less or none of that good, electing to purchase a different good as a substitute. Those who value the product more highly will still purchase the good, even at a high price. Similarly, when the price of the product decreases, some consumers who did not value the product highly enough to purchase it before will now be induced to purchase it, and some other buyers will be induced to buy a greater quantity.

Figure 1: Downward-sloping demand curve

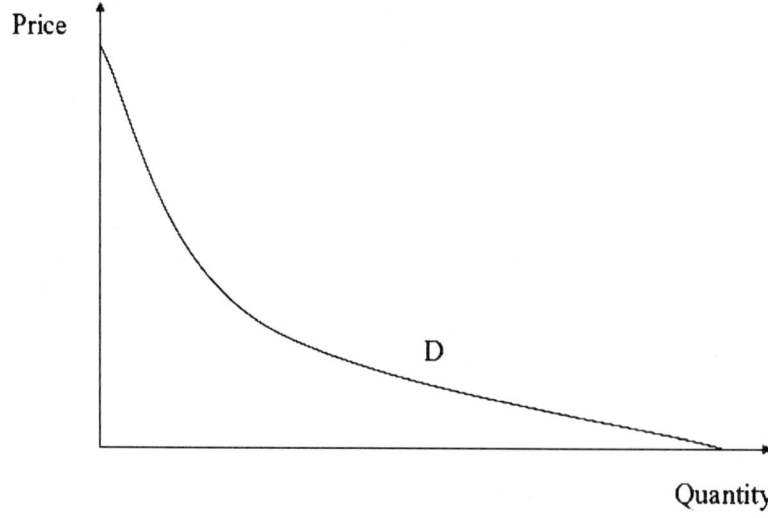

B. Elasticity

Another critical economic concept is elasticity of demand, which is a measure of how sensitive consumers are to a price change in the product. More precisely, elasticity is the absolute value (*i.e.*, ignore negative sign) of the quotient of a resulting percent change in quantity demanded to a percent change in price, expressed symbolically as

$$e_d = \left| \frac{\dfrac{\Delta Q}{Q}}{\dfrac{\Delta P}{P}} \right|$$

Points on the demand curve for which elasticity exceeds 1 are said to be relatively elastic, while those less than 1 are relatively inelastic. In the extreme cases, a product with a horizontal demand curve has infinite elasticity (*i.e.*, is perfectly elastic), while a product with a vertical demand curve has zero elasticity (*i.e.*, is perfectly inelastic). Note that, aside from these two special cases, a given demand curve will exhibit different values of elasticity at different points along the curve. (For additional details on elasticity values at various points along the demand curve, see the discussion below regarding the use of elasticity in measuring market power.) A useful related measure is the cross-elasticity of two products, x and y, which measures the percent change in demand of one product that results from a certain percent change in the price of another product. When the quotient of these two changes is high, we say that the pair of products exhibits high cross-elasticity and infer that the two products are close substitutes in the eyes of consumers. The formula for cross-elasticity is

$$e_{x,y} = \left| \frac{\dfrac{\Delta Q_x}{Q_x}}{\dfrac{\Delta P_y}{P_y}} \right|$$

Cross-elasticity is useful in defining the relevant market in which a firm operates, that is, determining which firms are actually competitors of that firm. The notion of elasticity captures the level of market power enjoyed by a firm. Intuitively, if as a result of raising prices only slightly above p*, a firm would lose a substantial amount of sales from its prior sales level of q* (this would correspond to a high value for e_d), then it does not have much power over the market when operating at the quantity-price combination (q*, p*). By contrast, if a firm can raise prices substantially and incur only a slight reduction in sales (which would correspond to a low value for e_d), then it does have a good deal of market power at that point on the demand curve. See below for a more technical discussion of the role of elasticity in measuring market power.

C.   Different Measures of Cost

In the short run, every firm faces several measures of costs. Fixed costs are those a firm incurs regardless of whether it produces anything at all. Examples of fixed costs include property taxes, management salaries, and interest payments on borrowed capital (or alternatively the opportunity cost of investing capital in that firm rather than elsewhere). Variable costs are those that vary with changing levels of production. Examples of variable costs include raw materials, advertising, and hourly wages of laborers. (If we take a long-run view rather than a short-run view, all costs are variable, because the owner of the would-be firm must decide whether to even enter the industry, and thus whether to invest any capital, build any facilities, hire any managers, etc. A short-run view assumes that such decisions have been made in favor of entering the industry, and thus some resources have been committed to this pursuit, resulting in positive fixed costs.)

Total cost is the sum of all fixed costs and variable costs. Average fixed cost per unit is the sum of the firm's fixed costs divided by the number of units produced, and average variable cost per unit is the sum of the firm's variable costs divided by the number of units produced. Average total cost is the sum of average variable cost and average fixed costs. Marginal variable cost is the incremental addition to variable cost caused by producing the last unit. The constancy of fixed costs implies that marginal variable cost necessarily equals marginal total cost, so referring simply to marginal cost creates no ambiguity.

Graphically, these cost functions exhibit certain predictable behaviors and relationships. We discuss a number of these relationships below, and invite the reader to think through each statement while studying the curves in Figure 2, in order to develop facility with these cost measures and the information they capture.

Fixed costs are constant for all levels of production, so the cost curve TFC is a horizontal line. Consequently, the total cost curve TC is simply an upward shift of the total variable cost curve TVC. Although TC and TVC are always increasing, the left-hand dotted vertical line highlights the fact that their growth rate slows as the marginal cost curve MC decreases and then begins to increase as MC passes its minimum point and begins increasing.

The average fixed cost curve (not pictured) is a strictly decreasing function, because the (constant) fixed costs are increasingly spread out over each unit as output grows. As a result, the average variable cost curve AVC approaches the average total cost curve ATC as output grows.

Finally, marginal cost intersects average variable cost at the latter curve's minimum, as highlighted by the middle vertical dotted line. This is because for units where MC < AVC, incorporating that last unit into the average pulls the average down. Similarly, for units where MC > AVC, incorporating that last unit into the average pulls the average up. At the exact point where MC = AVC, incorporating that last unit into the average leaves the average unchanged; that is, AVC is neither increasing nor decreasing at that intersection point. And because MC is an increasing function for sufficiently high levels of output (*i.e.*, after initial economies of scale have been exploited), we know MC is smaller than AVC to the left of the intersection point of the two curves, and greater than AVC to the right. Thus, AVC first decreases and then increases, so the intersection point is a minimum. By the same reasoning, MC intersects ATC at the latter curve's minimum, as highlighted by the right-hand vertical dotted line.

Figure 2: Cost curves

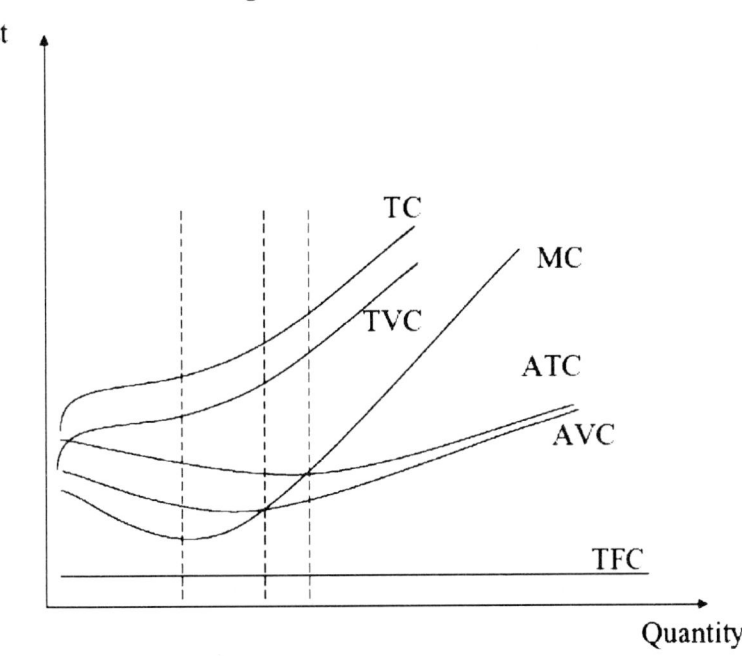

D. Determining the Profit–Maximizing Price and Output

For any firm, short-term profits are maximized by setting a level of production at which the marginal revenue MR gained by the last unit produced and sold equals the marginal cost MC of producing and selling that last unit. Because marginal cost increases as production increases, at a lower level of production marginal cost would be less than marginal revenue. Thus, producing and selling an extra unit would bring in more money than it would cost, resulting in increased profits, so a firm will continue to produce and sell so long as marginal cost is still less than or equal to marginal revenue. However, once marginal cost exceeds marginal revenue, producing and selling the last unit costs the firm more than the revenue the unit brings in, which causes total profits to decrease.

Thus, for any type of industry, a firm seeking to maximize short term profits will produce the level of output for which MR = MC. The industry type (*e.g.*, perfectly competitive versus monopolistic) merely affects the shape of the marginal revenue curve, as discussed below.

1. Perfect Competition

In perfect competition, there are so many sellers of virtually identical product, each producing such a small fraction of the total supply, that no one firm can influence the price of the product by changing its level of production, that is, by making the product slightly scarcer or more abundant. Charging the prevailing price, a firm in a perfectly competitive market can sell as many units as it chooses to produce. Due to the large number of competitors, the firm will sell no units if it attempts to charge a higher price, and it has no incentive to charge a lower price.

Thus, in perfect competition, the price a firm gets for its goods is constant regardless of the firm's level of production, so the marginal revenue curve is horizontal and is always equal to that fixed market price. For this reason, it is often said that a perfectly competitive firm will produce the level of output for which $P = MC$, where P is the market price, but this is just the universal formula of $MR = MC$ applied to the special case of perfect competition (in which marginal revenue is always the same as the market price). See Figure 3.

Figure 3: Short-term profit-maximizing output
for a firm in perfect competition

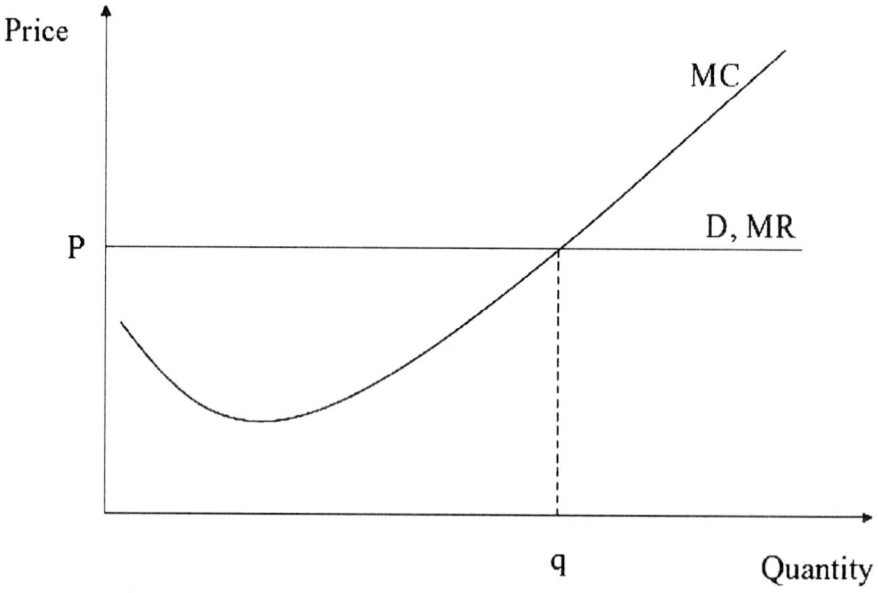

Note that in a perfectly competitive market, an individual firm's marginal cost curve coincides with its supply curve. For every quantity q^*, the curve MC gives a point (q^*, p^*) defining the price that would need to prevail, p^*, in order for the profit-maximizing firm to be willing to produce q^*. That is nothing but a supply schedule. Thus, to determine the supply curve of the industry as a whole, we horizontally sum the supply curves (*i.e.*, the MC curves) of all the individual firms in the industry. That is, the industry supply curve is the set of points

$$\left(\sum_{Firms} q_i^*, p^*\right) \text{ such that } MC\!\left(q_i^*\right) = p^* \text{ for some industry firm } i.$$

2. Monopoly

In a completely monopolized market, the monopolist firm *is* the industry. Thus, the firm's decision as to output level does affect the price it can charge. The less the firm produces, the higher a price it can charge, because scarcity will cause those consumers who value the product most to bid up the price. By contrast, the more the firm produces, the less it must charge for the product in order to induce existing customers to purchase addition units and capture additional consumers who don't value the product as highly as others do. We assume for now that the firm cannot price discriminate, that is, charge different prices to different consumers based on each consumer's willingness to pay. Thus, a decision to increase production by one unit requires a reduction in price not just for that marginal unit but for all units sold.

For this reason, the monopolist's marginal revenue curve starts at the same point on the vertical axis as the demand curve, but for all higher output levels MR lies below the demand curve—a portion of the price received for selling the last unit does not contribute to marginal revenue because it is used to cancel out the revenue hit the firm takes from the slight price reduction on all other units.

Not only does the marginal revenue curve lie below the demand curve, but, for a linear demand curve, elementary calculus shows that MR decreases twice as fast as demand; that is, its slope is twice as steep. This fact is also true in perfect competition, but there the individual firm's demand curve is horizontal, which means the slope is zero; two times zero is still zero, which explains why the MR curve for a perfectly competitive firm is also horizontal and in fact coincides with the firm's demand curve.

Once again, just like a perfectly competitive firm, a monopolist maximizing short-term profits will produce the level of output at which MR = MC, and then charge the price dictated by the demand schedule for that level of output. Below, we explore the economic consequences that arise when a monopolist exercises its market power to maximize short-term profits.

However, the monopolist may deviate from the MR = MC rule for long-run strategic reasons. Under certain circumstances, discussed below in the game theory section, predatory pricing may be a rational strategy for a monopolist focusing on long-term profits.

Figure 4: Short-term profit-maximizing price and output for a monopolist

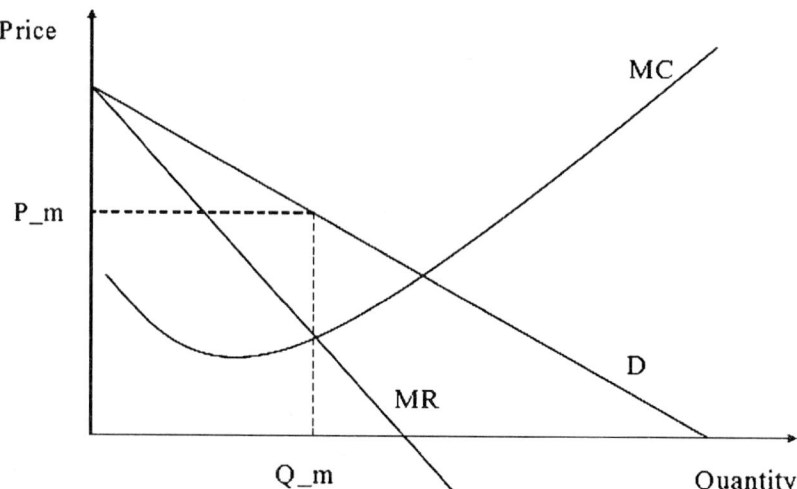

3.   Monopolistic Competition

A firm in such an industry faces a downward sloping demand curve because there is a lack of perfect substitutes for its product, and therefore a downward sloping marginal revenue curve as well. Its approach to choosing the profit-maximizing output level and corresponding price level is the same as a monopolist's.

4.   Oligopoly

A major firm in an oligopolistic industry also faces a downward sloping demand curve because the firm's substantial market share causes its output decisions to have a nontrivial effect on product supply and therefore on price. Its marginal revenue curve is therefore also declining (and twice as steeply as its demand curve). Once again, this firm will maximize its own short-term profits by setting production to the level where MR = MC and charging the corresponding price dictated by its demand curve.

However, such a strategy, if followed by all firms in the oligopolistic industry, would fail to maximize the industry's joint profits. Greater joint profits could be achieved if the industry as a whole restricted output somewhat and raised prices somewhat, as would happen in a one-firm monopoly (discussed below). Such an outcome requires cooperation among the firms. Although communicated agreements among competitors to fix prices are illegal *per se*, less explicit forms of coordination are treated more flexibly under antitrust law. In the game theory section below, we discuss a model for how cooperative understandings to raise prices can be reached among firms without resorting to explicit agreements.

5.   Dominant Firm and Competitive Fringe

As discussed earlier, in a situation in which there is a dominant firm (or a cartel whose joint market share is less than 100%) and a large set of small competitors (called the "competitive fringe"), the dominant firm can set the market price and the other small firms must accept that price. The only parameter the small firms determine is how much to produce at that price, and we know that each such firm will produce the number of units at which its marginal cost at that production level equals that price. Thus, for any hypothetical price the dominant firm might choose to set, we can sum the output supplied by each of the small firms, giving the competitive-fringe supply. We then derive the dominant firm's demand schedule by subtracting from the industry's demand schedule the competitive fringe supply at each price. The difference is the number of units the market still demands at each price, which the dominant firm will then make available, called the residual demand curve.

From the residual demand curve, we can determine the dominant firm's marginal revenue curve. To maximize short-term profits, the dominant firm will of course then choose the level of production at which its marginal revenue equals its marginal cost, and set the market price at the level dictated by the dominant firm's residual demand curve for this output level. At this set price, the amount supplied by the competitive fringe will exactly satisfy the remaining industry demand.

However, the dominant firm's short-run profit-maximizing price, which is of course adopted by the price-taking competitive fringe, might be high enough to allow even the competitive fringe to realize economic profits. This would induce other firms to enter the industry, which would eventually increase the competitive fringe supply and affect the dominant firm's residual demand curve and long-term profits. Thus, the dominant firm may choose to forego short-term profit maximization in favor of a more profitable long-term strategy, by setting the price low enough to slow down or eliminate expansion of the competitive fringe.

E.   Measuring Market Power

As mentioned above, elasticity is used to measure the degree of market power a firm possesses. (The details underlying the following discussion do require elementary calculus, but readers unfamiliar with calculus need not be concerned.) We start with the formula for total revenue (price charged times quantity sold), differentiate it with respect to quantity to derive the formula for marginal revenue, and substitute in the expression for elasticity of demand, giving us

$$MR = P * \left(1 - \frac{1}{e_d} \right)$$

As we know, a firm maximizing short-term profitability will operate at the production level at which the marginal revenue equals marginal cost. (As an aside, note also that such a firm would only produce a quantity at which MR was positive; otherwise it would be earning no profit and possibly even losing money by producing additional units. The formula above shows that MR is positive at output levels for which elasticity exceeds 1. Thus, a firm with market power will try to operate at the elastic portion of the demand curve.) Substituting MC for MR and manipulating terms, we get the following expression for market power in terms of elasticity:

$$\frac{P}{MC} = \frac{e_d}{e_d - 1}$$

This formula, capturing the ratio of the firm's profit-maximizing price to its marginal cost, is a sensible measure of the firm's relative market power. Under conditions of perfect competition, a product's price is equal to its marginal cost. Thus, a firm operating under such market conditions would have a ratio of 1. By contrast, the more the ratio exceeds 1, (*i.e.*, the more the profit-maximizing price diverges upward from marginal cost), the more market power the firm possesses.

F.   Consequences of Market Power

A monopolist (or any firm with some degree of market power, manifested by a downward-sloping demand curve) maximizes short-term profits by restricting output below what would be produced under perfect competition while at the same time charging a higher price than would prevail under perfect competition. Figure 5 shows the relevant cost and revenue functions for a monopolist and the profit-maximizing output Q_m and price P_m the monopolist will choose. If the monopolized industry were competitive, the marginal cost curve would also serve as the supply schedule, so the same figure also shows the price and output that would prevail under perfect competition.

The diagonally striped box represents the monopolist's supracompetitive profits. These profits are actually a wealth transfer from consumers to the producer, for if the competitive price were charged, the set of purchasers represented by this length on the Q-axis would have a substantial consumer surplus, because they value the product more highly than the price they have to pay to purchase it, as shown by the demand curve. Under monopoly pricing, they must pay more, so some of the consumer surplus is converted into producer surplus. If wealth distribution is of no concern as a matter of policy (a controversial position), then this aspect of monopoly pricing has no effect on overall societal welfare.

By contrast, the area under the demand curve and above the marginal cost curve, between Q_m and Q_c, represents value lost to society (often referred to as the deadweight loss) rather than a wealth transfer, because nobody appropriates this value. Under perfect competition, the quantity of goods $Q_c - Q_m$ would have been produced at price P_c. The vertically striped region would have been consumer surplus, since those consumers value the product more highly than the competitive price P_c which would have been charged. The horizontally striped region would have been producer surplus since the cost of production here is lower than the price charged. When a monopolist restricts output to the short-term profit-maximizing level, where MR = MC, the quantity of goods Q_c – Q_m is not produced so this societal value disappears.

Of course, maximizing short-term profits is not always the producer's goal, and different behaviors crop up when firms strategize for the long term. The next section examines such strategic behavior.

Figure 5: Comparing price and output under
monopoly and perfect competition

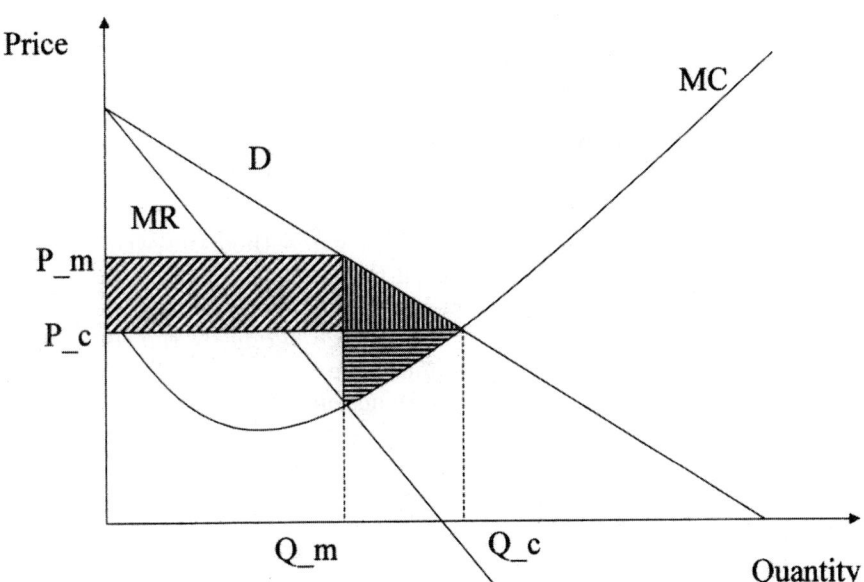

III.   Game Theory

Game theory, the study of strategic behavior, has found application in areas ranging from business to politics to biology to computer science. Recently, it has begun to gain influence in legal circles, notably among economics-minded antitrust scholars. Since game theory's emergence in the 1930s, its analytical tools have grown increasingly more technical and more powerful. While a thorough treatment is beyond the scope of this appendix, we hope to impart the flavor of this field by presenting a few simple illustrations. Our discussion here draws mainly from several applications of game theory to antitrust highlighted in *Game Theory and the Law*, by Douglas G. Baird, Robert H. Gertner & Randal C. Picker (Harvard University Press 1994).

A.   Market Preemption and Strategic Commitment

In the case In re E. I. duPont de Nemours & Co., 3 Trade Reg. Rep. (CCH) ¶ 21,770 (FTC Oct. 20, 1980), discussed on pp. ___ *supra*, the FTC considered duPont's plans to substantially expand capacity in anticipation of growth in demand (known as market preemption) and declined to condemn them as an attempt to monopolize. Although the Commission found in that case that the expansion was warranted by economies of scale rather than motivated by a desire to curb competition, game theory can illuminate how early expansion efforts might be used strategically to deter market entrants from competing with an incumbent firm.

Suppose a region has just one manufacturer of textiles, which we will refer to as Incumbent. Another firm, Entrant, plans to open a manufacturing plant in the region and must decide whether to compete with Incumbent by manufacturing textiles or go into an unrelated line of business, say, by producing ice cream. It would earn more by manufacturing textiles in competition with Incumbent than by making ice cream, provided Incumbent does not expand its own manufacturing capacity.

Incumbent, for its part, must decide whether to expand the capacity of its own plant. To do so would hurt both Entrant and Incumbent itself if Entrant competes with Incumbent, but would benefit Incumbent if Entrant does not compete.

To help predict people's likely actions, game theorists write down a "decision tree," which is a diagram of all the sequences of relevant actions that decision-makers ("players") can take. To start, we write down all actions the first player can take. For each such action by the first player, we write down all the actions the second player can take in response. This process continues until there are no more actions to be taken by any of the players. Figure 6 shows a decision tree of a game with two players. The first player must choose between two actions—making ice cream or making textiles—and the second player must then choose what to do if the first player makes ice cream and what to do if the first player makes textiles, leading to four different possible outcomes.

Each complete sequence of actions (or path down the decision tree) will result in consequences (or "payoffs") for all the players. In Figure 6, the leftmost path, where the first player makes ice cream and, in response, the second player expands, results in payoffs of 8 and 25, respectively. We can think of this as a gain of 8 dollars for the first player and 25 dollars for the second player. The units are unimportant, because the numbers are not very informative in isolation; rather, the payoffs from one sequence of actions must be compared to the payoffs from the other sequences. A rational player will seek to maximize her payoff, so we can use these numbers to predict the actions the players will take.

In Figure 6, if Entrant were to make ice cream, Incumbent's only choice is whether to expand and take a payoff of 25 or not expand and take a payoff of 20. Clearly, if Entrant chooses to make ice cream, Incumbent will choose to expand. At the same time, if Entrant were to compete by making textiles, Incumbent's only choice is whether to expand and take a payoff of 4 or not expand and take a payoff of 10. We see then that if Entrant chooses to make textiles, Incumbent will choose not to expand. So what previously looked like four possible outcomes boils down to two rational outcomes. Armed with this foresight, Entrant sees that his choices are between a payoff of 8 (from making ice cream while Incumbent expands) and a payoff of 13 (from making textiles while Incumbent declines to expand). Entrant prefers the payoff of 13 over the payoff of 8, so he will choose to compete with Incumbent, and Incumbent will respond by not expanding, thereby earning a payoff of 10.

Game theorists would call this method of solving the game "backwards induction." All this means is that we start with the last action, eliminate actions if the last mover will not take them, and proceed up the decision tree to the second-to-last mover, etc. Once we determine what the first mover will do, we can deduce the moves of the reactive players.

Figure 6: First mover = Entrant. Second mover = Incumbent.
Payoffs = (Entrant, Incumbent).

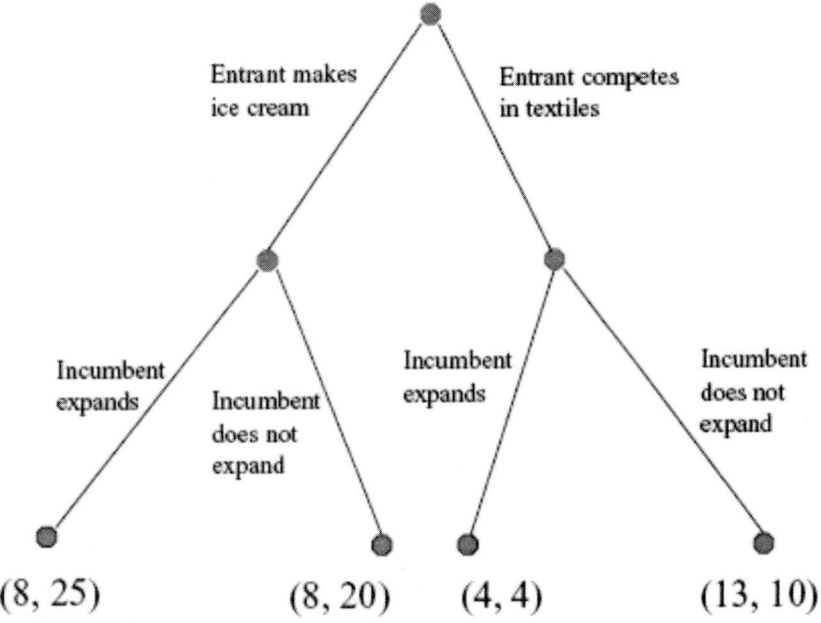

Note that the total payoff to the parties of the solution to this game is 23, which is less than the total payoff of 33 which would result if Entrant made ice cream and Incumbent expanded. Certainly Incumbent would be happier if it could induce Entrant not to compete. However, a threat to expand even if Entrant competes would not be credible, because once Entrant's decision to compete is made, Incumbent would only be shooting itself in the foot by expanding. Entrant knows this from the outset, and Incumbent knows that Entrant knows this, etc. Expanding is only helpful to Incumbent if the prospect of expansion can realistically influence Entrant before Entrant makes his decision. If Entrant really believes that Incumbent will expand no matter what Entrant chooses to do, then Entrant knows he is really choosing between a payoff of 8 from making ice cream while Incumbent expands, and a payoff of 4 by competing while

Incumbent expands. Preferring a payoff of 8 over a payoff of 4, Entrant will choose to make ice cream, and Incumbent will profitably expand.

Incumbent can make his expansion threat credible by taking early actions (*e.g.*, leasing land, buying machinery) that financially commit it to expansion (known as strategic commitment). Such actions have the effect of turning Incumbent into the first mover in the game. See Figure 7 below. Using the same reasoning process as before (beginning with the last action and working our way up the decision tree) we see that Incumbent will expand and Entrant will make ice cream instead of competing with Incumbent in the textile business.

Figure 7: First mover = Incumbent. Second mover = Entrant.
Payoffs = (Incumbent, Entrant).

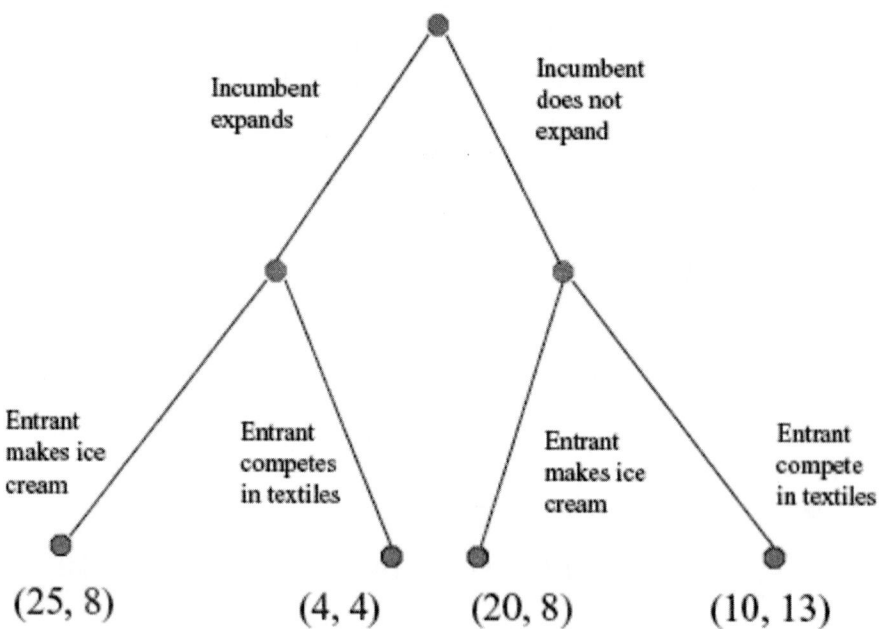

B.   Predatory Pricing and Reputation

Predatory pricing is the practice of lowering a firm's prices and foregoing short-term profits in the hope that competitors will leave the market (or be deterred from entering); at that point, the firm, now free from competition (or the threat of imminent market entrance), raises prices to extract monopoly profits and recoup losses incurred during the period of price reduction.

Some commentators argue that the threat of predation through price cuts is not credible because the cuts hurt the predator more than the prey, given that the predator is larger and hence sells a greater volume of reduced-price goods than the competitors who meet the price cut. However, game theory shows that if the face-off is repeated with different small opponents, and we do away with the assumption of complete information (where the structure of the game and the payoffs to every player are universally known, even if players' actions are secret), predation becomes credible. That is, under incomplete information, the dominant firm can build a reputation for predation, where the ongoing benefits of the reputation outweigh the initial costs of establishing it.

Consider a market with a large existing firm, Incumbent, and a smaller newcomer firm, Entrant. Initially, Entrant must choose whether to enter Incumbent's market or stay out. In response, Incumbent must choose whether to acquiesce to the Entrant's presence in its market or to predate against the Entrant. If the payoffs are written strictly in terms of profits, the game might resemble Figure 8 below. Entrant receives no payoff by not entering, while Incumbent continues to receive its prior payoff of 8. If Entrant enters and Incumbent acquiesces (declines to predate), Entrant earns a payoff of 3 and Incumbent earns a payoff reduced from 8 to 4, due to the new competition. On the other hand, if Entrant enters and Incumbent predates, Incumbent's payoff takes a bigger hit than Entrant's because Incumbent is bigger and sells more volume at the slashed price, as discussed in the preceding paragraph. Entrant suffers a payoff loss of 4, since his post-predation payoff is reduced from 3 to –1 when compared with entrance followed by acquiescence. Incumbent suffers a payoff loss of 6, since his post-predation payoff is reduced from 4 to –2 when compared with entrance followed by acquiescence.

If this set of payoffs is common knowledge to all the players, then Entrant knows that, if he enters, Incumbent will acquiesce, preferring a payoff of 4 to a payoff of –2. Thus, Entrant knows that his choice is between him entering and Incumbent acquiescing, yielding a payoff of 3 for Entrant, and him staying out, yielding a payoff of 0 for Entrant. Preferring 3 to 0, Entrant will enter and Incumbent will acquiesce.

Figure 8: Predation with a level-headed Incumbent

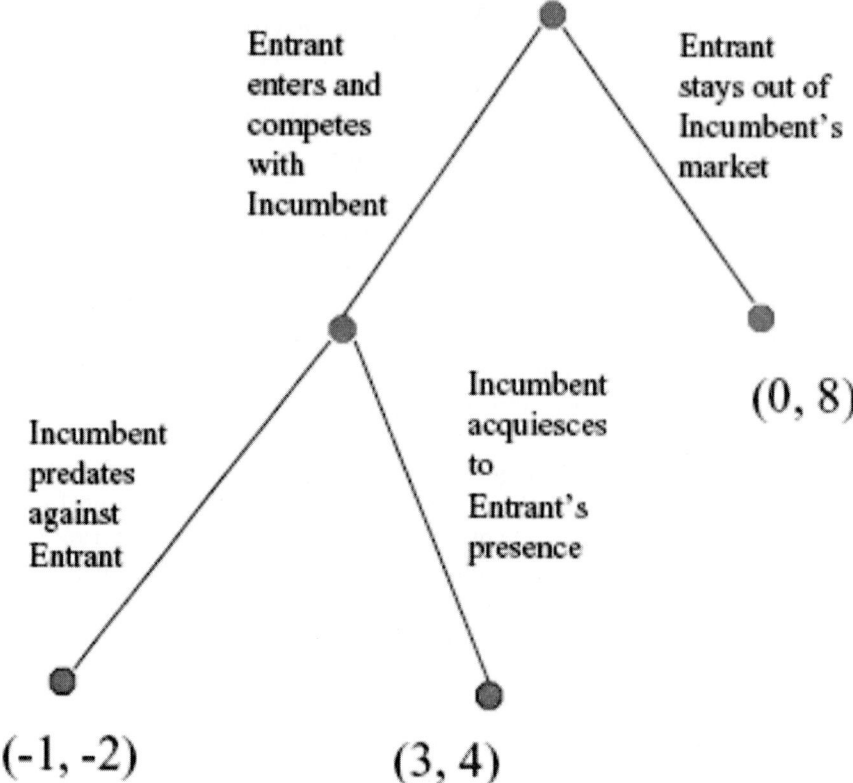

Entrant enters and competes with Incumbent

Entrant stays out of Incumbent's market

Incumbent acquiesces to Entrant's presence

(0, 8)

Incumbent predates against Entrant

(-1, -2)

(3, 4)

Suppose, however, that Entrant is not certain of all the payoffs involved in this game. Up until now we have implicitly assumed that payoffs depended only on monetary gain, and economic decisions were made on the basis of profitability. In real life, however, motivations to act may be influenced not only by financial gain but also by social custom, altruism, self-expression, and pride, to name a few. For all Entrant knows, the owner of the Incumbent firm might have a personality weighted toward pride and aggression, such that Incumbent might suffer a great deal of psychic pain from acquiescing. In such case, the payoffs might look like those in Figure 9 below, which is identical to Figure 8 in every way except for Incumbent's payoff from acquiescing. While a level-headed Incumbent would obtain a payoff of 4 from acquiescing, an aggressive Incumbent suffers, say, –7 units from the psychic pain, resulting in a net payoff of –3 from acquiescing. Under such circumstances, if Entrant enters, Incumbent will prefer to predate than acquiesce, preferring a payoff of –2 over a payoff of –3. Knowing, this, Entrant will prefer to stay out of the market and get a payoff of 0 rather than enter, be predated against, and wind up with a payoff of –1.

Figure 9: Predation with an aggressive Incumbent

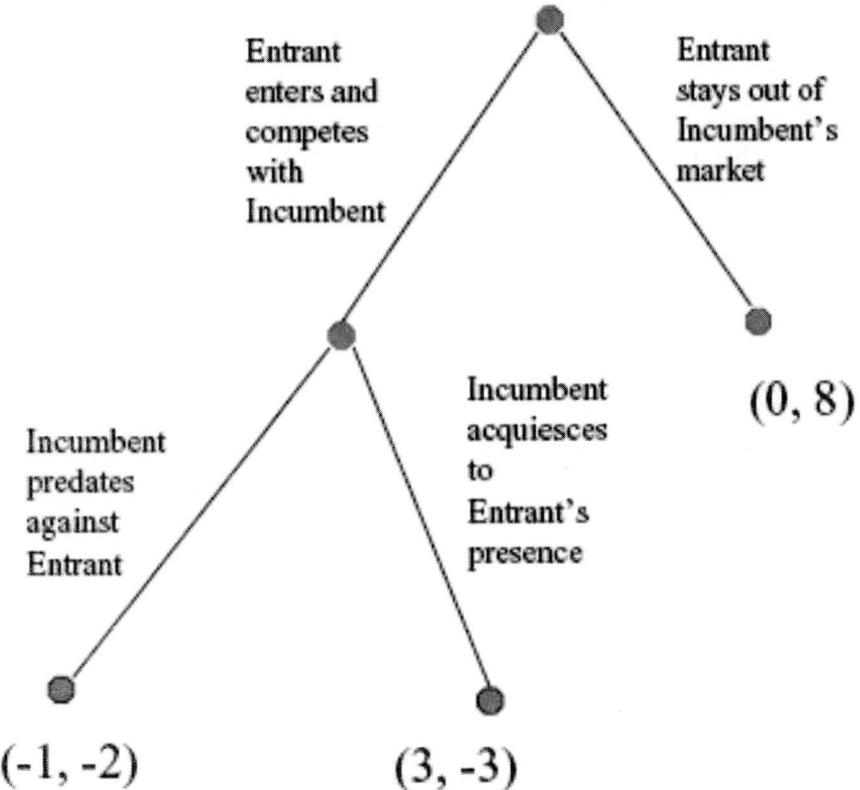

Entrant enters and competes with Incumbent

Entrant stays out of Incumbent's market

Incumbent predates against Entrant

Incumbent acquiesces to Entrant's presence

(0, 8)

(-1, -2)   (3, -3)

This result, no entrance by Entrant, is the one Incumbent prefers best of all, regardless of whether he is in reality level-headed or aggressive. Thus, it is in Incumbent's interest to fool Entrant into believing that Incumbent is, or very well might be, aggressive rather than level-headed— that is, to make the threat of predation credible. Assuming Incumbent is in reality level-headed, the payoff difference between having the market to himself and acquiescing to Entrant is $8 - 4 = 4$. The cost of predating is 6, the difference between the payoff of –2 from predating as compared to the payoff of 4 from acquiescing. Thus, if the large Incumbent confronts this game many times with different Entrants in different geographic regions, he can rationally afford to "spend" 6 units several times over by predating against the first few Entrants, in order to gain a reputation as an aggressive player. Each subsequent Entrant that is deterred from entering based on his acquired belief that Incumbent may well have an aggressive-type payoff structure results in a gain of 4 units to Incumbent. In the long run, therefore, Incumbent can gain financially by predating early. Of course, early predation must be consistent in order to cause the Entrants to think there is any chance that Incumbent is in reality aggressive, for even one instance of acquiescence would be inconsistent with the payoff structure of a true aggressive actor and would thus reveal Incumbent as a level-headed actor.

We note that the model of predation through reputation is distinct from the model of predation through signaling. In the latter, a dominant firm might slash prices below cost and simultaneously expand output, in the hope of signaling to small competitors that the dominant firm has lower cost than is true in reality, arising from economies of its new larger scale. Knowing that its own costs could never be that low, a small firm might then leave the market. Some have pointed out that this form of signaling is simply a classic bluff, and that small firms who are ignorant of what level of cost savings are actually possible and allow themselves to be fooled by a bluff should not be shielded from the results of their gullibility. Just as antitrust law must not deter the use of superior skill and foresight, it should not protect small firms that might suffer as a result of relying on their own inferior information or ill-honed instincts.

By contrast, the model of predation through reputation does not rely on gullibility of small firms. Each small firm may know just as much about the business as the big firm—it just does not know the personality type of the big firm. Indeed, the big firm itself may not know the personality type of the small firms, but their personality type is irrelevant. (The big firm does not fear predation by a small firm acting unilaterally because a small firm cannot accommodate much additional market share, so the large firm need not necessarily respond with a price cut in order to stay in the market.) Thus, it is merely the fact that the big firm has outlets in many geographical regions—and thus has arenas in which to express its genuine or feigned aggressive personality—that makes the small firm's lack of information a weakness; the big firm has the same lack of information, but its dominant size makes that information unimportant.

C.   Tacit Agreement through Repeated Games

Even people unacquainted with formal game theory may already have heard the term "prisoner's dilemma" and be familiar with the basic difficulty it captures with respect to coordinated action. We discuss here an analytically identical version of the game, relating to the pricing decisions of an oligopoly of two firms, also called a duopoly.

Suppose the two firms in a duopoly, Firm A and Firm B, sell a comparable product and each must decide what price to charge. For simplicity, we will assume that their choices are limited to a "low" price and a "high" price. Firm A knows that if both firms charge a high price, both will do well. However, if A charges high and B charges low, B will take away much of A's market share and A's profits will suffer. By the same token, A knows that he will reap a windfall by charging low if B charges high. If both firms charge low, they will maintain market share and do reasonably well, but not as well as if both charged high.

Because the players in this game make their decisions simultaneously rather than in sequence, the game can be represented by a two-by-two matrix of payoffs rather than a decision tree. The payoffs shown in Figure 10 are common knowledge to the players. A does not know what B will do, but A can see that if B charges high, A is better off charging low, and if B charges low, A is also better off charging low. Thus, A will charge low.

Given the symmetry in the payoffs, B reasons identically and concludes that its best strategy is to charge low, no matter what A chooses to charge. Thus, both players will charge low, even though joint payoffs would be higher if both charged high. Although both players know this, neither has sufficient assurance that the other will cooperate by charging high, given the temptation to undercut the competitor and obtain an even greater payoff. Indeed, even if one firm, say Firm A, had iron-clad assurance that B would charge high and that A would therefore not be left twisting in the wind, it would still be irrational—assuming this game is played only once— for A to charge high, since charging low under such circumstances would yield the maximum payoff.

Figure 10: Prisoner's dilemma applied to duopolistic
pricing Payoffs = (Firm A, Firm B)

Firm B

		Charge Low	Charge High
Firm A	Charge Low	(10, 10)	(16, 3)
	Charge High	(3, 16)	(13, 13)

The dynamics of the game change when we assume that the players face off an indefinite number of times, which is certainly more realistic than assuming that an oligopolist (or for that matter any firm) decides price on only one occasion. Repeated interactions allow the parties to bring in the element of trust, for each party knows that his conduct in this game can influence the other player's conduct in subsequent games. Relatedly, repeated play allows the players to communicate through patterns of behavior, for example, when one player punishes another player in a subsequent round for failing to cooperate in the prior round. This type of communication is slower and more ambiguous than sending a letter to a competitor warning him against lowering his price, but it has the power to promote relatively stable patterns of mutual high-pricing while avoiding the problem of *per se* illegality under the Sherman Act.

†